RAINBOW'S END

California Series on Social Choice and Political Economy
Edited by Brian Barry, Robert H. Bates, and Samuel L. Popkin

RAINBOW'S END

*Irish-Americans and the Dilemmas of
Urban Machine Politics, 1840–1985*

STEVEN P. ERIE

UNIVERSITY OF CALIFORNIA PRESS
BERKELEY   LOS ANGELES   LONDON

University of California Press
Berkeley and Los Angeles, California

University of California Press, Ltd.
London, England

© 1988 by
The Regents of the University of California

Library of Congress Cataloging-in-Publication Data

Erie, Steven P.
    Rainbow's end: Irish-Americans and the dilemmas of urban
machine politics, 1840–1985/Steven P. Erie.
    p. cm.—(California series on social choice and political
economy)
    Bibliography: p.
    Includes index.
    ISBN 0–520–06119–5
    1. Irish Americans—Political activity.   2. Politics, Prac-
tical—United States—History.   3. Municipal government—
United States—History.   4. Metropolitan government—
United States—History.
I. Title. II. Series.
E184.I6E75 1989
352'.000899162—dc19
                                                    87–35488
                                                         CIP

Printed in the United States of America
1   2   3   4   5   6   7   8   9

To My Grandparents
Delbert Vincent and Idamae Elizabeth O'Brien
and
To My Cousin Scott

Contents

List of Tables

Preface

San Diego, California, may strike the reader as a strange place to complete a book on the legendary Irish-American big-city political machines such as New York's Tammany Hall or the Dalcy organization in Chicago. Yet America's Finest City (as the local news commentators are so fond of saying) may not be so inappropriate a locale after all. Despite a reputation as a WASP bastion, the city has Irish political bloodlines. Mayor Maureen O'Connor is as Irish as they come. Former Mayor (and current U.S. Senator) Pete Wilson reportedly inherited his political talent from an Irish grandfather on the Chicago police force.

Underneath the veneer of nonpartisan reform, San Diego is also no stranger to the political corruption associated with the big-city eastern machines. In recent years a mayor, a city councilman, and a registrar of voters have resigned from office under shadow of an indictment or conviction.

In actuality, San Diego is but the final way station on a project that has enjoyed a long gestation period. My initial interest in Irish-American politics is a product of my own bloodlines. On my mother's side of the family are O'Briens, O'Neills, McGinleys, and Tobins—public payrollers all. Grandfather O'Brien was an assistant county assessor; Great Grandfather O'Brien, a county sheriff. Great Uncle Billy O'Neill was an "expediter" for the Daley machine, smoothing relations between North Side businesses and the party organization. In a literal sense, this book was "in the blood."

There have been other way stations and helpers. At UCLA, a dissertation on San Francisco ethnic and working-class politics in the late nineteenth century introduced me to Chris Buckley, an early West Coast Irish-American political boss, and to the methodological possibilities and pitfalls posed by the historical study of urban politics. I wish to thank Stephan Thernstrom, Francine Rabinovitz, Leo Snowiss, and Chuck Ries for encouraging (or at least acquiescing in) my interest in ethnic political history.

In a more immediate sense, this book is the outgrowth of a collaborative study of big-city political machines begun in the late 1970s with John Petrocik and Paul Sacks. John, Paul, and I spent a profitable year debating the nature of machine politics and how to study it. By their nature, triads are unstable, and ours was no exception. Tired of being on the perpetual short end of a two-to-one voting split and eager to study a political machine up close, I journeyed to Albany, New York.

There I found the powerful Irish-American Democratic organization of which an awed James McGregor Burns wrote a few years ago that "it is so well preserved that it should be put into the Smithsonian before we forget what a political machine looks like." I wish to thank the late Erastus Corning II, former mayor of Albany, William Kennedy, and my colleagues and friends at SUNY Albany for sharing their thoughts about the "house that Dan O'Connell built."

Next came a year's tour of duty with the U.S. Department of Health and Human Services in Washington, D.C. This sensitized me to the importance of the welfare state—critical for understanding the fate of the big-city machines in the twentieth century—and to the importance of intergovernmental politics.

San Diego, home of the largest St. Patrick's Day parade west of Chicago, has been a marvelous place to complete the work on this project. I would like to bestow honorary Celtic status on my colleagues, graduate students, and friends at UC San Diego for all the support they have shown. Vanessa Cunningham, Pete Irons, Sandy Lakoff, Tracy Strong, Sam Kernell, David Laitin, Neal Beck, Gary Jacobson, Priscilla Long, John Gilmour, Jim Ingram, Kathy Underwood, Mike Coste, Judy Johnson, Marilyn Wilson, and Nicole Moran read—and improved—innumerable drafts. Anita Schiller and Sue Galloway deserve special thanks for mobilizing the entire University of California library system to track down fugitive references. From afar, Clarence Stone, Stephan Thernstrom, David

Greenstone, Amy Bridges, Marty Rein, Norton E. Long, and Michael P. Smith have lent encouragement and constructive criticism. Michele Moran and Kelly Charter are to be thanked for their word-processing assistance. I owe to Michael K. Brown an example of how to pay professional and personal debts. He shall receive repayment in kind.

My most profound intellectual debt is owed to my friend Harold Brackman. Harold's sage and incisive comments on an early version of the manuscript enabled me to deepen the argument and to shape a flawed manuscript into a readable book. A free copy from the author is hardly adequate payment for his labors.

Del Mar, California
June 1987

Chapter One

The Irish and the
Big-City Machines

Rainbow's End is a study of Irish-American machine politics from
the mid-nineteenth century to the present in eight once heavily
Irish cities: New York, Philadelphia, Chicago, Boston, San Francisco, Pittsburgh, Jersey City, and Albany. Daniel Patrick Moynihan has observed that the Irish-American genius has been organizational rather than entrepreneurial or intellectual.[1] Displaying a
"distaste for commerce" and ideas, the Irish labored to build the
American Catholic church and the big-city Democratic machines.
Arguably the largest section in the pantheon of Irish-American he-
roes is reserved for the big-city party bosses, from Tammany Hall's
"Honest John" Kelly in the 1870s to Chicago's Richard Daley in
the 1970s.

Notwithstanding the demise of the old-time big-city machines,
Irish-American politicos are still larger-than-life figures. The departed Celtic party bosses continue to cast a long shadow over
contemporary urban minority groups, particularly blacks and Hispanics, who search for routes of group economic advancement.
The Irish are reputed to have used a political route to travel from
rags to riches, capturing the patronage-laden machines and turning public employment into an Irish preserve. Before today's ethnic
groups emulate the Irish, however, they would do well to carefully
examine the Irish experience with the big-city machines, separating historical fact from fiction. This study attempts such a task.

The machine emerged as the major urban political institution in the late nineteenth century; the Irish were among its leading architects and practitioners. A form of clientele politics, the party machine organized the electorate in order to control the tangible benefits of public office—patronage, services, contracts, and franchises. The machine employed these resources to maintain power. Bosses purchased voter support with offers of public jobs and services rather than by appeals to traditional loyalties or to class interests.

With roots in the second or Jacksonian party system of the 1820s and 1830s, the full-fledged or mature urban machine did not emerge until the third party system entered an advanced stage in the 1870s and 1880s. By 1890 centralized machines controlled one-half of the nation's twenty largest cities. Tammany Hall finally had consolidated its hold over Manhattan. Hugh McLaughlin's Democratic organization ruled neighboring Brooklyn. In Philadelphia, the McManes's Republican machine, which had governed the city since the end of the Civil War, was about to give way to the Durham and Vare GOP machines. Chris Magee ruled Republican Pittsburgh, and George Cox controlled Republican Cincinnati. Edward Butler had created a bipartisan machine to run St. Louis. San Francisco was controlled by the Democratic "Blind Boss" Christopher Buckley and the fire department, his political praetorian guard. Robert "Little Bob" Davis controlled Jersey City and surrounding Hudson County. Boss William F. Sheehan ran politics in Republican Buffalo. An entrenched Democratic machine, successor to Martin Van Buren's Regency, ruled Albany.[2]

Although the Irish did not control all of the big-city machines by 1890, they had captured most of the Democratic party organizations in the northern and midwestern cities. Lamenting the "Irish conquest of our cities," Yankee John Paul Bobcock furnished in 1894 a roll call of the late-nineteenth-century Celtic party bosses: John Kelly and Richard Croker in New York City, Hugh McLaughlin in Brooklyn, Mike McDonald in Chicago, Pat Maguire in Boston, Christopher Buckley in San Francisco, William Sheehan in Buffalo, and "Little Bob" Davis in Jersey City. In the twentieth century, more names would be added to the list: Charles Francis Murphy in New York City; Ed Kelly, Pat Nash, and Richard Daley in Chicago; James Michael Curley and Martin Lomasney in Boston; David Lawrence in Pittsburgh; Frank Hague in Jersey City; Dan O'Connell in Albany; and Tom and Jim Pendergast in Kansas City.[3]

The Irish, as Edward Levine argues, were "given to politics."[4] No other ethnic group made the same contribution to the building of the urban machines. Germans migrated to the United States in as large numbers as the Irish. The Germans were also nearly as urbanized as the Irish, settling in midwestern rather than eastern cities. Yet there were few German bosses or machines. Jews embraced reform and labor rather than machine politics. San Francisco's Abe Ruef and Chicago's Jake Arvey were among the few Jewish bosses. A few black bosses such as William Dawson in Chicago and Homer Brown in Pittsburgh ran sub-machines of white-controlled organizations. To the extent that the Irish-American bosses designated an ethnic heir apparent, it was the Italians. Italian bosses such as Carmine De Sapio of Tammany Hall took over many of the aging Irish machines in the late 1940s and 1950s. Yet the Italians were usually called on to preside over the machine's demise, not its rebirth. In more than one sense, the Italians were left "holding the bag."

Not only did the Irish predominate among urban ethnic party bosses, but they were also the architects of the strongest and most long-lived big-city machines. Compared with their Republican counterparts, Irish-run Democratic machines proved to be mobilizing and welfarist organizations. Republican machines, in Lincoln Steffens's phrase, were constructed "in the air."[5] As urban offshoots of state-level GOP machines, Republican big-city machines relied on the Yankee middle-class vote and did little to mobilize immigrant voters. With a middle-class constituency demanding low taxes, big-city GOP machines had little incentive to incorporate working-class immigrant groups and reward them with costly welfare services.

Big-city Democratic political machines, in contrast, were built "from the bottom up." Rooted in the institutional life of working-class ethnic neighborhoods—saloons, clubhouses, volunteer fire departments—Democratic organizations did a better job than their Republican counterparts of naturalizing and registering immigrants and rewarding them with patronage jobs and social services. The resulting longevity of Irish Democratic machines is remarkable. Under Celtic tutelage, Tammany Hall ran New York (with minor exceptions) from 1874 to 1933. The Hague machine controlled Jersey City from 1917 to 1949. Dan O'Connell built the Albany machine in 1922; it has yet to lose a city election. The Chicago machine ruled the Windy City from 1931 until Harold Washington's mayoral victory in 1983.

Yet the once mighty Irish machines are now in eclipse. Government bureaucracies and labor unions have assumed the welfare and employment functions once fulfilled by the machines. Civil service reform has limited their supply of patronage jobs. Their ethnic constituents have moved to the suburbs. Of the legion of Irish machines, only those of Chicago and Albany remain as relics of the past. In all likelihood, these two vestiges will soon pass from the scene. The powerful Chicago machine has been progressively weakened since 1976, losing the mayoral elections of 1979 and 1983. The Albany machine entered an interregnum phase with the death of Erastus Corning, O'Connell's successor, in 1983.

The Rainbow Theory of the Machine

Paradoxically, the demise of the Irish machine has been accompanied by a metamorphosis in our understanding of its achievements. During its heyday, it was castigated by progressives as corrupt and undemocratic. For muckraker Lincoln Steffens, the shame of machine politics was the "triumph of the commercial spirit" in public life.[6] Political reformer Frederick Howe scored the city boss for serving as a "majordomo" for large transportation and utility firms while ignoring the welfare of the working class.[7] For M. Ostrogorski, machine politics marked the triumph of "party formalism," the elevation of office over political principle.[8]

In the machine's twilight era, social scientists such as Robert Merton and Robert Dahl offered a much different understanding of its performance. The new view may be termed the "rainbow" theory of the old-style urban machine. The theory refers to both the *players* and the *prizes* of urban politics. In this view, urban machines, though corrupt and undemocratic, actively worked to incorporate working-class immigrant groups such as the Irish, Jews, and Italians. Machines supposedly fashioned multiethnic "rainbow" electoral coalitions, rewarding each group with jobs and services drawn from a sizable pot of municipal gold.[9]

The prizes awaiting ethnic capture in city politics appeared substantial. Urban machines controlled thousands of official and unofficial patronage jobs, the latter with firms franchised by or doing business with the city. More than 40,000 New York municipal jobs, for example, were at Tammany Hall's disposal in the late 1880s. Machines also controlled the awarding of public contracts, especially important in an era when cities were making their major capital improvements. Between 1900 and 1910, for example, San Francisco embarked on an ambitious program to make the city the "Paris of North America." Municipal expenditures rose threefold, from $5.6 to $17.4 million, to pay for new schools, hospitals, parks, playgrounds, sewers, and utilities. Local newspapers estimated that more than 6,000 contract jobs had been created by the program, considerably exceeding the combined city-county payroll.[10]

According to the rainbow theory, the Irish were the main beneficiaries of machine politics. Robert Dahl, for example, argues that the Irish used a political strategy to move from the working class into the middle class in the late nineteenth and early twentieth centuries. Celtic political activity—voter mobilization, participation in party politics, and municipal office holding—supposedly led to a disproportionate share of public sector resources, thereby accelerating the development of an Irish middle class. First- and second-generation Irish displayed a singular talent for electoral politics. In San Francisco, the proportion of adult Irish males registered to vote in 1900 was nearly double that of the city's other foreign-born adult males—70 percent versus 37 percent—and equaled that of the native-born.[11]

Group political mobilization seemingly brought economic results. Controlling such cities as New York, Chicago, Boston, and San Francisco by the 1880s, Irish bosses helped "Hibernianize" the public payroll. In the nation's fourteen largest cities between 1870 and 1900, the proportion of public employees of Irish parentage climbed from 11 percent to 30 percent while the proportion of the labor force of Irish parentage in these cities remained at 20 percent. Using public sector job opportunities, the Irish appeared to move into the urban middle class with surprising rapidity considering their meager job skills and the employment discrimination they encountered. Between 1870 and 1900 the proportion of first- and second-generation Irish in white-collar jobs in cities of more than 100,000 population, where over 40 percent of the nation's Irish-Americans lived, rose from 12 percent to 27 percent, while among the non-Irish in the big cities, the increase in white-collar ranks was relatively smaller, from 27 percent to 34 percent.[12]

The rainbow theory figured prominently in the ethnic revival movement of the 1960s and 1970s. Blacks and "unmeltable" whites drew on—and further embellished—the legend of Irish power. In particular, the legend served as a yardstick in the black power debates because it supposedly demonstrated the efficacy of local electoral strategies for capturing public sector resources, enabling significant numbers of an ethnic group to escape poverty. Blacks found the Irish model increasingly compelling as their political demands shifted from obtaining legal rights in the South to remedying economic conditions in the urban North. Black political leaders were called on to exchange nonelectoral skills—mass protest and constitutional litigation—for the electoral and organizational skills practiced by the Irish. As Charles Hamilton argues, "While other racial and ethnic leaders could spend time exploring the process of machine politics—learning how to recruit and deliver voters, and how to reward, punish and bargain for benefits— blacks had to spend time checking legal precedents and filing lawsuits. . . . Blacks, in other words, developed plaintiffs rather than precinct captains. . . . There were no black success models in the manner of Tammany Hall, Boss Crump, or the Cook County Democratic political machine."[13]

Notwithstanding its popularity, it is time to lay the rainbow theory of the urban machine to rest. In this study I argue that throughout most of their history, urban machines did *not* incorporate immigrants other than the Irish. The machine's arsenal of resources was far more modest than it sometimes appeared. Owing to the scarce nature of the machine's benefits, the Irish could not readily translate political power into group economic advancement. Limited as these prizes were, the Irish jealously guarded them, parsimoniously accommodating the later-arriving Southern and Eastern Europeans and blacks. The newcomers struggled constantly with their Irish political overlords. Their anti-Irish insurgency took varied forms: third parties, reform movements, and revolts within the machines. For the later ethnic arrivals, integration into the urban machines was a hard-won, delayed, and ultimately limited accomplishment.

My critique of the rainbow theory is based on a reassessment of both the machine's electoral strategies and its resource supply. In brief, the entrenched Irish machines were one-party regimes with few opponents. Having already constructed a minimal winning coalition among "old" immigrant—that is, Western European—voters, the established machines had little need to naturalize, register, and vote later ethnic arrivals. Moreover, machine bosses did not control an unlimited cornucopia of benefits. In particular, there was a limited supply of patronage with which to reward various ethnic claimants. So that the Irish could control the machine's scarce core resources of power and patronage, the Celtic bosses gave the slowly mobilizing "new" immigrants from Southern and Eastern Europe less valuable benefits—services, symbolic recognition, and collective benefits such as labor and social welfare legislation.

If power represented the "approved Irish secular value," as Edward Levine argues, there were limits to its use.[14] In this study, I address two interrelated dilemmas of the Irish machine, one economic, the other political. The first dilemma is that it was a poor mechanism for Irish economic advancement. Individual Irish bosses, contractors, and lawyers made fortunes off the machine. Tammany boss Richard Croker, for example, born penniless, retired from political life to enjoy the pleasures of raising horses on his baronial estate in Ireland. Yet I would argue that political machines could not serve as a route from rags to riches for the Irish working class. The first generation of machines built in the late nineteenth century controlled too little patronage to affect appreciably the life chances of the Irish. The twentieth-century machines created a much greater supply of patronage, and the Irish crowded into the public sector. On the eve of the Depression, more than one-third of the Irish workforce in machine cities depended on patronage for their livelihood. Yet the patronage created was blue-collar rather than white-collar, the wrong sort for group social mobility. As policemen, firemen, and city laborers, the Irish remained solidly lower-middle-class. Only with the machine's decline, forcing the Irish into higher education and private sector jobs, have the Irish been able to build a solid middle class rooted in business and the professions.[15] There were good political reasons for machines to prefer creating blue-collar jobs even though this hindered Irish economic advancement. Blue-collar jobs were cheaper, and more could be created for a given outlay. More jobs meant more votes for the machine.

The second dilemma of the Irish machine was political. The machine's organizational maintenance needs—building citywide electoral pluralities, securing necessary party financing, placating the business community—introduced a conservative strain into Irish-American urban leadership, resulting in lost opportunities to represent working-class political interests more fully. As they learned to manipulate the levers of urban power, Irish bosses turned their backs on more radical forms of working-class politics. The machine ultimately tamed Irish voters as well as leaders. The Irish working class was in the forefront of the labor insurgency against the machines in the 1870s and 1880s. Yet Irish enthusiasm for labor politics dimmed as ever-larger numbers were brought into the patronage system. The failure of labor parties in the big cities can thus partly be understood in terms of the threat they posed to the entrenched Irish machines and their ethnic beneficiaries.

The Life Cycle of the Urban Machine

Rainbow's End is a study of big-city machine politics as well as of ethnic politics. A second purpose of this study is to offer a new theory of the life cycle of the urban machine—its origins, longevity, and decline. Regarding the machine's origins, I offer a revision of the two leading theories. A "mass" theory, found in the work of Edward Banfield, James Q. Wilson, and Daniel Patrick Moynihan, argues that machines emerge as a reflection of an ethnic group's values and social structure. For Banfield and Wilson, the machine's trafficking in divisible benefits is a response to the "private-regarding" ethos of the European immigrants. For Moynihan, Celtic machines such as Tammany Hall are a reproduction of Irish village life.[16]

An "elite" theory, such as that found in the work of Martin Shefter, views the machine as an elite- rather than mass-created institution. Immigrant voters may demand divisible material benefits, but this demand pattern does not inevitably produce a centralized political machine. Party bosses build centralized machines by successfully resolving the organization's maintenance needs—a winning supply of votes, reward and discipline of the party's precinct and ward captains, control of public officials, and adequate party financing.[17]

This study poses a question that neither of these theories adequately answers: Why did cities such as New York produce powerful long-lasting machines whereas cities such as Boston, America's Dublin, never rose above factional ward politics? Mass and elite theories would predict that centralized machines would emerge in each city. Both cities had large Irish populations. Both cities had talented and ambitious Irish party leaders—John Kelly, Richard Croker, and Charles Francis Murphy in New York and James Michael Curley and Martin Lomasney in Boston.

I answer this question with an *intergovernmental* theory of big-city machines that highlights the pivotal role of local alliances with party leaders at the state and federal levels during the machine's fragile incubation period. In New York, unlike Massachusetts, Democratic governors friendly to Tammany Hall in the 1880s directed state patronage to the fledgling machine, seriously weakening Tammany's factional opponents by freezing them out of state assistance. Machine-building alliances extended to the federal level as well. During the 1930s, Irish party bosses such as Ed Kelly and Pat Nash in Chicago and David Lawrence in Pittsburgh used federal job programs such as the WPA to build a new generation of Democratic machines.

Once centralized machines emerged, how did they maintain themselves in power? The rainbow theory suggests they built multiethnic coalitions, enticing each group with the organization's apparent arsenal of jobs, services, and other tangible benefits. In this study I offer a different theory of the machine's longevity. Contrary to the rainbow theory, the political mobilization of ethnic groups entailed substantial risks. Newly enfranchised voters could demand more than the machine could offer. Moreover, throughout most of its history, there were sharp limits on the machine's supply of material inducements. For example, the willingness of voters and taxpayers to support an increase in city tax rates or indebtedness limited the number of municipal patronage jobs. The specter of middle-class tax revolts haunted Irish party bosses from John Kelly in the 1870s to Richard Daley in the 1970s. To these political constraints on the machine's patronage stock must be added legal constraints. State Republican machines and even a few reform Democratic governors fashioned constitutional straitjackets on the machine's ability to raise and spend public money.

Whereas the rainbow theory *assumes* a cornucopia of machine resources and concentrates on the question how machines distributed benefits to different claimants, I start with the premise that party bosses had to husband *scarce* resources. The demands of ethnic groups and the working class for jobs and services nearly always exceeded the machine's available supply. The secret of machine longevity, then, was bringing electoral demand into balance with resource supply.

How did machines manage electoral demand? I distinguish between two distinct stages of machine building: an embryonic stage, where fledgling machines face strong competitive electoral pressures from the opposition party and from rival factions within their own party; and a consolidation stage, where machines have triumphed over their opponents and have built minimal winning voter coalitions. Embryonic machines are mobilizers. They face competitive pressures to increase the number of partisan voters. Entrenched machines, in contrast, are selective mobilizers. Having defeated the other party's machine and rival factions, consolidated machines need only bring out their traditional supporters. There is little electoral incentive to mobilize newer ethnic arrivals.

Embryonic machines actively courted nonvoters. Tammany Hall's record naturalization of 41,000 immigrants in the 1868 gubernatorial campaign is testimony to the budding machine's weakness, not its strength. Similarly, late nineteenth-century Irish Democratic machines in San Francisco, Boston, Jersey City, and Albany naturalized and registered the "old," that is, Western European, immigrants. In cities controlled by fledgling machines, there was a dramatic increase in the size of the urban electorate and in voter participation rates.

The problem with the mobilization approach to managing electoral demand is that newly enfranchised voters must in some fashion be rewarded. Otherwise, their grievances against the machine mount and they are ripe for capture by the machine's opponents. Embryonic machines, however, often did not have the resources to pay off their new constituents. The mobilizing Irish machines of the late nineteenth century were forced by political and legal constraints to pursue conservative fiscal and patronage policies. The price of mobilizing the "old" ethnics was the continued threat of working-class insurgency. In the 1886 New York mayoral election, for example, Tammany Hall lacked the resources to buy off the ethnic working class and barely beat back the challenge of Henry George and the United Labor party.

Electoral mobilization without reward forced fledgling machines to develop a second set of voter management techniques. Electoral fraud and repression represented the major secondary techniques. In New York City's crucial 1886 mayoral election, Tammany Hall countered massive Irish and German working-class support for Henry George with thorough control of the city's police and thus of the ballot box. Uncounted ballots, nearly all for George, were seen floating down the Hudson for days after the election. In the twentieth century, the Chicago and Albany machines confounded the census takers by registering and voting the dead, the departed, and even the unborn. O'Connell's organization in Albany, for example, claimed the votes of 61 percent of the city's entire *population* of 131,000 in the 1940s.

Besides voter fraud, emerging machines used repression to weaken their opponents. Irish party bosses were famous for the ingenuity with which they systematically weakened labor and socialist parties. Machine-controlled bureaucrats and judges denied parade and meeting permits. The party's plug-uglies armed with brass knuckles waded into peaceful assemblies. Opposition leaders were frequently arrested on trumped-up charges. For insurgent Jews and Italians, the Irish machines specialized in rigorous enforcement of Sunday closing laws and in punitive denial of business permits.

Entrenched machines, in contrast, managed electoral demand in different ways. With little competitive electoral challenge, these machines turned a deaf ear to the pleas of newcomers for help with naturalization, registration, and voting. For example, what accounts for Tammany Hall's about-face in its treatment of immigrants between the 1860s and the early 1900s? The massive party-sponsored naturalization of the Irish and the Germans gave way to a not-so-benign electoral neglect of later-arriving Jews and Italians. Tammany's Yankee party chieftains in the 1860s had as much revulsion toward the Irish as Irish bosses after the turn of the century would have against the Southern and Eastern Europeans. The difference is that Tammany needed the immigrant vote in the 1860s and 1870s to fend off both a strong state Republican party and rival local Democratic organizations such as Irving Hall and the County Democracy. Having finally banished its opponents, except for an occasional reform mayor, the Tammany Hall of Charles Francis Murphy in 1910 no longer needed the new immigrant vote. Chicago's Irish Democratic party bosses Roger Sullivan and George Brennan worked far harder than their Tammany counterparts in the teens and twenties to naturalize and register the city's Poles, Czechs, Jews, and Italians. They had to, for Republican boss and mayor "Big Bill" Thompson was successfully mobilizing and wooing the same new ethnic voters.

The voter management strategy of the entrenched Irish machines—to mobilize the old but not the new immigrants—contributed to their short-term longevity. The machine's limited stock of patronage jobs and services would suffice to reward a smaller electorate of old but not new immigrants. This electoral strategy, however, had long-term costs. One of the chief reasons that the established Irish machines fell was that enterprising opposition leaders finally succeeded in mobilizing the new ethnics. For example, the Irish machines of New York and Jersey City fell in the 1930s and 1940s as reform leaders such as Fiorello La Guardia actively worked to naturalize, register, and win the votes of Italians, Jews, and Poles. In the 1980s, the Chicago machine staggered when finally challenged by the black community.

Electoral management is only half the story of the Irish machine's longevity. Machines also had to manage resources. The rainbow theory addresses the distributional strategies of the machines: how the Irish got police and fire jobs, the Jews teaching jobs, and the Italians lowly places in sanitation. Yet machines concentrated as much on *creating* resources as distributing them. Far too little attention has been given to what I would term a "supply-side" theory of the machine. What were the primary means machines used to enlarge the supply of tangible benefits, particularly new patronage jobs? What were the attendant political benefits *and* risks of different ways of enlarging the pie?

This study offers the beginnings of a "supply-side" theory of the machine. I consider such resource-enhancement strategies as tax increases, increases in public debt, annexation and incorporation, reliance on private sector patronage, and alliances with county, state, and federal bosses to capture additional public sector patronage. But each expansionary strategy had risks as well as benefits. For example, tax increases prompted middle-class tax revolts. Annexation enlarged the city's boundaries without increasing the tax rate. Yet annexation also enlarged the big-city electorate by including the outward-migrating and antimachine middle class.

Rainbow's End also presents a more complicated picture of the Irish machine's distributional decisions than that offered by conventional theory. The rainbow theorists posit an electorally "rational" distributional process: Machines allocate jobs and services to ethnic groups in proportion to their anticipated vote for the organization's candidates. This study argues that machine allocational decisions were more retrospective than prospective. Machines overrewarded previously incorporated groups and underrewarded newly incorporated groups. The Irish machine's supply of patronage jobs, for example, dramatically increased during the Progressive era. Remembering the old immigrants' antimachine insurgency in the 1870s and 1880s, the Celtic bosses gave the bulk of the new public sector jobs to the Irish rather than to Jews or Italians.

Rainbow theorists miss another dimension of the machine's allocational processes. The Irish machines developed elaborate ethnically differentiated benefit systems. The machine's core resources of power and patronage were reserved for the Irish, with minor shares given to the most serious challengers among the new ethnics, for example, Jews rather than Italians. Irish bosses preferred to give newcomers less valuable resources: services such as business licenses, symbolic recognition such as nomination to minor offices or machine observance of ethnic holidays such as Columbus Day, and labor and social welfare legislation.

Rainbow theorists also posit that machines trafficked primarily if not exclusively in divisible benefits rather than collective benefits. Divisible benefits such as patronage jobs could be rewarded or withheld from individuals in exchange for support for the machine. Collective benefits like Social Security checks, however, were distributed to program rather than political eligibles. Machines supposedly opposed collective benefits because they reduced the machine's monopoly over jobs and services for the working class. Machines could not control the allocation of collective benefits as readily as they could for divisible benefits.

This study, however, argues that machines actually supported collective benefit programs, ranging from the labor legislation of the Progressive era to the social welfare legislation of the New Deal and Great Society eras. The Irish machines lobbied for collective benefits in order to pay off junior ethnic coalitional partners at minimal cost to continued Irish control over the machine's divisible benefits of power and patronage. The machine's collective benefit strategy worked with Jews and Italians during the Progressive and New Deal eras and with blacks during the Great Society era.

The allocation of less valuable benefits to later ethnic groups represented a short-term machine distributional strategy. What happened when the new ethnics finally mobilized? In the long run, successful machines had to be more accommodating of the new ethnics' political demands. For working-class voters, demanding a great share of patronage jobs and welfare services, successful machines had to fashion a favorable exchange ratio between claimants and resources. Machines were in trouble when the ratio broke down because of rising numbers of voters or declining numbers of patronage jobs. Many of the established Irish machines fell precisely because they were unable to increase their resources as the big-city electorate grew.

The Depression and New Deal represented a watershed for big-city Irish machines. The machines' limited political incorporation of Southern and Eastern Europeans finally failed. Democratic presidential candidates Al Smith and Franklin D. Roosevelt brought

Jews, Italians, and Poles into the voting booth in record numbers. In cities such as New York and Chicago, the number of voters *doubled* between 1928 and 1936. What would happen if these new ethnic voters turned on the aging machines? Because of the Depression, the Irish machines found their resource base depleted at precisely the time they needed additional resources in order to court the new ethnics. The frenetic machine pursuit of federal patronage, particularly the WPA, can be understood as a strategy to increase the supply of machine benefits for the new voters.

To secure middle-class votes, however, machines had to devise a much different menu of policies. Middle-class voters were homeowners, sensitive to tax increases and less desirous of patronage jobs and welfare services. Middle-class voters demanded low taxes and homeowner services such as garbage collection and street repair. The longevity of the Irish machines of Chicago, Albany, and Pittsburgh well into the post–World War II era is attributable to their ability to shift from working-class to middle-class policies for white ethnics while piggybacking welfare-state programs for blacks and Hispanics.

This new theory of the machine's longevity in terms of an equilibrium between claimants and resources, particularly for working-class ethnic groups, is also a theory of the machine's demise. Middle-class reformers rarely destroyed machines. As Tammany sachem George Washington Plunkitt once observed, reformers were "shortlived morning glories."[18] Tammany Hall, for example, easily survived the reform administrations of Seth Low and John Purroy Mitchel. Machines were in trouble both when reformers increased the number of political participants by mobilizing the newer ethnic arrivals *and* when the machines lacked the resources to outbid them. Machines were in serious trouble when reformers rewarded as well as mobilized the newcomers. In New York City, Fiorello La Guardia permanently weakened Tammany Hall between 1933 and 1945 by mobilizing the city's Jews and Italians *and* by rewarding them. La Guardia tightened the city's civil service system in order to recruit Jews and Italians at the expense of the Irish while dramatically increasing the size of the city's human services bureaucracies. A new cohort of ethnic working-class voters had been politically indoctrinated and rewarded by Tammany's opponents. The Wigwam (as Tammany was called) would never be the same.

This study is particularly critical of one leading theory of the machine's demise. Rexford Tugwell in *The Brains Trust* and Edwin O'Connor in his magnificent *The Last Hurrah*, a barely fictionalized account of Boston's James Michael Curley, argue that New Deal social welfare programs destroyed the machines by breaking the organization's monopoly over the jobs and services distributed to urban working-class voters. With the advent of Social Security, Aid to Families with Dependent Children (AFDC), and unemployment compensation, urban voters no longer had to go to the machines for help.[19]

In some ways the New Deal did weaken local machines. FDR's mobilization of the urban ethnic vote destroyed or permanently weakened the established Republican machines in cities such as Pittsburgh and Philadelphia. The New Deal electoral coalition also turned on the entrenched Irish Democratic machines in cities such as New York and Jersey City. With many of the big-city machines reduced to rubble, New Deal labor legislation and social programs appeared to make it harder to build a *new* generation of machines. The Wagner Act, for example, strengthened labor as a political actor—in local as well as in national politics. In cities like Detroit with a strong reform rather than machine tradition, unions stepped into the political vacuum created by weak parties. The United Auto Workers' Committee on Political Education performed such party functions as getting out the vote. Union collective bargaining agreements took the place of the machine's patronage and welfare services. With unions performing traditional party functions, machines were harder to rebuild in the post–New Deal era. New Deal social programs, particularly Social Security, reduced the machine's control over the stream of government benefits going to voters and thus enabled some voters to be more politically independent.[20]

Yet for machines that survived the twin shoals of the New Deal electoral coalition and the Depression, the social programs of the New Deal and the Great Society represented potent tools for machine strengthening. In the postwar era, a third set of migrants came to northern cities. Poor blacks and Hispanics demanded the machine's traditional menu of patronage jobs and welfare services.

Yet machines could no longer supply these working-class benefits. Eroding tax bases and civil service reform cut deeply into the supply of patronage. Newly prosperous white middle-class voters demanded low taxes. Machines catered to the newer migrants with welfare-state programs, particularly public housing and AFDC, at minimal cost to the city treasury and to white taxpayers. Machine control of the black and Hispanic vote, however, now depended on a steady stream of social program benefits. With cutbacks in federal and state social programs in the Reagan era, this flow of benefits to the minority community was interrupted. The black revolt in the 1980s against the last of the machines was in large part fueled by welfare-state retrenchment. Social program retrenchment, not growth, has destabilized the few remaining big-city machines.

Overview of the Study

This interpretation of the machine's performance and beneficiaries is based on a comparative study of machine dynamics in eight once heavily Irish-American cities—New York, Philadelphia, Chicago, Boston, San Francisco, Pittsburgh, Jersey City, and Albany—from the mid-nineteenth century to the mid-1980s. As Table 1 shows, in 1870 these cities were among the eleven most heavily Irish of the twenty-five cities with more than 50,000 population. They ranged from Boston, with nearly one-quarter of its population born in Ireland, to Chicago, with almost one-eighth of its residents from the Emerald Isle. Of the ten most heavily Irish cities, only New Haven and Providence have been excluded from this study because of the paucity of data about their formative political histories. The existing studies of New Haven and Providence politics, however, suggest a replication of the patterns of machine and ethnic politics uncovered in the eight cities studied.[21]

This study is not based solely on a case study of a single machine. Nor is it based on case studies of only those cities where mature machines developed. Instead, I compare two sets of big cities with large Irish-American populations: those where Irish-controlled machines emerged and those cities where no strong citywide machine appeared or where a machine not controlled by

TABLE 1.   The Irish in the Cities, 1870

	Irish-Born as Percentage of Total Population	Foreign-Born as Percentage of Total Population	Total Population	Rank (by Total Population)	Number of Irish-Born	Number of Foreign-Born
Boston	22.7	35.1	250,526	7	56,900	87,986
Jersey City	21.5	38.6	82,546	17	17,665	31,835
New York	21.4	44.5	942,292	1	201,199	419,094
Albany	19.1	32.0	69,422	20	13,276	22,207
New Haven	18.9	28.2	50,840	25	9,601	14,356
Brooklyn	18.7	36.5	396,099	3	73,985	144,718
Providence	17.5	24.9	68,904	21	12,085	17,177
San Francisco	17.3	49.3	149,473	10	25,864	73,719
Pittsburgh	15.2	32.3	86,076	16	13,119	27,822
Philadelphia	14.3	27.2	674,022	2	96,698	183,624
Chicago	13.4	48.4	298,977	5	39,988	144,557
Newark	11.9	34.2	105,059	13	12,481	35,884
Cleveland	10.7	41.8	92,829	15	9,964	38,815
St. Louis	10.4	36.1	310,864	4	32,329	112,249
Rochester	9.7	34.0	62,386	22	6,078	21,184
Buffalo	9.6	39.3	117,714	11	11,264	46,237
Detroit	8.8	44.5	79,577	18	6,970	35,381
Cincinnati	8.6	36.8	216,239	8	18,624	79,612
New Orleans	7.7	25.3	191,418	9	14,693	48,475
Louisville	7.6	25.5	100,755	14	7,626	25,668
Allegheny	7.6	28.8	53,180	23	4,034	15,308
Washington, D.C.	6.4	12.6	109,199	12	6,948	13,757
Baltimore	5.7	21.1	267,354	6	15,223	56,484
Milwaukee	5.3	47.3	71,440	19	3,784	33,773
Richmond	2.4	7.4	51,038	24	1,239	3,778

Source: U.S. Census Office, Ninth Census, 1870 (Washington, D.C.: Government Printing Office, 1872), vol. 1, Table 8, pp. 386–391.
Note: This table includes the twenty-five cities with a population greater than 50,000 in 1870.

the Irish emerged. Table 2 shows that strong Irish-led Democratic machines were built in New York, Chicago, San Francisco, Pittsburgh, Jersey City, and Albany. In Philadelphia, as Dennis Clark argues, the Irish were handmaidens to a long-lived Republican machine they did not control.[22] Boston, the most Irish of the big cities, never rose above factional ward politics.

Mature machines exhibited certain characteristics. First, power was centralized in the hands of a single party boss. Second, the machine's power extended citywide. Despite pockets of opposition, mature machines commanded large electoral majorities. Consolidated machines also controlled most local offices and agencies and the patronage they commanded. Third, they exhibited staying power, winning several consecutive municipal elections and remaining in power for at least a decade. Fourth, machines trafficked primarily (but not exclusively) in divisible material benefits such as patronage jobs and welfare services. Political ideologies were foreign to the operation of the big-city machines. As a big-city machine politician remarked to James Bryce in 1880, "What are we here for except the offices?"[23]

Not only were there variations across cities in whether mature machines emerged, but there were also variations over time *within* machine cities in terms of the strength and longevity of the local party organization. In the late nineteenth century, Irish bosses built a first generation of Democratic machines in New York, San Francisco, Albany, and Jersey City. Of these four early machines, only Tammany Hall survived the debacle of 1896. During the Progressive era the Irish constructed a second generation of "reformed" machines in Albany and Jersey City. The New Deal realignment destabilized most of the entrenched Irish machines while spawning a third generation of more ethnically diverse Democratic machines in Chicago and Pittsburgh.

The temporal dimension of the Irish machines is of crucial importance. Each generation of machines embraced a distinct electoral coalition and set of policies. The four stages of Irish machine development considered in this study are as follows.

1840–1896. The Irish famine migration landed in the eastern cities in the late 1840s and early 1850s. By the late 1870s and early 1880s a first generation of Irish-run Democratic machines had emerged in New York (including Brooklyn, a separate city until

TABLE 2. *Machine Building in the Eight Cities, 1840–1985*

Political Regimes

	1840	1850	1860	1870	1880	1890	1900	1910	1920	1930	1940	1950	1960	1970	1980	1985
New York[a]	· · · Competitive Parties			Democratic Factionalism		Irish Democratic Machine (S) (Bosses Kelly, Croker, Murphy, Olvaney)					Fusion Reform	Italian Democratic Machine (W) (De Sapio)		Democratic & Fusion Reform		· · ·
Philadelphia			· · ·	Yankee Republican Machine (S)								Democratic Reform				· · ·
Chicago			· · ·	Democratic Factionalism						Yankee Republican Machine (W)	Irish Democratic Machine (S) (Kelly, Nash, Daley)			Democratic Factions		· · ·
Boston					· · · Irish Democratic Factionalism							Democratic Reform				· · ·

San Francisco	Nonpartisan Reform	Democratic and Labor Factions / Irish Democratic Machine (S) (Buckley) / Competitive Parties	Labor Machine (Ruef) (W)	Republican Reform		Democratic Reform
Pittsburgh	Yankee Republican Machine (S)			Republican Reform	Irish Democratic Machine (S) (Lawrence, Barr)	Democratic Reform
Jersey City	Irish Democratic Machine (W) (Davis)		Republican Reform	Irish Democratic Machine (S) (Hague)	Irish Democratic Machine (W) (Kenney)	Democratic Reform
Albany	Yankee-Irish Democratic Machine (W) (Herrick, McCabe)	Yankee Republican Machine (S)		Irish Democratic Machine (S) (O'Connell, Corning)		

Sources: Harold Zink, *City Bosses in the United States* (Durham, N.C.: Duke University Press, 1930); and Terry Nichols Clark, "The Irish Ethic and the Spirit of Patronage," *Ethnicity* 2 (1975): 327–343; as well as various sources cited in chapters 2–5.

Note: Regime typology based on (a) political structure; (b) dominant party; and (c) dominant ethnic group. Political structures: reform; competitive parties; one-party factionalism; weak machines (W); and strong machines (S).

[a] Manhattan until 1898; includes Brooklyn and the outer boroughs after 1898.

1898), San Francisco, Albany, and Jersey City. These cities featured large Irish voting populations *and* were in states with friendly Democratic governors. These early laissez-faire machines actively mobilized the Yankee and "old" immigrant—Irish, German, and English—working class. Because of the strength of their Republican opponents at both the local and state levels, these early machines pursued conservative fiscal, patronage, and labor policies. Lacking adequate patronage with which to co-opt the militant Irish working class, the early machines were plagued with working-class and immigrant insurgency.

1896–1928. A second generation of more long-lived Irish machines emerged during the Progressive era in Jersey City and Albany. The new machines differed from their nineteenth-century counterparts in key respects. First, they selectively mobilized the "old" but not the "new" immigrants, for example, the Irish but not the Jews or Italians. Second, they supported collective benefit programs such as Progressive-sponsored labor and social welfare legislation. Third, with the movement of the property-owning Yankee middle class to the suburbs, the ranks of the machine's opponents were reduced. The Irish machines could now pursue more expansionary fiscal policies with lessened risk of electoral reprisal. Expansionary fiscal policies increased the supply of patronage with which to reward restive working-class Irish voters. As ever-larger proportions of the Irish working class were drawn into the machine's patronage system, Irish enthusiasm for more radical labor politics diminished. The slowly mobilizing "new" ethnics were given services and symbolic recognition rather than patronage and power. However, the stability of the second-generation machines depended on restricting the newly arriving Southern and Eastern Europeans from electorally participating and making claims on the machine's resources.

1928–1950. The entrenched Irish machines became vulnerable to overthrow as the Depression depleted the patronage supply and as the New Deal party realignment finally mobilized the resentful Southern and Eastern Europeans. Yet the New Deal represented a machine-building as well as destabilizing force. In cities with weaker Democratic party organizations such as Chicago and Pittsburgh, the intraparty ethnic succession wars had been fought before the 1930s. In these cities, Irish bosses built a more ethnically diverse third generation of machines by capturing federal work relief patronage and by mobilizing and rewarding the new ethnics with power and jobs.

1950–1985. The postwar era marks a fourth and presumably final stage of machine development. Surviving Irish machines in Chicago, Pittsburgh, and Albany selectively mobilized middle-class white ethnics but not the newly arriving blacks and Hispanics. The postwar Irish machines offered a new set of locally financed policies: low taxes and homeowner services rather than the high taxes, massive patronage, and welfare services characteristic of earlier machines. As whites left the cities and the number of minorities grew, the postwar machines piggybacked federal welfare-state programs to appeal to the newer migrants. Welfare-state cutbacks politically galvanized blacks and threatened the remaining machines.

This study uses a wide variety of untapped data sources to study the electoral base, resources, and policies of big-city Irish machines. In terms of primary sources, I rely heavily on municipal reports, state blue books, federal census reports and program statistics, city directories, and newspaper almanacs. Municipal reports furnish valuable information on city revenue, spending and indebtedness patterns, patronage lists, voter registration, and election returns. State blue books yield lists of local public officials, public employees, and election returns. The dicennial federal census reports are a veritable gold mine of information on the big cities, particularly regarding ethnicity. They tell us about the ethnic composition of the big-city population, voting-age electorate, and specific groups of urban public employees such as policemen, firemen, teachers, and public officials. Federal program reports, such as those for AFDC and the WPA, furnish program expenditures and the number of recipients for various cities. Privately printed city directories provide rosters of local public officials and city employees. Finally, newspaper almanacs such as the New York World–Telegram *Almanac* and the Chicago Daily News *Almanac* yield big-city budgetary and electoral data in addition to lists of local party officials.

There are major reliability problems with many of these sources. The big-city machines were adept at their own version of double-entry bookkeeping: one set for the party bosses and one set for the public. Voter registration figures and election returns were padded for public consumption. City finances were systematically under-reported. Given these problems with primary sources, I have also used the massive secondary literature of books, articles, and dissertations on the politics of these machines, cities, and states.

The study is divided into two parts. The first part, consisting of Chapters 2 through 5, examines the four distinct stages of Irish-American machine politics: 1840–1896, 1896–1928, 1928–1950, and 1950–1985. The second part, consisting of Chapters 6 and 7, is theoretical. Chapter 6 examines machine building and the relation of party machines to the state. It focuses on the machine's life cycle: why centralized party organizations emerged in some cities and not in others, how machines maintained themselves, and what caused the machines' decline. The analysis also considers the clientelist perspective on the machine, placing the American big-city party organizations in broader comparative perspective. Chapter 7 addresses representational issues: the ways in which machines affected ethnic group political and economic life, and how machines shaped working-class politics. In particular, the chapter examines the machine's supposed "redistributional" function and the role of machines in producing America's muted version of working-class politics.

Chapter Two

Building the Nineteenth-Century Machines, 1840–1896

Introduction

Between 1846 and 1855 1.4 million Irish famine immigrants came to the United States. Though nearly all were rural cotters and laborers, more than 90 percent of the migrants would settle in the cities. The immigrants were field laborers, not farmers, in a single-crop economy. Only 6 percent of them would resettle on the land.

Because of the trans-Atlantic packet boat routes, most of the immigrants landed in the eastern port cities of Boston, New York, and Philadelphia. Lacking cash and the physical stamina to move inland, more than one-quarter of the famine immigrants would remain in these three cities. Parish priests encouraged them to stay in the eastern cities, where a network of Catholic churches already existed. Slowly, however, the uprooted followed canal and railroad projects, fanning out to the growing cities of New England, upstate New York, and the Great Lakes—New Haven, Providence, Albany, Buffalo, Cleveland, Detroit, and Chicago. Other port cities, particularly San Francisco, would also draw Irish immigrants. Not only had a rural people become overwhelmingly urban, they also settled in the largest cities. By 1870, 42 percent of the nation's 1.8 million Irish-born lived in the twenty-five cities with populations greater than 50,000. In contrast, only 10 percent of the country's 29 million native-born whites lived in the big cities.[1]

The Irish diaspora dramatically altered the complexion of the northern cities. In 1845, the Irish-born accounted for 2 percent of Boston's population; by 1855, 20 percent. By 1850 there were 133,730 Irish-born inhabitants of New York City, 26 percent of the total population. As of 1870, first-generation Irish constituted one-eighth of the population of the twenty-five largest cities. In 1870 the cities with the largest proportion of Irish-born residents included Boston, New York, Jersey City, Albany, New Haven, Brooklyn, Providence, San Francisco, Pittsburgh, and Philadelphia (see Table 1). If we add the American-born sons and daughters of Irish parents, the magnitude of the Celtic urban invasion becomes even more dramatic. In 1880, for example, an estimated one-third of New York City's residents were of Irish parentage.

The Irish migration to the cities soon took political form. The machine represented the dominant urban political institution of the late nineteenth century; the Irish were among its leading architects. The centralized big-city machines organized and linked the "input" and "output" dimensions of the local political system. On the input side, precinct captains mobilized the electorate. Local bosses controlled party caucuses and conventions and thus nominations to local office. By controlling voters and officeholders, the machine could control the output side of politics—patronage jobs, contracts, franchises, and services.

The machine maintained itself in power by skillfully deploying these resources. Bosses purchased voter support with individual economic inducements such as offers of public jobs or services rather than by appeals to traditional loyalties or to class-based interests. Tangible divisible benefits also disciplined the party's rank and file. Minor party officials were themselves municipal employees. Powerful ward chieftains were often rewarded with a share of the patronage commensurate with their district's share of the total party vote. Thus the machine sustained itself by exchanging material benefits for political support.[2]

The roots of the early big-city machines can be traced to the second or Jacksonian party system of the 1820s and 1830s. By the 1830s property requirements for voting in local elections had been relaxed. At the same time, the patronage or spoils system came to be perfected as an instrument of party discipline. By the 1840s party organization had taken on its modern geographical and hierarchical form. Battalions of precinct workers organized urban neighborhoods, reporting to precinct and ward captains, who in turn reported to the downtown bosses. In the 1840s party managers perfected new devices to swell the ranks of party loyalists. To capture the votes of the burgeoning immigrant population, Tammany Hall opened its famous Naturalization Bureau in 1840. An instant success, the department naturalized 11,000 foreigners by 1844.

In the 1850s embryonic and short-lived machines appeared in cities such as San Francisco and New York. In San Francisco, David Broderick, of Irish descent and recently arrived from Tammany Hall, briefly organized the city's Irish and German working class. Recognizing that voter loyalty could be purchased with a system of material payoffs, Broderick quickly tripled municipal expenditures and indebtedness. Broderick's tactics were emulated in New York City by Mayor Fernando Wood, the native-born darling of the city's foreign-born. During his administration, city outlays also tripled, from $3.2 to $9.8 million. Between 1855 and 1865, the number of naturalized voters in the city nearly doubled, from 43,000 to 78,000, while the number of native-born voters barely increased from 46,000 to 52,000. These embryonic machines dissolved in the party realignment and protean intraparty factionalism of the late 1850s. The mature long-lived machine would be a product of the third rather than the second party system.[3]

The Irish Role in Building the Early Machines: Four Questions

By 1890 Irish bosses ran most of the big-city Democratic machines constructed in the 1870s and 1880s. The Celtic bosses included Tammany Hall's Kelly and Croker, Brooklyn's McLaughlin, the Bay Area's Buckley, Buffalo's Sheenan, Jersey City's Davis, and Albany's Patrick McCabe. The Irish had also taken over the Democratic party in cities where centralized machines had not been built. For example, Mike McDonald led the Democrats in the Windy City, and Pat Maguire led them in the Hub. The Irish dominated the lower echelons of the urban Democratic party as well. By 1886, the Irish held 58 percent of the seats on the San Francisco Democratic party central committee. Sixty-nine percent of the members of Chicago's Democratic committee were Irish in 1890.

By 1892, the brogue had replaced Tammany's secret Indian hand-shake; 61 percent of the Tammany Society officers were Irish.[4]

Notwithstanding the prominence of the Irish in the early big-city machines, four issues can be raised regarding their role in machine building. First, what accounts for their unusually high group political participation rates? The Irish capture of the urban Democratic party depended on a large Irish voting bloc. In city after city the Irish mobilized politically much more quickly than other ethnic groups. Irish naturalization and voter registration rates were the highest of the immigrant groups. The Irish talent for electoral politics extended to high turnout rates and bloc voting for machine candidates. Some of the differences between ethnic groups in levels of group electoral participation can be attributed to the later arrival of the Southern and Eastern Europeans. By the 1880s most Irish-born adult males were voting; the "new" ethnics were barely getting off the boat. Yet even ethnic groups such as the Germans, who arrived at the same time as the Irish, had lower voter participation rates. To the extent that Irish power initially rested on group mobilization (and perhaps on the nonmobilization of other ethnic groups), what explains the differences in ethnic voter participation rates, particularly among the first wave of "old" European immigrants?

Second, although the Irish quickly mobilized in most cities, there was no one-to-one relationship between cities with large Irish-American populations (and thus numbers of voters) and cities in which Irish-run machines emerged in the late nineteenth century. In contrast with New York, Brooklyn, San Francisco, Jersey City, and Albany, where Irish machines were created, other cities with large Celtic populations did not produce centralized machines, or, if they emerged, they were controlled by other groups. Boston, the most Irish of the American cities, never produced a centralized machine. In Philadelphia and Pittsburgh, the state Republican machine built local Yankee-run GOP machines in the aftermath of the Civil War. In both of these cities, the Irish-American vote was split, the most enterprising shifting into the Republican camp. Save for a few contractors, Irish political influence was limited. In Chicago, another city with a large Irish population, competitive two-party politics and intraparty factionalism were the characteristic forms of politics in the late nineteenth century. In the twentieth century, it would take non-Irishman Anton Cermak to unite the various Irish factions in the Windy City and construct a citywide machine. Why did centralized Irish machines emerge in some of the cities with large numbers of Irish voters and not in others?

Third, why did the Irish urban machines of the late nineteenth century pursue politically risky conservative fiscal and patronage policies? In the Irish cities, the sharpest increases in city expenditures occurred in the 1860s and 1870s, *before* centralized machines were created and before the Irish controlled them. Once in power, the first generation of Irish bosses were guardians of Yankee fiscal orthodoxy. Yet conservative fiscal policies made the fledgling Irish machines extremely vulnerable to revolts from below. In cities such as New York and San Francisco, the early Irish machines had little patronage to dispense to immigrant working-class voters. With few rewards, working-class grievances against the machines mounted. As a consequence, the urban working class, the core constituency of the Democratic party, often revolted against the early machines, supporting local labor parties instead. Given the rainbow theory's account of substantial machine resources, their allocation to impoverished voters, and the supposed ensuing support of working-class voters for machine candidates, what accounts for the paucity of early machine resources and for the machine's inability to fully win the allegiance of the urban ethnic working class?

Fourth, notwithstanding the folklore about the ability of large numbers of Irish to use political routes of economic advancement, it appears that the early machine's fiscal conservatism limited the number of patronage jobs available for distribution. What were the resources of the early Irish-run machines? How much patronage was there and what share went to the Irish? In the absence of patronage, what kinds of appeals did the early Irish bosses make to working-class Irish voters? How successful were nonmaterial appeals?

Students of machine politics have grappled with these intertwined issues of ethnic political behavior and early machine building. "Mass" or group theorists trace the distinctive big-city political style of groups such as the Irish to their European background. Daniel Patrick Moynihan, for example, argues that early nineteenth-century Irish village life laid the foundations for later urban machines such as Tammany Hall.[5]

If Moynihan is correct about the Old World roots of the Irish machines, then how do we account for the fact that the same social conditions gave birth to much different patterns of Irish political participation in late nineteenth-century Ireland? In the context of an agrarian economy, Ireland produced a nationalist politics organized around the causes of land reform and home rule. In the context of an industrializing urban economy, Irish-Americans produced a mass politics of party, organization, and patronage. To understand Irish-*American* politics, one must look to New World as well as Old World roots.[6]

Likewise, group theorists would explain the fiscal conservatism of the first generation of Irish machines in terms of traditional Catholic values imported from Ireland. In subsequent pages I argue that there are weaknesses in this account of early machine fiscal behavior. The Irish-American community of the late nineteenth century was not monolithically conservative, as the group model would imply. In particular, the urban Irish working class grew increasingly militant and alienated from the early machines in the 1870s and 1880s. The conservatism of the Irish party bosses was as much a *consequence* as a cause of machine politics. I argue that the machine's maintenance needs, not a Catholic view of a static social order, introduced a cautious strain into early Irish political leadership.

Elite theorists have also addressed these questions. Martin Shefter, for example, has argued that machines emerged in some cities and not in others because of differences in local political alliances. Successful machine builders forged alliances with the conservative business community. I will argue that political alliances had to be developed vertically as well as horizontally, to the state capital as well as to the downtown business club. Machine fortunes heavily depended on which party or faction controlled the statehouse. State election laws affected the machine's ability to naturalize, register, and win the votes of the immigrants. State laws affected the machine's capacity to increase local taxes and indebtedness. State patronage significantly increased the machine's supply of public jobs.[7]

Irish-American Politics:
Old and New World Roots

For the Irish, there were Old World roots to their political skills, intense group solidarity, and the high value they placed on the economic rewards of politics. In Ireland, English Ascendancy produced the Penal Laws, a series of parliamentary acts passed between 1695 and 1746, which were designed to weaken Catholicism, the religion of 90 percent of Ireland's population, by reducing Catholics to a position of economic and political inferiority relative to Protestants. The Penal Laws restricted Catholic ownership and inheritance of land. Catholics were denied the privileges of voting, of holding public office, and of practicing law. The combined effect of these impositions was to forge a common bond of solidarity as Irish Catholics were reduced to penury and powerlessness.[8]

The struggle to repeal the Penal Laws, culminating in Catholic Emancipation in 1829, brought the Irish experience with mass political organization and with local electoral manipulation. In the early nineteenth century, Daniel O'Connell built the first Irish mass political organization. His Catholic Association sought religious and political emancipation, using parish priests to collect a "Catholic rent" from their parishioners to finance the organization's political activities. The association also pressured the recently enfranchised Catholic freehold voters to support the association's candidates in municipal elections. The Penal Laws' restrictions on Catholic voting and office holding had been somewhat relaxed in the 1790s. In 1793, the vote was given to Catholic tenants whose holdings yielded an annual interest of at least 40 shillings. Similar to English extraparliamentary organizations of the time, O'Connell's association secured votes and offices with promises of patronage. As Emmet Larkin has argued, by the late 1820s O'Connell's "unified national phalanx" of mobilized clergy and tenant farmers represented an "embryo Irish national state."[9]

The Irish would also benefit politically from the spread of the national educational system in the early nineteenth century. Although some argue that this nondenominational system was primarily designed to weaken its informal Catholic counterpart, the hedge schools, it is clear that the national system soon gained popularity with both the peasantry and the clergy. The Gaelic-speaking peasants wanted the economic and social advantages that speaking English might bring. The clergy wanted control of the financial and job patronage available from the system. With the increasing popularity of the educational system, the proportion of the population that spoke English rose dramatically, from an estimated 50 percent in 1800 to 95 percent in 1851. Literacy rates also rose. At least one-half of the famine emigrants were literate in English.[10]

Thus the Irish came to the New World with political advantages that other groups, such as the Germans, did not possess. German political unification would be achieved only in 1870. Class, regional, and religious differences divided the migrating Germans. Religion, especially, would split the German-American vote; German Catholics would gravitate to the Democratic party while German Lutherans would vote Republican. Language barriers would lengthen the process of naturalization and thus retard the development of potential voting strength. Finally, by arriving with farming, mercantile, and technical skills, the Germans, unlike the unskilled Irish, would not be as attracted by the economic payoffs of political participation.[11]

It would be a mistake, however, to view growing Irish-American involvement in urban politics, compared with groups such as the Germans, as solely the product of political values and skills imported from the struggle against the English. The development of the American party system also shaped the character of Irish-American political participation. The famine Irish arrived as the parties were entering their modern or mobilization phase. Urban Irish immigrants served as electoral cannon fodder in the competitive bidding wars among Democrats, Whigs, and Republicans. By the 1830s, internal improvements had become a "bipartisan obsession." The parties vigorously solicited Irish voters by offering them jobs on canal and highway projects.[12]

In the 1850s, after the Irish had been introduced to the electoral process and the patronage system, the party system buckled under the combined weight of sectionalism and nativism. The Irish migration was the largest Catholic migration to date. As Robert Kelley notes, "Few issues caused such continuing turbulence in the transatlantic Anglo-American community as the 'Irish Question.' . . . The Irish, in short, were the people who played the role of 'blacks' in British life, and in the United States, the same attitudes toward them persisted. . . . The arrival of the Catholic Irish, therefore, immediately shifted all political equations in America."[13] With the nativist reaction to Irish Catholics in the 1850s, signified by the rise of the Know-Nothing party and by the subsequent shift of many Protestant groups into the Republican party, Irish Catholic identification with the Democratic party was further solidified. In the years after 1860, the Irish Catholic vote would be heavily Democratic.

The Irish quickly mobilized in the big cities. Coming in the late 1840s, large numbers of Irish were soon naturalized and voting. By 1855, for example, more than one-fifth of New York's and Boston's voters were Irish, their numbers tripling since 1850. In the late nineteenth century, Irish naturalization, registration, and turnout rates regularly exceeded those of other groups, even the early-arriving Germans. Table 3 displays ethnic group voter registration rates for San Francisco in 1900. In the Bay Area, the proportion of Irish-born registered voters was nearly double that of the city's other foreign-born—70 percent versus 37 percent—and nearly equaled the rate for the native-born. In contrast, only 57 percent of the Germans were registered. The Irish also had higher turnout and bloc voting rates in San Francisco, further increasing their electoral leverage. In the five local and state elections held between 1894 and 1902, Democratic candidates received more than 60 percent of the total vote in the four most heavily Irish Assembly Districts (ADs 29–32) compared with less than 50 percent of the vote in the three heavily German districts (ADs 37, 39–40).[14]

The other Irish cities also featured higher rates of Irish electoral participation. In Boston, for example, 60 percent of the Irish-born males were registered voters in 1885 compared with 37 percent of the non-Irish. The midwestern cities, with alien suffrage laws allowing immigrants filing their first naturalization papers to vote, had higher immigrant voter registration rates than the eastern cities. Sixty-two percent of Chicago's foreign-born were registered to vote in 1892 compared with 39 percent of Boston's immigrants. Yet even in the Windy City the Irish were more politically active than other ethnic groups. Seventy-seven percent of the city's Irish-born were registered to vote in the 1892 presidential election compared with 64 percent of the Germans. Second-generation Irish

TABLE 3. *Gaining Political Leverage: Naturalizing and Registering the Immigrants, San Francisco, 1900*

Ethnic Group[a]	Citizens as Percentage of Voting-Age Males	Registered Voters as Percentage of Voting-Age Males	Total Number of Voting-Age Males	Total Number of Adult Male Citizens	Total Number of Registered Voters
Irish	95.3	69.6	11,871	11,310	8,261
Yankee[b]	100.0	72.6	62,251	62,251	45,189
Non-Irish immigrants	66.0	36.8	54,863	36,219	20,183
German	90.7	56.5	14,297	12,966	8,082
British	83.6	51.5	6,947	5,806	3,581
Scandinavian	85.0	37.9	6,311	5,367	2,390
Canadian	86.7	60.9	2,248	2,223	1,561
Italian	51.0	19.7	4,128	2,107	814
French	62.4	28.9	2,256	1,596	738
Chinese	4.3	0.1	9,601	414	7
Other immigrants	67.8	34.3	8,775	5,740	3,010
All voting-age males	71.2	57.1	128,985	109,780	73,633

Sources: U.S. Census Office, *Twelfth Census of the United States, 1900* (Washington, D.C.: Government Printing Office, 1901), vol. 1, Tables 82, 83, pp. 936–945; San Francisco Board of Supervisors, *San Francisco Municipal Reports, 1900–1901* (San Francisco: W. H. Hinton, 1901), pp. 373–374.
[a] By country of birth.
[b] Includes all native-born.

were even more politically active than their fathers, further augmenting Celtic voting strength. In New York City, for example, first- and second-generation Irish constituted one-quarter of the population but one-third of the registered voters in 1890.[15]

State Politics and the Building of the Early Irish Machines

A large Irish voting bloc was a necessary but not a sufficient condition for building the Irish machines. Irish voter registration and turnout rates were high throughout *all* eight cities surveyed. Irish machines, however, were built in the 1880s in some of these big cities and not in others. Irish bosses constructed strong centralized machines in New York (and soon-to-be-annexed Brooklyn), San Francisco, Jersey City, and Albany, but *not* in Boston, Philadelphia, Pittsburgh, or Chicago.

What accounts for machines emerging in some cities with large numbers of Irish voters and not in others? Two post–Civil War state party developments shaped urban machine building. First, in states such as New York and New Jersey, the Republicans unintentionally strengthened fledgling urban Democratic party organizations. In the late 1860s Radical Republicans embarked on a program of "urban reconstruction." Yet reconstruction backfired, further driving the immigrants into the Democratic party and enabling the Democrats to strengthen their formal party apparatus at the precinct and ward levels. Second, in New York, New Jersey, and California, pro-machine Democratic governors were elected in the 1870s and 1880s. Pro-machine governors strengthened the big-city party organizations in a variety of ways, particularly by channeling state patronage to them and by denying state resources to the machine's reform opponents. In other states, however, unfriendly Republican *and* Democratic governors and legislatures hindered the building of big-city machines.

The Radical Republican Attack

Near the end of the Civil War, Radical Republicans captured control of the New England and Middle Atlantic states. Their program of "reconstruction at home" attempted to weaken the emerging Democratic urban machines in two key ways: by making it harder for the Democrats to register immigrant voters and by loosening Democratic control over the saloons, the police, and the fire departments.

The Radicals tightened state suffrage laws in order to reduce the number of immigrant Democratic voters. In New York, the Radical-controlled state legislature passed a stringent voter registration law that applied only to New York City. At the 1867 state constitutional convention, Radicals such as Governor Reuben E. Fenton dominated the proceedings. The Radicals championed black suffrage but proposed lengthening the time period before naturalized immigrants would be eligible to vote. In New Jersey, the Republican-controlled state legislature passed a "sunset" act that closed the polls at dusk, making it more difficult for workers to vote. Adding insult to injury, the Garden State Republicans passed a voter registration law that applied only to the Democratic strongholds of Jersey City and Newark.[16]

At the national level, Radicals in Congress passed legislation designed to reduce fraudulent naturalization, registration, and voting by the urban Democrats. The Enforcement Act of 1870, passed to protect the constitutional rights of newly freed blacks, contained two sections designed to weaken the Democratic city organizations. Election frauds such as false registration and repeat voting were made federal offenses if perpetrated in federal elections. Furthermore, federal marshals were authorized to supervise these elections and to use federal troops if necessary to promote honest elections.

The Naturalization Act, also passed by Congress in 1870, posed an even greater threat to the Democratic city machines. The act tightened federal controls over the issuance of naturalization papers by *state* courts and extended to six months the period before which newly naturalized citizens were eligible to vote. The act also gave U.S. circuit court judges extraordinary powers over the conduct of national *and* state elections in cities with populations greater than 20,000. Federal judges were authorized to appoint commissioners to oversee voter registration, challenge voters, and count ballots in the cities.[17]

Suffrage restrictions and federal control over the electoral process were not the only means the Radicals employed to weaken the Democrats' ability to mobilize urban voters. In the nineteenth century, the cities did not have home rule charters and thus could be ruled by whichever party controlled the state. The Radicals used their control of the state executive and legislative branches to implement a program of urban institutional reform. State-controlled boards and commissions would supplant city agencies in performing such critical functions as public safety, health, and the licensing of saloons. The Radical program was largely designed to weaken the Democratic-controlled local institutions—the police and fire departments and saloons—responsible for organizing immigrant voters.

In New York there were prewar precedents for state interference in New York City's governance. In 1857, state Republicans had stripped the New York City police department, an important Tammany tool for revenue raising and for controlling the ballot box, from Democratic Mayor Fernando Wood's control and had placed the department under state control. The Republicans created the New York Board of Supervisors strictly as a state institution. Unlike similar boards in other counties of the state, the city board had no independent taxation authority. The board could levy only those taxes decreed by the Republican-controlled state legislature. The state legislature, in turn, was required yearly to pass a special act declaring the amount needed for the city's budget.[18]

New York's Radical Republican politicians adopted other measures to weaken the institutional base of the Democratic party in cities such as New York, Albany, and Buffalo. The Metropolitan Fire Department Act of 1865 created a state-controlled paid fire department in New York City, weakening the volunteer fire departments. As James Mohr notes, the local fire companies by the mid-1850s had become de facto Tammany ward organizations, particularly in Irish neighborhoods as the Irish had begun to man the fire lines. The Metropolitan Health Law of 1866 created a state-controlled metropolitan sanitary district to enforce health regulations and the city's excise laws. Besides stripping Tammany of street-cleaning contracts, the new law gave the health board liquor licensing power over the city's saloons, the heart of Tammany's ward organizations.[19]

Radicals in New York sought as well to neutralize upstate urban sources of Democratic strength with state boards and commissions. The Radical-dominated legislature created the Albany Capital Police District in 1865 and Buffalo's Niagara Police District shortly thereafter. Rochester, a more Republican city, received no state police commission.

Radical Republicans in other eastern states with big-city Democratic strongholds pursued similar programs of "urban reconstruction." To quell growing Irish influence in Jersey City, the Garden State's Republicans abolished the city's elected police chief and replaced the position with a state-appointed police commission. In 1871, the Republican-dominated state legislature abolished the city's government, replacing it with a series of state-appointed commissions. In Massachusetts, Radicals created state police and health boards, stripping the cities of their authority.[20]

Besides threatening the ability of the Democrats to mobilize urban voters, state-run commissions significantly reduced the number of patronage jobs controlled by local machines. In New York, for example, the Radicals succeeded in drying up most locally controlled patronage. By 1868 the Democratic-run city council controlled less than one-sixth of the city's expenditures.

Yet the Radical Republican attack on the Democratic machines backfired. Arguing that they were being treated like surrogate southerners, Tammany's leaders "work[ed] the naturalization mill full blast" and perfected their party organization. With its informal institutional base in the police department, volunteer fire departments, and saloons weakened, Tammany turned to strengthening the formal party organization. By the late 1860s representatives of the Wigwam manned all 230 election districts, linked by a strong chain of command.[21]

The Radical plan to institute black suffrage while tightening voter qualifications for foreign-born whites solidified immigrant support for the Democratic machines. In New York City, Irish support for Tammany had waned during the Civil War because the Irish felt they had not received a fair share of patronage in exchange for their votes. Tammany defused the incipient Irish rebellion by attacking the Radicals' new voter registration law. In Jersey City, the Republican attack forced the Irish to close ranks behind Robert Davis, ending middle-class Irish insurgency against the Democratic party leadership.

The Election of Pro-Machine Governors

A second and more important state party development affected urban machine building. With the waning of Radical Republican strength in the 1870s and the resurgence of the northern Democratic party, the embryonic city machines needed a prolonged gestation period protected by a sympathetic Democratic state administration. Friendly Democratic governors could strengthen machines in various ways. By channeling state patronage through the emerging machines, governors withheld vital resources from the machine's reform opponents. Pro-machine governors also minimized the harm done by Republican-controlled legislatures. But unsympathetic Democratic governors could seriously retard machine building. Antimachine governors could fuel the ambitions of local reformers by giving them state jobs.

The role of state Democratic politicians in successively promoting urban factionalism and then machine consolidation is illustrated in New York City politics in the 1870s and 1880s. Determined to resurrect Tammany Hall in the wake of Boss William Marcy Tweed's downfall in 1871, Irishman John Kelly invited Samuel Tilden and other respectable Democratic businessmen and lawyers into the Wigwam. Once Tammany was made respectable, Boss Kelly attempted to oust the so-called Swallow-tails, Tilden's wealthy entourage whom Kelly had brought in as window dressing. After supporting Tilden for governor in 1874, Kelly split with him after the election over matters of patronage. Tilden aligned himself with Irving Hall, an anti-Tammany Democratic club, and directed state patronage in that direction. Tilden's successor and friend, Lucius Robinson, also aligned himself with the anti-Kelly forces in the party. In a move reminiscent of his break with Tilden, Kelly later broke with newly elected Democratic Governor Grover Cleveland over state patronage allocations. Cleveland then aligned himself (and delivered state jobs) to the County Democracy, Tammany's most powerful rival club in the 1880s.

Thus a succession of anti-Tammany Democratic governors were elected in the 1870s and 1880s. They underwrote the anti-Tammany party factions, particularly Irving Hall and the County Democracy, with generous allocations of state patronage. Only with the election in 1885 of a more pro-Tammany governor, David B. Hill, was state assistance redirected. Governor Hill was originally intent on placating all factions in the city—the Tammany, Irving, County, and Brooklyn party organizations. Beset with leadership scandals and the defection of key supporters to Tammany, and weakened by attempted fusion with the Republicans, the County Democracy began to collapse in the late 1880s. Governor Hill immediately built an implicit alliance with Tammany by opposing state ballot reform—the replacement of party-printed and distributed ballots—and began redirecting state patronage to Tammany. By similar tactics, Hill also strengthened the Democratic machine being built upstate in Albany.[22]

Pro-machine governors were also elected in New Jersey and California in the 1880s, aiding Irish urban bosses in these states in consolidating their rule. In New Jersey, Democratic Governor Leon Abbett formed an alliance with the Irish boss of Jersey City, Robert Davis. Abbett gave state patronage to Davis rather than to his Yankee reform opponents and in other ways protected Davis and his organization from hostile action by the Republican-controlled state legislature.[23]

In California, San Francisco's Boss Chris Buckley strengthened his organization by adroit alignment with the ascendant wings of the state Democratic party. In 1882, Buckley joined the antimonopolist wing in electing George Stoneman as governor. As public support for Stoneman waned, Buckley switched to the conservative wing. In 1886, Buckley succeeded in securing the Democratic gubernatorial nomination for Washington Bartlett, the conservative mayor of San Francisco. With Bartlett's narrow victory, Buckley maintained his influence over the allocation of state patronage.[24]

Unfriendly State Administrations

In Massachusetts, Pennsylvania, and Illinois, however, the state party system hindered the building of Irish Democratic machines in Boston, Philadelphia, Pittsburgh, and Chicago in the late nineteenth century. In Massachusetts, Irish-born Pat Maguire had emerged by the mid-1870s as the "first among equals" in Boston's Democratic party. In 1885, under Maguire's tutelage, the city elected Hugh O'Brien as its first Irish Catholic mayor.[25]

The Radical Republicans unwittingly aided Maguire's machine-building efforts. As the Irish began to demand political power in the Hub after the Civil War, Radical Republicans such as Frank Bird and Governors Alexander Bullock and William Claflin pursued a program of urban reconstruction. The governor was given the power to appoint the Boston police commission and liquor licensing board. The Republican-controlled legislature established a taxation limit for Boston, the only city in the country where such a state-imposed limit existed. The state also strictly regulated the city's debt. Boston could not raise its debt above 2.5 percent of assessed valuation without permission from the state legislature.

Despite supporting legislation removing civil and political liabilities for blacks and Indians, the Radicals stalled on removing constitutional restrictions for white immigrants. In 1857, Republicans and Know-Nothings had joined to impose a literacy test on voting. In 1859, naturalized immigrants were barred from voting or holding office until they had been citizens for two years. Fearful of growing Irish voting strength in Boston, the Radicals refused to extend their antidiscriminatory campaign to the white immigrants.[26]

The Republican program to weaken Irish Democratic control of Boston succeeded in solidifying Irish support for the Democratic party. Yet Maguire's efforts to build a Boston Tammany were frustrated in the 1870s and 1880s by weaknesses in the state Democratic party. The state's Democrats entered the 1880s with a reputation that made the party a "byword for incapacity." In 1882, profiting from an economic downturn and from Republican factionalism at the state and national levels, Ben Butler, a born-again Democrat, was elected as only the second Democratic governor since the Civil War. Butler was unable to centralize the city's politics. Having campaigned primarily on the issue of retrenchment (accusing the Republicans of fiscal extravagance) and facing a hostile Republican-controlled legislature, Butler's short-lived administration was a negative and divisive one characterized by "government by veto." With little state patronage to reward the Boston Irish in return for their support, Butler was defeated by the Republicans in 1883. The Republicans, in turn, controlled the state for the rest of this crucial machine-building decade.[27]

Pat Maguire's only opportunity to use state patronage from a friendly Democratic administration to centralize the city's politics was briefly presented in 1890. Yankee Democrat William E.

"Billy" Russell was elected governor in that year. State patronage became the litmus test of Russell's relationship with the Boston Irish "saloon Democrats." Writing to Russell, Congressman Joseph H. O'Neill, a Maguire political ally, warned: "I hope you will not make the mistake of F. O. Prince [a Yankee who was elected Boston's mayor in the 1870s] who believed that there were [only] a half dozen men with Irish blood who had brains but that the balance was fit only to fill places with less than a thousand a year. You can well afford to divide even." Though handicapped by a Republican-controlled state legislature, Governor Russell gave as much state patronage as he could to the Boston Irish during his three one-year terms in office.[28]

Maguire's ability to construct a durable city machine with state patronage and to halt what one observer termed the "growing feudalization of the party" was interrupted by the depression of 1893 and the resulting loss of city hall and the statehouse. With Maguire's death in 1896, the process of feudalization accelerated. The remnants of the Maguire machine were liquidated, and the party was drawn and quartered by feuding Irish political chieftains. As early as 1892, John F. "Honey Fitz" Fitzgerald defeated Maguire ally O'Neill and seized control of the North End. Martin Lomasney was installed as the ward boss of the West End, and Patrick J. Kennedy (father of Joseph P.) took control of the East End. Soon James Michael Curley, later mayor and governor, emerged to control the South End. The Hub's Irish Democratic politics would be faction-ridden from this time onward.[29]

With the Boston Irish divided, Yankees from the western part of Massachusetts solidified control over the state party. When Democratic governors were occasionally elected, as was Yankee William Douglas in 1904, they did little to centralize Irish power in Boston. Governor Douglas actually worked to *reduce* the influence of the Irish in the state party and directed state patronage away from the Hub's contentious Irish ward bosses.[30]

A different set of state political forces hindered Irish machine building in the Middle Atlantic and North Central states that skirted the Mason-Dixon line, particularly in Pennsylvania and Illinois. In the post–Civil War era, the GOP normally controlled these states. Yet GOP state hegemony was threatened by a possible urban-rural Democratic alliance. There were large numbers of immigrants in cities such as Philadelphia, Pittsburgh, and Chicago. Large numbers of ex-southern Democrats lived in the rural southernmost counties of these states. In order to prevent an alliance between the urban foreign-born and the downstate native-born Democrats, the Republicans built their own machines in cities such as Philadelphia and Pittsburgh as offshoots of the state machine.[31]

In Philadelphia, Democratic factionalism in the 1850s encouraged a Republican machine to develop. The prewar Democracy (as the early Democratic party was called) was split between an American (i.e., native-born Protestant) and an Irish Catholic wing. As the Republicans rose to power, Irish Democrats were isolated in the First Congressional District in South Philadelphia. With the consolidation of a Republican urban machine in the 1870s, David Martin, the local protégé of Republican state boss Matthew Quay, began encouraging the recruitment of the Irish into the GOP machine. In particular, Martin wooed Irish contractors with public works contracts. The Irish contractors, in turn, delivered the votes of their Irish laborers to the machine.[32] In Pittsburgh, the state GOP also created a strong local machine during the Civil War. In the postwar era, the Steel City machine would serve as an integral part of the powerful state Republican machine run by Simon Cameron. As in Philadelphia, the large Irish vote was split as the politically ambitious joined the Republican party.

Even in cities with large Irish populations, late nineteenth-century Republican urban machines were decidedly different from their Democratic counterparts. Democratic machines were constructed from the bottom up. Rooted in the institutional life of ethnic neighborhoods—saloons, clubhouses, volunteer fire departments—Democratic machines extended upward to the city, county, and state levels. Republican machines were constructed, in Lincoln Steffens's phrase, "in the air," that is, from the top down. As adjuncts to state machines, GOP urban machines relied heavily on federal and state rather than local patronage. Designed to prevent Democratic control of the cities and a possible challenge to GOP state hegemony, Republican organizations encouraged political passivity and nonparticipation on the part of the immigrant working class.[33]

In Illinois, the state party system inhibited both Republicans and Democrats from constructing a Chicago machine in the nineteenth century. The Windy City's Mike McDonald, the Irish Democratic party leader, attempted to build a local machine in the 1870s. But McDonald's efforts were frustrated by Republican predominance in the state, which lasted from the Civil War to World War I. In the postbellum era, General John A. "Black Jack" Logan fashioned a Republican state machine by monopolizing federal patronage. Yet Chicago-downstate tensions plagued Republican state politics, and Logan was unable to construct a Republican machine in Chicago.[34]

Even with the state Republicans weakened by factionalism, the Windy City's Democrats were unable to use their occasional control of state government to construct a citywide machine. By the early 1890s, two major factions had emerged in the Chicago Democratic party. Mayors Carter Henry Harrison I and II both campaigned on a "personal liberty" (Sunday drinking) platform. Both developed a broad base of ethnic political support, including Germans, Slavs, and Irish saloonkeeper-politicians such as "Bathhouse John" Coughlin and "Hinky Dink" Kenna, bosses of the downtown First Ward. Yet the Harrisons' party leadership was challenged by John Hopkins and Roger Sullivan, leaders of the so-called gas crowd faction, because of Sullivan's presidency of the Ogden Gas Company. The Hopkins-Sullivan faction drew the support of most of the remaining Irish ward leaders.[35]

In the political upheavals of the early 1890s, radical Democrat John Altgeld was elected governor of Illinois. Rather than reducing party factionalism in Chicago through the adroit use of state patronage, Altgeld succeeded in further inflaming the factional divisions. The governor alienated the more conservative Sullivan faction by vetoing utility give-away legislation. He alienated the Harrison faction by opposing the younger Harrison's mayoral reelection bid in 1899. Lacking a friendly Democratic state administration, neither faction was able to consolidate its control over party and city. Chicago's Irish-controlled Democratic machine would emerge only in the twentieth century.[36]

Thus we have seen the importance of the state party system in shaping the fortunes of the early Irish machines. Radical Republicans pursued a program of electoral and institutional reform in the eastern states with urban Democratic (and Irish) strongholds. Rather than weakening the embryonic Democratic city organizations, the Radical attack succeeded in strengthening these machines. The election of pro-machine Democratic governors in states such as New York, New Jersey, and California further aided Irish machine building.

The Radical program of urban reconstruction was less necessary in the Middle Atlantic and North Central states where big-city GOP organizations were stronger. Yet in the northern states along the Mason-Dixon line, a possible alliance of city and country Democrats could have upset the consolidating Republican state machines. To prevent such an alliance, the Pennsylvania state GOP organization, for example, constructed adjunct urban machines in Philadelphia and Pittsburgh. In Illinois, however, where the Republican state organization was increasingly faction-ridden and where an antimachine Democrat was elected governor, neither party was able to build a centralized machine in the Windy City in the late nineteenth century.

Conservative Machine Policies and Revolts from Below

Once we understand how (to borrow Lincoln Steffens's phrase again) the early Irish machines were built both from the bottom up—by group mobilization—*and* from the top down—by state party alliances—a third question presents itself. Why did the new machines immediately embark on a program of retrenchment, thereby alienating working-class voters?

Table 4 examines changes in per capita spending for the big cities between 1880 and 1902. The Irish cities were far heavier spenders under Yankee than Irish rule. In 1880, before the Irish political conquest, outlays in the Irish machine cities of New York, San Francisco, Jersey City, and Albany averaged $30 per capita. In Boston, soon to be Irish-run but faction-ridden, the per capita outlay of $51 was among the highest in the country. Republican machines spent less, even where there were large numbers of Irish to feed. Per capita spending in the GOP strongholds of Philadelphia and Pittsburgh averaged $22. In competitive-party Chicago, where numerous boards and commissions performed traditional municipal functions, per capita outlays were significantly smaller ($12) than in Democratic or Republican machine cities. In the fourteen

TABLE 4.   *Machine Retrenchment, 1880–1902*

Cities and Regimes	Average Per Capita City Outlays ($)		Percentage Change from 1880 to 1902
	1880	*1902*	
Irish cities (8)	29	18	−37.9
Irish Democratic machine (New York, San Francisco, Jersey City, Albany)	30	17	−43.3
Irish Democratic nonmachine (Boston)	51	35	−31.4
Non-Irish Republican machine (Philadelphia, Pittsburgh)	22	16	−27.3
Non-Irish nonmachine (Chicago)	12	11	−8.3
Non-Irish cities (14)[a]	15	15	0

Sources: U.S. Census Office, *Report on Valuation, Taxation, and Public Indebtedness: 1880* (Washington, D.C.: Government Printing Office, 1884), Table 4, pp. 218–247; U.S. Bureau of the Census, *Special Reports: Statistics of Cities, 1902* (Washington, D.C.: Government Printing Office, 1902), Table 21, pp. 252–299.

[a] Includes all cities with more than 50,000 population *and* less than 13 percent Irish. See Table 1, p. 18.

remaining cities with populations of more than 50,000 (see Table 1), with smaller Irish populations and fewer machines, per capita municipal spending averaged only $15.[37]

The fledgling Irish machines soon performed a fiscal about-face. Between 1880 and 1902, average per capita outlays in the four Irish machine cities plummeted 43 percent, from $30 to $17. Public spending in politically fragmented Boston fell 31 percent, from $51 to $35. Even the Republican machines were not immune to retrenchment. Per capita outlays in Philadelphia and Pittsburgh dropped 27 percent, from $22 to $16. In the remaining cities, including Chicago, per capita spending remained relatively constant over this twenty-two-year period.

Spending *rose* during the machines' formative phase, in the 1860s and 1870s, when the immigrants were being mobilized, and fell as the machines consolidated power. Wary of tax revolts, Irish party bosses quickly built alliances with the Yankee middle class and business community. The propertied classes demanded cutbacks, after the excesses of the 1860s and early 1870s, and the early Irish bosses acquiesced. The early Irish machines, then, had all the trappings of Yankee reform administrations, complete with calls for municipal taxation limitations. Yet retrenchment posed severe hardship for the machine's natural constituency, the immigrant working class. The secret to the longevity of the early Irish machines was their ability to balance the contradictory demands of the middle class and the working class, for retrenchment and for patronage.[38]

The Irish bosses first heeded conservative Yankee businessmen, imposing retrenchment on the Irish working class as the price of assuming power. In New York City, anti-Tammany conservative William F. Havemeyer was elected mayor in 1872 in the wake of Tweed's downfall. Havemeyer quickly reduced the city budget from $36 million to $32 million. Notwithstanding the economic suffering caused by the panic of 1873, Havemeyer cut back on public works spending. Boss Kelly, dependent on the reformers to resurrect the Wigwam after Tweed's downfall, did little to moderate Havemeyer's fiscal policies. Kelly would soon demonstrate his own Irish brand of fiscal (and political) prudence. As city controller between 1876 and 1880, Kelly substantially reduced the city's massive Tweed-induced debt. As one close observer noted approvingly of Kelly's fiscal stewardship: "It requires a great man to stand between the City Treasury and this most dangerous mass."[39]

In San Francisco, Boss Chris Buckley also embarked on a program of fiscal retrenchment in the 1880s. In the 1882 municipal election, Buckley promised a "dollar limit" on the municipal taxation rate, that is, one dollar for each one hundred dollars of assessed valuation. Between 1882 and 1886 the Buckley-controlled Board of Supervisors succeeded in reducing the city tax rate from $1.50 to $1.05 while reducing inflated property values by one half, from $400 million to $200 million. With the machine's revenue sources drying up with fiscal reform, Buckley turned to ways of holding the line on public spending. Salaries were reduced and some positions were abolished. Between 1880 and 1890 San Francisco's population grew by 50 percent; public spending remained constant at $4.8 million.[40]

Conservative fiscal policies made the first generation of Irish

machines susceptible to revolts from below. In 1875 Tammany reduced city wages from $2.00 to $1.60 a day. As a result, John
Morrissey and the "short-hair" or lower-class faction in Tammany
broke with Kelley in 1875, claiming that Kelly was no longer sensitive to the needs of the working class, particularly the Irish. Tammany lost the 1875 mayoral election in part because of erosion in
its working-class support. In the 1886 New York mayoral election,
many working-class Irish and Germans deserted Tammany and
supported Henry George, the United Labor party candidate, nearly
toppling Tammany.[41]

In San Francisco, Chris Buckley experienced a critical loss of
working-class and ethnic support in the late 1880s. Retrenchment
angered the working class because it meant little patronage and
poor services. As labor revitalized in the 1880s—the number of
trade unions increasing from eighteen in 1878 to forty-five in
1883—Buckley failed to appeal to the growing labor movement.
The late 1880s brought worsening economic conditions to the city.
As the machine was unable to meet the needs of the working class,
estimated to account for one-third of the electorate, many workers
shifted their allegiance from the machine. Blue-collar workers
turned their energies to building the trade union movement, either
supporting antimachine candidates or withdrawing from party
politics. In the 1888 mayoral contest, Buckley's nominee, Edward
B. Pond, polled only 38 percent of the vote in a three-way contest
with Republican Charles R. Story and independent Democrat
C. C. O'Donnell. Though Pond barely won the election, thanks to
a split in the antimachine vote, he captured only 40 percent of the
Irish vote. Two years later, Buckley's candidate would lose the Irish
vote and the election, ending the "Blind Boss"'s control over Bay
Area politics.[42]

What accounts for the fiscal conservatism of the first generation
of Irish machines and for their inability to control their working-
class and immigrant constituency? Nathan Glazer and Daniel Patrick Moynihan have stressed the causal role of Irish Catholic political and social conservatism. They argue that "the Irish just
didn't know what to do with their [political] opportunity. They
never thought of politics as an instrument of social change—their
kind of politics involved the processes of a society that was not
changing."[43]

There are weaknesses, however, in the "group" interpretation of machine fiscal conservatism. The Irish-American community in the late nineteenth century was not monolithically conservative. Although critical political, economic, and social elites—machine politicians, the emerging "lace curtain" middle class, and the Catholic church hierarchy—were conservative on fiscal and labor issues, the rank and file was not. In fact, the urban Irish working class grew increasingly militant in the 1870s and 1880s. The working class formed the largest element in the Irish-American community, and its political support was essential to the urban Democratic machines. In cities such as New York, Jersey City, San Francisco, and Boston, more than 60 percent of the Irish-born workforce in 1870 was in unskilled and semiskilled occupations.

The depression of the 1870s brought a surge of Irish working-class support for local labor parties. In San Francisco, deteriorating economic conditions and increasing job competition between white and Chinese workers led in 1877 to the formation of the Workingmen's party of California. Led by Irish-born Denis Kearney, the labor party captured the city government and successfully pressured for a new state constitution. James Bryce argued that "the chief cause that made the new party grow, for grow it did, . . . was the support given their countrymen (Kearney and other WPC leaders) by the Irish, here a discontented and turbulent part of the population."[44] Most unskilled and semiskilled Irish workers deserted the Democratic party and formed the backbone of the new labor party, as they would again after the turn of the century with the Union Labor party. In Chicago, Irish working-class voters helped elect aldermen and state representatives of the socialist-backed Workingmen's party.[45]

The trade union movement also helped shape the growing class consciousness of urban Irish-American workers. In the late 1870s and early 1880s, the Knights of Labor drew strong support from Irish workers in the coal industry. The Knights spearheaded the national movement to create an independent labor party of trade unionists, socialists, and Greenbackers. The Irish were actively involved in the campaign to unionize the building trades, by 1900 the most highly unionized group of occupations in the country. Although the Irish did not predominate in the building trades rank and file, they quickly took over union leadership. By the turn of the century, nearly one-half of the presidents of the unions comprising the American Federation of Labor were Irish. Craft union leaders were committed to bread-and-butter or business unionism, entering local politics for such limited purposes as ensuring that city contracts involved union personnel. Cautious and conservative in local politics, the Irish-controlled building trades set a record for industrial conflict, generating nearly three times as many strikes, boycotts, and sympathy strikes as other industries such as mining.[46]

The Irish-American nationalist movement also helped shape the class consciousness of the Irish working class. The Fenian Brotherhood, organized in 1858, and the Clan na Gael, successor to the Fenians in the 1870s, represented working-class movements. Their republicanism, however, lacked a social program. Local leaders of the Land League, organized in 1880, sought reform of the American as well as Irish land systems. Radical Land League branches were conce. itrated in the anthracite coal region of Pennsylvania (where they functioned as surrogates for the Knights of Labor) and in the industrial cities of New England and the Middle Atlantic states. Even in cities such as New York and San Francisco, where moderates dominated the leadership of the local leagues, there was a strong conne ction between the local branches and the local labor movement. In New York, the Central Labor Union came into existence as a conse.juence of trade union rallies in support of tenant farmers' rights in Ireland. The Central Labor Union would challenge Tammany Hall's political hegemony in 1886 by nominating Henry George on a labor party ticket.[47]

With rising Irish working-class militancy, Irish party bosses frequently were more conservative than Irish voters on fiscal, labor, and social issues. The conservatism of Irish political leaders may have been as much a *consequence* as a cause of machine politics. In power, the machine's maintenance needs—building cross-class voting coalitions, placating the business community—introduced a conservative strain in early Irish machine leadership, resulting in lost political opportunities. As they learned to manipulate the levers of urban power, Irish politicians turned their backs on more radical working-class political ventures. As former Fenian revolutionary Jeremiah O'Donovan Rossa sadly observed: "We Irish of New York are American politicians before we are Irish, or anything else."[48]

Martin Shefter has suggested a second explanation of machine fiscal conservatism. Rather than drawing on Irish political culture as the explanatory factor, Shefter's "elite" model focuses on the nature of the local business groups supporting the machine. In New York, the speculators who supported Tweed and demanded expansionary fiscal policies gave way to the bankers, corporate lawyers, and independent businessmen who demanded that Kelly pursue "tight-fisted" economic policies.[49]

In order to understand why early Irish bosses sought alliances with business groups demanding retrenchment, one must distinguish between two distinct stages of machine building: a formative phase and a consolidation phase. In the machine's formative stage, which extended from the 1840s to the 1880s, party bosses expanded both the size of the electorate *and* the public sector. In New York City, Tammany Hall bosses Fernando Wood and William Marcy Tweed naturalized 9,207 immigrants per year between 1856 and 1867. The pace of naturalization soon quickened. In 1868, Tammany naturalized 41,112 foreign-born in order to swell the ranks of Democratic loyalists and to win the crucial gubernatorial contest in that year, freeing the city of state Republican control. The Wigwam hired the New York Printing Company, which Tweed owned, to print 105,000 blank naturalization applications and 69,000 certificates of naturalization. Immigrants fresh off the boat were given red tickets, allowing them to get their citizenship papers free. Tammany paid the required court fees and provided false witnesses to testify that the immigrants had been in the country the necessary five years.[50]

Running its naturalization mill "full blast," Tammany succeeded in dramatically increasing the number of voters. Table 5 traces the growth of the electorate and Tammany's electoral fortunes under four political bosses between 1855 and 1897: Fernando Wood, William Marcy Tweed, "Honest John" Kelly, and Richard Croker. During the Wood era, from the late 1840s to 1863, Tammany Hall worked its citizenship factory at "half blast," relying more on purchased and repeat voters than on the newly enfranchised. Voter fraud met with surprisingly little success. Between 1855 and 1863, as the city's electorate grew by one-fifth, Tammany managed to win only one of five mayoral elections as the artful Wood shuttled his army of fraudulent voters between the Wigwam and Mozart

TABLE 5. *The Tiger Lays Claim to New York: Voting and Turnout Under Four Tammany Bosses, 1855–1897*

Tammany Boss	Years	Mayoral Elections				Turnout		
		Number of Contests	Tammany Victories	Tammany Percentage of Total Vote		First Election	Last Election	Percentage Increase
Fernando Wood	1855–1863	5	1	38.6		59,643	71,101	19.2
William Marcy Tweed	1865–1872	3	2	51.8		71,101	134,878	89.7
"Honest John" Kelly	1874–1884	5	4[a]	53.1		134,878	226,035	67.6
Richard Croker	1886–1897	6	5	49.4[b]		226,035	300,939	33.1

Sources: For 1855–1886: New York Tribune, *Tribune Almanac and Political Register* (New York: G. Dearborn); for 1887–1897: New York State Legislature, *Red Book, State of New York.*
[a] Three Tammany victories were shared with its rivals, Irving Hall and the County Democracy.
[b] Includes three plurality victories in three-way contests with Republican, reform, or labor candidates.

Hall, Tammany's arch organizational rival in that era for control of the Democratic party.

Boss Tweed cranked up Tammany's naturalization mill. During Tweed's short tenure, the city's electorate nearly doubled, from 71,000 to close to 135,000 voters. A. Oakey Hall, Tweed's hand-picked candidate for mayor in 1868, received 75,000 votes, more than triple the number received five years earlier by Tammany nominee Francis I. A. "Boodle" Boole. Starting in the early 1870s, "Honest John" Kelly took up where Tweed had left off. Tammany's citizenship factory continued to churn out new voters. By Kelly's death in 1886, the Wigwam had naturalized nearly 80 percent of the city's Irish, German, and other "old" (Western European) immigrants. These new citizens swelled the ranks of the Tammany Tiger's voters, consolidating the machine's hold over party and city. Under Kelly, Tammany won (or shared victory with Democratic rivals Irving Hall and the County Democracy) in four of five mayoral contests, averaging 53 percent of the vote. However, an entrenched Tammany would no longer have to turn out newly minted voters. Under Kelly successor Richard Croker, the triumphant Tiger won five of six elections between 1886 and 1897 as the city's electorate grew at one-half the rate it had under Kelly—33 percent as opposed to 68 percent.

During this formative stage, the early Irish machines did more than mobilize immigrant voters. They also increased the size of the public sector in order to *reward* the new voters. In cities such as New York, per capita expenditures and debts soared from the 1850s to the early 1870s as *some* of the newly enfranchised voters were rewarded with newly created public jobs. Boss Tweed, for example, embarked on a program of massive deficit financing in the late 1860s in part to enlarge the city payroll. A contemporary observer estimated that there were 12,000 to 15,000 members of Tweed's "Shiny Hat Brigade," the holders of newly created municipal sinecures. Under Tweed the city's debt tripled, rising from $36 million in 1868 to $136 million at the end of 1870.[51]

But there were political limits on the fledgling machine's ability to expand its resource base. The nineteenth-century machine harnessed a system of municipal government organized primarily to promote economic growth and heavily dependent on local property taxes for revenue—the source of over two-thirds of city revenue in this era—in the context of fierce competition between cities for business location and capital investment.

In the machine's formative stage, soaring property tax rates and indebtedness resulted in a competitive disadvantage for business location and investment and in a political backlash by businessmen and middle-class property owners. As C. K. Yearley argues, the property-owning urban middle class was peculiarly affected by the machine's expansionary fiscal policies. The poor did not own property and thus escaped direct taxation. The rich shifted their wealth to more intangible forms of personal property—savings, securities, and credits—to escape taxation. Thus the machine's taxation burden largely fell on the property-owning middle class, which supplied the backbone of support for the antimachine municipal reform movements of the period from 1870 to 1910.[52]

In the nineteenth-century machine's mature or consolidation phase, extending from the mid-1870s to the turn of the century, a conservative fiscal strategy more acceptable to business and the middle class evolved. Tax rates and expenditures in machine cities such as New York and San Francisco stabilized as bosses such as Kelly and Buckley made peace with the business community. In the 1880s and 1890s population increases outpaced city expenditures, and per capita outlays in the Irish machine cities plummeted (see Table 4). Bosses had to find new ways of raising revenue and buying off the machine's rapacious working-class followers.

The Irish bosses first turned to indebtedness. Debt-financed public works projects finessed the conflicting political demands of the working class and middle class. Public works projects represented a valuable patronage source, particularly for the Irish-run building trades. At the same time, debt costs could be more easily hidden in the city budget, thereby placating the middle class, as long as the property tax rate remained constant.[53]

Yet the Irish bosses found their ability to borrow money severely hampered. Table 6 shows changes in the debt burden for the big cities between 1880 and 1902. The eight Irish cities were heavy borrowers in 1880. Per capita debts in these cities averaged $66 compared with $55 in the fourteen big cities with smaller Irish populations. After 1880, however, the Irish bosses were unable to borrow in order to pay for (and pay off) the "New Democracy" of

TABLE 6. *Going into Debt, 1880–1902*

Cities and Regimes	Average Per Capita City Debt ($)		Percentage Change from 1880 to 1902
	1880	*1902*	
Irish cities (8)	66	72	9.1
Irish Democratic machine (New York, San Francisco, Jersey City, Albany)	68	70	2.9
Irish Democratic nonmachine (Boston)	78	148	89.7
Non-Irish Republican machine (Philadelphia, Pittsburgh)	77	60	−22.1
Non-Irish nonmachine (Chicago)	25	29	13.8
Non-Irish cities (14)ª	55	58	5.5

Sources: U.S. Census Office, *Report on Valuation, Taxation, and Public Indebtedness: 1880* (Washington, D.C.: Government Printing Office, 1884), Table 22, pp. 883–890; U.S. Bureau of the Census, *Special Reports: Statistics of Cities, 1902* (Washington, D.C.: Government Printing Office, 1902), Table 38, pp. 443–449.

ª Includes all cities with more than 50,000 population *and* less than 13 percent Irish. See Table 1.

immigrant working-class voters. In the machine cities of New York, San Francisco, Jersey City, and Albany, the average debt burden increased by only 3 percent between 1880 and 1902. Boston's Irish ward bosses, in contrast, borrowed freely as the Hub's debt soared by nearly 90 percent. Compared with Boston's free spenders, the Republican bosses of Philadelphia and Pittsburgh succumbed to pay-as-you-go financing; their debt burden dropped by 22 percent.

The Irish Democratic machines wanted to borrow but could not. In the 1870s and 1880s their opponents succeeded in imposing constitutional restrictions on their ability to borrow money. Following the panic of 1873, which brought many cities to the verge of bankruptcy, conservative governors and state legislatures— Republican *and* Democratic—sought legal restrictions on the indebtedness powers of machine-controlled local governments. In New York, for example, anti-Tammany Democrat Governor Lucius Robinson accused the cities of a "disposition to play with debt and court taxation as if for a pastime." At Robinson's behest, the legislature proposed and voters approved a constitutional amendment that limited the borrowing power of local governments to 10 percent of their assessed valuation. Other constitutional restrictions on city borrowing powers included the requirement of local voter approval for municipal debts and the provision of a special tax or sinking fund for payment of city debts.[54]

With mounting constitutional limits on debt-financed capital improvement programs, machines turned to expanding the city as a whole rather than the relative size of the public sector. In particular, machine politicians pursued an aggressive annexation program to enlarge the city's boundaries and revenue base. Between 1880 and 1900, the twenty largest cities increased their territory by nearly one-third, with New York, Boston, and Chicago leading the way.[55]

Republican state governors and legislators also endorsed big-city annexation—but as a means of weakening the Democratic machines. In 1897, the Republican-controlled legislature of New York passed the Consolidation Act, uniting the five boroughs into the City of Greater New York. State GOP boss Thomas Platt proposed the act, believing that the city Republicans could win in 1898. In 1894 the GOP state ticket had carried the five boroughs. The Consolidation Act doubled the city's revenue base (and swelled the ranks of the patronage army to 60,000) without increasing the tax rate. The Republican stratagem backfired. Tammany won a resounding victory in the first consolidated election, capturing new patronage with which to cement working-class political allegiances.[56]

Annexation represented a double-edged sword for the Irish machines. On the one hand, annexation increased the machine's supply of jobs, always appealing to the working class, without necessarily increasing the property tax rate, of prime concern to the middle class. On the other hand, this strategy increased the number of nominally antimachine voters as it captured the outward-migrating Yankee middle class.

The fiscally starved Irish machines of the late nineteenth century also relied on a "vice tax" as a way of raising revenue. With the constant threat of middle-class tax revolts and the drying up of government revenue, machines offered police protection for gambling and prostitution in exchange for badly needed cash. In New

York City, for example, Richard Croker developed a police graft system in the late 1880s, substantially filling Tammany's coffers with the payoffs from gambling, drinking, and prostitution. Croker would soon learn the political risks as well as the benefits of a vice tax. In the early 1890s the Lexow Committee conducted a damaging investigation of the graft ring in the Tammany-controlled New York police department. Reformers capitalized on middle-class outrage to win the 1894 city elections.[57]

The fiscal conservatism of the first generation of Irish party bosses can thus be traced to the fragile machine's maintenance needs. Expansionary fiscal policies invited middle-class and business tax revolts. Conservative fiscal policies, in contrast, invited working-class insurgency. To temper the conflicting demands of the two classes for retrenchment and patronage, the Irish bosses chose conservative tax policies, were forced to adopt cautious borrowing programs, vigorously promoted annexation, and cashed in on vice.

Rewarding the Irish: The Limits of Early Machine Patronage

As Tammany boss Richard Croker candidly admitted, the machine needed to bribe the masses with spoils—"Here they take the shape of offices."[58] The lowly economic status of the Irish made them unusually susceptible to this form of machine flattery. In the late nineteenth century, the Irish lagged far behind other groups economically. In the eight cities surveyed, 67 percent of the Irish were unskilled or semiskilled laborers in 1870, compared with 28 percent of the Yankees and Germans. Few Irish were middle-class. In 1870 only 10 percent of the Irish in these eight cities held white-collar jobs, compared with 37 percent of the Yankees and 28 percent of the Germans.[59]

Did the Irish takeover of the Democratic machines dramatically improve their economic lot? A fourth question about the early machines involves the amount of patronage they actually controlled and how much they gave to the Irish. As I argue in Chapter 1, the prizes awaiting capture in city politics *appeared* substantial. Urban machines controlled thousands of public sector and private sector patronage jobs, the latter with firms franchised by or doing business with the city. Tammany Hall, for example, controlled 40,000 municipal jobs during Boss Kelly's rule. Machines also controlled the awarding of public works contracts, important in an era when cities were shifting their function from caretaking to providing amenities. For the Irish-controlled building trades, capital improvement projects were prizes indeed. Furthermore, the city payroll seemed to offer relatively greater advancement opportunities than did the private sector. In San Francisco, for example, 63 percent of all city workers in 1870 were in white-collar jobs compared with only 28 percent of those privately employed. Given the machine's apparent cornucopia of resources, it is small wonder that, as E. L. Godkin so acidly observed, the Irish undertook politics in a "predatory state of mind."[60]

Relative to the number of immigrant and working-class voters, however, the early machine's patronage supply was limited. Public jobs were the most important machine resource. How many of these political loaves and fishes were available to feed the party faithful? By today's standards, the public sector in the era of the nightwatchman state was quite small. Political constraints on increasing the property tax rate coupled with legal constraints on city borrowing powers restricted the nineteenth-century machine's ability to create patronage for the Irish. In 1870, the public sector accounted for only 3 percent of the big-city workforce, slowly climbing to 5 percent by 1900. Even Tammany's vaunted patronage army of more than 40,000 in the late 1880s was no more than platoon size in a labor force of nearly 1 million. In contrast, the public sector today comprises nearly 20 percent of the big-city labor force. The Irish would have to wait until the era of big government to use the public sector as a *group* route from rags to riches.[61]

Despite the limited amount of early machine patronage, the Irish grabbed what prizes there were. Table 7 traces Irish public employment gains in the big cities between 1870 and 1900. The four Irish machines successfully "Hibernianized" the public payroll. Despite falling per capita outlays, city employment in New York, San Francisco, Jersey City, and Albany rose from 10,950 in 1870 to 66,505 in 1900 as the number of Irish payrollers ballooned from 1,966 to 24,324. The Irish bosses had the Republicans to thank for much of their patronage coup. New York GOP boss Thomas Platt's miscalculation with the 1897 Consolidation

Act handed Tammany Hall 20,000 new patronage jobs—representing nearly 40 percent of the overall increase in the machine cities—on a silver platter. Aided by their foes, the Irish bosses could achieve both patronage and retrenchment.

Demonstrating an early and effective ethnic affirmative action policy, the four machines gave the Irish more than 40 percent of the newly created patronage. Yet the Irish did not always need friendly machines to place them on the city payroll. In Irish-controlled but nonmachine Boston, for example, the proportion of city workers of Irish descent rose from a paltry 5 percent in 1870 to 32 percent in 1900. In Chicago under Democratic party bosses Mike McDonald, Carter Harrison I, and Carter Harrison II, the Irish claim on the city payroll soared from 14 percent to 31 percent. Not to be outdone, the Republican machines of Philadelphia and Pittsburgh politically rebaptized the Irish and put them on the GOP payroll, though in smaller numbers.

Even with these dramatic public job gains, most Irish officeseekers in the late nineteenth century were bound to be disappointed. Because machines presided over governments of limited size and function, there were too few patronage plums for too many Irish jobseekers. As Table 7 shows, in 1900 only 6 percent of first- and second-generation Irish in New York, San Francisco, Jersey City, and Albany worked directly for government. In these four machine cities, 295,000 Irish entered the labor force between 1870 and 1900. The private sector, not the machine, generated up to 90 percent of the new urban job opportunities for these workers.

For the same reason, few middle-class gains were achieved by the Irish in the public sector during this period. San Francisco's Irish, for example, received one-third of the 2,500 white-collar public jobs created between 1870 and 1900. At the turn of the century, however, government employed fewer than 10 percent of all Irish white-collar workers. Here, too, the private sector was responsible for the vast majority of Irish middle-class job gains.[62]

Upwardly bound Irish had entered the public sector at the wrong time. Machines specialized in padding blue-collar payrolls in the police, fire, and public works departments. At the same time, the Irish machines deliberately limited white-collar job opportunities, particularly in the school system. More blue-collar than white-collar jobs could be created for a given financial outlay, an impor-

TABLE 7. How Many Plums? The Irish and Big-City Patronage, 1870–1900

Cities and Regimes	Municipal Employment, 1870[a]			Municipal Employment, 1900[a]			Percentage of Irish Workforce Employed by City Government	
	Irish[b]	All	Percentage Irish	Irish[b]	All	Percentage Irish	1870	1900
Irish cities (8)	2,994	21,697	13.8	42,841	129,463	33.1	1.3	5.6
Irish Democratic machine (New York, San Francisco, Jersey City, Albany)	1,966	10,950	17.9	24,324	66,505	36.6	1.4	5.8
Irish Democratic nonmachine (Boston)	132	2,660	5.0	3,227	10,143	31.8	0.5	3.8
Non-Irish Republican machine (Philadelphia, Pittsburgh)	535	5,566	9.6	6,516	24,750	26.3	1.2	4.5
Non-Irish nonmachine (Chicago)	361	2,521	14.3	8,774	28,065	31.3	1.8	8.7
Non-Irish cities (14)[c]	1,723	20,323	8.5	13,801	69,694	19.8	2.6	7.5

Sources: U.S. Census Office, Ninth Census, 1870 (Washington, D.C.: Government Printing Office, 1872), vol. 1, Table 32; U.S. Bureau of the Census, Special Reports: Occupations at the Twelfth Census (Washington, D.C.: Government Printing Office, 1904), Tables 41, 43.
[a]Based on more complete public employment information for the nation and for San Francisco, the 1870 figures have been increased by 20 percent; the 1900 figures, by 50 percent.
[b]For 1870, municipal employees born in Ireland; for 1900, municipal employees of Irish parentage.
[c]Includes all cities with more than 50,000 population and less than 13 percent Irish. See Table 1.

tant consideration for the vote-seeking Irish party bosses. White-collar patronage, in addition, did not have the same vote yield. Teachers represented the largest single source of white-collar public jobs, and most teachers were women, unable to vote in this era. Furthermore, middle-class political pressures limited machine influence over the hiring and firing of teachers. As a consequence, the heavily Catholic Democratic machines reached a concordance between church and state on limiting public school financing. A poorly financed public school system made the church-run parochial school system—where most Irish bosses had themselves been educated—all the more attractive. Given the machine's proletarianization of the public sector, greater job opportunities now loomed in the private sector, where growth in the white-collar service sector outpaced gains in blue-collar manufacturing. In the Bay Area, for example, the white-collar share of public employment dropped from 63 percent to 48 percent between 1870 and 1900; in the private sector, the white-collar share rose from 28 percent to 37 percent.[63]

Ironically, the relative security of blue-collar jobs in police, fire, and public works departments may have actually hindered the *early* development of an Irish-American middle class by encouraging long tenure in low-status positions. In San Francisco, the Irish garnered one-half of all blue-collar public jobs created between 1870 and 1900. However, compared with privately employed blue-collar workers— Irish and non-Irish—Celtic blue-collar civil servants were twice as likely to hold the same poor-paying job for twenty years.[64]

Perhaps the nineteenth-century machine's economic benefits for the Irish were more indirect than the public payroll. Bosses also controlled private sector patronage, particularly through the award of public works contracts or through control of "unofficial" patronage with firms dependent on the party organization for contracts and franchises. How did the Irish fare with the machine's stock of private sector jobs?

Some Irish clearly benefited from public works projects. The main beneficiaries were contractors, workers in the building trades, and the army of casual laborers. The Irish quickly gravitated into the urban contracting business. As early as 1870 nearly one-fifth of the nation's big-city contractors were Irish-born. As David Mont-

gomery notes, the characteristics of the construction industry—
low capital requirements, the important role of governmental action, and the complex social network of subcontracting—were
ideal for the Irish. Irish workers in the building trades particularly
benefited from public works projects because Irish contractors
preferred to hire Irish employees. But as unskilled and semiskilled
"new" immigrants flooded into the cities, they too began to demand employment on public works projects. By the turn of the
century, the organizationally blessed Irish dominated the union
leadership of the building trades but not the rank-and-file membership. Only in a few trades—such as plumbing and steamfitting—
did the Irish predominate. The majority of the Irish-American beneficiaries of public works projects were unskilled laborers. In cities
such as New York and San Francisco at the turn of the century,
fully 40 percent of the city's unskilled laborers were Irish. For this
sizable pool of Irish unskilled laborers, contract labor jobs represented poor-paying irregular employment, not a channel for ethnic
group economic progress.[65]

How did the Irish fare with the machine's supply of "unofficial"
patronage, that is, jobs in firms doing business with the machine
and filled by party workers in exchange for favorable governmental action? Financially starved machines had strong incentives to
expand the number of these positions, especially as civil service reforms protected increasing numbers of municipal employees. Yet
there were countervailing economic incentives encouraging businesses to resist machine encroachment on their payrolls. As Robert
Brooks observed, businesses preferred paying cash for political
favors rather than hiring inefficient party workers.[66] The lowly
character of private sector political jobs further limited advancement opportunities. Most utility jobs involved unskilled or semiskilled work. Although it is virtually impossible to estimate the
amount and ethnic distribution of this form of patronage, a survey
of the payrolls of private utilities and street railroads in San Francisco is revealing. In 1900, after twenty years of Irish rule, the Irish
were *not* overrepresented on these payrolls, contrary to what one
would expect had these jobs been machine-controlled and of economic value.[67]

Private sector patronage generated substantial economic opportunities for *individual* Irishmen. Irish contractors, in particular,

grew rich on padded public works contracts. It is questionable, however, whether these forms of patronage afforded economic advancement for large numbers of Irish workers. Regarding city capital improvement programs, the public payroll dwarfed the capital budget in size in late nineteenth-century municipal budgets. In Buckley's San Francisco, for example, more than one-half of the city budget of nearly $5 million in 1880 went for salaries. The remainder was divided evenly between capital improvements and expenses. In this era, public works projects generated only one-third to one-half the job opportunities of the public payroll. If the Irish had been employed on big-city public works projects at roughly the same rate as they were on the city payroll, then the machine's private sector jobs could have absorbed only an additional 3 to 4 percent of the Irish labor force. The early machine's combined public and private patronage could provide employment—much of it temporary or blue-collar—for only one out of ten Irish workers.[68]

Given this tale of machine parsimony, how do we account for the apparent rapid development of a sizable Irish middle class in the big cities? Between 1870 and 1900 the proportion of Irish in white-collar jobs in the eight cities surveyed rose from 10 percent to 24 percent. Could machines have improved the lot of the Irish in more indirect ways than patronage? If machines opened the private sector labor market to the Irish, the best they could do was provide entry-level positions. For the 90 percent of the Irish middle class in the private sector, economic progress was slow and uneven. As Stephan Thernstrom has carefully shown for Boston, most privately employed white-collar Irish were marginally middle class, having entered clerical and sales work rather than business and the professions. The Irish in America, as Daniel Patrick Moynihan accurately observed, would prove to be functionaries rather than entrepreneurs.[69]

In taking over the northern urban Democratic party and crowding into the machine's patronage enclave in the late nineteenth century, did the Irish significantly limit opportunities for *other* immigrant groups to seek fame and fortune—such as it was—in the public sector? At first glance, there appears to be little evidence for a so-called crowding effect. In the four Irish machine cities, non-Irish immigrants received one-third of the public jobs generated between 1870 and 1900. Before complimenting the Irish bosses on their political foresight in using patronage to reduce non-Irish discontent with Irish rule, it should be noted that these cities were steadily filling with the non-Irish during this period. By the turn of the century, the other immigrant groups constituted nearly 60 percent of the workforce in cities such as New York and San Francisco, yet they held only 36 percent of the public jobs. In the Irish machine cities, the non-Irish patronage "quota," that is, the share of public jobs allotted to non-Irish workers relative to their numbers in the labor force, rose from 39 percent in 1870 to 61 percent in 1900. By running the machines, the Irish bagged more than their fair share of patronage. In New York, San Francisco, Jersey City, and Albany, the ratio of public to overall employment for the Irish more than doubled from 64 percent in 1870 to 135 percent at century's end.[70]

What caused these early differences between Irish and non-Irish in the relative receipt of machine patronage? One obvious explanation lies in the different job skills ethnic groups brought to the New World. The largely unskilled Irish *needed* public employment; the skilled Germans generally did not. Even among the Germans, though, there were large numbers eager to do menial work. In the big cities, one-quarter of the German workforce in 1870 toiled as unskilled or semiskilled laborers.

A second explanation focuses on group voting strength rather than job demand. As Table 3 shows, the Irish had high naturalization, registration, and voting rates; other ethnic groups did not. Public employment allocations were highly sensitive to group electoral strength. In San Francisco between 1870 and 1900, differences in electoral mobilization rates (consisting of voter registration, turnout, and bloc voting) for the city's eight major ethnic groups accounted for 60 percent of the variance in group patronage shares.[71]

Yet more was involved than group muscle at the polls. Even when the non-Irish were naturalized, registered, and voting, they rarely received their fair share of public jobs. The Irish regarded politics and public employment as their secular calling. They hoarded as much patronage as they could, fending off other groups whether these groups voted or not. Thus in the Irish-run machine cities, the patronage yield of Irish votes far outstripped non-Irish votes. San

Francisco's machine, for example, added 15,172 new Irish voters and 2,286 new Irish payrollers between 1870 and 1900. During the same period, 13,238 Germans were added to the city's voter registration rolls, but only 611 found their way onto the public payroll. Irish votes in the Bay Area had more than three times the patronage yield of German votes. The ratio of new voters to new public jobs was seven to one for the Irish; for the Germans, twenty-two to one.[72]

Even by hoarding patronage from other ethnic groups, however, the first generation of Irish machines controlled too little gravy to fully satisfy the Irish working class. Unable to increase the machine's patronage supply any faster, Irish politicos chose two less costly ways of calming the Irish working class: heavy doses of labor rhetoric and recreational clubs.

In New York, fiscally conservative Tammany boss "Honest John" Kelly employed anticapitalist and antimonopolist rhetoric in the early 1880s to appeal to the city's increasingly restive working class. According to Eric Foner, the shift in Kelly's political rhetoric reflected the success of the Land League in propagating radical ideas among the Irish working class.[73] In San Francisco in the mid-1880s, conservative Boss Buckley belatedly realized the growing power of labor. Decrying the "cursed monopolists," the "Blind Boss" called for reduced transportation and utility rates for the city's working class.[74]

The Celtic machines also tried "circuses"—recreational clubs—in lieu of "bread"—patronage. As Shefter notes, in the close 1886 New York mayoral contest, pitting Tammany against organized labor, Henry George's United Labor party skillfully employed a popular network of labor recreational clubs affiliated with trade union locals to solicit working-class support. Tammany got the message and soon developed an equivalent with its year-round district recreational clubs. In San Francisco, the Buckley machine also opened district clubhouses in working-class and immigrant neighborhoods.[75]

Yet the symbolic and social appeals of the early budget-conscious Irish party bosses were never fully adequate to cement working-class and immigrant loyalties to the big-city machines. Social inducements such as district clubs were never as attractive to the working class as were economic benefits, whether patronage, welfare services, or labor legislation. In the late nineteenth century, revolts from below were the price paid for the machine's conservative fiscal policies. Under a new generation of Irish bosses in the twentieth century, machines would be constructed from sturdier materials. The second generation of Irish machines would figure out how to supply bread as well as circuses to the masses.

Chapter Three

Guardians of Power: The Irish Versus the New Immigrants, 1896–1928

Death, Transfiguration, and Machine Rebirth

The fragile penny-pinching Irish Democratic machines collapsed in the depression-ridden 1890s. As the panic of 1893 lengthened into depression, voters blamed the Democrats. The Democracy controlled the presidency, many governorships of northern states, and most of the big-city machines. Democratic politicians did little to alleviate the suffering of the growing army of unemployed. As leader of the Bourbon, or conservative, wing of the party, President Grover Cleveland remained committed to a balanced budget, laissez-faire economics, and federal nonintervention. Democrat Cleveland's nonintervention policy, however, did not extend to the Irish big-city bosses, his nominal allies. Ever the reformer, Cleveland joined forces with the Republicans as the economy worsened to attack the Democratic machines by denying them badly needed federal patronage.[1]

Fending off presidential attack from above and facing growing discontent from below, the Irish machines sought to soothe the masses on the cheap. Forced to choose the low-cost alternative, machines championed the workers' social—but not economic— demands: racetracks, gambling, and drinking. The Republicans, in contrast, promised bread rather than circuses. Campaigning on the issue of economic discontent, the GOP proposed government programs to put the jobless to work.

Capitalizing on the economic grievances of the urban working class, Republicans and reformers dethroned the reigning Irish Democratic bosses. In San Francisco, Republican boss Gavin Mc-Nab defeated "Blind Boss" Buckley in 1891 with substantial Irish and working-class support. During the turbulent 1890s, leadership of the Bay Area oscillated among Republicans, populists, and reform Democrats but not Democratic machine politicians. In Jersey City, the Davis machine succumbed to Republican reformer Mark Fagin in 1901. Reformers—Democratic as well as Republican—controlled Jersey City politics until World War I. In Albany, a reform fusion ticket triumphed over the Irish machine in the 1894 city election. Though the Democrats temporarily recaptured city hall, Republican boss William E. "Billy" Barnes took advantage of Democratic factionalism in 1899 to topple the incumbent machine. Wooing patronage-hungry Democratic politicians into his own organization, Billy Barnes would run Albany until 1921. Even Tammany did not emerge unscathed from the 1890s. The Wigwam lost the city elections of 1894 and 1902, prompting Boss Croker's resignation.

Despite the debacle of the 1890s, the Irish machines reemerged in strengthened form after the turn of the century. Following Boss Croker's resignation, Charles Francis Murphy took over Tammany Hall. Under Murphy and his successors, a revitalized Tiger ran the city (with minor exceptions) from 1903 to 1933. In 1917 Democrat Frank "I Am the Law" Hague was elected mayor of Jersey City. Hague built one of the most powerful—and repressive—machines in the country. Controlling the city, the county, and even the state, Hague ran Jersey City with an iron hand until 1949. Not to be outdone, Albany Democratic boss Dan O'Connell set the record for machine longevity. In the 1921 city elections, O'Connell capitalized on a rift between the Barnes machine and the Irish working class over an unsettled transit strike. Wooing the Irish back into the Democratic party, O'Connell routed Barnes at the polls and quickly consolidated power. As of 1987, the Albany Democratic machine had yet to lose a city election.

The second-generation Irish machines little resembled their

predecessors. Their strength lay in the provision of bread—lots of it—rather than circuses. Under the new machines, spending, borrowing, and patronage soared in the early twentieth century. Lavished on a single ethnic group, patronage tamed the restless Irish working class. With jobs and money, the new machines built a reliable electoral following. To win elections, machines merely mobilized the sizable Irish payroll army, Irish families, jobseekers, and, when needed, purchasable voters. With the machine's opponents reduced to a corporal's guard, the party bosses needed only a manageable rather than a large vote.

The electoral incentives of the new big-city party organizations differed considerably from their predecessors. Facing strong opposition, the late nineteenth-century machines had been mobilizers of the immigrant vote. With token opposition, the twentieth-century machines selectively brought out the vote. Having already fashioned a minimal winning electoral coalition among the earlier-arriving immigrants with the sturdiest of materials—jobs and money—the new machines turned their backs on later-arriving immigrants. Thus the second-generation party organizations did not naturalize, register, and vote the Southern and Eastern Europeans, who arrived from the late 1880s onward, at anything approaching the rate at which the Irish had been politically incorporated in the mid-nineteenth century.

Given the slowdown in immigrant assimilation, the twentieth-century Irish machines had little need to share power and jobs with the non-Irish. Instead, the newcomers were given less valuable rewards—social services, symbolic recognition, and collective benefits such as state labor and social welfare legislation. The strategy of parsimonious reward, however, would ultimately backfire. In the 1930s and 1940s, Southern and Eastern Europeans entered the voting booths in record numbers. Mobilizing the newcomers and seizing on their discontent with the machine's limited rewards, reformers succeeded in toppling many of the entrenched Irish machines.

There were important variations between cities in machine rebirth and policy transformation, raising several questions for analysis. First, as with the earlier machines, there was no one-to-one relationship between cities with large numbers of Irish-American voters and cities where Irish machines reemerged. The new ma-

chines did not invariably arise phoenix-like from the ashes of earlier organizations. In some machine cities, the ashes were hot; in
others, not. While New York, Jersey City, and Albany produced
both first- and second-generation machines, San Francisco did not.
The Bay Area's Democratic party remained moribund from the
turn of the century to the early 1960s. In New York, reformers
briefly interrupted Tammany's reign, enough to topple Boss Croker, but not the party organization. In Jersey City and Albany, a
generation would pass between the old and new Irish machines.

In the other four Irish cities, where first-generation Irish Democratic machines had not been built, the early twentieth century
would also prove inhospitable to rule by Irish Democratic bosses.
Irish-run Boston remained faction-ridden throughout this period.
Neither John F. "Honey Fitz" Fitzgerald, Martin Lomasney, nor,
later, James Michael Curley could centralize power in the heavily
Democratic Hub. Chicago's competitive and factional politics carried well into the twentieth century. Despite alternating periods of
Democratic and Republican rule in the Windy City, neither party
could consolidate power until the 1930s. And in a Republican era
bracketed by McKinley and Hoover, Yankee GOP machines would
run Philadelphia and Pittsburgh.

What explains the emergence of a new cohort of Irish machines
in some of the cities with large numbers of Irish voters and not in
others? Can the intergovernmental theory advanced to explain late
nineteenth-century machine building be extended into the twentieth century? Can the rebirth of some of the Irish machines be explained by alliances with pro-machine Democratic governors? Alternatively, can the failure to rebuild the San Francisco machine or
centralize power in Boston and Chicago be explained by hostile
state administrations?

Second, what explains the revolution in the machine's fiscal
policies? Nineteenth-century urban party bosses had not been able
to expand dramatically the size of the public sector and patronage
supply. Property tax increases invited middle-class tax revolts.
State constitutional restrictions hamstrung the machine's ability to
borrow money for public works projects. But twentieth-century
machines taxed and borrowed with political impunity. In the face
of mounting tax burdens, why did middle-class protest fizzle? In
the face of growing debt burdens, what remained of state financial
safeguards?

Third, what kind of patronage did the new machines control and what share went to the Irish? The nineteenth-century machine's limited and largely blue-collar patronage afforded the Irish opportunities for individual but not group social mobility. The twentieth-century machine's patronage policies, in contrast, appear to support the rainbow theory that politics served as an important route of group advancement for the Irish. As the new machine's prizes grew, ever larger numbers of Irishmen crowded into the public sector. Yet what accounts for the sluggish economic progress of the Irish well into the twentieth century? As Andrew Greeley has shown, the Irish, compared with the Jews, were slow to build a middle class anchored in business and the professions. The Irish middle class was just emerging on the eve of the Depression; its arrival would not occur until after World War II. In light of their political success, why was middle-class status so slow in coming for the Irish? Was there an *inverse* relationship between Irish political success and economic advancement? Did the second-generation Irish machines create white-collar job opportunities or did they continue to pad—with Paddys—blue-collar city payrolls?[2]

Fourth, why did the second-generation Irish machines do so little to assimilate and reward the Southern and Eastern Europeans? In the short run, this represented a rational electoral and allocational strategy. The fortunes of entrenched machines depended on the payroll and purchased vote, not the newcomers. Compared with the Irish, moreover, the Jews, Italians, Poles, and Czechs were slow to become citizens and exercise the franchise. With little muscle at the polls, they did not threaten—and thus could not bargain with—the Irish bosses. In the long run, however, the machine's strategy of minimal accommodation was self-defeating. As the newcomers slowly became citizens and voted, Irish prominence in urban public life rested on an increasingly fragile electoral base. Ultimately dealt a losing hand by demographic changes, the Irish bosses fought a brilliant rearguard action against the new ethnics. Yet the Celtic bosses could only delay—not prevent—the challenge of the newer arrivals to the continued Irish monopoly over power and patronage. With a sizable patronage infusion, the new machines could have afforded to incorporate and reward the Southern and Eastern Europeans. Why did the second generation of Irish-American party bosses fail to share the machine's now ample resources and thus risk another round of antimachine revolts from below? To these four questions about the early twentieth-century Irish machines we now turn.

State Politics and Machine Rebirth

The big-city Irish machines resurfaced during the brief period of national Democratic hegemony after 1912. The dominant Republican party had split between Regular and Bull Moose factions, allowing the Democrats to score victories at the national, state, and local levels. At the federal level, the Democrats effectively controlled the presidency and Congress for the first time in twenty years. At the state level, the Democrats won gubernatorial elections in major urban-industrial states such as New York, New Jersey, Massachusetts, and Illinois. Newly elected Democratic governors could assist machines in a variety of ways. Needing patronage to reward their followers, fledgling machines gratefully accepted state jobs. Friendly Democratic governors could also use their veto powers to prevent GOP-controlled state legislatures from interfering in urban affairs.[3]

Pro-Machine States

New Jersey and New York elected pro-machine Democratic governors between 1912 and 1921, allowing the reborn Jersey City and Albany machines to consolidate power. In Jersey City, would-be boss Frank Hague aligned himself in 1913 with Democratic Governor James F. Fielder. Serving as a city commissioner, Hague initially built his organization with Fielder's aid and protection, needed against Democratic Mayor Otto Wittpenn, Hague's rival and Fielder's gubernatorial opponent in 1913. Elected mayor of Jersey City in 1917, Hague moved immediately to control the governorship. Hague needed a pliable Democratic governor to shield his machine from the Republican-controlled state legislature, to increase his resources with state jobs, and, finally, to control the state Civil Service Commission and state Board of Taxes and Assessments in Trenton. A friendly civil service board would allow Hague to hire and fire city workers at will. A sympathetic state tax board, in turn, would permit Hague to expand his patronage army by increasing local property tax assessments for the city's railroads, oil companies, and public service corporations. In 1919, Hague succeeded in placing his friend Edward I. Edwards in the governor's chair. Hague then gave the gubernatorial nomination to George Silzer as Edwards was moved to the U.S. Senate. Replacing Silzer, Hague protégé A. Harry Moore was elected in 1925 to the first of three terms as governor of the Garden State. Controlling state patronage, civil service, and taxing authority, Hague consolidated his rule.[4]

In Albany, would-be boss Dan O'Connell launched his political career in 1919 by running for assessor on a reform platform, accusing GOP boss Barnes of high taxes and excessive public spending. Once elected, O'Connell forged ties with Democratic Governor Al Smith. Though Smith lost his gubernatorial rebid in the 1920 Republican landslide, the Albany Democrats were instrumental in his political comeback. At the 1921 state Democratic convention held in Syracuse, the Albany county delegation supported Smith. The 1921 election installed Smith in the statehouse and O'Connell across the street in city hall. Throughout the 1920s a grateful Smith would assist "Uncle Dan's" fledgling organization. Smith gave O'Connell 160 state jobs, particularly needed in light of the machine's low tax policies. O'Connell systematically padded the voter registration rolls to turn a two-to-one Republican advantage in 1921 into a two-to-one Democratic advantage by 1927. What O'Connell could not pad, he bought. Precinct captains purchased the flophouse vote on North Pearl Street on election day. The state did not intervene. O'Connell's tax policies, as Frank Robinson has observed, were "played like a violin." The machine sold lowered tax assessments to homeowners and deliberately overassessed businesses relative to residences. Again the state did not intervene. State noninterference in Albany affairs continued under Democratic governors Roosevelt and Lehman in the late 1920s and 1930s. Only with the election of Republican Thomas E. Dewey as governor in 1942 would the state finally investigate the city's voter registration and tax records. It was too late. O'Connell had fully consolidated power and easily derailed the former district attorney's antimachine crusade.[5]

Established machines such as Tammany Hall were less affected by state party politics than were the embryonic Hague and O'Connell organizations. After consolidating power in the late 1880s, the

Wigwam merely required the existence of a stable state political structure, regardless of the controlling party. Tammany bosses Croker and Murphy worked closely with state Republican boss Thomas Platt and his successor, Billy Barnes, to protect their respective political organizations. Murphy and Platt joined forces to defeat the direct primary bill sponsored by progressive GOP Governor Charles Evans Hughes. Even federal assault did not necessarily harm entrenched machines. Democratic President Woodrow Wilson's anti-Tammany federal patronage policies failed to weaken the Wigwam.[6]

Even though they were less buffeted by state politics, established machines still worked to control the governorship and state legislature. The governorship meant state patronage, the legislature, greater local autonomy and welfare legislation. With Tammany's help, Democrat John A. Dix was elected governor of New York in 1910, the first Democratic governor in years. A grateful Dix reciprocated by enlarging Tammany's patronage army with 300 state jobs. Dix's Democratic successor was William Sulzer, a protégé of Tammany boss Croker and a member of the Wigwam for twenty-five years, who became a born-again reformer in office. Tammany then worked as hard disposing of the turncoat Sulzer as it had in initially electing him. The Tiger also labored to control the state legislature. Tammany controlled the 1911 and 1913 sessions, the first controlled by the Democrats in twenty-five years. The machine helped pass important state social welfare legislation popular with the city's working class, particularly the Jews, who showed signs of political independence by supporting Socialist and Progressive candidates.[7]

Antimachine States

In contrast to New Jersey and New York, other state party systems were hostile to machine incubation. In the period 1896 to 1928, Republicans dominated California and Pennsylvania, preventing the rebirth of the Bay Area machine and any serious challenge to the GOP machines of Philadelphia and Pittsburgh. In Massachusetts and Illinois, however, Democratic governors were elected between 1910 and 1917. Yet these governors actively opposed the

Irish party bosses of Boston and Chicago as the bosses sought to consolidate power.

In San Francisco, an Irish successor to the Buckley machine did not emerge. The Democrats returned to power in 1897 as Irish reform Democrat James D. Phelan was elected mayor. Faced with a lockout and strike by the city's Irish teamsters in 1901, the conservative Phelan dispatched the Irish police force to convoy strikebreakers, break up picket lines, and disperse gatherings of strikers. Phelan's antilabor policies infuriated working-class Irish and contributed to the precipitous decline in Democratic party fortunes. In the 1901 city election, working-class Irish turned their backs on the Democrats and supported the newly organized Union Labor party. Skillfully using labor rhetoric, Abraham Reuf, a minor Republican party official, built a labor "machine" that ran San Francisco from 1901 to 1907. By 1907, however, the labor party's fortunes had fallen sharply as Reuf and other ULP leaders were indicted for graft. Patrick H. "Pinhead" McCarthy, the Irish-born head of the powerful Building Trades Council, breathed new life into the labor party, serving as mayor of the city between 1910 and 1912. Reuf and McCarthy relied heavily on the Irish vote. Having defected from the antilabor Democrats, the city's Irish gave the labor party nearly two-thirds of their votes in the six city elections held between 1901 and 1911. Yankees and Germans, in contrast, gave the ULP only one-third of their votes.[8]

Neither McCarthy nor the Irish leaders of the Democratic party could rebuild an Irish working-class machine, in part because they were outbid by the state Republicans. The Republicans controlled the Golden State from the late 1890s to the early 1930s. Elected governor in 1910, progressive Republican Hiram Johnson proposed state legislation significantly broadening the GOP's appeal to San Francisco's working-class Irish. Under Johnson's leadership, the state legislature passed far-reaching labor and social welfare legislation. As a result, Johnson brought many Bay Area working-class and Irish voters into the Republican party. The progressive platform also included such machine-weakening measures as the direct primary, nonpartisan local elections, and the initiative, referendum, and recall. The Bay Area's Irish Democratic politicians were stymied. Their constituents had first deserted them for labor candidates in city elections. Now Johnson was wooing the Irish working class into Republican politics at the state level. Electoral reforms, particularly nonpartisanship in city elections, made the task of machine building even more difficult. Republican politician James "Sunny Jim" Rolph quickly stepped into the political breach. Elected mayor in 1913, Rolph was a local version of Hiram Johnson. The progressive Rolph fashioned a broad-based bipartisan coalition of workers and businessmen that ruled the city into the 1930s. As in Philadelphia and Pittsburgh, the more politically ambitious Irish Democrats gravitated into the ruling camp.[9]

In contrast to GOP-controlled California, Massachusetts and Illinois elected Democratic governors during the Wilson era. But these governors did little to centralize Democratic or Irish power in Boston and Chicago. In Boston, Democrats John F. "Honey Fitz" Fitzgerald, elected mayor in 1905, and James Michael Curley, elected mayor in 1913, both tried their hand at building citywide machines. Growing Irish-Yankee friction in the state Democratic party, however, prevented Fitzgerald and Curley from eliminating each other and the remaining Irish ward bosses. Following Pat Maguire's death in 1896, Yankees from western Massachusetts consolidated their control over the state Democratic party organization as the contentious Boston Irish fought among themselves. The westerners would do little to relinquish control of the party.

In the early twentieth century, the Democrats finally broke the Republican stranglehold on the Bay State, electing three governors: William Douglas in 1904, Eugene Foss in 1910, and David A. Walsh in 1913. All three, however, came from the party's western wing and did little to centralize Boston's Irish politics. In 1905 Fitzgerald began building a citywide machine. The number of city employees multiplied as he hired temporary workers not covered by civil service. Governor Douglas did everything in his power to frustrate Fitzgerald, including giving state patronage to Fitzgerald's opponents. James Michael Curley would also use the powers of the mayor's office to try building a machine. Curley, like Fitzgerald before him, failed as relations between city hall and the statehouse soured. Even though Irishman Walsh had been elected governor, his primary allegiance was to the westerners. Walsh did little to help Curley in his quest to be a city boss.[10]

The Illinois Democratic party also experienced a resurgence during the Wilson years. Democrat Edward R. Dunne was elected governor in 1912. Elected on a reform platform, Dunne actually worked to *increase* rather than decrease Democratic factionalism in Chicago. A nominal protégé of Carter Harrison II, Dunne played the Harrison and Hopkins-Sullivan factions against each other, using state patronage to build an independent reform wing within the local party. Without state patronage, Mayor Harrison never moved beyond a personal following. When Hopkins and Sullivan began building a machine with county patronage, they found their efforts frustrated by Dunne's state patronage-based organization.[11]

In states such as Massachusetts and Illinois, *weak* state Republican machines paradoxically hurt Irish Democratic bosses trying to consolidate power in the cities. In the aftermath of the Civil War, the concerted Radical Republican attack on the emerging big-city Democratic machines had backfired. The urban Democratic party had been strengthened, not weakened. The Republican resurgence of the 1890s brought a new round of state attacks on the big-city Irish machines, directed by younger Republican bosses—Thomas Platt in New York, Murray Winthrop Crane in Massachusetts, and William Lorimer in Illinois. In contrast to Pennsylvania, the new state Republican machines were too faction-ridden to wrest control of the cities from the Democrats.

Weak state GOP bosses bolstered their position vis-à-vis Republican rivals by cutting deals with local Democratic politicians. GOP rivals, in turn, built alliances with other factions in the urban Democratic party. In the post-1896 era, Republican state dominance combined with factionalism meant that no machine, Republican or Democratic, could easily emerge in the cities. Interparty collusion reinforced intraparty factionalism.[12]

Republican state factionalism and collusion with the big-city Democrats were most advanced in Illinois. By 1900, the Republicans were split between a state faction headed by "Blond Boss" Lorimer, successor to "Black Jack" Logan, and an opposing federal faction fueled by patronage from the McKinley administration. Lorimer's strength lay in his control of the Cook County Republican organization, in ties to downstate Republican governors such as John R. Tanner, and in legislative henchmen such as Eddie Dwyer and "Fire Escape" Gus Nohe who controlled the General Assembly.

After the turn of the century, however, Lorimer's control of both state and county Republican organizations was seriously weakened. At the state level, the federal faction denied renomination to Lorimer ally Governor Tanner and forced Lorimer to accept downstate politician Richard C. Yates as the gubernatorial nominee. A limited alliance of convenience between Lorimer and Governor Yates broke down over Yates's renomination, and the Lorimer organization was denied state patronage. Lorimer's Cook County organization was then captured by States Attorney Charles S. Dineen, a former Lorimer protégé responsible for organizing the Swedes of southwest Chicago, who launched his own candidacy for the governorship. In a bitter contest in 1904, Dineen was elected governor.

Lorimer made deals with various Democratic city politicians to weaken his Republican opponents. In the 1908 gubernatorial election, Lorimer "knifed" Governor Dineen in Cook County, throwing his organization's votes to the Democratic nominee Adlai Stevenson. Still intent on revenge, Lorimer enlisted the aid of Hopkins and Sullivan to bolster his campaign in the state legislature for a U.S. Senate seat. Collusion between Lorimer and Hopkins-Sullivan reinforced factionalism among both the state Republicans and Chicago Democrats.[13]

Paradoxically, the *strengthening* of the Lorimer machine in the 1920s aided Democratic machine building in Chicago. In 1920, Lorimer's candidate, Len Small, won the governorship. In Cook County, Lorimer duplicated the feat by directing Republican "Big Bill" Thompson's victorious mayoral campaign. Lorimer and Thompson specifically targeted the city's newly arrived Southern and Eastern European immigrants. To remain competitive with Lorimer and Thompson, Democratic chieftain Roger Sullivan and his successor, George Brennan, broadened the base of the city's Democratic party by actively assimilating the new ethnics as citizens, voters, precinct captains, party committeemen, and public officeholders.

State politics thus continued to shape the destinies of the Irish machines and would-be Irish bosses well into the twentieth century. In New Jersey and New York, friendly Democratic governors nurtured the Hague and O'Connell machines during their fragile incubation period. In California and Pennsylvania, however, strong state Republican leaders or machines frustrated the urban Irish Democrats. The big-city Irish politicos missed their greatest opportunities in Massachusetts and Illinois during the Wilson years. Democratic governors in these two states did everything in their power to prevent the consolidation of urban and Irish power.

It is also important to note how state Republican machines shaped the fortunes of the urban Democracy. On the one hand, weak state GOP machines institutionalized interparty collusion and factionalism among the big-city Democrats. On the other hand, strong state Republican machines encouraged a political dialectic of challenge and response, forcing the big-city Democrats to strengthen their organizational apparatus and broaden the party's ethnic electoral base. Yet too much state Republican strength, as in Pennsylvania or California, relegated the urban Democrats to minority party status.

The Liberal Fiscal Policies of the New Machines

Unlike their predecessors, the new Irish machines went on a spending spree. Between 1880 and 1902, a period of generally stable prices, per capita spending in the four Irish machine cities had dropped from $30 to $17 (see Table 4). After the turn of the century, machines jettisoned their fiscal diet and went on a spree. Between 1902 and 1932, a period of rising prices until 1929, per capita outlays in New York, Jersey City, and Albany rose from $17 to $78. A portion of this increase was illusory, for the cost-of-living index doubled. Yet not all of the municipal spending increase was eaten by inflation. Table 8 compares big-city spending patterns from 1902 to 1932 in constant (1902) dollars. The Irish machines led the way on a big-city spending splurge. In New York, Jersey City, and Albany, real, that is, inflation-adjusted, per capita outlays rose by 112 percent after having dropped by 43 percent in the late nineteenth century.[14]

The reborn machines also went on a borrowing binge. In the nineteenth century, bosses Kelly, Croker, Buckley, Davis, and Mc-

TABLE 8. *Cities on a Spending Spree, 1902–1932*

Cities and Regimes	Average Per Capita City Outlays ($)		Percentage Change from 1902 to 1932
	1902	1932[a]	
Irish cities (8)	18	33	83.3
Irish Democratic machines (New York, Jersey City, Albany)	17	36	111.8
Irish Democratic nonmachine (Boston)	35	44	25.7
Non-Irish Republican machine (Philadelphia, Pittsburgh)	16	28	75.0
Non-Irish nonmachine (Chicago, San Francisco)	14	27	92.9
Non-Irish cities (13)[b]	15	29	93.3

Sources: U.S. Bureau of the Census, *Special Reports: Statistics of Cities, 1902* (Washington, D.C.: Government Printing Office, 1902), Table 21, pp. 252–299; U.S. Bureau of the Census, *Financial Statistics of Cities Having a Population over 100,000, 1932* (Washington, D.C.: Government Printing Office, 1934), Table 4, pp. 72–74.

[a] In 1902 dollars. For the cost-of-living measures used to adjust city spending and indebtedness for the period 1880 to 1932, see U.S. Bureau of the Census, *Historical Statistics of the United States: Colonial Times to 1957* (Washington, D.C.: Government Printing Office, 1960), series E 157–160, p. 127.

[b] Includes all cities with more than 50,000 population in 1870 *and* less than 13 percent Irish. See Table 1. (Allegheny annexed by Pittsburgh in 1907.)

Cabe had either been unwilling or unable to borrow. As Table 6 shows, the early machines' debt burden barely grew between 1880 and 1902. Bosses Murphy, Hague, and O'Connell, however, discovered that public debt was a many-splendored thing. Between 1902 and 1932, real per capita debt in New York, Jersey City, and Albany rose by 50 percent, from $93 to $140. The Irish bosses easily outpaced other big-city politicians in their early and enthusiastic commitment to Keynesian municipal financing. By the early 1930s, the three Irish machines' average debt burden was 41 percent higher—$140 versus $99 per capita—than that for the other nineteen big cities.[15]

Murphy, Hague, and O'Connell could spend and spend and borrow and borrow because members of the Yankee middle class were voting with their feet and leaving the cities, and because a financial modus vivendi had been reached with the state Republican bosses.

The Yankee middle class had formed the backbone of opposition to the taxing and spending schemes of the early Celtic machines. By the late nineteenth century, however, changes in urban transportation allowed the middle class to move to the streetcar suburbs.[16] Machine politicians used annexation and consolidation to enhance the organization's resources and to enlarge city boundaries by capturing the affluent migrants and their pocketbooks.

As the social and economic disparity between the suburbs and the cities grew, the affluent fought back. Continuing its suburban exodus, the middle class successfully pressured the state GOP bosses to lead it to the promised land. In response, Republican-controlled state legislatures made big-city annexation more difficult by imposing the requirement of dual voter approval in the city and to-be-annexed area. At the same time, the GOP made suburban incorporation easier. Machines could no longer swallow the suburbs. In the 1890s, the twenty largest cities had increased their territorial boundaries by 32 percent. Between 1900 and 1910, however, the big cities could increase their borders by only 11 percent.[17]

With middle-class suburbanization, the threat of big-city tax revolts evaporated. As impoverished Southern and Eastern Europeans replaced the Yankee middle class in the cities, bosses appealed to renters rather than homeowners. By 1920, more than three-quarters of all homes in New York, Jersey City, and Albany were rented.[18] Facing lower-class renters, bosses Murphy, Hague, and O'Connell could raise property taxes, the source of over two-thirds of municipal revenue, or pass bond referenda with little voter opposition. The machine's spending and borrowing spree would be paid for by nonvoting absentee landlords.

Disenfranchised urban landlords fought back at the state level. No longer able to stop the torrent of tax increases and bond elections with their votes, big-city property owners appealed to the state to limit the machine's fiscal appetite. Yet many of the state financial safeguards of the late nineteenth century had been torn down in order to heal divisions within the GOP's ranks. After 1896, the new Republican majority had quickly fractured into two camps. State Republican bosses such as New York's Platt confronted urban independents such as Theodore Roosevelt, who demanded an end to state interference in city affairs. To reduce the rift between independents and regular Republicans, GOP bosses reluctantly supported "home rule" for the cities. Finally recognizing the legal and financial independence of the cities, state machines removed many of the old constitutional barriers on local taxing, spending, and borrowing.[19]

Reform Republicans soothed the fears of urban property owners with *state* rather than local tax reform. Progressive GOP governors such as New York's Benjamin J. Odell, Jr., demonstrated their sympathy with property by lifting the double tax burden on real estate. In the late nineteenth century, both state and local governments relied heavily on property taxes. In 1890, for example, real property taxes accounted for 82 percent of local revenue and 64 percent of state revenue. This double burden heightened middle-class sensitivity to tax increases. After the turn of the century, tax reformers reduced the middle-class burden by separating local and state revenue sources. Local governments would continue to rely on the property tax. State revenues, however, were significantly diversified to include corporation, personal income, and gasoline taxes. By 1932 property taxes accounted for only 14 percent of state revenue compared with 72 percent of local revenue.[20]

Freed of the burden of financing both state and local government, the urban middle class jumped on the machine's spending bandwagon, demanding more public spending for parks, recreation, health, and education. In municipal bond elections, middle-class voters supported outlays for new parks, hospitals, and schools. Enthusiasm for capital improvements united the middle class and the working class. In ten bond elections held in San Francisco between 1899 and 1910, for example, middle-class and working-class voters approved by identical three-to-one margins an aggregate $151 million increase in the city's debt to pay for schools, hospitals, parks, sewers, and city-owned railroad and water systems.[21]

To Tax or To Borrow:
A Tale of Jersey City and Albany

Irish bosses could capitalize up to a point on the new middle-class enthusiasm for public spending. The pain threshold had been raised. But homeowners would still balk at massive property tax increases to pay for public projects employing the machine's pat-

ronage army. Debt financing concealed machine financing from
middle-class view: machines could absorb some public debts without necessarily increasing taxes. Nevertheless, machines had strong
organizational incentives to tax rather than borrow. Taxing enlarged the permanent city payroll—the machine's primary reward
to the cadre of party officials and voters. Borrowing, in contrast,
generated temporary patronage on public works projects for construction workers. For obvious reasons, bosses preferred permanent public sector patronage to temporary private sector jobs.

Some machines taxed; others borrowed. Machines taxed when
voters rented and property was absentee-owned. They borrowed
when large numbers of tax-conscious homeowners voted. Different property-owning patterns in Jersey City and Albany propelled
the Hague and O'Connell machines along different expansionary
fiscal routes. Boss Hague taxed. In the first ten years of his rule,
real per capita spending in Jersey City tripled, from $15 to $47. By
1930 Jersey City had the dubious honor of having the highest municipal tax rate in the country. O'Connell borrowed. During the
first ten years of Uncle Dan's rule, per capita spending in Albany
only rose from $14 to $28. Yet between 1902 and 1932, Albany's
per capita debt nearly tripled, from $45 to $118. By the early
1930s, nearly one-third of the entire city budget was devoted to
servicing the massive debt. In Jersey City, in contrast, the debt burden rose by a modest 50 percent.

Jersey City's economy of large absentee-owned corporations
shaped Hague's taxation policies. Serving as a major terminus for
railway traffic into New York City, the city had fourteen railroads
by 1875. The railroads soon owned one-third of the land in the
city. City politicians had cast covetous eyes on the railways. Railroad property taxes could fill city coffers, and their payrolls could
provide steady employment for the machine's precinct workers
and voters. To elude the grasp of rapacious local politicians, the
railroads successfully lobbied the state in 1884 for passage of
the Railroad Tax Act. The act forced the city to tax most railroad property at substantially lower rates relative to other taxable
property.[22]

Hague succeeded where other politicians had failed. He built his
party organization by boldly taxing the city's railroads, public service, and oil companies in order to pay for the largest per capita

city payroll in the country. Under Hague, the assessed evaluation
of railroad property ballooned from $67 million to $167 million.
For public service corporations, property values were raised from
$3 million to $30 million. Unintimidated by the Rockefellers,
Hague reassessed the city's Standard Oil property from $1.5 mil-
lion to $14 million. Claiming that Hague was a modern-day Robin
Hood, the big companies fought back, appealing the city's reassessments to the pro-railroad state Board of Taxes and Assessments. Predictably, the state board ruled against Hague, forcing
the Jersey City boss to consider how he planned to maintain his
massive patronage army. Hague decided to take over the state. A
pro-Hague governor would appoint a sympathetic tax board, and
the dramatic reassessments would stick.[23]

Grooming and electing a succession of Garden State Democratic
governors, who obliged Hague by appointing his men to the tax
and civil service boards, Hague passed the cost of the swollen city
payroll to the big corporations rather than to the city's voters, 80
percent of whom were renters and thus immune to the machine's
attack on property. Conceding defeat, the corporations passed the
Hague tax bill on to their customers as a cost of doing business in
Hudson County. With his windfall profits, Hague padded the city's
payroll from 1,745 in 1917 to 7,297 in 1930.[24]

Uncle Dan chose to borrow rather than tax. Compared with Jersey City, Albany's revenue base was more diversified and smaller.
Instead of national corporations, the city's economy consisted of
small family-owned retail businesses. Large parcels of tax-exempt
state property limited the upstate machine's opportunity for plun-
der. Most important, however, the city was fast becoming a haven
for homeowners rather than renters. Between 1920 and 1940, as
the machine discouraged apartment building, the city's homeownership rate rose from 28 percent to 41 percent.

As the ranks of tax-conscious homeowners grew, O'Connell's
fiscal policies became more circumspect. In the 1920s, the city's
public spending grew slowly, more comparable to the rates of non-
Irish or nonmachine cities than to New York and Jersey City. To
raise revenue, the machine sold low tax assessments to homeowners, a practice that continued into the 1970s. To further favor
homeowners, the machine created a two-tier system of assessments. The O'Connell organization assessed commercial property

at 64 percent of market value and residential property at 28 percent. Low taxes did not necessarily mean few patronage jobs. The Albany machine preferred quantity to quality, creating a welter of poor-paying blue-collar jobs in the parks and public works departments. Forced to keep the tax rate down, O'Connell keenly appreciated the ways public debt could be put to political use. The city's heavy borrowing created private sector patronage and helped finance the organization's tax auction scheme.[25]

Rewarding the Irish: The Patronage Possibilities of the New Machines

The taxing and borrowing policies of the second generation of Irish machines generated an enormous cache of patronage with which to reward the Irish and reduce working-class discontent. Between 1900 and 1930 the public sector nearly tripled in size in the three machine cities. Local government employment in New York City, for example, mushroomed from 54,386 to 148,421. The machines' primitive Keynesianism allowed the bosses to tighten their grip on the urban labor market as the public sector expanded more quickly than the private sector. Between 1900 and 1930 the booming public sector absorbed 10 percent of all job growth in New York, Jersey City, and Albany compared with only 5 percent between 1870 and 1900.[26]

Reformers fought the bosses with civil service plans designed to shield public personnel decisions from party influence. Yet the merit system did not appreciably affect the bosses' ability to staff the public payroll with the politically and ethnically deserving. The New York state constitution created civil service boards in New York and Albany as early as 1884 when Tammany and the McCabe machines were consolidating power. By state law in 1911, the New Jersey Civil Service Commission began administering the merit system in Jersey City. Bosses Murphy, O'Connell, and Hague easily circumvented these restraints. In New York City, for example, the Tammany-controlled civil service board rarely posted public notices of city job openings. Jobseekers were advised to visit their local ward boss instead. Irish civil service examiners gave essay rather than objective examinations to jobseekers in order to enhance their discretion over the choice of applicants. Exam scores were rarely posted. The city's antiquated merit system covered only a limited number of permanent positions, and Tammany hired, fired, and rehired an army of temporary workers exempt from civil service coverage. Before there were Kelly Girls, there were Tammany's "Kelly Boys."[27]

Twentieth-century machines soon uncovered other stores of public sector patronage. Urban machines particularly coveted county government. Machines needed to control the county prosecutor's office and court system as a buffer against attack by Democratic rivals and state Republicans. Control of the county tax assessor's office allowed bosses like O'Connell to manipulate and sell low assessments. Above all, the county represented a lucrative source of patronage. After passage of the 1897 Consolidation Act in New York, Manhattan-based Tammany quickly moved to capture county as well as city patronage, in part to weaken rival Democratic organizations in the outer boroughs, such as Brooklyn's McLaughlin machine. By 1930 Tammany controlled nearly 13,000 county jobs. In the tradition of "Little Bob" Davis, Boss Hague ruled Hudson County as well as Jersey City, adding 1,700 county positions to the machine's arsenal of 5,600 city jobs. O'Connell emulated Murphy and Hague by moving to control Albany County and its 346 patronage positions. As the number of urban voters grew relative to rural voters, big-city bosses moved to take over state politics and patronage as well. Pro-machine Democratic governors in New York and New Jersey gave the Irish bosses hundreds of state jobs.[28]

The machines' private sector patronage also ballooned, both in the construction industry and with firms doing business with the city. The machines' mounting debt generated sizable employment on public works projects. In San Francisco, for example, Boss Reuf's labor "machine" embarked on an ambitious program of capital improvements. Between 1900 and 1910 city outlays tripled as the proportion of the budget devoted to public works rose from 20 percent to nearly 40 percent. Local observers estimated that public projects had created more than 6,000 construction jobs, rivaling in size the combined city-county payroll.[29]

Murphy, Hague, and O'Connell also turned to large corporations as another source of jobs and profit. Tammany's Murphy called it his "businessmen's plan" to diversify the machine's resources as a hedge against fickle voters. Besides contractors, Murphy tithed city-regulated transportation and utility firms for patronage jobs and campaign contributions. Ironically, Tammany's reform opponents had significantly contributed to the machine's stock of private sector patronage by enlarging local government's regulatory responsibilities over privately owned street railways and utilities. Tammany quickly discovered the political uses of the regulatory state. In exchange for favorable franchise terms, public service corporations would make campaign donations and employ some of the machine's henchmen. Murphy's hedge paid off handsomely. In 1914, Tammany faced political disaster. Reformer John Purroy Mitchel was elected mayor, and the Wigwam lost city and county patronage. Martin Glynn, the Democratic gubernatorial nominee, was defeated. Claiming that he owed the organization nothing, President Wilson refused to give Murphy federal patronage. Even without public offices, Tammany prospered as campaign coffers remained filled with corporate contributions, and party workers were shuttled into the private sector.[30]

The second-generation Irish machines controlled patronage indeed. The expanding city and county payroll accounted for 10 percent of all urban job growth between 1900 and 1930; debt-financed public works projects added another 6 to 8 percent. State jobs and "unofficial" patronage further supplemented the machine's job roster. In all, the Irish machines created or controlled more than 20 percent of post-1900 job growth compared with less than 10 percent in the pre-1900 era.

Could the Irish now use the machines as a *group* route from rags to riches? Second-generation machines disappointed few Irish jobseekers. Table 9 estimates Irish employment gains in city and county government in New York, Jersey City, and Albany between 1900 and 1930. The Celtic surge into the public sector continued. Local government employment in the three machine cities rose from 59,202 in 1900 to 158,453 as the number of Irish payrollers increased from 21,749 to 82,116. Hiring their own, the Celtic bosses gave the Irish more than 60 percent of the new public jobs. Given the slow increase in the number of Irish workers and their continued ascent in public employment, the proportion of the Irish workforce employed by local government increased dramatically.

TABLE 9. *The Patronage Tree Bears Fruit: Machines Reward the Irish, 1900–1930*

Machine Cities	Local Government Employment, 1900[a]			Local Government Employment, 1930[a]			Percentage of Irish Workforce Employed by Local Government	
	Irish[b]	All	Percentage Irish	Irish[c]	All	Percentage Irish	1900[b]	1930[c]
New York	19,926	54,386	36.6	76,734	148,421	51.7	5.8	23.6
Jersey City	1,293	3,052	42.4	4,254	7,297	58.3	5.1	20.8
Albany	530	1,764	30.0	1,128	2,735	41.0	4.6	14.8

Sources: U.S. Bureau of the Census, *Special Reports: Occupations at the Twelfth Census* (Washington, D.C.: Government Printing Office, 1904), Tables 41, 43; U.S. Bureau of the Census, *Fifteenth Census of the United States, 1930* (Washington, D.C.: Government Printing Office, 1933), vol. 2, Table 11, vol. 4, Table 12; U.S. Bureau of the Census, *Statistical Abstract of the United States, 1938* (Washington, D.C.: Government Printing Office, 1938), Table 234, p. 229; New York World, *World Almanac, 1931* (New York: New York World, 1931), pp. 210, 545–549 (New York and Jersey City); Terry Nichols Clark, "The Irish Ethic and the Spirit of Patronage," *Ethnicity* 2 (1975): Fig. 3, p. 342 (Albany); and Table 7, above.

[a] Includes city and county employment.
[b] First- and second-generation Irish Americans.
[c] Estimated for first-, second-, and third-generation Irish. See Chapter 3, n. 31, p. 277, for estimating procedure.

In New York City, for example, the public sector employed nearly one-quarter of all first-, second-, and third-generation Irish workers in 1930, up from 6 percent in 1900.[31]

Machines also created private sector job opportunities for the Irish with their expanded menu of public works projects and their regulatory leverage over corporations. Although it is impossible to estimate precisely the machine's private sector patronage and the share received by the Irish, it is fair to assume that the construction industry and public service corporations employed at least half as many Irish as did local government. On the eve of the Depression, then, Tammany Hall and the Hague organization directly or indirectly employed at least one-third (and perhaps more) of the Irish workforce in the two cities.

The twentieth-century machines' patronage policies appear to support the contention that politics served as an important conduit of Irish economic advancement. Yet compared with Jews, the Irish were slow to build a professional and business class. The "lace curtain" Irish middle class, tied to civil service and the building trades, was just emerging by the late 1920s. With the coming of the Depression, Irish middle-class aspirations were set back until after World War II.

Paradoxically, Irish political success and economic failure were intimately related. Contrary to the conventional wisdom, machine patronage *reinforced* the lowly status of the Irish. In their endless quest to stretch the vote-getting value of patronage, bosses continued to proletarianize the public sector. In New York City, the blue-collar proportion of the public payroll rose from 54 percent in 1900 to 60 percent in 1930 as thousands of unskilled and semiskilled Irish took jobs in municipally owned subways, street railways, waterworks, and port facilities. Municipally owned utilities accounted for over one-half of Irish public sector job gains in New York in this era. Employment in the city's expanding police and fire departments accounted for another 21 percent of Irish government gains. In all, three-quarters of the Irish using Tammany's employment agency were shuttled into a blue-collar cul-de-sac.[32]

Nearly monopolizing blue-collar patronage, the Irish were forced to share white-collar patronage with other ethnic groups. The school system represented the largest and fastest growing source of white-collar public employment as Southern and Eastern

Europeans entered the classroom. Yet Jews soon displaced the Irish as teachers. In New York, Jews represented 11 percent of entering teachers in 1900 and 40 percent in 1930. The judicial and legal departments represented a prime source of white-collar patronage for Irish lawyers. After the turn of the century the Irish crowded onto the local bench and into the city and county corporation counsels' offices. Yet by the late 1920s Jews were also making an appearance as government attorneys and judges. Squeezed by the Jewish advance, upwardly mobile Irish filled low-paying clerkships.[33]

Thus the Irish in the early twentieth century crowded into the middling ranks of the public sector—in police and fire departments, utilities, and government clerkships. Yet as poorly paid policemen, firemen, and municipal clerks, the Irish were solidly lower-middle rather than middle class. By channeling so much economic energy into the public sector, the Irish forsook opportunities in the private sector, save for industries such as construction that depended on political connections. Ironically, as the public sector grew more blue-collar and Irish, the private sector grew more white-collar and non-Irish. In New York City, for example, the white-collar proportion of the private sector workforce rose from 34 percent in 1900 to 45 percent in 1930 as the Irish share of private employment dropped from 23 percent to 9 percent.[34]

Yet patronage and more patronage tamed the once wild Irish as city sinecures dampened the Celtic enthusiasm for labor politics. In New York, the last serious threat of working-class Irish insurgency against Tammany occurred in the 1905 mayoral election. Portraying himself as an urban populist, mayoral candidate William Randolph Hearst of the Municipal Ownership League attacked the unholy alliance between Tammany and private utility firms seeking public franchises. Irish-American labor leaders supported Hearst and his program of public ownership of the city's utilities. Hearst targeted the Irish vote, attacking George B. McClellan, Tammany's "silk-stocking" mayoral candidate, as an Anglophile—anathema to the Irish—and accusing Boss Murphy of "aristocratic habits." McClellan barely beat Hearst, 228,000 to 225,000, as the self-styled populist ran even with Tammany in working-class Irish districts. Tammany took the hint. After the election, the machine sponsored city ownership of utilities, creating thousands of sinecures for the Irish and bringing them securely into the organization's fold. Running on the Civic Alliance ticket in 1909, Hearst was badly trounced by Tammany's Gaynor as the Irish stayed in the Wigwam. Thereafter, Tammany would receive more than 75 percent of the working-class Irish vote. Celtic discontent with Tammany would now come from the reform-minded middle class rather than from labor.[35]

In Jersey City, Hague's pro-Irish patronage policies also paid off at the polls. As in other locales, the Jersey City Irish had grown militant in the late nineteenth century, experimenting with nationalism and unionism as alternatives to machine politics. In particular, the Irish Land League and Irish-run Central Labor Union led strikes and boycotts against the railroads, the major employers of the city's Irish working class. The League and labor forced the Davis machine leftward as Irish cops were sent to protect Irish strikers. The Irish reembraced the machine as Davis's policies earned corporate enmity. What Davis did with labor policies, Hague did with public jobs. Believing his fellow Irish had an innate political ability lacking in other groups, Hague gave the Irish a virtual franchise on public employment. The payroll Irish and their families returned the favor, treating their vote for Hague as a "religious obligation." In the Horseshoe district, a gerrymandered ward lumping most of the city's Irish together, the Hague organization regularly rolled up forty-to-one majorities.[36]

The New Immigrants: Old and New World Obstacles to Mobilization

Just as Bosses Murphy, Hague, and O'Connell learned how to subdue the Irish with patronage, they were confronted with the problem of how to incorporate the millions of "new" immigrants from Southern and Eastern Europe. Fleeing political and economic oppression, the new migrants began arriving in the cities in large numbers in the 1880s. Jews, Italians, and Poles predominated. For the Jews and Italians, New York City, the port of entry for three-quarters of all immigrants arriving between 1880 and 1914, would represent the urban mecca. New York counted 55,000 Russian and Polish Jews and 40,000 Italians among its residents in 1890, representing 5 percent of the overall population. By 1930, Gotham would be home to more than 2.5 million Jews and Italians, now representing 36 percent of the population. For the Poles, Chicago would be home. A trickle of Polish émigrés became a torrent as the number of Chicago Poles swelled from 24,086 in 1890 to 401,316 in 1930, constituting 12 percent of the city's population.

The second-wave immigrants arrived with none of the political advantages brought by the Irish from the Old World. Few Southern and Eastern Europeans spoke or read English. Most arrived with local and family rather than national identities, formed in the village and shtetl. In southern Italy and Sicily, for example, geographical and language barriers reinforced a web of local loyalties and identities known as *campanilismo*. Even residents of nearby villages were viewed as foreigners.

Return migration would also politically handicap the new immigrants, particularly the Italians. Coming to the United States primarily for economic reasons, single working-age males constituted 80 percent of all Italian immigrants arriving before 1914. Working for a *padrone* as casual labor on construction projects, the Italians scrimped and saved to return to their homeland. In all, 42 percent of all Italian immigrants arriving in America before World War I would return to Italy. Of the second-wave immigrants, Jews would stay. Fleeing the pogroms carried out after the assassination of Czar Alexander in 1881, Jews sought permanent refuge and brought their families with them. In contrast with the Italians, only 7 percent of the Jews would return to Europe.[37]

Fearful that the Irish bosses would claim the votes of the Southern and Eastern Europeans and threaten GOP control of state and federal government, Republicans hastily erected a series of legal barriers to citizenship and voting. At the federal level, the Republican majority passed the Naturalization Law of 1906 to tighten and lengthen the citizenship process. Radicals were disqualified. Naturalization courts began demanding literacy in English as a condition of citizenship. The act required more stringent proof of both lawful entry into the country and five years' continuous residence. Under the new law, the denial rate on naturalization petitions rose from an estimated 3 percent to 15 percent. Italians, in particular, were affected by the literacy test. On the eve of World War I, naturalization courts turned down nearly one out of every five Italians seeking citizenship. Under the 1906 act, the naturalization process doubled in average length—to eleven years—as would-be citizens were forced to provide witnesses testifying to the character of their entry into the United States and to the length of their residence.[38]

At the state level, Republican legislators were simultaneously tightening state voter qualifications to hamper the ability of the big-city Democratic machines to capitalize on the new supply of European votes. The state suffrage restriction movement took various forms. In the Midwest alien suffrage was abolished. In the mid-nineteenth century, thirteen predominately midwestern states had enticed settlers by permitting aliens who had filed their first naturalization papers to vote. Alien suffrage was an early casualty of the new immigration and the GOP resurgence in the 1890s. As early as 1894, Michigan's Republicans sponsored a constitutional amendment disenfranchising aliens. With the GOP surge, other states followed Michigan's lead; by 1910 alien suffrage was no more.[39]

Literacy tests represented a second way of restricting the vote, particularly in the Northeast. The literacy test movement began in Connecticut in the early 1890s as the state's GOP passed a constitutional amendment requiring that voters be able to read the Constitution. The reading requirement particularly affected the state's Italian-Americans. Literacy tests soon spread to nearly half the states, including Massachusetts. In New York, the GOP created a de facto literacy test by combining the secret ballot with voting machines or the "office" type of paper ballot. Secret voting by machine or office ballot required voters themselves to read the ballot.[40]

The ascendant Republicans also handicapped the new ethnics with personal registration laws applied only to urban voters. In the wake of charges of extensive ballot box stuffing leveled against the urban Democratic bosses, the New York Republicans in 1890 mandated that big-city voters register and reregister in person. While not directly aimed at the Southern and Eastern Europeans, the new registration requirements discouraged participation by making voting more difficult.[41]

The Republicans had small cause for worry. The entrenched Irish big-city bosses had no intention of churning out new citizens and voters. Although the Irish bosses did not support restrictions on citizenship and voting, once they had consolidated power they had little incentive to mobilize the newcomers. In the absence of competitive party pressures, machines relied on already constructed—and rewarded—electoral coalitions. Political assimilation of the new ethnics on the scale of the earlier machine-sponsored incorporation of the Irish would inevitably generate demands for an ethnic redistribution of power and patronage. With the middle class leaving the cities, state GOP bosses offering home rule and tax reform to stave off insurgency by urban progressives, and the new ethnics not participating, the Irish bosses faced the best of all political worlds: fewer potential opponents and more resources to reward the already mobilized.

The GOP had greater headaches where Irish machines had *not* consolidated power. Competitive electoral pressures, whether from the Republicans or from Democratic rivals, would force would-be Irish bosses to court the newcomers more actively. In order to outbid their opponents at the polls, fledgling machines would need to operate their citizenship and voting factories at full blast.

Table 10 shows the sensitivity of the citizenship process to local politics for the eight cities surveyed between 1900 and 1930. Contrary to the conventional wisdom that Irish politicos served as the most active brokers for the new immigrants, citizenship came slowest under entrenched Irish Democratic rule. In New York and Boston, barely one-half of the foreign-born had become citizens by 1930. In contrast, competitive party pressures hastened both Irish Democrats and Republicans to turn out new citizens in Jersey City, Albany, and Chicago. In Jersey City, Boss Hague's fledgling organization in the 1920s assisted the foreign-born in overcoming the hurdles to citizenship. The Barnes GOP machine in Albany had done the same between 1900 and 1920 to stave off a Democratic resurgence. In Chicago, Thompson's Republicans and Sullivan's and Brennan's Democrats engaged in the Great Naturalization Wars. In his pathbreaking study of the early Chicago Democratic machine, Harold Gosnell observed that more than 70 percent of Democratic precinct captains in 1928 reported assisting their constituents with naturalization. By 1930 the Windy City's politicians had secured citizenship for nearly two-thirds of the city's foreign-born. Even Yankee GOP bosses appeared to be better friends of the citizenship-seeking immigrants than did their Irish counterparts in New York and Boston. Reversing their nineteenth-century exclusionary habits, the Republican machines of Philadelphia and Pittsburgh by 1920 had registered more than two-thirds of the foreignborn.[42]

Yet not all of the intercity differences in naturalization rates can be traced to differences in ethnic and party hegemony. Ports of entry, whether New York, Boston, or San Francisco, had the lowest citizenship rates, in part because they had greater numbers of newly arrived immigrants. As Table 10 shows, New York was the great ethnic entrepôt; nearly half of the city's immigrants arrived after 1910. With the fewest new arrivals, Republican machines faced the lightest naturalization burden. In Pittsburgh, for example, two-thirds of the foreign-born had arrived before 1910.

Internal group dynamics also affected the rates at which the Southern and Eastern Europeans became citizens. Arriving with their families, Russian and Polish Jews were quickest to put down roots. Italians, however, were "birds of passage." Intending to return to their homeland, Italian laborers did not become citizens. With Tammany's naturalization mill working at half blast, 39 percent of New York's Russian-born—more than three-quarters Jewish—had become citizens by 1920 compared with only 27 percent of the Italian-born. In competitive Chicago, the two parties turned out new citizens at faster rates. Forty-five percent of the city's Russian-born and 35 percent of the Italian-born were citizens by 1920, even though larger numbers were newer arrivals compared with those in New York.[43]

Registration represented a second hurdle facing the new immigrants on the road to the ballot box. Here too the second-wave immigrants in cities such as New York and Boston suffered from the inertia of one-party and one-group rule. The Celtic party bosses registered the Irish en masse and the Southern and Eastern Europeans en individuel. Machine politicians sponsored the naturalization and registration of small numbers of "reliable" Southern and Eastern Europeans, for example, those on the public payroll and their families, those on public works projects, and the holders of machine-granted business licenses and contracts. This policy of not-so-benign electoral neglect became evident as the Irish consolidated power. In Boston, for example, an estimated 25 percent of the naturalized Italians and 39 percent of Russian-born citizens were registered to vote in the critical 1896 presidential election,

TABLE 10. At Half Blast: Naturalizing the New Immigrants, 1900–1930

	Percentage of Voting-Age White Immigrants Naturalized				Number of Voting-Age White Immigrants				Percentage Arriving Before 1910
	1900	1910	1920	1930	1900	1910	1920	1930	
New York	55.6	38.4	42.6	54.4	539,746	828,793	1,797,882	2,147,979	53.3
Jersey City	61.5	43.9	50.0	64.6	27,104	37,707	70,677	66,662	61.8
Albany	70.1	58.9	61.8	65.4	7,768	8,192	16,348	16,980	61.0
Boston	53.3	46.3	46.5	52.8	81,058	103,160	221,036	216,349	60.5
Chicago	68.6	50.2	54.8	64.2	271,962	379,850	743,803	800,515	60.1
San Francisco	68.4	48.0	52.3	55.3	56,102	75,768	128,791	145,606	57.3
Philadelphia	51.0	41.6	49.4	66.7	127,915	167,072	361,456	349,555	62.2
Pittsburgh	54.3	41.1	53.3	70.5	55,958	70,148	111,907	104,013	66.6

Sources: U.S. Census Office, Twelfth Census of the United States, 1900 (Washington, D.C.: Government Printing Office, 1901), vol. 1, Tables 82, 83; U.S. Bureau of the Census, Thirteenth Census of Population, 1910 (Washington, D.C.: Government Printing Office, 1913), vol. 3, Table 5; U.S. Bureau of the Census, Census of Population, 1920 (Washington, D.C.: Government Printing Office, 1923), vol. 3, Table 10; U.S. Bureau of the Census, Fifteenth Census of the United States, 1930 (Washington, D.C.: Government Printing Office, 1933), vol. 2, Tables 18, 19, 24, 25.
Note: Figures for 1900 and 1910 include males only; for 1920 and 1930, males and females are included.

compared with 88 percent of the naturalized Irish. Adding ethnic insult to injury, Irish bosses inflated the number of Southern and Eastern European voters by registering and voting newly arrived Irish under assumed names. "Big Tim" Sullivan, the Tammany district boss of the Lower East Side, regularly rounded up fresh Irish immigrants in saloons and had them vote under Jewish names.[44]

Heightened citizenship and registration requirements coupled with limited machine sponsorship meant that the new immigrants' actual voting strength lagged far behind potential influence. Between 1890 and 1920 the Jewish and Italian proportion of New York's voting-age population ballooned from 10 percent to 30 percent, whereas their share of the city's voters only rose from 2 percent to 13 percent.[45]

The growing potential vote of the Southern and Eastern Europeans should have been of some concern to the Irish bosses. Yet until the new immigrants began voting and displaying political independence from the machines, the party bosses concentrated on building a large-scale patronage-for-votes system in the Irish-American community. The first-generation machines did not have enough patronage to easily swing elections. In New York, for example, Boss Tweed's temporarily bloated patronage army of 12,000 to 15,000 in the late 1860s represented 16 to 20 percent of the Tammany vote. Bosses Kelly and Croker were forced to economize *and* naturalize and register the old immigrants in record numbers in order to beat back the strong challenge posed by reformers and rival Democrats. Between 1870 and 1890 the number of voters climbed from 132,000 to 274,000, growing at a rate one-third faster than the number of adult males. As the turnout rate rose from 53 percent of the voting-age males in 1870 to 62 percent in 1890, the payroll vote grew smaller. By 1892 the public retinue represented only 13 percent of the Wigwam's vote.[46]

After 1897 the "New Tammany" consolidated power by letting the Naturalization Bureau languish while expanding the vote-rich public payroll. Table 11 shows the changing shape of the New York City voting universe under Bosses Croker and Murphy between 1897 and 1925. Tammany reversed the relationship between the growth in the actual and potential electorates. Between 1897 and 1925 the actual electorate grew at *one-third* the rate of the potential electorate. Voter participation rates nose-dived as naturalization

TABLE 11. *The Tiger Conquers New York: Voting and Turnout Under Bosses Croker and Murphy, 1897–1925*

Mayoral Election	Tammany At The Polls			Voter Participation Rates		Total Adults[a] (thousands)	Total Citizens[a] (thousands)	Total Voters (thousands)	Tammany Voters (thousands)	Public Employees (thousands)
	Outcome	Vote Share (%)	Payroll Share of Tammany Vote (%)	Adults (%)	Citizens (%)					
1897	Win	44.7	19.5	61.2	81.2	855	645	524	234	46
1901	Loss	45.8	22.1	53.4	73.2	1,086	791	579	265	59
1903	Win	53.4	19.8	50.7	71.9	1,163	821	590	315	63
1905	Win	37.8	29.5	48.8	71.2	1,240	850	605	228	67
1909	Win	42.1	30.3	42.6	65.4	1,395	908	594	250	76
1913	Loss	37.3	36.0	40.6	60.6	1,544	1,035	627	234	84
1917	Win	46.8	28.8	40.5	60.5	1,654	1,108	671	314	91
1921	Win	64.2	14.0	31.6	44.4	3,696	2,633	1,168	750	105
1925	Win	65.8	16.6	28.0	37.8	4,058	3,010	1,138	750	124

Sources: U.S. Census Office, *Eleventh Census of the United States, 1890* (Washington, D.C.: Government Printing Office, 1895), vol. 1, pt. 1, Tables 34, 78, vol. 2, pt. 2, Tables 72, 74; U.S. Census Office, *Twelfth Census of the United States, 1900* (Washington, D.C.: Government Printing Office, 1901), vol. 1, pt. 1, Tables 80, 82, 83; U.S. Bureau of the Census, *Population at the Thirteenth Census, 1910* (Washington, D.C.: Government Printing Office, 1913), vol. 1, Tables 16, 34; U.S. Bureau of the Census, *Census of Population, 1920* (Washington, D.C.: Government Printing Office, 1923), vol. 3, Table 10; U.S. Bureau of the Census, *Fifteenth Census of the United States, 1930* (Washington, D.C.: Government Printing Office, 1933), vol. 2, Tables 24, 25, vol. 3, Table 15; New York World-Telegram, *World Almanac, 1940* (New York: World-Telegram, 1940), p. 795.

[a] Estimated for years between censuses.

and registration atrophied. Only 28 percent of New York's adults voted in the 1925 mayoral election compared with 61 percent in Greater New York's first mayoral election held in 1897.

As the electorate shrank in relative size, Tammany's share of the vote increased, testimony to the entrenched machine's interest in managing the *size* of the voting universe. In the seven mayoral contests held between 1897 and 1917, Tammany's candidates averaged only 44 percent of the total vote. Capitalizing on a large third party vote to split the opposition—Seth Low's Citizen Union in 1897, William Randolph Hearst's Municipal Ownership League in 1905 and Citizens' Alliance in 1909, and Morris Hillquit's Socialist party in 1917—Tammany won five of the seven elections. In the mayoral elections of 1921 and 1925, as women's suffrage doubled the size of the potential electorate, the Wigwam's "Red Mike" Hylan and Jimmy Walker averaged 65 percent of a still shrinking—in relative terms—voting universe.

Completing the shift from circuses to bread, Boss Murphy used the patronage vote to win city elections as the Consolidation Act and city-owned utilities handed Tammany fresh supplies of sinecures. On the eve of World War I, the 91,000 city payrollers represented nearly one-third of Democrat Hylan's overall vote. The Wigwam's private sector patronage further swelled the ranks of machine voters. To voters, patronage represented a more reliable material inducement than bribery. With their jobs at stake, city employees could be trusted to vote and to mobilize their relatives and friends. The number of bribed voters, however, depended on the machine's campaign fund, the funds available to the machine's opponents for counteroffers, and the amount of reform surveillance of the registration and voting processes. As reformers purged the number of venal voters in New York City, Tammany's electoral calculations increasingly hinged on the payroll vote. Across the Hudson, Boss Hague relied even more than Murphy on the patronage vote, while the leaner O'Connell organization upstate could not dispense with corruption as a vital tool for winning elections. With bread—jobs and money—now winning elections, the Irish machines reserved their circuses for the slowly mobilizing new ethnics.[47]

For the Southern and Eastern Europeans, the entrenched machine's limited assimilation accentuated the forms of political and

communal life brought over from the Old World. For Catholic subjects of European monarchies, machine exclusion reinforced political apathy and alienation. For the Jews, exclusion reinforced radical
and reform politics. Excluded as well from the Irish-controlled big-
city labor movement, Jews would turn to the needle trades as a
template for radical political organization. In New York City, Jewish trade unionism was intertwined with socialist politics. Socialist
Labor party leaders such as Morris Hillquit formed the United Hebrew Trades, the first Jewish union, in 1888. Jewish socialists organized the needle trades, which employed one-half of the city's
Yiddish-speaking immigrants by 1910, as the Irish leadership of the
skilled trades largely ignored less skilled workers. Between 1909
and 1913 union membership in the garment industry exploded
from 30,000 to 250,000. The United Garment Workers, the Amalgamated Clothing Workers, and the International Ladies' Garment
Workers were militant in the workplace, winning higher wages,
shorter hours, and safer working conditions. Under socialist and
union auspices, Jewish garment workers began thinking of themselves in terms of class and occupation rather than nationality and
religion.[48]

Machine exclusion encouraged the Southern and Eastern Europeans to strengthen their communal institutions. Jewish political
energies were channeled into the building of the *landsmann,* or
mutual aid societies, providing social activities, medical insurance,
and death benefits for their members. These ethnic social welfare
organizations were provincial, however, further isolating participants from the larger urban political system. *Landsmann* members, for example, came from the same town or shtetl. The subsequent development of nationality-based *landsmannshaften*
federations did little to break down the barriers between the ghetto
and the machine. As the new immigrants turned inward, the Irish
party bosses breathed easier.

Guarding the Spoils: Machines "Reward" the New Immigrants

Parsimonious machine accommodation of the new ethnics extended beyond the naturalization court and the ballot box. The
potential power of the newcomers threatened the economic well-

being and psychological security of the payroll Irish. In order to protect the interests of this core machine constituency, Celtic party bosses did little to share top party and governmental positions with the Southern and Eastern Europeans. In New York, Tammany leader "Big Tim" Sullivan ruled the Lower East Side, where the new immigrants congregated. As early as 1910, Sullivan's district was 85 percent Jewish and Italian and only 5 percent Irish. Yet the Irish maintained firm control over the party apparatus. As late as 1932, three-quarters of Tammany's district leaders on the Lower East Side were Irish while less than one-fifth were Jewish. The first Italian leader, Al Marinelli, was not selected until 1931. With a lock on the party organization, the Irish monopolized nomination to elective office. Between 1908 and 1933 every Tammany candidate for the Board of Aldermen, the State Assembly, and the Senate from the Lower East Side was Irish.[49]

Party and ethnic hegemony, not machines per se, encouraged parsimonious accommodation. Boston politics, for example, remained Irish, Democratic, and faction-ridden into the twentieth century. Yet the new immigrants fared little better in Boston than in New York in securing important party and government posts. By 1920, Italians constituted 95 percent of the residents of Boston's crowded North End. In the words of one observer, Honey Fitz's Jefferson Club ran the North End like an "Irish rotten borough." As the Italians joined the Jews in migrating to the city's West End, they were welcomed into Boss Martin Lomasney's Hendricks Club. Although Lomasney carefully recruited promising Italian and Jewish politicos as minor club functionaries, the key posts in the Hendricks Club remained in Celtic hands. Controlling the party apparatus, Boston's Irish Democratic ward bosses kept elective office an Irish preserve. Not a single Italian was elected to the city council or to the state legislature before 1930. As for the city's Jews, only in Dorchester's Fourteenth Ward were they able to control the ward committee and elect members to the city council.[50]

Competitive party pressures forced the Irish Democratic chieftains to more quickly share power and authority with the newcomers. In Chicago, the Southern and Eastern Europeans were partially incorporated into the embryonic Democratic machine during the period of intense party competition and factionalism. The factional cleavages among the Windy City Democrats slowly coalesced along Irish and non-Irish lines. Carter Harrison II pioneered the ethnically balanced ticket in the 1912 Democratic primary. For the nine major county offices, Harrison slated two Germans (one Jewish), two Bohemians, one Pole, an Englishman, and three Irish. Roger Sullivan, leader of the other faction, fielded a predominantly Irish ticket. With Harrison's defeat in the 1915 mayoral primary, Sullivan moved to reimpose Irish hegemony over the Cook County Democratic Central Committee. Purging the Southern and Eastern Europeans, the Irish restoration was soon completed. By 1916 more than 70 percent of the county committee members were Irish. Given the competitive nature of the city's politics, however, Sullivan's restoration of Irish power was short-lived. Aided by William Lorimer, Republican Mayor William Hale "Big Bill" Thompson began building a rival GOP machine during World War I. The Thompson machine incorporated Southern and Eastern Europeans, particularly Jews and Italians. Sullivan and his successor, George Brennan, took the hint and began sharing party posts with the newcomers. Between 1922 and 1930 the non-Irish share of the city's Democratic ward leadership rose from 39 to 50 percent.[51]

The sharing of power and patronage by the Irish Democratic bosses with the Southern and Eastern Europeans was not without risk. In Chicago, Brennan's parceling out of party power to the non-Irish provoked an intraparty revolt by rank-and-file Irish functionaries. The Celtic bosses were trapped between the conflicting demands of party and ethnicity. Incorporation of the new immigrants enhanced the machine's prospects but threatened the Irish. Any move to share the machine's core resources of power and patronage with the non-Irish threatened Irish party functionaries and the legion of working-class Irish dependent on the organization's largesse.

Deference to the machine's core ethnic constituency dictated that entrenched machines offer less valuable benefits such as services, "circuses," and symbolism to the newer arrivals. Tammany's "Big Tim" Sullivan perfected this minimal reward strategy. He and his Irish lieutenants distributed coal, food, and rent money to needy Jews and Italians on the Lower East Side. Tammany's police department opened up station houses as temporary shelters for the homeless. Sullivan expedited business licenses for ethnic shopkeepers and pushcart peddlers. He shamelessly "recognized" the new immigrants with symbolic gestures and donned a yarmulke to solicit Jewish votes. Sullivan solicited Italian votes by sponsoring legislation to make Columbus Day a holiday. Jews and Italians were accorded token nominations to minor party posts and judgeships.[52]

Not to be outdone, Boston's feudal—and feuding—Irish chieftains raised minimalist politics to a high art. Honey Fitz's Jefferson Club and Lomasney's Hendricks Club dispensed food, loans, and licenses to the newcomers but not city jobs, nominations to office, or major party posts. James Michael Curley inaugurated a new era in symbolic politics. Elected to Congress in 1911, Curley crusaded against literacy tests, immigration restriction, and commercial agreements with Russia, where pogroms were raging. Elected mayor in 1913, Curley made symbolic "League of Nations" politics a regular feature at flag-bedecked city hall.[53]

Yet social services and symbolic recognition failed as the slowly mobilizing Southern and Eastern Europeans experimented with alternatives to the Irish ward bosses and machines. Jews particularly resisted the limited blandishments of the Irish politicos. Writing in 1903, social worker Robert Woods observed that "the Jew is a thorn in the flesh of the Irish politician."[54] In New York, Jews actively supported Tammany opponents Henry George, William Randolph Hearst, and Seth Low. Jews were the chief supporters of the city's powerful Socialist party. In 1914, for example, the predominately Jewish Lower East Side sent a Socialist to Congress and several others to the state assembly. Whereas Jews embraced labor and reform politics, Italians went into the Republican camp. New York's GOP made strong inroads into the still-small Italian vote with candidates such as Fiorello La Guardia while the Hub's Yankee Republicans wooed Italians with minor state offices and their advocacy of sound money and high tariffs.[55]

Unwilling to share the core resources of power and patronage, yet recognizing the limited appeal of welfare services and "recognition," Irish bosses turned to collective benefits as a way both of securing the new immigrant vote and of maintaining the Irish monopoly over divisible benefits. In New York, Tammany was responsible for securing the passage of important state labor and social welfare legislation. The Wigwam's representatives controlled the state's Factory Investigating Commission, established in the wake of the disastrous Triangle Shirtwaist Company fire of 1911. The commission proposed fifty new laws affecting the wages and working and safety conditions of women and children. The Tammany-controlled state legislature enacted nearly all of the commission's proposals. The Wigwam's Al Smith, the Assembly's majority leader, and Robert Wagner, the Senate's majority leader, also secured passage of workmen's compensation, stricter tenement laws, a widows' pension plan, state utility and insurance regulation, and educational scholarships for the poor. In Jersey City, Frank Hague converted the city's public hospital into the nation's second largest medical center, providing free health care for the city's residents.[56]

The machine's embrace of the nascent welfare state produced a temporary cessation of hostilities between the Irish bosses and the new immigrants. Tammany's Al Smith, leader in the fight for progressive legislation, ran for governor of the Empire State in 1919 and 1921, cutting heavily into the Jewish Socialist vote in New York City. As Table 11 suggests, Tammany's progressive coattails extended to local office as Hylan and Walker received a majority vote from the city's Jews and Italians in the 1920s.

The growing weakness of the machine's opponents also contributed to the newcomers' belated support of the Irish bosses. In New York, New Jersey, and Massachusetts, the once-dominant state Republican party, originally intent on offering minor offices and patronage to the new ethnics, faltered in its ethnic recognition policies. In New York, for example, the GOP soured into nativism and conservatism, particularly alienating the city's Italians. The massive Tammany vote in the 1920s cut across ethnic and class lines, much as did Hearst's populist campaign of 1905, reflecting the weakness of the opposition as much as the effectiveness of the Wigwam's policies.[57]

The Irish machines played a much more active role in weakening working-class opponents, particularly the Socialists. As the Socialists gained strength among New York's Jews, Tammany struck back. In the 1917 mayoral election, Socialist Morris Hillquit ran a strong race against Tammany's "Red Mike" Hylan. Tammany dispatched wrecking crews to disrupt Hillquit's street rallies, closed public meeting halls to the Socialists, and even stuffed the ballot box to defeat Hillquit. When the Socialists still showed strength at the polls, electing four aldermen and four assemblymen, the machine retaliated by enforcing Sunday closing laws against Jewish businesses on the Lower East Side. The machine's antipathy to the Socialists was more political than cultural, a jurisdictional battle for working-class loyalties rather than a Catholic predilection for social stability and order.[58]

As the Jews, Italians, and Poles slowly mobilized in the 1920s, they finally demanded a greater share of the machine's core resources of power and patronage. Yet with so much of Irish economic well-being and group identity dependent on continued control of the machines and their resources, the Irish bosses were understandably loath to share. To preserve their hegemony, the Irish consciously pursued a divide-and-conquer strategy, pitting one ethnic group and leader against another. At critical moments, the Irish formed strategic alliances with some groups and not with others. As Jews and Italians began flexing their political muscle in New York in the 1920s, the Tammany Irish were forced to choose which group would become a junior coalitional partner, and thus eligible for a greater share of power and patronage. In New York, the Jews became Tammany's chosen people. The Wigwam offered Jews party posts on the Lower East Side, nomination to minor offices, and a greater share of municipal employment, particularly in the legal department and the rapidly expanding school system. Boss Murphy and his successors worked just as actively to reduce Italian influence by adroitly gerrymandering Italian neighborhoods. For all their new-found Tammany support, Italians received few party posts or political nominations and only the most menial jobs as garbagemen, street cleaners, and laborers on the politically sensitive docks.[59]

The failure of the Irish to share the machine's power and patronage with the newcomers ultimately encouraged anti-Irish insurgency. The machine's Achilles' heel would soon be revealed as Irish prominence in public life rested on an ever more fragile base. As Irish representation in the ranks of city employees, public works contractors, and construction workers grew in the twentieth century, Irish representation in the electorate declined. In New York City, first- and second-generation Irish constituted less than 10 percent of the eligible voters in 1930, down from one-third in 1900. In the late 1920s the tempo of naturalization and voting accelerated for the Southern and Eastern Europeans. By 1930 Jews and Italians constituted nearly one-third of New York's eligible voters. The day of reckoning would soon be at hand. In machine cities such as New York and Jersey City, an anti-Irish revolt would take the form of an independent reform movement against machine politics.

Even the greater sharing of power and patronage with the new immigrants in competitive-party cities would not prevent a challenge to Irish rule. Compared with their brethren in the Northeast, Chicago's Irish Democrats had incorporated the Southern and Eastern Europeans in the 1920s. Because the new ethnic party leaders had been given the requisite power and patronage with which to mount an intraparty challenge, the new immigrants' insurgency was channeled *within* the embryonic Democratic machine rather than into reform politics. Czech Anton Cermak was the leader of the anti-Irish dissidents in the city's Democratic party. As a member of the Cook County Board of Supervisors and later the city council, "Pushcart Tony" became a key patronage dispenser. Cermak skillfully employed patronage to factionalize the Irish, drawing important politicians such as Pat Nash into his camp, and to woo the Czechs, Jews, and Poles, all resentful of Irish rule. In the late 1920s, Cermak mounted his anti-Irish putsch and took over the Democratic County Central Committee.[60]

But the real challenge to the second-generation Irish machines would occur in the 1930s in response to national as well as local forces. The Depression and New Deal party realignment threatened the established machines by upsetting the equilibrium between the party's management of patronage and voters. The Depression depleted the machine's patronage stock while the national party realignment dramatically increased the number of new ethnic voters. The national mobilization of the Southern and Eastern Europeans presented a potential electoral challenge to the entrenched Irish Democratic bosses to the extent that the voter turnout surge in presidential elections spilled over into local contests and was captured by reformers. In order to survive the tandem economic and political crises, the Irish bosses would ransack the New Deal in search of more patronage.

Chapter Four

The Crisis of the 1930s: The Depression, the New Deal, and Changing Machine Fortunes, 1928–1950

Economic Crisis/Political Crisis

The 1920s represented the Irish machine's heyday. Freed from state interference, controlling a growing patronage supply, and temporarily shielded from electoral pressures from the new immigrants for a greater sharing of power and jobs, the Irish bosses could meet the demands of both party and ethnicity. Bread had replaced circuses in the machine's repertoire of electoral appeals to already mobilized voters. The swollen ethnic patronage vote now decided local elections. Where job advertisements had once said, "No Irish need apply," the machine's employment agency now proclaimed, "Only Irish need apply." A massive patronage network enveloped the solidly lower-middle-class Irish-American community.

But at the moment the Irish bosses thought they had hit upon a formula guaranteeing both ethnic power and prosperity, its premises unraveled. Starting in the late 1920s, national economic and political forces overtook the machines' destiny. The Depression and the New Deal upset the bosses' management of both patronage and the vote.

As the business slump deepened, entrenched machines faced a mounting fiscal crisis. Declining property tax revenues coupled with growing relief costs created enormous pressures to cut the public payroll and salaries. Yet retrenchment threatened the machine's vote-getting ability and the economic well-being of thousands of Irish payrollers. At the same time, the national political realignment of the 1930s mobilized the new immigrants. In the 1928 presidential election, Al Smith's candidacy brought Italians, Poles, Czechs, and other Catholic groups into the voting booth in record numbers. In 1932 and 1936 Franklin Delano Roosevelt brought Jews into the Democratic camp. With their supply of patronage decreasing rather than increasing, the big-city party bosses viewed the New Deal's voter turnout surge with considerable apprehension.

Nevertheless, the New Deal created *opportunities* for the Irish Democratic bosses. For the entrenched machines of New York, Jersey City, and Albany, the federal emergency jobs programs of the 1930s, particularly the Works Progress Administration (WPA), represented an important source of potential patronage with which to reward the Southern and Eastern Europeans and quell discontent. For Irish Democratic politicians in other cities, the Depression and party realignment had weakened entrenched Republican machines such as the Pittsburgh and Philadelphia organizations and had halted GOP machine building in cities such as Chicago. A new generation of aspiring Irish bosses was eager to fashion New Deal machines by using federal work relief patronage to woo the new immigrants into more broadly based electoral coalitions.

Not all machines responded similarly to the national economic and political upheavals of the 1930s. The twin crises weakened some machines while strengthening others, raising several important questions for analysis. First, why did the Depression represent a destabilizing force for machines in some of the eight cities and not in others? In general, older machines were most weakened by the business slump. Tammany Hall and the Jersey City Hague organization, for example, were forced to slash their public payrolls, angering Irish payrollers and disappointing the new immigrants seeking public jobs as unemployment mounted in the private sector. Retrenchment contributed to Tammany's massive defeat in the 1933 city elections and to Hague's desperate search for federal patronage in order to prevent a similar debacle. Embryonic machines, in contrast, were less politically weakened by the Depression. Although fledgling Irish machines in Chicago and Pittsburgh were forced to cut the city payroll, retrenchment delayed but did not thwart the building of a new generation of Irish-run machines. Why were old machines more politically buffeted by the Depression than were new machines?

Second, why did the national party realignment of 1928–1936 weaken some Irish Democratic machines and strengthen others? Again, the older machines were most destabilized. In New York, Fusion candidate Fiorello La Guardia fashioned a "crazy quilt" coalition of Italians, Jews, and Republicans to overthrow Tammany in 1933. In Jersey City, Hague could delay but not prevent insurgency by the Southern and Eastern Europeans first brought to the polls by Al Smith and Franklin Delano Roosevelt. In 1949 the city's Italians and Poles toppled the once mighty Hague organization. But not all entrenched machines were destabilized. In Albany, the O'Connell organization finessed the challenge of ethnic insurgency set in motion by national political forces. Why were some second-generation machines weakened by national realignment while others were not? Were there differences in the character of the realignment process in New York and Jersey City compared with Albany?

The New Deal coalition also strengthened a new generation of Irish machines being built in cities such as Chicago and Pittsburgh. In Chicago, Democrat Anton Cermak was elected mayor in 1931 with Southern and Eastern European—but not Irish—support. With Cermak's death in 1933, the Irish reasserted control over party and city. Bosses Edward Kelly and Pat Nash harnessed the New Deal's ethnic groups to build one of the country's most powerful and long-lasting machines. In Pittsburgh, the once mighty Republican organization was toppled in the early 1930s, a victim of retrenchment and of the New Deal realignment. Appealing to the Steel City's Southern and Eastern Europeans, Irish boss David Lawrence built a powerful patronage-based Democratic machine that governed the city until 1969. But not all would-be Irish bosses were equally successful. In Boston James Michael Curley could not reduce the long-standing enmity between Irish and non-Irish. Why were some aspiring Irish bosses in cities without entrenched Democratic machines better able than others to woo the Southern and Eastern Europeans?

Third, why were some machines able to capture badly needed

federal patronage, particularly the massive WPA program, while others were not? Of the second-generation machines, the Hague and O'Connell organizations converted the nominally nonpartisan WPA into machine-controlled patronage while in New York Tammany Hall failed to capture the city's 246,000 WPA jobs. In some nonmachine cities, Irish party leaders consolidated power using federal patronage. Kelly and Nash in Chicago and Lawrence in Pittsburgh used WPA jobs to reward the new immigrants and to centralize power. Yet federal patronage eluded other would-be Celtic bosses. In Boston, Mayor and later Governor Curley's machine-building efforts were frustrated by the Roosevelt administration's refusal to turn over control of the Hub's WPA program. Do the dynamics of presidential rather than local politics better explain which machines seized control of federal work relief programs and were thereby strengthened?

The use of federal jobs programs for local machine building raises important questions about the impact of New Deal social programs on the big-city machines. As popularized by Edwin O'Connor in *The Last Hurrah,* the conventional wisdom holds that New Deal programs hastened the demise of the old-time machines. Roosevelt's social programs supposedly weakened the machines because they offered the organization's constituents resources not controlled by the local party boss. National programs enacted in the mid-1930s such as Social Security, Aid to Families with Dependent Children, and federally insured state unemployment compensation featured collective benefits distributed to the categorically—not politically—eligible. In this view, urban machines were weakened because they could not convert collective benefits into divisible benefits—patronage—for which a political quid pro quo—the vote—could be exchanged.[1]

As Lyle Dorsett notes, the New Deal's programmatic effect on the urban machines was far more complex than the conventional wisdom allows. The New Deal's collective benefits *could* be converted into divisible benefits, and political eligibility requirements *could* be reinstated. The big-city bosses viewed the WPA program, ostensibly supplying collective benefits to the welfare-eligible unemployed, as a fresh source of patronage. If bosses controlled the selection of state and local WPA administrators, federal relief jobs could be turned into sub-rosa patronage. Control of the WPA would allow the Hague and O'Connell machines to navigate the shoals of the Depression and national party realignment and permit the Kelly-Nash and Lawrence machines to consolidate power.

Machines were less able to control the New Deal's permanent legacy of welfare and insurance programs than they were the WPA. However, federal social programs such as Aid to Families with Dependent Children and public housing were not beyond the bosses' grasp. In Chicago, for example, the machine's precinct captains expedited welfare applications and threatened recipients with loss of benefits if they voted for the machine's opponents. Thus the welfare state could strengthen as well as weaken local party organizations.[2]

Crisis I: The Depression and
Machine Retrenchment

The Depression ended the expansionary fiscal policies of the Irish machines. In New York City, the 1932 municipal budget stood at $631 million, having risen in real terms by 125 percent since 1918, whereas the city's population had climbed by only 15 percent. Gotham's debt stood at $1.9 billion, and more than one-third of the entire budget was devoted to servicing this massive debt.[3]

The budgetary spiral could no longer continue. During the prosperous 1920s, the value of taxable real estate, the source of more than two-thirds of city revenue, had soared. Riding the crest of an inflated real-estate market, machines could increase budgetary outlays substantially without increasing the tax rate. With the economic collapse of 1929, however, city revenues declined precipitously. Nationwide, the value of urban real estate declined by one-quarter between 1929 and 1933. Property tax collections also fell, compounding the cities' revenue shortfall. Between 1929 and 1933 the tax delinquency rate in the big cities rose from 10 percent to 33 percent. New York, Boston, and Chicago were among the hardest hit. In 1933 delinquent property taxes represented 42 percent of all their outstanding taxes.

Demands for greater welfare spending accompanied the revenue collapse as the big-city unemployment rate rose from 5 percent in 1929 to 33 percent in 1933. In New York City alone 1 million workers were in the bread lines during the winter of 1932. Local welfare systems buckled under the burden. New York's Home Re-

lief Bureau enrolled 100,000 families in late 1933 while the city's
Emergency Works Bureau placed 110,000 unemployed workers
on municipal public works projects. By 1934 New York City's welfare outlays of $121 million represented one-quarter of all general
government expenses, up from 3 percent in 1928.[4]

Yet the machine's capacity for economizing was severely limited.
In New York, Jersey City, and Albany, one-third of the budget serviced the debt in the early 1930s. The city payroll, accounting for
most of the remainder of the budget, represented the backbone of
the machine. There were strong organizational pressures to resist
cutbacks. A popular verse in New York City in the early 1930s accurately captured the sacrosanct character of the city's budget:
"Mayor, may we economize?" "Boys, I won't begrudge it—Hit the
depression between the eyes but don't go near the budget."[5]

Faced with the growing imbalance between revenues and outlays, the Irish bosses initially responded by borrowing money to
pay for the relief burden, thereby sparing the jobs of thousands of
machine payrollers. With large long-term debts, however, the Irish
machines quickly ran afoul of state debt limitations. The bosses
then entered the short-term money market, offering tax anticipation notes against projected—but not yet collected—tax revenues. In New York, Tammany Mayor John Patrick O'Brien, Jimmy
Walker's successor, negotiated a series of short-term bank loans to
finance the city's burgeoning home and work relief programs. In
Jersey City, saddled with the highest tax rates in the country, the
railroads proclaimed a tax strike. Boss Hague hurriedly met with
the city's bankers in order to meet the machine's massive payroll
and welfare obligations.[6]

With large payrolls and mounting debts, the once free-spending
Irish machines began to rely heavily on tax anticipation notes,
making them vulnerable to the spending priorities of the banks. By
the end of fiscal year (FY) 1933, repayment of short-term notes accounted for more than one-third of all general fund outlays in New
York and Jersey City compared with less than 10 percent of the
outlays in nonmachine cities. As the fiscal crisis worsened, bankers
raised interest rates on short-term municipal loans to reflect the
growing risk of default and to force the cities to retrench. New
York City paid 5.75 percent interest on short-term loans in 1932,
several times the interest rate paid by the banks to their depositors.[7]

In the spring of 1933 the bankers refused to extend additional short-term credit unless the machines substantially reduced city outlays. New York's banks demanded that the O'Brien administration reduce the city's budget by nearly one-fifth as a condition of further loans. In Chicago, a city particularly vulnerable because of a wholesale downward reassessment of real estate, the banks made further loans to the Cermak administration contingent upon a 10 percent reduction in city outlays.

Forced out of the short-term loan market, the Irish bosses turned to state government for financial relief. Tammany's leaders, for example, petitioned the New York Emergency Relief Administration for a state takeover of local relief costs. But assistance was not forthcoming, for the states were beset with a burgeoning fiscal crisis of their own. State income taxes, as well as gasoline and sales taxes, were highly elastic, rising and falling with the state of the economy. As the Depression deepened, state revenues eroded at a faster rate than city revenues. Facing state bankruptcy, Democratic Governor Herbert Lehman turned down Tammany's request.

The city bosses then approached the unsympathetic Hoover administration for federal assistance. Though Hoover opposed a federal bailout, he reluctantly signed the Emergency Relief and Construction Act of 1932. The ERC authorized the federal Reconstruction Finance Corporation to loan up to $300 million to states and localities at 3 percent interest. There was little federal "trickle down" to the cities as most ERC loans went to states as advances on future highway grants. Their hands tied by state borrowing restrictions, the cities received only $3.5 million in federal loans.[8]

As the machines' borrowing opportunities evaporated, the bosses sought new taxing authority. With the Depression's onset, property owners had successfully lobbied the states for tax limits. These restrictions generally took one of two forms. The most common was a rate limitation, expressed as a fixed percentage of the total assessed value of taxable property. States also imposed percentage limits on the maximum annual local budget increase. Unable to squeeze more tax revenue from property, machine politicians petitioned the states for new revenue sources. Tammany, for example, successfully lobbied Governor Lehman and the state legislature for emergency taxing powers to pay for relief. Tammany used its emergency powers to enact a regressive local sales tax—hitting poor families hardest—an inheritance tax, and a levy on public utilities. In New York and other machine cities, the new revenues failed to cover ever-rising welfare costs.[9]

The party was over. Tammany and the Hague organization finally had their backs to the wall as the banks made further loans conditional upon sizable reductions in the machine's twin vertebrae—the payroll and the capital budget. Working with the business community, New York City bankers forced the O'Brien administration to reopen the FY 1933 budget and reduce outlays by 18 percent. The so-called Bankers Agreement of 1933 also created a four-year $429 million ceiling on property taxes, the amount raised in FY 1933, and required a reserve fund against future tax nonpayments. In similar fashion, Jersey City banks made Hague walk the financial plank. The machine's payroll was cut by 10 percent, and city wages were reduced by one-quarter.[10]

Bank-sponsored retrenchment posed severe organizational maintenance problems for the established Irish machines. Payroll and salary reductions thinned the party's cadre of precinct and social service workers and eroded voter support, particularly in the Irish community. A dwindling patronage supply also made it difficult for the machines to reward the now-voting Southern and Eastern Europeans. Faced with bank retrenchment demands and countervailing resistance from the Irish payrollers, the Irish bosses cut back in ways least harmful to the machine and to the payroll Irish. In New York and Jersey City, the most draconian economy measures were directed at the public school system, the hospitals, and the relief agencies. These departments were the least beholden to the bosses, and their employees were increasingly Jewish rather than Irish. By 1934 Tammany had fired 11,000 of the city's 35,000 school teachers.[11]

No matter how cleverly the payroll was pared, retrenchment eroded voter support for the established machines. In New York City, the Wigwam's payroll and salary cutbacks angered municipal employees—Irish as well as Jewish—and paved the way for the breakup of the multiethnic machine coalition fashioned in the 1920s. The firing of Jewish teachers and health and social workers shifted the Jewish middle class away from Tammany and into the La Guardia camp in the crucial 1933 mayoral election that brought the reformers to power for twelve years. The machine's salary reductions also softened the previously monolithic Irish Tammany support. In the 1933 election Irishman John McKee, running for mayor on the Recovery party ticket initially with the combined blessing of FDR, Democratic National Committee Chairman James Farley, and Bronx political boss Ed Flynn, drew a substantial number of Irish voters away from Tammany nominee Mayor O'Brien. With a fractured Irish payroll vote and the new immigrants ripe for revolt, the starving Tiger's days were numbered.[12]

In Jersey City fresh patronage supplies mitigated the immediate effects of retrenchment. Hague shifted some displaced city workers onto the county payroll and quickly moved to control more state and federal patronage, particularly New Jersey's WPA program, in order to appease the city's Poles and Italians. Federal and state resources would soon slip from his grasp. With the coming of World War II, federal emergency jobs programs were terminated. Forced by Roosevelt in 1940 to accept reformer Charles Edison as governor, Hague also found state doors shut. His taxation policies now came back to haunt him. Railroad bankruptcies shifted the machine's onerous tax burden onto homeowners. Unable to create new public jobs and unwilling to fire the payroll Irish and replace them with Poles and Italians, Hague had sown the seeds of ethnic insurgency.[13]

Not all the entrenched machines were weakened by the Depression. In contrast to Tammany and the Hague organizations, the O'Connell machine in Albany was not forced to adopt a politically damaging retrenchment program. Because of the large number of property owners, the upstate machine had pursued cautious taxation and spending policies in the 1920s. Because a significant proportion of the city's labor force was employed by state government, and thus better shielded from the Depression, the city experienced only moderate unemployment levels and welfare demands in the 1930s. With lower taxation and fewer welfare burdens, the O'Connell organization weathered the economic upheaval with its patronage army intact.

As for the new machines, the Depression delayed but did not prevent their consolidation of power. In Chicago, Mayor Cermak succumbed to bankers turning the retrenchment screws. During his short eighteen-month tenure, Cermak reduced the number of city workers by 10 percent—to 18,000—and cut salaries by one-fifth.

The slimming of the public payroll heightened intraparty and inter-ethnic factionalism, particularly between the Irish and the Slavs. When the payroll Irish staged a revolt, Cermak maneuvered Henry Horner into the governor's chair and used state jobs to soften the blow of local retrenchment. Cermak's strained relations with the Irish city workers would also delay the delivery of federal patronage to the struggling Windy City machine. At the 1932 Democratic convention held in Cermak's Chicago, the mayor leaned toward Al Smith rather than FDR in order to placate the city's disaffected Irish Democrats. Unable to claim membership in the FRBC Club ("For Roosevelt Before the Convention") Cermak received little federal patronage. He traveled to Miami in 1933 to meet Roosevelt and plead for more federal aid. An assassin's bullet meant for the president mortally wounded the Chicago mayor instead. Cermak's Irish successors, Mayor Ed Kelly and Democratic County Chairman Pat Nash, expedited the receipt of federal patronage with a massive display of electoral might in the 1935 municipal elections designed to convince Roosevelt that the machine was indispensable to his reelection plans.[14]

The Depression also delayed the consolidation of the Lawrence machine in Pittsburgh. Since the Civil War, the Steel City had been run by a succession of Republican bosses—Squire Tommy Steele, Chris Magee, and William Flinn. With the death in 1921 of state boss Boise Penrose, the Pennsylvania GOP machine split into two factions, weakening the Pittsburgh organization. The Depression and national realignment completed the task of overthrowing Pittsburgh's GOP machine. The Steel City's break with the Republican party began at the national level in 1928 when Al Smith received nearly half of the city's vote. In 1932, the city went Democratic, the first time this had happened in a presidential contest since 1856. Seizing the opportunity, Democratic Party Chairman David Lawrence chose old-line progressive William McNair as the party's nominee in the 1933 mayoral election. McNair won and immediately embarked on an economy program, furloughing hundreds of city employees and reducing city salaries by 20 percent. Estranging Lawrence with his retrenchment program, McNair compounded his difficulties by appointing Republicans to head the patronage-rich departments of public works and public safety. Lawrence would have to force the economy-minded and bipartisan McNair out of office before a machine could be built.[15]

In heavily Democratic Boston, the business slump thwarted Mayor Curley's machine-building efforts. In the 1920s Curley had earned the reputation of being a monumental builder "unintimidated by public debt." In the early 1930s, as the Hub's unemployment rate soared and the welfare caseload increased sixfold, Curley proposed a massive public works program to put the unemployed to work. Curley's countercyclical project died in the Republican-controlled statehouse and in the Democratic-controlled city council. The city treasury's bipartisan guardians were watchful of both the growing fiscal crisis and Curley's political ambitions. The Hub's worsening finances further trimmed the mayor's spending plans. Reluctantly, Curley reduced city salaries by 10 percent and began laying off city workers. By the late 1930s the Boston payroll stood at 12,500, down from 21,000 before the Depression. With local patronage fast disappearing, Curley's machine-building plans would require an infusion of federal gravy.[16]

Yet the Depression's harshest effects were felt by old rather than new machines. For entrenched machines, there were greater organizational, ethnic, and electoral repercussions to payroll cutbacks. For Tammany Hall and the Hague organization, the public payroll employed an army of precinct captains and workers. If party workers were furloughed, established machines were less able to get out their customary vote and deliver expected welfare services. Moreover, the old machines had been most successful in placing the Irish on the city payroll. Cutbacks sent ripples of dissatisfaction through the party's core ethnic constituency. Because the old machines had not yet fought the ethnic wars of succession, unemployed Southern and Eastern Europeans demanded a fair share of public employment at the moment when the Irish bosses were least able to oblige.

Relying less on the public payroll, fledgling machines better survived austerity. In Pittsburgh, only 7 percent of the Democratic committeemen in 1934 were publicly employed. By firing Republican workers, the Lawrence machine could create job opportunities for Democratic workers even as the payroll was trimmed. Despite McNair's austerity program, Lawrence succeeded in placing one-half of the party's precinct captains on the public payroll by 1940. The new machines' retrenchment program produced less ethnic dissatisfaction. The Irish monopoly on public employment had not yet been established. With smaller numbers of Irish working for government, retrenchment did not fall as heavily on the Irish community. Because the Southern and Eastern Europeans had already been integrated into the Democratic party in two-party Chicago and Republican Pittsburgh, the new ethnic leaders had the power to ensure that their countrymen got a fair share of public jobs as the Republicans were purged. For a new generation of Irish bosses, austerity might not produce defeat at the polls as it did for the old bosses. Yet austerity programs rarely allowed nascent machines to consolidate power. For consolidation to occur, new sources of patronage would have to be found.[17]

Crisis II: The National Mobilization of the Southern and Eastern Europeans

Although the national realignment of 1928–1936 improved the Democratic party's prospects nationwide, it represented a destabilizing force for Democratic machines where the ethnic succession wars had not yet been fought. Southern and Eastern Europeans became citizens in record numbers in the late 1920s. Sixty-one percent of New York City's Russian- and Polish-born Jews had received their citizenship papers by 1930, up from 37 percent in 1920. Democratic presidential candidates targeted the new citizens. In the 1928 presidential election, Al Smith's candidacy mobilized nonvoting Italians, Poles, Jews, and other big-city immigrants. In 1932 and 1936 Roosevelt would build on the big-city ethnic coalition initially fashioned by Smith.

The surge in big-city turnout for presidential elections was remarkable. In New York City the number of voters increased by nearly 40 percent between 1924 and 1928—from 1.4 million to over 1.9 million—after having increased by only 15 percent between 1920 and 1924. The number of Gotham voters rose by another 26 percent between 1932 and 1936 as the city's immigrants ratified the New Deal. In all, the national realignment contributed to an effective doubling of the active electorate. Comparable increases in presidential election turnout between 1928 and 1936 occurred in Jersey City, Chicago, and Pittsburgh.

The Irish bosses temporarily breathed easier as the new immigrants embraced the party of Smith and Roosevelt. In New York City, three-quarters of the Italian and Jewish voters pulled the lever for Smith in 1928, up from fewer than one-half supporting Democratic candidate Davis in 1924. More than 70 percent of the Windy City's Poles and Czechs voted Democratic in 1928, up from fewer than 40 percent in 1924. The Southern and Eastern Europeans would line up as solidly for Roosevelt in 1932 and 1936 as they had for Smith in 1928.[18]

Yet the New Deal's electoral coattails did not necessarily extend to the big-city Democratic machines. The new immigrants had gained little from Irish bosses in the teens and twenties. As the Depression deepened, they added the denial of public jobs to their list of grievances against the Irish overlords. Given growing ethnic demands in the early 1930s for a reallocation of patronage and power, the national mobilization of the new immigrants presented a potential electoral challenge to the entrenched Irish machines. The presidential turnout surge could cut quite differently in local contests if captured by the machine's opponents.

Reform leaders in New York and Jersey City mobilized the Southern and Eastern Europeans, capitalizing on their long-standing grievances with Irish rule. In New York City, Fusionist candidate Fiorello La Guardia's strategy in the 1933 mayoral election was to unleash the Jews and the Italians. Jews now constituted one-quarter and the Italians one-sixth of the city's potential electorate. Yet the new immigrants, particularly Catholic women, rarely bothered to register and vote in local elections.

Enlisting fresh ethnic recruits, the Little Flower changed all that. Concentrating on groups such as the Italians with low registration and voting rates, La Guardia's Fusion organization joined other anti-Tammany reform groups in enrolling new voters at a record rate for a municipal election. By election day nearly 800,000 new recruits had been enrolled. The La Guardia organization pioneered the ethnically balanced ticket to woo the new voters. The Fusion "brotherhood" slate featured an Italian for mayor, a Jew for president of the Board of Aldermen, the obligatory Irishman for controller, and a WASP thrown in for good measure for district attorney. Tammany, in contrast, paraded its usual heavily Irish slate before the city's increasingly heterogeneous voters.[19]

La Guardia won in 1933, relegating Tammany to twelve years in the political wilderness, by capitalizing on a split in the traditional Irish machine vote and by mobilizing the new ethnics. Table 12

TABLE 12. *The Tiger Turns Tail: Voting and Turnout in New York City, 1925–1937*

Mayoral Election	Outcome	Candidate	Tammany At The Polls Vote Share (%)	Chief Opponent[a]	Opponents' Vote Share (%)	Voter Participation Rates Adults (%)	Citizens (%)	Total Adults[b] (thousands)	Total Citizens[b] (thousands)	Total Voters (thousands)
1925	Win	Walker	65.8	Waterman (R)	30.5	28.0	37.8	4,058	3,010	1,138
1929	Win	Walker	61.0	La Guardia (R)	25.8	31.6	42.1	4,512	3,379	1,424
1932	Win	O'Brien	63.0	Pounds (R)	26.5	35.1	47.5	4,777	3,532	1,676
1933	Loss	O'Brien	27.6	La Guardia (F)	40.9	43.9	58.0	4,837	3,667	2,125
1937	Loss	Mahoney	39.8	La Guardia (R, F, AL)	60.2	44.4	54.2	5,031	4,127	2,236

Sources: U.S. Bureau of the Census, *Census of Population, 1920* (Washington, D.C.: Government Printing Office, 1923), vol. 3, Table 10; U.S. Bureau of the Census, *Sixteenth Census of the United States, 1940* (Washington, D.C.: Government Printing Office, 1943), vol. 2, Table C–37, p. 157; New York World-Telegram, *World Almanac and Book of Facts for 1940* (New York: World-Telegram, 1940), pp. 794–795.
[a] Republican (R), Fusionist (F), American Labor (AL).
[b] Estimated for years between censuses.

shows the changing shape of New York City's voting universe between 1925 and 1937. As late as the 1932 special election to fill Jimmy Walker's unexpired term, Tammany had appeared impregnable, securing 63 percent of the vote. The drop in the Tiger's electoral fortunes was precipitous. In the three-way 1933 regular election, Tammany's share of the vote fell from its customary 60 percent to less than 30 percent as the Recovery party's McKee siphoned off 30 percent. La Guardia's mobilization campaign paid off handsomely. Having edged upward since 1928, voter participation rates took their sharpest jump between 1932 and 1933. Fifty-eight percent of Gotham's citizens voted in the 1933 mayoral election, up from 48 percent the year before.

Yet La Guardia had not fashioned a "Little New Deal" ethnic coalition *sans* Celts. As Arthur Mann notes, La Guardia's "crazy quilt" coalition ranged across the ideological, ethnic, and class spectrum. Old guard Republicans joined Socialists and reform Democrats in supporting Fusion. Eighty percent of the Italian voters cast their ballots for La Guardia, supplying one-quarter of his total vote. The crucial Jewish vote, however, was split along class lines. On the Irish-controlled Lower East Side, La Guardia received only one-third of the working-class Jewish vote. The Fusionists did best among middle-class Jews. As Tammany's economy measures fell heaviest on teachers and health and social workers, the Jewish middle class left the Wigwam. Nearly 60 percent would vote for La Guardia.[20]

La Guardia concentrated his first administration on solidifying new immigrant support to prevent Tammany's resurrection. Since the 1937 city election would be a contest for the Jewish vote, Fiorello immediately embarked on a campaign to increase the number of Jews and other new ethnics on the city's payroll. The city's antiquated civil service system was reformed in order to end job discrimination against the non-Irish. Municipal job openings were publicly advertised. Multiple-choice questions replaced essay examinations, reducing the discretion of Irish civil service examiners. A high school diploma replaced the traditional cursory entrance examination. La Guardia dispensed with the services of Tammany's temporary "Kelly Boys." Under his administration, the proportion of city positions covered by a strengthened civil service system rose from one-half in 1933 to three-quarters in 1940.[21]

The reform mayor also expanded the size of the city's human service agencies (and thus the number of job opportunities for the new ethnic claimants). Forced by the ever-watchful banks to cut the city's payroll by 6 percent in his first year in office, La Guardia subsequently increased employment in the departments of education, health, hospitals, and welfare. Propelled by human services funding as well as by population growth, the city payroll grew by 60 percent during his three terms.[22]

By the tandem tactics of civil service reform and bureaucratic expansion, La Guardia worked a dramatic alteration in the ethnic composition of the city's bureaucracy, particularly in the new human services agencies rather than in the old police, fire, and public works departments where the Irish remained firmly entrenched. The Jews, Tammany's chosen people in the 1920s, were the prime beneficiaries of La Guardia's personnel and social policies in the 1930s. In the city's school system, which the Irish had dominated until World War I, 56 percent of the entering teachers in 1940 were Jewish. The reform mayor's wooing of the new immigrants with the old benefits of patronage politics produced the desired electoral results. As Table 12 shows, La Guardia waltzed to victory in his 1937 reelection bid. A durable reform coalition of Southern and Eastern Europeans had been fashioned that would rule New York until the mid-1940s.[23]

A decaying Tammany remained out of power until 1945. Denied city patronage, it found its payroll reduced to county offices. Then when La Guardia turned to county civil service reform, the Irish Tiger's days were numbered. Denied county jobs in the 1940s, Tammany's aging Irish chieftains turned to the Italian-controlled underworld for desperately needed funding. The "Mafia plan" was not without risk, for the organization's ethnic balance of power soon shifted dramatically. Gangsters such as "Lucky" Luciano and Frank Costello decided to install their own Italian district leaders in Tammany's clubhouses. Led by Carmine De Sapio, an Italian bloc successfully challenged Irish party hegemony in the late 1940s.[24]

Using many of La Guardia's campaign tactics, a similar reform coalition of the new immigrants in Jersey City finally overthrew the Hague machine. Demographics and parsimony had finally caught up with the boss. By 1940 Italians and Poles constituted nearly one-half of Jersey City's eligible voters while the Irish ranks had thinned to one-fifth. Hague had done little to share power and patronage with the now numerous new immigrants. He defused an incipient Italian revolt in the mid-1930s by according greater ethnic representation on the state assembly ticket, the board of education, and the local judiciary. The machine's major patronage-dispensing and policy-making positions remained in Irish hands. Aided by control of the state's WPA and by a moribund Republican party, Hague stalled ethnic insurgency into the 1940s.

Disaster struck in 1949. Dissident Democrat John V. Kenney's mayoral campaign against incumbent Frank Hague Eggers, Hague's nephew and designated heir apparent, was lifted from La Guardia's playbook. Kenney practiced Fusion politics. The Fusionists enrolled a record 12,000 new voters—primarily Poles and Italians. Balanced slates crossed the Hudson as the new immigrants were nominated for major offices. Kenney followed La Guardia in splitting the Irish vote, though on generational lines, as returning Irish war veterans were drawn into the Fusion camp. Kenney's Freedom ticket won a resounding victory, securing 67 percent of the total vote.[25]

Kenney's first administration also drew inspiration from the Little Flower. The mayor quickly increased the payroll by 400—to 8,000—as Poles and Italians drew city paychecks. Unlike La Guardia, however, Kenney's ethnic accommodation policies were directed at machine building rather than reform. The new mayor soon moved to control the Democratic party. Kenney increased the number of ward leaders from sixteen to fifty, appointing loyal Poles and Italians.

Yet not all of the old machines were buffeted by the national political forces set in motion in the late 1920s. Albany's Dan O'Connell was not forced to fight the ethnic wars of succession produced by a rising tide of new immigrant voters. As Kristi Andersen notes, the character of the realigning process differed in Albany compared with New York and Jersey City. Tammany Hall and the Hague organization had faced *mobilization* realignments as the number of new Democratic voters expanded rapidly. In Albany, however, there was no flood of new ethnic voters. The Southern and Eastern Europeans had arrived earlier upstate than downstate. Table 10 shows that 61 percent of Albany's immigrants had arrived before 1910, compared with 53 percent of New York City's. As control of the state capital oscillated between competing machines in the late nineteenth and early twentieth centuries, both parties worked hard to naturalize and register the Southern and Eastern Europeans. As a consequence, Albany's immigrants were voting well before the 1928–1936 realignment. The upstate realignment would be one of *conversion* rather than of mobilization as the electorate grew by only 38 percent over this twelve-year period—only 40 percent of the growth rate in New York City. Uncle Dan assisted Smith and Roosevelt by inviting supporters of the defunct Barnes machine into the Democratic party. By the early 1930s a two-to-one Republican registration advantage had been transformed into a two-to-one Democratic lead.[26]

O'Connell's middle-class "service" machine more easily survived the economic and political upheavals of the 1930s than did the Tammany and Hague working-class "patronage" machines. In the 1920s Uncle Dan faced the task of politically converting a participating, home-owning, and Republican electorate. The Albany machine cultivated homeowners with a low tax rate—thus limiting the supply of patronage—and with the political manipulation of individual property tax assessments. As property changed hands, it was deliberately overassessed. The local ward leader would then graciously reduce the assessment, earning the new homeowner's gratitude *and* vote. For homeowners, the machine specialized in garbage delivery, street and pothole repair, and snow removal. The machine's middle-class menu of lowered taxes and homeowner services brought former GOP voters into the Democratic party in droves. O'Connell's occasional reform opponents would be denied a large pool of nonparticipating and unrewarded immigrant voters.[27]

Tammany Hall and the Hague organization, in contrast, relied more on patronage than on services to bring out the vote. Hague's massive public and private sector patronage army numbered nearly 20,000 in the late 1930s in a voting population of 120,000. The machine instructed each worker on the payroll to secure the votes of family and friends. If each retainer brought in two more votes, the machine was guaranteed victory—as long as the size of the voting population remained the same. Relying on the payroll vote, these machines had little incentive to expand the voting population.[28]

The twin crises of the 1930s fell far harder on machines that relied on jobs than on those relying on services. Because they were more financially extended, high-tax patronage machines were more vulnerable than low-tax service machines to the Depression. Retrenchment weakened the ability of patronage-based machines to mobilize their traditional constituency and to reward the new immigrants. By the early 1930s the neglected Southern and Eastern Europeans were voting in record numbers. Patronage machines were in electoral jeopardy because they had done little to curry favor with the newcomers.

The O'Connell machine learned an important lesson from the travails of the downstate patronage machines. The leaner Albany organization added to its margin of electoral safety in the 1930s and 1940s by systematically padding the lists of registrants and voters, testimony to Uncle Dan's control over the ballot box, the judiciary, and the political opposition. By the early 1940s the machine was defying the actuarial tables, claiming the votes of more than 60 percent of the entire population of men, women, and children.[29]

Although the national realignment played havoc with entrenched—particularly patronage-based—machines, it strengthened the fledgling Democratic organizations of Chicago and Pittsburgh. For the old machines, Irish power had preceded organizational consolidation. For the new machines, however, the ethnic succession wars had been fought *before* both the centralization of machine power and the national realignment. In Chicago Democratic leaders George Brennan and Anton Cermak had actively recruited Czechs, Jews, Poles, and Italians in the 1920s. In his victorious 1931 mayoral campaign, Cermak had carefully exploited national political forces. In presidential politics, the Windy City's realignment was mobilizing. Nearly 40 percent more voters went to the polls in 1928 than in 1924. Al Smith, scion of the Fulton Fish Market, received more than two-thirds of Chicago's new immigrant vote compared with one-third received by Democrat John W. Davis in the three-way 1924 contest. A countervailing local realignment, however, complicated Cermak's election bid. Between 1923 and 1927 the number of local voters had also soared by 40 percent—but into the hands of Republican "Big Bill" Thompson. In the 1927 city election, Thompson received more than one-half of the new ethnic vote. In his 1931 race against Thompson, Cermak wrapped himself in Smith's mantle and captured 65 percent of the new immigrant vote. Earlier than reformer La Guardia, machine politico Cermak had forged a "Little New Deal" coalition without the Celts. Republican Thompson received a sizable vote in normally Democratic wards controlled by disaffected Irish ward bosses.[30]

Although the national realignment was not the destabilizing force in Chicago Democratic politics that it would prove to be in New York and Jersey City, tensions between Irish and non-Irish persisted as Cermak and his successors consolidated power. After Cermak's death the restoration of Irish party leadership by Mayor Edward Kelly and County Chairman Pat Nash particularly rankled the new immigrants. The new Irish bosses avidly courted FDR for federal patronage to placate the ethnic dissidents. To demonstrate the machine's indispensability to Roosevelt, Kelly and Nash defeated the Republicans in the 1935 city election by a record 630,000 votes. The Democratic share of the 1935 local vote—83 percent—doubled the party's 1927 performance. Roosevelt got the message and hand-delivered the state's WPA to Kelly and Nash. The consolidating machine returned the favor. Naturalizing, registering, and voting the new immigrants, the machine's precinct captains pushed the city's presidential turnout rate to an unprecedented 89 percent in 1936, up from 76 percent in 1928.[31]

In Pittsburgh, the Democratic machine's ethnic succession wars were also fought before the new ethnics were mobilized. Though the Irish were the most active and influential group in the Steel City's Democratic party, minority party status encouraged them to share power. By the early 1930s, as the Lawrence machine was consolidating power, the Irish held fewer than one-third of the party's ward committee posts compared with one-fifth for the Germans and one-tenth for the Italians.[32]

Welcoming the newer ethnic arrivals into the revitalized Democratic party, Irish leader David Lawrence hoped to use FDR's coattails to build a Steel City machine. Between 1924 and 1936 Pittsburgh's electorate dramatically grew by 120 percent. The surge in voter turnout benefited the Democrats. In the three-way 1924 presidential election, Democrat Davis had received a paltry 9 percent of the one-quarter million votes cast in Allegheny County. Capitalizing on the 1924 La Follette progressive vote—32 per-

cent—and a rising tide of European Catholic voters, Al Smith in
1928 secured 48 percent of the county's vote. FDR built on Smith's
electoral foundations. By 1936 the Democratic standard bearer
had captured nearly 70 percent of the county's 562,000 votes. As
Bruce Stave has shown in his careful study of the emergence of the
modern Pittsburgh Democratic party, the city's polyglot new immigrants—Poles, Italians, Jews, Czechs, Yugoslavians, Hungari-
ans, and Lithuanians—were largely responsible for the resurgence
in the fortunes of national Democratic candidates.[33]

Local Democratic fortunes were another matter. Lawrence's
ability to harness the New Deal ethnic coalition for local machine
building was hampered by Democratic Mayor William McNair.
McNair was a progressive rather than a New Dealer. The mayor's
constituency, centered in the native-born middle class dissatisfied
with the aging and corrupt GOP machine, bore little relationship
to FDR's 1932 ethnic vote. Forcing McNair to resign in 1936, Lawrence installed Irish party regular Cornelius Scully in the mayor's
chair. Attracting both the Irish and the Southern and Eastern Europeans, Scully's landslide 1937 vote virtually duplicated the 1936
Roosevelt vote.[34]

The full consolidation of the ethnically heterogeneous Chicago
and Pittsburgh machines, however, would have to await local capture of federal resources. In both newly Democratic cities, local retrenchment programs had badly depleted the resources needed to
cement the allegiance of the new immigrants. Kelly, Nash, and
Lawrence would need to devise ways of harnessing the New Deal's
relief and recovery programs to their machine-building purposes.

In Boston the potential flood tide of new ethnic voters was not
captured by would-be Irish bosses. The city was already Democratic by the late 1920s—67 percent of the registered voters—and
heavily Irish. By 1930 more than half of the population was of Celtic
descent. Green Power in the Hub did not depend on long-lasting
interethnic alliances or a citywide machine. During the Progressive
era the city's Irish pols—Fitzgerald, Lomasney, and Curley—had
selectively used the new immigrants as a battering ram to challenge
Yankee political hegemony. With the arrival of Irish ascendancy in
the 1920s, the Irish politicians dispensed with the services of Jews
and Italians. The city's swollen bureaucracies—particularly the police and fire departments, water and public works, and the school

system—were turned into an Irish preserve. Frozen out of the solidly Irish Democratic party, many Jews became Republicans. The nominally Democratic Italians gave their votes grudgingly to Irish politicians.[35]

With majority party *and* ethnic status, Boston's Celtic politicos had little incentive to mobilize—or reward—the new immigrants. Irish hegemony served as the glue holding rampant Democratic factionalism together. Any bid by one of the feuding Irish ward bosses to mobilize the new immigrants entailed substantial risks of challenging Green Power and producing an Irish political backlash.

Hence the New Deal realignment was a curiously incomplete affair in Boston. Well into the 1930s, naturalization rates for the new immigrants in the Hub lagged (see Table 10). The Irish pols discovered a temporary use for the new ethnics in their love affair with Al Smith in 1928. Driven to the polls by the Celtic ward bosses in 1928, record numbers of new ethnics voted for Smith. Between 1924 and 1928 the Hub's presidential voters swelled by 40 percent—to 274,000. The Boston politicos never forgot Smith. With the coming of Roosevelt, however, the Irish spurned the new ethnics. Presidential turnout in the Hub dropped 6 percent—by 16,000—between 1928 and 1932 compared with a 27 percent increase nationwide. In all, Boston's voter participation rate rose by only 58 percent between 1928 and 1936—one-half New York City's increase.

Only one suitor remained—James Michael Curley. Curley was the beleaguered leader of the pro-Roosevelt forces in the 1932 Massachusetts Democratic primary. Lining up solidly behind Smith, the other Irish politicos easily carried the day. In the general election, as most of the city's Celtic politicians took a walk, Mayor Curley tried to mobilize the Jews and the Italians for Roosevelt—and himself. He failed. Curley's major voter registration drive netted a paltry 5,500 new voters. Distrustful of all Irish politicians, the new ethnics had also taken a walk.[36]

The New Deal Comes to the Cities: The WPA and Machine Building

The big-city Democratic bosses cast covetous glances at the New Deal's three major work relief programs. The Public Works Administration (PWA), created under the 1933 National Industrial Recovery Act, represented a $3.3 billion program of large-scale public works designed to stimulate recovery of the so-called heavy industries. Nationwide, by mid-1934 the PWA employed 542,000 individuals. The Civil Works Administration (CWA), created in late 1933, was designed to provide temporary employment on small-scale projects for 4.3 million individuals—half of whom were on relief—during the winter of 1933–1934.[37]

The Works Progress Administration (WPA) particularly caught the eye of the urban bosses. Created in 1935, the WPA represented a long-term $7.8 billion program to provide jobs for the welfare-eligible unemployed on small-scale locally initiated public works projects. By mid-1936 the WPA's highway, park, sewer, public building, and social service projects employed more than 3 million individuals nationwide.[38]

Although it was a national program, the WPA had a distinctive urban relief mission. The federal program's urban focus was a product both of jurisdictional battles with the rural-oriented Resettlement Administration and of the agency's decision to target funding in those areas with the highest unemployment rates and largest welfare caseloads—the big cities. As a result, half of all WPA workers nationwide were drawn from cities with populations of more than 100,000. In the cities, WPA expenditures quickly overshadowed all other welfare outlays. By 1936 the WPA accounted for two-thirds of all big-city relief expenditures.[39]

No wonder the big-city bosses coveted the WPA. Federal patronage dwarfed local resources. Table 13 shows the size of the 1936 WPA payroll relative to the municipal workforce and electorate for six of the once Irish cities. In most of the cities, the number of WPA workers more than doubled the municipal workforce. New York City's 246,000 WPA workers, for example, dwarfed the city payroll of 121,000. As Table 13 shows, relief workers and their families also meant a fresh source of machine votes.

This patronage windfall could be used both internally and externally to strengthen the party organization and to appeal to voters. Internally, white-collar supervisory and administrative jobs represented juicy plums for ward and precinct captains. As the Lawrence machine in Pittsburgh consolidated power in the late 1930s, one-third of its ward captains served as WPA project super-

TABLE 13. *Federal Relief for the Bosses: The WPA and the Cities, 1936*

	WPA Workers[a] (thousands)	City Employees[b] (thousands)	Registered Voters (thousands)	WPA Workers as a Percentage of City Employees	WPA Workers as a Percentage of Registered Voters
New York	246.0	121.4	2,324.4	202.6	10.6
Jersey City	5.2	3.7	151.2	140.5	3.4
Albany	3.9	1.9	72.0	205.3	5.4
Chicago	68.4	29.5	1,503.2	231.9	4.6
Pittsburgh	20.8	5.3	246.5	392.5	8.4
Boston	26.0	13.6	305.6	191.2	8.5

Sources: U.S. Works Progress Administration, *Final Report on the WPA Program, 1935–1943* (Washington, D.C.: Government Printing Office, 1946), Table 2, pp. 110–111; U.S. Bureau of the Census, *Sixteenth Census of the United States, 1940* (Washington, D.C.: Government Printing Office, 1943), vol. 3, pts. 1–5, Table 3; International City Managers' Association, *Municipal Year Book, 1937* (Chicago: International City Managers' Association, 1937), Table 2, pp. 183–184, Table 5, pp. 268–269.

[a]Estimated for the cities from state-level data.

[b]Excludes school system employees.

visors. Rank-and-file WPA workers could also be pressed into party service. In Chicago, the Kelly-Nash machine added party workers to the WPA payroll at election time for the sole purpose of canvassing precincts for Democratic candidates. The Jersey City machine found further political profit from relief, demonstrating that Hague could steal from the poor as well as the rich. The city's WPA workers were tithed a portion of their lowly wages for Hague's campaign war chest.[40]

Externally, the WPA meant machine votes as well as jobs. Table 13 shows that the WPA employed up to 10 percent of the big-city electorate. Bosses could extract gratitude from former—as well as current—reliefers. Over the program's life, 1935 to 1943, up to one-quarter of all big-city registered voters were on the WPA payroll at one time or another.[41] Tammany had a taste of federal relief patronage in 1933 with the CWA program. The Tiger's chieftains made party affiliation—not need—the test for employment on federal projects. Most applicants had to be cleared with their district leader. As one Tammany brave boasted, "This is how we make Democrats."[42] Tammany's blatant politicization of the CWA proved an embarrassment in the 1933 city elections. Bosses would have to be more discreet in their wooing of reliefers.

By providing popular neighborhood services, the WPA could win the hearts of other machine voters. For the bosses, the WPA represented a unique public works grant-in-aid—a federally financed, locally picked labor supply for machine-initiated neighborhood projects. WPA project sponsorship lay primarily with state and local governments. By judicious choice of the type, location, and even timing of WPA projects, machines could build neighborhood electoral support. Bosses used WPA funds for such popular projects as street and highway construction and improvements, sewer systems, parks, schools, and libraries. By locating WPA projects in areas of current or potential machine strength and by completing projects before municipal elections, the bosses could appeal for votes on the basis of neighborhood services rendered.[43]

The WPA also helped machines by easing pressure on their twin supports—the capital budget and the municipal payroll. The WPA allowed bosses to trim their capital budgets and keep the city payroll intact. In cities such as New York, the WPA accounted for more than half of all construction activity in the late 1930s.[44]

Yet the partisan conversion of the WPA was not easy. In its early days, the national Works Progress Administration was studiously nonpartisan in its policy-making and personnel decisions. Harry Hopkins, FDR's minister of relief, deliberately drew WPA district boundaries *across* congressional districts and county and city lines in order to minimize congressional and machine influences over the program. The program's initial nonpartisanship could be traceable to the dynamics of New Deal coalition building in Congress. Before his landslide 1936 reelection, Roosevelt needed the support of moderate Republicans and conservative Democrats to enact his domestic relief and recovery program. The president could not alienate these pivotal legislators with a blatant display of the partisan uses of relief.[45]

The WPA was politicized after the 1936 election. Roosevelt now had a solidly pro–New Deal majority in Congress. With less need to placate southern Democrats and moderate Republicans in Congress, Roosevelt could take the nonpartisan wrapping off relief and reward New Deal congressmen—and the men who selected them. Many of the New Deal legislators were beholden to the bosses. Frank Hague, for example, controlled the entire Garden State Democratic congressional delegation. Hague demanded federal patronage in exchange for his hand-picked legislators voting the New Deal line. As for federal relief, the bosses demanded the power to select state and district WPA administrators. Controlling the relief hierarchy, machines could politicize the key processes of project approval and worker eligibility. As federal relief czar Harry Hopkins moved over to become FDR's chief political adviser following the death of Louis Howe, the need to reward the urban New Deal congressmen and the bosses who selected them increasingly influenced WPA decision making.[46]

The puzzling question is why some Democratic bosses and machines and not others were able to control the WPA. Machine longevity does not explain the selective local capture of federal relief patronage. Roosevelt gave relief to some established machines but not to others. The Hague and O'Connell organizations became federal work relief dispensers. In fact, Boss Hague was made de facto relief czar for all of New Jersey. Allocated 18,000 temporary CWA jobs in 1933–1934, Hague was rewarded in 1937 with the state's allocation of 75,000 WPA slots and Hudson County's

10,000 positions. Nearing bankruptcy in the early 1930s when the railroads went on a tax strike, the Hague machine was revitalized by relief. By the late 1930s the organization was a gigantic federal employment and relief agency. More than $64 million in federal WPA and PWA funds poured into the machine's coffers. In upstate New York, the O'Connell machine also acquired valuable WPA patronage. Armed with federal relief, these machines brought the New Deal's newest ethnic recruits securely into the organization's fold.[47]

Roosevelt offered little relief for Tammany, however. By the mid-1930s the Tiger was wounded. After La Guardia's victory, Tammany was reduced to controlling county offices. Democratic Governor Lehman froze the Tiger out of state patronage, supporting Bronx boss Ed Flynn instead. When it came time to dole out federal patronage, Roosevelt also supported Flynn and, covertly, the progressive La Guardia. With New York City's share of national WPA outlays approaching one-seventh, Tammany's hungry braves circled the federal jobs program.[48]

Determined to deny Tammany badly needed WPA patronage, Mayor La Guardia successfully lobbied Washington for an unprecedented separate relief unit for the city, coequal with the forty-eight state agencies. La Guardia then helped select a succession of nonpartisan WPA chiefs for the city, many drawn from the Army Corps of Engineers—General Hugh Johnson, Victor Ridder, Colonel Brehon Somervell, and Oliver Gottschalk. The Wigwam's braves remained hungry.[49]

Some new machines succeeded where Tammany failed. The fledgling Democratic machines of Chicago and Pittsburgh were incubated with federal patronage. In Chicago, factional battles within the state Democratic party initially delayed the delivery of federal work relief. After Mayor Cermak's death, the struggling Kelly-Nash organization vied with Cermak protégé Governor Henry Horner for control of the state party and federal patronage. Roosevelt initially froze out the Chicago machine, remembering its love affair with Al Smith before the 1932 nominating convention. Ever the political realist, though, FDR knew how to count votes. The Kelly-Nash organization brought out the living—and dead—in record numbers for the president in 1936. A grateful FDR responded by delivering 68,000 Cook County WPA positions to the Irish co-bosses.[50]

Kelly and Nash deputized precinct captains as employment brokers for WPA jobseekers. The party's cadres also served as welfare brokers. To expedite Social Security and AFDC eligibility, the Windy City's precinct captains initiated client contacts with social service agencies. By 1936 two-thirds of the machine's lieutenants reported serving as employment and welfare brokers, up from one-third in 1928. Kelly and Nash particularly targeted the city's Southern and Eastern Europeans for jobs and relief. The new ethnics had flirted with the Republicans in the late 1920s and were still smarting over the Irish counter-putsch following Cermak's death.[51]

Relief patronage also served as the catalyst for building the Democratic machine in Pittsburgh. Rebuffed by old-line progressive McNair, Lawrence was denied control of the 5,300 city workers. Undaunted, the county chairman found WPA jobs—as supervisors and foremen—for his precinct committeemen. Controlling the dole, the nascent machine used Allegheny County's 21,000 WPA positions to good political effect. The job-hungry Southern and Eastern Europeans and the vote-hungry machine both found relief. Between 1930 and 1936 Democratic voter registration jumped from 5 percent to 56 percent. With McNair's long-awaited resignation and the election of party regular Cornelius Scully as mayor in 1937, the Lawrence organization captured the municipal payroll. By 1940 the WPA-based Steel City machine had consolidated power and would rule the city until shortly after Lawrence's death in 1966.[52]

The "Purple Shamrock" (as Boston's Curley was called) was not so lucky. In Massachusetts, Roosevelt appointed an independent state WPA administrator not beholden to any of the Boston ward bosses. Curley was outraged. The mayor had been the state's charter member in the FRBC Club, climbing on FDR's bandwagon in early 1932. After Roosevelt's election, Curley assumed his early support would result in his organization's being designated the clearinghouse for federal patronage in the Bay State.[53]

The president and his state relief administrator assumed otherwise. State WPA czar Arthur G. Rotch vigorously opposed the Shamrock's schemes for politicizing the WPA. Rotch so microscopically scrutinized Boston's WPA projects for possible signs of Curleyite influence that work relief in the Hub was nearly brought to a halt. Elected governor, Curley joined other state Democrats in forcing Rotch to resign in early 1936. The new relief administrator was no better. Federal WPA chief Hopkins named Paul Edwards, an out-of-state Democrat, to the state post. At Hopkins's urging, Edwards also resisted pressure from Curley and other Boston ward politicians to politicize the program.[54]

No federal relief meant no Curley machine. Yet the New Deal did not weaken Irish power in the Hub. It merely federalized it. In the vacuum created by the lack of a citywide machine, Irish power seeped up from the ward level and coalesced at the federal level. The Hub's New Deal hierarchy included congressmen and U.S. senators—vital to obtaining passage of Roosevelt-backed legislation, and not beholden to any big-city boss. Roosevelt and Hopkins wooed Irish congressmen such as John McCormack with WPA patronage. McCormack put the WPA to good use: a disproportionate number of federal public works projects were targeted in Irish neighborhoods in McCormack's district. McCormack's Irish campaign workers appeared on the WPA payroll. Armed with federal relief programs, the Hub's New Deal political hierarchy weakened the ward bosses and made later machine building more difficult.[55]

The WPA, the Bosses, and Presidential Coalition Building

What explains this puzzling pattern of federal relief going to some of the Irish bosses and not to others? Early support for Roosevelt's presidential ambitions, normally thought to be a key factor in federal patronage allocations, does not explain the pattern. The Hague, O'Connell, and Cermak-Kelly-Nash organizations were not members of the FRBC Club; each had supported Smith in the 1932 Democratic contest. Yet all three pro-Smith machines subsequently took over the local WPA programs. In Boston, however, Mayor Curley had been a Roosevelt loyalist from the beginning. Yet Roosevelt deliberately rebuffed the Shamrock in his efforts to politicize the Bay State relief program.

Much of the answer to the WPA patronage puzzle lies in the dynamics of presidential electoral calculation. By the early 1930s Democratic presidential coalition building depended on winning the Solid South and big northern urban-industrial states—New York, New Jersey, Pennsylvania, Illinois, California, Ohio, Michi-

gan, and Massachusetts. The South furnished 113 electoral college
votes while the eight northern states totaled 212 votes. The regional combination provided a winning 325 electoral college votes,
well over the magic number of 266.[56]

Yet the Democratic vote harvest in the big northern states was
problematic in the early 1930s. Seven of the eight had gone Republican in the presidential elections of 1920 through 1928. Enam-
ored with Smith, Massachusetts had strayed into the Democratic
column in 1928. Roosevelt would have to redouble his efforts to
woo the northern big-city voters.

Gavin Wright has found empirical support for the argument
that FDR's electoral calculations influenced the allocation of WPA
jobs. Wright argues that politically targeted New Deal spending
could increase voters' personal income, enhancing the likelihood
that those rewarded would support Roosevelt. A "rational" Roosevelt should have overallocated federal funding and WPA jobs to
pivotal states, defined in terms of their electoral college vote, the
uncertainty of the state's vote outcome, and the traditional closeness
of the state's Democratic vote to 50 percent of the total. Wright finds
these three electoral variables account for nearly 40 percent of the
per capita allotment of WPA jobs among the states.[57]

Wright is correct in his conclusion that presidential politics influenced the WPA. But he has misspecified the political and policy
processes involved. Regarding state WPA job quotas, there is little
evidence of presidential political influence. State job quotas were a
function of state relief caseloads. Each state's percentage of the national welfare caseload was multiplied by 3.5 million—the pre-
sumed maximum WPA employment—to arrive at its job quota.
Big urban-industrial states like New York had the highest per capita WPA job allotments not because of their electoral clout but because of their massive welfare caseloads. Their large relief burdens,
in turn, were a function of both the higher unemployment rates in
the big cities (relative to elsewhere) and their more developed welfare systems.[58]

Presidential politics intruded *after* state job quotas were determined. The politicization of the WPA was not a public auction
where presidential offers of WPA jobs purchased the individual
votes of work relief recipients. WPA employment nationwide rarely
exceeded 3 million, 4 percent of the country's registered voters in

1936. Most WPA workers were unskilled and unlikely to vote unless mobilized by local machines. A wholesale auction of work relief jobs had enormous political risks as well as a low payoff. Blatant program partisanship could backfire, alienating Congress and the public.

Partisan conversion of the WPA required discreet middlemen—the bosses. Work relief politics was a complicated intraparty bargaining process between FDR, Hopkins, and state and city bosses, not a crude auction with voters. In dealing with the bosses, Roosevelt's patronage policy was prospective, not retrospective. FDR rewarded those bosses and machines best able to enhance his reelection prospects. Because there were substantial costs to politicizing the WPA, FDR and Hopkins could only covertly reward a few bosses. They chose those bosses who could carry the crucial urban-industrial states.[59]

Big-city bosses could help carry their states for FDR in two ways—by the votes they controlled or by alliance with state bosses. The 1928 campaign had mobilized the big-city vote, changing the presidential political equation. Cities could now carry the state. By 1940 New York City's voters represented 51 percent of the Empire State's active voters. Chicago's voters constituted 45 percent of the Illinois electorate. In states where the city vote was smaller, FDR worked more directly with the state than with the city bosses. Urban machine alliances with the state boss or majority faction enhanced the chances of receiving federal relief.

Roosevelt had good reason to reward the city bosses. As Samuel Eldersveld has shown, the big-city vote determined Roosevelt's margin of victory, particularly in 1940 and 1944. In 1932, the nation's twelve largest cities supplied one-quarter of FDR's vote plurality. By 1944 the twelve cities supplied nearly two-thirds of Roosevelt's vote plurality. As for the electoral college vote, Eldersveld argues that Roosevelt would have lost the 1940 and 1944 elections without the votes supplied by the large cities. Roosevelt's 1940 landslide victory resulted in 449 electoral college votes. Had the twelve largest cities gone Republican, FDR would have lost with only 237 electoral votes, well below the minimum 266 needed to win. Without the cities in 1944, FDR's 432 electoral college votes would have been reduced to 239 votes.[60]

Given this electoral incentive, FDR allocated WPA patronage to

big-city bosses meeting the voting bloc or state party alliance criteria. The Kelly-Nash Chicago machine met the voting bloc criterion. The Illinois Democratic party was deeply split between the
Chicago machine and Governor Horner, leader of the downstate
Democrats. FDR initially designated the Horner organization as
the state clearinghouse for federal patronage, remembering the
Chicago machine's opposition to his nomination. After Kelly-Nash
showed itself capable of mobilizing the Windy City's voters and
carrying the state for Roosevelt, the president gave the machine
complete control over the Cook County WPA program.

The Hague and Lawrence machines met the party alliance criterion. Despite the fact that Jersey City represented only 10 percent
of the Garden State's voters, Hague became the chief dispenser of
federal patronage because he was the *state* boss. Pittsburgh's voters counted for even less, making up only 6 percent of the Keystone
State electorate. Yet the Lawrence machine received WPA patronage, in large part because of its initially close alliance with the state
Democratic boss, U.S. Senator Joseph Guffey.[61]

Tammany Hall and the Purple Shamrock flunked both patronage
tests. Though New York City's voters swayed the state, the weakened Wigwam could no longer deliver the big-city vote. Gotham's
vote could be delivered by independent progressives such as La
Guardia, particularly after the American Labor party was created
in 1936 to give the city's reform Democrats a ballot line for Roosevelt and the New Deal independent of the Tammany-controlled
Democratic line. Tammany also fell out of favor with the movers
and shakers in the state Democratic party—Governor Lehman,
U.S. Senator Robert Wagner, and Bronx boss Ed Flynn. With
powerful friends like these, Roosevelt could carry New York without the Tiger.

Boston's Curley also flunked both tests. The Purple Shamrock
could rally less than one-fifth of the state's voters. As for alliances,
the state Democratic party continued to be bitterly divided between a western Yankee and Boston Irish wing. Through the early
1930s the western wing was ascendant, sending David Walsh to the
U.S. Senate in 1927 and Joseph Ely to the governorship in 1930.
Without the western wing's active cooperation, Curley's weak
Boston organization could not deliver the state for Roosevelt. The
Bay State's 1932 Democratic primary demonstrated Curley's weak-

ness to FDR as the Walsh-Ely wing easily carried the primary for Smith. With neither faction able to single-handedly carry the state, the president decided to increase his leverage within a deeply divided party by using federal patronage—including the WPA—to build an independent Roosevelt wing. By the time Curley became governor, the die was already cast.[62]

Roosevelt's patronage treatment of the big-city Irish bosses demonstrated his reluctance to promote an ideological revolution within the Democratic party. Rather than a long-term strategy of turning the states into New Deal bastions, FDR was more interested in short-term electoral results. Far more than the Hudson separated Fiorello La Guardia and Frank Hague. Yet a self-interested Roosevelt could support both.[63]

For machines that successfully navigated the shoals of the Depression and New Deal, rough waters still lay ahead. The postwar era witnessed a new and enduring economic crisis—a structural decline in the economies of the aging northern cities, cutting sharply into the machine's resources. At the same time, the now prosperous white ethnics demanded a new menu of policies: low taxes and homeowner services. Migrating blacks and Hispanics, however, demanded the traditional fare of high taxes, patronage, and welfare services. To finesse contradictory voter demands with minimal resources, the postwar machines would enlist the services of the welfare state's permanent legacy.

Chapter Five

The Last Hurrah?
Machines in the Postwar Era,
1950–1985

The Twilight of Machines?

The Irish machines that marched out of the Great Depression and the New Deal were not the same ones that had marched in. Mighty Tammany was toppled, to be resurrected in weaker and temporary form after World War II. The Hague organization, the Tiger's Siamese twin across the Hudson, succumbed to the same diseases of reform fever, declining resources, and new ethnic insurgency. Only Albany's O'Connell organization smoothly navigated the fiscal crisis and accompanying party realignment. Yet the turbulent 1930s served as more than a graveyard for old-style urban politics. The New Deal also served as a maternity ward for a new breed of ethnically diverse and federally assisted machines in the Windy and Steel cities.

The postwar era, not the 1930s, represented the old-style party organization's Ice Age. The machine's traditional food supply of high taxes, patronage, and welfare services dwindled. The flight of industry and the middle class to the suburbs cut sharply into the tax base of the older Frostbelt cities. The introduction of big-city merit systems in the 1940s and 1950s cut further into the machine's patronage stock, strengthening bureaucracy at the expense of party. In the 1960s, new urban political actors—public sector unions and minorities—mounted a frontal assault on the remnants of the patronage system using the tools of collective bargaining and court-ordered affirmative action plans. By the 1970s, patronage could hardly serve as an instrument of reward and discipline for the party's cadre, let alone as an enticement to voters.

The machine's near-monopoly over welfare services to the urban working class collapsed in the face of competition from new providers—the federal government and labor unions. The New Deal's permanent legacy of social insurance and welfare programs such as Social Security, unemployment compensation, public housing, and Aid to Families with Dependent Children lay beyond the bosses' apparent reach. Guaranteeing union elections and collective bargaining, the Wagner Act underwrote labor's unionization of the big-city industrial labor force. In the competitive bidding wars with capital, labor offered prospective members job security and generous fringe benefits, particularly pensions and health insurance. Not to be outdone, corporations responded with their own lucrative benefit packages. The new social welfare triumvirate of labor, capital, and the federal government drove the big-city bosses with their Thanksgiving turkeys off the block.

Deprived of the leverage of patronage and welfare, machines sought new resources and allies. Growth became the new urban talisman as the machines enlisted business, labor, and the media to revitalize the aging Frostbelt cities. Lavish downtown redevelopment projects in Chicago, Pittsburgh, and Albany were designed to create new jobs and city revenue. Federal programs such as urban renewal, Community Development Block Grants, and Urban Development Action Grants financed the urban—and machine—renaissance. Yet intergovernmental economic aid created new political vulnerabilities. Growth required state enabling legislation and federal financial assistance. When state and national governments were captured in the 1950s by a resurgent GOP or reform Democrats, the big-city Democratic machines found their growth plans challenged.

The most serious dilemma of all for Irish machine builders was the changing character of the big-city electorate. The prewar machine's high-tax, job-creating, and welfare policies had attracted considerable ethnic working-class support. Wartime and postwar prosperity benefited the new ethnics, propelling large numbers into the property-owning middle class with less interest in high

taxes and public jobs. Many of the white ethnics joined the suburban exodus. Those who remained in the cities demanded new
machine policies: low property taxes and homeowner rather than
welfare services, for example, street repairs, garbage collection,
and the preservation of white neighborhoods and property values.

Postwar machines also faced the onslaught of a third wave of
lower-class ethnic migrants to the cities. Southern blacks came to
the northern cities in the largest domestic migration in history.
They were soon joined by Hispanics migrating from Puerto Rico,
Mexico, and Latin America. The newest migrants dramatically
changed the machine cities. In Chicago, for example, blacks and
Hispanics constituted 54 percent of the population in 1980, up
from one-quarter in 1960. The new migrants demanded the machine's traditional benefits—patronage and welfare services. Without the services of the welfare state, the Irish machines lacked the
resources to co-opt blacks and Hispanics and forestall demands
for a greater sharing of the organization's lifeblood—power.

Nevertheless, the Chicago, Albany, and Pittsburgh machines
showed remarkable resiliency in the face of declining resources and
shifts in the big-city electorate. The Chicago and Albany machines
reached their zenith in the 1960s—and survived in weakened form
into the mid-1980s. The powerful Lawrence organization in Pittsburgh faltered in 1969 only because of a leadership vacuum caused
by Lawrence's death and by the retirement of his designated successor, Irish Mayor Joseph Barr.

In a larger sense, though, the postwar era would prove to be an
Indian summer for the aging Irish machines. The powerful Chicago machine, progressively weakened since mayor and party boss
Richard Daley's death in 1976, lost the mayoral elections of 1979
and 1983. Long dormant in the Windy City's politics, blacks and
Hispanics elected Harold Washington mayor in 1983. Retreating
to the city council, machine regulars fought a stubborn rearguard
action against Washington's rainbow coalition before finally suc-
cumbing. In upstate New York, the Albany machine survived Dan
O'Connell's death in 1977 but faced a leadership vacuum following O'Connell successor Erastus Corning's death in 1983.

Winter came early for would-be machine builders in the other
once-Irish cities. In New York and Jersey City, citywide machines
reemerged under new ethnic ownership by the 1950s. Yet these

"fourth-generation" machines were weak and porous, unable to crack the whip over an increasingly powerful array of interest groups. By the early 1960s these rebuilt municipal engines over-heated as resources declined and as intergovernmental alliances frayed. The new machines also developed a crack in their electoral blocs. Democratic machines historically have depended on ethnic and working-class support. Yet in the 1960s antimachine insur-gents were able to enlist blacks and Hispanics in their crusade. As their electoral warranties expired, the new machines fell to reformers.

In Boston, San Francisco, and Philadelphia, where Irish Demo-cratic machines had not been built during the 1930s, the postwar resurgence in local Democratic fortunes produced middle-class re-form politics rather than a new generation of machines. In these cities, durable reform coalitions organized around the popular issues of downtown redevelopment, low taxes, civil service reform, and improved municipal service delivery. Patronage eluded the grasp of would-be bosses in these cities as reform tipped the bal-ance of power from party to bureaucracy. Kevin White in Boston and Frank Rizzo and William Green in Philadelphia tried their hands at machine building. All of them failed. None commanded the resources necessary to transform personal campaign organiza-tions into durable party machines.

The postwar era also marked the Ice Age for Irish leadership of the dying big-city Democratic machines. Demographics finally did the Celtic bosses in. Forced to accept the Southern and Eastern Eu-ropeans as junior coalitional partners in the 1930s, the aging Irish chieftains staged a brilliant and ever-so-slow retreat into the ma-chine's inner sanctum of patronage-dispensing and policy-making positions. Even there they were not safe from ethnic attack. A new rainbow coalition of blacks and Hispanics challenged white ethnic control of the machine's most coveted, scarcest, and zero-sum re-source—power.

This chapter examines the fall, Indian summer, and winter of the big-city Democratic machines and their Irish leaders. We shall proceed seasonally. First, fall. What were the dimensions and causes of the postwar machine crisis of declining resources, un-raveling intergovernmental alliances, and changing big-city voter demands? Second, Indian summer. How were the already consolidated Irish machines of Chicago, Albany, and Pittsburgh able to negotiate these changed and inhospitable conditions in the local political marketplace? The late nineteenth-century machine's conservative fiscal and patronage policies had fueled working-class insurgency. In the 1930s and 1940s the Southern and Eastern Europeans revolted against the financially pressed Tammany and Hague machines. In the postwar era, blacks and Hispanics would also demand the machine's traditional fare of patronage jobs and welfare services. Given new ethnic demands for material benefits in an era of declining machine resources, why were the revolts of minorities against the postwar machines so muted and late in coming?

Third, winter. If the entrenched machines found a niche in the barren postwar environment, why didn't a fourth generation of strong and durable machines emerge in the other once-Irish cities? New York and Jersey City both had robust traditions of political machines, for example, centralized party-based governance institutions, and of machine politics, that is, the trading in divisible material benefits.[1] Yet the final yield of the postwar era on both sides of the Hudson was machine politics at the ward or borough level rather than centralized citywide political machines. As for the other cities, Philadelphia had a strong tradition of GOP political machines while Boston and San Francisco traded in divisible benefits. Why did these three cities appear to embrace reform so suddenly and completely in the postwar era?

Finally, spring and the new big-city rainbow coalition. In the 1980s, blacks have infiltrated the walls of the once-Irish municipal Jericho, electing mayors in Chicago and Philadelphia and mounting a serious challenge to Irish rule in Boston. Taking their cue as much from Mayor Daley as from Jesse Jackson, big-city minority politicians such as Harold Washington have tried to build a new generation of black-led urban machines. Black would-be bosses seek to revitalize ward-based electoral systems as machine building blocks. Urban black politicians are also trying to forge cross-ethnic electoral coalitions with Hispanics and Asians. What is the future of political machines and machine politics in the hands of the new big-city minority politicians? Can machines be revitalized to serve the new minority poor, or have they suffered irreversible decline?

Fall: Dimensions of the Postwar Crisis

The Changing Urban Electorate

Two major changes in the big-city electorate threatened the post-war machines—the exodus of working-class white ethnics, the machine's traditional constituency, into the middle class and out of the city; and the massive influx of poor blacks and Hispanics. Machines had little control over these two shifts in the pool of big-city voters. Each had structural origins outside the city—in national and regional economies, in technology, and in federal policy. Yet machines had to respond as the electoral coalitions built in the 1930s and the policies that produced them unraveled.

White ethnics voted with their feet in record numbers in the postwar era. Between 1940 and 1980, 4 million whites, representing more than one-third of the white population, left the eight once-Irish cities for the suburbs and other regions. Many sirens lured them out of the big cities— the automobile, wartime and postwar prosperity, the decentralization of industry, and federal housing and highway policies.

The two-thirds of the white population that remained in these cities shared in postwar prosperity. Blue-collar workers became labor's new unionized aristocracy as collective bargaining agreements in the manufacturing sector guaranteed job security and rising wages. Other sectors of the growing central-city economy— business and financial services, government and nonprofit agencies—generated middle-class jobs for the machine's traditional ethnic constituents.[2]

As white ethnics moved into the middle class, they became homeowners, exchanging tenements in the inner wards for new homes in the outlying wards. Of the Irish machine cities, the process of embourgeoisement was more advanced in Albany with its 25,000 well-paid state employees. By 1940, 42 percent of the state capital's homes were owner-occupied. Postwar prosperity allowed other machine cities to catch up. In Chicago, 46 percent of whites owned their own homes in 1980, up from 30 percent in 1940. In the Steel City, 57 percent of the city's whites were property owners in 1980 compared with 39 percent in 1940.[3]

Rising homeownership rates affected the kinds of taxation and spending policies machines could pursue. Earlier machines had pursued expansionary fiscal policies with little fear of electoral reprisal. Working-class voters were renters, not homeowners; property tax hikes could be passed on to nonvoting absentee landlords. High taxes meant more public jobs, an important inducement to big-city voters.

The electoral risk of high-tax, job-creating policies ballooned during the prosperous 1950s. Middle-class homeowners no longer hungered for the old machine's working-class fare of patronage jobs and welfare services. The white ethnics now hankered for different machine policies—low property taxes, homeowner rather than welfare services, and the preservation of white neighborhoods and local institutions, particularly schools.

White taxpayer revolts were not the only electoral threat facing the postwar machines. The influx of blacks and Hispanics into northern cities represented a second major change in the urban electorate. Before World War II, black life had been rooted in tenant farming and sharecropping arrangements in the poorest southern states. After the war, its focus shifted northward and to the big cities. In the rural South, the mechanization of agriculture disrupted the tenant farming system, contributing to the massive exodus of blacks off the land. In the North, the wartime economy had created an unprecedented demand for labor. The postwar suburbanization of whites further encouraged rural southern blacks to move to the big cities.[4]

The black movement to the big cities was unprecedented in scale. Between 1940 and 1980, 5 million southern blacks packed their bags and moved north. Over 2.5 million of the migrants settled in the eight once-Irish cities. As minorities resettled and whites fled, the black share of these cities mushroomed from 8 percent of the population in 1940 to 30 percent in 1980.

Hispanics joined blacks in the northern cities, particularly in New York and Chicago. New York served as a magnet for Puerto Ricans and, more recently, for immigrants from Latin America. Chicago's diversified industrial base attracted Latinos from Mexico as well as Puerto Rico. By 1980, 1.4 million Hispanics resided in New York City, representing 20 percent of the city's population.

One-half million Latinos crowded into the Windy City, constituting 14 percent of the population.

Compared with white homeowners, poor blacks and Hispanics made different—and potentially conflicting—demands on the big-city machines. White homeowners demanded low taxes and limited public spending for homeowner services rather than patronage and welfare. Impoverished blacks and Hispanics, however, were renters who supported property tax increases to pay for needed city jobs and services. In the eight cities, fully three-quarters of blacks rented in 1980 compared with less than one-half of whites.

Big-city minorities particularly sought public jobs. The postwar suburbanization of private sector jobs contributed to chronically high unemployment rates for blacks. As industry decentralized, blacks were trapped by inner-city residential segregation and the consequent transportation costs imposed.[5] Public employment represented an attractive alternative. In the 1950s and 1960s government represented one of the fastest growing sectors of the central-city economy. City payrolls grew by 44 percent between 1947 and 1970 in the eight once-Irish cities. The heavily white-collar public sector offered higher wages, better fringe benefits, and greater job security than the private sector. Minorities had greater access to government jobs. The public sector pioneered antidiscrimination programs. As their voting strength grew, blacks and Hispanics could politically capture machine patronage.[6]

Minorities also demanded welfare services. Public housing represented a major demand—ironically created by the machine's own policies. Moving to the big cities, blacks confronted an acute housing shortage as machines such as the Daley organization collaborated with real-estate brokers to confine blacks to ghettos. The Chicago machine had a strong political incentive to maintain segregated housing patterns. By reinforcing racial residential patterns with housing, building code, and highway policies, the organization built electoral support in "protected" neighborhoods populated by white ethnics.[7]

Downtown urban renewal also contributed to the minority housing shortage. Machines collaborated with downtown businesses in slum clearance programs designed to revitalize the decaying central city. Uprooting thousands of blacks, urban renewal

TABLE 14. The Third Wave Arrives: Ethnicity and Race in the Eight Cities, 1980

	Total Population, 1980	First Wave, as Percentage of 1980 Population		Second Wave, as Percentage of 1980 Population		Third Wave, as Percentage of 1980 Population	
		Irish	Germans	Italians	Poles	Blacks	Hispanics
New York	7,071,639	9.2	6.4	14.2	4.8	25.2	19.9
Chicago	3,005,078	9.2	10.2	4.6	10.0	39.8	14.0
Philadelphia	1,688,210	18.1	13.2	11.4	5.9	37.8	3.8
San Francisco	678,974	12.7	11.0	6.2	1.9	12.7	12.2
Boston	562,994	26.8	5.3	12.3	3.1	22.4	6.4
Pittsburgh	423,938	19.3	24.8	11.6	9.9	24.0	0.7
Jersey City	223,532	15.2	7.1	13.8	8.9	27.7	18.8
Albany	101,727	26.0	15.7	14.8	7.0	16.1	2.0

Sources: U.S. Bureau of the Census, 1980 Census of Population, vol. 1, ch. C (Washington, D.C.: Government Printing Office, 1983), Table 69; U.S. Bureau of the Census, Statistical Abstract, 1981 (Washington, D.C.: Government Printing Office, 1981), no. 24, pp. 21–23.
Note: Self-reported ethnic ancestry.

programs substantially contributed to the inner-city housing shortage. As the northern ghettos filled, minorities pressured the big-city machines to build low-income public housing projects.

The dilemma of postwar machine coalition building involved the contradictory character of the demands of minorities and white ethnics. Poor blacks and Hispanics demanded large-scale and costly public investments in jobs and welfare services. Middle-class whites demanded low taxes, public spending for homeowner rather than welfare services, and the maintenance of white control over local institutions such as neighborhood schools and the police.

The changing character of the postwar urban electorate threatened not only the longevity of existing machines but also the Irish claim to party leadership. The Irish machines built during the 1930s had integrated the Southern and Eastern Europeans into the party's governing circle and onto the public payroll. Irish accommodation of the new ethnics, however, remained incomplete. Irish politicians in Chicago, Albany, and Pittsburgh monopolized key policy-making and patronage-dispensing positions well into the postwar era. As a consequence, tensions between Irish and non-Irish persisted. The Daley organization faced Polish insurgency in the early 1960s, and the O'Connell machine in Albany fought rebellious Italians.

Ironically, white suburban flight may have preserved Irish control over party and government as ethnic insurgents fled the city. In Chicago, the Irish held the mayor's office from 1933 to 1983 (with a three-year hiatus) and held between one-quarter and one-third of the seats on the city council into the 1970s. The Irish also retained effective control of the Cook County Democratic Central Committee into the early 1980s. In Albany, the machine regularly nominated a Protestant for mayor while the party organization and city council firmly remained in Irish hands.[8]

With the migration of blacks and Hispanics, however, Irish leadership both of the existing machines and of party-rebuilding efforts elsewhere rested on an ever-diminishing electoral base. Table 14 shows the ethnic composition in 1980 of the eight once-Irish cities. Residents of Irish ancestry averaged less than one-fifth of the cities' population compared with nearly one-third of Italian, Jewish, and Polish background. Yet the day of ethnic political reckoning would ultimately come from the newest minorities. By 1980, blacks and Hispanics made up more than 40 percent of the population of these cities. Minority leaders joined the ethnic chorus demanding a greater sharing of power and patronage from the entrenched Irish party bosses.

Declining Resources

The postwar era depleted the machine's arsenal of resources to meet this rising chorus of new electoral demands. The stock of patronage jobs dwindled under the combined pressures of civil service reform, union and minority challenge, and a shrinking local revenue base. Where prewar bosses had easily circumvented weak and antiquated civil service protections, postwar bosses found that civil service now had teeth. In New York City, for example, La Guardia tightened the merit system and expanded it to include three-quarters of the city's payroll by the end of his fourth administration, up from 55 percent at his inauguration. The dilemma posed for Carmine De Sapio, Tammany's postwar rebuilder, was substantial. While the city's population had climbed by 11 percent between 1930 and 1960, the number of "exempts"—patronage jobs—had fallen by 22 percent.[9]

Aided by the courts, civil service reformers in other machine cities followed suit. In 1946, the Chicago machine was on the verge of collapse. Party chairman Pat Nash had died in 1943. Mayor Edward Kelly's reputation sagged as city services deteriorated and charges of cronyism in the school board and other agencies mounted. Jacob Arvey took over as party chairman, enlisted the ward bosses to persuade Kelly to retire, and nominated Irish businessman and reformer Martin Kennelly for mayor, outflanking the Republicans who were planning to nominate their own blue-ribbon candidate.

Once elected, "Fartin' Martin" (as Alderman "Paddy" Bauler called him) proved politically inept—except for civil service reform. Uninterested in politics, the reform mayor let the aldermen—the so-called grey wolves—run the city. Yet Kennelly launched an assault on the patronage system, the source of the ward bosses' power. From 1947 to 1955, Kennelly cut the number of patronage jobs held by machine stalwarts by 40 percent, from 30,000 to 18,000.[10]

Reform governors joined reform mayors in attacking the patronage system. In New York, Republican Governor Thomas E. Dewey attacked the O'Connell machine in 1943, extending the stringent state civil service system to include county employment. By the stroke of a pen and several court fights, the Albany machine's public patronage supply was reduced by one-quarter, from 4,300 to 3,100 jobs.[11]

In the 1960s the patronage system came under attack not from reformers but from the machine's nominal allies—unions and minorities. In Chicago, Mayor Richard J. Daley, elected in 1955 as party regulars dumped reformer Kennelly, opposed public employee unionization and collective bargaining as a threat to the patronage system. The Windy City had long been a strong labor town, and the Chicago Federation of Labor was influential in the Democratic machine. Needing organized labor's votes and financial support, the machine returned the favor with massive downtown public works projects, the prevailing wage for craft union members on the city payroll, an elaborate and cost-escalating building code, and the appointment of labor representatives on most of the city's boards and commissions.[12]

Public sector unions were another matter. In the mid-1960s the city's public servants began organizing, posing a direct threat to the machine's cadre of 20,000 political workers masquerading as civil servants. The teachers were the largest of the city employee groups and the first to organize. Because the teachers had been outside the machine's patronage system for thirty years, Daley relented and agreed to collective bargaining. Union recognition meant no loss of party workers.

But the spoils system enveloped most other city employees; here Daley drew the line. Despite the mayor's opposition, public union militancy mushroomed in Chicago in the 1970s. In the hands of militant leaders since 1972, the teachers' union served as the vanguard. Teachers were soon joined by militant transit workers and firefighters, all demanding collective bargaining rights—and an end to patronage.[13]

Albany experienced a similar bitter fight over municipal unionization despite the machine's good relations with the city's traditional labor unions—teamsters, construction workers, and laborers. In the early 1960s the machine had crushed efforts to

unionize the police force. By the late 1960s, however, the firefighters were unionized, joined by police officers and municipal
blue-collar workers in 1973.[14]

Minorities also launched an attack on the patronage system. In
Chicago, blacks had served as Daley's margin of electoral victory
in the crucial 1955 and 1963 municipal elections when the machine had faced strong challenges. Yet blacks got little in return.
The party allocated patronage to ward leaders on the basis of the
number of Democratic votes received. Black wards got few patronage jobs because of low voter turnout levels.[15]

Federal civil rights legislation gave minorities another tool besides the vote for claiming their fair share of public jobs from the
machines—affirmative action. Title VII of the Civil Rights Act
of 1964, prohibiting job discrimination on the basis of race or
gender, was extended in 1972 to cover state and local government
employment. Blacks in the Windy City quickly brought suit in federal court to end the long-standing discriminatory hiring and pro-
motion practices of Daley's police and fire departments. After a
bitter court fight and lengthy negotiations, the machine relented.[16]

Minorities found reform allies in their attack on Chicago's patronage system. In the early 1970s, reformers filed a class action
suit in federal court against the machine's political sponsorship
system for county jobs. Drawn from the court testimony of the
machine's chief patronage job dispensers, Table 15 shows the magnitude of the spoils system in Cook County and Chicago city
government in the mid-1970s. More than one-half of the nearly
40,000 city and county jobs were given to party stalwarts. The federal courts upheld the class action suit filed by independent candidates, taxpayers, and voters. The Chicago machine was enjoined
from using partisan criteria in government job hiring and firing.
More nails had been driven into the patronage coffin.[17]

By the 1970s the machine's patronage system was further buffeted by an eroding local revenue base, the product of population
and capital flight. For the prewar machines, growth had been axi-
omatic. The population of the eight cities surveyed had increased
by an average 22 percent per decade between 1900 and 1930, permitting machines to pursue expansionary fiscal policies. The Irish
bosses had used the fiscal surplus to modestly redistribute resources from Yankee taxpayers to poor Irish payrollers.

TABLE 15. *"Civil Service" Chicago-Style:*
Public Employment and Machine Patronage, 1976

Public Employer	Total Full-Time Jobs	Percentage of Jobs Politically Sponsored[a]	Estimated Number of Patronage Jobs
City of Chicago	27,000[b]	50	13,500
Chicago Park District	3,869	50	1,935
President, Cook County Board	3,072	50	1,536
Clerk, county circuit court	1,700	75	1,275
Cook County clerk	264	75	198
Cook County sheriff	1,519[c]	—	1,188
Cook County recorder	303	75	228
Forest Preserve District	646	50	323
Cook County treasurer	210	75	158
Cook County assessor	390	50	195
Totals	38,973		21,546

Source: Shakman v. *the Democratic Organization of Cook County et al.,* no. 69 C 2145 (U.S. District Court for the Northern District of Illinois, Eastern Division), "Memorandum in Support of Plaintiffs' Motion for Partial Summary Judgment," p. 24.
[a] Based on court testimony of public officials.
[b] Excludes police and fire personnel.
[c] Excludes police and jail personnel.

In the postwar era urban growth was no longer automatic. Bosses found their local revenue base shrinking as population and industry fled from the cities. Aided and abetted by the automobile and federal housing and highway policies, the suburban exodus of big-city residents slowly accelerated. In the eight cities, the population dropped by an average 6 percent per decade between 1950 and 1970, the decline accelerating to 12 percent in the 1970s.

Industry followed. Corporate managers in manufacturing firms chose new suburban branch locations or relocated existing central-city plants in the suburbs rather than expanding antiquated and congested big-city production facilities. Federal defense spending fostered new industries such as aerospace and electronics, which built plants in suburban locations from the beginning.[18]

Population and capital flight significantly accelerated in the 1970s as foreign economic competition contributed to the de-industrialization of the Frostbelt cities. Chicago, for example, lost 10 percent of its population and 120,000 manufacturing jobs, representing more than one-tenth of all employment, during the decade. The Steel City, hard hit by Japanese steel imports and the slump in the American automobile industry, lost nearly 20 percent of its residents and employment during the traumatic 1970s.[19]

Machines desperately searched for additional revenue to cushion the blow of the fiscal crisis on the patronage system. Property taxes were exhausted. After twenty years of steady increase, intergovernmental assistance began declining in the late 1970s. Without new revenue, the party bosses had little choice but to pare the major budget outlay—the city payroll. In Chicago, municipal employment dropped from 45,000 in 1970 to 43,000 in 1980. In Albany, the city payroll declined from 3,300 in 1970 to 3,100 in 1980. In Pittsburgh, where reform Democrats filled the leadership vacuum created by Lawrence's death and Barr's retirement, independent Mayor Peter Flaherty embarked on a vigorous austerity program designed to remedy the city's finances and prevent the rebuilding of the Democratic machine. Between 1970 and 1977, Flaherty cut city employment by one-third, from 7,200 workers to 5,000.[20]

The postwar "patronage crisis" created severe organizational maintenance difficulties for the aging Irish machines. Fewer patronage jobs meant fewer controllable machine voters. Richard Daley, Dan O'Connell, and David Lawrence could not rely on the payroll vote as Charles Francis Murphy and Frank Hague had done so successfully in the 1920s. As the supply of patronage declined, machines would be forced to bring less precious metals to the electoral auction—municipal services and collective benefits. Fewer patronage jobs hampered the organization's ability to get out the vote by reducing the number of campaign workers. The political sponsorship system's decline also created severe morale problems within the party organization. Ambitious lower-level party functionaries now faced reduced career mobility opportunities.

Patronage had represented one element of the old machine's winning electoral formula; welfare services represented another.

With the coming of the New Deal, machines lost their franchise on social services to the urban working class. Federal social insurance and welfare programs distributed benefits to the categorically eligible, not the politically deserving. Welfare-state programs weakened the old-style urban party organizations to the extent the bosses could not convert collective benefits into divisible benefits for which working-class votes could be exchanged. As welfare participation rates for poor big-city black families skyrocketed in the 1960s, the bosses found themselves potentially deprived of control over the social services that had rewarded—and disciplined—previous generations of working-class ethnic voters.

The New Deal also strengthened organized labor as a rival provider of social services to the urban working class. The Wagner Act enabled labor to unionize much of the big-city manufacturing labor force. In the conservative political climate of the late 1940s, labor turned from new membership drives to the task of protecting and enlarging existing collective bargaining agreements. By the late 1940s, unions had won the battle to include fringe benefits such as health plans and pensions in labor contracts. Nonunion companies, in turn, were forced to respond with their own fringe benefit packages, reminiscent of the welfare capitalism of the 1920s. Unions, capital, and the federal government had ended the bosses' near monopoly control over social services to the urban working class.[21]

Machines were forced back on municipal service provision. Here too they began losing their grip. As Kenneth Mladenka argues, big-city bureaucracies such as street and sanitation departments competed with the machine as major actors in local service decisions. In Chicago, city agencies by the late 1960s actively intervened in answering citizen complaints, planning neighborhood service allocations on the basis of need, and reviewing compliance. Ward politicians were reduced to a service broker role, putting constituents in touch with the right public agency. In Daley's Chicago, bureaucratic routines rather than party vote-maximization imperatives appeared to shape municipal service delivery.[22]

Even the machine's ability to set local tax rates—of considerable importance to homeowners—was reduced as ever larger portions of the city budget became noncontrollable. By the 1960s, municipal unions and federal and state officials became major actors in the local budgetary process. Public employee unions wrested wage and salary decisions—the largest element of city budgets—from local elected officials. City workers secured automatic salary increases based on cost-of-living adjustments and comparable wage increases in the private sector. Federal and state regulatory mandates on local service delivery further reduced the budgetary authority of local elected officials. As a result, the city bosses watched helplessly as city budgets and local tax rates spiraled upward in the 1960s and 1970s. The bosses were quickly losing their grip over the major levers of urban power—jobs, services, and taxes.

Indian Summer: Machine Accommodation Strategies

Resources

How did machines respond to the tandem crises? In terms of resources, machines at first were slow to revise their winning ways. Chicago's Richard Daley, for example, came to power in the 1950s invoking the old formula of high taxes and ever more patronage. After defeating reform mayor Kennelly in the hotly contested 1955 Democratic primary, Daley tried to consolidate his power among the party rank and file by the traditional method of padding the city payroll. He was stymied, however, by state taxation powers and by the city council's control of the budget. Under the terms of the Illinois constitution, the state legislature, not the mayor or the city council, had the power to set municipal real-estate tax levies. Daley's first item of business was to secure an exemption for Chicago. His second item of business was to wrest budget-making power from the "grey wolves," the aldermen who had run the city during the Kennelly years. Here too he needed state assistance.

Like earlier generations of machine builders, Daley consolidated his power with intergovernmental alliances. Daley knew Springfield, having previously served as a state representative and a senator. His state connections paid off handsomely as the legislature and governor approved his plans for placing city taxation and budget-making powers in the mayor's office.[23]

Armed with new fiscal powers, Daley undid the civil service mischief of the Kennelly years but at the price of a taxpayers' revolt. Taxation and spending in the Windy City dramatically rose in the late 1950s and early 1960s as the new boss consolidated power.

Chicago's property tax rate rose faster than any other big city in the country. The number of city employees increased by one-third—to 40,000—during the mayor's first two terms as the machine padded the payroll with fresh patronage. The property tax rate ballooned further with revelations of a burglary ring in the police department. Daley appointed reformer O. W. Wilson as police superintendent with orders to clean house. Wilson did—for a price. The police budget skyrocketed from $75 million to $200 million.[24]

Daley invoked the machine's old spending formula, and it appeared to work until 1963. Angered by a 100 percent increase in taxes since 1955, white homeowners staged a major revolt against the machine. In the 1963 general election, Republican candidate Benjamin Adamowski charged that Daley had fattened the city payroll at the expense of homeowners. Heavily taxed property owners responded, particularly Polish-Americans also incensed by the failure of the Irish to share power. Adamowski won the middle-class ethnic wards on the North Side, receiving a majority of the white vote citywide. Daley narrowly defeated the Polish challenger only because of a massive black vote in machine-controlled South Side wards.[25]

A taxpayers' revolt also threatened the O'Connell machine in upstate New York. Between 1921 and 1969 the low-tax machine had routinely won city elections with between 70 and 86 percent of the vote. In 1972, however, the machine's high-debt policies and financial sleight of hand finally unraveled. A mounting city deficit forced O'Connell to increase real-estate taxes by 84 percent. Albany's Democratic taxpayers revolted. In the 1973 city election, protesting homeowners flocked to support Republican mayoral candidate Carl Touhy. Despite a sixteen-to-one Democratic voter registration edge, Touhy came within 3,500 votes of defeating eight-term Mayor Erastus Corning II.[26]

Tax revolts taught the modern Irish bosses the risks of too rapidly expanding the relative size of the public sector. As an alternative, bosses championed downtown redevelopment projects promoting the city's growth as a whole. In Chicago, the downtown area known as the Loop was stagnating by the early 1950s. Taking power, Daley launched an ambitious revitalization program using federal urban renewal funds, eminent domain, and zoning. Growth yielded political dividends as the machine fashioned a powerful coalition of developers, bankers, and unions.[27]

The other Irish bosses also embraced the talisman of growth. Pittsburgh was a decaying city in the mid-1940s, the downtown Golden Triangle in sharp decline. Party boss David Lawrence took office as mayor in 1946, pledging himself to carry out the Steel City's facelift. Wooing wealthy industrialists and financiers, his traditional Republican rivals, Lawrence launched the Pittsburgh Renaissance project. The Renaissance rebuilt downtown, cleared the slums, and attracted corporate headquarters. Tax revenues, falling in the early 1940s, rebounded. Between 1947 and 1955 property valuations rose from $961 million to $1.12 billion.[28]

Albany's downtown facelift would be public, not private, conducted under state Republican rather than local Democratic auspices. Embarrassed by the blighted neighborhoods adjoining the state capitol in the late 1950s, GOP Governor Nelson Rockefeller proposed and built the massive ten-year $2 billion Empire State Plaza government office complex. The plaza, popularly known as the South Mall, revitalized the city's decaying South End. Completed in the mid-1970s, the plaza launched Albany's urban renaissance as private investment and $27 million in federal housing money poured into the blighted South End.[29]

Downtown revitalization required federal and state assistance, creating new political dependencies and vulnerabilities for the Irish machines. In Chicago, Daley's Loop renewal program required a substantial infusion of federal financial assistance. The federal share of local capital outlays rose from 9 percent in 1955 to 32 percent in 1977. As federal financial involvement in local growth deepened, the Daley machine became prisoner to changing federal urban policy priorities. Welcoming the expansion of federal slum clearance to include commercial redevelopment and housing (1954), the machine later found itself saddled with the consolidation of federal urban renewal and social programs (1966); the merger of planning, housing, and physical development programs (1974); and the brokering of public and private sector investment funds for purposes of commercial development (1978).[30]

Downtown redevelopment also required state assistance, which was troubling to the Irish bosses when the GOP or reform Democrats controlled the statehouse. Republican William Stratton was governor of Illinois when Daley launched his ambitious revitalization program. When Daley later turned to the Crosstown Expressway project, he found reform Democrat and arch rival Dan Walker in the governor's chair. In Pittsburgh, David Lawrence needed a state legal package to restructure the city. The package included pollution control, waste disposal, highways, mass transit, parking, and new sources of revenue. Yet in the postwar era Pennsylvania had returned to its old Republican ways. The fate of the Pittsburgh Renaissance project would be in the hands of three successive state GOP administrations. In decaying Albany, the O'Connell machine faced a potentially hostile Governor Nelson Rockefeller and a resurgent Republican-Conservative party alliance in the late 1960s and early 1970s.

Irish bosses were able to make bipartisan redevelopment deals by enlisting powerful local Republican pro-growth interests—bankers, developers, and business owners. In the Windy City, the downtown GOP business establishment enthusiastically endorsed Daley's Loop renewal program, giving the mayor increased state political leverage. Led by the Mellon family, the Steel City's business and financial community was ready to remake the city with or without the Lawrence machine. Lawrence skillfully leveraged local business support to secure state approval of his rescue package.[31]

The O'Connell organization faced a different political threat posed by downtown renewal. Because Albany's facelift was at the behest of the state GOP, the machine had little need to curry favor with local business interests. Yet the 100 acres expropriated in 1962 for the South Mall project displaced the rooming-house population crucial to the machine's success. The machine could count one-fifth of its normal citywide vote among the 9,000 refugees. The project also cut into its revenue base as tenements and businesses were removed from the tax rolls, replaced by tax-exempt state property. Faced with this twin threat, the machine initially opposed the South Mall project.[32]

Notwithstanding these costs, the machine would eventually support the massive state office project in order to gain needed political influence with the powerful Republican governor. The billion-dollar project required unprecedented financing. Rockefeller knew that a statewide bond referendum of this magnitude benefiting only one locality would likely be defeated. The Albany Democrats came up with an innovative and politically shrewd alternative. Mayor Erastus Corning proposed that Albany County, not the state, sell the bonds to build the South Mall. The county would then lease the office complex to the state for ninety-nine years at rents high enough to retire the bonds and to make up for lost tax revenues. A desperate Rockefeller agreed.[33]

The O'Connell-Corning gamble paid off handsomely in 1971 when state Republicans and local reformers tried to pry the Albany school system, its $17 million annual budget, and 1,000 employees from machine control. The school board was appointed, and the mayor packed it with machine partisans. In 1971, the city's population officially fell below 115,000, the minimum population under state law for an appointed school board. Albany would have to have an elected board. Republicans wanted a high turnout general election in November for the school board when national and state political currents could neutralize machine strength. O'Connell and Corning wanted a low turnout election in May when their full weight could be brought to bear. The machine now used its control of county bonds for the South Mall project to pressure Rockefeller. The city quietly stalled construction by canceling the sale of $70 million in project bonds. Rockefeller got the message and introduced a bill mandating a May election—good machine weather.[34]

Downtown redevelopment projects helped machines manage the postwar fiscal crisis by creating jobs and shoring up the tax base. Yet the key *organizational* resource issue was dwindling patronage. Even though the payroll vote no longer carried elections, patronage remained an essential organizational commodity. Chicago's 3,500 precinct captains, for example, depended on public jobs. Precinct captains served as vote mobilizers on election day and as service brokers the rest of the year. The machine's lower-echelon functionaries had help. In the mid-1970s, there were 12,500 patronage precinct workers, an average of four workers for each of the city's 3,000 precincts. A $200 million precinct organization—at public expense—could yield substantial electoral results.[35]

Machines handled the patronage crisis in time-tested ways. In Chicago, Richard Daley evaded civil service regulations much as James Michael Curley had done in Boston three generations earlier. Entrance examinations were given infrequently and were deliberately made difficult so that only a few applicants could qualify for permanent positions. Pleading necessity, the machine would hire numerous temporaries—for the rest of their lives. As collective bargaining agreements and affirmative action plans cut deeply into the organization's stock of public sector jobs, Daley implemented a Chicago version of Charles Francis Murphy's "businessmen's plan." Regulated businesses such as utilities, bus companies, and racetracks added party workers to their rosters.[36] In Albany, Dan O'Connell also packaged patronage from a variety of sources—the city government, the school system, county-regulated nursing homes, and state government. Even Albany County, under state civil service since 1943, was not immune from the spoils system. The county's merit system compliance record was the worst in the state.[37]

White Ethnics

Dwindling patronage and loss of monopoly control over welfare services did not weaken the postwar machine's appeal to white ethnics. Middle-class whites no longer demanded machine-supplied patronage and social services. Instead, the ethnics demanded low taxes, homeowner services, and the preservation of white neighborhoods and schools.

The antimachine tax revolts of the 1960s and early 1970s taught the bosses a valuable lesson—the need to cater to the policy preferences of white homeowners. In Chicago, the Daley machine in the mid-1960s began shifting its policies and electoral base, replacing costly patronage and welfare services delivered to poor inner-city wards with efficient low-cost homeowner services delivered to outlying middle-class wards.[38]

Daley froze the property tax rate in 1970 to placate white homeowners. The machine diversified its local revenue portfolio to include taxes on vehicles and utilities. Yet the machine's primary fiscal strategy in the post–tax revolt era was intergovernmental. Daley used his power in state and national politics to generate new revenue. In the 1960s Daley placed Otto Kerner in the governor's chair. State financial aid to the city increased as did the city's share of the state sales tax. The machine's biggest revenue coup involved federal assistance. Between 1970 and 1978 public spending in Chicago doubled—to $10 billion—although the city budget rose by only 58 percent. By 1978 federal spending in Chicago was 430 percent greater than municipal outlays from local revenue sources, up from 250 percent in 1970.[39]

Machines catered to new service as well as tax demands. While bureaucracy competed with party in influencing postwar municipal service decisions, machine politicians demonstrated an uncanny ability to intervene on behalf of voters at all stages of the service delivery process. Machines were particularly interested in maintaining control over labor-intensive and discretionary homeowner services. In Chicago, the city's building and housing codes were among the strictest in the nation. In a study of property code enforcement in the Windy City, Bryan Jones has shown that the machine thoroughly controlled the policy-making process. Ward committeemen and precinct captains stimulated citizen service demands, invoked special attention rules for particular neighborhoods, and actively intervened in the compliance process. The machine also practiced the politics of code nonenforcement, holding a powerful club over recalcitrant property owners.[40]

More generally, Daley instructed his ward bosses to act as service brokers, expediting housekeeping services such as street and sidewalk repairs, tree trimming, and garbage removal. Improved neighborhood services contributed to growing white homeowner support for the machine. As John Petrocik has shown in his study of the 1975 Chicago mayoral election, machine-provided services to white ethnics accounted for nearly one-third of Daley's overall vote plurality. For white homeowners, Chicago was "the city that works."[41]

At the same time, Daley deliberately increased the power of bureaucrats over the delivery of municipal services, particularly capital-intensive and immobile projects such as parks, schools, police, and fire stations. The mayor worked tirelessly to professionalize the upper echelons of the local public sector. His talent scouts conducted nationwide personnel searches to discover top-notch professionals needed to run the agencies responsible for delivering basic public services.[42]

There were good political reasons for bureaucratizing municipal services. Quality services bought votes, as Daley discovered in 1975. Daley also remembered his early battle with the "grey wolves." Administrators were hired by the mayor and responsible to him, not to the aldermen. Daley could both raise the level of public services, popular with voters, and weaken the power of the ward politicians. Thus service equalization and enhanced bureaucratic discretion contained a political logic, maximizing the organization's vote potential *and* the mayor's power.

To maintain his power, the mayor adroitly played the ward politicians off against the professional bureaucrats. Daley deployed his army of temporary employees in city agencies providing homeowner services. The mayor carefully ladled this service-relevant patronage to the ward leaders, rewarding them for faithful party service while enhancing their ability to serve their constituents. These boss-controlled lower-level party-bureaucratic networks represented a check on top-level bureaucrats. As Milton Rakove has observed, Daley expected his administrators "to recognize political realities in Chicago and be sensitive to the built-in relationships among city agencies, the ward organizations, and voters."[43] In Chicago, the party ruled the bureaucracy, and the mayor ruled the party.

Middle-class whites demanded that machines supply more than low taxes and homeowner services. As the northern cities filled with blacks and Hispanics, whites also demanded the preservation of white neighborhoods and continued control over such "culture-transmitting" institutions as the schools. White hegemony, not divisible benefits, increasingly served as the machine's chief attraction for the ethnic middle class.[44]

In Chicago, housing and the schools served as the twin litmus tests for white voters. The Chicago Housing Authority represented a key machine mechanism for maintaining racial residential segregation—and the white vote. The Housing Authority practiced racial discrimination in both public housing site selection and tenant assignment. In particular, the agency had to choose whether to build low-density public housing on vacant land in white neighborhoods or high-density projects on cleared slum sites. The extension of heavily black housing projects into white neighborhoods threatened the machine's traditional ethnic constituency. As the white ward bosses rose in opposition to scattered-site projects, the agency turned to building inner-city high-rise projects. Segregated public housing projects were not the only weapons the machine used to maintain white neighborhoods. Freeway routes also served as racial barriers, as did the issuance of real-estate licenses to discriminating realtors. The Albany machine practiced similar racial containment policies, confining the city's 15,000 blacks to the South End and Arbor Hill ghettos.[45]

Segregated and poorly funded public schools represented a second element in the machine's bargaining agreement with white voters. The Irish bosses had never understood the public schools except as a source of patronage. Educated in parochial schools, the bosses deliberately underfunded the public schools to make the church's educational system more attractive—and to keep the property tax rate down. In Chicago, 40 percent of the city's tax dollar went for public education compared with an average 70 percent in the surrounding suburbs. The city's meager education funds hired patronage janitors rather than teachers. Blacks and Hispanics, then, were forced to fight a two-sided battle. Minorities demanded both integrated schools and a substantial increase in public funding.[46]

Machines had to resist minority demands in order to maintain white ethnic support and staunch the exodus to the suburbs. In Chicago, school superintendent Benjamin Willis failed to integrate the city's schools or equalize resources between predominately white and black schools. Racial conflict soon spilled over into the machine's appointments to the Board of Education. In Albany, where one-half of all students were enrolled in Catholic parochial schools, the O'Connell organization refused to spend more on public schools or desegregate the school system. The machine's educational policies won the endorsement of Irish, Italian, and Polish middle-class voters—and the powerful Catholic church.[47]

The machine's defense of white racial interests solved one organizational maintenance problem while creating another. Concerning Chicago, Paul Kleppner argues that a new type of exchange relationship had developed between the machine and white voters by the 1960s. Traditional material benefits—patronage jobs and welfare services—no longer bound whites to the machine. The postwar machines had fewer benefits to offer, and middle-class whites had less need to accept. The new transactions involved power and race. Machines guaranteed the preservation of white neighborhoods, schools, and other culture-transmitting institutions for a small price—the ballot.[48]

But the machine's new policy algorithm had a major down-side risk—the minority vote. Machines could concede little to blacks on housing and schools because whites perceived these issues as zero-sum. Black gains in integrated housing or school busing equaled white losses. As minorities tipped the city's population, machines had to come to a biracial accommodation. If housing and schools were declared off-limits to blacks, machines would have to offer instead the traditional menu of patronage jobs and social services to prevent minority insurgency. With patronage dwindling and welfare preempted, machines were in a quandary.

Minorities

Before the mid-1960s shift in policies and electoral base, Irish machines had avidly courted the minority vote. In Chicago and Pittsburgh, black sub-machines were created in the late 1930s and early 1940s. In Chicago, Congressman William Dawson, the only black in the Daley machine's inner circle, ran the massive South Side ghetto. Blacks on the South Side and on the racially changing West Side supplied the margin of victory in three of Mayor Daley's six victorious campaigns between 1955 and 1976. In the 1955 general election, for example, Daley defeated Republican Robert Merriam by 127,000 votes, receiving a 125,000 vote plurality in heavily black machine-controlled wards. Despite their electoral fealty, minorities received few material rewards from the Daley organization. Rather than giving Dawson significant power or patronage, Daley rewarded him with "policy," that is, control of the numbers racket. Blacks made up 40 percent of Chicago's population in 1970, but only 20 percent of the municipal workforce, largely in menial positions.[49]

In Pittsburgh, state representative Homer Brown ran the Lawrence organization's black sub-machine. Brown did yeoman service for Lawrence. Not only did Brown dependably supply the black vote; he also served as the key leader shepherding the Pittsburgh Renaissance project through the Pennsylvania House of Representatives. A grateful Lawrence bestowed real "policy" on Brown. The Steel City's boss pushed through a fair employment practices ordinance and appointed minorities to top-level jobs in his administration.[50]

Minority demands on the big-city party organizations escalated during the turbulent 1960s. In Chicago, the black movement started growing in the early 1960s, led by Saul Alinsky's Woodlawn organization seeking better schools. In 1966 Martin Luther King, Jr., took the civil rights movement north to Chicago, demanding an end to segregated housing and discrimination in employment. As King marched through Chicago's white suburbs, racial tension increased. Riots rocked the Windy City in 1966 in the Lawndale ghetto and in 1968 in the West Side ghetto. In Albany, black neighborhood groups such as Better Homes and activist groups such as the Brothers pressured the O'Connell machine for public housing, control of federal antipoverty funds, and an end to urban renewal.[51]

Machines like the Daley organization judiciously used welfare-state programs to control the minority vote and to siphon off discontent at minimal cost to the city treasury and to tax-conscious white homeowners. Both New Deal and Great Society social programs were used for these purposes. Public housing and Aid to Families with Dependent Children (AFDC) represented the two major New Deal programs that machines used to placate blacks.

Migrating blacks confronted an acute housing shortage as the northern machines collaborated with real-estate brokers to confine blacks to crowded inner-city ghettos. By uprooting thousands of blacks, urban renewal programs contributed substantially to the inner-city housing shortage. As the northern ghettos filled in the postwar era, the big-city machines lobbied for federal housing money to build low-income public housing projects. Segregated federal housing projects not only soothed the fears of white ethnics; they also served to concentrate the black vote and make it more controllable.[52]

The postwar suburbanization of private sector jobs and industry had contributed to chronically high unemployment rates for urban blacks. Rather than grant more substantial policy and municipal employment concessions to the restive black community (which would anger the machine's white ethnic constituency), machines chose welfare as a politically cheaper response. As Frances Fox Piven and Richard A. Cloward have argued, welfare limited the scope of urban racial conflict because existing white political prerogatives were not challenged.[53]

Machines exerted little control over determining AFDC eligibility. Yet there were ways of politicizing this collective benefit program. So that it could claim credit for increasing welfare benefit levels, the Chicago machine instructed its state legislative and congressional delegations to vote for welfare liberalization measures. At the local level, Chicago's precinct captains set up welfare information bureaus in public housing projects to put prospective welfare clients in contact with the appropriate social agency. Even though the Windy City's machine politicians did not control program eligibility, they threatened welfare recipients with loss of public assistance should they vote for the machine's opponents. Under machine auspices, the welfare participation rate for black families in Chicago rose from 18 percent in 1969 to 32 percent in 1979.[54]

Machines also commandeered Great Society programs to stabilize and build political support in the black community, particularly among the emerging middle class. While the federal antipoverty programs of the 1960s such as Community Action, Job Corps, and Model Cities ostensibly were targeted at the poor, they created considerable employment for human service providers. The $2.7 billion annual federal spending for Title I of the Elementary and Secondary Education Act, for example, created 275,000 teaching and administrative positions. Nationwide, Great Society programs generated 2 million new human services jobs, primarily in local government and in nonprofit community-based organizations.[55]

The big-city bosses had strong political incentive to use federally funded human services employment to respond to growing black demands. As with welfare, federally subsidized social employment limited the scope of interracial conflict. By channeling blacks into jobs in expanding social service agencies, machine politicians minimized conflict with whites in traditional city agencies such as police and fire departments. Social welfare employment also represented one of the most tangible and effective ways the bosses could respond to the threat of urban disorder. In Chicago, 54 percent of the black job gains between 1960 and 1980 occurred in social welfare agencies. By 1980, one-third of the Windy City's blacks and nearly 60 percent of the black middle class worked in human services and government.[56]

Welfare-state programs stabilized the big-city machines by creating a large-scale social welfare economy—of middle-class service providers and lower-class recipients—in the black community. As long as social programs grew, the welfare state represented a potent partisan tool. Machine politicians carefully ensured that the party organization and not the black community controlled local antipoverty agencies. Mayor Daley successfully resisted black political demands for control of the Community Action Program by demonstrating the machine's importance in Democratic presidential politics. In 1964, Daley delivered Chicago for Lyndon Johnson by a record 675,000 votes in order to highlight the president's dependence on the machine. The lesson was not lost on federal antipoverty director Sargent Shriver, who wanted to be governor of Illinois. The president and his antipoverty chieftain sued for peace. By this show of electoral clout, reminiscent of the Kelly-Nash machine's mobilization of Chicago voters in the mid-1930s to capture control of the local WPA program, Daley received $140 million in federal antipoverty funds.[57]

In Chicago, the machine used the welfare state to dismantle and control the black vote. By the late 1960s the Daley organization had developed a new formula for success: Mobilize the white ethnic vote, particularly in wards undergoing racial transition. The large black vote of 1963 was no longer needed for victory. In fact, the black vote now loomed as a risk, particularly if black independents could capture it and challenge the machine. The machine employed a series of strategies to dilute the now superfluous minority vote. Wards on the South Side were racially gerrymandered. When black sub-lieutenant William Dawson died in 1970, the machine groomed no replacement.[58]

Above all, the machine relied on the expanding welfare state to demobilize the black vote. Minority social service providers involved themselves in intergovernmental bureaucratic politics—the grants economy—rather than in community electoral politics. The expansion of means-tested antipoverty programs such as AFDC depoliticized welfare recipients by isolating them from the work experiences encouraging political participation. Federal social programs thus represented a potent machine tool for co-opting the black middle class and depoliticizing the underclass. As the welfare state penetrated the black community, voter participation rates declined sharply. In Chicago, the black turnout rate dropped from 60 percent to 37 percent between 1964 and 1976.[59]

The welfare state even captured the residual black vote. In the Windy City, public housing projects represented the most tightly controlled precincts in the inner city. As Don Rose, one of the city's leading political strategists, observed of the welfare-state "plantation provinces," "the Organization owns a lock on a solid 20 percent of the black vote. This is the vote the Machine would deliver for a George Wallace against Martin Luther King."[60]

Not all machines needed the black vote or the welfare state. Unlike Chicago, the minority vote loomed small in Albany. As Table 14 shows, in 1980 blacks and Hispanics constituted only 18 percent of Albany's population compared with 54 percent of Chicago's. Pursuing low-tax and homeowner-service policies from the 1920s onward, the O'Connell organization did not face white ethnic insurgency until 1973—after the turmoil of the 1960s. Not needing the black vote, the machine mounted no voter registration drives in the South End and Arbor Hill ghettos.

Uncle Dan did not suffer when he failed to capture the War on Poverty. In Albany, antipoverty funds initially flowed into the Trinity Institution, a South End Episcopal Settlement House, not into the machine's coffers. Unlike the Daley organization, the O'Connell machine could not deliver the New York state vote for Democratic presidential candidates. To cripple the community-controlled antipoverty program, the machine withdrew the city's subsidy to the Trinity Institution. As a result, Albany was the last major city in the country to launch an antipoverty program. As minority unrest grew in the South End ghetto, the machine skillfully deployed Albany County's Human Resources Department. The department gave out 15,000 jobs over ten years, building a solid base among the city's poor and minorities. The department deliberately chose manpower training and jobs over cash transfers. During the 1970s, the welfare participation rate for the city's black families remained at 24 percent.[61]

For heavy users of the welfare state such as the Chicago machine, federal programs bought the organization a twenty-year lease on life by rewarding and co-opting blacks. The Daley organization had constructed a winning electoral coalition of white ethnics in the late 1960s with low taxes, homeowner services, and white hegemony. The transformed machine required minority acquiescence. Yet the systematic demobilization of the black vote contained a hitch. Up to 60 percent of the city's registered voters didn't vote in local elections—reminiscent of Tammany Hall in the 1920s.[62] Black quiescence required the services of a growing welfare state. Welfare-state contraction, however, could destabilize machines by encouraging the threatened black middle class to register and mobilize the votes of the underclass. The Chicago machine would learn of the dangers of welfare-state dependence in the early 1980s. Light users of the welfare state such as the O'Connell organization, in contrast, could more easily weather social program retrenchment.

Winter: Failures of Machine Building

The entrenched Irish machines of Chicago, Albany, and Pittsburgh adapted to the postwar market conditions of lessened resources and changing voter demands. Would-be bosses in the other once-Irish cities were not so lucky. Weakened machines reemerged in New York and Jersey City in the 1950s, only to collapse in the 1960s and early 1970s. These pluralist regimes, as Martin Shefter has termed them, never managed to get their acts together.[63] Pale imitations of the Murphy and Hague organizations, the postwar successors were weaker and more porous, forced to bargain with a powerful array of new interest groups and independent power centers.

In Boston and Philadelphia, where Irish Democratic machines had never been built, Democratic mayors tried their hand at machine building in the late 1960s and early 1970s. But the mayors succeeded only in creating personal campaign organizations, not long-lived party-based institutions. When they left office, their personal followings disintegrated.

What accounts for the postwar experience of these ersatz machines, weaker forms of the classic Irish big-city organizations? Why couldn't machine builders in these cities imitate Chicago's Daley, delivering low taxes, efficient services, and racially segregated neighborhoods and schools to white ethnic homeowners and the welfare state to minorities?

Weakened Machines

In New York City, Carmine De Sapio slowly resurrected an Italian-run "New Tammany" after World War II. During the La Guardia years, Tammany had been badly wounded by civil service reform. Not only did the Little Flower blanket city employment with a strengthened merit system; he also succeeded in eradicating the patronage system in county government, the last bastion of the Wigwam's strength. Stripped of patronage and revenue, Tammany's aging Irish chieftains were forced to sell the organization's clubhouse and sue for peace with the new ethnics. The Southern and Eastern Europeans demanded surrender. The Italian-controlled underworld threw out Christy Sullivan, the last of the Irish Tammany bosses, in 1943 after Sullivan nominated an antiracket reformer to be district attorney. Completing the Italian putsch, De Sapio took over leadership of Tammany Hall in 1949.

De Sapio's leadership did not extend to city government until 1953. In 1945, La Guardia retired and independent Democrat William O'Dwyer was elected. Though O'Dwyer initially gave Tammany some patronage, he demonstrated his independence by dispensing top appointments to the other county party leaders, all resentful of the Manhattan-based Tammany. De Sapio was further thwarted in 1950 when O'Dwyer unexpectedly resigned to become ambassador to Mexico. In the ensuing special election, De Sapio's candidate, Ferdinand Pecora, was defeated by independent Vincent Impelliteri, endorsed by underworld leader Frank Luchese.

De Sapio finally consolidated power in 1953 as the Wigwam's candidates for mayor and governor—Robert F. Wagner, Jr., and Averill Harriman—both won. De Sapio employed both patronage and policy to rebuild Tammany. Municipal employment rose by nearly one-third between 1949 and 1957, from 199,000 to 262,000, as Tammany recaptured badly needed patronage. The refurbished Tiger embraced such popular reforms as public housing, rent control, civil rights, and even permanent voter registration. With Governor Harriman beholden, De Sapio reached the zenith of his power between 1955 and 1958.[64]

Yet Italian machine-rebuilding efforts failed in New York. Despite Tammany's metamorphosis from patronage to policy, the city's Jews remained firmly in the ranks of the reformers, organizing anti-Tammany political clubs throughout Manhattan in order to infiltrate and capture the party bureaucracy. Loss of state and federal patronage in the late 1950s and early 1960s seriously hampered Tammany's ability to fight the reformers. As Tammany weakened, Mayor Wagner severed his connection with De Sapio and joined the insurgents. In the crucial 1961 mayoral election, the reformers under the leadership of a born-again Bob Wagner defeated Tammany by capturing the non-Irish and non-Italian vote—Jews, Yankees, Puerto Ricans, and blacks. Tammany would not be resurrected as control of the city's politics passed to reformers such as John V. Lindsay and Ed Koch.[65]

Across the Hudson, insurgent leader John V. Kenney tried to construct a successor organization to the Hague machine in the 1950s. Like De Sapio, Kenney pursued expansionary policies to augment his fledgling organization's stock of resources. Between 1949 and 1957, Jersey City employment rose by one-fifth, from 6,900 to 8,300. As in Chicago, Kenney's fiscal policies backfired as local property taxes ballooned, arousing the opposition of ethnic homeowners. Kenney's ticket lost to a dissident Polish and Italian faction in 1957.

Despite his return in 1961, Kenney never fully consolidated power. After a brief fling with fiscal austerity, designed to soothe taxpayers' nerves, the would-be boss jacked up the property tax rate by 30 percent to enrich the party coffers—and the pockets of his henchmen. High taxes were the price white homeowners were willing to pay in the 1960s for the preservation of racial hegemony. By the 1960s blacks and Hispanics represented more than one-third of Jersey City's population. As minority unrest grew, law-and-order Mayor Thomas J. Whelan ordered police shotgun patrols in the ghetto. White homeowners were temporarily lulled. With another record tax increase in 1970, however, Kenney's days were numbered. As homeowners mobilized to overthrow the boss, the federal government intervened. Kenney and eleven other Jersey City politicians were indicted and convicted in federal court on charges of receiving $3.5 million in kickbacks on construction contracts. Thereafter, reformers Paul Jordan and Thomas F. X. Smith would rule the land of Hague.[66]

What accounts for the reemergence and decline of postwar ma-

chines in New York and New Jersey? Like Daley, De Sapio and
Kenney initially employed the same building blocks used by earlier
generations of machine builders: intergovernmental political alliances and expanding resources. In New York, De Sapio's relationship with Governor Harriman paid off handsomely with state
patronage and financial assistance. Both De Sapio and Kenney expanded the local public sector in order to create patronage for
their followers and improve the delivery of municipal services to
voters.

These strategies worked for a time. But a crucial difference separated New York and Jersey City from Chicago and Albany. In the
latter cities, machines maintained a continuous grip on the levers
of urban power, forcing interest groups both to moderate their demands and to channel them through the dominant party organization. In the former cities, machines had lost to reformers, opening
up a Pandora's box of escalating group demands eluding machine
recapture.

In New York, independent centers of power had grown during
Tammany's twelve-year hiatus—the outer borough party organizations, special districts such as the Triborough Authority, labor
unions, and, above all, a powerful reform movement. Reformers
had left the Tammany-run Democratic party in the 1930s and
early 1940s, channeling their energies into the American Labor
party and the La Guardia administration. With La Guardia's retirement and the splintering of the ALP, many returned home.
Tammany's metamorphosis in the 1950s from divisible benefits to
collective goods was a tribute to the power of the reformers.[67]

As group demands exploded, would-be bosses required an extra
infusion of resources. Intergovernmental alliances were particularly critical for the postwar machines. Yet vertical alliances created new political vulnerabilities as well as opportunities. In New
York, De Sapio's star rose with Democratic Governor Harriman
and set with Republican Nelson Rockefeller. De Sapio had used
his alliance with Harriman to contain the party's reform faction,
which was intent on organizing anti-Tammany clubs throughout
Manhattan. In 1958 Rockefeller beat Harriman. The loss of state
patronage hampered Tammany's ability to fight the reformers and
heightened the importance of federal patronage as the 1960 election loomed. Wanting to be a presidential kingmaker, De Sapio

committed a fatal error by maintaining his independence from the Kennedy organization until it was too late. The newly elected Irish-American president never forgot, deliberately depriving De Sapio of federal patronage. The Tiger's loss of state and federal aid emboldened local reformers. As Tammany weakened, Mayor Wagner severed his Tammany connection, realigning himself in the crucial 1961 city election with the party reformers led by ex-Governor Herbert Lehman and Eleanor Roosevelt.[68]

In Jersey City, Kenney's intergovernmental downfall was more ignominious. As the city's property tax rate soared in the 1960s to pay for machine building, Kenney turned to federal assistance. Federal grants and contracts eased pressure on local taxpayers, revitalized the decaying downtown area, rewarded the city's minorities, and enriched Kenney and his henchmen. The last purpose was impermissible. In 1970 the Nixon administration began investigating the awarding of federal construction contracts in Jersey City. A year later a federal grand jury indicted the machine's top leadership for its kickback scheme on federal projects.

True to form, new machines were more sensitive to external interventions than old machines. Yet there were higher start-up and maintenance costs for *all* machines in the Frostbelt cities in the postwar era, requiring larger dosages of external assistance. Postwar machines had to perform what James O'Connor has termed the capital accumulation and legitimation functions on an unprecedented scale.[69] Ambitious downtown revitalization projects were launched. Human service jobs and cash transfers flowed into the ghetto. With local revenue sources exhausted, the bosses tapped— and were trapped by—the intergovernmental system.

De Sapio and Kenney failed with intergovernmental alliances. Daley, Lawrence, and O'Connell succeeded. Faced with potentially hostile state and national Republican administrations in the 1950s, Daley and Lawrence fashioned local bipartisan growth coalitions to augment their intergovernmental leverage. With Democratic ascendancy in the 1960s, the two bosses took over their respective states. In Illinois, Daley put protégé Otto Kerner in the governor's chair and demonstrated his electoral indispensability to Presidents Kennedy and Johnson. In Pennsylvania, Lawrence himself moved from the mayor's office to the governor's office in 1959 and designated Irishman Joseph Barr his successor.[70]

In New York, Democratic state ascendancy came in the 1970s.

As the landlord of the Empire State Plaza project, Dan O'Connell had extracted crucial policy concessions from Governor Rockefeller. After its close escape in the 1973 city election, the Albany machine strengthened itself by actively supporting Democrat Hugh Carey for governor. Once elected, a grateful Carey diverted state patronage to the O'Connell organization. After Uncle Dan's death, successor Erastus Corning also dabbled in state politics. Corning was the first major upstate Democratic politician to support Mario Cuomo's candidacy for governor.[71]

Intergovernmental assistance allowed the strong Chicago, Pittsburgh, and Albany machines to contain their Republican and reform opponents. In strong machine cities, there was little resembling New York City's postwar machine/reform dialectic.[72] In weakened machine cities, the character of the dialectic underwent a significant transformation with the passing of citywide machines. In New York City, Tammany Hall's passing did not mean an end to political machines. No longer welcome at city hall, Democratic machines still resided at the sub-city level.

Gotham's powerful Democratic county organizations paid their last respects—and little more—to the deceased. The outer borough machines had grown in strength and organization to match their mushrooming populations. Tammany's Charles Francis Murphy had launched Ed Flynn's career as boss of the Bronx organization in 1922. Thereafter, the satellite Bronx, Brooklyn, and Queens organizations would slowly gravitate out of Tammany's orbit. Into the 1980s, the borough machines and local party organizations such as the Jefferson Democratic Club in racially embattled Canarsie would employ traditional material resources to keep their ethnic constituents in line in local races.[73]

With the demise of citywide machines, reform also underwent a transformation. In New York, Mayor Lindsay donned reformer Wagner's electoral mantle, fashioning a coalition of liberals—both WASP and Jewish—and minorities. The Wagner-Lindsay reform coalition collapsed in the early 1970s as white ethnic homeowners in the outer boroughs rebelled. Democratic Mayor Abe Beame, Lindsay's successor, proved to be no East Coast Richard Daley. Beame failed to refurbish the Democratic machine as a political home for the city's conservative-leaning white ethnic property owners.

As a result, a new type of reform—the personalized leadership of antimachine Mayor Ed Koch—became the dominant vehicle for protecting white hegemony and for expediting neighborhood services. Instead of consolidating a new citywide organization, Koch ultimately made his peace with borough power brokers in the Bronx, Brooklyn, and Queens. The price he paid became clear only after his 1981 and 1985 reelections when the scent of scandal involving these surviving county Democratic machines tainted the mayor.[74]

In New York, then, the postwar reform cycle began with a liberal cross-class Jewish-minority alliance against the machine Irish and Italians. It ended with a middle-class Jewish-Irish-Italian alliance against lower-class blacks and Hispanics presided over by a neoconservative Jew, the beau ideal of the grandchildren of the new immigrants.

Personal Organizations

In Boston, Philadelphia, and San Francisco, the postwar era would be fertile soil for the Democratic party but barren ground for machine building. The New Deal helped shape both outcomes. Where there was no preexisting machine useful to Roosevelt's reelection plans, the president could strengthen the reform wing of a revitalized local Democratic party. In Boston, FDR's patronage policies increased the influence of the anti-Curley reform forces in the faction-ridden party. In Philadelphia, the pre–New Deal Democratic ward politicians had served at the pleasure of the GOP machine. As Democratic fortunes waxed in the 1930s, Roosevelt spurned the kept ward bosses, directing federal patronage to the Democratic Warriors Club led by reformers Joseph Clark, Jr., and Richardson Dilworth.[75]

The fruit of New Deal reform would ripen slowly. In Boston, reformers suffered an apparent setback in 1946 when James Michael Curley was reelected mayor while serving time in federal prison for influence peddling. The Purple Shamrock's resurrection was short-lived as the anti-Curley forces in the city—the business community and homeowners, Yankees, Jews, and middle-class Irish and Italians—coalesced into a broad-based bipartisan reform coalition.

Representing producer interests, the reformers denounced the legacy of Curleyism—high taxes, corruption, and a depressed business climate. Failing to build a centralized political machine, the Shamrock and his allies had constructed an urban welfare state instead. In 1950, the Hub had the highest per capita expenditures in the country for welfare, health, and hospitals. Fifty-five thousand people (one out of every fourteen residents) lived in public housing, the highest proportion for any large city. The local welfare state extended to the police and fire departments. The city had the highest per capita expenditures for police and fire protection of any major city—but uniformed personnel were paid the least. Curley and his cronies had systematically padded the payroll with legions of low-paid Irish policemen and firemen. With the highest tax rate in the country, the city's property owners groaned under the weight of the local welfare state, Irish-style.[76]

Denouncing "Curleyism," the reformers captured city hall in 1951 and held on for sixteen years. Irish reform mayors John Hynes and John Collins promoted an ambitious downtown revitalization program (the "New Boston"), instituted austerity programs to lower the city's onerous tax burden, extended civil service coverage, and successfully lobbied for state assumption of welfare costs. Redevelopment was the centerpiece of the Hynes and Collins administrations. No new office building had been constructed in the downtown area between 1927 and 1958. Securing federal urban renewal funds, reformers razed blighted neighborhoods and secured construction of the Prudential and Government Center anchor projects.[77]

A challenge to Irish hegemony did not accompany the Hub's revolution in policymaking. The Irish remained the largest ethnic group, allowing Green Power and reform to coexist. The Irish dominated the city council and public payroll well into the 1960s. Yet demographic forces were at work to pick the Irish lock on local government. By 1970, the Irish share of Boston's population had dipped below one-third while the black and Hispanic share approached one-quarter. New ethnic coalitional possibilities now presented themselves—even to Irish politicians.

An enterprising Irish politico took the challenge in 1967. Kevin White fashioned an outgroup coalition of liberals, blacks, and Italians to beat Louise Day Hicks and the South Boston working-class Irish. Elected mayor, White proceeded to reward his supporters.

Between 1967 and 1979 the black proportion of the city payroll rose from 6 percent to 18 percent. Italians also entered the city workforce in record numbers. To minimize the resentment of Irish payrollers, White used federal grant funding to create job opportunities for blacks and Italians. The mayor offered other blandishments to his supporters—improved neighborhood services and "Little City Halls" to expedite service complaints to Big City Hall in Government Center.[78]

In the mid-1970s reformer White turned to machine building. White began courting the South Boston Irish, his previous foes, to create a machine. In his 1975 and 1979 reelection bids, White hired between 1,500 and 2,000 temporary city workers, many from South Boston, to staff his campaign organization. In 1977 White tried to institutionalize his power with an audacious city charter proposal. The White charter would have reinstituted the partisan ballot and increased the mayor's authority over the troubled but patronage-rich Boston school system.[79]

For all his efforts, White succeeded only in building a personal campaign organization, not a centralized party-based machine. Declining resources and state recalcitrance thwarted the mayor's plans. White's political designs on the city payroll were limited by the merit system and collective bargaining agreements. Reformers Hynes and Collins had strengthened the city's civil service system. Major municipal labor unions—the Police Patrolmen's Association, the Boston firefighters' union, and the locals of the Association of Federal, State, County, and Municipal Employees (AFSCME) and the Service Employees International Union (SEIU)—had won the right of collective bargaining the year White took office.[80]

An intertwined fiscal and racial crisis in 1975–1977 further complicated White's machine-building plans. The municipal credit market collapsed in 1975 in the wake of New York City's de facto bankruptcy. Court-mandated school desegregation cost the city an unexpected $70 million. As the city's financial woes mounted, White promised the powerful municipal unions no layoffs in exchange for no wage increases. With Morgan Guaranty Trust Company, the chief underwriter on the city's bond issues, looking over his shoulder, White was forced to dismantle his army of provisional city workers. After the 1975 election, the mayor laid off 1,200 temporary municipal employees, representing 8 percent of the city's overall workforce. In 1979, White's postelection plans included the layoff of 1,700 more temporary workers.[81]

The state also conspired against the would-be city boss. The mayor's charter proposal required state approval. Despite strenuous lobbying, White's proposal for a return to partisan patronage politics died in the state legislature. Proposition 2½, passed by Massachusetts voters in 1981, was the last nail in White's political coffin. Limiting local property taxes, the proposition cut deeply into Boston's revenue base and municipal payroll. A discouraged White announced his retirement in 1983, unable to pass his diminished campaign organization to a designated successor.

The New Deal's reform legacy also hindered Democratic machine building in Philadelphia. Strengthened with federal patronage, reformers Joe Clark, Jr., and Richardson Dilworth in the late 1930s wrested control of the local Democratic party organization from the kept ward bosses. The reformers then turned their sights on the scandal-ridden GOP Vare machine, which had suffered serious reverses in the 1930s. In 1934 Bill Vare had died with no successor in sight. The feuding Republican ward bosses temporarily united at election time as the organization lurched forward on its own momentum. In 1935 the machine narrowly averted defeat as Democrat John Kelly won at the polls but lost at the ballot counting. More trouble loomed as a New Deal coalition of Catholics, Jews, and blacks slowly took shape. Conceding defeat in national elections, the machine continued to woo the ethnics in local contests with low taxes and social services delivered by an army of precinct committeemen.[82]

The GOP machine finally succumbed in 1951. With the property tax rate frozen since 1936, basic municipal services had been deteriorating. Faced with the collapse of the city's infrastructure of streets, sewers, and public transportation, the business community called a halt. Mayor Bernard Samuel was forced to create a Committee of Fifteen to investigate the machine's fall from service—and business—grace. Philadelphia's modern-day Committee of Correspondence uncovered considerable scandal, prompting calls for a new city charter. The city's leading business, financial, and legal firms organized the Greater Philadelphia Movement to pressure for government reform. The machine reluctantly endorsed a new charter calling for home rule, the consolidation of city and county offices, a strong mayor-council system, and a sharp reduction in patronage.[83]

Philadelphia's voters approved the new charter in 1951 and called on the Democrats to implement it. Democratic mayors Joe Clark, Jr. (1952–1956), Richardson Dilworth (1956–1962), and James Tate (1962–1972) embraced much of Chicago machine-builder Daley's agenda—slum clearance and urban renewal, mass transit, and public housing. Yet the employment policies of the Chicago machine Democrats and the Philadelphia reformers diverged considerably. In the Windy City, Daley reinvigorated the patronage system to reward white ethnic partisans. In the City of Brotherly Love, reform Democrats accepted the new charter's civil service system and used it to recruit blacks. By 1970 blacks made up 43 percent of Philadelphia's municipal workforce—double their proportion in Chicago.[84]

The reformers' incorporation of blacks generated a white backlash in what became the City of Not-So-Brotherly Love. Elected mayor in 1971 with the blessing of James Tate and Democratic party chieftain Peter Camiel, former police commissioner Frank Rizzo cracked heads in the ghetto and vowed to protect white neighborhoods. Rizzo then turned to machine building to institutionalize his white ethnic political base à la Chicago's Richard Daley. Because the merit system severely limited the patronage yield of municipal employment, Rizzo invoked the intergovernmental connection. Entering into a marriage of convenience with the Nixon White House and mending his fences with liberal Democratic Governor Milton Shapp, the former police chief built a formidable campaign organization with urban renewal funding and patronage.

Like Kevin White in Boston, however, Rizzo could construct only a personal organization, not a durable party machine. His alliance with Nixon alienated Peter Camiel and the regular Democratic organization. Disbarred by the city charter from serving a third term, the law-and-order mayor was unable to designate a successor. Though William Green, the next chief executive, rose to power through the Democratic ward system, he also broke with the organization to become a Philadelphia Robert Wagner—a born-again antipatronage reformer.[85]

The postwar period, then, proved to be inhospitable for building a fourth generation of big-city machines but not for maintaining preexisting organizations. The Chicago, Pittsburgh, and Albany machines adapted to declining resources and changing voter demands by freezing the tax rate, promoting downtown revitalization, delivering homeowner services, and piggybacking the welfare state. In other cities, the postwar yield was short-lived ersatz machines. New York and Jersey City produced the closest postwar approximations to the machine ideal. Both De Sapio and Kenney took the traditional supply-side path of expanding the patronage stock and forging intergovernmental party alliances to augment and monopolize resources. As in the past, embryonic machines were most vulnerable to external shocks. The drying up of state and federal assistance hastened reform insurgency in New York City and De Sapio's early retirement. Across the Hudson, a federal indictment gave Kenney new vacation plans.

The supply-side path was available from the 1940s through the late 1960s as city payrolls grew. By the early 1970s, however, would-be bosses faced declining resources. In both Boston and Philadelphia, strong merit systems installed in the 1950s coupled with collective bargaining agreements with powerful municipal unions fashioned in the 1960s shielded the city payroll from Mayors White and Rizzo. The fiscal crisis of the 1970s further complicated the mayors' search for patronage. White, for example, was forced to slash Boston's payroll by nearly one-quarter. Both White and Rizzo turned to ersatz patronage—temporary city workers and federal project employees—to build personal campaign organizations. Yet the two mayors could not generate the resources needed to transform candidate-centered organizations into robust party-based machines.

Nor were state political alliances forthcoming to consolidate these two fledgling machines. In the postwar era, all machines were more dependent on external aid. Intergovernmental alliances were important even to entrenched organizations. During the turbulent 1960s, the Chicago and Pittsburgh machines had hitched up to workhorse Governors Otto Kerner and David Lawrence. In the 1970s and 1980s, New York Democratic Governors Hugh Carey and Mario Cuomo gave the O'Connell-Corning organization an extended lease on life with state patronage and protection.

In postwar Massachusetts, however, the statehouse remained predominately in Republican hands until 1974—the year of Watergate. Elected in 1974, Democratic Governor Michael Dukakis proved to be a defective helpmate for would-be boss Kevin White. During the Boston school busing crisis, White looked for a heavy hitter to intercede with federal judge Arthur Garrity. When Dukakis turned out to be a lightweight, White was forced to look beyond the state altogether to the establishment figure Cyrus Vance. White's machine-building plans were further frustrated in 1978 when Dukakis lost to insurgent conservative Democrat Edward J. King. King's ascension further hastened White's retirement. The mayor, who had attempted to go from John Lindsay North to Richard Daley East, called it quits.[86]

Pennsylvania politics frustrated Frank Rizzo. The state's patronage system had once been massive—50,000 jobs for the governor to dole out in the 1950s, ten times the gubernatorial patronage of New Jersey, the second leading state. Civil service reform and collective bargaining under Republicans and reform Democrats had sharply reduced the governor's patronage to 4,000 positions by the time Democrat Shapp was elected in 1971. A Philadelphia businessman, Shapp made a political career as a reformer in the 1960s, defeating the Lawrence organization's choice in the 1966 Democratic gubernatorial primary.[87]

Ideologically antagonistic to the conservative Rizzo, Shapp supported liberal opponent William Green in Philadelphia's 1971 mayoral election. Later, the reform governor and the mayor briefly aligned politically. Rizzo supported Shapp's ill-starred presidential bid while Shapp agreed to support Rizzo in ousting Peter Camiel as head of the regular Democratic organization. As Shapp's presidential campaign quickly became a fiasco, his reputation as a "Jewish Harry Truman" changed to that of a Democratic version of Harold Stassen. The strained union between the two Democratic politicians eventually helped discredit both as scandals rocked their respective administrations. In 1978, control of the statehouse passed back to the Republicans, hastening Rizzo's exit from Philadelphia politics. Weak Democratic governors had thwarted Mayors Rizzo and White as they attempted to build big-city machines by projecting a strong and continuing voice into state politics.[88]

Spring: The New Rainbow Politics

In the 1980s the new minorities would no longer work through white intermediaries in the once-Irish cities. Black mayoral candidates won in machine Chicago and reform Philadelphia and mounted a serious challenge to Irish rule in Boston. Reminiscent of the Jewish-Italian alliance of the 1930s, black challengers have tried their hand at building multiethnic coalitions uniting blacks, Hispanics, Asians, and white liberals.

What is the nature of the new big-city rainbow politics? Are today's challenging coalitions truly cross-ethnic or are they primarily black-based? The centerpiece of the new politics is the unprecedented remobilization of the black vote. What has caused this mass reentry into electoral politics? Is it the product of local forces or national developments such as welfare-state retrenchment? To what extent can black politicians continue to direct this electoral surge to buttress their claims to cross-ethnic and urban leadership? As for the treatment of their coalition partners, are today's black politicos modern-day Fiorello La Guardias or Boss Hagues? Are Hispanics and Asians being rewarded with a fair share of power, jobs, and services? Alternatively, are black politicians acting as traditional ethnic brokers, recasting themselves toward Hispanics and Asians in the parsimonious ways the Irish once accommodated Jews and Italians?

Moreover, what is the future of the new rainbow politics? Notwithstanding their reform rhetoric, are minority politicians actually seeking to build a new generation of political machines? Have the old-style machines such as Chicago's suffered irreversible decline, or can they be refurbished to serve the urban poor? To what extent is the character of the new minority politics conditioned by different big-city political traditions—machine politics in Chicago and reform in Philadelphia and Boston? To these questions we now turn.

The Indian summer of the Chicago machine ended in 1983. Black mayoral candidate Harold Washington fashioned a rainbow coalition of blacks, Hispanics, and lakeshore liberals to defeat Mayor Jane Byrne and State Senator Richard M. Daley, son of the late mayor, in the Democratic primary. In the general election, the city's white ethnics, the machine's traditional mainstays, flocked to

Republican candidate Bernard Epton, no longer a sacrificial lamb. The election was a referendum on race as a record 82 percent of eligible voters went to the polls. Eighty-eight percent of whites supported Epton while 95 percent of blacks voted for Washington. Washington barely nosed out Epton by 46,250 votes out of a record 1.3 million cast.[89]

Washington's razor-thin victory depended on a massive remobilization of the black vote. In 1979, only 35 percent of eligible blacks had voted; in 1983, an unprecedented 73 percent went to the polls. Cutbacks in federal programs contributed to the reentry of Chicago's blacks into electoral politics. In the 1960s, the welfare state had served as a crucial appendage of the Daley organization in the black community. By the late 1970s, however, social programs—and the machine—were in trouble. At the federal level, President Carter initiated cutbacks in welfare, health, and social service grants-in-aid to states and cities. At the state level, the election of Republican Governor James Thompson in 1976 signaled an era of fiscal austerity as the state cut back on social spending. By 1979 Chicago had exhausted its own revenue sources and was unable to make up for the intergovernmental shortfall.[90]

Ronald Reagan's election in 1980 led to an even more sustained attack on social programs providing employment for the black middle class and transfer payments for the poor. For fiscal year (FY) 1982, the Reagan administration reduced social outlays by $35 billion, primarily in means-tested programs for the poor. Budget reductions in subsequent years were directed at the social service programs providing minority employment—education, manpower and training, and health and social services. In FY 1983, for example, Great Society service programs were the target of more than $7 billion in cutbacks. "The 1983 budget for domestic programs," warned Henry Aaron of the Brookings Institution, "must be viewed . . . as the boldest and most controversial attempt in fifty years to roll back the place of the federal government as a guarantor of equal opportunity and provider of social services."[91]

Welfare-state retrenchment politically galvanized the black community. Threatened with job loss, minority service providers had the incentive to organize themselves and their welfare clientele to support liberal candidates. Threatened with benefit loss, welfare recipients also discovered the necessity of electoral action. The

1982 elections were the first opportunity for blacks to vote their bread-and-butter discontent with Reagan. By mid-1982, pollsters had uncovered sharp racial differences in evaluations of the Reagan domestic record. The preelection Gallup poll showed whites narrowly approving the president's job performance—47 percent to 43 percent—whereas nonwhites disapproved it by a resounding 77 percent to 12 percent margin. Blacks went to the polls in record numbers to register their disapproval of Reagan's policies. In Chicago, black Democrats flocked to the registration tables and voting booth. More than 100,000 new black voters were registered in early October. Nearly all went to the polls. For the city as a whole, 144,000 more votes were cast in 1982 than in 1978. The black electoral surge went overwhelmingly Democratic. Nationwide, the NBC News exit poll showed 93 percent of blacks voting Democratic. As Thomas Cavanagh has argued, for blacks the 1982 election was a referendum on Reagan.[92]

In Chicago, Reagan's cutbacks in social programs significantly accelerated the slowly growing black estrangement from the machine. The 1975 mayoral election had revealed the first major black disenchantment with the Daley regime. The machine's refusal to appoint blacks to top positions, coupled with charges of police brutality, not social program reductions, produced these initial stirrings of minority discontent. Daley died in late 1976 and was replaced by Alderman Michael Bilandic, a non-Catholic Croatian from Daley's Bridgeport neighborhood. Bilandic's hopes for reelection in 1978 died in a preelection blizzard, one of the worst in the city's history. The city's snow removal effort collapsed. As commuters turned from private to public transportation, Bilandic had the commuter trains bypass inner-city stations in favor of suburban locations. Blacks were outraged. With 63 percent of the black vote, Democratic maverick Jane Byrne defeated machine regular Bilandic.[93]

Despite rising discontent with the machine's policies, the black vote was not mobilized until *after* Reagan's attack on the welfare state. Before 1980, black voter participation rates remained low. As of 1979, only 520,000 out of 950,000 eligible blacks were registered. Cutbacks in federal social programs brought the black middle class back into local electoral politics. Blacks working in social service agencies, activists in community-based organizations hurt by funding reductions, and ministers orchestrated a large-scale voter registration drive in welfare agencies, unemployment offices, and the churches.

More than 200 grass-roots organizations and churches participated in the registration campaign. The welfare state was at the heart of the mobilization campaign. In mid-1982, POWER (People Organized for Welfare and Employment Rights), a coalition of sixteen community organizations, announced plans to register welfare recipients. POWER successfully fought the Chicago Board of Election Commissioners and the state public aid and labor departments in order to conduct on-site voter registration in public welfare and unemployment offices. Other minority groups joined POWER. Black United Communities, another important grass-roots umbrella organization, trained volunteers in the voter drive and enlisted the support of the Urban League and Jesse Jackson's Operation PUSH (People United to Save Humanity). Threatened with federal cutbacks in their own programs, the black churches joined the registration drive. Notwithstanding the national character of social program cutbacks, the black response was local. "All politics," as Irish-American House Speaker Tip O'Neill once observed, "is local."[94]

The black revolt against the Chicago machine forces a reconsideration of the relationship between machines and welfare-state programs. The conventional wisdom holds that the growth of social programs weakens machines by supplying voters with non-machine-controlled resources. Although the welfare state may have hindered the building of a fourth generation of machines in the postwar era, entrenched party organizations purchased a fifty-year lease on life by skillfully diverting federal social programs to the task of rewarding and co-opting minorities. However, the machine's harnessing of the welfare state was not without risk. In the postwar era, federal and state decision makers rather than local machine politicians controlled the supply of resources integrating minorities. The Reagan administration's domestic policies destabilized those big-city party organizations dependent on social programs. In Chicago, welfare-state contraction, not growth, fueled the black revolt.

The tide of black insurgency crested in other cities in 1983. In Philadelphia, Wilson Goode, the black City Managing Director, bested Frank Rizzo in the Democratic mayoral primary, going on to victory in the general election. Though the campaign was less racial in character than Chicago's, the electoral coalitions were remarkably the same. Goode received 98 percent of the high-turnout black vote while securing only 24 percent of the white vote.[95]

In Boston, former black militant Mel King mounted a voter registration campaign aimed at blacks and Latinos in his race for mayor against South Boston populist Ray Flynn. Enlisting such black leaders as Jesse Jackson and Harold Washington, the King campaign swelled the city's voter registration rolls by 25 percent in the months before the election. In the nonpartisan primary, King fashioned a rainbow coalition of blacks, Hispanics, Asians, and white liberals, forcing Flynn into a runoff election. More than 63 percent of the Hub's registered voters turned out, the highest proportion in more than two decades. Though King ultimately lost to Flynn, the Hub had witnessed the emergence of blacks and other minorities as a countervailing force to Irish rule.[96]

In crucial ways, the new big-city rainbow politics resembles the earlier mobilization of Southern and Eastern Europeans. National forces the Al Smith candidacy, the Depression, and the New Deal—had brought the new ethnics into the electoral process in record numbers. Big-city regimes, Democratic as well as Republican, were overthrown in mobilizing elections: Tammany Hall, the Hague machine, and the GOP organizations in Chicago and Pittsburgh. Today's rainbow politics represents an electoral surge of the third-wave migrants propelled by national forces.

The character of the ethnic insurgency in the 1930s had depended on the nature of the prevailing regime. So too in the 1980s. In cities run by entrenched Irish Democratic machines, the Southern and Eastern Europeans were drawn into antimachine reform movements. In competitive-party Chicago and GOP-controlled Pittsburgh, the new ethnic revolt was harnessed to Democratic machine building. Contemporary insurgency in Chicago—white (Byrne) as well as black (Washington)—has been defined by the presence of the machine. Both Byrne and Washington adopted campaign poses as antimachine reformers. Yet the mayors have not demonstrated that they can govern Chicago effectively without accommodating the ward bosses. In Philadelphia and Boston, with postwar reform traditions punctuated only by the failed machine-building schemes of Mayors Rizzo and White, the Goode and King campaigns have been reformist.

Despite these similarities, the new rainbow politics differs in major ways from earlier cross-ethnic coalitions. Regarding resources, the prizes and the means of ethnic capture are different. Mayoral patronage, even in Chicago, is now limited. Minority capture of municipal employment depends on affirmative action plans and revised civil service examinations, not on party sponsorship. The flow of welfare-state benefits, crucial to the minority community, eludes black control. In Chicago, the coalition built by Mayor Washington may have to make its peace with Republican administrations at the federal and state levels. It may also have to come to terms with the white Democrats who control Cook County. The welfare state passes through the county offices, not city hall. Having lost control of the city council in 1986 to Washington-backed candidates who won special elections ordered by the federal courts, the white-controlled remnant of the machine headed by Aldermen "Fast Eddie" Vrdolyak and Edward Burke may retreat to the county. Neglected by Daley, the suburban Democrats are the crucial force in the future of the Cook County organization.[97]

Today's rainbow politicians are also hindered by a mounting fiscal crisis. The consolidation of ethnic power has traditionally depended on expanding resources to incorporate and reward new groups. The Irish were brought into the embryonic Democratic machines during the expansionary 1850s and 1860s. Fiscal austerity in the 1870s and 1880s encouraged working-class Irish revolts against the early machines. With the return of flush times in the early twentieth century, the machines finally incorporated the Irish working class. In the 1930s and 1940s big-city politicians— reform as well as machine—parlayed federal programs to incorporate the Southern and Eastern Europeans.

Unlike earlier ethnic politicos, newly elected black politicians lack the means to reward their followers. In an era of domestic budget retrenchment, federal programs have been slashed. Chicago lost $200 million in federal funding for 1986. Under Gramm-Rudman, the Windy City was projected to lose an additional $527 million in 1987. National retrenchment compounded the burgeoning local fiscal crisis. Handed a $150 million budget deficit upon taking office, Mayor Harold Washington reluctantly increased property taxes by $80 million.

A hostile white-controlled city council frustrated the mayor's plans to seize control of patronage and reward his restless rainbow supporters. Chicago's "Council Wars" lasted three long years. As Washington finally took control of the council in 1986, he targeted the machine's patronage reserve. The Park District, with its 3,321 full-time employees and 1,500 summer positions, was the first to go. Under the guise of agency reorganization, the mayor appointed a black city department head to oversee fifteen-year-veteran Superintendent Edmund Kelly.[98]

With few loaves and fishes, black leaders resemble the nineteenth-century Irish bosses in terms of facing insurgency from within their own ranks. Militant Irish labor leaders had challenged the leadership of conservative Irish machine politicians. In the 1980s, a black protest elite headed by ministers such as Jesse Jackson challenged black elected officials such as Harold Washington. Diminished resources also heightened tensions among black elected leaders. In Chicago, black aldermen fought Mayor Washington and the black ward committeemen for control of $80 million in federal grant funding.[99]

In order to best their ethnic rivals, black elected officials may be forced to demobilize the volatile underclass—particularly if they can't deliver jobs and services. An electoral purge of the black poor may strengthen the leadership claims of elected officials within the minority community, but it also encourages ambitious white politicians. In Philadelphia, Wilson Goode beat Republican John Egan by 152,000 votes in the 1983 general election. Since then, 147,000 voters—mostly black Democrats—have been purged from the voter registration rolls, unable to vote in the 1987 municipal elections.[100]

Diminished resources also frustrate black politicos in their efforts to cement cross-ethnic alliances. In the 1983 general election, Washington received a majority of the Hispanic vote. Yet the black-brown alliance may be unraveling as Washington's organization doles out its limited supply of patronage to blacks, its core ethnic constituency. Latino representation on the municipal payroll remains minuscule. Hispanics are only slowly being recruited as precinct captains and ward committeemen. Lacking resources, black politicians may be forced to borrow a page from the Irish brokers in their parsimonious accommodation of other ethnic groups.

The new big-city rainbow coalition is also unstable because of the different demands of its partners. Asian-Americans are prosperous and politically conservative. The Hispanic community is fractured along nationality, class, and political lines. Poor and liberal, Puerto Ricans are natural allies for blacks. Split economically and politically, Chicanos are not natural allies. Unlike the black middle class, which is heavily employed in the public sector, the Chicano middle class is largely in small business, a breeding ground for political conservatism. There is little common ground between the new black power brokers and the prosperous and deeply conservative Cuban-American community.[101]

Underneath the umbrella of rainbow rhetoric, contemporary black politicians are practicing ethnic particularism à la the Irish power brokers. The old-style Irish machines did not fashion multi-ethnic rainbow coalitions, rewarding each group with a fair share of the prizes drawn from a sizable pot of municipal gold. Throughout most of their history, the big-city machines were as much instruments of voter demobilization as mobilization, of ethnic exclusion as inclusion. There is little reason to believe that black politicians can succeed at cross-ethnic rainbow politics where the legendary Irish bosses failed.

Chapter Six

Machine Building, Irish-American Style

The Life-Cycle Debate

The once-mighty Irish big-city machines are nearly extinct. Tammany Hall, the Buckley organization in the Bay Area, Frank Hague's powerful Jersey City organization, the Steel City Lawrence organization—all are gone. Only Chicago and Albany remain as relics of the past. In all likelihood, though, these two vestiges will soon pass from the scene.

After dominating Chicago for decades, the Daley machine is a shambles. With its leader dead and a black mayor elected, the organization's white regulars retreated to the city council where they fought a bitter, stubborn, three-year rearguard action to retain control of the machine's power and patronage. In the end they lost. Court-ordered reapportionment and new elections wiped out the old guard's four-vote majority on the council. Mayor Harold Washington used his razor-thin council majority to seize control of the Board of Education, the huge Chicago Transit Authority, and the Chicago Park District, an independent agency with 5,000 patronage jobs and a $130-million budget.[1]

This patronage infusion may not be enough to resuscitate the machine under black leadership. The city faces an unprecedented fiscal crisis. The white regulars still control county government and the stream of welfare-state benefits sustaining former Mayor Washington's minority constituency. Even the vaunted Albany machine is in trouble, having entered an interregnum phase in 1983 following the death of Erastus Corning, Dan O'Connell's chosen successor.

Though the urban machines are largely gone, machine politics—the trading in particularistic benefits—lives. In New York, the Bronx, Queens, and Brooklyn Democratic county organizations win elections through the use of patronage, contracts, and franchises. In reaction to the big-city Democratic organizations, suburban Republicans have also tried their hand at machine building. In Long Island, the Nassau County Republican organization has wooed the Italians and Irish fleeing New York. Controlling 20,000 patronage jobs, the Nassau Republicans have built an impressive suburban machine addressing neighborhood issues and delivering homeowner services.[2]

Although these county remnants have led some to claim that the reports of the death of the political machine have been greatly exaggerated, the era of the patronage-based centralized big-city machines *is* passing. The urban machine's demise has spawned a cottage industry devoted to debating the machine's nature, functions, and dynamics. Both domestic and foreign developments have propelled the search for a summary judgment.

Domestically, as Theodore Lowi argues, "new" machines—reformed bureaucracies—have replaced the old party machines, prompting comparisons of the two urban governing arrangements.[3] In light of the general unresponsiveness of reformed structures to the interests of minorities and the working class, the dying urban machine has been given a posthumous facelift. During its heyday, boss rule was castigated by progressives as corrupt and undemocratic. In its twilight era, analysis—much of it sympathetic—replaced pejorative evaluation, and causal inquiry superseded description. Suitably refurbished, the machine is now viewed as an early, informal version of the welfare state, responding to the needs of the immigrant working class.[4]

Studies of less developed countries have also prompted a reassessment of American big-city political machines. The myth of American political exceptionalism evaporated as postwar studies of Sicily and southern Italy, India, and the emerging African and Asian states showed startling similarities to the big-city American machines. In Third World countries, party politicians behaved like the big-city bosses, trading material benefits such as patronage jobs and welfare services for political support. Seen in the broader context of political development, then, machines represented a form of clientelist politics, superseding the traditional patron-client relation between landlord and peasant in rural society. Yet party-based clientelism was considered a transitional stage between traditional and modern society, destined to dissolve in the face of organized interest groups and class-based ideological parties.[5]

The writing of the urban machine's epitaph has generated considerable controversy. Americanists have been preoccupied with what can best be termed organizational life-cycle issues—the machine's origins, longevity, and decline. Here are some of the major theoretical hotspots in this debate.

Regarding the emergence of centralized machines, two competing theories have been advanced. Group theory depicts the machine as a mass-created phenomenon. Immigrant groups such as the Irish demanded material benefits such as patronage jobs and social services. By supplying these resources, bosses built winning electoral coalitions and strong machines.

Elite theory, in contrast, argues that centralized machines are leader-created. Voters may demand material benefits, but this demand pattern does not inevitably produce a centralized machine. To consolidate power, entrepreneurial party bosses have to create governing—not merely electoral—coalitions, forging strategic alliances with the local business community to ensure adequate party finances and to mute reform opposition.

Successful machines ultimately had to fashion winning electoral coalitions as well as ruling alliances. Much of the debate over the maintenance strategies of the big-city party organizations focuses on the character of the transaction between politicians and voters. For exchange theorists, the transaction is primarily economic. Bosses seek electoral support and voters try to improve their material well-being. In this view, bosses target past and prospective supporters with material benefits. Machine longevity depends on allocating sufficient divisible benefits to build a winning electoral coalition. This long-accepted exchange model is now under challenge. Recent studies of the Chicago and New Haven machines, for example, have shown that factors other than vote maximization influence the allocation of jobs and services. Voters, in turn, may support machines in the absence of direct economic reward.[6]

The machine's demise has also triggered a coroner's inquest. The conventional wisdom traced the machine's decline to two factors—first, to a decline in both the supply and the control of resources, as a result of the inroads made by reform and the welfare state; and, second, to changes in voter demand as the machine's traditional supporters moved into the middle class. In short, machines no longer commanded the tangible benefits to purchase votes, and middle-class voters no longer wanted the machine's traditional fare of lowly patronage jobs and welfare services. This received wisdom is currently under sustained attack as studies show reform and the welfare state strengthening machines and the big-city bosses adapting their policies to middle-class tastes.

Issues of party coalition building and resource distribution have preoccupied American students of the urban machine. Comparativists, however, have examined a broader set of questions raised by machine politics: the character of the political transition from traditional to modern society, machines as forms of clientelist politics, and the relationship of the party system to state building.

On one level, the clientelist perspective on the machine emphasizes similarities between the American big-city party organizations and their urban and rural counterparts in contemporary Third World countries. Throughout the world, machine politics flourishes in the democratic interstices separating traditional and modern society, where uprooted peasants demand concrete material benefits from party leaders in exchange for their votes. First comes "democracy," that is, participatory politics; later, urban-industrial development. Machine politics persists until the lag between political development and class formation is overcome.

On another level, comparativists have distinguished between U.S. and Third World machines. In the United States, economic development was rapid, but political democracy was even more precocious. Universal suffrage triumphed remarkably early in the American federal system, generations before thoroughgoing urban-industrial transformation. In this context, the big-city machines were quintessentially nineteenth-century American phenomena—localized party structures at the periphery of a fragmented political system with minimal political and programmatic linkages to the national core. Machines both reflected and helped sustain the decentralized, parochial, and particularistic character of American politics well into the late twentieth century.

In contrast, later developing urban and rural machines in Third World countries arose in an era of centralized nation-states featuring national entitlement and development programs. In this context, Third World machines reflected and helped reinforce strong national party and programmatic structures. In the comparative party and clientelist research, there is surprisingly little dissent from this comparison of the "advanced" character of Third World machines relative to the "backward" character of the American big-city machines, the cornerstone of party development from the late nineteenth century to the mid-twentieth century.

Our analysis of four generations of machine building in eight of the once most heavily Irish-American cities, 1840 to 1985, allows us to test these theories of machine building and of American political development. The eight cities produced six strong Irish Democratic machines—Tammany Hall, the Buckley organization, the Hague machine, the O'Connell organization, the Kelly-Nash-Daley machine, and the Lawrence organization—over a one-hundred-year period. It is true that our ability to generalize from these cases to all big-city machines is limited. After all, these six cases are not a representative sample of all urban machines; Republican machines—for example, in Philadelphia, Pittsburgh, and Cincinnati—and Democratic machines in the border states—for example, Boss Crump's machine in Memphis and the Pendergast organization in Kansas City—have been excluded. Nevertheless, though not representative of all machines, the Irish big-city party organizations best approximate the pure or classic immigrant-based and welfarist machines.

Not only do we test existing theories; we also offer a new theory of machine development. This new approach departs in two critical ways from existing theories. First, it places machine development in the context of the party system, particularly in terms of intergovernmental and intraparty alliances. Urban machine building required vertical alliances to sympathetic state and national leaders, especially in the fragile gestation period, in order to monopolize public sector resources, starve factional opponents, and reward party functionaries and voters. Group and elite theories, in contrast, treat the urban political system as a hermetically sealed environment. Machine building is seen as the product of such endogenous urban factors as a large pool of needy immigrant voters.

Second, the new view emphasizes the resource side of machine politics—a Say's Law of big-city bosses and organizations. For the urban bosses, resource problems were paramount, for voter demand almost always exceeded available supply. Hence bosses spent as much time creating resources such as patronage jobs as they spent distributing them. A revised theory of machine dynamics, then, needs to specify the strategies for increasing the supply of patronage and other tangible benefits. In the long run, the scarcity of machine benefits shaped both the character and the volume of electoral demand. Rather than catering to their supporters, bosses spent much of their time deflating demand, particularly for the organization's core resources of power and patronage. In contrast, conventional wisdom assumes a cornucopia of resources and treats demand as independent of supply.

In the following pages we shall apply the findings from our case studies of the classic Irish urban machines to the theoretical debates concerning the three phases of the machine's life cycle—gestation, maintenance, and decline—before considering their relevance to issues of clientelist politics and comparative party and political development.

The Origins of Machines

Group Approaches

There is not one but several group or mass theories of the machine's birth. Let us consider three leading models. Edward Banfield and James Q. Wilson argue that machines arose as a response to the "private-regarding" ethos of working-class European immigrants. Imported from the Old World, the immigrant outlook consisted of neighborhood rather than citywide attachments. The impoverished European arrivals viewed politics as the self-interested pursuit of material gain rather than as the disinterested search for the public good. According to this model, big-city machines were fueled by this chorus of particularistic ethnic demands. Lest Banfield and Wilson be accused of offering only a demand theory of machines, they caution that sheer numbers of needy immigrants were not a sufficient condition for the development of strong machines. Machines needed resources with which to reward immigrant party workers and voters. The greater the resources, ceteris paribus, the stronger the organization and its electoral coalition.[7]

Casting his theoretical net more narrowly, Daniel Patrick Moynihan has proposed an Irish variant of the ethos account of the machine's birth. Whereas Banfield and Wilson trace the demand for machine politics to working-class Catholic groups such as the Czechs, Poles, and Italians, Moynihan highlights the peculiarly Irish role in building the big-city Democratic machines such as Tammany Hall. For Moynihan, machines were a reproduction of the social structure and value system of Irish village life. Village saloons, for example, organized local political life as they later would in American cities. The structure of the Irish Catholic church—its hierarchy and neighborhood parishes—would also serve as a template for later urban party organization. Under centuries of English oppression, the Irish assimilated the political values of their conquerors. Politics was thought of in terms of material self-interest and hierarchical patron-client relations.[8]

James Scott offers an alternative mass theory of machine building. For Scott it is not Old World values or Irish rural custom that provides the fertile soil for machines. Comparing the similarities of today's African and Asian industrializing countries to nineteenth-century America, Scott argues that machinelike parties are not a unique American big-city phenomenon. Instead, they emerge in "transitional social contexts" where traditional patterns of peasant deference to landowners and local notables have broken down and the "modern" loyalties of occupation and class have not yet taken hold.[9]

How useful are group or mass theories for understanding the origins of machines in the eight cities surveyed? At first glance, the case studies seem to provide support for a group interpretation. Centralized Irish-led machines, after all, emerged in six of the eight cities with large Irish-American populations, lending credibility to Moynihan's village transplant argument. Yet the Irish were carriers of multiple strains of politics. Pace Moynihan, there were not one but several political exits out of the Irish villages. The same rural soil produced in late nineteenth-century America a conservative organizational politics of patronage and power and in Ireland an insurgent mass politics organized around the causes of nationalism, land reform, and home rule. Only in postindependence Ireland would the supposed Irish affinity for machine politics assert itself.[10]

For the early stages of American machine development, group theories better describe the attitudes and behavior of Irish political elites—party bosses and workers—than those of the mass of working-class Celtic voters. The Irish-American community of the late nineteenth century did not uniformly support the fledgling machines. Although the Celtic politicos functioned as a conservative, self-serving elite, the working class was open to radical, mass appeals. In the 1870s and 1880s, Irish workers channeled much of their political energy into antimachine labor parties, into a class-conscious trade union movement, and into the Irish nationalist movement—hardly grist for the "private-regarding" political mill.

In fact, the urban machine itself, not Old World traits, independently shaped political values and the structure of political possibilities in the early Irish-American community. Working-class Irish revolts against boss rule evaporated in the early twentieth century as ever larger numbers of Irish were brought into the patronage system. In this manner, the big-city party organizations were not passive reactors to particularistic group demands. They were active participants in helping create what Terry Clark calls the "Irish patronage ethic."[11] Both Moynihan's rural transplant hypothesis and the Banfield and Wilson ethos theory, then, fail to consider how the Irish bosses worked tirelessly to cultivate an exclusive demand for their privatized product in the Irish-American community.

Structural limitations on the machine's supply of resources forced the Celtic bosses to frustrate mass demands among other immigrant groups. The machine's parsimonious accommodation of the non-Irish helps explain a major anomaly in ethos theory: the persistent failure of the Southern and Eastern Europeans to support the Irish machines. Given their enthusiasm for radical and reform politics, Jews were beyond the private-regarding pale. Other second-wave groups revolted against their Irish overlords. New York City's Italians voted overwhelmingly for reformer La Guardia in the 1930s and 1940s. Jersey City's Polish and Italians overthrew the Hague machine in the late 1940s. In the Windy City, Poles represented a thorn in Richard Daley's side in the late 1950s and early 1960s.

How do we explain these episodes of antimachine insurgency on the part of the machine's supposed ethnic supporters? Southern and Eastern European Catholics may well have been private-regarding.

But the entrenched Irish machines did not automatically cater to their demands. Complementing the policy of not-so-benign electoral neglect of Southern and Eastern European immigrants, the bosses offered limited benefits to the new ethnics—social services, symbolic recognition, and collective benefits—rather than a greater sharing of the scarce core resources of power and patronage. Parsimonious accommodation produced antimachine revolts by the second-wave migrants.

As with the Irish, changes in the machine's policies—not traits imported from the Old World—transformed the political outlook and behavior of newer immigrants. Private-regardingness among big-city Catholics eventually blossomed in the postwar era as machines accommodated them with a greater sharing of jobs, services, and, yes, even power, but at the price of not rewarding later-arriving blacks and Hispanics.

Why did the machines so sparsely reward newcomers, whether Southern and Eastern Europeans or blacks and Hispanics? In contrast to the Panglossian view of resource creation advanced by today's supply-side economics, there were sharp structural limits on the machine's supply of resources. A major weakness of ethos theory is that it blurs the line between voter demand and machine response, treating the latter as if it were an almost automatic reflex of group cultural and political predispositions. In actuality, there were inherent conflicts in the machine's political economy between supply and demand. Machines were structurally constrained resource-generating and resource-allocating mechanisms, which accommodated voter demand only within certain class-imposed political limits.

Elite Approaches

Group theories have been challenged from another quarter. Elite theories, such as that found in the work of Martin Shefter, see leadership alliances, not electoral coalition building, as the key factor in machine building. Drawing on Raymond Wolfinger's distinction between machine politics—as the demand for particularistic benefits—and political machines—as centralized political structures—Shefter argues that voter demand for tangible benefits did not invariably produce a citywide machine. Boston's voters were as private-regarding as New York's, but the faction-ridden Hub never produced a Tammany Hall North.[12]

According to Shefter, machine incentives can yield a variety of political structures. Individual politicians may practice "rapacious individualism," looting the city treasury to build personal followings. Alternatively, enduring factions within the dominant party may vie with one another in using tangible benefits to compete for electoral favor. Finally, a centralized machine under the direction of a single boss can monopolize the allocation of benefits.[13]

For elite theorists, successful machine builders must solve various organizational dilemmas, for example, wooing voters, ensuring party finances, controlling elected officials, and rewarding and disciplining the machine's ward bosses and precinct captains. The party-building enterprise requires governing alliances, not merely temporary electoral coalitions constructed every few years. To govern successfully, bosses must win the support of key actors in the local business community.

Shefter's account of Tammany Hall's consolidation of power in the late nineteenth century illustrates the importance of party-business alliances. Protean factionalism characterized the city's Democracy from the 1840s to the 1870s. In this premachine era of "rapacious individualism," the immigrant working-class vote assumed increasing importance. Would-be bosses built electoral followings with the patronage produced by expansionary fiscal policies. To underwrite their expansionary policies, Tammany politicians such as Fernando Wood and Boss Tweed formed alliances with contractors and speculators benefiting from municipal spending and indebtedness.

A different pattern of elite alliances and fiscal policies accompanied John Kelly's reign as Tammany's chieftain following Boss Tweed's downfall in the early 1870s. Kelly quickly aligned himself with the "Swallow-tails," the reform-minded bankers, lawyers, and businessmen demanding "tight-fisted" fiscal policies. Yet the program of municipal retrenchment demanded by conservative business interests meant little "trickle down" to the immigrant working class. With little patronage, how could Tammany consolidate its electoral base? Borrowing a page from Henry George's 1886 labor campaign, Kelly and his lieutenants devised a cheaper way to organize Tammany voters, particularly the upwardly mobile second-generation ethnics: year-round district social clubs.[14]

By the tandem tactics of capturing reform-minded businessmen with fiscal retrenchment and the immigrant working class with social clubs, Kelly supposedly weakened both business and voter support for factional opponents, particularly the reform-minded County Democracy. With the County Democracy's collapse in the late 1880s, Tammany's arrival as an unchallenged machine was complete.

In elite theory, material resources play a minimal role in machine consolidation. Tammany monopolized city patronage in the 1870s and early 1880s yet factionalism persisted within the Democratic party. Factionalism declined after 1886 even though Tammany's supply of city patronage remained the same. What did change in the late 1880s was the nature of the machine's inducements: District clubs were added to the Tiger's arsenal of enticements.

Intergovernmental Alliances

Elite theory is correct in highlighting the importance of leadership alliances for machine building. The real question is whether alliances with the business community were sufficient for machine consolidation.

Elite theory must be expanded to include other machine-building alliances. In the preceding chapters I have argued that successful aspiring bosses had to forge alliances with state and national party leaders. Vital to organizational consolidation was the monopoly of all public patronage—county, state, and national as well as city—controlled by the machine's party in the metropolis. Each patronage cache could fuel a rival party faction. To cure the mischief of faction, would-be bosses had to be oligopolists, monopolizing the raw materials needed by their competitors.

Elite theory must also be modified to include patronage as a crucial party-building ingredient. The theory views the conflict between machine and reform factions as one involving different nonmaterial incentive systems. Machine politicians used social incentives to reward voters. Reformers relied on ideological appeals. By deemphasizing the importance of patronage, the theory anachronistically projects back into the late nineteenth century developments that did not occur until the mid-twentieth century. The Democratic reform clubs of the 1950s relied heavily on ideological and programmatic appeals. Postwar machine politicians also de-emphasized old-style job patronage (relative to their early counter-parts) because the organization's electoral support increasingly rested on the provision of homeowner and welfare-state services.

Unlike the elite approach, our theory places the fight over pat-ronage at the heart of early party factionalism. In contrast with to-day's reformers, the antimachine factions of the late nineteenth century relied heavily on patronage to reward both voters and campaign workers. Reform was but a thin veneer for Irving Hall and the County Democracy, Tammany's major rivals for control of the New York City Democracy in the 1870s and 1880s. All three shared the same office-for-gain ethos. In contrast, patronage was not the major axis along which Tammany fought Henry George and his followers. The labor party had to be disposed of in an ideo-logical war to the death before the various Democratic factions could indulge themselves in the luxury of party infighting.

Let us consider the evidence for an intergovernmental, party-based, and patronage-centered interpretation of Tammany's emer-gence as an undisputed machine. Does control of the statehouse rather than entrée into the downtown businessmen's club, and the use of patronage rather than availability of the clubhouse, better explain Tammany's triumph over Irving Hall and the County De-mocracy? Yes. "Honest John" Kelly's alliance with the "Swallow-tails" was short-lived as Tammany broke with Democratic reform governor Samuel Tilden in 1874 over matters of state patronage. Tilden then built an alliance with Irving Hall, funneling state re-sources to the reformers rather than to Tammany. The Tiger's mo-nopoly of city patronage meant little to the rival faction sustained with state resources.

Democrat Lucius Robinson succeeded Tilden as governor, also aligning himself with the party's reform wing. With Tammany's support, Democrat Grover Cleveland succeeded Robinson. Kelly's romance with the conservative Cleveland was brief; the dalli-ance predictably dissolved over the distribution of state patronage to the rival city factions. Cleveland funneled state patronage to the County Democracy, reform successor to Irving Hall.

Only with Democrat David B. Hill's election in 1885 was state patronage finally channeled to Tammany. Governor Hill initially tried to placate all factions in the local Democracy. The County Democracy's collapse began with leadership scandals and an abortive fusion attempt with the Republicans. As the County Democracy began to crumble, "I Am a Democrat" Hill hastened its collapse by redirecting the County's share of state patronage to Tammany. Monopolizing both state and local patronage, the Tiger's triumph over rival factions was complete.

Tammany was not alone in seeking intergovernmental assistance to consolidate power. In the 1880s, the fledgling Irish machines of Jersey City and San Francisco forged crucial alliances with pro-machine Democratic governors. In the 1910s and 1920s, Frank Hague in Jersey City and Dan O'Connell in Albany did the same. As the Democrats became the majority party in the 1930s, federal alliances shaped the fortunes of a third generation of Irish machines in Chicago and Pittsburgh.

Republican machines also required an intergovernmental assist. In a careful study of GOP machine building in Cincinnati, James Ingram has shown the importance of state party linkages. In the 1880s the city's Republican party was split into three factions headed by George Cox, Amor Smith, and George Moerlin. "Old Boy" Cox bested his rivals for control of the party and city in 1886 by forging an alliance with Republican Governor Joseph B. Foraker. "Fire Alarm" Foraker assisted Cox in two ways. Cox was appointed state oil gauger, allowing the would-be boss to make connections with Cincinnati's business elite. Foraker also provided Cox with 2,000 state patronage jobs. Cox's army of payrollers was platooned to the various wards, there to take over the neighborhood GOP organizations. Within two years the "Old Boy" had emerged as the city's undisputed leader.[15]

The case for intergovernmental party alliances is strengthened when we consider cities where centralized machines did not emerge. Hostile state and national administrations, not the absence of alliances with the economic elite or the lack of neighborhood clubhouses, explain the failure of machine consolidation. In the late nineteenth century, Irish politicos in Boston and Chicago replicated Tammany's alliance pattern with local economic notables and its social clubs for district voters. Yet neither the Hub's Pat Maguire nor the Windy City's Mike McDonald could build a citywide machine. In early twentieth-century Boston, John F. Fitzgerald's Jefferson Club and Martin Lomasney's Hendricks Club rivaled Tammany's district clubhouses. Neither Boston politician could turn neighborhood recreational programs into citywide power. Relying on patronage rather than clubs, the Hub's James Michael Curley came closer than Fitzgerald or Lomasney to building a centralized machine.

State party politics explains the failure of machine building in early Boston and Chicago. The GOP dominated Massachusetts politics after the Civil War. Bay State Republicans established stringent taxation and indebtedness limitations for Boston, limiting the patronage take of ambitious Irish Democratic politicians. As the Irish finally took over the city, the GOP invented other forms of damage control. The patronage-rich Boston police department, for example, was placed under state authority. Even the resurgence of the state's Democratic party in the early twentieth century did not bode well for would-be Hub bosses. Yankees from western Massachusetts solidified their control over the party and thus nomination for the governorship. In order to limit the influence of Boston's feuding Irish ward bosses in state party politics, Democratic governors aligned with the western faction turned their backs on the Hub.

Hostile state administrations also prevented Irish bosses from building a Chicago machine before the 1930s. In the late nineteenth century, Mike McDonald's efforts to construct a midwestern Tammany were frustrated by "Black Jack" Logan's state GOP machine. With McDonald's death, two factions—followers of the Carter Harrisons I and II and the Hopkins-Sullivan wing—arose in the Windy City's Democratic party. Occasional Democratic governors did little to centralize Chicago Democratic politics. In the 1890s radical Governor Altgeld's policies inflamed the city's factional divisions. In the early twentieth century, reform Governor Dunne employed state patronage to build an independent Dunne wing alongside the Harrison and Hopkins-Sullivan factions. The emergence of the modern Democratic machine in Chicago would await Franklin Delano Roosevelt and the New Deal.

In a recent and important analysis of local party systems in the twentieth century, David Mayhew has also highlighted the role of state party structures in explaining the distinctive geographical patterning of the big-city machines. Local machines were concentrated in the Middle Atlantic states (New York, New Jersey, Pennsylvania), not in New England (Massachusetts) or the West (California). To explain this regional pattern, Mayhew discounts such causal variables as the size of the immigrant population. Instead, he argues that urban machines arose from the 1890s onward in states with preexisting strong traditional party organizations (TPOs). Strong TPO states featured durable, autonomous, and hierarchical party systems, which slated candidates for office and used material incentives to enforce party discipline and woo voters. Where state TPOs were weak, urban machines either did not emerge (Boston) or did not last long (San Francisco).[16]

Mayhew's theory points us in the right local machine-building direction—the state party system. Yet even within states with strong patronage-based parties, there were variations in the emergence of local machines over time and between cities. Machine politics remained strong in New York, New Jersey, and Pennsylvania from the 1860s through the late 1960s. Consistent with Mayhew's theory, these hospitable state party systems early on spawned Democratic machines in New York City, Albany, and Jersey City, and GOP machines in Philadelphia and Pittsburgh.

From the 1930s through the early 1950s, however, four of these five big-city machines were toppled. Only one strong and durable replacement was constructed—the Lawrence organization in Pittsburgh. The De Sapio and Kenny successors to Tammany Hall and the Hague organization were weak and short-lived. In Philadelphia, Mayor Frank Rizzo could not transform a personal campaign organization into a party-based machine. Despite the fertile soil of patronage-based state party systems, would-be bosses in the postwar era found the machine-building task more difficult than Mayhew's theory suggests.

Our theory of intergovernmental alliances adds an active ingredient in the state party system equation—the character of the controlling party and faction. Mayhew emphasizes the facilitating role of overall state party structures, contrasting strong patronage-based systems with all others. Yet the existence of a hierarchical and patronage-based state party system did not automatically result in local machines. To consolidate power, local party bosses needed to monopolize all public sector resources in the metropolis to strengthen their organizations and starve their opponents. Within strong patronage-based state party *structures*, intraparty (factional) *cleavages* and interparty *competition* represented important variables explaining where and when local machines emerged. For would-be urban bosses, ruling parties and factions in state and national politics mattered.

Given the crucial role of intergovernmental, intraparty alliances in machine consolidation, what explains why some aspiring bosses were successful alliance builders and others were not? Much depended on what local bosses had to offer leaders at the state and federal levels. The quid pro quo for local receipt of intergovernmental assistance involved help in furthering the careers of political higher-ups.

The forms of local assistance varied according to the needs of state and national leaders. Big-city GOP bosses were particularly eager to please Republican U.S. senators, the linchpins of state machines. As Mayhew notes, senators were "in the thick of . . . [state party structures], induced into building or tending them because of their need for state legislative majorities in order to reach and hold office in Washington (before the Seventeenth Amendment switched the power to elect Senators from legislators to popular elections). Senators were supplied, especially on the Republican side, with federal patronage (notably in post offices and custom houses) that was helpful in supporting organizations back home."[17] In return for senatorial assistance and federal patronage, local Republican bosses elected and placed at the disposal of senators the requisite state legislative majorities.

Failing to capture the White House (and federal patronage) throughout most of the period between the Civil War and the Depression, the Democrats set their sights on the statehouse. For the big-city Irish Democratic bosses, the governorship—and state patronage—was a vital adjunct to early machine building. With the coming of Roosevelt and the New Deal, the presidency and federal resources replaced governorships and state resources as necessary building blocks of strong local Democratic party organizations.

Roosevelt's treatment of the Democratic big-city bosses in the 1930s illustrates the kinds of local assistance demanded. The urban bosses captured needed federal patronage (particularly the WPA) to the extent they contributed to Roosevelt's reelection prospects. FDR had the greatest incentive to hand over federal relief to state and local party leaders in the heavily populated urban-industrial states with the greatest electoral clout and with the greatest uncertainty regarding the vote outcome. In these states, big-city bosses enhanced their prospects for federal patronage either by delivering an urban voting bloc pivotal to the state electoral outcome or by aligning themselves with the dominant wing of the state Democratic party. The Irish machines of Chicago, Pittsburgh, Jersey City, and Albany met these criteria and captured the local WPA. Failing FDR's reelection tests, Irish politicians in New York and Boston were denied federal work relief. Without federal assistance, Tammany could not mount a challenge to La Guardia, and Curley could not consolidate power in the faction-ridden Hub.

Intergovernmental intraparty alliances and patronage monopolies were most crucial in the initial stages of machine building. Consolidated machines, in contrast, merely required the existence of stable state and national political structures, regardless of the controlling party. Dominating the local party and governmental systems, established machines substantially increased the start-up costs and risks for rival parties and intraparty factions, costs that could rarely be overcome by a temporary infusion of state or federal patronage. Tammany Hall, for example, easily beat back the challenge of President Woodrow Wilson, who was anxious to have reformers capture the city's Democratic organization.

Since the New Deal, however, intergovernmental alliances have assumed increasing importance at *all stages* of the machine's life cycle. Postwar machine builders lacked the local resources of their predecessors. The twin imperatives of economic revitalization and social welfare in the older cities have required massive and continued infusions of state and federal aid. Given greater organizational fragility, modern urban bosses are at the mercy of state and federal decision makers. The postwar downfall of De Sapio in New York and Kenney in Jersey City illustrates the heightened risks of federal intervention.

Yet with the population decline of the Frostbelt and the older cities, local bosses have less to offer in return. The quadrennial presidential sweepstakes has moved to the growing Sunbelt, rendering the one-time big-city kingmakers irrelevant. In the northern urban-industrial states themselves, big-city bosses have less to contribute to state political leaders as the suburbs grow at the expense of the central cities. The failure of Kevin White in Boston and Frank Rizzo in Philadelphia to turn personal campaign organizations into machines is in part attributable to their failure to command the resources needed to cement alliances to state leaders.

Conventional elite theory fails to illuminate these crucial intra-party and intergovernmental machine-building alliances. Elite theory is further weakened by its overestimation of the attractiveness of social inducements like clubhouses to voters. It is true that machine alliances with conservative business owners limited the supply of material inducements to voters. As a consequence, the early machines offered circuses in lieu of bread to working-class immigrant voters. But district clubhouses were never as attractive as economic benefits, whether patronage jobs, welfare services, or labor legislation. The early machine's limited patronage cache explains its failure to solidify its electoral base. Only with an expanding resource base could the bosses bring working-class voters securely into the political fold. The machine's search for intergovernmental and private sector patronage can be understood as an attempt to overcome the resource constraints imposed by alliances with the conservative business community.

Maintaining the Machine

Exchange Theories

Once machines consolidated power with intergovernmental assistance, how did they maintain themselves? The conventional wisdom holds that machines fashioned elaborate exchanges with key constituencies—the business community, labor, party functionaries, and voters. Consolidating power, machines assumed control over an impressive array of valued goods and services—patronage, social services, taxation and police powers, contracts and franchises, and regulatory oversight.[18] All could be cashed in for political support, particularly for votes and campaign contributions.

There is disagreement, however, among exchange theorists regarding the terms of the transaction between voters and the machine. For pluralists such as Robert Dahl, bosses offered valuable material benefits—patronage jobs and welfare services—for votes. Each recipient of the machine's job largesse, in turn, was responsible for bringing at least five machine voters to the polls.[19] But others have stressed the nonmaterial character of the relationship between the party organization and voters. For Shefter, circuses (clubhouses) were more decisive than bread (patronage). Banfield and Wilson argue that the purchase price of votes was even cheaper. Because patronage was scarce, it was used for party workers, not voters. To solicit votes, party workers primarily traded in the currency of friendship.[20]

The vote-getting value of patronage has been challenged in a number of studies. Frank Sorauf's early pathbreaking study of state highway jobs in a rural Pennsylvania county pointed to the limits of low-level patronage as a reward for past party service, let alone prospective party work such as getting out the vote.[21] James Q. Wilson pointed out the conflicting uses of patronage—to maintain the organization or to maximize the vote—and the inevitable trade-off between rewarding all ward bosses equally or disproportionately rewarding the most effective vote producers.[22]

Recent empirical studies of urban machines have concluded that bosses allocate patronage for purposes other than maximizing the vote. In a study of the allocation of summer CETA jobs in New Haven, Michael Johnston shows that the Italian bosses practiced ethnic particularism rather than vote maximization. Most of the federally funded jobs went to Italians rather than to blacks, the party's most loyal supporters.[23] In a similar study, Thomas Guterbock examined the job and service allocation decisions of Chicago machine politicians in a typical ward in the early 1970s. Guterbock found that the machine overrewarded the fickle and independent middle class and systematically underrewarded the faithful lower class.[24] Studies such as these have supplied the evidence for a mounting attack on a vote-maximizing exchange model of machines.

Our analysis of the methods used by the Irish urban bosses to maintain power enables us to shed some light on the utility of exchange theory. At the outset, three crucial points must be made. First, there were basic differences in the terms of the machine's transaction with working-class voters compared to its transaction with their middle-class counterparts. Patronage and welfare services, not clubhouses and friendship, were the essential ingredients needed to build working-class support. Machines could dispense with public jobs in accommodating middle-class voters, but the middle class demanded its own brand of neighborhood and homeowner services. Complicating the building of cross-class alliances in the postwar era was the overlapping issue of race. Middle-class whites also demanded the preservation of white neighborhoods and schools.

Second, the big-city bosses behaved much like the congressmen studied by Richard Fenno.[25] For purposes of allocating benefits and building electoral coalitions, both sets of politicians viewed their constituency as a set of concentric circles. The bosses divided voters into supporters and opponents. Among supporters, machine politicians further distinguished between primary and secondary constituencies. For the Irish bosses the primary constituents were, first, party workers and payrollers and, second, their fellow Irishmen. Needless to say, there was substantial overlap between these two core clientele groups.[26]

Third, exchange theories implicitly assume a fixed number of claimants and a fixed amount of resources. In actuality, bosses were constantly manipulating both the supply of and the demand for machine resources to achieve minimal winning electoral coalitions. Coalition building, particularly with working-class voters, depended on a favorable *exchange ratio* between resources and political supporters. As good oligopolists in the local political marketplace, bosses actively worked to keep competitors and newcomers out. They worked as fervently to pyramid their supply of material resources, particularly patronage jobs. In the following section we present a more sophisticated exchange model of machine behavior, one that considers the *relationship* of resources to claimants and the active role of bosses in managing both.

Managing Conflicting Constituency Demands

The behavior of the Irish big-city bosses can best be understood as the management of conflicting demands. From "Honest John" Kelly to Richard Daley, the Irish bosses deployed the machine's material resources in order to achieve three objectives: the building of winning electoral coalitions, the financing and discipline of a large-scale patronage-based party organization, and the maintenance of Irish power and prosperity.

These three goals were potentially contradictory because different claimants demanded different policy menus. For the immigrant working class, particularly the Irish, the machine represented a vast social service agency, dispensing jobs and welfare benefits. As the social service tax burden did not directly fall on their shoulders, ethnic working-class renters supported high taxes and indebtedness. Middle-class homeowners and much of the business community, however, demanded low taxes and different services. Ward bosses and precinct captains demanded expansionary resource policies. For these machine functionaries, greater patronage enhanced their power and prestige and expedited the delivery of both votes and services. But the tax burden needed to pay for the machine's patronage army was deeply resented by the middle class and the business community. Finally, continued Irish political hegemony in the face of demographic changes increased the risk of revolt by unrewarded ethnic groups.

Given these contradictory demands, how did the Irish bosses build winning electoral coalitions? Vote-getting strategies varied with the class composition of the electorate. Regarding the working class, machine politicians actively worked to create and maintain a favorable exchange ratio between voter demands and party-controlled resources. Bosses improved the terms of exchange in one of two ways: by increasing the supply of resources, or by limiting the number of voters.

Creating Resources. Bosses rarely possessed the cornucopia of benefits suggested by the rainbow theory of the machine and by exchange theorists. Machines generally faced conditions of resource scarcity as the number of claimants far exceeded available supply. Under these conditions, machines had a strong incentive to expand their resource base. Bosses possessed a hierarchy of resources with which to woo groups of voters: party and governmental offices, patronage, services, symbolic recognition, collective benefits, and, when all else failed, cash bribes. These goods can be arrayed along a continuum in terms of their value and their elasticity of supply.

Power—top party and elective offices—represented the machine's scarcest and most conflict-laden resource. Its supply was finite; its allocation, zero-sum. Nothing better illustrates the conflict between the machine's maintenance and vote-maximization goals. In the short run, the Irish monopoly of power preserved the machine. In the long run, the failure to share power with later-arriving ethnic groups eroded the organization's electoral base. The Celtic bosses developed several stratagems to forestall ethnic demands for a reallocation of power. Pliable new ethnic leaders were selected, for example, Mike Scaturchio in Jersey City and William Dawson in Chicago. As demographic changes forced the bosses' hand, the Irish retreated into the inner sanctum of major policy-making and patronage-dispensing positions, giving the new ethnic claimants lesser posts. But too rapid a sharing of power carried the risk of revolt by the machine's core Irish constituency.

Patronage represented a more elastic organizational resource than power. The size of the patronage pie could be increased, previously unrewarded groups could be given the newly created shares, and group conflict could be limited. To protect the Irish monopoly over power, the Celtic bosses encouraged the newcomers to seek patronage instead. But the redirection of group demands contained risks because the Irish also monopolized existing patronage. To protect the jobs of Irish payrollers and to minimize intergroup conflict, the bosses searched for additional job caches. Each inflationary strategy, however, had political risks as well as benefits.

Property tax hikes represented the most direct way of increasing the stock of local patronage jobs. Property taxes supplied the bulk of municipal revenue; wages and salaries represented the major budget outlay in labor-intensive local government. Yet the temptation to hike taxes to generate more patronage was tempered by the risk of homeowner-led tax revolts.

The risk of reprisal varied with the rate of homeownership. Low rates meant that absentee landlords and businesses, not local voters, would foot the machine's patronage bill. High rates meant that large numbers of voters were directly exposed to tax increases. The big-city bosses sculpted their tax policies accordingly.

The cyclical character of urban homeownership patterns—high in the late nineteenth century, low in the early twentieth century, and rising by mid-century—produced a corresponding machine taxation and patronage cycle. The low taxes and limited patronage of the first-generation machines gave way to the taxation and patronage explosion of the second-generation machines. Rising homeownership rates for white ethnics in the postwar era served as a damper on further tax hikes, a lesson learned the hard way by Chicago's Daley and Albany's O'Connell.

When machines could not tax, they went into debt. Relative to taxation, indebtedness solved an electoral problem while creating an organizational one. Machines could raise municipal debt levels without necessarily increasing the tax rate, thus reducing the risk of a taxpayers' revolt. But indebtedness created the wrong sort of patronage. Municipal bonds financed public works projects, generating temporary private sector patronage, primarily in the construction industry, rather than permanent public sector patronage, the backbone of the machine's ward and precinct organizations.

Taxation and indebtedness increased the relative size of the public sector in the local economy. But machines could also promote economic growth, siphoning off a share of the revenue added, without corresponding increases in levels of taxation and indebtedness. The tools used to promote growth were varied. Debt-financed public works projects, limited as they were as a source of permanent machine patronage, improved the urban infrastructure, encouraging business location and investment.[27] In the postwar era, federally financed downtown revitalization programs replaced locally financed public works projects as engines of growth.

Alternatively, the bosses pursued annexation to capture outward-bound businesses and residents. Annexation, while solving an organizational problem, created an electoral one. With the creation of Greater New York, for example, Tammany's patronage supply doubled. Extending the city's boundaries, however, also doubled the number of antimachine voters. The machine's outward-migrating middle-class opponents would continue to have a voice, not an exit.[28]

Given the political costs of these resource-enhancement strategies, the big-city bosses tried to piggyback other sources of patronage on the cheap. During the Progressive era, machines increasingly turned to "unofficial patronage," for example, private sector jobs with businesses franchised by or regulated by local authorities. By increasing the scope of the regulatory state, the machine's reform opponents had unwittingly created new dependencies for the bosses to exploit. Regulated firms such as private utilities and street railroads found themselves employing the machine's henchmen in exchange for favorable governmental action.

Yet there were limits to what Tammany's Murphy termed his "businessmen's plan." Businesses preferred to pay cash to the bosses rather than to hire inefficient party workers. Patronage workers in the private sector did not have the free time for party work enjoyed by their publicly employed counterparts.

Faced with these constraints, the bosses tried to capture other sources of public sector patronage. All six machines studied took over county government. Counties were a many-splendored thing. Crusading district attorneys could be silenced. The county tax assessor's and collector's offices served as vital adjuncts of machine rule. In friendly times, counties represented larger platforms than cities for projecting the bosses' voice into state politics. In unfriendly times, counties served as larger moats protecting machines from attack by state-level rivals. And, above all, counties meant more patronage.

Intergovernmental alliances could also produce state and federal patronage for the big-city bosses. Necessary for stamping out local factional opponents during the machine's embryonic phase, intergovernmental resources were also useful in the bosses' search for ways to maintain power, particularly during periods of economic crisis and local retrenchment. Yet intraparty alliances—and the resources they brought at little cost to local voters—were fragile, particularly in the postwar era as the number of suburban voters exceeded the big-city voting population. The aging machines no longer represented the balance of party or governmental power.

Cash bribes represented a less reliable material inducement than patronage to voters, particularly after the introduction of the Australian, or secret, ballot. With their jobs at stake, the machine's payrollers could be trusted to bring their friends and relatives to the polls. In contrast, the number of bribed voters depended on the machine's campaign fund, counteroffers by the bosses' opponents, and the extent of reform surveillance over the electoral process.

As Gary Cox and Morgan Kousser observe, the secret ballot changed the dynamics of electoral corruption.[29] How could the bosses tell whether bribed voters carried out their part of the bargain in the shrouded polling booth? Risk-averse bosses began bribing the machine's opponents not to vote. Some enterprising bosses like Albany's Dan O'Connell ingeniously penetrated the veil of vote secrecy. The well-oiled O'Connell machine literally refused to lubricate the Republican lever on the city's voting machines. Thus, an antimachine vote was a squeaky vote. With precinct captains listening outside, bribed electors learned to vote in silence.

The machine's core resources—job patronage and power—were given to its core constituency, the Irish. The overallocation of the machine's most valued benefits to the Irish solved group and organizational dilemmas. The Irish moved from the working class to the lower middle class. Bound by ties of ethnicity and material self-interest, Irish ward and precinct captains dutifully staffed the machine's clubhouses, dispensing services for votes. In the long run, though, the Irish resource monopoly created electoral problems as new groups demanded a reallocation of benefits.

But patronage reallocation in the interests of managing a growing electorate collided with the goals of organizational maintenance, Irish political power, and material well-being. As sources of additional patronage were exhausted, the bosses would have to take public jobs away from the Irish in order to reward the non-Irish. A zero-sum job allocation would and did provoke revolts among the machine's Irish foot soldiers.

To reconcile conflicting organizational, group, and electoral goals, the Irish bosses created new and cheap forms of patronage. The Celtic variant on the parable of the loaves and fishes involved a "patronage stretch" to include services, symbolic recognition, and collective benefits. Nearly all governmental resources and powers were converted into particularistic benefits. Nonjob forms of patronage placed fewer demands on tax-conscious city homeowners. With new resource elasticities, the Irish bosses could reward the non-Irish.

In lieu of power and jobs, the Irish bosses gave the Southern and Eastern Europeans services, for example, business licenses and in-kind welfare benefits such as food and shelter, in exchange for political support. Machines also catered to the newcomers' status and recognition needs. Tammany's "Big Tim" Sullivan, boss of the heavily Jewish Lower East Side, donned a yarmulke to solicit Jewish votes. Even the welfare state could be enlisted as a machine vote-getting device. Although the bosses exerted little control over collective benefit programs, they loudly claimed credit for passage of popular labor and social welfare legislation and actively intervened as informational and service brokers. In their quest for minority political support, the machines harnessed themselves to the New Deal and the Great Society.

But patronage elasticity did not mean fungibility. The machine's resource arsenal was pyramidal. Until the middle of the twentieth century, the great resource (and constituency) divide lay between power and patronage (for the Irish) and all other divisible benefits (for the non-Irish). As the Irish began losing the wars of ethnic succession, that divide was finally crossed—first by the Southern and Eastern Europeans, and later by blacks.

In the postwar era, the machine's core constituency shifted—and so did the forms of patronage. With the coming of civil service reform, collective bargaining, affirmative action, and the fiscal crisis, the supply of old-fashioned job patronage was depleted. No longer sufficient as a vote-getting device, job patronage was deployed to maintain the party's grass-roots service and campaign operations. As the machine's core constituency shifted from working-class Irish to white ethnic homeowners, bosses created middle-class patronage. With a sizable middle-class constituency by the 1920s, the Albany machine led the way, specializing in tax concessions and homeowner services. The Chicago machine would soon follow.

Over time, the machine's resource policies followed a cyclical pattern. Embryonic machines faced the greatest pressures to expand the public economy via old-fashioned job patronage. Consolidating machines were mobilizers, pressing newly enfranchised working-class ethnic voters into service to defeat their opponents. Political impressment was not without cost, for the new claimants lined up for the machine's employment and welfare services.

Established machines, particularly with middle-class supporters, faced fewer expansionary pressures. The new forms of middle-class patronage, particularly tax concessions to the machine's loyal voters, reduced the organization's revenue base. Expansionary pressures from the lower class could be met with other forms of new-fashioned patronage, particularly collective benefits provided from "on high" at no immediate expense to local taxpayers. As a consequence, the entrenched postwar machines had modest local public economies.[30]

Deflating Voter Demand.   The creation and distribution of resources was only part of the machine's success story. Machines also had to manage demand, particularly from the working class, in order to fashion favorable trading terms between its products and customers. Contrary to the conventional wisdom, the machine's lower-class clientele was not inert putty in the bosses' hands, susceptible to easy manipulation and low-cost bribery.

In actuality, the Irish machines were generally toppled from below, not from above. The general belief, of course, is that machines were most vigorously challenged by middle-class reform movements. It is true that reformers incessantly nipped at the bosses' heels, occasionally drawing blood and electing insurgent mayors such as New York's Seth Low and John Purroy Mitchel. But reform produced primarily short-term fluctuations in the machine's fortunes, not long-term realignments. In order to overthrow the ancien régime Celtique, reformers had to enlist ethnic and working-class helpers.

The threat of antimachine insurgency from below was real indeed. In the late nineteenth century, local labor parties, not reform movements, posed the most serious threat to the early Irish machines. In the twentieth century, insurgent leaders such as Fiorello La Guardia, John V. Kenney, and Harold Washington put together coalitions of unmobilized and unrewarded ethnic groups to topple once-powerful Irish machines.

Given the dangers to machines of failing to incorporate ethnic working-class voters, why didn't the bosses adopt a policy of total voter mobilization? Mobilization had advantages. Enlarging the size of the electoral universe allowed the bosses to preempt their opponents by reducing the pool of voters available for countermobilization. It also enhanced the bosses' ability to project a voice in state and national politics.

But full mobilization of all working-class ethnic groups was costly. It threatened to drain the organization's limited stock of stores and provoke a reallocation of power and patronage from Irish to non-Irish. Faced with supply-side constraints, the Irish bosses turned to the task of deflating demand from below.

Demand deflation took various forms. As oligopolists of the working-class market, the bosses drove rival producers and product lines out of town. Both repression and corruption were used to defeat the machine's labor and Socialist party rivals. The machine's henchmen intimidated labor party speakers and voters. The machine-controlled police force broke up Socialist meetings, revoked the business licenses of insurgent immigrant entrepreneurs, and enforced Sunday-closing laws to stifle Jewish dissidents. When all else failed, rivals for the labor vote were counted out at the polls, as New York's Henry George discovered in 1886. The antipathy shown by the Irish machine was more political than cultural, a jurisdictional battle for working-class allegiances rather than a conservative Catholic predilection for social stability and order.

The Irish machines also kept new ethnic customers out of the political marketplace. Once minimal winning coalitions had been constructed, the machines had little incentive to naturalize, register, and mobilize the votes of later ethnic arrivals. Mobilization of the newcomers, particularly the Southern and Eastern Europeans, would have been difficult for the bosses in any event. The new ethnics were handicapped by language and cultural barriers, contributing to their slow political mobilization. Tightened naturalization and suffrage laws created additional barriers to electoral participation.

The sharp post-1896 decline in voter participation rates in the large urban-industrial states has been the object of considerable debate. The big northern and midwestern states experienced 15 percent to 20 percent declines in voter turnout between 1896 and 1912. One leading theory of demobilization looks at the role of national economic elites in depressing political participation levels. Walter Dean Burnham has argued that the exigencies of corporate capitalism demanded that the political economy be insulated from working-class pressures during the brutal takeoff phase of industrialization.[31]

According to Burnham, the American industrial elite was particularly vulnerable because of the early extension of the franchise relative to other industrializing countries. Economic leaders brought the industrial workforce to heel by reducing interparty competition in the big urban states and by tightening the electoral rules of the game. The northern financial and industrial elite thus buffered itself from countervailing pressures from below.[32]

The Burnham corporate conspiracy thesis has been challenged by a political-institutional theory of demobilization. Philip Converse and Jerrold Rusk argue that legal-institutional changes such as personal registration laws, the secret ballot, and the direct primary were responsible for the drop in turnout (more modest than Burnham claims) in the big urban states. National economic elites displayed little interest in electoral reform and in shrinking the urban-industrial voting universe. Instead, state and local *political* leaders—urban reformers and rural party elites—led the battle for electoral rule changes in order to weaken the corrupt big-city machines. Restricted access to the ballot box, not the rise of one-party politics, represented the primary instrument causing turnout decline among the urban working class.[33]

Our case studies of the big-city Irish machines shed some light on the demobilization debate. They underscore its local and political character. Yet contrary to the Converse-Rusk argument, demobilization made strange political bedfellows—and beneficiaries. Although the big-city Irish Democratic bosses initially opposed the suffrage restriction movement, they welcomed its consequences. Entrenched machines had already fashioned minimal winning electoral coalitions. Voter restrictions weakened challengers, not supporters, of the machine by reducing the number of immigrant working-class voters available for countermobilization. Instead of strengthening the reformers' hand against the machine, electoral reform could do precisely the opposite.

Alongside these formal hurdles, the Irish Democratic bosses were busily constructing informal ones. Where Irish Democratic power was consolidated by the turn of the century, the big-city bosses actively worked to insulate local politics from challenges to *their* hegemony. Electoral calculations hinged on a manageable vote, not necessarily a large one. Party-sponsored naturalization and registration of the immigrants atrophied. Machine politicians used repression and corruption to discourage immigrant labor party opponents. The machine's electoral neglect of blacks and Hispanics in the 1970s would be a replay of its nonfeasance toward the Southern and Eastern Europeans in the early twentieth century. Only in competitive-party cities such as Chicago in the 1920s would the Irish politicos work tirelessly to help the new immigrants surmount the hurdles of naturalization, registration, and voting.[34]

A Reconsideration of Exchange Theory

Exchange theory does much to explain the behavior and success of the big-city Irish politicos. Throughout most of its history, the machine traded material benefits for electoral support. The most active trading stocks, however, varied between cities and socioeconomic classes. Where machines primarily relied on working-class constituents, patronage and welfare services were the essential bargaining chips. With the nationalization of American politics, the sources of patronage and welfare support shifted from the local to the federal government. To middle-class voters, in contrast, low taxes and local homeowner services mattered.

The machine's multiple streams of benefits and beneficiaries help explain seeming anomalies in its behavior. Studying the Daley organization in the early 1970s, Thomas Guterbock was puzzled by the "irrational" behavior of many precinct captains. The party lieutenants specialized in handling middle-class service demands, acting as brokers between homeowners and the street and sanitation departments. Local party officials devoted less attention to lower-class demands. Rather than expediting the delivery of social services to the poor, the machine's henchmen referred supplicants to the appropriate public or private social service agency. At election time, however, machine support was greater among lower-class than middle-class voters. Guterbock concluded that exchange theory does not capture the machine's behavior.[35]

Exchange theory may be equal to the task. The postwar Chicago machine had the greatest leverage over city departments such as streets and sanitation that handled homeowner demands. With high voting rates among the middle class, the machine was understandably solicitous of its needs and could do something about them. Conversely, the machine had less leverage over welfare-state programs. Here its function was largely informational, putting the needy in contact with the appropriate social agency. Yet the machine successfully claimed credit for the stream of welfare-state benefits to the poor, the organization's most loyal supporters.

Notwithstanding the general usefulness of an exchange model of machine politics, the approach needs to be broadened in two ways. First, although the conventional wisdom views machines as single-purpose institutions, relentlessly pursuing vote maximization to the exclusion of all other goals, the bosses in fact serviced multiple actors in the political marketplace—voters, party functionaries, state and federal leaders, particular ethnic groups. Each made demands on the organization's scarce resources. A revised theory needs to specify the terms and tradeoffs of these multiple transactions.

Second, exchange theory views distributional decisions as central to machine politics. Yet allocational choices were made in the broader context of resource and demand management. An adequate account of machine politics must analyze how the bosses created resources and how they managed the demands of multiple constituencies, not merely how they allocated portions of the pie to various claimants. The bosses were chefs and maître d's as well as servers.

The Machine's Decline

The machine's demise has also generated considerable controversy. Two general theories of machine decline have been advanced. *Resource* theories look at what the bosses offered to political supporters, for example, patronage jobs, welfare services, and clubhouses. In this view, diminished control over benefits hastened the end of the big-city machines. *Demand* theories look at what political supporters wanted from the machines. In this view, the assimilation of the machine's traditional ethnic supporters into the public-regarding middle class sounded the death knell of boss rule.

Resource Theories

There are several resource theories of the machine's decline. The most famous suggests that the municipal reform movement of the early twentieth century dried up the bosses' supply of enticements. In the standard progressive account, reforms such as civil service, nonpartisanship, and the direct primary brought the bosses to their knees by weakening the machines' control over both resources and voters.[36]

The reformers' victory statements were made prematurely, before all the returns were in on the machine's staying power. If reform had been successful in depleting the machine's resource supply, there should have been a subsequent decline in both the number and the strength of the big-city machines. Yet the heyday of machines was the 1920s, *after* the reform movement had crested. The postreform Tammany Hall of Charles Francis Murphy and the Hague organization in Jersey City, for example, easily outperformed their prereform predecessors as vote getters and as patronage dispensers.

At best, the urban reformers succeeded in driving the big-city bosses into temporary exile. In the eight cities studied, reform rarely produced an enduring coup d'état. Championing austerity programs unpopular with the working class, reform mayors rarely lasted more than one term. As Tammany ward chieftain George Washington Plunkitt observed, reformers "were [like] mornin' glories—looked lovely in the mornin' and withered up in a short time, while the regular machines went on flourishing forever." [37] Reform movements dethroned machines only when they produced long-lasting local electoral realignments. For this, progressives had to enlist the machine's traditional working-class ethnic supporters with a welfarist set of policy offerings.

Changes in the rules of the local game dampened the machines more than reform mayors did, particularly in the case of embryonic organizations. Already controlling government and the electorate, established bosses could circumvent such reforms as civil service and nonpartisanship. For prospective bosses, however, the task was more difficult. New machines had high start-up costs, requiring generous resource infusions to construct the requisite grassroots party organization and electoral coalition. Brand identification had to be established with voters. Ward and precinct organizations had to be created and staffed. Party henchmen had to infiltrate government so that services could be delivered on call to the machine's supporters. In the short run, would-be bosses could circumvent single reforms. In the long run, multiple reforms created barriers to machine building. Reform charters in San Francisco (circa 1898) and Philadelphia (circa 1951), for example, included strengthened civil service systems that depleted the patronage supply, making later machine building far more difficult. The gossamer threads of reform could tie down would-be Boss Gullivers.

Paradoxically, however, reform may have strengthened already established big-city machines by *increasing* the supply of particularistic benefits available for capture. The antimachine camp was divided into structural and social factions. Structural reformers such as New York Mayor Seth Low embraced changes in the formal rules of the game but not increased public expenditures. Pitted against fiscal conservatives were social reformers such as Detroit Mayor Hazen Pingree. Pingree lavishly spent public money on social and recreational programs for the working class and increased local government's regulatory oversight over public utilities and transportation companies.[38]

Social reform could be turned to the bosses' advantage. Increased spending for schools, hospitals, and parks meant more patronage once machines were reinstalled in power and civil service barriers were overcome. The regulatory state created new business dependencies on government, giving the bosses the leverage needed to demand private sector patronage and campaign contributions.

For the ethnic bosses, reform produced electoral cohesion as well as unexpected resources. Reformers tried to break up the unholy alliance between boss and immigrant. To accommodate popular demand and raise needed revenue, the machine tacitly sanctioned liquor, gambling, and prostitution. Led by Protestant ministers, the upper-middle-class Brahmin reformers attacked the trinity of machine-protected working-class pleasures. Championing literacy tests and personal registration, the reformers also attacked the immigrants at the polls. Like the Radical Republican anti-immigrant crusade of the 1860s, the progressive reform program backfired. Spurned by nativist reformers, the immigrants retreated into the bosses' embrace.

If the progressives did not bring down the big-city bosses, what did? A second resource theory argues that rival institutions, particularly the welfare state and labor unions, outbid the old-style bosses for working-class support. Presidential adviser Rexford Tugwell and novelist Edwin O'Connor have proposed the most famous version of this theory.[39] For Tugwell and O'Connor, the responsibility for the bosses' "last hurrah" was placed at the doorstep of the New Deal, which brought down the old-time urban machines by taking working-class handouts out of the bosses' hands and replacing them with Social Security and unemployment checks. With the welfare state's arrival, the bosses' monopoly over working-class benefits supposedly was broken.

Yet the New Deal's effects on the big-city machines were far more complex and contradictory than the broken-monopoly hypothesis allows. Three critical distinctions must be made. First, new machines were far more vulnerable to external shocks than were old machines. Second, the impact of the New Deal's electoral coalition needs to be distinguished from the impact of federal social legislation. Third, different pieces of the Roosevelt legislative program had different consequences for urban political organizations and the resources they controlled.

In some ways the New Deal did weaken the big-city machines. The New Deal electoral alliance overthrew or weakened established GOP machines in cities such as Pittsburgh and Philadelphia. Even the Irish Democratic machines were not immune to the new Democratic majority. Roosevelt's electoral coalition included previously nonvoting Southern and Eastern Europeans, eager to overthrow their Irish wardlords in cities like New York and Jersey City.

As with progressive reform, the New Deal's social welfare and labor legislation made it more difficult to build *new* machines. In particular, labor emerged from the 1930s a strengthened political actor in local politics. Unions began performing traditional party functions like preprimary endorsements and getting out the vote, making it more difficult for prospective bosses to build strong independent party organizations.

The New Deal also energized congressmen and senators as federal benefit dispensers, weakening postwar bosses in nonmachine cities. In faction-torn Boston, for example, welfare-state assistance and national public works projects were channeled through federal, not local, officials. Postwar machine builders in the Hub would confront a powerful and independent federal political hierarchy. In Chicago, however, the emerging local machine coalesced with the New Deal, capturing federal offices and programs in the process. The machine controlled the postwar selection of congressmen and retained control of federal benefits.[40]

Yet for the Irish Democratic machines that survived the New Deal's initial electoral onslaught and for the new generation of more ethnically heterogeneous machines built on the New Deal majority, Roosevelt's social programs represented a massive infusion of desperately needed resources. Machines contributing most to FDR's reelection prospects captured relief programs such as the WPA, more than doubling the patronage available for party distribution. The WPA meant popular neighborhood projects and services as well as patronage jobs, enhancing the machine's vote totals. As Daley demonstrated in Chicago, even the New Deal's permanent social welfare legacy of public housing and AFDC could serve as pillars of local party organization.

A third resource theory of urban party decline looks at the bosses' dwindling cache of social rather than material inducements. James Q. Wilson has argued that Tammany's clubhouses atrophied in the postwar era, presaging the Wigwam's defeat in 1961.[41] Unable to adapt to the arrival of Jews and Puerto Ricans, the aging Irish election district captains retreated to their clubhouses. For party regulars, camaraderie replaced the delivery of services and the mobilization of voters. Reformers stepped into the breach, organizing anti-Tammany clubs throughout Manhattan in order to infiltrate and capture the Democratic party.

Did the collapse of the machine's clubhouses hasten the bosses' demise? Of the Irish machines studied, there was no one-to-one relationship between the vitality of party clubhouses and electoral strength. Strong district clubs built by Tammany Hall and the Hague organization did not prevent the realigning elections of 1933 and 1949. In other cities, however, weakened machine clubhouses predated realignments. In the Bay Area, the Buckley machine's district clubs jettisoned their recreational activities by 1890, concentrating instead on voter registration and party record keeping. The San Francisco working class turned on Boss Buckley shortly thereafter.[42]

Is the clubhouse–electoral support linkage causal or casual? A decline in the bosses' material resources may have produced both the withering of local clubs and the shift of ethnic and working-class voters into the antimachine camp. In San Francisco, worsening economic conditions in the late 1880s reduced Buckley's patronage army, leading to a reduction in clubhouse manpower and responsibilities. In New York, De Sapio's loss of state patronage and prospective federal sinecures contributed to Tammany's in-

ability to prevent reform infiltration. Declining patronage also reduced each boss's appeal to working-class voters. Collapsing clubhouses were part of a more general decline in the machine's arsenal
of material inducements to voters.

Demand Theories

A second set of theories explains the machine's demise in terms of
changing voter demands. Banfield and Wilson, for example, argue
that machines—like the New Deal Democratic party coalition
generally—self-destructed. The bosses' very successes in raising
the standard of living of the immigrant working class proved their
undoing. As the ethnics moved into the middle class, they dropped
their private-regarding, machine-supporting ways.[43]

This so-called assimilation theory allows the immigrants—but
not the bosses—to change their ways. In actuality, postwar machines did adapt to middle-class tastes. As the number of middle-
class voters grew, machines switched their policy offerings from
high taxes, patronage, and welfare services to low taxes and homeowner services. The policy transformation was not smooth and automatic. The O'Connell and Daley organizations, for example,
needed the goad of taxpayer uprisings to shift policy gears.

Prosperity, particularly in the postwar era, may have inhibited
middle-class ethnic support for a *new* generation of big-city machines. Yet a middle-class ethnic backlash is not the key to the
downfall of the entrenched machines. The classic Irish Democratic
organizations were destabilized from below, not from above. The
unincorporated ethnic and minority working class, not the rising
middle class, brought down the bosses in San Francisco, New
York, Jersey City, and now in Chicago.

These machines may well have self-destructed, but in different
ways than those suggested by assimilation theory. The machine's
ethnically segmented electoral-mobilization and resource-allocation policies promoted interethnic conflict within the working
class rather than interclass cleavages. Exclusionary policies produced antimachine mobilization on the part of unincorporated
ethnic groups. Admittedly, the Lawrence organization in Pittsburgh is an outlier in this deprivation-mobilization theory of machine decline. Rather than machine exclusionary policies, a leader-

ship vacuum in the late 1960s ushered in an era of reform in the Steel City.

Upsetting the Terms of Exchange

Explaining the demise of the classic Irish-American big-city machines is more complicated than the resource and demand theories allow. Declining resources—particularly patronage and welfare services—hurt machines with heavily working-class constituencies. Machines with middle-class constituencies and policies were less buffeted by retrenchment. But the Progressive movement, the New Deal, and the Great Society did not necessarily weaken the bosses' hold over the working class. Far from reducing either the machines' supply or monopoly of jobs and social services, each "reform" movement actually added to the bosses' stock of material inducements.

What mattered for the machine's longevity was the overall *relationship* between resources and groups of claimants. In particular, bosses strove for a favorable exchange ratio between party-supplied resources and voter demands. As the ratio rose, larger proportions of the electorate were incorporated within the machine's material reward system. The organization's electoral cushion rose. As the ratio dropped, however, larger proportions of the active electorate were deprived of the machine's resources. The ratio could drop in two ways. First, the stock of resources could drop while voter demand remained constant. Second, increases in the size of the electoral universe could outpace growth in the stock of resources. Large pools of deprived voters could be enlisted against the machines.[44]

Bosses tried to manage both the level of resources and political demand to maintain favorable exchange terms. Yet *external* political and economic forces could upset the trading terms established by the bosses in the local political marketplace, setting the stage for insurgency. Consider the role of external forces in the three major episodes of ethnic and working-class insurgency against the Celtic machines. In the 1870s and 1880s, state political leaders employed constitutional fiscal restraints to starve the Irish urban Democracy. The voter-resource ratio dropped as the patronage supply failed to keep up with the growing number of newly enrolled immigrant voters. The Buckley machine fell in San Francisco. In cities like New York, the Irish bosses were forced to use corruption and repression to best their powerful labor party opponents.

The stable second-generation Irish machines stockpiled resources and shrank the relative voting universe, reversing the exchange ratio. Yet ethnic and working-class insurgency mounted in the 1930s and 1940s in response to national economic and political forces. The Depression forced local payroll retrenchment. The New Deal coalition mobilized the unrewarded Southern and Eastern Europeans. The terms of machine exchange became unfavorable again as the number of claimants grew faster than resources. Where federal resources were not given or were subsequently withdrawn, the second-wave migrants revolted against their Irish political patrons. Tammany Hall and the Hague organization fell to the new ethnic working class.

The third-generation Irish machines required a steady infusion of federal resources to maintain favorable exchange terms with lower-class minority voters. Welfare-state benefits replaced local patronage as the primary machine inducement to the third-wave migrants. Social program retrenchment in the early 1980s, however, produced a worsening trade balance between the machine and minorities. The threatened withdrawal of previously granted benefits remobilized the black community against the aging white big-city political organizations, which failed to protect their minority clientele against federal cutbacks.

To what extent can we generalize this theory of the urban machine's life cycle? The theory is derived from a study of the evolution of the classic Irish Democratic machines in the heavily ethnic northern cities. More research is needed to determine whether the same organizational dynamics were evident in other places without Irish bosses, new immigrant constituencies, and competitive state party politics. Southern and border cities such as New Orleans, Baltimore, Memphis, and Kansas City produced Democratic machines where these conditions were missing. With smaller Irish-American populations in the southern cities, the ethnic makeup of the machine's governing circle was different. Celtic machine politicians could participate as individual players but not as ethnic prime movers. How did the lessened Irish role affect the coalition-building and resource-allocation strategies of the southern machines? In the southern cities, racial and class polarization, not ethnic conflict, constituted the dominant political cleavages long before the influx of blacks and Hispanics into the northern cities. How did this cleavage pattern affect the machine's electoral appeals and policies? Finally, the "southern relations" of the northern machines emerged in one-party states where factionalism within the Democratic party represented the dominant political cleavage. How did intraparty factionalism affect the building of the southern machines? A more general theory of the urban machine's life cycle needs to compare the northern and southern Democratic variants.[45]

A more general theory of machine building should also address the northern Republican big-city relations. Powerful GOP organizations ran cities such as Philadelphia, Pittsburgh, and Cincinnati from the Civil War to the Great Depression. Although the Republican and Democratic machines have been treated as nearly identical except for the party label, there were major differences between them.

In the urban Republican scheme of things, politically rebaptized Irish were, at best, junior coalitional partners in Yankee-controlled organizations. More reliant than their Democratic counterparts on middle-class votes, the GOP big-city juggernauts had smaller public sectors and less local patronage. As a consequence, the local Republican bosses sought and received greater infusions of state and federal patronage to compensate for the local resource shortfall. Because the fulcrum of GOP power was state and national—not local—politics, these big-city organizations were enmeshed in state and national party structures to a far greater degree than were their more autonomous Democratic counterparts. A more general theory of machine building also needs to consider the distinctive ethnic, coalitional, resource, and party alliance patterns of the GOP big-city organizations.[46]

American Machines in Comparative Perspective

While American students of machine politics have been preoccupied with organizational life-cycle issues, students of comparative politics have addressed a broader set of relations between party, state, and society. This "clientelist" perspective on the machine emphasizes the historical shift from the "old" patron-client ties linking landlord and peasant in traditional society to the "new" party-directed patronage ties connecting political leaders and voters in modernizing urban-industrial society.[47]

The clientelist approach further distinguishes between two stages of machine politics associated with the evolution of the modern state. The first stage features local, patronage-based, "orthodox" party organizations at the periphery of a weak national state characterized by limited functional responsibility and geographical fragmentation. The second stage features "neotraditional" or "mass patronage" local party structures integrated into strong national political parties and into centralized welfare and economic development programs.[48]

The Christian Democratic (DC) party in southern Italy in the postwar era has served as the model for this two-stage theory of machine development. Studying the DC machine in Catania, Mario Caciagli and Frank Belloni argue that the political demands accompanying urbanization and industrialization overwhelmed pre-existing individualistic clientelist networks. In response, the Christian Democrats solidified power by creating a new form of mass clientelism linking groups to public power. Lacking local resources, the DC bosses turned to national resources, particularly economic development programs, to build the new clientelist system.[49]

In a parallel study of the postwar Christian Democratic machine in Palermo, Judith Chubb argues that the new "mass patronage" clientelism rested on the local party's monopoly of resources rather than on an ever-increasing supply of benefits. Given economic underdevelopment and limits on both local and national resources, the Palermo bosses maintained power by astutely monopolizing resource transfers from the core to the periphery. The DC controlled the local entrepreneurial class with its state-assisted urban development and credit programs. The machine appealed to the traditional middle class and to the poor with its licensing and discretionary law enforcement powers. Finally, the DC used job patronage to control government employees.[50]

Ironically, students of southern Italian machine politics such as Caciagli, Belloni, Chubb, and Rene Lemarchand have denied the applicability of the "mass patronage" model to the American case.

They view the modern American big-city machines as "orthodox" organizations, throwbacks to the weak, localistic, and limited nineteenth-century American state. Lemarchand, for example, argues that American machines like the Daley organization use local particularistic benefits such as city jobs and services, not nationally supplied collective benefits, to construct old-fashioned individualistic (rather than modern group) clientele networks. Lemarchand concludes that "the Daley machine in Chicago has a great deal more in common with the Radical machine of Argentina in the 1920s [another orthodox party organization] than they each have with the Christian Democratic machine in contemporary Italy."[51]

Clientelist theorists misunderstand the American case. Since the late nineteenth century the once-local machines have been progressively absorbed into broader party and programmatic structures. The life cycle of the Irish Democratic machines involved a two-stage expansion of linkages—first from local to state, then from state to national. Even the "classic" early Democratic machines such as Kelly's Tammany Hall, though unable to integrate into Republican-controlled national power networks, nevertheless were "mainstream" products of a national political culture that legitimated their acquisitive ethos and distributive logic. This national "patronage culture" actually predates the Jacksonian spoils system of the 1820s, going back to the Federalist patronage machine of the 1790s. Succeeding waves of immigrants injected a "mass" potential into this initially entrepreneurial or elite system.[52]

In the twentieth century, the classical Irish urban machines have served as engines of political modernization, highly integrated into both the modern Democratic party and the national welfare state. The big-city machines and unions were the key institutional building blocks of the national Democratic party of the 1930s and 1940s.[53] By their control of local electorates and congressional representatives, the Irish machines also served as pillars of the New Deal and the Great Society. Although wedded to a "patronage logic," machines actively supported the expansion of the welfare state in order to solve local coalition-maintenance problems. National resources could be used to reward previously unincorporated ethnic groups.

Richard Daley in Chicago and the local Christian Democratic party bosses of southern Italy had much in common after all. Both American and Italian bosses in the postwar era required national welfare-state and economic development programs to maintain power. Clientelist theorists misclassify the postwar American case because they are not aware of the machine's significant post–New Deal linkages with national trends in both party development and the welfare state. Instead, they project into the twentieth century the "localized" late nineteenth-century machines for whom core-vertical linkages were limited to the state level.

America's post–New Deal "mass patronage" machines need further study, particularly in terms of their relationship to national programs. Consider, for example, the current crisis of the welfare state. Clientelist theory views the evolution of modern local machines and national social programs as mutually reinforcing. Consistent with this theory, the American big-city bosses supported and subsequently benefited from Progressive-era social welfare reforms, the New Deal, and the Great Society. The building of the American welfare state made strange political bedfellows. Samuel Beer points out how the big-city politicians actively joined forces with social service advocates in the 1960s to promote "direct federalism"—local lobbying networks in Washington and social program linkages bypassing the states.[54]

But there was a dark side to this mutual symbiosis: potential mutual destruction. While the fate of machines increasingly hinged on the benefits provided by the welfare state, the fate of the welfare state hinged on the votes produced by the decaying big-city party organizations. Yet local politicians were lulled into political inertia by the seemingly automatic nature of social program gains achieved under both Republican (Nixon, Ford) and Democratic (Kennedy, Johnson, Carter) administrations. National bureaucratic incrementalism exacted a local political price. In Chicago, for example, voter turnout rates dropped in the late 1960s and early 1970s as the machine dispensed with mobilizing its welfare-state clientele. Yet this unraveling of the electoral base of the party system, as Claus Offe points out, accentuated the legitimation crisis of the Keynesian welfare state. Machines—and the party system generally—were no longer able to fulfill their mass mobilization function in support of government social programs.[55]

The contradictory relationship between the urban Democratic party and the welfare state deserves far more attention than it has received. In the 1980s it became fashionable to view postwar urban politics through the lens of "pro-growth" coalitions and federal economic development programs rather than through the prism of national social programs. But "pro-welfare" coalitions were as central to the making—and unmaking—of the postwar urban Democratic party as were the "pro-growth" coalitions so provocatively analyzed by John Mollenkopf. Mollenkopf argues that federal urban development programs since the 1930s have been the "principal means" through which the modern Democratic party was created.[56]

The single prism of national revitalization programs such as urban renewal is too narrow to do justice to postwar urban Democratic politics. The welfare state also had a significant political impact on the Democratic-controlled big cities, particularly on those cities dominated by machines (Chicago, Pittsburgh). Mollenkopf, however, studied reform cities (San Francisco, Boston) dominated by pro-growth coalitions and policies. Yet welfare politics affected even these reform cities, for although growth policies preoccupied local decision makers in Boston and San Francisco in the 1950s and 1970s, welfare policies dominated their decision making in the 1930s and 1960s.

By studying reform cities rather than machine cities, Mollenkopf overestimates the antiparty logic of national urban policy since the New Deal. He argues that the New Deal revolutionized the urban political landscape by substituting a program-based, nationally directed bureaucratic strategy for amassing power for a patronage-based, locally rooted party strategy. In this fashion, Roosevelt supposedly built a new reform coalition in the cities.[57]

But the New Deal was most creative in redirecting urban political reality by its *fusion* of party and bureaucracy, of patronage and policy. Far from being antiparty instruments to modernize local government, federal relief programs like the WPA were carefully calibrated to co-opt existing machines and even to help build new ones. Similarly, in machine cities like Chicago, Great Society programs were a complement, not a substitute, for local party organization.[58]

As for future urban coalition building, the welfare state—and local regimes grafted onto it—may contain a dark antigrowth side. Accepting pro-growth politics as an automatic given, Mollenkopf calls for building a new coalition of minority neighborhood organizations and young white professionals.[59] Harold Washington's initial victory by a coalition of South Side and lakefront voters and the recent downtown Chicago building boom seem to bear out this thesis.

Washington tried to ride two political horses—growth *and* welfare services—and was trapped by their contradictory pull. In power, the mayor jockeyed himself into a partnership with bankers and developers to construct a *governing* coalition. But the horse on which he first rode to power was a minority-welfare state clientele jeopardized by Reagan's cutbacks in social programs. This *voting* constituency represented the foundation of Washington's support and has benefited little from his growth policies. In an era of declining welfare, the late mayor also experienced difficulty maintaining existing social service levels to his core constituency.

The future does not augur well for big-city minority mayors such as Harold Washington. Economic trends in aging heartland cities like Chicago (rather than coastal oases like Boston and San Francisco) point toward continuing deindustrialization and accelerating racial and class polarization, not toward the building of multiethnic, cross-class growth coalitions.

Perhaps students of southern Italian politics can provide a lesson about the possible mutually reinforcing character of local economic backwardness and entrenched machines. In her study of the Palermo Christian Democratic party, Judith Chubb argues that economic underdevelopment enhanced the machine's power. Monopolizing national and local resources, the party became "the obligatory intermediary to all transactions involving individuals and public power." Economic growth, however, threatened the DC machine by "creating new sources of wealth and privilege and potential opposition groups."[60]

The post–New Deal American machines developed at the same time as their Italian counterparts and, more significantly, in regions characterized by increasing industrial backwardness. Under new ethnic ownership, the decaying big-city machines of the American rustbowl may turn out to be parasitic of the metropolitan industrial decay they promise to ameliorate, but just as regularly exacerbate, through redevelopment programs. The last of the Democratic machines are also parasitic of the welfare-dependent underclass. The talisman of unbridled growth may not be grabbed as eagerly by big-city minority politicians as some analysts would have us believe, particularly if it entails welfare-state cutbacks.

The political and economic situation of today's urban minorities raises questions about the historical use of local party and state structures to advance the interests of working-class ethnic groups. Paul Peterson has downplayed the political machine's "redistributional" role, arguing instead that the local bosses umpired modest ethnic group "allocational" contests over patronage. For Peterson, redistributional policies are best left to the federal government, not to city hall. Viewed historically, how accurate is the Petersonian model of limited local redistributional politics?[61]

More generally, how did the big-city machines contribute to the oft-noted pattern of American political exceptionalism—the failure to produce European-style social democratic political parties and universal social welfare programs? Ira Katznelson argues that the institutional separation of party machines and unions fragmented American working-class politics by encouraging different ways of thinking and behaving in the community and workplace. Machines encouraged ethnic divisions in the community; unions, class divisions in the workplace.[62] Is institutional incongruity the key to explaining America's muted working-class politics, as Katznelson would have it? Or did the big-city machines and unions work in tandem to fracture the working class along ethnic-racial lines, pitting older arrivals against newcomers? These questions about the machine's ability to *represent* ethnic group and working-class interests are the subject of the next chapter.

Chapter Seven

Rainbow's End:
Machines, Immigrants,
and the Working Class

Cui Bono? The Beneficiary Debate

The performance of the classic immigrant-based big-city machines has sparked a second controversy, which is concerned with the consequences of boss rule. During the machine's heyday, reformers had attacked the urban bosses for weakening democracy and promoting plutocracy. Traditional liberals such as James Bryce and M. Ostrogorski deplored the capture of the postbellum party system by professional officeseekers eager for patronage, power, and profit. For Bryce, America's corrupt spoilsmen were a far cry from the liberal democratic ideal of enlightened party statesmen involved in principled confrontation over the burning issues of the day. Bryce singled out the Irish-American big-city bosses for particular criticism. In their quest for power and spoils, the demagogic Celtic bosses supposedly manipulated the masses of ignorant foreign-born voters, thereby upsetting the counterbalancing role of public opinion over narrow, venal elites.[1]

Social welfare liberals such as Frederick Howe and Lincoln Steffens added a new dimension to Bryce's critique by attacking the unholy alliance between the big-city bosses and the utility and transportation magnates. For Howe, machine politics promoted plutocracy and the exploitation of the poor by the wealthy. Granted lucrative public franchises, monopolists charged the working class all that the traffic would bear. The machine's tax concessions to the wealthy limited the provision of public amenities and welfare services to the needy.[2] For progressive reformers, machine politics had produced the ultimate horror—"the rule of mob and money."[3]

In the machine's twilight era, however, a much different evaluation of its performance has been advanced. In the new pluralist or "rainbow" view, the machine, though imperfectly democratic, incorporated the immigrant working class. Facing competition in the electoral marketplace, big-city bosses found it in their interests to serve as ethnic middlemen, quickly naturalizing and registering successive waves of immigrants. In this fashion, machines ostensibly assimilated the newcomers, fashioning multiethnic "rainbow" coalitions.

For pluralists such as Robert Dahl, the resource-laden machines served as redistributional devices. The votes of lower-class immigrants could be traded for public jobs and other material benefits. The Irish were the machine's beneficiaries par excellence. Capturing the levers of urban power, the Irish could build a middle class on a base of patronage jobs. In the pluralist scheme of things, ethnic political assimilation and economic reward ameliorated working-class grievances. Ethnic-machine politics in this manner is said to have muted more radical forms of working-class political action.

Notwithstanding the big-city machine's decline, this rainbow theory has figured prominently in contemporary minority power debates, promising a pot of gold for today's ethnic groups. In the 1960s and 1970s, blacks mobilized to capture the big cities. The legend of the Irish machines served as an important yardstick in the black power debates, showing how group voting strength could be turned into local political power. Group power, in turn, promised to yield sizable economic rewards such as public jobs and contracts. In the 1980s, big-city minority politicians claim to have expanded their electoral constituency. One part Jesse Jackson and one part Boss Tweed, the new coalitional formula calls for multiethnic "rainbow" politics.[4]

But as the new minorities embraced the pluralist model of group power and coalition building, the model underwent academic revision. A variant interpretation emphasized the machine's symbolic, not material, accommodation of the immigrants. For revisionists such as Raymond Wolfinger, middle-class leadership, not working-class votes, represented the crucial building block of ethnic group power. Ethnic capture of city hall, in turn, promised very little group economic yield. In a recent and influential study, Paul Peterson has pointed out the sharp constraints on local redistributional politics.

At issue in the pluralist-revisionist debate was the machine's capacity to represent ethnic group and working-class interests. In this chapter we reconsider the pluralist and revisionist models, using the data from our analysis of the classic Irish-American big-city machines. Did the old-style urban party organizations politically assimilate the successive waves of immigrants, as the pluralists would have it? Were machines redistributional devices serving as a route of social mobility for groups such as the Irish? How did machines contribute to American political exceptionalism—the failure to produce strong labor parties with social welfare programs?

This debate over the machine's performance in redressing group inequalities is of compelling relevance for today's urban minorities. As blacks take over the citadels of once-Irish big-city power, the question again arises whether group political power can be translated into economic advancement. Though the terrain of urban politics has changed since the heyday of the Irish bosses, with reformed bureaucracies replacing party machines as the chief instruments of governance, the question of the machine's historical role in promoting ethnic assimilation and economic redistribution is still current.

To the extent that the controversy over the future of black, Hispanic, and Asian-American politics in the big cities is dominated by the long shadow of the legendary Irish machine, we need to understand the difference between historical fact and historical fiction. Hence, this chapter concludes by assessing the relevance of machine politics for today's urban minorities and by examining the political mechanisms for incorporating more recent ethnic arrivals to the cities.

Machines and Ethnic Assimilation
The Pluralist Approach

In the postwar era, social scientists eulogized the dying and much-maligned machine. In the 1940s and 1950s, a new generation of empirically trained sociologists such as William Foote Whyte, Robert K. Merton, and Daniel Bell used the machine as a test case to critique the middle-class Protestant value orientation that had dominated social analysis. Buttressing their claims for a value-neutral, functional approach to social science, the Young Turks argued that the censorious view of machine politics ignored the positive functions performed by lower-class ethnic institutions offering unconventional mobility routes. Finding their career opportunities blocked in the Protestant-controlled business world, the Irish had turned to the machine; the Italians, to the mob. Because it served the material needs of the immigrant working class, machine politics persisted, despite middle-class Protestant opposition.[5]

By the 1960s, political scientists such as Dahl, Fred Greenstein, Elmer Cornwell, and Edgar Litt had joined the chorus of machine defenders, arguing that the big-city party bosses had been both ethnic integrators and system stabilizers-transformers.[6] In the hands of the pluralists, the machine became a local precursor to the New Deal ethnic coalition and the welfare state; the boss, a new paradigm of democratic leadership and mass politics.

The pluralist locus classicus was *Who Governs?*, Robert Dahl's 1961 survey of New Haven's political development over two centuries. Dahl's treatment of the Irish party bosses represented part of a larger analysis of successful regime transformation. In nineteenth-century New Haven, an oligarchic system of cumulative inequalities and overlapping privileges (the same hands holding wealth, social standing, and power) gradually and peacefully gave way to a pluralist system of dispersed inequalities and advantages (in which different people controlled different resources).[7]

By the mid-nineteenth century, a new breed of Yankee businessmen-politicians had displaced the "Old Standing Order" of leading Federalist and Congregationalist families. From humble origins, the new self-made entrepreneurs fought to end property restrictions on voting in order to mobilize a new electoral majority of native-born artisans and laborers. But this insurgent elite's primary weapon of victory—the vote—would soon be turned against them. Successfully challenging Yankee leadership at century's end, Irish Democratic politicians naturalized, registered, and claimed the votes of their countrymen in order to forge a new electoral majority.[8]

The Irish bosses then turned to the task of group economic uplift. According to Dahl, politics and city jobs served as "major springboards" for the Irish into the middle class. Controlling the levers of urban power, the Irish traded votes for patronage, accelerating their movement out of the laboring classes. The early machine's patronage cache awaiting capture appeared sizable indeed. In the pre–New Deal era, the big-city machines controlled thousands of public sector and private sector patronage jobs. Tammany Hall, for example, had more than 40,000 patronage jobs at its disposal in the late 1880s. Furthermore, the public sector offered greater social mobility opportunities than did the private sector. In San Francisco at the turn of the century, nearly one-quarter of all public employees were in professional and managerial positions compared with only 6 percent of the privately employed workforce.[9]

Using machine patronage, the Irish supposedly built a middle class with surprising rapidity considering their meager job skills and the discrimination they encountered. In the big cities, the proportion of first- and second-generation Irish in white-collar jobs rose from 12 percent to 27 percent between 1870 and 1900. Among the non-Irish, the white-collar increase was smaller, from 27 percent to 34 percent. As Andrew Greeley has shown, Irish-Americans are now the most affluent of the country's non-Jewish ethnic groups, having translated their apparently early white-collar job gains into a solid middle and upper middle class anchored in business and the professions in the post–World War II era.[10]

Dahl's account of the rise of the Irish "ex-plebes" and the accompanying systemic shift from cumulative to dispersed inequalities is central to a larger pluralist theory of American politics. Placing himself in an Aristotelian-Machiavellian tradition, Dahl highlighted the creative role of political elites such as the Irish party bosses in promoting both change and stability in the modern city-state. In the hands of gifted leaders, the mechanisms of political equality—popular sovereignty, universal suffrage, competitive parties, and the patronage system—could be used to reduce social and economic inequalities.

Our case studies support the pluralist argument regarding the machine's *political* assimilation of the Irish. The English-speaking famine Irish arrived as the competitive second party system was entering its modern or mobilization phase. As the Irish allegiance to the Democratic party solidified, the embryonic machines actively worked to naturalize and enroll Irish voters. Group mobilization allowed the Irish to infiltrate and take over the helm of the big-city Democratic machines.

Yet the machine's *economic* assimilation of the Irish—and its redistributional potential generally—was smaller than pluralists allow. For one thing, early Irish economic progress was slower and more uneven than the growth in white-collar jobholders indicates. As Stephan Thernstrom has carefully shown for Boston, many middle-class gains by first- and second-generation Irish were marginal at best, signaling entry into poorly paid clerical and sales work rather than into business and the professions.[11]

Thernstrom also cautions that it is misleading to compare Irish economic progress with the sluggish performance of the new immigrants. The new immigration was made up of successive waves of impoverished Southern and Eastern Europeans. More instructive is his comparison of the progress of the politically powerful Irish in Boston's labor market relative to that of other early-arriving but politically weaker immigrant groups. First- and second-generation Germans, Scandinavians, and English all climbed the economic ladder more quickly than did their Irish counterparts.

Our case studies of the classic Irish machines suggest that the pluralist model overestimates the magnitude of machine resources and the Irish ability to use them for sizable group economic gain. The Democratic machines of the late nineteenth century offered impressive channels of advancement for *individual* Irish politicians and contractors. But the early machines could do only so much for Irish *group* mobility.

Political and class constraints hampered the early bosses in their search for greater resources. Middle-class Yankee Republicans had not yet migrated to the suburbs. They vigorously contested local elections, demanding fiscal retrenchment. The early Irish bosses like John Kelly also had to contend with opponents in their own ranks: Democratic businessmen-reformers advocating "tight-fisted" economic policies. This bipartisan conservative coalition forced the nascent Celtic machines to pursue cautious fiscal policies, limiting their patronage take.

Republicans dominated state politics during much of this era, reinforcing the fiscal conservatism of the early Irish machines. Republican governors and legislators imposed constitutional restrictions, severely limiting the bosses' ability to raise taxes, increase municipal debts, and reward their working-class ethnic followers. Consequently, as Chapter 2 has argued, only a small minority of the Irish working class in the late nineteenth century could crowd into the machine's patronage enclave.

The twentieth-century machines did a better job of economically aiding the Irish. Political and legal constraints on the bosses' ability to raise and spend money—and thus to create patronage jobs—began to ease as the machine's middle-class Republican and reform opponents moved to the suburbs, as home rule lifted state fiscal restraints, and as the millions of Southern and Eastern Europeans filling the cities demanded new services. Machines directly and indirectly controlled more than 20 percent of post-1900 urban job growth, double their pre-1900 share. In the Irish-run machine cities of New York, Jersey City, and Albany, the Irish were rewarded with more than 60 percent of this newly created patronage. As a result, on the eve of the Depression, at least one-third of the Irish-stock workforce toiled in machine-sponsored jobs.

The second-generation machine's patronage policies appear to support the pluralist argument that politics served as an important conduit of Irish economic advancement. Compared with Yankees, Germans, and Jews, though, the Irish were slow to build a middle class in business and the professions. Today's Irish affluence was latecoming, postdating the heyday of the machine. As even Greeley admits, the Irish middle class was only emerging on the eve of the Depression; its arrival would not occur until after World War II.[12]

In light of Irish political success, why was Irish middle-class status so slow in coming? Was there an *inverse* relation between political success and economic advancement? The Irish crowded into the largely blue-collar urban public sector in the late nineteenth and early twentieth centuries. Yet as low-paid policemen, firemen, and city clerks, the Irish were solidly lower-middle- rather than middle-class. The relative security of blue-collar jobs in public works, police, and fire departments may have hindered the building of an Irish middle class by encouraging long tenure in poorly paid bureaucratic positions. The pluralist machine's apparent cornucopia of resources could turn into a blue-collar cul-de-sac.[13]

It can be argued that by channeling so much of their economic energy into the public sector, the Irish forsook opportunities in the private sector save for industries such as construction that depended on political connections. As Moynihan has accurately observed, the economic rewards of America have gone to entrepreneurs, not to functionaries. Moreover, the Irish public sector job gains were fragile. The Depression forced the cities to cut their payrolls. The 1930s also witnessed the long-awaited revolt of the Southern and Eastern Europeans against their Irish overlords. Thousands of Irish-American payrollers lost their jobs as a result of retrenchment and machine overthrow. Only with lessened job dependence on the machine in the prosperous post–World War II era were the third- and fourth-generation Irish able to move rapidly into business and the professions.

The puzzling question is why the Irish embraced the machine's blue-collar patronage system with such enthusiasm. Dahl has advanced a "blocked mobility" explanation. In his account, the Irish quickly assimilated the American value of upward mobility. However, limited job skills and anti-Catholicism blocked Irish advancement in the private sector. Thus, the Irish, in Dahl's words, "eagerly grabbed the 'dangling rope' [of politics] up the formidable economic slope."[14]

If the Irish so easily assimilated the American success ethic, why did they allow the dangling rope of politics to become a noose? There are both cultural and resource explanations for the Irish overreliance on the patronage system. Moynihan has taken issue with Dahl, arguing that the Irish displayed a "distaste for commerce," valuing security over entrepreneurial success. Seeking safe bureaucratic havens, the Irish settled for marginal advancement through politics.[15]

Borrowing a page from Max Weber, Edward Levine similarly argues that the Irish working class consciously rejected the middle-class Protestant value of economic achievement. Alienated from Protestant values and institutions, the Irish constructed the Democratic party and the Catholic church as mutually reinforcing institutions rooted in working-class Irish Catholic values. For the Irish, power and security, not money or status, represented the highest values. In this scheme of things, social and geographical mobility meant apostasy. Reinforcing their separateness from the Protestant mainstream, politics enveloped the Irish, becoming *the* approved secular career. As the machines have declined, however, the Irish have gradually replaced the values of power and security with those of money and status.[16]

A resource explanation for limited Irish patronage mobility looks to the machine's maintenance needs. To win the jurisdictional battles for working-class support, machines quickly realized the potency of economic appeals. Yet scarce economic benefits had to be spread as widely as possible to realize their full vote-getting value. Thus the Irish bosses stretched patronage, creating large numbers of poorly paid blue-collar positions to maximize the number of working-class voters rewarded. The machine's job growth strategy created ever more blue-collar public employment for the Irish at a time when the cities were moving from a manufacturing to a service economy and when the greatest increases in private sector employment occurred in white-collar ranks.

The party's maintenance needs conflicted with the long-run goal of Irish prosperity. But patronage had short-run economic advantages. The machine's job system allowed unskilled and semiskilled Irish workers to move to the next rung above the working class. In fact, the ready availability of blue-collar patronage helped to *shape* Irish economic horizons, encouraging the values of security, seniority, and slow bureaucratic advancement.

The pluralist view of the machine as an integrator of the immigrants has been applied to the Southern and Eastern Europeans. Elmer Cornwell, for example, argues that the Irish bosses in the northern cities were forced to politically assimilate the second-wave immigrants in order to continue to win elections.[17] Competitive electoral pressures encouraged the Irish bosses to naturalize and register the newer arrivals. Our survey of the classic Irish machines found that the machine's invisible hand did not automatically embrace the newcomers. Mature machines were one-party regimes lacking the political incentive to mobilize the second-wave immigrants. The Irish Democratic bosses had already constructed winning electoral coalitions among early-arriving ethnic groups. The newcomers' political assimilation would only encourage demands for a redistribution of power and patronage.

In entrenched machine cities like New York and Jersey City, naturalization and voter registration rates for the Southern and Eastern Europeans remained quite low until the late 1920s. Electoral participation rates for the second-wave immigrants increased thereafter in response to national candidates and issues rather than to sponsorship by local party bosses.

In competitive party cities, however, the Irish party chieftains worked energetically to mobilize the Southern and Eastern Europeans. The fledgling Democratic machines of Chicago and Pittsburgh most successfully mobilized the newcomers. As the minority party in these cities in the 1920s, the Democrats were forced into actively courting the new ethnics. Chicago's Democratic precinct captains naturalized and registered the new immigrants far more quickly than did their counterparts in one-party New York, Jersey City, and Boston.

Entrenched machines did little to further economic assimilation among the Southern and Eastern Europeans before the latter mobilized in the 1930s. With so much of Irish well-being and group identity dependent on continued control of the machines, Irish politicos were understandably loath to share power and patronage. To preserve their hegemony, the Irish accommodated the slowly mobilizing newcomers in parsimonious fashion, dispensing social services, symbolic recognition, and collective benefits rather than the organization's core resources of power and patronage.

At critical moments the Irish were forced by electoral pressures to enter tactical alliances with some groups for a greater share of the machine's jealously guarded core resources. As Jews flexed their political muscle in New York in the 1920s, the Irish offered them minor offices and a greater share of municipal employment, particularly in the rapidly expanding school system. The Celtic bosses worked as actively to reduce Italian influence by gerrymandering Italian neighborhoods.

Postwar machines such as the Daley organization accommodated the Southern and Eastern Europeans in different and less costly ways than those in which the prewar machines had rewarded the Irish. Wartime and postwar prosperity benefited the second-wave immigrants and their children, propelling large numbers into the property-owning middle class. As homeowners, white ethnics objected to high property taxes to pay for patronage jobs they did not need. The Southern and Eastern Europeans demand a different set of machine policies: low property taxes, the preservation of property values and white neighborhoods, and homeowner rather than welfare services. The postwar Irish-led machines accommodated these taxation and service demands—as long as the Irish maintained control over key party positions and those city offices with major policy-making and patronage-dispensing responsibilities.

Machines did little to assimilate blacks and Hispanics. In the pre-1960 period, black sub-machines to the white machines had emerged in cities such as Chicago and Pittsburgh. Congressman William Dawson, the only black in the Daley machine's inner circle, ran the black sub-machine in the South Side ghetto. To counter the threat of Polish insurgency, Dawson and his lieutenants mobilized the minority vote for Mayor Daley. As the threat of white revolt diminished in the 1960s, the threat of black revolt grew. Using welfare-state benefits, the machine systematically demobilized the black vote.

Contrary to pluralist theory, the big-city machine's political and economic incorporation of ethnic groups was limited. The Irish represent the theory's par excellence case. The nascent Democratic machines actively assisted the Irish in acquiring citizenship, in voting, and in securing patronage jobs. Yet pluralist theory exaggerates the ability of the Irish to turn political into economic success. The economic disadvantages suffered by the Irish could not readily be overcome by politics; they may even have been aggravated. Celtic economic success came *after* the machine's heyday. Failing to consider the class and political constraints on the machine's creation and distribution of resources, pluralists overestimate the old-style party organization's redistributional capacity.

The pluralist case is further weakened when we consider the machine's limited assimilation of other ethnic groups. The entrenched Democratic machines did little to mobilize and reward the new arrivals from Southern and Eastern Europe, the South, the Caribbean, and Latin America. Deprived of machine sponsorship, the newcomers would have to rely on internal group resources to contest urban power.

The Revisionist Approach

Raymond Wolfinger recognizes that machines did little to aid ethnic assimilation. Rather than relying on majority party sponsorship, ethnic groups had to develop their own resources to amass power. Where votes represent the crucial group resource for pluralists, Wolfinger points to the importance of middle-class leadership.[18]

The revisionist critique posits an economic determinism wherein ethnic political power follows from the development of "bourgeois" economic power within the newcomer community. Ethnic power is an elite-driven process. Middle-class leaders possess the organizational and communication skills needed to press the group's demands. Because a middle class takes time to build, there is a generational time lag before group influence is achieved.[19]

The model also posits a political determinism in which middle-class ethnic demands must be "linked" to the political system for group influence to occur. Minority parties have greater incentive than majority parties to mobilize and reward the new ethnic group. Minority party bosses forge a group-party linkage by nominating middle-class ethnic leaders to major offices, particularly the mayorality. Only with this ethnic-party elite alliance does group political mobilization occur. The nomination of ethnic leaders seals the party-group "tie," encouraging the group to register and vote en masse.[20]

But ethnic power, even when finally achieved, had limited redistributional potential. Following Oscar Handlin, Wolfinger argues that ethnic group demands were not expansive but conservative, traceable to the immigrants' Catholic peasant origins.[21] Machines, in turn, controlled limited material benefits. As a consequence, machines gave immigrants few tangible benefits. "Politics," Wolfinger concludes, "has not been a pathway enabling ethnics to attain equality in social and economic life."[22] Instead, the party system specialized in symbolic inducements. Catering to the status needs of the emerging ethnic middle class rather than to the material needs of the working class, local bosses successively "recognized" aspiring groups with elite nominations to public office.

Wolfinger's theory accurately describes the case it is based on—New Haven's Republican-leaning Italians. In the early twentieth century, the Irish controlled the city's majority Democratic party and did little to assimilate the Italians. Led by the farsighted Ullman brothers, the Republican party actively courted the Italian vote. As the Italians moved from the working class into the middle class, the Republicans nominated William Celentano for mayor in

1939, the first Italian selected for a major public office. Celentano won in 1945 as thousands of newly registered Italian Republicans went to the polls, sealing the local ethnic-party alliance.

But New Haven's Italian Republicans were an atypical case. In other Democratic cities, the GOP was slow to pick up the ethnic slack. Republicans in New York and Boston soured into nativism and conservatism in the 1920s, turning their backs on the new immigrants. Tammany Hall got the Jewish and Italian vote by default. The Irish Democratic bosses complicated minority party challenges by grooming their own kept ethnic leaders. Ever on the lookout for potential opposition, the Hague machine gave the city's sanitation contract to Italian loyalist Mike Scaturcchio. In cities like Chicago and Pittsburgh, the national Democratic re-alignment of the 1930s overshadowed local party-group alliances as a prime energizer of new ethnic leaders and voters. Italian Fiorello La Guardia and Czech Anton Cermak, for example, rode the New Deal's ethnic turnout surge into the mayor's office in the nation's two largest cities.

In northern cities, the Italians lacked group voting power, as important for building group influence as a large middle-class and party sponsorship. High rates of return migration to Italy, limited familiarity with English, and literacy test barriers for naturalization and voting drastically limited the number of Italian-American voters, creating disincentives for *any* party to mobilize the newcomers. Growing Italian voting strength, however, changed the party calculus. In New Haven, rising Italian voter participation rates in the 1930s encouraged the GOP to first nominate Celentano for mayor in 1939.

The first-wave immigrants from Western Europe clearly represent confounding cases for Wolfinger's middle-class hypothesis. The Germans, English, and Scandinavians, who were the first to develop middle classes, had their politicization impeded precisely for this reason. For the Irish, in contrast, the possession of political power long predated the development of a middle class. As saloon-keepers, volunteer firemen, and foremen on public works projects, early Irish leadership emerged from the working class and lower-middle class. Green Power did not await elite nominations and recognition from on high. Instead, the Irish built power from the grass roots, infiltrating the bottom of the political hierarchy as precinct and ward captains and as nominees for minor public offices. Working-class Irish built a politics of group electoral mobilization, party activism, and patronage.

Machines and Working-Class Politics

The Pluralist Account

Both pluralists and revisionists agree that machines retarded the development of labor parties. However, they disagree about the mechanisms used to produce this outcome. For Dahl, machines rapidly mobilized and paid off ethnic groups with divisible benefits. It was precisely the machine's large-scale distribution of jobs and services to the immigrant working class that was responsible in the pre–New Deal era for defusing the potential of militant labor parties and for delaying demands for collective welfare benefits. The Irish party bosses simply outbid their rivals for working-class political support, beating back the challenge of local labor parties in the late nineteenth century and the Socialist party after the turn of the century.[23]

Our case studies suggest that the pluralist model accurately describes the patronage system's conservatizing effects on assimilated ethnic groups. Patronage helped quell Irish working-class radicalism. The late nineteenth-century machines had little patronage at their disposal to reduce working-class support for local labor parties. The patronage-rich machines of the early twentieth century, in contrast, put the Irish on the city payroll in droves, dimming their enthusiasm for labor politics.

Yet the machine's triumph over militant opponents was a product of more than ethnic assimilation and patronage. Other means of fending off challenges were employed. First, the Irish machines pursued a divide-and-conquer electoral strategy that set ethnic groups at one another's throats. Having discovered a winning electoral formula, mature machines fractured the working class into incorporated and unincorporated ethnic groups. In the pre–New Deal period, the Democratic machines mobilized and rewarded the Irish but not the Jews, Italians, and Slavs. In the post–New Deal period, machines systematically mobilized and rewarded white ethnics but not blacks and Hispanics. Selective incorporation by the machine heightened ethnic conflict, thereby inhibiting unified working-class political action.

In this fashion, the big-city bosses actively participated in reducing the size of the working-class voting universe, thereby increasing any challenger's mobilization costs. Rival parties would have to naturalize, register, and secure the votes of the working-class nonparticipants. In the post-1896 period, entrenched machines abetted capital in insulating the political system from pressures from below that might challenge their respective political and economic hegemonies.

Second, machines split off the ethnic masses from their potential leaders through the process of co-opting the emerging lower-middle class. Michael Rogin has accurately observed that ethnic party and union leaders were more conservative than the ethnic masses.[24] The fragile nineteenth-century machine's maintenance needs forced the early Celtic bosses to placate business by imposing retrenchment on the working class. But as the robust twentieth-century machines inducted ever-more Irish into the patronage system, elite prudence became mass conservatism. The bosses also used tangible benefits to co-opt aspiring non-Irish leaders, splitting emerging ethnic elites off from the masses.

Third, machines used both divisible *and* collective benefits to establish hegemony over the working class. The pluralist model views the two types of benefits as competing with each other; in fact, they were politically complementary. The Irish party bosses allotted their cache of divisible benefits—patronage—to their core constituency—the Irish. The limited divisible leftovers were given to the strongest ethnic challengers at the coalition's periphery. Yet the patronage-based big-city party organizations also supported welfare-state programs. The Irish party bosses lined up behind Progressive-era workman's compensation and factory safety legislation and supported New Deal labor and social welfare programs. Machines supported collective benefit initiatives in part to dampen new immigrant enthusiasm for progressivism, socialism, and anti-machine reform.

Fourth, the pluralist model ignores the machine's darker, repressive side. The bosses used nightsticks as well as patronage carrots to maintain power. Irish-controlled police departments were frequently used to break up labor party and socialist rallies and to discourage insurgents from going to the polls. Where repression failed, corruption succeeded. The machine's labor challengers were all too often counted out at the polls in close elections.

Ira Katznelson has developed an important neopluralist account of the machine's role in fracturing working-class politics. What is distinctive about the American workforce is its conservatism in the community and its militancy in the workplace. In the community, the rapid extension of the vote to white males in the 1820s and 1830s allowed the early machines to incorporate the immigrant working class. In the workplace, the union movement also developed in the permissive political climate of the antebellum period. Then during the postbellum period, ethnic ghettos reinforced the communal logic of machine politics while organized labor continued to woo successive waves of immigrant workers.[25]

Unlike their European counterparts, who struggled simultaneously to acquire the vote *and* to unionize, institutional dynamics, according to Katznelson, encouraged the American working class to develop different ways of thinking and acting in the community and workplace. Neighborhood-based machines encouraged ethnic and racial identification, demands, and organization. Workplace-based unions, however, encouraged a militant class consciousness. This institutional split created a fissure in working-class political attitudes and behavior, hindering the development of a party-class alignment on the European social democratic pattern.[26]

The problem with this "institutional separation" hypothesis is that neither big-city machines nor unions ever fully incorporated the immigrant working class. Both were ethnically exclusive institutions, fracturing the working class into assimilated and non-assimilated groups. As demonstrated in the case studies, machine-umpired ethnic wars of succession in the community pitted older working-class ethnic arrivals against newcomers. Katznelson's community-workplace dichotomy merely aggravated more fundamental ethnic-class discords orchestrated by political elites.

Organized labor also fought its own internal wars of ethnic succession. Wendy Mink has shown a similar pattern of newcomer exclusion practiced by unions in the late nineteenth and early twentieth centuries. "Trade union nativism" characterized the labor politics of the period. To protect existing union prerogatives and to guarantee jobs for Irish, Yankee, and German union members, the conservative craft union leadership excluded Southern and Eastern Europeans. With the Irish-led old immigrants dominating the big-city craft unions, Jews turned to organizing the needle trades. Later, the Southern and Eastern Europeans would be active participants in organizing the insurgent industrial unions (the CIO) that would challenge the craft unions of the AFL for leadership of the labor movement.[27]

The Katznelson hypothesis is further weakened when we consider the tacit alliance constructed between the Irish machines and the Irish-controlled trade unions. In the Democratic-controlled cities, machine-union ties were forged in the late nineteenth century, creating additional obstacles to party-class alignments. The partnership had a strong caste overlay. The Irish controlled the northern Democratic machines and headed more than half of the big-city American Federation of Labor locals.[28]

But the alliance was as much a product of mutual self-interest as it was an expression of ethnic primordialism. Bosses could do much for local unions. Sympathetic judges and police hampered the ability of capital to break strikes and boycotts. The construction industry, backbone of the early big-city labor movement, valued public works projects. Union officials appointed to public works boards ensured that these projects bore the union label. Unions could do much for the bosses. Tacit alliances co-opted organized labor and its vote, thereby weakening labor party challenges. In turn, machine protection strengthened labor's hand relative to capital, encouraging the very militancy in the workplace that the separation hypothesis takes as a given.

Structural tensions within the working class, then, were as much horizontal as vertical. Katznelson subscribes to a vertical conflict between party-based ethnic divisions in the community and union-based class divisions in the workplace. But there were cross-cutting cleavages. The early machines and craft unions worked in tandem to fracture the working class, pitting an ethnic "aristocracy of labor and politics" against later arrivals. Institutional and ethnic hegemony represented twin motive forces producing these horizontal political fissures.

The Revisionist Account

Pluralism's critics have developed a variant interpretation for the failure of working-class radicalism. Two arguments stand out in the revisionist model. First, the critics downplay the magnitude of the challenge by placing great store in the conservatism of the European peasant immigrants. For revisionists, the cautious immigrants eschewed radical politics. The uprooted also appeared unmoved by populist and progressive insurgency.

Second, the party system performed a different buffering role for the masses than bread-and-butter pluralism allows. For Wolfinger, the party system "horizontally divided" ethnic groups by accommodating in limited fashion the tangible demands of their emerging middle-class leadership strata while denying the masses anything but the intangibles of symbolic recognition. Placing ethnic leaders in high offices was the sine qua non of recognition politics. Recognition, in turn, muted class politics. Symbolic gratification diverted attention from material needs and demands. Group recognition also heightened the salience of ethnic consciousness, thus inhibiting the development of cross-ethnic class consciousness.[29]

There are problems with the revisionist argument. For one thing, it exaggerates the immigrants' conservatism. In the cities, the Irish and German working class supported local labor parties in the 1870s and 1880s. In the twentieth century, the new immigrants endorsed progressive candidates such as Theodore Roosevelt, Woodrow Wilson, and Hiram Johnson. New York City's Jews and Milwaukee's Germans were ardent supports of the Socialist party. In the countryside, Scandinavian farmers supported populism and progressivism.

For another thing, the theory underplays the machine's very real carrots and sticks. Machines specialized in supplying tangible benefits to their core ethnic supporters, reserving "recognition" for weak groups excluded from a meaningful share of power and patronage. If the manipulation of symbols was the essence of machine politics, why did the bosses work so tirelessly to increase their stock of material benefits? Machines also used repression and corruption to prevent leftist parties from winning elections. Far from eschewing radical politics, the immigrants were frequently denied the opportunity of choosing.

Finally, the theory overestimates the potency of symbolic appeals to ethnic groups. Riding the crest of group mobilization, aspiring ethnic elites found they had to satisfy group material needs as well as status yearnings. The carriers of symbolic politics were normally the status-conscious nouveau middle classes, not the huddled ethnic masses. Working-class immigrants demanded substantive, not merely formal, representation. La Guardia, for example, embarked on an ambitious program of civil service reform and human service spending to create the jobs and services needed to reward his ethnic supporters and to create a durable electoral coalition.

Machine Redistribution
Historically Reconsidered

In the 1980s, public choice economists joined the revisionist camp. Taking his cue from economic theory, Paul Peterson has made a powerful case against local redistributional politics machine-style. Peterson's approach can best be considered neorevisionist as he borrows from the revisionists the "output" argument that local institutions like the machine can do little to redistribute wealth from the rich to the poor, while taking from the pluralists the "input" argument of extensive ethnic group bargaining over allocational issues such as public employment.[30]

For Peterson, economics shapes policy, and policy shapes patterns of urban political decision making and participation. The Petersonian model divides urban policymaking into three parts: developmental, redistributional, and allocational.[31] Developmental policies promoting economic growth are the city's raison d'être. With permeable economies and mobile capital, cities find themselves in a competitive sweepstakes with other locales. To promote prosperity, local politicians offer investors favorable taxation and expenditure policies. Because capital can flee in reaction to unfavorable taxation-benefit ratios, local leaders avoid redistributional transfers from the rich to the poor. Public employment and service policies are allocational policies—the essence of machine politics. Unlike developmental and redistributional policies, their economic impact on the city's market position is limited and uncertain.[32]

Different patterns of political decision making and participation characterize the three policy arenas. Developmental policies feature covert business-political elite alliances. Decision making is done in private, and conflict is kept to a minimum. Redistributional policies represent a species of local nondecision making. Local elites keep them off the urban political agenda, kicking them upstairs to the state and national levels. With greater control of the economy, national decision makers can tax capital to pay for welfare-state programs for the needy. An intermediate category in the policy tug of war between the imperatives of growth and redistribution, allocational policies are the stuff of local public decision making. In the pluralist arena, community groups bargain with local decision makers over their relative shares of public jobs and services.[33]

In this neorevisionist model, the machine serves as the allocational device par excellence. Even for party bosses, economic priorities take precedence over political imperatives. The city's economic well-being has higher standing than the machine's maintenance needs. Accordingly, the machine heeds the business community more than the working class. The taxation and expenditure policies needed to promote development sharply constrain the machine's redistributional capacity. As a result, the machine uses ethnic-racial appeals as a strategy to convert redistributive demands into allocational contests over job and service distribution—group contests that can be won or lost without fundamental alteration in the urban capitalist political economy.[34]

Even the machine-reformer conflict is sanitized from the taint of redistributional class politics in this model. For reformers, the primary antimachine issues were corruption and patronage, not the bosses' predatory taxation of property owners. The merit system served as the reformers' consensual holy grail. In the Petersonian scheme of things, the reform-machine conflict over public employment practices was another group allocational issue. But contrary to Peterson the charge of machine corruption had indelible class components. The issue deeply split the business community, as entrepreneurs benefited from the bosses' easing of the legal obstacles to capital formation. Turning a blind eye to "white-collar crime" benefiting members of the business community, reformers instead excoriated the evils of the blue-collar ethnic patronage system.[35]

How accurate is the Petersonian model of the machine, its primarily allocational character, and the limited possibilities for local redistributional policies? The model is rooted in the post–New Deal present, yet claims to speak for the pre–New Deal past. Since the 1930s, developments have taken place that confirm essential elements of the approach. New Deal and Great Society welfare-state programs have highlighted the national government's redistributional role. The creation of national and international markets coupled with new technologies have given capital undreamed-of mobility opportunities. With the American economy stalled in the 1970s, growth became the centerpiece of the domestic political agenda. With highly permeable local economies, a new generation of municipal development specialists competed with one another to entice investors to their city with evermore favorable taxation and policy packages.[36]

But what of the past? Peterson freezes his subject matter in time, treats the transient present as permanent, and fails to appreciate the virtues of a dynamic view of the contingent relationship between present and past. Consider his intergovernmental theory of redistributional policy. For Peterson, nationals redistribute; locals do not. But in the pre–New Deal period, it was precisely the locals who did and the state and nationals who did not. The big-city Irish Democratic machines constantly faced redistributional pressures from below. State and national governments, particularly when controlled by the GOP or reform Democrats, were the biggest *obstacles* to local redistribution.

In the early twentieth century, the Irish machines did serve as limited redistributional devices, taxing business and the middle class in order to put lower-middle class Irish on the city payroll. The patronage practices of the Hague machine—and the taxes needed to support his Irish version of the welfare state—were, as his reform opponent argued, a redistributional issue.

Claiming to offer an intergovernmental perspective on urban politics, Peterson instead reifies the different governmental levels, treating them more like alien essences than as dynamic components of an ever-changing core-periphery system. His picture of how redistributional issues have been kept out of local politics distorts the historical record and accepts as a "given" emerging differences between local and national arenas that, instead, have to be explained.

A more historically oriented model would recognize how nine-teenth-century big-city politics significantly diverged from the Petersonian model. As Amy Bridges points out, during the heyday of the second party system, national policy debates and federal patronage sources were the very stuff of New York City politics.[37] With the breakup of the second party system and continuing after the Civil War, local politics developed its own autonomous partisan structure and policy agenda. Yet, contrary to Peterson, these changes, at least for a generation or two, made city governments more—not less—responsive than the federal government to redistributive pressures and initiatives.

Changes initiated during the Progressive era and accelerated during the New Deal period—the welfare state—gradually insulated city governments from redistributional pressures and moved urban political issues such as public employment within the "allocational" parameters that the Peterson model takes as an unchanging datum. If local politics "stayed the same"—and the lid was kept on local insurgent forces—the reason was that local political elites and newly mobilized lower-class claimants in the 1930s and 1960s generated political forces that made the federal government expand its role.

A more historically oriented model would also appreciate how big-city economies were more susceptible than at present to local redistributional politics. In the late nineteenth and early twentieth centuries, much of the urban economy was local. Business owners were captives of local markets and customers, unable to move freely as tax burdens shifted. It was precisely their geographical immobility that propelled them into active political involvement, making them guardians of the city treasury.

Capital tied to national markets was less interested in local politics. But even national businesses could be incorporated into local redistributional schemes. Some national businesses were geographically immobile and thus subject to local tax extortion. Needing terminal space in Jersey City in order to transfer freight to New York City, the country's major railroads were forced to pass along the high cost of Boss Hague's welfare state to their customers. In the postwar era, however, the growth of markets and technologies has given capital the upper hand vis-à-vis local political elites that it previously lacked.[38]

The real problem with the Peterson model is that it substitutes a reified citywide economic logic for political and institutional imperatives. Class interpretations of urban politics sometimes commit the sin of reductionism—reducing structures and policies to the mere reflex of the groups that articulate them. Peterson, however, surrenders to the opposite, hedgehog-like vice of economically reifying "the interests of the city, taken as a whole," independent of underlying political institutions and forces.[39]

Political machines are a cardinal case in point. The big-city bosses responded to contradictory economic pressures in terms of a political logic of building the governing alliances and electoral coalitions needed to maintain the organization in power. The weak nineteenth-century Irish bosses had bowed to business pressures, risking insurgency from below. The strong early twentieth-century bosses played to the "old" ethnic working class, imposing the cost of redistribution on property owners. Capital's position in the urban political economy had become increasingly precarious. Working-class renters could vote; absentee suburban property owners could not. Bosses increased the tax rate—supposedly injurious to the economic health of the city as whole—to maintain the political health of the party organization and its working-class electoral base. Bosses subsequently cut back on tax hikes when faced with political reprisal—taxpayer revolts—rather than investment strikes.

Having treated the highly circumscribed boundaries of contemporary city politics as a given, Peterson finally reverses himself, concluding that, after all, our federal system is an "aberration" and that "city limits" can be transcended by such tinkering as putting the full faith and credit of the federal government behind all state and local governmental indebtedness. However, he never ventures a searching historical explanation of why our aberrant federal system developed in the way it did.

From the Founding Fathers on, federalism has been, among other things, a strategy to kick class-based issues upstairs and thus keep them out of arenas—like local politics—that are "too close to home" to allow safe resolution. Creating a powerful national government that, ultimately, might become an instrument of redistribution as well as of growth was the risk taken by Hamiltonians intent on restricting the operation of redistributional forces such as the ethnically based machines in the state and local arenas.[40]

Today's Big-City Rainbow Politics:
Machines Revividus?

In the past twenty years the baton of urban power has slowly been passed to the third- and fourth-generation ethnic arrivals—blacks, Hispanics, and Asians. Black mayors have been elected in Los Angeles, Chicago, Philadelphia, Detroit, Atlanta, Washington, Cleveland, Gary, Newark, and New Orleans. Blacks have also been elected in large numbers to city councils and school boards. The new black power is bureaucratic as well as electoral. In the big cities, black administrators have been appointed to such top policy-making positions as city manager, police chief, and school superintendent.[41]

In the Sunbelt, Hispanics and Asians are beginning to transform urban political life. San Antonio's voters in 1981 elected Henry Cisneros as the first Mexican-American mayor of a major U.S. city. Miami has a Cuban-American mayor and a Hispanic majority on the city council. Reversing a century-old legacy of racism and discrimination against Asians, California's cities are witnessing the first stirrings of Asian-American power. Los Angeles's voters elected Michael Woo to the city council, and San Francisco Mayor Dianne Feinstein appointed Thomas Hsieh to the city's Board of Supervisors.[42]

As the new minorities mobilize, particularly the black and Mexican-American communities with large lower-class populations, they have searched for strategies of group uplift. The viability of the machine model was problematic for the new groups. Before the 1960s, minorities were deliberately kept out of the established system of "city trenches." Except for a few independent politicians such as New York's Adam Clayton Powell, the legacy of the machine era for blacks was "plantation politics" Chicago-style. When the minority assault finally came, the old-style party organizations were in the last stages of decline.[43]

In the postmachine era, the prizes of urban politics seemed hollow indeed. The northern cities where blacks had migrated in massive numbers had experienced economic decline, their treasuries nearing bankruptcy. The rapidly growing Sunbelt cities had small, lean public sectors (the legacy of conservative reformers), limiting government job opportunities. To make matters worse, white civil service commissioners and municipal union stewards zealously guarded the prerogatives of the heavily white public sector work-force, making it difficult for minorities to translate political gains into economic advancement.[44]

Even the means of ethnic capture were more difficult. The new minorities were the victims of reform. In the process of wresting power from the Irish, the Southern and Eastern Europeans had created additional barriers for later-arriving groups. The second-wave ethnics joined Yankee reformers in bringing to the eastern cities the reforms first implemented by progressives in the West and South: at-large city council elections, nonpartisanship, educa-tional requirements for public employment, and expanded civil service coverage. At-large electoral systems, in particular, made it harder for blacks to gain representation on city councils. Designed to prevent the machine's reemergence, reforms also made it more difficult for working-class blacks and Hispanics to gain group in-fluence and benefits.[45]

In this bleak age of reform, a possible return to machine politics didn't seem so bad after all. Black politicians in particular called for the machine's resurrection in part or in toto. During the 1960s, black moderates committed to "working within the system" had embraced the Irish model of group electoral politics to counter radical separatist demands. The radical rhetoric of militant nation-alism and community control ultimately proved an empty threat, revealing an incrementalist and patronage core that could be ac-commodated as the emerging black bourgeoisie took over such community institutions as schools and health clinics. By the 1970s, blacks of diverse ideological inclinations had moved "from protest to politics," emulating the strategy of ethnic group mobilization—registration, turnout, and bloc voting en masse—first perfected by the Irish.[46]

To appeal to both militants and moderates in the minority com-munity, contemporary black politicians disingenuously coupled radical-reformist rhetoric with venerable machine-building tech-niques designed to enhance group influence and payoffs. Claiming that at-large electoral systems discriminated against racial minor-ities, followers of rainbow "reformer" Jesse Jackson in cities such as Pittsburgh and Cincinnati have pursued the machine gambit of reviving the ward system. Chicago's "antimachine" Mayor Harold

Washington ransacked city hall and special district governments for additional patronage to pay off his supporters and consolidate power. Reformer Washington also vigorously opposed a move to make the city's elections nonpartisan.[47]

Are black politicians correct in looking to the machine past? What lessons could the departed Irish bosses offer today's minorities about group influence, electoral coalition building, and economic advancement through local politics? Moynihan has argued that the twentieth-century black experience needs to be understood in terms of a critical comparison with the nineteenth-century Irish experience.[48]

Both groups have tried their hand at public sector politics, seeking governmental channels of group mobility. The Irish political experience cannot fully be emulated by blacks because the big-city machines—centralized party structures—are unlikely to be revived in anything like their historical form. Yet machine politics—the trading in divisible benefits—has staying power in local politics. The Irish bosses were the undisputed masters of this game. Can their example educate today's minority power brokers about both the possibilities and the limits of ethnic politics?

On the positive side, the Irish experience demonstrates some potential for group economic uplift through the local political process. The votes of the Irish working class could be translated into group power and a major share of city jobs and services. The twentieth-century Celtic municipal engines served as modest redistributional devices, reallocating economic burdens and benefits within the middle of the class structure. To the extent that the Irish bosses were Robin Hoods, they were selective about their victims and beneficiaries. Rather than taking from the very rich and giving to the very poor, the Irish politicos took from the Yankee middle class and gave to the lower-middle-class payroll Irish.

On the negative side, the Irish machines were as much instruments of social control as of economic reward. The nineteenth-century Irish bosses imposed retrenchment on their followers as the price of keeping power. Black mayors are under the same fiscal constraints today. Retrenchment produced ideological-class schisms among the Irish in the 1880s and is doing the same for blacks in the 1980s. The conflict between Tammany's conservative "long-hair" Irish faction and the militant working-class "short-hairs" finds contemporary expression in the tensions between moderate black mayors and militant followers of the Jacksonian rainbow.

The early Irish bosses parsimoniously accommodated later arrivals on the rainbow bandwagon. With limited resources and pressing group demands, black politicians may have to do the same with Hispanics and Asians. The down-side risk of today's slow-growth politics is that the new rainbow coalition may produce a small pot of gold for the black political elite, while browns, yellows, and even the black underclass are left chasing the mirage.

Concluding the Irish-black comparison on an even more pessimistic note, what will urban politics look like at century's end if present trends in conservative national politics and uneven regional economic development continue? Will big-city minority politicians in declining Frostbelt cities be called on to implement an updated "System of '96"—for 1996? Will black leaders soothe the "mixed multitudes" with populist rhetoric while cutting deals with conservative national politicians? And will federally funded "urban enterprise zones" prove to be the newest species of "plantation politics" designed to discipline the have-nots? Big-city minority politicians might have to take a lesson from the Christian Democratic party bosses of stagnant Palermo after all.

Blacks are now emulating the Irish by using political strategies of group uplift. The means employed, however, are different. The Irish used the big-city party organizations; blacks use local and national bureaucracies. The locus of urban power has shifted from political machines to independent and semiautonomous bureaucracies, organized along functional lines. Furthermore, urban politics has been nationalized. In the post–New Deal era, the political access and economic distribution functions once monopolized by local machines now are nationally performed by the Democratic party and federal welfare-state bureaucracies.[49]

Peter Eisinger finds black mayors pursuing a dual strategy of group advancement in this new arena of urban politics. The first prong consists of the politics of public sector bureaucracies. Black leaders in cities such as Detroit and Atlanta have used their appointment powers to name minorities to head city personnel departments and other major agencies. Minority administrators, in turn, have launched aggressive affirmative action programs, producing a dramatic increase in the minority share of public employment. Black mayors are also using affirmative action to award city contracts to minority businesses. Newark's former Mayor Kenneth Gibson, for example, set aside 25 percent of all federal public works project monies for minority contractors.[50]

The second prong consists of a strategy of "trickle down" from private sector economic growth. Black mayors in Los Angeles, Chicago, Detroit, Washington, Atlanta, and Newark have formed alliances with the white business community to promote downtown redevelopment, hoping to create private sector job opportunities for minorities.

The Irish experience suggests the limits of this dual strategy. On the public sector side, the approach has a major down-side risk—retrenchment. The Irish were the principal beneficiaries of city payroll growth from 1900 to 1929; after 1929, however, they were also the victims of retrenchment. Blacks clearly benefited from the halcyon municipal employment growth of the 1960s and early 1970s. The late 1970s, however, brought municipal austerity, threatening to reverse black city payroll gains. As the last hired, minorities were frequently the first victims of budgetary cutbacks. Detroit's black Mayor Coleman Young, for example, was forced by budget-balancing pressures to fire hundreds of minority police, undoing in a single afternoon ten years of hard-fought affirmative action in police hiring.

Black politicians and civil servants may also face a political challenge to their power and prerogatives. In the 1930s and 1940s, the Irish machine's jerry-built rainbow coalition unraveled as the new immigrants countermobilized, jeopardizing the jobs of thousands of Irish payrollers. In the 1990s, Asian-Americans and Hispanics could challenge blacks for control of the big cities, particularly if black politicians are unable or unwilling to share power and patronage. With a large and prosperous middle class, Asian-Americans in particular might assume the broker role, financing and leading an Asian-Hispanic coalition that could threaten today's black municipal workers.

The Irish experience also suggests caution regarding the extent of "trickle down" to the black masses from publicly subsidized private sector growth. Public investment in urban infrastructure was the early equivalent of today's publicly assisted downtown redevelopment projects. Public works contracts benefited individual Irish contractors while providing temporary low-wage employment for the masses of unskilled and semiskilled Irish workers.

Today, black mayors offer public seed money, tax and zoning abatements, and lease-back arrangements to downtown developers. Ambitious redevelopment projects like Detroit's Renaissance Center and Atlanta's Peachtree Plaza are sold to minorities and the poor on the premise that economic benefits—primarily in the form of job opportunities—will filter down to them. But new convention centers, hotels, and shopping centers are not a viable vehicle of group uplift. Too few jobs are created to make an appreciable dent in inner-city poverty. The limited pool of high-paying professional and managerial positions disproportionately goes to upper-middle-class white suburbanites. Minority "trickle down" has primarily taken the form of a limited number of low-wage service jobs.[51]

There is a vital third element to today's black advancement strategy—federal social programs. Both Irish and black politicians have used the expanding welfare state to consolidate power. The nascent Irish Democratic machines of the 1930s fused with New Deal programs. A generation later, the Great Society served as a catalyst for black power. Studying minority politics in ten northern California cities, Rufus Browning, Dale Marshall, and David Tabb argue that the Great Society programs "provided the functional equivalent of earlier forms of patronage." In the Bay Area cities, federal social initiatives encouraged minority political mobilization, promoted their incorporation into local governing coalitions, and secured greater local governmental responsiveness to minority job and service demands.[52]

The expanding welfare state was more than a vehicle for black assimilation into local politics. It was a primary route of group *economic* advancement. Where the Irish had used machine patronage, blacks now relied on federally funded social programs. In the 1960s and early 1970s, the new black middle class found jobs in the expanding federally funded human services sector—health, education, and welfare. By the late 1970s, nearly half of all black professionals and managers worked in the social welfare sector, compared with less than one-quarter of comparably situated whites.[53]

The welfare state meant more than jobs for the black middle class; it also represented cash and in-kind welfare payments for the underclass. From the mid-1960s onward, the black poor increasingly relied on transfer payments. Two-thirds of poor black families received welfare in the late 1970s, up from one-third in the late 1960s. Economically, blacks were more integrated into the public sector in the late 1970s than the Irish had been during the machine's heyday—but under *federal* and *bureaucratic* auspices.[54]

But black politicians lack integrating mechanisms like the machine that can fuse together the disparate elements of today's urban politics—national versus local, bureaucratic versus electoral. As a result, big-city and minority politics reflect their unreconciled imperatives. The continued flow of welfare-state jobs, transfer payments, and social services, which sustain the black middle class and underclass, depend on group influence and alliance building at the national and state levels where social policy is made and funded. Blacks, however, are not as well organized to press their claims outside the local political arena.

In the absence of local machines capable of mobilizing voters, bureaucratic politics has acted as a depressant on electoral participation. The relationship between the bureaucratic service provider and the recipient differs from the relationship between the party cadre and the voter. Precinct workers are encouraged to mobilize loyal voters on election day. Human service workers, however, have little incentive to politically mobilize their clientele—as long as social programs and budgets grow. In the 1970s, minority service providers increasingly involved themselves in bureaucratic politics within the intergovernmental grant system rather than in mobilizing their clientele in local electoral politics. The expansion of means-tested programs such as AFDC depoliticized welfare recipients by isolating them from the work experiences encouraging political participation.[55]

Whatever the Great Society's initial mobilization effect, it soon acted as a brake on black voter turnout. During the period of welfare-state expansion, from 1964 to 1976, the mass electoral base of black politics in the northern cities eroded. The voting rate for young urban blacks plummeted, from 56 percent to 29 percent, while the rate for unemployed blacks dropped nearly as sharply, from 62 percent to 37 percent. Low turnout hurt big-city

black politicians seeking to challenge white-controlled machine
and reform regimes.[56]

Welfare-state contraction in the 1980s, however, reversed the
bureaucratic expansion-electoral decline cycle. Threatened with
job and benefit loss by the Reagan cutbacks, minority social service providers and recipients quickly rediscovered the value of electoral politics. Though primarily generated by national forces, the
remobilization drive could be used in local politics. In machine
Chicago and reform Philadelphia, black mayoral candidates rode
the electoral surge to victory.

It is ironic that the policies of a president who points to his Irish
ancestry during campaigns helped to produce the last hurrah for
the Irish Democratic machines. Black mayors have ridden the turbulent waves of Reaganite austerity into office. Yet the practitioners of the new ethnic politics are trying to consolidate power
with limited local resources and diminished welfare-state largesse.
Lacking the tangible benefits demanded by their supporters, the
new minority power brokers may discover what was learned the
hard way by the now-departed Irish bosses: the real lessons at rainbow's end.

Notes

All works that appear in abbreviated form in the
notes are cited in full in the bibliography.

Chapter One

1. Daniel Patrick Moynihan, "The Irish," in Nathan Glazer and Daniel Patrick Moynihan, *Beyond the Melting Pot,* pp. 217–287.

2. James Bryce, *The American Commonwealth,* pp. 101–135; Harold Zink, *City Bosses in the United States.*

3. John Paul Bobcock, "The Irish Conquest of Our Cities," pp. 186–195.

4. Edward M. Levine, *The Irish and Irish Politicians,* pp. 138, 142–143.

5. Lincoln Steffens, *The Shame of the Cities,* pp. 136–138.

6. Ibid., pp. 5, 16–18.

7. Frederick C. Howe, *The City: The Hope of Democracy,* pp. 61–91.

8. M. Ostrogorski, *Democracy and the American Party System,* pp. 225–281.

9. See Robert K. Merton, *Social Theory and Social Structure,* pp. 125–136; Robert A. Dahl, *Who Governs? Democracy and Power in an American City,* pp. 32–62. The rainbow theory of the machine also figures prominently in Elmer E. Cornwell, "Bosses, Machines, and Ethnic Groups," pp. 27–39; and in the Kerner Commission's findings in U.S. National Advisory Commission on Civil Disorders, *Report,* pp. 143–145.

10. Steven P. Erie, "Politics, the Public Sector, and Irish Social Mobility: San Francisco, 1870–1900," pp. 274–289.

11. Dahl, *Who Governs?* pp. 40–42; Steven P. Erie, "Two Faces of Ethnic Power: Comparing the Irish and Black Experiences," pp. 263, 272.

12. For evidence of Irish big-city public employment gains, see Carl Wittke, *The Irish in America,* pp. 108–110; Terry Nichols Clark, "The Irish Ethic and the Spirit of Patronage," pp. 327–343. The figures for 1870 and 1900 are reported in U.S. Census Office, *Ninth Census, 1870,* vol. 1, Tables 29, 32; and U.S. Bureau of the Census, *Special Reports: Occupations at the Twelfth Census,* Tables 41, 43.

13. Charles V. Hamilton, "Blacks and the Crisis of Political Participation," pp. 191–193. A sizable body of black power literature uses the

legend of Irish power in this fashion. For representative discussions, see Harold Cruse, *The Crisis of the Negro Intellectual: From Its Origins to the Present,* pp. 315–316; Chuck Stone, *Black Political Power in America,* pp. 110–118; James P. Comer, "The Social Power of the Negro," in Floyd B. Barbour, ed., *The Black Power Revolt,* pp. 72–84; and Robert M. Fogelson, *Violence as Protest,* pp. 128–137.

14. Levine, *Irish and Irish Politicians,* p. 185.

15. Andrew Greeley, *That Most Distressful Nation: The Taming of the American Irish,* pp. 122–128; Andrew Greeley, *Ethnicity, Denomination, and Inequality,* pp. 54–55.

16. Edward C. Banfield and James Q. Wilson, *City Politics,* pp. 33–46, 115–127; James Q. Wilson and Edward C. Banfield, "Public-Regardingness as a Value Premise in Voting Behavior," pp. 876–887; Glazer and Moynihan, *Beyond the Melting Pot,* pp. 223–229.

17. Martin Shefter, "The Emergence of the Political Machine: An Alternative View," in Willis Hawley et al., eds., *Theoretical Perspectives on Urban Politics,* pp. 14–44.

18. William L. Riordan, comp., *Plunkitt of Tammany Hall,* p. 17.

19. Rexford Tugwell, *The Brains Trust,* pp. 366–371; Edwin O'Connor, *The Last Hurrah,* pp. 329–330.

20. Regarding labor in Detroit politics, see J. David Greenstone, *Labor in American Politics,* pp. 110–140.

21. For New Haven, see Dahl, *Who Governs?* pp. 32–62; Raymond E. Wolfinger, *The Politics of Progress,* pp. 30–129; and Jerome K. Myers, "Assimilation in the Political Community," pp. 175–182. For Providence, see Elmer E. Cornwell, "Party Absorption of Ethnic Groups: The Case of Providence, Rhode Island," pp. 205–210; Elmer E. Cornwell, "Some Occupational Patterns in Party Committee Membership," pp. 87–98; and Leo E. Carroll, "Irish and Italians in Providence, Rhode Island, 1880–1960," pp. 67–74.

22. Dennis Clark, *The Irish in Philadelphia: Ten Generations of Urban Experience,* p. 172.

23. Bryce, *American Commonwealth,* p. 115.

Chapter Two

1. Oliver MacDonaugh, "The Irish Famine Emigration to the United States," pp. 430–433.

2. For representative definitions of the machine, see Edward C. Banfield and James Q. Wilson, *City Politics,* pp. 115–117; James C. Scott, "Corruption, Machine Politics, and Political Change," pp. 1143–1145;

Raymond E. Wolfinger, "Why Political Machines Have Not Withered Away and Other Revisionist Thoughts," pp. 374–375. For a definition stressing nonmaterial as well as material rewards, see Fred I. Greenstein, "The Changing Pattern of Urban Party Politics," pp. 2–3.

3. For an excellent analysis of the building of Tammany Hall in the antebellum era, see Amy Bridges, *A City in the Republic.*

4. Based on a surname analysis. For lists of Democratic party leaders, see *San Francisco Evening Bulletin,* September 15, 1886; Chicago Daily News, *Almanac, 1891,* p. 299; New York World, *World Almanac, 1893,* p. 331.

5. Daniel Patrick Moynihan, "The Irish," in Nathan Glazer and Daniel Patrick Moynihan, *Beyond the Melting Pot,* pp. 223–226.

6. For an analysis of the differences between Irish and Irish-American politics, see Thomas N. Brown, "The Political Irish: Politicians and Rebels," in David Noel Doyle and Owen Dudley Edwards, eds., *America and Ireland, 1776–1976,* pp. 133–150.

7. Martin Shefter, "The Emergence of the Political Machine: An Alternative View," in Willis Hawley et al., eds., *Theoretical Perspectives on Urban Politics,* pp. 14–44. Also see David R. Cameron, "Toward a Theory of Political Mobilization," pp. 140–142.

8. Robert E. Kennedy, Jr., *The Irish: Emigration, Marriage, and Fertility,* pp. 20–21.

9. Emmet Larkin, "Church, State, and Nation in Modern Ireland," pp. 1248–1251.

10. Donald H. Akenson, *The Irish Educational Experiment,* pp. 49–56, 202–213, 376–391.

11. On German-American politics, see Frederick C. Luebke, *Immigrants and Politics: The Germans of Nebraska, 1880–1900,* pp. 179–185; Carl Wittke, *Refugees of Revolution,* pp. 203–218.

12. Robert Kelley, *The Cultural Patterns in American Politics,* pp. 154–155, 172, 187. Tammany Hall is normally credited with using this patronage strategy to win Irish votes. However, it was first used against Tammany. In the 1820s, gubernatorial candidate DeWitt Clinton successfully outbid Tammany for Irish votes with promises of construction jobs on the Erie Canal.

13. Ibid., pp. 172–173.

14. Steven P. Erie, "The Development of Class and Ethnic Politics in San Francisco, 1870–1910: A Critique of the Pluralist Interpretation," Tables 5.11, 5.12, pp. 293–296.

15. Frederick A. Bushee, *Ethnic Factors in the Population of Boston,* Table 31, p. 124; Chicago Daily News, *Almanac, 1894,* p. 318 (nationality of registered foreign-born voters); U.S. Census Office, *Eleventh Cen-*

sus of the United States, 1890, vol. 1, pt. 1: Table 34, p. 670, Table 78, p. 752; vol. 1, pt. 2: Table 72, p. 282, Table 74, p. 288.

16. James C. Mohr, *The Radical Republicans and Reform in New York During Reconstruction*, pp. 208–209, 219–223, 235–238.

17. Jerome Mushkat, *The Reconstruction of the New York Democracy, 1861–1874*, pp. 145–146, 163–164.

18. Gustavus Myers, *History of Tammany Hall*, pp. 183, 187, 211.

19. Mohr, *Radical Republicans*, pp. 23–24, 84, 106–111; Mushkat, *Reconstruction*, pp. 64–65, 93.

20. Douglas V. Shaw, *The Making of an Immigrant City: Ethnic and Cultural Conflict in Jersey City, New Jersey, 1850–1877*, pp. 113, 217.

21. Jerome Mushkat, *Tammany: The Evolution of a Political Machine, 1789–1865*, pp. 82–83, 96–99, 110–111, 116, 128–135, 143–144; Herbert Bass, "The Politics of Ballot Reform in New York State, 1888–1890," pp. 253–272.

22. Herbert Bass, *"I Am a Democrat": The Political Career of David Bennett Hill*, pp. 82–83, 96–99, 110–111, 128–135, 143–144.

23. John Kincaid, "Political Success and Policy Failure: The Persistence of Machine Politics in Jersey City," p. 433.

24. R. Hal Williams, *The Democratic Party and California Politics, 1880–1896*, pp. 24–26, 102–105.

25. Geoffrey Blodgett, *The Gentle Reformers: Massachusetts Democrats in the Cleveland Era*, pp. 60, 64–69, 141, 143, 149–153. For accounts of the political mobilization of the Irish in Boston and of the nativist reaction, see Peter K. Eisinger, *The Politics of Displacement: Racial and Ethnic Transition in Three American Cities*, pp. 29–54; and Oscar Handlin, *Boston's Immigrants: A Study in Acculturation*, pp. 191–206.

26. John F. Stack, Jr., *International Conflict in an American City*, pp. 32–33; Richard H. Abbott, "Massachusetts: Maintaining Hegemony," in James C. Mohr, ed., *Radical Republicans in the North: State Politics During Reconstruction*, pp. 5–8, 18.

27. Richard Harmond, "The 'Beast' in Boston: Benjamin F. Butler as Governor of Massachusetts," pp. 267–268; Blodgett, *Gentle Reformers*, pp. 15, 18.

28. Harold U. Faulkner, *Politics, Reform, and Expansion, 1890–1900*, pp. 94–110; Blodgett, *Gentle Reformers*, pp. 84–93, 154 (O'Neill quote).

29. Murray B. Levin, *The Compleat Politician: Political Strategy in Massachusetts*, p. 17; Joseph F. Dineen, *The Purple Shamrock: The Honorable James Michael Curley of Boston*, pp. 17, 25, 29; Blodgett, *Gentle Reformers*, pp. 26–28, 30, 109–113, 166–170.

30. Richard M. Abrams, *Conservatism in a Progressive Era: Massachusetts Politics, 1900–1912*, pp. 44–45, 119, 168.

31. For a discussion of how state politics shaped the evolution of big-city machines, see Kincaid, "Political Success," pp. 24–26, 60, 95, 217–225.

32. Dennis Clark, *The Irish in Philadelphia: Ten Generations of Urban Experience*, pp. 120–121, 136–141, 172. For an analysis of the state Republican machine, see James A. Kehl, *Boss Rule in the Gilded Age: Matt Quay of Pennsylvania*.

33. Lincoln Steffens, *The Shame of the Cities*, pp. 138, 142–143.

34. Matthew Josephson, *The Politicos, 1865–1896*, pp. 87–99.

35. Paul Michael Green, "The Chicago Democratic Party, 1840–1920: From Factionalism to Political Organization," pp. 16, 33–34, 89–92; Lloyd Wendt and Herman Kogan, *Bosses in Lusty Chicago: The Story of Bathhouse John and Hinky Dink*, pp. 200–207, 239–241.

36. Ray Ginger, *Altgeld's America: The Lincoln Ideal Versus Changing Realities*, pp. 71–72, 168–169; Carter H. Harrison, Jr., *Stormy Years*, pp. 39–41.

37. For evidence of Irish-American preferences for higher urban public expenditures as compared with other ethnic groups, see Terry Nichols Clark, "The Irish Ethic and the Spirit of Patronage," pp. 327–343; James J. Vanecko and Jennie Kronenfeld, "Preferences for Public Expenditures and Ethno-Racial Group Membership: A Test of the Theory of Political Ethos," pp. 311–366; and John W. Foley, "Community Structure and Public Policy Outputs in 300 Eastern American Communities: Toward a Sociology of the Public Sector," pp. 222–234. For an analysis of turn-of-the-century expenditures in medium-sized cities, see J. Rogers Hollingsworth and Ellen Jane Hollingsworth, "Expenditures in American Cities," in William O. Aydelotte et al., eds., *The Dimensions of Quantitative Research in History*, pp. 347–389.

38. Martin Shefter, "New York City's Fiscal Crisis: The Politics of Inflation and Retrenchment," pp. 101–105.

39. M. R. Werner, *Tammany Hall*, p. 276; Myers, *History of Tammany Hall*, pp. 254–256.

40. William A. Bullough, *The Blind Boss and His City: Christopher Augustine Buckley and Nineteenth-Century San Francisco*, pp. 92, 136. For contemporary accounts of Buckley's rule, see Jeremiah Lynch, *Buckleyism: The Government of a State*; and *San Francisco Morning Call*, November 10, 1892.

41. Arthur Genen, "John Kelly: New York's First Irish Boss," pp. 126–128; Martin Shefter, "The Electoral Foundations of the Political Ma-

chine: New York City, 1884–1897," in Joel H. Silbey, et al., eds., *The History of American Electoral Behavior*, p. 290.

42. Bullough, *Blind Boss*, pp. 97, 160–163, 232–233.

43. Moynihan, "The Irish," pp. 229, 259–260. A similar argument is made by Raymond E. Wolfinger in "The Development and Persistence of Ethnic Voting," pp. 896–908.

44. James Bryce, *The American Commonwealth*, p. 434.

45. For an early and sympathetic account of the Workingmen's party of California by journalist Henry George, later nominated for mayor of New York City on a labor party ticket, see his article "The Kearney Agitation in California," pp. 433–453. On labor politics generally in San Francisco, see Alexander Saxton, *The Indispensable Enemy: Labor and the Anti-Chinese Movement in California*, pp. 113–156; and Erie, "Development of Class and Ethnic Politics in San Francisco," pp. 128–145. Regarding labor politics in Chicago, see Howard H. Quint, *The Forging of American Socialism*, p. 14.

46. David Montgomery, "The Irish and the American Labor Movement," in David Noel Doyle and Owen Dudley Edwards, eds., *America and Ireland, 1776–1976*, pp. 207, 211, 213; Daniel Bell, *Marxian Socialism in the United States*, pp. 24–25.

47. Eric Foner, "Radicalism in the Gilded Age: The Land League and Irish-America," pp. 8–15, 24–25, 28; Montgomery, "Irish and the American Labor Movement," p. 216. On the Irish nationalist movement in Chicago, see Michael F. Funchion, *Chicago's Irish Nationalists, 1881–1890*.

48. Florence E. Gibson, *The Attitudes of the New York Irish Toward State and National Affairs, 1848–1892*, p. 245 (Rossa quote).

49. Martin Shefter, "The Emergence of the Political Machine," in Willis Hawley et al., eds., *Theoretical Perspectives on Urban Politics*, pp. 29–32.

50. Alfred Connable and Edward Silberfarb, *Tigers of Tammany: Nine Men Who Ran New York*, p. 155; Myers, *History of Tammany Hall*, p. 217; Werner, *Tammany Hall*, pp. 135–136. For evidence of the success of San Francisco's Democratic politicians in naturalizing and registering the Irish in the late 1860s, see R. A. Burchell, *The San Francisco Irish, 1848–1880*, p. 18.

51. Werner, *Tammany Hall*, p. 170. By 1868 Boss Tweed controlled state as well as local government. Tweed broadened his appeal to immigrant and working-class voters by state subsidies to Catholic schools and to religious charities. See John W. Pratt, "Boss Tweed's Public Welfare Program," pp. 396–411.

52. C. K. Yearley, *The Money Machines: The Breakdown and Reform of Governmental and Party Finance in the North, 1860–1920*, pp. 3–74.

53. Yearley observes that demands for liberalized debt policies came from the top as well as the bottom of the class structure. "Men of substance, realtors, bankers, construction men, contractors, manufacturers, and suppliers of the varied equipage essential to urban growth . . . succumbed to tempting speculations which public indebtedness could and did abet; the roads, sewers, utilities, schools, and other public improvements useful to increasing the value of existing realty and attracting even larger populations to particular areas could thereby come more swiftly" (ibid., p. 264).

54. Horace Secrist, *An Economic Analysis of the Constitutional Restrictions upon Public Indebtedness in the United States*, vol. 8, no. 1, pp. 56–63. States also imposed constitutional limitations on city taxation powers. See Richard T. Ely, *Taxation in American States and Cities*, pp. 396–397.

55. Jon C. Teaford, *City and Suburb: The Political Fragmentation of Metropolitan America, 1850–1970*, pp. 39, 62, 77.

56. Werner, *Tammany Hall*, p. 451.

57. Yearley, *Money Machines*, pp. 97–118; Werner, *Tammany Hall*, pp. 348, 356–357.

58. Werner, *Tammany Hall*, p. 449.

59. U.S. Census Office, *Ninth Census, 1870*, vol. 1, Table 32; U.S. Bureau of the Census, *Special Reports: Occupations at the Twelfth Census*, Tables 41, 43. For the occupational ranking scheme, see Stephan Thernstrom, *The Other Bostonians: Poverty and Progress in the American Metropolis, 1880–1970*, Appendix B: "On the Socioeconomic Ranking of Occupations," pp. 289–302.

60. For an excellent summary of the scope of the machine's resources, see Charles Merriam, *The American Party System*, pp. 160–163. See also E. L. Godkin, "Criminal Politics," pp. 706–723.

61. Steven P. Erie, "Politics, the Public Sector, and Irish Social Mobility: San Francisco, 1870–1900," Table 2, p. 281.

62. Ibid., Table 4, p. 283.

63. Ibid. For a case study of an Irish machine's proletarianization of the public sector, see Frank S. Robinson, *Machine Politics: A Study of Albany's O'Connells*, pp. 166–168, 182.

64. Erie, "Politics, the Public Sector," Table 4, p. 283, and n. 37, pp. 287–288.

65. Montgomery, "Irish and the American Labor Movement," pp. 205–217.

66. Robert C. Brooks, *Political Parties and Electoral Problems*, p. 214. The machine's private sector patronage is also discussed in William Bennett Munro, *The Government of American Cities*, pp. 172–174.

67. U.S. Bureau of the Census, *Special Reports: Occupations at the Twelfth Census*, Table 43, pp. 720–725.

68. San Francisco Board of Supervisors, *San Francisco Municipal Reports, 1880–1881*, pp. 491–556.

69. Thernstrom, *Other Bostonians*, pp. 132–133, 142; Moynihan, "The Irish," pp. 229, 259–260. For a similar argument about sluggish Irish economic progress and the limited opportunities available in the public sector, see Dennis P. Ryan, *Beyond the Ballot Box: A Social History of the Boston Irish, 1845–1917*, pp. 148–153.

70. U.S. Census Office, *Ninth Census, 1870*, vol. 1, Table 32; U.S. Bureau of the Census, *Special Reports: Occupations at the Twelfth Census*, Tables 41, 43.

71. Erie, "Politics, the Public Sector," Table 5, p. 285.

72. San Francisco Recorder, *General List of Citizens of the United States Registered in the Great Register, 1867*, p. 2; San Francisco Board of Supervisors, *San Francisco Municipal Reports, 1900–1901*, pp. 373–374. For 1900, second-generation Irish and German voters have been included. See Erie, "Development of Class and Ethnic Politics in San Francisco," Table 4, p. 283.

73. Foner, "Radicalism in the Gilded Age," p. 29; Genen, "John Kelly," pp. 261–323.

74. Bullough, *Blind Boss*, p. 177.

75. Shefter, "Electoral Foundations," pp. 263–298.

Chapter Three

1. For studies of the impact of the 1893 depression on the fortunes of the Democratic party, particularly in the northern cities, see Samuel T. McSeveney, *The Politics of Depression: Political Behavior in the Northeast, 1893–1896*, pp. 43, 87–133, 163–221; and Carl N. Degler, "American Political Parties and the Rise of the City: An Interpretation," in Alexander B. Callow, Jr., ed., *American Urban History*, pp. 469–470.

2. Andrew Greeley, *That Most Distressful Nation: The Taming of the American Irish*, pp. 122–128; Andrew Greeley, *Ethnicity, Denomination, and Inequality*, pp. 54–55.

3. John Kincaid, "Political Success and Policy Failure: The Persistence of Machine Politics in Jersey City," pp. 233–234, 287–289.

4. Dayton David McKean, *The Boss: The Hague Machine in Action*, pp. 37–44.

5. Frank S. Robinson, *Machine Politics: A Study of Albany's O'Connells*, pp. 14, 49–54.

6. M. R. Werner, *Tammany Hall*, pp. 516–517.

7. Gustavus Myers, *History of Tammany Hall*, pp. 353–363.

8. Walton E. Bean, *Boss Ruef's San Francisco: The Story of the Union Labor Party, Big Business, and the Graft Prosecution;* Steven P. Erie, "The Development of Class and Ethnic Politics in San Francisco, 1870–1910: A Critique of the Pluralist Interpretation," pp. 196–216, 227, and Table 5.13, p. 300.

9. George Mowry, *The California Progressives;* Spencer Olin, *California's Prodigal Sons: Hiram Johnson and the Progressive Movement, 1911–1917;* Alexander Saxton, "San Francisco Labor and the Populist and Progressive Insurgencies," pp. 421–438; Michael Rogin, "Progressivism and the California Electorate," pp. 297–314; John L. Shover, "The Progressives and the Working-Class Vote in California," pp. 584–601.

10. Richard M. Abrams, *Conservatism in a Progressive Era: Massachusetts Politics, 1900–1912,* pp. 45–48, 105–107, 147–187, 287; Geoffrey Blodgett, *The Gentle Reformers: Massachusetts Democrats in the Cleveland Era,* pp. 256, 271. Even if Governor Walsh had wanted to centralize Boston's Democratic politics, as Governor "Billy" Russell had briefly attempted to do in 1890, his efforts might have been frustrated by federal patronage policies. The Wilson administration appointed New Yorker Dudley Field Malone as the state's chief patronage dispenser with express orders to wage warfare against Boston's Irish machine politicians. Malone used federal appointments to create more havoc in the Hub's already chaotic politics—all in the name of reform. Regarding Fitzgerald's patronage practices, see the Boston Finance Commission, *Reports and Communications,* vol. 2, pp. 194–227.

11. Alex Gottfried, *Boss Cermak of Chicago: A Study of Political Leadership,* pp. 70, 80–82.

12. Robert D. Marcus, *Grand Old Party: Political Structure in the Gilded Age,* p. 223.

13. Joel A. Tarr, *A Study in Boss Politics: William Lorimer of Chicago,* p. 196.

14. For the cost-of-living measures used to adjust city spending and indebtedness for the period 1880 to 1932, see U.S. Bureau of the Census, *Historical Statistics of the United States: Colonial Times to 1957,* series E 157–160, p. 127.

15. U.S. Census Office, *Special Reports: Wealth, Debt, and Taxation,* Table 86, pp. 452–612; U.S. Bureau of the Census, *Financial Statistics of Cities Having a Population over 100,000, 1932,* Table 18, pp. 176–179.

16. For an excellent study of the urban transportation revolution and

suburban growth in late nineteenth-century Boston, see Sam Bass Warner, Jr., *Streetcar Suburbs: The Process of Growth in Boston, 1870–1900*.

17. Jon C. Teaford, *City and Suburb: The Political Fragmentation of Metropolitan America, 1850–1970*, pp. 77, 90–94.

18. U.S. Bureau of the Census, *Census of Population, 1920*, vol. 2, Table 7, p. 1288.

19. Richard L. McCormick, *From Realignment to Reform: Political Change in New York State, 1893–1910*, pp. 120–134.

20. Ibid., pp. 168–171; U.S. Bureau of the Census, *State and Local Government Special Studies: Historical Review of State and Local Government Finances*, G-SS-no. 25, Table 1, p. 13. In some states, particularly where Republicans controlled the statehouse and Democrats city hall, the reform package included limits on city borrowing authority. For example, Massachusetts in 1921 placed a 2.5 percent debt ceiling (as a percentage of the total assessed value of taxable property) on the cities. Local borrowing in the Bay State also had to be approved by two-thirds of the voters. New Jersey in 1916 placed a 7 percent debt limit on the cities, while New York enacted a 10 percent debt ceiling. See Lance W. Lancaster, "State Limitations on Local Indebtedness," in International City Managers' Association, *Municipal Year Book, 1936*, pp. 313–327, esp. Table 8, pp. 319–323.

21. Steven P. Erie, "Progressivism and San Francisco Labor, 1899–1917," pp. 33–34.

22. Kincaid, "Political Success," pp. 414–415, 429.

23. McKean, *The Boss*, p. 44. Hague's tax policies were also shaped by New Jersey's 7 percent ceiling on municipal debts. In order to borrow, Hague increased the city's assessment base by taxing property at 100 percent of true value. See ibid., pp. 253, 259–260.

24. Ibid., pp. 249–259.

25. Robinson, *Machine Politics*, pp. 137–139.

26. For analyses of the growth of urban public employment, 1900–1930, see Steven P. Erie, "Politics, the Public Sector, and Irish Social Mobility: San Francisco, 1870–1900," Table 2, p. 281; Willford I. King, *The National Income and Its Purchasing Power*, pp. 360–363; William E. Mosher and Sophie Polah, "Public Employment in the United States," pp. 51–72; and Simon Kuznets, *National Income and Its Composition, 1919–1938*, vol. 2, Table G–7, p. 814.

27. For a survey of municipal civil service systems, see the International City Managers' Association, *Municipal Year Book, 1941*, Table 4–A, pp. 130–132. Regarding Tammany's personnel practices, see Charles Garrett, *The La Guardia Years: Machine and Reform Politics in New York City*, pp. 133–134.

28. U.S. Bureau of the Census, *Fifteenth Census of the United States, 1930,* vol. 2, Table 11, vol. 4, Table 12. For an analysis of the importance of counties for machine consolidation, see Kincaid, "Political Success," pp. 264–266.

29. Steven P. Erie, "Two Faces of Ethnic Power: Comparing the Irish and Black Experiences," p. 263.

30. Werner, *Tammany Hall,* p. 557. The other Irish bosses also relied heavily on private sector patronage. Hague, for example, milked the waterfront and large packing companies such as Swift and Armour. See Richard J. Connors, *A Cycle of Power: The Career of Jersey City Mayor Frank Hague,* p. 88.

31. Unlike the 1900 census, the 1930 census does not report the number of Irish-stock public employees for the cities. I used the following procedure to estimate the number of Irish public servants for 1930. Regarding Albany, Terry Clark has done a surname analysis of the city payroll from 1870 to 1970. For 1930, approximately 41 percent of the city's elected officials, policemen, firemen, and other employees were of Irish descent. See Clark, "The Irish Ethic and the Spirit of Patronage," Fig. 3, p. 342. For New York and Jersey City, I have used a conservative estimating procedure. The New York World's *World Almanac* for 1931 provides rosters of top officials for New York (N = 428) and Jersey City–Hudson County (N = 56). Fifty-two percent of New York City's officials and 58 percent of the leadership of Jersey City–Hudson County had Irish surnames. These proportions were used to estimate the Irish share of overall city and county employment. I believe this is a reasonable estimating procedure for the following reasons. First, as Theodore J. Lowi has shown for New York City, ethnic ticket-balancing considerations were most pronounced for top elective and appointive positions. See Theodore J. Lowi, *At the Pleasure of the Mayor: Patronage and Power in New York City, 1898–1958,* pp. 29–46, esp. Fig. 2.1, p. 36. Top leadership, then, should have included *fewer* Irish than the rank and file. If anything, the ethnicity of public employees should more closely reflect that of the chief patronage dispensers, the party central committee members and the ward bosses. In 1932, nearly 70 percent of Tammany's district leaders in Manhattan were Irish. Second, the New York City and Jersey City estimates are consistent with a sample survey of 1,600 family heads in New Haven conducted in 1931–1933. In Irish-run New Haven, 49 percent of all public workers in the survey were Irish. See John W. McConnell, *The Evolution of Social Classes,* pp. 82–84, 214. As a final check, I did a surname analysis of the 1927 and 1933 rosters of top New York City and Jersey City officials. The Irish share of top positions remained remarkably constant. One final estimation problem remained. The surname analysis cap-

tured all Irish regardless of generation while the 1930 census only included first- and second-generation Irish. Based on secondary literature estimates and on the generational dropoff resulting from mixed marriages, I have estimated the size of the third-generation Irish workforce at roughly one-half that of the second generation.

32. Thomas M. Henderson, *Tammany Hall and the New Immigrants: The Progressive Years,* pp. 83–87, 166; U.S. Bureau of the Census, *Special Reports: Occupations at the Twelfth Census,* Tables 41, 43; U.S. Bureau of the Census, *Fifteenth Census of the United States, 1930,* vol. 2, Table 11, and vol. 4, Table 12.

33. Ronald H. Bayor, *Neighbors in Conflict: The Irish, Germans, Jews, and Italians of New York City, 1929–1941,* p. 26; New York World, *World Almanac* for 1931, pp. 545–549.

34. U.S. Bureau of the Census, *Special Reports: Occupations at the Twelfth Census,* Tables 41, 43; U.S. Bureau of the Census, *Fifteenth Census of the United States, 1930,* vol. 2, Table 11, vol. 4, Table 12; and Alba M. Edwards, *A Socio-Economic Grouping of the Gainful Workers of the United States,* Appendix, p. 275.

35. Alfred Connable and Edward Silberfarb, *Tigers of Tammany: Nine Men Who Ran New York,* p. 243; Kenneth Finegold, "Progressivism, Electoral Change, and Public Policy in New York City, 1900–1917," Occasional Paper no. 83–1, pp. 18–28; Myers, *History of Tammany Hall,* p. 309; Henderson, *Tammany Hall,* pp. 91, 124. The slowly growing Irish middle class began experimenting with antimachine reform politics as labor insurgency died. In New York, the anti-Tammany fusion ticket of 1913 was heavily Irish—John Purroy Mitchel for mayor and Prendergast and McAneny for citywide office—and drew substantial Irish middle-class support.

36. Connors, *Cycle of Power,* p. 94; Kincaid, "Political Success," pp. 429–431.

37. John Palmer Gavit, *Americans by Choice,* pp. 77–142, 232–233.

38. Ibid., p. 241; U.S. Bureau of the Census, *Historical Statistics of the United States, Colonial Times to the Present,* series C 168–180, p. 115.

39. For the enterprising reader, state voter qualifications are reported annually in the New York World Telegram's *World Almanac.* For an analysis of the Michigan movement to abolish alien suffrage, see Melvin G. Holli, *Reform in Detroit: Hazen S. Pingree and Urban Politics,* p. 151.

40. William M. Johnson, "On the Outside Looking In: Irish, Italian, and Black Ethnic Politics in an American City," p. 185.

41. McCormick, *From Realignment to Reform,* p. 54.

42. Harold F. Gosnell, *Machine Politics: Chicago Model,* Table 8,

p. 71. For evidence of how Chicago's competitive parties also registered and voted the new immigrants, see Charles E. Merriam and Harold F. Gosnell, *Non-Voting: Causes and Methods of Control*, pp. 202, 228–230.

43. U.S. Bureau of the Census, *Census of Population, 1920*, vol. 2, Table 16. Chicago's higher naturalization rates relative to New York were not a function of an older, settled population. Chicago's immigrants were newer arrivals. Forty-three percent of the Windy City's Russian-born, for example, had arrived after 1910 compared with 38 percent of New York's. See U.S. Bureau of the Census, *Fifteenth Census of the United States, 1930*, vol. 2, Tables 18, 19.

44. Werner, *Tammany Hall*, p. 436; Frederick A. Bushee, *Ethnic Factors in the Population of Boston*, Table 31, p. 124 (nationalities of 1896 registered voters). Naturalization rates for the Hub's ethnic groups are estimated from the censuses of 1890, 1900, and 1910.

45. U.S. Census Office, *Eleventh Census of the United States, 1890*, vol. 1, pt. 1, Table 78, vol. 1, pt. 2, Tables 72, 74; U.S. Bureau of the Census, *Census of Population, 1920*, vol. 2, Tables 16, 34; New York World, *World Almanac*, and New York municipal reports, variously dated.

46. Sources for New York City voting returns, 1870 to 1890, are New York Tribune, *Tribune Almanac and Political Register;* and New York State Legislature, *Red Book, State of New York*. For voting-age males and municipal employment, see U.S. Census Office, *Ninth Census, 1870*, vol. 1, pt. 1, Table 78, and vol. 1, pt. 2, Table 118.

47. For contemporary estimates of the size of the payroll vote in the big cities, see William Bennett Munro, *The Government of American Cities*, pp. 265–293, 401–440; and Robert C. Brooks, *Political Parties and Electoral Problems*, pp. 190–251, 541–574. For an early account of vote buying in New York, see John Gilmer Speed, "The Purchase of Votes in New York City," pp. 386–387, reprinted in Arnold J. Heidenheimer, ed., *Political Corruption: Readings in Comparative Analysis*, pp. 422–426.

48. Irving Howe, *World of Our Fathers*, pp. 80–84, 101–115, 287–324; Thomas Kessner, *The Golden Door: Italian and Jewish Immigrant Mobility in New York City, 1880–1915*, pp. 28–31.

49. New York World Telegram, *World Almanac* for 1932, p. 920; Norman Martin Adler, "Ethnics in Politics: Access to Office in New York City," esp. pp. 20–23, 48, 88–100, 197–227; Connable and Silberfarb, *Tigers of Tammany*, pp. 307–311; Lowi, *At the Pleasure of the Mayor*.

50. Herbert J. Gans, *The Urban Villagers: Group and Class in the Life of Italian-Americans*, pp. 174–175; William M. DeMarco, *Ethnics and Enclaves: Boston's Italian North End*, pp. 22–23.

51. John M. Allswang, *A House for All Peoples: Ethnic Politics in*

Chicago, 1890–1936, pp. 35–36, 104, 161; Paul Michael Green, "The Chicago Democratic Party, 1840–1920: From Factionalism to Political Organization," pp. 156–158, 333.

52. Henderson, *Tammany Hall,* pp. 4–5, 137; Howe, *World of Our Fathers,* pp. 360–383.

53. Joseph F. Dineen, *The Purple Shamrock: The Honorable James Michael Curley of Boston,* pp. 85, 172; Charles Angoff, *The Tone of the Twenties and Other Essays,* pp. 150–155.

54. Robert A. Woods, ed., *Americans in Process,* p. 64.

55. Lawrence H. Fuchs, *The Political Behavior of American Jews,* pp. 56, 63, 123, 135–139; Howe, *World of Our Fathers,* pp. 310–321.

56. Nancy Joan Weiss, *Charles Francis Murphy, 1858–1924: Respectability and Responsibility in Tammany Politics,* pp. 81–85; J. Joseph Huthmacher, "Urban Liberalism and the Age of Reform," pp. 234–238; Mark S. Foster, "Frank Hague of Jersey City: The Boss as Reformer," pp. 106–116. For an account of Lomasney's sponsorship of progressive legislation in Massachusetts, see John D. Buenker, "The Mahatma and Progressive Reform: Martin Lomasney as Lawmaker, 1911–1917," pp. 404–405.

57. J. Joseph Huthmacher, *Massachusetts People and Politics, 1919–1933,* pp. 93, 119–120; Henderson, *Tammany Hall,* pp. 249–251, 264–270.

58. Fuchs, *Political Behavior,* p. 127; Henderson, *Tammany Hall,* pp. 212–231.

59. Bayor, *Neighbors in Conflict,* pp. 26–31; Adler, "Ethnics in Politics"; Henderson, *Tammany Hall,* pp. 4–5, 137. For an account of how Chicago's Irish politicians also gerrymandered Italian neighborhoods, see Humbert S. Nelli, "John Powers and the Italians: Politics in a Chicago Ward, 1896–1921," pp. 67–84.

60. Gottfried, *Boss Cermak,* pp. 169–199; Allswang, *House for All Peoples,* pp. 105–106, 152–156.

Chapter Four

1. See Edwin O'Connor, *The Last Hurrah,* pp. 329–330; and Rexford G. Tugwell, *The Brains Trust,* pp. 366–371.

2. Lyle W. Dorsett, *Franklin D. Roosevelt and the City Bosses,* pp. 1–8, 113–116.

3. Robert A. Caro, *The Power Broker: Robert Moses and the Fall of New York,* pp. 326–327.

4. James T. Patterson, *The New Deal and the States: Federalism in Transition,* pp. 26–31; International City Managers' Association, *Munic-*

ipal Year Book, 1934, Table 11, pp. 206–211; U.S. Works Progress Administration, *Family Unemployment,* Table 20, pp. 125–126; International City Managers' Association, *Municipal Year Book, 1937,* Table 9, pp. 356–357.

5. Quoted in William Whyte, *Financing New York City,* pamphlet series no. 2, p. 5.

6. Barbara Blumberg, *The New Deal and the Unemployed: The View from New York City,* p. 27; Richard J. Connors, *A Cycle of Power: The Career of Jersey City Mayor Frank Hague,* p. 159.

7. International City Managers' Association, *Municipal Year Book, 1934,* Table 12, pp. 212–217; Martin Shefter, "Economic Crises, Social Coalitions, and Political Institutions: New York City's Little New Deal," p. 23.

8. Donald S. Watson, "Financing Relief and Recovery: [The] Reconstruction Finance Corporation," in International City Managers' Association, *Municipal Year Book, 1937,* pp. 375–381, esp. Table 2, pp. 380–381.

9. William O. Suiter, "State Limits on Local Property Taxes," in International City Managers' Association, *Municipal Year Book, 1936,* pp. 328–339, esp. Table 10, pp. 334–337; Robert P. Ingalls, *Herbert H. Lehman and New York's Little New Deal,* p. 51.

10. Shefter, "Economic Crises," pp. 32–33; Connors, *Cycle of Power,* p. 159; International City Managers' Association, *Municipal Year Book, 1935,* Table 5, pp. 204–208.

11. Charles Garrett, *The La Guardia Years: Machine and Reform Politics in New York City,* p. 104; Caro, *Power Broker,* p. 327; Harold F. Gosnell, *Machine Politics: Chicago Model,* p. 17.

12. Arthur Mann, *La Guardia Comes to Power, 1933,* pp. 138–149.

13. John Kincaid, "Political Success and Policy Failure: The Persistence of Machine Politics in Jersey City," pp. 472–473; Connors, *Cycle of Power,* pp. 141–183.

14. Alex Gottfried, *Boss Cermak of Chicago: A Study of Political Leadership,* pp. 262–263, 304–305.

15. Bruce M. Stave, *The New Deal and the Last Hurrah: Pittsburgh Machine Politics,* pp. 27–29, 86–88, 94.

16. Charles H. Trout, *Boston, the Great Depression, and the New Deal,* pp. 30–40, 50–59, 99, 286.

17. Stave, *New Deal,* pp. 165–169.

18. David Burner, *The Politics of Provincialism: The Democratic Party in Transition, 1918–1932,* pp. 215–243; John M. Allswang, *A House for All Peoples: Ethnic Politics in Chicago, 1890–1936,* p. 42. For more general studies of the role of the new ethnics in the 1928–1936 re-

alignment, see Samuel Lubell, *The Future of American Politics*, pp. 43–55; Jerome M. Clubb and Howard W. Allen, "The Cities and the Election of 1928: Partisan Realignment?" pp. 1205–1220; and Kristi Andersen, *The Creation of a Democratic Majority, 1928–1936*, pp. 19–52. For evidence of a parallel 1928 mobilization of rural Protestant women for Hoover, see Allan J. Lichtman, *Prejudice and the Old Politics: The Presidential Election of 1928*.

19. Mann, *La Guardia Comes to Power*, pp. 26, 113; Garrett, *La Guardia Years*, p. 110.

20. Ronald H. Bayor, *Neighbors in Conflict: The Irish, Germans, Jews, and Italians of New York City, 1929–1941*, p. 127; Mann, *La Guardia Comes to Power*, pp. 124, 138–146.

21. Bayor, *Neighbors in Conflict*, p. 135; Garrett, *La Guardia Years*, p. 134.

22. Garrett, *La Guardia Years*, pp. 147, 366 (n. 6).

23. Bayor, *Neighbors in Conflict*, p. 26.

24. Warren Moscow, *The Last of the Big-Time Bosses: The Life and Times of Carmine De Sapio and the Rise and Fall of Tammany Hall*, pp. 54–59; Daniel Bell, "Crime as an American Way of Life," pp. 131–154.

25. Connors, *Cycle of Power*, pp. 142–183; Kincaid, "Political Success," pp. 502–511.

26. Andersen, *Creation of a Democratic Majority*, pp. 34–37.

27. Frank S. Robinson, *Machine Politics: A Study of Albany's O'Connells*, pp. 138–139.

28. Dayton David McKean, *The Boss: The Hague Machine in Action*, p. 127.

29. Imposing state oversight over Albany's registration and election procedures, Republican Governor Thomas E. Dewey was able slowly to reduce the O'Connell machine's padded registration and vote totals. Between 1940 and 1960 the city's 85,000 registered voters were trimmed to 58,000, despite only a slight drop in population. Robinson, *Machine Politics*, pp. 163–164.

30. Milton L. Rakove, *Don't Make No Waves, Don't Back No Losers: An Insider's Analysis of the Daley Machine*, pp. 1–5; Gottfried, *Boss Cermak*, p. 326; Gosnell, *Machine Politics*, pp. 13, 109, 173; Andersen, *Creation of a Democratic Majority*, pp. 31, 83–120; Allswang, *House for All Peoples*, pp. 40–47.

31. Gosnell, *Machine Politics*, pp. 52–53, 71.

32. Stave, *New Deal*, pp. 6, 180, Table 23.

33. Stave reports robust ward-level correlations between the foreign stock population and the 1928 Smith vote ($r = .87$) and the 1932 Roosevelt vote ($r = .67$). Ibid., p. 203.

34. Stave notes the anemic correlation between the 1932 Roosevelt vote and the 1933 McNair vote ($r = .16$) compared with the strong linkage between the 1936 vote for FDR and the 1937 vote for Scully ($r = .88$). Ibid., pp. 209, 222.

35. Trout, *Boston*, pp. 11, 258–267; John F. Stack, Jr., *International Conflict in an American City*, pp. 32–39.

36. Trout, *Boston*, p. 116.

37. Arthur W. MacMahon et al., *The Administration of Federal Work Relief*, pp. 3–18.

38. U.S. Works Progress Administration, *Summary of Relief and Federal Work Program Statistics, 1933–1940*, Table 1, pp. 46–49.

39. Donald S. Howard, *The WPA and Federal Relief Policy*, Table 20, p. 399; U.S. Social Security Board, "Relief in Urban Areas," in International City Managers' Association, *Municipal Year Book, 1939*, pp. 460–465, esp. p. 461.

40. Stave, *New Deal*, pp. 147–169; MacMahon, *Administration*, pp. 285–286; Gosnell, *Machine Politics*, p. 75.

41. Blumberg, *New Deal*, p. 282. Urban Democratic machines could build formidable public sector coalitions by mobilizing municipal employees, WPA workers, and direct relief recipients. In New York, Jersey City, Chicago, and Pittsburgh these three groups constituted one-quarter to one-third of all voters.

42. Caro, *Power Broker*, p. 325.

43. Blumberg, *New Deal*, p. 126; Trout, *Boston*, pp. 170–171, 301, and Table 8.2, p. 193; MacMahon, *Administration*, p. 303.

44. Blumberg, *New Deal*, p. 126.

45. Searle F. Charles, *Minister of Relief: Harry Hopkins and the Depression*, p. 175. Before the 1936 election the WPA issued regulations making partisan interference with WPA officials and workers illegal. Solicitation of campaign funds, voter canvassing, and votes from WPA personnel were prohibited. WPA enforcement of partisan prohibitions was spotty at best. Ibid., pp. 180–181.

46. Ibid., pp. 54, 74–78, 142–143; McKean, *The Boss*, p. 99.

47. Dorsett, *Roosevelt*, p. 103; Kincaid, "Political Success," p. 471; McKean, *The Boss*, p. 104.

48. Ingalls, *Lehman*, p. 12; Mann, *La Guardia Comes to Power*, p. 123.

49. Blumberg, *New Deal*, pp. 49–50, 70–71, 99–101, 266–267, 296–297.

50. Gosnell, *Machine Politics*, pp. 11, 19, 24, 75–78, 89.

51. Dorsett, *Roosevelt*, p. 91; Gosnell, *Machine Politics*, pp. 71, 78–80, 90.

52. Stave, *New Deal*, pp. 27–35, 64–88, 108–113, 139–144, 155,

162–181. For an account of Lawrence's political career, see Paul B. Beer, *Pennsylvania Politics Today and Yesterday: The Tolerable Accommodation,* pp. 239–266.

53. Harold Gorvine, "The New Deal in Massachusetts," in John Braeman et al., eds., *The New Deal: The State and Local Levels,* pp. 4–5; Dorsett, *Roosevelt,* pp. 15–16, 21–28.

54. Gorvine, "New Deal," pp. 24–25; Trout, *Boston,* pp. 164–168. Control of pre-WPA federal relief programs also eluded Curley's grasp. Both the PWA and Federal Emergency Relief Administration (FERA) grant-in-aid program required project approval by the state relief board. The Bay State's Emergency Relief Administration and the state Emergency Finance Board were both controlled by the Walsh-Ely western wing of the state Democratic party. As leader of the rival Boston wing, Curley found his proposed PWA and FERA projects blocked or delayed by state boards controlled by the Walsh-Ely faction. Curley briefly controlled some WPA patronage in 1936. During the superheated 1936 U.S. senatorial campaign, state relief boss Edwards relented and gave candidate Curley appointment power over a few lower-level WPA administrative positions. Curley exaggerated his relief influence, claiming to control 2,200 WPA project supervisors during his unsuccessful campaign for a U.S. Senate seat.

55. Trout, *Boston,* pp. 170–171, 278–279.

56. For an insightful analysis of how presidential elections after 1928 were influenced by the big-city vote in the urban-industrial states, see Samuel J. Eldersveld, "The Influence of Metropolitan Party Pluralities in Presidential Elections Since 1920: A Study of Twelve Cities," pp. 1189–1209.

57. Gavin Wright, "The Political Economy of New Deal Spending: An Econometric Analysis," pp. 30–38.

58. For a discussion of how state WPA job quotas were determined, see MacMahon, *Administration,* p. 101.

59. For an account of the "prospective" character of FDR's state patronage policies, see James T. Patterson, *The New Deal and the States: Federalism in Transition,* pp. 168–193.

60. Eldersveld, "Influence of Metropolitan Party Pluralities," pp. 1198–1202.

61. Regarding Lawrence's alliance with state Boss Guffey, see Richard C. Keller, "Pennsylvania's Little New Deal," in John Braeman et al., eds., *The New Deal: The State and Local Levels,* pp. 45–76; and Thomas H. Coode and John F. Bauman, "Democratic Politics and Pennsylvania, 1932–1938," in Thomas H. Coode and John F. Bauman, eds., *People, Poverty, and Politics: Pennsylvanians During the Great Depression,* pp. 224–250.

62. J. Joseph Huthmacher, *Massachusetts People and Politics, 1919–1933*, pp. 236, 250–263; Gorvine, "New Deal," pp. 4–13.

63. Patterson, *New Deal*, p. 171.

Chapter Five

1. For an analysis of the distinction between machine politics and political machines, see Raymond E. Wolfinger, "Why Political Machines Have Not Withered Away and Other Revisionist Thoughts," pp. 374–375.

2. John H. Mollenkopf, *The Contested City*, pp. 28–36.

3. U.S. Bureau of the Census, *Statistical Abstract of the United States, 1950*, Table 908, pp. 759–760; U.S. Bureau of the Census, *Census of Housing, 1980*, vol. 1, ch. A, Table 18.

4. Frances Fox Piven and Richard A. Cloward, *Regulating the Poor: The Functions of Public Welfare*, pp. 200–205.

5. John F. Kain, "Housing Segregation, Negro Employment, and Metropolitan Decentralization," pp. 175–197; John F. Kain, "The Distribution of Jobs and Industry," in James Q. Wilson, ed., *The Metropolitan Enigma*, pp. 23–30.

6. Bennett Harrison, *Urban Economic Development*, pp. 27–31; Bennett Harrison and Paul Osterman, "Public Employment and Urban Poverty: Some New Facts and a Policy Analysis," pp. 305–313, 363–366; Steven P. Erie, "Public Policy and Black Economic Polarization," pp. 308–309.

7. Mike Royko, *Boss: Richard J. Daley of Chicago*, pp. 136–137, 141; Arnold R. Hirsch, *Making the Second Ghetto: Race and Housing in Chicago, 1940–1960*.

8. Milton L. Rakove, *Don't Make No Waves, Don't Back No Losers: An Insider's Analysis of the Daley Machine*, pp. 34–37; Frank S. Robinson, *Machine Politics: A Study of Albany's O'Connells*, pp. 139–148.

9. Warren Moscow, *The Last of the Big-Time Bosses: The Life and Times of Carmine De Sapio and the Rise and Fall of Tammany Hall*, pp. 62–97.

10. Len O'Connor, *Clout: Mayor Daley and His City*, p. 85.

11. Robinson, *Machine Politics*, p. 169.

12. William J. Grimshaw, "The Daley Legacy: A Declining Politics of Party, Race, and Public Unions," in Samuel K. Gove and Louis H. Masotti, eds., *After Daley: Chicago Politics in Transition*, p. 64; John Waner, quoted in Milton L. Rakove, ed., *We Don't Want Nobody Nobody Sent: An Oral History of the Daley Years*, pp. 284–285.

13. Grimshaw, "Daley Legacy," pp. 69–71, 80.

14. R. L. McManus, Jr., "The Mayor's Stormy Pond," p. A–5.

15. Michael B. Preston, "Black Politics in the Post–Daley Era," in Gove and Masotti, eds., *After Daley*, pp. 101–107; Royko, *Boss*, pp. 67–68.

16. Grimshaw, "Daley Legacy," p. 77.

17. *Shakman* v. *the Democratic Organization of Cook County et al.*, no. 69 C 2145 (U.S. District Court for the Northern District of Illinois, Eastern Division), Memoranda and Stipulations. I am grateful to John Petrocik for sharing these materials with me.

18. Mollenkopf, *Contested City*, pp. 20–28.

19. U.S. Bureau of the Census, *1970 Census of Population*, vol. 1, Table 87; U.S. Bureau of the Census, *1980 Census of Population*, vol. 1, ch. C, Table 122.

20. U.S. Bureau of the Census, *Local Government Employment in Selected Metropolitan Areas and Large Counties, 1970*, Table 4; U.S. Bureau of the Census, *Local Government Employment in Selected Metropolitan Areas and Large Counties, 1981*, Table 4; Wendell Rawls, Jr., "Pittsburgh Nears End of Era as Flaherty Prepares to Move."

21. Michael K. Brown, "The Segmented Welfare State: The Political Origins and Consequences of U.S. Social Policy, 1938–1980," pp. 5–6.

22. Kenneth R. Mladenka, "The Urban Bureaucracy and the Chicago Political Machine: Who Gets What and the Limits to Political Control," pp. 991–998; Kenneth R. Mladenka, "Citizen Demands and Urban Services: The Distribution of Bureaucratic Response in Chicago and Houston," pp. 693–714.

23. O'Connor, *Clout*, pp. 172–173; Royko, *Boss*, p. 98; Samuel K. Gove, "State Impact: The Daley Legacy," in Gove and Masotti, eds., *After Daley*, p. 205.

24. O'Connor, *Clout*, pp. 149, 170–176.

25. Royko, *Boss*, pp. 129–132.

26. Alan C. Miller, "Corning: From the Shadow to 'Absolute King,'" p. A–19; Robinson, *Machine Politics*, pp. 139–140.

27. Ralph Whitehead, Jr., "The Organization Man," p. 352; O'Connor, *Clout*, p. 134.

28. Frank Hawkins, "Lawrence of Pittsburgh: Boss of the Mellon Patch," pp. 57–61.

29. Joann Crupi, "Corning: Last of the Traditional Political Bosses," pp. 12–13.

30. Donald H. Haider, "Capital Budgeting and Planning in the Post–Daley Era," in Gove and Masotti, eds., *After Daley*, pp. 161–165.

31. For a general analysis of postwar big-city pro-growth coalitions,

see Mollenkopf, *Contested City*. Regarding pro-growth politics in Chicago, see Royko, *Boss*, pp. 100–103; O'Connor, *Clout*, pp. 132–134, 149. Regarding Pittsburgh's growth politics, see Hawkins, "Lawrence of Pittsburgh," pp. 57, 60–61.

32. William Kennedy, *O Albany!* pp. 307–308, 316.

33. R. L. McManus, Jr., "Corning Dead: Last of the Traditional Political Machine Bosses," p. A–5.

34. Kennedy, *O Albany!* p. 316. In an interview a year before his death, Albany Mayor Erastus Corning revealed his method for handling Rockefeller: "When you're dealing with someone on a higher authority, you've got to deal from a position of strength. In other words, you've got to have something you can do to help, if you want them to help you. That's the art—to find something you can do, and then know what you'd like to trade for it." Quoted in McManus, "Mayor's Stormy Pond," p. A–5.

35. *Shakman* v. *the Democratic Organization of Cook County et al.*, no. 69 C 2145 (U.S. District Court for the Northern District of Illinois, Eastern Division), "Memorandum in Support of Plaintiffs' Motion for Partial Summary Judgment," pp. 23–41.

36. Royko, *Boss*, pp. 67–69, 78; O'Connor, *Clout*, pp. 128–129.

37. Robinson, *Machine Politics*, p. 169.

38. Roger E. Kasperson, "Toward a Geography of Urban Politics: Chicago, a Case Study," pp. 95–107; Whitehead, "Organization Man," pp. 355–356.

39. Len O'Connor, *Requiem: The Decline and Demise of Mayor Daley and His Era*, p. 134; "The City That Survives," *The Economist*, March 29, 1980.

40. Bryan Jones, "Party and Bureaucracy: The Influence of Intermediary Groups on Urban Public Service Delivery," pp. 688–689; Royko, *Boss*, p. 136. For evidence of political influence over municipal service delivery in Boston, see David L. Cingranelli, "Race, Politics, and Elites: Testing Alternative Models of Municipal Service Distribution," pp. 664–692; and Frederic N. Bolotin and David L. Cingranelli, "Equity and Urban Policy: The Underclass Hypothesis Revisited," pp. 209–219.

41. John Petrocik, "Voting in a Machine City: Chicago, 1975," p. 334. For evidence that citywide services represented a collective rather than an individual good in Chicago, see Ester R. Fuchs and Robert Y. Shapiro, "Government Performance as a Basis for Machine Support," pp. 537–550.

42. Milton L. Rakove, "Jane Byrne and the New Chicago Politics," in Gove and Masotti, eds., *After Daley*, p. 221.

43. Ibid.

44. For evidence of middle-class white demands for cultural dominance, see Anthony Downs, *Opening Up the Suburbs.*

45. Paul Kleppner, *Chicago Divided: The Making of a Black Mayor,* pp. 43–50; Royko, *Boss,* pp. 136–141; Kennedy, *O Albany!* p. 264.

46. John Hoellen, quoted in Rakove, *We Don't Want Nobody Nobody Sent,* pp. 300–301.

47. Grimshaw, "Daley Legacy," p. 69; Robinson, *Machine Politics,* pp. 179–182.

48. Kleppner, *Chicago Divided,* pp. 83–84; Kathleen A. Kemp and Robert L. Lineberry, "The Last of the Great Urban Machines and the Last of the Great Urban Mayors? Chicago Politics, 1955–1977," in Gove and Masotti, eds., *After Daley,* pp. 2–12, 18–20.

49. Martin Kilson, "Political Change in the Negro Ghetto, 1900–1940s," in Nathan I. Huggins et al., eds., *Key Issues in the Afro-American Experience,* pp. 182–189; O'Connor, *Clout,* pp. 120–121; Rakove, *Don't Make No Waves,* pp. 16, 110–111.

50. Constance A. Cunningham, "Homer S. Brown: First Black Political Leader in Pittsburgh," pp. 304–317; Hawkins, "Lawrence of Pittsburg," p. 61.

51. Royko, *Boss,* pp. 141–142; O'Connor, *Clout,* pp. 192–193; Kennedy, *O Albany!* pp. 166–167, 173, 260–264.

52. Hirsch, *Making the Second Ghetto;* Royko, *Boss,* pp. 136–144.

53. Piven and Cloward, *Regulating the Poor,* pp. 242–243.

54. Edward C. Banfield, *Political Influence: A New Theory of Urban Politics,* p. 74; Royko, *Boss,* p. 138; U.S. Bureau of the Census, *1970 Census of Population,* vol. 1, Table 94; U.S. Bureau of the Census, *1980 Census of Population,* vol. 1, ch. C, Table 137.

55. Michael K. Brown and Steven P. Erie, "Blacks and the Legacy of the Great Society: The Economic and Political Impact of Federal Social Policy," pp. 302–304; U.S. Bureau of Labor Statistics, *Manpower Impact of Federal Government Programs: Selected Grants-in-Aid to State and Local Governments,* Report 424, pp. 18–21.

56. U.S. Bureau of the Census, *Census of Population: 1960,* vol. 1, Table 129; U.S. Bureau of the Census, *1980 Census of Population,* vol. 1, ch. C, Tables 129, 135.

57. David L. Protess, "Banfield's Chicago Revisited: The Conditions for and Social Policy Implications of the Transformation of a Political Machine," pp. 184–202; O'Connor, *Clout,* p. 107.

58. Grimshaw, "Daley Legacy," p. 72; Rakove, *Don't Make No Waves,* pp. 110–111, 259.

59. Steven P. Erie, "Rainbow's End: From the Old to the New Urban

Ethnic Politics," in Joan W. Moore and Lionel Maldonado, eds., *Urban Ethnicity in the United States,* pp. 268–269; Charles V. Hamilton, "Public Policy and Some Political Consequences," in Marguerite R. Barnett and James A. Hefner, eds., *Public Policy for the Black Community,* pp. 239–255.

60. Quoted in Kleppner, *Chicago Divided,* p. 78.

61. Alan C. Miller, "His Honor, the Boss," p. 14; Kennedy, *O Albany!* pp. 173, 277–278, 328.

62. Kleppner, *Chicago Divided,* p. 83.

63. Martin Shefter, *Political Crisis/Fiscal Crisis: The Collapse and Revival of New York City.*

64. Wallace S. Sayre and Herbert Kaufman, *Governing New York City: Politics in the Metropolis,* Table 9, p. 48; Moscow, *Last of the Big-Time Bosses,* pp. 62–97, 105, 114–115, 127.

65. James Q. Wilson, *The Amateur Democrat: Club Politics in Three Cities,* pp. 32–64; Alfred Connable and Edward Silberfarb, *Tigers of Tammany: Nine Men Who Ran New York,* pp. 297–299.

66. Thomas F. X. Smith, *The Powerticians,* pp. 213, 226–227, 250–272.

67. Warren Moscow, *Politics in the Empire State,* pp. 97–109, 135; Shefter, *Political Crisis,* pp. 29–37.

68. Moscow, *Last of the Big-Time Bosses,* pp. 124–127, 159–183.

69. James O'Connor, *The Fiscal Crisis of the State.*

70. Royko, *Boss,* p. 58; O'Connor, *Clout,* pp. 180–181, 187; Hawkins, "Lawrence of Pittsburgh," p. 57.

71. Crupi, "Corning," pp. 12–13; Kennedy, *O Albany!* p. 316.

72. For an analysis of the machine-reform dialectic in New York politics, see Shefter, *Political Crisis,* pp. 13–104.

73. Jonathan Rieder, *Canarsie: The Jews and Italians of Brooklyn Against Liberalism,* pp. 51–54, 76–77, 123–129, 163–164, 216–263; Sayre and Kaufman, *Governing New York City,* p. 18.

74. For analyses of post–Tammany New York politics and mayoral coalition building, see Charles R. Morris, *The Cost of Good Intentions: New York City and the Liberal Experiment, 1960–1975;* Edward Koch, *Mayor;* Roger Starr, "John V. Lindsay: A Political Portrait," pp. 25–46; and Nat Hentoff, "Profile: The Mayor [Lindsay]."

75. John L. Shover, "The Emergence of a Two-Party System in Republican Philadelphia, 1924–1936," p. 1001.

76. Edward C. Banfield and Martha Derthick, *A Report on the Politics of Boston,* pp. VI-1–VI-13.

77. Ibid., pp. II-20–II-25, II-36, VI-14.

78. Martha Wagner Weinberg, "Boston's Kevin White: A Mayor Who

Survives," pp. 87–106; Alan Lupo, *Liberty's Chosen Home: The Politics of Violence in Boston*, p. 188.

79. Philip B. Heymann and Martha Wagner Weinberg, "The Paradox of Power: Mayoral Leadership on Charter Reform in Boston," in Walter Dean Burnham and Martha Wagner Weinberg, eds., *American Politics and Public Policy*, pp. 280–303; "Boston: White ex machina," p. 28.

80. Chris Black, "City, Unions Not the Best of Friends."

81. Peter Cowan, "1,600 Facing Hub Layoffs"; Black, "City"; Weinberg, "Boston's Kevin White," pp. 87–106.

82. Roger Butterfield, "Revolt in Philadelphia," November 15, 1952, pp. 40–41, 65–67, 70.

83. Ibid., November 1, 1952, pp. 19–21, 106–107; November 22, 1952, pp. 13, 36–39.

84. Melvin G. Holli and Peter d'A Jones, eds., *Biographical Dictionary of American Mayors, 1820–1980: Big City Mayors*, pp. 67–68 (Clark), 103–104 (Dilworth), 355–356 (Tate).

85. "Rizzo's Town"; "Philadelphia: Man or Machine?" For accounts of Rizzo's political career, see Fred Hamilton, *Rizzo*; and Joseph R. Daughen and Peter Binzen, *The Cop Who Would Be King*.

86. J. Anthony Lucas, *Common Ground: A Turbulent Decade in the Lives of Three American Families*, pp. 610–623; George V. Higgins, *Style Versus Substance: Boston, Kevin White, and the Politics of Illusion*, pp. 125–128, 179–187.

87. Reed M. Smith, *State Government in Transition: Reforms of the Leader Administration, 1955–1959*, pp. 80–85; Paul B. Beer, *Pennsylvania Politics Today and Yesterday: The Tolerable Accommodation*, pp. 210–215, 268, 348–349, 372–374.

88. Hamilton, *Rizzo*, pp. 162–163; Beer, *Pennsylvania Politics*, pp. 363–387.

89. Kleppner, *Chicago Divided*, pp. 149, 217–218.

90. "The City That Survives."

91. Henry Aaron, "Nondefense Programs," in Joseph A. Pechman, ed., *Setting National Priorities: The 1983 Budget*, pp. 149–150; Michael K. Brown, "Gutting the Great Society: Black Economic Progress and the Budget Cuts," pp. 11–24.

92. Thomas E. Cavanagh, *The Reagan Referendum: The Black Vote in the 1982 Elections*, pp. 3–6, 8.

93. O'Connor, *Requiem*, pp. 50, 121; Michael B. Preston, "Black Politics and Public Policy in Chicago: Self-Interest Versus Constituent Representation," in Michael B. Preston et al., eds., *The New Black Politics: The Search for Political Power*, pp. 168–174.

94. Manning Marable, "How Washington Won: The Political Econ-

omy of Race in Chicago," pp. 57–60; Ralph Whitehead, Jr., "The Chicago Story: Two Dailies, a Campaign—and an Earthquake," p. 30; Edward Thompson III, "Race and the Chicago Election," p. 4; Kleppner, *Chicago Divided*, p. 135 (O'Neill quote), pp. 146–147.

95. Kleppner, *Chicago Divided*, p. 250.

96. Fox Butterfield, "Signs of Change Appearing in Boston Electorate"; Higgins, *Style Versus Substance*, p. 179.

97. Rakove, *Don't Make No Waves*, pp. 3–14; Lawrence N. Hansen, "Suburban Politics and the Decline of the One-City Party," in Gove and Masotti, eds., *After Daley*, pp. 175–202.

98. Chinta Strausberg, "Mayor Asks Illinois' Cities to Battle Feds"; Chinta Strausberg, "Mayor Seizes Control of Park Board."

99. Adolph L. Reed, Jr., *The Jesse Jackson Phenomenon*, pp. 1–11; Chinta Strausberg, "Wallace Won't Quit"; Chinta Strausberg, "Hutch, Humes Answer Critics"; Chinta Strausberg, "Humes, Stroger Trade Blows."

100. *Philadelphia Tribune*, June 24, 1986. For evidence of white acquiescence to black rule in Detroit and Atlanta, see Peter K. Eisinger, *The Politics of Displacement: Racial and Ethnic Transition in Three American Cities.*

101. Joanne Jacobs, "Asian-American Political Muscle"; Bruce E. Cain and D. Roderick Kiewiet, *Minorities in California;* Kevin Phillips, "New Americans for the Next America"; Joanne Belenchia, "Latinos and Chicago Politics," in Gove and Masotti, eds., *After Daley*, pp. 118–145. For evidence of liberal cross-ethnic coalitions in California cities, see Rufus P. Browning et al., eds., *Protest Is Not Enough.*

Chapter Six

1. Larry Green, "Chicago's Mayor Finally Grasps Power and Spoils," pp. 1, 18.

2. Jeff Greenfield, "Payoffs Still Define Politics in Some Cities"; Tom Watson, "All Powerful Machine of Yore Endures in New York's Nassau," pp. 1623–1625.

3. Theodore J. Lowi, "Machine Politics—Old and New," pp. 83–92.

4. For a comparison of the two perspectives on the machine, see J. David Greenstone and Paul E. Peterson, "Reformers, Machines, and the War on Poverty," in James Q. Wilson, ed., *City Politics and Public Policy*, pp. 268–272. The revisionist theory of the machine is presented in Fred I. Greenstein, "The Changing Pattern of Urban Party Politics," pp. 1–13; Elmer E. Cornwell, "Bosses, Machines, and Ethnic Groups," pp. 27–39; and Robert K. Merton, *Social Theory and Social Structure*, pp. 125–136.

5. Alex Weingrod, "Patrons, Patronage, and Political Parties," pp. 377–400; James C. Scott, "Corruption, Machine Politics, and Political Change," pp. 1142–1158.

6. Thomas M. Guterbock, *Machine Politics in Transition: Party and Community in Chicago;* Michael Johnston, "Patrons and Clients, Jobs and Machines: A Case Study of the Uses of Patronage," pp. 385–398.

7. Edward C. Banfield and James Q. Wilson, *City Politics,* pp. 33–46; James Q. Wilson and Edward C. Banfield, "Public-Regardingness as a Value Premise in Voting Behavior," pp. 876–887. Regarding the debate over ethos theory, see Raymond E. Wolfinger and John Osgood Field, "Political Ethos and the Structure of City Government," pp. 306–326; Robert L. Lineberry and Edmund P. Fowler, "Reformism and Public Policies in American Cities," pp. 701–716; Timothy E. Hennessy, "Problems in Concept Formation: The Ethos 'Theory' and the Comparative Study of Urban Politics," pp. 537–564; and Edward C. Banfield and James Q. Wilson, "Political Ethos Revisited," pp. 1048–1062.

8. Daniel Patrick Moynihan, "The Irish," in Nathan Glazer and Daniel Patrick Moynihan, *Beyond the Melting Pot,* pp. 217–287. The role of the Catholic church as an organizational model for the machine is discussed in Edward M. Levine, *The Irish and Irish Politicians,* pp. 123–134.

9. Scott, "Corruption," pp. 1145–1148, 1155. For an application of the uprooted hypothesis to Irish-American politics, see Oscar Handlin, *The Uprooted,* pp. 201–226. Amy Bridges offers a similar account. In the United States, the franchise expanded at the beginning of industrialization, bringing the social conflicts created by economic transformation into the arena of party politics. In the cities the result was machine politics. According to Bridges, if England had had manhood suffrage in the early nineteenth century the outcome would have been machine politics in cities such as Manchester, Liverpool, and London (Amy Bridges, *A City in the Republic*). For the comparative argument, see Amy Bridges, "Rethinking the Origins of Machine Politics," in John Mollenkopf et al., eds., *Power, Structure, and Place.*

10. As Thomas N. Brown has observed, "The rebel resides in Ireland; the politician in America." For the differences between Irish politics in late nineteenth-century Ireland and America, see Thomas Brown, "The Political Irish: Politicians and Rebels," in David Noel Doyle and Owen Dudley Edwards, eds., *America and Ireland, 1776–1976,* pp. 133–150. Ireland's rebels turned politicians in the twentieth century. For case studies of local machine building in modern Ireland, see Paul Martin Sacks, *The Donegal Mafia: An Irish Political Machine;* and Max Bart, "The Political Machine and Its Importance in the Irish Republic," pp. 6–20.

America's Irish politicians turned rebels in the twentieth century. For evidence of Irish-American liberalism and public-regardingness, see Lawrence J. McCaffrey, *The Irish Diaspora in America*, pp. 146–147.

11. Terry Nichols Clark, "The Irish Ethic and the Spirit of Patronage," pp. 327–343.

12. Martin Shefter, "The Emergence of the Political Machine: An Alternative View," in Willis Hawley et al., eds., *Theoretical Perspectives on Urban Politics*, pp. 14–44.

13. Shefter, "Emergence of the Political Machine," pp. 21–27.

14. Martin Shefter, "The Electoral Foundations of the Political Machine: New York City, 1884–1897," in Joel H. Silbey et al., eds., *The History of American Electoral Behavior*, pp. 263–298.

15. James Warren Ingram III, "The 'Old Boy' Triggers the 'Fire Alarm': Boss Cox, Governor Foraker, and Machine Building in Cincinnati, 1885–1915," esp. pp. 45–48.

16. David R. Mayhew, *Placing Parties in American Politics*, pp. 20–21, 212–236.

17. Ibid., p. 212.

18. Regarding exchange theory, see George C. Homans, "Social Behavior as Exchange," pp. 597–606; Richard M. Emerson, "Power-Dependence Relations," pp. 31–40; Peter Blau, *Exchange and Power in Social Life*; R. L. Curry and L. L. Wade, *A Theory of Political Exchange*; Sidney Waldman, *Foundations of Political Analysis*; and the selections in *Sociological Inquiry* 42, nos. 3 and 4 (September and December 1972). For an estimate of the diverse kinds of resources machines could exchange for political support in a city of 100,000, see Charles Merriam, *The American Party System*, pp. 160–163.

19. Robert A. Dahl, *Who Governs? Democracy and Power in an American City*, pp. 32–51. The estimate of the vote yield of patronage is supplied by D. W. Brogan, *Politics in America*, pp. 114–115.

20. Banfield and Wilson, *City Politics*, pp. 117–118; Peter B. Clark and James Q. Wilson, "Incentive Systems: A Theory of Organizations," pp. 129–166.

21. Frank Sorauf, "State Patronage in a Rural County," pp. 1046–1056. See also Frank Sorauf, "The Silent Revolution in Patronage," pp. 28–34; and W. Robert Gump, "The Functions of Patronage in American Party Politics: An Empirical Reappraisal," pp. 87–107.

22. James Q. Wilson, "The Economy of Patronage," pp. 369–380.

23. Johnston, "Patrons and Clients," pp. 385–398.

24. Guterbock, *Machine Politics*, pp. 146–169. In another mid-1970s study of the Chicago machine, Ester R. Fuchs and Robert Y.

Shapiro argue that the Daley organization built voter support by efficiently delivering citywide services, not merely by providing individual benefits. See Fuchs and Shapiro, "Government Performance as a Basis for Machine Support," pp. 537–550.

25. Richard F. Fenno, Jr., *Home Style: House Members in Their Districts,* pp. 1–30.

26. For an application of Fenno's model of electoral coalition building to the big-city machines under conditions of risk aversion, see Gary W. Cox and Matt McCubbins, "Electoral Politics as a Redistributive Game," pp. 370–389. Cox and McCubbins argue that risk-averse bosses overreward primary constituencies and underreward secondary constituencies.

27. Regarding machine growth policies, see Roger W. Lotchin, "Power and Policy: American City Politics Between the Two World Wars," in Scott Greer, ed., *Ethnics, Machines, and the American Urban Future,* pp. 30–37.

28. The terms *voice* and *exit* are Albert O. Hirschman's; see his *Exit, Voice, and Loyalty.*

29. Gary W. Cox and Morgan Kousser, "Turnout and Rural Corruption: New York as a Test Case," pp. 646–663.

30. Regarding machine fiscal policies, see Mayhew, *Placing Parties,* pp. 262–307.

31. Walter Dean Burnham, "The Changing Shape of the American Political Universe," pp. 7–28.

32. Walter Dean Burnham, *Critical Elections and the Mainsprings of American Politics,* pp. 71–90; Walter Dean Burnham, "Theory and Voting Research," pp. 1002–1023.

33. Philip E. Converse, "Comment on Burnham's 'Theory and Voting Research,'" pp. 1024–1027; Jerrold G. Rusk, "Comment: The American Electoral Universe: Speculation and Evidence," pp. 1028–1049. Surprisingly, Converse and Rusk fail to note the role played by the 1906 Naturalization Act in dampening turnout rates (see Chapter 3).

34. For evidence of party-sponsored registration and voting of the immigrants in Chicago's 1923 mayoral election, see Charles E. Merriam and Harold F. Gosnell, *Non-Voting: Causes and Methods of Control,* pp. 202, 228–230. Not all entrenched machines were demobilizers. Bosses in noncompetitive cities but in competitive-party and critical states often pursued mobilization strategies. Walter Dean Burnham notes that the GOP "steamrollers" of Philadelphia and Pittsburgh rolled up massive vote pluralities in order to project their influence into state and national politics. See Burnham, *Critical Elections,* pp. 51–53.

35. Guterbock, *Machine Politics*, pp. 146–169.

36. For accounts of the early successes of the reformers, see Harold A. Stone et al., *City Manager Government in the United States: A Review After Twenty-Five Years;* Frank M. Stewart, *A Half Century of Municipal Reform;* Richard S. Childs, *Civic Victories: The Story of an Unfinished Revolution;* Richard Hofstadter, *The Age of Reform;* Lorin Peterson, *The Day of the Mugwump;* and George Mowry, *The California Progressives.* A model study of national civil service reform and its limits is Stephen Skowronek's *Building a New American State,* pp. 47–84, 177–211. For an overview of theories of machine decline, see Harvey Boulay and Alan DiGaetano, "Why Did Political Machines Disappear?" pp. 25–50.

37. William L. Riordan, comp., *Plunkitt of Tammany Hall,* pp. 17–20.

38. Melvin G. Holli, *Reform in Detroit: Hazen S. Pingree and Urban Politics,* pp. 393–403; C. K. Yearley, *The Money Machines: The Breakdown and Reform of Governmental and Party Finance in the North, 1860–1920,* pp. 253–269.

39. Rexford Tugwell, *The Brains Trust,* pp. 366–371; Edwin O'Connor, *The Last Hurrah,* pp. 329–330.

40. Leo M. Snowiss, "Congressional Recruitment and Representation," esp. pp. 629–631.

41. James Q. Wilson, *The Amateur Democrat,* pp. 32–64, 301–316.

42. William A. Bullough, *The Blind Boss and His City: Christopher Augustine Buckley and Nineteenth-Century San Francisco,* pp. 232–233.

43. Banfield and Wilson, *City Politics,* pp. 121–125. For a provocative analysis of the self-destructive tendencies of the post–New Deal Democratic party, see Thomas Byrne Edsall, *The New Politics of Inequality,* pp. 23–66.

44. James C. Scott and Benedict J. Kerkvliet, "How Traditional Rural Patrons Lose Legitimacy," in Steffen W. Schmidt et al., eds., *Friends, Followers, and Factions: A Reader in Political Clientelism,* pp. 439–458; Boulay and DiGaetano, "Why Did Political Machines Disappear?" pp. 36–38.

45. Here is a sampling of the research on the southern relations: Regarding New Orleans machine politics, see John R. Kemp, ed., *Martin Behrman of New Orleans: Memoirs of a City Boss;* Joy J. Jackson, *New Orleans in the Gilded Age: Politics and Urban Progress, 1880–1896;* George M. Reynolds, *Machine Politics in New Orleans, 1897–1926;* and Edward F. Haas, *DeLesseps S. Morrison and the Image of Reform: New Orleans Politics, 1946–1961.* On boss rule in Baltimore, see Edwin

Rothman, "Factional Machine-Politics: William Curran and the Baltimore City Democratic Party Organization, 1929–1946"; James B. Crooks, *Politics and Progress: The Rise of Urban Progressivism in Baltimore, 1895 to 1911;* and Henry Bain, "Five Kinds of Politics: A Historical and Comparative Study of the Making of Legislators in Five Maryland Constituencies," pp. 816–919. Regarding the Crump machine in Memphis, see William D. Miller, *Mr. Crump of Memphis;* D. Tucker, *Lieutenant Lee of Beale Street;* Alfred Steinberg, *The Bosses,* pp. 72–133; David M. Tucker, *Memphis Since Crump: Bossism, Blacks, and Civic Reformers, 1948–1968;* and Kenneth D. Wald, "The Electoral Base of Political Machines: A Deviant Case Analysis," pp. 3–29. On the Pendergast organization in Kansas City, see William Reddig, *Tom's Town: Kansas City and the Pendergast Legend;* A. Theodore Brown, *The Politics of Reform: Kansas City's Municipal Government, 1925–1950;* Lyle W. Dorsett, *The Pendergast Machine;* and Steinberg, *The Bosses,* pp. 307–366.

46. Regarding the northern GOP relations, consult the following sources: On Philadelphia machine politics, see Lincoln Steffens, *The Shame of the Cities,* pp. 134–161; Harold Zink, *City Bosses in the United States,* pp. 194–229; David Harold Kurtzman, *Methods of Controlling Votes in Philadelphia;* J. T. Salter, *Boss Rule: Portraits in City Politics;* Dennis Clark, *The Irish in Philadelphia: Ten Generations of Urban Experience,* pp. 117–179; John L. Shover, "The Emergence of a Two-Party System in Republican Philadelphia, 1924–1936," pp. 985–1002; and James Reichley, *The Art of Government: Reform and Organization Politics in Philadelphia.* On Pittsburgh GOP machine politics, see Steffens, *Shame of the Cities,* pp. 101–133; Zink, *City Bosses,* pp. 230–256; and Bruce M. Stave, *The New Deal and the Last Hurrah: Pittsburgh Machine Politics,* pp. 24–52. Regarding the Cox machine in Cincinnati, see Zink, *City Bosses,* pp. 257–274; and Zane L. Miller, *Boss Cox's Cincinnati: Urban Politics in the Progressive Era.*

47. For an introduction to the clientelist approach to machine politics, see Scott, "Corruption"; Weingrod, "Patrons"; James C. Scott, "Political Clientelism: A Bibliographic Essay," in Steffen W. Schmidt et al., eds., *Friends,* pp. 483–505; and René Lemarchand, "Comparative Political Clientelism: Structure, Process, and Optic," in S. N. Eisenstadt and René Lemarchand, eds., *Political Clientelism, Patronage, and Development,* pp. 7–31.

48. Weingrod, "Patrons," pp. 377–395; Lemarchand, "Comparative Political Clientelism," pp. 21–24.

49. Mario Caciagli and Frank Belloni, "The 'New' Clientelism in

Southern Italy: The Christian Democratic Party in Catania," in Eisenstadt and Lemarchand, eds., *Political Clientelism,* pp. 35–55.

50. Judith Chubb, "The Social Bases of an Urban Political Machine: The Case of Palermo," pp. 107–125; Judith Chubb, *Patronage, Power, and Poverty in Southern Italy.*

51. Lemarchand, "Comparative Political Clientelism," p. 22. On the supposed "backward" character of the American machines, see Caciagli and Belloni, "'New' Clientelism," p. 43; Judith Chubb, "The Social Bases of an Urban Political Machine: The Christian Democratic Party in Palermo," in Eisenstadt and Lemarchand, eds., *Political Clientelism,* pp. 84–85.

52. Matthew A. Crenson, *The Federal Machine: Beginnings of Bureaucracy in Jacksonian America,* pp. 11–17, 31–57, 72–101; Carl E. Prince, *The Federalists and the Origins of the U.S. Civil Service,* pp. ix–xiii, 1–20; Richard L. McCormick, "The Party Period and Public Policy: An Exploratory Hypothesis," pp. 279–298.

53. Mayhew, *Placing Parties,* p. 324.

54. Samuel Beer, "Political Overload and Federalism," pp. 5–17; Samuel Beer, "The Adoption of General Revenue Sharing: A Case Study in Public Sector Politics," pp. 127–195. For the pre–Great Society roots of direct federalism, see Philip Funigiello, *The Challenge to Urban Liberalism: Federal-City Relations During World War II,* pp. 52–55, 72–75, 234–242.

55. Claus Offe, *Contradictions of the Welfare State,* pp. 179–206.

56. John H. Mollenkopf, *The Contested City,* p. 3.

57. Ibid., pp. 44–48, 61–71. Mollenkopf's choices of San Francisco and Boston are open to question, given his intent of studying the antiparty logic of federal programs and its impact on the building of the modern urban Democratic party. Neither city had a strong Democratic machine in the 1930s and 1940s for federal programs to challenge. San Francisco, today's liberal bastion, was firmly in the grip of the Republican party from the Progressive era to the New Frontier. Boston's Democratic politics were faction-ridden, not centralized. In neither city did federal urban programs from the New Deal onward produce postwar reform coalitions. San Francisco's reform politics predate the New Deal, going back to the Progressive era. Boston's reform politics were a reaction to local forces—Curleyism—rather than to federal urban programs. Democratic cities like Chicago, Pittsburgh, Jersey City, and Albany with strong New Deal–era machines are more appropriate test cases for his thesis.

58. Greenstone and Peterson, "Reformers," pp. 267–292.

59. Mollenkopf, *Contested City,* pp. 267–268, 292–297.

60. Chubb, "Social Bases," pp. 123–124.
61. Paul Peterson, *City Limits*, pp. 150–166.
62. Ira Katznelson, *City Trenches*, pp. 1–72.

Chapter Seven

1. James Bryce, *The American Commonwealth*, pp. 3–167, 254–256, 302–303, 370–371; M. Ostrogorski, *Democracy and the American Party System*, pp. 225–281, 364–456.

2. Frederick C. Howe, *The City: The Hope of Democracy*, pp. 61–98, 116–118; Lincoln Steffens, *The Shame of the Cities*, pp. 4–5, 16–18. For early defenses of boss rule, see Henry Jones Ford, "Municipal Corruption," pp. 673–686; and William L. Riordan, comp., *Plunkitt of Tammany Hall*.

3. Reformer Albert Stickney, quoted in C. K. Yearley, *The Money Machines: The Breakdown and Reform of Governmental and Party Finance in the North, 1860–1920*, p. 17.

4. Regarding the treatment of the machine in the black power debate, see n. 13 in Chapter 1, above. The machine model also figured prominently in the Kerner Commission report; see U.S. National Advisory Commission on Civil Disorders, *Report*, ch. 9, "Comparing the Immigrant and Negro Experience," pp. 278–282.

5. William Foote Whyte, "Social Organization in the Slums," pp. 34–39; William Foote Whyte, *Street Corner Society: The Social Structure of an Italian Slum*, pp. 194–252; Robert K. Merton, *Social Theory and Social Structure*, pp. 125–136; Daniel Bell, "Crime as an American Way of Life," pp. 131–154; Jerome K. Myers, "Assimilation in the Political Community," pp. 175–182.

6. Fred I. Greenstein, "The Changing Pattern of Urban Party Politics," pp. 1–13; Elmer E. Cornwell, "Party Absorption of Ethnic Groups: The Case of Providence, Rhode Island," pp. 87–98; Elmer E. Cornwell, "Bosses, Machines, and Ethnic Groups," pp. 27–39; Edgar Litt, *Beyond Pluralism: Ethnic Politics in America*, esp. pp. 60–74, 155–168.

7. Robert A. Dahl, *Who Governs? Democracy and Power in an American City*, pp. 2–86.

8. Ibid., pp. 11–31. In support of his "springboard" thesis, Dahl cites a 1933 sample survey of 1,600 New Haven families conducted by Yale's Institute of Human Relations. Constituting 13 percent of the sample, Irish-Americans held nearly half of the public service jobs. Yet the city's public sector constituted only 5 percent of the local economy and employed only 15 percent of the Irish-stock workforce. The 1930 census reports that blue-collar jobs accounted for nearly half of all public em-

ployment. See John W. McConnell, *The Evolution of Social Classes*, pp. 84–85; and U.S. Bureau of the Census, *Fifteenth Census of the United States, 1930*, vol. 4, Table 12, pp. 280–283.

9. Dahl, *Who Governs?* pp. 40–44; Eric L. McKitrick, "The Study of Corruption," pp. 502–514; Steven P. Erie, "Two Faces of Ethnic Power," pp. 262–263.

10. U.S. Census Office, *Ninth Census, 1870*, vol. 1, Tables 29, 32; U.S. Bureau of the Census, *Special Reports: Occupations at the Twelfth Census*, Tables 41, 43; Andrew Greeley, *That Most Distressful Nation: The Taming of the American Irish*, pp. 122–128; Andrew Greeley, *Ethnicity, Denomination, and Inequality*, pp. 54–55.

11. Stephan Thernstrom, *The Other Bostonians*, pp. 132–133, 232.

12. Greeley, *That Most Distressful Nation*, pp. 122–128; Greeley, *Ethnicity*, pp. 54–55.

13. Dennis P. Ryan, *Beyond the Ballot Box: A Social History of the Boston Irish, 1845–1917*, pp. 106, 149.

14. Dahl, *Who Governs?* pp. 33–34, 40–41. Oscar Handlin argues that the acculturated second-generation Irish, not the transplanted first generation, saw politics as a route of personal and group advancement; see Handlin, *The Uprooted*, pp. 201–216.

15. Daniel Patrick Moynihan, "The Irish," in Nathan Glazer and Daniel Patrick Moynihan, *Beyond the Melting Pot*, pp. 229, 259–260.

16. Edward M. Levine, *The Irish and Irish Politicians: A Study of Cultural and Social Alienation*, pp. 134–138.

17. Cornwell, "Bosses."

18. Raymond E. Wolfinger, "The Development and Persistence of Ethnic Voting," pp. 896–908; Raymond E. Wolfinger, *The Politics of Progress*, pp. 30–73.

19. Wolfinger, *Politics of Progress*, p. 49; Stanley Lieberson, *A Piece of the Pie: Blacks and White Immigrants Since 1880*, pp. 77–119. For a test of the middle-class thesis, see Leo E. Carroll, "Irish and Italians in Providence, Rhode Island, 1880–1960," pp. 67–74.

20. Wolfinger, *Politics of Progress*, pp. 47–51. For a similar argument regarding the party system's role in politicizing ethnicity, see Michael Parenti, "Ethnic Politics and the Persistence of Ethnic Identification," pp. 717–726.

21. Raymond E. Wolfinger, "Some Consequences of Ethnic Politics," in M. Kent Jennings and L. Harmon Zeigler, eds., *The Electoral Process*, pp. 44–50; Handlin, *The Uprooted*, pp. 201–226.

22. Wolfinger, "Some Consequences," p. 50.

23. Dahl, *Who Governs?* pp. 52–59. In the Dahlian model, divisible material benefits represented the primary way the system muted class

conflict in the pre–New Deal era. Dahl also mentions the facilitating role of symbolic politics such as ethnic nomination to public office and, in the post–New Deal era, the role of collective benefits—redevelopment, neighborhood renewal, education, and recreation. Ibid., pp. 60–62.

24. Michael Rogin, "Nonpartisanship and the Group Interest," in Philip Green and Sanford Levenson, eds., *Power and Community: Dissenting Essays in Political Science*, pp. 112–141; Michael Rogin, *The Intellectuals and McCarthy: The Radical Specter*, pp. 193, 205.

25. Ira Katznelson, *City Trenches: Urban Politics and the Patterning of Class in the United States*, pp. 1–72. For an incisive analysis of the rise of "artisan insurgency" in the antebellum period, see Sean Wilentz, *Chants Democratic: New York City and the Rise of the Working Class, 1788–1850*.

26. Katznelson, *City Trenches*.

27. Gwendolyn Mink, *Old Labor and New Immigrants in American Political Development*, pp. 45–68, 113–157.

28. For a pioneering analysis of the forging of union-Democratic party ties, see Marc Karson, *American Labor Unions and Politics, 1900–1918*. Regarding the Irish-American role in the craft union movement, see David Montgomery, "The Irish and the American Labor Movement," in David Noel Doyle and Owen Dudley Edwards, eds., *America and Ireland, 1776–1976*, pp. 205–217.

29. Wolfinger, "Some Consequences," pp. 45–51.

30. Paul Peterson, *City Limits*, pp. 3–38, 150–166.

31. Theodore J. Lowi, "American Business, Public Policy, Case Studies, and Political Theory," pp. 677–715.

32. Peterson, *City Limits*, pp. 41–65.

33. Ibid., pp. 131–183.

34. Ibid., pp. 150–166, esp. pp. 156–158.

35. Ibid., pp. 152–156.

36. Robert Goodman, *The Last Entrepreneurs: America's Regional Wars for Jobs and Dollars*, pp. 1–31, 76–115.

37. Amy Bridges, *A City in the Republic*, pp. 24–29, 61–82, 131–137, 146–161.

38. Barry Bluestone and Bennett Harrison, *The Deindustrialization of America*, pp. 15–19.

39. Peterson, *City Limits*, pp. 17–38, 131–149. For a penetrating analysis of the "political juggling act" required of urban governance, see Martin Shefter, *Political Crisis/Fiscal Crisis: The Collapse and Revival of New York City*, esp. pp. 3–12.

40. Viewing federalism from this perspective, one questions Peterson's

assertion that "the federal system which limits the policies and politics of local governments in the United States is not an inevitable part of a capitalist system" (*City Limits*, p. 218). In a cross-national sense, the "aberration" may not be inevitable, but it is difficult to imagine the American political economy developing as it has without it.

41. Regarding urban black politics, see Leonard A. Cole, *Blacks in Power: A Comparative Study of Black and White Elected Officials;* William E. Nelson, Jr., and Philip J. Meranto, *Electing Black Mayors: Political Action in the Black Community;* John R. Howard and Robert C. Smith, eds., "Urban Black Politics," pp. 1–150; Peter K. Eisinger, *The Politics of Displacement: Racial and Ethnic Transition in Three American Cities;* Albert Karnig and Susan Welch, *Black Representation and Urban Policy;* and Michael B. Preston et al., eds., *The New Black Politics: The Search for Political Power.*

42. On Hispanic and Asian-American politics, see F. Chris Garcia and Rudolpho de la Garza, *The Chicano Political Experience: Three Perspectives;* Raymond A. Mohl, "Miami: The Ethnic Cauldron," in Richard M. Bernard and Bradley R. Rice, eds., *Sunbelt Cities: Politics and Growth Since World War Two,* pp. 58–99; David L. Clark, "Los Angeles: Improbable Los Angeles," in Bernard and Rice, eds., *Sunbelt Cities,* pp. 268–308; Joan Moore and Harry Pachon, *Hispanics in the United States;* Bruce E. Cain and D. Roderick Kiewiet, *Minorities in California;* and Judy Tachibana, "California's Asians: Power from a Growing Population," pp. 534–543.

43. Martin Kilson, "Political Change in the Negro Ghetto, 1900–1940s," in Nathan Huggins et al., eds., *Key Issues in the Afro-American Experience,* pp. 182–189; Hanes Walton, Jr., *Black Politics: A Theoretical and Structural Analysis,* pp. 56–69.

44. Roger E. Alcaly and David Mermelstein, eds., *The Fiscal Crisis of American Cities;* George Sternlieb and James W. Hughes, "The Uncertain Future of the Center City," pp. 455–572; Marilyn Gittell, "Public Employment and the Public Service," in Alan Gartner et al., eds., *Public Service Employment: An Analysis of Its History, Problems, and Prospects,* pp. 121–142.

45. Leonard Sloan, "Good Government and the Politics of Race," pp. 171–174; Albert Karnig, "Black Representation on City Councils: The Impact of District Elections and Socioeconomic Factors," pp. 223–242; Theodore P. Robinson and Thomas R. Dye, "Reformism and Black Representation on City Councils," pp. 133–142; Richard L. Engstrom and Michael D. McDonald, "The Election of Blacks to City Councils: Clarifying the Impact of Electoral Arrangements on the Seats/Popula-

tion Relationship," pp. 344–354; Peggy Heilig and Robert J. Mundt, "Changes in Representational Equity: The Effect of Adopting Districts," pp. 393–397.

46. Joyce Gelb, "Blacks, Blocs, and Ballots: The Relevance of Party Politics to the Negro," pp. 44–69; Charles V. Hamilton, "Blacks and the Crisis of Political Participation," pp. 191–193; Robert C. Smith, "The Changing Shape of Urban Black Politics: 1960–1970," pp. 16–28.

47. Linda M. Watkins, "Pittsburgh Blacks' Paucity of Political Clout Stirs Struggle over the City's At-Large Election System," p. 58; Marty Willis, "Jan. 6 Demonstration to Greet All-White City Council," pp. A–1, A–4; Gilbert Price, "Skirmish Begins 'At Large' Battle" [Cincinnati], p. H–8; Larry Green, "Chicago's Mayor Finally Grasps Power and Spoils," pp. 1, 18; Chinta Strausberg, "Mayor Seizes Control of Park Board," pp. 1, 18; Robert Davis and Joseph Tybor, "Mayor Wins Election Ruling," pp. 1, 10.

48. Daniel Patrick Moynihan, "Foreword" to Greeley, *That Most Distressful Nation*, p. xi.

49. Ira Katznelson, "The Crisis of the Capitalist City: Urban Politics and Social Control," in Willis D. Hawley et al., eds., *Theoretical Perspectives on Urban Politics*, pp. 223–226.

50. Peter K. Eisinger, "Black Employment in Municipal Jobs: The Impact of Black Political Power," pp. 380–392; Peter K. Eisinger, "The Economic Conditions of Black Employment in Municipal Bureaucracy," pp. 754–771; Peter K. Eisinger, "Black Mayors and the Politics of Racial Economic Advancement," in William C. McReady, ed., *Culture, Ethnicity, and Identity*, pp. 95–109; John J. Harrigan, *Political Change in the Metropolis*, pp. 129–139. For evidence that minority gains in elective office have not been translated into significant minority policy payoffs, see Susan Welch and Albert Karnig, "The Impact of Black Elected Officials on Urban Social Expenditures," pp. 707–714; and Edmond J. Keller, "The Impact of Black Mayors on Urban Policy," pp. 40–52.

51. Clarence N. Stone, *Economic Growth and Neighborhood Discontent: System Bias in the Urban Renewal Program of Atlanta*, pp. 90–185; Clarence N. Stone, "Atlanta: Protest and Elections Are Not Enough," in Rufus P. Browning and Dale Rogers Marshall, eds., "Black and Hispanic Power in City Politics: A Forum," pp. 618–625; Dennis R. Judd, *The Politics of American Cities: Private Power and Public Policy*, pp. 373–407; John Helyar and Robert Johnson, "Tale of Two Cities: Chicago's Busy Center Masks a Loss of Jobs in Its Outlying Areas," pp. 1, 22.

52. Rufus P. Browning et al., *Protest Is Not Enough: The Struggle of Blacks and Hispanics for Equality in Urban Politics*, pp. 207–238 (quote at p. 214).

53. Michael K. Brown and Steven P. Erie, "Blacks and the Legacy of the Great Society: The Economic and Political Impact of Federal Social Policy," pp. 302–309, esp. Table 3, p. 308; U.S. Equal Employment Opportunity Commission, *Minorities and Women in State and Local Government, 1977,* vol. 1; U.S. Civil Service Commission, *Minority Group Employment in the Federal Government, 1975.*

54. Steven P. Erie, "Public Policy and Black Economic Polarization," pp. 311–315, esp. Table 1, p. 313.

55. Charles V. Hamilton, "Public Policy and Some Political Consequences," in Marguerite R. Barnett and James A. Hefner, eds., *Public Policy for the Black Community,* p. 245; and Charles V. Hamilton, "The Patron-Recipient Relationship and Minority Politics in New York City," p. 224.

56. U.S. Bureau of the Census, *Voter Participation in the National Election, November, 1964,* pp. 11–13, 21–22; U.S. Bureau of the Census, *Voting and Registration in the Election of November, 1976,* pp. 14–23, 61–62.

Bibliography

Aaron, Henry. "Nondefense Programs." In *Setting National Priorities: The 1983 Budget,* edited by Joseph A. Pechman, pp. 101–150. Washington, D.C.: Brookings Institution, 1982.

Abbott, Richard H. "Massachusetts: Maintaining Hegemony." In *Radical Republicans in the North: State Politics During Reconstruction,* edited by James C. Mohr, pp. 1–25. Baltimore: Johns Hopkins University Press, 1976.

Abrams, Richard M. *Conservatism in a Progressive Era: Massachusetts Politics, 1900–1912.* Cambridge, Mass.: Harvard University Press, 1964.

Adler, Norman Martin. "Ethnics in Politics: Access to Office in New York City." Ph.D. dissertation, University of Wisconsin, 1971.

Akenson, Donald H. *The Irish Educational Experiment: The National System of Education in the Nineteenth Century.* London: Routledge and Kegan Paul, 1970.

Alcaly, Roger E., and David Mermelstein, eds. *The Fiscal Crisis of American Cities.* New York: Vintage Books, 1977.

Allswang, John M. *A House for All Peoples: Ethnic Politics in Chicago, 1890–1936.* Lexington: University Press of Kentucky, 1971.

Andersen, Kristi. *The Creation of a Democratic Majority, 1928–1936.* Chicago: University of Chicago Press, 1979.

Angoff, Charles. *The Tone of the Twenties and Other Essays.* New York: A. S. Barnes, 1966.

Bain, Henry. "Five Kinds of Politics: A Historical and Comparative Study of the Making of Legislators in Five Maryland Constituencies." Ph.D. dissertation, Harvard University, 1970.

Banfield, Edward C. *Political Influence: A New Theory of Urban Politics.* New York: Free Press, 1961.

Banfield, Edward C., and Martha Derthick. *A Report on the Politics of Boston*. Cambridge, Mass.: Joint Center for Urban Studies, MIT and Harvard, 1960.

Banfield, Edward C., and James Q. Wilson. *City Politics*. New York: Vintage, 1963.

———. "Political Ethos Revisited." *American Political Science Review* 65, no. 4 (December 1971): 1048–1062.

Bart, Max. "The Political Machine and Its Importance in the Irish Republic." *Political Anthropology* 1, no. 1 (March 1975): 6–20.

Bass, Herbert. *"I Am a Democrat": The Political Career of David Bennett Hill*. Syracuse, N.Y.: Syracuse University Press, 1961.

———. "The Politics of Ballot Reform in New York State, 1888–1890." *New York History* 42, no. 3 (July 1961): 253–272.

Bayor, Ronald H. *Neighbors in Conflict: The Irish, Germans, Jews, and Italians of New York City, 1929–1941*. Baltimore: Johns Hopkins University Press, 1978.

Bean, Walton E. *Boss Ruef's San Francisco: The Story of the Union Labor Party, Big Business, and the Graft Prosecution*. Berkeley and Los Angeles: University of California Press, 1952.

Beer, Paul B. *Pennsylvania Politics Today and Yesterday: The Tolerable Accommodation*. University Park: Pennsylvania State University Press, 1980.

Beer, Samuel. "The Adoption of General Revenue Sharing: A Case Study in Public Sector Politics." *Public Policy* 24, no. 2 (Spring 1976): 127–195.

———. "Political Overload and Federalism." *Polity* 10, no. 1 (Fall 1977): 5–17.

Belenchia, Joanne. "Latinos and Chicago Politics." In *After Daley: Chicago Politics in Transition*, edited by Samuel K. Gove and Louis H. Masotti, pp. 118–145. Urbana: University of Illinois Press, 1982.

Bell, Daniel. "Crime as an American Way of Life." *Antioch Review* 13 (Summer 1953): 131–154.

———. *Marxian Socialism in the United States*. Princeton: Princeton University Press, 1967.

Black, Chris. "City, Unions Not the Best of Friends." *Boston Globe*, October 4, 1979.

Blau, Peter. *Exchange and Power in Social Life*. New York: John Wiley, 1964.

Blodgett, Geoffrey. *The Gentle Reformers: Massachusetts Democrats in the Cleveland Era*. Cambridge, Mass.: Harvard University Press, 1966.

Bluestone, Barry, and Bennett Harrison. *The Deindustrialization of America: Plant Closings, Community Abandonment, and the Dismantling of Basic Industry*. New York: Basic Books, 1982.

Blumberg, Barbara. *The New Deal and the Unemployed: The View from New York City.* Lewisburg, Pa.: Bucknell University Press, 1979.

Bobcock, John Paul. "The Irish Conquest of Our Cities." *Forum* 17 (April 1894): 186–195.

Bolotin, Frederic N., and David L. Cingranelli. "Equity and Urban Policy: The Underclass Hypothesis Revisited." *Journal of Politics* 45, no. 1 (February 1983): 209–219.

Boston Finance Commission. *Reports and Communications.* Boston: Boston Printing Department, 1909.

"Boston: White ex machina." *The Economist,* December 18, 1978, p. 28.

Boulay, Harvey, and Alan DiGaetano. "Why Did Political Machines Disappear?" *Journal of Urban History* 12, no. 1 (November 1985): 25–50.

Bridges, Amy. *A City in the Republic.* Cambridge: Cambridge University Press, 1984.

———. "Rethinking the Origins of Machine Politics." In *Power, Structure, and Place,* edited by John Mollenkopf, Thomas Bender, and Ira Katznelson. Beverly Hills, Ca.: Sage Publications, 1988.

Brogan, D. W. *Politics in America.* Garden City, N.Y.: Doubleday, 1960.

Brooks, Robert C. *Political Parties and Electoral Problems.* 3d ed. New York: Harper and Brothers, 1933.

Brown, A. Theodore. *The Politics of Reform: Kansas City's Municipal Government, 1925–1950.* Kansas City, Mo.: Community Studies, Inc., 1958.

Brown, Michael K. "Gutting the Great Society: Black Economic Progress and the Budget Cuts." *Urban League Review* 7 (1982): 11–24.

———. "The Segmented Welfare State: The Political Origins and Consequences of U.S. Social Policy, 1938–1980." Paper presented at the meeting of the Western Political Science Association, Las Vegas, Nevada, March 28–31, 1985.

Brown, Michael K., and Steven P. Erie. "Blacks and the Legacy of the Great Society: The Economic and Political Impact of Federal Social Policy." *Public Policy* 29, no. 3 (Summer 1981): 299–330.

Brown, Thomas N. "The Political Irish: Politicians and Rebels." In *America and Ireland, 1776–1976,* edited by David Noel Doyle and Owen Dudley Edwards, pp. 130–150. Westport, Conn.: Greenwood Press, 1980.

Browning, Rufus P., Dale Rogers Marshall, and David H. Tabb. *Protest Is Not Enough: The Struggle of Blacks and Hispanics for Equality in Urban Politics.* Berkeley and Los Angeles: University of California Press, 1984.

Bryce, James. *The American Commonwealth.* Rev. ed. vol. 2. New York: Macmillan, 1921.

Buenker, John D. "The Mahatma and Progressive Reform: Martin Lomasney as Lawmaker, 1911–1917." *New England Quarterly* (September 1971): 397–419.

Bullough, William A. *The Blind Boss and His City: Christopher Augustine Buckley and Nineteenth-Century San Francisco.* Berkeley and Los Angeles: University of California Press, 1979.

Burchell, R. A. *The San Francisco Irish, 1848–1880.* Manchester, England: Manchester University Press, 1979.

Burner, David. *The Politics of Provincialism: The Democratic Party in Transition, 1918–1932.* New York: Alfred A. Knopf, 1968.

Burnham, Walter Dean. "The Changing Shape of the American Political Universe." *American Political Science Review* 59, no. 1 (March 1965): 7–28.

———. *Critical Elections and the Mainsprings of American Politics.* New York: W. W. Norton, 1970.

———. "Theory and Voting Research." *American Political Science Review* 68, no. 3 (September 1974): 1002–1023.

Bushee, Frederick A. *Ethnic Factors in the Population of Boston.* New York: Macmillan, 1903.

Butterfield, Fox. "Signs of Change Appearing in Boston Electorate." *New York Times,* October 13, 1983.

Butterfield, Roger. "Revolt in Philadelphia." *Saturday Evening Post* 225 (November 1, 1952): 19ff.; (November 15, 1952): 40ff.; (November 22, 1952): 36ff.

Caciagli, Mario, and Frank Belloni. "The 'New' Clientelism in Southern Italy: The Christian Democratic Party in Catania." In *Political Clientelism, Patronage, and Development,* edited by S. N. Eisenstadt and René Lemarchand, pp. 35–55. Beverly Hills, Ca.: Sage Publications, 1981.

Cain, Bruce E., and D. Roderick Kiewiet. *Minorities in California.* Pasadena, Ca.: California Institute of Technology, 1986.

Cameron, David R. "Toward a Theory of Political Mobilization." *Journal of Politics* 36, no. 1 (February 1974): 138–171.

Caro, Robert A. *The Power Broker: Robert Moses and the Fall of New York.* New York: Vintage Books, 1975.

Carroll, Leo E. "Irish and Italians in Providence, Rhode Island, 1880–1960." *Rhode Island History* 28 (August 1969): 67–74.

Cavanagh, Thomas E. *The Reagan Referendum: The Black Vote in the 1982 Elections.* Washington, D.C.: Joint Center for Political Studies, April 1983.

Charles, Searle F. *Minister of Relief: Harry Hopkins and the Depression.* Syracuse, N.Y.: Syracuse University Press, 1963.

Chicago Daily News. *Almanac.* Chicago: Daily News, 1891–1930.

Childs, Richard S. *Civic Victories: The Story of an Unfinished Revolution.* New York: Harper and Brothers, 1952.

Chubb, Judith. "The Social Bases of an Urban Political Machine: The Case of Palermo." *Political Science Quarterly* 96, no. 1 (Spring 1981): 107–125.

———. *Patronage, Power, and Poverty in Southern Italy.* Cambridge: Cambridge University Press, 1982.

———. "The Social Bases of an Urban Political Machine: The Christian Democratic Party in Palermo." In *Political Clientelism, Patronage, and Development,* edited by S. N. Eisenstadt and René Lemarchand, pp. 57–89. Beverly Hills, Ca.: Sage Publications, 1986.

Cingranelli, David L. "Race, Politics, and Elites: Testing Alternative Models of Municipal Service Distribution." *American Journal of Political Science* 25, no. 4 (November 1981): 664–692.

"The City That Survives." *The Economist,* March 29, 1980, pp. 5–28.

Clark, David L. "Los Angeles: Improbable Los Angeles." In *Sunbelt Cities: Politics and Growth Since World War Two,* edited by Richard M. Bernard and Bradley R. Rice, pp. 268–308. Austin: University of Texas Press, 1983.

Clark, Dennis. *The Irish in Philadelphia: Ten Generations of Urban Experience.* Philadelphia: Temple University Press, 1973.

Clark, Peter B., and James Q. Wilson. "Incentive Systems: A Theory of Organizations." *Administrative Science Quarterly* 6 (September 1961): 129–166.

Clark, Terry Nichols. "The Irish Ethic and the Spirit of Patronage." *Ethnicity* 2 (1975): 327–343.

Clubb, Jerome M., and Howard W. Allen. "The Cities and the Election of 1928: Partisan Realignment?" *American Historical Review* 64, no. 4 (April 1969): 1205–1220.

Cole, Leonard A. *Blacks in Power: A Comparative Study of Black and White Elected Officials.* Princeton: Princeton University Press, 1976.

Comer, James P. "The Social Power of the Negro." In *The Black Power Revolt,* edited by Floyd B. Barbour, pp. 72–84. Boston: Extending Horizons, 1968.

Connable, Alfred, and Edward Silberfarb. *Tigers of Tammany: Nine Men Who Ran New York.* New York: Holt, Rinehart and Winston, 1967.

Connors, Richard J. *A Cycle of Power: The Career of Jersey City Mayor Frank Hague.* Metuchen, N.J.: Scarecrow Press, 1971.

Converse, Philip E. "Comment on Burnham's 'Theory and Voting Research.'" *American Political Science Review* 68, no. 3 (September 1974): 1024–1027.

Coode, Thomas H., and John F. Bauman. "Democratic Politics and Pennsylvania, 1932–1938." In *People, Poverty and Politics: Pennsylvanians During the Great Depression,* edited by Thomas H. Coode and John F. Bauman, pp. 224–250. Lewisburg, Pa.: Bucknell University Press, 1981.

Cornwell, Elmer E. "Party Absorption of Ethnic Groups: The Case of Providence, Rhode Island." *Social Forces* 38 (March 1960): 205–210.

———. "Some Occupational Patterns in Party Committee Membership." *Rhode Island History* 20 (July 1961): 87–98.

———. "Bosses, Machines, and Ethnic Groups." *Annals* 353 (May 1964): 27–39.

Cowan, Peter. "1600 Facing Hub Layoffs." *Boston Globe,* November 11, 1979.

Cox, Gary W., and Morgan Kousser. "Turnout and Rural Corruption: New York as a Test Case." *American Journal of Political Science* 25, no. 4 (November 1981): 646–663.

Cox, Gary W., and Matt McCubbins. "Electoral Politics as a Redistributive Game." *Journal of Politics* 48, no. 2 (May 1986): 370–389.

Crenson, Matthew A. *The Federal Machine: Beginnings of Bureaucracy in Jacksonian America.* Baltimore: Johns Hopkins University Press, 1975.

Crooks, James B. *Politics and Progress: The Rise of Urban Progressivism in Baltimore, 1895 to 1911.* Baton Rouge: Louisiana State University Press, 1968.

Crupi, Joann. "Corning: Last of the Traditional Bosses." *Albany Times Union and Knickerbocker News,* June 3, 1983, pp. 12–13.

Cruse, Harold. *The Crisis of the Negro Intellectual: From Its Origins to the Present.* New York: Morrow, 1967.

Cunningham, Constance A. "Homer S. Brown: First Black Political Leader in Pittsburgh." *Journal of Negro History* 66 (Winter 1981–82): 304–317.

Curry, R. L., and L. L. Wade. *A Theory of Political Exchange.* Englewood Cliffs, N.J.: Prentice-Hall, 1968.

Dahl, Robert A. *Who Governs? Democracy and Power in an American City.* New Haven: Yale University Press, 1961.

Daughen, Joseph R., and Peter Binzen. *The Cop Who Would Be King.* Boston: Little, Brown, 1977.

Davis, Robert, and Joseph Tybor. "Mayor Wins Election Ruling." *Chicago Tribune,* September 3, 1986, pp. 1, 10.

Degler, Carl N. "American Political Parties and the Rise of the City: An Interpretation." In *American Urban History,* edited by Alexander B. Callow, Jr., pp. 465–479. New York: Oxford University Press, 1969.

DeMarco, William M. *Ethnics and Enclaves: Boston's Italian North End.* Ann Arbor, Mich.: UMI Research Press, 1981.

Dineen, Joseph F. *The Purple Shamrock: The Honorable James Michael Curley of Boston.* New York: W. W. Norton, 1949.

Dorsett, Lyle W. *The Pendergast Machine.* New York: Oxford University Press, 1968.

———. *Franklin D. Roosevelt and the City Bosses.* Port Washington, N.Y.: Kennikat Press, 1977.

Downs, Anthony. *Opening Up the Suburbs.* New Haven: Yale University Press, 1973.

Edsall, Thomas Byrne. *The New Politics of Inequality.* New York: W. W. Norton, 1984.

Edwards, Alba M. *A Socio-Economic Grouping of the Gainful Workers of the United States.* Washington, D.C.: Government Printing Office, 1938.

Eisenstadt, S. N., and René Lemarchand, eds. *Political Clientelism, Patronage, and Development.* Beverly Hills, Ca.: Sage Publications, 1981.

Eisinger, Peter K. *The Politics of Displacement: Racial and Ethnic Transition in Three American Cities.* New York: Academic Press, 1980.

———. "Black Employment in Municipal Jobs: The Impact of Black Political Power." *American Political Science Review* 76, no. 2 (June 1982): 380–392.

———. "The Economic Conditions of Black Employment in Municipal Bureaucracy." *American Journal of Political Science* 26, no. 4 (November 1982): 754–771.

———. "Black Mayors and the Politics of Racial Economic Advancement." In *Culture, Ethnicity, and Identity,* edited by William C. McReady, pp. 95–109. New York: Academic Press, 1983.

Eldersveld, Samuel J. "The Influence of Metropolitan Party Pluralities in Presidential Elections Since 1920: A Study of Twelve Cities." *American Political Science Review* 43, no. 6 (December 1949): 1189–1209.

Ely, Richard T. *Taxation in American States and Cities.* New York: Thomas Crowell, 1888.

Emerson, Richard M. "Power-Dependence Relations." *American Sociological Review* 27 (February 1962): 31–40.

Engstrom, Richard L., and Michael D. McDonald. "The Election of Blacks to City Councils: Clarifying the Impact of Electoral Arrangements on the Seats/Population Relationship." *American Political Science Review* 75, no. 2 (June 1981): 344–354.

Erie, Steven P. "The Development of Class and Ethnic Politics in San Francisco, 1870–1910: A Critique of the Pluralist Interpretation." Ph.D. dissertation, University of California, Los Angeles, 1975.

————. "Progressivism and San Francisco Labor, 1899–1917." Unpublished manuscript, University of Southern California, 1977.

————. "Politics, the Public Sector and Irish Social Mobility: San Francisco, 1870–1900." *Western Political Quarterly* 31, no. 2 (June 1978): 274–289.

————. "Public Policy and Black Economic Polarization." *Policy Analysis* 6, no. 3 (Summer 1980): 305–317.

————. "Two Faces of Ethnic Power: Comparing the Irish and Black Experiences." *Polity* 13, no. 2 (Winter 1980): 261–284.

————. "Rainbow's End: From the Old to the New Urban Ethnic Politics." In *Urban Ethnicity in the United States,* edited by Joan W. Moore and Lionel Maldonado, pp. 249–275. Beverly Hills, Ca.: Sage Publications, 1985.

Faulkner, Harold U. *Politics, Reform and Expansion, 1890–1900.* New York: Harper Torchbooks, 1959.

Fenno, Richard F., Jr. *Home Style: House Members in Their Districts.* Boston: Little, Brown, 1978.

Finegold, Kenneth. "Progressivism, Electoral Change, and Public Policy in New York City, 1900–1917." Center for American Political Studies, Harvard University, October 1983.

Fogelson, Robert M. *Violence as Protest.* New York: Doubleday, 1971.

Foley, John W. "Community Structure and Public Policy Outputs in 300 Eastern American Communities: Toward a Sociology of the Public Sector." *Ethnicity* 6 (September 1979): 222–234.

Foner, Eric. "Radicalism in the Gilded Age: The Land League and Irish-America." *Marxist Perspectives* 1 (Summer 1978): 6–54.

Ford, Henry Jones. "Municipal Corruption." *Political Science Quarterly* 19 (1904): 673–686.

Foster, Mark S. "Frank Hague of Jersey City: The Boss as Reformer." *New Jersey History* 86 (Summer 1968): 106–116.

Fuchs, Ester R., and Robert Y. Shapiro. "Government Performance as a Basis for Machine Support." *Urban Affairs Quarterly* 18, no. 4 (June 1983): 537–550.

Fuchs, Lawrence H. *The Political Behavior of American Jews.* Glencoe, Ill.: Free Press, 1956.

Funchion, Michael F. *Chicago's Irish Nationalists, 1881–1890.* New York: Arno Press, 1976.

Funigiello, Philip. *The Challenge to Urban Liberalism: Federal-City Relations During World War II.* Knoxville: University of Tennessee Press, 1978.

Gans, Herbert J. *The Urban Villagers: Group and Class in the Life of Italian-Americans.* New York: Free Press, 1962.

Garcia, F. Chris, and Rudolpho de la Garza. *The Chicano Political Experience: Three Perspectives.* North Scituate, Mass.: Duxbury Press, 1977.

Garrett, Charles. *The La Guardia Years: Machine and Reform Politics in New York City.* New Brunswick, N.J.: Rutgers University Press, 1961.

Gavit, John Palmer. *Americans by Choice.* Montclair, N.J.: Patterson Smith, 1971. Originally published in 1922.

Gelb, Joyce. "Blacks, Blocs, and Ballots: The Relevance of Party Politics to the Negro." *Polity* 3, no. 1 (Fall 1970): 44–69.

Genen, Arthur. "John Kelly: New York's First Irish Boss." Ph.D. dissertation, New York University, 1971.

George, Henry. "The Kearney Agitation in California." *Popular Science Monthly* 17 (August 1880): 433–453.

Gibson, Florence E. *The Attitudes of the New York Irish Toward State and National Affairs, 1848–1892.* New York: Columbia University Press, 1951.

Ginger, Ray. *Altgeld's America: The Lincoln Ideal Versus Changing Realities.* Chicago: Quadrangle, 1965.

Gittell, Marilyn. "Public Employment and the Public Service." In *Public Service Employment: An Analysis of Its History, Problems, and Prospects,* edited by Alan Gartner et al., pp. 121–142. New York: Praeger, 1973.

Glazer, Nathan, and Daniel Patrick Moynihan. *Beyond the Melting Pot.* Cambridge, Mass.: MIT Press, 1964.

Godkin, E. L. "Criminal Politics." *North American Review* 151 (1890): 706–723.

Goodman, Robert. *The Last Entrepreneurs: America's Regional Wars for Jobs and Dollars.* New York: Simon and Schuster, 1980.

Gorvine, Harold. "The New Deal in Massachusetts." In *The New Deal: The State and Local Levels,* edited by John Braeman, Robert H. Bremner, and David Brody, pp. 3–44. Columbus: Ohio State University Press, 1975.

Gosnell, Harold F. *Machine Politics: Chicago Model.* 2d ed. Chicago: University of Chicago Press, 1968. Originally published in 1937.

Gottfried, Alex. *Boss Cermak of Chicago: A Study of Political Leadership.* Seattle: University of Washington Press, 1962.

———. "Political Machines." In *International Encyclopedia of the Social Sciences.* Vol. 12. Edited by David L. Sills. New York: Crowell, Collier, and Macmillan, 1968.

Gove, Samuel K. "State Impact: The Daley Legacy." In *After Daley: Chicago Politics in Transition,* edited by Samuel K. Gove and Louis H. Masotti, pp. 203–216. Urbana: University of Illinois Press, 1982.

Gove, Samuel K., and Louis H. Masotti, eds. *After Daley: Chicago Politics in Transition*. Urbana: University of Illinois Press, 1982.

Greeley, Andrew. *That Most Distressful Nation: The Taming of the American Irish*. Chicago: Quadrangle, 1972.

———. *Ethnicity, Denomination, and Inequality*. Beverly Hills, Ca.: Sage Publications, 1976.

Green, Larry. "Chicago's Mayor Finally Grasps Power and Spoils." *Los Angeles Times*, August 2, 1986, pt. 1, pp. 1, 18.

Green, Paul Michael. "The Chicago Democratic Party, 1840–1920: From Factionalism to Political Organization." Ph.D. dissertation, University of Chicago, 1975.

Greenfield, Jeff. "Payoffs Still Define Politics in Some Cities." *Los Angeles Times*, April 13, 1986.

Greenstein, Fred I. "The Changing Pattern of Urban Party Politics." *Annals* 353 (May 1964): 1–13.

Greenstone, J. David. *Labor in American Politics*. New York: Vintage Books, 1970.

Greenstone, J. David, and Paul E. Peterson. "Reformers, Machines, and the War on Poverty." In *City Politics and Public Policy*, edited by James Q. Wilson, pp. 267–292. New York: John Wiley, 1971.

Grimshaw, William J. "The Daley Legacy: A Declining Politics of Party, Race, and Public Unions." In *After Daley: Chicago Politics in Transition*, edited by Samuel K. Gove and Louis H. Masotti, pp. 57–87. Urbana: University of Illinois Press, 1982.

Gump, W. Robert. "The Functions of Patronage in American Party Politics: An Empirical Reappraisal." *Midwest Journal of Political Science* 15, no. 1 (February 1971): 87–107.

Guterbock, Thomas M. *Machine Politics in Transition: Party and Community in Chicago*. Chicago: University of Chicago Press, 1980.

Haas, Edward F. *DeLesseps S. Morrison and the Image of Reform: New Orleans Politics, 1946–1961*. Baton Rouge: Louisiana State University Press, 1974.

Haider, Donald H. "Capital Budgeting and Planning in the Post-Daley Era." In *After Daley: Chicago Politics in Transition*, edited by Samuel K. Gove and Louis H. Masotti, pp. 159–174. Urbana: University of Illinois Press, 1982.

Hamilton, Charles V. "Blacks and the Crisis of Political Participation." *Public Interest* 34 (Winter 1974): 185–210.

———. "Public Policy and Some Political Consequences." In *Public Policy for the Black Community*, edited by Marguerite R. Barnett and James A. Hefner, pp. 239–255. New York: Alfred Publishing, 1976.

———. "The Patron-Recipient Relationship and Minority Politics in New York City." *Political Science Quarterly* 95 (Summer 1979): 211–227.

Hamilton, Fred. *Rizzo.* New York: Viking Press, 1973.

Handlin, Oscar. *The Uprooted.* New York: Grosset and Dunlap, 1951.

———. *Boston's Immigrants: A Study in Acculturation.* Rev. ed. New York: Atheneum, 1970. Originally published in 1941.

Hansen, Lawrence N. "Suburban Politics and the Decline of the One-City Party." In *After Daley: Chicago Politics in Transition,* edited by Samuel K. Gove and Louis H. Masotti, pp. 175–202. Urbana: University of Illinois Press, 1982.

Harmond, Richard. "The 'Beast' in Boston: Benjamin F. Butler as Governor of Massachusetts." *Journal of American History* 55 (September 1968): 266–280.

Harrigan, John J. *Political Change in the Metropolis.* Boston: Little, Brown, 1985.

Harrison, Bennett. *Urban Economic Development.* Washington, D.C.: Urban Institute, 1974.

Harrison, Bennett, and Paul Osterman. "Public Employment and Urban Poverty: Some New Facts and a Policy Analysis." *Urban Affairs Quarterly* 9 (March 1974): 305–313, 363–366.

Harrison, Carter H., Jr. *Stormy Years.* Indianapolis, Ind.: Bobbs-Merrill, 1935.

Hawkins, Frank. "Lawrence of Pittsburgh: Boss of the Mellon Patch." *Harper's Magazine* 213 (August 1956): 57–61.

Heidenheimer, Arnold J., ed. *Political Corruption: Readings in Comparative Analysis.* New York: Holt, Rinehart and Winston, 1970.

Heilig, Peggy, and Robert J. Mundt. "Change in Representational Equity: The Effect of Adopting Districts." *Social Science Quarterly* 64, no. 1 (June 1983): 393–397.

Helyar, John, and Robert Johnson. "Tale of Two Cities: Chicago's Busy Center Masks a Loss of Jobs in Its Outlying Areas." *Wall Street Journal,* April 16, 1986, pp. 1, 22.

Henderson, Thomas M. *Tammany Hall and the New Immigrants: The Progressive Years.* New York: Arno Press, 1976.

Hennessy, Timothy E. "Problems in Concept Formation: The Ethos 'Theory' and the Comparative Study of Urban Politics." *Midwest Journal of Political Science* 14, no. 4 (November 1970): 537–564.

Hentoff, Nat. "Profile: The Mayor [Lindsay]." *New Yorker* 45, no. 3 (May 3, 1969): 44ff.; (May 10, 1969): 42ff.

Heymann, Philip B., and Martha Wagner Weinberg. "The Paradox of Power: Mayoral Leadership on Charter Reform in Boston." In *Ameri-*

can Politics and Public Policy, edited by Walter Dean Burnham and Martha Wagner Weinberg, pp. 280–303. Cambridge, Mass.: MIT Press, 1978.

Higgins, George V. *Style Versus Substance: Boston, Kevin White, and the Politics of Illusion.* New York: Macmillan, 1984.

Hirsch, Arnold R. *Making the Second Ghetto: Race and Housing in Chicago, 1940–1960.* New York: Cambridge University Press, 1983.

Hirschman, Albert O. *Exit, Voice, and Loyalty.* Cambridge, Mass.: Harvard University Press, 1970.

Hofstadter, Richard. *The Age of Reform.* New York: Alfred A. Knopf, 1955.

Holli, Melvin G. *Reform in Detroit: Hazen S. Pingree and Urban Politics.* New York: Oxford University Press, 1969.

Holli, Melvin G., and Peter d'A Jones, eds. *Biographical Dictionary of American Mayors, 1820–1980: Big City Mayors.* Westport, Conn.: Greenwood Press, 1981.

Hollingsworth, J. Rogers, and Ellen Jane Hollingsworth. "Expenditures in American Cities." In *The Dimensions of Quantitative Research in History,* edited by William O. Aydelotte, Allan G. Bogue, and Robert William Fogel, pp. 347–389. Princeton: Princeton University Press, 1972.

Homans, George C. "Social Behavior as Exchange." *Journal of Sociology* 63 (May 1958): 597–606.

Howard, Donald S. *The WPA and Federal Relief Policy.* New York: Russell Sage, 1943.

Howard, John R., and Robert C. Smith, eds. "Urban Black Politics." *Annals* 439 (September 1978): 1–150.

Howe, Frederick C. *The City: The Hope of Democracy.* Seattle: University of Washington Press, 1967. Originally published in 1905.

Howe, Irving. *World of Our Fathers.* New York: Simon and Schuster, 1976.

Huthmacher, J. Joseph. *Massachusetts People and Politics, 1919–1933.* Cambridge, Mass.: Belknap Press, 1959.

———. "Urban Liberalism and the Age of Reform." *Mississippi Valley Historical Review* 49 (September 1962): 231–241.

Ingalls, Robert P. *Herbert H. Lehman and New York's Little New Deal.* New York: New York University Press, 1975.

Ingram, James Warren, III. "The 'Old Boy' Triggers the 'Fire Alarm': Boss Cox, Governor Foraker, and Machine Building in Cincinnati, 1885–1915." Senior honors thesis, Department of Political Science, University of California, San Diego, April 1986.

International City Managers' Association. *Municipal Year Book.* Chicago: International City Managers' Association, 1933–1941.

Jackson, Joy J. *New Orleans in the Gilded Age: Politics and Urban Progress, 1880–1896.* Baton Rouge: Louisiana State University Press, 1969.

Jacobs, Joanne. "Asian-American Political Muscle." *Wall Street Journal,* December 27, 1985.

Johnson, William M. "On the Outside Looking In: Irish, Italian, and Black Ethnic Politics in an American City." Ph.D. dissertation, Yale University, 1977.

Johnston, Michael. "Patrons and Clients, Jobs and Machines: A Case Study of the Uses of Patronage." *American Political Science Review* 73, no. 2 (June 1979): 385–398.

Jones, Bryan. "Party and Bureaucracy: The Influence of Intermediate Groups on Urban Public Service Delivery." *American Political Science Review* 75, no. 3 (September 1981): 688–700.

Josephson, Matthew. *The Politicos, 1865–1896.* New York: Harcourt, Brace and World, 1963. Originally published in 1938.

Judd, Dennis R. *The Politics of American Cities: Private Power and Public Policy.* 2d ed. Boston: Little, Brown, 1984.

Kain, John F. "Housing Segregation, Negro Employment, and Metropolitan Decentralization." *Quarterly Journal of Economics* 82 (May 1968): 175–197.

———. "The Distribution of Jobs and Industry." In *The Metropolitan Enigma,* edited by James Q. Wilson, pp. 23–30. Garden City, N.J.: Anchor Books, 1970.

Karnig, Albert. "Black Representation on City Councils: The Impact of District Elections and Socioeconomic Factors." *Urban Affairs Quarterly* 12, no. 2 (December 1976): 223–242.

Karnig, Albert, and Susan Welch. *Black Representation and Urban Policy.* Chicago: University of Chicago Press, 1980.

Karson, Marc. *American Labor Unions and Politics, 1900–1918.* Carbondale: Southern Illinois University Press, 1958.

Kasperson, Roger E. "Toward a Geography of Urban Politics: Chicago, a Case Study." *Economic Geography* 11, no. 2 (April 1965): 95–107.

Katznelson, Ira. "The Crisis of the Capitalist City: Urban Politics and Social Control." In *Theoretical Perspectives on Urban Politics,* edited by Willis D. Hawley et al., pp. 214–229. Englewood Cliffs, N.J.: Prentice-Hall, 1976.

———. *City Trenches: Urban Politics and the Patterning of Class in the United States.* Chicago: University of Chicago Press, 1982.

Kehl, James A. *Boss Rule in the Gilded Age: Matt Quay of Pennsylvania.* Pittsburgh: University of Pittsburgh Press, 1981.

Keller, Edmond J. "The Impact of Black Mayors on Urban Policy." *Annals* 439 (September 1979): 40–52.

Keller, Morton. *Affairs of State.* Cambridge, Mass.: Harvard University Press, 1977.

Keller, Richard C. "Pennsylvania's Little New Deal." In *The New Deal: The State and Local Levels,* edited by John Braeman, Robert H. Bremner, and David Brody, pp. 45–76. Columbus: Ohio State University Press, 1975.

Kelley, Robert. *The Cultural Patterns in American Politics.* New York: Alfred A. Knopf, 1974.

"The Kelly-Nash Political Machine." *Fortune* 14, no. 1 (August 1936): 47–126.

Kemp, John R., ed. *Martin Behrman of New Orleans: Memoirs of a City Boss.* Baton Rouge: Louisiana State University Press, 1977.

Kemp, Kathleen A., and Robert L. Lineberry. "The Last of the Great Urban Machines and the Last of the Great Urban Mayors? Chicago Politics, 1955–1977." In *After Daley: Chicago Politics in Transition,* edited by Samuel K. Gove and Louis H. Masotti, pp. 1–26. Urbana: University of Illinois Press, 1982.

Kennedy, Robert E., Jr. *The Irish: Emigration, Marriage, and Fertility.* Berkeley and Los Angeles: University of California Press, 1973.

Kennedy, William. *O Albany!* New York: Viking, 1983.

Kessner, Thomas. *The Golden Door: Italian and Jewish Immigrant Mobility in New York City, 1880–1915.* New York: Oxford University Press, 1977.

Kilson, Martin. "Political Change in the Negro Ghetto, 1900–1940s." In *Key Issues in the Afro-American Experience,* edited by Nathan I. Huggins, Martin Kilson, and Daniel M. Fox, pp. 182–189. New York: Harcourt Brace Jovanovich, 1971.

Kincaid, John. "Political Success and Policy Failure: The Persistence of Machine Politics in Jersey City." Ph.D. dissertation, Temple University, 1981.

King, Willford I. *The National Income and Its Purchasing Power.* New York: National Bureau of Economic Research, 1930.

Kleppner, Paul. *Chicago Divided: The Making of a Black Mayor.* DeKalb: Northern Illinois University Press, 1985.

Koch, Edward. *Mayor.* New York: Simon and Schuster, 1984.

Kurtzman, David Harold. *Methods of Controlling Votes in Philadelphia.* Philadelphia: Privately printed, 1935.

Kuznets, Simon. *National Income and Its Composition, 1919–1938.* New York: National Bureau of Economic Research, 1941.

Lancaster, Lance W. "State Limitations on Local Indebtedness." In *Municipal Year Book, 1936,* pp. 313–327. Chicago: International City Managers' Association, 1936.

Larkin, Emmet. "Church, State, and Nation in Modern Ireland." *American Historical Review* 80, no. 5 (December 1975): 1244–1276.

Lemarchand, René. "Comparative Political Clientelism: Structure, Process and Optic." In *Political Clientelism, Patronage, and Development,* edited by S. N. Eisenstadt and René Lemarchand, pp. 7–31. Beverly Hills, Ca.: Sage Publications, 1981.

Levin, Murray B. *The Compleat Politician: Political Strategy in Massachusetts.* New York: Bobbs-Merrill, 1962.

Levine, Edward M. *The Irish and Irish Politicians: A Study of Cultural and Social Alienation.* Notre Dame, Ind.: University of Notre Dame Press, 1966.

Lichtman, Allan J. *Prejudice and the Old Politics: The Presidential Election of 1928.* Chapel Hill: University of North Carolina Press, 1979.

Lieberson, Stanley. *A Piece of the Pie: Blacks and White Immigrants Since 1880.* Berkeley and Los Angeles: University of California Press, 1980.

Lineberry, Robert L., and Edmund P. Fowler. "Reformism and Public Policies in American Cities." *American Political Science Review* 61, no. 3 (September 1967): 701–716.

Litt, Edgar. *Beyond Pluralism: Ethnic Politics in America.* Glenview, Ill.: Scott, Foresman, 1970.

Lotchin, Roger W. "Power and Policy: American City Politics Between the Two World Wars." In *Ethnics, Machines, and the American Urban Future,* edited by Scott Greer, pp. 30–37. Cambridge, Mass.: Schenkman, 1981.

Lowi, Theodore J. "American Business, Public Policy, Case Studies, and Political Theory." *World Politics* 16 (July 1964): 677–715.

———. *At the Pleasure of the Mayor: Patronage and Power in New York City, 1898–1958.* New York: Free Press, 1964.

———. "Machine Politics—Old and New." *Public Interest* (Fall 1967): 83–92.

Lubell, Samuel. *The Future of American Politics.* 3d ed. New York: Harper and Row, 1965. Originally published in 1951.

Lucas, J. Anthony. *Common Ground: A Turbulent Decade in the Lives of Three American Families.* New York: Alfred A. Knopf, 1985.

Luebke, Frederick C. *Immigrants and Politics: The Germans of Nebraska, 1880–1900.* Lincoln: University of Nebraska Press, 1974.

Lupo, Alan. *Liberty's Chosen Home: The Politics of Violence in Boston.* Boston: Little, Brown, 1977.

Lynch, Jeremiah. *Buckleyism: The Government of a State.* San Francisco: N.p., 1889.

McCaffrey, Lawrence J. *The Irish Diaspora in America.* Bloomington: Indiana University Press, 1976.

McConnell, John W. *The Evolution of Social Classes.* Washington, D.C.: American Council on Public Affairs, 1942.

McCormick, Richard L. "The Party Period and Public Policy: An Exploratory Hypothesis." *Journal of American History* 66, no. 2 (September 1979): 279–298.

———. *From Realignment to Reform: Political Change in New York State, 1893–1910.* Ithaca: Cornell University Press, 1981.

MacDonaugh, Oliver. "The Irish Famine Emigration to the United States." *Perspectives in American History* 10 (1976): 357–448.

McKean, Dayton David. *The Boss: The Hague Machine in Action.* New York: Russell and Russell, 1967. Originally published in 1940.

McKitrick, Eric L. "The Study of Corruption." *Political Science Quarterly* 72 (December 1957): 502–514.

MacMahon, Arthur W., John D. Millett, and Gladys Ogden. *The Administration of Federal Work Relief.* New York: De Capo Press, 1971. Originally published in 1941.

McManus, R. L., Jr. "Corning Dead: Last of the Traditional Political Machine Bosses." *Albany Times Union,* May 29, 1983, p. A–5.

———. "The Mayor's Stormy Pond." *Albany Times Union,* May 29, 1983, p. A–5.

McSeveney, Samuel T. *The Politics of Depression: Political Behavior in the Northeast, 1893–1896.* New York: Oxford University Press, 1972.

Mann, Arthur. *La Guardia Comes to Power, 1933.* New York: J. B. Lippincott, 1965.

Marable, Manning. "How Washington Won: The Political Economy of Race in Chicago." *Intergroup Relations* 11, no. 2 (Summer 1983): 56–81.

Marcus, Robert D. *Grand Old Party: Political Structure in the Gilded Age.* New York: Oxford University Press, 1971.

Mayhew, David R. *Placing Parties in American Politics.* Princeton: Princeton University Press, 1986.

Merriam, Charles. *The American Party System.* New York: Macmillan, 1922.

Merriam, Charles E., and Harold F. Gosnell. *Non-Voting: Causes and Methods of Control.* Chicago: University of Chicago Press, 1924.

Merton, Robert K. *Social Theory and Social Structure.* Rev. ed. New York: Free Press, 1968. Originally published in 1949.

Miller, Alan C. "Corning: From the Shadow to 'Absolute King.'" *Albany Times Union,* October 21, 1979, p. A–19.

———. "His Honor, the Boss." *Albany Times Union,* October 25, 1979, p. 14.

Miller, William D. *Mr. Crump of Memphis.* Baton Rouge: Louisiana State University Press, 1964.

Miller, Zane L. *Boss Cox's Cincinnati: Urban Politics in the Progressive Era.* New York: Oxford University Press, 1968.

Mink, Gwendolyn. *Old Labor and New Immigrants in American Political Development.* Ithaca: Cornell University Press, 1986.

Mladenka, Kenneth R. "The Urban Bureaucracy and the Chicago Political Machine: Who Gets What and the Limits to Political Control." *American Political Science Review* 74, no. 4 (December 1980): 991–998.

———. "Citizen Demands and Urban Services: The Distribution of Bureaucratic Response in Chicago and Houston." *American Journal of Political Science* 25, no. 4 (November 1981): 693–714.

Mohl, Raymond A. "Miami: The Ethnic Cauldron." In *Sunbelt Cities: Politics and Growth Since World War Two,* edited by Richard M. Bernard and Bradley R. Rice, pp. 58–99. Austin: University of Texas Press, 1983.

Mohr, James C. *The Radical Republicans and Reform in New York During Reconstruction.* Ithaca: Cornell University Press, 1973.

Mollenkopf, John H. *The Contested City.* Princeton: Princeton University Press, 1983.

Montgomery, David. "The Irish and the American Labor Movement." In *America and Ireland, 1776–1976,* edited by David Noel Doyle and Owen Dudley Edwards, pp. 205–217. Westport, Conn.: Greenwood Press, 1980.

Moore, Joan, and Harry Pachon. *Hispanics in the United States.* Englewood Cliffs, N.J.: Prentice-Hall, 1985.

Morris, Charles R. *The Cost of Good Intentions: New York City and the Liberal Experiment, 1960–1975.* New York: McGraw-Hill, 1981.

Moscow, Warren. *Politics in the Empire State.* New York: Alfred A. Knopf, 1948.

———. *The Last of the Big-Time Bosses: The Life and Times of Carmine De Sapio and the Rise and Fall of Tammany Hall.* New York: Stein and Day, 1971.

Mosher, William E., and Sophie Polah. "Public Employment in the United States." *National Municipal Review* 21, no. 1 (January 1932): 51–72.

Mowry, George. *The California Progressives.* Chicago: Quadrangle, 1963.

Moynihan, Daniel Patrick. "The Irish." In *Beyond the Melting Pot,* by Nathan Glazer and Daniel Patrick Moynihan, pp. 217–287. Cambridge, Mass.: MIT Press, 1964.

Munro, William Bennett. *The Government of American Cities.* 3d ed. New York: Macmillan, 1920.

Mushkat, Jerome. *Tammany: The Evolution of a Political Machine, 1789–1865.* Syracuse, N.Y.: Syracuse University Press, 1971.

———. *The Reconstruction of the New York Democracy, 1861–1874.* Rutherford, N.J.: Fairleigh Dickinson University Press, 1981.

Myers, Gustavus. *History of Tammany Hall.* New York: Dover, 1971. Originally published in 1917.

Myers, Jerome K. "Assimilation in the Political Community." *Sociology and Social Research* 35 (January-February 1951): 175–182.

Nelli, Humbert S. "John Powers and the Italians: Politics in a Chicago Ward, 1896–1921." *Journal of American History* 57 (June 1970): 67–84.

Nelson, William E., Jr., and Philip J. Meranto. *Electing Black Mayors: Political Action in the Black Community.* Columbus: Ohio State University Press, 1977.

New York State Legislature. *Red Book, State of New York.* Albany: New York State Legislature, 1887–1897.

New York Tribune. *Tribune Almanac and Political Register.* New York: G. Dearborn, 1855–1886.

New York World. *World Almanac.* New York: New York World, 1893–1941.

O'Connor, Edwin. *The Last Hurrah.* New York: Bantam Books, 1956.

O'Connor, James. *The Fiscal Crisis of the State.* New York: St. Martin's Press, 1973.

O'Connor, Len. *Clout: Mayor Daley and His City.* Chicago: Henry Regnery, 1975.

———. *Requiem: The Decline and Demise of Mayor Daley and His Era.* Chicago: Contemporary Books, 1977.

Offe, Claus. *Contradictions of the Welfare State.* Cambridge, Mass.: MIT Press, 1984.

Olin, Spencer. *California's Prodigal Sons: Hiram Johnson and the Progressive Movement, 1911–1917.* Berkeley and Los Angeles: University of California Press, 1968.

Ostrogorski, M. *Democracy and the American Party System.* New York: Macmillan, 1921.

Parenti, Michael. "Ethnic Politics and the Persistence of Ethnic Identification." *American Political Science Review* 61, no. 3 (September 1967): 717–726.

Patterson, James T. *The New Deal and the States: Federalism in Transition.* Princeton: Princeton University Press, 1969.

Peterson, Lorin. *The Day of the Mugwump.* New York: Random House, 1961.

Peterson, Paul. *City Limits.* Chicago: University of Chicago Press, 1981.

Petrocik, John. "Voting in a Machine City: Chicago, 1975." *Ethnicity* 8 (1981): 320–340.

"Philadelphia: Man or Machine?" *The Economist,* August 8, 1981.

Phillips, Kevin. "New Americans for the Next America." *Los Angeles Times,* May 11, 1986.

Piven, Frances Fox, and Richard A. Cloward. *Regulating the Poor: The Functions of Public Welfare.* New York: Vintage Books, 1971.

Pratt, John W. "Boss Tweed's Public Welfare Program." *New York Historical Society Quarterly* 45, no. 4 (October 1961): 396–411.

Preston, Michael B. "Black Politics and Public Policy in Chicago: Self-Interest Versus Constituent Representation." In *The New Black Politics: The Search for Political Power,* edited by Michael B. Preston, Lenneal J. Henderson, Jr., and Paul Purycar, pp. 159–186. New York: Longman, 1982.

———. "Black Politics in the Post-Daley Era." In *After Daley: Chicago Politics in Transition,* edited by Samuel K. Gove and Louis H. Masotti, pp. 88–117. Urbana: University of Illinois Press, 1982.

Preston, Michael B., Lenneal J. Henderson, Jr., and Paul Puryear, eds. *The New Black Politics: The Search for Political Power.* New York: Longman, 1982.

Price, Gilbert. "Skirmish Begins 'At Large' Battle." *Cleveland Call and Post,* February 13, 1986, p. H–8.

Prince, Carl E. *The Federalists and the Origins of the U.S. Civil Service.* New York: New York University Press, 1977.

Protess, David L. "Banfield's Chicago Revisited: The Conditions for and Social Policy Implications of the Transformation of a Political Machine." *Social Service Review* 48, no. 2 (June 1974): 184–202.

Quint, Howard H. *The Forging of American Socialism.* Indianapolis, Ind.: Bobbs-Merrill, 1953.

Rakove, Milton L. *Don't Make No Waves, Don't Back No Losers: An Insider's Analysis of the Daley Machine.* Bloomington: Indiana University Press, 1975.

———. "Jane Byrne and the New Chicago Politics." In *After Daley: Chicago Politics in Transition,* edited by Samuel K. Gove and Louis H. Masotti, pp. 217–236. Urbana: University of Illinois Press, 1982.

Rakove, Milton L., ed. *We Don't Want Nobody Nobody Sent: An Oral History of the Daley Years.* Bloomington: Indiana University Press, 1979.

Rawls, Wendell, Jr. "Pittsburgh Nears End of Era as Flaherty Prepares to Move." *New York Times,* February 26, 1977.

Reddig, William. *Tom's Town: Kansas City and the Pendergast Legend.* New York: J. B. Lippincott, 1947.

Reed, Adolph L., Jr. *The Jesse Jackson Phenomenon.* New Haven: Yale University Press, 1986.

Reichley, James. *The Art of Government: Reform and Organization Politics in Philadelphia.* New York: Fund for the Republic, 1959.

Reynolds, George M. *Machine Politics in New Orleans, 1897–1926.* New York: Columbia University Press, 1936.

Rieder, Jonathan. *Canarsie: The Jews and Italians of Brooklyn Against Liberalism.* Cambridge, Mass.: Harvard University Press, 1985.

Riordan, William L., comp. *Plunkitt of Tammany Hall.* New York: E. P. Dutton, 1963. Originally published in 1905.

"Rizzo's Town." *The Economist,* November 4, 1978.

Robinson, Frank S. *Machine Politics: A Study of Albany's O'Connells.* New Brunswick, N.J.: Transaction Books, 1977.

Robinson, Theodore P., and Thomas R. Dye. "Reformism and Black Representation on City Councils." *Social Science Quarterly* 59, no. 1 (June 1978): 133–142.

Rogin, Michael. *The Intellectuals and McCarthy: The Radical Specter.* Cambridge, Mass.: MIT Press, 1967.

———. "Progressivism and the California Electorate." *Journal of American History* 55 (September 1968): 297–314.

———. "Nonpartisanship and the Group Interest." In *Power and Community: Dissenting Essays in Political Science,* edited by Philip Green and Sanford Levenson, pp. 112–141. New York: Vintage Books, 1970.

Rothman, Edwin. "Factional Machine-Politics: William Curran and the Baltimore City Democratic Party Organization, 1929–1946." Ph.D. dissertation, Johns Hopkins University, 1949.

Royko, Mike. *Boss: Richard J. Daley of Chicago.* New York: Signet, 1971.

Rusk, Jerrold G. "Comment: The American Electoral Universe: Speculation and Evidence." *American Political Science Review* 68, no. 3 (September 1974): 1028–1049.

Ryan, Dennis P. *Beyond the Ballot Box: A Social History of the Boston Irish, 1845–1917.* Rutherford, N.J.: Fairleigh Dickinson University Press, 1983.

Sacks, Paul Martin. *The Donegal Mafia: An Irish Political Machine.* New Haven: Yale University Press, 1976.

Salter, J. T. *Boss Rule: Portraits in City Politics.* New York: McGraw-Hill, 1935.

San Francisco Board of Supervisors. *San Francisco Municipal Reports.* San Francisco: W. H. Hinton, 1870–1915.

San Francisco Recorder. *General List of Citizens of the United States Registered in the Great Register, 1867.* San Francisco: County Recorder, 1867.

Saxton, Alexander. "San Francisco Labor and the Populist and Progressive Insurgencies." *Pacific Historical Review* 34 (September 1965): 421–438.

———. *The Indispensable Enemy: Labor and the Anti-Chinese Movement in California.* Berkeley and Los Angeles: University of California Press, 1971.

Sayre, Wallace S., and Herbert Kaufman. *Governing New York City: Politics in the Metropolis.* New York: Russell Sage, 1960.

Scott, James C. "Corruption, Machine Politics, and Political Change." *American Political Science Review* 63, no. 4 (December 1969): 1142–1158.

———. "Political Clientelism: A Bibliographic Essay." In *Friends, Followers, and Factions: A Reader in Political Clientelism,* edited by Steffen W. Schmidt, Laura Guasti, Carl H. Landé, and James C. Scott, pp. 483–505. Berkeley and Los Angeles: University of California Press, 1977.

Scott, James C., and Benedict J. Kerkvliet. "How Traditional Rural Patrons Lose Legitimacy." In *Friends, Followers, and Factions: A Reader in Political Clientelism,* edited by Steffen W. Schmidt, Laura Guasti, Carl H. Landé, and James C. Scott, pp. 439–458. Berkeley and Los Angeles: University of California Press, 1977.

Secrist, Horace. *An Economic Analysis of the Constitutional Restrictions upon Public Indebtedness in the United States.* Madison: University of Wisconsin, 1914.

Shaw, Douglas V. *The Making of an Immigrant City: Ethnic and Cultural Conflict in Jersey City, New Jersey, 1850–1877.* New York: Arno Press, 1976.

Shefter, Martin. "The Emergence of the Political Machine: An Alternative View." In *Theoretical Perspectives on Urban Politics,* edited by Willis D. Hawley et al., pp. 14–44. Englewood Cliffs, N.J.: Prentice-Hall, 1976.

———. "New York City's Fiscal Crisis: The Politics of Inflation and Retrenchment." *Public Interest* 48 (Summer 1977): 98–127.

———. "The Electoral Foundations of the Political Machine: New York City, 1884–1897." In *The History of American Electoral Behavior,* edited by Joel H. Silbey, Allan A. Bogue, and William H. Flanigan, pp. 263–298. Princeton: Princeton University Press, 1978.

———. "Economic Crises, Social Coalitions, and Political Institutions: New York City's Little New Deal." Paper presented at the annual meeting of the American Political Science Association, New York, September 3–6, 1981.

———. *Political Crisis/Fiscal Crisis: The Collapse and Revival of New York City.* New York: Basic Books, 1985.

Shover, John L. "The Progressives and the Working-Class Vote in California." *Labor History* 10 (Fall 1969): 584–601.

———. "The Emergence of a Two-Party System in Republican Philadelphia, 1924–1936." *Journal of American History* 60, no. 4 (March 1974): 985–1002.

Skowronek, Stephen. *Building a New American State.* Cambridge: Cambridge University Press, 1982.

Sloan, Leonard. "Good Government and the Politics of Race." *Social Problems* 17 (Fall 1969): 171–174.

Smith, Reed M. *State Government in Transition: Reforms of the Leader Administration, 1955–1959.* Philadelphia: University of Pennsylvania Press, 1959.

Smith, Robert C. "The Changing Shape of Urban Black Politics: 1960–1970." *Annals* 439 (September 1978): 16–28.

Smith, Thomas F. X. *The Powerticians.* Secaucus, N.J.: Lyle Stuart, 1980.

Snowiss, Leo M. "Congressional Recruitment and Representation." *American Political Science Review* 60, no. 3 (September 1966): 627–639.

Sorauf, Frank. "State Patronage in a Rural County." *American Political Science Review* 50, no. 4 (December 1956): 1046–1056.

———. "The Silent Revolution in Patronage." *Public Administration Review* 20, no. 1 (Winter 1960): 28–34.

Speed, John Gilmer. "The Purchase of Votes in New York City." *Harper's Weekly* 49 (1905): 386–387.

Stack, John F., Jr. *International Conflict in an American City.* Westport, Conn.: Greenwood Press, 1979.

Starr, Roger. "John V. Lindsay: A Political Portrait." *Commentary,* February 1970, pp. 25–46.

Stave, Bruce M. *The New Deal and the Last Hurrah: Pittsburgh Machine Politics.* Pittsburgh: University of Pittsburgh Press, 1970.

Steffens, Lincoln. *The Shame of the Cities.* New York: Hill and Wang, 1966. Originally published in 1903.

Steinberg, Alfred. *The Bosses.* New York: Macmillan, 1972.

Sternlieb, George, and James W. Hughes. "The Uncertain Future of the

Center City." *Urban Affairs Quarterly* 18, no. 4 (June 1983): 455–472.

Stewart, Frank M. *A Half Century of Municipal Reform.* Berkeley and Los Angeles: University of California Press, 1950.

Stone, Chuck. *Black Political Power in America.* Indianapolis, Ind.: Bobbs-Merrill, 1968.

Stone, Clarence N. *Economic Growth and Neighborhood Discontent: System Bias in the Urban Renewal Program of Atlanta.* Chapel Hill: University of North Carolina Press, 1976.

———. "Atlanta: Protest and Elections Are Not Enough." In "Black and Hispanic Power in City Politics: A Forum," edited by Rufus P. Browning and Dale Rogers Marshall. *PS* 19, no. 3 (Summer 1986): 618–625.

Stone, Harold A., Don K. Price, and Kathryn H. Stone. *City Manager Government in the United States: A Review After Twenty-Five Years.* Chicago: Public Administration Service, 1940.

Strausberg, Chinta. "Wallace Won't Quit." *Chicago Defender,* April 3, 1986.

———. "Mayor Asks Illinois' Cities to Battle Feds." *Chicago Defender,* May 24, 1986.

———. "Hutch, Humes Answer Critics." *Chicago Defender,* June 2, 1986.

———. "Humes, Stroger Trade Blows." *Chicago Defender,* June 3, 1986.

———. "Mayor Seizes Control of Park Board." *Chicago Defender,* June 17, 1986, pp. 1, 18.

Suiter, William O. "State Limits on Local Property Taxes." In *Municipal Year Book, 1936,* pp. 328–339. Chicago: International City Managers' Association, 1936.

Tachibana, Judy. "California's Asians: Power from a Growing Population." *California Journal* 17, no. 11 (November 1986): 534–543.

Tarr, Joel A. *A Study in Boss Politics: William Lorimer of Chicago.* Urbana: University of Illinois Press, 1971.

Teaford, Jon C. *City and Suburb: The Political Fragmentation of Metropolitan America, 1850–1970.* Baltimore: Johns Hopkins University Press, 1979.

Thernstrom, Stephan. *The Other Bostonians: Poverty and Progress in the American Metropolis, 1880–1970.* Cambridge, Mass.: Harvard University Press, 1973.

Thompson, Edward, III. "Race and the Chicago Election." *Journal of Ethnic Studies* 11, no. 4 (Winter 1984): 1–10.

Trout, Charles H. *Boston, the Great Depression, and the New Deal.* New York: Oxford University Press, 1977.

Tucker, D. *Lieutenant Lee of Beale Street*. Nashville: Vanderbilt University Press, 1971.

Tucker, David M. *Memphis Since Crump: Bossism, Blacks, and Civic Reformers, 1948–1968*. Knoxville: University of Tennessee Press, 1980.

Tugwell, Rexford. *The Brains Trust*. New York: Viking, 1968.

U.S. Bureau of the Census. *Special Reports: Statistics of Cities, 1902*. Washington, D.C.: Government Printing Office, 1902.

———. *Special Reports: Occupations at the Twelfth Census*. Washington, D.C.: Government Printing Office, 1904.

———. *Census of Population, 1920*. Washington, D.C.: Government Printing Office, 1922–1923.

———. *Fifteenth Census of the United States, 1930*. Washington, D.C.: Government Printing Office, 1933.

———. *Financial Statistics of Cities Having a Population over 100,000, 1932*. Washington, D.C.: Government Printing Office, 1934.

———. *Statistical Abstract of the United States, 1938*. Washington, D.C.: Government Printing Office, 1938.

———. *Sixteenth Census of the United States, 1940*. Washington, D.C.: Government Printing Office, 1943.

———. *State and Local Government Special Studies: Historical Review of State and Local Government Finances*. Washington, D.C.: Government Printing Office, 1948.

———. *Statistical Abstract of the United States, 1950*. Washington, D.C.: Government Printing Office, 1950.

———. *Historical Statistics of the United States: Colonial Times to 1957*. Washington, D.C.: Government Printing Office, 1960.

———. *Census of Population: 1960*. Washington, D.C.: Government Printing Office, 1963.

———. *Voter Participation in the National Election, November, 1964*. Washington, D.C.: Government Printing Office, 1965.

———. *Local Government Employment in Selected Metropolitan Areas and Large Counties, 1970*. Washington, D.C.: Government Printing Office, 1971.

———. *1970 Census of Population*. Washington, D.C.: Government Printing Office, 1973.

———. *Voting and Registration in the Election of November, 1976*. Washington, D.C.: Government Printing Office, 1977.

———. *Statistical Abstract, 1981*. Washington, D.C.: Government Printing Office, 1981.

———. *Census of Housing, 1980*. Washington, D.C.: Government Printing Office, 1982.

———. *Local Government Employment in Selected Metropolitan Areas and Large Counties, 1981.* Washington, D.C.: Government Printing Office, 1983.

———. *1980 Census of Population.* Washington, D.C.: Government Printing Office, 1983.

U.S. Bureau of Labor Statistics. *Manpower Impact of Federal Government Programs: Selected Grants-in-Aid to State and Local Governments.* Washington, D.C.: Government Printing Office, 1973.

U.S. Census Office. *Ninth Census, 1870.* Washington, D.C.: Government Printing Office, 1872.

———. *Report on Valuation, Taxation, and Public Indebtedness: 1880.* Washington, D.C.: Government Printing Office, 1884.

———. *Eleventh Census of the United States, 1890.* Washington, D.C.: Government Printing Office, 1895.

———. *Twelfth Census of the United States, 1900.* Washington, D.C.: Government Printing Office, 1901.

———. *Special Reports: Wealth, Debt, and Taxation.* Washington, D.C.: Government Printing Office, 1907.

U.S. Civil Service Commission. *Minority Group Employment in the Federal Government, 1975.* Washington, D.C.: Government Printing Office, 1977.

U.S. Equal Employment Opportunity Commission. *Minorities and Women in State and Local Government, 1977.* Washington, D.C.: Government Printing Office, 1977.

U.S. National Advisory Commission on Civil Disorders. *Report.* Washington, D.C.: Government Printing Office, 1968.

U.S. Social Security Board. "Relief in Urban Areas." In *Municipal Year Book, 1939,* pp. 460–465. Chicago: International City Managers' Association, 1939.

U.S. Works Progress Administration. *Family Unemployment.* Washington, D.C.: Government Printing Office, 1940.

———. *Summary of Relief and Federal Work Program Statistics, 1933–1940.* Washington, D.C.: Government Printing Office, 1941.

Vanecko, James J., and Jennie Kronenfeld. "Preferences for Public Expenditures and Ethno-Racial Group Membership: A Test of the Theory of Political Ethos." *Ethnicity* 4 (December 1977): 311–336.

Wald, Kenneth D. "The Electoral Base of Political Machines: A Deviant Case Analysis." *Urban Affairs Quarterly* 16, no. 1 (September 1980): 3–29.

Waldman, Sidney. *Foundations of Political Analysis.* Englewood Cliffs, N.J.: Prentice-Hall, 1972.

Walton, Hanes, Jr. *Black Politics: A Theoretical and Structural Analysis.* Philadelphia: J. B. Lippincott, 1972.

Warner, Sam Bass, Jr. *Streetcar Suburbs: The Process of Growth in Boston, 1870–1900.* Cambridge, Mass.: Harvard University Press, 1962.

Watkins, Linda M. "Pittsburgh Blacks' Paucity of Political Clout Stirs Struggle over the City's At-Large Election System." *Wall Street Journal,* April 1, 1986, p. 58.

Watson, Donald S. "Financing Relief and Recovery: [The] Reconstruction Finance Corporation." In *Municipal Year Book, 1937,* pp. 375–381. Chicago: International City Managers' Association, 1937.

Watson, Tom. "All Powerful Machine of Yore Endures in New York's Nassau." *Congressional Quarterly Weekly Report,* April 17, 1985, pp. 1623–1625.

Weinberg, Martha Wagner. "Boston's Kevin White: A Mayor Who Survives." *Political Science Quarterly* 96, no. 1 (Spring 1981): 87–106.

Weingrod, Alex. "Patrons, Patronage, and Political Parties." *Comparative Studies in Society and History* 10, no. 4 (July 1968): 377–400.

Weiss, Nancy Joan. *Charles Francis Murphy, 1858–1924: Respectability and Responsibility in Tammany Politics.* Northampton, Mass.: Smith College, 1968.

Welch, Susan, and Albert Karnig. "The Impact of Black Elected Officials on Urban Social Expenditures." *Policy Studies Journal* 7 (Summer 1979): 707–714.

Wendt, Lloyd, and Herman Kogan. *Bosses in Lusty Chicago: The Story of Bathhouse John and Hinky Dink.* Bloomington: Indiana University Press, 1967. Originally published in 1943 as *Lords of the Levee.*

Werner, M. R. *Tammany Hall.* Garden City, N.Y.: Doubleday, Doran and Co., 1928.

Whitehead, Ralph, Jr. "The Organization Man." *American Scholar* 46 (Summer 1977): 351–357.

———. "The Chicago Story: Two Dailies, a Campaign—and an Earthquake." *Columbia Journalism Review* (July–August 1983): 25–31.

Whyte, William. *Financing New York City.* New York: Annals of the Academy of Political and Social Science, 1935.

Whyte, William Foote. "Social Organization in the Slums." *American Sociological Review* 8, no. 1 (February 1943): 34–39.

———. *Street Corner Society: The Social Structure of an Italian Slum.* Chicago: University of Chicago Press, 1955. Originally published in 1943.

Wilentz, Sean. *Chants Democratic: New York City and the Rise of the Working Class, 1788–1850.* New York: Oxford University Press, 1984.

Williams, R. Hal. *The Democratic Party and California Politics, 1880–1896.* Stanford: Stanford University Press, 1973.

Willis, Marty. "Jan. 6 Demonstration to Greet All-White City Council." *Pittsburgh Courier,* January 11, 1986, pp. A–1, A–4.

Wilson, James Q. "The Economy of Patronage." *Journal of Political Economy* 69, no. 4 (August 1961): 369–380.

———. *The Amateur Democrat: Club Politics in Three Cities.* Chicago: University of Chicago Press, 1966.

Wilson, James Q. and Edward C. Banfield. "Public-Regardingness as a Value Premise in Voting Behavior." *American Political Science Review* 58, no. 4 (December 1964): 876–887.

Wittke, Carl. *Refugees of Revolution.* Philadelphia: University of Pennsylvania Press, 1952.

———. *The Irish in America.* Baton Rouge: Louisiana State University Press, 1956.

Wolfinger, Raymond E. "The Development and Persistence of Ethnic Voting." *American Political Science Review* 59, no. 4 (December 1965): 896–908.

———. "Some Consequences of Ethnic Politics." In *The Electoral Process,* edited by M. Kent Jennings and L. Harmon Zeigler, pp. 42–54. Englewood Cliffs, N.J.: Prentice-Hall, 1966.

———. "Why Political Machines Have Not Withered Away and Other Revisionist Thoughts." *Journal of Politics* 34, no. 2 (May 1972): 365–398.

———. *The Politics of Progress.* Englewood Cliffs, N.J.: Prentice-Hall, 1974.

Wolfinger, Raymond E., and John Osgood Field. "Political Ethos and the Structure of City Government." *American Political Science Review* 60, no. 2 (June 1966): 306–326.

Woods, Robert A., ed. *Americans in Process.* Boston: Houghton Mifflin, 1903.

Wright, Gavin. "The Political Economy of New Deal Spending: An Econometric Analysis." *Review of Economics and Statistics* 56, no. 1 (February 1974): 30–38.

Yearley, C. K. *The Money Machines: The Breakdown and Reform of Governmental and Party Finance in the North, 1860–1920.* Albany: State University of New York Press, 1970.

Zink, Harold. *City Bosses in the United States.* Durham, N.C.: Duke University Press, 1930.

Index

Aaron, Henry, 184
AFDC (Aid to Families with Dependent
 Children): and co-optation of black
 service providers, 168, 265; demobiliz-
 ing impact of, on welfare recipients,
 168, 265; exploited by Daley machine,
 225; politicization of, 167; used to
 placate urban blacks, 166
Affirmative action, 141; in Chicago,
 152
Albany: Barnes machine in, 68; homeownership in, 84; McCabe machine in,
 84; new immigrant voters in, 10,
 123–124; redevelopment in, 158–
 160; state government interference in,
 38; War on Poverty in, 169. See also
 O'Connell machine
Altgeld, John P. (governor of Illinois), 44,
 204
American Labor party, 138, 173
Andersen, Kristi, 123
Annexation: as double-edged sword, 57;
 and New York Consolidation Act of
 1897, 56; as resource-enhancement
 strategy, 13, 213; and suburban incorporation, 81
Asian-Americans, 259, 263. See also Minorities, contemporary

Banfield, Edward C., and mass theory of
 machine, 8, 196, 209, 226
Barnes, William E. (Republican boss of
 Albany), 68, 74
Beer, Samuel, 232
Bell, Daniel, 239
Belloni, Frank, 230
Black-Irish comparisons, 6, 237–238,
 260–265. See also Rainbow theory of
 machine

Black mayors, 258–262. See also names
 of individual mayors
Blacks: activism of, during 1960s, 166;
 in Boston, 178, 187; critical to Daley
 mayoral victories, 152, 154, 165; declining turnout in Chicago among
 (1964–1976), 169; disenchanted with
 Daley machine, 185; migration of, to
 northern cities, 146; political remobilization among, and rainbow
 coalition, 184–186, 260–262; and
 sub-machines in Chicago and Pittsburgh, 3, 165–166, 168; and welfare
 state dependence, 168–170. See also
 Minorities, contemporary
Bobcock, John Paul, 2
Border and Southern states, political culture and machine building in, 195,
 228–229. See also Sunbelt cities
Boston: blacks in postwar, 178, 187; factional ward politics in, 19, 42, 70; impact of Depression in, 117; Irish
 population in, 9, 177; new immigrants
 in, 128; postwar reform and redevelopment in, 143, 176–177; White's
 personal organization in, 177–179,
 182. See also Curley, James Michael
Brains Trust, The (Tugwell), 16
Brennan, George, and Hopkins-Sullivan
 faction, 12, 78, 102
Bridges, Amy, 257
Broderick, David, 27
Brooks, Robert, 62
Brown, Homer, 3, 165
Browning, Rufus, 264
Bryce, James, 19, 49, 236
Buckley, Christopher (boss of San
 Francisco): fall of, 228; fiscal conser-
 vatism of, 47–48

Compositor: G & S Typesetters, Inc.
Printer: Braun-Brumfield, Inc.
Binder: Braun-Brumfield, Inc.
Text: 11/13 Sabon
Display: Sabon

MACHINE LEARNING

An Artificial Intelligence Approach
Volume II

MACHINE LEARNING
An Artificial Intelligence Approach
Volume II

Contributors:

Saul Amarel
John R. Anderson
Ranan B. Banerji
Robert C. Berwick
Gary L. Bradshaw
Mark H. Burstein
Jaime G. Carbonell
Gerald DeJong
Nachum Dershowitz
Thomas G. Dietterich
Kenneth D. Forbus
Jean-Gabriel Ganascia
Dedre Gentner
John H. Holland
Smadar T. Kedar-Cabelli
Yves Kodratoff
Patrick Langley

Michael Lebowitz
Douglas B. Lenat
Sridhar Mahadevan
Ryszard S. Michalski
Donald Michie
Allen Newell
J. Ross Quinlan
Paul S. Rosenbloom
Claude Sammut
Bernard Silver
Herbert A. Simon
Robert E. Stepp III
Gail E. Thornburg
Paul E. Utgoff
Patrick H. Winston
Jan M. Zytkow

Editors:

Ryszard S. Michalski
University of Illinois
at Urbana-Champaign, IL

Jaime G. Carbonell
Carnegie-Mellon University
Pittsburgh, PA

Tom M. Mitchell
Rutgers University
New Brunswick, NJ

Morgan Kaufmann
Publishers, Inc.
95 First Street, Los Altos, California 94022

Printed in the United States of America

10   9   8   7   6   5   4   3   2

Library of Congress Cataloging-in-Publication Data
(Revised for vol. 2)
Main entry under title:

Machine learning.

    Vol. 2–   prepared by Saul Amarel . . . [et al.]
and published by M. Kaufmann Publishers, Los Altos, Calif.
       Bibliography; p. 511–549.
       Includes indexes.
       1. Machine learning.   2. Artificial intelligence.
   I. Anderson, John Robert, date. II. Michalski,
Ryszard Stanislaw, date. III. Carbonell, Jaime G.
(Jaime Guillermo) IV. Mitchell, Tom M. (Tom Michael), date.
V. Amarel, Saul
Q325.M32 1983   006.3′1   82-10654
ISBN 0-935382-05-4 (Volume 1)
ISBN 0-934613-00-1 (Volume 2)

Acknowledgments
The paper appearing as chapter 4 of this book originally appeared in the journal *Artificial Intelligence,* Volume 25, Number 2, pages 187–232, and is reprinted here with permission of North Holland Publishing, Amsterdam.

    Chapter 10 of this book is a portion of a book to be released soon by Kluwer Academic Publishers and is published here with the permission of Kluwer Academic Publishers, Hingham, Massachusetts.

    Chapter 17 is a modified version of an article published in *Artificial Intelligence Journal,* Volume 20, Number 10, and is published here with the permission of North Holland Publishing, Amsterdam.

CONTENTS

PREFACE

The recent extraordinary growth of artificial intelligence and its applications has been paralleled by a surge of interest in machine learning, a field concerned with the developing computational theories of learning processes and building learning machines. Because the ability to learn is clearly fundamental to any intelligent behavior, the concerns and goals of machine learning are central to the progress of artificial intelligence.

This book presents tutorial overviews and a selection of works representative of the state of the art in machine learning. It is the second basic text on this subject, following *Machine Learning: An Artificial Intelligence Approach* (Michalski, Carbonell, and Mitchell, 1983). The success of the first book and the rapid expansion of the field in recent years have encouraged the editors to put together the current collection. The individual chapters represent contributions of leading researchers in the field. Initial shorter versions of most of the chapters were presented at the Second International Workshop on Machine Learning, held June 22–24, 1983, at Allerton House in Monticello, the residential conference center of the University of Illinois.

The authors of the chapters have made a special effort to write their contributions in a readable tutorial fashion. It is hoped that this will make the book more accessible to a wide spectrum of readers with an interest in understanding the current state of machine learning. These might include researchers in artificial intelligence and cognitive science, knowledge engineers, computer scientists, data analysts, information scientists, philosophers, psychologists and linguists. The book is intended to serve both as a convenient source of information for them, and as a text for students taking courses in artificial intelligence, particularly in machine learning and knowledge acquisition.

Topics covered include

- A road-map and a classification of machine learning research
- Theoretical issues and methods for learning concepts and rules from examples
- Cognitive models of human learning
- Using analogy to learn concepts, to program, and to solve problems
- Quantitative discovery systems, theory formation, and conceptual clustering

- Learning in parallel rule-based systems
- Aspects of natural language learning
- Learning to solve equations

To facilitate instruction and further studies, an extensive indexed bibliography of recent contributions and landmarks of earlier research is provided, as well as an updated glossary of basic terms in machine learning.

It is our pleasant duty to thank many individuals who helped in various ways to make this book a reality. Our gratitude goes to Alan L. Meyrowitz from the Office of Naval Research and James N. Snyder and Richard Canaday from the Department of Computer Science at the University of Illinois at Urbana-Champaign for their support and contribution to the Second International Machine Learning Workshop. This Workshop provided the real impetus for the genesis of this book.

We thank the authors for their special efforts to make their chapters easy to read and consistent with other chapters. Crucial to the quality of this book were comments and criticism from the reviewers of individual chapters: Jeff Becker, Kaihu Chen, Jerry DeJong, Brian Falkenhainer, Bruce Katz, Heedong Ko, Steve Minton, Bob Reinke, Robert Stepp, and Bryan Stout. We are indebted to the copy editor Kate Engelberg for helping to smooth some sharp edges in the text, and to Debi Place for her adept secretarial assistance. Thanks go also to MIT's Artificial Intelligence Laboratory for providing support for the first editor while he worked on this book.

We present this new text on machine learning to its community of readers in the hope that it will prove to be a valuable messenger of progress in this important field.

—*Ryszard S. Michalski, Jaime G. Carbonell, Tom M. Mitchell*

PART
ONE

GENERAL ISSUES

1

UNDERSTANDING THE NATURE OF LEARNING:

Issues and Research Directions

Ryszard S. Michalski*
Massachusetts Institute of Technology

Abstract

This chapter presents an overview of goals and directions in machine learning research and serves as a conceptual road map to other chapters. It investigates intrinsic aspects of the learning process, classifies current lines of research, and presents the author's view of the relationship among *learning paradigms, strategies,* and *orientations.*

1.1 DO WE NEED LEARNING MACHINES?

Artificial intelligence (AI) is now experiencing extraordinary growth, and applications of its ideas and methods are appearing in many fields. Among its most visible and important successes are the development of expert systems, practical implementations of natural language–understanding systems, significant advances in computer vision and speech understanding, and new insights into building powerful inference systems. This rapid expansion of activities in AI leads one to believe that new successes are forthcoming.

---

*On leave of absence from the University of Illinois at Urbana-Champaign.

In this context, it is important to ask what the limitations of the current methods are and what new directions research in this field should take. One of the obvious limitations, and hence a direction for further research, relates to *machine learning*—a field concerned with developing computational theories of learning and constructing learning systems.

Except for experimental programs developed in the course of machine learning research, current AI systems have very limited learning abilities or none at all. All of their knowledge must be programmed into them. When they contain an error, they cannot correct it on their own; they will repeat it endlessly, no matter how many times the procedure is executed. They can neither improve gradually with experience nor learn domain knowledge by experimentation. They cannot automatically generate their algorithms, formulate new abstractions, or develop new solutions by drawing analogies to old ones, or through discovery. Generally speaking, these systems lack the ability to draw *inductive inferences* from information given to them. One might say that almost all current AI systems are *deductive,* as they are able to draw conclusions from knowledge incorporated and/or supplied to them, but they cannot acquire or generate new knowledge on their own.

By contrast, when we look at human intelligence we see that among its most striking aspects are the abilities to acquire new knowledge, to learn new skills, and to improve with practice. In time, use of these learning abilities can turn a young, inexperienced person into a journeyman engineer, educator, artist, or physician. Our common perception is that a person who would repeat the same error again and again could hardly be called intelligent. The ability to learn from error is considered fundamental to the individual and to the society at large (Popper, 1959, 1981; Kuhn, 1970; Lakatos, 1970; Berkson and Wettersten, 1984; Hayes-Roth, 1983—*Machine Learning I,* chap. 8, see below).

Because learning ability is so intimately entwined with intelligent behavior and research in AI gives us new insights and powerful tools to study it, many researchers postulate that one of the new central goals for research in artificial intelligence should be understanding the nature of learning and implementing learning capabilities in machines (McCarthy, 1983; Schank, 1983). Overcoming the above-mentioned limitations sets an agenda of research tasks.

Questions then arise about whether this goal is achievable, and if so, whether it is desirable. Let us start with the question of achievability. Answering it involves us immediately in questions of definition. Can we identify some general criteria such that, if satisfied by a machine, we would agree to call this machine a learning system?

As machine learning research has shown, learning ability manifests itself not as an all-or-nothing quality but as a spectrum of information-processing activities, ranging from the direct memorization of facts and acquisition of simple skills by imitation to very intricate inferential processes leading to creation of new concepts and discovery of new knowledge. It always involves a change in a system, whether human or machine, that makes it better in some sense.

For now, let us put the question of the definition of learning aside (it is discussed in more detail in the next section of this chapter) and observe that machine learning is experiencing a renaissance after its past steady but slow growth. Efforts to develop programs exhibiting some forms of learning have multiplied in recent years. This young field has already achieved a number of successes. A summary of some of these efforts is found in *Machine Learning: An Artificial Intelligence Approach* (Michalski, Carbonell, and Mitchell, 1983), henceforth referred to as *Machine Learning I*. The current book is a sequel; it reports some key subsequent efforts characteristic of the state-of-the-art in machine learning.

On the basis of the results achieved so far, it is clear that some rudimentary machine learning abilities are possible. Already there exist programs able to formulate new concepts and discover previously unknown regularities in data; develop decision rules that can outperform human rules; draw interesting analogies; automatically learn problem-solving heuristics; or develop generalized plans for achieving a goal. Many of these programs are discussed in *Machine Learning I*. What is less clear is the level of progress that can be achieved in machine learning using conventional computer hardware and present programming methods. As always in science, such questions can be answered only by conducting further research and continuing to develop experimental learning systems.

New dimensions of research in machine learning will open with the development of *connection machines, fifth generation computer systems,* and other novel computer architectures, currently under development (e.g., Hillis, 1981; Kawanobe, 1984). For example, Hinton, Sejnowski, and Ackley (1984) describe how learning may occur in *Boltzmann machines.* The knowledge acquired by such systems is represented by the strengths of the connections between simple, neuron-like elements. The research in this direction should address the problem of overcoming the limitations of early systems of this type, such as the *Perceptron* (Minsky and Papert, 1969). New potential for research in machine learning also emerges in connection with the development of new programming systems, in particular, logic programming and its first embodiment in PROLOG (Robinson, 1983).

Why is it desirable to develop learning machines? It appears that the development of such systems is necessary to ensure further progress in artificial intelligence or closely related disciplines. This seems to be particularly true in areas such as expert systems or any large-scale, knowledge-based systems; computer vision and speech understanding; natural language understanding; intelligent tutoring systems; and (truly) friendly human-machine interfaces. As more and more complex tasks are set for AI systems, more and more knowledge must be represented in them. Such knowledge must encompass domain-specific facts and rules, commonsense heuristics and constraints, and general concepts and theories about the world. The scope of knowledge in any system must be widened to avoid a common problem with the current systems, sometimes referred to as falling off the *knowledge cliff* (Feigenbaum, 1984) or *brittleness* (Holland, 1975, chap. 20; see also Larkin et al., 1985). The problem is that a system performs well within the scope of knowledge provided to it, but any slight move outside its narrow competence causes the performance to deteriorate rapidly.

Introducing all the required knowledge into any new system is a very complex, time-consuming, and error-prone process, requiring special expertise. For example, building an expert system involves a collaborative effort of highly trained experts—at least one *domain expert* and one *knowledge engineer* (Davis and Lenat, 1982; Hayes-Roth, Waterman, and Lenat, 1983; Buchanan and Shortliffe, 1984). This task can be simplified by using machine learning techniques. Such techniques would enable a system to develop decision rules from examples of experts' decisions and through the automated analysis of facts in a database.

With the rapid increase in the amount of data and knowledge that the society generates, there is a growing need not only for storing, organizing, and delivering this information but also for using it in new, creative ways. Knowledge can be viewed as *compressed information* (Rendell, 1983), and we now need machines that can compress databases and information systems into knowledge bases automatically via conceptual analysis of their contents. As envisioned by Michie (1982), *"the most technically gripping challenge, even if not immediately the most economically important, will be how to spread the computer wave from the front end of the scientific process, the telescopes, microscopes, . . . spark chambers and the like, back to the recognition and reasoning processes by which the chaos of data is finally consolidated into orderly discovery."*

This chapter's author might add that the computer will have a role not only as *scientists'* and *technologists'* intelligent assistant but also as an intelligent *personal* assistant. Individuals in the expanding information society will need such assistants to cope with the overwhelming amounts of available information and the complexities of everyday decision making. In order for such assistants to play the designated roles, their function and knowledge should by *dynamic.* These assistants should be able to adapt to changing demands and be self-modifiable; that is, they should be able to learn.

A similar need for learning abilities exists in the areas of computer vision and speech understanding. To build a computer vision system, one has to incorporate into it a variety of vision-specific transformations; concepts of geometry; physical and functional descriptions of visual objects the system is to recognize; and related information (e.g., Winston et al., 1983; Winston, 1984). To "handcraft" all this information into a system is difficult. It would be much easier to teach the system by showing it examples of given concepts and have it learn the appropriate generalizations and descriptions, just as we teach visual concepts to humans.

A system capable of understanding and interacting with humans in natural language has to be equipped with knowledge of syntactic properties of language (Marcus, 1980), as well as with many concepts and concept structures (such as frames, scripts, and schemata) capturing semantic and pragmatic aspects of the language (Winograd, 1981; Schank, 1982; see also chaps. 19 and 21 of this volume). One may estimate that in an advanced natural language understander, the number of such concepts and concept structures may easily reach tens of thousands or more. Programming all this knowledge into a computer is a monumental task. It is very desirable to simplify this task by employing a learning system. In addition, even if at some point all this knowledge were incorporated in a machine, a language understander would not work well for long without learning abilities. The meaning of human concepts is dynamic; it changes with time and adapts to new contexts and requirements. Novel concepts are continuously being created and developed, and some are being outgrown. Therefore, as in the cases above, we need a learning system capable of acquiring new concepts and concept structures by generalization from examples or by analogy to prior knowledge. Such a system should be able to modify, specialize, or generalize old concepts in a flexible fashion.

Intelligent tutoring systems must be able to present material at a level of difficulty and detail suited to the state of knowledge of the student. In order to do so, the system must know and follow the student's changing knowledge. A desirable way of acquiring this information is not by repeated direct testing but by learning from clues, behavior, and the implicit model of the student during tutorial sessions. Thus learning abilities are required not only from the student but from the tutor as well (Sleeman and Brown, 1982; Sleeman, 1983—*Machine Learning I,* chap. 16).

Through learning capabilities future computers should be able to acquire knowledge directly by using documents and books, by conversing with humans, and by generalizing observations of their environment, which they make with their artificial senses. They should be capable of improving through practice and experience. It is possible that future machine learning systems will suffer little, if at all, from some human limitations, such as poor memory, distracted attention, low efficiency, and the difficulty of transferring acquired knowledge from one learner to another. Once one learning system is developed, a theoretically limitless number of copies of it can be built, which, one hopes, can be employed to learn new knowledge in diverse domains. In addition, any new knowledge acquired by a learning system can be copied to other systems rapidly and relatively inexpensively (unlike human knowledge, which must be painstakingly reacquired by each new student).

Of course, we are still far away from such idealized vision, but it has now become conceivable that such learning systems might be developed in the future. It is then desirable to consider not only expected advantages but also possible undesirable consequences. The latter issue could be dismissed by observing that any new technology brings new opportunities for misuse, and that this has never stopped us from developing it. Moreover, such aspects are usually considered an issue outside scientific or technical research. Yet we need to examine this particular issue carefully, for the creation of machines that can self-acquire knowledge brings about new dimensions of complexity in the development of technology and reflects on the way the field of machine learning should be developed.

The first dimension of complexity is the predictive opacity of self-changing systems. Predicting the behavior of machines that can learn inductively is considerably more difficult than predicting the behavior of machines without such an ability. The key idea behind learning machines is that they should be able to create knowledge that can surprise their human creators. This might cause unexpected difficulties, or even dangers, if someone would apply such a system to solve important problems without understanding the system's limitations. In addition, the increased unpredictability of learning machines implies increased possibilities for their misuse.

Some experts argue that predicting behavior of complex computer systems is very difficult already. They look at the addition of learning capabilities to our computers as further amplification of these difficulties, but not as a quantum leap to a new state. Whether we see a leap or merely an amplification of unpredictability, a strong expectation is that potential benefits from this technology will amply compensate for such undesirable consequences. And with regard to the increased potential for its misuse, why not use these smart learning machines to "police" other machines to prevent or combat attempted misapplication?

In addition to the difficulty of predicting the behavior of learning machines, another dimension must be considered, which stems from the very nature of any knowledge other than factual observation. As has been observed by Hume (see, e.g., 1888) and later by Popper (1959) and others, such knowledge is *inherently conjectural;* that is, any knowledge created by generalization from specific observations or by analogy to known facts cannot in principle be proven correct, though it may be disproven.

This results from the fact that inductive inference is not *truth preserving* but only *falsity preserving* (Michalski, 1983). As an illustration, consider this statement: "All scientists at MIT's AI Laboratory are bright." A deductive conclusion from this statement can be that Roger Light, who works at the AI Laboratory, must be bright. If the original premise is true, then this conclusion must be true also. An example of inductive inference from the initial premise might be this statement: "All scientists at MIT are bright." In this case, even if the original premise were true, such an inductive conclusion might not be. However, if the original premise is false, then this inductive conclusion must be false also. Thus, in contrast with a deductive system, correct inputs to an inductive system do not guarantee the correctness of the outputs. Moreover, for any given input there is theoretically an infinite number of possible inductive conclusions. The ones we actually make reflect the preferences, assumptions, and constraints that we use in formulating our generalizations (Medin, Wattenmaker, and Michalski, 1985; Utgoff, chap. 5).

For the above reasons, if learning machines are to generate knowledge useful to us, it is important that they be equipped with knowledge of all the relevant human constraints and assumptions. As it is unlikely that *all* subtle human and societal constraints and preferences will ever be made known to machines, there is the possibility that machine-generated knowledge will violate some human constraints. A quote from Hofstadter (1980) is pertinent here: *"Unless* [the program] *had an amazingly faithful replica of human body . . . it would probably have enormously different perspectives on what is important, what was interesting, etc."* Because the perception of what is important and what is interesting is a necessary component in guiding creation of new knowledge (Lenat, 1983), such differences are significant. Thus when such machine-created knowledge is used, it may lead to solutions that are technically flawless but socially undesirable.

A related concern is that people may give too much credibility to the knowledge created by machines. This phenomenon has already been observed in related contexts, for example, when people are unduly influenced by results of computer statistical analysis without clearly understanding its assumptions, or when people ascribe personality to a computer consultation system, as in the case of ELIZA (Weizenbaum, 1976). Furthermore, even if it may be well known to scientists that inductively generated knowledge is inherently error-prone, this fact may be less obvious to nonexperts.

An important implication of the above discussion is that any new knowledge generated by machines should be subjected to close *human scrutiny* before it is used. This suggests an important goal for research in machine learning: If people have to understand and validate machine-generated knowledge, then machine learning systems should be equipped with adequate *explanation facilities.* Furthermore, knowledge created by machines should be expressed in forms closely corresponding to human descriptions and mental models of this knowledge; that is, such knowledge should satisfy what this author calls the *comprehensibility principle* (Michalski, 1983). When designing explanation capabilities for learning systems, one should strive to facilitate human understanding not only of the surface results but also of the underlying principles, assumptions, and theories that lead to these results.

One may hypothesize that although the existence of advanced learning machines would eliminate the current *knowlege acquisition* bottleneck, it could ultimately create a *knowledge ratification* bottleneck. In this situation so much new knowledge might be generated by machines that it could become difficult for human experts to test and approve it. Should this happen—well, future researchers will have an interesting problem with which to while away their idle hours. One may envision these researchers inventing sophisticated learning machines that would design experiments to test knowledge created by other sophisticated learning machines.

With these notes of concern, mixed with arguments stressing the importance of machine learning, let us now look more closely at the intrinsic properties of the learning process.

1.2 WHAT IS LEARNING?

As mentioned earlier, a common view holds that learning involves making changes in the system that will improve it in some way. In this description, the term *improve* needs more precision. Clearly, wine improves with time, but nobody would call such an improvement learning.[1] Simon (1983—*Machine Learning I,* chap. 2) gives a more precise characterization:

> *"Learning denotes changes in the system that are adaptive in the sense that they enable the system to do the same task or tasks drawn from the same population more effectively the next time."*

The requirement that a system improve performance for learning to take place is widely accepted. There are, however, activities that can be categorized as learning, in which the *improvement criterion* is difficult to apply (as will be seen in a discussion below). Minsky (1985) in his insightful theory of thinking, *The Society of Mind,* replaces this criterion with a more general one requiring that changes are merely useful:

> *"Learning is making useful changes in our minds."*

He subsequently observes that such a definition is too broad to be of any use. Let us then approach the problem of capturing the fundamental aspects of learning in another way. It may be observed that learning is often equated simply with acquiring *new* knowledge, as in the statement: "As the satellite burned in the atmosphere, the spacelab astronaut *learned* that the satellite had an auxiliary antenna." In this case, the astronaut simply acquired a piece of information, but this will never improve his performance with *this* satellite. The *knowledge acquisition* aspect of learning seems to be the *essence* of most learning acts. Those acts where it appears to play only a small role are cases of what is usually termed *skill acquisition.* The latter refers to gradual improvement of motor or cognitive skills through repeated effort, sometimes involving little or no conscious thought (Carbonell, Michalski and Mitchell, 1983— *Machine Learning I,* chap. 1). In this discussion, however, we will concentrate on the knowledge acquisition aspect of learning, a theme that recurs throughout the book.

In order to acquire knowledge of anything, one, obviously, has to represent this knowledge in some form, whether as declarative statements, procedures, a mixture of the two, or as something else (McCarthy, 1968). This fact and the above considerations lead us to the following characterization of learning:

> *Learning is constructing or modifying representations of what is being experienced.*

---

[1]This counterexample was suggested by Steve Tanimoto from the University of Washington in Seattle.

The concept of *experience* includes here any sensory stimuli, as well as internal *Gedanken* processes. These stimuli and internal processes are the vehicles through which the learning system perceives the reality that it is trying to represent. The internal thought processes can themselves be a subject of learning.

Thus, from the above view, the central aspect of learning is the process of constructing a representation of some reality, rather than improving performance. Performance improvement is considered to be a consequence and often the purpose of building the representation, but it can be asserted only in the context of the learner's goals. Because most learning acts indeed involve improvement of performance and because it is easier to measure performance than to read minds, naturally we link the two. Yet, performance improvement does not seem to be an invariable condition for every act of learning. There are situations in which it does not appear to be of primary relevance, as in learning to appreciate beauty. There are also situations in which it may even be misleading. The latter situations occur when it is difficult to accurately assess the learner's goal. For example, workers in a labor camp may want to learn how to do less and appear to do more, yet they keep this goal secret. From the viewpoint of an external observer, these workers will appear not to be learning, as their performance will be decreasing with practice. Thus it seems clear that to determine learning by measuring performance may not be possible without knowing the goals of the learner.

Three dimensions seem to be particularly important for evaluating the constructed representations: *validity, effectiveness,* and *abstraction level.* Validity (or truthfulness) refers to the degree of accuracy with which the representation fits the reality. It characterizes the precision of the mapping between the reality and the representation. The second criterion, effectiveness, attempts to capture the performance aspect of learning. It characterizes the usefulness of the representation for achieving a given purpose or goal. The more effective the representation, the better the performance of the system. Thus this criterion is central for tasks in which performance is of primary concern. The third criterion, abstraction level, reflects the scope, detail, and precision of concepts used in the description. It defines the *explanatory* power of the representation. These three dimensions together determine what may be called the *quality* of learning.

The representations can be in the form of symbolic descriptions, algorithms, simulation models, control procedures, plans, images, or general formal theories. If one stretches the concept of representation to include physical or physiological imprints occurring in the nervous system when one is acquiring a skill, the above view of learning seems also to cover skill acquisition.

From this viewpoint, a fundamental problem in any research on machine learning concerns the form and method used to represent and modify the knowledge or the skill being acquired. With regard to the question of modifying knowledge, it is important to identify the components and the properties of the representation that are modifiable by the system and those that are not.

In the taxonomy of machine learning research given in chapter 1 (Carbonell, Michalski, and Mitchell) of *Machine Learning I,* three criteria were suggested as especially useful for classifying and comparing machine learning investigations: *learning strategy, knowledge representation,* and *application domain.* The learning strategy refers to the type of inference employed by the system during learning. Some additional ideas reflecting recent progress on this topic are presented in section 1.4 below. The criteria of knowledge representation and application domain were well covered in the above-mentioned reference and will be omitted here. Instead, two other classification criteria will be discussed in some detail: *research paradigms* (section 1.3) and *learning orientations* (section 1.5). The research paradigm criterion refers here to the approach taken to construct a system, and the learning orientation refers to the scope and the subject of study.

1.3 RESEARCH PARADIGMS

Since the inception of machine learning in the fifties, research efforts have placed the emphasis at different times on different approaches and goals. One can distinguish three major research paradigms or approaches in this area: *neural modeling* and *decision theoretic techniques; symbolic concept acquisition;* and *knowledge-intensive, domain-specific learning.* These research approaches differ chiefly in the amounts of a priori knowledge *built into* the learning system and in the way knowledge is *represented* and *modified* in the system.

The neural modeling approach strives to develop general-purpose learning systems that start with little initial knowledge. Such systems are usually referred to as *neural nets* or *self-organizing* systems. A system of this type consists of a network of interconnected elements, typically neuron-like, that perform some simple logical function, usually a threshold logic function. Such a system learns by incrementally modifying the *connection strengths* between the elements, typically by changing continuous (i.e., non-discrete) weights associated with these connections. The system's initial knowledge is provided by the choice of the input elements that represent selected attributes of objects under consideration and by the structure and initial strength of the connections in the network. This can be a random structure, one prearranged by the designer, or a mixture of the two. Such learning systems include the *Perceptron* (Rosenblatt, 1958), *Pandemonium* (Selfridge, 1959), and any learning machine using *discriminant functions* (Nilsson, 1965). More recent examples stemming from this paradigm are various adaptive control systems (Tsypkin, 1972; Caianiello and Musso, 1984). Research in this area has led to the *decision-theoretic approach* in pattern recognition. Related to this approach is research on *evolutionary learning* (Fogel, Owens, and Walsh, 1966; Conrad, 1983) and on *genetic algorithms* (Holland, 1975; see also chap. 20). As mentioned earlier, there is a resurgence of interest in this learning paradigm with the recent efforts to develop *connection machines* (Hinton, Sejnowski, and Ackley, 1984).

Characteristic features of systems built under this paradigm include low levels of a priori built-in knowledge and the use of continuously changeable parameters to achieve learning. A related feature is the numerical character of learning methods and algorithms. This strongly contrasts this paradigm with the next two paradigms, in which the main emphasis is on creating and manipulating complex symbolic structures during the process of learning.

In *symbolic concept acquisition* (SCA), the system learns by constructing a symbolic representation of a given set of concepts through the analysis of examples and counterexamples of these concepts. The representations typically are in the form of a logical expression, a decision tree, production rules, or a semantic network. Some of the systems developed under this paradigm have multipurpose applicability and have demonstrated practical usefulness. Examples of such systems are Winston's ARCH program (Winston, 1975), the AQVAL program (Michalski, 1975), and ID3 (Quinlan, 1979). In this paradigm, the attributes or predicates relevant to the concept are provided to the system by the teacher.

In *knowledge-intensive, domain-specific learning* (KDL), the system contains numerous predefined concepts, knowledge structures, domain constraints, heuristic rules, and built-in transformations relevant to the specific domain for which the system is built. Not all the relevant attributes or concepts are proved initially; the system is expected to derive new ones in the process of learning (this author refers to such a process as *constructive induction*). Thus the main differences between the KDL and SCA paradigms lie in the amount and the kind of background knowledge supplied to the system and the richness of knowledge structures generated by the system. Learning systems based on this approach are typically developed for a specific domain and cannot be used directly in another domain. The research in this paradigm has explored not only the strategy of *learning from examples,* but also strategies such as *learning by analogy,* and *learning by observation and discovery* (see section 1.4). Examples of systems based on this approach are Meta-DENDRAL (Buchanan and Feigenbaum, 1978) and AM (Lenat, 1983—*Machine Learning I,* chap. 9).

Many systems developed in the past represent a certain mixture of the above-mentioned approaches. An interesting combination of the SCA and KDL approaches is a system based on the idea of an *exchangeable knowledge module.* Such a system combines general-purpose learning mechanisms with built-in facilities for defining and using domain-specific knowledge. When such a system is applied to a given problem, domain-specific knowledge is supplied to it by the teacher via the system's knowledge representation facilities. By separating general inference capabilities from the domain-specific knowledge, such a learning system can be applied to a wide spectrum of different domains and still take advantage of domain-specific knowledge in the process of learning. This philosophy underlies the INDUCE system, which learns structural descriptions of objects from examples (Michalski, 1980). Winston's program for learning by analogy is another example (Winston, 1982). The LEX system for acquiring and refining problem-solving heuristics (Mitchell, Utgoff, and Banerji, 1983—*Machine Learning I*, chap. 6) and the EURISKO program for discovering new heuristics (Lenat, 1983) are other examples. Several chapters in this volume describe learning methods that also fall into this category.

For a historical review of these three research paradigms the reader is referred to chapter 1 in *Machine Learning I*. A sample of contemporary research on self-organizing systems is found in Caianiello and Musso (1984). A recent review of approaches to machine learning has been made by Langley and Carbonell (1984). The primary concerns of this book are symbolic concepts acquisition and knowledge-intensive, domain-specific paradigms of learning.

1.4 LEARNING STRATEGIES

In every learning situation, the learner transforms information provided by a teacher (or environment) into some new form in which it is stored for future use. The nature of this transformation determines the type of learning strategy used. Several basic strategies have been distinguished: *rote learning, learning by instruction, learning by deduction, learning by analogy,* and *learning by induction.* The latter subdivides into *learning from examples* and *learning by observation and discovery.* These strategies are ordered by the increasing complexity of the transformation (inference) from the information initially provided to the knowledge ultimately acquired. Their order thus reflects increasing effort on the part of the student and correspondingly decreasing effort on the part of the teacher. In any act of human learning, a mixture of these strategies is usually involved. It is useful to distinguish these strategies not only for tutorial purposes but for the purpose of designing learning systems as well. Though most current systems focus on a single learning strategy, one may expect that machine learning research will give increasing attention to multistrategy systems. Chapter 1 of *Machine Learning I* describes these learning strategies in detail. Because of their importance to this book and because of some changes in their classification brought about by recent research, they will be reviewed briefly here.

In rote learning there is basically no transformation; the information from the teacher is more or less directly accepted and memorized by the learner. A major concern here is how to index the stored knowledge for future retrieval. In learning by instruction (or *learning by being told*), the basic transformations performed by a learner are *selection* and *reformulation* (mainly at a syntactic level) of information provided by the teacher. In deductive learning, the learner draws deductive, truth-preserving inferences from the knowledge given and stores useful conclusions (this strategy was identified as a separate category only recently; see Michalski, 1983, 1985). Deductive learning includes knowledge reformulation, knowledge compilation, creation of macro-operators, caching, chunking, equivalence-preserving operationalization, and other truth-preserving transformations (see Glossary).

If the transformation process involves generalization of input information and selection of the most plausible or desirable result, that is, the inductive inference, then we have inductive learning. Learning by analogy is deductive and inductive learning combined. Here, descriptions from different domains are matched to determine a common substructure, which serves as the basis for analogical mapping. Finding the common substructure involves inductive inference, whereas performing analogical mapping is a form of deduction. *Learning by being reminded,* described by Schank (1982), can be viewed as a form of learning by analogy. Learning by analogy is discussed in chapters 13 (Burstein), 14 (Carbonell), and 15 (Dershowitz).

Inductive learning can be subdivided into learning from examples and learning by observation and discovery. In *learning from examples* (also called *concept acquisition*), the task is to determine a general description explaining all positive examples and excluding all negative examples of the target concept. The examples are provided by a source of information, which can be a teacher who knows the concept or the environment on which the student performs experiments and from which it receives feedback. The latter case is called *learning by experimentation* (this includes *learning by doing* and *learning by problem solving*). *Stimulus-response* learning can also be classified as a form of learning from examples.

Recent research has revealed two interesting subdivisions within this form of learning: *instance-to-class* and *part-to-whole generalization.* In instance-to-class generalization, the system is given independent instances (examples) of some class of objects, and the goal is to induce a general description of the class. Most research done on learning from examples has concentrated on such instance-to-class generalization. The objects can be structured blocks, geometrical shapes, descriptions of diseases, stories, problem solutions, control operators, and so forth. Various aspects of this problem are discussed in chapters 3 (Winston), 5 (Utgoff), 6 (Quinlan), 7 (Sammut and Banerji), 8 (Lebowitz), and 9 (Kodratoff and Ganascia). For a review of earlier methods for such generalization, see Dietterich and Michalski (1983— *Machine Learning I,* chap. 3) and Cohen and Feigenbaum (1982).

In part-to-whole generalization, the task is to hypothesize a description of a whole object (scene, situation, process), given selected parts of it. For example, given a collection of snapshots of selected parts of a room, reconstruct the total view of that room. Another example is to determine a rule (a theory) characterizing a sequence of objects or a process from seeing only a part of this sequence or process. This type of learning problem is considered in chapter 4 (Dietterich and Michalski). A closely related area of research concerns the *qualitative process prediction* (Michalski, Ko, and Chen, 1985).

In learning by observation and discovery (also called *descriptive generalization*), one searches, without the help of a teacher, for regularities and general rules explaining all or at least most observations. This form of learning includes *conceptual clustering* (forming object classes describable by simple concepts), constructing classifications, fitting equations to data, discovering laws explaining a set of observations, and formulating theories accounting for the behavior of a system. *Genetic algorithms* (Holland, chap. 20) and *empirical prediction algorithms* (Zagoruiko, 1976) can be viewed as variants of this learning strategy. Various aspects of this strategy are discussed in chapters 16 (Langley et al.), 17 (Stepp and Michalski), 18 (Amarel), and 19 (DeJong).

The primary focus of this book is on learning by induction and analogy. Therefore, a few additional comments may be useful about inductive inference, which is at the heart of these strategies. Inductive inference starts with a set of facts (observations)—and optionally with an a priori hypothesis about these facts—and produces a preferred generalization explaining these facts. As mentioned before, it is a falsity-preserving inference accomplished by the application of *generalization inference rules* (Michalski, 1983a). As noted by Popper (1981) and others, "pure" induction, that is, direct inference from facts to theories without any *interpretive* (*explanatory*) concepts, is impossible. These concepts are needed to describe the observations and are part of the learner's *background knowledge*. This background knowledge is a necessary component of any inductive process. It also includes goals of learning, domain-specific constraints, causal relationships, heuristics and biases that guide the generalization process, and the criteria for evaluating competing hypotheses.

One can distinguish two techniques for guiding and constraining generalization: the *similarity-based* and the *constraint-based techniques*. The similarity-based technique explores *inter-example* relationships; that is, it examines the examples and counterexamples of a concept in order to create a concept description. It searches for features shared among facts or examples in the same class and looks for common causes and explanations of why different examples belong to the same class. It generalizes over the differences between examples either by ignoring the differing features or by formulating concepts that encompass the differences. Some early learning methods using this technique are reviewed by Dietterich and Michalski in chapter 3 of *Machine Learning I*.

The constraint-based technique exploits the *intra-example* relationships, which constrain the interpretive or explanatory concepts applied to one or more facts or examples. Any generalization of these facts or examples must satisfy these constraints. For example, when generalizing the fact that a box is on the table, one should satisfy the constraint that whatever is on the table cannot be so heavy that it would break the table or so large that it could not be placed on the table. A variant of this technique is described by Andreae (1984), who uses the concept of *justification* for a hypothesis. Another important variant, called an *explanation-based* generalization, puts the emphasis on the role of explanatory knowledge (Mitchell, Keller, and Kedar-Cabelli, 1986). It applies a system's background knowledge to formulate a high-level conceptual explanation or interpretation of a given fact or event. In chapter 19, DeJong discusses a method implementing such a technique in the context of story

understanding. The similarity-based and constraint-based techniques are complementary and can be used simultaneously in learning systems.

1.5 LEARNING ORIENTATIONS

The previous two sections discussed two important classifying criteria for
machine learning research: *learning paradigms* and *learning strategies,* respectively.
To recapitulate, the first criterion concerns the type of knowledge represented and
manipulated in the system, and the second criterion deals with the type of inference
performed on the knowledge. This section will briefly discuss one more classifying
criterion, the *research orientation,* which concerns the scope and subject of study. By
analogy, a *paradigm* corresponds to one's point of departure and the terrain through
which one travels, a *strategy* specifies the means of locomotion, and an *orientation*
indicates the destination.

As described in chapter 1 of *Machine Learning I,* research in machine learning
encompasses three interconnected orientations:

- Theoretical analysis and development of general learning algorithms
- The development of computational models of human learning processes (also
  called *cognitive modeling*)
- Task-oriented studies concerned with building learning systems for specific
  applications (also called an *engineering orientation*)

Research in the first orientation investigates theoretical learning tasks, or
simplified practical ones, and tries to develop algorithms that accomplish these tasks
independently of application. There is no restriction on the type of algorithm developed. The algorithm need not be similar to the one a human might use to perform the
given task. As a variation, some authors postulate that at least the knowledge structures generated as an end result of learning should be similar to those a human being
might create, although the process of their creation can be different (Michalski,
1983a). In this orientation researchers strive to chart the theoretical space of possible
learning algorithms. Chapters 3 (Winston), 5 (Utgoff), 7 (Sammut and Banerji),
and 9 (Kodratoff and Ganascia) represent a sample of work representative of this
orientation.

In the second orientation, human learning is the focus, and the development of
computational theories and experimental models of human learning is the goal. This
research will likely have important influence on human education as well as on the
techniques of implementing machine learning systems. Chapters 10 (Rosenbloom
and Newell), 11 (Anderson), and 14 (Carbonell) are characteristic of this orientation.

Finally, work in the third orientation undertakes specific practical learning
tasks and tries to develop engineering systems capable of performing these tasks. An
example here would be a program that learns to recognize dangerous conditions for
aircraft in flight. Such efforts usually have to address a host of other problems not

directly related to learning, such as the appropriate interpretation of the input signals or the development of problem-specific transformations of the data. Any useful ideas from the other two orientations are readily adopted in this orientation. Often, when a solution to a specific problem is found, it is generalized to a method for solving a class of similar problems. An example of such research is described by Dietterich and Michalski in chapter 4.

The above three research orientations make up a trichotomy of mutually dependent and supportive efforts that fuel the machinery of learning research. Such a trichotomy has come to pervade the whole of artificial intelligence.

1.6 READER'S GUIDE TO THIS BOOK

As indicated in sections 1.3 and 1.4 above, this book is concerned with the SCA (symbolic concept acquisition) and the KDL (knowledge-intensive domain-specific learning) paradigms and concentrates on inductive and analogical learning strategies. Both major types of inductive learning—that is, learning from examples and learning by observation and discovery—are represented. The chapters are grouped into six parts reflecting the major learning strategy or the research orientation employed in the work.

Part One provides an introduction and discussion of general issues in the field of machine learning. After the overview presented in this chapter, views from several researchers on important problems in this field for the decade of the eighties are presented in **chapter 2.** These topics emerged from a panel discussion held at the 2nd International Machine Learning Workshop at the University of Illinois in June 1983 (Michalski, 1983b).

Part Two describes a selection of results on *learning from examples.* In **chapter 3,** Winston integrates ideas about several interrelated topics: learning from precedents and exercises, using *near misses* in learning, generalizing *if-then* rules, and employing *unless* conditions to prevent incorrect rule application. The role of an unless condition is to block a given if-then rule whenever facts at hand satisfy this condition. Such a condition facilitates an incremental improvement of rules.

In **chapter 4,** Dietterich and Michalski present a theoretical framework and methodology for a certain type of *part-to-whole generalization.* They describe a general method using three models for discovering a rule that characterizes a sequence of objects and predicts a plausible sequence continuation. Each object in the sequence is described by discrete attributes, which are either given a priori or derived by applying various inference rules and sequence transformations.

Utgoff in **chapter 5** investigates the role of *bias* or *preference criterion* in determining a plausible hypothesis in inductive learning. He presents a methodology and a program—STABB—for shifting bias in the course of learning from examples.

In **chapter 6,** Quinlan examines the effect of noise in training examples on the discovery of classification rules and their accuracy. He makes several interesting conjectures about how to formulate the learning task when training examples are expected to contain noise.

Next, in **chapter 7,** Sammut and Banerji investigate the role of previously learned concepts in the learning of new ones and the problem of inductive learning with an *active* learner. Such a learner is not just passively accepting examples from a teacher but is also generating examples on its own and asking the teacher whether they represent the concept being learned.

In **chapter 8,** Lebowitz discusses a somewhat related problem. He explores the use of concepts stored in the memory for generalizing complex structural descriptions. His *Generalization-Based Memory* method determines what concepts to learn and formulates definitions of the concepts learned. The ideas are exemplified by two programs, one for concept evaluation, the other for generalization of complex structural descriptions.

Next, in **chapter 9,** Kodratoff and Ganascia discuss various theoretical aspects of the generalization process. They show how generalization is accomplished by creating links among training examples. These links are represented as variable bindings.

Part Three takes up *cognitive aspects of learning.* In **chapter 10,** Rosenbloom and Newell present ideas about modeling processes that underlie improvement of performance by practice. Their model of practice is based on the concept of *chunking,* that is, grouping subgoals into higher goals. They show that this model explains the known *power law* of human practice.

Next, in **chapter 11,** Anderson discusses learning mechanisms involved in *knowledge compilation,* that is, in the process by which subjects move from a declarative representation of a skill to a procedural representation. He shows how mechanisms of *composition* (collapsing multiple productions into a single production) and *proceduralization* (building into productions information that resides in declarative form in the long-term memory) can simulate the initial stages of skill acquisition in the domain of learning how to program.

In **chapter 12,** Forbus and Gentner present their work on a computational model of human learning of physical domains. They use *Qualitative Process Theory* to model human physical knowledge and *Structure Mapping Theory,* which characterizes analogy and other comparisons, to describe processes of changing knowledge representations.

Part Four focuses on the topic of *learning by analogy.* Burstein, in **chapter 13,** presents a model of learning by analogical reasoning. He describes it in the context of acquiring the semantics of assignment statements in the BASIC programming language. According to his model, the use of analogies to learn concepts in a new domain depends strongly on causal abstractions previously formed in a familiar domain. These analogies are extended incrementally to handle related situations.

In **chapter 14,** Carbonell presents his theory of *derivational analogy* and its implications for case-based reasoning and expertise acquisition. In essence, the derivation of solutions to related problems is replayed and modified to solve new and increasingly more complex problems. The method is proposed as a means of automating knowledge and skill acquisition for expert systems.

Dershowitz, in **chapter 15,** focuses on analogy as a tool for automatic programming. He shows how analogies between program specifications (as well as between their derivations) can be used to debug a program or to modify an existing program to perform a new task. These analogies can also be used to derive an abstract schema of a set of programs and to instantiate a schema in order to yield a particular program.

Part Five covers *learning by observation and discovery.* In **chapter 16,** Langley, Zytkow, Simon, and Bradshaw describe four systems addressing different aspects of scientific discovery. BACON.6 formulates empirical laws characterizing any numerical observational data. GLAUBER takes on discovery of qualitative laws of chemical reactions. STAHL undertakes the problem of determining components of substances involved in such reactions. Finally, DALTON focuses on the formulation of structural models for these reactions.

In **chapter 17,** Stepp and Michalski report on their recent work on *conceptual clustering,* that is, creating a classification of observations by identifying subclasses that correspond to simple concepts. Unlike previous work on generating goal-free classifications of unstructured objects, the new research takes on the construction of goal-oriented classifications of structured objects. The authors describe and illustrate by examples how a learner's concepts and inference rules are used in constructing such purposive classifications.

In **chapter 18,** Amarel discusses problems of theory formation in the context of program synthesis. He illustrates his method and ideas by a problem of inferring a program from input-output data associations in the domain of partially ordered structures. His method emphasizes the role of algebraic and geometric models and the importance of shifting problem representations in the program synthesis task.

Taking a different tack, DeJong in **chapter 19** discusses a method of learning from observation that exploits the inner constraints among explanatory concepts in the system's background knowledge to guide the process of generalization from a single example. His examples are stories about people's problem-solving behavior. This knowledge-based generalization process is used to propose new schemata.

Part Six explores some general aspects of learning. In **chapter 20,** Holland discusses general-purpose learning algorithms based on a parallel rule–based system architecture. He advances the theme that inductive processes in such rule-based systems are a way of overcoming the *brittleness* of current AI systems, which is due to the narrow scope of their domain-specific knowledge.

In **chapter 21,** Berwick explores the issues of general constraints underlying processes of natural language acquisition. He discusses the relative importance of general, domain-independent learning principles versus domain-specific learning, and presents the *subset principle* for guiding generalization from positive-only examples.

Finally, in **chapter 22,** Silver describes a learning technique called *Precondition Analysis* that allows a program to learn strategies for problem solving. He illustrates his method with examples from the domain of algebraic equations.

The book concludes with a bibliography of research in machine learning since 1980, with a few major landmarks representing earlier research. (A comprehensive bibliography of previous research in this field can be found in *Machine Learning I.*) The bibliography is indexed by underlying learning strategy, domain of application, and research methodology. An updated glossary of terms in machine learning is also provided, as well as a bibliographical note about each author.

ACKNOWLEDGMENTS

This research was done at the Artificial Intelligence Laboratory of the Massachusetts Institute of Technology, where the author worked while on leave of absence from the University of Illinois at Urbana-Champaign. The author wishes to thank Patrick Winston for inviting him to the Laboratory, for many fruitful and enjoyable discussions, and for comments on an earlier version of this chapter. The unique and stimulating environment of the MIT AI Laboratory and discussions at the Learning Group were helpful in shaping the ideas presented here. Support for the Laboratory's research is provided in part by the Advanced Research Projects Agency under the Office of Naval Research Contract N00014-80-C-0505.

The author thanks his coeditors, Jaime Carbonell and Tom Mitchell, for the collaboration and contributive comments. The discussion and remarks of Randy Davis from the MIT AI Laboratory were a valuable challenge and helped to improve this paper. He suggested the idea of using learning machines for protection against the misuse of learning machines. Richard Doyle, Michael Kashket, Boris Katz, and David Kirsh from the MIT AI Laboratory and Allan Collins from Bolt Beranek and Newman, Inc., provided important feedback and thoughtful comments on the earlier draft. The author expresses gratitude to Bob Stepp, Larry Rendell, Jeff Becker, Bruce Katz, and Brian Stout from the AI Laboratory at the University of Illinois for valuable suggestions and criticism. Useful comments and suggestions were provided by Ken Forbus from the UI Department of Computer Science. The author is indebted to Gail Thornburg from the UI Graduate School of Library and Information Science for her many insightful remarks and criticisms. Important suggestions were provided by

Jan Gorecki from the UI Department of Sociology. This work was supported in part by the National Science Foundation under Grant No. DCR-8406801 and the Office of Naval Research under Contract N00014-82-K-0186.

References

Andreae, P. M., "Constraint Limited Generalization: Acquiring Procedures from Examples," *Proceedings of AAAI-84,* Austin, Tex., pp. 6–10, 1984.

Berkson, W. and Wettersten, J., *Learning from Error,* Open Court, La Salle, Ill., 1984.

Buchanan, B. G., and Feigenbaum, E. A., "DENDRAL and Meta-DENDRAL: Their Applications Dimension," *Artificial Intelligence,* Vol. 11, pp. 5–24, 1978.

Buchanan, B. G., and Shortliffe, E. H. (Eds.), *Rule-based Expert Systems,* Addison-Wesley, Reading, Mass., 1984.

Caianiello, E. R., and Musso, G., *Cybernetic Systems: Recognition, Learning, Self-Organization,* Research Studies Press, Ltd., Letchworth, Hertfordshire, England; Wiley, New York, 1984.

Carbonell, J. G., Michalski, R. S., and Mitchell, T. M., "An Overview of Machine Learning," in *Machine Learning: An Artificial Intelligence Approach,* R. S. Michalski, J. G. Carbonell, and T. M. Mitchell (Eds.), Tioga, Palo Alto, Calif., 1983.

Cohen, P. R., and Feigenbaum, E. A. (Eds.), *The Handbook of Artificial Intelligence,* Vol. 3, Kaufmann, Los Altos, Calif., 1982.

Conrad, M., *Adaptability,* Plenum Press, New York, 1983.

Davis, R., and Lenat, D. B., *Knowledge-based Systems in Artificial Intelligence,* McGraw-Hill, New York, 1982.

Dieterich, T. G., and Michalski, R. S., "A Comparative Review of Selected Methods for Learning from Examples," in *Machine Learning: An Artificial Intelligence Approach,* R. S. Michalski, J. G. Carbonell, and T. M. Mitchell (Eds.), Tioga, Palo Alto, Calif., 1983.

Feigenbaum, A. E., Lecture at the First U.S.-China Joint Seminar on Automation and Intelligent Systems, Beijing, China, May 28–June 1, 1984.

Fogel, L., Owens, A., and Walsh, M., *Artificial Intelligence Through Simulated Evolution,* Wiley, New York, 1966.

Hayes-Roth, F., "Using Proofs and Refutations to Learn from Experience," in *Machine Learning: An Artificial Intelligence Approach,* R. S. Michalski, J. G. Carbonell, and T. M. Mitchell (Eds.), Tioga, Palo Alto, Calif., 1983.

Hayes-Roth, F., Waterman, D. A., and Lenat, D. B. (Eds.), *Building Expert Systems,* Addison-Wesley, Reading, Mass., 1983.

Hillis, W. D., "The Connection Machine (Computer Architecture for the New Wave)," AI Memo No. 646, MIT, September 1981.

Hinton, G. E., Sejnowski, T. J., and Ackley, D. H., "Boltzmann Machines: Constraint Satisfaction Networks That Learn," Technical Report CMU-CS-84-119, Department of Computer Science, Carnegie-Mellon University, 1984.

Hofstadter, D. R., *Godel, Escher, Bach: An Eternal Golden Braid,* Vintage, New York, 1980.

Holland, J., *Adaptation in Natural and Artificial Systems,* University of Michigan Press, Ann Arbor, 1975.

Hume, D., *A Treatise of Human Nature,* L. S. Selby-Bigge (Ed.), Clarendon Press, Oxford, 1888.

Kawanobe, K., "Current Status and Future Plans of the Fifth Generation Computer Systems Project," *Proceedings of the International Conference on Fifth Generation Computer Systems,* COT, Tokyo, pp. 3–36, 1984.

Kuhn, T. S., *The Structure of Scientific Revolutions,* 2d ed. en., University of Chicago Press, Chicago, 1970.

Lakatos, I., "Falsification and the Methodology of Scientific Research Programmes," in *Criticism and the Growth of Knowledge,* A. Musgrave and I. Lakatos (Eds.), Cambridge University Press, Cambridge, 1970.

Langley, P., and Carbonell, J. G., "Approaches to Machine Learning," *Journal of the American Society for Information Science,* Vol. 35, No. 5, pp. 306–331, 1984.

Larkin, J., Reif, F., Carbonell, J., and Gugliotta, A., "FERMI: Flexible Expert Reasoning with Multi-Domain Inferencing," submitted to *Cognitive Science,* 1985.

Lenat, D. G., "The Role of Heuristics in Learning by Discovery: Three Case Studies," in *Machine Learning: An Artificial Intelligence Approach,* R. S. Michalski, J. G. Carbonell, and T. M. Mitchell (Eds.), Tioga, Palo Alto, Calif., 1983.

Marcus, M. P., *A Theory of Syntactic Recognition for Natural Language,* MIT Press, Cambridge, 1980.

McCarthy, J., "Programs with Common Sense," in *Semantic Information Processing,* M. Minsky (Ed.), MIT Press, Cambridge, 1968.

————, "President's Quarterly Message: AI Needs More Emphasis on Basic Research," *AI Magazine,* Vol. 4, pp. 4–5, 1983.

Medin, D. L., Wattenmaker, W. D., and Michalski, R. S., "Constraints in Inductive Learning: An Experimental Study Comparing Human and Machine Performance," submitted to *Cognitive Science,* 1985.

Michalski, R. S., "Variable-Valued Logic and Its Applications to Pattern Recognition and Machine Learning," in *Computer Science and Multiple-Valued Logic: Theory and Applications,* D. C. Rine (Ed.), North-Holland, 1975.

————, "Pattern Recognition as Rule-Guided Inductive Inference," *IEEE Transactions on Pattern Analysis and Machine Intelligence,* Vol. PAMI-2, No. 4, pp. 349–61, July 1980.

————, "A Theory and Methodology of Inductive Learning," *Artificial Intelligence,* Vol. 20, No. 2, pp. 111–161, 1983, 1983a.

————, "Learning Strategies and Automated Knowledge Acquisition: An Overview,;" in *Knowledge-Based Learning Systems,* L. Bolc, (Ed.), Springer-Verlag, 1985.

Michalski, R. S., Carbonell, J. G., and Mitchell, T. M. (Eds.), *Machine Learning: An Artificial Intelligence Approach,* Tioga, Palo Alto, Calif., 1983.

Michalski, R. S., Ko, H., and Chen, K., "Qualitative Process Prediction: A Method and a Program SPARC/G," *Reports of the Intelligent Systems Group,* ISG-12, Department of Computer Science, University of Illinois, Urbana, 1985.

Michie, D., *Machine Intelligence and Related Topics,* Gordon and Breach, New York, 1982.

Minsky, M. *The Society of Mind,* MIT Press, Cambridge (draft, April 1985), forthcoming.

Minsky, M., and Papert, S., *Perceptrons,* MIT Press, Cambridge, 1969.

Mitchell, T. M., Keller, R. M., and Kedar-Cabelli, S. T., "Explanation-Based Generalization: A Unifying View," *Machine Learning,* Vol. 1, No. 1 (Jan 1986): in press.

Mitchell, T. M., Utgoff, P. E., and Banerji, R., "Learning by Experimentation: Acquiring and Refining Problem-Solving Heuristics," in *Machine Learning: An Artificial Intelligence Approach,* R. S. Michalski, J. G. Carbonell, and T. M. Mitchell (Eds.), Tioga, Palo Alto, Calif., 1983.

Nilsson, N. J., *Learning Machines,* McGraw-Hill, New York, 1965.

Popper, K. R., *The Logic of Scientific Discovery,* Basic Books, New York, 1959.

———, *Objective Knowledge: An Evolutionary Approach,* rev. ed., Oxford University Press, Oxford, 1981.

Quinlan, J. R., "Discovering Rules from Large Collections of Examples: A Case Study," in *Expert Systems in the Microelectronics Age,* D. Michie (Ed.), Edinburg University Press, Edinburgh, 1979.

Rendell, L. A., "Toward a Unified Approach to Conceptual Knowledge Acquisition," *AI Magazine,* Vol. 4, pp. 19–27, Winter, 1983.

Robinson, J. A., "Logic Programming—Past, Present and Future," *New Generation Computing,* Vol. 1, No. 2, pp. 107–24, 1983.

Rosenblatt, F., "The Perceptron: A Probabilistic Model for Information Storage and Organization in the Brain," *Psychological Review,* Vol. 65, pp. 386–407, 1958.

Schank, R. C., *Dynamic Memory: A Theory of Reminding and Learning in Computers and People,* Cambridge University Press, Cambridge, 1982.

———, "The Current State of AI: One Man's Opinion," *AI Magazine,* Vol. 4, No. 1, pp. 3–8, Winter/Spring 1983.

Selfridge, M., "Pandemonium: A Paradigm for Learning," *Proceedings of the Symposium on Mechanization of Thought Processes,* D. Blake, and A. Uttley (Eds.), HMSO, London, pp. 511–29, 1959.

Simon, H. A., "Why Should Machines Learn?" in *Machine Learning: An Artificial Intelligence Approach,* R. S. Michalski, J. G. Carbonell, and T. M. Mitchell (Eds.), Tioga, Palo Alto, Calif., 1983.

Sleeman, D. H., "Inferring Student Models for Intelligent Computer-Aided Instruction," in *Machine Learning: An Artificial Intelligence Approach,* R. S. Michalski, J. G. Carbonell, and T. M. Mitchell (Eds.), Tioga, Palo Alto, Calif., 1983.

Sleeman, D. H., and Brown, J. S. (Eds.), *Intelligent Tutoring Systems,* Academic Press, New York, 1982.

Tsypkin, J. Z., *Foundations of the Theory of Learning Systems* (in Russian), Publisher Nauka, Moscow, 1972.

Weizenbaum, J., *Computer Power and Human Reason,* Freeman, San Francisco, 1976.

Winograd, T., "What Does It Mean to Understand Language?" in *Perspectives on Cognitive Science,* D. A. Norman (Ed.), Ablex, Norwood, N. J., 1981.

Winston, P. H., "Learning Structural Descriptions from Examples," in *The Psychology of Computer Vision,* P. H. Winston (Ed.), McGraw-Hill, New York, 1975.

————, "Learning and Reasoning by Analogy," *Communications of the ACM,* Vol. 19, No. 3, 1982.

————, *Artificial Intelligence,* 2d ed., Addison-Wesley, Reading, Mass., 1984.

Winston, P. H.; Binford, T. O.; Katz, B.; and Lowry, M. R., "Learning Physical Descriptions from Functional Definitions, Examples and Precedents," *Proceedings of the AAAI-83,* Washington, D.C., pp. 433–39, 1983.

Zagoruiko, N., "Empirical Prediction Algorithms," in *Computer Oriented Learning Processes,* J. C. Simon (Ed.), Noordhoff, Leyden, 1976.

2

MACHINE LEARNING:

Challenges of the Eighties

Edited transcript of a panel discussion held at the 2nd International Machine Learning Workshop, Allerton House, University of Illinois, June 22–24, 1983

Ryszard S. Michalski
(Moderator)

Saul Amarel

Douglas B. Lenat

Donald Michie

Patrick H. Winston

Transcribed and edited by
Gail Thornburg and
Ryszard S. Michalski

Michalski:

Now that our Workshop is coming to a close, it is time to summarize our thoughts and discuss some of the issues important to our field. To start with, let me raise some questions particularly suitable for discussion. First of all, what are the most important tasks for machine learning research for the near and not-so-near future? Next, what is the role of machine learning in AI? How important and how feasible is automated knowledge acquisition for expert systems? Shouldn't we stress this area much more than we stressed it in the past?

Another interesting issue is the role of domain-specific versus general approaches to machine learning. As you know, for a long time many researchers avoided research that could be called general methods of learning. It was believed that such research was not going to bring any interesting results, that the resulting systems would be very inefficient, and that the whole area of general learning was a hopeless task.

As a result of such attitudes, many researchers started to explore learning issues in the context of specific problems. This domain-specific research led to interesting results and impressive learning systems. There was, however, a bad side to it; it led to a situation in which certain groups worked in their little niches, deeply involved with their favorite domain-specific problems and not communicating sufficiently with other groups. They often developed their own terminology, unaware that it was more or less isomorphic to the terminology of some other groups, and this hampered interaction and the progress of the field. Moreover, that kind of domain-specific research didn't lead to any more general understanding of the problems of the field and didn't lead to any new theories or principles. Certainly the time has come for us to identify more general principles in our field.

A related issue for discussion is the question of pure versus applied machine learning research. Should we stress the theoretical research, or should we be more oriented toward designing and implementing practical learning systems?

Another issue to consider is whether we should continue to study in depth single learning strategies, or whether we should now attempt to build integrated learning systems that employ several strategies. Clearly the existing embodiment of a learning system, a human being, can learn using a variety of strategies simultaneously. Moreover, the strategies that people use change with their accumulation of knowledge. We know that children learn differently than adults do. The major difference is that adults already have a large store of knowledge about the external world and so can use this knowledge when they learn new things. Therefore, using strategies involving analogy is generally more appropriate for them than for children, who don't yet have much knowledge and thus cannot use analogical reasoning to the same extent.

Another important topic for discussion concerns the terminology and description languages useful for machine learning research. I have already mentioned that one of the problems we face is that researchers in this field use a variety of terminologies, some of them isomorphic. Identification of some of those isomorphisms would be very useful for the further progress of the field and would make it easier for new researchers to enter the field. An interesting problem related to this is the role of formal languages such as predicate calculus in our field. What is their usefulness for representing program-generated knowledge versus their usefulness as well-defined formalisms for describing learning algorithms.

Finally, are we already a field? If so, what are our unifying principles and our goals? And one more issue: We are now facing the development of new computer architectures, so we may study learning problems using machines to be developed— connection machines, Boltzmann machines, and so forth. Will this new development in computer architectures bring us some important new tools that will help us in machine learning research?

I will end on this question and introduce to you our panelists: Saul Amarel, Rutgers University; Donald Michie, University of Edinburgh; Doug Lenat, Stanford University; and Patrick Winston, MIT. They will air their own views on these and other topics in this order. At the end, using my prerogative as moderator, I will make some final comments.

Amarel:

I understand that what we're supposed to talk about is a view of the field five to ten years from now. Ryszard has put many questions to us, and I'm going to address some of them.

First of all, on the issue of pure research versus applied research, I think we need both. I think we need both in parallel, and I think we should do both even on the same project. This has been my own philosophy for some time. We have to develop both parts of the activity. We need applications, specific explorations, to generate ideas about how to approach new problems and new challenges. We need the basic research part in order to tie things together and to see what is equivalent to what, what is superior to what, and why. We also need to see how things relate to each other as well as to other areas of AI and computer science, or to psychology.

My own sense is that problems of theory formation—and some problems of learning—are no different from other issues in the area of problem solving. I would very much like to see an integration and an overall framework to encompass problems in all domains, including domains of theory formation. To date, we have put a tremendous amount of emphasis on derivation problems, on pathfinding problems, on interpretation problems, and on other areas that we call problem solving. There are some areas of problem solving that have to do with constraint satisfaction, where the number of constraints to be satisfied is typically large; also, we have problems in which we must handle a large number of interacting goals. If you look carefully at the problem methodologies used in these areas, you will find them not very different from methodologies that we use in some areas of hypothesis generation, theory formation, and learning. I think we should do a little more work on relating these various areas to each other, from two points of view: what the problem formulation is and what the problem-solving processes are.

I don't think we should split these issues. We could of course split the problem-solving domain into subdomains, in accordance with certain ideas having to do with the methodology of solution, complexity, or the degree of dependence between problem conditions. In my mind the degree of dependence between problem conditions is probably the most fundamental parameter for thinking about different methods of problem solving. In many of the derivation problems—that is, many of the problems that are usually conceived as conventional problem solving—we usually work in one space. Here we talk about moving from state to state, of using operators, inference rules, and so on. The more you delve into theory formation problems, the more you see that you have to work in more than one space. In most instances we work in two spaces: in the space of solutions and in the space of problem conditions. And most of the time the difficulty arises because the languages and the sets of concepts that are available to us in these two spaces are different.

The best strategy we can then pursue, which indeed we pursue in a very intuitive way, is to try to establish early enough a link between one space and the other and to formulate the problem in just one space as much as possible, in order to be able to solve it with well-known methods. The entire issue of how to handle problems involving both a solution space and a problem condition space, as well as how to link the spaces and how to coordinate the two-space search, has been with us for some time. This was recognized in the early 1970s by several people; one might cite a very good paper by Simon and Lea in this area.[1] I think this issue will require more thinking.

As I said, I think the basic issue in choosing a problem-solving method is really the question of problem decomposability. If we can decompose a problem, we can assign a method to a goal, independently of other goals, making our problem-solving activity relatively easy. In most of the problem-solving efforts in AI we have taken this kind of approach. As soon as goals become very interdependent, we cannot reason very clearly from problem conditions to goals, and we have a difficult problem. This is what creates a major difficulty in problems of theory formation and learning: it's very difficult to decompose the problems. To the extent that we are able to decompose, or to the extent that we are going to be good in handling methodologies of decomposition, we will also improve our ability to develop effective methodologies for formation problems.

I was very interested in the many comments and the considerable amount of work being done in the area of analogical reasoning. Personally, I would very much like to have a moratorium on the term *analogy,* because it is regarded in somewhat different ways by different people. That's a problem that we have in the field, anyway—trying to determine how to use such terms as *intelligence* or *learning.* Since these terms have different connotations for different people, agreement is extremely difficult to accomplish. We have to be a little more precise in operational terms, in defining what we mean when we talk about a particular analogical reasoning methodology, and so on. As I was listening to various approaches, my own sense was as follows: As Ryszard was saying, studying learning in an environment with a tremendous amount of relevant knowledge is very important. Most of our learning is being done

---

[1] H. A. Simon and G. Lea, "Problem Solving and Rule Induction: A Unified View," in *Knowledge and Cognition,* L. Gregg (Ed.), Erlbaum, Hillsdale, N. J., 1974.

in a situation in which we know of many problems and of ways of solving them; we know the structures and methods in other domains, and in some way we try to import that knowledge and bring it to bear on the problem at hand.

Possibly the entire issue of analogy could be subsumed under the following mechanism: Given a problem, we must find some other problem known to us that is somehow similar to the initial problem. We use the "similar" problem as a focusing mechanism for selecting schemata that are promising, to start at least a part of the problem-solving activity. We import the "similar" problem, we use the method that worked for that problem, and then we go on to do a different kind of problem solving in order to complete our task. I cannot possibly conceive how analogical reasoning alone can do the entire job. The most difficult part is not the identification of the analogy but the assimilation of the analogy, the repair, and the additional work needed in order to finish the job, *after* the analogy has been imported.

And I would very much like to see more work done on the use of analogical reasoning and the use of repair strategies to finish a piece of analogical reasoning as a basis for solving a new problem. Also, in terms of theory formation, my recent work shows that the most difficult aspect of the problem is not encountered in the early stages of theory formation. The difficulty is at the end of the process, when you have "almost correct" theories and would like to converge on a solution. The amount of reasoning that is needed then is enormous, and the techniques used are much more demanding, which is precisely where I think domain knowledge in large quantities must come into play. I don't see how we can form theories in certain areas without already knowing quite a bit about the area itself. This is essentially Bill Martin's postulate, that you must know quite a bit about a domain if you want to do some learning in it. I think it's absolutely essential.

As for applications, I certainly think that we need much more work in the area of learning, in the creation of knowledge bases for expert systems. There's no doubt that this is the only way we can go. The field is asking for it, not only in terms of the expert systems of today, where we have a thousand rules or more, but also in terms of situations—and these are both fundamental problems and application problems—where a system is already working, but we would like to identify subdomains of the system where, on the basis of the active experience of a system, things could be done even better. We would like to be able to identify specialized methods in any given subdomain, as human experts do, and make them available to that particular subdomain. The entire movement from novice or average performance to expert performance requires this identification of special characteristics of subdomains and special methodologies that could be applied to them, so that the result will be increased expertise. The entire area of expertise acquisition in the context of expert systems is extremely interesting for learning, both in terms of basic kinds of problems and in terms of impact on the building of expert systems.

There are more specific things I want to say about current projects. It concerns me that I don't see any projects of the Meta-DENDRAL type around us today. What are we going to have after Meta-DENDRAL? This was a major, interesting, well-chosen domain, with very interesting challenges, where one could develop many ideas about theory formation. I would like us to find ways whereby any given group that did not have the interest and the staffing to continue such a project could develop arrangements so that some other group could continue the project (I know all the difficulties involved) and perhaps build on the experience of the first group, to try to move beyond the stage at which, for instance, Meta-DENDRAL was left. I would very much like to see more scientific theory formation going on, maybe in the biological sciences, or perhaps in areas of physics. This would be extremely important for us to pursue.

Now there is another area of learning that I find might be very useful for us and might relate a little more closely to psychological investigations. This has to do with developing environments for problem solving with appropriate graphics and monitoring capabilities, where one could watch the operation of an expert in a domain. It could be a designer (e.g., a designer of an engineering system), another kind of professional such as a manager, and at the same time it could give various aids to that professional. I am not talking yet about an automatic system. Rather, those professionals will have aids, and at the same time they will have monitoring facilities to record what they are doing. It would be an excellent thing to capture, in some gradual fashion, some of the ways in which those managers or professionals or designers do things—and learn how people actually do things—by using these kinds of environments. This has implications for experimental environments and facilities. That's where I can see those psychologists who are interested in human-machine interactions or in learning generally interacting with involved nonpsychologists.

A final thought: I have a feeling that if we want to advance in the area of concept discovery and in the area of theory formation in a deep way, then we should be doing more things of the kind that Doug Lenat did in the AM system. This means that we should be thinking *not* only about one specific learning problem but about a cluster of interconnected learning problems. The output of one can in some way be utilized as an input to another and can in some cases enable us to come back and revise ideas about concepts that we have been using in a component problem. Isolated, very simple formation or learning activities are very important to our understanding of some of the basic methodology. Yet how much more interesting it would be to have a set of activities in a specific domain—such as mathematics or physics—in which we could see how the various activities interact. No scientists work exclusively on one problem at one time. They always work on several problems, and they transfer knowledge from problem to problem; in addition, of course, they bring to each problem considerable knowledge from outside the problem domain.

At this point I think I should end my comments and let my other colleagues on the panel speak. Thank you.

Michie:

I should like to endorse a theme that I take from Saul Amarel's remarks, namely, the anchoring effect of a good choice of problem. AI work is now at a cross-roads. More accurately, it is at a Y-junction of the kind that experimental psychologists like to use to test animals. One arm of the Y-junction leads to a philosophy of free-floating work. The other leads to a sense of direction derived from well-defined, hard problems.

I see an analogy here to the early days of aeronautics. The use of balloons offers a useful caricature of the free-floating school. In a balloon one is happy to float wherever the wind blows and to exchange anecdotes with other balloonists about interesting glimpses of whatever terrain one happens to pass over.

The really hard problem in aeronautics was that of directional flight, which confronted the heavier-than-air school. Unfortunately, in every branch of systematic inquiry the free-floating approach has a fatal attraction for the administrators of science. They feel they really understand that kind of thing. So the first people to venture into the directional styles must not be too surprised if the political and administrative leaders of society give them a hard time and seek to coax or deflect them into unstructured explorations in which all concerned can relax.

Let me tell you about this as it worked out in the case of powered flight. Early experiments met success in the hands of two very hard-headed, scientifically trained engineers, the Wright brothers, followed almost immediately afterwards by Cody in the United Kingdom. By about 1908–1909 an infant technology had taken root, in many ways comparable to the infant technology of intelligent, computer-controlled robotics that characterized the late 1960s and the early 1970s in the AI field. The balloonists were still pottering on, and they were more successful than the heavier-than-air people in the higher reaches of science/political wisdom.

The British prime minister set up a subcommittee of the Imperial Defense Committee, chaired by Lord Escher. This committee worked for a few months in late 1908 and reported early in 1909. They took a variety of evidence from officers and politicians of the defense establishment on whether the heavier-than-air principle had a future.

After finely sifting the evidence, they came to the unanimous conclusion that it did not. The subcommittee's recommendation to the Imperial Defense Committee was that all work on heavier-than-air flight should be canceled and government resources redeployed to the study of balloons.

The prime minister of the time, H. H. Asquith, is on record in the minutes of the Imperial Defense Committee as pronouncing himself highly satisfied with this decision. Shortly after this, Bleriot flew the Channel, attracting a great deal of publicity. By good chance, Lord Escher was an intelligent man of high integrity. He began to worry that possibly his committee had made a terrible error. After further thought and study, he put a heavily documented case to the prime minister, to the effect that his committee had made a mistake and that it was in the national interest for Britain to arm herself with an effective fleet of heavier-than-air machines.

There is a moral in this story for artificial intelligence. The kind of work that was being done at SRI on the SHAKEY project was a typical hard problem on which all the intellectual and other resources of the AI craft had to be brought to bear to establish success. Along with similar projects at Stanford, MIT, and Edinburgh, this investigation into world modeling, recognition, and planning had to be discontinued because the world around us can understand coffee table talk about these topics, but it is repelled and mystified by sustained and detailed experiment.

Yet as far as our professional criteria are concerned, there is no way out but to select hard problems to act as forcing functions. The fact that a free-floating, liberal arts approach can warm the hearts of administrators should be taken not as a positive rallying point but as a point against.

In terms of practice, what does this mean? Our field, which is infant still and lacks a hardened skeleton on which to hang a definite morphology, needs a style of practice determined by the professional standards and rules of evidence customary in experimental and theoretical science. It should aim to supersede the standards and rules of evidence customary in the liberal arts and in some of the less developed engineering disciplines such as computer science.

For the future, let me humbly suggest that our next meeting be restricted to papers that report on completed results. Any philosophizing about future work that they may additionally contain will then at least be accompanied by a directional point of reference. In well-established branches of science, no one would consider operating to any more permissive criteria.

Lenat:

Now let me start off by agreeing, in a way, with something that Donald said earlier, that the field of machine learning can be anchored by working on hard, specific, very well-defined problems. In fact, I think that's the reason the field has looked at-anchor for so long.

Assuming that we want to progress from our relatively primitive state of technology, I think we will have to send out small craft and hope that some of them do make it back safely. More seriously, though, if we do want anchors of the kind that Donald was talking about, something that we can use productively, then those anchors should be the sources of power that our programs tap into and that we tap into in our research.

The first source of power is synergy. *Synergy* means getting out more than you put in, in dealings between programs and human beings. In the work we do with EURISKO—for example, the toy naval ship design—are things that neither we nor the program alone could do, and it's the human-machine synergy that I think we're really tapping. We're exploiting and technically combining the different capabilities of each of us. Then, of course, there's synergy between the programs we build and the work that other AI researchers do in areas other than machine learning. Putting learning modules onto the front of expert systems, for instance, is that sort of synergy. And finally, there is synergy with other machine learning researchers, so that we can get our programs to cooperate, work together, argue together. That's something that by and large has not been tapped, but I think it is a source of power just waiting there to be exploited.

The next source is analogy, with two types of uses, though Amarel wants to see that word banned. One use is to generate plausible, potentially true conjectures, ideas, conceptualizations, and ways of looking at the world, as well as ways to explore them (perhaps through other means) to see if they really are true.

The second use for analogy is in knowledge acquisition, for instance, in getting material into the knowledge base of an expert system. We do this all the time, by looking around for a unit or a frame or a rule that is similar to what we want to enter, getting the unit, copying it, and editing it. While the "copy and edit" process is a trivial kind of analogizing, less trivial analogizing would presumably provide less trivial kinds of knowledge acquisition aids.

The next source of power is heuristics, and I have nothing more to say about that right now. In case you aren't familiar with this, you can see Jerry DeJong's puzzle [a word puzzle distributed to all conference participants] for a clear definition of what it's good for, or my 1984 *AI Journal* articles.

Next is representation. Again, there are two issues here. One is having and finding natural representations, which I think is very important. The other is changing representations, also very important, one of the kinds of things that Saul mentioned.

Finally there is a certain catchall category, in which we find things like parallelism, morphological analysis, sources of power we haven't discovered yet.

What I really want to focus on is what we can do to exploit these sources of power in the coming decade. If we carry this exercise further, then somewhere up at the very top level would be the goals that we are trying to achieve—but I'm not interested in that high a level. At an intermediate level, one concern is the human-machine interface. This is something that can tap into the human-machine synergy, obviously. In the human-machine interface there are several aspects of concern. One of them is I/O, but that's not really part of our business—that's for people in hardware or other areas of AI to worry about. These are things like having snazzy forms of Ivan Sutherland's old helmet you can wear—that is, sunglasses that project separate CRT images on the inside of each eye; accelerometers that sense your head, neck, and eye movements, so that as you turn your head the scene changes in real time; nice things like that mean you're not limited by small screen sizes in what your display area can be. Of course with the hat it's natural to want accoutrements like gloves that sense your hands. . . . Anyway, we're not going to worry about that—but somebody else will.

Then, obviously, we'll want things like natural language and speech recognition and—remembering that we'll have these gloves and these funny glasses on—we might as well start using nonverbal cues as well. Again, let's let someone else worry about that, but keep in mind, it's going to happen.

The thing we *can* do to exploit the synergy with human beings is to start thinking about models of sessions at a terminal between a person and the program that's running, or in fact, models of individual people. One way to do that is to start taxonomizing sessions and taxonomizing groups of individuals; so, for instance, you know that if a user starts a sentence with the word *let* that user must be a mathematician—and we treat mathematicians differently from human beings.

Michie: The user could be a priest.

Lenat: Yes, but I suspect we would treat him as a phenomenon similar to a mathematician.

Next we have the synergy with the other AI researchers and their programs. The way we foster that is to build our systems as portable modules that can be plugged into various other sorts of systems. Similarly, if we build those modules in a very clean way so that they can plug into each other, then we can start getting synergy among various learning programs. This is one of the main directions that I see the work in EURISKO taking in the future. We're going to try to clean it up and get it into a form I can give to the world to look at or use, depending on the audience.

As for you-know-what [analogy], we could do the generation of plausible hypotheses that we'd like using it, if only we had a broad enough knowledge base. I think the thing that's held us back is that if the program only knows about plane geometry and has to come up with an analogy, it must be an analogy from plane geometry. What lets people do analogizing, or generation and exploitation of metaphors, so effectively is the enormous range of knowledge we have. This is not so much the depth but the breadth of knowledge, several orders of magnitude more than any system's program has. The kinds of tasks to work on there include putting an encyclopedia on-line, not in a textual sense, but actually in a knowledge base, so that it can be used. There is a group at Atari working with Alan Kay and myself doing that kind of project with roughly a 13- to 15-year time frame. There's an article on it at IJCAI this summer [1983], if you're interested.

Besides putting in encyclopedic facts about the world, you want to add commonsense facts about the world. Let's say there are a thousand "fact words" in basic English, maybe another thousand or two that should have been there. And if you're going to do such a project in any finite amount of time, you won't want to take the approach that Pat Hayes took with water, spending several years and doing it right. Instead you must take a day or so, think about what a two-year-old child knows about water, write it down, and go on to the next word. I think that's the right tack to take for ten years, to see what happens. Imagine—we get a little bit of knowledge about each of several thousand commonsense concepts into a program, and then, parenthetically, technical knowledge, the kind of knowledege one would find in expert systems.

If we had that for several different domains in one place, that might also lead to exploiting analogy.

Just as we want to have a broad knowledge base to exploit analogy, we want a broad heuristic base to exploit the power of heuristics and the way they organize. You need to consider all the world's heuristics, which you might do by looking at thousands of specific heuristics and starting to generalize them very slowly, to build up some huge tree of heuristics.

Once you have that kind of heuristic base you can tap into analogy and other things. And again, I think that this is something that's doable, just barely, in the coming decade—a moderate job, not a complete job.

And then I even have the nerve to put representation bases on our "list of knowledge to accumulate," though we only have about eight representations we know about—so you might as well have a program that knows about them and can choose among them and occasionally even augment them. I see that as one of the real opportunities for work in the future.

Another thing—if you took a look at the paper I have in the proceedings for this conference, you'll have noticed that I talk a lot about cognitive economy—programs that model, monitor, and modify themselves. That's another way of tapping into both change of representation and of heuristics.

Nowhere in my talk is there anything about theory, and so—since someone will probably ask—we *can* fit theory in here if you want. You can talk about work on the nature of learning, and if you do, then what you're really looking into is a kind of synthesis of all the things that are going on elsewhere in the picture, plus perhaps some idea of what's happening with human beings. And notice all the work on human cognition—just a very narrow fragment of what people could be working on. Why is that? Why not worry about societies, organizations, and machines instead of just organisms? Why not worry about organisms, why just worry about cognition? Learning goes on, on different time scales: by hours rather than minutes at the immune system level, by years at the corporate level, or even over millenia via evolution.

The final kind of learning theory that I think is worth doing is dimensions of learning, the kinds of things that Michalski, Carbonell, and Mitchell talk about in their chapter in *Machine Learning I*. It's very useful because it lets you do morphological analysis. You can start by saying, here are the ten dimensions along which learning systems can be categorized. Observe that all the systems that we've built so far cluster here and here and here, yet there are vast areas of the space that aren't populated by any system. Why is that?

Thinking about those sorts of issues can lead you to new insights about what's less easy and hard and why. Or, occasionally, they can lead you to say that someone ought to build a system that has these properties.

Before closing, let me respond to a couple of things that other people have said earlier. One of them related to the role of machine learning in AI. I see a kind of coroutine role, just as if I said, "Gee, I'd really like to have natural language and speech recognition modules in my learning system." Then suppose the natural language people say, "Gee, I'd really like to have a learning module in my natural language system." Those are both reasonable things to say, and I envision a kind of symbiosis—*maybe* synergy—developing there.

As for pure versus applied research, I think labels like that are a kind of red herring. When we build expert systems, for instance, the real problem in getting consensus among experts is that they have slightly different meanings for the terms they use. All the time gets wasted in arguments that involve mere syntactical disagreement. I think the same thing is likely to happen in the pure/applied issue, with a lot of time wasted arguing about various categories of what should and shouldn't be done. Let's not worry so much about terminology.

As for individual versus integrated learning systems, I think that integrated systems are almost going to be a necessity. Again, looking back over AI, we see lots of individual mechanisms that were originally *the* chief source of power in programs—Perceptrons, automatic backtracking, unification, and resolution. In all those cases, people got real excited and they developed programs that had this or that mechanism as their sole source of power, and they had some initial early successes. Then they "lost big" three to five years down the road, and everyone got turned off and went into other fields. Seven to ten years later, we started coming back with a new perspective, saying "Hey, these are really neat things to use as sub-sub-submechanisms all through our programs." The same thing is going to happen here, I think; we should start integrating before we find ourselves at the wrong end of another seven-year backlash.

Winston:

I propose to make a claim that we are faced with one danger and one opportunity, but first I want to say that I think things are basically in pretty good shape. This was a splendid meeting, an uplifting one in comparison with most I attend. It seems to me that there are four reasons why we should be happy to be in the position we are in.

Reason number one is that the research that we're doing is well balanced. The various dimensions—practical, applied, special, general, formal, informal—all look good to me in the sense that the dimensions are generally well balanced.

The second point is that we're not diverted much, in comparison with other parts of the field. I don't see very many people doing what I would consider silly recursions into noncritical problems. We don't see very many papers claiming that a new control structure is essential *before* we can do any work on learning, or that we have to invent new programming languages before we can get started. Some say we need these things, of course, but there's no general sense of futility for lack of some tool.

The third thing is that there are very few, if any, "snake oil salespeople" making ridiculous promises. If you look at other parts of artificial intelligence, that's not the case. We have an obligation to continue to insure that our little subfield maintains that kind of distinction.

Fourth, I think we're doing basically the right things. It's not just a matter of generalized balance, but the fact that there are now some new things that weren't being done, that should have been done, and that are, in fact, beginning to get done. We now see papers on guessing and confirming structure, work on quality and process, and new reflections on what we can say about the educational process. Those are all important pursuits that happily are now under way.

Now let me go back to my original two-point list of one danger and one opportunity. The danger is that our field is about to become too successful. If I may invoke a precedent and try to build an analogy, I would not be at all surprised to find that our specialty is going the way of expert systems. That is, vast public interest, hundreds of spin-off companies, depletion of university resources, industrial raids—the whole works. The usual corruption that all of that brings is a serious danger that I think we have to face. And I don't know what to do about it.

We could very well become the banner part of AI in the next few years, it seems to me, displacing expert systems. Again we need to go back to a kind of social pressure, I suppose, to insure that we're not corrupted by that popularity.

The opportunity has to do with ambition fueled by hardware. When I was doing computer vision, it was unthinkable to consider anything other than running a 3-by-3 operator over a 256-by-256 image. That was a procrustean bed on which to lie, and we didn't get very far as a consequence. So, what's the analog of that today? It *might* be fooling around with a single story instead of hundreds of stories.

What I'm driving at is that we have all this interest in supercomputers lying out there, and I don't think we've thought much about how to exploit it. I'm willing to argue both sides of this question, of course. I don't think we should dash off and build machines for learning. On the other hand, I think it's worth a little more thought than has gone into it so far—that is, thought about what we could do with supermachines by way of superuses. Doug Lenat of course thinks about using lots of machines, but very few of us, if any, have thought about how we might use unbelievably fast machines to do unbelievably quick matching and operations of that sort.

So, I think that's the opportunity. If things work out as they did in vision, then we'll be thinking much better thoughts in ten years as a consequence. Now it's laughable to run a 3-by-3 operator over *anything;* you view vision problems much differently. When you can run 30-by-30 operators over 1000-by-1000 pictures in a quarter of a second, you change the nature of your thinking. Similarly, when we can make hundreds of analogies, not just a few, our perspective will shift increasingly toward a more global view.

Michalski:

Thank you, Patrick. I find myself very much in agreement with other panelists; maybe I should feel a little disappointed.

Winston: I'll argue with you.

Michalski:

But there are a few issues that I feel were insufficiently discussed. One is theory: Are we anywhere close to building something that could be called the computational theory of learning? Well, certainly we are at an early stage in our research, and we cannot say that we are in a position to build any complete general theory of learning.

Still, I think that work toward a computational theory of learning has some good points. I am not saying that we should all go to work on a theory of learning, naturally, but I think a few of us should give some thought to this issue. Theory can give us a better understanding of the relationships existing among different directions and different techniques, can clean up terminology, and, most of all, can help us to teach the subject of machine learning. When we have a clean theory, although not complete—and actually not even "clean"—we can more easily discuss our problems and build upon what we have already done. We can also identify isomorphisms and relationships between different concepts and different methods.

I could identify several groups in the past whose methods were almost equivalent except for the terminologies they used. So while there was the appearance of something new and different, in substance it was not necessarily so. Another thing that I would like to argue—and I probably will be a minority here—is that there is a need for research on what could be termed *multi-purpose methods* (or *generic task* methods).

What do I mean by such multi-purpose methods? I don't mean methods that are, shall we say, quintessentially general techniques of learning, applicable to all problems. Rather, I mean the following: A certain sufficiently broad yet cohesive subdomain of problems is identified, and then an effort is made to develop a learning method applicable to any problem that falls into such a domain.

These multi-purpose methods can be equipped with knowledge of a particular domain to which the method applies, so this would not be a "knowledge-free" method. However, if the method is sufficiently robust, it could be adapted easily to a range of tasks, so we would not have just one method per task. That's my idea of a multi-purpose method.

You may ask for examples, and there are examples of such methods. The easiest thing for me to say is that some of the methods that we developed in Illinois, like those implemented in INDUCE, AQ11, or CLUSTER programs, represent, in my opinion, that kind of work. They are not general in the sense that they can solve every kind of problem, but they are multi-purpose as they can be useful for a range of problems of a specific type, occurring in many applications. In other words, if a problem satisfies certain constraints and criteria, then the method can be applied.

Finally, I was somewhat surprised that so few papers in this workshop were devoted to the area of knowledge acquisition for expert systems. We know that knowledge acquisition is the bottleneck in the development of AI systems—in particular, of expert systems. Using current methods, this painstaking process may take years, and I believe that we as researchers in machine learning should devote new efforts to this area. Although we had few talks on this subject, it is certainly an important research direction to explore.

With these remarks, I propose to close our discussion. To all panelists I extend the warmest thanks for their contribution.

PART
TWO

LEARNING CONCEPTS AND RULES FROM EXAMPLES

3

LEARNING BY AUGMENTING RULES AND ACCUMULATING CENSORS

Patrick H. Winston
Massachusetts Institute of Technology

Abstract

This chapter is a synthesis of several sets of ideas: ideas about learning from precedents and exercises, ideas about learning using near misses, ideas about generalizing if-then rules, and ideas about using censors to prevent procedure misapplication.

The synthesis enables two extensions to an implemented system that solves problems involving precedents and exercises and that generates if-then rules as a by-product. These extensions are as follows:

- If-then rules are augmented by *unless* conditions, creating *augmented if-then rules*. An augmented if-then rule is blocked whenever an unless condition is easily shown to be true. When one if-then rule is used to block another through an unless condition, the blocking rule is called a *censor*. Like ordinary augmented if-then rules, censors can be learned.

- *Definition rules* are introduced that facilitate graceful refinement. The definition rules are also augmented if-then rules. They work by virtue of *unless* entries that capture certain nuances of meaning that are different from those expressible by necessary conditions. Like ordinary augmented if-then rules, definition rules can be learned.

The strength of the ideas is illustrated by representative experiments. All of these experiments have been performed with an implemented system.

3.1 KEY IDEAS

This work builds primarily on a theory of learning from precedents and exercises using *constraint transfer* (Winston, 1981). The theory addresses the analogy process at work when we exploit past experience in fields like management, political science, economics, medicine, and law, as well as experience from everyday life.

Two extensions to the theory are described. Work on the first extension was motivated by some of the apparent blunders of the extant system. Work on the second extension was motivated by some problems encountered in making definitions.

First, a brief review of the overall theory is presented, followed by an example that shows how the rules generated by the unextended learning system can be misapplied. Next, various solutions to the misapplication problem are discussed, including the introduction of censors. At this point *augmented if-then rules* are explained. Each augmented if-then rule contains not only if and then parts, but also an *unless* part. Before a rule acts, censors determine if any existing facts directly demonstrate that an unless relation is true. If so, the rule is *blocked*.

This leads to the development of definition rules based on augmented if-then rules and a discussion of their relevance to the problem of concise definition versus unlimited nuance.

Next, it is shown that censors can block censors and that censors can be learned, both by precedent and exercise and by near miss.

Finally, precedents for this work itself are described, including ideas that stimulated what this author has done, such as Minsky's ideas on the role of censors in problem solving (Minsky, 1980), as well as other ideas that were reinvented or borrowed by the author as his work progressed, such as Goldstein and Grimson's ideas on generalizing if-then rules (1977).

There are references throughout to an implemented system that acquires and uses censors. This implemented system inherits the following key ingredients, all of which are explained in detail in previously published papers:

- *Analogy-based reasoning using constraint transfer.* Reasoning by analogy requires the ability to determine how two situations that are similar in some respects may be similar in other respects as well. Here the determination is done by transferring constraining cause relations from the precedent situation to the exercise situation.

- *Learned if-then rules.* In contrast to current practice in knowledge engineering, if-then rules emerge automatically as problems are solved. Teachers supply precedents and exercises, leaving the work of formulating the if-then rules to the system.

- *Rule-based reasoning.* Once learned, rules can be used. Since rules are viewed as simple situations, the constraint-transfer programs that work with the precedent situation also work with rules, doing simple rule-based reasoning. Thus learning and reasoning reside together harmoniously in the same system.

- *Actor-object representation.* Situations are represented using relations. Each relation has true, false, or unknown as its truth value, and any relation can be an object involved in another relation.
- *Importance-dominated matching.* The similarity between two situations is measured by finding the best possible match according to what is important in the precedent situation. A precedent relation is considered important if it is connected to another relation by an importance-determining constraint. At the moment, cause-relation connection is the only importance-determining constraint recognized.

3.2 WHAT IS TO BE UNDERSTOOD

Let us begin by reviewing the sort of task addressed by the theory as previously reported. Consider the following précis of *Macbeth*, given by a teacher as a precedent:

> MA is a story about Macbeth, Lady-Macbeth, Duncan, and Macduff. Macbeth is an evil noble, Lady-Macbeth is a greedy, ambitious woman, Duncan is a king, and Macduff is a noble.
>
> Lady-Macbeth persuades Macbeth to want to be king because she is greedy. She is able to influence him because he is married to her and because he is weak. Macbeth murders Duncan with a knife. Macbeth murders Duncan because Macbeth wants to be king and because Macbeth is evil. Lady-Macbeth kills herself. Macduff is angry. Macduff kills Macbeth because Macbeth murdered Duncan and because Macduff is loyal to Duncan.

Next, consider the following exercise:

> Let E be an exercise about a weak noble and a greedy lady. The lady is married to the noble. In E show that the noble may want to be king.

Told by a teacher that *Macbeth* is to be considered a precedent, the implemented system announces that the precedent suggests that the noble may want to be king. Then the system creates a principle-capturing if-then rule that suggests that the weakness of a noble and the greed of his wife can cause the noble to want to be king. The rule looks like this, printed as an if-then rule:

```
Rule
   RULE-1
if
   [LADY-4 IS GREEDY]
   [NOBLE-4 IS WEAK]
   [[NOBLE-4 IS MARRIED] TO LADY-4]
```

then
```
  [NOBLE-4 WANT [NOBLE-4 A-KIND-OF KING]]
```
case
```
  MA
```

Internally, the rule actually contains more information because the internal representation preserves the way cause relations tie everything together, which is merely summarized by the if-then form of the rule. Figure 3-1 illustrates this.

Here, however, it suits our purpose best to paraphrase the rules in English, as in
the following rendition of the sample rule:

> RULE-1   IF   There is a greedy lady
>   and there is a weak noble
>   and the noble is married to the lady
>   THEN   the noble may want to be king.

The exercise problem could have been handled by this rule directly, without recourse
to the *Macbeth* precedent, were it available when the problem was posed. Thus the
rule adds power. Unfortunately, it also adds blunder, as when the following exercise
is given:

> *Let E be an exercise about a weak noble and a greedy lady. The lady is married to
> the noble. He does not like her. In E show that the noble may want to be king.*

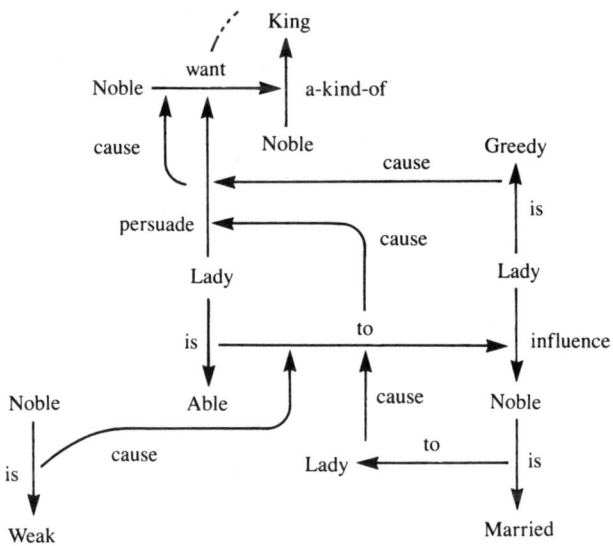

Figure 3-1: The internal representation of a rule.

This situation is different because we know that it is difficult for a person to influence someone who does not like him or her. Evidently, the rule is overly general, ready to reach conclusions when it should not.

This paper introduces extensions to the existing theory such that the implemented system acts correctly on the given example and many others. To be considered a success, however, a system should not just work, it should work because it embodies arguable ideas. The arguable ideas embodied in the improved system are the following:

- The *blocking principle.* Suppose a rule, derived from a precedent, seems to apply to a problem. Consider all the relations in that part of the precedent's causal structure involved in forming the rule. If any such relation corresponds to a relation that is either false or manifestly implausible in the problem situation, then the rule based on the precedent does not apply.
- The *prima facie conjecture.* A relation is manifestly implausible if its negation can be shown by a direct, one-step inference from relations already in place.

3.3 REASONING AND CREATING RULES USING ANALOGY

Let us review how rules are generated. A previous paper explains this in detail (Winston, 1981), as does the textbook treatment (Winston, 1984).

Consider the *Macbeth* precedent, given earlier, together with the exercise, both expressed in semantic-network form, as shown in figures 3-2 and 3-3. When asked to demonstrate that the man may want to be king, given the *Macbeth* precedent, the system proceeds as follows:

- The people in the precedent are matched with the people in the exercise. More generally, precedent parts are matched with exercise parts.
- The causal structure of the precedent is mapped onto the exercise.
- It is determined that the mapped causal structure ties the relation to be shown to relations known to be true.
- A rule is constructed, with generalizations of the exercise relations used becoming if parts and a generalization of the relation to be shown becoming the then part.

When a single precedent cannot supply the total causal structure needed, the system attempts to chain several together. In the example, if it were not known already that the woman was greedy, as required for application of the *Macbeth* precedent, greed might be established through another precedent or already-learned rule.

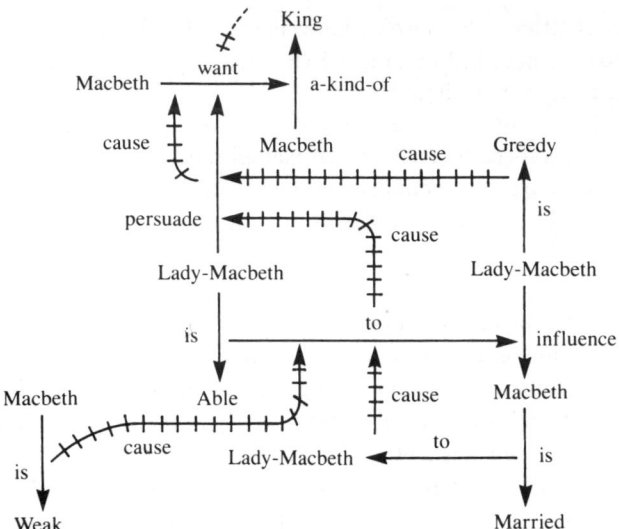

Figure 3-2: Problems are solved by transferring the existing cause relations of a precedent (crossed lines) onto the problem to be solved (figure 3-3).

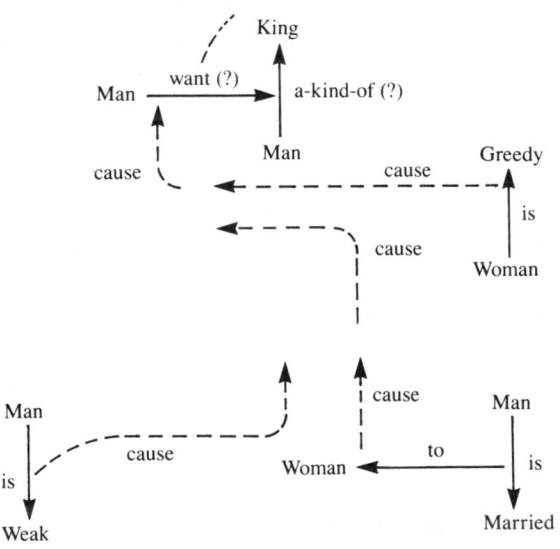

Figure 3-3: Problems are solved by transferring the existing cause relations of a precedent (figure 3-2) onto the problem to be solved (dotted lines).

3.4 IMPROVING PERFORMANCE BY ENABLING CENSORS

So far we have established that rules can be generated and that they need to be blocked in certain circumstances. There are three obvious ways to arrange for blocking.

First, expand the if part of an offending rule, restricting its use. One problem with this idea is that rules can become bloated with endless tests for increasingly unlikely minutiae. Such bloat makes rules obscure and hard to criticize, debug, and improve, both for us people and for reasoning programs.

Second, attach censors to each rule. Have the censors check the problem to be solved for contraindications to the rules to which the censors are attached. One problem is that the rules can become bloated with censor names; these censor names would give no explicit insight into when the rules do not apply.

Third, have censors watch for particular relations. Forbid any rule or precedent to work toward establishing a relation to which a censor objects. One problem is that the rules continue to look silly, containing no hint about when they do not apply.

3.4.1 Censors Can Block Augmented If-Then Rules

A better, less obvious idea is this:

- Augment each rule at the time it is generated with entries that correspond to negations of all the relations in the transferred causal structure, except of course for those relations that become the if and then parts of the rule. These augmenting entries constitute the unless part of the rule. According to the blocking principle, if any entry in the unless part of the rule corresponds to something that is manifestly true, then the rule does not apply.

Note that entries in the unless part of the rule are distinguished by the way that they are used, not by the fact that the truth value of many is false. In our examples, the unless entries usually will be false relations because they are negations of relations that are usually true. But a precedent's intermediate relations, those from which unless entries are made, may be false relations, leading to unless entries that are true relations.

Clearly, a relation is manifestly true if the existing facts indicate that the relation is true. But introspectively, it seems unreasonable to go deeply into reasoning about unless entries. Hence the implemented system adheres to the following specialization of the prima facie conjecture:

- If any entry in the unless part of a rule corresponds to a relation that can be shown to be true by another rule working directly from relations already in place, without further inference, then block the rule.

Note that the restriction to one-step inference is an attempt to translate *manifestly true* into a computationally precise mechanism. Doubtless there will be better translations.

Let us consider an example. Suppose that a rule's unless part is triggered when someone is unable to influence another. Such a rule will be blocked if the person to be influenced does not like the other. The augmented form of RULE-1 is as follows:

RULE-1   IF   There is a greedy lady
                   and there is a weak noble
                   and the noble is married to the lady
         THEN   the noble may want to be king
         UNLESS   the lady does not persuade the noble to want to be king
                   or the lady is not able to influence the noble.

The blocking rule is as follows:

RULE-2   IF   There is a person X who does not like another person Y
         THEN   Y is not able to influence X.

A rule becomes a *censor* when it blocks the application of another rule. Because censors look just like any other rules, they can be learned, stored, and retrieved in the same ways.

Note that when the illustrated rule is used to block another, the illustrated rule works only if it is known at the time of use that there is dislike. There is no attempt to demonstrate dislike when it is not already known.

Note that the viability of the prima facie conjecture depends on the existence of a rich vocabulary of relations. It would be difficult to demonstrate anything in one step if all relations were reduced to canonical constellations of small-vocabulary primitives. This opens the question of just how rich the vocabulary should be, a question answered operationally by the free use of those relations for which there are common natural language words.

The viability of the prima facie conjecture also depends on the availability of all solid facts before backward-chaining problem solving begins. This means that all solid facts are either given or deduced already by forward chaining from given facts using reliable, potentially relevant rules. Reliability is insured by forward chaining only with rules that reach unassailable conclusions. Relevance cannot be insured, but it can be rendered more likely. One way is to use the context mechanism described in an earlier paper (Winston, 1981).

3.4.2 Censors Can Block Censors

Actually, it is possible to be influenced by someone you dislike if for some reason you trust the person in spite of the dislike. Perhaps the real able-to-influence censor should look like this:

RULE-2   IF   There is a person X who does not like another person Y
         THEN   Y is not able to influence X
         UNLESS   X trusts Y.

Such a censor could be blocked by another censor that states that you believe a person if he or she has the ability to convince you:

CENSOR-1   IF   There is a person X who is able to convince another
                      person Y
            THEN   Y trusts X.

To illustrate how these can interact, consider the following situation:

> *Let E be an exercise about a weak noble and a greedy lady. The lady is married to the noble. He does not like her. However, the lady is able to convince the noble. In E show that the noble may want to be king.*

This produces the following scenario:

- First the problem is posed and RULE-1 is fetched. Its if parts are satisfied.
- Next, the unless part of RULE-1 is examined. The condition involving the ability to influence causes RULE-2 to be fetched. Its if parts are satisfied. RULE-1 is about to be blocked.
- But RULE-2's unless part must be examined. The line involving believing causes CENSOR-1 to be fetched. Its if parts are satisfied. Thus CENSOR-1 blocks RULE-2, preventing RULE-2 from blocking RULE-1.
- Finally, RULE-1 succeeds, establishing the relation originally in question.

3.4.3 Augmented If-Then Rules Are Not Rules of Inference

It is tempting to write censors in the following way:

$$A_1 \& \ldots \& A_n \& \sim (B_1 \lor \ldots \lor B_n) \Rightarrow C$$

or alternatively,

$$A_1 \& \ldots \& A_n \& \sim B_1 \& \ldots \& \sim B_n \Rightarrow C$$

where A's are in the if part of the rule and B's are in the unless part.

Logical notation is deceptive, however, for in the use of augmented if-then rules, the A's and B's are treated differently from each other, in contrast to the conventions of traditional logic: unlimited effort is to be put into showing the A's are true; only one-step effort is put into showing that the B's are true, with the B's assumed false on failure.

Note that rules used as censors are not permitted to create new objects. This insures that the amount of computation added by the application of censors to unless entries is bounded even though censors have their own unless parts that must be checked by censors. This author believes that it is likely that censor computations will prove in practice to be broad and shallow as well as bounded, suggesting parallel implementation.

3.4.4 Augmented Rules Suggest an Approach to Certain Definition Problems

Winograd has discussed the difficulty of definition using the word *bachelor* (1976). To be sure, a bachelor is an unmarried adult man, but Winograd notes that such definition can cause trouble if used when someone says, "Please invite some nice bachelors to my party," for it would be strange to invite certain kinds of bachelors. For example, Catholic priests and misogamists, although they satisfy the dictionary definition, are clearly not what a party giver has in mind.

Since the exception possibilities seem limitless, Winograd feels it is inappropriate to rest a definition of *bachelor* on a clearly defined, small set of primitive propositions. He argues that it is better to think of using some abstract measure of closeness to an extensible set of exemplars. Woods takes issue with Winograd's view, arguing that correct understanding must involve an explicit selection of a particular word sense, rather than closeness to a generally applicable exemplar set (Woods, 1981).

The augmented-rule idea may offer a slightly different approach to the problem. Consider the following definition of *bachelor,* stated as an augmented if-then rule:

RULE-2   IF   There is a man
                       and the man is not married
                       and the man is an adult
         THEN   the man is a bachelor
         UNLESS   the man is not expected to be married
                       or the man is not able to be married.

With this definition the conclusion can be avoided, even though the if part of the rule is fully satisfied, provided that the individual involved is not able to be married or is not expected to be married. This takes care of the priest and the misogamist problems, given the following censors:

CENSOR-1   IF   A man is a misogamist
           THEN   the man is not expected to be married.
CENSOR-2   IF   A man is a priest
           THEN   the man is not able to be married.

Evidently there can be a simple, stable definition of *bachelor* and at the same time an interaction between growing knowledge about bachelors and the definition, when appropriate, as the knowledge is accumulated. The definition is used more intelligently as more is learned, and in a sense, the definition is never closed.

How does capturing the meaning of *bachelor* with an augmented if-then rule compare with other approaches? One point of view is that Winograd's exemplars correspond to rule-generating precedents, and learned augmented if-then rules correspond to Woods's selectable word senses. Learning about bachelors from precedents will be discussed in section 3.5.1.

3.4.5 Censors Can Improve Precedent Reasoning

Although censors were originally investigated in this work in order to cure the apparent silliness of some learned rules, they help in another context too. When ordinary precedent-exercise problem solving is in progress, the analogy part of the system works back through the causal structure in the precedent, looking for relations that correspond to relations in the exercise. Each time the system fails to find a corresponding relation, it does a censor check before moving further through the causal structure.

Work with a precedent stops if a censor check exposes a relation in the precedent that corresponds to a relation in the exercise that is manifestly improbable. The precedent's intended conclusion is judged inoperable because the exercise supports the censor's blocking conclusion.

3.5 LEARNING AUGMENTED RULES

Since censor rules and definition rules are just rules used in a special way, they can be learned just like any other rules. This may be by direct telling, or it may be by precedent and exercise, or it may be by near miss.

3.5.1 Augmented Rules Can Be Learned by Precedent and Exercise

Here is a precedent and an exercise for learning the *bachelor* definition rule:

Let S be a story about Casanova. Casanova is a bachelor because he is a man and because he is expected to be married. He is expected to be married because he is able to be married. He is able to be married because he is an adult and because he is not married.

Let E be an exercise about Henry. He is a man and an adult. He is not married. In E show that Henry is a bachelor.

Of course, one might argue that providing the precedent involving Casanova is unrealistic spoon feeding. Indeed it may well be, so it is important to understand that the same *bachelor* rule can be learned using several independent precedents together:

Let S be a story about a man. He is a bachelor because he is expected to be married. He is a bachelor because he is a man.

Let S be a story about a man. He is expected to be married because he is able to be married.

Let S be a story about a man. He is able to be married because he is an adult and because he is not married.

Alternatively, the *bachelor* rule can be learned using several previously learned rules:

STORY-1	IF		There is a man
			and the man is an adult
	THEN		the man is expected to be married.
STORY-2	IF		A man is able to be married
	THEN		the man is expected to be married.
STORY-3	IF		A man is an adult
			and the man is not married
	THEN		the man is able to be married.

It is also possible to learn a rule that allows a married Muslim who is seeking an additional wife to be considered a bachelor.

3.5.2 Augmented Rules Can Be Learned by Near Miss

Of course, there should be some way of recovering if an impoverished definition is acquired early on. The near-miss idea seems useful in such situations. Consider this scenario:

- A teacher tells the system that a bachelor is an unmarried, adult man. This produces an impoverished definition of bachelor, one without anything in the unless part.
- The teacher complains when the system identifies a Catholic priest as a bachelor.
- The system notices that the only robust difference between the priest and other people who are correctly identified as bachelors is that the priest is not able to be married.
- The system guesses that bachelors must be able to be married and puts an appropriate entry in the unless part of the bachelor definition.

Of course, this is a particularly simple situation because there is but one object involved and the descriptions are such that the relation that causes the near miss is the only relation that is caused by something and not deemed plausible in a situation where the rule does not apply. It is not known how difficult it would be to identify the right difference in general, but recent work on *near-miss groups* suggests that the right difference can be identified, given that there are several situations for which the rule works and should, as well as several for which the rule works but should not (Winston, 1984).

In the event that there is no way to narrow down the possibilities conclusively, there are two approaches, both of which are under study and deserve attention. One approach is to do search, perhaps massive search. The other alternative is to do nothing. Work by Berwick on syntax acquisition (1982) and by Minsky on concept learning (draft) both suggest that if it is difficult to identify the right difference, a learning system should simply give up, waiting for more transparent examples to come along.

3.6 THE IMPLEMENTED SYSTEM

The example precedents, exercises, rules, and censors in this paper are shown in the exact English form used by the implemented system. Translation from English into the semantic net representation used by the system is done by a parser developed and implemented by Katz (Katz, 1980; Katz and Winston, 1982). The grammar used by the parser is also used by a generator, which produces English versions of the rules.

So far, the system knows a few dozen censors, most of which it has been told and of all of which it can learn from precedents or rules and exercises. Clearly, the number is enough to do surface-scratching experiments and to illustrate the ideas, but an order of magnitude or two more will be required to demonstrate the ideas.

3.7 OPEN QUESTIONS

It is plain that this work is only a beginning. Work is in progress on several related fronts:

- Exploiting several situations for which a rule works and should, together with several for which the same rule works but should not, in order to improve the rule.
- In collaboration with Ryszard Michalski: generalizing the notion *manifestly improbable* in order to devise a variable-precision logic (Michalski and Winston, 1985).
- In collaboration with Thomas O. Binford (Stanford University), Michael Lowry (Stanford University), and Boris Katz: creating appearance descriptions from functional descriptions, precedents, and examples (Winston et al., 1983).
- In collaboration with Peter Andreae: using abstractions in matching and in indexing and retrieving.
- In collaboration with Richard Doyle: the problem of incorporating time into the representation.
- In collaboration with Boris Katz and others: retrieving precedents from a database so that they need not be given by a teacher.
- In response to a suggestion by J. Michael Brady: augmenting the rules with an *if-relevant* part in addition to the unless part described in this paper. The idea is that the if-relevant part will somehow keep track of the ultimate goals to which a rule may be relevant, so that the rule is used in forward chaining only if one of

the potential ultimate goals is involved in the problem to be solved. This would make the rules look like this in logical notation:

$$A_1 \ \& \ \ldots \ \& \ A_n \ \& \ \sim (B_1 \lor \ldots \lor B_n) \ \& \ (G_1 \lor \ldots \lor G_n) \Rightarrow C$$

where the A's are in the if part of the rule, the B's are in the unless part, and the G's are in the if-relevant part; and where it is understood that only one-step effort is to be put into the B's and G's. This would complement the existing context mechanism explained previously (Winston, 1981).

In addition, the following questions, enumerated in a previous paper, remain open (Winston, 1981):

- There is no way to handle subcategories of cause such as those sketched by Rieger (1978).
- There is no way to summarize an episode in a story so as to make a general précis leading to more abstract rules. Lehnert's summarization work should be tried (1981).

3.8 CONCLUSION: SIMPLE IDEAS HAVE PROMISE

This chapter is about a set of ideas that enable improvement in the reliability of learned rules. The extended theory enables improved performance in those domains subject to problem solving by analogy. Such domains satisfy several restrictions:

- The situations in the domain can be represented by the relations between the parts together and the classes and properties of those parts.
- The importance of a part of a description is determined by the constraints in which it participates.
- Constraints that determine something once will tend to do so again.

Things that involve spatial, visual, and aural reasoning do not seem to satisfy all restrictions. Things that involve management, political science, economics, law, medicine, and ordinary common sense do seem to satisfy the restrictions, however, and are targets for the learning and reasoning ideas of the theory:

- Actor-object representation.
- Importance-dominated matching.
- Analogy-based reasoning using constraint transfer.
- If-then rules learned by solving problems.
- If-then rules improved by modifications based on near misses.
- If-then rules augmented by unless parts.
- Blocking censors that create fences around rules using prima facie evidence.

3.9 RELATED WORK

This work builds on the MACBETH system (Winston, 1979, 1981, 1984), which concentrated on analogy and rule acquisition. Minsky's views on censors also had a major influence (Minsky, 1980).

To a lesser extent, the idea of learning by near miss is involved (Winston, 1970). However, in this newer work, not only is there a different purpose, there is a much greater degree of participation by the learning system in the learning process, because many precedents, rules, and censors have to be accepted or retrieved and made to work together, not just a single model and near miss. Consequently, on the spectrum ranging from learning by being told to learning by discovery, this newer work lies further toward the learning-by-discovery end.

The augmented if-then rule is a special case of the annotated if-then rule introduced by Goldstein and Grimson in a paper on flight simulation (1977). They suggested that if-then rules should exhibit certain unlesslike conditions (which they called caveats) as well as rationales, plans, and control information. The work of Brown and VanLehn (1980) on explaining subtraction bugs is a more recent precedent for using censors to block rules, although their censors (which they call critics) are triggered by what a rule does, rather than by unless conditions.

The idea that censors should work only with the facts in hand is a variant on the theme of reasoning using limited resources, an idea that is discussed widely, particularly in the expert systems literature.

It was observed in conversation that the definition of *bachelor* really should say something about a man's being expected to be married (John Mallery, private communication) leading the author to try handling the bachelor problem with the unless framework. Another colleague pointed out that the prima facie conjecture does not make sense unless all reliable, potentially relevant forward chaining is done first (Boris Katz, private communication). Changing the designator *if-plausible,* used in a previous version of this chapter, to *unless* was also suggested by a colleague (Jonathan H. Connell, private communication).

And of course, analogy was first studied in Artificial Intelligence by Evans (1963); the matcher in his geometric analogy program ranked matches according to built-in, implicit importance criteria. Matches viewing two figures as rotations of one another, for example, were regarded as stronger than matches viewing the same two figures as reflections. Evans was able to use fixed, built-in importance criteria because he worked only with the world of simple figures.

ACKNOWLEDGMENTS

This paper was improved by comments from Robert C. Berwick, J. Michael Brady, Boris Katz, Michael Lowry, and Karen A. Prendergast.

The research was done at the Artificial Intelligence Laboratory of the Massachusetts Institute of Technology. Support for the Laboratory's artificial intelligence research is provided in part by the Advanced Research Projects Agency of the Department of Defense under Office of Naval Research Contract N00014-80-C-0505.

References

Berwick, R., "Locality Principles and the Acquisition of Syntactic Knowledge," Ph.D. diss., Department of Electrical Engineering and Computer Science, MIT, 1982.

Brown, J. S., and VanLehn, K., "Repair Theory: A Generative Theory of Bugs in Procedural Skills," *Cognitive Science,* Vol. 4, No. 4, pp. 379–426, 1980.

Davis, R., "Applications of Meta Level Knowledge to the Construction, Maintenance, and Use of Large Knowledge Bases," Ph.D. diss., Stanford University, 1979. (Published in *Knowledge-Based Systems in Artificial Intelligence,* R. Davis and D. Lenat (Eds.), McGraw-Hill, New York, 1980.

Evans, T. G., "A Heuristic Program to Solve Geometric Analogy Problems," in *Semantic Information Processing,* M. Minsky, (Ed.), MIT Press, Cambridge, 1968. (Based on Ph.D. diss., Department of Electrical Engineering, MIT, 1963.)

Goldstein, I. P., and Grimson, E., "Annotated Production Systems: A Model for Skill Acquisition," *Proceedings of the Fifth IJCAI,* Cambridge, Mass., pp. 311–17, 1977.

Katz, B., "A Three-Step Procedure for Language Generation," AI Memo No. 599, MIT, December 1980.

Katz, B., and Winston, P. H., "Parsing and Generating English Using Commutative Transformations," AI Memo No. 677, MIT, May 1982. See also "A Two-Way Natural Language Interface," in *Integrated Interactive Computing Systems,* P. Degano and E. Sandewall, (Eds.), North-Holland, Amsterdam, 1982.

Lehnert, W., "Plot Units and Narrative Summarization," *Cognitive Science,* Vol. 5, No. 4, pp. 293–331, 1981.

Michalski, R. S. and Winston, P. H., "Variable Precision Logic," AI Memo No. 857, MIT, 1985.

Minsky, M., "Jokes and the Logic of the Cognitive Unconscious," AI Memo No. 603, MIT, November 1980.

———, Draft on society of mind theory of thinking.

Rieger, C., "On Organization of Knowledge for Problem Solving and Language Comprehension," *Artificial Intelligence,* Vol. 7, No. 2, 1978.

Winograd, T., "Towards a Procedural Understanding of Semantics," AI Memo AIM-292, Stanford University, November 1976. (Also appears as Report No. STAN-CS-76-580, Department of Computer Science, Stanford University, 1976.)

Winston, P. H., "Learning Structural Descriptions from Examples," Ph.D. diss., MIT, 1970. (Published in a shortened version in *The Psychology of Computer Vision,* P. H. Winston (Ed.), McGraw-Hill, New York, 1975.)

———, "Learning by Creating and Justifying Transfer Frames," *Artificial Intelligence,* Vol. 10, No. 2, pp. 147–72, 1978.

———, "Learning and Reasoning by Analogy," *Communications of the ACM,* Vol. 23, No. 12, pp. 689–703, December 1980. (Available with details as "Learning and Reasoning by Analogy: The Details," AI Memo No. 520, MIT, April 1979.)

———, "Learning New Principles from Precedents and Exercises," *Artificial Intelligence,* Vol. 19, No. 3, pp. 321–50, 1982. (Available with details as "Learning New Principles from Precedents and Exercises: The Details," AI Memo No. 632, MIT, May 1981.)

———, "Learning by Augmenting Rules and Accumulating Censors: The Details," AI Memo No. 678, MIT, May 1982.

———, *Artificial Intelligence,* 2d ed, Addison-Wesley, Reading, Mass., 1984.

———, "Improving Learned Constraints Using Symbolic Correlation," forthcoming.

Winston, P. H.; Binford, T. O.; Katz, B., and Lowry, M. R., "Learning Physical Descriptions from Functional Definitions, Examples, and Precedents," *Proceedings of AAAI-83,* Washington, D.C., pp. 433–39, 1983.

Woods, W. A., "Procedural Semantics as a Theory of Meaning," Bolt Beranek and Newman Report No. 4627, March 1981. (Also published in *Computational Aspects of Linguistic Structures,* A. Joshi, I. Sag, and B. Webber (Eds.), Cambridge University Press, Cambridge, 1982.)

4

LEARNING TO PREDICT SEQUENCES

Thomas G. Dietterich
Oregon State University

Ryszard S. Michalski*
Massachusetts Institute of Technology

Abstract

This chapter considers the problem of discovering a rule characterizing a given sequence of events (objects) and able to predict a plausible continuation of the sequence. This prediction is nondeterministic because the rule doesn't necessarily tell exactly which events must appear next in the sequence but rather determines a set of plausible next events. It is assumed that the individual events in the sequence are characterized by a set of attributes and that the next event depends solely on the values of the attributes for the previous events in the sequence. The attributes are either initially given or derived from the initial ones through a chain of inferences. Three basic rule models are employed to guide the search for a sequence-generating rule: decomposition, periodic, and disjunctive normal form (DNF). The search process involves simultaneously transforming the initial sequences to *derived* sequences and instantiating general rule models to find the best match between the instantiated model and the derived sequence. A program called SPARC/E is described that implements most of the methodology as applied to discovering sequence-generating rules in the card game Eleusis. This game, which attempts to model the process of scientific discovery, is used as a source of examples illustrating the performance of SPARC/E.

---

*On leave of absence from the University of Illinois at Urbana-Champaign.

4.1 INTRODUCTION

Inductive learning—that is, learning by generalizing specific facts or observations—is a fundamental strategy by which we acquire knowledge about the world. Computer models of inductive learning have been studied from the AI perspective for several years now, and one result of this research has been the identification of several different kinds of inductive learning. At least three different types have been studied: (1) *instance-to-class induction,* (2) *part-to-whole induction,* and (3) *conceptual clustering.*

Instance-to-class induction has received the most attention. Here, the learning system is presented with independent instances representing some class, and the task is to induce a general description of the class. The instances can be specific physical objects, actions, processes, images, and so on. The learned class description (also called the *concept description*) can be used to classify new instances whose correct class is not known.

An example of this type of learning problem is determining diagnostic rules from a set of diagnosed cases of diseases. For example, Michalski and Chilausky (1980) describe a learning program, AQ11, that is presented with a set of independent training instances, each of which is an example of a soybean plant with a given disease. The AQ11 program then induces a general description of that disease. This description can be applied to diagnose the occurrence of this disease in other soybean plants. From several hundred such training instances covering nineteen different soybean diseases, AQ11 has inferred a set of nineteen diagnostic rules. Several other researchers have investigated instance-to-class learning problems (e.g., Winston, 1970; Buchanan and Mitchell, 1978; Mitchell, Utgoff, and Banerji, 1983). Reviews of various methods for such instance-to-class induction appear in Michalski, Carbonell, and Mitchell (1983) and Dietterich et al. (1982).

The second type of inductive learning—part-to-whole induction—has received less attention. Part-to-whole induction involves constructing a description of a whole object by observing only selected parts of it, for example, hypothesizing the description of a whole scene, given a set of fragments of the scene. An important part-to-whole induction problem is discovering a description of a sequence of objects where the "part" consists of the first k elements of the sequence and the "whole" is the total sequence.

This type of part-to-whole induction problem has been studied in the past under the name of *sequence extrapolation* or *letter-sequence prediction.* Simon and Kotovsky (Simon and Kotovsky, 1963; Simon, 1972; Kotovsky and Simon, 1973), for example, study problems in which a program (or a person) is given partial sequences such as

A   B   X   B   C   W   C   D   V   . . .

and asked to predict the next few letters in the sequence. Their program does this by first finding a sequence-generating rule and then applying that rule to predict the continuation of the sequence. In this case, the rule might state that the sequence is a periodically repeating subsequence of three letters in which the first two letters are successors of the letter appearing in the previous period and the third letter is the predecessor of the corresponding letter in the previous period. Related work on this type of learning has been done by Solomonoff (1964), Hedrick (1976), and Hofstadter (1983, 1985).

The third type of learning problem—conceptual clustering—has received very little attention. We mention it here only for completeness. Clustering problems arise when several objects (or situations) are presented to a learner and the learner must invent classes into which the objects can be usefully grouped. An example of such a problem is learning sound systems in spoken language. The human ear is capable of distinguishing among a wide variety of spoken sounds. However, any given human language groups all of these sounds into a relatively small number of equivalence classes (roughly fifty). All sounds within a given class are regarded as being identical for purposes of communication. Recently, Michalski (1980) and Michalski and Stepp (1983) developed a method and a computer program, CLUSTER, for *conjunctive conceptual clustering* that can solve such learning problems.

This chapter presents further research on the second type of inductive learning problem, that is, part-to-whole induction. We are particularly interested in sequence prediction problems that are much more complex than letter-series prediction. Letter-series prediction is a very simple problem for two reasons. First, in letter series, each object in the sequence has only one attribute—its name. Second, the desired sequence prediction rule is deterministic, because it is assumed that there is only one legal continuation of the sequence. This chapter presents a method for discovering sequence prediction rules in cases in which the objects may be described by many relevant attributes and the sequence prediction rule is nondeterministic. This type of learning problem is called a *nondeterministic prediction problem,* or an NDP problem.

In an NDP problem, the learner is presented with a finite sequence of events. Each event is characterized by the values of a number of discrete-valued attributes. The goal is to find a *sequence-generating rule* that, given the first k events, states the values of the attributes[1] that must be true of event $k + 1$. Since the sequence-generating rule may only state values for *some* of the attributes, the rule may not necessarily predict a unique event $k + 1$. This is what makes the rule nondeterministic. Because only a partial description of the original sequence is sought and because the description may involve new attributes not present in the initial set, a very large

---

[1]It is assumed that the rule is expressed in terms of attributes that are either observable attributes of objects present in the sequence up to the moment when a new object is generated or attributes that can be derived from such observable attributes by some known inference rules.

number of hypotheses may need to be examined. This makes this problem much more difficult than the previously studied letter-series extrapolation problems.

The card game Eleusis (Abbott, 1977; Gardner, 1977) represents a nondeterministic sequence prediction problem. We will use examples from this game to illustrate the proposed general methodology for discovering rules for event sequences.

4.1.1 Eleusis: An Exemplary Nondeterministic Prediction Problem

An interesting NDP problem arises in the card game Eleusis, invented by Robert Abbott (1977; Gardner, 1977). Eleusis is an inductive game in which players attempt to discover a generating rule (known only to the dealer) for a sequence of cards. This "secret rule" is invented and recorded by the dealer before the game. Each player, in his or her turn, adds one card to the sequence, and the dealer indicates whether the card is a correct (or incorrect) extension of the sequence (i.e., satisfies or does not satisfy the secret sequence-generating rule). Players who play incorrectly are penalized by having additional cards added to their hands. The goal of each player is to get rid of all the cards in his or her hand, which is only possible if correct cards are played. The cards played during the game are displayed in the form of a layout in which the correct cards form the "main line" and incorrect cards form "side lines" branching down from the main line at the card that they follow. Figure 4-1 shows a typical Eleusis layout for the sequence-generating rule "Play alternating red and black cards." In this game, the 3 of hearts was played first, followed by the 9 of spades and the jack of diamonds. All of these were correct. Following the jack, the 5 of diamonds was played. It appears on a sideline below the jack, because it was not a correct extension of the sequence. (At this point, a black card is required.) The 4 of clubs was then correctly played, and so on.

Below are several examples of sequence-generating rules for Eleusis:

- If the last card was a spade, play a heart; if the last card was a heart, play a diamond; if the last card was a diamond, play a club; and if the last card was a club, play a spade.
- Play a card one point higher or one point lower than the last card.
- If the last card was black, play a card higher than or equal to that card; if the last card was red, play lower or equal.
- Play alternating even and odd cards.

Main line:	3H	9S	JD	4C	JD	2C	10D	2C	5H
Side lines:			5D		AH	AS	8H		
					8H	10S	7H		
					QD		10H		

Figure 4-1:   A sample Eleusis layout.

- Play strings of cards such that each string contains cards all in the same suit and has an odd number of cards in it.

There are four important points to note about this game. First, observe that an Eleusis rule typically allows any of several cards to be played legally after each card. Hence, Eleusis provides an instance of the nondeterministic prediction problem.

Second, notice that the rules employ descriptors or terms that do not appear in the input sequence. The input data provides only the suit and rank (value) of each card and its position in the sequence. The sequence-generating rules, however, may include such terms as *even, odd, black, red*, and *strings of cards such that each string contains cards all in the same suit and has an odd number of cards in it*. The learning program must bridge this gap between the terms appearing in the input sequence and the terms needed for expressing the rules. To bridge this gap, one has to solve what is called the *description space transformation problem.*

The third point is that several different logical forms are employed to express the rules. Some rules take the form of a set of if-then rules: "If the last card was a spade, play a heart. . . . " Other rules are stated as simple disjunctions: "Play a card one point higher or one point lower than the last card." And still others describe the layout as a periodically repeating sequence: "Play alternating even and odd cards." The learning program must have the capacity to create descriptions that capture these different logical forms. The authors' approach to the solution is to divide different sequence-generating rules into a few general classes according to the logical form of the rules. Each class is represented by an abstract *model*, or logical schema, which can be parameterized and then instantiated to yield a particular sequence-generating rule. For this reason, this method is called a *multiple model learning method.*

Finally, it should be noted that the space of possible Eleusis rules is very large. Indeed, there is in principle no limit to the number of secret rules. However, to make the game interesting to human players, Eleusis has a point-scoring scheme that encourages the dealer to choose only fairly simple sequence-generating rules. The program SPARC/E described here is capable of representing more than 10^{137} rules.[2]

---

[2]This estimate is based on computing the space of all syntactically legal VL_{22} conjunctive statements (see section 4.3) containing the following set of descriptors (each descriptor is followed by the number of elements in its value set and the number of possible selectors that can be formed using those elements): SUIT (4,9), RANK (13,91), COLOR (2,3), FACEDNESS (2,3), PARITY (2,3), PRIMENESS (2,3), RANKMOD3 (3,7), D-SUIT01 (4,9), D-SUIT02 (4,9), D-RANK01 (25,300), D-RANK02 (25,300), S-RANK01 (25,300), S-RANK02 (25,300), D-COLOR01 (2,3), D-COLOR02 (2,3), D-FACEDNESS01 (2,3), D-FACEDNESS02 (2,3), D-PARITY01 (2,3), D-PARITY02 (2,3), D-PRIMENESS01 (2,3), D-PRIMENESS02 (2,3), D-RANKMOD3-01 (3,7), D-RANKMOD3-02 (3,7). The SUIT and RANKMOD3 descriptors are cyclically ordered, and the RANK descriptors are interval descriptors. All others are nominal. In a decomposition rule with a lookback of $L = 2$, the first seven descriptors appear three times—once for each card. Hence, the total number of possible conjuncts is $(9*91*3*3*3*3*7)^3 * (9*300*300*3*3*3*3*7)^2 = 2.11221*10^{34}$. If there are four conjuncts in a rule, then we obtain $[2.11221*10^{34}]^4 = 1.99*10^{137}$.

Now that these remarks have been made, the three main problems addressed in this chapter are pointed out:

- Transforming the original description space to aid induction
- Applying multiple rule models to discover sequence-generating rules
- Developing a strategy and overall system architecture for learning with multiple models

In the next two subsections, the first two problems are described along with a review of how each has been solved in existing systems. Discussion of the third problem, the overall system architecture, is postponed until section 4.4.

4.1.2 Transforming the Description Space

The problem of transforming the initial problem description arises in any domain in which the given data (e.g., the training instances in concept learning) are observations or measurements that do not include the information directly relevant to the task at hand. For example, in character recognition, the input typically consists of a matrix of light intensities representing a character, but the relevant information includes position-invariant properties of letters such as the presence of a line on the left or right of a character, occurrence of line endings, closed contours, and so on (e.g., Karpinski and Michalski, 1966). These position-invariant properties can be made explicit by applying description space transformations to the raw data.

An example of a learning program that performs description space transformation is INTSUM, which is part of the Meta-DENDRAL system (Buchanan and Mitchell, 1978). INTSUM is presented with raw training instances in the form of chemical structures (graphs) and associated mass spectra, represented as fragment masses and their intensities. For each fragment in the mass spectrum, INTSUM must determine the bonds that could have broken to produce that fragment. A simple mass spectrometer simulator is used to develop these hypothesized bond breaks. Each of the resulting transformed training instances has the form of a chemical structure and a set of bonds that broke when that structure was placed in the mass spectrometer. It is this information that is provided to the remaining parts of the Meta-DENDRAL system (programs RULEGEN and RULEMOD).

In character recognition programs and in Meta-DENDRAL, the data transformations are fixed in advance. In many learning programs, however, the proper transformations are not know a priori. In such cases, a learning system needs to select or invent appropriate description space transformations.

The type of description space transformation performed by a program is a useful criterion for characterizing learning methods. The simplest learning methods (e.g., linear regression) determine only the coefficients for an a priori determined, fixed set of variables arranged in a predetermined expression. More sophisticated are learning algorithms, such as the A^q algorithm (Michalski, 1969, 1972) and the candidate elimination algorithm (Mitchell, 1978, 1983), that are able to determine which attributes are relevant and how they should be combined. Another level of sophistication is obtained when a learning program applies a set of predetermined transformations to the data prior to inductive generalization (Buchanan and Mitchell, 1978; Soloway, 1978). These programs augment the basic inductive algorithms by applying a set of predetermined transformations to the data prior to inductive generalization. The next step of difficulty is represented by learning algorithms that select description space transformations under the guidance of special heuristics. Very few researchers have addressed this problem (e.g., Lenat, 1983; Michalski, 1983). The most sophisticated algorithms currently envisioned—but not yet developed—would be capable of discovering new data transformations. Figure 4-2 shows this spectrum of inductive learning problems.

The SPARC/E method presented in this chapter falls under category 4 of figure 4-2, as it selects transformations under heuristic guidance. The program has available four general classes of description space transformations (see section 4.2) from which it selects the appropriate ones to apply under the guidance of domain-specific heuristics.

4.1.3 Learning with Multiple Models

The second major problem that arises in the Eleusis prediction problem involves using multiple description models in the process of inductive learning. This problem has not received much attention in previous AI research. Almost all existing learning systems employ only a *single model* for determining the space of possible output descriptions (hypotheses). Many systems, for example, use conjunctive models to represent concepts; that is, they assume that the learned concept will be expressed as a conjunction of predicates. By constraining the search to consider only conjunctive descriptions, they greatly simplify the learning problem.

A more general approach, employed by Michalski (1969, 1972), constrains descriptions to be in disjunctive normal form with the *fewest* conjunctive statements. The induction algorithm first finds one conjunctive statement, then another, and so on until all of the training instances are covered. Meta-DENDRAL employs a fairly elaborate simulator of the operation of the mass spectrometer to guide its search for conjunctive cleavage rules (Buchanan and Mitchell, 1978). In general, current learning systems use a single model, and very few authors have made their models explicit.

1. Determine coefficients
2. Select relevant variables and combine them
3. Apply predetermined transformations
4. Select transformations under heuristic guidance
5. Discover new transformations

Figure 4-2: Spectrum of learning problems in order of increasing difficulty.

One researcher who has employed multiple models is Persson (1966). He applied four different models to the problem of extrapolating number and letter sequences. Briefly, these models were the following:

- A model that computes the coefficients and the degree of a polynomial by applying Newton's forward-difference formula (the degree can be arbitrarily large).

- An extended model that discovers exponential rules of the form AB^C, where A is a polynomial of degree 4 or less, and B and C are polynomials of degree 1 or less (i.e., B and C are of the form $ax + b$).

- A simple periodic model for periods of length 2 (i.e., intertwined sequences).

- A generalization of the Kotovsky and Simon model for Thurstone letter series that can discover simple periodic and segmented sequence-generating laws.

These models are applied by the program in a rather unusual learning situation in which the program is given a *sequence* of sequence extrapolation problems. Thus, in addition to attempting to solve each individual sequence extrapolation problem, Persson's program tries to predict the *kind* of sequence prediction problem that it will next receive.

Persson's work shows the value of employing multiple description models to search for sequence-generating rules. The major limitation of Persson's approach, however, is that it is specific to number- and letter-sequence prediction. His methods cannot solve the more general prediction problems described in this chapter in which events have multiple attributes (both numerical and nonnumerical) and the sequences are characterized by nondeterministic, logic-based sequence prediction rules.

One can conceive a spectrum of five model-based learning methods (see figure 4-3). The simplest approach is to use a single model. This has been the common approach in AI thus far. The next step is to provide a learning program with a set of models from which it would choose the most appropriate ones. This is the approach used by Persson. The third level of sophistication would be to have the program generate a predetermined set of models by applying a given set of data transformations. This method could be improved further by having the program decide which models to generate on the basis of special heuristics. Finally, an even more sophisticated program would be able to invent new models and apply them to guide the learning process.

1. Single model
2. Selection from a few models
3. Predetermined generation of models
4. Heuristically guided generation of models
5. Discovery of new models

Figure 4-3:   Spectrum of model-based methods in order of increasing difficulty.

The approach described in this chapter searches a predetermined space of possible models in a depth-first fashion and hence falls under category 3 of figure 4-3. The main theoretical contributions of this research include the development of techniques for (1) selecting description space transformations, (2) applying multiple description models, and (3) matching instantiated models to the transformed sequences using a bidirectional search.

4.1.4 Overview of Solution

This section gives an overview of the approach to solving NDP problems presented here. As described above, the learning program is given an input sequence of events. It is assumed that a sequence of events is given and that the task is to find a nondeterministic sequence-generating rule characterizing the input sequence and able to predict its plausible continuation. In the proposed solution, the learning program is supplied with various operators for sequence transformation and with specifications of different rule models. (The implemented method employs four sequence transformation operators and three rule models.)

The sequence transformation operators are repeatedly applied to the input sequence to yield *derived sequences* in which additional facts about the sequence are made explicit. This is a bottom-up process of elaborating and reformulating the data. Simultaneously, through a top-down process, the general rule models are specialized by filling in various parameters and formulas to obtain specific sequence-generating rules. Lastly, the learning program applies three model-fitting algorithms (one for each model) to fit the partially refined model to the transformed data. Thus, the learning program conducts both a bottom-up elaboration of the data and a top-down specialization of the rule models until one of the model-fitting algorithms can be applied to find a match between the elaborated sequence and some specialized rule model. One or more resulting specialized rules are output as candidate sequence-generating rules.

Figure 4-4 illustrates this process schematically. The top-down model specialization process occurs in parallel with the bottom-up data transformation process, thus constituting a kind of bidirectional search.

Model instantiation, as used in this chapter, is an extension of the well-known AI technique of schema instantiation. Schema instantiation has been applied, for example, by Schank and Abelson (1975) to interpret natural language, by Englemore and Terry (1979) to interpret X-ray diffraction data in protein chemistry, and by Friedland (1979) to plan genetics experiments. Model instantiation differs from schema instantiation in the complexity of the instantiation process. Model instantiation involves not only filling in predetermined slots or substituting constants for variables but also synthesizing a logical formula of an assumed type. For example, in order to instantiate each of the three models described below, the program must synthesize a conjunction of predicates or a disjunction of such conjunctions that satisfies

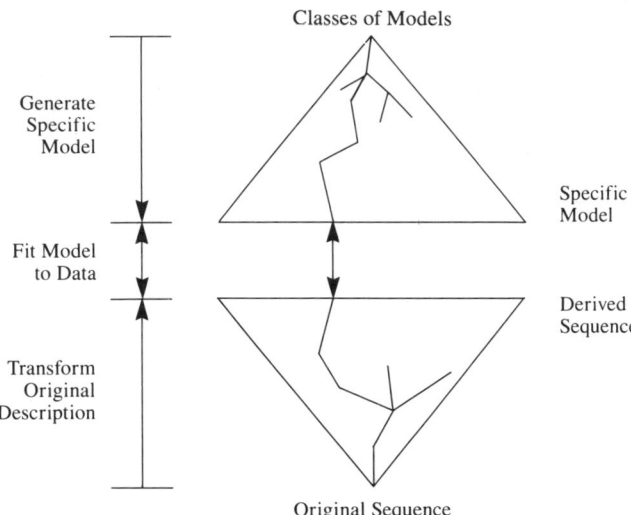

Figure 4-4:   Schematic description of the rule discovery process.

certain constraints. Model instantiation methods share with schema instantiation methods the advantage that they are efficient and also effective with noisy and uncertain data. The constraints provided by the models (or schemata) drastically reduce the size of the space that the program must search.

The principal disadvantage of model and schema instantiation methods is they require that substantial amounts of domain knowledge be built into the program. A ring architecture is employed in the design of the learning program, as described in section 4.4, to keep this domain knowledge explicit and easily modified. This architecture facilitates the application of the system to a variety of problems by simplifying the process of changing the domain-specific parts of the program.

The remaining sections of this chapter discuss the following: (1) the methods used for representing and transforming the initial training instances; (2) the techniques for representing the models and sequence-generating rules; and (3) the details of the program SPARC/E, which implements most of the described methodology. The model-fitting algorithms are presented and the program is illustrated by a few selected examples of its operation when applied to the inductive card game Eleusis.

4.2 TRANSFORMING THE ORIGINAL DESCRIPTION SPACE

Now that the problem to be solved (the NDP problem) has been defined and its solution sketched, the details of that solution can be presented. First, the language is presented for describing the original sequence. Then, the transformation operators are described for changing this initial representation into a form more amenable for discovering sequence-generating rules.

4.2.1 Representing the Initial Sequence

A sequence of objects is represented as an indexed list:[3]

$$\langle q_1, q_2, \ldots, q_k \rangle$$

Each object q_i is described by a set of attributes (also called *descriptors*) $f_1, f_2, \ldots, f_n$, which can be viewed as functions mapping objects into attribute values. To state that attribute f_i of object q_j has value r, we write

$$[f_i(q_j) = r]$$

This expression is called a *selector*. For example, if f_i is *color* and r is *red,* then the selector

$$[\text{COLOR}(q_j) = \text{red}]$$

states that the color of the jth object in the sequence is red.

Each attribute is only permitted to take on values from a finite value set, called the *domain* $D(f_i)$, of that attribute. This constraint is part of the background knowledge that has to be given to the program. For example, in a deck of cards, the domain of the SUIT attribute is {clubs, diamonds, hearts, spades}. Additional knowledge about the domain set can be represented. In particular, the domain set may be linearly ordered, cyclically ordered (i.e., have a circular, wraparound ordering), or tree ordered. We will see below how these domain orderings are applied to the problem of representing cards in an Eleusis game.

A complete initial description of a single object q_j, called an *event,* is an expression giving the values for all the attributes applicable to q_j. This is usually written as a conjunction of selectors:

$$[f_1(q_j) = r_1][f_2(q_j) = r_2] \ldots [f_n(q_j) = r_n]$$

It can also be represented as a vector of attribute values:

$$(r_1, r_2, \ldots, r_n)$$

This vector notation suggests that each object description can be viewed as a point in the *event space* **E:**

$$\mathbf{E} = D(f_1) \times D(f_2) \times \ldots \times D(f_n)$$

where $D(f_i)$ is the domain of attribute f_i. This event space contains all possible events.

---

[3]A summary of the notational conventions used in this chapter appears in the Appendix to this chapter.

A complete description of the initial sequence is a list of conjunctions of selectors (or alternatively, a list of attribute vectors)—one conjunction for each object in the sequence. Each sequence description can thus be viewed as a trajectory in the event space **E**. The space of all possible sequences is the set of all possible trajectories of events in **E**. It is important to note, however, that because of the discreteness of the space, these trajectories are not continuous; that is, two adjacent events in the sequence may not be "close" in the event space.

4.2.2 Transformation Operators

As mentioned in section 4.1, it is often necessary to transform the initial sequence into a derived sequence in order to facilitate the discovery of sequence-generating rules. Such a data transformation can be viewed as a mapping T from one set of sequences S, containing objects Q, described by attributes F, to another set of *derived sequences S'*, containing *derived objects Q'* and described by *derived attributes F'*.

$$T_{p,r,s} \ldots : \langle S, Q, F \rangle \rightarrow \langle S', Q', F' \rangle$$

where $p, r, s \ldots$ are parameters of the transformation that control its application. Each transformation may be applied iteratively; that is, the output of one transformation can be the input to a subsequent transformation. The authors have found four basic transformations to be especially useful for discovering sequence-generating rules: (1) *adding derived attributes*, (2) *segmenting*, (3) *splitting into phases*, and (4) *blocking*. Each of these will now be described in turn.

4.2.2.1 Adding Derived Attributes

The simplest transformation does not change the set of sequences S or the set of objects Q but only the set of attributes F. For example, in Eleusis, the initial set F contains only two attributes: the RANK and SUIT of a card. These can be augmented by deriving such attributes as COLOR (red or black), FACEDNESS (faced or nonfaced), PARITY (odd or even), and PRIMENESS (prime or not prime in rank). Although the adding-derived-attributes transformation has no parameters, in cases where many such attributes could be derived the program must use some heuristics to decide which attributes should be generated and added to the derived sequence.

4.2.2.2 Segmenting

The segmenting transformation derives a new sequence that is made up of a new set of objects Q', which are described by a new set of attributes F'. The new sequence is produced from the original sequence by dividing the original sequence into nonoverlapping segments. Each segment becomes a derived object in the new sequence. The only parameter of this transformation is the segmentation condition that specifies how the original sequence is to be divided into segments. Three types of segmentation conditions are distinguished: (1) those that use properties of the *original objects* to determine where the sequence *should* be broken, (2) those that use properties of the *original objects* to determine where the sequence should *not* be broken, and (3) those that use properties of *derived objects* to determine where the original sequence *should* be broken.

For example, suppose the original sequence consists of physical objects described by attributes such as WEIGHT, COLOR, and HEIGHT. An example of each type of segmentation condition follows:

1. Break when $[\text{WEIGHT}(q_{i-1}) > 10][\text{WEIGHT}(q_i) \leq 10]$.

   According to this condition, the original sequence is to be broken (between q_{i-1} and q_i) at the point where the weight of an object changes from above 10 to under 10.

2. Don't break as long as $[\text{COLOR}(q_{i-1}) = \text{COLOR}(q_i)][\text{WEIGHT}(q_i) > 10]$

   This condition states that the original sequence will not be broken (between q_{i-1} and q_i) if the color stays the same and the weight remains above 10. It will be broken at any point where either one of these conditions fails to hold.

3. Break so that $[\text{LENGTH}(q_i') = 2]$.

   This condition states that derived objects (q_i') should be subsequences of length 2 from the original sequence (i.e., pairs of adjacent objects from the original sequence).

The choice of attributes F' for describing the newly derived objects Q' depends on the segmentation condition used to segment the sequence. For example, if the segmentation condition is $[\text{length}(q_i') = 2]$, attributes of interest might include the sum of the VALUES of the two original objects, the maximum VALUE, the minimum VALUE, and so on. The LENGTH of the segment would not be of interest, since by definition it is a constant. However, if the segmentation condition is $[\text{color}(q_{i-1}) = \text{color}(q_{i-1})]$, the LENGTH of the segment could be an interesting attribute and should be derived. Also, the COLOR shared by all of the cards in the segment might be of interest. In the implementation described here, the user provides an a priori knowledge base that specifies which attributes should be derived. Every user-specified attribute is derived unless the program can prove from the segmentation condition that the attribute would not have a well-defined value for each segment in the sequence or else would be trivially constant for all segments.

Often, a segmentation condition leads to the creation of incomplete segments at the beginning and end of the original sequence. These boundary cases can create difficulties during model instantiation, so they are ignored during rule discovery but checked during rule evaluation.

4.2.2.3 Splitting

The splitting transformation splits a single sequence into a *sequence* of P separate subsequences called *phases:* $\langle ph_1, ph_2, \ldots \rangle$. Sequence ph_i starts with the object q_i (the object of the ith position in the original sequence) and continues with objects taken from succeeding positions at distance P apart in the original sequence. The objects in phase sequence ph_i are referred to as $\langle ph_{i,1}\ ph_{i,2}\ ph_{i,3} \ldots \rangle$. Hence, after splitting, derived object $ph_{i,j}$ is identical to original object $q_{i+P*(j-1)}$. P is the parameter of the splitting transformation and denotes the number of phases (the period length). Figure 4-5 shows the splitting operation with $P = 3$.

The objects within each phase retain the linear ordering that they had in the original sequence. The phases themselves can be considered to be cyclically ordered so that ph_1 precedes ph_2, which precedes ph_3, and so on, until ph_P, which is followed by ph_1 again. Consider, for example, the following sequence:

$$\langle 1\quad 8\quad 2\quad 9\quad 3\quad 10\quad 4\quad 11\rangle$$

The splitting transformation with P $= 2$ would produce the sequence $\langle ph_1\ ph_2 \rangle$ where

$$ph_1 = \langle 1\quad 2\quad 3\quad 4\rangle$$
$$ph_2 = \langle 8\quad 9\quad 10\quad 11\rangle$$

Since the splitting transformation simply breaks the original sequence of objects into subsequences of the same objects, no new descriptors are defined. The descriptors used to characterize objects in each of the phases are the same as those used to characterize the objects in the original sequence.

The splitting transformation can be applied to break one sequence prediction problem into several subproblems—one for each phase. This enables the system to discover periodic rules.

4.2.2.4 Blocking

The blocking transformation converts the original sequence into a new sequence made up of a new set of objects B' and a new set of attributes F'. The new sequence is created by breaking the original sequence into overlapping segments

Original sequence:	$\langle q_1$	q_2	q_3	q_4	q_5	q_6	q_7	q_8	$q_9\rangle$
Derived sequence:	$\langle ph_1\ ph_2\ ph_3\rangle$, where								
ph_1:	$\langle ph_{1,1}$			$ph_{1,2}$			$ph_{1,3}\rangle$		
ph_2:			$\langle ph_{2,1}$			$ph_{2,2}$			$ph_{2,3}\rangle$
ph_3:					$\langle ph_{3,1}$			$ph_{3,2}$	$ph_{3,3}\rangle$

(where $ph_{i,j} = q_k$ as indicated by vertical alignment, e.g., $ph_{1,2} = q_4$.)

Figure 4-5: Splitting transformation with $P = 3$.

called *blocks*. Each object b_i in the new sequence describes a block of $L + 1$ consecutive objects from the original sequence, starting at object q_i (called the *head*) and proceeding backwards to object q_{i-L} (where L is the *lookback* parameter of the blocking transformation). Figure 4-6 shows the blocking operation for $L = 2$ (block length of 3).

Several attributes are derived to describe each block. For each attribute A applicable to the objects in the original sequence, the attributes A0, A1, . . . , AL are defined that are applicable to the objects in the derived sequence. $A0(b_i)$ has the same value as $A(q_i)$; $A1(b_i)$ has the same value as $A(q_{i-1})$; and so on until $AL(b_i)$, which has the same value as $A(q_{i-L})$. In other words, the original attributes are retained in the new sequence, but they are renamed so that they apply to whole *blocks* rather than to individual objects in the original sequence. The numerical suffix on the new names encodes the relative position of the original object q_i in block b_j.

For example, suppose the original sequence of objects is $\langle q_1 \, q_2 \, q_3 \, q_4 \, q_5 \rangle$ with attributes RANK and SUIT, where

q_1: $[\text{RANK}(q_1) = 2][\text{SUIT}(q_1) = \text{H}]$

q_2: $[\text{RANK}(q_2) = 4][\text{SUIT}(q_2) = \text{S}]$

q_3: $[\text{RANK}(q_3) = 6][\text{SUIT}(q_3) = \text{C}]$

q_4: $[\text{RANK}(q_4) = 8][\text{SUIT}(q_4) = \text{D}]$

q_5: $[\text{RANK}(q_5) = 10][\text{SUIT}(q_5) = \text{H}]$

Suppose we apply the blocking transformation to this sequence with $L = 2$ to obtain the derived sequence of blocks $\langle b_3 \, b_4 \, b_5 \rangle$. Then the descriptors RANK0, RANK1, RANK2, SUIT0, SUIT1, and SUIT2 will be derived with the values

b_3: $[\text{RANK}2(b_3) = 2][\text{SUIT}2(b_3) = \text{H}]$ &
$\quad\;\; [\text{RANK}1(b_3) = 4][\text{SUIT}1(b_3) = \text{S}]$ &
$\quad\;\; [\text{RANK}0(b_3) = 6][\text{SUIT}0(b_3) = \text{C}]$

b_4: $[\text{RANK}2(b_4) = 4][\text{SUIT}2(b_4) = \text{S}]$ &
$\quad\;\; [\text{RANK}1(b_4) = 6][\text{SUIT}1(b_4) = \text{C}]$ &
$\quad\;\; [\text{RANK}0(b_4) = 8][\text{SUIT}0(b_4) = \text{D}]$

Original sequence: $\langle q_1 \quad\; q_2 \quad\;\; q_3 \quad\;\; q_4 \quad\;\; q_5 \quad\;\; q_6 \quad\;\; q_7 \quad\;\; q_8 \rangle$
Derived sequence: $\qquad\qquad\qquad\quad\;\; \langle b_3 \quad\;\; b_4 \quad\;\; b_5 \quad\;\; b_6 \quad\;\; b_7 \quad\;\; b_8 \rangle$
where b_i are derived objects defined as follows:
b_3: $\qquad\quad\; \langle q_1 \quad\; q_2 \quad\;\; \underline{q_3} \rangle$
b_4: $\qquad\qquad\qquad\; \langle q_2 \quad\;\; \underline{q_3} \quad\;\; q_4 \rangle$
b_5: $\qquad\qquad\qquad\qquad\qquad\; \langle q_3 \quad\;\; \underline{q_4} \quad\;\; q_5 \rangle$
b_6: $\qquad\qquad\qquad\qquad\qquad\qquad\qquad\; \langle q_4 \quad\;\; \underline{q_5} \quad\;\; q_6 \rangle$
b_7: $\qquad\qquad\qquad\qquad\qquad\qquad\qquad\qquad\qquad\; \langle q_5 \quad\;\; \underline{q_6} \quad\;\; q_7 \rangle$
b_8: $\qquad\qquad\qquad\qquad\qquad\qquad\qquad\qquad\qquad\qquad\qquad\; \langle q_6 \quad\;\; \underline{q_7} \quad\;\; q_8 \rangle$
The underlined objects are the head objects of each block.

Figure 4-6: The blocking transformation with lookback parameter $L = 2$.

b_5: $[\text{RANK2}(b_5) = 6][\text{SUIT2}(b_5) = \text{C}]$ &
        $[\text{RANK1}(b_5) = 8][\text{SUIT1}(b_5) = \text{D}]$ &
        $[\text{RANK0}(b_5) = 10][\text{SUIT0}(b_5) = \text{H}]$

This transformation leads to a highly redundant representation of the information in the original sequence. For example, the information about SUIT and RANK of the original object q_3 is repeated as SUIT0 and RANK0 of block b_3, SUIT1 and RANK1 of block b_4, and SUIT2 and RANK2 of block b_5. However, this derived sequence of blocks facilitates the representation of the relationships between objects in the original sequence. Many sequence prediction rules involve such relationships.

To represent relationships between objects, additional descriptors called *sum* and *difference* descriptors are defined. In the case of the above sequence, the descriptors S-RANK01, S-RANK02, D-RANK01, D-RANK02, D-SUIT01, and D-SUIT02 are created. The value of S-RANK01(b_i) is the sum of RANK0(b_i) and RANK1(b_i). The value of D-RANK01(b_i) is the difference between RANK0(b_i) and RANK1(b_i). Thus, in addition to the selectors shown above, the following selectors would also be derived for the new sequence:

b_3: $[\text{S-RANK01}(b_3) = 10][\text{S-RANK02}(b_3) = 8]$ &
        $[\text{D-RANK01}(b_3) = 2][\text{D-RANK02}(b_3) = 4]$ &
        $[\text{D-SUIT01}(b_3) = 1][\text{D-SUIT02}(b_3) = 2]$
b_4: $[\text{S-RANK01}(b_4) = 14][\text{S-RANK02}(b_4) = 12]$ &
        $[\text{D-RANK01}(b_4) = 2][\text{D-RANK02}(b_4) = 4]$ &
        $[\text{D-SUIT01}(b_4) = 1][\text{D-SUIT02}(b_4) = 2]$
b_5: $[\text{S-RANK01}(b_5) = 18][\text{S-RANK02}(b_5) = 16]$ &
        $[\text{D-RANK01}(b_5) = 2][\text{D-RANK02}(b_5) = 4]$ &
        $[\text{D-SUIT01}(b_5) = 1][\text{D-SUIT02}(b_5) = 2]$

Using this representation, it is relatively easy to discover that $[\text{D-RANK01}(b_i) = 2]$ is true for all blocks b_i.

Ordinarily, sum and difference attributes only make sense for attributes such as RANK whose domain sets are linearly ordered. We have extended the definition of difference to cover unordered and cyclically ordered domain sets as well. For an unordered attribute such as COLOR, whose domain set is {red, black}, D-COLOR01 takes on the value 0 if the COLOR0(b_i) = COLOR1(b_i) and 1 otherwise. For attributes with cyclically ordered domain sets, such as SUIT with values {clubs, diamonds, hearts, spades}, D-SUIT01 is equal to the number of steps in the forward direction that are required to get from SUIT1(b_i) to SUIT0(b_i). If SUIT1(b_i) = diamonds and SUIT0(b_i) = clubs, D-SUIT01(b_i) = 3.

The sum and difference attributes make the ordering of the original sequence explicit in the attributes that describe each block. Consequently, it is no longer necessary to represent the ordering between blocks. Hence, the model-fitting algorithms discussed below treat the derived sequence (of blocks) as an unordered set of events.

One difficulty with the above notation is that the numerical suffixes are not very easy to read, especially when they are combined with sum or difference prefixes. Hence, an alternative representation has been developed that is more comprehensible. In this notation, selectors that refer to blocks, such as [SUIT$1(b_i)$ = H], are written as selectors that refer to objects in the original sequence, such as [SUIT(q_{i-1}) = H]. Similarly, selectors such as [D-RANK$01(b_i)$ = 3] are written as [RANK(q_i) = RANK(q_{i-1}) + 3]. This notation makes the meaning of the selectors clear without the blocks b_i being explicitly mentioned.

For purposes of implementation, however, the first notation (which refers to blocks explicitly) is better because it enables the program to treat all sequences—including derived sequences—uniformly. In contrast to this, the second notation works only when one blocking transformation at most is applied. Multiple blocking transformations cannot be captured without the blocks being explicitly mentioned. Since it is rare that more than one blocking transformation is needed, and since the second notation is more understandable, it will be used for the rest of this chapter.

4.3 REPRESENTING SEQUENCE-GENERATING RULES AND MODELS

A *sequence-generating rule* is a function g that assigns to each sequence of objects $\langle q_1, q_2, \ldots, q_k \rangle$ a nonempty set of *admissible next objects* Q_{k+1}:

$$g(\langle q_1, q_2, \ldots, q_k \rangle) = Q_{k+1}$$

Q_{k+1} is the set of all objects that could appear as the next object in the sequence. For example, in the rule "Play a card whose rank is one higher than the previous card," the value of the function g when applied to a sequence whose last card is the 4C is the set of cards {5C, 5D, 5H, 5S}. This is written

$$g(\langle \ldots 4C \rangle) = Q_{k+1} = \{5C, 5D, 5H, 5S\}$$

Each set Q_{k+1} may contain only one event, or it may contain a large set of possible events. If for all k, the sequence $\langle q_1, q_2, \ldots, q_k \rangle$ is mapped by g into a singleton set, then the rule is a *deterministic* rule; otherwise, it is a *nondeterministic* rule. This chapter addresses the problem of discovering a nondeterministic sequence-generating rule, g, given the sequence $\langle q_1, q_2, \ldots, q_k \rangle$ where q_i are characterized by a finite set of discrete attributes.

The sequence $\langle q_1, q_2, \ldots, q_k \rangle$ can be viewed as the set of assertions

$q_1 \in g(\langle \rangle)$
$q_2 \in g(\langle q_1 \rangle)$
$\vdots$
$q_m \in g(\langle q_1, \ldots, q_{m-1} \rangle)$

(Recall that the value of $g(s)$, where s is a sequence, is a *set* of possible next objects.) These assertions are positive instances of the desired sequence-generating rule.

In Eleusis, negative instances are provided by the cards on the sidelines—that is, the cards indicated by the dealer as being incorrect continuations of the sequence. A sideline card q_4^- played after card q_3 provides a negative instance of the form:

$q_4^- \notin g(\langle q_1, q_2, q_3 \rangle)$

The goal is to find an expression for g that is *consistent* with these training instances and satisfies some preference criterion. (An expression g is consistent with the training instances if it characterizes all of the positive instances and excludes all of the negative instances.)

The preference criterion in this methodology, and generally in learning systems, attempts to evaluate a candidate rule in terms of its generality, predictive power, simplicity, and so on. These semantic properties are difficult to compute, however. Instead, virtually all learning systems employ syntactic criteria that correspond in some way to these semantic criteria. Syntactic criteria—such as the number of selectors in a conjunction and the number of conjuncts in a disjunction—will only correspond to the semantic criteria if the representational framework is well chosen (see McCarthy, 1958). As noted in the introduction, most previous AI research on learning has employed a single representational framework or model for describing the rules or concepts to be learned. In Eleusis, a single framework is insufficient. Instead, three basic models have been developed that were found to be useful: *the DNF model, the decomposition model,* and *the periodic model.* When these models are employed, syntactic criteria can be used to approximate semantic criteria during evaluation.

A *model* is a structure that specifies a general syntactic form for a class of descriptions (in our case, sequence-generating rules). A model consists of *model parameters* and a set of *constraints* that the model places on the forms of descriptions. The process of specifying the values for the parameters of a model is called *parameterizing* the model. The process of filling in the form of the parameterized model is called *instantiating* the model. A fully parameterized and fully instantiated model forms a sequence-generating rule. Models can be instantiated using the original sequence or, more typically, using a sequence derived by the application of some of the data transformations discussed in the previous section.

All three models use the variable-valued logic calculus VL_{22}[4] for representing sequence-generating rules. VL_{22} is an extension of the predicate calculus that uses the *selector* as its simplest kind of formula. The VL_{22} selector is substantially more expressive than the simple selector presented above in section 4.2.1. Recall that the simple selector has the form

$$[f_i(q_j) = r]$$

whereas the VL_{22} selector has the form

$$[f_i(x_1, x_2, \ldots, x_n) = r_1 \lor r_2 \lor \ldots \lor r_m]$$

In the VL_{22} selector, attributes f_i can take any number of arguments $(x_1, x_2, \ldots, x_n)$. Furthermore, the attributes f_i can take on any one of a *set* of values $\{r_1, r_2, \ldots r_m\}$. The $\lor$ denotes the *internal disjunction* operator, that is, the disjunction of values of the same attribute. Thus, the selector

$$[\text{RANK}(q_i) = 9 \lor 10 \lor J \lor Q \lor K]$$

indicates that the rank of object q_i can be either 9, 10, J, Q, or K. In this case, the same selector could be expressed alternatively as

$$[\text{RANK}(q_i) \geq 9],$$

since the domain of the RANK attribute is known to be linearly ordered with a maximum value of K (king). To aid comprehensibility, VL_{22} provides the operators $<$, $>$, $\leq$, $\geq$, and $\neq$, in addition to the basic $=$ operator.

Examples of typical selectors include:

- $[\text{RANK}(q_i) \neq \text{RANK}(q_{i-1})]$
  (paraphrase: the RANK of q_i is different from the RANK of q_{i-1})
- $[\text{SUIT}(q_i) = \text{SUIT}(q_{i-1}) + 1]$
  (paraphrase: the SUIT increases by one from q_{i-1} to q_i)
- $[\text{RANK}(q_i) + \text{RANK}(q_{i-2}) > 10]$
  (paraphrase: the sum of the RANKs of q_i and q_{i-2} is greater than 10)

Now that the basic notation of VL_{22} has been introduced, each of the three rule models is presented in turn.

4.3.1 The DNF Model

The DNF model supports the broad class of rules that can be expressed as a universally quantified VL_{22} statement in disjunctive normal form. The DNF model has one parameter, the degree of lookback L. An example of a DNF rule (with $L = 1$) is

---

[4]VL_{22} denotes version 2 of the variable-valued logic calculus system VL_2.

$$\forall\, i([\text{COLOR}(q_i) = \text{COLOR}(q_{i-1})] \,\vee\, [\text{RANK}(q_i) = \text{RANK}(q_{i-1})])$$

which can be paraphrased as "Every object (q_i) in the sequence has the same color or the same rank (or both) as the preceding object (q_{i-1})."

In general, a DNF rule is a collection of conjuncts (C_j) of the form

$$\forall i(C_1(q_i) \,\vee\, C_2(q_i) \,\vee\, \dots \,\vee\, C_k(q_i))$$

The universal quantification over i indicates that this description is true for all objects q_i in the sequence.

An additional constraint specified in the DNF model is that the number of conjuncts k should be close to the minimum that produces a description consistent with the data.

4.3.2 The Decomposition Model

The decomposition model constrains the description to be a set of implications of the form

$$L_1 \Rightarrow R_1$$
$$L_2 \Rightarrow R_2$$
$$\vdots$$
$$L_m \Rightarrow R_m$$

where the $\Rightarrow$ sign indicates logical implication.

The model states that the left- and right-hand sides, L_j and R_j, must all be VL$_{22}$ conjunctions. The left-hand sides must be mutually exclusive and exhaustive—that is, the following two statements are true:

$$L_1 \,\vee\, L_2 \,\vee\, \dots \,\vee\, L_m \quad \text{and}$$
$$\forall j,k\,(j \neq k) \Rightarrow\, \sim (L_j \,\&\, L_k)$$

The first statement says that at least one of the left-hand sides L_j is always satisfied. The second statement says that if j and k are different, then L_j and L_k cannot both be satisfied simultaneously.

A decomposition rule describes the next object in the sequence in terms of characteristics of the previous objects in the sequence. For example, the rule

$$\forall i(([\text{COLOR}(q_{i-1}) = \text{black}] \Rightarrow [\text{PARITY}(q_i) = \text{odd}])\,\&$$
$$([\text{COLOR}(q_{i-1}) = \text{red}] \Rightarrow [\text{PARITY}(q_i) = \text{even}]))$$

is a decomposition rule that says that if the last card was black, the next card must be odd and if the last card was red, the next card must be even.

The decomposition model has a lookback parameter L that indicates how far back in the sequence the sequence-generating rule must "look" in order to predict the next object in the sequence. The above rule has a lookback parameter of 1, because it examines q_{i-1} (the previous object in the sequence).

4.3.3 The Periodic Model

This model consists of rules that describe objects in the sequence as having attribute values that repeat periodically. For example, the rule "Play alternating red and black cards" is a periodic rule. The periodic model has two parameters: the period length P, and the lookback L. The period length parameter P gives the number of phases in the periodic rule. A periodic rule can be viewed as applying a splitting transformation to split the original sequence into P separate sequences. Each separate phase sequence has a simple description. The lookback parameter L tells how far back, within a phase sequence, a periodic rule "looks" in order to predict the attributes of the next object in that phase. The periodic model imposes the additional constraint (or preference) that the different phases be disjoint (i.e., any given card is only playable within one phase).

A periodic rule is represented as an ordered P-tuple of VL_{22} conjunctions. The jth conjunction describes the jth phase sequence. The rule

$$\langle[\text{COLOR}(ph_{1,i}) = \text{red}], [\text{RANK}(ph_{2,i}) \geq \text{RANK}(ph_{2,i-1})]\rangle$$

is a periodic rule with $P = 2$ and $L = 1$, which says that the sequence is made of two (interleaved) phases. Each card in the first phase is red; each card in the second phase has a rank at least as high as the preceding card in that phase. Hence, one sequence that satisfies this rule is $\langle$2H 3C 10H 5S AD 6S 6H 6C$\rangle$.

4.3.4 Derived Models

The three basic models can be combined to describe more complex rules. Basic models can be joined by conjunction, disjunction, and negation. For example, the rule "Play alternating red and black cards such that the cards are in nondecreasing order" is a conjunction of the periodic rule

$$\langle[\text{COLOR}(ph_{1,i}) = \text{red}], [\text{COLOR}(ph_{2,i}) = \text{black}]\rangle$$

and the DNF rule

$$[\text{RANK}(q_i) \geq \text{RANK}(q_{i-1})].$$

4.3.5 Model Equivalences and the Heuristic Value of Models

The reader may have noticed that the decomposition and periodic models appear to be special cases of the DNF model. In particular, assuming that the left-hand side clauses in a decomposition rule are mutually exclusive and exhaustive, the decomposition rule

$$L_1 \Rightarrow R_1$$
$$L_2 \Rightarrow R_2$$
$$\vdots$$
$$L_m \Rightarrow R_m$$

can be written as the DNF rule

$$[L_1 \ \& \ R_1] \ \lor \ [L_2 \ \& \ R_2] \ \lor \ \ldots \ \lor \ [L_m \ \& \ R_m]$$

Similarly, if the phases (C_i) of a periodic rule are mutually exclusive and exhaustive, then the periodic rule

$$\langle C_1, C_2, \ldots, C_k \rangle$$

can be reexpressed as a decomposition rule of the form

$$C_1 \Rightarrow C_2$$
$$C_2 \Rightarrow C_3$$
$$\vdots$$
$$C_{k-1} \Rightarrow C_k$$
$$C_k \Rightarrow C_1$$

This transformation from the periodic model into the decomposition model does not work when the phases of the periodic rule overlap. Consider, for example, the following periodic rule in which the phases are neither mutually exclusive nor exhaustive:

$\langle [\text{COLOR}(ph_{1,i}) = \text{red}], [\text{RANK}(ph_{2,i}) = \text{even}] \rangle$
(paraphrase: play alternating red and even cards)

Because the phases overlap, the transformation into a decomposition rule produces a slightly different rule:

$[\text{COLOR}(q_{i-1}) = \text{red}] \Rightarrow [\text{PARITY}(q_i) = \text{even}] \ \&$
$[\text{PARITY}(q_{i-1}) = \text{even}] \Rightarrow [\text{COLOR}(q_i) = \text{red}]$

To see how the two rules differ, consider the sequence of cards

$\langle \textbf{3D 2D 4C} \ldots \rangle$

This sequence satisfies the second rule (the first if-then clause can be applied twice), but not the first rule (since the 4C is not red).

Even when the constraints of mutual exclusion and exhaustion are violated, it is always possible to develop some equivalent DNF rule for any periodic or decomposition rule. This is so because one can always provide additional descriptors that capture the particular relationship. The resulting DNF rules are not always as succinct or comprehensible, however, as the same rule expressed using one of the other models.

Consider this same periodic rule. Suppose that a new descriptor, called POSITION, is defined whose value for each object q_i is the position i of the object in the sequence. With this descriptor, the above rule can be encoded as

$[\text{POSITION}(q_i) = \text{odd}] \Rightarrow [\text{COLOR}(q_i) = \text{red}]$ &
$[\text{POSITION}(q_i) = \text{even}] \Rightarrow [\text{PARITY}(q_i) = \text{even}]$

Since any sequence-generating rule can be expressed in the DNF model, it is reasonable to ask why multiple models should be used at all. The answer is that the primary value of multiple models is that they provide heuristic guidance to the search for *plausible* rules. Hence, though the DNF model is capable of *representing* all of these rules, it is not helpful for *discovering* them. In short, it is *epistemologically adequate* but not *heuristically adequate* (see McCarthy and Hayes, 1969; McCarthy, 1977). Each model directs the attention of the learning system to a small subspace of the space of all possible DNF VL_{22} rules. The next section shows how the constraints associated with each model are incorporated into special model-fitting induction algorithms.

4.4 ARCHITECTURE AND ALGORITHMS

Section 4.3 described the three basic processes involved in discovering sequence-generating rules: (1) transformation of the original sequence into a derived sequence, (2) selection of an appropriate model (and determination of its parameters) for the given sequence, and (3) fitting (instantiation) of the models to the derived sequence. Sections 4.2 and 4.3 presented the four data transformations and the three models. This section covers the third step of fitting specialized models to the transformed sequence. The model-fitting process is most easily understood in the context of the program architecture, so this section also discusses the system's architecture.

4.4.1 Overview of the System

The processes in the system (see figure 4-7) are structured into four components—the three basic ones mentioned above plus an evaluation component. The processes of transforming the initial sequence and of selecting and parameterizing a model are performed in parallel. Then model-fitting algorithms use the transformed sequence to instantiate the parameterized model to obtain a candidate sequence-generating rule. These candidate rules are then evaluated to determine the final set of rules.

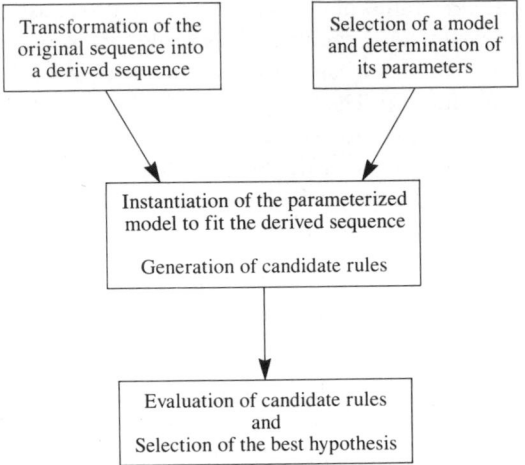

Figure 4-7: Basic processes in rule discovery.

The reason for performing data transformation and model selection in parallel is that these two processes are interdependent. For example, if a periodic model is selected (with period length P), then a splitting transformation (with number of phases P) needs to be applied to the sequence. These two processes can be viewed as simultaneous, cooperative searches of two spaces: the space of possible data transformations and the space of possible parameterized models.

4.4.2 Overview of the Concentric Ring Architecture

In order for the learning system to be easily modified to handle entire classes of NDP problems, the system is structured as a set of concentric knowledge rings (see figure 4-8). A knowledge ring is a set of routines that perform a particular function using only knowledge appropriate to that function. The procedures within a given ring may invoke other procedures in that ring or in rings that are inside the given ring. Under these constraints, the concentric ring structure forms a hierarchically organized system.

Ideally, the rings should be organized so that the outermost ring uses the most problem-specific knowledge and performs the most problem-specific operations and the innermost ring uses the most general knowledge and performs the most general tasks. Such an architecture improves the program's generality because it can be applied to increasingly different NDP problems by the removal and replacement of the outer rings. If the program is to be applied to radically different learning problems, all but the innermost ring may need to be replaced.

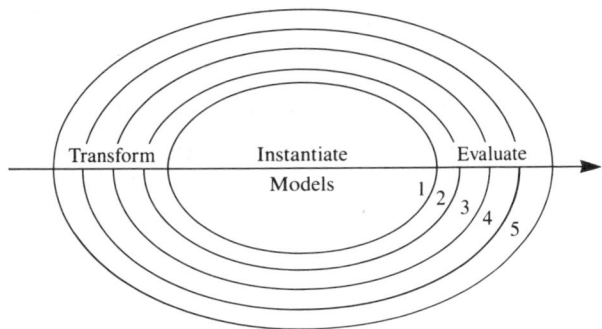

Figure 4-8: The knowledge ring architecture.

The ring architecture is used here as follows. The outermost rings perform user interface functions and convert the initial sequence from whatever domain-specific notation is being used into a sequence of VL_{22} events. The innermost ring performs the model-fitting functions. It expects the data to be properly transformed so that the data have the same form as the models to which they arc to be fitted. The intervening rings conduct the simultaneous processes of developing a properly parameterized model and transforming the input sequence into an appropriate derived sequence.

The intervening rings also evaluate the rules discovered by the innermost ring using the knowledge available in each ring.

4.4.3 The System SPARC/E

SPARC (Sequential PAttern ReCognition) is a general program designed to solve a variety of nondeterministic prediction problems using the ring architecture. So far, only a more specific version of the program, called SPARC/E, has been implemented. SPARC/E is tailored specifically to the problem of rule discovery in the game Eleusis. It is made up of five rings, as shown in figure 4-8.

This section describes the functions of each ring in SPARC/E. The Eleusis layout shown in figure 4-9 will be used to illustrate these ring functions. Recall that in an Eleusis layout, the main line shows the correctly played sequence of cards (positive examples). The side lines, which branch out below the main line, contain cards

Main line:	3H	9S	4C	JD	2C	10D	8H	7H	2C
Side lines:		JD		AH	AS			10H	
		5D		8H	10S				
				QD					

Figure 4-9: Sample Eleusis layout.

that do not satisfy the rule—that is, incorrect continuations of the sequence (negative examples).

4.4.3.1 Ring 5: User Interface

Ring 5, the outermost ring, provides a user interface to the program. It executes user's commands for playing the card game Eleusis, as well as commands for controlling the search, data transformation, generalization, and evaluation functions of the program. One command in Ring 5 is the INDUCE command that instructs SPARC/E to look for plausible NDP rules that describe the current sequence. When the INDUCE command is given, Ring 5 calls Ring 4 to begin the rule discovery process. Ring 5 provides Ring 4 with an initial sequence of VL_{22} events in which the only attributes are SUIT and RANK.

4.4.3.2 Ring 4: Adding Derived Attributes

Ring 4 applies the adding-derived-attributes transformation to the initial sequence of cards. This involves creating derived attributes that make explicit certain commonly known characteristics of playing cards that are likely to be used in an Eleusis rule: COLOR, PARITY, FACED versus NONFACED cards, and so on. The user of the program provides a definition for each descriptor that is to be derived. Figure 4-10 shows the layout from figure 4-9 after it has been processed by Ring 4. The plusses

VL_{22} event	Positive or negative
[RANK(card$_1$) = 3][SUIT(card$_1$) = H] & [PARITY(card$_1$) = odd][COLOR(card$_1$) = red] & [PRIME(card$_1$) = N][FACED(card$_1$) = Y]	+
[RANK(card$_2$) = 9][SUIT(card$_2$) = S] & [PARITY(card$_2$) = odd][COLOR(card$_2$) = black] & [PRIME(card$_2$) = N][FACED(card$_2$) = N]	+
[RANK(card$_3$) = J][SUIT(card$_3$) = D] & [PARITY(card$_3$) = odd][COLOR(card$_3$) = red] & [PRIME(card$_3$) = Y][FACED(card$_3$) = Y]	−
[RANK(card$_3$) = 5][SUIT(card$_3$) = D] & [PARITY(card$_3$) = odd][COLOR(card$_3$) = red] & [PRIME(card$_3$) = N][FACED(card$_3$) = Y]	−
[RANK(card$_3$) = 4][SUIT(card$_3$) = C] & [PARITY(card$_3$) = even][COLOR(card$_3$) = black] & [PRIME(card$_3$) = N][FACED(card$_3$) = N]	+
[RANK(card$_4$) = J][SUIT(card$_4$) = D] & [PARITY(card$_4$) = odd][COLOR(card$_4$) = red] & [PRIME(card$_4$) = Y][FACED(card$_4$) = Y]	+
etc.	

Figure 4-10:   Derived layout after Ring 4 processing of the layout in figure 4-9.

and minuses along the right-hand side of the figure indicate whether the event is a positive example or a negative example of the sequence-generating rule. These derived events are passed to Ring 3 for further processing.

4.4.3.3 Ring 3: Segmenting the Layout

Ring 3 is the first Eleusis-independent ring. It applies the segmenting transformation to the sequence supplied by Ring 4. In the present implementation, the end points of each segment are determined by applying a segmentation predicate $P(\text{card}_{i-1}, \text{card}_i)$ to all pairs of adjacent events in the sequence. When the predicate P evaluates to FALSE, the sequence is broken between card_{i-1} and card_i to form the end of a segment. Typical segmentation predicates used are the following:

$[\text{RANK}(\text{card}_i) = \text{RANK}(\text{card}_{i-1})]$
$[\text{RANK}(\text{card}_i) = \text{RANK}(\text{card}_{i-1}) + 1]$
$[\text{COLOR}(\text{card}_i) = \text{COLOR}(\text{card}_{i-1})]$
$[\text{SUIT}(\text{card}_i) = \text{SUIT}(\text{card}_{i-1})]$
$[\text{PARITY}(\text{card}_i) = \text{PARITY}(\text{card}_{i-1})]$

Other techniques for performing segmentation, such as providing a predicate that becomes TRUE at a segment boundary (see section 4.2.2.2), are not implemented in SPARC/E.

Ring 3 searches the space of possible segmentations using two search-pruning heuristics. After each attempt to segment the sequence, it counts the number of derived objects (segments) k in the derived sequence. If k is less than 3, the segmentation is discarded since there are too few derived objects to use for generalization. If k is more than half of the number of objects in the original sequence, the segmentation is also discarded because in this case many segments contain only one original object. Segmented sequences that survive these two pruning heuristics are passed on to Ring 2 for further processing.

One segmentation that Ring 3 always performs is the "null" segmentation— that is, it always passes the unsegmented sequence directly to the inner rings. Figure 4-11 shows a sample layout and the resulting derived layout after segmentation using the segmentation condition $[\text{SUIT}(\text{card}_i) = \text{SUIT}(\text{card}_{i-1})]$. The derived objects (segments) are denoted by variables segment_i. The negative event $[\text{SUIT}(\text{segment}_2) = \text{D}][\text{COLOR}(\text{segment}_2) = \text{red}][\text{LENGTH}(\text{segment}_2) = 3]$ is obtained from the segment ⟨**5D   2D   4D**⟩, which ends in a "side-line" card. Notice that the very last card in the sequence, the king of spades, is not included in any segment. This is because the king is the first card of a new segment, and it is impossible to know how long that segment will be until it is completed. Once a sequence-generating rule is found by the inner rings, Ring 3 will check to make sure that the king of spades is consistent with the rule.

The layout:

3H	5D	2D	7C	AC	9C	JH	6H	8H	QH	KS
	5S	4D		AH						
				7S						

The derived sequence:

Description of derived object	Positive or negative
[SUIT(segment$_1$) = H][COLOR(segment$_1$) = red] & [LENGTH(segment$_1$) = 1]	+
[SUIT(segment$_2$) = D][COLOR(segment$_2$) = red] & [LENGTH(segment$_2$) = 2]	+
[SUIT(segment$_2$) = D][COLOR(segment$_2$) = red] & [LENGTH(segment$_2$) = 3]	−
[SUIT(segment$_3$) = C][COLOR(segment$_3$) = black] & [LENGTH(segment$_3$) = 3]	+
[SUIT(segment$_4$) = H][COLOR(segment$_4$) = red] & [LENGTH(segment$_4$) = 4]	+

Figure 4-11: Sample layout and segmented sequence under segmentation condition [SUIT(card$_i$) = SUIT(card$_{i-1}$)].

SPARC/E derives the descriptors COLOR, SUIT, and LENGTH to describe each derived object. The choice of which descriptors to derive involves three steps. First, LENGTH is derived whenever the segmentation transformation is applied. Second, any descriptor that is tested in the segmentation predicate (in this case, SUIT) is also derived. Third, any descriptor is derived whose value can be proved to be the same for all cards in each segment. In this case, COLOR is derived because, if SUIT is a constant, then COLOR is also a constant. Using this segmentation, SPARC can use the DNF model to discover that the segmented sequence can be described as

[LENGTH(segment$_i$) = LENGTH(segment$_{i-1}$) + 1]

That is, the LENGTH of each segment of constant SUIT (in the main line) increases by 1.

4.4.3.4 Ring 2: Parameterizing the Models

Ring 2 searches the space of parameterizations of the three basic models. Each model is considered in turn. For each model, Ring 2 develops a set of derived events based on each allowed value of the lookback parameter L and the number of phases parameter P. The user can control which models should be inspected and what range of values for L and P should be investigated. By default, the program will inspect the decomposition model with $L = 0$, 1, or 2 and the periodic model with $P = 1$ or 2 or $L = 0$ or 1. The DNF model is not inspected under the default settings for the program.

Specifically, Ring 2 performs the actions listed below depending on which model is being parameterized:

The decomposition model. For the decomposition model with lookback parameter L, Ring 2 applies the blocking transformation to break the sequence received from Ring 3 into blocks of length L. After blocking, all of the attributes that described the original objects are converted into attributes that describe the whole block (as discussed in section 4.2.2.4 above). Furthermore, sum and difference descriptors are derived to represent the relationships between adjacent objects in the original sequence. The resulting derived events can be viewed as very specific if-then clauses of the following form:

Given an initial sequence of objects $\langle q_1, q_2, \ldots, q_m \rangle$, let us look at block b_i which describes the subsequence $\langle q_{i-L}, \ldots, q_{i-1}, q_i \rangle$. Let F_j, $j = 0, 1, \ldots, L$, denote the set of selectors describing object q_{i-j} renamed so that they apply to block b_i. For example, F_1 could be selectors [SUIT1(b_i) = H][RANK1(b_i) = 3]—selectors that originally referred to object q_{i-1}. Let $d(F_j, F_k)$ denote all of the difference selectors obtained by "subtracting" event F_k from event F_j, and let $s(F_j, F_k)$ denote all of the summation selectors obtained by "summing" events F_j and F_k. For example, $d(F_0, F_1)$ could include the selectors [D-SUIT01(b_i) = 2][D-RANK01(b_i) = -3] obtained from "subtracting" F_1 from F_0.

With these definitions, the derived events for the decomposition model have the following form:

$$F_1 \& \ldots \& F_L \Rightarrow F_0 \& d(F_0, F_1) \& \ldots \& d(F_0, F_L) \&$$
$$s(F_0, F_1) \& \ldots \& s(F_0, F_L)$$

Suppose, for example, that the initial sequence of cards is

$\langle$**2H   4D   6S   8C**$\rangle$

with only the SUIT and RANK descriptors being employed. Then suppose that Ring 2 applies the blocking transformation with a lookback of 2. Figure 4-12 shows the two derived events that will be produced by Ring 2 (the corresponding notation is shown to the right of each group of selectors).

These derived events no longer need to be ordered, since the ordering information is made explicit within the events. These events have the form of very specific if-then clauses. This facilitates the model-fitting process in Ring 1.

The DNF model. For the DNF model with lookback parameter L, the sequence derived in Ring 3 is blocked in a very similar manner, except that only the selectors

Derived event	Abbreviation
$[\text{RANK}1(q_{i-1}) = 4][\text{SUIT}1(q_{i-1}) = \text{D}]$	F_1
$[\text{RANK}2(q_{i-2}) = 2][\text{SUIT}2(q_{i-2}) = \text{H}]$	F_2
$\Rightarrow$	
$[\text{RANK}0(q_i) = 6][\text{SUIT}0(q_i) = \text{S}]$	F_0
$[\text{D-RANK}01(q_i,q_{i-1}) = 2][\text{D-SUIT}(q_i,q_{i-1}) = 2]$	$d(F_0,F_1)$
$[\text{D-RANK}02(q_i,q_{i-2}) = 4][\text{D-SUIT}(q_i,q_{i-2}) = 1]$	$d(F_0,F_2)$
$[\text{S-RANK}01(q_i,q_{i-1}) = 10]$	$s(F_0,F_1)$
$[\text{S-RANK}02(q_i,q_{i-2}) = 8]$	$s(F_0,F_2)$
$[\text{RANK}1(q_{i-1}) = 6][\text{SUIT}1(q_{i-1}) = \text{S}]$	F_1
$[\text{RANK}2(q_{i-2}) = 4][\text{SUIT}2(q_{i-2}) = \text{D}]$	F_2
$\Rightarrow$	
$[\text{RANK}0(q_i) = 8][\text{SUIT}0(q_i) = \text{C}]$	F_0
$[\text{D-RANK}01(q_i,q_{i-1}) = 2][\text{D-SUIT}(q_i,q_{i-1}) = 1]$	$d(F_0,F_1)$
$[\text{D-RANK}02(q_i,q_{i-2}) = 4][\text{D-SUIT}(q_i,q_{i-2}) = 3]$	$d(F_0,F_2)$
$[\text{S-RANK}01(q_i,q_{i-1}) = 14]$	$s(F_0,F_1)$
$[\text{S-RANK}02(q_i,q_{i-2}) = 12]$	$s(F_0,F_2)$

Figure 4-12: Sample events showing which sum and difference descriptors are derived.

describing q_i are retained in the description of block b_i. The derived events have the following form:

$$F_0 \ \& \ d(F_0, F_1) \ \& \ \ldots \ \& \ d(F_0, F_L) \ \& \ s(F_0, F_1) \ \& \ \ldots \ s(F_0, F_L)$$

These events are very specific conjuncts that are passed to the A^q algorithm (Michalski, 1969, 1972) in Ring 1, where they are generalized to form a DNF description.

The periodic model. For the periodic model with period length P and lookback L, Ring 2 performs a splitting transformation followed by a blocking transformation. First, the sequence obtained from Ring 3 is split into P separate sequences. Then each separate sequence is blocked into blocks of length $L + 1$. The derived events have the same form as the events derived for the DNF model. Note that because the blocking occurs after the splitting, the lookback takes place only within a phase.

To provide an example of the function of Ring 2, figure 4-13 shows some events from figure 4-10 after they have been transformed in preparation for fitting to a decomposition model with $L = 1$.

4.4.3.5 Ring 1: The Basic Model-fitting Algorithm

Ring 1 consists of three separate model-fitting algorithms: the A^q algorithm, the decomposition algorithm, and the periodic algorithm.

Derived event								Positive or
									negative

[RANK1(b_2) = 3][SUIT1(b_2) = H]
[PARITY1(b_2) = odd][COLOR1(b_2) = red]
[PRIME1(b_2) = Y][FACED1(b_2) = N]

$$\Rightarrow$$

[RANK0(b_2) = 9][SUIT0(b_2) = S][PARITY0(b_2) = odd]
[COLOR0(b_2) = black][PRIME0(b_2) = N]
[FACED0(b_2) = N][D-RANK01(b_2) = +6]
[D-SUIT01(b_2) = +1][D-PARITY01(b_2) = N]
[D-COLOR01(b_2) = Y][D-PRIME01(b_2) = Y]
[D-FACED01(b_2) = Y][S-RANK01(b_2) = 12]					+

[RANK1(b_3) = 9][SUIT1(b_3) = S]
[PARITY1(b_3) = odd][COLOR1(b_3) = black]
[PRIME1(b_3) = N][FACED1(b_3) = N]

$$\Rightarrow$$

[RANK0(b_3) = J][SUIT0(b_3) = D][PARITY0(b_3) = odd]
[COLOR0(b_3) = red][PRIME0(b_3) = Y]
[FACED0(b_3) = Y][D-RANK01(b_3) = +2]
[D-SUIT01(b_3) = +2][D-PARITY01(b_3) = N]
[D-COLOR01(b_3) = Y][D-PRIME01(b_3) = Y]
[D-FACED01(b_3) = Y][S-RANK01(b_3) = 20]					−

Figure 4-13: Some events of figure 4-10 transformed for decomposition $L = 1$.

The A^q algorithm (Michalski, 1969, 1972) is applied to fit the DNF model to the data. A^q attempts to find the DNF description with the fewest number of conjunctive terms that covers all of the positive examples and none of the negative examples. The algorithm operates as follows: First, a positive example, called the seed, is chosen, and the set of maximally general conjunctive expressions consistent with this seed and all of the negative examples is computed. This set is called a *star,* and it is equivalent to the G-set in Mitchell's (1978) version space approach (if the G-set is computed with the seed positive example and all of the negative examples). One element from this star is chosen to be a conjunct in the output DNF description, and all positive examples covered by it are removed from further consideration. If any positive examples remain, the process is repeated; some positive example that was not covered by *any* member of any preceding star is selected as a new seed. In this manner, a DNF description with few conjunctive terms is found. If the stars are computed without any pruning, then A^q can provide a tight bound on the number of conjuncts that would appear in the shortest DNF description (i.e., with the fewest conjunctive terms).

The decomposition algorithm is an iterative algorithm that seeks to fit the data to a decomposition model. The key task of the decomposition algorithm is to identify a few attributes, called *decomposition attributes,* from which the decomposition rule can be developed. A decomposition attribute is an attribute that appears on the left-hand side of an if-then clause of a decomposition rule. For example, the decomposition rule

$$[\text{COLOR}(\text{card}_{i-1}) = \text{black}] \Rightarrow [\text{PARITY}(\text{card}_i) = \text{odd}] \&$$
$$[\text{COLOR}(\text{card}_{i-1}) = \text{red}] \quad \Rightarrow [\text{PARITY}(\text{card}_i) = \text{even}]$$

decomposes on COLOR. Hence, COLOR is the single decomposition attribute.

The algorithm uses a generate-and-test approach of the following form:

```
decomposition-attributes := {}  The empty set

while rule is not consistent do
     begin

          generate a trial decomposition
          (based on positive evidence only)
          for each possible decomposition attribute

          test these trial decompositions against
          the data

          select the best decomposition attribute and
          add it to the set decomposition-attributes

     end
```

The process of generating a trial decomposition takes place in two steps. First, a VL_{22} conjunction is formed for each possible value of the decomposition attribute. All positive events that have the same value of the decomposition attribute on their left-hand sides are merged together to form a single conjunction of selectors. This VL_{22} conjunction forms the right-hand side of a single clause in the decomposition rule. Within this conjunction, a selector is created for each attribute by the formation of the internal disjunction of the values in the corresponding selectors in the events. For example, using all of the events derived in Ring 2 for the sample layout in figure 4-9, the decomposition algorithm generates the trial decomposition shown in figure 4-14 for the PARITY(card$_{i-1}$) attribute.

Since there are only two values (odd and even) for the decomposition attribute in the sequence shown in figure 4-9, two conjunctions are formed. The first conjunction is obtained by merging all of the positive events for which [PARITY(card$_{i-1}$) = odd]. There are four such events. The first selector in that conjunction, [RANK(card$_i$) = 9 $\lor$ 4 $\lor$ 2], is obtained by forming the internal disjunction of the values of RANK(card$_i$) in each of the four events.

$[\text{PARITY}(\text{card}_{i-1}) = \text{odd}]$

$$\Rightarrow$$

$[\text{RANK}(\text{card}_i) = 2 \lor 4 \lor 9]$
$[\text{SUIT}(\text{card}_i) = \text{S} \lor \text{C}][\text{PARITY}(\text{card}_i) = \text{even} \lor \text{odd}]$
$[\text{COLOR}(\text{card}_i) = \text{black}][\text{PRIME}(\text{card}_i) = \text{Y} \lor \text{N}]$
$[\text{FACED}(\text{card}_i) = \text{N}]$
$[\text{D-RANK}(\text{card}_i,\text{card}_{i-1}) = -7 \lor -5 \lor +6]$
$[\text{D-SUIT}(\text{card}_i,\text{card}_{i-1}) = 1 \lor 2 \lor 3]$
$[\text{D-PARITY}(\text{card}_i,\text{card}_{i-1}) = \text{Y} \lor \text{N}]$
$[\text{D-COLOR}(\text{card}_i,\text{card}_{i-1}) = \text{Y} \lor \text{N}]$
$[\text{D-PRIME}(\text{card}_i,\text{card}_{i-1}) = \text{Y} \lor \text{N}]$
$[\text{D-FACED}(\text{card}_i,\text{card}_{i-1}) = \text{Y} \lor \text{N}]$
$[\text{S-RANK}(\text{card}_i,\text{card}_{i-1}) = 12 \lor 13 \lor 9]$ &

$[\text{PARITY}(\text{card}_{i-1}) = \text{even}]$

$$\Rightarrow$$

$[\text{RANK}(\text{card}_i) = 7 \lor 8 \lor 10 \lor \text{J}]$
$[\text{SUIT}(\text{card}_i) = \text{H} \lor \text{D}][\text{PARITY}(\text{card}_i) = \text{even} \lor \text{odd}]$
$[\text{COLOR}(\text{card}_i) = \text{red}][\text{PRIME}(\text{card}_i) = \text{Y} \lor \text{N}]$
$[\text{FACED}(\text{card}_i) = \text{Y} \lor \text{N}]$
$[\text{D-RANK}(\text{card}_i,\text{card}_{i-1}) = -1 \lor -2 \lor 7 \lor 8]$
$[\text{D-SUIT}(\text{card}_i,\text{card}_{i-1}) = 0 \lor 1]$
$[\text{D-PARITY}(\text{card}_i,\text{card}_{i-1}) = \text{Y} \lor \text{N}]$
$[\text{D-COLOR}(\text{card}_i,\text{card}_{i-1}) = \text{Y} \lor \text{N}]$
$[\text{D-PRIME}(\text{card}_i,\text{card}_{i-1}) = \text{Y} \lor \text{N}]$
$[\text{D-FACED}(\text{card}_i,\text{card}_{i-1}) = \text{Y} \lor \text{N}]$
$[\text{S-RANK}(\text{card}_i,\text{card}_{i-1}) = 12 \lor 15 \lor 18]$

Figure 4-14:   Trial decomposition on the $\text{PARITY}(\text{card}_{i-1})$ attribute.

The second step in forming a trial decomposition is to generalize each clause in the trial rule. The generalization is accomplished by applying rules of generalization to extend internal disjunctions and drop selectors. (See Michalski, 1983, for a description of various rules of generalization.) Corresponding attributes in the different clauses of the decomposition rule are compared, and selectors whose value sets overlap are dropped. When these rules of generalization are applied to the trial decomposition of, for example, PARITY, the following generalized trial decomposition is obtained:

$[\text{PARITY}(\text{card}_{i-1}) = \text{odd}] \leftrightarrow [\text{SUIT}(\text{card}_i) = \text{C} \lor \text{S}][\text{COLOR}(\text{card}_i) = \text{black}]$ &
$[\text{PARITY}(\text{card}_{i-1}) = \text{even}] \leftrightarrow [\text{SUIT}(\text{card}_i) = \text{H} \lor \text{D}][\text{COLOR}(\text{card}_i) = \text{red}]$

This is a very promising trial decomposition. However, it has been developed using only positive evidence—without considering the possibility that it may cover some negative events. Hence, the trial decomposition must be tested against the negative events to determine whether or not it is consistent. It turns out that the generalized trial decomposition shown above is indeed consistent with the negative evidence.

After a trial decomposition has been developed for each possible decomposition attribute, the best decomposition attribute is selected according to a heuristic attribute-quality functional. The attribute-quality functional tests such things as the number of negative events covered by the trial decomposition, the number of clauses with nonnull right-hand sides, and the complexity of the trial decomposition (defined as the number of selectors that cannot be written with a single operator and a single value). The chosen trial decomposition forms a candidate sequence prediction rule.

If the candidate rule is not consistent with the data (i.e., still covers some negative examples), then the decomposition algorithm must be repeated to select a second attribute to add to the left-hand sides of the if-then clauses. This has the effect of splitting each of the if-then clauses into several more if-then clauses. For example, if we first decomposed on PARITY(card_{i-1}) and then on FACED(card_{i-1}), we would obtain four if-then clauses of the form:

[PARITY(card_{i-1}) = odd][FACED(card_{i-1}) = N] $\Rightarrow$ . . .
[PARITY(card_{i-1}) = odd][FACED(card_{i-1}) = Y] $\Rightarrow$ . . .
[PARITY(card_{i-1}) = even][FACED(card_{i-1}) = N] $\Rightarrow$ . . .
[PARITY(card_{i-1}) = even][FACED(card_{i-1}) = Y] $\Rightarrow$ . . .

The periodic algorithm is similar to the decomposition algorithm. For each phase of the period, it takes all of the positive events in that phase and combines them to form a single conjunct by forming the internal disjunction of all of the value sets of corresponding selectors. Next, rules of generalization are applied to extend internal disjunctions and drop selectors. Finally, corresponding attributes in different phases are compared, and selectors whose value sets overlap are dropped if this can be done without covering any negative examples.

4.4.3.6 Evaluating the NDP Rules

Once Ring 1 has instantiated the parameterized models to produce a set of rules, the rules are passed back through the concentric rings of the program. Each ring evaluates the rules according to plausibility criteria based on knowledge available in that ring. Ring 2, for example, applies knowledge of the fact that valid sequences can be continued indefinitely. It checks to see that the rule predicts that the sequence could be so continued. Ring 3, which applies the segmentation transformation, applies its knowledge about the tail end of the unsegmented sequence to make sure it is consistent with the rule. (Recall that the segmentation transformation is sometimes unable to segment the last few events in the sequence.) Ring 4 tests the rule using the plausibility criteria for Eleusis. These criteria are as follows:

1. Prefer rules with intermediate degree of complexity. In Eleusis, Occam's razor does not always apply. The dealer is unlikely to choose a rule that is extremely simple, because it would be too easy to discover. Very complex rules will not be

discovered by anyone, and since the rules of the game discourage such an outcome, the dealer is not likely to choose such complex rules either.

2. Prefer rules with an intermediate degree of nondeterminism. Rules with a low
   degree of nondeterminism lead to many incorrect plays, thus rendering them
   easy to discover. Rules that are very nondeterministic generally lead to few
   incorrect plays and are therefore difficult to discover.

Rules that do not satisfy these heuristic criteria are discarded. The remaining
rules are returned to Ring 5 where they are printed for the user.

4.5 EXAMPLES OF PROGRAM EXECUTION

In this section, some example Eleusis games are presented, along with the corresponding sequence-generating rules that were discovered by SPARC/E. Each of
these games was an actual game played among people, and the rules are presented as
they were displayed by SPARC/E (with minor typesetting changes).

The raw sequences presented to SPARC/E had only two attributes: SUIT and
RANK. SPARC/E was given definitions of the following derivable attributes:

- COLOR (red for hearts and diamonds; black for clubs and spades)
- FACE (true if the card is a faced, picture card, false otherwise)
- PRIME (true if the card has a prime rank, false otherwise)
- MOD2 (the parity value of the card, 0 if the card is even, 1 otherwise)
- MOD3 (the rank of the card modulo 3)
- LENMOD2 (when SPARC/E segments the main sequence into derived subse-
  quences, it computes the LENGTH of each of the subsequences modulo 2)

Three examples of the program execution are presented. Here are some points
to notice in reading the examples: First, each rule is assumed to be universally quantified over all events in the sequence. This quantification is not explicitly printed.
Second, when the value set of a selector includes a set of adjacent values—for
example, [RANK(card$_i$) = 3 $\vee$ 4 $\vee$ 5]—this is printed as [RANK(CARDI) =
3 . . 5]. The computation times given are for an implementation in Pascal on the
CDC CYBER 175.

4.5.1 Example 1

In this example, we show the program discovering a segmented rule. The program was presented with the following layout:

Main line:	AH	7C	6C	9S	10H	7H	10D	JC	AD
Side lines:			KD			5S		QD	
			JH						

continued:	4H	8D	7C	9S	10C	KS	2C	10S	JS
	3S			9H		QH			
				6H		AD			

The program only discovered one rule for this layout, precisely the rule that the dealer had in mind (1.2 seconds required):

```
RULE 1: LOOKBACK: 0 NPHASES: 1 PERIODIC MODEL
SEGMENTATION CONDITION = [COLOR(CARDI) = COLOR(CARDI-1)]:
                        PERIOD< [LENMOD2(PH1SEGMENTI) = 1] >
```

The rule states that one must play strings of cards with the same color. The strings must always have odd lengths. The segmentation condition states that a segment is a string of cards all of the same color. CARDI refers to the Ith card in the original sequence. SPARC/E discovered this rule as a degenerate periodic rule with a period length P of 1. Hence, PH1SEGMENTI refers to the Ith segment in phase 1 (the only phase) of the derived sequence. Actually, the rule that the dealer had in mind has one additional constraint: a queen must not be played adjacent to a jack or king.

4.5.2 Example 2

The second example requires the program to discover a fairly simple periodic rule. Here is the layout:

Main line:	JC	4D	QH	3S	QD	9H	QC	7H	QD
Side lines:	KC	5S				4S		10D	
		7S							

Main line continued:	9D	QC	3H	KH	4C	KD	6C	JD	8D

Main line continued:	JH	7C	JD	7H	JH	6H	KD

The program discovered three equivalent versions of the rule, which can be paraphrased as "Play alternating faced and nonfaced cards." Here are the rules (0.49 seconds required):

```
RULE 1: LOOKBACK: 1 NPHASES: 0 DECOMPOSITION MODEL

[FACE(CARDI − 1)=FALSE] =>
    [RANK(CARDI) ≥ JACK]
    [RANK(CARDI) > RANK(CARDI − 1)]
    [FACE(CARDI)=TRUE]                &
```

```
[FACE(CARDI − 1)=TRUE]  =>
   [RANK(CARDI)=3 . . 9]
   [RANK(CARDI) < RANK(CARDI − 1)]
   [FACE(CARDI) =FALSE]
```

RULE 2: LOOKBACK: 1 NPHASES: 1 PERIODIC MODEL

```
PERIOD<[RANK(PH1CARDI) ≥ 3]
        [RANK(PH1CARDI) ≠ RANK(PH1CARDI − 1)]
        [FACE(PH1CARDI) ≠ FACE(PH1CARDI − 1)]>
```

RULE 3: LOOKBACK: 1 NPHASES: 2 PERIODIC MODEL

```
PERIOD<[RANK(PH1CARDI) ≥ JACK]
        [RANK(PH1CARDI) ≥ − RANK(PH1CARDI − 1)+20]
        [FACE(PH1CARDI)=TRUE],

        [RANK(PH2CARDI)=3 . . 9]
        [RANK(PH2CARDI)=− RANK(PH2CARDI − 1)+5 . . 14]
        [FACE(PH2CARDI)=FALSE]>
```

Rule 1 is a decomposition rule with a lookback of 1. Rule 2 expresses the rule as a degenerate periodic rule with a single phase. Rule 3 expresses the rule in the "natural" way as a periodic rule of length 2.

Notice that, although the program has the gist of the rule, it has discovered a number of redundant conditions. For example, in rule 1, the program did not use knowledge of the fact that [RANK($card_i$) ≥ jack] implies [FACE($card_i$) = true], and therefore it did not remove the former selector. Similarly, because of the interaction of the two conditions in rule 1, [RANK($card_i$) > RANK($card_{i-1}$)] is completely redundant.

4.5.3 Example 3

The third example shows the upper limits of the program's abilities. During this game, only one of the human players even got close to guessing the rule, yet the program discovers a good approximation of the rule using only a portion of the layout that was available to the human players. Here is the layout:

Main line:	4H	5D	8C	JS	2C	5S	AC	5S		10H
Side lines:	7C	6S	KC	AH		6C		AS		
	JH	7H	3H	KD						
	4C	2C		QS						
	10S	7S								
	8H	6D								
	AD	6H								
	2D	4C								

The program produced the following rules after 6.5 seconds:

```
RULE 1: LOOKBACK: 1 NPHASES: 0 DNF MODEL
```

$$[\text{RANK(CARDI)} \leq 5][\text{SUIT(CARDI)} = \text{SUIT(CARDI} - 1) + 1] \quad \lor$$
$$[\text{RANK(CARDI)} \geq 5][\text{SUIT(CARDI)} = \text{SUIT(CARDI} - 1) + 3]$$

```
RULE 2: LOOKBACK: 1 NPHASES: 1 PERIODIC MODEL
```

$$\text{PERIOD}\langle[\text{RANK(PH1CARDI)} = \text{RANK(PH1CARDI} - 1) - 9]$$
$$[\text{RANK(PH1CARDI)} = -\text{RANK(PH1CARDI} - 1) + 4,5,7,11,13,17]$$
$$[\text{SUIT(PH1CARDI)} = \text{SUIT(PH1CARDI} - 1) + 1,2,3]\rangle$$

```
RULE 3: LOOKBACK: 1 NPHASES: 2 PERIODIC MODEL
```

$$\text{PERIOD}\langle[\text{RANK(PH1CARDI)} = \text{ACE},2,8,10]$$
$$[\text{RANK(PH1CARDI)} = -\text{RANK(PH1CARDI} - 1) + 1,8,9,10],$$

$$[\text{RANK(PH2CARDI)} = 5 \ . \ . \ \text{JACK}][\text{SUIT(PH2CARDI)} = \text{SPADES}]$$
$$[\text{RANK(PH2CARDI)} = \text{RANK(PH2CARDI} - 1) + -0 \ . \ . \ 6]$$
$$[\text{RANK(PH2CARDI)} = -\text{RANK(PH2CARDI} - 1) + 8 \ . \ . \ 14]$$
$$[\text{SUIT(PH2CARDI)} = \text{SUIT(PH2CARDI} - 1) + 0 \ . \ . \ 2]$$
$$[\text{COLOR(PH2CARDI)} = \text{BLACK}][\text{PRIME(PH2CARDI)} = \text{PTRUE}]$$
$$[\text{PRIME(PH2CARDI)} = \text{PRIME(PH2CARDI} - 1)]$$
$$[\text{MOD2(PH2CARDI)} = 1][\text{MOD2(PH2CARDI} - 1) = \text{MOD2(PH2CARDI} - 1) + 0]$$
$$[\text{MOD2(PH2CARDI)} = -\text{MOD2(PH2CARDI} - 1) + 0][\text{MOD3(PH2CARDI)} = 2]$$
$$[\text{MOD3(PH2CARDI)} = \text{MOD3(PH2CARDI} - 1) + 0]$$
$$[\text{MOD3(PH2CARDI)} = -\text{MOD3(PH2CARDI} - 1) + 1]\rangle$$

The rule that the dealer had in mind was the following:

$$[\text{SUIT}(\text{card}_i) = \text{SUIT}(\text{card}_{i-1}) + 3]$$
$$[\text{RANK}(\text{card}_i) \geq \text{RANK}(\text{card}_{i-1})] \quad \lor$$

$$[\text{SUIT}(\text{card}_i) = \text{SUIT}(\text{card}_{i-1}) + 1]$$
$$[\text{RANK}(\text{card}_i) \leq \text{RANK}(\text{card}_{i-1})].$$

There is a strong symmetry in this rule: the players may either play a lower card in the next "higher" suit (recall that the suits are cyclically ordered) or a higher card in the next "lower" suit. The program discovered a slightly simpler version of the rule (rule 1) that happened to be consistent with the training instances. Note that adding 3 to the SUIT has the effect of computing the next lower suit.

The other two rules discovered by the program are very poor. They are typical of the kinds of rules that the program discovers when the model does not fit the data very well. Both rules are filled with irrelevant descriptors and values. The current program has very little ability to assess how well a model fits the data. These rules should not be printed by the program, because they are highly implausible.

4.6 SUMMARY

A methodology has been presented for discovering sequence-generating rules for a class of nondeterministic prediction problems. The main ideas behind this methodology are (1) the use of description space transformations of the initial data and (2) the use of different rule models to guide the search for the candidate rules. Four different description space transformations (adding attributes, blocking, splitting into phases, and segmenting) and three models (DNF, periodic, and decomposition) have been presented.

The main part of the methodology has been implemented in the program SPARC/E and applied to the rule discovery problem in the card game Eleusis. The experiments with the program demonstrated that it can discover most of the Eleusis secret rules played in ordinary human games and that it often outperforms human players.

The methodology is quite general and can be applied to other nondeterministic prediction problems in which the objects in the initial sequence are describable by a set of finite-valued attributes. The main strengths of the method are that it can (1) solve learning problems in which the initial training instances require substantial description space transformation and (2) search very large spaces of possible rules using a set of rule models for guidance.

Many aspects of this methodology remain to be investigated. We have not considered NDP problems in which (1) the training instances are noisy, (2) the training instances have internal structure so that an attribute vector representation of these instances is not adequate, and (3) the sequence-generating rules are permitted to have exceptions. Application of this methodology to real-world problems will probably also require the development of additional sequence transformations and rule models. Also, more heuristics need to be developed that can be used to guide the application of transformations and models.

Despite its ability to outperform human players, the current implementation of SPARC/E has several shortcomings. The program presently conducts a nearly exhaustive depth-first search of the possible models and transformations. Much could be gained by having the program conduct a best-first, heuristically guided search instead. The present implementation does not include the ability to evaluate the plausibility of the rules it discovers. It is also not able to simplify rules by removing redundant selectors, nor is it able to estimate the degree of nondeterminism of the rule. The last two can be implemented without too much difficulty by the inclusion of inference routines that make more complete use of the background knowledge already available to the program. Finally, an important weakness of the current program is its inability to form composite models.

In addition to these specific problems, there are some more general problems that further research in the area of sequence-generating rules should address. First, in some real-world problems, there may not be one, but several example sequences that are governed by the same sequence-generating rule. Such problems occur, in particular, in describing the processes of disease development in medicine and agriculture. A specific problem of this type that has been partially investigated involves predicting the time course of cutworm infestation in a cornfield and estimating the potential damage to the crop (see Davis, 1981; Baim, 1983; and Boulanger, 1983). In this problem, several sequences of observations are available—one for each field— and there is a need to develop a general sequence-generating rule that predicts all of these sequences.

A second general problem for further research is handling processes in which time is a continuous variable. In particular, there is the problem of programs that perform qualitative modeling of such processes and qualitative evaluation of trends based on example event sequences. AI research has so far given little attention to these tasks.

ACKNOWLEDGMENTS

Earlier versions of this chapter appeared in the *Proceedings of the International Machine Learning Workshop* (1983) and subsequently in the *Artificial Intelligence Journal,* Vol. 24, No. 2, pp. 187–231, 1985. The authors wish to thank the referees of the Workshop and the Journal for their helpful suggestions and to North-Holland Publishing Company, Amsterdam, for permission to print this version here. Thanks also go to Danny Berlin for bringing several errors to our attention. The authors are grateful to Robert Abbott for inventing the game Eleusis, which was the original motivation for this research and the source of examples for SPARC/E. They also thank Donald Michie for challenging them to develop such a program.

A part of the work was done while the second author worked at the Artificial Intelligence Laboratory at the Massachusetts Institute of Technology. Support for MIT's Artificial Intelligence research is provided in part by the Advanced Research

Projects Agency under Office of Naval Research Contract No. N00014-80-C-0505. The authors gratefully acknowledge the partial support of the National Science Foundation under Grant DCR-84-06801 and the Office of Naval Research under Grant No. N00014-82-K-0186.

APPENDIX: NOTATIONAL CONVENTIONS

The following notational conventions are employed in this chapter. In general, lowercase letters denote objects in some sequence (q, ph, b) or index variables (i, j, k) or the lengths of sequences (m, n). Uppercase letters denote sets of objects, attributes, and so on (Q, F, S), as well as parameters of models and transformations (L, P). Small capitals denote attributes (COLOR, RANK).

$\langle \rangle$	Angle brackets denote sequences of objects, e.g., $\langle 2 \quad 4 \quad 6 \quad 8 \rangle$, as well as periodic rules, e.g., $\langle [\text{COLOR}(ph_{1,i}) = \text{red}], [\text{COLOR}(ph_{2,i}) = \text{black}] \rangle$
q_i	The ith object in an input sequence
q_i'	The ith object in a derived sequence
q_i^-	An object that constitutes an incorrect extension of the sequence after object q_{i-1}
b_i	The ith block in a sequence derived by the blocking transformation
ph_i	The ith phase derived by the splitting transformation
$ph_{l,j}$	The jth object in the lth phase after a splitting transformation
n	The number of descriptors
E	The space of possible events
F	The starting set of attributes for a transformation
S	The starting set of sequences for a transformation
Q	The starting set of objects for a transformation
F'	The set of derived attributes from a transformation
S'	The set of derived sequences from a transformation
Q'	The set of derived objects from a transformation
F_j	The set of selectors describing object q_{i-j} in block b_i
g	The sequence-generating function that maps a sequence into a set of objects Q_{k+1} that can appear as continuations of the sequence
Q_{k+1}	The set of objects that can appear as continuations of the sequence $\langle q_1, q_2, \ldots q_k \rangle$

P	The number of phases parameter of the splitting transformation and the periodic model
L	The lookback parameter of the blocking transformation and all three models
$[f_i(q_j) = r_k]$	A simple selector, which asserts that feature f_i of object q_j has the value r_k
$[f_i(q_j) = r_1 \lor r_2 \lor r_3]\}$	A selector containing an internal disjunction. It asserts that f_i can have the value r_1 or r_2 or r_3
D prefix	The D prefix on an attribute name indicates that it is a difference attribute. Hence, D-RANK(q_i,q_{i-1}) is equal to RANK(q_i) − RANK(q_{i-1})
s prefix	The s prefix on an attribute name indicates that it is a summation attribute. Hence s-RANK(q_i,q_{i-1}) is equal to RANK(q_i) + RANK(q_{i-1})
$d(F_i,F_j)$	The set of difference selectors obtained by "subtracting" selectors F_j from F_i
$s(F_i,F_j)$	The set of summation selectors obtained by "adding" selectors F_i and F_j
$\Rightarrow$	Logical implication

References

Abbott, R., "The New Eleusis," 1977. (Available from the author, Box 1175, General Post Office, New York, N.Y. 10116.)

Baim, P. W., "Automated Acquisition of Decision Rules: Problems of Attribute Construction and Selection," M.S. thesis, Department of Computer Science, University of Illinois, Urbana, 1983.

Boulanger, A. G., "The Expert System PLANT/CD: A Case Study in Applying the General Purpose Inference System ADVISE to Predicting Black Cutworm Damage in Corn," M.S. thesis, Department of Computer Science, University of Illinois, Urbana, 1983.

Buchanan, B. G., and Mitchell, T. M., "Model-directed Learning of Production Rules," in *Pattern-directed Inference Systems,* D. A. Waterman and F. Hayes-Roth (Eds.), Academic Press, New York, 1978.

Cohen, P. R., and Feigenbaum, E. A., *The Handbook of Artificial Intelligence,* Vol. 3, Kaufmann, Los Altos, Calif., 1982.

Davis, J., "CONVART: A Program for Constructive Induction on Time-Dependent Data," M.S. thesis, Department of Computer Science, University of Illinois, Urbana, 1981.

Dietterich, T. G., London, R., Clarkson, K., and Dromey, G., "Learning and Inductive Inference," in *The Handbook of Artificial Intelligence,* Vol. 3, P. R. Cohen and E. A. Feigenbaum (Eds.), Kaufmann, Los Altos, Calif., 1982.

Dietterich, T. G., and Michalski, R. S., "Inductive Learning of Structural Descriptions: Evaluation Criteria and Comparative Review of Selected Methods," *Artificial Intelligence,* Vol. 16, No. 3, pp. 257–94, 1981.

Englemore, R., and Terry, A., "Structure and Function of the Crysalis System," *Proceedings of the Seventh IJCAI*, Tokyo, pp. 250–56, 1979.

Friedland, P. E., "Knowledge-Based Experiment Design in Molecular Genetics," Report No. HPP-79-29, Department of Computer Science, Stanford University, 1979.

Gardner, M., "On Playing the New Eleusis, The Game That Simulates the Search for Truth," *Scientific American*, No. 237, pp. 18–25, October 1977.

Hedrick, C. L., "Learning Production Systems from Examples," *Artificial Intelligence*, Vol. 7, No. 1, pp. 21–49, 1976.

Hofstadter, D. R., "The Architecture of JUMBO," *Proceedings of the International Machine Learning Workshop*, R. S. Michalski (Ed.), Allerton House, University of Illinois at Urbana-Champaign, pp. 161–70, June 22–24, 1983.

———, "Analogies and Roles in Human and Machine Thinking," 1985, in press.

Karpinski, J., and Michalski, R. S., "A System That Learns to Recognize Hand-written Alphanumeric Characters," *Proce Institute Automatyki*, Polish Academy of Sciences, No. 35, 1966.

Kotovsky, K., and Simon, H. A., "Empirical Tests of a Theory of Human Acquisition of Concepts for Sequential Patterns," *Cognitive Psychology*, No. 4, pp. 399–424, 1973.

Langley, P. W., "Descriptive Discovery Processes: Experiments in Baconian Science," Report No. CMU-CS-80-121, Department of Computer Science, Carnegie-Mellon University, 1980.

Lenat, D. B., "The Role of Heuristics in Learning by Discovery: Three Case Studies," in *Machine Learning: An Artificial Intelligence Approach*, R. S. Michalski, J. G. Carbonell, and T. M. Mitchell (Eds.), Tioga, Palo Alto, Calif., 1983.

McCarthy, J., "Programs with Common Sense," in *Proceedings of the Symposium on the Mechanization of Thought Processes*, National Physical Laboratory, pp. 77–84, 1958.

———, "Epistemological Problems of Artificial Intelligence," *Proceedings of the Fifth IJCAI*, Cambridge, Mass., pp. 1038–44, 1977.

McCarthy, J., and Hayes, P., "Some Epistemological Problems from the Standpoint of Artificial Intelligence," in *Machine Intelligence 4*, B. Meltzer and D. Michie (Eds.), Edinburgh University Press, Edinburgh, 1969.

Michalski, R. S., "On the Quasi-Minimal Solution of the General Covering Problem," in *Fifth International Symposium on Information Processing, FCIP 69*, Yugoslavia, Vol. A3, 2–12, 1969.

———, "A Variable-valued Logic System as Applied to Picture Description," in *Graphic Languages: Proceedings of the IFIP Working Conference on Graphic Languages*, P. Nake and A. Rosenfeld (Eds.), Vancouver, B. C., pp. 20–47, 1972.

———, "Knowledge Acquisition Through Conceptual Clustering: A Theoretical Framework and an Algorithm for Partitioning Data into Conjunctive Concepts," *Journal of Policy Analysis and Information Systems*, Vol. 4, No. 3, pp. 219–44, September 1980.

———, "A Theory and Methodology of Inductive Learning," *Artificial Intelligence*, Vol. 20, 111–61, 1983.

Michalski, R. S., Carbonell, J. G., and Mitchell, T. M. (Eds.), *Machine Learning: An Artificial Intelligence Approach*, Tioga, Palo Alto, Calif., 1983.

Michalski, R. S., and Chilausky, R. L., "Learning by Being Told and Learning from Examples: An Experimental Comparison of the Two Methods of Knowledge Acquisition in the Context of Developing an Expert System for Soybean Disease Diagnosis," *Policy Analysis and Information Systems,* Vol. 4, No. 2, June 1980.

Michalski, R. S., and Stepp, R. E., "Learning from Observation: Conceptual Clustering," in *Machine Learning: An Artificial Intelligence Approach,* R. S. Michalski, J. G. Carbonell, and T. M. Mitchell (Eds.), Tioga, Palo Alto, Calif., 1983.

Mitchell, T. M., "Version Spaces: An Approach to Concept Learning," Report No. STAN-CS-78-711, Department of Computer Science, Stanford University, 1978.

Mitchell, T. M., Utgoff, P. E., and Banerji, R. B., "Learning by Experimentation: Acquiring and Refining Problem-Solving Heuristics," in *Machine Learning: An Artificial Intelligence Approach,* R. S. Michalski, J. G. Carbonell, and T. M. Mitchell (Eds.), Tioga, Palo Alto, Calif., 1983.

Persson, S., "Some Sequence Extrapolating Programs: A Study of Representation and Modeling in Inquiring Systems," Report No. CS50, Department of Computer Science, Stanford University, 1966.

Samuel, A. L., "Some Studies in Machine Learning Using the Game of Checkers," in *Computers and Thought,* E. A. Feigenbaum and J. Feldman (Eds.), McGraw-Hill, New York, 1963.

————, "Some Studies in Machine Learning Using the Game of Checkers II—Recent Progress," *IBM Journal of Research and Development,* Vol. 11, No. 6, pp. 601–17, 1967.

Schank, R., and Abelson, R., "Scripts, Plans, and Knowledge," *Proceedings of the Fourth IJCAI,* Tbilisi, Georgia, USSR, pp. 151–57, 1975.

Simon, H. A., "Complexity and the Representation of Patterned Sequences of Symbols," *Psychological Review,* Vol. 79, 369–82, 1972.

Simon, H. A., and Kotovsky, K., "Human Acquisition of Concepts for Sequential Patterns," *Psychological Review,* Vol. 70, pp. 534–46, 1963.

Solomonoff, R. S., "A Formal Theory of Inductive Inference," *Information and Control,* Vol. 7, pp. 1–22, 224–54, 1964.

Soloway, E. M., "Learning = Interpretation + Generalization: A Case Study in Knowledge-Directed Learning," Report No. COINS TR-78-13, Department of Computer and Information Science, University of Massachusetts, Amherst, 1978.

Winston, P. H., "Learning Structural Descriptions from Examples," Report No. AI-TR-231, MIT, 1970.

5

SHIFT OF BIAS FOR INDUCTIVE CONCEPT LEARNING

Paul E. Utgoff
University of Massachusetts at Amherst

Abstract

Programs that learn inductive generalizations from examples are guided not only by the training instances that they observe but also by *bias* that determines how generalizations are to be formed, given the observed training instances. This chapter examines the essential role of bias in inductive concept learning, argues that one bias can be better than another, and presents a program, STABB, that shifts its bias during the course of learning from examples. The main objective is to show that the search for a good bias, part of the learning task, can be performed mechanically. By-products of the research are a methodology for shifting bias and the two algorithms of STABB.

5.1 INTRODUCTION

Except for the presented examples and counterexamples of the concept being learned, all factors that influence hypothesis selection constitute *bias*. These factors include the following:

1. The language in which hypotheses are described
2. The space of hypotheses that the program can consider
3. The procedures that define in what order hypotheses are to be considered
4. The acceptance criteria that define whether a search procedure may stop with a given hypothesis or should continue searching for a better choice

5.1.1 Concept Learning as Searching a Hypothesis Space

A *concept* is a classification rule that partitions a domain of instances into those instances that satisfy the rule and those that do not. For example, the concept of a prime number is a partition of the set of numbers into those that are prime and those that are not. The classification rule is, "*x* is prime if and only if *x* is an integer and *x* is evenly divisible only by *x* and 1." A classification rule can serve as a set description. Hereafter, the terms *classification rule, concept description, and set description* are used synonymously.

Viewing concepts as sets provides a useful tool. For example, the concept "numerically less than" can be described as the set of ordered pairs that satisfy the "numerically less than" relation. The concept "threading a needle" can be described as the set of event sequences that result in a threaded needle.

In the paradigm of learning from examples, a learning program is shown examples and counterexamples of the target concept. The *target concept* is the one concept that correctly classifies all the instances in the domain. Examples of the target concept are referred to as *positive* instances. Similarly, counterexamples of the target concept are referred to as *negative* instances. If a classification rule is true for all observed (presented by a trainer) positive instances and is false for all observed negative instances, then the concept that corresponds to the classification rule is *consistent* with the observed data. The objective of the concept learner is to infer a classification rule that describes the target concept.

For a domain of instances **I** there are $2^{|I|}$ distinct subsets over **I**. The domain **I** may be infinitely large, in which case the set of $2^{|I|}$ distinct concepts is also infinitely large. The set of all subsets over a domain **I** is referred to as the set of *all distinct concepts* over **I**. If two descriptions refer to the same subset of instances, then the two referenced concepts are not distinct. Two concept descriptions that each describe the same concept are *synonyms*.

The problem of inferring a concept based on observation of positive and negative training instances is easily viewed as one of searching a space of concepts for one that best classifies the instances in the domain (Mitchell, 1982). As illustrated in figure 5-1, a concept **A** classifies the instances *better* than a concept **B** if and only if the concept **A** classifies more instances correctly than does **B**. An instance is classified *correctly* if and only if the classification is consistent with the target concept **T**. Note that this definition is based solely on the number of correctly classified instances. If it were the case that some misclassifications were worse than others—guilty versus innocent—then an alternate definition of *better* would be needed.

Ideally, the concept learner would immediately select the target concept as its hypothesis, but the learner does not know which concept is the target concept. Because the concept learner cannot know the target concept ahead of time, the learner cannot select a hypothesis based on closeness of fit with the target concept.

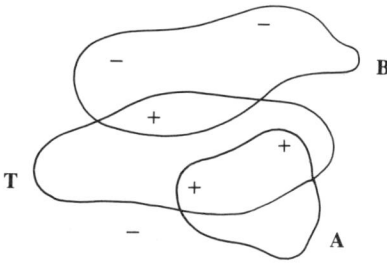

Figure 5-1: Concept **A** better than concept **B.**

Nevertheless, a concept-learning program requires some classification metric so that it will have a bias that allows it to evaluate whether one hypothesis is to be preferred to another. For example, consistency with the training instances is one feature of a hypothesis that is customarily included in a classification metric; a hypothesis that misclassifies some of the training instances cannot be the target concept, assuming correct classification by the trainer. A classification metric that includes the consistency feature guides the concept learner to prefer any consistent hypothesis to any inconsistent hypothesis. Additional features of hypotheses or their descriptions are necessary to define further how to choose from among consistent hypotheses.

5.1.2 Role of Bias in Concept Learning

A program that learns concepts from examples is guided toward an inductive generalization not only by the training instances but also by bias that determines how to choose from among the hypotheses. Without the bias, the program has no basis for selecting one hypothesis in favor of another. By selecting a hypothesis, a concept learner makes an inductive leap because the concept learner guesses that the hypothesis correctly classifies all the instances in the domain; that is, the concept learner assumes that the current hypothesis is the target concept. Had the bias been different, the learner would have selected a different hypothesis and as a result would have made a different inductive leap.

Consider two features of bias:

1. A *strong* bias is one that focuses the concept learner on a relatively small number of hypotheses. Conversely, a *weak* bias is one that allows the concept learner to consider a relatively large number of hypotheses.

2. A *correct* bias is one that allows the concept learner to select the target concept. Conversely, an *incorrect* bias is one that does not allow the concept learner to select the target concept.

A concept learner's task is simplest when bias is strongest and correct because the concept learner immediately selects the only choice available—the target concept.

A concept learner's task is most difficult when bias is weakest but incorrect because the concept learner cannot select the target concept and has no other guidance regarding hypothesis selection.

Figure 5-2 illustrates that induction in the learning-from-examples paradigm is a function of two arguments, the training instances, and the bias for hypothesis preference. Given any particular sequence of training instances, however, induction becomes a function of one argument, the bias. This chapter addresses the problem of selecting a bias, not the problem of selecting a training sequence.

Consider an example of a learning scenario that shows the role of bias. Person **A** is to learn a concept from examples presented by person **B**. Person **B** only presents correctly classified positive and negative instances of the concept. It is the job of person **A** to infer the target concept that person **B** is endeavoring to teach. Person **B** presents the first instance:

(3,4) is a positive instance

Person **A** may perhaps form a hypothesis of the concept such as "an ordered pair of numbers." Person **B** then presents the second instance:

(6,5) is a negative instance

Person **A** may perhaps revise his or her hypothesis of the concept to be "an ordered pair of numbers where the first is numerically less than the second." If person **A** has not made a random choice from among the set of distinct plausible hypotheses, then, by definition, he or she has been guided by bias to choose the "less than" hypothesis. Consider some alternative consistent hypotheses that **A** could have chosen:

1. An ordered pair of numbers in which the first is an odd integer
2. An ordered pair of numbers in which the second is an even integer
3. An ordered pair of numbers in which the first is an odd integer *and* the second is an even integer

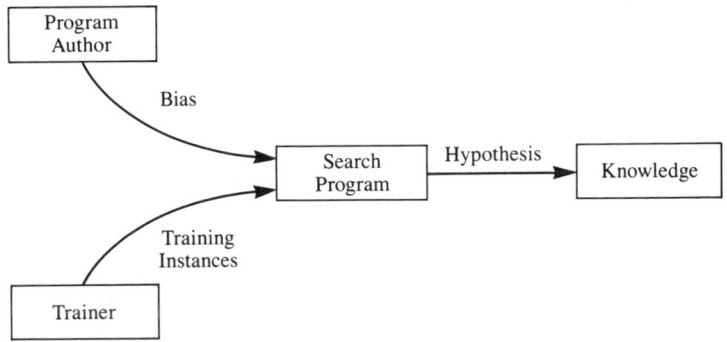

Figure 5-2:   Role of bias in inductive generalization.

4. An ordered pair of numbers in which the first is an odd integer *or* the second is an even integer
5. An ordered pair of numbers the binary sum of which has a 1 in the 4's place
6. An ordered pair of numbers the decimal sum of which has a 0 in the 10's place
7. A pair of numbers the sum of which is 7
8. An ordered pair of numbers in which the second is 1 more than the first
9. An ordered pair of numbers in which the first is not 1 more than the second

Note in the above example that the hypotheses make use of other concepts such as order, odd integer, even integer, logical *and,* logical *or,* logical *not,* addition, binary notation, decimal notation, digit's place, and the "one more than" relation. These are terms that are commonly associated with numbers and logical combinations of features. Other hypotheses are consistent that are difficult to state succinctly, for example, some apparently arbitrary set of pairs of numbers. When people are involved, human factors come into play. For example, one assumes that there is a vocabulary of concepts that the people share. Furthermore, person **A** may try to guess what kind of concept person **B** would try to teach.

5.1.3 Kinds of Bias

Several kinds of bias can be characterized at an abstract level.

1. There can be a *total* preference ordering over the hypotheses. In the above example involving pairs of ordered numbers, there are ten consistent hypotheses. An example of a total preference ordering would be to have the concept learner prefer those ten concepts, together with others, in some specified order. There are other methods for specifying a preference ordering. For example, one can prefer one hypothesis to another based on the syntax of the description; for example, one can prefer a hypothesis that does not use logical *or* to one that does.

2. There can be a *partial* preference ordering. One can select the most preferred hypothesis when there is exactly one, or choose randomly from the set of most preferred, or not choose at all and simply keep track of the set of most preferred.

3. It is possible to restrict the space of hypotheses through which the concept learner conducts its search. If a space is used in which not all hypotheses are represented, the concept learner is unable to select hypotheses that are not in the space. Use of a restricted hypothesis space is a very practical method for focusing the concept learner on a set of preferred hypotheses.

4. There can be a combination of kinds of bias. For example, one can use a restricted space of hypotheses *and* specify a preference criterion for those that are in the space.

5.1.4 Origin of Bias

The research in inductive concept-learning programs to date has contributed several good techniques for using a given bias to guide the way to choosing a hypothesis. These programs do not, however, include directed methods by which the program itself shifts the bias. Michalski has recognized the need to vary the bias and has provided a mechanism through which the user of his program can specify the bias to be used for a given run (Michalski, 1983). The program author spends considerable time and effort searching for a bias that will allow the program to perform satisfactorily. As the author repeatedly shifts the bias by hand and retests the learning program, a search for a better bias is taking place. Human authors use both their experience with previous bias failures and their knowledge as domain experts to guide their search for a better bias. Bias A is *better* than bias B if the hypotheses selected when bias A is used are better classifiers than those selected when bias B is used. This ability to search for a better bias is a major skill that researchers apply. As researchers work on getting good performances from learning programs, they do part of the learning task themselves by improving the bias employed by the concept-learning program. An inductive concept-learning program should be able to conduct its own search for an appropriate bias. Until programs have such capability, the search for an improved bias will continue to be done by hand. The lack of such techniques was the motivation for the research reported here.

An inductive concept-learning program that includes search for a better bias learns how to learn. By changing one's bias, one changes not only what is to be induced in the current learning task but also what is to be induced in future learning tasks. An open question is whether there are elements of bias that are useful across many learning domains. For example, is a bias toward comparative simplicity of hypothesis descriptions universally useful? No such universally useful bias has yet been positively identified. The orientation in this chapter is toward the ability to *shift* bias. Shift of bias is a less difficult problem because it is possible to observe cases of manual search for and shift to a better bias. An important experiment (taking many years) would be to observe many cases of concept-learning programs that shift bias and then try to generalize on the properties of the biases that were selected. This is a possible approach toward identifying characteristics of bias—for example, simplicity—that occur across many domains.

5.1.5 Another View of Bias

One kind of bias mentioned above in section 5.1.3 is use of a restricted hypothesis space. A standard method for defining a restricted hypothesis space is to use a description language in which not all concepts are describable. If a concept is not describable in the description language, then it does not exist as a hypothesis in the hypothesis space. For example, a restricted description language might include a description for the concept of a prime number and yet exclude any description for the concept of an odd integer. In such a case, the concept learner could select the hypothesis "prime number" and could not select the hypothesis "odd integer."

The description language defines the restricted hypothesis space and is therefore a contributor to bias. If one changes the description language, then one is also changing the bias. Thus, in the case of bias coming from a restricted hypothesis space, searching for a better bias is equivalent to searching for a better description language.

5.2 A FRAMEWORK FOR SHIFTING BIAS

This section lays out a three-step framework for building a procedure that can *shift* the bias used by the learning program. An approach to shift of bias is dependent on both the kind of bias that the learning program uses and the formalism in which the bias is encoded.

5.2.1 Encoding Bias

The remainder of this chapter focuses on bias that comes from using a restricted hypothesis space. The restricted hypothesis space is defined by a concept description language in which not all concepts over the instance domain are describable. A hypothesis space that does not include all distinct hypotheses is *incomplete*. There are two major reasons for choosing to study bias that comes from an incomplete hypothesis space:

1. An incomplete hypothesis space can be represented by a description language in which not all distinct concepts are describable. The problem of searching for a better bias becomes one of searching for a better description language. A description language is easily represented as a data structure, something that is far easier to manipulate than a control structure.

2. There already exists a concept-learning algorithm, Mitchell's candidate elimination algorithm (Mitchell, 1977, 1978), that encodes bias as a restricted hypothesis space. This permits the immediate study of methods for shifting bias.

For bias that comes from a restricted description language, there are two major contributors to the bias:

1. Bias comes from the *formalism* in which the description language is expressed. A formalism is a formal system in which a language is expressed. For example, a formal grammar of string substitution rules is a formalism for specifying a formal language. Predicate calculus is a formalism for expressing well-formed formulas that represent theories. A theory can be used as a description of all that is true or false according to the theory.

2. Bias comes from the *language* as expressed in a given formalism. A language is a set of sentences or descriptions. For a formal language, the set of sentences in

the language is the set of sentences that can be produced by applying some sequence of legal string substitutions that are specifically permitted by the grammar. If a sentence in the alphabet of symbols cannot be produced by following rules in the grammar, then the sentence is not in the language. Thus the definition of the language defines the restrictions—that is, bias—on what is describable within the formalism.

This chapter examines bias that comes from using a restricted language within a formalism; it does not examine bias that comes from a given formalism. Methods are developed for changing the language that is available to the concept learner within a given formalism but not for changing the formalism in which that language is expressed. Change of formalism and understanding of biases implied by a given formalism are open areas for further study. Section 5.3.3 shows an example of bias coming from the formalism.

A bias can be too strong or too weak. As mentioned in section 5.1.2, the extent to which a description language is restricted determines the strength of the bias. If a bias is strong and correct, then the concept-learning task is relatively easy because the concept learner will be guided to selection of the target concept. If the bias is strong and incorrect, then the concept learner may eliminate *all* hypotheses from the restricted space. If a bias is weak, the concept learner may do little better than random selection of a hypothesis. Given some fixed number of training instances and some fixed amount of time, a bias that is too weak may prevent the concept learner from eliminating enough hypotheses from the space to be able to isolate a single hypothesis, such as the target concept. Correctness of bias determines whether the concept learner is able to select the target concept as a hypothesis. Strength of bias determines how many hypotheses have been eliminated before *any* training instances are observed. With no bias, there is no induction.

This chapter focuses on the problem of shifting from a strong bias to one that is weaker. The problem of moving in the other direction, from a weak bias to one that is stronger, is briefly considered in section 5.3.2.7. The choice of designing a method for weakening a strong bias is based on the view that learning is itself a process of ruling out some hypotheses in favor of others that are to be retained, for example, Mitchell's candidate elimination algorithm. If a bias is too weak, then the concept learner can, in theory, continue to observe training instances until the space of consistent hypotheses is sufficiently pruned. On the other hand, if a bias is incorrect and too strong and the space of consistent hypotheses is emptied, the concept learner will not benefit from further training. The problem of an incorrect and overly strong bias is serious—just as in racism and other forms of prejudice. Program authors who design a restricted hypothesis space characteristically err toward defining too strong a bias because they include in the hypothesis space only those concepts that they know about and suspect may be useful in the domain. If the bias is incorrect, then a concept-learning program should be able to weaken its bias in a controlled manner in an attempt to make the bias correct yet not too weak.

5.2.2 When to Shift to a Weaker Bias

Before shifting to a weaker bias, one must determine that a shift is warranted. A sufficient condition is the following:

If the hypothesis space does not include a concept that is consistent with the observed training instances and the training instances have been correctly classified by the trainer, then the bias is too strong.

In general a shift to a weaker bias can be made whenever the concept learner is no longer willing to accept any of the hypotheses from which it must choose. For example, if a concept-learning algorithm allows some number of apparently misclassified instances in a hypothesis, then a shift to a new bias can be made when the number is exceeded. If the same instance is classified as positive on one occasion and as negative on another, then the two training instances can be discarded.

5.2.3 How to Shift to a Weaker Bias: A Three-Step Framework

The objective of shifting to a weaker bias is to enable the concept learner to select a hypothesis that is consistent with the training instances and that is as close to the target concept as possible. Because the concept learner cannot know which concept is the target concept, it is necessary to use *heuristic* methods for deciding exactly how to weaken the bias.

The framework for shifting to a weaker bias studied here consists of three steps:

1. *Recommend* (via heuristics) new concept descriptions to be added to the concept description language.
2. *Translate* recommendations into new concept descriptions that are expressed in the formalism of the concept description language.
3. *Assimilate* any new concepts into the restricted space of hypotheses so that the organization of the hypothesis space is maintained.

Step 1 determines a better bias to which to shift. Steps 2 and 3 are the mechanics for carrying out the shift. The resulting new concept description language is a superset of the former description language, and therefore it provides a strictly weaker bias.

5.2.3.1 Recommending a Better Bias

The task of step 1 is to formulate recommendations for new descriptions to be added to the space of hypotheses. The recommendations are then given as output to step 2. How does one identify a better bias to which to move?

In the framework, the concept learner shifts to a new bias only when the existing hypothesis space no longer contains any consistent hypotheses. The fact that the existing description language contains no consistent descriptions shows that the existing bias is incorrect. New descriptive capability is added to the description language to alter the bias so that the new space of hypotheses contains at least one consistent hypothesis.

Figure 5-3 shows two partitions of the space of all distinct hypotheses. The first partition consists of two subsets: those descriptions that are in the restricted space of hypotheses to be searched by the concept learner and those that are not. The second partition also consists of two subsets: those descriptions that are consistent with the training instances and those that are not. As concept learning takes place, the new knowledge of the classification of the training instance allows the concept learner to identify inconsistent hypotheses. Thus, the set of hypotheses consistent with the training instances shrinks during concept learning. When the set of consistent hypotheses within the restricted space—that is, the intersection—becomes empty, then a shift to a weaker bias is required. To weaken the bias, it is necessary to move the partition that defines the restricted hypothesis space so that there is again a nonempty set of consistent hypotheses within the now-less-restricted space of hypotheses. Thus the set of describable hypotheses grows during bias weakening.

Although the goal is to add consistent hypotheses to the restricted space, they should not be chosen at random. Recall from section 5.1.2 that the selection of a hypothesis by the concept learner constitutes an inductive leap because the hypothesis specifies the classification of the unobserved instances. If consistent hypotheses were to be added to the hypothesis space without regard to how they classify unobserved instances, then there would be no confidence in an inductive leap that results from selecting such a consistent hypothesis.

The problem for the concept learner is to move to a new bias that will cause the concept learner to make satisfactory inductive leaps based on the observed data. Because the concept learner cannot already know which concept is the target concept, the concept learner must make an intelligent guess based on heuristics for shifting to a weaker bias.

The problem of selecting the initial bias is customarily solved by the researcher. On the basis of the experience of this author and several colleagues, it can be stated

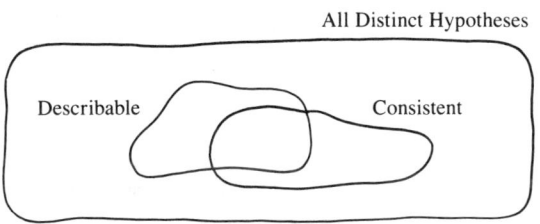

Figure 5-3:   Partitions of the space of all distinct hypotheses.

that the first choice for the bias will be incorrect. In the absence of a mechanism for correctly selecting an initial bias, the problem of shifting to a better bias will remain important. Human researchers can do a better job of choosing a bias on subsequent trials because they have learned something from the previous failures. Thus the problem of shifting to a new bias differs from the problem of initially selecting a bias because one shifts to a different bias with the added knowledge of those biases that have failed in the past.

Consider an example heuristic that corresponds to Vere's technique (1980) for constructing counterfactual descriptions:

> *If the description language does not contain a consistent description, then construct a new consistent description that is a counterfactual of existing descriptions.*

The heuristic relies on existing descriptions in the restricted hypothesis space, the training instances, and the set-difference operator " $-$ " to determine the classifications of unobserved instances. For example, one could define a new concept "negative number" as "a number that is not positive."

5.2.3.2 Translating Recommendations into New Concept Descriptions

The second step of the framework is to translate the recommendations into new descriptions within the formalism of the concept description language. The recommendations are received as input from step 1. The new descriptions are given as output to step 3.

The recommendations specify new descriptive capability to add to the description language. Step 1 uses a second language, a *recommendation language,* to specify new concepts that should become part of the concept description language. A recommendation is not itself part of the description language because a recommendation corresponds to descriptive capability that is not yet in the existing concept description language. A necessary step for acting on a recommendation is the identification of corresponding concepts that are describable in the formalism of the description language. The approach used in the framework is to translate each recommendation into one or more descriptions expressed in the formalism of the description language.

Again consider the counterfactual example. Suppose there is a recommendation to add a new concept "negative number," defined as "a number that is not positive." The recommendation may be of the form "add a new description N such that $N = R - P$," where R is the set of real numbers and P is the set of positive numbers. The description language may not contain the set difference operator " $-$." If " $-$ " is not in the description language, then one or more translation steps could be used to remove it from the " $R - P$ " part of the specification. One step could be to translate " $R - P$ " to " $R \cap \sim P$." A second step could be to evaluate " $\sim P$ " with a function that computes a complementary description within the formalism of the language. A third step could be to evaluate the intersection of " R " and the result of evaluating

" $\sim P$." By performing such translation steps, one can compute descriptions that are expressed in the formalism of the description language. Translation of unusable knowledge into usable knowledge via equivalence-maintaining transformations has been pursued by Mostow (1983) and by Keller (1983)

5.2.3.3 Assimilating New Concepts into the Hypothesis Space

The third and final step of the framework is to assimilate new descriptions expressed in the formalism of the description language into the space of hypotheses. The new descriptions are received as input from step 2.

Assimilation is essential because new descriptions must be made available to the concept-learning program while the integrity of the existing concept description language is maintained. For any new concept to become part of the description language, some change to the description language is necessary. In the framework, the concept learner *assimilates* a new concept by adding it to the restricted space of hypotheses that is searched by the concept learner.

There are two major problems:

1. *How* does one assimilate a new description? The mechanics depend on the formalism of the description language. For example, for a partially ordered space of descriptions, assimilating a new description corresponds to defining one or more new subset links between the new description and existing, more general descriptions. That is, a new description x is assimilated as a specialization of existing description y by asserting $x \subset y$.

2. *Where* in the description language does one assimilate a new description? This too depends on the organization of the hypothesis space. For example, for a partially ordered space of descriptions, deciding which sets are immediately more general than a new description is a nontrivial problem. Because a concept to be assimilated is not yet in the description language, one needs to be able to evaluate subset relationships based not on subset links and matching but instead on the definition of the new concept.

As an example, again consider the problem of assimilating a new description that originated from the construction of a counterfactual description. Assume that the space of hypotheses is organized by a partial order on the subset relation. How would one go about assimilating a new concept N defined as the set of negative numbers? If the definition of N was derived through translation by evaluating $R - P$, then it is known that $R - P \subset R$. N could then be assimilated by asserting $N \subset R$.

5.3 STABB: A Program That Shifts Bias

STABB (Shift To A Better Bias) is a program consisting of two procedures designed according to the framework described in section 5.2. One procedure is called *least disjunction,* the other, *constraint back-propagation.* STABB was incorporated into the existing LEX program (Mitchell, 1983), thereby giving LEX the ability to shift its bias. (STABB is presented in greater detail in Utgoff, 1984.)

5.3.1 Overview of LEX

LEX is a concept-learning program that creates and refines heuristics that suggest whether a given operator would be applied to a given problem state in a forward-search problem solver. Associated with each operator is a heuristic that represents the concept "set of states to which this operator *should* be applied." The problem for the concept learner is to determine this set correctly for each operator.

LEX learns heuristics in the domain of integral calculus. The program is initially given a set of problem-solving operators. Each operator has a domain of states to which the operator can be applied, a rewrite rule, and a range of states that can be produced by application of the operator. For each operator, the domain of applicability describes states to which the operator *can* be applied. In contrast, for each heuristic, the domain of applicability describes states to which the associated operator *should* be applied.

As shown in figure 5-4, LEX is a system that generates problems, solves problems, criticizes solutions, and learns heuristics that guide the problem solver to solutions of future problems with fewer wasted search steps. The generalizer is the module that does the actual concept learning by eliminating inconsistent hypotheses. STABB was added to LEX by modifying the generalizer so that, when no currently available hypothesis is consistent with the training instances, the generalizer invokes STABB to shift LEX to a new bias.

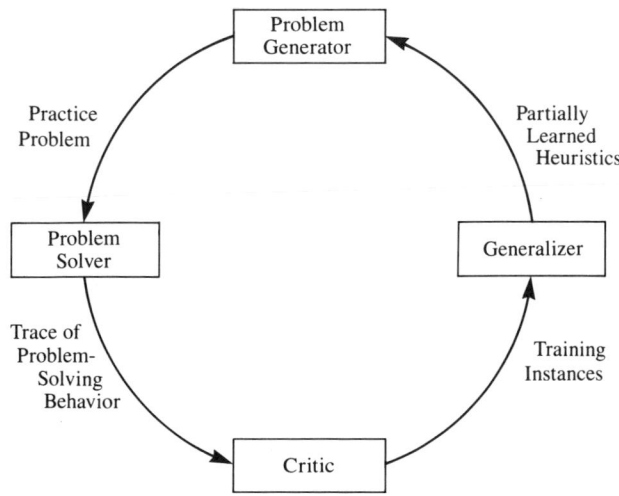

Figure 5-4:   Top-level flow of control in LEX.

The problem solver solves a problem by forward search until a state is produced that contains no integral. The critic then criticizes the solution tree that was produced by the forward search. For each operator application *along* the minimum cost solution path, the critic labels the operator application a *positive* instance showing a state to which the given operator should be applied. For each operator application that leads *away* from the minimum cost solution path, the critic labels the operator application a *negative* instance showing a state to which the given operator should not be applied. The critic then passes the set of training instances to the generalizer so the generalizer can update the heuristics being learned for the operators. For each heuristic, the generalizer uses Mitchell's candidate elimination algorithm to maintain a version space of all candidate versions of the heuristic that have not been refuted. If a version space becomes empty, then all hypotheses in the restricted space of hypotheses are inconsistent. That is the criterion used by STABB for determining when to move to a different bias. At that point, LEX calls STABB.

5.3.1.1 Description Language

Although LEX learns a heuristic for each operator, it has a single concept description language. In the one language there is need to be able to describe any heuristic that is to be learned.

LEX's description language uses the formalism of a context-free grammar. Customarily, grammars are used to specify a language of terminal sentences. As such, the set of all terminal strings defines the *instance language,* or the set of all describable instances. To define the concept description language, LEX uses a grammar, but the language consists of *all* sentential forms, nonterminal or terminal. A sentential form that contains only terminal symbols is a description of an instance in the domain and simultaneously a description of the singleton set that contains that instance. A sentential form that contains a nonterminal symbol is a description of a set of instances in the domain. For example, in the LEX grammar the nonterminal trig describes the set {sin, cos, tan, csc, sec, cot}, where trig is a nonterminal and each of sin, cos, tan, csc, sec, and cot is a terminal. The complete LEX grammar is shown in figure 5-5.

There are three points to note regarding LEX's grammar:

1. LEX uses a less familiar mathematical notation for function combinations. If $f(x) = g(x)$ OP $h(x)$, where OP is some combining operator such as " $+$," then one can also refer to the function using combined name $(g$ OP $h)$. For example, for sin$(x) + $ cos(x), the combined name would be (sin $+$ cos) or, using LEX's grammar, ($+$ sin cos). This was done for simplicity so that the argument variable, in this case x, appears only once in the expression, whatever the expression may be.

2. There are three descriptions—afr, r, and knmz—for which *recognition predicates* are defined. A recognition predicate is an algorithmic recognizer for the

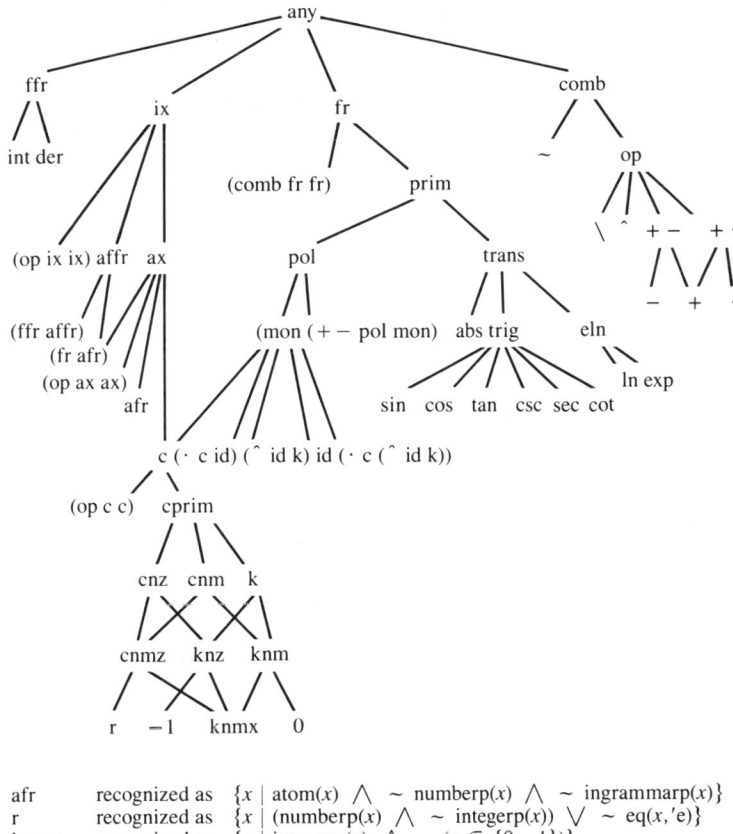

afr	recognized as	$\{x \mid atom(x) \land \sim numberp(x) \land \sim ingrammarp(x)\}$
r	recognized as	$\{x \mid (numberp(x) \land \sim integerp(x)) \lor \sim eq(x,'e)\}$
knmz	recognized as	$\{x \mid integerp(x) \land \sim (x \in \{0, -1\})\}$

Figure 5-5: LEX grammar for integral calculus.

elements of a given set. The predicate is true if and only if the argument is recognized as belonging to the given set. LEX uses selected recognition predicates for efficiency to take advantage of parsing already done by the LISP interpreter. Thus the vocabulary of symbols consists of LISP atoms and lists, not single characters. For all x such that recognition predicate (x), there is effectively a grammar rule "recognition predicate $\Rightarrow x$." In particular, the following rules apply:

    a. Something is an afr if and only if it is a nonnumeric atom that is not used explicitly elsewhere in the grammar.

    b. Something is an r if and only if it is a noninteger number or the atom e (Euler's constant).

    c. Something is a knmz if and only if it is an integer that is neither 0 nor −1.

3. Any nonnumeric symbol may have trailing digits appended to it. For example, the symbol sin can also be given as sin1. The digits are not part of the symbol. Instead, the digits simply make it possible to reference a particular symbol in an expression, for example (+ sin1 (* cos sin2)). LEX can observe or ignore such digits, depending on how it needs to use the expression. For example, when matching descriptions, LEX can ignore the digits. On the other hand, when rewriting a state, LEX can use the digits to insure that it operates on the intended symbols.

5.3.1.2 Matching Two Descriptions

The ability to determine whether one description is more general than or equal to another is central to many concept-learning algorithms. At a basic level is the classification task of determining whether an instance, a description of a singleton set, is included in a given concept. For many learning algorithms there is a need to determine whether one concept, not necessarily a singleton set, is included in another. The candidate elimination algorithm that LEX uses to maintain the version space for each heuristic specifically requires a matching predicate that tests the "more general than" relation.

For LEX, a description **a** is more general than or equal to a description **b** if and only if **a** grammatically derives **b** or **a** derives a sentential form within **b**. If description **a** derives **b**, then **a** matches *onto* **b**. If description **a** derives a sentential form properly within **b**, then **a** matches *into* **b**. For matching, LEX uses a function **match(a, b, flags)** that returns a list of derivation trees showing how **a** matches **b**. The flags argument is not pertinent to the discussion here. If **a** is not more general than **b**, then the match function returns a null list. For example, cos is more general than (+ sin cos) because cos grammatically derives (in zero steps) the cos within (+ sin cos). As a second example, trig is more general than (+ sin cos) in two ways. First, trig derives sin. Second, trig derives cos.

5.3.1.3 Operator Language

Each operator consists of the following set of items:

LHS	A concept description for the domain of the operator
RHS	A concept description for the range of the operator
FORWARD	A LISP expression that, when evaluated, computes the values for all atoms in RHS that are not used in LHS

BACKWARD   A LISP expression that, when evaluated, computes the values
            for all atoms in LHS that are not used in RHS

COMMENT   A description in English of what the operator does

The domain and range of each operator are describable in the concept description language. The operator may be applied in the forward or backward direction. This does not mean that every operator has an inverse. What it does mean is that for the *set* of states in the domain for one direction of the operator, the mechanics exist for defining how to compute the *set* of states in the range for that direction of the operator.

Some operator applications require calculation of new values. An example of one that does not require calculation is commutation, (* fr1 fr2) $\Rightarrow$ (* fr2 fr1), because all symbols in the range are bound in the domain. In general, extra calculation is necessary only when symbols are used in the range that are not bound in the domain. Note that the ability to provide each operator with a procedure for calculating values to be used in the range gives the operator language the full power of the LISP interpreter.

5.3.2 Least Disjunction: A Goal-Free Method

Least disjunction is one of the two procedures used by STABB. The procedure is designed according to the framework presented in section 5.2. The procedure uses the observed positive and negative training instances and the existing description language as inputs. The method does not make use of the learning goal; that is, it does not use the fact that the purpose of the learning is to find a domain of applicability for which the operator should be applied. The method only considers the observed instances as syntactic entities. As such the method is *goal free.*

The procedure shifts bias by adding a new concept description to the concept description language. The constructed description is equivalent to a least-specific disjunctive description that is consistent with the training instances.

5.3.2.1 Recommending a Better Bias

To recommend a better bias, the procedure employs the following heuristic:

If a consistent description is needed, then construct a least-specific disjunction of existing descriptions.

The motivation for building a new description from existing descriptions is that the existing descriptions probably already describe concepts that are useful in the domain. The reason for using a least-specific (most-general) form is that the most-specific form is exactly the set of positive instances, and the corresponding inference is therefore that all unobserved instances are negative instances. Defining a new description as a disjunction of existing descriptions allows the classification information in the existing descriptions to be incorporated into the new description.

The least disjunction procedure calculates a specification of a new concept by searching for a least-specific disjunction that is consistent with the training instances.

A least disjunction is a disjunction of minimally specific descriptions in the language such that each disjunct covers as many positive instances as possible without covering any negative instances, and every positive instance is covered by at least one of the disjuncts. A least disjunction is computed in four steps:

1. Create an initial disjunctive description that is the set of positive training instances. The set of positive training instances is the most-specific disjunctive description, and it is always consistent with the training instances, by definition. This fact guarantees that the least disjunction procedure can always find a new consistent description.

2. Search for all generalizations of the disjuncts that produce descriptions that are more general than *some* of the positive training instances but not more general than any of the negative instances. This generation step is done in a straightforward manner by efficient generation of combinations of two or more disjuncts, coupled with pruning of paths that produce inconsistent generalizations.

3. From the resulting list of generalizations (concept descriptions), eliminate any concept description that is more specific or equal to some other description in the list. The purpose of this step is to remove any description that is not needed in the disjunctive description being constructed.

4. Remove those embedding expressions of each disjunct that are identical for all the disjuncts. This step is included because all the disjuncts may share some single common context. If the disjunctive description under construction is to be as general as possible, any such common context must be discarded. The removal of such common context embodies a secondary heuristic:

> *If a concept is useful in one context, then it may also be useful in another context.*

For example, assume that the previous three steps produced a disjunctive description $\int x \cdot \sin(x) \cdot dx \lor \int x \mid \cos(x) \cdot dx$. Then, in this step, the procedure would remove the common context $\int x \cdot \ldots (x) \cdot dx$ from each disjunct, leaving sin $\lor$ cos. The mechanism for doing this step is as follows:

   a. Align the disjuncts according to how the domain of the operator matched each disjunctive term.

   b. For each disjunct, delete all embedding expressions of the disjunct that occur identically in *all* the disjuncts.

5.3.2.2 Translating Recommendations into New Concept Descriptions

The second step of the least disjunction procedure is to translate the disjunctive description, recommended by the first step, into a description using the formalism of the LEX description language. Specifically, it is necessary to create a new description that does not use the disjunction operator $\vee$ required for describing a least disjunction. The procedure does this simply by creating a new symbol for the vocabulary and then defining the new symbol as more general than each of the disjuncts in the disjunctive description. In the LEX grammar, this step corresponds to creating a new symbol NS and then for each disjunct d_i adding a new grammar rule NS $\Rightarrow$ d_i to the grammar that defines the concept description language. For example, to translate the new description sin $\vee$ cos, the procedure could create a new symbol, say, N16S, and then add two new grammar rules N16S $\Rightarrow$ sin and N16S $\Rightarrow$ cos. As a result of translation, the new concept is describable without explicit disjunction because the disjunction is implied by the grammar rules.

5.3.2.3 Assimilating New Concepts into the Hypothesis Space

The third step of the least disjunction procedure is to assimilate new descriptions, created by the second step, into the LEX description language. During the translation step, a new description NS was created by defining grammar rules from NS to other descriptions in the concept description language. The new description NS is not yet part of the description language, however, because NS itself is not yet derivable in the grammar.

The least disjunction procedure assimilates a new description NS in two steps:

1. Define a set of descriptions **mg** that consists of the most specific descriptions in the description language that are more general than *all* the disjuncts used to define the new concept NS. Each such description includes one or more negative instances, but that is all right; the objective is to splice the new description into the description language. For example, in the case of sin $\vee$ cos, the set **mg** is {trig}.

2. For each description mg_i, add a new grammar rule $mg_i \Rightarrow$ NS to the grammar. For example, as shown in figure 5-6 when **mg** is {trig}, assimilation is completed by adding the grammar rule trig $\Rightarrow$ N16S.

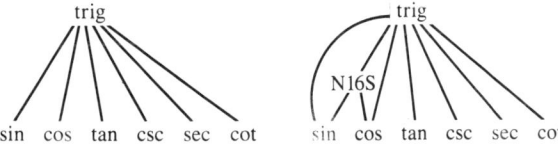

Figure 5-6:   Bias before and after shift.

5.3.2.4 Requirements

Three conditions must be met in order to guarantee that the least disjunction method can construct and assimilate a new concept description:

1. Every concept containing exactly one instance must be in the concept description language. This insures that it is always possible to construct a consistent disjunctive description.

2. The concept containing every instance must be in the description language. This insures that there will always be a description that is more general than any constructed disjunctive description.

3. There must be a method for asserting the "subset" predicate for two descriptions. This is necessary so that assimilation of a new description can be effected.

5.3.2.5 Experiment

Mathematical expressions are shown below in standard Leibniz notation. LEX was given three problems: $\int x \cdot \sin(x) \cdot dx$, $\int x \cdot \cos(x) \cdot dx$, and $\int x \cdot \tan(x) \cdot dx$. For the first problem, $\int x \cdot \sin(x) \cdot dx$, the problem solver found the solution shown in figure 5-7. The generalizer then refined the heuristic for op12, integration-by-parts, by using $\int x \cdot \sin(x) \cdot dx$ as a positive instance. The resulting version space was as follows:

G: $\{\int f(x) \cdot g(x) \cdot dx; u = f(x); dv = g(x) \cdot dx\}$
S: $\{\int x \cdot \sin(x) \cdot dx; u = x; dv = \sin(x) \cdot dx\}$

A version space is an efficient representation of all descriptions in the description language that are consistent with the training instances. All that needs to be stored explicitly is the set **G** of most-general consistent descriptions and the set **S** of most-specific consistent descriptions. All other consistent descriptions are stored implicitly between the boundaries.

$$\int x \cdot \sin(x) \cdot dx; \ u{=}x; \ dv{=}\sin(x) \cdot dx$$

op12: $\int u \cdot dv \Rightarrow u \cdot v - \int v \cdot du$

$$-x \cdot \cos(x) - \int -\cos(x) \cdot dx$$

op3: $\int c \cdot f(x) \cdot dx \Rightarrow c \cdot \int f(x) \cdot dx$

$$-x \cdot \cos(x) + \int \cos(x) \cdot dx$$

op10: $\int \cos(x) \cdot dx \Rightarrow \sin(x)$

$$-x \cdot \cos(x) + \sin(x)$$

Figure 5-7: Solution for $\int x \cdot \sin(x) \cdot dx$ using integration-by-parts.

LEX solved the second problem, $\int x \cdot \cos(x) \cdot dx$, also by starting with op12. LEX's generalizer updated the version space for op12 to the following:

G: $\{\int f(x) \cdot g(x) \cdot dx; u = f(x); dv = g(x) \cdot dx\}$
S: $\{\int x \cdot \text{trig}(x) \cdot dx; u = x; dv = \text{trig}(x) \cdot dx\}$

When LEX tackled the third problem, $\int x \cdot \tan(x) \cdot dx$, it tried to use the integration-by-parts approach as it did for the first two problems, but it did not work. As a result, the critic identified use of op12 on the state $\int x \cdot \tan(x) \cdot dx$ as a negative instance. The bias in the existing language prohibited the generalizer from finding a consistent description that could include sin and cos but exclude tan. Accordingly, STABB was called to shift LEX's bias.

The control strategy of STABB is first to try the constraint back-propagation procedure described below in section 5.3.3. That procedure does not always produce a recommendation. If constraint back-propagation does not recommend a shift, then STABB tries the least disjunction procedure, which can always recommend a new consistent description. In this experiment, the constraint back-propagation procedure did not produce a recommendation for a shift, so STABB used the least disjunction procedure.

The least disjunction procedure took the following steps:

1. Recommend that a description equivalent to sin $\vee$ cos be added to the description language.
2. Translate the recommendation that sin $\vee$ cos be describable into a new description N16S defined as being more general than sin and cos.
3. Assimilate the new concept N16S as more specific than trig.

Figure 5-6 shows the relevant portion of LEX's description language before and after the shift to the weaker bias. Following the shift, LEX reinitialized the version space for op12 and then reprocessed the training instances. After the training instances were reprocessed, the version space for op12 was as follows:

G: $\{\int f(x) \cdot N16S(x) \cdot dx; u = f(x); dv = N16S(x) \cdot dx\}$
S: $\{\int x \cdot N16S(x) \cdot dx; u = x; dv = N16S(x) \cdot dx\}$

5.3.2.6 Language Shift and Version Spaces

In general, it is necessary to adjust the version space boundary sets after the shift to a new bias. Recall that version space boundary sets are a compact representation of the set of all consistent hypotheses in a given description language. If the description language is enriched by the addition of new descriptions, the version space is *not* guaranteed to represent the set of *all* consistent hypotheses in the new language. It is only guaranteed to represent the set of all consistent hypotheses in the *old* language. There may be consistent descriptions in the enriched language that are incorrectly excluded from the version space that was calculated with the unenriched language. For this reason it is necessary to compute a new version space in the enriched language. An obvious method, the one used by STABB, is simply to start over and reprocess all the training instances.

An important ramification of shifting the concept description language is that the version spaces for the other heuristics, computed in the old language, may be affected as well. Even though the version spaces for the other heuristics are not empty (i.e., there are consistent descriptions), shift of the language removes the guarantee that the version spaces contain all consistent descriptions describable in the language. Thus it is necessary to recompute the version spaces for *all* the heuristics.

5.3.2.7 Obsolete Descriptions: Strengthening Bias

One problem that occurs with the least disjunction procedure is creation of descriptions that later become obsolete. For example, in subsequent activity a new description N17S, defined as more general than N16S and exp, was constructed and added to the concept description language. The creation of N17S to describe the heuristic for op12 rendered N16S unnecessary. That is, the original justification for the creation of N16S—to enable one to describe the heuristic of op12—was no longer present. This raises the problem of discarding obsolete descriptions, a form of strengthening bias. How does one identify a stronger bias? Three possible approaches are as follows:

1. Keep track of *why* a description was created. For example, one could associate with N16S the fact that it was created so that the heuristic for op12 would be describable. If the justification for the existence of a description becomes invalid, in this case that N16S ceases to be used in the description of the heuristic for op12, one could then remove the description (assuming no other justification exists—e.g., the description is not in use in describing some other heuristic). Thus, when N17S is created and N16S is no longer used to describe the heuristic for op12, the existence of N16S would no longer be justified.

2. As suggested by Banerji (Ranan Banerji, personal communication, 1984), associate with each description the number of places in which the concept learner currently uses it. A program could automatically discard descriptions that fall below some specified usage.

3. Conduct a search for candidate descriptions in the description language that can be removed from the language without causing any version space computed in such a language to be empty. This is uninteresting for any single version space because any candidate description can be eliminated as easily as another. For multiple version spaces based on a single description language, however, as in the case of LEX, the problem is interesting. One would attempt to search for a further restricted description language that would result in the overall smallest nonempty version spaces for all the heuristics.

5.3.2.8 Choosing Among Syntactic Methods

In the experiment above, a counterfactual method could have recommended a new concept "trig except tan." The least disjunction method recommended a new concept "sin or cos." There is no apparent advantage to either one. If the concept learner had some idea or clue about the syntactic properties of the target concept, then there might possibly be a criterion for preferring one method to another, but such a criterion is extremely weak.

Descriptions that are not based on *why* an instance is either positive or negative do not capture the essence of a concept. A disjunctive description that is a list of disjoined positive instances describes only that they are positive, *not* why they are. Similarly, a counterfactual description that is a list of excepted negative instances describes only that they are excepted, not why they are.

As an example, consider the problem of making the inductive leap that positive instance $\{2,4,6,8\}$ and negative instances $\{1,3,5,7\}$ are indicative of the set of even integers. Assume that there is a description for the set of integers but no subclasses of integers. Consider four possible descriptions:

1. Syntactic via disjunction: $2 \lor 4 \lor 6 \lor 8$
2. Syntactic via counterfactual: $(((\text{integers} \ \& \sim 1) \ \& \sim 3) \ \& \sim 5) \ \& \sim 7$
3. Analytic via division: $\{x \mid \text{remainder}(x,2) = 0\}$
4. Analytic via binary: $\{x \mid \text{logicaland}(x,1) = 0\}$

Syntactic methods are useful because they can lead to descriptions of useful sets. A preferable approach, however, is to attempt to draw on information that can drive an analytic method, for example, constraint back-propagation.

5.3.3 Constraint Back-Propagation: A Goal-Sensitive Method

Constraint back-propagation (Utgoff, 1982) is the other of the two procedures used by STABB. The procedure is designed according to the framework described in section 5.2. Unlike the least disjunction procedure, constraint back-propagation takes advantage of the fact that the concepts to be learned describe when and when not to apply given operators. In addition to the training instances and the description language, the procedure also uses a set of backward problem-solving operators, a description of the set of solved problems, and the solution sequence from which the training instances were extracted to help determine a shift to a new bias. As such, the method is *goal sensitive.*

5.3.3.1 Recommending a Better Bias

When LEX cannot find a consistent description to describe the domain of a heuristic, instead of examining individual training instances, the procedure analyzes a solution sequence for which the operator application was a positive instance to determine how to adjust LEX's bias. Each constructed description describes a constrained set that is needed to describe the constrained domain of the operator sequence. By deducing the domain of an operator sequence such that application of the operator sequence to a state in the domain will produce a solution, the procedure can identify useful new concepts to add to the description language.

To recommend a better bias, the procedure employs the following heuristic:

> *If an operator sequence leads to a solution, then create a new concept description that describes the domain of the operator sequence.*

This heuristic is chosen because of the a priori knowledge that the recommended domain of applicability for a given operator is the union of the domains of all useful operator sequences that start with a given operator. To describe the union, one can start by being able to describe identifiable subsets in that union.

To compute a specification of the domain of an operator sequence that produces a state in a given range, in this case the set of solved problems, one applies a deduction procedure known as *constraint propagation* or *goal regression*. Propagation of constraints through an operator sequence is a well-known technique; what is new in STABB is the use of constraint propagation as a heuristic method for identifying new concepts that should be describable in the description language. The STRIPS program (Fikes, Hart, and Nilsson, 1972) computes preconditions for macro-operators by reasoning about constraints. Waldinger's program for achieving simultaneous goals (Waldinger, 1976) uses goal regression to deduce a restricted domain of an operator such that application of the operator to a state in the restricted domain is guaranteed to produce a state in an intended restricted range. Stallman and Sussman's EL (Stallman and Sussman, 1977) computes values at various points in electrical circuits by reasoning from known values, a procedure analogous to solving a system of simultaneous equations. Stefik's MOLGEN (Stefik, 1980) plans experiments in molecular genetics. Whenever constraints become known or specialized during the planning process, actions that are inconsistent with the constraints are eliminated. The CRITTER program (Kelley and Steinberg, 1982) uses constraint propagation to reason about digital circuits. From a statement of output specifications and definitions of components in a circuit, the program deduces input specifications of one component and propagates them backward through the rest of the components in the circuit.

Constraint back-propagation is a procedure for deducing the domain of an operator sequence or macro-operator that produces some constrained range of states. The constraint back-propagation function, **cbp,** used by STABB is as follows:

```
cbp(seq) =
{ if length(seq)==0
    then
      solved
```

```
        else
          abop(head(seq),inter(dom(head(seq)),cbp(tail(seq))))
}
with abbreviations:
cbp             constraint-back-propagation
seq             operator-sequence
abop            apply-backward-operator
head            first-element-of-list
inter           set-intersection
dom             domain-description-of-operator
solved          set-of-all-solved-states
tail            list-with-first-element-removed
```

If an operator sequence *opseq* is of length 1, it means that the operator produced a *solved* problem. By intersecting the set of all solved problems, described by ax in the LEX grammar, with the range of the forward operator, the procedure calculates the subset of the range containing solved problems. As shown in figure 5-8, by applying the backward version of the operator to the subset, the procedure calculates a constrained domain of the forward operator such that application of the forward operator to any state in the constrained domain produces a solved problem. If an operator sequence is of length greater than 1, it means that the tail of the operator sequence produced a solved problem. By applying constraint back-propagation to the tail of the sequence, the procedure calculates a constrained domain for the tail. That constrained domain describes the set of states for which the tail of the sequence leads to a solved problem. As such, the constrained domain for the tail of the sequence can be intersected with the range of the operator at the head of the list, and the backward version of the operator at the head of the list can be applied to calculate the constrained domain of the entire sequence.

The constraint back-propagation procedure uses *backward* operators, as opposed to strict inverse operators. An inverse operator by definition undoes the effect of the corresponding operator. An operator that is a one-one or one-many mapping has a functional inverse. An operator that is a many-one or many-many mapping does not have a functional inverse, because there is not a unique value in the domain

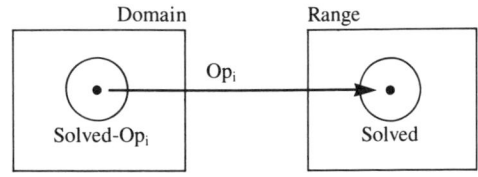

Figure 5-8: Constraint back-propagation.

that maps to the range. A backward operator differs from an inverse operator because it maps a state in the range to the *set* of states in the domain. Thus backward operators map sets of states to other sets of states.

Each LEX operator includes two LISP expressions for computing values as part of the operator application. One of those expressions, FORWARD, is straightforward because the forward operators are written to map a single problem state in the domain of the operator to a single problem state in the range. The other expression, BACKWARD, is of a different nature because it can map a set of states in its domain (the range of the forward operator) to a set of states in its range. Each LISP expression for how to apply the operator in the backward direction must encode how that is to be done. Consider three cases:

1. If no LISP evaluation is needed, as with commutation, $(+ \ fr1 \ fr2) \Leftrightarrow (+ \ fr2 \ fr1)$, then there will be no need to shift bias, because any description in the domain of the backward operator is immediately describable in the range of the backward operator.

2. If some LISP evaluation is required but the result of applying the backward operator is a single state, then the state is describable in the range of the backward operator.

3. If some LISP evaluation is required and the result of applying the backward operator is a set of states, then the operator calls a function named **look-up-or-make**. The **look-up-or-make** function constructs a recognition predicate, based on the LISP evaluation that is to be applied to the argument of the recognition predicate and the constrained set in which the result must be included if the argument is to be considered recognized. If a recognition predicate based on these two arguments already exists, then the corresponding symbol in the description language is returned. If such a recognition predicate does not exist, it is created and associated with a new symbol, assimilated into the description language (described below), and returned.

Consider an example. There is an operator op99c $\Rightarrow 2 \cdot (c/2)$, where c is any real number. The procedure is given the task of propagating $2 \cdot k$ backward through op99, where k is the set of integers. The intersection of $2 \cdot (c/2)$ and $2 \cdot k$ evaluates to $2 \cdot k$. If $2 \cdot k$ is passed through op99[backward], the constrained domain of the forward operator must be the set of numbers in which each is equivalent to 2 multiplied by some integer, that is, the even numbers. The set of even integers is, of course, a proper subset of the set of real numbers. This illustration is continued in the next two sections.

Although implementation of each of the three steps of the framework of section 5.2 is described separately below, the three steps are actually done for each operator in turn, as the constraints back-propagate through the solution sequence. That is, there can be a shift of bias via recommendation, translation, and assimilation at each step in the operator sequence.

5.3.3.2 Translating Recommendations into New Concept Descriptions

Step 2 of the constraint back-propagation procedure is to translate the recommendations produced by step 1 into descriptions using the formalism of the LEX description language. The **cbp** function manipulates expressions consisting not only of descriptions in LEX's description language but also of calls to the **intersection** function and to backward operator definitions. To translate such recommendations into LEX descriptions, the procedure must remove all references to intersection and backward operators. Such references are translated by evaluation. Thus the procedure depends on being able to evaluate the intersection of two descriptions and on being able to apply a backward operator. Certain backward operators were difficult to implement for LEX, for example, the backward operator for integration-by-parts. Any time that an intersection cannot be calculated or a backward operator cannot be applied, the procedure fails in the translation step.

New descriptions are created during the translation process when necessary. For example, applying op99^{backward} to $2 \cdot k$ requires creation of a description for the set of even integers. If the description of a constrained domain is computed by an operation found only in an operator, for example, multiplication, then the translation procedure constructs a new description in the form of a recognition predicate. In general, for some set $\mathbf{w}$ computed as $\mathbf{w} = f^{backward}(y)$, the corresponding recognition predicate is $\{x \mid \text{match}(y, f(x))\}$. The predicate defines those elements to which one can apply the operation and produce a result that satisfies the constraint. For example, for a description of the set in which each element is equivalent to $2 \cdot k$, for some k, the corresponding recognition predicate is $\{x \mid \text{match}('k, [x/2])\}$. The procedure creates a new description by generating a new symbol NS for the vocabulary of the language and then associating the definition of the new recognition predicate with the new symbol by adding a grammar rule of the form NS $\Rightarrow$ new-recognition-predicate.

Creation of a new definition for a recognition predicate does not necessarily mean that a new description will be incorporated into the concept description language. When a new definition is created, the translation algorithm first searches for a concept in the language with the same definition. Here, *same* means "syntactically equal"; testing functional equivalence is a classical nontrivial problem. However, because the procedure generates recognition predicates in only one way, any attempt to create a second identical definition will be thwarted by this test.

In addition to application of backward operators, there is the problem of evaluating intersection of descriptions. Intersection is evaluated with the following algorithm:

```
Intersection(x,y) =
If Match(x,y) then y,
  else
```

```
If Match(y,x) then x,
  else Most-General (Intersection(Next-More-Specific(x),y) ∪
                     Intersection(x,Next-More-Specific(y)))
```

Most-General is a function that returns the most general descriptions from its argument, and **Next-More-Specific** is a function that returns those descriptions in the language that are immediately more specific than the argument. When **Intersection** returns more than one description, then the intersection is the disjunction of those descriptions and the disjunction is not describable in the description language. For example, **Intersection**(sin,(+ trig (+ ℓn fr))) returns (+ trig (+ ℓn sin)) ∨ (+ sin (+ ℓn fr)) due to the multiple ways in which sin can specialize (+ trig (+ ℓn fr)) at trig or fr. Disjunction is not a problem, however, because the routines within the least disjunction procedure (section 5.3.2) can be called to translate and assimilate a disjunctive description.

5.3.3.3 Assimilating New Concepts into the Hypothesis Space

Step 3 of the constraint back-propagation procedure is to assimilate new descriptions, created by step 2, into the LEX description language. To assimilate a new description NS, the procedure must add the new description NS to the concept description language. Those concepts that are more specific than NS are well defined by the recognition predicate created during translation in step 2. The concept NS is not yet part of the language, however, because NS is not itself yet derivable in the grammar.

The constraint back-propagation procedure assimilates a new description NS by adding a new grammar rule of the form d ⇒ NS. The description d is the unconstrained description that was used in the domain of the corresponding operator. For example, for op99, the operator rewrites c as 2 · [c/2]. When a new description for even integers, say N22S, is assimilated, the new grammar rule would be c ⇒ N22S.

Using a description in an operator's domain as the generalization of the new description has two drawbacks, as follows:

1. Although the method does not incorrectly assert any subset relation, it is nevertheless weak because it does not assert all correct subset relations. For example, it is not incorrect to assert that the set of even integers is a specialization of the set of real numbers, but the assertion is weak because it does not tell the whole story. It would be much stronger to assert that the set of even integers is a specialization of the set of integers.

2. With this assimilation method, the extent to which the domain of an operator is large (general) is the extent to which the proper point of assimilation is poorly specified. A program author will want to write operators in as general a form as possible to maximize the number of legal transformations available to the problem solver. The task of assimilating a new concept description into a

partially ordered hierarchy of descriptions is done properly by making a new description immediately more specific than the most specific existing descriptions possible.

5.3.3.4 Requirements

Four conditions must be met in order to guarantee that the constraint back-propagation method can construct and assimilate a new concept description:

1. A description of the set of solved states is needed so that the procedure can intersect the range of an operator with the set of solved states to compute the set of solved states that can be produced by the operator.

2. A function to compute the intersection of two descriptions is necessary so that the range of an operator can be constrained as necessary. The case of intersecting the range of an operator with the set of solved problems is necessary so that application of the backward operator to the constrained range will lead to a constrained domain that describes the set of states "solved by application op_i."

3. For each operator, a definition of how to apply the operator in the backward direction is needed so that a constrained domain can be calculated by application of the operator.

4. For any operator that includes arithmetic computation, or other kinds of computation not modeled in the grammar, it is necessary that such computations be capable of being incorporated in a concept description.

5.3.3.5 Experiment

LEX found a solution for $\int \cos^7(x) \cdot dx$ similar[1] to that shown in figure 5-9. LEX was then given $\int \cos^6(x) \cdot dx$ for which the same solution failed and $\int \cos^5(x) \cdot dx$ for which the same solution worked. The description language did not contain a description that both included $\int \cos^7(x) \cdot dx$ and $\int \cos^5(x) \cdot dx$ and excluded $\int \cos^6(x) \cdot dx$. LEX called STABB to shift the bias so that the language could describe the heuristic for op51. STABB tried the constraint back-propagation procedure, and the back-propagation should have proceeded as shown in figure 5-10. However, one step was too difficult for the intersection algorithm, discussed below. Otherwise, the method worked.

STABB correctly handled the last two steps of the back-propagation sequence (first two steps of the solution sequence). In $\int (\cos^2(x))^k) \cdot \cos(x) \cdot dx$, the exponent k denotes that the exponent must be an integer. This constraint propagated earlier

---

[1]LEX does not have a multiply-polynomial operator, so the actual solution sequence was bizarre.

$\int \cos^7 (x) \cdot dx$

$\downarrow$ op51: $f^c \Rightarrow f^{[c-1]} \cdot f$

$\int \cos^6(x) \cdot \cos(x) \cdot dx$

$\downarrow$ op50: $f^c \Rightarrow (f^2)^{[c/2]}$

$\int (\cos^2(x))^3 \cdot \cos(x) \cdot dx$

$\downarrow$ op52: $\cos^2 \Rightarrow 1 - \sin^2$

$\int (1 - \sin^2(x))^3 \cdot \cos(x) \cdot dx$

$\downarrow$ op43: $\int f^c(g(x)) \cdot g'(x) \cdot dx \Rightarrow \int f^c(u) \cdot du;$
$\quad u = g(x)$

$\int (1 - u^2)^3 \cdot du,\ u = \sin(x)$

$\downarrow$ multiply polynomial

Figure 5-9:   Solution for $\int \cos^7(x) \cdot dx$.

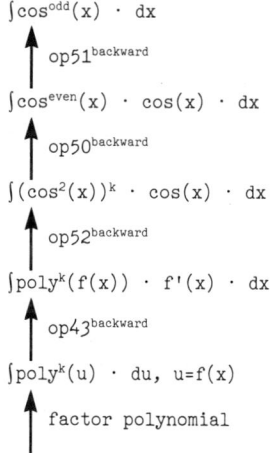

Figure 5-10:   Back-propagation for $\int \cos^7(x) \cdot dx$.

from the fact that the solution sequence works only if the polynomial can be multiplied out to remove the exponent. Back-propagation of the product of the set of integers k and 2 from the $\cos^2$ through the exponent in $op^{backward}50$ caused a new description to be created for the set of even integers, that is, the set of elements such that each element is the product of some integer and 2. Prior to this shift of bias, LEX could not describe the set of even integers. Back-propagation of the set of even integers through the exponent in $op^{backward}51$ caused a new description to be created for the set of odd integers, that is, the set of elements in which each is the difference of some even integer and 1. Prior to this shift of bias, LEX could not describe the set of odd integers.

These two shifts benefit LEX not only by enabling it to describe the heuristics for op51 and op50 but also by allowing it to consider and describe heuristics for future learning problems as well. For example, there is a similar solution method for problems of the form $\int \sin^{\text{odd}}(x) \cdot dx$.

The definition constructed for "even integer" was $\{x \mid \text{match}('k, [x/2])\}$. Because op50 is defined to operate on any real-valued exponent, the new concept was assimilated as a specialization of real. The new concept should have been assimilated as a specialization of integer. In section 5.3.3.6 below, a method for correct assimilation is discussed.

The third-from-last step in the back-propagation sequence failed. The description that would have propagated through op43^{backward} is $\int \text{poly}^k(f(x)) \cdot f'(x) \cdot dx$. Note that the expression uses $f(x)$ as well as $f'(x)$, indicating that $f'(x)$ is sensitive to the $f(x)$ of the same context. LEX can represent a similar description $\int \text{poly}^k(f(x)) \cdot g(x) \cdot dx$, but it is incapable of describing the constraint that the derivative of $f(x)$ be equal to $g(x) \cdot dx$. That is not a large problem for op43^{backward} if u is an instance of a function, because in such cases the derivative can simply be computed. If u corresponds to some larger set of functions, then the missing constraint—that derivative of $f(x)$ is equal to $g(x) \cdot dx$—cannot be tolerated. When the next propagation step through op52^{backward} is started, the lack of the constraint is fatal. In the experiment, it would be necessary to intersect sin(x) with $\int \text{poly}^k(f(x)) \cdot f'(x) \cdot dx$. There is an intersection, $\int \text{poly}^k(\sin(x)) \cdot \cos(x) \cdot dx$. The intersection algorithm computes trivially that $f \cap \sin$ is sin, but notice that f' must then be cos. LEX's description language (and the intersection function) cannot represent this kind of context sensitivity. This exposes the fact that the formalism, a context-free grammar, is biased against descriptions that include context sensitivity of this kind. This suggests that mechanisms for shift of bias must address choice and change of formalism. The ability to identify exactly those elements of bias that come from a given formalism is an important open research question. One possible solution is to use a bias-free formalism, but that is probably less preferable to using a formalism with a desirable bias. Thus shift of bias may also entail shift of formalism, a little-studied problem.

There are two points to note regarding op50:

1. Op50 is not mathematically correct when the value of function f is negative. Squaring the value of the given function will change a negative value to a positive value, and the principle nth root of a positive real is positive. However, LEX does not have knowledge regarding such limitations on the law of exponents. The experiment shows that STABB was able to define a useful concept "even integer" by deducing a class of problems for which the sequence does work. Application of op50 when the exponent is odd is mathematically illegal

when $f(x)$ has a negative value. LEX applies op50 illegally in such cases and simply cannot progress when, later on in the solution sequence, there is a polynomial raised to a noninteger power. Thus STABB learned about "even integer" from an operator sequence that reached a conclusion only when an exponent was even. An improvement to LEX would be to have it detect mathematical inconsistency in an operator. For example, if LEX could itself identify the mathematical problem with the law of exponents for a negative base and an even exponent, it would have a second method for learning about even integers as well as a method for detecting mathematical inconsistency in op50.

2. Op50 had to be added specifically so that the problem could be solved. This is due to the fact that LEX is a forward-search problem solver. The entire reason that LEX should rewrite $\cos^c(x)$ as $(\cos^2(x))^{c/2}$, mathematical correctness notwithstanding, is to allow op52 ($\cos^2 \Rightarrow 1 - \sin^2$) to be applied. The actual chain of reasoning used by a human is probably some form of means-ends analysis. For example, the reasoning steps could be as follows:

   a. To obtain a simple polynomial, work toward using the change of variable operator (op43).
   b. To set up the integrand for change of variable, work toward introducing sin.
   c. To introduce sin, work toward introducing a $\cos^2$ so that op52 can transform it into $1 - \sin^2$.
   d. To create a $\cos^2$, use the law of exponents.

LEX cannot do means-ends analysis, however, so op50 was necessary.

5.3.3.6 Knowledge-Based Assimilation

The description for "even integer" could have been assimilated correctly in the experiment in the following way: an alternative definition of "even integer" is $[y \mid (\exists x \in k \mid y = 2 \cdot x)\}$. This definition can be generated mechanically as easily as that generated by STABB. From the constraint back-propagation it is known that x and 2 are integers. If it were also known that the integers are closed under multiplication, then a procedure could easily prove that every y is also an integer. The critical piece of knowledge for the proof is that the integers are closed under multiplication.

For such an assimilation method to work, the learning program has first to formulate the right subproblem, and then it has to solve it. For the even integer example, the right subproblem is to determine whether the set of $k \cdot k$ is more specific than or equal to the set of integers.

To formulate good subproblems for the assimilation task, LEX can search for subproblems by generating expressions within a bounded space. The specific bound for the even integer example is the expression $2 \cdot k$. The general bound is the set of real numbers c.[2] The program could exhaustively consider generalizations of the specific bound that are not more general than the general bound. For the even integers example, using LEX's description langauge, some of those generalizations are [k · k], [2 · r], [k · r], and [r · r]. For each expression so generated, the learning program could use any knowledge it has about the set of objects implied by the generated expression. If the program has knowledge about a given set, it could query an expert. It would be a pleasant surprise if a learning program asked such intelligent questions as, "Are the integers closed under multiplication?" or, in mathematical terms, "Is the result of [k · k] always k?" This approach identifies knowledge worth having, an important problem for knowledge acquisition programs.

When the expert provides additional knowledge, the learning program could save the piece of knowledge for potential application in the future. One method for encoding such acquired knowledge is to embed it in the concept description language. For example, one could insert the set k · k as a specialization of k.

5.3.3.7 Bias in Formalism of Description Language

In section 5.3.3.5 the intersection algorithm was shown to be inadequate because it could not handle certain context-sensitive constraints. In the first experiment there was a need to intersect the description $\sin(x)$ with a description that included $f(x)$ *and* $g(x)$, where $g(x)$ was to be constrained to be the derivative of $f(x)$. The intersection of $\sin(x)$ and $f(x)$ was computed easily as $\sin(x)$, but as a result of the inability to specify the derivative constraint for the $g(x)$, there was no knowledge in the intersection algorithm that $g(x)$ depended on the $f(x)$. To finish the computation, the intersection algorithm would have had to calculate $g(x)$ by computing the derivative, in this case, of $\sin(x)$ as $\cos(x)$.

The correspondence between $f(x)$ and $g(x)$ could not be practically represented in LEX's grammar. In addition, intersection failed because it would have had to use the correspondence for its calculation. The LEX formalism is biased against such descriptions. Shift of bias can include shift of formalism as well. More work is needed on understanding the bias of formalism.

5.3.3.8 Interaction of Operator Language and Description Language

The grammar for LEX's concept description language uses string rewrite rules. The operators use string rewrites *and* arithmetic rewrites. Thus, through composition of symbolic and arithmetic transformations, it is possible to construct

---

[2]Note that although the description language does not contain the explicit axiom that [c · c] always evaluates to a real result, the operator for evaluating multiplication does. It would be a significant improvement for a program such as LEX to be able to use such knowledge already encoded in the operators.

descriptions that are not found in the LEX grammar. This is the reason that constraint back-propagation can be used to deduce new descriptions. The problem-solving experience shows which operator sequences should be followed. Back-propagation of constraints over such a sequence can yield useful compositions of symbolic and arithmetic transformations. The bias-shifting procedure translates any concepts that are defined through an arithmetic composition into recognition predicates that are added to the concept description language.

The operator language and the concept description language were written for different purposes. The experiment has shown an area in which they interact. Grammar rewrite rules *and* operator rewrite rules both define how one description can be transformed into another. Further consideration should be given to whether the present distinction between these two classes of transformation rules is worthwhile. It may be useful to provide a single formalism that permits string rewrites *and* arithmetic rewrites.

In addition to the problem of mixing the two classes of rewrite rules for constraint propagation, having a separate operator language and description language allows other inconsistencies. For example, because the interaction of the operator language and the concept description language was not originally well understood, certain liberties were taken when the operators were written. For example, the change of variable operator is

$$\int g(f(x)) \cdot f'(x)dx \Rightarrow \int g(u)du, u = f(x)$$

One may wonder how the domain of an operator can describe $g(f(x)) \cdot f'(x)$ when the concept description language cannot. This is possible only because the domain of the operator is described as $\int g(f(x)) \cdot h(x)dx$ and the code in the operator explicitly tests whether derivative($f(x)$) = $h(x)$. If the relation holds, the operator performs the change of variable. If the relation does not hold, the operator rewrites the problem state to include the symbol fail, which is not in LEX's grammar. At that point, the problem solver will never be able to proceed to a solution along that branch of the search tree because fail does not appear in the domain of any operator. Several other operators use this fail convention. This is counterproductive, however, because LEX then futilely tries to learn a heuristic without the ability to describe the domain of the heuristic in the formalism of the concept description language. It is a poor idea to permit descriptive capability in the operator language that cannot be described within the formalism of the concept description language.

5.3.3.9 A Method for Computing a Strong and Correct Bias

If the ability to do constraint back-propagation exists, it appears possible to compute an initial bias that is strong and correct for problems that can be solved within *n* steps. That is, an initial bias is computed prior to observation of *any* training instances. Consider $n = 0$. The set of states that is solved in 0 steps is the set of solved states. Consider $n = 1$. Intersection of the range of an operator with the set of solved states and application of the backward operator yield the set of states that can be solved with exactly $n = 1$ operator application. Any new descriptions needed for the constraint propagation step are added to the language during the propagation step. Consider $n > 1$. The constraint back-propagation technique would deduce the domains of the operators that lead to a state that is solvable in $n - 1$ steps. Thus it is possible to deduce the domains of all operator sequences of length less than or equal to n that lead to a solution. Descriptions other than those created during constraint back-propagation are unnecessary because the only descriptions ever needed are those of domains of operator sequences.

The major benefit of this approach is that the description language will become sufficiently enriched that the domain of a heuristic will be describable in the language (for any operator application involved in a solution sequence of not more than n steps). A drawback of the approach is that only good operator sequences justify heuristics, so many of the deduced descriptions will never be needed for a heuristic. Nevertheless, the approach does not introduce descriptions that are not needed for describing the domain of *some* operator sequence. In practical applications, the length of the longest operator sequence will be sufficiently small, for example, less than twenty steps, to make this approach computationally acceptable. For LEX, the longest operator sequence observed is approximately fifteen steps. Although there are potentially |set of operators|^n sequences of length n, there will be significant pruning whenever the domain of one operator does not intersect the range of another. Research on finding an initial bias that is strong and correct is an important unexplored area.

This technique can compute a bias that is too weak or, equivalently, a description language that is too rich. There are two reasons for this, as follows:

1. As mentioned above, the language will be able to describe concepts needed for operator sequences that a program like LEX would learn through experience not to use.
2. Useful operator sequences may have the same beginning subsequence and yet diverge at some point. As shown in figure 5-11, if two sequences diverge, then there is no need to distinguish between the two trajectories while they still share a common path. For example, there is no need to describe individually both the domain of operator sequence OpA-OpB *and* the domain of operator sequence OpA-OpC. It is sufficient to be able to describe the domain of operator sequence OpA-(OpB $\lor$ OpC).

Despite the fact that it computes a bias that is weaker than necessary for describing the heuristics that LEX will ultimately learn, the approach is promising because it computes only domains of applicability that LEX can ever consider, given some set of operators. LEX has no need to describe any other set.

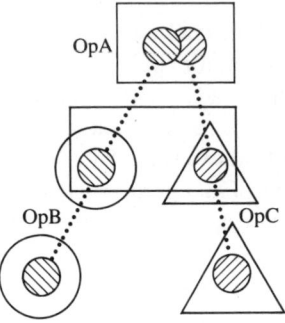

Figure 5-11: Diverging operator sequences.

5.3.3.10 Familiar Uses of Constraint Back-Propagation

Constraint propagation is a familiar process, but it is not always recognized as such. Banerji (1980) presents a form of constraint back-propagation for tic-tac-toe. There he shows deduction of the concept "fork."

Consider an example from the domain of chess, as illustrated in figures 5-12 through 5-15. It is white's move. In move 1, white elects to guard its unprotected knight$_1$ with its bishop (figure 5-13). In move 2, black's bishop captures white's knight$_1$ (figure 5-14). In move 3, white's bishop captures black's bishop (figure 5-15). White has removed its guard for its knight! Black's rook can now safely capture

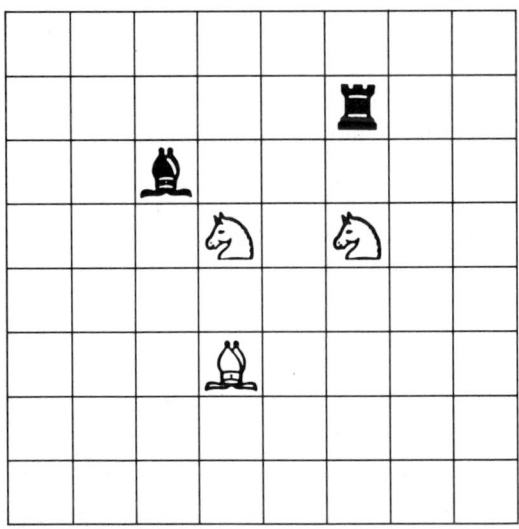

Figure 5-12: An example from the domain of chess.

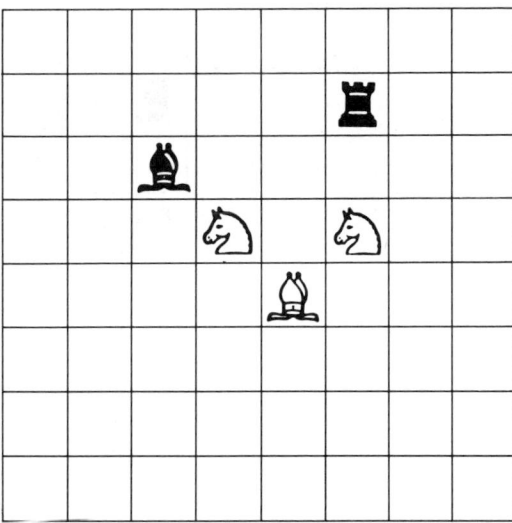

Figure 5-13: First move.

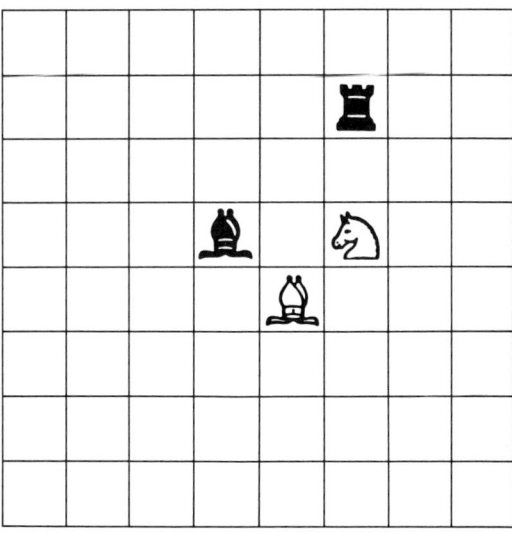

Figure 5-14: Second move.

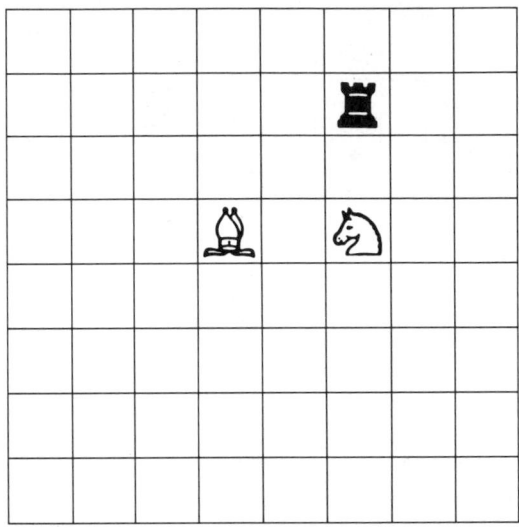

Figure 5-15:   Third move.

white's knight. White wants to understand what led to a free capture for its opponent in order to avoid giving away a free capture in future play.

Consider a reasoning process based on constraint back-propagation. Assume that white has the (conjunctive) concept of a "free capture":

```
freecapture (x,y,p1,p2)
    [ it is x's turn
      x has a piece at p1
      x's piece at p1 can move to p2
      y has a piece at p2
      y does not have a piece that can move to p2
    ]
```

White reasons backward through move 3 to see that when it made the capture, the piece it moved had been guarding another white piece. The concept of a "free capture that gives away a free capture" or, with a shorter name, "indirect trade," is deduced:

```
indirecttrade(x,y,p1,p2,p3,p4)
    [ freecapture(x,y,p1,p2)
    y has a piece at p3
    x has a piece at p4
    y's piece at p3 can move to p4
    x's piece at p1 can move to p4
```

```
   if x's piece at p1 were at p2,
     then it could not then move to p4
 ]
```

White reasons backward through move 2 to see that when black made its capture, black produced a position that was an indirect trade. The concept of a "capture that leaves an indirect trade" is deduced:

```
captureleavinganindirecttrade(x,y,p1,p2,p3,p4,p5)
 [ it is x's turn
   x has a piece at p3
   x's piece at p3 can move to p4
   y has a piece at p4
   y has a piece at p1
   y's piece at p1 can move to p4
   y has a piece at p5
   y's piece at p1 can move to p5
   if y's piece at p1 were at p5,
      then it could not then move to p4
   x has a piece at p2
   x's piece at p2 can move to p5
   ]
```

White reasons backward through move 1 to see that removing black's free capture by guarding a threatened piece with a guard that is already guarding some other piece will lead to a capture leaving an indirect trade for black.

A player that deduces these concepts and tests possible successor board positions with respect to these concepts becomes a better chess player. One endeavors to be able to predict consequences of moves based on recognition of patterns rather than generating and evaluating successor board positions. The main lesson from this example is that constraint back-propagation can serve as a fundamental mechanism for deducing useful classes that it is worthwhile to describe.

5.4 CONCLUSIONS

The primary objective of the research reported in this chapter was to show that the search for a good bias for inductive concept learning can be performed mechanically. A by-product was the program STABB and its two procedures, least disjunction and constraint back-propagation. More work is needed on the fundamental problem of shift of bias. Three research directions that emerge (see below) should be pursued further.

Assimilation Tasks Generating Knowledge Acquisition Problems. There is evidence
that assimilation tasks can point to new knowledge that it would be useful to acquire.
For example, the procedure described in section 5.3.3.6 for proving subset relationships for recognition predicates, created by constraint back-propagation, requires
knowledge that the concept learner may or may not have. The procedure can create
conditional statements of the form "if x then $y \subset z$." If the concept learner already
knows that x is true, then the subset relation $y \subset z$ is proved. If the concept learner
does not know x, then it must ascertain x. It would be a step forward to see LEX ask
questions such as, "Are the integers closed under multiplication?" while working on
an assimilation task.

Calculation of an Initial Bias. There is evidence that a strong bias can be deduced
when concept learning involves learning constrained domains for problem-solving
operators, as with LEX. A mechanical procedure for calculating an initial bias would
constitute an advance in machine learning. In section 5.3.3.9 a procedure was suggested that exhaustively applies constraint back-propagation to all operator sequences
that lead to a problem solution within an operator sequence of some specified length.
Solution paths will be pruned whenever the constrained domain of an operator
sequence becomes empty.

Goal-Free versus Goal-Sensitive Methods. There is evidence that goal-sensitive
methods are stronger than goal-free methods. The principal advantage of goal-
sensitive methods is that they attempt to use all available information instead of only
selected portions. The two procedures of STABB—least disjunction and constraint
back-propagation—contrast sharply in this regard. The least disjunction procedure
examines only the training instances and the current description language when it
searches for a better bias. In contrast, the constraint back-propagation procedure
takes advantage of the additional knowledge that the training instances are part of an
operator sequence that LEX's critic identified as good. Because it uses that knowledge of the learning context, the constraint back-propagation procedure is sensitive
to the learning goal at hand. As a result, the constraint back-propagation procedure is
able to deduce constrained domains of applicability, the original objective of the
learning process. Thus learning programs may be able to depend less on empirical
induction via observation of training instances and more on analytic deduction via
observation of solution sequences. Whatever the learning context—whether learning
that takes place in a problem-solving domain or learning that simply improves classification skills—a procedure for shifting bias should make use of the best information
available.

ACKNOWLEDGMENTS

The work reported here comes from the author's Ph.D. research conducted in the Computer Science Department at Rutgers University. This work was supported by National Science Foundation Grant No. GMCS80-08889, National Institute of Health Grant No. RR-64309, Rutgers University Laboratory for Computer Science Research, and Siemens Research and Technology Laboratories.

For their helpful input on this and related work, the author thanks Tom Mitchell, Ran Banerji, Saul Amarel, N. S. Sridharan, Bob Smith, Rich Keller, Donna Nagel, Pat Schooley, Tom Dietterich, Jaime Carbonell, Ryszard Michalski, Smadar Kedar-Cabelli, and Tony Bonner.

References

Banerji, R. B., *Artificial Intelligence: A Theoretical Approach*, Elsevier North-Holland, New York, 1980.

Fikes, R E., Hart, P. E., and Nilsson, N. J., "Learning and Executing Generalized Robot Plans," *Artificial Intelligence*, Vol. 3, pp. 251–88, 1972.

Keller, R. M., "Learning by Re-Expressing Concepts for Efficient Recognition," *Proceedings of the AAAI-83*, Washington, D. C., pp. 182-86, 1983.

Kelly, V. E., and Steinberg, L. I., "The Critter System: Analyzing Digital Circuits by Propagating Behaviors and Specifications," *Proceedings of the AAAI-82*, Pittsburgh, Pa., pp. 284–89, 1982.

Michalski, R. S., "A Theory and Methodology of Inductive Learning," *Artificial Intelligence*, Vol. 20, No. 2, pp. 118–61, 1983.

Mitchell, T. M., "Version Spaces: A Candidate Elimination Approach to Rule Learning," *Proceedings of the Fifth IJCAI*, Cambridge, Mass., pp. 305–10, 1977.

———, "Version Spaces: An Approach to Concept Learning," Ph.D. diss., Stanford University, 1978. (Also available as Report No. STAN-CS-78-711, HPP-79-2, Department of Computer Science, Stanford University, 1978.)

———, "Generalization as Search," *Artificial Intelligence*, Vol. 18, No. 2, pp. 203–26, 1982.

Mitchell, T. M., Utgoff, P. E., and Banerji, R. B., "Learning by Experimentation: Acquiring and Refining Problem-Solving Heuristics," in *Machine Learning: An Artificial Intelligence Approach*, R. S. Michalski, J. G. Carbonell, and T. M. Mitchell (Eds.), Tioga, Palo Alto, Calif., 1983.

Mostow, D. J., "Machine Transformation of Advice into a Heuristic Search Procedure," in *Machine Learning: An Artificial Intelligence Approach*, R. S. Michalski, J. G. Carbonell, and T. M. Mitchell (Eds.), Tioga, Palo Alto, Calif., 1983.

Stallman, R. M., and Sussman, G. J., "Forward Reasoning and Dependency-Directed Backtracking in a System for Computer-Aided Circuit Analysis," *Artificial Intelligence*, Vol. 9, No. 2, pp. 135–96, 1977.

Stefik, M. J., "Planning with Constraints," Ph.D. diss., Stanford University, 1980. (Also available as Report No. STAN-CS-80-784, Department of Computer Science, Stanford University, 1980.)

Utgoff, P. E., "Shift of Bias for Inductive Concept Learning," Ph.D. diss., Rutgers University, 1984.

Utgoff, P. E., and Mitchell, T. M., "Acquisition of Appropriate Bias for Inductive Concept Learning," *Proceedings of AAAI-82,* Pittsburgh, Pa., pp. 414–17, 1982.

Vere, S. A., "Multilevel Counterfactuals for Generalizations of Relational Concepts and Productions," *Artificial Intelligence,* Vol. 14, No. 2, pp. 138–64, 1980.

Waldinger, R., "Achieving Several Goals Simultaneously," in *Machine Intelligence,* E. W. Elcock, and D. Michie (Eds.), Wiley, New York, 1976.

6

THE EFFECT OF NOISE ON CONCEPT LEARNING

J. Ross Quinlan
New South Wales Institute of Technology

Abstract

Concept-learning systems are intended to discover general classification rules from the examination of a given set of examples described in terms of a collection of properties. This chapter looks at the effect of noise in these descriptions of the discovery of classification rules and on their accuracy. A modified form of an existing rule-building algorithm that can tolerate noisy descriptions is presented. After discussing the results of three sets of experiments, the author makes several conjectures about the way the classification task should be formulated when noise is expected.

6.1 INTRODUCTION

Michalski (1983) defines *inductive inference* as the process of going from specific observational knowledge about some objects and a (possibly null) initial inductive hypothesis to an inductive assertion that "strongly" or "weakly" implies or accounts for the observations. One subdomain of inductive inference is *concept learning from examples,* in which the specific knowledge consists of a set of objects belonging to known classes. The inductive assertion is expressed as a *classification rule* for assigning any object, seen or unseen, to a class. The strong implication requirement is satisfied if the rule correctly classifies all known objects.

These objects are known only through their *descriptions* in terms of a collection of properties, which might include measurements, yes-no indicators, and qualitative assessments. For example, the description of a man might include his weight (a measurement), whether or not he is healthy (a Boolean value based on judgment), and the color of his eyes (a subjective division into categories).

In real-world classification tasks, the description of an object will often contain errors. Some sources of these errors are faulty measurement, ill-defined threshholds (e.g., when is a person "tall"?), and subjective interpretation of a multitude of inputs (e.g., what criteria are used when describing a person as "athletic"?). Regardless of the source, however, these errors can be expected to affect the formation and use of classification rules in two ways.

First, inductive inference systems must employ some form of generalization to anticipate unseen objects. This is usually accomplished by identifying subsets in the given set of objects that share common properties. Errors in the description of these objects will tend to confuse any generalization mechanisms of this type. Suppose, for example, that the subset of red-haired people is classified differently from others; this information may be difficult to discover if many red-haired people have been erroneously described as "fair" or "brunette" and vice versa. Secondly, problems arise independently when the rule formed from the given objects is used to classify another object. The classification rule is couched in terms of the description of an object, and if this description contains errors, the result given by the classification rule for the object in question might well be incorrect also.

This paper investigates the effect of description errors on both the formation of classification rules and their use in classifying objects. The formalism is a relatively simple one in which objects are described in terms of a fixed list of properties, or *attributes,* each with its own small, unordered collection of discrete attribute values. A classification rule takes the form of a decision tree that examines the values of some attributes of an object in order to assign it to a class.

Since this work involves observing the effects of description errors, a way to control the error must be included. This has been handled here by introducing varying levels of noise into the correct description of an object. Specifically, suppose a noise level of n percent has been applied to some attribute A. Whenever an object's description is now generated, the true value of A for that object will be replaced with n percent probability by a randomly chosen value. This process models description errors as the occasional, nonrepeatable substitution of a possibly incorrect value for the true attribute value. Notice that this is not the same as replacing the value of an attribute with a different value. In the case of a binary attribute, the latter would give a situation in which a noise level of 100 percent in some attribute A would simply invert the value of A with no loss of information.

The effect of description errors is always to degrade the performance of the classification rules. In general, the decision tree produced when the given set of objects contains noise will not be the same as that produced in the noise-free case. When the tree is used to classify an object, it could then give a wrong result either because it is the wrong tree or because the description of the object being classified is incorrect. The noise model allows the error rate in descriptions to be varied at will to show the effect on the performance of the rule, measured in terms of the proportion of occasions on which it gives the correct classification of an object.

This chapter first describes an existing top-down algorithm for constructing classification rules in the form of decision trees and shows how it has been modified to deal with erroneous descriptions of this type. Three experiments are then discussed in which the level of noise applied to descriptions is varied and the degradation of performance of the classification rule is observed. The results of these experiments suggest several hypotheses relevant to concept learning with noisy data.

6.2 ALGORITHM FOR DEVELOPING CLASSIFICATION RULES

The basic aim of a concept-learning system is to construct a rule for classifying objects from knowledge of a *training set* of objects whose classes are given. In the formalism used here all objects are described by a fixed collection of attributes, each with its own set of discrete values. Each object belongs to one of two classes, denoted 0 and 1, respectively, although the extension to more than two classes is straightforward. A rule is expressed as a *decision tree:* each interior node consists of a test of an attribute with one subtree for every possible value of that attribute, and each leaf has an assigned class signaling the appropriate outcome of the classification rule.

If there are no two objects that have the same value for each attribute and yet belong to different classes, the attributes are *adequate* for the classification task. (If this property does not hold, there are pairs of objects belonging to different classes that cannot be distinguished on the basis of the information provided by the attributes.) Previous work (Quinlan, 1983) reported on a system called ID3 that was developed for this case. ID3 constructs a decision tree using a top-down, divide-and-conquer approach: select an attribute, divide the training set into subsets characterized by the possible values of the attribute, and follow the same procedure recursively with each subset until no subset contains objects from both classes. These single-class subsets correspond then to leaves of the decision tree and can be labeled with that class.

The method depends for its practicality on making a good choice of attribute to test at each stage. ID3 takes an information-theoretic approach as follows: Imagine a set S of objects and let p be the proportion of them that belongs to class 1. A decision tree formed from S is hypothesized that correctly classifies all objects in S. An arbitrary object passed to this decision tree will be assigned by it to class 0 or class 1, and if S is in some sense "typical" of the objects that might be passed to the rule, it seems reasonable to expect that the proportion of such objects assigned by the decision rule to class 1 would also be p. From another perspective, the decision tree can be regarded as a message generator that says "class 1" with probability p and "class 0" with probability $1 - p$. The information content of such a message is given by

$$M(S) = -p \log_2 p - (1-p) \log_2(1-p).$$

This $M(S)$ is a measure of the information that must be supplied by the hypothetical decision tree derived from S or, alternatively, serves as a predictor of its complexity.

For example, let A be an attribute with n possible values $A_1, A_2, \ldots, A_n$. If the decision tree were to have as its root a test on the value of A, S would be divided into subsets $S_1, S_2, \ldots, S_n$ so that S_i contained all objects from S with value A_i of A. The expected information requirement in this case can be expressed as

$$B(S,A) = \text{sum}_i(W_i \times M(S_i))$$

where the weight W_i is the proportion of the objects in subset S_i. The information gained by testing attribute A is then the difference

$$M(S) - B(S,A),$$

which, as might be expected, is always greater than or equal to zero. As the root of the decision tree for set S, ID3 chooses the attribute A that maximizes this information gain or, equivalently, that minimizes the expected residual information $B(S,A)$.

6.2.1 Modifications to Cope with Noise

The presence of description errors complicates this situation somewhat. If the descriptions of the object contain noise, it may be that the attributes are no longer adequate for the classification task. For example, if two objects belonging to different classes differ only in one attribute and that attribute is affected by noise, the perceived descriptions of the objects may be identical. The result may be one or more training (sub)sets containing objects with identical descriptions but different classes, in which case no amount of testing attributes will produce single-class subsets. What ought to be done in a situation of this kind?

Let us suppose that we decide to associate class c with this leaf. There are two values for c that suggest themselves. We could generalize our notion of class to a continuous value lying between 0 and 1; a class of 0.7, say, would be interpreted as meaning, "with probability 0.7, objects corresponding to this leaf belong to class 1." Each object at the leaf would then have an associated classification error given by

if the object is really class 0: $c - 0$;
if the object is really class 1: $1 - c$.

So, if the subset of objects at the leaf contained n_0 from class 0 and n_1 from class 1, the obvious choice for c would be

$$c = n_1/(n_0+n_1).$$

It is straightforward to verify that this choice for c minimizes the sum of the squares of the classification errors of all objects at the leaf. The alternative choice for c would be to adopt a voting model, assigning all objects to the class that has the most representatives at the leaf. In this case

if n_0 is greater than n_1: $c = 0$;
otherwise: $c = 1$.

It can be shown that this choice for c minimizes the sum of the classification errors rather than the sum of their squares. Both choices for the class c to associate with a leaf have been tried; for later reference they are called the *probability* and *majority* methods, respectively.

In building a decision tree, one may elect to stop testing an object's attributes when it appears that there are no further tests relevant to its class. The generalized procedure for building a decision tree $T(S)$ for the set S of objects can be stated as follows:

- If all objects in S belong to the same class, $T(S)$ is a leaf labeled with that class.
- If $M(S) = B(S,A)$ for all attributes A, testing further attributes seems unhelpful to determining the class of the objects. The decision tree $T(S)$ is again a leaf whose associated class is determined by either the probability or majority method mentioned above.
- Otherwise, find an attribute A that minimizes the residual information $B(S,A)$ and set $T(S)$ to the decision tree

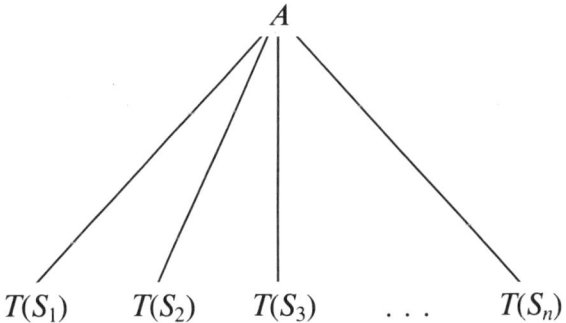

where $T(S_i)$ is the decision tree for the subset S_i of S consisting of the objects that have the ith value of the selected attribute A.

Although it looks reasonable, this approach yields nonsensically large decision trees. For example let S be a training set containing objects of both classes, and let us suppose that no further testing of attributes is relevant to S. Let A be a random binary-valued attribute. Unless the proportion of class 1 objects with each value of attribute A is *exactly* the same as the proportion of class 1 objects in all of S (a most unlikely event, statistically speaking), $B(S,A)$ will be less than $M(S)$, and it will appear that testing attribute A is worthwhile.

The obvious expedient of requiring that $B(S,A)$ be less than $M(S) - h$ for some threshold h does circumvent the problem, but trials found that values of h sufficiently large to prevent testing irrelevant attributes significantly degraded the performance of the procedure when the attributes were indeed adequate.

One solution to this problem comes from the chi-square test for stochastic independence. Consider again a set S of objects and an attribute A with m values. If the values of A for these objects are just noise, the values would be expected to be unrelated to the objects' classes, and thus the values of attribute A and of the class would be expected to be independent. The converse is not true, but if there is reason to suspect that class and attribute are independent, one explanation could be that A is noise. If one allows this tacit assumption that independence indicates noise, the development proceeds as follows:

Let $N[i,c]$ denote the number of objects in S with the ith value of attribute A that belongs to class c. If an object's class is independent of its value of attribute A, the number $N'[i,c]$ that we would expect to find is given by

$$N'[i,c] = N[i,*] \times N[*,c]/|S|$$

where $*$ denotes summation over a parameter; for example, $N[i,*]$ is $N[i,0] + N[i,1]$. Then the statistic

$$\text{sum}_i \text{sum}_c \{(N[i,c] - N'[i,c])^2/N'[i,c]\}$$

is approximately chi-square with $m - 1$ degrees of freedom. If this value exceeds a tabulated value, the hypothesis that an object's class and the value of A are independent over S (i.e., that A is useless for classifying S) can be rejected with known confidence (Hogg and Craig, 1970, 313ff.).

This is incorporated into the tree-building procedure by requiring that no attribute A will be considered for testing unless one can reject, with a high degree of confidence, the hypothesis that the value of A is independent of the class over the given set S. One minor difficulty is that the chi-square test is unreliable for very small values of the expectations N', so the common practice of using the test only when all values of N' are at least 4 has been followed. For these experiments, the chi-square test was used with a confidence level of 99 percent; its use resulted in a dramatic reduction in the size of the tree when noise levels were high, with no degradation in the noise-free case.

6.3 CLASSIFICATION TASKS

Since this study was intended to be an empirical investigation with practical applications, it was important to use real (as opposed to invented) classification tasks; artificial ones would almost inevitably contain built-in assumptions that might influence the results. For this reason, the data used in the experiments described in the following sections were taken without modification from previous work on classifying board positions in a small chess end game. Two domains were used. In the first, the universe consists of 551 objects described in terms of thirty-nine binary-valued attributes. About 74 percent of the objects belong to class 1, and the smallest known correct decision tree for the task contains 175 nodes. (As this indicates, the classification task is indeed a difficult one.) One of the attributes is redundant in the sense that a correct rule can be constructed without reference to it. The second domain exhibits a more skewed class distribution—only about 15 percent of the 428 objects belong to class 1. There are twenty-three binary-valued attributes, none of them redundant, and a much simpler correct decision tree of eighty-five nodes is known. The two classification tasks will be referred to as task 551 and task 428, respectively.

6.4 FIRST EXPERIMENT

The first experiment investigated the effect of noise on building and using a decision tree. In each trial, the whole collection of objects was corrupted to a predetermined level and used to form a decision tree. A different corrupted copy of all objects was then generated, and each object was classified by the decision tree. The results obtained were compared with the known classes of the objects, and a mean error was computed as the sum of the absolute difference between the real and computed classes expressed as a percentage of the total number of objects. Each experiment was repeated twenty times with different corruptions of the training set and test cases to give a more reliable average, together with an indication of its variance.

The form of the experiment was as follows: Each attribute in turn was individually corrupted with noise levels 5, 10, 15, 20, 30, 40, . . . , 100 percent, giving in all twelve average errors showing the effect of noise in that attribute alone. The same noise levels were then applied to all attributes simultaneously. Finally, the class information in the training set was corrupted to the same levels. These trials thus gave an indication of misclassification error under twelve levels of noise for each attribute in isolation, for all attributes together, and for the class information in the training set.

6.4.1 Task 551

The same procedure was followed with both classification tasks, but the first of them will be focused on here. As would be expected, the effects of the noise vary markedly from attribute to attribute. Figure 6-1 shows the degradation of performance as noise is added to attribute 2 (the most sensitive), attribute 32 (the least sensitive and, as it happens, the redundant attribute), and the average over the thirty-nine attributes. This agrees with our intuition that, in classification problems, some attributes are more important than others. In fact, the *importance* of an attribute can be defined without reference to noise as the unavoidable average classification error that results if the attribute in question is deleted altogether from the data, thus preventing its use in the decision tree. This quantity can be measured for any training set and is not tied to a particular concept-learning approach. If we remove attribute 2, for example, 146 pairs of objects give rise to identical descriptions in terms of the remaining attributes. Of these pairs, eight are both objects of class 0, ninety-four are both objects of class 1, and forty-four pairs contain one object from each class.

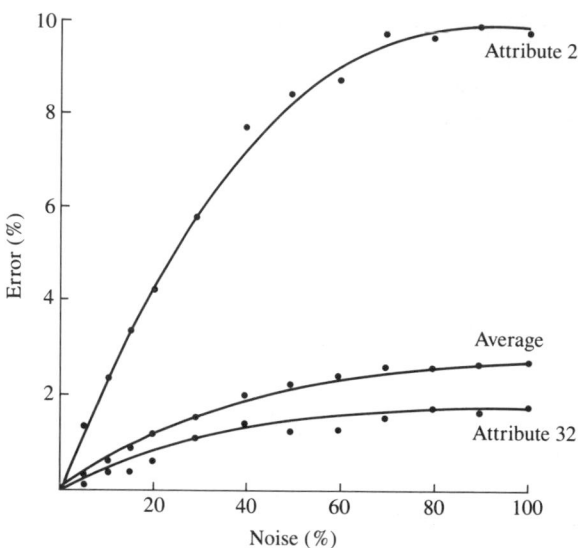

Figure 6-1: Classification error as a function of noise for attributes 2, 32, and the average for all attributes (first experiment, task 551).

It is only these last pairs that cause a problem because, given the (remaining) information available, no classification scheme could possibly differentiate between them. The importance of attribute 2 can then be calculated as the total error arising from deleting that attribute; this figure will be the same whether the probability or majority method is used. Expressed as a percentage of the number of objects, this figure is therefore 44/551, or 8 percent. Similarly, the importance of the redundant attribute 32 is zero, and the average of all attributes is 1.0 percent. The ranking of attributes by importance agrees well with their ranking by error with 100 percent noise. Notice that, in figure 6-1, the error with 100 percent noise for attributes 2, 32, and the average is very close to their respective importances plus 1.8 percent.

For the cases above where one attribute at a time was affected by noise, results using the two leaf-labeling methods (probability and majority) are indistinguishable. This can be explained by observing that, even when a single attribute is completely corrupted, it can cause only pairs of objects to share a common description. In this situation, both methods give the same expected error. When noise corrupts class information in the training set or several attributes, however, more than two objects can share the same description, and differences between the methods become apparent.

The effect of noise applied to class information will be considered first. If class is treated as a sort of attribute, its importance would necessarily be 50 percent for every two-class classification task. The reason for this is that, if the class information in the training set is replaced by a random variable, the resulting classification rule would also be random and so would be expected to be correct half the time. Figure 6-2 shows experimental agreement with this result, but it also demonstrates clearly that the degradation takes a different form from that appearing in the previous figure. The curve obtained using the probability leaf-labeling method is initially linear, then bulges slightly before returning to near the predicted 50 percent at very high noise levels. The corresponding curve for the majority method is similar at low noise levels, but it falls well below the other at intermediate values of noise before rejoining it when class information is completely random.

Figure 6-3 shows the effect of noise applied simultaneously to all attributes. Notice that the average error does not tend to 50 percent. It might seem that, if the description of all objects were random, we would get the same result as that produced by destroying class information. But in this case the training set still contains class frequency information that will be reflected in the resulting decision tree. If the entire training set were to become a single leaf, the probability method would assign this leaf a class c whose value is 410/551, or 0.74, giving an expected error of

$$0.74 \times 0.26 + 0.26 \times 0.74,$$

which comes to 38 percent. The majority method would assign c the value 1, since there are more class 1 objects than class 0 objects, giving an expected error of

$$0.74 \times 0 + 0.26 \times 1,$$

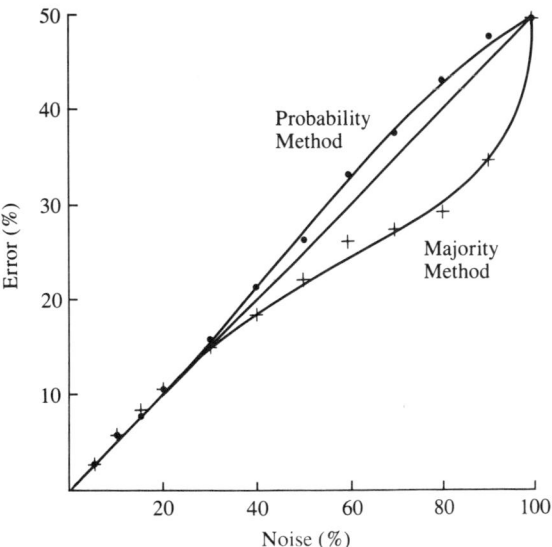

Figure 6-2: Classification error from noise in class information (first experiment, task 551).

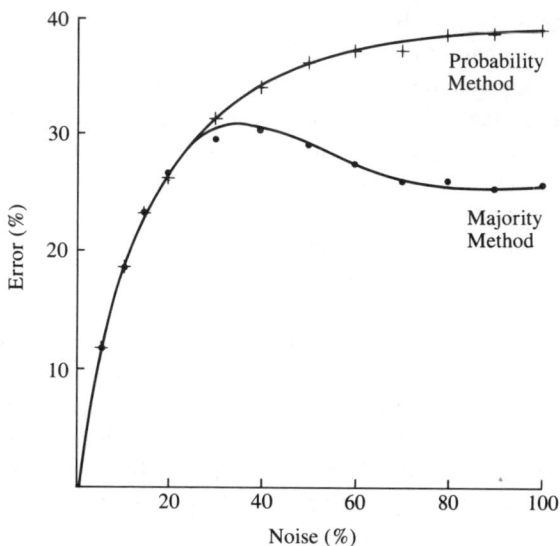

Figure 6-3: Classification error from noise in all attributes simultaneously (first experiment, task 551).

or 26 percent. The measured average errors were very close to these values. Notice that the two methods produce similar results initially, but the majority method actually leads to a *decline* in average error at higher noise levels.

After an initial increase, the size of the decision tree decreases as noise is increased, averaging only two nodes when the descriptions are completely random. This demonstrates the utility of the chi-square test mentioned earlier, as without it, the average number of nodes for decision trees obtained from random descriptions exceeded 500 nodes, even though they gave similar error rates.

6.4.2 Task 428

The same procedure was followed with the second classification task. The results, summarized in figures 6-4, 6-5, and 6-6, agree with those reported above.

Adding noise to single attributes produces saturation curves similar to those shown in figure 6-1. The most important attribute for this task is attribute 1, with value 5.1 percent, and figure 6-4 shows the increase in classification error as noise increases for this attribute and for the average single attribute. As before, it makes no difference in this case whether the probability or majority method is used to label leaves of the decision tree.

Error introduced by noise in the training set's class information again approaches 50 percent. This time, though, there are more marked bulges above and below the central linear trend (figure 6-5) due to the probability and majority methods, respectively.

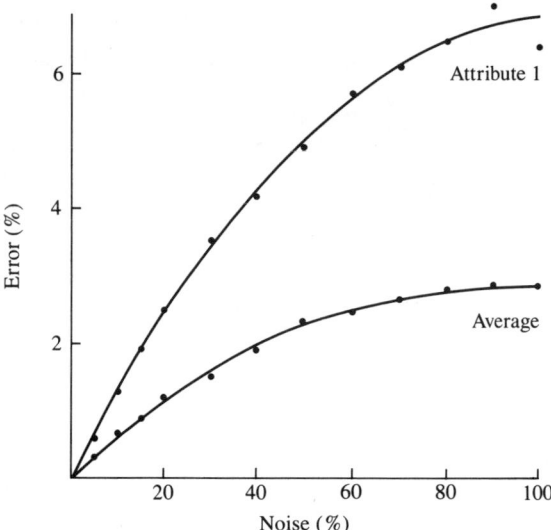

Figure 6-4: Classification error from noise in attribute 1 and average for all attributes (first experiment, task 428).

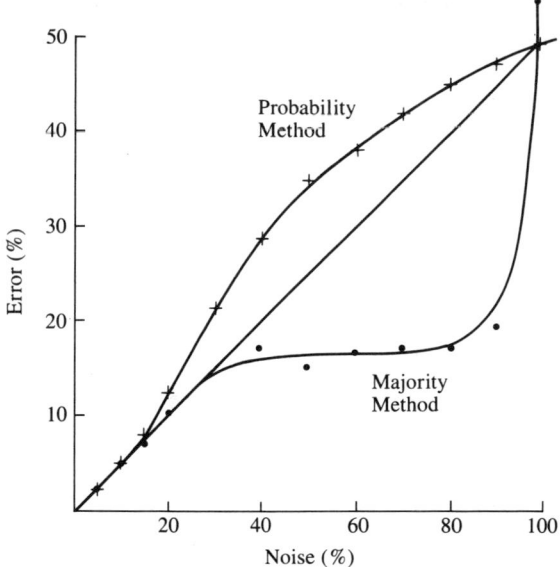

Figure 6-5: Classification error from noise in class information (first experiment, task 428).

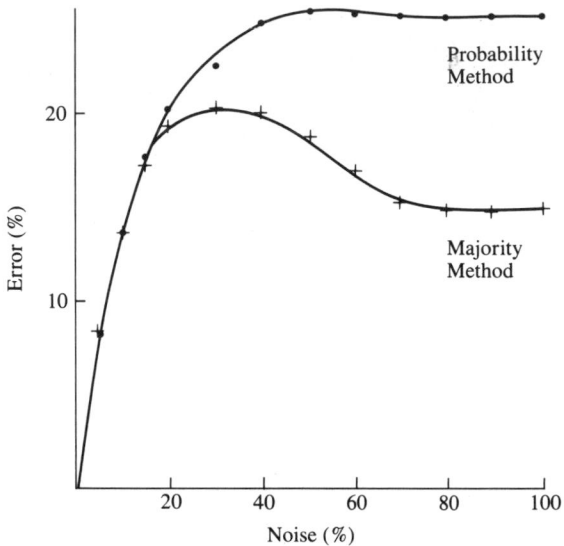

Figure 6-6: Classification error from noise in all attributes (first experiment, task 428).

Small-scale trials on a synthetic task suggest that these bulges are linked to the difference between the real class distribution and those substituted by noise, with larger discrepancies causing larger bulges.

The curves when all attributes are corrupted simultaneously (figure 6-6) closely match those of figure 6-3. For this task, the expected error at 100 percent noise using the probability method is 25 percent, and that for the majority method is 15 percent, as confirmed by the observed values.

6.5 SECOND EXPERIMENT

The first experiment treated noise as a uniform commodity that applied both to the construction and to the use of classification rules. Since noise was present in the training set, the decision tree itself contained errors, and further errors were introduced as a consequence of faulty attribute values when the tree was used to classify an object. The second experiment was designed to separate the effects of noise on forming a classification rule and on using that rule. A correct decision tree was first constructed using all objects with no added noise. (Since the training set was a noise-free one and the attributes were adequate, there were no leaves containing objects from both classes. Consequently, both the probability and the majority methods of labeling leaves give the same decision tree.) This correct tree was then used to classify objects corrupted in a manner similar to the manner in which it was done in the previous experiment.

As before, each trial was repeated twenty times. The same twelve noise levels were applied to each attribute individually and then to all attributes together. The measure of degradation was again the average classification error over all objects.

We will focus for the moment on task 551. Once more, the importance of an attribute was a good predictor of its sensitivity to noise, with the most important (attribute 2) being most affected. When single attributes were corrupted by noise, the degradation in classification performance now increased linearly. When all attributes were corrupted simultaneously, though, a different saturation curve was generated.

The solid curves of figure 6-7 show the consequences of applying noise to attribute 2 and the average single attribute. The broken curves are the corresponding results from the first experiment in which noise was also applied to the training set. Figure 6-8 shows similar curves for the trials in which all attributes were corrupted simultaneously. Very surprisingly, the degradation in classification performance when noise is excluded from the training set becomes considerably higher in all three cases. The effect is not entirely uniform, though, and the maximum degradation experienced with some less important single attributes is somewhat lower than before.

The same series of trials was repeated with task 428. The results in all respects mirrored those above.

This experiment demonstrates that noise has a different effect when the underlying classification rule is correct than when the rule itself was formed from a noisy

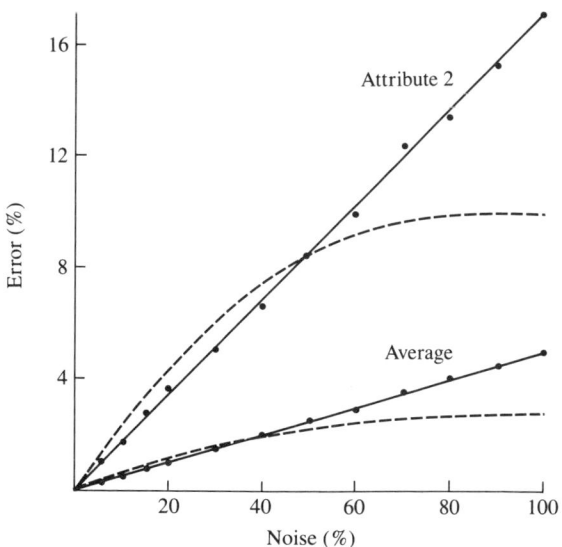

Figure 6-7: Classification error using correct decision tree (second experiment, task 551).

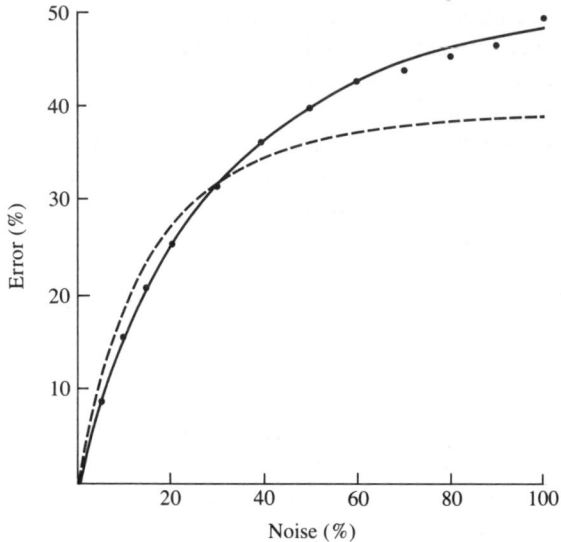

Figure 6-8: Classification error using correct decision tree, all attributes corrupted together (second experiment, task 551).

training set. The form of single-attribute degradation is different (linear versus saturation), and even though the classification rule is correct, higher levels of noise produce a significantly higher average misclassification rate than previously.

6.6 THIRD EXPERIMENT

The first two experiments both assumed that the whole universe of objects was available for construction of a classification rule. This third experiment was intended to check that the same results applied in the more usual case in which only a subset of the objects was used as a training set. The resulting decision tree was tested on both known objects (those in the training set) and unseen objects that were not taken into account when the tree was formed.

As with the second experiment, similar results were obtained for both task 551 and task 428, so only the former will be discussed here. Each trial was structured as follows: A subset containing one-fifth of the 551 objects was selected randomly (a different subset each time) and corrupted by the imposition of noise. A decision tree was formed using the corrupted objects as a training set. A new corrupted copy of all 551 objects was then generated and each object was tested using the decision tree. Each trial was again repeated twenty times. The corruptions used mimicked those of the first experiment: 5, 10, . . . , 100 percent noise applied to each attribute in turn, all attributes simultaneously, and to the class information in the training set.

Even when the training set is noise-free, the fact that it is not complete means that the decision tree generated from it will not correctly classify all objects. There is thus a base error before any effects of noise, found to be 13.2 ± 0.8 percent (or, to put it another way, a classification rule formed from about 20 percent of this universe correctly classified about 87 percent of the universe).

There was a considerably higher variance on the results for these experiments and correspondingly poorer curve fits. The effect of noise on attribute 2 again produced the highest degradation, with a peak value of 21 percent. The effects of noise on attribute 2, all attributes together, and the class information appear in figure 6-9. Generally speaking, the results with low noise levels are displaced by the base error, but the curves are similar in form to those obtained from the first experiment. The error due to class noise still approaches 50 percent, and the error due to noise in all attributes together again saturates toward 38 percent or 26 percent, depending on whether the probability or majority leaf-labeling method is used.

6.7 FINDINGS

The results of the experiments, especially the first and second, suggest several policy-level conjectures concerning the use of inductive inference machinery in noisy environments. These are conjectures because their applicability across classification problems and across rule-inducing systems has not yet been established.

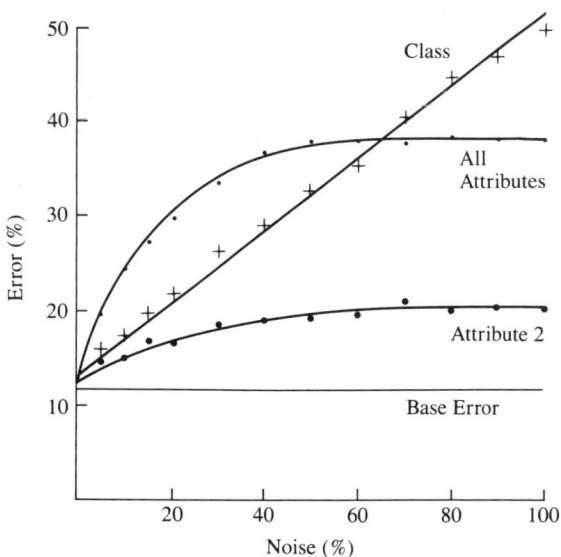

Figure 6-9: Classification error from incomplete training sets (third experiment, task 551).

• It is important to eliminate noise affecting the class membership of the objects in the training set.

The importance of the class information is 50 percent, as discussed under the first experiment. This figure is much higher than the importance of any attribute in either classification task studied here, where the maximum value was 8 percent for attribute 2 of task 551. The first experiment confirmed that noise in the class information degrades performance linearly for lower noise levels, and in particular the average classification error should then be half the noise rate even when all objects are included in the training set. Clearly, high levels of noise in the class information of the training set would generate unacceptable classification rules anyway.

• It is not worthwhile expending effort to eliminate noise from the attribute values of objects in the training set if there is going to be a significant amount of noise when the induced classification rule is used in practice.

This observation comes from figures 6-7 and 6-8. If the noise in the average attribute is greater than about 45 percent, the performance of the correct decision tree (formed from a noise-free training set) falls below that of the tree obtained when the same level of noise was also present in the training set. The same holds true when all attributes are affected together by noise. It would seem that the tree-forming algorithm tends to avoid using noisy attributes, but this feature is nullified if the training set is noise free and so gives no indication of the noise to be expected in practice. Even at the lower levels of noise, the performance of the correct tree is only marginally superior to that of the tree formed from the training set whose attributes were subject to the same level of noise experienced during the testing phase.

• We are better off dispensing altogether with noisy, less important attributes.

Consider again figure 6-1 for the first classification task. Since attribute 32 is redundant, its importance is zero; that is, if this attribute is excluded altogether, the decision tree will still perform correctly. On the other hand, including the attribute with even slight levels of noise allows the attribute to be used in the decision tree and leads to classification errors when it is used. Again, the average importance of the attributes is 1 percent, so dispensing with this "average" attribute will cause only 1 percent classification errors. The figure shows that fewer classification errors would be produced if this average attribute were excluded when its noise level exceeded 15 percent. Finally, performance would even be improved if attribute 2 with its highest importance (8 percent) were excluded if the noise level in this attribute exceeded 46 percent. In short, the less the importance of an attribute, the more readily it should be discarded altogether when it is corrupted by even low levels of noise.

- The payoff in noise reduction increases with the importance of the attribute.

This statement is not as obvious as it may appear. All the experiments have confirmed a strong relation between the degradation in performance as an attribute is corrupted and the importance of that attribute. Remember that *importance* of an attribute is not a subjective term but a value that can be computed over any given training set, noisy or otherwise. Therefore, if additional resources were available to minimize errors in describing objects, the importance model would indicate the attribute to which the extra effort could most profitably be applied.

- The majority method of assigning classes to leaves is preferable to the probability method.

Any concept-learning system operating in a noisy environment must face the problem of what to do when apparently indistinguishable objects in its training set belong to different classes. Any such system must decide to assign a subcollection of indistinguishable objects to some class, and this paper has explored two of the more obvious ways to make that assignment. The majority method, as noted earlier, leads to the minimum number of expected errors on retrial when the objects at a leaf are assigned to a single class. In some situations, such as when a single attribute is affected by noise, the majority and probability methods give identical results. However, figures 6-2, 6-3, 6-5, and 6-6 demonstrate that the majority method also gives lower error rates when the decision tree is used to classify new objects (or different corruptions of old objects), and the discrepancy between the methods can be substantial when noise rates are high.

6.8 CONCLUSION

The work reported here falls into three parts. First, a tree-building procedure has been developed that can cope with noisy data. Second, the procedure has been implemented (in the language C) and extensive trials carried out on two real classification tasks with controlled addition of noise. Finally, as a consequence of the experimental results obtained in these trials, conjectures have been advanced about the use of noisy attributes and the expected benefits of reducing noise.

This study has been almost entirely empirical. The next step is obviously to try to understand, at a more abstract level, some of the observed phenomena, such as the different degradation curve shapes for noise in attribute and class information. It would also be interesting to find out whether similar results are obtained with alternative systems for constructing classification rules.

References

Hogg, R. V., and Craig, A. T., *Introduction to Mathematical Statistics,* 3d ed., Macmillan, New York, 1970.

Michalski, R. S., "A Theory and Methodology of Inductive Learning," in *Machine Learning: An Artificial Intelligence Approach,* R. S. Michalski, J. G. Carbonell, and T. M. Mitchell (Eds.), Tioga, Palo Alto, Calif., 1983.

Quinlan, J. R., "Learning Efficient Classification Procedures and Their Application to Chess End Games," in *Machine Learning: An Artificial Intelligence Approach,* R. S. Michalski, J. G. Carbonell, and T. M. Mitchell (Eds.), Tioga, Palo Alto, Calif., 1983.

7

LEARNING CONCEPTS BY ASKING QUESTIONS

Claude Sammut
University of New South Wales

Ranan B. Banerji
Saint Joseph's University

Abstract

Two important issues in machine learning are explored: (1) the role that memory plays in acquiring new concepts and (2) the extent to which the learner can take an active part in acquiring these concepts. This chapter describes MARVIN, a program that uses previously learned concepts to learn new concepts. The program forms hypotheses about the concept being learned and tests the hypotheses by asking the trainer questions.

Learning begins when the trainer shows MARVIN an example of the concept to be learned. The program determines which objects in the example belong to concepts stored in the memory. A description of the new concept is formed by using the information obtained from the memory to generalize the description of the training example. The generalized description is tested when the program constructs new examples and shows them to the trainer, asking if they belong to the target concept.

7.1 INTRODUCTION

From personal experience we know that it is hard to learn new concepts unless we already understand quite a lot about the subject we are studying. For example, when mathematics is taught in school, the teacher begins with a simple problem like, What are numbers? Later, more complicated concepts, such as addition and then multiplication, are presented. Usually many years of patient accumulation of knowledge in a given field are required before one can fully understand the most complex concepts in that field. To be able to learn in stages, the student must have a memory he or she can use to integrate all the knowledge acquired. As new concepts are added to the memory, the student's vocabulary broadens, enabling him or her to describe still more complex concepts.

As well as using memory, a human student also asks questions to learn. Often a teacher will show the student an example to explain a new concept. However, a few examples are not always enough to define the concept completely. It is easy to generalize from a small number of examples and come up with an incorrect idea of the concept that the teacher wants the student to learn. Questions often help to identify those parts of the concept that have been misunderstood.

MARVIN is a program that can learn complex concepts by using its memory of simpler concepts to help describe the newer concepts. MARVIN also asks the trainer questions to check that its description of the concept is correct. A concept is informally defined as the description of a set of objects in some universe. An object is called a *positive example* of a concept if the object is in the set defined by the concept description. A *negative example* is an object not contained in the set.

MARVIN begins learning a new concept when the trainer shows it an object that is a positive example of the concept to be learned (the *target concept*). The description of the example represents a concept that contains only one object, the example itself. The target concept is a generalization of the example because it contains that object and perhaps many other objects. One concept P is a *generalization* of another concept Q if Q describes a subset of P. Alternatively, we say that Q is a *specialization* of P. MARVIN's task is to discover the description of the target. It will do this by searching for a generalization of the initial example that contains all the positive examples of the target and none of the negative examples.

Suppose P is a generalization of the initial example. Also suppose that P describes a subset of the target. That is, P only contains objects that are positive examples of the target. We say that P is a *consistent generalization* of the initial example. If Q is a generalization that contains an object not in the target, then we will say that Q is an *inconsistent generalization* of the target. A generalization of the initial example is called a *trial concept*.

MARVIN's search for the target concept is a *specific-to-general* search, that is, the program begins with the initial example and creates a new trial concept by generalizing the example slightly. If the generalization is consistent, then MARVIN creates a new trial that is a generalization of the previous one. To find out if a generalization is inconsistent, the program constructs objects that are contained in the trial and shows them to the trainer. If the trainer answers that one of the objects is not contained in the target, then the generalization is inconsistent. When this occurs, MARVIN tries to create a new trial that is more specific than the previous one; that is, it tries to create a concept that excludes the negative examples of the target. If specialization fails to produce a consistent trial, then a different generalization is tried.

MARVIN will continue to make as many generalizations as it can as long as it can maintain consistency. When it has run out of generalizations, the concept description is stored in the program's memory.

So far we have not specified how MARVIN describes concepts. The concept description language is a subset of first-order predicate logic very similar to PROLOG. MARVIN constructs example objects by taking a concept description and executing it as if it were a program. For MARVIN, learning a concept is equivalent to synthesizing a logic program.

The program consists of four major components:

- A memory containing the descriptions of concepts that have been learned or provided by the trainer as background knowledge
- A pattern matcher that determines if objects shown to the program belong to concepts stored in the memory
- A simple theorem prover that, given a concept description, generates objects that satisfy the conditions in the description
- A search strategy that directs the operation of the other components in order to find a description for the concept that the trainer is trying to teach the program

The work on MARVIN has grown out of earlier efforts by Banerji (1964) and Cohen (1978), who both stressed the importance of a learning system's being able to extend its power to describe concepts through learning. In the following section the representation language used by MARVIN is described.

7.2 REPRESENTING CONCEPTS IN FIRST-ORDER LOGIC

A concept is represented by a set of *Horn clauses.* These are expressions in first-order predicate calculus having the form

$$P(X) \leftarrow Q(X) \ \& \ R(X) \ \& \ S(X).$$

That is, an object X belongs to the concept P if the predicates Q and R and S are true. The clause will be called a definition of the concept P.

As an example, let us describe the concept *tee.* An object X is a *tee* if it consists of two objects. One object A may have any shape and lies on top of another object B, which is a brick and which is standing up.

$tee(X) \leftarrow$
        A is_part_of X &
        B is_part_of X &
        A is_on B &
        any_shape(A) &
        lying(A) &

brick(B) &
standing(B).

We can think of this clause as describing the set of all objects X that satisfy the conditions on the right-hand side of the arrow; *any_shape* is defined as

any_shape(X) ← brick(X).
any_shape(X) ← wedge(X).

That is, the shape of an object in this world may be a brick or a wedge.

MARVIN's *long-term* memory is a database of such clauses. The program also has a *short-term* memory containing the set of *facts* that describe individual objects presented by the trainer as examples. By *fact* we mean a *unit clause*, that is, a clause with no right-hand side. Thus an instance x of the concept *tee* would appear in the short-term memory as

a is_part_of x.
b is_part_of x.
b is_on a.
brick(a).
wedge(b).
standing(a).
lying(b).

This describes a wedge lying on top of a brick.

Originally generalization and specialization were defined in terms of sets of objects. These definitions help one to understand what those operations mean, but they do not give one an effective way of performing generalizations or specializations. To construct a description of a concept P that is more general than Q, the program must transform the expression in the description language that represents Q into another expression that represents P; that is, generalizations and specializations must be defined as operations that manipulate the description language.

7.3 GENERALIZATIONS

Suppose x is an object defined by the following predicates: $Q_1(x)$ & $R_1(x)$ & $S_1(x)$. If there is a concept represented by

$P(X)$ ← $Q_1(X)$ & $R_1(X)$ & $S_1(X)$.
$P(X)$ ← $Q_2(X)$ & $R_2(X)$ & $S_2(X)$.

then x is a positive example of the concept P. Note that the conjunction of predicates describing x matches the conjunction on the right-hand side of the first clause. Now suppose x is an object appearing in some visual scene shown to MARVIN. Since x is an example of P, the program can try to generalize the description of the scene by asking, "If I replace x with some other example of P, has the scene been changed in any essential way?" In the last example of the previous section, b was a wedge and also an instance of *any_shape*. The description of x can be generalized by replacing *wedge(b)* by *any_shape(b)*. Wedge(b) matches the right-hand side of one clause of *any_shape*.

When replacement operations are performed, clauses are thought of as rewrite rules. Rewrite rules are most commonly used to define the grammar of a language. In fact, the set of clauses stored in MARVIN's memory defines a language. Sentences in the language describe objects belonging to concepts known to MARVIN. A distinction should be maintained between the concept description language (i.e., Horn clauses in first-order logic) and the language that describes the set of all objects recognizable by the program. The latter is a subset of the description language. Shapiro (1981) gives a more rigorous discussion of the relationship between these two languages.

Replacement—such as changing *wedge(b)* to *any_shape(b)*—is the fundamental operation used in generalization. When there are a large number of concepts stored in the long-term memory, many such replacements are possible. The description of one instance of a concept may be transformed into many different generalizations. The main problem for the learning program is to search efficiently through the space of all such generalizations. Before a formal definition of generalization is given, let us consider another example.

Suppose we wish to describe a column of bricks as a brick standing on the ground or a brick standing on another column. This is a recursive description consisting of two clauses:

column(X) ←
    brick(X) &
    standing(X) &
    X is_on Y,
    ground(Y).

column(X) ←
    brick(X) &
    standing(X) &
    X is_on Y &
    column(Y).

It is implicit that variables such as Y are existentially quantified. Suppose that these clauses as well as others form the set of clauses in the long-term memory $S_i \leftarrow M_i$. Also assume that there is a set of facts C_0 in short-term memory that consists of the following unit clauses:

brick(a).   (1)
standing(a).   (2)

a is_on b.   (3)
brick(b).   (4)
standing(b).   (5)
b is_on c.   (6)
ground(c).   (7)

If b is substituted for the variable X and c for the variable Y, then predicates (4), (5), (6), and (7) match the right-hand side of the first clause in the definition of *column;* that is, b is an example of the concept *column*. The *substitution* for this match is the set of pairs $\{X/a, Y/B\}$. C_0 can be *elaborated* by the addition of the predicate *column*(b) to form C_1.

brick(a).   (1)
standing(a).   (2)
a is_on b.   (3)
brick(b).   (4)
standing(b).   (5)
b is_on c.   (6)
ground(c).   (7)
column(b).   (8)

Now predicates (1), (2), (3), and (8) match the right-hand side of the second clause of *column* with the substitution $\{X/a, Y/b\}$. Thus a new set C_2 can be constructed by the addition of *column*(a) to C_1.

The process called *elaboration* simply entails finding out which objects in the short-term memory are examples of concepts that MARVIN knows. This requires that the program match object descriptions with the right-hand sides of clauses and then add the left-hand side to the short-term memory.

The pattern-matching operations used in the elaboration will now be defined. It is convenient to think of conjunctions of predicates as being equivalent to sets of predicates. In what follows, sets will almost always contain predicates or clauses, not objects.

Definition 1: Given a set of clauses

$$S_1 \leftarrow M_1$$
$$\vdots$$
$$S_k \leftarrow M_k$$

and a set of predicates C, we say that C' is an *elaboration* of C if there is an M_i and a substitution σ such that

$$\sigma M_i \subseteq C \text{ and } C' = C \cup \sigma\{S_i\}.$$

The set C represents the set of facts that are presented to the program by the trainer as a description of an instance of the concept to be learned. The program expands or elaborates this definition by finding those clauses stored in memory whose right-hand sides match a subset of C. The left-hand sides of the clauses are added to C to form C'. The pattern matcher uses a simple unification procedure (Robinson, 1965) to construct substitutions for the variables in the clause. The effect of this elaboration is to augment the description of the example using the knowledge that MARVIN has acquired previously.

When predicate (8) was added to C, it enabled MARVIN to find more matches in memory. In this way, sets of predicates can be elaborated repeatedly, giving a sequence of new sets derived from C_0.

Definition 2: Given a set C_0, we define a sequence $C_0 \ldots C_n$ such that C_{i+1} is an elaboration of C_i and C_n cannot be elaborated further. We write

$$\text{All\_Elaborations}(C_0) = C_n,$$

representing the set of all predicates derived from C_0.

The information obtained through elaboration is used to construct hypotheses, or *trials,* for the concept being learned. The initial trial T_0 is always equivalent to C_0. The program may generalize T_i to a new trial T_{i+1} by replacing predicates in T_i that match the right-hand side of a clause with the predicate on the left.

Again using the column example, we begin with T_0 equivalent to C_0. The first trial T_1 may be obtained by replacing the predicates (4), (5), (6), and (7) with column (*b*), giving:

brick(*a*).	(1)
standing(*a*).	(2)
a is_on *b*.	(3)
column(*b*).	(8)

Clearly this is a generalization of T_0, since b may now be a column of any height. The following definition shows exactly how we arrive at a replacement operation such as the one above.

Definition 3: If T_i is a trial concept and M is a subset of T_i, and if there exists a clause in memory $S \leftarrow M'$ such that with the substitution of σ, $M = \sigma M'$, then we define a replacement operation that will create a new trial T_{i+1} such that

$$T_{i+1} = T_i - M \cup \sigma\{S\}.$$

T_{i+1} is called a *generalization* of T_i. If there is more than one clause in the definition of the concept S, the T_{i+1} is more general than T_i, since S describes a larger set of objects than M does.

In the example, T_i can be generalized further. All of the remaining predicates match the second clause in the description of *column.* They can all be replaced by the single predicate *column (a).* Thus, a sequence of more general trials can be produced.

Definition 4: If $T_0, \ldots T_k$ is a sequence of trials such that T_i generalizes to T_{i+1}, then we say T_0 satisfies T_k.

Notice that making generalizations is exactly the same as recognizing that an object belongs to a concept. Although the program may construct many generalizations, only those that are less general than or the same as the target are of interest. Once a generalization has been created, we must be able to test if it is consistent or not.

Definition 5: Trial T is consistent with the target T' if any object that satisfies T also satisfies T'.

The next section describes what is done when an inconsistent trial is constructed.

7.4 SPECIALIZATIONS

A generalization results in the replacement of a set of predicates in a trial by a single, more general predicate. The replacement operation throws away some specific information contained in the set M (i.e., those predicates that matched the right-hand side of the clause) in favor of the more general statement S (i.e., the left-hand side of the clause). If the new trial is consistent, then the information lost was not important. However, if the generalization is inconsistent, then too much information was lost. To make T_{i+1} more specific, MARVIN reexamines the predicates in M to determine which ones contain essential information.

Suppose we wish to teach MARVIN what an arch is. Assume that, among other things, MARVIN has already learned the concepts *any_shape* and *same_shape,* shown below.

$$\text{any\_shape}(X) \leftarrow \text{brick}(X).$$
$$\text{any\_shape}(X) \leftarrow \text{wedge}(X). \tag{1}$$

$$\text{same\_shape}(X,Y) \leftarrow \text{brick}(X) \,\&\, \text{brick}(Y).$$
$$\text{same\_shape}(X,Y) \leftarrow \text{wedge}(X) \,\&\, \text{wedge}(Y). \tag{2}$$

The following set of predicates describes the example of an arch shown by the trainer:

a is_part_of x.
b is_part_of x.
c is_part_of x.
a is_on b.
a is_on c.
b left_of c.
b does_not_touch c.
lying(a).
wedge(a).
standing(b).
brick(b). (3)

standing(c).
brick(c).   (4)

This forms the initial trial T_0. The final definition of *arch* should include the specification that the two columns b and c may have any shape as long as they are both the same. Now let us begin generating trial descriptions of *arch* by performing replacements.

1. Since b is a brick, it is an instance of *any_shape;* thus one possible trial T_1 replaces *brick(b)* above with *any_shape(b)*, using clause (1).

2. This generalization would allow b to be a wedge while c remains a brick. Note that the generalization is not totally incorrect since b may be a wedge; however, additional information must be added to qualify the generalization. This additional information is obtained by searching for another replacement that involves at least one of the predicates removed from the original trial.

3. Predicates (3) and (4) match the right-hand side of clause (2), and predicate (3) also matches the right-hand side of clause (1). A new trial T_2 may be formed by adding *some_shape(b, c)* to T_1. This specialization creates a consistent trial.

Note that since clause (2) completely subsumes the clause (1) predicate, *any_shape(b)* can be ignored in the new trial. In general, this would not be the case. *Specialization* can now be defined as follows:

Definition 6: Suppose T is a trial concept. Let

$$T^1 = T - M^1 \cup \sigma^1\{S^1\}$$

be a generalization of T obtained by replacing a subset of predicates, that is, M^1, with a reference to the concept S^1. Let

$$T^2 = T - M^2 \cup \sigma^2\{S^2\}$$

be another generalization of T, such that

$$M^1 \cap M^2 \neq \emptyset;$$

then $T^1 \cup T^2$ is *more specific* than either T^1 or T^2.

The purpose of the specialization operation defined above is to conjoin two generalizations of T; that is, specialization will force the program to search for conjunctions of generalizations. Without specialization, MARVIN could only discover generalizations that consist of single replacements. MARVIN will usually attempt one generalization—say, T^1—and if it finds the generalization to be inconsistent it will look for T^2 to make the trial more specific.

7.5 CONSTRUCTING EXAMPLES TO TEST HYPOTHESES

To find out if a trial T_{i+1} is consistent or not, MARVIN shows the trainer an instance of T_{i+1}. If the program can create an object that does not belong to the target but does belong to T_{i+1}, then T_{i+1} is inconsistent. However, since the program has not yet learned the description of the target concept, how can we guarantee that an object not in the target is shown to the trainer when the trial is inconsistent?

The set All_Elaborations(T_0) contains all predicates that can be inferred from T_0. If the target concept can be learned at all, then its description must be a subset of All_Elaborations(T_0). Any object that fails to satisfy any of the predicates in this set cannot belong to the target. To test the trial T_{i+1}, MARVIN constructs an object that does not satisfy any of the predicates in All_Elaborations(T_0), with the exception that T_{i+1} and anything that it implies must be satisfied. This guarantees that, if at all possible, an object will be constructed so that it belongs to the trial concept but not to the target. If the trial is consistent, then the object must belong to the target.

> **Definition 7:** *Let* T_{i+1} *be a generalization of* T_i. *Any object that satisfies* T_{i+1} *but negates each element of*
>
> $$\text{All\_Elaborations}(T_i) \; - \; \text{All\_Elaborations}(T_{i+1})$$
>
> *is called a* crucial *object. If* T_i *is consistent with the target and* T_{i+1} *is not, then no crucial object satisfies the target.*

Recall that in the example in section 7.3 the description T_0 of a column consisting of two blocks was generalized to the description T_1 of a block resting on another column. By Definition 7, an object that can be used to test the generalization may be constructed by the following procedure:

1. Find all elaborations of T_0:

brick(a).	(1)
standing(a).	(2)
a is_on b.	(3)
brick(b).	(4)
standing(b).	(5)
b is_on c.	(6)
ground(c).	(7)
column(b).	(8)
column(a).	(9)

2. Find the set of all predicates implied by T_1, that is, all elaborations of T_1:

brick(a).	(1)
standing(a).	(2)
a is_on b.	(3)
column(b).	(8)
column(a).	(9)

3. Find All_Elaborations (T_0) $-$ All_Elaborations(T_1):

brick(b).	(4)
standing(b).	(5)

b is_on c. (6)

ground(c). (7)

4. Construct an object that satisfies T_1 but does not satisfy any of the four predicates (4), (5), (6), or (7). The resulting object will consist of a brick on top of at least two more bricks. Negation of predicates (4), (5), (6), and (7) prevents the bottom of the column from being a single brick standing on the ground.

Methods for generalizing and specializing concept description have now been developed, as well as a way of testing whether those descriptions are consistent or not. In the following section, all of these elements will be brought together to create the complete MARVIN.

7.6 AN OVERVIEW OF THE LEARNING ALGORITHM

Let us now summarize MARVIN's learning algorithm:

To learn a new clause:

1. Receive an example of the concept from the trainer.
2. Find the list of all replacement operations obtainable from the primary predicates.
3. Use these operations to generalize the initial trial.
4. Store the resulting concept in memory.

To find the list of replacement operations:

1. Let C initially be the set of all facts describing the training example.
2. Find the set I of all concepts implied by C.
3. Append I to C.
4. Repeat this procedure until no more implied concepts can be found. The result is All_Elaborations(C). The list of replacement operations consists of all the clauses used to find the implied concepts in All_Elaborations(P) (see Definitions 1 and 2).

To generalize a trial T_i:

1. Choose the first concept in the list of replacement operations.
2. Perform the replacement to obtain T_{i+1} (see Definition 3).
3. Try to *qualify* T_{i+1}.
4. If T_{i+1} cannot be qualified, abandon this replacement.
5. Repeat this procedure with the next replacement operation in the list.

To qualify a trial, T_{i+1}:

1. Construct a crucial object that satisfies T_{i+1} but does not satisfy the set

   All_Elaborations(T_i) $-$ All_Elaborations(T_{i+1})

   (see Definition 7).
2. Ask trainer if object satisfies target. If it does, then T_{i+1} has been qualified.
3. If it does not, then specialize T_{i+1} to a new trial T_{i+2}.
4. Try to qualify T_{i+2}.

To specialize a trial T_{i+1}:

1. Search list of replacement operations for a clause $S \leftarrow M$ such that $M \cap M^{i+1} \neq \emptyset$; M^{i+1} comes from the replacement that produced T_{i+1}.
2. Perform replacement on T_{i+1} to obtain the new trial T_{i+2} (see Definition 6).

To construct an example from a trial T_{i+1}:

1. To construct an example from $P \& Q$: Construct P, Construct Q.
2. To construct an example from an atomic predicate P when there is a set of clauses $\{P \leftarrow B_i\}$ in memory:

   a. Select a B_i such that

   $B \cap$ (All_Elaborations(T_i) $-$ All_Elaborations(T_{i+1})) $= \emptyset$

   b. Construct an example using the selected B_i.
3. To construct an example from an atomic predicate P when there is no clause $P \leftarrow B$, add P to the set of predicates representing the example.

7.7 A TYPICAL LEARNING TASK

In this section the steps involved in learning the description of an arch will be discussed. This time the description will be slightly more involved than the version discussed in section 7.4. MARVIN will learn that an arch consists of an object of any shape lying on top of two columns of equal height. The columns are adjacent to each other, but they must not touch.

Initially the program's memory is empty. Since concepts stored in the memory are essential to performing generalizations, any object shown to MARVIN that it cannot recognize is simply remembered without any attempt at generalizations. If the trainer states that x is a brick and x is an example of the concept *any_shape,* MARVIN will remember this fact.

When MARVIN begins operation, it often starts by learning basic concepts by rote; *any_shape* and *any_orientation* will be learned in this way.

any_shape(X) $\leftarrow$ brick(X).
any_shape(X) $\leftarrow$ wedge(X).

any_orientation(X) ← standing(X).
any_orientation(X) ← lying(X).

These concepts may be written out to file at the end of one learning session and reloaded at a later time so that they need not be relearned.

The description of *arch* will contain references to two quite complex concepts, namely, *column* and *same_height*. A concept like *arch* cannot be learned unless the other concepts to which it refers are already in the memory. In an analogy to describing something in English, one cannot adequately describe a table unless one knows about words like *leg* and *flat*. After teaching MARVIN about shape and orientation, the trainer presents examples of columns.

The details of the learning session will not be discussed here until the program starts learning about arches. It is important to note that the description of *column* is recursive, that is, it refers to itself. Because of this, the trainer must take care in presenting examples of columns. The first example must teach MARVIN about the non-recursive disjunct of the description. That is the first clause shown below. Having learned this, the program is then able to recognize the recursive nature of more complex examples.

column(X) ←
    brick(X) &
    standing(X) &
    X is_on Y &
    ground(Y).

column(X) ←
    brick(X) &
    standing(X) &
    X is_on Y &
    column(Y).

In this learning session, columns will consist only of bricks. The same consideration for recursive concepts applies to learning *same_height*. The heights of two columns may be compared by scanning down both columns to see if the ground is reached at the same time.

same_height(X, Y) ←
    ground(X) &
    ground(Y).

same_height($X1, X2$) ←
    brick($X1$) &
    standing($X1$) &
    brick($X2$) &
    standing($X2$) &

*X*1 is_on *Y*1 &
*X*2 is_on *Y*2 &
same_height(*Y*1, *Y*2).

To complete MARVIN's background knowledge so that it can learn about arches, the trainer must also teach it the following concepts:

X adjacent_to *Y* ← *X* left_of *Y.*
X adjacent_to *Y* ← *Y* left_of *X.*

X may_touch *Y* ← *X* touches *Y.*
X may_touch *Y* ← *X* does_not_touch *Y.*

X may_be_on *Y* ← *X* is_on *Y.*
X may_be_on *Y* ← *X* is_not_on *Y.*

Assuming that all the above concepts are now present in MARVIN's memory, the trainer can begin to teach it what an arch is. The program is presented with the description of an instance of *arch*, shown below (see figure 7-1).

A part_of *X.*
B part_of *X.*
C part_of *X.*
A is_on *B.*
A is_on *C.*
B is_on *D.*
C is_on *E.*
ground(*D*).
ground(*E*).
B left_of *C.*
B does_not_touch *C.*
lying(*A*).
wedge(*A*).
standing(*B*).
brick(*B*).
standing(*C*).
brick(*C*).

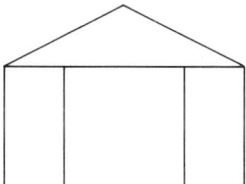

Figure 7-1:   An example of the concept *arch.*

Having seen an example of the concept, the pattern matcher determines which objects in the example belong to concepts in the memory. This recognition process results in the generation of all possible replacements. These are shown below with the predicates to be replaced on the right-hand side of the arrow and the predicate replacing them on the left.

any_shape(*B*) ← brick(*B*).   (1)
any_shape(*C*) ← brick(*C*).   (2)
any_shape(*A*) ← wedge(*A*).   (3)

any_orientation(B) ← standing(B).   (4)
any_orientation(C) ← standing(C).   (5)
any_orientation(A) ← lying(A).   (6)

column(B) ← brick(B) & standing(B) & B is_on D & ground(D). (7)
column(C) ← brick(C) & standing(C) & C is_on E & ground(E). (8)

same_height(D, E) ← ground(D) & ground(E).   (9)
same_height(B, C) ←   (10)
    brick(B) &
    standing(B) &
    brick (C) &
    standing(C) &
    B is_on D &
    C is_on E &
    same_height(D, E).

B adjacent_to C ← B left_of C.   (11)

B may_touch C ← B does_not_touch C.   (12)

A may_be_on B ← A is_on B.   (13)
A may_be_on C ← A is_on C.   (14)
B may_be_on D ← B is_on D.   (15)
C may_be_on E ← C is_on E.   (16)

The program takes each replacement in turn and attempts to create a consistent trial. The first replacement attempts to generalize the shape of B. This results in the following trial:

    A part of X.
    B part_of X.
    C part_of X.
    A is_on B.
    A is_on C.
    B is_on D.
    C is_on E.
    ground(D).
    ground(E).
    B left_of C.
    B does_not_touch C.
    lying(A).
    wedge(A).
    standing(B).
    standing(C).
    brick(C).
    any_shape(B).

To test this trial, the program asks if the following figure is an example of an arch (see figure 7-2):

A part_of *X.*
B part_of *X.*
C part_of *X.*
A is_on *B.*
A is_on *C.*
B is_on *D.*
C is_on *E.*
ground(*D*).
ground(*E*).
B left_of *C.*
B does_not_touch *C.*
lying(*A*).
wedge(*A*).
standing(*B*).
standing(*C*).
brick(*C*).
wedge(*B*).

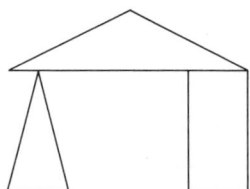

Figure 7-2:   Another example of the concept *arch.*

A new object has been created in which the shape of *B* has been changed to a wedge. The trainer responds no, indicating that this is an inconsistent trial.

Since the trial is inconsistent, another trial that is more specific must be constructed. This is done by finding another replacement that involves the predicate *brick(B)*. The program selects replacement (7), resulting in the following new trial:

A part_of *X.*
B part_of *X.*
C part_of *X.*
A is_on *B.*
A is_on *C.*
B is_on *D.*
C is_on *E.*
ground(*D*).
ground(*E*).
B left_of *C.*
B does_not_touch *C.*
lying(*A*).
wedge(*A*).
standing(*C*).
brick(*C*).
column(*B*).

This generates the following training example (see figure 7-3):

A part_of X.
B part_of X.
C part_of X.
A is_on B.
A is_on C.
C is_on E.
ground(E).
B left_of C.
B does_not_touch C.
lying(A).
wedge(A).
standing(C).
brick(C).
brick(B).
standing(B).
B is_on _1.
brick(_1).
standing(_1).
_1 is_on _2.
ground(_2).

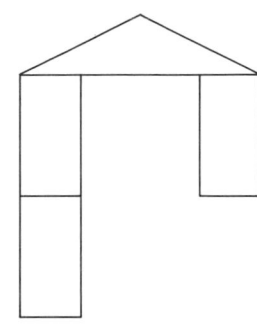

Figure 7-3:   A counterexample of the concept *arch*.

Since replacement (7) generalizes B to any column, MARVIN constructs a new example in which B is a column but not the same one as before. B is now a two-brick column. _1 and _2 are names generated by the program to stand for new objects. Since the left and right columns of the arch must be the same height, the trainer responds no again. Thus the trial must be specialized even further. Since the right-hand sides of replacements (7) and (10) have a nonempty intersection, replacement (10) is selected to make the trial more specific. This new trial is as follows:

A part_of X.
B part_of X.
C part_of X.
A is_on B.
A is_on C.
B left_of C.
B does_not_touch C.
lying(A).
wedge(A).
column(B).
same_height(B,C).

The program now constructs a new example in which both columns are two bricks high. The trainer indicates that this trial is consistent, so MARVIN can now resume generalizing.

The remaining questions asked by MARVIN will not be shown in detail. However, the program will go on to test the shape of *A,* which can be generalized to any shape. However, *A* cannot assume any orientation; it must be lying down. MARVIN will discover that *B* is adjacent to *C* but must not touch *C.* Finally it will conclude that the description of an arch is as follows:

> *A* part_of *X.*
> *B* part_of *X.*
> *C* part_of *X.*
> *A* is_on *B.*
> *A* is_on *C.*
> column(*B*).
> same_height(*B, C*).
> column(*C*).
> any_shape(*A*).
> lying(*A*).
> *B* adjacent_to *C.*
> *B* does_not_touch *C.*

In all, eight questions are asked before MARVIN is finished. However, it should be noted that in general the number of questions asked depends on the number of concepts in memory that match parts of the example. As the size of the memory increases, so will the number of questions.

7.8 CONCEPTS THAT MARVIN HAS LEARNED

In this section some of the concepts that MARVIN has been able to learn will be described.

Since concepts are represented as Horn clauses in first-order logic, they can be viewed as logic programs. Thus MARVIN is able to perform not only as a learning system, but also as an automatic programming system. The class of programs that can be synthesized is limited by the way in which variables are created. When the trainer presents an example to the program, each object in the example is given a name. When the description is generalized and turned into a concept, the object names become variables. MARVIN has no ability to invent existentially quantified variables other than those derived from the example, nor can it deal with universal quantification.

Some of the concepts MARVIN has learned are as follows:

- *List manipulation.* A list can be represented by a recursive concept similar to *column.* A column is an object with a top that is a brick and a bottom that is another column. Similarly, a list is an object with a head of some specified type and a tail that is another list. The trainer can teach MARVIN to append lists by showing it examples consisting of input/output pairs for the concept *append.* Using a PROLOG-like notation, the trainer might present an example like *append*([ ], [*1*], [*1*]). Another example might *append*([*1*], [*2*], [*1, 2*]). If these two examples were shown in that order, MARVIN would have enough information to synthesize both clauses of the recursive concept. Once it knows how to append lists, MARVIN can then learn to reverse them, again by seeing examples of input/output pairs.

- *Arithmetic on numbers represented as strings of binary digits.* A string of bits can be represented as a list of objects that can be either 0 or 1. MARVIN can learn to compare numbers by learning the concept *less.* As examples, the program would be shown pairs of numbers in which one was less than the other. Input/output pairs can also be presented to the program in order to teach it about addition and other arithmetic operations.

- *Sorting.* Once the program knows how to do arithmetic and manipulate lists, it can learn how to sort lists of numbers. It can learn a simple insertion sort. However, because of the program's inability to invent new existentially quantified variables, learning more efficient sorting algorithms, such as quicksort, is beyond its capabilities.

- *Grammar rules.* MARVIN is capable of learning to recognize sentences in context-free grammars. For example, the program has been taught to recognize a very limited subset of English. A string of words can be represented as a list. Concepts such as *verb, noun,* and so on, are taught first, so that the program can identify parts of speech. After that, MARVIN can learn to recognize noun phrases and verb phrases and so on until the representation of a complete sentence has been acquired. One of the interesting problems encountered in the course of teaching such grammatical concepts to MARVIN is that concepts such as *noun phrase* and *verb phrase* can refer to each other. Since the concepts are disjunctive, the concepts can be taught in steps. One concept is partially learned, then part of the second is learned, and then the description of the first concept can be completed. Sammut discusses this problem more fully (1981).

- *A more difficult language recognition problem* that MARVIN has learned to solve is that posed by Hayes-Roth and McDermott (1978). The task was to learn the rules to transform a sentence in the active form, such as "The little man sang a lovely song," to the passive form—"A lovely song was sung by the little man."

- *Geometrical concepts* as described by Michalski (1980) have also been learned.

MARVIN has proved to be capable of learning many concepts in a variety of domains. In the next section areas of possible improvement will be discussed.

7.9 DETECTING ERRORS IN CONCEPT DESCRIPTIONS

It has been seen that the trainer has the responsibility for teaching MARVIN all the necessary background knowledge required to describe any new concept that is to be learned. This means that the trainer must carefully choose the training examples and the order in which they are presented. To see what happens when concepts are not taught in the best order, let us return to the description of columns.

We now wish to make the definition slightly more general by allowing cylinders as well as bricks to make up a column, but not wedges. Suppose that *any shape* in our blocks world is defined as follows:

any_shape(X) ← brick(X).
any_shape(X) ← cylinder(X).
any_shape(X) ← wedge(X).   (R1)

If MARVIN is shown an example of a column without first being taught to distinguish wedges from bricks and cylinders, it will construct the wrong description for a column. Remember that to generalize a description, the program replaces predicates that match the right-hand side of a clause with the corresponding left-hand side. If the example of the column contained bricks, then MARVIN would recognize the brick as belonging to *any_shape* and attempt to generalize. To test the generalization, it would construct another instance of the concept. In this case, the program could construct a column with cylinders. This would be an instance of the target concept, even though the description it has created is too general.

If MARVIN had first learned a concept such as *flat_top* defined as

flat_top(X) ← brick(X).
flat_top(X) ← cylinder(X).

then the correct description of a column could be learned. The problem here is, How can we determine that a concept description has been learned incorrectly?

Let us suppose that we are carrying on an extended dialogue with MARVIN, and at some point we see that the program has stated that an object is a *tee* even though it is not. MARVIN's description of *tee* must be incorrect. However, supposing that *tee* is now defined as a brick lying on a column, is the bug the description of *tee* itself, or is it in one of the concepts that it refers to, such as *column?* We can "debug" the concept by using a method similar to Shapiro's backtrace (1981). To illustrate this

method, let us continue with the *tees* and columns. Assume that the concept description *any_shape,* above, has been learned, as well as the following:

column(X) ←   (R2)
    ground(Y).

column(X) ←   (R3)

    any_shape(X) &
    standing(X) &
    X is_on_Y &
    column(Y).

tee(T) ←   (R4)

    X is_part_of T &
    Y is_part_of T &
    brick(X) &
    lying(X) &
    X is_on Y &
    column(Y).

The first clause in this version of *column* has been simplified to make the explanation
easier.

    Now suppose that the following object, X, has been incorrectly recognized as a
tee (see figure 7-4):

A part_of X.	(1)
B part_of X.	(3)
A is_on B.	(4)
B is_on C.	(5)
brick(A).	(6)
lying(A).	(7)
wedge(B).	(8)
standing(B).	(9)
ground(C).	(10)

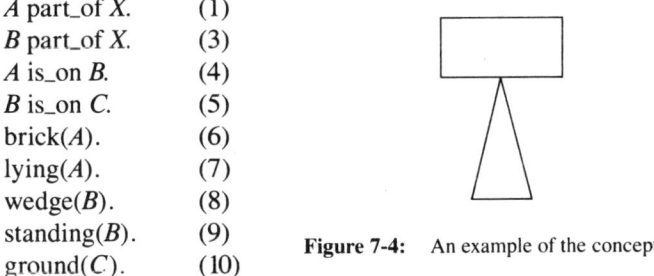

Figure 7-4:   An example of the concept *tee.*

    We will debug the concept descriptions by tracing through the steps MARVIN
took to recognize this object incorrectly as a *tee.* Let us first list those steps.

1. Predicate (8) matches (R1), the third clause of *any_shape.* Performing a
   replacement leaves us with the following:

A part_of X.	(1)
B part_of X.	(3)
A is_on B.	(4)
B is_on C.	(5)
brick(A).	(6)

lying(A).   (7)
standing(B).   (9)
ground(C).   (10)
any_shape(B).   (11)

2. Predicate (10) matches (R2), the first clause of *column*. Replacing predicate (10) with the corresponding predicate in the left-hand side of that clause leaves the following:

A part_of X.   (1)
B part_of X.   (3)
A is_on B.   (4)
B is_on C.   (5)
brick(A).   (6)
lying(A).   (7)
standing(B).   (9)
any_shape(B).   (11)
column(C).   (12)

3. Predicates (5), (9), (11), and (12) match (R3), the second clause of *column*. The replacement leaves the following:

A part_of X.   (1)
B part_of X.   (3)
A is_on B.   (4)
brick(A).   (6)
lying(A).   (7)
column(B).   (13)

4. All of the remaining predicates match (R4), the description of *tee,* leaving

   tee(X).   (14)

Thus, the object has been incorrectly recognized as a *tee.*

When the trainer has told MARVIN that this derivation is incorrect, the program retraces its steps, asking the trainer to confirm that each replacement should have taken place. The following questions correspond to each of the steps above.

1. MARVIN checks the first replacement for correctness by asking the trainer, "Is B an example of *any_shape?*" If the answer is yes, then the program continues. In this case, a wedge is an example of *any_shape.*

2. Checking step 2, MARVIN asks, "Is C an example of a *column?*" Again, the answer is yes.

3. Finally, checking the third replacement, MARVIN asks, "Is B an example of *column?*" This time, the trainer answers no. Thus the offending clause, (R3), has been identified.

Note that the description of *any_shape* is not incorrect. It is the definition of *column* that is too general. The next step in debugging the concept is to identify the predicate within the clause that is incorrect.

Since the object *B* was incorrectly classified as a column, MARVIN asks the trainer to change the description of *B* so that it becomes a column. The trainer should make the least number of changes possible. Assume that the description is changed to a brick standing on the ground. Now the program may consider why the new object *X* is a column and *B* is not. The two descriptions are:

wedge(*B*).	brick(*X*).
standing(*B*).	standing(*X*).
B is_on *C*.	*X* is_on *Y*.
ground(*C*).	ground(*Y*).

The properties that the two objects have in common can be ignored, leaving only the shape. The replacement (R1) caused *wedge(B)* to be generalized to *any_shape(B)*. Since this replacement resulted in a misclassification, it should not be used in clause (R3). MARVIN can now tell the trainer that it has located the bug and ask the trainer to teach it about columns again, this time not using *any_shape*. More specifically, the program can ask, "Is there a distinction between *brick(B)* and *wedge(B)* that you haven't explained yet?"

7.10 CONCLUSION

When we characterize learning as a search process, we make the following assumptions:

1. There is a language that is used to describe concepts.
2. A state in the search space is a collection of descriptions written in this language. Given a set of examples, a goal state is a set of descriptions such that each positive example satisfies some description and no negative example satisfies any description.
3. There is a set of generalization rules for transforming states into new states.
4. A strategy for using the set of examples as a guide to choosing the useful sequence of transformations that leads one to the goal state.

The problem of learning is to search through the space with a sequence of generalizations until a path to the goal is found. The search space is determined by the language used to describe concepts. Learning systems such as LEX (Utgoff and Mitchell, 1982) and MIS (Shapiro, 1981) have languages that are fixed at the start of the learning task. System INDUCE (Michalski, 1983) can automatically construct new terms in the language, but the rules for constructing them must be given. In programs such as MARVIN (Sammut, 1981) and its predecessor, CONFUCIUS (Cohen, 1978), learning systems have been investigated in which the description language changes depending on the state, that is, on the set of descriptions learned. Put another way, in previous work the transformations operated on single sentences in the state, but in the authors' work the rules take the whole state into consideration. This makes for a significant difference in the efficiency of the descriptions learned and, under many circumstances, in the efficiency of the search process itself.

MARVIN is able easily to extend its language because it uses sets of Horn clauses as descriptions, just as MIS does. The program is designed to emulate teacher/student learning. Unlike LEX, it is not initially given a hierarchy of concepts. The relationships among concepts are built up as the trainer presents new ones. As in human teacher/student interactions, it is expected that simple concepts will be taught before complex ones. For example, addition is taught as a concept before multiplication, since the description of multiplication may use addition. The collection of concepts as a whole forms a model of the world in which the program exists.

MARVIN does not passively accept data from the trainer. It "performs experiments" to test its hypotheses by constructing its own training examples. This provides the trainer with feedback indicating how well MARVIN has "understood" the concept. With improvements that will allow it to detect and correct misconceptions, a learning system like MARVIN could find applications in the interactive acquisition of knowledge for expert systems. However, its main contributions thus far have been in demonstrating a program whose language grows in descriptive power as it learns new concepts and in being able to use those concepts as procedures to perform actions, that is, to build objects.

ACKNOWLEDGMENTS

This paper was written while the first author was with the Department of Computer Science, University of Illinois at Urbana-Champaign. We thank R. S. Michalski for his help during the stay at Illinois. We also thank Ian Hayes for his helpful comments on a draft of this paper.

References

Banerji, R. B., "A Language for the Description of Concepts," *General Systems 9,* 1964.

Cohen, B. L., "A Theory of Structural Concept Formation and Pattern Recognition," Ph.D. diss., Department of Computer Science, University of New South Wales, Sydney, Australia, 1978.

Hayes-Roth, F., and McDermott, J., "An Interference Matching Technique for Inducing Abstractions," *Communications of the ACM,* Vol. 21, pp. 401–11, May 1978.

Michalski, R. S., "Pattern Recognition as Rule-Guided Inference," *IEEE Transactions on Pattern Analysis and Machine Intelligence,* Vol. 2, No. 4, pp. 349–61, July 1980.

————, "A Theory and Methodology of Inductive Learning," in *Machine Learning: An Artificial Intelligence Approach*, R. S. Michalski, J. G. Carbonell, and T. M. Mitchell (Eds.), Tioga, Palo Alto, Calif., 1983.

Robinson, J. A., "A Machine Oriented Logic Based on the Resolution Principle," *Journal of the ACM*, Vol. 12, No. 1, pp. 23–41, January 1965.

Sammut, C. A., "Learning Concepts by Performing Experiments," Ph.D. diss., Department of Computer Science, University of New South Wales, Sydney, Australia, 1981.

Shapiro, E. Y., "Inductive Inference of Theories from Facts," Technical Report No. 192, Yale University, 1981.

Utgoff, P. E., and Mitchell, T. M., "Acquisition of Appropriate Bias for Inductive Concept Learning," *Proceedings of AAAI-82*, Pittsburgh, Pa., pp. 414–17, August 1982.

8

CONCEPT LEARNING IN A RICH INPUT DOMAIN:

Generalization-Based Memory

Michael Lebowitz
Columbia University

Abstract

Automatic concept learning from large amounts of complex input data is an important and difficult process. This chapter discusses how the use of a permanent, generalization-based memory can serve as an important tool in developing programs that learn in rich input domains. The use of Generalization-Based Memory (GBM) allows programs to determine what concepts to learn as well as definitions of the concepts. The chapter presents two programs under development at Columbia that employ GBM, UNIMEM, and RESEARCHER, and explains how they perform concept evaluation and generalization of complex structural descriptions.

8.1 INTRODUCTION

Automatic concept learning in the form of generalization has been shown to be useful in interpreting and organizing large amounts of information about a domain (Lebowitz, 1980, 1983a; Schank, 1982). It is also an interesting task in its own right. Recently this author has been concerned with the development of new methods of concept formation that employ a permanent memory of previously determined concepts along with the examples that led to their creation. These methods involve the determination of what concepts to learn as well as the definitions of the concepts. In particular, the focus has been on the problems of concept formation from a stream of input that is complex in any of several different ways. This chapter details this class of problems, presents the basic learning technique used, known as Generalization-Based Memory (GBM), and indicates solutions to some of the specific problems involved.

Much of the concept-learning research that has been done in artificial intelligence has consisted either of supplying programs with examples, and possibly counterexamples, of specified concepts and having these programs determine definitions of the concepts (e.g., Winston, 1972; Mitchell 1982; Dieterich and Michalski, 1983); or of using largely analytic techniques to classify input (e.g., Michalski, 1980; Langley, 1981). In "real-world" settings, the crucial concepts to be learned—those that best help explain and organize information about a domain—are not presupplied; rather, it is necessary to determine these concepts from a stream of very complex input data. Consequently, this research concentrates not just on methods for comparing examples but also on methods for determining what examples to compare, which largely determines the concepts to create.

Taking examples from various programs he has worked on, the author looks here at how intelligent systems could extract generalizations to the same extent as human learners from complex input streams such as the following: "States that have large school expenditures have high per capita incomes" (from information about the states of the United States); "A large class of disk drives uses flexible (floppy) disks" (from patent abstracts about disk drives); or "Terrorist attacks in Northern Ireland are frequently carried out by the IRA" (from news stories about terrorism).

Generalization-Based Memory was developed for IPP, a computer program that read, remembered, and generalized from news stories (Lebowitz, 1980, 1983a, 1983b), based on intuitions about how complex episodes might be stored in memory by people in a manner analogous to Schank's MOPs (Schank, 1980, 1982; Riesbeck, 1981) and Kolodner's E-MOPs (Kolodner, 1984). The author believes it is advantageous to use the same techniques in more traditional concept-learning environments and for intelligent information systems that make use of complex streams of input. The presentation here of the problems of concept learning from complex input focuses on two intelligent information systems being developed at Columbia, UNIMEM and RESEARCHER, both of which use GBM.

UNIMEM is a program that can accept a large quantity of relatively unstructured facts about a domain, use generalization techniques to determine important concepts, and then use these concepts to organize the information in a fashion that allows further generalization and intelligent question answering. For example, if information about the states in the United States is given to such a program (a domain used in prototype testing), the program might determine that *New England states,* or *states with large education budgets* are useful concepts. UNIMEM is being used to study problems that can arise when the individual items used for learning are not highly structured but consist simply of a set of descriptive features.

The problems in forming concepts from complex input data involved in research with UNIMEM include the following: determining the impact of domain-dependent knowledge on concept learning; categorizing numeric input information so that generalization is possible; evaluating and refining concepts from further examples; using concepts that very slightly contradict new input items—those like Winston's "near misses" (1972) but that are not preidentified as such; dealing with concepts that change over time; and answering questions based on Generalization-Based Memory. In this chapter, the basic techniques for using GBM and for evaluating concepts in the context of UNIMEM are presented.

In contrast with UNIMEM, RESEARCHER (Lebowitz 1983c, 1983d) deals with highly structured physical descriptions of devices. RESEARCHER reads patent abstracts in natural language form and then remembers and generalizes information from these texts, automatically creating appropriate object classes. Complete understanding (and generalization) of patent abstracts requires many kinds of analysis. To date the focus has been on the complex physical descriptions of the objects described (e.g., part x is on top of part y), as opposed to, for example, functional characteristics. In this chapter RESEARCHER is used as a context in which to discuss the problems of comparing complex, highly structured representations.

Figure 8-1 shows some typical concepts generalized by each of the Generalization-Based Memory programs mentioned here. The IPP and UNIMEM generalizations were actually made by the programs (although the English was generated by hand), and the RESEARCHER examples are target concepts that can currently be learned from simplified input.

The remainder of this chapter describes how this research relates to other work in concept formation and presents an overview of the concept-learning methods employed in this research, concentrating on the use of Generalization-Based Memory. Finally, concept evaluation and generalization of complex structural descriptions, typical problems in this research, are described.

IPP Concepts:
Bombings in El Salvador cause damage but do not often hurt anyone.
Urban terrorists in Italy frequently use silencer-equipped pistols.

UNIMEM Concepts:
State class—High urban percentage, low minority percentage, moderate income, low taxes, manufacturing important (RI, NJ, TX, MI, FLA, OH)

State class—High value of farmland, fairly high population, manufacturing, agriculture, tourism important (NC, ARK, TENN, MINN, WISC, VA, MO)

RESEARCHER Concepts:
Floppy disk drive

Double density disk drive

Fully enclosed disk drive

Figure 8-1: Examples of GBM concepts.

8.2 COMPLEX INPUT DOMAINS

The intelligent information systems being developed by the author basically engage in what Michalski calls *multiple concept learning from observation (descriptive generalization)* (1983). These programs are given large numbers of examples with no prespecification of the concepts to generalize; they acquire sets of concepts by deciding what instances to compare and how such examples are similar. The concepts they derive are often overlapping; that is, many concepts can describe the same example.

The tasks of these programs also involve aspects of Michalski's *concept acquisition*. In addition to determining the properties of instances in the classes they create, they fit objects to those classes. There are elements in these programs both of observing patterns in data and of developing discriminant descriptions of the classes thereby derived.

This research is characterized by several other properties that are somewhat novel (particularly in combination) for working systems but that are, in the author's opinion, crucial to the development of useful, dynamic information systems. The first parameter characterizing this work is that it involves *"pragmatic" generalizations;* that is, the concepts describe what is *usually,* but *not necessarily always,* true. This means, crucially, that methods that invalidate generalized concepts on the basis of a single counterexample are not acceptable. In the same vein, it is not a requirement that every concept that could legitimately be generalized be found. The class of pragmatic generalizations provides more power and flexibility in representing what it is possible to learn about a rich domain.

The pragmatic nature of these generalizations is in sharp contrast with most other learning methods. Although there has been work dealing with noisy input data (e.g., Quinlan, 1983, and to some extent Mitchell, 1982), it has always been assumed that the generalizations themselves perfectly described the world, even if they were perhaps obscured in the input data. The need to deal with pragmatic generalizations strongly affects all aspects of the author's work.

Secondly, the learning discussed here is *incremental.* When systems are continually receiving input, it is not possible for them to wait for all examples to be available for inspection before they create concepts. In this work it is required that after every example is processed the systems have made the best possible generalizations based on the input that has been processed. Although it is possible to imagine the incremental application of many other methods, most other learning research has assumed that all the input is available to the learning process at once and that the process is rerun from scratch if new information is added. A notable exception is the work of Winston (1972), in which a concept is incrementally developed (although only a single concept at a time is learned from specially selected inputs).

Finally, it is expected that these systems will ultimately deal with *large numbers of examples.* It is the ability to deal with many examples and many concepts simultaneously that gives human learners the power that intelligent information systems should have. No method that requires comparison of a new instance with all, or a large portion of all, previous examples will be acceptable, for computational reasons. Even comparison with generalized concepts must be done in a principled way. Furthermore, these systems must deal with whatever examples they are given, not with input that is specially prepared (as by a teacher). In addition, there are sometimes cases in which the individual items to be generalized are themselves complex, as in RESEARCHER.

Although there has been learning research that involves large numbers of examples (e.g., Quinlan, 1979), much of it has been statistically oriented (see Cohen and Feigenbaum, 1982), and little of it has dealt with pragmatic generalizations (with the exception of Schank, 1982, and related research). The fact that all concepts are not guaranteed to be logically correct turns out to have a major effect on the learning process.

The author believes that methods for dealing with the type of input described here will be necessary in developing systems that take full advantage of the large quantities of complex information available. One area that has not been addressed but that will be important in the author's future work is the use of explanation-based generalization of the sort discussed in DeJong (1983), Mitchell (1983), Mostow (1983), and Riesbeck (1983).

8.3 GENERALIZATION-BASED MEMORY

This section provides an overview of the techniques used to form concepts as part of maintaining a Generalization-Based Memory. For clarity, the way the process works in UNIMEM is described, but the main techniques are identical in IPP and RESEARCHER.

The basic idea of Generalization-Based Memory is that a generalization system begins to create a hierarchy of concepts that describe a situation from a small number of examples, and then it records in memory specific items, both those examples from which the concepts are generalized and others, in terms of the generalized concepts. More specific generalizations are recorded along with specific examples under the more general cases. GBM involves identifying and defining multiple concepts, as opposed to maintaining a single model of a concept.

In order to standardize terminology, the objects stored in memory are used to build generalizations—that is, the input examples—are referred to as *instances*. In UNIMEM these are descriptions of objects in a domain. In UNIMEM an instance is described in terms of a set of *features* (essentially property/value pairs). As will be seen, RESEARCHER uses more complex descriptions of instances. The combinations of generalizations, themselves sets of features, and the events and subgeneralizations they organize are called *GEN-NODEs*.[1] GEN-NODEs form the basis of GBM. The structure of a typical GEN-NODE is shown in figure 8-2. The manner in which GEN-NODEs are combined to form a concept hierarchy is illustrated in figure 8-3.

Generalization-Based Memory basically consists of one or more hierarchies of GEN-NODEs that describe concepts of increasing specificity.[2] As shown in figures 8-2 and 8-3, instances and sub-GEN-NODEs are stored under each GEN-NODE using discrimination networks (D-NETs) (Charniak et al., 1980). (Note that a given GEN-NODE can organize both instances and more specific GEN-NODEs.) D-NETs provide an efficient way to retrieve any object stored with a given set of indices. In the GBM model, every feature of an instance or sub-GEN-NODE is initially used as an index, resulting in shallow, bushy D-NETs that allow retrieval of an object given any one of its features. The resulting plethora of indices is pruned by ceasing to use as indices features that pertain to a large number of objects in a given D-NET.

The use of a hierarchy of GEN-NODEs with D-NETs as a method of memory organization allows efficient storage of information, since information in a generalization does not have to be repeated for each instance that it describes. In addition, it allows relevant generalizations and instances—and *only* relevant generalizations and instances—to be found efficiently in memory during processing, allowing further generalizations. This property of GBM is largely independent of the specific knowledge representation being used.

The use of concept hierarchies to organize information about concepts intelligently and efficiently is not a new one. Semantic networks (Quillian, 1978), frame systems (Minsky, 1975), and MOPs (Schank, 1980, 1982), among many other formalisms, all include this property. A primary feature of the representation language

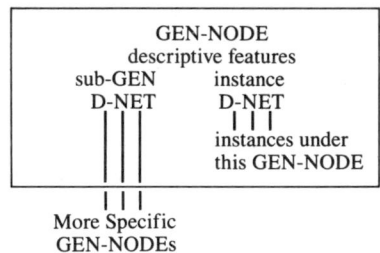

Figure 8-2:   GEN-NODE structure.

---

[1]GEN-NOTEs were called S-MOPs in IPP, since they are in some sense specialized versions of Schank's Memory Organization Packets (Schank, 1982).

[2]Technically, through methods not described in this paper, the set of GEN-NODEs may form not a tree but a directed acyclic graph.

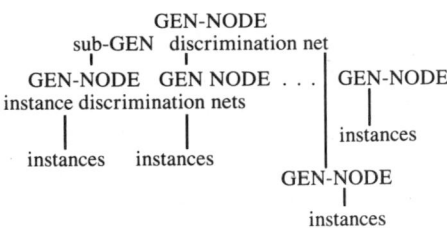

Figure 8-3:   Schematic structure of GBM.

KRL (Bobrow and Winograd, 1977) is its ability to allow inheritance to be implemented easily. Wasserman and Lebowitz (1983) show how frame-based schemes can be applied to physical object descriptions. What is new here is the dynamically changing nature of the concept hierarchy and its use to guide the development of further concepts. Only a limited amount of work has been done on automatically generalizing concept hierarchies, including Hayes (1977), Michalski and Stepp (1983), and Sammut and Banerji (1983), and this work has not dealt with pragmatic generalizations or particularly large numbers of examples.

The process of maintaining GBM is a relatively simple one, once the memory organization method has been defined. As each new instance is processed, the most specific GEN-NODE that describes it is found. This is done easily and efficiently, using the discrimination nets that index the GEN-NODEs in memory, starting with a very general node that covers the whole range of instances in the domain. Then, before the instance is actually indexed under that GEN-NODE, a check is made for instances already stored there that have additional features in common with the new instance; these can be found using the instance D-NET. If there are enough such features (one of many adjustable parameters of GBM[3]), a new concept is generalized and the contributing instances are indexed there. Otherwise, the new instance is simply stored under the existing GEN-NODE.[4]

Two further important features characterize GBM. Since concepts are generalized on the basis of only a few instances, they must be evaluated to eliminate overgeneralization (including the elimination of whole concepts). This is discussed in section 8.4. The second feature is the use of *predictability*. Space does not permit a discussion of predictability here (see Lebowitz, 1983a), but the basic idea is that the

---

[3]Future research may look at how the parameters of GBM could be adjusted automatically.

[4]The process is actually a bit more complex, since a given instance can be stored in multiple spots in memory for two different reasons. Either instance can be classified initially in several different ways, each of which would indicate a place to store it, or several different "most specific" GEN-NODEs might be found, each of which would lead to the processing described.

presence of some of the features of a concept in an instance indicates the relevance of the concept and that these features can be identified quite easily using GBM.

Further details of the algorithm used to maintain GBM are shown in figures 8-4, 8-5, and 8-6. Figure 8-4 shows that the addition of a new instance to GBM consists of finding the GEN-NODE (or GEN-NODEs) that best describes the instance (updating feature confidence factors as in section 8.4), followed by indexing the new instance (which includes a check for new generalizations). Figure 8-5 shows the process that searches for the GEN-NODE that best describes the new instance (essentially a depth-first search heuristically guided by features of the new instance that have not been explained), and figure 8-6 shows how the new instance is actually added to memory, possibly causing new concepts to be generalized.

The use of GBM as described in this section can successfully satisfy the domain characteristics described in section 8.2, as follows:

1. All concepts generalized in GBM are *"pragmatic."* No concept is removed by a single counterexample; instead, the process described in the next section is used to evaluate all concepts. The generalization process is also pragmatic because it can sometimes miss concepts that could be found by comparing instances that were stored in widely different parts of memory, but this seems a reasonable trade-off to avoid combinatoric numbers of comparisons.

2. GBM is inherently *incremental.* As each instance is added to GBM, the best possible concepts that can be generalized so far are made.

3. GBM is ideal for learning from *large numbers of examples.* The use of a hierarchy of concepts that organize specific instances allows only instances that might lead to generalizations to be compared to each other. Relevant concepts are easily found. It is also an efficient way to store the concepts.

The details of updating GBM are further illustrated with an example in section 8.5, following a discussion of concept evaluation.

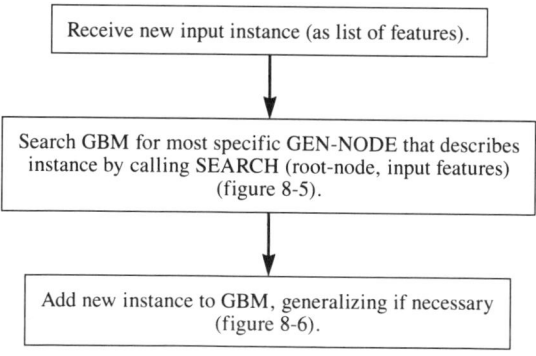

Figure 8-4:   GBM update algorithm.

SEARCH (GEN-NODE, unexplained-features)

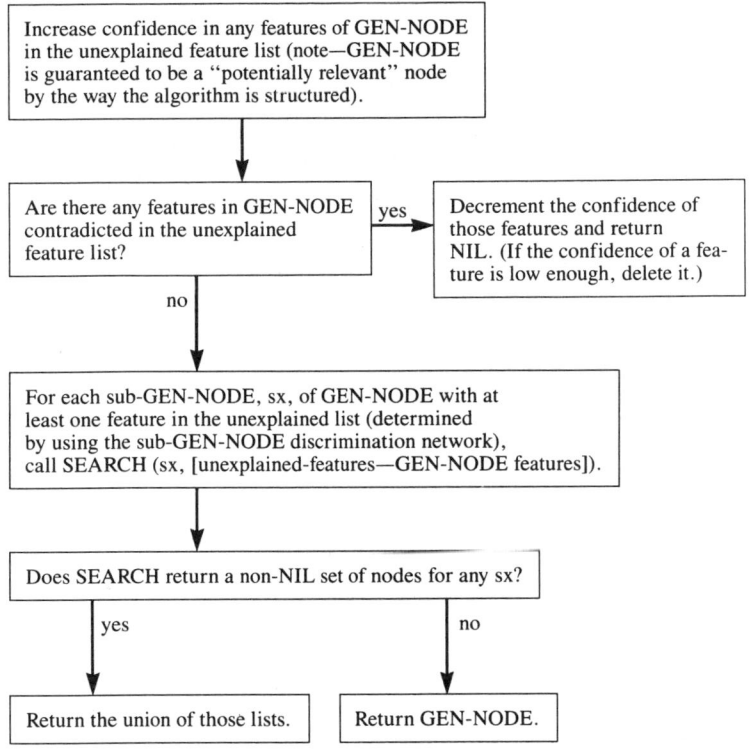

Figure 8-5: Searching GBM for most specific GEN-NODE.

8.4 CONCEPT EVALUATION

As mentioned in the previous section, the concept-learning process described here inherently leads to overgeneralization, particularly in a domain in which there is a large amount of information about each instance. For this reason, each concept learned is evaluated over time. For each generalization made by UNIMEM, an evaluation process continually looks for later instances for which the generalization might be relevant. This occurs as a normal part of the memory search process, since the generalizations to be evaluated are exactly those that might be used to store the new instances. UNIMEM checks whether a relevant generalization is confirmed or contradicted by each new instance.

A new instance found by UNIMEM is considered to contradict an applicable concept if it possesses a predictive feature indicating that the concept is relevant *and* another feature with the same property as the concept (such as the region of a state)

UPDATE (GEN-NODE, new-instance)

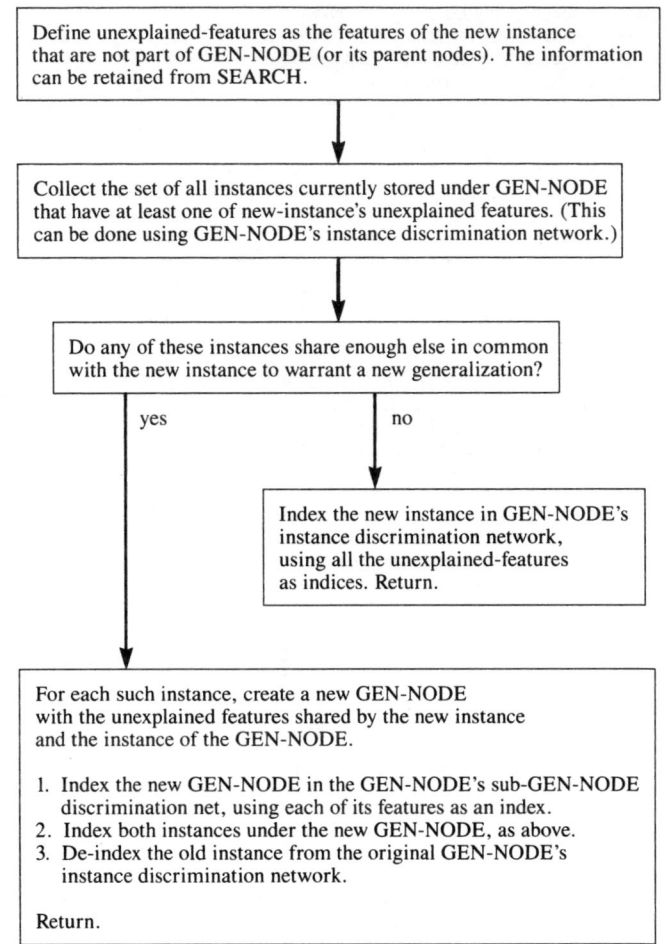

Figure 8-6: Updating GBM.

but with a different value (such as Midwest instead of East). Intuitively, when this condition occurs, confidence in the concept should be reduced.

Early versions of confidence for generalizations in GBM simply involved adding or subtracting points from a numeric confidence level for each GEN-NODE, resulting in a property much like the confidence in conclusions discussed in Collins (1978) or the confidence in rule application used in some expert systems, such as MYCIN (Shortliffe, 1978). In a domain rich in information, this technique will not suffice, since there will almost *always* be extraneous information in each generalized concept as the result of inevitable coincidences that will cause confidence in the concept to be undermined.

Ideally, when a generalization is disconfirmed the "bad" (overly specific) parts should be thrown away and the "good" parts kept. The problem then reduces to identifying the components of a generalization that are overly specific so they can be deleted, leaving intact a valid generalization. Furthermore, for this process to be useful, it must be done at a minimum cost, occurring as a natural part of the memory update process, one would hope, and requiring only a small amount of extra record keeping. The task is somewhat similar to that for which pattern recognition techniques are used (see Cohen and Feigenbaum, 1982, for an AI perspective on pattern recognition), but it deals with concrete, if pragmatic, concept definitions rather than statistical representations.

The solution devised for UNIMEM is straightforward. Instead of keeping a single confidence level as part of each GEN-NODE, UNIMEM tracks the number of times each feature of a concept is confirmed or contradicted. In effect, a confidence level is maintained for each feature of each concept rather than a single value for an entire concept.

Specifically, a counter is maintained for each feature of each generalization, and these counters are incremented or decremented as their features are confirmed or contradicted, respectively, in a situation in which a concept is deemed relevant. The counter modification occurs as UNIMEM determines which GEN-NODEs best describe a new instance, as explained in section 8.3. If a counter passes a negative threshold (another adjustable parameter), then the feature can be eliminated from the generalization, since it has been wrong much more often than right. If too many features of a generalization have been eliminated, the entire generalization is eliminated. Details of this process and an example of its application in the domain of football plays can be found in Lebowitz (1982).

When this scheme was added to UNIMEM, it proved quite effective in culling extraneous features from generalizations; it totally disconfirmed only those concepts that were completely the result of coincidence. In several test domains this procedure produced generalized concepts that made excellent intuitive sense. A simple example from the domain involving information about states in the United States is presented here. Use of this domain is fully explained in the detailed example in section 8.5.[5]

```
GND1:
INCOME          RANGE        INC3:4
TAXES           RANGE        TAX2:5
SCHOOL-EXP      RANGE        SCH3:3
MINORITY-PCT    RANGE        MIN1:2
Organizing: IOWA, KANSAS, MICHIGAN, MONTANA, NEBRASKA, PENNSYLVANIA, TEXAS
```

Figure 8-7:   Final UNIMEM generalization.

---

[5]A different run of the program is used for the example here.

Figure 8-7 illustrates a concept (GND1) generalized by UNIMEM. This concept describes states with moderately high per capita income, rather low taxes, high school expenditures, and fairly low minority population (the last is actually a broad category that covers most states). This concept can be used to describe the seven states listed.

Figure 8-8 shows how this concept was initially generalized from Iowa and Nebraska. Notice that these states are similar in a number of additional ways—for example, they are both farm states—so UNIMEM initially generalized an over-general, and not widely applicable, concept. These features, which are extraneous in the sense that they inhibit wider application of the concept, were ultimately removed by the evaluation process described in this section, leaving a much more useful concept.

8.5 A UNIMEM EXAMPLE

As a further illustration of how GBM is maintained, including the formation of new concepts, an example is presented here that is taken from an actual run of UNIMEM. In this run the program was provided with a number of facts about each state in the United States. Figure 8-9 shows a small portion of GBM after information from forty-two states (not including Oregon) had been added to memory. (The states were presented to UNIMEM in random order.[6])

Each GEN-NODE in figure 8-9 is shown in terms of a set of features. For features derived from numeric data, the third column of each feature (the value) indicates a category derived from the numeric value by a method described in Lebowitz (1985). For example, the fourth feature of GEN-NODE GND1, taxes, has the value TAX2:5, indicating that the tax rate for the states described by this GEN-NODE falls

```
GND1:
CRIME-RATE      RANGE        CRI3:5
STATE-DEBT      RANGE        DEB2:7
INCOME          RANGE        INC3:4
TAXES           RANGE        TAX2:5
MIGRATION-NET   RANGE        MIG1:9
SCHOOL-EXP      RANGE        SCH3:3
STATE           REGION       FARM
MINORITY-PCT    RANGE        MIN1:2
Organizing: IOWA, NEBRASKA
```

Figure 8-8: Initial generalization.

---

[6]Since UNIMEM has certain subjective aspects, in the sense used by Abelson (1973) and Carbonell (1981), the concepts formed in GBM vary depending on the order instances are added. However, the effect does not seem to be strong, and the concept evaluation process described in the next section tends to lead to similar, though not necessarily identical, concepts arising over time.

```
GNDO
[ARIZONA MASSACHUSETTS NEWMEXICO SOUTHDAKOTA WESTVIRGINIA]

    GND1
    INDUSTRY        TYPE              MANUFACTURING (20)
    INDUSTRY        TYPE              TOURISM       (-2)
    INDUSTRY        TYPE              AGRICULTURE   (16)
    TAXES           RANGE             TAX2:5        (14)
    MINORITY        RANGE             MIN1:2        (32)
    STATE           SIZE              SIZ4:6        (deleted)
    STATE           REGION            MT            (deleted)
    INDUSTRY        TYPE              MINING        (deleted)
    INDUSTRY        TYPE              ELECTRONICS   (deleted)
    []

        GND5
        INCOME          RANGE         INC3:4        (4)
        INDUSTRY        TYPE          MINING        (1)
        SCHOOL-EXP      RANGE         SCH3:3        (0)
        STATE           SIZE          SIZ4:6        (deleted)
        URBAN-PCT       RANGE         URB6:6        (deleted)
        [UTAH]

            GND7
            CRIME-RATE      RANGE         CRI5:5        (-1)
            STATE-DEBT      RANGE         DEB3:7        (1)
            INDUSTRY        TYPE          GOVERNMENT    (-1)
            STATE           SIZE          SIZ4:6        (0)
            URBAN-PCT       RANGE         URB6:6        (0)
            [COLORADO NEVADA]

            GND13
            STATE-DEBT      RANGE         DEB5:7        (0)
            FARM-VAL        RANGE         FAR5:6        (0)
            STATE           SIZE          SIZ4:6        (0)
            URBAN-PCT       RANGE         URB6:6        (0)
            [MICHIGAN MINNESOTA]
```

Figure 8-9:   A section of UNIMEM GBM without Oregon.

in the second of five categories; that is, it is rather low. The numeric value following each feature indicates UNIMEM's current confidence in that feature (as described in the previous section). These values start at zero. The threshold for eliminating a feature was −3 for this run. The features followed by "deleted" are no longer part of the generalizations but were originally included and then deleted by the concept evaluation algorithm. Listed under each GEN-NODE are the instances (states) indexed there.

The section of GBM shown in figure 8-9 includes five GEN-NODEs. The top-level node, GND0, has no features and hence describes all instances. It serves to organize the GBM hierarchy for states and index any instances not yet described by any generalization. GND1 describes states with fairly low taxes, low minority population, and industries that include manufacturing, tourism, and agriculture. Additional features present when it was created (from Idaho and Colorado, as it happens), have been deleted to make the GEN-NODE more widely applicable.

GND1 organizes several sub-GEN-NODEs, one of which, GND5, is shown in figure 8-9. This node describes middle-income mining states with large school expenditures. Utah is indexed under GND5. This GEN-NODE in turn organizes two yet-more-specific GEN-NODEs, GND7 and GND13. GND7 describes mid-sized states with relatively high crime rates, moderate state debt, government as a significant industry, and a high proportion of urban population. Colorado and Nevada are indexed under it.[7] GND13 describes mid-sized states with high-valued farm property, fairly high state debt, and a high proportion of urban population. It indexes Michigan and Minnesota. Notice how for the states at the bottom of the hierarchy, such as Colorado, Nevada, Michigan, and Minnesota, none of the information in GEN-NODEs GND1, GND5, and GND7 or GND13 will have to be repeated for the specific instance, since it can be inherited.

With GBM containing the information in figure 8-9, information about Oregon was next added to memory. Figure 8-10 shows the first phase of this addition

```
*(run-state 'oregon)

Features: OREGON (STATE)
    STATE           REGION      WS
    POPULATION      RANGE       POP5:7
    URBAN-PCT       RANGE       URB5:6
    MINORITY        RANGE       MIN1:2
    MIGRATION-NET   RANGE       MIG8:9
    STATE           SIZE        SIZ4:6
    SCHOOL-EXP      RANGE       SCH3:3
    CRIME-RATE      RANGE       CRI4:5
    STATE-DEBT      RANGE       DEB5:7
    MILITARY-MONEY  RANGE       MIL4:9
    INCOME          RANGE       INC3:4
    FARM-VAL        RANGE       FAR4:6
    TAXES           RANGE       TAX2:5
    INDUSTRY        TYPE        MANUFACTURING
                    TYPE        FORESTRY
                    TYPE        TOURISM
                    TYPE        FOOD-PROCESSING
                    TYPE        AGRICULTURE

Best existing S-MOP(s) --
GND5 -- potential remindings: UTAH
< and others >
```

Figure 8-10: UNIMEM finding a GEN-NODE that describes Oregon.

---

[7]Note that although the total number of urban residents in these states is probably small, the *proportion* of such residents is high.

procedure. Shown are the features given to describe Oregon. Also shown are the results of the search phase, in which UNIMEM determined that GND5 (as well as GEN-NODEs in other parts of GBM) best described the new instance. GND5 was selected because it contained at least one feature of Oregon (two, in fact—income and school expenditures), none of its features is contradicted by Oregon, and neither GND7 nor GND13 is appropriate (GND7 conflicts in state debt and urban percentage, and GND13 conflicts in farmland value and urban percentage).

Having decided that GND5 is the GEN-NODE that currently best describes Oregon, UNIMEM proceeds to update GBM by attempting to index Oregon under that node. The results of this process are shown in figure 8-11. During the indexing process, UNIMEM notices that Utah, which is already indexed under GND5, has the identical values for state size, crime rate, and region of the country as does Oregon. Thus a new GEN-NODE, GND50, can be created with these features. (It also inherits all the features of GEN-NODEs GND1 and GND5.)

Figure 8-12 shows how GBM has been changed by the addition of Oregon. GND50, the new GEN-NODE, has been added under GND5. Oregon and Utah have both been indexed there. Note also how the confidences of features supported by Oregon have been incremented and those contradicted have been decremented, using the algorithm described in the previous section. For example, in GND13 confidence in state debt and state size has increased and confidence in farm value and urban percentage has gone down.

8.6 RESEARCHER

As mentioned earlier in this chapter, RESEARCHER (Lebowitz, 1983c, 1983d) is a program that reads patent abstracts and adds information from them to a

```
Creating more specific STATE (GND50) than GND5 from events UTAH OREGON
with features:

STATE          REGION      WS
STATE          SIZE        SIZ4:6
CRIME-RATE     RANGE       CRI4:5
------
   SCHOOL-EXP  RANGE       SCH3:3
   INCOME      RANGE       INC3:4
   INDUSTRY    TYPE        MINING
   MINORITY    RANGE       MIN1:2
   TAXES       RANGE       TAX2:5
   INDUSTRY    TYPE        MANUFACTURING
               TYPE        TOURISM
               TYPE        AGRICULTURE

<processing for other GEN-NODEs that describe Oregon>
```

Figure 8-11: UNIMEM adding Oregon to GBM.

```
GNDO
[ARIZONA MASSACHUSETTS NEWMEXICO SOUTHDAKOTA WESTVIRGINIA]

    GND1
    INDUSTRY        TYPE            MANUFACTURING (21)
    INDUSTRY        TYPE            TOURISM       (-1)
    INDUSTRY        TYPE            AGRICULTURE   (17)
    TAXES           RANGE           TAX2:5        (15)
    MINORITY        RANGE           MIN1:2        (33)
    STATE           SIZE            SIZ4:6        (deleted)
    STATE           REGION          MT            (deleted)
    INDUSTRY        TYPE            MINING        (deleted)
    INDUSTRY        TYPE            ELECTRONICS   (deleted)
    []

        GND5
        INCOME      RANGE           INC3:4        (5)
        INDUSTRY    TYPE            MINING        (0)
        SCHOOL-EXP  RANGE           SCH3:3        (1)
        STATE       SIZE            SIZ4:6        (deleted)
        URBAN-PCT   RANGE           URB6:6        (deleted)
        []

            GND7
            CRIME-RATE  RANGE       CRI5:5        (-2)
            STATE-DEBT  RANGE       DEB3:7        (0)
            INDUSTRY    TYPE        GOVERNMENT    (-2)
            STATE       SIZE        SIZ4:6        (1)
            URBAN-PCT   RANGE       URB6:6        (-1)
            [COLORADO NEVADA]

            GND13
            STATE-DEBT  RANGE       DEB5:7        (1)
            FARM-VAL    RANGE       FAR5:6        (-1)
            STATE       SIZE        SIZ4:6        (1)
            URBAN-PCT   RANGE       URB6:6        (-1)
            [MICHIGAN MINNESOTA]

            GND50
            STATE       REGION      WS            (0)
            STATE       SIZE        SIZ4:6        (0)
            CRIME-RATE  RANGE       CRI4:5        (0)
            [OREGON UTAH]
```

Figure 8-12: The same section of GBM with Oregon.

Generalization-Based Memory so that it can effectively answer questions. This chapter looks only at the process of taking representations of two objects (or, equivalency, a generalized concept and concrete object) and forming a generalized concept. The representations compared here are framelike and primitive based, concentrating on the physical relations among the various parts of a complex object. (See Wasserman and Lebowitz, 1983, for a complete description of the representation scheme.)

In the disk drive domain, typical concepts that the generalization process might identify as being useful would be *floppy disk drives* and *double-sided disks*. As with UNIMEM, this must be done without specifically providing the program with examples of these concepts. Instead, instances stored together in Generalization-Based Memory are recognized as being similar and are generalized.

The use of GBM is more complex here than in the UNIMEM. The "features" that two objects have in common can only be determined by comparing two complex object representations. The matching problem is much the same as that faced by Winston in his blocks world learning work (1972). The problem here is in certain ways both more difficult and easier than Winston's. It is more difficult because much more complex representations are involved. However, the existence of an entire GBM rather than a model of a single concept will simplify the matching process. Both the complexity of matching object descriptions and the way in which GBM can simplify the process are described here.

The representations for two similar, slightly simplified disk drive patents, used to test the initial version of RESEARCHER's generalization module, are shown in figure 8-13. Clearly the two disk drives in figure 8-13 have much in common that can be the source of a new concept derived through generalization—an *enclosed disk drive*. Figure 8-14 shows the concept created by RESEARCHER's generalization module. The process that created this generalization, although conceptually similar to the GBM update algorithm shown in section 8.4, differs in many details, largely due to the impossibility of representing complex physical objects as simple sets of features.

The idea illustrated in figure 8-14 is that RESEARCHER finds the parts of two objects that are similar and abstracts them out into a generalized concept. In this example, the two devices contained similar disk drives and enclosures. Each had a cover on top of some other object. These similarities form the basis of a generalized enclosed disk drive. Only the additional parts and relations of each instance need be recorded in memory along with the generalization. Currently, the generalization

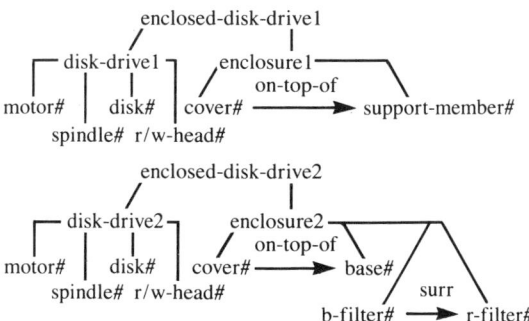

Figure 8-13: Similar disk drives.

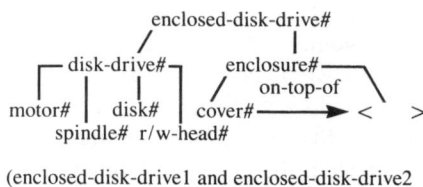

(enclosed-disk-drive1 and enclosed-disk-drive2
stored as variants of enclosed-disk-drive#)

Figure 8-14:   Generalized enclosed disk drive.

module of RESEARCHER, which is integrated with the parser, is able to handle a moderate number of simple examples, including indexing the new objects as variants of existing generalizations.

Adapting GBM for use on complex structural descriptions has proven to be a difficult problem, even when only the assorted relations among the objects in the descriptions are considered. One of the major problems in generalizing structural descriptions is the process of matching two representations (either of two objects or of an object and a generalized object), thereby determining what parts and relations correspond. (This was pointed out for simpler examples in Winston, 1972). Clearly, if there are two distinct disk drive representations and one wishes to determine that the disk mounts in them are similar, then one must determine that they should be compared with each other. (Note that if the similarity is strong enough, it may be desirable to modify the representations to point to a single disk mount representation in memory.) Since one part of the description of complex objects is a set of relations, the relations in one object must be associated with those in the other.

The matching process here is quite a difficult one. In structured objects that are involved, the parts of very similar objects may be aggregated differently in various descriptions. For example, a read/write head might be described as a direct part of a disk drive in one patent but as part of a read/write assembly in another. This makes the inherent similarity difficult to identify.

At the moment, this "level problem" is handled with simple heuristics that allow only a limited amount of "level hopping" during the comparison process (to avoid the need to consider every possible correspondence among levels), along with a bit of combinatoric force.

The ultimate solution to the level problem lies in more extensive use of Generalization-Based Memory. If a new object can be identified as an instance of a generalized concept with only a few minor differences (done with a discrimination net–based search of the sort described in section 8.3), then the levels of aggregation will be set. When GBM is used, only a small number of *differences* between objects have to be compared, rather than entire complex descriptions. This should allow RESEARCHER to meet all the performance constraints (i. e., generalize pragmatically, be incremental, and handle large numbers of objects), even when the complex representations needed to describe real-world objects are used.

In effect, what this work involves is using the generalized descriptions that have been created to form dynamically a canonical framework for describing new objects. Such an approach can help solve one of the major problems of canonical representations systems. Such representation schemes have many well-known advantages (see Schank, 1972, for example), including simplifying the inference process. However, it is often difficult to select the canonical primitives needed for such schemes, and in domains that change over time, it may be impossible. A dynamically created framework of the sort suggested here has the potential to combine the advantages of systems based on canonical primitives with the ability to adapt to the domain without the problems of initially selecting the primitives.[8] A similar approach for cognitive modeling–type tasks is taken in Schank (1982), and the issues of a dynamically changing canonical framework are a topic of this author's current research.

8.7 CONCLUSION

The work with Generalization-Based Memory described in this chapter suggests several important morals. The first is that the development of a dynamic set of concepts is a powerful approach to take when learning from a rich input domain. It is not realistic to hope to find the "right" set of concepts all at once, so it is crucial that the concepts already learned be constantly updated and new ones constantly sought. New information can thus be taken advantage of, and changes in the domain can be adapted to. Furthermore, the use of long-term memory, in the form of GBM, allows programs to deal with many concepts at once and still retain efficiency. In fact, as has been shown, considering many concepts at once often ends up being easier than learning them one at a time, and it certainly leads to more powerful systems. The author believes the development of UNIMEM and RESEARCHER indicates that the idea of Generalization-Based Memory is a sound one and that these programs can serve as valuable test-beds for the pursuit of important issues in concept learning.

ACKNOWLEDGMENTS

This research was supported in part by the Defense Advanced Research Projects Agency under Contract N00039-84-C-0165. Comments by Kathy McKeown and anonymous reviewers on an earlier draft of this chapter were most helpful. Work on RESEARCHER and UNIMEM has been greatly advanced by graduate students at

---

[8]Although an initial representation for the instances given to this system still has to be developed for each domain, it is not as crucial as in other systems, since many properties of the representation can change over time.

Columbia, including Michelle Baker, Andrea Danyluk, Tom Ellman, Larry Hirsch, Laila Moussa, Cecile Paris, Kenneth Wasserman, and Ursula Wolz.

References

Abelson, R. P., "The Structure of Belief Systems," in *Computer Models of Thought and Language,* R. C. Schank and K. Colby (Eds.), Freeman, San Francisco, 1973.

Bobrow, D. G., and Winograd, T., "An Overview of KRL, A Knowledge Representation Language," *Cognitive Science,* Vol. 1, No. 1, pp. 3–46, 1977.

Carbonell, J. G., *Subjective Understanding: Computer Models of Belief Systems,* UMI Research Press, Ann Arbor, Mich., 1981.

Charniak, E., Riesbeck, C. K., and McDermott, D. V., *Artificial Intelligence Programming,* Erlbaum, Hillsdale, N. J., 1980.

Cohen, P. R., and Feigenbaum, E. A. (eds.), *The Handbook of Artificial Intelligence,* Vol. 3, Kaufmann, Los Altos, Calif., 1982.

Collins, A., "Fragments of a Theory of Human Plausible Reasoning," TINLAP-2, Urbana-Champaign, Ill., 1978.

DeJong, G. F., "An Approach to Learning from Observation," *Proceedings of the International Machine Learning Workshop,* R. S. Michalski (Ed.), Allerton House, University of Illinois at Urbana-Champaign, pp. 171–76, June 22–24, 1983. (An updated version of this paper appears as chap. 19 of this volume.)

Dietterich, T. G., and Michalski, R. S., "Discovering Patterns in Sequences of Objects," *Proceedings of the International Machine Learning Workshop,* R. S. Michalski (Ed.), Allerton House, University of Illinois at Urbana-Champaign, pp. 41–57, June 22–24, 1983. (An updated version of this paper appears as chap. 4 of this volume.)

Hayes, P. J., "On Semantic Nets, Frames and Associations," *Proceedings of the Fifth IJCAI,* Cambridge, Mass., pp. 99–107, 1977.

Kolodner, J. L., *Retrieval and Organizational Strategies in Conceptual Memory: A Computer Model,* Erlbaum, Hillsdale, N.J., 1984.

Langley, P., "Data-driven Discovery of Natural Laws," *Cognitive Science,* Vol. 5, No. 1, pp. 31–54, 1981.

Lebowitz, M., "Generalization and Memory in an Integrated Understanding System," Technical Report 186, Department of Computer Science, Yale University, 1980. (Ph.D. diss., Yale University, 1980.)

———, "Correcting Erroneous Generalizations," *Cognition and Brain Theory,* Vol. 5, No. 4, pp. 367–81, 1982.

————, "Generalization from Natural Language Text," *Cognitive Science,* Vol. 7, No. 1, pp. 1–40, 1983a.

————, "Memory-based Parsing," *Artificial Intelligence,* Vol. 21, No. 4, pp. 363–404, 1983b.

————, "Intelligent Information Systems," *Proceedings of the Sixth International ACM SIGIR Conference,* Bethesda, Md., pp. 25–30, 1983c.

————, "RESEARCHER: An Overview," *Proceedings of the Third AAAI,* Washington, D.C., pp. 232–35, 1983d.

————, "Classifying Numeric Information for Generalization," *Cognitive Science,* 1985, in press.

Michalski, R. S., "Pattern Recognition as Rule-guided Inductive Inference," *IEEE Transactions on Pattern Analysis and Machine Intelligence,* Vol. 2, No. 4, pp. 349–61, 1980.

————, "A Theory of Methodology of Inductive Learning," *Artificial Intelligence,* Vol. 2., pp. 111–61, 1983.

Michalski, R. S., and Stepp, R. E., "Automated Construction of Classifications: Conceptual Clustering Versus Numerical Taxonomy," *IEEE Transactions on Pattern Analysis and Machine Intelligence,* Vol. 5, No. 4, pp. 396–409, 1983.

Minsky, M., "A Framework for Representing Knowledge," in *The Psychology of Computer Vision,* P. H. Winston (Ed.), McGraw-Hill, New York, 1975.

Mitchell, T. M., "Generalization as Search," *Artificial Intelligence,* Vol. 18, pp. 203–26, 1982.

————, "Learning and Problem Solving," *Proceedings of the Eighth IJCAI,* Karlsruhe, W. Ger., pp. 1139–51, 1983.

Mostow, J., "Operationalizing Advice: A Problem-solving Model," *Proceedings of the International Machine Learning Workshop,* R. S. Michalski (Ed.), Allerton House, University of Illinois at Urbana Champaign, pp. 110–16, June 22–24, 1983.

Quillian, M. R., "Semantic Memory," in *Semantic Information Processing,* M. Minsky (Ed.), MIT Press, Cambridge, 1978.

Quinlan, J. R., "Induction over Large Data Bases," Technical Report HPP-79-14, Computer Science Department, Stanford University, 1979.

————, "Learning from Noisy Data," *Proceedings of the International Machine Learning Workshop,* R. S. Michalski (Ed.), Allerton House, University of Illinois at Urbana-Champaign, pp. 58–64, June 22–24, 1983. (An updated version of this paper appears as chap. 6 of this volume.)

Riesbeck, C. K., "Failure-driven Reminding for Incremental Learning," *Proceedings of the Seventh IJCAI,* Vancouver, B.C., pp. 115–20, 1981.

————, "Knowledge Reorganization and Reasoning Style," Technical Report 270, Department of Computer Science, Yale University, 1983.

Sammut, C., and Banerji, R., "Hierarchical Memories: An Aid to Concept Learning," *Proceedings of the International Machine Learning Workshop,* R. S. Michalski (Ed.), Allerton House, University of Illinois at Urbana-Champaign, pp. 74–80, June 22–24, 1983. (An updated version of this paper appears as chap. 7 of this volume.)

Schank, R. C., "Conceptual Dependency: A Theory of Natural Language Understanding," *Cognitive Psychology,* Vol. 3, No. 4, 1972, pp. 532–631, 1972.

———, "Language and Memory," *Cognitive Science,* Vol. 4, No. 3, pp. 243–84, 1980.

———, *Dynamic Memory: A Theory of Reminding and Learning in Computers and People,* Cambridge University Press, Cambridge, 1982.

Shortliffe, E. H., *Computer-Based Medical Consultation: MYCIN,* Academic Press, New York, 1978.

Wasserman, K., and Lebowitz, M., "Representing Complex Physical Objects," *Cognition and Brain Theory,* Vol. 6, No. 3, pp. 333–52, 1983.

Winston, P. H., "Learning Structural Descriptions from Examples," in *The Psychology of Computer Vision,* P. H. Winston (Ed.), McGraw-Hill, New York, 1972.

9

IMPROVING THE GENERALIZATION STEP IN LEARNING

Yves Kodratoff
Jean-Gabriel Ganascia
Université de Paris-Sud

Abstract

This chapter discusses problems of generalizing expressions and changing description language. It considers a method of learning in which the inventive steps are accorded less attention then the deductive steps. It is shown that some seemingly inductive discoveries may well be realized by a deductive system, when this system does an in-depth analysis of the properties of the proposed examples. The forgetting operation, which is central in learning, can be viewed as a change of description. A good description keeps only the meaningful characteristics for the learning task. Regardless of the point at which the change of description takes place (either during or after the generalization process), and change that leads to forgetting something or to completing the description has to be preceded by an analysis of the generalization success or failure. The main idea of this chapter—that generalization discovers the significant links in the examples and expresses them as variable bindings—is shown to be surprisingly efficient when counterexamples are used.

9.1 INTRODUCTION

The problem of learning is central to artificial intelligence because intelligent behavior implies an ability to adapt to new situations. Our current robots need to acquire automatic learning capacities if they are to work in a world where changes may occur.

A description of the main ideas relevant to the field of machine learning has been given in a particularly accessible article by Dietterich and Michalski (1981). It is assumed that the reader is acquainted with this article, since this chapter criticizes and refines the generalization concept used by these authors. A comprehensive survey of concept learning can also be found in Cohen and Feigenbaum (1982) and Holte (1984).

Some of the ideas presented in this chapter were initially described by Hayes-Roth and McDermott (1978) and Vere (1981), but here a much more explicit version of these ideas is given, and their important consequences are shown. The authors describe the way one should deduce information from examples in order to find a suitable generalization, given a set of formulas describing the examples. Quite often, the formulas must be changed significantly because although they contain useful implicit information, it is usually difficult to deduce "all" the possible information without their becoming formulas of infinite length. This chapter shows what information must be deduced and what must be left implicit. The essential step of the "information adjustment" process is described in section 9.4.

As a demonstration of the usefulness of this approach, an example is given in section 9.6 illustrating how considerable confusion in generalization formulas may be avoided when some useful implicit information has *not* been forgotten. For this, an example similar to Vere's (see section 9.6) will be given, and the same description language will be used. Vere was able to find a formula that would recognize the examples and reject the counterexamples; however, the concept of "one block only on another block" was not discovered. The method described in this chapter can discover this concept. More generally, the authors consider it compulsory that a generalization algorithm be able to discover explicitly the concept that the examples are intended to illustrate. In case of failure, the description language or the generalization algorithm must be considered faulty.

The methodology used here relies on two main ideas, an intuitive explanation of which will be presented first. The first idea relates concept discovery to *variable binding*. In a set of examples of a concept, the links between the components of each example may be present by simple chance. The role of generalization is the discovery of those links that are significant and those that are not. For example, given the expression

(ON   B A) & (ON   C B) & (ON   D C),

where ON is a function that is not a subject of generalization and arguments A, B, C, and D are constants, one can notice the following:

1. B and C appear in two expressions in parentheses (literals).
2. Both B and C occur once in first position, once in second position.
3. The same argument never occurs twice in a literal (i.e., there is no literal like (ON   A A), for instance).

4. A and D appear only once.

5. Names of the arguments can be alphabetically ordered.

A generalization that takes into account these links is the following:

(ON x w) & (ON y x) & (ON z y) &
(DIFFERENT-FROM-EACH-OTHER w x y z) &
(ALPHABETIC-ORDERING w x y z).

Other examples will be used either for further generalization—for example, replacing the two occurrences of y by different variables—or for further specialization—for example, instantiating the variable z to D in all examples.

Following Hayes-Roth and McDermott (1978) and Vere (1981), the authors will state here that the information relative to the difference between two constants is always implicit in the example: for example, (ON   B A) really means (ON   B A) & (DIFFERENT A B). It may seem all too obvious to insist on this fact, but in many everyday situations the same object (or person) is called by different names and different objects are called by the same name. It is assumed here that in any description, different objects are given different names. For instance, "my efficient secretary, Viviane Bourotte," can be designated by many subsets of the above sentence, and one can find, at least in France, many "Pierres" who are different persons.

When these different names (constants) are generalized to different variables, it must be recalled that some information has been lost, since $f(x,y)$ may be instantiated by $f(A,B)$ as well as by $f(A,A)$, where A and B are constants. This explains, for instance, why $E_1 = $ (ON   A B) and $E_2 = $ (ON   C D) will be generalized to $E_g = $ (ON x y) & (DIFFERENT x, y) in order to recall that in the examples E_1 and E_2 the variables x and y are never instantiated to the same constant.

In these examples, one could also make the assumption that different variables represent different objects and cannot therefore be instantiated by the same constant. This would force us to specify the cases in which different variables may represent the same object and to introduce in this case a predicate MAY-BE-THE-SAME. Choosing DIFFERENT rather than MAY-BE-THE-SAME has no significance, except that the first choice is the one made by the logicians who say that $f(x,y)$ is more general than $f(x,x)$. They recognize that $f(x,y)$ has the meaning "$f(x,y)$ & (MAY-BE-THE-SAME x y)," MAY-BE-THE-SAME being implicit, as it is in this chapter.

What has been done in the above example, that is, detecting all the links of one example and afterwards checking their validity for the other examples, is usually a very difficult task. In reality, the algorithm described here detects links common to a set of examples.

The second idea derives from the first one. If all links are to be detected, then the *dropping condition rule* must be used with extreme care, as illustrated by the following example: Suppose that some examples exemplify a property P of a concept and some others exemplify a property Q. Suppose that everything relative to P is left, but the parts with property Q are dropped; then important information about the concept has been lost. In a "real" world, suppose that a camera pictures a scene of different blocks from three different directions, but in each picture some of the blocks (not necessarily the same ones) are not in sight. If the dropping condition rule is used, the missing information in each picture will lead to a loss of information about the scene.

The method described here, on the other hand, proposes to look for some stored information about the scene in order to fill up the "holes" of knowledge that may be present in some pictures. The authors plan to represent all the descriptions using the same structural pattern before starting the generalization process.

These two ideas have two main implications:

- *First implication.* Because a concept must be defined by the links between the variables contained in its formulation, a formula containing a disjunction describes two concepts rather than one, unless strong links between the variables of the two disjoints are found. A very important side effect of avoiding the dropping condition rule is that no disjunctive generalization can be obtained from the usually conjunctive form of the examples. This is because all examples are put under the same form (i.e., examples containing fewer literals than others are extended, if possible, up to the size of the longer ones), which is the form of the final generalized formula.

- *Second implication.* Although Vere (1980) and Mitchell (1983) use counterexamples in very different ways, they both use them as a specialization device. Vere specializes an overgeneralized formula, and Mitchell avoids overgeneralization by using counterexamples. However, the use of counterexamples described here is not specifically aimed at particularization. Counterexamples are used in order to check the existence of a link between some variables and some operators. These links must not be present in a final generalization; this fact has been called "pruning the generalization" (Kodratoff, 1983).

Counterexamples may be used to add further links to generalization. They are then used for particularization. For instance, suppose that a set of examples leads to the generalization

$G1 = (BLACK\ x)\ \&\ (SPHERE\ y)$

and that a counterexample to the set of examples is

$CG1 = (BLACK\ A)\ \&\ (SPHERE\ A).$

CG1 is an instance of G1 by the substitution $(x \leftarrow A, y \leftarrow A)$. In order to avoid this matching, it is enough to specify that x and y may not have the same instantiation. G1 is transformed into $G2 = (BLACK\ x)\ \&\ (SPHERE\ y)\ \&\ (DIFFERENT\ x\ y)$, which is more particular than G1.

Of course, another way to take into account the counterexample is to choose

G3 = (BLACK x) & (SPHERE y) & ($x \neq$ A).

Since G3 is more particular than G2, it could be possible to say that one is a "better" generalization than the other. A complete discussion of this point is outside the scope of this chapter, however, so let us simply (1) acknowledge it as an important problem; (2) remark that it comes from the fact that counterexamples are now being used in a way that may not be symmetrical to the way examples are used; and (3) understand that one cannot really decide which is the best with the present information. If (BLACK A) & (SPHERE C) is another counterexample, then G3 is the good generalization.

Another use of the counterexamples is for an "overgeneralization" that must take place when, on the contrary, counterexamples match or partly match the generalization, that is, when the descriptions of positive and negative examples intersect significantly. Suppose, for instance, that we obtain, for a given set of examples, the generalization

GG = (EDIBLE x) & (TASTY x) & (TASTY y) & (DIFFERENT x y),

which means, "there are two different objects: one is edible and tasty; the other one is tasty." Suppose also that the following negative example is given:

CGG = (EDIBLE beef) & (TASTY vegetables),

which says, "beef is edible and vegetables are tasty." In this case, CGG can be a partial instance of GG with the substitution {$x \leftarrow$ beef, $y \leftarrow$ vegetables} (notice that (TASTY x) in GG cannot match (TASTY vegetables) in CGG because of the (DIFFERENT x y) in GG).

This partial matching says that GG and CGG partially intersect, which indicates that x edibility and y tastiness are not very important, but, on the contrary, x tastiness fully characterizes the examples as opposed to CGG. This puts some emphasis on (TASTY x) in GG since it explains why CGG is a counterexample (because beef is not tasty).

The complete overgeneralization procedure is complicated and will not be detailed here. There are cases in which such an analysis of the partial matchings of the generalization of the examples and each counterexample may give an indication that some parts of this generalization are never used in order to explain the counterexample rejection, and therefore they have no interest.

The two main ideas presented in this chapter are as follows:

• Concept discovery is discovery of relevant variable bindings.

• Information should be dropped from a formula only with extreme care.

The following discussion will focus mainly on the first idea, describing methods for discovery of variable bindings. The authors will only hint, in section 9.6, at the kind of care that must be taken when information is dropped. (More details can be found in Kodratoff et al., 1984.)

9.2 CONCEPT LEARNING VERSUS THEOREM LEARNING

During generalization, one often replaces some constants by variables whose quantification is not usually explicitly defined. One may also consider that any variable is universally quantified as are, for instance, PROLOG variables. The authors maintain that this widely shared approach is not valid in some learning situations.

9.2.1 Theorem Generality

Stating that theorem T1 is more general than theorem T2 is simply a way of saying that T2 is a logical consequence of T1 or that T2 is proved as soon as T1 has been proved (see Plotkin, 1970; Michalski, 1983). When theorems are considered, the more general implies the more particular.

Example 1. Let T1 be a theorem stating that the operation * is commutative and T2 be a theorem stating that e is a constant that commutes with any elements:

$$T1 = \forall x \ \forall y \ [x * y = y * x]$$
$$T2 = \forall x \ [x * e = e * x]$$

It is clear that T2 is more particular than T1 since for a given *, the proof of T1 implies the proof of T2. On the contrary, T2 can be true when T1 is false. For instance, when * is function composition law and e is the identity function, T1 is false and T2 is true.

Example 2. Let T1′, T2′, and T3′ be three theorems:

$$T1' = \forall x \ \forall y \ \forall z \ [x * (y * z) = (x * y) * z]$$
$$T2' = \forall x \ \forall y \ [x * (y * e) = (x * y) * e]$$
$$T3' = \forall x \ [x * (x * e) = (x * x) * e]$$

T1′ is more general than T2′, which in turn is more general than T3′. Let x, y, z be lists and e be the empty list ( ), and let * be defined by $x * y =$ (APPEND x (REVERSE y)). For instance, if $x =$ (A B C) and $y =$ (D E), then $x * y =$ (A B C E D). One can see that T1′ is false (consider, e.g., the instance $x =$ ( ), $y =$ (A B), $z =$ (C)) and T2′ is true for any list. Since T2′ is true, one knows that T3′ is true.

Let us notice that T2 is obtained from T1 by substituting e for y (and deleting $\forall \ y$), that T2′ is obtained from T1′ by substituting e for z (and deleting $\forall \ z$), and T3′ is obtained from T2′ by substituting x for y (and deleting $\forall \ y$). Thus in this case one theorem can be obtained from another by simple substitutions.

9.2.2 Concept Generality

Let $P(x)$ be a logical formula that contains some unquantified variables. It is not a theorem; otherwise all of its variables would be quantified. Let X_1 be the set of the examples and X_2 be the set of counterexamples to $P(x)$.

$$X_1 = \{a/P(a) = \text{TRUE}\}, \qquad X_2 = \{b/P(b) = \text{FALSE}\}$$

where a and b are constants. $P(x)$ can be viewed as a recognition function. One says that it recognizes the x belonging to X_1 and "rejects" the x belonging to X_2.

Let us define a *concept* through the theorem

$$\forall\ x[P(x) \Rightarrow \text{Concept}(x)],$$

where Concept is the name of the concerned concept and $P(x)$ is its recognition function. If we define a concept as a theorem, it must follow the rules seen in section 9.2.1, and the more general concept implies the less general one (as proven in Michalski, 1983).

Let us now consider the recognition functions themselves. Suppose that $P(x)$ and $P'(x)$ are two recognition functions of the *same* concept. Let

$$X_1' = \{a/P'(a) = \text{TRUE}\}, \qquad X_2' = \{b/P'(b) = \text{FALSE}\}.$$

Suppose that X_1 contains X_1'; then one says that $P(x)$ is a *more general recognition function* than $P'(x)$. This definition does not contradict intuition, as the following example shows.

Example. Let F1 and F2 be two scenes (see figure 9-1; spatial relationships are not relevant) described by

F1: (SQUARE a) & (STRIPED a) & (TRIANGLE b)
F2: (SQUARE c) & (STRIPED d) & (TRIANGLE d)

The formula

$$G(x, y, z) = (\text{SQUARE } x) \ \& \ (\text{STRIPED } y) \ \& \ (\text{TRIANGLE } z)$$

is a generalization of F1 and F2 since the substitution $(x \leftarrow a, y \leftarrow a, z \leftarrow b)$ leads from G to F1, and the substitution $(x \leftarrow c, y \leftarrow d, z \leftarrow d)$ leads from G to F2.
The set X_1 for $P = G(x, y, z)$ is

$$X_1 = \{\text{F1,F2}\}$$

Consider now the formula $P' = G(x, y, d)$. It is clear that P' is an instance of P, since one obtains P' from P by replacing variable z of P by d. X_1' for P' is

$$X_1' = \{\text{F2}\}.$$

Therefore, X_1 contains X_1'.

Figure 9-1: Scene F1 represents a striped square under a triangle and scene F2 represents a striped triangle under a square.

The above (correct) definition of generality for recognition functions,

"P is more general than P' iff X_1 contains X_1',"

has been the cause of some misunderstandings. Since $X'1$ is included in X_1, it follows that P is TRUE whenever P' is TRUE, which recalls the definition of the implication. It can lead to the following (wrong) assertion:

"The more particular recognition function implies the more general one."

And, when concepts are identified with their recognition functions, the following (also wrong) assertion can result:

"The more particular concept implies the more general one."

The two above assertions are simply language misuses, since if x is a free variable, the validity of the formula $P' \Rightarrow P$ is not defined (see, for instance, Chang and Lee, 1973).

The appendix to this chapter contains a definition of the *i-implication,* which correctly formalizes the link between "truth domain" inclusion and implication.

9.2.3 What Is Learned During Concept Learning

Our definition of recognition function may seem incomplete since no information about the validity domain of the concept is introduced (otherwise some variables would be quantified). Let us further analyze the example in section 9.2.2.

F1 says that there are a striped square and a triangle. The concept $G(x, y, z)$ says that there are three objects, a triangle, a square, and a striped object. These three objects may be different, but they also may be the same. Therefore $G(x, y, z)$ states that the square may be striped, the triangle may be striped (all this information is contained in the examples and correctly generalized in $G(x, y, z)$), and that the triangle may be the square. This last bit of information is, of course, wrong. Looking at the possible instance of x, y, z, one sees that x and y may have the same instance (in F1) and that y and z may have the same instance (in F2), but that x and z never have the same instance. Therefore, a better way of generalizing F1 and F2 would have been

$$G'(x, y, z) = (\text{SQUARE } x) \ \& \ (\text{STRIPED } y) \ \& \ (\text{TRIANGLE } z)$$
$$\& \ (\text{DIFFERENT } x \ z),$$

which implicitly says that x and y or y and z may be the same.

Of course, G' is not the "best" generalization. For instance, one could also add the information that two forms are "blank," that the striped ones are convex polygons, and so on. Nevertheless, this example shows that G' makes the correct variable binding one can expect from the "constants binding" implicit in F1 and F2. Example F1 says implicitly that the triangle is different from the striped square, and example F2 says implicitly that the square is different from the striped triangle, and this information is kept in G'.

The concept G' (and, for that matter, F1 and F2) is not really of striking interest, but for those who accepted G as a correct generalization, it shows that finding the correct variable binding is not such a trivial task.

9.2.4 Concept Learning Is Not Enough

Once a set of concepts is learned, one has obtained recognition functions like G or G' above that contain free variables. One must now define to what kind of objects they are worth applying. For instance, the variables in G should never be instantiated by Christian names. The learning process should go on by finding the validity domains of these variables and the links among variables. But this is theorem learning, which is beyond the scope of this chapter.

9.3 GENERALIZATION: A DEFINITION

This section presents a definition of generality, albeit a somewhat weak one. The authors' aim is not to claim that it is the only good one but to illustrate that much useful information can be deduced by the use of this definition only.

Since this definition has been given in order to make use of all the deductive conclusions that can be drawn from the examples, it must be understood that it has points in common with other generalization systems. In particular, the language APC (Michalski, 1983) contains many deductive as well as inductive rules and has close relationships with the method presented here, which can be seen as a kind of amplified description of the "extending reference rule" (see Michalski, 1984) and the "inductive resolution rule."

9.3.1 Definitions

Terms. Let V be a countable set of variables and F a family of functions indexed by the natural integers. When a function f belongs to F_n, one says that the arity of f is n. The set F_0 of functions of arity zero is the set of the constants.

The set of terms on V and F is defined by

1. $v \in V$ is a term;
2. $f(t_1, \ldots, t_n)$ is a term iff $f \in F_n$ and $t_1, \ldots, t_n$ are terms.

It can be seen intuitively that the set of terms is a set of expressions built with functions of some arity, constants, and variables.

9.3.2 Term Generalization

Generalization. The term t_1 is more general than the term t_2, denoted by $t_1 \leq t_2$, iff there exists a substitution $\sigma t_1 = t_2$.

ϵ-generalization. This definition does not take into account the properties of the functions. Let ϵ be a set of axioms that expresses these properties. When one needs to use these axioms in order to recognize the equality of two terms, one says that they are "ϵ-equal." For instance, the two terms $t_1 = (2 + 3)$ and $t_2 = (3 + 2)$ are not considered "equal" but "ϵ-equal" because one needs to use the axiom of $+$ commutativity

$$\forall x \ \forall \ y \ [(x + y) = (y + x)]$$

in order to recognize that $t_1 =_\epsilon t_2$.

This definition may seem counterintuitive, but it is necessary to single out the use of axioms in the context of an automatic generation of generalizations because their use may lead to infinite computation loops (using the axiom in one direction and then in the other one). This kind of problem has been studied extensively (see, for instance, Stickel, 1981; Hsiang, 1982).

Let $=_\epsilon$ denote ϵ-equality. A term t_1 is more general than a term t_2 in the theory ϵ iff there exist t'_1, t'_2, σ such that

$$t'_1 =_\epsilon t_1,$$
$$t'_2 =_\epsilon t_2, \text{ and}$$
$$\sigma t'_1 = t'_2.$$

Depending on ϵ, it may be that the above definition of ϵ-generalization is not consistent. Using some of the properties, one may find t'_1 and t'_2 such that $t_1 =_\epsilon t'_1$ and $t_2 =_\epsilon t'_2$ and there exists σ_1 such that $\sigma_1 t_1 = t_2$. Using other properties, one may find t''_1 and t''_2 such that $t_1 =_\epsilon t''_1$ and $t_2 =_\epsilon t''_2$, but there exists σ_2 such that $\sigma_2 t''_2 = t''_1$ even when $t_1 \neq_\epsilon t_2$.

Since we want to use the properties of the functions and further define the generality of formulas (therefore using the properties of our connectors), it is necessary to find a definition of ϵ-generalization that avoids this difficulty.

Example of ϵ-generalization (where predicates are treated like terms). Let us suppose that we work in a world of objects with colors and that the following knowledge is available:

$$\forall \ x \ \exists \ y (\text{COLOR } y \ x)$$

This states that each object x has a color named y. In addition, RED is a kind of COLOR, and this information is also supposed to be known. This knowledge allows us to transform any predicate like $(\text{RED } x)$ into an instance of more general predicate $(\text{COLOR RED } x)$.

Let us compare the generality of the concept *red square* C_1 and *square* C_2:

$$C_1 = (\text{SQUARE } x) \ \& \ (\text{RED } x), \qquad C_2 = (\text{SQUARE } x)$$

Applying the above theorem, one knows that for any x of C_2, there is an unknown color, say y. Therefore C_2 is equivalent to $C'_2 = (\text{SQUARE } x) \ \& \ (\text{COLOR } y \ x)$. Based on the fact that RED is more particular than COLOR, one can find $C'_1 =_\epsilon C'_1$, $C'_1 = (\text{SQUARE } x) \ \& \ (\text{COLOR RED } x)$. Now the usual term definition of generality can be applied since $\sigma C'_2 = C'_1$ with $\sigma = (y \leftarrow \text{RED})$. Therefore C_2 is more general than C_1 in the theory containing the above information.

9.3.3 Formula Generalization

Let E_1 and E_2 be two formulas and ϵ an equational theory.

Generalized formula. We shall say that formula E_1 is a *generalization* of formula E_2 if Condition 1 is fulfilled.

Condition 1: $\exists E'_1$ such that
$$E'_1 =_\epsilon E_1 \qquad \text{and} \qquad \exists \sigma_2 \text{ such that } \sigma_2 E'_1 =_\epsilon E_2.$$

This condition states that there exists E'_1, equivalent to E_1, and that E'_1, considered as a term is more general than E_2 considered as a term.

The next definition gives another condition that insures that formula generality is a partial ordering.

Generality relation between two formulas. We shall say that E_1 is *more general* than E_2 when Condition 1 and Condition 2 are fulfilled.

Condition 2: $\forall E'_2$ such that
$$E'_2 =_\epsilon E_2 \qquad \text{and} \qquad \exists \sigma_1, \text{ such that}$$
$$\sigma_1 E'_2 =_\epsilon E_1$$
implies
$$E'_2 =_\epsilon E_1.$$

This second condition states that the first condition meets no contradictions. It says that if there is an E'_2 that is equivalent to E_2 and that is more general (as a term) than E_1, then all three—E_1, E_2, and E'_2—must be equivalent.

9.4 STRUCTURAL MATCHING

Let us recall the (restricted) definition of the generalization as given in section 9.3.3:

If E_g is a generalization of $E_1, E_2, \ldots, E_n$, then $\forall\ i \in [1,n]\ \exists\ E'_i \exists \sigma_i$ such that $E_i =_\epsilon E_i$ and $\sigma_i E_g = E'_i$.

The first step is to find for each E_i the appropriate E'_i. This step is called the detection of structural matching between $E_1, E_2, \ldots, E_n$, and when this step succeeds, the formulas $E'_1, E'_2, \ldots, E'_n$, are said to match each other structurally.

This section is devoted to the definition and the intuitive meaning of the structural matching. Also described here is a way of obtaining structural matching by using properties of the representation and theorems about the description language.

9.4.1 Definition of the Structural Match

Two formulas structurally match if they are identical except for the constants and the variables that instantiate their predicates.

Definition. E_1 and E_2 being two formulas, E_1 structurally matches E_2 iff $\exists\ C\ \exists\ \sigma_1, \sigma_2$ such that

1. $\sigma_1 C = E_1$ and $\sigma_2 C = E_2$;
2. σ_1 and σ_2 never substitute a variable by a predicate or a function.

Example

Let E_1 = (COLOR x y) & (FORM TRIANGLE y),
$\quad E_2$ = (COLOR GREEN z) & (FORM u t), and
$\quad E_3$ = (GREEN z)

E_1 and E_2 structurally match but E_2 and E_3 do not, although one can notice that $E_2 =_\epsilon E_3$ in the theory that says that each object has a form.

9.4.2 Determining the Structural Matching

Given a learning set $L = E_1, E_2, \ldots, E_n$, the first step of learning is to find, for each E_i belonging to L, a formula $E'_i =_\epsilon E_i$ such that all E'_i structurally match each other. The structural matching is obtained by progressive meaning-preserving transformations.

9.4.2.1 Using Representation Laws

A representation language (see the appendix to this chapter) is given when the properties of each connector in the expressions are known. For instance, let us assume that the unique connector of representation is the logical conjunction &. The properties of & are not only the commutativity and the associativity but also the idempotency and the existence of a neutral element (True). The following will show the importance of a systematic use of these last two properties.

Associativity and commutativity of &. It is quite evident that associativity and commutativity of & must be used for detecting structural matching. This fact has often been used, since it allows one to consider a conjunction of clauses as a set of clauses.

Example

$$E_1 = (((\text{RED A}) \, \& \, (\text{SQUARE A})) \, \& \, ((\text{TRIANGLE B}) \, \& \, (\text{GREEN E})))$$
$$E_2 = (((\text{RED C}) \, \& \, (\text{TRIANGLE C})) \, \& \, ((\text{SQUARE D}) \, \& \, (\text{GREEN D})))$$

Using associativity and commutativity of &, we may transform E_1 into $E'_1 = ((\text{RED A}) \, \& \, (\text{TRIANGLE E})) \, \& \, ((\text{SQUARE A}) \, \& \, (\text{GREEN B})))$, where E'_1 structurally matches E_2, since there exists a formula C and two substitutions σ_1 and σ_2 such that $\sigma_1 C = E'_1$ and $\sigma_2 C = E_2$:

$$C = (((\text{RED } x) \, \& \, (\text{TRIANGLE } y)) \, \& \, ((\text{SQUARE } z) \, \& \, (\text{GREEN } v)))$$
$$\sigma_1 = (x \leftarrow \text{A}, y \leftarrow \text{E}, z \leftarrow \text{A}, y \leftarrow \text{B})$$
$$\sigma_2 = (x \leftarrow \text{C}, y \leftarrow \text{C}, z \leftarrow \text{D}, v \leftarrow \text{D})$$

Because of associativity and commutativity of logical &, the parentheses are meaningless and will be omitted from now on.

& idempotency. Consider the learning set containing E_3 and E_4:

$$E_3 = (\text{SQUARE A}) \, \& \, (\text{RED A}) \, \& \, (\text{SMALL A})$$
$$E_4 = (\text{SQUARE B}) \, \& \, (\text{RED B}) \, \& \, (\text{SQUARE C}) \, \& \, (\text{SMALL C})$$

The classical way of generalizing applied on these formulas (Hayes-Roth and McDermott, 1978; Michalski, 1983) uses the dropping condition rule. It leads to two different generalizations:

$$E'_g = (\text{SQUARE } x) \, \& \, (\text{RED } x) \, \& \, (\text{SMALL } y)$$
$$E''_g = (\text{RED } x) \, \& \, (\text{SQUARE } y) \, \& \, (\text{SMALL } y)$$

These two formulas are not generalizations because there does not exist any transformation E'_4 of E_4 (where $E'_4 =_\epsilon E_4$) that is an instantiation of E'_g or E''_g. The aim here is to avoid as much as possible the use of the dropping condition rule during the generalization process because it abstracts some piece of information. But the dropping condition rule must be used after the generalization process, using counter-examples, to extract some common characteristics of the generalization that do not belong to the counterexamples. This second step in learning uses links between variables in the generalized formula (see section 9.6).

In order to detect the structural matching between E_3 and E_4 we must use the idempotency of &. E_3 may be rewritten as E'_3, which structurally matches E_4:

$$E'_3 = (\text{SQUARE A}) \ \& \ (\text{RED A}) \ \& \ (\text{SQUARE A}) \ \& \ (\text{SMALL A})$$

E'_3 structurally matches E_4 since there exists C,

$$C = (\text{SQUARE } x) \ \& \ (\text{RED } x) \ \& \ (\text{SQUARE } y) \ \& \ (\text{SMALL } y),$$

and there exist σ_3 and σ_4 such that

$$\sigma_3 C = E'_3 \text{ and } \sigma_4 = E_4,$$

where $\sigma_3 = (x \leftarrow \text{A}, y \leftarrow \text{A})$ and $\sigma_3 = (x \leftarrow \text{B}, y \leftarrow \text{C})$. No variable is substituted by a predicate.

Now let us consider the formula E'_3. E'_3 may not be represented by a set of clauses, as in Vere (1980) or Hayes-Roth and McDermott (1978), because the clause (SQUARE A) appears twice in E'_3. Therefore we must use a multiset of clauses (i.e., a set with multiple occurrences of clauses) to represent formulas when the representation is purely conjunctive. When representation is more complicated, more sophisticated data structures are required to represent formulas.

Neutral element. The existence of a neutral element (True) is used not by itself but with regard to semantical properties of the description language. It indicates that every theorem known as *True* may be conjuncted to any conjunctive formula in order to obtain the structural match. In case of pure disjunctive clauses, theorems known as *False* may be inserted.

9.4.2.2 Using Properties of the Description

The properties of the description language are given first by predicate taxonomies (hierarchies), which express generality relationships among predicates, and second by rewrite rules, which express theorems about the properties of the predicates.

Hierarchy of predicates. Generality relationships among predicates must be encoded as hierarchies. For instance, suppose that we are in a world where objects are plain geometrical figures. The form of the objects in such a world is one of their most important attributes. But their shapes may be specified with more or less generality depending on the precision of the initial description.

Example

Let us suppose we want to generalize two formulas:

$E_1 = $ (STRIPED A) & (SQUARE A)
$E_2 = $ (STRIPED B) & (TRIANGLE u v B)

E_1 is very different from E_2 because a square is, in a sense, a much better defined shape than a triangle.

In order to find a structural matching between E_1 and E_2, one must be aware that a square and a triangle have some common properties because both are polygons. This inference is allowed by the hierarchy of shape predicates shown in figure 9-2. This hierarchy has been used deliberately to show that "tangled hierarchies" must sometimes be used.

In order to use predicate taxonomies, one must look for a common ancestor in the hierarchy; this process has been called "climbing the generalization tree" (Michalski, 1983). It is used to find the desired new expressions E'_1 and E'_2 where $E'_1 =_\epsilon E_1$ and $E'_2 =_\epsilon E_2$:

$E'_1 = $ (STRIPED A) &
　　　　(POLYGON QUADRILATERAL RECTANGLE SQUARE A)
$E'_2 = $ (STRIPED B) & (POLYGON TRIANGLE u v B)

Now E'_1 and E'_2 structurally match.

Let

$C = $ (STRIPED x) & (POLYGON y z t x)

and

$\sigma_1 C = E'_1, \sigma_2 C = E'_2,$

where

$\sigma_1 = (x \leftarrow $ A, $y \leftarrow $ QUADRILATERAL, $z \leftarrow $ RECTANGLE,
　　　$t \leftarrow $ SQUARE)

and

$\sigma_2 = (x \leftarrow $ B, $y \leftarrow $ TRIANGLE, $z \leftarrow u, t \leftarrow v).$

Rewriting rules. Rewriting rules are used to encode both theorems and properties of predicates. These rules are themselves theorems, so they are bound formulas, that is, formulas quantified by existential or universal quantifiers. For instance, suppose we are in a block world and there are two predicates. The first expresses that one block is above another (e.g., (ON　A B) expresses that A is on B), and the second expresses that one block is near another (e.g., (NEAR　A B) expresses that A is near B). The predicate NEAR is commutative (i.e., $\forall$ x $\forall$ y [(NEAR x y) = (NEAR y x)]) but not transitive (i.e., (NEAR x y) and (NEAR y z) do not imply (NEAR x z)). In order

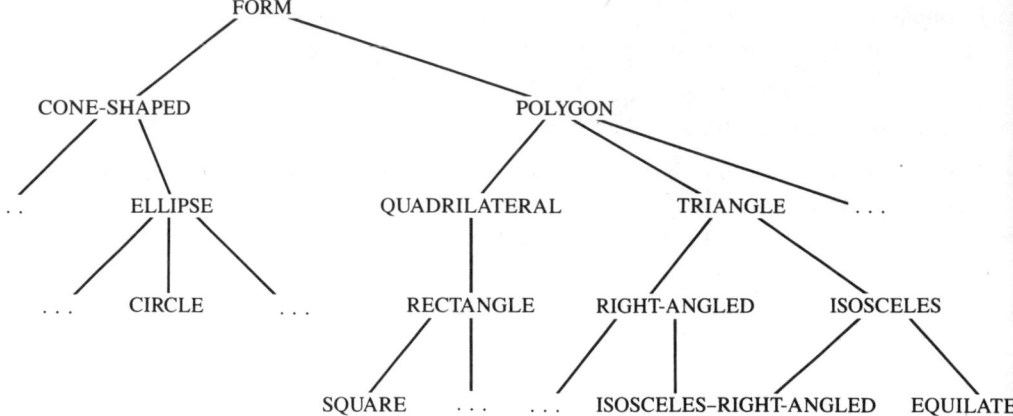

Figure 9-2:   One possible tangled hierarchy plane geometrical forms.

to take into account the commutativity of NEAR during the detection of the structural match, we must encode it as a rewrite rule:

$$\forall x \ \forall y \ [(\text{NEAR } x \ y) \ \rightarrow \ (\text{NEAR } y \ x)]. \tag{R1}$$

NEAR and ON are linked in any case since objects that are ON each other are also NEAR each other. One has

$$\forall x \ \forall y \ [(\text{ON } x \ y) \ \rightarrow \ (\text{ON } x \ y) \ \& \ (\text{NEAR } x \ y)]. \tag{R2}$$

These rules are not supposed to be applied carelessly—for instance, rule (R2) applied to itself may give a formula of infinite length. One applies them in order to obtain a structural matching; this fact will control the process of rule application and prevent infinite loops.

The rewrite rules may also be used to encode theorems. For instance, in a colored world each object has a color, but all objects do not have the same color; otherwise the information about color would be empty, and this would be equivalent to being in a noncolored world. This information may be expressed by

$$\forall x \ \forall y \ [\textit{True} \ \rightarrow \ (\text{COLOR } y \ x)] \tag{R3}$$

(i.e., each object x has a color named y).

In order to apply the quantified rewrite rules, we must remove the quantifier according to the following laws:

1. A variable that appears under the scope of a universal quantifier may be instantiated by any term, constant or variable.

2. A variable that appears under the scope of an existential quantifier may be instantiated only by a variable that does not belong to the formula in which the rule is applied.

Example

Let E_3 = (ON   E F) & (NEAR   E F) and
E_4 = (ON   G H).

Applying rule (R2) to E_4 leads to

E_4' = (ON   G H) & (NEAR   G H),

which structurally matches E_3.

Let E_5 = (RED C) & (NEAR   D C) and
E_6 = (NEAR   I J).

Applying rule (R3) in one of its correct instantiations,

True → (COLOR u J),

we obtain

E_6' = (COLOR u J) & (NEAR I J).

Using the color predicates hierarchy given in figure 9-3, we obtain

E_5' = (COLOR RED C) & (NEAR D C),

which structurally matches E_6'.

9.4.3 A Complete Example

In this section a less trivial example is presented. The aim is to prove that (LOWER x y) is more general than (EQ x 1) & (EQ Y 2). This statement is intuitively clear, but its proof is not so trivial. The needed semantic rules about the properties of the predicates LOWER and EQ are as follows:

$\forall$ x [*True* → (EQ x x)]   (R4)
True → (LOWER 1 2)   (R5)
$\forall x$ $\forall y$ $\forall z$ [(LOWER x y) & (EQ z x) → (LOWER z y)]   (R6)
$\forall$ x $\forall y$ $\forall z$ [(LOWER x y) & (EQ z y) → (LOWER x z)]   (R7)

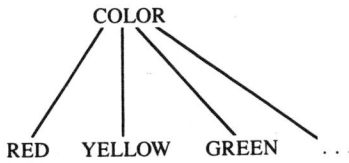

Figure 9-3: A simple "COLOR" hierarchy.

Let $T_1 = (\text{LOWER } x_1 z_1)$ and
$T_2 = (\text{EQ } x_2 \ 1) \ \& \ (\text{EQ } y_2 \ 2)$.

Using rule (R4) twice in T_1, we obtain

$T_1' = (\text{LOWER } x_1 \ y_1) \ \& \ (\text{EQ } x_1 \ x_1) \ \& \ (\text{EQ } y_1 \ y_1)$.

T_2 may be rewritten in T_2' by applying rule (R5):

$T_2' = (\text{LOWER } 1 \ 2) \ \& \ (\text{EQ } x_2 \ 1) \ \& \ (\text{EQ } y_2 \ 2)$.

T_1' and T_2' match structurally. The algorithm of section 9.5 will now detect that they generalize to

$T' = (\text{LOWER } x \ y) \ \& \ (\text{EQ } v \ x) \ \& \ (\text{EQ } w \ y)$.

Using rules (R6) and (R7), we can rewrite T' as T:

$T = (\text{LOWER } v \ w) =_\epsilon T_1$.

This shows that $T_1 \leq T_2$ as proven by the definition of generality relation between two formulas in section 9.3.

9.4.4 Conflicting Structural Matching

Structural matching does not have a unique solution in general, as the following example will show. Consider the following instances:

$E_1 = (\text{RED A}) \ \& \ (\text{RED B}) \ \& \ (\text{SQUARE B})$
$E_2 = (\text{RED C}) \ \& \ (\text{SQUARE D})$

A structural matching of E_1 and E_2 may be obtained in two ways. The first way is to use & idempotency to obtain

$E_2' = (\text{RED C}) \ \& \ (\text{RED C}) \ \& \ (\text{SQUARE D})$.

Now E_1 and E_2' structurally match, leading to the generalization

$E_g = (\text{RED } x) \ \& \ (\text{RED } y) \ \& \ (\text{SQUARE } z) \ \& \ (\text{DIFFERENT } x \ z)$.

The second way is to use rule (R3)

$\forall \ x \ \exists \ y \ [\text{TRUE} \rightarrow (\text{COLOR } y \ x)]$

with the instantiation $x \leftarrow D$ to obtain

$E_2'' = (\text{RED C}) \ \& \ (\text{COLOR } y \ \text{D}) \ \& \ (\text{SQUARE D})$.

Using the COLOR predicate hierarchy, one also obtains

$E_1' = (\text{RED A}) \ \& \ (\text{COLOR RED B}) \ \& \ (\text{SQUARE B})$.

This leads to the generalization

$E_g' = (\text{RED } x) \ \& \ (\text{COLOR } v \ z) \ \& \ (\text{SQUARE } z) \ \& \ (\text{DIFFERENT } x \ z)$,

where the fact that v must be different from both x and z is kept implicit.

The generalizations E_g and E'_g have their own qualities, and one cannot state that one is "better" than the other, since they both contain three variables.

The reader has probably noticed that the theorems are applied here in the most judicious way; for instance, instantiating x by C in rule (R3) would have led to

$$E'_2{}'' = (\text{RED C}) \ \& \ (\text{COLOR } y \text{ C}) \ \& \ (\text{SQUARE D}).$$

The generalization of $E'_2{}''$ and E'_1 gives

$$E''_g = (\text{RED } x) \ \& \ (\text{COLOR } v \ y) \ \& \ (\text{SQUARE } z) \ \& \ (\text{DIFFERENT } x \ z),$$

which is much too general as compared to E'_g or E_g.

Section 9.5 shows a way to detect the good instantiations. Nevertheless, the fact that incomparable generalizations may be obtained cannot be avoided, as the above example shows. From the "point of view" of the colors (i.e., keeping the colors as consistent as possible), E_g is the best generalization. From the "point of view" of the objects (i.e., introducing the minimum number of objects), E'_g is better.

The position of the authors is that the best point of view is one given "at a higher level," meaning that it is a metaknowledge that can be given at the same time that the theorems and the hierarchies are given.

9.5 GENERALIZATION ALGORITHM

As previously seen, the generalization process may be divided into two main steps. The first is intended to detect structural matchings among examples belonging to the learning set. Finding a structural matching is the most difficult, though preliminary, task of the generalization process, so a sketch of the structural matching detection algorithm will be produced. The second step, the actual generalization phase, may be easily realized; it involves simply detecting the common links between variables in all the structurally matching formulas.

9.5.1 Structural Matching Detection Algorithm

It has been shown that detection of structural matching is central in the generalization process. To solve this problem, the algorithm presented here operates progressively and in parallel on all examples.

9.5.1.1 Overview of the Algorithm

The algorithm may be roughly described as sequence of two alternate operations. The conjunction of these two operations leads to the introduction of new variables with common occurrences in all examples. Each of these variables is a generalization variable (GV). Links between variables, or between variables and constants, keep track of the instantiations of each variable in each example.

The first operation consists of choosing one constant or one variable that is not a GV in each example and turning it into a new GV. As will be seen, this choice is a crucial step in the process, and one therefore needs to use heuristics in order to lead it. Depending on the strategy, one may either make one choice at a time or build a tree of choices, each of them leading to a generalization formula.

In the present implemented state of this algorithm, the user has three choices. The first is to provide an ordering of the predicates, which the system then uses for finding generalizations that favor the "point of view" (see section 9.4) expressed by this ordering. The second is to choose directly the constant to be turned into a variable and to repeat this for each example. The third is to leave the system entirely free and let it choose the generalization that minimizes the combinatory search.

The second operation is a partial structural matching. One considers the set of predicates containing GVs and attempts to realize a structural matching of this subset of the example predicates. Each variable of the GV must be at the same occurrence of the same predicate in all the examples. Otherwise, the structural matching is considered faulty, and a new one is sought.

This operation usually leads to different, partially matching formulas. In this case one must either use a specific heuristic similar to the heuristic used in the first operation or build simultaneously different partially matching formulas. Operations 1 and 2 are repeated until there are no constants left.

The instantiations of each variable are not dropped, since this is very useful information to be used further in detecting the links between variables.

9.5.1.2 Description of the Algorithm

Each of the steps of the algorithm is exemplified by the following very simple example:

Let E_1 = (ON   A B)
E_2 = (ON   C D) & (NEAR   D F)

The predicates ON and NEAR are those defined in section 9.4.2.2 under *Rewrite rules*. Their properties are expressed by rules (R1) and (R2):

$\forall\, x\,\forall\, y\,[(\text{NEAR}\ x\ y)\ \rightarrow\ (\text{NEAR}\ y\ x)]$ (R1)
$\forall\, x\,\forall\, y\,[(\text{ON}\ x\ y)\ \rightarrow\ (\text{ON}\ x\ y)\ \&\ (\text{NEAR}\ x\ y)]$ (R2)

Operation 1 is divided into two steps:

Step 1: One constant (or non–GV variable) is chosen in each example according to some heuristics. Suppose that the heuristic requires one to choose first the second argument of the predicate ON, next the first argument of ON, and then the first and the second arguments of NEAR. Applying Step 1 to the example leads one to turn B and D into a GV.

Step 2: A new GV is created and substituted for the constants and the variables chosen in Step 1. One keeps track of this substitution by using links between variables. Applying Step 2 to the example, one obtains

$$E_1 = (\text{ON} \quad \text{A} \quad x_0)[(= x_0 \text{ B})]$$
$$E_2 = (\text{ON} \quad \text{C} \quad x_0) \ \& \ (\text{NEAR} \ x_0 \ \text{F})[(= x_0 \text{ D})]$$

where the formula inside [ ] states the links between variables.

Operation 2 is intended to force the partial structural matching between examples. Let us consider the example again: x_0 appears once in E_1 (as the second argument of the predicate ON) and twice in E_2 (as the second argument of the predicate ON and as the first argument of the predicate NEAR). There is one common occurrence of x_0 in E_1 and E_2, and there is one occurrence that appears in E_2 and not in E_1.
Operation 2 is also divided into two steps:

Step 3: The occurrence of the variables substituted in Step 2 is detected and the fact that these occurrences belong to all the examples is checked.

Step 4: If this is not the case, an attempt is made to generate them using the transformations introduced in section 9.4.

For instance since the first argument of NEAR is x_0 in E_2, an attempt is made to generate it in E_1. Rule (R2) with instantiation $x \leftarrow$ A and $y \leftarrow x_0$ is applied to E_1. One obtains

$$E_1 =_\epsilon E_1' = (\text{ON A } x_0) \ \& \ (\text{NEAR A } x_0) \ \& \ [(= x_0 \text{ B})].$$

x_0 appears now in E_1' as the second argument of NEAR, and we want to generate it as the first argument of x_0, which is possible using rule (R1). Therefore, E_1' will be rewritten as

$$E_1'' = (\text{ON A } x_0) \ \& \ (\text{NEAR } x_0 \text{ A}) \ \& \ [(= x_0 \text{ B})].$$

Finally, if Step 4 did not manage to generate some occurrence of the variable substituted in Step 2, then Step 4 kills this occurrence by introducing a new variable.
Let us go on applying this algorithm to the example.

Step 1: Suppose that A and C, the first arguments of ON, are chosen.
Step 2: $E_1'' = (\text{ON } y_0 x_0) \ \& \ (\text{NEAR } x_0 \ y_0) \ \& \ [(= y_0 \text{ A}) \ \& \ (\neq x_0 y_0)$
$\qquad\qquad \& \ (= x_0 \text{ B})]$
$\qquad E_2 = (\text{ON } y_0 x_0) \ \& \ (\text{NEAR } x_0 \text{ F}) \ \& \ [(= x_0 \text{ D}) \ \&$
$\qquad\qquad (= y_0 \text{ C}) \ \& \ (\neq x_0 y_0)]$
Step 3: Occurrence of y_0 shared by all examples: $(\text{ON } y_0 x_0)$. Occurrence of y_0 belonging to E_1'' and not to E_2 : $(\text{NEAR } x_0 y_0)$.

Step 4: In order to generate (NEAR x y_0) rules (R1) and (R2) are used so E_2 is rewritten as E_2'':

$$E_2'' = \text{(ON } y_0x_0) \text{ \& (NEAR } x_0y_0) \text{ \& (NEAR } x_0\text{F) \&}$$
$$[(= x_0 \text{ D}) \text{ \& } (= x_0 \text{ C}) \text{ \& } (\neq x_0y_0)].$$

Step 1: The last constant is F.

Step 2: $E_1'' = \text{(ON } y_0x_0) \text{ \& (NEAR } x_0y_0) \text{ \& } [(= x_0 \text{ B}) \text{ \& } (= y_0 \text{ A}) \text{ \&}$
$$(\neq x_0y_0)]$$

$E_2 = \text{(ON } y_0x_0) \text{ \& (NEAR } x_0y_0) \text{ \& (NEAR } x_0z_0) \text{ \& } [(= x_0 \text{ D}) \text{ \&}$
$$(= y_0 \text{ C}) \text{ \& } (= z_0 \text{ F}) \text{ \& } (\neq x_0y_0) \text{ \& } (\neq z_0x_0) \text{ \& } (\neq z_0y_0)]$$

Step 3: The only occurrence of z_0 is (NEAR x_0z_0) in E_2.

Step 4: A similar occurrence of z_0 in E_1'' can be obtained by the use of & idempotency and (NEAR x_0y_0) $=_\epsilon$ (NEAR x_0z_0) & $[(= z_0y_0)]$:

$E_1''' = \text{(ON } y_0x_0) \text{ \& (NEAR } x_0y_0) \text{ \& (NEAR } x_0z_0) \text{ \&}$
$$[(= x_0 \text{B}) \text{ \& } (= y_0 \text{A}) \text{ \& } (= z_0y_0) \text{ \& } (\neq x_0y_0) \text{ \& } (\neq z_0 \, x_0)]$$

$E_2'' = \text{(ON } y_0x_0) \text{ \& (NEAR } x_0y_0) \text{ \& (NEAR } x_0z_0) \text{ \& } [(= x_0 \text{ D}) \text{ \&}$
$$(= x_0 \text{ F}) \text{ \& } (= y_0 \text{ C}) \text{ \& } (\neq x_0y_0) \text{ \& } (\neq z_0x_0) \text{ \& } (\neq z_0y_0)]$$

Now the algorithm stops because there is no constant or variable that is not being a GV in formulas E_1''' and E_2''. One can easily verify the structural matching of E_1''' and E_2''.

9.5.2 Pure Generalization Algorithm

The pure generalization algorithm compares links between variables in this set of obtained formulas. If a link exists in all formulas, it remains in the generalized formula; if not, it must be suppressed. Therefore the set of links belonging to the generalized formula is the intersection of links belonging to each formula. For instance, E_g being the generalization of E_1 and E_2,

$$E_g = \text{(ON } y_0x_0) \text{ \& (NEAR } y_0x_0) \text{ \& (NEAR } x_0z_0) \text{ \& } [(\neq x_0y_0z_0)].$$

One can now see that the restricted definition of generalization, given in section 9.3, has been used to build up the algorithm of structural matching. This algorithm renders explicit the implicit information contained in the examples that is necessary for the construction of a good generalization.

Once this information has been gathered, the dropping rule can be used in order to obtain a generalization. The reader can now understand what was meant at the beginning of this chapter by the statement that the dropping rule should be used with extreme care. In other words, *the dropping rule can be used after an attempt has been made to put the example formulas into structural matching.*

9.6 LEARNING A CONCEPT FROM EXAMPLES AND COUNTEREXAMPLES

In this section an example is given that shows the importance of the information gathered during structural matching. Such information will allow us to find an explanation of the differences among examples and counterexamples.

The example used here is taken from Vere (1980) and involves "stacking, transfer, and unstacking actions for uniform cubic blocks on a table." The counterexamples "illustrate that block 1 cannot be moved on top of another block 2 if there is a block 3 already on block 2" (Vere, 1980). The formula generated by Vere's system is

$$[(\text{ON } t \text{ TABLE}) \& \sim ((\text{ON } u \text{ } z) \sim ((\text{ON } y \text{ } v) \& \sim ((\text{ON } z \text{ TABLE})$$
$$\& (\text{ON } w \text{ } u))))] (\text{ON } x \text{ } y) \rightarrow (\text{ON } x \text{ } z)$$

where x, y, z, t, u, v, and w are variables that can be instantiated by the name of a block or the constant TABLE; where the $\rightarrow$ shows the modification to be done to the blocks; and where the expression inside the brackets is the context in which this modification is allowed. This formula takes the value TRUE for all the examples and the value FALSE for all the counterexamples, but it is a poor illustration of the concept of stacking and unstacking wherein two blocks cannot be on a third one.

The examples used here (see figure 9-4) are not the same as Vere's because his are somewhat complicated, but it is easy to check that these examples convey the same idea.

In Vere's notation these examples would be described as follows:

E_1: [(ON   A TABLE)](ON   B TABLE) $\rightarrow$ (ON   B A)
E_2: [(ON   E TABLE) & (ON   F E)](ON   G F) $\rightarrow$ (ON   G TABLE)
E_3: [(ON   H TABLE) & (ON   I H)](ON   J TABLE) $\rightarrow$ (ON   J I)

Using the methodology described in this chapter, the reader will easily see that

$$\text{G: } [(\text{ON } t \text{ TABLE}) \& (\text{ON } t' \text{ } u) \& (\text{DIFFERENT}(x(y \text{ } z \text{ } t \text{ } t' \text{ } u))(y(z \text{ } t))$$
$$(z \text{ } u)(t' \text{ } u))] (\text{ON } x \text{ } y) \rightarrow (\text{ON } x \text{ } z)$$

is a generalization of E_1, E_2, E_3 where, for instance, (DIFFERENT$(y(z \text{ } t))(z \text{ } u)$) is a short way of saying (DIFFERENT $y \text{ } z$) & (DIFFERENT $y \text{ } t$) & (DIFFERENT $z \text{ } u$).

As will be seen, G also has no instance such that two cubes are over a third one. Of course, G is simpler than Vere's formula, but it is still not satisfactory, because much of its information is irrelevant to the concept.

Let us now consider the counterexample E_1' shown in figure 9-5. E_1' is written as:

$$E_1' = [(\text{ON   M TABLE}) \& (\text{ON   P M})](\text{ON   N TABLE}) \rightarrow (\text{ON   N M}).$$

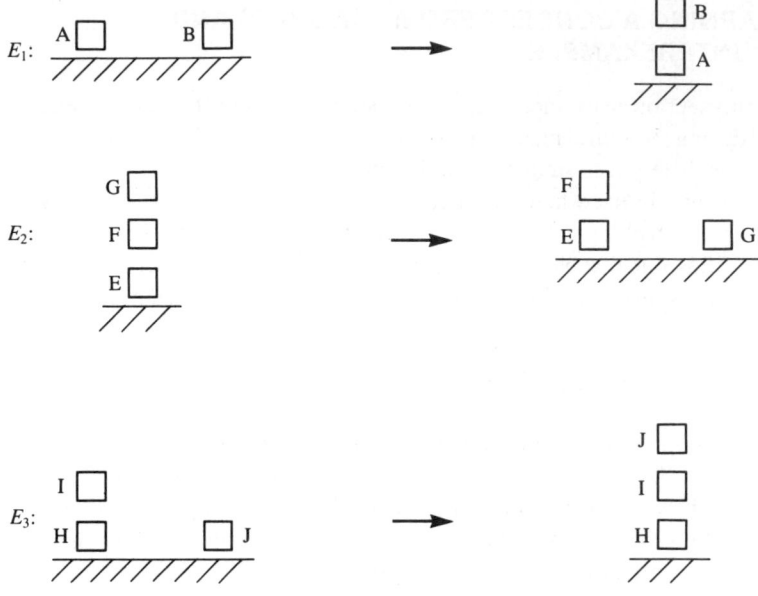

Figure 9-4: Examples of stacking and unstacking cubes.

Figure 9-5: A counterexample to the examples given in figure 9-4.

This counterexample is "nearly" an instance of G with the following instantiations:

$$x \leftarrow N, y \leftarrow \text{TABLE}, z \leftarrow M, t' \leftarrow P, u \leftarrow M, t \leftarrow M$$

This succeeds only if z, u, and t are the same. From the set of DIFFERENT in G, one sees that u and t may be the same and that therefore the link between the two M's in

$$[(\text{ON} \quad \text{M TABLE})(\text{ON} \quad \text{P M})]$$

may be present in both examples and counterexamples; that z and t may be the same and that therefore the link between the two M's in

$$[(\text{ON} \quad \text{M TABLE}) \,\&\, (\text{ON} \quad \text{P M})](\text{ON} \quad \text{N TABLE}) \rightarrow (\text{ON} \quad \text{N M})$$

may be present in both examples and counterexamples; and that z and u cannot be the same and that therefore the link between the two M's in

$$[(\text{ON} \quad M \text{ TABLE}) \ \& \ (\text{ON} \quad P\,M)](\text{ON} \quad N \text{ TABLE}) \ \rightarrow \ (\text{ON} \quad N\,M)$$

is the link that rejects the counterexample as the instance of G. This link expresses precisely that a new block cannot be put on another one that is not "clear."

Our concept is therefore described by the formula

$$G' = [(\text{ON } t \text{ TABLE}) \ \& \ (\text{ON } t' \ u) \ \& \ (\text{DIFFERENT } z \ u)]$$
$$(\text{ON } x \ y) \ \rightarrow \ (\text{ON } x \ z),$$

which is included in G.

A more detailed study of the possible matchings of G and other counterexamples would be necessary before one would find the correct generalization, which is actually more complicated than G'. More details are given elsewhere (Kodratoff et al., 1984), but it is hoped that the reader now tends to agree with the statement that concept learning is the discovery of relevant variable bindings.

9.7 CONCLUSION

The main goal of this chapter has been to describe an algorithm that detects variable bindings common to the examples. The importance of variable bindings has been exemplified by their use with counterexamples: they are a source of possible "near misses" (Winston, 1975) between examples and counterexamples, and they may therefore help us to find explanations for the validity of the generalization. In the example in section 9.6, the link (DIFFERENT $u \, z$) explains why two blocks cannot be put on top of the same third block. The discovery of these links can be made using deductive procedures and a very restricted definition of generalization.

One must be aware that several sets of links, that is, several independent structural matchings, can lead to different generalizations. Each of them favors the memorization of some aspect of the examples. Since it requires the knowledge of the relative importance of the predicates describing the examples, the algorithm described here helps to make explicit the relationships between a given generalization and the aspects it favors.

Finally, the authors would like to stress that acquiring the knowledge of the relative importance of the different predicates describing the examples may also be considered an act of learning. The authors are currently developing methods of applying the idea of structural matching in order to find hints about this importance by mixing symbolic and numerical information.

APPENDIX: GENERALIZATION AND "I-IMPLICATION"

1. Definitions

Terms. These have been defined in section 9.3.1.

Description language. Let P_i be a set of predicate symbols of arity i, and let us call $P = P_0 \cup P_1 \ldots \cup P_n$ where P_0 is TRUE or FALSE.

The predicates may be related by one or several generalization hierarchies. For instance, the predicates PLANE-FIGURE, POLYGON, and SQUARE are of decreasing generality.

Some predicates may have properties or may be related by theorems. For instance, the predicate (NEAR x y) (which states that x and y are near each other) is certainly commutative— $\forall x \forall y [(NEAR x y) \Rightarrow (NEAR y x)]$—but it is not transitive since

$$\exists x \exists y \exists z [\sim [(NEAR x y) \& (NEAR y z) \Rightarrow (NEAR x z)]].$$

Let H be the set of theorems concerning the predicate. Then the triplet (P,H,T) is called a description language.

Literal. Let $t_1, \ldots t_n$ be terms and $p \in P_n$; then $(p\ t_1 \ldots t_n)$ or $\sim (p\ t_1, \ldots t_n)$ are called *literals.*

Representation language. Expressions defined here are a little more general than the usual clauses because the authors allow more connectors than are allowed in classical predicate logic. A representation language is defined by a description language and connectors with their syntax and semantics. The connectors are those of logic as well as special connectors describing possible actions.

For instance, when Vere (1980) wants to describe a scene where blocks are transferred (see figure 9-6), which can be described by

[(ON   A TABLE)](ON   B TABLE) → (ON   B A),

he "invents" two connectors. One of them is the set of brackets which contains the context in which the action may be done. In this example the context is [(ON   A

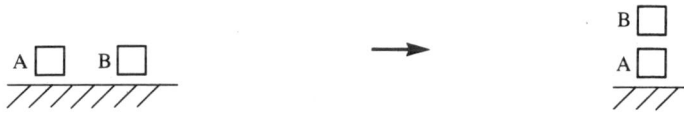

Figure 9-6:   An example of stacking two cubes.

TABLE)]. The other connector is the arrow, which describes the action that must be done. In this example the action is (ON B TABLE) $\rightarrow$ (ON B A).

The invention of new descriptors is certainly a part of learning, but it is an extremely difficult task. (For a solution see Kodratoff et al., 1984; Michalski, 1983).

Formula. A formula is an expression of the representation language obtained by connecting valid expressions of the description language.

2. Term Generalization

Term generalization has been defined in section 9.3.2.

3. Formula Generalization

Formula generalization has been defined in section 9.3.3.

Property of $\leq$ *("more general than").* This is a partial ordering. From its definition, $\leq$ is trivially reflexive and transitive. In order to avoid the ϵ-generalization difficulty described in section 9.3.2 we must prove its antisymmetry.

Suppose that one has together $E_1 \leq E_2$ and $E_2 \leq E_1$.

From $E_1 \leq E_2$ it follows (by Condition 2 of section 9.3.3) that if E_2' verifies $E_2' =_\epsilon E_2$ and there exists a substitution σ_1 such that $\sigma_1 E_2' =_\epsilon E_1$, then

$$E_2' =_\epsilon E_1.$$

From $E_2 \leq E_1$ it follows (by Condition 1 of section 9.3.3) that there is an E_2'' such that $E_2'' =_\epsilon E_2$ and there is a σ_2 such that $\sigma_2 E_2'' =_\epsilon E_1$.

It follows that $E_2'' =_\epsilon E_1 =_\epsilon E_2$, which proves antisymmetry.

4. Definition of the I-Implication

In section 9.2.2, the "truth domain" $X1$ of a predicate $P(x)$ was defined by

$$X1 = \{a/P(a) = \text{TRUE}\}.$$

This definition can be trivially extended to any formula containing free variables.

The i-implication formalizes the fact that the formula E_1 is more general than a formula E_2 iff the truth domain of E_1 contains the truth domain of E_2. In a sense, this expresses the fact that E_1 is more general than E_2 in a particular universe if E_1 is always TRUE when E_2 is TRUE in this universe. This is a kind of implication by the instantiations, and this is why it is called here the i-implication. As explained in section 9.3, formulas with free variables cannot really *imply* each other; i-implication is defined to formalize the intuitive feeling that truth value domain inclusion has something to do with implication.

Let us call the set of the possible constants C and the instantiations by constants I. It will be noted that the formula E has been instantiated by constants (i.e., all the variables of E are replaced by constants) and that this instantiation takes the value TRUE by $I(E)$. This is a substitution, and substitution composition is well defined.

Let E_1 and E_2 be two formulas; one says that E_1 i-implies E_2, $E_1 \Rightarrow_i E_2$, iff for all instantiation I_1 by constants of E_1 such that $I_1(E_1)$, there exists an instantiation I_2 of E_2 such that $I_2 \bigcirc I_1(E_1)$ and $I_2 \bigcirc I_1(E_2')$ where $E_2' = \varrho E_2$ and ϱ is a variable renaming.

Example.
Let $E_1 = f(x) \& f(y)$, $E_2 = f(y)$, $\varrho = (z \leftarrow x)$, $\varrho' = (x \leftarrow z)$. Trivially, $E_1 \Rightarrow E_2$ since any instantiation that gives the value TRUE to E_1 also gives the value TRUE to ϱE_2. One also has $E_2 \Rightarrow_i E_1$, since for any instantiation I_2 such that $I_2(E_2)$ one can find I_1 such that $I_1 \bigcirc I_2(E_2)$ and $I_1 \bigcirc I_2(\varrho' E_1)$.

Let I_2 be for instance $z \leftarrow C$ and suppose that $I_2(E_2) = f(C)$ is TRUE. One can find $I_1 = (y \leftarrow C)$ such that $I_1 \bigcirc I_2(E_2) = f(C)$ is TRUE and $I_1 \bigcirc I_2(\varrho' E_1) = f(C) \& f(C)$ is also TRUE.

5. Properties of the I-Implication

Property 1: $E_1 =_\epsilon E_2$ implies that $E_1 \Rightarrow_i E_2$ and $E_2 \Rightarrow_i E_1$.
Property 2: $\Rightarrow_i$ is transitive.
Property 3: $\sigma E_1 = E_2$ implies that $E_2 \Rightarrow_i E_1$

Lemma 1: $\forall\ E_1, E_2$ ($E_1 \leq E_2$ implies that $E_2 \Rightarrow_i E_1$).

Proof:
By definition of formula generalization, $E_1 \leq E_2$ implies that there is an E_1' such that $E_1' =_\epsilon E_1$ and a substitution σ, such that $\sigma E_1' =_\epsilon E_2$.
By Property 1, $\sigma E_1' =_\epsilon E_2$ implies that $E_2 \Rightarrow_i \sigma E_1'$.
By Property 3 (applied to the triviality $\sigma E_1' = \sigma E_1'$), one has $\sigma E_1' \Rightarrow_i E_1'$.
Since $E_1' =_\epsilon E_1$, the above implication can be rewritten as $\sigma E_1' \Rightarrow_i E_1$. Therefore, by Property 2,

$$E_2 \Rightarrow_i E_1$$

Lemma 2: Let E_1 and E_2 be two formulas that fulfill Condition 1 and Condition 2'.
Condition 1: $E_1 =_\epsilon E_1'$ and $E_2 =_\epsilon E_2'$, and there is a σ, such that $\sigma E_1' = E_2'$.
Condition 2': $\sim (E_1 \Rightarrow_i E_2)$(i.e., E_1 does not i-imply E_2).
Then

$$E_1 \leq E_2 \text{ (as defined in section 9.3.3).}$$

Proof
α Since $E_1 =_\epsilon E_1'$, Condition 2' also reads: $\sim (E_1' \Rightarrow_i E_2)$.
β Since $E_2 =_\epsilon E_2'$ this gives $\sim (E_1' \Rightarrow_i E_2')$, which will be written as

E_2'' such that $E_2'' =_\epsilon E_2$ one has: $\sim (E_1' \Rightarrow_i E_2'')$.

γ On the other hand, Property 3 states that

$\exists \sigma$ such that $\sigma E_2'' = E_1''$ implies $E_1' \Rightarrow_i E_2''$;

therefore

$\sim (E_1' \Rightarrow_i E_2'')$ implies that $\sim (\exists \sigma$ such that $\sigma E_2'' = E_1')$.
δ It follows that $\forall E_2''$ such that $E_2'' =_\epsilon E_2$, one has: $\sim (\exists \sigma$ such that $\sigma E_2'' = E_1')$.
Finally, since $\sim A \Rightarrow (A \Rightarrow B)$, where

$$A = (\exists \sigma \text{ such that } \sigma E_2'' = E_1') \text{ and } B = (E_2'' =_\epsilon E_1'),$$

one also has $A \Rightarrow B$, which is exactly Condition 2.

In conclusion, this last result and Condition 1 show that $E_1 \leq E_2$.

6. Formula Generalization (Second Version)

Recall the definition of generalization that was given in section 9.3.3. A formula was more general than another one provided it fulfilled two conditions, called Condition 1 and Condition 2. From Lemma 2, it follows that Conditions 1 and 2 of the first version (of section 9.3.3) are equivalent to Conditions 1 and 2' of Lemma 2.

Theorem. The two definitions using Conditions 1 and 2 or 1 and 2' are equivalent. One should notice that point δ of the proof of Lemma 2 explicitly states that there is no other substitution in the reverse direction when 2 or 2' is added to Condition 1.

The counterexample given in Kodratoff (1983), where one finds two terms t_1 and t_2 such that

$$t_1' =_\epsilon t_1,$$
$$t_2' =_\epsilon t_2,$$
$$\sigma_1 t_1' = t_2',$$
$$t_1'' =_\epsilon t_1,$$
$$t_2'' =_\epsilon t_2, \text{ and}$$
$$\sigma_2 t_2'' = t_1''$$

is precisely a case where 2 or 2' is not verified.

References

Chang, C. L., and Lee, R. C. T., *Symbolic Logic and Mechanical Theorem Proving,* Academic Press, New York, 1973.

Cohen, P. R., and Feigenbaum, E. A., *The Handbook of Artificial Intelligence,* Vol. 3, Pittman, London, 1982.

Dietterich, G. T., and Michalski, R. S., "Inductive Learning of Structural Descriptions: Evaluation Criteria and Comparative Review of Selected Methods," *Artificial Intelligence,* Vol. 16, pp. 257–94, 1981.

Hayes-Roth, F., and McDermott, J., "An Interference Matching Technique for Inducing Abstractions," *Communications of the ACM,* Vol. 21, pp. 401–11, 1978.

Holte, R. C., "Artificial Intelligence Approaches to Concept Learning," in *Advanced Digital Information Systems,* I. Alexander (Ed.), Prentice-Hall, Englewood Cliffs, N. J., 1984.

Hsiang, J., "Topics in Automated Theorem Proving and Program Generation," Ph.D. diss., Department of Computer Science, University of Illinois at Urbana-Champaign, 1982.

Kodratoff, Y., "Generalizing and Particularizing as Techniques of Learning," *Computers and Artificial Intelligence,* Vol. 2, pp. 417–41, 1983.

Kodratoff, Y.; Ganascia, J. G.; Clavieras, B.; Bollinger, T.; and Tecuci, G., "Careful Generalization for Concept Learning," *Proceedings of the Sixth European Conference on Artificial Intelligence,* Pisa, pp. 483–92, 1984.

Michalski, R. S., "A Theory and Methodology of Inductive Learning," in *Machine Learning: An Artificial Intelligence Approach,* R. S. Michalski, J. G. Carbonell, and T. M. Mitchell (Eds.), Tioga, Palo Alto, Calif., 1983.

———, "Inductive Learning as Rule-Guided Transformation of Symbolic Descriptions: A Theory and Implementation," *Automatic Program Construction Techniques,* A. Bierman, G. Guiho, and Y. Kodratoff (Eds.), Macmillan, New York, 1984.

Mitchell, T. M., "Learning and Problem Solving," *Proceedings of the Eighth IJCAI,* Karlsruhe, W. Ger., pp. 1139–69, 1983.

Plotkin, G. D., "A Note on Inductive Generalization," in *Machine Intelligence,* B. Meltzer and D. Michie (Eds.), American Elsevier, New York, 1970.

Stickel, M. E., "A Unification Algorithm for Associative-Commutative Functions," *Journal of the ACM,* Vol. 28, 423–43, 1981.

Vere, S. A., "Multilevel Counterfactuals for Generalizations of Relational Concepts and Productions," *Artificial Intelligence,* Vol. 14, pp. 139–64, 1980.

———, "Constrained N-to-1 Generalizations," Draft, 23 February 1981.

Winston, P. H., "Learning Structural Descriptions from Examples," in *The Psychology of Computer Vision,* P. H. Winston (Ed.), McGraw-Hill, New York, 1975.

PART
THREE

COGNITIVE ASPECTS OF
LEARNING

10

THE CHUNKING OF GOAL HIERARCHIES:

A Generalized Model of Practice

Paul S. Rosenbloom
Stanford University

Allen Newell
Carnegie-Mellon University

Abstract

This chapter describes recent advances in the specification and implementation of a model of practice. In previous work the authors showed that there is a ubiquitous regularity underlying human practice, referred to as the *power law of practice.* They also developed an abstract model of practice, called the *chunking theory of learning.* This previous work established the feasibility of the chunking theory for a single 1023-choice reaction-time task, but the implementation was specific to that one task. In the current work a modified formulation of the chunking theory is developed that allows a more general implementation. In this formulation, task algorithms are expressed in terms of hierarchical goal structures. These algorithms are simulated within a goal-based production-system architecture designed for this purpose. *Chunking* occurs during task performance in terms of the parameters and results of the goals experienced. It improves the performance of the system by gradually reducing the need to decompose goals into their subgoals. This model has been successfully applied to the task employed in the previous work and to a set of stimulus-response compatibility tasks.

10.1 INTRODUCTION

How can systems—both natural and artificial—improve their own performance? At least for natural systems (people, for example), we know that *practice* is effective. A system is engaged in practice when it repeatedly performs one task or a set of similar tasks. Recently, Newell and Rosenbloom (1981) brought together the evidence that there is a ubiquitous law—the *power law of practice*—that characterizes the improvements in human performance during practice. The law states that when human performance is measured in terms of the time needed to perform a task, it improves as a power-law function of the number of times the task has been performed (called the *trial number*). This result holds over the entire domain of human performance, including both purely perceptual tasks, such as target detection (Neisser, Novick, and Lazar, 1963), and purely cognitive tasks, such as supplying justifications for geometric proofs (Neves and Anderson, 1981).

The ubiquity of the power law of practice suggests that it may reflect something in the underlying *cognitive architecture.* The nature of the architecture is of fundamental importance for both artificial intelligence and psychology (in fact, for all of cognitive science; see Newell, 1973; Anderson, 1983a). It provides the control structure within which thought occurs, determining which computations are easy and inexpensive as well as what errors will be made and when. Two important ingredients in the recent success of expert systems come from fundamental work on the cognitive architecture; specifically, the development of *production systems* (Newell and Simon, 1972; Newell, 1973) and *goal-structured problem solving* (Ernst and Newell, 1969; Newell and Simon, 1972). This chapter discusses recent efforts to take advantage of the power law of practice by using it as a generator for a general production-system practice mechanism. This is a highly constrained task because of the paucity of plausible practice models that can produce power-law practice curves (Newell and Rosenbloom, 1981).

As a beginning, Newell and Rosenbloom (1981) developed an abstract model of practice based on the concept of *chunking*—a concept already established to be ubiquitous in human performance—and derived from it a practice equation capable of closely mimicking a power law. It was hypothesized that this model formed the basis for the performance improvements brought about by practice. In sections 10.2 and 10.3 this work on the power law and the abstract formulation of the chunking theory is briefly summarized.

Rosenbloom and Newell (1982a, 1982b) took the analysis one step further by showing how the *chunking theory of learning* could be implemented for a single psychological task within a highly parallel, activation-based production system called XAPS2. This work established more securely that the theory is a viable model of human practice by showing how it could actually be applied to a task to produce power-law practice curves. By producing a working system, it also established the theory's viability as a practice mechanism for artificial systems.

The principal weakness of the work done up to that point was the heavy task dependence of the implementation. Both the representation used for describing the task to be performed and the chunking mechanism itself had built into them knowledge about the specific task and how it should be performed. The work reported here is focused on the removal of this weakness by the development of generalized, task-independent models of performance and practice.

This generalization process has been driven by the use of a set of tasks that fall within a neighborhood around the task previously modeled. That task sits within an experimental domain widely used in psychology, the domain of *reaction-time* tasks (Woodworth and Schlosberg, 1954). Reaction-time tasks involve the presentation to a subject of stimulus display—such as an array of lights, a string of characters on a computer terminal, or a spoken word—for which a specific "correct" response is expected. The response may be spoken, manual (such as pressing a button, pushing a lever, or typing), or something quite different. From the subject's reaction time—the time it takes to make the response—and error rate, it is possible to draw conclusions about the nature of the subject's cognitive processing.

The particular task, as performed by Seibel (1963), was a 1023-choice reaction-time task. It involved ten lights (strung out horizontally) and ten buttons, with each button right below a light. On each trial of the task some of the lights came on while the rest remained off. The subject's task was to respond as rapidly as possible by pressing the buttons corresponding to the lights that were on. There were $2^{10} - 1$, or 1023, possible situations with which the subject had to deal (excluding the one in which all ten lights were off). Rosenbloom (1983) showed that a general task representation based on the concept of *goal hierarchies* (discussed in section 10.4) could be developed for the performance of this task.

In a goal hierarchy, the root node expresses a desire to do a task. At each level further down in the hierarchy, the goals at the level above are decomposed into a set of smaller goals to be achieved. Decomposition continues until the goals at some level can be achieved directly. This is a common control structure for the kinds of complex problem-solving systems found in artificial intelligence, but this is the first time they have been applied to the domain of reaction-time tasks.

Goal hierarchies also provided the basis for models of a set of related reaction-time tasks known as *stimulus-response compatibility* tasks. These tasks involve fixed sets of stimuli and responses and a mapping between them that is manipulated. The main phenomenon is that more complex and/or "counterintuitive" relationships between stimuli and responses lead to longer reaction times and more error. A model of stimulus-response compatibility based on goal hierarchies provides excellent fits to the human reaction-time data (Rosenbloom, 1983).

The generalized practice mechanism (described in section 10.5) is grounded in this goal-based representation of task performance. It resembles a form of store-versus-compute trade-off, in which composite structures (chunks) are created that relate patterns of goal parameters to patterns of goal results.

These chunking and goal-processing mechanisms are evaluated by implementing them as part of the architecture of the XAPS3 production system. The XAPS3 architecture is an evolutionary development from the XAPS2 architecture. Only those changes required by the needs of chunking and goal processing have been made. This architecture is described in section 10.6. From this implementation simulated practice results have been generated and analyzed for the Seibel and compatibility experiments (section 10.7).[1]

Following the analysis of the model, this work is placed in perspective by relating the chunking theory to previous work on learning mechanisms (section 10.8). The theory stakes out an intermediary position among four previously disparate mechanisms, bringing out an unexpected commonality among them.

Before concluding and summarizing (section 10.10), some final comments are presented on ways in which the scope of the chunking theory can be expanded to cover more than just the speeding up of existing algorithms (section 10.9). Specifically, the authors describe a way in which chunking might be led to perform other varieties of learning, such as generalization, discrimination, and method acquisition.

10.2 THE POWER LAW OF PRACTICE

Performance improves with practice. More precisely, the time needed to perform a task decreases as a power-law function of the number of times the task has been performed. This basic law, the power law of practice, has been known since Snoddy (1926). This law was originally recognized in the domain of motor skills, but it has recently become clear that it holds over a much wider range of human tasks, possibly extending to the full range of human performance. Newell and Rosenbloom (1981) brought together the evidence for this law from tasks involving perceptual-motor skills (Snoddy, 1926; Crossman, 1959), perception (Kolers, 1975; Neisser, Novick, and Lazar, 1963), motor behavior (Card, English, and Burr, 1978), elementary decisions (Seibel, 1963), memory (Anderson, 1980), routine cognitive skill (Moran, 1980), and problem solving (Neves and Anderson, 1981; Newell and Rosenbloom, 1981).

Practice curves are generated by plotting task performance against trial number. This cannot be done without assuming some specific *measure* of performance. There are many possibilities for such a measure, including such things as quantity produced per unit time and number of errors per trial. The power law of

---

[1] A more comprehensive presentation and discussion of these results can be found in Rosenbloom (1983).

practice is defined in terms of the *time* to perform the task on a trial. It states that the time to perform the task (T) is a power-law function of the trial number (N):

$$T = BN^{-\alpha} \tag{1}$$

As shown by the following log transform of Equation 1, power-law functions plot as straight lines on log-log paper:

$$\log(T) = \log(B) + (-\alpha)\log(N) \tag{2}$$

Figure 10-1 shows the practice curve from one subject in Kolers' study (1975) of reading inverted texts—each line of text on the page was turned upside down—as plotted on log-log paper. The solid line represents the power-law fit to this data. Its linearity is clear ($r^2 = 0.932$).

Many practice curves are linear (in log-log coordinates) over much of their range but show a flattening at their two ends. These deviations can be removed by using a four-parameter *generalized* power-law function. One of the two new parameters (A) takes into account that the asymptote of learning can be greater than zero. In general, there is a nonzero minimum bound on performance time, determined by basic physiological limitations and/or device limitations—if, for example, the subject must operate a machine. The other added parameter (E) is required because power laws are not translation invariant. Practice occurring before the official beginning of the experiment—even if it consists only of transfer of training from everyday experience—will alter the shape of the curve, unless the effect is explicitly allowed

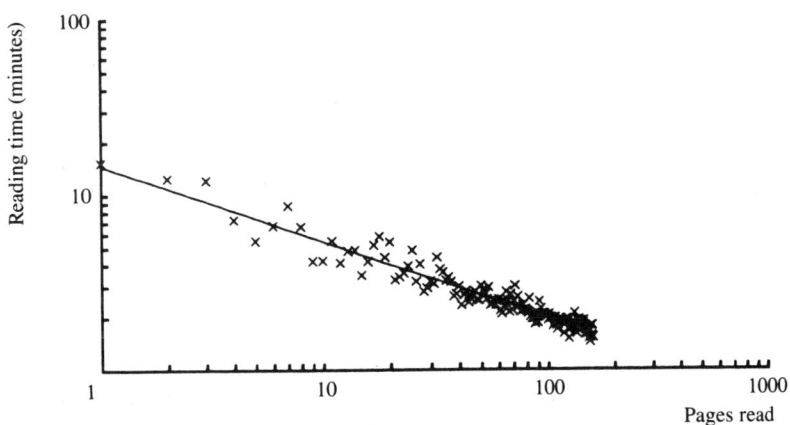

Figure 10-1: Learning to read inverted text (log-log coordinates). Plotted from the original data for Subject HA (Kolers, 1975).

for by the inclusion of this parameter. Augmenting the power-law function by these two parameters yields the following generalized function:

$$T = A + B(N + E)^{-\alpha} \qquad (3)$$

A generalized power law plots as a straight line on log-log paper once the effects of the asymptote (A) are removed from the time (T), and the effective number of trials prior to the experiment (E) are added to those performed during the experiment (N):

$$\log(T - A) = \log(B) + (-\alpha) \log(N + E) \qquad (4)$$

Figure 10-2 shows a practice curve from the Seibel task (Seibel, 1963), as fit by a generalized power-law function (each data point represents the mean reaction time over a block of 1023 trials). This curve, which shows flattening at both ends when plotted as a simple power law, is now linear over the whole range of trials. As stated earlier, similar fits are found across all dimensions of human performance. Though these fits are impressive, it must be stressed that the power law of practice is only an *empirical* law. The true underlying law must resemble a power law, but it may have a different analytical form.

10.3 THE CHUNKING THEORY OF LEARNING

The chunking theory of learning proposes that practice improves performance via the acquisition of knowledge about patterns in the task environment. Implicit in this theory is a model of task performance based on this pattern knowledge. These

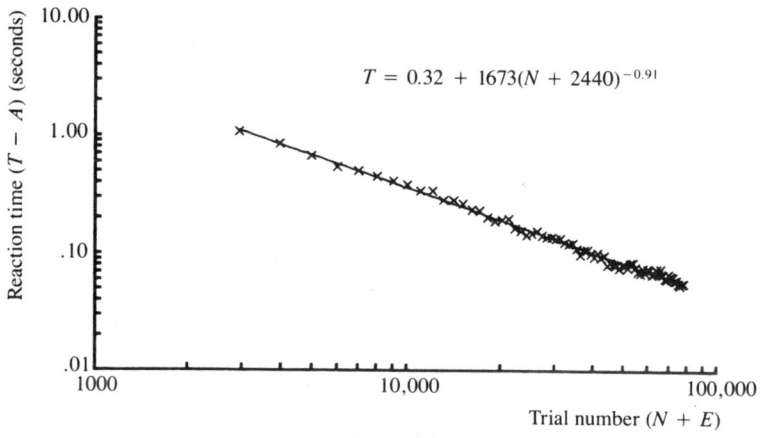

Figure 10-2:   Optimal general power-law fit to the Seibel data (log-log coordinates).

patterns are called *chunks* (Miller, 1956). The theory thus starts from the *chunking hypothesis:*

> **The chunking hypothesis:** A human acquires and organizes knowledge of the environment by forming and storing expressions, called *chunks,* that are structured collections of the chunks existing at the time of learning.

The existence of chunks implies that memory is hierarchically structured as a lattice (tangled hierarchy, acyclic directed graph, and so on) rooted in a set of preexisting *primitives.* A given chunk can be accessed in a top-down fashion, by *decoding* a chunk of which it is a part, or in a bottom-up fashion, by *encoding* from the parts of the chunk. Encoding is a recognition or parsing process.

The existence of chunks does not need to be justified solely on the basis of the practice curves. Chunks stand on their own as a thoroughly documented component of human performance (Miller, 1956; DeGroot, 1965; Bower and Winzenz, 1969; Johnson, 1972; Chase and Simon, 1973; Chase and Ericsson, 1981). The traditional view of chunks is that they are data structures representing a combination of several items. For example, in one set of classic experiments, Bower and colleagues (Bower, 1972; Bower and Springston, 1970; Bower and Winzenz, 1969) showed that recall of strings of numbers or letters is strongly influenced by the segmentation of the string. If the segmentation corresponds to a previously learned grouping of the items (for example, FBI-PHD-TWA-IBM), performance is better than if no such relation obtains (FB-IPH-DTW-AIB-M). These results were interpreted as evidence for segmentation-guided chunking of familiar strings. By replacing a string of several letters with a single chunk, the subject's memory load is reduced, allowing more letters to be remembered. At recall time the chunks are decoded to yield the original items to be recalled.

The chunking theory of learning proposes two modifications to this classical view. The first change is the assumption that there is not a single symbol (chunk) to which the items are encoded and from which they can later be decoded. As a simple example, the process of reading the string IBM out loud is more than just the encoding of the three letters into a chunk, followed by the subsequent decoding to the three letters. What needs to be decoded is not the visual representation of IBM, but the articulatory representation—allowing the subject to *say* "IBM."

Based on this consideration, the chunking theory assumes that there are two symbols for each chunk—a *stimulus* symbol and a *response* symbol. The process of using a chunk consists of encoding the stimulus items to the stimulus symbol (a many-one mapping), mapping the stimulus symbol to the response symbol (a one-one mapping), and decoding the response symbol to the response items (a one-many mapping) (see figure 10-3). Encoding and decoding are fast parallel hierarchical processes, and the mapping serves as a (serial) point of control at which the choice of response can be made. Acquisition of a chunk speeds up performance by reducing the number of mappings to be performed. In the example in figure 10-3, before the chunk

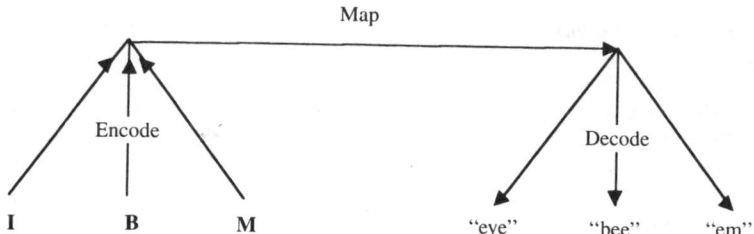

Figure 10-3:   A three-part chunk for the articulation of the visual string "IBM."

is acquired, three mappings (one for each letter) are required. After acquisition of the chunk, one mapping suffices.

The second difference between this proposal and the classical view of chunking is the idea that the chunk consists of the three processes (encoding, mapping, and decoding), not just the symbols. This is really just a shift of emphasis; chunks are viewed as the processes rather than just as the results of the processes.

10.4 GOAL-STRUCTURED PERFORMANCE MODELS

In its current formulation, chunking explains how performance on a task can be sped up with practice. It does not explain how the organism first learns to do the task (but see the discussion in section 10.9). Consequently, each task simulation must be initialized with a performance model for the task. What is needed—and is provided by the notion of a *goal hierarchy*—is a general, task-independent representation for these performance models. Goal hierarchies are frequently found in artificial intelligence systems, but they have not previously been employed in the modeling of the kinds of reaction-time tasks dealt with here.

Goal hierarchies are built out of *goals;* each goal is a data structure representing a desired state of affairs. A goal is not a procedure for bringing about that state; it is only a description of the state. In order for the goal state to be brought about, there must be a *method* associated with the goal. The method could be a rigid algorithm, or it could be one of the more flexible *weak methods* (Newell, 1969), such as means-ends analysis (Ernst and Newell, 1969) or heuristic search (Nilsson, 1971). In the discussion that follows, the properly distinct notions of goal and method will be conflated together into a single active concept for the sake of convenience. These conflated "goals" are active processes that take a set of *parameters* and return a set of *results*.

When a goal can be decomposed into a set of simpler goals (Nilsson, 1971) and those goals can be decomposed even further, a goal hierarchy results. In its simplest form, as an AND hierarchy, a goal is successful if all of its subgoals are successful. The structure to be described here more closely resembles an AND/OR hierarchy, in which some goals succeed only if all of their subgoals succeed, and others succeed if any one of their subgoals succeed. A *terminal* goal is reached when the goal can be fulfilled directly, without the need for further decomposition.

We use a *depth-first* strategy for processing a goal hierarchy, in which the most recently generated (the deepest) goal is always selected as the next goal to process. With a depth-first paradigm there is always exactly one goal being actively worked on at any point in time. We will refer to this goal as the *active* or *current* goal. When a subgoal becomes the active goal, the parent goal of that subgoal is *suspended* until control is returned to it by completion of the subgoal, at which point it again becomes the current goal. On completion, the subgoal will have either *succeeded* or *failed*. The *control stack* specifies the location in the hierarchy at which control currently resides. It does this by maintaining the path from the root goal of the hierarchy to the current goal. This path consists of the active goal and all of its suspended ancestors.

Figure 10-4 shows two different representations of a goal hierarchy for the Seibel (1963) 1023-choice reaction-time task. At the top of the figure, the hierarchy is shown as a tree structure. At the bottom of the figure, the goals are shown in their depth-first processing order. In both representations the boldface goals are the

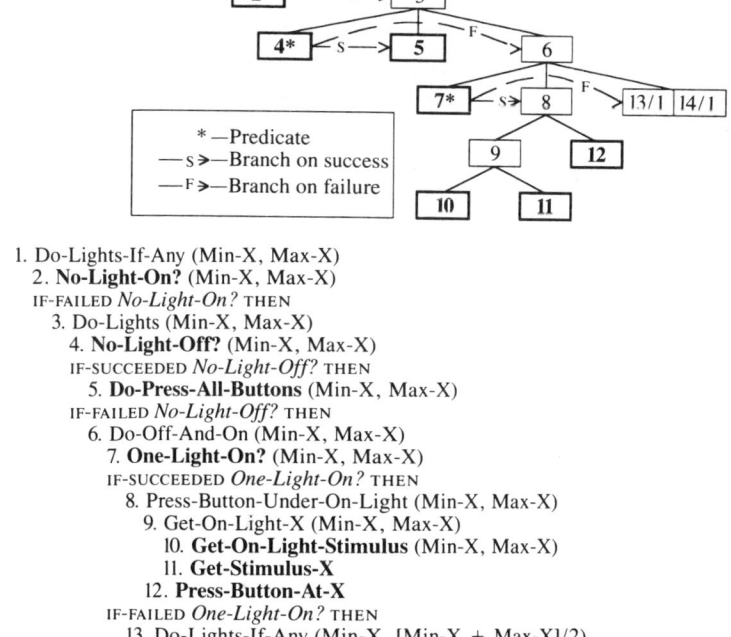

1. Do-Lights-If-Any (Min-X, Max-X)
2. **No-Light-On?** (Min-X, Max-X)
   IF-FAILED *No-Light-On?* THEN
   3. Do-Lights (Min-X, Max-X)
      4. **No-Light-Off?** (Min-X, Max-X)
      IF-SUCCEEDED *No-Light-Off?* THEN
         5. **Do-Press-All-Buttons** (Min-X, Max-X)
      IF-FAILED *No-Light-Off?* THEN
         6. Do-Off-And-On (Min-X, Max-X)
            7. **One-Light-On?** (Min-X, Max-X)
            IF-SUCCEEDED *One-Light-On?* THEN
               8. Press-Button-Under-On-Light (Min-X, Max-X)
               9. Get-On-Light-X (Min-X, Max-X)
                  10. **Get-On-Light-Stimulus** (Min-X, Max-X)
                  11. **Get-Stimulus-X**
               12. **Press-Button-At-X**
            IF-FAILED *One-Light-On?* THEN
               13. Do-Lights-If-Any (Min-X, [Min-X + Max-X]/2)
               14. Do-Lights-If-Any ([Min-X + Max-X]/2, Max-X)

Figure 10-4:   Goal hierarchy for the Seibel (1963) task.

terminals—those goals that can be fulfilled directly. The labeled arrows (either s or F) represent *branch* points in the hierarchy. With simple depth-first processing, the children of a node are processed in a strict left-to-right fashion. In this work, this style of control has been augmented by allowing the left-to-right processing to be conditioned on the success or failure of the previous child (actually, of any previous goal for which this information is still available). For example, goal 2 (**No-Light-On?**) tests whether there are any lights on within a specific region of the display of lights. Only if this goal fails should goal 3 (Do-Lights) be attempted. If goal 2 succeeds, then there are no lights on that need to be processed and the parent goal (goal 1: Do-Lights-If-Any) can be terminated successfully. Those goals that do not return a result are called *predicates* (denoted by an asterisk in figure 10-4) and are used to test the truth of various conditions. It is only the success or failure of predicates that matters (as the basis for a branch). If the predicate succeeds, then the condition is true. If it fails, the reason could be either that the condition is false or that something went wrong during the attempt.

The goal structure in figure 10-4 is based on a recursive divide-and-conquer algorithm in which the stimulus display is broken up into smaller and smaller horizontal segments until *manageable* pieces are generated. There are three types of horizontal segments that have been defined as manageable. The first type of manageable segment is one in which no lights are on. Such segments require no explicit processing, so the goal just returns with success. The opposite of the first type of segment—one in which no lights are off—is also manageable. For such a segment, the system generates a single response specifying that a *press* action must occur in the entire region defined by the segment (using the **Do-Press-All-Buttons** goal). Specifying a single button press is actually a special case of this, in which the region is just large enough to contain the one button. Allowing multi-on-light segments to be manageable implies that sequences of adjacent on-lights can be pressed simultaneously even before chunking has begun. Such behavior is seen very early in the trial sequence for some subjects. The remaining manageable segments are those that contain exactly one light on. These segments are processed (using the Press-Button-Under-On-Light goal) by finding the location of that light and generating a button press at that location. If a generated segment does not meet any of these three criteria, it is unmanageable and is split into two smaller segments.

The recursive aspect of the algorithm implies that many different instances of each goal will be simultaneously represented in the system, although at most one can actually be active. It is necessary to keep track of which goal instance is relevant to which segment of the stimulus display, so the segment (in terms of its minimum and maximum X values) is an *explicit* parameter to the goals. In addition to the explicit parameters, a goal can have *implicitly* defined parameters. Any object existing before the activation of the goal (i.e., as part of the goal's *initial state*) that is examined during the processing of the goal—such as a stimulus light—is an implicit parameter of the goal. Implicit parameters are dynamically determined by the actual processing of the goal.

A second implication of the recursion in this hierarchy is that the system does not start off with a constant built-in goal hierarchy. Instead, it has a generator of goal hierarchies. That chunking works on such a structure is important for any claims about the potential generality of the mechanism (for more on this, see section 10.9).

The recursion occurs at goals 13 and 14 in figure 10-4. They are repetitions of the topmost goal in the hierarchy (Do-Lights-If-Any), but the scope of each is limited to one-half of the display currently being processed. The numeric computation to obtain the middle of the segment (involving an addition and a division), while on the surface too powerful a computation to appear where it does, is only intended as an approximation to a process that divides the stimulus display into two (or three) roughly equal parts.

In addition to the goal hierarchy, the model assumes a *working memory* for the short-term storage of information relevant to the processing that is going on. For each goal, the working memory is logically partitioned into two components—the *initial state* and the *local state*. The initial state consists of the data existing at the time the goal is first activated. The remainder of the working memory—consisting of those pieces of data created during the processing of the goal—makes up its local state. Only the local state of a goal can be modified during the processing of that goal; the initial state can be examined, but it cannot be modified. The modularity resulting from this scoping rule increases the likelihood that an arbitrary set of goals can be pursued without their interfering with each other. This modularity is also important in insuring correct performance of the chunking mechanism.

Each datum in the working memory is relevant in a particular temporal *processing context*. As long as the datum's creator goal is in the control stack, the system is working either on that goal or on one of its descendants. The datum may be relevant at any point in this processing. However, once the goal disappears from the control stack, it is no longer being pursued. The datum will most likely no longer be relevant. The processing context of a datum is that period of processing during which its creator goal is in the control stack. Once a piece of information becomes *out of context*—its creator is no longer part of the control stack—it usually can be safely deleted from the working memory. Data that cannot be deleted—because they are needed outside of the context in which they were created—are called the *results* of the goal. Their continued presence in the working memory is insured by changing their context to be the context of the parent goal.

10.5 CHUNKING ON GOAL HIERARCHIES

Given a task-independent organization for performance models, it is possible to return to the original objective of describing a task-independent formulation of the chunking theory. In the chunking mechanism described by Rosenbloom and Newell (1982a, 1982b), chunks related patterns of stimuli (lights) to patterns of responses

(button presses). The goal-oriented formulation is obtained by altering this definition slightly so that chunks relate patterns of goal parameters to patterns of goal
results. Each chunk improves the performance of the system by eliminating the need
to process fully a specific instance (a combination of parameter values) of a particular goal. It replaces the normal processing (decomposition into subgoals for nonterminal goals and direct execution of an action for terminal goals) with a direct connection between the relevant parameter values and results. A goal can (and almost
certainly will) have more than one possible chunk; each combination of parameter
values requires its own chunk.

As with the abstract characterization of the chunking theory, each chunk consists of three components: encoding, decoding, and connection (or mapping). The
goal's parameter values form the basis for the encoding component. Given the presence of those values in the working memory, the encoding component generates a new
object representing their combination. Encoding is a parallel, goal-independent, data-
driven process. Every encoding component executes as soon as appropriate, irre-
spective of whatever else is happening in the system. The results of encoding components can themselves become parameter values of other goals, leading to a
hierarchical encoding process.

The results of the goal form the basis for the decoding component. Given the
presence of an encoded result-object in the working memory, the decoding component generates the actual results returned by the goal. Decoding occurs when the
results are needed. As with encoding, decoding is a parallel, goal-independent process. The set of decoding components forms a hierarchical structure in which complex results are decoded to simpler ones, which are then decoded even further.

The connection component of the chunk generates the encoded result from the
encoded parameter. Connections provide a locus of control by occurring serially,
under the control of the goals. Thus a connection can be made only when the system is
working on the goal for which the chunk was formed (and after the encoding component has executed). This insures that, even though encoding and decoding are uncon-
trolled, only appropriate results are generated.

A chunk can be created for a goal when the following two conditions are met:
(1) the goal has just completed successfully, and (2) all of the goal's subgoals were
themselves processed by chunks. The first condition insures both that chunks are created for appropriate goals and that the chunk is created at a time when the information
required for the chunk is available. The second condition causes chunks to be created
bottom up in the goal hierarchy. It is this bottom-up aspect of chunking that leads to
hierarchical encoding and decoding networks. However, notice that bottom-up
chunking does not imply that all low-level chunks are learned before any high-level
chunks are learned, or even that all of the chunks must be learned for a subgoal before
any can be learned for its parent goal. The second condition on chunk creation merely
states that chunks must exist for the goal's subgoals *in the current situation*. Whether
other chunks exist or do not exist for the subgoals is irrelevant.

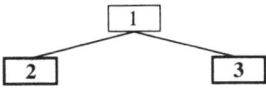

1. Compute-Average-Of-Two-Numbers
   2. **Compute-Sum-Of-Two-Numbers**
   3. **Divide-Sum-By-2**

Figure 10-5:   A simple three-goal hierarchy for the averaging of two numbers.

Given enough practice with enough task variations, all of the situations for all of the goals in the hierarchy will be chunked, and asymptotic behavior will be reached for the task. The amount of time this takes depends on the number of goals, the number of situations for each goal, how frequently the different situations arise, and whether chunks are created whenever they can be.

The three-goal hierarchy shown in figure 10-5 provides a simple example of how chunking works. This structure computes the average of two numbers. The top-level goal (Computer-Average-Of-Two-Numbers) takes as parameters the two numbers to be averaged and returns to a single result, which is their mean. The first sub-goal **(Compute-Sum-Of-Two-Numbers)** performs the first half of the computation. It takes the two numbers as parameters and returns their sum as its result. The second subgoal finishes the computation by taking the sum as a parameter and returning half of it as its result.

Suppose that the first task is to average the numbers 3 and 7. Control would pass from goal 1 to goal 2. When goal 2 finishes and returns its result of 10, a chunk of three components is created (bottom left of figure 10-6). An encoding component is created that encodes the two parameters (3 and 7) into a new symbol (E1). It executes as soon as it is created, because the parameters are in the working memory. A decoding component is created that decodes from a second new symbol (D1) to the result (10). A connection component (the horizontal line with the goal name above it and goal number below it) is created that generates the result symbol (D1) when it detects both the presence of the encoded parameter (E1) and that goal 2 is the active goal. The connection does not execute immediately because goal 2 is already complete when the chunk is created.

Following the termination of goal 2, goal 1 is reactivated but then is suspended in favor of goal 3 **(Divide-Sum-By-2)**. When this goal terminates successfully (returning the number 5), a chunk is created for it (bottom right of figure 10-6). The encoding component encodes the number 10 into the symbol E2; the decoding component decodes from the symbol D2 to the number 5; and the connection component connects E2 to D2 (in the presence of an active goal 3). In contrast to the chunk for goal 1, this chunk can be used in more than one task situation. It can be used whenever goal 1 generates a sum of 10, whether it does it by adding 3 and 7, 5 and 5, or any other pair of numbers. This is a form of transfer of training.

Following the termination of goal 3, goal 1 is reactivated and terminates successfully (returning the number 5). No chunk is created for goal 1 because its subgoals were not processed by chunks. At this point, the task is complete.

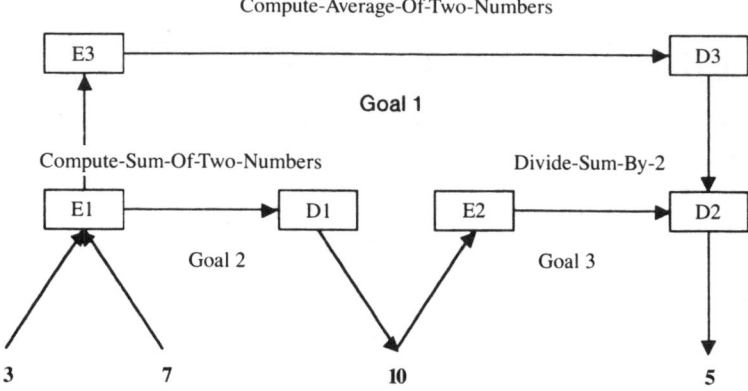

Figure 10-6: Sample chunks created for the hierarchy in figure 10-5.

Given what was learned during the performance of this task, the next time the same task is performed things will go differently. As soon as the task is restarted (again with the values 3 and 7), the encoding component from the chunk for goal 2 executes, placing E1 in the working memory. Goal 1 is activated and then suspended in favor of goal 2. At this point, the connection component for goal 2 executes, generating D1 and successfully completing goal 2. D1 is decoded to the number 10, which is then immediately reencoded to E2 by the encoding component for goal 3. Following the subsequent reactivation and suspension of goal 1, goal 3 is activated. The connection component for goal 3 executes, generating D2 and returning D2 as the result to goal 1. This time, when goal 1 terminates, a chunk is created (top of figure 10-6), because both of the subgoals were processed by chunks.

The encoding component for this chunk builds upon the existing encodings by encoding E1 to a new symbol (E3); it does not go straight from goal 1's primitive parameters (3 and 7). This happens (and causes hierarchical encoding) because, for this instance of goal 1, E1 is the implicit parameter, not 3 and 7. Recall from section 10.4 that the implicit parameters of a goal consist of those pieces of the goal's initial state that are examined during the goal's performance. E1 is generated before goal 1 is activated (so it is part of the goal's initial state) and examined by the connection component for goal 2. On the other hand, neither of the objects representing the numbers 3 and 7 is examined during the processing of goal 1. Therefore, E1 is an implicit parameter (and included in the chunk), and the numbers 3 and 7 are not.

The decoding component is created in an analogous hierarchical fashion. It decodes from a new symbol (D3) to D2. This occurs because D2 (and not the number 5) is the result of goal 1. It never became necessary to decode D2, so it was passed directly up as the result of both goals 3 and 1. The connection component of this chunk links E3 to D3 in a straightforward manner.

If the same task is performed yet again, the encoding components immediately generate E1, followed by E3. Goal 1 is activated, and its connection component executes, generating D3 and completing goal 1. If the result is needed by some part of the system outside of the hierarchy, it will be decoded to D2 and then to the number 5.

The example that we have just gone through outlines the basics of how the chunking mechanism works. The next step is to look at the more complex situation of the Seibel task (figure 10-4). Chunking starts in this structure with the terminal goals (numbers 2, 4, 5, 7, 10, 11, and 12). Consider goal 11 (**Get-Stimulus-X**), for example. Successful completion of this goal requires retrieving from the working memory the representation of a stimulus that has been perceived and then generating a piece of information representing the horizontal location (X) of that stimulus. The parameter for this goal is the stimulus—an implicit parameter—and the result is the location. In the chunk for this situation, the encoding and decoding components are trivial. They simply recode from the single parameter to a new symbol and from a second new symbol to the result. The connection component tests for the presence of an active **Get-Stimulus-X** goal and the encoding symbol and produces the decoding symbol.

Goal 10 (**Get-On-Light-Stimulus**) presents a slightly more complicated case than goal 11. The goal has both explicit and implicit parameters. The explicit parameters (Min-X and Max-X) define the region of the stimulus display in which an on-light should be found. The implicit parameter is the actual external representation (in the stimulus display) of the on-light that is found. The result of this goal is the internal representation of the on-light as it appears in the working memory. Just as before, the implicit parameter and the result form the basis for trivial encoding and decoding components. However, the explicit parameters are different. They do not exist as separate entities in the working memory; instead they act as if they were augmentations to the name of the goal. Therefore, they appear along with the name of the goal as part of the connection component.

As a final example of the workings of the chunking mechanism, consider how it creates chunks consisting of sequences of light-button pairs—the kind of chunks produced by the chunking mechanism in Rosenbloom and Newell (1982a). The locus of these chunks can be found at the recursive step in the goal hierarchy. The root (and recursive) goal in the hierarchy (Do-Lights-If-Any) has implicit parameters that represent lights in the stimulus display, and it generates results that are the button presses for those lights. The earliest chunks that can be created for this goal are those at the bottom of the recursion—that is, goals to process manageable segments of the display. Each of these chunks will represent a single on-light in a region, a region of solid on-lights, or a region with no on-lights. Once the chunks exist for goals 13 and 14 (and their sibling goal 7, the predicate **One-Light-On?**) in a single situation, the parent goal (goal 6: Do-Off-And-On) can be chunked. This yields a new chunk for the combined situation in both segments. This process continues up the hierarchy until goal 1 is chunked for that level of recursion. But goal 1 at that level is just goal 13 or 14 at the next level up. Therefore, gradually (since these chunks are acquired one at a time), the level of aggregation of segments covered by chunks increases.

This process always leads to light-button chunks for contiguous light-button pairs. It does not lead to chunks for disjoint patterns such as the two extreme right and left light-button pairs. This is not a limitation on the generality of the chunking mechanism. Instead, it is a function of the goal structure employed. A different goal structure (reflecting a different processing strategy) could lead to the creation of such disjoint chunk patterns.

One of the strong task dependencies present in the Rosenbloom and Newell (1982a) chunking mechanism was that encoding productions had to have a condition added to them that insured that no on-light appeared between the two patterns being chunked together. This was so even though the information that this condition was necessary appeared nowhere in the task algorithm. In the hierarchy in figure 10-4, such conditions are generated naturally from the goals for processing segments of the display with no on-lights in them. We see that the task dependencies show up in the goal hierarchy, not in the chunking mechanism.

The following list of points summarizes the key aspects of chunking as it applies to goal hierarchies:

- Each chunk represents a specific goal with a specific set of parameter values. It relates the parameter values to the results of the goal.
- Chunks are created through experience with the goals processed.
- Chunks are created bottom up in the goal hierarchy.
- Chunks consist of encoding, connection, and decoding components.
- Chunk encoding and decoding are hierarchical, parallel, goal-asynchronous processes that operate on goal parameters and results, respectively.
- Chunk connection is a serial, goal-synchronous process that generates (possibly encoded) results from (possibly encoded) parameters.
- Chunks improve performance by replacing the normal processing of a goal (and its subgoals) with the faster processes of encoding, connection, and decoding.

10.6 THE XAPS3 ARCHITECTURE

Modeling goal hierarchies and chunking requires an architecture with specific properties. The XAPS3 production-system architecture is one such architecture.[2] It is a new architecture, but it builds upon the work done in the development of the

---

[2]See Rosenbloom (1983) for a more detailed description of the XAPS3 architecture. A general introduction to production systems can be found in Waterman and Hayes-Roth (1978).

XAPS2 architecture (Rosenbloom and Newell, 1982a). The presentation of XAPS2 begins with a discussion of a set of *constraints* that must be met by any architecture within which the chunking theory of learning is implemented. These constraints state that the model must contain both parallelism and a bottleneck (the *parallel* and *bottleneck* constraints). The parallelism must appear in all aspects of the system's performance including cognitive processing (the *cognitive-parallelism* constraint), and the bottleneck must occur after chunk encoding and before chunk decoding (the *encoding* and *decoding* constraints). It is not claimed that these constraints are known to be necessary—the arguments are not that tight—but this permits (and encourages) attempts to show how the constraints can be circumvented.

The same constraints still hold—as they must if they are really constraints—for the design of the XAPS3 architecture. More recently, two new constraints have been formulated from the consequences of the chunking theory. These new constraints rule out XAPS2 and have led to the design of the XAPS3 architecture. Although XAPS3 is a direct descendent of XAPS2, the constraints have forced a number of significant changes in the XAPS3 design.

The first new constraint is the *crypto-information constraint:*

The crypto-information constraint: Any system that learns through experience cannot use crypto-information if it wants to guarantee correct learning.

Crypto-information—hidden information—is information that the architecture accesses while making performance decisions but that is not accessible to programs running within the architecture. The XAPS2 architecture employs a form of crypto-information in its use of *activation*—real-valued weights associated to portions of working memory. These activation values are used by the architecture to decide which of multiple instantiations of a production should execute on a cycle, among other purposes. It is crypto-information because knowledge about activation values cannot be represented in the productions executed within the architecture. Another example of crypto-information is the information about working memory recency used for conflict resolution in the OPS languages (Forgy, 1981).

The use of activation in XAPS2 is a good example of how crypto-information can lead to incorrect performance. Suppose there is an object A with an activation of 0.5 and an object b with an activation 0.3. Suppose also that there is a production that matches both A and B, generating two instantiations. When this situation first occurs, the instantiation that matches A will execute because of its greater activation. From this experience, the system learns what action to perform under these circumstances—that is, the action associated with the A instantiation. At some later point both A and B may again be represented, but this time with the activations reversed. Even though the action associated with B is now the correct one, its previous experience tells the system to do the action associated with A, because the information about relative levels of activation could not be represented in the record of the previous experience.

Not only would the previous information be incorrect, but there would in fact be no way ever to learn the correct information.

It is important to note that this constraint does not rule out all activation-based production-system architectures. If the activation is not used as a basis for an architectural decision, or if sufficient knowledge about activation levels is representable within productions, then activation is not a a problem, because it is no longer a form of crypto-information.

Though activation was a focal point of the XAPS2 design, XAPS3 has been designed to work without it to meet the demands of this constraint. It is thus a more traditional, purely symbolic, production-system architecture.

The second new constraint is the *goal-architecturality constraint:*

> **The goal-architecturality constraint:** The representation and processing of goals must be defined in the architecture itself; it cannot be left up to the discretion of productions.[3]

The reason behind this constraint can be traced to the chunking mechanism's need to understand how goals are represented and processed. This requirement implies that goals must be understood by the architecture, because the chunking mechanism is itself an architectural mechanism.

One way for the architecture to understand the processing of goals is for the goal-processing algorithm to be defined within the architecture itself. The obvious alternative—production-defined processing of goals—requires the chunking mechanism to be able to abstract the algorithm and representation from the productions and tune itself to whatever scheme is being used. This requires considerably more intelligence than the authors are willing to ascribe to the chunking mechanism or for that matter to any mechanism built into the architecture. For a system to exhibit truly adaptive behavior, it must be able to apply its full knowledge and learning capabilities to any task requiring intelligence. This is feasible at the program level but not at the architectural level.

In response to the goal-architecturality constraint, the goal processing that occurred at the level of productions in XAPS2 has been moved down into the architecture of XAPS3.

XAPS3 is one architecture sitting within the design space delimited by the constraints so far determined. The remainder of this section describes the XAPS3 architecture (for more details, see Rosenbloom, 1983). It is like XAPS2 in the structure of working memory objects and in the fact that it allows parallelism at the level of production execution, but it differs in its lack of activation and in its built-in mechanisms

---

[3]Anderson (1982a) has previously made a similar argument for the placement of goal processing in the architecture of the ACT* production system (Anderson, 1983a).

for goal processing and chunking.[4] This description is divided into sections on the standard components of a production system—working memory, production memory, and the cycle of execution—followed by sections on the processing of goals and the chunking mechanism.

10.6.1 Working Memory

The XAPS3 working memory consists of an unordered set of *objects* representing all of the types of information required in an information-processing system (except for the types of information represented in productions): goals, patterns of stimuli and responses, intermediate computations, and so forth. Each object is a token, in the sense of the classical type-token distinction. It is uniquely specified by a general *type* and a unique *identifier*. The type is a symbol that can be common among several objects, such as **Goal.** The identifier is a unique symbol for the object, which allows multiple objects of the same type to be present simultaneously in working memory. A new identifier is generated dynamically by the architecture whenever a new object is created.

XAPS3 objects also have an optional set of *attributes,* each of which has exactly one *value.* A successfully completed instance of a **Press-Button-At-Horizontal-Location** goal (with a type of **Goal** and an identifier of Object127) looks like the following example.[5]

> (**Goal** Object127
> [NAME *Press-Button-At-Horizontal-Location*]
> [STATUS *Succeeded*] [RESULT-TYPE *Response*])

The interpretation of the two attributes (NAME and STATUS) should be obvious. They tell the system that this goal is an instance of the **Press-Button-At-Horizontal-Location** goal that has completed successfully. The third attribute (RESULT-TYPE) specifies the type of object to be returned as the result of this goal (see section 10.6.4 for the details).

During the lifetime of a working memory object, two types of auxiliary tags are kept. The *created-by* tag marks the identifier of the goal that was active—there being one at most—when the object was created (if there was no goal active at the time, then the special symbol ⟨None⟩ is used). This tag is used for determining the object's status as part of either the local or the initial state of the current goal. The *examined-by* tag marks the identifier of the goal active when the object was last

---

[4]See Moran (1973), Anderson (1983a), and Sauers and Farrell (1982) for other attempts at integrating the processing of goals into the architecture of a production system.

[5]The format of this object and of subsequent objects and productions has been altered slightly for clarity of presentation.

examined by a production. This tag, in combination with the first one, allows the chunking mechanism to determine the implicit parameters of goals.

10.6.2 Production Memory

There is a single homogeneous production memory in XAPS3. The productions in it are similar to the productions in XAPS2 and to those in the OPS languages. They have three parts: a name, a list of one or more conditions, and a list of one or more actions. Here is an example production taken from the implementation of the Seibel task (figure 10-4):

> (DefProd SubGoal/Do-Lights/Do-Press-All-Buttons
> ((**Goal** ⟨Exists⟩ [NAME *Do-Lights*] [STATUS *Active*]
>   [MINIMUM-LOCATION = *?Min-Loc*]
>   [MAXIMUM-LOCATION = *?Max-Loc*])
> (**Goal** {⟨Local⟩ ⟨Exists⟩} [NAME *No-Light-Off?*]
>   [STATUS *Succeeded*]))
> →
> ((**Goal** ⟨New-Object⟩ [**Name** *Do-Press-All-Buttons*]
>   [STATUS *Want*] [RESULT-TYPE *Response*]
>   [MINIMUM-LOCATION = *?Min-Loc*]
>   [MAXIMUM-LOCATION = *?Max-Loc*])))

The name (SubGoal/Do-Lights/Do-Press-All-Buttons) is purely for the convenience of the programmer; it doesn't affect the processing of the system in any way. Each condition is a pattern to be matched against the objects in working memory. A condition pattern contains a type field (specifying the type of object to be matched), an identifier field (containing several different types of information), and an optional set of patterns for attributes. In the first condition in production SubGoal/Do-Lights/Do-Press-All-Buttons the type is **Goal,** the identifier is ⟨Exists⟩, and there are four attributes (NAME, STATUS, MINIMUM-LOCATION, and MAXIMUM-LOCATION) with associated values (*Do-Lights, Active,* = *?Min-Loc,* and = *?Max-Loc,* respectively).

Condition patterns are built primarily from *constants* and *variables.* Constants are signified by the presence of the appropriate symbol in the pattern and only match objects that contain that symbol in that role. Some example constants in production SubGoal/Do-Lights/Do-Press-All-Buttons are **Goal,** MINIMUM-LOCATION, and *Succeeded.* Variables are signified by a symbol (the name of the variable) preceded by an equal sign. They match anything appearing in their role in an object. An example is = *?Min-Loc* in the sample production. All instances of the same variable within a production must be bound to the same value in order for the match to succeed.

The identifier in the first condition of production SubGoal/Do-Lights/Do-Press-All-Buttons is specified by the special symbol <Exists>. Such a condition succeeds if there is any object in working memory that matches the condition. If there is more than one such object, the choice is conceptually arbitrary (actually, the first object found is used). Only one instantiation is generated. If the identifier is specified as a variable, the condition still acts like an exists condition, but the identifier can be retrieved, allowing the object to be modified by the actions of the production.

The complete opposite of an exists condition is a not-exists condition—commonly called a negated condition. When the symbol <Not-Exists> appears in the identifier field, it signifies that the match succeeds only if there is no object in working memory that matches the remainder of the condition pattern.

The second condition in the sample production contains the symbol <Local> as well as <Exists> in the identifier field (they are conjoined syntactically by braces). When this symbol is added to an identifier pattern of any type—constant, variable, exists, or not-exists—it signifies that the condition should be matched only against those objects in working memory that are local to the active goal. This information—provided by the objects' created-by tags—is a means by which the production that works on a goal can determine which objects are part of their local context.

The remainder of the condition specifies a pattern that must be met by the attribute-value pairs of working memory objects. These patterns are built out of constants, variables, built-in predicates (such as <Greater-Than>), and general LISP computations (via an escape mechanism). In addition, any of the above forms can be negated, denoting that the condition only matches objects that do not match the pattern.

There is only one kind of action in XAPS3—modifying working memory. The interface to the outside world is through working memory rather than through production actions. Actions can create new objects in working memory and, under certain circumstances, modify existing objects. When the action has an identifier of <New-Object>, a new object is created by replacing the identifier with a newly generated symbol, instantiating the variables with their values computed during the match, and replacing calls to LISP functions with their values (via another escape mechanism). An existing object can be modified by passing its identifier as a parameter from a condition. As discussed in section 10.4, only objects local to the current goal can be modified.

There are no production actions that lead to the deletion of values or objects from working memory. A value can be removed only if it is superseded by another value. As discussed in section 10.4, objects go away when they are no longer part of the current context.[6] No explicit mechanism for deletion has proved necessary, so none has been included.

---

[6]This mechanism is similar to the *dampening* mechanism in the ACT architecture (Anderson, 1976).

10.6.3 The Cycle of Execution

XAPS3 follows the traditional *recognize-act* cycle of production-system architectures, with a few twists thrown in by the need to process goals. The recognition phase begins with the *match* and finishes up with *conflict resolution*. The *cycle number*—simulated time—is incremented after the recognition phase, whether any productions are executed or not. During the act phase, productions are executed.

10.6.3.1 Recognition

The match phase is quite simple. All of the productions in the system are matched against working memory in parallel (conceptually). This process yields a set of legal instantiations with at most one instantiation per production, because each condition generates at most one instantiation. Each instantiation consists of a production name and a set of variable bindings for that production that yield a successful match. This set of instantiations is then passed in its entirety to the conflict resolution phase,[7] where they are winnowed down to the set to be executed on the current cycle. This winnowing is accomplished via a pair of conflict resolution rules.

The first rule is *goal-context refraction*. A production instantiation can fire only once within any particular goal context. It is a form of the standard OPS refractory inhibition rule (Forgy, 1981), differing only in how the inhibition on firing is released. With the standard rule, the inhibition is released whenever one of the working memory objects on which the instantiation is predicated has been modified. With goal-context refraction, inhibition is released whenever the system leaves the context in which the instantiation fired. If the instantiation could not legally fire before the context was established but could fire both while the context was active and after the context was terminated, then the instantiation must be based, at least in part, on a result generated during the context and returned when the context was left. Therefore, the instantiation should be free to fire again to reestablish the still-relevant information.

The second rule—the *parameter-passing bottleneck*—states that only one parameter-passing instantiation can execute on a cycle (conceptually selected arbitrarily). This rule first appeared in a slightly different form as an assumption in the HPSA77 architecture (Newell, 1980a). It will be justified in section 10.6.5.

10.6.3.2 Action

All of the instantiations that make it through the conflict resolution phase are fired (conceptually) in parallel. Firing a production instantiation consists of

---

[7]For purposes of efficiency, these two phases are actually intermingled. However, this does not change the behavior of the system at the level at which we are interested.

(1) overwriting the *examined-by* tags of the working memory objects matched by the instantiation, with the identifier of the active goal; (2) replacing all variables in the actions by the values determined during the match phase; (3) evaluating any LISP forms; and (4) performing the actions. This can result in the addition of new objects to working memory or the modification of existing local objects. If conflicting values are simultaneously asserted, the winner is selected arbitrarily. This does not violate the crypto-information constraint because the architecture is using no information in making the decision. If the performance system works correctly, even when it can't depend on the outcome of the decision, then the learned information will not lead to incorrect performance.

10.6.4 Goal Processing

In section 10.4, the processing of goals was described at an abstract level. In this section how that processing is implemented within the XAPS3 architecture is described. The goals themselves, unlike chunks, are just data structures in working memory. A typical XAPS3 goal goes through four phases in its life. The current phase of a goal is represented explicitly at all times by the value associated with the STATUS attribute of the working memory object representing the goal.

In the first stage of its life, the goal is *desired:* at some point, but not necessarily right then, the goal should be processed. Productions create goal desires by generating a new object of type **Goal.** Each new goal object must have a NAME attribute, a STATUS attribute with a value of *Want,* and a RESULT-TYPE attribute. In addition, it may have any number of other attributes, specifying explicit parameters to the goal. The value of the RESULT-TYPE attribute specifies the type of the results that are to be returned on successful completion of the goal. All local objects of that type are considered to be results of the goal. Results are marked explicitly so they won't be flushed when the context is left and so the chunking mechanism will know to include them in the chunks for the goal.

Leaving the expression of goal desires under the control of productions allows goals to be processed by the architecture, while the structure of the hierarchy is still left under program (that is, production) control. The architecture controls the transition to the second, *active* phase of the goal's life. At most, one goal is active at any point in time. The architecture attempts to activate a new goal whenever the system is at a loss about how to continue with the current goal. This occurs when there is an empty conflict set; that is, there is no production instantiation that can legally fire on the current cycle. When this happens, the system looks in working memory to determine if there are any subgoals of the current goal—those goals created while the current goal was active—that are desired. If such a subgoal is found, it is made the active goal, and the parent goal is *suspended* by replacing its STATUS with the identifier of the newly activated subgoal. If more than one desired subgoal is found, one is arbitrarily selected (actually, the last one found is used).

Suspension is the third phase in the life of a goal (it occurs only for nonterminal goals). Replacing the status of the parent goal with the subgoal's identifier accomplishes two things: it halts work on the goal, because the productions that process goals all check for a status of *Active,* and it maintains the control stack for the goal hierarchy. A suspended goal remains suspended until its active subgoal terminates, at which time it returns to being active. If a goal has more than one subgoal, the goal will oscillate between the active and suspended states.

If no progress can be made on the active goal and there are no desired subgoals, then the system has no idea how to continue making progress; it therefore terminates the active goal with a status of *Failed.* Following termination, the goal is in its fourth and final phase of life. In addition to a failure termination, goals can be terminated with a status of *Succeeded.* There are no uniform criteria for determining when an arbitrary goal has completed successfully, so it has been left to productions to assert that this has happened. This is done via the creation of an object of type **Succeeded.** When the architecture detects the presence of such an object in working memory, it terminates the current goal and reactivates its parent.

At goal termination time a number of activities occur in addition to the obvious one of changing the active goal. The first two activities occur only on the successful termination of a goal. As will be discussed in the following section, the first step is the possible creation of a chunk. The second step is to return the results of the terminating goal to its parent goal. This is accomplished by altering the created-by tags of the results so that it looks as if they were created by the parent goal. The third step is to delete all of the objects from working memory created during the processing of this goal. The fourth and final step is to enable result decoding if it is appropriate.

10.6.5 Chunking

As was seen in section 10.5, chunking improves performance by enabling the system to use its experience with previous instances of a goal to avoid expanding the goal tree below it. In this section is detailed how this has been implemented within the XAPS3 architecture—yielding a working, task-independent production-system practice mechanism. This section begins with a description of how chunks are used and concludes with a description of how they are acquired.

10.6.5.1 The Use of Chunks

The key to the behavior of a chunk lies in its connection component. When a goal is proposed in a situation in which a chunk has already been created for it, the connection component of that chunk substitutes for the normal processing of the goal. This is accomplished in XAPS3 by having the connection component check that the goal's status is *desired*. The connection is a production containing a condition testing for the existence of a desired goal, a condition testing for the encoding of the goal's parameters, and any relevant negated (`<Not-Exists>`) conditions. It has two actions: one marks the goal as having succeeded, and the other asserts the goal's encoded result. If there is a desired goal in working memory in a situation for which a connection production exists, the connection will be eligible to fire. Whether (and when) it does fire depends on conflict resolution. Connection productions are subject to the parameter-passing–bottleneck conflict resolution rule because they pass the identifier of the desired goal as a parameter to the action that marks the goal as having succeeded. This conflict resolution rule serves a dual purpose: (1) it implements part of the bottleneck constraint by insuring that only one goal can be connected at a time, and (2) it removes a source of possible error by insuring that only one connection can execute for any particular goal instance.

If the connection does fire, it removes the need to activate and expand the goal, because the goal's results will be generated directly by the connection (and decoding) and the goal will be marked as having succeeded. If instead no connection production is available for the current situation of a desired goal, then eventually the production system will reach an impasse—no productions eligible to fire—and the goal will be activated and expanded. Therefore, we have just the behavior required of chunks— they replace goal activation and expansion, if they exist.

This behavior is, of course, predicated on the workings of the encoding and decoding components of the chunk.[8] The encoding component of a chunk must execute before the associated connection can. In fact, it should execute even before the parent goal is activated, because the subgoal's encoded symbol should be part of the parent goal's initial state. Recall that encodings are built up hierarchically. If the parent goal shares all of the parameters of one of its subgoals, then the encoding of the parent goal's parameters should be based on the encoding generated for the subgoal. This behavior occurs in XAPS3 because the encoding components are implemented as goal-free productions that do not pass parameters. They fire (concurrently with whatever else is happening in the system) whenever the appropriate parameter values for their goal are in working memory (subject to refraction). If the parameters exist before the parent goal becomes active, as they must if they are parameters to it, then the encoded symbol becomes part of the parent goal's initial state.

As stated in section 10.4, the decoding component must decode an encoded result when it will be needed. Each decoding component is a production that keys off the nonprimitive result pattern generated by the connection production and off an

---

[8]For efficiency, the encoding and decoding components are not created if there is only one parameter or result, respectively.

object of type **Decode.** When the architecture determines that decoding should occur, it places a **Decode** object in working memory, with the type of the object to be decoded specified by the TYPE attribute.[9] The actions of the decoding production generate the component results out of which the nonprimitive pattern was composed.

10.6.5.2 The Acquisition of Chunks

A complete specification of the chunk acquisition process must include the details of when chunks can be acquired and from what information they are built. A chunk can be acquired when three conditions are met. The first condition is that some goal must have just been completed. The system can't create a chunk for a goal that terminated at some point in the distant past, because the information on which the chunk must be based is no longer available. Chunks also are not created prior to goal completion (on partial results). Chunks are simple to create in part because they summarize all of the effects of a goal. If chunks were created partway through the processing of a goal—for partial results of the goal—then a sophisticated analysis might be required in order to determine which parameters affect which results and how. This is not really a limitation on what can be chunked, because any isolable portion of the performance can be made into a goal.

The second condition is that the goal must have completed successfully. Part of the essence of goal failure is that the system does not know why the goal failed. This means that the system does not know which parameter values have lead to the failure; thus, it can't create a chunk that correctly summarizes the situation. Chunking is success-driven learning, as opposed to failure-driven learning (see for example, Winston, 1975).

The third and final condition for chunk creation is that all of the working memory modifications occurring since the goal was first activated must be attributable to that goal, rather than to one of its subgoals. This condition is implemented by insuring that no productions were fired while any of the goal's subgoals were active. All of the subgoals must either be processed by a chunk or fail immediately after activation—failure of a subgoal, particularly of predicates, does not necessarily imply failure of the parent goal.

To summarize, a chunk is created after the system has decided to terminate a goal successfully but before anything is done about it (such as marking the goal succeeded, returning the results, or flushing the local objects from working memory). At that point the goal is still active, and all of its information is readily available.

Most of the information on which the chunk is based can be found in working memory (but see below). The first piece of information needed for the creation of a chunk is the name (and identifier) of the goal that is being chunked. This information

---

[9]Matters are actually somewhat more complicated (Rosenbloom, 1983).

is found by retrieving the object representing the active goal. The goal's explicit parameters are also available as attribute-value pairs on the goal object. Given the goal's identifier, the system finds its implicit parameters by retrieving all of the objects in working memory that were part of the goal's initial state—that is, their created-by tag contains an identifier different from that of the active goal—and that were examined by a production during the processing of the active goal. This last type of information is contained in the objects' examined-by tags. The goal's results are equally easy to find. The architecture simply retrieves all of the goal's local objects that have a type equal to the goal's RESULT-TYPE.

Because the goal parameter and result information is determined from the constant objects in working memory, chunks themselves are not parameterized. Each chunk represents a specific situation for a specific goal. However, two forms of abstraction are performed during the creation of a chunk: (1) the inclusion of only the implicit parameters of a goal and not the entire initial state, and (2) the replacement of constant identifiers (found in the working memory objects) with neutral ⟨Exists⟩ specifications. These abstractions allow the chunks to be applicable in any situation that is relevantly identical, not merely totally identical. Different chunks are needed only for relevant differences.

The one complication in the clean picture of chunk acquisition so far presented involves the use of negated conditions during the processing of a goal. When a negated condition successfully matches working memory, there is no working memory object that can be marked as having been examined. Therefore, some of the information required for chunk creation cannot be represented in working memory. The current solution for this problem is not elegant, but it works. A temporary auxiliary memory is maintained, into which is placed each nonlocal negated condition occurring on productions that fire during the processing of the goal (local negated conditions can be ignored because they do not test the initial state). This memory is reinitialized whenever the goal that is eligible to be chunked changes. Before the conditions are placed in the memory they are fully instantiated with the values bound to their variables by the other conditions in their production. As discussed in Rosenbloom (1983), including a negated condition in an encoding production can lead to performance errors, so these conditions are all included in the associated connection production.

10.7 RESULTS

In this section some results derived from applying the XAPS3 architecture to a set of reaction-time tasks will be presented. A more complete presentation of these results can be found in Rosenbloom (1983). The first experiment described here is the Seibel task. Two different sequences of trials were simulated, of which the first sequence is the same as the one used in Rosenbloom and Newell (1982a). The simulation completed 268 trials before it was terminated.[10] A total of 682 productions was learned. On the second sequence of trials—from a newly generated random permutation of the 1023 possibilities—259 trials were completed before termination. For this sequence, 652 productions were learned.

Figure 10-7 shows the first sequence as fit by a general power law. Each point in the figure represents the mean value over five data points (except for the last one, which only includes three).[11] For this curve, the asymptote parameter (A) has no effect. Only E, the correction for previous practice, is required to straighten out the curve. At first glance, it seems nonsensical to talk about previous practice for such a simulation, but a plausible interpretation is possible. In fact, there are two independent explanations—either or both may be responsible.

The first possibility is that the level at which the terminal goals are defined is too high (complex). If the "true" terminals are more primitive, then chunking starts at a lower level in the hierarchy. One view of what chunks are doing is that they are turning their associated (possibly nonterminal) goals into terminal goals for particular parameter situations. During preliminary bottom-up chunking, the system would eventually reach the lowest level in the current hierarchy. All of the practice prior to that point is effectively previous practice for the current simulation.

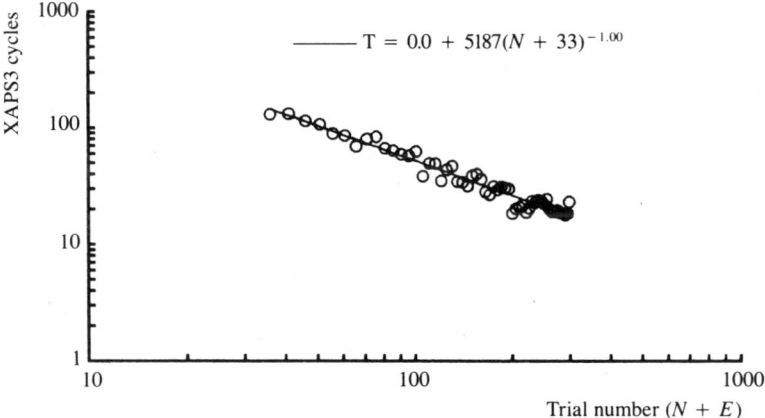

Figure 10-7:   General power-law fit to 268 simulated trials of the Seibel (1963) task.

---

[10]At this point the FRANZLISP system—which appeared not to be garbage collecting in the first place—refused to allocate any more memory for the simulation.

[11]These data appear noisier than the human data from Seibel (1963) shown in figure 10-2. This is accounted for by the fact that each point in figure 10-2 was the mean of 1023 data points and each point in this figure is the mean of five data points.

The other source of previous practice is the goal hierarchy itself. This structure is posited at the beginning of the simulation, hence it is already known perfectly. However, there must exist some process of *method acquisition* by which the subject goes from the written (or oral) instructions to an internal goal hierarchy. Though method acquisition does not fall within the domain of what is here defined as "practice," a scheme will be proposed in section 10.9 whereby chunking may lead to a mechanism for method acquisition.

In addition to the Seibel task, the system so far has been applied to fourteen tasks from three different stimulus-response compatibility experiments (Fitts and Seeger, 1953; Morin and Forrin, 1962; Duncan, 1977). As a sample of these results, figure 10-8 shows a pair of simulated practice curves for two tasks from Fitts and Seeger (1953). These curves contain fifty trials each, aggregated by five trials per data point.

This chapter is not the appropriate place to discuss the issues surrounding whether the simulated practice curves are truly power laws or something slightly different (such as exponentials). Suffice it to say that a mixture of exponential, power law, and ambiguous curves is obtained. These results roughly follow the predictions of the approximate mathematical analysis of the chunking theory appearing in Rosenbloom (1983). They also fit with the observation that the human curves tend to be most exponential for the simplest tasks—the compatibility tasks are among the simplest tasks for which we have human practice data. For more on this issue, see Newell and Rosenbloom (1981) and Rosenbloom (1983).

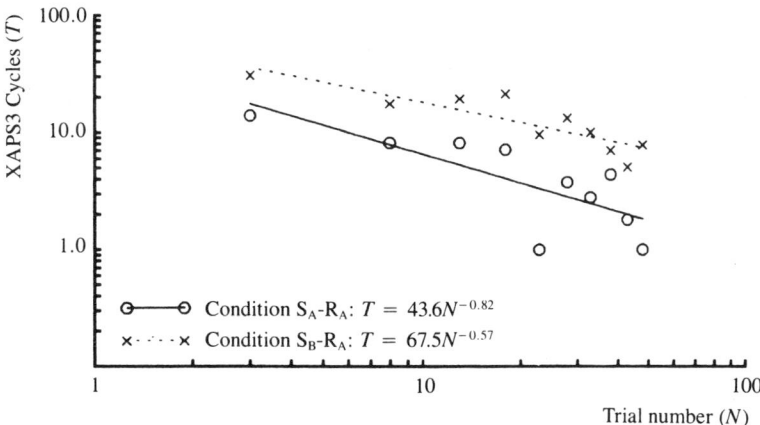

Figure 10-8: Simulated practice curves for conditions S_A-R_A and S_B-R_A from Fitts and Seeger (1953). The latter curve is the average over two hierarchy variations.

10.8 RELATIONSHIP TO PREVIOUS WORK

The current formulation of the chunking theory of learning provides an interesting point of contact among four previously disparate concepts: (1) classical chunking; (2) production composition (Lewis, 1978; Neves and Anderson, 1981; Anderson, 1982b); (3) table look-up—memo functions (Michie, 1968) and signature tables (Samuel, 1967); and (4) macro-operators (Fikes, Hart and Nilsson, 1972; Korf, 1983). Classical chunking has already been discussed in section 10.3, so this section covers only the latter three ideas, followed by a proposal about the underlying commonality among these concepts.

10.8.1 Production Composition

Production composition (Lewis, 1978; Neves and Anderson, 1981; Anderson, 1982b) is a learning scheme whereby new productions are created through the combination of old ones. Given a pair of productions that execute successively, the system creates their composition from their conditions and actions (figure 10-9). The condition side of the new production consists of all of the conditions of the first production (C_1, C_2, and C_3), plus those conditions from the second production that do not match actions of the first production (C_5). The conditions of the second production that match actions of the first production (C_4 matches A_4) are not included in the composition (removing the serial dependency between the two productions). All of the actions from both productions are combined in the action side of the new production (A_4 and A_6). The resulting composition is a single production that accomplishes the combined effects of the older pair of productions. As learning continues, composed productions can themselves be composed, until there is a single production for an entire task.

In some recent work with the GRAPES system (Saures and Farrell, 1982; Anderson, Farrell, and Saurers, 1982; Anderson, 1983b), production composition was integrated with goal-based processing. In GRAPES, specific goals are designated by the programmer to be ones for which composition will occur. When such a

$$C_1 \ C_2 \ C_3 \ \longrightarrow \ A_4$$

$$C_4 \ C_5 \ \longrightarrow \ A_6$$

$$C_1 \ C_2 \ C_3 \qquad\qquad C_5 \ \longrightarrow \ A_4 \ A_6$$

Figure 10-9: An example of production composition.

goal completes successfully, all of the productions that executed during that time are composed together, yielding a single production that accomplishes the goal.

Because the main effects of chunking and goal-based composition are the same—the short-circuiting of goals by composite productions—it is probably too early to know which mechanism will turn out to be the correct one for a general practice mechanism. However, there are a number of differences between them worth noting. We will focus on the three most important: (1) the knowledge required by the learning procedure: (2) the generality of what is learned; and (3) the hierarchical nature of what is learned.

10.8.1.1 Knowledge-Source Differences

With chunking, all of the information required for learning can be found in working memory (modulo negated conditions). With production composition, the information comes from production memory (and possibly from working memory). Being able to ignore the structure of productions has two advantages. The first advantage is that the chunking mechanism can be much simpler. This is both because working memory is much simpler than production memory—productions contain conditions, actions, variables, function calls, negations, and other structures and information—and because, with composition, the complex process of matching conditions of later productions to actions of previous productions is required, in order that conditions that test intermediate products not be included in the composition. Chunking accomplishes this by only including objects that are part of the goal's initial state.

The second advantage of the chunking strategy, of learning from working memory, is that chunking is applicable to any goal, no matter what its internal implementation is (productions or something else). As long as the processing of the goal leaves marks on the working memory objects that it examines, chunking can work.

10.8.1.2 Generalization Differences

The products of chunking are always constant productions (except for the identifiers of objects) that apply only for the situation in which they were created (although, as already discussed, two forms of abstractions are performed). With production composition, the variables existing in the productions to be composed are retained in the new production. The newly learned material is thus more general than that learned by chunking. The chunking mechanism definitely has more of a table look-up flavor. Section 10.8.2 contains a more thorough discussion of chunking as table look-up, and section 10.9 discusses how a chunking mechanism could possibly learn parameterized information.

10.8.1.3 Hierarchical Differences

Both mechanisms learn hierarchically in that they learn for goals in a hierarchy. They differ in how they decide about which goals to learn and in whether the learned material is itself hierarchical.

Chunking occurs bottom up in the goal hierarchy. Production composition—in GRAPES at least—works in isolation on any single goal in the hierarchy. For this to work, subgoals are kept as actions in the new productions. The composition approach is more flexible, but the chunking approach has two compensating advantages. The first advantage is that, with chunking, the encoding and decoding components can be themselves hierarchical, based on the encoding and decoding components of the previously chunked subgoals. Productions produced by composition tend to accumulate huge numbers of conditions and actions because they are flat structures.

The second advantage is again simplicity. When information is learned about a goal at an arbitrary position in the hierarchy, its execution is intermingled with the execution of its subgoals. Knowing which information belongs in which context requires a complete historical trace of the changes made to working memory and the goals that made the changes.

10.8.2 Table Look-up

It has been seen that from one point of view chunking resembles production composition. From another point of view it resembles a table look-up scheme, in which a table of input parameters versus results is gradually learned for each goal in the system. As such, it has two important predecessors—memo functions (Michie, 1968; Marsh, 1970) and signature tables (Samuel, 1967).

10.8.2.1 Memo Functions

A memo function[12] is a function with an auxiliary table added. Whenever the function is evaluated, the table is first checked to see if there is a result stored with the current set of parameter values. If there is, it is retrieved as the value of the function. Otherwise, the function is computed and the arguments and result are stored in the table. Memo functions have been used to increase the efficiency of mathematical functions (Michie, 1968; Marsh, 1970) and of tree searches (Marsh, 1970).

---

[12]Memo functions themselves are derived from the earlier work by Samuel (1959) on creating a rote memory for the values of board positions in the game of checkers.

Chunking can be seen as generating memo functions for goals. But these are hierarchical memo functions, and ones in which the arguments need not be specified explicitly. Chunking also provides a cleaner implementation of the ideas behind memo functions because the table is not simply an add-on to a different processing structure. It is implemented by the same "stuff" (productions) as is used to represent the other types of processing in the system.

10.8.2.2 Signature Tables

Signature tables were developed as a means of implementing nonlinearities in an evaluation function for checkers (Samuel, 1967). The evaluation function is represented as a hierarchical mosaic of signature tables. Each signature table had between two and four parameters, each of which had between three and fifteen possible values. The parameters to the lowest-level tables were measures computed on the checkerboard. For each combination of parameter values a number was stored in the table representing how good that combination was. There were nine of these tables arranged in a three-level hierarchy. The values generated by lower tables were fed into higher tables. The final value of the evaluation function was the number generated by the root (top) table.

Signature tables capture the table look-up and hierarchical aspects of chunking, though only for encoding. There is no decoding because signature tables are not a model of action; they act simply as a classifier of board positions. Another difference between chunking and signature tables is that information is stored in the latter not as a direct function of experience, but as correlations over a number of experiences.

10.8.3 Macro-Operators

A macro-operator is a sequence of operators that can be viewed as a single operator. One classical system that makes use of macro-operators is STRIPS (Fikes, Hart, and Nilsson, 1972). STRIPS works by taking a task and performing a search to find a sequence of operators that will accomplish the task. Given a solution, STRIPS first generates a highly specific macro-operator from the sequence of operators and then generalizes it by figuring out which constants can be replaced by variables. The generalized macro-operator is used as a plan to guide the performance of the task, and it can be used as a primitive operator in the generation of a macro-operator for another task.

Each STRIPS operator is much like a production: it has a set of conditions (a *precondition wff*) and a set of actions (consisting of an *add list* and a *delete list*). Each macro-operator is represented as a *triangle table* representing the conditions and actions for all subsequences of the operators in the macro-operator (preserving the order of execution). This process is very much like a production composition scheme that takes all of the productions that fire during the processing of a goal and creates a composition for every possible subsequence of them. STRIPS differs from the mechanisms described above in exactly how it represents, selects, and uses what it learns, but it shares a common strategy of storing, with experience, meaningful (based on the task/goal) composites that can reduce the amount of processing required by subsequent tasks.

Another form of macro-operators can be found in Korf's (1983) work on macro-operator–based problem solving. Korf presents a methodology by which a table of macro-operators can be found that can collectively solve all variations on a problem. For example, one table of macro-operators is sufficient for solving any initial configuration of Rubik's cube. Korf's technique is based on having a set of differences between the goal state and the current state. The differences are ordered and then solved one at a time. During the solution of a difference, solutions to previous differences can be destroyed, but they must be reinstated before the current difference is considered solved. Rather than learn by experience, Korf's system preprocesses the task to learn the macro-operator table capable of handling all variations of the task. It does this in time proportional to what it would take to search for a solution to one variation of the task without the table of macro-operators.

Even though the macro-operators are nonvariabilized, a single table with size proportional to the product of the number of differences and the number of values per difference is totally sufficient. This is because at each point in the solution what is to be done depends only on the value of the current difference and not on any of the other differences. It is possible to be more concrete and to bring out the relationship of this mechanism to chunking by viewing the sequence of differences as a goal hierarchy. The top-level goal is to solve all of the differences. In general, to solve the first $x + 1$ differences one first processes a subgoal for solving the first x differences; one then processes a subgoal for solving the first $x + 1$ differences given that the first x differences have been solved. These latter conditional goals are the terminal goals in the hierarchy. Moreover, each one has only one parameter that can vary—the value of difference $x + 1$—so only a very few macro-operators need be created for the goal (the number of values that the difference can take). Korf's macro-operators are essentially chunks for these terminal goals. They relate the parameters of a goal (the set of differences already solved and the value of the next difference) to the composite result (the sequence of operators to be performed). Korf avoids the combinatorial explosion implicit in the tasks by creating macro-operators only for these limited terminal goals. If the chunking mechanism were doing the learning, it would begin by chunking the terminals, but it would then proceed to learn about the nonterminal goals as well. Korf's work is a good example of how choosing the right goal hierarchy (and limiting the set of goals for which learning occurs) can enable a small set of nonvariabilized macro-operators (or chunks) to solve a large class of problems.

10.8.4 Summary

Although classical chunking, production composition, table look-up, and macro-operators were proposed in quite different contexts and bear little obvious relationship to each other, the current formulation of the chunking theory of learning has strong ties to all four. (1) It explains how classical chunks can be created and used; (2) it results in productions similar to those generated by goal-directed production composition; (3) it caches the results of computations, as in a table look-up scheme; and (4) it unitizes sequences of operators into higher-level macro-operators. The chunking theory differs from these four mechanisms in a number of ways, but at the same time it occupies a common ground among them. This leads the authors to propose that all five mechanisms are different manifestations of a single underlying idea centered on the storage of composite information rather than its recomputation. The chunking theory has a number of useful features, but it is probably too early to know what formulation will turn out to be the correct one in the long run for general practice mechanism.

10.9 EXPANDING THE SCOPE OF CHUNKING

In this work it has been shown how chunking can provide a model of practice for tasks that can already be accomplished. Performance is sped up but not qualitatively changed. It is interesting to ask whether chunking can be used to implement any of the other, more complex forms of learning, such as method acquisition, concept formation, generalization, discrimination, learning by being told, and expectation-driven learning. Chunking does not directly accomplish any of these forms of learning, and on first glance the table look-up nature of chunking would seem to preclude its use in such sophisticated ways. However, four considerations suggest the possibility that the scope of chunking may extend much further.

The first two considerations derive from the ubiquitous presence of both chunking and the power law of practice in human performance. Chunking is already implicated at least in higher-level cognitive processes, and the power law of practice has been shown to occur over *all* levels of human performance. Thus, if the current chunking theory turns out not to be extendable, the limitation will probably be in the details of the implementation itself rather than in the more global formulation of the theory.

The remaining two considerations stem from the interaction of chunking with problem solving. The combination of these two mechanisms has the potential for generating interesting forms of learning. The strongest evidence of this potential to date can be found in the work of Anderson (1983b). He has demonstrated how production composition (a mechanism that is quite similar to chunking, as has been shown here), when combined with specific forms of problem solving, can effectively perform both production generalization and discrimination. Generalization comes about through the composition of an analogy process, and discrimination comes from the composition of an error-correction procedure.

The final line of evidence comes from the work of Newell and Laird on the structure of a general problem-solving system based on the *problem space hypothesis* (Newell, 1980b), a *universal weak method* (Laird and Newell, 1983), and *universal subgoaling* (Laird, 1983). The problem space hypothesis states that intelligent agents are always performing in a problem space. At any instant, the agent will have a *goal* that it is attempting to fulfill. Associated with that goal is a *problem space* in which the goal can be pursued. The problem space consists of a set of *states,* a *problem* (initial and desired states), a set of *operators* that move the agent between states, and *search control* information that assists in guiding the agent efficiently from the initial to the desired state. Added to this problem space structure are (1) a universal weak method, which allows the basic problem-solving methods, such as generate-and-test and depth-first search, to arise trivially out of the knowledge of the task being performed; and (2) universal subgoaling, which enables a problem solver automatically to create subgoals for any difficulties that can arise during problem solving. The result of this line of work has been a problem-solving production-system architecture called SOAR2 that implements these three concepts (Laird, 1983).

To see the power of integrating chunking with such a problem-solving system, consider the problem of *method acquisition;* given an arbitrary task or problem, how does the system first construct a method (goal structure) for it? This is the prototypical case of "hard" learning. There are at least two ways in which chunking can assist SOAR2 in method acquisition: (1) by compiling complex problem-solving processes into efficient operators, and (2) by acquiring search control information that eliminates irrelevant search paths. A single goal-chunking mechanism can acquire both of these types of information; the difference is in the types of goals that are chunked.

The compilation process is analogous to the kinds of chunks that are created in XAPS3: inefficient subgoal processing is replaced by efficient operator application. Given a task along with its associated goals and problem spaces, SOAR2 attempts to fulfill the task goal through a repeated process of elaborating the current situation with information and selecting a new goal, problem space, state, or operator. The system applies operators to a state by creating a new state, elaborating it with the results of the operator, and selecting the new state. If the application of the operator requires problem solving itself, it will not be possible to apply it to a state directly via a set of elaborations. Instead, a difficulty will arise for which SOAR2 will create a subgoal.

One way this subgoal can be pursued is by the selection of a problem space within which the task of applying the problematic operator to its state can be accomplished. The subgoal is fulfilled when the operator has been applied and a new state generated. A chunk could be created for this subgoal that would be applicable in any state that defines the same set of parameters for that operator. The next time the operator is tried it will be applied directly, so the difficulty will not occur and the subgoal will not be needed.

Another way that a difficulty can arise in SOAR2 is if there is uncertainty about which operator to apply to a state. As with all such difficulties, SOAR2 automatically creates a subgoal to work on this problem. It then employs an *operator selection* problem space within which it can evaluate and compare the set of candidate operators. The difficulty is finally resolved when a set of *preferences*—statements about which operators are preferred to which other operators—has been created that uniquely determines which of the original operators should be selected.

A subgoal that deals with an operator selection problem has a set of parameters— those aspects of the goal and state that were examined during the generation of the preferences. It also has a set of results—the preferences. Should a chunk be created for this goal, it would be a piece of search control for the problem space that allows it to pick the appropriate operator directly. As the system acquires more search control, the method becomes more efficient because of the resulting reduction in the amount of search required.

One limitation of the current chunking mechanism that such a method acquisition scheme could alleviate is the inability of chunks to implement parameterized operators. Chunking always creates a totally specified piece of knowledge. As currently formulated, it cannot create the kinds of parameterized operators used as terminal nodes in the goal hierarchies. We have seen that chunking does create abstracted knowledge, and Korf's (1983) work shows that nonvariabilized macro-operators can attain a good deal of generality from the goal hierarchy itself (see section 10.8.3), but fully parameterized operators are outside the current scope. On the other hand, problem spaces are inherently parameterized by their initial and desired states. Therefore it may be that it is not necessary for chunks to create parameterized operators. These operators can come from another source (problem spaces). Chunks would only be responsible for making these operators more efficient.

In summary, the ubiquity of both chunking and power-law learning indicates that the chunking model may not be limited in its scope to simple speedups. Examining three "hard" types of learning reveals that generalization and discrimination are possible via the combination of a similar learning mechanism (production composition) and specific types of problem solving; additionally, method acquisition appears feasible via chunking in problem spaces. If this does work out, it may prove possible to be able to formulate a number of the other difficult learning problems within this paradigm. The complications would appear as problem solving in problem spaces, and the chunking mechanism would remain simple, merely recording the results generated by the problem-solving system.

10.10 CONCLUSION

At the beginning of this investigation the authors set out to develop a generalized, task-independent model of practice, capable of producing power-law practice curves. The model was to be based on the concept of chunking, and it was to be used as the basis (and a source of constraint) for a production-system practice mechanism. All of this has been accomplished. The generalized model that has been developed is based on a goal-structured representation of reaction-time tasks. Each task has its own goal hierarchy, representing an initial performance algorithm.

When a goal is successfully completed, a three-part chunk can be created for it. The chunk is based on the parameters and results of the goal. The encoding component of the chunk encodes the parameters of the goal, yielding a new symbol representing their combination. The connection component of the chunk ties the encoded parameter symbol to an encoded symbol for the results of the goal. The decoding component of the chunk decodes the new result symbol to the results out of which it is composed.

The chunk improves the performance of the system by eliminating the need to process the goal fully; the chunk takes care of it. The process of chunking proceeds bottom up in the goal hierarchy. Once chunks are created for all of a goal's subgoals in a specific situation, it is possible to create a chunk for the goal. This process proceeds up the hierarchy until there is a chunk for the top-level goal for every situation that it could face.

Mechanisms for goal processing and chunking have been built into a new production-system architecture that fits within a set of contraints developed for the architecture of cognition. This architecture has been applied to a number of different reaction-time tasks (though not all of these results are presented here). It is capable of producing power-law practice curves.

As currently formulated, the chunking theory stakes out a position that is intermediary among four previous disparate mechanisms: classical chunking, memo functions, production composition, and macro-operators. These five ideas are different manifestations of a single underlying idea centered on the storage of composite information rather than its recomputation.

And finally, a research path has been outlined by which the chunking theory, when integrated with a problem-solving system, can potentially be expanded to cover aspects of learning, such as method acquisition, outside of the domain of pure practice.[13]

---

[13]For follow-up work along this path, see Laird, Rosenbloom, and Newell (1984).

ACKNOWLEDGMENTS

This research was sponsored by the Defense Advanced Research Projects Agency (DOD), ARPA Order No. 3597, monitored by the Air Force Avionics Laboratory under Contract F33615-78-C-1551. The views and conclusions contained in this document are those of the authors and should not be interpreted as representing the official policies, either expressed or implied, of the Defense Advanced Research Projects Agency or the U.S. Government.

The authors would like to thank John Laird for innumerable helpful discussions about this material.

References

Anderson, J. R., *Language, Memory, and Thought,* Erlbaum, Hillsdale, N.J., 1976.

——, Private communication, 1980.

——, Private communication, 1982a.

——, "Acquisition of Cognitive Skill," *Psychological Review,* Vol. 89, pp. 369–406, 1982b.

——, *The Architecture of Cognition,* Harvard University Press, Cambridge, 1983a.

——, "Knowledge Compilation: The General Learning Mechanism," *Proceedings of the Machine Learning Workshop,* R. S. Michalski (Ed.), Allerton House, University of Illinois at Urbana-Champaign, pp. 203–12, June 22–24, 1983b. (An updated version of this paper appears as chap. 11 of this volume.)

Anderson, J. R., Farrell, R., and Sauers, R., "Learning to Plan in LISP," Technical Report, Department of Psychology, Carnegie-Mellon University, 1982.

Bower, G. H., "Perceptual Groups as Coding Units in Immediate Memory," *Psychonomic Science,* Vol. 27, pp. 217–19, 1972.

Bower, G. H., and Springston, F., "Pauses as Recoding Points in Letter Series," *Journal of Experimental Psychology,* Vol. 83. pp. 421–30, 1970.

Bower, G. H., and Winzenz, D., "Group Structure, Coding, and Memory for Digit Series," *Journal of Experimental Psychology Monograph,* Vol. 80, Pt. 2, pp. 1–17, May 1969.

Card, S. K., English, W. K., and Burr, B., "Evaluation of Mouse, Rate Controlled Isometric Joystick, Step Keys, and Text Keys for Text Selection on a CRT," *Ergonomics,* Vol. 21, pp. 601–13, 1978.

Chase, W. G., and Ericsson, K. A., "Skilled Memory," in *Cognitive Skills and Their Acquisition,* J. R. Anderson (Ed.), Erlbaum, Hillsdale, N.J., 1981.

Chase, W. G. and Simon, H. A., "Perception in Chess," *Cognitive Psychology,* Vol. 4, pp. 55–81, 1973.

Crossman, E. R. F. W., "A Theory of the Acquisition of Speed-Skill," *Ergonomics,* Vol. 2, pp. 153–66, 1959.

DeGroot, A. D., *Thought and Choice in Chess,* Mouton, The Hague, 1965.

Duncan, J., "Response Selection Rules in Spatial Choice Reaction Tasks," *Attention and Performance VI,* Erlbaum, Hillsdale, N.J., 1977.

Ernst, G. W., and Newell, A., *GPS: A Case Study in Generality and Problem Solving,* ACM Monograph, Academic Press, New York, 1969.

Fikes, R. E., Hart, P. E., and Nilsson, N. J., "Learning and Executing Generalized Robot Plans," *Artificial Intelligence,* Vol. 3, pp. 251–88, 1972.

Fitts, P. M., and Seeger, C. M., "S-R Compatibility: Spatial Characteristics of Stimulus and Response Codes," *Journal of Experimental Psychology,* Vol. 46, pp. 199–210, 1953.

Forgy, C. L., "OPS5 User's Manual," Technical Report CMU-CS-81-135, Department of Computer Science, Carnegie-Mellon University, July 1981.

Johnson, N. F., "Organization and the Concept of a Memory Code," in *Coding Processes in Human Memory,* A. W. Melton and E. Martin (Eds.), Winston, Washington, D.C., 1972.

Kolers, P. A., "Memorial Consequences of Automatized Encoding," *Journal of Experimental Psychology: Human Learning and Memory,* Vol. 1, No. 6, pp. 689–701, 1975.

Korf, R. E., "Learning to Solve Problems by Searching for Macro-Operators," Ph.D. diss., Carnegie-Mellon University, 1983. (Available as Technical Report No. 83-138, Department of Computer Science, Carnegie-Mellon University, 1983.)

Laird, J. E., "Universal Subgoaling," Ph.D. diss., Carnegie-Mellon University, 1983.

Laird, J. E., and Newell, A., "A Universal Weak Method," Technical Report No. 83-141, Department of Computer Science, Carnegie-Mellon University, 1983.

Laird, J. E., Rosenbloom, P. S., and Newell, A., "Towards Chunking as a General Learning Mechanism," in *Proceedings of AAAI-84,* Austin, Tex., pp. 188–192, 1984.

Lewis, C. H., "Production System Models of Practice Effects," Ph.D. diss., University of Michigan, 1978.

Marsh, D., "Memo Functions, the Graph Traverser, and a Simple Control Situation," in *Machine Intelligence 5,* B. Meltzer and D. Michie (Eds.), American Elsevier, New York, 1970.

Michie, D., "'Memo' Functions and Machine Learning," *Nature,* Vol. 218, pp. 19–22, 1968.

Miller, G. A., "The Magic Number Seven Plus or Minus Two: Some Limits on Our Capacity for Processing Information," *Psychological Review,* Vol. 63, pp. 81–97, 1956.

Moran, T. P., "The Symbolic Imagery Hypothesis: An Empirical Investigation via a Production System Simulation of Human Behavior in a Visualization Task," Ph.D. diss., Carnegie-Mellon University, 1973.

———, "Compiling Cognitive Skill," AIP Memo No. 150, Xerox PARC, 1980.

Morin, R. E., and Forrin, B., "Mixing Two Types of S-R Association in a Choice Reaction Time Task," *Journal of Experimental Psychology,* Vol. 64, pp. 137–41, 1962.

Neisser, U., Novick, R., and Lazar, R., "Searching for Ten Targets Simultaneously," *Perceptual and Motor Skills,* Vol. 17, pp. 427–32, 1963.

Neves, D. M., and Anderson, J. R., "Knowledge Compilation: Mechanisms for the Automatization of Cognitive Skills," in *Cognitive Skills and Their Acquisition,* J. R. Anderson (Ed.), Erlbaum, Hillsdale, N.J., 1981.

Newell, A., "Heuristic Programming: Ill-Structured Problems," in *Progress in Operations Research,* Vol. 3, J. Aronofsky (Ed.), Wiley, New York, 1969.

———, "Production Systems: Models of Control Structures," in *Visual Information Processing,* W. G. Chase (Ed.), Academic Press, New York, 1973.

———, "Harpy, Production Systems and Human Cognition," in *Perception and Production of Fluent Speech,* R. Cole (Ed.), Erlbaum, Hillsdale, N.J., 1980a. (Also available as Technical Report No. CMU-CS-78-140, Department of Computer Science, Carnegie-Mellon University, 1978.)

———, "Reasoning, Problem Solving and Decision Processes: The Problem Space as a Fundamental Category," in *Attention and Performance VIII,* R. Nickerson (Ed.), Erlbaum, Hillsdale, N.J., 1980b. (Also available as Technical Report CMU CSD, Department of Computer Science, Carnegie-Mellon University, 1979.)

Newell, A. and Rosenbloom, P. S., "Mechanisms of Skill Acquisition and the Law of Practice," in *Cognitive Skills and Their Acquisition,* J. R. Anderson (Ed.), Erlbaum, Hillsdale, N.J., 1981.

Newell, A., and Simon, H. A., *Human Problem Solving,* Prentice-Hall, Englewood Cliffs, N.J., 1972.

Nilsson, N. J., *Problem-Solving Methods in Artificial Intelligence,* McGraw-Hill, New York, 1971.

Rosenbloom, P. S., "The Chunking of Goal Hierarchies: A Model of Practice and Stimulus-Response Compatibility," Ph.D. diss., Carnegie-Mellon University, 1983. (Available as Technical Report No. 83-148, Department of Computer Science, Carnegie-Mellon University, 1983.)

Rosenbloom, P. S., and Newell, A., "Learning by Chunking: A Production-System Model of Practice," Technical Report No. 82-135, Department of Computer Science, Carnegie-Mellon University, 1982a.

———, "Learning by Chunking: Summary of a Task and a Model," *Proceedings of AAAI-82,* Pittsburgh, Pa., pp. 255–257, 1982b.

Samuel, A. L., "Some Studies in Machine Learning Using the Game of Checkers," *IBM Journal of Research and Development,* Vol. 3, pp. 210–29, 1959.

———, "Some Studies in Machine Learning Using the Game of Checkers, II—Recent Progress," *IBM Journal of Research and Development,* Vol. 11, pp. 601–17, 1967.

Sauers, R., and Farrell, R., "GRAPES User's Manual," Technical Report, Department of Psychology, Carnegie-Mellon University, 1982.

Seibel, R., "Discrimination Reaction Time for a 1,023-Alternative Task," *Journal of Experimental Psychology,* Vol. 66, No. 3, pp. 215–26, 1963.

Snoddy, G. S., "Learning and Stability," *Journal of Applied Psychology,* Vol. 10, pp. 1–36, 1926.

Waterman, D. A., and Hayes-Roth, F. (Eds.), *Pattern-Directed Inference Systems,* Academic Press, New York, 1978.

Winston, P. H., "Learning Structural Descriptions from Examples," in *The Psychology of Computer Vision,* P. H. Winston (Ed.), McGraw-Hill, New York, 1975.

Woodworth, R. S., and Schlosberg, H., *Experimental Psychology,* rev. ed., Holt, Rinehart and Winston, New York, 1954.

11

KNOWLEDGE COMPILATION:

The General Learning Mechanism

John R. Anderson
Carnegie-Mellon University

Abstract

The ACT learning mechanisms of knowledge compilation, consisting of composition and proceduralization, are discussed. Composition operates by collapsing multiple productions into a single production that has the effect of the set. Proceduralization operates by building into productions information that previously had to be retrieved from long-term memory. It is shown how these two mechanisms can simulate the initial stages of skill acquisition in the domain of learning how to program. It is also shown that these mechanisms can reproduce the effects that have been attributed to inductive learning mechanisms involving generalization and discrimination. Generalizations and discriminations emerge as consequences of compiling the processes of analogy formation and error correction.

11.1 INTRODUCTION

One of the oldest intellectual issues is whether all forms of learning can be accounted for by associative learning—that is, learning by associating co-occurring elements (see Anderson and Bower, 1973, for a historical review). One consequence of our new technical age has been to refine this question practically out of existence. However, the issue has received a new embodiment in the world of machine learning in which there is a set of proposals about learning by induction and discovery. These learning mechanisms assume implicitly that it is not possible for adequate learning to be achieved by means of association by contiguity. Approximately half the papers at the 1983 Machine Learning Conference had this character.

The basic assumption is that any adequate learning system has to have as part of its basic architecture the ability to compare noncontiguous examples, look for commonalities and differences, formulate hypotheses, and act on these hypotheses. Two papers, however, seemed to be the intellectual heirs to the association-by-contiguity position; one was by Rosenbloom and Newell, and the other was by this author. The two proposals were quite different in detail but similar in spirit. The common spirit consisted of two assumptions about the basic architecture. The first was that behavior was controlled according to hierarchical goal structure—that the basic category of behavior was problem solving, not induction. In both papers the problem solving was encoded in a production system. The second assumption was that the only form of learning consisted of creating one-step operators that had the same effect as the multiple steps of information processing in the original problem solution. The goal structure is used in deciding which steps belong together and should be collapsed into a single operator.

The purpose of this chapter is to argue that these two architectural assumptions are adequate to account for inductive learning. This argument will be made within the context of the ACT* theory of learning (Anderson, 1983a). The ACT* theory includes both inductive learning mechanisms and operator-collapsing mechanisms. It will be shown here that operator collapsing can account for the phenomena that were attributed to the inductive mechanisms in ACT*. Of course, this leaves open the question of whether there are other inductive processes, not in ACT*, that are beyond the scope of operator collapsing. However, it will be left to others to show that such phenomena exist.

Knowledge compilation is the name given to the principles in ACT that govern operator collapsing (Anderson, 1982, 1983a; Anderson, Sauers, and Farrell, 1982; Neves and Anderson, 1981). These principles are concerned with how a new skill is acquired, such as generating a proof in geometry (Anderson, 1983b). In the general framework a learner is viewed as beginning with declarative information relevant to the execution of a skill. For instance, in the case of geometry, the student might learn about the properties of two-column proofs and various theorems and postulates. This information is stored in declarative form—that is, as facts about the domain. For this knowledge to be used, general *interpretive* procedures must be applied to it. Two types of interpretive procedures commonly observed in human subjects are general problem-solving procedures and general analogy procedures. Knowledge compilation operates on the traces of such procedures, creating more efficient procedures that are specific to the task domain.

This chapter will discuss knowledge compilation and give an example of its use to simulate the learning of initial programming skills. The rest of the chapter will be devoted to discussing how knowledge compilation can produce inductive processes of discrimination and generalization (Anderson, Kline, and Beasley, 1979; Hayes-Roth and McDermott, 1976; Langley, 1985; Michalski and Stepp, 1983; Mitchell, 1978; Vere, 1975). It will be argued further that there is evidence in the human case that knowledge compilation is the process that underlies generalization and discrimination.

11.2 INTRODUCTION TO KNOWLEDGE COMPILATION

Knowledge compilation mechanisms are defined with respect to a production system like ACT (Anderson, 1983a), which has a separate long-term declarative memory to represent facts and a production memory to represent procedures. The knowledge compilation mechanisms operate on the traces of production applications to create new productions. Before the details of a full example or of the implementation are presented, a brief overview will be given.

The knowledge compilation processes in ACT can be divided into two subprocesses. The first, called *composition,* takes a sequence of productions that follow each other in solving a particular problem and collapses them into a single production that has the same effect as the sequence. The idea of composition was first developed by Lewis (1978). Composition speeds up the processing by creating new productions that embody the sequence of steps used in a particular problem domain. The second process, *proceduralization,* builds versions of the productions that no longer require the domain-specific declarative information to be retrieved into working memory so the information can be matched by the general interpretive productions. Thus it creates new productions that collapse the formerly separate processes of information retrieval and production matching.

The basic processes of compilation can be illustrated with the task of dialing telephone numbers. It has been noted (Anderson, 1976) that one develops a special procedure for dialing a frequently dialed telephone number. Sometimes declarative access to the number is lost, and the only access one has to the number is through a procedure for dialing it.

Consider the following two productions that might serve to dial a telephone number:

P1   IF the goal is to dial ?telephone-number
                and ?digit is the first digit of ?telephone-number
        THEN dial ?digit.

P2   IF the goal is to dial ?telephone-number
                and ?digit1 has just been dialed
                and ?digit2 is after ?digit1 in ?telephone-number
        THEN dial ?digit2.

Composition creates "macroproductions" that perform the operation of a pair of productions that occurred in sequence. Applied to the sequence of P1 followed by P2, composition would create

P1&P2   IF the goal is to dial ?telephone-number
               and ?digit1 is the first digit of ?telephone-number
               and ?digit2 is after ?digit1 in ?telephone-number
           THEN dial ?digit1 and then ?digit2.

Compositions like this will reduce the number of production applications to perform the task.

A composed production like P1&P2 still requires that the information (in this case, the telephone number) be retrieved from long-term memory, held in working memory, and matched to the second and third clauses in P1&P2. Proceduralization eliminates clauses in the condition of a production that require information to be retrieved from long-term memory and held in working memory. In P1&P2, the second and third condition clauses would be eliminated. The variables that would have been bound in matching these clauses are replaced by the values to which they are bound in the special case. If this production is applied in dialing Mary's telephone number, which is 432-2815, the variables in P1&P2 would be bound as follows:

>   ?telephone-number → Mary's number
>   ?digit1 → 4
>   ?digit2 → 3

Substituting these values for the variables and eliminating the second and third condition clauses transform the production into

P1&P2*   IF the goal is to dial Mary's number
           THEN dial 4 and then 3.

By further composition and proceduralization, a production can be built that dials the full number:

P*   IF the goal is to dial Mary's number
           THEN dial 4-3-2-2-8-1-5.

It should be emphasized that forming this production does not necessarily imply the loss of the declarative representation nor of the ability to use it interpretively. In the few reported cases where people can dial a number but not report it, the declarative knowledge probably has ceased to be used and has simply been forgotten.

Elsewhere (Anderson, 1982, 1983a; Neves and Anderson, 1981) the evidence for knowledge compilation from the literature of experimental psychology has been discussed. The major issue to be explained here is how these mechanisms are implemented and used in relatively complex problem-solving domains. The author's work on this topic has been done in the context of the GRAPES simulation of the ACT theory (Sauers and Farrell, 1982). GRAPES is a system devoted to simulating ACT in the context of novice LISP programming. It simulates the problem solving and programming of novices writing LISP functions, as well as the way novices learn from their problem-solving episodes. A typical GRAPES simulation of a subject will be described here first, and then the mechanisms of knowledge compilation underlying that simulation will be examined.

11.3 A SIMULATION OF LISP PROGRAMMING

One of our consistent observations about novices is that they are not able to read instructions of even modest complexity and then generate the instructed behavior without error. This is not surprising given the ACT theory. According to that theory, instructions are initially stored in a declarative form, but behavior requires procedures that are represented as productions. Instructions cannot directly set up procedures to perform the skill. General interpretive productions must convert this knowledge into behavior. Many of the problems arise because of the indirection through these interpretive productions.

The problem-solving episode described here is one of the early ones simulated by the author. (For simulations of more complex programming, see Anderson, Sauers, and Farrell, 1982.) The difficulties experienced in this episode are typical of the difficulties people have in making the transition from instruction to experience. The subject, BR, had read the instruction on pages 33 to 37 of Winston and Horn (1981) on function definition, but she extracted virtually nothing from the text instruction. What she did extract was a template for how to write a function definition:

```
(DEFUN < function name >
  ( <parameter 1> <parameter 2>  . . .  <parameter n>)
  <process description>)
```

Winston and Horn assert that "angle brackets delineate descriptions of things." She also studied some examples of function definitions to which she referred. The most important of these converted Fahrenheit to Celsius:

```
(DEFUN F-TO-C (TEMP)
  (QUOTIENT (DIFFERENCE TEMP 32) 1.8))
```

BR's first problem was to define the function FIRST, which returns the first element of a list. She knew the function CAR and how to use it when interacting with the monitor in LISP. CAR returns the first element of the list that is its argument. She knew, for instance, that if she typed (CAR '(A B C)), the monitor would return the answer A. Thus this problem is really an exercise in using the syntax of function definition rather than one in defining a novel function.

BR's method of solving these problems relied heavily on trying to use the structure of the template and the examples to guide her function writing. This process is referred to as *structural analogy*. A production system was created in GRAPES that would simulate this protocol. The only productions required for this simulation were productions that could do structural analogy and productions that could use the LISP functions CAR and CDR at the top level. The first type of production represents a general ability that can be used in many contexts (for instance, in filling out income tax forms). The second type was acquired from work with earlier chapters in Winston and Horn.

Figure 11-1 illustrates the goal tree generated in simulating this example. Each box in figure 11-1 represents a goal, and each arrow emanating from a box represents a GRAPES production trying to achieve the goal. If the production generates subgoals, it is connected to goal boxes below. The simulation starts with the goal of writing the function and chooses to use the template for function definition as a guide. This is referred to as *mapping* the template. The first subgoals that GRAPES processed in figure 11-1 involved mapping DEFUN and < function name > in the template. Productions responding to these goals wrote out ''(DEFUN FIRST'' without difficulty.

Like our subject, GRAPES was not able to write out the parameter part of the function template directly because GRAPES did not know what a "parameter" was. In cases like this, GRAPES' analogy productions will resort to a concrete example. The concrete example retrieved by GRAPES is the definition of F-TO-C given earlier. GRAPES solved the analogy as follows: X is to F-TO-C as the parameter list—that is, (< parameter 1 > < parameter 2 > . . . < parameter n >)—is to the abstract template, and it retrieved (TEMP) as the value for X. Thus it decided (TEMP) was serving the parameter role in F-TO-C. Then it solved the analogy X is to FIRST as (TEMP) is to F-TO-C and came up with the answer (LIST1), which it put into the function definition; that is GRAPES decided (LIST1) served the comparable role in the function it was defining as (TEMP) was serving in F-TO-C.

Then GRAPES turned to the process definition. Being unable to interpret directly what is meant by < process description >, it looked to its concrete example F-TO-C and saw that LISP code filled this slot, which performed the function operations. In analogy, GRAPES set its goal to write code that would perform the operations required by FIRST. A production for using CAR at the top level applied next in GRAPES, but there is no production to specify how to write the argument to the function CAR in this context. GRAPES and the subject know that CAR will operate on LIST1, but they do not know the syntax for specifying the argument LIST1. GRAPES again turns to its concrete example F-TO-C. It solves the analogy (CAR ARG) is to (QUOTIENT X) and retrieves (DIFFERENCE TEMP 32), which is the first argument to QUOTIENT. It then solves the analogy problem of what it must do to LIST1 to make it like (DIFFERENCE TEMP 32) and decides it should embed LIST1 in parentheses. The subject made the same error. The function definition at this point as written by both subject and GRAPES is

```
(DEFUN FIRST (LIST1)
  (CAR (LIST)))
```

There are two things to note at this point. First, the subject has read information in the text that would have enabled her to know that she should not embed LIST1

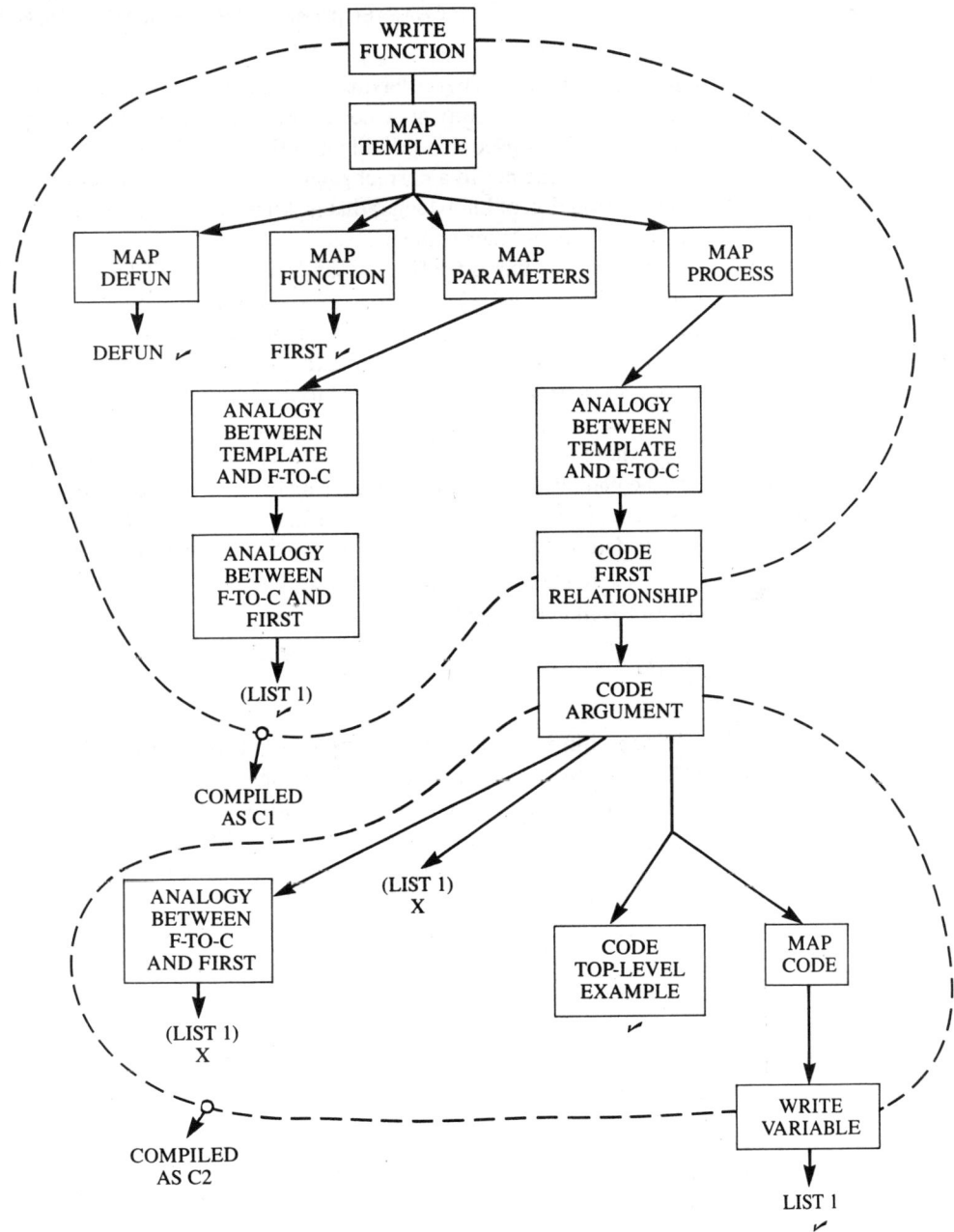

Figure 11-1: A representation of the goal structure in subject BR's solution to the problem of writing the function FIRST. The boxes represent goals, and the arrows indicate that a production has decomposed the goal above into the subgoals below. Checks indicated successful goals, and X's indicate failed goals. The dotted lines indicate parts of the goal tree combined in composition.

in parentheses, but this has no impact on her behavior. Second, on previous occasions she had correctly specified variable arguments when evaluating functions at the top level. Eventually, the experimenter used this second fact—that the subject could do it correctly at the top level—to guide her to a correct solution. Both of these observations illustrate the relative isolation of knowledge; that is, knowledge studied or used in one context is not available in another context.

When the subject tries her function definition, an error message is generated: ''LIST1: undefined function object.'' GRAPES received the same error message when it tried out the same function definition. The error occurred because LISP treats the first thing inside a parenthesized expression as a function. GRAPES associated this error with the failure to specify the argument to CAR correctly. On previous occasions BR had encountered the same error at the top level while typing in commands like (CAR (A)), where the argument to CAR is to be taken literally rather than evaluated. In the past she had always repaired these errors by *quoting* the argument; that is the argument is preceded by a single quotation mark: (CAR'(A)). It is assumed that both the subject and GRAPES have compiled from previous experience a rule and that the way to repress this error is by quoting the argument, which stops LISP from evaluating. The function definition at this point is

```
(DEFUN FIRST (LIST1)
  (CAR '(LIST)))
```

When this new function is tried on an example, LISP returns the CAR of '(LIST1), which is LIST1, rather than the first element of the value of LIST1. This is the point at which the experimenter intervened and reminded the subject of how she would solve the problem at the top level. If the subject were writing code at the top level she would have used (CAR LIST1) rather than (CAR (LIST1)) or (CAR '(LIST1)). This intervention was simulated in GRAPES by refocusing it on the code-argument goal in figure 11-1 and putting (CAR LIST1) as a top-level example in working memory. Then GRAPES and the subject both mapped this code to its current function definition and came up with the correct code.

11.3.1 Knowledge Compilation

After finally solving this problem, the knowledge compilation mechanism formed two productions that aided its solution of the second problem. These productions summarized much of the problem solving that took place:

C1   IF the goal is to write ?function defined on ?variable
          THEN write (DEFUN ?function (?variable)
                and set as a subgoal to code ?relation calculated by ?function
                and then write).

C2   IF the goal is to code ?argument
              and ?argument corresponds to ?variable of ?function
            THEN write ?variable.

The portions of the goal tree that are summarized by each of these productions are encircled in figure 11-1. The first production captures the top-level syntax of a function, and the second summarizes the search involved in discovering how to specify an argument to a function. With these productions, GRAPES was able to write a second function much more easily, as was the subject. This function, called SECOND, was to return the second element of a list.

11.3.2 Conclusions

There are a number of conclusions to be drawn from BR's protocol and the GRAPES simulation. The first concerns the importance of structural analogy in bridging the gap between current knowledge and the needed behavior. There are two sources for the structure from which the analogy is made. One is templates and worked-out problems provided in the text. The other is structures that the subject can generate; for instance, the subject generated (CAR LIST1) as a top-level solution and then used this in her function definition.

A second conclusion is that a problem-solving episode is organized as a hierarchical goal structure in which the goals are expanded in a depth-first and left-to-right fashion. Jeffries et al. (1981) note this hierarchical structure in the programming behavior of experts, although their subjects use breadth-first expansion in contrast to the depth-first expansion used by these novice subjects.

The third conclusion concerns the importance of knowledge compilation in extracting new production rules from an example problem. These rules streamline the solution of later problems. As the protocol shows, the learning can be accomplished on the basis of a single example. It should be stressed that the lessons of this example "stuck"; that is, BR on later days did not have the same difficulty with the basic syntax of function definition or with argument specification. It should also be stressed that compilation depends critically on the structure of goal trees; that is, the structure of the goal tree identifies what parts of the problem-solving episode belong together and what can be collapsed into a single rule.

In these three features—structural analogy, hierarchical goal trees, and knowledge compilation—we have one complete solution to the issue of how the learner is able to make the transition to a new cognitive behavior. The important question is whether there is anything in this transition that might be called induction. In the opinion of the author, there is not. The process of analogy formation is purely a problem-solving effort to make the structure of the current solution similar to the structure of the old solutions. Knowledge compilation just puts steps that had occurred in the original problem into single operators. The system does not try to form any generalization—and, indeed, how could it, working from a single example?

Still, the result is a pair of general operators for writing LISP functions. This almost has the flavor of "black magic." In later sections this black magic will be explained.

11.4 FURTHER DISCUSSION OF COMPILATION

Before a discussion of how generalizations occur is presented, some further examples of proceduralization and composition will be considered.

11.4.1 Proceduralization

Proceduralization can be illustrated in its pure form by the following example. In GRAPES there is a production that will retrieve function definitions from long-term memory and apply them as follows:

> IF the goal is to code ?relation on ?argument
> and there is ?function that codes ?relation
> THEN use ?function with ?argument
> and set as a subgoal to code ?argument.

In this production, ?relation, ?function, and ?argument are variables that allow the production to match different data. The second line of the condition might match, for instance, ''CAR codes the first member of a list'' with ?function bound to CAR and ?relation bound to first member. If this rule is proceduralized to eliminate the retrieval of the CAR definition, it becomes

> C3 IF the goal is to code the first member of ?argument
> THEN use CAR of ?argument
> and set as a subgoal to code ?argument.

This is achieved by deleting the second clause in the first production, which required memory retrieval, and making the rest of the production specific to the relation *first element* and the function CAR. Now a production has been created that can directly recognize the application of CAR. The amount of information that has to be maintained in working memory is thus reduced.

11.4.2 Composition

As an example of pure composition, let us suppose we wanted to add the first member of LIST1 to LIST2. Then the following two operators would apply in sequence:

> IF the goal is to add ?element to ?list
> THEN CONS ?element to ?list
> and set as subgoals to code ?element
> and to code ?list.
> IF the goal is code the first member of ?argument

THEN use CAR of ?argument
and set as a subgoal to code ?argument.

The first rule above would apply binding ?element to "the first member of LIST1" and ?list to "LIST2." The second production would apply binding ?argument to "LIST1." A simple case of composition would involve combining these two productions together to produce

C4   IF the goal is to add the first member of ?argument to ?list
      THEN CONS the CAR of ?argument to the ?list
           and set as subgoals to code ?argument
           and to code ?list.

Such compositions collapse repeated sequences of coding operations to create macro-operators. The result is a speedup in coding. A major issue concerns deciding which productions to compose together. The above example is a fairly simple case of collapsing two levels of a goal tree into one. However, in some cases, such as that presented in figure 11-1, many productions can be collapsed. GRAPES determines which productions to collapse by inspecting the goal tree. Composition distinguishes between two types of goals: *inherent goals* and *planning goals*. Inherent goals are intrinsic parts of the programming task. For current purposes, inherent goals are all variants of writing code. The important feature of inherent goals is that in achieving them one achieves part of the original task. Planning goals produce results that are used to guide the solution of the original problem, but the results themselves are not part of the original problem. In figure 11-1 the inherent goals are "code the function," "code the relationship," "code the argument," and "write the variable"; all the rest are planning goals.

Composition collapses productions in one of two ways. One is by eliminating the planning goals that are intermediate between two inherent goals. This is what happened when production C1, given earlier, was formed for figure 11-1. Composition formed a rule that went from the goal of "code the function" to the goal of "code the relationship." In doing this, it compiled out the planning process and simply left in the products of that planning. The same process underlies the formation of C2 from the goal tree in figure 11-1.

The second way composition collapses productions is illustrated in the case of C4. Here composition starts with the goal of adding the first element of one list to another, skips over the intermediate goal of coding the first element of the list, and sets the goals of coding the two lists. In doing this it is basically creating macro-operators similar to those in STRIPS (Fikes and Nilsson, 1971). This learning scheme requires that the learner be able to identify which subgoals are essential to the problem solutions and which are only intermediate to the final solution.

It needs to be emphasized that neither proceduralization nor composition eliminates the original production rules from which they were built. Rather, the new compiled rules just serve as supplemental rules that produce better performance in certain circumstances.

The effect of the knowledge compilation process is to create a set of productions that mirror the structure of LISP. They may explicitly involve LISP functions like CAR or COND or LISP programming techniques like tail-recursion. These productions will preserve the inherent goals that are specific to LISP and delete the planning goals involved in domain-general processes like structural analogy. Thus representative productions become the following (see Anderson, Sauers, and Farrell, 1982):

C5   IF the goal is to code the second member of ?list
      THEN use CADR and set a subgoal
                  to code ?list.

C6   IF the goal is to obtain all the elements which have
                  ?relation to any member of ?list
      THEN use MAPCONC and set as subgoals
                  1. To code ?function that will return all the elements that have
                  ?relation to ?argument.
                  2. To code ?list.

11.5 GENERALIZATION

Generalization is a mechanism for learning new productions in ACT*. It is the learning mechanism in ACT* that is most transparently inductive. As it is typically formulated (see, e.g., Anderson, Kline, and Beasley, 1980), it takes a pair of productions and generates what is called the *maximal common generalization*. This is the most specific production that will apply everywhere that the original productions would and that will have the same effect as the original productions. For a simple example, consider the following pair of productions:

S1   IF Fred is rich
                  and Fred is ugly
                  and Fred is smart
                  and Fred is of medium height
      THEN Fred is in club 1.

S2   IF Gail is rich
                  and Gail is ugly
                  and Gail is stupid
                  and Gail is of medium height
      THEN Gail is in club 1.

The following production would be formed as the generalization of the two:

G1   IF   ?person is rich
                  and ?person is ugly

and ?person is of medium height
THEN   ?person is in club 1

where ?person is a variable. The pair of productions can be viewed as specific observations and G1 as a generalization formed from these observations. Note that G1 is formed both by deleting condition clauses and by replacing constants by variables. These are the two transformations that occur when one moves to generalizations.

The interesting observation is that compilation results in clause deletion and replacement of constants with variables. Compilation deletes clauses associated with omitted goals and with planning. Variables from planning productions can remain in the compiled productions. This is how the effect of generalization is obtained through compilation.

Specifically, it appears that generalizations can be formed through the process of compiling analogies. The basic framework is as follows: The system has instances committed to memory as declarative facts. When a new instance is encountered, the system compares it to a memorized instance and uses the structure of the memorized instance to guide response. Compiling this compare-and-respond behavior produces a production that is a generalization from the two instances. This is basically what happened in the case of forming C1 and C2 from figure 11-1. A simpler example will be presented here to make this process more transparent. Then psychological evidence will be introduced indicating that this is the correct conception of generalization in humans.

Consider a very simple production set that will classify new instances according to their similarity to studied instances:

P1   IF the goal is to classify ?object
             and ?reference has been studied
          THEN initialize the measure of overlap.
             and set as subgoals to compare ?object to ?reference
             and to determine if ?object is in the same category as ?reference.
P2   IF the goal is to compare ?object to ?reference
             and ?object has ?feature
             and ?reference has ?feature
          THEN increment the measure of overlap.
P3   IF the goal is to compare ?object to ?reference
             and there are no more matching features
          THEN POP the goal.
P4   IF the goal is to determine if ?object is in the same category as
             ?reference
             and the measure of overlap is above threshold
             and ?reference is in ?category
          THEN ?object is in ?category.

P5   IF the goal is to determine if ?object is in the same category as
                ?reference
            and the measure of overlap is below threshold
        THEN POP failure.

This production set will keep comparing the object to be classified to candidate references from memory until a high-similarity reference is found. Then it will place the
object in the same category as the high-similarity reference.

Suppose the system has committed to memory that Fred is in category 1 and
that he is rich, ugly, smart, and of medium height. Then the system is asked to categorize Gail, who is rich, ugly, stupid, and of medium height. Figure 11-2 illustrates the
goal tree generated by GRAPES in applying this production set to the classification
problem. It found matches on three features and a mismatch on one, which, it will be
assumed, was sufficient to exceed threshold. The compilation process regarded all
the similarity comparisons as planning goals and compiled all of this out, forming
the following single production:

            IF the goal is to classify ?object
            and ?object is rich

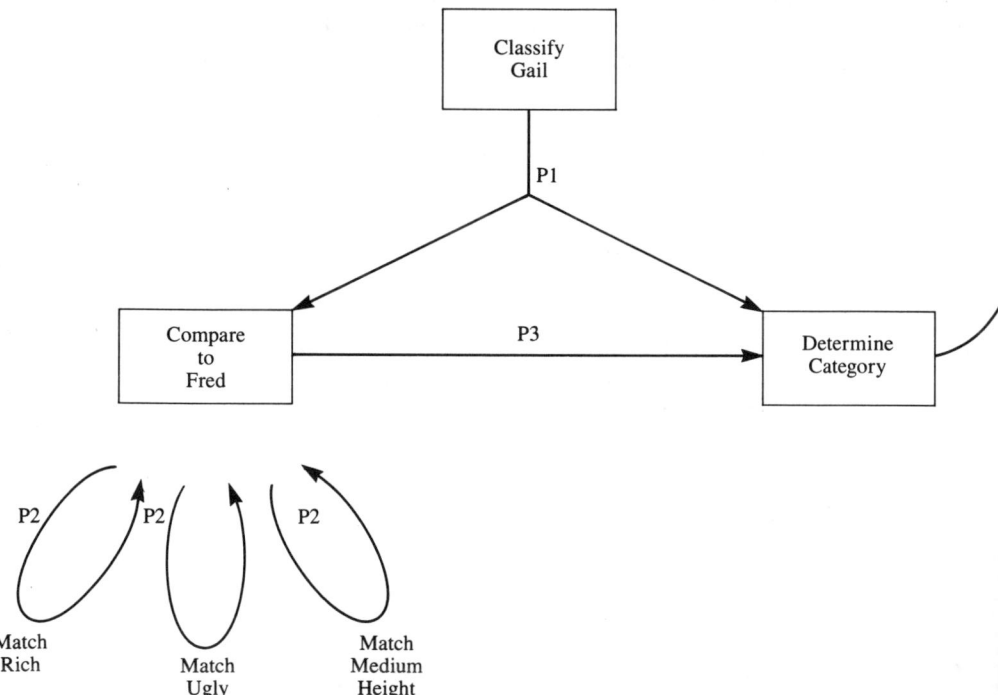

Figure 11-2: A representation of flow of control in the classification of Gail by analogy to Fred.

and ?object is ugly
and ?object is of medium height
THEN   ?object is in club 1.

This production is essentially identical to the generalization G1 given earlier. Thus compiling the process of making an analogy will result in generalization.

There are a number of features that distinguish this path to generalization from a standard induction paradigm such as the ACT* generalization mechanism. First, it is based on a single example. Second, being the result of conscious problem solving, it is more flexible. If the system thought certain features (such as appearance) should be discounted in analogy formation, this could be accommodated and a different analogy would appear. If the system thought that what was important was number of extremely positive features (e.g., rich, smart), again this could be accommodated and a different generalization would appear.

What has been described is a procedure for producing the same effect as generalization. What reason is there to believe that this procedure is the process underlying generalization rather than the more direct generalization mechanism? First, it is more plausible within the ACT production system framework. To produce a generalization in ACT it is necessary to start out with very specific productions like S1 and S2 given earlier. This is because the generalization mechanism only works on productions. These highly specific productions are patently nonintuitive, and moreover the ACT theory would claim it is not possible to form such productions directly. Thus an ACT theory that produces generalization through compilation is more plausible than one that uses the direct generalization mechanism.

Second, independent of the ACT framework, the evidence is against an automatic generalization mechanism that has no strategic component. Both Elio and Anderson (1984) and Kline (1983) have shown that the generalizations learners emerge with depend on both their problem-solving set and the order of the examples. Thus it does not seem that humans extract always and only the maximal common generalizations. The generalizations they do extract are determined by what they are looking for. This is better modeled by a system like the preceding one that leaves similarity detection at the strategic level.

Third, notice that the system can classify on the basis of a single studied instance. A generalization scheme requires at least two instances to form a generalization before novel instances can be classified. Elio and Anderson (1981) showed that subjects can classify novel instances on the basis of similarity to a single studied instance when there is no possibility of generalization. This is consistent with the current conception. In addition, Elio and Anderson showed that subjects could better classify a novel instance when there was a relevant generalization that could be formed from two studied instances—even when overall similarity of studied instances to novel instances was kept constant. This shows that generalizations also are made and that all classification is not a matter of analogy. Again the evidence is consistent with the current scheme.

Furthermore, experiments have been done in which subjects can classify novel instances after studying instances while unaware of their classification structure (Brooks, 1978). For instance, subjects learn to associate animals and cities to stimuli in a simple paired-associate experiment. After doing the paired-associate task, they are told that all the stimuli associated to new-world animals and cities form one category and all stimuli associated to old-world responses form another category. Subjects were unaware of the old-world/new-world dimension during study. They can now reliably classify new instances as old- or new-world stimuli. Since subjects were not aware of the classification structure at study there was no opportunity to form generalizations. The classification must be on the basis of comparing specific studied stimuli to specific test stimuli.

Carbonell provides an elaborate discussion of how analogy might be used to guide problem solving that goes beyond the discussion here (1983). He also speculates on how generalizations might emerge from the analogy process. He proposes that the learner would store analogical solutions and generalize from these in just the way one typically generalizes from example. This discussion shows that generalizations can emerge as a by-product of the analogy process without a separate generalization phase.

11.6 DISCRIMINATION

Less work has been done on discrimination in the knowledge acquisition literature, and there is less consensus about how discrimination is done. However, the general situation calling for discrimination is one in which there is an overly general rule and thus a need to restrict its range. It is doubtful that there is a single way to form discriminations, and this probably accounts for the lack of consensus in the literature. Certainly there is not a uniform discrimination process in humans. However, for purposes of discussion a kind of discrimination called *action discrimination* in the ACT theory (Anderson, 1982, 1983a) will be presented here. Again for clarity it will be illustrated with simple classifications, but Anderson (1982) can be consulted for more complex applications.

Suppose we have the following general production:

```
G2        IF   ?person is rich
               ?person is of medium height
        THEN   ?person is in club 1.
```

Suppose this rule is applied to David, who is smart, good-looking, rich, and of medium height. It would classify David as being in club 1. However, suppose it is subsequently learned that David is in club 2. Thus an error has been made, and the system sets out to form a discrimination that will correct this error.

In forming a discrimination the system looks for some past instance to which the rule correctly applied. Suppose in this case Fred, who is smart, ugly, rich, and of medium height, is retrieved as someone correctly classified by the rule. The discrimination mechanism looks for some feature that was true of the successful instance but not true of the unsuccessful instance. In this case, the only difference is that David is good-looking and Fred is ugly. Therefore, a new production is formed that has this added feature:

D1   IF   ?person is rich
                 and ?person is of medium height
                 and ?person is good-looking
            THEN ?person is in club 2.

This is called an action discrimination because it has a different action from the production (G2) from which it was formed. D1 does not replace G2, but because of the specificity ordering of productions in ACT, D1 will take precedence over G2 whenever both match. G2 will only apply when the person is not good-looking. Note that in forming an action discrimination the system both adds to the condition of a production and changes the action.

The interesting thing to note is that compilation can have the effect of adding to the condition of a production and changing the action. When we compose two productions, P1 followed by P2, we can add to the conditions of P1 some of the conditions of P2, and we can change the action of P1 to the action of P2. Thus it appears that we might be able to get the effect of discrimination through compilation.

The basic scheme for getting discrimination through compilation is to have the system consciously and deliberately go through the steps involved in forming a discrimination. Discrimination is done by problem-solving productions rather than as an automatic process above the production system. Thus a sequence of productions will compute a discrimination. Compiling that sequence will result in a discriminate production. As will be seen, doing this is not as straightforward technically as the generalization case. This is because it would be necessary to inspect the contents of productions to mimic perfectly the automatic discrimination process, whereas this is not necessary in order to mimic generalization. In the ACT theory one production cannot inspect the contents of another. Still, we can get nearly the effect of automatic discrimination in a fairly plausible way.

As noted earlier, there are multiple ways of forming discriminations. This section will focus on the action discrimination as just sketched out. However, this general scheme will probably extend to other types of discrimination. In this scheme the productions compute the discrimination and then compile that computation. After the compilation of an action discrimination is illustrated, the evidence that this view of discrimination is psychologically correct will be considered.

This example will be developed within the framework of productions P1–P6 given earlier for classifying objects by analogy. The learning situation here is one in which the learner makes a classification of an object, receives feedback, and if the classification is incorrect tries to find a discriminating feature. Assume the learner has compiled the following too-general production:

G2*   IF the goal is to classify ?object
             and ?object is rich
             and ?object is of medium height
        THEN ?object is in club 1.

This is a variant of G2 given earlier but now set up for the current framework. As earlier, assume it misapplies to classify David, who is smart, good-looking, rich, and of medium height, as being in club 1. An error is detected, and a goal is set to reclassify David.

The following three productions are relevant to the correction of a misclassification:

P7   IF the goal is to classify ?object
             and ?object is in ?category1
             but ?object was classified as in ?category2
             and ?reference is in ?category2
        THEN remove the classification of ?object
             and set as subgoals to find a difference between ?object and
              ?reference
             and then to reclassify ?object
             and then to correct the classification of ?object.
P8   IF the goal is to find a difference between ?object and ?reference
             and ?object is in ?category1
             and ?object has ?feature1 on ?dimension
             and ?reference has ?feature2 on ?dimension
             and ?feature1 is different from ?feature2
        THEN conclude ?object is in ?category1 because of ?feature1.
P9   IF the goal is to correct the classification of ?object
             and ?object has been classified as in ?category2
             but ?object is in ?category1 because of ?feature1
        THEN change the classified category of ?object to ?category1.

Production P7 will apply to correct the situation. It selects some instance that was in the incorrect category. Suppose again it selects Fred, who is rich, ugly, smart, and of medium height. This is an instance the overgeneral production G2* would have correctly classified. There is no guarantee that the instance selected by P7 will be one that fits the overgeneral production, because P7 cannot inspect G2*. However, the spreading activation retrieval mechanisms in ACT (see Anderson, 1983a) would tend to select an instance that overlaps highly with the current instance and hence the rule that classified the current instance. P7 sets goals to find a difference between David and Fred and then to reclassify David.

Production P8 will note that David is good-looking and Fred is ugly and so enter into memory the fact that "David is in club 1 because he is good-looking." Then the system will return to the goal of classifying David once again. Again G2* would apply to misclassify David as being in club 1, but now production P9 can apply to correct the classification of David. P7 followed by P8 followed by G2* followed by P9 constitutes a goal tree that can be composed together and proceduralized. The result will be the following production:

D1*   IF the goal is to classify ?object
             and ?object is rich
             and ?object is of medium height
             and ?object is good-looking
       THEN   ?object is in club 2.

This is essentially the same as D1 formed earlier by the automatic discrimination mechanism.

There are two essential features that distinguish this means to discrimination from the automatic discrimination of the current ACT theory. First, it requires that the learner initially make a classification of the object and then correct that classification if it is in error. Second, it requires that the learner make a conscious hypothesis about what distinguishes the current instance from prior instances that were in the hypothesized category. Both of these features have been confirmed in two series of experiments by Lewis and Anderson (1985). One series of experiments involved rules for proving triangles congruent in geometry, and the other series involved rules for traveling through a maze. In both series subjects were given overgeneral rules that had to be discriminated. Subjects who passively studied instances failed to learn the discriminating features. Subjects learned only when they made active hypotheses about the correct rule, which could then be disconfirmed. Furthermore, the only subjects to learn were those who had some conscious awareness of what the discriminating features were. Thus subjects discriminated only when both conditions of the current scheme of discriminating through compilation were satisfied.

The example illustrated above is somewhat unrealistic since it assumes the learner both finds the discriminating feature and uses it to reclassify the item. However, this is what is required if a discriminated production is to be formed on the same trial as the discriminating feature is identified. It seems more reasonable to assume that this is stretched out over multiple trials—on one trial the learner forms a declarative proposition about the importance of a discriminating feature like "good-looking," and on another trial the learner acts on this information. The discriminating production would be acquired on the later trial when the learner acted. There is no guarantee in this situation that the production learned would be identical to what is formally defined as an action discrimination in ACT*, but the learning would be in the general direction of discrimination.

11.7 GENERAL CONCLUSIONS

There is ample evidence for the existence of something close to knowledge compilation as a basic process of human learning (Anderson, 1982; Anderson, Farrell, and Sauers, 1983; Neves and Anderson, 1981). The evidence had always been rather scarce for the details of the ACT mechanisms of generalization and discrimination, and more recently some rather negative evidence has been gathered. Clearly, humans can approach the task of extending experience as typical problem solving. Generalized or discriminated productions appear as the product of compiling this problem solving.

It is something of an embarrassment that the author worked so long with the ACT mechanisms before realizing how the knowledge compilation mechanisms could be recruited to provide the effect of generalization and discrimination. This is because he thought of knowledge compilation as simply making existing paths of processing more efficient rather than enabling novel paths of processing. To get novel behavior it seemed that inductive mechanisms of learning such as generalization and discrimination were needed. What was not recognized was that if the results of acting on the basis of similarity detection and difference detection were compiled, productions could be produced that enabled novel behavior.

The fundamental point then is that the induction process occurs as a conscious problem-solving effort to find a basis for dealing with a new case. In compiling the results of this problem solution, productions are formed that will extend to the new situation. The fundamental category of behavior is problem solving, not induction. This theory is one of learning not by temporal contiguity but by contiguity in the problem-solving goal structure. There is no such thing as unconscious induction of features. Recently, Dulany, Carlson, and Dewey (1984) have demonstrated that in situations in which subjects are supposedly engaged in unconscious induction they can be shown to have conscious inductive hypotheses on which they are acting.

References

Anderson, J. R. *Language, Memory, and Thought*, Erlbaum, Hillsdale, N.J., 1976.

———, "Acquisition of Cognitive Skill," *Psychological Review*, Vol. 89, pp. 369–406, 1982.

———, *The Architecture of Cognition*, Harvard University Press, Cambridge, 1983a.

———, "Acquisition of Proof Skills in Geometry," in *Machine Learning: An Artificial Intelligence Approach*, R. S. Michalski, J. G. Carbonell, and T. M. Mitchell (Eds.), Tioga, Palo Alto, Calif., 1983b.

Anderson, J. R., and Bower, G. H., *Human Associative Memory*, Winston, Washington, D.C., 1973.

Anderson, J. R., Kline, P. J., and Beasley, C. M., "A General Learning Theory and Its Application to Schema Abstraction," in *The Psychology of Learning and Motivation,* Vol. 13, G. H. Bower (Ed.), Academic Press, New York, 1979.

———, "Complex Learning Processes," in *Aptitude, Learning, and Instruction,* Vol. 2, R. E. Snow, P. A. Frederico, and W. E. Montague (Eds.), Erlbaum, Hillsdale, N.J., 1980.

Anderson, J. R., Sauers, R., and Farrell, R., "Learning to Plan in LISP," Technical Report ONR82-1, Carnegie-Mellon University, 1982.

Brooks, L. "Nonanalytic Concept Formation and Memory for Instances," in *Cognition and Categorization,* E. Rosch and B. B. Lloyd (Eds.), Erlbaum, Hillsdale, N.J., 1978.

Carbonell, J. G., "Learning from Analogy: Formulating and Generalizing Plans from Past Experience," in *Machine Learning: An Artificial Intelligence Approach,* R. S. Michalski, J. G. Carbonell, and T. M. Mitchell (Eds.), Tioga, Palo Alto, Calif., 1983.

Dulany, D. E., Carlson, R. A., and Dewey, G. I., "A Case of Syntactic Learning and Judgment: How Conscious and How Abstract?" *Journal of Experimental Psychology: General,* Vol. 113, pp. 54–55, 1984.

Elio, R., and Anderson, J. R., "The Effects of Category Generalization and Instance Similarity on Schema Abstraction," *Journal of Experimental Psychology: Human Learning and Memory,* Vol. 7, pp. 397–417, 1981.

———, "The Effects of Information Order and Learning Mode on Schema Abstraction," *Memory and Cognition,* Vol. 12, pp. 20–30, 1984.

Fikes, R. E., and Nilsson, N. J., "STRIPS: A New Approach to the Application of Theorem Proving to Problem Solving," *Artificial Intelligence,* Vol. 2, pp. 189–208, 1971.

Hayes-Roth, F., and McDermott, J., "Learning Structured Patterns from Examples," *Proceedings of the Third International Joint Conference on Pattern Recognition,* Coronado, Calif., pp. 419–23, 1976.

Jeffries, R.; Turner, A. A.; Polson, P. G.; and Atwood, M. E., "The Processes Involved in Designing Software," in *Cognitive Skills and Their Acquisition,* J. R. Anderson (Ed.), Erlbaum, Hillsdale, N.J., 1981.

Kline, P. J., "Computing the Similarity of Structured Objects by Means of a Heuristic Search for Correspondence," Ph.D. diss., University of Michigan, 1983.

Langley, P., "A General Theory of Discrimination Learning," in *Self-modifying Production System Models of Learning and Development,* D. Klahr, P. Langley, and R. T. Neches (Eds.), Bradford Books, Cambridge, Mass., 1985, in press.

Lewis, C. H., "Production System Models of Practice Effects," Ph.D. diss., University of Michigan, 1978.

Lewis, M., and Anderson, J. R., "The Role of Feedback in Discriminating Problem-solving Operators," *Cognitive Psychology,* 1985, in press.

Michalski, R. S., and Stepp, R. E., "Learning from Observation: Conceptual Clustering," in *Machine Learning: An Artificial Intelligence Approach,* R. S. Michalski, J. G. Carbonell, and T. M. Mitchell (Eds.), Tioga, Palo Alto, Calif., 1983.

Mitchell, T. M., "Version Spaces: An Approach to Concept Learning," Ph.D. diss., Stanford University, 1978.

Neves, D. M., and Anderson, J. R., "Knowledge Compilation: Mechanisms for the Automatization of Cognitive Skills," in *Cognitive Skills and Their Acquisition,* J. R. Anderson (Ed.), Erlbaum, Hillsdale, N.J., 1981.

Sauers, R., and Farrell, R. "GRAPES User's Manual," Technical Report ONR-82-3, Carnegie-Mellon University, 1982.

Vere, S. A., "Induction of Concepts in the Predicate Calculus," *Proceedings of the Fourth IJCAI,* Tbilisi, Georgia, USSR, pp. 281–87, 1975.

Winston, P. H., and Horn, B. K. P., *LISP,* Addison-Wesley, Reading, Mass., 1981.

12

LEARNING PHYSICAL DOMAINS:

Toward a Theoretical Framework

Kenneth D. Forbus
Dedre Gentner
University of Illinois
at Urbana-Champaign

Abstract

This chapter presents a theoretical framework that is being developed in an attempt to construct a computational account of human learning of physical domains. Qualitative Process theory is used to model portions of people's physical knowledge, and Structural Mapping theory is used to characterize the computations that move a learner from one representation to another. The chapter outlines the component theories and proposes a learning sequence for physical domains.

12.1 INTRODUCTION

People use and extend their knowledge of the physical world constantly. Understanding how this fluency is achieved would be an important milestone in understanding human learning and intelligence, as well as a useful guide for constructing machines that learn. The authors' purpose is to construct a computational account of human experiential learning in physical domains.

This work is still at the stage where questions are being refined rather than answers provided. In many cases, there is no direct evidence for the claims made here. In other instances, support for the theory is obtained by combining evidence from several different areas, including developmental psychology, studies of learning, and other psychological research. No one of these is adequate by itself. When extrapolating from adult learning research, we must keep in mind that cases of pure experiential learning are rare in adult life; some sort of instruction or prior expectation is typically involved. Developmental research provides a good source of data, since much of young children's learning is truly from direct experience. Yet when developmental results are applied, it must be remembered that children are not only learning but also maturing. Therefore, in order to isolate and study experiential learning, the existing empirical findings must be examined, filtered, and carefully fitted together. Although space does not permit detailing all the relevant lines of evidence, the authors will try to give the reader some justification for our claims whenever possible.

As this volume attests, the past few years have seen significant progress in machine learning. However, to construct programs that learn as well as (or better than) people do, it is important to understand how human learning works. Ultimately both psychological studies and direct computational experiments (i.e., constructing programs) will be necessary to provide a full account. To this end, the authors will try when possible to indicate how techniques developed in machine learning might be used to implement such programs.

12.1.1 Overview

A brief prologue may help to organize the material. Three key ideas underlie the theory: (1) the centrality of *physical processes* in mental models of science; (2) the importance of analogy in learning; and (3) the primacy of rich, contextually specific representations. The idea that the notion of process is central to human knowledge about physical domains is the chief tenent of Qualitative Process (QP) theory (Forbus, 1981, 1984). This is not to say that notions of process are there from the beginning. Rather, it is hypothesized that a person's experiential knowledge of a domain begins as a collection of scenarios that describe particular phenomena, out of which is developed a vocabulary of processes that provides a notion of mechanism for the domain. The second key idea concerns the role of comparisons among related knowledge structures. The authors conjecture that much of experiential learning proceeds through spontaneous comparisons—which may be implicit or explicit— between a current scenario and prior similar or analogous scenarios that the learner has stored in memory. Structure Mapping theory (see Gentner, 1980, 1983) describes these kinds of comparisons.

The third idea is a rather paradoxical claim: in human processing, more is often easier.[1] Rich, perceptually based representations are acquired earlier in learning than

---

[1] It should be noted that psychologists by no means generally agree with this claim. Consequently, the authors tried to be fairly explicit in presenting evidence for this position.

sparse abstract representations. That is, early domain representations differ from more advanced representations of the same domain in containing more information, especially perceptual information specific to the initial context of use. A second aspect of the "more is easier" claim concerns comparisons: it is suggested that, for humans, similarity comparisons are easier when there is more overlap between the two knowledge structures being compared.

On the basis of these three ideas, the authors propose a canonical learning sequence. The claim is that human learning of physical domains can be viewed as a sequence of different mental models: (1) *protohistories,* (2) the *causal corpus,* (3) *naive physics,* and (4) *expert models.* Briefly, protohistories are rich, contextually specific, highly perceptual representations of phenomena, capturing expectations about typical phenomenological patterns—for example, "If I turn the key, the car will start." With the causal corpus, the expectations of mechanism enters; here the representation consists of simple statements that some sort of causal connection exists between variables—"If the car has no gas, it will not start." In the naive physics stage, processes are introduced to provide the mechanism underlying the causal corpus— "Gas must flow from the tank to the carburetor and mix with air so that the mixture can be ignited by the spark." The disparate local connections of the causal corpus are replaced with qualitative models organized around the notion of process. Finally, in the expert models stage, quantitative representations are created—for example, models of the effects of different mixtures of oxygen and gasoline.

In this chapter the authors discuss their conjectures about these models and about how a learner constructs one type of model from another. First, however, the component theories that underlie this framework are briefly summarized: Qualitative Process theory, which provides concepts needed to represent the models (particularly in the naive physics stage), and Structure Mapping theory, which characterizes the kinds of computations that move the learner from one representation to another. Then the overall role of structure-mapping comparisons is examined in the progression from rich to sparse representations. With these foundations in place, the four stages of learning for physical domains are then described.

12.2 QUALITATIVE PROCESS THEORY

The first requirement of this work is a language in which to describe people's commonsense knowledge about physical situations. People know about a great many kinds of physical changes: things move, collide, bend, break, heat up, cool down, flow, and boil. Intuitively we think of these as *processes.* Qualitative Process theory attempts to formalize this notion of process to provide a common form for qualitative theories of dynamics. As will become clear later on, the authors do not believe that the first models people construct of a domain take the form of process, nor even that they become knowledgeable enough to construct these models for every domain they experience. Nevertheless, some of the concepts of QP theory will be useful in describing models in other stages as well.

In QP theory, a physical situation is modeled as a collection of objects and relationships among them, with processes responsible for causing changes. The continuous parameters of an object, such as temperature and pressure, are represented by *quantities*. A quantity has two parts, an *amount* and a *derivative*. Amounts and derivatives are both *numbers*. The model to keep in mind for numbers is that of the reals, but it is important to note that in QP theory particular numerical values are never used. Instead, the value of a number is described in terms of its *quantity space*—a collection of inequalities that hold between it and other quantities. Figure 12-1 illustrates a quantity space for the level of liquid in a container. The quantity space is a useful qualitative representation because processes typically start and stop when inequalities between parameters change.

Figure 12-2 illustrates a typical process, called LIQUID-FLOW. A process has five parts: *individuals, preconditions, quantity conditions, relations,* and *influences.* Roughly speaking, the individuals part describes where instances of a process might occur, the preconditions and quantity conditions tell when it will be acting, and the relations and influences describe what holds as a consequence of it acting. In more detail, for any collection of objects that matches the individual specifications there is a *process instance* that represents the potential for that process to occur between those individuals in a particular way. For example, there will be two instances of LIQUID-FLOW between the liquid in the containers in figure 12-2, each corresponding to flow in a particular direction.

A process instance is *active* whenever both its preconditions and its quantity conditions are true. The distinction between preconditions and quantity conditions is that quantity conditions can be determined within QP theory but preconditions cannot. Quantity conditions concern what inequalities hold and what other processes (or individual views, which are introduced below) are active. Preconditions concern

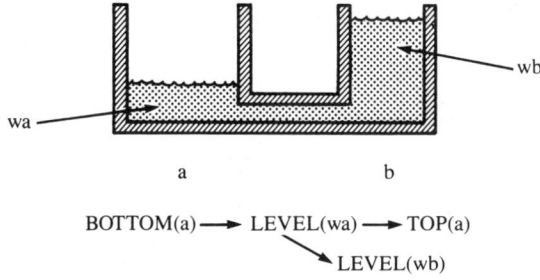

Figure 12-1: A quantity space describes the value of a number by the inequality relationships that hold between it and other numbers. An arrow indicates that the number at its head is greater than the number at its tail. Thus LEVEL(wa) is less than LEVEL(wb) and greater than BOTTOM(a), and LEVEL(wb) and TOP(a) are unordered.

```
Process LIQUID-FLOW

Individuals:
  source, a CONTAINED-LIQUID
dest, a CONTAINED-LIQUID
path, a FLUID-PATH, FLUID-CONNECTION(source, dest, path)

 Preconditions:
  ALIGNED(path)

Quantity Conditions:
  A[PRESSURE(source)] > A[PRESSURE(dest)]

Relations:
  Let flow-rate, diff be quantities
diff = PRESSURE(source) - PRESSURE (dest)
flow-rate ∝_{Q+} diff

Influences:
  I + (AMOUNT-OF(dest), A[flow-rate])
  I - (AMOUNT-OF(source), A[flow-rate])
```

Figure 12-2: A typical process. This process specification describes a simple kind of liquid flow. It can occur between two contained liquids that are connected by a fluid path, whenever the path is aligned—that is, all valves in the path are open—and the pressure in the one taken as source is greater than the pressure in the contained liquid taken as destination. The quantity type AMOUNT-OF represents how much "stuff" there is in an object. (Recall the function of A maps a quantity into the number that is its amount, a number, as opposed to AMOUNT-OF, which is a function that maps a piece of stuff into a quantity.)

any relevant factors other than quantity conditions, such as spatial boundaries. For example, in "real" physics we can solve equations to figure out how fast a ball will be moving when it hits the floor, but the equations will not tell us a priori where the floor is. Or, returning to the present example, if we know that all the valves in the fluid path between the two containers are open (i.e., the fluid path is aligned), then fluid will flow, but we cannot predict within QP theory when or if someone will walk by and turn off a valve. Because these factors still affect dynamical conclusions, preconditions must be explicitly represented.

Whenever a process instance is active, its influences and relations hold. The influences component of a process specifies the direct effects of a process; the relations component describes other facts that are true while the process is active. The direct effects—called *direct influences*—take the form

$$I + (Q, n)$$

or

$$I - (Q, n)$$

depending on whether n is a positive or negative contribution to the derivative of Q. If
a quantity is directly influenced, its derivative will be the sum of all the direct influences on it. Returning to the description of LIQUID-FLOW, for example, we see that
when an instance of LIQUID-FLOW is active, there will be a positive influence on the
amount of liquid in the destination and an equal, negative influence on the amount of
liquid in the source.

The relations field can describe new individuals that are created by virtue of the
process being active (such as the steam produced by boiling water), as well as properties needed by representations outside QP theory (such as the appearance of boiling
water). An especially important kind of fact expressed in the relations component is
functional dependency between quantities. Functional dependencies between quantities are expressed by

$$Q1 \propto_{Q+} Q2$$

(read "Q1 is *qualitatively proportional* to Q2," or informally, "Q1 q-prop Q2"),
meaning there exists a function that determines Q1 and is strictly increasing in its
dependence on Q2. $\propto_{Q-}$ indicates that the dependence is strictly decreasing. Note
that qualitative proportionalities express partial information, since the exact nature
of the function relating the parameters is not known and the function may or may not
depend upon other quantities.[2] If a quantity Q1 is functionally dependent on a quantity Q2, and if Q2 is influenced by a process P, then we will say that P *indirectly influences* Q1R; that is, when P is acting it can cause Q1 to change. If, for instance, the
PRESSURE and LEVEL of a liquid are qualitatively proportional to the AMOUNT-OF of the
liquid, then LIQUID-FLOW will indirectly influence both PRESSURE and LEVEL
because it directly influences AMOUNT-OF. It is important to note that the only way a
quantity can change is if it is directly or indirectly influenced. This means that one
can reason by exclusion: If nothing is influencing the amount of fluid in a container,
then it isn't changing, but if the amount is changing, something must be influencing
it. No changes happen by themselves. Furthermore, we can trace the possible paths of
influences in a situation and determine whether or not particular kinds of changes can
occur.

Two other important types of descriptions should also be mentioned here. *Individual views* are descriptions used to represent both objects whose existence are subject to dynamical constraints and states of objects. "The water in a cup," for example,
is described as a CONTAINED-LIQUID (see figure 12-3) because we can get rid of it by

---

[2]QP theory also provides ways to specify dependence on properties that are not quantities (such as shape, in
relating the level of a liquid in a container to its volume) and to make stronger statements about functional
relationships, such as "Q1 depends on Q2 directly, with no intervening parameters" and "Q depends on Q1
and Q2 and nothing else" when required for framing stronger hypotheses about a domain. However, pre-
cise specifications of functions (e.g., Q1 = |Q2|*2) are not permitted.

```
INDIVIDUAL-VIEW CONTAINED-LIQUID

Individuals:
  c a CONTAINER
  s a SUBSTANCE

Preconditions:
  CAN-CONTAIN-SUBSTANCE(c,s)

Quantity Conditions:
  A[AMOUNT-OF-IN(s, c)] > ZERO

Relations:
  THERE IS g, a PIECE-OF-STUFF
  HAS-QUANTITY(g, AMOUNT-OF)
  AMOUNT-OF(g) = AMOUNT-OF-IN(s, c)
  HAS-QUANTITY(g, LEVEL)
  LEVEL(g) ∝_{Q+} AMOUNT-OF(g)
  HAS-QUANTITY(g, PRESSURE)
  PRESSURE(g) ∝_{Q+} LEVEL(g)
```

Figure 12-3: This typical individual view describes a piece of liquid in a container, using the ontology for liquids described in Hayes (1979a). THERE IS is just "syntactic sugar" for stating that whenever the preconditions and quantity conditions are true, g will exist.

reducing its amount to zero (perhaps by making it the source of an instance of LIQUID-FLOW). Another example is a model of a spring. Springs have three states—relaxed, compressed, and stretched—each of which can be modeled by individual views. Individual views are specified in the same way as processes, in that they have individuals, preconditions, quantity conditions, and relations. However, they do not have an influence component; directly influencing quantities is the sole prerogative of processes.

The other kind of description is the *encapsulated history*. How an object changes through time is represented by its *history* (Hayes, 1979b). Histories are annotated pieces of space-time; thus they are object centered, have finite spatial extent, and extend over time.[3] As its name suggests, an encapsulated history is a schematized description of some fragments of histories for a collection of objects. Encapsulated histories are useful for summarizing behavior and for directly describing phenomena that have not been accounted for by process descriptions. An example of the latter usage is describing collisions between moving objects. A very simple way to model

---

[3]By contrast, the classic situational calculus description of change (McCarthy and Hayes, 1969) consists of *situations* that describe the whole universe at some particular instant of time.

collisions is to say that the very next thing that happens after, say, an object hits a wall is that its velocity reverses and it starts moving the other way. Given how rapidly collisions occur, this model is quite adequate for most purposes, and encapsulated histories allow it to be written this way.

A reasoner's theory of dynamics for a particular domain is characterized in terms of (1) a *process vocabulary* that describes the kinds of processes the reasoner believes can occur and (2) a *view vocabulary* that describes dynamical objects and relevant states of objects. All changes are assumed to be directly or indirectly caused by processes—the *sole mechanism* assumption—which provides a strong constraint on the form of dynamical theories. Importantly, the content of dynamical theories is not tightly constrained—incorrect theories can be expressed as easily (and sometimes more easily!) than correct theories. For example versions of Newtonian, Aristotelian, and Impetus theories of motion have all been encoded using QP theory.

QP theory sanctions several basic deductions. For example, the kinds of processes that might occur in a situation can be determined by using the process and view vocabularies to construct instances representing the different possibilities. The collection of processes acting at any time characterizes "what is happening" then in that situation, and these processes can be found by evaluating the preconditions and quantity conditions for these instances.

Consider again the example in figure 12-1. There will be two instances of the LIQUID-FLOW process, and since the level in wb is greater than wa, the LIQUID-FLOW instance representing flow from wb to wa will be active. By taking into account all the influences on each quantity (called *resolving* its influences), we can often determine the sign of its derivative. The sign of the derivative is important because it represents how the amount of the quantity is changing—increasing, decreasing, or remaining constant. In this example there is only one process instance acting, which makes things simple. AMOUNT-OF(wb) is directly influenced, and since this influence is negative, it will decrease. By the $\propto_{Q+}$ statements in the CONTAINED-LIQUID description, LEVEL(wb) and PRESSURE(wb) will be indirectly influenced and thus will also decrease. Similarly, AMOUNT-OF(wa), LEVEL(wa), and PRESSURE(wa) will increase.

From the ways the quantities are changing we can determine how the process and view structures themselves might change, since they depend in part on the inequalities stated as quantity conditions. This computation is called *limit analysis*. In the example two things might happen—the pressures in wb and wa might equalize, or AMOUNT-OF(wb) could become zero, thus ending wb's existence (the geometry of this example rules out the latter).

The basic deductions of QP theory can be combined to perform more complex reasoning tasks. Two examples of more complex deductions are qualitative simulation (Forbus, 1984) and measurement interpretation (Forbus, 1983). Qualitative simulation consists of performing limit analysis repeatedly. It is useful for making predictions, for instance, that boiling water in a sealed container could cause an explosion. Measurement interpretation provides a link between physical theories and observations; for example, it might be hypothesized that the level of a fluid in a container is dropping because the fluid is flowing out somewhere. Measurements taken at a single instant may be interpreted by searching through the space of process and view structures for situations in which the results of influence resolution match the observations. Algorithms for interpreting measurements taken over a span of time are still under development.

12.3 COMPARISONS AND STRUCTURE MAPPING

So far this chapter has considered how portions of a person's knowledge about the physical world might be represented. Let us now turn to the question of how such domain models might be learned. The authors conjecture that a major process in experiential learning is comparing the current situation with stored descriptions. Consider the example of a person who has just moved to a cold climate and is learning to operate a furnace. Suppose that at first he wrongly believes that the house will get warm faster if the thermostat is set to a temperature higher than the desired temperature. (Kempton shows that this view is quite common; Kempton, 1985.) How can he reach the correct conclusion that the *rate* of heating does not depend on the temperature setting? There are at least three different ways, each based on a different kind of implicit comparison. First, he could compare his past furnace experiences with each other and notice a regularity in the rate of heating that is independent of the thermostat setting. Second, he may compare the furnace situation with known abstractions and realize that it is best described as a positional-action controller (as opposed to a proportional-action controller). Third, he may use an analogy, comparing the furnace situation with a description from another domain, such as fluid flow, to suggest governing principles. Each of these ways of learning relies on some form of comparison, either with a stored record of literally similar events, with a stored abstraction, or with a stored description that can function as an analogy.

Structure Mapping theory is concerned with such comparisons (see Gentner 1980, 1982, 1983; Gentner and Gentner, 1983). The theory describes the rules that are used to import a descriptive structure from one domain (the *base* domain) into another (the *target* domain). The central intuition is that an analogy implies that a predicate structure from one domain can be applied in another domain with arbitrarily different objects and surface appearances. *Literal similarity, analogy, mere appearance mappings,* and *abstraction mappings* (applications of general laws) are viewed as different kinds of mappings between descriptions. The types of comparisons are defined syntactically, in terms of the form of the knowledge representation, not in terms of its content. Each type of comparison will be considered in turn.

1. An analogy is a comparison in which relational predicates, but few or no object attributes, are mapped from base to target. The particular relations mapped are determined by *systematicity,* as defined by the existence of higher-order

constraining relations that can themselves be mapped.[4] The correspondences between objects of the base and objects of the target are thus determined by the roles of the objects in the relational structure, not by any intrinsic similarity between the objects themselves.

2. A literal similarity statement is a comparison in which a large number of predicates, both attributes and relations, can be mapped from base to target. Here, the model is based on one proposed by Tversky (1977), which states that the similarity between A and B increases with the size of the intersection of their feature sets and decreases with the size of the intersection of the two complement sets.[5] Thus, there are many more shared predicates than nonshared predicates.

3. An abstract mapping is a comparison in which the base domain is an abstract relational structure. Predicates from the abstract base domain are mapped into the target domain. As in analogy, the mapped predicates are a relational structure. Abstraction differs from analogy in the nature of the base domain. There are almost no object attributes in the base, so there are few, if any, one-place predicates to be left behind. Applying a rule to a situation is an example of abstraction mapping. Sometimes the relational structure so mapped will also be referred to as an *abstraction*.

4. A mere appearance match is a comparison in which the object attributes match but the relational structure does not. In a sense it is the opposite of analogy. Such matches are easily made, but they guarantee nothing beyond similarity in appearance.

A series of related examples using the analogy between heat flow and water flow will illustrate these distinctions. Figures 12-4a and 12-4b show a water-flow situation and the corresponding heat-flow situation (adapted from Buckley, 1979, 15–25). Figure 12-5 shows a possible representation a person might have of the water situation. Notice that the description contains both object-attribute predicates, such as CYLINDRICAL(beaker), and relational predicates, such as GREATER-THAN

---

[4]Object attributes are predicates that take one object as an argument, such as RED(x). Relations are predicates that take two or more arguments, such as COLLIDE (x, y). We define the *order* of a proposition as follows: Constants have order zero, as do functions on them. The order of a proposition is one plus the maximum of the orders of its arguments. Thus COLLIDE(x, y) would be first order if x and y are domain objects, and CAUSE(COLLIDE(x, y), BREAK(x)) would be second order. Examples of higher-order relations are CAUSE and IMPLIES.

[5]Again according to Tversky, the negative effects of the two complement sets are not equal; for example, given the question How similar is A to B?, the set (B − A)—features of B not shared by A—counts more than the set (A − B).

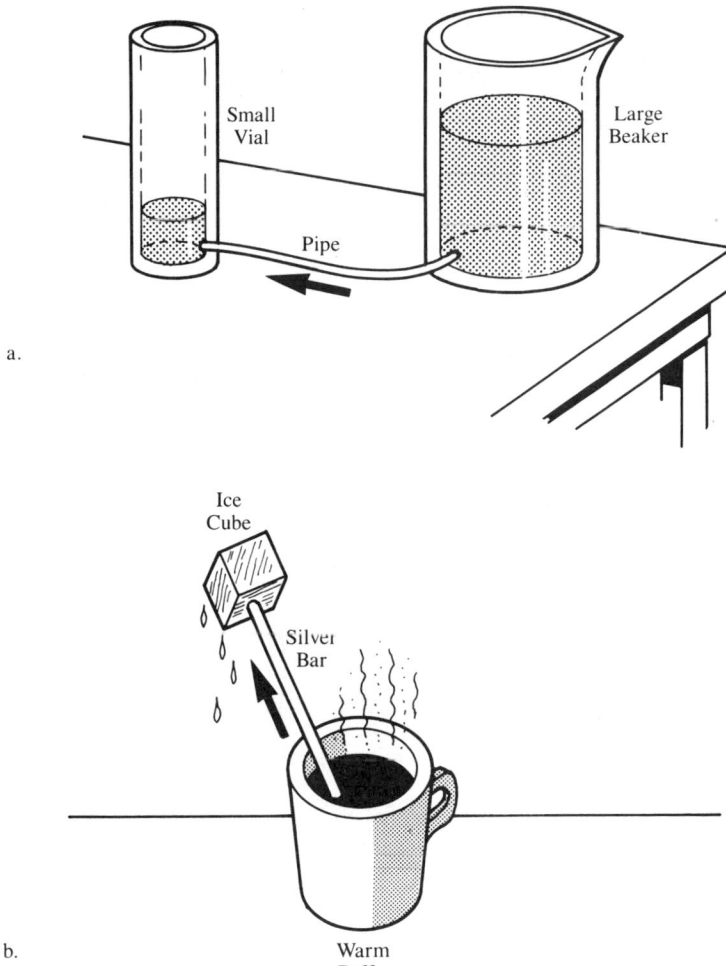

Figure 12-4: These two physical situations involving flow will be used to illustrate the kinds of comparisons sanctioned by Structure Mapping theory and later to illustrate how QP-style domain descriptions can be used in analogies: (a) A water-flow situation; (b) the corresponding heat-flow situation.

[PRESSURE(water, beaker), PRESSURE(water, vial)]. Let us consider the comparison types as exemplified here:

1. The analogy *Heat is like water* conveys that certain aspects of the water description can be mapped onto the heat domain. In particular, (1) object attributes should be dropped; (2) some relational predicates should be carried over; and (3) systematicity determines which relations should be mapped. Thus, CYLINDRICAL(beaker) is dropped, along with other object attributes;

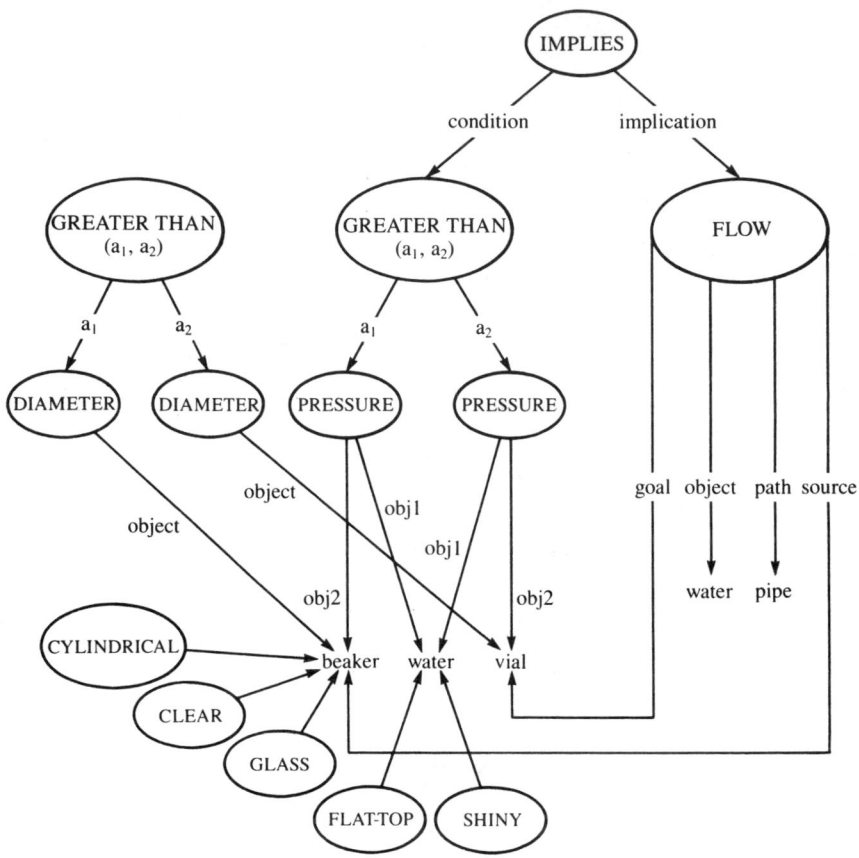

Figure 12-5:   A representation of the water situation. This network represents a portion of what a person might know about the water situation illustrated in figure 12-14. In this and other figures, predicates are written in upper case and circled. Objects are written in lower case and uncircled. A simplified representation is used to illustrate the rules of analogy. A more detailed model will be shown.

that is, the target objects do not have to resemble their corresponding base objects. Some relations are carried across, such as, GREATER-THAN [PRESSURE(water, beaker), PRESSURE(water, vial)]. Yet not all relations are carried across. By the systematicity principle, this GREATER-THAN relation is preserved because it is part of the mappable chain governed by the higher-order relation IMPLIES. In contrast, the relation GREATER-THAN[DIAMETER (beaker), DIAMETER(vial)] is not carried across, since it is not part of any mappable system of constraining relations in this representation of the base domain.

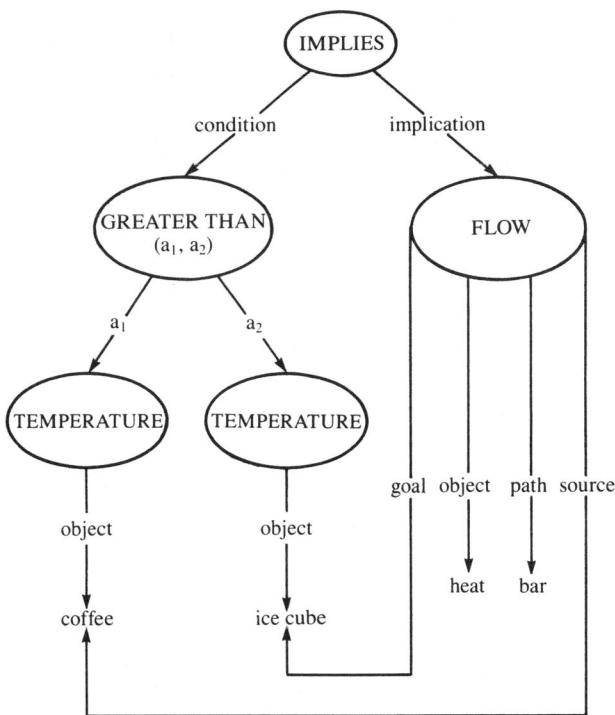

Figure 12-6: A representation of the heat situation that results from the heat/water analogy. This network represents the knowledge a person would map across into the heat domain from the water situation illustrated in figure 12-5. As in that figure, a simplified representation is used here. A more detailed treatment of this analogy is presented later.

Figure 12-6 shows the representation in the target domain of heat flow that results from the analogical mapping. Given the arbitrary object correspondences heat/water, beaker/coffee, vial/ice cube, pipe/bar, and PRESSURE/ TEMPERATURE,[6] systematicity operates to enforce a tacit preference for coherence and predictive power. The systematic relational structure in the water domain

---

[6]In this analogy, the first-order predicate of PRESSURE in the water domain must be replaced by TEMPERATURE in the heat domain. Although systems of relations can often be imported into the target without change, substitutions of lower-order relations, as well as of objects and their attributes, are sometimes made in order to permit mapping a larger systematic chain.

```
IMPLIES(GREATER-THAN[PRESSURE(water, beaker),
                    PRESSURE(water, vial)],
       FLOW(water, pipe, beaker, vial))
```

is mapped into

```
IMPLIES(GREATER-THAN[TEMPERATURE(heat, coffee),
                     TEMPERATURE(heat, ice cube)],
        FLOW(heat, bar, coffee, ice cube))
```

2. The literal similarity comparison *Kool-Aid is like water* conveys that most of the water description can be applied to Kool-Aid. In literal similarity, both object attributes, such as FLAT-TOP(water), and relational predicates, such as the systematic chain discussed above, are mapped over.

3. The abstraction *Heat is a through-variable* might be available to a student who knows some system dynamics. This abstraction conveys the idea that heat can be thought of as something that flows across a difference in potential (i.e., some sort of across-variable—in this case, temperature). This is much the same relational structure as conveyed by the analogy in 1, above; the difference is that in the abstract base domain of through-variables and across-variables, there are no concrete properties of objects to be left behind in the mapping.

4. A mere appearance match is a match with overlap chiefly in lower-order predicates, such as object attributes, but little or no relational match. An example is *The tabletop gleamed like water.* Such a match typically yields little or no useful information about the target; here, for example, little can be learned about the table by mapping across knowledge about water. These matches, however, cannot be ignored in a theory of learning, because a novice learner may be unable to tell them from true literal similarity matches.

Table 12-1 summarizes the kinds of predicate overlap that characterize literal similarity, analogy, abstraction, and mere appearance matches, as well as one other kind of comparison, *anomaly.* An anomaly is a match with little or no predicate overlap; it is included simply for completeness.

It should be clear that the contrasts described here are continua, not dichotomies. For example, analogy and literal similarity lie on a continuum. Given that two domains overlap in relational structure, then the comparison becomes more a literal similarity match to the extent that their object attributes also overlap and more an analogy to the extent that few or no object attributes overlap. A different sort of continuum exists between analogies and general laws. In both cases, a relational structure is mapped from base to target. If the base representation included concrete

Table 12-1: Kinds of Domain Comparisons

	OBJECT ATTRIBUTES	RELATIONS	EXAMPLE
Literal Similarity	Many	Many	Milk is like water.
Analogy	Few	Many	Heat is like water.
Abstraction	Few	Many	Heat flow is a through-variable.
Anomaly	Few	Few	Coffee is like the solar system.
Mere Appearance	Many	Few	The glass tabletop gleamed like a pool of water.

objects whose individual attributes must be left behind in the mapping, the comparison is an analogy. As the object nodes of the base domain become more abstract and variablelike, the comparison is seen more as a general law.

12.4 STRUCTURE MAPPING AND LEARNING

The role of a comparison in learning depends on at least two things: (1) *accessibility*—the likelihood that the match will be noticed—and (2) *usefulness*—what can be deduced from the match if it is accessed. Accessibility, in turn, depends at least on (a) the *familiarity* of the base description and (b) the overall *similarity* between the base description and the current target. The immediate usefulness of a match depends, of course, on whether the content of the match is appropriate to the task at hand. In addition, the usefulness of a match depends on the *inspectability* of the matching content—the degree to which it can be consciously analyzed and articulated. The comparisons discussed above behave very differently with respect to accessibility and inspectability.

For novice learners, literal similarity matches are the most accessible comparisons, and abstractions are the least accessible. In contrast, abstraction matches are far more inspectable than literal similarity matches. On both dimensions, analogies are intermediate. That is one reason that analogy is crucial in learning. Some evidence for these conjectures will now be reviewed.

Literal similarity matches are highly accessible. It has been shown in education and training literature that the more similar a new situation is to an original situation the more readily transfer of training occurs (cf. Brown and Campione, 1985). The term *generalization gradient* expresses the fact that a learned response generalizes more readily the more similar the new situation is to the original situation. In contrast, subjects are often quite slow to use an available analogy. In research done by

Reed, Ernst, and Banerji (1974) and later by Gick and Holyoak (1980, 1983), subjects were asked to solve a rather difficult problem, such as how to cure an inoperable tumor with radiation without killing the flesh along the path of the rays. Just prior to receiving the problem some of the subjects read material that contained an analogous solution, such as a story about a general who split his troops up so that they all converged simultaneously on a fortress he wished to capture

There are three interesting results here. First, a good analogy can be very powerful *if* it is noticed. Without the analogy, only about 10 percent of the subjects could solve the problem. Once the experimental subjects were told to use the prior story as an analogy, 80 to 90 percent of them solved the problem correctly. Second, a potentially powerful analogy can easily go unnoticed. Before the analogy was pointed out, only about a third of the subjects spontaneously noticed and used it. It cannot be taken for granted that a potential analogue will be spontaneously noticed and used. Third, literal similarity is far more accessible than true analogy. In one of their studies, Gick and Holyoak (1983) happened to set up a literal similarity match between the story and problem. Subjects had to solve a problem that involved tying two ropes together, and the story they were given involved tying two ribbons together. In this case, 70 to 80 percent of the subjects were able to access the matching story spontaneously.

There is also developmental evidence that literal similarity matches appear prior to analogies and abstraction matches in learning. One example is early word learning. In spontaneous labeling, one-year-old children frequently apply words to objects that closely resemble the original referent of the word; for example *doggie* will be applied to another dog or to a cat, and *car* to cars, trucks, or other vehicles (Clark, 1973). Truly analogous or metaphorical usages are seldom heard until the age of two or three years; for example, a three-year-old child remarks about his dirty bedraggled blanket, "It's out of gas" (Gentner and Stuart, 1984; Winner, 1979).

Children are said to move from rich, concrete representations to more abstract, rule-based systems (cf. Bruner, Olver, and Greenfield, 1966; Gibson, 1969). Even three-year-olds can sort objects into perceptually similar categories; for example, they can group a cat and a dog and exclude a hen. However, not until they are five or six years old can they succeed if the match is more abstract; for example, a category like "living thing" requires grouping perceptually dissimilar things.

In the same vein, research on the novice-expert shift in adult learning has demonstrated that whereas novice science students typically match situations on the basis of surface features, experts use deeper and more abstract criteria (Larkin, 1983). For example, Chi, Feltovich, and Glaser (1981) have shown that when novice physics students are asked to classify problems into similar groups they put together problems with similar surface features, such as "inclined planes" or "pulleys." Experts, on the other hand, use categories like "force problems" and "energy problems."

One final indication of the ease with which literal similarity matches are made involves an indirect, but very important, line of argument. In the realm of object concepts, there is some evidence that people automatically perform literal similarity comparisons to combine perceptually similar experiences into composite prototypes (see Posner and Mitchell, 1967; Rosch, 1973, 1975, 1978; Smith and Medin, 1981).[7] In the Posner and Mitchell study, people classified dot patterns into categories. After they had sorted the patterns, they were asked to remember which patterns they had seen. Although the task called simply for accessing verbatim memory, subjects showed systematic misrecognitions: they falsely remembered having seen prototypical patterns that were never presented. Thus without being told to do so, people formed composite mental representations, apparently based on implicit comparisons among the patterns that they saw. The virtually automatic nature of prototype learning is further evidence that the literal similarity matches on which they are based are highly accessible—indeed, evidence that making such comparisons is a passive, essentially automatic process (see also Reber, 1967, 1976).

However, prototypes also illustrate the limited usefulness of literal similarity matches. Although these implicit composites are often sufficient for recognizing and categorizing situations, they are of limited use in deriving causal principles. This is because (1) a match based largely on perceptual commonalities will often fail to contain the correct principles and (2) even when some of the correct relations are present, literal similarity matches are too rich to be inspectable. There is some evidence, albeit indirect, for this notion of rich, noninspectable representations. Nickerson and Adams (1979) studied people's memory of the common penny. Despite the overwhelming amount of experience that the subjects had with pennies, and despite their evident ability to recognize and categorize pennies, they were remarkably poor at recalling or recognizing the details of how pennies look. This demonstrates that possessing a description sufficient to recognize a class of objects is no guarantee that the description can be articulated.

Studies of young children show that similarity judgments can be difficult to decompose. Shepp (1978) has found that three- and four-year-olds appear to base their similarity judgments on some kind of overall comparison; they are typically unable to judge one dimension independently of another. For example, they cannot ignore height when judging width. Unlike adults, they are unable to treat length and width as separable.

By contrast an appropriate abstraction match is likely to be extremely useful in both respects: it should contain the correct principle, and the match should be inspectable. But abstractions are often not particularly accessible, especially for novices. Novice learners may not know the appropriate abstraction, or it may be so unfamiliar that they will not retrieve it when appropriate. Thus abstraction mappings,

---

[7]The term *prototype* has been used in various ways in psychology. Here it is used to refer to a *structured* composite object.

although ultimately important, are unlikely to play a major role in the early stages of learning.

Analogies lie between the highly accessible literal similarity matches and the highly useful abstraction matches. Potential analogies are less accessible in experiential learning than literal similarity matches. This is because analogy requires that the learner's database be accessed via relational matches; object matches are of little or no use. However, once found, an analogy should be more useful than a literal similarity match in deriving the key principles, since the shared data structure is sparse enough to permit analysis. (Of course, educators often explicitly introduce analogies in teaching beginners for exactly this reason. In this case, the problem of noticing the analogical match is bypassed.) Moreover, by the systematicity principle, the set of overlapping predicates is likely to include higher-order relations, such as causality and logical implication. Thus analogy can function to reveal principles in a domain that previously lacked the appropriate abstractions (Burstein, chap. 13 of this volume; Carbonell, chap. 14; Clements, 1982; Darden, 1983; Gentner, 1980, 1982, 1983; Gentner and Gentner, 1983; Gick and Holyoak, 1983; Hoffman, 1980). Winston's system (see Winston, 1980, 1982), which derives if-then rules by abstracting the predicates common to two analogues, is a case in point.

The *analogical shift hypothesis* concerns the role of these comparisons in experiential learning. In the earliest stages most of the spontaneous matches are either mere appearance matches (and thus erroneous) or literal similarity matches based on massive feature overlap. This is to say that initial learning is surface oriented and conservative, based on rich, specific-case kinds of matches. As the domain becomes familiar, more distant comparisons begin to occur; matches are made in which fewer object attributes are shared. These sparse comparisons lead to the kinds of binary connections that form the bulk of the causal corpus—for example "Lighter things go farther when thrown." Analogy also serves as a means of introducing structured mental models. Successful analogies may yield abstractions that can be stored and accessed (Gick and Holyoak, 1983; Winston, 1980, 1982). Thus, analogy plays an important role in the middle and later stages of learning. In the final stages, when learning is well advanced, abstraction mappings play a major role.

12.5 STAGES OF UNDERSTANDING

The authors suspect that four kinds of mental models are generated in the process of understanding physical domains. The sequence of models proposed here is developmental, in that the theories of each stage are generated both by the phenomena being understood and by the theories of the stage before it. It is not proposed that every person go through every stage for every domain, nor that a person is at the same stage in every domain at the same time.

12.5.1 Stage 1: Protohistories

Suppose some new physical phenomenon is being observed. If there is no prior model, all one can do is observe and remember what is happening. The authors conjecture that the simplest physical models of a domain are *protohistories*—prototype histories that serve as summaries of experience.[8] Like object prototypes, protohistories are the "most typical instances" of phenomena. The terms in these descriptions are observables, and their deductive import can be roughly expressed as, "If I see X, then Y will happen (has happened)."

Consider a balance beam or seesaw. If a weight is placed on each side of the fulcrum, the seesaw will either tilt counterclockwise, tilt clockwise, or not tilt at all. Most people have had enough experiences with seesaws to have formed protohistories concerning their behavior. By the conjecture described here, a protohistory is automatically available whenever they encounter a seesaw. From it, they can often predict which way the particular seesaw will move. For example, they may have a protohistory that describes what happens if a small person gets on the seesaw opposite a large person.

However, the predictive power of protohistories is quite limited. There is no guarantee that the features matched actually correspond to relevant factors. For example, an observer will be fooled when a large person sits close to the fulcrum if the observer's seesaw protohistories have been formed from watching people sitting at equal distances. Massive overlap in features is needed for reliable use, which means protohistories will yield conclusions in fewer situations than a true theory would. Consider, for example, two weights hung from opposite ends of a stick that is suspended by a string. The principle involved is the same, yet the situations look dissimilar enough that the protohistories for seesaws would not match. Furthermore, there is no certain way to decide between conflicting results if more than one protohistory matches a situation.[9]

12.5.1.1 Learning Protohistories

The process of constructing protohistories involves dividing up experience into classes according to literal similarity and abstracting a summary for each class. There has been little direct research on this process. However, investigations into the process of constructing object prototypes provide some hints. First, people seem to be able implicitly (i.e., unconsciously) to compute a kind of component match. Second, this intersection is not merely a simple feature intersection; rather, it appears

---

[8]Some of diSessa's *phenomenological primitives* (1983) appear to be representable as protohistories.

[9]There are of course heuristic criteria, such as using the protohistory that has worked most often. The problem with such heuristics is that little is learned from mistakes.

that configurations among features are important in the prototype. Third, once this prototype is computed, it has powerful effects on the subsequent processing of experience. As mentioned previously, once people abstract a prototype from a set of patterns, they may be more confident of having seen the prototype—which was never presented—than they are of having seen the patterns actually presented (Posner and Mitchell, 1967). Finally, people may not be aware of forming prototypes, except as a general sense of increased familiarity with a category.

In summary, if protohistories behave like object prototypes, then they should be found to (1) be computed implicitly; (2) act as composite concepts; (3) be sensitive to perceptual configurations among events; and (4), once computed, show the recognition strength and other psychological privileges of prototypes.

The machine learning research that most closely captures this type of learning is concerned with *conceptual clustering* (see Michalski and Stepp, 1983). So far, such research has focused on classifying objects that can be characterized mainly by differing attributes. Extending such techniques to describe situations that depend critically on relational descriptions could provide a method for computing protohistories (Stepp and Michalski, chap. 17).

12.5.2 Stage 2: The Causal Corpus

Protohistories summarize the phenomena, but they do not constitute a theory of them. Building a detailed theory directly can be quite difficult. The space of possible models connecting all observable (and possible) parameters in a typical situation can be quite large. The authors conjecture that weaker theories, theories that characterize which parts of the situation are relevant to desired conclusions, are formed first. In particular, it is conjectured that a collection of CAUSE statements, the causal corpus, is computed from prototype objects and protohistories.

CAUSE is viewed here as an approximate concept, a weak form of ontological commitment. In particular, saying CAUSE(A, B) expresses belief in the existence of some mechanism, specified by some theory T, such that IMPLIES [(AND A T), B]. Many, perhaps most, of the causal corpus relations are binary relations among variables—for example, "Bigger objects weigh more" (Piaget, 1951; Carey, 1985), or "Smaller objects have higher pitch when struck" (diSessa, 1983).

The notion of mechanism in the causal corpus is quite primitive: the causal beliefs need be neither explicit nor internally consistent. Later in the learning sequence, as will be seen, *processes* will assume the role of mechanisms for physical domains. Nevertheless, the authors conjecture that even at this early stage, the learner makes a distinction between mechanistic connections and, say, definitional connections.[10] Further, they suspect that many of the initial causal connections are

---

[10]For example, the statement CAUSE(TRIANGLE(f), HAS-THREE-SIDES(f)) is not a legitimate use of CAUSE by this account, since the required axioms of geometry do not specify a mechanism.

incorrect. Novices often include diagnostic and correlational relations in their causal corpus. For example, asked if an increase in the evaporation rate will cause a change in the temperature of the water, a novice may reply, "Yes, because it would have to be hotter to evaporate more."

CAUSE, then, is a statement of belief in some mechanistic connection. The distillation of experience from protohistories into the causal corpus serves three purposes. First, it serves as a means of data reduction. Second, it provides a collection of heuristics that can be used directly to draw inferences. Even if the learner doesn't have firm grounds to consider the CAUSE statements complete or correct, the CAUSE statements may often suffice for the desired class of inferences. Third, the collection of CAUSE relations can be used to guide the search for a deeper theory of the domain. The CAUSE statements suggest connections among various aspects of the domain that a deeper theory must either explain or explain away.

Returning to the seesaw example, suppose the causal corpus is now applied to a balance beam built out of blocks. Suppose the two blocks on it are called a and b. The causal corpus might be as follows:

```
CAUSE(BIGGER(a, b), TILT-TOWARDS(a))
CAUSE(FARTHER(a, b), TILT-TOWARDS(a))
```

These statements can be interpreted as rules in several ways: If block a is bigger than block b, one can predict tilt, and if one sees tilt, one may hypothesize that one block is farther out than another. These statements are more broadly applicable than protohistories since they refer to fewer properties. Unlike protohistories, the causal corpus is sparse enough to be debugged to some degree.

However, the approximate nature of the CAUSE relation limits the learner's ability to discriminate between conflicting predictions. With the causal corpus above, for instance, if block a is bigger and block b is farther out, we will have two predictions. Inhelder and Piaget (1985) and Siegler (1976, 1981) have documented such a stage in the development of understanding about the balance beam (with analogous developmental sequences in other domains). Initially, children focus only on weight. But there is an interesting second stage when they come to realize that both weight and distance are important but they do not yet know the interrelations. They can manage either property by itself if the other is constant; but if both properties vary, they tend to focus on one or the other inconsistently. Eventually they become able to coordinate weight and distance in the balance beam problem. At this stage, if not before, they have gone beyond the causal corpus. As will be discussed, in order to make more precise inferences the learner must eventually uncover the mechanisms whose behavior is described by causal corpus.

12.5.2.1 Learning the Causal Corpus

The authors suspect that there are three techniques for computing and debugging a causal corpus. The first technique is to hypothesize causality from co-occurrence:

```
If you always see A before B,
   then hypothesize CAUSE (A, B)
```

and

```
If A is true whenever B is true,
   then hypothesize CAUSE (A, B)
```

These rules make certain assumptions about the form of memory, namely, that some number of circumstances can be remembered and that they can be remembered in sufficient detail that A and B are either explicitly stored or computable from what is stored. Protohistories should serve as a means of initial data reduction from which a causal corpus can be constructed.

It is not clear exactly how the learner abstracts out particular variables from the rich representation of the protohistory stage. However this is done, the simplification achieved with the causal corpus is considerable. Another study by Siegler (1978) shows the power of focusing on particular variables. Three-year-old children were shown a balance beam, asked to predict which way it would tilt, and then shown what actually occurred. Even after large numbers of trials, their performance failed to improve. But when they were taught to think of the domain in terms of a few relevant variables—weight and length—their performance did improve with experience. The moral to be drawn is that the pace of learning is greatly accelerated when a small number of variables can be abstracted from all the possibly relevant factors.

As suggested earlier, many of the early causal relations will be incorrect. The authors suspect that there exists a class of rules that are used to debug a causal corpus in the face of new information (cf. Sussman, 1976). Each rule corresponds to a hypothesis about a bug in the structure of the causal corpus, such as a missing precondition. The authors believe that the task of judging a causal corpus for consistency is an example of an important but relatively neglected kind of learning, *coherence-driven learning*. Coherence-driven learning is learning that is driven not by a mismatch between the model and the world but by inconsistencies within the model itself. Williams, Hollan, and Stevens (1983) found evidence of such learning. They studied a subject who was learning about a heat exchanger and noted that one source of insight was a "boggle" experience, in which the person noticed that a current inference contradicted a prior belief. The authors are still examining the criteria for judging the consistency of a causal corpus.[11] Such criteria will play a major role in controlling the dubugging rules and the mixture of generation and debugging that occurs.

Analogy provides the third technique for extending a causal corpus (see Gentner and Gentner, 1983; Stevens, Collins, and Goldin, 1979). The CAUSE relations from one domain can be mapped into another, since CAUSE qualifies as a higher-order constraining relation (see also Winston, 1982).

12.5.3 Stage 3: Naive Physics

The naive physics models replace CAUSE statements with theories about the specific mechanisms of change. The ontology is extended by adding processes to explain observed changes. The ontology also includes properties and objects that are not directly observable (for example, heat and heat flow) and the new relationships (such as fluid path and heat path) required to reason about them.

An important advantage of these models is that they allow one to reason by exclusion. Unlike the previous stages, predictions that fail still yield information about the situation. For instance, if fluid is flowing into a container and the level is not rising, then it is reasonable to hypothesize that fluid is flowing out of it through some unknown path.

Returning to the balance beam example, a process SWING might be used to describe rotation around a contact point (see figure 12-7). The preconditions describe the geometric configuration of the system, and the quantity condition says that SWING will occur whenever there is a nonzero angular velocity. SWING directly influences the angular position of the beam. Thus a prediction concerning tilt becomes a prediction about which instance, if any, of the SWING process will be active.[12]

What influences ANGULAR-VELOCITY? The existence of an ANGULAR-ACCELERATION process (see figure 12-8) that directly influences ANGULAR-VELOCITY whenever there is a net torque will be assumed. It is further assumed that

```
For-All (x) For-All (y)
 PHYSOB(x) and CONTACT-POINT(cp)
 implies NET-TORQUE(x, cp) = SUM-OF(TORQUES-ON(x, cp))
```

---

[11]With Lance Rips of the University of Chicago, the authors are investigating the role of intransitives in debugging causal descriptions.

[12]An alternate, and equally good, representation for SWING would leave directions implicit in the sign of the velocity. In that vocabulary, the balance beam would give rise to only one instance of SWING, and determining which way the beam moves requires that one determine first whether the instance of swing is active and if it is, what the sign of the angular velocity is.

```
        Process SWING
Individuals:
  b a PHYSOB
  c a PHYSOB
  cp a CONTACT-POINT
  dir a DIRECTION

Preconditions:
  MOBILE(b)
  not MOBILE(c)
  CONNECTED(b, c, cp)
  ROTATION-FREE(b, c, cp)
  DIRECTION-OF(dir, ANGULAR-VELOCITY(b, cp))

Quantity Conditions:
  An[ANGULAR-VELOCITY(b, cp)] > ZERO

Influences:
  I + (ANGULAR-POSITION(b, cp), A[ANGULAR-VELOCITY(b, cp)])
```

Figure 12-7: A SWING process describes rotation of an object around another object. For the balance beam there will be two instances of this process, differing only in their bindings for the direction dir. In each instance b will be bound to the beam, c will be bound to the fulcrum, and cp will be bound to the contact point between them.

It is assumed that each physical object (PHYSOB) has quantities to represent its angular position and velocity with respect to each point of contact with other objects. Directions will be noted by the symbols CW, CCW, and NULL, corresponding to clockwise rotation, counterclockwise rotation, and no rotation.

In other words, the net torque on an object around a contact point is the sum of the torques on that object measured around that contact point. The mass of the beam will be ignored, and the pull of gravity on the blocks on each side of the fulcrum will be assumed to be the only source of torques. Figure 12-9 describes this induced torque by means of an individual view. Notice that the factors illuminated in the causal corpus of BIGGER and FARTHER have become the quantities MASS and DISTANCE, and their role in producing swinging has been explicated. In particular, these properties determine how much torque each block places on the beam. The sum of the torques determines the net torque, which can cause the beam to accelerate and thus swing.

This model comes one step closer to a model that can always determine which way something will tilt. There will still be cases in which exactly what will happen cannot be determined (e.g., if the mass on one side is increased and it is brought closer to the pivot), but this is a precise hypothesis about what all the relevant factors are.

12.5.3.1 Learning Naive Physics

The major problem in learning a naive physics is constructing a vocabulary of processes that consistently describes experience. The learner must strip away the

```
Process ANGULAR-ACCELERATION

Individuals:
  b  a PHYSOB
  c  a PHYSOB
  cp a CONTACT-POINT
  dir a DIRECTION

Preconditions:
  MOBILE(b)
  not MOBILE(c)
  CONNECTED(b, c, cp)
  ROTATION-FREE(b, c, cp)
  DIRECTION-OF(dir, NET-TORQUE(b, cp))

Quantity Conditions:
  Am[NET-TORQUE(b, cp)] > ZERO

Relations:
  Let acc be a quantity
  acc ∝Q+ NET-TORQUE(b, cp)
  acc ∝Q  MASS(b)

Influences:
  I + (ANGULAR-VELOCITY(b, cp), A[acc])
```

Figure 12-8: An ANGULAR-ACCELERATION process.

irrelevant predicates that are part of his or her protohistories and causal corpus and construct more appropriate descriptions. In addition, the learner must sometimes hypothesize the existence of objects and properties that are not directly observable. Research in machine learning has developed several techniques for inductive learning that should prove useful (see Dietterich and Michalski, 1983; Mitchell, 1982; Michalski, 1983). These problems are starting to be addressed directly in the study of scientific discovery (Langley, et al., 1983).

The causal corpus provides a search space for potential process vocabularies. Each statement in the causal corpus must be elaborated into a consequence of a process vocabulary. It appears that there are only a small number of distinct ways to perform the elaboration, depending on the particular form of the arguments. For example, the statement

```
The decrease in AMOUNT-OF q
 causes the LEVEL OF Q to fall
```

```
Individual View GRAVITY-INDUCED-TORQUE

Individuals:
  b  a  PHYSOB
  c  a  PHYSOB
  d  a  PHYSOB
  cp a  CONTACT-POINT

Preconditions:
  CONNECTED(b, c, cp)
  ON(d, b)

Relations:
  Let f be a quantity
  f ELEMENT-OF TORQUES-ON(b, cp)
  f ∝_Q+ DISTANCE(C-M(d), cp)
  f ∝_Q+ MASS(d)
  ;Assign positive torques to CW, negative torques to CCW
  ON(C-M(d), SIDE-OF(CW, b, cp)) iff As [f] = 1
  ON(C-M(d), SIDE-OF(CCW, b, cp)) iff As [f] = -1
  ON(C-M(d), SIDE-OF(NULL, b, cp)) iff As [f] = 0
```

Figure 12-9:   A description of gravity-induced torque.

indicates that some active process (or individual view) in the situation contains the statement

$$LEVEL(q) \propto_{Q+} AMOUNT\text{-}OF(q)$$

in its relations.

Hypothesizing a process vocabulary from a causal corpus should be much simpler than working from protohistories or direct observation. Yet it still appears difficult. The authors conjecture that there are several constraints that make the problem more tractable. First, people are apparently *conservative* in the introduction of unobserved properties. For example, some subjects have a model of a domain that appears to be organized around one parameter—a "generalized strength" attribute. In reasoning about fluids, for instance, they appear to use *pressure, flow rate,* and *velocity* as different names for the same thing. In electricity, they use *voltage, current, power, potential,* and *velocity of electrons* interchangeably. The advantage of this theory generation strategy is, of course, that simpler models will be explored first, with further distinctions made only when necessary. Second, some physical laws are used as constraints on what process vocabularies are possible. Conservation of energy, for example, demands that if a process directly influences a quantity representing some form of energy, it must also directly influence some other quantity representing some form of energy, but in the opposite direction.

Once again, analogy can provide a constructive mechanism. It can be used to import candidate processes from previously understood domains—for example, when one understands heat flow in terms of fluid flow. This is an especially powerful mechanism because if the model for the previous domain is consistent with physical laws, then it suggests that the model for the new domain may be so as well. Recall the liquid flow model presented in section 12-2. Figure 12-10 illustrates a collection of assertions that describes the consequences of a particular instance of LIQUID-FLOW. [13]

Suppose a person hypothesizes that there is a process of heat flow analogous to the process of liquid flow. By Structure Mapping theory, this means that the person suspects that a similar relational structure holds among the objects in the heat-flow situation (the coffee, the ice cube, the silver bar, and the instance of heat flow) as holds among the objects in the liquid-flow situation (the water in the beaker, the water in the vial, the pipe, and the instance of liquid flow). Mapping the systematic relational structure (see figure 12-11) leads to several predictions that the person can check to see whether the analogy is correct. For example, it can be determined whether or not the temperature of the ice cube is rising and the temperature of the coffee falling. The structure-mapping rules for analogy have provided an initial model for the process of heat flow; in particular, the preconditions, quantity conditions, relations, and influences are all carried across from liquid flow. Note that to make the analogy really work, a new kind of object—a HEAT-PATH—must be postulated. Thus analogy can provide candidates for extending ontologies. [14]

12.5.4 Stage 4: Expert Models

The models generated so far have two important limitations. First, they still contain fundamental ambiguities, ambiguities that are inherent in the nature of qualitative representations. [15] Second, they lack domain-independent generalizations (except in the raw form of the representation—CAUSE statements, processes, and so on). The final stage of learning consists of overcoming these limitations, of discovering ways to resolve ambiguities and to construct powerful generalizations.

Clearly several kinds of knowledge are involved, and the potential complexity of the models in this stage is open-ended (it includes the whole of mathematical physics, for example). Examples of the kinds of knowledge involved include

---

[13]The assertions were generated by an early version of GIZMO, a computer program being constructed to explore the computational aspects of QP theory. GIZMO was designed to make predictions and interpret measurements, not to be a learning system. In particular, these descriptions were not generated with learning or analogy in mind.

[14]Of course, such extensions are not to be made lightly. The authors suspect that new types of objects are postulated in the target domain only when necessary to preserve a much larger systematic structure.

[15]The nature of ambiguity in qualitative descriptions is discussed by deKleer (1979) and Forbus (1984).

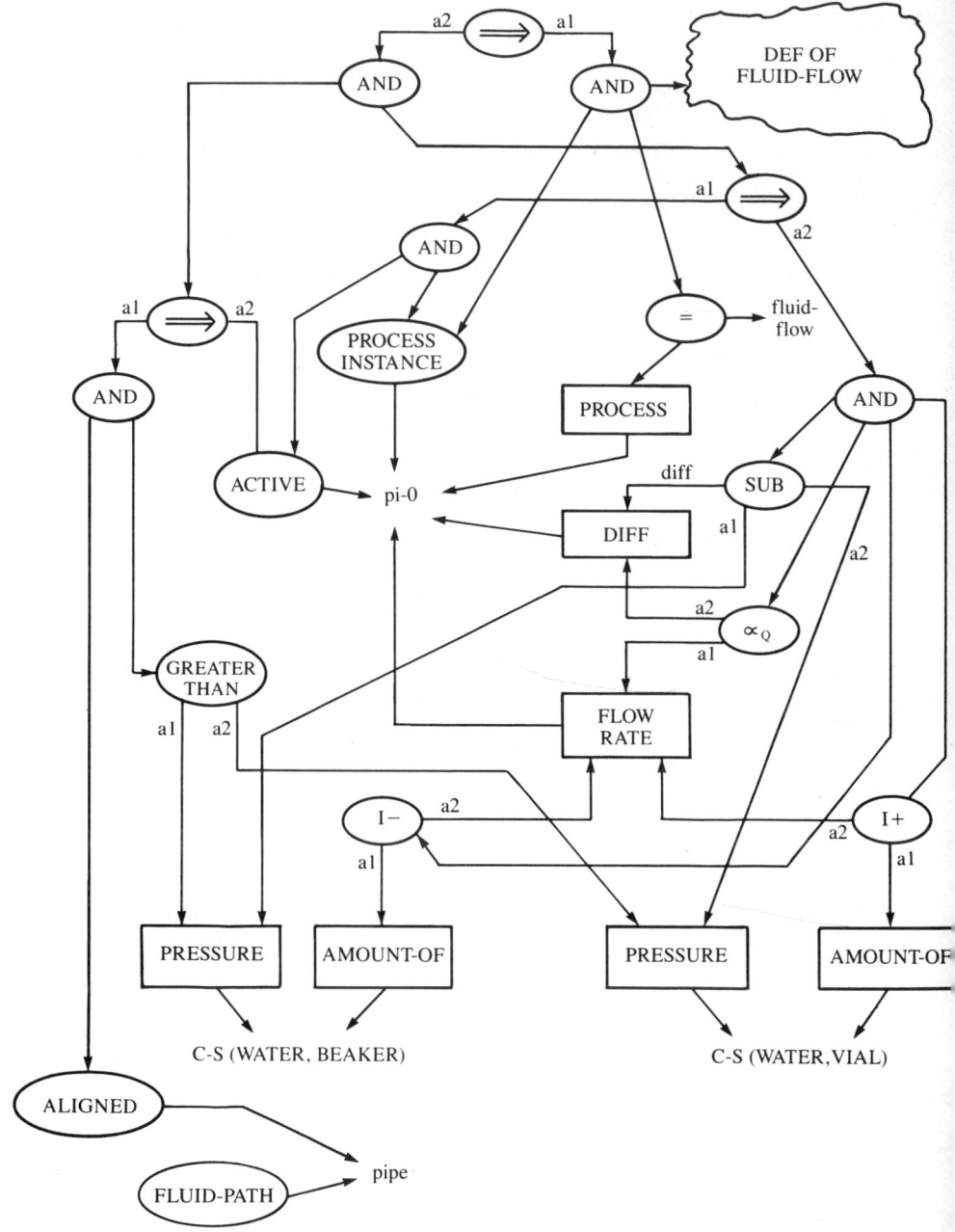

Figure 12-10: Relational structure for an instance of liquid flow. These important conclusions follow from the definition of liquid flow presented in figure 12-2 and the assumption that an instance of liquid flow exists involving the liquids in the two containers. Specifically, they describe the conditions for and consequences of the process instance pi = 0's being active.

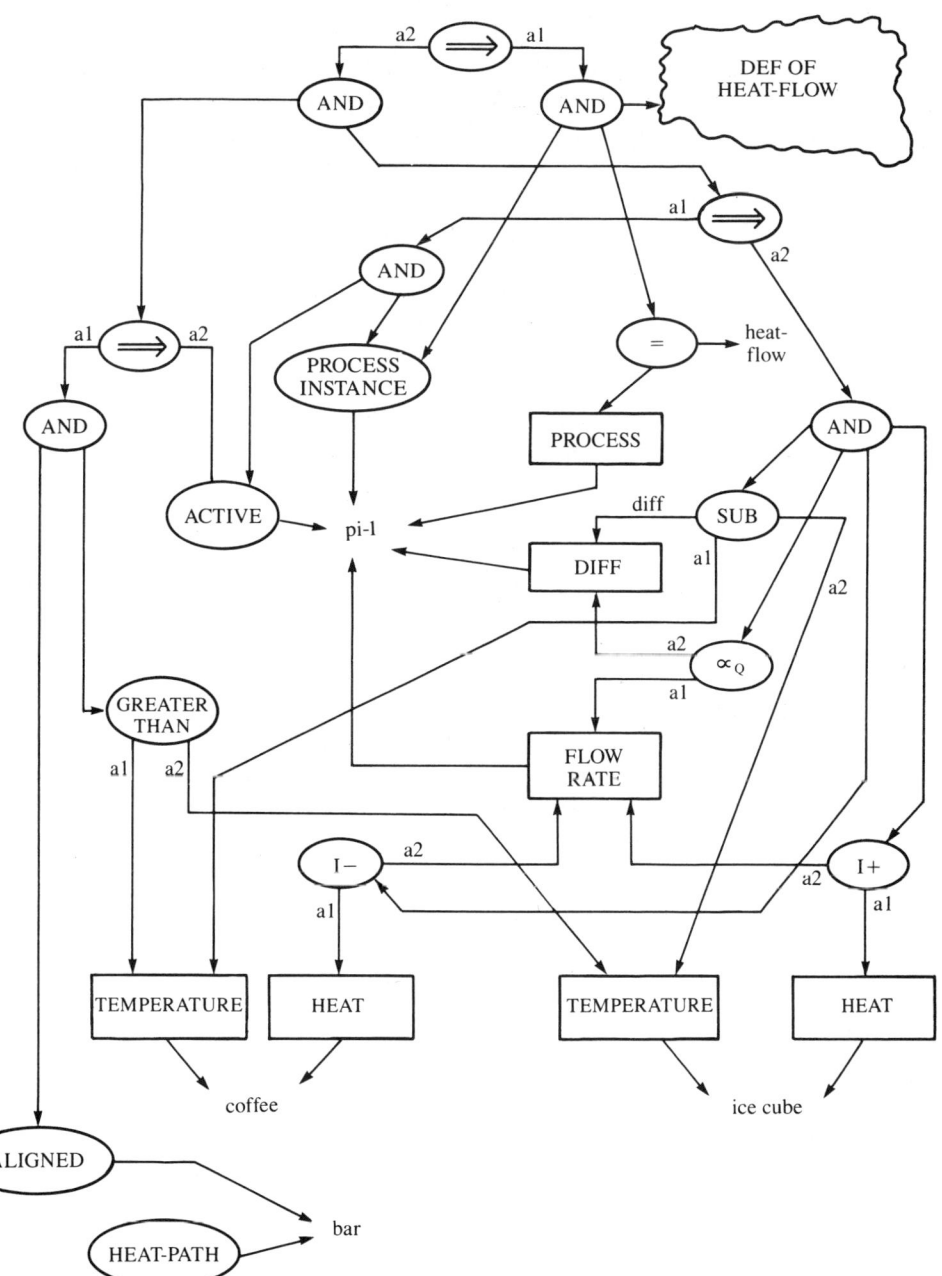

Figure 12-11: Relational structure transferred to heat flow. Here the relational structure describing a situation involving liquid flow has been transferred to a situation involving heat flow. Notice the systematicity of the relational structure, as indicated by the nested chains of implications.

equations to describe relationships between parameters, "rules of thumb" to specify useful default resolutions for ambiguities, and new ontologies to allow reasoning about more complex systems. The importance of mathematical models is fairly obvious. The rules of thumb are less obvious but equally important (see, e.g., Lenat, 1982). In physical domains they include empirical knowledge about the circumstances under which certain processes can be ignored (such as evaporation when water is poured from one glass to another) and what their net effect is (such as Black's law for the temperature of mixtures). Finally, different ontologies are sometimes necessary to deal with certain types of complex systems. In the process-oriented physics discussed here, describing flow requires finding flow paths. Finding flow paths in complex networks such as electrical circuits can quickly become computationally intractable; switching to a device-centered physics such as that described in deKleer and Brown (1983) can reduce the computational burden to manageable proportions for such systems.

In the balance beam example, it is known that the force of a block on the beam is qualitatively proportional to the mass of the block and to the distance from the fulcrum. If it is also known that the torque is the product of distance and weight, then providing numerical values for these quantities will allow an unambiguous prediction about tilt.

12.5.4.1 Learning Expert Models

The transition to expert models involves several kinds of learning. Some aspects of this transition probably lie outside the scope of experiential learning; for example, people typically learn mathematical models by being taught rather than by discovery. Some aspects of this learning—such as developing new ontologies—involve improving the content of the representations. Other aspects of the transition from a naive physics to an expert physics are better described as translating the existing qualitative representations into quantitative statements, using mathematics to express laws. By converting a physical theory into a mathematical model, the learner gains the ability to make precise predictions and to recognize powerful generalizations more easily. An important part of this refinement is to elaborate $\propto_Q$ statements into constraint equations. Langley (1979; Langley, Zytkow, Simon, and Bradshaw, 1983) describes techniques that should be useful for converting qualitative laws into mathematical relations.

Developing rules of thumb means knowing not just what is possible but what is probable. The learner must discover which outcomes raised by qualitative reasoning are likely or unlikely and which potential interactions can be ignored. The techniques developed in machine learning for acquiring heuristics should be directly applicable (cf. Lenat, 1982; Mitchell et al., 1981). In addition, the authors suspect the possible behaviors raised by naive physics are compared against known protohistories. Hypothesized outcomes that have no corresponding protohistory are judged unlikely, and those corresponding to a highly familiar and accessible protohistory are judged very likely (see Tversky and Kahneman, 1973).

Further, it seems likely that at least some expert rules of thumb derive from learning new protohistories. This intuition is based in part on research in automaticity (Schneider and Fisk, 1983). It has been demonstrated that, given an orderly domain and sufficient practice, adult subjects can learn a new response pattern well enough so that it becomes essentially effortless (see also Anderson, 1982; Rumelhart and Norman, 1978). Moreover, there is some transfer from the learned material to new similar material. These learned sequences have many of the essential qualities of protohistories. First, they are triggered by recognition (in the terms used here, by a literal similarity match between the present situation and a stored situation). Second, computing and carrying out the procedures that follow from the match are automatic; virtually no attentional resources are required. Third, these computations are implicit; subjects are typically poor at introspecting about what they are doing, and when they do introspect, it can interfere with the response (Brooks, 1978; Reber, 1967, 1976). It may be too simplistic to view protohistories as a special case of automatic pattern-response combination, but there is enough overlap to allow some confidence that protohistories can continue to be learned at all stages of expertise. Of course, the *contents* of expert protohistories may be different from those of novices, since experts' protohistories may reflect a more advanced ontology, as discussed below. However, the mechanism of a perceptually triggered automatic match should be the same.

The authors suspect that ontological shift is driven both by the desire to understand more complex physical systems and by the emergence of domain-independent mathematical abstractions. As an example of the first kind, consider the problem of reasoning about fluid flow in a complex system, such as a steam plant. Hayes (1979b) has distinguished two separate ontologies for liquids: a *contained-liquid* ontology, in which liquid is thought of as the fluid in a place, and a *molecular collection* ontology, in which water is thought of as little bits of fluid that move around inside the system. The contained-liquid ontology is appropriate if the goal is to determine what flows can occur. However, this view of water is not useful if one wants to know how changes in the properties of the working fluid in one part of the system (say, the rising temperature of the inlet water in a boiler) affect properties of the fluid in another part of the system (say, temperature of the steam coming out of the boiler's superheater). In this case, liquid must be viewed in terms of molecular collections that move around inside the system. Conversely, establishing flows using the molecular collection view is very difficult. A learner with only one of these two ontologies will have a difficult time with certain questions, and such difficulties may drive the search for a new ontology.

Mathematical abstractions provide another important driving force in ontological change. In system dynamics, for example, physical systems involving fluid elements, mechanical elements, thermal elements, and acoustical elements are viewed as variations on a common, abstract theme. This means that the analysis and synthesis tools developed for abstract mathematical models can be used to solve problems in several domains. This is a powerful motivation, as evidenced by the wave of interest in attempting diverse applications evoked by the publication of certain new mathematical formalisms (e.g., catastrophe theory and fractal geometry).

12.6 SUMMARY

The authors have described their progress in weaving together Structure Mapping theory and Qualitative Process theory into a framework that aims to account for learning in physical domains. The learning sequence is built around three ideas. First, development proceeds from rich to sparse and from concrete to abstract—that is, initial representations differ from later representations in containing more, and more context-specific, information. Second, after sufficient experience people develop experiential models that are centered around the notion of physical process, as described by Qualitative Process theory. Third, the process of comparing and mapping between stored knowledge and the current situation, as described in Structure Mapping theory, is central to experiential learning.

Four stages of experiential learning have been laid out: protohistories, the causal corpus, naive physics, and expert models.[16] The first stage, that of protohistories, embodies the idea that early representations are rich and context specific; this stage attempts to capture a combination of evidence from developmental patterns, similarity judgments, basic-level categories, and object prototypes. The third stage is the process-centered stage described by Qualitative Process theory. The fourth stage builds on the third-stage models, adding domain-independent generalizations and in some cases mathematical models. There is some evidence for the third and fourth stages in the research on the novice-expert shift (Chi, Feltovich, and Glaser, 1981; Larkin, 1983).

The second stage, the causal corpus, is the most speculative. There is no direct evidence for its existence, nor do the authors currently have a detailed theory of the kinds of causal statements that can enter into the representations. Moreover, detailing how the causal corpus emerges from protohistories will not be easy. But something like the causal corpus seems necessary: a collection of simplistic, mostly binary, directed regularities among dimensions and quantities that begin to be differentiated

---

[16]In deriving this sequence of learning stages, the authors have been influenced by Piaget's well-known theory of cognitive development (see Piaget, 1954; or for an introduction to the work, see Flavel, 1963). However, the four stages of learning presented here differ considerably from Piaget's four-stage account. One difference, for example, is that the authors view their stages as domain specific, whereas Piaget's stages are intended as general stages of intellectual development.

out of the tangled representations of the protohistory stage. The learner can now use these simple assertions as grist for further progress.

What happens to prior stages as new stages occur? First, stored representations have to be distinguished from new learning. The authors conjecture that learners retain much of their stored knowledge even when they go beyond the stage at which it was formed. Thus, a hydraulics engineer still uses the same protohistory he or she formed as a toddler to decide how fast one can carry a glass of water without spilling it. And, as deKleer points out (1979), expert physicists do not always resort to quantitative models (fourth stage); frequently the answer they want can be obtained by using a good qualitative model (third stage).

But what about new learning? Does new learning occur only at the leading edge, or do people continue to learn at levels below the most advanced stage they have attained? The authors suspect that even experts continue to learn at all prior stages, with the possible exception of the causal corpus. As described earlier, there is evidence that even experts continue to lay down new protohistories. Similarly, learners who are operating at the fourth stage, that of expert models, may continue to learn and refine their naive physics. This is because the mathematical models of the fourth stage are not a substitute for the process models of the third stage.[17] Improvements to a naive physics are useful whether or not mathematical models are also available. As expertise increases the least new learning is expected within the causal corpus.

Of the four levels, the causal corpus has the least claim to continued independent existence in an advanced expert. The causal corpus is not reliable for prediction, nor does it possess the advantages of automaticity.[18] In summary, the overall picture is that a learner moves from rich, perceptual protohistories to the sparser representation of the causal corpus. The causal corpus serves as a staging area in which rough connections among variables can be stored until they can be subsumed into a true system. If learning continues, a person develops a process-centered naive physics and, for some domains, expert models.

---

[17]Historically, philosophers of science have differed about whether the best conception of a domain is provided by a mathematical model or by a mechanical model. For an extended discussion of this historical debate, see Hesse (1966). The position taken here is that both mathematical models and mechanical models are important to full understanding of a domain.

[18]This discussion, of course, concerns domains for which the learner eventually acquires expert knowledge. We suspect that people rely heavily on causal corpus knowledge in domains in which they are inexpert. Further, there are many domains, such as child-rearing or getting rich, that lack definitive models. Collins's work on plausible reasoning (1978) suggests that in these domains, people rely heavily on this causal corpus knowledge. See also Salter's work (1983) on tacit theories of economics.

ACKNOWLEDGMENTS

The authors gratefully acknowledge the intellectual and financial support of Schlumberger-Doll Research. They thank Allan Collins, Dave Chapman, Ed Smith, Albert Stevens, and Dan Weld for their insightful comments on an earlier draft of this paper.

References

Anderson, J. R., "Acquisition of Cognitive Skill," *Psychological Review,* Vol. 89, No. 4, pp. 369–406, 1982.

Brooks, L., "Nonanalytic Concept Formation and Memory for Instances," *Cognition and Categorization,* B. B. Lloyd and E. Rosch (Eds.), Erlbaum, Hillsdale, N.J., 1978.

Brown, A. L., and Campione, J. C., "Three Faces of Transfer: Implications for Early Competence, Individual Differences, and Instruction," in *Advances in Developmental Psychology,* M. Lamb, A. Brown, and B. Rogoff (Eds.), Erlbaum, Hillsdale, N.J., 1985, in press.

Bruner, J. S., Olver, R., and Greenfield, P., *Studies in Cognitive Growth,* Wiley, New York, 1966.

Buckley, S., *Sun Up to Sun Down,* McGraw-Hill, New York, 1979.

Burstein, M. H., "Concept Formation by Incremental Analogical Reasoning and Debugging," *Proceedings of the International Machine Learning Workshop,* R. S. Michalski (Ed.), Allerton House, University of Illinois at Urbana-Champaign, pp. 19–25, June 22–24, 1983. (An updated version of this paper appears as chap. 13 of this volume.)

Carbonell, J. G., "A Computational Model of Problem-Solving by Analogy," *Proceedings of the Seventh IJCAI,* Vancouver, B.C., pp. 147–52, 1981.

———, "Derivational Analogy in Problem Solving and Knowledge Acquisition," *Proceedings of the International Machine Learning Workshop,* R. S. Michalski (Ed.), Allerton House, University of Illinois at Urbana-Champaign, pp. 12–18, June 22–24, 1983. (An updated version of this paper appears as chap. 14 of this volume.)

Carey, S., "Are Children Fundamentally Different Kinds of Thinkers and Learners Than Adults?" in *Thinking and Learning Skills,* Vol. 2, S. Chipman, J. Segal, and R. Glaser (Eds.), Erlbaum, Hillsdale, N.J., 1985, in press.

Case, R., "Intellectual Development from Birth to Adulthood: A Neo-Piagetian Interpretation," in *Children's Thinking: What Develops?* R. S. Siegler (Ed.), Erlbaum, Hillsdale, N.J., 1978.

Chi, M. T. H., Feltovich, P. J., and Glaser, R., "Categorization and Representation of Physics Problems by Experts and Novices," *Cognitive Science,* Vol. 5, No. 2, pp. 121–51, April-June 1981.

Clark, E. V., "What's in a Word? On the Child's Acquisition of Semantics in His First Language," in *Cognitive Development and the Acquisition of Language,* T. E. Moore (Ed.), Academic Press, New York, 1973.

Clements, J., "Analogical Reasoning Patterns in Expert Problem-solving," *Proceedings of the Fourth Annual Conference of the Cognitive Science Society,* Berkeley, Calif., pp. 137–40, 1982.

Collins, A., "Fragments of a Theory of Human Plausible Reasoning," in *Theoretical Issues in Natural Language Processing II*, D. Waltz (Ed.), University of Illinois at Urbana-Champaign, 1978.

Collins, A.; Warnock, E. H.; Aiello, N.; and Miller, M. L., "Reasoning from Incomplete Knowledge," in *Representation and Understanding: Studies in Cognitive Science*, D. Bobrow and A. Collins (Eds.), Academic Press, New York, 1975.

Darden, L., "Reasoning by Analogy in Scientific Theory Construction," *Proceedings of the International Machine Learning Workshop*, R. S. Michalski (Ed.), Allerton House, University of Illinois at Urbana-Champaign, pp. 31–40, June 22–24, 1983.

deKleer, J., "Causal and Teleological Reasoning in Circuit Recognition," Technical Report No. 529, AI Lab, MIT, 1979.

deKleer, J., and Brown, J. S., "Assumptions and Ambiguities in Mechanistic Mental Models," in *Mental Models*, D. Gentner and A. L. Stevens (Eds.), Erlbaum, Hillsdale, N.J., 1983.

Dietterich, T., and Michalski, R. S., "A Comparative Review of Selected Methods for Learning from Examples," in *Machine Learning: An Artificial Intelligence Approach*, R. S. Michalski, J. G. Carbonell, and T. M. Mitchell (Eds.), Tioga, Palo Alto, Calif., 1983.

diSessa, A., "Phenomenology and the Evolution of Intuition," in *Mental Models*, D. Gentner and A. L. Stevens (Eds.), Erlbaum, Hillsdale, N.J., 1983.

Flavell, J. H., *The Developmental Psychology of Jean Piaget*, Van Nostrand Reinhold, New York, 1963.

Forbus, K., "Qualitative Reasoning about Physical Processes," *Proceedings of the Seventh IJCAI*, Vancouver, B.C., pp. 326–30, 1981.

———, "Measurement Interpretation in Qualitative Process Theory," *Proceedings of the Eighth IJCAI*, Karlsruhe, W. Ger., pp. 315–20, 1983.

———, "Qualitative Process Theory," Technical Report No. 789, AI Lab, MIT, 1984.

Garner, W. R., "Aspects of Stimulus: Features, Dimensions, and Configurations," in *Cognition and Categorization*, B. B. Lloyd and E. Rosch (Eds.), Erlbaum, Hillsdale, N.J., 1978.

Gelman, R., "Counting in the Preschooler: What Does and Does Not Develop," in *Children's Thinking: What Develops?* R. S. Siegler (Ed.), Erlbaum, Hillsdale, N.J., 1978.

Gentner, D., "The Structure of Analogical Models in Science," Technical Report No. 4451, Bolt Beranek and Newman, Cambridge, Mass., 1980.

———, "Are Scientific Analogies Metaphors?" in *Metaphor: Problems and Perspectives*, D. Miall (Ed.), Harvester Press, Ltd., Brighton, England, 1982.

———, "Structure-Mapping: A Theoretical Framework for Analogy," *Cognitive Science*, Vol. 7, No. 2, pp. 155–70, 1983.

Gentner, D., and Gentner, D. R., "Flowing Waters or Teeming Crowds: Mental Models of Electricity," in *Mental Models*, D. Gentner and A. L. Stevens (Eds.), Erlbaum, Hillsdale, N.J., 1983.

Gentner, D., and Stuart, P., "Metaphor as Structure-Mapping: What Develops," Technical Report No. 315, Center for the Study of Reading, University of Illinois, 1984.

Gibson, E. J., *Principles of Perceptual Learning and Development*, Prentice-Hall, Englewood Cliffs, N.J., 1969.

Gick, M. L., and Holyoak, K. J., "Analogical Problem Solving," *Cognitive Psychology,* Vol. 12, pp. 306–55, 1980.

———, "Schema Induction and Analogical Transfer," *Cognitive Psychology,* Vol. 15, pp. 1–38, 1983.

Hayes, P. J., "The Naive Physics Manifesto," in *Expert Systems in the Microelectronic Age,* D. Michie (Ed.), Edinburgh University Press, Edinburgh, 1979a.

———, "Naive Physics 1: Ontology for Liquids," Memo, Centre pour les etudes semantiques et cognitives, Geneva, Switzerland, 1979b.

Hesse, M. B., *Models and Analogies in Science,* University of Notre Dame Press, Notre Dame, Ind., 1966.

Hoffman, R. R., "Metaphor in Science," in *The Psycholinguistics of Figurative Language,* R. P. Honeck and R. R. Hoffman (Eds.), Erlbaum, Hillsdale, N.J., 1980.

Inhelder, B., and Piaget, J., *The Growth of Logical Thinking from Childhood to Adolescence,* Basic Books, New York, 1958.

Kahneman, D., and Tversky, A., "Subjective Probability: A Judgment of Representitiveness," *Cognitive Psychology,* Vol. 3, pp. 430–54, 1972.

Kempton, W., "Two Theories Used for Home Heat Control," in *Cultural Models in Language and Thought,* D. Holland and N. Quinn (Eds.), Cambridge University Press, Cambridge, 1985, in press.

Langley, P., "Rediscovering Physics with BACON.3," *Proceedings of the Sixth IJCAI,* Tokyo, pp. 505–7, 1979.

Langley, P.; Zytkow, J.; Simon, H.; and Bradshaw, G., "Mechanisms for Qualitative and Quantitative Discovery," *Proceedings of the International Machine Learning Workshop,* R. S. Michalski (Ed.), Allerton House, University of Illinois at Urbana-Champaign, June 22–24, 1983. (An updated version of this paper appears as chap. 16 of this volume.)

Larkin, J., "The Role of Problem Representation in Physics," in *Mental Models,* D. Gentner and A. L. Stevens (Eds.), Erlbaum, Hillsdale, N.J., 1983.

Lenat, D., "The Nature of Heuristics," *Artificial Intelligence,* Vol. 19, pp. 189–249, 1982.

———, "The Nature of Heuristics II," *Artificial Intellgence,* Vol. 20, pp. 31–59, 1983.

———, "The Nature of Heuristics III," *Artificial Intelligence,* Vol. 20, pp. 61–98, 1983.

McCarthy, J., and Hayes, P., "Some Philosophical Problems from the Standpoint of Artificial Intelligence," in *Machine Intelligence 4,* Edinburgh University Press, Edinburgh, 1969.

Michalski, R. S., "A Theory and Methodology of Inductive Learning," *Artificial Intelligence,* Vol. 20, pp. 111–61, 1983.

Michalski, R. S., and Stepp, R. E., "Learning from Observation: Conceptual Clustering," in *Machine Learning: An Artificial Intelligence Approach,* R. S. Michalski, J. G. Carbonell, and T. M. Mitchell (Eds.), Tioga, Palo Alto, Calif., 1983.

Mitchell, T. M., "Generalization as Search," *Artificial Intelligence,* Vol. 18, pp. 203–26, 1982.

Mitchell, T. M.; Utgoff, P. E.; Nudel, B.; and Banerji, R., "Learning Problem-solving Heuristics Through Practice," *Proceedings of the Seventh IJCAI,* Vancouver, B.C., pp. 127–34, 1981.

Nelson, K., "How Children Represent Knowledge of Their World in and out of Language: A Preliminary Report," in *Children's Thinking: What Develops?* R. S. Siegler (Ed.), Erlbaum, Hillsdale, N.J., 1978.

Nickerson, R. S., and Adams, M. J., "Long-term Memory for a Common Object," *Cognitive Psychology,* Vol. 11, pp. 287–307, 1979.

Palmer, S. E., "Fundamental Aspects of Cognitive Representation," in *Cognition and Categorization,* B. B. Lloyd and E. Rosch (Eds.), Erlbaum, Hillsdale, N.J., 1978.

Piaget, J., *The Child's Conception of Physical Causality,* Routledge & Kegan Paul, London, 1951.

———, *The Construction of Reality in the Child,* Basic Books, New York, 1954.

Posner, M. I., and Mitchell, R. F., "Chronometric Analysis of Classification," *Psychological Review,* Vol. 74, pp. 392–409, 1967.

Reber, A. S., "Implicit Learning of Artificial Grammars," *Journal of Verbal Learning and Verbal Behavior,* Vol. 6, pp. 855–63, 1967.

———, "Implicit Learning of Synthetic Languages: The Role of Instructional Set," *Journal of Experimental Psychology: Human Memory and Learning,* Vol. 2, pp. 88–94, 1976.

Reed, S. K., Ernst, G. W., and Banerji, R., "The Role of Analogy in Transfer Between Similar Problem States," *Cognitive Psychology,* Vol. 6, pp. 436–50, 1974.

Rosch, E., "On the Internal Structure of Perceptual and Semantic Categories," in *Cognitive Development and the Acquisition of Language,* T. E. Moore (Ed.), Academic Press, New York, 1973.

———, "Cognitive Representations of Semantic Categories," *Journal of Experimental Psychology: General,* Vol. 107, pp. 192–233, 1975.

———, "Principles of Categorization," in *Cognition and Categorization,* E. Rosch and B. B. Lloyd (Eds.), Erlbaum, Hillsdale, N.J., 1978.

Rumelhart, D., and Norman, D. A., "Accretion, Tuning, and Restructuring: Three Modes of Learning," in *Semantic Factors in Cognition,* J. W. Cotton and R. L. Klatzky (Eds.), Erlbaum, Hillsdale, N.J., 1978.

Schneider, W., and Fisk, A. D., "Attention Theory and Mechanisms for Skilled Performance," in *Memory and Control of Action,* R. A. Magill (Ed.), North-Holland, New York, 1983.

Shepp, B. E., "From Perceived Similarity to Dimensional Structure: A New Hypothesis about Perspective Development," in *Cognition and Categorization,* E. Rosch and B. B. Lloyd (Eds.), Erlbaum, Hillsdale, N.J., 1978.

Siegler, R. S., "Three Aspects of Cognitive Development," *Cognitive Psychology,* Vol. 8, pp. 481–520, 1976.

———, "The Origins of Scientific Reasoning," in *Children's Thinking: What Develops?* in R. S. Siegler (Ed.), Erlbaum, Hillsdale, N.J., 1978.

———, "Developmental Sequences Within and Between Concepts," *Monographs of the Society for Research in Child Development,* Vol. 46, No. 2, 1981.

Smith, E. E., and Medin, D. L., *Categories and Concepts,* Harvard University Press, Cambridge, 1981.

Stepp, R. E., and Michalski, R. S., "How to Structure Structured Objects," *Proceedings of the International Machine Learning Workshop,* R. S. Michalski (Ed.), Allerton House, University of Illinois at Urbana-Champaign, pp. 156–60, June 22–24, 1983. (An updated version of this paper appears as chap. 17 of this volume.)

Stevens, A., Collins, A., and Goldin, S. E., "Misconceptions in Students' Understanding," *Journal of Man-Machine Studies,* Vol. 11, pp. 145–56, 1979.

Sussman, G. J., *A Computational Model of Skill Acquisition,* Springer-Verlag, New York, 1976.

Tversky, A., "Features of Similarity," *Psychological Review,* Vol. 84, pp. 327–52, 1977.

Tversky, A., and Gati, I., "Similarity, Separability and the Triangle Inequality," *Psychological Review,* Vol. 89, No. 2, pp. 123–54, 1982.

Tversky, A., and Kahneman, D., "Availability: A Heuristic for Judging Frequency and Probability," *Cognitive Psychology,* Vol. 5, pp. 207–32, 1973.

Williams, M., Hollan, J., and Stevens, A. L., "Human Reasoning about a Simple Physical System," in *Mental Models,* D. Gentner and A. L. Stevens (Eds.), Erlbaum, Hillsdale, N.J., 1983.

Winner, E., "New Names for Old Things," *Journal of Child Language,* Vol. 6, pp. 469–91, 1979.

Winston, P. H., "Learning and Reasoning by Analogy," *Communications of the ACM,* Vol. 23, No. 12, pp. 689–703, 1980.

————, "Learning New Principles from Precedents and Exercises," *Artificial Intelligence,* Vol. 19, pp. 321–50, 1982.

PART
FOUR

LEARNING BY
ANALOGY

13

CONCEPT FORMATION BY INCREMENTAL ANALOGICAL REASONING AND DEBUGGING

Mark H. Burstein
Yale University

Abstract

This chapter presents a model of learning by analogical reasoning. The model is based on two main ideas, namely, (1) that the analogies used in learning about an unfamiliar domain depend heavily on the use of previously formed causal abstractions in a familiar or base domain; (2) that these analogies are extended *incrementally* to handle related situations. CARL is a computer program that learns about the semantics of assignment statements for the BASIC programming language. It is described as an illustration of causally driven analogical reasoning and learning. The model maps and debugs inferences drawn from several commonly used analogies to assignment in response to presented examples.

13.1 INTRODUCTION

It has often been said among AI researchers that learning something new requires knowing a lot about it already. This is certainly true for learning by analogy. This chapter shows how prior knowledge can be applied in one specific kind of learning by analogy, namely, the formation of new concepts in an unfamiliar domain from analogies presented in a text or by a teacher. A computer program, CARL, will be described to illustrate this kind of learning. CARL learns about the semantics of assignment statements for the BASIC programming language when given analogies like those found in introductory computer programming textbooks. The model was

motivated in part by observations of how students behaved when they were first introduced to BASIC using these analogies. In fact, it was often the *errors* made by these
students that provided the most useful insights into analogical reasoning processes.

Some unresolved problems with earlier models of analogical reasoning are
addressed here. Because of the close relationship between everyday notions of
analogy and similarity, several models of analogical reasoning in AI have been developed around forms of partial pattern matching. Algorithms like those developed by
Evans (1968) and Winston (1980) were based on the assumption that a best partial
match could be found by accumulating evidence for each of a number of possible
object-to-object mappings between representations of two situations and then
choosing the one that scored highest. In these systems, evidence for a match consisted
essentially of the number of relational connections preserved between corresponding
objects for a given alignment of objects. The object alignment that placed the largest
number of relations and attributes in correspondence was considered the best match
and thus the "correct" analogical interpretation.

This approach has several major drawbacks as a model for analogical *learning*.
First, it presupposes that well-defined, bounded representational models of the situations in both the *base* (i.e., familiar) domain and the *target* domain are available as
inputs. In a learning situation, however, the required prior representations of objects
and relations in the target domain may be wrong or inconsistent with the analogy. If
the domain is totally unfamiliar, there may not even be any fragments of a useful representation available. The point of presenting an analogy to students is to aid them in
the *construction* of a representation of a target situation or to correct problems in a
prior representation. Since matching cannot be used to construct such a representation where there was none before, it cannot be the basis of a general theory of learning
by analogy.

Another problem with theories based principally on the matching of descriptions, particularly as the complexity of these descriptions increases, is that conceptual representations for real situations may contain many objects that don't take part
in a specified analogy. Winston has suggested that attention to important relations,
such as those involving causal links, can reduce the number of links and thus the computational complexity of the matching process to some degree (Winston, 1980,
1982). Yet even in strictly causal models, subsystems can quite often be usefully
expanded to greater and greater levels of detail (de Kleer and Brown, 1981; Collins
and Gentner, 1982); new objects and relationships that may or may not play roles in
the analogy are thus introduced. A system that takes as input incomplete descriptions
of analogical situations, such as those presented in texts, but that has a large body of
background causal knowledge and other knowledge for "filling out" such descriptions, would still need methods for narrowing the focus of the comparison. In particular, it must be possible to find analogical relationships between situations without
pairing detailed specifications of *all* of the objects potentially present in representations of each situation.

To address these objections, we have replaced bottom-up matching with an approach based on analogical *mapping*. Such an approach uses a set of heuristics to delimit what is to be "imported" from a base to a target domain at a given time. One such heuristic involves mapping previously formed abstractions, such as those embodying causal and planning rules. It has been argued independently that such structures are necessary when one is interpreting, planning, and reasoning about situations in familiar domains (Wilensky, 1983; Sacerdoti, 1975). Focusing on such structures and their associated special cases and known problems allows for a much more top-down form of analogical reasoning. This is exactly what is required when prior knowledge of the target domain is severely impoverished.

13.2 Student Protocols Used as Guidelines

Analogies found in typical introductory texts generally include statements suggesting correspondences between classes of objects in the domains to be related. To be useful, these stated correspondences must be presented along with a target domain situation described *in terms of* a plausible situation in the familiar domain. This is illustrated in figure 13-1, which depicts the method used by one author to introduce the notion of a computer variable.

The analogy shown in figure 13-1 can be paraphrased as follows: "A *variable* is like a *box* in that numbers can be *inside* variables similar to the way objects can be inside boxes." If this analogy is to be applied effectively by a student learning about assignment, it will be helpful if some valid actions involving variables in this relationship are explicitly introduced, as by the statement "To *put* the number 5 in the variable X, type '$X = 5$'." Regardless of how it is presented, however, this kind of given information must be combined with a student's ability to access knowledge of the "box" domain, including many specific concepts and inferences developed from

A	B	C	D	E	F	G	H	I
3				12				
J	K	L	M	N	O	P	Q	R
		7						
S	T	U	V	W	X	Y	Z	
					5			

To illustrate the concept of *variable,* imagine that there are 26 little *boxes* inside the computer. Each box can *contain* one number at any one time (Albrecht, Finkel, and Brown, 1978).

Figure 13-1:   A textbook introduction to variables.

experience in that domain. In this simple case, a student must at least be able to interpret statements about *putting* objects in boxes and to predict the effects of such actions under varying conditions.

This author found that students learning introductory BASIC generated a number of *plausible,* though incorrect, explanations when asked to predict the effects of presented examples or to solve simple problems using what they had been told about the "programming" domain. Their answers were plausible in the sense that they were based on valid or plausible scenarios for events in one of the analogical base domains that they knew. The errors occurred even when they were analyzing extremely simple assignment statements. For example, statements like "$X = Y$" were misinterpreted as indicating that the variable Y was to be "placed inside" the variable X. This can be seen as a mapping of the plausible scenario that a box can be placed inside another, larger box.

Errors of this type are almost inevitable when one is extrapolating from an analogical base domain, since analogies are, almost by definition, useful but imperfect correspondences between situations. Although these errors were not the intended effects of the teacher who presented the analogy, they may nevertheless be taken as examples of analogical reasoning in humans with limited knowledge of a target domain. They were therefore included in the data treated by the process model presented here.

Such examples make it clear that an important part of the process of developing new concepts by analogy must be the incremental debugging of the inferences derived from the analogy. Sources of alternate hypotheses, including *additional analogies,* can also be quite useful in this debugging process. The following protocols with one subject (Perry, age ten) illustrate this quite clearly. After Perry read a paragraph containing the box analogy, taken from a textbook, the dialogue shown in figure 13-2 occurred.

Here, three common analogies to variables and assignment are mentioned (shown in italics in the figure): (1) *putting* numbers *in* variables is like putting objects

Teacher: Suppose there's a box called X and we're going to store the number 5 in there. How would you do that?
Pupil: The variables . . . uh X . . . X . . . no . . .
Teacher: You have to tell it . . .
Pupil: Put the number 5 in the variable X.
Teacher: You have to give it a command that will make it do that. Now, here we have an example . . . suppose I type "$B = 10$."
Pupil: Oh, and if you want to store this 10 you write . . .
Teacher: Now I typed that in, so now it's going to *remember* that, ok?
Pupil: That *B equals 10.*
Teacher: It's got a box called *B,* and inside it is 10.
Pupil: So you write the box and then the number that you want to store it in?
Teacher: Yes, and you put in an equal sign to tell it to do that.

Figure 13-2: An informal introduction of several related analogies.

in boxes, (2) computers use variables to *remember* things they are *told*, and (3) assignment statements are like *algebraic equalities*. At first glance, this might seem to be more confusing than helpful. Yet each analogy can be shown to play a useful, often complementary, role in developing a working understanding of the idea of assignment. Tutorial textbooks often use at least two of these analogies. If they are not presented explicitly as analogies, their presence is suggested by the normal language of the computer science domain. Computer *memory* is often referred to, and the equal sign is used in a number of languages to denote assignment.

The real test of a tutorial analogy is how it affects one's understanding of new situations. The following example shows one way in which having several analogies can be more helpful than having just one. As the dialogue above continued, a point about transferring values from one variable to another was illustrated. The teacher typed "$P = 10$" and then "$Q = P$." Figure 13-3 shows what happened. Perry clearly seems to have made the inference that if "$Q = P$" was analogous to moving an object from one box to another, then the number that had been in P must now be in Q. Since objects, when moved, are no longer at their original location, P must now be "empty."

When pressed, Perry was uncertain about this conclusion and came up with an alternate explanation based on an entirely different line of reasoning, using a different analogy. If typing "$Q = P$" is treated as a statement to the computer that the two variables have equal values, then, according to the normal algebraic interpretation, one can conclude from the fact that P was originally 10 that Q is also 10, while P's value stays the same.

Applying his knowledge of algebra in this explanation did not stop Perry from further use of the box analogy. He continued to use both models in analyzing new situations. Algebra simply provided what seemed like a more satisfactory answer to this particular problem.

Teacher: So what's in P now?
  Pupil: Oh. Nothing.
Teacher: Nothing?
  Pupil: 10! and then Q is also.
Teacher: What do you think it is? Is it nothing or 10?
  Pupil: Let's find out. First let's see . . .
Teacher: Well, what do you think it is?
  Pupil: If you have two boxes, and you moved . . .
         You moved or it equals to? You moved what's in P to Q so there's nothing in it, or did you
         only put the same number in Q that's in P? I think it's 10.
Teacher: You think it's 10?
  Pupil: Because you don't say that, uh, move P at all . . . take P out. You only said that Q equals the
         same as P. So if it equals, it has to be 10, because if there's no 10 in it, Q wouldn't be equal to
         it.

Figure 13-3:   Two analogies involving conflicting predictions.

Such errors and their explanations played an important role in the development of the process model implemented in CARL. Because these incorrect hypotheses were arrived at by extending existing analogies to cover plausible, related base-domain situations, they were assumed to have been produced by the same analogical reasoning process that produced correct answers in other cases. Thus the analogical reasoning model described below was developed in an attempt to account for these errors as well as for correct analogical inferences.

13.3 A PROGRAM THAT LEARNS ABOUT ASSIGNMENT

Many aspects of the overall learning model are illustrated in the behavior of the computer program CARL, which learns about different kinds of assignment statements by building and combining inferences drawn from several different analogies. Figure 13-4 is the equivalent in English of one portion of a dialogue with CARL (actual inputs are in an extended version of Conceptual Dependency; see Schank and Abelson, 1977).

With the aid of a tutor CARL develops semantic representations for most common types of assignment statements. It forms rules concurrently about how to parse them, how to infer the logical results of their execution, and how to generate them as components of simple plans. In the process, it makes a number of the same mistakes made by people learning the same material. (See Burstein, 1981, for other examples.)

Teacher:	The computer remembers a number by putting it in a variable.
Teacher:	A variable is like a box.
Teacher:	To put the number 5 in the variable named X, type "$X=5$."
Teacher:	How do you get the computer to remember the number 9?
CARL:	Type "$X=9$."
Teacher:	Suppose I then type "$X=6$."
Teacher:	Now what's in the variable X?
CARL:	6 is in X and 9 is in X.
Teacher:	No, the 6 replaces the 9 in X.
CARL:	OK.
Teacher:	Suppose I type "$Y=5$." and then "$X=Y$."
Teacher:	Now what's in the variable X?
CARL:	Y is in X.
Teacher:	No, it means put the number in Y into X.
CARL:	OK.
Teacher:	Now what's in the variable Y?
CARL:	Nothing.
Teacher:	Guess again.
CARL:	5 is in Y (by analogy to equality).
Teacher:	Correct.
CARL:	OK.

Figure 13-4:   A dialogue with CARL.

13.4 AN INITIAL STRUCTURE MAPPING THEORY

The analogical reasoning process used in CARL was strongly influenced by some psychological studies of analogical learning. Gentner has outlined a cognitive model of learning from scientific or "explanatory" analogies involving some of the problems mentioned here, though not others (Gentner, 1982; Gentner and Gentner, 1982; see also chap. 12 of this volume). The analogies considered by Gentner included such statements as:

The hydrogen atom is like the solar system.
Electricity flows through a wire like water through a pipe.

The model Gentner proposed for learning from such analogies, unlike those based principally on pattern matching, did not require a full description of the target domain beforehand. In her model, relations, or predicates connecting several objects or concepts, are mapped *identically* from one domain to the other under a prespecified object-object correspondence. After identical first-order relations have been mapped to relate corresponding objects in a target situation, second-order predicates, such as causal links between relations, are also mapped.

Although this model does suggest a way to map new structures into an unfamiliar domain, it does not give a good account of how corresponding objects are first identified, nor does it constrain *which* relations are mapped. It also does not allow for mappings between nonidentical relations, which is often necessary.

The need to constrain the set of relations mapped by an analogy can be seen by examining Gentner's representation of a mental model for the solar system and the mapping her system predicts to an analogous model for the atom (fig. 13-5). In the diagram, the sun is related to each planet by the predicate HOTTER-THAN, as well

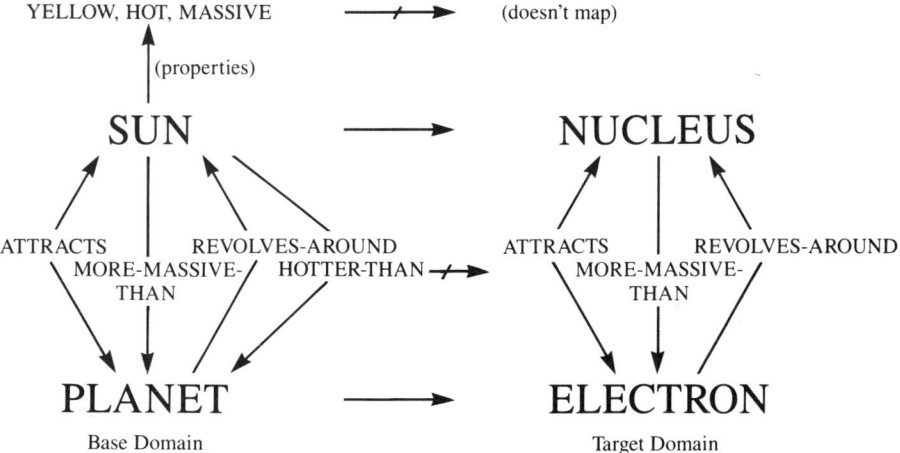

Figure 13-5: Gentner's representation of Rutherford's atomic model.

as by ATTRACTS and REVOLVES-AROUND, two predicates that are themselves causally related (not shown). The problem Gentner noticed was that the HOTTER-THAN relation does *not* seem to be mapped to the atomic model; that is, people don't generally believe that the analogy implies that the nucleus of an atom must be hotter than its surrounding electrons. Gentner's formal specification of the mapping process could not predict this failure to map certain relations. This is a potentially large problem, since many other attribute comparisons, such as BRIGHTER-THAN, YELLOWER-THAN, and so on, could also be part of a description of the solar system. Presumably, those relations are not being mapped either.

The explanation provided by Gentner for this phenomenon was in terms of a general condition on the mapping process, which she called the *systematicity condition.* This condition is essentially that "predicates are more likely to be imported into the target if they belong to a system of coherent, mutually constraining relationships, the others of which are mapped" (Gentner and Gentner, 1982). In this case, the constraint system is the causal relationship connecting the relations ATTRACTS and MORE-MASSIVE-THAN to the motion REVOLVES-AROUND. Since these predicates are related together, the systematicity condition predicts that they are more likely to be mapped. Although this example clearly shows the need to constrain the mapping to a subset of all the possible relations between a given set of objects, Gentner's systematicity condition is not easily integrated into her proposed process model, as stated.

In CARL, this general condition is reformulated as part of a set of top-down constraints on the relations considered for mapping. When a causally connected structure can be found in memory to support a described base-domain situation, only relations taking part in that structure are considered for mapping. By this rule, the only relations considered for mapping in an analysis of the solar system analogy are those contributing to the learner's prior causal model of the relative movement of the planetary bodies. The rule is not simply a restatement of Gentner's condition, since the discourse context and the active goals of the learner may influence the type of causal explanation retrieved for a given situation and hence the effect of the rule. For example, this model suggests that there will be times when a description of an analogy is underspecified (no causal structure found) or ambiguous (several causal structures found).[1]

A second mapping constraint used in CARL operates on the structured sets of relations retrieved from memory. This constraint states that simple attribute compar-

---

[1]Interpreting the solar system analogy when given the statement "Each atom is like a solar system" is presumably made easier if one is also given some statement like "Electrons *move about* the nucleus the way planets move about the sun," or if an accompanying diagram is provided that focuses one's attention directly on the similar *motions* of the two systems.

isons (like HOTTER-THAN, LARGER-THAN, and so on) are not mapped if the objects in the target domain cannot be compared on the same relational scale and no corresponding attributes have been suggested by the teacher. For example, in applying the analogy between boxes and variables, CARL decides that the precondition that numbers must "fit" inside variables should be dropped from the causal structure for assignment because there is no common size scale for numbers and variables.

Of course, limiting the set of relations considered for mapping in this way requires that the causal structures governing base-domain situations are made available to the analogical reasoning system at the appropriate time. All of this is made easier in the context of a language-understanding system that activates such memory structures as a normal part of its language interpretation process. When CARL is presented with a statement of a novel analogy, it uses the object and predicate assumptions given in the analogy statement to turn an analogical description of a target-domain event into a description of a base-domain situation that it can support as plausible with causal and goal/plan structures retrieved from memory in that domain. It then maps the retrieved causal structure to the target domain.

The result of mapping a causally connected structure found under these conditions is the formation of a new, parallel, causal structure characterizing the target example. Objects in the target example are made to fill roles in the newly formed structure; known object correspondences between the domains are used when available. When known correspondences are not available, object correspondences between the domains are only formed by virtue of role correspondences between the mapped structures. So, for example, from a causal structure indicating that the result of putting a physical object in a container is the state "the object is INSIDE the container," CARL concludes that one result of an assignment is a parallel relationship between variable and numbers. On the basis of corresponding roles in these relations, an indirect correspondence is formed between physical objects (that go into boxes) and numbers. This causally directed mapping process forms new target-domain causal structures where none existed before, while allowing correspondences between relations to be formed with some consideration of what is known of the objects and relations in the target domain.

The approach to analogical reasoning and concept formation taken here parallels Carbonell's work on analogical problem solving (Carbonell, 1983; see also chap. 14 of this volume). Carbonell outlined a problem-solving process whose first step was to be *reminded* of a solution to a similar problem. The process model he proposed then modified the components of the recalled plan to satisfy the needs of the new problem using a set of operators that preserved, as much as possible, the temporal and logical goal/subgoal structure of the original solution. Both Carbonell's model and that of the author were strongly influenced by Schank's theory of human memory organization (Schank, 1982) and the effects of that organization on the processes of interpreting, planning, and learning about new situations.

13.5 MAPPING TO NONIDENTICAL RELATIONS

Gentner's model also claimed that all relations are mapped "identically" between analogous situations. Although this might be true in analogies between purely spatial descriptions of situations, including the standard geometric analogies discussed by Evans (1968), it is much too strong a claim in general. When analogies are formed between physically realizable situations and purely abstract ones, as in mathematics and computer programming, it is impossible to maintain the "identical predicate" mapping model.

Probably the most important thing implied by the analogy between boxes and variables is the fact that variables can "contain" things; that is, the relationship between a box and an object inside the box is, in some ways, similar to the relationship between a variable and the number associated with that variable. Yet it is not the physical properties of boxes that are preserved by this analogy. Variables don't have sides and a bottom that a contained object can rest on. The relations related by mapping are similar primarily because of the actions and plans in which each is involved. One can *put* things *in* boxes, and assignment provides a way to "put" numbers "in" variables as well. The principle function of the containment relation for variables is its role in abstract plans like STORE-OBJECT.

Students learning to program are generally aware that computers can manipulate numbers and that the reason one learns to program is to be able to direct the computer's actions. This knowledge may be used to infer that the action of putting a number in a variable will be used in plans to manipulate numbers. Whether or not this inference occurs immediately, however, the fact that the analogy between boxes and variables relates physical objects to abstract concepts (numbers) suggests that the actual preconditions and side effects of assignment in the programming domain may be quite different from the conditions on placing objects in boxes. Although students only *gradually* discover how these situations differ, it is important that such differences not invalidate the analogy entirely. In a computational inference system, this must be reflected in the predicates representing the relations in each domain.

The problem from the standpoint of Gentner's model is that the relationship that is mapped from the "box world" to the "computer world" is exactly that of *physical containment*. When this relation is copied into the programming domain, the interpretation that results is that a number is physically INSIDE of a variable. Under normal circumstances, people learning to program may have no idea what computer variables are, but they should know that numbers are not physical objects and they should not expect that all the inferences involving the relation INSIDE will apply when numbers are placed "in" variables.

This problem can be characterized as one of *levels of abstraction*. Depending on how much is known about the objects in the target domain when the analogy is presented, it may or may not be reasonable to map the most specific version of a relation from one domain to another. When mapping a relation identically leads to the violation of a constraint on one of the slots in that relation, then the relation meant in the target domain must be one sharing some of the properties of the base-domain relation but not others.

When an attempt to map a relation directly results in such a constraint violation, CARL forms a *virtual relation* in the target domain that is a "sibling" of the corresponding base-domain relation or an ancestor at some higher level in the generalization hierarchy of relational predicates. The constraints initially placed on the slots in virtual relations are determined primarily from the classes of the objects related in the target-domain examples presented.

When CARL is given the box analogy, it finds that mapping objects to numbers violates a normal constraint on the INSIDE relation. Instead, CARL forms a new predicate to relate variables and their "contents." This relation, hereafter called INSIDE-VAR, is initially given the constraints that the "contents" slot be a number and the "container" slot be a variable, based on the types of the objects in the accompanying example, "$X = 5$." Inferences are associated with this new relation as they are successfully mapped from the box domain, learned independently in the new domain, or inherited from other analogies.

The final result of mapping the structure PUT-IN-BOX, describing the causal relations involved in putting an object in a container, looks roughly as shown in figure 13-6. Notice particularly that the PTRANS predicate indicating *physical* transfer was also replaced by the more general predicate TRANS (general state change) because the object "moved" in the target domain was not a physical object.

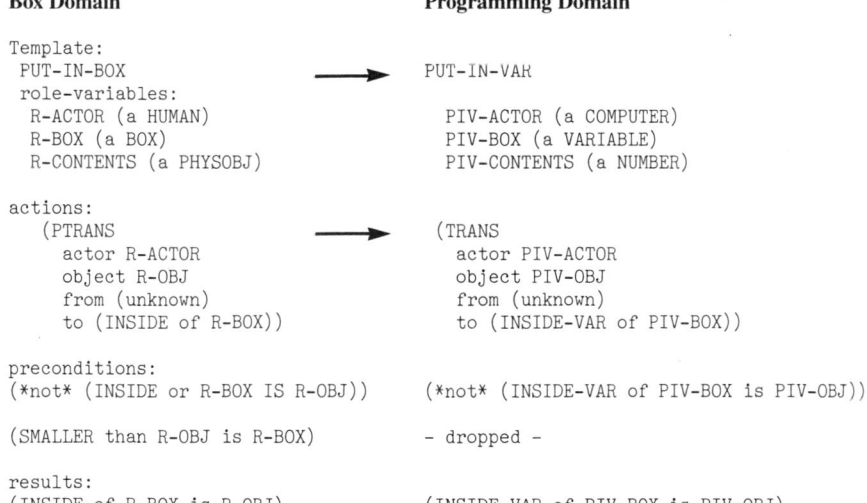

Box Domain   **Programming Domain**

```
Template:
 PUT-IN-BOX                   ──────▶       PUT-IN-VAR
  role-variables:
   R-ACTOR (a HUMAN)                         PIV-ACTOR (a COMPUTER)
   R-BOX (a BOX)                             PIV-BOX (a VARIABLE)
   R-CONTENTS (a PHYSOBJ)                    PIV-CONTENTS (a NUMBER)

 actions:
   (PTRANS                    ──────▶        (TRANS
     actor R-ACTOR                             actor PIV-ACTOR
     object R-OBJ                              object PIV-OBJ
     from (unknown)                            from (unknown)
     to (INSIDE of R-BOX))                     to (INSIDE-VAR of PIV-BOX))

 preconditions:
 (*not* (INSIDE or R-BOX IS R-OBJ))        (*not* (INSIDE-VAR of PIV-BOX is PIV-OBJ))

 (SMALLER than R-OBJ is R-BOX)              - dropped -

 results:
 (INSIDE of R-BOX is R-OBJ)                 (INSIDE-VAR of PIV-BOX is PIV-OBJ)
```

Figure 13-6: Mapping a simple causal structure.

13.6 OVERVIEW OF THE ANALOGY–MAPPING PROCESS

In general, CARL develops simple causal or inferential structures in a target domain by retrieving structures in memory from a familiar domain and adapting them using a top-down mapping process that preserves the causal/temporal links explicitly specified in those structures. The predicates mapped are subject to transformation within their abstraction hierarchy, as described above. Subsequent use of an analogy may occur when new examples are presented for which no explanation can be found in the target domain or when problems are presented requiring the retrieval of plans or actions to achieve specific, analogically stated goals. The latter, in CARL's subset of the programming domain, is generally a request for the generation of an assignment statement satisfying some specific goals or constraints.

In answering a question, CARL always looks first for memory structures in the domain it is learning about. If this fails, it tries known analogies. Thus subsequent access to base domains is always for the purpose of mapping new, related structures: related action situations or more detailed, context-specific versions of previously mapped structures that account for additional predications or results.

The mapping process tries to form structures in the target domain under the following general constraints:

- Corresponding predicates must be of the same class (action, relation, plan step, plan, goal, and so on).
- Corresponding predicates in the target structure are related together by causal or temporal links corresponding to those in the base-domain structure.
- Corresponding case slots of analogically related predicates must consistently be filled by corresponding *roles* of the two structures related.

CARL keeps a record called an AMAP detailing all of the object, role, and predicate correspondences developed. AMAPS are extended as needed to include new correspondences as they are found.

Because the AMAP uses *role* correspondences as well as object class correspondences, the relationships between objects of two domains can actually change quite subtly when new problems are being handled. Several bugs in protocols observed by the author depend on this distinction. The question "How would you put one more in X?" has been answered with "$X = 1$" by a student, and the question "What is in X after you type '$X = 7$' and then '$X = 6$'?" has been answered, "13." These responses can be interpreted in terms of a variant of the box analogy, by which the number assigned to the variable corresponds to the *number of objects* placed in a box. Thus, for the first problem, "$X = 1$" simply places an object in a box that already contained some objects, causing it to contain "one more," while putting six objects in a box that contained seven others results in one with thirteen.

These solutions can both be explained by an analogical correspondence between contents of boxes and contents of variables that maps a *set* of objects to the *cardinality* of that set rather than mapping an object to a number. This is a slightly different analogical mapping, though the same roles ("contents") of each base- and target-domain situations are being related. Modeling these responses requires that the analogy formation process primarily relate objects in terms of their functional roles in specific situations and only secondarily determine how object features correspond.

13.7 INCREMENTAL ANALOGICAL REASONING

Even when analogies are based on simple actions, the specific inferences retrieved in support of new examples may vary considerably, depending on the context. For example, throwing a rock at a brick wall and throwing one at a glass wall are immediately known to have very different consequences. Although an analogy to a thrown rock might imply indirectly that each of these alternate contexts had a correlate in a target domain, in practice each potential class of target domain situations must be explored.

Extending analogies in this fashion is an error-prone process. In the protocols examined by the author, attempts to extend analogies to variant target-domain situations occurred both when subjects were responding to presented problems and examples and also when they were generating examples in independent attempts to find out more about what was possible in the programming domain. Perry displayed the latter behavior early in his first session when he began asking questions to find out what could go "inside" a variable. He asked whether it was possible to put one "box" in another. This is clearly a reasonable thing to do with real boxes, but it's impossible in BASIC.

CARL extends analogies by mapping context-specific inferences like this one, but only when they form part of the interpretation of a presented example. In the computer dialogue shown in figure 13-4, CARL first tries using the box analogy to interpret "$X = Y$" in terms of the action "move one box into another." When this is corrected by the tutor's statement that the *contents* of Y are moved, CARL tries mapping a causal chain describing the transfer of an object from one container to another, much as Perry did in figure 13-3.

Both of these hypotheses about statements like "$X = Y$" are generated *after* CARL's initial application of the box analogy to the BASIC statement "$X = 5$." Each subsequent use of the analogy also involves the mapping of a causal description from the base to the target domain. Information saved in the AMAP from that earlier mapping of the causal prototype "put an object in a box" is first used in a "reverse mapping" process to construct a base-domain description of the new problem. This base-domain description is used to trigger the retrieval of a base-domain causal structure explaining it. The AMAP is then used again to map the new causal chain into the programming domain. This results in a model for "$X = Y$" containing the "bug" that the "moved" number is no longer in Y.

The memory organization and retrieval system used in CARL for knowledge of simple action-based domains involving familiar objects is an extension of an object-based indexing system described by Lehnert (1978; Lehnert and Burstein, 1979) for natural language–processing tasks. So that CARL could also retrieve a variety of special case situations, its memory retrieval process was augmented using discrimination networks based on the specification hierarchy model of episodic memory developed by Lebowitz (1980) and Kolodner (1980). In addition, precondition and result indices were added so that actions and simple plans could also be retrieved in response to requests for the achievement of specific goals. Any or all of these forms of indexing may be used in finding a suitable structure to map. For familiar domains, the system assumes that a large set of fairly specific causal inference structures exists in memory at the beginning of the learning process. No attempt is currently being made to construct composite causal structures on the fly, although clearly that might be necessary with more complex analogies.

Figure 13-7 shows part of CARL's network of causal structures describing the effects of some simple actions involving containers.

In the computer session shown in figure 13-4, an initial mapping from the box domain was formed from the causal structure PUT-IN-BOX. Thereafter, specializations of that structure were available for use when new examples were presented. In addition, once the new containment relation was formed for variables, expectations were established for the other "primitive" situations involving containers. Thus, from the fact that variables can "contain" numbers, CARL expected that they might also be "put in" or "removed."

After considering a number of examples, CARL develops a similar network of causal structures in its target domain. Many of the structures formed by the mapping process contain erroneous inferences at first. These structures are "debugged" in the target domain, if possible, or replaced, depending on the nature of the correction suggested by the tutor. Once a structure describing some class of assignment statements has been debugged, corrections made to that structure propagate downward to any subsequently formed specializations of it. Thus, once there is a debugged prototype for statements like "$X = 5$," the fact that prior values of X are *replaced* rather than accumulated also applies to causal structures mapped when cases like "$X = Y$" are analyzed. The inheritance mechanism in CARL that handles this is active only when new structures are formed, so it was important in "teaching" CARL to show it these

Situations with BOX as a CONTAINER:

(PUT-IN-BOX   OBJ-IN-BOX   TAKE-FROM-BOX)
    / | \\   /
   / | TRANSFER-OBJ-BETWEEN-BOXES
  | PUT-BOX-IN-BOX   \\
  PUT-MORE-IN-BOX   SWAP-OBJ-IN-BOXES

Figure 13-7:   Part of the specialization network for things "INSIDE" boxes.

bugs early on. This model seems to suggest at least one reason why it is best to keep initial analogical prototypes as simple as possible and to correct problems with them quickly.

CARL also develops parsing and generation rules for each class of assignment statement successfully represented. These rules are developed during the final stage of the analysis of each example.

13.8 USING MULTIPLE ANALOGIES

CARL is often able to predict the effects of assignments better by using the similarity of assignment statements to equalities than by using the box model. In general, the box model does not help much in interpreting statements containing arithmetic expressions. However, many assignment statements can be interpreted correctly if they are first considered as algebraic equalities, particularly if all of the variables appearing to the right of the equal sign have known values and the variable on the left has none.

CARL first notices that algebra might be useful in learning about an assignment when it sees the "$=$" sign in statements like "$X = 5$." As it builds a new meaning for "$=$," it discovers this earlier definition in its dictionary. Reparsing "$X = 5$" as an equality, CARL forms an interpretation with the conclusion that the value of the algebraic variable X is 5. However, because the statement is also a communicative act, the effect of the statement on the "BASIC computer" is to cause it to *store* a new fact, namely, that "the value of the variable X is 5." This interpretation thus depends both on the algebraic rule that statements of the form *"variable = number"* imply that the value of the variable *is* the specified number and on a partially formed analogical model of the computer as a humanlike interpreter of facts and requests.

It should be emphasized here that a causal/temporal element must be introduced when CARL moves from algebra to assignment. In algebra, variables do not have changeable values. However, for the algebraic and box models to be related to each other successfully, a comparable causal effect had to be found. For this reason, it was important that the algebra model be applied in conjunction with a model of the machine as an active agent or interpreter of statements.

Since CARL represents the inference about X's value as occurring as a result of the statement being typed into a computer, it has a causal/temporal effect that can be related to an effect of the "physical" model of the same assignment statement developed using the box analogy; that is, both interpretations of the statement cause an association to be formed between a variable and a value. By comparing these two descriptions of the causal effects of interpreting this one statement, CARL forms a mapping from the predicate VAR-VALUE in the algebra domain to the predicate INSIDE-VAR that it had previously constructed using another analogy.

Once this analogical association is formed, CARL can interpret the effects of assignment statements involving arithmetic expressions by first parsing them as equalities. When it does this during an attempt to determine the effect of an unfamiliar kind of assignment, it uses rules of algebra to determine the value of the variable on the left. The result is then mapped onto a causal structure describing that effect on a corresponding programming variable. Structures from alternate analogies in this fashion may be used either to replace erroneous inferences developed using other analogies or to model situations that had no direct counterparts in the other analogical domains. However, since the relationship between algebraic equalities and assignments was based only on the discovery of similar causal *effects,* CARL's representation of the "storing action" in these new descriptions of classes of assignments is still based on the action model developed primarily from the box analogy and the corrections made to it. The result is a "mixed" model, but one that enables CARL to interpret correctly assignment statements of the form "$X = X + 1$," which it could not do using any of its analogies independently.

The foregoing analysis depends on a causal model of actions involving objects like containers, rules of equality and arithmetic from algebra, and rules about agents and information processors that are used primarily in interacting with other human beings. Each contributes a piece to the puzzle. In learning about assignment, CARL makes only limited use of the third analogy, relating computers to *humans* as information processors with an ability to communicate, manipulate numbers, and *remember* things. However, the author has argued that this analogy does play a role in relating knowledge of algebra to its causal model for assignment. This may explain why references to these last two analogies often appear together, both in textbooks and in informal dialogues like that shown in figure 13-2.

The interactions among the three analogies used by CARL are roughly summarized in figure 13-8. It should be noted that each analogy is represented and related at several levels of description but that the functions served by the analogies are quite different. The box model provides the initial causal model of the assignment domain. The algebra domain provides knowledge of numbers, the operations that can be performed on them, and the symbols for representing them. The human processor model is active primarily at the planning level, providing *reasons* for many of the operations that computers can perform and expectations that it will be capable of others. It also plays a role in early models of many of the computer commands, especially input and output functions. For example, when Perry wanted to check the value of a variable, which he knew was done with the PRINT command, he would often say, "Let's ask him."

13.9 CONCLUSIONS

CARL illustrates how analogical learning in a new domain can be accomplished by a combination of incremental analogical reasoning and the use of multiple analogical models. The author has also argued that effective analogical mapping for learning requires focusing on previously known abstractions in a base domain. This was found to be necessary in forming rules about assignment in CARL, both to limit the analogical reasoning required to create initial models of concepts in the new domain and to allow for incremental debugging of the many errors that can result from the use of analogies. The process described here is heavily teacher directed, but it allows for fairly rapid development of a working understanding of basic concepts in a new domain.

This chapter describes an attempt to model the learning of a common human cognitive task, given the kinds of information that students often receive when learning the same task. It also investigates a number of potential problems in prior models of analogical reasoning and their role in learning. There are several problems that must be addressed more closely before the algorithms used in CARL can be applied in a general machine learning system, even one operating in a similar, "tutorial" mode. One of the most important and potentially useful of these is the continued investigation of the ways that multiple analogies interact and contribute to the formation of a coherent target system. Analogical reasoning and hypothesis generation are intrinsically error-prone processes, requiring continuous monitoring and debugging. Because of this, effective analogical learning systems can benefit from the use of multiple analogies. The ability of a system to make effective use of several analogies in learning should reduce the number of detailed explanations and corrections that need to be supplied by a teacher. This alone would improve the viability of these systems.

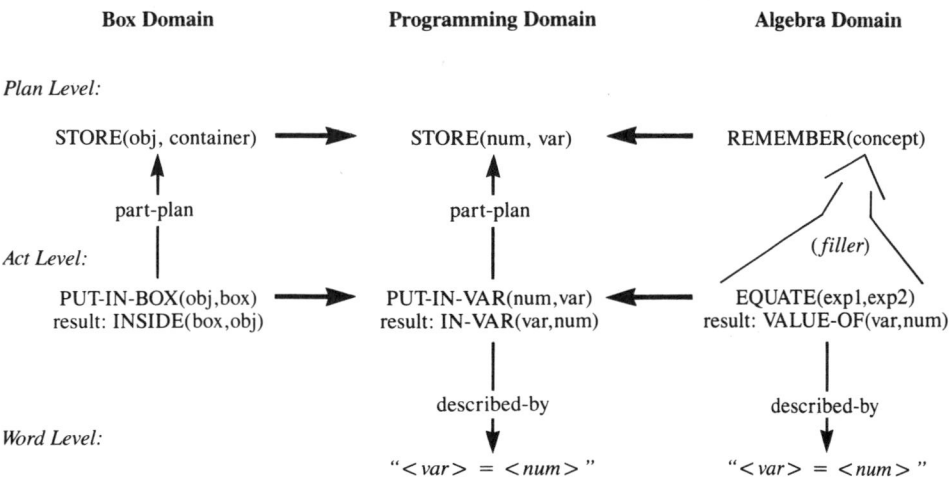

Figure 13-8: Interactions among three analogies.

ACKNOWLEDGMENTS

The author would like to thank Dr. Chris Riesbeck and Larry Birnbaum for many helpful comments on drafts of this paper.

The work reported in this chapter was supported in part by the Advanced Research Projects Agency of the Department of Defense and monitored by the Office of Naval Research under Contract No. N00014-75-C-111.

References

Albrecht, R., Finkel, L., and Brown, J. R., *BASIC for Home Computers,* Wiley, New York, 1978.

Burstein, M. H., "Concept Formation through the Interaction of Multiple Models," *Proceedings of the Third Annual Conference of the Cognitive Science Society,* pp. 271–74, August 1981.

Carbonell, J. G., "Learning by Analogy: Formulating and Generalizing Plans from Past Experience," in *Machine Learning: An Artificial Intelligence Approach,* R. S. Michalski, J. G. Carbonell, and T. M. Mitchell (Eds.), Tioga, Palo Alto, Calif., 1983.

Collins, A., and Gentner, D., "Constructing Runnable Mental Models," *Proceedings of the Fourth Annual Conference of the Cognitive Science Society,* pp. 86–89, August 1982.

de Kleer, J., and Brown, J. S., "Mental Models of Physical Mechanisms and Their Acquisition," *Cognitive Skills and Their Acquisition,* J. R. Anderson (Ed.), Erlbaum, Hillsdale, N.J., 1981.

Evans, T. G., "A Program for the Solution of Geometric Analogy Intelligence Test Questions," *Semantic Information Processing,* M. L. Minsky (Ed.), MIT Press, Cambridge, 1968.

Gentner, D., "Structure Mapping: A Theoretical Framework for Analogy and Similarity," *Proceedings of the Fourth Annual Conference of the Cognitive Science Society,* pp. 13–15, August 1982.

Gentner, D., and Gentner, D. R., "Flowing Waters or Teeming Crowds: Mental Models of Electricity," in *Mental Models,* D. Gentner and A. L. Stevens (Eds.), Erlbaum, Hillsdale, N.J., 1982.

Kolodner, J. L., "Retrieval and Organizational Strategies in Conceptual Memory: A Computer Model," Technical Report No. 187, Department of Computer Science, Yale University, 1980.

Lebowitz, M., "Generalization and Memory in an Integrated Understanding System," Ph.D. diss., Yale University, 1980.

Lehnert, W. G., "Representing Physical Objects in Memory," Technical Report No. 131, Department of Computer Science, Yale University, 1978.

Lehnert, W. G., and Burstein, M. H., "The Role of Object Primitives in Natural Language Processing," *Proceedings of the Sixth IJCAI,* Tokyo, pp. 522–24, 1979.

Sacerdoti, E. D., "A Structure for Plans and Behavior," Technical Report No. 109, SRI Artificial Intelligence Center, 1975.

Schank, R. C., *Dynamic Memory: A Theory of Learning in Computers and People.* Cambridge University Press, Cambridge, 1982.

Schank, R. C., and Abelson, R., *Scripts, Plans, Goals and Understanding,* Erlbaum, Hillsdale, N.J., 1977.

Wilensky, R., *Planning and Understanding: A Computational Approach to Human Reasoning,* Addison-Wesley, Reading, Mass., 1983.

Winston, P., "Learning and Reasoning by Analogy," *Communications of the ACM,* Vol. 23, No. 12, pp. 683–703, December 1980.

————, "Learning New Principles from Precedents and Exercises," *Artificial Intelligence,* Vol. 19, pp. 321–50, 1982.

14

DERIVATIONAL ANALOGY:

A Theory of Reconstructive Problem Solving and Expertise Acquisition

Jaime G. Carbonell
Carnegie-Mellon University

Abstract

Derivational analogy, a method of solving problems based on the transfer of past experience to new problem situations, is discussed in the context of other general approaches to problem solving. The experience transfer process consists of recreating lines of reasoning, including decision sequences and accompanying justifications, that proved effective in solving particular problems requiring similar initial analysis. The role of derivational analogy in case-based reasoning and in automated expertise acquisition is discussed.

14.1 INTRODUCTION: THE ROLE OF ANALOGY IN PROBLEM SOLVING

The term *problem solving* in artificial intelligence has been used to denote disparate forms of intelligent action to achieve well-defined goals. Perhaps the most common usage stems from the work of Newell and Simon (1972) in which problem solving consists of selecting a sequence of operators (from a preanalyzed finite set) that transforms an initial problem state into a desired goal state. Intelligent behavior consists of a focused search for a suitable operator sequence involving analysis of the states resulting from the application of different operators to earlier states.[1] Many researchers have adopted this viewpoint (Fikes and Nilsson, 1971; Sacerdoti, 1974; Nilsson, 1980).

However, a totally different approach has been advocated by McDermott (1967) and by Wilensky (1978, 1983) that views problem solving as plan instantiation. For each problem posed there are one or more plans that outline a solution, and problem solving consists of identifying and instantiating these plans. In order to select, instantiate, or refine plans, additional plans that tell how to instantiate other plans or how to solve subproblems are brought to bear in a recursive manner. Traditional notions of search are totally absent from this formulation. Some systems, such as the counterplanning mechanism in POLITICS (Carbonell, 1981b, 1981c), provide a hybrid approach, instantiating plans whenever possible and searching to construct potential solutions in the absence of applicable plans.

A third approach is to solve a new problem by analogy to a previously solved similar problem. This process entails searching for related past problems and transforming their solutions into solutions potentially applicable to the new problem (Pólya, 1945). Such a method was developed and advocated by the author (Carbonell, 1982, 1983) primarily as a means of bringing to bear problem-solving expertise acquired from past experience. The analogical transformation process itself may require search, as it is seldom immediately clear how a solution to a similar problem can be adapted to a new situation.

A useful means of classifying different problem-solving methods is to compare them in terms of the amount and specificity of domain knowledge they require.

- If no structuring domain knowledge is available and there is no useful past experience to draw upon, weak methods such as heuristic search and means-end analysis are the only tools that can be brought to bear. Even in these knowledge-poor situations, information about goal states, possible actions, their known preconditions, and their expected outcomes is required.

- If specific domain knowledge in the form of plans or procedures exists, such plans may be instantiated directly, recursively solving any subproblems that arise in the process.

- If general plans apply but no specific ones do, the general plans can be used to reduce the problem (by partitioning the problem or providing islands in the search space). For instance, in computing the pressure at a particular point in a fluid statics problem, one may use the general plan of applying the principle of

---

[1] In means-ends analysis, the current state is compared to the goal state, and one or more operators that reduce the difference are selected, whereas in heuristic search, the present state is evaluated in isolation and compared to alternate states resulting from the application of different operators (to states generated earlier in the search), and the search for a solution continues from the highest-rated state.

equilibrium of forces at the point of interest (the vector sum of the forces = 0). But the application of this plan only reduces the original problem to one of finding and combining the appropriate forces, without hinting at how that may be accomplished in a specific problem (Carbonell, Larkin, and Reif, 1983; Larkin, Reif, and Carbonell, 1985).

• If no specific plans apply but the problem resembles one solved previously, analogical transformation can be applied to adapt the solution of that similar past problem to the new situation. For instance, in some studies it has proven easier for students to solve mechanics problems by analogy to simpler, solved problems than by appealing to first principles or by applying general procedures presented in a physics text (Clements, 1982). As an example of analogy involving composite skills rather than pure cognition, consider a person who knows how to drive a car and is asked to drive a truck. Such a person may have no general plan or procedure for driving trucks but is likely to perform most of the steps correctly by transferring much of his or her automobile-driving knowledge. Would that we had robots that were so self-adaptable to new, if recognizably related, tasks!

Clearly, these problem-solving approaches, illustrated in figure 14-1, are not mutually exclusive; for instance, a "first-principles" approach can be used to reduce a problem to simpler subproblems, which in turn can be solved by analogy to recognizably similar past problems or by any of the other methods. In fact, a general inference engine for problem solving in the natural sciences that combines all four

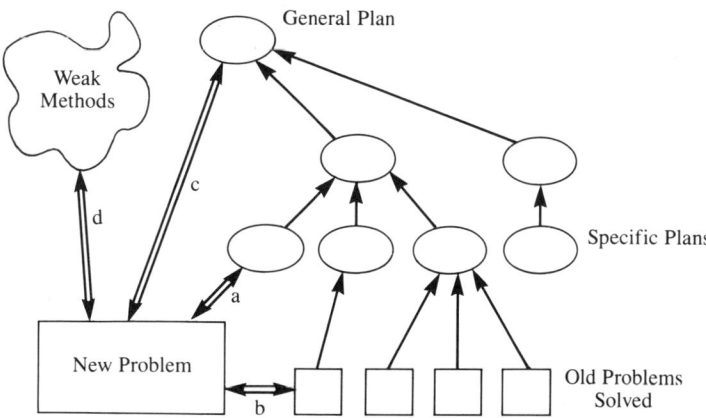

Figure 14-1:   Problem solving may involve the following: (a) instantiating specific plans, (b) using analogical transformation to a known solution of a similar problem, (c) applying general plans to reduce the problem, (d) applying weak methods to search heuristically for a possible solution, or (e) using a combination of these approaches.

approaches is being developed (Carbonell, Larkin, and Reif, 1983; Larkin, Reif, and Carbonell, 1985).

As discussed earlier, only direct plan instantiation and weak methods have received substantial attention by AI practitioners. For instance, Laird and Newell's recent formulation of a universal weak method (Laird and Newell, 1983) as a general problem-solving engine is developed completely within the search paradigm. Expert systems, for the most part, combine aspects of plan instantiation (often broken into small rule-size chunks of knowledge) and heuristic search in whatever manner best exploits the explicit and implicit constraints of the specific domain (Feigenbaum, Buchanan, and Lederberg, 1971; Shortliffe, 1976; Duda et al., 1979; McDermott, 1980, 1982). The author is more concerned with the other two approaches, as they could conceivably provide powerful reasoning mechanisms not heretofore analyzed in the context of automating problem-solving processes and of allowing the problem solver to learn from experience. The rest of this chapter focuses on a new formulation of the analogical problem-solving approach and its role in automating the knowledge acquisition process.

14.2 ANALOGY AND EXPERIENTIAL REASONING

The term *analogy* often conjures up recollections of artificially contrived problems in various psychometric exams, such as, "*X* is to *Y* as *Z* is to ?" This aspect of analogy is far too narrow and independent of context to be useful in general problem-solving domains. Instead, the following operational definition of analogical problem solving is proposed consistent with past AI research efforts (Kling, 1971; Winston, 1978, 1979; Gentner, 1980; Carbonell, 1981a, 1983):

> **Definition:** *Analogical problem solving consists of transferring knowledge from past problem-solving episodes to new problems that share significant aspects with corresponding past experience and using the transferred knowledge to construct solutions to the new problems.*

In order to make this definition operational, the problem-solving method must specify the following:

- What it means for problems to "share significant aspects"
- What knowledge is transferred from past experience to the new situation
- Precisely how the knowledge transfer process occurs
- How analogically related experiences are selected from a potentially vast long-term memory of past problem-solving episodes.

There are two distinct approaches to analogical problem solving. The first approach, called *transformational analogy,* has been successfully implemented in ARIES (Analogical Reasoning and Inductive Experimentation System) (Carbonell, 1983). The second approach, called *derivational analogy,* is a reconstructive rather than a transformational method, and it is the topic of this chapter. Both methods are analyzed with respect to the four criteria listed above.

14.2.1 Analogical Transformation of Past Solutions

If a particular solution has been found to work on a problem similar to the one at hand, perhaps it can be used, with minor modification, for the present problem. By *solution* is meant only a sequence of actions that if applied to the initial state of a problem brings about its goal state. Simple though this process may appear, an effective computer implementation requires that many difficult issues be resolved, namely:

1. Descriptions of past problems and of their solutions must be remembered and indexed for later retrieval.
2. The new problem must be matched against a large number of potentially relevant past problems to find closely related ones, if any. An operational similarity metric is required as a basis for selecting the most suitable past experiences.
3. The solution to a selected old problem must be transformed to satisfy the requirements of the new problem statement.

In order to achieve these objectives, the initial analogical problem solver (Carbonell, 1983) required a partial matcher with a built-in similarity criterion, a set of possible transformations to map the solution of one problem into the solution to a closely related problem, and a memory-indexing mechanism based on a MOPs-like memory encoding of events and actions (Schank, 1982). The solution transformation process was implemented as a set of atomic transform operators and a means-ends problem solver that searched for sequences of atomic transformations that, when applied to the retrieved solution, yielded a solution to the new problem. The resultant system, called ARIES, turned out to be far more complex than was originally envisioned. Partial pattern matching of problem descriptions and searching in the space of solution transformations are difficult tasks in themselves. Figure 14-2 illustrates the transformational analogy process.

In terms of the four criteria, the solution transformation process may be classified as follows:

1. Two problems share significant aspects if they match within a certain preset threshold in the initial partial matching process, according to the built-in similarity metric.
2. The knowledge transferred to the new situation is the sequence of actions from the retrieved solution, whether or not that sequence is later modified in the analogical mapping process.
3. The knowledge transfer process is accomplished by copying the retrieved solution and perturbing it incrementally according to the primitive transformation

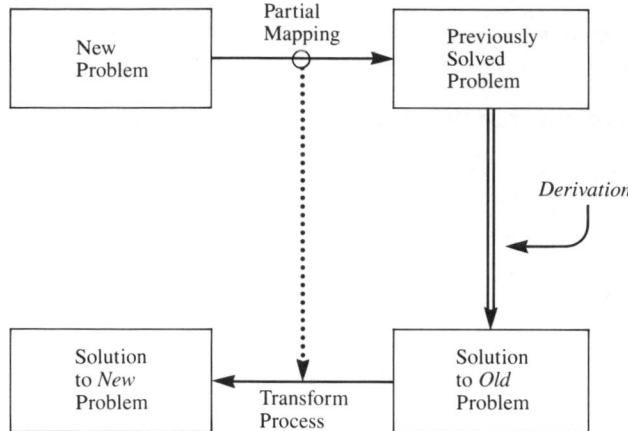

Figure 14-2: The transformational analogy process. Solutions to closely related problems are retrieved and modified to satisfy the requirements of the new problem.

steps in the heuristically guided manner until it satisfies the requirements of the new problem. (See Carbonell, 1983, for details.)

4. The selection of relevant past problems is constrained by the memory-indexing scheme and the partial pattern matcher.

Since a significant fraction of problems encountered in mundane situations and in areas requiring substantial domain expertise (but not in abstract mathematical puzzles) bears close resemblance to past solved problems, the ARIES method proved effective when tested in various domains, including algebra problems and route-planning tasks. An experiential learning component was added to ARIES that constructed simple plans (generalized sequences of actions) for recurring classes of problems, hence allowing the system to solve new problems in this class by the direct plan instantiation approach. However, no sooner was the solution transformation method implemented and analyzed than some of its shortcomings became strikingly apparent. In response to these deficiencies, more sophisticated methods of drawing analogies were analyzed, as discussed in the following section.

14.3 THE DERIVATIONAL ANALOGY METHOD

In formulating plans and solving problems, a considerable amount of intermediate information is produced in addition to the resultant plan or specific solution. For instance, formulation of subgoal structures, generation and subsequent rejection of alternatives, and access to various knowledge structures all typically take place in the problem-solving process. But the solution transformation method outlined above ignores all such information, focusing only upon the resultant sequence of actions and disregarding the reasons for selecting those actions. Why should one take such extra information into account? It would certainly complicate the analogical problem-solving process; nevertheless, what benefits would accrue from such an endeavor? Perhaps the best way to answer this question is by analysis of the shortcomings of the simple solution transformation process and of ways that such problems may be alleviated or circumvented by preserving more information from which qualitatively different analogies may be drawn. The general idea of derivational analogy is depicted in figure 14-3 and examined in greater detail below.

14.3.1 The Need for Preserving Derivation Histories

Consider, for instance, the domain of constructing computer programs to meet a set of predefined specifications. In the automatic programming literature, perhaps the most widely used technique is one of progressive refinement (Barstow, 1977; Balzer, 1975; Kant, 1981). In brief, progressive refinement is a multistage process that starts from abstract specifications stated in a high-level language (typically English or some variant of first-order logic) and produces progressively more operational or algorithmic descriptions of the specification committing to control decisions, data structures, and eventually specific statements in the target computer language. However, humans (at least this writer) seldom follow such a long and painstaking process, unless perhaps the specifications call for a truly novel program

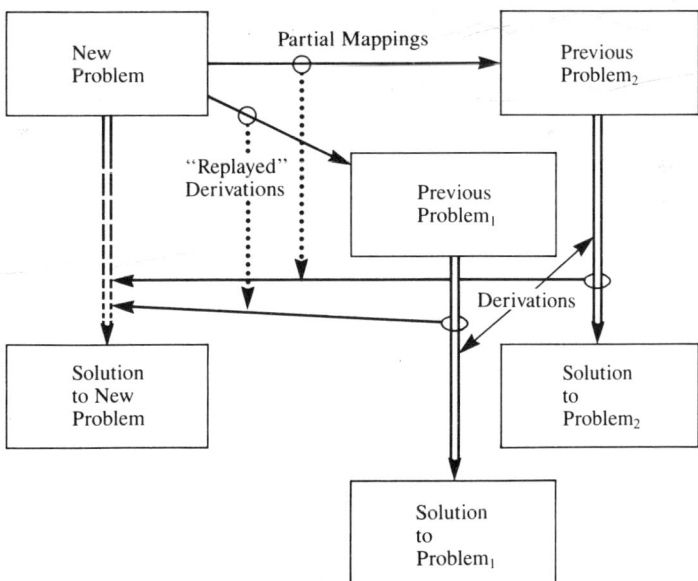

Figure 14-3: The derivational analogy process. The derivational traces of similar past problems are replayed and where necessary modified to construct a solution to a similar new problem.

unlike anything in their past experience. Instead, a common practice is to recall similar past programs and reconstruct the new programming problem along the same lines. For instance, one should be able to program a quicksort algorithm in LISP quite easily if one has recently implemented quicksort in Pascal. Similarly, writing LISP programs that perform tasks centered around depth-first tree traversal (such as testing equality of S-expressions or finding the node with maximal value) are rather trivial for LISP programmers but surprisingly difficult for those who lack the appropriate experience.

The solution transformation process proves singularly inappropriate as a means of exploiting past experiences in such problems. A Pascal implementation of quicksort may look very different from a good LISP implementation. In fact, attempting to transfer corresponding steps from the Pascal program into LISP is clearly not a good way to produce any reasonable LISP program, let alone an elegant or efficient one. Although the two problem statements may have been similar, and although the problem-solving processes may preserve much of the inherent similarity, the resultant solutions (i.e., the Pascal and LISP programs) may bear little if any direct similarities.

The useful similarities lie in the algorithms implemented and in the set of decisions and internal reasoning steps required to produce the two programs by successively refining the general specification of the problem. Therefore, the analogy must take place starting at earlier stages of the original Pascal implementation, and it must be guided by a reconsideration of the key decisions in light of the new situation. In particular, the derivation of the LISP quicksort program starts from the same specifications, retaining the same divide-and-conquer strategy, but it may diverge in the selection of data structures (e.g., lists versus arrays) or in the method of choosing the comparison element, depending on the tools available in each language and their expected efficiency. However, future decisions (e.g., whether to recurse or iterate, what mnemonics to use as variable names, and so on) that do not depend on earlier divergent decisions can still be transferred to the new domain rather than recomputed. Thus, the derivational analogy method walks through the reasoning steps in the construction of the past solution and considers whether they are still appropriate in the new situation or whether they should be reconsidered in light of significant differences between the two situations.

The difference between the solution transformation approach and the derivational analogy approach just outlined can be stated in terms of the operational knowledge that can be brought to bear. The former corresponds to a person who has never before programmed quicksort and is given the Pascal code as an aid in constructing the LISP implementation; whereas the latter is akin to a person who has programmed the Pascal version and therefore has a better understanding of the issues involved before undertaking the LISP implementation. Swartout and Balzer (1982) and Reif and Scherlis (1982) have argued independently in favor of working with program derivations as the basic entities in tasks relating to automatic programming. The advantages of the derivational analogy approach are quite evident in programming because of the frequent inappropriateness of direct solution transformation; but even in domains in which the latter is useful, one can envision problems that demonstrate the need for preserving or reconstructing past reasoning processes.

14.3.2 The Process of Drawing Analogies by Derivational Transformation

Let us examine in greater detail the process of drawing analogies from past reasoning processes. The essential insight is that useful experience is encoded in the reasoning process used to derive solutions to similar problems, rather than just in the resultant solution. Additionally, a method of bringing that experience to bear in the problem-solving process is required in order to make this form of analogy a computationally tractable approach. Here we outline such a method:

1. When solving a problem by any means, store each step taken in the solution process, as illustrated in figure 14-4, including the following:

   - The subgoal structure of the problem
   - Each decision made (whether a decision to take action, to explore new possibilities, or to abandon present plans), including the following:
     - Alternatives considered and rejected
     - The reasons for the decisions taken (with dependency links to the problem description or information derived therefrom)
     - The start of a false path taken (with the reason why this appeared to be a promising alternative and the reason why it proved otherwise, again with dependency links to the problem description. Note that the body of the false path and other resultant information need not be preserved).
     - Dependencies of later decisions on earlier ones in the derivation.
   - Pointers to the knowledge that was accessed and that proved useful in the eventual construction of the solution
   - The resultant solution itself
     - In the event that the problem solver proved incapable of solving the problem, store the closest approach to a solution, along with the reasons why no further progress could be made (e.g., a conjunctive subgoal that could not be satisfied).
     - In the event that the solution depends, perhaps indirectly, on volatile assumptions not stated in the problem description (such as the cooperation of another agent or time-dependent states), store the appropriate dependencies.

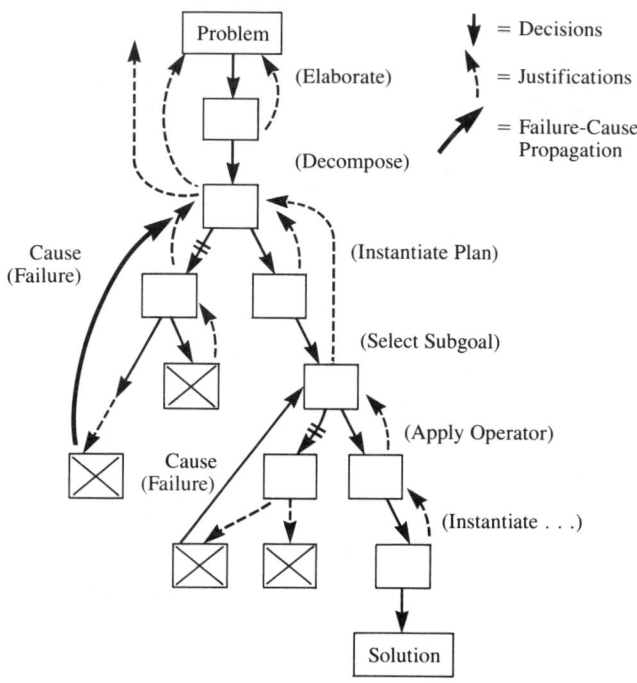

Figure 14-4: A derivational trace. Each reasoning step is justified in terms of previous reasoning steps or external knowledge. When a solution attempt fails, the cause of failure is propagated back to the branching point from the successful path and retained.

2. When a new problem is encountered that does not lend itself to direct plan instantiation or other direct recognition of the solution pattern, start to analyze the problem by applying general plans or weak methods, whichever is appropriate to the situation.

3. If after the analysis of the problem is commenced, the reasoning process (the initial decisions made and the information taken into account) parallels that of past problem situations, retrieve the full reasoning traces and proceed with the derivational transformation process. If not, consider the possibility of solution transformation analogy or, failing that, proceed with the present line of non-analogical reasoning.

   • Two problems are considered similar if their analysis results in equivalent reasoning processes, at least in its initial stages. This replaces the more arbitrary context-free similarity metric required for partial matching among problem descriptions in drawing analogies by direct solution transformation. Hence, past reasoning traces (henceforth called *derivations*) are retrieved if their initial segment matches that of the first stages of the analysis of the present problem.

- The retrieved reasoning processes are then used much as individual relevant cases in medicine are used to generate expectations and drive the diagnostic analysis. Reasoning from individual cases has been recognized as an important component of expertise (Schank, 1983), but little has been said of the necessary information that each case must contain, let alone providing a simple method of retrieving the appropriate cases in a manner that does not rely on arbitrary similarity metrics. The stand is taken here that cases must contain the reasoning process used to yield an answer, together with dependencies to the particular circumstances of the problem, pointers to data that proved useful, a list of alternative reasoning paths not taken, and failed attempts (coupled with both reasons for their failure and reasons for their having been tried). Case-based reasoning is nothing more than derivational analogy applied to domains of extensive expertise.

- It is important to know that although one may view derivational analogy as an interim step in reasoning from particular past experiences as more general plans are acquired, it is a mechanism that remains forever useful, since knowledge is always incomplete, and exceptions to the best formulated general plans require representation and use of individual reasoning episodes.

4. Apply a retrieved derivation to the current situation as follows: For each step in the derivation, starting immediately after the matched initial segment, check whether the reasons for performing that step are still valid by tracing dependencies in the retrieved derivation to relevant parts of the old problem description or to volatile external assumptions made in the initial problem solving.

- If parts of the problem statement or external assumptions on which the retrieved situation rests are also true in the present problem situation, proceed to check the next step in the retrieved derivation.

- If there is a violated assumption or problem statement, check whether the decision made would still be justified by a different derivation path from the new assumptions or statements. If so, store the new dependencies and proceed to the next step in the retrieved derivation. The idea of tracing causal dependencies and verifying past inference paths borrows heavily from TMS (Doyle, 1979) and some of the nonmonotonic logic literature (McDermott and Doyle, 1980). However, the role played by data dependencies in derivational analogy is somewhat different and more constrained than it is in maintaining global consistency in deductive data bases.

- If the old decision cannot be justified by the new problem situation, proceed as follows:

    ○ Evaluate the alternatives not chosen at that juncture and select an appropriate one in the usual problem-solving manner, storing it along with its justifications, or

    ○ Initiate the subgoal of establishing the right supports in order for the old decision to apply in the new problem[2] (clearly, any problem-solving method can be brought to bear in achieving the new subgoal), or

    ○ Abandon this derivational analogy in favor of another, more appropriate problem-solving experience from which to draw the analogy or in favor of other means of problem solving.

- If one or more failure paths are associated with the current decision, check the cause of failure and the reasons these alternatives appeared viable in the context of the original problem (by tracing dependency links when required). In the case that their reasons for failure no longer apply but the initial reasons for selecting these alternatives are still present, consider reconstructing this alternate solution path in favor of continuing to apply and modify the present derivation (especially if quality of solution is more important than problem-solving effort).

- In the event that a different decision is taken at some point in the rederivation, do not abandon the old derivation, since future decisions may be independent of some past decisions or may still be valid (via different justifications) in spite of the somewhat different circumstances. This requires that dependency links be kept between decisions at different stages in the derivation.

- In the event that a preponderance of the old decisions are invalidated in the new problem situation, abandon the derivational analogy. Exactly what the perseverance threshold should be is a topic for empirical investigation, as it depends on whether there are other tractable means of solving this problem and on the overhead cost of reevaluating individual past decisions that are no longer supported and that may or may not have independent justification.

---

[2]This approach works only if the missing or violated premise relates to that part of the global state under control of the problem solver, such as acquiring a missing tool or resource, rather than that part under the control of an uncooperative external agent or a recalcitrant environment. The discussion of strategy-based counterplanning gives a more complete account of subgoaling to rectify unfulfilled expectations (Carbonell, 1981b, 1981c).

5. After an entire derivation has been found to apply to the new problem, store its divergence from the parent derivation as another potentially useful source of analogies and as an instance from which more general plans can be formulated if a large number of problems share a common solution procedure (Carbonell, 1983).

14.3.3 Efficiency Concerns

An important aspect of the derivational analogy approach is the ability to store and trace dependency links. It should be noted that some of the inherent inefficiencies in maintaining global consistency in a large deductive database do not apply, as the dependency links are internal to each derivation with external pointers only to the problem description and to any volatile assumptions necessitated in constructing the resultant solution. Hence, the size of each dependency network is quite small compared to a dependency network spanning all memory. Dependencies are also stored among decisions taken at different stages in the temporal sequence of the derivation, thus providing the derivational analogy process access to causal relations computed at the time the initial problem was solved.

The analogical rederivation process is not inherently space inefficient, although it may so appear at first glance. The sequence of decisions in the solution path of a problem is stored, together with necessary dependencies, the problem description, the resultant solution, and alternative reasoning paths not chosen. Failed paths are not stored; only the initial decision that was taken to embark upon that path and the eventual reason for failure (with its causal dependencies) are remembered. Hence, the size of the memory for derivational traces is proportional to the depth of the search tree rather than to the number of nodes visited. Problems that share large portions of their derivational structure can be so represented in memory, saving space and allowing similarity-based indexing. Moreover, when a generalized plan is formulated for recurring problems that share a common derivational structure, the individual derivations that are totally subsumed by the more general structure can be permanently masked or deleted. Those derivations that represent exceptions to the general rule, however, are precisely the instances that should be saved and indexed accordingly for future problem solving (Hayes-Roth, 1983).

14.3.4 Summarizing the Derivational Process

Derivational analogy bears closer resemblance to Schank's reconstructive memory (1980, 1982) and Minsky's K-lines (1980) than to traditional notions of analogy. Although derivational analogy is less ambitious in scope than either of these theories, it is a more precisely defined inference process that can lead to an operational method of reasoning from particular experiential instances. The key notion is to reconstruct the relevant aspects of past problem-solving situations and thereby transfer knowledge to the new scenario, where that knowledge consists of decision sequences and their justifications rather than individual declarative assertions. In summary, consider how the process of derivational analogy can be described in terms of the four criteria for analogical reasoning presented in the previous section:

1. Two problems share significant aspects if their initial analysis yields the same reasoning steps, that is, if the initial segments of their respective derivations start by considering the same issues and making the same decisions.

2. The earlier derivation may be transferred to the new situation, in essence recreating the significant aspects of the reasoning process that solved the past problem.

3. Knowledge transfer is accomplished by reconsidering old decisions in light of the new problem situation, preserving those that apply, and replacing or modifying those whose supports are no longer valid in the new situation.

4. Problems and their derivations are stored in a large episodic memory along the line of Schank's MOPs (1982), and retrieval occurs by replication of initial segments of decision sequences recalling the past reasoning process.

14.4 INCREMENTAL EXPERTISE ACQUISITION

Derivational analogy is a fertile computational paradigm that supports various knowledge acquisition and skill refinement strategies. Thus far the focus here has been on the basic problem-solving aspects, but a major motivation behind the reconstructive derivational strategy is the natural manner in which it can be extended to include incremental acquisition of domain expertise. First, case-based reasoning as a major component of human expertise will be briefly considered. Then, some concrete methods for acquiring and refining expertise from experience will be examined, based upon the derivational analogy model.

14.4.1 Case-Based Reasoning as a Model of Human Expertise

The vast majority of present-day expert systems encode their knowledge as a large, amorphous set of domain-specific rules (Feigenbaum, Buchanan, and Lederberg, 1971; McDermott, 1980, 1982; Shortliffe, 1976; Waterman, Hayes-Roth, and Lenat, 1983). The "knowledge engineering" task is defined as one of extracting from the human expert the set of rules that comprise his or her expertise in particular, well-defined domains. The task is by no means easy—quite the contrary. It can take years of laborious efforts by teams of domain experts and AI researchers in an iterative process of formulating, evaluating, reformulating, discarding, and refining a set of rules to develop the knowledge base of a particular expert system. Observing this phenomenon, Edward Feigenbaum uttered his now-famous proclamation, "In the knowledge lies the power." How right he was! Fortunately, however, the tacit assumption that domain knowledge must necessarily be represented as large sets of context-independent rules is proving to be only an early engineering decision, and a very limiting one at that. The knowledge must be captured, but the question of the best means of acquiring and representing it in a computationally effective manner remains.

What then would be an alternative means of representing and acquiring domain knowledge? In order to address this question, the author set out to build an expert system and gain first-hand experience, keeping in perspective all the different problem-solving methods and machine learning paradigms. In less than a year, with the help of one programmer and two domain experts, SMOKEY (Carbonell, 1985), a prototype fire diagnosis expert system, was produced. In essence, SMOKEY polls multiple remote sensors (heat detectors, smoke detectors, air pressure detectors, and so on), and calculates the location, expected spread, and critical nature of a fire on a building or a ship. From this assessment it recommends actions, such as signaling safe exit routes free of smoke, closing down air circulation ducts before they spread toxic smoke to unaffected areas, selecting equipment for the fire-fighting team appropriate to the nature of the fire, and so on. Several lessons were learned from this endeavor, and here the focus will be on the central one: the utility of case-based reasoning.

When naval experts were interviewed about on-board fire diagnosis situations, it was found that for sizable fires, they are swamped with too much information coming from all the potentially relevant sensors. Therefore, videotape simulations of several fires were played at much-reduced speeds. The results were amazing: previously sloppy decisions ignoring crucial information vanished, and elaborate problem-solving protocols were recorded, including fairly complete justifications for each action or decision taken. Unfortunately, real fires cannot be played in slow motion to allow for human reaction time and memory limitations. Thus, the need for a SMOKEY-like system on a fast processor was established. Now the question remained of how the excellent (slow-motion) problem-solving traces could be converted into the knowledge base of an expert system. The key insight was that perhaps they need not be converted—only encoded appropriately and fed to a derivational analogy problem solver and learning module. SMOKEY was built concurrently with the development of the derivational analogy method, so the expertise acquisition steps discussed below were carried out largely by hand, rather than in a completely automated fashion.

Human experts are incredibly poor at producing general deductive rules that account for their behavior. When forced to do so by insistent knowledge engineers, they try hard and produce faulty rules. When they are later faced with a problem in which the rule fails, the typical response is: "Well, I didn't think of *that* situation, but perhaps I can fix the rule . . . or add a new one . . . ." This ad hoc iterative process, slow and frustratingly inefficient as it may be, usually converges upon an acceptable knowledge base. However, a much more efficient and humane approach is to let the experts do what they do best: solve problems in their domain of expertise. The only added burden is a reporting requirement. Each problem-solving step, including references to static domain knowledge or to heuristics of the domain, must be reported explicitly, along with the reason why such knowledge was used. This process provides external derivational traces that a derivational analogy inference engine can use to solve similar future problems in an effective manner. Although the derivational method was originally conceived as a means to reason and learn from one's own past experience, a more knowledgeable external source, such as a human expert or a worked-out problem example in a textbook, can prove even more effective.

Case-based reasoning is particulary prevalent in law—at least in the British and American systems of jurisprudence—and in medical diagnosis and treatment. The idea of case-based reasoning in expert systems is not new. Schank (1983), for instance, advocates this method as superior and closer to human reasoning than present expert systems. Doyle (1984) proposes the notion of emulating the human master-apprentice process as a means whereby the latter (human or computer) can acquire expertise by replicating the reasoning processes of the former. Here, a concrete computational mechanism—the derivational analogy process—is proposed as a means of providing expert systems with the ability to reason from cases, whether the cases be past experience or externally acquired knowledge. However, human experts can solve problems progressively more quickly and effectively with repeated experience. Whereas case-based reasoning may reflect accurately a crucial intermediate stage in the learning process and may account for problem-solving behavior in infrequently recurring situations, some knowledge is gradually compiled into more general processes abstracted from the concrete cases. That is to say, for the most routine, recurring problems, the derivational analogy process should produce general plans that can be instantiated directly. The following section explores learning techniques in derivational analogy.

14.4.2 Automatic Acquisition of Plans and Strategies

The standard behavioral definition for learning can be paraphrased as follows:

Definition: *A system (biological or mechanical) is said to learn if it can modify its behavior after a set of experiences such that it can perform a task more accurately or more efficiently than before or perform a new task beyond its previous capabilities.*

What can be learned in the derivational analogy process, according to this definition? Learning can occur at many levels and in many forms.

14.4.2.1 Enrichment of Case-Based Memory

As a system solves problems or is presented with fully annotated derivations of solutions, its repertoire of cases increases. Thus it will be able to derive analogical solutions from these new experiences. This incremental, monotonic increase in its experiential knowledge base provides a powerful argument in favor of a method such as derivational analogy, which can utilize the experience directly to solve new problems.

14.4.2.2 Generalized Plans

If only the resultant solutions to a large set of analogically related problems are used (rather than the entire derivations), generalized operator sequence plans can be abstracted. This process requires that solutions derived from a common analogical parent form a set of positive exemplars, and unrelated or failed solutions form a set of negative exemplars. These sets are given to a general inductive engine (Michalski, 1983) or to an incremental one such as Mitchell's version space method (Mitchell, 1978; Mitchell, Utgoff, and Banerji, 1983), which abstracts a generalized plan from the recurring common aspects of these solutions. Later, the generalized plan can be instantiated directly—or refined further if more instance solutions are derived. Figure 14-5 summarizes this process. (For a longer discussion, see Carbonell, 1983.)

14.4.2.3 Strategy Acquisition

The same method for inducing generalized plans from positive and negative exemplars can be applied to different parts of the full derivational trace.

Considerations of alternate decision points in derivationally related solutions can lead to the compilation of domain-specific heuristics for making future choices

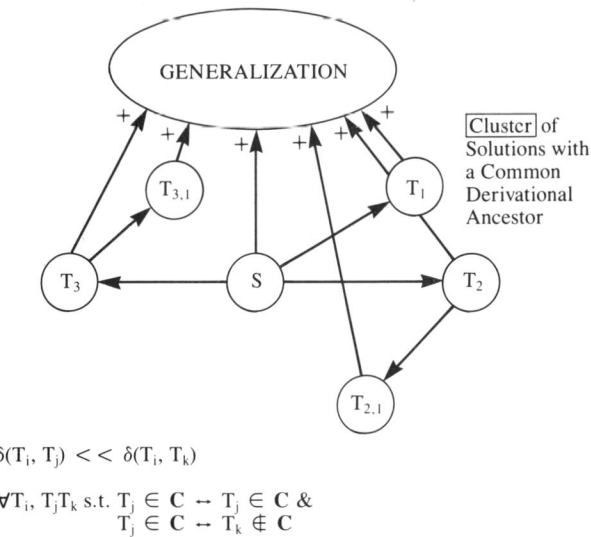

$$\delta(T_i, T_j) << \delta(T_i, T_k)$$

$$\forall T_i, T_jT_k \text{ s.t. } T_j \in C \rightarrow T_j \in C \ \&$$
$$T_j \in C \rightarrow T_k \notin C$$

Figure 14-5: Generalizing plans from analogically related solutions. Solutions derived from common transformational ancestors form a cluster of positive exemplars. Failed attempts and members of other clusters provide the negative exemplars to an induction engine.

of the same nature. If a particular decision was part of a successful derivation in several related solutions but led to a false path under other problem solutions, the requisite grist for the induction engine again exists: a set of positive exemplars in the justifications of the successful decision and a set of near-miss negative exemplars in the cases where the same decision proved ineffective. In fact, the cause of failure (propagated back to the causally related decision point and retained in the derivational trace, as discussed earlier) provides a set of necessary—but perhaps not sufficient—conditions to discriminate between the positive and negative instances of the decision.

Consider, for instance, the selection of a means of transportation in various problem-solving situations that involve travel. If an automobile was successfully selected three times to travel between cities in the continental United States but was erroneously suggested as a means of traveling between Boston and London, the strategy for selecting a means of transportation can be refined. The cause of failure (no land route between the source and destination) serves to add a necessary condition to the strategy, and the fact that automobile travel proved successful independent of the exact compass orientation or identity of the cities within the United States serves to assert the independence of the strategy from such considerations. In fact, a trial implementation in the route-finding domain has yielded planning strategies increasingly more appropriate to the task domain.

Applying the same technique to problem decomposition tasks, plan selection tasks (when multiple generalized plans exist for a given subproblem), and methods of avoiding the causes of failure under similar circumstances can also yield automated refinement of the system's behavior. In all cases, the internal and external justifications provide the means for the system to focus on the functionally relevant aspects of the phase in the derivation from which it is attempting to learn. However, in contrast to the strategy selection task above, there is no empirical validation of the utility or feasibility of attempting to produce better problem decomposition criteria, plan selection methods, or generalized avoidance of recurring pitfalls. This is currently an active area of exploration.

14.4.2.4 Fractioning Derivations into Rules

A process akin to "decomposition" is the formulation of generally applicable rules from more problem-specific derivational sequences. Contrary to Anderson (1983) and others who view knowledge compilation as perhaps the most significant learning strategy, this author considers the decompilation process to be at least as important. Recall that in case-based reasoning one is given compiled but fully annotated audit trails of the reasoning process—the derivational traces. The fractioning task is one of axiomatizing the long, problem-specific traces into individual rules that are applicable to a much wider range of situations, although each rule solves only part of the new problem. The difficult aspect of the task is to bundle the derivationally related steps into useful rules, insuring that the necessary (and only the necessary) preconditions are associated with each rule. But its utility lies in its ability to permit the learning of more generally applicable knowledge from specific experiences. The knowledge engineers may yet have their precious rule sets, but they will be rule sets generated automatically after extended experience with derivational traces rather than rules produced and gradually refined by hand at the cost of much time and frustration.

Let us see how rules would be fractioned off from longer derivational traces. The process described below has been tested only in the route-finding domain thus far, but there it has proven useful.

1. *Find relevant candidates.* The first step in the formulation of rules from derivational traces is to search for candidate subsequences of actions that recur in different, possibly unrelated, derivational traces in the domain. For instance, the sequence

   ```
   LOCATE(bridge),
   PLAN-ROUTE(here,bridge),
   PLAN-ROUTE(bridge,destination)
   ```

   occurred with high frequency and it was proposed as a rule kernel.

2. *Trace justifications.* Why must one plan a route or locate a bridge? The justification for the former comes from the supergoal goal PLAN-ROUTE (here, destination), and the justification for the latter comes from the fact that the presence of a river between "here" and "destination" violates a precondition for land travel.

3. *Formulate rule.* Computable predicates must first be found to establish the justifications. These become the condition side of the rule. Then the justified subsequences of actions, parameterized to the most general justifiable class of actions or objects, becomes the action side of the rule. In the present example, the resultant rule is:

   ```
   IF  GOAL(x) is LOC(x,time-2) = destination
       & LOC(x,time-1) = here
       & BETWEEN (here,destination) = river
       & TRANSPORTATION(x) = land-vehicle
   THEN  FIND(bridge,river)
         PLAN-ROUTE(here,bridge)
         PLAN-ROUTE(bridge,destination)
   ```

Thus it can be seen that from multiple planning episodes the following rule can be induced: If one must cross a river, then one should first worry about finding a bridge and plan the route according to this constraint. The rule-fractioning process truly requires all three phases: finding relevant sequences, determining the justifications for these sequences, and actually formulating the rule from this information. Without a derivational trace it would not be possible to fraction rules reliably, because the justifications provided in the trace are needed for searching out the *necessary and useful* conditions for the left-hand side of the rule. Otherwise, one would have to postulate that the recurrent subsequence was either totally independent of context (a terrible assumption—the system would be searching for bridges when there were no rivers to cross) or completely dependent on context, requiring that the entire trace up to that point be included in the condition side, rather than just the causally relevant conditions indicated by the justifications.

14.5 CONCLUDING REMARK

Derivational analogy is a powerful reasoning mechanism, one that provides the information necessary for learning to occur in many different forms, from accumulation of cases to formulation of domain-oriented strategies and sets of deductive rules. It has been remarked that heuristics are "compiled hindsight" and as such can prove useful in guiding future behavior. But how can one take advantage of hindsight unless one recalls past experiences, including aspects of one's state of mind that are necessary in order to reconstruct past problem-solving behaviors in new situations? There must be a retrospective process capable of exploiting past experience and a gradual, incremental learning process that abstracts more generally applicable chunks of knowledge from that experience. The derivational analogy process is one concrete method for realizing the former, and the strategy and rule acquisition process are a means of implementing the latter. Together they form a computational theory of incremental expertise acquisition, a theory that is still in the process of being implemented, tested, refined, and reformulated.

ACKNOWLEDGMENTS

This research was supported in part by the Office of Naval Research (ONR) under grants Nos. N00014-79-C-0661 and N00014-82-C-50767 and in part by a grant from IBM. The author thanks the following colleagues for their enlightening discussions that helped to clarify the ideas presented in this chapter: Jon Doyle, Jill Larkin, Steve Minton, and Allen Newell.

References

Anderson, J. A., "Acquisition of Proof Skills in Geometry," in *Machine Learning: An Artificial Intelligence Approach*, R. S. Michalski, J. G. Carbonell, and T. M. Mitchell (Eds.), Tioga, Palo Alto, Calif., 1983.

Balzer, R., "Imprecise Program Specification," Technical Report RR-75-36, USC/Information Sciences Institute, 1975.

Barstow, D. R., "Automatic Construction of Algorithms and Data Structures Using a Knowledge Base of Programming Rules," Ph.D. diss., Stanford University, 1977.

Carbonell, J. G., "Counterplanning: A Strategy-Based Model of Adversary Planning in Real-World Situations," *Artificial Intelligence,* Vol. 16, pp. 295–329, 1981a.

————, "A Computational Model of Problem Solving by Analogy," *Proceedings of the Seventh IJCAI,* Vancouver, B.C., pp. 147–52, 1981b.

————, *Subjective Understanding: Computer Models of Belief Systems,* UMI Research Press, Ann Arbor, Mich., 1981c.

————, "Experiential Learning in Analogical Problem Solving," *Proceedings of AAAI-82,* Pittsburgh, Pa., pp. 168–71, 1982.

————, "Learning by Analogy: Formulating and Generalizing Plans from Past Experience," in *Machine Learning: An Artificial Intelligence Approach,* R. S. Michalski, J. G. Carbonell, and T. M. Mitchell (Eds.), Tioga, Palo Alto, Calif., 1983.

————, "The SMOKEY Fire-Diagnosis System," Technical Report, Computer Science Department, Carnegie-Mellon University, 1985.

Carbonell, J. G., Larkin, J. H., and Reif, F., "Towards a General Scientific Reasoning Engine," Technical Report, CIP No. 445, Computer Science Department, Carnegie-Mellon University, 1983.

Clements, J., "Analogical Reasoning Patterns in Expert Problem Solving," *Proceedings of the Fourth Annual Conference of the Cognitive Science Society,* 1982.

Doyle, J., "A Truth Maintenance System," *Artificial Intelligence,* Vol. 12, pp. 231–72, 1979.

————, "Expert Systems Without Computers," *AI Magazine,* Vol. 5, No. 2, pp. 59–63, 1984.

Duda, R. O.; Hart, P. E.; Konolige, K.; and Reboh, R., "A Computer-Based Consultant for Mineral Exploration," Technical Report 6415, SRI, 1979.

Feigenbaum, E. A., Buchanan, B. G., and Lederberg, J., "On Generality and Problem Solving: A Case Study Using the DENDRAL Program," in *Machine Intelligence 6,* D. Michie (Ed.), Edinburgh University Press, Edinburgh, 1971.

Fikes, R. E., and Nilsson, N. J., "STRIPS: A New Approach to the Application of Theorem Proving to Problem Solving," *Artificial Intelligence,* Vol. 2, pp. 189–208, 1971.

Gentner, D., "The Structure of Analogical Models in Science," Technical Report 4451, Bolt Beranek and Newman, 1980.

Hayes-Roth, F., "Using Proofs and Refutations to Learn from Experience," in *Machine Learning: An Artificial Intelligence Approach,* R. S. Michalski, J. G. Carbonell, and T. M. Mitchell (Eds.), Tioga, Palo Alto, Calif., 1983.

Kant, E., *Efficiency in Program Synthesis,* UMI Research Press, Ann Arbor, Mich., 1981.

Kling, R. E., "A Paradigm for Reasoning by Analogy," *Artificial Intelligence,* Vol. 2, pp. 147–78, 1971.

Laird, J. E., and Newell, A., "A Universal Weak Method," *Proceedings of the Eighth IJCAI,* Karlsruhe, W. Ger., pp. 771–73, 1983.

Larkin, J., Reif, F., and Carbonell, J. G., "FERMI: A Flexible Expert Reasoner with Multi-Domain Inference," *Cognitive Science,* Vol. 9, 1985, submitted.

McDermott, D. V., "Planning and Acting," *Cognitive Science,* Vol. 2, No. 2, pp. 71–109, 1967.

McDermott, D. V., and Doyle, J., "Non-Monotonic Logic I," *Artificial Intelligence,* Vol. 13, pp. 41–72, 1980.

McDermott, J., "R1: A Rule-Based Configurer of Computer Systems," Technical Report, Computer Science Department, Carnegie-Mellon University, 1980.

———, "XSEL: A Computer Salesperson's Assistant," in *Machine Intelligence 10,* J. Hayes, D. Michie, and Y-H. Pao (Eds.), Ellis Horwood Ltd., Chichester, U.K., 1982.

Michalski, R. S., "A Theory and Methodology of Learning from Examples," in *Machine Learning: An Artificial Intelligence Approach,* R. S. Michalski, J. G. Carbonell, and T. M. Mitchell (Eds.), Tioga, Palo Alto, Calif., 1983.

Minsky, M., "K-Lines: A Theory of Memory," *Cognitive Science,* Vol. 4, No. 2, pp. 117–33, 1980.

Mitchell, T. M., "Version Spaces: An Approach to Concept Learning," Ph.D. diss., Stanford University, 1978.

Mitchell, T. M., Utgoff, P. E., and Banerji, R. B., "Learning by Experimentation: Acquiring and Refining Problem-Solving Heuristics," in *Machine Learning: An Artificial Intelligence Approach,* R. S. Michalski, J. G. Carbonell, and T. M. Mitchell (Eds.), Tioga, Palo Alto, Calif., 1983.

Newell, A., and Simon, H. A., *Human Problem Solving,* Prentice-Hall, Englewood Cliffs, N. J., 1972.

Nilsson, N. J., *Principles of Artificial Intelligence,* Tioga, Palo Alto, Calif., 1980.

Pólya, G., *How to Solve It,* Princeton University Press, Princeton, N. J., 1945.

Reif, J. H., and Scherlis, W. L., "Deriving Efficient Graph Algorithms," Technical Report, Computer Science Department, Carnegie-Mellon University, 1982.

Sacerdoti, E. D., "Planning in a Hierarchy of Abstraction Spaces," *Artificial Intelligence,* Vol. 5, No. 2, pp. 115–35, 1974.

Schank, R. C., "Language and Memory," *Cognitive Science,* Vol. 4, No. 3, pp. 243–84, 1980.

———, *Dynamic Memory,* Cambridge University Press, Cambridge, 1982.

———, "The Current State of AI: One Man's Opinion," *AI Magazine,* Vol. 4, No. 1, pp. 1–8, 1983.

Shortliffe, E., *Computer Based Medical Consultations: MYCIN,* American Elsevier, New York, 1976.

Swartout, W., and Balzer, R., "On the Inevitable Intertwining of Specification and Implementation," *Communications of the ACM,* Vol. 25, No. 7, pp. 438–40, 1982.

Waterman, D., Hayes-Roth, F., and Lenat, D. (Eds.), *Building Expert Systems,* Addison-Wesley, Reading, Mass., 1983.

Wilensky, R., "Understanding Goal-Based Stories," Ph.D. diss., Yale University, 1978.

———, *Planning and Understanding,* Addison-Wesley, Reading, Mass., 1983.

Winston, P., "Learning by Creating and Justifying Transfer Frames," Technical Report AIM-520, AI Laboratory, MIT, 1978.

———, "Learning and Reasoning by Analogy," *Communications of the ACM,* Vol. 23, No. 12, pp. 689–703, 1979.

15

PROGRAMMING BY ANALOGY

Nachum Dershowitz
*University of Illinois
at Urbana-Champaign*

Abstract

Analogy is one tool that automatic programming systems can use to learn from experience, just as programmers do. This chapter illustrates how analogies between program specification (and derivations) can be used to debug incorrect programs, modify existing programs to perform different tasks, derive abstract schemata from given sets of cognate programs, and instantiate schemata to solve new problems.

An analogy between the specification of a given program and that of a new problem is used as the basis for modifying the given program to meet the new specification. Debugging is a special case of modification: if a program computes wrong results, it must be modified to achieve the intended results. For program abstraction, an analogy is sought between the specifications of the given programs; it may then be used to transform an existing program into an abstract schema that embodies the shared technique. When the specification of the derived schema is compared with a given concrete specification and an analogy between them is formulated, an instantiation of the schema may be found that yields the desired concrete program.

> *Analogy pervades all our thinking, our everyday speech and our trivial conclusions as well as artistic ways of expression and the highest scientific achievements.*
>
> —*George Pólya*

15.1 INTRODUCTION

Programming begins with a specification of what the envisioned program ought to do. It is the programmer's job to develop an executable program that satisfies that specification. Yet only a small fraction of a programmer's time is typically devoted to the creation of original programs *ex nihilo*. Rather, most of the programmer's effort is normally directed at debugging incorrect programs, adapting known techniques to specific problems at hand, modifying existing programs to meet amended specifications, extending old programs to include expanded capabilities, and abstracting ideas of general applicability into "subroutines."

The goal of research in automatic programming is to formalize the methods and strategies used by programmers so that they may be incorporated in automatic and interactive programming environments. In the author's view, program development systems should incorporate formal tools for transforming and manipulating programs. This work investigates how analogies might be used by such a system for that purpose.

The importance of analogical reasoning has been stressed by many, from Descartes to Pólya. For a discussion of the role of analogy in the sciences, see Hesse (1966); for a review of psychological theories of analogical reasoning, see Sternberg (1977); other works on analogy include Rumelhart and Norman (1981), VanLehn and Brown (1980), Gentner (1983), and Holyoak (1983). An early work on automating analogical reasoning is Evans (1968). The use of analogy in automated problem solving in general and in theorem proving in particular was proposed in Kling (1971). Other works employing analogy as an implement in problem solving include Moore and Newell (1973), Brown (1976), Chen and Findler (1976), Brown and Tärnlund (1979), McDermott (1979), Winston (1980), Carbonell (1983b), and Burstein (1983). The use of analogies to guide the modification of programs was suggested in Manna and Waldinger (1975) and pursued further in Dershowitz and Manna (1977), Ulrich and Moll (1977), and Amarel (chap. 18 of this volume). Recently, Carbonell (1983a) has stressed the importance of considering the history of a program's derivation, not just the "polished" final product.

Programmers improve with experience by assimilating programming techniques they encounter and judiciously applying the ideas they learn to new problems. One way a programmer can apply knowledge is by modifying a known program to achieve some new goal. For example, a program that uses the binary-search technique to compute square roots might be transformed into one that searches an array. This chapter shows how one can modify programs by finding an analogy between the specification of the existing program and that of the desired program and then using the analogy as a basis for transforming the existing program to meet the new specification. Program debugging is a special case of modification: if a program computes wrong results, it must be modified to achieve the intended results.

The idea that programs should be constructed by a series of transformations has been widely promoted. The difference between such transformations and modification is that in modification correctness with respect to the original specification is *not* preserved. Rather, it is necessary that the resultant program be correct with respect to the *transformed* specification. Correctness-preserving transformations and specification-changing modifications are thus complementary. A scenario of computer-aided programming and debugging appeared in Floyd (1971). The HACKER system (Sussman, 1975) constructed programs by trying out alternatives and attempting to debug them when necessary; other knowledge-based or plan-based debugging systems have been designed as well.

All the programs described here are annotated with an *output specification* (stating the desired relationship between the input and output variables upon termination of the program), an *input specification* (defining the set of legal inputs on which the program is intended to operate), and *invariant assertions* (relations that are known always to hold at specific points in the program for the current values of variables) demonstrating its correctness. The invariant assertions play an important role in the derivation of analogies. Katz and Manna (1975) and Sagiv (1976) describe debugging techniques based—like the method described here—on invariant assertions.

Program modification is not the only way programmers use previously acquired knowledge. After coming up with several modifications of their first "wheel," they are likely to formulate for themselves (and perhaps for others) an abstract notion of the underlying principle and reuse it in new, but related, applications. Program schemata are a convenient form for remembering such knowledge. A schema may embody basic programming techniques and strategies (e.g., the *generate-and-test* paradigm or the *binary-search* technique) and contains abstract, uninstantiated symbols, in terms of which its specification is stated.

The abstraction of a set of concrete programs to obtain a program schema and the instantiation of abstract schemata to solve concrete problems may be viewed from the perspective of modification methods. This perspective provides a methodology for applying old knowledge to new problems. Beginning with a set of programs sharing some basic strategy and their correctness proofs, one can derive a program schema that represents their analogous elements. Preconditions for the schema's applicability are derived from the correctness proofs. The resultant schema's abstract specification may be compared with a given concrete specification to suggest an instantiation that yields a concrete program when applied to the schema. If the instantiation satisfies the preconditions, the correctness of the new program is guaranteed.

To date there has been a limited amount of research on program abstraction. The STRIPS system (Fikes, Hart, and Nilsson, 1972) generalized the loop-free robot plans that it generated; HACKER (Sussman, 1975) "subroutinized" and generalized the "blocks-world" plans it synthesized, executing the plan to determine which program constants could be abstracted; Winston (1983) generalizes rules using analogical reasoning. Dershowitz and Manna (1975) suggested using the proof of correctness of a program to guide the abstraction process; that idea was followed up in Dershowitz (1985). Gerhart (1975) and others have advocated and illustrated the use of schemata as a powerful programming tool. A collection of such schemata, along with a catalog of correctness-preserving program transformations, could serve as part of an interactive program development system.

In the following sections the life-cycle of an example program is traced. The example illustrates some of the kinds of transformations programs undergo and how analogy can be used as a guide. First, an imperfect program for computing the quotient of two real numbers is analyzed. After the program is *debugged,* it is *modified* to approximate the cube root of a real number and to search an ordered array. Underlying all three programs is the binary-search technique; a binary-search schema is obtained by *abstracting* the programs. This schema is then *instantiated* to obtain another program, one to compute the square root of an integer. The instantiated program is then modified once more to perform integer division with remainder and then is subjected to a series of transformations to take advantage of properties specific to division.

Further details of the methodology advocated here may be found in Dershowitz (1983), where a partial implementation of some of the analogical aspects of programming is also described, including debugging, modification, and instantiation (but not abstraction).

15.2 AN EXAMPLE

Consider the problem of computing the quotient q of two nonnegative real numbers c and d within a specified (positive) tolerance e. These requirements are conveniently expressed in the form of the following skeleton program:

D_1: **begin comment** *real-division specification*
    assert $0 \le c < d, e > 0$
    achieve $| c/d - q | < e$ **varying** q
    end

The **achieve** statement,

    achieve $| c/d - q | < e$ **varying** q,

contains the *output specification* giving the relation among the variables $q, c, d,$ and e that should be attained at the end of program execution: the (absolute value of the) difference between the exact quotient c/d and the result q should be less than e. The clause **varying** q indicates that of the variables in the specification, only q may be set by the program; the other variables, $c, d,$ and e, contain input values that remain fixed. The *input specification* defines the set of input values on which the program is intended to operate. Assuming that we wish the program to handle the case when the quotient is in the range 0 to 1, that is, when the numerator c is smaller than the denominator d, the appropriate input specification is contained in the **assert** statement,

    assert $0 \le c \le d, e > 0$,

attached to the beginning of the program. For the problem at hand, it is assumed that no general real-division operator / is available, though division by powers of 2 ("shifts") is permissible.

Now let us imagine that a programmer went ahead and constructed the following program:

T_1: **begin comment** *suggested real-division program*
    B_1: **assert** $0 \le c < d,\ e > 0$
    purpose $|\ c/d - q\ | < e$
      purpose $q \le c/d < q + s,\ s \le e$
        $(q,s) := (0,1)$
        loop L_1: **suggest** $q \le c/d < q + s$
            until $s \le e$
            purpose $q \le c/d < q + s,\ 0 < s < s_{L_1}$
              if $d \cdot (q + s) \le c$ **then** $q := q + s$ **fi**
            $s := s/2$
        repeat
      suggest $q \le c/d < q + s,\ s \le e$
    E_1: **suggest** $|\ c/d - q\ | < e$
    end

The **purpose** statement,

    purpose $|\ c/d - q\ | < e,$

is a comment describing the intent of the code following it. The statement

    suggest $|\ c/d - q\ | < e$

contains the programmer's contention that the preceding code actually achieves the desired relation; that is, the relation $|\ c/d - q\ | < e$ holds for the value of q when control reaches the end of the program. The comment

    purpose $q \le c/d < q + s,\ s \le e$

indicates that the programmer's intention is to achieve the desired relation $|\ c/d - q\ | < e$ by achieving the subgoals $q \le c/d \le q + s$ and $s \le e$. Achieving these relations is sufficient for $|\ c/d - q\ | < e$ to hold. For this purpose the programmer constructed an iterative loop intended to keep the first relation invariantly true while progress was being made towards the second. The suggested invariant is contained in the statement

    suggest $q \le c/d < q + s$

at label L_1. The goal of the loop body is

    purpose $q \le c/d < q + s,\ 0 < s < s_{L_1},$

where s_{L_1} denotes the value of the variable s when control was last at the label L_1. This means that the value of s is to be less than it just was at the head of the loop. The two loop-body statements are accordingly repeated (zero or more times) until the test $s \le e$ becomes true, at which point the loop will be exited.

We know what the above program was intended for, but in fact it does not always fulfill those intentions. However, before we can debug it, we need to know more about what it actually does. This can be accomplished by examining the code and annotating the program with the discovered invariant relations. (See Dershowitz and Manna, 1981, for one collection of annotation rules.) Here a few necessary invariants are derived informally.

The loop terminates when the exit test $s \leq e$ becomes true. It follows that the relation $s \leq e$ must hold when control reaches the label E_1. This can be asserted in an invariant

E_1: **assert** $s \leq e$.

Similarly, if the exit test is not taken and the loop body is executed, then the exit test must have been false, that is, $s > e$. Neither branch of the conditional statement affects s, and therefore the relation $s > e$ holds after the conditional statement as well. At that point s is divided by 2. If before the division we had $s > e$, then at the end of the loop body we have $2s > e$. Thus whenever the loop body is executed, control returns to the head of the loop with the relation $2s > e$. holding. Since that relation does not necessarily hold when the loop is first entered with $s = 1$, it itself is not a loop invariant. Nevertheless, the disjunction of the relations $s = 1$ and $2 \cdot s > e$ is a loop invariant, since one relation holds when the loop is first entered and the other holds every time the loop is repeated; that is, we have

L_1: **assert** $s = 1 \ \lor \ 2s > e$.

Turning now to the body of the loop, let us consider the conditional statement

if $d \cdot (q + s) \leq c$ **then** $q := q + s$ **fi**.

The **then**-path of the conditional statement is taken when $d \cdot (q + s) \leq c$; therefore, after resetting q to $q + s$, we have $d \cdot q \leq c$. Since conditional statements are often intended to achieve the same purpose in different cases, it is plausible that the relation $d \cdot q \leq c$—achieved by the **then**-path of the conditional—is meant to hold also when the **then**-path is not taken. This suggests the "candidate" invariant

L_1: **suggest** $d \cdot q \leq c$.

Indeed, since $d \cdot q \leq c$ is true initially, when $q = 0$ and $c \geq 0$, and it is unaffected when the conditional test is false (since the value of q is not changed), it invariantly holds when control reaches the head of the loop. We have derived the loop invariant

L_1: **assert** $d \cdot q \leq c$.

The **then**-path is not taken when $c < d \cdot (q + s)$. In that case s is divided in half and q is left unchanged, yielding $c < d \cdot (q + 2s)$ at the end of the current iteration. It turns out that this relation holds before the loop is entered and is preserved by the **then**-path. Thus, we have the additional invariant

L_1: **assert** $c < d \cdot (q + 2s)$.

The loop invariants $d \cdot q \leq c$ and $c < d \cdot (q + 2s)$ remain true when the loop exit is taken; along with the exit test $s \leq e$, they imply that upon termination of the program the output invariant

E_1: **assert** $| c/d - q | < 2 \cdot e$

holds. Note that the desired relation $| c/d - q | < e$ is *not* implied.

The annotated program—with invariants that correctly express what the program does—is as follows:

T_1: **begin comment** *annotated buggy real-division program*
    B_1: **assert** $0 \leq c < d, e > 0$
    purpose $| c/d - q | < e$
       purpose $q \leq c/d < q + s, s \leq e$
          $(q,s) := (0,1)$
          loop L_1: **assert** $d \cdot q \leq c, c < d \cdot (q + 2 \cdot s), s = 1 \bigvee 2 \cdot$
                                     $s > e$
                suggest $c/d < q + s$
                until $s \leq e$
                purpose $q \leq c/d, c/d < q + s, 0 < s < s_{L_1}$
                   if $d \cdot (q + s) \leq c$ **then** $q := q + s$ **fi**
                $s := s/2$
          repeat
       assert $q \leq c/d < q + 2 \cdot s, s \leq e$
       suggest $c/d < q + s$
    E_1: **assert** $| c/d - q | < 2 \cdot e$
    suggest $| c/d - q | < e$
    end

Now that something is known about what the program does, debugging can be attempted.

15.3 DEBUGGING

The task now is to find a correction to the program that will achieve the desired output invariant

    suggest $| c/d - q | < e$.

The first step is to look for a way to transform the actual invariant into the desired one; then the same transformation is applied to the program, thereby, it is hoped, correcting the error. Accordingly, an analogy is sought between the actual output invariant and the desired specification; we write

$$| c/d - q | < 2e \Rightarrow | c/d - q | < e$$

The obvious difference between the two expressions is that where the first has $2 \cdot e$, the second has just e. So, the analogy can be reduced to simply

$$2e \Rightarrow e.$$

The insufficient $| c/d - q | < 2e$ can therefore be transformed into the desired $| c/d - q | < e$ by replacing e with $e/2$, that is, by applying the transformation $e \Rightarrow e/2$.

So far it has been determined that the transformation $e \Rightarrow e/2$, applied to the output invariant $| c/d - q | < 2e$, yields the desired output specification $| c/d - q | < e$. That same transformation is now applied to the whole annotated program. The symbol e appears once in the program text: the exit clause $s \leq e$ accordingly becomes $s \leq e/2$. It also appears four times in the invariants; for example, the input assertion $e > 0$ transforms into $e/2 > 0$, which is equivalent to $e > 0$. The transformed program is

$$(q,s) := (0,1)$$
loop L_2: **assert** $d \cdot q \leq c < d \cdot (q + 2s)$
        until $s \leq e / 2$
        purpose $q \leq c/d < q + 2s, 0 < s < s_{L_2}$
        if $d \cdot (q + s) \leq c$ **then** $q := q + s$ **fi**
        $s := s/2$
    repeat
assert $q \leq c/d < q + 2s, 2s \leq e.$

(The **purpose** statement has also been changed to reflect what the loop body does in reality, as opposed to what was intended.) It can be shown that a transformation such as $e \Rightarrow e/2$ preserves the relation between the program text and invariants; that is, the transformed assertions are invariants of the transformed program (see Dershowitz, 1983).

In this manner the program is modified to achieve the intended result $| c/d - q | < e$. But note that the loop invariant still differs from that suggested by the programmer. The difference between the two is that although the programmer intended $c < d \cdot (q + s)$ to be true, in fact $c < d \cdot (q + 2s)$ holds. If desired, this can be remedied by applying the transformation

$$s \Rightarrow s/2.$$

Applying this global transformation affects the five occurrences of s in the program code. The exit clause becomes

until $s/2 \leq e/2$,

or equivalently,

until $s \le e$;

the conditional statement becomes

if $d \cdot (q + s/2) \le c$ **then** $q := q + s/2$ **fi**.

The assignment statement

$s := 1$

transforms into

$s/2 := 1$,

which, unfortunately, is not a legal assignment, since an expression appears on the left-hand side. The intent of this illegal statement, however, is to

achieve $s/2 = 1$ **varying** s

which is the same as

achieve $s = 2$ **varying** s,

and may be accomplished by the assignment

$s :- 2$.

Similarly, the assignment

$s := s/2$

gives rise to the goal

achieve $s/2 = (s'/2)/2$ **varying** s,

where s' represents the value of the variable s prior to this goal. This is the same as the goal $s = s'/2$, which is achieved by the original assignment

$s := s/2$

At this point, the loop body contains the two statements

if $d \cdot (q + s/2) \le c$ **then** $q := q + s/2$ **fi**
$s := s/2$.

Since the expression $s/2$ appears three times in these two statements, this program may be slightly improved by transforming them into

$s := s/2$
if $d \cdot (q + s) \le c$ **then** $q := q + s$ **fi**.

When all of the above changes are incorporated, the final real-division program is as follows:

D_2: **begin comment** *real-division program*
   B_2: **assert** $0 \le c < d,\ e > 0$
   purpose $|\ c/d - q\ | < e$

purpose $q \leq c/d < q + s, s \leq e$
    $(q,s) := (0,2)$
loop L_2: **assert** $d \cdot q \leq c < d \cdot (q + s), s = 2 \lor 2s > e$
    until $s \leq e$
    purpose $q \leq c/d, c/d < q + s, 0 < s < s_{L_2}$
    $s := s / 2$
    if $d \cdot (q + s) \leq c$ **then** $q := q + s$ **fi**
    repeat
  assert $q \leq c/d, c/d < q + s, s \leq e$
E_2: **assert** $|c/d - q| < e$
end

Note that this program is almost the same as the original "buggy" program. It differs in two ways: the two loop-body assignments are interchanged (this presumably was the programmer's error), and s is initialized to 2 rather than 1 (either initialization works).

Now, consider the following specification:

C_3: **begin comment** *cube-root specification*
   assert $a \geq 0, e > 0$
   achieve $|a^{1/3} - r| < e$ **varying** r
   end

We would like to use the corrected real-division program as a basis for the construction of the specified program for computing cube roots. (It is assumed, of course, that the cube-root operator is not primitive.) To this end, the specifications of the two programs are first compared. The output specification of the division program is

    assert $|c/d - q| < e$,

and the output specification of the desired program is

    achieve $|a^{1/3} - r| < e$ **varying** r.

The obvious analogy between the two is

    $q \Rightarrow r$
    $c/d \Rightarrow a^{1/3}$;

that is, where the former specification has q, the other has r, and where the former has c/d, the other has $a^{1/3}$. One way to obtain a cube-root program from the division program is via the transformations

    $q \Rightarrow r$
    $u/v \Rightarrow u^{1/3}$
    $c \Rightarrow a,$

where by $u/v \Rightarrow u^{1/3}$ is meant that every occurrence of the (general) division operator / is replaced by the cube-root operator applied to what was the numerator. (The operator /2 is not transformed into a cube root, since—unlike general division—it is a primitive operation. If such a distinction were not made, the program derivation would have to be examined more carefully.) Transformations that involve specific functions, such as division, are not, however, guaranteed to yield a correct program, since the program may be based on some property that holds for division but not for extracting roots. Such transformations are heuristic in nature; they only suggest a possible analogy between the two programs. Indeed, when this transformation is applied to the division program D_2, the result is a program that computes a/d, not $a^{1/3}$. What must be done in such cases is to review the derivation of the program, expressed by the programmer in **purpose** statements, and see where the analogy breaks down.

The purpose of the division program was $| c/d - q | < e$, which transformed into $| a^{1/3} - r | < e$ as desired. The programmer achieved $| c/d - q | < e$ by breaking it into the subgoals given in the statement

purpose $q \leq c/d < q + s, s \leq e,$

part of which became the exit test for the loop, and part of which became a loop invariant. These subgoals transform into

purpose $r \leq a^{1/3} < r + s, s \leq e,$

which indeed imply the transformed goal $| a^{1/3} - r | < e$. The purpose of the loop body of the division program was

purpose $q \leq c/d < q + s, 0 < s < s_{L_2}.$

In other words, the loop body reachieves the invariant while making progress towards the exit test by decreasing s. The loop-body subgoal of the transformed program, then, is

purpose $r \leq a^{1/3} < r + s, 0 < s < s_{L_3}.$

At this point the division program halves s and introduces a conditional with the following purpose:

purpose $q \leq c/d < q + s.$

It is here that the analogy breaks down. The division program achieves the above purpose in two cases, by testing if $d \cdot (q + s) \leq c$ or not. For example, if $d \cdot (q + s) \leq c$ does not hold, then $c/d < q + s$, as desired. On the other hand, the fact that $d \cdot (r + s) \leq a$ does not hold in the cube-root program reveals nothing about $a^{1/3} < r + s$. Therefore, a transformation is sought that makes $d \cdot (r + s) > a$ imply $a^{1/3} < r + s$ or the equivalent $a < (r + s)^3$. Matching the outcome of the test with the desired invariant tells us that the implication would hold if we could transform $d \cdot (r + s) \Rightarrow (r + s)^3$. Thus, where the division program has the function $u \cdot v$, the cube-root program requires v^3. The analogy is completed by adding the transformation

$u \cdot v \Rightarrow v^3,$

which is applied to the conditional test.

There remains one problem: a transformed program can only be expected to satisfy the output specification for those inputs that satisfy the *transformed* input specification, which is unfortunately more restrictive than the given input specification. In the case presented here, this can be solved if we find an alternative manner by which to initialize the invariant $r \leq a^{1/3} < r + s$ prior to entering the loop. To achieve the subgoal $r \leq a^{1/3}$, we can let $r = 0$. Then to achieve $a^{1/3} < r + s = s$, we can let $s = a + 1$ (given the fact that $a^{1/3} < a + 1$). The complete cube-root program is:

C_3: **begin comment** *cube-root program*
  B_3: **assert** $a \geq 0$, $e > 0$
  $(r,s) := (0, a + 1)$
  loop L_3: **assert** $r \leq a^{1/3} < r + s$
       until $s \leq e$
       $s := s/2$
       if $(r + s)^3 \leq a$ **then** $r := r + s$ **fi**
       repeat
  E_3: **assert** $| a^{1/3} - r | < e$
  end

15.4 A MORE PROBLEMATIC EXAMPLE

In the previous examples, the two given specifications were syntactically similar, and the transformations applied were relatively straightforward. This next example will illustrate some of the difficulties that may be encountered when analogies are used to guide the modification of programs.

In this example, it is shown how the correct cube-root program C_3 may be used as a basis for constructing a program that searches for the position z of an element b known to occur in an array segment $A[1:n]$. The array is assumed to contain integers sorted in nondescending order. Our goal is

A_4: **begin comment** *array-search specification*
  assert $u \leq v \supset A[u] \leq A[v]$, $A[u] \in \mathbf{Z}$, $b \in A$
  achieve $A[z] = b$ **varying** z
  end

where $b \in A$ means that the element b occurs in the array segment $A[1:n]$. That A is an array of nondecreasing integers is expressed in the input conditions $A[u] \in \mathbf{Z}$ and $u \leq v \supset A[u] \leq A[v]$ (where the variables u and v are universally quantified). Arrays may be indexed by any real number, and the convention is adopted that the intended element may be found by truncating the index, that is,

$A[u] = A[\lfloor u \rfloor]$

for all u. (In a similar manner, one could develop a program following the ALGOL 60 convention of rounding off the index.) The desired goal

> **achieve** $A[z] = b$ **varying** z

is not directly comparable with the output specification

> **assert** $| a^{1/3} - r | < e$

of the given program. Therefore, the goal must be decomposed somewhat.
   As a first try, the desired goal is replaced with the equivalent goal

> **achieve** $A[z] \leq b \leq A[z]$ **varying** z.

This replacement is guided by the fact that an equality is desired and the given program achieves an inequality. Since only integers are involved, this is the same as

> **achieve** $A[z] \leq b < A[z] + 1$ **varying** z.

Also, it is known that the cube-root program actually achieves the output invariants

> **assert** $r \leq a^{1/3} < r + e$.

Accordingly, a transformation

> $r \leq a^{1/3} < r + e \Rightarrow A[z] \leq b < A[z] + 1$

is sought and the subgoal $r \leq a^{1/3}$ is compared with $A[z] \leq b$. Matching the two sides of the inequality produces

> $r \Rightarrow A[z]$
> $a^{1/3} \Rightarrow b$.

To obtain $a^{1/3} \Rightarrow b$, we can let

> $a \Rightarrow b^3$.

Applying these transformations to the whole goal leaves $A[z] \leq b < A[z] + e \Rightarrow A[z] \leq b < A[z] + 1$, suggesting the additional transformation

> $e \Rightarrow 1$.

   Applying the three transformations

> $r \Rightarrow A[z]$
> $a \Rightarrow b^3$
> $e \Rightarrow 1$

to the given cube-root program yields the following program:

> X_4: **begin comment** *proposed array-search program*
> B_4: **assert** $b^3 \geq 1, 1 > 0$
> $(A[z],s) := (1,b^3 - 1)$
>   **loop** L_4: **assert** $A[z] \leq b < A[z] + s$
>   **until** $s \leq 1$

$s := s/2$
if $(A[z] + s)^3 \leq b^3$ **then** $A[z]: = A[z] + s$ **fi**
repeat
E_4: **assert** $A[z] \leq b < A[z] + 1$
end

There are, however, a number of problems with this program, the insurmountable one lying in the **then**-branch assignment $A[z] := A[z] + s$. The original goal stated that only z is an output variable; the array A is an input variable that may not be modified by an assignment. Furthermore, there is *no* way to

achieve $A[z] = A[z'] + s$ **varying** z

(where z' denotes the previous value of z), since the value $A[z'] + s$ might not appear in A at all.

So another alternative must be sought. Since $A[u] = A[\lfloor u \rfloor]$, the goal

achieve $A[z] = b$ **varying** z

is equivalent to

achieve $A[\lfloor z \rfloor] = b$ **varying** z.

At this point it would be appropriate to extract z from the expression $A[\lfloor z \rfloor]$, as the output variable r appears by itself in the output invariants of the given program C_3. To facilitate this, we need to make temporary use of an inverse of the array-indexing function. (The inverse function serves only as a formal mechanism for expressing transformations; it will be eliminated from the final version of the program.) The function $pos(U, u)$ gives the (integral) position of the (rightmost) occurrence of the element u in the array U. Thus, $A[pos(A,b)] = b$, and, in order to

achieve $A[\lfloor z \rfloor] = b$ **varying** z,

it suffices to

achieve $pos(A,b) = \lfloor z \rfloor$ **varying** z.

Applying now the definition of $\lfloor u \rfloor$, we obtain the conjunctive goal

achieve $pos(A,b) \leq z < pos(A,b) + 1, pos(A,b) \in \mathbf{Z}$ **varying** z.

Since the conjunct $pos(A,b) \in \mathbf{Z}$ follows from the definition of pos (and the fact that $b \in A$), we are left with the goal

achieve $pos(A,b) \leq z < pos(A,b) + 1$ **varying** z.

The current goal is still not readily comparable with the output invariants

assert $r \leq a^{1/3} < r + e$

of the cube-root program. Whereas for the array-search program the output variable z appears on the right-hand side of the $\leq$ relation and on the left-hand side of the $<$

relation, for cube-root program the sides are reversed. One possible solution is to transform the predicates $\leq$ and $<$. To get

$$r \leq a^{1/3} \Rightarrow z \geq pos(A,b),$$

the transformations

$$r \Rightarrow z$$
$$\leq \Rightarrow \geq$$
$$a^{1/3} \Rightarrow pos(A,b)$$

may be applied. To obtain the third transformation, we let

$$a \Rightarrow pos(A,b)^3.$$

(This latter transformation hides the real analogy between $u^{1/3} \Rightarrow pos(A,u)$. Its advantage, however, is that it is guaranteed to preserve correctness with respect to the specifications.) Applying these transformations to the subgoal $a^{1/3} < r + e$ leaves

$$pos(A,b) < z + e \Rightarrow pos(A,b) + 1 > z.$$

Transposing to isolate $pos(A,b)$ on both inequalities gives

$$pos(A,b) < z + e \Rightarrow pos(A,b) > z - 1,$$

so the transformations $< \Rightarrow >$ and $e \Rightarrow -1$ are added. Altogether this gives

$$r \Rightarrow z$$
$$\leq \Rightarrow \geq$$
$$a \Rightarrow pos(A,b)^3$$
$$< \Rightarrow >$$
$$e \Rightarrow -1.$$

Applying these five transformations to the given cube-root program C_3 and simplifying yields the program

$$(z,s) := (1, pos(A,b)^3 + 1)$$
loop L_5: **suggest** $z \geq pos(A,b) > z + s$
  until $s \geq -1$
  $s := s/2$
  if $z + s \geq pos(A,b)$ **then** $z := z + s$ **fi**
  repeat
E_5: **suggest** $z \geq pos(A,b) > z - 1.$

(The transformed invariants are only suggestions, since the constants $\leq$ and $<$ are being transformed.) Before the nonprimitive function *pos* is eliminated from the transformed program, an attempt is made to verify the correctness of the program as is. The suggested loop invariants

suggest $z \geq pos(A,b) > z + s$

along with the exit condition

until $s \geq -1$

clearly imply the desired output invariant

    suggest $pos(A,b) \leq z$, $z < pos(A,b) + 1$.

Furthermore, the loop-body path preserves the loop invariants for both cases of the conditional.

    The problem is with the verification condition for the initialization path: the assignment $(z,s) := (1, pos(A,b)^3 + 1)$ does not initialize the loop invariants. Since the transformed initialization does not work, it must be replaced with an unachieved subgoal

    assert $u \leq v \supset A[u] \leq A[v]$, $A[u] \in \mathbf{Z}$, $b \in A$
    achieve $z \geq pos(A,b)$, $pos(A,b) > z + s$ **varying** z,s.

The purpose of this goal is to set the variables z and s so that the loop invariants $z \geq pos(A,b)$ and $pos(A,b) > z + s$ hold when the loop is entered for the first time. Since it is given that b appears within the segment $A[1:n]$, the relation $z \geq pos(A,b)$ can be achieved by letting $z = n$. Now $pos(A,b) > z + s$ can be achieved by the insistence that $z + s = 0$, for which s is initialized to $-z = -n$.

    Replacing the initialization requires rechecking the verification condition for termination. It must be the case that when the initial value $-n$ of s is repeatedly halved, the exit test $s \geq -1$ becomes true at some point. Since this is insured, all the verification conditions hold and the transformed program is correct.

    Finally, the conditional test $z + s \geq pos(A,b)$ containing the nonprimitive function pos may be replaced by $A[z + s + 1] > b$. That the two tests are equivalent may be deduced from the input specification $u \leq v \supset A[u] \leq A[v]$ and the definition of pos. The program now is as follows:

    A_5: **begin comment** *array-search program*
      B_5: **assert** $u \leq v \supset A[u] \leq A[v]$, $A[u] \in \mathbf{Z}$, $b \in A$
      $(z,s) := (n, -n)$
      loop L_5: **assert** $A[z + s + 1] \leq b < A[z + 1]$
             until $s \geq -1$
             $s := s / 2$
             if $A[z + s + 1] > b$ **then** $z := z + s$ **fi**
             repeat
      E_5: **assert** $A[z] = b$
      end

    The above array-search program is certainly not the most obvious one. But that is to be expected, since it was derived by analogy with a different program, not from scratch. If desired, it could be given a more conventional appearance by replacing $z + s$ (the lower bound of the search) with a new variable y and following up with additional program transformations.

15.5 ABSTRACTION

At this point there are three programs, D_2 for finding quotients, C_3 for finding cube roots, and A_5 for searching ordered arrays, all utilizing the binary-search technique. It would be nice if one could extract an abstract version of the programs that captures the essence of the technique but is not specific to any one problem. The resultant abstract program schema could be used as a model of binary search for the solution of future problems.

For this purpose, consider the complete analogy that was found between the specifications of D_2 and C_3:

$$q \Leftrightarrow r$$
$$u/v \Leftrightarrow u^{1/3}$$
$$c \Leftrightarrow a$$
$$u \cdot v \Leftrightarrow v^3.$$

Since both u/v and $u^{1/3}$ are functions, they can be generalized to an abstract function $\gamma(u,v)$. Similarly the generalization of $u \cdot v$ and v^3 is another function $\delta(u,v)$. Both q and r are output variables and are generalized to an abstract output variable z; the input variables c and a are generalized to an abstract input variable x. This gives the following set of transformations for generalizing the division program:

$$q \Rightarrow z$$
$$u/v \Rightarrow \gamma(u,v)$$
$$c \Rightarrow x$$
$$u \cdot v \Rightarrow \delta(u,v).$$

Applying these transformations to the specification

achieve $| c/d - q | < e$ **varying** q

of the division program yields

achieve $| \gamma(x,d) - z | < e$ **varying** z.

This will be the abstract output specification of the schema. Substituting the abstract functions γ and δ into their respective positions in the division program D_2 does not, however, result in a schema that will work for all instantiations of γ and δ. This is because the original program relied upon facts specific to multiplication and division. It must therefore be determined under what conditions the abstract schema does achieve its specifications.

To begin with, the transformed initialization assignment does not achieve the desired loop invariant. The loop initialization is therefore replaced with the subgoal

achieve $\delta(d,z) \le x < \delta(d,z + s)$ **varying** $z,s,$

leaving unspecified—for the time being at least—the details of how to initialize the loop invariant. For the loop-body path to be correct, the truth of the invariant must imply that the invariant will hold next time around; this can easily be shown to be the case for any function δ. For the loop-exit path to be correct, the loop invariants, plus exit test, must imply that the output invariant holds. For this to be the case, it suffices to establish the condition

$$\delta(w,u) \le v \equiv u \le \gamma(v,w).$$

In this manner, a general program schema has been derived for a binary search for the value of $\gamma(x,d)$ within a tolerance e:

> S_6: **begin comment** *binary-search schema*
> B_6: **assert** $e > 0,\ \delta(w,u) \le v \equiv u \le \gamma(v,w)$
>   **achieve** $\delta(d,z) \le x < \delta(d,z + s)$ **varying** z,s
>   **loop** L_6: **assert** $\delta(d,z) \le x < \delta(d,z + s)$
>   **until** $s \le e$
> $s := s/2$
>   **if** $\delta(d,z + s) \le x$ **then** $z := z + s$ **fi**
>   **repeat**
> E_6: **assert** $|\ \gamma(x,d) - z\ | < e$
>   **end**

Of course, for this schema to be executable, the function δ appearing in it must be primitive; otherwise, it should be replaced. Similarly, the unachieved subgoal

> **achieve** $\delta(d,z) \le x < \delta(d,z + s)$ **varying** z,s

must be reduced to primitives. If the analogy with A_5 had also been considered, a somewhat more general schema would have resulted.

15.6 INSTANTIATION

The binary-search schema just derived from the division program may be applied to the computation of the square root of an integer. The goal is to construct a program that finds the integer square root z of a nonnegative integer a:

> R_7: **begin comment** *integer square-root specification*
>   **assert** $a \in \mathbf{N}$
>   **achieve** $z = \lfloor\sqrt{a}\rfloor$ **varying** z
>   **end**

where the function $\lfloor u \rfloor$ yields the largest integer not greater than u.

This goal cannot be directly matched with the output specification of the schema

> **assert** $|\ \gamma(x,d) - z\ | < e$ **varying** z.

However, if the goal $z = \lfloor\sqrt{a}\rfloor$ is expanded using the definition of $\lfloor u \rfloor$, the equivalent goal

achieve $z \le \sqrt{a} < z + 1$, $z \in \mathbf{Z}$ **varying** z

(where $\mathbf{Z}$ is the set of all integers) is obtained; that is, z should be the largest integer not greater than $\sqrt{a}$. Since it is known that the schema achieves the output invariants

assert $z \le \gamma(x,d) < z + e$,

these invariants can be compared with the above goal. This suggests the transformation

$$\gamma(u,v) \Rightarrow \sqrt{u}$$
$$x \Rightarrow a$$
$$e \Rightarrow 1$$

to achieve $z \le \sqrt{a} < z + 1$. In addition, the program will have to be extended to insure that the final value of z is an integer.

The precondition for the schema's correctness is

assert $e > 0$, $\delta(w,u) \le v \equiv u \le \gamma(v,w)$;

instantiating it yields

assert $1 > 0$, $\delta(w,u) \le v \equiv u \le \sqrt{v}$.

This condition may be satisfied by taking $\delta(w,u)$ to be u^2 (and requiring $u \ge 0$). This completes the analogy and suggests the additional transformation

$$\delta(w,u) \Rightarrow u^2.$$

Applying the instantiation mapping to the schema, we obtain the following partially written program:

P_7: **begin comment** *incomplete integer square-root program*
    B_7: **assert** $a \in \mathbf{N}$
    achieve $z^2 \le a < (z + s)^2$ **varying** z,s
    loop L_7: **assert** $z^2 \le a < (z + s)^2$
            until $s \le 1$
            $s := s/2$
            if $(z + s)^2 \le a$ **then** $z := z + s$ **fi**
            repeat
    assert $| \sqrt{a} - z | < 1$
    achieve $z \in \mathbf{Z}$ **protecting** $z \le \sqrt{a} < z + 1$ **varying** z
    end

This program still contains two unachieved subgoals. The first can be achieved by assigning $(z,s) := (0, a + 1)$. For the second, the current value of z may be perturbed just enough to make it an integer, leaving the relation $z \le \sqrt{a} < z + 1$, already achieved by the instantiated schema, still "protected." This can be done by assigning

if $\lceil z \rceil^2 \le a$ **then** $z := \lceil z \rceil$ **else** $z := \lfloor z \rfloor$ **fi**.

15.7 EXTENSION

An alternative approach to completing the above program is to insist that $z \in \mathbf{Z}$ hold *throughout* execution of P_7. This is the avenue pursued, for example, in the "structured programming" derivations in Dijkstra (1976) and Blikle (1978).

Note that actually $z \in \mathbf{N}$ must be achieved, since the invariant $\sqrt{a} < z + 1$ implies that z is nonnegative. To this end, the goal

achieve $z \in \mathbf{N}$ **in** R_7 **varying** z

is set up, meaning that $z \in \mathbf{N}$ is to be "globally" invariant in P_7. Accordingly, $z \in \mathbf{N}$ must be established initially and then preserved throughout the loop computation. Letting $z = 0$ initially gives $z \in \mathbf{N}$, as is desired. Since z is sometimes incremented by s, the latter should also be a nonnegative integer. Finally, in order to preserve the invariant $s \in \mathbf{N}$ while it is repeatedly halved until it is no longer greater than 1, it is necessary and sufficient that $s \in 2^{\mathbf{N}}$ be invariant, where $2^{\mathbf{N}}$ denotes the set of nonnegative powers of 2. Accordingly, the conjunct $s \in 2^{\mathbf{N}}$ is added to the initialization subgoal $a < s^2$.

At this point, we have an unachieved subgoal

achieve $a < s^2$, $s \in 2^{\mathbf{N}}$ **varying** s.

To achieve this conjunctive goal, we transform it into an iterative loop,

> **purpose** $a < s^2$, $s \in 2^{\mathbf{N}}$
> **achieve** $s \in 2^{\mathbf{N}}$ **varying** s
> **loop** L_8': **assert** $s \in 2^{\mathbf{N}}$
>   **until** $a < s^2$
>   **achieve** *approach*($a < s^2$) **protecting** $s \in 2^{\mathbf{N}}$ **varying** s
>   **repeat**
> **assert** $a < s^2$, $s \in 2^{\mathbf{N}}$

choosing first to achieve $s \in 2^{\mathbf{N}}$ and then to keep it true while the loop is being executed until the remaining conjunct $a < s^2$ is also satisfied.

To initialize $s \in 2^{\mathbf{N}}$, we let $s = 2^0$ and assign

$s := 1.$

Within the loop we have the subgoal

achieve *approach*($a < s^2$) **protecting** $s \in 2^{\mathbf{N}}$ **varying** s;

that is, we wish to preserve the invariant $s \in 2^{\mathbf{N}}$ while progress is made towards the exit test $a < s^2$. Since it is known that initially $s = 1$, and since ultimately $0 \leq \sqrt{a} < s$ is desired, it follows that s increases within the loop. Presuming that s increases *monotonically,* it follows that s must be multiplied by some positive power of 2, for example,

$s := 2 \cdot s.$

When all the pieces are put together, the following program is obtained:

R_8: **begin comment** *integer square-root program*
  B_8: **assert** $a \in \mathbf{N}$
  $z = 0$
  purpose $a < s^2, s \in 2^N$
    $s := 1$
    loop L_8': **assert** $s \in 2^N$
          until $a < s^2$
          $s := 2 \cdot s$
          repeat
  purpose $z^2 \le a, a < (z + s)^2, s \le 1$
    loop L_8: **assert** $z^2 \le a, a < (z + s)^2, z \in \mathbf{N}, s \in 2^N$
          until $s \le 1$
          $s := s/2$
          if $(z + s)^2 \le a$ **then** $z := z + s$ **fi**
          repeat
  E_8: **assert** $z = \lfloor \sqrt{a} \rfloor$
  end

In the above program, the exit test $a < s^2$ and conditional test $(z + s)^2 \le a$ are the most expensive expressions computed. They can be replaced by cheaper operations by a series of correctness-preserving program transformations (see, e.g., Wensley, 1959; Dijkstra, 1976; Blikle, 1978; Dershowitz, 1983). In the following example, something similar is done:

Suppose now that we wish to construct a program to compute the quotient q and remainder r of two integers c and d. The formal specification is

Q_9: **begin comment** *integer division specification*
  assert $c \in \mathbf{N}, d \in \mathbf{N} + 1$
  achieve $q \le c/d < q + 1, q \in \mathbf{N}, r = c - d \cdot q$ **varying** q, r
  end

Of course, the general-division operator is meant not to be a primitive; in fact it would be preferable that the program not use multiplication by other than a constant.

In order for the above goal to be achieved, program R_8 must be modified. The first step is to attempt to discover an analogy between the specifications of the two programs. In this case the output specification

  E_8: **assert** $z = \lfloor \sqrt{a} \rfloor$

of the square-root program bears little external resemblance to the goal

  achieve $q \le c/d < q + 1, q \in \mathbf{N}, r = c - d \cdot q$ **varying** q, r.

But, if it is also known that the output invariants

E_8: **assert** $z \le \sqrt{a} < z + 1, z \in \mathbf{Z}$

hold, then the analogy is more readily apparent. One possible set of transformations is

$z \Rightarrow q$
$\sqrt{a} \Rightarrow c/d.$

The latter transformation can be accomplished by letting

$a \Rightarrow (c/d)^2.$

These transformations will achieve the desired conjuncts $q \le c/d$ and $c/d < q + 1$; in addition the program will have to be extended to achieve $r = c - d \cdot q$.
When these transformations are applied, the exit test of the first loop, $a < s^2$, becomes $(c/d)^2 < s^2$. Since $c, d,$ and s are all positive, this is the same as $c/d < s$ or $c < d \cdot s$. Similarly, the conditional test $(z + s)^2 \le a$ becomes $d \cdot (q + s) \le c$. The transformed program accordingly is

$(q,s) := (0,1)$
loop L_9': **assert** $s \in 2^{\mathbf{N}}$
        until $c < d \cdot s$
        $s := 2 \cdot s$
        repeat
loop L_9: **assert** $q \le c/d, c/d < q + s, q \in \mathbf{N}, s \in 2^{\mathbf{N}}$
        until $s \le 1$
        $s := s/2$
        if $d \cdot (q + s) \le c$ **then** $q := q + s$ **fi**
        repeat

When the transformation $a \Rightarrow (c/d)^2$ is applied to the given input specification $a \in \mathbf{N}$ of the integer square-root program, the condition $(c/d)^2 \in \mathbf{N}$ on the inputs c and d is obtained. The problem is that this is stronger than the specification $c \in \mathbf{N}$ and $d \in \mathbf{Z} + 1$ for integer division. However, all that is actually needed for the correctness of the square-root program is $a \ge 0$; the input specification $a \in \mathbf{N}$ is unnecessarily restrictive. Applying the transformation to $a \ge 0$ instead yields $(c/d)^2 \ge 0$. Since this is implied by $c \in \mathbf{N}$ and $d \in \mathbf{N} + 1$, the above program is correct for all legal inputs.
At this point, the program achieves most of the requirements in the output specification of Q_9. The additional requirement $r = c - d \cdot q$ can be achieved if the above program is extended by incorporating the output variable r and maintaining the desired relation throughout the program. This requires that whenever q is assigned to, the new variable r be updated in tandem. Thus, when q is initialized to 0, r is set to $c - d \cdot 0 = c$. When q is incremented by s, r is updated to $c - d \cdot (q + s) = r - d \cdot s$.

With the new assignments to r included, the program is as follows:

$(q,s,r) := (0,1,c)$
loop L_9': **assert** $s \in 2^N$
             until $c < d \cdot s$
             $s := 2 \cdot s$
             repeat
loop L_9: **assert** $q \leq c/d < q + s$, $q \in$ **N**, $s \in 2^N$
             $s := s/2$
             if $d \cdot (q + s) \leq c$ **then** $(q,r) := (q + s, r - d \cdot s)$ **fi**
             repeat

Note that the conditional test $d \cdot (q + s) \leq c$, which is equivalent to $d \cdot s \leq c - d \cdot q$, can be replaced by $d \cdot s \leq r$ now that r is available. Furthermore, the expression $d \cdot s$ involves multiplication and appears several times. The program can be improved by the introduction of a new variable u and the extension of the program once more to maintain the new relation $u = d \cdot s$ globally invariant. Substituting u for all occurrences of $d \cdot s$ and updating it whenever the value of s is changed produces the following program:

Q_9: **begin comment** *integer division program*
   B_9: **assert** $c \in$ **N**, $d \in$ **N** $+ 1$
   $(q,s,r,u) := (0,1,c,d)$
   loop L_9': **assert** $s \in 2^N$, $u = d \cdot s$
                until $c < u$
                $(s,u) := (2s,u)$
                repeat
   loop L_9: **assert** $q \leq c/d$, $c/d < q + s$, $q \in$ **N**, $s \in 2^N$,
                      $r = c - d \cdot q$, $u = d \cdot s$
                until $s \leq 1$
                $(s,u) := (s/2,\ u/2)$
                if $u \leq r$ **then** $(q,r) := (q + s, r - u)$ **fi**
                repeat
   E_9: **assert** $q \leq c/d < q + 1$, $q \in$ **N**, $r = c - d \cdot q$.
   end

This is the desired "hardware" integer-division program (see Wensley, 1959). Its only operations are addition, subtraction, comparison, and shifting—hardware instructions on binary computers.

15.8 DISCUSSION

The examples in this chapter have illustrated how an imaginary automated programming system might use analogical reasoning to perform some of the varied tasks of program construction. The author imagines that a future programmer faced with the task of developing a new program (or subprogram) to meet a set of specifications might first search for an applicable schema. After instantiating that schema appropriately, the programmer might have to perform various other transformations to satisfy remaining specifications or to increase efficiency. If no applicable schema can be found, the programmer might still be able to find a program solving an analogous problem and modify it. Those two programs together could then be used to formulate a schema for future use. (Using a schema is preferable to modifying a related program because correctness is ensured if the preconditions are satisfied. The extraction of appropriate preconditions, however, is what makes abstraction more complex a task than either modification or instantiation.) Naturally, some steps taken in these examples were more intuitive than others and more easily implementable. An attempt has been made here to highlight, rather than to hide, the difficulties that may be encountered in finding and applying analogies.

The work presented here lies at the confluence of machine learning and automatic programming. As such, it illustrates the potential value of analogical reasoning in the programming domain. This domain differs from many others in that (1) it is well defined, (2) reasoning is "monotonic," and (3) formal tools are available. Some of the problems encountered in the examples, such as the need to analyze and transform programs, are typical for automatic programming. Their resolution requires powerful tools, large libraries, and efficient search mechanisms.

The analogical methods described here are meant to complement other program transformation techniques and program synthesis and analysis tools. For example, the decision to split a search range down the middle can only be justified by the neatness of the resultant program, as in Dijkstra (1976), by the desire to minimize the number of variables, as in Manna and Waldinger (1985), or by the efficiency of the algorithm (necessitating *ex post facto* analysis). But once the idea of binary search has been developed in one context, it can be applied—by analogy—to other contexts. In general, an instantiated schema would be transformed to take the specifics of the problem domain into account. In the process, program statements may be moved, changed, or deleted, to a point where the transformed program bears little resemblance to the schema. For example, Newton's faster method for calculating square roots is in large measure analogous to the binary method, but splits the range at a point other than the center.

Analogies between different objects can be sought on several levels—the levels of external appearance, of outward performance, and of inner workings. Generally, one can dramatically change the external appearance of a program, that is, the code, without affecting the underlying algorithm. At the opposite end of the spectrum, input/output specifications, which define the outward performance of a program but not how it accomplishes what it does, can be identical for very disparate programs. Between the two extremes, comments about the program's inner workings—its correctness and efficiency—are perhaps a better guide when one is looking for similarities between programs. Therefore, it makes sense to begin by formulating an analogy between program specifications and then to extend that analogy by examining how the different programs achieve their analogous desiderata. The more one knows about the "rhyme and reason" of a program, the more likely one is to be able to profit from comparing it with other programs.

The problems inherent in the use of analogies for program modification and abstraction include *hidden* analogies, *misleading* analogies, *incomplete* analogies, and *overzealous* analogies. Hidden analogies arise when given specifications (of the existing program and the desired problem in the case of modification; of the two or more existing programs in the case of abstraction) that are to be compared with one another have little in common syntactically. Since the pattern-matching ideas employed here are syntax based, the underlying analogy is hidden when the specifications are not syntactically similar. Then it is necessary to rephrase the specifications in some equivalent manner that brings their similarity out before an analogy can be found. This is clearly a difficult problem in its own right; in general some form of means-end analysis seems appropriate.

At the opposite extreme, a syntactic analogy may be misleading. The same symbol may appear in the specifications of two programs but play nonanalogous roles in them. Two programs might even have exactly the same specifications but employ totally different methods of solution. This kind of situation would be detected when correctness conditions are analyzed. Other work on "repairing" analogies includes Burstein (1983), Carbonell (1983a), and Winston (1983).

Knowing how a program was constructed can help one avoid overzealously applying transformations to unrelated parts of a program. Like Carbonell (1983a), the author believes that it is necessary in general to look for analogies between derivations. An example has been given here of how comments on the purpose of code segments help complete an analogy between two programs when only part of it was found by a comparison of specifications.

In summary, programming by analogy may be thought of as including the following (nonindependent) steps:

- *Find relevant programs.* The question of how one knows which programs are worth looking at in detail has not been addressed. One would presumably begin by looking for some kind of broad similarity before continuing with the next step.
- *Analyze the given program.* If necessary, the given program can be annotated with invariant assertions. In particular, the relation between input and output variables achieved by the program should be determined so it may be compared with the desired relation. It would be better yet if the programmer (human or machine) has provided an annotated history of the decisions made in deriving the given program. Annotation is particularly essential for debugging, since what the incorrect program actually does is unspecified.

- *Rephrase the specifications to bring out their similarity.* The specifications of the given and desired programs may be given in a form that obscures any analogy. Thus it may be necessary to express the specifications in some equivalent form that makes their similarity more pronounced. In general this may be a very difficult task.

- *Discover an analogy between the specifications.* This analogy suggests a set of transformations that yield the desired specification when applied to the specification of the given program.

- *Check the validity of the proposed transformations.* For those types of transformations that do not necessarily preserve correctness, the verification conditions are examined.

- *Extend the analogy.* When the program derivations are examined, it often becomes clear that the analogy must be extended with additional transformations.

- *Localize the transformations.* Other times, transformations must be localized to specific occurrences of symbols. One does this by looking at the dependencies of symbols in a program proof.

- *Apply the transformations.* The transformations found in the previous steps are applied to the given program.

- *Rewrite any unexecutable statements.* Any nonprimitive statements or expressions introduced into the program by the transformations must be reexpressed in terms of primitives.

- *Synthesize new segments.* If necessary, new program segments can be written to replace parts of the program that cannot be modified.

- *Extend the modified program.* Code is integrated into the program for any unachieved parts of the desired specification.

- *Optimize the transformed program.* At this point, domain-specific transformations can be applied. One may be able to optimize the new program by taking advantage of properties it has that may not have held for the old program.

The author does not have a full implementation, but he envisions the possibility of such methods being embedded in a semiautomated program development environment in which the system performs the more straightforward steps in a consistent manner. The reasoning ability needed by such a system is similar to that required by, say, a program verification system; the program manipulation abilities are comparable to those required of transformation systems. All require the same knowledge of the subject domains and need similar logical arithmetic capabilites. It may be that logic-based programming languages (see Kowalski, 1974) will provide a relatively convenient environment for this kind of research. The identity of specification and programming languages and the potential availability of suitable general-purpose theorem provers should aid the design of program manipulation systems. Of course, such methods as those described by the author (or by others) would not suffice to produce large-scale, complex programs. Still, top-down programming methodology favors small, easily comprehensible modules, each of which should be amenable to the kind of manipulations presented here. The larger a program, the more convoluted it is, and the deeper the ideas that went into it, the more difficult it is—for humans or machine—to reason about it.

In conclusion, the author has endeavored to show how analogies may be exploited to allow a program development system to profit from past experience. But analogical reasoning is only one mode of thought, albeit an important one; it must be combined with other techniques as well.

ACKNOWLEDGMENT

This research was supported in part by the National Science Foundation under Grants MCS 79-04897 and MCS 83-07755.

References

Amarel, S., "Program Synthesis as a Theory Formation Task: Problem Representations and Solution Methods," chap. 18 of this volume, 1985.

Blikle, A., "Towards Mathematical Structured Programming," in *Formal Descriptions of Programming Concepts,* E. J. Neuhold (Ed.), North-Holland, Amsterdam, 1978.

Brown, R. H., "Reasoning by Analogy," Working Paper 132, AI Lab, MIT, October 1976.

Brown, F. M., and Tärnlund, S. Å, "Inductive Reasoning on Recursive Equations," *Artificial Intelligence,* Vol. 12, No. 3, pp. 207–29, November 1979.

Burstein, M. H., "Concept Formation by Incremental Reasoning and Debugging," *Proceedings of the International Machine Learning Workshop,* R. S. Michalski (Ed.), Allerton House, University of Illinois at Urbana-Champaign, pp. 19–25, June 22–24, 1983. (An updated version of this paper appears as chap. 13 of this volume.)

Carbonell, J. G., "Derivational Analogy in Problem Solving and Knowledge Acquisition," *Proceedings of the International Machine Learning Workshop,* R. S. Michalski (Ed.), Allerton House, University of Illinois at Urbana-Champaign, pp. 12–18, June 22–24, 1983a. (An updated version of this paper appears as chap. 14 of this volume.)

———, "Learning by Analogy: Formulating and Generalizing Plans from Past Experience," in *Machine Learning: An Artificial Intelligence Approach,* R. S. Michalski, J. G. Carbonell, and T. M. Mitchell (Eds.), Tioga, Palo Alto, Calif., 1983b.

Chen, D. T. W., and Findler, N. V., "Toward Analogical Reasoning in Problem Solving by Computers," Technical Report 115, Department of Computer Science, State University of New York, Buffalo, December 1976.

Dershowitz, N., "Program Abstraction and Instantiation," *ACM Transactions on Programming Languages and Systems,* Vol. 7, No. 3, July 1985.

————, *The Evolution of Programs*, Birkhäuser, Boston, 1983.

Dershowitz, N., and Manna, Z., "On Automating Structured Programming," *Proceedings of the Colloque IRIA on Proving and Improving Programs*, Arc-et-Senans, France, pp. 167–93, July 1975.

————, "The Evolution of Programs: Automatic Program Modification, " *IEEE Transactions on Software Engineering*, Vol. SE-3, No. 6, pp. 377–85, November 1977.

————, "Inference Rules for Program Annotation," *IEEE Transactions on Software Engineering*, Vol. SE-7, No. 2, pp. 207–22, March 1981.

Dijkstra, E. W., *A Discipline of Programming*, Prentice-Hall, Englewood Cliffs, N.J., 1976.

Evans, T. G., "A Program for the Solution of Geometric-Analogy Intelligence Test Questions," in *Semantic Information Processing*, M. L. Minsky (Ed.), MIT Press, Cambridge, 1968.

Fikes, R. E., Hart, P. E., and Nilsson, N. J., "Learning and Executing Generalized Robot Plans," *Artificial Intelligence*, Vol. 3, No. 4, pp. 251–88, Winter 1972.

Floyd, R. W., "Toward Interactive Design of Correct Programs," *Proceedings of the Information Processing Congress*, Ljubljana, Yugoslavia, pp. 7–10, August 1971.

Gentner, D., "Structure-mapping: A Theoretical Framework for Analogy," *Cognitive Science*, Vol. 7, pp. 155–70, 1983.

Gerhart, S. L., "Knowledge about Programs: A Model and Case Study," *Proceedings of the International Conference on Reliable Software*, Los Angeles, Calif., pp. 88–95, April 1975.

Hesse, M., *Models and Analogies in Science*, University of Notre Dame Press, Notre Dame, Ind., 1966.

Holyoak, K. J., "Analogical Thinking and Human Intelligence," in *Advances in the Psychology of Human Intelligence*, Vol. 2, R. J. Sternberg (Ed.), Erlbaum, Hillsdale, N.J., 1983.

Katz, S. M., and Manna, Z., "Towards Automatic Debugging of Programs," *Proceedings of the International Conference on Reliable Software*, Los Angeles, Calif., pp. 143–55, April 1975.

Kling, R. E., "Reasoning by Analogy with Applications to Heuristic Problem Solving: A Case Study," Ph.D. diss., Stanford University, 1971.

Kowalski, R. A., "Predicate Logic as Programming Language," *Proceedings of the IFIP Congress*, Amsterdam, pp. 569–74, 1974.

Manna, Z., and Waldinger, R. J., "Knowledge and Reasoning in Program Synthesis," *Artificial Intelligence*, Vol. 6, No. 2, pp. 175–208, Summer 1975.

————, "The origin of the binary-search paradigm," *Proceedings of the Ninth IJCAI*, Los Angeles, Calif., August 1985.

McDermott, J., "Learning to Use Analogies," *Proceedings of the Sixth IJCAI*, Tokyo, pp. 568–76, August 1979.

Moore, J. A., and Newell, A., "How Can MERLIN Understand?" in *Knowledge and Cognition*, L. Gregg (Ed.), Erlbaum, Hillsdale, N.J., 1973.

Rumelhart, D. E., and Norman, D. A., "Analogical Processes in Learning," in *Cognitive Skills and Their Acquisition*, J. R. Anderson (Ed.), Erlbaum, Hillsdale, N.J., 1981.

Sagiv, Y., "A Study of the Automatic Debugging of Programs," Master's thesis, Weizmann Institute of Science, Rehovot, Israel, 1976.

Sternberg, R. J., *Intelligence, Information Processing, and Analogical Reasoning,* Erlbaum, Hillsdale, N.J., 1977.

Sussman, G. J., *A Computer Model of Skill Acquisition,* American Elsevier, New York, 1975.

Ulrich, J. W., and Moll, R., "Program Synthesis by Analogy," *Proceedings of the ACM Symposium on Artificial Intelligence and Programming Languages,* Rochester, N.Y., pp. 22–28, August 1977.

VanLehn, K., and Brown, J. S., "Planning Nets: A Representation for Formalizing Analogies and Semantic Models of Procedural Skills," in *Aptitude, Learning and Instruction: Cognitive Process Analyses,* R. E. Snow, P. A. Federico, and W. E. Montague (Eds.), Erlbaum, Hillsdale, N.J., 1980.

Wensley, J. H., "A Class of Non-analytical Iterative Processes," *Computer Journal,* Vol. 1, No. 4, pp. 163–67, January 1959.

Winston, P. H., "Learning and Reasoning by Analogy," *Communications of the ACM,* Vol. 23, No. 12, pp. 689–703, December 1980.

————, "Learning by Augmenting Rules and Accumulating Censors," *Proceedings of the International Machine Learning Workshop,* R. S. Michalski (Ed.), Allerton House, University of Illinois at Urbana-Champaign, pp. 2–11, June 22–24, 1983. (An updated version of this paper appears as chap. 3 of this volume.)

PART
FIVE

LEARNING BY OBSERVATION AND DISCOVERY

16

THE SEARCH FOR REGULARITY:

Four Aspects of Scientific Discovery

Pat Langley
Jan M. Zytkow
Herbert A. Simon
Gary L. Bradshaw
Carnegie-Mellon University

Abstract

Scientific discovery is a complex activity involving many different components. Our interest in discovery has led us to construct four AI systems that address different facets of this process. BACON.6 focuses on the discovery of empirical laws that summarize numerical data. This program searches a space of data and a space of numerical laws, and includes methods for postulating intrinsic properties and noting common divisors. GLAUBER is concerned with discovering laws of qualitative structure, such as the hypothesis that acids react with alkalis to form salts. It searches a space of qualitative laws, using evaluation functions to focus attention on laws covering the greatest number of observed facts. STAHL attempts to determine the components of substances involved in reactions, and has been used to model the reasoning that led to the phlogiston theory. This system searches through the space of componential models, using heuristics to make plausible inferences. The final system, DALTON, is concerned with formulating structural models of chemical reactions. It searches the space of possible models, considering simple models before more complex ones and using a conservation assumption to constrain possibilities. While each of these discovery systems is interesting in its own right, we are also exploring ways in which the systems can interact to help direct each other's search processes.

Key Terms: scientific discovery, empirical laws, structural models, explanation, qualitative laws, theory of acids and bases, theory of phlogiston, atomic theory

16.1 EXPLORING THE SCIENTIFIC PROCESS

Science is a multifaceted process, concerned both with the collection of data and with their explanation. Within these two basic components additional subdivisions exist. The first process ranges from exploratory data gathering to the design of specific experiments to test explicit hypotheses. Similarly, the explanatory process ranges from the induction of simple empirical laws to the formulation of complex structural and process models. These components are not independent, since the relation between data and theory is all-important in science. Still, the relations between the various components are complex, and if the scientific process is ever to be understood, powerful methods must be used.

In this chapter we apply the methodology of AI to explore the processes of scientific discovery. Our goal is not to explain the details of historical science, though the history of science is fascinating and we will certainly draw upon it in our efforts. Rather, we hope to understand the processes by which scientific discoveries *could* have been made; in other words, our goal is to develop methods that are *sufficient* for making such discoveries. To this end, we will draw upon the AI technique of implementing one's theory as a running computer program. Thus, we will devote much of this chapter to describing particular AI programs and their behavior in specific domains.

One of the central insights of AI is that intelligence involves the ability to *search*—and the ability to direct that search in profitable directions. Search involves the exploration of some space of possibilities, which Newell and Simon (1972) have called a *problem space*. A problem space is defined by two components: (1) one or more *initial* states from which search begins; and (2) one or more *operators* for generating new states from existing ones. Taken together, these components determine a set of states that can be systematically searched. In order to search such a space, one also needs some search control scheme to direct search down one path or another, and some test to determine when the goal state has been reached. The notion of problem spaces is important for each of our discovery systems, and we will describe each system in terms of its search characteristics.

We have organized this chapter around four AI systems that address different aspects of the discovery process. First we describe BACON, a system that is concerned with discovering empirical laws of a quantitative nature. We will begin with BACON since it is the first discovery system we constructed, and many readers may have some familiarity with it. More important, our recent work has been largely motivated by BACON's limitations, so a consideration of the system's capabilities and limits will lay a solid foundation for the rest of the chapter. After this we describe GLAUBER, a system that is also concerned with empirical laws, but in this case laws having a qualitative form. Next we examine STAHL, a program that infers the components of substances from reactions, followed by DALTON, a system that constructs simple structural models. Since these systems address complementary aspects of the discovery process, we close the chapter by discussing some possible interactions among the programs, and the possibility of constructing an integrated discovery system.

16.2 DISCOVERING QUANTITATIVE EMPIRICAL LAWS

At the very end of the eighteenth century and the beginning of the nineteenth century, three fundamental discoveries were made that shaped the directions of chemical research for several generations thereafter. The first of these was Proust's statement of the law of constant proportions (1799). Proust conducted a painstaking analysis of chemical compounds, finding that the ratio of the combining weights of the constituent elements was always constant for a particular compound. The second fundamental advance was Dalton's introduction of the law of multiple proportions (1804). This law asserts that when two elements combine to form several different compounds, the ratios of their combining weights are always small integer multiples of one another. The third advance was Gay-Lussac's discovery of the law of combining volumes for gaseous reactions (1809), which states that gases combine with each other in very simple ratios by volume.

These three discoveries provided the foundation for a quantitative theory of chemical reactions, and ultimately led to the determination of relative atomic weights. To some extent, Dalton's and Gay-Lussac's laws were motivated by an atomic hypothesis, but there were strong empirical components to the discoveries as well. Although Proust's law might be dealt with using traditional curve-fitting techniques, the other laws involve more complex relations. Thus, the history of early chemistry provides a challenging domain for testing AI methods for empirical discovery. Below we describe a discovery system that focuses on quantitative discovery, and examine its approach to finding these chemical laws, as well as other laws from the history of science.

16.2.1 Searching the Space of Data

We have explored the process of quantitative discovery through BACON.6, the sixth in a line of programs named after Sir Francis Bacon (1561–1626). The system is given a set of independent and dependent variables, and based on data it gathers, the program generates empirical laws that relate these variables to each other. In order to achieve this goal, BACON varies one of the terms, looking for relations between that term and the dependent variables. Once a functional relation has been found, the parameters in that function are given the status of dependent terms at a higher level of description. The system then repeats this process with a different value for the second independent term, arriving at a new set of parameters. When all values of the second independent term have been considered, BACON has a set of higher-level dependent values (based on the parameters) associated with each of the independent values. The system finds a numeric relation between these terms, and again the parameters become dependent values at the next higher level of description. This process continues until all the independent terms have been incorporated into a complex quantitative relationship.

BACON can be viewed as searching two distinct problem spaces—the space of *data* and the space of *laws*. These searches interact in a complex manner, but before we examine this interaction, let us examine each of the search schemes independently, starting with search through the data space (see table 16-1). As noted, BACON is provided with a set of independent terms, along with possible values for each term. Using these values, the system generates a complete factorial design involving all combinations of independent values, and then it examines the values of the known dependent terms for each combination. BACON's generation of all independent combinations can be viewed in terms of search, with states containing partially specified experimental combinations. The initial state has no independent values specified, while goal states include values for all of the independent terms. The operator for moving through this space inputs a partially specified experimental combination and decides on the value for one of the unspecified terms. Search control is depth first, but since many combinations must be generated, the system must backtrack and explore many different paths.

For instance, suppose BACON is given three independent terms—the pressure P on a gas, the temperature T of that gas in degrees Celsius, and the quantity N of the gas—along with the single dependent term V, the volume of the gas. Further suppose that BACON is told to examine N with values 1, 2, and 3, T with values 10, 20, and 30, and P with values 1000, 2000, and 3000. In order to generate an experimental combination, the system begins with an initial state in which no values have been specified, which we may represent as [ ]. Next, the SPECIFY-VALUE operator applies, generating a new state in which the value of N is determined, say [$N = 1$]. Upon its next application, the operator generates a third state in which the value of P is given, say [$N = 1, T = 10$]. When BACON applies the operator a third time, the complete

Table 16-1: BACON's data-gathering method viewed in terms of search.

Initial state: The null combination [ ]

Goal state: A complete experimental combination of independent values

Intermediate state: A partial combination of independent values

Operators:
  Specify-value: Specifies the value of an undetermined independent value

Heuristics/Evaluation functions: None; search is exhaustive

Search control: Exhaustive depth-first search with backtracking; generates all goal states

---

experimental combination $[N = 1, T = 10, P = 1000]$ is generated, and the program can examine the volume associated with this combination.

However, if BACON is to gather sufficient data on which to base its laws, it must continue the search. Accordingly, the system backs up to the previous state $[N = 1, T = 10]$ and applies the operator with different arguments, generating the second goal combination, $[N = 1, T = 10, P = 2000]$. This allows a second value of the volume to be observed and associated with an experimental combination. At this point, the system again backtracks to $[N = 1, T = 10]$ and then generates a third goal state, $[N = 1, T = 10, P = 3000]$, thus gathering a third observation of the volume. Having exhausted the potential values of T, BACON then proceeds to back up two steps to $[N = 1]$. From here it generates the states $[N = 1, T = 20]$ and finally $[N = 1, T = 20, P = 1000]$, another complete experimental combination. BACON continues in this fashion until it has generated all experimental combinations of the independent values it was given and observes the volumes associated with each combination. Figure 16-1 shows the tree that results from this search through the space of data; the numbers on each state represent the order in which that state is generated.[1]

16.2.2 Searching the Space of Laws

Now let us turn to BACON.6's method for searching the space of numeric laws (see table 16-2). Given a set of independent values and a corresponding set of dependent values, the system attempts to find one or more laws that predict the observed values as accurately as possible. In order to achieve this goal, BACON requires some information about the *form* that plausible laws may take. For instance, for the independent term x and the dependent term y, the user may tell the program to consider laws having the form $y = ax^2 + bx + c$, as well as those with the form $\sin(y) = ax + b$. These forms define the space of the laws that BACON will explore in its attempt to summarize the observed data.[2]

Given a set of forms, BACON generates a set of initial states from which to begin the search. This is done by inserting the abstract parameters in each form with the values 1, 0, or -1. For simplicity, let us consider only for form $y = ax + b$ and examine the resulting initial states. In this case, there are $3^2 = 9$ possible initial states: $[a = 1, b = 1], [a = 1, b = 0], [a = 1, b = -1], [a = 0, b = 1], [a = 0, b = 0], [a = 0, b = -1], [a = -1, b = 1], [a = -1, b = 0]$, and

---

[1] An earlier version of BACON (Langley, Bradshaw, and Simon, 1982) was capable of modifying this search based on discoveries it had made. The current system does not include this ability.

[2] Earlier versions of BACON were restricted to particular forms. For instance, BACON.5 (Langley, Bradshaw, and Simon, 1982) only considered laws of the form $y^i = ax^2 + bx + c$, where i took on small integral values, and thus was less flexible than the current system.

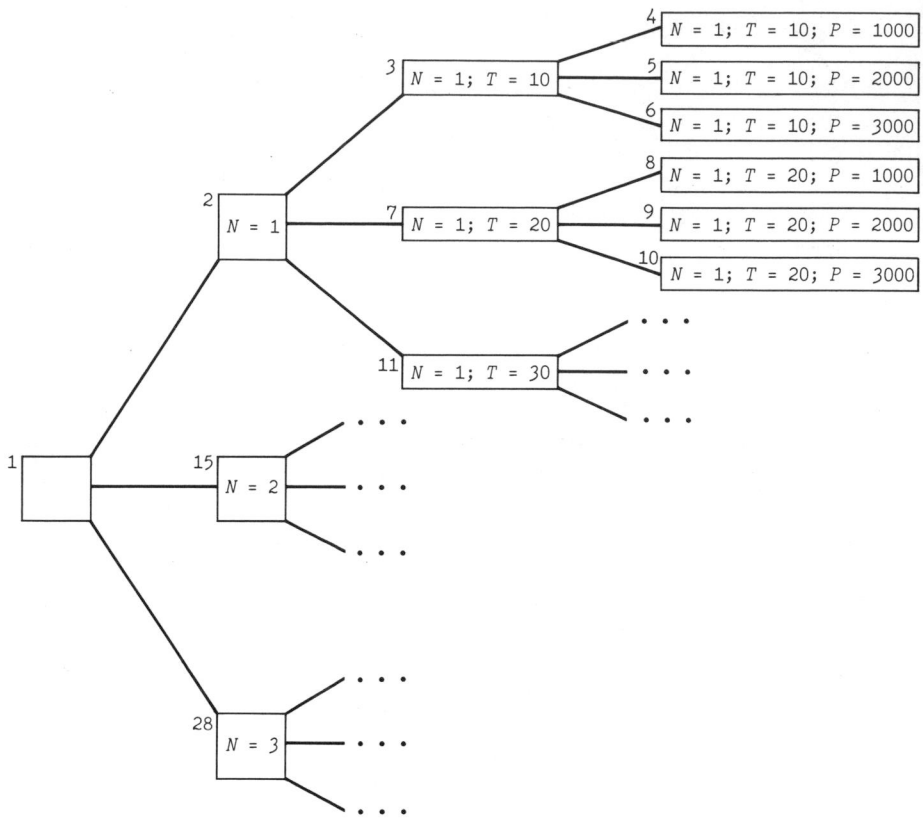

Figure 16-1: BACON's search through the space of data.

Table 16-2: BACON's law-finding method viewed in terms of search.

Initial states: Sets of parameters consisting of 1, 0, and −1
Goal state: A set of parameters that maximally predicts the observed data
Intermediate states: Sets of parameters that account for some of the data
Operators:
Add/Subtract: Adds or subtracts from one parameter value
Evaluation function: Select states that lead to higher correlations, thus better predicting the data
Search control: Hill climbing using a beam search

$[a = -1, b = -1]$. These parameters are chosen because they are evenly distributed throughout the space of parameters, so that the best set of parameters should be near one of them. Starting from these idealized parameters, BACON attempts to determine the optimum state through a process of successive approximation.

BACON.6 employs a single operator for moving through the space of parameters. This operator accepts one of the current sets as input, and generates a new parameter combination by adding or subtracting some number from one of the existing values. The amount that is added or subtracted decreases as the system's search progresses. For instance, the system begins by adding/subtracting 0.5 from the various values. On the second step, this amount is reduced to 0.25, and so on. BACON's strategy for exploring the parameter space is best described as a beam-search version of hill climbing. At the outset, the N best states are selected for further attention, and the remainder are abandoned. The addition/subtraction operator is then applied to these N states in all possible ways, generating a new set of M states. Of these $N + M$ states, the N best are selected (some of the originals may be retained), and the process is repeated. When none of the new states show any improvement over the preceding states, the search is terminated.

In selecting some states in favor of others, BACON considers the ability of each parameter set to predict the observed values. In order to estimate this ability, the system substitutes the parameter values into the form of the law and computes the correlation between the observed independent and dependent values. A high correlation means that the parameters predict the data well, while a low correlation implies that the state's predictive ability is poor. Since correlations are insensitive to absolute values, only the *relative* values of the parameters are important. It is for this reason that the initial values of 1, 0, and -1 were able to "cover" the space of parameters. In any case, this evaluation function is used to direct search toward sets of parameters that account for as much of the data as possible.

Since this search strategy uses the data only to *test* hypotheses and not to generate them, it is robust with respect to numerical noise. BACON.6 is guaranteed to find some law that summarizes regularity in the data, even if this regularity is only partial. Of course, when the data are very noisy, there may not be one set of parameters (or even one form of law) that is clearly superior to its competitors. In such cases, the program returns a number of laws. One of BACON's interesting features is that the system carries out the same amount of search regardless of the amount of noise occurring in the data.

16.2.3 Relation Between the Search Methods

Now that we have examined BACON's two search schemes in isolation, it is time to consider their relation to one another. Basically, the system's search for laws is *embedded* within its search for data. To understand this statement, let us return to figure 16-1, which presents the order in which BACON gathers its data. Consider the three highest terminal nodes, $[N = 1, T = 10, P = 1000]$, $[N = 1, T = 10, P = 2000]$, and $[N = 1, T = 10, P = 3000]$. For each of these combinations, the system observes some value of the dependent volume V. When all three values have been noted, BACON attempts to find a law relating them to the three values of the pressure P, using the search strategy just described. The result of this search is one or more parameters (let us assume that one law is obviously better than all others), and these are stored at the next higher state in the data search tree. For instance, for $P = 1000, 2000$, and 3000, the observed values for V would be 2.35, 1.18, and 0.78. For these data, the form $V^{-1} = aP + b$ gives the best fit, with the parameter values $a = 0.000425$ and $b = 0$. The value for a is stored with the state $[N = 1, T = 10]$ for future use; however, the system treats 0 as a special value, so the result for b would not be stored.

Upon observing a second set of values, BACON attempts to find a second law. For the experimental combinations $[N = 1, T = 20, P = 1000]$, $[N = 1, T = 20, P = 2000]$, and $[N = 1, T = 20, P = 3000]$, the system finds the values 2.44, 1.22, and 0.81 for the volume. Again the form $V^{-1} = aP + b$ proves useful, this time with the values $a = 0.000410$ and $b = 0$, and again these values are stored at a higher state, in this case $[N = 1, T = 20]$. Very similar events occur when the value of T is 30, giving the parameter values $a = 0.000396$ and $b = 0$, which are stored with $[N = 1, T = 30]$. At this point, BACON has three sets of values for the higher-level dependent terms a and b. Moreover, these values are stored with the abstracted combinations $[N = 1, T = 10]$, $[N = 1, T = 20]$, and $[N = 1, T = 30]$. Given the values 10, 20, and 30 for T, along with the values 0.000425, 0.000410, and 0.000396 for a, the program attempts to find a law relating these two terms. In this case, it finds the form $a^{-1} = cT + d$ to best summarize the data, with $c = 8.32$ and $d = 2271.4$. These values are stored with the next higher state in the data tree, $[N = 1]$, for future use.

This process is continued as more data are gathered. First BACON finds three additional laws relating the variables P and V. Based on the resulting parameter values, the form $a^{-1} = cT + d$ is again found to be useful, this time with $c = 16.64$ and $d = 4542.7$. These higher-level dependent values are stored with the state $[N = 2]$. Similar steps lead to three more laws of the form $V^{-1} = aP + b$ and then to a third law of the form $a^{-1} = cT + d$. This time BACON finds the best fit with $c = 24.96$ and $d = 6814.1$ and stores these values with $[N = 3]$. Now the system has three values of N, along with three associated values of both c and d. For each of these dependent terms, BACON searches the space of laws, arriving at the two laws $c = eN$ and $d = fN$, with $e = 8.32$ and $f = 2271.4$. These two parameter values are stored at the initial data state $[\ ]$ and represent invariant parameters that are not conditional on any independent terms. By substituting these values into the forms found at each level in BACON's search, we arrive at the relation $V^{-1} = (8.32NT + 2271.4N)^{-1}P$. This expression can be transformed into $PV = 8.32NT + 2271.4N$ if we divide through by P and invert the equation. If we then factor out 8.32 N on the right side of the relation, we arrive at $PV = 8.32N(T + 273)$, which is the standard form of the ideal gas law. Note that in some sense, BACON has determined that the Celsius temperature scale is insufficient for describing the relation among the four terms, and has effectively introduced the Kelvin scale by adding 273 to the observed Celsius values.

From this example, we see that BACON carries out as many searches through the law space as there are nonterminal states in the data space. Figure 16-2 summarizes the parameter values resulting from each of these searches, along with the data states at which they are stored. The number next to each state represents the order in which that law was discovered. Note that this order is different from the order in

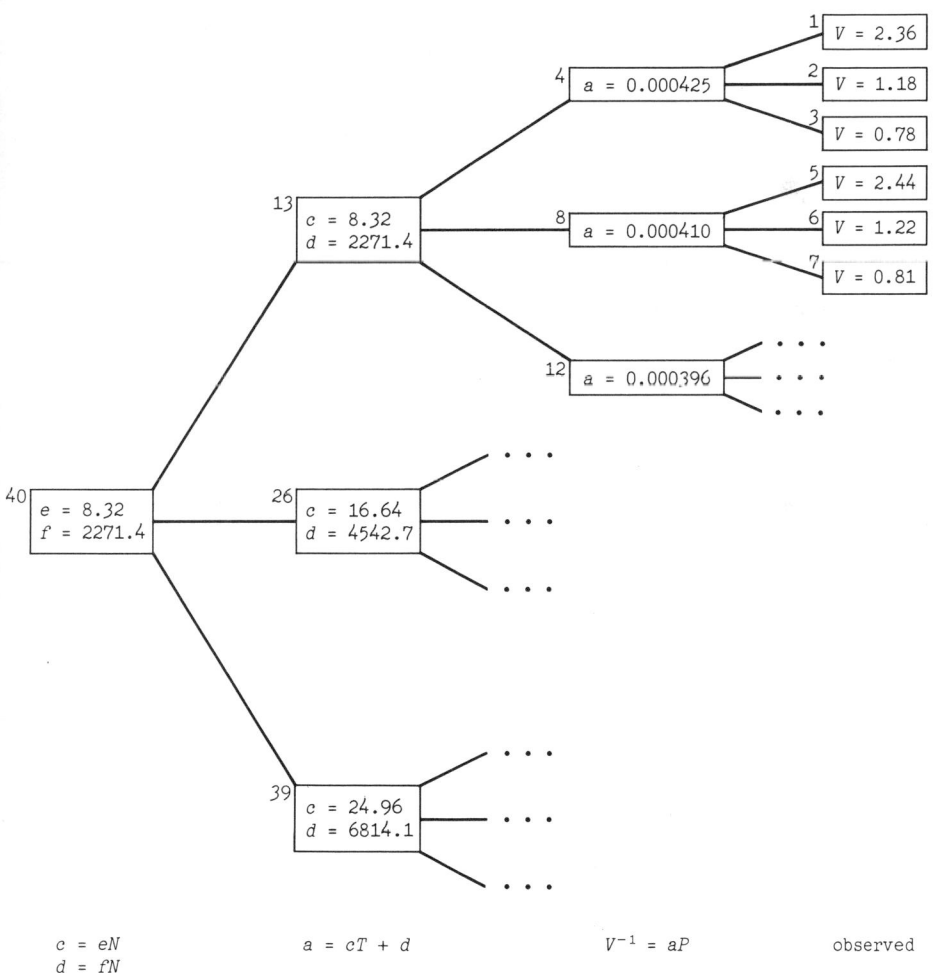

Figure 16-2:   BACON's rediscovery of the ideal gas law.

which the data space itself was searched. In an important sense the search for data provides structure to BACON's search for laws, since it provides both direct observations and a place to store parameters so they can be used as data at later stages. This process is somewhat similar to Rosenbloom's model of the chunking process (1983). In this cognitive simulation, a goal hierarchy provides the top-down control that determines the *types* of chunks that should be formed. However, a data-driven learning mechanism determines the particular chunks that are acquired from the bottom up. Thus BACON's search through the data space can be viewed as providing top-down constraints on the types of laws that will be discovered (e.g., which variables are related), while the system must still search through the resulting law space to determine the particular laws that best summarize the data.

We should mention in passing that once BACON discovers that a particular form of law is useful in one context, it uses that information to constrain search in similar contexts. For instance, when the system finds that only the form $V^{-1} = aP + b$ is useful when $[N = 1, T = 10]$, it considers only this form when $[N = 1, T = 20]$, $[N = 1, T = 40]$, and so forth. In addition, since it found $b = 0$, this parameter was removed from the form, leaving the simplified expression $V^{-1} = aP$. In other words, BACON redefines its problem space in the light of its previous experience, so that considerably less search results. Now that we have examined BACON's basic methods for discovering empirical laws, let us examine some additional methods that let it deal with the chemical domain.

16.2.4 Intrinsic Properties and Common Divisors

While BACON's basic methods are useful for discovering relations between numerical terms, they cannot be used to relate *nominal,* or symbolic, independent terms to numeric dependent variables, and this is precisely the situation in which the early chemists found themselves. For instance, the independent terms in Proust's, Dalton's, and Gay-Lussac's chemical experiments were the elements or compounds involved, while the dependent terms were numerical measures such as weight or volume. In such cases, BACON defines *intrinsic properties* that take on numeric values and then associates these properties with the nominal terms.

Let us consider the role of intrinsic properties in BACON's rediscovery of the early chemical laws. Given control over the substances entering and resulting from a reaction, as well as the weight of the first substance that is used, the system gathers data like those shown in table 16-3. Upon varying the amount of oxygen used to form nitric oxide (NO), the program discovers that the two weights w_1 and w_2 are linearly related with a slope of 1.14 and an intercept of zero. Upon varying the output of the reaction, BACON.6 then examines the weight relations for the compound nitrous oxide (N_2O). In this case, the law is also linear, but the slope has changed to 0.57. A similar result is obtained when the system examines the values for nitrogen dioxide, and in this case the slope is 2.28.

Table 16-3: Determining the combining weights for reactions.

Element$_1$	Element$_2$	Compound	W_1	W_2	W_2/W_1
Nitrogen	Oxygen	NO	1.0.	1.14	1.14
Nitrogen	Oxygen	NO	2.0	2.28	1.14
Nitrogen	Oxygen	NO	3.0	3.42	1.14
Nitrogen	Oxygen	N_2O	1.0	0.57	0.57
Nitrogen	Oxygen	N_2O	2.0	1.14	0.57
Nitrogen	Oxygen	N_2O	3.0	1.71	0.57
Nitrogen	Oxygen	NO_2	1.0	2.28	2.28
Nitrogen	Oxygen	NO_2	2.0	4.56	2.28
Nitrogen	Oxygen	NO_2	3.0	6.84	2.28

The slopes that BACON.6 finds in these experiments are closely related to the weight ratios found by Proust. Having found these ratios, the program stores its results at a higher level of description, as shown in table 16-4, and treats these summaries as data. The table also includes the results obtained for two reactions of oxygen and carbon. In this case, the system finds three nominal independent terms and a single numeric dependent variable, so it defines an intrinsic property (say p) whose values are associated with the three nominal values under which they occur. Thus, the value of p for the triple nitrogen/oxygen/nitric oxide would be set to 1.14, the value for nitrogen/oxygen/nitrous oxide would be 0.57, and the value for nitrogen/oxygen/nitrogen dioxide would be 2.28. As stated, these intrinsic values simply store an already-known fact, and in this sense they are tautological. However, they can be retrieved in future experiments involving the same chemicals and used to make predictions or to discover new empirical laws.

As we have seen, Proust's insight about combining weights laid the groundwork for Dalton's law of multiple proportions. This law stated that in cases where two elements combine to form *different* compounds, the ratios of their combining weights were always small integer multiples of one another. BACON includes a method that lets it discover just such a relation in the data from table 16-4. This

Table 16-4: Noting common divisors for chemical reactions.

Element$_1$	Element$_2$	Compound	W_2/W_1	P	W_2/W_1P
Nitrogen	Oxygen	NO	1.14	2	0.57
Nitrogen	Oxygen	N_2O	0.57	1	0.57
Nitrogen	Oxygen	NO_2	2.28	4	0.57
Carbon	Oxygen	CO	1.33	1	1.33
Carbon	Oxygen	CO_2	2.66	2	1.33

method operates whenever the system defines a new intrinsic property, and examines the values of the new property to see if they (or their inverses) have a common divisor. This technique is especially useful when intrinsic values are associated with a conjunction of nominal values, as often occurs in chemistry. We have described both the intrinsic property and common divisor methods at length in earlier papers (Bradshaw, Langley, and Simon, 1980; Langley, Bradshaw, and Simon, 1983).

In this case, BACON notes that 1.14, 0.57, and 2.28 have the common divisor 0.57, and would replace these intrinsic values with their corresponding integers 2, 1, and 4. In addition, the program defines a higher-level intrinsic property based on the divisors it finds in different situations, and associates the divisors with those cases. Thus, the common divisor 0.57 would be associated with the nitrogen/oxygen pair, while the divisor 1.33 would be associated with carbon and oxygen. These relations are formally equivalent to Dalton's law of multiple proportions. BACON takes a similar path in discovering Gay-Lussac's common divisors for combining volumes, and has even arrived at the correct relative atomic weights for hydrogen, oxygen, and nitrogen from data similar to those in table 16-3. Thus, BACON's discovery mechanisms account for the major quantitative laws found by chemists in the early nineteenth century. Note that neither the intrinsic property method nor the common divisor method involve any significant search themselves. Rather, their role is to transform symbolic data into numeric data, so that BACON's law-finding method can be used to discover relationships.

16.2.5 Comments on BACON.6

In the preceding pages, we have described BACON's methods for gathering data, discovering numeric laws, and postulating new properties. All in all, BACON provides an interesting and useful account of the discovery of quantitative empirical laws. However, the system leaves some important questions unanswered. For example, how do scientists decide which variables to employ in their experiments? Similarly, how do they use their newly discovered laws once they have found them? In BACON, the relevant variables are provided by the programmer, and the laws are simply printed on a terminal screen. One can imagine a version of BACON with an improved user interface, serving as a scientist's aide in analyzing data and fulfilling a useful function while still requiring its user to design its input and interpret its output. This is one direction in which the system might be extended, and such an interactive version could be very useful in some areas of science.

However, if one's goal is to understand the nature of scientific discovery, then a more serious answer to the above questions is required. For instance, we know from the history of science that empirical laws eventually lead to theories and explanations, and BACON has little to say about such aspects of discovery. We also know that even vague theories can have important impacts on the data one gathers. This suggests that we will find answers to both questions only by studying other facets of the discovery process. Although constructing AI models of these components would undoubtedly be interesting even in isolation, the true advantage will come from exploring the interrelations among different forms of discovery. Our long-range goal, then, should be to understand components of the discovery process whose outputs can be used as BACON's inputs and to uncover other components that can employ BACON's outputs as their inputs. In the remainder of this chapter, we focus on three different models of discovery that we have constructed to this end, and we close with some speculations on possible interactions among the various systems.

16.3 DISCOVERING QUALITATIVE EMPIRICAL LAWS

Upon examining the history of science, one finds that the discovery of quantitative laws is generally preceded by the discovery of qualitative relations. For instance, early physicists noted that colliding objects tended to change velocities before they determined the exact form of this relationship. Similarly, plant and animal breeders knew that certain traits were passed on to offspring long before Mendel formulated the quantitative principles of inheritance. One of the best examples of this trend may be found in the history of chemistry, where early scientists discovered qualitative laws of reaction decades before numeric relations were determined. In particular, the history of the theory of acids and bases provides useful insights into the discovery of qualitative empirical laws.

By the seventeenth and eighteenth centuries, chemists had made considerable progress in classifying substances on the basis of qualitative properties. During this period, researchers focused on features such as the taste and texture of substances, as well as the interactions between substances. Thus, they knew that the substance we now call hydrochloric acid had a sour taste, and that it combined with ammonia to form NH_4Cl (though the structure of this compound was not known). Moreover, they knew that sulfuric acid also tasted sour, and that it combined with ammonia to form $(NH_4)_2SO_4$. From such facts as these, the early chemists defined classes such as *acids, alkalis,* and *salts* and formulated laws involving these terms, such as "acids taste sour" and "acids react with alkalis to form salts." Eventually, they came to view both alkalis and metals as special cases of the more abstract concept *base,* and they arrived at the more general law "acids react with bases to form salts." Although some exceptions to these statements were known, chemists found the laws sufficiently general to use in making predictions as well as in classifying new substances. We shall see that the two processes—defining classes like acid and alkali and formulating laws involving these classes—play a central role in the qualitative discovery process.

16.3.1 The GLAUBER System

In our efforts to understand the process of scientific discovery, we have implemented GLAUBER,[3] an AI system that formulates qualitative empirical laws. The program is named after Johann Rudolph Glauber (1607–1670), a seventeenth-century German chemist who played an important role in developing the theory of acids and bases. Table 16-5 summarizes GLAUBER in terms of search concepts. The system accepts as input a set of qualitative facts, which are represented in terms of a simple framelike structure. Each fact contains a *predicate* that specifies the type of fact it is, along with one or more attribute-value pairs. For example, the fact that HCl reacts with NH_3 to form NH_4Cl would be stored as (reacts inputs {HCl NH_3} outputs {NH_4Cl}). Here the predicate is *reacts,* the attributes are *inputs* and *outputs,* and the sets {HCl NH_3} and {NH_4Cl} are the values for these attributes.[4] The knowledge that HCl tastes sour would be stored as (has-quality object {HCl} taste {sour}). In this case the values are enclosed in braces for consistency with other predicates (such as *reacts*), which may have multiple symbols as values.

GLAUBER's goal is to transform these facts into a set of qualitative laws having the same *form* as the original facts, but in which specific substances have been replaced by abstract classes, such as the concepts of *acid* and *alkali.* In addition, these classes must have an associated list of members; for instance, HCl and H_2SO_4 would be examples of acids, while NaOH and KOH would be members of the alkali class.

Table 16-5: GLAUBER viewed in terms of search concepts.

Initial state: A list of facts containing only constant terms

Goal state: A list of laws relating classes, along with definitions of those classes

Intermediate states:
  A list of laws relating some classes, along with definitions of classes; some facts remain

Operators:
  Form-law: Defines a class and substitutes it into facts
  Determine-quantifier: Specifies existential or universal quantifiers

Heuristics:
  For Form-law: Select that object occurring in the most analogous facts
  For Determine-quantifier: Quantify universally if the data justify it

Search control: Best-first search with no backtracking

---

[3]The current version of GLAUBER differs from the earlier version described by Langley, Zytkow, Simon, and Bradshaw (1983). Although the state descriptions are very similar in the two systems, both the operators and the search control differ considerably.

[4]GLAUBER knows that the order of symbols contained in a set does not matter, so that (reacts inputs {NH_3 HCl} outputs {NH_4Cl}) would be considered identical to the above fact.

Taken together, the qualitative laws relating classes and the extensional definitions of these classes let one predict the original facts, along with other facts that have not yet been observed.

GLAUBER's two operators are concerned with transforming the original data into such laws and classes. The first of these operators, FORM-LAW, inputs a set of facts having the same predicate and at least one common argument; it replaces these with a single law in which some arguments have been replaced by a class name, and it defines each of the new classes in terms of their members. For example, given the two facts (reacts inputs {HCl NaOH} outputs {NaCl}) and (reacts inputs {HNO_3 NaOH} outputs {$NaNO_3$}), the FORM-LAW operator would define two classes, say x and y, and replace the facts with the law (reacts inputs {x NaOH} outputs {y}). The operator would also note that HCl and HNO_3 are members of the newly created class x, while NaCl and $NaNO_3$ are members of the y class. Finally, the FORM-LAW operator iterates through the current set of facts and laws, replacing occurrences of these substances with their class names. For instance, if the facts (has-quality object {HCl} taste {sour}) and (has-quality object {HNO_3} taste {sour}) were known, they would be replaced by the pattern (has-quality object {x} taste {sour}).

When GLAUBER formulates a new set of laws, the system must decide the appropriate level of generality for each law. To this end, the second operator (DETERMINE-QUANTIFIER) iterates through the set of laws and determines whether each class mentioned in a law should be existentially or universally quantified. If an existential quantifier is settled on, then the law is interpreted as holding for only a *single* member of the class. If a universal quantifier is selected, the law is interpreted as holding for *all* members of the class. If a single class is introduced, then this class is universally quantified in the resulting law; in this case, the level of quantification is not an issue, since this is tautologically determined by the manner in which the classes were defined. However, if N classes are introduced, then N versions of the law result, each containing one universally quantified class and with the quantifiers for the remaining classes undetermined. For instance, in the above example, two variations on the reaction law would be formulated— $\forall x?y$ (reacts inputs {x NaOH} outputs {y}) and $\forall x?y$ (reacts inputs {x NaOH} outputs {y}).[5] The first of these states that all members of class x react with at least one member of the class y; the second states that all members of the class y can be formed by at least one member of x in reaction with NaOH. The first quantifier in each law follows from the class definition, but the second quantifier must be determined empirically.

---

[5]In this chapter, expressions of the form $\forall x\, P(x)$ are intended as shorthand for longer expressions of the form $\forall y \mid y \in x\, P(y)$, where x is a class name and y is a member of that class. Expressions of the form $\exists x\, P(x)$ should be interpreted in a similar fashion.

A similar issue arises when the FORM-LAW operator generates additional laws by replacing substances with classes in other facts. In these cases, all of the quantifiers must be tested against observations. For example, the pattern (has-quality object $\{x\}$ taste $\{$sour$\}$) might hold for all members of x, or for only a few members of this class. Thus, the DETERMINE-QUANTIFIER operator examines the known facts and decides on the appropriate quantifier. If more than one class is involved, the possibility of multiple forms of the law must be considered. Thus if a pattern were formed by substituting both x and y for members of these classes, GLAUBER might decide on a single law in which both were universally quantified, a single law in which both were existentially quantified, or two laws involving both existential and universal quantifiers.

Once GLAUBER has applied the FORM-LAW and DETERMINE-QUANTIFIER operators, it has a revised set of facts and laws to which these operators can be applied recursively. The FORM-LAW operator may apply to laws as well as to facts, provided these laws have identical quantifiers. For example, given the two laws $\forall x \exists y$ (reacts inputs $\{x$ NaOH$\}$ outputs $\{y\}$) and $\forall x \exists y$ (reacts inputs $\{x$ KOH$\}$ outputs $\{y\}$), this operator would generate the more abstract pattern $\forall x \exists w$ (reacts inputs $\{x\,u\}$ outputs $\{w\}$). In addition, it would define the class u to have the members NaOH and KOH and define the class w with the classes y and z as subsets. DETERMINE-QUANTIFIER would then proceed to decide on the generality of this pattern, and the process would be repeated on the revised set of facts and laws. GLAUBER continues this alternation between finding laws and determining their generality until the goal state has been reached—this is a set of maximally general laws that account for as many of the original facts as possible.

Using its two operators, GLAUBER carries out a *best-first* search through the space of possible laws and classes. The system's search control does not include back-up capability, since its evaluation functions are sufficiently powerful to direct search down acceptable paths. In determining which law to formulate (and thus which classes to define), GLAUBER considers all known substances and classes and selects that symbol occurring in the largest number of analogous facts. Thus, if two facts having the *reacts* predicate were found to include NaOH in the inputs slot, then NaOH would receive a score of two, unless it occurred in some other set of facts more often. In the case of laws, GLAUBER uses the total number of facts covered by those laws. GLAUBER indexes its facts and laws in terms of their arguments, so these scores are easily computed for each substance and class. Once this has been done, the system applies the FORM-LAW operator to those facts containing the highest scoring symbol, with the constraint that existentially quantified classes are not considered.

In determining the placement of universal and existential quantifiers, GLAUBER examines the facts (or lower-level laws) on which the current law is based. The system generates all of the laws/facts that would be produced by a universal quantifier for a given class, and if enough of these have been observed (or inferred), then the universal quantifier is retained for that class; otherwise an existential quantifier is used. Thus, the system can be viewed as looking ahead one step in order to determine which move is most desirable. A certain percentage of the predicted facts must be observed before GLAUBER generalizes over a class; this percentage is specified by the user. The program interprets missing facts as unobserved; the current system cannot handle disconfirming evidence, such as $\sim \exists$ salt (reacts inputs {HCl HNO$_3$} outputs {salt}).

16.3.2 Rediscovering the Concepts of Acids and Alkalis

Now that we have described GLAUBER in the abstract, let us examine its behavior given a particular set of facts as input. These facts are presented at the top of table 16-6 and are very similar to facts known by seventeenth-century chemists

Table 16-6: States generated by GLAUBER in discovering acids and alkalis.

Initial state S1:	
(reacts inputs {HCl NaOH} outputs {NaCl})	(has-quality object {NaCl} taste {salty})
(reacts inputs {HCl KOH} outputs {KCl})	(has-quality object {KCl} taste {salty})
(reacts inputs {IINO$_3$ NaOII} outputs {NaNO$_3$})	(has-quality objcct {NaNO$_3$} tastc {salty})
(reacts inputs {HNO$_3$ KOH} outputs {KNO$_3$})	(has-quality object {KNO$_3$} taste {salty})
(has-quality object {HCl} taste {sour})	(has-quality object {NaOH} taste {bitter})
(has-quality object {HNO$_3$} taste {sour})	(has-quality object {KOH} taste {bitter})

FIND-LAW and DETERMINE-QUANTIFIER lead to state S3:	
SALTS: {NaCl, KCl, NaNO$_3$, KNO$_3$}	
$\exists$ salt (reacts inputs {HCl NaOH} outputs {salt})	(has-quality object {HCl} taste {sour})
$\exists$ salt (reacts inputs {HCl KOH} outputs {salt})	(has-quality object {HNO$_3$} taste {sour})
$\exists$ salt (reacts inputs {HNO$_3$ NaOH} outputs {salt})	(has-quality object {NaOH} taste {bitter})
$\exists$ salt (reacts inputs {HNO$_3$ KOH} outputs {salt})	(has-quality object {KOH} taste {bitter})
$\forall$ salt (has-quality object {salt} taste {salty})	

FIND-LAW and DETERMINE-QUANTIFIER lead to state S5:	
SALTS: {NaCl, KCl, NaNO$_3$, KNO$_3$}	
ACIDS: {HCl, HNO$_3$}	
$\forall$ acid $\exists$ salt (reacts inputs {acid NaOH} outputs {salt})	(has-quality object {NaOH} taste {bitter})
$\forall$ acid $\exists$ salt (reacts inputs {acid KOH} outputs {salt})	(has-quality object {KOH} taste {bitter})
$\forall$ salt (has-quality object {salt} taste {salty})	
$\forall$ acid (has-quality object {acid} taste {sour})	

FIND-LAW and DETERMINE-QUANTIFIER lead to state S7:
SALTS: {NaCl, KCl, NaNO$_3$, KNO$_3$}
ACIDS: {HCl, HNO$_3$}
ALKALIS: {NaOH, KOH}
$\forall$ alkali $\forall$ acid $\exists$ salt (reacts inputs {acid alkali} outputs {salt})
$\forall$ salt (has-quality object {salt} taste {salty})
$\forall$ acid (has-quality object {acid} taste {sour})
$\forall$ alkali (has-quality object {alkali} taste {bitter})

before they formulated the theory of acids and bases. As we shall see, GLAUBER arrives at a set of laws and classes very similar to those proposed by the early chemists. The data in the table are intentionally simplified for the sake of clarity. However, we have tested the system on larger sets of data as well as on sets with less regularity.

Given the twelve facts as inputs, GLAUBER begins by examining the symbols used as arguments in the propositions and determining which of these occur in the greatest number of analogous facts. It notes that the symbols HCL, HNO$_3$, NaOH, and KOH are each arguments of the *inputs* slot for two facts involving the *reacts* predicate. Similarly, the symbols *sour* and *bitter* each occur as arguments of the *taste* slot in two *has-quality* facts. However, the highest scoring symbol is *salty,* which occurs in four *has-quality* facts as the value for *taste.* As a result, these four facts are replaced by the pattern (has-quality object {salt} taste {salty}), which has the same form as the original propositions, but in which the differing values of the *object* slot have been replaced by the class name *salt.* Also, the four substances NaCl, KCl, NaNO$_3$, and KNO$_3$ are stored as members of the new class.

In addition to proposing this hypothesis, the FORM-LAW operator generates four additional patterns by substituting the symbol *salt* for members of this class into other facts. Thus, the facts (reacts inputs {HCl NaOH} outputs {NaCl}) and (reacts inputs {HCl KOH} outputs {KCl}) are replaced by the hypotheses (reacts inputs {HCl NaOH} outputs {salt}) and (reacts inputs {HCl KOH} outputs {salt}). Similarly, the facts (reacts inputs {HNO$_3$ NaOH} outputs {NaNO$_3$}) and (reacts inputs {HNO$_3$ KOH} outputs {KNO$_3$}) are replaced by (reacts inputs {HNO$_3$ NaOH} outputs {salt}) and (reacts inputs {HNO$_3$ KOH} outputs {salt}). Although the first of these patterns is guaranteed to be universally quantified by the manner in which the *salt* class was defined, the generality of the other laws must be empirically determined. For example, if the hypothesis (reacts inputs {HCl NaOH} outputs {salt}) were universally quantified over the class of salts, then four facts would be predicted. Since only one of these predictions has been observed, GLAUBER includes an existential quantifier rather than a universal one. The same decision is made for the other patterns formed by substitution, leading to the laws and facts shown in the second section of the table.

Given this new state of the world, GLAUBER again determines which of the known symbols occur in the most analogous facts. In this case, the set of alternatives is slightly different from that on the earlier cycle, since the class name *salt* has replaced the individual members of that class. Given the current set of facts and laws, six symbols tie for the honors—NaOH, KOH, HCl, HNO$_3$, sour, and bitter. For example, the first of these occurs in the laws ∃salt (reacts inputs {HCl NaOH} outputs {salt}) and ∃salt (reacts inputs {HNO$_3$ NaOH} outputs {salt}), while the second occurs in the laws ∃salt (reacts inputs {HCl KOH} outputs {salt}) and ∃salt (reacts inputs {HNO$_3$ KOH} outputs {salt}). The *salt* symbol actually occurs in all four of these laws, but the class name is not considered, since it is existentially quantified in the laws. Since all of the viable options involve two laws (each based on one fact apiece), GLAUBER selects one of them at random. Let us follow the course events take when the system chooses the pair of facts involving the symbol NaOH.

Based on these facts, the FORM-LAW operator generates the pattern (reacts inputs {acid NaOH} outputs {salt}), and defines the new class *acid* as containing the elements HCl and HNO_3. Two additional hypotheses result from substitution—(reacts inputs {acid KOH} outputs {salt}) and (has-quality object {acid} taste {sour})—each replacing two directly observed facts. After substitution, GLAUBER has four laws and two facts in memory. However, the system must still determine the generality of these laws. The DETERMINE-QUANTIFIER operator proceeds to consider the predictions made by each law when universally quantified over the new class of *acids*. Since all of the predicted facts have been observed, the universal quantifier is retained for each of the new laws, giving the set of facts and laws shown in the third section of the table.

At this point, only five symbols remain to be considered—NaOH, KOH, bitter, and the classes *salt* and *acid*. The first two occur only in single laws, while the third occurs in two analogous facts. The class name *salt* appears in two analogous laws but is ignored due to its existential quantifier. However, the class name *acid* occurs in two analogous laws that are based on two facts apiece, giving *acid* a score of four. As a result, the two laws are passed to the FORM-LAW operator and a higher-level pattern—(reacts inputs {acid alkali} outputs {salt})—is formed on this basis. In addition, the class *alkali* is defined as having the members NaOH and KOH. A second hypothesis—(has-quality object {alkali} taste {bitter})—is formed by substitution, and both laws are universally quantified over the new class, the first by definition and the second empirically. At this point, GLAUBER has reached its goal of specifying a maximally general set of laws that summarizes the original data. The final laws (shown in the fourth section of table 16-6) are very similar to those proposed by the early chemists. When GLAUBER is given reactions involving metals as alkalis, it defines the broader class *bases* (containing both metals and alkalis as members) and arrives at the central tenet that acids combine with bases to form salts.

16.3.3 Comments on GLAUBER

In its present form, GLAUBER has some important limitations, and these should be remedied in future versions of the system. The first difficulty involves the system's evaluation function for directing search through the space of classes and laws. The current version iterates through the set of known symbols and selects the symbol that occurs in the greatest number of analogous facts. This leads GLAUBER to prefer large classes to small ones, which in turn leads to laws with greater generality in the sense that they cover more of the observed facts. However, recall that once GLAUBER defines a new class on the basis of some law, it then creates additional laws by substituting the class for its members in other facts. This suggests a broader definition of generality, including all facts predicted by any law involving the new class. This analysis leads to two methods for preferring one class over another. The most obvious approach involves computing the percentage of predictions that are actually borne out by observations; we shall call this the *predictive power* of a class and its associated laws. The second method involves computing the total number of facts predicted by a class and its related laws; we shall call this the *predictive potential* of the class.

Obviously, a set of laws that predicts a few observations but predicts many unobserved ones is undesirable; this suggests that predictive power should be used to weed out grossly unacceptable classes. However, given roughly equal scores on this dimension, sets of laws with greater predictive potential should be preferred, since these lead to many predictions, which, if satisfied, will lead to an increase in predictive power. One difficulty in implementing this scheme is that GLAUBER would have to generate the potential classes and their associated laws in order to determine their predictive power and potential. Moreover, it would have to consider whether these laws should be existentially or universally quantified in order to maximize their scores. In other words, the system would have to apply the FIND-LAW operator in all possible ways, and then apply the DETERMINE-QUANTIFIER operator in all possible ways in order to determine the best path to follow. This is equivalent to doing a two-step look-ahead in the search tree, and it would involve considerably more computation time than the current simple strategy. The details of this scheme remain to be elaborated, but the basic idea of defining classes that account for the most data seems a plausible approach.

A second limitation involves the possibility of alternative divisions of substances into classes. In some cases, two or more branches in the search tree may lead to equally (or almost equally) good descriptions of the data. These competing paths may ultimately lead to the same state, or they may lead to completely different organizations of knowledge. In the latter case, one would like the system to discover both frameworks. However, since the current version of GLAUBER carries out a depth-first search without back-up, it must select one of the paths at random, thus ignoring what may be an equally useful summary of the data. Future versions of the system should be able to consider multiple alternatives while still using evaluation functions to keep search to a minimum.

In order to understand the last of GLAUBER's limitations, we must review some related work on machine learning. Wolff (1978) has explored an approach to grammar learning that incorporates methods very similar to those used in GLAUBER. Wolff's system begins with a sequence of letters and, based on common sequences of symbols, defines *chunks* in terms of these sequences. For example, given the sequence "thedogchasedthecatthecatchasedthedog . . . ," the program defines chunks like *the, dog, cat,* and *chased.* Whenever a chunk is created, the component symbols are replaced by the symbol for that chunk. In this case, the sequence "the-dog-chased-the-cat-the-cat-chased-the-dog" would result. In addition, when a number of different symbols (letters or chunks) are found to precede or follow a common symbol, a disjunctive class is defined in terms of the first set. For instance, in the above sequence the sub-sequences "the-dog-chased" and "the-cat-chased" occur. Based on this regularity, Wolff's program would define the disjunctive class *noun* = {*dog, cat*}. The symbol for this new class is then substituted into the letter sequence for the member symbols. In this case, the sequence "the-noun-chased-the-noun-the noun-chased-the-noun" would be generated. These two basic methods are applied recursively, so that chunks can be defined in terms of disjunctive classes and vice versa. Thus, given the last sequence, the chunk *sentence* = *the-noun-chased-the-noun* would be defined, giving the final sequence "sentence-sentence."

From this description we see that Wolff's learning system employs two operators—one for forming disjunctive classes such as *noun* and another for defining chunks or *conjunctive* classes, such as *dog*. The first of these is identical to GLAUBER's operator for forming disjunctive classes like *acid* and *alkali*.[6] The main difference between the two systems lies in the *heuristics* for forming such disjuncts. Wolff employs adjacency criteria well suited to the language acquisition domain, while GLAUBER uses the notion of shared arguments, which is more appropriate for relational domains. In contrast, the second operator in Wolff's method has no analog in GLAUBER's repertoire, and this suggests a gap in our discovery system's capabilities. Upon reflection, one would like GLAUBER to note recurring relations between *conjunctions* of facts as well as those involving isolated propositions. Let us consider an example from the domain of genetics that requires this form of reasoning. Suppose the system observed (as did Mendel) that when certain green garden peas were self-fertilized, they produced only green offspring, but that when other green peas were self-fertilized, they produced both green and yellow children. In this case, we would like GLAUBER to divide the green peas into two classes based not on their own directly observable features (since these are identical) but on the features of their offspring. Thus, in looking for patterns, the system would have to examine not only single facts, but pairs of facts, triples of facts, and so forth. Such a strategy, though much more expensive than the current one, would enable the program to note that some green peas have only green offspring, while others have mixed offspring, and to classify them on this basis. This would be equivalent to defining *chunks* based on co-occurring facts and could be viewed as a relational version of the chunking method used in Wolff's system.

We should also briefly consider some other discovery systems with similar concerns. First, Michalski and Stepp (1983) have studied the task of conceptual clustering, in which one forms a hierarchical taxonomy for classifying objects. Since

---

[6]Rather we should say that GLAUBER's operator is identical to Wolff's operator, since Wolff's work preceded our own by many years. Although the original version of GLAUBER was developed independently of Wolff's approach, the current system borrows considerably from his results in the domain of grammar learning.

GLAUBER also divides objects into classes, it can be viewed as carrying out a form of conceptual clustering, even though its methods differ significantly from those used by Michalski and Stepp. GLAUBER also bears some resemblance to Brown's discovery system (1973), which also generated abstract laws covering a set of facts. However, this early system's search methods also differed considerably from those in GLAUBER, and it did not define new classes in the process of stating laws. Finally, we should mention some recent work by Emde, Habel, and Rollinger (1983) that involves the discovery of qualitative laws. In this case, the focus is on determining whether predicates obey certain relations, such as transitivity or inversivity. Although this approach leads to laws very similar to those found by Brown, the model-driven discovery method contrasts with the data-driven approach used in the other systems. To summarize, we find that GLAUBER bears some relation to other systems for qualitative discovery but is most similar to Wolff's grammar-learning system in both spirit and method.

16.4 DETERMINING THE COMPONENTS OF SUBSTANCES

We have already seen that early chemists were concerned with both qualitative and quantitative descriptions of chemical reactions. However, another one of their primary goals was to determine the *components* of various substances, and information about chemical reactions proved quite useful in this regard. The goal of determining such components assumed an important facet of the atomic theory in that it postulated primitive building blocks for the observed substances, even though no stance was taken on whether these building blocks were particulate or continuous in nature. Thus the formulation of componential models embodied a simple form of explanation that is clearly distinct from the descriptive summaries generated by BACON and GLAUBER.

During the eighteenth century, chemists developed models of many substances, but they devoted considerable attention to explaining combustion and related phenomena. As a result, two different componential models were eventually proposed to account for this process. The first assumed that combustion involved the decomposition of two substances, and was known as the theory of *phlogiston*. The second assumed that combustion involved the combination of two substances, and was called the *oxygen* theory. Although the phlogiston theory was eventually rejected in favor of its competitor, it provided a plausible account of the known reactions and was well respected for decades. This suggests an important constraint on computational models of scientific discovery: such models should be able to arrive at plausible laws or models even if they were ultimately rejected in favor of others. This makes the area of combustion reactions an ideal test for systems concerned with formulating componential models, since we know two models that can usefully account for the observations.

16.4.1 The STAHL System

Our interest in componential models has led us to construct a third AI system that infers such models from a set of known reactions. The program is named STAHL, after G. E. Stahl (1660–1734), one of the principle formulators of the phlogiston theory. Like GLAUBER, this program accepts qualitative information as input and generates qualitative statements as output (see table 16-7). However, since STAHL's conclusions relate to the internal structure of substances, they can be viewed as simple explanations rather than descriptive summaries. The system's initial state consists of a set of reactions, represented in the same framelike format used by GLAUBER. For instance, the reaction of hydrogen and oxygen to form water would be represented as (reacts inputs {hydrogen oxygen} outputs {water}). STAHL's goal is to determine the components of all nonelemental substances involved in the given reactions. This information is represented in the same formalism as the initial reactions. Thus, the conclusion that water is composed of hydrogen and oxygen would be stated as (components of {water} are {hydrogen oxygen}). Intermediate states consist of inferences about the components of some substances, along with transformed versions of the initial reactions.

STAHL incorporates four operators for moving through the space of possible componential models. These operators are closely linked to the heuristics that propose them, so they are best discussed together. The most basic of these operator/ heuristics deals with simple synthesis and decomposition reactions and lets the system unambiguously infer the components of a compound. It can be stated as follows:

INFER-COMPOSITION
If A and B react to form C
     Or if C decomposes into A and B
Then infer that C is composed of A and B.

Table 16-7:   STAHL viewed in terms of search concepts.

Initial state: A list of reactions relating substances

Goal state: The components of each compound substance

Intermediate states: Components of some substances, modified reactions

Operators/Heuristics:
  Infer-composition: Decides on the components of substance
  Reduce: Cancels substances occurring on both sides of a reaction
  Substitute: Replaces a substance with its components in a reaction
  Identify-components: Identifies two components as the same
  Identify-compounds: Identifies two compounds as the same

Search control: Depth-first search with no backtracking

An obvious example of this rule's use involves determining the components of water. Given the information that hydrogen reacts with oxygen to form water, STAHL would infer that the latter substance is composed of the first two. Note that STAHL does not draw any conclusions about the *amount* of hydrogen and oxygen contributing to water, but only infers that they contribute something. Of course, the INFER-COMPOSITION rule is not limited to reactions involving pairs of elements; it can also deal with cases in which three or more substances unite to form a single compound.

If all chemical reactions were of the form shown above, STAHL's task would be simple indeed. However, more complex reactions are common in chemistry, so STAHL includes additional operators for dealing with these more complex situations. The purpose of these operators is to transform complex reactions into simpler forms so they can eventually be matched by the INFER-COMPOSITION rule shown above. One such operator is responsible for "canceling" out substances occurring on both sides of a reaction; the "reduction" heuristic that proposes this operator can be paraphrased as follows:

REDUCE
If A occurs on both sides of a reaction
Then remove A from the reaction.

This heuristic leads directly to a simplified version of a reaction. For instance, if STAHL is told that "A, B, and C react to form D and C," the REDUCE rule would apply, giving the simplified reaction "A and B react to form D." This revised relation would then be used to the INFER-COMPOSITION rule to infer that D is composed of A and B. One can imagine cases in which this approach would lead to errors, as when different amounts of a substance are observed before and after a reaction. However, similar errors were commonly made by early chemists, and we are interested in explaining these reasoning errors rather than avoiding them.

STAHL incorporates a third operator that initially leads to more complex statements of reactions, but may make it possible for the REDUCE rule to apply. The heuristic for proposing this operator draws on information about the components of a substance that have been inferred earlier; it can be stated as follows:

SUBSTITUTE
If A occurs in a reaction
    And A is composed of B and C
Then replace A with B and C.

For instance, the system may know that X is composed of Y and Z, and that "*x* reacts with W to form V and Z." In this case, the SUBSTITUTE rule would rewrite the second relation as "Y, Z, and W react to form V and Z." Given this formulation, the REDUCE rule would lead to "Y and W react to form V," and the INFER-COMPOSITION rule would lead to the conclusion that V is composed of Y and W.

As before, the SUBSTITUTE rule is not restricted to substances composed of two elements but works equally well for more complex structures.

A final operator is responsible for postulating that two substances that were originally thought to be different are in fact identical. Two separate heuristics propose when to apply this operator; the first of these rules may be stated as follows:

IDENTIFY-COMPONENTS
If A is composed of B and C
    And A is composed of B and D
Then identify C with D.

This heuristic matches when STAHL learns that a compound can be decomposed in two different ways, but in which those decompositions differ by only a single substance. The second heuristic is very similar, except that it applies when two apparently different compounds are found to have the same components. It can be paraphrased as follows:

IDENTIFY-COMPOUNDS
If A is composed of C and D
    And A is composed of C and D
Then identify A with B.

The history of chemistry abounds with cases in which a new substance was discovered in two different contexts, was originally thought to be two distinct substances, and was eventually combined into a single concept. We will see an example of such identification shortly.

STAHL can be viewed as carrying out a depth-first search through the space of componential models, relying entirely on its heuristics to select the appropriate path. In general, these heuristics are sufficiently powerful that the system need never backtrack, though we will discuss some situations later where this capability is required. In some cases, more than one heuristic (or more than one instantiation of the same heuristic) can be applied to the current state. Different choices may lead STAHL to quite different componential models, and the system employs a sophisticated strategy to resolve such conflicts, which we have described elsewhere (Zytkow and Simon, 1986).

One of the interesting features of STAHL is the manner in which its heuristics interact. Note that the substitution rule requires knowledge of a substance's composition, so that some inferences about composition must be made before it can be used. However, we have also seen that complex reactions must be rewritten by the reduction and substitution rules before some composition inferences can be made. This interdependence leads to a "bootstrapping" effect, in which inferences made by one of the rules enable further inferences to be made, these allow additional inferences, and so forth, until as many conclusions as possible have been drawn. This process generally begins with one or more simple reactions, but after this the particular path taken depends on the data available to the system.

Let us consider STAHL's heuristics in operation on the relatively simple task of inferring the composition of lime and magnesia. In order to formulate models of these two substances, the system requires two initial reactions: (reacts inputs {lime} outputs {quick-lime fixed-air}) and (reacts inputs {quick-lime magnesia} outputs {lime calcined-magnesia}). Given this information, the INFER-COMPOSITION rule applies first, leading to the inference that lime ($CaCO_3$) is composed of quick-lime (CaO) and fixed-air (CO_2). This result enables the SUBSTITUTION heuristic to match, leading to a temporarily more complex version of the second reaction, (reacts inputs {quick-lime magnesia} outputs {quick-lime fixed-air calcined-magnesia}). However, since the substance quick-lime occurs in both sides of the modified reaction, the REDUCTION rule applies, transforming it into the simpler form (reacts inputs {magnesia} outputs {fixed-air calcined-magnesia}). Finally, this reduced form allows the INFER-COMPOSITION rule to infer that magnesia is composed of the substances fixed-air (CO_2) and calcined-magnesia (MgO). At this point, since no more of its heuristics seem applicable, STAHL concludes that it has formulated as many componential models as the data allow and halts its operation. The system's behavior on this example is summarized in table 16-8. Now that we have presented an overview of STAHL's inference methods, let us examine their application to a historically more interesting example—discovering the phlogiston theory.

16.4.2 Discovering the Phlogiston Theory

The theory of phlogiston originated early in the eighteenth century, and after undergoing several transformations, it was widely accepted until the 1780s. This

Table 16-8:   Inferring the composition of lime and magnesia.

Initial state S1:
(reacts inputs {lime} outputs {quick-lime fixed-air})
(reacts inputs {quick-lime magnesia} outputs {lime calcined-magnesia})

INFER-COMPOSITION leads to state S2:
(components of {lime} are {quick-lime fixed-air})
(reacts inputs {quick-lime magnesia} outputs {lime calcined-magnesia})

SUBSTITUTE leads to state S3:
(components of {lime} are {quick-lime fixed-air})
(reacts inputs {quick-lime magnesia} outputs {quick-lime fixed-air calcined-magnesia})

REDUCE leads to state S4:
(components of {lime} are {quick-lime fixed-air})
(reacts inputs {magnesia} outputs {fixed-air calcined-magnesia})

INFER-COMPOSITION leads to final state S5:
(components of {lime} are {quick-lime fixed-air})
(components of {magnesia} are {fixed-air calcined-magnesia})

---

theory adopted the ancient view that fire, heat, and light are different manifestations of a common principle that leaves a body during combustion. Therefore, any reaction involving combustion was viewed as a decomposition; for instance, burning coal was interpreted as decomposing into the matter of fire (another term for phlogiston) and ash.[7] Early phlogistians were not able to isolate phlogiston, but the disengagement of fire during combustion seemed to be a good observational reason for admitting that some substance was given off by the burning body. Later, as the notion of phlogiston proved useful in explaining many additional reactions, the existence of this substance was supported by a substantial body of evidence.

After they began to study combustion within closed vessels, chemists realized that air was necessary for combustion to occur. However, they did not assume that air changed its chemical identity during this process. Rather, they decided that air played an auxiliary role, similar to that played by water in reactions involving acids, alkalis, and salts. Thus, even starting with empirically more complete descriptions of combustion, such as "in the presence of air, carbon burns to release phlogiston and to form ash," they employed the reduction heuristic to remove air and simplify the relation. Given such data, STAHL makes similar "errors" in reasoning, so that it provides a simple explanation of the process by which chemists developed phlogiston-based models of combustion reactions. Such confusions are common in the history of chemistry, and a similar error led the followers of Lavoisier to believe (approximately 1810) that sodium was a compound of soda and hydrogen.

Lets us examine the path taken by STAHL in arriving at one version of the phlogiston theory. The system is presented with two facts: (reacts inputs {coal air} outputs {matter-of-fire ash air}) and (reacts inputs {calx-of-iron coal air} outputs {iron ash air}).[8] One may question the exact representation of these facts, but clearly something very much like them was believed during the period in which the phlogiston theory was developed. Given this information, STAHL immediately applies its REDUCE operator to the first fact, giving the revised reaction (reacts inputs {coal} outputs {matter-of-fire ash}). The system then applies the same operator to the second fact, giving the reduced reaction (reacts inputs {calx-of-iron coal} outputs {iron ash}). After this, the INFER-COMPOSITION rule is applied to the first revised reaction, giving the inference that coal is composed of matter-of-fire (or phlogiston) and ash, one belief of the early phlogiston theorists. Having arrived at this conclusion, STAHL applies the SUBSTITUTE rule, generating the expanded relation (reacts inputs {calx-of-iron ash matter-of-fire} outputs {iron ash}). At this

---

[7]Several decades later, in the second half of the eighteenth century, fixd air (carbon dioxide) was discovered and recognized as the product of burning coal in place of ash.

[8]Calx of iron was the current name for iron oxide; we have used the original terminology because the modern term is based on the oxygen theory developed by Lavoisier.

point, the REDUCE rule is used to remove ash from both sides of the equation, giving (reacts inputs {calx-of-iron matter-of-fire} outputs {iron}). Finally, the INFER-COMPOSITION operator leads STAHL to infer that iron is a compound of calx-of-iron and the matter of fire. Table 16-9 summarizes the states visited by the system in arriving at these conclusions, along with the operators used to generate them.

Let us now consider how STAHL employs its identification heuristics with respect to the phlogiston theory. Suppose the system is given the following additional data: (reacts inputs {iron sulfuric-acid water} outputs {vitriol-of-iron inflammable-air water}) and (reacts inputs {calx-of-iron sulfuric-acid water} outputs {vitriol-of-iron water}).[9] Given these facts, STAHL removes the water from both reactions using the REDUCE operator. This sufficiently simplifies the second reaction so that it can apply the INFER-COMPOSITION rule, inferring that vitriol-of-iron is composed of calx-of-iron and sulfuric-acid. This fact is substituted into the first reaction, giving (reacts inputs {iron sulfuric-acid} outputs {calx-of-iron sulfuric-acid inflammable-air}). After using the REDUCE operator to eliminate sulfuric-acid from both sides

Table 16-9: STAHL's steps in formulating the phlogiston model.

Initial state S1:
(reacts inputs {coal air} outputs {matter-of-fire ash air})
(reacts inputs {calx-of-iron coal air} outputs {iron ash air})

REDUCE leads to state S2:
(reacts inputs {coal} outputs {matter-of-fire ash})
(reacts inputs {calx-of-iron coal air} outputs {iron ash air})

REDUCE leads to state S3:
(reacts inputs {coal} outputs {matter-of-fire ash})
(reacts inputs {calx-of-iron coal air} outputs {iron ash})

INFER-COMPOSITION leads to state S4:
(components of {coal} are {matter-of-fire ash})
(reacts inputs {calx-of-iron coal} outputs {iron ash})

SUBSTITUTE leads to state S5:
(components of {coal} are {matter-of-fire ash})
(reacts inputs {calx-of-iron matter-of-fire ash} outputs {iron ash})

REDUCE leads to state S6:
(components of {coal} are {matter-of-fire ash})
(reacts inputs {calx-of-iron matter-of-fire} outputs {iron})

INFER-COMPOSITION leads to final state S7:
(components of {coal} are {matter-of-fire ash})
(components of {iron} are {calx-of-iron matter-of-fire})

---

[9] The formula for vitriol of iron is $FeSO_4$, while the modern name for inflammable air is hydrogen.

of this expression, STAHL infers that iron consists of calx-of-iron and inflammable air. However, the system knows from the other reactions described earlier that iron can also be decomposed into calx-of-iron and phlogiston. Using the first of its identification heuristics (IDENTIFY-COMPONENTS), the system infers that inflammable air and phlogiston are identical. Both the reasoning and conclusions of STAHL in this example are very similar to those of Cavendish and other phlogiston theorists during the 1760s.

16.4.3 Comments on STAHL

Earlier we mentioned one case in which STAHL's heuristics might lead to erroneous inferences, but we did not pursue the matter. In fact, there are a number of ways in which the system's heuristics can lead it astray. One situation involves the notion of infinitely recursing componential models. For instance, given certain reactions involving mercury, calx-of-mercury, and oxygen,[10] STAHL eventually makes two inferences: (components of {mercury} are {calx-of-mercury phlogiston}) and (components of {calx-of-mercury} are {mercury oxygen}). Taken together, these two inferences imply that mercury is composed of itself, and this seems an undesirable characteristic for an explanatory model.

Ultimately, such infinite recursions must be due to the faulty description of one or more reactions. Given trace information about which heuristics proposed which inferences, STAHL is able to track down the responsible reaction and call it into question. Historically, chemists introduced conceptual distinctions to explain such inconsistencies. For instance, to avoid the difficulty mentioned above, they formulated the concept *calx-of-mercury-proper* as distinct from calx-of-mercury, and STAHL introduces an analogous distinction. In some sense, this is similar to BACON's introduction of new intrinsic properties when it encounters a situation in which its numeric methods fail to apply. As with BACON, such concepts may appear tautological when first introduced, but they become respectable to the extent that they prove useful in dealing with other situations besides the one leading to their introduction.

STAHL's heuristics can lead to other forms of inconsistency as well. For instance, the system may infer that A consists of B and C and later infer that A also consists of B, C, and D. Alternatively, the program may reduce a reaction to the form (reacts inputs {X} outputs {   }), which contains inputs but no outputs. In both cases, STAHL is able to trace back through its chain of inferences to determine the source of the problem and either reject the offending observation or restate it using a new concept. This process can be viewed as a form of backtracking through the search space, though not in any simple sense. It is better described as rejecting the current state and

---

[10]Later versions of the phlogiston theory actually included oxygen as an element, but they retained phlogiston as their central feature.

moving sideways through the problem space to another state at approximately the same depth. Such reformulations occurred many times in the early days of chemistry, and STAHL's methods for error recovery parallel the historical developments in many ways. Zytkow and Simon (1986) have described this aspect of the system in more detail.

16.5 FORMULATING STRUCTURAL MODELS

As an area of science matures, researchers progress from descriptions to explanations. Although the dividing line between these forms of understanding is fuzzy, some examples clearly lie at the explanatory end of the spectrum. For instance, the kinetic theory of heat provides an explanation of both Black's law and the ideal gas law. A simpler example, though no less impressive at the time it was proposed, is Dalton's atomic theory. Both examples involve some form of structural model in which macroscopic phenomena are described in terms of their inferred components. Although this is not the only form of scientific explanation, the notion of structural models seems significant enough to explore in some detail. Let us review the history of the atomic theory as a prelude to our computational analysis of this aspect of discovery.

We have seen that a portion of the atomic hypothesis was implicit in componential models such as the phlogiston theory, but the full version of the atomic model was first proposed by John Dalton in 1808. In his attempt to explain the law of multiple proportions, Dalton assumed that substances were composed of particles called atoms, and he focused on the *numbers* of particles making up each substance. Following his lead, chemists adopted the design of such atomic models as one of their central concerns. Dalton employed his *rule of greatest simplicity* to apply the atomic theory to specific cases, and although this heuristic worked in many cases, it led him to incorrect conclusions in others. For instance, it led him to conclude that water was composed of a single hydrogen atom and a single oxygen atom. In contrast, Avogadro (1811) employed Gay-Lussac's data on combining volumes, along with the assumption that equal volumes of gases contained equal numbers of particles. Using this information, he inferred diatomic models for hydrogen and oxygen and a different structure for water. Although we accept Avogadro's hypothesis today, it was rejected by his contemporaries, since they believed that different atoms of the same element would repel, rather than attract, each other. This is another case in which two hypotheses provided plausible accounts of phenomena, making the area an ideal one for testing a discovery system concerned with formulating structural models.

16.5.1 The DALTON System

Our interest in structural models has led us to construct a fourth discovery system concerned with this issue. Since John Dalton was one of the earliest proponents of such models, we have named the system DALTON. The system accepts a set of reactions as input, along with information about the components of the substances involved in these reactions. For instance, DALTON would be told that hydrogen reacts with oxygen to form water, and that hydrogen reacts with nitrogen to form ammonia. Along with this information, the system would be told that water has hydrogen and oxygen as its components, while ammonia has hydrogen and nitrogen as its components.[11] Finally, it would be informed that hydrogen, oxygen, and nitrogen are elements, implying that they have no components other than themselves.

DALTON knows that two quantities are important in a reaction—the number of *molecules* of each substance that takes part (in the simplest form of the reaction) and the number of *particles* of each type in a given molecule.[12] The system's goal is to devise a model for each reaction that specifies the number of molecules and particles for each of the substances involved. Given this goal, the reactions from which DALTON begins its search are best viewed as very abstract models in which these numbers have not yet been specified. In its search through the space of models, the program generates intermediate states in which some amounts have been specified but others have not. Table 16-10 summarizes the program in terms of search concepts.

The system incorporates three operators for instantiating these models and thus moving through the problem space. The first of these inputs a reaction in which the number of molecules for a particular substance is unknown and outputs a revised reaction in which this amount is specified. For instance, this routine must

Table 16-10: DALTON viewed in terms of search concepts.

Initial state: A list of reactions and the components of the substances involved

Goal state: A model of each reaction, specifying the number of molecules and the number of particles in each compound

Intermediate states: Partial models of some reactions

Operators:
  Determine-molecules: Specifies the number of times a compound occurs in a reaction
  Determine-atoms: Specifies the number of atoms of a given type in a molecule
  Conserve-particles: Determines remaining numbers based on conservation principle

Heuristics:
  For Determine-molecules: Consider only multiples of the combining volumes
  For Determine-atoms: Select simpler models first

Search control: Depth-first search with backtracking

---

[11] Thus, DALTON accepts as input the type of information that STAHL generates as output, suggesting that these systems could easily be linked together. We will discuss this possibility in a later section.

[12] This means that the DALTON program begins with a better notion of the true situation than did its namesake, since John Dalton did not make the distinction between atoms and molecules.

hypothesize the number of oxygen molecules involved in the water reaction. A second operator is responsible for specifying the number of times a given element occurs in a particular molecule. For example, given the information that oxygen is one of the components of sulfuric acid, this operator would hypothesize the number of oxygen atoms involved in the acid. A final operator also determines the number of atoms in a substance, but in a much more efficient manner. This routine assumes that for each element taking part in a reaction, the total number of particles is conserved. The operator is given the number of molecules on both sides of a reaction, along with the number of particles on one side of that reaction. From this information, it determines whether the conservation assumption can be satisfied, and if so, it specifies the number of particles on the other side of the reaction necessary to balance the equation. If conservation cannot be satisfied under the existing assumptions, it returns this information instead.

Using these three operators, DALTON carries out a depth-first search through the space of possible models. The system focuses on one reaction at a time, first determining the number of molecules and then the number of particles in each molecule. Simpler models are considered before more complex ones. Thus models involving one molecule for some substance would be proposed before one specifying two or three molecules. Similarly, models incorporating one occurrence of an element (monatomic models) would be considered before models involving two occurrences of that element (diatomic models). The conservation assumption is employed as soon as the model for a reaction is sufficiently constrained for it to be used. Since some partial models cannot be instantiated in any way that will satisfy the conservation constraint, DALTON must be able to backtrack and consider other paths to a complete model.

One additional constraint makes the process of constructing models challenging. Consistency requires that the model for a substance be the same for all reactions in which it occurs. For example, if hydrogen is assumed to be monatomic for the water reaction, it must also be monatomic in the ammonia reaction. In general, this assumption will simplify the search process, since models completed earlier will constrain those dealt with at later points. However, it is possible that the model for a substance results in a conservation-consistent model for one reaction but leads to difficulties for another reaction. In such cases, DALTON must revise its earlier model in order to construct a consistent explanation for both reactions. This involves a form of backtracking, though not the simple form discussed above, since some existing models may be retained. We will present an example of this back-up method shortly.

16.5.2 A Monatomic Model of the Water Reaction

Now that we have examined DALTON's problem space and search control in the abstract, let us consider their use in an example. Suppose the system is asked to construct a model of the water reaction, given the information that water is composed of hydrogen and oxygen and that hydrogen and oxygen are primitive elements (and thus composed of themselves). In this case, the program must determine the number of hydrogen, oxygen, and water molecules and the number of particles of each type in the various molecules. As we have seen, DALTON begins with a very abstract model in which no commitments are made and successively refines this model as it proceeds. Let us examine what happens at each state in the search through the space of models.

Starting with an abstract model of the form (H O → W), the program first considers the number of hydrogen molecules involved. Lacking any theoretical bias, the system chooses the simplest hypothesis and assumes a single hydrogen molecule is required. If this choice later causes difficulty, the model builder can back up and try another path. Similar initial choices are made for oxygen and water, so that the partially specified model includes one molecule for each. This is represented by the proposition ((H) (O) → (W)), in which each molecule is enclosed in parentheses.

Now DALTON must determine the internal structure of each type of molecule, and it decides to assume initially that both hydrogen and oxygen consist of a single elementary particle (say h and o), giving the model ((h) (o) → (W)). At this point, the program invokes its conservation-based operator. This routine checks to see if the model can be finalized in such a way that conservation is obeyed. If this is possible, DALTON outputs the completed model and halts, but if the conservation principle cannot be satisfied the system backs up and considers other possibilities. In this case, the conservation operator tells DALTON that the water molecule must be composed of one h particle and one o particle, and that the final model must have the form ((h) (o) → (h o)). This model is equivalent to the one originally formulated by the human chemist John Dalton. Figure 16-3 presents some of the paths available in the space of molecular models. In arriving at the monatomic model just described, DALTON takes the left path, and since this leads to an acceptable solution, no backtracking is required.

16.5.3 A Diatomic Model of the Water Reaction

As we have seen, DALTON's basic strategy is to carry out a depth-first search through the space of models, ordering the search so that simple models are considered first. However, when enough of the model has been specified, a theory-driven heuristic (implementing the conservation assumption) takes over and finalizes the model. DALTON can also employ theory-driven methods at other stages in its search process, and these methods can alter the system's behavior in significant ways. Thus, in the above run, the system had no theoretical biases other than a belief in conservation of particles and a desire to construct as simple a model as possible. However, if we give DALTON some additional information about the water reaction, its behavior changes significantly. Avogadro was aware of Gay-Lussac's results, and he firmly

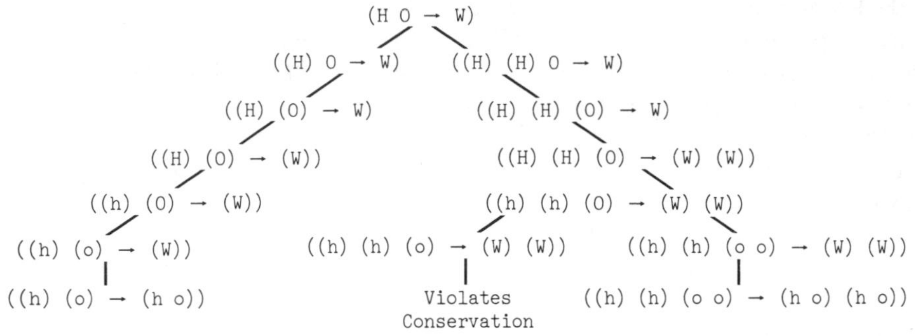

```
                              (H O → W)
                             ╱        ╲
                  ((H) O → W)          ((H) (H) O → W)
                  ╱                            ╲
          ((H) (O) → W)                        ((H) (H) (O) → W)
          ╱                                            ╲
    ((H) (O) → (W))                            ((H) (H) (O) → (W) (W))
    ╱                                                   ╲
((h) (O) → (W))                                 ((h) (h) (O) → (W) (W))
╱                                               ╱
((h) (o) → (W))            ((h) (h) (o) →  (W) (W))        ((h) (h) (o o) → (W) (W))
     |                            |                              |
((h) (o) → (h o))            Violates            ((h) (h) (o o) → (h o) (h o))
                           Conservation
```

Figure 16-3: DALTON's search for a model of the water reaction.

believed that the combining volumes he observed were related to the number of molecules involved in the reaction. To model this knowledge, we can add the heuristic:

INFER-MULTIPLES

If you want to know the number of molecules of X that are involved in a reaction
    And the combining volume of X was V
Then consider only multiples of V as possibilities.

Given this assumption (and knowledge of the combining volumes), the program (let us call it DALTON') instead postulates two molecules of hydrogen and water (and if this was later found to be unsatisfactory, four and then six), while retaining the assumption of one oxygen molecule. Thus, at the third level in the search tree, DALTON' has the partially specified model ((H) (H) (O) → (W) (W)).

    At this point the revised system moves to consider the internal structure of the hydrogen molecule, assuming it is composed of a single particle (say h), and makes a similar assumption for oxygen. However, for the resulting model, ((h) (h) (o) → (W) (W)), there exists no decomposition of water in terms of h and o that satisfies the conservation assumption, so the program backs up and considers some other alternative. DALTON' next hypothesizes that the oxygen molecule is composed of two particles, and since this does allow conservation to be satisfied, a final model is constructed in which oxygen is diatomic and hydrogen is monatomic: ((h) (h) (o o) → (h o) (h o)). (These two search paths are shown on the right side in figure 16-3.) While this model differs from the modern-day one, it is consistent with Gay-Lussac's data and encounters difficulty only when other reactions are considered. For example, the monatomic assumption for hydrogen does not work for the ammonia reaction.

    Like most of the programs we have described, DALTON is stated as a production system. In default mode, the system uses a few simple rules to formulate simpler models first and more complicated ones as necessary. However, if new condition-action rules are added to the system, they take precedence over the default rules and can direct search down paths that might otherwise not be considered. Thus, one can insert a rule that would match if the combining volume of some substance is known, and use this information to determine the number of molecules used for that substance in the model. The conservation assumption is implemented in a similar fashion, so that it generates a molecular structure for a reaction's output that uses all particles occurring in the input.

Once DALTON has generated a successful model for a reaction, it converts this knowledge into productions. For instance, having arrived at the diatomic explanation of water given above, the program would store one rule concerning the molecules of hydrogen involved, another for oxygen molecules, and a third for the water molecules. If the system is asked to explain the water reaction at a later date, it will be able to recall the number of molecules without search. DALTON also constructs productions describing the internal structure of various molecules; this knowledge is useful not only in reexplaining the water reaction but in explaining other cases as well. For instance, when asked to model the ammonia reaction, the system would immediately propose that hydrogen was monatomic, based on the success of this assumption in its model of water. None of the models incorporating this assumption satisfy conservation, so the system would back up, hypothesize that hydrogen is instead diatomic, and eventually arrive at the correct model for ammonia.

However, DALTON must also update its model of the water reaction. Since the system knows that its monatomic hydrogen rule was responsible for leading it astray, it removes this rule from memory and replaces it with a diatomic rule for hydrogen. It then focuses on the reaction that led it to construct the monatomic production and checks to see if the replacement rule works here as well. In this case it does, but had it run into difficulty, the DALTON would have repeated the process, considering ever-more-complicated molecular structures (up to a limit), until both the water and the ammonia reaction had been successfully explained by a single rule.

16.5.4 Comments on DALTON

Although DALTON's methods are concerned with reactions, they are not limited to the chemical domain. For example, the field of elementary particle physics is also concerned with reactions and with the formulation of structural models to explain those reactions. The most widely accepted theory in this domain accounts for the internal structure of protons, neutrons, and other hadrons in terms of a small set of hypothesized particles called *quarks*. In its present form, DALTON cannot discover the quark theory, but two relatively simple extensions should enable the system to arrive at the basic tenets of this framework.

First, the current version of DALTON requires either knowledge of the components of a substance or knowledge that a substance is elementary, such as hydrogen or oxygen. However, there are no directly observable "elements" in the field of particle physics, and in order to explain particle interactions, one must postulate entirely new substances that have never been seen. For example, the basic proton "molecule" is viewed as composed not of three proton "atoms," but as composed of two *u* quarks and one *d* quark. In order to regenerate the quark theory, DALTON must be modified to search the larger space of models in which such decompositions can occur. Alternatively, one can imagine a modified version of STAHL capable of determining the unseen components of hadrons, with DALTON retaining its focus on the number of particles involved. In any case, the issue of inferred particles must be addressed in one system or the other.

An equally important aspect of the quantum theory involves the conservation of mass and of the various quantum numbers, such as spin and electric charge. In order to generate these features of the theory, DALTON must attempt to explain quantitative attributes of directly observable substances (such as protons and neutrons) in terms of attributes associated with inferred substances (such as quarks). Presumably, these constraints can be stated as theory-driven heuristics, much as the conservation of particles assumption is implemented in the current version. Once the system has been given this capability, it may also be able to rediscover the basic version of the caloric theory, in which the conserved properties of mass, heat, and heat quantity are used to explain changes in the nonconserved quantity temperature.

A less obvious application of DALTON involves the field of classical genetics. For example, the rules of heredity for garden peas, first enumerated by Mendel in 1866, can be viewed as reactions in which characteristics of the parents are transformed into characteristics of the offspring. Given the first extension described above, along with a suitable replacement for the conservation assumption (since this does not apply in reproductive systems), DALTON should be able to arrive at the two-trait model originally formulated by Mendel. For example, let us suppose that the system is provided with genotypic statements of the result of inbreeding and crossbreeding, which might be induced by another discovery system (like GLAUBER) from phenotypic descriptions of these reactions.

If we let G stand for green peas that produce only green offspring, Y stand for yellow peas that produce only yellow offspring, and G' stand for green peas that produce mixed offspring, then four basic reactions suffice to describe Mendel's observations: G G → G, Y Y → Y, G Y → G', and G' G' → G G' Y. Given these reactions, an extended version of DALTON should be able to infer that two primitive traits (say g and y) are required and to decide that the genotype G can be modeled by the "molecular" pair (g g), that Y can be modeled by the pair (y y), and that G' can be modeled by the pair (g y). As we envision it, the system's explanation of these reactions would not involve the notion of dominance, nor would it predict the proportions in which the various genotypes are observed, but it would account for the basic qualitative relations between parents and offspring.

Before closing our discussion of DALTON, we should briefly examine its relation to DENDRAL (Feigenbaum, Buchanan, and Lederberg, 1971), a well-known AI system that was also concerned with formulating structural models of substances, in this case, complex organic molecules. Rather than using reactions for its basic information, DENDRAL searched for models that would account for mass spectrogram data. In addition, the system employed considerable knowledge of organic chemistry to direct its search through the space of possible models. There is no doubt that this early program could effectively search spaces in which DALTON would be quickly overwhelmed, and could generate structural models more complex than our system could begin to consider. However, this analysis misses an important point. DENDRAL was concerned primarily with imitating twentieth-century organic chemists who draw upon centuries of accumulated knowledge about chemicals and their reactions. In contrast, DALTON is concerned with an earlier stage in the discovery process, such as we find with the early chemists in their attempt to formulate atomic models with very little available knowledge. Thus, DALTON and DENDRAL can be viewed as lying at two ends of a spectrum, with the first studying simple discoveries in a knowledge-poor environment and the second focusing on more complex discoveries in a knowledge-rich environment. Ultimately, we may understand both approaches as special cases of a more general method for creating structural models, but that remains a topic for future research.

16.6 TOWARD AN INTEGRATED DISCOVERY SYSTEM

In this chapter, we examined four AI systems that address different aspects of the discovery process. Although each of these programs is interesting in its own right, they should ultimately be combined into a single, integrated discovery system. One advantage of this approach is that it will increase our understanding of the relations among the various forms of discovery. This understanding will in turn constrain the component systems, since the outputs of one program would have to conform to the inputs of another. This will lead to revisions of the existing systems, and more robust and plausible discovery programs will result. Another benefit is that the resulting system would be more self-contained, relying less on the programmer and more on its own devices. To the extent that this can be achieved, an integrated discovery system would be much less susceptible to the criticism that one is "building in discoveries" by providing the necessary inputs.

Since the notion of search is central to all four discovery systems, let us explore the role of search in the proposed integrated system. Clearly, the operators used by each of the systems will remain the same, as will the heuristics for applying those operators. The initial states for each system will be largely the same, but they will no longer be provided by the programmer. Instead, they will be generated by other systems as output. Given a set of operators and rules for applying those operators, the specification of an initial state effectively defines a problem space. Thus, to the extent that discovery system A's initial state is created by another system B, we can claim that B has defined the problem space that A will search. This may lead A to specify a new initial state for B, thus defining a new space for it to search. The dream of the AI learning system that "pulls itself up by its own bootstraps" is an old one, and we do not expect it to be achieved in the near future. However, we do believe that it lies in the direction we propose to explore, in which individual learning systems are combined to form a whole that becomes greater than the sum of their parts.

In this section, we examine some scenarios in which significant interactions might take place among BACON, GLAUBER, STAHL, and DALTON. In each case, we will treat the individual systems as black boxes, and focus on the relation between their inputs and outputs. Although we are far from actually combining these programs into a unified system, we hope that these examples will convince the reader that such a system is not only possible but necessary if the complex process called scientific discovery is ever to be understood.

16.6.1 Designing Experiments and Generalizing Laws

Earlier in the chapter, we noted that the discovery of qualitative laws often precedes the discovery of quantitative relations. This suggests that GLAUBER should be able to contribute something to BACON's search for numeric laws. However, the most obvious connection involves the search through the space of *data* rather than the space of laws. The reader will recall that BACON relies on the programmer to provide a set of variables and values, leading the system to run particular factorial experiments. Our hope is that GLAUBER will give BACON enough information to let it design its own experiments. For instance, suppose BACON were told by GLAUBER that nitric oxide, nitrous oxide, and nitrogen dioxide were all substances that resulted from reactions between nitrogen and oxygen. Given knowledge of this class of compounds, an extended version of BACON might design an experiment in which the substances entering a reaction (oxygen and nitrogen) were held constant, while the output of the reaction was varied. If quantitative variables such as the weights of the substances were examined, the resulting experiment would lead BACON to Dalton's law of multiple proportions, as described earlier.

The second use of GLAUBER's output relates to BACON's generalization process. As it is currently implemented, BACON initially associates intrinsic values with all potentially relevant symbolic conditions and generalizes by removing conditions whenever it finds that a set of intrinsic values is useful in a new context.

However, the availability of the classes generated by GLAUBER presents an alternative generalization method. Rather than removing conditions entirely, one can generalize by replacing the symbol in a condition with the class containing that symbol. For instance, suppose BACON has stored a set of intrinsic values, with one condition for retrieval being that one of the substances entering the reaction is HCl. Next, suppose that the system finds the same intrinsic values useful when the substance is HNO_3 instead of HCl. Rather than inferring that this condition is irrelevant, BACON might decide that the intrinsic values should be retrieved whenever an *acid* is involved in the reaction (provided that GLAUBER had already defined this concept). This is a more conservative approach to generalization, and it would allow BACON to express a larger class of hypotheses than it currently can. Of course, the system could eventually decide to remove this condition entirely, should the intrinsic values prove useful for nonacids as well.

This approach to generalization suggests that GLAUBER might find a use for BACON's output as well. Imagine an alternative scheme for generalizing intrinsic values, in which BACON iterates through all symbolic values, collecting those for which a set of intrinsic values is useful. Suppose the connection between symbols and values is stored in propositions, such as (intrinsics of {HCl} are {1.23 2.76 4.35}) and (intrinsics of {HNO_3} are {1.23 2.76 4.35}). Given such a set of propositions, GLAUBER could define a class (say A) based on those substances for which the values were useful and formulate a law summarizing this knowledge, such as (intrinsics of {A} are {1.23 2.76 4.35}). If this class corresponded to another class, such as *acids,* so much the better. Thus, one can imagine GLAUBER aiding BACON's generalization process, or BACON's generalization method providing data for GLAUBER's discoveries, depending on which system is allowed to operate first.

16.6.2 Determining the Components of Acids

The fact that both STAHL and GLAUBER are capable of dealing with reactions between substances suggests that there is room for interaction between these systems. If GLAUBER is given reactions such as (reacts inputs {HCl NaOH} outputs {NaCl}) as inputs, it generates abstract reactions like (reacts inputs {acid alkali} outputs {salt}) as output. If such laws are passed to STAHL as data, the program will attempt to determine the components of the "substances" involved. In this case, the system would infer that all salts are composed of an acid and an alkali. This conclusion is not very surprising, though it is an inference one would like a discovery system to make.

More complex interactions become possible when one realizes that concepts such as HCl and NaOH are not primitive at all, but are based upon lower-level observations much like the higher-level concepts of acid and alkali. For instance, GLAUBER might be given many facts about the taste and color of a large set of substances (let us call them o1, o2, and so forth). Some of these substances would have very similar tastes, as well as very similar colors. Based on such shared properties, these chemicals would be grouped into the classes we know as hydrogen (H), chlorine (Cl), and others. If the primitive substances had been involved in reactions such as (reacts inputs {o1 o2} outputs {o3}), GLAUBER would rewrite these in terms of the new classes, giving reaction "laws" like (reacts inputs {H Cl} outputs {HCl}). Such laws would then be processed by GLAUBER to determine still-higher-level classes and laws. However, they could also be passed as inputs to the STAHL system.

Given inputs such as (reacts inputs {H Cl} outputs {HCl}), STAHL would apply its rules to infer the components of the substances involved. In this case, it would immediately infer that {HCl} is composed of hydrogen and chlorine. By itself, this inference is not very interesting. However, suppose STAHL then proceeded to pass this result back to GLAUBER as additional data. In order to do this, it must represent the inference in GLAUBER's terms, but the existing (components of {HCl} are {H Cl}) will serve quite well. Given this fact and similar facts, such as (components of {HNO_3} are {H NO_3}), and given examples of reactions involving acids and alkalis, GLAUBER would formulate the class of acids and generate by substitution the laws (components of {acid} are {H Cl}) and (components of {acid} are {H NO_3}). Taken together, these laws would lead to a new class (let us say *acid-components*) with members like Cl and NO_3, along with the law (components of {acid} are {H acid-component}). This law (appropriately quantified) states that all acids have hydrogen as one of their components. This conclusion can be reached through a complex interaction in which GLAUBER affects STAHL's search through the space of componential models, and STAHL in turn affects the GLAUBER search through the space of classes and qualitative laws. A similar line of reasoning would lead the GLAUBER/STAHL combination to the conclusion that all metals have phlogiston as one of their components.

16.6.3 Building Structural Models

As we have seen, STAHL focuses on determining the *components* of chemical substances, while DALTON is concerned with the *number* of particles involved in a reaction. Thus, STAHL can be viewed as laying the groundwork for a detailed structural model, with DALTON being responsible for finalizing the model. Moreover, DALTON requires knowledge about the components of a substance in testing its conservation assumption, and it is natural to assume that this information comes from STAHL. In fact, the coupling between these programs is already sufficiently close to view them as successive stages of a single system, and we expect to merge them in our future research. Let us explore the form such a combined system might take.

One can identify three distinct stages in the process of building structural models. The first involves identifying the components of substances, and is the focus of the STAHL system. We have discussed some potential extensions of this system, such as providing the ability to postulate unobserved components, but this would not alter the basic goal of the system. The second stage involves determining the number of times each component occurs in some substance, and is the focus of DALTON. Again, we have discussed some possible extensions, such as determining numeric attributes of the components, but the basic task remains the same. The final stage, which we have so far ignored, involves specifying the manner in which the various components are *connected* to each other. Early chemists were able to avoid this issue, but the discovery of organic molecules eventually forced them to deal with the problem. Kekule's insight about the structure of the benzene ring was essentially an insight about the connections between the components of that compound. Search in this stage would involve selecting a pair of components to connect and selecting a type of bond to connect them.

We envision a single discovery system that searches the space of structural models, first determining the components involved, then identifying the number of particles taking part, and finally modeling the connections between these particles. Starting with completely abstract models, this system would successively instantiate them until their complete structure had been determined. At each stage in this instantiation process, the system would employ constraints, such as the conservation assumption, to reject some models in favor of others. Although the space of models would be quite large, search through this space would be relatively constrained. Although considerable work would be involved in constructing such a program, it would be an important step toward integrating the four discovery systems we have described.

16.6.4 Discovering the Principles of Inheritance

Earlier in this chapter, we outlined an extended version of GLAUBER that would be able to note patterns among conjunctions of facts. We discussed the application of this system to Mendel's data on heredity, showing how it could be used to infer genotypic classes (e.g., pure-breeding green peas G, mixed green peas G′, and pure-breeding yellow peas Y) from observations about phenotypes (e.g., green and yellow peas). In another section, we proposed an extended version of DALTON that, given genotypic descriptions of the offspring resulting from various matings, would be able to infer Mendel's two-trait model to account for those descriptions.[13] This suggests a straightforward relation between the two programs that should extend to other domains besides genetics. We envision GLAUBER starting with directly observed reactions and, based on regularities among those reactions, rewriting them at a higher level of description. DALTON would then take the higher-level reactions and devise structural models to account for them. According to this view, GLAUBER

---

[13]In fact, this could best be accomplished by the integrated version of STAHL and DALTON just described.

would serve mainly as a preprocessor for DALTON, transforming direct observations into an initial state upon which the structural modeler could operate.

However, information can flow in the opposite direction as well. Once DALTON has constructed models for a set of genotypic classes (such as {g g} for G, {y y} for Y, and {g y} for G'), this information could be passed back to GLAUBER. For instance, suppose GLAUBER begins with the following knowledge, some of which would be provided by DALTON:

> (components of {Y} are {y y})
> (components of {G} are {g g})
> (components of {G'} are {g y})
> (has-property object {Y} color {yellow})
> (has-property object {G} color {green})
> (has-property object {G'} color {green})

Given this information, an extended version of GLAUBER would note two "facts" involving green-colored classes and observe that both of these classes (G and G') have the symbol g as one of their components. As a result, the following two laws would be formulated:

> $\forall Q \exists P$ (components of {Q} are {g P})
> $\forall Q$ (has-property object {Q} color {green})

In addition, the class Q would be defined as the union of the classes G and G', while P is defined as having the members y and g.[14] Taken together, these laws state that all green peas contain at least one instance of g in their list of components. This example is similar to the earlier case in which GLAUBER noted hydrogen as a component of acids, but one can interpret it somewhat differently. In the context of genetics, the above law is stating that g is a *dominant* trait, since it leads to green plants whenever it occurs as a component. Again, we have seen that complex feedback between two discovery methods can lead to laws that could not be discovered by either method alone.

16.6.5 Constraining the Search for Structural Models

We have seen how DALTON's search through the space of structural models can be altered by heuristics, such as the combining volume rule that led to Avogadro's model of the water reaction. However, we have not discussed the origin of the information used by such rules. For instance, Avogadro's heuristic must know the combining volumes for a reaction before it can be used to constrain search. Since this

---

[14]The current version of the system cannot handle situations in which a substance like g is treated as both a constant and a member of a class. This capability would have to be added before GLAUBER could work as proposed.

information is numeric, it is natural to consider BACON as a possible source, and upon reviewing BACON's chemical discoveries, we find that the system's common divisor method generates the combining volumes required by DALTON. Thus BACON's output can be used to direct DALTON's search through the space of possible models.

We have discussed an extended version of DALTON that would determine numeric properties of the components in its models. For example, the system might estimate the relative atomic weights of elements taking part in a set of reactions. (This was a major concern of the early chemists.) Given such estimates, one can imagine DALTON placing additional constraints on its models and using these constraints to reject some models in favor of others. For example, the system might require that the estimated atomic weights be consistent across different reactions. However, in order to estimate the relative weights of the components in a model, DALTON would have to know the combining weights of the substances involved in a set of reactions. Again, BACON is the obvious source for such knowledge, since it generates combining weights at the same time that it produces combining volumes. In summary, BACON has the potential to place significant constraints on DALTON's search process. It is interesting to observe that data-driven methods, like those used in BACON, can be such an aid to theory-drive behavior of the type found in DALTON.

16.6.6 Structure of the Proposed System

The above scenarios provide some idea of the *behavior* we expect from the integrated discovery system, but we have not discussed the *structure* of the proposed system. In particular, we should consider how closely linked the systems will be to one another. In considering the relation between STAHL and DALTON, we decided that the coupling should be very close, since these systems can actually be viewed as dealing with different stages in the same search process. However, it is not clear that the same conclusion holds for BACON, GLAUBER, and STAHL/DALTON, since these systems seem to address genuinely different aspects of discovery—the search for quantitative laws, the search for qualitative laws, and the search for structural models. More likely, the systems should be given access to a common blackboard, and care should be taken to insure compatible representations.

If we assume that the systems should be loosely coupled, we must still specify whether interaction occurs occasionally or continuously. The first approach assumes that one system would begin, run its course, and then deposit its results on the common blackboard, to be followed by another system that takes advantage of these results to define its search space. This fits in well with the current version of GLAUBER, which requires all facts at the outset of a run. An alternative scheme would have the systems running concurrently, with each depositing results on the blackboard and with these results dynamically affecting the paths taken by other systems. This approach is well suited to the STAHL program, which already uses an incremental approach to formulating componential models. Although an incremental system like STAHL (and to some extent BACON) can be provided with all the data at the outset, an all-at-once system like GLAUBER cannot be run in incremental mode. Thus, if we decide to pursue an incremental version of the integrated discovery system, GLAUBER will have to be substantially revised in order to fit into this framework.

16.6.7 Conclusions

In this chapter, we examined four aspects of the diverse activity known as scientific discovery—finding quantitative laws, generating qualitative laws, inferring the components of substances, and formulating structural models. Our approach involved constructing AI systems that focused on these different facets of science and testing them on their ability to replicate historical discoveries. We drew out examples mainly from the history of chemistry, since this area provided useful tests for each of the systems and since it allowed us to explore potential connections among the discovery programs. We found that each of the systems could be usefully viewed as carrying out search through a space of laws or models, and we examined the operators and heuristics used to direct search through these spaces. We also found that each of the systems has some important limitations, and we proposed some extensions that should lead to improved future versions.

Although the four systems—BACON, GLAUBER, STAHL, and DALTON—have each contributed to our understanding of discovery, we believe that an even greater understanding could result from exploring the *relations* among the systems. As a result, we plan to construct an integrated discovery system that will incorporate the individual systems as components. As we have noted many times, scientific discovery is a multifaceted process, and even within such an expanded framework, we must omit many of its important aspects. For instance, we have not addressed the formulation of mechanistic explanations such as the kinetic theory of gases, the role of structural analogies as studied by Winston (1980) and Gentner (1983), or the design of new measurement devices. Thus, even our goal of an integrated discovery system is limited in some important respects. However, limiting one's focus of attention is a venerable and useful tradition in the history of science, and there will be ample time to incorporate these additional facets of discovery after we better understand the relations among the four existing systems.

ACKNOWLEDGMENTS

The research described in this chapter was supported by contract N00014-82-0168 from the Office of Naval Research, Division of Information Science.

References

Bradshaw, G. L., Langley, P., and Simon, H. A., "BACON.4: The Discovery of Intrinsic Properties," *Proceedings of the Third Biennial Conference of the Canadian Society for Computational Studies of Intelligence,* Victoria, B.C., pp. 19–25, 1980.

Brown, J. S., "Steps Toward Automatic Theory Formation," *Proceedings of the Third IJCAI,* Stanford, Calif., pp. 20–23, 1973.

Emde, W., Habel, C. H., and Rollinger, C., "The Discovery of the Equator or Concept Driven Learning," *Proceedings of the Eighth IJCAI,* Karlsruhe, W. Ger., pp. 455–58, 1983.

Feigenbaum, E. A., Buchanan, B. G., and Lederberg, J., "On Generality and Problem Solving: A Case Study Using the DENDRAL Program," in *Machine Intelligence 6,* Edinburgh University Press, Edinburgh, 1971.

Gentner, D., "Structure Mapping: A Theoretical Framework for Analogy," *Cognitive Science,* Vol. 7, pp. 155–70, 1983.

Langley, P., Bradshaw, G. L., and Simon, H. A., "Data-driven and Expectation-driven Discovery of Empirical Laws," *Proceedings of the Fourth Biennial Conference of the Canadian Society for Computational Studies of Intelligence,* Sasketoon, Saskatchewan, pp. 137–43, 1982.

————, "Rediscovering Chemistry with the BACON System," in *Machine Learning: An Artificial Intelligence Approach,* R. S. Michalski, J. G. Carbonell, and T. M. Mitchell (Eds.), Tioga, Palo Alto, Calif., 1983.

Langley, P., Zytkow, J., Bradshaw, G. L., and Simon, H. A., "Mechanisms for Qualitative and Quantitative Discovery," *Proceedings of the International Machine Learning Workshop,* R. S. Michalski (Ed.), Allerton House, University of Illinois at Urbana-Champaign, pp. 12–32, June 22–24, 1983. (An updated version of this paper appears as Chap. 16 of this volume.)

Michalski, R. S., and Stepp, R. E., "Learning from Observation: Conceptual Clustering," in *Machine Learning: An Artificial Intelligence Approach,* R. S. Michalski, J. G. Carbonell, and T. M. Mitchell (Eds.), Tioga, Palo Alto, Calif., 1983.

Newell, A., and Simon, H. A., *Human Problem Solving,* Prentice-Hall, Englewood Cliffs, N.J., 1972.

Rosenbloom, P., "The Chunking Model of Goal Hierarchies: A Model of Practice and Stimulus-Response Compatibility," Ph.D. diss., Carnegie-Mellon University, 1983.

Winston, P. H., "Learning and Reasoning by Analogy," *Communications of the ACM,* Vol. 23, pp. 689–703, 1980.

Wolff, J. G., "Grammar Discovery as Data Compression," *Proceedings of the AISB/GI Conference on Artificial Intelligence,* Hamburg, W. Ger., pp. 375–79, 1978.

Zytkow, J. M., and Simon, H. A., "A Theory of Historical Discovery: The Construction of Componential Models." To appear in *Machine Learning,* Vol. I, 1986.

17

CONCEPTUAL CLUSTERING:

Inventing Goal-Oriented Classifications of Structured Objects

Robert E. Stepp III
University of Illinois at Urbana-Champaign

Ryszard S. Michalski*
Massachusetts Institute of Technology

Abstract

An important form of inductive learning is inventing a meaningful classification of given objects or events. This chapter extends the authors' previous work on this problem that was based on *conceptual clustering,* that is, grouping objects into conceptually simple classes. In contrast to the past work, the new method deals with classifying objects represented by structural descriptions rather than by sequences of attribute values. These descriptions are expressed in *Annotated Predicate Calculus* (APC), which is a typed predicate logic calculus with additional operators.

It is shown that in order to create a meaningful classification, a system must be equipped with *background knowledge,* which includes goals of classification, classification evaluation criteria, and deductive and inductive inference rules. The goals and goal-relevant descriptive concepts are organized into a *Goal Dependency Network* (GDN). Inference rules permit the system to derive high-level descriptive concepts such as functional and causal attributes from lower-level descriptive concepts provided initially. Example classifications created by the program CLUSTER/S and by people are presented.

*On leave of absence from the University of Illinois at Urbana-Champaign.

17.1 INTRODUCTION

Creating a classification[1] is typically the first step in developing a theory about a collection of observations or phenomena. This process is a form of learning from observation (learning without a teacher), and its goal is to structure given observations into a hierarchy of meaningful categories. The problem of automatically creating such a hierarchy has so far received little attention in AI. Yet creating classifications is a very basic and widely practiced intellectual process.

Past work on this problem was done mostly outside AI under the headings of numerical taxonomy and cluster analysis (Anderberg, 1973). Those methods are based on the application of a mathematical measure of similarity between objects, defined over a finite, a priori given set of object attributes. Classes of objects are taken as collections of objects with high intraclass and low interclass similarity. The methods assume that objects are characterized by sequences of attribute/value pairs and that this information is sufficient for creating a classification. The methods do not take into consideration any *background knowledge* about the semantic relationships among object attributes or global concepts that could be used for characterizing object configurations. Nor do they take into consideration possible goals of classification that might be indicated by background knowledge.

As a result, classifications obtained by traditional methods are often difficult to interpret conceptually. The problem of interpreting the results has remained a challenging task for the data analyst. In addition, traditional classification-building methods describe objects by attribute value sequences and therefore are inadequate for creating classifications of structured objects. The description of such objects must involve not only attributes of objects as a whole but also attributes of object components and relationships among these components.

This chapter describes a method for automated generation of classifications of structured objects through a process of *conceptual clustering*. This process generates classes (clusters of objects) by first generating conceptual descriptions of the classes and then classifying the objects according to these descriptions. The method is illustrated by a sample problem, and classifications produced by machine are compared to those produced by people.

17.2 THE GOAL OF THIS RESEARCH

The idea of conceptual clustering leads to an entirely new approach to the problem of creating classifications (Michalski, 1980a; Michalski and Stepp, 1983a, 1983b; Stepp, 1984). This idea states that objects should be arranged into classes that

---

[1]Creating or building a classification involves two subprocesses: (1) generating an appropriate set of categories and (2) classifying all given entities according to the generated categories.

represent simple concepts rather than classes defined solely by a predefined measure of similarity among their members.

In the earlier work on conceptual clustering, objects or events were described by attribute-value sequences. The method arranged the objects into a hierarchy of classes described by *conjunctive concepts*. These concepts are expressed as logical products of relations on selected object attributes. The generated sibling classes of any node in the hierarchy represented the most preferred (sub)classification from this node according to a given *preference criterion*. The background knowledge included the definitions of the attributes used in object descriptions, their domains and types, and the classification preference criterion.

This research extends the previous work in three ways:

- Objects and classes are described by structural descriptions, which are expressed in *Annotated Predicate Calculus* (APC), a typed predicate calculus with additional operators.
- The background knowledge includes inference rules for deriving high-level descriptive concepts from the low-level concepts initially provided.[2]
- The system is supplied with a general goal of the classification, which provides the means for identifying relevant descriptors and inference rules for deriving new descriptors. This avoids the necessity of defining them explicitly, as in the previous method.

An important aspect of this approach is the emphasis placed on the role of background knowledge for constructing meaningful and useful classifications. In this method the background knowledge consists of a network of goals of the classification, inference rules and heuristics for deriving new descriptors, definitions of attribute domains and types, and the classification preference criterion. The network of goals, called the *Goal Dependency Network* (GDN), is used for guiding the search for relevant descriptors and inference rules.

The necessity of using background knowledge in any form of inductive learning is indicated in the theory of inductive learning (Michalski, 1983). Important work involving background knowledge has been done by Winston (see chap. 3 of this volume), who describes an incremental learning process in which the background knowledge contains relevant precedents, exercises, and *unless conditions*. In chapter 19 DeJong presents a method of using background knowledge to acquire explanatory schemata that describe sequences of events presented as stories. Background knowledge has also been used by Mitchell and Keller (1983) to guide an inductive learning program for acquiring a problem-solving heuristics in integral calculus. In learning

---

[2]The descriptive concepts are called *descriptors* and include attributes, n-ary functions, and relations used to characterize objects or events.

by analogy, described by Burstein in chapter 13, a large body of causal knowledge is used to "fill out" incomplete descriptions and guide analogical inference. Carbonell (1983, and chap. 14 of this volume) developed a method for acquiring problem-solving strategies by analogy to solutions to similar problems. Rendell's Probabilistic Learning System demonstrated the usefulness of clustering points in the solution space for reducing the search required in problem solving (Rendell, 1983). As for the problem of learning structural descriptions from examples, various aspects of this problem are discussed in Winston (1984) and Dietterich and Michalski (1983).

To provide the necessary background, section 17.3 presents a brief overview of the authors' earlier method of attribute-based conjunctive conceptual clustering. Section 17.4 focuses on the role of background knowledge and goals in building classifications. Following that, section 17.5 presents a sample problem involving building a classification of structured objects. Finally, section 17.6 presents two methods for constructing classifications of structured objects that employ background knowledge.

17.3 ATTRIBUTE-BASED CONJUNCTIVE CONCEPTUAL CLUSTERING (PREVIOUS WORK)

This section briefly describes the authors' previous work on classifications using the method of *attribute-based conjunctive conceptual clustering* (AC^3), which is the sorting basis of the method presented here. The main idea behind AC^3 is that a configuration of objects forms a class only if it can be described by a conjunctive concept involving relations on object attributes. AC^3 is a special case of general conceptual clustering that generates a network of concepts to characterize a collection of objects. The problem posed in the framework of AC^3 is defined as follows:

Given: A set of objects (physical or abstract),

   A set of attributes to be used to characterize the objects, and

   A body of background knowledge, which includes the problem constraints, properties of attributes, inference rules for generating new attributes, and a criterion for evaluating the quality of candidate classifications;

Find: A hierarchy of object classes, and their descriptions in the form of conjunctive statements. Subclasses that are descendants of any parent class should have logically disjoint descriptions and maximize a *clustering preference criterion*.

As mentioned before, in conventional data analysis classes of objects are formulated solely on the basis of a measure of object similarity. The similarity between any two objects is characterized by a single number: the value of a similarity function applied to symbolic descriptions of objects. These symbolic descriptions are vectors, whose components are scores on selected object attributes. Such measures of similarity are *context free;* that is, the similarity between any two objects A and B depends solely on the properties of the objects and is not influenced by any context (the *environment* surrounding the objects). Consequently, methods that use such measures are fundamentally unable to capture the *gestalt* properties of object clusters, that is, properties that characterize a cluster as a whole and are not derivable from properties of individual entities. In order to detect such properties, the system must be equipped with the ability to recognize configurations of objects representing certain global concepts.

This idea is the basis of conceptual clustering. Instead of similarity between objects, say, A and B, the method uses *conceptual cohesiveness* of A and B, which depends not only on those objects and surrounding objects E (the *environment*) but also on a set of concepts C that are available for describing A and B together. Thus, the conceptual cohesiveness between two objects A and B is a four-argument function $f(A,B,E,C)$ in contrast to an ordinary two-argument similarity function $f(A,B)$.

The conjunctive conceptual clustering method consists of two phases: a *clustering* phase and a *hierarchy-building* phase. The clustering phase arranges objects into classes using conceptual cohesiveness, so that the obtained clustering maximizes the given context-based clustering preference criterion. The hierarchy-building phase starts with building first-level conceptual classifications of all objects (at the *root* of the hierarchy). Then it recursively builds a classification for each sibling group of objects from the previous classification until the *stop growth* criterion is met.

The clustering phase algorithm works by alternately selecting a set of *seed* objects (one per class) and using the seeds to guide inductive inference over positive-only events to produce generalized, but mutually disjoint, descriptions of object classes. This process insures that each seed object is placed into a separate class. Each cluster description is as general as possible (various generalization transformations are exhaustively applied) so that it covers the given seed but no other seeds. Different seeds are used over several iterations while the clustering preference criterion is monitored. The algorithm halts when the clustering preference criterion does not improve for a dynamically determined number of iterations. The algorithm is described in detail in Michalski and Stepp (1983b).

17.4 THE USE OF BACKGROUND KNOWLEDGE AND GOALS

Suppose that we are observing a typical restaurant table on which there are such objects as food on a plate, a salad, utensils, salt and pepper, napkins, a vase with flowers, a coffee cup, and so on, as illustrated in figure 17-1. Suppose a person is

Figure 17-1:   A typical restaurant table.

asked to build a meaningful classification of objects on the table. One way to create a classification is to perform the following chain of inferences:

- Salt and pepper are seasonings
  Seasonings are used to add zest to food
  Seasoned food is something to be eaten
  Things that are to be eaten are edible
  Salt and pepper are edible

- Salad is a vegetable
  Vegetables are food
  Food is something to be eaten
  Things that are to be eaten are edible
  Salad is edible

A similar chain of inferences applied to *meat on a plate* and *cake on a dessert plate* will also lead to the concept *is edible.* On the other hand, a napkin is not food and is therefore not edible. A vase containing flowers is not food and is therefore not edible. Consequently, one meaningful classification of objects on the table is simply *edible* versus *inedible.*

One may observe that when the background knowledge contains many such rules of inference, a large number of different but equally meaningful classifications can be created. The problem is then how to decide which of the classifications is best or most appropriate. For example, if inference rules about food types, suppliers, processing, and packaging were contained in the knowledge base, they could be used for generating other classifications. Some new classifications might produce categories such as *domestic* versus *imported* or *perishable* versus *nonperishable*. The problem of which classification to select can be resolved by assuming a general goal or purpose to be served by the classification. Assume, for example, that the classification is to be useful to an agent who wants to *survive*. Such a behavioral goal to *survive* dictates that a person has to ingest food and liquids, and be safe. Furthermore, the subgoal *ingest* can be linked to the two modes of ingestion, that is, consuming food and drinking liquids. In the context of the subordinate goals reached by links from the most general goal node, the relevant attributes are, for example, *is_edible,* and *is_potable, tastes_good.* The attribute *tastes_good* is linked by the implication relation to *is_edible* or *is_potable* (if something tastes good then it is either edible or potable).

Thus there is a general goal leading to subgoals and then to one or more attributes that are relevant in the context of the goal. Such relationships are captured in the Goal Dependency Network (GDN) mentioned earlier. This network links goals, subgoals, and relevant attributes together. Part of a hypothetical GDN headed by the *survive* goal is shown in figure 17-2. In the illustration, main goals are denoted by double

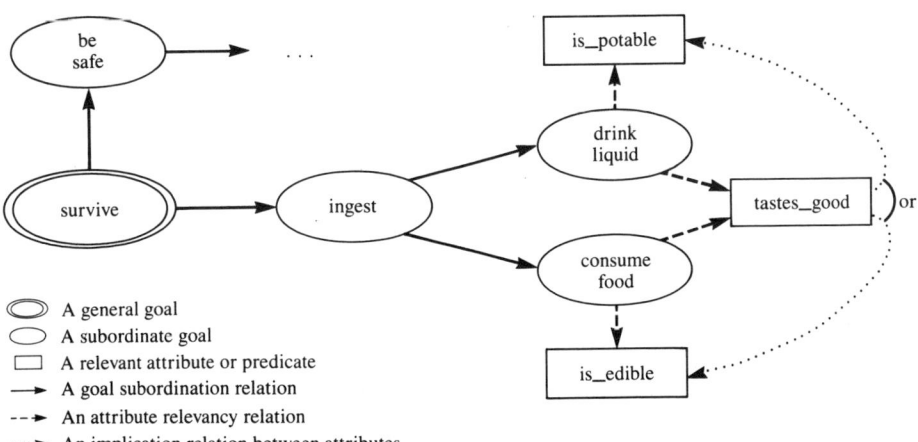

Figure 17-2:   A GDN headed by the goal *survive.*

ellipses, and subgoals and relevant descriptors are denoted by regular ellipses and rectangles, respectively. The solid arcs between nodes are directed from goal nodes towards subordinate goal nodes. The dashed arcs between nodes and attributes are directed from goal nodes to relevant attribute nodes, and the dotted arcs link an attribute with an implied attribute.

Suppose that the goals of the agent include not only *survive* but also *be healthy and beautiful*. When both goals are involved, a GDN such as the one in figure 17-3 is used. Here, the links from the two top-level goals converge at the *consume dietary food* subgoal which links to the subordinate goals *consume lean foods* and *consume balanced diet*. Attached to these latter nodes are the relevant descriptors *fat content*

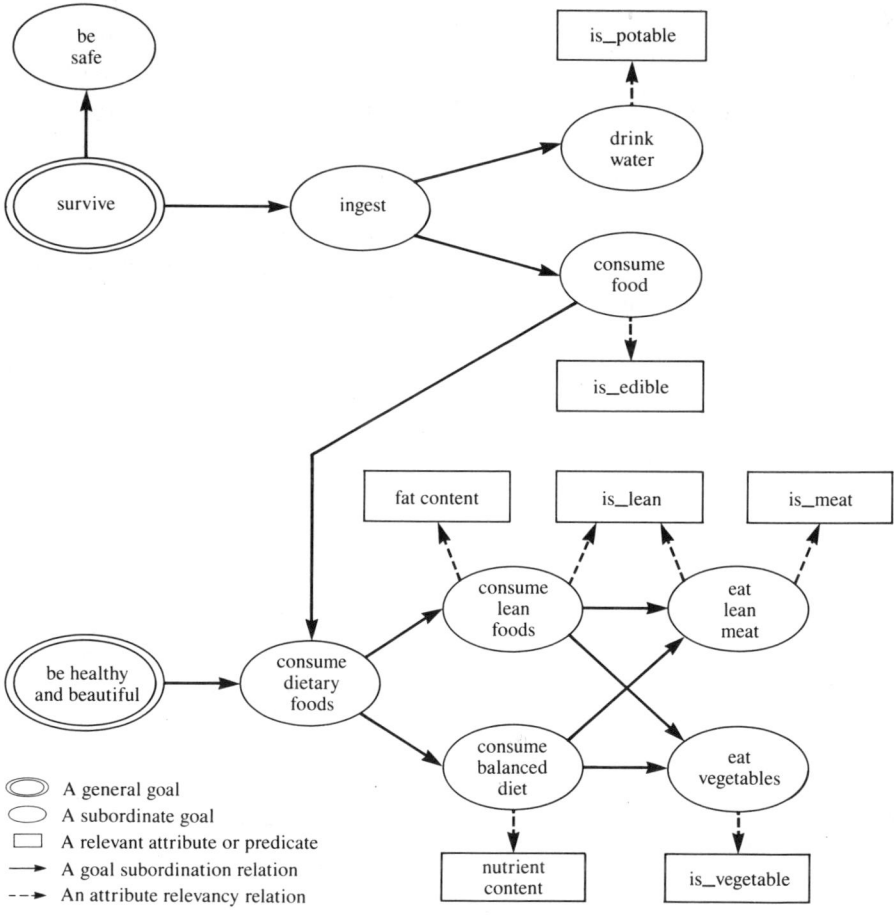

Figure 17-3:   A GDN for the goals *survive* and *be healthy and beautiful*.

and *is_lean,* and *nutrient content,* respectively. The two subgoal nodes mentioned above have subordinate goal nodes of their own. These include *eat lean meat* and *eat vegetables.* The relevant descriptors attached to these nodes include the predicates *is_lean, is_meat,* and *is_vegetable.* Thus, by the addition of the top-level goal *be healthy and beautiful,* five additional relevant attributes are proposed by the GDN.

Adding a top-level goal may reduce the number of attributes thought to be relevant. Suppose we add a *vegetarian life-style* goal. Link paths from the three top-level goals converge at the subordinate goal *eat vegetables.* This increases the relevancy of the *is_vegetable* predicate which now dominates in relevancy over the other attributes. The GDN for this last situation is illustrated in figure 17-4.

Let us now consider a specific problem: the system is given symbolic descriptions of objects on the table in terms of their physical attributes (including structure) along with *survive* as a general goal of classification, and we want it to create the classification into edible versus inedible objects. Notice first that creating such a classification solely on the basis of original attributes is practically impossible, because objects that are in the same functional class (edible or inedible) can be vastly different in terms of their physical properties (see Winston, 1984, for a discussion of this problem). A program that could classify objects on a table as edible or inedible would have to be equipped with background knowledge consisting of the previously described inference rules and with the ability to use them in a goal-directed way.

Background knowledge built into the program can be divided into *general purpose* and *domain specific.* General-purpose knowledge consists of fundamental constraints and criteria specifying general properties of classifications. This includes a specification of the domain of each descriptor, the type of the domain (unordered, linearly ordered, or tree-structure ordered), and a sequence of elementary criteria to be applied lexicographically with tolerances to evaluate classifications. The *Lexicographical Evaluation Functional with tolerances,* or LEF (see section 17.6.2), is used to select from among candidate classification schemes the one that is the most preferred viewpoint of the given goal.

Domain-specific background knowledge consists of inference rules for deriving values for new descriptors and GDN to infer which descriptors (attributes, functions, or predicates) are relevant to the goal of classification.

Event descriptors can be divided into *initial descriptors* and *derived descriptors.* Both kinds of descriptors can appear attached to goal nodes in the GDN. The initial descriptors can be divided into those that are relevant with respect to the goals and those that are irrelevant. In some problems, the relevant descriptors are unknown and not necessarily provided as initial descriptors. A solution can still be obtained in such cases if background knowledge can be used to derive relevant descriptors from those that are initially given. Inference rules in the knowledge base are used to infer the values of the derived descriptors. Domain-specific knowledge in the GDN is used to guide the application of inference rules toward descriptors that are likely to be relevant and thus worth the computational cost of their derivation.

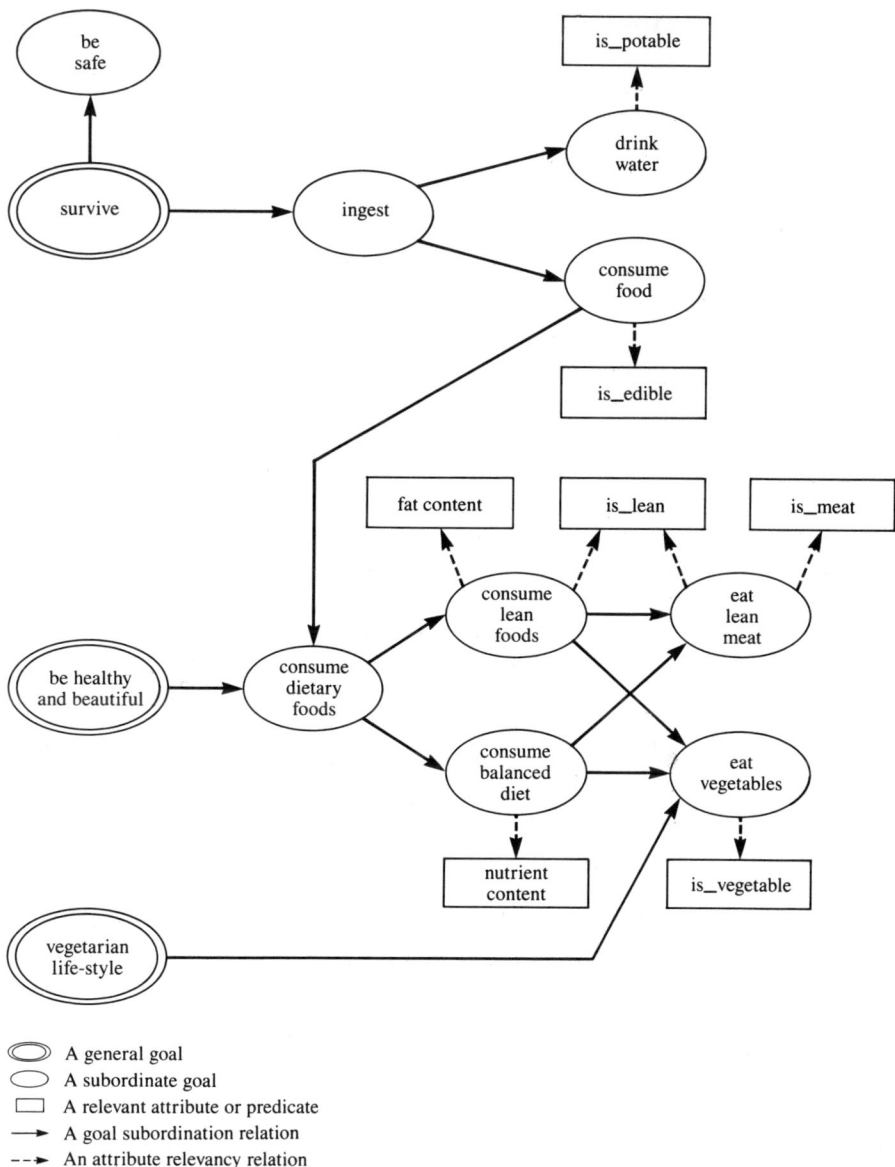

Figure 17-4: A GDN for the goals *survive, be healthy and beautiful,* and *vegetarian life-style.*

Derived descriptors can be divided into two categories:

- *Descriptors derived by logical inference.* These descriptors are predicates and functions obtained by the application of general and problem-specific inference rules to the initial descriptions of the objects. In this work, inference rules consist of a condition part and a consequence part. Whenever an object description matches the condition portion of a rule, the consequence portion is applied to the object description. The consequence may be composed either of new predicates and functions to be asserted or of arithmetic expressions that are evaluated. In either case, the new descriptors (unless already present) are appended to the object description and become available as attributes that are potentially relevant for building classifications of the objects.

- *Descriptors derived by special computations, experiments, or devices.* These descriptors are obtained from the initial descriptors by the application of specialized descriptor generation procedures, by running experiments, or by activating some external device, that is, any procedure other than the application of condition-consequence rules. Examples of such descriptors generated by the INDUCE/2 program (Hoff, Michalski, and Stepp, 1983) are "the number of object subparts," "the number of subparts with some specific property," "the number of different values observed for an attribute," and "properties common to all subparts." The program can also automatically generate multiplace predicates to assert "same function value" for several parts—for example, samecolor($p1,p2$)—and single-place predicates to assert head and tail positions in a chain of properties—for example, to assert most-ontop($p1$) and least-ontop($p1$) when given ontop($p1,p2$) and ontop($p2,p3$).

17.5 BUILDING CLASSIFICATIONS OF STRUCTURED OBJECTS

Let us turn now to the problem of classifying structured objects. Consider, for example, the problem of classifying trains,[3] shown in figure 17-5. The trains are structured objects, each consisting of a sequence of cars of different shapes and sizes. The individual cars carry a variable number of items of different shapes. The problem presented is in a class of learning problems known as *learning from observation,* or *concept formation.* It is interesting to both AI researchers and cognitive psychologists.

---

[3]This example is a reformulation of a problem known as "East- and Westbound Trains" (Michalski and Larson, 1977). In the original formulation, two collections of trains were given, those that were eastbound (A to E) and those that were westbound (F to J); the problem was to learn a simple rule for distinguishing between the eastbound and the westbound trains. Thus the original problem was that of *learning from examples,* or *concept acquisition.*

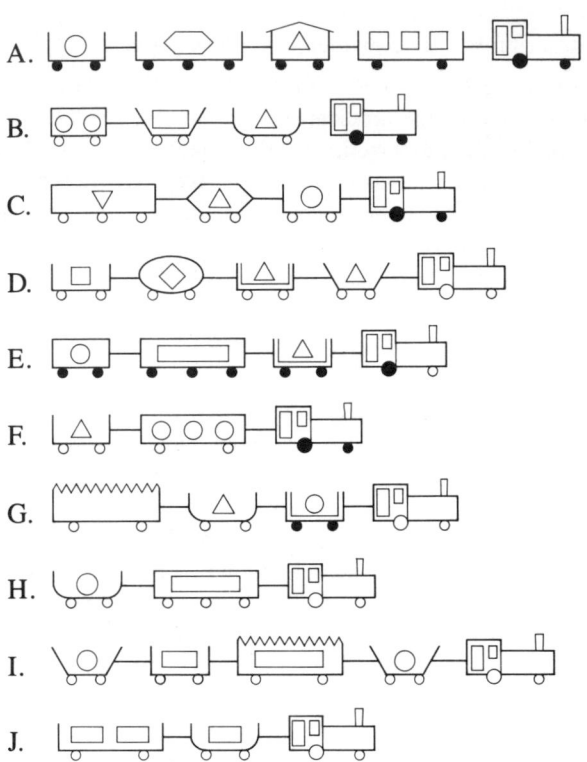

Figure 17-5:   How would you classify these trains?

Human classifications of the trains shown in figure 17-5 have been investigated by Medin, Wattenmaker, and Michalski (1985). The ten trains were placed on separate index cards so they could be arranged into groups by the subjects in the experiment. Each subject was instructed to partition the trains according to three methods and to state the rationale used:

1. Arrange the trains into any number of groups.
2. Arrange the trains into two equal groups.
3. Arrange the trains into any number of groups of conceptually similar objects plus an "other" group to hold any unusual or hard-to-classify trains.

The experiment was completed by thirty-one subjects who made a total of ninety-three classification schemes for partitioning the objects. The most popular basis for classification (seventeen repetitions) was the number of cars in the trains (a simple attribute that characterizes each train as a whole). The three clusters formed were the following: "trains containing two cars," "trains containing three cars," and "trains containing four cars." The second most frequent classification (seven repetitions) was based on the engine wheel color. These two classifications are shown in figure 17-6. Of the ninety-three classifications produced, forty of them were unique. Thus, although there was no explicit goal for classification given, there was a pattern of uniformity among the subjects. The pattern was not a very strong one, however, as witnessed by a wide spectrum of singleton solutions.

This problem is an example of a class of problems for which the implicit classification goal is to generate classes that are conceptually simple and based on easy-to-determine visual attributes. When people are asked to build such classifications, they typically form classes with *disjoint* descriptions, as in the study by Medin. People typically do not suggest intersecting classifications, and it is for this reason that we focus on methods that produce disjoint descriptions.

Classification problems such as this one occur when one wants to organize and classify observations that require structural descriptions—for example, when one wants to classify physical or chemical structures, analyze genetic sequences, build taxonomies of plants or animals, characterize visual scenes, or split a sequence of temporal events into episodes with simple meanings. As an example of the latter problem, consider splitting a kidnapping story into episodes such as kidnapping, bargaining, and exchange (DeJong, 1981).

One problem of concern here is to develop a general method that when applied to the collection of structured objects, such as trains, could potentially generate the conjunctive concepts occurring in human classifications or invent new concepts having similar appeal. We first assume that there is only a very general goal for a classification, such as *simplicity of descriptions of categories* or *good fit of the categories to the examples.* The method should be able to generate conceptual categories that can be described by a conjunction of predicates. These conjunctions should represent a minimal overgeneralization of observed events in the class so as to insure a good "fit" between each class description and the events.

Figure 17-7 shows a hypothetical GDN for a classification for which the general goal is to find simple visual patterns. A subordinate goal is to look for simple geometrical regularities in object descriptions. For the trains problem, this goal node leads to the relevant variables such as *number of cars, color of wheels, number of wheels, number of items carried,* and so on. The *simple geometrical regularities* goal links to the two subordinate goals *shape of components* and *similarity of components.* The first of these subgoals leads to relevant attributes involving shape (*cargo shape, engine shape, car shape*). The second subgoal leads to a variety of relevant attributes relating one component of a train to other components. The *number of different shapes* attribute gives the count of the different car shapes in a train. A count of the number of different cargo shapes in a car would be another attribute of this same type. The *same car shape* or *same color of wheels* attributes are predicates of two or more variables that denote the equality of feature values across several components in the train. If all components have the same value for some attribute, then a *forall*

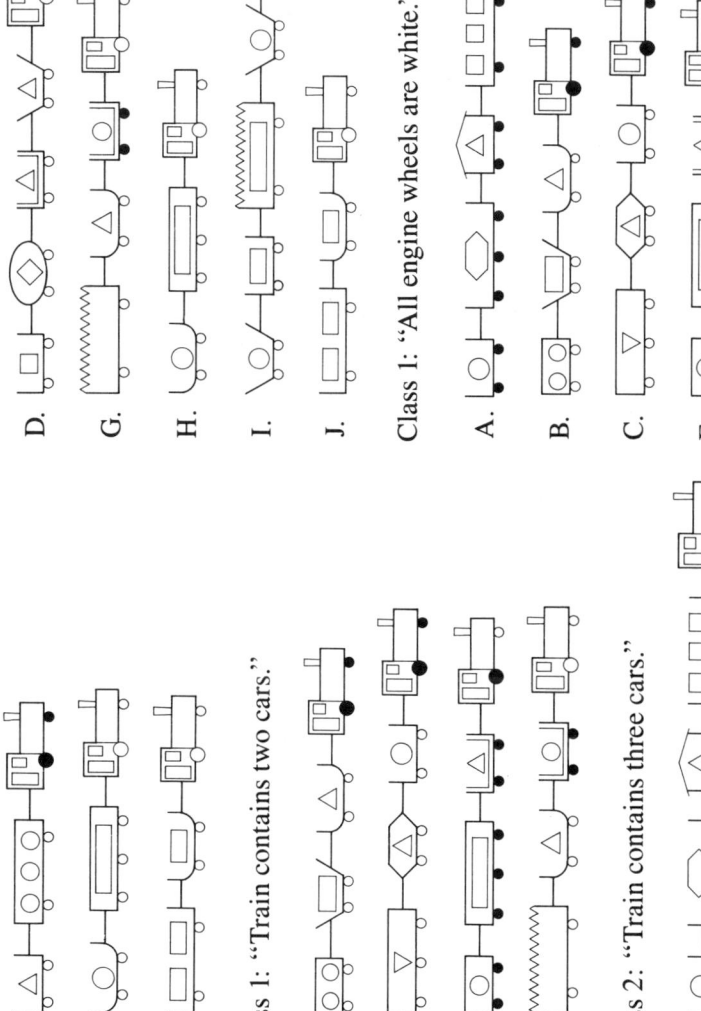

F.

H.

J.

Class 1: "Train contains two cars."

B.

C.

E.

G.

Class 2: "Train contains three cars."

A.

D.

I.

Class 3: "Train contains four cars."

D.

G.

H.

I.

J.

Class 1: "All engine wheels are white."

A.

B.

C.

E.

F.

Class 2: "Not all engine wheels are white."

Figure 17-6: The two most popular classifications produced by people.

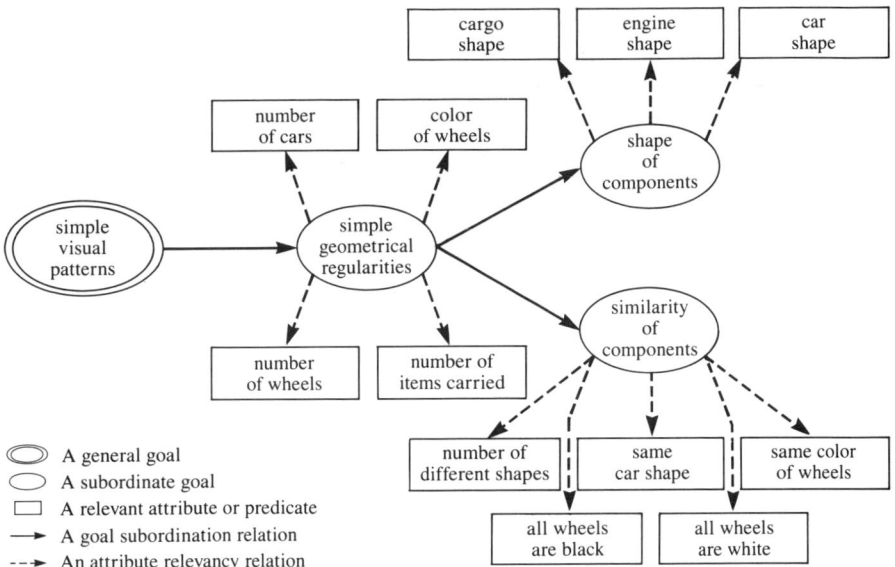

Figure 17-7: A GDN for the goal of finding simple visual patterns.

predicate, such as *all wheels in the train are black,* is a relevant attribute for describing the situation.

As examples of solutions obtained by the program CLUSTER/S implementing the method, figure 17-8 shows two classifications created for the trains problem. For this problem, the structured descriptions of each train involve the descriptors *contains, infront, car shape, number of wheels, wheel color, cargo shape,* and *number of items carried.* The program determined several new descriptors that were not in the initial descriptions, such as *number of different shapes, same-shape* predicates, *same-color-of-wheels* predicates and so on.

The generated attribute vectors were processed using a classification evaluation criterion that attempts to minimize the number of attributes used in a description, maximize the number of attributes that singly discriminate among all classes, and maximize the number of attributes that take different values in different classes. Minimizing the number of attributes used tends to conflict with the other two elementary criteria. This was handled by specifying a high tolerance (90 percent) for the first elementary criterion and zero tolerances for the second and third elementary criteria in the LEF evaluation criterion described in section 17.6.2.

B

A.

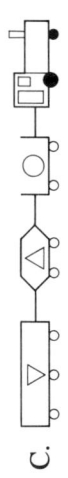
D.

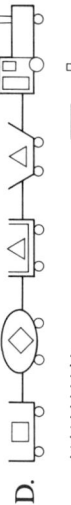
H.

I.

J.

Class 1: "Wheels on all cars have the same color."

B.

C.

E.

F.

G.

Class 2: "Wheels on all cars do not have the same color."

A

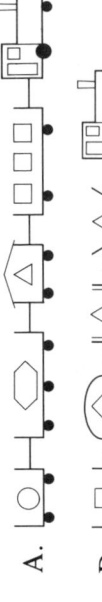
A.

E.

F.

H.

J.

Class 1: "There are two different car shapes in the train."

B.

C.

D.

G.

I.

Class 2: "There are three or more different car shapes in the train."

Figure 17-8: Two simple classifications found by the program CLUSTER/S.

Classification A in figure 17-8 was generated by the program with two different sets of class descriptions. The top class ("There are two different car shapes in the train") was also described as "The third car from the engine (if it exists) has black wheels." The bottom class ("There are three or more different car shapes in the train") was also described as "The third car from the engine exists and has white wheels." Classification B in figure 17-8 is based on the derived predicate *samecolor*. Both classifications received the same evaluation criterion score and were considered to be alternative classifications. Solutions of the kind shown in figure 17-8 are appealing because the differences between classes is striking yet not obvious from casual inspection.

17.6 TWO METHODS FOR BUILDING CLASSIFICATIONS

This section describes two methods for solving problems of the kind posed in the preceding section, that is, building a classification of a collection of structured objects. One method is called RD, which stands for *repeated discrimination,* and the other is called CA, which stands for *classifying attributes.* The RD method is based on the authors' previous work and reduces the problem of building a classification into a sequence of concept acquisition problems, specifically, problems of determining discriminant descriptions of objects with given class labels (Michalski and Stepp, 1983b). The CA method is based on generating candidate *classifying attributes* either from the initially given pool of attributes or from derived attributes generated with the aid of inference rules and the Goal Dependency Network.

The two methods are similar in that they both use the same representation language (APC) for describing objects, classes of objects, and general and problem-specific background knowledge. Both methods use the LEF as the general-purpose criterion for measuring the *quality* of generated candidate solutions. The APC and LEF are described in the next two sections, respectively.

17.6.1 The Description Language: Annotated Predicate Calculus

The Annotated Predicate Calculus (APC) is an extension of predicate calculus that uses several novel forms and attaches an *annotation* to each predicate, variable, and function (Michalski, 1983). The annotation is a store of information about the given predicate or atomic function, such as the type and structure of its legal value set, related (more general or more specific) descriptors in descriptor hierarchy, and other information. In addition to all the forms found in predicate calculus, the language also uses a special kind of predicate called a *selector.* A simple selector is in the form

[atomic-function   REL   value-of-atomic-function]

where REL (relation) stands for one of the symbols $= \neq < > \leq \geq$. An example of such a selector is

[weight(box) > 2kg]

which means "the weight of the box is greater than 2 kg." A more complex selector may involve *internal disjunction* or *internal conjunction*. These two operators apply to terms rather than to predicates and are illustrated by the two corresponding examples:

[color(box) = red & purple]   "The color of the box is either red *or* purple."

[color(box1 & box2) = red]   "The color of box 1 *and* box 2 is red."

The meaning of the internal disjunction operator is defined by

$$[f(x) = a \ \& \ b] \Rightarrow [f(x) = a] \ \& \ [f(x) = b]$$

and the meaning of the internal conjunction operator is defined by

$$[f(x \ \& \ y) = a] \Rightarrow [f(x) = a] \ \& \ [f(y) = a].$$

Selectors can be combined by standard logical operators to form more complex expressions. Background knowledge is expressed as a set of APC implicative rules:

CONDITION $\Rightarrow$ CONSEQUENCE

where CONDITION and CONSEQUENCE are conjunctions of selectors. Thus a rule in APC is more general than the Horn clause used in PROLOG. If CONDITION is satisfied, the CONSEQUENCE is asserted. To understand the implicative statement, consider the assertion "vegetables are food" from the example in section 17.4. It can be expressed in APC by the following statement, which says, "if an object is a vegetable then it is also a food":

[is_vegetable(object)] $\Rightarrow$ [is_food(object)]

An alternative way to express this idea in APC is

[object-type(object) = vegetable] $\Rightarrow$ [object-type(object) = food]

which says, "if the type category of an object is *vegetable* than the type category is also *food*." In this latter statement *vegetable* and *food* are treated as elements of the structured domain of the attribute *object-type*. This implication expresses a generalizing inference rule called *climbing the generalization tree*. Further details on the APC language are given in Michalski (1983).

17.6.2 Directing the Process by Measuring Classification Quality

Creating a classification is a difficult problem because there are usually many potential solutions with no clearly correct or incorrect answers. This proliferation of answers was seen in the experiment with human classification building presented in section 17.5. The decision about which classification to choose can be based on some perceived set of goals (Medin, Wattenmaker, and Michalski, 1985), a goal-oriented, statistic-based utility function (Rendell, 1983), or some measure of the *quality* of the classification.

One way to measure classification quality that has been successful in both INDUCE/2 and CLUSTER/2 is to define various elementary, easy-to-measure criteria specifying desirable properties of a classification and to assemble them together into one general criterion, called the *Lexicographical Evaluation Functional with tolerances* (LEF) (Michalski, 1980b). Each elementary criterion measures a certain aspect of the generated classifications. Examples of elementary criteria are the relevance of descriptors used in the class descriptions to the general goal, the fit between the classification and the objects, the simplicity of the class descriptions, the number of attributes that singly discriminate among all classes, and the number of attributes necessary to classify the objects into the proposed classes (Michalski and Stepp, 1983b).

The LEF consists of an ordered sequence of elementary criteria along with tolerances that control to what extent different solutions are considered equivalent. First, all classifications are evaluated according to the first elementary criterion. Those that score best or within the given tolerance range from the best are retained. Those retained are then evaluated according to the next elementary criterion, and so on, until either a single classification remains or the list of elementary criteria in the LEF is exhausted. In the latter case, all classifications that remain are judged equal and the algorithm picks one arbitrarily. To control combinatorial explosion, the LEF is also applied during the search process that generates classifications. The LEF provides a powerful heuristic for searching the huge space of hypothetical classifications to find a classification that optimizes several criteria at once.

17.6.3 Using Background Knowledge

Building a meaningful classification relies on finding good classifying attributes (high-level attributes used to define classes). For example, the attribute *is_edible* discussed in section 17.4 is such a high-level classifying attribute. The repeated discrimination and classifying attributes methods, described in sections 17.6.4 and 17.6.5, both use background knowledge in the search for such attributes. The Goal Dependency Network is traversed to find the interactions between the classification goal(s) and the potential descriptors. Background knowledge rules enable the system to perform a chain of inferences to derive values for new descriptors for inclusion in object descriptions. The new descriptors are tested to determine if they make good classifying attributes by applying the LEF to the classification defined by the classifying attribute.

As described in section 17.4, the background knowledge rules can represent both the built-in general-purpose knowledge and the domain-specific knowledge provided by the data analyst. In the latter case, knowledge for generating inferentially derived descriptors is supplied in the form of an inference rule (called a background rule, or *b-rule*). Special types of b-rules include expressions of arithmetic relationships (*a*-rules), such as

$$\forall \text{ object, girth(object)} = \text{length(object)} + \text{width(object)}$$

and implicative rules that specify logical relationships (*l*-rules), such as:

$$\forall p1,p2,p3, [\text{above}(p1,p2)][\text{above}(p2,p3)] \Rightarrow [\text{above}(p_1,p_3)]$$

or

$$\forall p_1,p_2,p_3, [\text{mother } (p_1,p_2) \text{ \& } ([\text{mother}(p_2,p_3)] \vee [\text{father}(p_2,p_3)])$$
$$\Leftrightarrow [\text{grandmother}(p_1,p_3)].$$

Each rule is associated with a condition defining the situations to which it is applicable.

17.6.4 Concept Formation by Repeated Discrimination: Method RD

This section explains how a problem of concept formation (here, building a classification) can be solved via a sequence of controlled steps of concept acquisition (learning concepts from examples). We start with a brief description of the program INDUCE/2, which solves concept acquisition tasks involving structured objects.

Given a set of events (by which we mean symbolic descriptions of objects or situations) arranged into two or more classes, INDUCE/2 induces a general description of each class in the form of an annotated predicate calculus expression. First, all events are divided into two sets: set $F1$ of events belonging to the class currently being considered and set $F0$ of events belonging to any other class (counterexamples to set $F1$). One event at a time is selected from set $F1$ (the *seed* event) and a *star* is built that *covers* the seed event *against* all events in set $F0$. The star is the set of all alternative most general descriptions that describe the seed event (and possibly other events from $F1$) and no events from $F0$ (Michalski, 1983; Michalski and Stepp, 1983b).

To control combinatorial explosion, INDUCE/2 determines *bounded* stars rather than complete stars. A bounded star contains only a fixed number of descriptions selected as most promising according to LEF. The highest-rank description in the bounded star is chosen as a part of the solution. The events covered by the resulting description are removed from set $F1$. If any events remain in $F1$, another seed event (from among those not yet covered) is selected and the whole process is repeated. When all events in the set $F1$ have been covered, the solution is complete; it is the disjunction of the descriptions selected in each iteration.

This algorithm for concept acquisition can be adapted for solving classification construction problems. Given a set of unclassified objects, k seed objects are selected randomly and treated as individual representatives of k imaginary classes. The algorithm then generates descriptions of each seed that are maximally general and do not cover any other seed. These descriptions are then used to determine the most representative object in each newly formed class (defined as the set of objects satisfying the class description). The representative objects are used as new seeds for the next iteration. The process stops either when consecutive iterations converge to some stable solution or when a specific number of iterations pass without improving the classification (from the viewpoint of the criterion LEF).

This approach requires the selection of a defined number of representative objects (corresponding to the number of classes). Since the best number of classes to form is usually unknown, two techniques are used: (1) varying the number of classes and (2) composing the classes hierarchically.

Since the classification to be formed should be simple and easy to understand, the number of classes that stem from any node of the classification hierarchy was assumed to be in the range of two to seven. Since this range is small, it is computationally feasible to repeat the whole process for every number in this range. The solution that optimizes the score on the LEF (with appropriate adjustment for the effect of the number of classes on the score) indicates the best number of classes to form at this level of the hierarchy.

The above idea of repeated discrimination for performing concept acquisition has been implemented in the program CLUSTER/2 for a subset of annotated predicate calculus involving only attributes (zero-argument functions). Besides its relative computational simplicity, this approach has other advantages stemming from descriptions (for both objects and classes) that are quantifier free. Specifically, it should be noted that classifications normally have the property that they can unambiguously classify any object into its corresponding class. To have this property, the class descriptions must be mutually disjoint.

For conjunctive descriptions involving relations on attribute/value pairs, the disjointness property is easy to test and easy to maintain. For the larger subset of APC involving existentially quantified variables, predicates on these variables, and function/value relationships over quantified variables, the test for mutual disjointness of descriptions and the maintenance of disjointness are difficult. As a result of this difficulty, the approach taken for concept acquisition from structured objects involves two processing steps. The first step, using algorithms of INDUCE/2, finds an optimized characteristic generalization of the entire collection of events and then applies it to generate a quantifier-free description of each object (a vector of attribute values). The second step processes the quantifier-free object descriptions with the

CLUSTER/2 algorithm to form optimized classifications. These two processes are combined in the program CLUSTER/S.

A characteristic generalization expresses a common substructure in all structured objects that facilitates the binding of a subset of the free variables (representing object parts) to specific parts. That portion of the structure of each object that is described by the characteristic generalization is called the *core* of each object. With corresponding parts identified in all objects, the cores may be described by a vector of attribute values. Thus the descriptions of object cores need neither quantified variables nor multiplace predicates in their descriptions (i.e., such descriptions can be handled by the CLUSTER/2 program).

It is recognized that structural differences between objects would be lost by the above approach since it focuses on the *common* substructure found in all given objects. To retain some unique structural features of individual objects, an inspection is made of the connections between object subparts within the core and object subparts outside the core. New predicates are automatically generated and added to object descriptions to denote the attachment of different kinds of additional structures to the core of each object.

The descriptions of each substructure connected to the cores of objects are collected and classified by recursive application of the conjunctive conceptual clustering procedure. The resulting types of substructures are given labels (e.g., a unique class number) which are used in the generated predicates that show *what* kind of additional structure is attached *where* to the core structure. The final object descriptions contain attributes for core parts and predicates denoting the kind of attached substructures, as well as derived descriptors for both core subparts and the object as a whole. After this transformation, objects are describable (with reduced detail) by attribute vectors.

The following extension of the trains problem will further illustrate the use of a GDN and problem-specific background knowledge. Suppose that the knowledge base includes an inference rule that can identify trains carrying toxic chemicals. Suppose also that the general goal *survive* has a subordinate goal to *monitor dangerous shipments*. The additional background knowledge can be used to help build a classification.

In the illustrations of the trains a toxic chemical container will be identified as a single sphere (circle) riding in an open-top car. The logical inference rule (*l*-rule) supplied to CLUSTER/S is

[contains(trains,car)][car-shape(car) = opentop]
[cargo-shape(car) = circle][items-carried(car) = 1]
   ⇔ [has_toxic_chemicals(train)]

In the above rule, equivalence is used to indicate that the negation of the condition part is sufficient to assert the negative of the consequence part. After this rule is applied, all trains will have descriptions containing either the toxic-chemical predicate or its negation. The characteristic description generated by CLUSTER/S will now contain the additional predicate *has_toxic_chemicals(train)* or its negation.

In the GDN we find the main goal *survive* and a chain of subordinate goals beginning with *be safe* and *monitor dangerous shipments*. Two additional subgoals are *monitor chemicals shipments* and *monitor toxic chemicals shipments*. Attached to these nodes are relevant attributes such as *is_explosive, is_radioactive, is_flammable, is_corrosive, has_toxic_chemicals*, and so on. The GDN is illustrated in figure 17.9. The GDN signals the relevancy of these descriptors to the goal *survive*. Assuming that this goal takes precedence over the goal *find simple visual patterns*, classifications that make use of the *has_toxic_chemicals* descriptor in formulating conceptual classes score higher than those that use descriptors. The classification produced in this case is shown in figure 17-10.

17.6.5 Concept Formation by Finding Classifying Attributes: Method CA

This section describes another approach for building classifications called *classifying attributes* (briefly, CA). This approach attempts to find one or more *classifying* attributes whose value sets can be split into ranges that define individual classes. The important aspect of this approach is that the classifying attribute can be derived through a goal-directed chain of inferences from the initial attributes. The

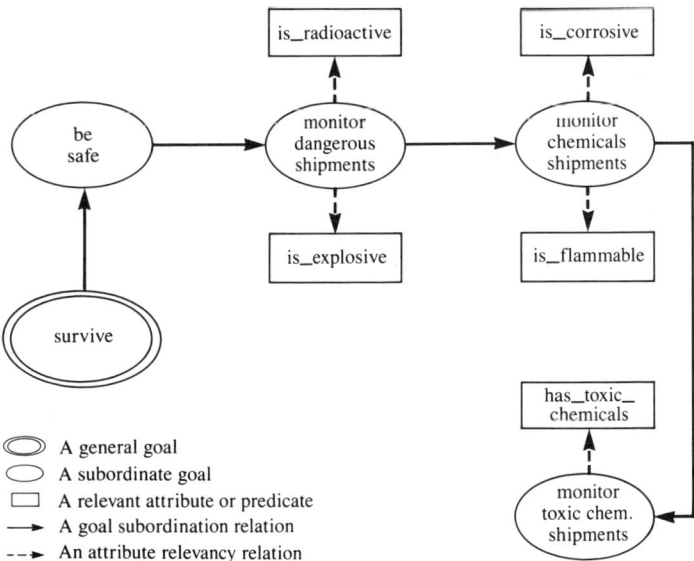

Figure 17-9: A hypothetical GDN for dangerous train shipments.

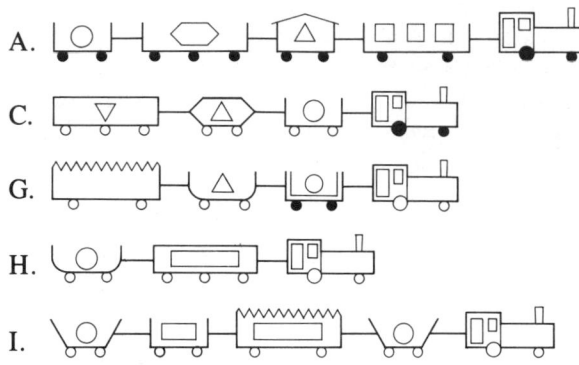

"These trains are carrying toxic chemicals."

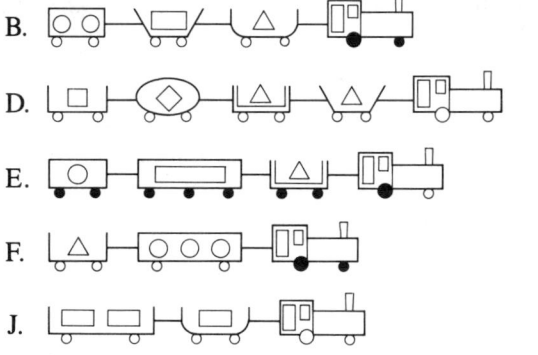

"These trains are not carrying toxic chemicals."

Figure 17-10: A classification produced using the *toxic chemicals* inference rule.

classifying attributes sought are the ones that lead to classes of objects that are best according to the classification goal.

The promise of a descriptor to serve as a classifying attribute is determined by consulting the GDN and by considering how many other descriptors it implies. For example, if the goal of the classification described in section 17.4 is *finding food*, the attribute *edibility* might be a classifying attribute. The second way of determining the promise of an attribute can be illustrated by the problem of classifying birds. The question of whether *color* is a more important classifying attribute than *is_waterbird* is answered in favor of *is_waterbird*, because the latter implicatively leads to more implied attributes than does the attribute *color* in a given GDN network (e.g., *is_waterbird* implies *can_swim, has_webbed_feet, eats_fish,* and so on) (Medin, 1982).

There are two fundamental processes that operate alternately to generate the classification. The first process SEARCH searches for the classifying attribute whose value set can be partitioned to form classes such that the produced classification scores best according to the LEF. The second process GENERATE generates new descriptors by a chain of inferences using two forms of background knowledge rules: logical implicative rules (l-rules) and arithmetic rules (a-rules). Descriptors that can be inferred are ordered by relevancy indicated by the GDN and the goals of the classification.

SEARCH can be performed in two ways. When the number of classes to form (k) is known in advance, the process searches for attributes having k or more different values in the descriptions of the objects to be classified. These values are called the *observed values* of the attribute. Attributes with the number of observed values smaller than k are not considered. For attributes with observed value sets larger than k, the choice of the mapping of value subsets to classes depends on the resulting LEF score for the classification produced and the type of the value set. When the number of classes to form is not known, the above technique is performed for a range of values of k. The best number of classes is indicated by the classification that is best according to the LEF.

GENERATE constructs new attributes from combinations of existing attributes. Certain heuristics of attribute construction are used to guide the process. For example, two attributes that have linearly ordered value sets can be combined using arithmetic operators. When the attributes have numerical values (as opposed to symbolic values such as *small, medium,* and *large*), a trend analysis can be used to suggest appropriate arithmetic operators, as in the BACON system (see chap. 16). Predicates can be combined by logical operators to form new attributes through l-rules. For example, a rule that says an animal is a reptile if it is cold-blooded and lays eggs can be written in APC as

$$[\text{cold-blooded}(a1)][\text{offspring birth}(a1) = \text{egg}] \Rightarrow [\text{animal-type}(a1) = \text{reptile}].$$

The application of this rule to the given animal descriptions yields the new attribute *animal-type* with the specified value *reptile.* Using this rule and similar ones, one might classify some animals into reptiles, mammals, and birds even though the type of each animal is not stated in the original data.

17.7 SUMMARY

This chapter has discussed the problem of building classifications of structured objects using goal-directed inferences from background knowledge. Two methods for performing this task were described. The first method, RD (repeated discrimination), transforms concept formation into a sequence of concept acquisition tasks. The second method, CA (classifying attributes), forms classes by generating new descriptors using a chain of inferences and testing them as candidate classifying criteria. The criterion selected is the one that partitions the set of events in the way most preferred according to a Lexicographical Evaluation Functional (LEF).

The classifying attributes are generated with the aid of a Goal Dependency Network, which relates goals to subgoals and to relevant attributes. The ability to incorporate domain-specific background knowledge in the form of inference rules and Goal Dependency Networks adds a new dimension to the process of concept formation and data analysis.

This work could be further extended through the investigation of alternative representations for describing classes in a classification. These could include the use of logical operators such as implication, equivalence, and exception in a class description. The exception operator appears to be especially interesting because of its frequent use by people. Exception clauses in logical rules can be introduced by using *unless* conditions to handle the cases that are not frequent or ordinary (see chap. 3).

Another extension of this work could be the development of a system capable of characterizing a collection of observations (facts, events, and so on) not just by a hierarchy of concepts but by a *concept network*, in which nodes represent conceptual classes and links represent various relations among them. In the kind of hierarchy considered here, any two generated concepts are related by the relation *is a generalization of* or *is a specialization of* or *is a disjoint of.* In a concept network (a form of semantic network) a much larger set of relations would be allowed.

ACKNOWLEDGMENTS

This research was done in part at the Department of Computer Science Artificial Intelligence Laboratory at the University of Illinois and in part at the Artificial Intelligence Laboratory at the Massachusetts Institute of Technology. Support for the University of Illinois Laboratory is provided in part by grants from the National Science Foundation under grant No. NSF DCR 84-06801 and the Office of Naval Research under grant No. N00014-82-K-0185. Support for the Massachusetts Institute of Technology Laboratory is provided in part by the Advanced Research Projects Agency of the U.S. Department of Defense under the Office of Naval Research contract number N00014-80-C-0505.

The authors wish to thank Tom Mitchell at Rutgers University and Larry Rendell at the University of Illinois for remarks and criticisms on earlier versions of the manuscript. They also thank Peter Andreae at the Massachusetts Institute of Technology Artificial Intelligence Laboratory and Doug Medin at the University of Illinois Department of Psychology for useful discussions and valuable comments.

References

Anderberg, M. R., *Cluster Analysis for Applications,* Academic Press, New York, 1973.

Burstein, M. H., "Concept Formation by Incremental Analogical Reasoning and Debugging," chap. 13 of this volume, 1985.

Carbonell, J. G., "Derivational Analogy in Problem Solving and Knowledge Acquisition," *Proceedings of the International Machine Learning Workshop,* R. S. Michalski (Ed.), Allerton House, University of Illinois at Urbana-Champaign, pp. 12–18, June 22–24, 1983. (An updated version of this paper appears as chap. 14 of this volume.)

DeJong, G., "Generalizations Based on Explanations," *Proceedings of the Seventh IJCAI,* Vancouver, B.C., pp. 67–69, 1981.

————, "An Approach to Learning from Observation,"chap. 19 of this volume, 1986.

Dietterich, T. G., and Michalski, R. S., "A Comparative Review of Selected Methods for Learning from Examples," in *Machine Learning: An Artificial Intelligence Approach,* R. S. Michalski, J. G. Carbonell, and T. M. Mitchell (Eds.), Tioga, Palo Alto, Calif., 1983.

Hoff, W., Michalski, R. S., and Stepp, R., "INDUCE/2: A Program for Learning Structural Descriptions from Examples," Technical Report No. UIUCDCS-F-83-904, Department of Computer Science, University of Illinois at Urbana-Champaign, 1983.

Langley, P.; Zytkow, J.; Simon, H. A.; and Bradshaw, G. L., "The Search for Regularity: Four Aspects of Scientific Discovery," chap. 16 of this volume, 1986.

Lingle, J. H., Altom, M. W., and Medin, D. L., "Of Cabbages and Kings: Assessing the Extendibility of Natural Object Concept Models to Social Things," in *Handbook on Social Cognition,* R. Wyer, T. Srull, and J. Hortwick (Eds.), Erlbaum, Hillsdale, N.J., 1983.

Medin, D. L., "Structural Principles in Categorization," in *The Developments of Perception and Cognition,* T. Tighe, B. Shepp, H. Pick (Eds.), Erlbaum, Hillsdale, N.J., 1982.

Medin, D. L., Wattenmaker, W. S., and Michalski, R. S., "Constraints in Inductive Learning: An Experimental Study Comparing Human and Machine Performance," submitted to *Cognitive Science,* 1985.

Michalski, R. S., "Knowledge Acquisition Through Conceptual Clustering: A Theoretical Framework and an Algorithm for Partitioning Data into Conjunctive Concepts," *Policy Analysis and Information Systems,* Vol. 4, No. 3, pp. 219–44, 1980a.

————, "Pattern Recognition as Rule-Guided Inductive Inference," *IEEE Transactions on Pattern Analysis and Machine Intelligence,* Vol. PAMI-2, No. 4., pp. 349–61, July 1980b.

————, "A Theory and Methodology of Inductive Learning," in *Machine Learning: An Artificial Intelligence Approach,* R. S. Michalski, J. G. Carbonell, and T. M. Mitchell (Eds.), Tioga, Palo Alto, Calif., 1983.

Michalski, R. S., and Larson, J. B., "Inductive Inference of VL Decision Rules," Paper presented at Workshop in Pattern-Directed Inference Systems, Hawaii, May 1977. (Published in *SIGART Newsletter,* ACM, No. 63, pp. 38–44, June 1977.)

Michalski, R. S., and Stepp, R. E., "Automated Construction of Classifications: Conceptual Clustering versus Numerical Taxonomy," *IEEE Transactions on Pattern Analysis and Machine Intelligence,* Vol. PAMI-5, No. 4, pp. 396–410, July 1983a.

————, "Learning from Observation: Conceptual Clustering," in *Machine Learning: An Artificial Intelligence Approach,* R. S. Michalski, J. G. Carbonell, and T. M. Mitchell (Eds.), Tioga, Palo Alto, Calif., 1983b.

Mitchell, T. M., and Keller, R. M., "Goal Directed Learning," *Proceedings of the 2nd International Machine Learning Workshop,* R. S. Michalski (Ed.), Allerton House, University of Illinois at Urbana-Champaign, June 22–24, 1983.

Rendell, L. A., "Toward a Unified Approach for Conceptual Knowledge Acquisition," *AI Magazine,* Winter 1983.

Stepp, R. E., "Conjunctive Conceptual Clustering: A Methodology and Experimentation," Ph.D. diss., Department of Computer Science, University of Illinois at Urbana-Champaign, 1984.

Winston, P. H., *Artificial Intelligence,* Addison-Wesley, Reading, Mass., 1984.

————, "Learning by Augmenting Rules and Accumulating Censors," chap. 3 of this volume, 1985.

18

PROGRAM SYNTHESIS AS A THEORY FORMATION TASK:

Problem Representations and Solution Methods

Saul Amarel
Rutgers University

Abstract

This chapter is concerned with theory formation processes in the context of a program synthesis task. The problem is to synthesize a program, in a given programming language, that satisfies a given set of input-output data associations. The input-output associations are drawn from some data space, whereas the possible solutions/programs (i.e., the programming language) define a program space. Several different formulations of the theory formation problem are presented that impact the difficulty of solving the problem. The movement to more effective problem formulations involves structuring the program space in a way that facilitates the establishment of links to data space and an increase in the amount of reasoning that takes place in data space. The use of models (algebraic and geometric) was found to be essential in the reasoning that takes place in the more effective problem formulations.

Three main procedural formulations are discussed, two of which were developed in previous work. One is based on heuristic hill climbing in program space. The second is more goal oriented and involves "navigating" in program space under the guidance of an algebraic model. The third formulation, a more recent one, is based on detailed reasoning in data space. Two methods are presented in connection with this third formulation: a combination method and an elimination method. When the reasoning is shifted toward the data space, several interesting domain-dependent problems of concept specialization and generalization are encountered. Basic AI issues that are identified and on which more work is needed include formation of macromoves in "appropriate" representations of program space and data space; development of methods for combining "partially correct" programs and for modifying "almost correct" programs; and exploration of the interplay between choosing a domain for which to construct a theory and the formation of an "interesting" theory for that domain.

18.1 INTRODUCTION: MOTIVATION AND ASSUMPTIONS

The main objective of this research is to understand theory formation processes and to develop effective methods of mechanizing them. A secondary objective is to develop approaches for the design of certain automatic program synthesis systems. In particular, situations are considered in which functional properties of a computer program are specified in the form of explicit input-output associations, and the problem is to synthesize a program, in a given programming language, that satisfies the given associations. Although this is a rather uncommon formulation of realistic program synthesis problems, it provides an excellent task environment for the study of certain types of theory formation processes.

There is another, more fundamental objective that motivates this work. Theory formation processes are central to an understanding of the *problem of representation in problem solving;* this problem has been recognized by now as being of basic importance to AI (Newell, 1969; Amarel, 1970). The questions of how to choose an appropriate problem formulation and how to change it to fit the special characteristics of a task are at the heart of this problem. One of the ways in which the study of theory formation processes contributes to our understanding of these questions of representational choice is simply by the fact that it adds to our corpus of knowledge in this area *another important case* of a problem solving situation in which the nature of relationships between alternative problem formulations and problem solving efficiency has been examined in some depth. In previous work, the author analyzed several cases of problem solving activity in specific domains in an attempt to elucidate issues of choice of formulation and mechanisms for shifting from one formulation to another. The focus of most of this work has been on derivation problems (Amarel, 1968, 1981). This chapter concentrates on a similar analysis of alternative representations of a formation problem. The emphasis is on the various bodies of knowledge that are associated with different formulations of the problem and on the various ways in which this knowledge can be used in problem solving. Of special interest in the present case is the use of models in guiding the formation process. It is also important to know whether there are any substantial differences between the mechanisms that are needed for shifting between formulations of theory formation problems and the mechanisms that mediate shifts between formulations of other types of problems.

The latter question is of special significance in light of recent studies of *expertise acquisition* via shifts in problem representation (Amarel, 1982) that suggest the following: *The ability to shift problem representations in an "appropriate" direction requires theory formation capabilities for discovering "interesting" regularities in some body of problem solving experience and program synthesis capabilities for exploiting these regularities in the development of specialized, high-performance procedures.*

But theory formation and program synthesis problems face representation problems themselves as questions of improving their performance arise. Shifts in representation may be required to improve theory formation processes, and theory formation processes may be required in turn to effect these shifts, and so on. It is important to recognize and to clarify these relationships. The first step is to recognize the centrality of theory formation processes to the task of mechanizing shifts between problem formulations and to focus not only on the development of effective schemes for theory formation but also on the study of "first-order" mechanisms for improving theory formation schemes via shifts in representation.

It has been clear for some time that progress is needed in various aspects of theory formation processes—conceptual approaches as well as specific design techniques—if AI applications are to be developed that will have serious impact on the "doing of science." However, progress in this area has been slow. The main development during the seventies, which was most promising in terms of exploration of AI ideas in the context of an empirical science application, was the Meta-DENDRAL project at Stanford (Lindsay et al., 1980). The work on BACON at Carnegie-Mellon (Langley, Bradshaw, and Simon, 1983) and Lenat's work on AM and EURISCO (Davis and Lenat, 1982) are more recent contributions to theory formation. These projects are introducing promising new ideas into this area of study, and they are providing a certain momentum in this field that is important to maintain.

In general, theory formation involves both the *choice of a domain of phenomena* that are to be expressed within some conceptual framework *and* the *finding of an expression within the framework* for explaining/defining the domain. The interplay between domain choice and the formulation of a theory for the domain is an interesting and complex process that is difficult to capture at present. At this stage of knowledge of theory formation, it is useful to focus attention on each of these parts separately and to gain some insight into the nature of dependencies between them. This is the approach taken in the work presented here.

More specifically, it is assumed that the initial statement of the theory formation problem includes a fundamental *supposition* about the domain of the theory, namely, that the elements of the domain are to be considered as belonging to a distinct class for which a theory, within the given conceptual framework, can be constructed. The supposition can be regarded as an exploratory one—to be confirmed or denied. The effort to find a coherent theory for the given domain can be seen as an attempt to validate the supposition. Only in the course of this attempt may it be possible to find out whether changes should be made to the supposition and what they may be. The process of setting and resetting the domain of a theory is closely related to *concept discovery processes.* These processes are discussed below in the context of certain knowledge-rich formulations of the theory formation problem.

A theory in an empirical science is *about a domain of phenomena,* and it has the function of an intellectual mechanism for explaining and predicting in that domain of the science. The *form* of the theory that can emerge in a scientific culture depends on the basic concepts, the languages, and the schemas/paradigms that are available in the culture. There is a strong analogy between this situation and the process of trying to synthesize a computer program that can embody a given set of data associations in terms of a programming language that the computer can effectively use. If as a result of such an effort a program is obtained that "satisfies" all the data associations that are given up to a certain point in time, then the program is considered to be *acceptable.* If a new set of associations is presented, then the program might still be acceptable or it might not be. In the latter case, the problem is how to modify the previous program in order to attain a new program that is acceptable over the new extended domain. It may be extremely difficult to accommodate the domain extensions within a single program/theory. In such a case it would be appropriate to consider partitioning the problem into subdomains for each of which acceptable programs can be obtained within certain bounds of available effort.

The question of whether a given program that is known to satisfy a subdomain of some domain will be able to satisfy extensions of the subdomain is of importance to *inductive logic* but *not to AI.* What matters from the point of view of AI is to create and study schemes whose behavior is that of a theoretician who seeks to integrate all current evidence in a certain domain within a theory that he invented, and whose distinguishing characteristics is that he never "leaves the game" despite evidence refuting his previous theory, but he attempts to construct new theories that would accommodate the new evidence.

In accordance with this view, the problem of program formation can be characterized as a *constraint satisfaction* problem. A finite set of functional conditions is imposed on a desired structure, and the problem is to synthesize the structure using a specified repertoire of construction material and assembly techniques. In this case, functional conditions are in the form of data associations that the desired theory/program must satisfy, and the set of possible solution structures is defined in terms of a language of programs.

The problem faced here is how to search in the given language of programs for a program that satisfies the constraints imposed by the given set of data associations. The constraints are presented in a *data space,* and the possible solutions are presented in a *program space;* furthermore, the initial body of available knowledge is not in a form that permits the establishment of useful links between the two spaces. Thus this is a characteristic *problem of formation* (Amarel, 1970). In problems of this type, the solution process cannot proceed through the use of reasoning from the problem constraints to specific parts of possible solutions. The bulk of search is being done in program space, where candidate solutions are generated, and the data is used mainly to *test* the solution candidates. If the power of the process is to be increased, it is essential that the a priori control that problem constraints—that is, the data associations—can have on the generation of candidate programs also be increased. This requires the development of strong links between data space and program space, as well as a strategy for good coordination between the search/reasoning activities in the two spaces. The significance of the two-space model for the studying of problems of theory formation is discussed in detail by Simon and Lea (Simon and Lea, 1974).

In this chapter several formulations of a specific program formation problem are presented. The movement to formulations of higher effectiveness involves the structuring of program space in such a way that links with data space are facilitated, *and* the amount of reasoning that takes place in data space is increased. The role of models (algebraic, geometric) is extremely important in the stronger problem formulations. Three main approaches to the problem are discussed. The first approach, developed about twenty years ago (Amarel, 1962a, 1962b) is based on heuristic hill climbing in program space. The second approach, developed in the early seventies (Amarel, 1971), is more goal oriented and involves searching the program space under the guidance of an algebraic model. Work on the third approach is more recent and is based on detailed reasoning in data space. Two methods are presented for using the results of the detailed analysis of individual data associations in the construction of a program/solution for the entire domain. The first is a combination method in which it is crucial to have effective techniques of program modification in order to proceed to a successful assembly of a solution. The second is a method of elimination that can be seen as a variant of the "version space" approach to learning (Mitchell, 1978). If a geometric representation of data space is introduced, it is possible to move to a very strong formulation of the formation problem in which a small set of macro-moves and of well-chosen intermediate concepts provides the basis for highly effective ways of constructing solutions. In the following sections, the first two approaches to the formation problem will be briefly described, and the third approach and the relationships among the approaches will be more fully discussed.

Before the detailed discussion is begun, a word about the choice of domain is in order. The tasks considered are in the relatively simple mathematical area of finite, partially ordered structures. This area has proven to be an excellent environment in which certain *essential aspects* of program formation problems can be studied. Since an important objective of this work is to analyze *various approaches* to the same problem and to identify the effects of representational changes on performance, it is necessary to keep the problem domain as stable as possible. Thus no effort was made to "diversify" the domain over the various stages of work in this area. The initial choice of domain was much influenced by Piaget's work (Piaget, 1936, 1952) on the mental development of children. As suggested by Piaget's theory, the next stage of development after that involving the classification of concrete objects into sets and the formation of relational concepts is that involving the formation of algebraic structures—in particular, those related to the propositional calculus. Thus the initial choice of domain and the specific assumptions about the task environment were intended to provide a setting for an exploration of the mechanization of this stage of development. From the present perspective it is now clear that the difficulty of mechanizing this stage of development was greatly underestimated twenty years ago, although it is probably easier to approach this task now. In any event, even though the original reason for choosing the domain is largely irrelevant now, this domain can still be used fruitfully in the exploration of theory formation processes in program synthesis.

18.2 A CLASS OF PROGRAM FORMATION PROBLEMS: INITIAL STAGES OF PROBLEM FORMULATION

Let us suppose that a problem solver[1] with a given (limited) knowledge of sets, elementary relations, and programming is presented with the following statement of a *problem* π_1 (see figure 18-1):

> *Given* (1) a database in the form of a finite, partially ordered structure $\Sigma_1 = (\sigma_1, I, E)$, where σ_1 is a set of five elements, I is a proper inclusion relation defined for

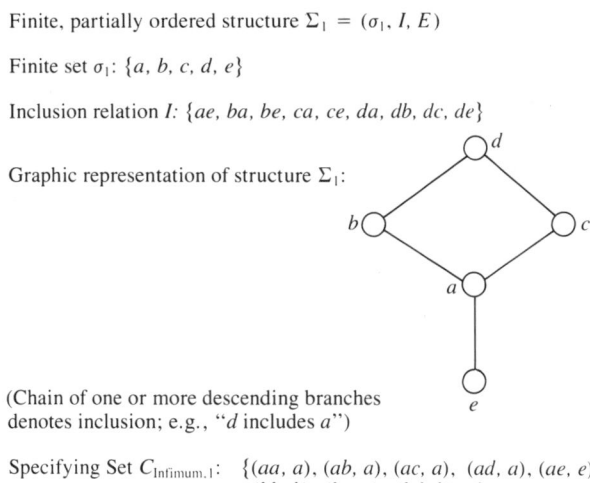

Finite, partially ordered structure $\Sigma_1 = (\sigma_1, I, E)$

Finite set σ_1: $\{a, b, c, d, e\}$

Inclusion relation I: $\{ae, ba, be, ca, ce, da, db, dc, de\}$

Graphic representation of structure Σ_1:

(Chain of one or more descending branches denotes inclusion; e.g., "d includes a")

Specifying Set $C_{\text{Infimum.1}}$: $\{(aa, a), (ab, a), (ac, a), (ad, a), (ae, e),$
$(bb, b), (bc, a), (bd, b), (be, e), (cc, c),$
$(cd, c), (ce, e), (dd, d), (de, e), (ee, e)\}$

Figure 18-1: Data for program formation problem π_1.

---

all the elements of σ_1, and E is the equality relation); (2) a language for specifying programs, in which input values for the programs can be taken from σ_1, and the language can handle at the basic level set operations and the relations I, E, and the converse of I (called "is-included-by" and denoted by $\hat{I}$); and (3) a finite set of associations (Called the specifying set $C_{\text{Infimum},1}$) between pairs of elements of the set σ_1 and elements of the same set.

Find a simple program in the given language of programs that computes the right side of an association from its left side for each of the associations in the given specifying set.

In essence, the problem solver is asked to *discover an effective procedure* for assigning to each left side of a given association its specified right hand and to express this procedure as a program in the given program language. Another view is that he is asked to *form a theory* that explains the given set of associations in terms of the concept in the program language.

The set of associations is a specification of the *Infimum* function, explicitly defined for the partially ordered structure. Thus the task of the problem solver is to discover a program for computing the Infimum in the given finite structure. The program sought can also be seen as a theory for the given set of associations.

The requirement that the solution to the problem be simple can be easily appreciated in the theory formation context. The more simple a theory is, the easier it is to test it and use it. More importantly, a simple theory is more manageable when it has to be analyzed and modified, that is, when it has to be "debugged." And it should be recalled that the bulk of the process of theory formation consists of debugging.

In order to proceed with the solution of the problem, the problem solver must recognize it as a member of a *problem class* for which he has available one or more problem solving schemas. Such recognition leads to an internal formulation that represents an *assimilation of the problem* by the problem solver; that is, the problem solver "understands" the problem and knows *what to do* with it.

The formulation of a *problem class* in declarative form can be presented in general as a 4-tuple (Amarel, 1982)

$$(D, X, C, \Delta),$$

where D is the *domain specification* (i.e., a body of knowledge within which problems in the class are conceptualized and handled); X is the set of *possible solutions; C* specifies the type of *problem conditions* that are characteristic of problems in the class; and Δ is a *problem-data domain*. Each element in Δ represents specific problem data that identify an individual problem in the class. Thus a *specific problem* in the class can be formulated by providing (1) the class formulation, that is, the above 4-tuple, and (2) the specific problem-data, that is, an element in Δ that identifies the problem. A solution to the problem must be an element of X that satisfies the class conditions C as specialized by the individual problem-data.

Let us consider now an initial declarative formulation F_{d1} for a class of program formation problems in which it is assumed that the problem π_1 is embedded.

18.2.1 Initial Declarative Problem Formulation

18.2.1.1 Initial Domain Specification D_1

The specification of a domain includes descriptions of concepts in the domain and of relationships among them. It is assumed that D_1 has at its *basic level* the following concepts: sets, relations, functions; predicates of set membership, set inclusion, and set equality, as well as predicates for testing whether a set is empty or is a singleton; set operations of union, intersection, and complementation; relational operations of disjunction, conjunction, product, converse-of, and negation; and properties of these concepts.

In addition to its basic concepts, it is assumed that D_1 has some knowledge of the concept of a *finite, partially ordered structure* Σ. In particular a definition of finite, partially ordered structures is assumed to exist in terms of basic concepts in D_1, and the problem solver is assumed to be currently engaged in an *exploration* of key properties of these structures (Infimum, Supremum, and their relationships). Actually, the problem π_1 can be seen as part of this exploration; and eventually a solution to π_1 and to related problems can be expected to add procedural definitions of the "Infimum" concept to the domain. More specifically, the problem solver is assumed to be now at a stage of trying to define operationally the concepts of Infimum and Supremum in terms of the inclusion relation and its properties. This is a task that has both mathematical significance (Birkhoff and MacLane, 1953) and psychological significance (Piaget, 1952).

A finite, partially ordered structure is a tuple $\Sigma = (\sigma, I, E)$, where σ is a finite set of n elements, I is a proper inclusion relation (dyadic, antisymmetric, transitive) defined over σ, and E is the equality relation for elements of σ. Partial orderings are extremely important mathematical concepts. Boolean algebras, the system of all subgroups of a finite group, and finite sets of positive integers under the divisibility relation are examples of such structures. Many information structures handled in computers can also be seen as partially ordered structures.

For any inclusion relation I, a new relation I_ℓ (for local inclusion) may be defined, such that $bI_\ell a$ (read, b includes-locally a) if bIa (i.e., b includes a) and there is no x such that bIx and xIa. The term used commonly for the concept of "local-includes" is *covers*. Now, finite, partially ordered structures may be represented in graphic form by diagrams of the type shown in figure 18-1. In such diagrams, each element of σ is represented by a node so placed that the node for b is *above* the node for a if bIa, and there is a descending branch from b to a in case that $bI_\ell a$. It can be established that the relation bIa holds from the diagram if it is possible to climb from a to b along an ascending chain in the diagram. The diagram shown in figure 18-2

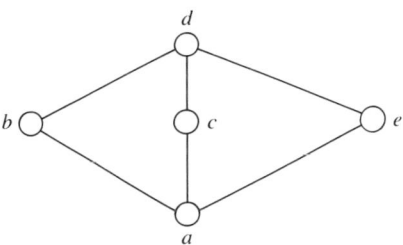

Figure 18-2: Example of a five-element, partially ordered structure.

represents a second example of a finite, partially ordered structure with five elements that defines the structure of all subgroups of the four-group.

The geometric representation is shown here *for convenience of exposition.* It is not assumed that the concept of local inclusion or the geometric representation of finite partially ordered structures is part of the D_1 that is available to the problem solver in the initial stages of his solution-finding activity. However, as will be seen later, the geometric representation of partially ordered structures plays an important role in the formulation of certain strong methods of program formation in the present domain.

Relative to the given finite, partially ordered structure, there are in D_1 three types of *data objects:*

u-type: These are elements of σ.
(They are implementable as LISP atoms.)

q-type: These are elements of 2^σ, that is, they are subsets of σ.
(They are implementable as lists of atoms without repetition.)

g-type: These are bags whose elements are of *q*-type.
(They are implementable as lists of lists.)

A *computational action* can be defined as a transition between one or more data objects (the input of the action) and some other data object (the output of the action). Such an action can be seen as the application of a basic function on specified input data. As will be seen below, computational actions provide the atomic elements (the vocabulary) for the language of constructible programs. The computational actions in D_1 can be conveniently represented in the form of special simple graphs.

The data objects are represented as nodes of various types. Data of *u*-type are represented by $\bigcirc$; of *q*-type by $|$; and of *g*-type by $|\,|$.

The available computational actions are shown in figures 18-3, 18-4, and 18-5.

Each of these special graphs represents a process that when executed, transforms the data at the left of the arrow to the right in accordance with the function that labels the graph.

Figure 18-3: The leftmost graph stands for the functional expression $\eta(u) = q$, where η denotes a function that corresponds to the relation I in the following way: If a is the value of the argument u, then q is the set of all elements x in σ for which aIx holds. Its LISP representation is

> (lambda (u) (I-function u)),

where I-function is the LISP function corresponding to η. Similarly, the LISP representation of the $\hat{\eta}$ computational action is (lambda (u) (Icap-function u)), where Icap-function is the LISP function corresponding to $\hat{\eta}$, and $\hat{\eta}$ corresponds to $\hat{I}$ in a manner similar to the correspondence between η and I. The LISP representation of the ϵ computational action is (lambda (u) (E-function u)), where E-function corresponds to ϵ, and it returns for an input u the list (u) that represents the singleton $\{u\}$.

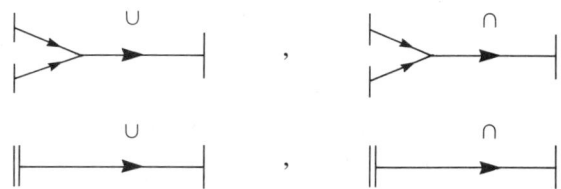

Figure 18-4: The upper two graphs denote the union and intersection functions over two sets. In the bottom graphs, union and intersection are defined as iterative operations over any number of sets that are contained in an input bag.

Figure 18-5: These graphs stand for list-processing functions, in particular, for *selecting* elements from a set (left graph) and for *collecting* elements into a bag (right graph). They will be further defined below in the context of constructible action sequences or programs.

For a given finite, partially ordered structure, the set of all data objects in D_1 and the set of all computational actions define a *data space.* As in all problem solving situations, this is an extremely important concept. Given a set of input data objects and an output data object, the output is *directly obtainable* from the inputs if there exists a computational action that can effect the transition from the given inputs to the output. A *computational path* from a set of input data objects to an output data object is defined as a finite aggregate of computational actions that can effect a transition from the inputs to the output. The notion of a "computational path" is equivalent to the notion of a "computational trace" of a program for given input data.

It is important to stress that the definition of the data space is given *implicitly* in D_1—via the specification of the set of all data objects and the set of computational actions.

18.2.1.2 Specification of the Set X_1 of Problem Solutions—That Is, of the Constructible Programs

In the problem class described here, the possible solutions are *constructible programs*. The set X_1 is the language of constructible programs. The initial definition of the language, which is assumed to be part of the initial declarative problem formulation, is presented in detail in previous work (Amarel, 1971). The main elements of this definition are summarized below.

The language of constructible programs is given in terms of available (permissible) program statements and of conditions for combining such statements into programs.

The set of program statements is identical with the set of basic computational actions defined in D_1. Each program statement can be implemented as a simple LISP function. In this implementation, data of u-type are atoms, data of q-type are lists without repetition, and data of g-type are lists of lists.

Programs can be represented as graphs that are constructed by aggregating program statement graphs in certain ways. This representation is especially suitable for describing (and for reasoning about) the *data flow* in the program. There are two kinds of branches in program graphs: solid branches $\rightarrow$ for the flow of data and dashed branches $\dashrightarrow$ for the flow of control. In most cases, the flow of control can be determined in a straightforward way from the flow of data. Explicit specification of control is needed only when loops involving list-processing statements (selection and collection statements) must be specified. However, the *loop structure* of constructible programs for our problem class is assumed to be severely constrained. Only simple nesting of iterative loops is permitted. A loop has the characteristic structure shown in figure 18-6.

In this structure, p_1 denotes a *program variable* that can take as values programs that have a u-type input and a q-type output. The input to the overall structure is of q-type, and its output is also of q-type. The structure can be regarded as a *loop macrostatement* that does the following: each element of the input q_1 is operated upon by p_1, and the results are collected in a bag g; the output q_o is obtained by applying the specified set operation ($\cup$ or $\cap$) on the elements of g. To clarify further the notion of a loop macrostatement, let us represent it in LISP for a specific assignment of values

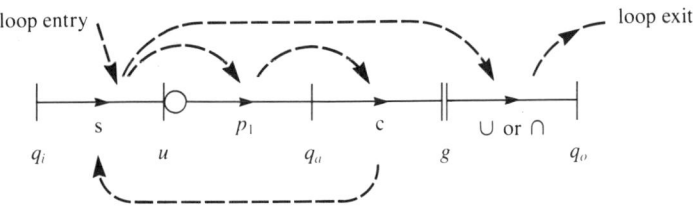

Figure 18-6: Loop structure of constructible programs.

to p_1 and to the set operation. Specifically, let the program P_1 be the value of p_1, and let the set operation be an iterated intersection operation, which will be denoted by Intersection-*. The LISP function Intersection-* takes as input a list of lists in which the lists stand for sets to be intersected and the result is to be returned as an output list. The convention used here for this function is that if the input list is empty, then the output list is also empty; and if the input list has a single list as its element, then this list is the function's output. With these assumptions, a LISP representation of the loop macrostatement is a follows:

```
(lambda (q) (Intersection-* (Mapcar 'P₁ q)))
```

Now consider a set of program statements that is made of loop macrostatements and of the previously specified basic program statements except s-statements and c-statements; let us call this set T_ℓ. Suppose also that the input and output structure of constructible programs is specified; that is, the number and type of input variable and the type of the output variable are given. A program input can be made to correspond to the input of a statement from T_ℓ if their data types match; the same is true for outputs. Further, two statements from T_ℓ can be concatenated if the output type of the first matches the input type of the second.

A constructible program can be defined recursively as a directed graph made of aggregations of statements from T_ℓ that establish some kind of connective tissue between the program input and the output; and furthermore, any loop macrostatement in such a graph can have as values of its program variable only graphs representing constructible programs. It can be seen that a graph representing a constructible program is a data flow graph without loops. This type of graph has been called a *riverlike graph* (Amarel, 1971), because it has the general form of water flow in a river system. In such a system, river channels merge, diverge, and run side by side in a pattern of motions whose general direction is from river sources (the program inputs) to the river mouth (the program output).

It can be shown that riverlike graphs can be partitioned into equivalence classes, each represented by a *decoupled graph* as its normal form representative. In a constructible program that is represented by a decoupled graph, the output variable of a component statement (unless it corresponds to the program output) is used precisely once as an input variable in another statement of the program. Under these conditions, it is possible for the program to specify the same computation more then once if the result of the computation is to be used more than once as input of subsequent computations. Clearly it is possible in this case to simplify the program by eliminating the redundant computations and by using intermediate results more then once. However, for purposes of program synthesis it is more desirable to work with representations in the form of decoupled graphs. It is assumed therefore, that the specification of the set X_1 of constructible programs amounts to a characterization of the set of decoupled riverlike graphs that are made from elements (program statements) taken from the set T_ℓ. Note that the specification of X_1 is not in a generative form. Membership in X_1 can be determined by *testing* whether a given candidate graph satisfies the required conditions. Further, associated with X_1 are procedures for expanding a riverlike graph that is not decoupled into a functionally equivalent decoupled form and for simplifying decoupled graphs.

Clearly there is a connection between the notion of a constructible program and that of a computational path, which was introduced as part of the domain specification D_1. As indicated previously, each computational trace of a constructible program for any input data is equivalent to a computational path in data space. However, because of some of the constraints imposed on the language of programs, it is not the case that for every computational path in data space there exists a computational trace of a constructible program in X_1.

Now, a member of X_1 is acceptable as a solution to a problem in our class if it satisfies in addition the problem class conditions as specified by the individual problem-data.

18.2.1.3 General Conditions C_1 Imposed on the Problem Class

The conditions C_1 are as follows:

1. Given a "specifying set" in the form of a finite set of associations, where each association has the form (u_1u_2, u_3) and u_1, u_2, u_3 are elements of the set σ of some partially ordered structure Σ. A solution program P must satisfy $P(u_1u_2) = u_3$ for each association in the specifying set.
2. The structure of the program should be the simplest possible. (This will be made clearer below.)

18.2.1.4 Problem-Data Domain Δ_1: Initial Internal Formulation of the Specific Problem π_1

The problem-data domain consists of all the finite, partially ordered structures; and for each structure Σ with a set σ of n elements, it consists of a set of possible associations in the form of pairs (u_1u_2, u_3). The set of possible associations is characterized by a *domain of associations,* which is the set of all the possible left sides in associations, and a *range of associations,* which is the set of all the possible right sides. In the problem class now under consideration, the domain of associations consists of *all unordered pairs* taken from σ. Let us call this domain $d1$. The range of associations is the set σ. Thus the size of the domain set $d1$ is $n(n + 1)/2$, and the size of the range is n.

The problem-data for an individual problem is given by defining a specific structure Σ and a specific "specifying set" of associations. Thus the initial internal formulation of the problem π_1 in declarative form consists of the problem class formulation $(D_1, X_1, C_1, \Delta_1)$, augmented by the specific problem-data that is shown in figure 18-1.

18.2.2 Transforming the Initial Formulation of the Formation Problem into Procedural Form

For a problem solver to proceed with a solution finding/constructing activity, he needs to transform (parts of) the declarative formulation of the problem into *procedural form;* that is, he needs to define a solution construction process that is controlled by the problem formulation. Basically, the problem solver must reformulate knowledge about the problem in a form suitable for defining a generative process for producing candidate solutions. Thus it is of central importance to find ways of describing the language of programs in terms of some *generative grammar.* The choice of a grammar for specifying the language of programs and the development of methods for using such a grammar in theory formation processes have been major components of previous work in this area.

If there is a generative grammar for the language of programs, then a *structural description* can be assigned to each program in the language with respect to the grammar. The structural description would articulate the structure of the program in terms of types of combinations of program statements that are defined in the grammar. The basic approach used here from the early stages of exploration of the program formation problem was to represent and manipulate programs in terms of their structural descriptions. This approach is guided by the expectation that certain regularities exist between features of a structural description of a program and its functional characteristics and also that such regularities can be exploited in the formulation of efficient procedures for search over the program language.

Since there is no unique way of describing the language of programs in terms of a grammar, then the question must be faced of *how to choose an "appropriate" grammar,* that is, a grammar that assigns "appropriate" structural descriptions to programs. Appropriateness here is meant in the sense of leading to the establishment of structure-function regularities that can be fruitfully used in problem solving. The problem of choosing among possible grammars of the language of programs proved to be at the crux of the *problem of representation* in the present formation problem (Amarel, 1970, 1971).

Previous work on the program formation problem resulted in two major approaches to solving the problem. During work with the *first approach* (Amarel, 1962a, 1962b), several grammars were tried and used with varying degrees of success as parts of heuristic "generate-and-test" procedures for solution finding. It became clear very soon that performance was highly sensitive to the choice of program grammar. Small changes in the way of specifying the grammar had strong effects on overall system performance—over a range of parameters of the heuristic search strategy. This experience provided convincing evidence of how central the problem of representation was in the program formation process; and it led to a *second approach* (Amarel, 1971), which concentrated on conditions for choosing a program grammar and—more generally—on ways of formulating a useful concept of *program space.*

A useful definition of program space requires a definition of the set of programs (i.e., of the program language) *and,* in addition, a definition of some relations between programs that can provide *added structure* that can be used for reasoning about program behaviors. When the additional relational structure on the set of programs is defined, additional conditions on how to represent this set are introduced, which amounts to added guidance on the choice of program grammar. In the second approach to the program formation problem, the following condition was used as a guide to the choice of program grammar:

> The grammar should be such that each structural description constructed in the grammar must have an interpretation in a mathematical system in which there exists a structure of relationships that can be used for reasoning about programs in terms of their functional properties.

This condition was satisfied by the construction of an algebraic model of program space in which for each structural description of a program there corresponds an expression in the algebra. The algebraic model will be discussed later. First the program grammar G_1 that was obtained under guidance of the model will be described briefly. (A more detailed description is given in Amarel, 1971.)

Although this is one of several grammars that were used in the past in this research, it illustrates the main characteristics of all the grammars used in the first approach to program formation, and it can be used to describe the strategy of search in that approach. It can also be used to describe the second approach to the problem as well as more recent work with a third approach.

18.2.2.1 The Program Grammar G_1: Structural Descriptions of Programs and Program Schemes

A program grammar can easily embody the part of the declarative problem formulation that specifies the set X_1 of constructible programs, that is, the possible (legal) solutions to the formation problem. In the case described here, a grammar may also be constrained to some (small) extent by the problem class conditions C_1 and by the characteristics of the data domain Δ_1. Specifically, the grammar G_1 is limited to two-input problems where each input accepts data of u-type; it is also limited to programs that treat each input symmetrically; and it assigns to each generated program a measure of structural cost, a weight w, that can be used in handling the condition of program simplicity.

As indicated previously, programs are represented as graphs that obey certain local rules of articulation and that have certain boundary (input-output) characteristics. These graphs can be viewed as analogs of strings in ordinary languages, and they are called *aggregates*. An aggregate is a combination of graph elements each of which can be either a *terminal* or a *nonterminal* in the program grammar: it is assembled in accordance with the *rules of aggregation* in the grammar. These rules are analogs of rules of replacement in grammars of ordinary languages. The grammar has a *starting nonterminal element,* and aggregates can be generated by repeated applications of rules of aggregation starting from the starting element.

An aggregate that consists exclusively of terminal elements is called a *terminal aggregate;* and it represents a completely specified program. The terminal elements of the program grammar G_1 are the *set of computational actions,* represented in graph form, that were defined previously in section 18.2.1.1 as part of the domain specification D_1.

The nonterminal elements of G_1 are the elementary graphs shown in figure 18-7.

The graph at left is called a (u_1u_2, q)-program, and the graph at right is called a (u, q)-program. These nonterminal elements play the usual syntactic role of representatives for program types. In the present grammar, nonterminals classify programs (or part of programs) by their input-output structure. This is a rough characterization that provides necessary conditions for possible connectivities, or compositions, between program parts.

The rules of aggregation of G_1 are shown in figure 18-8. Each rule has a name, a *transition* part, and an associated tree, which is called a *unit of structural description.* The transition part of a rule represents a possible replacement of its left side, that is, of a nonterminal element, by its right side, which is in the form of an aggregate that contains one or more terminal elements. The application of a rule of aggregation amounts to specifying a part of the structure of a graph that represents a program. The *structural description* of a (graph representing a) program consists of the record of rule applications that collectively specify the program (graph). Thus every rule application can be seen as building a piece of structural description, and this is represented by the elementary tree shown in the right side of a rule. In such a tree, the upper node corresponds to the nonterminal element in the left side of the rule's transition; the dark node below it corresponds to the rule name; and nodes below the dark node (if they exist) correspond to the nonterminals in the right side of the rule's transition.

Each rule represents a specific mode of combining nonterminals or the instantiation of a nonterminal by a definite program statement. The name of a rule reflects the specific rule action. For example, $R_{2,\varnothing}$ is a rule that specifies the structure of a two-input program (of a (u_1u_2, q)-type) as being in the form of a cascade of a

Figure 18-7:   Nonterminal elements of G_1.

Rule name
(Least-expected Weight w^*) Transition Unit of Structural Description

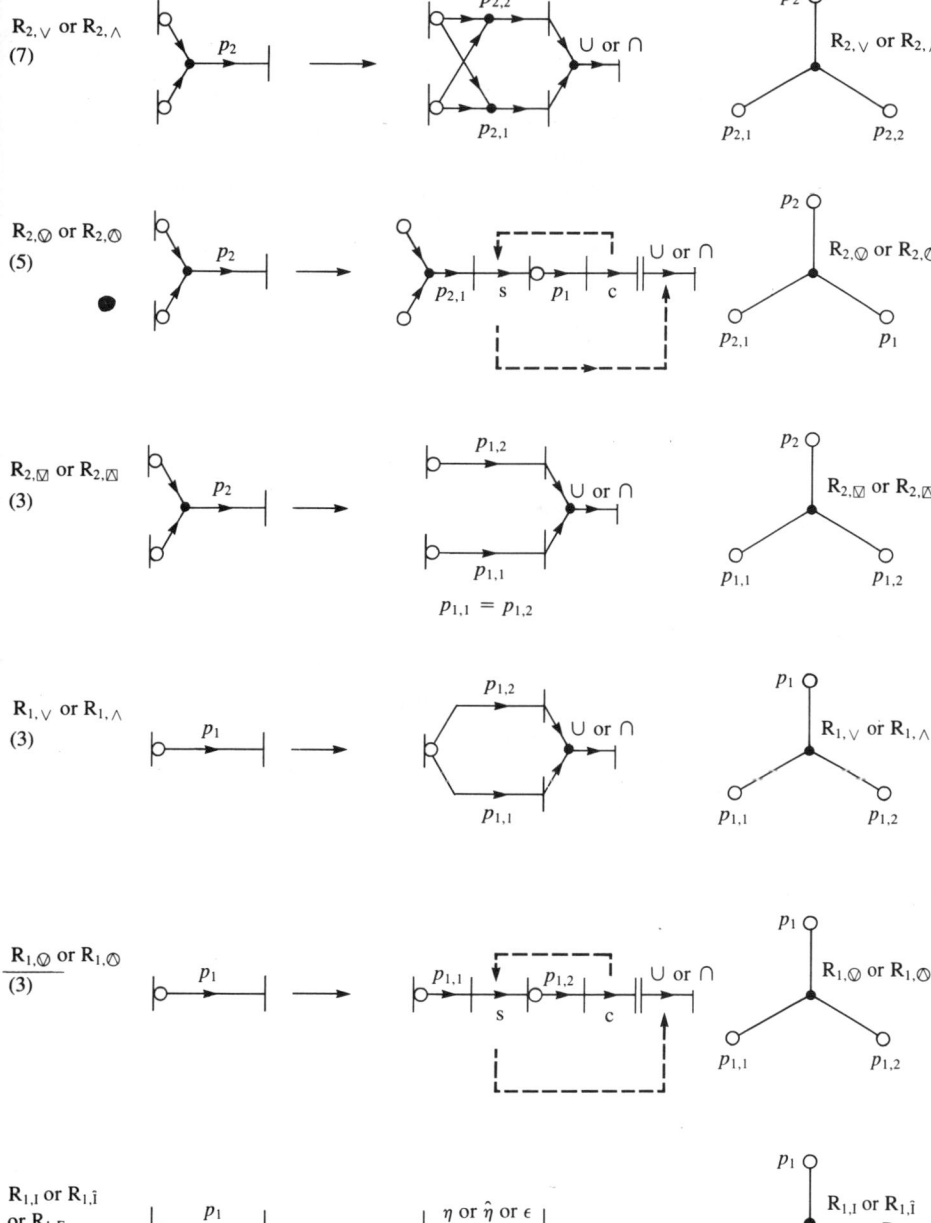

Notes: For simplicity, several rules are combined in one row. The assignment of names, $p_2, p_{2,1}, \ldots, p_1$, $p_{1,1}, \ldots$, to the nonterminals has been introduced in order to indicate the correspondence between parts of program graphs in the transition part of a rule and parts of the associated structural description. These notations are not necessary for describing the transitions (except for rules $R_{2,\boxtimes}$, $R_{2,\boxtimes}$, where some naming mechanism is needed to express the condition that the aggregates corresponding to the two "arms" of the graph are identical).

Figure 18-8: Rules of aggregation of grammar G_1.

two-input program and a one-input program followed by a set-union operation. The symbol $\oslash$ is used to represent this type of cascade + union combination. The choice of this symbol and of the other symbols for rules derives from the algebraic model interpretation, as will be seen later.

Together with each rule name in figure 18-8 there is a number that denotes the least-expected weight, w^*, of a terminal aggregate that would result if the rule were applied. This is the weight of the simplest program that can be structured in accordance with the rule. This notion will be discussed further below.

Note that in Rules $R_{2,\square}$ and $R_{2,\triangle}$, a condition $p_{1,1} = p_{1,2}$ is associated with the transition. This reflects the requirement that a two-input program should treat its inputs symmetrically.

The rules $R_{1,I}$, $R_{1,\hat{I}}$, $R_{1,E}$ are called *terminal rules,* since their application results in the production of terminal aggregates. They are represented by special nodes, $\bullet$, in structural descriptions.

For two-input programs, where each input is of u-type, the starting nonterminal element is a (u_1u_2, q)-program graph (see figure 18-9).

The notion of *derivability in the grammar* can be readily transferred from the conventional linguistic context into the present situation.

The language of constructible programs for the problem class can now be defined in terms of the grammar G_1. This language, call it L_1, is the set of terminal aggregates that are derivable in G_1 from the starting (u_1u_2, q)-program graph.

The structural description of a program P in G_1 is a tree that can be obtained from the derivation (construction) of P in G_1 by putting together in an appropriate manner the units of structural description that correspond to the rule applications in the derivation. The structural description, call it $\delta(P)$, contains all the information needed to construct the program P in accordance with the rules of aggregation in G_1.

Basically, the grammar determines how a candidate solution (a program) *can* be constructed from component substructures and from elementary parts. Since the grammar rules are nondeterministic, each time a rule is applied a specific *choice* must be made among alternative applicable rules. From the point of view of a formation process, a candidate program is completely determined by the pattern of choices of aggregation rules that collectively specify the program's structural description. Now, the white nodes in a structural description correspond to the choice points that determine the program. Thus the number of white nodes in the structural description of a program is a significant measure of formation complexity for the program, called

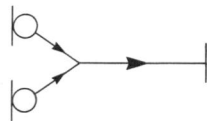

Figure 18-9:   Starting nonterminal element for two-input programs.

the *program's weight, w.* The weight of a program is also closely related to the count of statements in the program; it equals the count of all program statements with the exception of the list-processing statements (i.e., the s-statements and c-statements). Note that w can also be seen as the count of black nodes (rule applications) in a structural description.

These concepts are illustrated in figure 18-10, which shows a program for the Infimum function—both its structural description in G_1 and its graph representation as a terminal aggregate in the language L_1. This program is the solution of the problem π_1 specified in figure 18-1. Note that the weight of this program is 19.

An examination of the structural description of P_{Infimum} or of its corresponding graph representation shows that it has a redundant substructure marked as P_F in figure 18-10b. Clearly a simplification can be obtained by eliminating the redundant P_F and by reorganizing the data paths in an appropriate way. Although this would result in a program that is more efficient for execution purposes, it would be an inferior representation for purposes of program formation, where reasoning with programs in the form of decoupled riverlike graphs is more desirable.

It is possible to abbreviate the structural description of a program by retaining only the nodes for rule names and by eliminating all but the essential information in a rule name. This yields an *abstract description*, $\delta_A(P)$ of P. Such an abstract description captures the essence of a plan for constructing a program. The abstract description of the program P_{Infimum} is shown in figure 18-11.

The following is a LISP representation of the program P_{Infimum}:

```
P_Infimum:  (lambda (u₁ u₂)
            (Intersection
            [Intersection-* (Mapcar
                            '(lambda (x) (Union
                                        (Icap-function x)
                                        (E-function x)))

                (Intersection
                (Union (I-function u₁) E-function u₁))
                (Union (I-function u₂) (E-function u₂)))]
            [Intersection (Union (I-function u₁) (E-function u₁)
                          (Union (I-function u₂) (E-function u₂))]))
```

The functions I-function, Icap-function, E-function, and Intersection-* are specific to the domain language; they were defined previously.

The concepts of *program variable* and *program scheme* are useful for the representation and manipulation of programs during the formation process. A program scheme is an incompletely specified program that has a given structure, parts of which are well defined and other parts of which are identified by program variables.

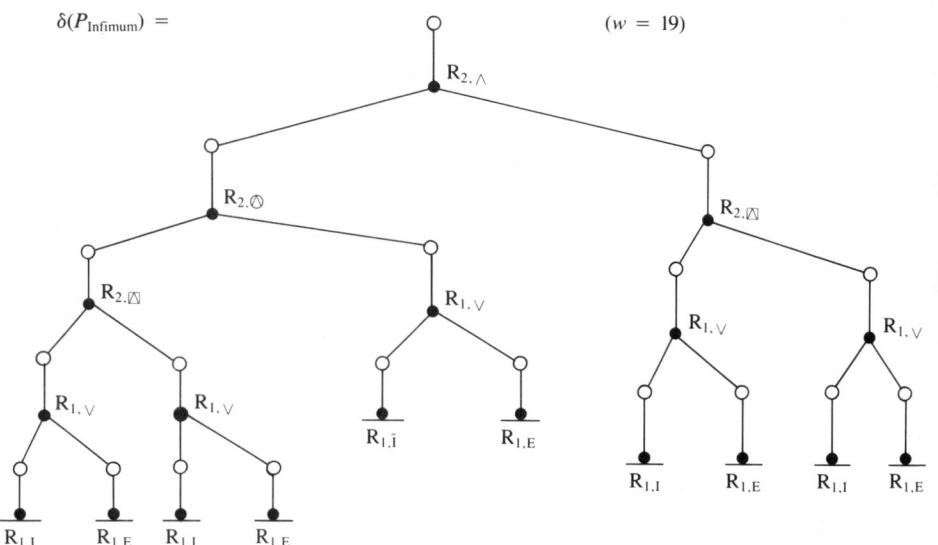

a. Structural description of the Infimum program in G_1.

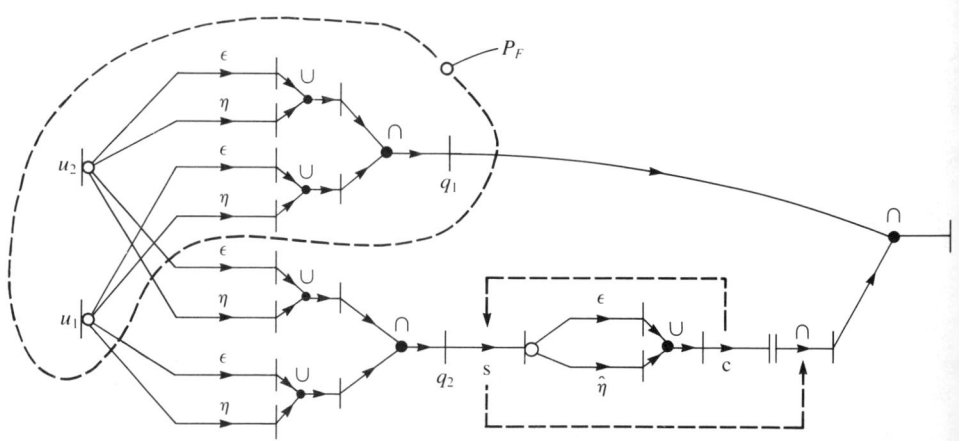

b. Representation of the Infimum program in the graph language L_1.

Figure 18-10:   Representations of solution to problem π_1:   the Infimum program.

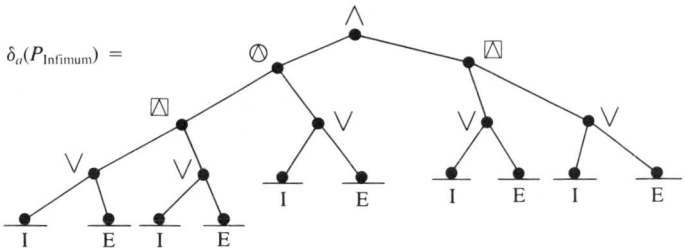

Figure 18-11: Abstract description of the Infimum program in G_1.

The *values* of a program variable can be either completely specified programs or program schemes that are themselves expressed in terms of (other) program variables.

The set of constructible two-input program schemes can easily be defined as an extension of the language L_1 of two-input programs via the introduction of program variables as terminal elements in an extension of the grammar G_1.

18.2.3 Initial Procedural Formulation of the Formation Problem: Heuristic Search in Program Space

The formulation of a program grammar such as G_1 provides a key element for the specifications of problem solving procedures for program formation.

Let us review the way in which the program grammar, together with an associated body of control knowledge, was used in the first approach to a solution of the formation problem (Amarel, 1962b), which was based on heuristic "hill climbing" in program space.

The program grammar provides the basis for specifying a generator of candidate solutions in a typical "generate-and-test" loop. The behavior of the generator can be conveniently represented by an AND-OR *search tree.* The tree has decision (choice) nodes and rule applications nodes. The decision nodes are OR nodes, and the rule application nodes are AND nodes. A solution candidate (a program) is generated as a structural description, which is a special kind of subtree of the search tree. A solution tree has a single descendant at each decision node and a characteristic number of descendants (two or one, depending on the rule) at each rule application node; its terminal nodes are all rule application nodes of type $R_{1,I}$, $R_{1,\bar{I}}$, or $R_{1,E}$. It can be seen in figure 18-10a that the structural description of the Infimum program is a tree of this type. The white nodes in the structural description tree correspond to decision nodes in the search tree.

After the generation of a candidate solution in the form of a structural description of a program, the formation procedure translates it into an executable program, possibly simplifies it, and then *tests* the program by running it over a *sample* of the given table of data associations. The test provides an estimate of the proportion of data associations that are satisfied by the candidate program. This estimate is called the program *value v*. The v of a program is intended as a measure of the functional worth of the program relative to the given set of problem conditions. This measure provides an evaluation of the set of decisions that codetermine the structural description of the candidate solution/program from the point of view of the problem conditions that the solution is asked to satisfy. Therefore, the procedure associates the v of a program to each decision node in the search tree that participates in the specification of its structural description. This assignment of values to decision points in the search tree is then used in subsequent decisions of the formation process.

In the formulation of the hill-climbing heuristics, the following additional concepts are being used: the *least expected weight* of a program that would result from choosing a certain grammar rule at a decision node of the search tree (this is the w^*, discussed previously); a measure of *accumulated search effort* associated with a decision node (call it e)—this is a count of the choices made at the decision node up to the present as the system is trying to build candidate programs; and a *value decrement* associated with a decision node, which provides a measure of *sensitivity* of program value to decision changes at the node (call it δv).

The generation process proceeds by experimenting with simple program (small w) first and by moving gradually to more complex programs. The system attempts to build a *locally stable program* at a given level of program complexity: it focuses then on a decision node of such a program, and it "grows" a program substructure of increased complexity below that node; it then attempts to find a locally stable program at the increased level of complexity, and so on until a solution is obtained or a certain predetermined level of available effort is reached.

A program is considered to be locally stable if, for all its decision nodes, changing a decision one at a time does not yield a program of higher v. Using this notion saves considerable search effort and storage capacity, as search proceeds mainly in a "best first" manner by modifications of the most promising locally stable programs.

The most important heuristic choice in this process is the choice of where to focus next on the structure of a "high-v" program for the generation of new (more complex) program substructures and then what initial assignments of structure and program elements to make at that point. The heuristics that control focus of attention on decision nodes are guided by largest δv, smallest w^*, and smallest e, in that order of priority. After attention has focused on a decision node, the system must decide what structure to "grow" below that node. The initial assignment of program elements to the new structure is made by an *"associative transfer"* of nearby structures in the search tree, with priority given to structures that participated in relatively successful "locally stable" programs. (Details of these heuristics are given in Amarel, 1962b.)

Application of the heuristic "generate-and-test" approach to the formation problem π_1 resulted in a process that can be summarized by the "learning curve" (or "formation curve") of figure 18-12. The abscissa represents numbers of programs

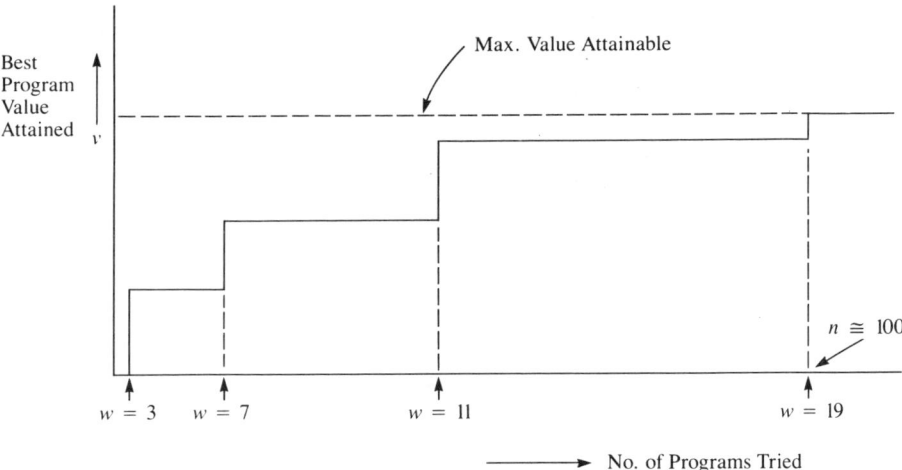

Figure 18-12: Formation curve for Infimum programs (first "top-down" approach).

tried so far. Clearly the improvements in v come in sudden jumps. At each point of improvement, the weight w of the "best" program attained is shown in the figure.

In experiments with the heuristic hill-climbing search process, some of the heuristics postulated/used appeared to be successful. However, it is very difficult to understand their strengths and limitations, and thus it is difficult to have any consistent expectations about system performance for different problems in the given class.

18.2.4 Comments on the Heuristic Search Approach

Finding a solution to the Infimum problem by a simple exhaustive search strategy requires trying roughly 10^9 programs. This is a rather large search space. In the heuristic search approach just outlined, a solution is found after about 10^2 program tries (see figure 18-12). This clearly represents a strong improvement. However, the solution is quite unstable. If the problem-data is given in terms of a different partially ordered structure (not Σ_1 as in our problem π_1), or if small changes are made in the definition of program grammar, then the search effort needed to find a solution may grow appreciably. What is more disturbing is that it is difficult to see how is it possible to improve performance within the present approach. These issues and concerns led to the formulation of a second approach, in which new knowledge is introduced in the form of a model of program space that helps in developing search plans that are "better informed." This approach results in an improved—and more stable— method of solution.

18.3 IMPROVED PROCEDURAL FORMULATION OF THE FORMATION PROBLEM: MODEL-GUIDED REASONING IN PROGRAM SPACE

18.3.1 Algebraic Model of Program Space

This section will describe the mathematical model of program space that plays a key role in the second approach to the program formation problem. The model and its formal properties are presented in detail in previous work (Amarel, 1971).

The model is a *modified algebra of relations.* It consists of a system $\mathscr{R}$ for handling one-input programs and an extended system $\mathscr{R}_{d1}$ for handling two-input programs.[2]

18.3.1.1 Introduction to the Algebraic Model

Given a finite set σ of n elements, let us call a dyadic relation R on σ a *one-input relation.* Let us represent R by an $n \times n$ binary matrix and denote the matrix by $\mathbf{R}$.

To build the matrix $\mathbf{R}$, let us associate with each element of σ a numerical index from 1 to $n;$ and let the i-row and i-column of the matrix correspond to the i-element of σ. The value of the $\mathbf{r}_{ij}$ component of the matrix $\mathbf{R}$ is 1 if $\mathbf{R}$ holds between the i-element and the j-element of σ: otherwise, it is 0. For example, the matrix corresponding to the proper inclusion relation I on the set σ_1 of the problem shown in figure 18-1 is as shown in figure 18-13.

In the specification of this matrix, the assignment of indices is

$$1 \to e, 2 \to a, 3 \to b, 4 \to c, 5 \to d.$$

Elements of the sets σ and 2^σ can be represented by n-dimensional row vectors, as follows: An element of σ to which there corresponds a numerical index i is represented by a vector with a 1 at its i-component and a 0 elsewhere; a subset of elements of σ is represented by a vector with a 1 at each component that corresponds to an element of the subset and 0 elsewhere. Now, it can easily be seen that program statements in the language of constructible programs can be modeled by ordinary vector-matrix multiplications. For example, the program statement shown in figure 18-14

$$\mathbf{I} = \begin{bmatrix} 0\,0\,0\,0\,0 \\ 1\,0\,0\,0\,0 \\ 1\,1\,0\,0\,0 \\ 1\,1\,0\,0\,0 \\ 1\,1\,1\,1\,0 \end{bmatrix}$$

Figure 18-13: Relation matrix for proper inclusion relation I.

---

[2]The subscript $d1$ comes from the definition of the domain of associations in the problem class (see section 18.2.1.4).

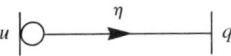

Figure 18-14: A one-input program statement.

can be modeled by the expression $\mathbf{q} = \mathbf{u}\,\mathbf{I}$, where $\mathbf{u}$, $\mathbf{q}$ are the vector representations of u and q respectively, $\mathbf{I}$ is the matrix corresponding to I, and the multiplication can be defined as

$\mathbf{q} = \mathrm{row}_i\,(\mathbf{I})$ if $\mathrm{comp}_i\,(\mathbf{u}) = 1$ and $\mathrm{comp}_j\,(\mathbf{u}) = 0$ for all $j \neq i$
$\quad\ \ \mathrm{row}_i\,(\mathbf{0})$ if all the components of $\mathbf{u}$ are 0.

In this definition, $\mathrm{comp}_i\,(\mathbf{u})$ denotes the i-component of the vector $\mathbf{u}$, and $\mathbf{0}$ denotes the matrix of zeros that corresponds to the *null* relation.

In addition to the usual operations of the algebra of relations, a *new product operation*, denoted by $\oslash$, is introduced here. The ordinary product of relations is denoted by $\oslash$. The new operation, $\oslash$, is needed in order to obtain a complete model for the set of constructible programs; its introduction is responsible for the deviation between the system described here and the ordinary algebra of relations. The two product operations can be defined as follows:

For any relations X, Y, Z, and for all indices i from 1 to n,

$(Z = X \oslash Y) \equiv (\mathrm{row}_i\,(\mathbf{Z}) = \bigvee \mathrm{row}_k(\mathbf{Y})$
$\qquad\qquad\qquad\qquad\qquad k \in \tau\,[\mathrm{row}_i\,(\mathbf{X})]$

$(Z = X \oslash Y) \equiv (\mathrm{row}_i\,(\mathbf{Z}) = \&\ \mathrm{row}_k(\mathbf{Y})$
$\qquad\qquad\qquad\qquad\qquad k \in \tau\,[\mathrm{row}_i(\mathbf{X})],$

where $\tau\,[\mathrm{row}_i(\,\mathbf{X})]$ denotes the set of coordinates in the i-row of $\mathbf{X}$ whose value is 1; and $\bigvee$ and $\&$ are used for iterated disjunction and conjunction, respectively.

The logical interpretation of these operations is as follows:

$\oslash$-product: uZv holds if there is a w in σ such that (uXw) and (wYv) both hold. (This is the ordinary product of relations.)

$\oslash$-product: uZv holds if for all w in σ such that (uXw) holds, the relations (wYv) hold also. (This is the new, more restrictive, product introduced in the present modified algebra of relations.)

It can easily be verified that there exists a simple correspondence between any constructible program of (u,q)-type and a one-input relational expression made of the relations I, $\hat{I}$, E, the products $\oslash$, $\oslash$, and the Boolean operations $\bigvee$, $\&$. Consider in particular the aggregations of (u,q)-type statements that are defined by the rules $R_{1,\vee}$, $R_{1,\wedge}$ and $R_{1,\oslash}$, $R_{1,\oslash}$ of the program grammar G_1 (see figure 18-8):

To the aggregates[3] shown in figure 18-15 there corresponds the relational expressions $(X \vee Y)$, $(X \mathbin{\&} Y)$, respectively, where X, Y are one-input relations; and to the aggregates shown in figure 18-16 there correspond the expressions $(X \oslash Y)$, $(X \oslash Y)$, respectively.

18.3.1.2 The Algebra of One-Input Programs $\mathcal{R}$

The algebra of one-input programs has as atomic elements the relations I, $\hat{I}$, E, and 0, and as operations the Boolean operations $\vee$ and $\&$ and the relation products $\oslash$ and $\oslash$. The terms of $\mathcal{R}$ are relational expressions made from these atomic elements, relation variables, and the given operations (used here in infix form). For each term in this algebra there is a corresponding relation matrix as well as a corresponding one-input program in our language.

The terms of $\mathcal{R}$ are partially ordered under an *implication relation,* denoted by $\rightarrow$. For any two terms X, Y, the implication $X \rightarrow Y$ holds when the relation matrix corresponding to X *is included in* the relation matrix corresponding to Y. The logical interpretation of $X \rightarrow Y$ is that for any pair of elements u and v in σ, if uXv holds then uYv also holds. Now, if $X \rightarrow Y$ and $Y \rightarrow X$, then X and Y are *equivalent* and we write $X \leftrightarrow Y$.

From our point of view, the usefulness of the model is determined by the degree to which it provides some structure in program space that can help one to reason about programs in functional terms. The implication relation induces a rich structure in $\mathcal{R}$, which proves to be useful in developing a more goal-oriented strategy for program formation.

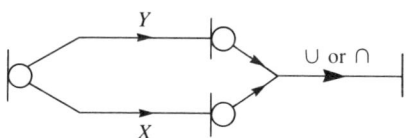

Figure 18-15: A one-input "parallel" program aggregate.

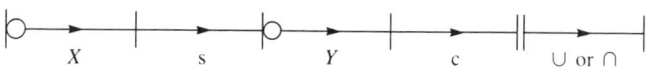

Figure 18-16: A one-input "cascade" program aggregate.

---

[3]For simplicity of exposition, no distinction is made here between a relation X and the function (call it χ) whose value for any element u of σ is the set of all v in σ such that uXv holds. In a strict sense, the label X in the graph representation of the program should be changed to χ.

Key features of the structure of $\mathcal{R}$ are summarized below:

1. *Properties of Boolean Operations:* The usual properties of idempotency, commutativity, distributivity, and associativity

2. *General Properties of Product Operations*

   $(X \triangle Y) \to (X \nabla Y)$, for any terms X, Y

   $(X \nabla 0) \leftrightarrow (0 \nabla X) \leftrightarrow (X \triangle 0) \leftrightarrow (0 \triangle X) \leftrightarrow 0$

   $(X \nabla E) \leftrightarrow (E \nabla X) \leftrightarrow (E \triangle X) \leftrightarrow X$

   $(X \triangle E) \to X$

   if $X \to Y$, then $(Z \nabla X) \to (Z \nabla Y)$

   $\qquad\qquad\qquad\ (X \nabla Z) \to (Y \nabla Z)$

   $\qquad\qquad\qquad\ (Z \triangle X) \to (Z \triangle Y)$

   $\qquad\qquad\qquad\ (X \triangle Z) \leftarrow (Y \triangle Z)$,

   for any X, Y, Z.

3. *Associative Properties of Product Operations*
   a. General: For any one-input relations X,Y,Z,

   $((X \nabla Y) \nabla Z) \leftrightarrow (X \nabla (Y \nabla Z))$

   $((X \triangle Y) \nabla Z) \to (X \triangle (Y \nabla Z))$

   $((X \nabla Y) \triangle Z) \leftarrow (X \triangle (Y \triangle Z))$.

   b. Special case: If $Y = E \lor W$, for any W (including $W = 0$) then $((X \nabla Y) \triangle Z) \leftrightarrow (X \triangle (Y \triangle Z))$.

4. *Distributive Properties of Products with Boolean Operations*
   a. Right distributivities: For any one-input relations X,Y,Z,

   $((X \lor Y) \nabla Z) \leftrightarrow ((X \nabla Z) \lor (Y \nabla Z))$

   $((X \& Y) \nabla Z) \to ((X \nabla Z) \& (Y \nabla Z))$

   $((X \lor Y) \triangle Z) \leftarrow ((X \triangle Z) \& (Y \triangle Z))$

   b. Left Distributivities: For any one-input relations X,Y,Z,

   $(X \nabla (Y \lor Z)) \leftrightarrow ((X \nabla Y) \lor (X \nabla Z))$

   $(X \triangle (Y \lor Z)) \leftarrow ((X \triangle Y) \lor (X \triangle Z))$

   $(X \nabla (Y \& Z)) \to ((X \nabla Y) \& (X \nabla Z))$

   $(X \triangle (Y \& Z)) \leftrightarrow ((X \triangle Y) \& (X \triangle Z))$

5. *Specific Properties of Atomic Relation I, $\hat{I}$, E*

$$(I \,\&\, \hat{I}) \leftrightarrow (I \,\&\, E) \leftrightarrow (\hat{I} \,\&\, E) \leftrightarrow 0$$

$$(I \,Ⓥ\, I) \rightarrow I; (I \,⊘\, I) \leftrightarrow 0$$

$$(\hat{I} \,Ⓥ\, \hat{I}) \rightarrow \hat{I}; (\hat{I} \,⊘\, \hat{I}) \leftrightarrow 0$$

$$(E \,Ⓥ\, E) \leftrightarrow (E \,⊘\, E) \leftrightarrow E$$

$$((I \vee E) \,\&\, (\hat{I} \vee E)) \leftrightarrow E$$

$$((I \vee E) \,Ⓥ\, (I \vee E)) \leftrightarrow (I \vee E)$$

$$((\hat{I} \vee E) \,Ⓥ\, (\hat{I} \vee E)) \leftrightarrow (\hat{I} \vee E)$$

$$((I \vee E) \,⊘\, (\hat{I} \vee E)) \leftrightarrow (\hat{I} \vee E)$$

$$((\hat{I} \vee E) \,⊘\, (I \vee E)) \leftrightarrow (I \vee E)$$

18.3.1.3 The Algebra of Two-Input Programs $\mathcal{R}_{d1}$

Consider now triadic relations on a finite set σ of n elements. A triadic relation is a rule that specifies for each pair taken from the set $\sigma \times \sigma$ if the relation holds between this pair and any element of σ. In general, the domain size of such a relation is n^2. In accordance with the specification of our problem-data domain Δ_1 (see section 18.2.1.4), the domain of triadic relations in the model is restricted to the set of $n(n + 1)/2$ unordered pairs of elements taken from σ, that is, to the domain of associations $d1$. Let us call the triadic relations in our model *two-input relations* and mark them with a subscript $d1$, for example, R_{d1}.

A two-input relation R_{d1} can be represented by a binary matrix of $n(n + 1)/2$ rows and n columns. Let us denote the matrix by $\mathbf{R}_{d1}$. The ij-row of the matrix corresponds to an input pair made of the i-element of σ and the j-element of σ (in accordance with some indexing of elements of σ); and the k-column of the matrix corresponds to the k-element of σ. The value of the $\mathbf{r}_{ij,k}$ component of the matrix $\mathbf{R}_{d1}$ holds between the ij-pair of σ and the k-element of σ; otherwise it is a 0.

For a given indexing of the elements of σ, let us arrange input pairs in accordance with the ordering $\langle (1, 1), (1, 2), \ldots, (1, n), (2, 2), \ldots, (2, n), (n - 1, n - 1), (n - 1, n), (n, n) \rangle$. Now, let us order the rows of two-input relation matrices in accordance with this ordering, and let us establish a correspondence between the components of row vectors (with $n(n + 1)/2$ dimensions) and this ordering. In analogy with the one-input case, an element of the input domain $d1$ to which there corresponds a pair of elements of σ with indexes ij can be represented by a row vector with a 1 at its ij-component and 0 elsewhere.

If u_1, u_2 are variables that take as values elements of σ, then let $\mathbf{u}_1\mathbf{u}_2$ denote the vector representation of the input pair. The expression $\mathbf{q} = \mathbf{u}_1\mathbf{u}_2 \, \mathbf{R}_{d1}$ denotes an ordinary multiplication of the $n(n + 1)/2$-dimensional row vector $\mathbf{u}_1\mathbf{u}_2$ and the matrix $\mathbf{R}_{d1}$, which produces the n-dimensional row vector $\mathbf{q}$, under the rule:

$\mathbf{q} = (\text{row}_{ij} (\mathbf{R}_{d1}))$, if ij is the component of the vector $\mathbf{u}_1\mathbf{u}_2$ whose value is 1.

Two operations, ☑ and ◺, are introduced for composing two-input relations from one-input relations. They are called *cross products,* and they are defined as follows:

For any pair of one-input relations X, Y, any two-input relation Z_{d1}, and any pair of indices i, j,

$$(Z_{d1} = X \boxdot Y) \equiv (\text{row}_{ij} (Z_{d1}) = \text{row}_i (\mathbf{X}) \vee \text{row}_j (\mathbf{Y})),$$
$$(Z_{d1} = X \boxtimes Y) \equiv (\text{row}_{ij} (Z_{d1}) = \text{row}_i (\mathbf{X}) \,\&\, \text{row}_j (\mathbf{Y})).$$

Cross-product operations behave in the same way as Boolean operations. Their compositions can be shown to be equivalent to Boolean operations between matrices that are special *extensions* of the matrices that represent the composing relations.

The two product operations $\oslash$, $\obslash$ can be extended in a natural way from one-input relations to two-input relations. The Boolean operations between relations can also be used here in the usual way.

It can easily be verified that there exists a simple correspondence between any constructible program of (u_1u_2,q)-type and a two-input relational expression made of the relation I, $\hat{I}$, E, the products $\oslash$, $\obslash$, the Boolean operations $\vee$, $\&$, and the cross products $\boxdot$, $\boxtimes$. Consider in particular the aggregates involving (u_1u_2,q)-type programs that are produced by the rules $R_{2,\boxdot}$, $R_{2,\boxtimes}$, $R_{2,\oslash}$, $R_{2,\obslash}$, $R_{2,\vee}$ and $R_{2,\wedge}$ of the program grammar G_1 (see figure 18-8).

To the aggregates shown in figure 18-17 there correspond the relational expressions $(X \boxdot Y)$, $(X \boxtimes Y)$, respectively, where X, Y are any one-input relations; to the aggregates shown in figure 18-18 there correspond the relational expressions $(X_{d1} \oslash Y)$, $(X_{d1} \obslash Y)$, where X_{d1} is any two-input relation and Y is any one-input

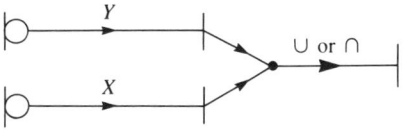

Figure 18-17:   A two-input "parallel" program aggregate.

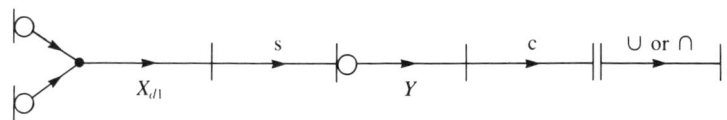

Figure 18-18:   A two-input "cascade" program aggregate.

relation; and to the aggregates shown in figure 18-19 there correspond the relational expressions $(X_{d1} \lor Y_{d1})$, $(X_{d1} \,\&\, Y_{d1})$, where X_{d1}, Y_{d1} are any two-input relations.

Consider as an example the relational expression that corresponds to the Infimum program shown in figures 18-10 and 18-11. The expression is

$$[[(I \lor E) \boxtimes (I \lor E)] \oslash (\hat{I} \lor E)] \,\&\, [(I \lor E) \boxtimes (I \lor E)].$$

Note that this expression is the infix representation of the "abstract description" of the Infimum program that derives from the structural description of the program in G_1 (given in figure 18-11).

In general, for any two-input constructible program there is a corresponding relational expression that can be obtained in a straightforward way from the structural description of the program obtained in the grammar G_1. The program and its corresponding relational expression are functionally equivalent—in the sense that their input-output behaviors are the same. This correspondence is the basis for the modeling relationship between the set of constructible programs described here and the relational expressions of the modified algebra of relations $\mathcal{R}_{d1}$.

The algebra of two-input programs $\mathcal{R}_{d1}$ is an extension of the algebra $\mathcal{R}$, with the two operations $\boxtimes$, $\boxtimes$ added. The terms of $\mathcal{R}_{d1}$ are the two-input relational expressions described previously. These terms are partially ordered under the implication relation, $\rightarrow$, as described above in connection with $\mathcal{R}$.

The properties of the operations $\lor$, $\&$, $\oslash$, $\oslash$ carry over from $\mathcal{R}$ to $\mathcal{R}_{d1}$ with appropriate replacements of one-input relation variables by two-input relation variables. The associativities of $\boxtimes$, $\boxtimes$ are the same as the associativities of the Boolean operations $\lor$, $\&$, respectively; the operations $\boxtimes$, $\boxtimes$ distribute with Boolean operations in the same way as $\lor$ or $\&$, respectively; and the right distributivities of the products $\oslash$, $\oslash$ with respect to the cross products $\boxtimes$, $\boxtimes$ are the same as those between $\oslash$, $\oslash$ and the Boolean operations $\lor$, $\&$, respectively.

18.3.1.4 The Program Space Induced by the Algebraic Model: Distances in the Space

In view of the modeling correspondence that was established between the set of constructible programs and the algebraic system $\mathcal{R}_{d1}$, the algebraic model induces

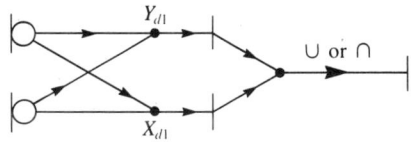

Figure 18-19: Another form of a two-input "parallel" program aggregate.

an implicational structure on the set of programs—thus providing a more useful definition of program space than had been available before. For any two-input programs P_1, P_2 with projections R_1, R_2, respectively, in the model $\mathcal{R}_{d1}$, if the implication $R_1 \rightarrow R_2$ holds, then we can also say that $P_1 \rightarrow P_2$. There now exists a calculus of programs in which one can reason about program equivalence and inclusion. Furthermore these behavioral concepts are related to structural features of programs.

The number of two-input programs in L_1—and correspondingly the number of terms in $\mathcal{R}_{d1}$—is not finite. However, there is a finite number of functions that these programs can compute, since there is a finite number of relation matrices that correspond to terms of $\mathcal{R}_{d1}$. For our problem class, this number is certainly smaller than $2^{n^2(n+1)/2}$, where n is the number of elements in the set σ. We can visualize all the two-input constructible programs sorted into a finite number of equivalence classes, each defined by a relation matrix that expresses the functional behavior of any program in the class. To each of these equivalence classes, that is, to each relation matrix that corresponds to some constructible program, there corresponds a point in our new program space. Let us call this space $M_1(n)$.

The points of $M_1(n)$ are partially ordered under the inclusion relation, $\rightarrow$. They are a subset of the full lattice of relations that is defined by the set of all the $2^{n^2(n+1)/2}$ relation matrices. Let us call this Boolean lattice $B_1(n)$.

The set of associations given in the statement of the formation problem can be seen as a specification of the "goal program" in terms of its relation matrix. (Each association corresponds to a row of the relation matrix of the goal program.) This is a functional specification, and it can always be represented as a point in the Boolean lattice $B_1(n)$. If the desired program is representable in the language of constructible programs, then it can also be represented as a point in the program space $M_1(n)$. If the desired program is not representable in the program language, which means that the problem has no solution, then it cannot be represented as a point in $M_1(n)$. The problem solver has no way of knowing that the problem has no solution by analyzing the problem statement. He can only try to come as close as possible to the point in the Boolean lattice that represents the desired function—by constructing candidate program structures whose functional behavior is "close" to the desired function. If an endless search in the unsolvable cases is to be avoided, a predetermined ceiling must be set on available problem solving effort so that the system can stop when the ceiling is reached.

In order that a strategy may be developed for moving from points in program space that represent known program structures to the desired point, that is, to the goal program, it is important to introduce a notion of *distance* between programs that can be used to guide *distance-reducing moves*.

The notion of distance is defined here as follows: For any program P, let $m(P)$ denote the number of 1's in the relation matrix that represents P. Then, the distance $D(P_1, P_2)$ between two programs P_1, P_2 in the lattice $B_1(n)$ is

$$D(P_1, P_2) = m(P_1 \vee P_2) - m(P_1 \,\&\, P_2).$$

This distance is a measure of the symmetric set difference between the relation matrices that correspond to the programs P_1, P_2.

Since the algebra $\mathcal{R}_{d1}$ has a rich implicational structure (i.e., the structure of inclusions between relation matrices) and this structure can provide considerable guidance on how to move "vertically" in the lattice $B_1(n)$, it is useful to define the distance D in terms of a "vertical" component D_v and a "horizontal" component D_h. Thus we have

$$D(P_1, P_2) \overset{\text{def}}{=} D_v(P_1, P_2) + D_h(P_1, P_2), \text{ where}$$

$$D_v(P_1, P_2) = m(P_1) - m(P_2),$$

$$D_h(P_1, P_2) = 2(m(P_2) - m(P_1 \,\&\, P_2)),$$

under the assumption that $m(P_1) \geq m(P_2)$.

The notion of verticality is induced from a commonly used geometric representation of the lattice $B_1(n)$. In this representation, the null program[4] is shown at the bottom, the unit program[5] is at the top, and for any pair of programs P_1, P_2, if $P_1 \rightarrow P_2$, then P_1 is portrayed below P_2 in the lattice. As we move up in the lattice, the value of m increases. The distance relationships between two programs P_1, P_2 in a lattice $B_1(n)$ are schematically shown in figure 18-20. The relationship between the relation matrices that correspond to the programs P_1, P_2 of figure 18-20 are shown schematically in figure 18-21.

Note that the smaller the horizontal distance between two programs, the more a situation is approached in which one program includes the other.

The distances as defined here do not provide detailed information about the difference sets in the outputs of the two programs; they provide only measures of size of the difference sets. This is adequate for the present approach, but it has certain disadvantages and limitations, which will be discussed later.

18.3.2 Goal-Oriented Method of Solution That Uses Properties of the Model

In view of the structure of program space that is induced by the algebraic model, the process of solution finding can now take a more *goal-oriented* form. The goal to be achieved can be seen as a point in the lattice $B_1(n)$ of programs that is defined by its specifying set of input-output associations. Clearly this set represents the relation matrix of the desired goal program P_g.

---

[4]The null program has a relation matrix filled with zeros.

[5]The unit program has a relation matrix filled with ones.

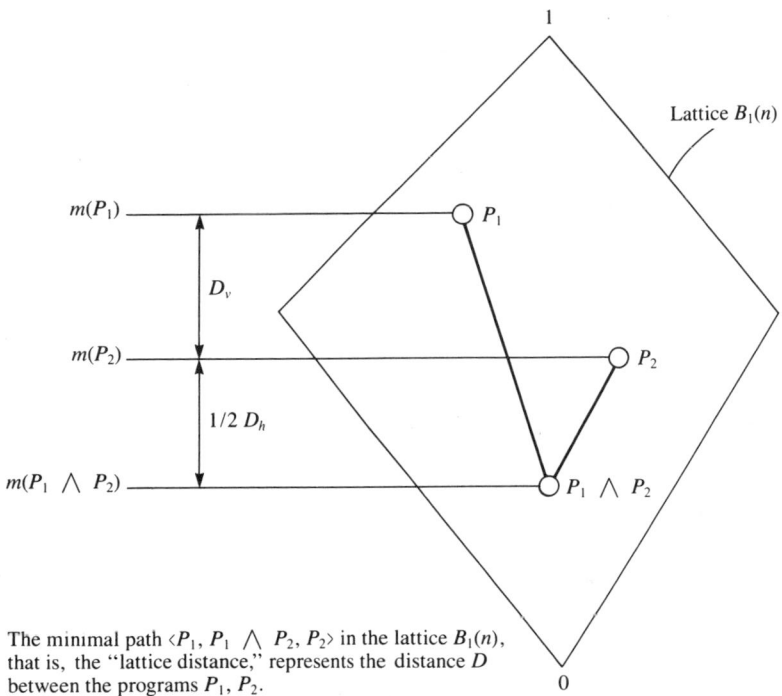

The minimal path $\langle P_1, P_1 \wedge P_2, P_2\rangle$ in the lattice $B_1(n)$, that is, the "lattice distance," represents the distance D between the programs P_1, P_2.

Figure 18-20: Distance between programs in lattice of programs $B_1(n)$.

The solution process is again based on a generate-and-test scheme, but the sequence of candidate programs that are being generated is more strongly guided (relative to the previous approach, described in section 18.2.3) by the problem-data. More specifically, the problem-data are seen as the specification of the goal program P_g in the lattice $B_1(n)$; and the distance from a candidate program P and the program P_g can be used to reason in a more informed way about the generation of subsequent program candidates whose distance to P_g should be (one hopes) smaller.

At any stage of the problem solving process, the *problem state* is defined as the set of pairs

$$\langle \varrho(P), (D_v\,(P,\,P_g),\,D_h(P,\,P_g))\rangle$$

for all candidate programs P that have been generated and tested so far. Here, $\varrho(P)$ denotes the relational expression that represents the structure of P in the algebraic model.

The problem solver must use the information in the current problem state, together with general knowledge about program space, in deciding what move to

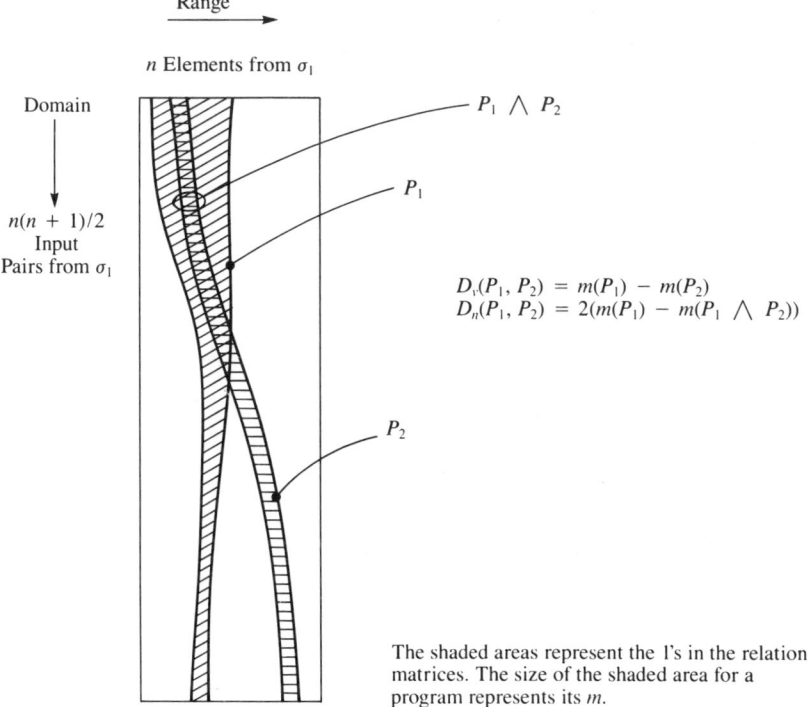

Figure 18-21:   Relation matrices corresponding to programs P_1, P_2 shown in figure 18-20.

take, that is, what next program to generate, in order to reach the desired point P_g by generating (and testing) as small a number of candidate programs as possible. The problem can be regarded as *navigating* in problem space. Appropriate navigating actions can be taken on the basis of knowledge in the algebraic model. A dominant direction in the program lattice is the vertical, determined by inclusion relations in the algebra. Thus a reasonable plan of navigation is to move first into a roughly vertical alignment with the desired goal point P_g by trying to reduce the horizontal distance to the goal and then to slide (to ascend or to descend) into P_g by using the rich set of inclusion relations in the algebraic model. This plan has to be further refined, especially at the *terminal stage* of the formation process, where more subtle and "local" reasoning is needed in order to reach the goal. At the terminal stage, something akin to a delicate maneuver is needed: a pair of program structures must be found from among those that evolve in accordance with the vertical alignment plan— each at zero horizontal distance to P_g but at a substantial horizontal distance relative to each other—whose intersection "falls on" P_g.

The entire generation process is under the overall control of the grammar G_1, with initial preference given to low-weight program structures. As the process moves to the vertical alignment stage and to the preparation of candidates for the terminal intersection maneuver the algebraic model provides much of the guidance for the specific choices of generation.

18.3.3 The Model-Guided Approach Applied to the Formation Problem π_1

Let us illustrate the model-guided approach to formation via an outline of the solution process for our problem π_1 (which is described in figure 18-1).

A candidate program P is specified here in terms of its structure $\varrho(P)$ and its distance $D(P,P_g)$ from the goal program $P_g = P_{\text{Infimum}}$. The distance is given as a pair of components (D_v, D_h). The value v' of a program (which is a modified notion of the value v of a program, defined here as the count of associations that are satisfied by the program) is also given, for purposes of comparison. The relation matrices of the key programs during the present process are shown in figure 18-22.

Goal Program		Candidate programs						
		P_1	$P_{1,1}$	$P_{1,2}$	$P_{2,1}$	$P_{2,2}$ $((I \vee E) \triangle (I \vee E))$	$P_{2,3}$ $(P_{2,2} \oslash (\hat{I} \vee E))$	$P_{3,1}$
Inputs	P_{Infimum}	$E \triangle E$	$I \triangle I$	$\hat{I} \triangle \hat{I}$	$P_1 \vee P_{1,1}$	$(I \vee E)$	$(\hat{I} \vee E)$	$P_{2,2} \wedge P_{2,3}$
ee	e	ⓔ	—	abcd	ⓔ	ⓔ	eabcd	ⓔ
ea	e	ea	ⓔ	abcd	ea	ⓔ	eabcd	ⓔ
eb	e	eb	ea	abcd	eab	ⓔ	eabcd	ⓔ
ec	e	ec	ea	abcd	eac	ⓔ	eabcd	ⓔ
ed	e	ed	eabc	abcd	eabcd	ⓔ	eabcd	ⓔ
aa	a	ⓐ	e	bcd	ea	ea	abcd	ⓐ
ab	a	ab	ea	bcd	eab	ea	abcd	ⓐ
ac	a	ac	ea	bcd	eac	ea	abcd	ⓐ
ad	a	ad	eabc	bcd	eabcd	ea	abcd	ⓐ
bb	b	ⓑ	ea	d	eab	eab	bd	ⓑ
bc	a	bc	ea	d	eabc	ea	abcd	ⓐ
bd	b	bd	eabc	d	eabcd	eab	bd	ⓑ
cc	c	ⓒ	ea	d	eac	eac	cd	ⓒ
cd	c	cd	eabc	d	eabcd	eac	cd	ⓒ
dd	d	ⓓ	eabc	—	eabcd	eabcd	d	ⓓ
m	15	25	36	37	52	32	54	15
D		12	31	52	37	17	39	0
D_v		10	21	22	37	17	39	0
D_h		2	10	30	0	0	0	0
v'		5	1	0	1	5	0	15

Note: The entries in circles show parts of candidate programs that match the goal program.

Figure 18-22: Relation matrices of main programs generated in model-guided approach.

The following are the main steps in the process of formation:

1. A set of simple programs (with $w = 3$) is generated and tested. This is an *initial exploration* stage.

    $P_1 = (E \boxdot E)$, $(10,2)$; $v' = 5$
    $P_{1,1} = (I \boxdot I)$, $(21,10)$; $v' = 1$
    $P_{1,2} = (\hat{I} \boxdot \hat{I})$, $(22,30)$; $v' = 0$

    The programs $P_1, P_{1,1}$ have the smallest horizontal distance from P_g, and they are chosen for the next step.

2. Combinations of promising programs from the previous step are tried in order to bring the horizontal distance to zero. This is a stage whose objective is to reach vertical alignment with the goal program. By using P_1, $P_{1,1}$, a zero horizontal distance is obtained.

    $P_{2,1} = ((E \boxdot E) \vee (I \boxdot I))$, $(37,0)$; $v' = 1$, $w = 7$

    From the algebra, the structure of $P_{2,1}$ is equivalent to $((I \vee E) \boxdot (I \vee E))$.

3. Algebraic properties are used to find programs with zero horizontal distance that have a smaller vertical distance from P_g by manipulation of previous promising programs. This represents the stage of "sliding vertically." Here, a change of the cross product $\boxdot$ in $P_{2,1}$, to $\boxslash$, takes us in the right direction.

    $P_{2,2} = ((I \vee E) \boxslash (I \vee E))$, $(17,0)$; $v' = 5$, $w = 7$

4. In *preparation for the terminal intersection maneuver,* programs are formed that have zero horizontal distance to P_g and large horizontal distances among themselves.

    $P_{2,3} = [((I \vee E) \boxslash (I \vee E))] \oslash (\hat{I} \vee E)]$, $(39,0)$;
    $v' = 0$, $w = 11$

    Note that while the horizontal distance of $P_{2,3}$ to P_g is zero, its horizontal distance to $P_{2,2}$ is large: $D_h(P_{2,2}, P_{2,3}) = 34$

5. A *terminal intersection maneuver* is tried among previously developed programs. The desired goal program is reached by the intersection of $P_{2,2}$ and $P_{2,3}$.

    $P_{3,1} = ([(I \vee E) \boxslash (I \vee E)] \, \& \, [((I \vee E) \boxslash (I \vee E)) \oslash (\hat{I} \vee E)])$, $(0,0)$; $v' = 15$, $w = 19$

    Thus $P_{3,1} = P_g = P_{\text{Infimum}}$.

A graphic representation of the main stages in the model-guided formation process is shown in figure 18-23.

The most difficult part in the present process is the choice of candidates for the terminal intersection maneuver. A good heuristic, which was found empirically, is as follows: Suppose that at step 3 a good program P_a is obtained and we wish to use it as

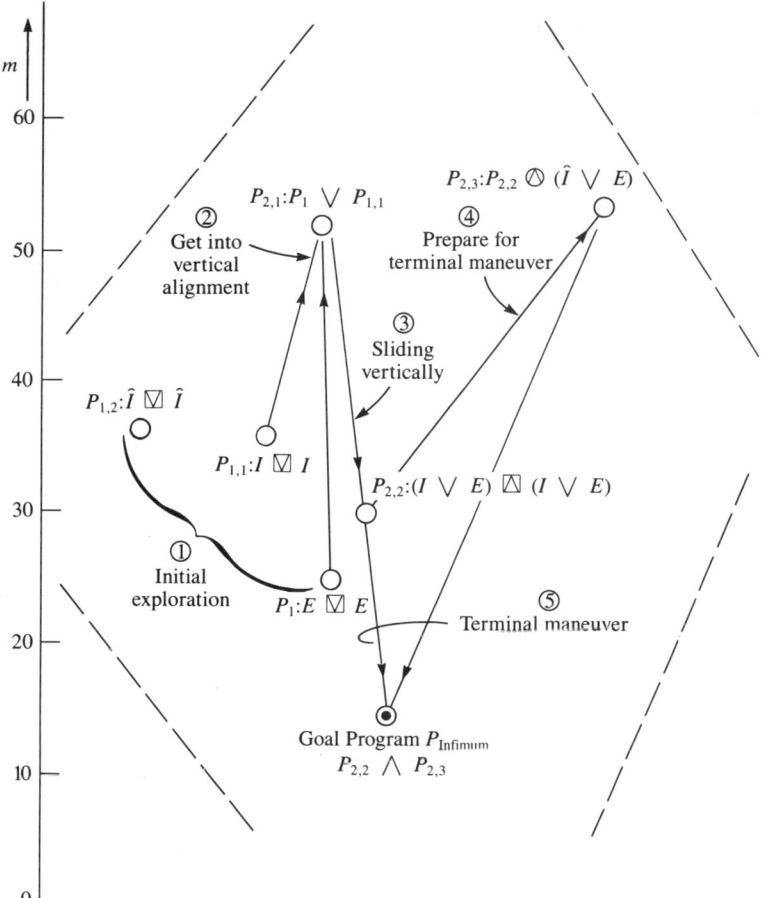

Figure 18-23: Graphic representation of stages in model-guided formation process—shown in lattice of programs.

one of the pair of programs to intersect in the terminal maneuver; construct a cascade structure $P_a \oslash P_{a1}$ for some P_{a1} and use it as the second program in the intersection. Such a structure has a good chance of success. Even with the guidance of this heuristic, considerable search may be needed to find "appropriate" structures P_a, P_{a1}.

The number of major decisions made during this formation process is approximately twenty. The situation is clearly more selective and more goal oriented than in the previous heuristic hill-climbing approach. However, the present distance-guided approach does not provide the detailed type of "local" information that is needed in the terminal stage of reasoning for achieving the goal. Furthermore, without a better understanding of the grounds for the heuristics that guide the terminal intersection maneuver, it is very difficult to restrict the search involved and to see how the process can be improved.

It is interesting to examine the relation matrices that correspond to the main programs formed in the present path to solution (see figure 18-22). There is much detailed structure in the pattern of deviations between a candidate program and the goal program that is not captured by the coarse concept of distance in program space. It makes sense to consider using this structure more directly in order to understand the domain-specific nature of the terminal phase in the present formation process and to develop improved approaches to formation. These considerations led to a third approach to the formation problem, which relies on more detailed reasoning with individual items of problem-data.

Before a description of current work with the third approach is presented, some general comments about the model-guided approach will be made.

18.3.4 Comments on the Model-Guided Approach: Relationship to the Previous Approach and Open Problems

The model-guided method of constructing candidate solutions differs appreciably from the heuristic hill-climbing method. In the hill-climbing method, a solution candidate (a program) is built from top to bottom—first the global structure is specified, and gradually choices of substructures and of terminal elements are made. Only in the first, exploratory, stage of the model-guided approach is such a method of solution construction used. In the subsequent stages, candidate programs are gradually built from the bottom up—first some of the terminal substructures are built, and then they are combined into bigger structures. The grammar of the program language determines the program units and their possible mode of aggregation, but it is the overall plan of formation—which is based on the algebraic model—that determines the specific manner in which candidate programs are put together.

It should be emphasized that the central representational choice in this problem has been the choice of program grammar. This choice was guided by the introduction of the algebraic model. However, the model made a more direct contribution to the formulation of a method of solution. Properties of the model led to a new overall plan for solution and to the introduction of new problem solving moves for effecting transitions in program space.

The key steps that are required for a transition from the previous formulation (described in section 18.2.3) to the present model-guided formulation are the following:

1. Find a model of program space.
2. Find "useful" properties of the model.

3. Use the model properties to formulate a method of solution (overall plan, detailed moves, control heuristics).

These steps were made "by hand" in the present work. One of the important objectives of future work in this area is to examine these steps in considerable detail in order to clarify the problems that one must face in mechanizing them. The mechanization of step 3 is approachable at present. The work of Mostow (1981) on "operationalizing" problem solving knowledge is relevant here. Similar problems are found in other problem reformulation studies (Amarel, 1981, 1982). The mechanization of step 2 is more difficult, but Lenat's work on AM and EURISCO (Davis and Lenat, 1982; Lenat, 1983a) has resulted in several ideas and methods that are relevant to this task.

Mechanization of the model-finding task (step 1) continues to appear very difficult. The problem of finding, adapting, and extending existing mathematical systems, to be used as models of a domain, was discussed in previous work (Amarel, 1971). No major progress has been made in this area over the last decade. If advances are to be made in the area of model-finding processes, a better understanding of *model-utilizing* processes must be reached. This is an area of AI in which more research is needed. It is also an area in which good progress is possible in the near future.

18.4 A THIRD APPROACH TO PROCEDURAL FORMULATIONS OF THE FORMATION PROBLEM: REASONING IN DATA SPACE

In the third approach to the program formation problem, the solution-finding process is strongly guided by the detailed analysis of individual data associations. In contrast to the previous two approaches, in which the main thrust of reasoning is from candidate programs to *the entire set of data associations,* the present approach goes from *individual associations* to candidate programs. Although the search for solution is tightly constrained by the program grammar and by the algebraic properties of the model of program space, an increased amount of reasoning takes place in *data space.* Given a data association, a derivation problem is solved to obtain a "computational path" that links the two elements of the association. The derivation is constrained by the program grammar. Only computational paths that can be generated by a constructible program are considered. The goal program is obtained by reasoning with the set of programs that are generated as candidates for producing the computational paths for all the data associations.

Two alternative methods have been explored within the present data-driven approach, called the *combination method* and the *elimination method.* These methods differ mainly in the way in which they obtain the overall solution from partial solutions. A partial solution is a program that satisfies one or more data associations but not all the associations in the domain. For example, in the problem π_1 a partial solution may be a program that satisfies the data association (ab, a) in the problem's specifying set (i.e., it returns $\{a\}$ for the input pair (ab)) but does not "satisfy" some other data association (bc, a), as in this case the program returns $\{ae\}$ for the input pair (bc) instead of the desired $\{a\}$. (See figure 18-1 where the specifying set of data association for the problem π_1 is shown.)

18.4.1 Knowledge Available in the Data-Driven Approach

Before the description of the solution methods is given, it is important to summarize the bodies of knowledge that are available in the new formulation and the form in which this knowledge is available. The program space is defined in terms of the program grammar G_1 and the algebraic model $\mathcal{R}_{d1}$. For our present purposes, the structure of inclusion relations in the algebra is not important. However, *equivalence* properties between relational expressions are very important, and so is the matrix interpretation of algebraic properties, which provides the basis for reasoning about "partial equivalences," that is, equivalences that hold only for parts of the domain of input pairs $d1$.

As indicated previously in section 18.2.1.1, the domain specification D_1 of the problem class includes a definition of *data space*. For a given finite, partially ordered structure, this definition is in terms of all the data objects in D_1 and the set of all available computational actions. A computational path in data space from a set of input data objects to an output data object is an aggregate of computational actions that effects the transition from input to output. In the present data-driven approach to formation, effective ways are needed of finding/constructing a computational path between a given pair of input data and output data. This requires the solution of a derivation problem, for which there are well-known methods in AI. To solve derivation problems effectively, it is important to have a good representation of the available actions; this includes not only a description of effects of actions but also appropriate applicability conditions for actions. In our problem, these conditions can be obtained from knowledge about the available computational actions, that is, knowledge about the relations I, $\hat{I}$, E, about the set operations $\vee$, $\&$, and about the list-processing operations s, c. In the previous two procedural formulations of the formation problem, the availability of this knowledge was not necessary. In the present formulation it is.

The following is a partial list of the properties of computational actions that are needed by the formation process in its present approach.

18.4.1.1 Properties of Computational Actions

1. $I: x \notin Ix$, for all x in σ.

   if $Ix = \{y, \alpha\}$, then $x \in \hat{I}y$; x, y are in σ.

   (For convenience, the notation Ix is used here instead of the proper functional notation ηx which was introduced in section 18.2.1.1., where the value of ηx

(here Ix) is the set of all elements in σ that stand in relation I to x; the notation $\{y, \alpha\}$ denotes a set where one of the elements is y and the *rest* of the elements is represented by α).

2. $\hat{I}$: $x \notin \hat{I}x$, for all x in σ.

   if $\hat{I}x = \{y, \alpha\}$, then $x \in Iy$; x, y are in σ.

3. E: $x \in Ex$, for all x in σ.

   The set $Ex = \{x\}$ is a singleton.

4. $\cap$: if $\cap x_1 x_2 \ldots x_n = y$, where $x_1, x_2, \ldots, x_n$ are in 2^σ and y is a singleton set $\{u\}$, then the input sets $x_1, x_2, \ldots, x_n$ must have the form $x_1 = \{u, \alpha_1\}$, $x_2 = \{u, \alpha_2\}, \ldots, x_n = \{u, \alpha_n\}$, where $\alpha_1, \alpha_2, \ldots, \alpha_n$ represent disjoint sets (and one or more of them may be empty). In the special case $\cap x$, then x must be $\{u\}$.

5. $\cup$: if $\cup x_1, x_2 \ldots x_n$, where $x_1, x_2, \ldots x_n$ are in 2^σ and y is a singleton set $\{u\}$, then the input sets $x_1, x_2, \ldots, x_n$ must have the form $\{u\}$, or they must be empty; but at least one of the input sets must be nonempty.

It is assumed that this knowledge about properties of computational actions is available to the formation process and furthermore that the knowledge is in a form that can be conveniently applied depending on the direction of reasoning—forward from the inputs or backwards from the output.

18.4.2 The Data-Driven Combination Method

The following is a general outline of the method. For a given data association, the process requests from the grammar G_1 candidate program schemes, starting from the lowest weight schemes and gradually increasing the weight. Given a program scheme, an effort is made to instantiate it in a way that would solve the computational path problem for the given data association. When a program is found that satisfies the data association, it is tested over the remaining associations. If all the associations are satisfied, then the process terminates with success. If not, then attention focuses on an association that is not satisfied by this program, and a process of finding a program that solves the computational path problem for this association is carried out. Given a set of programs, each partially satisfying the given set of data associations, an effort is made to *combine* them so as to achieve a solution for the entire set.

18.4.2.1 Application of the Data-Driven Combination Method to the Formation Problem π_1

A good way of describing the formation method and its properties is to show how it applies to a specific problem. The following is an outline of the process of applying the method to the formation problem π_1.

1. Consider the *data association* (*ee, e*).

   Assume Scheme $S_1 = (p \; \triangle \; p)$ with $w = 3$.

   The program variable p can take values I, $\hat{I}$, or E. Options can be determined by (1) *trial assignment and evaluation* (i.e., running a candidate program with the left side of the data association as input and checking whether the computed output matches the right side of the data association) or (2) *reasoning backwards* from the right side of the data association and propagating data constraints in the direction of the input. In the present case, trial assignments yield a program[6]

   $$P_{1,3} = (E \; \triangle \; E); \; w = 3$$

   that satisfies the given data association.

   In a LISP paraphrase, $P_{1,3}$ corresponds to

   (lambda $(u_1 \; u_2)$ (intersection (E-function u_1) (E-function u_2))),

   where E-function is the functional form of E (see section 18.2.1.1 above).

   The program $P_{1,3}$ is tried over the entire data domain $d1$. It satisfies a total of five from among the fifteen associations; these are (*ee, e*), (*aa, a*), (*bb, b*), (*cc, c*), (*dd, d*). Furthermore, the program behavior has an *"interesting"* pattern: it has null values outside the subdomain of $d1$ in which its behavior matches the desired program behavior. As will be seen later, this behavior is considered interesting because it facilitates the combination of partially successful programs—which is a highly valued property in the present method.

2. Now attention is focused on one of the data associations that are not satisfied by $P_{1,3}$.

   Consider the *data association* (*ab, a*).

   A. Assume scheme $S_1 = (p \; \triangle \; p)$ with $w = 3$.

   By the use of trial assignments and evaluations it can be determined that *there is no solution of type S_1*, that is, there is no instantiation of this scheme that satisfies the given data association.

   Retain this failure of S_1.

   B. Assume scheme $S_2 = (p \; \triangledown \; p)$ with $w = 3$.

   By similar method, S_2 *fails. Retain* this fact.

   C. Move now to schemes with $w = 5$. Assume scheme $S_3 = ((p_1 \; \triangle \; p_1) \; \oslash \; p_2)$.

   In the graph language of programs, the structure is as shown in figure 18-24.

---

[6]For purposes of comparison across methods, a single name for a program structure is used throughout this chapter. This explains the rather odd choice of subscripts. The relation matrices of the program $P_{1,3}$ as well as of other key programs generated via this method are shown in figure 18-27.

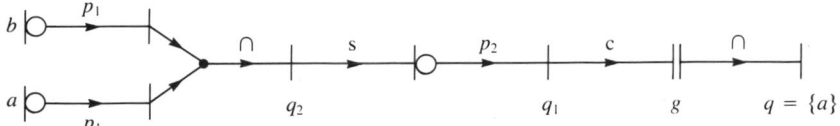

Figure 18-24:   Graph representation of scheme S_3.

Data constraints are propagated from the output backwards. Since the output set q should be $\{a\}$, then in view of the properties of $\cap$, the elements of the bag g should be of the form $\{a, \alpha_1\}, \{a, \alpha_2\}, \ldots, \{a, \alpha_n\}$, where $n > 1$, and the sets $\alpha_1, \alpha_2, \ldots, \alpha_n$ should be disjoint. In the special case in which g has only one element, then it should be $\{a\}$. Thus the values of q_1 should be in the form $\{a, \alpha\}$, where α may be empty.

Consider the possible value assignments to p_2.

$$p_2 = E?$$

(Output of p_2 can be $\{a\}$. Then, input to p_2 must be a. Input to s must be one or more a. But since q_2 is a set it must be a singleton, $\{a\}$. But we know from previous work with S_1 that there is no solution for the front block $(p_1 \;\boxtimes\; p_1)$, when the input-output of the block is (ab, a). Thus $p_2 = E$ fails. This fact and the reason for failure—that is, failure of S_1 for the given data association—are *retained*.)

$$p_2 = I?$$

(Inputs to p_2 must be b or c or d (from general properties of I and the specific definition of I in the present problem (see figure 18-1)). But in each of these cases, output of p_2 includes a and e. This violates the data constraint on the bag g. Thus $p_2 = I$ fails. This fact and the reason for failure—that is, properties of I—are *retained*.)

$$p_2 = \hat{I}?$$

(By similar reasoning, this assignment *fails* also. Thus, scheme S_3 fails. *Retain* this fact and its reasons. Note that this conclusion is obtained without looking into assignments for p_1.)

D. The scheme $S_3^1 = ((p_1 \;\boxtimes\; p_1) \;\oslash\; p_2)$ is also found to *fail*. Here much of the reasoning for S_3 can be "borrowed."

E. Assume now scheme $S_4 = ((p_1 \;\boxtimes\; p_1) \;\varnothing\; p_2)$.

By reasoning similar to that used in the S_3 case, scheme S_4 *fails*. It is interesting to note how an algebraic property can be used in the present analysis: Checking for the assignment $p_2 = E$, we have $S_4 = S_1 \;\varnothing\; E$; but it is known from the algebra that $X \;\varnothing\; E \leftrightarrow X$ (see section 18.3.1.2, 2); thus S_4 is reduced to S_1, which has already failed.

F. Move now to schemes with $w = 7$.

By analysis, *the four following schemes fail:*

$$S_5 = ((p_1 \boxtriangle p_1) \oslash (p_2 \lor p_3))$$
$$S_6 = ((p_1 \boxtriangle p_1) \oslash (p_2 \,\&\, p_3))$$
$$S_7 = ((p_1 \boxtriangle p_1) \obar (p_2 \lor p_3))$$
$$S_8 = ((p_1 \boxtriangle p_1) \obar (p_2 \,\&\, p_3));$$

and the schemes obtained by changing $(p_1 \boxtriangle p_1)$ into $(p_1 \boxvee p_1)$ in these schemes also *fail*. It is interesting to discuss one part of this analysis which illustrates the use of the algebra and the possibility of obtaining *"serendipitous" solutions.* Consider the scheme S_6: By the left distributivity properties of the algebra (see section 18.3.1.2, 4b) the scheme S_6 is equivalent to

$$((p_1 \boxtriangle p_1) \oslash p_2) \,\&\, ((p_1 \boxtriangle p_1) \oslash p_3).$$

Propagation of the output constraint requires that the two partial outputs of this decomposition be in the form $\{a, \alpha_1\}$, $\{a, \alpha_2\}$, where α_1, α_2 represent disjoint sets. Pursuing an analysis of the subschemes in a manner similar to S_3 shows that there are no possible assignments for p_2, p_3, p_1 that satisfy the output constraints. However, if *one* of the front blocks $(p_1 \boxtriangle p_1)$ is changed to $(p_1' \boxvee p_1')$, then a solution exists. The solution is

$$P_4 = ((I \boxtriangle I) \oslash \hat{I}) \,\&\, ((\hat{I} \boxvee \hat{I}) \oslash I); \quad w = 11.$$

This program cannot be "simplified" into a form of type S_6 (with $w = 7$), because changing the connective in the front block has spoiled the possibility of using the left distributivity property of the algebra in reverse. Evaluation of P_4 over the entire data domain shows that it satisfies four of the fifteen associations (see figure 18-27). This happens not to be an especially strong program. However, the program is *retained*.

It should be noted that in the present case P_4 was obtained by deviating slightly from a specific goal-oriented task and by exploring opportunistically a "local neighborhood" when the goal-directed analysis returned failure. This may be an interesting source of serendipitous findings. More work in this area is needed.

G. Exploration continues now with other schemes that have $w = 7$.

Work on the scheme $S_9 = ((p_1 \boxtriangle p_1) \,\&\, (p_2 \boxtriangle p_2))$ returns *failure*. However, work on the scheme $S_{10} = ((p_1 \boxvee p_1) \,\&\, (p_2 \boxvee p_2))$ yields a solution in the form

$$P_2 = ((E \boxvee E) \,\&\, (I \boxvee I)); \quad w = 7.$$

Evaluation of P_2 over the entire data domain shows that it satisfies nine of the fifteen associations (see figure 18-27). Furthermore, the program behavior has the same interesting pattern that was observed previously in $P_{1,3}$; that is, it has null values outside the subdomain of $d1$ in which its behavior matches the desired program behavior. This is considered a strong program.

By algebraic manipulation, the program P_2 can be shown to be equivalent to the following program, P_2' with $w = 9$.

$$P_2' = [(E \boxdot E) \, \& \, ((E \boxdot E) \oslash I)].$$

This derives from the following:

$$(I \boxdot I) \leftrightarrow ((E \oslash I) \boxdot (E \oslash I)) \leftrightarrow ((E \boxdot E) \oslash I).$$

Establishing such an equivalence is motivated by (1) the possibility of simplifying the program and (2) the usefulness of the formation process's having several structures that are functionally equivalent. Program simplification is helped by identifying common subblocks that handle the same data. Functionally equivalent structures provide different "starting points" in program space around which it may be fruitful to explore for promising solution candidates. It should be noted that the generation of candidates takes place in the space of program structures.

The problem solver is now at a point at which he must handle the issue of how to combine partially successful programs. This is a key problem in the present process, and it will be given special attention in the next section—at the risk of introducing some discontinuity in the description of the problem solving process for π_1.

3. *A key part of the process: How to combine programs.*

Examination of the programs obtained so far shows that the two interesting programs $P_{1,3}$ and P_2 jointly cover a very large part of the data domain $d1$. Actually, their *union* covers fourteen out of the fifteen associations. The only data association not covered is (bc, a). In this situation, it is natural to propose the following program as a new candidate:

$$P_5 = P_{1,3} \vee P_2 = [(E \boxtimes E) \vee ((E \boxdot E) \, \& \, (I \boxdot I))]; \; w = 11.$$

By algebraic manipulation, the program P_5 can be shown to be equivalent to the following program, whose weight is also 11:

$$P_3 = [(E \boxdot E) \, \& \, ((E \boxdot E) \oslash (I \vee E))]; \; w = 11.$$

The use of a union operator for combining two programs in the way just done is a very powerful and simple method of solving the *program combination problem.* It was possible in this case because of the "interestingness" property of the two component programs; that is, for every input, such a program returns the correct output or the null set.

However, it is not always possible to find a way of combining partly correct programs in this simple way. Actually, the most difficult and central problem in this area is how to combine/merge programs that provide partial solutions to the formation problem by satisfying subdomains of the given function. This is an instance of the difficult AI problem of how to handle *conjunctive goals.* The formation problem can easily be seen as a problem of finding a plan to satisfy a set of conjunctive goals. This problem is especially difficult if there is no way of designing a plan that is *decomposable*—that is, that can be divided into parts each of which can be seen as devoted to satisfying one of the goals. This is certainly the situation in the program formation program, and it is common in many other theory formation or design tasks. The nature of this problem and the importance of working with "nearly decomposable systems," are discussed in depth by Simon in his book *Sciences of the Artificial* (Simon, 1969).

There has been a certain amount of progress in AI on methods for problem solving and plan generation in conjunctive goal situations. The earliest work in this area was by Ernst and Newell (1969) on GPS, which was pursued further by Ernst and Goldstein (1982) and by Korf (1982) in connection with approaches for handling interacting goals. The work described by Sacerdoti (1977), Stefik (1981), Waldinger (1977), and Warren (1974, 1976) has further advanced our understanding of the problem.

In the area of program synthesis, the problem of conjunctive goals has received some attention from Manna and Waldinger (1975, 1977). This was recognized by them as an especially difficult problem, one in which methods of solution seem to be very domain specific. However, they suggest two very general approaches in their work that are relevant to the present task. The first approach involves the notion of *program modification*. This approach was also proposed by Sussman (1975) and Mostow (1981). The main idea is that in order to achieve goals C_1 *and* C_2 simultaneously, one should first write a program to achieve C_1 and then modify that program to achieve C_2 as well. Of course, in the course of modification one must keep in mind that the achievement of C_1 must be protected while an effort is being made to achieve the goal C_2.

The second approach involves some variant of the notion of *generalization*. The main idea here is to make the solution of the first goal as "general" as possible, so that some "special case" of the solution might satisfy the second goal as well. The key step in this approach is to develop an appropriate notion of a "generalization hierarchy." Mitchell's approach to learning, in which the notion of "version space" is used (Mitchell, 1977, 1978) is closely related to this general approach.

In the present data-driven combination method of program formation, a strategy of *program modification* has been explored. A key decision here is choosing a specific program on which modifications are to be made. Good candidates for modification are any of the interesting programs obtained so far, that is, either the elementary interesting programs such as $P_{1,3}$ or P_2 or the compound interesting program P_3 that was obtained by combining other interesting programs via a union operator.

The generalization approach to the handling of conjunctive goals will be discussed further below in connection with the second data-driven method of formation, which is based on a process of elimination.

Let us return now to the solution process, which we left after obtaining the strong interesting program

$$P_3 = [(E \boxed{\vee} E) \& ((E \boxed{\vee} E) \oslash (I \vee E))]; w = 11,$$

which satisfies all the data associations but one, namely, the (bc, a) association (see figure 18-27). A LISP representation of the program P_3 is as follows:

```
P₃ = (lambda(u₁ u₂) (Intersection)
                    [Union (E-function u₁)(E-function u₂)]
                    [Intersection-* (Mapcar
                        '(lambda (x)
                            (Union (I-function x
                             E-function x)))
                            (Union (E-function u₁)
                                   (E-function u₂)))])).
```

18.4.2.2 Continuation of the Problem-Solving Process for π_1: Program Modification Stage

It is possible that a statistical approach to formation, in which much weight is ordinarily given to the *number* of satisfied associations, may decide to stop here and to neglect the "troublemaking" association (bc, a). However, such process would completely miss an important part of the concept of Infimum that the program/theory must capture. In particular, in the partially ordered structure Σ_1, this is the only association that illustrates the case of Infimum for *noncomparable* elements (i.e., elements not on the same chain). The number of situations that exemplify an important case within the domain of a theory can easily be changed. For example, the structure Σ_2 in figure 18-25 has the same number of elements as Σ_1, but it presents more associations than in Σ_1 that illustrate the case of Infimum for noncomparable elements, namely, (bc, a) (eb, a), (ec, a). The main point of this comment is that an effective theory formation process should be able to approach *each* item of data in its domain and try to "understand" it. A lone item, as exemplified by the (bc, a) data association in this problem, may be representative of an important facet of a phenomenon, and it should receive attention unless there is good reason for it not to—including, for example, the lack of resources to pursue the investigation.

It happens that considerable "modification effort" is needed in order to go from the strong program P_3 to a goal program that satisfies the association (bc, a) as well as the other fourteen associations. Let us now outline the reasoning involved as we pursue the solution of π_1.

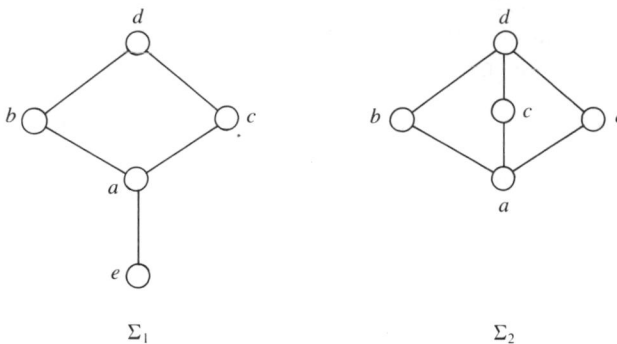

Figure 18-25: Two partially ordered structures with the same number of elements but with different proportions of noncomparable elements.

The structure of the program P_3 is shown in figure 18-26a in the graph language. If the input pair (b, c) is applied, the output is the empty set, and the distribution of data at various parts of the program is as shown in the figure. We would like the output to be $\{a\}$. The inputs to the last intersection operation in the program should be $\{a, \alpha_1\}$, $\{a, \alpha_2\}$, for α_1, α_2, representing disjoint sets. One of the branches of P_3 (the lower one in the figure) produces an output $\{a, e\}$ that matches the desired form. Let us try to change the other branch so that its output will be (a, α_2), such that α_2 and $\{e\}$ have a null intersection. We now have the following *subproblem:* Find a computational path from the set $\{b, c\}$—that is, from the present output of the "delinquent" program part—to the desired output $\{a, \alpha_2\}$. An attempt can be made to obtain a solution to this problem via a systematic search of the type presented earlier. However, a more goal-directed approach based on reasoning in data space is also possible. The reasoning can be seen best in the context of the geometric representation of the partially ordered structure Σ_1, which is shown in figure 18-26b.

The reasoning is as follows: To obtain from the elements b, c a set that includes the element a, one should apply the I operation on both b and c and combine the results by union or intersection; this will produce a set $\{a, e\}$. The e must be "filtered out" of that set; this can be obtained by applying the $\hat{I}$ operation on the set $\{a, e\}$ and by producing as output the union of the results. Alternatively, the $(\hat{I} \vee E)$ operation may be applied on the set $\{a, e\}$, and the output may be obtained from the intersection of the results. This argument results in four possible programs for patching the delinquent part of P_3, shown in figure 18-26c. Unfortunately, although a patched program satisfies the association (bc, a), it loses ground in several of the associations that were previously satisfied by P_3.

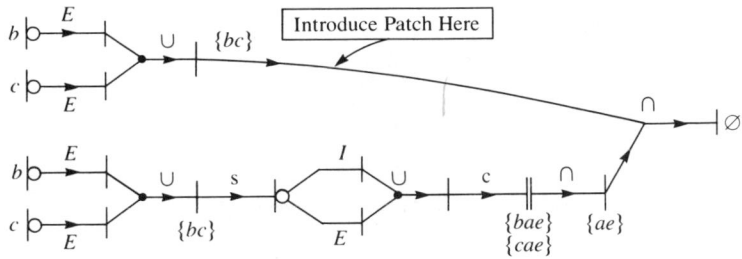

a. Initial strong program P_3, which is to be modified.

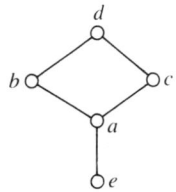

b. The partially ordered structure Σ_1.

c. Development of possible "patches" for modifying P_3.

Figure 18-26: Approach to program modification.

Actually, the best patched program, call it P_5, satisfies only five of the fifteen associations in the domain (see figure 18-27). The structure of this program is

$$P_5 = [(((E \boxtimes E) \oslash I) \oslash \hat{I}) \& ((E \boxtimes E) \oslash (I \lor E))]; \ w = 15.$$

Now, additional modification of P_5 is needed. Attention remains focused on the part that was recently patched. After a certain amount of search, the part

$$((E \boxtimes E) \oslash I) \oslash \hat{I}$$

	Infimum	$P_{1,3}$ E ⟎ E	P_4 [(I ⟎ I) ⊘ Î] ∧ (Î ⟏ Î) ⊘ I]	P_2 (E ⟏ E) ∧ (I ⟏ I)	P_3 [(E ⟏ E) ∧ ((E ⟏ E) ⊘ (I ∨ E))]	P_5 [((E ⟏ E) ⦸ I) ⦸ Î) ∧ ((E ⟏ E) ⊘ (I ∨ E))]	$P_6 = P_{3,1}$ [((E ⦸ E) ⊘ (I ∨ E)) ⊘ (Î ∨ E)) ∧ ((E ⟏ E) ⊘ (I ∨ E))]
ee	e	ⓔ	—	—	ⓔ	—	ⓔ
ea	e	—	—	ⓔ	ⓔ	—	ⓔ
eb	e	—	—	ⓔ	ⓔ	—	ⓔ
ec	e	—	—	ⓔ	ⓔ	—	ⓔ
ed	e	—	—	ⓔ	ⓔ	—	ⓔ
aa	a	ⓐ	ⓐ	—	ⓐ	ⓐ	ⓐ
ab	a	—	ⓐ	ⓐ	ⓐ	ⓐ	ⓐ
ac	a	—	ⓐ	ⓐ	ⓐ	ⓐ	ⓐ
ad	a	—	ⓐ	ⓐ	ⓐ	ⓐ	ⓐ
bb	b	ⓑ	bc	—	ⓑ	ab	ⓑ
bc	a	—	bc	—	—	ⓐ	ⓐ
bd	b	—	bc	ⓑ	ⓑ	ab	ⓑ
cc	c	ⓒ	bc	—	ⓒ	ac	ⓒ
cd	c	—	bc	ⓒ	ⓒ	ac	ⓒ
dd	d	ⓓ	—	—	ⓓ	abcd	ⓓ

Figure 18-27: Relation matrices of important programs generated in the data-driven approach with a strategy of program combination/modification.

is modified into

$$[((E \boxveebox E) \oslash (I \vee E)) \oslash (\hat{I} \vee E)],$$

and this results in the following program, which satisfies all the data associations:

$$P_6 = [((E \boxveebox E) \oslash (I \vee E)) \oslash (\hat{I} \vee E)) \& ((E \boxveebox E) \oslash (I \vee E))]; w = 19.$$

It can easily be seen that the program P_6 is equivalent to the program $P_{3,1}$, which was the solution obtained in previous approaches.

A LISP representation of the program P_6 is as follows:

```
P₆ = (lambda (u₁ u₂)
          (Intersection
              [Intersection-* (Mapcar
                  '(lambda (x)(Union
                              (Icap-function x)
                              (E-function x)))
                  (Intersection-* (Mapcar
                      '(lambda (y) (Union
                                  (I-function y) (E-function y)))
                      (Union (E-function u₁)
                             (E-function u₂)))))]
              [Intersection-* (Mapcar
                  '(lambda (z) (Union
                              (I-function z) (E-function z)))
                  (Union (E-function u₁) (E-function u₂)))])).
```

Note that while P_6 is functionally equivalent to the program P_{Infimum} which was shown in section 18.2.1.1, their structures (and LISP representations) are different. The functional equivalence of the two programs can easily be established within the algebraic model.

18.4.2.3 Comments on the Data-Driven Combination Method: Discovery of New Concepts Defined over Subdomains

In general, although the data-driven program combination/modification approach is more controlled and better guided than the previous approaches, it still involves a considerable amount of search. The problem of combining partial solutions and of modifying programs in effective ways remains a formidable one. This is an area where more research is needed.

The notion of "interesting" programs that was introduced here induces the idea that these programs may be used to define *new concepts* in the problem under investigation. These are concepts of *interesting subdomains of the domain* d1 of input data that was originally given. The concepts are identified by subdomains of $d1$ for which interesting special solutions to the Infimum problem were found. These subdomains can be defined as follows:

$d_{1,1}$: Pairs from $d1$ for which application of the program $P_{1,3} = (E \ \boxtimes \ E)$ returns a nonnull value (In our case, the pairs are *ee, aa, bb, cc, dd*).

$d_{1,2}$: Pairs from $d1$ for which application of the program $P_2 = ((E \ \boxdot \ E)$ & $(I \ \boxdot \ I))$ returns a nonnull value (In our case, the pairs are *ea, eb, ec, ed, ab, ac, ad, bd, cd*).

$d_{1,3}$: Union of $d_{1,1}$ and $d_{1,2}$. Elements of this set are characterized by a nonnull value of the program $P_3 = [(E \ \boxdot \ E) \ \& \ ((E \ \boxdot \ E) \ \oslash \ (I \ \vee \ E))]$.

Thus the present approach to theory formation can provide the basis for *concept discovery* processes. In these processes, a domain of a phenomenon is redefined so that it can be captured by a program with certain special characteristics, such as simplicity in a given language. This is a promising area of investigation, and it should be explored further.

There is an interesting connection between this notion of concept discovery and the notion of performance improvement in expert problem solving systems. Improvement in problem solving performance is often obtained by specializing a method to a subdomain of a class of problems. This is an important approach to *expertise acquisition;* it involves the formation of the concept of an interesting subdomain of specialization *and* of an efficient solution method for handling problems in the subdomain (Amarel, 1982). The issues of defining a subdomain in terms of an interesting solution method are similar to those encountered in the present program formation task.

In view of the subdomain concepts just discussed, it is possible to express the program for $P_{Infimum}$ in the general form of a conditional statement,[7] as follows:

$$P_{\mathrm{Infimum}} = \begin{array}{l} \textit{If } \mathrm{NOT\ NULL}\ P_{1,3} = (E\ \boxtimes\ E),\ \textit{then }P_{1,3} \\ \textit{If } \mathrm{NOT\ NULL}\ P_2 = ((E\ \boxdot\ E)\ \&\ (I\ \boxdot\ I)),\ \textit{then }P_2 \\ \textit{Else }P_6 = [(((E\ \boxdot\ E)\ \oslash\ (I\ \vee\ E))\ \oslash\ (\hat{I}\ \vee\ E))\ \& \\ ((E\ \boxdot\ E)\ \oslash\ (\hat{I}\ \vee\ E)).] \end{array}$$

Of course, a suitable augmentation in the program language is needed in order to obtain statements in this form.

18.4.3 The Data-Driven Elimination Method

18.4.3.1 Geometric Representation of Data Space

Before proceeding with a discussion of the data-driven elimination method, let us briefly introduce a geometric representation of data space that is extremely useful

---

[7]The syntax used here is informal, but the statement is meant to be read as a LISP conditional.

in expressing and understanding the concepts involved in the method. The representation is based on the well-known graphic representation of finite, partially ordered structures, that is, the structure diagram discussed in section 18.2.1.1 above. Now, each point in data space can be represented as a *geometric region* that covers parts of the structure diagram. A computational action that takes one or more data objects to another can be seen as a transformation between regions that correspond to the data objects. The idea is very similar to that of Venn diagrams, except that the geometry helps in the handling of the inclusion structure of the sets involved. As an example, figure 18-28 shows on the geometric representation of data space for the problem π_1 the data point $\{ea\}$ obtained from the intersection of all the elements included by the element *b and* all those included by *c*. Several other examples of uses of the geometric representation of data space will be seen below.

18.4.3.2 General Description of the Elimination Method: Assumptions Made on the Basis of Specialized Knowledge About Problems in the Class

For a given data association, the process finds all the constructible programs up to a specified weight ceiling that satisfy the association. If no program is found, then the condition on the weight ceiling is relaxed and search continues for programs of higher weight, and so on, until a specified ceiling of available computational effort is reached; then the process stops. Suppose now that a set of programs is obtained that satisfies the first association. This set is checked over a second association; and the programs that do not satisfy the new association are *eliminated*. The remaining programs are checked over a third association, and so on, until all the data associations are considered. If one or more programs remain after this elimination process, then a solution to the problem has been found. If not, then the process is repeated with further relaxation of the program weight ceiling until all the computational effort that was allocated to this problem has been spent.

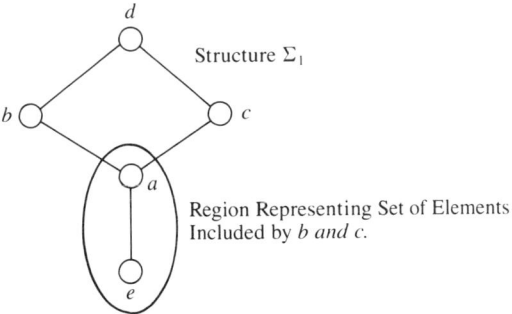

Figure 18-28:   Example of use of geometric representation of data space.

In addition, in the present formulation it is assumed that certain restrictions are imposed on the process of finding a program that satisfies a given data association. Let us assume that an association in the form (x_1x_2, y) is under consideration.

Except in cases in which a solution has the form of an elementary scheme with $w = 3$ (e.g., $(E \ \square \ E)$), the structure of candidate solutions is restricted to the form $P_a \vee P_b$. This means that for a desired output of the solution/program in the form of a singleton $\{y\}$, the outputs of P_a and P_b are sets that have the forms $\{y, \alpha_1\}$, $\{y, \alpha_2\}$, respectively, and the parts α_1, α_2 of these sets are disjoint (or one or both may be empty).

Furthermore, an assumption is made that there is a very restricted number of points in data space that can instantiate the sets $\{y, \alpha_1\}$, $\{y, \alpha_2\}$ whose intersection produces the desired output. These are (1) the set $\{x_1, x_2\}$ made of the inputs to the program, provided that at least one of the x's is identical with y (let us call it the *input set*); (2) the set of all elements u in σ, such that $u = y$ or y/u; (3) the set of all elements u in σ such that $u = y$ or $y\hat{/}u$. It is useful to see an interpretation of the last two sets in the geometric representation of data space (see figure 18-29). The second set is made of all the elements that can be reached from y by descending along the chains in Σ that go through y; it is suggestive to call this set the *cone of y*. The third set is made of all the elements that can be reached from y by ascending along all the chains in Σ that go through y; it is suggestive to call it the *inverted cone of y*.

Now, the process of finding a program that satisfies a given data association can proceed as a search in data space moving *forward* from the left side of the given association (the input pair of the program) toward the sets that are possible candidates

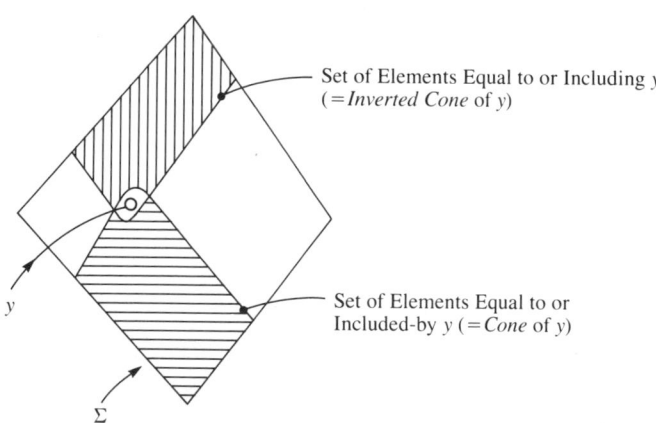

Figure 18-29: The two "cone sets" of an element y of a partially ordered structure Σ, shown in the geometric representation of data space.

for a terminal intersection. Alternatively, the search in data space can proceed backward from the sets that are candidates for terminal intersection toward the given input pair.

Clearly the assumption on restricting the points in data space that are possible candidates for the terminal intersection represents an important introduction of *specialized knowledge* of the problem domain into the solution method. This knowledge can be derived from analysis of properties of computational actions and of their aggregates in the problem domain and/or by empirical exploration of properties of solutions in the domain. The geometric representation of data space facilitates enormously *our* understanding of the properties of the domain. Mechanizing the discovery of the geometric representation and of uses of the representation in finding properties of the domain that are useful for solving problems in a given class remains an important open problem in AI.

Let us proceed now with an outline of an example of application of the present method to the problem π_1.

18.4.3.3 Application of the Data-Driven Elimination Method to the Formation Problem π_1

1. Assume the weight cciling is set at $w = 7$.

   A. Consider the *data association* (ab, a).

   In the present case, the candidate sets for terminal intersection are the input set $\{ab\}$ and the "cone sets" $\{ae\}$, $\{abcd\}$ (see figure 18-30a).

   The input set $\{ab\}$ can be produced from the input pair by the program $(E \boxtimes E)\,(w = 3)$.

   The cone set $\{ae\}$ can be produced from the input pair by the following programs:

   $$w = 3: (I \boxtimes I)$$
   $$w = 5: ((\hat{I} \boxtimes \hat{I}) \oslash I)$$
   $$w = 7: ((I \vee E) \boxtimes (I \vee E))$$

   The inverted cone set $\{abcd\}$ can be produced from the input pair by the following programs:

   $$w = 5: ((I \boxtimes I) \oslash \hat{I}),\ ((I \boxtimes I) \oslash \hat{I}),\ ((I \boxtimes I) \oslash \hat{I})$$
   $$w = 7: ((\hat{I} \vee E) \boxtimes (\hat{I} \vee E)),\ ((I \boxtimes I) \oslash (\hat{I} \vee E))$$

   In this listing of the programs, if a new program is found that is known to be functionally equivalent to a program that is already in the list (i.e., the previously generated/listed program has w lower than or equal to the new program), then a new program is not added to the list. For example, the program $(E \boxtimes E) \oslash (I \vee E))$ with $w = 7$ is not added to the list of "producers" of the set $\{ae\}$ after the program $((I \vee E) \boxtimes (I \vee E))$, which is its equivalent, has been listed there. The test for equivalence is based on the known

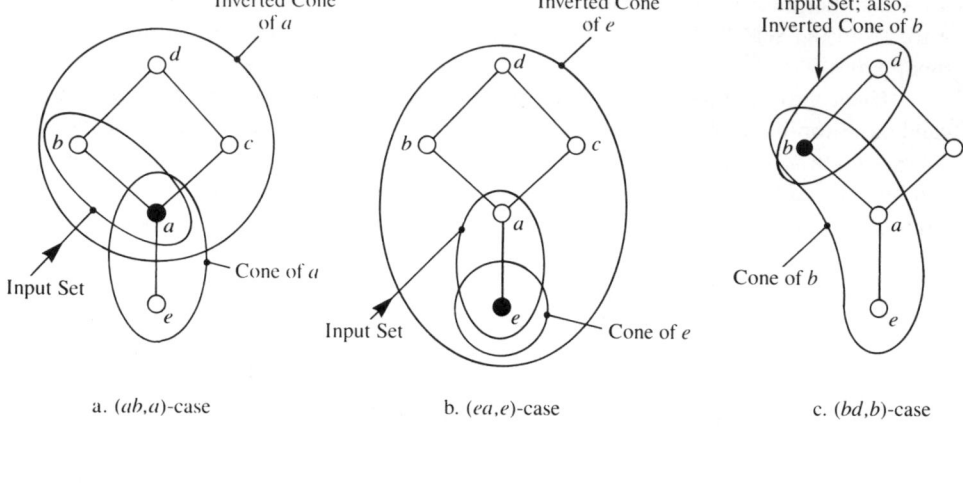

a. (ab,a)-case

b. (ea,e)-case

c. (bd,b)-case

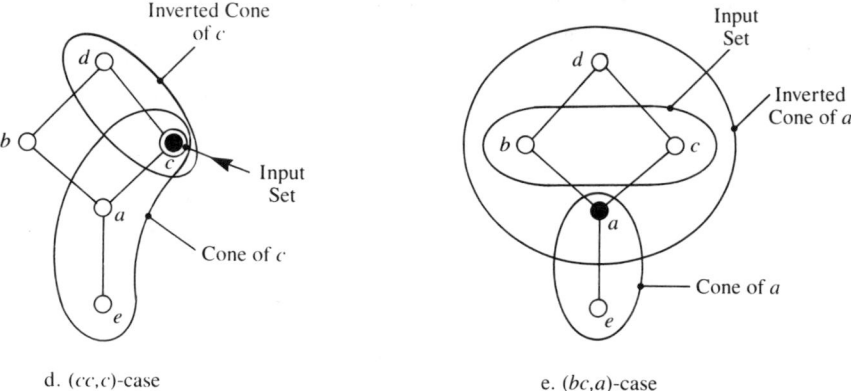

d. (cc,c)-case

e. (bc,a)-case

Note: The desired output in each case is shown as a darkened node.

Figure 18-30: Important sets used for finding solutions in individual cases, shown in the geometric representation of data space.

properties of the algebraic model. Note that the pruning of functionally equivalent programs is not necessary, but it may help with efficiency.

The objective of these program listings is to produce a *sufficient amount of functional variety* in the form of a set of programs, all of which satisfy the data association under consideration. The hope is that within this functional variety a program will be found that satisfies all the other associations in the domain. This is a special instance of the approach to solving conjunctive goal problems by generalization. In this approach, an attempt is made to find a set of solutions for the first goal which is *as general* as possible, so that a subset of this set might satisfy the second goal, and then the third goal, and so on.

On the basis of the previous analysis, three solutions are obtained that are based on a terminal intersection of the sets $\{ab\}$, $\{ae\}$, and fifteen solutions that are based on a terminal intersection of the cone sets $\{ae\}$, $\{abcd\}$. For example, the first three solutions are as follows:[8]

$$P_2 = [(E \boxtimes E) \ \& \ (I \boxtimes I)]$$
$$P_7 = [((E \boxtimes E) \ \& \ (\hat{I} \boxtimes \hat{I}) \oslash I)]$$
$$P_3 = [(E \boxtimes E) \ \& \ ((I \vee E) \boxtimes (I \vee E))]$$

B. Consider now the *data association* (ea, e).

In the present case, the candidate sets for terminal intersection consist of the input set $\{ea\}$ and the cone sets $\{e\}$, $\{eabcd\}$ (see figure 18-30b).

As in the previous case, the input set $\{ea\}$ can be produced from the input pair by the program $(E \boxtimes E)$.

The cone set $\{e\}$ can be produced from the input pair by the same three programs that produced the set $\{ae\}$ in the previous case.

The inverted cone set $\{eabcd\}$ can be produced from the input pair by using only two of the five programs that were used to produce the set $\{ae\}$ in the previous case. The three programs that are *eliminated* are $((I \boxtimes I) \oslash \hat{I})$, $((I \boxtimes I) \oslash \hat{I})$, $((I \boxtimes I) \oslash \hat{I})$.

Thus a total of nine solutions are obtained, three by intersection with the input set and six by intersection between the two cone sets.

C. Consider next the *data association* (bd, b).

The candidates for terminal intersection are the input set $\{bd\}$ and the cone sets $\{eab\}$ and $\{bd\}$ (see figure 18-30c). Note that in this case the input set and the inverted cone set of the output are equal. Despite this, the process continues to consider alternate *ways* of constructing the set $\{bd\}$.

The first way of constructing $\{bd\}$ from the input pair is via the program $(E \boxtimes E)$ which, as before, produces/characterizes the input set.

The second way of constructing the set $\{bd\}$ is by viewing it as the inverted cone set of the output b and checking whether any of the remaining programs

---

[8]If a program received a name previously in this chapter, it is given the same name here. Thus P_2, P_3 can be recognized as programs that were encountered previously.

for producing inverted cone sets can produce it. From the two remaining programs, only one can do it; it is $((\hat{I} \vee E) \boxtimes (\hat{I} \vee E))$. The other program— $((I \boxtimes I) \oslash (\hat{I} \vee E))$—is eliminated. Thus one out of the five initial programs for producing inverted cone sets is left.

The cone set $\{eab\}$ can be produced from the input pair by using only one of the three remaining programs for producing cone sets. This program is $((I \vee E) \boxtimes (I \vee E))$. The other two programs are eliminated. Thus at this point only two complete programs remain as possible solutions to our program. They are

$$P_3 = [(E \boxtimes E) \,\&\, ((I \vee E) \boxtimes (I \vee E))]; \; w = 11$$
$$P_8 = [((I \vee E) \boxtimes (I \vee E)) \,\&\, ((\hat{I} \vee E) \boxtimes (\hat{I} \vee E))];$$
$$w = 15.$$

The program P_3 is based on an intersection of the input set and the cone set of the output. P_3 was encountered previously in work with other approaches. It is a very strong program; it satisfies all but one of the fifteen data associations (see figure 18-27). The program P_8 is new. It is based on an intersection of the two cone sets of the output. Examination of this program shows that it is as strong as P_3; actually, it is functionally equivalent to P_3.

The process can continue now by going from other individual data associations toward the set of remaining programs and by eliminating programs as needed. Alternatively, as in the present case in which a small number of programs remain, the remaining programs are run over the entire data domain, and data associations that are not satisfied by any of the programs are noted. Proceeding with the latter approach shows that the only data association not satisfied by either P_3 or P_8 is (bc, a). Attention focuses now on this association.

2. Assume now that the weight ceiling is raised to $w = 9$.

In the *data association* (bc, a), the input set does not include the output a. Thus the only candidates for terminal intersection are the cone sets of a, that is, $\{ae\}$ and $\{abcd\}$ (see figure 18-30e).

Let us first consider programs that can produce the cone set $\{ae\}$ from the input pair (bc). The remaining program $((I \vee E) \boxtimes (I \vee E))$ with $w = 7$ can do it. No additional programs with $w = 8, 9$ can be found that can satisfy this goal.

Consider next programs that can produce the inverted cone set $\{abcd\}$ from the input pair (bc). The program $((\hat{I} \vee E) \boxtimes (\hat{I} \vee E))$ with $w = 7$ that remained from previous work fails; thus it is eliminated. No new programs with $w = 8, 9$ can be found that can satisfy the present goal.

Thus at this point *no program exists* as a possible solution to our problem.

3. Assume finally that the weight ceiling is raised to $w = 11$.

There are now two programs that can produce the cone set $\{ae\}$ from the input pair (bc):

$w = 7$: $((I \vee E) \boxtimes (I \vee E))$ (This is the "old" program.)
$w = 11$: $((E \boxvee E) \oslash ((\hat{I} \vee E) \oslash (I \vee E)))$.

Note that the second program is functionally equivalent to the first.[9] Thus it does not contribute extra functional variety. The formation process can devote some time to such recognition of equivalence and drop the new candidate program, or it can ignore this issue. This does not have a fundamental effect on whether a solution can be found. However, the issue should be considered from the point of view of solution-finding efficiency. Since efficiency is important for the formation process, some heuristic guidance is needed on the question of pruning functionally equivalent program candidates. In general, if the number of candidates is large, it pays to devote some effort to this pruning process.

Let us move now to the search for programs with weights $w = 10, 11$ that can produce the inverted cone set $\{abcd\}$ from the input pair (bc). The only programs that can be found are

$(((I \vee E) \boxtimes (I \vee E)) \oslash (\hat{I} \vee E))$; $w = 11$, and
$(((E \boxvee E) \oslash (I \vee E)) \oslash (\hat{I} \vee E))$; $w = 11$.

These two programs are functionally equivalent.

From the component programs for the two cone sets, several functionally equivalent solutions to the problem π_1 can now be obtained. Two of these solutions are as follows:

$P_{3,1} = [((I \vee E) \boxtimes (I \vee E)) \& ((I \vee E) \boxtimes (I \vee E) \oslash (\hat{I} \vee E))]$; $w = 19$,
$P_6 = [((E \boxvee E) \oslash (I \vee E)) \& ((E \boxvee E) \oslash (I \vee E) \oslash (\hat{I} \vee E))]$; $w = 19$.

(The first program can be recognized as $P_{3,1}$, which was obtained as the solution to the problem π_1 in the course of work with the first two approaches to formation. The second program can be recognized as P_6, which was the solution obtained in the data-driven combination method.)

In work so far with the present method, no special attention was given to the *order* in which input associations are considered. Clearly order has an effect on the efficiency of the process, and it should be studied in the context of the present

[9]From the algebraic model it can be seen that $((I \vee E) \boxtimes (I \vee E)) \leftrightarrow ((E \boxvee E) \oslash (I \vee E))$; and in view of the property $((\hat{I} \vee E) \oslash (I \vee E)) \leftrightarrow (I \vee E)$ (see section 18.3.1.2, 5) we obtain that $((E \boxvee E) \oslash (I \vee E)) \leftrightarrow ((E \boxvee E) \oslash ((\hat{I} \vee E) \oslash (I \vee E)))$.

approach. There has been a considerable amount of work on the ordering of constraints in constraint satisfaction problems (Nudel, 1983). Much of this work will probably be relevant to the present problem.

18.4.3.4 Discussion of the Data-Driven Elimination Method

The viewpoint from relation matrices. Let us examine the process of elimination in the framework of the relation matrices of programs. The set of data association has a domain of $n(n + 1)/2$ possible inputs and a range of n possible outputs. Thus there are at most $n^{n(n+1)/2}$ possible functions; and if it is assumed that a function is specified for k point of its domain, then the functional variety drops to $n^{[n(n+1)/2]-k}$. Only a small part of the functional variety can be realized in the language of constructible programs.

Now, given the first data association, a set of programs—up to a given complexity ceiling—is generated that satisfies the association. This set can be seen as the "version space" (Mitchell, 1977, 1978) of all possible solutions that are consistent with the given data association. When the second association is processed, only those programs from the previous set that also satisfy the new association are retained. This process may result in the elimination of some possible solutions and thus in the trimming down of the version space of possible solutions. In general, at some intermediate stage in the process, after several data associations have been handled that cover a subdomain d_{1a} of the total domain, a version space of possible solutions is obtained that represents all programs with weight up to a certain maximum that are *functionally equivalent with respect to the subdomain d_{1a}.* Unfortunately, convenient ways of characterizing these version spaces and of reasoning with them do not at present exist. An extension of the algebraic model that would handle *partial functions* and their relationships would be very helpful here.

The process of solution elimination is illustrated schematically in figure 18-31. After the first association is processed, the version space of solutions includes the programs P_u, P_v, P_w. These programs are represented by their graphs, that is, by the distribution of 1's in their relation matrix representation. After the second association is processed, one of the programs, P_w, is eliminated because it does not satisfy the new association; and the remaining version space is made of P_u and P_v.

The viewpoint from the geometrical representation of data space. It is very revealing to interpret the solution obtained for the problem π_1 and some of the "almost correct" solutions from the viewpoint of the geometric representation of data space.

Let us consider first the correct solution to the Infimum problem. Given a data association (x_1x_2, y), the solution program can be seen to produce the output y from the input pair (x_1x_2) in three major steps (see figure 18-32).

1. The cone set of the output y is formed from the input pair (x_1x_2). (This is achieved by first forming the cone sets of x_1 and of x_2 and then intersecting

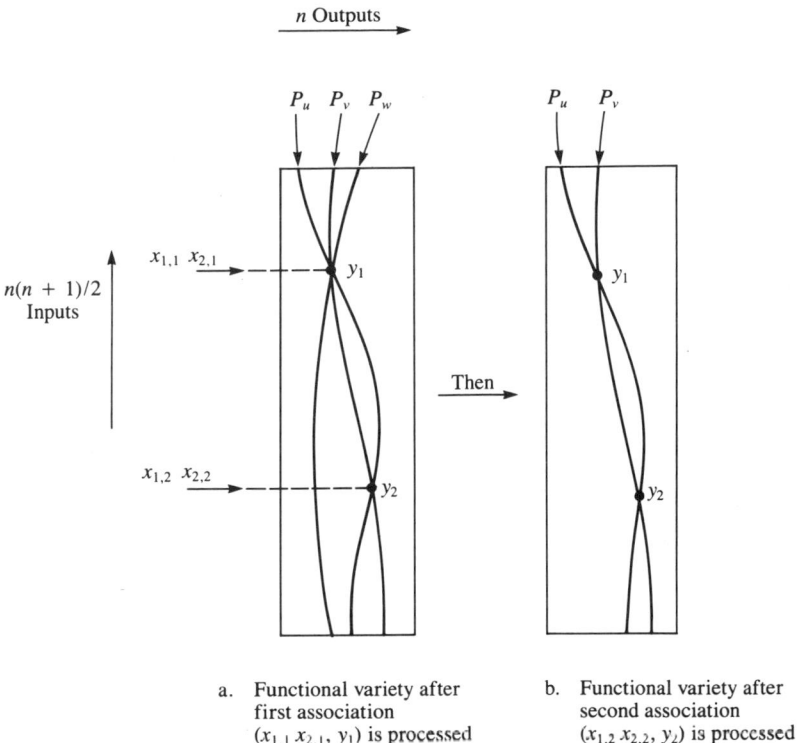

a. Functional variety after
   first association
   $(x_{1,1}\, x_{2,1},\, y_1)$ is processed

b. Functional variety after
   second association
   $(x_{1,2}\, x_{2,2},\, y_2)$ is processed

Figure 18-31: Illustration of the functional elimination process on the matrix representation of programs.

them. The subprogram $((I \vee E)\ \boxtimes\ (I \vee E))$ applied to the input pair $(x_1 x_2)$ implements this step. It should be noted that for any element x, application of the program $(I \vee E)$ on x produces the cone of x.)

2. The inverted cone set of the output y is formed from the cone set of y. (This is achieved by first forming the inverted cone set for each element in the cone set of y and then intersecting the results. This step is implemented by the second part of the cascade subprogram $[((I \vee E)\ \boxtimes\ (I \vee E)) \oslash (\hat{I} \vee E)]$. This part applies the program $(\hat{I} \vee E)$ to each element of the set that is produced by $((I \vee E)\ \boxtimes\ (I \vee E))$ in the first step of this process, and it intersects the results. It should be noted that for any element x, application of the program $(\hat{I} \vee E)$ produces the inverted cone of x.)

3. The cone set and the inverted cone set of y are intersected to obtain y. (It can easily be seen that this is implemented by the main intersection operation of the solution program $P_{3,1}$.)

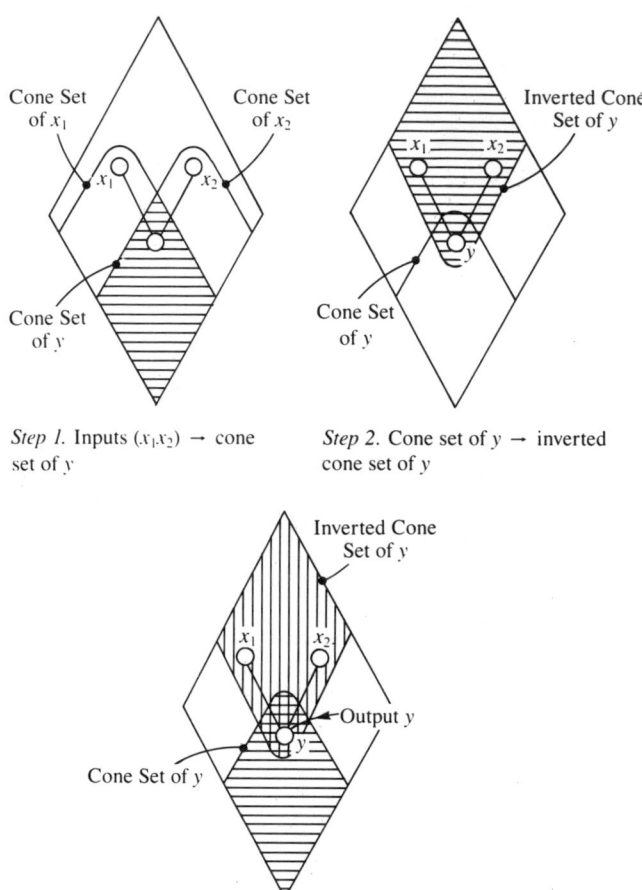

Step 1. Inputs $(x_1, x_2) \rightarrow$ cone set of y

Step 2. Cone set of $y \rightarrow$ inverted cone set of y

Step 3. Cone set of y, inverted cone set of $y \rightarrow y$

Figure 18-32: Interpretation of solution to the Infimum problem as a three-step process on the geometrical representation of data space.

Let us review now the previous model-guided process of formation (which was summarized in figure 18-23 above) in light of the present interpretation in the geometric representation. Steps 1, 2, and 3 of the previous process correspond to the search of a program for achieving present step 1. Step 4 of the previous process corresponds to the building of a program for achieving present step 2. Previous step 5, in which a *terminal maneuver* was used to obtain the desired goal program, corresponds to building a program that implements present step 3, that is, the intersection of the cone sets of the output. Although the model-guided approach to navigating in a structured program space was useful for coming close to the desired solution, it was inadequate for guiding the terminal maneuver in that process. The terminal maneuver must be seen from a completely different viewpoint in order to understand it and to devise strong ways of implementing it. The present geometric representation of data space, in which data and their relationships are presented in an especially appropriate way, provides the right framework.

Evaluation functions that measure the proportion of inputs satisfied or that estimate distance from the goal program in some program space have limited value in the formation process. They can help the process in the task of producing some promising fragments of a solution, but they leave open the extremely difficult problem of how to combine these fragments into a successful solution assembly. A considerable amount of specific domain knowledge and strong methods of reasoning are needed in order to approach the latter problem. Above all, it is clearly essential to handle the problem within an appropriate conceptual framework. The data space representation that was used to guide and interpret the present formation method appears very promising in this respect.

18.5 FURTHER IMPROVEMENT IN PROCEDURAL FORMULATION: FORMATION OF MACROMOVES AND OF NEW RELATED CONCEPTS; DOMAIN EXTENSION

An improved formulation of the program formation problem can be obtained by explicitly forming the concepts of *macromoves* for computing the *cone set* and the *inverted cone set* of an element in the finite set σ. The compound computational action $(I \lor E)$ will compute the former, and $(\hat{I} \lor E)$ will compute the latter. The automatic formation of these macromoves is an approachable task at present. It involves the identification of useful regularities in records of problem solving activity in the problem class.

A stronger macromove would consist of the computation that takes as input a set of elements q and produces as output the *intersection of all the cone sets* of the elements in q. In the graphic language of constructible programs, such a macromove is represented as shown in figure 18-33.

In the algebraic model for two-input programs, the operator sequence $\oslash (I \lor E)$ in an expression of the form $(P \oslash (I \lor E))$ for any P represents the macromove. Let us denote the macromove by its operator sequence. In the geometric representation of data space, the macromove can be seen as in figure 18-34.

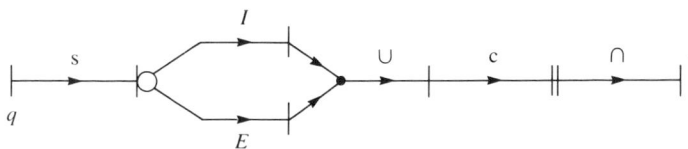

Figure 18-33: Macromove $\oslash (I \lor E)$.

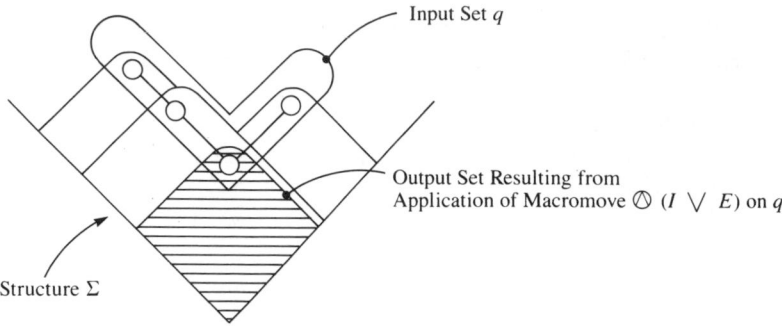

Figure 18-34:   Effect of macromove $\oslash$ $(I \lor E)$ shown in geometric representation of data space.

Thus if a set q can be represented as a region with a minimum point in the diagram of a structure Σ, then the macromove produces a cone whose apex touches from below the minimum point of the region representing the set q.

Actually, in terms of conventional mathematical concepts, the macromove $\oslash$ $(I \lor E)$ when applied to a set q produces the *set of all lower bounds* of q. A lower bound of the set q is an element u in σ satisfying xIu or xEu for all elements x in q.

A LISP representation of this macromove, call it *Lower-bounds-of-set,* is as follows:

```
Lower-bounds-of-set: (lambda (q) (Intersection-* (Mapcar
                     '(lambda (x) (Union (I-function x)
                     (E-function x)))q)).
```

A macromove $\oslash$ $(\hat{I} \lor E)$ for computing the *set of all upper bounds* of a set q can be defined and interpreted in a manner similar to the $\oslash$ $(I \lor E)$ macromove. Its LISP representation is:

```
Upper-bounds-of-set: (lambda (q) (Intersection-* (Mapcar
                     '(lambda (x) (Union (Icap-function x)
                     (E-function x)))q)).
```

The automatic formation of the strong macromoves and of the related concepts of the set of all lower bounds of a set and of the set of all upper bounds of a set is an interesting, but approachable, AI task at present. Mechanizing these concept discovery and macromove formation processes is a prerequisite for moving automatically to strong formulations of the program formulation problem. It should be noted that, as in the case of the interesting programs introduced above in section 18.4.2.1 (and their related subdomain concepts), discovery processes are being encountered here that are aimed at two mutually interdependent notions: the concept of an "interesting set," which depends on the existence of a "good method" for computing it, and a "good method" worthy of being singled out and given a separate identity which depends on the ability to focus on the interesting set as a good candidate of a new concept. This is the type of concept discovery problems that were identified in other studies of problem reformulation (Amarel, 1982). Preliminary work in this area shows that it would be promising to pursue some of Lenat's approaches (Lenat, 1983b) in the present context.

Assuming that the above macromoves $\oslash$ $(I \vee E)$, $\oslash$ $(\hat{I} \vee E)$ and their related concepts are available, then it is possible to define the following simple but powerful *maneuver* in our data space: Given a set q in 2^{σ} with a "smallest" element u, then u can be extracted by computing from q the set of all lower bounds of q and then intersecting the latter set with q.

This maneuver can be easily seen in the geometric representation of data space (see figure 18-35). The smallest element in q is obtained by pointing from below a cone that touches it and by intersecting q and the cone.

This maneuver can be represented by the following LISP function:

```
Smallest-of-set: (lambda (q) (Intersection
                              (Lower-bounds-of-set q) q)).
```

A similar maneuver can be defined for obtaining the "greatest" element of a set in the partially ordered structure.

Its LISP representation is

```
Greatest-element-of-set: (lambda (q) (Intersection
                              (Upper-bounds-of-set q) q)).
```

Clearly these two maneuvers can themselves be seen as macromoves that are defined in terms of previously defined macromoves.

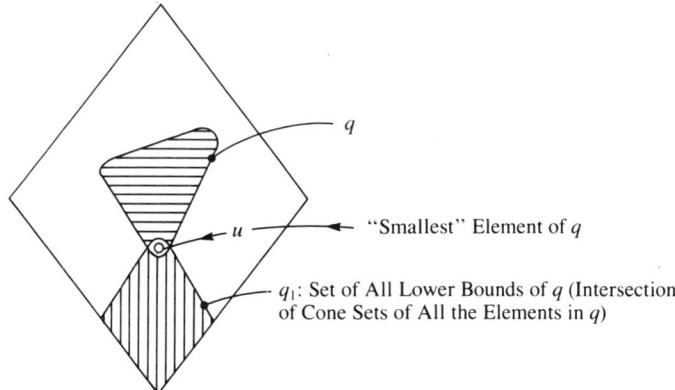

q

"Smallest" Element of *q*

q_1: Set of All Lower Bounds of q (Intersection of Cone Sets of All the Elements in q)

Figure 18-35: The "minimum extraction maneuver" $(q \wedge q_1) = \{u\}$.

Now a three-step process for computing the Infimum can be expressed in terms of our macromoves as follows:

1. Given an input pair (x_1x_2), form the input set $q = \{x_1x_2\}$.
2. Apply the macromove "Lower-bounds-of-set" on q. This produces the set q_1 of lower bounds of q.
3. Apply the macromove "Greatest-element-of-set" on q_1. This produces the desired output.

Note that this process is identical with the three-step process described in section 18.4.3.4 (in which a geometric interpretation of the solution process is presented), except that the individual steps are defined differently; present steps 1 and 2 correspond to the single step 1 in that process, and present step 3 corresponds to previous steps 2 and 3.

A LISP representation of a program that expresses the present three steps is as follows:

```
P'₆: (lambda (x₁x₂) (Greatest-element-of-set
            (Lower-bounds-of-set (Union (E-function x₁)
                                        (E-function x₂))))))
```

Note that P'_6 is a summary representation of the program P_6 for the Infimum (which was shown previously in section 18.4.2.2) with several program operations chunked together into bigger aggregates defined by the macromoves.

Clearly the chunking of structure embodied in the macromoves and the formation of related intermediate concepts of lower-bound and upper-bound sets result in a most appropriate representation for handling the Infimum formation problem. One can reason effectively with the elements of the representation, and these elements are of the right *grain* for the formation task.

Experience of problem solving within the improved formulation induces attention on the definition of programs whose inputs are sets (i.e., subsets of σ). For example, the macro-operations $\oslash (I \vee E)$, $\oslash (\hat{I} \vee E)$ have as their domain the set 2^σ. Although the initial problem formulation was to find a definition of a mapping (in a given language of programs) that was specified over a domain $d1$ of unordered pairs from σ, the solution that was obtained is made mostly of components that are specified over the more extended domain of 2^σ. Actually, the only part of the program P'_6 that directly handles elements of σ is the "front part"

```
(Union (E-function x₁)
       (E-function x₂))
```

that transforms an input pair (x_1x_2) into an input set. Under these conditions, it is possible to define an *extension* of the Infimum concept by redefining the domain of the function; the new domain is 2^σ. The new definition of the extended concept of Infimum can be seen as the first step in the *discovery* of a new concept, where a plausible domain extension of an existing concept is proposed as a concept candidate. It turns out that the proposed new concept is an important and useful mathematical concept; it is the *greatest lower bound of a set* in a partially ordered structure. A LISP representation of this concept is as follows:

```
Greatest-lower-bound-of-set: (lambda (q)
        (Greatest-element-of-set (Lower-bounds-of-set q))).
```

The methods developed by Lenat are relevant to the mechanization of this concept extension. Representation of the new concept requires that several modifications be introduced in the program language and in its related algebraic model. These are fairly straightforward, and they will not be described in detail here.

It should be noted that the algebraic model is still available (with only minor changes relative to the model that is used for handling programs over the domain $d1$) for handling programs over the extended domain 2^σ.

18.6 CONCLUDING COMMENTS

The evolution of methods described in this chapter shows that an effective theory formation process needs *large amounts of knowledge of various kinds* and careful choice of representations. Although a considerable amount of progress toward a solution can take place by intelligent searches in program space, it seems essential to pursue the terminal stages of solution via *detailed data-driven reasoning supported by domain-specific knowledge.* More work is needed on methods for effective coordination of reasoning in program space and in data space.

The exploration of data-driven methods of program formation has brought out forcefully the fundamental importance of the *degree of dependence between problem conditions* on the choice of method of problem solving. The problems of combining several "partially correct" programs into a desired program and of modifying "almost correct" programs into a correct one are closely related to the problems of *constructing plans for satisfying several interacting goals.* This is a basic problem in AI that needs much more research.

It is becoming evident that the notion of problem formulation in theory formation is somehow fluid and open-ended. More specifically, although attention may focus initially on some domain of phenomena to be "covered" by a theory, the attempt to construct the theory may lead to a redefinition of the domain of the theory (partitions of the initial domain or extensions) that creates new theory formation tasks. The processes of redefining a domain are closely related to concept discovery processes of the type studied by Lenat; they are precipitated/guided by knowledge gathered in the course of attempting to solve the theory formation problem for the initial domain. A promising approach, which is also of direct relevance to the automatic *acquisition of expertise* in other types of problems, is to define a domain as "interesting" if a specialized method is discovered that is especially effective for solving problems in that domain. The interplay between domain choice and the formation of a theory for the domain is an interesting and difficult problem. Much more work is needed in this area.

The discovery and use of *appropriate models* plays an important role in the theory formation processes presented in this chapter. The algebraic model of program space provides sufficient structure to the space to enable a major change in the method of solution—from a heuristic hill-climbing method to a goal-oriented method in which it is possible to develop a plan in program space for moving in the direction of the goal. An interesting, and approachable, problem in this area is to mechanize the process of developing a solution method on the basis of known properties of a relevant model. The problem of *finding* a relevant model (or of adapting a given model to the needs of a task) and of finding interesting properties of the model on the basis of which a good solution method can be formulated, continues to be beyond the present capabilities of AI. However, further progress in theory formation processes will bring us closer to a point where the mechanization of these capabilities can be contemplated.

In order to discover the strong formulation of the program formation problem, where macromoves and high-level intermediate concepts could be defined, it was essential to work within an *"appropriate" representation of data space.* The geometric model, which is based on the diagrammatic representation of partially ordered structures, has proved to be extremely fruitful in this respect. There are similarities between the present situation and the impact of geometric representations on the solution of other problems studied in AI, for example, in the Missionaries and Cannibals problem (Amarel, 1968). There are also similar open questions. Is the appropriateness of the geometric representation, where several properties of a complex situation are conveyed in a single structure, due solely to certain properties of the perceptual and reasoning processes of people? In what way should the geometric representation be encoded in a machine, and what processes of analysis and interpretation should be used to make the representation as appropriate for machines as it is for people? These are important questions for theory formation problems as they are for other areas of problem solving, and they require much more study. Given an appropriate representation of data space, the problem of *discovering useful regularities* in solutions that lead to a problem reformulation in terms of higher-level concepts, such as macromoves, is approachable at present. Processes of macromove formation are of general relevance to problems of improving performance in problem solving (expertise) via problem reformulations. Progress in this area requires the applications of theory formation techniques of the type described here.

A few final comments about research methodology. In the course of this work, several computer-based experiments were made. Most of the experiments were concerned with properties of searches in program space and used the heuristic hill-climbing method and the model-guided method. Work on a system for doing experiments with data-driven methods has begun recently. Because of the relative simplicity of our domain (and its formal properties) it has been possible to carry out several detailed hand simulations in order to probe possible methods of formation and the effects of various assumptions about representations and models on these methods. In this area major emphasis still needs to be place on the *conceptual clarification of approaches;* the computer provides the necessary means for selective experimentation in support of the conceptual work.

ACKNOWLEDGMENTS

The research presented in this chapter was supported in part by the Division of Research Resources, NIH, Grant RR00643 to the Rutgers Research Resource on Computers in Biomedicine.

An early version of this chapter was written while the author was a Visiting Research Fellow at the Artificial Intelligence Center, SRI International, Menlo Park, Calif., during the spring of 1983. The support of SRI International is gratefully acknowledged.

References

Amarel, S., "An Approach to Automatic Theory Formation," in *Principles of Self-Organization*, H. Von Foerster and G. Zopf (Eds.), Pergamon Press, New York, 1962a.

———, "On the Automatic Formation of a Computer Program Which Represents a Theory," in *Self-Organizing Systems-1962*, M. Yovits, G. Jacobi, and G. Goldstein (Eds.), Spartan Books, Washington, D.C., 1962b.

———, "On Representation of Problems of Reasoning About Action," In *Machine Intelligence 3*, D. Michie (Ed.), University of Edinburgh Press, Edinburgh, 1968.

———, "On the Representation of Problems and Goal-Directed Procedures for Computers," in *Theoretical Approaches to Non-Numerical Problem Solving*, R. B. Banerji and M. Mesarovic (Eds.), Springer Verlag, Heidelberg, W. Ger., 1970.

———, "Representations and Modeling in Problems of Program Formation," in *Machine Intelligence 6*, B. Meltzer and D. Michie (Eds.), University of Edinburgh Press, Edinburgh, 1971.

———, "Problems of Representation in Heuristic Problem Solving: Related Issues in the Development of Expert Systems," Technical Report CBM-TR-118, Rutgers University, 1981. (Also published in *Methods of Heuristics*, R. Groner, M. Groner, and W. F. Bischof (Eds.), Erlbaum, Hillsdale, N.J., 1983.

———, "Expert Behavior and Problem Representation," Technical Report CBM-TR-126, Rutgers University. 1982. (Also published in *Artificial and Human Intelligence*, A. Elithorn and R. B. Banerji (Eds.), North-Holland, Amsterdam, 1984.

Birkhoff, G., and MacLane, S., *A Survey of Modern Algebra*, Macmillan, New York, 1953.

Davis, R., and Lenat, D., "AM: Discovery in Mathematics as Heuristic Search," in *Knowledge-Based Systems in Artificial Intelligence, Part One*, McGraw-Hill, New York, 1982.

Ernst, G., and Goldstein, M., "Mechanical Discovery of Classes of Problem-Solving Strategies," *Journal of the ACM,* Vol. 29, No. 1, pp. 1–23, January 1982.

Ernst, G., and Newell, A., *GPS: A Case Study in Generality and Problem Solving,* Academic Press, New York, 1969.

Korf. R., "A Program That Learns to Solve Rubik's Cube," in *Proceedings of AAAI-82,* Pittsburgh, Pa, pp. 164–67, 1982.

Langley, P., Bradshaw, G. L., and Simon, H. A., "Rediscovering Chemistry with the BACON System," in *Machine Learning: An Artificial Intelligence Approach,* R. S. Michalski, J. G. Carbonell, and T. M. Mitchell (Eds.), Tioga, Palo Alto, Calif., 1983.

Lenat, D., "EURISCO: A Program That Learns New Heuristics and Domain Concepts. The Nature of Heuristics III: Program Design and Results," *Artificial Intelligence,* Vol. 21, Nos. 1, 2, pp. 61–98, March 1983a.

———, "Theory Formation by Heuristic Search. The Nature of Heuristics II: Background and Examples," *Artificial Intelligence,* Vol. 21, Nos. 1, 2, pp. 31–59, March 1983b.

Lindsay, K.; Buchanan, B. G.; Feignebaum, E. A.; and Lederberg, J., *The Dendral Project: Applications of Artificial Intelligence for Organic Chemistry,* McGraw-Hill, New York, 1980.

Manna, Z., and Waldinger, R., "Knowledge and Reasoning in Program Synthesis," *AI Journal,* 1975.

Manna, S., and Waldinger, R., *Synthesis: Dreams—Programs,* Technical Report No. 156, SRI International, 1977.

Mitchell, T. M., "Version Spaces: A Candidate Elimination Approach to Rule Learning," *Proceedings of the Fifth IJCAI,* pp. 305–10, Cambridge, Mass., 1977.

———, "Version Spaces: An Approach to Concept Learning," Ph.D. diss., Stanford University, 1978. (Also published as Stanford CS Report STAN-CS-78-711, HPP-79-2, Stanford University, 1978.)

Mostow, D. J., "Mechanical Transformation of Task Heuristics into Operational Procedures," Ph.D. diss., Carnegie-Mellon University, 1981.

Newell, A., "Heuristic Programming: III Structured Problems," in *Progress in Operations Research,* Vol. 3, J. S. Aronofsky (Ed.), Wiley, New York, 1969.

Nudel, B., "Consistent-Labeling Problems and Their Algorithms: Expected-Complexities and Theory-Based Heuristics," *Artificial Intelligence,* Vol. 21, Nos. 1, 2, pp. 135–78, March 1983.

Piaget, J., *The Origins of Intelligence in Children,* M. Cook (Trans.), International University Press, New York, 1936.

———, "La Logistique Axiomatique ou pure La Logistique Operatoire ou Psychologique et les Realites Auxquelles Elles Correspondent," *Methodos* IV, 1952.

Sacerdoti, E. D., *A Structure for Plans and Behavior,* American Elsevier, New York, 1977. (Ph.D. diss., Stanford University, 1975.)

Simon, H. A., *The Sciences of the Artificial,* MIT Press, Cambridge, 1969.

Simon, H. A., and Lea, G., "Problem Solving and Rule Induction: A Unified View," in *Knowledge and Cognition,* Erlbaum, Hillsdale, N.J., 1974.

Stefik, M., "Planning With Constraints," *Artificial Intelligence,* 1981.

Sussman, G., *A Computer Model of Skill Acquisition,* American Elsevier, New York, 1975.

Waldinger, R. J., "Achieving Several Goals Simultaneously," in *Machine Intelligence 8,* E. Elcock and D. Michie (Eds.), Ellis Horwood, Chichester, England, 1977.

Warren, D. H. D., "WARPLAN: A System for Generating Plans," Technical Report 76, University of Edinburgh, Edinburgh, 1974.

———, "Generating Conditional Plans and Programs," *Proceedings of the AISB,* Edinburgh, 1976.

19

AN APPROACH TO LEARNING FROM OBSERVATION

Gerald DeJong
*University of Illinois
at Urbana-Champaign*

Abstract

Learning from observation requires that a system appreciate the significance of an event (or set of events) that is either fortuitous or part of another's planning process and then generalize the new events into a new concept. A framework is presented in which these processes can occur. The approach is called *explanatory schema acquisition*. It involves knowledge-based generalization that can construct a first-pass generalized concept from just one input example. A natural language system that acquires new schemata has been implemented. When presented with a story that illustrates new problem-solving behavior in a character, the system generalizes its understanding of the technique and remembers the general form to aid in processing later stories.

19.1 INTRODUCTION

This chapter discusses an approach to learning concepts from observation. The concepts learned are problem-solving schemata. The approach taken is not the standard correlational one, in which one examines a number of events and constructs a new concept by noting the commonalities and differences that emerge among the events. In the correlational approach the certainty that a new concept is correct and useful increases with the number of events; with only a few events some observed commonalities may be chance similarities.

By contrast, in explanatory schema acquisition (ESA) feature significance is judged through the use of background knowledge rather than correlational similarity.

Thus a new concept can be constructed from just one event. New concepts can be incomplete and require later refinement based on other events. However, they are full schemata and can be used immediately to aid in processing. The approach requires much background knowledge; the domain knowledge is used both to judge the significance of an event and to generalize it into a schema.

As mentioned above, the concepts learned are problem-solving schemata. Therefore much of the knowledge must be problem-solving knowledge: knowledge of the operators in the domain and knowledge about goals and how they interact. The motivation for this work has thus far been entirely computational. This kind of learning is driven by the system's explanation of an observed event (DeJong, 1981). The author's intuition is that real-world human adult learning is largely explanation driven, but no psychological experiments have as yet been performed to test this hypothesis; therefore, the author is not in a position to defend it.

19.1.1 Problem Solving with Schemata

In this section the task of problem solving will be cast in terms necessary for ESA learning to take place. Problem solving can be viewed as the process of transforming some initial state of the world into a goal state by the application of a sequence of known operators. The operators define a search space that must be explored in order for one to discover how the goal state can be achieved. The complexity of a blind search is $O(m^n)$, where m is the number of operators available and n is the number of steps in the solution path. Figure 19.1 shows such a search tree for $m = 3$ and $n = 4$. This complexity prohibits the use of blind search in all but the most trivial of tasks. Instead methods such as means-ends analysis (Newell and Simon, 1972), heuristic searches like A* (Nilsson, 1980), and schematic problem solving are used. This chapter will concentrate on the last alternative.

Schematic problem solving involves the use of schemata to augment the set of operators the system can use. Schemata are prestored, canned solutions to general problems. These solutions are sequences of the original operators. The hope is to simplify greatly the search space by the use of only a few (often just one or two) of these schemata or macro-operators to solve the problem.

Consider figures 19-2 and 19-3. Figure 19-2 represents the same problem as figure 19-1, but here it is simplified to show only the solution path through the search tree. Suppose the system has a schema Sch 1 composed of a sequence of original operators Op_1, Op_2, Op_1, Op_3. This schema solves the problem immediately. As figure 19-3 shows, the depth of the search tree is just one.

Schematic problem solvers can be relatively untroubled by rich domains. However, two new difficulties are raised that stem from the great number of schemata that must be a part of the system. The first is the schema selection problem. Little will be said about this here; the problem has been discussed elsewhere (Minsky, 1974; Charniak, 1977; Schank and Abelson, 1977; DeJong, 1979; Lebowitz, 1980). The

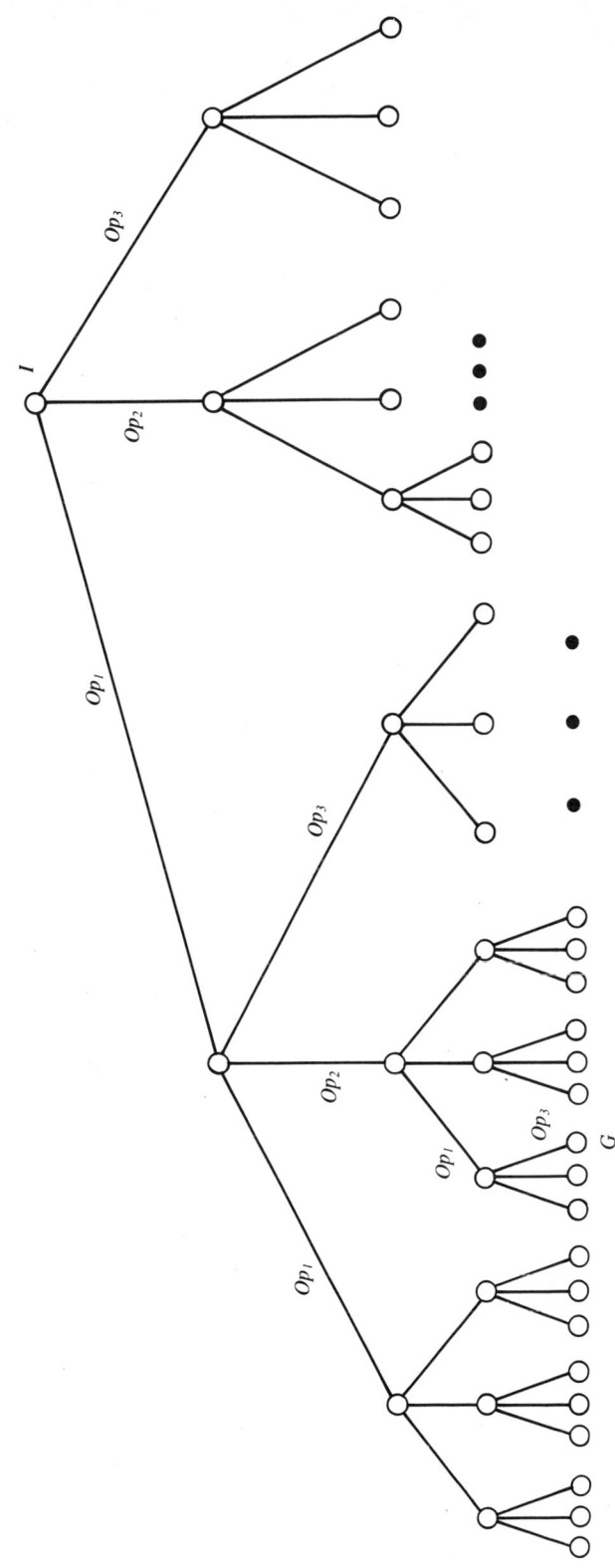

Figure 19-1: A search tree for $m = 3$ and $n = 4$.

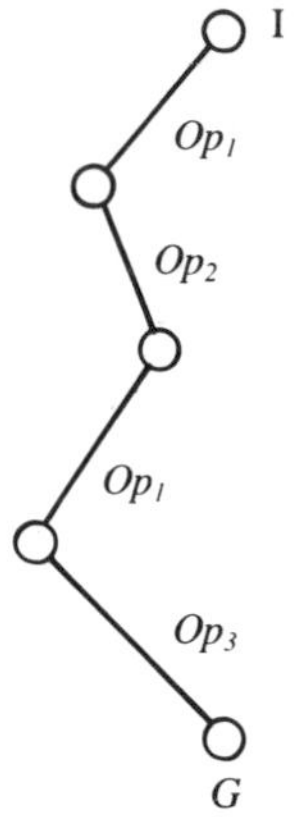

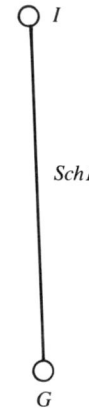

Figure 19-2:   Solution using operator.

Figure 19-3:   Solution using schemata.

second difficulty is how to get an extensive and useful set of schemata into the system. This is the problem addressed in the remainder of this chapter.

19.1.2 Constraint-Based Learning

Suppose we have some initial state I that must be transformed into a goal state G. The system must select a schema that is capable of the desired transformation. If no single schema transforms I to G then the system must combine a few schemata sequentially to do the job. However, the system must not be permitted to look for sequences of arbitrary length. Unconstrained searching must be avoided since this would reduce the schema system to a search problem solver with its concomitant inefficiencies in rich domains.

Now assume that G can be achieved from I only through the application of many schemata in sequence; that is, no single schema nor any short sequence of schemata can transform I into G. In this case the problem is *intractable* for the system even though there is, in principle, a solution. In rich domains such intractable problems are, for all practical purposes, just as insoluble as impossible problems. Without the appropriate schemata, searching for a solution is a bit like the monkey recreating Shakespeare's *Hamlet* from random keystrokes on a typewriter.

All is not lost, however. True, the system cannot solve the problem of transforming I to G, but it can verify (and in some sense "understand") a solution presented to it. The system has knowledge of all the operators necessary for the solution. It can, when given a solution, verify that all the preconditions for each operator are satisfied and that each operator application yields the desired effects. The time complexity of this verification is polynomial in n (linear in n with a reasonable simplifying assumption), where n is the number of operator steps in the solution transformation.

Verification of a proposed solution involves two parts. First, the sequence of operators must be viable; that is, at the time of application of each operator all of the preconditions for that operator must be satisfied. Second, the resulting state after the application of the last operator of the sequence must be demonstrated to contain the goal state.

A state is made up of a collection of features (or propositions). Each precondition can also be viewed as a required feature (or proposition). It will be assumed that the cost of checking whether a precondition is satisfied in a state is proportional to the number of features in that state.

Let p_j be the number of preconditions for the jth operator,

a_j be the number of features added by the jth operator,

r_j be the number of features removed by the jth operator,

E be the number of features in the initial state.

The cost C of verifying the viability of the sequence is

$$C = K \sum_{j=1}^{n} p_j \left(E + \sum_{l=1}^{j-1} (a_l - r_l) \right) \tag{1}$$

where K is a constant of proportionality. If p is the largest p_j and a is the largest a_j, we have

$$C \leq K \sum_{j=1}^{n} p \left(E + \sum_{l=1}^{j-1} a \right) \tag{2}$$

Simplifying, the cost of demonstrating the viability of a solution is

$$C \leq KpEn + Kpa \frac{n(n-1)}{2} \tag{3}$$

Testing that the goal state is satisfied by the final state is at worst linear in n. The number of features in the final state is no greater than

$$E + \sum_{j=1}^{n} a \quad \text{or} \quad E + na \tag{4}$$

Each feature of the goal must be checked against this state. However, since the number of features composing the goal state is independent of n, the cost is at most a constant multiplied by expression (4).

If it is assumed that each operator deletes on the average about as many features from a state as it adds, then the inner summation in (1) approaches zero and the cost becomes $O(n)$; the cost of testing the goal state against the final state becomes independent of n. $O(n)$ is also a trivial lower bound since one must at least consider each operator to verify the sequence.

Thus, understanding a solution is very efficient even if the original problem is intractable for the system.

Once a solution is verified it can be used by the system to solve the same problem should it occur again. To do this the system must file away the verified solution indexed by the initial and final states. When the system is presented with the same problem it can simply retrieve and execute the stored solution as illustrated in figure 19-3. Such a stored structure might be considered the beginning of a schema.

However, more things are possible than just solving very similar problems. The new verified solution can be generalized to apply to a broad *class* of similar problems. Generalization can be driven by inspection of the verified example using world knowledge about the component operators. This process is called *constraint-based generalization* because it is driven by the preservation of the underlying verification steps composing the explanation of why the solution worked in the first place. A schema (or set of schemata) is then constructed to remember the generalization and to serve as an organization point for retrieval in later problem solving.

Briefly, the process of explanatory schema acquisition can be summarized as (1) verifying or "understanding" the input, (2) deciding whether this example warrants generalization, and (3) if so, generalizing the input to a new schema. The verification phase can be more involved than previously indicated. In particular, complete solutions are seldom apparent from the observation of the problem-solving behavior of others. Generally only a few overt actions are apparent. To complete the solution the system must infer many missing steps and fill in causal inferences. The domain largely determines how difficult the inference process is. In a simplified robot world nearly all important state changes can be observed, and therefore, very few inferences need to be added. However, in a natural language task domain the system might have to hypothesize missing but implied actions and infer mental and other internal states of characters. It is essential that the representation of the solution be augmented with these missing inferences; without them the explanation would be incomplete and no generalization would be possible. Although the inference problem is indeed difficult, it is common to all natural language systems and has been addressed else-where (Schmidt and Sridharan, 1977; Cullingford, 1978; DeJong, 1979; Kolodner, 1980; Lebowitz, 1980; Granger, 1980).

The understanding phase is not significantly different from most planning-type understanders, with one exception: the understander must maintain data dependency supports (Fikes, 1975; Doyle, 1979) for all the inferences necessary to make sense of the input. This dependency network drives the generalization process. The particular input representation is generalized as far as possible without violating the depen-dency support structure. Violating the dependency support structure would under-mine the solution's verification (i.e., the reasons the system has for believing the input makes sense).

Generalization can be done in a number of different ways. The particular gen-eralization constructed is determined by fitting the input into a taxonomy of general-ization techniques. In the next section this taxonomy of generalization is presented, followed by a brief discussion of when to generalize. Finally, an example is given demonstrating a working ESA system.

19.2 TAXONOMY OF GENERALIZATIONS

There are four situations that when recognized in the text either individually or in combination ought to invoke the generalization routines. They are the following:

Schema Composition
Secondary Effect Elevation
Schema Alteration
Volitionalization

In the first part of this section each of these situations will be illustrated with an example.

19.2.1 Schema Composition

The first situation is called *schema composition.* Basically, it involves com-posing known schemata in a novel way. This will typically involve a primary schema, essentially unchanged, with one or more of its preconditions satisfied in a novel way by other known schemata.

To clarify the procedure let us consider an example. This example is a story about a kidnapping. Let us assume that we, the readers of this example, do not yet have a schema for kidnapping or extortion or any similar notion. However, the knowledge of a considerable quantity of background information about stealing, bar-gaining, the use of normal physical objects, and goals of people and institutions is assumed.

Paris police disclosed Tuesday that a man who identified himself as Jean Maraneaux abducted the twelve-year-old daughter of a wealthy Parisian businessman
Michel Boullard late last week. Boullard received a letter containing a snapshot
of the kidnapped girl. The next day he received a telegram demanding that one
million francs be left in a lobby wastebasket of the crowded Pompidou Center in
exchange for the girl. Asking that the police not intervene, Boullard arranged for
the delivery of the money. His daughter was found wandering blindfolded with
her hands bound near his downtown office on Monday.

In this story the primary schema is BARGAIN, a schema that we assumed the
system already knew. One of the preconditions specified in the BARGAIN schema is
that both parties to the bargain must convince each other that they can indeed deliver
their sides of the bargain. For Maraneaux, this corresponds to making Boullard
believe that he (Maraneaux) has control of Boullard's daughter and can therefore
relinquish the girl to him. Maraneaux achieves this by actually establishing control
over the daughter (via an instance of the STEAL schema) and then sending Boullard a
photograph. To the system, this is a novel way to satisfy BARGAIN's preconditions.

19.2.2 Secondary Effect Elevation

Consider the following scenario:

Fred wanted to date only Sue, but Sue steadfastly refused his overtures. Fred was
on the verge of giving up when he saw what happened to his friend, John: John
wanted to date Mary but she also refused. John started seeing Wilma. Mary
became jealous, and the next time he asked her, Mary eagerly accepted. Fred told
Sue he was going to make a date with Lisa.

Here Fred has used an existing schema (DATE) in a new way. This is called *secondary effect elevation*. Fred's DATE schema already contains all of the knowledge
necessary for resolving his dilemma. The problem is that the normal DATE schema is
organized in the wrong way. In secondary effect elevation situations a new schema
can be constructed by modifying an existing schema to indicate that the schema may
be used to achieve a result that is normally neutral or negative.

The main purpose of the DATE schema is to satisfy certain recurring social
goals (like companionship, sex, and so on). DATE contains secondary effects as well.
These are often undesirable effects accompanying the main, planned effects. For
example, one is usually monetarily poorer after a date. Another secondary effect is
that an old girlfriend may become jealous of the new date. What Fred learned from
John's experience is that it is occasionally useful to invoke the DATE schema in order
to cause one of its secondary effects (jealousy) while completely ignoring the usual
main goal.

Just as with schema composition, the existing schema is changed to reflect a
generalization made from a specific instance. In this case, the specific instance is
John's interactions with Mary. Notice, however, that Fred did not simply copy John's

actions. John actually made a date with Wilma, but Fred only expressed an intention to date Lisa. This is not an earth-shaking difference, but in the context of dating it is extremely significant. In the normal DATE situation, expressing an intention to date someone is not nearly so satisfying as an actual date. Once dating is modified for the purpose of causing jealousy, however, expressing an intention to date and actually carrying it out can be equally effective.

One might argue that the distinction between main and secondary effects of a schema is otiose and, in situations such as this, even deleterious. After all, DATE already had all the information necessary for solving Fred's problem. If a system simply treats all the effects of a schema the same, then any effect can be singled out during the planning process to be used as the main goal. There is, however, a strong argument against this position. The possible desired effects of a schema do not exist only within the schema itself. They are used to organize and select among schemata in both understanding and planning applications. Many effects (like feeling more tired after a date than before) will not be used in the normal planning or understanding process. If they are treated the same as legitimate main goals the system will be swamped in a combinatorial quagmire of undifferentiated possibilities, most of which are wildly implausible.

For example, we do not want the understanding process to predict that John will take a nap when it is told that John dated Mary. Given the input "John took a nap," the system ought to be able to justify it. However, it ought not actively predict it. There is a multiplicity of individual actions making up the DATE schema (each with its own set of effects), and the vast majority of the effects from this schema (and any other schema) are simply irrelevant to overall planning and understanding processes. Instead, we would like the system to single out the plausible volitional effects of its schemata and use only those for schema organization and selection. Thus in the example, Fred has constructed, via secondary effect elevation, a new use of the DATE schema.

19.2.3 Schema Alteration

Schema alteration involves modifying a nearly correct schema so that it fits the requirements of a new situation. The alteration process is guided by the system's world model. This is illustrated by the following anecdote:

> I had occasion to replace temporarily a broken window in my back door with a plywood panel. The plywood sheet from which the panel was to be cut had a "good" side and a "bad" side (as does most raw lumber). The good side was reasonably smooth, but the bad side had several ruts and knot holes. I automatically examined both sides of the sheet (presumably as part of my SAWING or CUTTING-A-BOARD-TO-FIT schema) and selected the good side to face into the house, leaving the bad side to be exposed to the elements. After I had cut the panel and fitted it in place I noticed that several splinters had been torn out, leaving ruts in the good side. I immediately saw the problem. Hand saws only cut

in one direction. With hand saws, the downward motion does the cutting and the upward motion only repositions the cutting blade for another downward motion. I had cut the wood panel with the good side facing down. The downward cutting action has a tendency to tear splinters of wood out of the lower surface of the board. Since the good side was the lower surface, it suffered the loss of splinters.

If I had to perform the same action again, I would not make the same mistake. I would cut the board with the good side facing up. However, what I learned was not just a simple specialized patch to handle this particular instance of splintering. Since I knew the cause of the splintering, I knew that it would not always be a problem: it is only a problem when (1) the lumber is prone to splintering, (2) there is a good side of the board that is to be preserved, and (3) one is making a crosscut (across the wood's grain) rather than a rip cut (along the grain). Moreover, the solution is not always to position the wood with the good side up. My electric saber saw (also a reciprocating saw) cuts during the upward blade motion rather than during the downward motion. Clearly, the solution when using the saber saw is the opposite: to position the board with the good side down. Now, these are not hard-and-fast rules: with a sheet of plywood of sufficiently poor quality, splintering would likely always be a problem. Rather, these are useful heuristics that lead to a refinement of the SAWING schema.

Note that this refinement to the SAWING schema is far more general than required to handle the particular problem that gave rise to it. The refinement contains contingencies relevant to the use of saber saws even though no saber saw was used in the immediate problem. This is possible because the refinement is driven by a world model, not just the problem. The SAWING schema was altered by identifying and eliminating the offending cause in the underlying knowledge-based explanation of the phenomenon.

19.2.4 Volitionalization

This situation involves transforming a schema for which there is no planner (like VEHICLE-ACCIDENT, ROULETTE, etc.) into a schema that can be used by a planner to attain a specific goal. Consider the following story:

Herman, who was married to Joy for fifteen years had fallen in love with his secretary, Heather. When Joy refused to divorce him, Herman cut a hydraulic brake hose in Joy's car. The next time she drove down the winding road to town she lost control of her car and struck a tree. The car burst into flames.

This story describes a vehicle accident. However, unlike most vehicle accidents, this one has an active agent. The VEHICLE-ACCIDENT schema is normally nonvolitional; that is, it dictates what to expect in a vehicle accident situation, but it does not allow planned invocation. This schema cannot be involved in problem-solving planning.

The story illustrates that an event that was previously only attributable to accidental causes can, in fact, be controlled. Thus a volitional counterpart can be constructed for the previously nonvolitional schema. The new volitional schema has certain effects that can be labeled as its main goals, new constraints on the actors and objects, and so on. It is, in fact, a new schema in its own right. Furthermore, using the underlying explanation of the story to drive the generalization process, the schema can encompass situations significantly different from the one described in the story. For example, it could handle a story about a student weakening the steering rod of a professor's car after receiving a failing grade.

19.3 TO GENERALIZE OR NOT TO GENERALIZE

There are five aspects to consider when one is deciding whether or not to generalize an input into a new schema. By hypothesis it will be assumed that the input did not match an existing schema. (If it had, then the system would have already possessed the desired schema, and indeed that schema would have been used to process the story.) If any of these five conditions does not hold, constructing a new schema from this input is inappropriate.

The criteria are as follows:

1. Is the main goal of a character achieved?
2. Is the goal a general one?
3. Are the resources required by the goal achiever generally available?
4. Is this new method of achieving the goal at least as effective as the other known volitional schemata to achieve this goal?
5. Does the input match one of the known generalizable patterns?

These criteria are tested for all goals in the story. The first criterion—Was the goal achieved?—is self-explanatory and easily judged. The second—Is it a general goal?—and the third—Are the resources generally available?—require some discussion.

Novelty alone in an approach to achieving a goal is not sufficient to warrant the construction of a new schema. Consider, for example, the plots in the "Mission Impossible" television series. These plots are noteworthy in that they are very novel. They all use bizarre methods to achieve rather peculiar goals. Furthermore, they are always successful. However, the goals achieved are not the type that arise in ordinary life, and the resources and skills needed are so specialized and uncommon that the same solution would never be applicable again. Clearly a new schema should be constructed only if there is a reasonable expectation that it will be helpful in future processing. If a schema will never be used again, it should not be constructed in the first place.

How can the utility of a particular goal be judged? The answer to this is closely tied to where goals come from. Achieving a goal that arises from general conditions important to an individual's well-being and that uses readily available resources is likely to result in an interesting new schema, one that will arise again and again. For the solution, an aspect of Schank and Abelson's theory of planning (1977) is used. In their view *themes* give rise to the highest-level goals (goals that are not simply subgoals in the achievement of other goals). *Interpersonal* and *life* themes are of interest here. An example of the former is a husband's offering (and therefore, at some level, wanting) to type a term paper for his overworked student wife. This exemplifies the theme of taking on goals of others whom one cares for. It is not necessary to go beyond this theme in explaining the husband's actions. Examples of life themes are attempting to satisfy one's hunger, to gain money, or to relieve boredom. Themes give rise to goals that require no further justification.

The fourth criterion is self-explanatory. The idea is that the system should not bother constructing schemata that are much less efficient than similar already-known schemata. In a natural language input this would occur only if a character were using a highly suboptimal plan.

The fifth criterion—Does the input match one of the known generalizable patterns?—simply states that the input must be identified within the taxonomy of generalization techniques, as given in the previous section. This is necessary to allow the system to bring its technique-specific generalization knowledge to bear.

19.4 AN EXAMPLE

Here an example of the first-pass implementation of the system is given. It illustrates a new schema acquired by volitionalization. The system does not have a natural language front end. Rather, the inputs are given in an internal conceptual form. This is the representation that would be the output of a natural language front end. Inputs are denoted by lines starting with "Processing— . . . " There are just four inputs. English versions of the inputs are given below. For readability, this output is a slightly altered form of the program's output. The system generates many more GEN-SYMed atoms and refers to them by the GENSYM names. The GENSYMs have been replaced with mnemonic symbols.

```
ENGLISHIFIED INPUT:
 1)CLAUDIUS OWNED AN ISLAND ESTATE.
 2)AGRIPPINA FED CLAUDIUS POISONED MUSHROOMS.
 3)CLAUDIUS DIED.
 4)AGRIPPINA INHERITED THE ISLAND ESTATE.

The first input:
Processing---($POSS(ACTOR*CLAUDIUS*)(OBJECT(*ESTATE*)))
```

```
New Schema---S00001 ($POSS(ACTOR*CLAUDIUS*)(OBJECT*ESTATE*))
Setting bindings and links
```

*The first proposition is input. The internal story representation is ini-
tially empty. Thus, no processing is required to integrate this input. However, an instance of the $POSS schema is created. It is called S00001.
Pointers to *CLAUDIUS* and *ESTATE* are established. These are the
variables, or bindings, of the new instance of the POSSess schema.*

```
New Schema---S00002 ($DESIRE-FOR-MATERIAL-THINGS
                (ACTOR*CLAUDIUS*)
                (OBJECT*ESTATE*))
Setting bindings and links
```

*A new schema S00002, which is an instance of $DESIRE-FOR-
MATERIAL-THINGS, is created and activated in a bottom-up response
to the first input. This schema represents the knowledge that people usually act so as to preserve their possessions. Links are constructed to tie
this instance to schema S00001.*

```
The second input:
 Processing---($FEED(ACTOR*AGRIPPINA*)
                (OBJECT*POISON*TYPE*MUSHROOM*))

 New Schema---S00003($FEED(ACTOR*AGRIPPINA*(OBJECT*POISON*)
                (TO*CLAUDIUS*))
Setting bindings and links
New Schema---S00005($EAT(ACTOR*CLAUDIUS*)(OBJECT*POISON*)
Activated by S00003
Setting bindings and links

 New Schema---S00006($NAIVE-POISON(ACTOR*AGRIPPINA*)
                (INSTRUMENT*MUSHROOM*)(OBJECT*CLAUDIUS*))
Activated by S00003
Setting bindings and links
```

*$EATing poison brings in the poison schema. We call it NAIVE-POISON
to remind ourselves that it is an incomplete schema containing little more
than what is needed for this story.*

```
New Schema---S00007($MOVE(ACTOR*AGRIPPINA*)
               (OBJECT*MUSHROOM*)(FROM(OUTSIDE*CLAUDIUS*)
               (TO(INSIDE*CLAUDIUS*)))
```

The system infers that the $NAIVE-POISON involves INGESTing an object that must be a poison, which in turn involves a physical MOVEment to the inside of the person, and that the person has some initial $HEALTH state.

```
Activated by S00006
Setting bindings and links
```

```
New Schema---S00008($BODILY-HARM(OBJECT*CLAUDIUS*))
Activated by S00006
Setting bindings and links
```

```
New Schema---
S00009($HEALTH(CREATURE*CLAUDIUS*)(STATE(*VAR*S1)))
Activated by S00008
Setting bindings and links
```

```
New Schema---S00010($INGEST(ACTOR*AGRIPPINA*)(OBJECT*POISON*)
               (TO*CLAUDIUS*))
Activated by S00006
Setting bindings and links
```

```
New Schema---S00011($DEATH(OBJECT*CLAUDIUS*))
Activated by S00006
Setting bindings and links
```

This $DEATH is predicted by the poisoning. POISON has two possible outcomes. One is that the person may survive, the other is that the person may die. Both are predicted, but only one is allowed to be eventually satisfied.

```
Old Schema---S00009($HEALTH(CREATURE*CLAUDIUS*)
(STATE*ALIVE*))
Activated by S00011
Setting bindings and links
```

```
New Schema---S00012($HEALTH(CREATURE*CLAUDIUS*)(STATE*DEAD*))
Activated by S00011
Setting bindings and links
```

If he survives, Claudius might become ill. This is also predicted.

```
New Schema---S00013 ($NAUSEA(ACTOR*CLAUDIUS*))
Activated by S00006
Setting bindings and links
```

If Claudius dies, Agrippina, the volitional actor of S00006 ($NAIVE-POISON) might have had this outcome as a goal. This activates a murder schema.

```
New Schema---S00014($NAIVE-PREMEDITATED-MURDER
              (ACTOR*AGRIPPINA*)(OBJECT*CLAUDIUS*))
Activated by S00006
Setting bindings and links

Old Schema---S00011($DEATH(OBJECT*CLAUDIUS*))
Activated by S00014
Setting bindings and links

Old Schema---S00006($NAIVE-POISON(ACTOR*AGRIPPINA*)
              (INSTRUMENT*MUSHROOM*)(OBJECT*CLAUDIUS*))
Activated by S00014
Setting bindings and links

New Conjunction Node---S00015(AND($DEATH(ACTOR*CLAUDIUS*))
                      (NOT($PUNISH(OBJECT*AGRIPPINA*)))))
```

The murder schema contains information that the killer will probably have the goal of escaping punishment for the crime.

```
Old Schema---S00011($DEATH(OBJECT*CLAUDIUS*))
```

```
The third input:
Processing---($DEATH(OBJECT*CLAUDIUS*))
Old Schema---S00011($DEATH(OBJECT*CLAUDIUS*))
```

This matches the dying prediction. Thus, very little processing need be done here.

```
The fourth input:
 Processing---($NAIVE-INDIVIDUAL-INHERIT(HEIR*AGRIPPINA*)
                (BEQUESTS*ESTATE*))
```

The system must justify that the conditions for INHERITance are indeed fulfilled.

```
New Schema---S00018($NAIVE-INDIVIDUAL-
              INHERIT(HEIR*AGRIPPINA*)
              (BEQUESTS*ESTATE*))
Setting bindings and links

Old Schema---S00001($POSS(ACTOR*CLAUDIUS*)(OBJECT*ESTATE*))
Activated by S00018
Setting bindings and links

Old Schema---S00011($DEATH(OBJECT*CLAUDIUS*))
Activated by S00018
Setting bindings and links

New Schema---S00021($HEALTH(CREATURE*AGRIPPINA*)
(STATE*ALIVE*))
Activated by S00018
Setting bindings and links

Old Schema---S00012($HEALTH(CREATURE*CLAUDIUS*)(STATE*DEAD*))
Activated by S00018
Setting bindings and links

New Schema---S00022($TRANSFER-OF-POSSESSION(FROM*CLAUDIUS*)
(TO*AGRIPPINA*)(OBJECT*ESTATE*))
Activated by S00018
Setting bindings and links
```

Since the conditions are all true, the conclusions of INHERIT are asserted.

```
Old Schema---S00001($POSS(ACTOR*CLAUDIUS*)(OBJECT*ESTATE*))
Activated by S00022
Setting bindings and links
```

```
New Schema---S00025($POSS(ACTOR*AGRIPPINA*)(OBJECT*ESTATE*))
Activated by S00022
Setting bindings and links

New Schema---S00026($MATERIAL-DESIRE(ACTOR*AGRIPPINA*)
             (OBJECT*ESTATE*))
             Activated by S00025
             Setting bindings and links
```

Finally, the system has a motivation for the murder. General background knowledge about people dictates that everyone may be assumed to desire material objects. An action of Agrippina has just resulted in Agrippina's acquisition of a new material object. The explanation of how she achieved this result is examined. The minimal necessary conditions to preserve the validity of the explanation are propagated to the initial state of the world. A new schema is then constructed with these general requirements as preconditions.

```
VOLITIONALIZATION TRIGGERED

NEW SCHEMA V00035:
 (FORM SCHEMA
 (VARS(BENEFACTOR(*VAR*V00031)
   PRIOR-HEIRS(*VAR*V00033)
   BEQUESTS(*VAR*V00029)
   HEIR(*VAR*V00030)
   ACTOR(*VAR*V00030)
   OBJECT(*VAR*V00031))
 (POINT-OF-VIEW(*VAR*V00030))
 (GOAL V00032)
 (ACTIVATE
  (V00032($POSS(ACTOR(*VAR*V00030))
         (OBJECT(*VAR*V00029)))
      V00033
      ($NAIVE-INDIVIDUAL-INHERIT(BENEFACTOR(*VAR*V00031))
                   PRIOR-HEIRS(*VAR*V00033)
                   BEQUESTS(*VAR*V00029)
                   HEIR(*VAR*V00030))
      V00034
      ($NAIVE-PREMEDITATED-MURDER ACTOR(*VAR*V00030)
                   OBJECT(*VAR*V00031))
 (COMPLEX(V00033 V00034)))))
```

19.5 CONCLUSION

The example shows a new schema acquired by the system. The form of this schema is identical to those preprogrammed into the system. The only difference is in the lack of mnemonic naming of variables. There are several problems with this implementation that are the subject of current research. First, there is an inadequate treatment of time. The system assumes (whenever it cares) that the inputs are presented in the same order as the events they report. The system performs (through schema expansion) a good deal of causal analysis. This also implies some temporal orderings. However, by and large, difficult time problems do not surface for this simple story.

A second problem is with variable constraints. This implementation does very little reasoning about objects. Most of its generalization is performed on constituent events rather than the objects participating in those events. These generalizations (such as generalizing POISON to MURDER) seemed less obvious and therefore more interesting. Furthermore, there has been previous work on generalizing objects (Fikes, Hart, and Nilsson, 1972). Finally, there is a good deal of work to be done on goal manipulation of story characters on schema representation. The representations used here are ad hoc and cannot easily handle the next task the author has chosen (a sequence of kidnapping stories).

Unlike the similarity-based approaches (Fox and Reddy, 1977; Michalski, 1977; Langley, 1981) and many other knowledge-based approaches (Soloway, 1977; Lebowitz, 1980; Schank, 1982; Michalski and Stepp, 1983), this procedure is capable of constructing a schema from one input example. The procedure is not "failure-driven" (Kolodner, 1980; Lebowitz, 1980; Schank, 1982). Nor is it primarily analogical (Winston, 1980; Carbonell, 1982). The LEX system (Mitchell, Utgoff, and Banerji, 1983) is also a significantly different approach. In that system concepts are acquired that are judged to be useful through search and experimentation, not through an analysis of why an operator was useful. In ESA concepts are formed entirely on the basis of this kind of analysis. Finally, it must be acknowledged that the knowledge-based concept approach owes much to the earlier works of Fikes, Hart, and Nilsson (1972), Lenat (1976), and Soloway (1977).

ACKNOWLEDGMENTS

This work was supported in part by the Air Force Office of Scientific Research under Grant F49620-82-K-0009 and in part by the National Science Foundation under Grant NSF IST 81-20254.

The author is indebted to the members of the Coodinated Science Laboratory Learning Group at the University of Illinois: Alberto Segre, Paul O'Rorke, and Ashwin Ram. Paul O'Rorke implemented the system that performed the example.

References

Carbonell, J., "Experiential Learning in Analogical Problem Solving," *Proceedings of the NCAI*, Pittsburgh, Pa., pp. 168–71, 1982.

Charniak, E., "MS. MALAPROP, a Language Comprehension System," *Proceedings of the Fifth IJCAI*, Cambridge, Mass., pp. 1–7, 1977.

Cullingford, R., "Script Application: Computer Understanding of Newspaper Stories," Research Report No. 116, Department of Computer Science, Yale University, 1978.

DeJong, G., "Generalizations Based on Explanations," *Proceedings of the Seventh IJCAI*, Vancouver, Canada, pp. 67–70, 1981.

DeJong, G., "Prediction and Substantiation: A New Approach to Natural Language Processing," *Cognitive Science*, Vol. 3, pp. 251–73, 1979.

Doyle, J., "A Truth Maintenance System," *Artificial Intelligence*, Vol. 12, No. 2, pp. 231–72, 1979.

Fikes, R., "Deductive Retrieval Mechanisms for State Description Models," *Proceedings of the Fourth IJCAI*, Tiblisi, Georgia, USSR, pp. 99–106, 1975.

Fikes, R., Hart, P., and Nilsson, N., "Learning and Executing Generalized Robot Plans," *Artificial Intelligence*, Vol. 3, No. 2, pp. 251–88, 1972.

Fox, M., and Reddy, R., "Knowledge-guided Learning of Structural Descriptions," *Proceedings of the Fifth IJCAI*, Cambridge, Mass., pp. 318–19, 1977.

Granger, R., "Adaptive Understanding: Correcting Erroneous Inferences," Research Report No. 171, Department of Computer Science, Yale University, 1980.

Kolodner, J., "Retrieval and Organizational Strategies in Conceptual Memory: A Computer Model," Research Report No. 187, Department of Computer Science, Yale University, 1980.

Langley, P., "Data-driven Discovery of Physical Laws," *Cognitive Science*, Vol. 5, pp. 31–54, 1981.

Lebowitz, M., "Generalization and Memory in an Integrated Understanding System," Research Report No. 186, Department of Computer Science, Yale University, 1980.

Lenat, D., "AM: An Artificial Intelligence Approach to Discovery in Mathematics as Heuristic Search," AIM-286, AI Laboratory, Stanford University, 1976.

Michalski, R., "A System of Programs for Computer-aided Induction: A Summary," *Proceedings of the Fifth IJCAI*, Cambridge, Mass., pp. 319–20, 1977.

Michalski, R., and Stepp, R., "Automated Construction of Classifications: Conceptual Clustering Versus Numerical Taxonomy," *IEEE Transactions on Pattern Analysis and Machine Intelligence*, Vol. 5, No. 4, pp. 396–410, July 1983.

Minsky, M. "A Framework for the Representation of Knowledge," AI Report TR-306, MIT, 1974.

Mitchell, T., Utgoff, P., and Banerji, R., "Learning by Experimentation: Acquiring and Refining Problem-solving Heuristics," in *Machine Learning: An Artificial Intelligence Approach*, R. S. Michalski, J. G. Carbonell, and T. M. Mitchell (Eds.), Tioga, Palo Alto, Calif., 1983.

Newell, A., and Simon, H., *Human Problem Solving*, Prentice-Hall, Englewood Cliffs, N. J., 1972.

Nilsson, N., *Principles of Artificial Intelligence*, Tioga, Palo Alto, Calif., 1980.

Schank, R., *Dynamic Memory,* Cambridge University Press, Cambridge, 1982.

Schank, R., and Abelson, R., *Scripts, Plans, Goals, and Understanding,* Erlbaum, Hillsdale, N. J., 1977.

Schmidt, C., and Sridharan, N., "Plan Recognition Using a Hypothesize and Revise Paradigm: An Example," *Proceedings of the Fifth IJCAI,* Cambridge, Mass., pp. 480–86, 1977.

Soloway, E., "Knowledge-directed Learning Using Multiple Levels of Description," Ph.D. diss., Computer Science Department, University of Massachusetts, Amherst, 1977.

Winston, P., "Learning and Reasoning by Analogy," *Communications of the ACM,* Vol. 23, No. 12, pp. 689–702, 1980.

PART
SIX

AN EXPLORATION OF
GENERAL ASPECTS OF
LEARNING

20

ESCAPING BRITTLENESS:

The Possibilities of General-Purpose Learning Algorithms Applied to Parallel Rule–Based Systems

John H. Holland
University of Michigan

Abstract

Message-passing, rule-based production systems in which many rules are active simultaneously offer attractive possibilities for the exploitation of general-purpose machine learning algorithms. In such systems each rule can be looked upon as a tentative hypothesis about some aspect of the task environment, competing against other plausible hypotheses being entertained at the same time. In this context there are two major tasks for machine learning algorithms: (1) apportionment of credit and (2) rule discovery.

The apportionment-of-credit algorithm(s) must assign "strength" to rules on the basis of their observed usefulness to the system. The problem is complicated by the difficulty of determining which of a cluster of rules active in an early, "stage-setting" capacity has contributed to a later useful outcome (e.g., rules controlling early moves that make possible a later triple jump in checkers). If strengths can be assigned appropriately, then they can be used to determine a rule's ability to win against competing rules, and they can be used to determine the rule's likelihood of being used as a "parent" for new rules. Surprisingly, for credit apportionment algorithms of the *bucket-brigade* variety, one can prove fixed-point theorems that provide some guarantees of an appropriate apportionment.

The task of rule discovery depends critically upon the discovery of good "building blocks" for generating plausible rules (hypotheses). A parallel system designed with machine learning in mind must permit a constant flux of new rules to be tested and exploited or discarded. Moreover this flux must not disturb the system's behavior in task environments for which it has well-practiced, effective procedures. *Genetic algorithms,* using the strengths as "fitnesses," offer subtle ways of discovering good building blocks, and there are new versions of theorems from mathematical genetics that enable us to understand this discovery process.

20.1 INTRODUCTION

The research that has culminated in the design of expert systems is a solid achievement for artificial intelligence: Given appropriately restricted domains, expert systems display the reasoned consideration of alternatives that one expects of an expert. The source of this success, the domain-specific character of the systems, is also a source of limitations. The systems are *brittle* in the sense that they respond appropriately only in narrow domains and require substantial human intervention to compensate for even slight shifts in domain (see Duda and Shortliffe, 1983). This problem of brittleness and ways to temper it are the main concern of this chapter. The overall theme is that *induction* is the basic—and perhaps only—way of making large advances in this direction.

To gain a clearer idea of the scope of the overall problem, consider some of the specific problems induction faces in this context. At the top of the list is the task of generating useful ways of categorizing input. In complex domains there is a perpetual novelty to the input so that experience can guide future action only if the system discovers regularities or recurrences in the input. The categories induced must be broad enough to "cover" the likely possibilities parsimoniously; at the same time they must be specific enough to distinguish situations requiring different behaviors. Categories must be incorporated into rules that "point" both to actions and to an aura of associated categories. That is, as the categories are induced, they must be arranged in a "tangled hierarchy" (see Fahlman, 1979) that enables the system to model its environment appropriately.

On a larger scale induction must provide plausible alternatives and changes in the hierarchies and models based upon these categories. In this structure, credit must be apportioned to the all-important categories that point to "stage-setting" actions necessary for later success. Because of the uncertainty of any induction, the process must be carried out in such a way that the system can absorb new, tentative rules without destroying capabilities in well-practiced situations. In all but the simplest situations a complex combination of competing rules will be activated so that the system must select a subset of rules that provides a coherent "picture" (model) of the situation. This picture in turn directs behavior and attempts at confirmation. At the highest level, the system must make effective use of metaphor and analogy to transfer inferences from familiar to unfamiliar situations (a capacity only touched upon in this chapter). The first two sections of the chapter will expand upon these problems.

Section 20.2 takes a closer look at the notions of domain and environment, and section 20.3 examines (informal) criteria bearing on the escape from brittleness.

The approach advocated in this chapter is based upon a class of message-passing, rule-based systems, called *classifier systems,* in which large numbers of rules can be active simultaneously. Individual rules can be kept simple and standardized because combinations of rules are used to define complex situations. This approach results in both parsimony and flexibility, because the same rule can be used in many contexts (see criterion 1 in section 20.3). Moreover, it gives a different slant to the induction task—the object becomes that of finding rules that serve well in a variety of tasks.

All rules are in condition/action form. Each condition specifies the set of messages satisfying it, and each action specifies the message sent when the condition part is satisfied. Because messages are kept to a standard length, it is possible to define conditions using strings of standard length, and this is done in such a way that it is simple to set the generality of a condition. As a consequence default hierarchies are easy to generate and use. Rules can be tied together into networks of various kinds by appropriate use of tagging. Section 20.4 describes classifier systems in detail.

Simplicity of the component rules also eases the tasks of the learning algorithms. First among these tasks is that of rating the usefulness of existing rules. This is the task of the *bucket-brigade* algorithm; it assigns a *strength* to each individual rule, modifying the strength on the basis of the rule's overall usefulness as the system accumulates experience. In effect the algorithm treats each rule as a middleman in a complex economy, its survival being dependent upon "making a profit" in its local interactions. In the long run, such profits will recur only if the rule is tied into chains of interactions leading to successful actions. Bucket-brigade algorithms are defined and described in the first part of section 20.5.

The most difficult inductive task is that of generating plausible new rules. Here that task is carried out by a *genetic algorithm.* It uses high-strength classifiers as the "parents" of new classifiers to be tested under the bucket brigade. Although the genetic algorithm acts directly upon the strings defining classifiers, it can be shown that it is implicitly searching and using a space of "building blocks." Moreover, it is searching this space orders of magnitude more rapidly than would be indicated by the rate at which it is processing strings. Rules generated by the genetic algorithm do not displace their parents; rather they displace low-strength rules, entering into competition with the other rules in the system. This competition gives the overall system a graceful way of handling conflicts and tentative hypotheses. The latter part of section 20.5 describes genetic algorithms and their effects upon classifiers.

Systems organized along these lines have been tested successfully in a variety of contexts. For example, a poker-playing version of the system (Smith, 1980), starting with classifiers embodying only the rules of the game, competed with overwhelming success against Waterman's learning poker player (Waterman and Hayes-Roth, 1978). Recently Goldberg (1983) tested a system that, starting with a clean slate (randomly generated classifiers), confronted a gas pipeline transmission problem involving diurnal variation, seasonal variation, and leaks. The system generated successful control procedures embedded in a (discovered) default hierarchy distinguishing normal operation from "leaky" operation. Additional tests are discussed in section 20.6.

20.2 DOMAINS AND ENVIRONMENTS

A closer look at the role of induction begins with a closer look at the domains—the *environment*—in which the system is to operate. The environment provides the grist for the inductive mill, thereby setting the possibilities for, and the ultimate limitations on, the inductive process. An environment with no regularities (however defined) offers no opportunities for induction. Human experience indicates that real environments abound in regularities. The problem is to uncover and exploit them.

This chapter will restrict itself to environments that, implicitly or explicitly, present problems in terms of goals to be attained. In this context the system "closes the loop" through the environment, receiving information from the environment and acting upon the environment to bring about changes therein. The environment signals the solution of a problem by feeding back a quantity called *payoff*. (This term from game theory, chosen for its neutrality, is the cognate of *utility* in economics, *error signals* in control theory, *fitness* in genetics, *reward* in psychology, and so on.) This format cleanly exposes most of the difficult problems in planning and problem solving, ranging from game playing though the design of mobile robots to abstract tasks such as the production of a corpus of useful theorems. The system uses the states of the environment as "stepping stones" to reach goal states that feed back payoff. The problem, simply, is to go efficiently from "here," a nongoal state, to "there," a goal state. The subtleties underlying this simple statement increase rapidly as the complexity of the state graph of the environment increases. One need go no further than the game trees and simply defined goals of chess or go to see deep subtleties; real-world situations typified by the design of flexible robots or interactive information retrieval systems offer even deeper problems.

The system can be thought of as receiving information about the current state of its environment in the form of *messages* generated by an input interface. The input interface typically consists of a set of feature detectors, and the message consists of a string of feature values. The systems dealt with here generally do *not* have high-level interpreters for these messages. That is, the rules of the system work directly on the message strings, acting on the presence or absence of certain bits. Whatever meanings there are, are supplied by the actions of the rules and, ultimately, by the effects produced on the environment.

The contrast between this "environment-oriented" approach and a "language-oriented" approach is worth pointing up. Consider the game of checkers. A language-oriented approach would use a language (symbols, grammar, etc., based, say, on standard checkers move notation) to specify legal moves, desirable configurations, and so on. The language, with an interpreter providing properties of board configurations and the like, would then be used, along with deductive inference, to develop a goal-oriented plan. The environment-oriented approach uses detectors (cf. the "parameters" used by Samuel, 1959) to generate bit strings based on the checkerboard configuration. These messages are processed by rules (arranged in a complex default hierarchy; see below) to determine plans and moves. An environment-oriented approach does not explicitly assign abstract symbols to board configurations, nor does it explicitly search for and apply grammatical rules to such symbols.

Note that the environment-oriented approach is *not* more restricted in its powers of definition than the language-oriented approach. The ultimate limits on the definitional powers of either approach are set by the input interface. The system cannot distinguish environmental state configurations assigned identical values by the input interface, be they symbols or feature strings. (This sets aside certain sequential tests, but the argument remains the same even if these are used. More formally, the input interface groups environmental states into equivalence classes; elements of the same equivalence class are the same as far as the system is concerned.) All that definition can do under either approach is to categorize the distinguishable. It divides the distinguishable elements into two classes—those that satisfy the definition and those that do not.

If the system is computationally complete (can define any procedure) with respect to sorting the input messages into classes, then it has reached the limits of what definition can do for it relative to distinguishability. Stated another way, if two systems are computationally complete with respect to input interfaces that set identical restrictions on distinguishability, then the systems have the same limits on their powers of definition. This is true even if one system is language-oriented and the other is environment-oriented. The environment-oriented systems that will be examined shortly accomplish definition by a combination of conditions, tags, and recoding (see section 20.4.3); they are computationally complete relative to the set of messages produced by any input interface.

20.3 CRITERIA

This investigation of ways of avoiding brittleness has been guided by several informal criteria derived primarily from ruminations about flexible natural systems and consideration of various landmarks in machine learning. The systems defined in the next section are intended as procedural implementations of these criteria, which are as follows:

1. Recombination and parallelism. In order to avoid a distinct rule for each situation (a "visiting grandmother" rule, a "yellow Volkswagon with a flat tire" rule, etc.), it is imperative that the system's response to any situation be mediated by the concurrent activation of a *set* of relevant rules. By activating several elementary rules in response to a complex set of conditions, rather than relying on anticipation of the overall situation by provision of a single preformed rule, the system sets combinatorics to work for it rather than against it. As a simple example, by selecting one each from ten hairlines, ten eye configurations, ten noses, ten mouths, and ten jawlines, the system can match any one of one hundred thousand distinct faces at the cost of retaining only fifty elementary rules. Under this criterion, it is incumbent upon induction and learning to search for rules that are useful "building blocks" in a variety of contexts. If the building blocks are well chosen, the system may be able to function well in situations not previously encountered. For instance, if the system has rules categorizing and handling input messages according to the usual notions of *hooved, four-legged,* and *horned,* it is conceivable that it would infer that a unicorn (observed for the first time) is *herbivorous.*

2. Categorization and default hierarchies. Categorization is the system's major weapon for combating the environment's perpetual novelty. The system must readily generate categories for input messages, and it must be able to generate categories relevant to its internal processes. These candidates must be tested repeatedly for usefulness and used with increasing or decreasing frequency in accord with the outcome (see criterion 5, "Competition, confirmation, and gracefulness," below).

Moreover, there must be some criterion of plausibility so that the system is not overwhelmed with poor candidates. Appropriate bottom-up procedures (e.g., generalization of input messages) and top-down procedures (e.g., recombination of parts of the definitions of extant categories) can go far toward implementing this constraint. The categories generated should spontaneously arrange themselves into a default hierarchy (much like the skeleton of Fahlman's NETL, 1979), so that details invoke "sketches" of the situations, allowing transfer of information between experiences activating similar sketches. (The more rules held in common by the clusters of rules defining two sketches, the more similar they are.) High-level interpreters for determining categories should be avoided where possible because they impose complex relations between syntax and semantics, greatly complicating the induction of categories.

3. Association. The use of categories as building blocks is much enhanced if, as the categories develop, an aura of associations with other categories also develops. Various "triggers," such as the co-occurrence of a pair of categories in a given environmental situation, can limit the formation of associations to plausible candidates. Associations are recorded by *synchronic pointers*—pointers that do *not* imply temporal sequence—and these pointers must be tested repeatedly for usefulness (see criterion 5). The generation and selection of the categories and pointers that serve as building blocks are processes that provide the system with a wide range of structures that act much like *virtual copies* (Fahlman, 1979). To use a biological analogy, these virtual copies play the role of "species" filling the "niches" defined by the regularities (opportunities for exploitation) uncovered in the system's experience. The meaning of the virtual copies stems from the process of competition and selection that determines their emergence. This contrasts strongly with attempts to arrive at such structures a priori, which is much like attempting to develop a taxonomy for species without understanding their ontogeny.

4. Diachronic pointing, models, and prediction. Although Samuel's paper (1959) is often cited in machine learning, his use of model building to solve problems is almost always overlooked. (This may be because he modeled strategies by using linear forms, forms that typically serve only as linear pattern recognition devices.) Because of the model building, Samuel's checkers player can refine its strategy while playing the game, when there is no payoff from the environment. This greatly enhances the system's flexibility. When a system uses a model to generate expectations or predictions, it can use subsequent verification or falsification of the predictions to guide revisions of the model (toward better prediction) even in the absence of payoff.

In the present context, the construction of a model requires that the system include a second kind of pointer—the *diachronic pointers*—to indicate temporal sequences of categories. In short, the system forms temporal associations. Trigger conditions serve to restrict the generation of candidates, as they did in the case of synchronic pointers. For example, if a well-established category Y consistently follows well-established category X when the system makes response R, then it is plausible to induce a diachronic pointer between X and Y. (Note that a general category will often describe an environmental situation that persists over an extended period, as in the case of a *going home* or *pursuit of prey* category, allowing the trigger to link categories well separated in time.) As in the case of synchronic pointers, the diachronic pointers must be subjected to continued selection for usefulness.

5. Competition, confirmation, and gracefulness. The previous criteria have exploited parallelism to provide clusters of rules that serve both as virtual copies and as models. Parallelism neatly sidesteps the priority issues of one-rule-at-a-time systems but leaves open questions concerning conflict and consistency. Of all the elementary rules that are candidates for activation in a given situation, which ones get the nod?

The foundation for an answer is set by an effective apportionment-of-credit algorithm. Strengths must be assigned to rules in accord with their past usefulness in the situations in which they have been invoked. Once again Samuel (1959) leads the way. The problem is one of strengthening stage-setting rules that make possible later actions yielding payoff. The exploitation of predictions provides a mechanism. Let us assume, following Samuel, that the strength of a rule amounts to a prediction of the average payoff the system will receive *later* if the rule is invoked *concurrently* as part of a cluster. Assume further that a second rule is coupled to the given rule by a diachronic pointer. If this second rule has a strength (prediction) very different from that of the first rule, then the strength of the first rule can be revised to bring it into line with the later prediction (see discussion in Samuel, 1959, and the definition of the bucket-brigade algorithm in section 20.5). When the system has such an algorithm for revising strengths, then the invocation of rules can be decided by a competition based on strength and the degree to which the rule's conditions are satisfied by the current situation.

In effect the various rules held by the system are treated as competing hypotheses. The winners are the system's estimate of the current situation. It is critical to the system's performance and flexibility that its rules represent a wide range of competing, even conflicting, hypotheses. The competition replaces a criterion of global consistency—a criterion that is infeasible for any very large system of rules—with one of progressive confirmation under the apportionment-of-credit algorithm. With this outlook, rules that consistently make poor predictions when invoked have their strength steadily decreased to the point that they are displaced by newer candidates. The newer candidates must in turn compete, usually doing well in "niches" not well handled by rules already in the system. The combination of competition and confirmation contributes to the system's *gracefulness:* Large numbers of new candidates can be injected without disturbing performance in well-practiced domains.

20.4 CLASSIFIER SYSTEMS

20.4.1 Overview

Classifier systems are general-purpose programming systems designed to meet the objectives and criteria set forth in sections 20.2 and 20.3. They have been designed from the outset to be amenable to modification by learning algorithms. Particular attention has been given to questions of gracefulness and to the provision of "natural" building blocks. The systems have already been tested in a variety of contexts (see section 20.6).

Classifier systems have many affinities to the rule-based (production system) approach to expert systems (see, for example, Davis and King, 1977, or Waterman and Hayes-Roth, 1978) but with the following major differences:

1. Any number of rules, called *classifiers,* can be active at the same time. There can be no direct conflict between classifiers because the only action of a classifier is to post a message to a global message list—the more classifiers activated, the more messages on the message list. The resulting conflict-free concurrency sidesteps the difficult conflict resolution problems of one-rule-at-a-time systems (see McDermott and Forgy, 1978), allowing the system to use many rules concurrently to summarize and act upon a situation. The rules become building

blocks that can be combined to handle a wide variety of situations. Moreover, the parallelism makes it easier to specify and control the parallel processes that pervade the real world.

2. Messages are strings of fixed length k over a fixed alphabet, taken to be $\{1,0\}$ in the definitions that follow. Classifiers, as is usual with production systems, consist of a *condition* part and an *action* part, but the conditions are all specified by strings of length k over the alphabet $\{1,0,\#\}$. With this provision it is possible to use a simple matching operator to test whether or not some message satisfies a condition. From the architectural viewpoint, the fixed lengths encourage organizations exploiting fixed-length registers, an important consideration in simulations or physical realizations.

3. When the condition part of a classifier is satisfied by some message on the message list, the action part uses the message to form a new message, which is posted on the new message list. Thus the basic procedure of the *system* is a simple loop in which all classifiers access the current message list, determine if their conditions have been satisfied, and if so, post messages to the message list for the next time-step. As mentioned earlier, any number of classifiers can be active simultaneously without conflict, because actions only add messages to the new message list.

4. All external communication (input and output) is via messages to the message list. As a result, all internal control information and external communication reside in the same data structure.

5. Because the order in which classifiers are executed is independent of the order in which the classifiers are stored, and because satisfaction of conditions is determined by a simple matching operation, there is no need for an interpreter. This makes it possible to design local syntactic operators that modify systems of classifiers ("programs") in useful ways, something difficult to do for standard languages or production systems but very important if the system is to be modified by learning algorithms or expert advice.

6. Because of the global nature of the message list, tagging and related techniques become efficient ways of "coupling" classifiers, forcing predetermined execution sequences, and so on. The combination of concurrency and a global list avoids the limitations on tagging discussed by Davis and King (1977) in their review of production systems.

20.4.2 Definition of the Basic Elements: Classifiers and Messages

Classifiers have the same role in classifier systems that instructions have in computer language. They are called classifiers because they can be used to classify messages into general sets, but they are broader in concept and application than this name would indicate, providing both processing and recoding. The message specified by the action part of the classifier changes the internal state of the system, thereby influencing later action, and it may cause external (effector) action. Provided with some simple message-processing capabilities, classifiers can carry out arbitrary operations on messages, including recursions. It follows that there are classifier systems that are computationally universal.

The major technical hurdle in implementing a message-processing version of a production system is that of providing a simple way of defining conditions in terms of messages. Each condition specifies a subset of the set of all possible messages—the set of messages that *satisfies* the condition. There is no simple and compact way of specifying an arbitrary subset of a large set; that is, most subsets must be specified element by element. Nevertheless there is one large and important class of subsets that *can* be simply specified, and any other subset can be defined as a union of these subsets. Each subset in this special class is specified by a string of length k over the three-letter alphabet $\{1,0,\#\}$. (Recall that messages, for present purposes, are strings of length k over the alphabet $\{1,0\}$.) The $\#$ symbol plays the role here of a "don't care" in the sense that wherever a $\#$ occurs in the specifying string one can substitute either a 1 or a 0 and still have a member of the subset. For example, the string 11 . . . 1# specifies the subset of exactly two elements, namely, the messages $\{11 \ldots 11, 11 \ldots 10\}$, and the string 1## . . . ## specifies the subset consisting of all messages that start with a 1.

More formally, let

$$\langle s_1, s_2, \ldots, s_j, \ldots s_k \rangle, \quad s_j \in \{1,0,\#\}$$

be a string of k symbols specifying a subset, and let

$$\langle m_1, m_2, \ldots, m_k \rangle, \quad m_j \in \{1,0\}$$

be a k-bit message. The message belongs to the specified subset just in case

1. if $s_j = 1$ or $s_j = 0$, then $m_j = s_j$
2. if $s_j = \#$, then m_j can be either 1 or 0.

The subset consists of all messages satisfying this requirement; that is, each subset is a hyperplane in the space of messages.

In this notation, classifier conditions are specified using strings of length k over the alphabet $\{1,0,\#\}$. We extend the notation by allowing the string to be prefixed by a minus sign $(-)$, with the intended interpretation that the prefixed condition is satisfied only if *no* message of the given subset is present on the message list. That is, if string c specifies subset S of the set of all messages, the condition $-c$ is *not* satisfied just in case the message list contains a message belonging to S. Combinations of classifiers can be used to implement conditions over arbitrary subsets in much the same way that AND, OR, and NOT can be combined to yield arbitrary Boolean functions (see section 20.4.3).

When the condition part of a classifier is satisfied, it produces a message specified by its action (or message specification) part. The action part, like the condition part, is specified by a string of length k that contains the # symbol, but the # has a different meaning. Now it plays the role of a "pass through" in the sense that wherever the # symbol occurs in the action part, the corresponding bit in a message satisfying the condition part is passed through into the outgoing message. For example, consider the message specification 11 . . . 1# in the action part of the classifier, and assume the message 00 . . . 00 satisfies the condition part of the classifier. Then the outgoing message will be 11 . . . 10.

More formally, let

$$\langle a_1, a_2, \ldots, a_j, \ldots a_k \rangle, \quad a_j \in \{1, 0, \#\}$$

be a string of k symbols in the action part of a classifier, and let

$$\langle m_1, m_2, \ldots, m_j, \ldots, m_k \rangle, \quad m_j \in \{1, 0\}$$

be a message satisfying the condition part of the classifier. Then the outgoing message, at position j, has value

1. a_j, if $a_j = 1$ or 0
2. m_j, if $a_j = \#$.

In brief, if a message satisfies the condition of a classifier, a new message is generated from the action portion of the classifier by using the 1's and 0's of the action part and passing through bits of the satisfying message at the pass through positions of the action part.

It is useful to generalize the notion of a classifier to allow an arbitrary number of conditions. Condition i of an r-condition classifier C is specified by a string c_i of length k over the symbols $\{1, 0, \#\}$, possibly prefixed by a $-$; the action part is specified by a single string a of a length k over the symbols $\{1, 0, \#\}$. Notationally, the conditions in the condition part are separated by "," and the action part is separated from the condition part by "/". Thus the specification of an r-condition classifier will have the form

$$c_1, c_2, \ldots, c_r / a.$$

The condition part of the classifier C is *satisfied* if each condition c_i is satisfied by some message M_j on the current message list. When the classifier is satisfied, an outgoing message M^* is generated as before using the message M_j satisfying condition c_1 and the action part a. At each position where a has a bit 0 or 1, M^* gets that bit; at each position where a has a pass through #, M^* gets the corresponding bit of M_j.

These definitions are sufficient to define the basic elements of a classifier system. A *classifier system* consists of a list of classifiers $\{C_1, C_2, \ldots, C_N\}$, a message list, an input interface, and an output interface. The *basic execution cycle* of this system proceeds as follows:

1. Place all messages from the input interface on the current message list.
2. Compare all messages to all conditions and record all matches.
3. For each match generate a message for the new message list.
4. Replace the current message list by the new message list.
5. Process the new message list through the output interface to produce system output.
6. Return to step 1.

A classifier system may be augmented by algorithms for "look-ahead," inference, and learning. Several methods for doing these things will be described in the next two subsections and in section 20.5. For some of these, weights are associated with classifiers and messages, and wherever a match is made a record is kept of the classifier that is satisfied and of the combinations of messages that satisfied it so that these weights can be modified periodically. Such enriched systems will still be called classifier systems unless there is some distinction to be pointed up by using a different name.

Because matching messages against conditions is a simple process, the central loop of the process (step 2 above) proceeds rapidly even on standard von Neumann architectures. One simulation currently in operation executes a time-step involving 256 conditions and thirty-two messages in less than 0.1 second. Parallel architectures offer speedups in proportion to the parallelism.

20.4.3 Tagging and Networks

Pointers, action sequences, and other processes dependent upon "addressing" are attained using *tags* to *couple* classifiers.

A classifier C_2 is coupled to a classifier C_1 if some condition of C_2 is satisfied by the message(s) generated by the action part of C_1. Note that a classifier with very specific conditions (few #'s) will typically be coupled to only a few other classifiers, and a classifier with very general conditions (many #'s) will be coupled to many other classifiers. When used to implement part of a "semantic network" or neural network, a classifier with very specific conditions has few incoming branches, and a classifier with very general conditions has many incoming branches.

Tags are a simple way of providing coupling. For example, any message with the prefix 1101 will satisfy a condition of the form 1101# . . . #, so a classifier with this condition in effect has an address: to send a message to this classifier one employs the prefix 1101. Since b bits yield 2^b tags and tags can be placed anywhere in a condition, a great number of conditions can be addressed uniquely.

By using appropriate prefixes, one can define a classifier that attends to a specific set of classifiers. Consider a pair of classifiers C_1 and C_2 that send messages

tagged with 1101 and 1001, respectively. A classifier with the condition 1101## . . . ##
will attend only to C_1, whereas a classifier with the configuration 1#01## . . . ## will
attend to both C_1 and C_2. Using a combination of pass throughs (#'s in the action
parts) and recodings (in which the prefix on the outgoing message differs from that of
the satisfying messages), one can circumvent, usually with little effort, the limitation
that the conditions be hyperplanes in the message space.

Boolean compounds of conditions—and hence the specification of conditions
satisfied by arbitrarily chosen subsets of messages—are readily achieved by tags. An
AND-condition is expressed by a single multicondition classifier such as $M_1, M_2/M$,
for M is only added to the list if *both M_1 and M_2* are satisfied. An OR-condition is
expressed by a set of classifiers such as $\{M_1/M; M_2/M\}$, for M is added to the list if
either M_1 or M_2 is satisfied. With these primitives, any Boolean form can be
expressed by a set of classifiers. For example,

$$(M_1 \ \& \ M_2) \ \lor \ [(M_3 \ \& \ (-M_4)]$$

is achieved by the classifiers

$$\{M_1, M_2/M_5 \ ; \ M_3, -M_4/M_5\}.$$

The judicious use of #'s and recoding again reduces the number of classifiers
required when the Boolean expressions are complex. By assigning tags to the input,
internal, and output states of a finite system, one can realize arbitrary state transition
diagrams.

The use of tags to couple classifiers for purposes of control and sequencing is
illustrated in detail in the next subsection. The example also illustrates the use of concurrency and distributed control in classifier systems.

20.4.4 A Simple Classifier Control System

Figure 20-1 gives the schematic of a simple control routine for a classifier
system operating in a two-dimensional environment. When there is an object of a
specified type anywhere in the system's field of vision, this classifier routine acts to
bring the system next to the object and hold it there.

The environment contains objects distributed over a planar surface. The input
interface produces a message for an object in the field of vision. This message indicates the relative position of the object in the field of vision (left-of-center, center,
right-of-center) and whether it is distant from or adjacent to the system. The classifiers process this information and issue commands to the output interface (ROTATE
VISION VECTOR [LEFT, RIGHT], COUPLE MOTION VECTOR TO VISION
VECTOR, MOVE FORWARD, STOP). The control routine proceeds by stages, first
centering the object, then aligning the direction of motion to that vision direction,
next moving forward in that direction, and finally stopping when adjacent to the
object. The operations of the system take place over successive execution cycles or
time-steps.

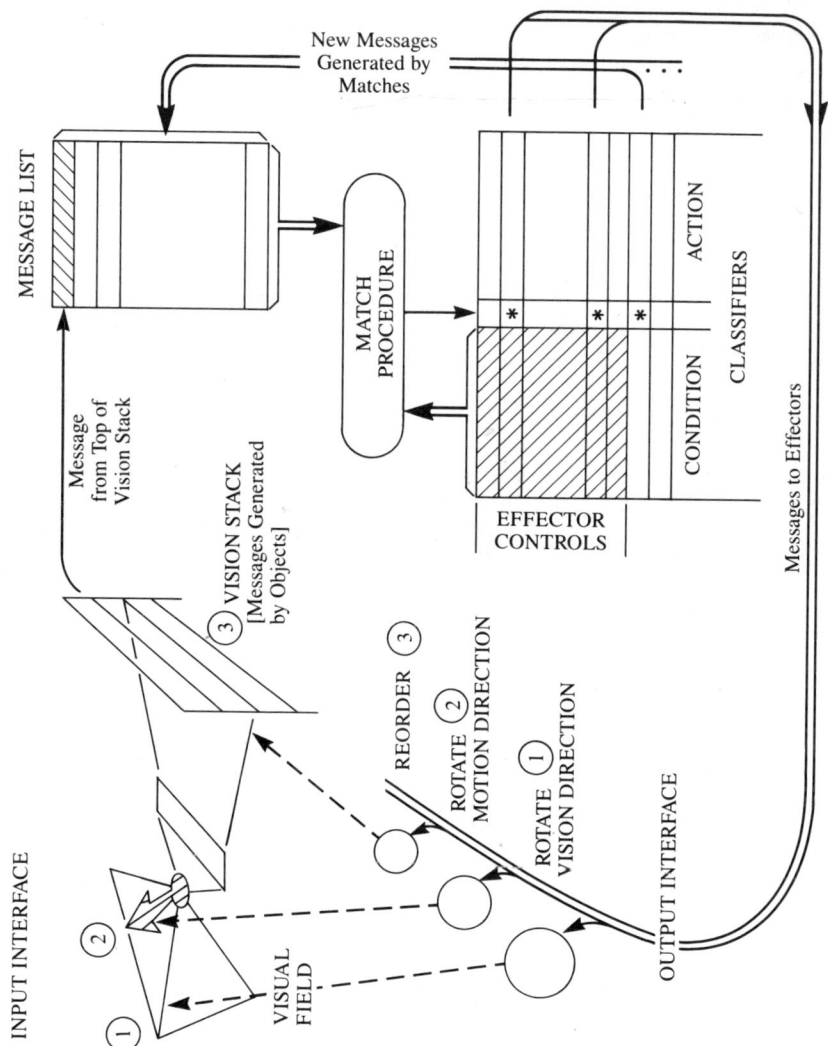

Figure 20-1: Schematic for a classifier-based cognitive system.

To define the classifier system, one first defines the input messages, then the condition parts of classifiers, and then the action parts of classifiers. Each of these is 16 bits long, though the present example is based on actual simulation in which they are 32 bits long.

The leftmost bit of a message is a tag, 1 for an input message and 0 for any other kind of message. The next 12 bits of an input message specify the properties of an object. (Note that these 12 bits can be used for entirely different purposes for messages with initial tag 0.) There are twelve independent properties, with 1 indicating the presence and 0 indicating the absence of a property in an object. For concreteness we will stipulate that the system is searching for objects—goal objects—that satisfy the condition #111000# ########. That is, it is searching for objects that have the first three properties and lack the next three, whether or not they have the remaining six properties.

The last 3 bits in an interface message give information about the relative position of the object in the field of vision. They are interpreted as follows:

bits 14, 15:   1,0 object left-of-center
               0,1 object right-of-center
               0,0 object centered
bit 16:   1 object adjacent
               0 object not adjacent.

Thus, the message 11110001 01011100 indicates the presence in the visual field of a goal object that is left- of center and not adjacent, only the underlined bits being relevant to this interpretation.

Classifier *conditions* will be abbreviated as follows:

x = desired object x is present in the field of vision
c = object is centered
l = object is left-of-center
r = object is right-of-center
a = object is adjacent
$-a$ = object is not adjacent

Following these conventions, $[x,l,-a]$ specifies the condition 1111000# #####100, and so on.

The action part of each classifier specifies a 16-bit message issued when the conditions of the classifier are satisfied. Each such message will simply be abbreviated as the corresponding 16-bit integer. That is, "[4]" abbreviates the *message* 00000000 00000100, the tag 0 at the first position indicating that this is *not* an input message.

The classifier routine controls three effectors: an effector to move the direction of vision incrementally (15 degrees in the simulation) to the left or right, a second effector to set the direction of motion parallel to the direction of vision, and a third effector to cause the system to move forward one unit in the direction of motion. If no command is issued to a given effector during an execution cycle, that effector retains its last setting. In presenting the action effected by messages to effectors we will use

$L=$ rotate vision vector 15 degrees to the left
$R=$ rotate vision vector 15 degrees to the right
$P=$ set the move vector parallel to the vision vector
$G=$ move one unit forward in the move vector direction

There are nine classifiers in this illustrative system. The first four lead to operations by the remaining five, the next three cause output actions, the eighth causes the system to halt, and the ninth will be explained shortly.

$C1$ $[x,1]/[4]$
$C2$ $[x,r]/[5]$
$C3$ $[x,c,-a]/[6]$
$C4$ $[x,c,a]/[7]$
$C5$ $[4]/[8]$ [8] causes effector action L
$C6$ $[5]/[9]$ [9] causes effector action R
$C7$ $[6]/[10]$ [10] causes effector actions P and G
$C8$ $[7]/[11]$ [11] causes the cycling to halt
$C9$ $[4or5or6or7]/[0]$

(Note that the condition [4or5or6or7] is specified by the string 00000000 000001##.)

If an object of the desired type x appears at the far left of the field of vision at execution cycle t, classifier $C1$ is activated, placing message [4] on the message list at cycle $t + 1$. Assuming the object x is still left-of-center, the classifiers $C1$, $C5$, and $C9$ become active at cycle $t + 1$ and the message list consists of 4 messages: [4], [8], [0], and the message from the input interface. This list of messages continues until x is centered as a result of the repetitions of the L command, whereupon $C3$ would be activated, and so on (see table 20-1).

Note that message [4] provides a recording of the message from the input interface, coupling this information to the classifier $C5$ ([4]/[8]), which causes effector action L. Any message [m] could have been used for this purpose; for example, the pair of classifiers $[x,1]/[m]$ and $[m]/[8]$ would have produced the same action L. It is this "internal" recoding that permits the classifier systems to carry out arbitrary computations, so that formally speaking classifier languages are computationally complete.

In detail, the execution sequence of the classifier system proceeds as shown in table 20-1. It is clear that the classifier [4or5or6or7]/[0] plays no role in this example. It is inserted to illustrate the concept of a *support* classifier, which is useful when the bucket-brigade algorithm (see section 20.5) is incorporated into this classifier

Table 20-1: Example of a typical execution sequence.

Major Cycle (Time)	Active Classifiers	Message List
t	$C1$	11110001 10000100 [4]
$t + 1$	$C1, C5, C9$	11110001 10000100 [4] [8] [0]
$t + 2$	$C1, C5, C9$	11110001 10000100 [4] [8] [0]
⋮		
($t + c$ is the time at which object x is first centered.)		
$t + c$	$C3, C9$	11110001 10000000 [6] [0]
$t + c + 1$	$C3, C7, C9$	11110001 10000000 [6] [10] [0]
⋮		
($t + a$ is the time at which the system is first adjacent to object x.)		
$t + a$	$C4, C9$	11110001 10000001 [7] [0]
$t + a + 1$	$C4, C8, C9$	11110001 10000001 [7] [11] [0]
(The system has now halted adjacent to object x.)		

system. In that case the classifier [4or5or6or7]/[0] serves to reinforce the whole set of classifiers. With further additions such a classifier can be used to call the whole routine when an object x appears.

20.4.5 Use of Classifiers to Define Complex Entities and Hierarchies

The introduction to this chapter made the point that the ultimate limitations on definition are no greater for the environment-oriented approach than for the language-oriented approach, that limit being set by distinguishability. Section 20.4.3 showed that clusters of coupled classifiers can be arranged to respond to any chosen subset of the set of possible messages. Because messages are the unifying element of classifier systems—providing internal communication as well as communication from the environment—this capability provides broad powers of definition. There is not room here for a detailed exposition, but the possibility of defining objects involving complex combinations of categories and relations—Winston's definition of an *arch* (1975) is a simple example—can at least be made plausible.

First, networklike interactions of coupled classifiers, through the use of tags and conditions of varying generality, have already been discussed (section 20.4.3). When the condition part of a rule is satisfied and it is coupled into such an array, it acts by pointing to other classifiers that are to have their condition parts tested in turn. That is, the outgoing message is tagged so that it is attended to by the classifiers to which the rule is to be coupled. This operation is quite analogous to passing a marker over a link in NETL (Fahlman, 1979) or to moving down one of the links in a linked list.

Because messages are involved, not just markers, a great deal of information can be carried from point to point in the network. For instance, the tag of a message can indicate its point of origin, and other bits carry information passed through or recoded (see section 20.4.2). Because of the parallelism of classifier systems, clusters of coactive rules can be used to define categories and objects (see section 20.4.3 and 20.4.4). The pointing technique can be extended to include relations, coupling some classifiers in a cluster to other related clusters. Finally, default hierarchies develop naturally under the bidding process discussed in section 20.5. Under the bidding process, when two classifiers are satisfied, say by the same message, the one with the more specific condition (fewer #'s) usually becomes active. As the induction procedures add new candidates to the system (see section 20.5), the "specialists" (fewer #'s) serve as exceptions to the "generalists" (more #'s) under the competition induced by the bidding process. A specialist may in turn serve as a default for a still more specific classifier, whence the developing default hierarchy arises.

The combination of the default hierarchy, so realized, with the clusters of coupled classifiers provides an effect much like Fahlman's virtual copy (1979). Environmental messages cause the activation of a cluster of classifiers that provides the "frame" and specifics wherein the system builds its responses to the situation. The tag on the outgoing message from a cluster can indicate the presence of some complex object, such as an *arch,* while the pass through bits (see section 20.4.2) carry incidental information (color, size, etc.) possibly relevant to further processing. The processing can include expectations (classifiers satisfied by messages from the virtual copy but not yet supported by messages from the environment) and plans (coupled sequences of classifiers wherein only the first element of the sequence is activated by messages from the environment).

The object of the next section is to show how such structures can emerge, in response to experience, under the impetus of competition and learning and induction rules. Some early uses of classifier systems for realistic problems (Wilson, 1982; Goldberg, 1983) show that default hierarchies do emerge and that sequences of coupled classifiers sensitive to stage-setting situations do develop.

20.5 LEARNING AND INDUCTION

The essence of classifier systems is a parallelism and a standardization that permit both a "building block" approach to the processing of information and the use of competition to resolve conflicts. It is the latter property, competition, that makes possible an approach to learning that is both general and powerful.

Two kinds of learning algorithms are required if a classifier system is to adapt to changes in the domains and goals presented to it. The first is an algorithm that reinforces or apportions credit to rules already available to the system. (Samuel's 1959 paper is full of insights concerning this problem.) The second is an algorithm for generating new, plausible rules when the rules available prove inadequate. (Samuel calls this "the parameter problem," and it is the one problem on which he did not really make progress. Recently both Lenat [1983] and Hofstadter [1983] have offered interesting approaches to it.) Here, in order to exploit competition between classifiers, two new kinds of algorithm are introduced. The first, the apportionment-of-credit algorithm, is called a *bucket-brigade algorithm.* The second, the rule generation algorithm, is called a *genetic algorithm.*

20.5.1 Bucket-Brigade Algorithms

The bucket-brigade algorithm is designed to assign credit to each classifier in the system according to its overall usefulness in attaining system goals. To this end, each classifier in the system is assigned a value, called its *strength,* and it is this value that the bucket-brigade algorithm adjusts. The problem is easy enough when a classifier participates directly in goal-achieving action that produces payoff, but it is quite difficult to decide which of the classifiers active early in a sequence sets the stage for later successful actions. (In Samuel's terms, it is easy enough to credit classifiers that combine to produce a triple jump at some point in the game; it is much harder to decide which classifiers active earlier were responsible for changes that made the later jump possible.) By a combination of analysis, and simulation (Wilson, 1982; Goldberg, 1983), we can show that the bucket-brigade algorithm actually accomplishes this task.

The algorithm works, via a modification of the basic execution cycle, by introducing a competition between classifiers. Recall that, during the execution cycle, each classifier scans all the messages on the global message list, producing a new message from each message satisfying its conditions. That procedure is now modified so that satisfied classifiers must compete to get their messages on the message list. Each satisfied classifier makes a *bid* based on its strength, and only the highest bidding classifiers get their messages on the list. The size of the bid depends not only on the classifier's strength but also on its specificity. (Recall that the specificity of a classifier is measured by the number of non-#'s in its condition part.) Specifically, the bid produced by a classifier is proportional to the product of its strength ("past usefulness") and its specificity ("relevance"—the amount of information about the current situation incorporated in its condition part).

Formally, when the condition part of a classifier C is satisfied, it makes a bid

$$\text{Bid}(C,t) = cR(C)\text{Strength}(C,t)$$

where $R(C)$ is the specificity, equal to the number of non-#'s in the condition part of C divided by the length thereof; $S(C,t)$ is the strength of C at time t, and c is a constant considerably less than 1 (e.g., 1/8 or 1/16).

The *winning* (high) bidders place their messages on the message list and have their strength *reduced* by the amount of the bid (they are paying for the privilege of posting a new message):

$$\text{Strength}(C,t + 1) = \text{Strength}(C,t) - B(C,t)$$

for a winning classifier C. The classifiers $\{C'\}$ that sent the messages matched by this winner have their strengths *increased* by the amount of the bid (it is shared among them in the simplest version):

$$\text{Strength}(C',t + 1) = \text{Strength}(C',t) + a\text{Bid}(C,t)$$

where $a = 1/(\text{number of members of } \{C'\})$. (The senders are rewarded for setting up a situation usable by C.)

The bucket-brigade algorithm treats each classifier as a kind of middleman in a complex economy, the strength of a classifier measuring its ability to turn a "profit." As a middleman, the classifier only deals with its suppliers—the classifiers that send messages satisfying its conditions—and its consumers—the classifiers that are in turn satisfied by the messages it sends. Whenever a classifier wins a bidding competition, it initiates a transaction in which it pays out part of its strength to its suppliers and then receives similar payments from its consumers.

The classifier's strength is a kind of capital. If a classifier receives more from its consumers than it paid out, it has made a profit, that is, its strength is increased. This is likely to occur only if the consumer in turn is profitable. This chain leads to the ultimate consumers, the classifiers that attain goals directly and receive payoff directly from the environment. That is, certain actions are immediately rewarded or reinforced by the environment; this payoff for goal attainment is added to the strengths of all classifiers active at that time. The profitability of other classifiers depends upon their being coupled into sequences leading to payoff. Thus, the bucket-brigade assures that early-acting, stage-setting classifiers receive credit if they (on average) make possible later, overtly rewarding acts.

It is worth noting that some of the fixed-point theorems of mathematical economics provide a way of proving the above for environments that have "stable" statistics.

20.5.2 Genetic Algorithms

Once strengths can be assigned to classifiers, a basis exists for generating new classifiers to enter the competition. In broadest terms the genetic algorithm uses high-strength classifiers as progenitors for new classifiers to be tested under the bucket brigade. Because of the parallelism of classifier systems, newly generated classifiers can be inserted into the "population" without the system's repertoire in well-practiced situations being seriously disrupted (see below). It is vital to the understanding of genetic algorithms to know that even the simplest versions act much more subtly than "random search with preservation of the best" (contrary to common misreading of genetics as a process primarily driven by mutation). Genetic algorithms have been studied intensively through analysis (Holland, 1975; Bethke, 1980) and simulation (DeJong, 1980; Smith, 1980; Booker, 1982; and others).

Although genetic algorithms act subtly, the basic execution cycle (the "central loop") is quite simple:

1. Select pairs from the set of classifiers according to strength—the stronger the classifier, the more likely its selection.
2. Apply genetic operators to the pairs, creating "offspring." Chief among the genetic operators is crossover, which simply exchanges a randomly selected segment between the pairs (see figure 20-3).
3. Replace the weakest classifiers with the offspring.

The effect of this procedure is to emphasize various combinations of defining elements—schemata—as building blocks for the construction of new classifiers. The tentative nature of the classifiers constructed in this way is pointed up by step 3 above. They will be displaced if they do not acquire strength under the bucket-brigade algorithm. Note that a newly constructed classifier gains or loses strength (aside from certain "taxations") only when its condition is satisfied and it wins the bidding competition to become active. As will be seen, this has much to do with the overall system's gracefulness relative to the insertion of new rules.

20.5.2.1 Definitions

To begin, let us consider the set C of all strings of length k over an alphabet of n letters. For example, the alphabet could be $\{1,0,\#\}$ so that the strings designate condition parts or message parts for classifiers. In the standard terminology of genetics these strings would be called *genotypes* and the values for individual letters in a string would be called *alleles*. The *set* of strings being tested at a given time (e.g., a classifier system) is called a *population*. In brief, and very roughly, a genetic algorithm can be looked upon as a sampling procedure that draws samples from the set **C**; each sample drawn has a value, the *fitness* of the corresponding genotype. From this viewpoint, the classifier system at time t—call it $B(t)$—is a set of classifiers drawn from **C**, and the fitness of each classifier is its strength. The genetic algorithm uses the fitnesses of the genotypes in $B(t)$ to generate new genotypes for test.

As will soon be seen in detail, the genetic algorithm uses the familiar "reproduction according to fitness" in combination with certain genetic operators (e.g., crossover; see below) to generate the new genotypes (classifiers). This process progressively biases the sampling procedure toward the use of *combinations* of alleles (building blocks) associated with above-average fitness. Surprisingly, in a population of size M, the algorithm effectively exploits some multiple of M^3 combinations in exploring **C**. (How this happens will be seen in a moment.) For populations of more than a few individuals this number, M^3, is vastly greater than the total number of alleles in the population. The corresponding speedup in the rate of searching **C**, a property called *implicit parallelism*, makes possible very high rates of adaptation. Moreover, because a genetic algorithm uses a distributed database (the population) to generate new samples, it is all but immune to some of the difficulties—false peaks, discontinuities, high-dimensionality, and so on—that commonly attend complex problems.

The task now is to give some substance—and intuition—to this outline. An understanding of some of the advantages and limitations of genetic algorithms can be reached via three short steps. First, in order to describe the nonuniform sampling procedure generated by a genetic algorithm, a special class of subsets of **C** is defined. Then, in the second step, an explicit sampling procedure emphasizing the sampling of combinations is used to examine the role of these special subsets in the nonuniform sampling procedure. The final step is to show how the genetic algorithm accomplishes implicitly and rapidly what is an intolerable computational burden for the explicit procedure.

For the first step, the subsets (combinations) of interest, called *schemata*, can be characterized as follows: Much as in the definition of conditions for classifiers (see section 20.4.2), values are first fixed at a selected set of positions in the k-position strings. Note that for classifiers the strings are over the alphabet $\{1,0,\#\}$ rather than the alphabet $\{1,0\}$. By using a (new) "don't care" symbol * for positions not fixed, one can specify schemata quite compactly. Thus *0**#** . . . ** is the set of *all* conditions (or actions) having a 0 at position 2 and a # at position 5. The set of schemata is the set of all collections that can be defined in this way. Note that schemata for classifiers define subsets of the *space of possible conditions* (or actions), in contrast to the conditions themselves, which define subsets of the *space of messages*. Thus a schema constitutes a building block from which one can construct classifiers.

Parenthetically, schemata can also be characterized in a way familiar to mathematicians: If we look upon the k-position strings as vectors in a k-dimensional space (each component having one of n values $0, 1, \ldots, n - 1$), then the schemata are hyperplanes of the k-dimensional space. Schemata name particular subsets of the set **C** of k-position strings. These subsets are of interest because they correspond to particular combinations of letters and because they are easily and compactly defined by strings on an $n + 1$-letter alphabet $\{0, 1, \ldots, n - 1, *\}$.

(For simplicity, $n = 2$, implying binary strings, will be used throughout the rest of this subsection. For theoretical reasons it is usually advantageous to recode strings over large alphabets, $n > 2$, into binary strings. To apply the discussion directly to classifiers, simply increase n to 3, using the particular alphabet $\{1,0,\#\}$.)

Now it is time for the second step. For a better illustration of the way in which schemata can aid a search, an algorithm will be considered that manipulates schemata explicitly. Although this algorithm is an aid to understanding, it is impractical from the computational point of view because of the enormous amounts of time and storage it would require. The genetic algorithm, to be described in the third step accomplishes the same actions concisely and rapidly via an implicit manipulation. The explicit version involves the following steps:

1. Set $t = 0$ and generate, at random, a set $B(t)$ of M strings.
2. Observe the value of $v(C)$, the "fitness," of each string C in $B(t)$.

   (From a more formal point of view, steps 1 and 2 amount to sampling the random variable v, using a sample of size M taken from **C**.)
3. Let $M(\mathbf{s}, t)$ be the number of strings in $B(t)$ belonging to the schema **s** (i.e., the strings are instances of **s**). If $M(\mathbf{s}, t) > 0$ for **s**, calculate the average value $\hat{v}(\mathbf{s}, t)$ of the strings in $B(t)$ belonging to that schema. Calculate, also, the average value $\hat{v}(t)$ of the set of M samples.

   (There will be somewhere between 2^k and $M*2^k$ schemata with one or more instances in $B(t)$. More formally, $\hat{v}(\mathbf{s}, t)$ is the marginal sample average of v over the subset **s**.)
4. Select a new set $B(t + 1)$ of M strings so that the number of instances of each schema s in the new set is equal to

$$M(\mathbf{s}, t + 1) = [\hat{v}(\mathbf{s}, t)/\hat{v}(t)]*M(\mathbf{s}, t)$$

   for as many schemata as possible.

   (Informally, this recursion says that schemata observed to be above average, $\hat{v}(\mathbf{s}, t) > \hat{v}(t)$, receive more samples on the next time-step. Similarly, below-average schemata receive fewer samples. At first sight it may seem impossible to meet this requirement in any meaningful way because there are so many schemata, but see below.)
5. Set t to $t + 1$ and return to step 2.

It is difficult to satisfy the requirement of step 4 because the schemata (hyperplanes) intersect each other over and over again. In fact there are so many intersections that *each* string belongs to 2^k distinct schemata. Thus any sample allocated to one schema is as well a sample of $2^k - 1$ other schemata. However, a little thought and some calculation show that it *is* possible to distribute M new samples so that all schemata *with more than a few elements* receive the requisite number of samples. (Note that this means that schemata with more than a few *'s in their defining strings can be sampled according to the dictates of step 4.) Actually to carry out the distribution explicitly, allocating samples schema by schema so that step 4 is satisfied, would require an enormous amount of computation.

Setting aside the difficulties of implementation, we find that the algorithm uses very plausible inferences in generating "fit" strings. Most importantly, it samples with increasing intensity schemata that contain strings of above-average strength. The net effect of increasing the proportion of samples allocated to above-average schemata is to move the overall average $\hat{v}(t)$ upward. Because the average $\hat{v}(t)$ increases with time, this sampling procedure is a global "force" driving the search into subsets observed to contain valuable strings. Moreover, because the algorithm works from a database of M points distributed over **C,** it is not easily caught on "false peaks" (local optima). (Standard optimization procedures work well only with single-peak functions, relying on a uniform random search for "starting points" when there are multiple peaks.) Overall, this algorithm is much more globally oriented than standard optimization procedures, searching through a great many schemata for regularities and interactions that can be exploited. This point has been established, for the algorithm described next, by extensive experimental comparisons between that algorithm and standard procedures (Bethke, 1980; DeJong, 1980).

Figure 20-2 illustrates the use of schemata to locate the global optimum of a function $v(x)$ on the interval [0,1]. The arguments of the function are represented as binary fractions so that, for example, the argument $x = 1/2$ is represented as $0.100 \ldots 0$. If we look upon the binary representations as strings, then the schema $1** \ldots *$ is the subset of all arguments greater than or equal to 1/2, that is, the interval [1/2,1]. Similarly, the schema $**1* \ldots *$ is a set of intervals (see top half of figure 20-2) corresponding to all the binary fractions that have a 1 in the third place. Other schemata are determined accordingly. Regularities of the function, such as periodicities, trends, and so on, are readily exploited by the biasing of samples toward appropriate schemata. The genetic algorithm automatically takes advantage of such schemata, as will be seen in a moment.

From an intuitive point of view, good schemata (schemata containing strings of above-average fitness) can be thought of as useful building blocks for constructing new strings. For example, if the schemata $1*0** \ldots **$ and $***001** \ldots **$ are both good, then it seems reasonable to investigate strings constructed with these building blocks, namely, strings belonging to the schema $1*0001** \ldots **$. The power of this

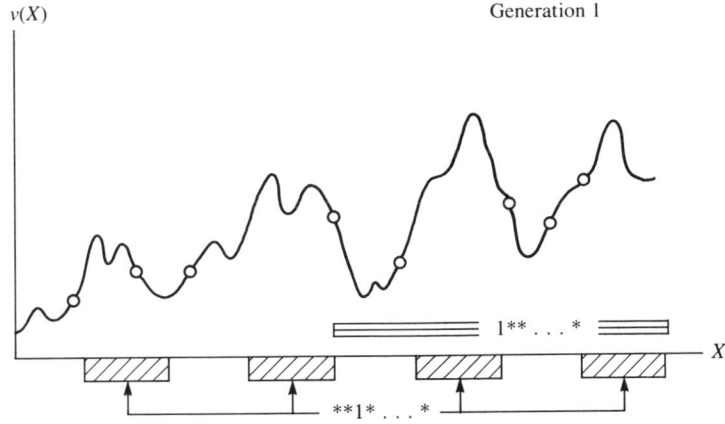

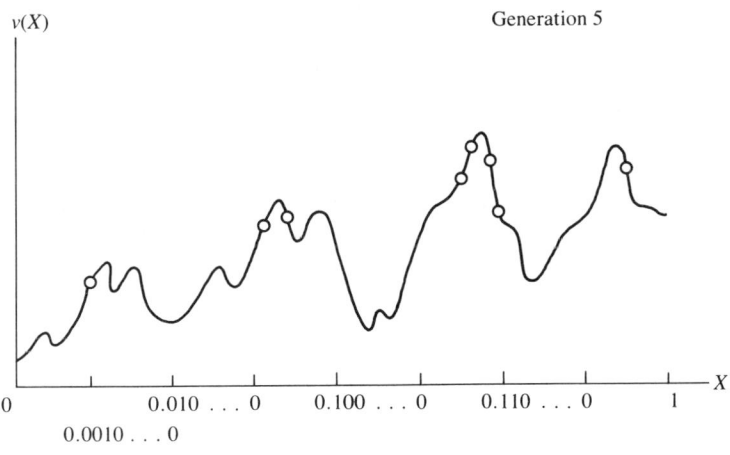

O Trials (individuals)

Figure 20-2: Example of function optimization by genetic algorithm.

kind of algorithm lies in its rapid accumulation of large numbers of better-than-average building blocks—building blocks that exploit regularities and interactions in the sample space **C**. By carefully choosing TM samples over T iterations, the algorithm accumulates information about a large number of potential building blocks, a number somewhere between 2^k and $TM2^k$.

Our objective now is to see how we can obtain the effects of this direct algorithm without paying the tremendous computational costs. This third step of the explanation involves, first, a specification of the genetic algorithm and, second, an explanation of its implicit manipulation of schemata (see figure 20-3).

The specification is as follows:

1. Set $t = 0$ and generate, at random, a set $B(t)$ of M strings.
2. Observe the value $v(C)$ of each string C in $B(t)$.
3. Compute the average strength $\hat{v}$ of the M strings in the database $B(t)$ and assign a normalized value $v(C)/\hat{v}$ to each string C in $B(t)$.
4. Assign each string in $B(t)$ a probability proportional to its normalized value and then select n, $n < < M$, pairs of strings from $B(t)$ using this probability distribution.
5. Apply genetic operators to each pair, forming $2n$ new strings. The most important of the genetic operators is crossover (see figure 20-3): A position along the

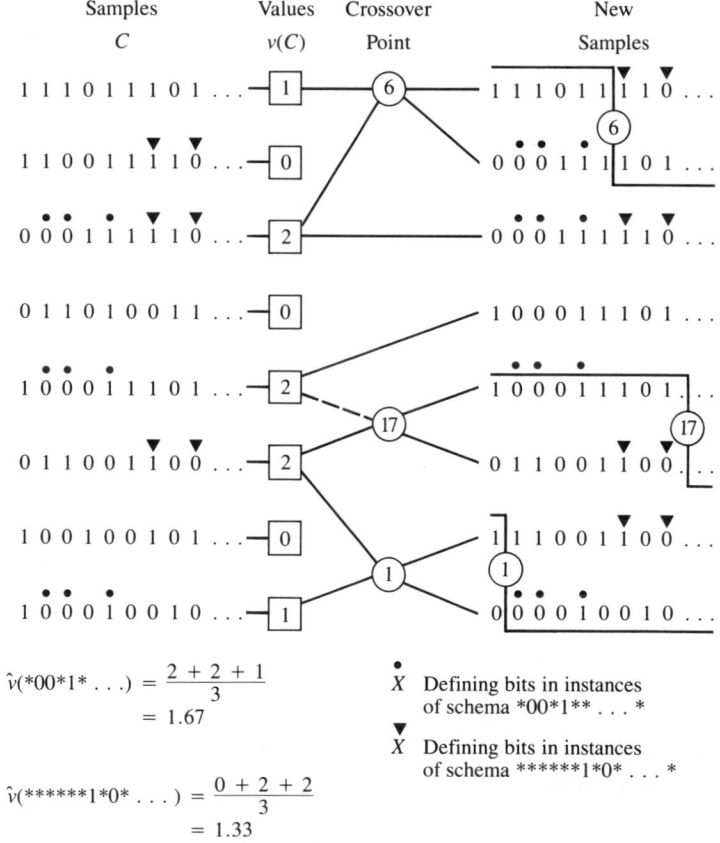

$$\hat{v}(*00*1* \ldots) = \frac{2 + 2 + 1}{3}$$
$$= 1.67$$

$$\hat{v}(******1*0* \ldots) = \frac{0 + 2 + 2}{3}$$
$$= 1.33$$

$\overset{\bullet}{X}$ Defining bits in instances of schema $*00*1** \ldots *$

$\overset{\blacktriangledown}{X}$ Defining bits in instances of schema $******1*0* \ldots *$

Figure 20-3:   Example of the genetic algorithm's effect on schemata.

string is selected at random, and then, in the pair being operated upon, the segments to the left of this position are exchanged. This simple operation has subtle effects when used in combination with the "emphasis" provided by step 3 as will be seen shortly. The other operators, such as *mutation* and *inversion*, have lesser roles in this use of the algorithm, mainly providing "insurance" against overemphasis of a given kind of schema. (See Holland, 1975, chap. 6, secs. 2, 3, and 4, for details.)

6. Select $2n$ strings from $B(t)$ and replace them with the $2n$ new strings resulting from step 4. (There are some technical issues involved in the selection of the strings to be replaced. These issues primarily concern limitations on the portion of the database allocated to strings of a given type. In effect each string belongs to a niche in the database and its spread is to be limited to the size—i.e., carrying capacity—of that niche. See Bethke, 1980, and DeJong, 1980, for details.)

7. Set t to $t + 1$ and return to step 2.

Unlike the earlier direct algorithm, the genetic algorithm never deals directly with schemata—it only manipulates the strings in $B(t)$. If one wishes to explore the action of the algorithm relative to schemata, it is helpful to divide the algorithm's action into two phases: Phase 1 consists of steps 2–4; phase 2 consists of steps 5–6.

Consider first what would happen if phase 1 were iterated without the execution of phase 2 (but with the replacement of strings in $B(t)$). In particular, let phase 1 be iterated $M/2n$ times (assuming for convenience that M is a multiple of $2n$). It is not difficult to show that the expected number of instances of a schema s at the end of this iteration is just $\hat{v}(s)$ times the number of instances at the outset (see Holland, 1975). This is true of *every* schema with instances in B, and this is just what was required of the direct algorithm in step 4.

What, then, is accomplished by phase 2? The problem is that phase 1 introduces no *new* strings into B; it merely introduces additional copies of strings already there. Phase 1 provides emphasis, but no new trials. The genetic operators, applied in phase 2, obviously modify the strings in B. It is a fundamental property of genetic algorithms (Theorem 6.2.3, Holland, 1975) that the emphasis provided by phase 1 is little disturbed by phase 2. That is, after phase 2, schemata with instances in B will largely have the *number* of instances provided by phase 1 *but they will be new instances*.

Thus the genetic algorithm as a whole generates new samples of *schemata* already present, increasing or decreasing the sampling rate according to the multiplier $\hat{v}(s,t)/\hat{v}(t)$, as desired. From the point of view of sampling theory, these new samples increase confidence in the estimates $\hat{v}(s)$ for each above-average schema s in B. Some calculation (Holland, 1975, chap. 4) shows that considerably more than M^3 schemata are so treated every $M/2n$ time-steps. Moreover, samples are generated for schemata not previously tried without this procedure being disrupted. All of this comes about through simple—and fast—manipulations of $2n$ strings per step. This implicit manipulation of a great many schemata via operations on relatively few strings is called *implicit parallelism*.

20.5.2.2 Application to Classifiers

How does all this apply to the generation of new classifiers? As mentioned, the strengths assigned by the bucket-brigade algorithm serve as the fitnesses of the classifiers. Because the parts of the classifier are strings of standard length k over a fixed alphabet $\{1,0,\#\}$, three possible alleles per locus, the procedures of the genetic algorithm are directly applicable. A combination of alleles that occurs in several strong classifiers—for example, a particular tag, or part of a message, or a combination of properties—automatically becomes a building block for the construction of new classifiers. Such combinations amount to schemata that are subject to the theorems concerning implicit parallelism.

If the classifier system is using M classifiers, it can be shown that, as the genetic algorithm generates new classifiers, it is effectively selecting amongst more than M^3 building blocks, each rated on the basis of past experience! The building blocks so manipulated determine important properties, such as classifier coupling and control sequencing (see section 20.4.3 and 20.4.4). Thus the genetic algorithm can encourage variants of useful subroutines, and it can generate hierarchical substructures for testing. In sum, the genetic algorithm offers an inductive procedure that is (1) fast (because of the implicit parallelism), (2) relatively immune to misdirection (because of the distributed database provided by the population), and (3) capable of sophisticated transfer of knowledge from one situation to another (because of the role of schemata).

It is important to note that, in general, the candidate rules generated by the genetic algorithm do *not* displace the parent rules. The parent rules simply supply copies of their parts for use by the genetic operators (such as crossover); they remain in the system in their original form. The offspring rules typically displace rules of low strength, thus eliminating rules that have not proved valuable to the system. As a consequence the parent rules, because of their high strength, will tend to remain in control of situations in which they acquired their strength. New rules typically get their chance in situations where none of the high-strength rules have their conditions satisfied. That is, they tend to fill new niches corresponding to domains in which the system has inadequate sets of rules. (This feature goes hand in hand with Scott's (1983) use of "play" as a means of reducing uncertainty about the environment.)

Ultimately, of course, new rules may outcompete their parents (or other relatives) if they prove superior under the bucket-brigade algorithm. The *explicit* parallelism, under which a variety of rules is active simultaneously, encourages the competition. The result is a system that can explore without disturbing well-established capabilities. In short, the system is graceful rather than brittle.

20.6 TESTS AND PROSPECTS

Several years ago a series of tests of simplified classifier systems (Holland and Reitman, 1978) demonstrated simple transfer of learning from problem to problem and showed that the genetic algorithm yielded learning, in that context, an order of magnitude faster than weight-changing techniques alone. The results were encouraging enough to spark a variety of subsequent tests at several places. Smith (then at the University of Pittsburgh, now at Carnegie-Mellon University) completed a classifier system (1980) that competed against Waterman's poker player (Waterman and Hayes-Roth, 1978)—also a learning program—with overwhelming success. Wilson (then at Polaroid, now at the Rowland Institute) used a classifier system (1982) with a genetic algorithm in a series of experiments involving TV-camera–mechanical-arm coordination, culminating in a successful demonstration of the segregation of the classifiers, under learning, into sets (Wilson calls them *demes*) corresponding to control subroutines. Booker has done an in-depth simulation study (1982) of classifier systems as cognitive models, with particular emphasis on the generation of cognitive maps under experience. More recently, Goldberg (1983) has demonstrated emergence of a default hierarchy in a study of the use of classifiers, under the genetic algorithm, as adaptive controls for gas pipeline transmission. There are several ongoing projects, including one that uses a classifier system to deal with the classification problem in KL-ONE (Forrest, 1982).

The more advanced properties of classifier systems are being tested with the help of a program, CS1, that is both a "compiler," allowing design and simulation of classifier systems on a serial computer, and a "test-bed," providing the means of simulating a wide range of environments for testing the learning algorithms. The current version provides the following facilities:

1. Simulation of a task environment consisting of up to 256 objects, each with up to thirty-two distinct features, emplaced on a 65,000-by-65,000 grid. Any or all of the objects may be mobile.

2. An input interface that consist of an arbitrarily shaped "vision cone" that views a local part of the surface (typically less than 1000 grid points) and uses feature detectors to generate an input message for each object in the vision cone.

3. An emulator for the classifier system that can retain, in random access memory, the description of over 1000 classifiers and a message list of up to thirty-two messages. This part of the system is written in machine language and can execute a basic time-step (all classifiers matched against all messages) in about 0.1 second. The overall system runs in close to real time, making it convenient to run long learning sequences in the simulated environment.

4. An output interface that permits manipulation of objects on the grid, movement over the grid, rotation of a visual cone, and in fact any other effector action conveniently specifiable by a subroutine.

5. Parameterized versions of both the bucket-brigade and genetic algorithms, including provisions for contingent activation of these algorithms (such as activation of the genetic algorithm when no classifier responds to an input message).

Studying full-fledged classifier systems is much like studying an ecology. There are niches, adaptations exploiting them, and shifting hierarchies of interaction—the emergence of parasitic classifiers has even been observed! Questions abound. Most pressing is the question of limitations. What is it that such systems *cannot* learn from experience? The author's observations to date indicate that general-purpose learning algorithms, given the right grist, can produce organizations that are detailed, appropriate, and subtle. This contradicts accepted wisdom in AI; somewhere there is a boundary (or set of them) that marks the limits of what can be accomplished reasonably with so-called weak methods. The author's impression is that the domain of such methods is *much* larger than is usually believed. Within this domain brittleness is no longer a bête noire.

Although most of the studies to date have dealt with systems that start with a tabula rasa—the most difficult test for a general-purpose learning procedure—this would not be the typical use of such systems. Classifier systems are general-purpose systems that can be programmed initially to implement whatever expert knowledge is available to the designers and their consultants. Learning then allows the system to expand, correct errors, and transfer information from one domain to another. In this context the question becomes one of how flexible—and graceful—such a system can be. It is important to provide ways of instructing such systems so that they can generate rules—hypotheses to be held tentatively—on the basis of advice. Little has been done in this direction.

Much more remains to be discovered about conditions that induce a classifier system to construct models of its environment for purposes of planning and look-ahead. It is particularly important to understand how look-ahead and virtual explorations can be incorporated without other activities of the system being disturbed. Ultimately the question is whether such systems can develop symbols (cf. Hofstadter, 1983) and use them, via abstract models, to generate plans and expectations.

ACKNOWLEDGMENT

This research was supported in part by the National Science Foundation under grants IST-8018043, MCS-7826016, and MCS-8305830.

References

Bethke, A. D., "Genetic Algorithms as Function Optimizers," Ph.D. diss., Department of Computer and Communication Sciences, University of Michigan, 1980.

Booker, L., "Intelligent Behavior as an Adaptation to the Task Environment," Ph.D. diss., Department of Computer and Communication Sciences, University of Michigan, 1982.

Davis, R., and King, J., "An Overview of Production Systems," in *Machine Intelligence 8*, E. W. Elcock, and D. Michie (Eds.), American Elsevier, New York, 1977.

DeJong, K. A., "Adaptive System Design—A Genetic Approach," *IEEE Transactions: Systems, Man, and Cybernetics*, Vol. 10, No. 9, 1980.

Duda, R. O., and Shortliffe, E. H., "Expert Systems Research," *Science*, Vol. 220, pp. 261–68, 1983.

Fahlman, S. E., *NETL: A System for Representing and Using Real-World Knowledge*, MIT Press, Cambridge, 1979.

Forrest, S., "A Parallel Algorithm for Classification of KL-ONE Networks," Consul Note No. 15, USC/ Information Sciences Institute, 1982.

Goldberg, D., "Computer Aided Gas Pipeline Operation Using Genetic Algorithms and Rule Learning," Ph.D. diss., Department of Civil Engineering, University of Michigan, 1983.

Hofstadter, D. R., "Artificial Intelligence: Subcognition as Computation," in *The Study of Information*, F. Machlup and U. Mansfield (Eds.), Wiley, New York, 1983.

Holland, J. H., *Adaptation in Natural and Artificial Systems*, University of Michigan Press, Ann Arbor, 1975.

Holland, J. H., and Reitman, J. S., "Cognitive Systems Based on Adaptive Algorithms," in *Pattern-Directed Inference Systems*, D. A. Waterman and F. Hayes-Roth (Eds.), Academic Press, New York, 1978.

Lenat, D. B., "The Role of Heuristics in Learning by Discovery: Three Case Studies," in *Machine Learning: An Artificial Intelligence Approach*, R. S. Michalski, J. G. Carbonell, and T. M. Mitchell (Eds.), Tioga, Palo Alto, Calif., 1983.

McDermott, J., and Forgy, C., "Production System Conflict Resolution Strategies," in *Pattern-Directed Inference Systems*, D. A. Waterman, and F. Hayes-Roth (Eds.), Academic Press, New York, 1978.

Samuel, A. L., "Some Studies in Machine Learning Using the Game of Checkers," *IBM Journal of Research and Development*, Vol. 3, pp. 211–32, 1959.

Scott, P., "Knowledge-Oriented Learning," *Proceedings of the Eighth IJCAI*, Karlsruhe, W. Ger., pp. 432–35, 1983.

Smith, S., "A Learning System Based on Genetic Algorithms," Ph.D. diss., Department of Computer Science, University of Pittsburgh, 1980.

Waterman, D. A., and Hayes-Roth, F. (Eds.), *Pattern-Directed Inference Systems*, Academic Press, New York, 1978.

Wilson, S., "Adaptive 'Cortical' Pattern Recognition," Internal Report, Research Laboratories, Polaroid Corporation, 1982.

Winston, P. H., "Learning Structural Descriptions from Examples," in *The Psychology of Computer Vision*, P. H. Winston (Ed.), McGraw-Hill, New York, 1975.

21

LEARNING FROM POSITIVE-ONLY EXAMPLES:

The Subset Principle and Three Case Studies

Robert C. Berwick
Massachusetts Institute of Technology

Abstract

A key issue for learning theory has been the relative importance of domain-independent learning versus domain-specific learning. How much of learning is attributable to general learning methods like inductive generalization, and how much is attributable to particular techniques and representations that apply only to specific domains? This chapter explores this issue through an analysis of the role of one general principle in the context of several very specific domains. Angluin (1978) established a necessary and sufficient condition for the acquisition of a (recursive) language (in the sense used by Gold, 1967) from positive-only evidence. The effect of this condition is to impose an ordering on possible sequences of guesses about the target language combined with the array of possible data sequences in such a way that the acquisition system always guesses the narrowest possible language compatible with the data given so far. In this chapter, this "Subset Principle" is applied to three areas in which extensive domain-specific knowledge is present. First, concept acquisition in children, as studied by Keil (1979), is considered, followed by an examination of the area of natural language, where syntactic constructions and phonological distinctive feature systems are explored. Constraints on these systems are shown to follow the Subset Principle, providing some evidence that natural learning systems are designed to be easily learnable.

21.1 INTRODUCTION

What are the scope and power of "general" learning principles? General methods like inductive generalization or analogy have figured prominently in any discussion of learning. Those who have embraced such general principles range across the scientific spectrum, from Skinner and Piaget to Newell and Simon. More recently, however, the very existence of general learning principles has been questioned:

> What I intend to signify in referring to the doctrine of uniformity of mind is . . . that there are general principles of learning that underlie all of these systems, accounting for their development: "multipurpose learning strategies," as they are called, that apply "across the board." In contrast, it might be proposed that various "mental organs" develop in specific ways . . . and that multipurpose learning strategies are no more likely to exist than general principles of "growth of organs" that account for the shape, structure, and function of the kidney, the liver, the heart, the visual system, and so forth. (Chomsky, 1980, 245)

Chomsky claims that there are no general principles of human learning. Each domain, be it language, motor control, vision, or mathematics, has its own particular constraints. Even if this were true, however, there would still be room for a domain-independent learning theory; it would consist of general principles supplementing the particular constraints of each domain.

As a simple example, consider Winston's classic program that learned the descriptions of scenes made from toy blocks, such as *arch* or *house* (Winston, 1975). Here the domain-dependent constraints include those of the *representation language* primitives, that is, the basic vocabulary used to describe blocks world scenes, such as the predicates *touch* or *is-a-brick,* and the way that these basic predicates can be pasted together. The presumably domain-independent principles of the blocks world include generalization heuristics such as "require link," a descriptor-modification introduced when a negative example shown by a teacher establishes that a particular feature of a block model *must* be present. For instance, if Winston's program was shown a nonarch with its top (or lintel) lying on the ground, it could apply the require link heuristic to the descriptor that the two arch columns *must* support the lintel. The require link heuristic is part of general learning theory.

The question still remains of the relative contribution of general learning theory to the explanation of human learning; that is, can it help us account for observed patterns of human cognitive development? The answer is often assumed to be yes, but matters are far from clear. The aim of this chapter is to show that there is a viable general learning theory that helps explain why human learning proceeds the way it does. It will be shown that there is a powerful constraint on the order in which a learner should consider hypotheses, called here the *Subset Principle.* Armed with this principle, the author then shows how to explain some observed patterns in human learning in the domains of language and concept acquisition.

To see just why the explanatory power of general learning theory can be questioned at all, let us consider the example of language. Modern linguists generally make the idealization that language acquisition is "instantaneous"—that is, they imagine that the language learner is presented with all the "input data" (sentences of their language to learn) at once. This is clearly false. Children hear sentences strung out over time. Linguists know that this idealization is false, just as physicists know that there are no frictionless planes. Yet the idealization has proved remarkably successful: so far, no generalizations about the properties of natural languages have been lost because of the idealization of instantaneous acquisition. At least the linguists would claim that this is true. In fact, it is widely assumed that there is no theory of language learning at all. John Marshall has put things this way:

> There is, however, a very general problem with practically all studies of language development, whether investigated from the standpoint of rule acquisition, strategy change, or elaboration of mechanism. The problem arises both for accounts that postulate "stages" of development (i.e., a finite number of qualitatively distinct levels of organization through which the organism passes en route from molecule to maturity) and for accounts that view development as a continuous function of simple accumulation. The difficulty is this: No one has seriously attempted to specify a mechanism that "drives" language acquisition through its "stages" or along its continuous function. Or more succinctly: there is no known learning theory for language. (Marshall, 1979, 443)

This chapter provides just such a theory. The Subset Principle heuristic "drives" language acquisition through its stages. It is not a constraint particular to language, just as the require link heuristic is not particular to the domain of toy blocks. What is the Subset Principle? Intuitively, it is a strategy of "timid acquisition": If possible guesses can be arranged in a subset relationship, then the learner should make the smallest possible guess about what it should learn consistent with the evidence it has seen so far. This is an exceedingly simple idea, yet it is quite powerful. As it happens, this constraint is necessary and sufficient for successful acquisition given only positive training examples, where successful acquisition is defined as convergence to the correct target description or language after some finite number of training examples. (Recall that a positive training example is an example of the concept to be learned. In the Winston toy blocks world, if one is learning about arches, then a positive example is an example of an arch. A negative example is an example of a nonarch.)

This chapter will focus on two natural learning systems, language and concept development. The Subset Principle can account for a wide variety of constraints in these systems. In the case of concept development, the way that children learn about what kinds of things there are in the world will be examined. The analysis is based on work by Keil (1979). It will be seen that the Subset Principle actually explains the developmental stages that children go through as they learn. Language will be considered next, and two subareas will be examined. The first is phonology, that part of linguistics that studies the inventory of sounds in a language. Linguists know that the possible sounds in a given natural language are actually quite limited—out of fifty or so possible sounds, there will be at most a handful of vowels (like *a* or *u*) and a few dozen consonants (like *p, t,* or *k*). Many languages have far fewer consonants. The vast majority of possible combinations of consonants and vowels is never found. For example, no natural language lacks so-called voiceless consonants (consonants pronounced without the vocal cords vibrating, as in a hissed *s*). Why is this so? The Subset Principle explains why: the gaps are an artifact of timid acquisition. The second subarea of language examined here is syntax. Here too the Subset Principle accounts for a wide variety of otherwise inexplicable constraints.

Finally, the Subset Principle has had two "practical" applications. First, it has been used in a computer model for language acquisition (Berwick, 1980, 1982). This model has successfully acquired a large complement of rules for analyzing English sentences and is now being extended to Chinese and German. Second, recent psycholinguistic evidence has probed for evidence of the Subset Principle in young children's acquisition of syntax; preliminary results confirm the principle.

Before applications of the Subset Principle in specific learning situations are considered, the principle will be described in the abstract.

21.2 THE SUBSET PRINCIPLE

The Subset Principle is actually quite simple. The intuition behind it will be presented first. Let us use the Winston blocks world setting as an example of a typical learning situation. We assume that the learner has at its disposal a fixed representation language with which to describe observed scenes of blocks. The learner is presented with examples and nonexamples of some target concept to learn, such as *arch*. In the case of language, the target concept is the rule system of the language itself, such as English or German. Acquisition proceeds via the presentation of a sequence of positive and negative examples. After each example the learner may make some response and change its current model of the target concept or language. A change is prompted by some difference between the current model and an example. If after some finite sequence of presentations the learner does not change its model and has settled on the correct target model or language, we say that acquisition has succeeded.

Consider how this works in the toy blocks world. If the system's current model of an arch includes two columns supporting a wedge, and if it now receives as an example of an arch a set of blocks with two columns supporting a rectangular brick, then the difference prompts a generalization. Perhaps the top of the arch can be any prismatic solid. Positive examples (examples of arches) induce generalizations. They rule out descriptions that are too specific. On the other side, negative examples rule out certain overgeneralizations. If we present as an example of a nonarch two blocks that touch each other (so that there is no hole between them) plus a wedge on top, then the discrepancy between this and the current model forces the learner to add a *must-*

not-touch or *must have a hole between* descriptor to the properties of the two supporting columns. In Mitchell's version space framework (1978), positive examples force the boundary of the "specific descriptions" frontier toward more general descriptions, and negative examples force the boundary of the "maximally general descriptions" toward more specific descriptions.

An important variant of this learning situation restricts the learner to positive examples. This is a crucial assumption for models of language acquisition, where the existence of negative evidence is problematic. Children do not seem to learn their native language through explicit, Berlitz-like training sequences (see Brown and Hanlon, 1970; Wexler and Culicover, 1980). No one tells them that "sentence X is *not* a sentence in English," corresponding to the "this is *not* an arch" examples in the toy blocks world.

Unfortunately, a restriction to positive evidence makes learning harder. The danger is overgeneralization. Suppose a learning program gets only positive examples of a concept or a language. If the program's model of the concept becomes too general, no further positive evidence can dislodge it from its incorrect perch. This is simply because there can be no inconsistency between a too-general model and a positive example. We have no negative examples that tell us that we have gone beyond the correct target description. Remember, it is the negative examples in Mitchell's framework that tell us when we have overgeneralized. In the arch example, if we are limited to examples of arches, and if after seeing two columns supporting a brick we generalize to say that the columns may or may not touch, then no further examples where the columns do not touch will disagree with our description.

A solution is to avoid ever hypothesizing an overly general description. We should *order* our hypotheses in such a way that at each step we are guaranteed never to have formed too general a description. This way, if our description is incorrect, say, too specific, then a later positive example will correct it. If we say that arches can have only wedges on top, then an arch example with a brick on top tells us that we are wrong. If our description is just right and arches always have wedges on top, then we simply never change our original hypothesis. In a word, we want our hypotheses to be maximally *disconfirmable*. In the arch example, again, we see that the right choice to make after seeing an arch where the two columns do not touch each other is to use the descriptor *must-not-touch* to begin with. This description is refutable by a positive example if we are wrong: if someone shows us an arch with the two supporting columns touching, then we change to *may-or-may-not-touch*. In this case, of course, our original description is correct. Note how a description of *may-or-may-not-touch*" is wrong to begin with, since it cannot be disconfirmed by positive examples if the correct target descriptions is *may not touch*.

Consider what it means to have a hypothesis that can be disconfirmed by positive examples. Call M_{hypo} the hypothesized model (like the arch description). Let $\mathbf{M}_{hypo}$ be the set of arches describable by M_{hypo}. Similarly, let M_{true} and $\mathbf{M}_{true}$ be the true description and set of arches so describable, respectively. If M_{hypo} is wrong, then for it to be disconfirmable by positive examples, some example in $\mathbf{M}_{\text{true}}$ should show this; that is, there should be some finite set of examples that is not covered by $\mathbf{M}_{\text{hypo}}$. This is just like the brick-topped arch example that tells us that our description of arches as all wedge-topped is wrong. Mathematically, then, we can disconfirm our hypothesis if $\mathbf{M}_{\text{true}}$ is *not* a proper subset of $\mathbf{M}_{\text{hypo}}$. Disconfirmation fails only if any example covered by $\mathbf{M}_{\text{true}}$ is also covered by $\mathbf{M}_{\text{hypo}}$. But this is just to say that disconfirmation fails if $\mathbf{M}_{\text{true}}$ *is* a subset of $\mathbf{M}_{\text{hypo}}$. In this case, $\mathbf{M}_{\text{hypo}}$ is too general, unless it happens to be exactly correct.

Of course, in any actual learning situation we do not know what the true description is. However, we can still arrange for a sequence of hypotheses to meet the condition of disconfirmability. Consider any two hypotheses h_i and h_{i+1}, where the subscripts mean that the hypothesis $i + 1$ is put forth after hypothesis i. Once again, hypothesis $i + 1$ should *not* be a proper subset of hypothesis i. If we guess first that column supports for an arch *may-or-may-not-touch* then we cannot disconfirm this, since the hypothesis *may-touch* is a proper subset of this first guess. Reversing the logic, what we should do is order our guesses so that each pair $(i, i + 1)$ is disconfirmable. We say that this arrangement of hypotheses satisfies the Subset Principle.

It is not hard to see why the Subset Principle is dubbed "timid acquisition." If a learning system follows the principle, then it most often makes the smallest generalization possible at any given step. (It need not be so timid if it can be certain of receiving disconfirming evidence at some later point. For example, suppose the learner had to choose between two languages, $L_1 = \{a^i, i \text{ is odd}\} + \{a, a^2, \ldots, a^{10}\}$ and $L_2 = \{a^i, i \text{ is even}\} + \{a, a^2, \ldots, a^{10}\}$. Then just a single positive example, say, a^3, can spark an inductive leap to the guess of L_1, even though this may be wrong. For if the learner is wrong, it will eventually get an example such as a^{12} that will prove this to be so. On the other hand, a timid generalizer would not be able to make such a leap.)

It is also not hard to see that the Subset Principle is sufficient to guarantee successful acquisition after some finite number of positive examples. (We might not know how many examples this would take, however.) This is because any step at all is a step in the right direction, as stimulated by a positive example. After some finite number of steps, the system must guess the correct target language or description.

More strikingly, Angluin (1978) has shown that this principle is actually necessary for acquisition given positive-only evidence. Angluin proves this result using the techniques of recursive function theory. In her framework, the "hypotheses" are a family of languages, $\mathcal{L} = \{L_1, L_2, \ldots, L_j, \ldots, L_i, \ldots L_n\}$. The "examples" are finite collections of positive examples, perhaps singleton sets or perhaps not, defined as T_i, where T_i is a positive set of examples for hypothesis L_i. Finally, Angluin uses the term *identifiable* to mean that after some finite number of positive example presentations, the learning procedure (1) guesses the right target language and (2) never changes its guess after this. This is Gold's (1967) traditional definition of identifiability in the limit. The theorem proved is the following:

Theorem 1: Given a family of languages $\mathscr{L}$, $\mathscr{L}$ is identifiable from positive-only evidence if and only if for each target language L_i in $\mathscr{L}$ there exists a computable procedure that enumerates finite sets T_1, $T_2, \ldots$, such that

    (1) $T_i \subseteq L_i \subseteq \mathscr{L}$ and

    (2) For all $j > i$, if $T_i \subseteq L_j$, then L_j is not a proper subset of L_i.

The Subset Principle is a very general and abstract restriction on acquisition using positive examples. Suppose that hypotheses may be nested, so that each one completely covers the next. This is usually the case in natural languages, when one has a rich theoretical vocabulary and is trying to find a correct description of some target grammar. In this situation, Angluin's result says that one must find the smallest generalization covering the samples seen so far or otherwise one risks overgeneralizing. This kind of problem is also discussed in a more general context by Diettrich and Michalski (1983).

However, there is another way for hypothesis $i + 1$ not to be a proper subset of hypothesis i and so meet the Subset Principle. Hypotheses could partially overlap; in this case, that would mean that there is some example not covered by one guess that is in the second. Then the learner need not subscribe to minimal generalization, as discussed earlier. Angluin's theorem covers both sorts of cases.

Since the subset arrangement is the focus in the next two sections, it will be described in more detail. Suppose that all the possible target concepts or languages can be arranged in a nested order, like concentric circles. Then to meet the Subset Principle the acquisition procedure must order its hypotheses so that it always guesses the narrowest possible hypothesis or language at each step. This is because if all hypotheses are so nested then the only way for the hypothesis guessed at step $i + 1$ *not* to be a proper subset of that guessed at step i is for it to contain hypothesis i. The right sequence of guesses will be monotonically increasing—each description will cover the one before it in the sequence. This is what is meant by "timid acquisition"; at each step the system will take the smallest possible step consistent with evidence seen in order to avoid the possibility of guessing too large a language. It corresponds to an incremental search through the space of hypotheses, starting from the most specific first. The power of this principle suggests that we look for evidence that it is applied in natural learning settings. In the next two sections we shall see if we can find such evidence. As far as can be determined, the Subset Principle exhausts what can be said about ordering constraints in language acquisition and perhaps in other domains as well.

21.3 CONCEPT DEVELOPMENT AND THE SUBSET PRINCIPLE

The first example presented here is drawn from research on conceptual development initiated by Sommers (1971) and pursued by Keil (1979). It will be seen that children's developing knowledge about the world obeys the Subset Principle. But first let us summarize Keil's research. Keil claims that if one arranges a person's judgments of whether a set of "predications" of terms "makes sense" or not, then one obtains a characteristically hierarchical tree. By *predication* here Keil means such things as *is loved, is an hour long, can be thought about, is green,* and so forth. Thus, an apple can be green but not an hour long; a recess can be an hour long but not green; and both can be thought about. This is really just a way of describing how people categorize things. For instance, a recess and an apple are different things, because apples can be green but recesses cannot be. As Keil suggests, following Sommers, these facts can be represented by predicates placed at the nodes of a graph in such a way that interior nodes of the graph denote predicates and leaf nodes of the graph (those nodes not dominating any other nodes) denote things in the world like recesses and apples. A leaf is dominated by the predicate nodes that it makes sense to apply to that leaf. For example, since *recess* can be an hour long or can be thought about but cannot be green, it is placed below the first two nodes but not the last. But since an *apple* can be green or thought about but not an hour long, *apple* is placed below the nodes *can be thought about* and *is green.* Finally, predicates (the interior nodes of the graph) are placed according to the leaves they span. A node is dominated by another node if the leaves the first node dominates are a proper subset of the leaves the second node dominates. Applying this to the example produces the graph shown in figure 21-1. Objects in the world (tree leaves) are shown in italics.

Note that the predicate *is thought about* will typically be at the root of such a graph. More interestingly, the graph is almost always a tree. The key point is that one rarely finds a natural conceptual structure where the resulting graph forms M- or W-shaped patterns—that is, a case where a single term is subsumed by predicates from two separate hierarchical trees. This is because such a structure leads to indeterminate things in the world, as Keil notes. This is dubbed the *M-constraint.*

For example, suppose that a *zorch* was a word denoting either a blue pyramid or a red cube. Further suppose that *pyramids* could be blue or thought about and that *cubes* could be red or colored or thought about. The predication tree would then look like the one shown in figure 21-2.

According to the M-constraint, *zorch* could not stand for a natural concept, at least not in the vocabulary of blocks used earlier. This is because *zorch* would fall

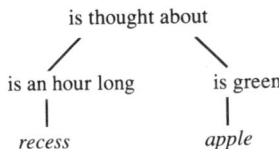

Figure 21-1:   A simple predication tree.

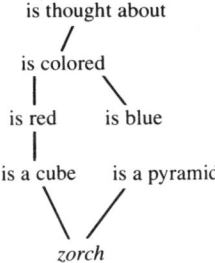

Figure 21-2:   An unnatural concept results in an M-constraint violation.

under two separate hierarchy trees, violating the M-constraint; note the distinctive partial W-shaped arrangement of the links of the graph at the bottom.

Keil developed a method to describe the trees of developing children. Basically, he asked children whether recesses could be green, or if they could be an hour long, and so forth. He found that predication trees "grow" by the refinement of existing tree links without the destruction of existing domination relationships. No radical surgery occurs in which a pattern of domination links is completely destroyed. To see what this means, consider figures 21-3 and 21-4, which show a

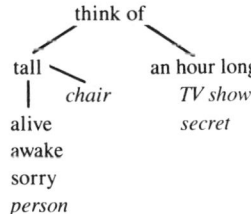

Figure 21-3:   Sample predication tree at age five–six. (This is a single individual's tree.)

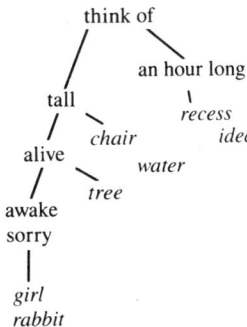

Figure 21-4:   Foliated predication tree at age seven–eight.

sample of evidence that Keil obtained of children's predication trees at ages five to six and then at ages seven to eight.

At the earliest ages studied (five–six years), some children's predictability trees looked like the one in figure 21-3.

The trees of second graders were foliated versions of initial trees of this kind; that is, the new predication trees developed without existing domination links being destroyed; new links were simply inserted between existing predicates. Figure 21-5 illustrates this. Note how the class {alive, awake, sorry} is split into two. This is not a necessary condition for the development of predication trees; for example, trees could develop by a general rearrangement of predicate links. It could have been that children first consider *an hour long* to fall between *tall* and *alive,* only to move it from this position to the position shown in figure 21-4. But this evidently does not happen.

What Keil did not explain was *why* predication trees develop by branching. The Subset Principle can tell us why. Basically, this kind of branching corresponds to a "timid" refinement strategy, in the sense that there are no other refinements that could be interposed between the new tree and the old one. In other words, the children construct minimal extensions of their ways of categorizing objects in the world. Presumably the extensions are minimal in order to avoid overgeneralization. For example, a first-grade child could take the tree in figure 21-4 and make an "inductive leap" to a tree of the kind shown in figure 21-5 that splits apart *alive, awake,* and *sorry* all in one step.

If the child made this leap in one step, it might go astray: the correct tree could be one where *sorry* and *awake* were collapsed together. Note how this tree can be interposed between the current tree and the overly general guess. To avoid this possibility, children stick their ontological necks out as little as possible—at least, that is what is suggested by this evidence. Incremental refinement is not necessary, but apparently it is observed. The Subset Principle dictates what the next possible set of predication trees looks like: it should be some minimal refinement of existing trees.

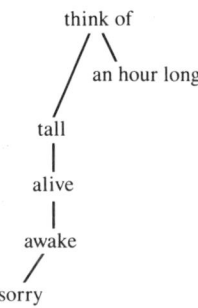

Figure 21-5:   A predication tree that is possibly too general.

21.4 LEARNING SOUND SYSTEMS AND THE SUBSET PRINCIPLE

Let us now turn to the question of how the sound systems of language are acquired. Once again, some relevant background material and terminology will be presented first, and it will then be shown that the Subset Principle can actually help explain why only certain sound systems exist in the world's languages. This is an example of how a *general* learning principle may be used to account for a domain-specific constraint, in this case a constraint on what is a possible human language.

According to the distinctive feature theory of sound systems originally developed by Prague school structuralists such as Jakobson and pursued by Chomsky and Halle in *The Sound Pattern of English* (1968), all natural sounds such as *a* or *p* can be described via a small number of binary-valued distinctive features. By and large these features have an articulatory or an acoustic grounding, with names suggestive of how the tongue and lips are placed as they are pronounced, such as *high, back, anterior,* and the like. *Back* refers to a vowel sound produced in the back of the mouth; *anterior,* in the front of the mouth; *high,* with the tongue raised high. There are about twenty-four features in all. Given binary values for distinctive features ($+$ or $-$), there are 2^{24} possible single language sounds or *segments* (about sixteen million) and even more possible subsets of these segments, what are called *segmental systems.* However, most of these segmental systems are not attested in human languages. Why is this?

In part, the reason for this is that distinctive features are not determined independently of one another. Rather, certain distinctive features can be fixed *only after* certain other features are set. For instance, according to the theory of Kean (1974), the distinctive feature *consonantal* must be set before the feature *back* or *continuant.* (*Consonantal* is simply a binary feature that is $+$ if a sound is consonant and $-$ if the sound is not a consonant. *Continuant* is a sound produced like a continuous tone.)

Kean developed this theory as a way to explain some of the observed restrictions on possible sound systems and possible phonological rule systems. But there is another way to interpret such a theory, and that is as a developmental program for how a sound system is acquired. By construing the theory in this new way, one can in fact exhibit an acquisition system in which large numbers of developmental pathways are eliminated because of the *order* in which a small number of parameters are set. Kean's theory of markedness for phonological sounds (or segments) will be outlined here to show how this approach works in detail. Kean states the basic aim of her theory as follows:

> It is assumed here that there is a relatively small set of distinctive features with binary specifications in terms of which all the members of every segmental system can be characterized at every stage of phonological representation. The postulation of such a set of features makes a substantive claim as to the class of possible elements in phonological systems.
>
> Of the set of possible segments characterized by the distinctive features, it is evident that some are present in nearly every language, with others only occasionally occurring. For example, the segments *t* and *a* are nearly ubiquitous in segmental systems; they are

found at all stages of phonological representation in an overwhelming majority of languages, but the segments *kp* and *u* only occasionally enjoy a place in segmental systems. The simple postulation of a set of features cannot account for such facts. (1974, 6)

To explain the relative frequency or rarity of certain sounds, Kean posits "a hierarchy of features which is derivable from the intrinsic ordering . . . of markedness conventions" (1974, 81). For example, vowels are usually − anterior, consonants are + anterior. It is therefore highly unusual, or *marked,* for a vowel to have the feature + *anterior.* But vowels also have the feature − *consonantal* and consonants the feature + *consonantal.* Therefore, the feature *anterior* is correlated with that of *consonantal;* in the usual or unmarked case the following rule applies:

unmarked anterior → + anterior (if we already have determined the feature + *consonantal* for the segment)

unmarked anterior → − anterior (if we already have determined − *consonantal*)

From the complement of this rule, we obtain the convention for determining what the value of *anterior* should be if it is marked:

marked anterior → − anterior (if we already have determined + *consonantal*)

unmarked anterior → + anterior (if we have determined − *consonantal*)

Determining whether a sound segment is marked for anterior or not logically demands that the feature *consonantal* be determined first. If the sound is − consonantal, then the sound will usually be − anterior (the unmarked case); if + consonantal, the sound will usually be + anterior. Pursuing this approach, Kean goes on to show that whether the feature *back* is unmarked (expected) or marked (unexpected) depends on the value of the distinctive feature *anterior.* One obtains the following hierarchy of distinctive features: *consonantal, anterior, back.* If this analysis is applied to all twenty-four distinctive features that Kean considers, one arrives at the dependency diagram shown in figure 21-6. This gives a complete picture of the *order* in which features must be set for the feature values for any sound segment like *p* or *t* to be determined.

Here is what the other feature names mean: *sonorant* is, literally, a sonorous sound; *low* is a sound produced with the tongue low; *labial,* with the lips; *lateral,* with the tongue at the side of the lips and mouth; *coronal,* midway up; *flap* and *trill,* by vibrating the tongue; *delayed release,* by blocking air and then exploding it outwards. The other feature names are mostly self-explanatory.

Each distinctive feature in the network depends on those features immediately *above* it to determine whether it is marked or not. For example, to determine whether the feature *continuant* is marked or unmarked we must know the values of the features *coronal* and *nasal;* to know whether *continuant* is marked or not, we must know the values of the features *coronal* and all features above *coronal, nasal,* and *sonorant.*

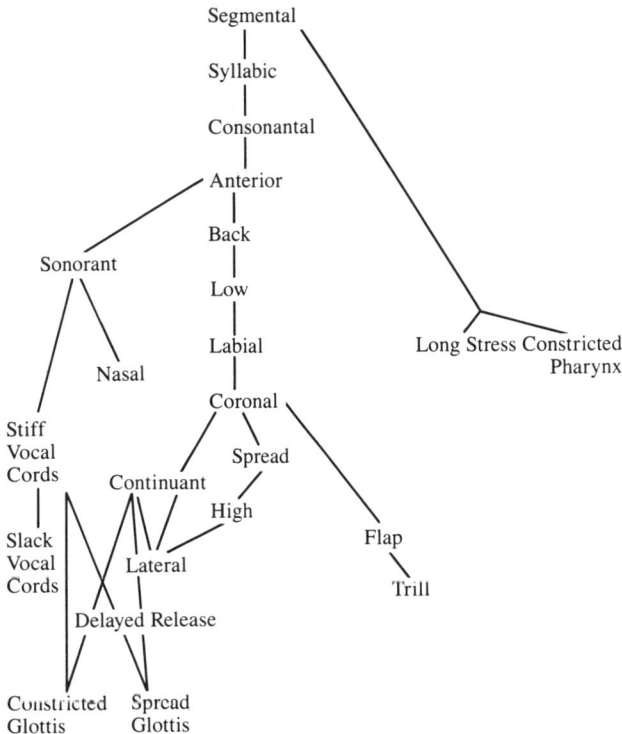

Figure 21-6: Hierarchy diagram for distinctive features.

Although Kean did not choose to do so, we may interpret this hierarchical structure as the specification of an acquisition procedure for learning a sound system. The key point is that this procedure follows the Subset Principle, and this explains the appearance of the dependency diagram. We now describe how this works.

According to distinctive feature theory, sounds can be distinguished only if they have different values for at least one of the twenty-four distinctive features. For example, the sounds *a* and *i* are distinguishable given a sound system that sets all distinctive features for the two sounds to the same value save for the feature *back*. The sound *a* is unmarked for back, but *i* is marked for back (i.e., is expected). As another example, the sound *ae* is also marked for back (− *back*) but is distinguishable from *i* because it is additionally marked + *low*.

We see then that a sound must be explicitly marked in order for it to be distinguished from the default set of plus and minus values. Otherwise, all sound would be unmarked for all distinctive features, and hence all would possess the same array of distinctive feature values. In other words, if the array of distinctive feature marks is regarded as partitioning the universe of possible sounds into equivalence classes, then if no sounds were marked there would be just one class of sounds, the totally unmarked one.

This remark is not quite accurate, however, since Kean also assumes a basic syllabic/nonsyllabic distinction in addition to purely distinctive feature contrasts. As a result, there is always an initial division of all possible sounds into two classes, consonants and vowels, according to the following rules:

unmarked consonantal → + consonantal (if segment is already − syllabic)

marked consonantal → − consonantal (if segment is already + syllabic)

Given the initial partition defined by the feature *syllabic,* we can thus distinguish two classes of sounds, even if no other distinctive features are used for marking sounds:

$\{i, e, ae, u, o, oe, i, e, a\, u, o\}$ (+ syllabic)

$\{p, t, t^y, \ldots\}$ (− syllabic)

At this stage then, there are in effect just two sounds, "consonants" and "vowels," as defined by local sound context. To generate new classes, we must mark additional distinctive feature values. The key idea here is that there is a definite order in which new features are used to form new sound classes. New classes may be formed by splitting established classes, with the split based on the order given by the distinctive feature hierarchy. Suppose we start with a division into just two classes of sounds, consonants and vowels. The next partition is based on the next *unused* (previously unmarked) feature in the hierarchy. This is a natural assumption. We cannot get a new class of sounds unless we explicitly mark a distinctive feature contrary to its expected value—otherwise, we would simply obtain the default feature settings for all later features in the feature hierarchy. So we must mark at least one new distinctive feature. Further, since features lower down in the hierarchy depend on the values of features above them, the natural place to look for the next distinctive feature to mark or not is the next feature below *consonantal* in the hierarchy, i.e., either the feature *anterior* or the feature *sonorant.* We cannot skip either of these features to try to mark, say, the feature *labial,* because the value of *labial* depends upon whether *low* and *labial* were marked or not, and these features have not yet been evaluated. So let us say that, in general, a new partition must be formed by marking exactly one of the distinctive features immediately below the last feature that was marked.

How is a split triggered? This choice must be "data driven" since different sound systems will have different sounds (from the adult point of view) that are marked for a particular distinctive feature. For example, as Kean observes, in Hawaiian only the sound *n* is marked for *sonorant,* but in Wichita, it is *r* that is so marked (1974, 57). A split must therefore be triggered by a detectable difference between at least one of the members of an existing sound class and the rest of the members of that class. Presumably, this difference could be detected on a variety of grounds, articulatory or acoustic. The new sound might just *sound* different. Nothing more will be said here about just how this might occur. What one can say, however, is just *where* the next distinction will be made. The Subset Principle states that the next available unused distinctive feature in the Kean hierarchy must be used as the point of refinement. Otherwise the learner could guess too large a language and go astray.

As an example, consider again the class of vowels $\{i, e, ae, eu, \ldots\}$. According to the feature hierarchy diagram, the next split of this class must be described by the value of the next feature below *consonantal*, namely, *anterior*. As it turns out, the feature combination $[- \ consonantal + anterior]$ is physically impossible (the mouth and tongue cannot produce both features simultaneously) so that in fact the feature *anterior* cannot be freely varied given that the value of the feature *consonantal* is minus. So the candidate distinctive features that may be used to split the class $\{i, e, a, \ldots\}$ become the features just below *anterior*, namely, *back* or *sonorant*. The combination $[- \ consonantal, - \ sonorant]$ is also impossible, however, so that a potential split must be pursued by considering *back*. Features such as *strident* or *continuant* would not be used as this point.

Suppose then that the feature *back* is selected for marking, forming the basis for a new partition of sounds. By marking *back* we obtain the following potential classes: *marked back* $\{i. \ e, ae, u, \ldots\}$ and *unmarked back* $\{a,$ etc.$\}$. Kean's marking convention *unmarked back* $\rightarrow + back$ given $- anterior$ establishes that *marked back* must be $- back$ in this case, and *unmarked back,* $+ back$. In effect, two kinds of "vowels" have been established, corresponding to two possible pathways through the hierarchy diagram.

The important feature of the partitioning process is that splitting occurs at the leading edge of the directed hierarchy graph by successive refinement of exiting classes of sounds. This is a powerful constraint on possible natural sound systems. Suppose that this constraint did not exist. Then it would be possible to have a sound system in which the feature *sonorant* was not used—not set as either marked or unmarked—but the feature *labial* was used. There would be a "gap" in the feature hierarchy skipping over the use of a feature. No such system exists among the world's languages.

Because extension of classes occurs solely via the refinement of existing partitions, the set of sound classes at step i will be a refinement of all of those before it in the developmental sequence. This is simply the same constraint we saw with the predication trees, now repeated in a quite different domain. In particular, this restriction means that just *one* distinctive feature will be set as either marked or unmarked at any single acquisition step. Again, this is not a necessary constraint, since it is not clear why one could not develop a new class by marking two or more features in one step.

The effect of this constraint is to guarantee incremental acquisition. At any step i in the development of a sound system, the classes of sounds will be at most one mark (m) different. For instance, this constraint excludes the array of marks described in figure 21-7, where m stands for a marked feature and u for an unmarked feature.

	X1	**X2**	**X3**	**X4**
Consonantal	*m*	*u*	*u*	*u*
Anterior	*m*	*u*	*u*	*u*
Back	*m*	*u*	*u*	*u*
Low	*u*	*m*	*u*	*u*
Labial	*u*	*u*	*m*	*u*
Sonorant	*u*	*u*	*m*	*u*

Figure 21-7:   An impossible configuration of *u* and *m* marks.

From one point of view the one-mark constraint is a puzzling one. It is not at all obvious why sound systems should be designed so that the alteration of a single distinctive feature could convert an *a* into an *i*. This would seem to be an unwise design choice from the standpoint of error detection or error correction; as is well known, in order to be able to correct errors of k bits, then sounds would have to be separated by a ball of radius $2k + 1$ (since one must guarantee that changes of up to k bits in any two sounds still leave one able to determine the original sound).

Importantly, natural sound systems do seem to obey the one-mark constraint, as Kean observes. In other words, the matrices of *m*'s and *u*'s of natural sound systems cannot look like the one depicted in figure 21-7, with no sound more than one *m* away from any other. That this is so may be attributed to a design that follows the Subset Principle. Let us see why this is so.

As the way in which the hierarchy can be interpreted as an acquisition model has been described here, only one feature can be used to form a new partition of sounds—only one *mark* (*m*) is ever added at any given step. As a result, at any stage in the acquisition of a sound system the partitions correspond to sounds that are at most one *m* apart, automatically satisfying the distinguishability constraint. So Kean's observation might well be explained as a side effect of the acquisition of sound systems. Even so, it seems as though a stipulation about the well-formedness of segmental systems has merely been replaced with a stipulation about the acquisition of segmental systems. Why should acquisition be incremental?

Suppose that acquisition is not incremental and that two or more marks can be added at a single step. It would then be possible to form a new class partition based on marking both the features *labial* and *sonorant* without having first used the feature *sonorant* to form any sound classes.

There would be no class that would correctly accommodate a sound that is labeled [*unmarked labial, marked sonorant*]. One way to remedy this problem would be to allow the procedure to go back and rebuild classes that have already been formed, but this would violate the developmental ordering that has been assumed. The fringe of the hierarchy tree would no longer summarize the possible next states that could be hypothesized, since there could be sounds such as *n* that would demand the interpolation of new classes between older partitions and the current partition. In other words, the one-*m* constraint amounts to the demand that new classes be the minimally specific refinements of existing classes. It is impossible to guess an overly general sound system, because each new guess is the smallest possible refinement of preceding guesses. But this is just the Subset Principle again. At each step, the narrowest language is hypothesized, consistent with positive evidence seen so far.

21.5 LEARNING SYNTAX AND THE SUBSET PRINCIPLE

The Subset Principle subsumes a variety of proposals that have been advanced in the linguistic literature that order hypotheses for language acquisition. In fact, it appears as though the Subset Principle exhausts what can be said about ordering constraints in acquisition. In support of this claim several proposals that have been made regarding the ordering of hypotheses in the acquisition of syntactic constructions will be reviewed. It is not important that the reader appreciate all the details of these examples. The intent is to give a feel for the variety of different kinds of grammatical constructions that fall under the Subset Principle.

21.5.1 An Adjacency Requirement in English

In English, noun phrase direct objects must be adjacent to verbs: *I gave a book quickly to Bill* is fine, but *I gave quickly a book to Bill* is not. (In some languages, such as French, this constraint is weakened so that an adverb may be interpolated between verb and object; in other languages, such as Japanese, this constraint is so weak that the object can be quite distant from the verb.)

How is the adjacency requirement acquired? Once again, the Subset Principle may be invoked. The most restrictive assumption possible is that adjacency holds since it generates the *narrowest* class of language possibilities. To assume otherwise would be to guess a language that could be too large, hence a possible Subset violation. A language satisfying the adjacency condition could be a proper subset of one that was not and yet cover the same triggering data. The acquisition procedure thus assumes an adjacency requirement as the default, unmarked case, loosening it only if positive examples are encountered that indicate violations of adjacency. Since examples violating adjacency (*I hit hardly Bill*) will never be encountered in English, this strict requirement will never be dropped.

In other languages (like French) positive examples exhibiting adjacency violations would prompt a relaxation of these conditions, perhaps along a continuum of possibilities. Thus one might expect to find languages where strict adjacency was relaxed according to a hierarchy of phrasal types. This prediction seems to be confirmed.

21.5.2 Arguments of Verbs

Verbs differ in the number of noun phrase objects (or arguments) that they require and in whether those arguments are obligatory or optional. For example, *eat* may or may not take an argument denoting the thing eaten: *John ate an ice cream cone, John ate.* In contrast, *take* must take an argument: *John took an ice cream cone* is fine, but *John took* is not. Note that a language where a verb may or may not take an argument is a superset of a language where that verb must take an argument. If hypotheses are to be ordered by the Subset Principle, the first guess to make about any verb is that if it appears with an argument, then that argument must be assumed obligatory until a positive example appears in which that argument is not present at all; if such an example appears, the argument is optional. This strategy is observed in children (Roeper, 1982).

21.5.3 Bounding Nodes for Subjacency (Rizzi, 1978)

In most current theories of generative grammar, it is assumed that grammatical rules obey a certain "locality principle," in that a movement cannot cross more than a single sentence boundary. For example, in the first sentence below, *John* is understood as the subject of the embedded sentence *to like ice cream.* The second sentence is ill formed if interpreted this way. The only difference is that the second sentence interposes an additional sentence boundary via the *it is certain* clause. Square brackets mark these boundaries.

1. John is certain [$_S$ trace to like ice cream]
2. John seems [$_S$ it is certain [$_S$ trace to like ice cream]]

This called the subjacency constraint. This constraint is also what makes the following sentence poor, where the *who* words are linked to positions as indicated by subscripts *i* and *j*. For example, the first *who* is the object of *know.* Unfortunately, two S's must be crossed to link up to this position—hence the sentence is no good.

The man who I don't know who knows.

The man [who$_i$[$_S$ (first S) I don't know [who$_j$ [$_S$ (second S) *j* knows *i*]]]]

Interestingly, this last sentence is grammatical in Italian, as discussed by Rizzi (1978):

L'uomo [*wh$_i$* che non so [chi$_j$ [$_S$ *j* conosca *i*]]]]

According to Rizzi, this is because it is a *full* clause with *that* or *for* in it that counts for subjacency in Italian, not just a simple "S" or sentence. (A full "S" in English would be something like *For John to go . . . .*) This kind of phrase is called an S-bar. Rizzi claims that S-bar, not S, is what counts in Italian. Therefore, the *who* in the sentence above can be the object of *conosca* (know) because it crosses only a single full clause boundary that starts at *chi.* The second boundary is an S, not an

S-bar. Apparently, the choice of a bounding node is yet another parameter that must be set in order to learn a language.

Suppose Rizzi's analysis is correct. How could the choice of bounding node be determined on the basis of evidence received by an acquisition procedure? Once again, let us apply the Subset Principle. If the bounding node for subjacency is S, then a narrower class of languages is generated than if the bounding node for subjacency is S-bar. Therefore, by the Subset Principle, the acquisition procedure's first hypothesis should be to set the bounding node for subjacency to S. In other words, the default assumption is that all languages are like English in this regard. If this assumption is wrong, then a positive example will appear that violates S-bounding—as in the Italian example above. Then the acquisition procedure can reset the subjacency parameter to the next "largest" value, namely, S-bar.

21.6 SUMMARY AND CONCLUSIONS

This chapter has shown that there is at least one quite general principle of learning, the Subset Principle, that applies "across the board" in a domain-independent fashion. The Subset Principle arranges the order of hypotheses that a learner should advance in the face of positive-only evidence. The principle has wide applications, showing up in such diverse domains as the acquisition of category concepts, sound systems, and syntax. It has been used explicitly in at least one model for the acquisition of language (Berwick, 1982) and implicitly in the version space model of acquisition.

The Subset Principle makes strong predictions about the order of events in human language acquisition. Are any of these predictions confirmed? In fact, recent experimental tests have been made of the ordering constraints implied by the acquisition proposals described in this section. Children are asked to "act out" certain situations with toy animals in order to see if they understand particular sentences of the sort described above. The results are preliminary (Wexler, 1984), but so far correspond exactly to the predictions of the Subset Principle.

It has already been seen that Keil's work in concept acquisition points to confirmation of the Subset Principle. What of the acquisition of language sound systems? Results here are sketchy. However, there is at least one "classic" piece of evidence, namely, the observations of Jakobson (1968). The Subset Principle ordering predicts that t, p, and k would be among the first consonants acquired and a, i, the first vowels. This sequencing appears to be *roughly* verified by empirical work, though there has been controversy regarding Jakobson's more restricted and probably overly strong proposal.

It remains to be seen whether other kinds of human learning, such as the acquisition of arithmetic skills, abide by the Subset Principle. There is at least some suggestive evidence (see VanLehn, 1983) that they do. Several natural learning systems, then, obey the Subset Principle, in which positive-only example evidence plays a dominant role. Machine learning systems would do well to follow this successful design.

ACKNOWLEDGMENTS

This chapter describes research carried out at the Artificial Intelligence Laboratory at MIT. Support for the Laboratory's artificial intelligence research is provided in part by the Advanced Research Projects Agency under Office of Naval Research Contract N00014-80-C-0505.

References

Angluin, D., "Inductive Inference of Formal Languages from Positive Data," *Information and Control,* Vol. 45, pp. 117–35, 1978.

Berwick, R., "Computational Analogs of Constraints on Grammars," *Proceedings of the Eighteenth Annual Meeting of the Association for Computational Linguistics,* Philadelphia, Pa., pp. 49–54, 1980.

————, "Locality Principles and the Acquisition of Syntactic Knowledge," Ph.D. diss., Department of Electrical Engineering and Computer Science, MIT, 1982.

Brown, R., and Hanlon, C., "Derivational Complexity and the Order of Acquisition in Child Speech," in *Cognition and the Development of Language,* J. R. Hayes (Ed.), Wiley, New York, 1970.

Chomsky, N., *Rules and Representations,* New York, Columbia University Press, 1980.

Chomsky, N., and Halle, M., *The Sound Pattern of English,* New York, Harper and Row, 1968.

Dietterich, T., and Michalski, R., *"A Comparative Review of Selected Methods for Learning from Examples,"* in *Machine Learning: An Artificial Intelligence Approach,* R. S. Michalski, J. G. Carbonell, and T. M. Mitchell (Eds.), Tioga, Palo Alto, Calif., 1983.

Gold, E., "Language Identification to the Limit," *Information and Control,* Vol. 10, pp. 447–74, 1967.

Jakobson, R., *Child Language, Aphasia, and Phonological Universals,* The Hague, Mouton, 1968.

Kean, M., "The Theory of Markedness in Generative Grammar," Ph.D. diss. Department of Linguistics, MIT, 1974.

Keil, F., *Semantic and Conceptual Development: An Ontological Perspective,* Harvard University Press, Cambridge, 1979.

Marshall, J., "Language Acquisition in a Biological Framework," in *Language Acquisition,* P. Fletcher, and M. Garman (Eds.), Cambridge University Press, New York, 1979.

Mitchell, T., "Version Spaces: An Approach to Concept Learning," Computer Science Report CS-78-711, Stanford University, 1978.

Rizzi, L., "A Restructuring Rule in Italian Syntax," in *Transformational Studies in European Languages,* S. J. Keyser (Ed.), MIT Press, Cambridge, 1978.

Roeper, T., "On the Deductive Model and the Role of Productive Morphology," in *The Logical Problem of Language Acquisition,* C. Baker and J. McCarthy (Eds.), MIT Press, Cambridge, 1982.

Sommers, F., "Structural Ontology," *Philosophia,* Vol. 1, pp. 79–85, 1971.

VanLehn, K., "Validating a Model of Children's Arithmetic Skills: Sierra," *Proceedings of the International Machine Learning Workshop,* R. S. Michalski (Ed.), Allerton House, University of Illinois at Urbana-Champaign, June 22–24, 1983.

Wexler, K., "Independence and the Subset Principle," University of Massachusetts *Conference on Formal Models of Language Acquisiton,* Amherst, 1984, forthcoming.

Wexler, K., and Culicover, P., *Formal Principles of Language Acquisition,* MIT Press, Cambridge, 1980.

Winston, P., "Learning Structural Descriptions of Blocks World Scenes from Examples," in *The Psychology of Computer Vision,* P. H. Winston (Ed.), McGraw-Hill, New York, 1975.

22

PRECONDITION ANALYSIS:

Learning Control Information

Bernard Silver
University of Edinburgh

Abstract

This chapter describes a learning technique called *Precondition Analysis*. A program using this technique learns from the worked example of a correctly executed task. In this sense, Precondition Analysis is a form of "learning from examples," but it differs from most such learning methods in two ways:

1. Precondition Analysis is principally used to learn strategies for problem solving. This contrasts with the more classical uses of learning from examples, in which the program learns concepts or decision rules.

2. The technique allows a program to learn from a single example, whereas most other systems require several examples.

Precondition Analysis is described in the context of a program called LP that learns new techniques for solving symbolic equations. Precondition Analysis has been successfully used by LP to learn several new equation-solving strategies.

22.1 INTRODUCTION

This chapter uses symbolic equation solving as an example domain. The program LP uses questions taken from A-level mathematics papers, such as[1]

$$\sin(2*x) + \sin(3*x) + \sin(5*x) = 0. \tag{1}$$

---

[1] A-levels are taken at age eighteen in England and Wales and are used as a criterion in selection for university.

The task of solving an equation consists of taking an equation and transforming it using legal algebraic operations until a solved state is obtained. The equation is solved when it is of the form x = ans, where x is the unknown and ans doesn't contain x, or if it is a disjunction of such terms.

Equation solving is a difficult task because at each step a large number of possible legal operations can be performed. Bundy (1975) shows that ten is a conservative figure for the branching rate in this domain. Possible operations include the use of commutativity, identity, and functional reflexive axioms. For example, equation (1) can be transformed to many forms, including the following:

$$\sin(2*x) + \sin(3*x) = -\sin(5*x)$$
$$\sin^{-1}(\sin(2*x) + \sin(3*x) + \sin(5*x)) = \sin^{-1}0$$
$$\sin(2*x) + 2*\sin(4*x)*\cos(x) = 0 \tag{2}$$

Of the three examples shown, only the transformation to (2) is a good choice, as this equation lies on an optimal solution path. The same kind of choice occurs at every step of the solution; that is, there are many ways of transforming equation (2), including one that transforms it back to (1).

The average length of the solution path for the problems used by LP is about ten steps. This implies that the average search space contains ten billion nodes at the depth at which the solution occurs. Some of the paths rejoin, so the actual search space won't contain this number of different nodes. However, the number will still be very large. A program that had to examine all these possibilities would soon get bogged down in what is known as the *combinatorial explosion.* As the number of steps in the solution increases, the number of possible paths increases exponentially. What is needed is some way of pruning the search space. The program should only consider a small subset of possible operators at various points in the search.

Skilled humans can find the correct solution path with almost no search at all. Apparently these people are using some technique of search constraint. The LP project is an attempt to build a program that can learn this type of search constraint information so that it can be taught to solve new types of equations.

22.1.1 Precondition Analysis

A program using Precondition Analysis works in two phases, the *learning cycle* and the *performance phase.* During the learning cycle, the program is given a *worked example.* The worked example shows how to solve an equation. The example consists of a sequence of problem states, snapshots of the equation-solving process. No other information is given; for example, the program isn't told how one state arises from the previous one.

LP learns three kinds of things during the learning cycle:

1. *Rewrite rules.* These are algebraic facts, such as

   $$\cos(x) + \cos(y) \rightarrow 2*\cos((x + y)/2)*\cos((x - y)/2).$$

   These are supplied by the user (see section 22.4.2.1.)

2. *Methods.* LP has a set of problem-solving operators, called *methods.* Methods apply rewrite rules. They have conditions indicating how and when various rules should be used. Methods are described in more detail in section 22.3.1.

3. *Schemata.* These are equation-solving plans and are used by the performance element.

   The learning cycle consists of four phases:

1. *Operator Identification.* In this phase, LP tries to discover which methods were used in the worked example. The question is, How was each step in the worked example performed? LP may discover that a step in the worked example uses some method that it doesn't have. In this case, LP must learn a new method.

2. *Precondition Analysis.* Here the question is, What is the purpose of each step?

3. *Method creation.* In this phase, LP creates and stores new problem-solving methods.

4. *Schema creation.* Finally, LP stores all this information in a *schema.* The schema records the sequence of methods that were used to solve a worked example. The schema also contains the strategic information indicating why each method was used.

The schema is executed in a flexible way by the performance element. LP tries to use the same sequence of methods as are used in the worked example. Usually the sequence can't be executed exactly. As the schema records the strategic reasons for each step, the program is able to patch the plan in a sensible way.

LP is able to learn a new technique by examining a single worked example. As Neves points out (1978), many textbooks present just one worked example before proceeding to the exercises. This consideration rules out many concept-learning methods (see, e.g., Mitchell, 1978; Winston, 1975), as these programs generally need to process several instances before the concept is learned.

The learning cycle is described in more detail in section 22.4, and the performance phase is discussed in section 22.5. Various parts of the precondition analysis technique are similar to parts of the learning method used by other researchers, particularly Mitchell (1978, 1983) and DeJong (1983).

22.2 BACKGROUND TO LP

LP is built on the equation-solving program PRESS[2] (Bundy and Welham, 1981; Sterling et al., 1982). Both programs are written in PROLOG (Clocksin and Mellish, 1981). PRESS is a nonlearning program; the only way to increase its ability is to write new code. There is a test set of equations, and each version of PRESS is primarily judged by how many of these equations it can solve. The test set contain question from A-level mathematics papers.

Other research has dealt with learning equation-solving methods, but this author's interests are somewhat different. Most of the other fairly recent work in this field (e.g., Brazdil, 1978; Langley, 1983; Neves, 1978) has concentrated on very simple equations, such as

$$2*x + 3 = 5.$$

Such work has demonstrated that computer programs can learn to solve equations, building up from very little knowledge. However, the strategies used to solve such equations are rather simple; the difficult part is to teach the program algebraic rules.

The A-level standard questions used by LP are much harder than those considered by other researchers. Knowledge of algebraic rules is no longer sufficient to solve such equations; the search space is too large. The solver requires some strategic guidance, knowledge of *how* and *when* to apply the rules.

22.3 THE PROBLEM-SOLVING METHODS

Many learning programs work in domains in which the basic operators are similar to those of STRIPS (Fikes, Hart, and Nilsson, 1972). LEX (Mitchell, 1983; Mitchell, Utgoff, and Banerji, 1983), and ALEX (Neves, 1978) are examples.

The equivalent of operators in LP are the *methods*. However, methods do not have one of the desirable properties of STRIPS-type operators. The preconditions of a method represent necessary but not sufficient conditions, whereas the preconditions of STRIPS-type operators are both sufficient and necessary. In general, a method is not certain to succeed even if the preconditions are applicable. This is because the preconditions are too general, but stronger preconditions cannot be given that do not involve actually applying the method to test if it is applicable! Similarly, it is difficult to specify effects of the operator. It seems that this might be a problem in many domains.

The fact that LP methods lack these properties is important. If the methods were as well behaved as STRIPS operators, it would be possible to build a much more powerful planning system, and a lot of the heuristic nature of LP would be unnecessary.

---

[2]PRolog Equation Solving System. LP stands for Learning Press.

22.3.1 The Methods of LP

LP begins with about fifteen methods. Each method has (1) a set of preconditions; (2) a set of postconditions; (3) and associated set of rewrite rules; and (4) some information indicating how to apply the rewrite rules—for example, information about whether the rewrite rule should be applied to the whole equation or just to some special subterms. The postconditions are used to specify what must be true after a method has been applied in the *desired* way, but there is no guarantee that the method will make these true; that is, it may be possible to apply the method in an undesirable way, where the postconditions are false. Postconditions are used to check that the method has been applied in the right way.

Each LP method has an associated set of rewrite rules. A method can only use the rules in its associated set. The rules in a set are related in that they may be able to achieve a particular kind of effect. Some examples are given below.

In the following sections, one method, Isolation, is described in detail, and four others are described briefly.[3]

22.3.1.1 Isolation

Isolation is a method that solves equations containing exactly one occurrence of the unknown. Consider the following (very simple) example, showing the solution of the equation

$\log_e(2*x) = 1.$

$$\log_e(2*x) = 1 \qquad\qquad\qquad (3)$$
$$2*x = e \qquad\qquad\qquad (4)$$
$$x = e/2 \qquad\qquad\qquad (5)$$

The last line of the example, line (5), is the solution to the equation. There is a single occurrence of x, isolated on the left-hand side.

The previous line (4) also has the only occurrence of x on the left-hand side, but in this case it appears as the first argument of the multiplication function. The last line is obtained from (4) by applying the inverse of this function to both sides.

In the case of line (4), it can be said that multiplication is the *outermost* function.

Similarly, line (4) is obtained from line (3) by removing the outermost function, which is the logarithmic function in this case. A function is removed by applying the inverse of that function to both sides of the equation. In this case this is done by exponentiating both sides.

---

[3] All of the LP methods except for Factorization Preparation, described in section 22.3.1.5, are also PRESS methods. PRESS methods are described in Langley (1983) and Sterling et al. (1982).

This process of removing the outermost function is called *Isolation*. Isolation works on equations containing exactly one occurrence of the unknown. At each application it removes the outermost function surrounding the occurrence of the unknown, until the unknown appears alone.

The precondition of Isolation is that the equation Eqn contains exactly one occurrence of the unknown X, written as **single-occ(X,Eqn)**. The postcondition is that the resultant equation is solved. Isolation rules are of the form

$$C(U_1, U_2, \ldots, U_n, B) \ \& \ F(U_1, U_2, \ldots, U_n) = B \Rightarrow U_i = F_i^{-1}(B),$$

where C is a (possibly empty) set of conditions, U_i contains the unknown, and F_i^{-1} is the inverse of F with respect to the ith argument of F.[4] For example, the first Isolation step above uses the rule

$$B > 0 \ \& \ U_1^{U_2} = B \Rightarrow U_2 = \log_{U_1} B.$$

(Here F is the two-argument exponentiation function ($F(X, Y) = X^Y$), i is 2, and C is the single condition that B must be positive.) Isolation rules are applied in a restricted manner. At any stage Isolation strips off only the outermost function dominating the unknown. For example, given the equation

$$\sin(\cos(x)) = \tan(a),$$

Isolation strips off the sin function rather than the tan one.

22.3.1.2 Collection

If the equation contains more than one occurrence of the unknown, Isolation cannot be applied. In such cases LP may be able to use another method, Collection, that tries to reduce the number of occurrences of the unknown.

Collection rules include the following:

$$U*N + U*M \rightarrow U*(N + M)$$
$$U^2 + 2*U* V + V^2 \Rightarrow (U + V)^2$$

In the first case the term corresponding to U must contain the unknown. Either U or V can contain the unknown in the second case.

Like Isolation, Collection applies its rules selectively. Collection applies its rules to subterms of the equation that have two immediate subterms containing the unknown. (These are called *least-dominating subterms* in Bundy and Welham, 1981.)

Collection can only be applied to equations containing two or more occurrences of the unknown, and its effect is to reduce the number of occurrences. Note

---

[4] In some cases there will be a disjunction of terms on the right-hand side. For example, if F is the square function:

$$x^2 = a \Rightarrow x = a^{1/2} \ \bigvee \ x = -(a^{1/2}).$$

that Collection need not reduce the number to one, so Isolation may not apply after Collection. Sometimes a sequence of Collection applications will be needed to reduce the number of occurrences to one so that Isolation can be applied; in other cases totally different methods will be needed.

The precondition of Collection is that the equation Eqn contain more than one occurrence of the unknown. The postcondition is that the new Eqn has fewer occurrences than the original equation.

22.3.1.3 Attraction

Attraction is a method that moves occurrences of the unknown "closer" together[5] in the hope that Collection will then be applicable. Attraction has the same precondition as Collection. Its postcondition is that the unknowns are closer in the resultant equation than in the original one. Attraction rules include the following:

$$\log_w U + \log_w V \rightarrow \log_w(U*V)$$
$$U*W + V*W \rightarrow (U + V)*W$$

In these rules the terms U and V are attracted, so these terms must contain the unknown and the other terms must not. Like Collection rules, Attraction rules are applied to least-dominating subterms.

22.3.1.4 Factorization

An equation of the form

$$a*b*c \ldots * k = 0 \tag{6}$$

can be transformed to the disjunctive set of equations

$$a = 0 \lor b = 0 \lor \ldots \lor k = 0. \tag{7}$$

Each member of the disjunct (7) can be solved as an independent equation. The solution of the original equation (6) is the disjunction of the solutions to the individual equations in (7).

LP is able to perform this type of transformation using its Factorization method. The preconditions of Factorization can be expressed as the set {rhs-zero(Eqn), lhs-prod(x,Eqn)}; that is, the right-hand side must be zero, and the left-hand side must be a product in the unknown X.

Factorization has the effect of splitting a complex equation into several simpler ones. The new equations contain fewer occurrences of the unknown than the original

---

[5]The concept of "closeness" has been defined in a precise way; see Bundy and Welham (1981) for details.

one, and thus it is possible that Isolation can apply to the individual factors. For example, Factorization splits

$$\cos(x)*\sin(x)*\tan(x) = 0$$

into three factors, each of which can then be solved by Isolation.

Key methods. Factorization should be used whenever it is applicable. It is one of the *key methods,* methods that should be applied whenever possible. Isolation is another key method. Key methods play a special role in Precondition Analysis.

22.3.1.5 Factorization Preparation

The last method to be described is Factorization Preparation. As the name suggests, Factorization Preparation transforms the equation so that Factorization can be applied.

This method takes an equation of the form

$$e_1 + e_2 + \ldots + e_n = 0$$

and transforms it to

$$f*(e'_1 + e'_2 + \ldots + e'_n) = 0, \tag{8}$$

where f is a common factor of the e_i and

$$f*e'_i = e_i$$

The e_i and f must contain the unknown; f is called the *common subterm* of the left-hand side.

This method uses the distributive law (backwards)

$$A*B + A*C + \ldots + A*M \rightarrow A*(B + C + \ldots + M). \tag{9}$$

Note that Factorization can now be applied to equation (8).

The preconditions of Factorization Preparation are

{rhs-zero(Eqn), mult-occ(X,Eqn), lhs-sum(X,Eqn),
common-subterms(X,Eqn)}.

Note that the common subterm must contain the unknown and must be a (top-level) multiplicative factor of each member of the sum. This last condition, expressed as common-subterms (X,Eqn), implies that the distributive law can be applied and prevents x from being counted as a common factor of

$$\cos(x) + \cos(2*x) + \cos(3*x).$$

22.3.2 Using the Methods

Now that some of the methods have been described, this section will describe how LP uses the methods to solve equations *before* learning has taken place.[6] Learning modifies the behavior; see section 22.5.

The technique used by LP is similar to that used in the Boyer-Moore theorem prover. Boyer and Moore (1979) use the term *waterfall* to describe their top-level process. This terminology will be followed here: the term *heuristic waterfall* will be used to describe the control flow of LP.

The waterfall consists of a number of methods. At the top of the waterfall, LP checks to see if the equation is already solved. If it is, LP returns the answer, and the equation is removed from the waterfall. Otherwise, the equation is passed over the waterfall. As the equation goes down, the methods try to transform it. If a method succeeds in transforming the equation, the new equation is sent to the top of the waterfall and the process is repeated. If a method such as Factorization creates more than one equation, all such equations are sent to the top.[7] If a method fails to transform the equation, the equation falls to the next level, where the next method is tried. The process terminates with success when there are no more equations to be processed. If an equation falls right through the waterfall—that is, no method can transform the equation—LP backtracks. Finally, if all possibilities have been tried and equations still remain in the waterfall, the process terminates with failure; that is, LP fails to solve the equation.

Generally, the key methods (such as Isolation and Factorization) should be attempted first, and this is reflected in the ordering. The rest of the ordering was determined experimentally. Various different orderings were tried on some test problems, and the output was evaluated on several criteria. These criteria included considerations of efficiency and of whether the output resembled the output that humans would produce when solving the problems themselves.

This ordering can be viewed as implementing a kind of plan. For example, LP first tries to apply Isolation. If this fails, it tries Collection and then attempts to apply Isolation to the result.

Note that the waterfall is a very simple control mechanism. Such a simple device can be used because the search space of the methods is small and well behaved. By *well behaved* is meant that if a method is applicable, it will usually be right to apply it, and if this decision is wrong, dead ends are quickly reached.

On more complex problems, however, the waterfall is just too simple. The program requires more guidance than that provided by the ordering of the waterfall.

---

[6]PRESS uses the technique described here.

[7]All these subproblems have to be solved; the program attempts to solve them in an arbitrary order.

Such information is provided by worked examples. LP uses these to build a schema that provides a more flexible control.

22.4 THE LEARNING CYCLE

The learning cycle falls into four phases:

1. *Operator Identification*
2. *Precondition Analysis*
3. *Method creation*
4. *Schema creation*

Each of these phases will be described after the characteristics of the worked examples used by LP are examined.

22.4.1 Worked Examples

A worked example shows the steps involved in the solution of an equation. The example shows various points in the solution process. It is arranged as a sequence of *lines,* each line being an equation or a disjunction or conjunction of equations. Generally, each line can be transformed into the next by the application of a sequence of legal algebraic operations. Such a sequence is called a *step.*

A worked example should contain enough detail so that the reader (either a human or a program) can understand the technique being demonstrated, but there should not be so much detail that the important points are swamped.

Figure 22-1 shows a typical instance of the type of worked example used by LP. The example shows the solution of the equation

$$\cos(x) + 2*\cos(2*x) + \cos(3*x) = 0.$$

$$
\begin{array}{ll}
\cos(x) + 2*\cos(2*x) + \cos(3*x) = 0 & (1) \\
2*\cos(2*x)*\cos(x) + 2*\cos(2*x) = 0 & (2) \\
2*\cos(2*x)*(\cos(x) + 1) = 0 & (3) \\
\cos(2*x) = 0 \ \bigvee \ \cos(x) + 1 = 0 & (4) \\
\cos(2*x) = 0 & (5) \\
x = 180*n_1 = 45 & (6) \\
\cos(x) + 1 = 0 & (7) \\
\cos(x) = -1 & (8) \\
x = 180*(2*n_2 + 1) & (9)
\end{array}
$$

Figure 22-1: A worked example.

The angle measure is degrees, and n_1 and n_2 are arbitrary integers. This example will be used in the discussion here. This worked example is typical of those used by LP. Note that the examples contain no annotations or grouping information.

Generally, it is assumed that each line in the worked example follows from the previous one; for example, the step from (3) to (4) is recognized as a Factorization step. However, this assumption breaks down if the example is presented linearly in the way adopted here: line (5) doesn't really follow from line (4), and line (7) certainly doesn't follow from line (6).

LP overcomes such problems by looking out for special situations. It knows that some examples fall into distinct *sections*. Examples that use Factorization form one such category. The first section of a Factorization example consists of the steps leading up to the Factorization step. In figure 22-1, lines (1) to (4) form this section. If the Factorization step gives rise to n factors, the example then falls into n more sections, each section containing the steps that solve one factor.

Each of the factor sections is considered separately back to the "parent" Factorization step that formed it. In figure 22-1, lines (5) to (6) form one section, and lines (7) to (9) form another. The parent step is (4). LP needs to know how to divide examples into sections; such knowledge can be given explicitly.

Each type of section has a *purpose*. The purpose of the first section of a Factorization example is to allow Factorization to apply. The purpose of the other sections is simply to solve a factor. The concept of sections and their purposes is used during the performance phase (see section 22.5).

22.4.2 Operator Identification

After sectioning the example, LP has to discover *how* each line in the worked example is transformed into the next.

The program examines consecutive pairs of steps within each section; that is, it examines line (1) and line (2), then line (2) and line (3), and so on. Note that for Operator Identification the example is examined in a forward direction, from the initial equation. This contrasts with the backward examination that takes place during the Precondition Analysis phase.

Suppose that LP is working on the step from a line l to the next line, say m. LP first tries to see if an existing method can account for the step. To do this, LP tries to find a method whose preconditions are satisfied by l and whose postconditions are satisfied by m.

If LP finds a method, it attempts to use it to transform l into m. If the method is successful, LP records that the step from l to m was performed by that method and proceeds to the step from m to the next line.

For example, consider the worked example shown in figure 22-1. Suppose that LP is working on the step from line (2) to line (3), that is,

$$2*\cos(2*x)*\cos(x) + 2*\cos(2*x) = 0 \tag{2}$$
$$2*\cos(2*x)*\cos(x) + 1) = 0 \tag{3}$$

LP discovers that Factorization Preparation can transform line (2) to line (3).

In the interesting case, the program cannot find a method that would account for the step and marks the step as *not immediately parsed*.

Suppose that the program has a step that it cannot account for; that is, no known method would produce the transformation between lines l and m. There are two distinct cases. The first case is when LP finds a method, say, **M**, whose preconditions and postconditions are satisfied by the two lines, but it finds that M can't produce the transformation. In this case it informs the user that it is probably missing a rewrite rule for the method M. At a later stage the user is asked to provide the missing rule, and this rule is then made available to M.

The second case is when no apparently applicable method is discovered. The program then assumes that an unknown rewrite rule (i.e., an identity) has been used. Once it has been given the rule by the user, it will need to create a new method that can apply the rule.

In either case, the program can use the worked example to conjecture the particular instance of the rule. To do this, LP makes use of a very obvious but extremely effective heuristic. The heuristic can be paraphrased as follows: Given two consecutive lines of an example, delete all terms common to both and conjecture that the remaining expressions are equal.

For instance, given

$$A + B = C$$
$$B + D = C$$

as two consecutive lines of a worked example, it is reasonable to conjecture that $A = D$.[8]

Consider the worked example shown in figure 22-1. For example, suppose that the program does not understand the step from (1) to (2), that is,

$$\cos(x) + 2*\cos(2*x) + \cos(3*x) = 0 \tag{1}$$
$$2*\cos(2*x)*\cos(x) + 2*\cos(2*x) = 0 \tag{2}$$

---

[8]LP knows facts about the commutative nature of $+$, etc., so it is not confused by the changing argument position of *B*.

Using the heuristic, the program notes that both lines contain the additive term $2*\cos(2*x)$. It deletes this and considers the rest. Nothing else is common, so it produces the correct conjecture

$$\cos(x) + \cos(3*x) = 2*\cos(2*x)*\cos(x) \tag{10}$$

The heuristic is not perfect; there are examples on which LP can make errors. Neves (1978) uses a similar heuristic in his program ALEX. However, ALEX is *not* given the rule; it guesses the rule by generalizing the conjecture and replacing numbers with variables where this appears to be appropriate. ALEX can be misled by spurious correlations.

22.4.2.1 Assimilating the Rule

LP has conjectured a specific instance of the rewrite rule. It now asks the user to confirm the conjecture. If the conjecture is not true, the program exits with failure. If the conjecture is true, the user is asked to provide the general rule. For example, if the conjecture was (10) above, the user would provide the rule

$$\cos(A) + \cos(B) \rightarrow 2*\cos((A + B)/2)*\cos((A - B)/2). \tag{11}$$

Now the rule must be assimilated. Recall that there are two possible reasons why a step may not be immediately parsed. First, the step may use an existing method M,[9] but LP may lack the necessary rewrite rule or, second, the step may use an entirely new method.

In the first case LP adds the new rule to the rule set of M. Now method M should be able to perform the step. This process allows LP to add new rules to methods, thereby increasing their scope. Otherwise, LP must create the new method. The new rule will eventually be placed in the rule set of this new method.

22.4.3 The Precondition Analysis Phase

Figure 22-2 shows the example of figure 22-1 after Operator Identification. Each line is preceded by the name of the method that produced it or an explanatory comment.

Now the Precondition Analysis phase begins. The method is essentially simple. Basically the idea is to find the *major aim* of each step, that is, to answer the question, Why was the step performed? As indicated earlier, this analysis is expressed in terms of the satisfaction of preconditions of the subsequent steps. In the simplest case, the first method is applied to satisfy some preconditions of the second method so that

---

[9]Note that M need not be one of the original methods. It can be a method created by LP earlier in the session.

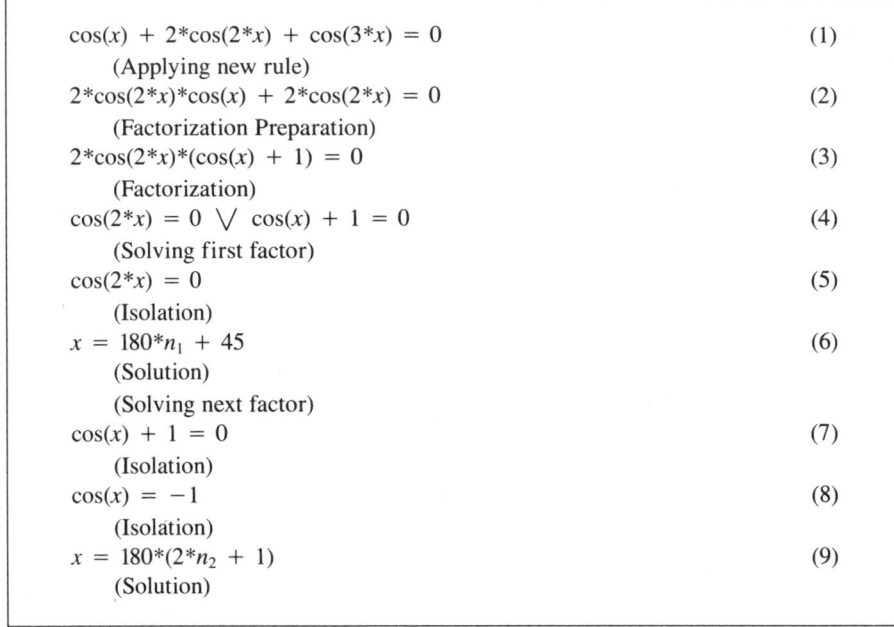

$$\cos(x) + 2*\cos(2*x) + \cos(3*x) = 0 \tag{1}$$

(Applying new rule)

$$2*\cos(2*x)*\cos(x) + 2*\cos(2*x) = 0 \tag{2}$$

(Factorization Preparation)

$$2*\cos(2*x)*(\cos(x) + 1) = 0 \tag{3}$$

(Factorization)

$$\cos(2*x) = 0 \;\bigvee\; \cos(x) + 1 = 0 \tag{4}$$

(Solving first factor)

$$\cos(2*x) = 0 \tag{5}$$

(Isolation)

$$x = 180*n_1 + 45 \tag{6}$$

(Solution)

(Solving next factor)

$$\cos(x) + 1 = 0 \tag{7}$$

(Isolation)

$$\cos(x) = -1 \tag{8}$$

(Isolation)

$$x = 180*(2*n_2 + 1) \tag{9}$$

(Solution)

Figure 22-2: The worked example after Operator Identification.

that method can be applied.[10] The second method is applied in turn in order to satisfy some preconditions of the third method, and so on. Finally, the last method is applied in order to produce a solution. Sometimes the situation is somewhat more complicated (see section 22.4.4.1).

The analysis takes place for each section of the example. In general the problem is to find the purpose of the application of method M at line i to produce line $i + 1$. The step from (1) to (2) in figure 22-2 will be used as an example:

$$\cos(x) + 2*\cos(2*x) + \cos(3*x) = 0 \tag{1}$$

$$2*\cos(2*x)*\cos(x) + 2*\cos(2*x) = 0 \tag{2}$$

The following step is Factorization Preparation.

---

[10]Note that some of the preconditions of the second method may already be satisfied by the original state, so in general there is no need for the first method alone to satisfy *all* the preconditions of the second method.

LP first finds the preconditions **P** of the method M' applied at line $i + 1$ to give line $i + 2$. In this case, M' is Factorization Preparation. The set **P** is

{rhs-zero(Eqn),lhs-sum(X,Eqn),common-subterms(X,Eqn)}.

LP then finds which of the members of **P** are satisfied at line i. Call these preconditions **S**. In the example, the first two elements of **P** are satisfied but the last isn't.

S is therefore {rhs-zero(Eqn), lhs-sum(X,Eqn)}. the set difference **P** \ **S** is the set of preconditions not satisfied at line i but satisfied at $i + 1$; call this set ME.[11] In this case, ME is {common-subterms(X,Eqn)}. If ME is nonempty, LP assumes that the aim of applying M is to satisfy ME so that M' can be applied. The set ME is called the *major effects* of the step (the major aim of a step is to satisfy the major effects). If LP finds that all the preconditions of M' were satisfied at line i—that is, ME is empty—it looks for another explanation (see section 22.4.4.1).

The above analysis is performed for each "real" step in the worked example. (Real steps exclude those steps that are artifacts, such as partial applications of Isolation.)

The final analysis is shown in table 22-1. Note that Eqn in each line refers to the *current* equation, that is, a different equation in each case. Similarly X refers to the current unknown, which happens to be x for every line. The first column corresponds to the lines in figure 22-2. Note that not all lines appear, such as line (8); those that do not appear are superfluous to the analysis. The last column of the last three entries is blank. In the case of the Isolation entries, each entry ends its section so no next method follows. Factorization is a key method, so no detailed analysis of the preconditions is required. The analysis is used by LP to create new methods and schemata.

22.4.4 Creating New Methods

The next stage involves creating new methods. New methods are created if the program has been given new rules by the user. Since LP is method based rather than

Table 22-1:   Analysis of worked example.

Line	Method	Major Effects (ME)	Satisfied Preconditions (S)
(2)	Application of new rule	common-subterms(X,Eqn)	rhs-zero(Eqn) lhs-sum(X,Eqn)
(3)	Factorization Preparation	lhs-prod(X,Eqn)	rhs-zero(Eqn)
(4)	Factorization	(Key method)	
(6)	Isolation	(Solves equation)	
(7)	Isolation	(Solves equation)	

---

[11]ME must be satisfied at $i + 1$ or M' could not be applied.

rule based—that is, it learns *control* rather than factual knowledge—it must create new methods that apply the new rules. The new methods can be used in the same way as the original methods. By creating new methods, the program increases its ability to solve problems.

A new rule was applied at line (1) in figure 22-2. The above analysis gives the aim of this step, expressed as the set ME in table 22-1. LP creates a new method that can apply the rule. The new method allows LP to apply the rewrite rule whenever this is appropriate.

Finding the preconditions. There is a choice for the preconditions of the new method. The preconditions can be obtained from the analysis above, from the lines in the worked example, or from some combination of the two. LP adopts the first approach and makes the preconditions of the method **S**. It is hoped that applying the operator won't undo the satisfaction of this set.[12] When LP eventually applies the new operator, if it succeeds in satisfying the major effect ME and **S** is also satisfied, *all* the preconditions of the following method M will be satisfied.

The postconditions of the method are the preconditions of the following method M. When LP later applies the new operator, it will therefore test to see if the application of the operator does in fact preserve the satisfaction of **S**. In this way, LP is able to create a method with preconditions that are probably necessary, although they aren't sufficient. The preconditions are only probably necessary because it may be that the rules used will automatically satisfy some of **S** anyway, even if these preconditions aren't satisfied already.

In the example above, a new method is created that has as preconditions

{lhs-sum(X,Eqn), rhs-zero(Eqn), mult-occ(X,Eqn)},

where mult-occ(X,Eqn) is satisfied when there are multiple occurrences of X in Eqn.
The postconditions of the new method are

{lhs-sum(X,Eqn), rhs-zero(Eqn), mult-occ(X,Eqn), common-subterms(X,Eqn)}.

22.4.4.1 When the Set ME Is Empty

Sometimes LP will find that the step it is trying to analyze satisfies no missing preconditions of the following method. In the terms used above, the set ME is empty. LP is able to recognize two cases in which this happens:

Manipulating the equation. One possibility is that the rule is used to manipulate the equation so that M′ can be applied, although no new preconditions are satisfied. This

---

[12]LP checks for this—see next paragraph.

kind of behavior occurs because, in general, the preconditions are necessary but not sufficient conditions. The vocabulary of LP is insufficient to express the necessary conditions.

In general, if a step from line i to line $i + 1$ doesn't satisfy any new preconditions of the method M' applied at line $i + 1$, no existing method can produce the step and M' couldn't be applied at line i. LP then creates a new method M in the following way:

The user has already supplied the rule R that allows the step to be performed. If the preconditions of M' are P, the method M has P as *both* its preconditions and postconditions. M uses rule R and has M' as its indicated next method. The major effects of M are empty, and LP informs the user that this step doesn't appear to satisfy any new preconditions of the following method but it appears to be essential anyway! The fact that M has no major effects can be used when LP is solving new equations.

Parallel steps. The other case is that in which two (or more) steps have to be applied before a third, but the order of the first two is arbitrary. In this case, when LP comes to analyze the first step, it will find that ME is empty. This seems similar to the case above, but there is an important difference. In the former, M' can't be applied at line i, so some manipulation is needed. In the case described here, M' can be applied at line i. LP notes that the two steps can be applied in either order and creates a method that applies both, telescoping the two steps.

22.4.5 Creating the Schema

After the above work is done, the schema can be created easily. The schema contains three main parts. These are (1) the generating equation, (2) the unknown that is being solved *for,* and (3) the *body* of the schema.

The body is a list consisting of all the methods used in the worked example. Each step is tagged with the following:

1. The method used
2. The preconditions that it is used to satisfy, that is, the major effects
3. Any conditions that must also be maintained, that is, the set **S.**

The schema is divided in the same way as the worked example; that is, all the sectioning is preserved.

The schema "summarizes" the worked example and is used to solve new equations. The schema isn't a perfect plan. LP hasn't analyzed the example completely and has made simplifying assumptions. Before it could analyze the example completely. LP would need extensive modification. For example, the solution method of the standard example used here works *exactly* only on equations of the form

$$\cos(A*x) + 2*\cos(B*x) + \cos(C*x) = 0,$$

where *A, B,* and *C* don't contain *x* and are in arithmetic progression. If LP were to be able to derive this condition, either it would have to have concepts such as arithmetic progression in its description space and use some form of concept learning or it would have to use a technique such as Mitchell's goal-directed learning (1983). However, the nature of the operators of LP make the latter approach difficult (see section 20.6). Instead, LP has produced an approximate plan that it executes flexibly.

Part of the schema produced by LP for the worked example of figure 22-1 is shown in table 22-2. The schema is stored as a method, called a *schema method.* The preconditions of the method are the preconditions of the first method in the schema. The postconditions are that the equation is solved.

22.5 SOLVING NEW EQUATIONS

The user gives LP a new equation to solve, called the *given equation.* The program first tries to find a schema method that might help it solve the given equation. To do this, the program finds a schema method whose preconditions are satisfied by the given equation. This insures that at least the first operator in the schema *might* be applicable (recall that the preconditions are necessary but not sufficient).

Once the schema has been selected, LP uses it to guide the attempt to solve the given equation. The schema lists the methods used to solve the generating equation, together with other information about preconditions and purposes.

In essence, LP tries to apply the methods listed in the schema to the given equation. LP tries to use the schema from the top; that is, it tries to apply the first method first, and if it succeeds, it tries to apply the second method, and so on. LP works down the schema, at any point working on a particular step of the schema. The method in this step is called the *current indicated method,* and it can be said that LP is trying to apply the current indicated method.

Table 22-2: Part of the schema.

Name	Preconditions	Purpose
Method New	{rhs-zero(Eqn), lhs-sum(X,Eqn), mult-occ(X,Eqn)}	Produce common sub-terms for Factorization Preparation
Factorization Preparation	{rhs-zero(Eqn), lhs-sum(X,Eqn), common-subterms(X,Eqn)}	Produce product on lhs equation so that Factorization can be applied
Factorization	{rhs-zero(Eqn), lhs-prod(X,Eqn), mult-occ(X,Eqn)}	(Major step)
Isolation	{single-occ(X,Eqn)}	(Solution)
Isolation	{single-occ(X,Eqn)}	(Solution)
$\cos(x) + 2*\cos(2*x) + \cos(3*x) = 0, x.$		

If it succeeds in applying the current indicated method, LP moves on to the next step, trying to apply the new schema method, and so on. By trying to apply the steps it learned from the worked example in exactly the same sequence, LP is using the results of a form of learning called *learning by rote*. This is a reasonable first strategy: the steps solved the generating equation, and the given equation and generating equation both satisfy the preconditions of the first method in the schema. If the given equation is very similar to the generating equation, the attempt may succeed. More usually, there will come a point when a method listed in the schema can't be applied to the transformed given equation.

If LP has only learned the list of steps, it would now be stuck. This illustrates the weakness of learning by rote. Since there is no understanding of the reasons for various decisions, it is very difficult to recover from unexpected failure.

However, the schema contains other information as well. The most important parts are its division into sections and the major aims of each step. This information enables LP to modify the linear execution of the schema.

Basically, LP uses the "algorithm" for **solve(Eqn,*X*,Ans,Sch,MN,SN)**, shown in table 22-3, which defines how to solve Eqn for *X* to get Ans starting at

Table 22-3: The **solve** algorithm.

Test	Action
1. Is Eqn solved?	Exit with success, with Ans = Eqn.
2. Is the purpose of the current section (number SN) achieved?	Proceed to next section, i.e., call **solve(Eqn,*X*,Ans,Sch,1,NewS)**, where NewS is SN + 1.
3. Can the current indicated method (number MN) be applied?	Proceed to next method, i.e., call **solve(New,*X*,Ans,Sch,NewM,SN)**, where NewM is NM + 1, and New is the result of applying method number MN to Eqn.
4. Can a method (M′) that achieves the same purpose as method number MN be applied?	Proceed to next method, i.e., call **solve(New,*X*,Ans,Sch,NewM,SN)**, where NewM is NM + 1, and New is the result of applying M′ to Eqn.
5. Can another method (M′) be applied that doesn't undo any already satisfied preconditions of method number MN?	Try again with transformed equation, i.e., call **solve(New,*X*,Ans,Sch,NM,SN)**, where New is the result of applying M′ to Eqn.
6. Is the set of major effects of method number MN empty?	Omit method, i.e., call **solve(Eqn,*X*,Ans,Sch,NewM,SN)**, where NewM is NM + 1.
7. Otherwise	Fail; backtrack if possible

method number MN of section number SN of the schema Sch. The process starts at the first method of the first section of Sch; that is, the original call is **solve(Eqn,X,Ans,Sch,1,1)**.

LP tries each test in order, starting from the top, until one succeeds. It then performs the action specified for that test. The first test is obvious; if the equation is solved LP has finished.

Note that the first two tests allow LP to omit large numbers of steps. These tests look for states that are unexpectedly "good." Placing these tests first allows LP to take advantage of such fortuitous circumstances. The planner of STRIPS, PLANEX (Fikes, Hart, and Nilsson, 1972), also does this, but there are differences. PLANEX always tries to apply the last step in a plan, then the last two, and so on. This allows STRIPS to execute the smallest part of the plan that is applicable. Such an approach isn't useful for LP, since the methods aren't well behaved.

The third test is the obvious one; try to apply the same operator that was used in the worked example.

The fourth test allows LP to replace one operator in the plan with another that achieves the same effect. If such an operator can be found, things may still go wrong, since the original operator may have had an undetected effect, but this substitution action is a reasonable heuristic.

The fifth test is less directed. LP can't apply the operator it wants to, and it can't substitute for the operator. LP tries to find an operator that won't undo any already satisfied preconditions but that might manipulate the equation in some unspecified way so that the desired operator may then be applicable. LP wouldn't need to perform such actions if the methods were better behaved. Note that this procedure can be applied over and over again, allowing LP to *add* an indefinite number of steps to the plan.

The sixth test allows LP to omit an operator if it has no major effects. This is risky, since the operator did something in the original worked example—LP just couldn't describe what it was! Nevertheless, as a last resort, this method is reasonable.

22.5.1 An Example

As an example, suppose that LP is given the equation

$$2*\cos(x) + 3*\cos(2*x) + 2*\cos(3*x) = 0 \tag{12}$$

to solve and that it chooses to use the schema shown in table 22-2. This schema was generated by the equation

$$\cos(x) + 2*\cos(2*x) + \cos(3*x) = 0 \tag{13}$$

The first step is to see if the equation is completely solved. It isn't, so the next step is to see if the purpose of the current schema section has been attained. The purpose of the current section is to allow Factorization to apply. Equation (12) isn't a product, so Factorization can't be applied; therefore the purpose of the current section hasn't been attained yet. Consequently, LP attempts to apply the current indicated method.

The first method in the schema is New, which applies the rule

$$\cos(A) + \cos(B) \rightarrow 2*\cos((A + B)/2)*\cos((A - B)/2)$$

in order to provide common subterms for Factorization Preparation.

The rule can't be applied directly to equation (12) as the cosine terms have multiplicative factors dominating them. The attempt to apply New to this equation therefore fails.

LP now tries to find a method that would achieve the major effects of New; that is, it tries to find a method that produces common subterms for Factorization Preparation. Suppose that it can't find such a method.[13] LP now tries to use other methods, in the hope that it will then be able to apply New. These methods must not alter any preconditions of New that are already satisfied by the equation (12). There are three such preconditions: the right-hand side is 0, the left-hand side is a sum, and the equation contains multiple occurrences of the unknown.

Many methods can be ruled out quickly. Either their preconditions aren't satisfied, or they have already been tried, or their postconditions don't satisfy the preconditions of New. In fact, only two methods remain, Collection and Attraction. Collection fails to transform the equation, so Attraction is tried. This succeeds, transforming the equation to

$$2*(\cos(x) + \cos(5*x)) + 3*\cos(3*x) = 0 \qquad (14)$$

The equation has been transformed. LP first checks to see if the equation is solved. It isn't, so LP tests to see if the purpose of the current schema section has been attained. In this case, as Factorization can't be applied to equation (14), the purpose still hasn't been achieved. LP now tries to apply the current indicated method, New. This attempt succeeds on the new equation, (14), and from then on the schema can be applied exactly.

The schema has been modified by adding an initial extra step. Note that if equation (12) had initially been given as a worked example, the schema would have contained Attraction as the first step. This step in fact has no major effect. If LP had then been given equation (13) to solve, it would eventually omit this step. The schema would then apply exactly.

---

[13]This will be the case if LP has seen only the one worked example before being given the new equation. Other worked examples might cause LP to create other methods with this major effect.

22.6 RELATION TO OTHER WORK

LP is related in many ways to the work of DeJong and of Mitchell et al. DeJong's explanatory schema acquisition technique (1983) works in the domain of story understanding. DeJong is concerned with knowledge-based generalization rather than problem solving. His program builds new concepts from the examples; for example, kidnapping is seen as a novel way of combining stealing with bargaining. These concepts are then used to understand later stories, but there is no sense in which they are executed. Nevertheless, DeJong's work shows that it is possible to analyze preconditions to produce useful results in domains very different from equation solving.

Mitchell's LEX2 (Mitchell, 1983; Mitchell, Utgoff, and Banerji, 1983) learns heuristics—that is, control information—for symbolic integration. His technique and Precondition Analysis are both *analytic* rather than *empirical* as defined by Mitchell (1983). However, LEX2 has nothing corresponding to a schema and doesn't learn *sequences* of operator applications; it only learns when to apply individual methods.[14] LEX2 also has the restriction that the operators are "invertible;" that is, given the state after the application of an operator, it should be possible to discover the state before the operator application. The LP methods don't satisfy this condition, as a method may have used any of a large number of rules. LEX2 also uses several examples to learn, although in theory it need not.

22.7 RESULTS

LP has successfully learned many equation-solving methods. These have allowed LP to solve problems that can't be solved by PRESS. It has also been able to learn some of its initial methods,[15] thus "rebuilding" itself from a lower level. The methods it learns are not quite as efficient as the original methods (which have been handcrafted for PRESS), but they are quite usable.

Thus Precondition Analysis has proved useful in the domain of equation solving. However, the author believes that the technique can be applied in many other domains. He plans in the near future to build a Precondition Analysis shell to which domain knowledge can be added.

---

[14]While learning when to apply an individual operator, LEX2 in effect assumes that the operator is to be used as part of a certain given sequence. However, it retains no information about the sequence and has to rederive it during the problem-solving phase.

[15]The user can turn off any of LP's methods. The program then effectively has no knowledge of these methods.

22.8 CONCLUSIONS

This chapter has presented the learning technique of Precondition Analysis, which has been implemented in the equation-solving program LP. Precondition Analysis learns control information in the form of new methods and learns strategies in the form of schemata. This knowledge can be obtained from a single example.

LP is a version of PRESS that learns new methods and constructs equation-solving plans. LP has successfully learned a number of methods and plans that it has used to solve new equations. Precondition Analysis and LP are described in more detail in Silver (1984).

ACKNOWLEDGMENTS

The author would like to thank all members of the Mathematical Reasoning Group at Edinburgh for their help with this work. Alan Bundy, Leon Sterling, Lawrence Byrd, and Lincoln Wallen have been particularly helpful. He would also like to thank Tom Mitchell for his useful comments on a draft of this paper.

This work was supported by the Science and Engineering Research Council, who provided grant GR/C/20826 and a Research Studentship for the author.

References

Boyer, R. S., and Moore, J. S., *A Computational Logic,* ACM Monograph Series, Academic Press, New York, 1979.

Brazdil, P., "Experimental Learning Model," *AISB/GI,* Society for the Study of Artificial Intelligence and the Simulation of Behavior, pp. 46–60, 1978.

Bundy, A., "Analysing Mathematical Proofs (or Reading Between the Lines)," Research Paper 2, Department of Artificial Intelligence, University of Edinburgh, 1975.

Bundy, A., and Welham, B., "Using Meta-level Inference for Selective Application of Multiple Rewrite Rules in Algebraic Manipulation," *Artificial Intelligence,* Vol. 16, No. 2, pp. 189–212, 1981.

Clocksin, W. F., and Mellish, C. S., *Programming in Prolog,* Springer Verlag, Berlin, 1981.

DeJong, G., "An Approach to Learning from Observation," *Proceedings of the International Machine Learning Workshop,* R. S. Michalski (Ed.), Allerton House, University of Illinois at Urbana-Champaign, pp. 171–76, June 22–24, 1983. (An updated version of this paper appears as chapter 19 of this volume.)

Fikes, R. E., Hart, P. E., and Nilsson, N. J., "Learning and Executing Generalized Robot Plans," *Artificial Intelligence,* Vol. 3, pp. 251–88, 1972.

Langley, P., "Learning Effective Search Heuristics," *Proceedings of the Eighth IJCAI,* Karlsruhe, W. Ger., pp. 419–21, 1983.

Mitchell, T. M., "Version Spaces: An Approach to Concept Learning," Ph.D. diss., Stanford University, 1978.

————, "Learning and Problem Solving," *Proceedings of the Eighth IJCAI,* Karlsruhe, W. Ger., pp. 1139–52, 1983.

Mitchell, T. M., Utgoff, P. E., and Banerji, R., "Learning by Experimentation: Acquiring and Refining Problem-Solving Heuristics," in *Machine Learning: An Artificial Intelligence Approach,* R. S. Michalski, J. G. Carbonell, and T. M. Mitchell (Eds.), Tioga, Palo Alto, Calif., 1983.

Neves, D. M., "A Computer Program That Learns Algebraic Procedures by Examining Examples and Working Problems in a Textbook," *Proceedings of the Second National Conference, Canadian Society for Computational Studies of Intelligence,* Toronto, pp., 191–95, 1978.

Silver, B., "Using Meta-Level Inference to Constrain Search and to Learn Strategies in Equation Solving," Ph.D. diss., Department of Artificial Intelligence, University of Edinburgh, 1984.

Sterling, L.; Bundy, A.; Byrd, L.; O'Keefe, R.; and Silver, B., "Solving Symbolic Equations with PRESS," *Computer Algebra,* Lecture Notes in Computer Science, No. 144, Springer Verlag, Berlin, 1982.

Winston, P., "Learning Structural Descriptions from Examples," in *The Psychology of Computer Vision,* P. Winston (Ed.), McGraw-Hill, New York, 1975.

BIBLIOGRAPHY OF RECENT MACHINE LEARNING RESEARCH

Smadar T. Kedar-Cabelli
Sridhar Mahadevan
Rutgers University

1. INTRODUCTION

The aim of this bibliography is to provide a resource consisting mainly of recent research contributions in machine learning (1980–1984). It is patterned closely after the bibliography in *Machine Learning: An Artificial Intelligence Approach* (Michalski, Carbonell, and Mitchell, 1983), referred to here as *Machine Learning I*. The current bibliography complements the earlier bibliography by emphasizing recent additions to machine learning research. The emphasis is primarily on research in machine learning from the artificial intelligence perspective, although some contributions from related disciplines such as psychology, cognitive science, philosophy, and mathematics are also included. The selection is representative rather than exhaustive. To round out the bibliography, several classics in machine learning (seminal papers published prior to 1980) and a few carefully selected overviews and background materials have been included. It is hoped that the reader will find the bibliography a handy reference to machine learning research.

The editors of this bibliography gratefully acknowledge the help of all those who provided useful suggestions. In particular they thank Tom Mitchell, Ryszard Michalski, Jaime Carbonell, Tom Dietterich, Paul Utgoff, and Rich Keller. In addition, they would like to thank Paul Utgoff for his help in all phases of the bibliographic process.

As with any work of this kind, some references are inevitably overlooked. The editors apologize in advance to the authors of those works, and to the readers, for any omissions.

2. A ROAD MAP TO THE LITERATURE

Much machine learning research is published in conference proceedings on artificial intelligence. These include the *Proceedings of the International Joint Conference on Artificial Intelligence* (*IJCAI*), published biannually and the *Proceedings of the National Conference on Artificial Intelligence* (*AAAI*), published annually. In addition, research has been presented at two workshops on machine learning: the First International Machine Learning Workshop, held in 1980 in Pittsburgh, Pennsylvania, and the Second International Machine Learning Workshop, held in 1983 in Allerton House, Urbana, Illinois. Selected papers from the first workshop were revised and collected into *Machine Learning I*. Papers from the second workshop were initially published in 1983 as the *Proceedings of the International Machine Learning Workshop*. Selected papers from the second workshop were revised and collected to produce this volume. In addition, the reader will find the chapter "Learning and Inductive Inference" in *The Handbook of Artificial Intelligence* (Cohen and Feigenbaum, 1982) an important source material, particularly for earlier work. Machine learning articles are also found in various AI journals, the most prominent being *Artificial Intelligence*.

3. EXPLANATION OF THE CATEGORIES

Each bibliographic entry is categorized along three dimensions: the *learning strategy* it is describing (or how the learning is done); the *domain of application* (or what is being learned); and the *research methodology* (or how the research is performed). Each of these dimensions is divided into several categories. Each category is identified by a code letter, followed by a brief explanation and a list of key words commonly used in the field to describe work in this category. (In addition, categories under "learning strategy" are collected into three supercategories, explained in chapter 1 of this book.) For example, in the reference "A Computational Model of Problem Solving by Analogy" by J. G. Carbonell, the learning strategy is "analogy" (code letter **a**), the domain of application is "problem solving" (code letter **s**), and the research methodology is "experimental AI" (which is given no code letter since it is assumed to be the default methodology in machine learning).

A list of the categories is provided below. Under each category are listed the numbers of the references belonging to this category. Following that are the references. Next to each reference in the left margin are the code letters of the categories to which the reference belongs. For example, "A Computational Model of Problem Solving by Analogy" will be mentioned under both the **a** and the **s** categories, and the code letters **as** will appear next to this reference.

One final note: The categorization used here differs slightly from that used in the bibliography of *Machine Learning I*. This is due partly to the fast evolution of the field and partly to the editors' differing views of how the field is organized. A rough correspondence of the code letters of the categories in the two bibliographies is as follows:

Categories *Machine Learning I*	Categories *Machine Learning II*	Meaning
a	a	Learning by analogy
b	b	Background material
c	e	Learning from examples
d	d	Learning by discovery
e	i	Intelligent computer-assisted instruction
g	n	Learning of natural language
h	s	Learning of skills
k	k	Knowledge acquisition for expert systems
l	n	Learning of natural language
m	m	Cognitive modeling
o	o	Overviews
p	p	Learning of procedures
q	c	Learning from observation
r	c	Conceptual clustering
–	t	Learning by being told
–	r	Learning by reformulation
–	g	Genetic algorithms
–	l	Research employing formal logic
–	f	Philosophical aspects of learning

4. THE CATEGORIES

LEARNING STRATEGY

Learning by Induction:

Category **e. Learning from examples:** The learner uses training examples provided by a teacher or the environment in order to learn. Some commonly used key words are *learning from examples, inductive inference, inductive learning, generalization, concept acquisition, characterization, learning by experimentation, empirical generalization,* and *concept learning.*

{2, 13, 14, 15, 17, 18, 22, 23, 24, 25, 26, 27, 29, 30, 36, 48, 59, 61, 62, 63, 66, 67, 68, 70, 71, 74, 92, 106, 108, 111, 112, 115, 117, 118, 141, 151, 163, 172, 173, 174, 176, 180, 184, 190, 195, 196, 197, 198, 200, 201, 203, 215, 225, 226, 230, 231, 232, 233, 234, 235, 243, 246, 253, 254, 255, 256, 271, 272, 273, 281, 283, 286, 288, 289, 291, 293, 294, 295, 297, 298, 304, 305, 308, 310, 311, 312}

Category **c. Learning from observation:** The learner is provided with unclassified examples and must itself classify examples by observing similarities and differences among them. Some commonly used key words are *learning from observation, learning by classification, taxonomic classification, conceptual clustering, statistical approaches to clustering,* and *unsupervised learning.*

{148, 149, 150, 151, 162, 171, 173, 175, 176, 177, 178, 181, 232, 233, 234, 235, 236, 237, 238, 239, 290, 291, 305}

Category **d. Learning by discovery:** The learner investigates a domain in an unguided, exploratory fashion and discovers new concepts and relationships among them. Some commonly used key words are *discovery* and *theory formation.*

{2, 3, 4, 28, 55, 58, 70, 72, 73, 77, 132, 133, 136, 137, 139, 140, 142, 144, 149, 152, 153, 154, 156, 157, 159, 160, 161, 241, 268, 269, 270}

Learning by Deduction:

Category **t. Learning by being told:** The learner uses knowledge provided to it, such as a theory of the domain, advice, or instructions, in order to learn. Some commonly used key words are *learning by being told, learning by taking advice, operationalization, goal-directed generalization, explanation-based generalization, model-driven learning, learning from instructions,* and *supervised learning.*

{8, 10, 11, 72, 81, 94, 95, 99, 100, 110, 164, 166, 174, 194, 204, 206, 207, 208, 209, 210, 221, 251, 252, 289}

Category **r. Learning by reformulation:** The learner reformulates and restructures already-available knowledge in order to learn. Some commonly used key words are *problem reformulation, creating macro-operators, chunking, knowledge compilation, caching (memo functions), proceduralization, reconstructive memory, failure-driven learning,* and *shifts in representation.*

{1, 19, 54, 59, 61, 62, 63, 82, 86, 103, 119, 120, 121, 122, 123, 124, 126, 127, 151, 155, 158, 169, 212, 214, 218, 227, 242, 244, 245, 246, 247, 251, 252, 255, 257, 258, 259, 263, 264, 291, 294, 295, 297, 298}

Learning by Analogy:

Category **a. Learning by analogy:** The learner reasons by analogy in order to learn concepts and problem-solving strategies. Some commonly used key words are *concept learning by analogy, analogical problem solving, structure mapping, case-based reasoning* and *reminding.*

{16, 37, 38, 41, 42, 43, 45, 47, 51, 55, 65, 75, 78, 83, 86, 88, 89, 90, 102, 104, 107, 109, 116, 130, 131, 169, 170, 205, 248, 249, 300, 309, 310, 311, 312}

DOMAIN OF APPLICATION:

Category **s. Learning of skills:** Strategies, heuristics, production rules, in problem solving, planning, game playing, theorem proving.

{7, 8, 10, 11, 15, 16, 17, 19, 32, 34, 36, 39, 41, 42, 43, 45, 47, 49, 51, 66, 74, 75, 77, 82, 85, 89, 93, 99, 110, 111, 112, 122, 123, 124, 126, 127, 128, 134, 135, 141, 145, 146, 163, 164, 194, 195, 196, 198, 201, 202, 203, 204, 206, 207, 208, 209, 210, 213, 215, 218, 221, 230, 231, 234, 236, 237, 238, 239, 240, 245, 247, 249, 256, 262, 271, 272, 273, 280, 281, 284, 292, 294, 295, 298, 300, 301, 302, 303}

Category **k. Learning and knowledge acquisition for expert systems:** Expertise acquisition.

{12, 22, 34, 50, 51, 56, 57, 58, 85, 94, 95, 98, 101, 113, 125, 174, 182, 190, 191, 204, 226, 227, 250, 277}

Category **n. Learning of natural language:** Natural language acquisition, syntax acquisition, grammatical inference, learning of word meanings.

{6, 23, 24, 25, 54, 59, 60, 61, 62, 63, 80, 92, 102, 130, 131, 150, 222, 242, 257, 258, 259, 266, 267, 286}

Category **p. Learning of procedures:** Program synthesis, automatic programming learning of robot procedures.

{3, 4, 13, 27, 30, 65, 72, 73, 81, 134, 212, 223, 292, 301}

Category **i. Instruction:** Intelligent computer-assisted instruction (ICAI).

{31, 39, 50, 250, 278, 279, 282}

RESEARCH METHODOLOGY

Unless otherwise indicated, the research methodology is experimental AI. Typically this involves the development of computer models of learning (often in specific task domains) and the creation of computer programs with learning capabilities as the primary means of validating the research.

Category **l.** Research employing formal **logic,** automata theory, or other formal systems as its primary means of validation.

{24, 26, 48, 91, 92, 116, 118, 147, 168, 222, 268, 269, 270, 299}

Category **m.** Research employing psychological experiments of human learning as its primary means of validation. Some common key words are *cognitive modeling* and *cognitive psychology.*

{5, 6, 7, 8, 9, 10, 11, 15, 32, 33, 37, 38, 39, 49, 64, 75, 80, 83, 87, 88, 89, 90, 97, 107, 114, 115, 119, 120, 121, 135, 138, 145, 146, 147, 213, 214, 215, 217, 218, 220,

244, 246, 248, 249, 257, 258, 259, 266, 267, 280, 282, 283, 284, 287, 301, 302, 303}

Category **g.** Research influenced by biological models, in particular **genetic** or neural models. Some commonly used key words are *genetic algorithms, neural models,* and *adaptive systems.*

{40, 96, 105, 165, 224, 239, 285}

OTHER:

Category **f. Philosophical** or epistemological discussions of machine learning.

{52, 55, 91, 129, 168, 229, 241, 263, 264}

Category **b. Background** and general material: Selected material in artificial intelligence and related disciplines needed as background for machine learning research.

{20, 21, 33, 53, 76, 79, 87, 93, 101, 104, 128, 129, 130, 131, 166, 167, 168, 179, 188, 192, 193, 203, 205, 216, 217, 219, 220, 223, 228, 229, 257, 258, 261, 265, 274, 275, 306, 307}

Category **o. Overviews,** critiques, and surveys of work in machine learning.

{7, 9, 14, 18, 35, 36, 40, 44, 46, 67, 68, 69, 71, 84, 106, 113, 114, 117, 138, 143, 153, 179, 180, 183, 185, 186, 187, 188, 189, 199, 200, 202, 211, 224, 228, 240, 241, 260, 273, 276, 287, 296}

5. References

br   1. **Amarel, S.,** "On Representation of Problems of Reasoning about Actions," in *Machine Intelligence 3,* D. Michie (Ed.), University of Edinburgh Press, Edinburgh, 1968.

de   2. **Amarel, S.,** "Problems of Representation in Heuristic Problem Solving: Related Issues in the Development of Expert Systems," in *Methods of Heuristics,* R. Groner, M. Groner, and W. F. Bischof (Eds.), Erlbaum, Hillsdale, N.J., 1983.

dp   3. **Amarel, S.,** "Expert Behavior and Problem Representation," in *Human and Artificial Intelligence,* A. Elithorn and R. Banerji (Eds.), North–Holland, Amsterdam, 1984.

dp   4. **Amarel, S.,** "Program Synthesis as a Theory Formation Task: Problem Representations and Solution Methods," In *Machine Learning: An Artificial Intelligence Approach,* Vol. II, R. S. Michalski, J. G. Carbonell, and T. M. Mitchell (Eds.), Morgan Kaufmann, Los Altos, Calif., 1986. (An earlier version appeared in

Proceedings of the International Machine Learning Workshop, R. S. Michalski (Ed.), Allerton House, University of Illinois at Urbana-Champaign, June 22–24, 1983).

m   5. **Anderson, J. R., Kline, P. J., and Beasley, C. M.,** "A General Learning Theory and Its Application to Schema Abstraction," in *The Psychology of Learning and Motivation,* G. H. Bower (Ed.), Academic Press, New York, 1979.

mn   6. **Anderson, J. R.,** "A Theory of Language Acquisition Based on General Learning Principles," *Proceedings of the Seventh IJCAI,* Vancouver, B.C., pp. 97–103, 1981.

mos   7. **Anderson, J. R.** (Ed.), *Cognitive Skills and Their Acquisition,* Erlbaum, Hillsdale, N.J., 1981.

mst   8. **Anderson, J. R., Greeno, J. G., Kline, P. J., and Neves, D. M.,** "Acquisition of Problem-Solving Skill," in *Cognitive Skills and Their Acquisition,* J. R. Anderson (Ed.), Erlbaum, Hillsdale, N.J., 1981.

mos   9. **Anderson, J. R.,** *The Architecture of Cognition,* Harvard University Press, Cambridge, 1983.

mst   10. **Anderson, J. R.,** "Acquisition of Proof Skills in Geometry," in *Machine Learning: An Artificial Intelligence Approach,* R. S. Michalski, J. G. Carbonell, and T. M. Mitchell (Eds.), Tioga, Palo Alto, Calif., 1983.

mst   11. **Anderson, J. R.,** "Knowledge Compilation: The General Learning Mechanism. " In *Machine Learning: An Artificial Intelligence Approach,* Vol. II, R. S. Michalski, J. G. Carbonell, and T. M. Mitchell (Eds.), Morgan Kaufmann, Los Altos, Calif., 1986. (An earlier version appeared in *Proceedings of the International Machine Learning Workshop,* R. S. Michalski (Ed.), Allerton House, University of Illinois at Urbana-Champaign, June 22–24, 1983.)

k   12. **Andreae, J. H.,** "The Development of Intelligent Interfaces Between Operator Environments," Technical Report Man-Machine Studies, Progress Report UC-DSE-24, Department of Electrical and Electronic Engineering, University of Canterbury, Christchurch, New Zealand, November 1984.

ep   13. **Andreae, P. M.,** "Constraint Limited Generalization: Acquiring Procedures from Examples," *Proceedings of AAAI-84,* Austin, Tex., pp. 6–10, 1984.

eo
14. **Angluin, D., and Smith, C. H.,** "Inductive Inference: Theory and Methods," *ACM Computing Surveys,* Vol. 15, No. 3, pp. 237–70, September 1983.

ems
15. **Anzai, Y., and Simon, H. A.,** "The Theory of Learning by Doing," *Psychological Review,* Vol. 86, No. 2, pp. 124–40, March 1979.

as
16. **Araya, A. A.,** "Learning by Controlled Transference of Knowledge between Domains," *Proceedings of the Eighth IJCAI,* Karlsruhe, W. Ger., pp. 439–43, 1983.

es
17. **Araya, A. A.,** "Learning Problem Classes by Means of Experimentation and Generalization," *Proceedings of AAAI-84,* Austin, Tex., pp. 11–15, 1984.

eo
18. **Banerji, R. B., and Mitchell, T. M.,** "Description Languages and Learning Algorithms: A Paradigm for Comparison," *International Journal of Policy Analysis and Information Systems,* Vol. 4, No. 2, pp. 124–40, June 1980.

rs
19. **Banerji, R. B.,** "GPS and the Psychology of the Rubik Cubist: A Study in Reasoning About Actions," in *Human and Artificial Intelligence,* A. Elithorn and R. B. Banerji (Eds.), North–Holland, Amsterdam, 1984.

b
20. **Barr, A., and Feigenbaum, E. A.** (Eds.), *The Handbook of Artificial Intelligence,* Vol. 1, Kaufmann, Los Altos, Calif., 1981.

b
21. **Barr, A., and Feigenbaum, E. A.** (Eds.), *The Handbook of Artificial Intelligence,* Vol. II, Kaufmann, Los Altos, Calif., 1982.

ek
22. **Benjamin, D. P., and Harrison, M. C.,** "A Production System for Learning Plans from an Expert," *Proceedings of AAAI-83,* Washington, D.C., pp. 22–26, 1983.

en
23. **Berwick, R. C.,** "Learning Word Meanings from Examples," *Proceedings of the Eighth IJCAI,* Karlsruhe, W. Ger., pp. 459–61, 1983.

eln
24. **Berwick, R. C.,** "Locality Principles and the Acquisition of Syntactic Knowledge," Ph.D. diss., Department of Computer Science, MIT, 1983.

en
25. **Berwick, R. C.,** "Domain-Independent Learning and the Subset Principle," in *Machine Learning: An Artificial Intelligence Approach,* Vol. II, R. S. Michalski, J. G. Carbonell, and T. M. Mitchell (Eds.), Morgan Kaufmann, Los Altos, Calif., 1986. (Original version appeared in *Proceedings of the International*

Machine Learning Workshop, R. S. Michalski (Ed.), Allerton House, University of Illinois at Urbana-Champaign, June 22–24, 1983.)

el   26. **Blum, L., and Blum, M.,** "Toward a Mathematical Theory of Inductive Inference," *Information and Control,* Vol. 28, pp. 125–55, 1975.

ep   27. **Bond, A. H., and Mott, D. H.,** "Learning of Sensory-Motor Schemas in a Mobile Robot," *Proceedings of the Seventh IJCAI,* Vancouver, B.C., pp. 159–61, 1981.

d   28. **Bradshaw, G. L., Langley, P. W., and Simon, H. A.,** "BACON. 4: The Discovery of Intrinsic Properties," *Proceedings of the Canadian Society for Computational Studies of Intelligence,* Victoria, B.C., pp. 19–25, 1980.

e   29. **Brazdil, P.,** "Experimental Learning Model," *Proceedings of the Society for the Study of AI and Simulation of Behavior (AISB) Conference,* 1978.

ep   30. **Brazdil, P.,** "A Model for Error Detection and Correction," Ph.D. diss., Department of Computer Science, University of Edinburgh, 1981.

i   31. **Brown, J. S., and Burton, R. R.,** "Multiple Representations of Knowledge for Tutorial Reasoning," in *Representation and Understanding,* D. G. Bobrow and A. Collins (Eds.), Academic Press, New York, 1975.

ms   32. **Brown, J. S., and VanLehn, K.,** "Repair Theory: A Generative Theory of Bugs in Procedural Skills," *Cognitive Science,* Vol. 4, No. 4, pp. 379–426, October-December 1980.

bm   33. **Bruner, J. S., Goodnow, J. J., and Austin, G. A.,** *A Study of Thinking,* Wiley, New York, 1956.

ks   34. **Buchanan, B. G., and Mitchell, T. M.,** "Model-Directed Learning of Production Rules," in *Pattern-Directed Inference Systems,* D. A. Waterman and F. Hayes-Roth (Eds.), Academic Press, New York, 1978.

o   35. **Buchanan, B. G., Mitchell, T. M., Smith, R. G., and Johnson, C. R., Jr.,** "Models of Learning Systems," Technical Report STAN-CS-79-692, Department of Computer Science, Stanford University, 1979.

eos   36. **Bundy, A., and Silver, B.,** "A Critical Survey of Rule Learning Programs," *Proceedings of the Fifth European Conference on AI,* Paris, pp. 151–57, 1982.

am   37. **Burstein, M. H.,** "A Model of Learning by Incremental Analogical Reasoning and Debugging," *Proceedings of AAAI-83,* Washington, D.C., pp. 45–48, 1983.

am   38. **Burstein, M. H.,** "Concept Formation by Incremental Analogical Reasoning and Debugging," in *Machine Learning: An Artificial Intelligence Approach,* Vol. II, R. S. Michalski, J. G. Carbonell, and T. M. Mitchell (Eds.), Morgan Kaufmann, Los Altos, Calif., 1986. (An earlier version appeared in *Proceedings of the International Machine Learning Workshop,* R. S. Michalski (Ed.), Allerton House, University of Illinois at Urbana-Champaign, June 22–24, 1983.)

ims   39. **Burton, R. R.,** "Diagnosing Bugs in a Simple Procedural Skill," in *Intelligent Tutoring Systems,* D. H. Sleeman and J. S. Brown (Eds.), Academic Press, New York, 1982.

go   40. **Caianiello, E. R., and Musso, G.,** *Cybernetic Systems: Recognition, Learning, Self-Organization,* Wiley, New York, 1984.

as   41. **Carbonell, J. G.,** "A Computational Model of Problem Solving by Analogy," *Proceedings of the Seventh IJCAI,* Vancouver, B.C., pp. 147–52, 1981.

as   42. **Carbonell, J. G.,** "Experiential Learning in Analogical Problem Solving," *Proceedings of AAAI-82,* Pittsburgh, Pa., pp. 168–71, 1982.

as   43. **Carbonell, J. G.,** "Learning by Analogy: Formulating and Generalizing Plans from Past Experience," in *Machine Learning: An Artificial Intelligence Approach,* R. S. Michalski, J. G. Carbonell, and T. M. Mitchell (Eds.), Tioga, Palo Alto, Calif., 1983.

o   44. **Carbonell, J. G., Michalski, R. S., and Mitchell, T. M.,** "An Overview of Machine Learning," in *Machine Learning: An Artificial Intelligence Approach,* R. S. Michalski, J. G. Carbonell, and T. M. Mitchell (Eds.), Tioga, Palo Alto, Calif., 1983.

as   45. **Carbonell, J. G.,** "Derivational Analogy and Its Role in Problem Solving," *Proceedings of AAAI-83,* Washington, D.C., pp. 64–69, 1983.

o   46. **Carbonell, J. G., Michalski, R. S., and Mitchell, T. M.,**
     "Machine Learning: A Historical and Methodological Analysis,"
     AI Magazine, Vol. 4, No. 3, pp. 69–79, Fall 1983.

as   47. **Carbonell, J. G.,** "Analogy in Problem Solving. " In *Machine
     Learning: An Artificial Intelligence Approach,* Vol. II, R. S.
     Michalski, J. G. Carbonell, and T. M. Mitchell (Eds.), Morgan
     Kaufmann, Los Altos, Calif., 1986. (An earlier version appeared in
     Proceedings of the International Machine Learning Workshop,
     R. S. Michalski (Ed.), Allerton House, University of Illinois at
     Urbana-Champaign, June 22–24, 1983.)

el   48. **Case, J., and Smith, C.,** "Comparison of Identification Criteria
     for Mechanized Inductive Inference," *Theoretical Computer Sci-
     ence,* Vol. 25, No. 2, pp. 193–220, March 1983.

ms   49. **Chi, M. T. H., Feltovich, P. J., and Glaser, R.,** "Categorization
     and Representation of Physics Problems by Experts and Novices,"
     Cognitive Science, Vol. 5, No. 2, pp. 121–51, April-June 1981.

ik   50. **Clancey, W. J.,** "Transfer of Rule-Based Expertise Through a
     Tutorial Dialogue," Ph. D. diss., Department of Computer Science,
     Stanford University, 1979. (Also available as Technical Report
     STAN-CS-79-769, Department of Computer Science, Stanford Uni-
     versity, 1979.)

aks 51. **Clements, J.,** "Analogical Reasoning Patterns in Expert Problem
     Solving," *Proceedings of the Fourth Annual Meeting of the Cogni-
     tive Science Society,* Ann Arbor, Mich., 1982.

f   53. **Cohen, B., and Murphy, G. L.,** "Models of Concepts," *Cognitive
     Science,* Vol. 8, No. 1, pp. 27–58, January-March 1984.

b   52. **Cohen, P. R., and Feigenbaum, E. A.** (Eds.), *The Handbook of
     Artificial Intelligence,* Vol. 3, Kaufmann, Los Altos, Calif., 1982.

nr   54. **Cullingford, R. E., Krueger, M. W., Selfridge, M., and
     Bienkowski, M. A.,** "Towards Automating Explanations," *Pro-
     ceedings of the Seventh IJCAI,* Vancouver, B.C., pp. 362–67, 1981.

adf 55. **Darden, L.,** "Reasoning by Analogy in Scientific Theory Con-
     struction," *Proceedings of the International Machine Learning
     Workshop,* R. S. Michalski (Ed.), Allerton House, University of
     Illinois at Urbana-Champaign, June 22–24, 1983.

k   56. **Davis, R.,** "Applications of Meta Level Knowledge to the Con-
     struction, Maintenance and Use of Large Knowledge Bases,"

Ph.D. diss., Department of Computer Science, Stanford University, 1976. (Also appears in *Knowledge-Based Systems in Artificial Intelligence,* R. Davis and D. Lenat, Eds., McGraw-Hill, New York, 1981.)

k

57. **Davis, R.,** "Interactive Transfer of Expertise: Acquisition of New Inference Rules," *Proceedings of the Fifth IJCAI,* Cambridge, Mass., pp. 321–28, 1977.

dk

58. **Davis, R., and Lenat, D. B.,** *Knowledge-Based Systems in Artificial Intelligence.* McGraw-Hill, New York, 1981.

enr

59. **DeJong, G.,** "Automatic Schema Acquisition in a Natural Language Environment," *Proceedings of AAAI-82,* Pittsburgh, Pa., pp. 410–13, 1982.

n

60. **DeJong, G.,** "Skimming Stories in Real Time: An Experiment in Integrated Understanding," Ph.D. diss., Department of Computer Science, Yale University, 1979.

enr

61. **DeJong, G.,** "Generalizations Based on Explanations," *Proceedings of the Seventh IJCAI,* Vancouver, B.C., pp. 67–69, 1981.

enr

62. **DeJong, G.,** "Acquiring Schemata through Understanding and Generalizing Plans," *Proceedings of the Eighth IJCAI,* Karlsruhe, W. Ger., pp. 462–64, 1983.

enr

63. **DeJong, G.,** "An Approach to Learning from Observation," in *Machine Learning: An Artificial Intelligence Approach,* Vol. II, R. S. Michalski, J. G. Carbonell, and T. M. Mitchell (Eds.), Morgan Kaufmann, Los Altos, Calif., 1986. (An earlier version appeared in *Proceedings of the International Machine Learning Workshop,* R. S. Michalski (Ed.), Allerton House, University of Illinois at Urbana-Champaign, June 22–24, 1983.)

m

64. **DeKleer, J., and Brown, J. S.,** "Mental Models of Physical Mechanisms and Their Acquisition," in *Cognitive Skills and Their Acquisition,* J. R. Anderson (Ed.), Erlbaum, Hillsdale, N.J., 1981.

ap

65. **Dershowitz, N.,** "Programming by Analogy," in *Machine Learning: An Artificial Intelligence Approach,* Vol. II, R. S. Michalski, J. G. Carbonell, and T. M. Mitchell (Eds.), Morgan Kaufmann, Los Altos, Calif., 1986. (An earlier version appeared in *Proceedings of the International Machine Learning Workshop,* R. S. Michalski (Ed.), Allerton House, University of Illinois at Urbana-Champaign, June 22–24, 1983.)

es   **66. Dietterich, T. G.,** "Applying General Induction Methods to the Card Game Eleusis," *Proceedings of AAAI-80,* Stanford, Calif., pp. 218–20, 1980.

eo   **67. Dietterich, T. G., and Michalski, R. S.,** "Inductive Learning of Structural Descriptions: Evaluation Criteria and Comparative Review of Selected Methods," *Artificial Intelligence,* Vol. 16, No. 3, pp. 257–94, July 1981.

eo   **68. Dietterich, T. G., and Buchanan, B. G.,** "The Role of the Critic in Learning Systems," Technical Report No. HHP-81-19, (also No. STAN-CS-81-891), Department of Computer Science, Stanford University, 1981.

o   **69. Dietterich, T. G., London, B., Clarkson, K., and Dromey, G.,** "Learning and Inductive Inference," in *The Handbook of Artificial Intelligence,* Vol. 3, P. R. Cohen and E. A. Feigenbaum (Eds.), Kaufmann, Los Altos, Calif., 1982.

de   **70. Dietterich, T. G., and Buchanan, B. G.,** "The Role of Experimentation in Theory Formation," *Proceedings of the International Machine Learning Workshop,* R. S. Michalski (Ed.), Allerton House, University of Illinois at Urbana-Champaign, pp. 147–55, June 22–24, 1983.

eo   **71. Dietterich, T. G., and Michalski, R. S.,** "A Comparative Review of Selected Methods for Learning from Examples," in *Machine Learning: An Artificial Intelligence Approach,* R. S. Michalski, J. G. Carbonell, and T. M. Mitchell (Eds.), Tioga, Palo Alto, Calif., 1983.

dpt   **72. Dietterich, T. G.,** "Constraint Propagation Techniques for Theory-Driven Data Interpretation," Ph.D. diss., Department of Computer Science, Stanford University, 1984.

dp   **73. Dietterich, T. G.,** "Learning About Systems That Contain State Variables," *Proceedings of AAAI-83,* Washington, D.C., pp. 96–100, 1984.

es   **74. Dietterich, T. G., and Michalski, R. S.,** "Learning to Predict Sequences," in *Machine Learning: An Artificial Intelligence Approach,* Vol. II, R. S. Michalski, J. G. Carbonell, and T. M. Mitchell (Eds.), Morgan Kaufmann, Los Altos, Calif., 1986. (An earlier version appeared in *Proceedings of the International Machine Learning Workshop,* R. S. Michalski (Ed.), Allerton House, University of Illinois at Urbana-Champaign, June 22–24, 1982.)

ams **75. Douglas, S. A., and Moran, T. P.,** "Learning Operator Semantics by Analogy," *Proceedings of AAAI-83,* Washington, D.C., pp. 100–103, 1983.

b   **76. Doyle, J.,** "A Truth Maintenance System," *Artificial Intelligence,* Vol. 12, No. 3, pp. 231–72, November 1979.

ds   **77. Ernst, G. W., and Goldstein, M. M.,** "Mechanical Discovery of Classes of Problem-Solving Strategies," *Journal of the ACM,* Vol. 29, No. 1, pp. 1–23, January 1982.

a   **78. Evans, T. G.,** "A Program for the Solution of a Class of Geometric Analogy Intelligence Test Questions," in *Semantic Information Processing,* M. Minsky (Ed.), MIT Press, Cambridge, 1968.

b   **79. Feigenbaum, E. A., and Feldman, J.** (Eds.), *Computers and Thought,* McGraw-Hill, New York, 1963.

mn   **80. Feigenbaum, E. A.,** "The Simulation of Verbal Learning Behavior," In *Computers and Thought,* E. A. Feigenbaum and J. Feldman (Eds.), McGraw-Hill, New York, 1963.

pt   **81. Fickas, S.,** "Automatic Goal-Directed Program Transformation," *Proceedings of AAAI-80,* Stanford, Calif., pp. 68–70, 1980.

rs   **82. Fikes, R. E., Hart, P. E., and Nilsson, N. J.,** "Learning and Executing Generalized Robot Plans," *Artificial Intelligence,* Vol. 3, No. 4, pp. 251–88, Winter 1972.

am   **83. Forbus, K. D., and Gentner, D.,** "Learning Physical Domains: Toward a Theoretic Framework," in *Machine Learning: An Artificial Intelligence Approach,* Vol. II, R. S. Michalski, J. G. Carbonell, and T. M. Mitchell (Eds.), Morgan Kaufmann, Los Altos, Calif., 1986. (An earlier version appeared in *Proceedings of the International Machine Learning Workshop,* R. S. Michalski (Ed.), Allerton House, University of Illinois at Urbana-Champaign, June 22–24, 1983.)

o   **84. Forsyth, R.,** "Machine Learning Systems," *Proceedings of the Association for Library and Information Management (ASLIB),* London, pp. 219–27, 1984.

ks   **85. Friedland, P. E.,** "Acquisition of Procedural Knowledge from Domain Experts," *Proceedings of the Seventh IJCAI,* Vancouver, B.C., pp. 856–61, 1981.

ar   **86. Genesereth, M. R.,** "Metaphors and Models," *Proceedings of AAAI-80,* Stanford, Calif., pp. 208–11, 1980.

bm   87. **Gentner, D., and Stevens, A. L.** (Eds.), *Mental Models,* Erlbaum, Hillsdale, N.J., 1983.

am   88. **Gentner, D.,** "Structure Mapping: A Theoretical Framework for Analogy," *Cognitive Science,* Vol. 7, No. 2, pp. 155–70, April-June 1983.

ams   89. **Gick, M. L., and Holyoak, K. J.,** "Analogical Problem Solving," *Cognitive Psychology,* Vol. 12, pp. 306–55, 1980.

am   90. **Gick, M. L., and Holyoak, K. J.,** "Schema Induction and Analogical Transfer," *Cognitive Psychology,* Vol. 15, pp. 1–38, 1983.

fl   91. **Glymour, C., Kelly, K., and Scheines, R.,** "Two Programs for Testing Hypotheses of Any Logical Forms," *Proceedings of the International Machine Learning Workshop,* R. S. Michalski (Ed.) Allerton House, University of Illinois at Urbana-Champaign, pp. 96–98, June 22–24, 1983.

eln   92. **Gold, E. M.,** "Language Identification in the Limit," *Information and Control,* Vol. 10, pp. 447–74, 1967.

bs   93. **Groner, R., Groner, M., and Bischof, W. F.** (Eds.), *Methods of Heuristics,* Erlbaum, Hillsdale, N.J., 1983.

kt   94. **Haas, N., and Hendrix, G. G.,** "An Approach to Acquiring and Applying Knowledge," *Proceedings of AAAI-80,* Stanford, Calif., pp. 235–39, 1980.

kt   95. **Haas, N., and Hendrix, G. G.,** "Learning by Being Told: Acquiring Knowledge for Information Management," in *Machine Learning: An Artificial Intelligence Approach,* R. S. Michalski, J. G. Carbonell, and T. M. Mitchell (Eds.), Tioga, Palo Alto, Calif., 1983.

g   96. **Hampson, S. E.,** "A Neural Model of Adaptive Behavior," Ph.D. diss., Department of Computer and Information Sciences, University of California, Irvine, 1983.

m   97. **Hanson, S. J., and Timberlake, W.,** "Regulations During Challenge: General Model of Learned Performance Under Schedule Constraints," *Psychological Review,* Vol. 90, pp. 261–82, 1983.

k   98. **Hayes-Roth, F., Klahr, P., and Mostow, D. J.,** "Knowledge Acquisition, Knowledge Programming, and Knowledge Refinement," Technical Report R-2540-NSF, Rand Corporation, 1980.

st   99. **Hayes-Roth, F., Klahr, P., and Mostow, D. J.,** "Advice-Taking and Knowledge Refinement: An Iterative View of Skill

Acquisition," in *Skill Acquisition and Development,* J. A. Anderson (Ed.), Erlbaum, Hillsdale, N.J., 1981.

t   **100. Hayes-Roth, F.,** "Using Proofs and Refutations to Learn from Experience," In *Machine Learning: An Artificial Intelligence Approach,* R. S. Michalski, J. G. Carbonell, and T. M. Mitchell (Eds.), Tioga, Palo Alto, Calif., 1983.

bk   **101. Hayes-Roth, F., Waterman, D. A., and Lenat, D. B.** (Eds.), *Building Expert Systems,* Addison-Wesley, Reading, Mass., 1983.

an   **102. Hobbs, J. R.,** "Metaphor Interpretation as Selective Inferencing," *Proceedings of the Eighth IJCAI,* Karlsruhe, W. Ger., pp. 85–91, 1983.

r   **103. Hofstadter, D. R.,** "The Architecture of Jumbo," *Proceedings of the International Machine Learning Workshop,* R. S. Michalski (Ed.), Allerton House, University of Illinois at Urbana-Champaign, pp. 161–70, June 22–24, 1983.

ab   **104. Hofstadter, D.,** "Analogies and Roles in Human and Machine Thinking," in *Metamagical Themas,* D. Hofstadter (Ed.), Basic Books, New York, 1985.

g   **105. Holland, J. H.,** "Escaping Brittleness: The Possibilities of General-Purpose Learning Algorithms Applied to Parallel Rule-Based Systems," in *Machine Learning: An Artificial Intelligence Approach,* Vol. II, R. S. Michalski, J. G. Carbonell, and T. M. Mitchell (Eds.), Morgan Kaufmann, Los Altos, Calif., 1986. (An earlier version appeared in *Proceedings of the International Machine Learning Workshop,* R. S. Michalski (Ed.), Allerton House, University of Illinois at Urbana-Champaign, June 22–24, 1983.)

eo   **106. Holte, R. C.,** "Artificial Intelligence Approaches to Concept Learning," In *Digital Information Systems,* I. Alexander (Ed.), Prentice-Hall International, Englewood Cliffs, N.J., 1984.

am   **107. Holyoak, K. J.,** "Analogical Thinking and Human Intelligence," in *Advances in the Psychology of Human Intelligence,* R. J. Sternberg (Ed.), Erlbaum, Hillsdale, N.J., 1984.

e   **108. Iba, G. A.,** "Learning Disjunctive Concepts from Examples," Master's thesis, MIT, 1979. (Also available as AI Memo 548, MIT, 1979.)

a   **109. Kedar-Cabelli, S. T.,** "Purpose-Directed Analogy," *Proceedings of the Cognitive Science Society,* Irvine, Calif., pp. 150–159, 1985.

st   110. **Keller, R. M.,** "Learning by Re-expressing Concepts for Efficient Recognition," *Proceedings of AAAI-83,* Washington, D.C., pp. 182–86, 1983.

es   111. **Kibler, D., and Porter, B.,** "Episodic Learning," *Proceedings of AAAI-83,* Washington, D.C., pp. 191–96, 1983.

es   112. **Kibler, D., and Porter, B.,** "Perturbation: A Means for Guiding Generalization," *Proceedings of the Eighth IJCAI,* Karlsruhe, W. Ger., pp. 415–18, 1983.

ko   113. **Kitakami, H., Kunifuji, S., Miyachi, T., and Furukawa, K.,** "Methodology for Implementation of a Knowledge Acquisition System," Technical Report ICOT TR-037, ICOT, Institute for New Generation Computer Technology, Tokyo, 1983.

mo   114. **Klahr, D., Langley, P., and Neches, R. T.** (Eds.), *Self-Modifying Production System Models of Learning and Development,* Bradford Books, Cambridge, Mass., 1983.

em   115. **Kline, P. J.,** "The Superiority of Relative Criteria in Partial Matching and Generalization," *Proceedings of the Seventh IJCAI,* Vancouver, B.C., pp. 296–303, 1981.

al   116. **Kling, R. E.,** "A Paradigm for Reasoning by Analogy," *Artificial Intelligence,* Vol. II, No. 2, pp. 147–78, Fall 1971.

eo   117. **Knapman, J.,** "A Critical Review of Winston's Learning Structural Descriptions from Examples," *AISB Quarterly,* Vol. 31, pp. 319–20, September 1978.

el   118. **Kodratoff, Y., and Ganascia, J. G.,** "Improving the Generalization Step of Learning," in *Machine Learning: An Artificial Intelligence Approach,* Vol. II, R. S. Michalski, J. G. Carbonell, and T. M. Mitchell (Eds.), Morgan Kaufmann, Los Altos, Calif., 1986. (An earlier version appeared in *Proceedings of the International Machine Learning Workshop,* R. S. Michalski (Ed.), Allerton House, University of Illinois at Urbana-Champaign, June 22–24, 1983.)

mr   119. **Kolodner, J. L.,** "Retrieval and Organizational Strategies in Conceptual Memory: A Computer Model," Ph.D. diss., Department of Computer Science, Yale University, 1980. (Also available as Technical Report 187, Yale University, 1980.)

mr   120. **Kolodner, J. L.,** "Maintaining Organization in a Dynamic Long-Term Memory," *Cognitive Science,* Vol. 7, No. 4, pp. 243–80, October-December 1983.

mr   121. **Kolodner, J. L.,** "Reconstructive Memory: A Computer Model,"
                 Cognitive Science, Vol. 7, No. 4, pp. 281–328, October-December
                 1983.

rs   122. **Korf, R. E.,** "Toward a Model of Representation Changes," *Artifi-*
                 cial Intelligence, Vol. 14, No. 1, pp. 41–78, August 1980.

rs   123. **Korf, R. E.,** "Operator Decomposability: A New Type of Prob-
                 lem Structure," *Proceedings of AAAI-83,* Washington, D.C., pp.
                 206–9, 1983.

rs   124. **Korf, R. E.,** *Learning to Solve Problems by Searching for Macro-*
                 Operators, Pitman, Marshfield, Mass., 1985. (Also available as
                 Ph.D. diss., Department of Computer Science, Carnegie-Mellon
                 University, 1983.)

k   125. **Kulikowski, C. A.,** "Knowledge Acquisition and Learning in
                 EXPERT," *Proceedings of the International Machine Learning*
                 Workshop, R. S. Michalski (Ed.), Allerton House, University of
                 Illinois at Urbana-Champaign, pp. 71–73, June 22–24, 1983.

rs   126. **Laird, J. E., and Newell, A.,** "A Universal Weak Method: Sum-
                 mary of Results," *Proceedings of the Eighth IJCAI,* Karlsruhe,
                 W. Ger., pp. 771–73, 1983.

es   127. **Laird, J. E., and Rosenbloom, P. S.,** "Toward Chunking as a
                 General Learning Mechanism," *Proceedings of AAAI-84,* Austin,
                 Tex., pp. 188–92, 1984.

bs   128. **Laird, J. E.,** "Universal Subgoaling," Ph.D. diss., Department of
                 Computer Science, Carnegie-Mellon University, 1984.

bf   129. **Lakatos, I.,** *Proofs and Refutations: The Logic of Mathematical*
                 Discovery, Cambridge University Press, Cambridge, 1976.

abn   130. **Lakoff, G., and Johnson, M.,** *Metaphors We Live By,* Chicago
                 University Press, Chicago, 1980.

abn   131. **Lakoff, G., and Johnson, M.,** "The Metaphorical Structure of
                 the Human Conceptual System," *Cognitive Science,* Vol. 4, No. 2,
                 pp. 195–208, April-June 1980.

d   132. **Langley, P. W.,** "BACON. 1: A General Discovery System," *Pro-*
                 ceedings of the Canadian Society for Computational Studies of
                 Intelligence, Toronto, pp. 173–80, 1978.

d   133. **Langley, P. W.,** "Descriptive Discovery Processes: Experiments
                 in Baconian Science," Ph.D. diss., Department of Psychology,
                 Carnegie-Mellon University, 1979.

ps **134. Langley, P. W., Neches, R., Neves, D., and Anzai, Y.,** "A Domain-Independent Framework for Procedure Learning," *Journal of Policy Analysis and Information Systems,* Vol. 4, No. 2, pp. 163–97, June 1980.

ms **135. Langley, P. W., Nicholas, D., Klahr, D., and Hood, G.,** "A Simulated World for Modelling Learning and Development," *Proceedings of the Third Annual Conference of the Cognitive Science Society,* Berkeley, 1981.

d **136. Langley, P. W.,** "Data-Driven Discovery of Physical Laws," *Cognitive Science,* Vol. 5, No. 1, pp. 31–54, January-March 1981.

d **137. Langley, P. W., Bradshaw, G., and Simon, H. A.,** "BACON. 5: The Discovery of Conservation Laws," *Proceedings of the Seventh IJCAI,* Vancouver, B.C., pp. 121–26, 1981.

mo **138. Langley, P. W., and Simon, H. A.,** "The Central Role of Learning in Cognition," in *Cognitive Skills and Their Acquisition,* J. R. Anderson (Ed.), Erlbaum, Hillsdale, N.J., 1981.

d **139. Langley, P. W., Bradshaw, G., and Simon, H. A.,** "Data-Driven and Expectation-Driven Discovery of Empirical Laws," *Proceedings of the Canadian Society for Computational Studies of Intelligence,* Saskatoon, Saskatchewan, pp. 137–43, 1982.

d **140. Langley, P. W., Zytkow, J., and Simon, H. A.,** "Three Facets of Scientific Discovery," *Proceedings of the Eighth IJCAI,* Karlsruhe, W. Ger., pp. 465–68, 1983.

es **141. Langley, P. W.,** "Learning Effective Search Heuristics," *Proceedings of the Eighth IJCAI,* Karlsruhe, W. Ger., pp. 419–21, 1983.

d **142. Langley, P. W., Simon, H. A., and Bradshaw, G. L.,** "Rediscovering Chemistry with the BACON System," in *Machine Learning: An Artificial Intelligence Approach,* R. S. Michalski, J. G. Carbonell, and T. M. Mitchell (Eds.), Tioga, Palo Alto, Calif., 1983.

o **143. Langley, P. W., and Carbonell, J. G.,** "Approaches to Machine Learning," *Journal of the American Society for Information Science,* Vol. 35, No. 5, pp. 306–16, September 1984.

d **144. Langley, P. W., Zytkow, J., Simon, H. A., and Bradshaw, G. L.,** "The Search for Regularity: Four Aspects of Scientific Discovery," in *Machine Learning: An Artificial Intelligence Approach,* Vol. II, R. S. Michalski, J. G. Carbonell, and

T. M. Mitchell (Eds.), Morgan Kaufmann, Los Altos, Calif., 1986. (An earlier version appeared in *Proceedings of the International Machine Learning Workshop,* R. S. Michalski (Ed.), Allerton House, University of Illinois at Urbana-Champaign, June 22–24, 1983.)

ms   **145. Larkin, J. H., McDermott, J., Simon, D. P., and Simon, H. A.,** "Models of Competence in Solving Physics Problems," *Cognitive Science,* Vol. 4, pp. 317–45, 1980.

ms   **146. Larkin, J. H.,** "Enriching Formal Knowledge: A Model for Learning to Solve Textbook Physics Problems," in *Cognitive Skills and Their Acquisition,* J. R. Anderson (Ed.), Erlbaum, Hillsdale, N.J., 1981.

mn   **147. Lebowitz, M.,** "Generalization and Memory in an Integrated Understanding System," Ph. D. diss., Department of Computer Science, Yale University, 1980.

c   **148. Lebowitz, M.,** "The Nature of Generalization in Understanding," *Proceedings of the Seventh IJCAI,* Vancouver, B.C., pp. 348–53, 1981.

cd   **149. Lebowitz, M.,** "RESEARCHER: An Overview," *Proceedings of AAAI-83,* Washington, D.C., pp. 232–35, 1983.

cn   **150. Lebowitz, M.,** "Generalization from Natural Language Text," *Cognitive Science,* Vol. 7, pp. 1–40, 1983.

cer   **151. Lebowitz, M.,** "Concept Learning in a Rich Input Domain: Generalization-Based Memory," in *Machine Learning: An Artificial Intelligence Approach,* Vol. II, R. S. Michalski, J. G. Carbonell, and T. M. Mitchell (Eds.), Morgan Kaufmann, Los Altos, Calif., 1986. (An earlier version appeared in *Proceedings of the International Machine Learning Workshop,.* R. S. Michalski (Ed.), Allerton House, University of Illinois at Urbana-Champaign, June 22–24, 1983.)

d   **152. Lenat, D. B.,** "AM: An Artificial Intelligence Approach to Discovery in Mathematics as Heuristic Search," Ph. D. diss., Department of Computer Science, Stanford University, 1976.

do   **153. Lenat, D. B.,** "The Ubiquity of Discovery," *Artificial Intelligence,* Vol. 9, No. 3, pp. 257–85, December 1977.

d   **154. Lenat, D. B.,** "Automated Theory Formation in Mathematics," *Proceedings of the Fifth IJCAI,* Cambridge, Mass., pp. 833–42, 1977.

r   155. **Lenat, D. B., Hayes-Roth, F., and Klahr, P.,** "Cognitive
        Economy in Artificial Intelligence Systems," *Proceedings of the
        Sixth IJCAI,* Tokyo, pp. 531–36, 1979.

d   156. **Lenat, D. B.,** "The Role of Heuristics in Learning by Discovery:
        Three Case Studies," in *Machine Learning: An Artificial Intelli-
        gence Approach,* R. S. Michalski, J. G. Carbonell, and T. M.
        Mitchell (Eds.), Tioga, Palo Alto, Calif., 1982.

d   157. **Lenat, D. B.,** "The Nature of Heuristics," *Artificial Intelli-
        gence,* Vol. 19, No. 2, pp. 189–249, October 1982.

r   158. **Lenat, D. B., Hayes-Roth, F. and Klahr, P.,** "Cognitive Economy
        in a Fluid Task Environment," *Proceedings of the International
        Machine Learning Workshop,* R. S. Michalski (Ed.), Allerton
        House, University of Illinois at Urbana-Champaign, pp. 133–46,
        June 22–24, 1983.

d   159. **Lenat, D. B.,** "Theory Formation by Heuristic Search: The Nature
        of Heuristics II: Background and Examples," *Artificial Intelli-
        gence,* Vol. 21, Nos. 1 and 2, pp. 31–59, March 1983.

d   160. **Lenat, D. B.,** "EURISKO: A Program That Learns New Heuris-
        tics and Domain Concepts: The Nature of Heuristics III: Program
        Design and Results," *Artificial Intelligence,* Vol. 21, Nos. 1 and 2,
        pp. 61–98, March 1983.

df   161. **Lenat, D. B., and Brown, J. S.,** "Why AM and Eurisko Appear to
        Work," *Artificial Intelligence,* Vol. 23, No. 3, pp. 269–94, August
        1984. (Also appears in *Proceedings of AAAI-83,* Washington, D.C.,
        1983.)

c   162. **Loisel, R., and Kodratoff, Y.,** "Learning (Complex) Structural
        Descriptions from Examples," *Proceedings of the Seventh IJCAI,*
        Vancouver, B.C., pp. 141–43, 1981.

es   163. **MacDonald, B. A., and Andreae, J. H.,** "The Competence of a
        Multiple Context Learning System," *International Journal on
        General Systems,* No. 7, pp. 123–50, 1981.

st   164. **Mahadevan, S.,** "Verification-Based Learning: A Generalization
        Strategy for Inferring Problem-Reduction Methods," *Proceedings
        of the Ninth IJCAI,* Los Angeles, Calif., pp. 616–23, 1985.

g   165. **Mauldin, M. L.,** "Maintaining Diversity in Genetic Search," *Pro-
        ceedings of AAAI-84,* Austin, Tex., pp. 247–50, 1984.

bt   166. **McCarthy, J.,** "The Advice Taker," in *Semantic Information Pro-
        cessing,* M. Minsky (Ed.), MIT Press, Cambridge, Mass., 1968.

b   167. **McCarthy, J.,** "Programs with Common Sense," in *Semantic Information Processing,* M. Minsky (Ed.), MIT Press, Cambridge, Mass., 1968.

bfl   168. **McCarthy, J., and Hayes, P. J.,** "Some Philosophical Problems from the Standpoint of Artificial Intelligence," in *Machine Intelligence 6,* B. Meltzer and D. Michie (Eds.), Edinburgh University Press, Edinburgh, 1969.

ar   169. **McCarthy, L. T., and Sridharan, N. S.,** "The Representation of an Evolving System of Legal Concepts: II. Prototypes and Deformations," *Proceedings of the Seventh IJCAI,* Vancouver, B.C., pp. 246–53, 1981.

a   170. **McDermott, J.,** "Learning to Use Analogies," *Proceedings of the Sixth IJCAI,* Tokyo, pp. 568–76, 1979.

c   171. **Medin, D. L.,** "Linear Separability and Concept Naturalness," *Proceedings of the International Machine Learning Workshop,* R. S. Michalski (Ed.), Allerton House, University of Illinois at Urbana-Champaign, pp. 213–17, June 22–24, 1983.

e   172. **Michalski, R. S.,** "Discovering Classification Rules Using Variable-Valued Logic System VL1," *Proceedings of the Third IJCAI,* Stanford, Calif., pp. 162–72, 1973.

ce   173. **Michalski, R. S.,** "Pattern Recognition as Rule-Guided Inductive Inference," *IEEE Transactions on Pattern Analysis and Machine Intelligence,* Vol. PAMI-2, No. 4, pp. 349–61, July 1980.

ekt   174. **Michalski, R. S., and Chilausky, R. L.,** "Learning by Being Told and Learning from Examples: An Experimental Comparison of the Two Methods of Knowledge Acquisition in the Context of Developing an Expert System for Soybean Disease Diagnosis," *Policy Analysis and Information Systems,* Vol. 4, No. 2 (special issue on knowledge acquisition and induction), June 1980.

c   175. **Michalski, R. S.,** "Knowledge Acquisition Through Conceptual Clustering: A Theoretical Framework and an Algorithm for Partitioning Data into Conjunctive Concepts," *Policy Analysis and Information Systems,* Vol. 4, No. 3, pp. 219–44, September 1980.

ce   176. **Michalski, R. S., and Stepp, R. E.,** "An Application of AI Techniques to Structuring Objects into an Optimal Conceptual Hierarchy," *Proceedings of the Seventh IJCAI,* Vancouver, B.C., pp. 460–65, 1981.

c   **177. Michalski, R. S., Stepp, R., and Diday, E.,** "A Recent Advance in Data Analysis: Clustering Objects into Classes Characterized by Conjunctive Concepts," in *Progress in Pattern Recognition,* L. Kanal and A. Rosenfeld (Eds.), North-Holland, Amsterdam, 1981.

c   **178. Michalski, R. S., and Stepp, R.,** "Learning from Observation: Conceptual Clustering," in *Machine Learning: An Artificial Intelligence Approach,* R. S. Michalski, J. G. Carbonell, and T. M. Mitchell (Eds.), Tioga, Palo Alto, Calif., 1983.

bo   **179. Michalski, R. S., Carbonell, J. G., and Mitchell, T. M.** (Eds.), *Machine Learning: An Artificial Intelligence Approach,* Tioga, Palo Alto, Calif., 1983.

eo   **180. Michalski, R. S.,** "A Theory and Methodology of Inductive Learning," *Artificial Intelligence,* Vol. 20, No. 2, pp. 111–61, February 1983. (A modified version appears in *Machine Learning: An Artificial Intelligence Approach,* R. S. Michalski, J. G. Carbonell, and T. M. Mitchell (Eds.).)

c   **181. Michalski, R. S., and Stepp, R.,** "Automated Construction of Classification: Conceptual Clustering Versus Numerical Taxonomy," *IEEE Transactions on Pattern Analysis and Machine Intelligence,* Vol. 5, No. 4, pp. 396–410, July 1983.

k   **182. Michalski, R. S., and Baskin, A. B.,** "Integrating Multiple Knowledge Representations and Learning Capabilities in an Expert System: The ADVISE System," *Proceedings of the Eighth IJCAI,* Karlsruhe, W. Ger., pp. 256–58, 1983.

o   **183. Michalski, R. S.** (Ed.), *Proceedings of the International Machine Learning Workshop,* Allerton House, University of Illinois at Urbana-Champaign, June 22–24, 1983.

e   **184. Michalski, R. S.,** "Inductive Learning as Rule-Guided Generalization of Symbolic Descriptions: A Theory and Implementation," in *Automatic Program Techniques,* A. W. Bierman, G. Guiho, and Y. Kodratoff (Eds.), Macmillan, New York, 1984.

o   **185. Michalski, R. S.,** "Learning Strategies and Automated Knowledge Acquisition: An Overview," in *Knowledge-Based Learning Systems,* L. Bolc (Ed.), Springer-Verlag, New York, 1986 (forthcoming).

o   **186. Michalski, R. S.,** "Understanding the Nature of Learning," in *Machine Learning: An Artificial Intelligence Approach,* Vol. II,

R. S. Michalski, J. G. Carbonell, and T. M. Mitchell (Eds.), Morgan Kaufmann, Los Altos, Calif., 1986.

o 187. **Michalski, R. S., Amarel, S., Lenat, D. B., Michie, D., and Winston, P. H.**, "Machine Learning: Challenges of the Eighties," in *Machine Learning: An Artificial Intelligence Approach,* Vol. II, R. S. Michalski, J. G. Carbonell, and T. M. Mitchell (Eds.), Morgan Kaufmann, Los Altos, Calif., 1986.

bo 188. **Michalski, R. S., Carbonell, J. G., and Mitchell, T. M.** (Eds.), *Machine Learning: An Artificial Intelligence Approach,* Vol. II, Morgan Kaufmann, Los Altos, Calif., 1986.

o 189. **Michie, D.**, "The State of the Art in Machine Learning," in *Introductory Readings in Expert Systems,* D. Michie (Ed.), Gordon and Breach, U. K., 1982.

ek 190. **Michie, D.**, "Inductive Rule Generation in the Context of the Fifth Generation," *Proceedings of the International Machine Learning Workshop,* R. S. Michalski (Ed.), Allerton House, University of Illinois at Urbana-Champaign, pp. 65–70, June 22–24, 1983.

k 191. **Michie, D.**, "Automating the Synthesis of Expert Knowledge," *ASLIB Proceedings,* London, pp. 337–43, September 1984.

b 192. **Minsky, M.**, "A Framework for Representing Knowledge," in *The Psychology of Computer Vision,* P. H. Winston (Ed.), McGraw-Hill, New York, 1975.

b 193. **Minsky, M.**, "Society of Mind," Technical Report, Department of Computer Science, MIT, 1985.

st 194. **Minton, S.**, "Constraint-Based Generalization: Learning Game-Playing Plans from Single Examples," *Proceedings of AAAI-84,* Austin, Tex., pp. 251–54, 1984.

es 195. **Mitchell, T. M.**, "Version Spaces: A Candidate Elimination Approach to Rule Learning," *Proceedings of the Fifth IJCAI,* Cambridge, Mass., pp. 305–10, 1977.

es 196. **Mitchell, T. M.**, "Version Spaces: An Approach to Concept Learning," Ph.D. diss., Department of Electrical Engineering, Stanford University, 1978. (Also available as Report STAN-CS-78-711, HPP-79-2, Department of Computer Science, Stanford University, 1978.)

e 197. **Mitchell, T. M.**, "The Need for Biases in Learning Generalizations," Technical Report CBM-TR-117, Rutgers University, 1980.

es   198. **Mitchell, T. M., Utgoff, P. E., Nudel, B., and Banerji, R.,** "Learning Problem-Solving Heuristics Through Practice," *Proceedings of the Seventh IJCAI,* Vancouver, B.C., pp. 127–34, 1981.

o   199. **Mitchell, T., Carbonell, J. G., and Michalski, R.,** "Special Section on Machine Learning," *SIGART Newsletter,* No. 76, pp. 25–64, April 1981.

eo   200. **Mitchell, T. M.,** "Generalization as Search," *Artificial Intelligence,* Vol. 18, No. 2, pp. 203–26, March 1982.

es   201. **Mitchell, T. M., Utgoff, P. E., and Banerji, R. B.,** "Learning by Experimentation: Acquiring and Refining Problem-Solving Heuristics," In *Machine Learning: An Artificial Intelligence Approach,* R. S. Michalski, J. G. Carbonell, and T. M. Mitchell (Eds.), Tioga, Palo Alto, Calif., 1983.

os   202. **Mitchell, T. M.,** "Learning and Problem Solving," *Proceedings of the Eighth IJCAI,* Karlsruhe, W. Ger., pp. 1139–51, 1983.

es   203. **Mitchell, T. M.,** "Toward Combining Empirical and Analytic Methods for Learning Heuristics," in *Human and Artificial Intelligence,* A. Elithorn and R. Banerji (Eds.), North-Holland, Amsterdam, 1984.

kst   204. **Mitchell, T. M., Mahadevan, S., and Steinberg, L.,** "LEAP: A Learning Apprentice for VLSI Design," *Proceedings of the Ninth IJCAI,* Los Angeles, Calif., pp. 573–80, 1985.

ab   205. **Moore, J., and Newell, A.,** "How Can Merlin Understand?" in *Knowledge and Cognition,* L. W. Gregg (Ed.), Erlbaum, Hillsdale, N.J., 1974.

st   206. **Mostow, D. J., and Hayes-Roth, F.,** "Operationalizing Heuristics: Some AI Methods for Assisting AI Programming," *Proceedings of the Sixth IJCAI,* Tokyo, pp. 601–9, 1979.

st   207. **Mostow, D. J.,** "Mechanical Transformation of Task Heuristics into Operational Procedures," Ph.D. diss., Department of Computer Science, Carnegie-Mellon University, 1981.

st   208. **Mostow, D. J.,** "Machine Transformation of Advice into a Heuristic Search Procedure," in *Machine Learning: An Artificial Intelligence Approach,* R. S. Michalski, J. G. Carbonell, and T. M. Mitchell (Eds.), Tioga, Palo Alto, Calif., 1983.

st   209. **Mostow, D. J.,** "Operationalizing Advice: A Problem-Solving Model," *Proceedings of the International Machine Learning*

Workshop, R. S. Michalski (Ed.), Allerton House, University of Illinois at Urbana-Champaign, pp. 110–16, June 22–24, 1983.

st   **210. Mostow, D. J.,** "A Problem-Solver for Making Advice Operational," *Proceedings of AAAI-83,* Washington, D.C., pp. 279–83, 1983.

o   **211. Mostow, D. J.,** "1983 International Machine Learning Workshop: An Informal Report," *SIGART Newsletter,* No. 86, pp. 24–31, October 1983.

pr   **212. Neches, R. T.,** "HPM: A Computational Formalism for Heuristic Procedure Modification," *Proceedings of the Seventh IJCAI,* Vancouver, B.C., pp. 283–88, 1981.

ms   **213. Neches, R.,** "Models of Heuristic Procedure Modification," Ph.D. diss., Department of Computer Science, Carnegie-Mellon University, 1982.

mr   **214. Neves, D. M., and Anderson, J. R.,** "Knowledge Compilation: Mechanisms for the Automatization of Cognitive Skills," in *Cognitive Skills and Their Acquisition,* J. R. Anderson (Ed.), Erlbaum, Hillsdale, N.J., 1981.

ems   **215. Neves, D. M.,** "Learning Procedures from Examples," Ph.D. diss., Department of Computer Science, Carnegie-Mellon University, 1981.

b   **216. Newell, A., and Simon, H.,** *Human Problem Solving.* Prentice-Hall, Englewood Cliffs, N.J., 1972.

bm   **217. Newell, A.,** "Reasoning, Problem Solving and Decision Processes: The Problem Space as a Fundamental Category," in *Attention and Performance VIII,* R. S. Nickerson (Ed.), Erlbaum, Hillsdale, N.J., 1980. (Originally appeared in *Proceedings of the International Symposium on Attention and Performance,* 1978.)

mrs   **218. Newell, A., and Rosenbloom, P.,** "Mechanisms of Skill Acquisition and the Law of Practice," in *Cognitive Skills and Their Acquisition,* J. R. Anderson (Ed.), Erlbaum, Hillsdale, N.J., 1981.

b   **219. Nilsson, N. J.,** *Principles of Artificial Intelligence,* Tioga, Palo Alto, Calif., 1980.

bm   **220. Norman, D. A.** (Ed.), *Perspectives on Cognitive Science,* Erlbaum, Hillsdale, N.J., 1981.

st   **221. O'Rorke, P.,** "Generalization for Explanation-Based Schema Acquisition," *Proceedings of AAAI-84,* Austin, Tex., pp. 260-63, 1984.

ln   222. **Osherson, D. N., and Weinstein, S.,** "Criteria of Language Learning," *Journal of Information and Control,* Vol. 52, No. 2, pp. 123–37, February 1982.

bp   223. **Paige, R.,** "Supercompilers—Extended Abstract," in *Program Transformation and Programming Environment,* P. Pepper (Ed.), Springer-Verlag, New York, 1984.

go   224. **Pettit, E., and Swigger, K. M.,** "An Analysis of Genetic-Based Pattern Tracking and Cognitive-Based Component Tracking Models of Adaptation," *Proceedings of AAAI-83,* Washington, D.C., pp. 327–32, 1983.

e   225. **Plotkin, G. D.,** "A Note on Inductive Generalization," In *Machine Intelligence 5,* B. Meltzer and D. Michie (Eds.), Edinburgh University Press, Edinburgh, 1970.

ek   226. **Politakis, P. G.,** "Using Empirical Analysis to Refine Expert System Knowledge Bases," Ph.D. diss., Department of Computer Science, Rutgers University, 1982. (Also available as Technical Report CBM-TR-130, Rutgers University, 1982.)

ek   227. **Politakis, P., and Weiss, S. M.,** "Using Empirical Analysis to Refine Expert System Knowledge Bases," *Artificial Intelligence,* Vol. 22, No. 1, pp. 23–48, February 1984.

b   228. **Pólya, G.,** *How to Solve It,* 2d. ed., Doubleday, New York, 1957.

bf   229. **Popper, K.,** *The Logic of Scientific Discovery,* 2d ed., Harper and Row, New York, 1968.

es   230. **Porter, B.,** "Learning Problem Solving," Ph.D. diss., Department of Computer and Information Sciences, University of California, Irvine, 1984.

es   231. **Porter, B., and Kibler, D.,** "Learning Operator Transformations," *Proceedings of AAAI-84,* Austin, Tex. pp. 278–82, 1984.

ce   232. **Quinlan, J. R.,** "Discovering Rules from Large Collections of Examples: A Case Study," in *Expert Systems in the Micro Electronic Age,* D. Michie (Ed.), Edinburgh University Press, Edinburgh, 1979.

ce   233. **Quinlan, J. R.,** "Semi-Autonomous Acquisition of Pattern-Based Knowledge," *Australian Computer Bulletin,* April 1980. (Also appears in *Machine Intelligence 10,* D. Michie, J. E. Hayes, and Y.-H. Pao (Eds.), Ellis Harwood Ltd., New York, 1982.)

ces   234. **Quinlan, J. R.,** "Learning Efficient Classification Procedures and Their Application to Chess End-Games," in *Machine*

Learning: An Artificial Intelligence Approach, R. S. Michalski, J. G. Carbonell, and T. M. Mitchell (Eds.), Tioga, Palo Alto, Calif., 1983.

ce   235. **Quinlan, J. R.,** "The Effect of Noise on Concept Learning," in *Machine Learning: An Artificial Intelligence Approach,* Vol. II, R. S. Michalski, J. G. Carbonell, and T. M. Mitchell (Eds.), Morgan Kaufmann, Los Altos, Calif., 1986. (An earlier version appeared in *Proceedings of the International Machine Learning Workshop,* R. S. Michalski (Ed.), Allerton House, University of Illinois at Urbana-Champaign, June 22–24, 1983.)

cs   236. **Rendell, L. A.,** "An Adaptive Plan for State-Space Problems," Ph.D. diss., Department of Computer Science, University of Waterloo, Waterloo, Canada, 1981.

cs   237. **Rendell, L. A.,** "A Learning System Which Accommodates Feature Interactions," *Proceedings of the Eighth IJCAI,* Karlsruhe, W. Ger., pp. 469–72, 1983.

cs   238. **Rendell, L. A.,** "A New Basis for State-Space Learning Systems and a Successful Implementation," *Artificial Intelligence,* Vol. 20, No. 4, pp. 369–92, July 1983.

cgs   239. **Rendell, L. A.,** "A Doubly Layered, Genetic Penetrance Learning System," *Proceedings of AAAI-83,* Washington, D.C., pp. 343–47, 1983.

os   240. **Rendell, L. A.,** "Toward a Unified Approach for Conceptual Knowledge Acquisition," *AI Magazine,* Vol. 4, No. 4, pp. 19–27, Winter 1983.

dfo   241. **Richie, G. D., and Hanna, F. K.,** "AM: A Case Study in AI Methodology," *Artificial Intelligence,* Vol. 23, No. 3, pp. 249–68, August 1984.

nr   242. **Riesbeck, C. K.,** "Failure-Driven Reminding for Incremental Learning," *Proceedings of the Seventh IJCAI,* Vancouver, B.C., pp. 115–20, 1981.

e   243. **Rissland, E. L., and Soloway, E. M.,** "Constrained Example Generation: A Testbed for Studying Issues in Learning," *Proceedings of the Seventh IJCAI,* Vancouver, B.C., pp. 162–64, 1981.

mr   244. **Rosch, E., and Mervis, C. B.,** "Family Resemblances: Studies in the Internal Structure of Categories," *Cognitive Psychology,* Vol. 7, No. 4, pp. 573–605, October 1975.

rs   **245. Rosenbloom, P. S., and Newell, A.,** "Learning by Chunking: Summary of a Task and a Model," *Proceedings of AAAI-82,* Pittsburgh, Pa., pp. 255–58, 1982.

emr   **246. Rosenbloom, P. S.,** "The Chunking of Goal Hierarchies: A Model of Practice and Stimulus-Response Compatibility," Ph.D. diss., Department of Psychology, Carnegie-Mellon University, 1983.

rs   **247. Rosenbloom, P. S., and Newell, A.,** "The Chunking of Goal Hierarchies," in *Machine Learning: An Artificial Intelligence Approach,* Vol. II, R. S. Michalski, J. G. Carbonell, and T. M. Mitchell (Eds.), Morgan Kaufmann, Los Altos, Calif., 1986. (An earlier version appeared in *Proceedings of the International Machine Learning Workshop,* R. S. Michalski (Ed.), Allerton House, University of Illinois at Urbana-Champaign, June 22–24, 1983.)

am   **248. Rumelhart, D. E., and Abrahamson, A. A.,** "A Model for Analogical Reasoning," *Cognitive Psychology,* Vol. 5, pp. 1–28, 1973.

ams   **249. Rumelhart, D. E., and Norman, D. E.,** "Analogical Processes in Learning," in *Cognitive Skills and Their Acquisition,* J. R. Anderson (Ed.), Erlbaum, Hillsdale, N.J., 1981.

ik   **250. Rychener, M. D.,** "The Instructible Production System: A Retrospective Analysis," in *Machine Learning: An Artificial Intelligence Approach,* R. S. Michalski, J. G. Carbonell, and T. M. Mitchell (Eds.), Tioga, Palo Alto, Calif., 1983.

tr   **251. Salzberg, S.,** "Generating Hypotheses to Explain Prediction Failures," *Proceedings of AAAI-83,* Washington, D.C., pp. 352–55, 1983.

rt   **252. Salzberg, S., and Atkinson, D. J.,** "Learning by Building Causal Explanations," *Proceedings of the Sixth European Conference on AI,* Pisa, Italy, pp. 497–500, 1984.

e   **253. Sammut, C.,** "Learning Concepts by Performing Experiments," Ph.D. diss., Department of Computer Science, University of New South Wales, 1981.

e   **254. Sammut, C.,** "Concept Learning by Experiment," *Proceedings of the Seventh IJCAI,* Vancouver, B.C., pp. 104–5, 1981.

er   **255. Sammut, C., and Banerji, R. B.,** "Learning Concepts by Asking Questions," In *Machine Learning: An Artificial Intelligence Approach,* Vol. II, R. S. Michalski, J. G. Carbonell, and

T. M. Mitchell (Eds.), Morgan Kaufmann, Los Altos, Calif., 1986. (An earlier version appeared in *Proceedings of the International Machine Learning Workshop,* R. S. Michalski (Ed.), Allerton House, University of Illinois at Urbana-Champaign, June 22–24, 1983.)

es   256. **Samuel, A. L.,** "Some Studies in Machine Learning Using the Game of Checkers," in *Computers and Thought,* E. A. Feigenbaum and J. Feldman (Eds.), McGraw-Hill, New York, 1963.

bmn   257. **Schank, R. C., and Abelson, R. P.,** *Scripts, Plans, Goals and Understanding,* Erlbaum, Hillsdale, N.J., 1977.

bmnr   258. **Schank, R. C.,** "Language and Memory," *Cognitive Science,* Vol. 4, No. 3, pp. 243–84, July-September 1980.

mnr   259. **Schank, R. C.,** *Dynamic Memory: A Theory of Reminding and Learning in Computers and People,* Cambridge University Press, Cambridge, 1982.

o   260. **Schank, R. C.,** "Looking at Learning," *Proceedings of the Fifth European Conference on AI,* Paris, pp. 11–18, 1982.

b   261. **Schank, R. C.,** "The Current State of AI: One Man's Opinion," *AI Magazine,* Vol. 4, No. 1, pp. 3–8, Winter/Spring 1983.

s   262. **Schmidt, C., Sridharan, N., and Goodson, J.,** "The Plan Recognition Problem," *Artificial Intelligence,* Vol. 11, Nos. 1 and 2, pp. 45–83, August 1978.

fr   263. **Scott, P. D., and Vogt, R. C.,** "Knowledge Oriented Learning," *Proceedings of the Eighth IJCAI,* Karlsruhe, W. Ger., pp. 432–35, August 1983.

fr   264. **Scott, P. D.,** "Learning: The Construction of Aposteriori Knowledge Structures," *Proceedings of AAAI-83,* Washington, D.C., pp. 359–63, 1983.

b   265. **Selfridge, O. G.,** "Pandemonium: A Paradigm for Learning," *Proceedings of the Symposium on the Mechanization of Thought Processes,* D. Blake and A. Uttley (Eds.), London, pp. 511–29, 1959.

mn   266. **Selfridge, M. A.,** "A Process Model of Language Acquisition," Ph.D. diss., Department of Computer Science, Yale University, 1980.

mn   267. **Selfridge, M. A.,** "A Computer Model of Child Language Acquisition," *Proceedings of the Seventh IJCAI,* Vancouver, B.C., pp. 92–95, 1981.

dl   **268. Shapiro, E. Y.,** "Inductive Inference of Theories from Facts,"
Research Report 192, Yale University, 1981.

dl   **269. Shapiro, E. Y.,** "An Algorithm That Infers Theories from Facts,"
Proceedings of the Seventh IJCAI, Vancouver, B.C., pp. 446–51,
1981.

dl   **270. Shapiro, E. Y.,** *Algorithmic Program Debugging,* MIT Press,
Cambridge, 1983.

es   **271. Silver, B.,** "Learning Equation Solving Methods from Examples,"
Proceedings of the Eighth IJCAI, Karlsruhe, W. Ger., pp. 429–31,
1983.

es   **272. Silver, B.,** "Precondition Analysis: Learning Control Information," in *Machine Learning: An Artificial Intelligence Approach,*
Vol. II, R. S. Michalski, J. G. Carbonell, and T. M. Mitchell
(Eds.), Morgan Kaufmann, Los Altos, Calif., 1986. (An earlier
version appeared in *Proceedings of the International Machine
Learning Workshop,* R. S. Michalski (Ed.), Allerton House, University of Illinois at Urbana-Champaign, June 22–24, 1983.)

eos   **273. Simon, H. A., and Lea, G.,** "Problem Solving and Rule Induction: A Unified View," in *Knowledge and Cognition,* L. W. Gregg
(Ed.), Erlbaum, Hillsdale, N.J., 1974.

b   **274. Simon, H. A.,** "Artificial Intelligence Systems That Understand,"
Proceedings of the Fifth IJCAI, Cambridge, Mass., pp. 1059–73,
1977.

b   **275. Simon, H. A.,** *The Sciences of the Artificial,* MIT Press, Cambridge, 1982.

o   **276. Simon, H. A.,** "Why Should Machines Learn?" in *Machine
Learning: An Artificial Intelligence Approach,* R. S. Michalski,
J. G. Carbonell, and T. M. Mitchell (Eds.), Tioga, Palo Alto,
Calif., 1983.

k   **277. Sleeman, D. H.,** "A Rule-Based Task Generation System," *Proceedings of the Seventh IJCAI,* Vancouver, B.C., pp. 882–87, 1981.

i   **278. Sleeman, D. H., and Brown, J. S.,** "Intelligent Tutoring Systems:
An Overview," in *Intelligent Tutoring Systems,* D. H. Sleeman and
J. S. Brown (Eds.), Academic Press, New York, 1981.

i   **279. Sleeman, D. H., and Brown, J. S.** (Eds.), *Intelligent Tutoring Systems,* Academic Press, New York, 1981.

ms   **280. Sleeman, D. H., and Smith, M. J.,** "Modeling Students' Problem Solving," *Artificial Intelligence,* Vol. 16, No. 2, pp. 171–87, May 1981.

es   **281. Sleeman, D. H., Langley, P., and Mitchell, T. M.,** "Learning from Solution Paths: An Approach to the Credit Assignment Problem," *AI Magazine,* Vol. 3, No. 2, pp. 48–52, Spring 1982.

im   **282. Sleeman, D. H.,** "Inferring Student Models for Intelligent Computer-Aided Instruction," in *Machine Learning: An Artificial Intelligence Approach,* R. S. Michalski, J. G. Carbonell, and T. M. Mitchell (Eds.), Tioga, Palo Alto, Calif., 1983.

em   **283. Sleeman, D.,** "Inferring (MAL) Rules from Pupils' Protocols," *Proceedings of the International Machine Learning Workshop,* R. S. Michalski (Ed.), Allerton House, University of Illinois at Urbana-Champaign, pp. 221–27, June 22–24, 1983.

ms   **284. Smith, R. L., Jr.,** "Modeling Student Acquisition of Problem Solving Skills," *Proceedings of AAAI-80,* Stanford, Calif., pp. 221–23, 1980.

g   **285. Smith, S.,** "A Learning System Based on Genetic Algorithms," Ph.D. diss., Department of Computer Science, University of Pittsburgh, 1980.

en   **286. Smith, D.,** "Focuser: A Strategic Interaction Paradigm for Language Acquisition," Ph.D. diss., Department of Computer Science, Rutgers University, 1982.

mo   **287. Snow, R. E., Fredrico, P. A., and Montague, W. E.** (Eds.), *Aptitude, Learning, and Instruction,* Vols. 1 and 2, Erlbaum, Hillsdale, N.J., 1980.

e   **288. Soloway, E. M., and Riseman, E. M.,** "Knowledge-Directed Learning," *SIGART Newsletter,* Vol. 63 (*Proceedings of the Workshop on Pattern-Directed Inference Systems*), pp. 49–55, 1977.

et   **289. Soloway, E. M.,** "Learning = Interpretation + Generalization: A Case Study in Knowledge-Directed Learning," Ph.D. diss., Department of Computer and Information Science, University of Massachusetts, Amherst, 1978. (Also available as Computer and Information Science Report COINS TR-78-13, U. Mass., 1967.)

c   **290. Stepp, R. E.,** "Conjunctive Conceptual Clustering: A Methodology and Experimentation," Ph.D. diss., Department of Computer Science, University of Illinois, Urbana, 1984.

cer   **291. Stepp, R. E., and Michalski, R. S.,** "Conceptual Clustering: Inventing Goal-Oriented Classifications of Structured Objects," in *Machine Learning: An Artificial Intelligence Approach,* Vol. II, R. S. Michalski, J. G. Carbonell, and T. M. Mitchell (Eds.), Morgan Kaufmann, Los Altos, Calif., 1986. (An earlier version appeared in *Proceedings of the International Machine Learning Workshop,* R. S. Michalski (Ed.), Allerton House, University of Illinois at Urbana-Champaign, June 22–24, 1983.)

ps   **292. Sussman, G. J.,** *A Computer Model of Skill Acquisition,* American Elsevier, New York, 1975.

e   **293. Techuci, G.,** "Learning Hierarchical Descriptions from Examples," *Computers and Artificial Intelligence,* Slovenska Akademia Vied, Romania, Vol. 3, No. 3, pp. 211–22, 1984.

ers   **294. Utgott, P. E., and Mitchell, T. M.,** "Acquisition of Appropriate Bias for Inductive Concept Learning," *Proceedings of AAAI-82,* Pittsburgh, Pa., pp. 414–17, 1982.

ers   **295. Utgoff, P. E.,** "Adjusting Bias in Concept Learning," *Proceedings of the Eighth IJCAI,* Karlsruhe, W. Ger., pp. 447–49, 1983.

o   **296. Utgoff, P. E., and Nudel, B.,** "Comprehensive Bibliography of Machine Learning," in *Machine Learning: An Artificial Intelligence Approach,* R. S. Michalski, J. G. Carbonell, and T. M. Mitchell (Eds.), Tioga, Palo Alto, Calif., 1983.

er   **297. Utgoff, P. E.,** "Shift of Bias for Inductive Concept Learning," Ph.D. diss., Department of Computer Science, Rutgers University, 1984.

ers   **298. Utgoff, P. E.,** "Shift of Bias for Inductive Concept Learning," in *Machine Learning: An Artificial Intelligence Approach,* Vol. II, R. S. Michalski, J. G. Carbonell, and T. M. Mitchell (Eds.), Morgan Kaufmann, Los Altos, Calif., 1986. (An earlier version appeared in *Proceedings of the International Machine Learning Workshop,* R. S. Michalski (Ed.), Allerton House, University of Illinois at Urbana-Champaign, June 22–24, 1983.)

l   **299. Valiant, L. G.,** "A Theory of the Learnable," *Communications of the ACM,* Vol. 27, No. 11, pp. 1134–42, November 1984.

as   **300. VanLehn, K., and Brown, J. S.,** "Planning Nets: A Representation for Formalizing Analogies and Semantic Models of Procedural Skills," in *Aptitude Learning and Instruction: Cognitive Processes of Learning and Problem-Solving,* R. E. Snow,

P. A. Frederico, and W. E. Montague (Eds.), Erlbaum, Hillsdale, N.J., 1980.

mp   **301. VanLehn, K.,** "Human Procedural Skill Acquisition: Theory, Model, and Psychological Validation," *Proceedings of AAAI-83,* Washington, D.C., pp. 420–23, 1983.

ms   **302. VanLehn, K.,** "Validating a Theory of Human Skill Acquisition," *Proceedings of the International Machine Learning Workshop,* R. S. Michalski (Ed.), Allerton House, University of Illinois at Urbana-Champaign, June 22–24, 1983.

ms   **303. VanLehn, K.,** "Felicity Conditions for Human Skill Acquisition: Validating an AI-Based Theory," Ph.D. diss., Department of Computer Science, MIT, 1983.

e   **304. Vere, S. A.,** "Multilevel Counterfactuals for Generalizations of Relational Concepts and Productions," *Artificial Intelligence,* Vol. 14, No. 2, pp. 138–64, September 1980.

ce   **305. Waterman, D. A.,** "Generalization Learning Techniques for Automating the Learning of Heuristics," *Artificial Intelligence,* Vol. 1, No. 1/2, pp. 121–70, 1970.

b   **306. Waterman, D. A., and Hayes-Roth, F.** (Eds.), *Pattern-Directed Inference Systems,* Academic Press, New York, 1978.

b   **307. Webber, B. L., and Nilsson, N. J.** (Eds.), *Readings in Artificial Intelligence,* Tioga, Palo Alto, Calif., 1981.

e   **308. Winston, P. H.,** "Learning Structural Descriptions from Examples," in *The Psychology of Computer Vision,* P. H. Winston (Ed.), McGraw-Hill, New York, 1975.

a   **309. Winston, P. H.,** "Learning and Reasoning by Analogy," *Communications of the ACM,* Vol. 23, No. 12, pp. 689–702, December 1980.

ae   **310. Winston, P. H.,** "Learning New Principles from Precedents and Exercises," *Artificial Intelligence,* Vol. 19, No. 3, pp. 321–350, November 1982.

ae   **311. Winston, P. H., Binford, T. O., Katz, B., and Lowry, M.,** "Learning Physical Descriptions from Functional Definitions, Examples, and Precedents," *Proceedings of AAAI-83,* Washington, D.C., pp. 433–39, 1983.

ae 312. **Winston, P. H.**, "Learning by Augmenting Rules and Accumulating Censors," in *Machine Learning: An Artificial Intelligence Approach,* Vol. II, R. S. Michalski, J. G. Carbonell, and T. M. Mitchell (Eds.), Morgan Kaufmann, Los Altos, Calif., 1986. (An earlier version appeared in *Proceedings of the International Machine Learning Workshop,* R. S. Michalski (Ed.), Allerton House, University of Illinois at Urbana-Champaign, June 22–24, 1983.)

UPDATED GLOSSARY OF SELECTED TERMS IN MACHINE LEARNING

This glossary is a modified and updated version of the glossary included in *Machine Learning I*. It was prepared by the editors with the help of some leading researchers in the field. The angle brackets "⟨ ⟩" indicate that the term used in a definition is itself an entry in the glossary. In a few cases, terms in the glossary have not been widely used in the literature but were included because they seem to be particularly descriptive of the important ideas they represent.

Adaptive Systems: Control systems or pattern recognition systems that achieve desired performance by adjusting their internal parameters.

Advice Taking: A form of learning in which the learner modifies its (procedural) behavior according to the (declarative) advice given by an instructor.

Analogical Inference: Mapping information from a known object or process to a less known but similar one.

Analogical Means-ends Analysis: A problem-solving process operating in the ⟨Analogical Problem Space⟩ akin to ⟨Means-ends Analysis⟩. A solution to a new problem is obtained via the transformation of the solution of a similar problem using operators that reduce differences between corresponding solution descriptions.

Analogical Problem Space: A problem space whose states are descriptions of problem solutions and whose operators transform one problem solution into a closely related one.

Attribute: A variable or one-argument ⟨Descriptor⟩ used to characterize an object or a process. For example, the *color* (of an object) or the *duration* (of a process) are attributes.

Caching (Memo Functions):   Storing the answer to frequently occurring questions (problems) in order to avoid a replication of past efforts; an example of ⟨Rote Learning⟩.

Causal Analysis: Tracing the probable causes of observed events, occasionally used in ⟨Credit (Blame) Assignment⟩.

Characteristic Description: A ⟨Concept Description⟩ that states properties characterizing all instances of a given concept (or class). (Cf. Discriminant Description).

Chunking: Grouping lower-level descriptions (patterns, operators, goals) into higher-level descriptions.

Complete Generalization: A description characterizing all ⟨Positive Examples⟩ of a given class, whether or not it also characterizes some ⟨Negative Examples⟩.

Composition: Grouping a sequence of ⟨Production Rules⟩ or operators into a single rule or operator.

Computer Assisted Instruction (CAI):   The study of computer-based teaching and testing.

Concept Acquisition: See ⟨Learning from Examples⟩.

Concept Description: (also Description, Generalization): A symbolic data structure defining a concept describing the class of all known instances of the concepts.

Concept Formation: A form of learning in which the learner generates concepts useful in characterizing a given collection of objects or facts or a subset of them.

Conceptual Clustering: A form of ⟨Learning from Observation⟩ concerned with arranging objects (situations, facts, etc.) into classes characterized by simple descriptive concepts rather than into classes defined by a predefined measure of similarity among their members, as in conventional clustering.

Consistent Generalization: A description of some or all ⟨Positive Examples⟩ of a class that does not include any ⟨Negative Examples⟩ of that class.

Consistent Hypothesis: See ⟨Consistent Generalization⟩

Constraint: A property or relation that restricts the space of possible solutions to a problem.

Constraint-based Generalization: A method of generalization that explores constraints binding descriptive concepts characterizing or explaining a given example (*intraexample* constraints) and produces a generalization of that event that satisfies these constraints. (Cf. ⟨Similarity-based Generalization⟩.)

Constructive Induction: An ⟨Inductive Learning⟩ process that generates new ⟨descriptors⟩ not provided in the description of initial facts or observations.

Credit (Blame) Assignment: Identifying the steps (decisions, operators, etc.) chiefly responsible for a success (failure) in the overall process of achieving a goal.

Decision Tree: A ⟨Discrimination Network⟩ in the form of a tree structure.

Deductive Inference: A mode of reasoning that starts with certain assertions (premises) and concludes with logical consequences of these assertions. It employs ⟨Deductive Inference Rules⟩.

Deductive Inference Rule: An ⟨Inference Rule⟩ that, given one or more assertions, produces a logically equivalent or more specific assertion. A deductive inference rule is a truth-preserving transformation of assertions. (Cf. ⟨Inductive Inference Rule⟩.)

Derivational Analogy: A case-based problem-solving method in which derivations of solutions to similar problems are replayed and modified to solve new problems.

Descriptor: An attribute, function, or predicate used as an elementary concept for describing objects or situations.

Discriminant Description: A ⟨Concept Description⟩ that states properties that distinguish the given concept from other concepts under consideration. (Cf. ⟨Characteristic Description⟩.)

Discrimination Network: A network encoding a set of tests to classify a collection of objects (situations, events, etc.) into fixed categories according to predetermined features of the objects.

Domain of a Descriptor: (also Value Set of a Descriptor): The set of admissible values that a ⟨Descriptor⟩ may take as a component of a ⟨Concept Description⟩.

Expert System: A computer system that achieves performance comparable to a human expert at solving problems in some task domain by utilizing a large amount of domain-specific knowledge. Because of the substantial amounts of knowledge required, the ⟨Knowledge Acquisition⟩ task assumes major proportions.

Expertise Acquisition: See ⟨Knowledge Acquisition⟩.

Feature: See ⟨Attribute⟩.

Generalization: Extending the scope of a concept description to include more instances (the opposite of ⟨Specialization⟩). This term is sometimes also used as a noun, synonymous with ⟨Concept Description⟩.

Generalization Rule: An ⟨Inductive Inference Rule⟩ used in generalizing examples in ⟨Learning from Examples⟩.

Grammatical Inference: A form of ⟨Inductive Inference⟩ concerned with inferring the grammar of a language from a set of sentences labeled "grammatically correct" and a second (optional) set labeled "grammatically incorrect."

Heuristics: Imperfect but useful pieces of knowledge employed in reasoning and problem-solving tasks, such as ⟨Plausible Inference⟩, discovery, and so on, in lieu of precise knowledge. Also, an approximate ⟨Inference Rule⟩.

Heuristic Search: A problem-solving method for finding a sequence of operators that transforms an initial state into a desired goal state. ⟨Heuristics⟩ are used to generate, test, and prune operator sequences.

Incremental Learning: Multistage learning in which knowledge learned at one stage is modified to accommodate new facts provided in subsequent stages.

Inductive Inference: A mode of reasoning that starts with some assertions, e.g., specific observations, and concludes with more-general and -plausible assertions, i.e., hypotheses explaining the initial assertions. It employs ⟨Inductive Inference Rules⟩.

Inductive Inference Rules: An ⟨Inference Rule⟩ that, given one or more assertions, produces an assertion that logically implies the original assertion(s). An inductive inference rule is a falsity-preserving transformation of assertions. (Cf. ⟨Deductive Inference Rule⟩.)

Inductive Learning: Learning by drawing ⟨Inductive Inferences⟩ from facts and observations obtained from a teacher or environment (that is, learning by ⟨Inductive Inference⟩).

Inference Rule: A rule that produces new assertions from old, either by the application of strict logical principles or by more imperfect, plausible methods. (See also ⟨Inductive Inference Rule⟩ and ⟨Deductive Inference Rule⟩.)

Intelligent CAI (ICAI):   The application of AI techniques in building ⟨Computer Assisted Instruction⟩ systems.

Knowledge Acquisition: (also Expertise Acquisition): A form of machine learning concerned with transferring knowledge from humans or a task environment into computers; often associated with constructing or augmenting the knowledge base of an ⟨Expert System⟩.

Knowledge Compilation: (also ⟨Operationalization⟩ of Knowledge): Translating knowledge from a declarative form that cannot be used directly into an effective procedural form; for example, converting the advice "Don't get wet" into specific instructions that recommend *how* to avoid getting wet in a given situation. (See also ⟨Skill Acquisition⟩.)

Learning by Being Told: See ⟨Learning from Instruction⟩.

Learning from Examples: Inferring a general ⟨Concept Description⟩ from examples and (optionally) counterexamples of that concept. This is a form of ⟨Inductive Learning⟩.

Learning from Instruction: (also Advice Taking, and Learning by Being Told): The process of transforming and integrating instructions from an external source (such as a teacher) into an internally usable form.

Learning from Observation: (also Learning without a Teacher, Unsupervised Learning): Constructing descriptions, hypotheses or theories about a given collection of facts or observations. In this form of learning there is no *a priori* classification of observations into sets exemplifying desired concepts.

Machine Learning: A subdomain of artificial intelligence concerned with developing computational theories of learning and constructing machines with learning capabilities.

Macro-operator: An operator composed of a sequence of more primitive operators. Appropriate macro-operators can simplify problem solving by allowing a more "coarse-grained" problem-solving search.

Means-ends Analysis: A problem-solving method that searches at each step for operators that maximally reduce the difference between the current state and a known goal state.

Near Miss: A counterexample of a concept that is quite similar to positive examples of this concept. Near misses are very useful in isolating significant features in ⟨Learning from Examples⟩.

Near-miss Analysis: The process of exploiting ⟨ Near Misses⟩ to bound the scope of ⟨Generalization⟩ in learning from examples.

Negative Example: In ⟨Learning from Examples⟩, a counterexample of a concept that may bound the scope of ⟨Generalization⟩.

Neural Network: A network of neuron-like elements that performs some simple logical function, typically a logic threshold function.

Operationalization: See ⟨Knowledge Compilation⟩.

Parameter Adjustment: Changing the relative weight of different terms in a mathematical expression, as a function of credit (blame) for past successes (failures); a kind of incremental curve fitting.

Partially Learned Concept: In concept learning, an underdetermined concept; that is, a concept whose precise description cannot be inferred on the basis of the learner's current data, knowledge, and assumptions. (See also ⟨Incremental Learning⟩ and ⟨Version Space⟩.)

Partial Matching: A technique for comparing structural descriptions by identifying their corresponding components; useful in various kinds of inference, such as ⟨Analogical Inference⟩.

Path Constraint   In problem solving, a ⟨Predicate⟩ that must be satisfied by any solution sequences; a type of ⟨Constraint⟩.

Plausible Inference: A derivation of likely conclusions from incomplete, imperfect, assumed, or indirectly relevant premises. This includes ⟨Inductive⟩, approximate, default, and ⟨Analogical⟩ inference.

Positive Example: In ⟨Learning from Examples⟩, an example or instance of a concept to be learned in ⟨Learning from Examples⟩.

Predicate: A statement that is either true or false; a basic building block of predicate logic.

Problem Reformulation: Translating a problem statement into an alternative logically equivalent form so that an appropriate solution method can be applied. This may include reformulating data representations and restating problem constraints.

Production Rule: A condition-action pair, stating that the action is to be performed if the condition is matched or satisfied.

Production System: An inference system comprised of a large set of ⟨Production Rules⟩, a working memory against which productions are matched, and the control structure to apply the productions to working memory.

Proceduralization: The conversion of declarative knowledge into procedural form (see also ⟨Knowledge Compilation⟩).

Rote Learning: Learning by direct memorization of facts without generalization (see also ⟨Caching⟩).

Schema: A symbolic structure that can be filled in by specific information ("instantiated") to denote an instance of the generic concept represented by the structure.

Similarity-based Generalization: A method of generalization that explores similarities and differences between examples of the same concept (*interexample similarities*) in order to create a description characterizing or explaining all examples of that concept (Cf. 〈Constraint-based generalization〉).

Similarity Metric: Either (1) a context-free mathematical measure on properties of object descriptions used in clustering—minimized for objects within a cluster and maximized for objects spanning clusters, or (2) a context-sensitive symbolic expression capturing relevant similarities between two object or process descriptions—used to establish mappings in 〈Analogical Inference〉.

Skill Acquisition: (and Refinement): Acquiring or improving a procedural skill (such as touch typing) by 〈Knowledge Compilation〉 and repeated practice.

Specialization: Narrowing the scope of a 〈Concept Description〉, thus reducing the sets of instances it describes (opposite of 〈Generalization〉).

Structural Description: A symbolic representation for objects and concepts based on descriptions of their parts and the relationships among them.

Supervised Learning: A term usually used in the context of 〈Adaptive Systems〉 or 〈Neural Networks〉 to denote learning processes in which input signals are accompanied by a classification decision provided by a teacher (see 〈Learning from Examples〉).

Transformational Analogy: A problem-solving method in which a solution to a similar problem is transformed incrementally into a solution to the new problem.

Unsupervised Learning: See 〈Learning from Observation〉.

Version Space: (of a concept): The set of alternative candidate 〈Concept Descriptions〉 that are consistent with the training data, knowledge, and assumptions of the concept learner. This set defines a 〈Partially Learned Concept〉 and can be represented in terms of its maximally general and maximally specific members.

Weak Methods: General methods for problem solving applicable in the absence of specific knowledge of the problem domain required for more direct or efficient algorithmic solutions. For example, see 〈Means-ends Analysis〉 and 〈Heuristic Search〉.

ABOUT THE AUTHORS

Saul Amarel is Professor of Computer Science at Rutgers University. He received his B.S. in Electrical Engineering (1948) from Technion, Israel, Institute of Technology and his M.S. (1953) and D. Eng. Sci. (1955) from Columbia University. From 1957 to 1969 he was Head of Computer Theory Research at RCS Laboratories, Princeton, N.J., and from 1969 to 1984 he was Chairman of Computer Science at Rutgers. He organized the Laboratory for Computer Science Research at Rutgers and founded the Rutgers Research Resource on Computers in Biomedicine, which has been a major center for research on knowledge-based systems since 1971. He has been involved in artificial intelligence research since the early sixties. In 1983 he was General Chairman of the International Joint Conference on Artificial Intelligence. His current research interests include problems of representation in problem solving, theory formation processes, model-guided reasoning, learning and expertise acquisition, planning and design problems, and applications of AI to medicine, engineering, and science. He is the author of numerous journal articles and book chapters. His current address is Department of Computer Science, Rutgers University, New Brunswick, NJ 08903.

John R. Anderson is Professor of Psychology and Computer Science at Carnegie-Mellon University. He received his B.A. from the University of British Columbia in 1968 and his Ph.D. from Stanford University in 1977. Before joining the faculty at CMU, Dr. Anderson was a Professor at Yale University. His research interests are in human learning and memory and intelligent tutoring. His books include *Human Associative Memory* (with G. Bower, 1973), *Language, Memory, and Thought* (1976), *Cognitive Psychology and Its Implications* (1980), *Cognitive Skills and Their Acquisition* (1981), and *The Architecture of Cognition* (1983). His current address is Department of Psychology, Carnegie-Mellon University, Pittsburgh, PA 15213.

Ranan B. Banerji is Professor of Mathematics and Computer Science at St. Joseph's University. He received his Ph.D. from the University of Calcutta in Physics and has worked on ionospheric physics and propagation, coding theory, languages, and automata theory prior to his present research in AI. His major interest is in mathematical models of problems and inductive logic involved in learning heuristics for problem solving. He is the author of two books on the subject. His current address is Department of Mathematics and Computer Science, St. Joseph's University, 5600 City Avenue, Philadelphia, PA 19131.

Robert C. Berwick is Assistant Professor of Computer Science and Engineering at the Massachusetts Institute of Technology in the Artificial Intelligence Laboratory. He received his A.B. in 1976 from Harvard College and his S.M. and Ph.D. from MIT in 1980 and 1982, respectively. His current research centers on the learning of syntax, word meaning, and the semantics of tense; formal models of inductive inference; and the relationship between computational complexity and language processing. Professor Berwick is the author of over fifty technical articles in the areas of computational linguistics and learning. He has published two books: *Computational Models of Discourse,* edited with J. Michael Brady (1983) and, with A. Weinberg, *The Grammatical Basis of Linguistic Performance* (1984). His current address is MIT Artificial Intelligence Laboratory, Room 820, 545 Technology Square, Cambridge, MA 02139.

Gary L. Bradshaw is Assistant Professor in Psychology at the University of Colorado, Boulder. He received his B.A. from the University of Missouri, Columbia, in 1974 and his Ph.D. from Carnegie-Mellon University in 1984. His research interest is in building intelligent systems capable of discovering knowledge through experience. Two major projects include BACON, a program capable of discovering scientific laws, and NEXUS, a program that identifies important components of speech and incorporates this information into a working speech recognition system. He has authored or coauthored fourteen technical papers in the areas of human learning, human memory, infant motor behavior, scientific discovery, and speech recognition. His current address is Psychology Department, Campus Box 345, University of Colorado, Boulder, CO 80309.

Mark H. Burstein is a Research Scientist at Bolt Beranek and Newman, Inc. He received his B.S. in Mathematics from the Massachusetts Institute of Technology in 1976 and his Ph.D. in Computer Science from Yale University in 1984. He is interested in cognitive modeling, learning, and knowledge representation. His dissertation describes a cognitive model of analytical processes by which students apply and integrate knowledge from several domains in learning new concepts. His current address is BBN Laboratories, 10 Moulton Street, Cambridge, MA 02238.

Jaime G. Carbonell is Associate Professor of Computer Science at Carnegie-Mellon University. Prior to joining the faculty at Carnegie-Mellon in 1978, he was a research fellow at Yale University, where he received his M.S. and Ph.D. in Computer Science, specializing in Artificial Intelligence and Natural Language Processing.

Previously, he had received degrees in Mathematics and Physics at the Massachusetts Institute of Technology. His research interests span various aspects of artificial intelligence, computational linguistics, knowledge engineering and cognitive science, especially natural language interfaces, machine learning, and analogical reasoning. Dr. Carbonell is the author of *Subjective Understanding: Computer Models of Belief Systems,* the coeditor of *Machine Learning: An Artificial Intelligence Approach* (1983) and *Machine Learning: An Artificial Intelligence Approach,* Vol. II (1986), and the author or coauthor of over eighty technical papers and reports. He is a founder and director of Carnegie Group, Inc., one of the nation's leading AI firms. He is chairman of SIGART (the Special Interest Group in Artificial Intelligence of the ACM). His current address is Department of Computer Science, Carnegie-Mellon University, Pittsburgh, PA 15213.

Gerald DeJong is Associate Professor of Electrical Engineering and Computer Science at the University of Illinois. He also has a research appointment at the Coordinated Science Laboratory. He received his B.S. from the University of South Dakota in 1974 and his Ph.D. from Yale University in 1979. After a year's postdoctoral work at Yale he began his current appointment in 1981. In 1982 he received an Exxon Junior Faculty Award and in 1984, an Arnold O. Beckman Award. His research interests include natural language processing, machine learning, and robotics. He designed the FRUMP natural language system, one of the few AI systems to work well on unconstrained novel inputs. More recently he has been working on explanation-based learning. Along with his graduate students he is currently working on AI projects in natural language processing, robotics, theorem proving, and physics problem solving. His current address is Coordinated Science Laboratory, University of Illinois at Urbana-Champaign, Urbana, IL 61801.

Nachum Dershowitz is Associate Professor of Computer Science at the University of Illinois at Urbana-Champaign. He studied in Israel, receiving his B.S. and Ph.D. in Applied Mathematics from the Weizmann Institute in 1975 and 1979, respectively. His doctoral research in automated program development took him to the Stanford Artificial Intelligence Laboratory; that work is described in his book *The Evolution of Programs* (1983). His research interests also include program verification and logic programming. His current address is Department of Computer Science, University of Illinois at Urbana-Champaign, 1304 West Springfield Avenue, Urbana, IL 61801.

Thomas G. Dietterich is Assistant Professor of Computer Science at Oregon State University in Corvallis, Oregon. He received his A.B. from Oberlin College in 1977, his M.S. from the University of Illinois in 1979, and his Ph.D. from Stanford University in 1984. He has written a number of articles on machine learning, including a survey entitled "Learning and Inductive Inference," which constitutes chapter 14 of volume 3 of *The Handbook of Artificial Intelligence* (1982). Dr. Dietterich's research concerns machine learning from the perspective of scientific theory formation. He is currently investigating issues that involve forming theories about systems that contain state variables, including the relationship between theory formation and experiment design. His current address is Department of Computer Science, Oregon State University, Corvallis, OR 97331.

Kenneth D. Forbus is Assistant Professor of Computer Science at the University of Illinois at Urbana-Champaign. He received his degrees from the Massachusetts Institute of Technology (B.S., 1977, M.S., 1981, Ph.D., 1984). His research concerns commonsense and qualitative reasoning, with a focus on reasoning about physical processes and space as well as learning. His current address is Department of Computer Science, University of Illinois, 1304 W. Springfield Ave., Urbana, IL 61801.

Jean-Gabriel Ganascia is Assistant Professor at the University of Paris-Sud, Orsay, where he is working in the Laboratoire de Recherche en Informatique. He obtained a degree as Docteur Ingenieur in 1983. His research involves modeling experts' behavior in domains in which data may be uncertain and reasoning inexact, such as medicine or geology. At present Professor Ganascia is completing a Doctorat d'Etat degree in Computer Science, concentrating on machine learning as applied to expert systems. His current address is Laboratoire de Recherche en Informatique, Université de Paris-Sud, Orsay, 91405, France.

Dedre Gentner is Associate Professor of Psychology at the University of Illinois at Urbana-Champaign. She received her A.B. from the University of California at Berkeley in 1969 and her Ph.D. from the University of California at San Diego in 1974. Her work is in cognitive psychology and cognitive development, with a focus on analogy, learning, and acquisition of meaning. Prior to joining the faculty at the University of Illinois, she was a senior scientist at Bolt Beranek and Newman, Inc. She is the coeditor of *Mental Models*. Her current address is Department of Psychology, University of Illinois, 603 E. Daniel, Champaign, IL 61801.

John H. Holland is Professor of Computer Science and Engineering at the University of Michigan. He received his B.S. in Physics from the Massachusetts Institute of Technology (1950), his M.A. in Mathematics from the University of Michigan (1954), and his Ph.D. in Communication Sciences (now Computer Science and Engineering) from the University of Michigan (1959). Dr. Holland's research interests center on adaptive systems, both natural and artificial, including genetic processes, economic systems, cognitive processes, induction, cellular automata, machine learning, and relevant computer architectures. He has published *Adaptation in Natural and Artificial Systems* and is currently completing, with three coauthors, *Induction: Learning, Discovery, and the Growth of Knowledge.* Dr. Holland has published over thirty papers in these areas, including several book chapters. His current address is Department of Electrical Engineering and Computer Science, University of Michigan, Ann Arbor, MI 48109.

Smadar T. Kedar-Cabelli is a doctoral candidate at Rutgers University, pursuing research in machine learning under the direction of Dr. Tom Mitchell. Her dissertation explores techniques for concept learning by analogy, guided by explicit knowledge of the purpose of the analogy. Her other interests in machine learning include analogy in legal reasoning, the relationship of learning and nonmonotonic reasoning, and goal-directed learning. She received a B.A. in Mathematics (1976) and an M.Sc. in Computer Science (1982) from Rutgers University. Her current address is Department of Computer Science, Rutgers University, New Brunswick, NJ 08903.

Yves Kodratoff is Associate Professor (maître de recherche) at the Laboratoire de Recherche en Informatique, University of Paris-Sud, Orsay. He obtained his Doctorat d'Etat in 1967 in the field of paramagnetic resonance applied to chemistry. At present Professor Kodratoff heads a group working on inference, learning, and automatic programming. His current address is Laboratoire de Recherche en Informatique, Université de Paris-Sud, Orsay, 91405, France.

Pat Langley is Associate Professor of Computer Science at the University of California at Irvine. His research focuses on computational methods for learning and discovery. He is the author of BACON, an AI system that has rediscovered a number of laws from the history of science; SAGE, a system that learns heuristics for directing search; and a number of other machine learning systems. His current research focuses on combining the results of previous efforts into integrated models of the learning process. Dr. Langley has published over thirty-five papers in the areas of artificial intelligence and cognitive science. He is Executive Editor of the journal *Machine Learning,* and he is coauthoring a book describing the results of the BACON Project. His current address is Department of Information and Computer Science, University of California, Irvine, CA 92717.

Michael Lebowitz is the Herbert M. Singer Assistant Professor of Computer Science at Columbia University. He received his S.B. (1975) from the Massachusetts Institute of Technology and his M.S. (1977) and Ph.D. (1980) from Yale University, all in Computer Science. At Columbia University he leads a research group studying intelligent information systems involving the automatic construction of large information bases from assorted kinds of data. His current research interests include learning, natural language processing, human memory models, and extended story generation. His current address is Department of Computer Science, Columbia University, New York, New York 10027.

Douglas B. Lenat is Principal Scientist at the Microelectronics and Computer Technology Corporation (MCC) and is a faculty member at Stanford University. His research has focused on machine learning through automated discovery and on the nature of heuristics, and it has earned IJCAI's Computers and Thought Award and AAAI's Best Paper Award. He coedited the book *Building Expert Systems* and coauthored the book *Knowledge Based Systems in Artificial Intelligence.* Dr. Lenat's numerous articles include the September 1984 overview of AI in *Scientific American*. His current address is Microelectronics and Computer Technology Corporation, 9430 Research Boulevard, Echelon Building #3, Austin, TX 78759.

Sridhar Mahadevan is a doctoral candidate in the Computer Science Department at Rutgers University. He received his M.Tech. in Electrical Engineering from the Indian Institute of Technology, Kanpur, in 1983. He is a research assistant in the Learning Apprentice Project at Rutgers University. He has written a number of articles in machine learning on generalization techniques for learning apprentice systems. His current address is Department of Computer Science, Rutgers University, New Brunswick, NJ 08903.

Ryszard S. Michalski is Professor of Computer Science and Medical Information Science and Director of the Artificial Intelligence Laboratory at the University of Illinois at Urbana-Champaign. He studied at the Cracow and Warsaw Technical Universities and received his M.S. from the Leningrad Polytechnic Institute and his Ph.D. from the University of Silesia in Poland. Prior to coming to the United States in 1970, he was a Research Scientist at the Polish Academy of Sciences in Warsaw. His research interests include machine learning, inductive inference, expert systems, modeling of human plausible reasoning, computer vision, and application of artificial intelligence to life sciences, particularly to medicine and agriculture. Dr. Michalski authored or coauthored over ninety research and technical papers on these topics. He coedited *Machine Learning: An Artificial Intelligence Approach* (1983) and *Machine Learning: An Artificial Intelligence Approach,* Vol. II (1986). He coorganized, with Carbonell and Mitchell, three International Workshops on Machine Learning (1980, 1983, and 1985). Dr. Michalski is coeditor of the *Machine Learning Journal.* His current address is Department of Computer Science, University of Illinois, 1304 W. Springfield, Urbana, IL 61801.

Donald Michie is Director of Research and Advanced Study at the Turing Institute, an Academic Associate of the University of Strathclyde, and Professor Emeritus of the University of Edinburgh. He received his M.A., D. Phil., and D.Sc. from Balliol College, Oxford. During the Second World War he joined the Bletchley Park code-breaking establishment, and after pursuing a postwar career in experimental genetics and immunology, he returned to machine intelligence in the early 1960s. In 1967 he was elected to a Personal Chair of Machine Intelligence in the University of Edinburgh. He has been Visiting Professor at several universities in the United States and is Adjunct Professor of Computer Science at the University of Illinois. He is editor-in-chief of the *Machine Intelligence* series and the author of books on machine intelligence and of scientific publications in biology and computer science. His most recent work has been concerned with the structured induction of situation-action plans from example decisions. His current address is the Turing Institute, George House, 36 North Hanover Street, Glasgow G12AD, Great Britain.

Tom M. Mitchell is Associate Professor of Computer Science at Rutgers University. He earned his B.S. degree (1973) from MIT and his M.S. (1975) and Ph.D. (1978) degrees from Stanford University. He is the recipient of the 1983 IJCAI Computers and Thought Award in recognition of his research on machine learning and of a 1984 NSF Presidential Young Investigator Award. Dr. Mitchell has taught Artificial Intelligence at Rutgers and in tutorial courses for the past six years. He is coeditor of *Machine Learning: An Artificial Intelligence Approach* (1983) and *Machine Learning: An Artificial Intelligence Approach,* Vol. II (1986). His current research lies in the areas of learning heuristics through experimentation, knowledge-based aids for circuit design, and frameworks for incorporating learning into knowledge-based systems. His current address is Department of Computer Science, Rutgers University, New Brunswick, NJ 08903.

Allen Newell is the U. A. and Helen Whitaker University Professor of Computer Science at Carnegie-Mellon University. He received his B.S. in physics in 1949 from Stanford University, did one year of graduate work at Princeton in 1950, and received his Ph.D. in industrial administration in 1957 from Carnegie Institute of Technology (now CMU). From 1957 to 1961 he was a member of the scientific staff at the Rand Corporation, and he subsequently joined Carnegie-Mellon University. Dr. Newell is a recipient of several distinguished awards, among them the 1971 Harry Goode Award of the American Federation of Information Processing Societies (AFIPS) and the 1975 A.M. Turing Award of the Association of Computing Machinery (jointly with Herbert S. Simon). He is a member of the National Academy of Sciences and the National Academy of Engineering. He has authored or coauthored several books and approximately 200 publications. His active research interests are artificial intelligence, human cognition, human-computer interaction, and the social impact of computers. His current address is Computer Science Department, Carnegie-Mellon University, Pittsburgh, PA 15213.

J. Ross Quinlan is the Head of the School of Computing Sciences at the New South Wales Institute of Technology in Sydney. He obtained his B.Sc. from the University of Sydney in 1965 and his Ph.D. from the newly formed Computer Science Group at the University of Washington in 1968. Dr. Quinlan spent the 1968–1969 academic year as a Visiting Assistant Professor at Carnegie-Mellon University, the 1970–1980 period in the Basser Department of Computer Science at the University of Sydney, and 1981–1982 as a Computer Scientist at the Rand Corporation in Los Angeles. He has worked in the area of artificial intelligence since 1965, first in problem solving and learning and more recently in expert systems, inductive inference, and plausible reasoning. His current address is School of Computing Sciences, N.S.W. Institute of Technology, Broadway, N.S.W. Australia 2007.

Paul S. Rosenbloom is Assistant Professor of Computer Science and Psychology at Stanford University. He received his B.S. (1976) in Mathematical Sciences from Stanford University and his M.S. (1978) and Ph.D. (1983) in Computer Science from

Carnegie-Mellon University. He spent the 1978–1979 academic year as a visiting graduate student in Psychology at the University of California, San Diego, and the year 1983–1984 as a Research Computer Scientist at Carnegie-Mellon University. His current research focuses on the design of cognitive architectures as both psychological models and artifically intelligent systems, with particular attention to the interactions among knowledge, learning, and problem solving. His current address is Heuristic Programming Project, Stanford University, 701 Welch Road (Building C), Palo Alto, CA 94304.

Claude Sammut is a Lecturer in Computer Science at the University of New South Wales. He received his B.Sc. from the University of New South Wales in 1978, and his Ph.D. from the same institution in 1982. After receiving his Ph.D. Dr. Sammut took a postdoctoral fellowship at Saint Joseph's University in Philadelphia and in 1983 was a Visiting Assistant Professor in the Department of Computer Science at the University of Illinois, Urbana-Champaign. His current research interests are in knowledge acquisition for expert systems and in logic programming. Dr. Sammut is the author of the UNSW PROLOG system. His current address is Department of Computer Science, University of New South Wales, P.O. Box 1, Kensington, N.S.W. Australia 2033.

Bernard Silver is a Senior Member of the Technical Staff at GTE Laboratories, Inc., in Waltham, Mass. He received his B.Sc. in Mathematics from Imperial College, London, in 1980, and his Ph.D. in Artificial Intelligence from the University of Edinburgh in 1984. His interests include controlling search, computer algebra, PROLOG, and strategy learning. His doctoral dissertation, "Using Meta-Level Inference to Constrain Search and to Learn Strategies in Equation Solving," supervised by Dr. Alan Bundy, combined these fields in the LP program. Dr. Silver is currently at GTE, continuing his research on machine learning. His current address is Information Sciences, Fundamental Research Laboratory, GTE Laboratories, Inc., 40 Sylvan Road, Waltham, MA 02254.

Herbert A. Simon is Professor of Computer Science and Psychology at Carnegie-Mellon University, where he has taught since 1949. He was educated at the University of Chicago (B.A., 1936, Ph.D., 1943). He is a member of the National Academy of Sciences, has honorary doctorates from a number of universities in the United States and abroad, and has received awards for distinguished service from the American Psychological Association, the Association for Computing Machinery, and the American Economic Association. In 1978 he received the Alfred Nobel Memorial Prize in Economics. Among his numerous books are *Administrative Behavior, Human Problem Solving* (with Allen Newell), *The New Sciences of Management Decision, Models of Thought, The Sciences of the Artificial, Models of Bounded Rationality* (vols. 1 and 2), *Reason in Human Affairs,* and *Protocol Analysis* (with K. A. Ericsson). His current address is Department of Psychology, Carnegie-Mellon University, Pittsburgh, PA 15213.

Robert E. Stepp III is Assistant Professor of Electrical and Computer Engineering at the University of Illinois at Urbana-Champaign. He received his A.B. (1970) and M.S. (1971) from the University of Nebraska and his Ph.D. in Computer Science from the University of Illinois (1984). Dr. Stepp has authored or coauthored several publications in the areas of inductive learning and conceptual clustering. His interests include machine learning, conceptual data analysis, software engineering, and applications of personal computers for helping the blind. His current address is University of Illinois, Coordinated Science Laboratory, 1101 W. Springfield Avenue, Urbana, IL 61801.

Gail E. Thornburg is a doctoral candidate in the Department of Library and Information Science at the University of Illinois at Urbana-Champaign. She received her M.S. from Kent State University in 1982 and is expected to receive her Ph.D. in 1986. Her interests include expert systems, information retrieval, and structure of knowledge. Her dissertation involves development of an advisory system for on-line bibliographic information retrieval. Her current address is Graduate School of Library and Information Science, University of Illinois, 1407 W. Gregory, Urbana, IL 61801.

Paul E. Utgoff is Assistant Professor in the Department of Computer and Information Science at the University of Massachusetts at Amherst. He received his B.Mus. (1974) from Oberlin College Conservatory of Music and his M.S. (1979) and Ph.D. (1984) in Computer Science from Rutgers University. His current research focuses on generalizing relations from examples. Additional research interests include learning from explanations, apprentice systems, deductive learning, and distributed systems. His current address is Department of Computer and Information Science, Lederle Graduate Research Center, University of Massachusetts, Amherst, MA 01003.

Patrick H. Winston is Professor of Electrical Engineering and Computer Science and Director of the Artificial Intelligence Laboratory at the Massachusetts Institute of Technology. He received his B.S. in 1965, his M.S. in 1967, and his Ph.D. in 1970, all from the Massachusetts Institute of Technology. His current research interests are concentrated in artificial intelligence and allied fields. He is particularly involved in the study of learning by analogy, commonsense problem solving, expert systems, and robots. He is the author of *Artificial Intelligence* (two editions), coauthor of LISP, editor of *The Psychology of Computer Vision,* and coeditor of *Artificial Intelligence: An MIT Perspective* and *The AI Business.* His current address is MIT Artificial Intelligence Laboratory, 545 Technology Square, Cambridge, MA 02139.

Jan M. Zytkow is Associate Professor of Computer Science at Wichita State University and Associate Professor of Philosophy of Science at the University of Warsaw, Poland. He received his M.S. in Physics (1967), Ph.D. in Philosophy (1972), and Habilitation in Philosophy of Science (1979), all at the University of Warsaw. His research interests include semantics of scientific theories, patterns of change and choice of scientific concepts and theories, systems of scientific discovery, expert systems, and philosophical foundations of artificial intelligence. In 1982–1984 he was a Visiting Professor at Carnegie-Mellon University in Pittsburgh. He has published some twenty-five research papers. His current address is Computer Science Department, Wichita State University, Wichita, KS 67208.

AUTHOR INDEX

SUBJECT INDEX

A* search, 572
Abstraction level of knowledge representation, 11
Abstraction mapping, 319, 320, 324, 326
Abstraction of programs, 395, 409-10
AC³, 474
Accessibility (of structure matches), 325-28
Achieve statement (in program specification), 396
Acids, discovery of theory of, 437-46
ACT, 291, 292, 293, 303-8
ACT* theory, 290, 300, 303
Action discrimination, 304
Adjacency requirement (of English syntax), 641
Aeronautics, history of, compared to ML, 33-34
ALEX, 650, 659
Algebraic equality (analogy for assignment),
    355-56, 365-66
Alkalis, discovery of theory of, 437-46
AM, 32, 501, 537
AMAPs, 362
Analogical mapping, 353
Analogical problem solving, 374-76
    needs of, 374, 375-76, 384
Analogical reasoning, 46, 49-50, 394
    using censors, 55
Analogical shift hypothesis, 328
Analogical transformation, 372-74
Analogy, 290, 304, 351-67
    assimilation and repair strategies of, 31

Note: In this index, ML is an abbreviation for machine learning, AI for artificial intelligence.

in automatic programming, 394-96, 402-4,
    408, 415-19
in automatic programming, problems in, 417
in automatic programming, steps of, 417-18
and classification, 305-6
debate on use of term, 30-31
and knowledge acquisition, 35
with multiple models, 354-56, 365-66
by pattern matching, 352
problems with, 25
role of, in problem solving, 371-74
in Structure Mapping theory, 319-24, 326,
    328, 333
use of, in human learning, 312, 319
See also Analogical reasoning
AND/OR hierarchy, 254, 519
Annotated Predicate Calculus, 473, 487-88
Annotation, 487
Anomaly, 324
Anterior (phonology feature), 635-40
Applications of ML, 31
Aq algorithm, 68, 93
AQ11, 64
Arch (blocks world concept), 178-84
Architectures, computer, in ML, 5, 28, 39
Arguments of verbs, 642
Arithmetic concepts learned, 185
Array-search, 404-8
Artificial intelligence, role of ML in, 37-38
A-rules, 490, 495
Assert statement (in program specification), 396
Assimilation of new concept descriptions, 118,
    125, 134-35, 138-39, 146

Managerial Accounting

First Canadian Edition

Managerial Accounting

First Canadian Edition

Lester E. Heitger, Ph.D., C.P.A.
Indiana University

Serge Matulich, Ph.D., C.P.A.
Texas Christian University

Turgut Var, M.B.A., Ph.D.
Simon Fraser University

McGraw-Hill Ryerson Limited

Toronto Montreal Auckland Bogotá Guatemala
Hamburg Johannesburg Lisbon London Madrid
Mexico New Delhi Panama Paris San Juan
São Paulo Singapore Sydney Tokyo

MANAGERIAL ACCOUNTING,
First Canadian Edition

ISBN: 0-07-548552-4

1 2 3 4 5 6 7 8 9 0   D   2 1 0 9 8 7 6 5 4 3

Printed and bound in Canada by John Deyell Company

Canadian Cataloguing in Publication Data

Heitger, Lester E.
    Managerial accounting

Includes index.
ISBN 0-07-548552-4

1. Managerial Accounting.   I. Matulich, Serge.
II. Var, Turgut.   III. Title.

HF5635.H446 1983   658.1'5   C83-094044-8

Contents

Preface

This book is the managerial accounting volume of a coordinated two-volume financial/managerial set designed for introductory accounting courses. The financial and managerial volumes together offer well-integrated and comprehensive coverage of the fundamentals of financial and managerial accounting in a Canadian setting. Either volume, however, may be used alone or with other texts. Both books have been used by the authors and other teachers in several courses and are therefore thoroughly class-tested both in Canada and the United States.

This book is suitable for schools that cover undergraduate or graduate managerial accounting either as a complete course in a semester or quarter, or in combination with financial accounting over the academic year. Both books have been carefully designed to cover a range of material that is sufficiently comprehensive to accommodate various course objectives. The level of coverage in this volume is designed to satisfy the needs of the potential accounting major as well as of those who will not continue with additional accounting courses. The approach provides a careful balance between conceptual and technical material and is based on the philosophy that future managers need a solid grasp of managerial accounting concepts before they can integrate business data into a decision-making framework.

Organization of the book

The book is divided into five major parts. Part 1, **Developing a Management Accounting Data Base**, introduces students to the managerial accounting environment, the basic concepts of costing, and relevant terminology that students must understand prior to proceeding through the remainder of the book. Part 2, **Cost Behaviour and Decision Making**, introduces students to the concept of cost behaviour patterns and how cost behaviour is used in cost measurement and management planning, analysis, and decision making. A variety of alternative-choice decisions is illustrated.

After students obtain the relevant background in the first five chapters, they are introduced in Part 3 to the major tasks of **Management, Planning, Control, and Responsibility Reporting**. Here such topics as budgeting, standard costs, and variance reporting for both manufacturing and nonmanufacturing operations are discussed. Further discussion includes managerial performance reporting, decentralized business operation, pricing of products and services, and capital budgeting. The planning, control, and reporting necessary in not-for-profit organizations is discussed, as is the influence of governmental actions on businesses.

Part 4, **Advanced Managerial Accounting Topics**, introduces students to some managerial tools that managers need in today's complex business environment. These include methods of inventory management, advanced concepts of standard costing, and a variety of quantitative tools used in planning and forecasting future business operations.

Many managerial accounting students have an incomplete financial accounting background. Part 5 of the book, **Financial Accounting Foundation for Managerial Accounting**, is intended to fill the gap left by financial accounting courses that do not use the **Financial Accounting, Canadian Edition** volume of this series. It consists of the statement of changes in financial position and financial statement analysis, two topics that are an important part of a manager's accounting background.

Special features of the book

Although the initial costing discussions in Chapters 2–4 deal primarily with manufacturing operations, other chapters include a reasonable mix of material on service, merchandising, and not-for-profit organizations so that students can obtain a broad general background in managerial accounting and understand the universal applicability of managerial accounting information. Moreover, the material is organized to enable students to integrate their learning into a coherent body of knowledge, rather than to learn what appear to be a number of unrelated topics. For example, cost-volume-profit material in Chapter 5 is integrated with a study of alternative choice decisions in Chapter 6, showing students how the analysis is used in decision making. The application of managerial accounting to other than manufacturing operations in Chapter 10 provides the breadth students need to understand the general application of the concepts they study. Difficult topics such as standard costing and process costing are presented clearly at a basic level using easy-to-understand examples. They are then followed by more complex discussions for those who desire more complete coverage.

The chapter dealing with quantitative techniques is especially useful because it focuses on managerial tools that can be used to identify cost behaviour patterns and to plan and control costs. Although the treatment is elementary, students' basic understanding of these quantitative concepts gives them an edge in other managerial courses and in their professional work.

The financial accounting material in the last two chapters presents topics that are frequently omitted in financial courses and that are often covered in other accounting textbooks in less than comprehensible terms. Users of this book will find both teaching and learning of the statement of changes in financial position greatly enhanced as a result of the approach used to present this material here.

Learning aids

Each chapter of the book is preceded by a brief **chapter overview** and a list of **learning objectives. Marginal notes** throughout the book help to focus attention or place emphasis on important items in the chapters. The wide margins allow students to insert their own marginal notes as they deem necessary. Numerous examples and figures illustrate key concepts.

A comprehensive **summary** at the end of each chapter reinforces important material and provides a quick review of the chapter. The summary is followed by a **list of important terms** introduced in the chapter, each referenced to the page number where it is first used. We purposely omit definitions at the end of the chapter so that students will look for unfamiliar terms in their appropriate context. However, a complete **glossary** is provided at the end of the book, and terms may be found there without having to know in which chapter they are introduced. Each glossary definition is referenced to the chapter in which it is first used.

End-of-chapter material

The questions, exercises, problems, and minicases at the end of each chapter are generally arranged in the same sequence as the chapter material, and they cover all topics in the chapter. To the extent possible, the exercises, problems, and minicases are also arranged in order of difficulty, with the shorter and easier problems occurring first, and the more demanding ones found in the later part of the chapter.

The exercises are generally short and relatively easy, and they typically cover a single topic or concept. The problems and minicases are longer and more challenging, usually integrating several topics or concepts. The problems are divided into two groups, roughly parallel in topic coverage and level of difficulty, enabling users to assign problems from one group in one term and from the other group in the following term. Far more exercises, problems, and case material are provided than can possibly be covered in one course, adding flexibility in problem selection and the option to use the book many times without repeating the same assignments in successive terms.

One of the important features of the exercises and problems is their thorough coordination with chapter material, thus enabling students to obtain guidance from the chapter when attempting a solution. Many students who have used the textbook have commented favourably on this integration of problem and text material. In addition, the questions, exercises, and problems range over a wide variety of topics, present students with interesting situations, and offer a variety of learning experiences.

All questions, exercises, problems, and their solutions have been designed by the authors and are thoroughly compatible with the text material. Solutions have been prepared by the authors and checked carefully for accuracy by two independent accounting instructors.

Minicases, a unique feature of the Canadian Edition, are carefully selected from examinations of the Society of Management Accountants of Canada, Certified General Accountants of Canada, Canadian Institute of Chartered Accountants, Institute of Management Accounting of the National Association of Accountants and, finally, the American Institute of Certified Public Accountants. They are simplified and adapted for use in introductory level undergraduate and graduate courses in Canada. Their solutions are checked and expanded in order to aid the prospective instructors.

Managerial Accounting—Canadian Edition also is unique in providing examples in the metric system, a system that Canada is committed to adopt in its entirety.

A complete set of student and instructor supplements is available with the text. Each supplement has been developed and written by the authors to ensure complete integration with the text. Below we discuss supplements available to students and to instructors.

Student supplements

A **Study Guide** is available that provides guidance and practice for each chapter of the book. It is designed to give students a maximum learning experience with a minimum of effort, focusing on the important aspects of each chapter and reinforcing chapter material by means of objective and practical exercises and self-tests. To minimize time lost in learning to solve new problems, students are given suggestions on how to approach the problem and what steps to take in arriving at the correct solution. Solutions explaining the steps needed to arrive at answers or the logic of a particular solution are provided for all study guide materials.

Two Practice Sets are available with the book and may be used to strengthen the knowledge of materials studied in the text. One practice set covers the product cost cycle in a manufacturing operation using a job order cost system, and the other presents a profit planning and performance measurement problem. The job order cost practice set is fully Canadianized by keeping various accounting programs that exist in Canada in mind. The profit planning practice set encompasses budgeting, standard costs, performance reports, and cost-volume-profit analysis. Either or both practice sets may be assigned, or they may be alternated for different terms. The practice sets contain all forms necessary for a complete solution, and the Solutions Manual to the text contains the complete solution to each practice set.

Instructor's supplements

A comprehensive **Solutions Manual** contains solutions to all questions, exercises, problems, and minicases in the book, as well as solutions to both practice sets. The manual also provides the instructor with a wealth of information useful for planning courses, choosing assignments, and preparing materials for use in classes. Each exercise and problem is described, the time necessary to complete each solution is estimated, the level of difficulty is specified, and an indication is given if a transparency is available for the exercise or problem. The manual contains specific suggestions on approaches to each chapter and guidance on using the chapter.

An important feature of the Solutions Manual is a topic-problem grid that provides a complete cross-reference between all exercises, problems and minicases and the topics covered in the chapter, enabling instructors to identify topic coverage of assigned material. The topic-problem grid can be invaluable in preparing course assignments and in advising students who request additional practice material.

Other supplements include a set of **Transparencies** and a comprehensive **Examination Questions** booklet. The Transparencies, for use with overhead projectors, consist of solutions to selected exercises and problems in the book. The Examination Questions consist of objective questions and practical problems covering all chapter material. All examination material is accompanied by solutions and time estimates and may be used to develop many different types of tests and quizzes, depending on the coverage of text material selected by the instructor. The quantity of test material far exceeds the requirements of a single course, allowing for the design of many different tests on any topic in the book.

Flexibility

One of our goals has been to make the book as flexible as possible, so that it may be adapted to a variety of course objectives. We have arranged the material in a sequence that we consider most logical for the first course in managerial accounting. Instructors may, however, arrange their courses differently. It is unlikely that anyone using the book will cover all 19 chapters during the course of one semester or quarter. The quantity of material available permits the instructor to choose those topics that best satisfy specific course objectives and to omit those topics that are deemed less important. A number of topics or entire chapters may be omitted without loss of continuity, as discussed in the Solutions Manual available to adopters.

The combination of textbook, student supplements, and instructor's supplements makes the book flexible and adaptable to many classroom situations. The material constitutes a complete package with timesaving aids for the experienced teacher and it is equally suitable for schools that use student teachers. The book is certainly suitable for self-study, because it explains difficult concepts clearly and leaves room for the instructor to digress, elaborate, and discuss material in the classroom. The pronoun "he" embraces both genders when used in this book without reference to a specific person.

Lester E. Heitger
Serge Matulich
Turgut Var

part 1

Developing a Management Accounting Data Base

Organizations need accounting information to function efficiently and effectively. Department heads are responsible for budgets built upon such things as the costs of materials, office space, and personnel. Production people need to know how efficiently they are using materials and labour in manufacturing products. Marketing managers need to know how effective their marketing programs are in generating sales revenue — is the expense of selling the product too high; should the product line be dropped; what is the cost of increasing production capacity? Financial managers need information on the organization so that they can report profitability and financial position to investors, creditors, taxing authorities, and regulatory agencies. The primary source of information is accounting information, much of which is derived from detailed cost data that accountants develop from daily business activities. The cost data base is particularly useful in developing managerial reports for internal decision making.

In Chapter 1 we describe the environment of managerial accounting and introduce basic concepts and terms essential to understanding the material that follows. In Chapter 2 we present the basic concepts of costing and cost flows. Chapters 3 and 4 describe product costing and the development of the cost accounting data base.

Chapter 1

The Managerial Accounting Environment

This chapter provides an overview of the management accounting function and its environment. When you have completed study of the chapter, you should understand:

1 The distinction between financial and managerial accounting.

2 The nature of decision making and the steps in the decision process.

3 The role of accounting information in the decision process.

4 The function of cost accounting and how it relates to financial and managerial accounting.

5 The characteristics of accounting information and how they are interrelated.

6 The activities involved in cost accounting.

7 What effect external organizations have on a company's data base.

8 What factors affect the complexity of a firm's cost accounting system.

9 Accounting organizations involved in cost accounting: Society of Management Accounting, Canadian Institute of Chartered Accountants, Certified General Accountants of Canada.

All organizations require accounting information to manage daily operations, plan future operations, and evaluate past performance. In addition, most organizations must provide external financial information to taxing authorities, shareholders, regulatory agencies, labour unions, and other special interest groups.

Financial accounting is concerned with providing information to external users. Volume I of this series is about the fundamentals of the external reporting process.[1] The accounting process that provides information primarily for internal use is called **managerial accounting.** This text is concerned primarily with managerial accounting activities for internal reporting to managers.

In this chapter we discuss the decision-making process and the role of accounting information in making decisions. The nature of managerial accounting is examined along with the environment in which management accounting functions. We also introduce the subject of **cost accounting,** which is the process of determining the cost of a product or activity, and we discuss its role in external and internal reporting. The chapter concludes with an overview of some of the regulatory groups that have an influence on the development of the cost accounting data base.

The decision-making process

We are faced with decisions almost continuously in our personal lives and in business. Many decisions are so routine that we may not even realize they are decisions, such as what clothes to wear each day or what to have for breakfast. Others cause us to be more conscious of the decision process because the decision is made less frequently and is of greater consequence, such as buying a car or choosing a job.

Decisions vary in complexity

Like personal decisions, business decisions vary in complexity and importance. Many decisions require no action at all. For instance, a stockholder may ask a broker for the market price of a stock and as a result of the reply may decide not to sell the stock. Similarly, a production supervisor looks at hourly quality control data and determines that production performance is within acceptable limits, so no action is necessary. Other business decisions, however, are much more complex, such as plant-expansion decisions or new-product decisions.

Decision making is both an art and a science. It is an art because decisions are made using both subjective and objective data. Decision makers must decide how to combine a variety of inputs into a logical decision framework. Decision making is a science because many complex decisions can be reduced to simpler components by means of quantitative methods. For example, many firms examine only a small portion of production output, using statistical techniques to determine whether production processes are operating within acceptable tolerance limits.

Decision theory

Decision making has been the subject of many research studies, most of which have centred on the structure of the decision process and the role of information in decision making. The body of knowledge concerning decision making is called **decision theory.** An in-depth discussion of decision theory is beyond the scope of this book. However, decision theory directly affects many

[1] Serge Matulich, Lester Heitger, and Turgut Var, *Financial Accounting, First Canadian Edition,* (Toronto: McGraw-Hill Ryerson, 1982).

of the managerial accounting concepts discussed here, and at various points in the text decision theory concepts are mentioned. Since so many business decisions are based on accounting information, it is important to understand the decision-making process and the relationship that accounting information bears to it.

The structure of decisions

Each individual makes decisions in a slightly different way. However, most people agree that the decision-making process includes the following:

1. Defining the problem
2. Identifying alternatives
3. Accumulating relevant information
4. Making the decision

Defining the problem. Perhaps the most important phase of decision making is **problem definition** because all of the other activities in the process depend upon this phase. If managers do not have a clear understanding of the

Identify specific problems

specific problem at hand, they may spend considerable time and effort identifying alternatives and gathering information that is irrelevant to solving the real problem. For example, a year-end inventory count reveals a substantial inventory shortage. The plant superintendent immediately suspects employee theft and asks his assistant to develop alternatives that will eliminate employee theft of inventory. A more careful study of the situation reveals that inventory shortages pertain only to materials used in the production of one of the firm's products. After additional analysis it is discovered that the problem stems from the use of different systems for recording product cost and for transferring inventory items into production. One type of document, issued by the production engineering department, is used as the basis for transferring inventory items into production. Another document, from the accounting department, is used to record the transfer of inventory costs. A clerk in the inventory storeroom prepares the accounting document based on production requirements no longer in effect. The document used for transferring inventory to production is based on current production engineering requirements. As a result, the two documents do not show the same quantities of inventory for the production of this particular product. Consequently, more inventory goes into production than is recorded, and the shortage is the result of faulty record keeping and not theft.

Incorrectly defined problems waste time and resources, so decision makers should not be too hasty in moving on to the alternatives phase of the decision process. Very complex problems may require much analysis before a clear definition is reached.

Identifying alternatives. Now that we know the problem, how do we solve it? Usually there is more than one feasible solution. Identifying alternatives is the idea phase of decision making in which managers can use their ingenuity.

The idea stage of decision making

Creativity is the watchword in identifying alternatives, and there is no need to be cautious or inhibited in this process since the alternatives are evaluated at a later phase. Unfortunately previous experience and bias often limit the variety of alternatives that managers consider.

Accumulating relevant information. Decision makers may desire a variety of information to assist in making decisions. Some information may be subjective and some objective; some may be internal to the organization, and some may be external. Some information may be based on past costs or events, and some may be based on management's expectations about future costs or events.

Only relevant information should be selected

Whatever the nature of the information, it must be relevant to the decision at hand. The idea is to select only those items of information that affect the decision and discard those that do not. In this age of information explosion,[2] decision makers may be inundated with data. Decision theorists refer to this phenomenon as **information overload.** Managers must cautiously select only those items of information that can be assimilated into a logical decision framework.

Information should increase knowledge or decrease uncertainty

Information should increase decision makers' knowledge or reduce their uncertainty. For example, a company manufactures ball bearings which it sells to companies A, B, C, and D. One day a customer calls and says he wants to double his normal monthly order, but the clerk who takes the message cannot remember which company called. Without information the sales manager has a 25 percent chance of guessing which company called and a 75 percent chance of guessing the wrong company. When the clerk recalls that he is certain it was not Company A, this bit of information increases the chance of guessing correctly to one-third and **reduces the risk** of an incorrect decision to two-thirds. Later in the day Company C calls to reaffirm its regular monthly order; this additional information reduces the risk of error to 50 percent since only B and D remain as possible choices. The same day a new customer, Company E, calls to place an order. This bit of data is not relevant to the question of which company wants to double its order. You can see that relevant information increased knowledge of the situation and reduced the risk of selecting the wrong company that wants to double its order.

Making the decision. It may appear that once the problem is defined, alternatives are identified, and relevant information is selected, the making of the decision is simple. Seldom is that the case, particularly for complex decisions. Often no single variable dominates in making the decision. Instead several important decision criteria interact and affect one another. For example, in choosing a career you may consider economic potential, job satisfaction, lifestyle, advancement potential, geographic location, and other variables. Some

---

[2]The term **information explosion** refers to the expansion of available information of all sorts, primarily due to tremendous advances in data processing and storage capabilities.

careers may rank high for some variables and low for others. The final decision depends on the decision model that you decide to use.

A **decision model** is a description of the way that a decision is made. Often decision models are quite simple. For example, an investor may decide to buy stock of a company if its earnings per share have increased at least 10 percent a year for the last three years. Other variables that may be included in the decision model are earnings ratios or dividend yields. Occasionally even complex problems are decided with simple decision models because managers are unwilling to try more complex techniques or because more complex models have not produced better results in the past. Many routine decisions are made with precise decision models. For example, quality control is performed with sampling procedures that determine when the production process is unsatisfactory and should be investigated. The decision model may be quite simple: Stop production and investigate if more than 3 percent of the products are defective. Whether the decision model is very sophisticated or very simple, it should be designed to further the goals of the organization or individual. Simple as that idea is, it is sometimes lost in the heat of dealing with complex problems. In the final analysis the **quality** of a decision is determined by how the decision affects the achievement of the organization's goals.

Decision models must further the goals of the organization

The role of accounting information in decision making

Accounting information is objective

The role of accounting information, as well as other types of information, is to increase knowledge or reduce risk. Unlike subjective information, accounting information is quantitative, verifiable information that often is very effective in aiding decision makers. For example, a supervisor with 20 years of work experience is of the opinion that assembly line productivity has declined over the last year. Although he may be right, much more useful information is obtained from an accounting report that documents an 8 percent decline in production efficiency, which has increased product cost by $.30 a unit and decreased annual profits by $60,000. As a result, managers frequently assign significant weight to the importance of accounting information even when it is supplemented with more subjective data. In short, few organizations can survive, let alone thrive, without reliable accounting information.

The demand for accounting information has grown significantly over the last decade. An important factor in the demand for more information in general has been the declining cost of computer equipment and the increased use of more sophisticated management planning and decision methods. Managers are demanding more detailed accounting data than ever before, particularly cost accounting data. The increase in demand for information in general has mushroomed in all organizations; the pressure for more accounting information in particular comes from managers' desire to satisfy both internal information needs and the needs of external information users, especially government. Some of the specific external demands for information are discussed later in the chapter.

<table>
<tr><td>

Accounting information characteristics

</td><td>

Useful accounting information has the following characteristics:

1. Relevance
2. Timeliness
3. Accuracy

</td></tr>
</table>

Relevance is a very important characteristic of accounting information. It means that accounting information must be useful in considering the specific problem or decision at hand. Relevance is important to external and internal accounting reports, but it particularly affects internal reports. External reports, such as income statements and balance sheets, serve a variety of users for many different types of decisions and are in general relevant for many different purposes.

Relevance has a specific influence on internal accounting reports. Internal reports are intended to assist managers in making individual decisions and in evaluating specific problems. Managers may accumulate and report any kind of accounting information they deem useful, and they may use their ingenuity in determining what internal accounting reports are prepared and how frequently—daily, weekly, monthly. The primary limitation on internal reporting is the cost of preparing such reports. **Cost-benefit** refers to the concept that organizations are willing to generate information only if the benefit derived from the information is greater than the cost of providing the information.

The benefits of accounting information must exceed the cost of providing it

Timeliness refers to the need for accounting information to be current. Many types of information lose value very rapidly. Financial information is particularly sensitive to the passage of time. Knowing how much a business is currently earning may enable an investor to decide whether or not to invest in the business. If the information is old, the investor's decision may not be made wisely. Similarly, a department store manager may find daily sales information very useful in assessing the value of advertising programs as long as the sales information is reported on a timely basis. If the sales information is a month old when the manager receives it, the information may have little value. Most internal accounting information is very sensitive to timing because much of it is used to monitor and control daily operation. Sometimes it is more important to have approximate information immediately than to have precise information later. Precision may have to be sacrificed to achieve timely reporting of relevant information.

Approximate information now or precise information later

Accuracy is important because even the most timely information is of little value if it is not accurate. For instance, very poor estimates of bad debt losses may cause a manager to take inappropriate action in connection with credit-granting policies. Accuracy is a major prerequisite of timely and relevant accounting information. It is important to distinguish between accuracy and precision. A report stating that a company earned $560,000 last year may be accurate, although the precise amount of earnings may be $560,386. On the other hand, earnings reported at $864,932.17 may appear very precise, but the information is of little value if the actual amount is $150,000.

The distinction between accuracy and precision

Many people believe that accounting information is accurate to the last penny. In fact, accounting information involves much estimation and approximation. It should, however, be accurate within the constraints imposed on the methods of measurement and the standards applied in producing information.

In summary, the three characteristics of accounting information are interrelated. Together the characteristics provide guidelines for evaluating the usefulness of accounting reports. Such evaluations are particularly appropriate for internal accounting reports.

Data and information

The terms *data* and *information* are used frequently in general conversation as well as in many technical disciplines. To ensure a common understanding of the terms, we briefly describe our use of the terms in this book.

In decision theory **information** is data that has been put together into a usable form. This definition of information creates a very individualistic concept of information. For example, a report showing departmental labour costs for one month may be useful to one departmental supervisor, but not to another. With the above definition, the report is information in one case, but not in the other. The term **data** is used to refer to the raw material or building blocks of an information system. **Data base** refers to the foundation of data supporting the information system and drawn on by users to meet information needs.

In this book we do not adhere to a strict definition of data and information. Usually we use the term data in reference to the accumulation and recording of costs. Information is used to refer to specific reports or cost analyses. You should not be concerned with the use of the terms in our discussions, but you should be aware of the more specific meanings of the terms.

Characteristics of managerial accounting reports

Accounting is typically divided into financial accounting and managerial accounting. This dichotomy is made primarily on the grounds of the orientation of the reports. Financial accounting refers to reports that are prepared primarily for external users, such as investors, creditors, regulatory agencies, and taxing authorities. We do not mean to imply that managers of organizations have no use for external reports. For example, net income, earnings per share, and balance sheet ratios are all of interest to many managers. However, external financial statements are prepared primarily to satisfy external reporting requirements.

Managerial accounting refers to reports designed to meet the needs of internal users. Managerial accounting reports are characterized by the fact that they are situation-specific, which means that the reports attempt to fill the information needs of managers with respect to specific problems, decisions, or situations. Since relatively few individuals use each managerial accounting report, such reports can be more specific than the general purpose financial statements that are intended to meet the information needs of many users.

Managerial reports are specific; financial reports are general

Another characteristic of managerial reports is that they are more detailed than external reports. For internal reporting a firm may develop detailed cost information for each product it produces, but in the external financial statements the firm reports only the total cost of all products produced. Aggregation of more detailed internal accounting reports is a common characteristic of most external reports.

A third characteristic of managerial reports is frequency. Many internal reports are prepared monthly, weekly, or even daily. For example, accountants may prepare weekly reports identifying the cost of producing products and may prepare daily reports on cash receipts and disbursements.

The cost accounting data base

In addition to the classifications of financial accounting and managerial accounting, accountants identify cost accounting activities. Unlike financial and managerial accounting, cost accounting does not refer to the reporting process. **Cost accounting** refers to the process of determining the cost of some particular product or activity. Cost accounting data are used for both internal and external reports. Many internal reports present detailed cost information on the production of specific products, such as lamps or knives, or they contain information on the cost of performing some activity, such as preparing a sales invoice. In external reports cost data are summarized and presented in aggregate. For example, the cost of producing all products sold during the period usually appears as a single number in the income statement.

Since cost data are used in both financial and managerial accounting reports, cost accounting is really part of both classifications of accounting. We present this relationship graphically in Figure 1-1. Notice that cost accounting underlies and supports both financial and managerial reporting. The **cost accounting data base** is the foundation of cost data that supports many accounting activities, particularly in manufacturing firms.

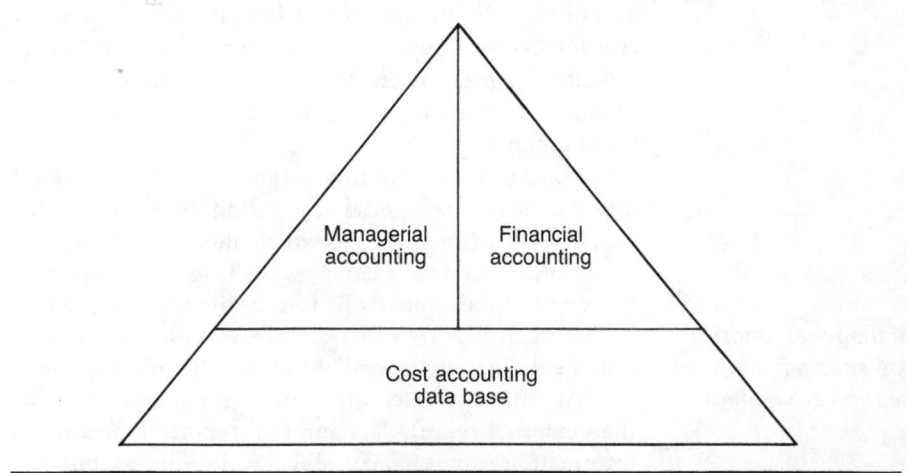

Figure 1-1
The cost accounting data base is the foundation from which many internal and external accounting reports emerge.

Occasionally cost accounting is referred to as manufacturing accounting. The need for detailed cost information was first noticed in manufacturing firms where product cost data were needed to control production costs and to determine selling prices. Many cost accounting concepts and techniques were developed in manufacturing industries. However, as product costing methods became more sophisticated, managers turned their attention to determining costs for nonmanufacturing activities. The process of determining costs for things other than tangible products is sometimes called **activity costing.** Finding the cost of programs and activities is very important in business and government. Chapters 10 and 16 discuss costs of nonmanufacturing activities.

Cost data are vital in preparing and understanding accounting reports, particularly managerial accounting reports. Therefore, Chapters 2 through 4 describe important cost accounting terminology and the fundamentals of determining costs. In this text we highlight only the fundamentals of cost accounting as they relate to the reporting function of managerial accounting. A later course devoted entirely to cost accounting is necessary for those interested in a comprehensive cost background. However, our treatment of cost concepts is sufficient to provide the necessary background for understanding many of the intricacies and problems associated with managerial accounting analysis and reporting. Here we describe basic cost accounting activities and those factors that determine the complexity of a cost system and the volume of cost data generated.

Cost accounting activities

Cost accounting is frequently classified into four different activities. They are:

1. Cost finding
2. Cost recording
3. Cost analyzing
4. Cost reporting

Cost finding. The first step in a cost accounting system is cost finding, which is just what it sounds like: determining cost for some specific product or activity. Although all activities in a cost system are important, cost finding is critical since all other activities depend on it. In most cost accounting courses a great deal of time is spent on cost finding procedures and techniques. A substantial part of the next three chapters is devoted to cost finding.

Cost recording. Most accounting systems are an integral part of a firm's formal accounting system with costs recorded in the journal and posted to the ledger. Specific cost recording procedures are not emphasized in this text, although some basic entries are shown in the three chapters dealing with the development of the cost data base.

Cost analyzing. Because accountants develop the cost data, they are usually most capable of analyzing cost information to solve problems, plan operations, or provide advice to managers. Meaningful cost analysis depends heavily upon a clear understanding of the cost finding methods used in cost accounting. People often attribute totally incorrect characteristics to costs. Throughout this book we describe many common errors caused by incorrect cost assumptions.

Cost reporting. Costs are reported in detail in many internal accounting reports and in aggregate in most external accounting reports. In terms of volume and frequency, by far the largest number of cost-based reports is for internal purposes. Many cost-related managerial accounting reports are presented throughout the book.

Factors affecting cost accounting systems

Many different factors determine the complexity of a cost system and the volume of cost data generated. Some of the most important factors are:

1. Size of the firm
2. Type of production process
3. Number of different products produced
4. Management's attitude toward cost information
5. External variables

Size of the firm. The amount of cost data necessary to manage a firm varies with the size of the firm. A firm in which two people manufacture fishing lures in a garage does not require as much cost data as a firm manufacturing fishing lures with 100 employees. In addition, the process of developing cost data is more complex in the larger firm because as an organization gets larger, some costs become more difficult to trace to specific products or activities. In general, the volume of cost data and the complexity of the cost system increases with firm size.

Type of production process. In cost accounting, costs are assigned to products on the basis of physical production activity. For example, the labour cost of a product is determined by the amount of time employees work on the product and on the wage rate of employees. As long as labour can be identified with specific products, accountants are able to assign labour costs to the products. However, some production processes are so complex that it is difficult to trace production costs to specific products. In such situations accountants have difficulty in assigning costs to products. As a general rule, the more complex the production process, the more difficult and complex is the cost system.

Number of different products produced. If a firm produces only one product, all manufacturing costs can be assigned to it. However, when a firm produces more than one product, the accountant must distribute the manufacturing costs among the various products. Some manufacturing costs, such as the cost of materials, clearly relate to specific products, but other costs of production, such as utilities and property taxes, are not so clearly identified with specific products. Usually the number of costs that is not identifiable with specific products increases with the number of products produced.

Management's attitude toward cost information. Some cost data are required by virtually all organizations. For instance, even a small manufacturing firm requires some measure of product cost to satisfy taxing authorities when filing tax returns. However, there is a tremendous difference between the bare minimum requirement for cost data and the amount of cost data that is or could be developed in firms using extensive managerial reporting procedures. The difference between the minimum and optimum cost system is a function of management's attitude toward cost information. Cost information is not free; it should be produced only when the value of the information is perceived to be greater than the cost of developing it. If managers have little use for cost information, the value assigned to the information does not warrant the expenditure of many resources to develop cost information. Management's attitude toward cost information is a major factor in the volume and sophistication of the cost system.

External variables. Cost data are used for external and internal reporting. Internal reporting is fundamentally unaffected by external variables. However, cost data for external reports may be affected by a wide variety of regulatory agencies, such as Revenue Canada, Transport Canada, the Canadian Radio and Telecommunications Commission (CRTC), and the provincial security exchange commissions. Some of these organizations are discussed later in the chapter. For now we just note that these and other external variables are having a growing influence on the frequency, detail, and structure of cost data and related reports.

External organizations and the cost data base

Since cost data are used for both internal and external accounting reports, external reporting requirements can have an influence on the kind of data base generated by Canadian businesses. For example, businesses involved with utilities are required to conform with certain rules in setting rates which are subject to governmental approval. The Combines Investigations Act also requires companies to provide information about their internal reports. Statistics Canada obtains a wealth of data from all kinds of businesses. In general, both federal and provincial governments exercise an important and growing influence over the volume, detail, and form of the cost data base of many firms. In this section we discuss some of the more important organizations that affect cost accounting data bases.

Revenue Canada

Revenue Canada, Taxation Division, is charged with the responsibility of ensuring that individuals and organizations pay the amount of federal and provincial income taxes that they are legally obliged to pay. In dealing with businesses, Revenue Canada must sometimes determine accounting procedures for tax purposes. Basically, Revenue Canada allows firms to use generally accepted accounting principles (GAAP) in determining taxable net income, but Revenue Canada also establishes certain rules and procedures that affect costs.

For instance, Revenue Canada defines product costs as the total cost of production. Revenue Canada sets various capital cost allowances, encourages consistency in the use of alternative accounting procedures, and requires proper maintenance of relevant records. Generally, Revenue Canada attempts to avoid tampering with GAAP, but it takes action when it perceives that tax obligations under the law may be misstated.

Provincial Securities and Exchange Commissions

As opposed to the United States Securities and Exchange Commission, Canada does not have a federal regulatory agency designed to protect individual investors. This function is carried out by various provincial securities and exchange commissions and other similar agencies serving the same purpose. The requirements of these agencies, although they heavily rely on generally accepted accounting principles, may change from one province to the other. Some of the releases of these organizations relate to cost accounting activities.

In addition to Canadian requirements, those firms that have shares registered on the U.S. exchanges are required to conform with the U.S. Securities and Exchange Commission (SEC) accounting pronouncements.

Canadian Institute of Chartered Accountants

Accounting and Auditing Research Committees of the Canadian Institute of Chartered Accountants (CICA) are responsible in publishing Accounting and Auditing Recommendations for the *CICA Handbook*, which constitutes the generally accepted accounting principles in Canada. The recommendations are primarily concerned with financial accounting, or the external reporting process. However, cost accounting information in summary form is part of the external financial statements of most organizations. Some of the pronouncements of the CICA therefore have a direct impact on the cost accounting systems of firms. The CICA confers **chartered accountant** (CA) designation in Canada.

Segmented Reporting

One of the most important requirements of the CICA directly affects the cost accounting systems of the firms whose shares trade publicly. This requirement is known as segmented information, line of business reporting, or segmented reporting. According to Section 1700 of the *CICA Handbook*, issued in 1979, the financial statements of an enterprise whose securities are traded in the public market are required to disclose information by industry and geographical area. A company's consolidated financial statements provide valuable information about its performance as a whole. However, more specific information about its performance in a particular industry or area might be needed for better comparison with the other companies. This more detailed information, called segmented information, requires a sound cost accounting data base.

Other Organizations

From time to time the Canadian government has established certain price and wage control programs. These programs, in general, require a prescribed set of rules that affect the cost accounting data base of the firms in Canada. For example, the last price and wage control measurements in the mid 1970s permitted price increases to those firms that could verify their cost increases. Certainly, this requirement meant maintenance of a good cost accounting data base.

As mentioned earlier, there are a number of regulatory agencies on both the federal and provincial levels that affect the cost accounting data base of Canadian firms.

Accounting organizations like the Certified General Accountants Association of Canada and the Society of Management Accountants are actively engaged in research, publication, and education of accountants in Canada. The latter organization is discussed in detail in this chapter because it is primarily related to management accounting. The reader is urged to refer to the *Financial Accounting* volume of this series for background information about the Canadian and U.S. accounting organizations.

Society of Management Accountants

The Society of Management Accountants of Canada (SMA) was formed by the provincial CA institutes in 1920. Since then it has become an independent entity. The SMA has several basic objectives:

a. To ensure that there are a sufficient number of qualified professional management accountants to meet the needs of business and government. The RIA (Registered Industrial Accountant) study program and continuing graduate services are designed to fulfill this requirement.
b. To set the standards for granting the professional accreditation in management accounting.
c. To promote, through cooperation with universities and colleges, the development of the RIA body of knowledge, and to ensure that it is available through the educational system.
d. To provide a continuing research in management accounting and related fields; to refine the role of the management accountant.
e. To inform members of developments in their profession; to provide educational courses and programs which help members keep pace with innovations in their field and foster personal and career growth.
f. To maintain the standards of competence of its members and enhance the status of the profession.

In line with these objectives the Society of Management Accountants confers the designation RIA (Registered Industrial Accountant) and publishes *Cost and Management*, the SMA journal that was established in 1924. The RIA program is divided into five levels that contain a various number of courses that progress in terms of difficulty. Candidates are required to complete all assignments and examinations. The candidate for professional accreditation as an RIA must meet the following requirements:

1. Successful completion of the prescribed RIA examination.
2. Successful completion of a period of relevant work experience, the length of such period to be determined by the provincial society. In practice, the student has usually fulfilled the work requirements by the time he or she has completed the program of instruction.

Finally, in order to retain the right to use the RIA designation, graduates must maintain their society membership in good standing.

Recently the Society of Management Accountants has issued an exposure draft on management accounting guidelines[1] similar to CICA exposure drafts on financial accounting.

Summary   Organizations require accounting information for internal management and to meet external reporting requirements. **Financial accounting** is concerned with providing accounting information to external users. **Managerial accounting** refers to the internal reporting process.

Decision making is a frequent activity, but many decisions are so routine that we fail to think of them as decisions. Major decisions, such as the purchase of expensive items, make us aware of the decision process. Decision making should be approached in a logical and systematic manner. Although each individual may have a different decision-making style, most people agree that the process includes **defining the problem, identifying alternatives, accumulating relevant information,** and **making the decision.** The body of knowledge encompassing decision making is called **decision theory.** A formal description of the way that a decision is made is called a **decision model.**

The role of information is to increase knowledge or decrease risk. Accounting information is often very useful in fulfilling this role because it is quantitative and verifiable. The demand for accounting information continues to grow.

Accounting information should be relevant, timely, and accurate. **Relevance** means accounting data must satisfy the specific information needs of the user. **Timeliness** relates to the decline in information value over time. Financial information is particularly sensitive to loss in value due to the passage of time. **Accuracy** deals with the correctness of accounting reports.

The terms *data* and *information* are often used interchangeably. In some disciplines **information** is data put together in usable form for a decision maker. **Data** are the raw materials or source elements of the information system. A **data base** is the total data foundation that supports the information system.

Cost accounting deals with the determination of cost for some specific product or activity. Cost data are used in both internal and external reports. Internal reports are more detailed and more frequent than external reports. Although a great deal of detailed cost data is used for internal reports, cost accounting and managerial accounting are not identical. Cost accounting provides data base support for both the financial and managerial reporting functions.

[1]Society of Management Accountants, January 1983, Hamilton, Ontario.

Cost accounting acitivity is divided into **cost finding, cost recording, cost analyzing,** and **cost reporting.** An understanding of cost accounting is necessary to understand many important aspects of managerial accounting.

The volume of cost data generated and the complexity of a cost system are affected by a number of important variables, including the size of the firm, the type of production process, the number of different products produced, management's attitude toward cost accounting information, and external variables. The major external variables are governmental agencies and regulatory bodies.

Revenue Canada monitors the operation of federal tax laws. Basically, Revenue Canada uses generally accepted accounting principles (GAAP) as the basis for determining taxable income. However, Revenue Canada determines accounting procedures for tax purposes whenever the use of GAAP results in taxable income that is unfair in the eyes of the taxing authorities.

The **provincial securities and exchange commissions** and other similar regulatory agencies do require certain information that relate to firms' cost accounting systems and procedures.

The Canadian Institute of Chartered Accountants is responsible for publishing the *CICA Handbook* which constitutes the generally accepted accounting principles in Canada. Although the recommendations are primarily concerned with financial accounting, they influence the cost accounting data base of companies. For example, requirement of **segmented information** disclosure for certain companies forces those affected companies to design their data base in such a way that it would facilitate this reporting requirement.

Among the other organizations that affect the data base of companies are **Transport Canada, Canadian Radio and Telecommunications Commission, Statistics Canada,** and a number of other federal and provincial regulatory bodies. Accounting organizations like the **Society of Management Accountants** (SMA), which confers **Registered Industrial Accountant** (RIA) designation, and the **Certified General Accountants Association of Canada** through research, publication, and education programs affect the cost accounting practices.

List of important terms
Many new terms commonly used in business and accounting have been introduced in this chapter. Most of them are used and explained in subsequent parts of the book. You should become familiar with the ones in the list that follows. The italic numbers in parentheses indicate the pages on which the terms first appear.

accuracy   *(8)*
Certified General Accountant
   (CGA)   *(15)*
Chartered Accountant (CA)   *(14)*
cost accounting   *(10)*
cost accounting data base   *(10)*
cost analyzing   *(11)*
cost benefit   *(8)*
cost finding   *(11)*
cost recording   *(11)*
cost reporting   *(12)*
data   *(9)*
data base   *(9)*

decision model   *(7)*
decision theory   *(4)*
financial accounting   *(4)*
information   *(9)*
managerial accounting   *(4)*
Provincial securities and
   exchange commissions   *(14)*
Registered Industrial Accountant
   (RIA)   *(15)*
relevance   *(8)*
Revenue Canada   *(13)*
Society of Management
   Accountants (SMA)   *(15)*
timeliness   *(8)*

Questions

1. Distinguish between financial accounting and managerial accounting.
2. Define decision theory. How does it relate to accounting?
3. Identify and briefly describe the basic steps in the decision process.
4. What does the term *information overload* mean?
5. Give an example of a decision model you have used in the last six months.
6. Where does accounting information fit into the decision process?
7. Describe the characteristics of accounting information.
8. Contrast managerial accounting and cost accounting.
9. Identify four cost accounting activities.
10. What factors affect the complexity of a cost accounting system?
11. What is segmented information? Why is it needed?
12. Describe the role of Revenue Canada in affecting cost accounting systems.
13. What are the objectives of CICA and SMA in Canada? In what ways are they similar and in what ways are they different?
14. You are enrolled in a college or university. Why? Briefly outline the steps you took (or might have taken) to make that decision.

Exercises

Ex. 1-1 **Understanding the role of accounting.** You are treasurer of a large state university. A decline in student enrollments for the second semester has caused tuition payments to fall $800,000 short of expectations. You prepare a report showing the effect of the tuition shortage on operations and suggest an immediate hiring freeze for nonessential positions. You take the report to the new university president, who does not have a business background. His response is, "Why did you bring me this? We are not a business. Costs make little difference here. When are people like you going to understand that the almighty dollar has no place on a college campus?"

Required:
Defend yourself.

Ex. 1-2 **Selecting accounting information.** Jackie Walker just recieved a degree in horticulture and plans to open a flower and gift shop. Although she is very skilled in her discipline, she has never had any accounting or business courses. She asks you, a friend, to tell her what kind of information she might need.

Required:
Answer Jackie, emphasizing the purpose of such information.

Ex. 1-3 **The role of accounting information.** As controller of the High Seas Waterbed Company, you are called before the executive committee. The president asks you, "How come our accounting system costs are growing as fast as our company? Here we are adding new products and new stores, and you're adding new people just as fast. An accounting system is an accounting system; the cost should remain constant from period to period. And what's this note about Statistics Canada forms? We don't have anything to do with Statistics Canada, do we?

Required:
Respond to the executive committee.

Ex. 1-4   Identifying decision-making activities. Below are descriptions of selected activities that occurred recently in a department store.

	Defining the Problem	Identifying Alternatives	Accumulating Information	Making the Decision
a. The store manager receives the sales report for the month of July and notes that sales are off by 5 percent from last July and 8 percent from expected sales for this July.				
b. A meeting of department heads and the controller indicates that July sales in sporting goods are off nearly 50 percent from what was expected. Sporting goods normally has the second-highest departmental sales volume in the store. Excluding sporting goods, July sales in the other departments are only 2 percent short of expected levels.				
c. The head of the sporting goods department points out that a new sporting goods discount store was opened only a block away on June 28. Heavy advertising and grand opening specials have drawn away many of the department store's customers.				
d. The head of the sporting goods department suggests that the store run a mid-summer sale on sporting goods matching or bettering the prices at the new store.				
e. The director of marketing thinks a significant reduction in prices in one department would change the flavour of the store and set a dangerous trend. She suggests that a vigorous newspaper and television advertising campaign be launched, emphasizing the reputation and service of the sporting goods department of the store.				
f. The head of another department says the store is fighting a losing battle against the tough new competition in sporting goods and recommends that the sporting goods department be eliminated altogether.				
g. The controller presents a departmental performance report which indicates that sporting goods still contributed something to the store's profit in July, even though it was not nearly as much as normal.				
h. A week after the meeting the director of marketing reports to the store manager on the cost of the proposed advertising program. A large advertising campaign would reduce the cost of the normal advertising program by 20 percent because of quantity discounts.				

	Defining the Problem	Identifying Alternatives	Accumulating Information	Making the Decision
i. The assistant controller prepares a cost study showing the reduction in profit margin per dollar of sales if the proposed price reductions are implemented.				
j. After careful study of the information, the store manager decides that sporting goods has been an integral part of the store for too long to eliminate the department. Also, it is difficult to measure the effect on business of wives shopping in other departments when their husbands come to shop for sporting goods.				
k. The store manager decides that discounts of about half the proposed amount would be acceptable in light of previous sale pricing guidelines. Larger discounts would require the elimination of certain store services.				
l. The store manager decides to increase advertising significantly for the next six months and periodically to run special discounts on selected items within the store's pricing policy.				

Required:

Indicate by a check mark in the appropriate column how each activity should be classified in terms of its role in the decision process.

Ex. 1-5   Classifying accounting activities. Following is a variety of accounting activities or events for the Curiali Corporation.

	Managerial Accounting	Financial Accounting	Cost Accounting
a. Daily time cards are tabulated to determine the amount of time employees spent on each activity.			
b. The cost of maintenance supplies is recorded.			
c. Weekly labour use reports are sent to production supervisors.			
d. A quarterly production output report is sent to the plant manager.			
e. The company's quarterly income statement is summarized in the financial news.			
f. The company president receives a quarterly profit report for each product line.			

	Managerial Accounting	Financial Accounting	Cost Accounting

g. The company's independent auditors discuss the need for several financial statement footnotes with the controller.

h. A list of materials put into production during the preceding day is sent to the accounting department by the inventory storeroom manager.

i. The controller presents a special report on the cost of building a new plant in Ontario at the board of directors' meeting.

j. The controller holds a special meeting of his staff to discuss the proper treatment on the balance sheet of the company's new lease on computer equipment.

Required:
Indicate by a check mark in the appropriate column how each activity or event should be classified.

Problem Set A

P. 1A-1   Identifying decision-making activities. Following are descriptions of activities that occurred recently at the Jones Manufacturing Company.

	Defining the Problem	Identifying Alternatives	Accumulating Information	Making the Decision
a. The plant manager noticed that the labour cost per unit of product has increased by 20 percent during the second quarter of the year.				
b. The chief engineer reports that no changes have been made in the production process during the second quarter.				
c. When asked about the situation, the production supervisor complained about the large amount of lost production time caused by the slow repair of machines that broke down.				
d. The maintenance supervisor defended the slow repair time by noting that no machinery had been replaced in several years. A large block of metal shearing and forming machines was all rapidly wearing out. Extensive maintenance on these machines was causing delays in repairs to plant machinery in general.				
e. The plant manager thinks the problem can be solved by replacing most of the old machines, hiring 20 new maintenance employees, or entering into a maintenance agreement with an outside firm to service all hydraulic machines.				
f. The accounting department prepares a study of expected costs for hiring 10 new maintenance employees.				
g. The finance department prepares a report evaluating the replacement of 10 shearing machines and 12 forming machines.				
h. The purchasing agent reports on the contract options available from the three qualified hydraulic maintenance companies in town.				
i. The plant manager decides he should not choose an alternative that requires a major cash outlay because lagging sales have made the company short of cash throughout the last year.				
j. The plant manager decides to hire 20 new maintenance employees.				

Required:
Indicate by a check mark in the appropriate column how each activity should be classified in terms of its role in the decision-making process.

Problem Set B

P. 1B-1   Classifying accounting activities. Below are a number of accounting-related activities of Benjamin's Manufacturing Company.

	Managerial Accounting	Financial Accounting	Cost Accounting
a. Company sales personnel are provided with reports showing their sales-to-date for the year compared with their target sales for the same period.			
b. Sales personnel turn in their weekly expense data to the accounting department.			
c. The controller and assistant controller discuss how to report the lease for the sales personnel's portable computer terminals on the balance sheet.			
d. The vice president of sales receives a report on the cost of selling each type of product.			
e. Weekly payroll costs are summarized and identified with specific activities.			
f. The company's annual report is issued.			
g. The year-end inventory count is taken, and adjustments are made to correct errors.			
h. A quarterly update on the profitability of a new line of business is sent to the bank providing financing for the project.			
i. A special labour efficiency report is prepared for the company negotiator to be used in upcoming contract negotiations.			
j. The company's independent auditor requested a list of product cost data to be used in the audit that starts next month.			

Required:
Indicate by a check mark in the appropriate column how each activity should be classified.

Minicases

Minicase 1-1

Identifying relevant accounting information. Nolan's department store has used a delivery service to make all local deliveries for many years. The cost of the service averages $.20 per kilogram this year for the 600 000 kilograms of merchandise delivered. The delivery service company plans to raise the rate by 15 percent for next year. The management of the department store is not pleased with the rate increase and thinks of starting the store's own delivery service. The following data have been gathered. An affiliate store in another city currently spends $.18 a kilogram for local deliveries. Two new delivery trucks would cost $80,000 each, have a delivery capacity of 500 000 kilograms each per year, and would have a salvage value of $5,000 each at the end of five years. Other truck costs would average $.01 per kilogram for insurance, $.04 for gas and oil, $.02 for maintenance, and $.06 for personnel. Other costs associated with loading, storing, and delivering merchandise would amount to $.05 a kilogram. If the trucks had been purchased last year, they would have cost only $65,000 each.

Required:
a. Determine the per-kilogram cost of deliveries if the store starts making its own deliveries. Should the store switch to its own delivery service?
b. Would your answer to part *a* change if deliveries for the next year were 800 000 kilograms instead of 600 000 kilograms?
c. What items of data did you choose to ignore in your analysis of parts *a* and *b*? Why?

Minicase 1-2   (Certified Accountants—U.K. adapted)

During 1980 Alfred Williams retired from the army and with his gratuity purchased a small retail wool shop which he called Olive's Wool Shop, after his wife. Since then he has run the shop with no assistance other than that from his wife Olive. During 1983 he was asked by the Retail Association of Wool Shops whether he would be prepared to submit his annual accounts, for these to be combined in an anonymous manner with those of other firms, to enable comparisons of trading results to be made.

Mr. Williams agreed and sent along his accounts for the year ended 31st March, 1983, which were as follows:

Olive's Wool Shop

Profit & Loss Account for the year ended 31st March, 1983

Sales		$101,450
Less: Cost of goods sold		60,870
Gross Profit		40,580
Expenses		
Wages	$3,250	
Rates	1,250	
Heating and light	3,700	
Insurance	800	
Advertising, print, stationery	5,100	
Miscellaneous expense	2,750	
Depreciation	4,000	
		20,850
Net Profit (before taxation)		$19,730

The following additional information had to be supplied:

i Whether the premises were owned or rented, and if the latter, the amount of the rent.

ii Details of the time that the owner and other members of his family spent working in the shop. In their case, Mr. Williams worked for 40 hours each week and his wife for 30 hours.

iii Details of equipment used in the shop (cost, date of purchase, estimated life).

iv The amount shown on the capital account. This was $47,500 at the commencement of the year in question.

Subsequently, Mr. Williams received the following statement of the "average" accounts for the wool shops contributing to the scheme, with his own results as "adjusted" by the Association.

	Olive's Wool Shop		Average Wool Shop	
Sales		$101,450		$124,400
Less: Cost of goods sold		60,870		64,700
Gross Profit		$40,580		$59,700
EXPENSES				
Management expenses	$20,000		$18,500	
Wages	8,650		6,100	
Rates	1,250		1,200	
Heating and light	3,700		3,450	
Insurance	800		900	
Advertising, printing, etc.	5,100		2,800	
Miscellaneous expenses	2,750		2,500	
Depreciation	4,000		4,000	
Interest on capital	4,750		4,800	
Rent	5,000		5,000	
	—	56,000	—	49,250
Net Profit (Loss) (before taxation)		$15,420		$10,450

Mr. Williams and his wife were perplexed at these figures as from their own accounts they had felt that they were doing very well.

Required:

a. An explanation of the purpose of the exercise and of the reasons for each of the adjustments to the original profit statement.

b. A comparison of the results of Olive's Wool Shop with those for similar shops which indicates those areas which Mr. Williams should investigate. How should Mr. Williams view these individual problem areas in order to improve the overall performance of his business?

Chapter 2

Cost Flows and Concepts

This chapter presents fundamental cost concepts and terminology that are essential in developing cost information and understanding cost reports. When you have completed this chapter, you should understand:

1 The definition of cost objective and the different types of cost objectives.

2 The types of costs included in product cost.

3 The relationship between cost flows and production flows.

4 The role of product costs in the income statements of various types of businesses.

5 The basic accounting activities associated with the acquisition and use of production resources.

6 The nature and composition of direct materials, direct labour, and manufacturing overhead.

7 The use of periodic and perpetual inventories.

8 The nature of unit costs.

9 That some costs change proportionately with the volume of activity and some costs remain constant.

In Chapter 1 we emphasized the importance of cost data in developing accounting reports and the concept that costs of all sorts play an important role in management accounting and in the decision-making process. You also learned that an important function of managerial accounting is to provide cost information in a meaningful way so that managers can make decisions intelligently. The next step in the study of managerial accounting is to become familiar with cost accounting terminology and how costs are determined. The purpose of Chapter 2 is to describe the flow of costs in the production of products and to present basic terminology commonly used in cost accounting and managerial accounting reports. With this foundation you will be ready for subsequent chapters in which many different kinds of costs are used for preparing managerial accounting reports. Upon completing this chapter, you should have a good understanding of how costs are related to the actual physical activity of producing products. You should also have an understanding of the basic terminology of cost accounting.

The concept of cost

Cost defined

Perhaps no accounting term is used more widely in everyday conversation than cost. As a result, cost may have many different meanings to different people. From an accounting point of view, cost is the amount of resources given up in exchange for some good or service. The resource given up is usually money, but if not, it is still expressed in monetary units.

The cost of purchased products

Sometimes determining costs is a simple process. The cost of many products and services can be found merely by asking a vendor or an agent selling the product or service. If you are interested in finding out how much it will cost to buy a boat, many boat dealers will provide you with the purchase price of various types of boats. The cost of many items, however, is not so readily available. When goods or services are not purchased but instead are produced, determining the cost may be difficult. Instead of a single quoted amount for an item, the cost of a manufactured product is a combination of the cost of many resources. For example, if you decide to build a boat, you have to determine the cost of all resources used in the production of the boat, such as the cost of materials, labour, and depreciation on production equipment, all of which are necessary to produce the boat. Some of the production costs, such as fibreglass, resin, and wood, are relatively easy to trace to the boat. Likewise, the cost of employees who work directly on producing the boat is readily identifiable as part of the cost of the boat. However, other costs, such as heating and electricity for the production plant and maintenance for the manufacturing plant and production machinery, are not very easy to identify with each boat. Moreover, the cost estimate for making the boat is less certain than the quotes received from boat dealers.

The cost of manufactured products

The fact that determining the cost of manufactured products can be difficult does not deter organizations from producing goods and services. Well-established cost accounting systems and procedures provide the means of measuring costs for a wide variety of uses. A large number of managerial accounting reports and related management decisions rely on cost data as the basic input.

Defining cost objectives

Cost objectives must be described clearly

The first step in determining the cost of any product or activity is to define the cost objective precisely. The cost objective is the product or activity whose cost is to be determined. For instance, if you want to know the cost of a boat, you must describe what type of boat you want. The dealer may have boats priced from $500 to $50,000. The more precise your description of the boat, the better the chance of obtaining the correct price quotation. In business it is just as essential for the accountant to know precisely what the cost objective is. Often it is a product, such as a tire, refrigerator, or backpack. Cost objectives may also be activities, such as the cost of an advertising campaign or the monthly cost of operating the company's computer. Identifying the cost objective sounds easy and often is, but great care must be exercised to describe what costs should be included in measuring the cost of some item. For example, the cost of a year at university might include:

1. Tuition, room and board.
2. Tuition, room and board, and books.
3. Tuition, room and board, books, and spending money.
4. Tuition, room and board, books, spending money, and transportation.
5. All expenditures for university plus the loss of income that would be earned if the student did not attend university.

Each of these definitions of the cost of a year at university may be appropriate depending on the way a person plans to use the information. For example, a parent trying to determine the total cash outlay for a year on campus might find item 4 to be the most useful measure of costs. On the other hand, item 1 best describes the contractual amount the university will charge. You can probably think of many personal examples of cost objectives, such as a car, a house, a vacation, or food costs. In each case a variety of different costs can be included. Consequently, it is very important that the cost objective for each situation is clearly and completely described. This is especially true in businesses that must use cost information for making many decisions. Cost objectives must state not only the nature of the cost, but also the amount of detail needed or desired. For example, management might be interested in the cost of:

1. The total advertising program.
2. Advertising for a specific product.
3. Advertising for a specific sales region.
4. Advertising by region for a specific product.
5. A variety of other combinations of advertising cost.

Each of these measures of cost would be useful to managers in planning and managing activities.

Product costing

A logical starting point for discussing costing concepts and procedures is with tangible products, such as tables, radios, baseballs, or washing machines. Often the costs associated with the production of a tangible product are easy to understand because one can visualize the flow of the product through the manufacturing process. In Chapters 2 through 4, product costing is emphasized. Later chapters cover costing of activities, such as marketing, computer services, and personnel services.

Manufacturing cost elements

Three basic types of manufacturing costs are identified with the production of goods. They are called cost elements and include:

The three types of manufacturing costs

1. Direct materials.
2. Direct labour.
3. Manufacturing overhead.

Material directly identifiable with products

Direct materials are the raw materials that can be directly identified with the production of a specific product. Direct materials become part of the product, such as the handle of a hammer, the wood frame of a sofa, or the steel in an automobile. For many products direct material is the largest manufacturing cost element. In some cases it is not possible or economically feasible to identify all raw material costs with individual products. For example, the amount of glue used to mount the insignia on an automobile is so insignificant in comparison with the total cost of manufacturing the car that accountants do not identify it as direct material. Such raw material items are called **indirect material** and are part of manufacturing overhead costs discussed below.

Labour directly identifiable with products

Direct labour is labour that can be specifically identified with the production of a particular product and contributes directly to completion of the product. Employees putting together the parts of a television set as it moves along the assembly line provide direct labour. Similarly, the cost of an employee painting the outside panels of an air conditioner and of a drill press operator drilling bolt holes in an automobile frame would be classified as direct labour. Some labour necessary for the efficient operation of manufacturing activities cannot readily be identified with specific products. For example, employees who move materials from one work centre to another and employees who repair and maintain the plant and production equipment are a necessary part of the production process, but their cost cannot be identified as direct labour. This indirect labour is part of manufacturing overhead cost discussed below.

Indirect manufacturing costs

Manufacturing overhead (MOH) consists of all manufacturing costs other than direct material and direct labour. It contains all of the indirect costs in the manufacturing process. Indirect manufacturing costs are necessary production costs, but they cannot be identified with specific products. Many different kinds of manufacturing overhead costs exist depending on the type of product and the type of production processes used. Although the specific composition of the MOH account varies from firm to firm, there are many common types of costs found in most manufactuing firms. Indirect materials and indirect labour have already been mentioned. Many other overhead costs are occupancy or capacity costs. They include:

1. Building rental or depreciation.
2. Machinery and equipment depreciation or lease cost.
3. Heat, light, and power costs.
4. Maintenance costs.
5. Insurance and taxes on the manufacturing facilities.

Other common manufacturing overhead costs are employee fringe benefits, such as health insurance, vacation pay, and pension benefits, supervisory salaries for manufacturing personnel, and inventory handling costs. Overhead costs are indirect costs of production and by their very nature are not directly identifiable with specific products. Overhead costs are, however, important and necessary manufacturing costs, and accountants must be able to assign them to products. Later in this chapter and in Chapter 4 we discuss the process of assigning overhead costs to products.

Manufacturing overhead is also called factory overhead, manufacturing burden, factory burden, or simply burden or overhead. All of these terms are used in business, but manufacturing overhead is most common and is used throughout this text.

No cost element is generally more important than the others

None of the three basic cost elements is generally more important than either of the others. The relative importance of each depends on the type of product and the way it is produced. One product may require more costly material or less skilled labour than another. Many products can be produced in a variety of ways. Some production methods may require much manual labour, whereas others may be highly automated. Frequently, managers change production methods, causing a shift in the relative importance of cost elements. For example, automation may reduce the relative amount of direct labour cost and increase the relative amount of manufacturing overhead cost. Lower product cost, increased production capacity, more production flexibility, and better production control are but a few reasons why managers alter the mix of production resources.

In discussing direct materials, direct labour, and manufacturing overhead, business managers sometimes combine terms. Direct materials and direct labour together are called prime cost. Prime refers to the directly traceable nature of the two costs. Direct labour and manufacturing overhead together are called conversion costs because together they are costs of converting raw materials into the finished product.

Production flows and cost flows

Production flow is a physical concept, and cost flow is an accounting concept. Production supervisors are primarily interested in monitoring and controlling production flows. Accountants are especially interested in determining and reporting the cost flows associated with the production process. The flow of

*Cost flows parallel
production flows*

product costs parallels the physical flow of the product through the production process. Accountants assign to products the costs that occur as a result of production activities. The causal relationship between production activity and product cost is most obvious with direct materials and direct labour costs, but the assignment of indirect manufacturing costs is essential as well and is guided by the matching concept, which requires the matching of expenses with associated revenues. With manufactured products, production costs are assigned to products and when the product is sold, the expense of producing the product is matched with the revenue generated by the sale of the product. Throughout this

*The matching
principle is the key to
product costing*

book the matching concept is stressed as the most important accounting principle in product costing and management reporting.

Visualize the production of a simple product, such as a sledge hammer. A worker picks up a wooden handle and inserts it in the hole of the hammer's head. He then drives a wedge into a slot to keep the handle from falling out of the head. You see that there are three raw materials: the head, the handle, and the wedge, and a certain amount of labour time is required to put the three together. With the help of labour the three materials flow together to make up the finished product. Each of the materials has a specific cost, as does the labour time of the worker. When the hammer head is joined to the handle, the sledge hammer's cost is the total of the two separate material costs. When the wedge is added, the cost of the sledge hammer increases by the cost of the wedge. At the same time, the cost of labour also increases the costs of the hammer. The flow of product costs parallels the physical flow of the materials and labour into the product through the production process.

As previously noted, production supervisors are primarily interested in controlling production flows. Are enough handles available? Is the wedge tight enough in each hammer? Is the amount of time spent on assembly excessive? Accountants, on the other hand, are especially interested in determining and reporting the cost flows associated with the production process. How much does each handle cost? Is the cost of the hammer head excessive? What is the wage of the employee? With direct material and labour costs the causal relationship between the production activity and product costs is clear. The assignment of indirect manufacturing costs is also important, however, and it is guided by the same matching concept that governs direct costs. The accountant is concerned with such questions as: How much of the factory depreciation should be assigned to each sledge hammer? How much electricity cost does each require?

As the sledge hammer example illustrates, materials are placed into production and converted into a product. As the product and costs change during the manufacturing process, the accountant must keep track of them in various inventory accounts.

**Manufacturing
inventories**

Typically inventories play a more important role in manufacturing firms than in other types of business. Service firms have little or no inventory that they hold for resale to customers. Operating supplies and convenience items are carried only to facilitate the main function of providing services. Merchandising firms acquire inventory for resale to customers. A merchandising firm may have many different classifications of inventory and many items within each inventory classification, but all inventory items are ready for sale. They do not require any major modifications, although assembly or other convenience services may be performed in connection with their sale.

A manufacturing firm has three major levels of inventory:

The three levels of manufacturing inventories

1. Raw materials
2. Work in process
3. Finished goods

The basic materials

Raw materials are the basic inputs or ingredients that are converted into final products through the production process. The term raw materials does not necessarily mean the most basic of resources, such as lumber and iron ore. Instead raw material for a manufacturing firm may be a partially manufactured product that is processed further. For example, pig iron is the raw material of the forging company that makes sledge hammer heads and sells them to the sledge hammer manufacturer. The final product of the forge is a raw material of the hammer manufacturer. The finished iron hammer head is the raw material of the sledge hammer manufacturer who buys the heads and wood handles used in the manufacture of the hammers. Most raw material inventory is used as direct material. A small portion appears as indirect material. A single product may require a large number of different raw materials, and a manufacturer that produces many different products may have thousands of different raw material items.

Partially completed products

Work in process is the second level of inventory in a manufacturing firm. It consists of unfinished products that are in the process of being converted into final products, such as the sledge hammer with head and handle joined, but not yet wedged. Many different items can be in work in process simultaneously. For example, a bakery can have a variety of breads, cakes, and doughnuts in process at any given time.

Products ready for sale

Finished goods is the final level of inventory consisting of products ready for sale, such as the completed sledge hammers. Finished goods inventory in a manufacturing firm is similar to the merchandise inventory in a merchandising firm. In a multiple-product manufacturing firm, there are many different finished goods inventory items.

Production cost cycle illustrated

The process of accounting for the cost of manufactured products closely parallels the actual physical flow of a product through production. Figure 2-1 shows the physical flow of products through the production process and the corresponding flow of costs through the ledger accounts, from the start of production through the sale of the product. It illustrates a complete cycle for the product cost of a manufacturing firm. The process summarized here is discussed in more detail later in the chapter.

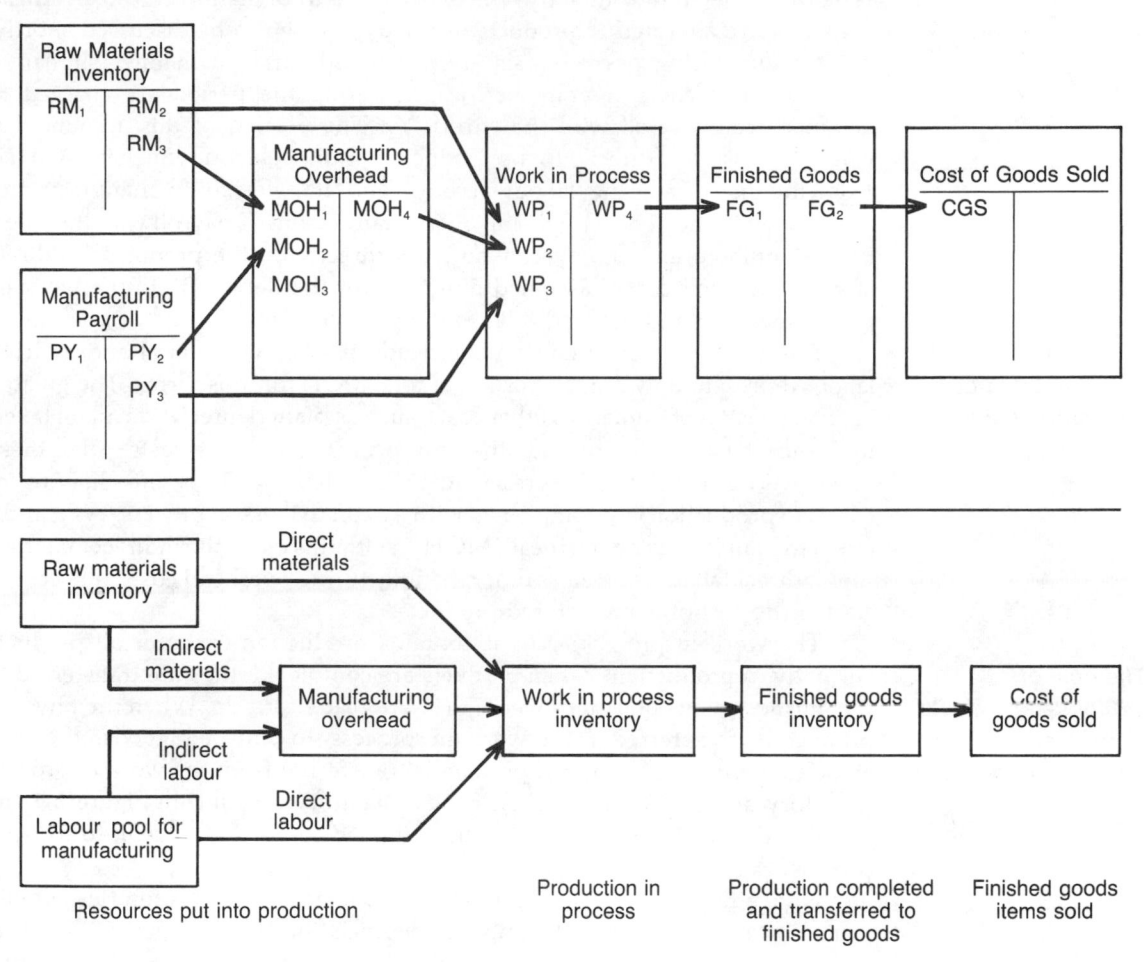

Figure 2-1
The physical flow of products through the production process is paralleled by
the flow of costs through the ledger accounts. The matching concept guides
accountants in assigning costs to products.

Raw material purchases are recorded in the raw materials inventory
account with a debit, represented in Figure 2-1 by RM_1. The transfer of raw
material cost to production occurs in two ways. The largest amounts of raw
materials are direct materials, recorded with a debit to work in process, WP_1,
and a credit to raw materials inventory, RM_2. When an indirect material is put
into production, it is recorded with a debit to manufacturing overhead, MOH_1,
and a credit to raw materials inventory, RM_3. Indirect materials cannot be

assigned to the product directly so they become part of manufacturing overhead costs that are allocated to products in a separate step to be discussed shortly.

Manufacturing payroll costs are accounted for in a manner similar to materials. The costs of employee wages during the period are charged to manufacturing payroll with the entry PY_1. The portion of this account that cannot be assigned directly to the products is indirect labour which is removed from the manufacturing labour account and transferred to manufacturing overhead with the debit MOH_2 and out of manufacturing payroll with the credit PY_2. Manufacturing employees who work directly on the products are direct labour, and their cost is assigned directly with the debit WP_3 to the work in process account and the credit PY_3 to the payroll account.

Manufacturing costs are charged to work in process

The debits to manufacturing overhead for indirect material and indirect labour represent only a small portion of total MOH for most firms. The greater portion consists of numerous other costs, such as plant depreciation, plant taxes, insurance, heat, electricity, and other indirect manufacturing costs. All of these other overhead items are represented by the debit MOH_3. The charging of MOH to production is accomplished with a debit to work in process, WP_2, and a credit to manufacturing overhead, MOH_4. With this entry the indirect materials and indirect labour, as well as other manufacturing overhead costs, all become part of the cost of manufactured products.

The cost of completed products is charged to finished goods

The work in process account contains production costs for all products currently in production. When products are completed, they are transferred to the finished goods inventory where they are **ready** for sale. When the physical product is transferred from work in process to finished goods, the cost associated with producing the product is transferred from the work in process inventory account to the finished goods inventory account. In Figure 2-1 the entry is represented by a debit to finished goods, FG_1, and a credit to work in process, WP_4.

Notice that both work in process and finished goods inventories contain some costs, such as payroll, utilities, depreciation, and property taxes that appear as period expenses in nonmanufacturing operations. In nonmanufacturing activities they are expensed because their value is gone. In a manufacturing firm, however, these costs enhance the value of the products on hand. Direct labour and production facilities have converted raw materials into goods that are more valuable than the raw materials from which they were made. This enhancement of value is not realized, however, until the product is sold. Since all of the costs that flow into production increase the value of the product, the costs are said to be inventoriable. Inventoriable costs are costs that legitimately can be added to the cost of a manufactured product because they are necessary for the production of the product.

Product costs become expenses at the time of sale

The sale of the product is the final step in the product cost-flow cycle. It is the event that causes the product cost to be transferred from the asset account, finished goods, to the expense account, cost of goods sold. The cost transfer is dictated by the matching principle, which requires the matching of expenses with associated revenues. The product cost is matched with the revenue generated from the sale of the product. This is accomplished by debiting cost of goods sold, CGS, and crediting finished goods inventory, FG_2, as shown in Figure 2-1. Regardless of how simple or complex the production process, the basic flow is the same as the one just described.

Product costs and the income statement

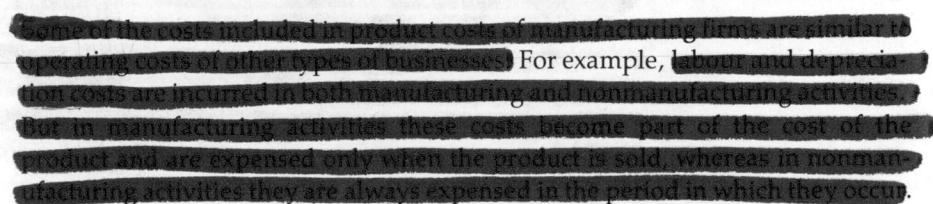 For example, labour and depreciation costs are incurred in both manufacturing and nonmanufacturing activities. But in manufacturing activities these costs become part of the cost of the product and are expensed only when the product is sold, whereas in nonmanufacturing activities they are always expensed in the period in which they occur. The income statement is convenient for comparing the cost characteristics of the three basic types of business: service firms, merchandising firms, and manufacturing firms.

Service firms

Doctors, lawyers, chartered accountants, realtors, and lawn-care companies are examples of businesses that sell services rather than products in order to generate revenue. The income statements of service firms are characterized by the fact that they have no product cost. The only deductions from revenue are operating expenses, which are costs that expired during the current accounting period and must be matched with the current period's revenues. The income statement of a service firm may also contain nonoperating revenues and expenses, income taxes, and extraordinary items that we omit to avoid unnecessary details. Figure 2-2 illustrates the income statement of a service business.

Service firms have no product expense

Fraser Williams, CA Income Statement For the Year Ended December 31, 1984		
Revenue from services		$88,000
Operating expenses:		
Salaries and wages	$38,000	
Office rent	4,800	
Depreciation on furniture and fixtures	2,400	
Professional and educational expenses	2,500	
Supplies	1,600	
Insurance	900	
Utilities	2,200	
Contributions to educational and charitable organizations	1,800	
Total operating expenses		54,200
Net income		$33,800

Figure 2-2
The income statement for a service firm has no product expense. Only operating expenses are deducted from revenue to determine net income.

Merchandising firms

Merchandising firms have a product cost

Department stores, drug stores, gift shops, and grocery stores are all common examples of merchandising businesses. The Canucks Sporting Goods Store, whose income statement is shown in Figure 2-3, is used to illustrate a merchandising income statement. Like all merchandising firms, it must first buy products before it can sell them to its customers. ~~The cost incurred by the merchandising firm in buying products is called product cost. When products are sold, the product cost becomes an expense called cost of goods sold. At the end of an accounting period, the cost of unsold products is considered an asset because the goods on hand have future economic value. This asset is called merchandise inventory and appears in the current asset section of the balance sheet.~~ The matching concept determines when the product cost becomes an expense. If the revenue from the sale of a product is reported in the income statement, then the corresponding cost of that product should be part of cost of goods sold in the same income statement.

In a merchandising firm the main revenue account is called sales. Associated with sales revenue is the product cost of the sold merchandise. The

Figure 2-3
A merchandising firm must buy inventory that it plans to sell for a profit. When the merchandise is sold, it becomes an expense called cost of goods sold. The difference between the cost and the selling price of units sold is called gross margin.

Canucks Sporting Goods Store Income Statement For the Year Ended December 31, 1984		
Sales		$236,500
Cost of goods sold:		
Beginning inventory 1/1/84	$ 74,000	
Purchases	$142,600	
Less: Purchase returns	(6,200)	
Add: Freight-in	2,400	
Net purchases	138,800	
Total goods available for sale	$212,800	
Less: Ending inventory 31/12/84	88,300	
Cost of goods sold		124,500
Gross margin		$112,000
Operating expenses:		
Salaries	$ 42,900	
Commissions	4,730	
Building rent	9,600	
Equipment rent	4,800	
Depreciation of furniture and fixtures	3,200	
Advertising	4,400	
Insurance	5,000	
Supplies	2,800	
Utilities	6,000	
Total operating expenses		83,430
Net income		$ 28,570

difference between sales revenue and cost of goods sold is called gross margin, and it is calculated before operating expenses are deducted. ~~Gross margin is the excess of the selling price over the cost of the product. For example, if a product sells for $5 and costs $2, the gross margin is $3.~~

Once the gross margin is determined, operating expenses are deducted, including all expenses of the period except product expense. The operating expenses of a merchandising firm are basically the same as those of a service firm. Differences in operating expenses occur because of the varying nature of operating activities of businesses. For instance, a merchandising firm has inventory handling expenses and usually more advertising expense than a service firm. However, many of the operating expense account classifications are similar.

Manufacturing firms

Like a merchandising firm, a manufacturing firm has a product cost that must be subtracted from sales revenue to arrive at gross margin. However, in a manufacturing firm the computation of the product cost is more complex than in a merchandising firm. The next two chapters are devoted to the determination of product cost for manufacturing businesses. Figure 2-4 illustrates a manufacturing business income statement.

Unlike a merchandising firm, a manufacturing company does not purchase products ready for sale. Instead it purchases a variety of production resources

Figure 2-4
Manufacturing firms convert raw materials into finished products in the production process. The cost of manufacturing the product becomes the product expense in the income statement when the product is sold.

Grenhurst Manufacturing Company Income Statement For the Year Ended December 31, 1984		
Sales		$792,000
Cost of goods sold:		
Beginning finished goods inventory 1/1/84	$ 82,000	
Add: Cost of goods manufactured in 1984	442,300	
Total goods available for sale	$524,300	
Less: Ending inventory 31/12/84	74,200	
Cost of goods sold		450,100
Gross margin		$341,900
Operating expenses:		
Salaries, sales and administrative personnel	$144,300	
Commissions	34,200	
Depreciation on selling and administrative furniture, fixtures, building, and equipment	68,400	
Advertising	15,000	
Insurance, office	8,600	
Supplies, office	26,500	
Utilities, office	19,900	
Total operating expenses		316,900
Net income		$ 25,000

that are assimilated into a salable product. The flow of costs from raw materials through finished goods to cost of goods sold is more difficult to identify than the product cost flow of a merchandising firm. Particularly the indirect costs of production are difficult to trace to products. In spite of these difficulties, it is important to develop accurate product costs for a variety of management uses. Cost data are the foundation for a multitude of management decisions and accounting reports, as discussed later in this book.

The operating expenses of a manufacturing firm may not be significantly different from those of a merchandising or service firm. In a manufacturing firm all operating expenses are nonmanufacturing costs, such as marketing and administrative expenses. All manufacturing costs appear as cost of goods sold if the product is sold, or as ending inventory if the product is not sold.

The schedule of cost of goods manufactured

Before it is possible to determine the amount of gross margin in the income statement, it is necessary to have the cost of goods manufactured for the period. This item, consisting of $442,300 in Figure 2-4, is not simply an account balance, but it is instead calculated from a schedule of cost of goods manufactured, an entirely new concept. Like the income statement, it covers a specific time period. The example in Figure 2-5 covers the calendar year 1984. Sometimes the schedule covers other time periods, such as a month or quarter.

The cost of manufactured products

The cost of goods manufactured schedule describes the cost of the products transferred from work in process to finished goods. It summarizes the flow of product costs through the work in process account for a specified time period. The cost of goods manufactured schedule starts with the beginning

Grenhurst Manufacturing Company Schedule of Cost of Goods Manufactured For the Year Ended December 31, 1984			
Beginning work in process 1/1/84			$ 46,800
Direct materials		$103,450	
Direct labour		152,900	
Manufacturing overhead:			
Depreciation, building	$ 46,000		
Depreciation, machinery	38,000		
Indirect labour	22,350		
Indirect materials	9,400		
Insurance	12,000		
Salaries	88,100		
Taxes, property	4,200		
Utilities	10,800	230,850	
Total manufacturing cost, 1984			487,200
Total manufacturing costs in production, 1984			$534,000
Less: Ending work in process 31/12/84			91,700
Cost of goods manufactured, 1984			$442,300

Figure 2-5
This schedule summarizes the total cost of manufacturing during the period, the cost of products transferred to finished goods during the period, and the cost of beginning and ending work in process inventories.

work in process inventory. To this amount are added the **production costs for the period** — direct materials, direct labour, and manufacturing overhead. ~~The costs added during the period represent new manufacturing costs for the period and are called total manufacturing cost for the period.~~ The total manufacturing cost for the period plus the beginning work in process inventory together represent the total manufacturing costs in production during the period. ~~At the end of the period, the remaining work in process inventory is subtracted from total manufacturing costs in production to find the cost of goods transferred to finished goods during the accounting period. This number is referred to as the cost of goods manufactured.~~ Do not confuse the term **cost of goods manufactured** with **total manufacturing cost for the period.** The former term describes the cost of the goods actually transferred to finished goods from work in process during the period. The latter term identifies the total manufacturing cost of the current period. The two numbers are identical only when the beginning and ending work in process inventory costs are identical.

The significance of product cost

Product cost is an important element in measuring the achievement of merchandising and manufacturing businesses. Variations in product costs can have a significant impact on key measures of performance, such as net income. To illustrate, a condensed income statement is presented below.

Sales	$1,000
Cost of goods sold	600
Gross margin	$ 400
Operating expenses	300
Net income	$ 100

Now assume that the product cost increases by 10 percent or $60 ($600 × .10). All other costs and revenues remain the same. The new income statement is:

The impact of product costs

Sales	$1,000
Cost of goods sold	660
Gross margin	$ 340
Operating expenses	300
Net income	$ 40

Note that the product cost has increased by 10 percent ($60/$600) and gross margin has declined by 15 percent ($60/$400). However, the really significant change is the 60 percent ($60/$100) decline in net income. ~~You can see that a relatively small change in product cost can cause a very significant change in net income.~~

Cost elements expanded

Earlier in the chapter we identified the three basic product cost elements—direct materials, direct labour, and manufacturing overhead—followed by a description of the cost flows in manufacturing activities. With these concepts understood, the discussion of the three cost elements can be expanded to present a more complete picture of the costing of manufactured products. The discussion is preceded by a brief description of control accounts that are used extensively in cost accounting.

Control accounts

Control accounts summarize detailed individual accounts

Control accounts are used to summarize the individual balances in a particular class of accounts. For example, control accounts are used to summarize the individual balances of accounts receivable of each customer and accounts payable to each supplier. The control account balance appears on the balance sheet rather than all the individual accounts receivable and accounts payable. All control accounts are supported by detailed subsidiary accounts that are maintained in a subsidiary ledger. The total of the individual balances in the subsidiary accounts is the balance in the general ledger control account. For example, a company has the following balances in its individual accounts receivable:

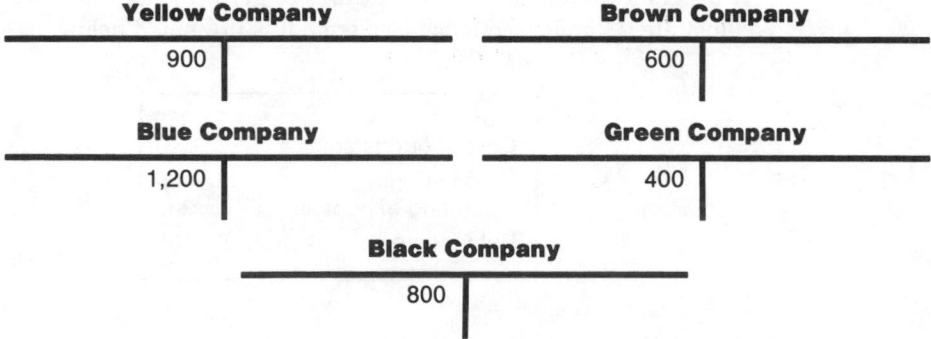

Yellow Company	Brown Company
900	600

Blue Company	Green Company
1,200	400

Black Company
800

The total of these accounts receivable is $3,900 and can be summarized in a control account for accounts receivable. If this is done, the control account replaces the individual accounts receivable in the general ledger, and the individual accounts become the subsidiary ledger for the control account.

Control accounts are used both for convenience and for control. For example, it would not be convenient to list all of a firm's individual accounts receivable on a balance sheet, although control over individual accounts is important. The subsidiary accounts provide the necessary control, and the control account balance is sufficient for balance sheet reporting and for situations in which managers need to know only the total amount of receivables.

Control accounts are widely used in managerial accounting, especially in the manufacturing area. Usually they are maintained for raw materials, work in process, finished goods, and manufacturing overhead. Control accounts facilitate the recording and reporting of cost flows, and they provide a ready framework for summarizing cost data.

Materials   The raw materials inventory is a major asset in most manufacturing firms and requires careful management. A discussion of inventory management is found in Chapter 15. Here we discuss the role of raw materials in the production process and trace the flow of costs associated with raw material flow.

~~There are two basic activities associated with the flow of raw materials in a manufacturing firm. The first is inventory acquisition and the second is inventory distribution. Inventory acquisition includes all of the activities necessary to purchase raw materials and move them into the inventory storage area called a storeroom or stores area. Inventory distribution refers to the process of distributing raw materials from inventory into production.~~

Acquiring inventory

Inventory acquisition. Figure 2-6 illustrates the activities associated with inventory acquisition and shows the major documents associated with the process. ~~These important source documents are valuable in identifying costs and providing an audit trail. A good audit trail enables the accountant to trace transactions and activities if problems or errors arise, and to verify that the accounting system is functioning properly.~~

The inventory acquisition process begins when someone determines that an item of raw material is needed. ~~Often someone in the inventory storeroom discovers that some inventory item is at an unacceptably low level and prepares a purchase requisition that is sent to the purchasing department.~~ This starts the purchasing process by notifying the purchasing department of the need for some item.

~~In the purchasing department a purchase order is prepared; this is a document used to place an order with a supplier.~~ The person in charge of the purchasing department is called a **purchasing agent.** In large organizations

Inventory acquisition activities

| A need for some raw material item is recognized. | → | Purchasing agent orders the required inventory item. | → | Inventory item is received. | → | Inventory item is transferred to the inventory storeroom control. |

Inventory acquisition documents

| Purchase requisition is prepared. | Purchase order is prepared. | Receiving report is prepared. | Inventory records are updated. |

Figure 2-6
Flow of inventory acquisition activities and the source of major inventory acquisition documents. Each activity results in a source document.

purchasing may be a highly specialized operation with a large purchasing department. In small firms it may be only one of several important functions performed by an individual. In either case the purchasing agent has prime responsibility for all purchasing activities.

When new materials arrive, a receiving report is issued. This document indicates receipt of the item or items and the amount received. The storeroom personnel then update the inventory records. Updating methods vary widely depending on the record-keeping system. With a manual system, entries are made by hand on inventory cards. In other systems, inventory records might be updated with a computer by using a remote terminal in the storeroom.

Putting inventory into production

Inventory distribution. It might seem that inventory distribution is simple. After all, it merely involves the transfer of materials from the inventory storage area to the production area. However, it is not always easy to have the proper quantity and quality of raw materials in the right place at the right time. The more complex the production activities, the more difficult is the inventory distribution process. A poor inventory distribution system can cost a company a great deal of money in lost producton and inefficient use of production facilities. The inventory distribution process is presented in Figure 2-7.

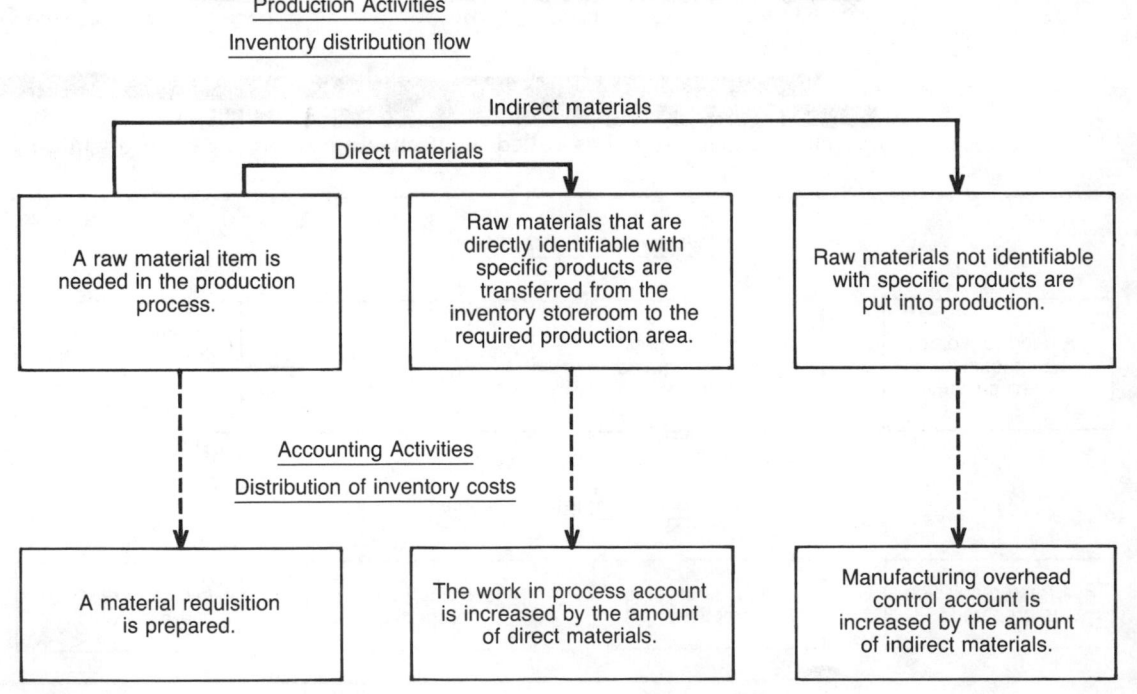

Figure 2-7
Inventory distribution activities result in source documents used to account for the activities.

A materials requisition initiates the flow of raw materials into production. This document indicates the type, quantity, and production location of the required material. Be careful to differentiate between a purchase requisition and a materials requisition. One initiates the purchasing process, the other initiates the internal inventory distribution process.

Labour   Accounting for manufacturing labour is not difficult, but it can be tedious. Many variables are involved in accounting for payrolls, and federal and provincial governments require a variety of detailed reports. Figure 2-8 summarizes graphically the process of accounting for manufacturing labour cost flows.

An important cost accounting activity is that of identifying manufacturing labour with specific products and assigning labour costs to production. Accountants must determine what activities manufacturing employees performed during their time at work so that labour costs can be identified with products. Documents for identifying employee time, such as daily time tickets and job time tickets, summarize the work activities of employees.

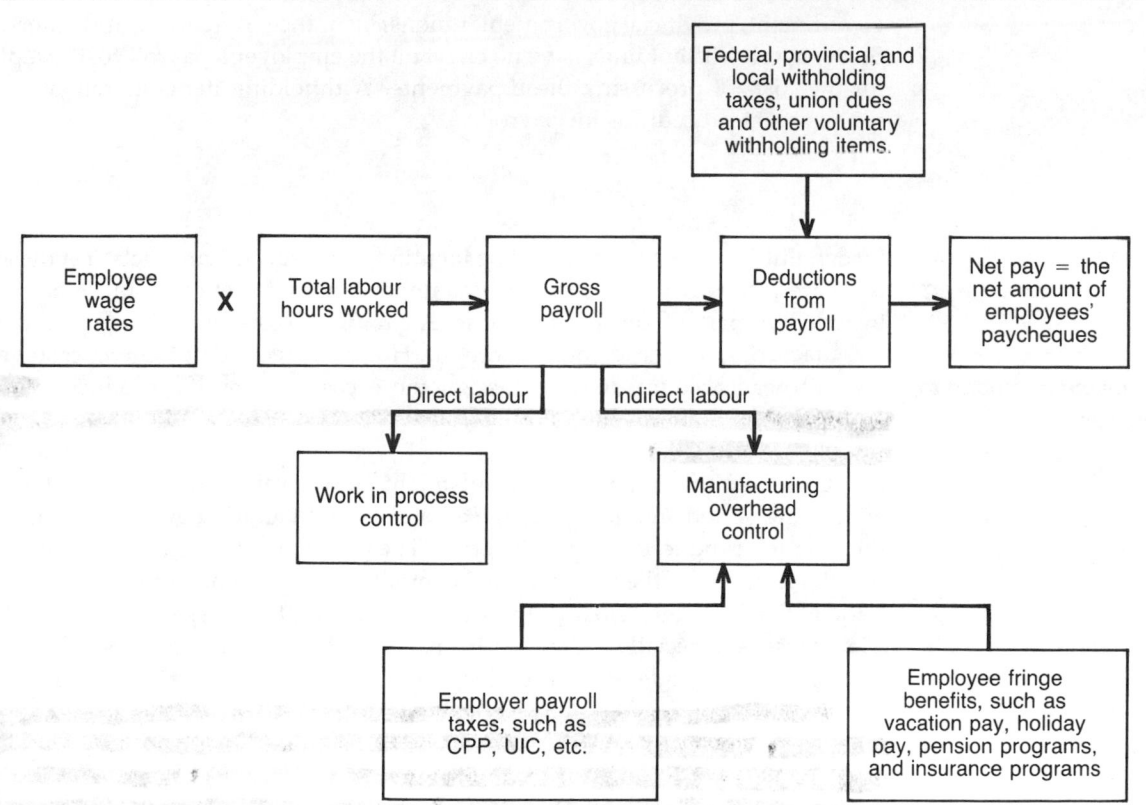

Figure 2-8
Manufacturing labour cost flows.

*Identifying labour
with products*

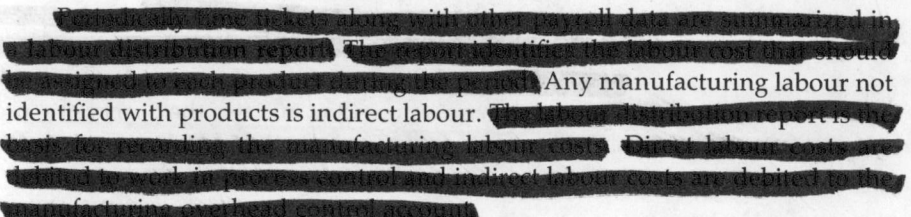

~~Periodically time tickets along with other payroll data are summarized in a labour distribution report. The report identifies the labour cost that should be assigned to each product during the period.~~ Any manufacturing labour not identified with products is indirect labour. ~~The labour distribution report is the basis for recording the manufacturing labour costs. Direct labour costs are debited to work in process control and indirect labour costs are debited to the manufacturing overhead control account.~~

The total cost of manufacturing labour is not just gross payroll. Clearly it is the most visible element of manufacturing labour, but two other elements are important also. Employer payroll taxes and employee fringe benefits are important and growing parts of labour cost. These two items have grown significantly in the last 20 years so that now they add 35 to 45 percent of the total payroll cost in many large businesses. ~~Payroll taxes and employee fringe benefits are usually treated as indirect costs and are charged to manufacturing overhead.~~ The problem with this approach is that managers may view gross payroll as the total cost of labour since these figures are the most visible, when actual manufacturing labour cost is much higher.

Amounts withheld from employees' cheques must be paid to the federal government, provincial government, unions, insurance companies, and others. Such payroll withholdings have no effect on the employer's payroll cost except for the costs of processing these payments. Withholding items merely affect the payment procedures for payroll.

Manufacturing overhead

Applying overhead to products

By definition indirect costs cannot be identified with specific products. Yet these costs are just as real, and often just as important, as direct costs and must be included as part of the product cost. All indirect costs are recorded in the manufacturing overhead control account. However, recording indirect costs in the overhead account does not assign these costs to specific products. ~~The process of assigning (charging) manufacturing overhead to products is called applying overhead.~~

One way of applying overhead might be to wait until the end of the accounting period and then to assign all of the manufacturing overhead costs to the products produced during the period. The problem with such an approach is that the total cost of the product is not computed until the end of the accounting period. This certainly violates the timeliness concept discussed in Chapter 1. Timeliness is especially important in managerial accounting reports affecting daily production and cost control decisions.

~~A better approach is to assign overhead costs to products as they are produced. However, since overhead costs are not known at the time of production, the amount to be applied must be estimated. To do this, the accountant determines an overhead rate. A manufacturing overhead rate is a predetermined amount derived from the expected manufacturing overhead cost and the expected quantity of production.~~ For example, the accountant may estimate that overhead costs for the year will be $400,000 and direct labour hours will be 100 000. In this case the predetermined overhead rate is $4 per direct labour hour. Four dollars of manufacturing overhead will be applied to a product for every hour of direct labour used to manufacture the product. Other examples of overhead rates are $6 per hour of machine use and $10 per unit of production. The process for determining overhead rates is discussed in Chapter 4.

~~The primary consideration in deciding on an overhead rate is the matching concept, which states that expenses should be matched with revenues generated by business operations.~~ In manufacturing firms, revenues result from the sale of the manufactured products. The largest expense usually is the cost of producing the products, and a major portion of this cost may be overhead. Therefore, ~~the rate used to apply overhead to production should do the best possible job of matching indirect manufacturing costs with products.~~ The selection of a proper overhead application base, such as direct labour hours or machine hours, is an important decision because it directly affects the matching of costs with products. Various application bases are discussed in Chapter 4.

~~The overhead rate is usually decided upon before the accounting period starts.~~ Once the rate is determined, indirect manufacturing costs can be charged to production on a timely basis along with direct materials and direct labour. ~~As production takes place, overhead is recorded using the predetermined rate by debiting work in process and crediting manufacturing overhead applied. The overhead applied account accumulates the total amount of overhead assigned to products, but this is not the actual amount of overhead incurred. Actual overhead costs are debited to a manufacturing overhead control account as they are identified.~~ For example, ~~when indirect materials are requisitioned, the cost of such materials is debited to manufacturing overhead control and credited to raw materials inventory.~~

~~Notice that there are two overhead accounts. Manufacturing overhead control contains a debit balance representing actual overhead incurred. Manufacturing overhead applied contains a credit balance representing overhead applied to products.~~ The cost flow of manufacturing overhead is illustrated in Figure 2-9.

Underapplied and overapplied overhead

~~At the end of the accounting year, the debit balance in the manufacturing overhead control account should be about the same dollar amount as the credit balance in the manufacturing overhead applied account.~~ However, the two accounts seldom have identical balances. ~~If the balance in the control account is greater than the balance~~ in the applied account, overhead is underapplied, ~~which is the case in Figure~~ 2-9. That means that actual overhead cost was somewhat greater than the amount of overhead assigned to products. Conversely, ~~if the control account balance is less than the balance in the applied account, overhead is overapplied.~~ The actual overhead cost is less than the amount of overhead charged to products.

Usually the amount underapplied or overapplied is relatively small. ~~The difference is eliminated by adjusting cost of goods sold in the income statement.~~

Indirect Manufacturing Costs

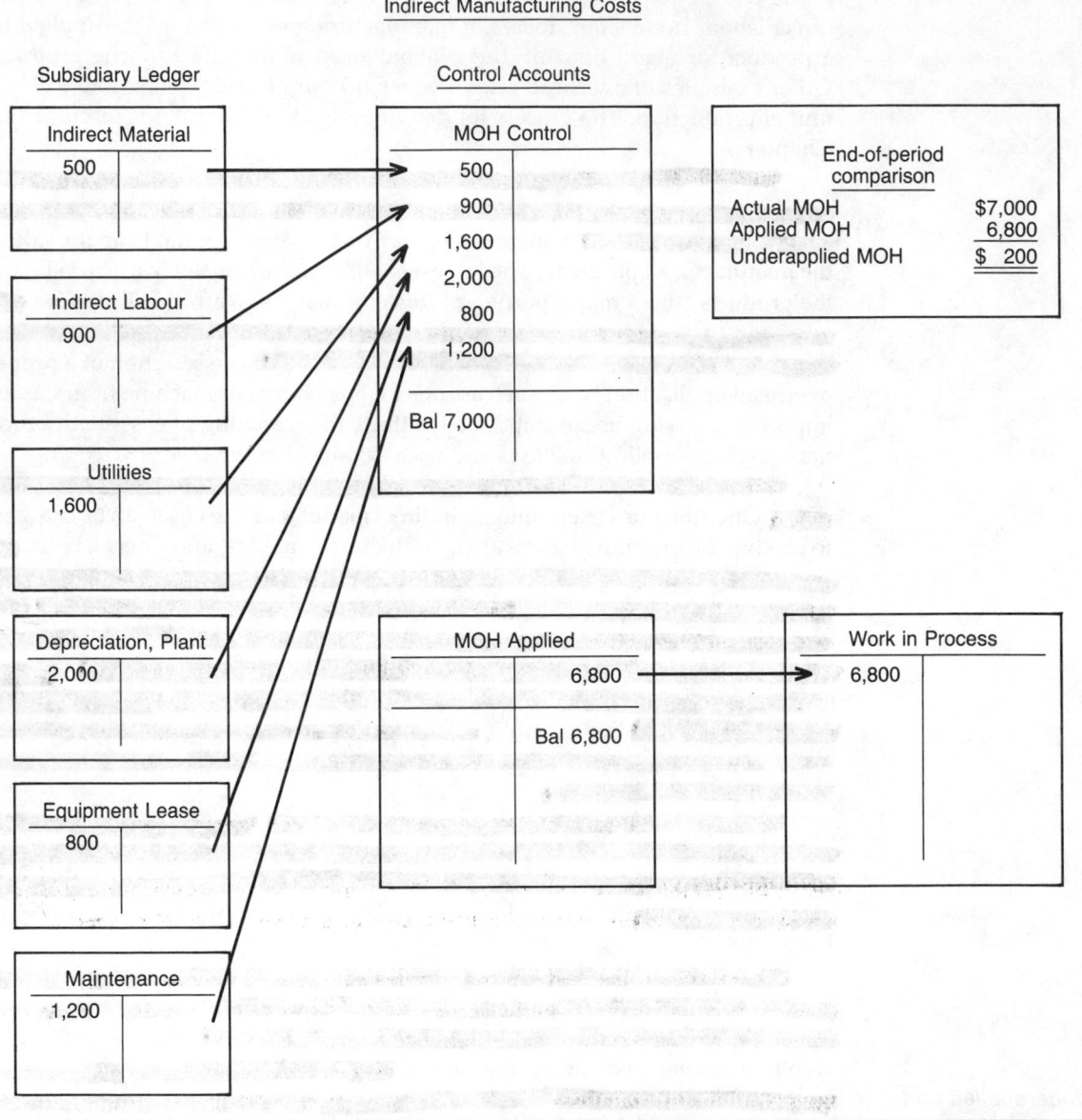

Figure 2-9
Manufacturing overhead cost flows.

Underapplied overhead increases cost of goods sold and overapplied overhead decreases cost of goods sold. The justification for this simple disposition of underapplied or overapplied overhead is twofold:

1. The amounts are immaterial.
2. Typically most of the goods produced during the year are sold by year-end.

If underapplied or overapplied overhead is large, financial statements may be distorted when the entire amount is assigned to cost of goods sold. In such cases the product costs should be adjusted to reflect the actual overhead cost. Product costs are found in three accounts—work in process inventory, finished goods inventory, and cost of goods sold. These three accounts are adjusted to reflect the actual manufacturing overhead cost by spreading the underapplied or overapplied overhead to the accounts in proportion to the relative amount of overhead remaining in each account at year-end. For instance, during the year a company incurs $140,000 in actual manufacturing overhead costs and applies $100,000 in overhead to products. Overhead is underapplied at year-end by $40,000. Of the $100,000 that has been applied to production during the year, $10,000 remains in work in process at year-end, $15,000 is in finished goods inventory, and $75,000 has been applied to the products already sold. Therefore, 10 percent, or $4,000, of the underapplied overhead is added to the work in process account; 15 percent, or $6,000, of the underapplied overhead is added to finished goods; and 75 percent, or $30,000 is added to cost of goods sold. The determination of whether underapplied or overapplied overhead is large enough to require prorating to inventory and cost of goods sold depends on the judgment of management. Figure 2-10 illustrates graphically the distribution of underapplied and overapplied overhead.

Additional cost concepts

In addition to the cost flow concepts presented earlier, there are a number of other concepts that should be discussed before moving on to the actual determination of product costs in Chapter 3.

Cost and expense

Frequent confusion arises in distinguishing between costs and expenses. Cost is the total amount of resource expended for some good or service, and expense is the amount of good or service used during a given accounting period. For example, a one-year fire insurance policy is purchased on August 1 for $2,400. At the end of the year, five months of the insurance protection have been used and seven months of protection remain. The **cost** of the one-year insurance policy is $2,400, but the **expense** of the protection used this year is $1,000 (5/12 × $2,400), leaving an unexpired cost of $1,400. Similarly a building is purchased for $100,000; it has an expected useful life of 10 years with no salvage value, and straight-line depreciation is used. The **cost** of the building is $100,000, but the **expense** of the building for the first year is $10,000 of depreciation.

Expense is a timing concept

Notice that expense is a timing concept indicated by the matching principle, whereas cost is a valuation concept.

Unit costs

One of the most widely used pieces of information from a product cost system is the unit cost. It is the cost of producing one unit of product or providing one unit of service. Some examples are:

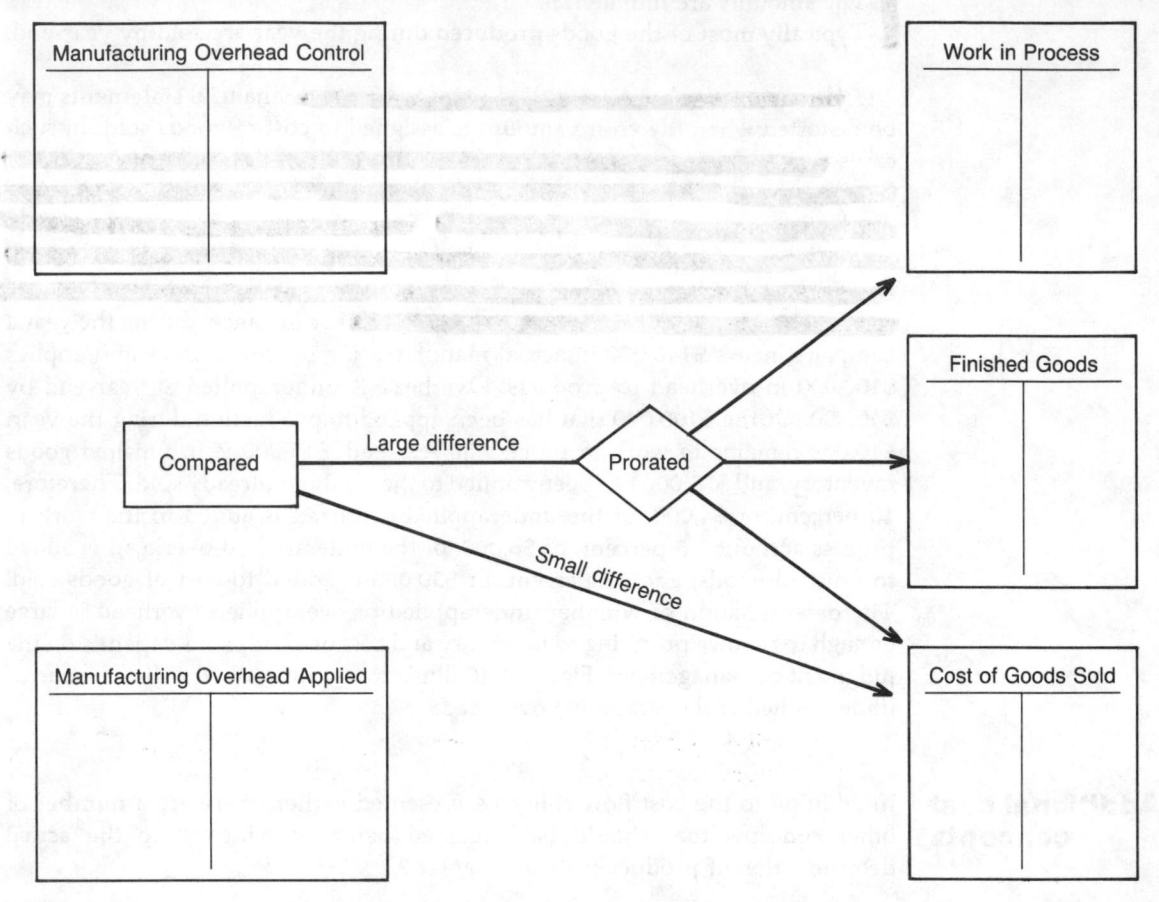

Figure 2-10
Distribution of underapplied and overapplied manufacturing overhead costs.

1. $4.50 to give one haircut
2. $9.22 to produce a pair of nylon running shoes
3. $5.81 to process each sales invoice, or
4. $.48 to produce a 25-cm plastic toy truck

Unit costs are convenient for planning and decision making, but caution is necessary in dealing with them. The fact that accountants have reduced all of the production cost flows to a single unit cost does **not** mean that it can be used like an external price from vendors. Unit costs, although convenient, have some special characteristics that must be understood.

The first characteristic of unit costs is that they are almost always averages.

Unit costs are averages

██████. They represent the average cost of producing a product over some time period or during a production run. For example, a production run has an output of 5000 kilograms of chocolate candy with total production cost of $6,250. The unit cost is $6,250/5000 kilograms = $1.25 per kilogram which is the average cost of producing a kilogram of the chocolate candy. Little can be said about the cost of producing a single kilogram of candy or about the cost per kilogram of candy with larger or smaller production runs. A few production processes, such as construction of a bridge, a dam, or a ship, result in a single unit of product, but most unit costs represent averaging to some degree. ██ ██ A 5000-kg batch of candy produced at another time may cost more or less than $1.25 per kilogram. ████ ██ ██ ████████ Caution must be exercised to avoid giving long-range predictive characteristics to unit costs.

At this stage in your study of managerial accounting, it is difficult to appreciate the strengths and limitations of unit cost figures. For now merely remember the basic characteristics of unit costs. Other important points about unit costs are presented where appropriate throughout this book.

Cost of periodic and perpetual inventories

In *Financial Accounting* we introduced periodic and perpetual inventories. Here we review these topics and note their importance in costing. ██ ████████████████████ All purchases of inventory are recorded in a separate purchases account. Reductions in inventory are not recorded during the period. At the end of the period, total net purchases are added to beginning inventory to find total inventory available for sale or use. Next, ending inventory is subtracted from total inventory available to arrive at inventory sold or used. Figure 2-3 shows the income statement of a merchandising firm that uses a periodic inventory system. To find the ending inventory figure, an inventory count must be taken and the units in inventory must be costed. Usually FIFO, LIFO, or weighted average methods are used as the cost flow assumption for costing inventories. ██ ██ ████████████████████████████ Costing the outflow of inventory requires the use of FIFO, LIFO, moving average, or specific identification methods. ██ ██ ██ ████████████████ In a periodic system, the amount of inventory used is the residual of an arithmetic operation. In a perpetual system, continuous inventory records are maintained, and inventory counts can be used to verify inventory records.

Common costs

Accountants try to identify costs with specific cost objectives because identifiable costs lend themselves well to analysis and evaluation by management. However, many costs are not readily identifiable with specific cost objectives; instead they are the common costs of two or more cost objectives. For example, a research laboratory supervisor may have responsibility for managing 10 different research projects. The cost of the supervisor's services is shared by all projects and is therefore a common cost of the projects.

Often it is necessary or desirable to assign part of a common cost to each cost objective benefitting from it. For example, Revenue Canada requires that the product costs used in determining a company's taxable income include all necessary costs of production, both direct and indirect. Thus costs common to more than one product must be assigned to the various products to determine product cost for reporting net income. Managers may find that, in a certain situation, direct costs represent only a small portion of total costs, and it may be necessary to assign common costs to cost objectives to aid in the analysis of the cost data in making some decisions. The assignment of common cost to various objectives is called cost allocation. Sometimes cost allocation is a simple and logical process. For example, the laboratory supervisor may keep good records of the time he spends on each project. Then the total cost of the supervisor can be allocated to the ten projects in proportion to the time spent on each. In situations where cost allocations are based on questionable relationships, the resulting cost data may be of little value.

Cost allocations and associated problems are crucial to the study of many different managerial accounting topics. Chapter 4 deals in depth with common costs and cost allocations.

Common costs may be allocated to products

Controllable costs

One of the most important concepts in managerial accounting is the concept of controllable cost. This concept strongly influences the development of many managerial accounting reports.

Ideally a controllable cost is one over which a manager has direct and complete decision authority. The term *controllable* has a nice management-oriented ring to it. Theoretically all costs are controllable by somebody in the organization. The chief executive officer of a firm should be responsible for all company costs. However, identifying responsibility for every cost is difficult at lower levels in the organization's management structure. Therefore, in practice a controllable cost is defined as a cost over which a manager has some influence or control. In spite of the difficulty of identifying controllable costs, the concept of controllability strongly influences many managerial accounting activities, such as planning, management reporting, and analysis of performance.

Managers have some influence or control over controllable costs

Cost behaviour

An important element in determining controllable costs is cost behaviour. The term refers to the way costs change with respect to some variable, such as time, units of output, or hours of labour. Usually cost behaviour is related to an activity variable, such as units of output. Costs that vary directly and proportionately with the activity level are called variable costs or directly variable costs. For example, if the production of each metal bookcase requires 2 hours of direct labour time at $6 per hour, the direct labour variable cost is $12 per unit. If 400 metal bookcases are produced in March, the total variable direct labour cost is \$4,800.

Fixed costs remain constant

A cost that does not change with the activity level is called a fixed cost. For example, the cost of leasing the building used in producing the metal bookcases is \$500 a month. It is a fixed cost because it does not change if the production volume changes. The \$500 monthly charge is related to the passage of time rather than to the number of bookcases produced.

Cost behaviour is important in management planning and decision making and in developing managerial accounting reports. The two broad categories of variable and fixed cost can be very useful, but they do not describe cost behaviour adequately for all managerial accounting purposes. Cost behaviour patterns, discussed further in Chapters 5 and 17, influence many types of managerial analyses presented throughout the book.

Summary

Cost accounting provides a data base for a wide variety of accounting reports. In particular, cost data provide detailed support for managerial accounting reports. Cost information is universally applicable to many economic and personal decisions. Cost data are used by all types of business firms and in all types of activities, but are particularly useful in manufacturing operations.

Costs can be developed for a variety of products and activities called **cost objectives.** Typical cost objectives include product costs, departmental costs, and the cost of performing various services.

Product costs consist of **direct materials, direct labour**, and **manufacturing overhead (MOH)**. Direct materials and direct labour are identifiable directly with products and together are referred to as **prime costs**. Manufacturing overhead includes all necessary costs of production other than the prime costs. Included are **indirect material, indirect labour**, and all capacity costs, such as plant depreciation, equipment depreciation, insurance and taxes on the production facilities, and utility costs for the manufacturing operations. Manufacturing overhead and direct labour together are called **conversion costs** because they combine to convert raw materials into finished products. Prime costs are called direct manufacturing costs. Manufacturing overhead costs are referred to as indirect manufacturing costs.

Manufacturing firms have three levels of inventory—raw materials, work in process, and finished goods. **Raw materials** are the basic ingredients of manufactured products. **Work in process** consists of products in the process of being produced. **Finished goods** are manufactured products that the firm sells, similar to merchandise inventory in a merchandising firm.

The physical flow of production is paralleled by the flow of costs through the ledger accounts. All production costs are recorded first in the work in process account. When products are completed, their costs are transferred to the finished goods inventory account. All production costs remain assets as long as the product remains in an inventory account. The cost of products that are sold is transferred from finished goods to **cost of goods sold.** At the time of sale, the

product cost becomes an expense. The expense is matched with the revenue from the sale of the product, satisfying the matching principle.

The **cost of goods manufactured schedule** is a summary of manufacturing costs incurred during the accounting period. The schedule starts with the beginning work in process, then current period production costs are added, and ending work in process is subtracted. The resulting amount is called **cost of goods manufactured,** and it represents the total cost of products transferred to finished goods during the accounting period.

Control accounts are used widely in product costing. Raw materials, work in process, and finished goods are common inventory control accounts and **manufacturing overhead control** and **manufacturing overhead applied** are common overhead control accounts. All control accounts are supported by **subsidiary ledgers** that provide the necessary detail not found in the control accounts. Materials purchases are recorded in the **inventory control** account. Raw materials acquisition documents consist of **purchase requisitions, purchase orders,** and **receiving reports.** A **materials requisition** form is used to start materials into production from inventory control. Raw materials inventory documents are used as a basis for accounting entries and to provide an audit trail. Labour cost entries for recording direct labour and indirect labour are prepared from a **labour distribution report**, which is prepared from payroll records and **daily time tickets** or **job time tickets**.

Manufacturing overhead includes all indirect costs of production. Actual overhead costs are accumulated in the **manufacturing overhead control** account. Typically overhead is applied to production using a **predetermined manufacturing overhead rate** and is recorded in the **manufacturing overhead applied** account. The overhead rate provides timely product cost data and usually is a close approximation of actual overhead costs. Any difference between actual and applied overhead is reconciled at the end of the accounting period. Small differences go to the cost of goods sold account. Large differences are prorated among work in process, finished goods, and costs of goods sold.

The term **cost** has a very specific meaning in accounting. Cost is the amount of resource given up for some good or service. **Expense** is the amount of resource used during a given accounting period. For some items cost and expense are the same because the good or service is used in the period purchased. However, some items such as fixed assets benefit many periods, and their annual expense is quite different from their cost.

A **perpetual inventory system** is used to maintain a continuous record of all inventory transactions and is essential in providing timely cost data for managerial accounting reports. With a **periodic inventory system** all inventory purchases are recorded in a separate purchases account. The product expense is not recorded until year-end when an inventory count is taken to see how much inventory is left. The product expense is determined by subtracting the ending inventory from the total goods available.

The **unit cost** of manufactured products is an **average** unit cost for some **time period** or production run. Therefore, managers must be cautious when using unit costs for decision purposes.

Controllable costs refer to costs over which managers have decision authority. This concept is important to many management reporting activities. **Cost behaviour** is important in determining controllable costs. **Variable costs** change proportionately with the level of activity. **Fixed costs** remain constant at all levels of activity.

List of important terms

Much new terminology is introduced in this chapter. The list below consists of terms that you should understand before proceeding to the next chapter. Other new terms are discussed more thoroughly in later chapters. The italic numbers in parentheses indicate the pages on which the terms first appear.

common cost *(52)*
control account *(42)*
controllable cost *(52)*
conversion cost *(32)*
cost *(29)*
cost allocation *(52)*
cost behaviour *(52)*
cost elements *(29)*
cost objective *(31)*
cost of goods manufactured *(40)*
cost of goods manufactured
  schedule *(40)*
costs of goods sold *(36)*
daily time ticket *(45)*
direct labour *(31)*
direct material *(31)*
expense *(53)*
finished goods *(34)*
fixed cost *(53)*
gross margin *(39)*
indirect labour *(29)*
indirect material *(31)*
inventoriable cost *(36)*
job time ticket *(44)*

labour distribution report *(46)*
manufacturing overhead
  (MOH) *(31)*
manufacturing overhead
  applied *(46)*
manufacturing overhead
  control *(49)*
manufacturing overhead rate *(46)*
materials requisition *(45)*
merchandise inventory *(38)*
periodic inventory system *(51)*
perpetual inventory system *(51)*
prime cost *(32)*
product cost *(31)*
purchase order *(43)*
purchase requisition *(43)*
purchasing agent *(43)*
raw materials *(34)*
receiving report *(44)*
subsidiary ledger *(42)*
total manufacturing cost *(41)*
unit cost *(49)*
variable cost *(52)*
work in process *(34)*

Questions

1. What is a cost objective? Give two examples from business and two from your personal life.
2. Describe the three basic cost elements of a manufactured product.
3. What do the terms *prime cost* and *conversion cost* mean?
4. Which is the most important of the cost elements?
5. Describe the different levels of inventory in a manufacturing firm.
6. What is meant by the term *inventoriable cost*?

7. Why is the determination of product cost different in a merchandising firm than in a manufacturing firm?
8. What is the product cost called in the income statement of a service firm?
9. What is the function of the cost of goods manufactured schedule?
10. Distinguish between a cost and an expense. Give an example of each.
11. Distinguish between a perpetual inventory system and a periodic inventory system. Which is used more often in manufacturing and why?
12. Of what significance is the concept of controllable cost in managerial accounting?
13. What is the function of control accounts? Name the most common control accounts used in manufacturing activities.
14. Distinguish between the inventory acquisition and inventory distribution functions.
15. Identify the primary inventory acquisition documents and describe their purpose.
16. The union negotiator says to the company negotiator, "We just agreed on a $7-an-hour contract. What do you mean it's costing the company $10 an hour for workers?" To what does the $10 figure refer?
17. What is the difference between the manufacturing overhead control account and the manufacturing overhead applied account?
18. What does it mean, in terms of product cost, when manufacturing overhead is underapplied?
19. What is the usual financial statement treatment of small amounts of underapplied or overapplied manufacturing overhead?

Exercises

Ex. 2-1 **Computing net income.** Below are selected financial data of Febo Company for two consecutive years.

1983	
Beginning finished goods	$ 15,000
Cost of goods manufactured	185,000
Ending finished goods	30,000
Sales	290,000
Operating expenses	75,000
1984	
Beginning finished goods	$ 30,000
Cost of goods manufactured	220,000
Ending finished goods	39,000
Sales	325,000
Operating expenses	110,000

Required:
Prepare income statements for both years.

Ex. 2-2   Determining period and product costs.

	Product Cost	Period Cost
a. Sales salaries	____	____
b. Indirect labour	____	____
c. An assembly line supervisor's salary	____	____
d. Vacation pay for factory workers	____	____
e. The controller's salary	____	____
f. Sales commissions	____	____
g. Storage and handling costs for the finished goods inventory	____	____
h. Office equipment lease cost	____	____
i. The cost of a maintenance contract for hydraulic equipment in the plant	____	____
j. Property taxes, factory	____	____
k. Property taxes, office	____	____
l. Factory fire insurance premiums	____	____
m. First aid room for factory employees	____	____
n. Depreciation, factory building	____	____
o. Depreciation, office building	____	____
p. Computer lease cost	____	____

Required:
Identify each of the items in the list above as either a product cost or a period cost for Quar's Manufacturing Company.

Ex. 2-3   Accounting for manufacturing labour. Mark DeSloover is employed as a skilled welder for Saskatoon Air Moving Systems Company. His wage rate is $9 an hour, and for each employee the company pays $8 a week for health insurance coverage, $10 a week into a guaranteed annual wage fund, and an additional 15 percent of gross wages for federal and provincial payroll taxes. During the first week of August Mark worked 40 hours. He worked 20 hours welding a 240-cm ventilation fan and 12 hours welding a 135-cm ventilation fan. The other eight hours he cleaned and serviced his welding equipment.

Required:
a. How much direct labour cost typically would be assigned to each fan this week for Mark's welding?
b. How much cost typically would be assigned to manufacturing overhead this week for Mark's work?
c. If this is a typical week, what is the total hourly cost of one direct labour hour of Mark's time if all labour-related costs are included in the computation?

Ex. 2-4   Cost of goods manufactured. The ledger balances presented below are for Bridgewater, Ltd. The firm uses a periodic inventory system for its raw materials. All materials used were direct materials.

Beginning work in process	$ 75,000
Direct labour	320,000
Sales salaries	180,000
Factory lease cost	36,000
Beginning finished goods	110,000
Sales	900,000
Indirect labour	20,000
Factory equipment depreciation	35,000
Purchases	350,000
Ending raw materials	70,000
Ending finished goods	150,000
Factory supervision	90,000
Ending work in process	130,000
Beginning raw materials	30,000

Required:
a. Prepare a schedule of cost of goods manufactured.
b. Calculate cost of goods sold for the period.

Ex. 2-5 **The nature of overhead costs.** The new executive vice president is very interested in evaluating personnel by monitoring controllable costs in each manager's sphere of responsibility. The vice president says, "From now on, all prime costs will be considered controllable and all manufacturing overhead costs will be noncontrollable."

Required:
a. Do you agree with this statement? Use some examples to support your answer.
b. Can you foresee any problems with such a definition of controllable costs?

Ex. 2-6 **Cost of goods manufactured schedule.** Goodwin Textiles needs information about the cost of its manufacturing operations. A bookkeeper at Goodwin has gathered the following data from the company's ledger.

Ending work in process	$ 43,000
Sales commissions	19,500
Office depreciation	16,000
Manufacturing plant depreciation	40,000
Production supervisors' salaries	85,000
Direct materials	180,000
Indirect labour	25,000
Property taxes (60% factory, 40% office)	30,000
Insurance on finished goods inventory	4,000
Insurance on raw materials	2,000
Utilities (80% factory, 20% office)	20,000
Indirect materials	15,000
Direct labour	200,000
Administrative salaries	120,000

Beginning work in process	26,000
Sales	950,000
Sales returns	10,000
Beginning finished goods	45,000
Ending finished goods	85,000
Maintenance (90% factory, 10% office)	40,000

Required:
Use the data provided to prepare a cost of goods manufactured schedule.

Ex. 2-7   Identifying types of costs. Following is a list of costs that you are to classify into various categories.

	Fixed	Variable	Product	Period
a. Direct labour	___	___	___	___
b. Indirect materials	___	___	___	___
c. Plant superintendent's salary	___	___	___	___
d. Depreciation, factory	___	___	___	___
e. Depreciation, office	___	___	___	___
f. Computer lease cost	___	___	___	___
g. Property taxes, office	___	___	___	___
h. Property taxes, factory	___	___	___	___
i. Fire insurance, factory	___	___	___	___
j. President's salary	___	___	___	___
k. Controller's salary	___	___	___	___
l. Indirect labour	___	___	___	___
m. Direct materials	___	___	___	___
n. Utilities, factory	___	___	___	___
o. Utilities, office	___	___	___	___

Required:
Assign each cost listed to the appropriate classification, fixed or variable cost and product or period cost.

Ex. 2-8   Changing product costs. Below is the condensed income statement of the November Company.

November Company Income Statement	
Sales (10 000 units)	$100,000
Cost of goods sold	70,000
Gross margin	$ 30,000
Operating expenses	20,000
Net income	$ 10,000

The cost of the units sold is composed of $3.00 of direct material, $1.50 of direct labour, and $2.50 of manufacturing overhead.

Required:
Determine the percentage change in net income caused by **each** of the following **independent** situations:

a. Direct material cost increases by 10 percent.
b. Direct labour cost increases by 10 percent.
c. Manufacturing overhead cost increases by 10 percent.
d. Selling price increases by 10 percent.
e. Selling price increases by 10 percent and all product costs increase by 10 percent.

Ex. 2-9 **Distinguishing between cost and expense.** Following are descriptions of various resource acquisitions for Armstrong, Inc.

	Cost	Expense
a. Purchase of a two-year fire insurance policy on May 1 at a cost of $6,000.	_____	_____
b. Purchase of a metal lathe for $16,000 on January 2. It has an eight-year useful life with an expected salvage value of $4,000. Straight-line depreciation is used.	_____	_____
c. Purchase of a six-month supply of computer printer ribbons on December 1 for $900.	_____	_____
d. Purchase of a delivery truck on July 2 with a five-year expected life. The company traded in an old truck with a market value of $4,000 and paid $21,000 in addition. The new truck has an expected salvage value of $5,000.	_____	_____
e. Purchase of a six-month maintenance agreement on hydraulic equipment on February 1 for $4,400.	_____	_____
f. A maintenance agreement on computer equipment for the next calendar year is purchased on November 29 for $16,500.	_____	_____
g. On December 31 the company receives a bill of $2,200 for repairs on the roof of the office building.	_____	_____

Required:
For each of the items above, determine the cost and the expense of Armstrong, Inc., for the calendar year ending December 31.

Ex. 2-10 **Underapplied and overapplied overhead.** Javais, Ltd., has the following balances in overhead accounts at year-end:

Manufacturing Overhead Control	Manufacturing Overhead Applied
150 000 ← actual OH	180 000

Company policy requires that if applied overhead is different from actual overhead by 10 percent or more, the difference should be prorated among work in process, finished goods, and cost of goods sold. At year-end the amounts of applied overhead still remaining in the three accounts are:

Work in process	$ 50,000
Finished goods	37,500
Cost of goods sold	162,500
Total	$250,000

Required:

a. Determine underapplied or overapplied overhead.

b. Prepare an entry to adjust overhead.

c. After necessary adjustments have been made, what are the amounts of overhead in the work in process, finished goods, and cost of goods sold accounts?

Problem Set A

P. 2A-1 Missing cost and sales data. Below are four sets of income statement data, with some items omitted. The situations are independent.

	Situation			
	A	**B**	**C**	**D**
Sales	$98,000	$80,000	$65,000	85,000
Beginning finished goods	6,000	9,000	5,000	$12,000
Beginning work in process	4,000	11,000	9,000	8,000
Direct materials	20,000	16,000	15,000	25,000
Direct labour	30,000	20,000	20,000	17,000
Manufacturing overhead	40,000	18,000	25,000	20,000
Ending work in process	12,000	9,000	4,000	7,000
Cost of goods manufactured	82,000	56,000	65,000	63,000
Ending finished goods	21,000	15,000	22,000	23,000
Cost of goods sold	67,000	50,000	49,000	52,000
Gross margin	31,000	30,000	17,000	33,000
Operating expenses	25,000	18,000	19,000	24,000
Net income	6,000	12,000	(2,000)	9,000

Required:

For each situation fill in the missing data.

P. 2A-2 **Identifying product costs.** Harvey Gamefisher has made fishing lures as a hobby for several years. He sold some lures to friends who were very impressed with his craftsmanship. At the suggestion of several trusted friends Harvey decided to retire from his $15,000-a-year job and manufacture fishing lures full-time. During the first year of business Harvey did the following:

1. Leased an old building for $4,800 a year.
2. Bought paint and other materials for $15,500.
3. Incurred monthly utility bills of $640.
4. Leased production machinery for $3,600 a year.
5. Hired an employee for $6 an hour who worked a total of 1660 hours.
6. Bought for $600 a typewriter that is expected to last four years.
7. Produced 20 000 lures.
8. Sold 18 000 lures for $2.50 each.
9. Had ending raw materials of $1,500.

Required:
a. What did it cost Harvey to produce the lures?
b. What was the cost of goods sold for the year?
c. What was Harvey's net income the first year in business? Should Harvey have retired from his old job?

P. 2A-3 **Cost of goods manufactured and the income statement.** Presented below are the ledger account balances of Decaver Corporation on 31/12/84.

Administrative salaries	$125,000
Beginning finished goods	44,000
Ending work in process	46,000
Sales	994,000
Sales salaries	110,000
Production salaries	85,000
Direct materials	240,000
Indirect materials	25,000
Factory utilities	22,000
Office utilities	8,000
Advertising	38,000
Factory depreciation	28,000
Office equipment depreciation	9,000
Factory machinery depreciation	19,000
Direct labour	181,000
Indirect labour	36,000
Office fire insurance	4,000
Factory property taxes	8,000
Factory fire insurance	12,000
Beginning work in process	52,000
Ending finished goods	70,000

Required:
a. Prepare a schedule of cost of goods manufactured.
b. Prepare an income statement.

P. 2A-4   Cost of goods sold and the income statement.

Bagley Department Store Trial Balance December 31		
	Debit	**Credit**
Cash	$ 26,000	
Accounts receivable	165,000	
Merchandise inventory 1/1	120,000	
Building	1,000,000	
Depreciation, building		$ 320,000
Equipment	250,000	
Depreciation, equipment		110,000
Accounts payable		72,000
Mortgage payable		240,000
Capital stock		400,000
Retained earnings		360,000
Sales		900,000
Sales returns and allowances	15,000	
Purchases	500,000	
Purchase returns and allowances		10,000
Advertising expense	90,000	
Bad debts expense	6,000	
Commissions expense	27,000	
Depreciation expense, store	32,000	
Depreciation expense, equipment	14,000	
Equipment lease expense	6,000	
Salaries expense	151,000	
Utilities expense	10,000	
	$2,412,000	$2,412,000

The Bagley Department Store operates on a calendar-year accounting period. The firm uses a periodic inventory system, and on each January 1 and 2 an inventory count is taken. The inventory count shows an ending cost of $150,000 for the year just completed. Other account balances are shown in the year-end trial balance.

Required:
a. Prepare an income statement using a schedule of cost of goods sold in good form.
b. Prepare a post-closing trial balance.

P. 2A-5   Identifying labour costs. The managers of the Colestone Products Company have just received a labour contract proposal from union leaders. The president wants to make a thorough analysis of the impact of the proposed contract on labour costs. You are the controller for Colestone, and you are asked to prepare an itemized listing of labour-related costs for the current contract and the proposed contract. You prepare the following:

Item	Current	Proposed
Wage rate	$ 6.00/h	$ 6.30/h
Vacation	2 weeks	3 weeks
Paid holidays	10 d	15 d
Pension fund contribution per employee per week	$24.00	$ 46.00
Education program contribution per employee per year	0	$144.00

Employees work 40 hours a week at Colestone and 20 percent of manufacturing labour is indirect labour. The letter accompanying the union's latest contract proposal states that the union is "interested in the quality of life for its employees rather than monetary issues and consequently is only seeking a 5 percent increase in the wage rate."

Required:
a. Determine the total cost per hour of manufacturing labour for the current contract and the proposed contract.
b. Respond to the union letter that accompanied the most recent union contract proposal.
c. What is the **total** labour cost for an hour of direct labour under the current contract? Proposed contract? (Ignore payroll taxes.)

P. 2A-6 **The effect of overhead on product costs.** Freireich Manufacturing Company applied overhead to products using an overhead rate of $6 per direct labour hour. At year-end actual manufacturing overhead was $345,600 and 60 000 direct labour hours had been worked. One product produced during the year, a special-order packaging machine, required 500 hours of direct labour.

Required:
a. What is the amount of underapplied or overapplied manufacturing overhead?
b. How much overhead was applied to the packaging machine?
c. How much overhead cost should have been applied to the packaging machine based on actual overhead cost?
d. What overhead rate would have provided no underapplied or overapplied overhead?

Problem Set B

P. 2B-1 **Missing cost and sales data.** Shown below are data from four independent income statements with some items omitted.

Required:
Fill in the missing data for each statement.

	Situation			
	A	**B**	**C**	**D**
Sales	$60,000	$75,000	_____	$80,000
Beginning finished goods	10,000	_____		4,000
Beginning work in process	5,000	9,000	$14,000	2,000
Direct materials	16,000	20,000	10,000	28,000
Direct labour	15,000	_____	18,000	30,000
Manufacturing overhead	22,000	25,000	27,000	_____
Ending work in process	10,000	16,000	_____	26,000
Cost of goods manufactured	_____	53,000	55,000	74,000
Ending finished goods	17,000	12,000	12,000	_____
Cost of goods sold	_____	57,000	65,000	60,000
Gross margin	_____	_____	29,000	_____
Operating expenses	23,000	_____	21,000	_____
Net income	_____	(4,000)	_____	3,000

P. 2B-2 **Identifying product costs.** For the last five years Sadie Williams has made homemade fudge for her friends and relatives for the holiday season. Her fudge is very delicious, and many people have told her that she should make fudge and sell it. One of Sadie's friends is insistent and offers to invest $2,500 in the business for 30 percent of the profits. Sadie is to supply another $500 in cash and provide a place to produce fudge. Sadie is to be paid $3.50 per hour for the time she works in the business and is to receive 70 percent of the profits. The money is invested, and on January 1 the business is started. During the year the following occurs:

1. Sadie buys kettles, utensils, a stove, and kitchen equipment needed for large-batch processing. The equipment and installation cost $2,000. The equipment has a five-year useful life with no salvage value.
2. Sugar, salt, cocoa, vanilla, and other supply purchases for the year cost $16,000.
3. Sadie works a total of 1000 hours.
4. 8000 kilograms of fudge are completed.
5. The candy is sold for $3 a kilogram to various candy stores and sweet shops within a 30-mile radius of Sadie's production facility. All candy produced during the period is sold and payment received.
6. Delivery charges amounting to $.05 a kilogram are paid, and Sadie pays $3,600 for advertising in local newspapers and on radio programs.
7. Sadie notes that her electricity bills were a total of $500 higher this year than last year.
8. Sadie pays $500 to a secretarial service to handle occasional correspondence, filing of records, and assorted bookkeeping activities.
9. At year-end a physical count shows that $5,200 of supplies inventory is on hand.

Required:

a. Calculate the average unit cost of producing 1 kilogram of candy during the period.

b. Calculate net income for the business.

c. Determine the amount each partner is entitled to receive as her share of the profits.

d. How much per hour did Sadie actually earn during the nine-month period?

e. How much cash is available at year-end for distribution to owners?

f. How can the cash balance be less than the profit, particularly when the beginning cash balance was $3,000?

P. 2B-3   Cost of goods manufactured and the income statement. Presented below are account balances from the general ledger of the Burkette Industrial Products Company on December 31, 1984.

Sales	$2,218,000
Sales salaries	145,000
Sales returns and allowances	43,000
Direct materials	420,000
Ending finished goods inventory	160,000
Beginning work in process inventory	80,000
Administrative salaries	350,000
Indirect labour	60,000
Office fire insurance	2,000
Delivery expense for finished products	12,000
Factory property tax	18,000
Direct labour	480,000
Factory fire insurance	7,000
Indirect materials	33,000
Factory supervision	120,000
Office equipment depreciation	4,000
Production equipment depreciation	26,000
Employee fringe benefits (70%, factory employees)	200,000
Advertising	70,000
Beginning finished goods inventory	120,000
Ending work in process inventory	110,000

Required:

a. Prepare a schedule of cost of goods manufactured.

b. Prepare an income statement.

P. 2B-4   Merchandising product cost. Shown below is the year-end trial balance of the Santanae Discount Store. The year-end inventory count reveals an ending inventory balance of $286,000.

Santanae Discount Store Trial Balance December 31		
	Debit	**Credit**
Cash	$ 38,000	
Accounts receivable	88,000	
Merchandise inventory 1/1	172,000	
Long-term investments	265,000	
Building	900,000	
Accumulated depreciation		$ 385,000
Accounts payable		74,000
Taxes payable		16,000
Notes payable		260,000
Common stock		360,000
Retained earnings		400,000
Sales		990,000
Sales returns and allowances	25,000	
Purchases	560,000	
Purchase returns and allowances		15,000
Freight-in	10,000	
Advertising expense	78,000	
Sales commissions	70,000	
Bad debt expense	16,000	
Equipment rental expense	12,000	
Depreciation expense	40,000	
Administrative salaries	135,000	
Maintenance expense	40,000	
Utilities expense	51,000	
	$2,500,000	$2,500,000

Required:

a. Prepare a cost of goods sold schedule in good form.

b. Prepare an income statement in good form. Use the product expense figure computed in part *a* for cost of goods sold.

c. Calculate the balance in retained earnings after closing all temporary accounts.

P. 2B-5   Evaluating labour costs. Mayfield Manufacturing Corporation recently negotiated a new labour contract calling for an average hourly wage rate of $8 per hour for manufacturing employees. Mayfield's chief accountant has assembled the following additional data relating to payroll costs:

1. Employer payroll taxes amount to 10 percent of the gross wages paid to employees during the year.

2. On average, employees work eight hours per day, five days a week, and have two weeks paid vacation per year.

3. Employees receive ten paid holidays a year.
4. Mayfield pays $18 into the employee guaranteed annual wage plan for each week an employee works.
5. On average, 90 percent of manufacturing employees' time can be identified as direct labour and the rest is indirect labour.

Required:
a. Determine the total annual labour cost per employee.
b. Determine the cost per hour worked of wages and other labour-related costs.
c. Compute the total cost of labour per direct labour hour.
d. Typically, what amount of direct labour cost would be assigned to a product of the Mayfield Manufacturing Corporation requiring 20 hours of direct labour?

P. 2B-6 **The effect of overhead on product costs.** Stradele Electric Motors, Inc., manufactures a heavy-duty 15 000-W motor that has the following production costs:

Direct materials	$180
Direct labour	120
Manufacturing overhead	150
	$450

The motor sells for $540, generating a gross margin of $90. During the accounting period just completed, actual manufacturing overhead was 16 percent more than the amount of overhead applied.

Required:
a. What is the actual amount of overhead for the motor?
b. What is the percentage change in product cost caused by the underapplied overhead?
c. Compute the actual gross margin for 15 000-W motors.
d. Compute the percentage change in gross margin caused by the underapplied overhead.

Minicase

Minicase 2-1

Mr. Smith has just been appointed as accountant for manufacturing operations of Burnaby Widgets Manufacturing, Ltd., a small company serving mainly the local market. The company manufactures spare parts for heavy construction machinery. These parts can not be obtained from regular channels and therefore they must be manufactured on order. In the past, Burnaby Widget Manufacturing, Ltd., used an overhead application rate 50 percent of direct labour cost. The labour cost has dramatically changed in 1983 as a result of the new collective bargaining agreement. However, the actual overhead, according to the records, has increased only 10 percent over the 1982 level. There has been no significant change in volume of production because Burnaby Widget Manufacturing, Ltd., deals with well-established firms in the area.

Required:
Briefly explain what would be the impact of the new collective agreement? What would you suggest to your new boss if you were Mr. Smith?

Chapter 3

Product Costing

This chapter presents the fundamentals of determining costs for specific products. Product cost data are an important part of many discussions and analyses later in the book. When you have completed the chapter, you should understand:

1 What job order and process costing are and when each is used.

2 How product costs are determined in each type of cost system.

3 The preparation and use of a job cost sheet.

4 The preparation and use of a cost of production report.

5 The meaning and use of unit costs in the two types of product costing systems.

6 How manufacturing costs are recorded in the company's accounting system.

One of the most important and interesting topics you will study in accounting is product costing. Virtually all physical items that you encounter daily, such as your car, home, food, textbooks, and clothes, have costs associated with them. There is a cost to produce each item, a cost to market it, and a cost to distribute it. In this chapter we discuss primarily the cost to produce products. Other types of costs are discussed in later chapters.

A study of product costing should provide you with an understanding of how costs are determined. This knowledge is a necessary prerequisite to comprehending and using much of the managerial accounting material in the following chapters.

The nature of the production process determines the type of costing system

There are two basic categories of product costing systems, **job order costing** and **process costing.** The type of cost system used depends primarily on the way the product is manufactured.

Job order costing is used for single items or batch processing

Job order costing is used for products that are produced in batches or intermittent production runs. Large construction projects use job order costing. Special-order items, such as specialized machinery or personalized products, and certain food products, like some baked goods, are produced in batches and are typical examples of production activity in which job order costing is used. Some businesses produce a certain amount of a product, for example, 1000 units, and then do not produce any more until inventory of the product reaches a level that requires more production. Job order production activities have definitely determinable starting and completion times. Accountants start accumulating costs for a job as soon as production is started, and the cost per unit of product is computed as soon as the job is complete.

Process costing is used for continuous flow production

Process costing is used for products that are produced in continuous flow production processes, e.g., on assembly lines. Unlike job order costing, there is usually no identifiable starting and completion time for the production activity. Automobiles, petroleum products, chemicals, and many appliances are examples of products typically costed using process costing systems. We discuss and illustrate job order costing first and then discuss process costing. Subsequently we illustrate the process of recording cost accounting activities in the formal records of the company. In an appendix to the chapter we extend the discussion of process costing.

Job order costing

Production costs are accumulated on a job cost sheet

Both job order and process costing systems are used to accumulate all of the direct materials, direct labour, and manufacturing overhead costs of production. In job order costing the costs of producing a product are accumulated on a document called a **job cost sheet,** an example of which is shown in Figure 3-1.

Job cost sheets vary significantly in style and form, but all contain the basic cost data required in Figure 3-1. At a minimum manufacturing costs are separated into the three basic cost elements. In addition to cost data, job cost sheets provide descriptive information, such as the dates the job was started and completed, the type of product produced, and the number of units produced. An important item in the job cost sheet is the **job number.** Sometimes job numbers are simple sequential reference numbers, or they may be more complex code numbers providing much useful processing information. For example, part number, customer number, production priority codes, and production sequencing codes are sometimes included in job numbering systems.

Job order cost sheet illustrated

To illustrate the use of a job cost sheet, we use the Blenford Air Moving Systems Company, which manufactures a variety of parts for fans and air conditioning units for commercial use. The company makes some products to fill specific customer orders. Smaller, general purpose products are produced for stock. No product or part requires continuous production runs, so all production is accounted for using job order costing.

In this example Blenford produces a 90-centimetre fan housing that it sells to a fan manufacturer. Two hundred fan housings are produced, and the costs are accumulated on the job cost sheet shown in Figure 3-2 (p. 73).

Job Cost Sheet

Date started _____   Job number _____
Date completed _____   Stock number _____
Units completed _____   Item _____

Direct Materials			Direct Labour			Manufacturing Overhead		
Date	Reference	Amount	Date	Reference	Amount	Date	Reference	Amount

Summary of Costs

	Total Cost	Unit Cost
Direct materials		
Direct labour		
Manufacturing overhead		
Total		

Figure 3-1
An example of a job cost sheet.

The starting date is entered on the job sheet, and a job number is assigned. Here the job number indicates the type of product, the intended use of the product, and a sequential number. In the top section of this job report, the only pieces of information unavailable on August 7 are the completion date and the units completed. These must be filled in after the job is finished on August 22.

Costs associated with the production of the 200 fan housings are recorded in the cost columns of the job cost sheet. The direct material costs are entered along with the material requisition numbers that provide a convenient cross-reference for auditors and for checking errors. Other firms may provide different information in the reference column, such as the type, quantity, or unit cost of the material.

The information is dictated by managers' needs

Direct labour costs are assigned to jobs on the basis of Blenford's weekly labour distribution report. The weekly labour cost for each job is entered in the amount column of the direct labour section of the job cost sheet. The date and reference columns indicate the particular labour distribution report that was the source for the entry. The 200 fan housings took 16 days to complete; this time period included labour costs from three different weekly labour distribution reports. Some businesses indicate in the reference column the hours worked on the job rather than the source document for the entry.

Blenford Air Moving Systems Company

Job Cost Sheet

Date started	7/8/83	Job number 6JL4741
Date completed	22/8/83	Stock number 3L17
Units completed	200	Item 90-cm fan housing

Direct Materials			Direct Labour			Manufacturing Overhead		
Date	**Reference**	**Amount**	**Date**	**Reference**	**Amount**	**Date**	**Reference**	**Amount**
7/8/83	MRQ 2112	$3,440	10/8/83	LD 201	$ 482	10/8/83	LD 201	$ 723
12/8/83	MRQ 2189	670	17/8/83	LD 202	1,488	17/8/83	LD 202	2,232
18/8/83	MRQ 2205	230	24/8/83	LD 203	1,250	24/8/83	LD 203	1,875
		$4,340			$3,220			$4,830

Summary of Costs

	Total Cost	Unit Cost
Direct materials	$ 4,340	$21.70
Direct labour	3,220	16.10
Manufacturing overhead	4,830	24.15
Total	$12,390	$61.95

Figure 3-2
An example of a completed job cost sheet.

Blenford uses an overhead rate of 150 percent of direct labour cost to apply manufacturing overhead to jobs. Since the application of manufacturing overhead depends on the amount of direct labour cost, overhead is assigned to the job whenever direct labour cost is charged to the job. Consequently, in this example manufacturing overhead is applied each week. In other firms manufacturing overhead may be applied using some other base, such as the number of machine hours used on the job. In that case a machine utilization report may be the basis for determining the amount of overhead to be applied to each job, and the overhead may be charged daily, weekly, monthly, or at some other time interval. Regardless of the application base, manufacturing overhead is charged to the job cost sheet in some systematic and timely fashion.

Costs are summarized when the job is completed

The summary of costs section of the job cost sheet is prepared when the job is completed. The costs for direct materials, direct labour, and manufacturing overhead are each totaled, and unit costs are computed for each cost element. The unit costs are averages. For example, $21.70 is the average unit cost for materials for the 200 fan housings. Some of the fan housings may have had

Unit costs are computed

material costs of $20.50 and others $22.80, but the average material cost for units produced in this job is $21.70 a unit. Also, the unit costs are for Job 6JL4741 only. Previous production runs and future production runs of 90-centimetre fan housings may have higher or lower unit costs. Unit costs are useful and convenient accounting information, but some caution must be exercised to ensure that unit costs are used intelligently in planning and controlling activities and making decisions.

Once a job is started, the cost sheet is referred to as an open job cost sheet. It remains open until the job is completed. After the summary of costs has been prepared, the cost totals are transferred from work in process to finished goods. The journal entry to accomplish the transfer for Job 6JL4741 is

Aug. 22	Finished Goods Inventory Control	12 390	
	Work in Process Control		12 390
	To record the transfer of costs to finished goods inventory for Job 6JL4741		

The open job cost sheets equal the work in process control account

The entry must be posted to the specific subsidiary accounts as well as to the two control accounts. The subsidiary ledger for work in process consists of all **open** job cost sheets. At any point in time the balance in the work in process control account should be equal to the total of the costs in the job cost sheets for jobs currently in production. Figure 3-3 (p. 75) illustrates graphically the relationship between the open job costs sheets and the work in process control account. When a job is completed and transferred to finished goods, the summarized job cost sheet is said to be closed. Closed job cost sheets are no longer part of work in process, but they may be used for such things as checking product costs, determining cost trends, setting product prices, or evaluating employee performance.

Departmental product cost data

Departmental job cost sheets provide more detail than a general job cost sheet

The amount of detail in product cost data depends on the information requirements of management. Typically, more cost detail means more expense, but the additional expense is justified in many situations.

When more detailed product cost data are needed, a **departmental job cost sheet** can be used. A departmental job cost sheet is similar to the job cost sheet shown in Figure 3-2. However, in addition to identifying costs by element, a departmental job cost sheet identifies costs by the department in which the cost occurred. If Blenford accumulated product costs by department, the departmental job cost sheet would appear as illustrated in Figure 3-4 (p. 76).

In this example the product is produced in three departments: cutting and welding, assembly, and painting. In other production situations there could be a larger or smaller number of production departments necessary to complete a job. Departmentalization facilitates cost control, aids in achieving the matching concept, and is important in evaluating the performance of departmental production supervisors.

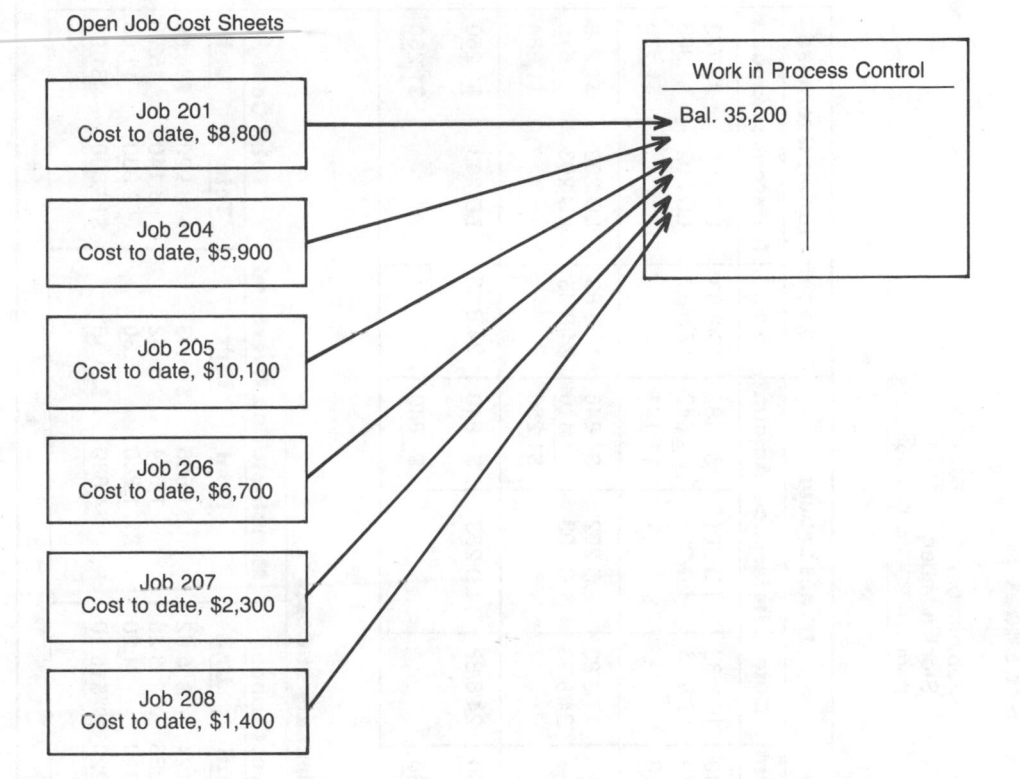

Figure 3-3
The balance in the Work in Process Control account equals the sum of the costs in all the open job cost sheets. When a job is completed, the job cost sheet is closed by summarizing the cost data and transferring the costs to finished goods.

In addition to the total and unit costs for materials, labour, and overhead, the total and unit costs for each cost element in each department are calculated at the bottom of the departmental job cost sheet. Changes in production efficiencies or other cost patterns are therefore much easier to identify.

Process costing

In job order costing each job or batch has a specific starting and completion time. Whether the job takes a day, a week, or a month, when it is completed, unit costs can be computed. Unlike batch processing, continuous flow production may continue for the entire year or longer without a break in the production activity. A process costing system is used to compute unit costs for goods produced in a continuous production process. The most obvious example is an assembly line where resources flow continuously along the line. At the

Blenford Air Moving Systems Company
Job Cost Sheet

Date started ___7/8/83___ Job number ___6JL4741___
Date completed ___22/8/83___ Stock number ___3L17___
Units completed ___200___ Item ___90-cm fan housings___

Department	Direct Materials			Direct Labour			Manufacturing Overhead		
	Date	Reference	Amount	Date	Reference	Amount	Date	Reference	Amount
Cutting and welding	7/8/83	MRQ 2112	$3,440	10/8/83	LD 201	$ 482	10/8/83	LD 201	$ 723
	12/8/83	MRQ 2189	670	17/8/83	LD 202	642	17/8/83	LD 202	963
			$4,110			$1,124			$1,686
Assembly			0	17/8/83	LD 202	$ 846	17/8/83	LD 202	$1,269
				24/8/83	LD 203	410	24/8/83	LD 203	615
						$1,256			$1,884
Painting	18/8/83	MRQ 2205	$ 230	24/8/83	LD 203	$ 840	24/8/83	LD 203	$1,260
			$ 230			$ 840			$1,260

Summary of Costs

Department	Direct Materials		Direct Labour		Manufacturing Overhead		Total Cost	
	Total	Unit	Total	Unit	Total	Unit	Total	Unit
Cutting and welding	$4,110	$20.55	$1,124	$ 5.62	$1,686	$ 8.43	$ 6,920	$34.60
Assembly	0	0	1,256	6.28	1,884	9.42	3,140	15.70
Painting	230	1.15	840	4.20	1,260	6.30	2,330	11.65
Total	$4,340	$21.70	$3,220	$16.10	$4,830	$24.15	$12,390	$61.95

Figure 3-4

An example of a departmental job cost sheet. Note the total cost of the product is the same as that on the general job cost sheet in Figure 3-2, but more detailed cost analysis is possible with the departmental report.

same time that materials are started at the beginning of the line, finished products are coming off at the end of the line.

Automobiles, petroleum products, and many food items are some common examples of goods that are produced using continuous flow production activities. There is no specific time when production starts and is completed. Managers cannot wait until year-end for cost data. Therefore, process costing is used to calculate product costs at desired time intervals, which may be daily, weekly, monthly, or any interval desired by management.

Production costs are reported periodically

A number of steps are necessary to create and operate a process costing system:

1. Establish specific process costing centres.
2. Determine the desired time interval for reporting product costs.
3. Gather manufacturing costs for each process centre for the reporting period.
4. Determine the amount of production for each process centre in terms of the output units of that process centre.
5. Using the data from steps 3 and 4, compute unit costs in each process centre.
6. Prepare the desired managerial accounting reports.

Process costing production activities are divided into process centres

In process costing the accountant divides the production process for each product into specific identifiable processing activities. Each separate processing activity is called a **process centre**. Each process centre is characterized by a homogeneous output, and the work performed in the process centre is the same for each unit processed. For example, a manufacturer of chocolate candy bars divides production into four process centres: mixing, cooking, moulding, and packaging. The output of the first two process centres is litres of liquid chocolate. Output of the last two process centres is units of 28-gram candy bars. In each process centre there is only one type of output, and no other product is produced in that centre.

A process centre in process costing is different from a production department in job order costing. A process centre only has one type of output during the accounting period, whereas many different products may be worked on in a job shop production department during an accounting period.

The total cost of a product is determined by adding the unit costs incurred in each process centre. The production of a product may require a few or many separate process centres. The number is determined by the production requirements for the product and by management's need for detailed cost data.

Production cost data are accumulated for each process centre and reported periodically to managers. The timing of reports depends on management's information needs and the cost of accumulating and reporting the cost data. Timeliness is an important attribute of relevant product cost data, so reports may be frequent. Monthly and weekly process centre cost reports are common, and even more frequent reports are possible with computerized accounting systems.

The first two steps in developing a process costing system are prerequisites to the operation of the system. Although steps 3 through 6 may require periodic evaluation, they are the repetitive steps necessary to operate a process costing system.

Cost reports for each process centre are called cost of production reports

The basic data gathered and computed in steps 3 through 5 are summarized and reported in a cost of production report. This report is similar to a job cost sheet in job order costing. The primary difference is the orientation of the reports. **Cost of production reports** summarize production costs for a particular time interval at a specific process centre. Complete cost data for a particular product include cost of production reports for all process centres involved in producing the product. On the other hand, a job cost sheet summarizes the cost data for the entire production run of the product regardless of the number of departments involved in the production. The job cost sheet is summarized when the job is completed. Cost of production reports are prepared at fixed intervals, such as weekly or monthly.

Cost of production reports cover a period of time

Process costing illustrated

The Fergus Valve Company is used to illustrate the basic procedures in developing product costs in a process costing system. In this example we examine the June 1983 production activity for a product called an R2 gas valve. The company purchases rough iron castings that are ground, drilled, and polished in a single process centre named the machining department. A cost of production report for June 1983 is presented, based on the June production and cost data that follow.

June production and cost data. On June 1, 1983, there is no beginning work in process inventory in the process centre. During June 10 000 valves are put into production, of which 9000 are completed and transferred out of the process centre. On June 30, 1983, 1000 valves remain in ending work in process inventory, with all material added and 40 percent of the direct labour and manufacturing overhead completed. The term **conversion** is often used in place of direct labour and manufacturing overhead when the percentage of completion in ending work in process inventory is identical for the two. We can state that in the machining department conversion is 40 percent complete, meaning that 40 percent of the total required labour is done, and 40 percent of the total overhead has been applied to the product. Production costs for the month are direct materials $12,000, direct labour $7,520, and manufacturing overhead $9,400.

The physical flow of products is described first

Using the above data, the June cost of production report is prepared and presented in Figure 3-5. Note the organization of the report. The top portion describes the physical flow of units, and the bottom portion summarizes the associated cost flows. The physical flow is divided into **units to account for** and **units accounted for.** The former tells the source of the units in production, and the latter describes their disposition. Since there is no beginning work in process inventory in June, the only source of units is the 10 000 units started, and they are the total units to account for. The units accounted for must equal the units to account for. The 10 000 total units are divided between the 9000 units transferred to the next department and the 1000 in ending work in process inventory on June 30, 1983.

Fergus Valve Company
Cost of Production Report
June 1983

Machining Department

Units to account for:			Units accounted for:		
Units started in June	10 000		Transferred out	9 000	
			Ending work in		
			process inventory	1 000	
	10 000			10 000	

	Cost	Equivalent Units	Unit Cost
Costs to account for:			
Materials	$12,000	10 000	$1.20
Labour	7,520	9 400	.80
Manufacturing overhead	9,400	9 400	1.00
	$28,920		$3.00
Costs accounted for:			
Transferred to next department	9000 @ $3.00 =		$27,000
Ending work in process inventory			
Materials	1000 @ $1.20 =	$1,200	
Labour	400 @ .80 =	320	
Manufacturing overhead	400 @ 1.00 =	400	1,920
			$28,920

Figure 3-5
The June cost of production report for the machining department of the Fergus Valve Company. Carefully observe the general format of the report.

Unit costs are computed

The cost section of the report is also divided into two parts. The first part is called **costs to account for.** This section contains a summary of all the costs incurred in the process centre during the period, and it shows the computed unit costs.

To compute unit costs it is necessary to determine the amount of costs and the number of units produced in the process centre during the period. The amount of costs is derived from various sources, such as material requisitions and labour distribution reports, just as in job order costing; however, the determination of the quantity of production is somewhat different. In job order costing the number of units produced is measured when the job is completed. In process costing it is not so simple because the production is continuous. Some units are started and completed during the period, and some units are only partially completed during the period. Obviously partially completed units cannot be counted the same as whole units. Accountants solve the problem by computing **equivalent units,** which is a measure of how many whole units of production are represented by the units completed plus the units partially

Equivalent units is the measure of production output

completed. In other words, if the entire production effort had been directed toward starting and completing all units, rather than partially completing some of the units, how many whole units would have been produced? The answer to this question represents equivalent units of production.

Since there was no beginning inventory in the process centre, the 9000 units transferred out must have been started and completed during the month. In addition to the 9000 whole units of production, some work has been done on the 1000 units in ending work in process inventory. Forty percent conversion means that two-fifths of the required labour and overhead has already been expended on the partially completed units. Another way of viewing the situation is that 60 percent of the conversion process is still required to complete the 1000 units. For direct labour and manufacturing overhead the equivalent units are 9000 started and completed plus 400 (1000 × .4) in ending work in process inventory, or 9400 equivalent units. The rough iron casting is the only direct material, and since it is added at the beginning, in terms of materials, all 10 000 units are complete.

Dividing the equivalent units for each cost element into their respective costs yields the unit cost for each cost element. These unit costs are the average unit costs for the month of June. Unit costs for prior or future periods may be different. Typically, managers compare cost of production reports from month to month to identify cost fluctuations.

Some costs are transferred out of the process centre

Some costs remain in ending work in process inventory

The **costs accounted for** section of the report describes what happened to the costs identified in the costs to account for section. Costs are accounted for in two ways. First, the cost of completed goods is transferred to the next production department or to finished goods. Second, the cost of goods not completed remains in the process centre as ending work in process inventory.

In the machining department 9000 units are completed and transferred out at a cost of $3.00 per unit. That accounts for $27,000 of the $28,920 total cost. Ending inventory of 1000 units consists of 1000 equivalent units of material and 400 equivalent units of labour and overhead. Multiplying the equivalent units in ending inventory by their appropriate unit cost, the cost of ending inventory is $1,920. The cost transferred out plus the cost of ending inventory is $28,920, the total cost to account for. The cost accounted for must always equal the cost to account for. Occasionally small rounding errors arise because of unit costs that are not even numbers, and a small rounding adjustment may be necessary so that the two totals balance.

The above example illustrates many of the fundamentals of a process costing system, including the basic nature and format of the cost of production report. This introduction to process costing should give you an understanding of the basic differences and similarities between job order costing and process costing. The appendix to the chapter extends the discussion of process costing to include beginning work in process inventories and summary product cost reports. The appendix is intended for those who want a somewhat deeper understanding of process costing concepts and procedures.

Recording cost flows

Cost data are part of a firm's accounting system

Both job order and process costing systems have been discussed and illustrated. The job order cost sheet and the cost of production report have been presented as the primary means of summarizing and reporting product costs. In addition to identifying costs, it is necessary to record the cost data in the company's formal accounting records. In this section of the chapter we illustrate the journal entries for basic manufacturing activities. Ruddington Industrial Products, Incorporated, is used in the illustration. First, a set of manufacturing activities is listed. Then, each activity is journalized and briefly discussed. Finally, a partial general ledger is presented in Figure 3-6 with all journal entries posted.

a. Ruddington purchased four different materials from a supplier at a total cost of $62,000 on open account.

b. $40,000 of direct materials are transferred from the inventory storeroom into production.

c. Indirect materials costing $4,640 are transferred from the inventory storeroom into production.

d. The weekly payroll for the manufacturing plant is $120,000.

e. $108,000 of the weekly manufacturing payroll can be identified with the production of specific products. The remaining $12,000 is indirect labour cost.

f. Additional weekly payroll costs include Canada Pension Plan and UIC taxes of $6,900, other taxes of $350, and provincial payroll taxes of $2,200.

g. Utility bills for the manufacturing plant of $16,500 are received and paid.

h. Depreciation for the period on manufacturing facilities includes $18,000 for plant and $14,600 for equipment.

i. Property taxes of $9,860 for the manufacturing facility are paid.

j. Manufacturing overhead is applied at the rate of $4.00 per direct labour hour. During the period 21 600 actual direct labour hours are used in production.

k. Products costing $210,000 are completed during the period and transferred to finished goods inventory.

l. Ruddington sold products costing $195,000 during the period for a total of $310,000.

m. At year-end the overhead applied account is closed into the overhead control account.

n. Any underapplied or overapplied overhead is closed into cost of goods sold.

Each of the preceding items is analyzed separately below. Like most manufacturing firms, Ruddington uses a perpetual inventory system.

a.	Inventory Control	62,000	
	Accounts Payable		62,000
	Purchased raw materials on open account.		

Whenever inventory control is debited, the amount must be posted to the control account in the general ledger and to the individual inventory accounts in the subsidiary ledger. For example, the $62,000 purchase of raw materials shown in *a* above might consist of the following inventory items:

$ 4,800 of JL2—black silicone sealer
$26,400 of KY6 – 185-W electric motors
$28,200 of LB9 – 12-gauge rolled aluminum
$ 2,600 of XX3—cleaning compound

Each of these individual inventory accounts in the subsidiary ledger is increased by the amount indicated.

Direct costs are charged to work in process control

b.	Work in Process Control	40,000	
	Inventory Control		40,000
	Issued direct materials to production.		

Indirect costs are charged to manufacturing overhead control

c.	Manufacturing Overhead Control	4,640	
	Inventory Control		4,640
	Issued indirect materials to production.		

Transactions *b* and *c* both illustrate transfers of raw material from inventory to production. The material in *b* can be identified with specific products and is recorded in work in process as direct materials. The indirect materials in *c* are included in overhead as part of the indirect cost of manufacturing.

d.	Payroll	120,000	
	Income Tax Withholding Payable		19,000
	Provincial Payroll Taxes Payable		3,900
	Canada Pension Plan and UIC Payable		6,900
	Union Dues Payable		1,200
	Cash		89,000
	Recorded the weekly payroll and withholding items		

Journal entry *d* records the manufacturing payroll. The amounts withheld from the employees' paycheques result from various tax rules and contractual agreements that are not of great concern here. The most important number in the above journal entry is the debit of $120,000. That debit is the gross payroll assigned to products for the pay period. The amounts withheld from employees' paycheques do not affect the payroll cost of the company.

e.	Work in Process Control	108,000	
	Manufacturing Overhead Control	12,000	
	Payroll		120,000
	Distributed the payroll.		

The gross payroll of $120,000 is assigned to direct and indirect labour by using the labour distribution report. Note that the amount of cash paid directly to employees does not affect the amount of labour cost distributed to production.

f.	Manufacturing Overhead Control	9,450	
	Canada Pension Plan and UIC Payable		6,900
	Provincial Withholding Taxes Payable		2,200
	Other Taxes Payable		350
	Recorded payroll taxes imposed on the employer.		

In addition to employee wages, businesses must match and pay various payroll taxes as shown in *f*.

g.	Manufacturing Overhead Control	16,500	
	Cash		16,500
	Paid utility bills for manufacturing.		
h.	Manufacturing Overhead Control	32,600	
	Accumulated Depreciation, Plant		18,000
	Accumulated Depreciation, Equipment		14,600
	Recorded annual depreciation for manufacturing.		
i.	Manufacturing Overhead Control	9,860	
	Cash		9,860
	Paid property tax bills on the production facility.		

Transactions *g* through *i* illustrate actual manufacturing overhead costs. In each case the cost is charged to the overhead control account. Throughout the period the overhead control account continues to accumulate a debit balance that represents the total actual overhead cost.

j.	Work in Process Control	86,400	
	Manufacturing Overhead Applied		86,400
	Applied overhead to products.		

Manufacturing overhead is applied to products using a predetermined overhead rate of $4.00 per direct labour hour. During the period 21 600 actual direct labour hours were used in production. Therefore, $86,400 (21 600 hours

× $4.00 per hour) is charged to work in process to apply overhead to production. In practice overhead is applied to production on a timely basis during the accounting period, such as daily or weekly, but here we use one summary entry to illustrate the accounts used.

When products are completed, costs associated with their production are transferred from work in process to finished goods inventory. For example, during the period Ruddington completed products costing $210,000, leaving a balance of $24,400 in ending work in process inventory.

k.	Finished Goods Inventory	210,000	
	Work In Process Control		210,000
	Transferred completed products to finished goods.		
l.	Cash	310,000	
	Cost of Goods Sold	195,000	
	Sales		310,000
	Finished Goods Inventory		195,000
	Recorded sale of finished goods and removed their cost from inventory.		

Products costing $195,000 are sold for $310,000. With a perpetual inventory the sale **and** the cost of the products sold are recorded at the same time.

At the end of the accounting period, the overhead control account balance is a debit of $85,050. The overhead applied account balance is a credit of $86,400. Actual overhead is $1,350 less than the amount applied. This relatively small difference, 1.5 percent of actual overhead, is credited to the cost of goods sold account at year-end when the two overhead accounts are closed. The necessary entries are

m.	Manufacturing Overhead Applied	86,400	
	Manufacturing Overhead Control		86,400
	Closed overhead applied into overhead control.		
n.	Manufacturing Overhead Control	1,350	
	Cost of Goods Sold		1,350
	Closed the overapplied balance left in MOH control into cost of goods sold.		

Overapplied overhead reduces product cost

The resulting cost of goods sold for the period decreases to $193,650. Figure 3-6 shows a partial set of ledger accounts of Ruddington Industrial Products after all of the above journal entries have been posted.

Cash

Debit		Credit	
l.	310,000	g.	16,500
		i.	9,860
		d.	89,000
Bal	194,640		

Inventory Control

Debit		Credit	
a.	62,000	b.	40,000
		c.	4,640
Bal	17,360		

Work in Process Control

Debit		Credit	
b.	40,000	k.	210,000
e.	108,000		
j.	86,400		
Bal	24,400		

Finished Goods Inventory

Debit		Credit	
k.	210,000	l.	195,000
Bal	15,000		

Accumulated Depreciation, Plant

Debit		Credit	
		h.	18,000

Accumulated Depreciation, Equipment

Debit		Credit	
		h.	14,600

Union Dues Payable

Debit		Credit	
		d.	1,200

Other Taxes Payable

Debit		Credit	
		f.	350

Accounts Payable

Debit		Credit	
		a.	62,000

Income Tax Withholding Payable

Debit		Credit	
		d.	19,000

Provincial Payroll Taxes Payable

Debit		Credit	
		d.	3,900
		f.	2,200
		Bal.	6,100

Canada Pension Plan Payable

Debit		Credit	
		d.	6,900
		f.	6,900
		Bal	13,800

Manufacturing Overhead Control

Debit		Credit	
c.	4,640	m.	86,400
e.	12,000		
f.	9,450		
g.	16,500		
h.	32,600		
i.	9,860		
Bal	85,050		
n.	1,350		

Manufacturing Overhead Applied

Debit		Credit	
m.	86,400	j.	86,400

Payroll

Debit		Credit	
d.	120,000	e.	120,000

Sales

Debit		Credit	
		l.	310,000

Cost of Goods Sold

Debit		Credit	
l.	195,000	n.	1,350
Bal	193,650		

Figure 3-6
Ruddington Industrial Products, Incorporated, partial ledger showing the account balances after posting all journal entries.

Appendix: Process costing extended

Earlier in the chapter the basic concepts and procedures of a process costing system were presented. An example illustrated a single process centre that had no beginning work in process inventory. However, most products are produced in more than one process centre, and most process centres have beginning and ending work in process inventories. In this appendix the discussion of process costing is extended to include beginning work in process inventories and multiple process centres. These additional concepts provide a more realistic picture of process costing systems, but they also increase the complexity of the costing process.

Process costing illustration continued

To illustrate the discussion, we continue to use the example of the R2 gas valve produced by the Fergus Valve Company. Assume the R2 gas valve is **not** complete when it is transferred out of the machining department process centre. Instead the valve goes from machining to the assembly department where washers and fittings are installed on the valve. Then the valve is transferred to the finishing department where it is completed by treating it with rust inhibitors and by buffing it. The valves are transferred from the finishing department to the finished goods inventory.

Earlier in the chapter a cost of production report was prepared for the month of June 1983 for the machining department (see Figure 3-5). Now we continue by providing production cost data for the other two processing centres used in the production of R2 valves. Following are June data and cost of production reports for assembly and finishing.

Assembly department. In the assembly department the castings transferred in from machining are combined with the necessary washers and fittings. The materials are added early in the assembly process. Completed units are transferred to the finishing department. In addition to the 9000 units transferred into assembly from the machining department, there are 3000 units of beginning work in process inventory in assembly on June 1.

The primary accounting difference between the machining and assembly departments is that assembly has a beginning work in process inventory. That may seem like a small difference, but it creates a problem of accounting for the inventory cost flow. In machining all costs were June production costs. In assembly there are June production costs, of course, but in addition there are costs in beginning inventory that have been carried over from the previous month's production costs. If the unit costs in beginning inventory are identical to unit costs in the current period, there is no difficulty. All units transferred out and units in ending inventory are accounted for using the same unit costs. However, identical unit costs are seldom the case. Even minor fluctuations in resource costs and production efficiencies create differing unit costs from one period to the next. All differences, major or minor, require the accountant to decide which costs should be transferred out of the process centre and which costs should remain in ending work in process inventory. Accountants use the

Beginning work in process requires the use of some inventory flow assumption

same inventory cost flow methods found in merchandising businesses. First in, first out (FIFO) and weighted average are the two most commonly used methods of costing production flows in process costing systems. We use FIFO to complete the Fergus Valve Company example, and we illustrate weighted average later in the appendix.

The June 1 beginning work in process inventory (WIP) consists of 3000 units with all materials and 30 percent conversion. These units have $8,700 of costs transferred in from the machining department last month. In addition, beginning inventory consists of $5,250 of material cost, $1,404 of labour cost, and $1,728 of manufacturing overhead cost, all incurred in the assembly department last month.

During June 9000 units are transferred in from the machining department. The $27,000 of costs transferred in with these units appeared in the machining department cost of production report as costs transferred out. Costs added in the assembly department during June consist of materials $16,200, labour $17,808, and manufacturing overhead $22,260. On June 30, 2000 units are in process with all assembly materials added and 75 percent of conversion completed.

Figure 3-7 is the assembly department June cost of production report. The units to account for section includes the 3000 units in June 1 beginning WIP in the assembly department plus the 9000 units transferred in from machining during June. The 12000 units are accounted for as follows: 10 000 units were completed during June and transferred to the finishing department; 2000 units are partially completed and remain in ending WIP. The costs to account for section looks much larger than it did in the machining department. This is caused by the fact that there were no beginning inventory costs in the machining department. Beginning inventory costs are computed separately so that FIFO can be used to account for the cost flows. Of course, the beginning inventory of one month is the ending inventory of the previous month, so the beginning inventory cost figures for June can be read directly from the May cost of production report of the assembly department. Another difference between

Costs flow from one process centre to the next

assembly and machining is the prior department costs. In process costing, costs are transferred from one process centre to the next process centre following the physical flow of production. Since production begins in the machining department, there is no prior department cost in the cost of production report in Figure 3-5. The $27,000 transferred out of the machining department appears as prior department cost for June in the assembly department report.

In the costs to account for section of the report, the computation of unit costs is the same in the assembly department as it was in the machining department. Each category of cost is divided by equivalent units to find unit cost. When there is a beginning inventory and the FIFO inventory method is used, unit costs are computed first for beginning work in process inventory and then for current-period production. In practice the unit costs for beginning work in process inventory in June can be read as ending work in process unit costs in the May cost of production report. In the example, the May cost of production report is not presented, so unit costs must be computed. Each cost in beginning inventory is divided by its equivalent units of production. For example, prior department costs and materials costs are divided by 3000 equivalent units. Prior department costs are always 100 percent complete; otherwise, the units would not have been transferred to the current production centre. All materials added in the assembly department are added early in the production process, so the 3000 units in beginning inventory are 100 percent complete as to materials. Direct labour and manufacturing overhead are only 30 percent complete in beginning work in process. Thus, the equivalent units for each is 900 (3000 × .3). Total cost in beginning inventory in assembly is $17,082, and the average unit cost of a whole unit is $8.13.

Current-period production consists of work done to complete the units in beginning work in process plus work done on the units transferred in during the month. First in, first out inventory assumes beginning inventory units are completed and transferred out first, followed by units transferred in during the period. The current-period costs for each cost category are divided by the equivalent units of production for the period to determine unit costs. The $27,000 prior department cost in June in assembly is the transferred-out cost from the June cost of production report for machining. It is divided by the 9000 units transferred into the department. Beginning inventory was already complete in terms of prior department costs on June 1. Similarly, the beginning inventory was complete in terms of material added in the assembly department. Therefore, June material costs in assembly pertain only to the 9000 units transferred in during June.

Labour and overhead were used to complete beginning inventory and to process units transferred in during the month. Equivalent units for labour and overhead represent the amount of effort, measured in whole units of output, expended on completing the beginning work in process, starting and completing units during the month, and working on units in ending work in process. In the assembly department in June the computation is:

Measuring the quantity of production output

	Units
Conversion required to complete beginning WIP (3000 × .70)	2 100
Units started and completed (9000 − 2000)	7 000
Conversion done on ending WIP (2000 × .75)	1 500
Equivalent units for labour and overhead	10 600

The units started and completed during the period can be computed in two ways. One way is to subtract the ending inventory from the units transferred in during the period (9000 − 2000 in this example). This approach works if no units are lost or spoiled in the production process. Another method is to subtract the units in beginning work in process from the units transferred out during the period (10 000 − 3000). The equivalent units for each cost element are divided into their corresponding cost to determine current-period unit costs.

```
┌─────────────────────────────────────────────────────────────────┐
│                    Fergus Valve Company                           │
│                  Cost of Production Report                         │
│                         June 1983                                 │
├─────────────────────────────────────────────────────────────────┤
│                    Assembly Department                            │
└─────────────────────────────────────────────────────────────────┘
```

Units to account for: Units accounted for:
  Beginning WIP   3000   Transferred out   10 000
  Transferred in, June 9000   Ending WIP   2 000
                       12 000   12 000

	Cost	Equivalent Units	Unit Cost
Costs to account for:			
Beginning work in process inventory			
Prior departments	$ 8,700	3000	$2.90
Materials	5,250	3000	1.75
Labour	1,404	900	1.56
Manufacturing overhead	1,728	900	1.92
	$ 17,082		$8.13
Current-period production			
Prior departments	$ 27,000	9 000	$3.00
Materials	16,200	9 000	1.80
Labour	17,808	10 600	1.68
Manufacturing overhead	22,260	10 600	2.10
	$ 83,268		$8.58
	$100,350		

Costs accounted for:
  Transferred to next department
    Prior departments   3000 @ $2.90 = $ 8,700
    Prior departments   7000 @ 3.00 = 21,000
    Materials   3000 @ 1.75 =   5,250
    Materials   7000 @ 1.80 = 12,600
    Labour   900 @ 1.56 =   1,404
    Labour   9100 @ 1.68 = 15,288
    Manufacturing overhead   900 @ 1.92 =   1,728
    Manufacturing overhead   9100 @ 2.10 = 19,110 $ 85,080

  Ending work in process inventory
    Prior departments   2000 @ $3.00 = $ 6,000
    Materials   2000 @ 1.80 =   3,600
    Labour   1500 @ 1.68 =   2,520
    Manufacturing overhead   1500 @ 2.10 =   3,150   15,270
                                                          $100,350

Figure 3-7
The June cost of production report for the assembly department. Compare
this report with the machining department report in Figure 3-5 and notice the
differences that arise because there is beginning inventory in assembly.

In the assembly department current-period units cost is $8.58, which is somewhat higher than unit cost in beginning inventory. The total cost to account for is $100,350, which includes beginning inventory costs and current-period production costs.

The costs accounted for section describes the disposition of the $100,350 of cost. Most of it is transferred on to the finishing department, but some remains in ending work in process. A total of 10 000 units is transferred out of assembly. Using FIFO, the costs of beginning inventory are the first transferred out, followed by current-period production costs until the cost of 10 000 units has been transferred to finishing. If beginning inventory was comprised of completed units, 3000 units would be transferred at $8.13 a unit and 7000 units would be transferred at the current-period cost of $8.58. However, beginning inventory is only 30 percent (900 equivalent units) complete in terms of labour and overhead. Since 10 000 units are transferred out, 9100 equivalent units of conversion cost must be transferred out, at the current-period cost. Therefore, the first 3000 equivalent units of prior department costs and material costs are transferred out at beginning inventory costs, and the next 7000 equivalent units are transferred out at current-period costs. The first 900 equivalent units of labour and overhead costs are transferred out at beginning inventory costs and the next 9100 equivalent units at current period costs. In total, 10 000 equivalent units of each cost element is transferred out at a total cost of $85,080.

What remains are the partially completed units in ending work in process inventory. These units are costed at the current period costs since all beginning inventory costs have already been transferred out. There are 2000 equivalent units of prior department costs and material costs and 1500 equivalent units of labour and overhead costs. The current-period unit cost for each cost element is multiplied by its number of equivalent units in ending inventory. The cost of ending work in process inventory in assembly is $15,270 which, when combined with the cost transferred out, accounts for all $100,350 of the costs to account for.

Finishing department. The last process centre in the production of R2 gas valves is the finishing department. Here the castings transferred in from the assembly department are completed by treating them with rust inhibitors and buffing them. Beginning WIP in June is 5000 units with all materials and 40 percent conversion. Ending WIP for June is 3000 units with all materials and $33^1/_3$ percent conversion. Completed valves are transferred to finished goods. Departmental costs for beginning inventory are: prior department costs $41,670, materials $1,400, labour $3,560, and overhead $4,450. Current-period costs are: prior department costs $85,080, materials $3,100, labour $22,440, overhead $28,050. The cost of production report for the finishing department is presented in Figure 3-8.

The format and computation of the finishing department report are similar to that of the assembly department report. Notice that the unit cost for current-period prior department costs is $8.508. The cost transferred out of the assembly

Fergus Valve Company
Cost of Production Report
June 1983

Finishing Department

Units to account for:		Units accounted for:	
Beginning WIP	5 000	Transferred out	12 000
Transferred in, June	10 000	Ending WIP	3 000
	15 000		15 000

	Cost	Equivalent Units	Unit Cost
Costs to account for:			
Beginning work in process inventory			
Prior departments	$ 41,670	5000	$ 8.334
Materials	1,400	5000	.28
Labour	3,560	2000	1.78
Manufacturing overhead	4,450	2000	2.225
	$ 51,080		$12.619
Current-period production			
Prior departments	$ 85,080	10 000	$ 8.508
Materials	3,100	10 000	.31
Labour	22,440	11 000	2.04
Manufacturing overhead	28,050	11 000	2.55
	$138,670		$13.408
	$189,750		

Costs accounted for:		
Transferred to finished goods		
Prior departments	5 000 @ $8.334 = $41,670	
Prior departments	7 000 @ 8.508 = 59,556	
Materials	5 000 @ .28 = 1,400	
Materials	7 000 @ .31 = 2,170	
Labour	2 000 @ 1.78 = 3,560	
Labour	10 000 @ 2.04 = 20,400	
Manufacturing overhead	2 000 @ 2.225 = 4,450	
Manufacturing overhead	10 000 @ 2.55 = 25,500	$158,706
Ending work in process inventory		
Prior departments	3 000 @ 8.508 = $25,524	
Materials	3 000 @ .31 = 930	
Labour	1 000 @ 2.04 = 2,040	
Manufacturing overhead	1 000 @ 2.55 = 2,550	31,044
		$189,750

Figure 3-8

The June cost of production report for the finishing department is similar to the assembly department report.

department was part beginning inventory cost at $8.13 per unit and part current-period cost at $8.58 per unit. The cost transferred into finishing totals $85,080 and represents 10 000 units from the assembly department. Dividing the cost by the number of units yields an average of $8.508. In other words, although FIFO is used to transfer costs out of a department, the transferred costs are averaged in the next department.

Using FIFO, $158,706 is transferred to the finished goods inventory representing the production cost of the 12 000 R2 gas valve units completed in June, and $31,044 is the cost of the 3000 units in ending inventory. The average unit cost of the units transferred to finished goods is $13.2255 ($158,706/12 000 units). That information by itself may not be enough to satisfy management's information needs. More detailed cost information may be desired. The cost of production report for each process centre identifies the unit cost of production for each cost element in that process centre. However, any costs incurred in other departments are merely identified as prior department costs. If management wants to know the unit cost of materials, labour, and overhead for producing R2 gas valves in June, the unit cost data from the cost of production reports must be summarized, as in Figure 3-9.

The data for Figure 3-9 are taken directly from the individual cost of production reports. Current-period cost data are used; therefore, the total unit cost of $13.48 is somewhat higher than the $13.2255 per unit cost transferred to finished goods. The difference occurs because the unit costs in beginning inventories were lower than current-period production costs. The beginning inventory costs were part of the costs transferred through the process centres

Figure 3-9
This managerial accounting report summarizes the physical flow of units and the current-period unit cost data found on the cost of production reports of the departments. The report provides information similar to that found on a departmental job cost sheet used in a job order cost system.

Fergus Valve Company
R2 Gas Valve Cost Report
June 1983

Physical Flow	Units			
	Machining	Assembly	Finishing	Total
Beginning inventory	0	3 000	5 000	8 000
Started/transferred in	10 000	9 000	10 000	—
Ending inventory	1 000	2 000	3 000	6 000
Transferred out	9 000	10 000	12 000	—

Cost Flow	Unit Costs			
	Machining	Assembly	Finishing	Total
Materials	$1.20	$1.80	$ .31	$ 3.31
Labour	.80	1.68	2.04	4.52
Manufacturing overhead	1.00	2.10	2.55	5.65
Total	$3.00	$5.58	$4.90	$13.48

```
┌─────────────────────────────────────────────────────────────────────────┐
│                         Fergus Valve Company                              │
│                       Cost of Production Report                           │
│                              June 1983                                    │
└─────────────────────────────────────────────────────────────────────────┘
```

Finishing Department

Units to account for:			Units accounted for:	
Beginning WIP	5,000		Transferred out	12,000
Transferred in, June	10,000		Ending WIP	3,000
	15,000			15,000

	Cost	Equivalent Units	Unit Cost
Costs to account for:			
Prior departments			
Beginning WIP	$ 41,670	5 000	$ 8.334
Current period	85,080	10 000	8.508
	$126,750	15 000	$ 8.45
Materials			
Beginning WIP	$ 1,400	5 000	$ .28
Current period	3,100	10 000	.31
	$ 4,500	15 000	$ .30
Labour			
Beginning WIP	$ 3,560	2 000	$ 1.78
Current period	22,440	11 000	2.04
	$ 26,000	13 000	$ 2.00
Manufacturing overhead			
Beginning WIP	$ 4,450	2 000	$ 2.225
Current period	28,050	11 000	2.55
	$ 32,500	3 000	$ 2.50
	$189,750		$13.25

Costs accounted for:			
Transferred to finished goods	12 000 @ $13.25 =		$159,000
Ending work in process inventory			
Prior department	3000 @ $ 8.45 =	$25,350	
Materials	3000 @ .30 =	900	
Labour	1000 @ 2.00 =	2,000	
Manufacturing overhead	1000 @ 2.50 =	2,500	30,750
			$189,750

Figure 3-10
The June cost of production report for the finishing department using a weighted average inventory cost flow rather than FIFO. The total cost is the same as in Figure 3-8, but the amounts transferred to finished goods and remaining in ending work in process are somewhat different from those obtained with FIFO.

to finished goods. However, beginning inventory costs are not used in the cost report in Figure 3-9; instead only current-period production costs are reported.

Weighted average inventory. In the R2 valve example, FIFO cost flow was used whenever there was a beginning inventory. Although FIFO is used frequently, weighted average is also common. To illustrate the use of the weighted average inventory method, the June cost of production report for the finishing department is prepared again, but the weighted average inventory method is used.

Figure 3-10 presents the June cost of production report for the finishing department using the weighted average approach. Notice that the total cost to account for is the same as with the FIFO inventory method. The choice of inventory costing methods does **not** affect the total cost to account for, nor does it affect the computation of equivalent units, which is the measurement of the physical quantity of production. What is affected is the way that unit costs are computed and the way that costs are assigned to units transferred out of the department and units in ending work in process inventory.

Weighted average is an accounting concept, not a production concept

The format of the unit cost computations in the cost of production report is somewhat different with a weighted average cost. Instead of grouping beginning inventory costs together and current-period costs together, the costs are grouped by cost element. This is necessary to compute a weighted average cost for each cost element. The average cost is determined in the same way that any weighted average is found. For each cost element, the cost in beginning inventory is added to the current-period cost, and that total is divided by the sum of the beginning inventory and current-period equivalent units. For example, material cost in beginning inventory was $1,400. Current-period material cost was $3,100. The total of $4,500 is divided by the 15,000 total equivalent units for material, yielding a weighted average unit cost of $.30 per unit.

Weighted average is used to cost the inventory flows

In the finishing department average unit costs are $8.45 for prior department costs, $.30 for materials, $2.00 for labour, and $2.50 for overhead. The total is $13.25 per unit. The **weighted average cost figure** is used to cost the units transferred out of the department during the period **and** to cost ending work in process inventory. Note that in addition to the weighted average unit costs, unit costs have been computed for each cost element in beginning inventory and current-period production. These unit costs are **not** used for transferring costs out of the department or costing ending inventory, **but** the costs are useful in helping managers evaluate performance from one period to another. Although cost of production reports provide the product cost data used in financial statements, they are also very useful in providing detailed cost data for many internal accounting reports and are valuable to managers in evaluating performance and making cost control decisions. Therefore, this information should appear on the cost of production report. Carefully compare the weighted average report in Figure 3-10 with the FIFO report in Figure 3-8 and identify the similarities and differences between these two reports.

Summary

There are two fundamental product costing systems. They are **job order costing** and **process costing.** The choice of the costing system depends on the nature of the production processes.

Job order costing is used for products that are produced in batches or intermittent production runs and are summarized on a **job cost sheet.** Costs are gathered for each cost element, and when a job is completed, unit costs are determined for each cost element and in total. Typically cost sheets contain **job number**, starting date, completion date, product number, product description, and units produced. Other information may be included on the job cost sheet if managers deem it desirable.

Costs of production are charged to the work in process control account. At the same time, the costs are entered on the appropriate individual job cost sheet. Any job currently in production has an **open job cost sheet.** All open job cost sheets comprise the subsidiary ledger for the work in process control account. When a job is completed, the cost sheet is summarized and costs are transferred from work in process control to finished goods control resulting in a **closed job cost sheet** which is **not** part of work in process control.

A **departmental job cost sheet** identifies costs by department as well as by cost element. It provides management with more detailed cost data and a better basis for control.

A process costing system is used to determine product costs for goods manufactured in a continuous flow production process. Production is divided into separate activities called **process centres** for which product cost data are accumulated. Periodically the cost data are summarized in reports called **cost of production reports**. These describe the physical flow of production in the process centre and the corresponding flow of production costs for a specific time period. Costs are identified for each cost element, and production quantities called **equivalent units** are divided into costs to find unit costs. Costs associated with completed units are transferred to the next department or finished goods, and ending work in process costs remain in the process centre.

The product cost flows identified in job order cost sheets and cost of production reports must be recorded with journal entries and posted to ledger accounts. Direct costs are charged to work in process and identified with specific jobs or process cost centres. Indirect costs are charged to manufacturing overhead and assigned to production when overhead is applied. The cost of completed products is debited to finished goods inventory, and work in process is credited. Product expense is recorded at the time of sale with a debit to cost of goods sold and a credit to finished goods inventory.

Appendix summary

Most process centres in continuous flow production activities have beginning and ending work in process inventories. If the unit cost of beginning inventory is different from the unit cost of current-period production, the accountant must decide how to account for the costs of units transferred out and the cost of units in ending work in process inventory. Either first in, first out (FIFO) or weighted average is used to account for the production cost flows. Sometimes managers may want data from cost of production reports summarized into other types of managerial accounting reports.

List of important terms
Following are important terms that have been defined and discussed in this chapter. You should be thoroughly acquainted with the meaning of these terms before proceeding to the next chapter.

> cost of production report *(78)*
> equivalent units *(79)*
> job cost sheet *(71)*
> job number *(72)*
> job order costing *(71)*
> process centre *(77)*
> process costing *(75)*

Questions[1]

1. Compare and contrast a job order cost system and a process cost system.
2. What is a job order cost sheet? What relationship does it have to the work in process control account?
3. Explain the function of a job number.
4. Explain to the president of the company why a departmental job cost sheet should be used when it yields an identical total product cost as a nondepartmental job cost sheet.
5. Describe the steps necessary to create and operate a process cost system.
6. Describe the purpose, format, and use of the cost of production report.
7. Explain what equivalent units are.
8.* Why must we deal with inventory pricing methods, such as FIFO, with process costing, but not with job order costing?
9.* Refer to the Fergus Valve Company example. What is the cost of ending work in process inventory on June 30, 1983, for the R2 gas valve production activity?
10. At the end of the accounting period, the manufacturing overhead control account has a debit balance of $145,250, and the manufacturing overhead applied account has a credit balance of $148,155. What is underapplied or overapplied overhead in this case, and what does it mean in terms of product cost?

[1]Questions marked with an asterisk (*) refer to material presented in the appendix to the chapter.

Exercises[2]

Ex. 3-1 **Journal entries for a manufacturing firm.** Following are selected data on the manufacturing operation of Budley Company, which uses a perpetual inventory system.

a. Materials are purchased on account at a cost of $80,000.

b. Material requisitions are filled for direct materials costing $18,000 and for indirect materials costing $4,000.

c. Weekly machine hours totaled 1600. Manufacturing overhead is applied at $6 per machine hour.

d. Job 411 is completed. It consists of 100 units, $4,000 direct materials cost, $5,000 direct labour cost, and $8,000 manufacturing overhead cost.

e. Job 411 is sold to a customer for $21,000 cash.

f. The property tax bill for the year in the amount of $12,000 is received; 80 percent is charged to manufacturing.

Required:
Journalize the above events and transactions.

Ex. 3-2 **Job cost sheet.** The data presented below pertain to Job 1162.

Job: 1162 Started: January 5	Units produced: 500 Completed: January 22		
Material requisitions:	**Date**	**Requisition Number**	**Amount**
	7/1	12227	$1,200
	11/1	12341	1,900
	16/1	12389	1,100
Labour distribution reports:	**Date**	**Hours**	**Amount**
	9/1	120	$ 960
	16/1	160	1,280
	23/1	70	560

Overhead is applied at the rate of $12 per direct labour hour.

Required:
Prepare a job cost sheet for Job 1162.

Ex. 3-3 **Job cost sheet.** Below are a material requisitions schedule and a payroll distribution schedule for the first week in May. Manufacturing overhead is applied at the rate of 200 percent of direct labour cost. Job 1511 was started and completed during the week. Four hundred units were produced.

[2]Exercises marked with an asterisk (*) are based on material presented in the appendix to the chapter.

Material Requisitions			Labour Distribution 8/5	
Date	Job Number	Amount	Job Number	Amount
2/5	1511	$2,200	1510	$3,600
2/5	1513	2,700	1511	4,200
3/5	1514	700	1512	2,000
3/5	1512	1,300	1513	1,600
4/5	1511	900	1514	900
4/5	1513	300	1515	600
5/5	1515	3,300		
6/5	1511	1,100		

Required:

Prepare a job cost sheet in good form for Job 1511.

Ex. 3-4 **Accounting for labour costs.** Jamison Custom Metal Work manufactures ornate gates, fences, and other decorative metal items on a made-to-order basis. Each order is costed using a job order cost system. Labour costs are assigned to jobs each week on the basis of a labour use schedule taken from daily time tickets. Any time not specifically identifiable with jobs is indirect labour. Below are manufacturing payroll data for the first week of October.

Hours worked	2000
Hourly rate	$7/h
Payroll tax rate (6%)	10%
Income tax withholding	15%
Provincial payroll taxes withholding	4%
Union dues withholding	2%

Labour time data from daily time tickets are as follows:

Job Number	Hours
106	220
107	160
108	90
109	450
110	340
111	110
112	480

Required:

a. Record the payroll and payroll taxes for the week.

b. Distribute the payroll costs to production.

c. If manufacturing overhead is applied to jobs at the rate of 80 percent of direct labour cost, how much overhead was applied to Job 109 this week?

Ex. 3-5 **Departmental job cost sheet.** The Colorado Manufacturing Company produces special machines made to customer specifications. The data presented below pertain to Order 1106.

Customer: Markworth Machine Shop   Date started: November 4
Description: 20 drill presses   Date finished: November 18
                                          Total cost to manufacture: ?

	Week Ending 11/11	Week Ending 18/11
Department 1:		
Materials	$4,400	$3,300
Direct labour rate	$6.00/h	$6.00/h
Labour hours	600	400
Department 2:		
Direct labour rate	$5.00/h	$5.00/h
Labour hours	300	140
Manufacturing overhead rate	$7.00/labour h	$7.00/labour h

Required:

a. Prepare a departmental job cost sheet using the above data.

b. If the 20 drill presses are sold for a total of $36,000, what is the percentage gross margin on sales for this job?

Ex. 3-6 **Computing equivalent units.** Below are data pertaining to the quantity of production in five different process centres. Each situation described is completely **independent** of the other situations. None of the process centres listed has beginning work in process.

	Process Centre				
	1	**2**	**3**	**4**	**5**
Units started or transferred in	10 000	50 000	40 000	30 000	60 000
Ending work in process	2 000	8 000	10 000	12 000	25 000
Percentage complete, conversion	50	75	20	65	25

Required:

Compute the equivalent units of conversion for the period for each process center.

Ex. 3-7 **Cost of production report.** The Rainbow Industrial Products Company manufactures paints and rust inhibitors that it sells by the barrel. Below are September cost data for the first production process of white gloss paint.

Beginning work in process inventory	0
Units started	20 000
Material costs	$65,000
Direct labour costs	$85,500
Manufacturing overhead costs	$51,300
Ending work in process inventory	4000 units, all materials, 3/4 conversion

Required:

Prepare a cost of production report for September.

Ex. 3-8   Cost of production report. Weston-Winton Company manufactures products in a continuous flow processing environment. Below are April data for the moulding department where the production of 15-centimetre diameter cast iron pipe elbows begins.

Beginning work in process	0
Units started	20 000
Cost of material added at the beginning	$75,000
Direct labour costs	$57,000
Manufacturing overhead costs	$85,500
Ending work in process	2000 units, all materials, 1/2 conversion
Finished units are transferred to the finishing department	

Required:

Prepare a cost of production report for April for the moulding department.

Ex. 3-9*   Computing equivalent units. Below are inventory flow data for five **independent** situations.

	Situation				
	A	**B**	**C**	**D**	**E**
Beginning inventory	0	2 000	4 000	10 000	1 000
Percentage complete	—	25	50	60	80
Units transferred in	15 000	12 000	20 000	50 000	25 000
Ending inventory	5 000	0	6 000	8 000	5 000
Percentage complete	40	—	30	25	80

Required:

For each situation above compute the equivalent units of production for the period.

Ex. 3-10* **Computing equivalent units.** Below are inventory flow data for five **independent** situations.

	Situation				
	1	**2**	**3**	**4**	**5**
Beginning WIP:	0	6 000	10 000	2 000	7 000
Percentage complete materials	0	40	100	50	80
Percentage complete conversion	0	60	40	60	90
Units transferred in	12 000	34 000	80 000	8 000	42 000
Ending WIP:	3 000	4 000	5 000	1 200	9 000
Percentage complete materials	100	60	100	75	60
Percentage complete conversion	75	90	80	80	70

Required:
For each situation compute the current-period equivalent units for materials and conversion.

Ex. 3-11* **Cost of production report.** Below are May production data for the blending department, which is the first process centre in the production of a cleaning compound.

a. Beginning work in process consists of 5000 litres, all materials, 60 percent conversion.
b. Beginning WIP costs include $5,050 materials, $1,860 labour, and $1,410 overhead.
c. Units started in May are 40 000 litres.
d. Material costs in May are $44,000.
e. Labour costs in May are $27,000.
f. Overhead costs in May are $21,600.
g. Ending work in process is 10 000 litres, all materials, 40 percent conversion.
h. Weighted average inventory method is used.

Required:
Prepare a May cost of production report for the blending department.

Problem Set A[3]

P. 3A-1 **Product costing journal entries.** Mayville Products produces men's clothing goods. It uses a perpetual inventory system. Below are transactions that occurred during September.

---

[3]Problems marked with an asterisk (*) are based on material presented in the appendix to the chapter.

a. The weekly manufacturing payroll of $150,000 is paid. Withholding items include $25,000 for income tax, $9,000 for CPP tax, $8,000 for provincial payroll taxes, and $1,500 for union dues.

b. All but $18,000 of the payroll is direct labour. Distribute the payroll.

c. In addition to its share of CPP taxes, the company must pay $3,000 in unemployment taxes.

d. Manufacturing overhead is applied to products at the rate of 120 percent of direct labour cost.

e. Raw materials are purchased on open account for $220,000.

f. Utility bills of $9,600 are received and paid; 80 percent of the utilities costs pertain to manufacturing activity.

g. Material requisitions are filled for $106,000 of which 90 percent is direct materials.

h. A bill of $3,600 for service on hydraulic metal presses is received and paid.

i. Job 4792 is completed. Total manufacturing costs were $16,840.

j. Job 4792 is sold for $25,000.

Required:
Journalize the above transactions.

P. 3A-2   **Departmental and single job cost sheets.** Shown below are data for two jobs. The manufacturing overhead rate is $5 per direct labour hour.

Required:
a. Prepare a departmental job cost sheet in good form for Job 211.
b. Prepare a nondepartmental job cost sheet for Job 212.

	Job 211	Job 212
Units produced	100	200
Department A:		
Direct labour hours	210	60
Direct labour cost	$ 940	$280
Prime costs	$1,290	$560
Department B:		
Direct labour hours	100	—
Direct labour cost	$ 500	—
Department C:		
Direct labour hours	320	100
Direct labour cost	$1,300	$410
Direct materials cost	$ 150	$100

P. 3A-3   **Departmental production cost information.** Winthrop Manufacturing is a job shop manufacturing operation. The company produces a number of different products and has five production centres: cutting, machining, assembly, finishing, and painting. Selected data are presented below.

Department	Direct Materials Cost		Direct Labour Hours		Hourly Direct Labour Rate, Both Jobs
	Job 522	Job 523	Job 522	Job 523	
Cutting	$3,600	$4,420	150	210	$7.00
Machining	800	–	180	190	6.00
Assembly	1,200	–	120	220	5.00
Finishing	–	420	–	100	6.50
Painting	100	200	50	40	5.00

On both jobs the manufacturing overhead rate is 150 percent of direct labour costs. The number of units produced is 200 on Job 522 and 100 on Job 523.

Required:
Prepare the summary of costs section of a departmental job cost sheet for Job 522 and for Job 523. Include per-unit and total costs by cost element for each department.

P. 3A-4 Analyzing product cost data. Gardenqueen Lawn Products produces a variety of lawn and garden products that it sells through franchised distributorships. Although the firm produces goods for its sales inventory, volume for most products is not large enough to warrant a full-time continuous production process. Therefore, job lots are produced for inventory. One popular product, the Gardenqueen 55-centimetre self-propelled mower, has had a selling price of $160 for the past two years during which time costs have fluctuated. In the last 18 months the firm has produced six job lots of this mower. Marketing costs are substantial for this type of product. Therefore, the managers of Gardenqueen think a minimum gross profit margin is 40 percent on sales. Below is a summary of the job cost sheets.

Job No.	Date Completed	Units Produced	Direct Materials	Direct Labour	Overhead Applied	Total Cost
2216	9/ 5/82	1,000	$ 35,000	$ 26,000	$ 39,000	$ 100,000
2409	30/10/82	600	22,800	15,600	23,400	61,800
2492	18/ 1/83	1,800	72,000	54,000	81,000	207,000
2629	14/ 4/83	2,500	105,000	80,000	120,000	305,000
2794	30/ 6/83	2,200	94,600	74,800	112,200	281,600
2930	22/10/83	1,900	85,500	68,400	102,600	256,500
Total		10,000	$414,900	$318,800	$478,200	$1,211,900

Required:
a. Has the cost of the mowers fluctuated enough to cause concern about the price of the product? Analyze the cost data presented and support your answer with cost analysis data.

b. What should the price of the mower be to meet the minimum gross margin requirement?

P. 3A-5   **Job cost sheet.** Below are data pertinent to the production of 400 9000-watt garden tractors in Job 13964. Overhead is applied at the rate of $9 per direct labour hour. The labour rate is $7 per hour. Material requisitions pertaining to Job 13964 include:

Date	Requisition Number	Amount
7/2	1477	$24,800
19/2	1524	19,200
2/3	1590	16,700
21/3	1634	13,300

Labour distribution data pertaining to Job 13964 are:

Date	Amount
15/2	$16,800
28/2	29,400
15/3	32,900
31/3	25,200

Required:
a. Prepare a job cost sheet for Job 13964.
b. What should the price of the tractor be if the company wants to earn a 29 percent gross margin on sales?

P. 3A-6   **Cost of production report.** The Standish Paper Products Company uses process costing to account for the production costs of all its products. Below are September production and cost data for the first process centre in the production of one of its products.

Beginning work in process inventory	0
Units started in September	25 000
Material costs	$46,250
Labour costs	$17,250
Overhead applied	$34,500
Ending work in process inventory	5000 units, all materials, 60 percent conversion

Required:
Prepare the September cost of production report in good form for the first process centre.

P. 3A-7* **Cost of production report.** Zanton Products, Inc., uses a process costing system to cost its products. September data for the metal fabricating department are presented below.

a. Beginning inventory: 10 000 units all materials, 1/2 conversion.
b. Costs of beginning inventory: materials, $13,000; labour $8,000; manufacturing overhead, $6,000.
c. Started 90 000 units in September.
d. Material costs for September: $126,000.
e. Labour costs for September: $140,000.
f. Manufacturing overhead applied in September: $104,000.
g. Ending inventory: 20 000 units, all materials, 1/4 conversion.
h. FIFO inventory method is used.

Required:
Prepare a cost of production report for the department.

P. 3A-8* **Cost of production report.** Below are March cost data for a finishing department of Redrocks Manufacturing Company. This department is the final production department in the manufacture of a certain type of bearing.

a. Beginning work in process: 6000 units, 2/3 materials, 1/4 conversion.
b. Costs of beginning work in process: prior departments, $48,000; materials, $10,000; labour, $3,000; overhead, $3,600.
c. Transferred in 30 000 units; cost, $243,000.
d. Materials are added periodically; cost for March, $81,200.
e. Labour costs in March, $65,600.
f. Overhead costs in March, $79,360.
g. Ending work in process: 5000 units, 2/5 materials, 1/2 conversion.
h. FIFO inventory method is used.

Required:
Prepare a March cost of production report in good form for the finishing department.

Problem Set B

P. 3B-1 **Recording cost activities.** Eckler Company uses a perpetual inventory system. Below are some transactions for the first week in March.

a. The company purchases $90,000 of raw materials on open account.
b. Material requisitions are filled for $42,000 of which $39,000 is direct materials.
c. The weekly payroll for manufacturing is $75,000. Withholding items include income withholding tax, $10,000; provincial payroll taxes withholding, $2,000; CPP withholding, $4,500; and union dues of $900.

d. All but $8,000 of the manufacturing payroll is direct labour. Distribute the payroll costs.

e. In addition to its share of CPP taxes, the company must pay $3,500 in unemployment taxes for manufacturing employees.

f. Overhead is applied at the rate of 150 percent of direct labour cost.

g. Utility bills of $3,500 for the manufacturing plant are received and paid.

h. Property taxes of $9,400 are paid; 70 percent is for manufacturing activities.

i. Jobs 981 and 982 are completed. They have costs of $10,420 and $8,200, respectively.

Required:
Journalize the above transactions.

P. 3B-2 **Departmental product cost information.** The chief salesperson for Stay-Solvent Industries just sold 500 cases of "Xzlocmuk," the company's secret vitality drug. Xzlocmuk is produced in job-lot batches for special orders and is not carried in general inventory ready for sale. Job production data are presented below.

Job. 5446 (500 cases of Xzlocmuk)				
Production Department	**Direct Materials**	**Direct Labour**		**Manufacturing Overhead Rate**
		Hours	**Rate**	
Mixing	$2,400	60	$5.00/h	150% of prime cost
Cooking	600	100	4.00/h	150% of prime cost
Settling	100	40	3.50/h	$4.00 per DLH
Packaging	200	10	4.00/h	$4.00 per DLH

Required:
Prepare the summary of costs section of a departmental job cost sheet for this production run of Xzlocmuk.

P. 3B-3 **Using product cost data.** Stichler Custom Storm and Awning Company uses a job cost system to accumulate manufacturing costs for its products. At the end of each week a schedule of active jobs is prepared showing the total cost assigned to each job to date. Data from the schedule are used as the basis for transferring costs of jobs completed during the week to finished goods. Below is the job cost schedule for the current week.

Job No.	Direct Materials	Direct Labour	MOH Applied	Total Cost
703	$ 4,200	$1,800	$2,700	$ 8,700
705	3,100	2,000	3,000	8,100 × .4
706	7,200	2,800	4,200	14,200
707	900	1,200	1,800	3,900
708	1,100	600	900	2,600
709	2,000	800	1,200	4,000
710	12,000	2,200	3,300	17,500
711	1,300	400	600	2,300
712	600	200	300	1,100

Required:

a. Jobs 703, 705, and 707 are completed during the week. Record their transfer to finished goods.

b. After the entry in part *a* is posted, what is the balance in the work in process control account?

c. If Stichler's pricing policy is to earn a 40 percent gross profit on sales, what will be the selling price of Job 705?

d. Do the data suggest what the manufacturing overhead rate is? If so, what is it?

P. 3B-4 Using product cost data. Denton Custom Products manufactures various utility and convenience items for off-the-road vehicles and pickup trucks. The company's policy is to evaluate the price of each product once a year. The policy is to price as low as possible to maintain a competitive sales position, but not to sell at a nonprofitable price. The desired target price for products provides a 40 percent gross margin although competition sometimes forces less profitable pricing. However, the minimum acceptable gross margin on sales is 30 percent.

One of the company's popular products, a swing-out spare tire carrier used on four-wheel drive vehicles, should have its price reevaluated based on production costs of the last year. The current selling price is $125. Below are cost data for the five production runs of the product during 1983.

Job No.	Date Completed	Units Produced	Materials	Labour	Overhead	Total Cost
3840	27/1/83	2 500	$ 75,000	$ 62,500	$ 50,000	$187,500
3912	05/3/83	1 000	31,000	30,000	24,000	85,000
3975	29/4/83	3 500	108,500	87,500	70,000	266,000
4101	04/8/83	2 000	62,000	54,000	44,000	160,000
4209	15/10/83	1 000	32,000	32,000	26,000	90,000
Total		10 000	$308,500	$266,000	$214,000	$788,500

Required:
a. Use the above data to determine what the price should be, based on:
   1. The cost of the first production run (Job 3840).
   2. Average unit cost for the year.
   3. Unit cost of the most recent production run.
b. Do the cost data suggest to you any trends in costs or significant variables that may affect the cost of the product? Explain.
c. Of the prices computed in part *a*, which one would you select? Explain.

P. 3B-5 **Job cost sheet.** Below are materials and labour data for the month of May for Coalrite Industries. Overhead is applied at the rate of 80 percent of direct labour cost.

				Material Requisitions During May			
Date	Requisition Number	Job Number	Amount	Date	Requisition Number	Job Number	Amount
1/5	248	112	$1,200	10/5	258	122	$ 850
1/5	249	119	2,100	14/5	259	120	1,400
2/5	250	116	900	16/5	260	123	600
2/5	251	118	400	17/5	261	119	400
3/5	252	120	4,200	20/5	262	124	1,840
6/5	253	119	800	21/5	263	121	660
6/5	254	115	200	24/5	264	120	600
7/5	255	117	750	26/5	265	125	900
8/5	256	119	500	28/5	266	122	1,100
9/5	257	121	1,100	29/5	267	123	300

	Labour Distribution, 1/5 through 15/5		
Job Number	Amount	Job Number	Amount
112	$ 450	120	$1,850
117	1,140	121	600
118	960	122	200
119	1,600		

	Labour distribution, 16/5 through 31/5		
Job Number	Amount	Job Number	Amount
118	$ 680	122	$1,340
119	800	123	490
120	1,450	124	930
121	1,020	125	190

Required:
a. Prepare a job cost sheet for Job 119, which was started and completed during May. Two hundred typing tables were produced.
b. How much overhead was applied to production in May?

P. 3B-6   **Cost of production report.** The Fairchild Chemical Company produces a very strong industrial adhesive in a continuous flow production process. The product is manufactured in a series of six processing centres, the last of which is the curing department. In January 40 000 kilograms of product were transferred into curing from the preceding department at a cost of $138,400. All but 6000 kilograms were completed and transferred to finished goods inventory. Ending work in process in the curing department has all materials and 70 percent conversion. January cost for materials in the process centre was $18,800, and labour cost was $21,392. Manufacturing overhead is applied at the rate of 150 percent of direct labour cost. There was no beginning WIP inventory in January.

Required:
Prepare a cost of production report in good form for the curing department for January.

P. 3B-7 *   **Cost of production report.** Jamaica Foods produces various gourmet delights that are sold primarily to restaurants and institutions. One of them, a rum sauce for meats and poultry, is produced in a three-department production process. The **last** department is the cooking department. January production data for the cooking department are presented below.

a. Beginning inventory: 10 000 kilograms, 2/5 materials, 3/5 conversion.
b. Costs of beginning inventory: prior departments, $9,000; materials, $1,360; labour, $2,400; MOH, $1,200.
c. Units transferred in during January: 60 000 kilograms; cost, $52,800.
d. Cost of material added in cooking department in January: $16,500.
e. Labour cost in January: $27,280.
f. MOH cost in January: $13,640.
g. Ending WIP inventory: 8000 kilograms, all materials, 3/4 conversion.
h. First in, first out inventory valuation is used in the cooking department.

Required:
Prepare a January cost of production report for the cooking department.

P. 3B-8 *   **Two department process costing.** Larry Lombard's Lasagna Factory produces high-quality lasagna noodles in a five-process production operation. The last two processes are cutting and packaging. Output in cutting is in kilograms and output in packaging is in cases. There are 20 kilograms of lasgna per case. Production data for March for these last two processes are presented below.

Cutting Department

a. Beginning WIP consists of 20 000 kilograms, all materials, 30 percent conversion.

b. Costs of beginning WIP include materials, $800; direct labour, $300; MOH, $150; prior departments, $4,200.

c. Transferred in, 80 000 kilograms at a cost of $17,600.

d. Materials, added at beginning at a cost of $4,000.

e. Direct labour, $4,600.

f. MOH, $2,300.

g. Ending WIP is 10 000 kilograms, all materials, 80 percent conversion.

h. FIFO inventory valuation is used.

Packaging Department

a. Beginning WIP consists of 1500 cases, all materials, 1/2 conversion.

b. Costs of beginning WIP include materials, $570; direct labour, $490; MOH, $620; prior departments, $10,570.

c. Transferred in?

d. Materials added at a cost of $1,890.

e. Direct labour, $2,500.

f. MOH, $3,750.

g. Ending WIP is 1000 cases, all materials, 3/4 conversion.

h. Average cost inventory method is used.

Required:

Prepare a cost of production report in good form for each department.

Minicases

Minicase 3-1 (CGA adapted)

You have just been appointed as the new accountant of the Dekker Company, Ltd. Unfortunately, the former accountant was killed in a fatal traffic accident, and his assistant is on vacation in Hawaii. The president of the Dekker Company calls you and requests a report on the activities of the most recent month. From the discussions you find out that the company uses a job order cost system and applies overhead at a predetermined rate of 50 percent of direct labour cost.

After a long night's search you have been able to obtain the following account balances for the most recent month, November 1984:

	November 1	November 30
Stores	$20,000	$15,000
Work in Process	7,000	unknown
Finished Goods Inventory	34,000	30,000
Accrued Payroll	13,000	9,000
Accounts Receivable	54,000	22,000
Accounts Payable	18,000	6,000
Sales		500,000

You were also able to obtain the following additional information from various people in the company:

1. All sales are on account.
2. The Accounts Payable account is used for the purchase of materials and supplies only.
3. Dekkers markup is 30 percent of sales.
4. There was one job in process on November 30th. To date, $2,000 of materials and $6,000 of direct labour have been charged to this job.
5. Actual overhead costs incurred during November were:

Supplies	$20,000
Indirect labour	55,000
Depreciation	10,000
Insurance	2,000

6. Materials and supplies purchased on account were $65,000.

Required:

Prepare a short report for the president. As a guideline the president indicated the following points that he would like you to stress in your report. These are:
a. Materials issued to production
b. Direct labour
c. Overhead applied
d. Cost of goods manufactured
e. Cost of goods sold
f. Payment of Accounts Payable
g. Collection of Accounts Receivable
h. Payment of payroll
i. Amount of over-or-underapplied overhead

Reproduced with permission from *Final Examination 1979*, published by CGA Canada, Vancouver, B.C.

Minicase 3-2 (CMA Examination Question)

Aknar Company manufactures high-quality leather products. The company's profits have declined during the past nine months. Aknar has used unit cost data which were developed 18 months ago in planning and controlling its operations. In an attempt to isolate the causes of poor profit performance, management is investigating the manufacturing operations of each of its products.

One of Aknar's main products is fine leather belts. The belts are produced in a single, continuous process in the Bluett Plant. During the process leather strips are sewn, punched, and dyed. Buckles are attached by rivets when the belts are 70 percent complete as to direct labour and overhead (conversion costs). The belts then enter a final finishing stage to conclude the process. Labour and overhead are applied continuously during the process. Aknar uses the weighted average method to calculate its unit costs.

The leather belts produced at the Bluett Plant wholesale for $9.95 each. Management wants to compare the current manufacturing costs per unit with the prices which exist on the market for leather belts. Top management has asked the Bluett Plant to submit data on the cost of manufacturing the leather belts for the month of October. This cost data will be used to evaluate whether modifications in the production process should be initiated or whether an increase in the selling price of the belts is justified. The cost per equivalent unit which is being used for planning and controlling purposes is $5.35 per unit.

The work-in-process inventory consisted of 400 partially completed units on October 1. The belts were 25 percent complete as to conversion costs. The costs included in the inventory on October 1 were as follows:

Leather strips	$1,000
Conversion costs	300
	$1,300

During October 7600 leather strips were placed in production. A total of 7300 good leather belts was completed. The work-in-process inventory on October 31 consisted of 700 belts which were 50 percent complete as to conversion costs.

The costs charged to production during October were as follows:

Leather strips	$20,600
Buckles	$4,550
Conversion costs	20,700
	$45,850

Required:
Do you think that the October production can meet the $5.35 per unit? Support your answer.

Chapter 4

Manufacturing Overhead and Cost Allocation

This chapter discusses manufacturing overhead and the role of common costs in product costing. Common costs occur in many manufacturing and nonmanufacturing activities. When you have completed the chapter, you should understand:

1 The nature of common costs.

2 Basic cost allocation procedures.

3 The computation and use of overhead rates.

4 The computation and use of departmental overhead rates.

5 The concept of joint products.

6 Methods of allocating joint costs.

In Chapter 2 we introduced common costs, which are costs that cannot be identified readily with specific cost objectives. Such costs create problems in product costing because they are difficult to assign accurately to individual cost objectives. The assignment of common costs to cost objectives is called cost allocation.

In this chapter we discuss the nature of common costs and common cost allocation procedures in manufacturing businesses. A manufacturing overhead example is used to illustrate cost allocations in developing and using overhead rates. Also, we examine the process of allocating common costs among joint products.

The nature of common costs

Causes of common costs

Common costs occur for a variety of reasons and often represent a large portion of total manufacturing costs. Some are caused by the organizational structure of the company, others by manufacturing processes that make it impossible to identify some manufacturing costs directly with specific products. For example, some common costs arise because managers choose to divide the business into separate departments to permit the accumulation of more detailed cost data for management purposes. Costs such as the premium on a fire insurance policy for a manufacturing plant are part of the total cost of operating the plant. If the plant is separated into several producing departments for costing purposes, then part of the fire insurance cost may be allocated to the departments that share the insurance protection. In this case the cost objectives are the departments, and the fire insurance premium is the common cost to be allocated.

All indirect manufacturing costs are common to the production of various products since they cannot be identified directly with individual products. Some products, such as gasoline and fuel oil, are not distinguishable as separate products early in the production process. Instead they appear as one product until some point in the manufacturing process where the products separate. Such products are called joint products. All manufacturing costs incurred before the products separate are identifiable only with the group of products, but not with specific products from the group. Therefore, all production costs before the point of separation are common to the group of products being produced.

Cost allocations in management reporting

Cost allocations should be guided by the matching principle

Many types of cost data serve managers

Cost allocation consists of deciding what part of indirect costs belongs to each cost objective. Allocation of common costs to cost objectives should not be arbitrary but should be based on the matching principle. In order to satisfy the matching principle, the accountant must find a meaningful causal relationship between the cost objective and the cost that is to be allocated to the objective. For example, heating costs may be allocated to departments based on the square metre of floor space occupied by each department because, in general, heating cost is directly related to the amount of space that is heated.

Decision makers need a variety of cost figures to assist in making different management decisions. For example, external users of accounting information, such as investors, require cost information that is condensed and summarized, whereas corporate managers need very detailed cost data for daily operating decisions. Managers may find that no single cost figure will suffice for making all types of managerial decisions. Decisions concerning production, pricing, purchasing, performance evaluation, and budgeting may each require accounting information containing somewhat different cost data. Allocated common costs often play an important role in the development of cost data. Some situations require full cost allocation; others require partial allocation. In some cases the decision by management is most easily made when no cost allocation is made. For example, full cost allocation is used for product costs in most external financial statements and in income tax returns as required by Revenue Canada. On the other hand, managers sometimes ignore common costs in making certain decisions about product pricing and in determining whether to make or buy a product. These and many other decisions affected by cost allocations are discussed in later chapters.

Manufacturing overhead costs

Cost allocations play an important role in the assignment of manufacturing overhead costs to products. Manufacturing overhead costs, such as depreciation on plant and equipment, utilities, maintenance, indirect material, and indirect labour, are necessary but indirect costs of production that are incurred to provide and maintain the necessary production facilities and in general to facilitate the manufacturing process. Yet these costs cannot be identified directly with specific products, and accountants must develop methods of assigning overhead costs to products in some logical fashion. The assignment of overhead starts with the development of appropriate overhead rates.

Manufacturing overhead rates

The application of manufacturing overhead to products would be simplified if managers were able to wait until the end of an accounting period to assign overhead costs. However, two problems would arise from such a policy. If the accounting period is long, such as a year, product costs are not timely enough to be of much use in decision making. If the period is short, such as a month, timely measures are obtained, but they are often distorted by seasonal factors. For example, heating and lighting costs are much higher in January than in July. Consequently, accountants need to develop a timely method of assigning overhead to products, but one that minimizes the problem of short-run or seasonal overhead cost fluctuations. To accomplish this, managers estimate the overhead costs and the amount of production for the accounting period and establish an overhead application rate based on the estimated overhead costs and estimated production activity. The application rate is used to assign overhead costs to products during the accounting period. Typically the amount of overhead applied to products in this manner is not identical to the amount of actual overhead cost incurred, but it is close enough to be helpful in making management decisions. Any discrepancies between actual and applied overhead can be adjusted at the end of the accounting period.

Predetermined overhead rates provide timely cost data

Differences between applied and actual overhead are adjusted at year-end

The development of a manufacturing overhead application base requires the following steps:

Prior to the beginning of the accounting period, estimates are made of the expected production level and the expected overhead cost for the next period, usually a year. From these estimates a budgeted overhead rate is established. Sometimes this rate is called the predetermined overhead rate to emphasize

The overhead cost cycle

the fact that such rates are based on estimates of the future year's activities. For example, the budgeted overhead rate for the next accounting year might be $6 per machine hour or 150 percent of direct labour cost.

Manufacturing overhead is applied to products using the predetermined overhead rate and actual measures of production, and the total applied is accumulated in the MOH Applied account.

Actual overhead costs are accumulated during the accounting period in the MOH Control account.

At the end of the accounting period, the applied overhead is compared with the actual overhead to determine the amount of overhead that has been overapplied or underapplied.

Developing the manufacturing overhead rate

A predetermined manufacturing overhead rate is calculated from estimated figures. First the total manufacturing overhead cost for the accounting period is estimated (budgeted overhead cost). Then the level of production for the period must be estimated to arrive at the budgeted activity level.

Estimates of future costs and activities involve uncertainty and sometimes are difficult to make accurately. Nevertheless, experienced managers are able to develop predetermined overhead rates that provide a close match between actual overhead and applied overhead. Once the estimates of costs and activities have been made, the calculation of the overhead rate is simple:

$$\text{Manufacturing overhead rate} = \frac{\text{Estimated manufacturing overhead cost}}{\text{Estimated activity level}}$$

The estimated activity level may be expressed in terms of various measures of activity. Units of output, direct labour hours, and machine hours are activity measures frequently used. The activity measure is referred to as the overhead application base.

The overhead application base

To illustrate the computation of a manufacturing overhead rate, assume that during the next year a manufacturing firm expects to produce 20 000 wooden porch swings, each requiring five hours of direct labour. Manufacturing overhead costs of $300,000 are expected for the year. With these estimates it is possible to calculate the overhead rate, based either on units of production or on direct labour hours. If the application base is to be units of production, the calculation is

$$\frac{\text{Total estimated MOH}}{\text{Total estimated units of production}} = \frac{\$300,000}{20\,000\ \text{units}} = \$15\ \text{per unit}$$

If the number of direct labour hours is considered a better application base than units of production, the rate can be calculated as follows:

$$\begin{aligned} \text{Total estimated labour hours} &= \text{Units of production} \times \text{Labour hours per unit} \\ &= 20\,000\ \text{porch swings} \times 5\ \text{hours per swing} \\ &= 100\,000\ \text{labour hours} \end{aligned}$$

$$\frac{\text{Total estimated MOH}}{\text{Total estimated labour hours}} = \frac{\$300,000}{100\,000\ \text{hours}} = \$3\ \text{per direct labour hour}$$

Selecting an overhead application base

Overhead application bases must satisfy the matching concept

The selection of an appropriate application base is critical in developing good product costs. The most important principle in selecting the application base is the matching principle. The direct costs of production are easily matched with products. It is just as desirable to match the indirect costs with products to ensure the proper measurement of income and proper balance sheet valuations. The very fact that manufacturing overhead is an indirect cost causes some people to believe that the matching principle does not apply, but overhead costs often are significant costs of production and should be matched with the revenue from the completed product just as direct costs are. The application of overhead is an attempt to match the indirect costs of manufacturing with the benefits derived from those costs. The benefits are, of course, the revenue from the sale of manufactured products whose completion is made possible, in part, by the indirect costs of production.

In addition to satisfying the matching principle, the choice of an application base should take into consideration both the ease of computing the overhead rate and the ease of understanding the rate that results from the computation. The following discussion describes some of the more common overhead application bases.

Direct labour hours (DLH). A popular application base that is easy to understand and apply is direct labour hours. Often it does a good job of matching overhead costs with products, and it is used as an application base by a large number of manufacturing firms. Some overhead costs, such as employer payroll taxes and employee fringe benefits, are related directly to the quantity of labour. Others, such as machinery operating costs and machine maintenance costs for equipment operated by direct labour, are related to some degree to the quantity of labour time. To illustrate, if total overhead costs are estimated at $260,000 and direct labour hours are estimated at 40 000, the calculation of the overhead rate is

$$\frac{\text{Total budgeted MOH}}{\text{Total budgeted direct labour hours}} = \frac{\$260,000}{40\ 000\ \text{DLH}} = \$6.50 \text{ per direct labour hour}$$

The above calculation means that for every hour of direct labour that is charged to a product, $6.50 is added to the cost of the product for overhead. Notice that the term **budgeted** is substituted for estimated in the above equation. Both terms refer to a projected cost of future activity level.

Direct labour cost (DLC). Similar to direct labour hours is the direct labour cost application base. Often this application base satisfies the criteria of matching, ease of understanding, and ease of application. Typically the choice between a labour hour base and a labour cost base is made on convenience considerations rather than on theoretical grounds. Using the same example of $260,000 for budgeted MOH and a budget of $200,000 for direct labour cost, the calculation of the overhead rate is

$$\frac{\text{Total budgeted MOH}}{\text{Budgeted direct labour cost}} = \frac{\$260,000}{\$200,000} = 1.3 \text{ or } 130\% \text{ of direct labour cost}$$

The above rate states that overhead cost is added to products at the rate of 130 percent of direct labour cost. In other words, for every $1 of direct labour cost, $1.30 of overhead is added to the product cost.

Units of production. In some production situations an overhead rate based on units of production may be desirable. This base should be used only if production consists of a single product or a relatively homogeneous set of products. For example, if a manufacturer builds 12-metre fibreglass boat hulls, all of which are similar, and this is the only product the company makes, an overhead rate based on units of production is acceptable. On the other hand, if the company produces boats ranging in size from 4-metre prams to 15-metre cruisers, a rate based on units of production would assign a disproportionate amount of overhead to the 4-metre prams. The 15-metre cruisers use significantly more manufacturing overhead resources, but both boats receive the same overhead cost with a units-of-production application base. To illustrate a units-of-production base, assume an estimated production of 10 000 units of product. The overhead rate is calculated as follows:

$$\frac{\text{Estimated MOH}}{\text{Estimated units of production}} = \frac{\$260{,}000}{10\ 000\ \text{units}} = \$26\ \text{per unit}$$

Machine hours (MH). An overhead rate based on machine hours is used when production is performed primarily on machines or when machine-related costs make up a large portion of overhead costs. This application base requires clerical work to gather the machine hour data. In some cases the collection of such data may be automated. In either case the additional cost of data collection is warranted if the result is an overhead rate that does a good job of matching. With an estimated 25 000 machine hours budgeted for the period, the calculation of the overhead rate is

$$\frac{\text{Estimated MOH}}{\text{Estimated machine hours}} = \frac{\$260{,}000}{25\ 000\ \text{MH}} = \$10.40\ \text{per machine hour}$$

This calculation indicates that for every hour of machine time used in producing the product, $10.40 is added to its cost for overhead.

Material cost. Sometimes manufacturing overhead costs are related closely to direct material costs. In that case a rate calculated on the basis of direct materials is warranted. The rate is usually expressed as a percentage of direct material cost. There are relatively few situations that lend themselves to a direct material application base in comparison to the other bases discussed. An example is a drug manufacturing process requiring many specialized materials that result in high material handling and storage costs. In some situations a direct material base can yield a good MOH rate. If the direct material cost is estimated at $160,000, the rate is

$$\frac{\text{Estimated MOH}}{\text{Estimated direct material cost}} = \frac{\$260{,}000}{\$160{,}000} = 1.625\ \text{or}\ 162.5\%\ \text{of direct material cost}$$

For every dollar of direct materials assigned to production, $1.625 of overhead is added to the cost of production.

Applying overhead

As can be seen from the above discussion, the entire process of determining overhead rates is accomplished with budgeted or estimated data. No actual costs or activity levels are used in calculating the overhead rate. However, in applying overhead to products, the overhead rate is multiplied by some actual amount of production. For example, before the accounting year begins, an overhead rate of 150 percent of direct labour cost is established. After the accounting period starts, $60 of direct labour cost is charged to a product. In that case $90 of overhead ($60 × 1.5) is charged to the product. The predetermined overhead rate is 150 percent of direct labour cost, and the measure of actual production is $60 of direct labour cost. The entry would be:

Applied overhead equals the overhead rate times the actual measure of activity

Work in Process Control	90	
Manufacturing Overhead Applied		90
Applied overhead to production.		

Departmental overhead rates

The managers of a business may find that one overhead rate for an entire manufacturing plant does a satisfactory job of applying overhead costs to all products. However, in some cases a single overhead rate may not do a good job of matching overhead costs with products. Some activities may require very expensive production facilities. For instance, the machining and metal fabricating department may require expensive production machinery with large utilities, maintenance, and insurance costs, whereas the assembly department may be very labour-intensive, requiring relatively inexpensive facilities. One overhead rate for a facility containing some very costly production equipment and also some relatively inexpensive equipment may provide a poor match of overhead costs. Products requiring a relatively large amount of production time in costly production facilities would not be charged enough overhead cost, and products requiring the less costly equipment would be charged too much overhead cost. To solve this problem, managers may create more than one overhead rate for a manufacturing plant, with each rate designed to match overhead costs with products accurately.

Departmental overhead rates may better match overhead costs with products

Separate overhead rates may be developed for each department or production activity, or for groups of departments that have similar overhead cost characteristics. For example, all machining production activities might have one overhead rate, all assembly activities another rate, and product painting yet another rate. The number of separate manufacturing overhead rates is limited only by management's information needs and the cost of creating and using separate rates.

Producing departments and service departments. Most departments in a manufacturing plant are directly involved in the production of the firm's products and are classified as producing departments. Typical production activities include metal fabrication, machining, drilling, assembly, and painting. Some departments are not involved directly in the production of products of the firm, but they provide services that are essential to the production activities. These service departments might include maintenance, tool room, inventory storeroom, and first aid. Since service departments make production possible or more efficient, their costs are considered part of the total cost of the product.

Using departmental overhead rates. The development and use of departmental overhead rates is similar to the development of a single comprehensive rate. The following steps are required:

1. The overhead rate is determined in advance for each department.
2. Overhead is applied to production during the accounting period using departmental overhead rates.
3. Actual overhead costs are accumulated for each department during the accounting period.
4. At the end of the period, underapplied and overapplied overhead are computed for each department as well as in total.

Departmental overhead rate procedures

The first step is the creation of departmental overhead rates. The budgeted overhead cost for each department is divided by the budgeted activity level in that department. Some overhead costs, such as depreciation or lease cost of machinery in a particular department, are easily identifiable as overhead costs of that department. Many other overhead costs are not so readily identifiable with individual departments. For example, the salary of the production plant manager is common to all of the departments in the manufacturing plant. Similarly the costs of utilities, insurance, property taxes, and plant depreciation are common to the various departments. These common overhead costs must be allocated to the various departments if departmental overhead costs are to be used.

Before the accounting period starts, budget estimates of utilities, plant depreciation, property taxes, etc. are allocated to departments to determine departmental overhead costs so that the departmental overhead rates can be computed. At year-end **actual** departmental overhead costs are determined by allocating actual departmental overhead costs to departments. Cost allocations to departments should reflect a causal relationship between the department and the cost. For example, factory heating costs often are closely related to the number of square metres of the building that is heated. Therefore, factory heating costs may be allocated based on the amount of square metres in each department. The cost of the plant's first aid room may be allocated to departments in proportion to the number of employees in each department. Fire insurance premiums may be allocated to departments in proportion to the value of the insured assets representing the investment in each department. When square metres, number of employees, investment value, or other variables are used

Allocation bases

to allocate costs to departments, they are called allocation bases. Allocation bases are used to allocate budgeted costs to departments so that departmental overhead rates can be computed. Allocation bases are also used to assign actual costs to departments to determine actual overhead costs. Be careful to distinguish between allocation bases and application bases. The former are used to allocate actual or budgeted costs to departments or other cost objectives, whereas the latter are used to apply overhead costs to products.

Comprehensive example

Understanding the complete cycle in developing and using departmental overhead rates is made easier with a comprehensive example. We use the Winthrop Manufacturing Company as an illustration. Winthrop has two service departments—maintenance and inventory storeroom—and three producing departments—metal fabricating, assembly, and finishing. In this example:

1. Budgeted manufacturing overhead is allocated to the departments, and departmental overhead rates are computed.
2. Predetermined overhead rates and actual measures of production activity are used to determine the amount of applied overhead.
3. The amount of underapplied or overapplied overhead is calculated by department at the end of the accounting period.

In this example there is a total of nine cost items, each representing a cost that must be allocated to the five departments. The total budgeted manufacturing overhead costs for the period and the allocation bases to be used are presented in Figure 4-1.

Setting departmental overhead rates

Budgeted data are used in developing overhead rates

The budgeted overhead costs presented in Figure 4-1 must be allocated to five departments using the allocation bases selected by management. Budgeted amounts for each allocation base are used to allocate the budgeted overhead costs to departments. Therefore, managers must estimate the number of employees in each department for the coming year, the number of square metres of floor space in each department, etc. The budgeted data in Figure 4-1 and the budgeted amounts for each allocation base presented in Figure 4-2 are used to determine the amounts of budgeted overhead in each department.

Allocation of budgeted overhead. The budgeted overhead costs in Figure 4-1 and the estimated allocation bases in Figure 4-2 are used to prepare the departmental cost allocations in Figure 4-3.

Figure 4-1
Manufacturing overhead costs must be allocated to the individual factory departments to determine budgeted departmental overhead. The allocations should be made using allocation bases that best satisfy the matching principle.

Winthrop Manufacturing Company Budgeted Manufacturing Overhead Costs For the Year Ending December 31, 1983		
Cost Item	**Amount**	**Allocation Base**
Indirect materials	$ 20,000	Past utilization ratios
Indirect labour	40,000	Past utilization ratios
Fuel oil (heating)	10,000	Square metres of floor area
Electricity	20,000	Square metres of floor area
Payroll fringe benefits	100,000	Number of employees
Fire insurance	4,000	Value of the investment
Property taxes	12,000	Value of the investment
Plant depreciation	40,000	Square metres of floor area
Machine depreciation	54,000	Specific identification
Total	$300,000	

Winthrop Manufacturing Company
Budgeted Activity Levels and Allocation Bases
For the Year Ending December 31, 1983

Allocation Base	Service Departments		Producing Departments			Total
	Maintenance	Inventory Storeroom	Metal Fabricating	Assembly	Finishing	
Past indirect material use	30%	5%	20%	30%	15%	100%
Past indirect labour use	5%	7.5%	37.5%	37.5%	12.5%	100%
Square metres of floor area	1000	2000	8000	5000	4000	20 000
Number of employees	6	4	15	15	10	50
Value of the investment	$100,000	$150,000	$500,000	$100,000	$150,000	$1,000,000
Maintenance hours	—	—	6000	2000	2000	10 000
Material requisitions	—	—	400	400	200	1000
Machine hours			20 000	25 000		
Direct labour hours						
Direct labour cost					$100 000	

Figure 4-2
Once allocation bases have been selected, the activity level must be estimated
for each allocation base. Each item of data in this schedule is an estimate of a
future level of activity or a future value.

Each cost in Figure 4-1 is first allocated to the two service departments and the three producing departments. The first two cost items are indirect materials and indirect labour. Each is allocated on the basis of past utilization ratios that are obtained from historical data. Of course, it is necessary to decide what past data to use. For example, the quantity of indirect materials used last year might be the basis for the allocation, or the ratio might be computed as the average quantity used in several past years. Historical data are useful in forecasting only if the current situation is similar to those from which the historical data originated. ~~If necessary, past data should be modified to reflect any expected changes in the production environment.~~

In this example the utilization ratios for indirect materials and indirect labour are expressed as percentages. The allocation of the $20,000 of budgeted indirect material cost is shown below.

Department	Budgeted Indirect Material Cost (See Figure 4-1)	× Department Allocation (See Figure 4-2)	= Allocated Departmental Cost for Indirect Materials (See Figure 4-3)
Maintenance	$20,000	30%	$ 6,000
Inventory storeroom	20,000	5	1,000
Metal fabricating	20,000	20	4,000
Assembly	20,000	30	6,000
Finishing	20,000	15	3,000
Total		100%	$20,000

Allocation base ratios are used to assign costs to departments

The indirect material allocation in the last column of the table is entered on the first line of Winthrop's departmental overhead worksheet in Figure 4-3. Indirect labour is allocated in a similar manner using past indirect labour utilization as an allocation base.

The cost of fuel oil used for heating is allocated on the basis of budgeted square metres of floor space for each department. In this case there is no convenient ratio as for indirect materials and indirect labour. However, the budgeted data for departmental space in square metres are readily available, and the allocation ratios are easily computed. Figure 4-2 shows that the plant has a total of 20 000 square metres for all departments. The allocation ratio is found by dividing each department's area estimate by the total number of square metres.

Department	Ratio		Department Allocation
Maintenance	1000/20 000	=	5%
Inventory storeroom	2000/20 000	=	10
Metal fabricating	8000/20 000	=	40
Assembly	5000/20 000	=	25
Finishing	4000/20 000	=	20
Total		=	100%

Winthrop Manufacturing Company
Schedule of Budgeted Overhead Costs
For the Year Ending December 31, 1983

Cost Item	Amount from Figure 4-1	Service Departments		Producing Departments		
		Maintenance	Inventory Storeroom	Metal Fabricating	Assembly	Finishing
Indirect materials	$ 20,000	$ 6,000	$ 1,000	$ 4,000	$ 6,000	$ 3,000
Indirect labour	40,000	2,000	3,000	15,000	15,000	5,000
Fuel oil	10,000	500	1,000	4,000	2,500	2,000
Electricity	20,000	1,000	2,000	8,000	5,000	4,000
Payroll fringe benefits	100,000	12,000	8,000	30,000	30,000	20,000
Fire insurance	4,000	400	600	2,000	400	600
Property taxes	12,000	1,200	1,800	6,000	1,200	1,800
Plant depreciation	40,000	2,000	4,000	16,000	10,000	8,000
Machine depreciation	54,000	4,900	3,600	27,000	13,900	4,600
Total	$300,000			$112,000	$ 84,000	$ 49,000
Maintenance department cost allocation to producing departments based on estimated maintenance hours		$30,000		18,000	6,000	6,000
Inventory storeroom cost allocations to producing departments based on estimated material requisitions			$25,000	10,000	10,000	5,000
Total estimated departmental overhead divided by estimated activity level				$140,000	$100,000	$ 60,000
				20,000 MH	25,000 DLH	$100,000
Budgeted overhead rate				$7 / machine hour	$4 / direct labour hour	60% of direct labour cost

Figure 4-3

Using the budgeted overhead costs in Figure 4-1 and the budgeted allocation bases in Figure 4-2, budgeted overhead costs are computed for each service department and each producing department. Next, service department costs are allocated to the producing departments to arrive at the budgeted departmental overhead costs. Finally, the budgeted overhead costs are divided by the budgeted activity levels to find the overhead rates.

Note that all allocation percentages sum to 100 percent. Once we have these percentages, we proceed as we did with indirect materials and indirect labour. The fuel oil allocations are on line 3 of the departmental overhead worksheet in Figure 4-3.

Square metreage is the allocation base for electricity and plant depreciation as well as for fuel oil. The square metreage ratios just calculated can be used to allocate the budgeted costs for electricity and plant depreciation by multiplying each cost by the square metreage percentage.

Payroll fringe benefits constitute a large overhead item for Winthrop. An allocation based on the number of employees in each department is logical. The allocation percentages are again computed from the data in Figure 4-2. When the total of 50 employees is divided into each department's budgeted number of employees, the departmental allocation percentages are 12 percent, 8 percent, 30 percent, 30 percent, and 20 percent, respectively, for the five departments. Using these percentages, you should calculate the allocation of budgeted payroll fringe benefit costs and compare them with the results in Figure 4-3.

Fire insurance and property taxes are closely related to the investment value of the tangible assets that are insured and taxed. Consequently, the estimated value of the investment in each department can be used to allocate these two costs. You may want to compute the allocation ratios for value of the investment and calculate the allocation for fire insurance and property taxes and compare your answers with the amounts in Figure 4-3.

The last cost is machine depreciation. Most machinery is identifiable with specific departments, so depreciation can be assigned to the department where each asset resides. Depreciation data are found in fixed asset records. In our example they are given, so there is no way for you to verify the amounts.

The sum of the five columns in Figure 4-3 represents the departmental overhead allocation for the five departments. At this point, however, we are not yet ready to compute the overhead rates. Since the service departments perform no direct production functions, there is no way to charge their overhead costs to products. Therefore, all service department costs must now be allocated to the three producing departments.

Allocating service department costs. Service department costs are allocated to producing departments in much the same way that we allocated manufacturing costs to all five cost departments. As always the allocations should be strongly influenced by the matching principle. Winthrop Manufacturing uses maintenance hours as its measure of the amount of maintenance service performed for each department. Similarly the number of material requisitions filled for each department is used to measure inventory storeroom services. These two allocation bases are used to distribute maintenance department costs and inventory storeroom costs to producing departments.

Service department cost must be allocated to producing departments

The allocation process used in this example is called direct allocation, meaning that service department costs are allocated directly to producing departments. No service department costs are allocated to other service departments, even though the maintenance department may perform some work for the inventory storeroom, and the inventory storeroom may fill material requisitions for the maintenance department. When interservice department activities are significant, some cost distortions can occur with direct allocation. Accountants try to minimize such distortions by using reciprocal allocation, which is a more complicated approach requiring the use of linear algebra and yielding more accurate results. Although we use only direct allocation in this text, you should be aware that sometimes other techniques are used in practice.

Computing the overhead rate

As indicated at the bottom of Figure 4-3, the allocated service department costs are added to the producing department totals to arrive at total budgeted overhead costs for production departments. The budgeted overhead cost of each producing department is divided by the department's budgeted activity level to determine the departmental overhead rates. For example, in the metal fabricating department the budgeted overhead cost of $140,000 is divided by the budget application base of 20 000 machine hours, yielding an overhead rate of $7 per machine hour. In a similar manner the assembly department overhead rate of $4 per direct labour hour and the finishing department overhead rate of 60 percent of direct labour cost are computed. In the Winthrop example the overhead application base is different for each department. We remind you that the entire process of determining departmental overhead rates is done with budgeted data.

Using departmental overhead rates

Applied overhead is accumulated for each department

Departmental overhead rates are determined before the accounting period begins. Once the accounting year starts, these rates are used to apply overhead to production. Each hour of machine time incurred in the metal fabricating department means $7 of overhead is applied to production, and every hour of direct labour time actually used in assembly causes $4 of overhead to be applied. Each time overhead is applied to production, work in process control is debited for the amount applied and the overhead applied account is credited. With departmental rates there is a manufacturing overhead applied account for each departmental overhead. For example, assume that during one day of production at Winthrop Manufacturing 100 machine hours are worked in the metal fabricating department, 120 hours of direct labour are worked in the assembly department, and $500 of direct labour cost are incurred in finishing. The journal entries to record overhead applied in each department for the day are

Work in Process Control (metal fabricating)	700	
MOH Applied (metal fabricating)		700
Applied overhead in metal fabricating (100 × $7).		
Work in Process Control (assembly)	480	
MOH Applied (assembly)		480
Applied overhead in assembly (120 × $4).		
Work in Process Control (finishing)	300	
MOH Applied (finishing)		300
Applied overhead in assembly ($500 × .6).		

Allocation of
actual overhead
to departments

*Actual departmental
overhead costs are
determined in a
similar way*

In addition to applying overhead, actual overhead costs are incurred during the accounting period. These costs must be assigned to the various departments so that actual overhead can be compared with applied overhead in each department. Some costs, such as a repair bill for a specific piece of machinery, may be directly identifiable with a department, but frequently actual overhead costs are common to all departments and have to be allocated just as budgeted costs.

The process of allocating actual overhead costs to departments is virtually identical to the process that we just discussed of allocating budgeted overhead costs to departments. The only difference is that **actual** data are used instead of **budgeted** data. The overhead costs that are allocated are the actual costs that have been incurred and accumulated in the overhead control account. Also, the amounts used for the allocation bases to assign costs to departments are actual measures. For example, management can actually measure the amount of square metres that each department has and count the number of employees in each department.

To illustrate the process of determining actual overhead costs for departments, we present actual overhead costs in Figure 4-4 and actual allocation base amounts in Figure 4-5. The data presented in Figures 4-1 and 4-2 and the data presented in Figures 4-4 and 4-5 are similar except that the former are budgeted data and the latter are actual data.

The worksheet showing the allocation of actual overhead costs to departments is presented in Figure 4-6. You may want to compute the cost allocations for several of the cost items to verify your understanding of cost allocation procedures. Of course, the actual costs in Figure 4-6 parallel the budgeted data in Figure 4-3. The actual service department costs are allocated to the three producing departments so that all actual overhead costs are assigned to the producing departments.

Figure 4-4
This figure is identical
to Figure 4-1 except
here actual rather
than budgeted over-
head costs are
presented.

Winthrop Manufacturing Company		
Actual Manufacturing Overhead Costs		
For the Year Ending December 31, 1983		
Cost Item	**Amount**	**Allocation Base**
Indirect materials	$ 25,000	Actual material requisitions
Indirect labour	40,000	Actual payroll reports
Fuel oil	16,000	Square metres of floor area
Electricity	24,000	Square metres of floor area
Payroll fringe benefits	120,000	Number of employees
Fire insurance	4,000	Value of the investment
Property taxes	16,000	Value of the investment
Plant depreciation	40,000	Square metres of floor area
Machine depreciation	55,000	Specific identification
	$340,000	

Winthrop Manufacturing Company
Actual Activity Levels and Allocation Bases
For the Year Ending December 31, 1983

Allocation Base	Service Departments		Producing Departments		
	Maintenance	Inventory Storeroom	Metal Fabricating	Assembly	Finishing
Indirect material usage	28.40%	3.60%	20.00%	32.00%	16.00%
Indirect labour usage	5.00%	3.75%	35.00%	40.25%	16.00%
Square metreage of floor area	1000	2000	8000	5000	4000
Number of employees	6	6	20	18	18
Value of the investment	$100,000	$150,000	$500,000	$100,000	$150,000
Maintenance hours			7000	2000	1000
Material requisitions			600	400	200
Machine hours			24 500	26 000	
Direct labour hours					
Direct labour cost					$102,000

Figure 4-5
This schedule contains actual measures of activity levels for the allocation bases.

Winthrop Manufacturing Company
Schedule of Actual Overhead Costs
For the Year Ending December 31, 1983

Cost Item	Amount from Figure 4-4	Service Departments		Producing Departments		
		Maintenance	Inventory Storeroom	Metal Fabricating	Assembly	Finishing
Indirect materials	$ 25,000	$ 7,100	$ 900	$ 5,000	$ 8,000	$ 4,000
Indirect labour	40,000	2,000	1,500	14,000	16,100	6,400
Fuel oil	16,000	800	1,600	6,400	4,000	3,200
Electricity	24,000	1,200	2,400	9,600	6,000	4,800
Payroll fringe benefits	120,000	12,000	12,000	40,000	36,000	20,000
Fire insurance	4,000	400	600	2,000	400	600
Property taxes	16,000	1,600	2,400	8,000	1,600	2,400
Plant depreciation	40,000	2,000	4,000	16,000	10,000	8,000
Machine depreciation	55,000	4,900	4,600	27,000	13,900	4,600
Total	$340,000	$32,000	$30,000	$128,000	$ 96,000	$54,000
Maintenance department cost allocations to producing departments based on **actual** maintenance hours		$32,000		22,400	6,400	3,200
Inventory storeroom cost allocations to producing departments based on **actual** material requisitions			$30,000	15,000	10,000	5,000
Total **actual** departmental overhead				$165,400	$112,400	$62,200

Figure 4-6
Actual departmental overhead costs are determined following the same procedures used to find budgeted departmental overhead. The only difference is that this figure contains actual data, whereas Figure 4-3 shows budgeted data.

Total applied overhead

Earlier we illustrated journal entries for applying overhead to production in each of the three producing departments at Winthrop. Such journal entries are made on a timely basis throughout the accounting period. The credits to the manufacturing overhead applied accounts for each department accumulate throughout the year, and at year-end the amount of overhead applied in each department can be read from the ledger account balances for each department.

In the Winthrop example, the overhead application process is summarized for the entire year. In each department the amount of applied overhead is equal to the departmental overhead rate times the actual activity level for the period as measured by the application base in the department. For example, the metal fabricating department used 24 500 actual machine hours (Figure 4-5), and the overhead rate is $7 per machine hour, as calculated in Figure 4-3. Multiplying the actual machine hours used by the $7 rate results in $171,500 of overhead applied to production in the metal fabricating department during the accounting period. Applied overhead in assembly and finishing is computed in a similar way, as shown in Figure 4-7.

Underapplied and overapplied overhead

At the end of the accounting period, the actual overhead in each department is compared with the applied overhead in each department to determine underapplied or overapplied overhead.

Comparing actual and applied overhead. It is a simple process to compare actual overhead in Figure 4-6 with applied overhead to find underapplied or overapplied overhead for each department. In the metal fabricating department the actual amount of overhead cost incurred is $165,400, and the amount applied is shown in Figure 4-7 as $171,500. The difference of $6,100 is the amount of overapplied overhead, and it means that the amount of overhead applied to products in the metal fabricating department was too large. It was 3.7 percent ($6,100/$165,400) more than the actual overhead cost in metal fabricating. In effect the **actual** cost of the products produced in the department is somewhat lower than the cost reflected by the applied overhead. The final column of Figure 4-7 indicates the underapplied or overapplied overhead in each department and in total.

Adding the departmental underapplied and overapplied overhead, we find net underapplied overhead of $3,300. Since actual overhead is $340,000, overhead is underapplied by only about 1 percent. Underapplied overhead is unfavourable because the department incurred more actual overhead than was applied to products. Overapplied overhead is favourable since the department incurred less actual overhead than was applied.

Typically, 1 percent of variance is considered to be small, but the individual departmental fluctuations are much greater. Metal fabricating is 3.7 percent overapplied, and assembly is 7.5 percent underapplied. You can now see one of the advantages of departmental data as compared with one comprehensive figure. Some sizable underapplied and overapplied overhead can be netted

Underapplied and overapplied overhead is computed for each department

Winthrop Manufacturing Company
Schedule of Underapplied and Overapplied Overhead
December 31, 1983

Department	Overhead Rate	×	Actual Activity Level	=	Applied Manufacturing Overhead	−	Actual Manufacturing Overhead from Figure 4-6	=	Underapplied/ (Overapplied) Overhead
Metal fabricating	$7/MH		24 500 MH		$171,500		$165,400		($6,100)
Assembly	$4/DLH		26 000 DLH		104,000		112,400		8,400
Finishing	60% of DLC		$102,000 DLC		61,200		62,200		1,000
Total					$336,700		$340,000		$3,300

Figure 4-7

In each department applied overhead is equal to the overhead rate times the actual level of activity for the overhead application base. Underapplied or overapplied overhead is the difference between the actual overhead and the applied overhead in each department.

out when only one total overhead figure is calculated. But when departmental overhead variances are available, managers can investigate the reasons for any discrepancy between applied and actual overhead and can deal with problems that may occur. One reason for the difference may be the use of inappropriate budgeted overhead rates.

Joint products and by-products

In some cases it is not possible to produce a single product without obtaining other products. For example, in the wood products industry it is not possible to produce plywood without producing sawdust. There was a time when sawdust was burned as a waste product, but now it is pressed into particle board and sold. Similarly in the food industry a beef carcass provides hide and internal organs in addition to the main cuts of meat. Crude oil is processed into gasoline, kerosene, fuel oil, and other oil products. When more than one product results from the production process, the products are either joint products or by-products.

The distinction between joint products and by-products is not always clear, but it is usually made on the basis of relative economic value. Joint products have relatively large economic value and are the main products in the production process. By-products have relatively small economic value and are less significant in comparison with the value of the main products. In some cases the distinction is difficult. A general rule, but one that cannot be applied in every situation, is:

* If the value of the product is so small that it has no effect on the decision to produce or not to produce the entire product group, it is a **by-product;** if it does affect the decision to produce, it is a **joint product.**

In the above examples particle board would probably be considered a by-product and plywood a main product. Gasoline, kerosene, and fuel oil would all normally be considered joint products. Because joint products are significantly more important than by-products, we limit our discussion in this chapter to the former.

Joint products cannot be identified separately until the split-off point

Joint costs are common to joint products

Common costs occur with joint products because some of the manufacturing costs occur prior to the time that the products can be identified individually. The split-off point is the point in the production process where products separate. At this point individual products become identifiable, and their production costs can be measured separately. Prior to the split-off point, all production costs are common to all of the joint products. These common costs are called joint costs.

Figure 4-8 illustrates the production flows for a company producing three joint products and a by-product. In the first two processes, blending and settling, the products are indistinguishable. Therefore, all production costs in the two process centres are common to all three products and are called the joint costs of the products. At the end of production in the second process centre, the three products split off or separate. All costs incurred after the split-off point are

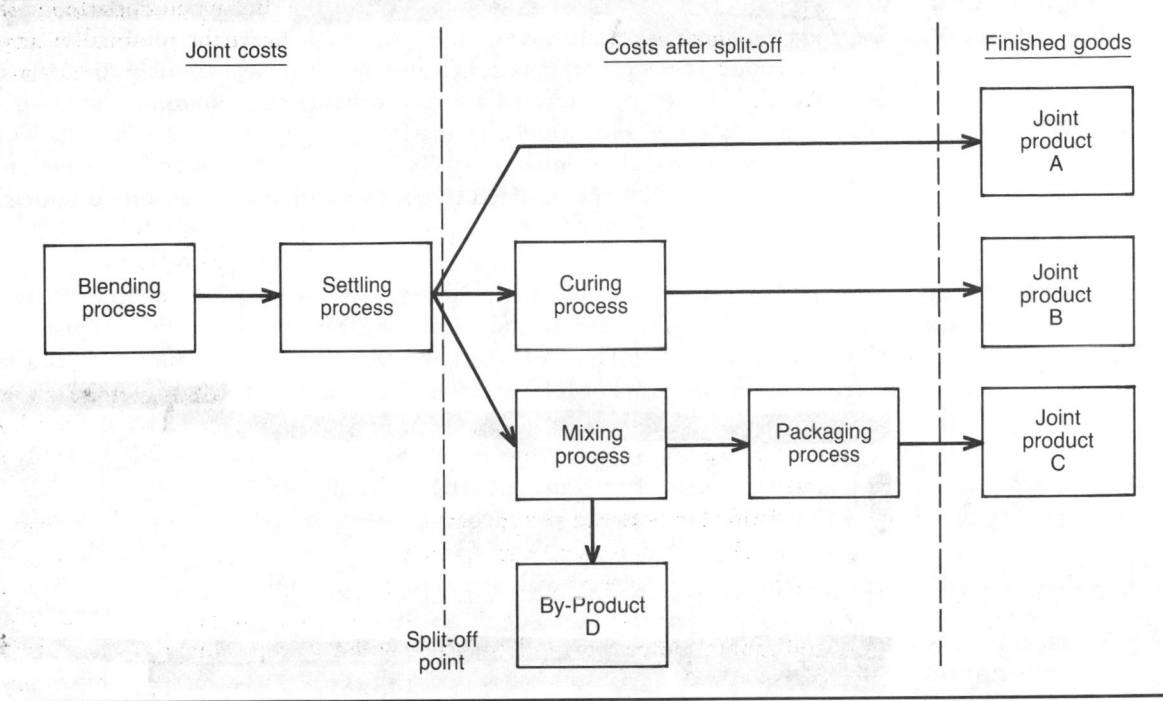

Figure 4-8
The split-off point is critical in joint product costing because all production
costs incurred before the split-off point are indistinguishable between products.

identifiable with each individual product. Product A goes right from split-off to
finished goods inventory. Product B goes to a curing process after split-off and
then to finished goods. Product C requires two additional processes before
reaching finished goods; one of the processes results in a by-product.
The total cost of joint products includes both joint costs and costs after
split-off. The latter costs are the type of product costs discussed in Chapters 2
and 3. The manufacturing costs can be identified with the individual products.
Joint costs, however, cannot be identified with each product and therefore must
be allocated to joint products to determine the total product cost. The cost of the
by-product may be minor and is not separated from the cost of Product C. If it is
significant, the by-product might be treated as another joint product with its
own separate cost.

The inability to identify joint costs with specific joint products does not
reduce the importance of the costs. However, joint costs entail the additional
step of allocating joint costs in determining product costs. Also, the resulting
product costs require careful interpretation. Since the full cost of products is
required for many accounting purposes, such as external reporting, some
method of allocating joint costs is necessary.

Joint product cost allocation Ideally the allocation of joint costs to individual products should be governed by the matching principle. However, the association between joint costs and specific product revenues often is not clear. It is not always possible to obtain a good match between product revenue and product cost; therefore, joint cost allocation procedures vary widely. In this chapter we present two methods of joint cost allocation and examine their effect on product costs. In later chapters we discuss other aspects of manufacturing activities that produce joint products.

Illustrative example Greengrow Company manufactures three types of fertilizers in a joint production process. The production and sales data for the month of August are tabulated in Figure 4-9. These data can be used to develop product costs for the three fertilizers in terms of total costs and costs per unit. The product costing process for joint products can be divided into two general steps:

Steps in joint product costing

1. Identify the costs of each product after split-off, and
2. Allocate the joint costs of production to the products.

We are primarily concerned with step 2 in this example.

Physical units allocation method One common approach is to allocate joint costs using the physical units allocation method, sometimes called the units of output method. In this example a bag of fertilizer is the output unit, so the $240,000 joint cost is allocated to the three products in proportion to the number of bags produced. With total production of 100 000 bags, the joint cost is allocated according to the following computations on page 135.

Greengrow Company Schedule of Production and Sales Data For the Month of August 1983				
Item	**Grow**	**Grow-U**	**Grow-U-Plus**	**Total**
Produced	60 000 bags	30 000 bags	10 000 bags	100 000 bags
Sold	60 000 bags	30 000 bags	10 000 bags	100 000 bags
Sales price	$4 per bag	$8 per bag	$12 per bag	
Cost after split-off	$60,000	$120,000	$30,000	$210,000
Joint cost = $240,000				

Figure 4-9
Three products are manufactured in this joint production process. Over half of the total manufacturing cost is joint cost that must be allocated to the three products to get a full cost for the products.

Grow	$\dfrac{60\,000 \text{ bags}}{100\,000 \text{ bags}} \times \$240,000 = \$144,000$
Grow U	$\dfrac{30\,000 \text{ bags}}{100\,000 \text{ bags}} \times \$240,000 = \$\ 72,000$
Grow-U-Plus	$\dfrac{10\,000 \text{ bags}}{100\,000 \text{ bags}} \times \$240,000 = \$\ 24,000$

Next, the costs after split-off are assigned to the products, and the total product cost is found. The solution is illustrated in Figure 4-10. The distinction between joint cost and cost after split-off is important because joint cost is an allocated cost and is treated differently from cost after split-off in many management decisions. Such decisions are discussed in Chapter 6. Here we focus only on the methods of allocation.

Each product has an identical joint cost per unit

As shown in Figure 4-10, the total joint cost allocated to each product is different, but the joint cost per unit of each product is $2.40 for all products. Costs after split-off are identified with specific products and added to the joint cost to arrive at total product cost. The total cost is used for many external reporting purposes. However, one must interpret such costs cautiously. To illustrate why, let us consider a second common method of allocating joint costs.

The physical units method of joint cost allocation is easy to use and understand, but it can yield questionable product costs if the sales values of the joint products are significantly different or if the costs after split-off are significantly different. An alternative method of joint cost allocation is the gross profit method.

	Greengrow Company					
	Product Cost Schedule Using Physical Units Allocation Method					
	For the Month of August 1983					

	Joint Cost		Cost after Split-off		Total Product Cost	
Product	**Total**	**Per Unit**	**Total**	**Per Unit**	**Total**	**Per Unit**
Grow	$144,000	$2.40	$ 60,000	$1.00	$204,000	$3.40
Grow-U	72,000	2.40	120,000	4.00	192,000	6.40
Grow-U-Plus	24,000	2.40	30,000	3.00	54,000	5.40
Total	$240,000		$210,000		$450,000	

Figure 4-10
The physical units allocation method is easy to understand and use: Each product receives an identical unit cost for joint costs.

Gross profit allocation method

The gross profit allocation method is used to allocate joint costs so that all products in the group of joint products have the same percentage gross profit. For example, if a group of joint products generates a 30 percent gross profit on sales, then each product would be assigned a **total cost** of 70 percent. Thus a product selling for $10 would have a total unit cost of $7 per unit, and a product with a price of $6 would have a total unit cost of $4.20. Each product has a gross profit of 30 percent, ($10 − $7)/$10 = 30 percent and ($6 − $4.20)/$6 = 30 percent.

Each product contributes the same percentage gross profit

The idea of the gross profit method is to determine the overall gross profit for the group of joint products and to assign joint costs to products so that each has the same percentage gross profit. The first step in the process is to determine the gross profit of the group of joint products by estimating the sales revenue of the entire product group and deducting the total cost of the products. To illustrate, the total cost of Greengrow Company's August production is $450,000 ($240,000 joint cost and $210,000 cost after split-off). Total sales value is the amounts produced times the selling prices, computed as follows:

Units	× Sales Price	= Total Sales Value
60 000 bags	$ 4 per bag	$240,000
30 000 bags	8 per bag	240,000
10 000 bags	12 per bag	120,000
Total sales value		$600,000

The total sales value of the group of joint products is $600,000. Therefore, the ratio of total product costs to sales value is 75 percent ($450,000/$600,000), which means that gross margin from the entire group of products is 25 percent of sales. To assign the appropriate joint cost to each product, it is first necessary to decide what the product's total cost should be to yield a gross margin of 25 percent. The cost after split-off is then deducted from the total cost to arrive at the amount of joint cost to be allocated to each product. The total cost of each product, based on the gross margin percentage, is calculated as follows:

Product	Sales Value	Ratio	Total Product Cost
Grow	$240,000	× .75 =	$180,000
Grow-U	240,000	× .75 =	180,000
Grow-U-Plus	120,000	× .75 =	90,000
Total	$600,000	× .75 =	$450,000

The total cost of each product includes both joint cost and cost after split-off. Since the cost after split-off is identified with each product, it is a simple process to allocate joint cost to each product. Either of the following basic relationships may be used:

$$\text{Allocated joint cost} + \text{Cost after split-off} = \text{Total cost}$$

or

$$\text{Allocated joint cost} = \text{Total cost} - \text{Cost after split-off}$$

Total cost is shown above, and cost after split-off is given in Figure 4-9. The amount of joint cost to be allocated to each product is

Product	Total Product Cost	Cost after Split-off	Allocated Joint Cost
Grow	$180,000	$ 60,000	$120,000
Grow-U	180,000	120,000	60,000
Grow-U-Plus	90,000	30,000	60,000

The results of the above computations are summarized in a product cost chart in Figure 4-11.

An argument in favour of the gross profit allocation method is that it often parallels management's decision to produce the group of joint products rather than a single product or one product at a time. Therefore, the product costs should reflect a single profit margin.

Compare the difference between the two allocation methods. Which of the product costs is correct? Depending on management's use of the product cost information, both costs can be correct. If some other method of joint cost allocation were used, it might yield still different product costs. (We have illustrated only two methods of joint cost allocations; many other methods are also used in practice.) The allocation of joint costs to products makes total unit

	Greengrow Company					
	Product Cost Schedule Using Physical Units Allocation Method					
	For the Month of August 1983					
	Joint Cost		Cost after Split-off		Total Product Cost	
Product	Total	Per Unit	Total	Per Unit	Total	Per Unit
Grow	$120,000	$2.00	$ 60,000	$1.00	$180,000	$3.00
Grow-U	60,000	2.00	120,000	4.00	180,000	6.00
Grow-U-Plus	60,000	6.00	30,000	3.00	90,000	9.00
Total	$240,000		$210,000		$450,000	

Figure 4-11
Under the gross profit allocation method, joint costs are allocated in a way that yields identical percentage gross margins. Here each product has a gross profit that is 25 percent of sales.

product costs difficult to evaluate and use in some types of management decisions. ~~The greater the proportion of allocated joint costs to total production cost, the more caution managers must exercise when using total product cost figures.~~ We shall elaborate on this problem when we discuss other aspects of joint product costs in Chapter 6.

Joint product inventory mix

In addition to the problem of allocating joint product costs, managers are also faced with the problem of managing joint product inventories. In many joint product manufacturing situations, the product mix cannot be changed significantly. The result is that some of the joint products may be selling well, while others are experiencing weak markets. For example, a petroleum company may experience a high demand for fuel oil and lower demand for gasoline during the winter months. In the summer the reverse may be true. To the extent possible management may try to change the production mix in order to obtain more of the product that is in demand. ~~Changing the production mix for joint products is not always possible, however, and often when it is possible, it is not economically feasible.~~ For example, in spite of the strong market for chicken breasts and legs, it is impossible to increase the production of these two products without increasing the production of wings, backs, necks, hearts, and gizzards proportionately.

Summary

A **common cost** is a cost shared by more than one cost objective. Common costs occur with many types of cost objectives. Sometimes they are a large portion of total product cost and must be assigned to cost objectives in a logical manner. The assignment of common costs is called **cost allocation.** Allocations should reflect a meaningful causal relationship between the cost objective and the cost.

Manufacturing overhead is a major common cost item. Typically overhead is applied using a **budgeted overhead rate,** also called a **predetermined overhead rate.** The overhead rate is obtained by dividing the **budgeted overhead cost** by the **budgeted activity level.** Many different activity levels can be used, including direct labour hours, direct labour cost, units of production, machine hours, and material cost. The choice of an **application base** is influenced strongly by the matching principle.

Sometimes a single overhead rate for an entire plant does a poor job of matching overhead costs with products. Therefore, **departmental overhead rates** may be used.

Departmental overhead rates require the allocation of all overhead costs to departments. Any **service department** costs must be allocated to **producing departments. Direct allocation** of service department costs is not as accurate as **reciprocal allocation,** but it is simpler to perform. The departmental cost allocations must be done twice: once, before the accounting period starts, with **budgeted** data to set the departmental overhead rates. A second allocation is necessary at the end of the accounting period with **actual** data to find actual departmental overhead costs. **Actual overhead** is compared with **applied overhead** to find **underapplied** and **overapplied** overhead for each department.

Joint products are indistinguishable in the production process until a point in the production process called the **split-off point.** Costs incurred prior to the split-off point are called **joint costs.** Beyond the split-off point they are called **costs after split-off.** Joint costs are common to all the products that pass beyond the split-off point and must be allocated to the products. Costs after split-off can be identified with specific products. The method of joint cost product allocation can have a major influence on the final product costs. Two typical allocation methods are used, one called the **physical units allocation method,** also called the **units of output method;** the other is the **gross profit allocation method.**

Total product costs resulting from different allocation methods should not be viewed as correct or incorrect because alternative joint cost allocation methods can yield strikingly different product costs.

Managers are concerned with joint product mix as well as product cost allocation. Changing the product mix is not always feasible or possible, even if some of the products are hard to sell.

List of important terms

Following are important terms introduced or discussed in the chapter. You should understand the meaning of these terms before working exercises and problems or proceeding to the next chapter.

allocation base   *(120)*
application base   *(117)*
budgeted activity level   *(116)*
budgeted overhead cost   *(116)*
budgeted overhead rate   *(115)*
by-product   *(132)*
common cost   *(113)*
cost after split-off   *(133)*
cost allocation   *(113)*
departmental overhead
   rates   *(120)*
direct allocation   *(125)*
gross profit allocation
   method   *(136)*

joint cost   *(132)*
joint product   *(114)*
physical units allocation
   method   *(134)*
predetermined overhead
   rate   *(115)*
producing department   *(119)*
reciprocal allocation   *(126)*
service department   *(119)*
split-off point   *(132)*

Questions

1. What are common costs and why do they occur?
2. Give some examples of common costs.
3. Discuss the relationship between common costs, cost objectives, and cost allocation.
4. What is a predetermined manufacturing overhead rate and why is it used?
5. Name three overhead application bases and give an example of where each might be appropriate.

6. What factors should managers consider in selecting an overhead application base?

7. Why should managers consider using departmental overhead rates?

8. Distinguish between producing and service departments.

9. To what does the term *direct allocation* refer?

10. A manager in a company comments, "I understand these product cost figures, but I don't know what this $5,500 underapplied overhead figure means." As the controller, explain in understandable terms.

11. Distinguish between budgeted overhead, actual overhead, and applied overhead.

12. Describe joint products and joint costs.

13. Is there any reason to separate joint costs from cost after split-off in developing product costs?

14. What kind of inventory problem may arise from the production of joint products?

15. Is the gross profit method or the physical units method the correct way of allocating joint cost?

Exercises

Ex. 4-1   **Determining allocation bases.** The following costs are incurred:

1. Supervision
2. Electricity
3. Maintenance
4. First aid room
5. Personnel
6. Heating
7. Real estate taxes
8. Indirect materials

Required:
a. Suggest an allocation base for each cost.
b. What is the most important criterion in selecting an allocation base?

Ex. 4-2   **Computing underapplied and overapplied overhead.** The Scotch Company has established its predetermined overhead rate for the year at $6.10 per machine hour. In May a total of 60 000 machine hours was clocked, and actual overhead amounted to $420,000. In June 54 000 machine hours were clocked, and actual MOH amounted to $320,000.

Required:
a. What is the amount of overapplied or underapplied overhead for May?
b. Calculate overapplied or underapplied MOH for June.

Ex. 4-3 **Using overhead rates.** Bluesky Manufacturing Company uses direct labour hours to apply overhead to products. In 1984 budgeted overhead was $900,000, and budgeted direct labour was 150 000 hours.

Job 1447 uses 250 hours of direct labour and yields 200 units of product. At year-end 160 000 direct labour hours have been used, and actual overhead amounts to $910,000.

Required:
a. What was the 1984 overhead rate?
b. What, if any, was the underapplied or overapplied overhead for the year?
c. How much overhead was charged to Job 1447?
d. What was the per-unit cost of overhead for products produced in Job 1447?

Ex. 4-4 **Computing overhead rates.** Below are budgeted data for the next accounting year for the Gablin Tool Supply Company.

Budgeted costs:	
Manufacturing overhead:	
Indirect materials	$ 45,000
Indirect labour	60,000
Utilities	75,000
Employee fringe benefits	60,000
Property taxes	40,000
Plant depreciation	70,000
Equipment depreciation	50,000
Total	$400,000
Direct materials	$200,000
Direct labour cost	$300,000
Other budgeted data:	
Machine hours	40 000
Direct labour hours	50 000
Units of output	20 000

Required:
Compute a manufacturing overhead rate based on:

a. Machine hours.
b. Direct labour hours.
c. Direct labour cost.
d. Direct material cost.
e. Prime cost.
f. Units of output.

Ex. 4-5 **Underapplied and overapplied overhead.** Meltcher Marine Products uses departmental overhead rates for each of its three producing departments — drilling, assembly, and painting. Below are 1984 year-end balances in the overhead accounts.

Overhead Control, Drilling		Overhead Applied, Drilling	
450,000			477,000

Overhead Control, Painting		Overhead Applied, Painting	
210,000			193,200

Overhead Control, Assembly		Overhead Applied, Assembly	
560,000			504,000

Required:
Prepare a schedule identifying the amount of underapplied and overapplied overhead for each department and in total. For each department and in total, express underapplied and overapplied overhead as a percentage of actual overhead.

Ex. 4-6   Overhead rates and product costs. Halston, Inc. has budgeted overhead of $500,000. Three possible application bases are budgeted:

Direct labour hours	62 500
Direct labour cost	$312,500
Machine hours	40 000

Following are data for Job 1472X:

Units produced	100
Direct materials cost	$2,450
Direct labour cost (500 h)	$4,000
Machine hours	420

Required:
a. Compute the overhead rate using each application base.
b. Compute the unit cost of the product using each of the three application bases.

Ex. 4-7   Allocating departmental overhead costs. The Manta Factory has two service departments, personnel and quality control, and two production departments, assembly and finishing. The following data are actual measures of activity in the departments during the year just completed.

	Personnel	Quality Control	Assembly	Finishing
Number of employees	4	6	30	10
Asset valuation in $	50,000	150,000	500,000	300,000
Number of machine hours	—	5000	30 000	15 000
Number of square metres	4000	8000	12 000	16 000
Number of jobs processed	—	—	280	120
Number of direct labour hours	—	—	30 000	20 000

The following overhead costs were incurred during the year:

	Cost Incurred	Allocation Base
Supervision	$24,000	Number of employees
Insurance	5,000	Asset valuation
Equipment depreciation	8,000	Machine hours
Building depreciation	12,000	Square metres
Material handling	15,000	Jobs processed

Allocations of service department costs to producing departments are based on direct labour hours for the personnel department and number of jobs processed for the quality control department.

Required:
Prepare a schedule of departmental overhead cost allocations so that all overhead costs are allocated to the two producing departments.

Ex. 4-8 **Overhead computations.** Wainwright Whitewater Canoes identifies three separate producing departments, each with its own manufacturing overhead rate. Below are budget data for 1984:

Department	Budgeted Activity	Budgeted Overhead Cost
Forming	30 000 machine hours	$240,000
Assembly	50 000 direct labour hours	200,000
Finishing	$120,000 direct labour cost	180,000

During 1984 actual activity levels were:

Department	Activity Level
Forming	34 000 machine hours
Assembly	56 000 direct labour hours
Finishing	$150,000 direct labour cost

Required:

a. What is the overhead rate for each department?

b. How much overhead was applied in each department?

c. If actual overhead costs were $250,000, $270,000, and $195,000, respectively, compute underapplied or overapplied overhead by department and in total.

Ex. 4-9 **Allocating common costs.** The Systems-Aid Corporation has an information systems development contract with a local government. The fee for the development service is determined by a contract that provides for coverage of all costs associated with the contract plus a profit margin of 15 percent. Most of the costs associated with this contract are direct costs, such as the salary of employees assigned to the project, supplies, and computer time used in the project. However, some costs are common to several contracts and must be allocated to the local contract to determine the fee. Below are data on costs that should be allocated to the contract.

Cost	Total Amount	Allocation Base
Supervision	$80,000	Hours of direct supervision
Insurance	20,000	Direct labour costs
Utilities	25,000	Direct costs of contracts
Building lease	20,000	Direct costs of contracts

Allocation base measures are presented below.

	Contract			
	Local	102R	104R	105R
Hours of supervision	400	300	100	200
Direct labour cost	$30,000	$40,000	$35,000	$ 45,000
*Direct costs of contracts	$60,000	$80,000	$40,000	$120,000

*Including direct labour costs.

Required:

a. Prepare a schedule of cost allocations to the local government contract.

b. Calculate the fee for the project.

Ex. 4-10 **Physical unit joint cost allocation.** The Petro Products Company manufactures two lubricants in a joint production process. One product, Lub-1, may be sold immediately after split-off. The other product, Lub-ez, requires further processing before it is ready for sale. There was no beginning inventory. The following production data are provided:

Total joint cost = $720,000
Additional cost of processing Lub-ez = $76,250

	Sales		
	Quantity	**Price**	**Ending Inventory**
Lub-1	2 000 000 L	$.40	75 000 L
Lub-ez	1 500 000 L	$.50	25 000 L

Required:
Determine the cost of the ending inventories using the physical unit method of joint cost allocation.

Ex. 4-11 **Gross profit joint cost allocation.** The Buzbee Honey Company produces artificial sweeteners to be used as sugar supplements. A continuous flow production process is used that yields four joint products. The products split off at the end of production in department 5, and three products go on for more processing before being transferred to finished goods. Cost data and other details for the month of February are presented below.

Joint cost = $180,000

Product	Quantity in litres	Sales Price per litre	Cost after Split-off
Buzie I	200 000	$.40	$40,000
Buzie II	100 000	.60	0
Buzie III	80 000	2.00	12,000
Buzie-Whamo	20 000	5.00	28,000

Required:
Using the gross profit method of joint cost allocation, compute the joint cost per unit, cost after split-off per unit, and total cost per unit.

Problem Set A

P. 4A-1 **Computing overhead costs.** Starfoam Insulating Company provides foam insulation for industrial products, such as heating and cooling units as well as refrigerators and freezers. Customers ship products to Starfoam, and the company processes orders using a job order accounting system. Insulation is sprayed into units using high-pressure spray guns; then the units are dried in huge ovens. Overhead is applied at the rate of $15 per machine hour in the spraying department and $10 per machine hour in the drying department.

Three jobs are completed the first week of July. Their production cost data are summarized below.

	Job		
	514	**516**	**517**
Direct materials cost	$12,000	$6,000	$8,000
Direct labour cost	$ 3,000	$2,000	$2,500
Spraying department, machine hours	375	250	310
Drying department, machine hours	200	150	150
Units produced	100	200	300

Required:

a. Calculate the amount of manufacturing overhead applied to each job.

b. Compute the per-unit cost of each job.

c. Compute the percentage of total product cost represented by overhead in Job 514.

P. 4A-2   Overhead costs. Omega Enterprises applies overhead to production using an overhead rate based on direct labour hours. The following cost and production estimates were made before the year started:

Direct labour cost	$160,000
Manufacturing overhead	$280,000
Machine hours	20 000
Units produced	500 000
Direct labour hours	40 000

At the end of the year, the accounts showed the following information:

Units produced	400 000
Machine hours	17 000
Direct materials	$500,000
Direct labour hours	35 000
Direct labour cost	$140,000
Manufacturing overhead	$231,000

Required:

a. Calculate the overhead rate.

b. Calculate the total amount of cost assigned to production during the year.

c. Determine the amount of overapplied or underapplied overhead.

d. How small would the actual activity level have to be in order to have underapplied factory overhead when actual overhead is $231,000?

P. 4A-3 Comprehensive departmental overhead. Following are budgeted data for three production departments—machining, forging, and milling.

Cost Item	Budgeted Amount	Allocation Base
Fire insurance	$ 6,000	Value of investment
Plant depreciation	15,000	Square metreage
Telephone	5,000	Number of extensions
Payroll taxes (CPP, UIC, etc.)	10,000	Number of employees
Indirect labour	36,000	Past utilization rate
Utilities	18,000	Square metreage

Budgeted Overhead Allocation Bases

	Service Departments		Production Departments		
	Repair Shop	Supply Department	Machining	Forging	Milling
Past indirect labour use	10%	10%	25%	35%	20%
Square metreage	1000	1000	4000	2000	2000
Number of phone extensions	3	7	5	5	5
Value of investment	$30,000	$20,000	$60,000	$ 40,000	$50,000
Number of employees	8	5	17	10	10
Repair shop service hours			10 000	6000	4000
Number of supply requisitions			460	160	370
Machine hours			19 000		
Direct labour cost				$100,000	
Direct labour hours					16,000

Repair shop service hours are used to allocate repair shop costs to producing departments, and number of supply requisitions is used for supply department allocations.

The following information is available at year-end:

	Machining	Forging	Milling
Actual activity level	17 000 machine hours	$97,000 DLC	15 000 DLH
Actual MOH cost	$35,000	$32,000	$19,400

Required:

a. Prepare a schedule of cost allocations to departments.

b. Calculate overhead rates for each of the three production departments using machine hours, direct labour cost, and direct labour hours, respectively, as the application bases.

c. Calculate the amount of underapplied or overapplied overhead for the three producing departments and in total.

P. 4A-4   Departmental overhead rates. Below are budgeted and actual manufacturing overhead data for a firm using departmental overhead rates. The firm has two service departments and three producing departments. Service department costs are assigned to producing departments using direct allocation. Budgeted and actual activity levels are presented for three possible application bases.

| | | Budgeted MOH Costs | | | |
	Stores	Tool Room	Department 1	Department 2	Department 3
Distributed MOH costs	$46,000	$26,000	$57,500	$ 86,250	$ 80,000
Service department distributions			28,000	24,000	20,000
Production department totals			$85,500	$110,250	$100,000

| | Budgeted Application Bases | | |
Production Department	Direct Labour Hours	Direct Labour Costs	Machine Hours
1	25,000	$ 90,000	19,000
2	31,500	100,000	29,400
3	60,000	200,000	24,500

| | | Actual MOH Costs | | | |
	Stores	Tool Room	Department 1	Department 2	Department 3
Distributed MOH costs	$39,000	$22,000	$78,000	$79,000	$60,000
Service department distributions			17,000	30,000	14,000
Production department totals			$95,000	$109,000	$74,000

| | Actual Application Bases | | |
Production Department	Direct Labour Hours	Direct Labour Costs	Machine Hours
1	23 000	$ 90,000	19 200
2	32 000	102,000	27 100
3	51 000	178,000	23 000

Management decides to use as application bases machine hours for department 1, direct labour hours for department 2, and direct labour cost for department 3.

Required:
a. Calculate the departmental overhead rates.
b. What was the amount of overhead applied in each department during the year?
c. What was the amount of underapplied or overapplied manufacturing overhead by department and in total?
d. What would your answer be to part c if the application bases had been direct labour hours, machine hours, and direct labour cost, respectively, for the three producing departments?

P. 4A-5 **Physical units and gross profit joint cost allocation.** The High Spirits Company produces the following three beverages for which joint costs are $240,000:

1. Apple juice: Sold immediately at the split-off point for $.70/L.
2. Apple cider: Processed further at an additional cost of $.50/L. Sold for $1.50/L.
3. Apple jack: Processed at a cost of $.75/L above that required for apple cider. Sold for $6.00/L.

The following data apply for the year:

Beverage	Litres Produced	Litres Sold
Apple juice	150,000	130,000
Apple cider	90,000	75,000
Apple jack	60,000	50,000

Required:
From the above information calculate joint cost per litre, cost after split-off per litre, and total product cost per litre using:

a. The physical units method of joint cost allocation.
b. The gross profit method of joint cost allocation.

P. 4A-6 **Computing joint product costs.** The following data pertain to four joint products of the Merville Manufacturing Company.

Product Code Name	Cost after Split-off	Kilogram Output	Ultimate Sales Price/Kg
PR I	$ 40,000	5 000	$30
PR II	60,000	10 000	12
PR III	35,000	20 000	5
PR IV	65,000	65 000	2
Total	$200,000	100 000	

Joint cost = $200,000

Required:
Calculate the total and per-unit cost of each product for joint cost, cost after split-off, and total product cost using:

a. The physical units method of joint cost allocation.
b. The gross profit method of joint cost allocation.

Problem Set B

P. 4B-1   Using overhead cost data. Saskatoon Catalogue Sales Company uses a centralized pool of secretaries to handle typing, filing, and other clerical activities. Many different departments use this central pool. Users of the secretarial pool are charged $10 an hour for a secretary's time. The charge is based on $4 an hour for wages plus $6 an hour for overhead. Overhead includes depreciation on office equipment and furniture and other occupancy costs. During the year the secretarial pool had actual labour cost of $126,000, actual overhead cost of $195,000, and 30 000 hours of labour time.

The director of marketing recently used the pool to have long personalized letters typed to 50 distributors. The charges for the service are as follows:

Materials and postage	$ 18
Typing	200
	$218

The director of marketing is upset about the amount of the charge. He says, "I can understand the salary charge, but that overhead charge is a lot of accounting funny money. After all we already own the building and typewriters."

Required:
a. Calculate any underapplied or overapplied overhead.
b. What was the total cost of an hour of time in the secretarial pool based on actual costs?
c. How would you justify the charges to the marketing director?
d. If overhead cost is expected to increase 10 percent from this year's actual cost and labour cost is expected to increase 15 percent from the budget figures, what should the new hourly rate be for secretarial services?

P. 4B-2   Departmental overhead rates. Below are data pertaining to the departmental operations of Digital Data Company. In departments A and C the manufacturing overhead application base is direct labour hours, whereas in B it is direct labour cost. The budgeted and actual data are for the current fiscal year.

	Department A	Department B	Department C
Budgeted direct labour hours	50 000	10 000	75 000
Actual direct labour hours	51 000	10 000	74 000
Budgeted manufacturing overhead	$240,000	$400,000	$300,000
Budgeted direct labour cost	300,000	80,000	400,000
Actual direct labour cost	319,000	82,000	420,000
Actual manufacturing overhead	256,000	392,000	300,000

Required:

a. Compute the manufacturing overhead rate for each department.

b. Compute the applied manufacturing overhead in each department for the fiscal year.

c. Determine the underapplied and overapplied overhead for each department and in total.

d. Answer part *c* again, assuming departments A and C base their overhead rates on direct labour cost and department B bases its overhead rate on direct labour hours.

P. 4B-3 **Departmental overhead rates.** Following are budgeted overhead cost data and budgeted activity levels for Plastiside Products. The company has two service departments—maintenance and inventory storeroom—and three production departments–casting, moulding, and finishing. The schedule of budgeted costs indicates the allocation base to be used in assigning overhead costs to departments. Maintenance hours is used to allocate maintenance department costs to producing departments, and number of material requisitions is used to allocate the inventory storeroom costs to producing departments.

Plastiside Products
Budgeted Manufacturing Overhead Costs
For the Year 1984

Cost	Allocation Base	Budgeted Indirect Costs
Electricity	Square metreage of floor space	$ 75,000
Plant depreciation	Square metreage of floor space	50,000
Fire insurance	Value of investment	50,000
Employee services	Number of employees	225,000
Indirect materials	Direct labour hours	100,000
Fuel oil	Square metreage of floor space	100,000
Total		$600,000

Plastiside Products
Budgeted Activity Measures
For the Year 1984

Allocation Base	Maintenance	Inventory Storeroom	Casting	Moulding	Finishing	Total
Number of employees	5	5	15	10	15	50
Square metreage	2000	8000	15 000	15 000	10 000	50 000
Value of investment	$140,000	$260,000	$580,000	$820,000	$200,000	$2,000,000
Machine hours			10 000	5 000	10 000	25 000
Maintenance hours			5 000	4 000	1 000	10 000
Material requisitions			200	200	600	1 000
Direct labour hours			15 000	10 000	25 000	50 000

Required:

a. Prepare a schedule of budgeted departmental overhead costs.

b. Compute departmental overhead rates using the following application bases:
   1. Casting—machine hours
   2. Moulding — direct labour hours
   3. Finishing — direct labour hours

P. 4B-4   **Departmental overhead and product costs.** Rayline Products, Inc., has always used a single manufacturing overhead rate for the entire production plant. The new controller has been pushing for a departmental overhead rate for the last six months. The president has been somewhat swayed by the controller's arguments, but believes that product costs will be about the same whether departmental or single overhead rates are used. The controller wants to show the president he is wrong, so he pulls two recently completed job cost sheets from the file and asks you to prepare a schedule showing the difference in product cost between departmental and single overhead rates. Pertinent data are presented below.

	Job 6113	**Job 6114**
Units produced	100	50
Machining department:		
Direct materials	$5,000	$3,500
Direct labour at $10/h	$3,500	$1,000
Machine hours	320	80
Assembly department:		
Direct labour at $10/h	$ 600	$1,200
Finishing department:		
Direct labour at $7/h	$1,050	$ 700

With a single rate Rayline uses direct labour hours as an application base for the entire plant. If departmental overhead rates are used, the controller suggests machine hours for the machining department, direct labour hours for assembly, and direct labour cost for finishing. Below are the pertinent overhead data.

	Department			
Budgeted	**Machining**	**Assembly**	**Finishing**	**Total**
MOH cost	$500,000	$300,000	$200,000	$1,000,000
Machine hours	25 000	10 000	20 000	55 000
Direct labour hours	30 000	60 000	35 000	125 000
Direct labour cost	$300,000	$600,000	$250,000	$1,150,000

Required:

a. Prepare a schedule showing the product costs using a single overhead rate.

b. Prepare a schedule of product costs using departmental overhead rates.

c. What is your conclusion based on the two jobs you evaluated?

P. 4B-5 **Joint product costs.** The Timberline Paper Company produces three basic products—cardboard, sheet paper, and wallpaper—from pulp it purchases at $120 per ton. Conversion costs amount to $105 per ton of input. The products sell for the following prices:

Cardboard	$1.75/10 kg
Sheet paper	2.25/10 kg
Wallpaper	3.25/10 kg

During a given accounting period, the output and sales were as follows:

Product	Production	Sales	Costs after Split-off
Cardboard	100 000 kg	90 000 kg	$ 8,000
Sheet paper	300 000 kg	280 000 kg	12,000
Wallpaper	200 000 kg	150 000 kg	10,000

There was no beginning inventory of raw materials, 400 tons of pulp were purchased and used to produce the above quantities, and none of the raw material purchased is left over.

Required:
Calculate the cost of the ending inventory using:

a. The gross profit allocation method.
b. The physical units allocation method.

P. 4B-6 **Gross profit joint cost allocation.** The Far West Milling Company processes various grains. The company processes soybeans into meal, oil, and animal feed. A 60-kg bag yields an average of 45 kilograms of meal, 10 kilograms of oil, and 5 kilograms of animal feed. Before split-off average processing costs are $.50 per bag and the average cost of soybeans is $7 per bag. After split-off additional processing costs are $35 per ton for meal, $50 per ton for oil, and $25 per ton for animal feed. The selling prices of the products are $230 per ton for meal, $.45 per kilogram for oil, and $130 per ton for animal feed. The company processed 1200 tons of soybeans in August. There are 1000 kilograms in a ton.

Required:
Prepare a schedule of product costs for soybean processing in August using the gross profit method of joint cost allocation.

Minicase 4-1

(SMA of Canada adapted)

Quality Department Stores, Ltd., has always followed the policy of fully allocating *all* costs to its various stores. Such costs have included head office central and administrative costs, consisting of executive and office salaries, travel expenses, accounting costs and audit fees, legal fees, office supplies, charitable donations, rentals, depreciation and postage.

All of these costs have been difficult to trace directly to the individual stores benefited; therefore, the basis of allocation has been that of the total revenue of each store. For example, during fiscal and calendar 1983, the following allocations were made:

Store	Revenue (in millions)	Costs Allocated on the Basis of Revenue (in millions)
Alpha	$ 75	$ 8.25
Beta	15	1.65
Gamma	45	4.95
Delta	45	4.95
	$180	$19.80

In 1983, the Alpha store's revenue was expected to rise; however, the store encountered severe competitive conditions and its revenue remained at $75 million. In contrast, the Delta store enjoyed unprecedented growth in business because of large influxes of population to that city. Its revenue rose to $105 million. Beta and Gamma revenues remained unchanged. Staff cutbacks and careful supervision and control reduced the total costs allocated on the basis of revenue to $18.0 million.

Required:

a. What costs were allocated to each store in 1983?

b. Using the results in part *a.* above, fully explain the limitations of using revenue as a basis for cost allocations, and describe a more appropriate alternative approach which Quality Department Stores, Ltd. might adopt.

Minicase 4-2

(SMA of Canada adapted)

A pharmaceutical company manufactures two products, A and B, in a common process. The joint costs amount to $12,000 per batch of finished goods. Each batch amounts to 10 000 litres, of which 25 percent are Product A and 75 percent are Product B. The two products are processed further, but without any gain or loss in volume. The costs of additional processing are $0.30 per litre for

Product A and $0.40 per litre for Product B. After the additional processing, the selling price of Product A is $2.10 per litre, and the selling price of Product B is $1.60 per litre.

Required:

a. If the joint costs are to be allocated on the basis of the net realizable value of each product at the split-off point, what amount of joint costs will be allocated to each product?

b. Prepare a schedule of gross profit by product and by batch using the preceding allocation and assuming that 80 percent of Product A and 60 percent of Product B were sold, with no opening inventories of either product.

c. The company has discovered an additional process by which Product A can be transformed into Product AA which could be sold for $6 per litre. On the other hand, this additional processing would increase costs by $2.10 per litre. Assuming that there is no other change in costs, should the company use the new process? Show supporting calculations.

part 2

Cost Behaviour and Decision Making

The development of a cost accounting data base is a prerequisite to the preparation of managerial accounting reports, but merely having a data base does not ensure useful reports. Different decisions require different types of accounting information. The key criterion in selecting accounting data for managerial reports is relevance. The behaviour of costs is important in determining whether they are relevant for decision making.

Chapter 5 presents typical cost behaviour patterns and characteristics and discusses how the behaviour of costs and their relationship to the volume of business activity determine the amount of profit earned by a business. In Chapter 6 common types of business decisions involving the use of cost behaviour information are discussed, showing how managers choose between alternative choices of action. Making correct choices often means the difference between profits and losses.

Chapter 5

Cost Behaviour and Cost-Volume-Profit Analysis

This chapter presents basic material on cost behaviour patterns and cost-volume-profit analysis. Both topics are important in management decision making and are used in other chapters of the book. When you have completed the chapter, you should understand:

1 The meaning of the term **cost behaviour pattern** and its importance in cost analysis and decision making.

2 The most common types of cost behaviour patterns.

3 Cost behaviour assumptions.

4 Simple methods of estimating costs.

5 The nature and use of cost-volume-profit analysis.

6 Break-even analysis and target net incomes.

7 Graphic Cost-volume-profit analysis.

8 Multiple product break-even analysis.

To provide the variety of cost information needed by management, accountants classify cost information along functional lines and behavioural lines. In earlier chapters we described costs classified according to functions, such as manufacturing, administration, or marketing. Functional cost classifications are useful for many purposes including external reporting. Classifying costs according to their behaviour, such as fixed or variable, refers to the way costs change with respect to changes in the volume of activity. Many management decisions are affected by cost behaviour patterns. For example, the management of a company is evaluating the possibility of eliminating fibreglass canoes from the line of boats it produces. Information that describes which costs will be eliminated totally, eliminated partially, or remain unchanged may be very relevant to the decision. Numerous business decisions require managerial accounting information on costs by behaviour patterns. Consequently, accountants must identify and report cost behaviour patterns, and managers must be able to relate the information to specific decision situations.

The purpose of this chapter is to describe typical cost behaviour patterns and to discuss how they may be useful in business analysis. Much of the chapter is devoted to cost-volume-profit analysis, which is a systematic examination of the relationships between costs, activity levels, and profit.

Cost behaviour

The term cost behaviour refers to the way costs change with respect to a change in the activity level. Some costs remain constant, some change proportionately, and others change in different patterns. Although costs behave in many different ways, for most purposes cost behaviour can be classified into a few common patterns. These include:

Typical cost behaviour patterns

1. Fixed costs.
2. Variable costs.
3. Mixed costs.
4. Semivariable costs, and
5. Semifixed costs.

Fixed costs

Fixed costs remain constant for all activity levels

Fixed costs are costs that do not change with changing levels of activity, that is, they are fixed for all activity levels. For example, the annual rental cost of a manufacturing plant is $24,000, and it remains unchanged regardless of the activity level. Other costs, such as property taxes and depreciation on equipment, typically are unaffected by changing activity levels and are therefore classified as fixed costs.

Figure 5-1 shows graphically the behaviour pattern of a fixed cost. With the activity level on the horizontal (X) axis and total cost on the vertical (Y) axis, a fixed cost is plotted as a horizontal line because total cost does not change regardless of the level of activity. The amount of fixed cost determines how high the line is on the vertical axis. In this case *a* represents the amount of the fixed cost and can be expressed as the equation

$$Y = a$$

This equation says that total cost Y equals a constant fixed cost represented by the letter *a*. Some costs that usually are fixed include:

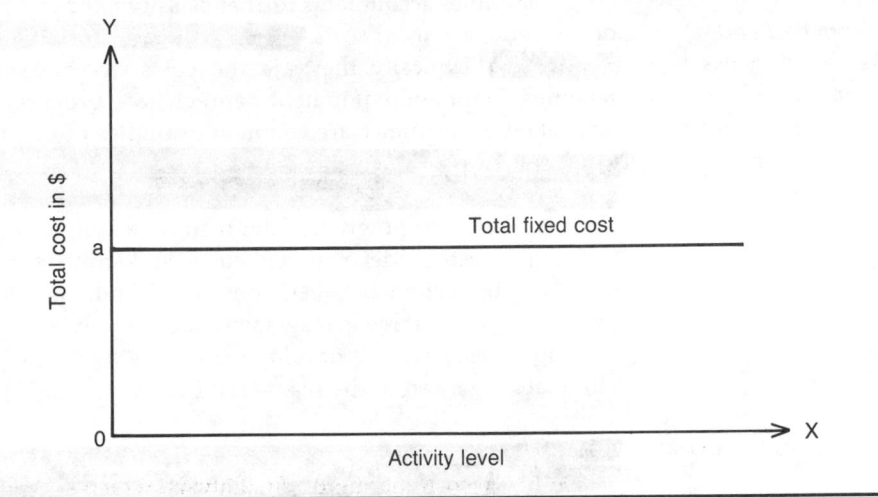

Figure 5-1
Fixed costs remain
constant for all
levels of activity
and therefore appear
as a horizontal
straight line. The
amount of fixed cost
is represented by *a*.

Some manufacturing overhead costs, such as:
    Plant depreciation
    Equipment depreciation
    A portion of utility costs
    Property taxes
    Plant and equipment insurance
    Production supervisory salaries
Depreciation on office facilities
Office equipment lease costs
Supervisory salaries
Property taxes on office
Advertising
Insurance on office

Often fixed costs are assigned to specific cost objectives, such as a product, a department, or an activity like marketing. If the fixed cost is allocated to products, the amount assigned to each unit of product depends on the number of units produced. If production activity is low, each unit of product receives a relatively large amount of the fixed cost, and if production activity is high, each unit of product receives a relatively small amount of the fixed cost. To illustrate, $2,000 of monthly rent on the manufacturing plant is allocated to the products produced in the manufacturing plant. If 500 toboggans are manufactured in the plant, $4 of the fixed rental cost ($2,000/500 toboggans) is allocated to each toboggan. However, if the output is 800 toboggans, each toboggan is assigned only $2.50 of plant rental cost ($2,000/800 toboggans). The plant rental cost is **fixed** at $2,000 for the period, but the amount allocated to each unit of output depends on how many units share the fixed cost.

Committed and discretionary fixed costs

Sometimes accountants further classify fixed costs as committed fixed costs or discretionary fixed costs. Committed fixed costs cannot be easily or quickly eliminated. Typically they are the costs necessary in providing plant and facilities. Plant and equipment depreciation, property taxes, long-term leases, and facilities insurance are common examples of committed costs. Discretionary fixed costs are costs that can be discontinued at management's discretion in a relatively short time in comparison with committed costs. Typical examples include marketing programs, administrative salaries, research and development costs, new systems development costs, and short-term renewable leases.

The distinction between committed and discretionary fixed costs is an important one in some management decisions. It is a far easier task to eliminate or reduce research and development costs during a business decline than to eliminate a portion of the plant facilities.

Variable costs

Total variable costs increase proportionately with increases in the level of activity

Variable costs are costs that increase directly and proportionately with the level of activity. There is a constant ratio between the change in the cost and the change in the level of activity. For example, if the direct material cost for a 2-metre wooden toboggan is $6.80, then for each additional toboggan manufactured the direct material cost is an additional $6.80. The total amount of direct material cost is determined by the number of units produced. One hundred toboggans have a direct material cost of $680. One hundred and one toboggans have a direct material cost of $686.80. The $6.80 increment for materials is the same at all levels of production. The total variable cost increases as the level of activity increases, but the variable cost per unit remains the same. This proportional relationship distinguishes variable cost patterns from other cost behaviour patterns and gives rise to the term directly variable costs that is used sometimes.

Figure 5-2 shows graphically the behaviour pattern of variable costs. The horizontal axis is the activity level and the vertical axis represents the total cost. For every unit of increase in activity there is a proportionate increase in the cost. The distance X on the horizontal axis represents the activity level. The distance Y on the vertical axis depicts the total variable cost caused by the level of activity. The ratio of Y to X is the proportional relationship between the variable cost and the activity level. This ratio is the same for all levels of activity. Therefore, a one-unit change in activity level causes the same total cost change anywhere within the firm's operating capacity.

Variable costs are graphed as a straight line that starts at the origin ($X = 0$ and $Y = 0$) and slopes upward to the right. The general form for the equation for a variable cost line is

$$Y = bX$$

where　　　　Y = the total variable cost
b = the variable cost per unit of activity
X = activity level measured in some unit such as direct labour hours or units of output

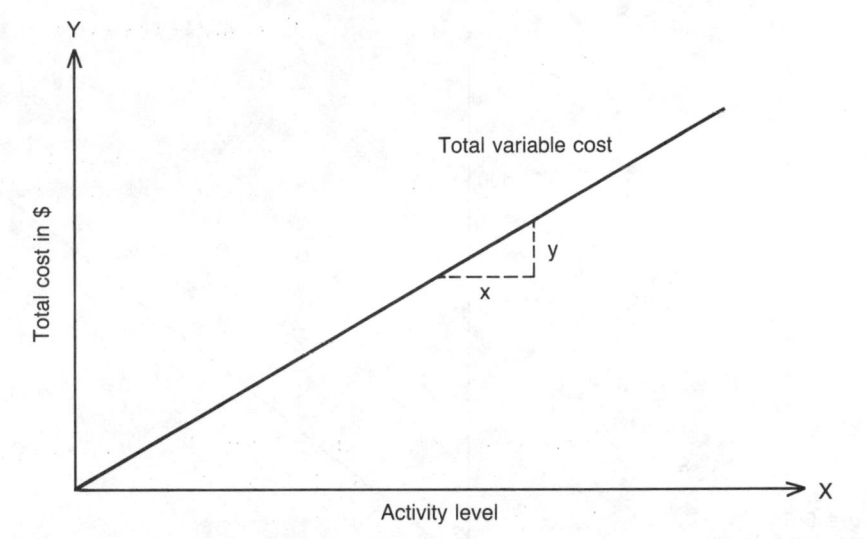

Figure 5-2
Variable costs are shown as a straight line sloping upward to the right. The ratio of *Y* to *X* is the rate of increase in the cost caused by the increase in activity.

Using the toboggan example mentioned earlier, with a direct material cost of $6.80 per unit, the variable cost would be represented by the equation

$$Y = \$6.80X$$

The above equation says that the total variable cost for materials (*Y*) for any number of toboggans produced (*X*) is equal to $6.80 times *X*. Notice that the ratio of *Y* to *X* is equal to *b* (*Y/X* = *b*), which in this case is $6.80, and *b* is called the slope of the line. If the level of production increases to 125 toboggans from 100, the change in the activity level is 25 units, and the change in total variable cost *Y* is (125 × $6.80) − (100 × $6.80) = $170. The ratio is $170/25 units, or still $6.80 per unit. The higher the ratio between total variable costs and the level of activity, the steeper the slope of the line. For example, if the direct material cost is $12 per toboggan, the equation for direct material cost is *Y* = $12*X*. The cost increases more quickly than before and is represented by a line that slopes more steeply, as shown in Figure 5-3.

Cost relationships expressed as equations can be very useful

Expressing cost relationships as equations can be very useful in analyzing costs and making decisions. It is important for you to understand the concepts of cost behaviour patterns as well as the mathematical representations of the cost patterns.

Many different types of costs are classified as variable costs including:

Direct materials
Direct labour
Variable MOH, such as:

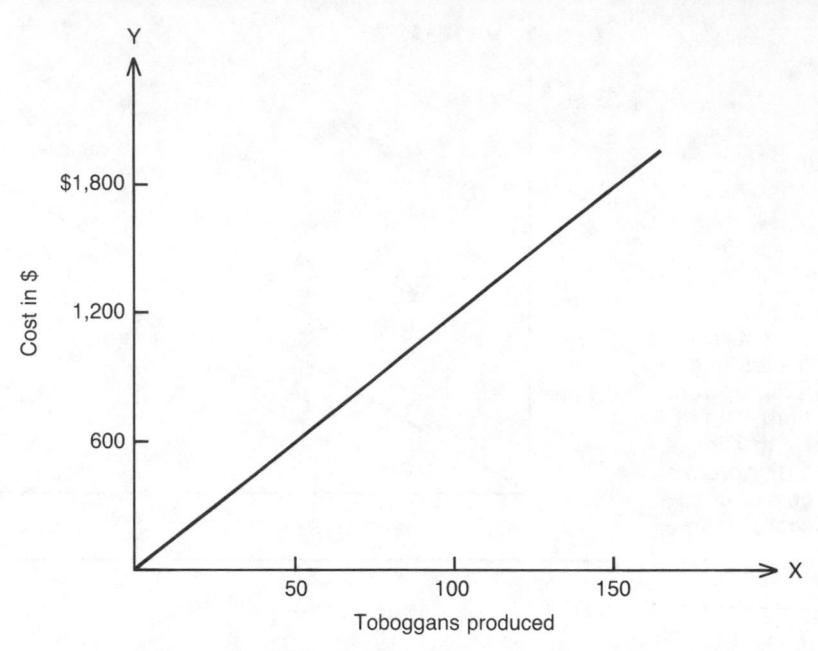

Figure 5-3
A graph of direct
material cost for
toboggans with a
unit material cost of
$12 per toboggan.

Factory supplies
Indirect materials
Payroll taxes on direct labour
Employee fringe benefits on direct labour
Sales commissions
Office supplies
Some utility costs

Directly variable costs sometimes are referred to as manageable costs because managers often determine whether the costs are incurred. Although many variable costs are controllable by managers, the terms controllable costs and variable costs are not synonymous. Some variable costs in a manager's sphere of responsibility may not be controllable. For instance, factory supplies used in servicing and maintaining production equipment may vary with the amount of production activity in the department, but the departmental production manager may have no control over the amount of factory supplies used. Conversely some controllable costs may have cost behaviour patterns other than directly variable. For instance, a manager may acquire a one-year maintenance agreement for hydraulic press equipment. The cost of the maintenance agreement became fixed for the year when the manager made the decision to incur the cost of the service.

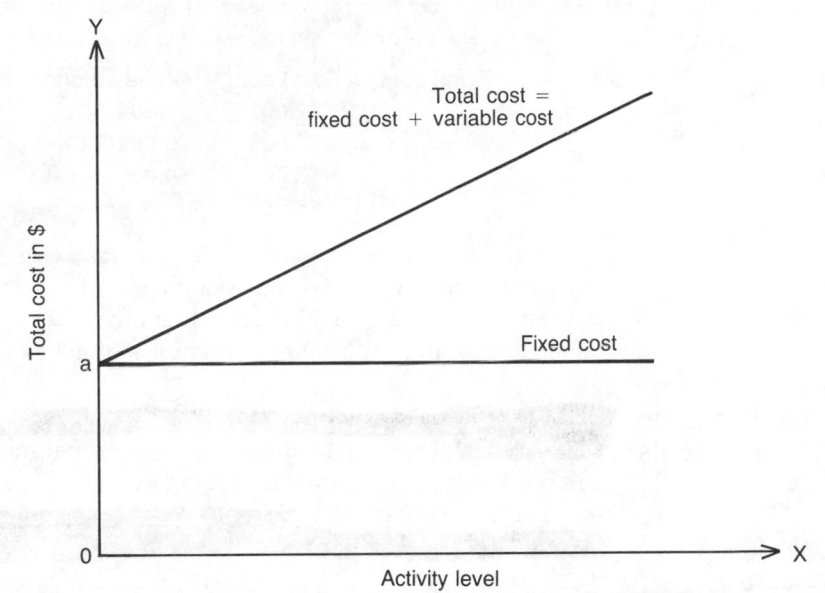

Figure 5-4
Mixed costs contain fixed and variable cost components that may be separated for managerial planning and control purposes.

Mixed costs

Mixed costs have both fixed and variable components

Many costs cannot be described by a single cost behaviour pattern and are called mixed costs. For purposes of decision analysis managers find it convenient to separate mixed costs into fixed and variable components.

Figure 5-4 illustrates a mixed cost. Fixed costs are shown by a straight line horizontal to the X axis. Total cost is equal to the fixed cost, *a*, plus the variable cost. To graph total costs, the line starts on the Y axis at point *a*, which is the amount of fixed cost. The total cost line slopes upward, indicating that variable costs are added to the fixed costs to equal total costs. Since the total amount of variable cost changes with the level of activity, the total cost line slopes upward as the activity level increases.

The equations for a fixed cost and a variable cost are combined to find the equation for a mixed cost.

Fixed cost	$Y = a$
Variable cost	$Y = bX$
Mixed cost	$Y = a + bX$

The mixed cost equation states that the total cost is equal to the fixed cost plus the variable cost. By substituting values for *a* and *b*, we can describe various mixed costs mathematically which is very useful in analyzing costs.

The total cost equation for the toboggan example is

$$\text{Total cost} = \text{Fixed cost} + \text{Variable cost}$$
$$Y = a + bX$$
$$Y = \$2{,}000 + \$6.80X$$

To find total cost for any level of toboggan production, it is merely necessary to insert a value for X. For instance, for 600 toboggans the total cost is

$$
\begin{aligned}
\text{Total cost} &= \text{Fixed cost} + (\text{Variable cost per unit} \times \text{Units}) \\
Y &= \$2,000 \quad + \$6.80X \\
&= \$2,000 \quad + \$6.80\,(600) \\
&= \$2,000 \quad + \$4,080 \\
&= \$6,080
\end{aligned}
$$

A graph showing total cost in the toboggan example appears in Figure 5-5. There are many costs that exhibit mixed cost characteristics, with some portions of the costs variable and others fixed. The costs of electricity, maintenance, and indirect labour are examples of mixed costs.

Semivariable costs

Semivariable costs increase with increasing levels of activity, but not at a constant rate. They can be divided into costs that increase at a decreasing rate and costs that increase at an increasing rate.

The left-hand graph in Figure 5-6 shows a semivariable cost that increases at a decreasing rate. This type of cost is referred to as a learning curve cost. The

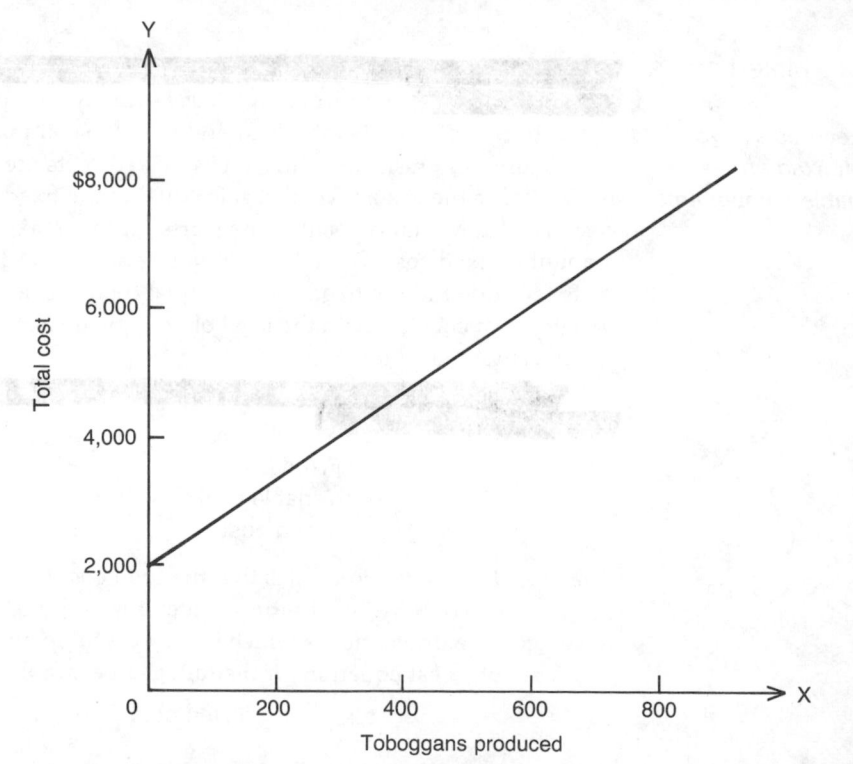

Figure 5-5
The total cost line for the production of toboggans. Fixed cost is $2,000, and variable cost is $6.80 per toboggan.

Learning curve costs result from improving labour efficiency

term originates from the observed decrease in labour costs that sometimes occurs as employees become more familiar with a new task. For example, it may require three hours of direct labour to assemble a lawn mower for the first production run of a new type of mower. However, employees may assemble the mowers in two hours and fifty minutes on the next run and in two hours and forty minutes on the third run.

The right-hand graph in figure 5-6 shows a semivariable cost that increases at an increasing rate. This type of cost behaviour is characterized by larger costs per unit of output as the activity level rises. For example, some forms of energy may be priced to encourage conservation. The price of energy rises as more and more energy is consumed; therefore, the per-unit cost of energy used in production rises. Managers should be very cautious of this type of cost because it can get out of control quickly. Semivariable cost curves are discussed further in Chapter 17.

Semifixed costs

Semifixed costs increase with the level of activity, but by intermittent jumps rather than continuously. Many different costs exhibit semifixed cost behaviour. For example, a firm may increase its production by working overtime or adding a night shift without increasing its cost for production facilities. But when

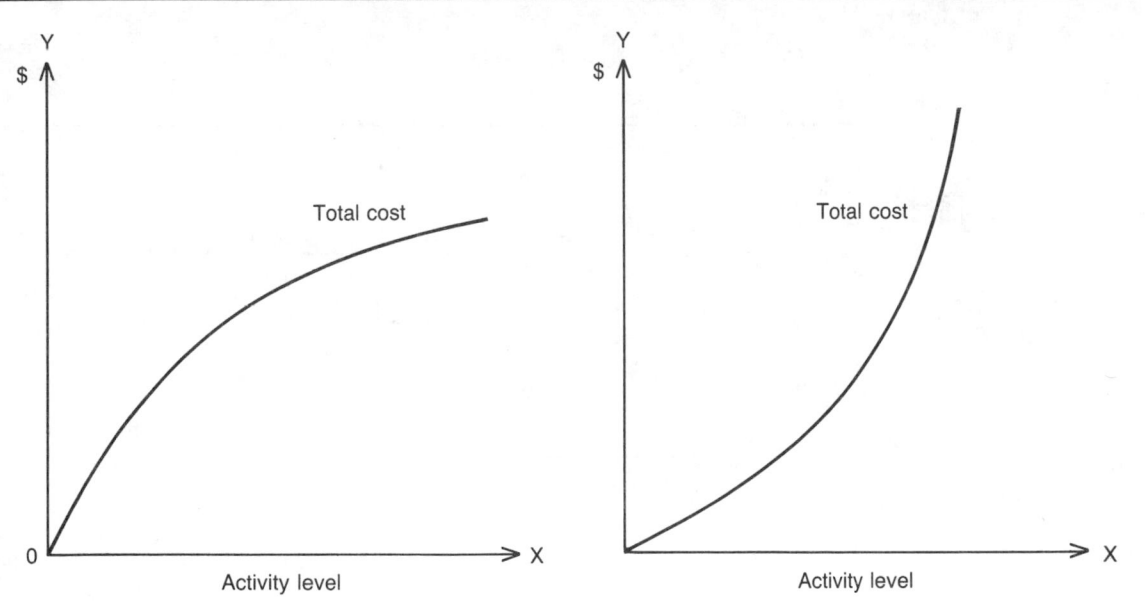

Figure 5-6
Semivariable costs that increase at a decreasing rate are called learning curve costs and are illustrated in the left-hand graph. Semivariable costs that increase at an increasing rate are shown in the right-hand graph.

maximum capacity is reached, increased production can be achieved only by expanding the plant. This causes a jump in the cost of production facilities. Similarly a firm has a delivery truck that is used to deliver large appliances sold in the store. Currently the truck is being utilized at capacity. Any increase in sales would result in the need for a new truck. The firm's policy of 10 percent sales growth a year will cause a jump in delivery equipment cost. The cost behaviour pattern of a semifixed cost is graphed in Figure 5–7.

Semifixed costs have some characteristics of both fixed and variable costs

Figure 5-7 illustrates why the term step function is used for semifixed costs. The semifixed cost pattern has characteristics of both variable costs and fixed costs. Like variable costs, semifixed costs increase with activity although not proportionately, and like fixed costs, they remain constant for stretches of activity levels although not for all levels of activity.

The graph of the cost is represented by solid horizontal line segments. The vertical dashed lines, labeled A, B, and C, represent the increase in cost at each step as the level of activity increases. In this illustration the cost increases are not equal. Likewise the intervals of activity between the increases in cost are not equal. The graph of semifixed costs is not continuous; it is broken whenever the amount of cost shifts to another level. Consequently, we cannot describe semifixed costs by a simple mathematical equation as we did variable and fixed costs. However, this does not prevent managers from identifying and using semifixed costs in decision making.

Figure 5-7
Semifixed costs jump intermittently from one level to another. They remain constant until another jump occurs at a higher level of activity. They are often called step function costs.

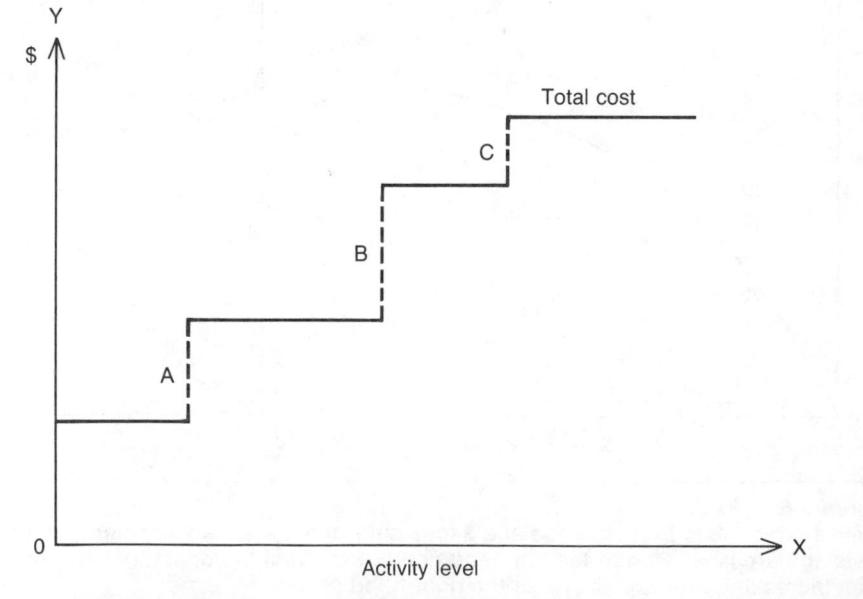

Cost behaviour assumptions

The discussion of cost behaviour rests on two very important assumptions: the relevant range assumption and the time assumption.

The relevant range covers levels of activity that are likely to occur

The relevant range assumption states that the identified cost behaviour patterns are correct only for a certain range of activity. Any level of activity above or below the relevant range may have different cost behaviour patterns. For example, Figure 5-8 shows cost curves with several different behaviour patterns. The left-hand graph depicts a curve of a semivariable cost with a learning curve slope from the origin to activity level A. From A to B the cost is directly variable, and above activity level B the cost is semivariable, increasing at an increasing rate. The right-hand graph shows a cost that is initially a mixed cost. Between activity levels C and D the cost is fixed. At D the cost jumps to a higher amount, exhibiting a semifixed cost pattern.

In each of the situations described in Figure 5-8, a **simple** description of the cost curves is not possible. However, very low and very high levels of activity often are not relevant to decision making because there is very little chance that those activity levels will occur. The important range covers the levels of activity that are likely to occur. This range of activity is called the relevant range. For example, if the activity level between A and B is the relevant range of activity in

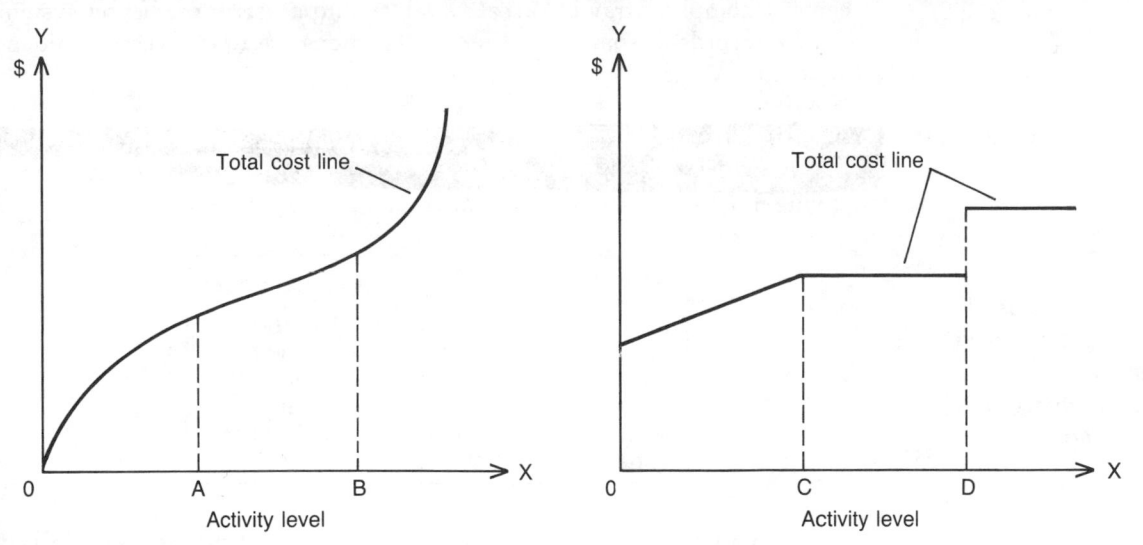

Figure 5-8
Cost behaviour patterns are seldom the same for an infinite range of activity.
In the left-hand graph the cost is semivariable outside of the relevant range
A to B. In the right-hand graph the fixed cost is semifixed or mixed outside the
relevant range C to D.

the left-hand graph of Figure 5-8, then managers can consider the cost to be directly variable. The fact that the cost exhibits other behaviour patterns outside the relevant range is unimportant as long as the estimate of the relevant range is correct. If the activity level between C and D is the relevant range for the cost in the right-hand graph, then managers can consider that cost to be a fixed cost.

The time assumption states that the identified cost behaviour patterns hold true only for a certain period of time. Many cost behaviour patterns may change over time, and few costs classified as fixed are fixed over the long run. Although they may be fixed for the current year, they may change over a period of years. For example, a one-year lease on a building is a fixed cost for the year, but it is not as yet fixed for subsequent years. Similarly a food processor may cause the cost of raw materials to shift from variable to fixed costs by entering into long-term purchase contracts for perishable food products used in production.

Cost behaviour patterns may change over time

Cost estimation techniques

A number of techniques have been developed for identifying the cost behaviour patterns of specific costs. We discuss some simple common approaches to cost estimation.

Intuition and professional experience

Sometimes there is no substitute for experience. Personnel with extensive service and a proven record of successful cost prediction are often invaluable in identifying cost patterns and predicting cost levels. They are often able to integrate a complex array of causal variables into a useful prediction system. The track records of some individuals' predictions are too successful to deny such nonmathematical prediction techniques.

High-low method

A simple and widely used cost estimation technique is the high-low method, which is used to isolate the fixed and variable costs of a mixed cost. Consider the following monthly cost and activity data for a six-month period:

High-low is used to estimate the fixed and variable components of mixed costs

Month	Cost	Labour Hours
January	$54,000	2100
February	$56,000	2300
March	$62,000	2400
April	$58,000	1900
May	$44,000	1500
June	$50,000	1700

The data indicate some cost variability with activity changes. The costs at low levels of activity are less than the costs at high levels of activity. However, it is not evident what the relationship is between the cost and the activity level. In an effort to distinguish the fixed and variable components of the cost, the high-low method is used. We select the highest cost and the lowest cost that occur in March and May, respectively, and divide the change in the cost ($62,000 – $44,000) by the corresponding change in the activity level (2400 hours – 1500 hours). The computation yields the per-unit variable cost b in the total cost formula $Y = a + bX$, where Y is the total cost.

$$b = \frac{\$62,000 - \$44,000}{2400 \text{ hours} - 1500 \text{ hours}}$$

$$= \frac{\$18,000}{900 \text{ hours}}$$

$$= \$20 \text{ per labour hour}$$

The solution indicates that for every labour hour used, the cost increases by $20. In March the total cost was $62,000 at 2400 hours of activity. Substituting the variable cost of $20 per hour and the total cost of $62,000 into the total cost formula allows us to solve for the fixed cost a.

$$
\begin{aligned}
\text{Total cost} &= \text{Fixed cost} + \text{Variable cost} \\
Y &= a + bX \\
\$62,000 &= a + \$20(2400 \text{ hours}) \\
\$62,000 &= a + \$48,000 \\
a &= \$14,000
\end{aligned}
$$

The same amount of fixed cost is derived by using the May data. The 1500 hours of direct labour is multiplied by $20 per hour to find variable cost of $30,000. Total cost of $44,000 minus variable cost of $30,000 yields the fixed cost, $14,000.

The high-low method provides a simple way of estimating the fixed and variable components of mixed costs, but the method may not be precise. It is possible that the actual fixed and variable cost components are significantly different from the ones estimated with the high-low method. More sophisticated statistical techniques of estimating fixed and variable cost components are available, and some of them are discussed and illustrated in Chapter 17.

Scatter diagram

Scatter diagrams help managers identify cost patterns and trends

Sometimes it is useful to plot cost data on a graph. With total cost on the vertical axis and activity level on the horizontal axis, each item of cost data appears as a dot on the graph as shown in Figure 5-9. Such a graph is called a **scatter diagram** because of the way that the data points scatter across the graph. The purpose of a scatter diagram is to aid in identifying the cost behaviour pattern for a set of cost data. Plotting the cost data may disclose relationships that are not apparent by merely listing the data.

The data used to estimate the fixed and variable costs by the high-low method are plotted in Figure 5-9. The strong linear relationship among the six data points is evident. The variable cost rate b can be approximated by drawing a line through the points so that it intersects at point a on the vertical axis. Point a in Figure 5-9 represents the graphic estimate of the fixed cost component. As you can see, it is very close to the $14,000 fixed cost estimate obtained by the high-low method.

In this example it was easy to draw a cost estimation line through the set of data points because the costs are strongly associated with the activity level.

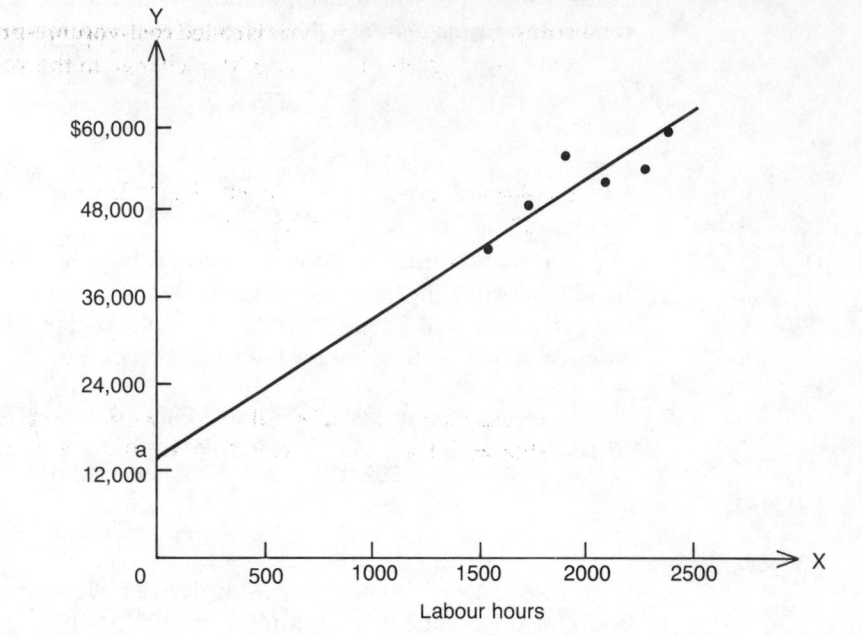

Figure 5-9
Scatter diagrams help managers spot cost behaviour patterns by visual observation of the data points. This example shows a mixed cost situation with a strong linear relationship.

Sometimes the association between costs and the activity level is not so obvious, and it may be difficult to draw an accurate line that closely fits the data set. Figure 5-10 presents a set of such data.

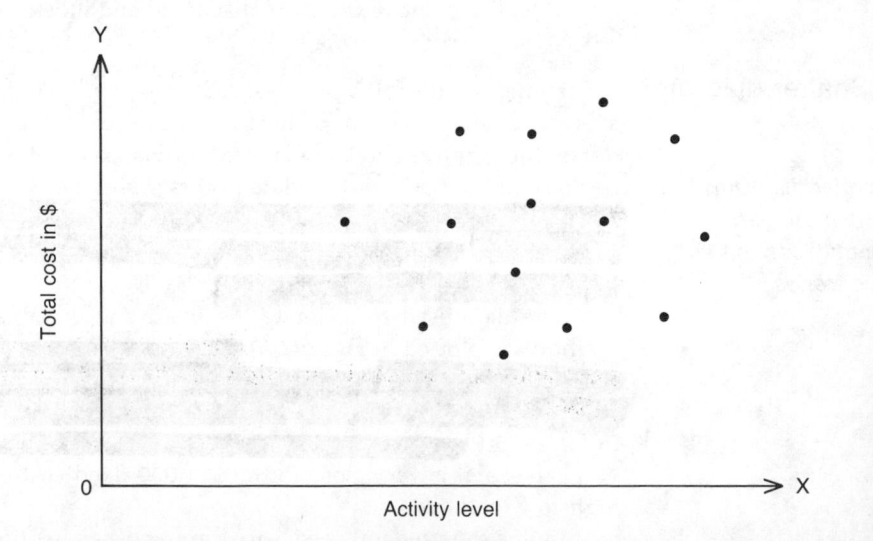

Figure 5-10
This scatter diagram shows no obvious cost pattern. Other analyses are required to determine the cost behaviour.

Cost-volume-profit relationships

Managers can perform many useful analyses with cost behaviour information. A very important type of analysis is called cost-volume-profit (CVP), which deals with how cost and profit change with a change in the volume of activity. There are many different CVP relationships that we discuss in this and the next chapter.

Break-even analysis

The break-even point occurs when revenue equals total cost

The break-even point is the level of activity where total costs equal total revenues, leaving no profit or loss. A break-even point may be computed for a product, a group of products, a division, an entire company, or any other carefully defined objective. At the break-even point revenues from the product are the same amount as the total costs of producing, selling, and distributing the product. Both the fixed and variable costs of manufacturing and nonmanufacturing operations must be included in the calculation of the break-even point. The unifying characteristic of all costs used in the analysis is that all are identifiable with the product or other cost objectives being considered in the analysis.

To illustrate, assume Samson Company, a manufacturer of gardening equipment, is considering the introduction of a new lawn sprinkler with an expected selling price of $5 per unit, variable cost of $3 per unit, and fixed cost of $10,000. Revenue is computed as the number of units sold times $5 per unit. Total variable cost is equal to $3 per unit times the number of units sold. The break-even point occurs when profit is zero. Therefore, breaking even means

or

$$
\begin{aligned}
\text{Revenue} &= \text{Total costs} \\
&= \text{Fixed cost} + \text{Variable cost}
\end{aligned}
$$

$$
\begin{aligned}
R &= TC \\
&= FC + VC
\end{aligned}
$$

Revenue is equal to the selling price times the number of units (X) and total variable cost equals the unit variable cost times the number of units (X).

Substituting, we have

$$\$5X = \$10,000 + \$3X$$

Solving for X:

$$\$5X - \$3X = \$10,000$$
$$\$2X = \$10,000$$
$$X = \frac{\$10,000}{\$2}$$
$$= 5000 \text{ units}$$

The break-even point is 5000 units. The answer is expressed in units because the variable (X) represents units. It is a simple matter to convert the break-even point into sales dollars by multiplying the answer in units by the selling price, yielding

$$5000 \text{ units} \times \$5 \text{ per unit} = \$25,000$$

Another approach to solving break-even problems is to subtract the unit variable cost from the unit selling price to find the unit contribution margin

Contribution margin is the difference between the selling price and variable cost

(CM). The unit contribution margin is the amount of revenue that the sale of each unit contributes toward the payment of fixed costs and the generation of profits. It is the difference between the selling price and the variable cost of the product. When fixed costs are fully covered by contribution margin, the break-even point is reached. Each additional unit sold above the break-even point contributes its margin toward net income. Thus the break-even point can be computed as follows:

$$\text{Contribution margin} = \text{Selling price} - \text{Variable cost}$$
$$= \$5 - \$3 = \$2$$
$$\text{Break-even point} = \frac{\text{Fixed cost}}{\text{Contribution margin}}$$

Substituting:

$$= \frac{\$10,000}{\$2} = 5000 \text{ units}$$

Sometimes specific unit selling price and unit variable cost data are not available. For instance, our illustration might have been stated as follows: Fixed cost = \$10,000 and variable cost = 60 percent of selling price. These data cannot be used in the break-even formulas presented above. However, the break-even point can be computed in dollars of sales with only a minor change in the formula. Instead of solving for units, we solve for dollars of sales, which is what the unknown term Y represents in the following equation:

$$\text{Revenue} = \text{Total cost}$$
$$= \text{Fixed cost} + \text{Variable cost}$$
$$Y = \$10,000 + .6Y$$

In other words, the break-even point occurs when total sales revenue (Y) equals the variable cost (60 percent of Y) plus the fixed cost (\$10,000).

Solving for Y:

$$Y - .6Y = \$10,000$$
$$.4Y = \$10,000$$
$$Y = \$10,000/.4$$
$$= \$25,000$$

Graphic presentations are common in managerial accounting reports, and we use many graphic reports throughout this text. One of the most useful graphic reports is a **cost-volume-profit chart,** also called a CVP chart. The CVP chart for the above example is illustrated in Figure 5-11. The chart has a total cost line and a total revenue line. The cost line is composed of fixed cost of \$10,000 plus variable cost of \$3 a unit. The total revenue line is \$5 a unit. Graphic analysis is discussed in detail later in the chapter.

Simple break-even analysis is interesting and important, but businesses are seldom interested in merely breaking even. Managers use many other CVP analyses which address such situations as:

Cost-volume-profit analysis involves much more than break-even analysis

1. Achieving a target net income.
2. Changing fixed costs.

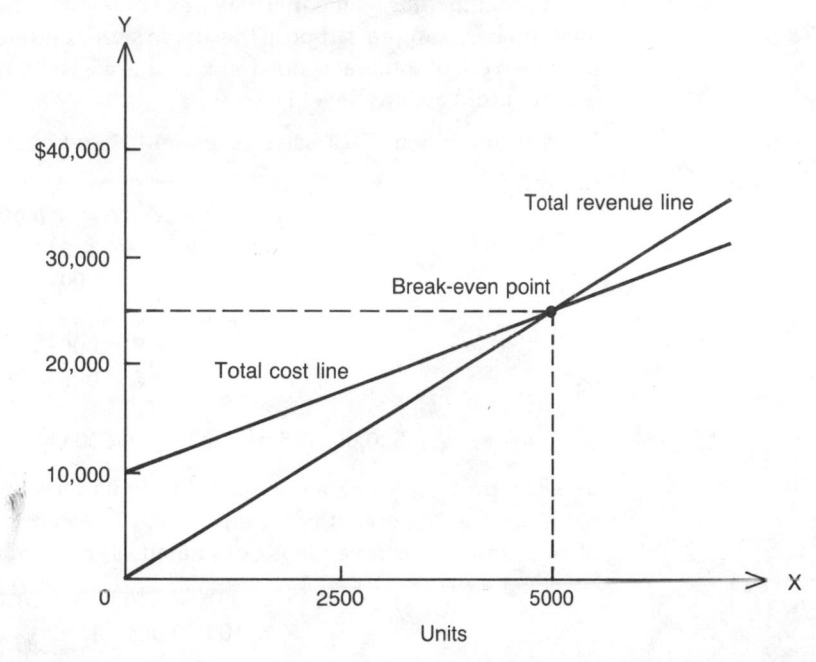

Figure 5-11
A graph is useful in showing the break-even point. The fixed cost is eventually covered because the revenue line has a steeper slope than the variable cost line. The difference between the slope of the revenue line and the variable cost line is the contribution margin, which is $5 − $3 = $2 in this example.

3. Changing variable costs.
4. Changing selling prices.
5. Changing management strategies.

Target net income

Although breaking even is a desirable hurdle, it is not the ultimate goal of a profit-seeking enterprise. Investors do not commit resources to businesses that promise a zero return. Instead firms strive to earn a level of profit that yields an acceptable return. CVP analysis can be used to determine the necessary level of activity to cover both fixed costs and a target net income. If the target net income is expressed in a dollar amount, it is merely added to the fixed cost and the required activity level is computed. For example, if Samson Company decides that an $8,000 net income is desired, the computation of the required number of lawn sprinklers is as follows:

$$\text{Sales} = \text{VC} + \text{FC} + \text{Profit}$$
$$\$5X = \$3X + \$10,000 + \$8,000$$
$$\$5X - \$3X = \$18,000$$
$$\$2X = \$18,000$$
$$X = 9000 \text{ units}$$

or

$$9000 \times \$5 = \$45,000 \text{ sales}$$

Sometimes target income may be expressed in some way other than a dollar amount. For example, suppose the above situation stated that net income should be 20 percent of total sales dollars. Variable cost is 60 percent of the selling price. The required activity level is

Sales revenue = 60% of sales revenue + Fixed costs + 20% of sales revenue

Substituting:

$$Y = .6Y + \$10,000 + .2Y$$
$$Y = .8Y + \$10,000$$
$$Y - .8Y = \$10,000$$
$$.2Y = \$10,000$$
$$Y = \$10,000/.2$$
$$= \$50,000 \text{ sales}$$

or

$$\$50,000/\$5 \text{ per unit} = 10\,000 \text{ units}$$

The problem can also be solved in units directly by noting that the target net income is 20 percent of selling price; 20 percent of $5 = $1. That means $1 of each unit's sales revenue is designated as required net income. Then

$$\$5X = \$3X + \$10,000 + \$1X$$
$$X = 10\,000 \text{ units}$$

Changing fixed costs

The term **fixed costs** implies costs that do not change. However, many fixed costs are discretionary and can be changed in the near future if management desires. Managers may use cost-volume-profit analysis when evaluating discretionary cost decisions or planning for a new committed fixed cost, such as a property tax increase.

The analysis is accomplished very easily by using the new fixed cost in the CVP equation. Continuing our example, assume that fixed costs for the next year are expected to increase by $5,000. The new fixed cost is $15,000, and the new break-even point is

$$\$5X = \$15,000 + \$3X$$
$$\$2X = \$15,000$$
$$X = 7500 \text{ units}$$

Since the contribution margin is $2 per unit, an increase in fixed cost of $5,000 will require an **additional** 2500 units to cover the **additional** fixed costs.

Changing variable costs

Frequently raw material cost, labour cost, or some other variable costs change, requiring a simple modification in the variable cost component of the break-even equation. If variable costs increase by $.75 per unit giving a new unit variable cost of $3.75 in the illustration, break-even volume is

$$\$5X = \$10,000 + \$3.75X$$
$$\$1.25X = \$10,000$$
$$X = \$10,000/\$1.25$$
$$= 8000 \text{ units}$$

The $.75 increase in variable cost represents 15 percent of the selling price; but it is also 37.5 percent of the $2 contribution margin. The new lower contribution margin results in a higher break-even volume. It takes more units of sales to cover the $10,000 of fixed costs.

Changing selling price

A change in the selling price has an effect similar to that caused by a change in variable cost. They both affect the contribution margin that is needed to cover fixed cost. If market conditions require a drop in the price of the product by $.40 to $4.60, the new break-even point is:

$$\$4.60X = \$3X + \$10,000$$
$$\$1.60X = \$10,000$$
$$X = 6250 \text{ units}$$

or

$$6250 \text{ units} \times \$4.60/\text{unit} = \$28,750 \text{ of sales}$$

Changing management strategies

By considering a change in one element of the cost-volume-profit model at a time, it is easy to see its effect on the break-even point. In practice, however, several variables may change simultaneously. Multiple changes are not difficult to analyze, but sometimes it is difficult to visualize the impact of several changes at once.

Often several variables change at the same time

To illustrate multiple changes, we assimilate several individual changes into a single computation. For example, management finds itself faced with a prospective increase in labour costs, which would increase variable costs of production. The company has two alternatives that will allow it to maintain its target level of profit of $9,000. It can increase the price to compensate for the increased cost, but an increase in price may cause a decrease in the volume of sales. The other alternative is to acquire a new piece of equipment that will automate some of the production and thus reduce variable labour costs. The new equipment would **add** $20,000 to the current fixed costs of $10,000, but variable costs would **decrease** from $3.00 to $2.60 per unit. The required level of sales to achieve the target profit of $9,000 with this alternative is computed as follows:

Increase fixed costs from $10,000 to $30,000.
Decrease variable costs from $3.00 to $2.60 per unit.
Target profit of $9,000, with no change in selling price.

$$\$5X = \$2.60X + \$30,000 + \$9,000$$
$$\$5X - \$2.60X = \$39,000$$
$$\$2.40X = \$39,000$$
$$X = \$39,000/\$2.40$$
$$= 16\ 250 \text{ units}$$

An alternative strategy to the one described above is to increase the selling price to $5.50 per unit. To counteract any decline in sales volume that may result, a new advertising and marketing campaign would be required that would raise fixed costs by $8,000 and raise variable costs to $4.25. Using these data, we have:

Increase fixed costs from $10,000 to $18,000.
Increase variable costs from $3.00 to $4.25 per unit.
Target profit of $9,000, with an increase in selling price
from $5.00 to $5.50.

$$\$5.50X = \$4.25X + \$18,000 + \$9,000$$
$$\$1.25X = \$27,000$$
$$X = 21\ 600 \text{ units}$$

The required sales to meet the target net income in the first alternative is $81,250, calculated as target volume of 16 250 units times the $5 selling price. In the second alternative target revenue is $118,200 (21 600 × $5.50). The obvious question is: Which of the two alternatives should management choose? The mere computation of the two target sales levels does not provide a ready basis for choosing between alternatives. Other analyses and information may be necessary. For example, if the target profit can be reached in either case, the second alternative may be the better one to select because it has a greater margin of safety. The concept of margin of safety is discussed later in this chapter. In addition, further insight into this type of decision making is provided in Chapter 6. Managerial accounting information provides managers with much relevant information for decision making, but it seldom provides the decision itself. Instead managers must use the data from accounting reports and mold them together with other information to make intelligent decisions.

Graphic solution to CVP

CVP charts allow visual analyses of cost-volume-profit relationships

Visual presentation of information sometimes is more useful and informative than verbal or mathematical descriptions. Some advantages of graphic presentations are:

1. Managers with a low tolerance for financial data often are able to understand financial information presented graphically.
2. A range of activity rather than a static situation can be presented.
3. Much more information can be presented and understood without information overload.
4. The solutions to some complex analyses are made simpler and more understandable.

In its simplest form a CVP graph looks like the chart in Figure 5-11, which depicts the CVP relationships described earlier in our example: Fixed cost is $10,000, variable cost is $3 per unit, and selling price is $5 per unit. The break-even point can be read on the horizontal axis in units or on the vertical axis in sales dollars. The 5000 units and $25,000 coincide with the answers computed before. In addition to the break-even information, the graphic solution can show the profit and loss possibilities at various activity levels. For instance, in Figure 5-12 you can see that at 8000 units there is a $6,000 profit, equal to the vertical distance between the total revenue line and the total cost line.

Charts illustrating CVP changes. Figure 5-13 illustrates graphically the changes in break-even point or target profit caused by changing the value of various cost and revenue elements used in cost-volume-profit analysis. The four

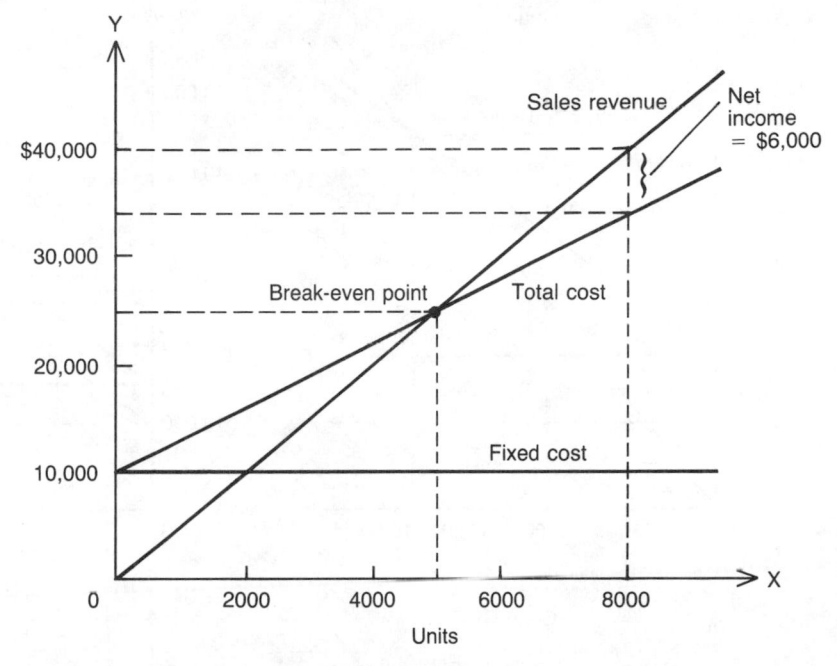

Figure 5-12
This cost-volume-profit chart illustrates the relationships of the cost data used earlier in our break-even computations. Notice how easy it is to evaluate a wide range of activity levels with a visual presentation of the data.

charts illustrate each of the changes discussed earlier in the chapter. Each chart shows the original example of breaking even with fixed cost of $10,000, variable cost of $3 per unit and a selling price of $5 per unit. In addition, each chart illustrates one change in the example and the effect on the break-even point or target profit. Chart A illustrates the addition of $8,000 of target profit to the analysis; B shows an increase in fixed cost of $5,000; C illustrates an increase in variable cost of $.75 per unit; and D shows the decrease in selling price from $5.00 to $4.60. These graphic solutions can be verified by comparing them with computational analyses of the changes presented earlier in the chapter.

A limitation of graphs is the lack of precision. It is often difficult to determine a precise answer to break-even or other CVP analyses. Poorly drawn graphs are almost useless. However, many managers use CVP charts for planning if visualizing CVP relationships is more important than computing precise answers.

Frequently, CVP charts are prepared in more detail. A common extension is to provide more fixed and variable cost details, as in Figure 5-14. Fixed costs are $150,000, and variable costs are 50 percent of selling price. The break-even point is at $300,000 of sales, or 50 percent of plant capacity. Of course, plant capacity could be expressed in some other activity measure, such as units of production. In addition to showing several classifications of variable costs, this chart shows income taxes. The income tax line starts at the break-even point since income taxes are levied on net income. Like other internal management

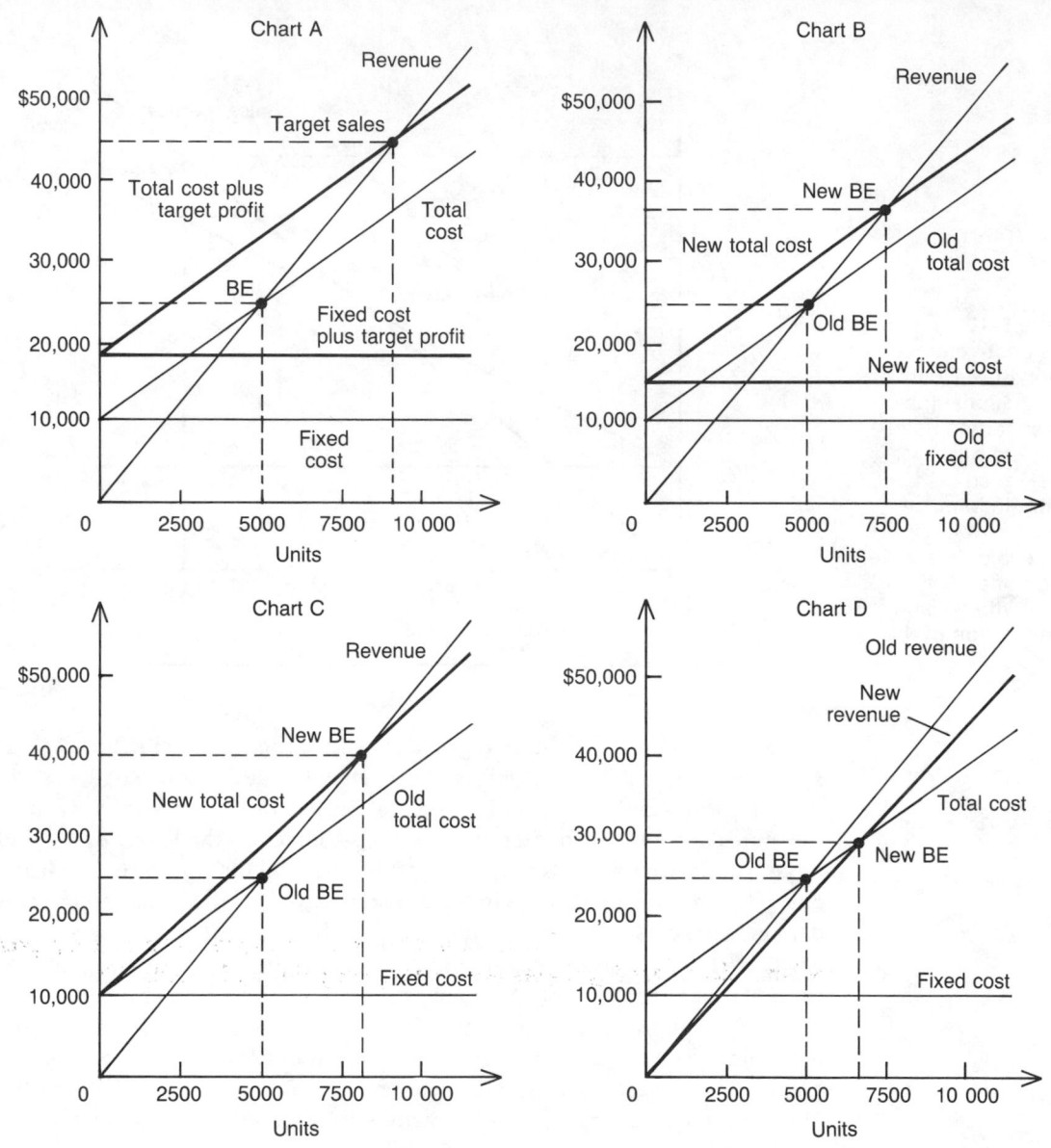

Figure 5-13
CVP charts depicting the effect on the break-even point of changes in the data used to compute cost-volume-profit analyses. The four charts illustrate: A. adding a target profit, B. increasing the amount of fixed cost, C. increasing the per-unit variable cost, and D. decreasing the selling price.

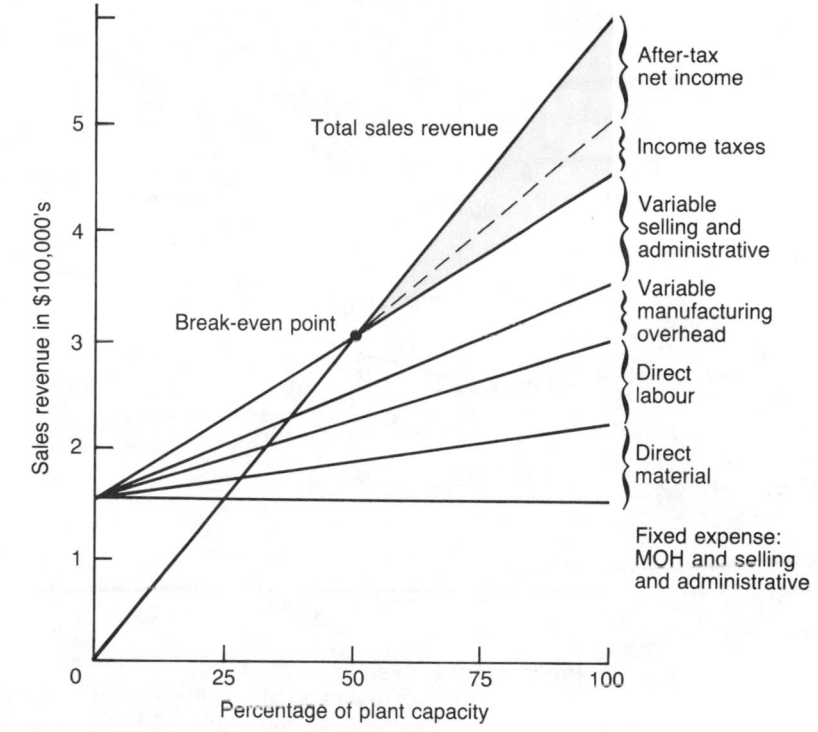

Figure 5-14
More detailed CVP charts provide managers with more analytic capabilities. Charts may be colour coded, crosshatched, or in other ways enhanced to provide better user-comprehension of the data.

reports, CVP charts are limited only by the ingenuity of the preparer and the cost-benefit relationship between the information in the report and the cost of preparing the report.

Profit-volume chart. A variation of cost-volume-profit charts is the profit-volume chart that highlights the break-even point and profitability. A profit-volume chart is presented in Figure 5-15 using the same cost and revenue data found in Figure 5-12. The horizontal axis represents activity levels, and the vertical axis is the profit in dollars. Since any activity level below the break-even point yields a loss, the vertical axis must have negative as well as positive values. With a zero level of activity, revenue is zero and variable cost is zero. Since fixed cost is $10,000, a loss appears as −$10,000 on the vertical axis. The same information can be obtained from the traditional CVP chart in Figure 5-12 by comparing the vertical distance between total cost of $10,000 and total revenue of zero. The advantage of the profit-volume chart is that the profit and loss information is more readily apparent.

A profit-volume chart highlights the break-even point and profit

The profit line is the difference between total revenue and total cost. It touches the vertical axis at the point where the activity level is zero. The value of the vertical axis intercept in our example is

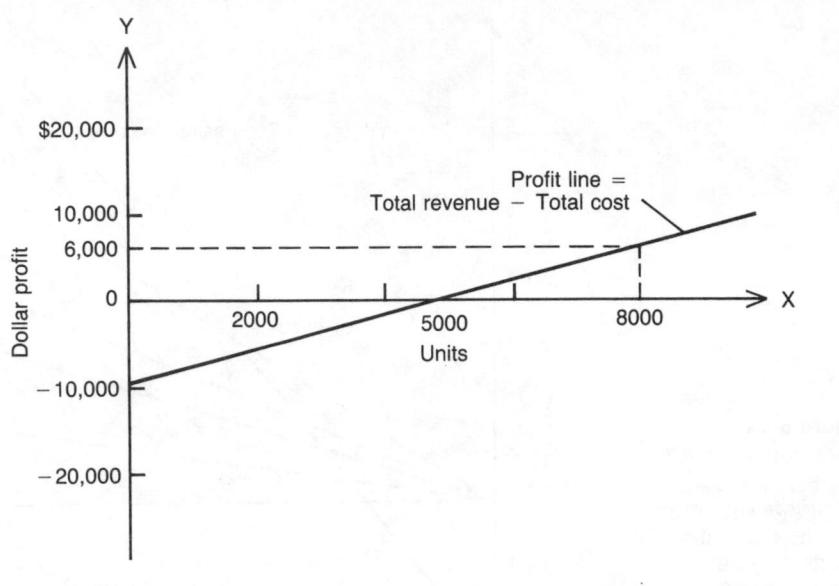

Figure 5-15

Profit-volume charts provide quick visual responses to break-even and profitability questions, although they lose much of the detailed cost and revenue information found on the CVP chart in Figure 5-14.

$$\begin{aligned}
\text{Profit} &= \text{Total revenue} - \text{Total cost} \\
&= (\text{Units} \times \text{Sales price}) - (\text{Fixed cost} + [\text{Units} \times \text{Variable cost/Unit}]) \\
&= (0 \times \$5) - (\$10,000 + (0 \times \$3)) \\
&= 0 - (\$10,000 + 0) \\
&= -\$10,000
\end{aligned}$$

As you see, the profit line intercepts the profit axis at an amount equal to the negative value of the fixed cost. In fact this relationship is always true because both revenue and variable cost equal zero at the zero activity level. Therefore, at that point the loss (negative profit) is equal to the fixed cost that is incurred whether or not any activity takes place.

From its origin the profit line slopes upward and to the right. The angle of the slope is determined by the contribution margin. The higher the contribution margin, the steeper the slope. The profit line crosses the horizontal axis at zero profit, which is the break-even point. At any activity level above the break-even point, a profit is earned. The profit for any activity level can be read from the chart. At the 8000-unit activity level, the profit-volume chart shows a profit of $6,000, just as in Figure 5-12.

Break-even analysis and the relevant range assumption

Earlier we discussed the relevant range assumption in connection with cost behaviour. In cost-volume-profit analysis, the relevant range assumption is especially important. All costs are assumed to fall into fixed or variable categories in CVP analysis. Some accountants maintain that this practice is an unrealistic representation of costs and that a better description is provided by a graph such as the one in Figure 5-16. This graph shows a curvilinear total cost line and a total revenue line with changing behaviour patterns. As a matter of fact,

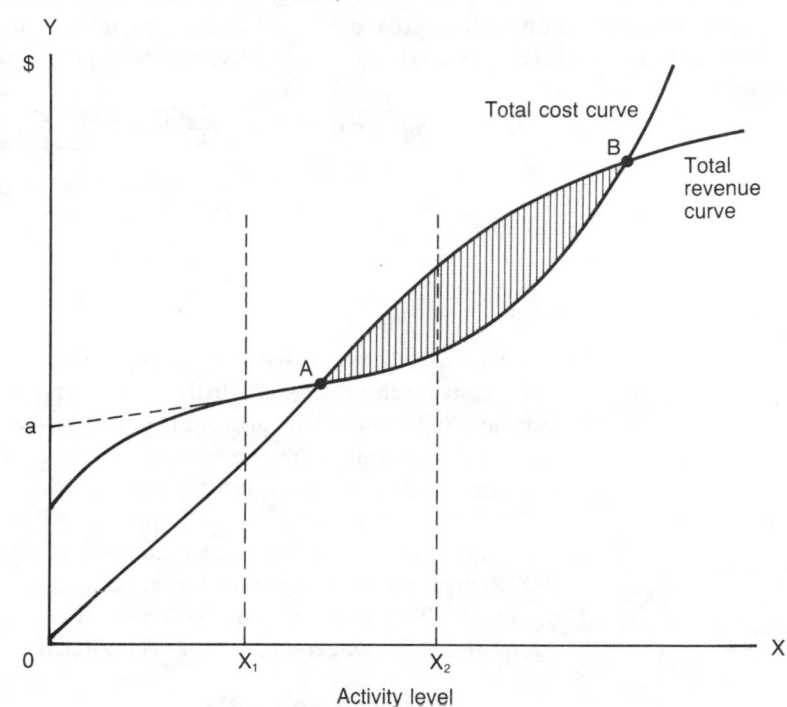

Figure 5-16
The accountant's view of the total cost and revenue curves may be somewhat limited, but it has proved very useful in a wide variety of management planning, control, and decision activities. Note the relevant range between the two broken lines.

the two curves cross twice and yield two different break-even points, A and B. The shaded area represents the profitable operating range.

Although the curves in Figure 5-16 may represent realistic cost behaviour, the graph includes activity levels that are outside of the relevant range, which means they have little or no chance of occurring. The relevant range is between X_1 and X_2 on the activity scale. In that range the two curves approximate straight lines, and the total cost curve can be extended to the vertical axis to graph a mixed cost function.

Margin of safety ratio

The margin of safety ratio is a measure of the difference between the actual level of activity and the break-even point expressed as a percentage of sales. The ratio is computed as follows:

$$\text{Margin of safety (MS)} = \frac{\text{Actual sales} - \text{Break-even sales}}{\text{Actual sales}}$$

The range of possible values for the ratio is from $-\infty$ to $+1$. A positive value means the firm is operating above the break-even level of activity. To illustrate, a firm has actual sales of 24 000 units and a break-even point of 15 000 units.

$$\text{Margin of safety} = \frac{24\ 000 - 15\ 000}{24\ 000} = .375 \text{ or } 37.5\%$$

The margin of safety ratio may also be computed using projected data rather than actual data. For example, a company projects sales of $400,000 and a break-even sales level of $260,000; the expected margin of safety ratio is

$$\text{Margin of safety} = \frac{\text{Budgeted sales} - \text{Break-even sales}}{\text{Budgeted sales}}$$

$$= \frac{\$400,000 - \$260,000}{\$400,000}$$

$$= \frac{\$140,000}{\$400,000} = .35 \text{ or } 35\%$$

To illustrate the use of the margin of safety ratio, we refer to the multiple changes example on page 177. In the first alternative the $5 price was maintained, and new equipment was acquired. Fixed cost was $30,000, and variable cost was $2.60 per unit. With the second alternative the price was raised to $5.50 per unit, and a new marketing program was implemented. Fixed cost was $18,000, and variable cost was $4.25 per unit. The required sales level to achieve the target profit was 16 250 units with the first alternative and 21 600 units with the second alternative. If the target sales levels for both alternatives seem attainable, is there a difference between their margin of safety ratios? First we compute the break-even point for each alternative.

Alternative 1	**Alternative 2**
Break-even sales = FC + VC	Break-even sales = FC + VC
$5X = \$30,000 + \$2.60X$	$5.50X = \$18,000 + \$4.25X$
$2.40X = \$30,000$	$1.25X = \$18,000$
$X = \underline{12\,500}$ units	$X = \underline{14\,400}$ units

Solving for the margin of safety ratios:

Alternative 1

$$MS = \frac{\text{Expected sales} - \text{Break-even sales}}{\text{Expected sales}}$$

$$= \frac{16\,250 - 12\,500}{16\,250} = \underline{.23} \text{ or } 23\%$$

Alternative 2

$$MS = \frac{\text{Expected sales} - \text{Break-even sales}}{\text{Expected sales}}$$

$$= \frac{21\,600 - 14\,400}{21\,600} = \underline{.33} \text{ or } 33\%$$

Figure 5-17 illustrates the margin of safety ratio concept. The left-hand graph presents alternative 1. Both the break-even point and the target profit level are identified. The difference in activity level between the two, represented by the distance **m,** is divided by the total amount of activity, represented by the distance **n,** to calculate the margin of safety ratio. Alternative 2 is presented in the right-hand graph of Figure 5-17. The margin of safety for alternative 2 is **m'/n'.**

If managers feel equally confident about achieving the level of sales required to meet the target profit, they may adopt the second alternative. Its

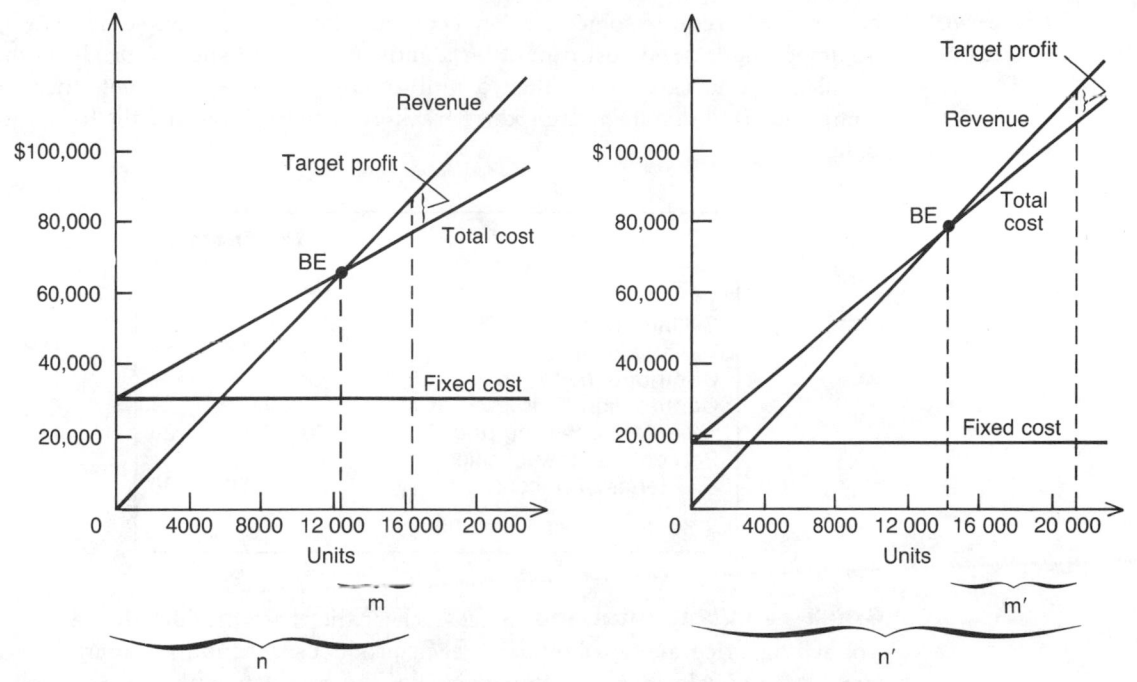

Figure 5-17
A graphic description of the margin of safety ratio. The two graphs show the
break-even point and expected activity level for two decision alternatives. The
activity levels used to compute the margin of safety for each situation are
identified on the X axis.

level of expected sales is further above its break-even level of activity. Managers
may consider alternative 2 less risky than alternative 1. Often the margin of
safety ratio is used as a measure of risk since it measures the relative amount of
actual activity level above or below the break-even activity level. The larger the
margin of safety ratio, the safer the situation, as there is less risk of reaching the
break-even point.

The value of the margin of safety ratio depends on the individual using
it and the type of decision being made. Like all ratio analysis, no absolute
parameters can be set for the ratio. The significance of any particular value
for a margin of safety ratio varies among industries, managers, and decision
situations. Nonetheless, as the ratio approaches the value 1, the situation is very
safe in terms of breaking even. As the ratio approaches 0, break-even safety is
low. Negative ratios mean that the break-even point has not yet been reached.
For example, if actual sales are 7500 units and break-even sales are 9000 units,
the ratio is

$$\frac{7500 - 9000}{7500} = \frac{-1500}{7500} = -.20 \text{ or } -20\%$$

Multiple product break-even analysis

When a firm produces more than one product, break-even and other CVP analyses may require some additional computations and involve some limiting assumptions. If fixed cost cannot be identified with the specific products the business produces or sells, then a multiproduct break-even point must be computed. To illustrate multiproduct break-even analysis, we use the following data:

	Products		
	A	**B**	**C**
Selling price	$10	$21	$25
Variable cost	8	14	18
Contribution margin	2	7	7
Contribution expressed as a percent of selling price	20	33.3	28
Percentage of total sales in terms of units	20	50	30
Total fixed cost = $42,000			

Break-even computations. Since each of the three products has a different selling price and variable cost, each product's contribution margin as a percentage of sales differs, although two of the products have identical dollar amounts of contribution margin. Clearly one problem in computing the break-even point is the lack of a single contribution margin that can be divided into the $42,000 fixed cost to find the break-even point.

The average contribution margin must be computed

The contribution margin problem is solved by computing an average contribution margin based on the expected percentage of total sales for each product. The unit contribution margin of each product is multiplied by its expected percentage of sales as follows:

A	$2 × .20 = $ .40
B	7 × .50 = 3.50
C	7 × .30 = 2.10
Average contribution margin	$6.00

The $6 average contribution margin represents a weighted average of the individual product contribution margins weighted by their expected portion of total sales. No single sale results in a $6 contribution margin, but the average contribution margin based on the expected sales mix is $6 per unit.

An alternative method of finding the average contribution margin is to compute the weighted average selling price and weighted average variable cost. Then subtract variable cost from selling price to find the average contribution

Product	Sales Frequency	Sales Price	Expected Value
Average Sales Value			
A	.20	$10	$ 2.00
B	.50	21	10.50
C	.30	25	7.50
			$20.00
Average Variable Cost			
A	.20	$ 8	$ 1.60
B	.50	14	7.00
C	.30	18	5.40
			14.00
Average contribution margin			$ 6.00

Figure 5-18
This figure shows the computation of expected contribution margin using the expected selling price and expected variable cost.

margin. Figure 5-18 shows the computations. Both methods yield the same result. If the computations are based on historical sales and cost data, the results are weighted averages. If expected sales and cost data are used in the computations, the results are called expected values. A great deal of CVP analysis is used for planning and is therefore future-oriented. Even when historical data are used, they are often assumed to be estimates of future activities.

It should be pointed out that the expected sales price of $20 and the expected contribution margin of $6 are not equal to any of the prices or contribution margins of specific products. The expected price of $20 is an **average.** In other words, when all of the revenues are totaled and divided by the units sold, the result is an average price of $20 per unit, although no product may have been sold for $20. The same is true of the $6 expected contribution margin. The $6 contribution margin is 30 percent of the $20 sales price. We can compute the break-even point as before:

$$\text{Break-even point} = \frac{\$42,000}{\$6} = 7000 \text{ units}$$

or in sales dollars:

$$\text{Break-even point} = \frac{\$42,000}{.30} = \$140,000$$

The sales mix estimate is critical in computing multiple product break-even

A multiple product break-even point rests upon the critical assumption that the relative sales frequencies will occur. If the sales mix is different from the 20 percent, 50 percent, and 30 percent used in the computations, the calculated break-even point will be wrong.

The 7000-unit break-even point represents sales of all three products. Management planning may require a break-even point expressed in individual product quantities. That is easily accomplished by multiplying the total units required to break even by the relative sales frequencies.

```
A        7000 units × .20 = 1,400
B        7000 units × .50 = 3,500
C        7000 units × .30 = 2,100
                            7,000
```

The computation in sales dollars is as follows:

```
1400 units × $10 = $ 14,000
3500 units × $21 = $ 73,500
2100 units × $25 = $ 52,500
                   $140,000
```

The discussion of multiproduct break-even analysis has assumed thus far that fixed costs cannot be specifically identified with the products. This assumption may be true particularly for nonmanufacturing fixed costs. In our example the $42,000 fixed cost is assumed to be common to all three products. Where fixed costs can be identified with products, each product is assigned its appropriate fixed cost, and multiproduct break-even analysis is reduced to a set of single product break-even computations.

Summary

An understanding of cost behaviour patterns is very important in making a wide variety of decisions. Although many different cost behaviour patterns can be identified, for accounting purposes several major classifications are most useful in management planning and control. **Fixed costs** remain constant at all levels of activity. **Variable costs** change directly and proportionately with activity level. Direct materials, direct labour, and sales commissions are common examples of variable costs. **Mixed costs** are composed of fixed and variable costs. **Semifixed costs** are called step function costs because they increase by intermittent jumps. **Semivariable costs** increase with activity, but at a changing rate. Those that increase at a decreasing rate are called **learning curve costs** and reflect increased efficiency as employees become more familiar with new tasks. Some semivariable costs increase at an increasing rate.

All cost behaviour analysis rests on two important assumptions. The **relevant range assumption** states that the identified cost behaviour patterns are correct only for a certain range of activity. Outside of that range other cost behaviour paterns may prevail. The **time assumption** states that identified cost behaviour patterns pertain to a specific period of time. During other time intervals the cost behaviour patterns may be different.

Sometimes it is difficult to identify a cost pattern for a specific cost. In addition to using the knowledge of experienced employees, the high-low and scatter diagram techniques may be used. The **high-low method** compares the change in cost and corresponding change in activity between the highest and lowest cost data elements to obtain the variable cost rate and the fixed cost. **Scatter diagrams** are plots of cost data used to identify cost patterns.

Cost-volume-profit analysis is a powerful management tool that is used to relate activity levels to changing costs and profits. **Break-even analysis** is used to compute the **break-even point** where total cost equals total revenue. Computationally it is: selling price times units equals fixed cost plus unit variable cost times units. The selling price minus variable cost is called the **contribution margin,** which can be divided into fixed cost to find the break-even point. Increased fixed cost and target net income can be integrated into the analysis merely by adding them to the initial fixed costs. Changing variable cost or selling price requires an adjustment of the contribution margin. All of these changes can be combined into a single analysis. Graphic presentations of CVP analysis provide managers with valuable assistance in understanding and using the information. The **profit-volume chart** highlights the break-even point and profitability.

The **margin of safety ratio** measures the difference between the actual activity level and the break-even activity level expressed as a percentage of actual activity. The ratio is computed as (sales − break-even)/sales. The possible range of margin of safety values is from $-\infty$ to $+1$.

When multiple products must be considered simultaneously in break-even analysis, a single contribution margin is computed. With historical data it is a weighted average contribution margin; when using projected data, it is an expected contribution margin. The average contribution margin is used to compute the break-even point in total units or sales dollars. The total number of units is divided among the individual products by applying the sales mix data used in computing the contribution margin. Multiple product break-even analysis rests heavily upon the accuracy of the sales mix information.

List of important terms

Following are important terms introduced or discussed in the chapter. You should understand the meaning of these terms before working exercises and problems or proceeding to the next chapter.

break-even point *(173)*
committed fixed cost *(162)*
contribution margin *(174)*
cost behaviour *(160)*
cost-volume-profit *(172)*
cost-volume-profit chart *(174)*
discretionary fixed cost *(162)*
fixed cost *(160)*
high-low method *(170)*
learning curve cost *(164)*

margin of safety ratio *(183)*
mixed cost *(165)*
profit-volume chart *(181)*
relevant range assumption *(169)*
scatter diagram *(171)*
semifixed cost *(167)*
semivariable cost *(166)*
time assumption *(170)*
variable cost *(162)*

Questions

1. What is meant by *cost behaviour patterns* and why would managers be concerned with such a thing?
2. Distinguish between fixed and variable costs.
   a. Give a brief definition of each.
   b. Identify the appropriate formula and its components.
   c. Provide two examples of each cost.
3. The plant manager is having trouble distinguishing between controllable and variable costs. As a cost accountant, how would you explain this issue?
4. Describe what is meant by committed and discretionary fixed costs and why it is important for management to be able to identify such costs.
5. "Semifixed and semivariable costs are one and the same, the words are just changed," says the new junior accountant just hired by the firm. As controller for the firm, what would you tell him?
6. What is the rationale behind calling a semivariable cost curve that increases at a decreasing rate a learning curve?
7. Discuss the importance of the relevant range and time assumptions as they relate to cost behaviour.
8. Using the last five years of monthly factory maintenance cost data, the cost accountant determined that there is a $40,000 fixed maintenance cost each month and a variable cost of $15 for each 10 direct labour hours worked.
   a. Graph the maintenance costs.
   b. Describe the maintenance costs in equation form.
9. What is a scatter diagram and of what use is it to business managers?
10. While walking through the cost accounting department, the vice president of finance hears you mention the *high-low method* to a coworker. He asks you if that is a horse-race betting system. What is your response?
11. "Cost-volume-profit analysis and break-even analysis are two names for the same thing." React to that statement.
12. What is the purpose of using graphic presentations of accounting information? What specific advantages are there to using CVP charts?
13. How does a profit-volume chart differ from a CVP chart?
14. Why does the graph in Figure 5-16 show two break-even points? Is the accountant's view of break even incorrect?
15. What effect does the relative sales frequency of products have on multiple product break-even analysis?
16. What is the formula for the margin of safety ratio and what information does the margin of safety ratio provide?

Exercises

Ex. 5-1 **Cost behaviour patterns.** The Quebec Waterbed Company is evaluating its marketing activities. In analyzing cost and volume data for the last six years, the accountant found a fixed marketing cost of $80,000 per year and a variable cost of $.08 per dollar of sales.

Required:
a. Write a cost equation to describe the company's total annual marketing cost.
b. Based on your equation in *a*, estimate marketing costs for annual sales of $2,000,000.
c. Carefully graph the marketing total cost line.

Ex. 5-2 **Scatter diagram.** During the past two years Howell Corporation experienced the following manufacturing overhead costs and production activity:

Quarter	Direct Labour Hours	MOH Cost
1st	36 000	$244,000
2nd	39 000	255,000
3rd	45 000	270,000
4th	52 000	295,000
5th	37 000	260,000
6th	40 000	265,000
7th	50 000	300,000
8th	55 000	320,000

Required:
Carefully plot the above data on a scatter diagram and draw a cost estimation line.

Ex. 5-3 **Cost estimation, high-low method.** Use the data from exercise 5-2.

Required:
a. Using the high-low method, compute the fixed and variable cost components for manufacturing overhead.
b. If activity is expected to jump to 70 000 direct labour hours in the fourth quarter of the current year, what would you project as total MOH costs for Howell?

Ex. 5-4 **CVP chart.** Following are cost behaviour data:

> Fixed costs = $3,000
> Variable costs = $.75/unit
> Sales price = $1.00/unit

Required:
a. From the above data provide a cost-volume-profit (CVP) graph identifying all parts.

b. Compute the break-even point in units and verify the answer with the graph.

Ex. 5-5   Cost estimation, high-low method. Quant, Incorporated, is in the process of preparing the budget for the maintenance department and asks you to make an estimate of fixed and variable costs for the coming year. They have provided you with the following data for the past five years:

Year	Units of Output	Repair Costs
1980	11 000	$160,000
1981	21 000	210,000
1982	19 000	190,000
1983	26 000	250,000
1984	14 000	175,000

Required:
Determine the variable and fixed repair costs using the high-low method.

Ex. 5-6   Break-even point and margin of safety. The income statement for Dryden Corporation as of year-end is as follows:

Sales (20 000 units)	$180,000
Variable expenses	110,000
Contribution margin	$ 70,000
Fixed expenses	52,500
Net income	$ 17,500

Management is dissatisfied with the results and plans the following changes for the coming year:

1. Implement a new marketing program that would increase fixed costs by $9,600 and variable cost by $.50 per unit. The new program is expected to increase unit sales by 15 percent.
2. A 5 percent increase in sales price to help meet the additional marketing expense.

You have been hired as a consultant to determine the feasibility of such changes.

Required:
a. Calculate the old and new break-even points and margin of safety ratios.
b. Calculate the net income with the proposed changes.

Ex. 5-7   Computing the break-even point. Below are data for a company that is contemplating some changes in its operations.

Fixed expenses per month:	
Rent	$1,500
Legal expenses	1,000
Advertising	3,000
Utilities	620
Variable expenses per unit:	
Variable manufacturing expenses	24
Variable selling expenses	2
Sales price	46

In order to increase sales, management is contemplating one of the following changes:

1. Increase sales commissions which would raise variable selling expense to $5 per unit.
2. Increase advertising to $3,800 per month.
3. Implement both of the above.

Required:
a. Find the present break-even point in terms of units and in dollars of sales.
b. Analyze each change independently to find the new break-even point.

Ex. 5-8   Break-even point and target profit. The Merrill Company produces a single product that it sells for $75 per unit. The product requires $45 per unit in variable costs to produce, and the firm has $720,000 in fixed costs. The management of Merrill Company has a stated goal of a 15 percent return on equity. Shareholders' equity consists of $100,000 of common stock and $300,000 of retained earnings.

Required:
From the above data determine:

a. The unit and sales dollar volume necessary to break even.
b. The unit and sales dollar volume necessary to attain management's profit goal.

Ex. 5-9   Break-even volume and margin of safety. Wiley Company sold 60 000 units of small transformers for electric trains at $10 per unit in 1984. Variable costs were $4 per unit, and fixed costs were $300,000.

Required:
a. Compute the break-even volume in units.
b. Compute the break-even volume in dollars.

    c. What does the unit contribution margin show?

    d. What was Wiley Company's margin of safety ratio in 1984?

Ex. 5-10   **CVP analysis.** The Sunset Tavern is open Monday through Saturday. It does a good business after 9 P.M. Monday through Thursday and after 5 P.M. on Friday and Saturday. The owner and operator of the tavern would like to increase business during the 5-to-9 period on Monday through Thursday. One suggestion is to have a "happy hour" those four days from 5 to 9 when all drinks would be two-for-the-price-of-one. In analyzing the situation, the owner has gathered the following data:

1. Average sales from 5 to 9 each Monday through Thursday are $100.
2. Variable cost of drinks averages 35 percent of price.
3. Fixed costs equal $3,575 a month.
4. Friday and Saturday sales average $400 a day for the 5-to-9 period.

Required:

a. Compute Sunset's break-even point in annual sales using the current pricing system.

b. To what level would sales have to increase to warrant the "happy hour"?

c. What other variables might the owner evaluate?

Ex. 5-11   **Multiple product break-even point.** Dynamic Tape Company produces two types of blank recording tapes that it distributes through wholesalers or sells directly to large retailers. The following data apply to these products:

Product	Sales Price	Variable Costs	Contribution Margin	Expected % of Units Sold
Cassette	$2.00	$ .60	$1.40	60
Cartridge	3.00	1.10	1.90	40
				100
Fixed costs:				
Sales personnel			$ 500,000	
Advertising and other promotion			2,000,000	
Other fixed costs			500,000	
Total fixed costs			$3,000,000	

Required:

a. Calculate the break-even point for each product in units and in dollars.

b. Calculate the unit volume and sales necessary to achieve a 20 percent return on sales.

Problem Set A

P. 5A-1   **Using CVP information.** Rob Henniger earns $12,000 a year as a lathe operator in an industrial plant. In his spare time he has invented a line of foolproof fishing lures. He would like to quit his job and start manufacturing fishing lures provided that he can remain at least as well off as he is now. He makes the following estimates:

> Annual lease cost for a business facility = $5,000
> Annual lease cost for production equipment = $7,000
> Fringe benefit costs now paid by Rob's employer that Rob will have to pay
>   if he quits his current job = $3,000
> Variable manufacturing cost = $.50 per lure
> Variable selling expense = $.10 per lure
> Selling price = $1.40 per lure

Required:

a. How many lures must Mr. Henniger produce and sell to meet his minimum requirements?

b. Rob believes sales will total 35 000 lures a year, but with an advertisement in each of the three top outdoor magazines, sales would double. The advertising campaign would cost $3,000 a month. Should he advertise?

c. Rob believes he can increase sales by 60 percent from 35 000 to 56 000 by lowering the price to $1.20. Should he lower the price?

P. 5A-2   **Unit cost CVP analysis.** The following annual income statement has been prepared by Lenox Company:

Sales (60,000 units)		$540,000
Cost of sales:		
Direct labour	$120,000	
Direct materials	90,000	
Variable MOH	30,000	
Fixed MOH	80,000	320,000
Gross margin		$220,000
Variable selling expenses	$ 50,000	
Fixed selling expenses	37,000	
Variable general and administrative expenses	70,000	
Fixed general and administrative expenses	33,000	190,000
Net income		$ 30,000

Management estimates that a new marketing campaign which would add $50,000 of fixed costs and $.50 per unit of variable cost would double sales next year. Raw material cost increases of 20 percent are expected next year. Also, the new labour agreement will increase direct labour costs by 10 percent next year.

Required:
Compute the following:

a. The current unit contribution margin.
b. The current break-even point in units and sales.
c. The current margin of safety ratio.
d. Excluding the marketing campaign, what effect do the expected cost changes have on the break-even point?
e. Should Lenox use the marketing campaign?

P. 5A-3 Identifying CVP relationships. Below are cost and price data for five **independent** situations.

	Situation				
	1	**2**	**3**	**4**	**5**
Sales price	$ 50	$_____	$ 20	$ 70	$ 28
Unit variable cost	34	45	13	_____	20
Fixed cost	_____	120,000	80,000	400,000	240,000
Target profit	12,000	30,000	_____	100,000	80,000
Required activity level in units	3250	10 000	20 000	12 500	_____

Required:
Provide the missing values.

P. 5A-4 Break-even point and CVP chart. Cordova Company manufactures basketballs that are sold to retailers at a price of $10 each. Unit variable costs are

Direct materials	$2.50
Direct labour	1.50
Variable MOH	1.00
Variable selling	1.50
Variable administrative	.50
Total	$7.00

Fixed costs are

Manufacturing overhead	$400,000
Selling	300,000
Administrative	200,000
Total	$900,000

This year's Cordova's sales were 350 000 units. The company's desired net income is $600,000 before taxes. The firm is evaluating a marketing program designed to help achieve the firm's target net income. The program would increase fixed costs by $145,000 and variable costs by $.25 a unit.

Required:
a. Calculate the break-even point in units and dollar sales.
b. Prepare a **detailed** cost-volume-profit chart, carefully labeled, based on the current situation.
c. Compute the margin of safety ratio for the current year.
d. Ignoring the marketing program, compute the sales level that will satisfy Cordova's net income requirement.
e. Compute the break-even point with the marketing program.
f. If the marketing program is implemented and sales precisely achieve the firm's minimum net income requirement, what is the margin of safety ratio?

P. 5A-5 **Multiple product break-even analysis.** Tandum Company produces four products with the following unit data:

	A	**B**	**C**	**D**
Selling price	$10	$ 8	$12	$15
Variable costs	$ 7	$ 3	$ 5	$ 9
Percentage of sales in units	40	15	20	25
Fixed costs = $295,850				

Required:
a. From the above information compute the break-even point in total units and total dollar sales.
b. Compute the break-even volume in units and dollar sales for each product.

P. 5A-6 **CVP analysis.** J. Bagley wants to start a business and goes to a bank for a loan. A major part of Bagley's presentation to the bank is the first-year projected income statement for the proposed company, as shown on page 198.

Beth Morgan, the bank loan officer, is not convinced the estimates are realistic for the first year of this type of business. She raises the following additional points that you must address:

1. What would be the expected net income for a sales level 20 percent below the projected level?
2. It may be possible to eliminate all but $6,000 of the fixed selling cost by paying sales people totally on commission. The variable selling expense would increase to 15 percent of selling price.
3. A 50 percent increase in unit sales can be achieved by lowering the selling price to $12.

Bagley, Inc.
Projected Income Statement
For the Year 1984

Sales (20 000 units)	$300,000
Less expenses:	
Variable manufacturing	$100,000
Fixed manufacturing	50,000
Variable selling	30,000
Fixed selling	30,000
Variable administrative	10,000
Fixed administrative	60,000
Net income	$ 20,000

Required:

a. If the estimated data are correct, what is the break-even point and margin of safety ratio in 1981?

b. Prepare a new income statement with the sales level lowered by 20 percent.

c. Calculate the margin of safety for the new sales level.

d. Find the new break-even point in response to Beth's second point.

e. Compute the effect on net income using Beth's third proposal assuming the original fixed and variable selling expenses.

P. 5A-7 Multiproduct CVP analysis. The Bluewater Fishing and Supply Company produces a variety of fishing equipment. The fishing rod division has three products. Unit price and cost data are presented below.

	Product		
	Graphite	Lightweight Fibreglass	Regular Fibreglass
Selling price	$40.00	$25.00	$15.00
Variable production costs	15.00	11.00	7.50
Variable selling costs	3.00	2.00	1.50
Variable administrative costs	2.00	2.00	2.00

The fishing rod division has the following fixed costs:

Fixed manufacturing overhead	$ 65,000
Fixed selling	25,000
Fixed administrative	45,000
Total	$135,000

The new president of Bluewater is very interested in seeing that each division of the company contributes its fair share to the profit of the firm. Recent quarterly profit reports have raised serious doubts in the president's mind about the operations of the fishing rod division. Below are the quarterly reports:

Fishing Rod Division
Quarterly Income Statement
First Quarter, 1984

	Product			
	Graphite	Lightweight Fibreglass	Regular Fibreglass	Total
Sales in units	1000	1200	900	3100
Sales revenue	$40,000	$30,000	$13,500	$83,500
Less variable costs:				
Variable manufacturing	15,000	13,200	6,750	34,950
Variable selling	3,000	2,400	1,350	6,750
Variable administrative	2,000	2,400	1,800	6,200
Product contribution margin	$20,000	$12,000	$ 3,600	$35,600
Less fixed costs:*				
Fixed manufacturing				($16,250)
Fixed selling				(6,250)
Fixed administrative				(11,250)
Division net income				$ 1,850

*One-fourth of the annual fixed costs for the division is assigned to each quarter.

Fishing Rod Division
Quarterly Income Statement
Second Quarter, 1984

	Product			
	Graphite	Lightweight Fibreglass	Regular Fibreglass	Total
Sales in units	500	1000	3000	4500
Sales revenue	$20,000	$25,000	$45,000	$90,000
Less variable costs:				
Variable manufacturing	7,500	11,000	22,500	41,000
Variable selling	1,500	2,000	4,500	8,000
Variable administrative	1,000	2,000	6,000	9,000
Product contribution margin	$10,000	$10,000	$12,000	$32,000
Less fixed costs:				
Fixed manufacturing				($16,250)
Fixed selling				(6,250)
Fixed administrative				(11,250)
Division net income				($1,750)

The fishing rod divisional manager estimates the sales mix in units for the third quarter will be 20 percent for graphite rods, 30 percent for lightweight fibreglass rods, and 50 percent for regular fibreglass rods. The marketing manager estimates that a new advertising campaign emphasizing the more expensive products would provide a sales mix of 30 percent graphite rods, 40 percent lightweight rods, and 30 percent regular rods. The advertising program would increase annual fixed costs by $16,200. The variable selling costs are comprised entirely of sales commissions.

The president of Bluewater was not pleased with the first-quarter profit in the fishing rod division. The profit was only 2.2 percent of sales. However, in the second quarter a net loss was incurred in spite of the fact that unit sales increased 45 percent and dollar sales increased 7.8 percent. The president suspects gross mismanagement of the production operations, but before he takes action he calls you in, as an expert, to evaluate the situation.

Required:
a. Explain the lower profit yet higher sales of the second quarter.
b. Compute the break-even point for the third quarter in total sales and unit sales assuming the divisional manager's estimated sales mix.
c. Compute the annual break-even point for each product assuming the advertising program is implemented.
d. Compute an estimated margin of safety ratios for 1984 for situations *b* and *c*. Expected sales in 1984 are 16 000 units.
e. Evaluate the division's sales commission structure.

Problem Set B

P. 5B-1   Sales percentage CVP analysis. Simple Simon Industries had the following revenue and expense data during the last year:

Sales		$1,000,000
Less:		
Variable manufacturing	$400,000	
Variable selling	100,000	
Variable administrative	100,000	
Fixed manufacturing	200,000	
Fixed selling	40,000	
Fixed administrative	60,000	900,000
Net income		$ 100,000

Required:
Consider each of the following **independently:**

a. Calculate the break-even point and the margin of safety ratio for Simple Simon Industries based on the current data.

b. What would be the new break-even point if fixed manufacturing cost increased by 20 percent?

c. If the selling price is raised 10 percent, variable manufacturing increased 20 percent, fixed selling increased 20 percent, and the same level of unit sales is maintained, what would be the net income?

d. If the sales price is raised 25 percent, all variable costs increased 20 percent, and fixed selling cost increased by $102,800, calculate the new break-even point.

P. 5B-2   CVP analysis. The following annual sales and expense data are for the Steinsford Manufacturing Company:

Sales		$800,000
Variable manufacturing	$360,000	
Fixed manufacturing	300,000	
Variable selling and administrative	120,000	
Fixed selling and administrative	120,000	900,000
Net income (loss)		($100,000)

This is the company's third year of operation. Management had targeted a $150,000 net income for the year. In the coming year the company expects variable manufacturing costs to increase by 12 percent and variable selling and administrative costs to increase by 4 percent. Fixed manufacturing costs are expected to increase by $9,000, and fixed selling and administrative costs are expected to increase by $30,000.

Required:

a. Compute the break-even level of sales for Steinsford Manufacturing for last year.

b. Compute the level of sales last year that would have provided the company with its target net income.

c. Compute the break-even point for the coming year assuming the expected cost increases occur.

d. The company president believes the company's product is underpriced. He believes a 20 percent price increase would have little effect on the number of units sold. Compute break-even volume assuming both the price and costs increase.

P. 5B-3   Identifying CVP relationships. Below are cost and price data for five **independent** situations.

	Situation				
	1	**2**	**3**	**4**	**5**
Fixed costs	$485,000	$137,000	$293,000	$164,000	$_____
Sales price	53	_____	14	21	39
Variable costs/unit	26	17	_____	16	31
Target profit	_____	55,000	32,000	21,000	12,000
Required activity level in units	18 740	16 000	65 000	_____	6000

Required:
Provide the missing values.

P. 5B-4   **Cost behaviour patterns.** As a new controller for a heavy manufacturing firm you have been concerned about rising overhead costs, particularly in some of the service areas. You have asked your assistant, a bright accounting graduate, to investigate three service functions: maintenance, first aid, and the tool room. After carefully analyzing 60 months of cost and production data, your assistant reports the following:

$$\text{Maintenance cost} = \$60,000 + \$2.00X$$
$$\text{First aid cost} = \$45,000 + .40X$$
$$\text{Tool room cost} = \$30,000 + .80X$$

X is the monthly activity expressed in units of production. All other overhead costs can be described by the equation

$$Y = \$165,000 + \$4.80X$$

September production is projected at 25 000 units.

Required:
a. Explain the meaning of the maintenance cost equation.
b. Graph the three service department equations on a single graph.
c. What is the expected cost for each service area in September?
d. Write the equation that would describe total manufacturing overhead costs.
e. What are total expected overhead costs for September?

P. 5B-5   **Multiple Product CVP analysis.** 1984 sales and cost data for a firm that manufactures three products are presented at the top of page 203.

Required:
a. Compute 1984 net income.
b. Compute the 1984 break-even point in total units and units of each product.
c. What is the average sales revenue from the sale of one unit?
d. What is the 1984 margin of safety ratio?

Product	Selling Price	Variable Cost	1980 Sales Volume in Units
X	$ 5	$3	5000
Y	10	5	3000
Z	20	8	2000

Total fixed costs = $39,200.

P. 5B-6 **Cost-volume-profit analysis.** Julia Johnson, chief investment analyst for Crafton Company, has a file on a local doughnut shop that is for sale. The revenue and expense data for the most recent year are as follows:

Sales (30 000 dozen doughnuts)	$60,000
Less:	
Variable costs	24,000
Fixed costs	39,000
Net loss	($ 3,000)

The purchase price for the shop is $50,000. It is estimated that sales could be increased by 15 percent if the shop remained open three more hours each night. This would have no effect on unit variable cost, but fixed costs would increase by $6,000 per year. The baking process has been a bottleneck in the production of doughnuts. An automatic doughnut machine would greatly increase productive capacity and reduce variable cost to $.40 a dozen. The machine would add $20,000 to annual fixed costs.

Required:
Julia gives you the file and asks you to:

a. Compute the current break-even point.
b. Compute the current margin of safety ratio.
c. Compute the minimum acceptable sales level for Crafton to purchase the doughnut shop assuming current operating conditions and that Crafton requires a 30 percent before-tax profit on sales.
d. Determine whether the doughnut shop should stay open three hours later each night.
e. Compute the new break-even point assuming the new machine is purchased.

P. 5B-7 **Multiple product CVP analysis.** The Birchbark Guide Service offers packaged 3-day, 6-day, and 12-day canoe and hiking trips into wilderness areas of Canada. A good deal of preparation, such as equipment packing, trip planning, customer equipment orientation, and administrative correspondence and scheduling, precedes each of these trips regardless of length. The result is that the per-day cost of the trips is lower for the longer trips. All of the cost difference cannot be reflected in the pricing system, or prices would appear unfair to many potential customers. In addition, many 12-day-trip customers are former customers from the shorter trips. Management therefore looks on the 3-day trip as something of a service to generate customer loyalty and repeat-trips that are longer. Below are the current price and cost data for the trips.

	3-Day Trip	6-Day Trip	12-Day Trip
Price	$75	$140	$250
Variable costs:			
Food	15	30	60
Supplies	9	18	36
Packing, cleaning, orientation, correspondence, etc.	36	42	49
Total variable cost	$60	$ 90	$145

Fixed costs include:	
Depreciation on canoes, tents, sleeping bags, and other equipment	$13,000
Depreciation on store facilities and equipment	9,000
Property taxes, power costs, and other facility fixed costs	7,000
Administrative, marketing, and supervisory fixed costs	31,000
Total fixed costs	$60,000

The owners of Birchbark Guide Service have accumulated some trip data for the past five years. During that period 45 percent of the trips sold were 3-day trips, 30 percent were 6-day trips, and 25 percent were 12-day trips. Last year Birchbark sold 1500 trips that generated $207,375 in revenue, but yielded only a $12,000 net income before tax. The owners are not very happy with the performance, and they hire you to help analyze the situation.

Required:

a. Compute the unit contribution margin of each product.
b. Compute the price per day of each length trip. Compute the average variable cost per day of each length trip.
c. Using the average sales mix described above, compute the break-even point in total trips, trips of each length, and in sales dollars.
d. The owners believe that the trip mix would change to 20 percent, 40 percent, and 40 percent, respectively, for the 3-, 6-, and 12-day trips if the prices were dropped to $120 for the 6-day trip and $225 for the 12-day trip. If the owners' predictions are true, should the pricing changes be made?
e. The owners believe that many customers are afraid to chance a long trip into the wilderness without experience. A better advertising brochure could assist in convincing potential customers that longer trips are more economical and interesting. The owners think the 20 percent, 40 percent, 40 percent sales mix mentioned in d can be achieved with the new brochures without a price reduction. The cost of the advertising program would be $15,000 a year. Should Birchbark use the advertising brochure?

Minicases

Minicase 5-1   (Certified Accountants—U.K. adapted)

Part Works, Ltd., is a publishing company which specializes in the production of flyer publications. The company recently introduced special single publications to enable it to extend the life of some of its more successful ventures. One such publication is to follow on from the extremely successful *Silver Fingers* part work.

The costing for this single publication, which as yet is unnamed and referred to as Silver Fingers A, is as follows:

  i Preparation costs—commissioning authors, photographers, composition, blocks, etc., for whatever quantity of the publication is produced—will be $3,000.

 ii Printing costs are $8 per hundred up to 25 000 and then $4 per hundred for any further copies—the reduction in costs resulting from less spoilt work and scrapping of paper during longer print runs.

iii Binding and other finishing costs $100 per 5000, whatever quantity is produced.

The publication is to be sold direct to newsagents and similar retailers at a fixed price of 20¢ each, to retail at a price of 25¢.

Required:

a. A table showing the production costs of 15 000, 20 000, 25 000, 30 000 and 35 000 of Silver Fingers A, together with the average costs per 5000 copies of each quantity. Show the marginal costs for each increment.

b. Draw a break-even chart for the publication and from this derive the break-even point. Check the accuracy of your graph by calculating the break-even point.

c. Part Works, Ltd., has already printed 35 000 copies of a publication with similar costs to Silver Fingers A. This has not sold as well as expected and the firm has 10 000 copies left, which seem likely to remain unsold. A dealer who specializes in market trading offers to buy these for $600. What factors should be considered before deciding whether or not to accept the offer? What difference would it have made if the offer had been for $100?

Minicase 5-2   (CMA Examination Question)

CEM Electronics manufactures two products—tape recorders and electonic calculators—and sells them nationally to wholesalers and retailers. The CEM management is very pleased with the company's performance for the current fiscal year. Projected sales through December 31, 1984 indicate that 70 000 tape recorders and 140 000 electronic calculators will be sold this year. The projected earnings statement, which appears below, shows that CEM will exceed its earnings goal of 9 percent on sales after taxes.

The tape recorder business has been fairly stable the last few years, and the company does not intend to change the tape recorder price. However, the competition among manufacturers of electronic calculators has been increasing. CEM's calculators have been very popular with consumers. In order to sustain this interest in their calculators and to meet the price reductions expected from competitors, management has decided to reduce the wholesale price of its calculator from $22.50 to $20.00 per unit effective January 1, 1985. At the same time, the company plans to spend an additional $57,000 on advertising during fiscal year 1985. As a consequence of these actions, management estimates that 80 percent of its total revenue will be derived from calculator sales, as compared to 75 percent in 1984. As in prior years, the sales mix is assumed to be the same at all volume levels.

The total fixed overhead costs will not change in 1985, nor will the variable overhead cost rates (applied in a direct labour hour base). However, the cost of materials and direct labour is expected to change. The cost of solid state electronic components will be cheaper in 1985. CEM estimates that material costs will drop 10 percent for the tape recorders and 20 percent for the calculators in 1985. However, direct labour costs for both products will increase 10 percent in the coming year.

CEM Electronics
Projected Earnings Statement
For the Year Ended December 31, 1984

	Tape Recorders		Electronic Calculators		
	Total Amount (000 omitted)	Per Unit	Total Amount (000 omitted)	Per Unit	Total (000 omitted)
Sales	$1,050	$15.00	$3,150	$22.50	$4,200.0
Production costs:					
Materials	$ 280	$ 4.00	$ 630	$ 4.50	$ 910.0
Direct labour	140	2.00	420	3.00	560.0
Variable overhead	140	2.00	280	2.00	420.0
Fixed overhead	70	1.00	210	1.50	280.0
Total production costs	$ 630	$ 9.00	$1,540	$11.00	$2,170.0
Gross margin	$ 420	$ 6.00	$1,610	$11.50	$2,030.0
Fixed selling and administrative					1,040.0
Net income before income taxes					$ 990.0
Income taxes (55%)					544.5
Net income					$ 445.5

Required:

a. How many tape recorder and electronic calculator units did CEM Electronics have to sell in 1984 to break even?

b. What volume of sales is required if CEM Electronics is to earn a profit in 1985 equal to 9 percent on sales after taxes?

c. How many tape recorder and electronic calculator units will CEM have to sell in 1985 to break even?

Chapter 6

Relevant Costs and Alternative Choice Decisions

This chapter continues the cost-volume-profit analysis introduced in Chapter 5 and extends the analysis specifically to the decision-making process. Concepts from this chapter are used, at least in part, in many chapters that follow. When you have completed this chapter, you should understand:

1 The concept of alternative choice decisions.

2 The nature and use of relevant costs.

3 The general analysis approach for two-alternative decisions.

4 The computation and use of cost indifference points.

5 The analysis of make-buy, joint product, and pricing decisions.

6 The computation and use of price indifference points.

7 The analysis of multiple alternative decisions.

Relevance is one of the three basic characteristics of accounting information discussed in Chapter 1. Relevance refers primarily to the usefulness of accounting information in making decisions. Since different individuals make decisions differently, there is no universal measure of relevance for all types of accounting information. However, certain types of accounting information generally are useful to many managers in making various kinds of business decisions. The purpose of this chapter is to present the concept of relevant costs and relate it to decision making. Some of the more common types of business decisions are used to illustrate how relevant cost data are identified and used in decision making. In this chapter we define relevant costs and then discuss how they are used in choosing among alternative choices of action. Decisions involving two alternatives are discussed and illustrated first, followed by decisions involving three alternatives.

Relevant costs

A wide variety of accounting information may be useful to managers. For example, sales data in units sold or in sales dollars may be useful in planning an advertising campaign. Balance sheet ratios may influence dividend payment decisions and earnings per share figures may influence capital-raising decisions. Cost data are of major importance in many decisions. But as you learned in previous chapters, there are many different types of cost. Some costs are classified according to function, such as manufacturing or nonmanufacturing. Some are classified according to cost behaviour patterns, such as fixed or variable. Sometimes cost classifications are combined, such as fixed marketing costs or variable manufacturing costs. Not all costs are of equal importance in making decisions, and managers must identify those that are useful in making each type of decision. Such costs are called relevant costs. The kinds of costs that are relevant to a decision vary with the type of decision and the person making the decision. However, most people attribute two basic characteristics to relevant costs.

Relevant costs are useful in making decisions

1. They are expected future costs.
2. They differ between decision alternatives.

Relevant costs are expected future costs

Expected future costs means that the costs are expected to occur during the time period covered by the decision. For example, a manager evaluating the cost of producing a new product during the next year uses the labour, material, and overhead costs expected during the next year. Past or historical costs are relevant to the decision only if they are expected to continue in the future.

Relevant costs are different between decision alternatives

Costs that are different between decision alternatives often are useful in analyzing decisions, but costs that are identical for each alternative have no impact on the decision. For example, if management is evaluating the purchase of either a manual or an automated drill press, both of which require skilled labour costing $8 per hour, then the labour rate is not relevant since it is the same for both alternatives. If, however, the manual drill press requires semiskilled labour at $6 per hour and the automated drill press requires skilled labour at $8 an hour, then the labour rate may be relevant because it is different between the alternatives. The difference between the amount of the two costs is called differential cost. In the above example differential cost is computed as follows:

$$\text{Differential cost} = \text{Cost of one alternative} - \text{Cost of the other alternative}$$
$$= \$8 - \$6 = \$2$$

Alternative choice decisions

Many of the decisions discussed in this chapter are frequently referred to as alternative choice decisions. Alternative choice decisions involve situations with two or more courses of action from which the decision maker must select the best alternative. In the broadest sense virtually all decisions are alternative choice decisions. For instance, should you continue watching television or start doing your homework? This decision involves choosing between two alternatives. Similarly, during spring vacation should you go to Hawaii to sunbathe, Jasper to ski, or home to relax? A decision involving more than two alternatives is called a multiple-alternative choice decision.

Many factors enter into the selection of the best alternative. Some decisions are based primarily on judgment, with little or no analytical data. Others involve systematic decision models. In most business decisions, some accounting data are useful in reaching a decision, and cost data are particularly useful in analyzing many alternative choice decisions.

The variety of alternative choice decisions is limitless. Some business examples are:

1. Should we manufacture or buy automobile windshields?
2. Should we sell a joint product at the split-off point or process it further?
3. Should we raise the price of a product or maintain the current price?
4. Should we keep our copying machine or acquire a faster one?
5. Should we produce the new fan wheels with semiautomated welding equipment or should we use fully automated welding equipment?
6. Should we accept a special order for a product below our normal selling price?

The analyses of these and other types of alternative choice decisions are often aided by relevant cost data. The discussions that follow illustrate a variety of alternative choice decisions and the types of costs relevant to each decision.

Two-alternative decisions

Many decisions involve choosing between two alternative courses of action. For instance, a sales manager is evaluating the choice of purchasing either special purpose electronic calculators or programmable electronic calculators for all sales personnel. Sometimes one of the alternatives being evaluated is the current situation. For example, a plant manager is evaluating a sophisticated new telephone and intercom system. The new system offers several advantages, but the current telephone system is far less expensive.

To illustrate some important concepts in analyzing two alternative decisions, we use the example of Endline Corporation, which produces a variety of toy products. The firm is planning to produce a plastic dump truck to sell for $5. The management of Endline must decide between two methods of producing the dump trucks.

Method A requires leasing a plastic moulding machine for $6,000 per year and purchasing a $2,000 annual maintenance contract on the equipment. Method B requires a more expensive automatic machine that has a higher maintenance contract but requires less labour to operate. The expected costs of the two production methods are listed in Figure 6-1.

All of the costs listed for the two plans are expected future costs, and they therefore satisfy one of the criteria for relevant costs. However, not all of the costs are different between production method A and production method B. Costs that are the same for each production method are not relevant costs. Both occupancy costs and unit material costs are expected to be identical for the two methods. Three costs are expected to be different, and the differential amounts for these three costs are shown in the far right column of Figure 6-1. The three differential costs in our example meet both relevant cost characteristics.

Only relevant costs are used in evaluating alternatives

Since the occupancy and material costs are the same whether management adopts method A or B, they should not affect the decision. However, the other three costs should be useful in making the decision. The maintenance contract and machine lease cost for production method B is $24,000 a year higher than with method A, but the variable cost of labour is $1.50 per unit less. The management of Endline Corporation has a choice between lower fixed cost and higher variable cost for A or higher fixed cost and lower variable cost for B.

If the decision is based solely on profits, the company will choose the plan that yields the higher net income. Since the selling price is the same for both

Endline Corporation
Expected Production Costs for Plastic Dump Trucks
For Two Possible Production Methods

	Method A	Method B	Differential Fixed Cost
Fixed costs:			
Occupancy costs	$ 4,000	$ 4,000	0
Maintenance contract	2,000	3,000	$ 1,000
Machine lease costs	6,000	29,000	23,000
Total	$12,000	$36,000	$24,000

	Method A	Method B	Differential Variable Cost
Variable costs:			
Materials	$1.00	$1.00	0
Labour	2.50	1.00	$1.50
Total	$3.50	$2.00	$1.50

Figure 6-1
The relevant costs in comparing alternative courses of action are the costs that differ between alternatives. Here the differential costs are shown in a separate column.

production methods, production costs determine any difference in profit between the two. For example, if Endline expects sales of 13 000 trucks in the first year of production, the following analysis can be made:

		Method A		Method B
Sales	13 000 @ $5.00	$65,000		$65,000
Less: Fixed costs		(12,000)		(36,000)
Variable costs	13 000 @ $3.50	(45,500)	13 000 @ $2.00	(26,000)
Profit		$ 7,500		$ 3,000

At the 18 000-unit level of sales, the results are as follows:

		Method A		Method B
Sales	18 000 @ $5.00	$90,000		$90,000
Less: Fixed costs		(12,000)		(36,000)
Variable costs	18 000 @ $3.50	(63,000)	18 000 @ $2.00	(36,000)
Profit		$15,000		$18,000

A comparison of the two situations shows that at 13 000 units method A provides the higher profit, and at 18 000 units method B is more profitable. In each case the profit is determined by applying the activity level to the cost data found in Figure 6-1. Although this approach provides an answer for both activity levels, it does **not** yield a general solution to the problem of selecting the appropriate production method for all activity levels.

The cost indifference point

The total cost of two alternatives is equal at the cost indifference point

A general solution is possible by using the relevant costs in Figure 6-1. At low levels of activity Endline should use method A because the lower fixed costs more than compensate for higher variable costs. Eventually, however, the lower fixed costs are more than offset by the higher variable costs, and then B becomes more profitable. The question is, At what level of activity does the choice shift from one production method to the other? The answer is the point where the lower fixed costs of A are offset exactly by its higher variable costs. This point is called the cost indifference point and is the activity level at which the cost is identical for the two alternatives. The cost indifference point can be computed by setting the cost formulas for each production method equal to each other as follows:

$$\text{Total cost of method A} = \text{Total cost of method B}$$
$$\text{Total fixed cost A} + \text{Total variable cost A} = \text{Total fixed cost B} + \text{Total variable c}$$
$$\$12,000 + \$3.50X = \$36,000 + \$2.00X$$
$$\$1.50X = \$24,000$$
$$X = 16\ 000 \text{ units}$$

Figure 6-2
The indifference point findings can be verified by substituting into each cost function values a little above and a little below the indifference point. With method A the total cost is higher above the indifference point, whereas with method B total cost is higher below the indifference point.

	Method A		
Activity level	15,990	16,000	16,010
Sales	$79,950	$80,000	$80,050
Less:			
Fixed costs	(12,000)	(12,000)	(12,000)
Variable costs	(55,965)	(56,000)	(56,035)
Profit	$11,985	$12,000	$12,015

	Method B		
Activity level	15,990	16,000	16,010
Sales	$79,950	$80,000	$80,050
Less:			
Fixed costs	(36,000)	(36,000)	(36,000)
Variable costs	(31,980)	(32,000)	(32,020)
Profit	$11,970	$12,000	$12,030

At 16 000 units both methods provide identical production costs and therefore yield the same profit. The lower fixed costs make A the more profitable production method up to 16 000 units. Beyond 16 000, production method B is more profitable. At 16 000 units management is indifferent between the two plans. By calculating the profit for each plan at 16 000 units and also just above and below this level of production, we can verify that 16 000 units is the point of indifference. Figure 6-2 shows the calculations.

The cost indifference point is presented graphically in Figure 6-3. The lower fixed cost of production method A means that initially the total cost line for A is lower than the total cost line for B. However, the higher variable cost of A causes the total cost line of A to have a steeper slope. Eventually, at the cost indifference point, the lower fixed cost of method A is entirely offset by its higher unit variable cost.

An alternative method of calculating the cost indifference point is to use the costs that are different between the two production alternatives. The differential costs are identified in the far right column of Figure 6-1. The calculations are as follows:

$$\text{Cost indifference point} = \frac{\text{Differential fixed cost}}{\text{Differential variable cost}}$$

$$= \frac{\$36,000 - \$12,000}{\$3.50 - \$2.00 \text{ per unit}}$$

$$= \frac{\$24,000}{\$1.50}$$

$$= \underline{16\ 000} \text{ units}$$

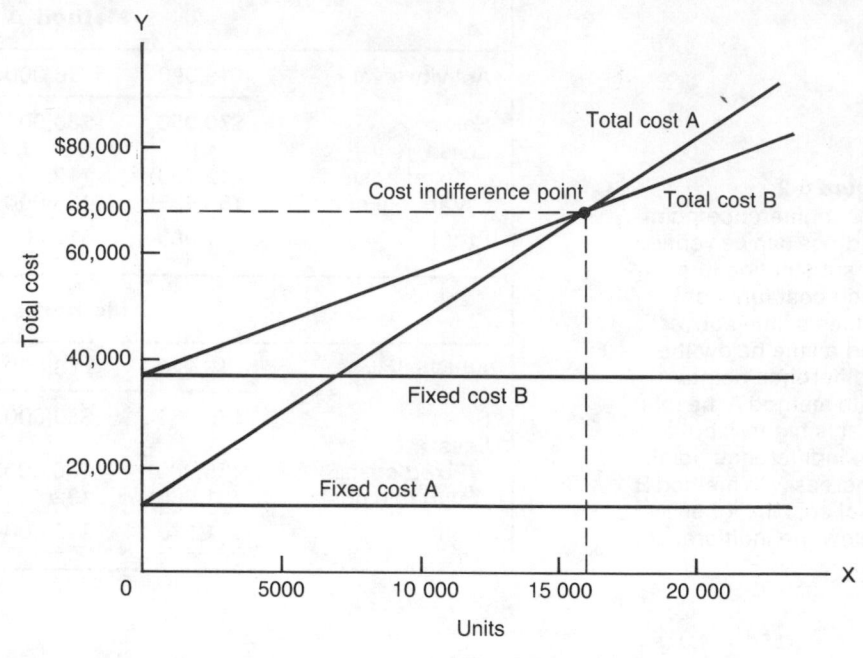

Figure 6-3
The total cost lines
cross at the cost
indifference point. The
higher fixed cost of B
is eventually offset by
its lower variable cost.

The graphic solution of the cost indifference point using differential costs is presented in Figure 6-4. The differential fixed cost is $24,000 ($36,000 − $12,000). The slope of the differential variable cost line is $1.50 per unit ($3.50 − $2.00). The differential variable cost exactly offsets the differential fixed cost at 16 000 units.

Notice that when the total cost equation is used to solve for the cost indifference point, the algebraic computations reduce variables to the differential costs, consisting only of the differential variable cost of $1.50 and the differential fixed cost of $24,000.

$$\$1.50X = \$24,000$$

Cost indifference points are useful in analyzing many types of alternative choice decisions, such as choosing between alternative production methods, marketing plans, or quality control programs. Likewise, whether to make or buy a product, to process a product further or sell at split-off, and to accept or reject a product order at a selling price below normal are all examples of decision alternatives that may, in part, require the use of relevant costs and cost indifference points. Before illustrating several types of alternative choice decisions, we briefly discuss the distinction between break-even points and cost indifference points.

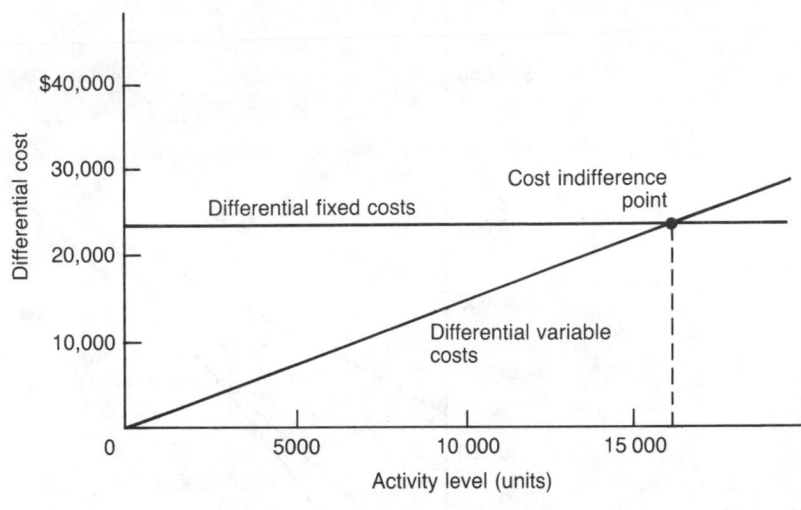

Figure 6-4
The advantage of lower fixed costs for production method A is eventually offset by its higher variable costs. At 16 000 units the two production methods have identical costs. Above 16 000 units method B has the lower total cost.

Break-even point compared with cost indifference point

In Chapter 5 we define the break-even point as the activity level at which total revenue equals total cost. The fixed and variable cost of the product and its selling price are used to compute the break-even point using the formula

Selling price × Units = Fixed cost + Variable cost × Units

On the other hand, the cost difference formula is

Total cost of one alternative = Total cost of the other alternative

Using the Endline Corporation data, two break-even points must be computed, one for each production method.

Production method A:

$$\$5X = \$12,000 + \$3.5X$$
$$\$1.5X = \$12,000$$
$$X = \underline{8000} \text{ units}$$

Production method B:

$$\$5X = \$36,000 + \$2X$$
$$\$3X = \$36,000$$
$$X = \underline{12\ 000} \text{ units}$$

The computation of the cost indifference point is made by equating the total costs of the two plans or by dividing the differential variable costs into the differential fixed costs. Using either approach we find that the cost indifference point of 16 000 units for the toy dump trucks is well above either break-even

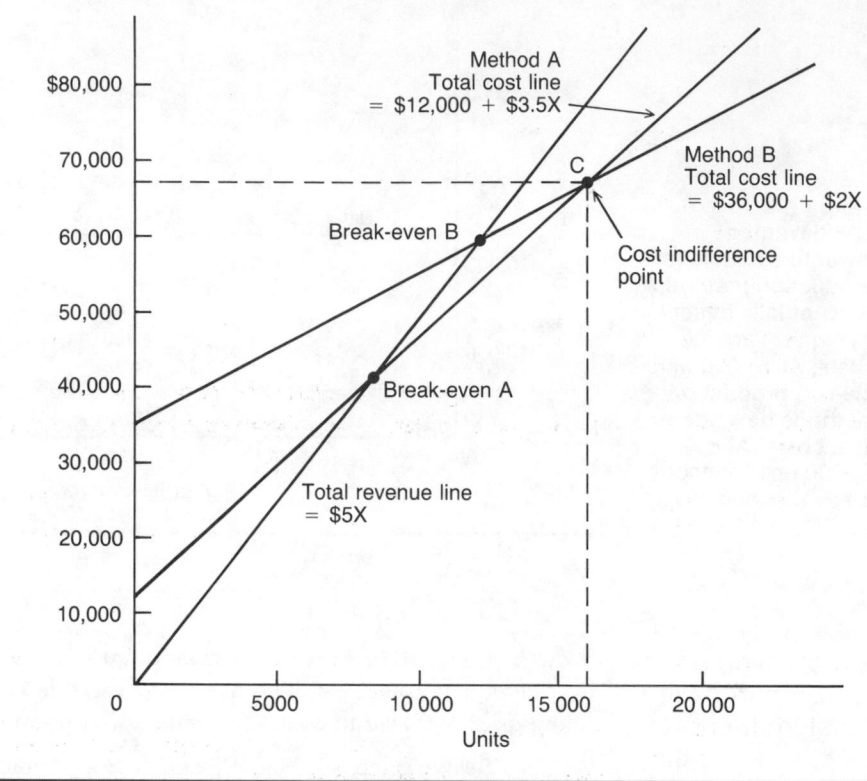

Figure 6-5
The break-even points occur where the revenue line crosses the total cost line of each alternative. The cost indifference point occurs where the two total cost lines intersect.

Cost indifference point analysis compares the costs of two alternatives

Break-even analysis compares total cost and total revenue for a single alternative

point in this example. The two break-even points and the cost indifference point are diagramed in Figure 6-5.

The graph in Figure 6-5 illustrates several important characteristics of cost indifference points. Indifference point C occurs where the two cost lines intersect, that is, where the total cost is identical for the two alternatives. Above 16 000 units the advantage of the lower fixed cost of A is offset by the lower variable cost rate of B.

Break-even points A and B occur where the total revenue line intersects each of the total cost lines. Note that the break-even points are completely different from the cost indifference point. The two analyses provide complementary, but different, information. Both may be useful in reaching a decision. For example, if expected sales are 17 000 units, the cost indifference analysis indicates that method B should be selected because it yields a higher net income than method A. However, if the risk of operating below the break-even point is very high, managers may choose A because it has a greater margin of safety. The margin of safety ratios for the two plans are:

$$\text{Method A margin of safety ratio} = \frac{17\,000\text{ units} - 8000\text{ units}}{17\,000\text{ units}} = .53\text{ or }53\%$$

$$\text{Method B margin of safety ratio} = \frac{17\,000\text{ units} - 12\,000\text{ units}}{17\,000\text{ units}} = .29\text{ or }29\%$$

Management may be willing to forego the expected extra income from B for the added safety of A.

Using relevant costs

The above discussion gives some indication of how cost indifference points are used to select between two decision alternatives and how break-even points enter into the decision-making process. Now we turn to several specific types of decisions and illustrate the use of relevant costs.

Make-buy decisions

A common type of alternative choice situation is a make-buy decision in which the decision maker chooses between buying an item or manufacturing it. Often the item is a raw material used in producing a product. For example, should a furniture manufacturer buy seat cushions for chairs it produces or should the cushions be manufactured by the firm? Most make-buy decisions involve tangible products, but some deal with administrative or service activities. For example, if a firm buys a new computer system, it may choose to service the computer with its own personnel, or the company can contract with an outside service firm to maintain and service the system.

Whether the make-buy decision deals with a tangible product or not, the analytical process is similar. Managers attempt to isolate the costs relevant to the decision at hand. As with other decisions, relevant costs are expected future costs that differ between alternatives. In make-buy decisions many cost data are presented in the form of unit costs, such as expected unit cost if manufactured and expected unit price if purchased. Since unit manufactured costs contain both fixed and variable costs, it may be difficult to determine the costs that differ between alternatives. In such situations unit costs must be used with caution to ensure that any comparisons of costs are valid.

To illustrate, Mighty-Mite Tractors manufactures a line of garden tractors. Currently the company purchases transmission subassemblies used in production. The current purchase price of $80 a unit is expected to increase to $90 next year. The company is operating at 70 percent of capacity and could manufacture the transmission subassemblies with its excess capacity. Additional fixed costs of $25,000 a year would be required for leasing machinery and equipment. Management estimates a need of 5000 units for next year. Estimated cost data for the manufacture of the transmissions are presented in Figure 6-6.

The unit cost data indicate that manufacturing the transmissions would cost $2 per unit more than buying them. However, the unit cost figure contains some costs that are not relevant to the decision, namely, the allocated fixed cost. Capacity cost of $60,000 will be incurred whether the transmissions are manufactured or purchased. Such costs are called sunk costs because they have already been incurred and cannot be changed. Most committed fixed costs are

Sunk costs are not relevant to decision making

Mighty-Mite Tractors
Estimated Production Costs
Transmission Subassemblies

Cost Item	Units	Unit Cost	Total Cost
Direct material	5000	$25	$125,000
Direct labour	5000	30	150,000
Variable MOH	5000	20	100,000
Additional fixed MOH	5000	5	25,000
Allocated fixed MOH	5000	12	60,000
Total		$92	$460,000

Purchase alternative = 5000 @ $90 = $450,000

Figure 6-6
Estimated production
cost data for 5000
transmission
subassemblies.

sunk costs and are not relevant to the decision process. In the Mighty-Mite Tractor example, allocated fixed overhead costs are neither differential costs nor expected future costs and therefore fail both tests of relevant costs. The relevant unit cost is $92 − $12, or $80. The company can save $10 per unit by producing rather than buying. Notice that the expected purchase price is used in the analysis. Historical costs are used for many types of internal and external reports, but for decision analysis historical costs are useful only as indicators of future costs. In the example the cost of the transmissions was expected to increase by $10 a unit.

Opportunity cost is the benefit foregone by rejecting one alternative to accept another

An additional type of relevant cost is opportunity cost. An opportunity cost is the benefit given up by rejecting one alternative and selecting another. For example, if the management of Mighty-Mite Tractors decides to manufacture transmission subassemblies, it must forego the use of the space for some other production alternative. The $10 per-unit saving created by producing rather than buying transmissions results in a $50,000 annual saving ($10 × 5000 units). However, another alternative use of the facilities may be to produce engine blocks at a saving of $15 per unit over the expected purchase price. If management expects to produce 5000 units, the cost-savings would be $75,000 for the year ($15 × 5000 units). In this situation the opportunity cost of producing the transmissions is $75,000 because the company must forego the production of engine blocks, which would save $75,000.

Opportunity costs are relevant costs. Sometimes managers are so interested in adopting a favourite project that they overlook important alternatives that may be even more attractive than the project being evaluated.

Joint product decisions

The existence of joint costs often involves situations that require choosing among alternatives. In Chapter 4 we discussed joint product costing and distinguished between allocated joint costs and cost after split-off. Now we discuss how these costs are used in decision making. To illustrate joint product decision making, we use Placerton Products Company, which produces two cleaning products in a joint production process. Both products require additional processing beyond the split-off point before they are ready for sale. A product cost schedule is presented in Figure 6-7 showing product costs using both the physical units and gross profit methods of allocating joint costs.

As with other alternative choice decisions, relevant costs play an important role in making decisions related to joint products. In general, joint product decisions can be categorized as those affecting single products and those affecting the entire group of joint products. Typically allocated joint costs are not relevant in making single product decisions, but they are relevant in analyzing decisions affecting the group of joint products. To illustrate, assume that another company markets a new product that competes directly with Muscle-X. To remain competitive, the price of Muscle-X must be reduced to $3.25. Should Placerton continue to produce Muscle-X? The total product cost data in the last column of Figure 6-7 indicate two different conclusions.

Allocated joint costs are not relevant to single product decisions

Total Product Cost for Muscle-X			
Joint Cost Allocation Method	Unit Cost	New Price	Decision
Physical units method	$2.45	$3.25	Keep producing
Gross profit method	3.50	3.25	Stop producing

The two decisions are conflicting because irrelevant cost data have been used in the analysis. If the company continues to produce the other product, the allocated joint cost is not relevant because the entire joint cost will still be incurred and will all be allocated to the single product. Therefore, joint costs should not be used in this type of decision analysis. In this case the relevant cost for the production of Muscle-X is the cost after split-off of $1.20 per unit. It is the only cost that is different between producing or not producing the product. The decision to stop or continue production should be made by comparing the new selling price of $3.25 with the cost after split-off of $1.20. The decision is to continue producing Muscle-X since it contributes $2.05 ($3.25 − $1.20) per litre toward covering joint costs. If Muscle-X were discontinued, the cost after split-off of $12,000 would be eliminated, but all joint costs would remain. The resulting gross margin calculation would be

	Both Products	Single Product
Revenue	$132,500	$100,000
Less: Joint cost	(75,000)	(75,000)
Cost after split-off	(30,000)	(18,000)
Gross margin	$ 27,500	$ 7,000

Placerton Products Company
Schedule of Joint Product Costs
For the Month of February

Physical Units Method

Product	Sales Price	Litres Produced	Joint Cost Total	Joint Cost Per Unit	Cost after Split-Off Total	Cost after Split-Off Per Unit	Total Product Cost Total	Total Product Cost Per Unit
Kleen-O	$2	50,000	$62,500	$1.25	$18,000	$ .36	$ 80,500	$1.61
Muscle-X	5	10,000	12,500	1.25	12,000	1.20	24,500	2.45
			$75,000		$30,000		$105,000	

Gross Profit Method

Product	Sales Price	Litres Produced	Joint Cost Total	Joint Cost Per Unit	Cost after Split-Off Total	Cost after Split-Off Per Unit	Total Product Cost Total	Total Product Cost Per Unit
Kleen-O	$2	50,000	$52,000	$1.04	$18,000	$ .36	$ 70,000	$1.40
Muscle-X	5	10,000	23,000	2.30	12,000	1.20	35,000	3.50
			$75,000		$30,000		$105,000	

Figure 6-7
This figure illustrates the difference between unit costs of joint products as a consequence of using different methods of allocating joint costs. As with other decisions, the relevant costs for joint product decisions are future-oriented differential costs.

The difference of $20,500 in gross margin is the 10 000 litres of Muscle-X produced times the $2.05 per litre difference between the product selling price and the per-unit cost after split-off. Not only is the allocated joint cost not relevant to the decision, but if it is used, it leads to an incorrect solution to the problem and the subsequent loss of $20,500 of income.

Another type of joint product decision requiring similar relevant costs is the choice between selling a product after split-off or processing it further. In the above example no sales occurred immediately after the split-off point. Now assume that the product Kleen-O can be sold for $1 a litre without processing beyond the split-off point. As we noted before, allocated joint cost has no relevance to individual product decisions; only differential costs are relevant. If Placerton sells Kleen-O at split-off, the revenue declines from $2 a litre to $1, and cost declines by $.36 a litre because there is no processing after split-off. Since the decline in revenue is greater than the decrease in cost, the appropriate decision is to process the product to completion. This is seen clearly by comparing a simple gross margin statement for Placerton Products Company both for the original situation and for selling Kleen-O at split-off.

	Process after Split-Off	Sell at Split-Off	Difference
Revenue	$150,000	$100,000	$50,000
Less: Joint cost	(75,000)	(75,000)	–
Cost after split-off	(30,000)	(12,000)	(18,000)
Gross margin	$ 45,000	$ 13,000	$32,000

The decline in revenue is $.64 a litre ($1.00 − $.36) more than the decline in cost. Since 50 000 litres are produced, total gross margin would decline by $32,000 ($.64 × 50 000 litres).

Let us assume a different situation. Muscle-X can be sold at split-off for $2.75 per litre, or after further processing for $3.25 per litre. If it is sold at split-off, the cost after split-off can be eliminated. In this situation revenue would decline by $.50 per litre, but cost after split-off would decline by $1.20 per litre. The net effect is a $.70 per litre increase in gross profit, or $7,000 ($.70 × 10 000 litres). Therefore, the product should be sold at split-off. This can be verified as before by preparing a schedule of gross margin.

	Process after Split-Off	Sell at Split-Off	Difference
Revenue	$132,500	$127,500	$ 5,000
Less: Joint cost	(75,000)	(75,000)	–
Cost after split-off	(30,000)	(18,000)	(12,000)
Gross margin	$ 27,500	$ 34,500	($7,000)

Discontinue production of all joint products in the group

Joint costs become relevant when one of the alternatives is to discontinue production of all the joint products in the group. For instance, Placerton Products Company has a policy of producing only products whose gross margin is at least 22 percent of selling price since a smaller margin does not cover marketing and administrative expenses. If the price of Muscle-X declines to $3.25, the total revenue from all products is

Product	Units	Price	Revenue
Kleen-O	50 000 L	$2.00	$100,000
Muscle-X	10 000 L	3.25	32,500
			$132,500

The required gross margin on this group of joint products is $29,150 ($132,500 × .22). To satisfy company policy, the revenue must cover all product costs plus $29,150 of required gross margin. The analysis is as follows:

Revenue	$132,500
Less: Joint costs	(75,000)
Cost after split-off	(30,000)
Target gross margin	(29,150)
Revenue deficit below minimum gross margin	($1,650)

In this situation the joint cost becomes a relevant cost because it is differential between producing both products or neither product. Given the company's policy on gross margin, the two products should not be produced.

Pricing decisions

Another type of important business decision involves the pricing of products or services. All profit seeking firms must establish and revise the prices they charge to their customers. Even not-for-profit organizations may have to make pricing decisions, such as a university setting tuition or Parks Canada determining user fees. Pricing is such an important topic that we devote all of Chapter 12 to pricing concepts and decisions. Here, however, we introduce the concept of relevant accounting information as it relates to pricing decisions.

A price increase usually causes a reduction in the number of units demanded

A decision to change a price typically affects the number of units sold, the total sales revenue for the product, and product profitability. Usually managers change a price to increase product profitability even though the sales volume might decline. Other times a price change may be required to respond to competition. Whatever the reason for the price change, the important question is, What will be the effect on sales volume and product profitability?

Often it is very difficult to anticipate the effect of a price change. However, some general comments about pricing may be useful. A price increase makes the product less desirable to consumers, usually causing a decrease in the number of units sold. If the increase in price and the decrease in demand result in an increase in total revenue, the demand for the product is said to be **inelastic.** If an increase in the price and the corresponding decrease in the number of units sold results in a decrease in total revenue, the demand for the product is said to be **elastic**. For example, the demand for liquor in Canada is very inelastic because the quantity sold does not change significantly with increases in the price. The demand for tobacco products, basic food staples, and electric energy is relatively inelastic. Products with ready substitutes are very price elastic. For instance, if one oil company raised the price of gasoline significantly above prices for the same grade of gasoline of other companies, most customers would switch to the lower-priced brands. In many situations it is difficult to predict the precise impact of a change in the selling price of a product. For example, a manufacturer of basketballs sells them for $12 each. A price increase of $2 each is being evaluated. Management expects some decrease in the number of units sold, but there is controversy over the amount of the decline in sales because the **price elasticity** of the product is not known. In such cases it is desirable to provide managers with data that may be useful in deciding whether to raise a price or continue the current price. One important type of information is the price indifference point.

Price indifference point

The **price indifference point** is the level of sales with the new selling price that provides the identical profit achieved with the old selling price and old unit sales volume. For example, if the basketball manufacturer earned a $20,000 profit by selling 10 000 basketballs at $12 each, the price indifference point for the $14 selling price is the minimum sales volume that will provide the $20,000 profit.

To illustrate price indifference, we use the example of Steadler Manufacturing Company, whose income statement is presented in Figure 6-8. The company manufactures lightweight backpacking stoves that it sells to dealers for $8.00 per unit. The company is contemplating an increase in the selling price to $9.00 per unit. If the selling price is increased, the volume of sales is expected to decline. The company is willing to increase the price if the resulting net

Figure 6-8
Price indifference is based on the net income figure, which is $30,000 in this example.

Steadler Manufacturing Company		
Income Statement		
For the Year Ended December 31, 1984		
Sales	25 000 units @ $8	$200,000
Less: Variable cost	25 000 units @ $5	(125,000)
Fixed cost		(45,000)
Net income		$ 30,000

income is greater than the $30,000 the company currently earns on the stoves. The question is, How far can the volume of sales decline before the price indifference point is reached?

The solution is obtained using CVP concepts from Chapter 5. The $30,000 current net income is the target net income. The solution is as follows:

(New selling price) (Units sold) = (Variable cost) (Units sold)
+ Fixed cost + Target net income

Substituting and solving for X, the number of units sold, we get

$$\$9X = \$5X + \$45,000 + \$30,000$$
$$\$4X = \$75,000$$
$$X = 18\ 750 \text{ units}$$

To check the answer, we compute net income at 18 750 units with the new selling price:

Revenue	18 750 × $9 = $168,750
Less: Variable cost	18 750 × $5 = (93,750)
Fixed cost	(45,000)
Net income	$ 30,000

The price indifference point indicates the volume of sales at which the new price generates a profit equal to the profit of the old sales volume and price. If management expects the sales volume with the new price to be below the price indifference point, the price increase should be rejected because profit will decline. Conversely the price change should be implemented if the expected sales volume with the price increase is greater than the price indifference point because profit will increase. For example, if 21 000 units of sales are expected at the new $9 selling price, profits for Steadler Manufacturing would be $39,000 or $9,000 higher than at the old price. As with cost indifference points, there may be other factors affecting the decision, such as the firm's public image, employee job security, or competitor actions.

The price indifference point is shown graphically in Figure 6-9. It occurs where net income with the new $9 price is identical to the $30,000 net income with the old $8 price. Both the new and the old price lines are graphed. The $30,000 profit is realized with the old price at 25 000 units. The profit is denoted as the distance n on the graph. Profit of $30,000 with the new price is achieved at a sales volume of 18 750 units. The new price profit is denoted by m on the graph. Of course, m and n are identical.

Another way of graphing this problem is presented in Figure 6-10. Here the fixed cost plus current or target net income is shown as a horizontal line representing the amount that must be covered by the contribution margin. The

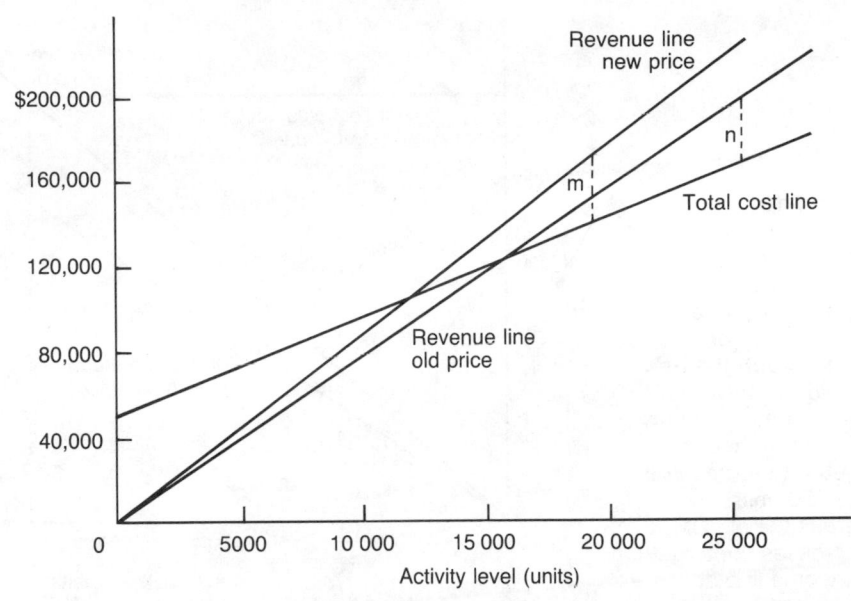

Figure 6-9
At the current price of $8, the net income of $30,000 is reached at a volume of 25 000 units. The same profit is achieved at a volume of 18 750 units with the new $9 price. Thus, 18 750 units is the price indifference point for the price increase.

new price of $9 provides a contribution margin of $4 ($9 selling price − $5 variable cost). The old price of $8 provides only a $3 contribution margin. Both contribution margin lines start at the origin on the graph in Figure 6-10. However, the new contribution margin line increases faster than the old one and intersects the fixed cost plus net income line at 18,750 units. The old CM line intersects at 25 000 units. Figure 6-10 yields the same results as Figure 6-9; however, the contribution margin graph is often easier to read.

The effect of multiple changes on the price indifference point

A variety of other factors may be included in the analysis. For example, Steadler plans to raise the price of the stoves to $10 but will improve the reliability of the stoves by using a better burner element. The company estimates the proposed changes will increase marketing and production fixed costs by $5,000 and variable costs by $1 a unit. The analysis is performed as before.

(New price) (Number of units) = (New variable cost) (Number of units)
+ Old fixed cost + Additional fixed cost + Target profit

Substituting values and solving:

$$\$10X = \$6X + \$45,000 + \$5,000 + \$30,000$$
$$\$4X = \$80,000$$
$$X = 20\ 000 \text{ units}$$

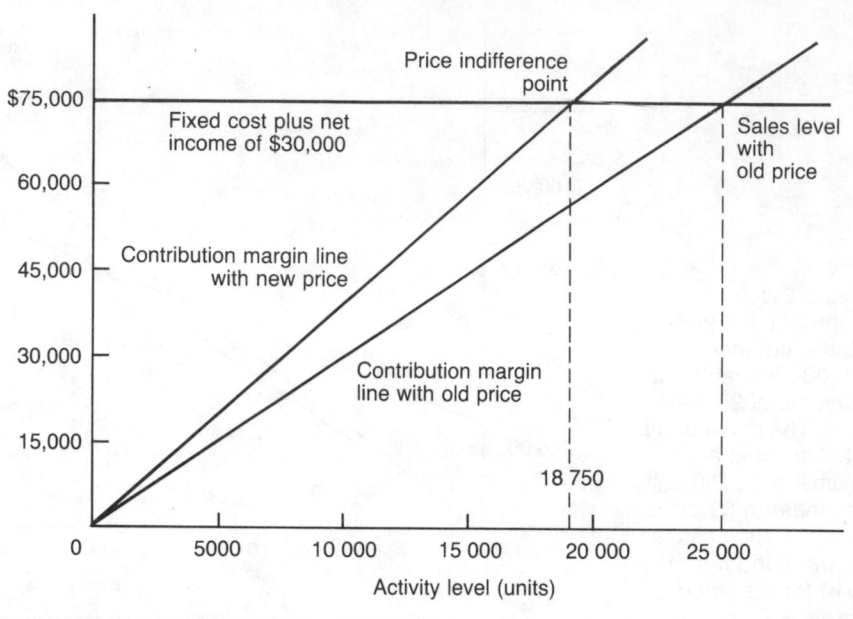

Figure 6-10
An alternative graphic approach to Figure 6-9 is to add the target net income to the fixed cost and then to graph the new and old contribution margin lines. The new CM line reaches the target net income line at 18 750 units, whereas the old CM line crosses the target net income line at 25 000 units.

Here the price indifference point tells us that if expected sales, at the new price and cost, are greater than 20 000 units, then the new price and associated costs should be implemented. Often it is difficult to estimate accurately the sales level with a new selling price, but with a price indifference point, a pricing decision can be made without a precise estimate of sales level. For example, in evaluating the situation with a $10 selling price and additional production and marketing costs for the stove, Steadler management may be uncertain of a specific sales estimate but believes that a range of 21 500 units to 23 000 units is reasonable. In spite of the inability to settle on a specific sales estimate, the management of Steadler can accept the new pricing and production plan because the lowest point in the range of sales estimates is still above the price indifference point.

The price indifference point is a two-alternative analysis

Again notice that the comparison is between two pricing alternatives, the old and the new price. Although we add some cost changes, there are still only two distinct alternatives being evaluated. The price indifference point does **not** establish a price, but it assists managers in evaluating two distinct pricing alternatives.

Special orders

All business opportunities should not be evaluated in the same way. For example, special orders or one-time orders often have different characteristics than recurring orders. As a result, each order should be evaluated based on costs relevant to the situation and the goals of the company.

SINFUL

For example, the ~~Divine~~ Fudge Company is operating at only 60 percent of capacity due to slow holiday season sales. A national organization of high school bands approaches Divine Fudge with a proposal that the firm produce 1 000 000 100-gram fudge bars to be sold for $1 by high school band members to raise money. The proposal calls for a $.55 purchase price for the bars. The fudge bars can be produced with the firm's current excess capacity. The company's chief accountant prepares the following cost estimates associated with the production and sale of the bars:

	Total Cost	Unit Cost
Direct materials	$250,000	$.25
Direct labour	100,000	.10
MOH (60% is allocated fixed MOH)	250,000	.25
Variable selling and administrative cost	50,000	.05
Total	$650,000	$.65

A glance at the unit cost data indicates that Divine Fudge would lose $.10 a bar, or $100,000, by accepting this special order. But allocated fixed overhead costs are not relevant to this decision since fixed overhead will exist whether the order is accepted or rejected. A more relevant cost analysis is

Direct materials	$.25
Direct labour	.10
Variable MOH (40% of total)	.10
Variable selling and administrative cost	.05
Total	$.50

Here we see that accepting the order adds $.05 per bar, or $50,000 in total, to the firm's profit. If no other factors affect the decision, the order should be accepted.

Other factors influencing special-order pricing decisions

Other factors may influence special-order pricing decisions. A major concern is the effect on regular customers. If regular customers are paying more for products and services, they may demand price reductions or quit buying from the firm. Another problem is that some special-order customers may decide to become regular customers, and changes in the price may become necessary. The Combines Investigation Act serves as another obstacle to special-order pricing. This law basically states that price differentation between customers is illegal unless the price differences can be justified by quality differences.

Multiple-alternative decisions

Decisions involving more than two alternatives are called multiple-alternative decisions

The previous discussion has centered on decisions with two alternatives. But frequently more than two alternative courses of action must be evaluated. Now we introduce the concept and procedures for decision making with multiple alternatives.

Multiple alternatives make the decision process more complicated for two reasons. First, the decision maker must gather more information and assimilate it into a logical decision framework. With a large number of alternatives, **information overload** may occur which means that the decision maker has more information than can be reasonably absorbed. A second problem is that the computation and interpretation of the cost analyses become more complicated.

Although multiple alternatives introduce some complications, an analysis is still possible. Break-even points and cost indifference points can still be determined. However, with multiple alternatives several cost indifference points may exist. Remember that a cost indifference point is the activity level at which total cost is identical between two alternatives. With multiple alternatives each alternative is compared with every other alternative to determine the cost indifference point. To illustrate the analysis of multiple alternatives, we use the example of the Lost City Municipal Court System. For each person brought before the court, a search of criminal records is made, and a case report is prepared. Currently the entire process is done manually. Two other methods of doing the work have been suggested. One method requires the use of semiautomatic equipment and reduces labour time. A second method is almost fully automated and reduces labour even more. Both of the proposed methods require the leasing of equipment. In addition, the equipment requires periodic maintenance and repair, which are covered by a maintenance agreement. The court administrator must choose between keeping the current system or switching to one of the two new systems. Data for the three alternatives are presented in Figure 6-11.

The first step is to compute the cost indifference point for each possible combination of alternatives using relevant cost data. Comparing the current manual system (alternative A) with the semiautomatic system (alternative B) yields cost indifference point AB. As before we are interested in expected future costs that differ between the two alternatives under consideration.

$$\text{Cost indifference point AB} = \frac{\text{Differential fixed cost}}{\text{Differential variable cost}}$$

$$= \frac{\$4,500 - \$1,500}{\$24/\text{case} - \$14/\text{case}}$$

$$= \frac{\$3,000}{\$10/\text{case}}$$

$$= 300 \text{ cases}$$

This indifference point provides precisely the same type of information obtained in the two-alternative situations discussed earlier. However, with three alternatives there are two other possible cost indifference points that must be calculated. Therefore, we compute the cost indifference points for the manual system compared with the fully automated system, denoted AC, and for the

Lost City Municipal Court System
Cost Analysis of Three Case Processing Methods

	Alternatives		
	A **Manual**	**B** **Semi-** **automatic**	**C** **Fully** **Automatic**
Monthly fixed costs:			
Occupancy	$1,500	$1,500	$ 1,500
Maintenance contract	0	500	1,000
Equipment lease	0	2,500	10,000
Total	$1,500	$4,500	$12,500
Unit variable costs:			
Supplies	$ 4	$ 8	$2
Labour	20	6	2
Total	$24	$14	$4

Description of the Alternatives

Alternative A: Current manual system
    Supply cost is $4 per report.
    Each report requires 5 hours labour.
    Labour rate is $4 per hour.

Alternative B: Semiautomated system
    Supply cost is $8 per report.
    Machine must be leased for $2,500 a month.
    Each report requires 1 hour of labour.
    Labour rate is $6 per hour.

Alternative C: Automated system
    Supply cost is $2 per report.
    Machine lease cost is $10,000 a month.
    Each report requires 15 minutes of labour.
    Labour rate is $8 per hour.

Figure 6-11
These are cost data for three alternative ways of processing the clerical work for cases brought before the Lost City Municipal Court System. With three choices the alternatives must be compared two at a time. Therefore, A must be compared with B, B with C, and A with C.

semiautomated system compared with the fully automated system, denoted BC. After the three cost indifference points have been computed, they may be used in the analysis of the alternatives.

The second cost comparison, between the current manual system and the fully automated system, yields indifference point AC.

$$\text{Cost indifference point AC} = \frac{\$12,500 - \$1,500}{\$24/\text{case} - \$4/\text{case}}$$

$$= \frac{\$11,000}{\$20/\text{case}}$$

$$= 550 \text{ cases}$$

The final comparison, between the semiautomated system and the fully automated system, yields indifference point BC.

$$\text{Cost indifference point BC} = \frac{\$12,500 - \$4,500}{\$14/\text{case} - \$4/\text{case}}$$

$$= \frac{\$8,000}{\$10/\text{case}}$$

$$= 800 \text{ cases}$$

With two alternatives it is fairly easy to see that at activity levels below the indifference point the alternative with lower fixed costs and higher variable costs should be used. Above the indifference point there is a shift to the alternative with higher fixed costs because these costs are more than offset by lower variable costs. With multiple alternatives the concept is the same, but the comparison must be made for all the alternatives, not just two.

Benefits are identical for the three alternatives, but the costs differ, so the objective is to select the alternative with the lowest total cost. However, computations of the cost indifference points show that each of the alternatives has the lowest total cost at **some** level of activity. The selection of the best alternative is made by determining the range of activity for which each alternative has the lowest cost. The decision depends upon the expected level of activity. If the choice is based solely on cost, management should select the alternative that provides the lowest total cost at the expected activity level.

The graph in Figure 6-12 shows the total cost line for each of the three alternatives. The intersections of the total cost lines are the cost indifference points. From 0 to 300 cases alternative A, the current manual system, has the lowest cost since the other two cost lines are above it. From 300 to 800 cases alternative B, the semiautomated system, provides the lowest cost in processing the reports. Above 800 cases the low variable cost of the fully automated system makes it the most economical. The lowest cost decision path is indicated with a heavy colored line that is the lowest total cost at all levels of activity. Notice that indifference point AC is irrelevant because at that level of activity the lower cost of alternative B renders the AC comparison meaningless.

At this point in the analysis there is not yet sufficient information to arrive at a decision. The cost information says:

With 0 to 300 cases use alternative A.
With 300 to 800 cases use alternative B.
Above 800 cases use alternative C.

To make the decision, the administrator must determine the most likely activity level that will occur in the future. Past history of the court's report-processing activity may be a good indicator of what can be expected. If the number of reports processed in the past remained fairly stable or showed a smoothly increasing trend, it may be possible to make good projections of future activity. Analysis of the past may, however, indicate that the number of reports processed fluctuates in a wide range, spanning more than one of the

> Select the alternative with the lowest total cost at the expected level of operations

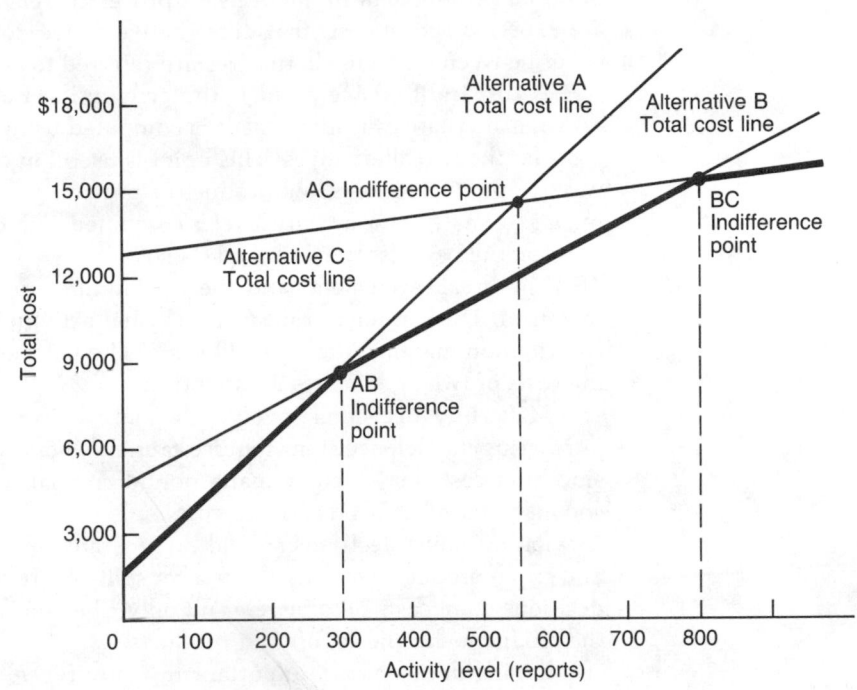

Figure 6-12
The three cost functions are graphed here. To find the minimum cost, follow the lowest cost line at all times. Here we start with plan A, switch to plan B at the AB cost indifference point, and switch to plan C at the BC indifference point. A switch always occurs at a cost indifference point. The lowest cost path is highlighted with a heavier line.

alternatives analyzed above. In that case the analysis may be only marginally useful. In addition, the decision maker must determine whether judgmental factors modify the above findings. For example, alternative C may be the most desirable, but it may be politically unfeasible to eliminate the jobs of current employees. If the present case load is 600 cases, alternative B appears most desirable, but C may be the better choice due to expected growth in the case load. At higher case levels alternative C would save money over the current manual system and would become the most cost-effective system at 800 cases. Whatever the other factors, cost analysis for multiple alternatives is usually very beneficial.

The complexity of the analysis of decisions involving more than three alternatives grows rapidly

Additional alternatives add complexity to cost analysis at a geometric rate. For instance, four alternatives may have six cost indifference points and five alternatives may have ten cost indifference points. The possible number of separate cost indifference points for multiple alternatives is $n(n-1)/2$ where n equals the number of alternatives. In this text we do not exceed three decision alternatives.

Summary   **Alternative choice decisions** involve situations with two or more courses of action from which the decision maker must select the best alternative. One important component in the decision process is relevant costs. **Relevant costs** are expected future costs that differ between decision alternatives. Costs that differ between decision alternatives are referred to as **differential costs**.

A **cost indifference point** is the activity level at which the cost for two decision alternatives is identical. It is computed using total costs or differential costs for the two alternatives. This point is useful in comparing two alternative ways of producing the same product or providing the same service. Management's estimate of the activity level is combined with the cost indifference point to select the best alternative based on cost.

The break-even point and the cost indifference point are two different measures. The former is a measure of what activity level is necessary for the contribution margin to cover fixed costs. The latter expresses the point where the costs of two alternatives are identical.

Make-buy decisions involve choosing between producing an item or purchasing it. Such decisions require caution when using unit production costs since unit costs may include many nondifferential costs. The correct decision should be based only on relevant costs.

Joint product decisions should be separated into single product decisions and group product decisions. Costs after split-off are relevant for single product decisions. Joint costs become relevant only when one alternative is to terminate the production of the set of joint products.

Pricing decisions are important to many types of organizations. A **price elastic** product is one whose total revenue falls with a price increase. A **price inelastic** product produces a rise in total revenue with a price increase. A **price indifference point** is the sales level at which the company's net income is identical between two pricing alternatives. The pricing decision is made by estimating the unit sales volume and comparing it with the price indifference point.

Multiple-alternative choice decisions involve comparing more than two alternatives. The first step is to compute the cost indifference points. There are three cost indifference points for three alternatives and six for four alternatives. The number of different cost indifference points increases geometrically with the number of different alternatives. The manager selects the alternative that yields the lowest cost at the expected level of activity. However, the computation of multiple indifference points is complicated, and the additional data may lead to information overload, making it hard to integrate the data into a logical decision model.

List of important terms

alternative choice decisions   *(210)*
cost indifference point   *(212)*
differential cost   *(209)*
information overload   *(228)*
make-buy decisions   *(217)*
multiple-alternative choice
   decision   *(210)*

opportunity cost   *(218)*
price elasticity   *(223)*
price indifference point   *(223)*
relevant cost   *(209)*
sunk cost   *(217)*

Questions

1. What does the term *relevant* mean in reference to accounting information?
2. What are relevant costs? How are they distinguishable from other costs?
3. What is meant by alternative choice decisions? Give some business and personal examples.
4. What is meant by the term *multiple alternatives*? If a manager is deciding between five alternatives, how many separate cost indifference points are possible?
5. Describe cost indifference points and explain their usefulness in decision making.
6. As the company controller, you provide the company president with relevant cost data concerning the purchase of ten new lathes. He says, "What do you mean, the $9 an hour we pay lathe operators is not relevant? I don't care what kind of lathes we buy, I am going to be interested in the amount we pay our lathe operators." Respond to the president.
7. Distinguish between a cost indifference point and a break-even point.
8. Why must managers use product costs cautiously when evaluating make-buy decisions?
9. When deciding between selling a joint product at the split-off point or processing further, what costs are relevant?
10. How is a price indifference point different from a cost indifference point?
11. A price indifference point tells us what price should be used for a product. Comment.

Exercises

Ex. 6-1   **Cost indifference point.** Following are data on two methods of producing an electronic watch.

	Method 1	Method 2
Direct material	3.10	$ 4.25
Direct labour	7.30	5.50
Variable MOH	6.20	5.10
Sales price	30.00	30.00
Yearly rental expense	22,000.00	26,000.00
Yearly insurance expense	5,300.00	9,700.00

Required:
a. Calculate the cost indifference point.
b. What is the significance of the indifference point calculated for part *a*?
c. At what levels of operations should each method be used?

Ex. 6-2   Make-buy decision. Stow-Dent Company accumulates the following cost data on the manufacture of 5000 pool filters last year. The filters are used with above-ground swimming pools manufactured by the company.

Direct materials	$25/unit
Direct labour	20/unit
Variable MOH	10/unit
Allocated fixed MOH	20/unit
Variable administrative	2/unit
Total unit cost	$77/unit

The company has an opportunity to buy the filters for $70 each. The company expects to need 600 units during the next year. Direct materials and labour costs will increase 10 percent, and other costs will stay the same. Seventy percent of the fixed manufacturing overhead cost allocated to the pool filters will remain if the filters are purchased; 30 percent of the fixed MOH cost is discretionary and can be eliminated. There is no alternative use for any excess capacity generated by eliminating production of pool filters.

Required:
Determine whether Stow-Dent should buy the filters or continue to manufacture them.

Ex. 6-3   Price indifference point. Given:

Variable costs	$6/unit
Fixed costs	$120,000
Current sales volume	50 000 units
Current price	$9/unit
New price	$11/unit

Required:
What is the price indifference point for the new selling price?

Ex. 6-4   Sell at split-off or process further. Do-Rite driveway sealer is manufactured in a joint product manufacturing process. Cost data for the driveway sealer are presented on page 235.

Manufacturing Costs	
Allocated joint cost	$ 6/can
Cost after split-off	4/can
Total unit cost	$10/can

Currently the product sells for $15 per 5-litre can. The sealer could be sold right after the split-off point for $10 a can. In addition to saving manufacturing costs, the company would save $1.50 a can in variable selling and administrative costs.

Required:
Should Do-Rite driveway sealer be sold at split-off or processed to completion? Support your decision with numerical data.

Ex. 6-5   Cost indifference point. Following are expected costs of production under two alternative plans:

	Production Plans	
	Plan 1	Plan 2
Variable costs:		
Direct materials	$ 4.60	$ 5.20
Direct labour	1.60	4.40
Variable MOH	1.00	2.00
Fixed costs:		
Insurance premiums	$10,000	$7,000
Utilities	12,600	4,000
Maintenance costs	15,400	2,000
Equipment rent	25,000	6,000

Required:
a. Compute the cost indifference point.
b. Describe the decision you would make based solely on the cost indifference point.
c. Present a graphical analysis of the indifference point you calculated.

Ex. 6-6   Break-even point and cost indifference point. Nutty World, Inc., is evaluating two alternative methods of processing roasted cashew nuts. One method is a fully automatic shelling, roasting, and packaging machine, and the other method is partially automated with some manual operations. Both methods will produce the identical product, a 1-kilogram tin of cashews that sells for $6. Below are cost data for the two processing methods.

	Automated	Semiautomated
Variable cost per 1-kg tin	$2.80	$3.60
Fixed expenses	$42,000	$27,000

Required:
a. Compute the break-even point in units for both alternatives.
b. Calculate the cost indifference point for the two production methods.
c. Prepare a complete graphical analysis of the alternatives.

Ex. 6-7   Price indifference point. Canadian Woods Treasures Company manufactures wool blankets that it sells for $80 each. At that price the company was able to earn a profit of $90,000 last year on sales of 8000 units. Variable costs during the year were $50 a blanket, and fixed costs were $150,000. The demand for these quality blankets is high, and the company is evaluating a price increase to $90.

Required:
a. What is the price indifference point?
b. Should the price be raised if sales with the new price are expected to be 7000 units?
c. If the price is increased and the expected sales level occurs, what is the net income for the year?

Ex. 6-8   Break-even point and cost indifference point. Following are cost data pertaining to different methods of mining road salt:

	Continuous Mining Equipment	Brine Solution Method
Variable costs per ton:		
Labour	$10.00	$ 4.00
Materials	.50	.80
Overhead	4.50	5.20
Total	$15.00	$10.00
Fixed costs:		
Equipment depreciation	$400,000	$ 600,000
Maintenance	200,000	300,000
Other overhead	200,000	300,000
Total	$800,000	$1,200,000

Salt is sold for $35 per ton. Last year the salt mine operated 225 days, with average production of 400 tons a day. The company expects the same volume of activity this year.

Required:
a. Compute the break-even point for each method.
b. Compute the cost indifference point.
c. Based on last year's production, which method should be used?

Ex. 6-9   Price indifference point. Steadfast Foods sells hot dogs for $1.50 a kilogram. The hot dogs cost $.90 a kilogram in variable costs to produce, and the fixed cost associated with the production and sale of the hot dogs is $120,000. The division manager is not happy with the profitability of this product, and he thinks the price should be raised by 20 percent. Current sales are 350 000 kilograms of hot dogs a year.

Required:
a. What is the price indifference point for the new price?
b. Show your analysis graphically.
c. If the new selling price causes a 25 percent drop in unit sales, should the price increase be implemented?

Ex. 6-10   Multiple-alternative decisions. Wiggley Company is evaluating three alternative methods of painting parts in its refrigerator manufacturing plant. Cost data for the alternatives are presented below.

	X	Y	Z
Variable costs per refrigerator:			
Direct materials	$10	$10	$12
Direct labour	15	9	5
Variable MOH	11	7	4
Total	$36	$26	$21
Fixed costs per year:			
Equipment lease costs	$24,000	$40,000	$60,000
Maintenance contract on equipment	6,000	10,000	15,000
Total	$30,000	$50,000	$75,000

Required:
a. Compute the cost indifference points for the three alternatives.
b. Graph the costs for each of the alternatives. Draw a dark line along the lowest-cost path of the three alternatives.
c. Describe the range of activity for which each alternative should be used.

Problem Set A

P. 6A-1 **Two-alternative graphic analysis.** This year Woodfair Hospital is using two different admitting procedures for each patient. The parallel admitting procedures are being used to provide the hospital's administrator with actual data on the two admitting methods. One procedure is almost fully automated, requiring the lease of computer equipment and using little labour time. The other admitting procedure is entirely manual, except for typewriters, and requires many documents and forms. At year-end one of the two admitting procedures will be adopted and the other dropped. Management expects to admit 4500 patients next year. Below are some cost data:

	Automatic	Manual
Variable costs per admittance:		
Forms and documents	$1.00	$3.00
Labour	3.00	8.00
Fixed admitting costs:		
Occupancy	$ 4,000	$4,000
Machine lease	36,000	2,000
Other	5,000	4,000

Required:
a. Graph the cost data.
b. At what level of admittance should Woodfair use the manual system and at what level should it use the automated system?
c. The administrator of Woodfair believes computers are the wave of the future for health care. He selects the automated system without considering the cost indifference point. Comment on the cost consequences of his decision.

P. 6A-2 **Special-order decision.** The Ripple Waterbed Company manufactures several types of waterbeds. Expecting a jump in demand for its product, the company built a large plant that currently is being utilized at 60 percent of capacity. A salesman brings in an offer from a large motel chain to purchase 100 heated king-size waterbeds for a price of $450 each. Normal selling price for the bed is $800 each. The schedule at the top of the following page presents costs of the king-size waterbeds for the current year's production. Acceptance of the order would cause no increase in any fixed cost.

Required:
a. Should the company accept the offer? Support your answer.
b. Would your answer to *a* change if sales commissions of $20 a bed could be eliminated on this special order?
c. Assume that 75 percent of the variable marketing costs can be eliminated. What would be the effect on net income from accepting this order?

	Costs for 1000 Units	Unit Cost
Direct materials	$260,000	$260
Direct labour	80,000	80
Manufacturing overhead (40% variable)	160,000	160
Marketing (1/3 variable)	120,000	120
Administrative (10% variable)	100,000	100
Total	$720,000	$720

P. 6A-3 **Make-buy decision.** Harper Company produces 7000 timing controls a month that it subsequently uses in its production of microwave ovens. The costs per unit of the timers are as follows:

Direct material	$ 3.20
Direct labour	4.40
Variable MOH	.60
Fixed MOH—discretionary	1.30
Fixed MOH—allocated	1.50
Total	$11.00

The company is considering purchasing the control for $9.75 per unit. Discretionary fixed costs can be eliminated if the timers are purchased. Committed fixed factory overhead in the amount of $10,500 is allocated to the 7000 units. If the timers are purchased, the factory space currently used in producing the timers can be used for warehouse space, thus reducing warehouse rental by $2,100 a month.

Required:
Determine whether the company should purchase the controls or continue to manufacture them.

P. 6A-4 **Joint product decisions.** Industrial Chemicals, Inc., produces products that are used by industrial firms to treat metals and wood. Three different types of exterior wood preservatives, X-Mol, Y-Mol, and Z-Mol, are produced as joint products. The per kilogram selling prices of the products are $14, $9, and $8, respectively. Below are quantity and cost data for the products for the year just completed. These cost relationships are expected to continue for the coming year.

All costs after split-off can be eliminated for any product that is not processed beyond split-off.

Product	Quantity Produced	Unit Cost		
		Joint	Cost after Split-Off	Total
X-Mol	5 000 litres	$4	$6	$10
Y-Mol	10 000 litres	4	3	7
Z-Mol	25 000 litres	4	2	6

Required:

Answer the following questions. Each situation is **independent** of the others.

a. A competitor introduces a new product that competes directly with Y-Mol. To sell Y-Mol, the price must be reduced to $6 a litre. Should Industrial Chemicals continue to produce Y-Mol?

b. X-Mol can be sold at split-off without further processing for $8.50 a litre. Should the product be sold at split-off?

c. A significant decline in the demand for Z-Mol forces a reduction in the price of the product to $4 a litre. What effect does this price decline have on production and sales decisions?

P. 6A-5 **Two-alternative analysis.** The McClellen Fence Company has been in business 40 years selling and installing chain link fences. The company employs four full-time installers as well as three part-time employees who supplement their other income by working for McClellen during busy periods. During the last year McClellen sold and installed 15 000 metres of chain link fence at an average price of $4 per metre. The company expects sales to increase by 10 percent this year, with prices and costs remaining the same. Recently the company hired a consulting firm to suggest methods of improving the company's shrinking profit margin. The consultants returned with a plan that involved leasing new, more efficient installation equipment that would greatly reduce the amount of manual labour involved in setting posts and stretching fence. The owner of the company is concerned about any actions that would require terminating part-time or full-time employees. Following are data on the current and proposed systems:

	Current	Proposed
Variable cost per 100 m of fence:		
Labour	$120	$ 40
Materials	180	210
Total	$300	$250
Fixed costs:		
Equipment	$3,000	$15,000
Other	2,000	3,000
Total	$5,000	$18,000

Required:

a. Compute the break-even point for both the current and proposed installation methods.

b. Compute the cost indifference point for the two alternatives.

c. Given the sales expectations, what is the cost effect of keeping the employees and continuing use of the old system instead of the proposed system?

d. A reevaluation of the labour estimates indicates that the estimated labour cost should be 25 percent higher than originally estimated for both alternatives. What is the effect on the cost indifference point?

P. 6A-6   Two-alternative comprehensive problem. Jolly Jaws Amusement Park charges $.40 each for all rides in the park. Variable costs amount to $.08 per ride, and fixed costs are $320,000. Last season the net income was $64,000 on sales of $480,000. Rising costs have cut sharply into Jolly Jaws' net income the last two years. This season management again expects cost increases of 25 percent for variable costs, and 10 percent for fixed costs. To help offset these increases, management is considering raising the price of a ride to $.50.

Required:

a. How many rides did Jolly Jaws sell last year?

b. If the price increase is **not** implemented, what is the expected net income for this season assuming the same volume of activity?

c. Compute the price indifference point for the new ride price.

d. Compute the break-even point for this season using (1) the old price, (2) the new price.

e. Should management raise the price of a ride if the price increase will reduce ride volume 10 percent from last season's level?

f. What is Jolly Jaws' expected net income for this year based upon your decision in *e*?

P. 6A-7   Multiple-alternative decision. The accounting department of Chauser Company uses the copying machines in the engineering graphics department of the firm for all of its copying needs. Accounting is charged for this service at cost. Soon the entire engineering graphics department will move to a new office building, and the move will terminate the accounting department's use of the copying service. The accounting department decides to acquire its own copying equipment and is currently evaluating several alternatives. Each alternative provides the same quality of copy although there are considerable differences in cost and speed. At the top of the facing page are cost data.

Required:

a. Compute the cost indifference points for the three alternatives.

b. What do the cost indifference points suggest as a course of action in this case?

	Cost per 100 Copies		
	Speed-O-Copy	Zip-O-Copy	Zap-O-Copy
Material cost	$5	$3	$2
Labour cost	6	2	1
Annual lease cost	$2,000	$5,000	$8,000

c. If management expects to need 72 800 copies next year, which copier would be most economical?

d. If management estimates a need for 72 800 copies in making its selection and only 45 000 copies are actually made, what is the cost of estimating the demand incorrectly?

e. Graph the costs for the three copiers, identifying the cost indifference points.

Problem Set B

P. 6B-1 Cost indifference points. The controller of Melburn Products seeks your advice on whether to replace its current manual assembly operation with an automated assembly line. The automated system would be much faster, use fewer employees, and reduce waste caused by errors. However, more skilled personnel would be needed to operate the system, and it involves a sizable annual lease cost. The data for the manual and automated systems are given below.

	Manual	Automated
Variable costs:		
Materials	$ 8.00/unit	$6.00/unit
Labour	16.00/unit	9.00/unit
Variable MOH	6.00/unit	5.00/unit
Fixed costs:		
Occupancy	$150,000/year	$160,000/year
Machinery lease	–	290,000/year

There is some concern that it is too late in the model year to change the assembly operation. If the company waits until the beginning of next year, it is expected the variable costs will rise by 10 percent and the fixed costs by 6 percent. Next year's sales estimate is 33 000 units.

Required:

a. At what level of production should Melburn Products switch to the automated system based on current costs?

b. Graph the current year cost data for the two alternatives.

c. Given the expected cost increases and sales for next year, decide if the assembly operation should be automated next year.

P. 6B-2   Special-order decision. Carbella Enterprises manufactures a variety of office furniture items, including a beautiful mahogany desk. A representative of a Middle-Eastern nation approaches the firm with an offer to buy 200 desks at a price of $450 each. Normal price is $600. The production of the 200 desks would not require the addition of any production facilities or other fixed costs. The following schedule presents cost data pertaining to the production and sale of mahogany desks:

	Total Costs for 5000 Desks	Unit Cost
Direct materials	$1,250,000	$250
Direct labour	500,000	100
Manufacturing overhead (40% variable)	750,000	150
Variable selling (all commissions)*	240,000	48
Fixed selling	50,000	10
Administrative (all fixed)	75,000	15
Allocated corporate expenses	100,000	20
Total	$2,965,000	$593

*The sales commission is based on a flat fee of $48 per desk sold.

Required:

a. If there is no commission expense, should Carbella accept this special order?

b. If the order is accepted, what would be the effect on company profitability?

c. Should the order be accepted if a commission fee must be paid to the sales representative covering the Middle East?

P. 6B-3   Service make-buy decision. Mumbly Drum Department Store is interested in providing a sales and management training program for its employees. Management is evaluating two alternatives. One is to use company personnel to develop materials and teach the classes. The second plan is to hire a management consulting firm to develop and teach the course. The two programs are expected to provide training experiences of equal quality to the employees. The controller has gathered some data on the two alternatives (shown on page 244).

Required:

a. If Mumbly Drum expects 140 employees a year to take the course, which alternative should the firm choose?

	Company Personnel	Management Consulting Firm
Variable costs:		
Materials cost per student	$ 15	–
Tuition per student	–	$100
Student salary while in class	160	160
Per-student cost of instructor	25	–
Fixed costs:		
Annual cost of developing materials	$16,000	–
Classroom occupancy cost*	2,000	–
Fixed part of fee for the course	–	$7,200

*Executive training room that would be used for other purposes if the class is held elsewhere.

b. What will the total cost of the program be in the first year under the alternative selected?

c. If the actual material cost is $25 per student, what effect does it have on your decision in part *a*?

P. 6B-4   **Joint product decisions.** The Pearly Waters Perfume Company manufactures various qualities of perfumes and colognes. One popular line of colognes includes three products that result from a joint product production process. Below are data from the most recent month of production:

Product	Price	Quantity	Joint Cost	Cost after Split-Off	Total Cost
Evergreen	$ 4	10 000	$2.80	$2	$4.80
Morning Flower	10	6 000	2.80	4	6.80
Evening Flower	15	4 000	2.80	5	7.80

As the new controller, you are called into the president's office along with the director of marketing. The president says, "I don't understand your product cost report. Either we are selling our largest-volume product for a loss, or the product cost data are all wrong. Now which is it?"

Required:

a. Respond to the president's question.

b. Another company has just introduced a product that competes directly with Morning Flower. To compete successfully with the other company's product, the price of Morning Flower cologne must be reduced to $6. Should the company do so and sell below cost?

c. If Pearly Waters has a policy of maintaining a gross margin of 20 percent on sales, what would your answer be in response to the price decline mentioned in *b*?

d. What is the minimum price for which Morning Flower can sell and still meet the 20 percent product gross margin for the group of products?

P. 6B-5 **Cost and price indifference points.** The production engineer of a manufacturing company is evaluating two methods of manufacturing metal typing strands that sell for $30. Expected first year sales are 15 000 units. Below are data relating to alternatives under consideration.

	Manual	Automated
Material	$10/unit	$13/unit
Labour	2h	1/2 h
Labour rate	$6/h	$8/h
Other variable costs	$3/unit	$2/unit
Fixed costs	$40,000	$121,000

Required:
a. Compute the break-even point for each alternative.
b. Compute the cost indifference point for the two alternatives.
c. What production method should be selected?
d. Given your decision in part *c*, what is the price indifference point of a $5 price increase?

P. 6B-6 **Two-alternative decision comprehensive problem.** A private university with a current enrollment of 12 000 students is reviewing cost and revenue data for the past academic year. Student tuition is $3,600 a year. Tuition normally covers 75 percent of university expenditures. The remaining 25 percent comes from endowments and contributions. During the last academic year fixed costs amounted to $30,000,000. The rest of the costs varied with student enrollment. Costs have been rising more rapidly than tuition or contributions, and the university just broke even last year. A tuition increase is being contemplated. The budget committee thinks endowment revenues and contributions will remain constant at last year's level for the next several years.

The fixed costs are expected to increase $3,000,000, and variable costs are expected to increase 10 percent. The president of the university tells the budget committee that he expects a new $5,000,000 grant in addition to the normal contributions for each of the next five years from a large corporation that is owned by an alumnus of the university. The university has been postponing a number of major capital improvement and building projects.

Required:
a. How much could student enrollment drop and the university still break even if tuition is raised to $4,200 a year and the grant is not received? Ignore the expected cost increases.

b. How would receipt of the grant affect your answer to part *a*?

c. If the grant is received and tuition is raised to $4,200, how much money would the university have available the first year for capital improvements and building with student enrollment of 11 200 and the expected cost increases?

d. If the grant is received and costs increase as predicted for the coming academic year, what tuition should the university charge to break even with its current enrollment of 12 000 students?

e. Compute the required tuition rate as in *d*, but provide $4,040,000 for capital improvements.

P. 6B-7   Multiple-alternative decision. The Morefield Salt Company mines road salt year-round and stores it in huge piles on a 40-ha storage site. During eight months of the year demand for road salt can be handled at the main warehouse storage facility. However, during four winter months the company must use the salt stored in the field to meet most of the demand.

Last winter the Morefield Salt Company used front-end loaders to load the salt into highway department salt trucks. Morefield rented the loaders since they are used heavily only for four months of the year. In past years the company rented whatever was available. Last year the company used three GW-6 and two GW-9 loaders. This year it is making a systematic analysis of the alternatives. Management has narrowed the choice to three whose data are presented below.

	Front-End Loaders		
	GW-6	**GW-9**	**GW-12**
Capacity in tons per hour	80	160	240
Operator wages per hour	$8	$10	$12
Other hourly operating costs	$4	$6	$8
Monthly lease cost per machine	$1,350	$3,700	$6,600
Monthly diesel/hydraulic maintenance agreement per machine	$ 150	$ 300	$ 400

During the peak four-month period the truck loading operation runs two 8-hour shifts, 25 days a month. The company expects to load an average of 192,000 tons a month during the four winter months. A systems engineer suggests that the firm look into an automated loading system to handle the loading activities for the 40-ha storage site. The automated system would require several gigantic hoppers and a sophisticated conveyor belt system. A system large enough to handle current demand would require an annual fixed cost of $95,000 and would have a variable loading cost of $.02 per ton.

Required:

a. Analyze the three alternatives for front-end loaders and suggest the best alternative.

b. What is the total and per-ton cost of loading salt for the four-month period using the alternative you recommended in *a*?

c. Assuming last year's costs were the same as this year's, how much more did the company pay for winter loading activities than was necessary assuming all machines were run full-time?

d. Analyze the automatic loading system and decide if it should be implemented.

Minicases

Minicase 6-1
(CGA adapted)

CGA Manufacturing Company, Ltd., has been in business for several years. It was founded by the late C.G. Adams, the father of George L. Adams, the president, and has been engaged in manufacturing quality French provincial furniture for the Canadian market. Since the production was very limited in the earlier years of the company, most of the accounting and tax matters were handled by George L. Adams and Mrs. Adams. During the 1970s the business has grown very rapidly and new export markets were tapped by the new marketing manager, Mr. Jim Johnson. As a result of this rapid development, last year a new accounting department was organized and Mr. Charlie D. Robertz was given full responsibility for this department.

The capacity of CGA Manufacturing Company through new investments has grown to 16 000 units of Type A chairs. However, current plans call for monthly production and sales of 10 000 units at $150 each. Mr. Robertz provided the following per unit cost for Type A chairs:

Unit Cost for Type A Chair	
Materials	$ 50.00
Direct labour	30.00
Variable manufacturing overhead	7.50
Fixed manufacturing overhead	15.00
Variable selling expenses	2.50
Fixed administrative expenses	10.00
Total unit cost	$115.00

Mr. Jim Johnson, after a lengthy business trip to British Columbia, informed the president that he had received a special order for 4000 chairs at $100.00.

Mr. George L. Adams called a meeting of Jim Johnson, Charlie D. Robertz, and himself to prepare an answer to the new customer.

Required:

Should the company accept a special order for 4000 units at $100.00 each? Explain fully.

Reproduced with permission from *Final Examination 1974*, published by CGA Canada, Vancouver, B.C.

Minicase 6-2   (SMA of Canada adapted)

Sun, Inc., manufactures cabinets for its own radios and for sale to outsiders in a plant which is separate from the radio operation. Management expects that during the third quarter of 1984—the three months ending September 30th—the cabinet facility will be operating at 80 percent of normal capacity. Because a higher utilization of plant capacity is desired, acceptance of a special order would be considered. Cost data for the Sun, Inc., cabinets now being manufactured are as follows:

Regular selling price to outsiders	$9.00
Cost per unit:	
Raw materials	$2.50
Direct labour — .5 hour @ $6.00	3.00
Overhead — .25 machine hour @ $4.00	1.00
Total costs	$6.50

Sun, Inc., has received special order inquiries from two companies, as follows:

1. Pluto, Ltd., would like to order a cabinet similar to that of Sun's. The Pluto cabinet requirement is for 25 000 to be shipped by October 1, 1984 for a price of $6.00 each. The cost data for this order would be similar to that of Sun cabinets, with one exception. According to the specifications provided by Pluto, Ltd., the special cabinet requires less expensive raw materials. These will cost only $2.25 per cabinet. It is estimated by management that the remaining costs, labour time, and machine time will be the same as the Sun, Inc., cabinet.

2. Saturn, Inc., has submitted another special order to Sun, Inc., for 8000 cabinets at $7.50 per cabinet. This order also would have to be shipped by October 1, 1984. However, the Saturn cabinet is different from any cabinet in the Sun line. The estimated unit costs of this cabinet are:

Raw materials	$3.25
Direct labour — .5 hour @ $6.00	3.00
Overhead — .5 hour @ $4.00	2.00
Total costs	$8.25

In addition Sun, Inc., will incur $1,800 in additional set-up costs and will have to purchase a special device costing $2,600 to manufacture these cabinets; this device would be discarded once the special order is completed.

Sun, Inc.'s manufacturing capabilities are limited to the total machine hours available. The maximum plant capacity available under normal operating conditions is 87 000 machine hours per year or 7250 machine hours per month. The budgeted fixed overhead for 1984 amounts to $208,800. All manufacturing overhead costs are applied to production at the predetermined rate of $4.00 per hour.

Sun, Inc., will have the entire third quarter—July 1, 1984 to September 30, 1984—to work on the special orders. It is not expected that any repeat business will be generated from either special order.

It is Sun, Inc.'s company practice not to subcontract any portion of an order when special orders are not expected to generate repeat sales.

Required:
Should Sun, Inc., accept either special order?
Justify your answer and show your calculations.

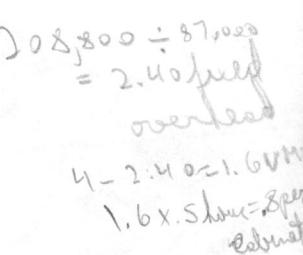

Minicase 6-3 (Certified Accountants—U.K. adapted)

Pattons, Limited produce a single product—the Patt. For the year commencing 1 July 1984, it budgets to produce 5000 Patts and sell them at $15.00 each.

The following Total Cost Card is drawn up for the production of one Patt on 1 July 1984:

	$
Direct materials	5
(10 kilograms @ $.50 per kilogram)	
Direct labour	
(4 hours @ $1.00 per hour)	4
Variable manufacturing overhead	2
(Note 1)	
Total variable cost	11
Fixed overhead (Note 2)	1
Total cost	$12

Notes

1. Variable manufacturing overheads are applied on the basis of labour hours.
2. Fixed overheads are applied on the basis of kilograms of material consumed.
3. Patts are produced using special equipment which can only be leased. The rental rates for this machinery are 50¢ per unit produced, with a minimum

rental charge of $3,000 per annum. As Pattons, Limited has never produced anywhere near sufficient Patts to cause this minimum rental charge to be exceeded, the minimum rental fee is classified as a fixed cost.

4. All materials used in the production of Patts are purchased from a single supplier who offers all his customers a discount of 20 percent in the form of an annual rebate on **all** purchases provided that these exceed 55 000 kilograms per annum.

5. Based on the budget for the year, direct labour will be working at full capacity. Once full capacity is exceeded overtime has to be paid to direct labour at time-and-a-half.

6. For budgeting purposes Pattons Limited ignores taxation and inflation. On August 1, 1984 a large organization asks Pattons whether it would be prepared to produce 1000 Patts for them at a price of $10 each. They would require these to be labeled as Ttaps, their brand name. The sales manager of Pattons asks the cost department to produce cost figures to help him decide whether to accept the order. Two sets of figures are produced by the cost department—the first working from the standard cost card, and the second using variable production costs. In both cases the figures show that to accept the order would cause the firm a $2,000 loss. However, the marketing director has desired an opening into this large organization for some time and persuades the managing director of Pattons to let him accept the order as a loss leader, saying that he is prepared to allocate $2,000 from his advertising budget to cover the expected loss.

Required:

a. Draw up the original budget for Pattons, Limited for the year commencing 1 July 1984.

b. Show how the cost department probably compiled the two sets of figures which indicated that acceptance of the order would cause a loss.

c. In the form of a table showing the company's position both with and without the order, exhibit how marginal costs and any contribution associated with the order would be calculated.

d. If any of the methods used in *b* and *c* above to calculate costs and income differ in content, explain with reference to the figures concerned why the differences occur. What principle should guide the preparation and presentation of information for decision making?

Reproduced from Certified Accountants Questions and Suggested Answers, including papers for Scottish and Irish Students, Professional Examination, June 1976. With permission of The Association of Certified Accountants.

part 3

Planning, Control, and Responsibility Reporting

Managing a business in today's economic environment is a complex and difficult task. Professional managers plan every phase of business operations in advance and must ensure, by means of carefully developed control procedures, that plans are carried out. Managers accomplish the planning and control function by assigning to different persons the responsibility for specific segments of business operations. Information must be provided concerning the accomplishment of goals and progress toward achieving predetermined managerial plans. Such information is provided by specialized managerial reports, many of which are accounting reports discussed in this part of the book.

Much managerial planning and control involves short-range business goals such as the number of units of a product to be produced next year. Chapter 7 discusses the way such business goals are developed by means of combining many separate budgets into a master budget. Once the budget is prepared, control over operations is accomplished by comparing the budgeted plans with actual operating results and by taking corrective action when necessary. Chapter 8 discusses the use of standards in measuring the costs of materials and labour used to produce goods and services. Chapter 9 deals with the more difficult problems of measuring and controlling the indirect costs of goods and services and the preparation of budgets at several levels of activity.

Measuring and reporting accomplishments often must be done for many separate segments of a business. Chapter 10 discusses the measurement of a specific business segment's contribution to overall business profits. Chapter 11 discusses the various approaches to dividing a business into specific centres of responsibility.

In addition to the short-range plans that deal with immediate problems of day-to-day business operations, long-range plans are also prepared by managers. Pricing of products, or planning a new production facility, may require looking many years into the future. Chapter 12 discusses the many factors that enter into the determination of the price of a product or service. Chapter 13 is devoted to capital budgeting, which involves the planning of new products and investment in production facilities. Chapter 14 discusses some of the aspects of planning, control, and responsibility reporting of not-for-profit organizations such as governments or hospitals. It also illustrates how the actions of government influence business operations ranging from current production to price setting and capital budgeting.

Chapter 7

Basic Budgeting Concepts

This chapter presents the basic concepts of budgeting and the procedures used in developing a budget. When you have completed this chapter, you should understand:

1 The nature and characteristics of budgets.

2 The functions of budgeting.

3 The composition and use of a master budget.

4 The nature and use of each component of the master budget.

5 The basic procedures used in developing a budget.

6 The budget review process.

7 The purpose of budget performance reports.

Virtually everyone has heard the term **budgeting** and has some concept of its meaning. Like many accounting terms, budgeting is used commonly in our everyday language. The news media discuss budgets of federal, provincial, and municipal governments, and many people describe a variety of resource allocation decisions, ranging from vacation planning to the purchase of food and clothing, as budgeting. The purpose of this chapter is to introduce the basic framework of the budgeting process, define budgeting terms, and provide a clear understanding of the concepts of budgeting. The primary emphasis in this chapter is business budgeting, but many of the concepts are applicable to nonbusiness activities.

The fundamentals of budgeting

Budget defined

A **budget** is a comprehensive quantitative plan for utilizing the resources of an entity for some specified period of time. Note that a budget:

1. Is quantitative.
2. Deals with some specific entity.
3. Covers a period of time in the future.

Budgets include both the inflow of revenue and the outflow of expenses.

Quantitative

Plans are expressed in quantitative measures

A significant amount of descriptive material may accompany a budget. From an accounting point of view, however, we are interested primarily in the quantitative description of activities expressed by the budget. All planned projects and activities for the organization are reduced to the common denominator of money or some other quantitative measure, such as units of input or output.

Budget entity

A budget must apply to a specific, clearly defined entity

The entity concept that is so important in financial accounting is essential to budgeting also. A specific budget must apply to a clearly defined accounting entity. For budgeting purposes, however, the entity may consist of a small part of a business entity, and budgets may be prepared for a section, division, or department of a business, or for a specific activity of an entity. For example, a student interested in budgeting the cost of a first year's college education should not include in the budget the cost of a three-week Banff vacation or the purchase of an $800 guitar. While these two expenditures may be costs of the period, they are not college education expenses.

Assume that Mary Drummer plans a trip to Florida over Christmas vacation. In making her plans, she estimates the amounts she expects to spend for the trip, as shown in Figure 7-1. Her plan is a budget divided into four basic cost categories. It is important to note that this budget is only for Mary's trip to Florida in December 1983. It does not include the cost of others who might travel with her or other trips or activities that Mary may plan for December 1983.

Note that a budgeting entity can be as specific as a single project, such as Mary's Florida trip, or it can be a broader activity, such as the cost of a year at

Figure 7-1
A very simple budget. Most people find it necessary to do some personal budgeting although the budgeting process may be very informal.

Mary Drummer **Budget for a Christmas Vacation to Florida** **December 10-21, 1983**	
My share of the gas	$ 40.00
My share of the lodging	85.00
Food costs	60.00
Souvenirs and miscellaneous	30.00
Total vacation budget	$215.00

college. Of course, a budget might well cover a much broader situation than either of the above examples, such as the budget for an entire manufacturing firm or for the Canadian government. The important concept here is that one must first define precisely the budget entity and only then can one start preparing the budget.

Organizations must clearly define each entity for which they prepare budgets. For example, if a firm prepares departmental budgets, the functions and activities of each department must be carefully delineated. Figure 7-2 presents a departmental labour budget for Murphy Manufacturing Company that shows the amount to be paid for labour in each department and the total for the entire company. Note that here the budget is just for departmental labour. A budget for the entire departmental entity would include amounts for labour, materials, maintenance, and many other items.

Future time period

Many financial figures are meaningless unless they are couched in some time reference. Income statements are annual, quarterly, or monthly. Likewise, a person receiving a $10,000 job offer would want to know if the figure represents pay for a month, a year, a lifetime, or some other time period. We may assume the $10,000 is an annual salary. However, in accounting time references should be clearly stated and not left for assumption.

Budgets are estimates of future economic events

Budgets should represent the expected financial consequences of planned programs and activities for a specified period of time. Annual budgets are widespread and important. Since most organizations prepare annual reports to satisfy reporting requirements of the Revenue Canada, provincial governments, lending institutions, and others, annual budgets provide a convenient framework for comparing planned results with actual results.

Murphy Manufacturing Company **Departmental Labour Budget** **1984**				
Department	**Shearing**	**Machining**	**Finishing**	**Assembly**	**Total**
Direct labour	$126,000	$220,000	$142,000	$108,000	$596,00
Indirect labour	44,000	80,000	30,000	18,000	172,00
Allocated service department labour	21,000	34,000	28,000	15,000	98,000
Total	$191,000	$334,000	$200,000	$141,000	$866,000

Figure 7-2
Budgets for businesses require systematic procedures for developing and reviewing the budget. Departmental budgets require managers to delineate carefully the functions and activities of each department.

In addition to annual budgets, many other time periods are used in budgeting as well. Long-term plans may be prepared for two, three, five, or even more years in the future. Longer-term budgets are usually less detailed than annual budgets. It is more difficult to prepare detailed plans as one moves farther away from the present.

Frequently annual budgets are divided into shorter time periods, such as quarters or months. Some critical areas, such as cash flow planning, may require weekly or daily budgets. Short-range budgets make possible quicker reponses to problems that may arise. Remember that all budgets, whether short-term or long-term, are estimates of the future. Most accounting reports deal with measuring the financial consequences of past events. There is a sharp contrast between measuring historical accounting data and making estimates of future economic events.

Reasons for budgeting

People budget for a variety of reasons. Some common reasons are that budgeting:

1. Requires periodic planning.
2. Fosters coordination, cooperation, and communication.
3. Forces quantification of proposals.
4. Provides a framework for performance evaluation.
5. Creates an awareness of business costs.
6. Satisfies legal and contractual requirements.
7. Orients a firm's activities toward organizational goals.

There are many reasons for budgeting

Periodic planning

Virtually all activities require some planning to ensure efficient and effective use of scarce resources. Some people are compulsive planners who continuously update plans that have already been made and plan for new activities and functions. At the other extreme are people who do not like to plan and therefore find little or no time to get involved in the planning process. The budgeting process closes the gap between these two extremes by creating a formal planning framework that provides specific, uniform periodic deadlines for each phase of the planning process. People who are not attuned to the planning process must still meet budget deadlines. Of course, planning does not guarantee success. People must execute the plans, but the planning process is an important prerequisite to many successful activities.

Coordination, cooperation, and communication

Planning by individuals does not ensure an optimum plan for the entire organization. The budgeting process, however, provides a vehicle for the exchange of ideas and objectives among people in the various organizational segments. The budget review process and other budget communication networks should minimize redundant and counterproductive programs by the time the final budget is approved.

Quantification

Since we live in a world of limited resources, virtually all individuals and organizations must ration their resources. The rationing process is easier for some than for others. Each person and each organization must compare the costs and benefits of each potential project or activity and choose those that result in the most appropriate resource allocation decisions.

Measuring cost and benefit requires some degree of quantification. Profit-oriented firms make dollar measurements for both costs and benefits. This is not always an easy task. For example, the benefits of an advertising campaign are increased sales and a better company image, but it is difficult to estimate the additional sales revenue caused specifically by an advertising campaign, and it is even more difficult to quantify the improvements in the company image. In not-for-profit organizations, such as governmental agencies, quantification of benefits can be even more difficult. For example, how does one quantify the benefits of better police protection, more music programs at the city park, or better fire protection, and how should the benefits be evaluated in allocating resources to each activity? Despite the difficulties, resource allocation decisions necessitate some reasonable quantification of the costs and benefits of the various projects under consideration.

Performance evaluation

Since budgets are estimates of future events, they also serve as realistic estimates of acceptable performance for each entity. Managerial performance in each budgeting entity may be appraised by comparing actual performance with budget projections. Most managers want to know what is expected of them so that they may monitor their own performance. Budgets help to provide that type of information. Of course, managers can also be evaluated on other criteria, but the value of having some quantifiable measure of performance should not be minimized.

Cost awareness

Accountants and financial managers are by nature concerned with the cost implications of decisions and activities, but many other managers are not. Production supervisors are concerned primarily with output, marketing managers with sales, and so forth. It is easy for people to ignore costs and cost-benefit relationships. At budgeting time, however, all managers with budget responsibility must think in terms of costs and benefits as they evaluate their projects and activities. This cost awareness provides a common ground for communication among the various functional areas of the organization.

Legal and contractual requirements

Many organizations are legally required to budget. Local fire departments, for example, cannot ignore budgeting even if it seems too much trouble, and the school boards would soon be out of funds if trustees decided not to submit a budget this year. Even in the absence of other reasons for budgeting, a large number of entities would prepare budgets simply because they are required to do so. Some firms commit themselves to a budgeting requirement when signing loan agreements or other operating agreements. For example, a bank may require a firm to submit an annual operating budget and monthly cash budgets throughout the life of a bank loan.

Goal orientation

Budgets should reflect plans to achieve organizational goals

Resource allocation decisions should be made considering the effect of proposed projects and activities on the achievement of goals. Simple as this may sound, it is sometimes difficult to relate general organizational goals to specific projects or activities. The reason is that many general goals are not operational—that is, it is difficult to determine the impact of specific projects on the achievement of the general goals of the organization. For example, organizational goals may be stated as follows:

1. Generate a satisfactory profit.
2. Maintain sufficient liquidity.

The terms *satisfactory* and *sufficient* may have different meanings for different people. A major prerequisite to goal-oriented budgeting is the development of a formal set of operational goals. Some organizations have no formally defined goals, and even those that do often have only general goals for the entire organization. Major operating units may function without written or clearly defined goals or objectives. Sometimes the unwritten objectives of the unit supervisor or a group of top managers represent a set of undefined objectives which may or may not dovetail with the general objectives of the organization, but which are nevertheless being implemented, if only subconsciously. Such informal structures may jeopardize the firm's ability to utilize its scarce resources optimally. Therefore, a logical first step toward effective budgeting is to formalize the goals of the organization. Starting at the top, general organizational goals should be as specific as possible, carefully established, and written. Next, each major unit of the organization should develop more specific operational goals. The process should continue down the organizational structure to the lowest level of budget responsibility. This goal-development process is difficult because it requires management at all levels to resolve difficult issues, but it results in a budgeting framework that is much more likely to be effective.

Organizational goals and objectives should be created and formally stated

It is not necessary for all goals to be defined with precision, and at high levels of management numerous goals may be stated in very general terms. For example, the loosely defined goals listed above may be stated more precisely to make them operational, and they may be combined with additional goals as follows:

1. Generate a return on investment of 15 percent or more.
2. Maintain a current ratio of 1.8 or more.
3. Provide valuable products to society.
4. Provide jobs for the community.

The last two items on the above list can be satisfied whether or not the organization achieves the first two goals, which are now stated in operational terms. The two operational goals can be used to establish organizational goals at lower levels that are compatible with the main objectives. For example, budget proposals for the acquisition of computer equipment can be evaluated more easily if detailed operating objectives are available. The goals of the data processing department should be consistent with the objective of earning a 15 percent return and maintaining a 1.8 current ratio. It is, of course, entirely possible that some goals are not relevant to all departments. Some examples of goals for the computer department are:

1. Provide corporate users with data processing services of quality equal to or greater than services that could be purchased from external time-sharing firms.
2. Provide corporate users with data processing services at a cost equal to or less than the cost of comparable services from external vendors.
3. Provide data processing services to any internal corporate user who can justify the cost of the service.
4. Charge (through the budget process) all corporate users the total cost of the services they use.

Defining goals for not-for-profit organizations is often more difficult than for profit seeking firms due to the inability to quantify many objectives. For example, the goals of a governmental agency may be stated as:

1. Maximize community benefits, given the amount of available resources.
2. Minimize the cost of providing a given level of service.

When budgets are prepared, however, the decision must still be made on the actual amount to be spent on a particular service or the amount of resources to be used for a specific project.

Functions of budgeting

There are two basic functions of budgeting:

1. Planning
2. Control

Planning

Planning is what most people think of when the term *budgeting* is mentioned. It encompasses the entire process of preparing the budget from the initial ideas through the development of the budget. The majority of the time and effort devoted to budgeting is expended in the planning stage. Careful planning provides the framework for the second function of budgeting.

Control

*In the control phase
of budgeting, actual
results are compared
with budget data*

The control phase in budgeting is the comparison of actual results with the budget. This comparison can occur only after some actual accounting data are available. For example, January production and cost data are necessary to compare with the January production budget to measure any difference between the two for the month. The comparison of actual results with budget expectations is often referred to as **performance reporting.** The term **control** does not merely refer to cost minimization, but instead it refers to the ability to monitor activities and take corrective action when actual results differ from expectations. The budget acts as a gauge against which managers measure actual costs and revenues.

While the planning function of budgeting may seem tedious and undesirable to some managers, it may still be more agreeable than the control phase. Typically it is more pleasant to plan for the future than to explain what went wrong when comparisons show unfavourable performance. However, the control phase is where managers can learn from the mistakes indicated by the performance reports.

The master budget

The total budget package

The **master budget** is the total budget package for an oganization; it is the end product of the budget preparation process. The master budget consists of all the individual budgets for each part of the organization aggregated into one overall budget for the entire organization. The exact composition of the master budget depends somewhat on the type and size of the business. However, all master budgets represent the organization's overall plan for the budget period in question.

Figure 7-3
A typical master budget for a manufacturing firm. Master budgets for other types of organizations also include an operating budget and a financial budget, although the components of each may vary. For example, a merchandising firm does not prepare a production budget.

Manufacturing Firm
Master Budget

Operating budget
  Sales budget
  Budget of ending inventories
  Production budget
    Materials budget
    Direct labour budget
    Manufacturing overhead budget
  Budgeted cost of goods sold
  Administrative expense budget
  Marketing expense budget
  Budgeted net income from operations
  Budgeted nonoperating items
  Budgeted net income
Financial budget
  Capital expenditure budget
  Cash budget
  Budgeted statement of financial position (balance sheet)
  Budgeted statement of changes in financial position

Figure 7-3 describes the basic components of a master budget for a manufacturing firm. The component parts fit together in a systematic fashion to form the firm's detailed operating plan for the coming year. Below we examine each of the components individually, followed by a comprehensive illustration of a master budget. The master budget is divided into two major categories, the operating budget and the financial budget. The operating budget covers operating expenses and revenues for the period; these result in budgeted net income. The financial budget includes the budgeted statement of financial position and other budgets used in financial management. A large part of the financial budget is determined by the operating budget and the beginning statement of financial position.

Operating budget

The **operating budget** is composed of the income statement elements. A manufacturing business budgets both manufacturing and nonmanufacturing activities. Below we discuss the various elements of the operating budget of a manufacturing firm.

The sales budget is prepared first

Sales budget. The **sales budget** is the first budget to be prepared, and it is usually considered the most important budget because so many other budgets are directly related to sales and are therefore largely derived from the sales budget. Inventory budgets, production budgets, personnel budgets, marketing budgets, administrative budgets, and other budget areas are all affected significantly by the amount of revenue that is expected from sales.

Sales budgets are influenced by a wide variety of factors. General economic conditions, pricing decisions, competitor actions, industry conditions, and marketing programs are just some of the items that must be evaluated. In an effort to develop a very accurate sales budget, firms employ many experts to assist in sales forecasting.

Often the sales budget starts with individual sales representatives or sales managers predicting sales in their particular area. The basic sales data are aggregated to arrive at a raw sales forecast that is then modified to reflect many of the variables mentioned previously. The resulting sales budget is expressed in dollars and must include sufficient detail on product mix and sales patterns to provide the information necessary for making decisions about changes in inventory levels and production quantities.

Budget of ending inventories. Inventories comprise a major portion of the current assets of many manufacturing firms. Separate inventory level decisions must be made for inventories of raw materials, work in process, and finished goods. Raw material scarcities, management's attitude about inventory levels, inventory carrying costs, inventory ordering costs, and other variables may all affect inventory level decisions. Managers may use the inventory management techniques discussed in Chapter 15, or they may make simple "seat of the pants" decisions about inventory. In either case decisions on inventory levels must be made before production budgets can be finalized.

Production budget. The production quantity budget is the starting point for developing the entire production budget. The materials budget, direct labour budget, and manufacturing overhead budget are all derived from the production quantity budget. Taken together, these budgets are referred to as the **production budget.** Managers must consider current and expected inventory levels as well as sales estimates when preparing the materials budget. Monthly **materials budgets** reflect any cyclical sales patterns and the time required between ordering and receiving material.

The **direct labour budget** is useful for production planning as well as for personnel management. Consideration must be given to any changes in the type of labour talent needed as a result of changes in the mix of products manufactured and sold. Likewise, firms must plan for changing labour requirements caused by cyclical production patterns. Significant swings in production demand during the year cause much greater problems in planning for labour than for inventory and manufacturing overhead.

The **manufacturing overhead budget** includes all indirect costs of manufacturing discussed in Chapters 3 and 4. Included are indirect material, indirect labour, capacity costs for the production facility, and indirect production support costs. It is important to separate the fixed and variable components of manufacturing overhead costs so that the cost estimates are reliable at the expected production level.

Budgeted cost of goods sold. For a manufacturing firm cost of goods sold represents the production cost of products that are sold. Consequently, the **cost of goods sold budget** follows directly from the production budget. The cost of goods sold figure is different from the production budget figure because of the effect of beginning and ending inventories.

Administrative expense budget. The **administrative expense budget** contains the administrative costs for nonmanufacturing business activities. Often the administrative expense budget contains many fixed costs, some of which may be avoidable if subsequent operations indicate some cost cuts are necessary. These avoidable costs, sometimes called discretionary fixed costs, include such items as research and development, employee educational and training programs, and portions of the personnel budget. Fixed costs that cannot be avoided during the period are called committed fixed costs. Mortgage payments, bond interest payments, and property taxes are classified as committed costs. Variable administrative costs may include some personnel costs, a portion of the utility costs, computer service bureau costs, and supplies costs.

Marketing expense budget. The marketing effort is an important determinant of sales volume. Consequently, the **marketing expense budget** should be prepared, at least in part, early in the budgeting process when the sales budget is being prepared. Of course, many marketing costs do not vary directly with sales volume. Some marketing costs, such as marketing management salaries, are fixed, and others behave in different ways. Marketing costs for some consumer products are very high and may exceed the cost of producing the product. In such cases the marketing budget is obviously a very important budget.

Expected net income

Budgeted net income. Once all of the preceding budgets are completed, budgeted net income from operations can be computed. This key figure is the target net income from normal operations. It is the major component of the firm's profit objective and as such should reflect the vast majority of the firm's activities for the budget period.

Sometimes a firm expects to have nonoperating items that affect the income statement, such as interest on investments or losses on the sale of fixed assets. These can be either revenue or expense items. Usually they are relatively small, although in large firms the dollar amounts can be sizable. If nonoperating items are expected, they should be included in the firm's total budgeted net income. A final operating budget item consists of income taxes expected on the budgeted net income. Income taxes are levied on actual, not budgeted, net income, but the budget plan should include expected taxes; therefore, the last figure in the **budgeted income statement** is budgeted after-tax net income.

The operating budget described in Figure 7-3 is for a manufacturing firm, but in many respects it is quite similar to operating budgets for other types of organizations. For example, a merchandising firm, such as a department store, has a similar operating budget, but there is no production budget. The cost of goods sold budget comes directly from merchandise inventory and the merchandise purchases budget. The rest of the operating budget is very similar, although the exact nature of the various budget elements may be somewhat different. For example, the type of marketing costs and the relative amount of marketing cost per dollar of sales may be different in a merchandising firm.

Operating budgets are important in all types of organizations

Operating budgets of service firms are slightly different because service firms have no product cost. The major components are revenue from services and operating expenses. For example, an optometrist's office would budget service revenue and operating expenses.

The operating budgets for public-sector organizations such as governmental agencies, and not-for-profit institutions, such as charities, are also similar in form to the one described. Of course, the nature of the revenues and costs is different. Public-sector budgeting is discussed in Chapter 14.

The financial budget

Although there are some differences in operating budgets of manufacturing, merchandising, and service firms, very little difference exists among **financial budgets** of these entities. The relative importance of the various accounts may differ, but there is little difference in the basic nature of the budgets.

Capital investment decisions

Capital expenditure budget. Capital budgeting usually refers to the acquisition of major items like plant and equipment, but many other types of projects fall into this category. A long-term employee education program is an example. The **capital expenditure budget** contains some of the most critical budgeting decisions of an organization. Typically, capital expenditures are relatively large in comparison with operating expenditures and have a long-term impact on the organization and the achievement of its goals.

Capital expenditure projects have useful lives in excess of one accounting period. Like other budgets, capital expenditure budget proposals are evaluated in light of organization goals and objectives. However, the length of the time period of capital budgeting projects and the relative size of the expenditures warrant detailed and careful analysis. A number of specialized analytical tools have been developed for making capital budgeting decisions. These are discussed in some detail in Chapter 13.

Cash budget. A major goal of virtually all organizations is liquidity, which means the ability to pay debts when they come due. Even governmental organizations must pay their bills and other obligations on time. Meeting cash obligations is not as simple as it may appear. Profitability and liquidity do not necessarily go hand in hand. Many firms experience their most critical liquidity problems when they go from a break-even position to profitability. At that time growing receivables, inventories, and capacity cost requirements may create cash shortages.

A very useful tool in cash management is the **cash budget.** Managers estimate all expected cash flows for the budget period. The typical starting point is cash from operations, which is net income adjusted for noncash items, such as depreciation. All nonoperating cash items are also included. Purchase of land and equipment, sales of bonds and common stock, and the acquisition of treasury stock are a few examples of nonoperating items affecting the cash budget. The net income figure and net cash flow for an accounting period may be very different because of nonoperating cash flow items or changes in working capital.

Annual cash budgets may cover too long a period of time to meet management's cash planning needs. Monthly, weekly, and even daily cash budgets may be more suitable for meeting management information requirements. The frequency of cash budgets depends on management's planning needs and the potential for cash management problems.

Cash management is intended to optimize cash balances; this means having enough cash to meet liquidity needs **and** not having so much cash that profitability is sacrificed. Excess cash should be invested in earning assets and should not be allowed to lie idly in the cash account. Cash budgeting is useful in dealing with both types of cash problems.

Statement of financial position. The budgeted statement of financial position or budgeted balance sheet is derived from the budgeted balance sheet at the beginning of the budget period and the expected changes in the account balances reflected in the operating budget, capital expenditure budget, and cash budget. The budgeted statement of financial position is more than a collection of residual balances resulting from other budget estimates. Undesirable projected balances and account relationships may cause management to change the operating plan. For instance, if a lending institution requires a firm to maintain a

Planning cash flows is important for all types of organizations

The budgeted balance sheet may reflect important account balance relationships

certain minimum current ratio and debt-equity ratio, the budget must reflect these requirements. If it does not, the operating plan must be changed until the agreed requirements are met.

Statement of changes in financial position. The final element of the master budget package is the statement of changes in financial position. It has emerged as a useful tool for managers in the financial planning process. This statement is usually prepared from data in the budgeted income statement and changes between the estimated balance sheet at the beginning of the budget period and the budgeted balance sheet at the end of the budget period.

Graphic depiction of the budgeting process

Figure 7-4 shows graphically the flow process in the development of the master budget for a manufacturing firm. The master budget example that follows should clarify the steps required to prepare the budget package. After studying the entire example, return to Figure 7-4 and follow the example through the flow diagram.

Master budget illustrated

Even for a small organization, the master budget can be a sizable document. The simple example that follows gives some indication of the potential size and complexity of the master budget of a business. The example illustrates a fixed or static budget prepared for a single expected level of activity. Flexible budgeting, which involves various activity levels, is discussed in Chapter 9.

The example is the master budget for Fable Manufacturing Company for the year 1984. Fable produces and sells two products, a birch captain's chair and an oak rocking chair. Each product requires one raw material and some direct labour for production. Production requirements are given below.

		Quantity per Unit of Product	
Resource	Price	Captain's Chair	Rocking Chair
Birch lumber	$1.60/bd m	10 bd m	—
Oak lumber	$2.00/bd m	—	12 bd m
Direct labour	$6.00/h	2h	3h

Sales are budgeted first

The first step is to prepare the sales budget in terms of both quantities and dollars, as shown in Figure 7-5. The sales dollars appear in the budgeted income statement, and the quantities are essential to the production budget. We have divided the budget into quarters. It is common to prepare monthly or quarterly budgets as well as the annual budget. Short-term budgets allow management to plan and control resources better. Note that Fable Manufacturing produces two products that have cyclical sales patterns as is evident from the quarterly figures but not from the yearly total. A single annual budget would not be very useful for planning Fable's production in 1984.

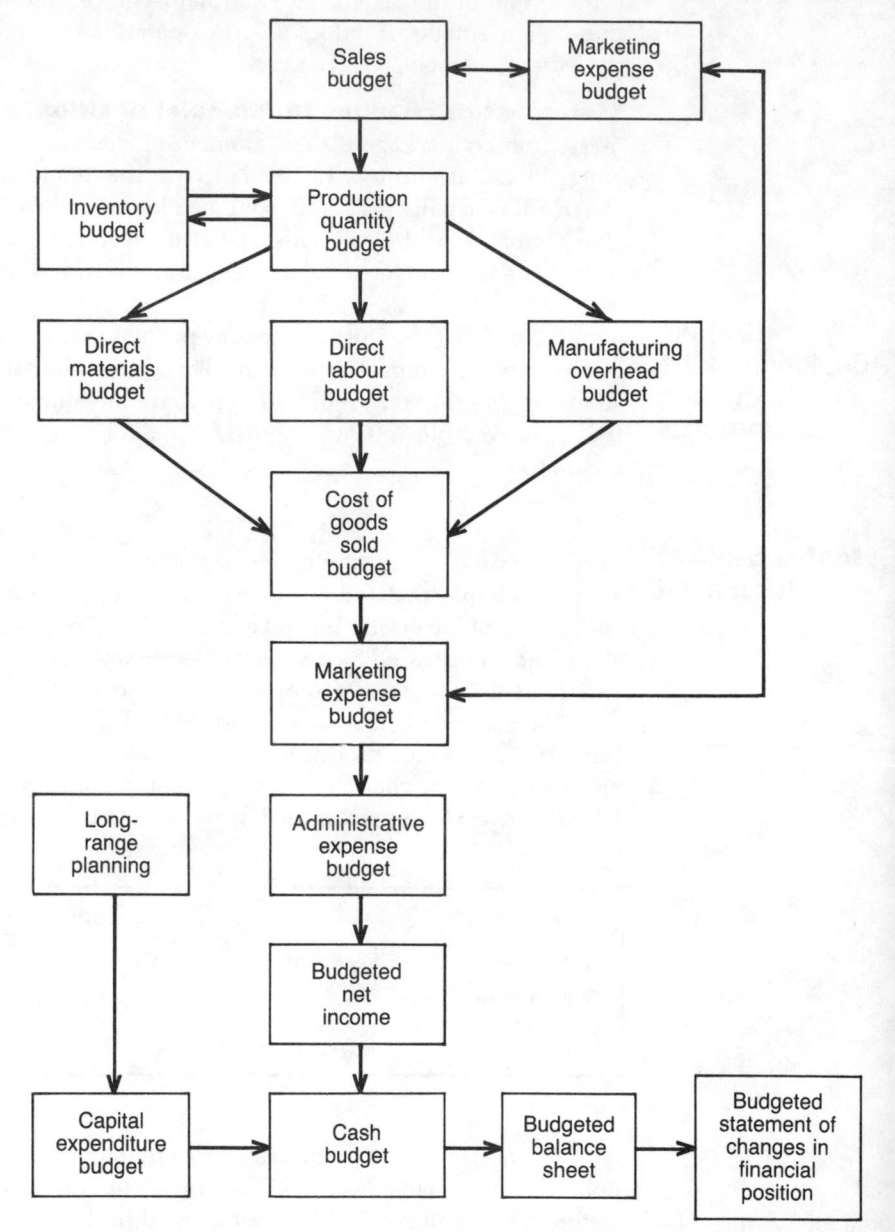

Figure 7-4
The development of the master budget is a somewhat sequential process in which information from one budget is input for another budget. However, some elements of the budgeting package such as the capital expenditure budget are somewhat independent.

Ending finished goods inventory budget

The ending inventory budget in Figure 7-6 is based on expected sales and management's policy toward inventory levels. Fable's policy is to have enough

Fable Manufacturing Company
Sales Budget
For the Year Ended December 31, 1984

	Captain's Chairs		Rocking Chairs		Company Total	
	Units	Amount	Units	Amount	Units	Amount
Quarter 1	2 000	$ 120,000	5 000	$ 450,000	7 000	$ 570,000
Quarter 2	6 000	360,000	2 000	180,000	8 000	540,000
Quarter 3	5 000	300,000	1 000	90,000	6 000	390,000
Quarter 4	4 000	240,000	7 000	630,000	11 000	870,000
Yearly total	17,000	$1,020,000	15,000	$1,350,000	32,000	$2,370,000

Figure 7-5
Sales budget prepared by quarters in units and in dollars. The fluctuations in
the quarterly amounts would be hidden if only annual figures were presented.

ending inventory to meet 25 percent of next quarter's budgeted sales. For
instance, the budgeted finished goods inventory of captain's chairs for the end
of the first quarter is 25 percent of budgeted second-quarter sales, or .25 ×
6,000 = 1500 chairs. The budgeted inventory for the end of the second quarter
is 25 percent of budgeted third-quarter sales, or .25 × 5000 = 1250 chairs. The
budgeted ending inventories for rocking chairs are computed in the same way.

Production quantity budget

The production quantity budget in Figure 7-7 is determined from budgeted
sales plus ending inventory requirements minus beginning inventory. Since
this company has two products, production quantities must be computed for
both. To illustrate, the production quantity budget for rocking chairs for the
first quarter is prepared as shown on page 268.

Figure 7-6
Budgeted ending
finished goods inven-
tory for each quarter
are determined by
expected sales levels
and desired supplies
of each inventory item.
Inventory levels may
be determined using
inventory manage-
ment techniques dis-
cussed in Chapter 15.

Fable Manufacturing Company
Ending Inventory Budget—Finished Goods
For the Year Ended December 31, 1984

	Quarter			
Finished Goods*	1	2	3	4[†]
Captain's chairs	1500	1250	1000	500
Rocking chairs	500	250	1000	1250

*25% of budgeted sales for the next quarter.
[†]Sales for the first quarter 1985 are expected to be the same as for first quarter 1984.

Fable Manufacturing Company					
Production Quantity Budget					
For the Year Ended December 31, 1984					

	Quarter				
	1	**2**	**3**	**4**	**Year Total***
Captain's Chairs					
Budgeted sales in units	2000	6000	5000	4000	17 000
Desired ending inventory	1500	1250	1000	500	500
Total requirements	3500	7250	6000	4500	17 500
Beginning inventory	800†	1500	1250	1000	800†
Budgeted production	2700	5750	4750	3500	16 700
Rocking Chairs					
Budgeted sales in units	5000	2000	1000	7000	15 000
Desired ending inventory	500	250	1750	1250	1 250
Total requirements	5500	2250	2750	8250	16 250
Beginning inventory	1200†	500	250	1750	1 200†
Budgeted production	4300	1750	2500	6500	15 050

*Figures in the rows for budgeted sales and budgeted production add across to the "year total" column, but those in the inventory rows and the total requirements row do not. Ending inventory is the same as the fourth-quarter figure, and beginning inventory is the same as the first-quarter figure.
†Estimated beginning inventory.

Figure 7-7
The production quantity budget. It is determined from beginning and ending inventory requirements and quarterly sales estimates. This budget is the primary determinant of the amounts in all the other production budgets.

Budgeted first-quarter sales of rocking chairs	5000 units
Add: Budgeted finished goods ending inventory	500
	5500
Less: Beginning finished goods inventory	(1200)
Total budgeted quantity for the quarter	4300 units

The first-quarter beginning finished goods inventory is estimated. In the other three quarters the beginning finished goods inventory for the quarter is the ending finished goods inventory of the preceding quarter. In the second quarter the production quantity is calculated as follows:

Budgeted second-quarter sales of rocking chairs	2000 units
Add: Budgeted finished goods ending inventory	250
	2250 units
Less: Beginning inventory (ending inventory of previous quarter)	(500)
Budgeted production quantity for the quarter	1750 units

The production quantity for captain's chairs is prepared in the same manner. Note the fluctuation in production from quarter to quarter caused by the fluctuation in sales. Clearly an annual production budget would be inadequate for the company.

Ending raw materials inventory budget

Sometimes the ending inventory budget for raw materials can be prepared when the finished goods ending inventory budget has been prepared. But Fable Manufacturing's policy for ending raw materials inventory is based on the production quantity budget. Consequently, the production quantity budget is prepared first, and then the budgeted ending inventory levels for raw materials are determined, as shown in Figure 7-8. Company policy is to maintain ending raw materials inventories equal to 50 percent of the amount required for the next quarter's production. To illustrate, the budgeted ending inventory for birch lumber for the first quarter is:

Second-quarter budgeted production of captain's chairs	5750 units
Required amount of birch lumber per chair	10 bd m
Required amount of birch lumber for second-quarter production	57 500 bd m
Fifty percent inventory requirement	.50
Required first-quarter ending inventory of birch lumber	28 750 bd m

Fable Manufacturing Company
Ending Inventory Budget—Raw Materials
For the Year Ended December 31, 1984

Raw Material*	Quarter			
	1	2	3	4[†]
Birch lumber (bd m)	28 750	23 750	17 500	13 500
Oak lumber (bd m)	10 500	15 000	39 000	25 800

*Ending raw materials each quarter must equal 50% of the raw material needed for the next quarter's budgeted production. Quantities are in board metres.
[†]Assume first-quarter production in 1985 will equal first-quarter production in 1984.

Figure 7-8
Raw materials inventory levels. Each item must be estimated from expected production and must comply with company policy on minimum levels of inventories.

Ending inventories for oak lumber are computed the same way. The first-quarter ending inventory of oak lumber is:

Second-quarter budgeted production of rocking chairs	1750 units
Required amount of oak lumber per rocking chair	12 bd m
Required amount of oak lumber for second-quarter production	21 000 bd m
Fifty percent inventory requirement	.50
Required first-quarter ending inventory of oak lumber	10 500 bd m

Materials purchases budget

The materials budget in Figure 7-9 indicates the expected material purchases for the period, given the budgeted production quantity and the required quantity of raw materials in ending inventory. Of course, some of the materials requirement will be met with beginning inventory. The computation is:

> Required material for budgeted current-quarter production
> + Required ending inventory
> − Beginning inventory
> _____
> = Budgeted purchases

The amount of material required for budgeted production during the quarter is the number of units of budgeted production for the quarter multiplied by the amount of raw material needed for each unit. Since there are two raw materials, the company must make the computation for each raw material for all four quarters.

Direct labour budget

The direct labour budget in Figure 7-10 follows directly from the production quantity budget. The budgeted quantity of production for each quarter is multiplied by the required amount of labour needed to produce each unit. Two hours of direct labour are required to produce one captain's chair and three hours of direct labour are needed to produce one rocking chair. These required labour hours are multiplied by the quarterly production quantity of each product to compute the direct labour budget.

We have ignored numerous factors that could complicate the direct labour budget, such as differing labour costs and the inability to increase or decrease the labour pool significantly. These are very real budgeting variables, but we omit them to simplify this illustration in order to concentrate on the basic budgeting concepts.

Fable Manufacturing Company
Materials Budget
For the Year Ended December 31, 1984

	Quarter				Year Total
	1	2	3	4	
Birch Lumber					
Material requirements in bd m for current quarter's production*	27,000	57,500	47,500	35,000	167,000
Ending inventory requirements	28,750	23,750	17,500	13,500	13,500
Total requirements	55,750	81,250	65,000	48,500	180,500
Less: Beginning inventory	10,500†	28,750	23,750	17,500	10,500†
Current-period purchases	45,250	52,500	41,250	31,000	170,000
Unit purchase price	×$1.60	×$1.60	×$1.60	×$1.60	×$1.60
Total cost of purchases, birch lumber	$ 72,400	$ 84,000	$ 66,000	$ 49,600	$272,000
Oak Lumber					
Material requirements in bd m for current quarter's production‡	51,600	21,000	30,000	78,000	180,600
Ending inventory requirements	10,500 ×2	15,000	39,000	25,800	25,800
Total requirements	62,100	36,000	69,000	103,800	206,400
Less: Beginning inventory	24,600†	10,500	15,000	39,000	24,600†
Current-period purchases	37,500	25,500	54,000	64,800	181,800
Unit purchase price	×$2.00	×$2.00	×$2.00	×$2.00	×$2.00
Total cost of purchases, oak lumber	$ 75,000	$ 51,000	$108,000	$129,600	$363,600
Total cost of material purchases	$147,400	$135,000	$174,000	$179,200	$635,600

*Budgeted production for the quarter times 10 bd m of birch lumber for each captain's chair.
†Estimated beginning inventory.
‡Budgeted production for the quarter times 12 bd m of oak lumber for each rocking chair.

Figure 7-9
The material purchases budget is based on required beginning and ending inventory levels and production during each quarter. Material quantity purchased is converted to dollars by multiplying by the purchase price for each raw material.

		Quarter			
Fable Manufacturing Company **Direct Labour Budget** **For the Year Ended December 31, 1984**					
	1	**2**	**3**	**4**	**Year Total**
Captain's Chairs					
Budgeted production	2,700	5,750	4,750	3,500	16,700
Direct labour hours per unit	×2	×2	×2	×2	×2
Required direct labour hours	5,400	11,500	9,500	7,000	33,400
Hourly rate	×$6	×$6	×$6	×$6	×$6
Direct labour cost	$ 32,400	$ 69,000	$ 57,000	$ 42,000	$200,400
Rocking Chairs					
Budgeted production	4,300	1,750	2,500	6,500	15,050
Direct labour hours per unit	×3	×3	×3	×3	×3
Required direct labour hours	12,900	5,250	7,500	19,500	45,150
Hourly rate	×$6	×$6	×$6	×$6	×$6
Direct labour cost	$ 77,400	$ 31,500	$ 45,000	$117,000	$270,900
Total direct labour hours	18,300	16,750	17,000	26,500	78,550
Total direct labour cost	$109,800	$100,500	$102,000	$159,000	$471,300

Figure 7-10
The direct labour budget is merely an extension of the production quantity
budget found in Figure 7-7. Production quantities are multiplied by the labour
requirement of each product produced.

Manufacturing overhead budget

Manufacturing overhead is divided between fixed and variable components, as shown in the manufacturing overhead budget in Figure 7-11. The total
variable cost fluctuates with the production level. Fable uses direct labour hours
as its measure of production activity. The budgeted amounts of variable overhead costs are based on the following estimated relationships:

	Estimated Variable Overhead Cost per Direct Labour Hour
Indirect materials	$ .50
Indirect labour	1.00
Employee fringe benefits	2.00
Payroll taxes	.50
Utilities	.60
Maintenance	.40
Total	$5.00

Fable Manufacturing Company
Manufacturing Overhead Budget
For the Year Ended December 31, 1984

Manufacturing Overhead	Quarter				Year Total
	1	2	3	4	
Variable costs:					
Indirect materials	$ 9,150	$ 8,375	$ 8,500	$ 13,250	$ 39,275
Indirect labour	18,300	16,750	17,000	26,500	78,550
Employee fringe benefits	36,600	33,500	34,000	53,000	157,100
Payroll taxes	9,150	8,375	8,500	13,250	39,275
Utilities	10,980	10,050	10,200	15,900	47,130
Maintenance	7,320	6,700	6,800	10,600	31,420
Total variable costs *18300 NS.00*	$ 91,500	$ 83,750	$ 85,000	$132,500	$392,750
Fixed costs:					
Supervision	$ 18,000	$ 18,000	$ 18,000	$ 18,000	$ 72,000
Depreciation	24,000	24,000	24,000	24,000	96,000
Maintenance	9,000	9,000	9,000	9,000	36,000
Property taxes*	4,912	4,913	4,912	4,913	19,650
Insurance	3,000	3,000	3,000	3,000	12,000
Total fixed costs	$ 58,912	$ 58,913	$ 58,912	$ 58,913	$235,650
Total manufacturing overhead costs	$150,412	$142,663	$143,912	$191,413	$628,400

$$\text{Manufacturing overhead rate} = \frac{\$628,400}{78\ 550\ \text{DLH}} = \$8.00/\text{h}$$

For cash flow purposes it is assumed that expenses are paid evenly over the four quarters as follows:

$$\frac{\$628,400 - \text{Depreciation of }\$96,000}{4\ \text{quarters}} = \frac{\$532,400}{4} = \$133,100/\text{quarter}$$

*The budgeted property tax of $19,650 amounts to $4,912.50 per quarter. Budgets are made up of estimated figures, and managers often round them to whole dollars; therefore, the quarterly amounts of $4,912 and $4,913 are alternated for the four quarters.

Figure 7-11
Variable manufacturing overhead budget based on the number of units produced each quarter. The overhead rate contains fixed and variable components.

Budgeted variable overhead is computed for each overhead item by multiplying the budgeted activity level for the quarter times the estimated amount of cost per direct labour hour for the overhead item. For example the budgeted indirect material cost of $9,150 the first quarter, as shown in Figure 7-11, is computed by multiplying 18 300 budgeted direct labour hours (Figure 7-10) times $.50 per direct labour hour. The other variable overhead costs are computed the same way. For example, the costs of three overhead items for the second quarter are computed as follows:

	Indirect Materials	Indirect Labour	Employee Fringe Benefits
Budgeted DLH for the second quarter	16,750	16,750	16,750
Estimated cost per direct labour hour	×$.50	×$1.00	×$2.00
Budgeted overhead amount	$8,375	$16,750	$33,500

Fixed overhead is determined by using past experience and knowledge of any expected changes. In this example it is just given as $58,912 a quarter. Notice that depreciation of $24,000 is not a cash expense. To estimate cash outflow caused by overhead costs, depreciation is subtracted from total

Fable Manufacturing Company
Cost of Goods Sold Budget
For the Year Ended December 31, 1984

	Captain's Chairs		Rocking Chairs		Total
Beginning inventory in units*	800		1,200		
Unit cost†	×$42		×$65		
Cost of beginning inventory		$ 33,600		$ 78,000	$ 111,600
1984 production*	16,700		15,050		
Unit cost‡	×$44		×$66		
Total production cost		734,800		993,300	1,728,100
Total available		$768,400		$1,071,300	$1,839,700
Less: Ending inventory in units§	500		1,250		
Unit cost	×$44		×$66		
Cost of ending inventory		22,000		82,500	104,500
Cost of goods sold		$746,400		$988,800	$1,735,200

*Production quantity budget (Figure 7-7).
†Estimated unit cost for beginning inventory.
‡Budgeted product costs are computed as follows:

	Captain's Chairs		Rocking Chairs	
Direct material	10 bd m @ $1.60	$16	12 bd m @ $2	$24
Direct labour	2 h @ $6	12	3 h @ $6	18
Manufacturing overhead	2 h @ $8	16	3 h @ $8	24
Total		$44		$66

§Ending finished goods inventory budget (Figure 7-6).

Figure 7-12
The cost of goods sold budget is derived from the cost of beginning inventory and the budgeted costs of production for the period. A FIFO inventory flow is assumed.

overhead. The remaining overhead cost is divided by four to spread the cash outflow evenly over the four quarters. The overhead cash outflow of $133,100 per quarter appears in the cash flow budget presented in Figure 7-17. In this example we spread the cash outflow from overhead evenly over the four quarters merely for the sake of convenience. In practice the budget should reflect the expected cash flow, and some quarters may have greater cash outflows than others. For example, winter heating costs may cause higher overhead cash outflows during the winter quarter.

Cost of goods sold budget

To arrive at the cost of goods sold budget (Figure 7-12), the budgets for total production, direct materials, direct labour, and manufacturing overhead plus beginning and ending finished goods inventory are used. Beginning inventory must be estimated because the end of the current year has not yet been reached when the budget is prepared. However, since year-end is near, the estimates may be quite accurate. The basic format for computing cost of goods sold is:

> Estimated finished goods inventory at the beginning of the budget year
> + Expected production during the budget year
> = Total cost of units available
> − Cost of expected ending finished goods inventory
> = Cost of goods sold

Administrative expense budget

The administrative expense budget in Figure 7-13 is not divided into quarters. Many of the administrative expenses are fixed or semivariable, so

Figure 7-13
In this budget administrative expenses are assumed to be spread equally over all four quarters, but in some cases they may vary throughout the year. A budget should reflect the expected cost behaviour.

Fable Manufacturing Company
Administrative Expense Budget
For the Year Ended December 31, 1984

Administrative salaries	$120,000
Clerical salaries	55,000
Insurance	8,000
Maintenance	17,000
Office supplies	9,000
Property taxes	7,000
Depreciation on office and equipment	24,000
	$240,000

It is assumed that administrative expenses are paid evenly over the four quarters as follows:

$$\frac{\$240,000 - \$24,000\ \text{depreciation}}{4\ \text{quarters}}$$

$$= \$54,000 \text{ per quarter cash outflow}$$

Fable Manufacturing Company
Marketing Expense Budget
For the Year Ended December 31, 1984

Marketing salaries and commissions	$110,000
Clerical salaries	46,000
Advertising	30,000
Entertainment	11,000
Insurance	4,000
Maintenance	12,000
Office supplies	9,000
Property taxes	4,000
Travel	16,000
Depreciation on office equipment	18,000
	$260,000

It is assumed that marketing expenses are paid evenly over the four quarters as follows:

$$\frac{\$260,000 - \$18,000 \text{ depreciation}}{4 \text{ quarters}}$$

$$= \$60,500 \text{ per quarter cash outflow}$$

Figure 7-14
The marketing expense budget includes some costs, such as commissions, that vary with sales. However, here we assume a constant marketing cost for each quarter to simplify the illustration.

quarterly budgets may not improve cost control for this cost area. For convenience we assume that the administrative expenses are paid evenly over the four quarters.

Marketing expense budget

The budgeting of marketing expense is similar to the budgeting of administrative expense. Some marketing expenses, such as sales commissions, vary directly with sales; others are fixed. In this example marketing expenses are spread evenly over the four quarters, as shown in Figure 7-14.

Fable Manufacturing Company
Budgeted Income Statement
For the Year Ended December 31, 1984

	From Figure		
Sales	7-5		$2,370,000
Cost of goods sold	7-12		1,735,200
Gross margin on sales			$ 634,800
Administrative expense	7-13	$240,000	
Marketing expense	7-14	260,000	
			500,000
Before-tax net income			$ 134,800
Income tax*			60,660
Net income†			$ 74,140

*A 45% effective tax rate is assumed.
†There are no nonoperating items.

Figure 7-15
The budgeted income statement is a key document in the profit plan. If the net income is unsatisfactory, management may revise the budget.

Budgeted income statement

One of the most eagerly awaited budgets is the income statement, shown in Figure 7-15. It is the end product of the profit plan and provides useful numbers in evaluating target net income or other measures of expected performance. If the budgeted net income figure is disappointing to management, it may be necessary to revise all of the budgets in an effort to generate a profit plan that satisfies management's expectations.

The basic elements of the budgeted income statement come from other budgets already prepared. Detailed information about sales, product cost, and administrative and selling expense can be found in the supporting budgets. The budgeted income tax is estimated and in this example is based on a rate of 45 percent.

Capital expenditure budget

Fable's capital expenditure budget, shown in Figure 7-16, is small, but it illustrates the process of determining the impact of capital expenditures on cash flow. A more extensive treatment of this topic is found in Chapter 13.

Cash budget

The cash budget in Figure 7-17 is critically important because it helps managers to avoid cash shortages or cash surpluses. The data for the cash budget are taken from many of the budgets previously prepared. Assumptions have to be made about the timing of receivable collections and expense payments based on past experience and expected changes in the future. For problems such as this example, the assumptions must be stated.

Budgeted balance sheet

The budgeted income statement ties together the December 31, 1983, and the December 31, 1984 balance sheets. At the time the budget is prepared, the current operating year has not yet ended. Therefore, the balance sheet for the end of the current year must be estimated. The Fable Manufacturing Company's December 31, 1983 balance sheet is presented in Figure 7-18, and the budgeted

Fable Manufacturing Company
Capital Expenditure Budget
For the Year Ended December 31, 1984

Project	Quarter 1	2	3	4	Year Total
Delivery equipment*	$43,000			$86,000	$129,000
Office equipment†	6,000	$ 6,000	$6,000	6,000	24,000
Manufacturing equipment‡	22,000	22,000			44,000
Total expenditures§	$71,000	$28,000	$6,000	$92,000	$197,000

*Purchase one delivery truck in the first quarter and two more in the fourth quarter to help with peak sales.
†Replace all desk calculators with new printout calculators and acquire new electric typewriters during the year.
‡Purchase four new high-speed welders as soon as they can be delivered.
§We assume cash outlays for capital expenditure items. Financing portions of major projects is common. That topic is covered in Chapter 13.

Figure 7-16
Capital expenditure budgets reflect the company's long-range planning strategy.

		Quarter			
	1	**2**	**3**	**4**	**Year Total**
Beginning balance	$ 31,000[a]	$ 82,200	$120,100	$ 25,500	$ 31,000[a]
Collections from sales[b]:					
Prior quarter .3	228,000	171,000	162,000	117,000	678,000
Current quarter .7	399,000	378,000	273,000	609,000	1,659,000
Total cash available					
without financing	$658,000	$631,200	$555,100	$751,500	$2,368,000
Less: Disbursements:					
Direct materials[c]	$147,400	$135,000	$174,000	$179,200	$ 635,600
Direct labour[d]	109,800	100,500	102,000	159,000	471,300
Manufacturing overhead[e]	133,100	133,100	133,100	133,100	532,400
Administrative expense[f]	54,000	54,000	54,000	54,000	216,000
Marketing expense[g]	60,500	60,500	60,500	60,500	242,000
Total disbursements	$504,800	$483,100	$523,600	$585,800	$2,097,300
Net cash available	$153,200	$148,100	$ 31,500	$165,700	$ 270,700
Capital expenditures[h]	71,000	28,000	6,000	92,000	197,000
Ending cash balance	$ 82,200	$120,100	$ 25,500	$ 73,700	$ 73,700

Fable Manufacturing Company
Cash Budget
For the Year Ended December 31, 1984

[a]Estimated beginning balance.
[b]From Figure 7-5; it is assumed that 70% of cash is collected during the quarter of the sale and the remaining 30%, the following quarter. Estimated fourth quarter sales, 1983 = $760,000.
[c]From Figure 7-9; it is assumed that materials are paid for in the quarter in which they are purchased.
[d]From Figure 7-10; it is assumed that labour is paid for in the quarter in which it is utilized.
[e]From Figure 7-11; $157,100 − $24,000 depreciation = $133,100.
[f]From Figure 7-13.
[g]From Figure 7-14.
[h]From Figure 7-16.

Figure 7-17
Cash budgets are critically important. Here we present quarterly cash budgets,
but many firms prepare monthly or weekly cash budgets.

balance sheet for the end of the budget year, December, 1984, is presented in
Figure 7-19. The account balances in the latter statement show the modification
made in the account balances in the beginning balance sheet, as reflected in the
operating budget and other financial budgets. Finally the budgeted statement of
changes in financial position, shown in Figure 7-20, is prepared from the
beginning and ending balance sheets, the income statement, and from data
in other budgets, such as the capital expenditure budget, that show expected
cash flows.

The Fable Manufacturing Company master budget example is not a very
large or complicated example. Still, the number of individual budgets is large

Fable Manufacturing Company
Budgeted Balance Sheet
December 31, 1983

Assets

Current assets:			
Cash		$ 31,000	
Accounts receivable		228,000	
Raw materials inventory		66,000	
Finished goods inventory		111,600	
			$ 436,600
Fixed assets:			
Land		$ 60,000	
Buildings	$780,000		
Less: Accumulated depreciation, building	200,000	580,000	
Equipment	$383,000		
Less: Accumulated depreciation, equipment	96,000	287,000	927,000
Total assets			$1,363,600

Liabilities and Stockholders' Equity

Stockholders' equity:		
Common stock	$600,000	
Retained earnings	763,600	$1,363,600
Total liabilities and stockholders' equity		$1,363,600

Figure 7-18
The December 31, 1983, budgeted balance sheet is the basis for preparing
the December 31, 1984, budgeted balance sheet.

and requires many computations. It should be clear that preparation of a complete master budget for an actual organization is a major task.

The profit plan

Profit plan best describes the operating part of the master budget

The term **profit plan** is sometimes used to refer to a master budget. Profit plan probably best describes the operating part of the master budget of a profit-oriented firm. However, it can be argued that the entire master budget of profit-oriented firms is the total profit plan for the firm. The operating budget shows details of budgeted net income, but the financial budgets, such as cash and capital expenditure budgets, are also an integral part of the overall profit planning of the firm.

Naturally the term *profit plan* is not suitable for public-sector firms. Organizations such as a fire department do not generate a net income. For public-sector organizations, **master budget** is the more logical term for the total budget package. Since we are concerned with both public- and private-sector

Fable Manufacturing Company
Budgeted Balance Sheet
December 31, 1984

Assets

Current assets:	From Figure		
Cash	7-17	$ 73,700	
Accounts receivable	7-5	261,000*	
Raw materials inventory	7-8	73,200†	
Finished goods inventory	7-6	104,500‡	
Total current assets			$ 512,400
Fixed assets:			
Land		$ 60,000	
Buildings	$780,000		
Less: Accumulated depreciation, building	290,000	490,000	
Equipment	$580,000		
Less: Accumulated depreciation, equipment	144,000	436,000	986,000
Total assets			$1,498,400

Liabilities and Stockholders' Equity

Current liabilities:		
Taxes payable		$ 60,660
Stockholders' equity:		
Common stock	$600,000	
Retained earnings	837,740	1,437,740
Total liabilities and stockholders' equity		$1,498,400

*30% of fourth-quarter budgeted sales.
†13 500 bd m of birch lumber @ $1.60/ bd m = $21,600 + 25 800 bd m oak lumber
@ $2.00/bd m = $51,600, for a total of $73,200.
‡500 captain's chairs at a cost of $44 each + 1250 rocking chairs at a cost of $66 each
(500 + $44) + (1250 + $66) = $104,500.

Figure 7-19
The budgeted balance sheet may identify problems of unsatisfactory relationships
caused by the profit plan, such as a poor current ratio or an unsatisfactory
debt-equity ratio.

organizations, we use *master budget* predominantly. However, be aware of *profit plan* because it is used occasionally in practice.

The budget review process

The budget plan is a plan that determines the allocation of resources within the organization. Typically the resources available are less than the demand for the resources. Consequently, there should be some systematic process for evaluating all proposals relating to the budget. The process of systematically evaluating budget proposals is referred to as the **budget review process.**

Fable Manufacturing Company
Budgeted Statement of Changes in Financial Position
For the Year Ended December 31, 1984

Sources of cash from operations:		
Net income		$ 74,140
Add: Items not requiring the use of cash		
Depreciation	$138,000	
Decrease in finished goods inventory	7,100	
Increase in taxes payable	60,660	205,760
Total		$279,900
Less: Items not providing cash		
Increase in accounts receivable	$ 33,000	
Increase in raw materials inventory	7,200	40,200
Total cash provided by operations		$239,700
Uses of cash:		
Purchase of new equipment		197,000
Increase in cash balance		$ 42,700

Figure 7-20
A budgeted statement of changes in financial position.

The budget review process determines the allocation of resources

In the early planning stages budget review may not be a formal process. Sometimes a few people or even a single individual makes the budgeting decisions. For example, production line supervisors may determine resource allocations within their department. Next a plant budget committee may evaluate budget proposals for all production supervisors. The budget proposals for the entire plant go to a division budget committee, and the final budget review is made by a budget committee of the controller and corporate vice presidents.

The budget review process varies among organizations. Even within a single firm, different budget review processes may be used in various segments of the firm and at various levels of responsibility. However, the basic review process is fairly standard. Figure 7-21 shows the general flow in the budget review process.

Control through budgeting

Performance reports are used to compare actual results with budgets

An important part of the control function of budgeting is the comparison of budgeted data with actual operating results. The comparisons are presented in periodic budget **performance reports.** The reports may be prepared as frequently as management desires but, as with other types of information, they are costly. Consequently, reports should be prepared only when the information can be cost-benefit justified. In the Fable Manufacturing Company example quarterly budgets were prepared. To illustrate performance reporting, we present hypothetical cost data for the first quarter of 1984 for manufacturing overhead. The report appears in Figure 7-22.

During the quarter Fable produced 3200 captain's chairs and 5200 rocking chairs. The budget figures and the actual cost figures for the year are presented

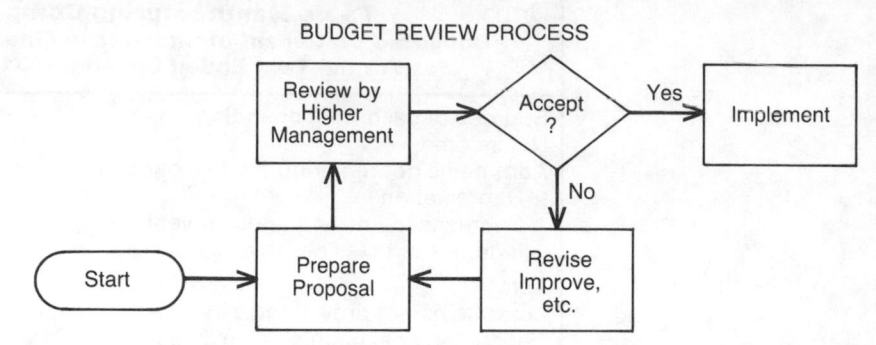

Figure 7-21
There are many types of budget review systems. This example is typical of the budget review process.

in Figure 7-22. The actual cost figures are a product of the accounting system and can be obtained only after the budget time period has elapsed. The right-hand column shows the differences between the budget and actual data. These differences are called **variances** because they show the variation between expected and actual results. Variances are favourable if actual costs are less than budgeted costs, and variances are unfavourable if actual costs are greater

Figure 7-22
A manufacturing overhead quarterly performance report. Detailed timely performance reports provide managers with a framework for identifying potential problem areas.

Fable Manufacturing Company
Manufacturing Overhead Performance Report
First Quarter 1984

Manufacturing Overhead	Budget	Actual	Variance (Favourable) Unfavourable
Variable costs:			
Indirect materials	$ 9,150	$ 10,800	$ 1,650 U
Indirect labour	18,300	19,000	700 U
Employee fringe benefits	36,600	45,200	8,600 U
Payroll taxes	9,150	11,400	2,250 U
Utilities	10,980	13,500	2,520 U
Maintenance	7,320	7,100	(220) F
Total variable costs	$ 91,500	$107,000	$15,500 U
Fixed costs:			
Supervision	$ 18,000	$ 18,000	0
Depreciation	24,000	24,000	0
Maintenance	9,000	9,500	$ 500 U
Property taxes	4,912	5,200	288 U
Insurance	3,000	3,300	300 U
Total fixed costs	$ 58,912	$ 60,000	$ 1,088 U
Total manufacturing overhead costs	$150,412	$167,000	$16,588 U

Vigero Municipality Health Department Performance Report October 1983			
Cost Classification	**Budget**	**Actual**	**Variance**
Clerical salaries	$ 5,400	$ 5,700	$300 U
Professional salaries	3,500	3,500	0
Rent expense	800	800	0
Electricity	160	190	30 U
Heating	220	200	(20) F
Computer time-sharing	800	520	(280) F
Maintenance	500	540	40 U
Employee fringe benefits	1,100	1,280	180 U
Total	$12,480	$12,730	$250 U

Figure 7-23
Performance report of a service organization. Total variance is small, but several individual accounts have relatively large variances.

than budgeted costs. Variances are used extensively in management accounting in performance reporting.

We use a *U* to designate unfavourable variances and an *F* and parentheses () to denote favourable variances. In practice the U and F are usually omitted since the parentheses are well understood. The total variance is $16,588 unfavourable, indicating an unfavourable overhead variance of approximately 11 percent of actual overhead cost. Part of the explanation of this variance may be the fact that the actual production level was different than expected during the quarter. Variances caused by changes in the level of activity are discussed in Chapter 9.

Another example of a budget performance report is presented in Figure 7-23. This report for the Vigero Municipality Health Department is an example of a service organization performance report. The total variance is $250 unfavourable. This total net variance may have little value for cost control purposes without more detailed information. Individual favourable and unfavourable variance may net out large variances of real importance. Therefore, the item-by-item variance information must be evaluated in detail to determine managerial performance and make specific cost control decisions.

The mere existence of a performance reporting system does not assure existence of a true control process. Control suggests a means for encouraging successful budget performance and discouraging unfavourable performance. Performance reporting alone does not assure that employees will strive toward budget objectives. Instead budget performance must be tied to the organization's reward structure. That means promotions, pay raises, bonuses, fringe benefits, and other rewards must be determined, at least in part, by employee budget performance.

Participative budgeting   Most budgeting experts agree that budgets should not be imposed by top-level management but instead should be prepared with the active participation of middle- and lower-level managers who are responsible for their individual

Budgets should not be imposed

budgets. **Participative budgeting** does not mean that each manager can choose exactly what goes into the budget; it means that managers with budget responsibility have an opportunity to explain and defend their respective budget proposals.

Human behaviour and budgets

It is difficult to discuss the control aspect of the budgeting process without mentioning behavioural implications. Budget control is based on the concept that managers should be held responsible for activities they manage. Performance reports reflect the degree of achievement of plans as embodied in the budget. However, there can be a variety of human reactions to even the most carefully prepared performance reports. To minimize adverse behavioural problems, care should be taken to develop and administer budgets appropriately. Budgets should not be used as a hammer to demand unattainable performance from employees. The best safeguard against unrealistic budgets is participative budgeting.

Selling the budget

Accountants are concerned primarily with the process of budget preparation, but this is not true of the majority of business managers. Although marketing managers, production supervisors, purchasing officers, and so forth, are all involved in the preparation of their budget, their primary concern must be **selling the budget.**

Budget proposals must be sold to the budget review committee

Selling the budget does not mean peddling it door to door. Instead it means convincing the budget review committee that a particular budget proposal should be accepted. For some managers selling the budget is the single most important activity in their entire job because if they fail at this task, even a tremendous management effort cannot obtain desired results.

With such an awesome description of the importance of selling the budget, one might conclude that it must be an exceedingly difficult process. Not so! Actually the process requires a mixture of logic and diligence. There is no precise formula for success, but some common suggestions are:

1. Know your audience.
2. Make a professional presentation.
3. Quantify the material.
4. Avoid surprises.
5. Set priorities.

Know your audience

A large part of the budget selling strategy may be determined by the nature of the budget review audience, whether it be one person or a group of people. Information that may prove essential to the successful budget approval effort includes:

1. Strategies that have succeeded or failed in the past.
2. Pet peeves or special likes of review members.
3. A variety of other committee characteristics.

Make a professional presentation

All managers are not delighted with the budget and the budgeting process. By the time budget review arrives, some managers just want to get it over with. Such an attitude can easily show during the budget review process. Review committees may interpret such attitudes as disdain for their job and their management function in general. Often the result is unfavourable action on the budget proposals under review.

A professional presentation includes:

An enthusiastic and polished presentation.
A neat, concise, and understandable budget proposal.
Ample supporting documentation.
A willingness and ability to answer relevant questions.

Quantify the material

Since most resource allocation decisions are in some way affected by their cost-benefit relationships, it is necessary to quantify both the costs and benefits of virtually all budget proposals. While cost estimation is seldom easy, it is usually far easier than the measurement of benefits. Even in the private sector, benefits are not always easy to measure in terms of the corporate goals of profitability and liquidity. In the not-for-profit sector, benefit measurement is even more difficult. For example, how does one measure the benefits of 20 new park rangers, 10 new police cars, or a decorative fountain in the city park? Obviously the quantification process would be different for each of these, and direct comparisons could be inconclusive. Yet, often just such comparisons must be made in arriving at final budget allocations.

It is easy to dismiss the value of quantification when the resulting numbers are hard to compare with other budget proposals, or the numbers are hard to verify. Nevertheless, some quantitative support typically is better than just general statements about the desirability of the budget proposal. Budget salesmanship should be approached with the same ingenuity that is found in the external marketing effort. If certain budget proposals have benefits that are difficult to quantify directly, various types of statistics might support the projects in an indirect way. For example, if a police department wants to justify 10 new police officers, it might offer supporting statistics on rising population in the community, rising crime rates, or relatively low per-capita police cost ratios. None of the suggested statistics measure direct benefits, but they may be more useful in swaying a budget review committee than some vague statement about the value of more officers. Statistics that are not direct measures of benefits can be used widely in both the public and private sector when supporting budget proposals.

Avoid surprises

Avoiding surprises means surprises to the review committee as well as surprises to the ones presenting the budget. Brand new proposals and information are hard to sell to a budget review committee. Anything startlingly new should be introduced and developed long before the final review process.

Surprises to managers presenting the budgets most often occur during the questioning process or when a budget proposal is more detailed than prior budgets. To minimize this problem, budget presentations should be carefully rehearsed in great detail. The rehearsal might include a realistic or even pessimistic mock review committee. The mock review should ask pointed and difficult questions. Sometimes knowing the answer to a relatively immaterial question is enough to secure a favourable opinion.

Set priorities

Few managers receive a totally favourable response to all budget requests. In a world of limited resources, wants exceed available resources, and managers should be prepared for a budget allocation that is somewhat different from the initial request. Typically all proposed budget items are not equally desirable. Some projects and activities are essential; others are highly desirable. Some would be nice but are really not essential.

Priority systems established by the managers of each budgeting entity before the review process starts aid in structuring the budget proposal so that important items are funded first. Setting priorities avoids embarrassing questions and last-minute decision crises that affect the quality of a professional presentation.

Summary

A **budget** is a comprehensive quantitative plan for the utilization of an entity's resources for some specific time period. Individuals and organizations must each define carefully the activity or function represented by the budget. The amount of detail provided in a budget is determined by the information needs of the user. Budgets force periodic planning, improve coordination and communication, and require quantification of plans. In addition, a budget provides a performance measurement framework, creates cost awareness, and provides goal orientation.

Planning and control are the two basic functions of budgeting. **Planning** involves the entire budget development process. **Control** is exercised by comparing actual results with budgeted data. The reporting process alone does not ensure control; it merely provides performance measures. Control is exercised by tying budget performance to the organization's reward structure.

The total budget package for an organization is called the **master budget.** It includes the operating budget and the financial budget. The **operating budget** describes the expected results of future operations of the organization. For a manufacturing firm it includes budgeted sales, inventories, materials, direct labour, manufacturing overhead, cost of goods sold, administrative expenses, marketing expenses, and net income. The **financial budget** includes budgeted capital expenditures, cash flows, balance sheet, and changes in financial position.

Participative budgeting refers to the active involvement of lower- and intermediate-level managers in the budgeting process. Budgets should not be imposed but rather should be developed with the input of all managers with budget responsibility. Budgets should never be used purely as pressure devices.

Selling the budget refers to the process of securing approval for budget proposals. Some suggestions for selling the budget include knowing the audience, making professional presentations, quantifying the material, avoiding surprises, and setting priorities.

List of important
terms

administrative expense
   budget *(262)*
budget *(254)*
budget review process *(280)*
budgeted balance sheet *(264)*
budgeted income
   statement *(263)*
budgeted statement of financial
   position *(264)*
capital expenditure budget *(263)*
cash budget *(264)*
control *(260)*
cost of goods sold budget *(262)*
direct labour budget *(262)*
financial budget *(263)*

manufacturing overhead
   budget *(262)*
marketing expense budget *(262)*
master budget *(260)*
materials budget *(262)*
operating budget *(261)*
participative budgeting *(283)*
performance reporting *(281)*
planning *(259)*
production budget *(262)*
profit plan *(279)*
sales budget *(261)*
selling the budget *(284)*
variance *(282)*

Questions

1. What are the basic characteristics of budgeting?
2. Define and describe the budget review process.
3. Explain the functions of budgeting.
4. How do long-term budgets differ from annual budgets?
5. What is meant by the term *goal-oriented budgets*? What practical implications does the term have in the budgeting process?
6. Define, compare, and contrast the terms *master budget* and *profit plan*. What significance does the term *profit plan* have for public-sector organizations?
7. Which budget is prepared first and why?
8. "Budgets are important in profit planning for private-sector firms, but budgets are costly and time-consuming frills in not-for-profit organizations." Respond.
9. Describe and illustrate the concept of a budgeting entity.
10. What is participative budgeting?
11. "Since the capital expenditure budget is not part of the budgeted income statement, it would not be considered part of the profit plan." Respond.
12. What factors would affect the frequency of production budget preparation?
13. Of what value is budget performance reporting? What behavioural implications are there with performance reports?
14. What is meant by selling the budget? Describe the budget selling process.

Exercises

Ex. 7-1   **Quarterly purchase budget.** Nite-Rider Auto Sales, a western auto-mobile and truck dealer, sells more four-wheel drive pickup trucks than any other vehicle. Budgeted sales of this type of vehicle for the coming model year are

Quarter	Trucks
1	250
2	350
3	200
4	150

Because of lead time between purchase orders and shipment of the trucks from the manufacturer, the company policy is to have an ending inventory each quarter equal to 30 percent of next quarter's estimated sales. Trucks cannot be purchased before the model year starts. There is no beginning or ending inventory for the model year.

Required:
Prepare a purchase quantities budget for the model year.

Ex. 7-2   **Direct labour budget.** The Yellowwood Ceramic Arts Company produces hand-moulded and painted ceramic pieces for lawn and garden decorations. Below are budgeted quarterly production quantity data for 1984 along with labour requirements for each of the three products produced.

Budgeted production in units is

Product	Quarter				Total
	1	2	3	4	
Fawn	2000	4000	8000	6000	20 000
Deer	1000	4000	6000	4000	15 000
Raccoon	500	1000	2000	1500	5 000

Labour requirements at the rate of $6 per hour are

Product	Labour Hours
Fawn	2
Deer	3
Raccoon	4

Required:
Prepare a direct labour budget by quarter for the company for 1984 assuming no beginning and ending inventories.

Ex. 7-3 **Production quantity and labour budget.** A manufacturer has the following labour requirements for the production of electric golf carts:

Labour Classification	Required Time	Hourly Rate
Moulding	8 h	$7
Machining	4 h	8
Assembly	12 h	6

Expected sales for March, April, May, and June are 800, 600, 500, and 400 units, respectively. March 1 beginning inventory of golf carts is 250. The desired ending inventory level each month is 50 percent of the expected sales for the following month.

Required:
a. Prepare production quantity budgets for the months of March, April, and May.
b. Prepare a direct labour budget for the months of March, April, and May, identifying each classification of labour.

Ex. 7-4 **Manufacturing overhead budget.** Geo-Scan Industries is developing its manufacturing overhead budget for the coming year. Relevant data from past experience and current budget expectations are given below.

	Type I Scanner	Type II Scanner
Sales budget	2000	5000
Labour requirement per unit	15 h	10 h

Manufacturing overhead expected cost relationships are

Fixed costs:	
Depreciation—manufacturing facilities	$35,000
Supervision—manufacturing	30,000
Fixed portion of other manufacturing costs	15,000
Variable costs:	
Indirect materials $.10 per direct labour hour	
Indirect labour .15 per direct labour hour	
Utilities .30 per direct labour hour	
Maintenance .05 per direct labour hour	

Required:

a. Prepare a manufacturing overhead budget at the expected level of activity.

b. Prepare a manufacturing overhead rate using direct labour hours as the application base.

Ex. 7-5 **Budget performance report.** The Nagley Municipality Park Board prepared the following budget for its 1983 parks operations and gathered the following actual data for 1983:

	Budget	Actual
Resources:		
Appropriations	$45,000	$43,000
Fees from admissions	6,000	6,300
Fees from programs	2,500	2,600
Total resources	$53,500	$51,900
Expenditures:		
Salaries	$14,500	$14,500
Seasonal wages	18,000	17,400
Equipment	8,500	8,400
Supplies	6,000	7,700
Utilities	2,500	3,100
Miscellaneous	4,000	3,550
Total expenditures	$53,500	$54,650

Required:

Prepare a budget performance report for the year 1983.

Ex. 7-6 **Budgeted cash receipts.** Unlimited Sales, Inc., has the following experience with sales: 40 percent of all sales are for cash, and a 2 percent discount is given for cash sales; the other 60 percent of sales are on credit. Fifty percent of the credit sales are collected in the month of the sale, 30 percent are collected the next month, 15 percent are collected two months after the sale, and 5 percent are never collected.

Budgeted monthly gross sales data are

January	February	March	April	May	June
$200,000	$250,000	$300,000	$400,000	$500,000	$400,000

Required:

Prepare a monthly budget of cash collection on sales for the second quarter of the year.

Ex. 7-7 **Monthly cash receipts.** Six months of budgeted sales for the Duckworth Department Store are presented below.

Month	Budgeted Sales
January	$100,000
February	90,000
March	120,000
April	150,000
May	160,000
June	160,000

The store sells 60 percent of the merchandise on credit. Credit collections are as follows: 40 percent, the month of the sale; 30 percent, the month after the sale; 26 percent, two months after the sale, plus a 2 percent late charge. Four percent of credit sales are never collected. A $12,000 bank note must be paid April 14. A note receivable of $32,000 will be collected on June 29 along with 10 percent annual interest for a six-month period.

Required:
Prepare a schedule of cash receipts for April, May, and June.

Ex. 7-8 **Purchase quantity budget.** The Markland Tire Store is a retail tire distributor selling three basic tires—nylon cord, steel-belted radials, and fibreglass-belted radials. Expected sales for the first four months of 1984 are

Tire	Quantity			
	January	February	March	April
Nylon cord	100	200	300	400
Steel-belted	500	600	800	900
Fibreglass-belted	200	200	300	400

The December 31, 1983, inventory of tires is 60 nylon cords, 100 steel-belted radials, 180 fibreglass-belted radials. The company policy for 1984 is to have inventory at month-end equal to 40 percent of next month's expected demand.

Required:
Prepare a purchase quantity budget for each of the first three months of 1984.

Ex. 7-9 **Labour budget.** An air conditioning company manufactures two basic types of coil assemblies for use in its air conditioning units. Labour requirements for the production of the two coils are presented on page 292.

	Labour Time Requirements		
Type of Labour	Class 1 Coil	Class 2 Coil	Labour Rate
Machining	4 hr	6 hr	$7
Welding	6 hr	10 hr	9
Finishing	2 hr	3 hr	6

The production quantity budget for the fourth quarter is

Product	October	November	December
Class 1 Coil	600	500	350
Class 2 Coil	400	350	300

Required:
Prepare monthly labour budgets, identifying each type of labour.

Ex. 7-10 **Quarterly materials purchase budget.** Fernald Company manufactures and sells liquid fertilizer in 5-litre bottles. Two raw materials, powdered nitrate and a mineral solution, are used in the production of the fertilizer. The nitrate sells for $.60 a kilogram, and the mineral solution is $.80 a litre. The production of a 5-litre bottle of fertilizer requires 4 kilograms of nitrate and 2 litres of mineral solution. January 1, 1984 inventories include 4800 kilograms of nitrate and 2400 litres of mineral solution. The company policy is to maintain inventory at the end of each quarter equal to 20 percent of the required quantity for next quarter's production. Budgeted production for the first quarter of 1985 is 5000 units (bottles of fertilizer). Budgeted quarterly production for 1984 is listed below.

Quarter	Budgeted Production
1	3000 units
2	8000 units
3	5000 units
4	4000 units

Required:
Prepare Fernald Company's 1984 materials purchase budget by quarters for each raw material.

Problem Set A

P. 7A-1 **Sales, ending inventory, and production quantity budgets.** Fetzer Automotive manufactures automobile generators and alternators that are sold to automobile manufacturers and parts dealers. Management expects to sell 120 000 generators and 180 000 alternators in 1982. Alternators are sold for $12

each and generators for $50 each. Annual sales are expected to be spread over
the 12 months of the year in the following percentages:

Month	Percentage of Annual Sales
January	.06
February	.06
March	.08
April	.06
May	.04
June	.02
July	.10
August	.12
September	.14
October	.14
November	.10
December	.08

The company policy is to have enough ending inventory each month to fill
30 percent of expected sale orders in the next month. Beginning inventory
January 1, 1982 is expected to be 4500 generators and 6000 alternators. Expected
sales for January 1983 are 8000 generators and 12 000 alternators.

Required:
a. Prepare a sales budget by month for each product and in total.
b. Prepare an ending inventory quantity budget for each product for each
month.
c. Prepare a monthly production quantity budget for each product.

P. 7A-2   Quarterly sales budget by sales region. Miserly Manufacturing Limited prepares a quarterly sales budget by sales territory. The company produces
and sells two products. Sales are divided into five sales regions. Each regional
sales manager prepares a sales forecast in units. When necessary, the sales
forecast is sometimes modified at company headquarters. The products PR1 and
PR2 sell for $20 and $30, respectively. The regional sales managers' forecasts for
1984 are presented below:

Region	PR1	PR2
Northeast	4 000	8 000
Southeast	9 000	5 000
Midwest	10 000	15 000
Southwest	5 000	2 000
Northwest	6 000	10 000

Corporate management thinks poor weather in the Midwest and Northeast
will reduce regional sales levels by 10 percent in the Northeast and 20 percent

in the Midwest. Annual sales for both products are spread over the four quarters in the following percentages:

	Percentage of Annual Sales				
	Quarter				Total Percentage
	1	2	3	4	
Northeast	10	40	30	20	100
Southeast	20	20	20	40	100
Midwest	15	30	30	25	100
Southwest	25	20	20	35	100
Northwest	10	50	30	10	100

Required:
Prepare a quarterly sales budget for each product by sales region and for the company in total.

P. 7A-3   **Materials and labour budgets.** The Citrus-Aid Corporation manufactures a powdered lemonade mix. The product sells for $2.50 per 2-kg can. The company expects to sell 40 000 cans the first quarter of 1984 and 60 000 cans, 56 000 cans, and 36 000 cans, respectively, in the following three quarters of the year. The production of a can of lemonade mix requires the following resources:

Dehydrated lemon juice	.6 kg @ $ .90/kg
Sugar	1.2 kg @ .25/kg
Labour	.06 h @ 6.00/h

Expected beginning inventories on January 1, 1984, are:

Item	Quantity
Lemonade mix	6 000 cans
Dehydrated lemon juice	6 720 kg
Sugar	33 600 kg

Management's policy is to have enough finished goods inventory at the end of each quarter to satisfy 25 percent of expected demand for the next quarter. The policy for raw materials is to have enough of each raw material to meet 40 percent of the quantity needed for next quarter's production.

Expected sales are 44 000 cans of lemonade mix for the first quarter of 1985 and 48 000 cans for the second quarter.

Required:
a. For each quarter of 1984, prepare a production quantity budget,
b. prepare a materials use budget,

c. prepare a materials purchases budget,
d. prepare a direct labour budget.

P. 7A-4 **Quarterly cash budget.** The Haley Dry Goods Company runs a chain of general merchandise department stores in northern Ontario. The average markup on merchandise inventory is 50 percent. Haley prepares quarterly sales budgets and their policy is to have an ending merchandise inventory equal to 1¼ times the next quarter's budgeted sales. Haley's budget committee has developed the following data:

1. Budgeted quarterly sales for 1984:

Quarter	Sales
1	$ 600,000
2	900,000
3	750,000
4	1,200,000

2. January 1, 1984, expected beginning merchandise inventory, at cost, $500,000.
3. Sales:
   40% for cash (2% cash discount).
   60% on credit of which:

   60% paid in quarter of sale.
   30% paid in following quarter after sale.
   6% paid in second quarter after sale.
   4% never collected.

4. Merchandise inventory purchases:
   30% paid in quarter of purchases.
   70% paid in following quarter.
5. Other budgeted expenses for 1984:

Quarter	Cost
1	$180,000
2	220,000
3	200,000
4	260,000

Of the other budgeted expenses, 90 percent are paid in the quarter in which they are incurred, and the remaining 10 percent are paid in the following quarter. The 1983 quarterly data are:

Quarter	Sales	Other Costs
1	$ 540,000	$170,000
2	820,000	205,000
3	700,000	190,000
4	1,000,000	240,000

6. Bank loan payments of $25,000 must be made at the end of the second and fourth quarters.
7. Estimated first-quarter sales, 1985 = $660,000.
8. Expected cash balance on January 1, 1984 = $160,000.
9. Fourth-quarter merchandise purchases in 1983 are: $500,000.

Required:
Prepare a quarterly cash budget for Haley Dry Goods Company.

P. 7A-5 **Comprehensive manufacturing budget.** Figby Corporation manufactures and sells two products. The director of budgeting provides the following sales and production data:

Sales Forecast for 1984			Expected	Desired
Product	Units	Price	Beginning Inventory	Ending Inventory
Y	5000	$ 80	800	1000
Z	2000	100	500	300

Manufacturing Resources	Unit	Cost	Production Use Y	Z
RS1	kilogram	$2/kg	2 kg	—
RS2	kilogram	3/kg	3 kg	2 kg
RS3	litre	5/L	1 L	2 L
RS4	litre	3/L	—	2 L
General labour	hour	5/h	4 h	2 h
Skilled labour	hour	8/h	—	3 h

Raw Materials	Expected Beginning Inventory	Desired Ending Inventory
RS1	600 kg	800 kg
RS2	1 000 kg	1 500 kg
RS3	2 000 L	1 000 L
RS4	200 L	200 L

The manufacturing overhead rate is $4 per direct labour hour. Assume FIFO inventory.

Required:

a. Prepare a sales budget.
b. Prepare a production quantity budget.
c. Prepare a direct materials use budget.
d. Prepare a direct materials purchases budget.

e. Prepare a direct labour budget.

f. Prepare a cost of goods sold budget assuming beginning inventory unit cost of $38 for Y and $70 for Z.

P. 7A-6 **Comprehensive budget for a manufacturing firm.** Nefultone Industries manufactures four types of cleaning compound with special grease-cutting abilities. All four products, which are sold in cans, are manufactured from basic inputs of petroleum distillates and ketones, but each product is cooked and distilled various lengths of time to bring out certain cleaning properties. For inventory identification purposes, petroleum distillates are called M1 and ketones are called M2. Budgeted production and sales data for 1984 are presented below. The company uses a FIFO inventory system.

Product	Sales Forecast In Cans	Unit Price	Expected Inventory, 1/1/84	1/1/84 Inventory, Expected Cost/Can
Nefle	30 000	$11	2000	$ 4
Nefle-Plus	11 000	14	1000	7
Nefle-Pro	8 000	16	500	8
Nefle-Whamo	7 000	19	500	11

Product	Direct Materials Quantity M1	M2	Direct Labour
Nefle	2 L	—	.4 h
Nefle-Plus	2 L	1 L	.7 h
Nefle-Pro	3 L	—	.9 h
Nefle-Whamo	3 L	1 L	1.2 h

Direct labour cost = $6 per h

Material costs:
  M1 = $1.00/L
  M2 = $1.50/L

Manufacturing overhead = $3 per labour hour

Expected beginning inventories of raw materials on 1/1/84:
  M1 = 20 000 units @ $1.00/L
  M2 = 2000 units @ 1.50/L

Desired ending inventories:
  Finished goods—15% of 1984 budgeted sales
  Raw materials—20% of 1984 budgeted use for production

Marketing and administrative expense budget data:
  Fixed costs:
    Marketing $40,000
    Administrative   60,000
  Variable costs:
    Marketing   10% of sales
    Administrative   5% of sales + 10% of direct labour cost

Required:

a. Prepare a sales budget.
b. Prepare a finished goods ending inventory budget.
c. Prepare a production quantity budget.
d. Prepare a materials use budget.
e. Prepare a materials purchases budget.
f. Prepare a direct labour budget.
g. Prepare a cost of goods sold budget.
h. Prepare a marketing and administrative expense budget.
i. Prepare a budgeted income statement.

Problem Set B

P. 7B-1 **Sales and production budget.** Wilderness Way Manufacturing produces hiking boots and mountaineering boots. The hiking boots sell for $50 a pair, and the mountaineering boots sell for $95 a pair. Management expects to sell 20 000 pairs of hiking boots and 5000 pairs of mountaineering boots during 1984. Annual boot sales are distributed over the year as follows:

Quarter	Percentage of Annual Sales
1	10
2	30
3	40
4	20

Since all boots are hand-made, the company finds it difficult to adjust to periodic jumps in demand. To avoid shipping delays and customer dissatisfaction, management's policy is to carry a finished goods inventory that at the end of each quarter is equal to 40 percent of the next quarter's expected demand. Expected beginning inventory for the year is 800 pairs of hiking boots and 200 pairs of mountaineering boots. In 1985 boot sales are expected to be the same as in 1984.

Required:

a. Prepare a sales budget by quarters for each product and in total.
b. Prepare an ending inventory quantity budget for each product.
c. Prepare a quarterly production quantity budget for each product.

P. 7B-2 **Quarterly sales budget by sales region.** The Green Valley Canoe Company sells 5-metre, 6-metre, and 7-metre aluminum canoes for $350, $400, and $500, respectively. The company's sales territory is divided into four regions. Regional sales managers supply the following estimates of unit sales for 1985:

Canoe	Region			
	Northeast	Midwest	Southeast	South
5-m	600	1000	300	200
6-m	1200	1250	700	600
7-m	300	625	200	200

The northern sales regions experience very seasonal sales patterns. The company uses quarterly sales and production budgets for planning and control. Annual sales for the three products are expected to occur in the following percentages over the four quarters for each region:

Region	Percent of Annual Sales per Quarter			
	1	2	3	4
Northeast	20	30	40	10
Midwest	15	40	35	10
Southeast	20	30	30	20
South	25	40	20	15

The northeast regional sales manager is usually very conservative with his sales estimate. The budget committee adjusts his sales estimates upward by 10 percent. The midwest regional sales manager is always overly optimistic; therefore the midwest sales estimates are decreased by 20 percent. Other regional sales estimates are usually reliable.

Required:
Prepare a quarterly sales budget for each product for each sales region and sales revenue for the company in total.

P. 7B-3 **Materials and labour budgets.** Donnybrook Furniture Company manufactures a high-quality, large, oval oak table. Below are data relevant to the production of an oak table.

Resource	Quantity	Unit Cost
Oak lumber	40 bd m	$ 3.20/m
Stain	.5 L	12.00/L
Finishing compound	.1 L	19.00/L
Cutting labour	1.5 h	7.00/h
Assembly labour	6 h	8.00/h
Finishing labour	5 h	9.00/h

Expected monthly sales for the first four months of 1984 are

Month	Sales
January	200
February	250
March	300
April	400
May	400

The company's policy is to have finished goods ending inventories each month equal to 20 percent of expected sales for next month and raw materials ending inventory equal to 30 percent of expected production needs for next month. Expected inventories for January 1, 1984 are:

Item	Quantity	Unit Cost
Oak tables	40 tables	$300/table
Oak lumber	8400 bd m	3/bd m
Stain	45 L	12/L
Finishing compound	120 L	19/L

Required:
a. Prepare a production quantity budget for January, February, and March.
b. Prepare a materials use budget for January, February, and March.
c. Prepare a materials purchases budget for January, February, and March.
d. Prepare a direct labour budget for January, February, and March.

P. 7B-4 **Monthly cash budget.** The Davis Lumber Company sells lumber and building supplies to builders and the general public. Cash-and-carry sales receive an 8 percent discount from the regular price. Typically sales are 30 percent cash-and-carry and 70 percent credit. Of the credit sales, 50 percent are collected in the month of the sale, 40 percent are collected the following month, 7 percent are collected two months after the sale, and 3 percent are never collected. Twenty percent of merchandise purchases are paid in the month of purchase; 80 percent are paid the following month. Other pertinent data include:

Month	Budgeted Sales	Budgeted Labour	Budgeted Other Expenses	Budgeted Purchases
January	$ 60,000	$10,000	$3,000	$ 40,000
February	90,000	12,000	3,600	60,000
March	120,000	16,000	4,500	70,000
April	150,000	20,000	5,000	110,000
May	180,000	20,000	5,000	120,000
June	165,000	18,000	5,000	100,000
July	150,000	18,000	4,500	90,000
August	135,000	14,000	4,000	80,000

All labour costs are paid in the month in which they are incurred. Other expenses include $800 a month depreciation. Eighty percent of the total other expenses are paid in the month in which they are incurred, and the remaining cash amount is paid the following month. A $60,000 bank note must be paid on June 10, 1984. The expected cash balance on April 1, 1984, is $28,000.

Required:
Prepare cash budgets for the months of April, May, and June.

P. 7B-5 **Comprehensive budget.** Rec-Furniture produces redwood picnic tables and benches. Below are forecasted data on sales, production requirements, and inventory levels. Assume FIFO inventory is used.

1984 Sales Forecast		
Product	**Units**	**Price**
Picnic tables	1200	$180
Benches	3000	45

Manufacturing Requirements

		Quantity	
Resource	**Cost or Rate**	**Table**	**Bench**
Redwood	$2.50/bd m	36 bd m	10 bd m
Sealer	9.00/L	1 L	.25 L
Bolts	.20 each	15 bolts	6 bolts
Assembly labour	7.00/h	3 h	1 h
Finishing labour	5.00/h	1 h	0.25 h

Inventory Item	Expected Beginning Inventory	Expected Cost
Picnic tables	70 tables	$125.00/table
Benches	100 benches	35.00/bench
Redwood	18 000 bd m	2.50/bd m
Sealer	600 L	9.00/L
Bolts	8800 bolts	.20 each

The manufacturing overhead rate is $2 per direct labour hour. Desired ending inventory levels in 1984 are 10 percent of 1984 budgeted demand for finished goods and 20 percent of 1984 budgeted use for raw materials.

Required:
a. Prepare a sales budget.
b. Prepare a production quantity budget.
c. Prepare a direct materials budget.
d. Prepare a direct labour budget.
e. Prepare a cost of goods sold budget assuming a FIFO inventory flow.

P. 7B-6 **Comprehensive budgeting problem.** In 1985 Nutro-Corp. will begin production of two brands of dog food. Expected sales for the year are 60 000 cases of Dog-Go at $10 a case and 25 000 cases of Dog-Pro at $16 a case. There are no beginning inventories, but the desired level of ending inventories of finished products is 20 percent of 1985 budgeted sales. Production requirements and costs for the two products are estimated below. Assume FIFO inventory.

	Production Input Requirements per Case				
	Direct Materials			Direct Labour	
Product	Beef	Beef By-products	Meal	Cooking	Packaging
Dog-Go	2 kg	4 kg	10 kg	0.2 h	0.2 h
Dog-Pro	4 kg	8 kg	4 kg	0.4 h	0.2 h

Material Costs:
Beef $.90/kg
Beef by-products .40/kg
Meal .20/kg

Labour costs:
Cooking $5.00/h
Packaging 4.00/h

Manufacturing overhead cost:
$2 per labour hour variable cost plus fixed overhead of $46,800

Marketing and administrative expenses:
Fixed expenses:
Marketing $30,000
Administrative 60,000
Variable expenses:
Marketing 6% of sales
Administrative 2% of sales

Desired ending inventory of raw materials is 10 percent of budgeted use in 1985.

Required:
a. Prepare a sales budget.
b. Prepare a production quantity budget.
c. Prepare a materials use budget.
d. Prepare a materials purchase budget.
e. Prepare a direct labour budget.
f. Compute the manufacturing overhead rate based on direct labour hours.
g. Prepare a schedule of product costs.
h. Prepare a cost of goods sold budget.
i. Prepare a marketing and administrative expense budget.
j. Prepare a budgeted income statement.

Minicases

Minicase 7-1 (Certified Accountants of U.K. adapted)

In cases where sales is the principal budgeting factor the sales forecast is a crucial part of the budgeting process. Frequently firms base their forecast of future sales on some relationship of past sales, which at the simplest level is mere extrapolation. However, attempts are often made to refine any such extrapolation by considering the factors which affect the sales of an organization.

The marketing director of the Four Casts Fishing Tackle Company has found that the sales of his firm can be predicted with some accuracy from:

$$S_{(t+1)} = K(S_t + S_{(t-1)} + S_{(t-2)})$$

where S is the sales figure for a period; t the period just completed; $(t - 1)$ etc., the previous period; and $(t + 1)$ the next period, the one for which the forecast is required. K is some constant which is used to combine the effect of the major variables which affect the company's sales and is itself a function of five variables (v), that is:

$$K = f(v_1, v_2, v_3, v_4, v_5)$$

Thus, in simple terms, the next year's sales forecast for the Four Casts Fishing Tackle Company is found from the sum of the last three years sales multiplied by some constant.

The only disadvantage found from this approach is that the constant has to be revised every three or four years.

Sales for the company over the past ten years have been increasing as follows: 24; 25; 27; 33; 40; 52; 65; 81; 116; 150.

Required:

a. Calculate three values for K (working to one decimal place), each of which gives a reasonable forecast of the company's sales for a period during years 4 to 10.

Use these values of K to prepare three sets of sales forecasts for years 4 to 10.

b Draw a graph which shows for the last seven years the company's actual sales and the forecasts that you obtained in part *a*. Comment upon the results.

c. What sort of factors do you think would go to make up the five variables (v) in the functional relationship which provides the company with its constant, K?

d. Briefly comment upon this method of sales forecasting.

Reproduced from Certified Accountants Questions and Suggested Answers, including papers for Scottish and Irish Students, Professional Examination, December 1975. With permission of The Association of Certified Accountants.

Minicase 7-2

The Alberta Division of Reid Corporation produces an intricate component part used in Reid's major product line. The division manager has been concerned recently by a lack of coordination between purchasing and production personnel and believes that a monthly budgeting system would be better than the present system.

Alberta's division manager has decided to develop budget information for the third quarter of the current year as a trial before the budget system is implemented for an entire fiscal year. In response to the division manager's request for data which could be used to develop budget information, the division controller accumulated the following data.

Sales

Sales through June 30, 1983, the first six months of the current year, are 24 000 units. Actual sales in units for May and June and estimated unit sales for the next four months are detailed as follows:

May (actual)	4000
June (actual)	4000
July (estimated)	5000
August (estimated)	6000
September (estimated)	7000
October (estimated)	7000

Alberta Division expects to sell 60 000 units during the year ending December 31, 1982.

Direct Material

Data regarding the materials used in the component are shown in the schedule below. The desired monthly ending inventory for all direct materials is to have sufficient materials on hand to produce the next month's estimated sales.

Direct material	Units of direct materials per finished component	Cost per unit	Inventory level 30/6 – 83
#101	6	$2.40	35 000 units
#211	4	3.60	30 000 units
#242	2	1.20	14 000 units

Direct Labour

Each component must pass through three different processes to be completed. Data regarding the direct labour is presented below:

Process	Direct labour hours per finished components	Cost per direct labour hour
Forming	.80	$8.00
Assembly	2.00	5.50
Finishing	.25	6.00

Factory Overhead

The division produced 27 000 components during this six-month period through June 30, 1983. The actual variable overhead costs incurred during this six-month period are shown below. The division controller believes the variable overhead costs will be incurred at the same rate during the last six months of 1983.

Supplies	$ 59,400
Electricity	27,000
Indirect labour	54,000
Other	8,100
Total variable overhead	$148,500

The fixed overhead costs incurred during the first six months of 1983 amounted to $93,500. Fixed overhead costs are budgeted for the full year as follows:

Supervision	$ 60,000
Taxes	7,200
Depreciation	86,400
Other	32,400
Total	$186,000

Finished Goods Inventory

The desired monthly ending inventory in units of completed components is 80 percent of the next month's estimated sales. There are 5000 finished units in the inventory on June 30, 1983.

Required:

a. Prepare a production budget in units for the Alberta Division for the third quarter ending September 30, 1983.

b. Without prejudice to your answer in Requirement *a*, assume the Alberta Division plans to produce 18 000 units during the third quarter ending September 30, 1983 and 60 000 units for the year ending December 31, 1983.

   1. Prepare a Direct Materials Purchase Budget in units and dollars for the third quarter ending September 30, 1983.

   2. Prepare a Direct Labour Budget in hours and dollars for the third quarter ending September 30, 1983.

3. Prepare a Factory Overhead Budget for the six-month period ending December 31, 1983.

c. Assume Alberta Division actually produced 38 000 components during the six-month period of July 1-December 31, 1983, and incurred variable overhead of $203,300 and fixed overhead of $95,000. Evaluate Alberta Division's performance for the last six months of 1983 with respect to its control of factory overhead costs. Show and explain briefly any supporting calculations used in your evaluation.

Minicase 7-3   (Certified Accountants of U.K. adapted)

The planned production and sales shown in the quarterly budget for Flexibility, Limited is 100 000 units at a sales price of $1 each.

The company only produces to order and its costs are:

Production costs

Depreciation of plant and machinery on a straight line basis $2,500 per quarter

Direct materials @ 25¢ per unit

Direct labour @ 10¢ per unit

Sales Costs

Advertising contracts $5,000 per annum.

Commission to agents on sales delivered at 10 percent of selling price.

Distribution of sales through a distributer equivalent to 5 percent of sales value delivered.

The company also has occupancy and administration costs of $20,000 per quarter which are divided equally between production and sales.

During the quarter just finished only 50 percent of the budgeted sales were achieved. The management committee, on appraising the current economic situation, feels that in the immediate future sales are likely to be at the lower level of recent performance.

Bigforest, the well-known mail order house, has recently offered to contract to take 200 000 units of Flexibility's production each year at the company's prevailing list price, less 50 percent. As the goods will be sold under the Bigforest's house brand, mail order sales are not expected to affect sales of the company's regular brand, as shown by the revised budget figure. Sales to the mail order house will not incur agents' commission and distribution costs are expected to be at the distributor's existing terms.

On examination of the budgeted and actual performance figures of Flexibility, Limited for the last quarter, the production manager says that to accept the order would make the company no better off. He reasons that although the acceptance of the order would enable the original budgeted production to be achieved, the 50 percent discount to be given on sales to Bigforest would reduce the profit shown in the original budget by $25,000, which would cause the company to make exactly the same loss as with current operations.

Required:

a. Statements which show the budgeted and actual performance during the quarter just completed.

b. Show how the production manager surmised that acceptance of the order would make the firm no better off and comment upon his analysis and conclusions.

c. What additional factors should a company in such a situation take into consideration before making a final decision on whether or not to accept such a contract?

Reproduced from Certified Accountants Questions and Suggested Answers, including papers for Scottish and Irish Students, Professional Examination, December 1975. With permission of The Association of Certified Accountants.

Minicase 7-4   (Certified Accountants—U.K. adapted)

Textiles, Limited operates a subsidiary, The Sunny Textile Company, Limited, which manufactures ladies swimwear. Following the success of this subsidiary it has been decided to expand it by diversifying into the production of swimwear for all the family. An extension to the Sunny Textile Company, Limited's factory is now being built for this purpose. The contract of this extension is for $100,000. Ten percent of the contract price had to be paid on signing the contract in December 1984. Another $50,000 has to be paid on the 30 March 1985, with the balance due on the later of May 30, 1985 or completion.

The financial year of the Sunny Textile Company, Limited runs from April 1 and budgeted figures for the 1985 calendar year have been produced as follows

Month	Sales (before discounts allowed) $	Purchase of raw materials (before discounts received) $	Wages $	Fixed manufacturing overhead (including depreciation $1,000 per month) $
Jan.	6,000	10,000	5,000	2,000
Feb.	6,000	10,000	5,000	2,000
Mar.	24,000	10,000	5,000	2,000
Apr.	48,000	10,000	5,000	2,000
May	48,000	10,000	5,000	2,000
June	48,000	10,000	5,000	7,000
July	24,000	10,000	5,000	2,000
Aug.	12,000	—	4,000	2,000
Sept.	2,000	10,000	5,000	2,000
Oct.	4,000	10,000	5,000	2,000
Nov.	4,000	10,000	5,000	2,000
Dec.	2,000	10,000	6,000	7,000
Total	$228,000	$110,000	$60,000	$34,000

In budgeting cash at bank on April 1, 1985 at $50,000 the company has overlooked the contract payment for the factory extension due on March 30, 1985.

Although the Sunny Textile Company, Limited requires payment for its sales in the month following that in which the sale is made, and offers a settlement discount of 5 percent for accounts settled within this period, experience has taught it to expect only half the payments when due. One-quarter of the payments follow during the second month after sale and the balance comes in the third month. Bad debts average $2^{1}/_{2}$ percent of sales.

It is the company's policy to pay for supplies during the month in which they are delivered in order to take advantage of a 10 percent prompt settlement discount offered by all its suppliers.

The level of inventories at the end of December 1985 are expected to remain unchanged from those prevailing in January. These are valued on a variable cost basis. The architect issued a final certificate for the factory extension on April 19th.

Required:

a. Prepare for the Sunny Textile Company, Limited:
  i a budgeted income statement,
  ii a cash budget on a monthly basis, both for the six months commencing April 1, 1985, stating clearly any assumptions that you need to make.
b. Discuss the value of cash budgets to management, illustrating the points that you make by reference to any implications that you can derive from the cash budget that you have prepared.

Reproduced from Certified Accountants Questions and Suggested Answers, including papers for Scottish and Irish Students, Professional Examination, June 1976. With permission of the Association of Certified Accountants.

Chapter 8

Standard Costs

This chapter presents the fundamentals of a standard cost system. Standards are very important in cost control, performance measurement, pricing decisions, and other managerial concepts that follow. When you have completed this chapter, you should understand:

1 The nature and use of standard costs.

2 The types and purpose of standard costs.

3 The development of standards.

4 The operation of a standard cost system.

5 The computation of direct material and direct labour variances.

6 The concept and procedures of reporting standard cost variances.

Standards are used as a basis for measuring performance or achievement. We use many types of standards in all walks of life. For example, in sports a .300 batting average is used to measure a baseball player's batting ability, or par on a golf course is used to measure golfing skill. Similarly a college may use a 3.0 grade-point average or inclusion on the dean's list as an indication of high academic achievement. In each of these examples an individual's performance is measured against some predetermined standard. The standard provides a quick and convenient means of performance appraisal.

In business situations standards provide much of the framework necessary for detailed and timely performance reporting, which is so important in monitoring and controlling daily business activities. The emphasis in this chapter is on the use of standards in business. We discuss the purpose of standards, the development of standards, and the operation of a standard cost system.

Standard costs defined

Standard costs are carefully predetermined costs that management establishes and uses as a basis for comparison with actual costs. Like all standards, standard

*Standard costs
are carefully
predetermined costs*

costs are measures of achievement. Consequently, management must use care to ensure that the standards are appropriate measures of performance that encourage attainment of organizational goals.

Standard costs are composed of two parts, a quantity and a cost. To illustrate, assume a firm named Kindell Machine Tool Company must produce plywood packing crates to package a new product. A manager estimates that the crates should require the following resources:

Resource	Quantity	Cost
2-cm plywood	20 m² per crate	$ .40/m²
Labour	30 min per crate	$6.00/h

In determining the quantity and cost for material and labour, management has set some **standards** on the cost of producing the crates. The estimates represent management's idea of what **should** be required to produce a crate. As the crates are constructed, these standards can be compared with the **actual** quantity and cost of material and labour, and management can determine whether production performance is different from the standards.

The standard cost of one crate is easily computed by multiplying the standard quantity of inputs times their standard costs and adding them up.

Resource	Quantity	Unit Cost	Total Cost
Plywood	20 m²	$ .40/m²	$ 8.00
Labour	.5 labour h	$6.00/h	3.00
Standard cost of direct material and direct labour			$11.00

During the first month of production 500 crates are manufactured. The actual resources used to produce the 500 crates are

Resource	Quantity	Cost
Plywood	10 400 m²	$ .38/m²
Labour	240 h	$6.20/h

It is evident from the data that the firm was able to pay less than standard for the plywood but had to pay more than the standard cost for labour. The difference between the standard and actual cost is called a **material price variance** for materials and a **labour rate variance** for labour. Both highlight the

*Unfavourable
variances mean
actual costs are
higher than standard*

same kind of cost difference. Since the purchase price of plywood was less than the standard price, the material price variance is **favourable.** The labour rate variance is **unfavourable** in this case because the amount paid to employees was $.20 per hour more than standard.

A second type of variance deals with the quantity of resources used rather than their cost. Quantity variances are not quite as obvious as price variances because the quantity standards are expressed in terms of one unit of output, but during the month many units are produced. It is therefore not obvious whether the 10 400 square metres of plywood used is more or less than the standard quantity. To determine the variance, we must first multiply the number of units produced by the standard quantity per unit.

	Units Produced	Unit × Standard Quantity	Total = Standard Quantity	Actual Quantity	Difference
Plywood	500	20	10 000	10 400	400
Labour	500	.5	250	240	10

The 500 crates require 20 square metres of plywood each, or a total of 10 000 square metres. Actual plywood utilization was 10 400 square metres. The company used 400 square metres too much. The difference is called the **material quantity variance.** Since the amount of material used is greater than the standard, the quantity variance is **unfavourable** in this case. Unfavourable variances mean actual costs are greater than standard costs.

*Favourable variances
mean actual costs
are lower than
standard*

The standard quantity of labour is 250 hours this month (500 crates × .5 hour per crate). Actual hours worked are only 240. The difference of 10 hours is called the **labour efficiency variance.** It is a **favourable** variance because the firm was able to produce the 500 crates with less labour time than was called for by the standards. Favourable variances cause actual costs to be lower than standard costs.

The material quantity variance and labour efficiency variance both measure the difference between the standard and actual quantity for resources. Before going on to a more detailed examination of variances later in this chapter, we first discuss concepts and conventions associated with the creation and operation of a standard cost system.

Recording costs in a standard cost system

Many manufacturing firms incorporate standard costs into their formal accounting system of journals and ledgers. All costs are recorded at the standard amount, and variances are recorded when they can be identified. For example, when Kindell Machine Tool Company purchased 10 400 square metres of plywood at $.38 per square metre on open account, the journal entry to record the purchase is

Materials Inventory (plywood)	4,160	
Material Price Variance		208
Accounts Payable		3,952

Bought 10 400 square metres of plywood at
$.38 per square metre for a total cost of $3,952.
Recorded at standard cost of $.40.

The purchase is recorded at the **standard** cost of $.40 per square metre of plywood rather than the actual cost of $.38 a square metre. Accounts payable is credited for the amount owed because the vendor is not concerned with Kindell's standard cost for plywood but only with the amount agreed upon as a purchase price. The difference between the standard cost and actual cost is the variance that is recorded in a variance account. In this case Kindell paid less than the standard price for plywood, so the variance is favourable and is recorded with a credit. On the other hand, unfavourable variances are recorded with debits. If a variance account contains some favourable variances (credits) and some unfavourable variances (debits) during an accounting period, the debits and credits are netted out to find an ending balance. A debit balance means a net **unfavourable variance** and a credit balance indicates a net **favourable variance.**

Unfavourable variances are debited and favourable variances are credited

The debit and credit relationship of variance accounts can be logically derived from your study of financial accounting. An unfavourable variance means that actual costs are greater than standard. The debit balance in the variance account is in effect an **extra** expense. Expense accounts normally have debit balances. Just the reverse is true for favourable variances.

The purpose of standards

Many business functions are facilitated by the use of standards. Earlier we mentioned the value of standards in the monitoring and controlling of business activities in general. More specifically, standard costs provide important benefits for a business, such as:

1. Cost control
2. Pricing decisions
3. Performance appraisal
4. Cost awareness
5. Management by objective

Cost control

Among the primary functions of managers are monitoring and controlling the costs of production, marketing, and administrative activities. Typically cost control does not refer merely to the minimization of costs. Cost control means identifying costs with their benefits and ensuring that the costs are justified, given the benefits that are derived. Standard costs provide a very useful framework for cost control.

Standards are often expressed in terms of one unit of output. For instance, in the crate manufacturing example just discussed, standards are defined as the quantity and cost of direct material and direct labour per crate. When standards are expressed in terms of a single unit of output, they can be used to measure cost performance for any number of units. Management can compare actual costs with standard costs as frequently as desired—once a month, once a week, once a day, or each work shift. As long as production output can be measured and actual cost accumulated, cost performance can be measured.

> *Standards allow comparison of actual costs with desired costs on a timely basis*

The great value of standards in cost control is that they provide the ability to compare actual costs with desired costs on a timely basis. Timely reporting of differences between actual and standard costs allows managers to take appropriate action to correct problems and maintain desired performance. Without standards many cost control problems would go undetected until considerable damage is done.

Pricing decisions

Frequently costs have an important influence on a company's product pricing decisions. Some products, such as certain agricultural commodities, sell at prices determined by the market in which they are traded. A seller of products, such as wheat, oats, soy beans, and hogs, decides whether or not to sell at the market price, but he does not determine the price. In this type of market costs affect only the decision to produce or not to produce, but not a specific pricing decision. However, most products do not sell in the same type of market as agricultural products. Instead companies attempt to differentiate their products from those of other companies in order to be able to sell their product at a price that will cover all costs of producing and distributing the product and earn an acceptable rate of return on capital invested. Claims that a product is bigger, better, prettier, more efficient, or in some other way more desirable than other products are designed to convince customers that a product is worth the asking price. Patent rights, advertising campaigns, and other techniques are used to differentiate products in the minds of the buying public. When the cost of a product is used in determining its selling price, standard costs often are used instead of actual costs in making the pricing decision because standard costs reflect the desired or expected cost of a product, whereas actual costs may include efficiencies or inefficiencies of production that are not expected to prevail and that cannot be anticipated when the pricing decision is made.

Standard costs are also used for the **internal pricing** of goods and services, often called **transfer pricing.** A transfer price is the amount charged by one segment of a business to another segment for a product or service. For example, one division of a company manufactures wheels that are transferred to another division of the company to be used in the manufacture of lawn carts. The wheels are an output of the first division and an input to the second division.

The transfer price is the amount used to record the transfer of wheels from one division to the other, as if the first division sold the wheels and the second one purchased them. The pricing of such transfers within the company allows managers to evaluate the operations and performance of divisions. Transfer prices may be based on actual costs, standard costs, market prices, or other bases. When cost is used as the transfer price, the best basis is standard costs because they eliminate the transfer of inefficiencies from one division to another. In Chapter 11 we discuss transfer pricing in more detail.

Performance appraisal

Evaluating employee performance is a difficult task, involving many different variables, some of which may be extremely subjective and therefore difficult or inappropriate to use in comparing employees. When standards are established for performance evaluation, they provide tangible measurement inputs that can be applied uniformly to all personnel. For example, the standard amount of labour time for performing various production activities may be used in evaluating the efficiency of employees working in each of the production activities. Similarly all production department supervisors may be evaluated on how close the department came to achieving standards. Standards can provide an effective type of evaluation, but if they are to be effective in performance evaluation, employees must have a clear understanding of the standards and the way they are to be used. In addition, employees must be provided with timely reports evaluating their performance. The timely reports are possible because the standards are readily available for quick comparison and reporting.

> *Standards provide a framework for evaluating performance*

Cost awareness

Accountants and financial managers are aware of the costs associated with the activities of the business, since they deal with them daily. Many other employees, however, have little or no awareness of costs. They may be concerned with such things as increasing daily production, improving employee morale, and improving production efficiency. All of these have an impact on costs, but often employees fail to relate costs to these business activities. Standard costs and standard cost performance reports often inform employees about the cost implications of their actions. Such cost awareness may result in better employee efforts at cost control.

Management by objective (MBO)

Management by objective is a simple yet powerful concept. In essence it means that managers establish specific objectives for all business activities. When activities fall within the desired performance levels, little management action is necessary. When performance varies significantly from desired levels, management takes appropriate action.

Many organizations find that MBO works best when a detailed standard cost system is used. Standards provide the quick, ready reference for identifying and reporting variances from acceptable performance levels.

Types of standards

Several different types of standards are used by managers. They are

1. Ideal standards
2. Basic standards
3. Currently attainable standards

Ideal standards

Ideal standards reflect the most optimistic expectations of management. Ideal standards can be achieved only with perfect operating conditions, such as no idle time, no breakdowns, no inventory shortages, and no employee errors—in other words, no production problems of any sort. Such production utopias are very rare, if they exist at all. Managers use ideal standards as a measure of optimum performance. Personnel are not expected to achieve the standards, but rather to come as close as possible. Sometimes ideal standards are used as a basis for setting more realistic performance measures.

Basic standards

Basic standards provide a framework for comparing performance over a period of years. They are sometimes called long-range standards because once created, they are used for a period of several years or longer. Performance trends are easier to spot when standards remain the same. However, rapidly rising resource costs and changing production technology often make basic standards difficult to use. As a result, not many firms use basic standards.

Currently attainable standards

Currently attainable standards are the most commonly used standards. They represent benchmarks for **efficient** production **in the current environment.** They are not as stringent as ideal standards because currently attainable standards allow for normal production problems, such as equipment maintenance, down time, random employee errors, and occasional inventory shortages. Still, currently attainable standards represent desirable performance.

The standard cost system

There are three basic activities in a standard cost system:

1. Standard setting
2. Accumulation of actual costs
3. Variance analysis

Standard setting

The first step in a standard cost system is the creation of the standards to be used as a basis for measuring performance. **Standard setting** is a very important activity because poorly conceived standards result in inappropriate measures of performance. Standard setting is not a one-time activity. As resource costs and production methods change, revision of the standards becomes necessary. In many firms standards are evaluated on a regular basis, such as annually or every six months.

Accumulation of actual costs

A standard cost system does not eliminate the need for accumulating actual production costs. Actual costs must be available for comparison with standard costs to determine if variances are occurring. Therefore, in manufacturing operations a standard cost system is used in conjunction with a job order cost system or a process cost system, which were discussed in Chapter 3. When standards are used in nonmanufacturing activities, they also become part of the system of cost measurement that is established for such activities.

Variance analysis

A **variance** occurs when actual costs differ from standard costs. Variances are typically expressed in terms of total dollar amount of variance and separated into more specific classifications of variances to facilitate cost analysis and control. **Variance analysis** is a systematic process of identifying variances and reporting them to management. Variance reports provide management with a great deal of detailed data useful in making daily decisions. For example, when the material and labour variances mentioned earlier in connection with plywood packing crates are reported, managers can use the reports to determine whether the company may be better off purchasing finished crates instead of building them.

Setting standards

Standard setting is not an easy task. The determination of standard costs requires some individual value judgments along with engineering data and historical cost data. All of these inputs must be combined logically to arrive at standards that will be most useful to management.

The process of setting standards

There is wide diversity among firms in methods of setting standards. The possibilities range from a single person setting all standards by intuition to firms with committees that use a variety of management science and engineering tools in setting standards. A number of methods and techniques are commonly used in most large organizations. We discuss some of these to give you a flavour of the standard setting process.

The standards committee. It is unlikely that any one individual can understand all of the issues relevant to setting standards in all parts of a business. Therefore, it is common to form a **standards committee** that establishes and monitors standards for the firm. Ideally the committee represents a cross-section of all segments of the firm that are affected by the standards. A key member of the committee is often the controller or some other member of the accounting department.

Technical input. When standard costs are mentioned, some people immediately visualize an industrial engineer with a stopwatch, carefully observing every move of a production employee in a manufacturing plant. Although such **time and motion** study data are used as aids in setting some standards, they are but one type of input. Other technical inputs are **simulation studies,** which involve models of the activity or operation being studied by the standards committee. Another approach involves **pilot production projects** whereby a small amount of product is made to generate some actual production data that are used to assist in setting the standards. Pilot production projects are used most frequently for new products that have no historical production data. New production methods may be subjected to learning curve analysis, discussed in Chapter 17. **Learning curves** are mathematical models that describe the decreasing labour time, and corresponding cost, required for the production of a product or service. Learning curve effects are experienced most often in the production of new products or the providing of new services.

Past experience. One should not overlook the importance of past experience in standard setting. Often the immediate past is the best predictor of the near future. If nothing else, past results are tangible and verifiable. Therefore, although many sophisticated prediction tools may be available, managers may give heavy weight to past experience in setting standards for future production.

Other inputs. Few management decisions are made without considering the effects on employees, consumers, and the general public. Standard setting is no exception. In particular, employees and labour unions are keenly interested in standards relating to labour efficiency. Many labour-management confrontations arise over standard-setting decisions, such as the amount of labour time allowed to assemble a product. Unresolved disputes about standards may result in strikes or other job actions by employees. Standard-related disputes must be settled before workable standards are created. The resulting standards represent management's belief of what costs **should be,** tempered by the environment within which management and the firm operate.

Standard cost variance analysis

Variances occur whenever actual costs are different from standard costs. As noted earlier, the term *variance analysis* refers to the systematic evaluation of variances in an attempt to provide managers with useful information for measuring efficiency and improving performance. Variance analysis is performed in order to answer two general questions:

Variance analysis addresses two questions

1. What is the amount of difference between actual and standard costs?
2. Why did the difference occur?

The first question deals with the measurement of the variance, which is basically a computation process. Accountants accumulate the actual cost data and compare them with the standards to compute the variances.

The second question concerns the cause of the variances. For instance, in the packing crate example discussed earlier, why was the labour cost $6.20 per hour rather than the standard rate of $6.00 per hour? Did the personnel manager hire a new, more expensive worker, or was a more expensive worker taken from another task and assigned to producing crates? Or was it yet another reason? Often the question of why the variance occurred is the more difficult of the two questions to answer. Sometimes variances result from a complex interaction of human and physical variables. For instance, the unfavourable material quantity variance of 400 square metres resulted from the following sequence of events:

Many variables may interact to cause variance

1. Inventory control personnel overlooked the reorder point for 2-cm plywood, and the company ran out of plywood.
2. The production supervisor decided to substitute 2-cm particle board for the plywood. Employees in the cutting department are not used to working with particle board and made many more cutting mistakes.

3. The supervisor in the cutting department was angry because he was not consulted about the material substitution. He told his employees not to worry about mistakes because they should not have to work with particle board.
4. The large circular saw with many automatic precision features was broken during the month; therefore, the work had to be done on smaller manual machines. The result was a significant increase in mistakes.

The fact that many variables affected the use of materials does not complicate the computation of the material quantity variance, but it complicates the process of explaining the variances and of taking the necessary action to correct the problem. Although accounting reports help, much more is needed. The analyst must have a clear understanding of the operations and personnel affecting each variance. To achieve this understanding, a firm may assign an accountant to a specific location in the plant. The accountant is then responsible for identifying, measuring, and reporting variances for the particular location. Such decentralization of the accounting activity is designed to provide more meaningful accounting information by making the accountant more familiar with specific production activities.

In this text we discuss primarily the computation and reporting of variances. The more complex issue of explaining their cause is beyond the scope of this text.

The computation of variances

Standard cost systems enable isolation of variances on a timely basis

One of the important benefits of a standard cost system is the ability to isolate detailed variances on a timely basis. Variances can be computed for all three of the basic cost elements—direct materials, direct labour, and manufacturing overhead. The computation of material and labour variances is quite similar. Manufacturing overhead requires different and somewhat more complex computations. In this chapter we discuss variance analysis for direct materials and direct labour. Manufacturing overhead variances are discussed in the next chapter together with flexible budgets.

Variances are expressed in dollar amounts and are denoted as favourable or unfavourable. For example, $350 favourable and $500 unfavourable are two variances. The $350 and $500 are the sizes or amounts of the variances, and the favourable and unfavourable express the direction of the variance. A variance is not complete without both types of information. Sometimes the symbols *F* and *U* are used to designate favourable and unfavourable variances in variance analysis reports.

Variances must be designated as favourable or unfavourable

The omission of an indication of whether a variance is favourable or unfavourable is a serious oversight in a managerial report. Often managers attach significantly different weights to variances depending on whether the variance is favourable or unfavourable. For example, a company policy may be to investigate any unfavourable variances greater than $100 and any favourable variances greater than $400.

To illustrate variance analysis, we use an example of a hypothetical firm called the Natural-Wood Products Company. Two of its products are oak

Natural-Wood Products Company Standard Cost for One Oak Coffee Table			
Resource	Standard Input Quantity	Standard Input Price	Standard Output Cost
Direct materials:			
Oak lumber	8 bd m	$ 2.50/bd m	$20.00
Finishing varnish	.5 L	18.00/L	9.00
Standard cost of direct materials			$29.00
Direct labour:			
Cutting and Assembly Department	3 h	$ 8.00/h	$24.00
Finishing Department	2 h	6.00/h	12.00
Standard cost of direct labour			$36.00
Manufacturing overhead	5 DLH	$ 6.00/DLH	$30.00
Total standard cost of an oak coffee table			$95.00

Figure 8-1
Management establishes standards for each resource used in production.
These detailed standards provide the basis for management's evaluation of the
product costs on a timely basis. Here the product consists of oak coffee tables.

coffee tables and redwood table lamps. The April 1983 production of these two
products is used to illustrate the computation and reporting of variances. The
discussion of the computation of variances is illustrated with production data
for oak coffee tables. The discussion of the reporting of variances is illustrated
with production data for both products. The standard costs for the two products
are presented in Figures 8-1 and 8-2.

Variances are computed for the month of April by comparing actual April
cost data with the standard costs for the products. Actual cost data are presented
in Figure 8-3.

During April 2000 oak coffee tables and 1500 redwood lamps are produced
by the Natural-Wood Products Company. Using the standard costs from Figures
8-1 and 8-2 and the actual cost data from Figure 8-3, it is easy to calculate the
total variance.

(Units produced × Unit standard cost) − Actual cost = Total variance

Oak tables:

$$(2000 \times \$95) - \$189{,}720 = \text{Total variance}$$
$$\$190{,}000 \quad - \$189{,}720 = \$280 \text{ F}$$

Redwood lamps:

$$(1500 \times \$47) - \$72{,}460 = \text{Total variance}$$
$$\$70{,}500 \quad - \$72{,}460 = \$1{,}960 \text{ U}$$

Natural-Wood Products Company Standard Cost for One Redwood Table Lamp			
Resource	**Standard Input Quantity**	**Standard Input Price**	**Standard Output Cost**
Direct materials:			
Redwood lumber	4 bd m	$3.00/bd m	$12.00
Electrical fixture	1 unit	9.00/unit	9.00
Standard cost of direct materials			$21.00
Direct labour:			
Forming and Finishing Department	2 h	$8.00/h	$16.00
Manufacturing overhead	2 machine h	$5.00/machine h	$10.00
Total standard cost of a redwood table lamp			$47.00

Figure 8-2
The standard cost of redwood lamps is $47, which is the expected cost of producing each lamp. Significant differences between standard and actual costs signal management to investigate.

The total standard cost for the 2000 oak coffee tables manufactured in April is $190,000. Actual April cost of $189,720 is slightly less, yielding a $280 favourable total variance for the product. The actual cost of redwood table lamps is greater than the standard cost during April, resulting in a $1,960 unfavourable variance for redwood lamps. These total variances provide some information about production efficiency. However, more detailed variance information is needed by management. The total variance can be divided into separate variances for each element of cost.

Material and labour variances

Typically two variances are identified for direct materials and two for direct labour. The variances are called **price** and **quantity variance** for direct materials and **rate** and **efficiency variance** for direct labour. Although the names of the material and labour variances are different, the computation of the variances is similar. Figure 8-4 shows the cost relationships used in computing direct material and direct labour variances.

Direct material variances

The discussion of material variances is separated into price and quantity variances followed by a graphic presentation of the variances. In addition to computing the variances, standard costs and variances are recorded in the books of account.

| Natural-Wood Products Company |
| Schedule of Actual Costs for the Month of April |

Oak Coffee Tables

Resource	Actual Input Quantity	Total Cost
Oak lumber	16 800 bd m	$ 45,360
Finishing varnish	1 040 L	17,160
Cutting and assembly labour	5 400 h	40,500
Finishing labour	3 900 h	29,100
Manufacturing overhead	9 300 h	57,600
Total actual costs for oak coffee tables		$189,720

Redwood Table Lamps

Resource	Actual Input Quantity	Total Cost
Redwood lumber	5600 bd m	$14,950
Electrical fixtures	1550 each	13,950
Forming finishing labour	3300 h	27,060
Manufacturing overhead	3300 h	16,500
Total actual costs for redwood table lamps		$72,460

Figure 8-3
Actual costs for oak tables and redwood lamps must be accumulated so that they can be compared with standards. Actual product costs are developed, as described in Chapter 3.

Price variance

The **material price variance** measures the amount of variance from standard that occurs because the price paid for raw materials is different from the standard cost. If the actual material cost is greater than standard, there is an unfavourable variance. A favourable price variance occurs if the cost of materials is lower than standard. The computation of the price variance comes directly from the cost relationships presented in Figure 8-4.

$$\left(\begin{array}{c}\text{Actual quantity} \\ \times \text{ Actual price}\end{array}\right) - \left(\begin{array}{c}\text{Actual quantity} \\ \times \text{ Standard price}\end{array}\right) = \text{Material price variance}$$

Since the actual price and standard price are both multiplied by the actual quantity, the formula can be simplified to

Actual quantity $\times$ (Actual price $-$ Standard price) = Material price variance

or   Actual quantity $\times$ Difference in price = Material price variance

In Figure 8-1 we find the standard quantities and standard prices for the resources used in the production of oak coffee tables. Actual materials used in April (as shown in Figure 8-3) are 16 800 board metres of oak lumber at $2.70 per board metre and 1040 litres of varnish at $16.50 a litre.

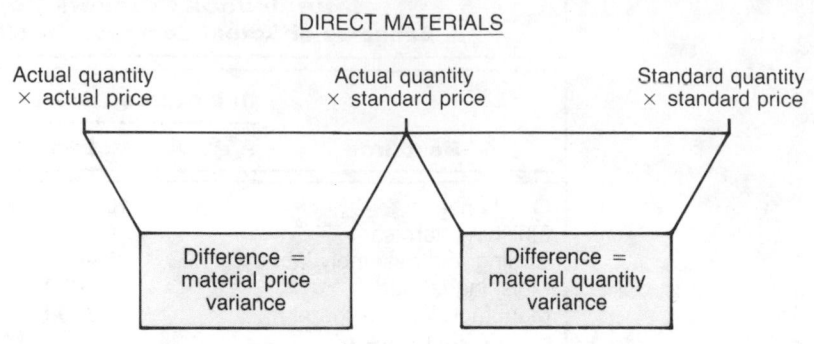

Figure 8-4
The same types of computations are used to calculate direct material variances and direct labour variances, although slightly different names are used for the variances.

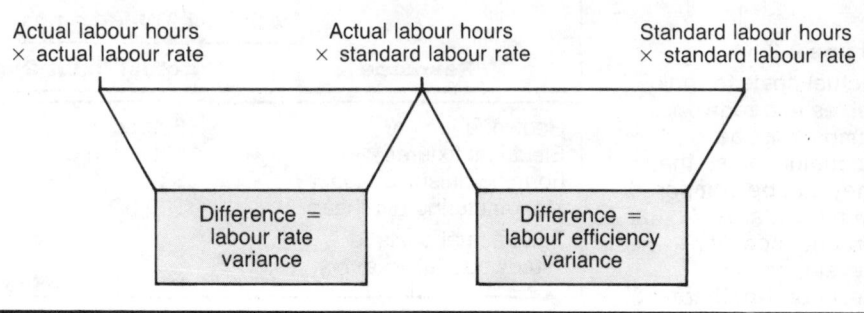

Actual quantity × (Actual price − Standard price) = Material price variance
Oak lumber: 16 800 bd m × ($2.70 − $2.50) = $3,360 U
Varnish: 1040 L   × ($16.50 − $18.00) = $1,560 F

The journal entries to record the purchase of the two raw materials on open account are

Recording material variances

Inventory Control (oak lumber)	42,000	
Material Price Variance	3,360	
Accounts Payable		45,360
Purchased 16 800 bd m of oak lumber at $2.70/bd m; standard cost, $2.50/bd m		
Inventory Control (varnish)	18,720	
Material Price Variance		1,560
Accounts Payable		17,160
Purchased 1040 L varnish at $16.50/L; standard cost, $18.00/L		

The material is recorded in the inventory account at the standard cost. Any variance from the standard cost is recorded in the material price variance account. The debit to the material price variance account for the purchase of oak lumber indicates that the material cost is $3,360 more than standard, and the credit of $1,560 indicates the varnish price was less than standard.

In this example only one material price variance account is used, which now has a debit balance of $1,800, indicating a net unfavourable material price variance in April for materials used in the production of oak coffee tables. Sometimes a separate variance account is used for each type of material. The amount of detail used in classifying and recording variances depends on the information needs of management and on the cost of gathering the additional cost data.

Sometimes it is not convenient to compare the actual and standard price of materials because the material is purchased for varying prices during the period. To illustrate, Figure 8-2 identifies the standard quantities and costs for redwood lamps. During the month of April 5600 board metres of redwood lumber are purchased and used. The total cost is $14,950, so the average cost per board metre of the redwood is $2.6696428. Instead of using a long decimal fraction, it is easier to use the general price variance formula stated earlier.

Price variance formula

$$\left(\begin{array}{c}\text{Actual quantity}\\ \times \text{ Actual price}\end{array}\right) - \left(\begin{array}{c}\text{Actual quantity}\\ \times \text{ Standard price}\end{array}\right) = \text{Material price variance}$$

Redwood lumber: $14,950 - (5600 \times \$3.00) = \text{Material price variance}$
$$\$14,950 - \$16,800 = \$1,850 \text{ F}$$

There are two general types of material price variances. One occurs because the purchase price of a raw material is different from its standard cost. This type of price variance typically is identified and recorded at the time of purchase. The second type of price variance occurs because a raw material of a different price is substituted for the standard raw material. For example, the standard for the production of packing crates calls for C–D–grade plywood with a cost of $.40 per square metre, but a temporary inventory shortage of this item necessitates the use of B-C–grade plywood at a standard cost of $.45 per square metre. The $.05 per square metre difference causes an unfavourable material price variance in the production of the packing crates. Typically this type of variance is identified and recorded when the material is put into production, whereas the former type is recorded at the time of purchase.

Quantity variance

The **material quantity variance** measures the amount of variance caused by using more or less materials than standard. More than standard is an unfavourable variance and less than standard is a favourable variance.

The computation of the material quantity variance is quite simple and is taken directly from the general cost relationships in Figure 8-4:

Quantity variance formula

$$\left(\begin{array}{c}\text{Actual quantity}\\ \times \text{ Standard price}\end{array}\right) - \left(\begin{array}{c}\text{Standard quantity}\\ \times \text{ Standard price}\end{array}\right) = \text{Material quantity variance}$$

This can be shortened to

$$\left(\begin{array}{c} \text{Actual quantity} \\ - \text{ Standard quantity} \end{array}\right) \times \text{Standard price} = \text{Material quantity variance}$$

or   Difference in quantity $\times$ Standard price = Material quantity variance

The standard quantity is the amount that should have been used for the number of units produced during the period. For example, if 2,000 oak coffee tables are produced in April, the standard quantities of the two raw materials are

Oak lumber: $2000 \times 8 \text{ bd m} = 16\,000 \text{ bd m}$
Varnish: $2000 \times .5 \text{ L} = 1000 \text{ L}$

Actual material quantities in April are 16 800 board metres of oak lumber and 1040 litres of varnish. The material quantity variances are computed as follows:

$$\left(\begin{array}{c} \text{Actual quantity} \\ - \text{ Standard quantity} \end{array}\right) \times \text{Standard price} = \text{Material quantity variance}$$

Oak lumber: $(16\,800 \text{ bd m} - 16\,000 \text{ bd m}) \times \$2.50/\text{bd m} = \$2,000 \text{ U}$
Varnish: $(1040 \text{ L} - 1000 \text{ L}) \times \quad \$18.00/\text{L} = \$ \quad 720 \text{ U}$

Like other variances, the material quantity variance should be isolated and recorded as soon as possible. If quantity variances can be identified at the time that materials are put into production, the entries for April production of oak coffee tables are as follows:

Work in Process (materials)	40 000	
Material Quantity Variance	2 000	
Inventory Control (oak lumber)		42 000
Put oak lumber into production and		
recorded material quantity variance.		
Work in Process (materials)	18 000	
Material Quantity Variance	720	
Inventory Control (varnish)		18 720
Put varnish into production and recorded		
material quantity variance.		

Sometimes it is not possible to identify material quantity variances at the time that materials are put into production. A quantity variance can be calculated only when the amount of production for the period can be measured. That may not be possible until the end of the period or at least until well after the materials have been added. If that was the case in the production of coffee tables, the input of raw materials is recorded at actual cost as follows:

Work in Process (materials)	42 000	
Inventory Control (oak lumber)		42 000
Put oak lumber into production.		
Work in Process (materials)	18 720	
Inventory Control (varnish)		18 720
Put varnish into production.		

Then when production is completed and transferred to finished goods, the entries for the materials portion of the product are

Finished Goods Inventory	40 000	
Material Quantity Variance	2 000	
Work in Process (materials)		42 000
Transferred work in process to finished goods and recorded material quantity variance.		
Finished Goods Inventory	18 000	
Material Quantity Variance	720	
Work in Process (materials)		18 720
Transferred work in process to finished goods and recorded material quantity variance.		

In practice the amount transferred to finished goods also includes direct labour and manufacturing overhead. However, here we identify only the materials to highlight the material quantity variance. Notice that the amount charged to the product and the amount of the variances are the same in the end regardless of the time the variance is identified. The timing of variance recognition affects management's ability to use the variances, but not the size of the variances. Timely variance information may, however, increase efficiency.

Graphic solution

Graphic analysis of variances

The variances discussed in the previous examples are illustrated graphically in Figure 8-5, which shows in the left graph the standard and actual costs for oak lumber used in April for the production of coffee tables. Standard and actual prices are plotted on the vertical axis, and standard and actual quantities on the horizontal axis. The standard cost is the coloured area formed by the standard price of $2.50 and the standard quantity of 16 000 board metres of lumber.

Actual price is greater than the standard price, and the actual quantity of material used is greater than the standard quantity. Therefore, actual cost is greater than standard as shown by the rectangle formed by the actual price of $2.70 and the actual quantity of 16 800 board metres of oak lumber. The difference in area between the standard cost rectangle and actual cost rectangle is the total material variance for oak lumber. It is composed of the price variance and quantity variance. The price variance is the difference between standard and actual prices multiplied by the actual quantity ($.20 × 16 800 board metres =

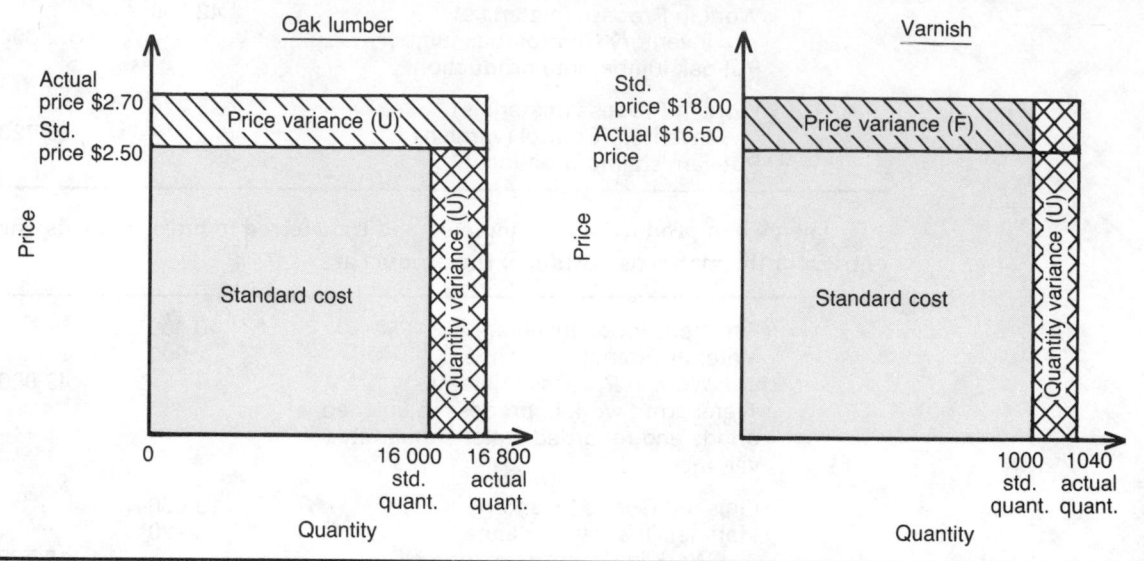

Figure 8-5
The total standard cost for any quantity of production is merely the unit
standard cost multiplied by the production quantity. The total standard cost
is represented by the clear rectangle. All **unfavourable** variances lie outside the
standard cost area. All **favourable** variances lie within the standard cost area.

$3,360) and is the cross-hatched area at the top of the rectangle. The material
quantity variance is the difference between standard and actual quantities times
the standard price (800 board metres × $2.50 = $2,000) and is represented by
the double cross-hatched area on the right side of the rectangle.

The variances for varnish are presented in the right graph in Figure 8-5.
The form is similar to the left graph except that the price variance is favourable.
The price variance is the difference between standard and actual prices multiplied by the actual quantity ($1.50 × 1040 litres = $1,560). Note that this
variance extends beyond the total standard cost area shown in colour. This
occurs because more than the standard quantity of material was used, but the
purchase price was favourable on the entire quantity used, not just the standard
quantity. Since the material quantity used was more than standard, the quantity
variance was unfavourable. The quantity variance is the difference between
the standard and actual quantities times the standard price (40 litres × $18.00
= $720). Some of the favourable price variance is offset by part of the unfa-
vourable quantity variance. As a result, the total variance for varnish is $1,560
F − $720 U = $840 F.

**Direct labour
variances**

The computation of direct labour variances is very similar to that of direct
material variances. However, there are some differences between labour and

materials in the setting of standards, the controllability of the variances, and the timing of the variance reports. Consequently, we treat labour and material separately and give different names to their variances in order to reflect better the specific information they convey.

Labour rate variance

The **labour rate variance** isolates the portion of the total labour variance that is caused by the actual labour rate being different from the expected (standard) labour rate. It is computed the same way as the material price variance. The formula is

Rate variance formula

$$\left(\begin{array}{c} \text{Actual hours} \\ \times \text{ Actual rate} \end{array} \right) - \left(\begin{array}{c} \text{Actual hours} \\ \times \text{ Standard rate} \end{array} \right) = \text{Labour rate variance}$$

The formula can be shortened to

$$\text{Difference in rate} \times \text{Actual hours} = \text{Labour rate variance}$$

To illustrate, we continue with the example of the April production of oak coffee tables. The amount of labour used in cutting and assembly was 5400 hours at $7.50 per hour; the finishing department used 3900 hours at a total cost of $29,100. Computing the rate variances we have

$$(\text{Actual rate} - \text{Standard rate}) \times \text{Actual hours} = \text{Labour rate variance}$$

Cutting and Assembly Department: $(\$8.00 - \$7.50) \times 5400 \text{ h} = \$2,700 \text{ F}$

If the 3900 hours of finishing department labour is divided into the total cost of $29,100, the result is $7.4615384 per hour. Rather than struggle with rounding problems, we go back to the general form of the rate variance formula.

$$\left(\begin{array}{c} \text{Actual hours} \\ \times \text{ Actual rate} \end{array} \right) - \left(\begin{array}{c} \text{Actual hours} \\ \times \text{ Standard rate} \end{array} \right) = \text{Labour rate variance}$$

Finishing Department : $\$29,100 - (\$6.00 \times 3900 \text{ h}) = \text{Labour rate variance}$
$\$29,100 - \$23,400 \qquad \qquad = \$5,700 \text{ U}$

Labour efficiency variance

The **labour efficiency variance** identifies the amount of the total labour variance caused by using more or less labour than the standard quantity. The term efficiency relates to the idea that labour is used efficiently if fewer hours than standard are required. Conversely, labour is used inefficiently if more labour hours than standard are required.

As with material, the standard hours cannot be determined without knowing the quantity of production for the period. In our example, 2000 coffee tables are produced in April, so the standard amounts of labour hours for the two types of labour are

$$\text{Units produced} \times \text{Standard hours per unit} = \begin{array}{l} \text{Standard quantity of} \\ \text{direct labour hours} \end{array}$$

Cutting and Assembly Department: $\quad 2000 \times 3 \text{ h} = 6000 \text{ labour h}$
Finishing Department: $\qquad \qquad \qquad 2000 \times 2 \text{ h} = 4000 \text{ labour h}$

The computation of the efficiency variance is very similar to the computation of the material quantity variance. The formula is

Efficiency variance formula

$$\left(\begin{array}{l}\text{Actual hours}\\ \times\text{ Standard rate}\end{array}\right) - \left(\begin{array}{l}\text{Standard hours}\\ \times\text{ Standard rate}\end{array}\right) = \text{Labour efficiency variance}$$

The formula can be shortened to

$$\text{Difference in hours} \times \text{Standard rate} = \text{Labour efficiency variance}$$

The labour efficiency variances for coffee tables are calculated as follows:

$$\left(\begin{array}{l}\text{Actual labour hours}\\ -\text{ Standard labour hours}\end{array}\right) \times \text{Standard rate} = \text{Labour efficiency variance}$$

Cutting and Assembly Department: (5400 h − 6000 h) × \$8.00 = \$4,800 F
Finishing Department: (3900 h − 4000 h) × \$6.00 = \$ 600 F

If the efficiency variances can be determined at the time the payroll is distributed to production (recorded in work in process), the journal entries to record the direct labour and the rate and efficiency variances are

Recording labour variances

Cutting and Assembling Labour:

Work in Process (labour)	48 000	
Labour Efficiency Variance		4 800
Labour Rate Variance		2 700
Payroll		40 500
Recorded direct labour and the labour variances.		

Finishing Labour:

Work in Process (labour)	24 000	
Labour Rate Variance	5 700	
Labour Efficiency Variance		600
Payroll		29 100
Recorded direct labour and the labour variances.		

If the labour efficiency variance cannot be determined at the time that labour cost is charged to production, the entries would be as follows:

Cutting and Assembling Labour:

Work in Process (labour)	43 200	
Labour Rate Variance		2 700
Payroll		40 500
Recorded direct labour and the labour rate variance.		

Finishing Labour:

Work in Process (labour)	23 400	
Labour Rate Variance	5 700	
Payroll		29 100
Recorded direct labour and the labour rate variance.		

Later, when the efficiency variances have been determined, the entries to transfer the labour portion of WIP to finished goods are

---

Cutting and Assembling Labour:

Finished Goods Inventory	48 000	
Labour Efficiency Variance		4 800
Work in Process (labour)		43 200

Transferred work in process to finished goods and recorded the labour efficiency variance.

Finishing Labour:

Finished Goods Inventory	24 000	
Labour Efficiency Variance		600
Work in Process (labour)		23 400

Transferred work in process to finished goods and recorded the labour efficiency variance.

Graphic Solution

The labour rate and efficiency variances just computed are presented graphically in Figure 8-6. Since both the rate and efficiency variances are favourable in the Cutting and Assembly Department, the variances appear

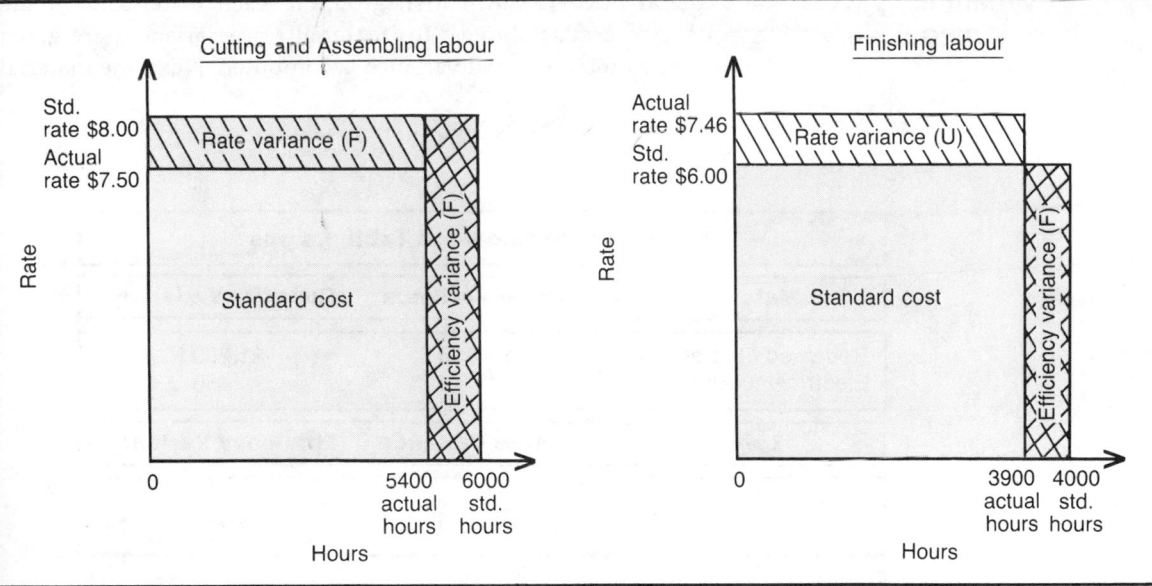

Figure 8-6

Labour variances appear similar to material variances except for slightly different terminology for the variances. Notice that both the rate and efficiency variance are within the clear standard cost area for the Cutting and Assembly Department because both variances are favourable. In the Finishing Department only the efficiency variance is favourable.

within the clear area of the total standard cost. The Finishing Department has a favourable efficiency variance and unfavourable rate variance, so the efficiency variance is cross-hatched, but the rate variance lies outside the clear standard cost area.

Variance analysis reporting

As with most internal reports, the preparation of variance analysis reports is not guided by a rigid set of reporting requirements. Instead variance reports are developed to meet the specific information needs of management. The content, format, and timing of variance reports differ widely among firms. As with all accounting information, variance reports must be cost-benefit justified, but that is the only limitation.

To illustrate variance reporting, we continue the Natural-Wood Products example. Oak coffee tables were used in discussing the computation of direct material and direct labour variances. These variances, together with April variances for redwood table lamps, are used to illustrate common production variance reports for manufacturing operations. April variances for redwood lamps are derived from standard and actual cost data presented in Figures 8-2 and 8-3 and are summarized in Figure 8-7, but the calculations are not shown.

Direct material variance reporting

The direct material variance report is illustrated in Figure 8-8. This report presents the material price variance first, grouping each material with the product for which it is used. Subtotals for material price variances are given for each product, and a total material variance is computed. Next, the material

Variances for Redwood Table Lamps		
Material	**Price Variance**	**Quantity Variance**
Redwood lumber	$1,850 F	$1,200 F
Electrical fixtures	0	450 U
Labour	**Rate Variance**	**Efficiency Variance**
Forming and Finishing Department	$660 U	$2,400 U

Figure 8-7
The material and labour variances for redwood table lamps are summarized in this figure. The variances were computed in the same way as the variances for oak tables. Using the standards from Figure 8-2 and the actual costs from Figure 8-3, you should compute several of the lamp variances to be certain you understand the procedure.

quantity variances are presented using a similar grouping to highlight the variances for each product. Finally, the price and quantity variances are summed to show a total direct material variance. The exact format of this report is not critical. The report shows one of many possible logical organizations of direct material variance data.

Natural-Wood Products Company
Performance Report—Direct Materials
April 1983

Material Price Variance

Material	Actual Quantity @ Actual Price	Actual Quantity @ Standard Price	Material Price Variance	
Oak Coffee Tables				
Oak lumber ~~each dept.~~	$45,360	$42,000	$3,360 U	
Varnish	17,160	18,720	1,560 F	
Material price variance for oak coffee tables			$1,800 U	
Redwood Table Lamps				
Redwood lumber	$14,950	$16,800	$1,850 F	
Electrical fixtures	13,950	13,950	0	
Material price variance for redwood table lamps			1,850 F	
Total material price variance during April				$ 50 F

Material Quantity Variance

Material	Actual Quantity @ Standard Price	Standard Quantity @ Standard Price	Material Quantity Variance	
Oak Coffee Tables				
Oak lumber	$42,000	$40,000	$2,000 U	
Varnish	18,720	18,000	720 U	
Material quantity variance for oak coffee tables			$2,720 U	
Redwood Table Lamps				
Redwood lumber	$16,800	$18,000	$1,200 F	
Electrical fixtures	13,950	13,500	450 U	
Material quantity variance for redwood table lamps			750 F	
Total material quantity variance in April				1,970 U
Total direct material variance in April				$1,920 U

Figure 8-8
This is a typical direct material performance report. The exact form of the report is not critical as long as the report is logical, understandable, and meets the information needs of managers.

Direct labour variance reporting

The direct labour variance report is illustrated in Figure 8-9. This report is organized similarly to the direct material report. The labour rate and efficiency variances are grouped according to product. Product subtotals are shown, as are totals for the monthly labour rate variance and monthly labour efficiency variance. The final figure is the total direct labour variance for April.

Natural-Wood Products Company
Performance Report—Direct Labour
April 1983

Labour Rate Variance

Department	Actual Hours @ Actual Rate	Actual Hours @ Standard Rate	Labour Rate Variance	
Oak Coffee Tables				
Cutting and assembly	$40,500	$43,200	$2,700 F	
Finishing	29,100	23,400	5,700 U	
Labour rate variance for oak coffee tables				$3,000 U
Redwood Table Lamps				
Forming and finishing	$27,060	$26,400	$ 660 U	
Labour rate variance for redwood table lamps				660 U
Total labour rate variance during April				$3,660 U

Labour Efficiency Variance

Department	Actual Hours @ Standard Rate	Standard Hours @ Standard Rate	Labour Efficiency Variance	
Oak Coffee Tables				
Cutting and assembly	$43,200	$48,000	$4,800 F	
Finishing	23,400	24,000	600 F	
Labour efficiency variance for oak coffee tables				$5,400 F
Redwood Table Lamps				
Forming and finishing	$26,400	$24,000	$2,400 U	
Labour efficiency variance for redwood table lamps				$2,400 U
Total labour efficiency variance				3,000 F
Total direct labour variance in April				$ 660 U

Figure 8-9
The labour performance report is similar to the direct material report. Variances should be reported on a timely basis so that problems can be investigated and solved before they cause significant losses.

Manufacturing overhead variance reporting

Computing total overhead variance

A manufacturing example is not complete without manufacturing overhead as a cost element. Consequently, we include overhead cost data in this example. The total overhead variance for each product is presented without a detailed analysis of the variance at this time. The analysis of overhead variances is postponed until the next chapter.

Figure 8-10 shows the computation of standard overhead for each product and a comparison of standard overhead with the actual manufacturing overhead given in Figure 8-3. The standard amount of overhead cost is merely the overhead rate multiplied by the standard number of hours of the application base for the number of units produced. To illustrate, direct labour hours are used to apply overhead to the oak coffee tables. Adding up the standard hours of cutting and assembling labour and finishing labour required to produce 2000 units yields a total of 10 000 standard hours. Multiplying by the overhead rate of $6/DLH for coffee tables gives a standard overhead cost of $60,000. Since actual MOH is $2,400 less, there is a $2,400 favourable variance. The same procedure is used to find the manufacturing overhead standard cost and variance for redwood lamps. The presentation in Figure 8-10 is by no means a method of overhead variance analysis but is merely an identification of the total manufacturing overhead variance.

Comprehensive variance reporting

Material, labour, and overhead variances are summarized in the product variance analysis report

The variance information in Figures 8-8 through 8-10 may be organized into a single comprehensive report, as shown in Figure 8-11, which presents a monthly product variance analysis report.

The product variance analysis report summarizes all of the production variances associated with each product. Although some detail is lost in comparison with the other variance reports, much variance information is concentrated in one report and is identified with specific products. Product variance reports may be very useful for some management decisions, such as product pricing, make-buy decisions, or evaluating managers with specific product responsibility. In later chapters we discuss the use of variance data and other managerial information in making these types of decisions.

Standard costs and the financial statements

Actual costs are the only costs that are generally accepted for external financial reporting. Therefore, even though standards are used in determining product costs internally, the standard cost cannot be used for costing inventories on the balance sheet or for costing products in the income statement. Often actual costs and standard costs are very close, yielding relatively small variances. In such situations standard costs may be used in the financial statements because the standard costs **closely approximate** the actual costs, and the difference is not material. Any small variances usually are netted out against cost of goods sold in the income statement.

Occasionally variances are very large. Perhaps a firm's raw materials become scarce, or fuel costs rise sharply, or some other major cost increase

Natural-Wood Products Company
Schedule of Manufacturing Overhead Variance
April 1983

Product	Standard Hours	MOH Rate	Standard Amount of MOH	Actual Amount of MOH	MOH Variance
Oak coffee tables	10 000 DLH	$6/DLH	$60,000	$57,600	$2,400 F
Redwood table lamps	3 000 machine h	$5/machine h	15,000	16,500	1,500 U
Total manufacturing overhead variance for April					$ 900 F

Figure 8-10

Manufacturing overhead is often a significant manufacturing cost. Overhead variances should be reported on a timely basis so that costs can be monitored and controlled. A schedule of total overhead variance is presented here. Detailed variance analyses for manufacturing overhead are presented in Chapter 9.

Natural-Wood Products Company Product Variance Analysis Report April 1983			
Variance	Oak Tables	Redwood Lamps	Total
Material price variance	$1,800 U	$1,850 F	$ 50 F
Material quantity variance	2,720 U	750 F	1,970 U
Total material variance	$4,520 U	$2,600 F	$1,920 U
Labour rate variance	$3,000 U	$ 660 U	$3,660 U
Labour efficiency variance	5,400 F	2,400 U	3,000 F
Total labour variance	$2,400 F	$3,060 U	$ 660 U
Manufacturing overhead variance	$2,400 F	$1,500 U	$ 900 F
Total April variance	$ 280 F	$1,960 U	$1,680 U

Figure 8-11
This report summarizes all of the production variances for the two products.
The report provides managers with a quick overview of production performance
in a single report.

occurs. Whatever the reason, standard costs may not be reported in financial
statements when actual costs vary significantly from standards. Instead the
accounts must be adjusted to reflect **actual cost.** That means the variance
accounts must be closed into the accounts that are affected by the variances.
Material variances typically affect raw materials inventory, work in process
inventory, finished goods inventory, and cost of goods sold. Labour and
overhead variances affect only the latter three accounts.

Disposition of large variances

Closing variance accounts

When variance accounts are closed into inventory and cost of goods sold, the
amount assigned to each account is determined by the relative amount of the
resource remaining in each account at year-end. For example, $1,000,000 of
direct labour was charged at standard to production during the year. At year-
end the following amounts of direct labour costs remain in the accounts:

Work in process	$100,000 = 10%
Finished goods	200,000 = 20%
Cost of goods sold	700,000 = 70%

If direct labour variances for the year were labour rate $160,000 unfavourable
and labour efficiency $180,000 unfavourable, the accounts would be closed as
follows:

Work in Process Inventory	34,000	
Finished Goods Inventory	68,000	
Cost of Goods Sold	238,000	
Labour Rate Variance		160,000
Labour Efficiency Variance		180,000
Allocated unfavourable variances to the affected accounts (10% of $340,000); (20% of $340,000); (70% of $340,000).		

Each of the accounts affected by the labour variance receive pro rata cost adjustments. When all variance accounts are closed with entries such as the one above, the inventory and cost of goods sold accounts reflect actual costs.

Summary

Standard costs are carefully predetermined costs. They are convenient measures of performance. A standard is composed of two parts, a quantity and a cost. Standards are used for cost control, pricing decisions, performance appraisal, cost awareness, and management by objective. Several types of standards are used. **Ideal standards** are very tight, reflecting a production utopia. **Basic standards** are created for use over periods of several years. **Currently attainable standards** reflect desirable performance, given normal production problems. Currently attainable standards are the most widely used type of standard.

There are three basic activities in a standard cost system. They are **standard setting, accumulation of actual costs,** and **variance analysis.** Standard setting is an important and difficult task involving many variables. Typically standards are set by a **standards committee** with representation from all parts of the organization affected by the standards. Inputs from engineering and techno-logical studies assist the committee in setting standards. Management's desires in setting standards are tempered by its environment, particularly employees and labour unions. Standards must be revised frequently to remain current if they are to be used for performance evaluation.

Most firms incorporate their standard cost system into their formal ac-counting system. Costs are recorded at standard, and any difference is recorded in a variance account. Unfavourable variances have debit balances, and fa-vourable variances have credit balances.

Variance analysis is the systematic evaluation of variances to provide managers with useful information. Variance analysis is performed for all three types of manufacturing cost elements. Variance analysis answers two questions: What is the amount of the variance? Why did the variance occur?

The first question is answered by performing computations on data gathered in the standard cost system. The answer to the second question requires more subjective evaluations of the operations and cost data, and the answer often is more art than science.

A variance is expressed as a dollar amount and is identified as favourable or unfavourable. **Favourable variances** mean that actual costs or quantities are less than standard. **Unfavourable variances** mean actual costs or quantities are greater than standard. A **material price variance** measures the amount of variance from standard caused when the actual price of material is different from the standard price. A **material quantity variance** results from using more or less material than the standard amount. The **labour rate variance** is similar to the material price variance and the **labour efficiency variance** is like the material quantity variance.

Once computed, variances should be reported in a manner that provides management with a maximum amount of useful information. There is no rigid set of reporting requirements. Instead variance reports are tailored to the information requirements of management, and many formats are possible.

Technically only actual costs may be reported in external financial statements. However, if variances are small, standard costs may be used for the financial statements since they closely approximate actual costs. Any minor variance is netted against cost of goods sold. If variances are large, the affected accounts must be adjusted to reflect actual costs.

List of important terms		
basic standards *(315)*	**material price variance** *(310)*
currently attainable standards *(315)*	**material quantity variance** *(311)*
favourable variance *(311)*	**standard cost** *(315)*
ideal standards *(315)*	**standards committee** *(316)*
labour efficiency variance *(311)*	**standard setting** *(315)*
labour rate variance *(310)*	**unfavourable variance** *(311)*
management by objective *(314)*	**variance analysis** *(317)*

Questions

1. Define what is meant by the term *standard cost* and explain its relevance with respect to internal and external reporting.
2. Identify and discuss the major reasons for using a standard cost system.
3. Differentiate between ideal, basic, and currently attainable standards.
4. What are the functions of a standards committee?
5. When and how are standards revised?
6. What two main questions are addressed by variance analysis?
7. What variances are computed for direct materials and direct labour? What do they mean?
8. How are standard costs treated for purposes of external financial reporting?
9. What is the normal balance in a material price variance account?
10. Comment on the following statement made by an assembly worker to his supervisor: "Standards are just pressure devices used by management to criticize employees. Nobody ever achieves the standards anyhow."
11. Briefly describe the three basic activities of a standard cost system.

12. Discuss the disposition of the balances in variance accounts in the closing of the books at year-end.

13. Identify which of the four variances—material price, material quantity, labour rate, labour efficiency—would be most useful in evaluating the following and explain why.
    a. Purchasing manager
    b. Production supervisor
    c. Personnel manager

14. Compare and contrast the application of manufacturing overhead to products in a standard cost system and in an actual cost system.

15. Comment on the following statements:
    a. All variances are bad.
    b. All variances should be investigated.
    c. Only unfavourable variances should be investigated.

16. As a new corporate controller, respond to a manager's remarks made at your first Monday morning meeting. "These weekly variance reports must be costing us a lot of money. Let's just prepare them once a quarter. As long as the information on the reports is correct, who cares when we get them."

Exercises

Ex. 8-1   Material variances. Sandra is a college student who operates a house-painting service in the summer time. She took accounting last semester and decided to establish material standards for her painting business. The standards are

Material	Standard Quantity per 10 Square Metres of Painting Surface	Standard Price
Primer	.20 L	$10/L
Finish paint	.25 L	15/L

During July the following actual results occurred:

Surface painted	2000 m²	
Materials used:		
Primer	48L @ $10.50 =	$ 504
Finish paint	46L @ $14.00 =	644
Total		$1,148

Required:
Compute the material price and quantity variances.

Ex. 8-2   Direct labour variances. Dandridge Company had the following standard and actual labour cost for the month:

Standard labour rate: $7/hour
Actual labour rate: $8/hour
Standard amount of labour for the output produced: 10 000 labour hours
Actual labour hours: 10 500

Required:
Compute the direct labour variances for Dandridge Company.

Ex. 8-3 **Graphing direct labour variances.** Refer to the standard and actual data provided for Dandridge Company in Exercise 8-2.

Required:
Using the data provided, prepare a graph of labour variances similar to the one in Figure 8-6.

Ex. 8-4 **Direct labour variances.** Jade Hydro Rural Electric Company has established a standard time of $1\frac{1}{2}$ hours for installing a new electric meter. The standard wage rate for meter installers is $8 per hour. In May 1100 labour hours were used at a cost of $8,690 to install 700 meters.

Required:
Compute the labour rate and efficiency variances and the total labour variance for meter installation in May.

Ex. 8-5 **Identifying standard and actual cost.** The following journal entries were made to assign direct material and direct labour cost to production for the week:

Work in Process (materials)	47,900	
Material Quantity Variance		400
Inventory Control		47,500
Work in Process (labour)	62,000	
Labour Efficiency Variance	2,500	
Labour Rate Variance		1,000
Payroll		63,500

Required:
Examine the above entries and answer the following questions:
a. What was the standard cost of the direct materials put into production?
b. Was the material quantity variance favourable or unfavourable?
c. What was the actual cost of direct labour?
d. What was the standard cost of direct labour?
e. What was the total direct labour variance?
f. Is the labour efficiency variance favourable or unfavourable?

Ex. 8-6   **Product costs and the revision of standards.** Adanac Corporation, which produces 15 000-watt electric motors, is currently negotiating a new labour agreement with its employees. The new wage rate is agreeable to both labour and management and calls for increases of $.50 an hour in each of the next two years. However, a major disagreement in the negotiations is the speed of the assembly line. Union negotiators are demanding a decrease in the assembly line speed from 5 metres a minute to 4 metres a minute. All direct labour activities are performed on the assembly line.

Current standard costs for one electric motor are

Direct material			$ 44
Direct labour	4 h	@ $6/h =	24
MOH	4 DLH @ $8/DLH =		32
Total			$100

Union negotiators point out that in the second year of the contract the labour rate will be only $7 an hour, a 16.7 percent increase over the current rate. Since labour accounts for only 24 percent ($24/$100) of the current product cost, the cost increase of the product caused by labour is really 4 percent (.24 × .167). Furthermore, the union argues that management should not be so concerned with the assembly line speed, which is a nonfinancial item that has no effect on product cost. Material costs and the MOH rate are expected to remain constant even with increased production hours.

Required:

a. Prepare management's case on the impact of the union's proposal on the standard cost of the product.

b. The current selling price of each motor is $160. What price would the company have to charge to achieve the same percentage gross margin that it is earning on the current price, if the union's proposed standards are accepted?

Ex. 8-7   **Using standard costs.** Following are basic and supplementary data on the mowing operations of Green-Yard:

1. Green-Yard Lawn Care Company has set a labour standard of 1.25 hours per 5000 square metres of lawn for mowing and trimming the lawn. The standard wage rate is $4.50 per hour. During the first two months of the mowing season Green-Yard mowed 4 800 000 square metres of lawn; 1420 hours of labour were used at a cost of $7,100.

2. Green-Yard computes labour hours for mowing by having employees record starting and finishing times for each lawn. Employees spend some time driving the equipment trucks between jobs. On the average, employees mow lawns only $62\frac{1}{2}$ percent of their workday. In addition to wages, employees receive vacations and fringe benefits amounting to 20 percent of their salary.

Required:

a. Compute the labour rate and efficiency variances based only on the data in paragraph 1.

b. With the additional information in paragraph 2, calculate the total standard labour cost for mowing a 5000-square metre of lawn.

Ex. 8-8 **Direct material variances.** Below are standard and actual material cost data on the production of oak barrels.

	Standards for Material		
Material	**Input Quantity**	**Input Price**	**Standard Cost per Barrel**
Oak lumber	10 bd m	$1.60/bd m	$16.00
Wood treatment chemical	.5 L	12.00/L	6.00
Iron rings	4	.60 each	2.40
Total standard material cost			$24.40

Actual Results

Production = 1200 barrels

Material	**Quantity**	**Total Cost**
Oak lumber	14 000 bd m	$24,500
Wood treatment chemical	500 L	5,500
Iron rings	4 800	2,640
Total actual material cost		$32,640

Required:

From the data presented compute the direct material price and quantity variances for each material.

Ex. 8-9 **Material and labour variances.** Following are standard and actual data on the production of an industrial cleaning compound that is sold by the barrel.

	Standard	**Actual**
Quantity of raw material purchased (kg)	—	40 000
Number of barrels of compound produced	—	10 000
Per kg purchase price of raw material	$4.00	$3.75
Raw material (kg) per barrel produced	8.80	8.65
Labour hours per barrel	2.00	2.25
Wage rate per hour	$5.00	$5.10

Required:
Use the data provided to calculate:
a. Material price variance
b. Material quantity variance
c. Labour rate variance
d. Labour efficiency variance

Ex. 8-10 **Computing and recording variances.** The Avco Company manufactures dining room tables with the following standard prime costs per unit:

Direct material	10 bd m @ $3/m
Direct labour	5h @ $5/h
Total	$55

The following events took place in May:
1. Purchased 60 000 board metres of lumber on open account at $2.80 a board metre.
2. Put 116 000 board metres of lumber into production for 11 000 tables.
3. Direct labour used in producing the tables cost $249,100 for 53 000 actual hours worked.
4. The 11 000 tables are completed and transferred to finished goods.

Required:
Prepare journal entries for the above transactions identifying variances when possible.

Ex. 8-11 **Setting and evaluating standards.** Dunnlevy Manufacturing Company is in its first year of production of a new line of outdoor gas grills. Unfamiliar with this type of product, Dunnlevy management is worried about the appropriateness of labour standards. Four production process centres are used to manufacture the gas grills. Labour standards are presented below along with actual hours used for the first six months of production.

Process	Hours per Unit	Total Actual Hours Used
Machining	1.5	4 500
Drilling	.5	1 900
Painting	.5	1 200
Assembling	2.0	4 000
Total	4.5	11 600

The number of gas grills produced during the six-month period is 2500.

Required:

a. Compute the total number of standard direct labour hours.

b. Compute the direct labour variances in terms of labour hours for each process and express the variances as a percentage of standard hours.

c. Evaluate the labour standards management established for the production of gas grills.

Problem Set A

P. 8A-1 **Direct material and direct labour performance reports.** Cravens Chemical Company has established the following standards for the production of an industrial solvent, ZT12. The solvent is sold in 50-litre drums.

Input Quantities	Input Cost	Standard Product Cost
Direct materials:		
30 L of X	$.40/L	$12.00
10 L of Y	.80/L	8.00
15 kg of Z	.60/kg	9.00
Standard direct material cost		$29.00
Direct labour ³/₄ h @ $6/h		4.50
Standard material and labour cost of one 50-L drum of solvent		$33.50

During August 10 000 drums of solvent were produced and sold. Actual material and labour costs are shown below.

1. Materials purchased and used:

```
280 000 L of X  @$.36/L  = $100,800
105 000 L of Y  @ .85/L  =   89,250
160 000 kg of Z @ .56/Kg =   89,600
```

2. Direct labour was 7000 hours at a total cost of $40,600.

Required:

a. Prepare a direct materials performance report for August.

b. Prepare a direct labour performance report for August.

P. 8A-2 **Interpreting standard cost variances.**

Refer to the trial balance below.

Required:

Use the data provided to calculate:

a. The standard cost of products sold.

b. The actual cost of products sold.

```
┌──────────────────────────────────────────────────────────┐
│                  Hawthorne Company                         │
│                    Trial Balance                           │
│                  December 31, 1983                         │
│                                                            │
│                                  Debit          Credit     │
│                                                            │
│  Cash                         $   60,000                   │
│  Accounts receivable              80,000                   │
│  Inventory                       120,000                   │
│  Plant and equipment             800,000                   │
│  Accumulated depreciation                    $  300,000    │
│  Accounts payable                                 30,000   │
│  Notes payable                                    70,000   │
│  Common stock                                    100,000   │
│  Retained earnings                               530,000   │
│  Sales                                           500,000   │
│  Cost of goods sold              275,000                   │
│  Administrative expenses          85,000                   │
│  Marketing expenses               60,000                   │
│  Material price variance          24,000                   │
│  Material quantity variance       12,000                   │
│  Labour rate variance                              8,000   │
│  Labour efficiency variance       22,000                   │
│  Total                        $1,538,000     $1,538,000    │
└──────────────────────────────────────────────────────────┘
```

   c. Net income based on standard cost.
   d. Net income based on actual cost.
   e. Total variance expressed as a percentage of total standard cost.
   f. The percentage decrease in income caused by the variances.

P. 8A-3 **Unit standard and actual costs and variance analysis.** During 1983
Weston Company produced 8000 down sleeping bags. Two materials, nylon
cloth and goose down, are used in the production process. Raw material standards are five metres of nylon at $6 per metre and three kilograms of down at
$12 per kilogram for each sleeping bag. The direct labour standards are four
hours at $6 per hour for each bag. Manufacturing overhead is applied at the rate
of $3 per direct labour hour. There were no beginning or ending work in process
inventories.
   During 1983 the following production costs were incurred:

	Nylon	Down
Direct material:		
Beginning inventory	4 000 m	2 000 kg
Ending inventory	3 000 m	1 000 kg
Purchases	38 000 m	25 000 kg
Purchase price	$6.40/m	$11.40/kg
Direct labour	36 000 h @ $5.90/h	
MOH	$92,000	

Required:
Use the preceding data to calculate:

a. The material price and quantity variances
b. The labour rate and efficiency variances
c. The total overhead variance
d. The standard unit cost of sleeping bags
e. The actual unit cost of sleeping bags

P. 8A-4 **Unit standard and actual costs and variance analysis.** Rudyards Bakery is famous for its all-natural-ingredients sour cream coffee cake. Standard data for a 100-cake batch are presented below for materials and labour.

Direct Material	Quantity	Cost	Total
Sugar	25 kg	$ .20/kg	$ 5.00
Eggs	12 dozen	.80/dozen	9.60
Flour	50 kg	.22/kg	11.00
Sour cream	8 L	6.00/L	48.00
Baking soda	.5 kg	.40/kg	.20
Salt	1 kg	.20/kg	.20
Standard cost for direct material			$ 74.00
Direct labour		4 h @ $6.50/h	26.00
Total standard direct material and direct labour cost			$100.00

During June Rudyards Bakery produced 2500 sour cream coffee cakes with the following production costs:

Direct Material	Quantity	Cost	Total
Sugar	650 kg	$ .22/kg	$ 143
Eggs	300 dozens	.75/dozen	225
Flour	1300 kg	.25/kg	325
Sour cream	220 L	6.25/L	1,375
Baking soda	12.5 kg	.40/kg	5
Salt	10 kg	.20/kg	2
Actual cost for direct material			$2,075
Direct labour		96 h @ $6.25/h	600
Total actual direct material and direct labour cost			$2,675

Required:
a. What is the standard direct material and direct labour cost for one sour cream coffee cake?
b. What is the actual prime cost for one coffee cake?
c. What is the total material variance for June?

d. What is the total labour variance for June?

e. Calculate material price and quantity variances for sugar, eggs, flour, and sour cream.

f. Calculate the labour rate and efficiency variances.

P. 8A-5 **Direct labour variances.** Kapecky, Inc., a furniture manufacturer, establishes the following labour standards for the production of its 105 cm × 165 cm birch dining room tables:

Cutting and assembling	8h @ $ 8/h =	$ 64
Finishing	6h @ 10/h =	60
Total		$124

Actual results for the month are:

1. The number of tables produced is 200.

2. Cutting and assembling labour is 1700 hours at a total cost of $14,450.

3. Finishing labour is 1150 hours at a total cost of $11,270.

Required

a. Calculate the total labour variance.

b. Compute the direct labour rate and efficiency variances for both departments.

c. Graph the cutting and assembly department variances.

P. 8A-6 **Comprehensive standard cost variance reporting problem.** Herbert Company is a major manufacturer of leather coats and boots and has developed standard costs for each which are shown below.

Since a different quality of leather is used for the two products, the standard price for the two types of leather is different. Similarly, the types of labour skills required for each product vary, resulting in different standard hourly rates for the two products even though they are produced in the same processing departments.

During June 1983, 11 000 units of leather coats and 11 000 pairs of leather boots were produced. The actual costs incurred are presented below.

Required:

From the data on actual and standard costs, prepare the following reports in good form:

a. Performance report—direct materials

b. Performance report—direct labour

c. Schedule of manufacturing overhead variance

d. Comprehensive product variance analysis report

Standard Cost	Input Quantity	Input Cost	Standard Cost of Output
Coats			
Direct materials:			
Leather	3 m²	$12.00/m²	$36.00
Buckles	1 unit	1.50/each	1.50
Standard cost of direct materials			$37.50
Direct labour:			
Cutting	2 h	$ 5.50/h	$11.00
Sewing	1 h	7.00/h	7.00
Standard cost of direct labour			18.00
Manufacturing overhead		$ 3.00/DLH	9.00
Total standard cost of a leather coat			$64.50
Leather boots (per Pair)			
Direct materials:			
Leather	2 m²	$ 5.00/m²	$10.00
Soles	2 units	1.00/each	2.00
Standard cost of direct materials			$12.00
Direct labour:			
Cutting	1 h	$ 4.00/h	$ 4.00
Sewing	1 h	5.00/h	5.00
Standard cost of direct labour			9.00
Manufacturing overhead		$ 1.00/DLH	2.00
Total standard cost of a pair of leather boots			$23.00

Herbert Company
Schedule of Actual Costs
June 1983

	Actual Input Quantity	Total Input Cost
Leather coats:		
Leather	36 000 m²	$417,600
Buckles	11 200 units	18,480
Cutting labour	21 000 h	130,200
Sewing labour	11 500 h	77,050
Manufacturing overhead	32 500 h	91,000
Total actual cost of leather coats		$734,330
Leather boots		
Leather	24 000 m²	$115,200
Soles	22 500 units	24,750
Cutting labour	10 500 h	43,575
Sewing labour	12 000 h	63,600
Manufacturing overhead	22 500 h	20,250
Total actual cost of leather boots		$267,375

P. 8A-7 **Comprehensive standard cost variance analysis.** I-M-Cool, Inc., manufactures industrial roof-top air conditioning units. Their largest seller, the XB410, accounts for 40 percent of their total sales revenue. However, recent increases in XB410 sales volume have not improved quarterly earnings reports. You have been called in to investigate the problem and provide your expert opinion on the situation. XB410 standard cost data are presented below along with actual production cost data for the last six months.

Standards for an XB410 Air Conditioner				
Direct materials:				
Galvanized steel	2 t	@ $ 500/ton	=	$1,000
Copper	.6 t	@ 2,200/ton	=	1,320
Paint	12 L	@ 4/L	=	48
Controls	1 unit	@ 260/unit	=	260
Motor	1 unit	@ 550/unit	=	550
Standard cost of direct materials				$3,178
Direct labour:				
Cutting and forming department	45 h	@ $ 8/h	=	$ 360
Coil department	15 h	@ 9/h	=	135
Painting department	3 h	@ 7/h	=	21
Assembly department	50 h	@ 8/h	=	400
Standard cost of direct labour				$ 916
Manufacturing overhead applied at the rate of $10/direct labour hour				$1,130
Total standard cost of XB410 unit				$5,224

Production Cost XB410—January through June		
	Quantity	**Cost**
Direct materials:		
Galvanized steel	720 t	$ 388,800
Copper	270 t	648,000
Paint	2880 L	9,360
Controls	305 units	76,250
Motors	300 units	186,000
Actual cost of direct materials		$1,308,410
Direct labour:		
Cutting and forming department	15 200 h	$ 110,700
Coil department	5 000 h	45,000
Painting department	840 h	5,712
Assembly department	17 000 h	121,500
Actual cost of direct labour		$ 282,912
Actual manufacturing overhead		$ 390,000
Total actual cost of production for XB410		$1,981,322

January through June operating data are

1. Altogether 300 XB410 units are produced and sold at a price of $9,400 each.
2. Commissions to sales people on XB410 are 5 percent of selling price rather than the normal company rate of 3 percent.
3. Advertising cost for the six-month period is $120,000.
4. The XB410 unit is a very sophisticated air conditioning system that requires a heavy commitment of time by the engineering department and key administrative people. For most products of I-M-Cool, engineering and administrative costs amount to about 15 percent of the selling price. For XB410 management feels the percentage is about 20 percent.

Required:
a. Prepare a direct materials performance report.
b. Prepare a direct labour performance report.
c. Prepare a manufacturing overhead schedule of variance.
d. Prepare a product variance analysis report
e. What is the actual unit product cost of the XB410 unit?
f. Prepare a product income statement for January through June for the XB410 product.
g. If the company requires a 15 percent profit on sales including all costs, what should be the selling price using the above actual cost data?

Problem Set B

P. 8B-1 **Material and labour variances.** Cajon Enterprises manufactures a rust-inhibiting paint that sells in 5-L cans. July production of 6000 cans of paint resulted in the following direct costs:

Materials:				
Base	25 000 L	@ $ 2.80/L	=	$70,000
Drying agents	1 600 L	@ 11.00/L	=	17,600
Colouring agents	5 500 kg	@ 2.20/kg	=	12,100
Total material costs				$99,700
Direct labour	5500 h	@ 6.80/h	=	$37,400

Standards for direct costs for one 5-L can of paint are as follows:

Materials:				
Base	4 L	@ $ 2.50/L	=	$10.00
Drying agents	.25 L	@ 12.00/L	=	3.00
Colouring agents	1 kg @	2.00/kg	=	2.00
Total material				$15.00
Direct labour	1 h	@ $ 7.00/h	=	7.00
Direct cost standards				$22.00

Required:

a. Calculate material price and quantity variances.

b. Calculate the labour rate and efficiency variances.

c. Calculate the actual per-unit direct cost of paint in July.

P. 8B-2 **Identifying and using variances.** Below is a somewhat summarized trial balance for the Diebolt Manufacturing Company at the end of its June 30 fiscal year.

Diebolt Manufacturing Company Trial Balance June 30		
	Debit	**Credit**
Cash	$ 26,000	
Accounts receivable	80,000	
Inventory	170,000	
Plant and equipment	500,000	
Accumulated depreciation		$ 220,000
Patents	33,000	
Accounts payable		40,000
Mortgage payable		120,000
Capital stock		100,000
Retained earnings		210,000
Sales		850,000
Cost of goods sold	442,000	
Administrative expenses	145,000	
Marketing expenses	110,000	
Material price variance	18,000	
Material quantity variance		6,000
Labour rate variance		2,000
Labour efficiency variance	24,000	
Total	$1,548,000	$1,548,000

Required:

a. What is the standard cost of the products sold?

b. What is the actual cost of the products sold?

c. Prepare an income statement in good form for the fiscal year.

d. What are standard and actual cost of goods sold expressed as a percentage of sales?

e. After closing entries have been posted, what will be the new balance in the retained earnings account if Diebolt has an effective tax rate of 40 percent?

P. 8B-3 **Computing and using variances.** Neat-N-Green provides a variety of lawn care services including lawn fertilizing. The company has developed standards for its services to help control costs and provide information for pricing decisions. For fertilizing lawns the following standards are used:

```
Per 5000 square metres of lawn:
    Labour time          1 h
    Labour rate          $4.40/h
    Material quantity    50 kg
    Material cost        $18/100 kg
```

During the second quarter of the year actual data for Neat-N-Green were

Total area fertilized: 2 100 000 square metres
Labour: 540 hours at a cost of $1,974
Material: 25 200 kilograms at a cost of $4,284

Required:
a. Compute the material price and quantity variances.
b. Compute the labor rate and efficiency variances.
c. If the average lawn size is 7500 square metres, what should Neat-N-Green charge for fertilizing if it wants to set the price at double the standard cost for labour and material?
d. What would your answer be to part c if actual costs were used in place of standard costs?
e. Do the variances indicate that any activities should be evaluated?

P. 8B-4   **Unit standard and actual costs and variance analysis.** Roth Manufacturing produces men's clothing in a job-shop production environment. Roth attaches the appropriate store label to the clothes during production and sells directly to several retail stores. A major product of Roth's is wool sport coats that have the following standards:

```
Wool material                          3 m   @$8.00/m = $24.00
Lining material                        2 m   @ 1.50/m =   3.00
Direct labour                          3 hr  @ 6.00/h =  18.00
MOH applied at the rate of $5 per direct labour hour  =  15.00
```

A recent job run of 1000 sport coats was completed with the following costs:

```
Wool material                  2900 m  @ $7.80/m = $22,620
Lining material                2200 m  @   1.40/m =   3,080
Direct MOH actual labour  3300 h  @   6.20/h =  20,460
                                                      16,500
Total cost of job                                    $62,660
```

Required:
a. What is the standard cost of one sport coat?

b. What is the actual cost of one sport coat for the job just completed?

c. Compute the material price and quantity variances.

d. Compute the labour rate and efficiency variances.

P. 8B-5 **Computing variances.** Following are standards for a product manufactured by Rosier Brothers:

Material	3 kg	@ $6.00/kg
Labour	5 h	@ $4.00/h
Overhead	5 h	@ 2.00/h

Actual production data are

1. Direct material cost $6.50 per kilogram.

2. Factory workers were paid $4.10 per hour.

3. Manufacturing overhead was $109,000.

Table of Variances				
			Variance	
	Actual	**Standard**	**Quantity/Efficiency**	**Price/Rate**
Material	$236,600	$216,000	_____	_____
Labour	225,500	240,000	_____	_____

Required:

a. How many units were produced?

b. Complete the table above and indicate whether each variance is favourable or unfavourable.

c. Compute the amount of overhead variance.

P. 8B-6 **Single product variance reporting.** Cranert Building Supply manufactures an asphalt sealer that it sells in 5-litre cans. The standards per can are as follows:

Material:			
Base	4 L	@ $ .75/L =	$ 3.00
Hardener	2 L	@ .50/L =	1.00
			$ 4.00
Labour	.75 h	@ $6.00/h =	$ 4.50
MOH	.75 h	@ $4.00/h =	$ 3.00
Total standard cost			$11.50

During May Cranert produced 10 000 cans of the asphalt sealer with the following total cost:

Material:				
Base	42 000 L	@ $80/L	=	$ 33,600
Hardener	19 000 L	@ .473684/L	=	9,000
Total actual material cost				$ 42,600
Labour	8000 h			50,000
MOH				32,000
Total actual cost				$124,600

Required:

From the data above prepare in good form:

a. A direct materials performance report.
b. A direct labour performance report.
c. A schedule of manufacturing overhead variance.
d. A product variance analysis report.

P. 8B-7 Comprehensive standard cost variance reporting problem. A. J. Frankfurter and Co. produces two types of meat products, sausage and bologna. The standard costs for a 500-kg batch of each of these products are shown in the following table:

	Table 8-1 *					
	500 kg Batch of Sausage			**500 kg Batch of Bologna**		
Resource	**Standard Quantity**	**Standard Price**	**Product Cost/Batch**	**Standard Quantity**	**Standard Price**	**Product Cost/Batch**
Direct materials:						
Pork meat	460 kg	$1.30	$598.00	450 kg	$1.15	$517.50
Spice	34 kg	2.50	85.00	40 kg	1.60	64.00
Casing	6 kg	2.00	12.00	10 kg	1.50	15.00
Direct labour						
Grinding department	2 h	$4.00/h	$ 8.00	2 h	$5.50/h	$ 11.00
Stuffing department	2 h	4.50/h	9.00	1.5 h	6.00/h	9.00
Packing department	1 h	3.50/h	3.50	.5 h	4.00/h	2.00
MOH	5 DLH	$15/h		4 DLH	$14/h	

*Although both products use the same type of raw materials and are processed by the same departments, different varieties of materials and labour are used for each product. Thus input price per kilogram and rates per hour are not the same for the two products.

Actual cost and production data appear below.

Table 8-2 *		
	Sausage	**Bologna**
Purchases, May 1983:		
Pork meat	46 000 kg @ $1.35	90 000 kg @ $1.20
Spice	4 000 kg @ 2.45	7 000 kg @ 1.70
Casings	600 kg @ 2.00	3 000 kg @ 1.40
Inventory, 30/4/83 (beginning)		
Pork meat	5000 kg	11 000 kg
Spice	700 kg	600 kg
Casings	100 kg	850 kg
Inventory, 31/5/83 (ending):		
Pork meat	6800 kg	8500 kg
Spice	1550 kg	750 kg
Casings	250 kg	1800 kg
Actual payroll, May 1983		
Grinding	185 h @ $3.90	415 h @ $5.40
Stuffing	175 h @ 4.60	275 h @ 6.15
Packing	87 h @ 3.70	105 h @ 3.80
Actual MOH, May 1983	$6,200	$11,900
Production output, May 1983	44 000 kg	90 000 kg

*Although both products use the same type of raw materials and are processed by the same departments, different varieties of materials and labour are used for each product. Thus input price per kilogram and rates per hour are not the same for the two products.

Required:

From the information provided in Tables 8-1 and 8-2, develop and present in good form the following reports for May 1983:

a. Performance report—direct materials.
b. Performance report—direct labour.
c. Schedule of MOH variance.
d. Product variance analysis report.

Minicases

Minicase 8-1   (CMA Examination Question)

Eastern Company manufactures special electrical equipment and parts. Eastern employs a standard cost accounting system with separate standards established for each product.

A special transformer is manufactured in the Transformer Department. Production volume is measured by direct labour hours in this department and a flexible budget system is used to plan and control department overhead.[1]

Standard costs for the special transformer are determined annually in September for the coming year. The standard cost of a transformer for 1983 was computed at $67.00 as shown below.

Direct material			
Iron	5 sheets	@ $2.00	$10.00
Copper	3 spools	@ $3.00	9.00
Direct labour	4 hours	@ $7.00	28.00
Variable overhead	4 hours	@ $3.00	12.00
Fixed Overhead	4 hours	@ $2.00	8.00
Total			$67.00

Overhead rates were based upon normal and expected monthly capacity for 1983, both of which were 4000 direct labour hours. Practical capacity for this department is 5000 direct labour hours per month. Variable overhead costs are expected to vary with the number of direct labour hours actually used.

During October 1983, 800 transformers were produced. This was below expectations because a work stoppage occurred during contract negotiations with the labour force. Once the contract was settled, the department scheduled overtime in an attempt to catch up to expected production levels.

The following costs were incurred in October, 1983.

Direct material	Direct materials purchased	Materials used
Iron	5000 sheets @ $2.00/sheet	3900 sheets
Copper	2200 spools @ $3.10/spool	2600 spools
Direct labour		
Regular time:	2000 hours @ $7.00	
	1400 hours @ $7.20	
Overtime:	600 of the 1400 hours were subject to overtime premium. The total overtime premium of $2,160 is included in variable overhead in accordance with company accounting practices.	
Variable overhead:	$10,000	
Fixed overhead:	$ 8,800	

[1] The concept of flexible budget, that is budgeting more than one level of activity, is fully discussed in Chapter 9.

Required:

Prepare a report to be submitted to the president of the Eastern Company. In your report indicate some of the possible causes of variances.

Minicase 8-2   (Certified Accountants—U.K. adapted)

Dropgoal, Ltd., manufactures rugby balls. As each ball is completed it is booked out to a subsidiary company, Try, Ltd. Dropgoal's budget for the seventh four-weekly control period of its financial year was as follows:

Sales (6000 units @ $8 each)		$48,000
Variable Costs		
Bladders (6000 @ $0.50 each)	$ 3,000	
Leather (200 ten hide bales @ $76.00 each)	15,200	
Sundry and packaging materials	1,300	
Direct labour (5000 hours @ 90¢ per hour)	4,500	
	24,000	
Fixed Costs		
Administrative and establishment expenses	4,239	
Staff and directors' salaries	$28,261	
		36,500
Budgeted net profit		$11,500

Due to power shortages during the "three-day week," Dropgoal was only able to manufacture during 60 percent of the budgeted production hours and was unable to sanction any overtime. Despite this the direct labour force was paid in full for the budgeted hours. Various other differences from budget occurred and the following are the actual figures for the period:

Sales (4000 units @ $9 each)		$36,000
Variable Costs		
Bladders (4000 @ $0.70 each)	$ 2,800	
Leather (100 ten hide bales @ $133.33 each)	13,333	
Sundry and packaging materials	867	
Direct labour (5000 hours @ $1.00 per hour)	5,000	
	22,000	
Fixed Costs		
Administrative expenses	4,385	
Staff and directors' salaries	8,315	
		34,700
Actual net profit		$ 1,300

Required:

a. Prepare a statement reconciling the budgeted contribution with the actual contribution, stating the variances in the way which you think will be most helpful to management. Present your calculations as schedules with references to the main statement.

b. Comment briefly on any apparent interrelationships between the variances.

Reproduced from Certified Accountants Questions and Suggested Answers, including papers for Scottish and Irish Students, Professional Examinations, June 1975. With permission of The Association of Certified Accountants.

Minicase 8-3   (Certified Accountants—U.K. adapted)

The Blendyarn Company, Limited operate a number of overseas subsidiaries which spin at 50/50 blend of wool/synthetic hosiery yarn, supplying this to their respective local knitwear manufacturers.

One of these subsidiaries which operates in the Far East is called Blendyarn Berhad. Blendyarn Berhad produces a budget for a four-week operating period (during which 40-hour, five-day weeks are worked) as follows:

Blendyarn Berhad		
Budget for the four weeks ended 30 October 1984		
Sales	$	$
(10 000 kg @ $10 per kg)		100,000
Direct Production Costs		
Wool (5000 kg @ $6)	30,000	
Synthetics (5000 kg @ $4)	20,000	
Oil, Dyestuffs, etc.	5,000	
Machine operators (9600 hours @ $1)	9,600	
Supervisors (320 h @ $1.25)	400	
	65,000	
Fixed Costs		
Administrative staff	1,000	
Sales staff	4,000	
Rent, taxes, power, etc.	10,000	
	15,000	
Total costs		80,000
Budgeted Net Profit		$ 20,000

Note: Rent, taxes, and power costs are divided on the ratio of three to one between production and administration/marketing.

Blendyarn Berhad only produces to order, and into the foreseeable future it has full order books, so any lost production directly reduces sales.

In October the Far Eastern subsidiary faced operating difficulties ensuing from monsoon rains which flooded its factory during the second week of the operating period. Although no damage was caused to materials, the management incurred additional expenses by hiring contract cleaners for three days at $500 per day to clean up the mess. As the operators could not work while the cleaning up was in progress, 60 percent of the week's production was lost. At the end of the three days' cleaning, management said that conditions within the factory had returned to normal, but on inspecting the factory themselves the operators disagreed and walked out. Management brought the contract cleaners back for two more days and at the same time negotiated with the operators to return to work. During the negotiations management offered to increase wages, although they refused to pay operators for the period during which they had walked out. The operators accepted the management's offer and at the commencement of the following week the factory was working normally. At the end of the four-week period during which the monsoon rains had caused the factory to be flooded, actual performance was as follows:

Blendyarn Berhad		
Actual performance for the four weeks ended 30 October 1984		
Sales	$	$
2500 kg @ $10		25,000
2500 kg @ $12		60,000
		85,000
Direct Production Costs		
Wood (3750 kg @ $8)	30,000	
Synthetics (3750 kg @ $4)	15,000	
Oil, Dyestuffs, etc.	4,456	
Machine operators 3840 h @ $1 = $3840		
4800 h @ $1.1 = 5280		
	9,120	
Supervisors 160 @ $1.25 = $200		
160 @ $1.40 = $224		
	424	
	59,000	
Fixed costs		
Administrative staff	1,250	
Sales staff	4,750	
Rent, taxes, power, etc.	10,000	
Contract cleaners (5 days @ $500)	2,500	
Total costs		77,500
Actual Net Profit		$ 7,500

Required:

As management accountant from the holding company who visited Blendyarn Berhad shortly after the monsoon, write a report to the management of the subsidiary explaining the differences between the actual and the budgeted figures as you see it, in a way which will enable Blendyarn's management to trace and eliminate any inefficiency.

Note: Your report does not necessarily have to follow traditional variance analysis if you feel that either there is insufficient information for that approach or that it would be clearer and more helpful to present the information in a different way.

Reproduced from Certified Accountants Questions and Suggested Answers, including papers for Scottish and Irish Students, Professional Examinations, June 1976. With permission of The Association of Certified Accountants.

Chapter 9

Flexible Budgeting and Manufacturing Overhead Variance Analysis

This chapter uses cost behaviour concepts from Chapter 5 and basic budgeting concepts from Chapter 7 to develop the concept of preparing budgets for more than one level of activity. Also, overhead variance analysis, introduced in Chapter 8, is discussed in depth in this chapter. When you have completed this chapter, you should understand:

1 The distinction between fixed and flexible budgets.

2 The purpose and procedures in developing a flexible budget.

3 Flexible budget performance reporting.

4 The effect of fixed cost on manufacturing overhead rates.

5 Overhead variance analysis.

Most well-managed businesses use an effective budgeting system to aid in the achievement of company goals. Budgets are useful planning tools and provide managers with a framework for evaluating performance. Fixed budgets, discussed in Chapter 7, are prepared for a single level of activity. If actual activity is close to that budgeted, the fixed budget can help managers plan business activities and provide a basis for measuring performance.

Actual activity may differ significantly from budgeted activity, however. An unexpected strike, cancellation of an order, an unexpected large new production contract, or other factors may cause the actual activity of a business to fall far short or exceed by a significant margin the level that was expected when the budget was prepared. In such situations a fixed budget may be of little use for measuring performance, and for that reason it may be desirable to prepare a flexible budget that covers a range of activity. Such budgets may provide managers with more useful information for planning and a better basis for comparing performance.

The purpose of this chapter is to discuss and illustrate the preparation and use of flexible budgets. In the last part of the chapter we cover the use of flexible budgets in analyzing manufacturing overhead variances.

Fixed budgeting

A **fixed budget,** sometimes called a **static budget,** provides cost and revenue estimates for one level of activity. For example, the master budget for the first quarter developed in Chapter 7 was based on expected production activity of 2700 captain's chairs and 4300 rocking chairs. Fixed budget performance reports compare data from actual operations with the single level of activity reflected in the budget. Figure 9-1 presents a fixed budget performance report taken from Chapter 7 (Figure 7-22). For many organizations the estimate of

Fixed budgets are prepared for one level of activity

Fable Manufacturing Company
Manufacturing Performance Report
First Quarter 1984

Manufacturing Overhead	Fixed Budget	Actual Cost	Variance (Favourable) Unfavourable
Variable costs:			
Indirect materials	$ 9,150	$ 10,800	$ 1,650
Indirect labour	18,300	19,000	700
Employee fringe benefits	36,600	45,200	8,600
Payroll taxes	9,150	11,400	2,250
Utilities	10,980	13,500	2,520
Maintenance	7,320	7,100	(220)
Total variable costs	$ 91,500	$107,000	$15,500
Fixed costs:			
Supervision	$ 18,000	$ 18,000	—
Depreciation	24,000	24,000	—
Maintenance	9,000	9,500	$ 500
Property taxes	4,912	5,200	288
Insurance	3,000	3,300	300
Total fixed costs	$ 58,912	$ 60,000	$ 1,088
Total manufacturing overhead	$150,412	$167,000	$16,588

Figure 9-1
Fixed budget performance report for manufacturing overhead activities.

activity level is close enough to the actual activity level to make the fixed budget a good basis for performance measurement.

However, if the actual level of activity turns out to be significantly different from the fixed budget level of activity, the performance report may provide very little useful information and may in fact be misleading. For example, the first quarter overhead budget of $150,412 presented in Figure 9-1 is based on estimated production of 2700 captain's chairs and 4300 rocking chairs. The actual overhead costs of $167,000 resulted from production of 3200 captain's chairs and 5200 rocking chairs, as noted in Chapter 7. Does the $16,588 unfavourable variance provide a useful measure of performance when actual production of chairs was 19 percent higher than budgeted and rocker production was 21 percent higher? You may remember from Chapter 5 that fixed costs remain constant at all levels of activity, and variable costs change with changing activity levels. Therefore, with higher activity levels costs can be expected to be higher also. The fixed budget provides little help in determining what first quarter overhead costs should be at activity levels that are higher than those used to prepare the budget. The performance data merely indicate that actual costs were higher than budgeted for the expected level of activity. The inability of fixed budget performance reports to provide useful information when actual activity differs significantly from expected activity is a major reason for using a flexible budgeting system. A flexible budget eliminates variances caused by volume changes and isolates cost variances due to changes in efficiency or other factors.

Flexible budgeting

Flexible budgets cover a range of activity

A **flexible budget,** also called a **dynamic budget,** is one that is prepared for more than one level of activity. For example, a firm may prepare budgets for 10 000, 11 000, and 12 000 units of production. The purpose of preparing budgets for multiple levels of activity is to provide managers with information about a range of activity in case the actual level of activity is different from the expected level. Managers continue to rely heavily on the budget based on the expected level of activity for planning material acquisitions, labour needs, and other resource requirements, but the flexible budget provides additional information useful in modifying plans if operating data indicate that some other level of activity will occur. When performance reports are prepared, actual results are compared with a budget based on the actual level of activity that the firm experienced.

Characteristics of flexible budgets

Flexible budgets have several desirable characteristics. They

1. Cover a range of activity.
2. Are dynamic.
3. Facilitate performance measurement.

Cover a range of activity. Forecasts of future events always involve some uncertainty. Managers want to minimize the effect of uncertainty in planning and decision making. Unlike a fixed budget, which provides only one estimate of expected outcomes, a flexible budget reflects expected results for a number of activity levels. A flexible budget does not reduce the probability that fluctuations in activity level will occur, but it does provide managers with information about the effect of changes in activity levels. Accurate predictions of activity level are sometimes hard to make, and many managers find they make more effective decisions with the aid of flexible budgets.

Some organizations experience very stable activity levels or activity levels that are very predictable. For example, a firm may have a sales growth rate of 9 to 10 percent a year for 10 years in a row. In such a case the expected activity level and associated revenues and costs may be relatively easy to estimate, and a fixed budget may be all that is needed. Other firms may experience widely fluctuating business activity, with some years of dramatic growth and other years of declining business. Among the most important factors influencing business stability is type of business. For example, tourist businesses are strongly affected by weather conditions and general economic conditions. Staples industries, such as food, are influenced less by economic conditions. Of course, individual food businesses, such as a single grocery store, may experience significant fluctuations due to growing or declining neighbourhood populations, managerial actions, or other variables. For businesses with widely fluctuating activity, flexible budgets are very useful.

An important step in developing a flexible budget is the selection of the range of activity covered by the flexible budget. Managers want information about several possible levels of activity that are likely to occur. Unlikely activity levels are not included. Often one activity level at each extreme of the activity range is selected, with one or more in between. The most likely activity level is the primary source of data for planning business operations.

Are dynamic. Flexible budgets allow managers to adjust plans more easily if activity differs from expected levels. With flexible budget data it is easy to adjust budget estimates on a timely basis to reflect fluctuations from the expected activity level. Such budgets address "what is" rather than "what was" or "what was expected." This dynamic nature of flexible budgets makes them a very useful decision-making tool for management.

> *Easy to adjust plans to changing activity levels*

Facilitate performance measurement. An important role of performance reporting is efficiency measurement. Often a fixed budget is useful for effectiveness measures, such as the achievement of a sales goal of 10 000 units, but in some cases it is not very helpful in identifying efficiency measures, such as the per-unit cost of marketing a product. A flexible budget is very useful for efficiency measurement because it answers the question, "What should the results be, given the actual level of activity?" To illustrate, refer to Figure 9-1. The report shows an unfavourable overhead variance of $16,588 for the first quarter of the year. The fixed budget is based on estimated production of

2700 captain's chairs and 4300 rocking chairs. The actual cost of $167,000 resulted from the production of 3200 captain's chairs and 5200 rocking chairs. Naturally, overhead is more than planned, but how much more than the original fixed budget should the cost be? The answer to this question is determined by preparing a new budget for the actual level of activity (3200 chairs and 5200 rockers) using the cost relationship used in developing the original budget. This new budget based on the activity level that occurred is compared with actual costs in the budget performance report.

A flexible budget performance report uses a budget based on the actual activity level

To illustrate a flexible budget and the variance report resulting from it, we use the Fable Manufacturing Company example from Chapter 7 and the company's first quarter overhead report shown in Figure 9-1. On the basis of the expected production of 2700 captain's chairs and 4300 rocking chairs, the company calculated the following number of direct labour hours, which were used to apply overhead and develop the overhead budget.

Captain's chairs	2700 × 2 h =	5 400
Rocking chairs	4300 × 3 h =	12 900
Total budgeted direct labour h		= 18 300

Using the same standard hours per unit, the expected labour hours for the actual production activity is 22 000 hours, as shown below.

Captain's chairs	3200 × 2 h =	6 400
Rocking chairs	5200 × 3 h =	15 600
Total budgeted direct labour h		= 22 000

The fixed budget in Figure 9-1 was prepared using 18 300 direct labour hours, and a flexible budget can be prepared using 22 000 direct labour hours. Both the fixed and flexible overhead budgets are prepared using fixed overhead cost data from Chapter 7 as well as the variable overhead data presented below.

	Cost per Direct Labour Hour
Indirect materials	$ .50
Indirect labour	1.00
Employee fringe benefits	2.00
Payroll taxes	.50
Utilities	.60
Maintenance	.40
	$5.00

With the fixed budget, each variable cost item was multiplied by 18 300 direct labour hours. For instance, indirect material was budgeted at $9,150 ($.50 × 18 300 DLH). With the flexible budget, each variable overhead item is multiplied by 22 000 direct labour hours. For example, indirect material is budgeted at $11,000 ($.50 × 22 000 DLH). The flexible budget for the actual level of activity is shown in Figure 9-2 and is computed by multiplying each of the variable cost items by 22 000 direct labour hours and adding the fixed costs given in Figure 7-22 of Chapter 7 and shown in Figure 9-1. The performance report is completed by listing the actual costs and comparing them with the flexible budget data.

Compare the variance report in Figure 9-1 with the one in Figure 9-2. The two reports show very different results. The fixed budget report identifies an unfavourable total variance of $16,588, which is 11 percent of total budgeted overhead costs. The flexible budget variance report shows a favourable variance of $1,912, which is 1.3 percent of total budgeted overhead cost in the flexible budget. In this case the flexible budget variance report provides a better measure of efficiency, since its budgeted costs are based on the actual activity level of 22 000 direct labour hours. Efficiency measures answer the question, "How good was performance, given the actual level of activity?" Whenever

Flexible budgets provide a better measure of efficiency than fixed budgets

Fable Manufacturing Company Manufacturing Overhead Performance Report First Quarter 1984			
Manufacturing Overhead	**Flexible Budget**	**Actual Cost**	**Variance (Favourable) Unfavourable**
Variable costs:			
Indirect materials	$ 11,000	$ 10,800	($200)
Indirect labour	22,000	19,000	(3,000)
Employee fringe benefits	44,000	45,200	1,200
Payroll taxes	11,000	11,400	400
Utilities	13,200	13,500	300
Maintenance	8,800	7,100	(1,700)
Total variable costs	$110,000	$107,000	($3,000)
Fixed costs:			
Supervision	$ 18,000	$ 18,000	—
Depreciation	24,000	24,000	—
Maintenance	9,000	9,500	500
Property taxes	4,912	5,200	288
Insurance	3,000	3,300	300
Total fixed costs	$ 58,912	$ 60,000	$1,088
Total manufacturing overhead	$168,912	$167,000	($1,912)

Figure 9-2
Flexible budget performance report for manufacturing overhead activities for the same period covered by the fixed budget report in Figure 9-1.

actual and budgeted activity are significantly different, a flexible budget variance analysis report provides a better measure of efficiency.

Flexible budgeting illustrated

The preceding discussion illustrated the need for flexible budget performance reports and how the reports are prepared using actual costs and the actual activity level. Now we illustrate the development of a flexible budget before the year begins. The student health centre of New Barrie University is used to illustrate the complete cycle in the development of a flexible budget and the preparation of a flexible budget variance analysis report. The health centre serves students enrolled in the university. Most patients require outpatient services, but facilities are available for students requiring hospitalization. The centre has a small permanent professional staff that is supplemented by doctors and nurses from the area who work part-time as needed. As a result, a portion of the salaries is fixed, while some of the medical salary cost varies with the number of students served.

Steps in the flexible budgeting process

The following steps are needed to develop a flexible budget:

1. Determine the range of activity the budget should cover.
2. Determine the cost behaviour patterns for each cost included in the budget.
3. Select the activity levels for which budgets will be prepared.
4. Prepare the flexible budget using the cost behaviour pattern data and the selected activity levels.

Determine the activity range of the flexible budget

Step 1. The first step in the budgeting process is to determine the range of activity the budget will cover. The activity range is important because cost behaviour patterns may be different in different ranges of activity. For example, the building lease cost may be fixed from 0 to 25 000 student visits a year, but beyond 25 000 visits additional space must be leased, causing a jump in the lease cost from $18,000 to $30,000 annually. This is the relevant range concept discussed in Chapter 5. It makes little sense to analyze costs and revenues for activity levels that have little chance of occurring.

Determine the cost behaviour patterns

Step 2. The cost behaviour pattern must be determined for each cost included in the budget. Typically firms analyze historical cost data using techniques discussed in Chapters 5 and 17, such as high low, scatter diagram, linear regression, or other methods. Behaviour patterns suggested by historical cost data analyses are modified to reflect known or expected changes, such as increased payroll taxes, new pension fund contributions, and increased property tax rates. Usually the behaviour pattern for each cost is described in terms of fixed and variable components.

In this example the activity measure is the number of student visits to the health centre. Other measures of activity, such as the number of medical staff hours, could have been used, but in this case management felt that student visits is the most appropriate measure. The health centre manager selects an activity range of 12 000 to 20 000 student visits for the budget year. This relatively wide activity range is selected because student enrollment figures for the coming year are not yet available. Also, the national health service is predicting a major flu epidemic during the year. If the flue epidemic strikes the campus, health service visits will be noticeably higher than this year's level of 15 000.

The health centre identifies ten different costs and determines the behaviour pattern of each. For example, Figure 9-3 shows a scatter diagram analysis of health centre maintenance costs for the last ten years. Analysis indicates that $20,000 of maintenance cost is fixed, and $1.50 per student visit is variable. Figure 9-4 summarizes the results of the cost behaviour analysis for each cost.

Select the activity levels for which budgets will be prepared

Step 3. Using the above data, budgets are prepared for the activity levels that management selects within the relevant range. In this example budgets are prepared for three activity levels—12 000, 16 000, and 20 000 student visits. The number of budgets prepared for different activity levels is a matter of managerial performance, which is influenced by the cost-benefit relationship of preparing more budgets. However, the cost of preparing budgets for different activity levels is not high once cost behaviour data have been developed. The

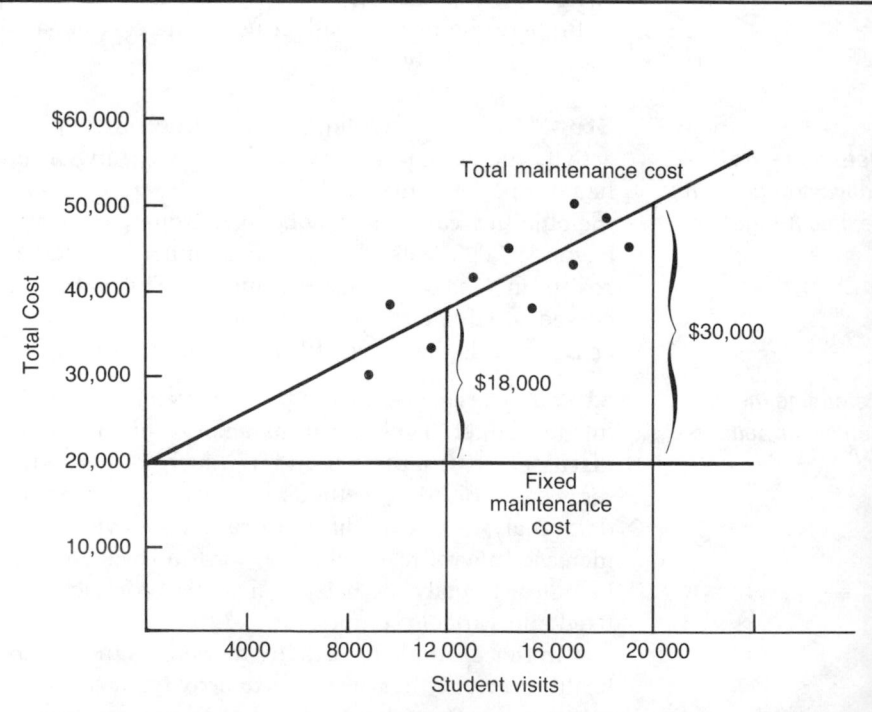

Figure 9-3
Scatter diagram of maintenance costs for the health centre of New Barrie University.

New Barrie University **Student Health Service** **Estimated Cost Behaviour Patterns** **For the Fiscal Year 1984–1985**		

Cost	Fixed Cost	Variable Cost per Student Visit
Administrative salaries	$35,000	—
Medical and nursing salaries	80,000	$8.00
Other salaries	28,000	2.50
Medical supplies	6,000	5.00
External laboratory fees and other medical fees	—	1.00
Building lease	18,000	—
Utilities	6,500	.50
Maintenance	20,000	1.50
Computer services	12,000	.75
Employee fringe benefits	34,500	1.75

Figure 9-4
Cost formula for the 10 cost pools used by the health centre for budgeting and costing purposes. Most are mixed costs.

health centre could have prepared a budget with increments of 1000 visits, but for our purposes three activity levels are sufficient.

Step 4. The actual preparation of a flexible budget is not difficult once the cost behaviour patterns are determined and data, such as that in Figure 9-4, are developed. These data are used to develop the flexible budget for each selected activity level, as shown in Figure 9-5. Note that the maintenance costs in the flexible budget are precisely as indicated by the total cost line for the three activity levels in Figure 9-3. The fixed and variable components for this and all other costs are separated in Figure 9-5 to highlight the composition of each cost at each activity level.

Prepare the budget for each selected activity level

Administrative salaries are entirely fixed and are therefore constant at $35,000 for all three activity levels. Medical and nursing salaries have a fixed component of $60,000 **and** a variable component of $8 per student visit. Therefore the variable part of this cost is $8 × 12 000, or $96,000, at the 12 000-visit level, $8 × 16 000, or $128,000, at the 16 000-visit level, and $8 × 20 000, or $160,000, for 20 000 visits. Similarly, the cost category, other salaries, has a fixed component of $28,000 plus a variable amount that increases at the rate of $2.50 per student visit to the health centre.

Other costs have fixed and variable elements just as medical and nursing salaries do. The total cost is found in each case by combining the fixed and variable costs as described above. Like administrative salaries, building lease cost is completely fixed, whereas external laboratory and other medical fees are entirely variable.

New Barrie University
Student Health Service
Flexible Budget
For the Fiscal year 1984-1985

Cost	Activity Level (Number of Student Visits)					
	12 000		16 000		20 000	
	Fixed	Variable	Fixed	Variable	Fixed	Variable
Administrative salaries	$ 35,000	—	$ 35,000	—	$ 35,000	—
Medical and nursing salaries	80,000	$ 96,000	80,000	$128,000	80,000	$160,000
Other salaries	28,000	30,000	28,000	40,000	28,000	50,000
Medical supplies	6,000	60,000	6,000	80,000	6,000	100,000
External laboratory fees and other medical fees	—	12,000	—	16,000	—	20,000
Building lease	18,000	—	18,000	—	18,000	—
Utilities	6,500	6,000	6,500	8,000	6,500	10,000
Maintenance	20,000	18,000	20,000	24,000	20,000	30,000
Computer services	12,000	9,000	12,000	12,000	12,000	15,000
Employee fringe benefits	34,500	21,000	34,500	28,000	34,500	35,000
Total	$240,000	$252,000	$240,000	$336,000	$240,000	$420,000

Figure 9-5

A flexible budget for the health centre, identifying fixed and variable cost components.

	Activity Level (Number of Student Visits)		
New Barrie University Student Health Service Flexible Budget For the Fiscal Year 1984-1985			
Cost	**12 000**	**16 000**	**20 000**
Administrative salaries	$ 35,000	$ 35,000	$ 35,000
Medical and nursing salaries	176,000	208,000	240,000
Other salaries	58,000	68,000	78,000
Medical supplies	66,000	86,000	106,000
External laboratory fees and other medical fees	12,000	16,000	20,000
Building lease	18,000	18,000	18,000
Utilities	12,500	14,500	16,500
Maintenance	38,000	44,000	50,000
Computer services	21,000	24,000	27,000
Employee fringe benefits	55,500	62,500	69,500
Total	$492,000	$576,000	$660,000

Figure 9-6
The fixed and variable cost data in Figure 9-5 are combined into a single amount for each cost at each activity level.

Fixed and variable costs are totaled for each activity level when all of the costs have been budgeted. The fixed costs remain constant for all levels of activity, and the variable costs increase with the level of activity. Usually fixed and variable costs are combined in the final version of a flexible budget, as illustrated in Figure 9-6, which combines the fixed and variable cost data in Figure 9-5.

The form of the flexible budget presented in Figure 9-6 is very common, but with this format it is not obvious what the fixed and variable cost components are. However, it is simple to compute the cost behaviour data from the flexible budget. For each cost merely take the difference in cost and divide it by the difference in activity level to find the variable cost. Then substitute the variable cost for one activity level to find the fixed cost. To illustrate, we use the medical and nursing salaries from the flexible budget in Figure 9-6.

Identifying fixed and variable cost from a flexible budget

$$\text{Variable cost} = \frac{\text{Cost at one activity level} - \text{Cost at another activity level}}{\text{Difference in activity level}}$$

$$= \frac{\$208,000 - \$176,000}{16\ 000 \text{ students} - 12\ 000 \text{ students}}$$

$$= \$8 \text{ per student visit}$$

Using the total cost formula for 12 000 student visits and substituting the variable cost figure, we have

$$
\begin{aligned}
\text{Total cost} &= \text{Fixed cost} + \text{Variable cost} \\
\$176{,}000 &= \text{Fixed cost} + (12\,000\ \text{students} \times \$8) \\
\$176{,}000 &= \text{Fixed cost} + \$96{,}000 \\
\$\ 80{,}000 &= \text{Fixed cost}
\end{aligned}
$$

The variable cost per student could be substituted into the total cost formula for medical and nursing salaries at 16 000 or 20 000 student visits, and the same $80,000 fixed cost would result. The fixed and variable cost component for other costs can be computed in the same way. For example, the computation for medical supplies is

$$
\begin{aligned}
\text{Variable cost} &= \frac{\$86{,}000 - \$66{,}000}{16\,000\ \text{students} - 12\,000\ \text{students}} \\
&= \frac{\$20{,}000}{4000\ \text{students}} = \$5\ \text{per student}
\end{aligned}
$$

$$
\begin{aligned}
\text{Fixed cost} &= \$66{,}000 - (12\,000\ \text{students} \times \$5) \\
&= \$66{,}000 - \$60{,}000 \\
&= \$6{,}000
\end{aligned}
$$

When the budget year is over, actual results are compared with the budget. But which budget is used? In flexible budgeting operating results are compared with a budget prepared for the level of activity actually achieved. For example, during the year the student health centre had 18 500 student visits. If a budget for this level of activity already exists, then a performance report is prepared from the budget data already available. If the actual activity level was not budgeted previously, a new budget is prepared. It may appear strange that a budget is prepared after an activity has already taken place, but you must keep in mind that this budget is not a plan for future operations; it is needed for analysis and reporting of performance. Since it was not possible to predict the precise activity level, a budget for this activity level was not prepared; now one is required to prepare the performance report. The data in Figure 9-4 are used to develop a new budget for 18 500 visits. That budget is presented in Figure 9-7 along with actual cost data for the period.

Prepare the budget performance report

The right column of Figure 9-7 shows variance computed for each cost and in total. Several costs show relatively large variances, although the total variance of $2,500 favourable is quite small.

The need for a budget at the actual level of activity is clear when the data are analyzed. If the actual cost of $626,000 is compared with the budget based on 16 000 visits (see Figure 9-6), the variance is $50,000 unfavourable. A comparison of actual data with the budget based on 20 000 visits yields a favourable variance of $34,000. The two comparisons provide widely differing results. The logical approach is to compare actual results with a budget based on the actual level of activity.

	New Barrie University Student Health Service Flexible Budget Performance Report For the Fiscal Year 1984-1985		
Cost	**Budget for 18 500 Students***	**Actual Cost**	**Variance (Favourable) Unfavourable**
Administrative salaries	$ 35,000	$ 37,000	$2,000
Medical and nursing salaries	228,000	236,900	8,900
Other salaries	74,250	67,000	(7,250)
Medical supplies	98,500	96,000	(2,500)
External laboratory fees and other medical fees	18,500	21,250	2,750
Building lease	18,000	18,000	—
Utilities	15,750	19,250	3,500
Maintenance	47,750	39,250	(8,500)
Computer services	25,875	21,375	(4,500)
Employee fringe benefits	66,875	69,975	3,100
Total	$628,500	$626,000	($2,500)

Figure 9-7
A flexible budget performance report is developed by preparing a budget for the actual activity level of 18 500 student visits and comparing budgeted with actual cost data for the year.

*Actual activity level = 18 500 student visits.

Manufacturing overhead flexible budgeting

Flexible budgets are used in planning and controlling all types of business activity, but they are particularly useful in developing manufacturing overhead rates and in analyzing overhead variances. A flexible budget allows managers to see the effect of different activity levels on the manufacturing overhead rate and resulting product costs. This point is discussed further with an illustration later in this chapter.

Developing an overhead flexible budget

We use the example of Hornebrook Structural Steel Company to illustrate the development of a manufacturing overhead rate and also to discuss overhead variance analysis in the next section. As with the previous example, the first step is estimation of the range of activity for the flexible budget. Hornebrook uses direct labour hours as its measure of activity. The range of activity selected is 15 000 to 30 000 direct labour hours. Hornebrook's products are used primarily in the construction industry, and the company experiences rather large sales fluctuations. Sales tend to be depressed during periods of little construction activity and high when construction activity picks up. The range of 15 000 to 30 000 direct labour hours is management's best estimate of the range of activity

Estimating the range of activity

the company might experience, with 25 000 hours being the expected activity level. Using this range of activity, cost behaviour patterns are analyzed for each manufacturing overhead cost. Figure 9-8 shows the cost behaviour patterns for Hornebrook's overhead costs.

Hornebrook Structural Steel Company Estimated Cost Behaviour Patterns For Manufacturing Overhead For the Year 1984		
Cost	Fixed Cost	Variable Cost per Direct Labour Hour
Indirect materials	—	$.50
Indirect labour	—	.70
Factory supplies	$12,000	.30
Maintenance	25,000	.60
Utilities	4,000	.80
Computer service charges	6,000	.10
Property taxes	5,000	—
Insurance	3,000	.10
Supervision	25,000	.90
Depreciation, production plant	30,000	—
Depreciation, production equipment	40,000	—

Figure 9-8

Cost formula data for Hornebrook's manufacturing overhead costs. Three costs are fixed, two are directly variable, and six are mixed costs.

The cost behaviour data from Figure 9-8 are used to develop a budget for each level of activity that management chooses to use in the flexible budget. In this example, four activity levels are illustrated, consisting of 15 000, 20 000, 25 000, and 30 000 direct labour hours. Fixed and variable costs are budgeted for each level of activity for each overhead cost. The flexible budget is presented in Figure 9-9.

Selecting budget activity levels

The flexible budget in Figure 9-9 is useful because it shows both fixed and variable costs and facilitates understanding of the budgeting process. As expected, the total cost remains constant for all levels of activity, and the total variable cost increases with the activity level. The rate of increase is $4 per direct labour hour, which can be determined by totaling variable cost data for each cost item in Figure 9-8 or by dividing the increased cost by the increased activity level between any two activity levels in the flexible budget.

The manufacturing overhead rate is determined by dividing the budgeted activity level into the budgeted overhead cost, as we discussed in Chapter 4. For example, at the 15 000-hour level, the budgeted amount ($150,000 + $60,000) divided by 15 000 hours yields an overhead rate of $14/per direct labour hour. In Chapter 4 a fixed budget was used to arrive at overhead cost, and only one set of budgeted data was available. Now we have budgeted data for four activity levels. Which should be used to compute the overhead rate?

Typically, the overhead rate is based on the firm's **normal capacity,** which is the expected activity level for the period, assuming normal operating conditions. In the Hornebrook example normal capacity is 25 000 direct labour hours. Therefore, the overhead rate is as shown below.

Hornebrook Structural Steel Company
Manufacturing Overhead Flexible Budget
For the Year 1984

Activity Level (Direct Labour Hours)

Cost	15 000 Fixed	15 000 Variable	20 000 Fixed	20 000 Variable	25 000 Fixed	25 000 Variable	30 000 Fixed	30 000 Variable
Indirect materials	—	$ 7,500	—	$10,000	—	$ 12,500	—	$ 15,000
Indirect labour	—	10,500	—	14,000	—	17,500	—	21,000
Factory supplies	$ 12,000	4,500	$ 12,000	6,000	$ 12,000	7,500	$ 12,000	9,000
Maintenance	25,000	9,000	25,000	12,000	25,000	15,000	25,000	18,000
Utilities	4,000	12,000	4,000	16,000	4,000	20,000	4,000	24,000
Computer service charges	6,000	1,500	6,000	2,000	6,000	2,500	6,000	3,000
Property taxes	5,000	—	5,000	—	5,000	—	5,000	—
Insurance	3,000	1,500	3,000	2,000	3,000	2,500	3,000	3,000
Supervision	25,000	13,500	25,000	18,000	25,000	22,500	25,000	27,000
Depreciation, production plant	30,000	—	30,000	—	30,000	—	30,000	—
Depreciation, production equipment	40,000	—	40,000	—	40,000	—	40,000	—
Total	$150,000	$60,000	$150,000	$80,000	$150,000	$100,000	$150,000	$120,000
Manufacturing overhead per direct labour hour	$10/DLH	$4/DLH	$7.50/DLH	$4/DLH	$6/DLH	$4/DLH	$5/DLH	$4/DLH
Manufacturing overhead rate	$14/DLH		$11.50/DLH		$10/DLH		$9/DLH	

Figure 9-9

A manufacturing overhead flexible budget separating fixed and variable costs.
The amount of the overhead rate depends on the level of activity used to allocate
fixed overhead costs.

$$\text{MOH rate} = \frac{\text{Budgeted manufacturing overhead}}{\text{Budgeted activity level}} = \frac{\$250,000}{25\ 000\ \text{DLH}} = \$10/\text{DLH}$$

Determining the overhead rate

In most previous discussions of overhead, no attempt was made to separate the overhead rate into its fixed and variable components. With a flexible budget such a separation is a simple task. Figure 9-9 indicates that the $250,000 budgeted overhead cost is composed of $100,000 variable cost and $150,000 fixed. Therefore, the overhead rate of $10 per direct labour hour is $4 an hour variable overhead ($100,000/25 000 DLH) and $6 fixed overhead ($150,000/25 000 DLH). The total variable cost changes proportionately with activity, which means that in this example variable overhead is $4 per hour for any activity level within the relevant range. However, the total amount of fixed manufacturing overhead remains constant throughout the relevant range, and the amount of fixed overhead assigned to each direct labour hour is determined by the estimated number of direct labour hours for the period. The larger the number of hours over which fixed cost is spread, the lower the hourly rate. For example, the fixed part of the overhead rate for Hornebrook is $10 per direct labour hour ($150,000/15 000 DLH) if normal capacity is 15 000 direct labour hours. If normal capacity is about 20 000 direct labour hours, the fixed overhead rate is $7.50 per DLH ($150,000/20 000 DLH). When the fixed overhead rate is added to the $4 per DLH variable rate, the total overhead rate is determined for each level of activity expressed in the flexible budget. Hornebrook's overhead rate would be $14/DLH if normal capacity were 15 000 hours, $11.50/DLH at 20 000 hours, and $9/DLH at 30 000 hours, as shown in Figure 9-9. The difference in the amount of the overhead rate is caused **entirely** by the amount of fixed overhead prorated over each direct labour hour.

Separating the overhead rate into its fixed and variable components

The overhead rate data from the flexible budget provide some useful information for analysis. For instance, the estimated normal capacity is 25 000 direct labour hours, but what if normal capacity turns out to be 20 000 hours? Then the correct overhead rate is $11.50/DLH, not $10/DLH. A product requiring 12 direct labour hours would be charged $120 of manufacturing overhead cost at the 25 000-hour level of activity, when $138 is the correct amount. The correct product cost would be $18 a unit higher than with the $10 overhead rate.

Flexible budgets allow analyses such as the one above. With a fixed budget one knows that the overhead rate would change if estimated normal capacity is incorrect, but the effect of the change on factors such as product cost is not clear.

In addition to providing valuable information for establishing overhead rates and analyzing the effect of different activity levels on product costs, flexible budgets are useful in analyzing manufacturing overhead variances.

Manufacturing overhead variance analysis

In Chapter 8 we discussed the purpose and use of standard costs. Variance analysis, the process of analyzing the difference between standard and actual costs, was discussed for direct materials and direct labour. Total variance was computed for manufacturing overhead, but no attempt was made to analyze overhead variance in more detail. Both direct materials and direct labour are directly variable costs, but overhead often includes relatively large amounts of fixed costs. If fixed costs are present, flexible budgets help to provide a basis for analyzing variances. Overhead variance analysis was postponed until flexible budgets were discussed because without flexible budgets it is difficult to assess the impact on overhead costs of activity levels that differ from the budgeted level. The purpose of overhead variance analysis is the same as that of other types of variance analysis: to determine how much actual results differ from expected outcomes and why the variance occurred. To illustrate **manufacturing overhead variance analysis,** we continue to use the example of Hornebrook Structural Steel Company. The following additional information is necessary:

1. The normal capacity of 25 000 direct labour hours is based on production of 12 500 tons of steel at 2 direct labour hours per ton.
2. Actual production in 1984 is 12 000 tons.
3. Actual manufacturing overhead cost in 1984 is $242,000.
4. Actual direct labour hours worked is 24 400.

In a standard cost system the total overhead variance is the difference between actual overhead and applied overhead. Actual overhead of $242,000 is found in the overhead control account. Applied overhead in a standard cost system is based on the standards and the amount of production. In this example applied overhead and total overhead variance are computed as follows:

Computing total overhead variance

$$
\begin{aligned}
\text{Applied overhead} &= \text{Actual output} \times \text{Standard hours per} \\
&\quad \text{Unit of output} \times \text{Overhead rate} \\
&= 12\ 000 \text{ tons} \times 2 \text{ h/t} \times \$10/\text{h} \\
&= \$240,000 \\
\text{Actual overhead} &= \underline{\$242,000} \\
\text{Manufacturing overhead variance} &= \$\ \ 2,000 \text{ unfavourable}
\end{aligned}
$$

The overhead variance can be diagrammed as follows:

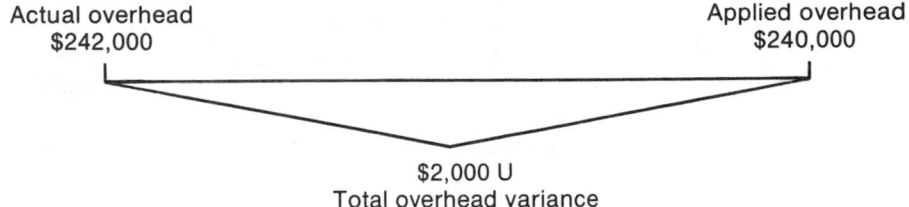

Actual overhead
$242,000

Applied overhead
$240,000

$2,000 U
Total overhead variance

In practice the total variance can be determined by comparing actual overhead, which is the ending balance in the ledger for the manufacturing overhead control account, with the balance in the manufacturing overhead applied account. For this example the account balances are

MOH Control	MOH Applied
242,000	240,000

As with other standard cost variance calculations, the standard cost for the period is computed from the actual quantity produced and the standard cost per unit. The variance is unfavourable for Hornebrook because actual overhead is greater than the standard amount of overhead.

Computing only the total variance is not very useful in analyzing overhead variances. Often it is helpful to separate the total overhead variance into more detailed measures. Just as direct material variance was split into price and quantity variances and direct labour was divided into rate and efficiency variances, so too can overhead be divided into more specific measures of variance. There are various approaches to overhead variance analysis. We describe two common approaches that use flexible budgets in the analysis process. They are called the two-variance method and the three-variance method.

Two-variance method

The **two-variance method** is an attempt to isolate the variance that is controllable by management and the variance caused by operating at an activity level other than the budgeted level of activity. The computations can be diagrammed as follows:

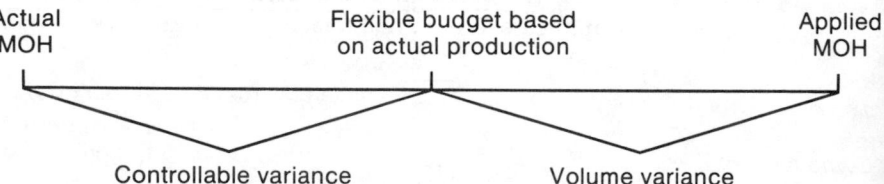

Actual MOH	Flexible budget based on actual production	Applied MOH

Controllable variance   Volume variance

Actual manufacturing overhead of $242,000 is given. A flexible budget based on actual output is determined as follows:

Actual production	=	12 000 tons
Standard direct labour h/t	=	2 h/t
Total standard direct labour hours given the amount of actual production =		24 000 h
Flexible budget based on output = Standard hours × Variable overhead cost per hour + Fixed overhead cost		
Variable cost	= 24 000 h × $4/h =	$ 96,000
Fixed cost	=	+ 150,000
Flexible budget based on actual production	=	$246,000

Applied overhead in a standard cost system is standard hours times the overhead rate. In this example applied overhead is 24 000 h × $10/h = $240,000. Substituting numbers from the example:

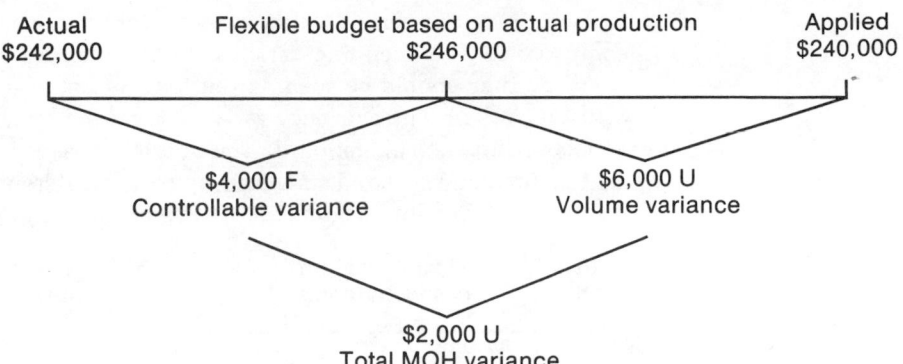

The **controllable variance** is the difference between actual overhead and a flexible budget based on actual output. The variance is called controllable because standards are benchmarks of performance, and a flexible budget based on output reflects expected achievement for managers. In this case the $4,000 controllable variance is favourable because the budgeted cost for the 24 000-standard-hour level of activity is $4,000 higher than the actual overhead cost. In other words, Hornebrook spent less for overhead than expected, given the amount of product produced.

Controllable variance

The **volume variance** describes the amount of variance that occurs because actual production is different from the budgeted amount of production. It arises when standard hours are different from the budgeted activity level. Remember that the $10 per hour overhead rate of Hornebrook was based on a budgeted activity level of 25 000 direct labour hours. The rate was composed of two parts, a $4 per-hour variable component and a $6 per-hour fixed component, as shown in Figure 9-9. The variable component is $4 per hour throughout the relevant range, but the fixed component of $6 per hour is $150,000 of fixed cost spread over 25 000 hours of expected activity. But if 25 000 standard hours are not worked, then a sum other than $150,000 in fixed overhead is applied to production. If only 24 000 standard hours are worked, as in the Hornebrook example, less than $150,000 of fixed overhead is prorated to production. The amount assigned to production in this case is $144,000 ($6 per hour × 24 000 standard hours). Activity is 1000 hours short of the budgeted activity level, and the variance of $6,000 is 1000 times the $6 per hour fixed overhead component. The variance is unfavourable because the standard amount of fixed overhead is $144,000 and the actual fixed overhead is $150,000, or $6,000 greater than standard. When the standard activity level is lower than the budgeted activity level, not enough was accomplished for the cost expended, and the volume variance is unfavourable. When the standard activity level is higher than the budgeted activity level, the volume variance is favourable.

The volume variance results from actual production being different from budgeted production

Three-variance method

The **three-variance method** is used to isolate a spending variance, an efficiency variance, and a volume variance. The spending and efficiency variances result from dividing the controllable variance in the two-variance method into two components. The spending variance results from spending more or less for overhead than should be spent, given the amount of input—in this case hours actually worked. The efficiency variance is caused by using a different number of labour hours than standard. The volume variance measures the variance that occurs because standard labour hours are different from budgeted labour hours. The following diagram shows the variance computations:

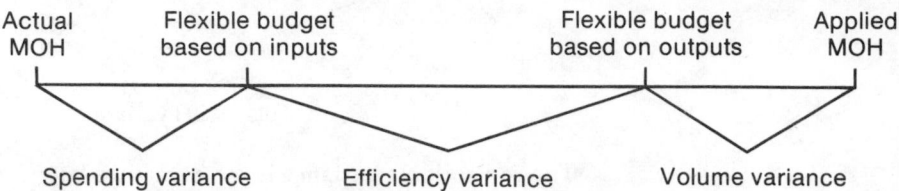

Frequently activity level is measured in terms of direct labour hours, machine hours, or some other activity variable. In our example direct labour hours is the activity level measure for the budget. Thus outputs are measured in terms of standard direct labour hours and inputs in terms of actual direct labour hours. A budget based on inputs means a budget based on actual direct labour hours, and a budget based on outputs means a budget based on standard direct labour hours.

As before, actual overhead cost is found in the overhead control account. A flexible budget based on actual hours is computed as follows:

Flexible budget based on input	= Actual hours × Variable overhead cost per hour + Fixed overhead cost
Variable cost	= 24 400 h × $4/h = $ 97,600
Fixed cost	= + 150,000
Flexible budget based on actual hours =	$247,600

A flexible budget based on standard hours was computed as $246,000 in the discussion of the two-variance method. Applied overhead is $240,000, the same as before. Substituting these numbers into the analysis:

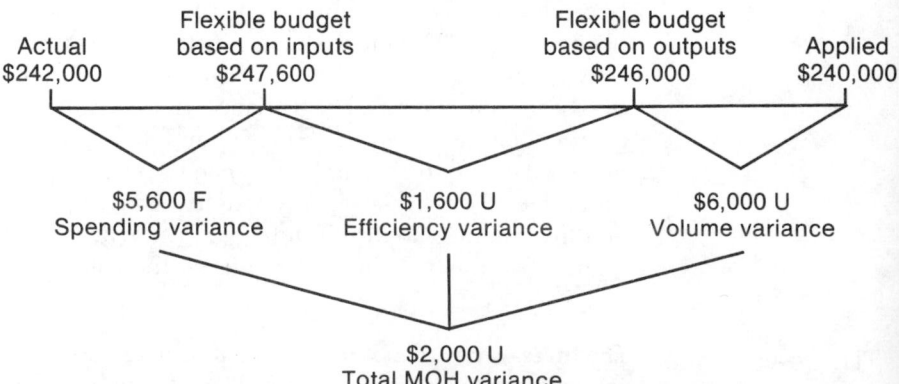

Spending variance

The **spending variance** addresses the question, "How much should have been spent on overhead, given the actual input?" It is a comparison of actual overhead with a flexible budget based on actual hours. In this example the actual overhead is $5,600 less than the budget amount and therefore is favourable.

Efficiency variance

The **efficiency variance** measures the amount of overhead variance attributable to using more or less inputs than allowed by the standards, given the amount of production. If actual hours worked are fewer than standard hours, the efficiency variance is favourable. An unfavourable variance occurs when actual hours exceed standard hours; this is the case in the Hornebrook example. Actual hours are 24 400, whereas standard hours are 24 000. The difference of 400 hours is multiplied by the variable overhead rate of $4 per hour, yielding an unfavourable efficiency variance of $1,600.

The volume variance is the same as the one computed and discussed before in the two-variance analysis. The terms **capacity variance** and **denominator variance** sometimes are used to describe the volume variance. Summing the three variances results in a $2,000 unfavourable total overhead variance, as with the two-variance method. Of course, the two-variance and three-variance methods always yield the same total variance for any particular set of data. The different variance analysis methods merely divide the total variance in different ways. The controllable variance measures the amount that actual overhead cost differs from the budget based on the output produced. The spending variance measures the amount that actual overhead differs from a budget based on the inputs. The difference between the spending and controllable variances is the efficiency variance that results when inputs differ from outputs. The two-variance method centers on measures of performance using a budget based on standard hours as a basis for measurement. The three-variance method uses a budget based on actual hours as a basis of performance measurement. Neither method is necessarily better than the other. Both are widely used in business, and the choice rests with managers' preferences and information needs. Other ways of measuring and interpreting the fixed overhead variance are advocated by some accountants. The two different overhead variance methods just discussed are sufficient for our purposes.

The two- and three-variance methods, their calculation, and their interpretation are summarized and illustrated in Figure 9-10.

Analysis of individual overhead accounts

In our discussion we have analyzed the overhead variances for the total manufacturing overhead account. However, the same analysis can be prepared for each cost included in the overhead account. In the Hornebrook example the overhead control account consists of 11 different costs that are maintained in a subsidiary ledger. The balance in the 11 accounts at year-end total to the control account balance of $242,000. An analysis identical to the analysis of the total overhead account can also be prepared for each individual overhead account. For example, assume the year-end balance in the overhead subsidiary ledger account for maintenance is $41,500. We can use the two- or three-variance method to analyze overhead variance for this one overhead cost. The three-variance method is shown below.

Type of Analysis	Calculation		Variance	Explanation
Two-Variance Method				
Controllable variance	Actual MOH	— Flexible budget, standard hours		Spent less on overhead than planned, given the number of units actually produced.
	$242,000	— $246,000	$4,000 F	
Volume variance	Flexible budget, standard hours	— Applied MOH		The volume in terms of standard hours was 1000 hours below normal capacity.
	$246,000	— $240,000	$6,000 U	
Total variance			$2,000 U	
Three-Variance Method				
Spending variance	Actual MOH	— Flexible budget, actual hours		Spent less on overhead than planned for the amount of input (hours worked).
	$242,000	— $247,600	$5,600 F	
Efficiency variance	Flexible budget, actual hours	— Flexible budget, standard hours		Used more hours than allowed by the standards for the quantity of goods produced.
	$247,600	— $246,000	$1,600 U	
Volume variance	Flexible budget, standard hours	— Applied MOH		The volume in terms of standard hours was 1000 hours below normal capacity.
	$246,000	— $240,000	$6,000 U	
Total variance			$2,000 U	

Figure 9-10
A comparison chart describing the computation and meaning of the different overhead variances.

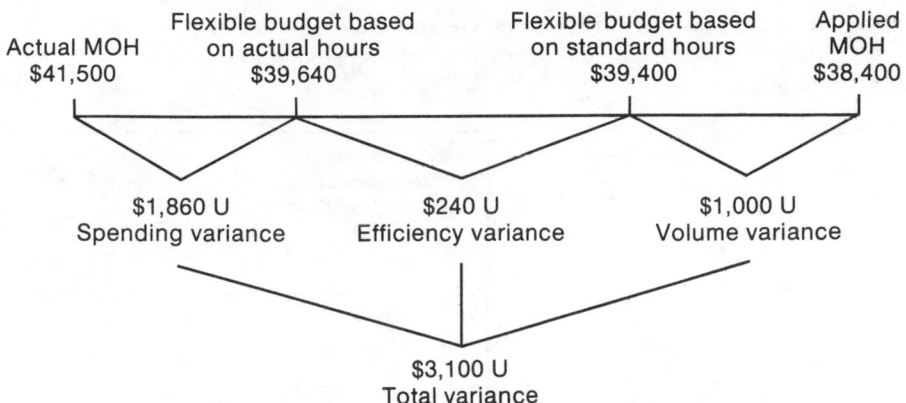

The actual overhead of $41,500 is the balance in the overhead subsidiary ledger for maintenance. The budget based on actual hours is 24 400 hours times the variable rate for maintenance, which is $.60 per hour, plus the fixed maintenance of $25,000. The same procedure is used to compute the budget based on 24 000 standard hours. The fixed and variable components for each cost in the Hornebrook example are found in Figure 9-8. When a single cost item is being analyzed, the overhead rate refers to the rate for that single item. Here maintenance has a fixed cost of $25,000 plus a variable rate of $.60 per hour. Dividing the fixed cost by the normal capacity of 25 000 hours yields a fixed rate of $1 per hour; adding the variable component, we have a rate of $1.60 for maintenance. Using this rate, we compute applied overhead at $38,400 (24 000 hours × $1.60 per hour). Note that here applied overhead refers to the amount of maintenance overhead applied. Overhead is applied for ten other overhead costs as well.

The other overhead costs can be analyzed in the same way. For instance, Figure 9-8 shows the cost behaviour formula for utilities cost, and the actual cost is $22,800. The variance analysis using the three-variance method is

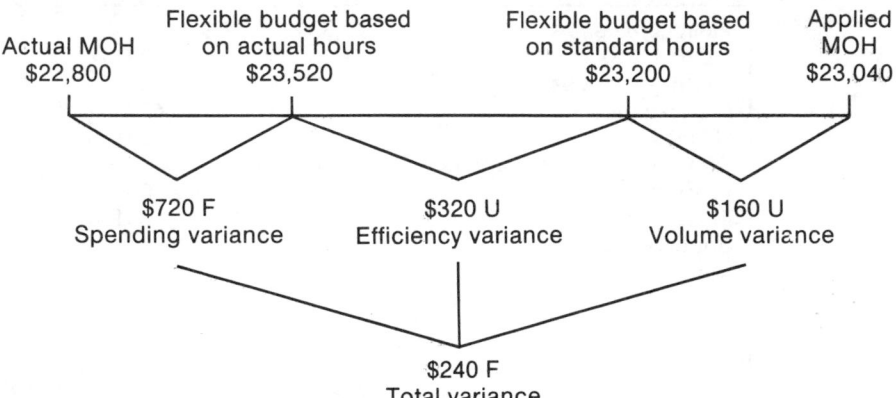

If each cost is analyzed in the same way as maintenance and utilities and the variances are totaled, the net variance is identical to the amounts computed

earlier when we analyzed the total overhead variance. To illustrate, each of the actual overhead costs is listed below:

Indirect materials	$ 9,700
Indirect labour	16,000
Factory supplies	18,600
Maintenance	41,500
Utilities	22,800
Computer service charges	7,600
Property taxes	5,100
Insurance	4,700
Supervision	46,000
Depreciation, production plant	30,000
Depreciation, production equipment	40,000
Total	$242,000

The variance analysis for each overhead cost is summarized in Figure 9-11. If you wish, you may use the data above to compute the variances for one or more of the overhead cost accounts to be certain that you understand the process.

Hornebrook Structural Steel Company
Detailed Analysis of Overhead Variances
For the Year 1984

Cost	Variance Spending	Variance Efficiency	Variance Volume	Variance Total
Indirect materials	$2,500 F	$ 200 U	$ 0	$2,300 F
Indirect labour	1,080 F	280 U	0	800 F
Factory supplies	720 F	120 U	480 U	120 F
Maintenance	1,860 U	240 U	1,000 U	3,100 U
Utilities	720 F	320 U	160 U	240 F
Computer service charges	840 F	40 U	240 U	560 F
Property taxes	100 U	0	200 U	300 U
Insurance	740 F	40 U	120 U	580 F
Supervision	960 F	360 U	1,000 U	400 U
Depreciation, production plant	0	0	1,200 U	1,200 U
Depreciation, production equipment	0	0	1,600 U	1,600 U
Total	$5,600 F	$1,600 U	$6,000 U	$2,000 U

Figure 9-11
A detailed variance analysis report for manufacturing overhead costs.

Summary   A major benefit of budgeting is the control over operations that is exercised through the comparison of actual results with the budget by means of **budget performance reporting.** Performance reports are most useful when budget data are based on an activity level that closely approximates the level of activity actually achieved. A useful method of developing relevant budget data is **flexible budgeting,** which means that budgets are prepared for more than one level of activity. Performance reports can then be prepared from a budget based on the actual level of activity. Flexible budgets are dynamic because they cover a range of activity, and they facilitate efficiency measurement.

The first step in flexible budgeting is to determine the range of activity to be covered by the budget. Next, cost behaviour patterns are identified for all costs for the activity range of the budget. Management selects a number of activity levels within the range of the budget, and budgets are prepared for each selected activity level. Actual operating data are accumulated for the period and compared with budget data for the activity level achieved.

Flexible budgets are very useful in developing manufacturing overhead rates and analyzing overhead variances. A flexible budget allows managers to distinguish between the variable and fixed components of overhead cost. Total variable overhead costs move proportionately with activity levels and therefore are a component of the overhead rate that is constant throughout the relevant range of the flexible budget. The total fixed overhead cost is constant throughout the relevant range and results in a declining overhead rate as the activity base is increased.

As with other variance analyses, manufacturing overhead variance analysis addresses the issues of the magnitude and cause of the variance. Total overhead variance may be divided into several components. The **two-variance method** isolates a controllable and a volume variance. The **controllable variance** measures the amount that actual overhead differs from the standard amount, given the number of units produced. It is the difference between actual overhead and a flexible budget based on actual output. The **volume variance** is the difference between a flexible budget based on standard hours and applied overhead. It shows the result of operating at a volume above or below normal capacity.

The **three-variance method** identifies spending, efficiency, and volume variances. The **spending variance** is a comparison between actual overhead and a flexible budget based on actual input. It measures the amount that actual overhead differs from planned overhead for the number of hours actually worked. The **efficiency variance** is the difference between standard and actual hours times the variable overhead rate. It describes the amount of overhead variance attributable to using more or fewer labour hours than standard. The volume variance is the same as the one computed in the two-variance method.

List of important terms

controllable variance *(377)*
dynamic budget *(361)*
efficiency variance *(379)*
fixed budget *(360)*

flexible budget *(361)*
manufacturing overhead variance analysis *(374)*
normal capacity *(372)*

Questions

1. Define fixed budgeting and flexible budgeting.
2. Briefly describe the characteristics of a flexible budget.
3. What are the steps involved in the flexible budgeting process?
4. What is meant by the relevant range and how does it affect the development of a flexible budget?
5. What does the volume variance measure? How do you determine whether the volume variance is favourable or unfavourable?
6. "Why are you having Jones waste time and money preparing a budget for last quarter's operations? We already know what happened last quarter, and three months earlier you convinced me that we should waste our time preparing four budgets for the quarter instead of one. I gave in then, but this is too much." Explain to the new vice president why another budget is needed in addition to the flexible budget already prepared earlier.
7. What variance is identified by comparing a flexible budget based on inputs with a flexible budget based on output?
8. Distinguish between the spending variance and the controllable variance.
9. What is the efficiency variance? Why does it occur?
10. Are the overhead efficiency variance and the labour efficiency variance the same thing? Explain.
11. "Tell the new accountant I just hired that he made a mistake. This variance report shows an efficiency variance for direct labour and another one for manufacturing overhead. Doesn't he know where the efficiency variance belongs?" Respond to this statement.

Exercises

Ex. 9-1 Overhead flexible budget. Eichner Machine Tool Company describes its overhead costs as follows:

	Fixed Costs	Variable Costs
Indirect labour	$10,000	$1.00 per DLH
Utilities	8,000	.50 per DLH
Maintenance	22,000	1.20 per DLH
Depreciation	30,000	—
Employee fringe benefits	6,000	2.10 per DLH
Factory supplies	4,000	.20 per DLH

Required:

a. Prepare a flexible budget at 20 000 and 25 000 direct labour hours.

b. If 20 000 direct labour hours is normal capacity, what is the overhead rate?

Ex. 9-2   **Flexible budget for a service activity.** Below are cost behaviour data for the medical laboratory of the Conklin City Medical Centre.

	Fixed	**Variable per Direct Labour Hour**
Supervisory salaries	$70,000	—
Laboratory labour cost	—	$9.00
Medical supplies	1,000	6.00
Maintenance	20,000	.10
Utilities	2,000	.50
Depreciation	12,000	—
Clerical	10,000	.40

Required:

Prepare a flexible budget using activity levels of 10 000, 12 000, and 14 000 direct labour hours.

Ex. 9-3   **Identifying favourable and unfavourable overhead and labour variances.** Below are budgeted, actual, and standard hour data of four different **entirely independent** firms.

	W	**X**	**Y**	**Z**
Budgeted hours	10 000	20 000	15 000	30 000
Actual hours	9 000	21 000	14 000	32 000
Standard hours	9 500	19 500	16 000	31 000

Required:

For **each** case above indicate the direction (favourable or unfavourable) of the volume variance and the efficiency variance.

Ex. 9-4   **Understanding overhead cost relationships.** Overhead cost data for the Frazer Corporation, shown below, uses a flexible budget to plan operations and evaluate alternatives. Normal capacity is 50 000 direct labour hours. Ten hours of direct labour are required to produce one unit of Frazer's product.

Required:

a. Compute the manufacturing overhead rate based on normal capacity.

	Percentage of Normal Capacity			
	80	**90**	**100**	**110**
Direct labour hours	40 000	45 000	50 000	55 000
Total manufacturing overhead	$178,000	$189,000	$200,000	$211,000

    b. If the normal capacity estimate is too high and the actual normal capacity is 40 000 hours, what is the overhead rate?

    c. What would be the effect on the overhead part of product cost if the normal capacity estimate of 50 000 is used to determine the overhead rate, but 40 000 is the true normal capacity?

Ex. 9-5 **Analyzing overhead variances.** The Dover Cliffs Manufacturing Company applies overhead at the rate of $10 per direct labour hour. At the end of the most recent business year, the firm experienced a large unfavourable overhead variance in spite of the fact that numerous efficiency measures had been adopted to reduce overhead costs. You have been called in to analyze the situation and you start by evaluating the following data:

Budgeted variable overhead	$400,000
Budgeted fixed overhead	600,000
Actual manufacturing overhead	900,000
Actual labour hours	79,000
Standard labour hours	80,000

Required:
Explain to Dover management the nature of the large unfavourable overhead variance that has occurred. Support your discussion with variance analysis information.

Ex. 9-6 **Overhead variances.** Below are data pertaining to manufacturing overhead for the Dahl Corporation:

Manufacturing overhead rate:	
Variable overhead	$3 per direct labour h
Fixed overhead	$5 per direct labour h
Budgeted activity level	20 000 direct labour h
Actual activity level	19 800 direct labour h
Standard hours	20 500 direct labour h
Actual manufacturing overhead	$161,000

Required:
a. Compute the overhead efficiency variance.
b. Compute the volume variance.

c. How much overhead was applied to production during the period?
d. Calculate the total overhead variance.

Ex. 9-7   Flexible budget for a service organization. Nelson Memorial Hospital uses flexible budgeting for all departments that experience fluctuating service demands. One such department is the hospital cafeteria where the average price of a meal is $3.00. The hospital's chief accountant has gathered the following data:

Costs	Fixed Costs	Variable Cost per Dollar of Sales
Food costs	–	$.40
Personnel wages	$10,000	.26
Depreciation	25,000	–
Utilities	6,000	.06
Maintenance	14,000	.03
Insurance	5,000	–

Required:
Prepare a flexible budget for the hospital cafeteria using 75 000, 80 000, and 85 000 meals as the activity levels.

Ex. 9-8   Flexible budget performance report. The Mexican Hat Pottery Company manufactures quality earthenware dishes. The company uses a flexible budgeting system for planning and controlling costs. Below are budgeted production data for the year just completed

	Budgeted	
Sets of dishes	10 000	12 000
Materials	$120,000	$144,000
Labour	300,000	350,000
Maintenance	70,000	72,000
Depreciation	40,000	40,000
Utilities	30,000	34,000

Actual production was 11 300 sets of dishes, and production costs were

Materials	$140,000
Labour	324,000
Maintenance	78,000
Depreciation	40,000
Utilities	34,000

Required:

Prepare a flexible budget variance analysis report.

Ex. 9-9   Fixed and flexible budget performance reports. Seidler University Student Bookstore made the following cost estimates for budgeting purposes:

Cost Item	Fixed	Variable per Dollar of Sales
Product cost	—	$.60
Employee wages	$16,000	.14
Supervisory salaries	25,000	.02
Supplies	1,000	.01
Utilities	3,000	.02
Rent	6,000	.01
Insurance	4,000	—

In 1984 the bookstore experienced the following results:

Sales	$350,000
Product cost	217,000
Employee wages	66,000
Supervisory salaries	33,000
Supplies	4,000
Utilities	8,500
Rent	9,500
Insurance	4,000
Profit	$ 8,000

Required:

a. Prepare a fixed budget performance report based on an estimated sales level of $300,000.

b. Prepare a flexible budget performance report.

Ex. 9-10   Developing a flexible budget. Meadow-Hill University operates a cafeteria in the student union from 11 A.M. until 7 P.M. Monday through Saturday. Student union management is interested in developing a flexible budget for the cafeteria operation. Number of meals served is the activity variable used for the cafeteria. The assumptions on which the flexible budget is to be developed are shown below.

	Costs	
	Fixed	**Variable**
Wages	$180,000	$ .15 per meal
Rental expense	20,000	—
Food costs	—	1.10
Utilities	3,000	.10
Maintenance	12,000	.10
Insurance	6,000	—
Supplies	5,000	.15
Average revenue per meal served is $2.25.		

Required:

a. Prepared a flexible budget for the cafeteria using 300 000, 350 000, and 400 000 meals served as activity levels.

b. At what level of activity does the cafeteria break even?

Problem Set A

P. 9A-1 **Flexible budget for a merchandising business.** The following sales and cost data pertain to the Sun-Tan City Ski Shoppe:

	Fixed Cost	**Variable Cost per Unit of Sales**
Product cost	—	$40
Utilities	$ 3,000	2
Building rent	7,200	—
Administrative	25,000	3
Marketing	15,000	8
Supplies	2,000	4
Sales price = $80 per unit.		

Required:

a. Prepare a flexible budget for the company using sales of 2000, 2500, and 3000 units as the activity levels.

b. At what sales level does the ski shop cover all of its costs?

P. 9A-2 **Flexible budget performance report.** The city of Hershfield owns and operates its own electric power company, which supplies electricity for the area. The company is not intended to earn a normal profit, but rates are set so as to meet all costs, with a small surplus remaining to cover unexpected costs or other contingencies. Budget and actual data for 1984 are shown below.

Hershfield Municipal Power Company Flexible Budget For the Year 1984			
	Budgeted Kilowatt Hours		**Actual Results Kilowatt Hours**
	60 million	**80 million**	**75 million**
Revenue	$2,700,000	$3,600,000	$3,375,000
Labour	580,000	740,000	665,000
Maintenance	240,000	260,000	240,000
Coal	1,200,000	1,600,000	1,615,000
Depreciation	250,000	250,000	250,000
Supplies	110,000	140,000	128,500
Supervision	150,000	160,000	146,500
Insurance	20,000	20,000	21,000
Miscellaneous	90,000	110,000	126,000
Profit	$ 60,000	$ 320,000	$ 183,000

Required:

Prepare a flexible budget variance analysis report.

P. 9A-3 **Flexible budget for a manufacturing business.** Malstrom Industries plans to start using flexible budgeting for its three-year-old farm grain wagon manufacturing division. Costs that are completely fixed are depreciation, $160,000; property taxes, $40,000; and insurance, $18,000. Completely variable costs include direct material of $700 per wagon and direct labour of $400 per wagon. Forty direct labour hours are required per wagon. Wagons sell for $1,800 each. Other costs are mixed, with fixed and variable components. Below are 1983 and 1984 data for the mixed cost items.

	1983	1984
Direct labour hours	100 000	120 000
Indirect materials	$ 60,000	$70,000
Indirect labour	105,000	121,000
Utilities	85,000	99,000
Maintenance	100,000	108,000
Supervision	200,000	204,000
Miscellaneous overhead	60,000	64,000
Administrative	430,000	436,000
Marketing	370,000	424,000

Required:

a. Prepare a schedule showing the cost behaviour pattern of each mixed cost.

b. Prepare a flexible budget for the division for 1985 using production levels of 3000, 3200, and 3400 wagons. Assume these activity levels are within the relevant range of the cost behaviour patterns experienced in 1983 and 1984.

c. Actual sales for 1985 were 3,350 wagons, yielding a profit of $682,000. Using flexible budget data, determine total variance from expected profit.

P. 9A-4   Computing manufacturing overhead variances. Magley, Inc., bases its overhead rate on machine hours. For the 1984 budget year, machine hours are estimated at 20 000. Four machine hours are required at standard to produce one unit of product. Variable overhead is expected to be $3 per hour, and the fixed overhead budget is $80,000. Actual production for the period is 4800 units, which were produced with 20 400 actual direct labour hours. At the end of 1984, the overhead control account has a balance of $142,800.

Required:
a. Compute manufacturing overhead variances using the two-variance method.
b. Compute manufacturing overhead variances using the three-variance method.

P. 9A-5   Using overhead cost relationships. Below are standard cost data for the production of wheelbarrows for Ramshee Corporation:

Labour time	$1^1/_2$ h per wheelbarrow
Labour rate	$8 per hour
Overhead rate	$10 per labour hour
Fixed manufacturing overhead	$90,000
Normal capacity	15 000 direct labour hour

During the year actual production was 10 500 wheelbarrows, actual overhead cost was $152,000, and actual hours worked was 15 200.

Required:
a. Calculate the variable part of the overhead rate.
b. Calculate the standard conversion cost of the wheelbarrow.
c. Compute the manufacturing overhead variances using the three-variance method.
d. Compute the direct **labour** efficiency variance.
e. Explain why the labour efficiency variance and the overhead efficiency variance are different.

P. 9A-6   Interpreting overhead variances. During the past year Trumpy Company had actual manufacturing overhead cost of $454,000. The overhead budget was based on a normal capacity of 50 000 direct labour hours. Standard hours were 51 000. Manufacturing overhead variances for the period are

Spending	$10,000 U
Efficiency	9,000 F
Volume	6,000 F

Required:
From the data above compute:

a. Applied manufacturing overhead.
b. Fixed manufacturing overhead rate.
c. Variable manufacturing overhead rate.
d. Actual hours.
e. The controllable variance of the two-variance method.

P. 9B-1 Problem Set B

Flexible budget for manufacturing overhead. Below are cost behaviour data for the Pollet Company's manufacturing overhead costs:

	Fixed	Variable per Machine Hour
Indirect labour	$10,000	$1.00
Depreciation	60,000	—
Utilities	12,000	1.50
Maintenance	30,000	1.00
Supervision	50,000	.50
Insurance	13,000	—
Property taxes	35,000	—

Required:
a. Prepare a flexible budget using 35 000, 40 000, and 45 000 machine hours as the activity levels.
b. If 40 000 machine hours is the normal capacity, what is the manufacturing overhead rate?

P. 9B-2 Flexible budget performance report.
The Snyder Shoe Shop uses a flexible budget to plan operations and measure performance. At the top of the facing page are budgeted and actual data for the shop for 1984. The company uses sales dollars as its measure of activity.

Required:
Prepare a flexible budget variance analysis report.

	Budget		Actual
Sales	$800,000	$1,000,000	$850,000
Cost of goods sold	480,000	600,000	493,000
Depreciation	15,000	15,000	15,000
Supervisory salaries	45,000	45,000	42,000
Commissions	120,000	150,000	119,000
Advertising	36,000	40,000	42,000
Maintenance	20,000	23,000	21,000
Utilities	18,000	20,000	24,000
Insurance	14,000	15,000	14,000
Profit	$ 52,000	$ 92,000	$ 80,000

P. 9B-3 **Flexible budget for a manufacturing business.** Top Banana Toys is planning to use a flexible budgeting system this year. To facilitate the preparation of the budget, the accountant has listed the last two years' operating data below.

	1983	1984
Direct labour hours	40 000	50 000
Sales	$1,800,000	$2,250,000
Direct labour	320,000	400,000
Direct materials	480,000	600,000
Depreciation	80,000	80,000
Property taxes	30,000	30,000
Maintenance	140,000	160,000
Utilities	55,000	65,000
Supervision	120,000	125,000
Administration	208,000	210,000
Marketing	270,000	315,000

Required:
a. Prepare a schedule showing the cost behaviour formula for each of the costs presented above.
b. Prepare a flexible budget for 45 000, 48 000, and 51 000 direct labour hours for 1985.
c. Actual activity for the year was 49 500 direct labour hours, which provided a profit of $260,000. Using flexible budgeting analysis, what is the total variance from expected profit?

P. 9B-4 **Computation of overhead variances.** Rico Concrete Products manufactures concrete garden ornaments and figures. The company uses a standard cost system and applies overhead using a direct labour hours application base. Normal capacity is 10 000 direct labour hours. The overhead rate of $6 per hour is split on a $\frac{1}{3}$ to $\frac{2}{3}$ basis between variable and fixed overhead costs, respectively. During the accounting year just completed, the following occurred:

Actual overhead cost	$60,000
Actual direct labour hours	9800
Standard direct labour hours	10 300

Required:
a. Prepare a two-variance analysis of overhead variance.
b. Prepare a three-variance analysis of overhead variance.

P. 9B-5 **Understanding overhead variance concepts.** Fenton Manufacturing uses a standard cost system and bases its overhead rate on expected normal capacity of 50 000 direct labour hours. Following are computations of the current-year overhead rate:

Budgeted variable overhead	$200,000
Budgeted fixed overhead	250,000
Total	$450,000
Overhead rate = $450,000/50,000 DLH = $9 per DLH	

During the year 40 000 actual hours were worked, and the overhead efficiency variance was $4,000 U.

Required:
a. What is the number of standard hours?
b. How much overhead was applied to products during the year?
c. What is Fenton's volume variance for the year?
d. If Fenton finds that 40 000 direct labour hours is its normal capacity, what effect does that have on the production cost of a product requiring 25 direct labour hours?

P. 9B-6 **Interpreting overhead variances.** Following are overhead data for the Blackwell company:

Manufacturing overhead rate:	
Variable	$2 per direct labour h
Fixed	3 per direct labour h
Budgeted direct labour hours	30 000

The three-variance method of analyzing overhead yields the following:

Spending variance	$6,000 U
Efficiency variance	3,000 U
Volume variance	1,500 U

Required:
From the partial data above determine:

a. Standard hours.
b. Actual hours worked.
c. Applied overhead.
d. Actual overhead.
e. Controllable variance.

Minicases

Minicase 9-1 (SMA of Canada adapted)

The Good Humour Company, Ltd., manufactures an internationally known line of umbrellas. Management has recently established a standard cost system in order to control costs and to set the selling price of its umbrellas at 150 percent of standard cost.

The standard cost per unit based on a monthly production of 1200 units is as follows:

Raw materials, 12 parts per unit @ $1.12
Direct labour, 2 hours per unit @ $5.50 per hour
Manufacturing overhead:
   Variable: $1.40 per direct labour hour
   Fixed: $4.10 per direct labour hour

During the month of June 1983, 1000 units were put into production and completed. The company accountant, John M. Barr, has gathered the following additional information concerning production.

a. Inventory—at June 1: Nil
                at June 30: Nil
b. Raw materials: 14 000 parts used at a total cost of $14,280.
c. Direct labour: cost for the month of June of $16,000.
d. Actual direct labour hours: 2500 hours.
e. Manufacturing overhead incurred for the month of June:
   Variable: $3,600
   Fixed: $10,000

Required:
a. Determine the unit selling price and all the variances resulting from production for the month of June, 1983 including raw materials, labour and

overhead. (Use the three-way variance method for manufacturing overhead.)

b. Comment on the possible causes of each manufacturing overhead variance.

c. Explain why it is preferable to compare actual data to standards rather than to historical data.

Minicase 9-2

The Yukon Plant of Ontario Corporation has been in operation for 15 months. Yukon employs a standard cost system for its manufacturing operations. The first six months' performance was affected by the usual problems associated with a new operation. Since that time the operations have been running smoothly. Unfortunately, however, the plant has not been able to produce profits on a consistent basis. As the production requirements to meet sales demand have increased, the profit performance has deteriorated.

The plant production manager, Mr. Aron Maples, commented at a staff meeting in which the plant general manager, Mr. Armand Persimmons, the corporate controller, Ms. Aylin Doublecheck, and Mr. John Johnson, the corporate budget director, were in attendance that the changing production requirements make it more difficult to control manufacturing expenses. He further noted that the budget for the plant included in the company's annual profit plan was not useful for judging the plant's performance because of the changes in the operating levels. The meeting resulted in a decision to prepare a report which would compare the plant's actual manufacturing expense performance with a budget of manufacturing expense based on actual direct labour hours in the plant.

Mr. Aron Maples, the plant production manager, and Mr. Thomas Abacus, the plant accountant, studied the cost patterns for recent months, and volume and cost data from other Ontario plants. Then they prepared the following flexible budget schedule for a month with 200 000 planned production hours

	Amount	Per Direct Labour Hour
Manufacturing Expenses		
Variable		
Indirect labour	$160,000	$0.80
Supplies	26,000	.13
Power	14,000	.07
		$1.00
Fixed		
Supervisory labour	64,000	
Heat and light	15,000	
Property taxes	5,000	
Total	$284,000	

which at standard would result in 50 000 units of output. The corporate controller, Ms. Aylin Doublecheck, reviewed and approved the flexible budget.

The manufacturing expense reports prepared for the first three months after the flexible budget program was approved were pleasing to Mr. Aron Maples, the plant production manager. They showed that manufacturing expenses were in line with the flexible budget allowance. This was also reflected by the report prepared for November, presented below, when 50,500 units were manufactured. However, the plant was still not producing an adequate profit because the variances from standard costs were quite large.

Yukon Plant Manufacturing Expenses November 1983 220 000 Actual Direct Labour Production Hours			
	Actual Costs	Allowed Costs	(Over) Under Budget
Variable			
Indirect labour	$177,000	$176,000	$(1,000)
Supplies	27,400	28,600	1,200
Power	16,000	15,400	(600)
Fixed			
Supervisory labour	65,000	64,000	(1,000)
Heat and light	15,500	15,000	(500)
Property taxes	5,000	5,000	0
	$305,900	$304,000	$(1,900)

Required:

a. Explain the advantages of flexible budgeting over fixed budgeting for cost control purposes.

b. Calculate the excess amount over standard spent on manufacturing expense items during November 1983. Analyze this excess amount into those variances due to: efficiency; spending.

c. Explain what the management of Yukon Plant should do to reduce: the efficiency variance; the spending variance.

Minicase 9-3 (CICA adapted)

Z. Mfg., Ltd., has several divisions and has just built a new plant which is capable of making up to 20 000 units of a raw product, HW. Management has introduced a standard cost system to aid it in performance evaluation of its various managers and for establishing a selling price for HW. At the present time, product HW does not have any competition and management has priced it at standard variable and fixed manufacturing cost, plus 60 percent. Management hopes that this price can be maintained for several years.

For the first year of operations, ending July 31, 1983, management plans to make 1000 units of product HW in each month. In 1984 and subsequent fiscal years production is expected to be 1500 units per month. In the first month of operations, August 1982, management expected that employees would not be familiar with the production methods. Thus, management budgeted for direct labour hours to be 20 percent in excess of standard hours per unit. In September 1982 and subsequent months management is expecting standard direct labour to be attained.

The company's experience in its other plants and with similar products indicates that variable manufacturing overhead will vary in proportion to actual direct labour dollars. For the first several years only product HW will be manufactured in the new plant. Fixed manufacturing costs of the new plant year are expected to be $990,000 and incurred evenly throughout the year.

The standard variable manufacturing cost per unit of product HW has been set at:

Direct Material	4 pieces @ $10 per piece	$ 40.00
Direct Labour	10 hours @ $15 per hour	150.00
Variable Manufacturing Overhead	50% of direct labour cost	75.00
		$265.00

At the end of August 1982, the actual costs incurred in making 950 units of HW were:

Direct Material	3850 pieces @ $9.80	$ 37,730
Direct Labour	12 000 hours @ $16.00	192,000
Variable Manufacturing Overhead		97,350
Fixed Manufacturing Overhead		86,110

Management now wishes to compare actual costs to budget and standards so as to ascertain what corrective action can be taken.

Required:

a. What selling price should Z Mfg., Ltd., set for product HW in accordance with the pricing formula set forth above? Explain.

b. Compute all variances between actual and standard cost of direct labour using a flexible budget. Indicate which person(s) (that is, position in the company) ought to be held accountable for each type of variance, and briefly state why.

c. Compute all variances between actual and applied manufacturing overhead. Indicate which person(s) (that is, position in the company) ought to be held accountable for each type of variance, and briefly state why.

Reprinted, with permission, from Uniform Final Examination, 1977, published by the Canadian Institute of Chartered Accountants, Toronto, Canada.

Minicase 9-4   (CICA adapted)

Sportech, Ltd., manufactures and sells baseball spikes and hockey skates. The baseball spikes are produced from January until the end of April. From May to December the company produces exclusively its three skate models sold under the brand names XL 100, XL 200, XL 300.

At the beginning of April 1984 the president analyzed the new budget revised by the controller on the basis of the new sales forecast prepared by the sales manager.

Budgeted Income Before Income Taxes

	XL 100	XL 200	XL 300	Total
Sales				
Number of pairs	20 000	18 000	10 000	
Price per pair	$ 14.00	$ 15.00	$ 25.00	
	$280,000	$270,000	$250,000	$800,000
Manufacturing Cost	200,000	207,000	180,000	587,000
Gross Margin	$ 80,000	$ 63,000	$ 70,000	$213,000
Selling expenses				
Delivery	$ 5,000	$ 4,500	$ 2,500	$ 12,000
Salaries and commissions	16,800	16,200	15,000	48,000
Salesmen's expenses	5,600	5,400	5,000	16,000
Advertising	15,000	15,000	15,000	45,000
Other (fixed costs)	7,000	6,750	6,250	20,000
Administrative expenses (fixed)	14,000	13,500	12,500	40,000
	$ 63,400	$ 61,350	$ 56,250	$181,000
Income	$ 16,600	$ 1,650	$ 13,750	$ 32,000
Underabsorbed manufacturing overhead				20,800
				$ 11,200

Budgeted Manufacturing Cost (per pair)

	XL 100	XL 200	XL 300
Direct materials			
Blades	$ 2.00	$ 2.00	$ 3.00
Other (leather, cap, etc.)	3.00	3.50	5.00
Direct labour	2.00	2.40	4.00
Applied overhead (150% of direct labour)	3.00	3.60	6.00
	$ 10.00	$ 11.50	$ 18.00

These budgeted figures are accompanied by the following explanatory notes:

i The burden rate has been determined on the following bases:

—The fixed costs ($144,000) are applied on the basis of the practical capacity of the plant, that is 36 000 direct labour hours for the last eight months.

Budgeted direct labour hours:

XL 100	20 000 × .5 h	= 10,000
XL 200	18 000 × .6 h	= 10,800
XL 300	10 000 × 1.0 h	= 10,000
		30,800

Manufacturing overhead to be applied:

Variable		$ 61,600
Fixed	$144,000 × $\dfrac{30\ 800}{36\ 000}$ h	123,200
		$184,800

Burden rate:

$$\frac{\text{Manufacturing overhead}}{\text{Direct labour cost}} \times 100\% = \frac{\$184,800}{\$123,200} \times 100\% = 150\%$$

ii Each of the five salesmen receives a monthly salary of $400 and a commission of 4 percent of all sales to the customers he visits regularly, even if they order directly.

iii Variable salesmen's expenses, fixed selling costs, and administrative expenses have been allocated as a percentage of sales.

iv Advertisements in newspapers, on radio, and on television always mention the three models. Therefore, the expense has been split evenly among the three models.

The president realized that the plant would not operate at practical capacity for the first time in many years, and that idle capacity would be costly for the company.

A few days later he received a letter from the purchasing agent of Sunset, Ltd., which operates a chain of department stores in the metropolitan area where Sportech's plant is located. This letter stated that Sunset would buy 10 000 pairs of each model of skates before the end of the year on the following conditions:

i Sportech would deliver one-quarter of the order on the last day of each of the last four months of the year at Sunset's central warehouse.

ii Sunset would pay for the goods before the 10th of the month following the delivery.

iii Cash and quantity discounts would amount to 15 percent of regular prices.

The president immediately called a meeting with the production manager, the sales manager, and the controller. The production manager saw an opportunity to wipe out the unabsorbed overhead. He mentioned that there would be no problem in hiring enough workers to operate at full capacity. He recalled that the union contract provided for an overtime premium of 50 percent after the regular 8-hour day or 40-hour week. Overtime is limited to three hours a day during the week, but employees can work four hours on Saturday mornings. He added that fixed manufacturing costs would increase by $3,000 a month, but that some savings may be realized, because the blades manufacturer would agree to a price reduction of 10 percent on all blades if the annual purchases totalled 60 000 pairs. The sales manager would take care personally of all relations with Sunset, but he insisted that all regular orders be accepted.

After a brief discussion, the controller and the sales manager agreed to prepare an analysis of all the important factors, qualitative as well as quantitative, that might affect the decision.

Required:

a. Calculate the effect on income before income taxes of this offer.

b. Discuss briefly the other factors that may have a bearing on the decision.

Reprinted, with permission, from Uniform Final Examination, 1975, published by the Canadian Institute of Chartered Accountants, Toronto, Canada.

Chapter 10

Costing Nonmanufacturing Activities and the Use of the Contribution Approach in Costing

This chapter presents material on costing nonmanufacturing activities and the use of the contribution approach in costing and reporting both manufacturing and nonmanufacturing activities. The costing and reporting of nonmanufacturing activities are important because such activities constitute a major segment of the economy. When you have completed this chapter, you should understand:

1 The similarities and differences between costing manufacturing and nonmanufacturing activities.

2 The two basic approaches to segmental reporting.

3 The form and content of the different types of segmental performance reports.

4 The concept of variable costing.

5 The similarities and differences between variable costing and absorption costing.

6 The determination of product costs using both variable and absorption costing.

7 The cause of any difference in net income between variable and absorption costing for a particular year.

Up to this point, our discussions of cost accounting concepts and procedures have dealt almost entirely with the determination of the cost of manufactured products. However, a great deal of economic activity involves nonmanufacturing operations. Service firms and merchandising firms have no manufacturing costs, and even manufacturing firms may have a significant amount of costs for nonmanufacturing activities. Marketing, general administration, engineering, and accounting are examples of nonmanufacturing activities. In the first part of this chapter we discuss the costing of nonmanufacturing activities, noting the similarities and differences between costing for manufacturing and nonmanufacturing activities. The two types of activities are combined when we turn to segmental reporting. The concept of contribution margin, introduced in Chapter 5, is extended to segmental reporting and product costing.

Costing nonmanufacturing activities

The cost of both manufacturing and nonmanufacturing activities must be monitored and controlled

Unit cost computations are similar for manufacturing activities and repetitive nonmanufacturing activities

The costs of all business activities must be monitored and controlled. Unfortunately not all activities lend themselves equally well to cost measurement. Most manufacturing activities are systematic and repetitive. The output is a single product or a set of homogeneous products. Many **nonmanufacturing activities** are not repetitive. For example, administrators, marketing managers, engineers, and other office personnel spend considerable time monitoring activities, analyzing problems, and making decisions. Although the types of problems and decisions may recur, these activities are not nearly as systematic and repetitive as most manufacturing activities.

On the other hand, some types of nonmanufacturing activities are repetitive and do generate a relatively homogeneous product. Examples are the preparation of purchase orders, sales invoices, and cheques or making phone calls in a telephone marketing survey. Repetitive activities lend themselves to cost measurement and the determination of unit costs in the same way that manufactured products do. The process is similar to product cost measurement. First, the cost objective must be carefully defined. Next, all direct costs are assigned to the cost objective. Finally, any indirect costs necessary to provide the service are allocated to the cost objective.

We illustrate activity costing with the Home Market Sales Company, a catalogue mail-order sales business. Each day orders received in the mail are sent to the order processing department where product descriptions and numbers are verified with catalogue information and a sales invoice is prepared. Management is interested in determining the cost of processing an order. The data on the following page have been accumulated for the order processing department for the year. Using these data, we can compute the average unit cost of processing orders. The direct costs include the sales invoice and direct labour. In addition, there are a number of indirect costs necessary to the order processing operations that cannot be identified with individual orders. Indirect costs for nonmanufacturing activities are treated similarly to indirect manu-

Orders processed	30 000
Hours worked	18 000
Hourly rate	$ 5
Invoice forms cost (31 200 invoices)	7,800
Indirect supplies and materials	4,000
Utilities cost	6,000
Depreciation, building	4,000
Depreciation, equipment	2,000
Payroll fringe benefits	18,000
Other departmental indirect costs	8,000

facturing costs. The cost of processing the 30 000 orders is summarized in Figure 10-1.

Notice that the computation of unit costs for processing a sales order is similar to the computation of unit costs for a manufactured product. The direct costs are similar to prime costs, and the indirect costs are similar to manufacturing overhead. The resulting unit cost is an average unit cost of processing orders during the year.

Standards for nonmanufacturing activities

The cost report shown in Figure 10-1 identifies an average unit cost, but it says nothing about how the cost compares with management's expectations for the order processing activity. Repetitive homogeneous activities, such as order processing, may be monitored and evaluated in much the same manner as

Home Market Sales Company
Order Processing Costs
For the Year Ended December 31, 1984

	Total Cost	Unit Cost*
Direct costs:		
Direct materials, invoice forms	$ 7,800	$ .26
Direct labour	90,000	3.00
Total direct costs	$ 97,800	$3.26
Indirect costs:		
Indirect supplies and materials	$ 4,000	
Utilities	6,000	
Depreciation, building	4,000	
Depreciation, equipment	2,000	
Payroll fringe benefits	18,000	
Other departmental indirect costs	8,000	
Total indirect costs	$ 42,000	1.40
Total cost of processing orders	$139,800	$4.66

*Based on a total of 30 000 orders processed

Figure 10-1
Order processing is a repetitive activity at Home Market Sales Company, and therefore unit costs can be determined in the same way as for a manufactured product. The unit costs are average unit costs for the year.

manufacturing activities. To illustrate, assume that the Home Market Sales Company has established the following standards for the order processing activity:

Direct materials: 1 invoice form per order @ $.20 each.
Direct labour: 35 minutes per order @ $5.25 per hour.
Indirect cost: Allocated at the rate of $2.30 per labour hour.

Using the actual cost data presented earlier and the standards just listed, it is a simple matter to prepare a variance analysis report similar to the ones presented in Chapter 8. Figure 10-2 illustrates a variance analysis report for the order processing activity.

The actual purchase price of invoices was $.25 ($7,800/31 200 invoices). Standard cost is $.20 a unit. The difference in cost times the 31 200 invoices used yields a $1,560 unfavourable material price variance. The quantity variance is the difference between the standard quantity of 30 000 invoices and the 31 200 actually used times the standard cost of $.20 an invoice. The result is a $240 unfavourable quantity variance.

The labour rate variance is the difference between the standard and actual rates times the number of hours worked. Here the actual rate is $.25 an hour lower than standard, yielding a $4,500 favourable rate variance. The standard quantity of labour is 35 minutes per order. However, 18 000 actual hours were used to process the 30 000 orders. That is .6 of an hour per order, or .6 × 60 minutes = 36 minutes per order. The efficiency variance is one minute unfa-

---

Home Market Sales Company
Variance Analysis Report for Order Processing
For the Year Ended December 31, 1984

Direct materials:		
Material price variance	($.20 − $.25) × 31 200	= $1,560 U
Material quantity variance	(30 000 forms − 31 200 forms) × $.20	= 240 U
Total material variance		$1,800 U
Direct labour:		
Labour rate variance	($5.25 − $5.00 × 18 000 h	= $4,500 F
Labour efficiency	{[(35 min − 36 min) × 30 000] / 60 min/h} × $5.25	= 2,625 U
Total labour variance		$1,875 F
Indirect costs:		
Standard indirect cost	17 500 h × $2.30 = $40,250	
Actual indirect cost	42,000	
Indirect cost variance		$1,750 U
Total variance for the year for order processing activities		$1,675 U

Figure 10-2
Standards are useful for both manufacturing and nonmanufacturing activities. Standard cost variance analysis reports are important management tools for all repetitive activities.

vourable times the 30 000 orders processed, which is 30 000 minutes. Converted into hours, that is 30 000 minutes/60 minutes per hour = 500 hours. Multiplying by the standard rate of $5.25 an hour yields a $2,625 unfavourable labour efficiency variance.

Indirect costs are allocated to order processing activities at the rate of $2.30 per labour hour. The 30 000 orders require 35/60 hours × 30 000 orders, or 17 500 standard hours. Multiplying 17 500 hours by the rate of $2.30 per hour yields $40,250, the standard amount of indirect cost for the year. Actual indirect costs are $42,000, so there is a $1,750 U variance for indirect costs. Total variance for the year in order processing is $1,675 unfavourable.

Although variance analysis reports are not as common in nonmanufacturing activities, such reports are very useful to managers. The detailed variance analysis data are useful for controlling order processing costs. The variance report presented in Figure 10-2 covers an entire year, but more timely reports, such as weekly or monthly, can be prepared. If the variance for any cost component indicates that management's attention is needed, action can be taken before serious problems develop. For example, the reason for the high price of order forms may have to be investigated with the possible aim of finding a cheaper source of supply. Management may also find that labour is not as efficient as expected because the department hired less skilfull employees who are paid less than the standard rate. However, using less skillful, and hence less efficient, employees at below-standard wages yields a net favourable labour rate variance, which may cause management to take no action on the unfavourable efficiency variance. On the other hand, if it is found that the unfavourable efficiency variance is due to employees taking 30-minute coffee breaks instead of 15 minutes, the problem can be corrected, leading to an even more favourable net labour variance.

Segmental reporting

Many nonmanufacturing activities are not repetitive or do not result in a homogeneous set of services. In such cases detailed standards and unit cost determinations are not feasible or even possible. Nonetheless, nonrepetitive activities require monitoring and controlling just as repetitive activities do. In many cases cost control is achieved by accumulating costs for the various segments of the firm, such as a department, a division, a marketing region, or any other part of an organization that management chooses to identify as a cost objective.

Segmental reporting defined

Segmental reporting* refers to the process of reporting the activities of various parts of an organization. The parts or segments of the organization for which reports are prepared depend on the information needs of management. Some examples of segmental reports are

> Income statements for each division of a company
> Product profitability reports
> Product profitability reports for sales districts
> Departmental cost reports

*Here the term segmental reporting and segmented reporting are used interchangeably.

Segmental reports often combine the costs of manufacturing and non-manufacturing activities. For example, divisional income statements and product profitability reports include product costs as well as the costs of some marketing and administrative activities. Often, in segmental reports product costs are in a more summarized form than in the detailed product cost reports discussed in earlier chapters.

The segmental reporting process

The variety and frequency of accounting reports for business segments is limited only by management's information requirements and the ability and desire to pay the cost of preparing the accounting reports. Although the variety of segmental reports is substantial, some functions are basic to the preparation of all segmental cost reports: The functions are

Functions in the segmental reporting process

1. Identify the cost objective.
2. Assign direct costs to the cost objective.
3. Allocate indirect costs to the cost objective.

Identify the cost objective. When dealing with a single manufactured product or a repetitive homogeneous activity, it is not difficult to define the cost objective. When the cost objective is a segment of the business, the objective is not always as easy to define. For example, if management is interested in determining the cost of marketing a particular product in one sales region of the country, the costing process may be clouded by the fact that some marketing efforts promote several products and some marketing programs affect more than one region. Therefore, each cost objective must be identified and described as precisely as possible to ensure that only appropriate costs are assigned to the objective.

Cost objectives are not always easy to define

Assign direct costs. Direct costs are those which are specifically identifiable with the cost objective. Direct materials and direct labour typically constitute the direct costs of manufactured products. They are variable costs that change directly with the number of units produced. However, direct costs are not necessarily variable. Many cost objectives for nonmanufacturing activities have fixed direct costs. For example, if management is interested in the total cost of the marketing activity, a $2,000,000 annual contract for television advertising is a fixed cost directly identifiable with the cost objective. Many cost objectives have fixed costs that are directly traceable to the specific activity being considered.

Some direct costs are fixed costs

Allocate indirect costs. Indirect costs are those which are not directly traceable to the cost objective, but which are necessary to the activity described by the cost objective. Some nonmanufacturing activities may have large amounts of indirect costs. A good example is the data processing activity, which typically has a significant amount of fixed indirect cost. Indirect costs should be allocated to segmental cost objectives using the matching principle as a guide.

Once the cost objective has been identified, assigning direct costs and allocating indirect costs must be accomplished in some systematic manner. There are two approaches commonly used to assign and allocate costs to segments. Both the full cost approach and the contribution approach are used for segmental reporting, the choice depending on the needs of management. The two approaches are discussed below.

The full costing approach to segmental reporting

Chapters 2, 3, and 4 discuss **full costing** in which all costs of production—direct and indirect, fixed and variable—are assigned to the product. The emphasis in such a cost system is on the functional classification of costs into categories, such as direct labour, indirect labour, utilities, and depreciation, or manufacturing and nonmanufacturing. If full costs are used in segmental reports, cost data are accumulated as discussed in Chapters 2 and 4 and are reported by the segments that the management of the firm desires to evaluate.

Longmount Diversified Products
Divisional Sales and Cost Data
For the Fiscal Year Ended August 31, 1984

	Business Machines	Home Products
Units sold	10 000	31 000
Average unit sales price	$ 86.00	$ 40.00
Average unit manufacturing costs:		
Direct materials	12.00	8.00
Direct labour	10.00	5.00
Manufacturing overhead	23.00	7.81
Operating expenses:		
Marketing	$126,000	$174,000
Distribution	60,000	102,000
Administrative	82,000	152,000
Corporate expenses not directly identifiable with divisions		$180,000

Figure 10-3
The unit sales price and unit cost data are the weighted average for the products manufactured in each division. For example, the $86 price in the Business Machines Division is the weighted average selling price of the business calculators and programmable calculators sold by that division. Also, note that some company expenses assigned to the two divisions are not identifiable with a specific division. These expenses are classified as corporate expenses.

The full costing approach illustrated

We use Longmount Diversified Products to illustrate segmental reporting using full costing. Longmount is a manufacturing firm whose products are manufactured in two divisions. The Business Machines Division produces a business calculator and a programmable scientific calculator. The Home Products Division manufactures toaster ovens and blenders. The company's management uses segmental reports to assist in evaluating performance of various activities. Among the reports used are a divisional income statement and a product profitability statement.

A divisional income statement identifies net income by division

A **divisional income statement** identifies the amount of net income generated by each division. Revenue and expenses are identified with the appropriate division, and corporate totals are accumulated. Divisional data for the fiscal year are presented in Figure 10-3.

A divisional income statement is shown in Figure 10-4. All revenues and expenses are identified with a division where possible. Expenses not identifiable with a specific division are deducted from the corporate total to arrive at corporate net income.

Isolates profit by product line

A **product profitability statement** isolates profits by product or product line using full product cost as the basis for measuring profit. In Figure 10-5 cost and quantity data of the Business Machines Division are segmented according to products and various direct and indirect costs are allocated to the two types of calculators. As an organization is divided into smaller and smaller

Figure 10-4
A divisional income statement highlights the profit contributed to the company's total profit by each division. Net income of the divisions does not equal total company profit because some expenses that cannot be identified with divisions must be deducted from the company total to find corporate net income.

Longmount Diversified Products
Divisional Income Statement
For the Fiscal Year Ended August 31, 1984

	Division		
	Business Machines	Home Products	Company Total
Sales	$860,000	$1,240,000	$2,100,000
Less: Cost of goods sold	450,000	645,000*	1,095,000
Gross margin on sales	$410,000	$ 595,000	$1,005,000
Less: Operating expenses:			
Marketing	$126,000	$ 174,000	$ 300,000
Distribution	60,000	102,000	162,000
Administrative	82,000	152,000	234,000
Total operating expenses	$268,000	$ 428,000	$ 696,000
Divisional net income	$142,000	$ 167,000	$ 309,000
Corporate expenses			180,000
Net income			$ 129,000

*Rounded.

	Longmount Diversified Products Business Machines Division Product Sales and Cost Data For the Fiscal Year Ended August 31		
	Product		
	Business Calculator	**Programmable Calculator**	**Division Expenses***
Units sold	8000	2000	
Sales price/unit	$ 70.00	$150.00	
Average unit manufacturing costs:			
Direct material	15.00	25.00	
Direct labour	8.00	20.00	
Manufacturing overhead	14.50	30.00	
Operating expenses:			
Marketing	$68,000	$40,000	$18,000
Distribution	29,000	9,000	22,000
Administrative	23,000	19,000	40,000
Total divisional expenses			$80,000

*Expenses identifiable with the division, but not with specific products.

Figure 10-5
Product cost and sales data for each product are necessary to prepare product profitability reports. Longmount's Business Machines Division has only two products, business calculators and programmable calculators.

parts, more and more of the costs become common costs and not identifiable with specific segments of the business. For example, the Business Machines Division has $80,000 of costs that are identifiable with the division, but not with specific products within the division. The report in Figure 10-4 indicates $126,000 marketing costs for the division. Of this amount $108,000 can be identified with the two calculators and assigned to them, as shown in Figure 10-5. The remaining $18,000 of marketing costs cannot be identified with either calculator and is therefore made part of the divisional expenses of $80,000.

Figure 10-6 illustrates the divisional product profitability statement. Here divisional expenses must be subtracted from total product profit to arrive at divisional profit. Naturally this figure must be the same as the division's profit shown in the divisional income statement in Figure 10-4.

The contribution approach to segmental reporting

Although the full cost approach is widely used, many people believe that much valuable management information is buried in full costs and therefore not available to managers. They suggest that costs should be reported by behaviour patterns, such as fixed and variable, because behavioural cost classifications are far more useful to managers for internal decision making.

Longmount Diversified Products Business Machines Division Product Profitability Statement For the Fiscal Year Ended August 31			
	Business Calculator	Programmable Calculator	Division Total
Sales	$560,000	$300,000	$860,000
Less: Cost of goods sold	300,000	150,000	450,000
Gross margin on sales	$260,000	$150,000	$410,000
Less: Operating expenses:			
Marketing	$ 68,000	$ 40,000	$108,000
Distribution	29,000	9,000	38,000
Administrative	23,000	19,000	42,000
Total operating expenses	$120,000	$ 68,000	$188,000
Product profitability	$140,000	$ 82,000	$222,000
Less: Divisional expenses*			80,000
Divisional net income			$142,000

*Divisional expenses not identifiable with products consist of $18,000 marketing, $22,000 distribution, and $40,000 administrative.

Figure 10-6
Here product profitability is measured using the full cost of products, which means both fixed and variable manufacturing costs are included in the product cost.

The contribution approach reports costs by behaviour pattern

In Chapter 5 we discussed the classification of costs by behaviour patterns, such as variable, fixed, semivariable, and semifixed. Behavioural cost classifications are used in Chapters 5 and 6 to analyze various business decision situations. Behavioural cost classification can be very useful in reporting segmental performance. Many managers believe reports based on the **contribution approach** are more useful than full cost reports. For example, often managers find contribution approach information very helpful in making decisions, such as whether to drop a product line or whether to make or buy a product.

The contribution approach illustrated

We continue the Longmount Diversified Products illustration to present the contribution approach to segmental reporting. Additional data are provided so that three different contribution approach reports can be prepared. These are

1. A divisional contribution statement
2. Product contribution statements
3. Sales region contribution statements

A **divisional contribution statement** describes the amount of contribution margin generated by each division of a firm. The concept of **contribution margin** used here is similar to the one used in cost-volume-profit analysis.

Longmount Diversified Products Divisional Sales and Cost Data For the Fiscal Year Ended August 31		
	Division	
	Business Machines	**Home Products**
Units sold	10 000	31 000
Average unit sales price	$ 86.00	$ 40.00
Average unit variable costs:		
Manufacturing	30.00	15.00
Marketing	8.60	4.00
Distribution	3.00	2.00
Administrative	1.20	2.00
Fixed costs directly identifiable with the division:		
Manufacturing	$150,000	$180,000
Marketing	40,000	50,000
Distribution	30,000	40,000
Administrative	70,000	90,000

Figure 10-7
It is necessary for all costs to be divided into fixed and variable components in order to prepare contribution approach reports. Here are the fixed and variable costs by division for Longmount. The unit variable costs are the weighted average unit variable costs for the products manufactured in each division.

The concept of contribution margin applied to divisional reporting

The only difference is that here we apply contribution margin to a division, whereas with CVP it was used primarily in reference to a single product. Sales and cost data are presented for Longmount's two divisions in Figure 10-7.

Data from Figure 10-7 are used to prepare the divisional contribution statement presented in Figure 10-8. First, variable manufacturing costs for each division are deducted from divisional sales revenue to yield the **manufacturing contribution margin.** Next, the variable expenses of nonmanufacturing activities are deducted, yielding the **contribution margin.** Finally, fixed expenses directly identifiable with each division are subtracted to arrive at the divisional contribution. This is the amount the division contributes toward covering corporate expenses and generating corporate profit. Corporate expenses include the general administrative expenses of operating the corporate offices. These expenses are necessary in the operations of the company, but they are not identifiable with specific divisions.

Contribution margin applied to products

A **product contribution statement** presents an analysis of the contribution margin by each product of a division. Such reports are useful in making many management decisions relating to product pricing, sales strategy, and production scheduling, or discontinuing a product line. The form of the product contribution statement is very similar to that of the divisional contribution statement. The primary difference is the cost objective, which is the product line instead of a division of the business.

A product contribution statement requires sales and cost data for each product included in the report. The example presented here is the Business

	Business Machines	Home Products	Company Total

Longmount Diversified Products
Divisional Contribution Statement
For the Fiscal Year Ended August 31

	Division		
	Business Machines	**Home Products**	**Company Total**
Sales	$860,000	$1,240,000	$2,100,000
Less: Variable manufacturing expenses	300,000	465,000	765,000
Manufacturing contribution margin	$560,000	$ 775,000	$1,335,000
Less: Other variable expenses:			
Variable marketing	$ 86,000	$ 124,000	$ 210,000
Variable distribution	30,000	62,000	92,000
Variable administrative	12,000	62,000	74,000
Total	$128,000	$ 248,000	$ 376,000
Contribution margin	$432,000	$ 527,000	$ 959,000
Less: Divisional fixed expenses:			
Fixed manufacturing	$150,000	$ 180,000	$ 330,000
Fixed marketing	40,000	50,000	90,000
Fixed distribution	30,000	40,000	70,000
Fixed administrative	70,000	90,000	160,000
Total	$290,000	$ 360,000	$ 650,000
Divisional contribution	$142,000	$ 167,000	$ 309,000
Corporate expenses			180,000
Net income			$ 129,000

Figure 10-8
A divisional contribution statement highlights the contribution margin provided by each division. Cost behaviour information by division is useful for many managerial decisions, such as determining whether to close a marginally profitable division.

Machines Division of Longmount Diversified Products, which produces a business calculator and a programmable calculator. Product data for the year are presented in Figure 10-9.

Figure 10-10 shows the product contribution statement prepared from the data in Figure 10-9. Since the Business Machines Division produces only two products, the sales and variable cost figures total to the amount shown in the Business Machines column of the divisional contribution report. If only part of the division's products were analyzed in the product contribution report, the amounts would not have the same total.

The computations of the manufacturing contribution margin and the contribution margin are precisely the same as they were in the divisional contribution statement except that in the product contribution statement both are

		Product		

Longmount Diversified Products
Business Machines Division
Product Sales and Cost Data
For the Fiscal Year Ended August 31

	Business Calculator	Programmable Calculator	Division Expenses*
Sales units:			
Eastern region	4500	1000	
Western region	3500	1000	
Sales price	$ 70	$ 150	
Unit variable costs:			
Manufacturing	$ 25	$ 50	
Marketing	7	15	
Distribution	3	3	
Administrative	1	2	
Fixed costs directly identifiable with the product:			
Manufacturing	$70,000	$60,000	$ 20,000
Marketing	12,000	10,000	18,000
Distribution	5,000	3,000	22,000
Administrative	15,000	15,000	40,000
Total divisional expenses			$100,000

*Fixed expenses identifiable with the division, but not with specific products.

Figure 10-9
Product contribution reports require cost behaviour data for individual products. Here we present cost and sales data for the Business Machines Division.

computed for each product. The next step, the computation of the product contribution, is somewhat different from the computation of the divisional contribution. The difference occurs because some of the fixed expenses that can be directly identified with the division cannot be specifically identified with the individual products. For instance, administrative cost pertains to the general administration of the division rather than to specific products. Similarly some advertising may promote the division's calculators in general rather than a specific product. The result is that only a part of the divisional fixed expenses is assigned to products, and some divisional expenses remain that are common to all divisional products. These divisional expenses are similar to the corporate expenses in the divisional contribution statement. After divisional expenses are deducted, the divisional contribution remains. This amount is equal to the amount shown in the divisional contribution statement for the Business Machines Division.

Contribution margin by sales region   A **sales region contribution statement** shows the amount of contribution margin generated in each sales region. Sometimes the cost of marketing and

	Products		
	Business Calculator	**Programmable Calculator**	**Division Totals**

Longmount Diversified Products
Business Machines Division
Product Contribution Statement
For the Fiscal Year Ended August 31

	Business Calculator	Programmable Calculator	Division Totals
Sales	$560,000	$300,000	$860,000
Less: Variable manufacturing expenses	200,000	100,000	300,000
Manufacturing contribution margin	$360,000	$200,000	$560,000
Less: Other variable expenses:			
Variable marketing	$ 56,000	$ 30,000	$ 86,000
Variable distribution	24,000	6,000	30,000
Variable administrative	8,000	4,000	12,000
Contribution margin	$272,000	$160,000	$432,000
Less: Fixed direct expense:			
Fixed manufacturing	$ 70,000	$ 60,000	$130,000
Fixed marketing	12,000	10,000	22,000
Fixed distribution	5,000	3,000	8,000
Fixed administrative	15,000	15,000	30,000
Product contribution	$170,000	$ 72,000	$242,000
Less: Divisional fixed expenses*			100,000
Divisional contribution			$142,000

*Divisional fixed expenses not identifiable with products consist of $20,000 manufacturing, $18,000 marketing, $22,000 distribution, and $40,000 administrative.

Figure 10-10
Product contribution reports help managers to evaluate cost-volume relationships and to make decisions about marketing, production priorities, and dropping product lines. Compare this report with the product profitability report in Figure 10-6.

distribution vary significantly between sales regions. For example, a sales office servicing the western provinces may have a significantly higher marketing and distribution costs than the Ontario sales office because of the travel and shipping costs caused by low population densities. Cost data by sales regions are useful in planning sales strategies and supervising marketing activities in general.

Longmount divides its sales activity into an Eastern and a Western region. Unit sales data by region appear in Figure 10-9 and are used in Figure 10-11 to present an analysis of contribution margin by sales region.

Selling price and variable manufacturing costs are identical for each region. However, variable marketing and distribution costs are significantly higher in the Western region than in the Eastern region. The average variable costs

Longmount Diversified Products Business Machines Division Sales Region Contribution Statement			
	Region		**Division Total**
	Eastern	**Western**	
Sales	$465,000	$395,000	$860,000
Less: Variable manufacturing expenses	162,500	137,500	300,000
Manufacturing contribution margin	$302,500	$257,500	$560,000
Less: Other variable expenses:			
Variable marketing	$ 33,500	$ 52,500	$ 86,000
Variable distribution	7,500	22,500	30,000
Variable administrative	6,500	5,500	12,000
Total	$ 47,500	$ 80,500	$128,000
Contribution margin	$255,000	$177,000	$432,000
Less: Fixed expenses:			
Fixed marketing	$ 6,000	$ 6,000	$ 12,000
Fixed distribution	6,000	12,000	18,000
Total	$ 12,000	$ 18,000	$ 30,000
Regional contribution	$243,000	$159,000	$402,000
Less: Divisional fixed expenses not assignable to regions*			260,000
Divisional contribution			$142,000

*Divisional fixed expenses not assignable to sales regions consist of $150,000 manufacturing, $28,000 marketing, $12,000 distribution, and $70,000 administrative.

Figure 10-11
Differential marketing, distribution, and administrative costs for different sales regions can cause a significant difference in the contribution margin of products sold in those regions. Sales region contribution reports often present important contribution data that are buried in divisional contribution reports.

shown in Figure 10-9 for marketing and distribution activities result from the following unit variable costs in each region:

	Eastern Region	**Western Region**
Business calculator		
Marketing	$ 4.67/unit	$10.00/unit
Distribution	1.44/unit	5.00/unit
Programmable calculator		
Marketing	12.50/unit	17.50/unit
Distribution	1.00/unit	5.00/unit

The result is a lower per-unit contribution margin for products sold in the Western region. Given a choice, management would prefer to sell units in the Eastern region, and during periods of peak production, priorities may be set in filling orders.

An important point is illustrated by the fixed expenses section of the report in Figure 10-11. Notice that very few divisional expenses are assignable to the sales regions. In this example none of the fixed manufacturing expenses or administrative expenses are identifiable with the sales regions, and only a small portion of the marketing and distribution fixed expenses is assigned to the regions. Typically fewer divisional fixed costs are identifiable with sales regions than are identifiable with products because costs are incurred to manufacture or sell a product in general rather than to manufacture and sell it in a specific region. In some cases a larger portion of the marketing and distribution costs may be identified with the regions than in our example, and occasionally some fixed manufacturing costs may be assigned to a sales region when a plant serves a specific region. However, the general statement holds that fewer divisional fixed costs are identifiable with sales regions than with product lines.

The contribution approach to product costing: variable costing

The above discussion described full costing and the contribution approach in reporting segmental performance with examples that included both products and operating costs. However, we did not examine in detail the effect of these two basic costing methods on product cost. Below we explore the impact of each method on product cost and the determination of net income. Each method is illustrated with an extensive example. The primary difference between the segmental reporting discussion and the one that follows is the amount of detail. In the section on segmental reporting we dealt with two products, whereas below we discuss the impact of the two costing methods on determining product cost for a specific product. Data on product costs may then be aggregated into segmental or corporate reports.

Absorption costing

Absorption costing, also referred to as **full costing,** is the generally accepted method of product costing for purposes of external reporting. Although the terms *full costing* and *absorption costing* are used interchangeably, *absorption costing* is the more common of the two, and we use it in the discussion that follows. Most of the product costs computed in Chapters 2, 3, and 4 are absorption costs. With absorption costing product costs include both direct and indirect costs of production. Direct materials, direct labour, and **all** manufacturing overhead are elements of the product cost. Fixed overhead costs are absorbed by the product and are part of cost of goods sold and ending inventories.

All production costs including fixed manufacturing overhead are assigned to products

Variable costing

Variable costing, often called **direct costing,** is a method of product costing that charges only the variable costs of manufacturing to the product. Direct materials, direct labour, and **variable** manufacturing overhead are included in inventory, and fixed manufacturing overhead costs are expensed during the period in which they are incurred together with all nonmanufacturing expenses. Although the term *direct costing* is frequently used, variable costing describes the process more accurately, because **indirect** variable overhead costs are part of the product cost.

What costs should be assigned to products?

The main controversy between the two methods centres on what costs should be inventoried (assigned to products). Variable costing advocates maintain that costs should be inventoried only if incurring the cost now eliminates the necessity of incurring the cost in the future. For example, adding direct materials to a unit of product now eliminates the need of adding the same materials to the same unit later. On the other hand, fixed capacity costs, such as depreciation on plant and equipment, are not avoidable in future periods because of current-period production.

A variable costing income statement highlights cost behaviour characteristics. The comparison of variable costs with revenue provides contribution margin information. Variable costing is one of several reporting methods generally classified as **contribution approach reporting.**

Variable and absorption costing illustrated and compared

We use Higgens Industries, Ltd., to illustrate variable and absorption costing. Figure 10-12 presents four years of production, cost, and sales data. In this example selling price, fixed costs, and per-unit variable costs remain constant during the four-year period, although the number of units produced and sold varies. Such cost and price stability is somewhat unrealistic, but price and cost

Higgens Industries, Ltd.
Sales and Cost Data
Years 1 through 4

	Year			
	1	2	3	4
Sales in units	45 000	50 000	55 000	50 000
Production in units	55 000	55 000	45 000	45 000
Direct materials per unit	$4	$4	$4	$4
Direct labour per unit	$5	$5	$5	$5
Variable MOH per unit	$3	$3	$3	$3
Fixed MOH	$400,000	$400,000	$400,000	$400,000
Variable selling and administrative per unit	$2	$2	$2	$2
Fixed selling and administrative	$220,000	$220,000	$220,000	$220,000
Sales price per unit	$32	$32	$32	$32
Beginning inventory in units	0	10 000	15 000	5 000

Figure 10-12
Sales and cost data for a four-year period are shown. All costs are identified as fixed or variable. In this example per-unit variable costs and total fixed costs remain constant.

stability makes it easier to understand the differences and similarities between variable and absorption costing. A later example has varying costs and selling prices.

The first step in preparing variable and absorption costing income statements is to compute the unit cost of the product for both costing methods. The computations are shown in Figure 10-13 with cost data obtained from Figure 10-12. The variable manufacturing costs consist of direct material, direct labour and variable manufacturing overhead. In this example variable manufacturing costs are $12 a unit in each of the four years. With the variable costing method, the $12 is the entire unit cost of the product. With the absorption costing method, a portion of the fixed manufacturing overhead cost must be allocated to the product in addition to the $12 variable cost.

The amount of fixed overhead allocated to each unit of product is determined by the amount of fixed cost and the number of units used in estimating the level of activity. Higgens uses 50 000 units as its estimate of the normal annual production level during the four-year period. The fixed overhead cost per unit is $400,000/50 000 units, or $8 per unit. Adding the fixed overhead component to the variable unit cost of $12 yields a total unit cost of $20.

The unit cost is identical for all four years because the fixed and variable costs remained constant. If the costs change, the unit costs are different each year, but the computational procedures are the same. A later example illustrates changing costs. The income statements in Figure 10-14 are prepared from the product cost data in Figure 10-13 and the sales and cost data in Figure 10-12.

In the absorption costing income statement, the sales revenue in each year is the number of units sold times the selling price of $32 per unit. Cost of goods sold is the number of units sold times $20 per unit. The variable selling expense is units sold times $2 per unit, and the fixed selling expense is a

Product cost using variable costing

Product cost using absorption costing

Absorption costing income statements

Higgens Industries, Ltd.
Unit Product Cost Data
Years 1 through 4

	Year			
	1	2	3	4
Variable manufacturing costs:				
Direct materials	$ 4	$ 4	$ 4	$ 4
Direct labour	5	5	5	5
Variable MOH	3	3	3	3
Product cost using variable costing	$12	$12	$12	$12
Add: Prorated fixed overhead cost	8	8	8	8
Product cost using absorption costing	$20	$20	$20	$20

Figure 10-13
Unit variable manufacturing costs constitute the total product cost in variable costing income statements. Product cost with absorption costing includes a prorated portion of fixed manufacturing overhead costs.

Higgens Industries, Ltd.
Absorption Costing Income Statement
For Years 1 through 4
(All figures in thousands)

	Year			
	1	2	3	4
Sales	$1,440	$1,600	$1,760	$1,600
Cost of goods sold	900	1,000	1,100	1,000
Gross margin	$ 540	$ 600	$ 660	$ 600
Variable selling and administrative	$ 90	$ 100	$ 110	$ 100
Fixed selling and administrative	220	220	220	220
Underapplied (overapplied) MOH	(40)	(40)	40	40
Total operating expenses	$ 270	$ 280	$ 370	$ 360
Net income	$ 270	$ 320	$ 290	$ 240

Higgens Industries, Ltd.
Variable Costing Income Statement
For Years 1 through 4
(All figures in thousands)

	Year			
	1	2	3	4
Sales	$1,440	$1,600	$1,760	$1,600
Variable product cost	540	600	660	600
Manufacturing contribution margin	$ 900	$1,000	$1,100	$1,000
Variable selling and administrative	90	100	110	100
Contribution margin	$ 810	$ 900	$ 990	$ 900
Fixed MOH	$ 400	$ 400	$ 400	$ 400
Fixed selling and administrative	220	220	220	220
Total fixed costs	$ 620	$ 620	$ 620	$ 620
Net income	$ 190	$ 280	$ 370	$ 280

Figure 10-14

The difference in net income in any particular year between absorption costing and variable costing is caused by the fixed manufacturing overhead costs that are carried from one period to the next through inventory. Fixed overhead costs included in ending inventory using absorption costing are transferred out of the period, thus reducing period expenses and increasing net income. Fixed manufacturing overhead costs in beginning inventory increase period expenses and reduce net income.

constant $220,000 per year regardless of the sales volume. The underapplied and overapplied overhead occur because actual production levels are different from the normal level of 50 000 units used for setting the overhead rate. In years 1 and 2, 55 000 units are produced and $440,000 (55 000 units × $8/unit) of **fixed** overhead is applied to production. Actual fixed MOH is $400,000, or $40,000 less. Therefore, $40,000 must be deducted from total product costs to report actual costs. In years 3 and 4, production is only 45 000 units. As a result, less overhead was applied than was actually incurred. Actual fixed overhead is $400,000, but only $360,000 (45 000 units × $8/unit) was applied, causing underapplied overhead of $40,000. As discussed in Chapters 4 and 8, these overhead variances typically are charged or credited to the cost of goods sold account for the year unless variances are very large.

Variable costing income statements

The variable costing income statement shows the same annual revenue amounts as the absorption costing income statement, since revenue is not affected by the choice of costing methods. However, the rest of the income statement looks quite different. The variable product cost of $12 per unit is subtracted from sales to find the **manufacturing contribution margin.** Variable selling and administrative costs are deducted to arrive at the **contribution margin** (CM). This is the same contribution margin discussed in connection with cost-volume profit analysis; only here it appears in total. The average unit contribution margin could be computed by dividing the total CM by the units sold. For instance, in year 1 the average contribution margin is $810,000/45 000 units = $18 per unit.

All fixed expenses are subtracted from the contribution margin to determine net income. Absorption costing and variable costing result in different net incomes for each of the four years. With absorption costing net income is higher in years 1 and 2 and lower in years 3 and 4 than variable costing net income.

The reason for the difference in net income between the two methods is the fixed manufacturing overhead cost included in absorption costing inventories

The difference in net income in any given year between the two costing methods is caused **entirely** by the **fixed** manufacturing overhead of $8 per unit that is absorbed by the products and included in beginning and ending inventories when absorption costing is used. With this method fixed MOH is assigned to products and is expensed only when the products are sold. The ending inventory therefore contains current fixed overhead costs that are not expensed until a future period.

To illustrate, refer to Figure 10-15, which shows the quantity and cost of beginning and ending inventory for both absorption and variable costing. The physical quantity of ending finished goods inventory is identical for both costing methods. However, the unit cost is $8 higher using absorption costing. At the end of year 1, when 10 000 units remain in inventory, $80,000 (10 000 units × $8/unit) of fixed overhead is transferred from year 1 to year 2.

With variable costing fixed overhead is expensed each year

With variable costing all of the fixed overhead cost is expensed in the year in which it is incurred, resulting in an $80,000 lower net income in year 1.

Each year the difference in net income between absorption and variable costing can be explained by the amount of fixed overhead in inventory that is transferred from one accounting period to another using the absorption costing

Higgens Industries, Ltd.
Schedule of Beginning and Ending Inventory
Under Absorption Costing and Variable Costing

		Year		
	1	**2**	**3**	**4**
		Absorption		
Beginning inventory:				
Number of units	0	10 000	15 000	5 000
Unit cost	—	$20	$20	$20
Total cost	—	$200,000	$300,000	$100,000
Ending inventory:				
Number of units	10 000	15 000	5 000	0
Unit cost	$20	$20	$20	—
Total cost	$200,000	$300,000	$100,000	—
		Variable Costing		
Beginning inventory:				
Number of units	0	10 000	15 000	5 000
Unit cost	—	$12	$12	$12
Total cost	—	$120,000	$180,000	$ 60,000
Ending inventory:				
Number of units	10 000	15 000	5 000	0
Unit cost	$12	$12	$12	—
Total cost	$120,000	$180,000	$ 60,000	—

Figure 10-15
The difference in the value of the ending inventory between absorption costing and variable costing is due entirely to the fixed manufacturing overhead cost that is assigned to products under absorption costing. In this example the fixed overhead cost is $8 per unit.

method. The fixed overhead costs that are in beginning and ending inventory are summarized in Figure 10-16.

Since there is no beginning inventory in year 1, no fixed overhead cost is transferred in from prior periods. Ending inventory of 10 000 units with $8 per unit fixed overhead has the effect of transferring $80,000 of fixed overhead out of year 1. Since all fixed overhead was expensed with variable costing, absorption costing net income is $80,000 higher. The $80,000 in fixed overhead transferred out of year 1 is transferred into year 2 in beginning inventory. This alone would make absorption costing net income $80,000 lower than variable costing net income in year 2, but $120,000 of year 2 fixed overhead is transferred out of year 2 via ending inventory. The result is a $40,000 higher net income in year 2 using absorption costing. Similarly the $120,000 of fixed overhead transferred into year 3 is partially offset by the $40,000 of fixed overhead included in year 3 ending inventory using absorption costing. The result is an $80,000 lower net income in year 3 with absorption costing. Finally in year 4, $40,000 of fixed overhead costs is transferred into the period, but none can be transferred out because there is no ending inventory. The result is a $40,000

Higgens Industries, Ltd.
Schedule of Fixed Overhead Costs Included in
Beginning and Ending Inventory under Absorption Costing

	Year			
	1	**2**	**3**	**4**
Fixed MOH transferred into the period in ending inventory	0	$ 80,000	$120,000	$40,000
Fixed MOH transferred out of the period in ending inventory	$80,000	120,000	40,000	0
Causes absorption costing net income to be	$80,000 higher	$ 40,000 higher	$ 80,000 lower	$40,000 lower

Figure 10-16
The difference in net income in any particular year between absorption costing and variable costing is caused by the fixed manufacturing overhead costs that are carried from one period to the next through inventory. Fixed overhead costs included in ending inventory are transferred out of the period, thus reducing period expenses and increasing net income. Fixed manufacturing overhead costs in beginning inventory increase period expenses and reduce net income.

lower net income in year 4 using absorption costing. Notice that the total net income for the four-year period is identical with both methods because there is no beginning inventory in year 1 and no ending inventory in year 4.

	Net Income	
Year	**Absorption**	**Variable**
1	$ 270,000	$ 190,000
2	320,000	280,000
3	290,000	370,000
4	240,000	280,000
Total	$1,120,000	$1,120,000

If there are no beginning and ending inventories, net income is the same for both variable and absorption costing

There is no fixed overhead to be transferred into year 1 or out of year 4. This situation holds for a single year as well. If there is no beginning and no ending inventory in an accounting period, the net income is the same for absorption and variable costing.

To show that inventoried fixed MOH costs are the only cause of differences between absorption and variable costing net income, we use the example of Higgens II Industries, Ltd. The production and sales quantities are

Higgens II Industries, Ltd.
Sales and Cost Data
Years 1 through 4

	Year			
	1	2	3	4
Sales in units	45 000	50 000	55 000	50 000
Production in units	55 000	55 000	45 000	45 000
Direct materials per unit	$3	$3	$4	$5
Direct labour per unit	$4	$5	$5	$6
Variable MOH per unit	$3	$4	$5	$5
Fixed MOH	$400,000	$400,000	$450,000	$450,000
Variable selling and administrative per unit	$2	$2	$3	$3
Fixed selling and administrative	$200,000	$220,000	$240,000	$250,000
Sales price per unit	$30	$32	$34	$35
Beginning inventory in units	0	10 000	15 000	5 000

Figure 10-17
Higgens II parallels the Higgens example, but in this illustration the fixed and variable costs and sales price fluctuate. This figure presents data similar to those found in Figure 10-12.

identical to those in the first example, but costs and selling prices fluctuate. Figures 10-17 through 10-21 exactly parallel Figures 10-12 through 10-16. In the final analysis the entire difference in net income in any particular year is caused by fixed overhead being transferred from one accounting period to another by absorption-costed inventories.

Higgens II Industries, Ltd.
Unit Product Cost Data
Years 1 through 4

	Year			
	1	2	3	4
Variable manufacturing costs:				
Direct materials	$ 3	$ 3	$ 4	$ 5
Direct labour	4	5	5	6
Variable MOH	3	4	5	5
Product cost using variable costing	$10	$12	$14	$16
Add: Prorated fixed MOH cost	8	8	9	9
Product cost using absorption costing	$18	$20	$23	$25

Figure 10-18
Product costs change from year to year in this example. However, the computation procedures for product costs and net income remains the same.

Higgens II Industries, Ltd.
Absorption Costing Income Statement
For Years 1 through 4
(All figures in thousands)

	Year			
	1	**2**	**3**	**4**
Sales	$1,350	$1,600	$1,870	$1,750
Cost of goods sold	810	980	1,220	1,240
Gross margin	$ 540	$ 620	$ 650	$ 510
Variable selling and administrative	$ 90	$ 100	$ 165	$ 150
Fixed selling and administrative	200	220	240	250
Underapplied (overapplied) MOH	(40)	(40)	45	45
Total operating expenses	$ 250	$ 280	$ 450	$ 445
Net income	$ 290	$ 340	$ 200	$ 65

Higgens II Industries, Ltd.
Variable Costing Income Statement
For Years 1 through 4
(All figures in thousands)

	Year			
	1	**2**	**3**	**4**
Sales	$1,350	$1,600	$1,870	$1,750
Variable product cost	450	580	740	790
Manufacturing contribution margin	$ 900	$1,020	$1,130	$ 960
Variable selling and administrative	90	100	165	150
Contribution margin	$ 810	$ 920	$ 965	$ 810
Fixed MOH	$ 400	$ 400	$ 450	$ 450
Fixed selling and administrative	200	220	240	250
Total fixed costs	$ 600	$ 620	$ 690	$ 700
Net income	$ 210	$ 300	$ 275	$ 110

Figure 10-19
This figure parallels Figure 10-14. The primary difference is that a number of cost and revenue elements are changing from year to year, whereas only production and sales quantities changed in the earlier example.

Higgens II Industries, Ltd. Schedule of Beginning and Ending Inventories Under Absorption Costing and Variable Costing				
	Year			
	1	**2**	**3**	**4**
	Absorption Costing			
Beginning inventory:				
Number of units	0	10 000	15 000	5000
Unit cost	—	$18	$20	$23
Total cost	—	$180,000	$300,000	$115,000
Ending inventory:				
Number of units	10 000	15 000	5000	0
Unit cost	$18	$20	$23	—
Total cost	$180,000	$300,000	$115,000	—
	Variable Costing			
Beginning inventory:				
Number of units	0	10 000	15 000	5000
Unit cost	—	$10	$12	$14
Total cost	—	$100,000	$180,000	$70,000
Ending inventory:				
Number of units	10 000	15 000	5000	0
Unit cost	$10	$12	$14	—
Total cost	$100,000	$180,000	$70,000	—

Figure 10-20
Again the sole difference in ending inventory values between variable and absorption costing are the fixed production costs assigned to absorption costing inventories. Here the amounts are $8 a unit in years 1 and 2 and $9 a unit in years 3 and 4.

Summary

Nonmanufacturing activities are an important part of the economy and require the same type of monitoring and control as manufacturing activities. Activities, such as order processing, invoice preparation, and keypunching, are repetitive and can be costed in much the same way as a manufactured product. Standards can be established for repetitive nonmanufacturing activities and timely variance reports can be prepared.

Nonrepetitive activities require cost control as well. Often costs are accumulated for specific segments of the firm. **Segmental reports** assist managers in evaluating performance in the various parts of the firm. As with other cost objectives, the basic approach in segmental cost reporting is to identify the cost objective, assign direct costs, and allocate the indirect costs. Full cost segmental reports use the basic full costing approach to cost determination.

An alternative method of segmental reporting uses the **contribution approach**. With this method the emphasis is on cost behaviour rather than functional cost classifications. Variable costs are subtracted from revenue to find the **contribution margin.** Fixed costs are deducted from the contribution margin to arrive at the **division** or **product contribution.** Advocates of the

Higgens II Industries, Ltd. Schedule of Fixed Overhead Costs Included in Beginning and Ending Inventory Under Absorption Costing				
	Year			
	1	**2**	**3**	**4**
Fixed MOH transferred into the period in beginning inventory	0	$ 80,000	$120,000	$45,000
Fixed MOH transferred out of the period in ending inventory	$80,000	120,000	45,000	0
Causes absorption costing net income to be	$80,000 higher	$ 40,000 higher	$ 75,000 lower	$45,000 lower

Figure 10-21

As with the earlier example, the total difference in net income in any given year is caused by the amount of fixed manufacturing costs transferred into the period through beginning inventory and out of the period through ending inventory.

contribution approach believe that this method provides managers with cost data that are more useful for decision making.

The contribution approach may be used for product costing as well as for segmental reporting. Products may be costed using **absorption costing,** sometimes called **full costing,** in which all production costs including fixed overhead costs are assigned to the product. Costs that are assigned to products are called **inventoriable costs.** With the contribution approach, only variable costs are assigned to products. Direct materials, direct labour, and variable manufacturing overhead constitute the product cost. All fixed overhead costs are expensed in the period in which they are incurred. This method of product costing is called **variable costing** or **direct costing.**

Differences in reported net income between variable and absorption costing occur because fixed overhead costs are carried from one accounting period to the next through ending inventory. If there are no beginning or ending inventories, the two costing methods yield identical net income, although the income statement format and information content are different.

List of important terms

absorption costing *(417)*
contribution approach *(411)*
contribution margin *(411)*
direct costing *(417)*
divisional contribution
  statement *(411)*

divisional income statement
  (409)
full costing *(408)*
manufacturing contribution
  margin *(403)*
nonmanufacturing statement
  (403)

product contribution
   statement *(412)* product
profitability
   statement *(409)*

sales region contribution
   statement *(414)*
segmental reports *(406)*
variable costing *(417)*

Questions

1. Costs for nonmanufacturing activities are of no concern to manufacturing firms. Comment.
2. Name some common nonmanufacturing activities.
3. What characteristics should an activity have in order for accountants to compute unit costs for the activity?
4. President to the controller, "Today I received a report from the standards setting committee indicating it was creating standards for our order processing department. Why? Aren't standards for manufacturing departments?" Respond to the president.
5. What is segmental reporting? Give some examples.
6. What are the basic functions in the segmental reporting process?
7. What is meant by the contribution approach to reporting?
8. How does a product contribution statement differ from a product profitability statement? Which is more useful?
9. A manager said to the chief cost accountant, "If contribution margin is so important, why do you bother to include fixed expenses in the contribution reports at all?" Answer for the chief cost accountant.
10. Describe absorption costing.
11. Describe variable costing.
12. Contribution margin and manufacturing contribution margin are the same thing. Comment.
13. What is the cause of a difference in net income between variable and absorption costing in any particular year?
14. What effect do fluctuating fixed and variable production costs have on the difference in the net income between variable and absorption costing?

Exercises

Ex. 10-1 **Costing service activities.** The Portage Amusement Company operates a series of amusement parks in Ontario. In an effort to control rising costs, management has undertaken a program of costing all activities. One activity, selling tickets for rides, is of particular interest because many managers thought of the activity as almost costless. At the top of the facing page are cost data for the last three-month period when 5 000 000 tickets were sold.

Required:
a. What is the cost of selling 10 000 tickets?

Wages of ticket sellers	$25,000
Printing cost per 1000 tickets	1
Depreciation and maintenance on ticket booths	2,500

b. If tickets sell for $.50 each, what is the cost of ticket selling expressed as a percentage of ticket revenue?

Ex. 10-2 Costing service activities. Westside Distillery has computerized all of its accounting, production, and marketing information systems. Keypunching of data is done internally by a keypunching department. Currently ten people—some part-time—are working in the department. There is one supervisor. Below are cost and output data for the keypunching department for the month of September.

Keypunchers' wages	$ 7,200
Supplies	3,600
Supervisory salary	1,600
Heat, light, and power	720
Depreciation on office space	400
Lease cost on equipment	1,600
Allocated corporate costs	2,880
	$18,000

Required:
a. Prepare a cost report for the keypunching activity, assuming there were 360 000 cards punched in September.
b. If Westside can get keypunching done outside the firm at a cost of 4.5¢ a card, should the company do so?

Ex. 10-3 Using service activity costs. Rugout Carpet Cleaning Company accumulates activity and cost data for its home rug-cleaning service. Activity is measured in square metres of rugs cleaned. Data for the fiscal year ended August 31 are presented below.

Square metres of rugs cleaned	120 000
Labour cost	$48,000
Cleaning compound	12,000
Other supplies	6,000
Depreciation on cleaning equipment	3,600
Insurance	2,400
Lease cost of company trucks used for home rug service	9,600
Other operating expenses	2,400

Required:

a. Prepare a cost report for the home rug-cleaning service using a square metres of rug as the unit for costing purposes.

b. If the average job size is 80 square metres of rug, what is the average cost of a job?

Ex. 10-4 **Labour variances for a service business.** The Fast-Tax Service Company prepares tax returns for the general public. Although there is a wide range in the complexity of the returns, the vast majority are very similar in form and degree of complexity. Consequently Fast-Tax management has the following labour standards for the preparation of returns:

	Standard Quantity	Standard Cost
Average preparation time	2 h	$9/h

Actual data from two regions for January to March show the following results:

	Region	
	Eastern	Midwest
Returns prepared	25 000	18 000
Hours worked	59 000	32 000
Salary expense	$566,400	$294,400

Required:

Prepare a labour variance report for each region.

Ex. 10-5 **Variable costing Income statement.** Below are data on the operation of Lopo Wagon Company for the year ending December 31, 1984

Units sold	60 000
Units manufactured	80 000
Selling price/unit	$ 12
Direct materials/unit	3
Direct labour	2
Variable MOH	2
Variable selling and administrative	1
Fixed manufacturing	140 000
Fixed selling and administrative	80 000
Normal capacity in units	80 000
No beginning inventory	

Required:
Prepare a variable costing income statement in good form.

Ex. 10-6   Absorption costing income statement. Refer to the data in Exercise 10-5 for the Lopo Wagon Company.

Required:
Prepare an absorption costing income statement in good form.

Ex. 10-7   Absorption and variable costing income statements for two years. During 1984, Exxo Corporation's first year of business, it manufactured 10 000 bottles of spray cologne. Fixed manufacturing costs were $10,000, variable manufacturing costs were $2/unit, and variable selling costs were $.20 per bottle sold. Sales for 1984 were 8000 bottles at $4/unit. In 1985 the number of units produced and the unit costs were the same as in 1984, but sales were 12 000 bottles at $4.20/unit. Fixed selling and administrative costs were $6,000 both years.

Required:
Prepare income statements for 1984 and 1985 using both variable and absorption costing.

Ex. 10-8   Absorption and variable costing income statements. Star Corporation has a maximum capacity of 360 000 solar-powered calculators per year, and a normal capacity of 250 000 units per year. Variable manufacturing costs are $14/unit, and variable selling and administrative expenses are $2/unit. Annual fixed manufacturing costs are $1,050,000/year, while fixed selling and administrative costs are $440,000/year. The sales price is $23/unit.

During 1984 the firm had a beginning inventory of 60 000 units, produced 220 000 units, and had total sales of 240 000 units. Assume beginning inventory costs are the same as 1984 production costs.

Required:
From this information provide in good form:

a. Income statement for 1984 using the absorption costing method.
b. Income statement for 1984 using the variable costing method.

Ex. 10-9   Variable and absorption costing income statements. Presented below are two years of sales and production data for Lynstrom, Inc., which uses FIFO inventory valuation.

Required:
a. Prepare a variable costing and an absorption costing income statement for both years.
b. Prepare a schedule that reconciles the net income between the two methods for both years.

	Year 1	Year 2
Production in units	100 000	30 000
Sales in units	50 000	100 000
Prime cost per unit	$ 11	$ 11
Variable MOH per unit	5	5
Variable selling and administrative	3	3
Fixed MOH	300,000	300,000
Fixed selling and administrative	100,000	100,000
Selling price per unit	30	30
Normal capacity in units	75,000	75,000
Beginning inventory in units	30,000*	8? 000

*Cost of beginning inventory is the same as the cost of production in year 1 for both direct costing and absorption costing.

Ex. 10-10 **Variable and absorption costing net income for two years.** Presented below are two years of sales and production data for Tree-Lite Industries, which uses FIFO inventory valuation. Normal production volume is 80 000 units.

	Year 1	Year 2
Production in units	80 000	60 000
Sales in units	50 000	80 000
Prime cost per unit	$ 13	$ 13
Variable MOH per unit	5	5
Variable selling and administrative	3	3
Fixed MOH	400,000	400,000
Fixed selling and administrative	300,000	300,000
Selling price per unit	40	40
Beginning inventory in units	30,000*	?

*Cost of beginning inventory is the same as the cost of production in year 1 for both the variable costing and absorption costing methods.

Required:

a. Complete the following schedule:

	Net Income	
	Year 1	Year 2
Variable costing	_____	_____
Absorption costing	_____	_____

b. Reconcile the difference in net income for year 2.

Problem Set A

P. 10A-1 Divisional income statement. The Halstead Boat Company produces and sells boats in two separate divisions, a canoe division and a fishing boat division. Below are divisional sales and cost data for the year.

	Division	
	Canoe	Fishing Boat
Units sales	1500	2000
Average unit selling price	$ 400	$ 700
Average unit manufacturing costs:		
Direct materials	120	240
Direct labour	50	80
Manufacturing overhead	50	120
Operating expenses:		
Marketing	80,000	140,000
Distribution	25,000	60,000
Administrative	60,000	110,000

Corporate expenses not directly identifiable with divisions are $140,000.

Required:
Prepare a full cost divisional income statement in good form.

P. 10A-2 Product profitability report. Product sales and cost data are presented below for the canoe division of the Halstead Boat Company mentioned in Problem 10A-1. The company produces three different canoes.

	Canoes		
	Lightweight	Standard	Camp
Unit sales	200	1000	300
Selling price	$ 380	$ 395	$ 430
Average unit manufacturing costs:			
Direct materials	90	117	150
Direct labour	59	47	54
Manufacturing overhead	59	47	54
Operating expenses:			
Marketing	3,800	19,750	6,450
Distribution	2,500	12,000	3,800
Administrative	8,000	16,000	8,000

Divisional expenses not identifiable with individual products are $84,700.

Required:
Prepare a product profitability report in good form.

P. 10A-3   Standard cost variance analysis for a service activity. The Smooth-water Water Softening Company has established standards for the installation of water softeners. Below are standard cost data and actual costs for the month of October.

Resource	Standard Quantity	Standard Cost
Copper pipe	30 m	$ .80/m
Salt pellets	102 kg	8.00/100 kg
Labour	4 h	9.00/h

Actual results: 125 installed

Resource	Actual Quantity	Actual Cost
Copper pipe	4000 m	$3,800
Salt pellets	12 000 kg	912
Labour	560 h	4 900

Required:

a. Prepare a variance analysis report for the month of October.

b. What is the standard cost for the installation of a water softener?

P. 10A-4   Variable and absorption costing over a four-year period. The Extra-Dri Spirits Company has always used traditional full costing methods to report net income. The company president has heard about variable costing and would like to know what effect variable costing would have on the company's reported net income. Normal capacity is 50 000 units. Below are four years of sales and cost data.

	Year 1	Year 2	Year 3	Year 4
Sales in units	50 000	50 000	50 000	50 000
Production in units	60 000	80 000	20 000	50 000
Fixed MOH	$400,000	$400,000	$400,000	$400,000
Fixed selling and administrative	$100,000	$100,000	$100,000	$100,000
Direct materials	$2/unit	$2/unit	$2/unit	$2/unit
Direct labour	$4/unit	$4/unit	$4/unit	$4/unit
Variable MOH	$4/unit	$4/unit	$4/unit	$4/unit
Variable selling and administrative	$3/unit	$3/unit	$3/unit	$3/unit
Unit price	$25	$25	$25	$25
Beginning inventory in units	0			

Required:

a. Prepare a schedule of product costs for the four years using variable and absorption costing.

b. Prepare a schedule of beginning and ending inventories for both methods for each of the four years.

c. Prepare a schedule of net income for the four-year period using both variable and absorption costing.

d. Prepare a schedule reconciling the difference in net income between the two methods.

P. 10A-5   **Using variable and absorption costing product cost data.** Wood-B-Gone Chain Saw Company manufactures a small chain saw that it sells through distributors. Below are sales and cost data for the most recent year of operations. Normal production and sales activity are 10 000 units. There is no beginning inventory.

	Variable	Fixed
Units produced	100 000	
Units sold	80 000	
Selling price per unit	$60	
Costs:	**Variable**	**Fixed**
Direct materials	$1,500,000	
Direct labour	1,100,000	
Production supervision		$ 120,000
Office salaries		300,000
Depreciation, production plant and equipment		450,000
Depreciation, office		120,000
Property taxes, 80% production facilities		100,000
Insurance, production facilities		20,000
Insurance, office		10,000
Indirect labour	160,000	140,000
Indirect material	70,000	50,000
Selling expense	200,000	250,000
Other administrative expenses		380,000
Utilities, 90% production facilities	300,000	100,000
Total costs	$3,330,000	$2,040,000

Required:

a. Calculate the cost of ending inventory using variable costing.

b. Calculate the cost of ending inventory using absorption costing.

c. Calculate the gross margin as a percentage of sales.

d. Calculate the contribution margin as a percentage of sales.

e. Find the difference in net income for the year between variable costing and absorption costing.

f. Calculate the net income for the year using variable costing.

P. 10A-6   **Quarterly product costs and income statements using variable and absorption costing.** Donaldson, Inc., has just completed its 1984 fiscal year, and the controller provides you with the following data:

	Quarter			
	1	2	3	4
Units produced	75 000	35 000	75 000	40 000
Units sold	50 000	60 000	60 000	45 000
Sales price/unit	$20	$22	$22	$25
Direct material/unit	4	3	3	5
Direct labour/unit	6	8	7	7
Variable MOH/unit	3	4	4	5

Fixed manufacturing overhead costs were $200,000 for each of the four quarters, and normal capacity is 50 000 units a quarter. Variable selling and administrative expenses totaled 4 percent of the sales price. Fixed selling and administrative expenses were $50,000 for each of the first two quarters and $40,000 for each of the last two quarters. Assume no beginning inventory for the year.

Required:
a. Prepare a schedule of the product costs for each quarter using variable and absorption costing.
b. Prepare a schedule of beginning and ending inventories for each quarter.
c. Prepare quarterly income statements using both variable and absorption costing.
d. Prepare a schedule reconciling the differences in net income between the two methods.

Problem Set B

P. 10B-1   **Divisional contribution statement.** The Melotone Musical Instruments Company manufactures stringed musical instruments in two divisions, the guitar division and the violin division. Sales and cost data are presented below for the fiscal year ended September 30.

Corporate expenses not identifiable with divisions are $14,000.

Required:
Prepare a divisional contribution statement for the Melotone Musical Instruments Company.

	Division	
	Guitar	**Violin**
Units sold	1000	250
Average unit sales price	$ 300	$ 600
Average unit variable costs:		
Manufacturing	120	220
Marketing	27	55
Distribution	13	30
Administrative	5	5
Fixed expenses identifiable with divisions:		
Manufacturing	$54,000	$26,000
Marketing	16,000	9,500
Distribution	8,000	3,000
Administrative	19,000	16,000

P. 10B-2 **Product contribution analysis.** Melotone Musical Instruments Company prepares product contribution analysis reports on a monthly basis. Below are product sales and cost data for September for the guitar division.

	Type of Guitar	
	Melotone Standard	**Melotone Classic**
Unit sales	800	200
Selling price	$ 225	$ 600
Unit variable costs:		
Manufacturing	90	240
Marketing	18	63
Distribution	10	25
Administrative	5	5
Fixed expenses identifiable with products:		
Manufacturing	$30,000	$16,000
Marketing	6,000	8,000
Distribution	2,500	2,000
Administrative	3,000	2,000

Divisional expenses not identifiable with individual products are $27,500.

Required:

Prepare a product contribution statement for the guitar division of Melotone.

P. 10B-3 **Sales region contribution analysis.** Melotone Musical Instruments Company divides its marketing effort into three sales regions. The sales regions have varying marketing, distribution, and administrative expenses. Below are relevant data for the Melotone Standard guitar in the three regions. Refer to Problem 10B-2 for manufacturing costs and selling price.

	Sales Region		
	Northern	Southern	Western
Unit sales	100	300	400
Variable expenses:			
Marketing	$ 24	$ 20	$ 15
Distribution	20	8	9
Administrative	9	5	4
Fixed expenses:			
Marketing	$4,000	$8,000	$10,000
Distribution	2,000	2,500	3,000
Administrative	1,000	1,000	2,000

Fixed expenses identifiable with the Melotone Standard guitar, but not identifiable with sales regions, are $8,000.

Required:
Prepare a sales region contribution analysis for the Melotone Standard guitar.

P. 10B-4   Variable and absorption costing net income and inventory costs.
DCG Limited manufactures a quality three-person rubber raft. Below are two years of production and sales data.

	Year 1	Year 2
Sales in units	50 000	50 000
Production in units	80 000	30 000
Unit selling price	$ 68	$ 68
Fixed manufacturing	$1,200,000	$1,200,000
Fixed selling	300,000	300,000
Fixed administrative	400,000	400,000
Prime costs per unit	10	10
Variable MOH per unit	6	6
Variable selling per unit	4	4
Variable administrative per unit	2	2
Beginning inventory in units	20,000	?

Variable administrative expense varies with production, whereas variable selling expense varies with units sold. Beginning inventory has unit variable manufacturing costs of $15 and allocated fixed manufacturing overhead costs of $22 per unit. Normal capacity is 50 000 units. Use FIFO inventory.

Required:
a. What is the total cost of ending inventory in year 1 using (1) variable costing, (2) absorption costing?
b. What is the difference in net income in year 1 between variable and absorption costing and why did it occur?
c. Prepare a variable costing and an absorption costing income statement in good form for year 2.

P. 10B-5   Using absorption and variable costing information. Below is a partial listing of sales and cost data for Leadville Manufacturing, Ltd.

Sales (25 000 units)	$1,250,000
Direct materials	240,000
Direct labour	180,000
Variable MOH	120,000
Fixed MOH	270,000
Variable selling expense	90,000
Fixed selling expense	150,000
Fixed administrative expense	290,000

Production this year equaled the normal level of 30 000 units. There was no beginning inventory.

Required:
a. What is the cost of ending inventory using variable costing?
b. What is the cost of ending inventory using absorption costing?
c. What is Leadville's gross margin on sales?
d. What is Leadville's manufacturing contribution margin as a percentage of sales?
e. What is Leadville's contribution margin as a percentage of sales?
f. What is the difference in net income between variable and absorption costing this year?

P. 10B-6   Comprehensive variable and absorption costing problem. Grogen Industries manufactures depth finders used primarily by fishermen. The product is sold to retail establishments. Normal production and sales levels are 20 000 units a year. Early in 1984 the company's union contract expired. A long strike ensued that lasted into the spring of 1985. Anticipating the strike, Grogen used a lot of overtime in 1983 to accumulate a large inventory by the time the strike occurred. The management of Grogen has always used absorption costing for financial reporting. There is some interest, however, in knowing what effect direct costing would have on reported income, particularly during unusual times, such as the long strike. Presented below are sales and cost data for the years 1982–1986.

	1982	1983	1984	1985	1986
Production in units	20 000	35 000	1 000	15 000	20 000
Sales in units	20 000	20 000	20 000	20 000	20 000
Selling price	$ 45	$ 48	$ 50	$ 52	$ 56
Prime cost	10	13	11	12	13
Variable MOH	6	6	7	7	8
Variable selling and administrative	4	4	5	5	6
Fixed MOH	$210,000	$210,000	$180,000	$240,000	$280,000
Fixed selling and administrative	200,000	200,000	200,000	210,000	240,000

Beginning inventory in 1982 was 10 000 units with an absorption cost of $245,000. With variable costing the inventory cost was $150,000.

Required:

a. Prepare a schedule of product costs for the five-year period using both variable and absorption costing.

b. Prepare a schedule of beginning and ending inventories using both variable and absorption costing.

c. Prepare income statements in schedule form for the years 1982–1986 using both variable and absorption costing.

d. Prepare a schedule to reconcile the difference between variable and absorption costing net income.

Minicases

Minicase 10-1   (CICA adapted)

POR, Ltd., sells two different products in three different regions. The products are made at a single factory, where all fixed costs are incurred. Fixed costs are allocated equally per unit to both products. Costs incurred by regions are all variable. Both products are in quite competitive markets, but the regions can set their own selling prices in accordance with local costs and market conditions.

The company's accountant decided to do an analysis to help determine whether the company's net income ($47,000 last month) could be improved. He first constructed the following matrix of last month's sales in units:

MATRIX I	Region 1	Region 2	Region 3	Total
Product A	10 000	20 000	10 000	40 000
Product B	30 000	10 000	20 000	60 000
Total	40 000	30 000	30 000	100 000

He then gathered the following data for last month:

Total sales revenue last month	$1,457,500
Total costs last month	1,410,500
Net income last month	$ 47,000

The accountant then constructed the following matrix:

MATRIX II	Region 1	Region 2	Region 3
Product A			
Selling price per unit	$12.00	$11.00	$15.00
Total cost per unit	14.25	10.30	12.40
Net income (loss) per unit	(2.25)	.70	2.60
Product B			
Selling price per unit	16.00	14.75	17.00
Total cost per unit	16.05	13.85	15.90
Net income (loss) per unit	(.05)	.90	1.10

Looking at this matrix, the accountant decided that it was clear that Product A should no longer be sold in Region 1 because the loss per unit is quite large. So hypothetically discontinuing Product A in Region 1, he recalculated total unit costs and income and discovered that the company's net income would indeed improve, by $7,500, but that, according to his analysis, the loss per unit of Product B in Region 1 would now increase.

Therefore, it seemed Product B should also be discontinued in Region 1, shutting down Region 1 altogether. However, if this were done the company's net income would decline from $54,500 to $11,000, and when total costs per unit were recalculated the unit costs of both products in Region 2 would exceed their selling prices. But if Region 2 were also shut down the company's net income would become a loss because the total costs per unit of both products in the remaining region, Region 3, would exceed their selling prices.

Thus it was obvious from the analysis that the company should go out of business altogether, yet its net income last month was $47,000! The accountant, in frustration, gave up his analysis.

Required:
a. In a few words, explain precisely what was conceptually wrong with the accountant's analysis. Do not use numbers in your answer.
b. Which, if any, products should probably be discontinued in which regions? Submit your answer in tabular form showing how you evaluated each of the six product/region combinations.

Reprinted, with permission, from Uniform Final Examination, 1974, published by the Canadian Institute of Chartered Accountants, Toronto, Canada.

Minicase 10-2

The Fable of the Accountant and the President*

ACT I:
Once upon a time a company was operating at a loss. Although its plant had a normal capacity of 30 000 widgets, it was selling only 10 000 a year, and its operating figures looked like this:

Price per unit	$ 1.00
Total fixed cost	6,000.00
Fixed manufacturing cost per unit	.60
Variable cost per unit	.65
Total unit cost	1.25
Total manufacturing cost	12,500.00
Cost of closing inventory	—
Cost of goods sold	12,500.00
Sales revenue	10,000.00
Operating loss	2,500.00

ACT II:
Then one day a bearded stranger came to the board of directors and said "Make me president, pay me half of any operating income I produce, and I'll make you all millionaires."

"Done," they said.

So the bearded stranger set the factory running at full capacity, making 30 000 widgets a year. His figures looked like this:

*Source unknown.

Total fixed cost	$ 6,000.00
Fixed manufacturing cost per unit	.20
Variable unit cost	.65
Total unit cost	.85
Total manufacturing cost	25,500.00
Cost of closing inventory	17,000.00
Cost of goods sold	8,500.00
Sales revenue	10,000.00
Operating income	1,500.00

"Pay me," said the bearded stranger. "But we're going broke," said the directors.

"Oh!" said the stranger. "You can read the income figures, can't you? You have never been more profitable!"

ACT III:

But just as everything seemed lost, an accountant in a gleaming eyeshade charged into the room.

"Hold," he cried. "I have just changed to the system called *variable costing*. We charge only variable manufacturing costs to inventory. So now the figures look like this:

Variable cost per unit	$ .65
Cost of manufacturing 30 000 units	19,500.00
Cost of closing inventory	13,000.00
Variable cost of goods sold	6,500.00
Sales revenue	10,000.00
Contribution margin	
(Here's where the trick comes in; we'll explain later.)	3,500.00
Total fixed costs	$ 6,000.00
Operating loss	$ 2,500.00

So the bearded stranger was foiled and the directors are once again looking for a way to earn income—and to sell off the inventory the stranger left them with.

Required:

Given the above information, prepare two income statements—one using absorption costing, the other variable costing—and reconcile the income figures of the bearded stranger and the accountant.

Minicase 10-3

(CMA Examination Question)

The vice president for sales of New Brunswick, Ltd., has received the Income Statement for November 1983. The statement has been prepared on the variable cost basis and is reproduced below. The firm has just adopted a variable costing system for internal reporting purposes.

New Brunswick Limited **Income Statement for the month of November 1983** **($000 omitted)**		
Sales		$2,400
Less: Variable standard cost of goods sold		1,200
Manufacturing margin		$1,200
Less: Fixed manufacturing costs at budget	$600	
Fixed manufacturing cost spending variance	0	600
Gross margin		$ 600
Less: Fixed selling and administrative costs		400
Net income before taxes		$ 200

The controller attached the following notes to the statements.

1. The unit sales price for November averaged $24.
2. The standard unit manufacturing costs for the month were:

Variable cost	$12
Fixed cost	4
	$16

The unit rate for fixed manufacturing costs is a predetermined rate based upon a normal monthly production of 150 000 units.
3. Production for November was 45 000 units in excess of sales.
4. The inventory at November 30 consisted of 80 000 units.

Required:
a. The vice president for sales is not comfortable with the variable cost basis and wonders what the net income would have been under the prior absorption cost basis.

   i. Present the November Income Statement on an absorption cost basis.

   ii. Reconcile and explain the difference between the variable costing and the absorption costing net income figures.
b. Explain the features associated with variable cost income measurement that should be attractive to the vice president for sales.

Minicase 10-4   (CMA Examination Question)

Quebec, Ltd., is a manufacturer of electrical components. The company maintains a significant inventory of a broad range of finished goods because it has built its business upon prompt shipments of any stock item.

The company manufactured all items it sold until recently when it discontinued the manufacturing of five items. The items were dropped from the manufacturing process because the unit costs computed by the company's absorption cost system did not provide a sufficient margin to cover shipping and selling costs. The five items are now purchased from other manufacturers at a price which allows Quebec, Ltd., to make a very small profit after shipping and selling costs. Quebec, Ltd., keeps these items in its product line in order to offer a complete line of electrical components.

The president, M. Claud Turgot, is disappointed in recent profitability performance. He thought that the switch from manufacture to purchase for the five items would improve profit performance. However, the reverse has occurred. All other factors affecting profits-sales volume, sales prices, and incurred selling and manufacturing costs were as expected, so the profit problem can be traced to this decision. The president has asked the controller's department to reevaluate the financial effects of the decision.

The task was assigned to Madame Barr, a recently hired assistant controller. She has reviewed the data used to reach the decision to purchase rather than manufacture. Her conclusion is that the company should have continued to manufacture the item. In her opinion the incorrect decision was made because absorption cost data rather than variable cost data were used to make the decision.

Required:
a. Explain what features of variable costing as compared to absorption costing make it possible for her conclusion to be correct.
b. For internal measurement purposes compare the income, return on investment, and inventory values under absorption costing and variable costing for periods where
   i. inventory quantities are rising
   ii. inventory quantities are declining
   iii. inventory quantities are stable
c. What advantages arc said to accrue to decision making if variable costing is used?

Minicase 10-5

Charles Adams, accountant, and his staff were recently sent to the offices of a new client, a manufacturer of furniture. Charles Adams's firm had been engaged to perform an audit for the year ended August 31, 1983. E, Ltd., has not had an audit before, and its unaudited financial statements and income tax returns for previous years were prepared by an external accountant. In the course of the audit, one of Charles Adams's junior staff raised the following points with Charles Adams: "E, Ltd., uses a standard cost system based on standards set for maximum efficiency. It also employs direct costing for fixed factory overhead. Won't we have to convert their cost of goods sold to actual costs and closing inventory to the lower of actual costs or replacement costs? That will be a big job! If we don't, we'll have to qualify our report as to the valuation of closing inventory—and the client doesn't want this. And didn't we give the client a rough estimate of the cost of an audit? He'll have to do the converting schedules for us. We'll lose money on the job if we have to do them. . . ."

Charles Adams asked his junior staff member to wait for an answer until the matter could be discussed with the client. Charles Adams thereupon raised the issue with the client and received the following response:

"Look, Revenue Canada has accepted that we cost our inventory at standard, using direct costs for income tax purposes; I'm certainly not going to change them and have to pay more income taxes. We need the cash for expansion. Also, we set up our present costing system for our internal uses. We need the variances in order to judge foremen's performance, and direct costing helps with pricing, and so on. We can't operate without the system, and I'm not going to mess it up for an auditor. Besides, our accounting staff is grossly overworked and cannot handle more needless bookkeeping. I think that you are being unreasonable and are ignoring the basics of what makes this business successful."

Required:
As Charles Adams, what response would you give to your client? What additional comments would you give to your junior staff member?

Reprinted, with permission, from Uniform Final Examination, 1977, published by the Canadian Institute of Chartered Accountants, Toronto, Canada.

Chapter 11

Decentralized Operations and Responsibility Accounting

This chapter deals specifically with the measurement of performance of business segments and incorporates many of the cost and performance reporting concepts of previous chapters. It addresses the problem of measuring segmental performance when there is a lot of business activity between segments of a firm. When you have completed this chapter, you should understand:

1 The concepts of decentralization and the reasons for decentralizing.

2 The nature and purpose of responsibility accounting.

3 The types of responsibility centres and when each is used.

4 How to prepare various responsibility reports.

5 The role of transfer pricing in performance reports.

6 The computation and use of the different types of transfer prices.

In many small organizations decision making is characterized by one individual making virtually all the important decisions. As an organization grows, it becomes difficult, even impossible, for a single person to make all decisions. Instead some decisions must be delegated to other managers by giving them authority over a given area of operations. For example, the owner of a small variety store employing four salesclerks may make all purchasing, pricing, advertising, personnel, and other decisions. As the store grows into a department store, some of the inventory purchasing decisions are assigned to department heads because the owner cannot be knowledgeable about all product lines sold in the store and must devote more time to the growing amount of accounting data and to financial planning. When a new store is opened in a neighbouring town, the new store manager may be assigned authority to make even more decisions. With authority comes responsibility, which means that managers are held accountable for their decisions. Ideally, managers are granted decision authority commensurate with their responsibility.

Decentralization defined

The need to delegate decision authority and responsibility to subordinates occurs because as organizations grow, centralized decision making can become unwieldy. Often it becomes necessary to separate the organization into more manageable units. This separation is known as **decentralization.** Managers of decentralized operations are given decision authority and must be held responsible for the results of their decisions. An important function of managerial accounting in decentralized organizations is reporting the performance of managers. The term **responsibility accounting** refers to the accounting process that reports how well managers meet their responsibility.

The purpose of this chapter is to introduce the concepts of decentralization and responsibility accounting. Many costing concepts from previous chapters and income measurement concepts from financial accounting are utilized in the discussion of responsibility reporting. Some of the more common responsibility accounting reports are illustrated and practical problems are discussed. We also cover transfer pricing, which can cause major difficulties in divisional performance measurement.

Responsibility accounting

Responsibility accounting rests on the premise that individuals should be held accountable for their performance and the performance of their subordinates. This concept guides accountants in the accumulation and reporting of operating results by areas of responsibility. Responsibility accounting embodies a number of important assumptions:

Assumptions embodied in responsibility accounting

1. Managers should be held responsible for the activities occurring in the area of the organization over which they exercise control.
2. Managers should strive to meet the goals and objectives established for them and for their segment of the organization.
3. Managers should participate in establishing the goals against which their performance is measured.
4. Goals should be attainable with efficient and effective performance.
5. Performance reports and feedback to managers should be timely.
6. It should be clearly stated what role responsibility accounting plays in the company's reward structure.

For small organizations responsibility reporting may have little importance, but as firms get larger, control and evaluation become more difficult. In such situations decentralization and responsibility accounting are beneficial because:

Benefits of decentralization and responsibility accounting systems

1. Organizations are separated into units of manageable size.
2. Decisions are made at the level at which managers are uniquely aware of the problems and information relevant to the decision.
3. Decisions can be made on a more timely basis.
4. Managers' morale and level of job satisfaction are higher because of their active participation in decision making.
5. Responsibility centre managers have an opportunity to gain valuable managerial skills that in turn provide the firm with a pool of potential top management personnel.
6. Managers are motivated to act in a manner most beneficial to the firm.

Types of responsibility centres

Responsibility centres can be classified in a variety of ways. In general, however, three classifications are commonly used:

1. Cost centre
2. Profit centre
3. Investment centre

The type of responsibility centre used for responsibility accounting depends on the type of business situation. The report should measure appropriately the performance of responsibility centre managers. For example, if a manager is responsible for the costs of a department but has no control over revenues, the responsibility report should be limited to costs and should not include profits. Below we discuss the nature of the different types of responsibility centres.

Cost centres

A **cost centre** is a segment of an organization in which managers are held responsible for the costs incurred in the segment. Cost centre managers have control over some or all of the costs in their segment of the business, but not over revenues. Cost centres are the most widely used form of responsibility centre because many different types of organizational segments can be identified as cost centres. For example, an entire marketing department, a sales region, or a single sales representative can be defined as a cost centre.

To illustrate further, the customer service department of a retail store provides valuable services that help generate and maintain profits. The fact that the customer service department is an important element in the successful operation of the store does not change the fact that it is difficult, if not impossible, to measure the effect of the department on profits. Consequently, a customer service department should be viewed as a cost centre, since this may be the only logical basis for responsibility reporting. The most important characteristic of a cost centre is that costs **controllable** by the management of the cost centre can be identified because the managers of cost centres are held responsible for the costs over which they have control.

Managers are held responsible for the costs incurred in their segment of the organization

It seems reasonable to expect cost centre managers to accept responsibility for the costs that they or their subordinates control. However, it is not always easy to identify costs with individual cost centres. The problem of determining what costs should be charged to cost centres is a critical problem in evaluating cost centre managers, and it certainly influences the control of corporate costs in general. The importance of this topic is underlined by the attention it has been given by accounting organizations. The Committee on Cost Concepts and Standards of the American Accounting Association considered this problem and formulated the following guides for deciding what costs should appropriately be charged to responsibility centre managers:

1. The person having authority over both the acquisition and the use of the service should be charged with the cost of such service.
2. The persons who can significantly influence the amount of cost through their own action may be charged with such costs.
3. Persons who cannot significantly influence the amount of cost through their own direct action may be charged with those elements with which the management desires them to be concerned, so that they will help to influence those who are responsible.[1]

As mentioned earlier, one desired benefit from decentralization and a responsibility accounting system is the motivation of managers to act in a way most beneficial to the firm as a whole. Thus costs should be identified and assigned in a way that has the most desired impact on employee motivation. The American Accounting Association Committee on Cost Concepts and Standards commented on this problem:

> The basis of measurement used in providing cost data for control is often a matter of management discretion and an important consideration in motivation. Different bases may significantly affect the way in which different individuals are motivated. For this reason, the basis of measurement selected should be consistent with the type of motivation desired. For example, different types of motivation may result when maintenance costs are charged to a responsibility centre on the basis of: (1) a rate per maintenance labour hour, (2) a rate per job, or (3) a single amount per month.[2]

Cost responsibility is so common in organizations that it forms a large portion of managerial accounting reports. For example, departmental product cost reports frequently are used for both product costing and for the evaluation of managers. Similarly a major use of the variance analysis reports discussed in Chapter 8 is the evaluation of managers based on cost responsibility. The number and variety of cost responsibility reports is very large. One example of a cost responsibility report is presented in Figure 11-1. In this example a

---

[1]"Committee on Cost Concepts and Standards," *Accounting Review*, April 1956, p. 189.
[2]Ibid.

Marine Products Production Division Divisional Performance Report For the Fiscal Year Ended October 31			
Department	**Standard Costs**	**Actual Costs**	**Variance**
Machining	$ 540,000	$ 620,000	$ 80,000
Welding	380,000	440,000	60,000
Assembly	450,000	480,000	30,000
Finishing	190,000	160,000	(30,000)
Painting	220,000	200,000	(20,000)
Total	$1,780,000	$1,900,000	$120,000

Marine Products Assembly Department Departmental Performance Report For the Fiscal Year Ended October 31			
Cost Item	**Standard Costs**	**Actual Costs**	**Variance**
Direct materials	$200,000	$245,000	$45,000
Direct labour	160,000	150,000	(10,000)
Manufacturing overhead	90,000	85,000	(5,000)
Total	$450,000	$480,000	$30,000

Figure 11-1
Segmental reports are prepared with the level of detail required by the managers using the reports. The total variances used in the divisional performance report are separated into variances by cost component in the departmental reports. Even more detail might be used in reporting the activities of a particular production operation within a department.

summarized variance report is shown at the top of the figure for each of five production departments of the Marine Products Company's Production Division. The bottom portion of the report shows the production variances for each cost element for the assembly department of the Production Division. In practice a complete set of departmental production reports is prepared. In addition, detailed variance reports are prepared for each product. Each report is at least part of the basis for managerial cost performance measurement.

Profit centres

Both cost and revenue responsibility

A **profit centre** is a segment of a business in which managers are held responsible for both costs and revenues. A profit centre may be viewed as a business within a business. The chief aim of the business as a whole—earning a profit—is also the main concern of each profit centre manager. Ideally if each of the profit centres optimizes its profits, then the profit of the firm as a whole will be optimized. However, the idea that each division maximizing its own profits will lead to maximizing the profits of the entire company is not necessarily true. Sometimes the maximization of profits by one division causes harm to another division. If interdivisional activities are impaired by profit-maximizing actions of divisions, the entire company may suffer.

Many departments or other segments of a business do not have the necessary characteristics to be evaluated as profit centres. For example, the home appliance department of a department store may be treated as a profit centre, since both costs and revenues are identifiable with the department and to a large degree controllable by departmental personnel and management. The key is to determine the type and amount of authority and responsibility that is assigned to a responsibility centre manager and to develop the type of responsibility reports that best measure the performance of the manager. Three criteria should be present for a company to have decentralized profit responsibility:

Criteria for profit responsibility

1. It must have two or more units for which separable measures of revenue and expense are obtained.
2. The management of these units must have considerable control over the units' expense and revenue. (Presumably authority to influence profit must accompany any true responsibility for the size of the profit.)
3. Each unit's profit must be calculated and reported regularly to top management, and the results of this calculation must be considered by top management as part of its evaluation of the unit's performance.[3]

The calculation of a profit centre's profit is very similar to the calculation of profit for an individual firm. The primary difference is that there are often some costs that are difficult to identify with individual profit centres because the costs are common to several profit centres. For example, some of the costs of corporate administration, research and development, and centralized computer services may be common to all of the divisions of the firm. These common costs are sometimes allocated to each of the profit centres, but if the allocations are made arbitrarily, the resulting profit figures may not be very useful. Consequently, divisional profit reports often present profit before allocation of corporate common costs and then profit after allocations have been computed and made.

Dealing with common costs

Figure 11-2 illustrates a divisional income statement of a company with three profit centres. All expenses specifically identifiable with a particular division are deducted from the division's sales revenue to find divisional net income before allocated corporate expenses are deducted. Next, corporate expenses common to the three divisions are allocated to each division using a logical allocation base. In this case the relative amount of sales is used to allocate common costs to each division. For instance, Division X had 45 percent of total company sales. Therefore, $36,000 of administrative expense and $18,000 of research and development expense, representing 45 percent of the total amount of each cost, are allocated to Division X. Notice that Division X has the highest dollar sales volume and the second-highest divisional net income before allocation of corporate common costs, but after the allocation

---

[3]John Mauriel and Robert Anthony, "Misevaluation of Investment Center Performance," *Harvard Business Review*, March–April, 1966, p. 99.

Ramjet Fuel Corporation Divisional Income Statement For the Fiscal Year Ended October 31				
	Division			**Company Total**
	X	**Y**	**Z**	
Sales	$450,000	$250,000	$300,000	$1,000,000
Less: Cost of goods sold	225,000	88,000	105,000	418,000
Gross margin	$225,000	$162,000	$195,000	$ 582,000
Less: Operating expenses:				
Advertising	$ 26,000	$ 15,000	$ 23,000	$ 64,000
Commissions	18,000	11,000	9,000	38,000
Rent	20,000	18,000	8,000	46,000
Salaries	90,000	70,000	60,000	220,000
Utilities	12,000	8,000	4,000	24,000
Divisional net income	$ 59,000	$ 40,000	$ 91,000	$ 190,000
Less: Allocated corporate expenses:				
Administrative	$ 36,000	$ 20,000	$ 24,000	$ 80,000
Research and development	18,000	10,000	12,000	40,000
Before-tax net income	$ 5,000	$ 10,000	$ 55,000	$ 70,000
Income tax (40%)	2,000	4,000	22,000	28,000
Net income	$ 3,000	$ 6,000	$ 33,000	$ 42,000

Figure 11-2
A profit centre manager directs a business within a business. The key ingredient
in establishing successful profit centres is that authority is commensurate with
responsibility. Typically comparison of profit centre performance is most
meaningful if allocated corporate expenses are excluded from the analysis.

Division X has the lowest profit. Shifts in relative profit performance caused
by common cost allocations should be viewed with caution. For example,
Division X covers $54,000 (that is, $36,000 + $18,000) in allocated corporate
expenses. If Division X were eliminated, the remaining two divisions would
have an additional $54,000 expense to cover before any profit was earned.

**Investment
centres**

*Performance
measurement based
on rate of return on
investment*

An **investment centre** is a segment of a business in which managers are held
responsible for the return on the resources invested in the segment. Many
people feel that a profit figure alone is not a good measure of a division's
performance because the amount of assets invested in a division are ignored.
Large and small divisions are viewed with one primary measure, dollar amount
of profits. However, the profit figure may be viewed in a different perspective.
To illustrate the problem and potential solution, assume that Division A reports
an annual profit of $100,000 and Division B reports a profit of $50,000 for the
same year. It appears that the management of A performed better than the

management of B. However, Division A has $1,000,000 in assets and Division B has $200,000 in assets. Division A has a return on assets of 10 percent, whereas Division B's return is 25 percent. This kind of situation gives rise to the extension of profit centres to investment centres.

In an investment centre the evaluation emphasis shifts from the profit figure to a measure of rate of return. The computation of an investment centre's rate of return on assets is simple.

$$\text{Return on assets} = \frac{\text{Investment centre earning}}{\text{Investment centre assets}}$$

For example, if earnings are $60,000 and assets are $400,000, the rate of return on investment is $60,000/$400,000 = 15 percent. Clearly the division's profit figure is a basic element in calculating the investment centre's rate of return, and the problems of isolating revenues and expenses are still of great importance. The other basic element in calculating an investment centre's rate of return is the investment base. Many different investment bases may be used, including the following:

Common investment bases

1. Total gross assets, which includes all assets of the division without regard to contra asset accounts, such as accumulated depreciation.
2. Total net assets, which includes all assets of the division less any contra asset accounts.
3. Total net assets employed, which includes all of the division's net assets that are employed in the production of divisional profit. Investments and other nonoperating assets are excluded from this base.
4. Stockholders' equity, which highlights the return to investors and includes contributed capital as well as earnings retained in the business. This asset base is applicable only to wholly owned subsidiaries if they are operated as a division of the parent company.
5. Others. Almost any other measure of investment base can be used if it is deemed appropriate by management. Working capital and fixed assets are two examples of other possible bases for measuring return on investment.

Clearly many different return on investment figures can be calculated for a single investment centre depending upon which investment base is selected. To illustrate, we use the example of the Downtown Department Store, which is a wholly owned subsidiary corporation of Consolidated Department Stores. Downtown is operated as a division of Consolidated, which uses return on investment (ROI) as a measure of divisional performance, but the firm is not certain which investment base should be used. The trial balance for the Downtown division is found in Figure 11-3.

Income is computed first and an asset base is selected

The first step is to compute the divisional net income. Here it is simply $1,000,000 revenue less $800,000 in expenses, yielding a net income of $200,000. Next, an investment base must be chosen. In the department store example all of the investment bases are illustrated in the order in which they were described.

Downtown Department Store Trial Balance October 31, 1983		
	Debit	Credit
Cash	$ 25,000	
Accounts receivable	75,000	
Merchandise inventory	250,000	
Land held for investment	100,000	
Building	500,000	
Accumulated depreciation, building		$ 250,000
Equipment	200,000	
Accumulated depreciation, equipment		150,000
Patents	50,000	
Accounts payable		40,000
Taxes payable		10,000
Mortgage payable		50,000
Capital stock		250,000
Retained earnings		250,000
Sales		1,000,000
Cost of goods sold	450,000	
Advertising expenses	50,000	
Commissions expenses	80,000	
Machine rental expenses	40,000	
Insurance expenses	20,000	
Salaries expenses	120,000	
Utilities expenses	40,000	
Total	$2,000,000	$2,000,000

Figure 11-3
This is the year-end trial balance of a department store that is a wholly owned subsidiary of Consolidated Department Stores. The subsidiary is operated as a division of the parent company.

Total gross assets. An investment base that is easy to use and understand is gross assets. This base includes all asset accounts without deducting contra asset accounts, such as accumulated depreciation. The investment base is found by adding up the balances in the asset accounts of the division. For Downtown Department Store the total assets are $1,200,000. The return on investment using gross assets is

$$\text{ROI} = \frac{\text{Net income}}{\text{Investment base}} = \frac{\$200,000}{\$1,200,000} = 16.67\%$$

Total net assets. Sometimes a more useful measure of investment base is total net assets, particularly when facilities are old and almost fully depreciated. The asset base is computed by totaling the balances in the asset accounts and subtracting the balances in the contra asset accounts. For Downtown Department Store total net assets are $1,200,000 minus the two accumulated depreciation accounts of $250,000 and $150,000, or $800,000. The rate of return on investment for total net assets is as follows:

$$ROI = \frac{\$200,000}{\$800,000} = 25\%$$

Total net assets employed. Occasionally a division owns assets that are not used in the normal productive activities of the division. For example, a company may invest excess cash in land that it intends to sell in several years. If such assets constitute a relatively large amount of total assets, they may distort the division's rate of return on the amount invested in operations of the division. To eliminate the problem, the asset base may be limited to assets employed in normal operating activities. To illustrate, assume Downtown's ROI is based on net assets employed. Net assets are $800,000, but that amount includes $100,000 of land held for investment that is not used in the division's normal activities as a department store. Therefore, the investment base using net assets employed is $800,000 minus $100,000, or $700,000, and the rate of return on net assets employed is

$$ROI = \frac{\$200,000}{\$700,000} = 28.6\%$$

Stockholders' equity. A popular measure of investment base is stockholders' equity. It is composed of contributed capital and earnings retained in the business. Depending on the organization of the firm, stockholders' equity may or may not be a possible investment base. For example, a department or other segment of an organization does not have its own owners' equity accounts. Instead, only the corporation as a whole has owners' equity. Downtown Department Store is a wholly owned subsidiary of Consolidated Department Stores and is operated as a divisional investment centre. Here stockholders' equity consists of capital stock and retained earnings totaling $500,000. The return on stockholders' equity is

$$ROI^* = \frac{\$200,000}{\$500,000} = 40\%$$

Other bases. Many other investment base measures are possible. Management should use whatever measure is most useful for such purposes as performance appraisal and decision making. For example, rapidly rising costs of production facilities or other major assets may render historical cost asset values meaningless as measures of investment bases for return on investment performance appraisal. To illustrate, assume that Downtown Department Store estimates a current market value of $2,500,000 for its assets. The return on investment using current market values is

$$ROI = \frac{\$200,000}{\$2,500,000} = 8\%$$

The rate of return based on current market values is dramatically different from the rate using total net assets, which is a historical cost measure.

*For convenience sake we use the beginning balance in owners' equity to compute the ROI. The ending balance or an average of the beginning and ending balance in owners' equity can be used also.

This type of measurement problem is very common among firms with heavy fixed cost investments. In recent years the cost of building a facility has doubled every three or four years in some areas of the country, and the current values of many facilities are many times higher than book value, or even original cost, for some plant assets.

Residual income

Residual income: income in excess of a target rate of return or target profit

The **residual income** method is a form of investment centre analysis. With residual income management establishes a desired or target rate of return for the division, and income above that amount is the residual income. Divisional management is evaluated on the amount of the division's residual income. To illustrate, assume the target net income for Downtown Department Store is 20 percent on total net assets. Total net assets are $800,000, so the target net income is $800,000 × .2 = $160,000. The residual income for the store is

Actual net income − Target net income = Residual income

$200,000   − $160,000   = $40,000

Residual income is a combination of the investment centre concept and the profit centre concept. An investment base is used as a part of the analysis, but the residual income figures may still be difficult to evaluate in comparing several divisions. For example, a company has three divisions, each of which earns a 25 percent return on its total net assets. However, the residual incomes of the divisions are dramatically different. Below are the data for the three divisions.

	Division		
	X	Y	Z
Total net assets	$100,000	$500,000	$1,000,000
Net income	25,000	125,000	250,000
ROI on net assets	25%	25%	25%
Target net income (15% of net assets)	$ 15,000	$ 75,000	$ 150,000
Residual income (net income − target net income)	10,000	50,000	100,000

Each division earned the same rate of return on net assets, and each has the same percentage target net income requirement. Still the residual income measures are dramatically different among the divisions. Thus this approach does have a tendency to highlight the divisions that generate the largest dollar profits for the firm.

Transfer pricing

One of the primary obstacles to meaningful divisional performance measurement is caused by the transfer of goods and services between divisions. If each division dealt only with organizations external to the firm, all transactions

Pricing interdivisional products and services

would be "arm's length" transactions, and prices for the goods and services would be determined by the market. However, in many decentralized businesses divisions deal with other divisions of the firm. Often some or all of the output of one division is the raw material input of another division, and so on until the final product of the company is sold to customers outside the firm. The issue raised by interdivisional transfers of products and services is, What should be the amount used to record the transfer of the product or service between divisions? This amount is called a **transfer price**. The transfer pricing dilemma has been described very well as follows:

The transfer pricing dilemma

> If a divisionalized company could arrange its affairs so that its divisions had no dealings of any kind with each other it would have removed one of the principal complexities of divisional profit measurement. It would also, however, have lost a valuable feature of decentralization, namely, the capacity to enjoy the fruits of division of labour and of specialization while simultaneously benefiting from integration to a greater or lesser degree. The fact that a divisionalized company is more than the sum of its parts is evidenced through the intricate pattern of interdivisional relationships which can establish itself within a large decentralized company.[4]

A transfer price is the amount at which goods and services are transferred between segments of a business. It is an internal price—the amount one responsibility centre charges another responsibility centre within the firm for a product or service. The importance of transfer prices for a given firm depends primarily on the importance of the transactions between the segments of the firm. If interdivisional transfers are minimal, the transfer price has little effect on the measurement of segmental performance. Substantial amounts of interdivisional transfers mean that the type of transfer price can have a dramatic effect on reported performance.

Many different transfer pricing methods are used in practice. The selection of a transfer pricing method is determined by the reporting needs of the business. For instance, one company may treat its automobile pool for executives and employees as a profit centre and use a market price for car rentals in charging for the use of vehicles. Another company may treat its automobile pool as a cost centre and charge a transfer price based on cost for the use of vehicles. No one method is better than the others, although market price seems to be the method cited most often as being closest to the ideal transfer price. The most commonly used transfer pricing methods are

Transfer pricing methods

1. Market price
2. Modified market price
3. Actual cost
4. Standard cost

[4]David Solomons, *Divisional Performance: Measurement and Control*, Financial Executives Research Foundation, New York, 1965, p. 160.

5. Modified cost
6. Negotiated price
7. Target profit
8. Other

Market price

Market price defined

Market price is often considered to be the ideal transfer price because it is determined by parties that are external to the firm and dealing at arm's length with one another. Therefore, when market price is used for internal transfers, the most objective measure of value is employed in charging for the goods or services exchanged. The market price is considered to be the one that would prevail if profit centres were in fact separate firms. It is the price that the selling division would receive if it sold to external customers, and it is the price that the buying division would have to pay if it bought from external suppliers.

A major problem with market price is that some goods and services that are transferred between divisions do not have a ready market price. The product or service may be specially made or have special characteristics that make any outside market price only a rough estimate of the market value for the specific product or service. For example, a patented circuit board for a calculator produced by one division of a firm and sold to another division may not be manufactured anywhere else in the world. Similarly, the supplying division may provide a more personalized service than the buying division could expect from an external supplier. Sometimes centralized corporate data processing centres provide other segments of the firm with far more personalized information processing services than could be obtained from an external time-sharing firm. Faster turnaround from data input to reports and more relevant report information are two commonly mentioned features attributed to corporate data processing centres. This specialized service differentiates the in-firm data processing service from an external service.

Sometimes even when there is a market price for a product or service sold between divisions, the market price is not used as the transfer price. Instead the market price is modified to reflect the specific situation involved in the intracompany transfers of products and services.

Modified market price

Market price plus appropriate adjustments

When there is an appropriate outside market, the market price is sometimes reduced to make allowance for the reduced selling effort and transportation expense that often characterize an interdivisional transfer. The justification is that if the selling division incurs less cost in making a sale to another division, some of the saving should be passed on to the buying division. In addition, other variables, such as special production requirements or inventory carrying costs, may be factors considered in charging a **modified market price.**

When there is no outside market for a product, a market price for a close substitute product is sometimes used. Typically, the market price of the substitute product is somewhat modified to reflect a realistic estimate of a market price for the firm's product. For example, if a firm uses high-quality material to manufacture specialized cold-weather-resistant bearings, the transfer price for the bearing may be set above the market price of a similar but lower-quality bearing to reflect the difference in production costs.

Actual cost

Pros . . .

And cons

Actual cost, sometimes called historical cost, is a popular transfer pricing method when market price is not feasible. Two frequently cited advantages of a historical cost transfer price are that it is definitely determinable and readily available. Given the discussion of costs in previous chapters, an obvious question is, Which costs are used for actual cost transfer prices? Typically actual cost refers to an absorption cost transfer price, meaning that all direct and indirect costs—both fixed and variable—are included in product cost. Exceptions are discussed later in the chapter.

Historical cost transfer prices are limited by the fact that a profit centre cannot be evaluated on a profit basis if its revenue is merely a recovery of cost. It is even difficult to evaluate a cost centre using historical cost transfer prices because all efficiencies and inefficiencies are passed on to the buying segments of the firm.

Standard cost

Standard costs isolate efficiency variances in the selling division

A **standard cost** transfer price has the advantage of isolating efficiency measures in the producing division. The price to the buying division is based on expected efficient performance. Standard costs reveal inefficient operations early so that they are not carried through to the final product. Compared to actual costs, standard costs are particularly effective with interdivisional transfers because an actual cost transfer price allows the seller to recover all costs, including inefficiencies. There may be little incentive to operate efficiently with actual cost transfer prices, and standard costs provide the incentive.

Modified cost

Cost plus appropriate adjustments

Partial cost

Many variations of cost are used as a basis for establishing transfer prices. A common transfer pricing model is **cost-plus** where some amount is added to the cost of the product or service in arriving at the transfer price. The amount added to cost may be a fixed amount, such as $5 a unit, or it may be a percentage, such as 15 percent of cost.

When actual costs are used as the basis for a cost-plus transfer price, there is little incentive for efficiency on the part of the selling division. In fact, if the model is expressed in terms of cost plus a percentage, the selling division can generate greater profits by incurring more costs. If standard costs are used as the base for cost-plus transfer prices, the problem of the selling division profiting from its own inefficiencies is eliminated. The amount of the transfer price is determined by the standard cost plus the additional amount.

Another form of modified cost transfer price is **partial cost,** which charges buying divisions only part of the total cost of providing the product or service being sold. Many partial cost transfer prices are used, such as marginal cost, prime cost, or variable cost. In theory partial cost includes all values between full cost and zero cost. Often partial cost transfer prices are used to encourage the use of some service or facilities. For example, many firms with large centralized computer installations have substantial excess capacity when a new computer is acquired. The computer represents a large commitment of fixed costs with relatively small amounts of variable operating costs. To increase the utilization of computer resources to a satisfactory level, users are charged a low attractive rate for computer services. The amount charged usually represents only a portion of total cost of the computer.

Most partial cost transfer prices are intended to encourage use, but only to a point. For example, if a low transfer price for computer services increases computer use too much, another larger computer may have to be acquired, thus causing another large cash outlay. Therefore, partial cost transfer prices must be monitored closely to ensure that organizational goals are not violated. Beyond a desired level of use, a new form of transfer pricing system may be adopted. To illustrate, let us expand on our discussion of a partial cost transfer price for computer services. At first management is pleased that more users are purchasing computer services because the variable cost of providing more computer services is very small when the firm has excess capacity. However, as the use of computer resources reaches full capacity, major fixed cost outlays are required for significant expansion of services. Consequently, many firms change their transfer price from partial cost to full cost, or even to cost-plus, as excess capacity dwindles. Typically the switch to full cost slows the growth in demand for services but does not eliminate the growth altogether.

Negotiated price

Bargaining between divisions

A **negotiated** transfer price is one that is determined by bargaining between buyer and seller. A negotiated price suggests an arm's length bargaining process such as one would encounter when dealing with entities external to the firm. For the process to work appropriately, the entities must have complete freedom to bargain. If agreement is not reached on the transfer price, the entities should have the ability to enter external markets. In the absence of such power, the negotiation approach may break down. If the buying and selling divisions must deal solely with each other, a bilateral monopoly exists. Economic analysis indicates that such a situation is indeterminant, which means no logical solution can be derived. In such cases management may impose the transfer price on the parties in question.

Target profit

A transfer price designed to provide a reasonable profit

Sometimes a transfer price is based on a target profit, such as 15 percent of standard costs or 10 percent of actual costs. **Target profit** transfer prices attempt to provide reasonable or desired profit levels for divisions when a market price is not available or when other transfer pricing methods would yield unsatisfactory results. To illustrate, refer to the following data for a manufacturing division of a corporation:

	Cost	
	Standard	**Actual**
Units produced	—	10 000
Manufacturing expenses	$80,000	$98,800
Operating expenses	20,000	30,000

*Profit measured
against standard
cost*

If company policy is to provide a divisional profit of 20 percent on sales with standard cost as the base, then the transfer price is obtained by first computing the total revenue required to yield the target profit and then dividing total revenue by units produced to find the transfer price. In this example the computation is

$$
\begin{aligned}
\text{Total revenue (TR)} &= .2 \text{ TR} + \text{Total standard cost} \\
\text{TR} &= .2 \text{ TR} + \$80{,}000 + \$20{,}000 \\
.8 \text{ TR} &= \$100{,}000 \\
\text{TR} &= \$125{,}000
\end{aligned}
$$

Thus $125,000 is the total revenue required to generate a 20 percent profit on sales using standard cost as the basis for measuring profit. The transfer price is total required revenue divided by the number of units produced.

$$
\begin{aligned}
\text{Transfer price} &= \$125{,}000/10\,000 \text{ units} \\
&= \$12.50 \text{ per unit}
\end{aligned}
$$

*Profit measured
against actual cost*

If the profit is measured against actual cost, the computational process is the same except that actual cost is substituted for standard cost. To illustrate, assume that company policy is to base the transfer price on a target profit of 8 percent of sales using actual cost as the base. The total required revenue is

$$
\begin{aligned}
\text{TR} &= .08 \text{ TR} + \text{Total actual cost} \\
\text{TR} &= .08 \text{ TR} + \$98{,}800 + \$30{,}000 \\
.92 \text{ TR} &= \$128{,}800 \\
\text{TR} &= \$140{,}000
\end{aligned}
$$

The transfer price is

$$
\begin{aligned}
\text{Transfer price} &= \$140{,}000/10\,000 \text{ units} \\
&= \$14.00 \text{ per unit}
\end{aligned}
$$

*Target profit transfer
price with some
outside sales*

The process of computing target profit transfer prices is slightly more difficult if the division sells part of its output in an outside market. To illustrate, assume in the preceding example that 20 percent of the division's output is sold in an outside market at $16.50 per unit and the remaining 80 percent is sold internally. What transfer price would yield a 20 percent profit on sales using standard costs to measure profit? Since standard costs and the target profit percentage have not changed from the original example, the total required revenue is still $125,000.

$$
\begin{aligned}
\text{TR} &= .20 \text{ TR} + \$80{,}000 + \$20{,}000 \\
\text{TR} &= \$125{,}000
\end{aligned}
$$

However, now some of the revenue will be generated from sales in the outside market. The amount of revenue is

$$
\begin{aligned}
&10\,000 \text{ units} \times 20 \text{ percent} \times \$16.50 \text{ per unit} \\
&\text{Revenue from outside market} = \$33{,}000
\end{aligned}
$$

The amount of revenue that must be generated by the transfer price from sales to other divisions is the total amount of required revenue less the sales generated in the outside market.

$$\text{Required internal sales revenue} = \$125,000 - \$33,000$$
$$= \$92,000$$

The transfer price is computed by dividing the required revenue from internal sales by the number of units sold to other divisions.

$$\text{Transfer price} = \$92,000/8000 \text{ units}$$
$$= \underline{\$11.50} \text{ per unit}$$

Others We have discussed the most common methods of transfer pricing, but managers may use any type of transfer price deemed useful in motivating employees toward achieving organizational goals. Some firms have developed sophisticated mathematical models for transfer pricing. Such methods as linear programming produce transfer prices whose apparent precision promotes favourable motivation among employees.

Transfer pricing illustrated To illustrate some of the more common transfer pricing methods, assume that Peachgrove Appliance Manufacturing produces refrigerators and stoves in a divisional organization. The motor division supplies motors to the refrigerator division. In the open market similar motors can be purchased for $70 each. Below are some recent cost data for the motor division.

Cost Item	Standard Cost	Actual Cost
Direct materials	$10	$14
Direct labour	15	18
Variable MOH	5	8
Fixed MOH	20	20

Using market price, the division transfers the motors at $70 per unit. If management thinks market price should be reduced 20 percent to reflect the absence of marketing costs, the transfer price is

$$\$70 - (\$70 \times .2) = \$70 - \$14 = \$56$$

With actual cost as a transfer price, we merely sum the costs of production and get a transfer price of $60. Based on standard cost, the transfer price is $50. The difference results from the unfavourable variances of $10 per motor.

If we use actual product cost plus 20 percent, the transfer price using actual cost is

$$\$60 + (\$60 \times .2) = \$72$$

and using standard product cost plus 20 percent the transfer price is

$$\$50 + (\$50 \times .2) = \$60$$

Other types of transfer prices might be used, for example, actual variable cost or standard prime cost. Respectively they yield:

Direct materials + Direct labour + Variable overhead
$14   + $18   + $8   = $40

Direct materials + Direct labour
$10   + $15   = $25

Summary

As an organization grows, centralized decision making can become unwieldy. Often it is necessary to separate the decision process into more manageable units. This separation is known as **decentralization.** Managers of decentralized operations are given decision authority and are held responsible for the results of their decisions. **Responsibility accounting** is used to report on segmental activity. It rests on the premise that managers should be responsible for the activities over which they have decision authority.

Cost centres, profit centres, and investment centres are the three basic forms of responsibility centres. **Cost centres** are decentralized units in which managers are responsible for the cost of operating the unit. Cost centres are very common because they can be used for any kind of segment in large or small organizations. The major problem is identifying the **controllable costs** in each centre.

In **profit centres** managers are held responsible for expenses **and** revenues. Each profit centre is a business within a business. Ideally the maximization of segmental profits results in maximization of corporate profit.

Investment centres carry the profit centre approach one step further by measuring the rate of return on the resources invested in the business segment. Often it is difficult to decide what investment base to use. Some common bases are **total gross assets, total net assets, total net assets employed,** and **stockholders' equity.**

Use of **residual income** to analyze the performance of investment centres is a variation of the rate of return methods. Each division is assigned a target profit in a dollar amount or percentage of investment base. Any profit above the target level is the residual income.

A major problem in segmental performance measurement is the intersegmental transfers of goods and services. If such transfers are significant, the question of how much to charge for the transferred goods and services is crucial in evaluating management performance. Many different **transfer prices** are used, and none is accepted as universally correct.

Market price is determined by pricing mechanisms external to the firm. **Modified market price** is the market price of an identical or similar product changed to reflect a more realistic estimate of the situation. **Actual cost** is the historical cost of producing the product or service transferred. It allows inefficiencies to be transferred out of the producing segment of the firm. **Standard costs** eliminate the problem of transferring the cost of inefficiency from one department to the next. **Modified cost** uses either historical or standard cost as a base from which to adjust for target profits or other factors. **Negotiated prices** allow the trading parties to participate directly in price setting. However, a bilateral monopoly may occur in which case top management must intercede to set the transfer price. **Target profit** transfer prices are based on a desired level of net income or return on investment. The transfer price is set at a level that is intended to yield the target profit.

List of important terms

actual cost *(460)*	**residual income** *(457)*
controllable cost *(449)*	**responsibility accounting** *(448)*
cost centre *(449)*	**responsibility centres** *(449)*
decentralization *(448)*	**standard cost** *(460)*
investment centre *(453)*	**stockholders' equity** *(456)*
market price *(459)*	**target profit** *(461)*
modified cost *(460)*	**total gross assets** *(455)*
modified market price *(459)*	**total net assets** *(455)*
negotiated price *(461)*	**total net assets employed** *(456)*
profit centre *(451)*	**transfer pricing** *(458)*

Questions

1. Why do firms decentralize?
2. What is meant by the term *responsibility accounting?* What assumptions are embodied in responsibility accounting?
3. Briefly describe the basic types of responsibility centres. Which type is most widely used? Why?
4. What is a controllable cost and how does this concept affect the assignment of costs to responsibility centres?
5. "Profit centres are great, a business within a business. Each minibusiness maximizes its profits, so the entire business maximizes profit." Do you agree?
6. Why might divisional performance evaluation be better using investment centres rather than profit centres?
7. Identify five investment bases that are used in investment centre analysis.
8. What is residual income?
9. Define transfer pricing and explain why it is necessary in responsibility reporting.
10. Name five methods of transfer pricing. Which method is correct?
11. "My performance report might mean something if my division did not have to buy all our raw material from other divisions and then get charged those ridiculous prices that someone in corporate headquarters sets. It is just a funny money game we play." Comment.

Exercises

Ex. 11-1 Computing rate of return on investment. The Fickle Pen Division of Allied Office Supplies generates the following data for the fiscal year ended November 30:

Sales	$ 900,000
Direct materials	200,000
Direct labour	150,000
MOH	250,000
Marketing	80,000
Administration	120,000
Assets (gross)	1,000,000
Accumulated depreciation	600,000

Assume no beginning and ending inventory.

Required:
a. Compute return on investment using total net assets as the base.
b. Compute return on investment using total gross assets as the base.

Ex. 11-2 Residual income. Duffers Tavern is a franchised chain of taverns, each of which is operated as a division. Performance is measured by residual income that is based on a target profit of 5 percent of sales. The Duffers Tavern in Endington City had yearly sales of $300,000, cost of goods sold of $120,000, and operating expenses of $155,000.

Required:
What is residual income for the tavern?

Ex. 11-3 Divisional performance measures. Rayburn Corporation is a decentralized specialized sales company. Each division competes with the other divisions for resources and for management rewards. Below are some summarized data.

	Division		
	X	**Y**	**Z**
Sales	$1,000,000	$800,000	$500,000
Net income	100,000	120,000	80,000
Assets	600,000	600,000	320,000

Required:
a. For each division compute sales as a percentage of assets.
b. For each division compute the rate of return on assets.
c. Which division had the best performance? Why?

Ex. 11-4   **Measures of segmental performance.** The Keertown branch of Fit-N-Trim Health Spa gathers the following data for the year just completed:

Current assets	$ 10,000
Fixed assets (gross)	250,000
Accumulated depreciation	50,000
Sales	140,000
Operating expenses	100,000

Required:

a. Compute return on investment using total gross assets as the base.
b. Compute return on investment using total net assets as the base.
c. Compute residual income using 15 percent of net assets as the target profit.

Ex. 11-5   **Measuring divisional performance.** Below is the year-end trial balance of Able Plastic Products.

	Debit	Credit
Current assets	$ 80,000	
Fixed assets	420,000	
Accumulated depreciation		$150,000
Land held for investment	210,000	
Current liabilities		20,000
Long-term liabilities		190,000
Capital stock		120,000
Retained earnings		160,000
Sales		300,000
Cost of goods sold	140,000	
Operating expenses	90,000	
Total	$940,000	$940,000

Required:
Compute return on investment using:

a. Total gross assets.
b. Total net assets.
c. Total gross assets employed.
d. Total net assets employed.
e. Stockholders' equity.

Ex. 11-6   **Measuring divisional performance.** Below is the trial balance of the Shin-Guard Division of Hockey Unlimited. This wholly owned subsidiary is treated as a division and evaluated by its return on investment.

	Debit	Credit
Current assets	$ 50,000	
Fixed assets	200,000	
Accumulated depreciation		$ 50,000
Land held for investment	50,000	
Liabilities		40,000
Owners' equity		150,000
Sales		300,000
Expenses	240,000	
Total	$540,000	$540,000

Required:
Compute return on investment for the division using as a base:

a. Total net assets.
b. Total net assets employed.
c. Total gross assets.
d. Stockholders' equity.

Ex. 11-7 Ranking divisional performance. Presented below are the net income and investment base data of four divisions.

Division	Net Income	Investment Base
Blue	$160,000	$1,000,000
Green	300,000	2,400,000
Red	200,000	1,000,000
Yellow	50,000	200,000

Required:
Rank the four divisions by net income, ROI, and residual income. Use 15 percent of the investment base for target net income in computing residual income.

Ex. 11-8 Computing transfer prices. The Hiawatha Doll Division of the Fine Toys Company produces dolls that it sells to the company's franchised retail outlets. Below are cost and production data for the past year.

Dolls produced	20 000
Direct materials	$40,000
Direct labour	30,000
MOH (40% variable)	50,000
Administrative (90% fixed)	60,000

Required:
What is the transfer price per unit for the dolls using:

a. Absorption costing?
b. Manufacturing cost plus 60 percent?
c. Variable cost plus 80 percent?
d. Variable manufacturing cost plus 80 percent?
e. A desired divisional income of 10 percent on sales?

Ex. 11-9 **The effect of the asset base on performance measurement.** Hoppleworth Products started operations eight years ago on the East Coast. Business grew rapidly, and soon product demand outstripped production facilities. Two years ago the company opened a new plant of identical size and capacity on the West Coast. Each plant serves its geographical area and is operated as a separate division. Below are operating data for the most recent year.

	Division	
	Eastern	**Western**
Sales	$1,000,000	$1,000,000
Manufacturing expenses	500,000	600,000
Marketing expenses	100,000	100,000
Administrative expenses	200,000	200,000
Current assets	200,000	200,000
Fixed assets (gross)	1,000,000	2,000,000
Accumulated depreciation	800,000	400,000

Since the East Coast plant was built, construction costs have doubled. The entire difference in manufacturing costs is due to higher depreciation costs at the West Coast plant.

Required:
a. Compute return on investment for each division based on total net assets.
b. Compute return on investment for each division based on total gross assets.
c. What is your evaluation of the two divisions?

Ex. 11-10 **Calculating and using transfer prices.** Central Data Systems of Big City, a government agency, provides data processing services for all branches of the city government. The city uses a full cost transfer price to charge for the use of intracity services. However, a continuing debate centres on the base to be used in the full cost charge for data processing services. During the year just ended, Central Data Systems incurred total costs of $2,000,000. The following measures of service activity were accumulated for the year:

Activity Measures	Total Annual Use for the Activity Measure
Core hours of time	4 000
Pages of printed output	10 000 000
Punch cards processed	20 000 000
Tape drive hours	10 000
Disc drive hours	20 000
Terminal connect hours	250 000

Below are total computer-utilization data for the year for two departments of city government.

	Department	
	Police	City Planning
Core hours of time	500	100
Pages of printed output	200 000	1 000 000
Punch cards processed	100 000	1 500 000
Tape drive hours	1 000	5 000
Disc drive hours	4 000	500
Terminal connect hours	100 000	10 000

Required:

a. Compute the transfer price for services rendered by Central Data Systems using **each** of the activity measures as a charging base.

b. Calculate the computer charge to the police department and city planning department based on each of the transfer prices computed in part *a*.

c. What observations and suggestions do you have concerning the transfer price?

Problem Set A

P. 11A-1 **Measuring divisional performance.** Presented below is the year-end trial balance of Seestring, Inc., a wholly owned subsidiary division of Seabrook International Corporation.

Required:
Calculate the following:

a. Return on investment using total gross assets as a base.

b. Return on investment using total net assets as a base.

c. Return on investment using total net assets employed as a base.

d. Return on investment using stockholders' equity as a base.

e. Residual income using a target profit of 20 percent of net assets employed.

	Debit	Credit
Cash	$ 10,000	
Marketable securities	20,000	
Accounts receivable	20,000	
Inventory	50,000	
Plant and equipment	320,000	
Accumulated depreciation		$100,000
Investments in nonoperating assets	80,000	
Current liabilities		20,000
Long-term liabilities		100,000
Capital stock		90,000
Retained earnings		110,000
Sales		250,000
Cost of goods sold	100,000	
Operating expenses	70,000	
Total	$670,000	$670,000

P. 11A-2 Divisional performance measurement. Dalton Enterprises has two divisions. Below are data for each of the divisions for the fiscal year ended October 31.

	Division	
	A	B
Sales	$400,000	$600,000
Cost of goods sold	200,000	250,000
Operating expenses	100,000	150,000
Current assets	150,000	200,000
Fixed assets	300,000	400,000
Current liabilities	50,000	20,000

Required:
Calculate the following:

a. Divisional net income.
b. The rate of return on total assets for each division.
c. The rate of return on fixed assets for each division.
d. The rate of return on working capital.

P. 11A-3 Determining transfer prices. The Pop-Up Popcorn Company is separated into three divisions: popcorn production, popcorn preparation, and caramel corn. The production division sells 60 percent of its products to the other two divisions and the rest to outside customers. The price to outside customers is $.80 per kilogram. Below are data relevant to popcorn production for the past year.

Production	500 000 kg
Direct materials	$ 80,000
Direct labour	100,000
Indirect production costs	60,000
Marketing expenses	25,000
Administrative expenses	75,000

Required:
a. Compute the transfer price for the sale of popcorn to the preparation division and caramel corn division assuming:
1. The objective of the production division is just to cover all costs.
2. The objective of the production division is to generate a profit of 15 percent on sales.
3. The transfer price is market price less the marketing expense, all of which is for external sales.
b. What is the production division's profit using the transfer price computed in part 3?

P. 11A-4 **Measuring divisional performance.** The Grand Island Auto Equipment Company is organized into three divisions operated as investment centres. Presented below are data for three years for the shock absorber division.

	1984	**1983**	**1982**
Sales	$1,210,000	$1,100,000	$1,000,000
Cost of goods sold	700,000	600,000	500,000
Operating expenses	300,000	250,000	200,000
Current assets	150,000	120,000	100,000
Fixed assets	2,000,000	2,000,000	2,000,000
Accumulated depreciation	1,400,000	1,100,000	800,000

Required:
For each year:

a. Compute net income.
b. Compute return on investment using total gross assets.
c. Compute return on investment using total net assets.
d. What is the trend in the division's performance?

P. 11A-5 **Transfer pricing of services.** Paradise City Park has been plagued by vandalism recently. There are no funds available to hire permanent security officers to patrol the park. However, there is a general contingency fund with enough resources to hire temporary security people to patrol the park for a while until the vandalism is controlled. Private security firms have bid for the job, with a low bid of $25 per patrol hour including patrol vehicles. The city police have heard of the situation and offered to patrol the park. In return the park must pay the city police out of the special contingency fund. City police cost and activity data for the year are

	Police Hours	Cost	
City police in total	1 000 000	$15,000,000	$15
City police patrol division —	400 000	7,200,000	$18

Sixty percent of the patrol division's cost is variable.

Required:

a. Compute the transfer price for the city police patrol service if:
  1. Park officials can convince the city police that full cost for city police activities in general is the appropriate transfer price.
  2. City police can convince park officials that full cost for the patrol division is the appropriate transfer price.
  3. City police can convince park officials that outside market price less a normal profit of 20 percent is the appropriate transfer price.
  4. Park officials can convince the city police that the appropriate transfer price is the variable part of the patrol division cost plus an incentive of 20 percent of the variable cost.

b. If the contingency fund can provide $27,000 for this project, how many patrol hours can the park purchase using each of the transfer prices computed above?

P. 11A-6 Determining transfer prices. The Do-Rite Company is a decentralized corporation with two divisions feeding all of their production into one division that processes inputs further and sells its output to an outside market. Below are standard and actual cost data for the two feeder divisions.

	Division M		Division N	
	Standard	Actual	Standard	Actual
Units produced	—	10 000	—	50 000
Direct materials	$100,000	$120,000	$200,000	$210,000
Direct labour	150,000	180,000	100,000	140,000
MOH	110,000	125,000	200,000	220,000
Administration	150,000	124,000	180,000	168,000

Required:

Given the data above, compute the transfer price for each division using:

a. Standard product cost plus 25 percent.
b. Actual product cost plus 20 percent.
c. A profit of 15 percent on sales using total standard costs.
d. A profit of 10 percent on sales using total actual costs.

Problem Set B

P. 11B-1 **Measuring divisional performance.** Below is the December 31 trial balance for a wholly owned subsidiary of a manufacturing company. The company operates the subsidiary as a division and is interested in evaluating the performance of each of its decentralized divisions.

	Debits	Credits
Cash	$ 10,000	
Marketable securities	20,000	
Accounts receivable	60,000	
Inventory	70,000	
Plant	520,000	
Accumulated depreciation, plant		$ 150,000
Land held for investment	170,000	
Patents	40,000	
Current liabilities		70,000
Long-term liabilities		180,000
Common stock		50,000
Retained earnings		320,000
Sales		300,000
Cost of goods sold	140,000	
Operating expenses	40,000	
Total	$1,070,000	$1,070,000

Required:
a. What is the rate of return on investment using:
1. Total net assets employed.
2. Total gross assets.
3. Owners' equity.
b. Calculate the residual income, assuming a target return of 15 percent on gross assets employed.

P. 11B-2 **Measuring divisional performance.** McDaniels Department Store divides its operations into three divisions for purposes of management and performance evaluation. Below are operating data for the three divisions.

	Division		
	P	Q	R
Sales	$10,000	$20,000	$30,000
Cost of goods sold	5,000	12,000	21,000
Operating expenses	2,000	4,000	6,000
Investment base	20,000	25,000	10,000

Required:
a. What is net income as a percentage of sales for each division?

b. What is net income as a percentage of investment base for each division?

c. What is divisional residual income if target net income is 10 percent of the investment base?

P. 11B-3 **Computing and using transfer prices.** The Power-Lite Division of Outside Products manufactures batteries that it sells primarily to the Lantern Division for inclusion with that division's main product. Last year 20 percent of the batteries were sold to other companies at a price of $1 each. The remaining batteries went to the Lantern Division. Cost data for the year are presented for Power-Lite.

Units produced	500 000
Manufacturing costs	$300,000
Marketing costs	10,000
Administrative costs	50,000

Required:

a. What should be the transfer price for the batteries if the company uses:
   1. Market price?
   2. Market price less marketing costs?
   3. A transfer price that will yield a net income of 10 percent on sales for Power-Lite?
   4. Product cost plus 40 percent?

b. Prepare a schedule showing the Power-Lite Division's net income for each of the transfer pricing alternatives computed.

P. 11B-4 **Return on investment.** Gun-Notch Outfitters runs a lodge on Great Slave Lake in Canada. It is one of several lodges the firm owns and operates. Each lodge is operated as a separate division. Below are relevant data for the past four years of operations.

	1984	1983	1982	1981
Revenues	$ 500,000	$ 470,000	$ 440,000	$ 400,000
Float plane expenses	20,000	16,000	14,000	10,000
Food expenses	70,000	64,000	56,000	50,000
Other operating expenses	330,000	300,000	260,000	200,000
Assets (gross)	1,000,000	1,000,000	1,000,000	1,000,000
Accumulated depreciation	800,000	600,000	400,000	200,000

Required:

a. Compute net income for each year.

b. Compute the return on investment for each year using total gross assets.

c. Compute the return on investment for each year using total net assets.

P. 11B-5 **Computing transfer prices.** The Jennison Chemical Company has three operating divisions. The chemical products division sells raw materials to the industrial products division and to the farm products division. The management of Jennison believes in profit responsibility and has established a transfer price of total standard cost plus 18 percent. Below are relevant data.

	Standard	Actual
Units produced	—	40 000 tons
Direct materials	$1,000,000	$1,200,000
Direct labour	400,000	360,000
MOH	600,000	650,000
Administrative expenses	800,000	920,000

Required:

a. What is the transfer price established by management?

b. What is the chemical products division's net income?

c. Would the chemical products division have been better off with a transfer price of total actual cost plus 8 percent?

P. 11B-6 **Determining and using transfer prices.** The Hot Iron Steel Company has a mining division and a steel production division. Currently the mining division sells 60 percent of its output to the steel production division and 40 percent in the outside market. The market price for iron ore is $100 a ton. Production and cost data for the mining division are presented below.

Output	500 000 tons
Direct labour	$12,000,000
Depreciation and depletion	10,000,000
Other production costs	10,000,000
Marketing	1,000,000
Administration	8,000,000

Required:

a. Compute the transfer price for iron ore, assuming:

   1. A total cost transfer price is used for all iron ore sold to the steel division.
   2. The objective of the mining division is to recover all divisional costs.
   3. A market price less marketing cost.
   4. The objective of the mining division is to earn 10 percent on sales.

b. What is the mining division's net income using each of the transfer prices computed above?

Minicases

Minicase 11-1   (SMA of Canada adapted)

The Greld Company has one product which is produced by two of its divisions. The Alpha division produces a major subassembly which the Omega division incorporates into the final product. There is a market for both the subassembly and the final product. Each of the divisions is a profit centre and the subassembly has a transfer price based on the long-run average market price.

The Controller, Ms. Leduc, has made the following data to each division manager

Final product selling price	$450
Long-run average selling price for the intermediate product	300
Outlay cost of completion in the Omega division	225
Outlay cost in the Alpha division	180

Required:

a. Should transfers be made to Omega if there is no excess capacity in the Alpha division? Is market price the correct transfer price? Give reasons.

b. Assume that Alpha division's maximum capacity for this product is 1000 units per month, and sales to the intermediate market are presently 800 units. Should 200 units be transferred to Omega division? At what relevant transfer price? Give reasons or calculations. Assume for a variety of reasons that Alpha will maintain the $300 selling price indefinitely; that is, Alpha is not considering cutting the price to outsiders, regardless of the presence of idle capacity.

c. Suppose Alpha quoted a transfer price of $300. What would be the contribution to the firm as a whole if the transfer price was $300. What would be the contribution to the firm as a whole if the transfer was made? Show calculations.

d. Suppose the manager of Alpha has the option of: (i) cutting the external price to $290, with the certainty that sales will rise to 1000 units or; (ii) maintaining the outside price of $300 for the 800 units and transferring the 200 units to Omega at some price that would produce the same income for Alpha. Which transfer price would produce the same income for Alpha? Show calculations.

e. What alternative bases can be used for establishing transfer prices in this case? Which basis would you recommend to the Greld Company in the above situation?

Minicase 11-2   (SMA of Canada adapted)

The Caplow Company is a multidivisional company, and its managers have been delegated full profit responsibility and complete autonomy to accept or reject transfers from other divisions. Division A produces a subassembly with a ready competitive market. This subassembly is currently used by Division B for a final product which is sold outside at $1,200. Division A charges Division B market price for the subassembly which is $700 per unit. Variable costs are $520 and $600 for Divisions A and B respectively.

The manager of Division B feels that should Division A transfer the subassembly at this price, Division B is unable to make a profit.

Required:

a. Compute Division B's profit contribution if transfers are made at the market price, and also the total contribution to profit for the company.

b. Assume that Division A can sell all its production in the open market. Should Division A transfer goods to Division B? If so, at what price?

c. Assume Division A can sell in the open market only 500 units at $700 per unit out of the 1000 units which it can produce every month, and that a 20 percent reduction in price is necessary to sell full capacity. Should transfers be made? If so, how many units should it transfer and at what price? Support your decision.

Minicase 11-3 (CICA adapted)

Turvar Company, Ltd., consists of five operating divisions located throughout the country and a central corporate office. Each operating division produces and markets its own line of products and sells the product line of other divisions within its region of the country. Each division prepares its own financial statements, and its manager is evaluated on the basis of the rate his division has earned on its investment (ROI). The division's investment figure used in the calculation has, since the system was started, included all the assets controlled by each divisional manager.

Until last year, the investment figure of each division did not include two classes of assets: headquarters' assets and research department's assets. The associated headquarters and research expenses were not included in the calculation of ROI. Headquarters' assets were not material (2 percent of the company's total assets) since most of headquarters' facilities were rented. Until recently, research assets also had been small, but by the spring of 1984 had grown to just over 10 percent of the company's total assets. It was expected that more funds would be invested in research facilities in the near future.

In late 1984, the president of Turvar, Ltd., suggested that all the company's assets be distributed in some way to all operating divisions. This would, he stated, make the reported return on investment by the divisions more realistic as indicators of how well the company was doing as a whole.

Required:

a. Outline the arguments for and against using ROI to measure divisional performance.

b. Evaluate the suggestion made by the president of Turvar Ltd.

Reprinted, with permission, from Uniform Final Examination, 1975, published by the Canadian Institute of Chartered Accountants, Toronto, Canada.

Chapter 12

Accounting Data and Pricing Decisions

This chapter discusses the economic framework and accounting concepts that are used in establishing selling prices for the products and services sold by a firm. In most organizations pricing is an important activity that requires an understanding of relevant concepts as well as an ability to apply these concepts in the complex economic environment of business. When you have completed this chapter, you should understand:

1 The fundamental economic framework in price determination.

2 The four basic market models.

3 The variables that affect the pricing decision.

4 The different types of pricing models in business.

5 The computation of prices with the most commonly used pricing models.

6 That each pricing situation must be evaluated separately.

One of the most important and interesting decisions that managers make is the pricing decision. **Pricing** refers to the assignment of a selling price to a product or service provided by the firm. Sometimes the term **price** is used to refer to the **purchase price** of some resource acquired by a firm, but this is more precisely a **cost** to the purchasing firm. In this chapter we discuss **selling price,** which is the amount charged customers for some product or service sold by the firm.

Selling price is the amount charged customers for some product or service

Pricing activities are more extensive than many people realize. It is easy to visualize the need to price each product in a department store or sporting goods store, but all organizations that provide a service for a fee or sell a product must decide on the amount to charge for each service or product. Included are dentists, who must establish prices for periodic checkups, X-ray services, teeth cleaning, filling, and extraction. A construction firm must decide how much to bid (price) on a bridge construction project or a new school gymnasium. Even not-for-profit organizations must set prices for services and products. The Post Office sets prices on mail services, Parks Canada establishes fees for park users, and local governments set prices for dog licence tags.

The number of products and services that must be priced is extensive, but pricing does not stop with a single pricing decision for each product or service. Prices must be continuously reevaluated to ensure that they reflect management's desires in light of current costs, market conditions, and competitor actions. Some prices may remain in effect for a year or more; others may change rapidly. Stamp and coin dealers change some prices daily. Canadian and U.S. automobile manufacturers have raised prices several times in one year. Some food prices fluctuate throughout the year. Pricing decisions are not static, but instead are part of a necessary continuing activity.

The purpose of this chapter is to provide you with an understanding of pricing. The first part of the chapter is a discussion of the nature of pricing decisions and of the entities that set prices. We introduce the economic framework in which pricing decisions take place so that you understand the reasons or rationale in establishing prices. The basic economic concepts play a role in production and pricing decisions discussed in the second part of the chapter in which we illustrate specific pricing models commonly used by businesses.

The economics of pricing

Pricing decisions may be influenced by internal factors, such as costs and profit objectives, and by external factors, such as competitors' pricing actions or regulatory pricing or profit guidelines. Some common factors that may influence pricing decisions are

Factors influencing pricing decisions

Cost data
Revenue and profit objectives
Type of product or service
Type of industry
Public image
Governmental influence
Management style
Competitor actions
Type of market
Economic trends
Other factors

How do all of these factors interact and result in a pricing decision? The answer depends on the individual making the pricing decision. Each decision maker incorporates pricing variables into the decision process in a different way. One person may weigh economic trends and industry averages heavily and may ignore government pressure for price restraint. Another may use government pricing guidelines as the primary variable in establishing new prices. Whatever the decision style and environment of the individual, many pricing decisions are couched, at least in part, in the general framework of economic pricing theory. The discussion that follows should provide you with a brief overview of the economic factors that affect pricing decisions. The discussion is only a brief presentation of the economic theory underlying pricing decisions. Entire textbooks are devoted to these concepts. We merely present relationships between the important economic factors in pricing decisions without an in-depth analysis of the economic theory underlying the relationships. In addition, many complicating factors are not discussed.

Economic models are only general frameworks for pricing decisions

The way prices are established depends on the market in which goods are traded. Economists describe several types of markets, including:

1. Perfectly competitive market
2. Monopolistic competition
3. Oligopoly
4. Monopoly

Perfectly competitive market

To be classified as a **perfectly competitive market,** the following characteristics must be met:

Characteristics of perfectly competitive markets

1. The goods traded must be homogeneous, which means that the product of one seller must be identical, in the opinion of purchasers, to the product of other sellers.
2. Market participants, whether buyers or sellers, cannot individually influence the market price of the product by their actions.
3. Resources must be able to move in and out of the market freely.
4. Buyers, sellers, and resource owners must have complete and perfect knowledge of prices and resource costs.

Very few products have perfectly competitive markets if all of the four characteristics are strictly interpreted. However, if the last two assumptions are slightly relaxed, a number of products are traded in markets that can be classified as perfectly competitive. Such a classification is useful in analyzing pricing and production decisions. Probably the most notable group of products selling in almost perfectly competitive markets are farm products, such as corn, wheat, rye, rapeseed, hogs, cattle, etc.

The prices of perfectly competitive products are determined by supply and demand. **Supply** is the total amount all suppliers are willing to sell at each possible selling price, and **demand** is the total amount all purchasers are willing to buy at each possible price. To illustrate the concept of supply, refer to the supply schedule for soybeans in Figure 12-1, which shows the amount of product that producers are willing to supply at each possible selling price. At a price of $10 a bag, suppliers are willing to produce 180 million bags of soybeans. At $9 a bag, suppliers are willing to produce only 170 million bags of beans. At lower prices even fewer soybeans will be supplied.

Graphically the supply schedule slopes up and to the right, showing a willingness on the part of producers to supply greater quantities of soybeans as the price increases. The graph of the supply schedule is called a **supply curve.** Figure 12-2 shows a supply curve for soybeans using the data from the supply schedule in Figure 12-1.

The demand for a product is inversely affected by price, which means that as the price increases, demand for the product decreases. For example, Figure 12-3 presents the demand schedule for soybeans. At $10 a bag purchasers are willing to buy only 70 million bags of soybeans. At $9 buyers are willing to purchase 100 million bags. As the price declines, demand increases because purchasers are willing to buy a larger quantity at the lower prices.

Data from the demand schedule in Figure 12-3 are graphed in Figure 12-4, which is called a **demand curve.** Notice that the demand curve slopes down and to the right, indicating an increasing demand for a product as the price declines.

The supply and demand curves for soybeans indicate that at high prices producers are willing to supply more soybeans than buyers are willing to purchase. Just the reverse is true at low prices. The only point where the buyers and sellers are in total agreement is where the two curves intersect. To illustrate, the supply and demand curves for soybeans are shown in a single

Figure 12-1
A supply schedule shows the quantity of a product supplied at each possible selling price. The quantity supplied declines with decreases in price because fewer and fewer suppliers find it economically feasible to supply the product.

Supply Schedule for Soybeans	
Price per Bag	Quantity Supplied (In millions of Bags a year)
$10	180
9	170
8	160
7	140
6	120
5	100
4	80
3	50
2	30
1	5

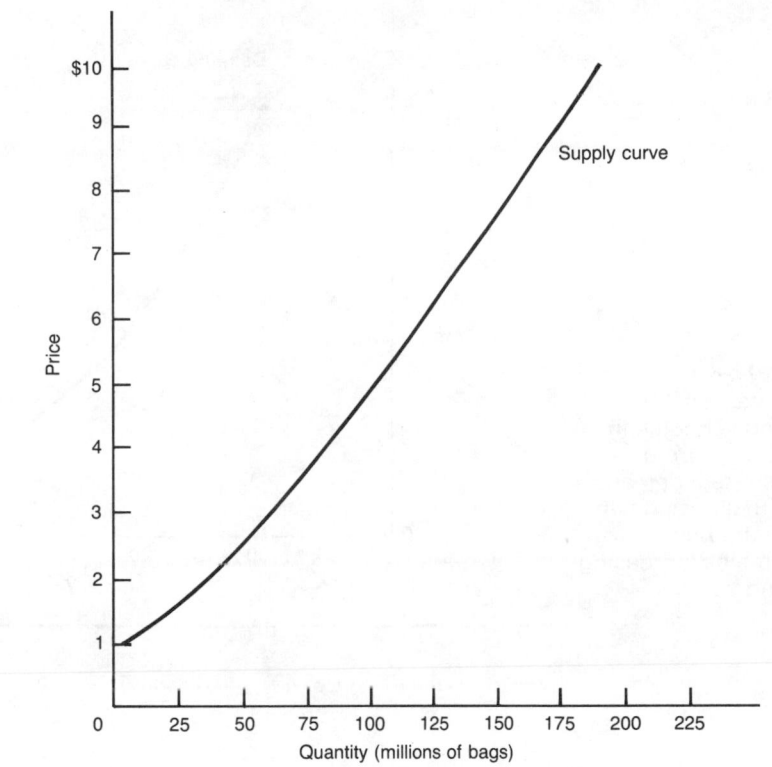

Figure 12-2
A supply curve is a graph of the data from a supply schedule. A supply curve slopes up and to the right, indicating the willingness of suppliers to increase supply as price increases.

Figure 12-3
A demand schedule shows the quantity demanded at various possible prices for a product. Demand increases as price decreases, showing the willingness of buyers to purchase more at lower prices.

Demand Schedule for Soybeans	
Price per Bag	**Quantity Demanded (in millions of Bags a year)**
$10	70
9	100
8	120
7	140
6	165
5	190
4	220
3	260
2	300
1	350

Note: One bag of soybean weighs 40 kilograms.

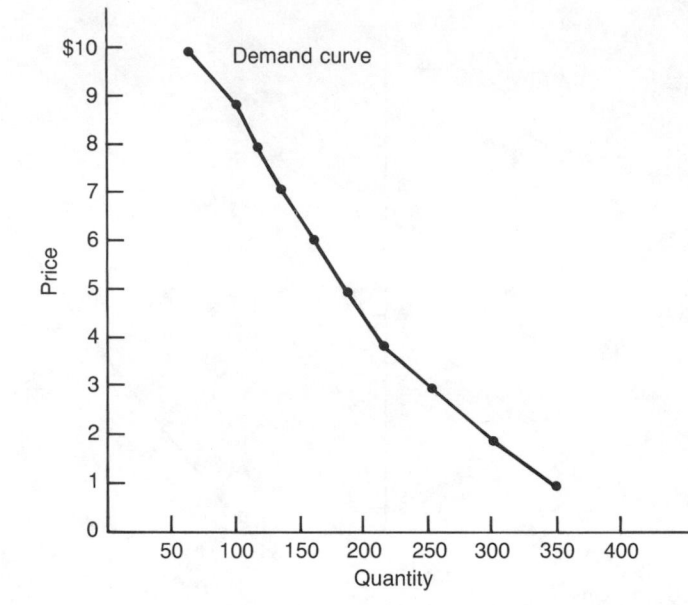

Figure 12-4
The data from the demand schedule in Figure 12-3 are used to illustrate a demand curve. It slopes down and to the right, showing the increasing demand as price declines.

Market equilibrium occurs when the quantity supplied and demanded are equal at a particular price

graph in Figure 12-5. The point of intersection, called the **market equilibrium point,** yields the market price *P*, $7 a bag in this example, and the quantity purchased *Q*, 140 million bags.

The $7 selling price and 140 million bags quantity are determined by all participants in the market. By definition no single buyer or seller can influence the market. If a seller attempts to charge more than $7 for a bag of soybeans, the purchaser will buy from someone else. A price lower than $7 makes no sense because individual suppliers can sell their entire supply at the market price in a perfectly competitive market. Therefore, the demand curve for an individual supplier in a perfectly competitive market is a horizontal straight line at the selling price, $7 in this case. This demand curve is illustrated in Figure 12-7. Be careful to note that here we have switched to a demand curve for an **individual** seller rather than a demand curve for **all** sellers in the market, as illustrated in Figure 12-4.

In a perfectly competitive market, a supplier can only decide the amount to produce and sell

Since individual suppliers cannot affect the price of a product, what decision do they have to make? Each supplier must decide how much to produce. Using the selling price and production cost data, each supplier must determine the optimum amount to produce and sell, which is the production level where profit is greatest. To illustrate, Figure 12-6, on page 486, presents cost data for a supplier with 20 hectares available for soybean production.

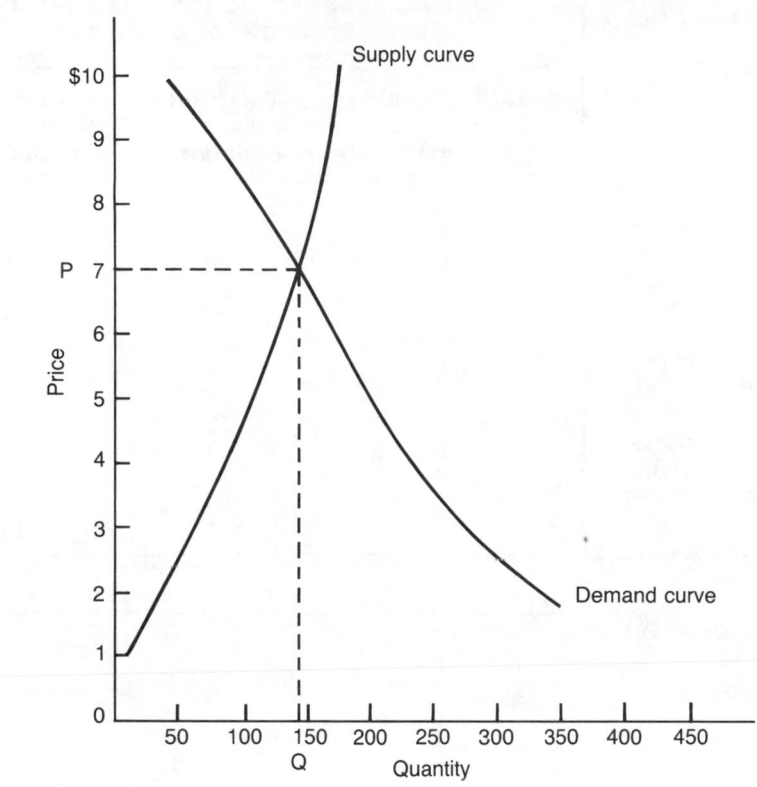

Figure 12-5
The intersection of
the supply and demand
curve is called the
market equilibrium
point. It is the point
where suppliers and
buyers agree on price
and quantity.

*Marginal cost
defined*

*Marginal revenue
defined*

The supplier has certain fixed costs, such as property taxes and some
production costs. The soybean yield can be varied by planting different amounts
of the land and by using more or less fertilizer and labour. The cost data for
various levels of production appear in Figure 12-6. The **marginal cost** is
the amount of cost increase caused by a unit increase in output. For example,
if production increases from four to five units, total cost increases from $2,700
to $3,200, or an increase of $500. The $500 marginal cost applies only to the
five-unit production level. At other production levels, the marginal cost is
different. The optimum strategy is to produce at the level where marginal
cost equals marginal revenue. **Marginal revenue** is the additional revenue
obtained by selling one additional unit of product. In a perfectly competitive
market, marginal revenue is equal to price so that the optimum strategy is to
produce at the level where marginal cost equals price. Beyond this point the
next unit of 100 bags of soybeans produced will cost more than the price it will
bring in the market. This strategy is shown graphically in Figure 12-7 and is
verified in Figure 12-8, which is a schedule of revenue, costs, and net income.

Schedule of Production Costs for a Single Producer of Soybeans		
Quantity Produced (In hundreds of bags)	Total Cost (In hundreds of dollars)	Marginal Cost (In hundreds of dollars)
0	$ 10	—
1	16	$ 6
2	20	4
3	23	3
4	27	4
5	32	5
6	38	6
7	45	7
8	53	8
9	63	10
10	75	12
11	89	14
12	105	16

Figure 12-6
Individual producers must determine the best course of action by evaluating the market price and the costs of production. A production schedule presents production costs at various levels of production. Higher levels of production generate larger marginal costs.

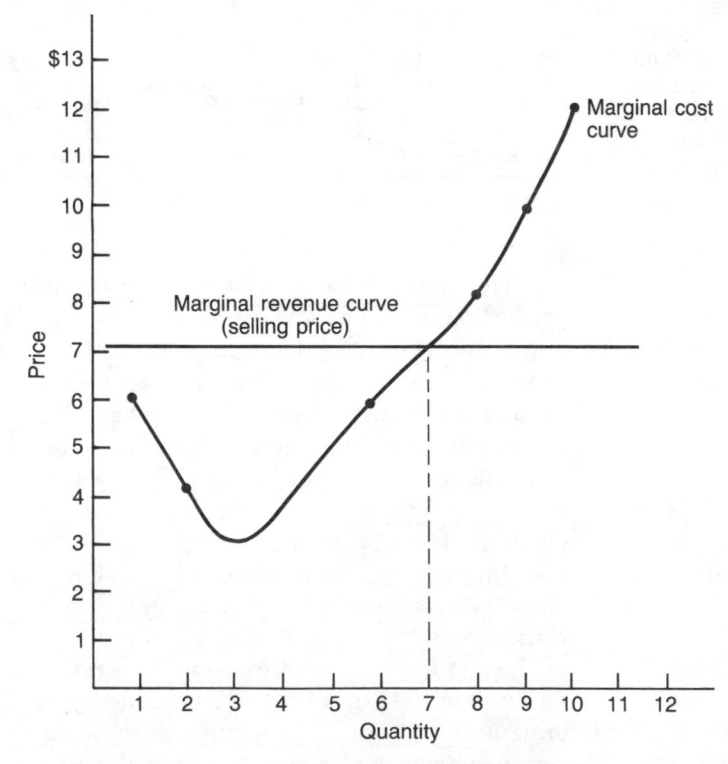

Figure 12-7
Each supplier maximizes profits by supplying products until marginal cost equals marginal revenue. In a perfectly competitive market, marginal revenue for an individual is the selling price. Therefore, the supplier should continue to supply products until marginal cost equals the market price.

Schedule of Revenue, Costs, and Net Income			
Quantity Sold (In hundreds of bags)	Total Revenue (In hundreds of dollars)	Total Cost (In hundreds of dollars)	Net Income (Loss) (In hundreds of dollars)
0	0	$10	$(10)
1	7	16	(9)
2	14	20	(6)
3	21	23	(2)
4	28	27	(1)
5	35	32	3
6	42	38	4
7	49	45	4
8	56	53	3
9	63	63	0
10	70	75	(5)
11	77	89	(12)
12	84	105	(21)

Figure 12-8
A schedule of revenues, costs, and net income verifies the graphic solution. Net income is maximized where marginal revenue equals marginal cost.

Monopolistic competition, monopoly, and oligopoly

Most products are not sold in perfectly competitive markets because they do not satisfy the homogeneous-product characteristic. Businesses spend a great deal of money advertising and promoting their products in an attempt to differentiate them from the products of other companies. "Our product is bigger, better, prettier, faster, more colourful, easier to use, easier to pay for, and so forth." Such differentiation creates a somewhat different type of market and pricing framework, including monopolistic competition, monopoly, and oligopoly.

Other types of markets defined

Monopolistic competition occurs when there are many sellers of similar, but not identical, products in the market. No single seller is able to exercise perceptible influence over the market price of the similar products. Breakfast cereals and many other food products are examples of monopolistic competition. **Monopoly** occurs when a firm is the sole supplier of some product. There are no competing products in the market. Electric utilities, telephone companies, and gas utilities are common examples. An **oligopoly** exists when there are several large sellers that dominate the market and basically compete against one another. The Canadian automobile market is an oligopolistic market.

The economic solution to the product pricing decision in other than perfectly competitive markets rests on the same principle of maximizing net income that is achieved when marginal revenue equals marginal cost. The difference between a perfectly competitive market and other market types is the shape of the revenue curves. In a perfectly competitive market, a single firm faces a horizontal demand curve. That means the firm can sell as many units of product as it chooses at the market price. The horizontal demand

Individual demand curves in other than perfectly competitive markets

curve is also the marginal revenue curve. Each additional unit of sales adds the same amount to total revenue as the last unit sold. In other types of markets **each** supplier faces a demand curve that slopes down and to the right similar to the demand curve facing the producers in aggregate in a perfectly competitive market.

The downward-sloping individual demand curve occurs because the firm attempts to differentiate its product from competing products by providing different features for the product, such as a different appearance, more functions, or less complicated controls, and by advertising in order to make a larger number of consumers aware of the product's existence and to build brand-name loyalty. When products are differentiated, the ability of the consumer to substitute one product for another is reduced because the competing product may not have quite the same features. For example, one automatic dishwasher costs more than another, but it is also quieter. A buyer may be willing to pay the higher price to obtain less noise, but if the price is much higher, the customer may forgo quiet operation in order to save money. Consequently, there is a range of price variation within which customers will not switch from one product to another. As the price increases, some, but not all, customers may switch to other products, reducing the amount demanded. If the price decreases, some competitors' customers will be attracted. The following examples illustrate the general pricing model for monopolistic competition and monopolies. Oligopolies must consider an additional characteristic mentioned later.

To illustrate the demand curve facing a single producer, we present quantity and revenue data in Figure 12-9. The quantity demanded by purchasers varies inversely with the product price. High prices mean few units

Figure 12-9
In markets that are not perfectly competitive, suppliers face a demand curve similar to the one faced by suppliers in aggregate in a perfectly competitive market. The demand declines as price increases, indicating that a supplier must reduce prices to increase unit sales.

Schedule of Demand, Total Revenue, and Marginal Revenue			
Price	Quantity Demanded	Total Revenue	Marginal Revenue
$12	0	0	0
11	1	$11	$11
10	2	20	9
9	3	27	7
8	4	32	5
7	5	35	3
6	6	36	1
5	7	35	−1
4	8	32	−3
3	9	27	−5
2	10	20	−7
1	11	11	−9

are purchased, and low prices result in more units being purchased. The total revenue column in Figure 12-9 is merely the selling price times the number of units demanded at each price. Marginal revenue is the amount added to total revenue by the sale of one additional unit.

Data from Figure 12-9 are graphed in Figure 12-10. Total revenue starts at 0 and rises to a peak at 6 units. Marginal revenue is $11 at 1 unit and declines throughout since the selling price must be lowered to generate more demand for the product. The demand curve shows how many units will be sold at a given price.

As with perfectly competitive markets, the supplier sells units of the product as long as the marginal revenue is greater than the marginal cost. Figure 12-11 presents cost data for the firm at each level of activity. The total cost and marginal cost data are graphed in Figure 12-12.

The marginal revenue and marginal cost curves are combined in Figure 12-13, where the vertical scale has been changed from Figure 12-12 to accentuate the slope of the curves. At four units of output marginal cost equals marginal revenue, and at this volume net income is maximized. If the producer raised or lowered the price, net income would decrease. Using the cost and revenue data in Figures 12-9 and 12-11, the producer can set the optimal price.

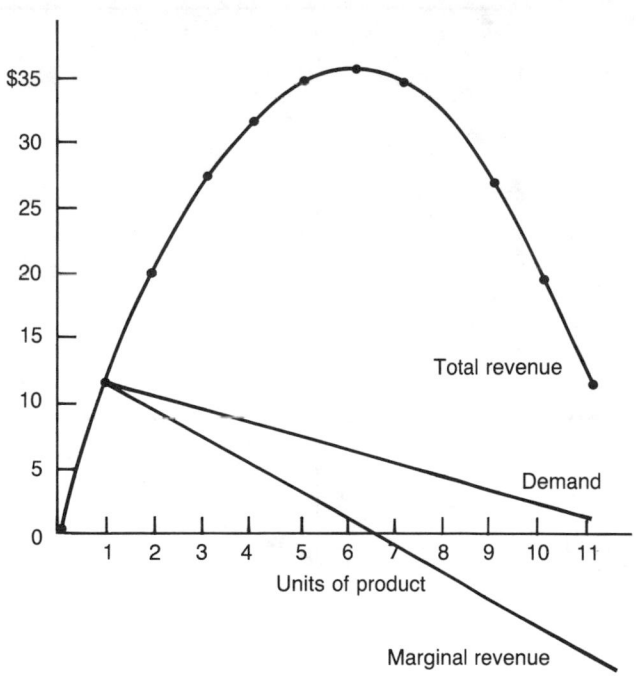

Figure 12-10
Marginal revenue declines throughout the range of activity. As selling price declines total revenue rises to a maximum point and then begins to decline at the point where marginal revenue is zero.

Schedule of Production, Total Cost, and Marginal Cost		
Quantity Produced	**Total Cost**	**Marginal Cost**
0	$10	—
1	13	$ 3
2	16	3
3	20	4
4	25	5
5	31	6
6	38	7
7	46	8
8	55	9
9	65	10
10	76	11
11	88	12

Figure 12-11
A schedule of production quantities and costs. The difference in total cost between any two levels of activity is marginal cost.

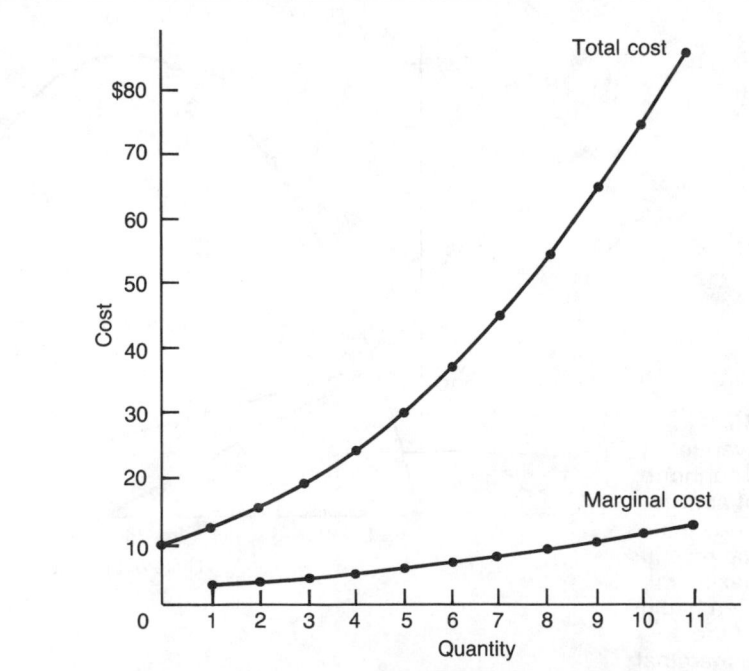

Figure 12-12
The costs graphed here come from data in Figure 12-11. If marginal cost is increasing, the total cost curve increases at an increasing rate.

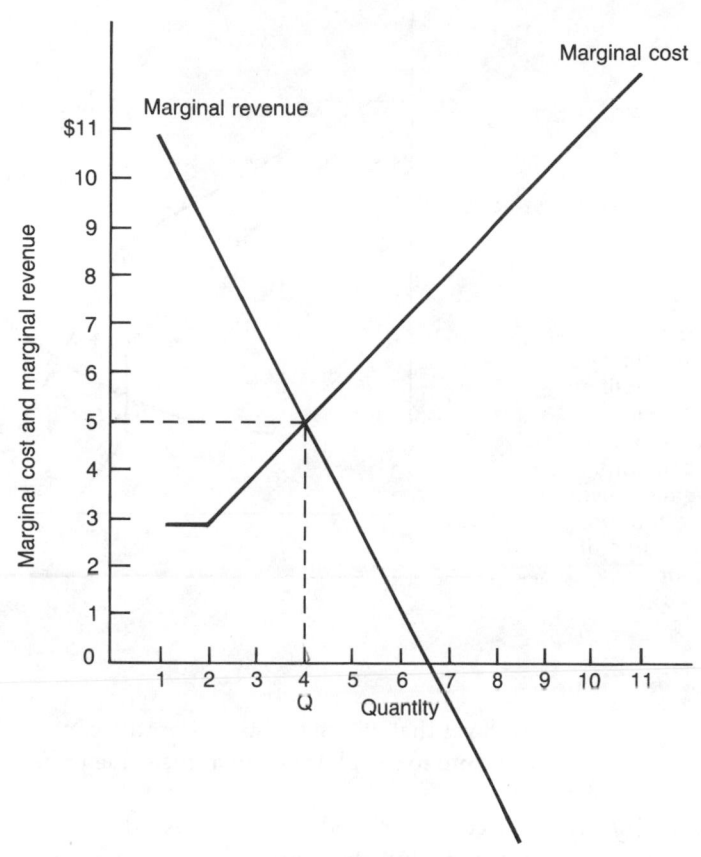

Figure 12-13
The market equilibrium point occurs where marginal cost and marginal revenue curves intersect.

Oligopolies described

Oligopolies have the characteristic that a single seller is large enough to affect the market price. As a result, the demand curve of one firm may be directly affected by the pricing actions of other sellers in the market. For example, if one producer of aluminum lowers the price, the demand for other producers' aluminum declines when buyers shift to the lower-priced producer. The result is that the demand curve for an oligopolistic firm may undergo sharp changes when going from one price to another, resulting in the **kinked demand curve** illustrated in Figure 12-14. There are various solutions to determining price in oligopolistic markets, depending upon the nature of the firms in the market, their relationship to one another, and the attitude of each firm's management about pricing. In some oligopolistic markets there are price leaders and price followers. Price leaders in effect establish the price, and the price followers merely adopt the price set by the leader. With this approach a price follower is basically confronted with a horizontal demand curve, as in a perfectly competitive market. The problem for the price leader is to set prices at

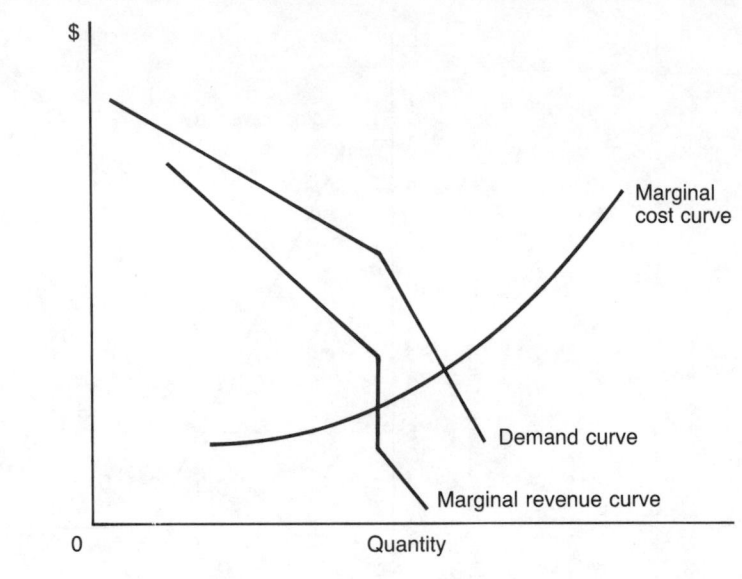

Figure 12-14
A kinked demand curve is caused by the direct competition between several oligopolistic firms. The pricing actions of one firm may have a dramatic effect on the demand curve of its competitors.

the level that will maximize its profits considering that the price followers will be trying to sell all they can at the same price.

Some modifying variables

The economic models just discussed are useful to managers in making pricing decisions, but the models are only a basic framework. Many variables affect the pricing of any particular product. Some important variables that have a modifying effect on economic models are

Profit satisfaction
Government influence
Model limitations
Inferior goods

Profit satisfaction. One of the primary assumptions in economic theory is that managers attempt to maximize profits. Without such an assumption many types of economic analysis are impossible, but in the modern environment of business, profit maximization may not be possible. Even the word **profit** elicits unfavourable comments from some people, and the term **profit maximization** sometimes has the connotation of unwarranted or excessive profits. Economists argue that excessive profits cannot last long because new resources would flow into the market to take advantage of the high profits, thus increasing supply and forcing down prices and profits. In our economy the free flow of resources from one market to another does not exist in all markets. For example, utilities have an exclusive franchise to serve certain geographical areas, and some industries, such as steel, require such huge capital investments that resources do not flow freely into the industry. Therefore, many people argue that excessive or unfair profits sometimes do occur.

Acceptable levels of profit

Unfavourable public sentiment toward excessive profits and direct intervention by governmental agencies have led firms from a goal of profit maximization to a more tempered description of profit objectives. The terms **satisfactory profit** or **target profit** are used to describe a level of profits that provides a reasonable return on invested capital, but not an excessive return. Some people maintain that the goal of management historically has been to earn a satisfactory profit in light of the business and social environment within which the firm operates. Target profit levels may reflect the maximum profit the firm strives to achieve, given the constraints of the business' environment, and such profit objectives may result in a product price somewhat different from the price suggested by an economic model.

Governments may affect pricing decisions in many different ways

Government influence. Some firms sell products whose prices are directly or indirectly affected by federal, provincial, or municipal governments. In the mid-1970s Canadians experienced wage and price controls imposed by the government in order to stabilize the economy and fight inflation. In this era of price and wage controls certain goods and services were exempted, while certain others required governmental approval for justified changes.

More recently, price for domestically produced crude oil is determined on a formula reached by federal and provincial governments. Electric utilities and telephone companies, typically, are required to secure approval for rate increases from rate-setting governmental organizations. Doctors' fees in Ontario, British Columbia, and other provinces are good examples of the extent of governmental interference in pricing goods and services. On occasion governmental representatives have indirectly affected prices by criticizing industries for price increases. This action, called **jaw boning,** has sometimes been used effectively by governments to discourage proposed price increases.

The list of products and services whose prices are affected by one or more agencies of government is lengthy. The important point here is that businesses are part of a total economic environment in which government plays an important and expanding role. The intelligent manager stays abreast of government actions affecting the operation of the business, including those actions affecting pricing decisions.

Models should be good representations of the item or activity modeled

Modeling limitations. A **model** is an abstract representation of something in the real world. Models are useful because they allow us to cut away details and get at the fundamental issues of the subject being modeled. However, modeling has some serious limitations. A model must be a good representation of the item or activity being modeled. The most sophisticated model can be totally useless if great care is not taken to ensure a proper fit with the subject. This limitation holds for pricing models as well as for other types of models.

Perhaps a more serious limitation is one of gathering appropriate and accurate data for use in the model. Pricing models require cost and revenue data that are projections of the future. Revenue data require estimations of consumer behaviour with changing prices. Any projection is difficult and risky, but estimates resting primarily on the actions of others are even more difficult than internal projections. The economic models described earlier in this chapter require a knowledge of supply and demand functions in order to set optimal prices. Because the exact form of these functions is usually not known, managers often set prices that are above or below optimal. A wide variety of prices may therefore be found for similar goods in markets that are characterized by monopolistic competition, and even in markets that approach perfect competition.

Inferior goods and other strange phenomena. Not all supply and demand situations can be described satisfactorily by the general economic models already discussed. Various special cases occur. One is referred to as **inferior goods,** or Giffen's paradox. An inferior good is a product whose quantity demanded varies directly with changes in price for the product. A price increase causes an increase in the quantity demanded, and a price decrease causes a decline in the quantity demanded. No class of products can be generally classified as inferior goods, but some products occasionally seem to possess such demand characteristics.

Giffen's paradox

One plausible explanation for the inferior goods effect is the adage "you get what you pay for." Many consumers equate quality and price. High-priced items are assumed to be high-quality items. Although such a relationship is often true, it is by no means universally true. There are numerous cases of firms that raised the price of a product significantly without changing the product, and they experienced a sharp increase in the number of units sold. One case involved a service firm that was having trouble selling its services. As a desperation measure the firm tripled its service rates, and sales volume increased 400 percent.

These exceptions, although interesting, should not be used in the general analysis of pricing decisions. The exceptions should be used only where they are known to apply, or their existence is strongly suspected.

Pricing models in business

Armed with the general economic relationships described by the economic models, managers must make pricing decisions for specific products. Typically managers select specific product pricing models that they feel will convert the relationships of the general economic models into a usable model for pricing individual products. Some of the more common pricing models are discussed below.

Cost-based pricing models

Many pricing models are based on cost relationships. For example, a merchant may add 50 percent to the cost paid for products to arrive at a selling price. A university may estimate its total operating cost for the coming academic year and set tuition rates by dividing the estimated student enrollment into the total estimated cost.

Cost bases are popular in making pricing decisions because they are easy to use and easy to understand. Prices can be explained easily to management and governmental agencies if necessary. Cost data are readily available from the accounting system, and little if any additional data need be gathered and assimilated to utilize cost-based pricing models. In addition, cost-based models are intuitively logical to many people. It seems reasonable that there should be a strong relationship between the cost of a product or service and the price charged. Although the cost-price relationship does not always exist, economic theory tells us that it should exist over the long run.

Frequently cost is an important variable in making pricing decisions

Cost-plus models

Price is set at cost plus some amount or percentage

A very simple and widely used cost-based pricing model is referred to as **cost-plus.** A cost-plus model uses the cost of the product or services and adds on a certain amount or percentage to arrive at the selling price. The obvious question is, Which cost should be used? You have seen that the term **cost** refers to a variety of possible costs, such as full cost, variable cost, standard cost, or others. Thus any cost-plus model must clearly identify the cost to be used.

Product cost plus a markup

Product cost. A common cost-plus model uses product cost as the basis for pricing. For example, Darwan Sporting Goods Store prices all products at cost plus 60 percent. The following products just received are priced below.

Product	Invoice Cost	Markup (60%)	Selling Price
Baseballs	$ 2.50	$1.50	$ 4.00
Basketballs	10.00	6.00	16.00
Footballs	9.00	5.40	14.40
Soccer balls	12.00	7.20	19.20

The same type of calculations can be used in pricing a manufactured product except that the manager cannot merely refer to an invoice. Instead the manager must use the firm's cost records for the manufacturing of the product. To illustrate, below are the summarized data from a job cost sheet for the production of 80 pop-up camping trailers. The manufacturer sells these trailers to recreational vehicle dealers for cost plus 40 percent.

Resource	Total Cost	Units Produced	Unit Cost
Direct materials	$43,200	80	$540
Direct labour	24,000	80	300
Applied manufacturing overhead	28,800	80	360
Total manufacturing cost	$96,000	80	$1,200

Selling price per unit = $1,200 + ($1,200 × .4) = $1,200 + $480 = $1,680

When product cost is used as the basis for pricing, the addition to cost (the 60 percent for the merchandising firm and the 40 percent for the manufacturing firm) must cover all operating expenses and generate a satisfactory level of profit. Often managers must experiment with the values used in the pricing model until a satisfactory level of profit is achieved.

Total cost. Sometimes the cost base used in pricing includes both product costs and operating costs. This is a common approach to pricing government contracts. For example, a contract may establish a price of total cost plus 15 percent. The cost part of the price allows the firm to recover all costs associated with the contract, and the 15 percent is the profit on the contract.

Price is set at product cost plus operating expenses plus a markup

Total cost pricing models are popular for government contracts because the government frequently purchases goods or services for which there is no ready market. For example, jet fighter airplanes that the Canadian government is committed to purchase cannot be sold to the general public. Frequently it is impossible to predict accurately the cost of such new and specialized products. If a price is established when the contract is signed, it may be much too high in order to allow for unknown production problems, or it may be much too low, causing the manufacturer to suffer a loss. The purpose of a total cost–based contract is to provide a fair price and a fair profit that is considered advantageous to both parties.

Costs must be identified with cost objectives

An obvious difficulty with a total cost–based pricing model is the determination of total cost. If the producing firm manufactures only a single product for the purchaser, the costing process is simplified, but most firms produce a variety of products for different customers. For instance, De Havilland Corporation produces aircraft for the federal government, and it sells a variety of products to private-sector customers. Although multiple customers and multiple products complicate the process of determining costs, the total cost of the contract can be computed. As discussed in Chapter 10, cost can be determined for repetitive nonmanufacturing activities and assigned to the contract for services utilized. Costs for nonroutine nonmanufacturing activities must be assigned using cost allocation procedures discussed in Chapter 4. As always, the guiding principle for the cost allocation is the matching principle. Even relying on the matching principle, cost determination problems sometimes arise. In order to deal with these problems in the United States, a board called Cost Accounting Standards Board (discussed in Chapter 1) was created to standardize the cost determination process and to minimize costing problems for federal government cost-plus contracts. No such board exists in Canada.

Cost-plus pricing illustrated

We illustrate cost-plus contracts with the example of Missile Magic, Inc., which has a contract to produce missile guidance systems for the government. The contract establishes a price of total cost plus 12 percent. Total cost is defined as manufacturing costs plus 30 percent of the firm's administrative costs. Production data for the contract are presented below along with administrative costs for the company in total.

Manufacturing costs:	
Direct materials	$ 330,000
Direct labour	620,000
Applied MOH	930,000
Total administrative costs	2,400,000

The contract price for the missile guidance systems is

Manufacturing cost	$1,880,000
Allocated administrative cost ($2,400,000 × .3)	720,000
Total contract cost	$2,600,000
Contract profit ($2,600,000 × .12)	312,000
Contract price	$2,912,000

Standard cost. Cost-plus models using actual cost figures as a base have a strange managerial characteristic: The more inefficient the manufacturer is, the larger the profit. For example, if a contract price is set at total cost plus 20 percent, $300,000 of total cost yields a contract profit of $60,000. However, if more inefficient operations yield a total cost of $400,000, the contract profit rises to $80,000. There is a double incentive to assign unnecessary costs to contracts. First, the costs are covered by the contract rather than by other activities of the firm, making the other activities less costly. Second, these extra costs raise the profit on the cost-plus contract. Even contracts using fixed fees, such as total cost plus $100,000 or product cost plus $160,000, provide little incentive for cost control when cost coverage is a basic part of the contract.

To minimize some of the problems just mentioned without eliminating the advantages of cost-plus pricing, standard costs can be used as the cost base. Standard cost pricing models place the burden of production efficiency on the manufacturer. The price to the buyer reflects only costs from efficient operations plus the agreed profit. Even standards are not always successful, however, since it is difficult to establish standards for new and complicated products and activities. An example of a standard cost–plus pricing system is presented below. The pricing model is standard manufacturing cost plus 75 percent.

Standard cost pricing models isolate efficiencies and inefficiencies of the manufacturing firm

	Unit Cost		
Resource	**Standard Cost**	**Actual Cost**	**Variance**
Direct materials	$10	$12	$ 2 U
Direct labour	18	24	6 U
Applied MOH	12	16	4 U
Total	$40	$52	$12 U

$$\text{Price} = \$40 + (\$40 \times .75) = \$40 + \$30 = \underline{\underline{\$70}}$$

If the model had been actual manufacturing cost plus 75 percent, the price would be $91 [$52 + ($52 × .75)]. The difference of $21 makes the price 30 percent higher than the price based on standard costs. When using standard cost pricing models, variances must be monitored carefully to ensure that prices reflect realistic production costs. If sizable variances persist, the pricing model may have to be modified.

Contribution approach pricing models

Only variable costs are used as the basis for pricing

Contribution approach pricing is also a cost-plus type of pricing, but the concept of the contribution approach is significantly different from full cost pricing. As with other applications of the contribution approach in managerial accounting, we are concerned with identifying all costs that vary with the product or service being priced. Fixed costs are **not** allocated to the product, service, or contract.

The contribution approach is appealing for a variety of reasons. One is that managers can more readily visualize the relationship between prices and costs that vary directly with sales. Since variable costs are used in segmental contribution reports and variable costing income statements, they are often very visible. Cost allocations that may be complicated or that may be based on questionable causal relationships are not necessary with the contribution approach. This pricing method often appeals to customers who are suspicious of allocated fixed costs. Often a customer would rather pay some multiple of variable costs than a much smaller percentage of a cost figure that includes fixed cost allocations. Whatever the reason, many products are priced using the contribution approach. A simple example follows. Knightlite Sleep Products manufactures beds and other sleep products. Variable cost data for the king-size waterbed are presented.

Resource	Unit Variable Cost
Direct materials	$ 80
Direct labour	50
Variable MOH	70
Variable selling	35
Variable administrative	5
Total variable cost	$240

Selling price equals variable costs plus 125 percent, so the selling price of the king-size waterbed is

$$\$240 + (\$240 \times 1.25) = \$240 + \$300 = \underline{\underline{\$540}}$$

The contribution approach to pricing ignores fixed costs in the pricing model. There is some danger of overlooking fixed costs altogether. Although fixed costs are not assigned to cost objectives under the contribution approach, they must be taken into account in determining the amount to be added to variable costs to arrive at the price. The amount added must provide enough revenue to cover all of the fixed costs and still provide a satisfactory profit. Fixed costs are important in the contribution approach to pricing, but they are treated in a different manner than with full cost pricing models.

Target profits

Establish prices aimed at earning a satisfactory profit

Earlier we discussed the concept of **satisfactory profits** as profit maximization within the current business environment. Satisfactory profit levels represent **target profits** that managers may use as a general guide in establishing prices or as the prime pricing variable, as in utility rate setting. Targets may be established in dollar amounts, such as $2,000,000, or in relation to other variables, such as 10 percent of sales or 15 percent return on net assets, as discussed in Chapter 11. Once the target profit is determined, prices are computed by dividing the expected activity level into the target profit.

To illustrate this pricing method, assume three new attorneys are trying to determine an appropriate hourly fee for their services. The three form a partnership and estimate that they will incur the following expenses during the coming year:

Secretarial salaries	$20,000
Building and equipment lease expenses	11,000
Utility expenses	4,000
Other expenses	10,000
Total expenses	$45,000

In addition, each of the three attorneys wants to earn $25,000 the first year. They expect a total of 3000 hours of billable time during the year.

The rate required to cover all expected expenses and reach the target profit is calculated as follows:

Total expenses	$ 45,000
Target profit	75,000
	$120,000/3000 hours = $40 per hour

The partners must now examine the $40/hour price to determine whether it is feasible. If competing firms charge much less, the attorneys may have to lower their profit expectations; on the other hand, they may find $40 to be so low that potential clients stay away, thinking that such low-priced services cannot be very good. The latter situation is an example of Giffen's paradox, discussed earlier in the chapter.

Special orders

All business opportunities should not be evaluated in the same way. The specific characteristics of each opportunity must be considered when evaluating the opportunity. For example, a one-time order or **special order** may provide a company with an opportunity to utilize some excess capacity. The selling price of the units in the special order may be different from the normal selling price, but that does not necessarily mean the order should be rejected. Instead it should be evaluated carefully to see how it impacts on total company profitability and other company goals.

To illustrate, Dunnlevit Auto Equipment Company produces a variety of auto parts for new cars and for replacement parts. The normal selling price for its automobile generator is $72 each. Recently an automobile manufacturer offered to buy 2000 generators from Dunnlevit for $55 per unit. The following cost estimates were prepared for the production of the 2000 generators:

Cost Item	Total Cost	Unit Cost
Direct materials	$ 60,000	$30
Direct labour	20,000	10
Manufacturing overhead (60% fixed overhead)	30,000	15
Selling and administrative (80% fixed)	20,000	10
Total	$130,000	$65

Dunnlevit currently has excess capacity, and the generators could be produced without incurring any additional fixed costs. This would be a one-time order. The automobile manufacturer normally produces its own generators, but new production equipment is being installed in the generator division, causing a temporary interruption of production.

Identifying and analyzing relevant data

A glance at the unit cost data indicates Dunnlevit Auto Equipment would lose $20,000 ($10 per unit × 2000 generators) if the special order is accepted. But fixed overhead cost and fixed selling and administrative costs are irrelevant to this decision since they will exist whether the order is accepted or rejected. A more relevant analysis of costs is to identify those which would occur only if the project is accepted:

Cost Item	Unit Cost
Direct materials	$30
Direct labour	10
Variable overhead (40% of $15)	6
Variable selling and administrative (20% of $10)	2
Total variable cost	$48

Accepting the order would provide a $7-per-unit ($55 selling price–$48 variable cost) contribution margin. Therefore, the special order would increase company profit by $14,000 ($7 × 2000 generators).

Other factors may influence special-order pricing decisions. A major concern is the effect on regular customers. If regular customers are paying more for products and services, they may demand price reductions or stop buying from the firm. Another problem is that some special-order customers may decide to become regular customers, and changes in the price may become necessary. Finally, various legislation similar to the Combines Investigations Act may restrict discriminatory special-order pricing practices of companies.

Loss leader pricing

Sell some products at or below cost to attract customers to the store to buy normally priced products

An old merchandising joke states, We may lose a little on every unit we sell, but we make it up in volume. It does not require any business experience to realize that such a merchandising policy quickly leads to disaster. However, the policy of selling a product at a small loss may be an effective approach in some circumstances. For example, most grocery stores offer weekly specials on certain items that temporarily are priced well below normal prices, perhaps even below cost. Products priced below cost are called **loss leaders,** and their function is to attract customers to the store. Hopefully customers will purchase enough regularly priced products along with the loss leaders to warrant the low prices on special products. Of course, some people purchase only the specially priced items, but in aggregate customers usually purchase a satisfactory mix of products.

Not all businesses are capable of using loss leader pricing. Ideally the business should sell a large variety of products that customers purchase on a regular basis. Firms selling expensive products, such as appliances and automobiles, typically are not able to use loss leaders. Most people do not buy one car below dealer cost and several more at the regular price. A form of loss leader pricing is attempted when dealers or manufacturers offer common options, such as power steering, power brakes, or air conditioning, well below regular prices. The hope is that customers will be attracted by the low prices on desirable options and will buy the automobile.

Summary

Pricing refers to the assignment of a selling price to a product or service provided by an organization. Pricing decisions are necessary in all profit-oriented organizations, and many not-for-profit organizations set prices on services, such as university tuition or city licence fees. Many factors affect prices, but pricing decisions are made within the framework of general economic models. The type of pricing model used depends upon the type of market in which the product is traded.

A **perfectly competitive market** is characterized by homogeneous products, free mobility of resources, and perfect information among market participants, none of whom can influence market prices. Price is determined by supply and demand. **Supply** is the total aggregate quantity of goods or services that suppliers are willing to provide at each possible price. The graph of a supply function is called a **supply curve. Demand** is the total aggregate quantity of goods or services that purchasers are willing to buy at each possible price. The graph of a demand function is called a **demand curve.** The **market**

equilibrium point is the price and quantity at which supply equals demand; it is the intersection of the supply and demand curves.

Since no individual supplier can affect market price in a perfectly competitive market, each supplier faces a horizontal demand curve at the market price. That means that individual suppliers can sell as many units of product as they choose at the market price. The quantity a supplier will provide is determined by the firm's cost schedule. Each firm maximizes its net income if it sells its products until the marginal cost of supplying the last unit equals the marginal revenue. **Marginal cost** is the amount of cost increase caused by a unit increase in output. **Marginal revenue** is the amount of increase in revenue caused by the sale of one additional unit. In a perfectly competitive market, marginal revenue is the selling price.

Most products are not sold in a perfectly competitive market. Monopolistic competition, monopoly, and oligopoly are three other market types. **Monopolistic competition** occurs when there are many sellers of similar, but not identical, products, and no single seller can influence market prices. **Monopoly** exists when a firm is the sole supplier of a product. **Oligopoly** results when several large sellers dominate a market and compete against one another. The economic solution to the pricing decision in each of these three markets is to maximize profits at the level of sales where marginal cost equals marginal revenue. The difference from a perfectly competitive market is that the seller faces a downward sloping demand curve rather than a horizontal one. Therefore, to increase the volume of sales, a seller must lower its price. Oligopolies may face a **kinked demand curve.** A price decrease by one firm causes a sharp drop in the quantity demanded from other firms. Prices are often set by the largest oligopolistic firm, which is usually a **price leader,** and the same price is charged by the remaining firms, which are **price followers.**

Business pricing decisions are not always made with exact adherence to economic models. Most firms do not maximize profits in the strict sense of the word. Instead firms strive to earn satisfactory profits that yield a desirable return on capital invested in the company. Government influence directly and indirectly affects some pricing decisions. For example, government agencies control prices of utilities. Indirect influence over prices of products, such as steel and other raw materials, occurs through government threats of sanctions. Economic models have limitations since they are abstract representations of something in the real world. If the model is a poor representation or the data used in the model are inaccurate or inappropriate, the model is of little value. Additionally the demand for some products does not take the form of a typical demand curve in economics. With some products, called **inferior goods,** the quantity demanded decreases as price decreases.

Within the general economic pricing framework, managers must select specific models for making pricing decisions. A variety of pricing models is used in business. **Cost-plus** models use the cost of the product or service and add a certain amount or percentage to arrive at the selling price. The cost base may be the product cost, total cost, or standard cost. Total cost is product cost plus nonmanufacturing cost. Full costs are used frequently in government cost-plus contracts. Standard costs are popular in pricing models because the buyer is not charged for seller inefficiencies.

Contribution approach pricing uses only variable costs in establishing prices. Although fixed costs do not enter directly into the computation of prices, they must be covered by the price before profits can be realized.

Prices may be established with reference to desired corporate profit levels. **Target profits** can be expressed in dollar amounts or as return on investment, but the target profit measure must be converted to expected sales quantities and mix to establish prices.

In setting prices for **special orders,** management may choose to sell below full cost as long as variable costs are covered. Caution must be exercised to guard against antagonizing regular customers or violating the law. Some businesses, such as grocery stores, may entice customers into their stores by offering **loss leaders** at a very low price, perhaps even below cost. Customers usually purchase enough regularly priced merchandise while in the store to make the loss leaders worthwhile.

List of important terms	
contribution approach pricing *(498)*	monopoly *(487)*
cost-plus pricing *(495)*	monopolistic competition *(487)*
demand *(481)*	oligopoly *(487)*
demand curve *(482)*	perfectly competitive market *(481)*
inferior goods *(494)*	pricing *(479)*
kinked demand curve *(491)*	purchase price *(479)*
loss leaders *(501)*	selling price *(479)*
marginal cost *(485)*	special orders *(499)*
marginal revenue *(485)*	supply *(481)*
market equilibrium *(484)*	supply curve *(482)*
	target profit pricing *(499)*

Questions

1. Distinguish between purchase price and selling price.
2. Give several examples of pricing decisions in not-for-profit organizations.
3. Identify six factors that often influence pricing decisions.
4. Identify the basic types of product markets.
5. What characteristics must a market have to be classified as perfectly competitive?
6. Describe a supply schedule and a supply curve.
7. "Don't give me any of the economics stuff, we set our own prices around this company." Comment.
8. What is a market equilibrium point and what information does it provide?
9. In a perfectly competitive market, how do individual suppliers determine the quantity of product they will supply?

10. What are the characteristics of a monopolistic competition market?
11. What is a monopoly market? Give an example.
12. Define marginal revenue.
13. Define marginal cost.
14. What is a kinked demand curve and to what kind of market does it apply?
15. Briefly describe several variables that modify the general economic pricing models.
16. Identify and briefly describe the basic cost-oriented pricing models.
17. What is meant by the contribution approach to pricing?
18. "I do not like to bother with fixed costs, so I really like the contribution approach pricing models." Comment.
19. President to the sales manager, "Special orders should be priced like all other orders; we cannot show any favouritism in this company." Do you agree? Explain.
20. "Loss leader pricing! Are you crazy? We cannot make any money selling below cost. We may need a new pricing specialist." As the pricing specialist, defend yourself.

Exercises

Ex. 12-1 **Graphing a supply curve.** Below are price and supply data for an ore market.

Price per Ton	Quantity Supplied (In thousands of tons)
$20	400
18	380
16	360
14	330
12	300
10	260
8	220
6	160
4	100
2	20

Required:
Use the data provided to graph a supply curve.

Ex. 12-2 **Graphing a demand curve.** At the top of the facing page are price and demand data for a mineral ore market.

Required:
Use the data provided to graph a demand curve.

Price per Ton	Quantity Demanded (In thousands of tons)
$20	20
18	50
16	75
14	100
12	130
10	160
8	220
6	270
4	340
2	450

Ex. 12-3 Graphic solution of market equilibrium. Refer to the supply and demand data in Exercises 12-1 and 12-2.

Required:
Determine the market equilibrium point and graph your solution.

Ex. 12-4 Using economic data. Below are production cost data for an individual firm producing ore in a perfectly competitive market. The market price for the ore is $12 per ton.

Quantity Produced in Tons	Total Production Costs	Marginal Cost
0	$ 2,000	—
100	2,400	$ 400
200	2,900	500
300	3,500	600
400	4,200	700
500	5,000	800
600	5,900	900
700	6,900	1,000
800	8,000	1,100
900	9,200	1,200
1000	10,600	1,400
1100	12,200	1,600
1200	14,000	1,800

Required
a. What is the optimum strategy for this producer?
b. What is the supplier's net income with the optimum strategy?
c. What is the supplier's net income if 1000 tons are produced and sold?

Ex. 12-5 Cost-plus pricing. The Shiny Coat Cat Food Company prices its products at full product cost plus 80 percent. Shown below are data on three of its products.

	Dry Food in a Bag	Canned Seafood Dinners	Moist Pouch Dinners
Units produced	10 000	6000	4000
Direct materials	$6,500	$900	$ 800
Direct labour	1,000	300	400
Manufacturing overhead	1,500	600	1,000
Marketing	4,000	500	500
Administrative	2,000	500	500

Required:
Use the data above to determine selling prices for each product.

Ex. 12-6   Pricing services. The Sweetswing Racket Shoppe sells tennis equipment, supplies, and apparel. As a service to customers, Sweetswing restrings tennis rackets. During the last six months the following data were accumulated:

Rackets restrung	400
Labour time	500 h
Labour rate	$6.00/h
Material cost	$2,200

Required:
a. What should Sweetswing charge for restringing if recovery of direct costs is the only objective?
b. What should the price be if recovery of full costs is the objective and Sweetswing estimates indirect costs are 40 percent of direct costs?
c. What should the price be if the objective is to include a normal markup of 25 percent above full cost?

Ex. 12-7   Special-order pricing. The Deep-Beep Depth Finder Company manufactures depth finders for fishermen and people seeking the Loch Ness monster. The most inexpensive model sells for $80, has variable production costs of $40 per unit, commission cost of $6 per unit, and variable distribution cost of $4 per unit. Fixed manufacturing costs associated with this model of depth finder are $100,000. Sales of the depth finders are 4000 units a year. A bass-boat manufacturer has offered to buy 1200 units at $60 each. This order would require a one-time cost of $18,000 to lease extra space and equipment until the order is completed. However, the normal commission of $6 per unit and the variable distribution cost would be eliminated.

Required:
a. Decide whether the special order should be accepted and support your decision with calculations.
b. If the regional distribution representative for the bass-boat manufacturer's area demands his commission, should the order be accepted?

Ex. 12-8 **Cost-plus pricing.** A retired man builds beautiful wooden dollhouses as a hobby and to supplement his income. He charges enough to cover lumber costs and give himself a little for his efforts. His wife tells him he is not charging enough to cover his costs, so he accumulates the following data:

	Expected Costs per House	Actual Costs per House
Lumber	$20	$35
Paint	2	1
Glue, fittings, and miscellaneous supplies and expenses	—	6
Total material cost	$22	$47
Labour time	20 h	30 h
Equipment cost	$2,500	
Expected useful life of equipment	10 yr	
Dollhouses produced per year	25	

The man had been charging $45 each for the dollhouses and had a long waiting list of customers. Several people have suggested the price could be more than doubled without a noticeable decline in the demand for the dollhouses.

Required:
a. If the man merely wants to recover all his actual costs, what should be the price?
b. If the man wants $1.50 an hour for his time plus actual costs, what should be the price for his product?
c. If an alternative use of the man's basement workshop is to rent the space as a small apartment for $1,200 a year, what is the full cost price for each dollhouse including the required labour rate?

Ex. 12-9 **Pricing analysis.** Janice has a $700-a-month summer job offer as a cost analyst for a construction company. An alternative is to offer swimming lessons to children, in her neighbour's pool. The neighbour will let Janice use the pool for lessons during the day for $180 a month. Janice likes the outdoors and would rather give swimming lessons than work in an office, but she needs all the money she can earn to return to college in the fall. Janice can schedule four 1-hour lessons per weekday in groups of five children each and can give lessons 22 days per month.

Required:
a. How much does Janice have to charge each student per lesson to equal her summer job offer?
b. If the maximum rate for group swimming lessons is $1.25 an hour and four group lessons are all that can be scheduled during a day, how large must the group be for Janice to match her salary offer?

Ex. 12-10   **Price analysis.** The Brown and White Lightning Factory manufactures a brew of amazing flavour called White Lightning. No other firm has a product of similar character. The firm seems to be able to sell all it can produce at the current price of $12 a litre. Variable costs are $4 a litre, and fixed costs are $25,000 a year. At current capacity the firm is able to produce 5000 litres a year. An increase of $15,000 a year in fixed costs would double capacity. However, price would have to be lowered to $10.50 a litre to sell all of the output.

A national distributor approaches Brown and White Lightning with an offer to buy 50 000 litres at $9 a litre. If the offer is accepted, an investment in plant and equipment of $1,000,000 would be required, adding $135,000 in annual fixed costs to the original amount of $25,000. The company requires an 8 percent return on the newly invested capital.

Required:
a. Should the firm expand the operations to 10 000 litres? Support your answer.
b. If the company doubles its present capacity, what is the minimum the company can charge for White Lightning and be at least as well off as before the expansion?
c. Should the company accept the offer to sell 50 000 litres at $9? Support your answer.

Problem Set A

P. 12A-1   **Graphic analysis in a perfectly competitive market.** A farmer produces wheat on a small farm. Below is the cost schedule for his wheat production.

Bags Produced	Total Cost	Marginal Cost
0	$1,000	—
100	1,300	$300
200	1,600	200
300	1,700	100
400	1,850	150
500	2,050	200
600	2,300	250
700	2,600	300
800	2,950	350
900	3,350	400
1000	3,800	450
1000	4,300	500

Required:
a. If the market price for wheat is $4.30 a bag, how much wheat should the farmer supply?

b. What is the farmer's net income at the optimum production level?

c. Graph the solution to this problem.

P. 12A-2   Cost-price analysis. Kool-Komfort Air Conditioning Company manufactures a full line of home air conditioners. Management is contemplating entering the recreational vehicle air conditioning market with a new model designed for use in travel trailers and motor homes. The model would have a maximum selling price of $500, given the size and quality of the unit. At that price marketing estimates indicate a sales level of 5000 units. Product engineers estimate new fixed manufacturing costs of $300,000 annually if the product is produced. Any new product must generate a minimum pretax profit of 15 percent of sales to be accepted. Management estimates variable marketing and administrative expenses of 10 percent of sales and fixed marketing and administrative costs of $225,000.

Required:

a. What is the maximum per-unit variable manufacturing cost that would still justify production of the new product?

b. If variable manufacturing costs are 10 percent less than the maximum computed in part *a* and the variable MOH costs amount to ⅙ of the total variable manufacturing costs, how much is prime cost per unit?

c. Assuming the variable manufacturing cost data in part *b*, what is the net income?

P. 12A-3   Cost-plus pricing. Store-All Products manufactures metal storage sheds using a standard cost control system for all products. Standard and actual cost data are presented for the MS10-12 model for the first quarter of the year when 1000 units were produced.

	Unit Cost	
	Actual Cost	**Standard Cost**
Direct materials	$280	$240
Direct labour	90	100
Variable MOH	30	20
Allocated fixed MOH	50	40

The management of Store-All is evaluating a number of possible pricing formulas. Assume marketing and administrative costs identifiable with the product are $190,000.

Required:

Using the above data, compute a price for the MS10-12 storage shed based on each of the following:

a. Full product cost plus 60 percent.
b. Standard cost plus 60 percent.
c. Variable product cost plus 100 percent.
d. Standard variable cost plus 120 percent.
e. Prime cost plus 150 percent.
f. Total cost plus 20 percent.

P. 12A-4   **Special order.** Fridgstrom, Inc., manufactures quality redwood picnic tables that it sells to garden stores for $120 each. Last year the company produced and sold 8000 picnic tables. Following are sales and cost data for the year:

Sales 8000 units @ $120		$960,000
Manufacturing costs:		
Direct material	$480,000	
Direct labour	200,000	
Manufacturing overhead		
(20% variable)	120,000	800,000
Gross margin		$160,000
Operating expenses:		
Marketing (80% variable)	$ 70,000	
Administrative (all fixed)	64,000	134,000
Net income		$ 26,000

Fridgstrom, Inc., received an offer from a department store chain to purchase 2000 picnic tables for $95 each. This special order would require the temporary lease of some production space and equipment. The building and equipment lease cost and setup costs for the special order would amount to $8,000.

Required:
a. Should the special order be accepted if there are no marketing and administrative costs associated with the order?
b. What is the effect on net income of accepting the special order?
c. Should the special order be accepted if only half of the variable marketing cost can be eliminated?
d. Assuming the situation described in part *c*, what is the effect on net income of accepting the order?

P. 12A-5   **Sales volume, pricing, and target profits.** For many years Ye Ole Corner Drug Store has used a pricing formula of product cost plus 120 percent. In the last several years the store has lost sales volume and experienced sharply declining profits. Following is the income statement for the most recent year:

Ye Ole Corner Drug Store
Income Statement
For the Year Ended October 31

Sales		$88,000
Less: Cost of goods sold		40,000
Gross margin		$48,000
Operating expenses:		
Advertising	$ 4,000	
Depreciation, store	3,600	
Equipment rental	2,100	
Insurance	1,800	
Miscellaneous	1,500	
Salary and wages	30,000	
Utilities	4,000	47,000
Net income		$ 1,000

The owner of the store thinks profits may be increased by reducing the product prices and increasing sales volume.

Required:
For parts *a, b,* and *c* assume operating expenses remain at $47,000.

a. If a new pricing formula of product cost plus 80 percent increases sales quantity by 30 percent, should this new pricing formula be used?
b. What would your answer be to part *a* if the new pricing formula resulted in a 60 percent increase in sales?
c. What is the required sales volume to generate a target net income of $15,000 if the pricing formula is product cost plus 80 percent?
d. Someone suggests that the store could become a small discount drugstore for the area by pricing all products at product cost plus 40 percent. This pricing strategy would require additional operating expenses of $23,000 a year, and the owner wants an annual profit of $30,000 to make such major changes. What sales volume is required to accept the proposed change?

P. 12A-6   **Cost analysis and target profit pricing.** White Rim Outfitters runs pack and float trips into the foothills of the Fraser River. The company offers 3-, 7-, and 14-day trips. Cost per day varies with the length of the trip due to large front-end costs for organizing and outfitting each trip, whether it lasts 3, 7, or 14 days. At the top of the following page are cost data for last year:
White Rim has the philosophy of keeping the 3-day-trip price as low as possible in the hope of generating repeat business for the longer trips.

Required:
a. Compute the price for each trip using 200 percent of direct costs as a model.

| | Trip Length | | | |
	3 Days	7 Days	14 Days	Total
Number of customers	200	100	50	350
Direct cost of trips:				
Outfitting costs	$10,000	$ 6,000	$ 4,000	$ 20,000
Guide costs	8,400	10,500	11,600	30,500
Supplies costs	3,600	4,200	4,200	12,000
Miscellaneous costs	2,000	1,000	500	3,500
Total direct costs	$24,000	$21,700	$20,300	$ 66,000
Other expenses:				
Marketing				$ 16,000
Trip research				8,000
Licences, taxes, etc.				2,000
General administrative				28,000
Total other expenses				$ 54,000
Total expenses				$120,000

b. Use the average daily direct cost of all trips as a basis for pricing each trip and apply the 200 percent model used in part *a*.

c. Using last year's volume and mix of trips, compute the required daily price for trips and the price of each type of trip, assuming a $30,000 target profit is required. Assume all costs remain the same.

d. If the company sets the price of the 3-day trip at direct costs plus 50 percent, what must be the prices for the other trips to generate the $30,000 target profit?

Problem Set B

P. 12B-1   **Graphic analysis of supply and demand.** Below are data for the Johnson Shirt Company.

Price	Quantity Demanded	Quantity Supplied
$20	100	1750
19	200	1700
18	300	1650
17	450	1550
16	550	1450
15	750	1350
14	900	1250
13	1150	1150
12	1400	1050
11	1700	900
10	2000	600
9	2400	300
8	2900	0

Required:

Carefully draw a supply and demand curve using the data above. Label the curves and the equilibrium point and show the market price and quantity demanded.

P. 12B-2 Cost analysis and pricing. Personal Security Products manufactures burglar alarm systems and other security products. The Car-Guard product is a small electronic alarm system for cars, boats, and other mobile items. The product was introduced at a bargain price of $180, which is standard cost plus 20 percent. Now the product is very successful, and the company is evaluating a more realistic price. Management is analyzing the production cost data summarized below.

Resource	Standard Unit Cost	Percentage Variance
Direct materials	$ 50	20.0 U
Direct labour	60	25.0 U
Manufacturing overhead	40	12.5 F
Total	$150	

The rest of the products at Personal Security are priced at standard cost plus 40 percent. Standard cost variance averages 5 percent unfavourable for the rest of the company's products.

Required:

a. If the price were actual product cost plus 20 percent, what would be the price of Car-Guard?

b. What price would be charged for Car-Guard using the company's normal pricing formula?

c. What price for Car-Guard would represent a close measure of the relationship between price and actual cost for the rest of the company's products?

P. 12B-3 Cost-base pricing. The Gourmet Heaven Restaurant specializes in prime rib dinners. In an effort to control costs and generate higher profits, the restaurant management established standards and accumulated detailed cost data for the prime rib dinner.

Until now the restaurant had merely picked some price for the prime rib dinner that sounded reasonable to management. Currently the price is $8.75. The cost data at the top of page 514 cause some concern among managers who are now interested in some cost-based method of pricing.

Required:

a. Determine the price of the prime rib dinner using:

1. Actual food cost plus 120 percent.

	Actual Unit Cost	Standard Unit Cost
Prime rib	$3.75	$2.80
Labour cost to cook and serve	.65	.50
Other direct food costs	.80	.70
Allocated indirect costs	3.80	3.00
Total costs	$9.00	$7.00

    2. Standard food cost plus 150 percent.
    3. Actual direct cost plus 125 percent.
    4. Standard direct cost plus 125 percent.
    5. Total actual cost plus 15 percent.
    6. Total standard cost plus 15 percent.
  b. Comment on your assessment of whether standard or actual costs should be used for pricing in this firm.

P. 12B-4   **Special-order analysis.** Smithberg Pharmaceutical manufactures general-purpose daily vitamins that it sells for $105 per 100-bottle case to several distribution companies which sell the product under their own brand names. An agency of the government offers to buy 10 000 cases of vitamins at $70 per case for use in an overseas nutrition program. This one-time special-order offer occurred because the agency's regular supplier suffered a long strike. Below are data for the year just completed.

Cost Item	Per Case
Direct materials	$40
Direct labour	8
MOH (40% variable)	30
Marketing and distribution costs (60% variable)	10
Administrative costs (10% variable)	10

    Currently Smithberg is operating at 60 percent of capacity, and the special order could be handled with additional equipment lease cost and setup costs of $40,000.

Required:
a. Should the special order be accepted if variable marketing and distribution costs on the order are half of normal?
b. What is the effect on Smithberg's net income if the order is accepted?
c. Should the order be accepted if all variable marketing and administrative costs apply to the special order?

d. Using part *c* assumptions, what is the effect on net income of accepting the special order?

P. 12B-5   **Target profits and pricing.** The Green Garden Tool Company manufactures a variety of garden tools including push-type and self-propelled lawn mowers. Management had decided to enter the garden tractor business with a 7500-watt tractor. Standard cost data for the tractor are presented below.

	Cost per Unit
Direct material	$300
Direct labour	150
Variable MOH	100
Variable marketing	50
Variable administrative	20

	Total Cost
Fixed MOH	$360,000
Fixed marketing	135,000
Fixed administrative	220,000

The company expects to produce and sell 2000 tractors the first year of operations and is trying to determine an appropriate selling price. Historically the firm has used a pricing formula of standard full product cost plus 40 percent. A new manager suggests full costs be abandoned as a pricing base. He suggests the price be set at 180 percent of standard variable product cost.

Required:
a. What would be the price for the tractor using the company's normal pricing formula?
b. What would be the price using the new manager's suggestion?
c. The firm generates a 15 percent profit on sales with its current products. What tractor selling price is necessary to achieve the same profit-sales relationship for the new product?
d. If market conditions limit selling price to $1,050, what level of tractor sales must be achieved to generate a 15 percent profit on sales?

P. 12B-6   **Analyzing cost and pricing data.** Beachfront Provincial Park requested funds from the Provincial legislature to build a badly needed breakwater to prevent further beach erosion. The estimated cost of the proposed project is $298,800. The legislature made a special appropriation of $200,000 to start the project, but park officials believe the project must be completed this year to prevent irreversible damage. Currently the park charges $.50-a-person admission to the park.

Park management has the power to raise fees up to $1.25 without special permission. Below are cost and revenue data for the park for last year when 150 000 people visited the park.

Revenue:	
Admission fees	$ 75,000
Legislative appropriations	300,000
Expenses:	
Normal maintenance	90,000
Park personnel salaries	202,000
Supplies	40,000
Utilities	25,000
Miscellaneous	18,000

This year appropriations and all costs are expected to rise 8 percent. The number of visitors has risen by 20 percent in each of the last three years, and a similar increase is expected this year. However, it is anticipated that for every $.05 increase in price, the increase in visitors will be 1 percent less than expected (for example, a $.05 increase in price means the increase in visitors would be 19 percent, and a $.10 price increase would mean an increase in park visitors of 18 percent).

The additional funds required to build the breakwater must come from higher fees from park users and cost savings in other areas. To minimize the impact on park users, $35,000 of normal maintenance programs will be postponed, and $8,000 of utilities and miscellaneous expenses will be eliminated. The funds saved will be used in the breakwater project.

Required:
a. What admission price must each park visitor be charged to pay for the breakwater if all of the above assumptions hold?
b. What would your answer to part *a* be if actual cost savings from operations totaled only $35,725 instead of $43,000?

Minicases

Minicase 12-1
(SMA of Canada adapted)

The Havero Company produces a high-quality product in one of its manufacturing plants. The product has been sold at a price of $1.60, and Havero's management has decided to investigate the availability of increasing the selling price to better compensate the company for increases in costs.

Havero's controller has developed the following estimates of costs:

Monthly Output (Units)	Operating Costs	
	Fixed Cost	**Marginal Cost per Unit**
50 000 and less	$20,000	$1.20
50 001 – 60 000	20,000	1.22
60 001 – 70 000	20,000	1.24
70 001 – 80 000	22,000	1.28
80 001 – 90 000	22,000	1.34
90 001 – 100 000	22,000	1.42
100 001 – 110 000	24,000	1.50
110 001 – 120 000	24,000	1.48
120 001 – 130 000	26,000	1.70

The marketing manager has completed studies of the possible effect of selling price on sales volume and provided the following estimates:

Selling Price per Unit	Monthly Sales in Units
$1.50	100 000
1.60	90 000
1.70	80 000
1.80	70 000
1.90	60 000
2.00	50 000

Required:
Prepare a schedule which will indicate the most profitable price at which to sell the product and indicate which price is the most profitable.

Minicase 12-2
(Certified Accountants U.K. adapted)

Wizard, Ltd., which is a good customer of Witch, Ltd., has asked Witch to produce 400 units of a special variation of one of the standard products that it buys from Witch. It costs $10 to produce each unit of the standard product which is sold at $12.

Although Witch is not geared up to make the modifications and variations required, it decides for "customer relationship" reasons to agree to go ahead and supply the order. It will be able to produce 100 of the special units each 40-hour week, but will require special machinery for the purpose. There are three alternative ways of obtaining this machinery, and these, and the costs associated with them, are as follows:

1. *Adapting existing machinery*
The existing machinery which could be adapted is not being used at present,

although it is envisaged that in approximately three months it will be required in its present form for a contract currently being negotiated.

Costs of adapting this machinery would be $500, and after the order has been completed it would cost $600 to remove the adaptations and replace worn parts, etc., in order to return the machine to its current value. The machinery which could be adapted originally cost $10,000 five years ago and is being depreciated at $1,000 per annum. A special insurance policy would have to be held while it was operated in its adapted form, the fixed annual premium associated with this being 2 percent of the value of the machine when adapted. The current value of the machine is $3,000.

Variable operating costs associated with using the adapted machinery would be: labour $1 per hour and maintenance 50¢ per hour.

2. *Leasing specialist machinery*

The charge for leasing suitable machinery, which includes maintenance and insurance, but no labour costs, is $5 per hour with a minimum lease charge of $300 per week.

3. *Purchasing specialist machinery.*

To buy a new machine would cost $5,000. Operating, maintenance and insurance costs would be the same as for the adapted one.

The manufacturers of the machinery estimate that it loses value at the rate of $2.00 for every unit produced and on this basis they are prepared to repurchase any machinery sold by them, after deducting a further 10 percent of the residual value to cover transaction expenses.

Required

a. A report to the management of Witch, Ltd., advising them of which of the alternative courses of action would be most beneficial, based upon the previous information. Indicate ways in which your recommended course of action might be further improved.

In your report suggest a price to be charged to Wizard, Ltd., for the modified product, mentioning the factors which should be considered before a final decision is taken.

b. Suppose that Wizard, Ltd., was willing to place a continuing order for the modified product. In this new situation broadly explain the alterations needed to produce a long-run cost analysis of the alternatives.

Note: You should ignore the cost of capital, taxation and inflation in your deliberations.

Reproduced from Certified Accountants Questions and Suggested Answers, including papers for Scottish and Irish Students, Professional Examination, December 1975. With permission of The Association of Certified Accountants.

Minicase 12-3 (SMA of Canada adapted)

Leanne Rose operates a small machine shop. She manufactures one standard product available from many similar businesses as well as manufacturing products to customer order. Her accountant prepared the annual income statement below:

	Custom Sales	Standard Sales	Total
Sales	$50,000	$30,000	$80,000
Expenses:			
Direct material	$10,000	$ 9,000	$19,000
Direct labour	20,000	11,000	31,000
Depreciation	6,300	3,600	9,900
Power	700	400	1,000
Rent	6,000	1,000	7,000
Heat and light	600	100	700
Total Expenses	$43,600	$25,100	$68,700
Net Income	$ 6,400	$ 4,900	$11,300

The depreciation charges are for machines used in the respective product lines. The power charge is allocated based on the estimate of power consumed. The rent is for the building space which has been leased for ten years at $7,000 per year. The rent, heat and light are allocated to the product lines based on amount of floor space occupied.

Leanne is planning operations for the coming year and faces a problem. A valued custom-order customer has asked Leanne if she would produce 5000 special units for her. Leanne has contracts with her other customers requiring delivery of the same number of custom and standard units as last year. Leanne is working at capacity and would have to reduce other production in order to manufacture the special units. She cannot reduce production of custom units but could purchase 50 percent of the required standard products for $14,000 from another machine shop, allowing sufficient capacity for the special order. The customer is willing to pay $8 for each special unit. The direct material cost will be $2 per unit and the direct labour will be $3.40 per unit.

Total power usage will increase by 20 percent if the special order is accepted. Leanne will have to spend $4,000 for a special device which will be discarded when the special job is done. These are the only extra costs of the special order.

Required:
a. Calculate total company net income if Leanne accepts the order. Based on profitability should Leanne accept?
b. Briefly discuss three other factors that should be considered before Leanne decides to accept or reject the special order.

Minicase 12-4   (SMA of Canada adapted)

The Elray Furniture Company has been incurring a loss of about $90,000 per year from normal operations. This loss is likely to occur again next year unless the company can increase sales. The company's factory has a capacity of 10 000 machine-hours per month, but has been operating at only 60 percent of capacity.

The company's fixed overhead costs total $840,000 per year. Overhead is allocated to production on the basis of machine-hours. The overhead rate for the coming year will be $12 per machine-hour and is calculated using a practical capacity (denominator) activity level.

Elray has received an order from a large department store chain for 15 000 bookshelf units. Although Elray does not normally produce bookshelf units, it is considering the offer since the company is anxious to increase the utilization of its plant. The following information relates to the order:

Machine time per unit	three machine-hours
Direct material per unit	$75
Direct labour per unit	$30
Shipping and selling costs per unit	$12
Administrative expenses will increase by	$24 000

If the company accepts the order, total fixed overhead will not change. The department store chain has offered a price of $135 per unit.

Required:

a. Should Elray accept the order for bookshelf units? Show calculations to support your answer.

b. What is the minimum price per bookshelf unit that Elray would require if the company is to break even this year?

Chapter 13

Capital Budgeting

This chapter is devoted to capital budgeting, which is the process of determining what capital expenditures a company should make. Capital expenditures often are long-term commitments of significant amounts of resources and involve long-range policy decisions. When you have completed this chapter, you should understand:

1 The nature and characteristics of the capital budgeting process.

2 The activities involved in capital budgeting.

3 The types of capital budgeting evaluation models and their characteristics.

4 How to use each of the capital budgeting evaluation models.

5 Factors other than the capital budgeting evaluation models that may enter into capital budgeting decisions.

6 What effects taxes and government assistance have on project evaluation.

Capital budgeting is the process of identifying, evaluating, planning, and financing major investment projects of an organization. Decisions to expand production facilities, acquire new production machinery, buy a new computer, or remodel the office building are all examples of capital expenditure decisions. Capital budgeting decisions made now determine to a large degree how successful an organization will be in achieving its goals and objectives in the years ahead. Capital budgeting plays an important role in the long-range success of many organizations because of several characteristics that differentiate it from most other elements of the master budget.

521

First, most capital budgeting projects require relatively large commitments of resources. Major projects, such as plant expansion or equipment replacement, may involve resource outlays in excess of annual net income. Relatively insignificant purchases are not treated as capital budgeting projects even if the items purchased have long lives. For example, the purchase of 40 electronic calculators at $35 each for use in the office would probably be treated as a period expense by most firms, and the purchase decision would be made by a manager with responsibility for office operating expenses.

Second, most capital expenditure decisions are long-term commitments; projects last more than one year, and many extend over five, ten, or even twenty years. The longer the time period affected by the project, the more difficult it is to predict revenues, expenses, and cost savings. Typically, the longer the life of the project, the more uncertain the budget estimates.

A third characteristic is that capital budgeting decisions involve long-term policy decisions and should rest firmly on organizational policies concerning growth, marketing, industry share, social responsibility, and others.

In this chapter we discuss in general the capital budgeting process and then concentrate on the most common methods of evaluating proposed capital budgeting projects. We also examine capital rationing, which deals with the issue of making capital budgeting decisions with a limited amount of available resources.

The capital budgeting process

The long-range effect that many capital expenditures have on an organization and the required size of the investment of many capital expenditures dictate a careful, systematic analysis of investment alternatives. A business often has far more investment alternatives than it has funds to invest. A capital expenditure evaluation system is necessary to ensure that all capital investment proposals are evaluated in light of organizational goals so that the most desirable investments are undertaken. Capital budgeting procedures vary among firms, but the process generally involves the following activities:

1. Identification of potential capital budgeting projects
2. Estimation of project benefits and costs
3. Evaluation of proposed projects
4. Development of the capital expenditure budget based on project acceptance criteria
5. Reevaluation of projects after acceptance

Identification of projects

The first phase of capital budgeting is the identification of capital budgeting projects. In many large organizations investment proposals are prepared by each segment of the firm. Each manager attempts to satisfy the most pressing capital investment needs of his department. For example, a production division may request new drill presses because the machines now in use are old and require frequent repairs. The marketing division may propose the acquisition of portable computer terminals for sales representatives to speed up the order entry process. Top management may propose a new companywide computer-based information processing system to improve decision making throughout the company. Together all capital investment proposals comprise the set of potential investments from which management attempts to select the optimum investments, given the organization's goals and available investment funds.

Estimation of project benefits and costs

Capital budgets may include such projects as plant expansions, employee education programs, replacement of major items of equipment, acquisition of a new computer, and many others. To be acceptable, each project must meet some minimum criteria established by a company. For example, a plant supervisor wants to replace an existing punch press with a new model that is faster. To justify the replacement, the supervisor must show not only that the new equipment is faster, but also that it provides sufficient savings over its useful life to justify its cost. The analysis of the new equipment is based on estimates of cost and future benefits. Such estimates are not always easy to make. Long-term projects are particularly difficult to estimate. For example, a house that cost $60,000 five years ago may cost $95,000 today, and the cost of constructing a 1870 square metres production plant may have increased from $1,000,000 to $1,800,000 in the last five years. What is your estimate of the change in housing prices over the next 20 years? Many plant facilities projects involve 20-year forecasts, yet the estimates must be made now so that the project may be evaluated along with other investment proposals.

Project evaluation

Capital investment projects may cover a short period of time or range beyond 20 years; they may involve a few thousand dollars or millions of dollars. Some projects are expected to improve profits directly through higher sales or lower costs, while others promise more indirect benefits, such as improvement in employee morale when a new employee cafeteria is built. Capital expenditure projects may impact on an organization in many different ways, consequently all projects must be systematically evaluated and each project's costs and benefits measured so that the most desirable projects are accepted. The evaluation process should include as much relevant project data as possible. With a diversity of investment projects there is also a diversity of project evaluation methods.

Development of the capital expenditure budget

The capital expenditure budget consists of all investment proposals that have been approved for the budget period. The budget may simply be a listing of the projects and the amounts of the investments, or it may provide additional descriptive data about the projects. Regardless of the format of the budget, it is the end result of management's decisions on capital investments.

The decisions that result in the budget are strongly influenced by information obtained during the evaluation phase of the capital budgeting process, but the evaluation process seldom provides the actual selection decision for investment proposals. Managers must decide on the amount of resources to be used for capital expenditures and must set priorities to meet company objectives.

An analysis of each proposal's costs and benefits may be supplemented by an analysis of other variables, such as the behavioural impact of accepting or rejecting a project. For example, rejecting all investment proposals of a particular division may have undesirable consequences even if the proposals do not meet the firm's criteria of acceptability. Approving several proposals of a particular division may appear to some managers as favouritism, although all proposals offered by the division meet the criteria of the firm. In addition, to evaluate a particular project, other criteria may have to be examined to prevent an undesirable consequence from what might appear to be a desirable project. For example, a proposal to automate the assembly process may be economically feasible, but employee productivity in other production functions may decline because of support for assembly employees who would lose their jobs.

Reevaluation of projects

All estimates of future events are risky, and capital expenditure predictions are particularly so, because of the long-term nature of the projects. Consequently, once projects are accepted, they should be reviewed periodically to determine if they are achieving original expectations.

Many firms are so busy evaluating new investment proposals and managing daily activities that they find little time to reevaluate projects accepted during prior periods. Basically, reevaluation can assist in two ways. One is that accuracy of past estimates may be useful in making new estimates or in estimating the accuracy of new proposals. For example, one supervisor may always underestimate project costs or overestimate labour productivity. A second use of project reevaluation is the comparison of operating projects with other investment alternatives. It may happen that an operating project should be liquidated and the funds invested in a new project. A formal system for evaluating the feasibility of terminating an operating project is called **capital abandonment analysis.**

Project evaluation methods

Project evaluation provides managers with information relevant for making capital budgeting decisions but, as we discussed in Chapter 1, relevance depends upon the person making the decision. Different decision makers may require different types of information. In capital budgeting, decision makers may use one or more of several available project evaluation methods in order to secure various types of project information. In this chapter we discuss the following evaluation methods:

Commonly used methods of evaluating capital budgeting projects

1. Discounted cash flow methods
   a. Internal rate of return
   b. Net present value
   c. Profitability index
2. Payback
3. Payback reciprocal
4. Accounting rate of return

Discounted cash flow methods

Discounted cash flow (DCF) methods of project evaluation depend on the time value of money for evaluating capital budgeting projects. The term *discounted cash flows* refers to the fact that all projected cash inflows and outflows for a capital budgeting project are discounted to their present value using an appropriate interest rate. Two discounted cash flow models are generally used in capital budgeting. One is called the internal rate of return (IRR) method, and the other is called the net present value (NPV) method. Both methods focus on the timing of the cash flows over the entire life of the project. The spotlight is on the cash flows as opposed to accounting measures of revenue and expense.

Discounted cash flow project evaluation methods are based on the time value of money

All discounted cash flow methods are based on the **time value of money,** which means that an amount of money received now is worth more than an equal amount of money received in the future. Money in hand can be invested to earn a return. For example, if money can be invested at 6 percent and $100 is invested now, it will accumulate to $106 by the end of one year [$100 + ($100 × .06)]. At the end of the second year, it accumulates to $112.36 [$106 + ($106 × .06)]. Clearly, then, $100 today is worth more than $100 two years from today. To be precise $89 invested now at 6 percent interest will accumulate to $100 at the end of two years. Therefore, $89 is the **present value (PV)** of $100 received two years from now if money can be invested at 6 percent. The time value of money is a very important concept involving compound interest. If you are not familiar with time value of money concepts, study the appendix at the end of this chapter before proceeding further.

Cash flow assumption

To simplify the process of evaluating proposals using discounted cash flows, the assumption is often made that any cash flows or cost savings from a project occur at the end of an accounting period. Although the assumption sometimes is unrealistic, because a project may offer cash flows or cost savings throughout the year over its lifetime, the assumption simplifies calculations and allows the use of present value tables. The results obtained are usually close enough to those that might be obtained by more realistic estimates of the precise timing of cash flows.

Internal rate of return (IRR)

IRR is the interest rate that discounts a project's cash inflows and cash outflows to the same present value

The **internal rate of return (IRR)** is the interest rate that discounts an investment's future cash flows to the present so that the present value of those cash flows exactly equals the cost of the investment. For example, if a project costs $10,000 and is expected to yield cash inflows of $2,000 per year for the next eight years, the internal rate of return is that interest rate which discounts the future cash inflows of $2,000 for eight years to a present value of $10,000. The IRR is not given; it must be computed. Once it is found for a specific project, management can decide whether the rate is sufficiently high to warrant acceptance of the project. When using the IRR method, management must have in mind some rate of return commonly referred to as the minimum acceptable rate of return, below which projects are not acceptable.

IRR computations with uniform cash flows

To illustrate, Joplin Products Company is contemplating the purchase of an automatic package-labeling machine. The new machine would eliminate the manual labeling process now used by the company. The net cash saving is estimated at $10,000 a year for five years. At the end of five years, the machine will be obsolete and will have no salvage value.

The purchase price of the machine is $32,000. If the machine is acquired, a part of the plant's electrical wiring system would have to be modified at a cost of $242. The purchase is subject to a 4 percent sales tax. The initial cash outflows represent the cost of the machine, which amounts to $33,522 calculated as follows:

Machine price	$32,000
Sales tax @ 4%	1,280
Electrical wiring	242
Total cost	$33,522

The objective is to determine the interest rate that will discount the present value of the expected cash savings for the machine to a present value that is equal to the machine's cost. The cash outflows of $33,522 all occur at the time of purchase. Therefore, the present value of the outlay is the actual amount of the cash paid. The inflows, or in this case cash savings, occur over a period of five years. Since the cash inflows are the same for all five years of the investment, they represent an annuity. Graphically the situation is as follows:

Cash outflow		Cash inflows				
− $33,522	$10,000	$10,000	$10,000	$10,000	$10,000

```
O---------O---------O---------O---------O---------O
          1         2         3         4         5      years
```

We want to find the interest rate i at which the present value of an annuity of five rents of $10,000 is equal to $33,522.

$$\text{Present value (PV)} = \text{Rent} \times f\,(i = ?, n = 5)$$
$$\$33,522 = \$10,000 \times f\,(i = ?, n = 5)$$
$$f = \frac{\$33,522}{\$10,000} = 3.3522$$

Using the value of f, the annuity factor, and the table for the present value of an annuity, we find for $n = 5$ the value 3.3522 in the 15 percent column. Therefore, 15 percent is the IRR.

Interpreting the internal rate of return

What does the 15 percent rate mean in evaluating the project? It tells management that the labeling machine project yields an investment return of 15 percent. If Joplin Products is evaluating other investment proposals, the IRR may be used as a ranking system. For instance other projects may yield estimated returns of 9 percent, 11 percent, 12 percent, and 17 percent. The labeling project yields the second highest estimated return. If Joplin accepts projects based on their rate of return, the labeling machine would be the second project accepted.

However, the mere ranking of projects by rate of return does not determine which projects to accept or reject. Management should accept only those projects which yield an acceptable rate of return. They are projects that yield a higher rate of return than the company pays for the capital it uses. A business must pay for the use of money in the form of interest and dividend payments to investors. The cost of using funds is called the **cost of capital.** Any investment that yields a rate of return greater than the cost of capital should be accepted since the project will increase the value of the firm. In the above example, the labeling machine would be an acceptable investment if Joplin's cost of capital is less than 15 percent.

The cost of capital is typically expressed as an interest rate. Businesses have many sources of funds, such as common stock, several classes of preferred stock, bonds, mortgages, notes payable, and other debt. Theoretically, a firm should be able to compute its weighted average cost of capital at any point in time, but many factors affect the cost of each of the sources of funds. Economic conditions or government actions may quickly change the cost of borrowing or raising equity capital. Consequently, cost of capital can only be estimated, but not measured precisely. In most textbook discussions, cost of capital is given as a certain amount, but in practice cost of capital is not easy to determine.

Many investment projects do not conveniently coincide with an annuity factor in the table. Instead the computed annuity factor falls somewhere between two numbers in the table. To illustrate, we use the labeling machine example and assume the annual cash savings are $8,000 a year instead of $10,000. The computed annuity factor is

$$\frac{\$33,522}{\$8,000} = 4.1903$$

The table for the present value of an annuity of five rents shows that the factor lies between 6 and 7 percent. Management may use the nearest whole percent as the IRR, in this case 6 percent. If this is not sufficiently precise, a more exact return can be calculated by interpolation as follows:

	Annuity Factors	
At 6%	4.2124	4.2124
Computed		4.1903
At 7%	4.1002	
Difference	.1122	.0221

The total difference between the factors for 6 and 7 percent is .1122. The annuity computed for the investment proposal is .0221 different from the 6 percent annuity and .0901 different from the annuity for 7 percent. The portion of interest that is above the 6 percent value is .0221/.1122 = .2 percent. Adding .2 percent to 6 percent, we get 6.2 percent as the IRR for this project. This, of course, is an approximation. A precise computation of the internal rate of return is easy to get with the aid of a computer or a fairly sophisticated electronic calculator.

Nonuniform cash flows. Some projects yield cash flows that are not equal for all periods of the project's life. For example, a project may cost $40,000 and provide cash savings of $10,000, $20,000, and $24,000, respectively, in each of the next three years. When cash flows are not uniform, an interest rate cannot be found using annuity tables. Instead trial-and-error methods or a computer can be used to find the IRR. If computed manually, the first step is to select an interest rate that seems reasonable and compute the present value of the individual cash flows using that rate. If the present value of the cash inflows is greater than the present value of the cash outflows, then the interest rate used is too low—that is, the IRR is higher than the interest rate selected. A higher interest rate is then chosen, and the present value of the cash flows is computed again. If the new interest rate yields a negative value, then a lower interest rate is selected. The process is repeated until the present value of the cash inflows is equal to the present value of the cash outflows. Finding the rate of return using trial-and-error methods can be tedious, but a computer can accomplish the task quite easily.

To illustrate finding the internal rate of return with unequal cash flows, we assume that the labeling machine in the previous example will yield the following savings:

Year	Cash Savings
1	$18,000
2	12,000
3	10,000
4	5,000
5	5,000

First an interest rate is selected. There is no formula for making a good first estimate of the interest rate, but experience in solving this type of problem greatly enhances the quality of initial estimates. For this example we choose a rate of 16 percent. Each future cash flow must be evaluated separately, requiring the use of the present value of $1 table. We assume that the cash saving occurs at the end of each year. Therefore, we must find the present value of $18,000 discounted for one year at 16 percent, the present value of $12,000 discounted for two years at 16 percent, and so on.

	Discount Factor (16%)	× Cash Savings	= Present Value of Cash Savings
Year 1	.8621	$18,000	$15,518
Year 2	.7432	12,000	8,918
Year 3	.6407	10,000	6,407
Year 4	.5523	5,000	2,762
Year 5	.4761	5,000	2,381
Present value of cash savings			$35,986
Present value of cash outflow			33,522
Difference			$ 2,464

If the present value of cash inflows is greater than the present value of cash outflows, the rate selected is lower than IRR

The present value of the cash inflow is $2,464 higher than the present value of the cash outflow. Therefore, the rate of return on the project must be higher than 16 percent.

The next interest rate chosen is 22 percent. Once again this is just a guess at the IRR. We proceed as before.

	Discount Factor (22%)	× Cash Savings =	Present Value of Cash Savings
Year 1	.8197	$18,000	$14,755
Year 2	.6719	12,000	8,063
Year 3	.5507	10,000	5,507
Year 4	.4514	5,000	2,257
Year 5	.3700	5,000	1,850
Present value of cash savings			$32,432
Present value of cash outflow			33,522
Difference			($ 1,090)

The present value of the cash savings is $1,090 lower than the present value of the cash outflow. Consequently, the IRR must be somewhere between 16 and 22 percent. Since the 22 percent rate provides a smaller absolute difference between the present values of the cash flows, the rate is closer to 22 percent than to 16 percent. Next we try 20 percent.

	Discount Factor (20%)	× Cash Savings =	Present Value of Cash Savings
Year 1	.8333	$18,000	$14,999
Year 2	.6944	12,000	8,333
Year 3	.5787	10,000	5,787
Year 4	.4823	5,000	2,412
Year 5	.4019	5,000	2,010
Present value of cash savings			$33,541
Present value of cash outflow			33,522
Difference			$ 19

The 20 percent interest rate discounts the cash savings to within $19 of the initial cash outflow, which means that 20 percent is a close approximation of the IRR for the project.

Internal rate of return characteristics. The IRR method specifically addresses the time value of money and the timing of cash flows. The important variable is cash flows, and accounting concepts of income measurement, such as depreciation, play no role in evaluating projects except as they affect cash flows. Furthermore, the method assumes that cash receipts are reinvested at the

The IRR method
assumes cash inflows
are reinvested at the
IRR of the project

internal rate of return of the project. For example, cash received from a project with a rate of return of 35 percent is assumed to be reinvested at the rate of 35 percent. This reinvestment assumption may be optimistic for high-yielding investments since cash received from one project may have to be reinvested in less profitable new projects.

Net present value (NPV)

NPV is the difference
between the present
value of the project
cash inflows and
outflows discounted
at the cost of capital

The **net present value (NPV)** method is another type of discounted cash flow project evaluation method. With net present value, all cash inflows and outflows are discounted at a minimum acceptable rate of return. If the present value of the cash inflows is greater than the present value of the cash outflows, the project is acceptable. Management must decide on the minimum acceptable rate of return, which is usually the firm's cost of capital.

To illustrate the net present value method, we return to the Joplin Products Company example in which a labeling machine could be purchased for $33,522 and would provide annual cash savings of $10,000 for each of five years. Joplin's cost of capital is 12 percent. The present value of the cash outflow is $33,522. The present value of the cash inflows is $10,000 each year discounted at the rate of 12 percent.

Net present value
computations with
uniform cash flows

When the cash flows are uniform for the life of the project, the present value of the cash flows can be computed as an annuity using the present value of an annuity of five payments of $10,000 each at 12 percent; the NPV is calculated as follows:

$$PV = \$10,000 \times f(n = 5, i = 12\%)$$

$= \$10,000 \times 3.6048 =$ Present value of cash inflows	$36,048
Less: Present value of cash outflows	33,522
Net present value of the project	$ 2,526

The net present value of the project is $2,526, which means the labeling machine is an acceptable project given Joplin's cost of capital. A positive net present value means that the company will earn a higher rate of return on its investment than it has to pay for the use of its capital. The net effect is that the present value of the earnings exceed by $2,526 the amount paid for the use of the funds to finance the investment. If Joplin's cost of capital were higher than 12 percent, the decision might be to reject the project. For instance, if the cost of capital is 16 percent, the net present value of the labeling machine project is

Present value of cash inflows $10,000 × 3.2743	$32,743
Less: Present value of cash outflows	33,522
Net present value of the project	($ 779)

In this case the new present value of the proposed project is negative, indicating the project should be rejected. Here the return from the investment is less by $779 than the cost of the funds used for the project. Notice that the reason the net present value is negative in this case is because the cost of capital is 16 percent instead of 12 percent. The cash inflows from the investment remained constant, but the company had to pay more for the capital to finance the project. Therefore the project is also discounted using a higher interest rate. This result should be expected if you recall the earlier computation of the internal rate of return for the project. The IRR is 15 percent, but the cost of capital is 16 percent, so the project does not meet this minimum return. Both methods provide a reject decision, given the 16 percent cost of capital and the cash flow data for the machine.

 If an investment has a salvage value, the money received from the sale of the investment is a cash inflow in addition to any revenues or cost savings generated by the project during the final year of use. For example, if the labeling machine had a salvage value of $3,000 at the end of five years, the cash inflow would be $10,000 in cost saving for year five **plus** $3,000 of salvage value. The entire $13,000 is discounted at the cost of capital of 12 percent. A salvage value increases the value of an investment, but since the cash from the sale of the investment is received at the time the investment is sold, the present value of the salvage may be small. In the case of the labeling machine, the $3,000 salvage value has a present value of $1,702 ($3,000 × .5674). High discount rates and long-lived projects may cause even a large salvage value to have a very insignificant present value.

Net present value computations with nonuniform cash flows
Unlike the internal rate of return method, no additional complexities are encountered with the net present value method when cash flows are irregular. All cash flows are discounted at the firm's cost of capital whether the cash flows are identical each year or different. To illustrate, assume a cost of capital of 12 percent and annual cash savings of $18,000, $12,000, $10,000, $5,000, and $5,000, respectively, for the five years. The computation of the net present value is

	Discount Factor	Cash Savings	Present Value of Cash Savings
Year 1	.8929	$18,000	$16,072
Year 2	.7972	12,000	9,566
Year 3	.7118	10,000	7,118
Year 4	.6355	5,000	3,178
Year 5	.5674	5,000	2,837
Present value of cash inflows			$38,771
Present value of cash outflows			33,522
Net present value of the project			$ 5,249

With irregular cash flows, the computations using the NPV method are easier than the IRR method.

Net present value characteristics. As with the internal rate of return, the net present value method relies on the time value of money and the timing

The NPV method assumes all cash inflows are reinvested at the cost of capital

of cash flows in evaluating projects. The key variable is the cash flows associated with the project. Since all cash flows are discounted at the cost of capital, the net present value method assumes that all cash inflows from projects are reinvested at the cost of capital. Net present value is simple to use and is especially convenient with nonuniform cash flows.

Profitability index (PI)

The net present value of a project is a function of the discount rate, the timing of the cash flows, and the size of the cash flows. Other things being equal, large investment proposals yield larger net present values. For example, two projects have the following cash flows:

Year	Small Machine	Large Machine
0	− $25,000	− $100,000
1	+ 10,000	+ 40,000
2	+ 10,000	+ 40,000
3	+ 10,000	+ 40,000
4	+ 10,000	+ 40,000

With a cost of capital of 14 percent, the net present values of the two machines are $4,137 and $16,548, respectively, so the large machine appears to be the more attractive project. Logic tells us, however, that the projects should be equally attractive investments since the cash flows of the larger machine are merely a multiple of four of the smaller machine. To adjust the analysis for the size of the cash flows we can calculate a **profitability index (PI)**, which is the ratio of the present value of the cash inflows to the present value of the cash outflows. In the example above, the profitability indexes are

$$\text{Profitability index} = \frac{\text{Present value of cash inflows}}{\text{Present value of cash outflows}}$$

$$\text{Profitability index of small machine} = \frac{\$29,137}{\$25,000} = \underline{1.17}$$

$$\text{Profitability index of large machine} = \frac{\$116,548}{\$100,000} = \underline{1.17}$$

The profitability index provides a basis for comparing investment projects of different sizes

The purpose of the profitability index is to provide a basis for comparison between projects of differing sizes. The higher the profitability index, the more desirable the project in terms of return per dollar of investment. A profitability index of 1.0 is the cutoff point for accepting projects. A profitability index less than 1.0 indicates a negative net present value for the project.

Other methods of evaluating capital expenditure projects

Discounted cash flow methods are popular for evaluating capital expenditure projects, but some managers prefer to use other evaluation methods. Three other methods that are used by many managers are payback, payback reciprocal, and accounting rate of return. None of these three methods uses discounted cash flows in the analysis.

Payback

The **payback** method, sometimes called the **payout** method, is a computationally simple project evaluation approach that has been used for many years. The procedure is to determine how long it takes for a project to return the cost of the original investment. For example, a retail store currently uses a delivery service to make all deliveries. The store can purchase two delivery trucks at a cost of $35,000 each. After deducting operating and maintenance expenses, the two trucks will save a total of $20,000 a year in delivery expenses for the next six years. After six years the trucks will be worn out and will be scrapped without any salvage value. The computation of payback is

$$\text{Payback} = \frac{\text{Initial cost}}{\text{Annual cash savings}}$$

$$= \frac{\$70,000}{\$20,000 \text{ per year}} = 3.5 \text{ years}$$

The cost of the trucks will be recovered in $3\frac{1}{2}$ years. The payback period itself does not provide an accept-reject decision for a project. Managers must assess the significance of the payback period in selecting investment alternatives. If several projects are being evaluated, projects may be accepted in the order of quickest payback. Alternatively the firm may decide to invest only in projects with a certain maximum payback period, such as three years or less. During periods of economic instability or when it is hard to raise money by borrowing or selling stock, some businesses choose capital investment projects that are expected to return the invested funds in a year or two. The payback method seems to become more popular during periods of economic instability.

Many managers feel that payback provides a measure of risk. Often cash flows expected in the near future are more certain than more distant cash flows; therefore, a quick payback period indicates a less risky project. An additional argument for payback is that earlier payback is desirable because cash is more valuable now than later.

Payback with nonuniform cash flows

Payback computations are slightly different if cash inflows are not identical from one year to the next. For instance, assume the truck example mentioned earlier has higher cash savings in earlier years because of lower maintenance costs on new trucks.

Year	Yearly Cash Savings	Cumulative Cash Savings
1	$30,000	$ 30,000
2	30,000	60,000
3	20,000	80,000
4	20,000	100,000
5	10,000	110,000
6	10,000	120,000

Payback period = $30,000 for year 1 + $30,000 for year 2
+ $10,000 for $\frac{1}{2}$ of year 3
= $2\frac{1}{2}$ years

The process is merely to add up the cash savings until the investment is recovered, starting with year 1. Only half of the cash saving available in year 3 is needed to pay back the original investment.

The payback method of project evaluation is particularly sensitive to the recovery of investment outlays. A logical extension of payback is the bailout concept. The basic idea of **bailout** is to determine how quickly the investment outlay for a project can be recovered from the combination of cash savings and the salvage value of the investment at any point in time. To illustrate, refer to the original truck example with a cost of $70,000 and annual cash savings of $20,000 a year. At the end of six years, the salvage value of the trucks is zero, but clearly when the trucks are new, they have a market value, which continues to decline throughout their useful life. Below is a chart that summarizes the estimated annual cash savings and salvage values for the trucks each year.

Year	Yearly Cash Savings	Total Cash Savings	Year-End Salvage Value	Total of Salvage Value + Cash Savings
1	$20,000	$ 20,000	$45,000	$ 65,000
2	20,000	40,000	30,000	70,000
3	20,000	60,000	20,000	80,000
4	20,000	80,000	10,000	90,000
5	20,000	100,000	5,000	105,000
6	20,000	120,000	0	120,000

At the end of two years, the cash savings of $40,000 and the salvage value of $30,000 allow the firm to recover its original investment. The cost recovery period of two years can only be achieved by terminating the project, hence the term *bailout*. Payback assumes the continuation of the project until the payback period has been reached.

Payback characteristics. A primary advantage of the payback method is its simplicity. No interest rates need to be estimated, and present value computations are not required. The only question is, "How soon will the investment be recovered?" An additional strength cited by supporters of payback is that it is a reasonable surrogate for risk. The longer one must wait for cash, the less certain it is that the cash will be received. Therefore, quick investment recovery is one measure of a low-risk project.

The payback method does not consider the time value of money or cash flows after the payback period

One criticism of payback is that no provision is made for the time value of money. All cash received during the payback period is of equal value in analyzing the project. A second problem is that cash flows occurring after the payback period are totally ignored. For example, two projects have the following cash flows:

| Project X | −$80,000 | $10,000 | $30,000 | $40,000 | $15,000 | 0 | 0 |
| Project Y | −$80,000 | $25,000 | $25,000 | $25,000 | $25,000 | $25,000 | $25,000 |

| | 1 | 2 | 3 | 4 | 5 | 6 | years |

A manager using the payback method would prefer project X with a payback of three years over project Y with a payback of more than three years. But in the payback computation, the timing of the cash flows during the payback period is ignored. The larger early cash receipts for project Y can be reinvested. Also, project Y has $70,000 of cash receipts after the payback period, and project X has only $15,000. Yet these cash flows never enter into the project evaluation using payback.

The payback reciprocal

An estimate of the internal rate of return

A simple method of estimating the internal rate of return from a project is the payback reciprocal, which is 1 divided by the payback period. For example, a project has an initial cash outlay of $20,000 followed by 10 years of annual cash savings of $5,000. The payback period is $20,000/$5,000 per year, or four years. The payback reciprocal is

$$\text{Payback reciprocal} = \frac{1}{\text{Payback period}} = \frac{1}{4} = 25\%$$

An initial cash outlay of $20,000 followed by 10 years of $5,000 cash inflows yields an internal rate of return of 21.4 percent, computed by using the table for the present value of an annuity of $1. The internal rate of return of 21.4 percent is 3.6 percent lower than the estimated internal rate of return computed by using the payback reciprocal. The payback reciprocal is always higher than the internal rate of return. However, if the life of the cash flows is at least twice the payback period, the payback reciprocal is a reasonable estimate of the rate of return. If the life of the cash flows is less than twice the payback period, the IRR estimate is very poor. To illustrate, the payback on the original labeling machine example is $33,522/$10,000 per year = 3.35 years. The payback reciprocal is 1/3.35 = 29.9 percent compared with the IRR of 15 percent, computed earlier. The life of the cash flows is only 1½ years beyond the payback period, which is significantly less than the required minimum of twice the payback period for a reasonable estimate of IRR.

Payback reciprocal characteristics. The payback reciprocal is easy to calculate and provides a reasonable estimate of the internal rate of return under some conditions. If the payback period is short and the investment period long, the method can save computation time. However, a limitation of the method is that it should be used only with uniform cash flows. With nonuniform cash flows, the payback reciprocal can be a very poor estimate of the internal rate of return regardless of the length of the investment project.

Cash flows must be uniform, and the life of the project must be at least twice the payback period

Accounting rate of return (ARR)

Rate of return based on accounting measures of income and investment

The **accounting rate of return (ARR)** method of evaluating capital budgeting projects is so named because it parallels traditional accounting concepts of income and investment. A project is evaluated by computing a rate of return on the investment using accounting measures of net income. The formula for accounting rate of return is

$$\text{ARR} = \frac{\text{Annual revenue from project} - \text{Annual expenses of project}}{\text{Project investment}}$$

For example, Wort Doughnut Company is contemplating the acquisition of a second automatic doughnut-making machine. The machine costs $20,000 and has a five-year useful life, with no salvage value. It is expected to add $10,000 of incremental revenue and $2,600 of additional operating expenses annually. Straight-line depreciation is used. Incremental net income is

Revenue		$10,000
Less: Operating expenses	$2,600	
Depreciation expenses	4,000	6,600
Incremental income		$ 3,400

All of the other capital budgeting evaluation methods discussed in the chapter are based on cash flows rather than accounting measures of income. Consequently, noncash items, such as depreciation, did not enter into the analysis. With the accounting rate of return method, however, accounting income is used as a prime element in the evaluation process. Therefore, depreciation must be used in determining income.

$$\text{ARR} = \frac{\text{Annual revenue from project} - \text{Annual expenses of project}}{\text{Project investment}}$$

$$= \frac{\$10,000 - \$2,600 - \$4,000}{\$20,000} = \frac{\$3,400}{\$20,000} = 17\%$$

Some advocates of the accounting rate of return method argue that the investment should not be measured at its initial cost of $20,000, but rather at the average investment for the life of the project. The average investment is the average book value of the asset over its useful life. It is easily calculated by adding the beginning and ending book value and dividing by 2. The beginning value is the cost of $20,000, and the ending value is the salvage value of $0. Therefore, the average investment is ($20,000 + $0)/2, or $10,000. Using this investment base the accounting rate of return is

$$\text{ARR} = \frac{\$10,000 - \$2,600 - \$4,000}{\$10,000} = 34\%$$

Clearly there is a significant difference between the computed rate depending on the choice of investment base. The controversy over the appropriate investment base is much the same as discussed in Chapter 11 in connection with determining the investment base for investment centre evaluation. A firm must select the most appropriate investment base, given its reasons for measuring the investment rate of return.

The accounting rate of return method provides managers with a basis for comparing investment alternatives. Projects may be ranked according to their accounting rates of return. Capital budgeting funds may be allocated to projects starting with the highest rate of return and going down the ranking until all of the investment funds are allocated. An alternative is to establish a minimum accounting rate of return for all projects. Each division or department is assigned a certain amount of investment funds as long as each project satisfies a minimum accounting rate of return.

Accounting rate of return characteristics. The accounting rate of return method is supported on the grounds that it closely parallels accounting concepts of income measurement and investment return. However, strong criticism is leveled against this method because it totally ignores the timing of cash flows, the duration of cash flows, and the time value of money.

ARR totally ignores the timing and duration of cash flows

Other factors influencing capital budgeting decisions

The discussion of the internal rate of return and net present value methods implied that all investment projects meeting the minimum return criteria are accepted where minimum return means a rate of return greater than the cost of capital, or a positive net present value. However, most managers use the information provided by the evaluation methods only as general guidelines in making capital expenditure decisions. The decision is really more than just a matter of ranking the alternatives or selecting those that qualify. Many other factors are usually examined and considered by management before the final decision is reached. Some of the considerations that may modify capital budgeting decisions are discussed below.

Economic conditions

Changes in economic conditions affect business operations and the way managers make business decisions. If managers believe that the economy is slowing down, they may be reluctant to make capital investments because it may mean that they have invested funds in capital projects that cannot be used effectively. A decline in economic activity may mean a reduction of sales and an increase in idle capacity, with a corresponding decrease in earnings. On the other hand, during good economic conditions, managers may perceive the need to expand capital investments in order to take advantage of the increase in demand for products and the resulting increase in sales, which may require expanded productive capacity. Managers may also build substantial excess productive capacity now to avoid expected large construction cost increases in the future.

Economic conditions may have a significant influence on capital budgeting decisions

The way economic changes affect a business often depends on the nature of the business. For example, luxury items and recreational products typically experience a decline in demand during economic downturns, whereas staples, such as food and fuel, tend to be relatively unaffected and experience stable demands. On the other hand, the demand for staples does not increase significantly during economic upturns when luxury goods experience strong demand. The demand for some products is affected by particular economic conditions even when the economy is booming. For example, during gasoline shortages sales of recreational vehicles are strongly curtailed.

Each firm must evaluate the effect of its own economic situation on capital budgeting decisions. For example, a grocery store pressed by competition from a new nearby store may experience falling sales and profits. Consequently, management may postpone a decision to install new electronic cash registers until it is clear the store can survive the competition. Similar actions are common among individuals. If you just started a new job and really want and need a new car, you may postpone the purchase until you are confident you will succeed in the job.

If cash shortages loom on the horizon, management often looks to the capital expenditure budget for spending cuts. During severe economic downturns the news media carry many reports of companies that have sharply curtailed capital expenditures from originally planned levels.

Growth policies

Many progressive companies have a significantly larger number of profitable investment projects than can be managed successfully. Rather than accept all profitable projects, the firm accepts as many as it can effectively manage, starting with the most profitable projects. Some managers find it hard to reject investment projects that look profitable, especially if they evaluate each proposal independently. However, unmanaged growth can turn potentially profitable investments into unprofitable mistakes. Managers must ascertain the volume of growth that can be effectively managed by the firm and must develop a capital budgeting policy accordingly.

Risk evaluation

Risk is an integral part of all business and professional activities. Business risk refers to the possibility that desired outcomes may not be achieved. In analyzing capital expenditures, expected cash flows are discounted at a target rate of return to find the net present value or internal rate of return, or perhaps the payback period is computed. In any case the estimated cash flows are the basis for the evaluation. Cash flows are easier to predict for some projects than for others. For example, the management of a fast-food chain with 40 restaurants in operation can probably predict cash flow better for a proposed new restaurant than the management of another restaurant chain just beginning business.

In capital budgeting, risk is usually defined in terms of the potential amount of fluctuations in cash inflows for a project. The more potential variability of the cash flows, the riskier the project. A problem is that none of the capital budgeting models have an explicit adjustment for risk. About the only feature is that most of the models discussed place a premium on earlier rather than later cash receipts. However, there is no measure of the possible variability

Most capital budgeting analysis models do not adjust for risk

of the cash flows in the models. Two projects may have identical expected cash flows; one project's cash flows may be virtually certain, and the other project's cash flows may be very volatile. The projects would be ranked equal using each of the evaluation methods, although one is clearly more desirable from a risk point of view. Profitable projects that managers think are too risky may be dropped from the capital expenditure budget. Most managers prefer a less risky investment over a more risky investment if the rates of return are equal. Risky projects must offer potentially greater returns in order to be viewed as attractive investment alternatives. Sometimes firms consider high-risk, high-return projects as a separate investment category. For instance, companies that invest in other businesses may create a separate investment analysis group to evaluate new potentially profitable companies that are seeking capital. Money invested in new high-risk firms is called **venture capital.** People providing venture capital accept the high risk of losing their investment but also expect the opportunity for large returns.

Intuitive factors

Capital budgeting project evaluation methods do not necessarily provide optimum capital budgeting decisions. Some managers believe that years of experience in a business plus good business intuition are the most valuable elements in capital budgeting decision making. Consequently, the capital expenditure budget may reflect decisions based on inputs other than the capital budgeting models. Many times, less structured methods of project evaluation are referred to as "seat-of-the-pants" techniques, intuitive techniques, or "by-gut-and-by-golly" techniques. Whatever their name there are many managers with good performance records who do not use formal capital budgeting evaluation models.

Capital rationing

Maximize the benefits from scarce resources

An illustration of capital rationing

The process of selecting the more desirable projects among many profitable investments is called capital rationing. Like any rationing it is designed to maximize the benefits available from using scarce resources. In this case the scarce resources are funds available for capital investments, and the benefits are returns on the investments. The process sounds simple enough. Rank the investments in order of profitability and accept the most profitable projects until the investment funds are exhausted. The problem is how to rank the projects. To illustrate, refer to Figure 13-1, which shows expected cash flows of five different projects that the company is evaluating.

The Connelly Company has approximately $140,000 to invest in the five potential projects. Cash flow data are presented for the projects labeled A through E. The projects have lives that range from three to ten years. Connelly estimates its cost of capital at 15 percent.

The management of Connelly wants as much data as possible to assist in making the investment decisions. Therefore, four different evaluation methods are used. Figure 13-2 shows the internal rate of return, net present value, profitability index, and payback period for all five projects.

	Project				
Year	A	B	C	D	E
0	−$52,189	−$50,197	−$40,000	−$20,000	−$89,882
1	+ 10,000	+ 5,000	+ 30,000	+ 15,000	+ 20,000
2	+ 10,000	+ 5,000	+ 20,000	+ 10,000	+ 20,000
3	+ 10,000	+ 10,000	+ 10,000	+ 5,000	+ 20,000
4	+ 40,000	+ 10,000	—	—	+ 20,000
5	—	+ 20,000	—	—	+ 20,000
6	—	+ 20,000	—	—	+ 20,000
7	—	+ 20,000	—	—	+ 20,000
8	—	+ 50,000	—	—	+ 20,000
9	—	—	—	—	+ 20,000
10	—	—	—	—	+ 20,000

Figure 13-1
Estimated cash flows for five investment projects. Only project E has uniform cash flows.

Different evaluation methods provide different rankings

A careful analysis of the data in Figure 13-2 indicates that there is no consensus about which is the most desirable and which is the least desirable project. On the whole, the five projects vary significantly in rank with each evaluation method. The data in Figure 13-2 are used to develop the ranking chart presented in Figure 13-3.

The projects with the highest internal rate of return rank third and fourth using net present value. The most desirable project using NPV ranks last using payback. Other interesting relationships can be found by scrutinizing Figures 13-2 and 13-3.

The obvious question is, Which ranking is correct? Unfortunately there is no obvious answer. Each evaluation method has some advocates who believe

	Project Evaluation Method*			
Project	Internal Rate of Return	Net Present Value	Profitability Index	Payback
A	10%	($6,485)	.88	3.55 year
B	20%	12,678	1.25	5.01 year
C	28.9%	7,785	1.19	1.50 year
D	28.9%	3,893	1.19	1.50 year
E	18%	10,494	1.12	4.49 year

Figure 13-2
Evaluation data for the five projects using four different evaluation methods. Notice the relative desirability of each project.

*Neither the payback reciprocal nor the accounting rate of return method was used because four of the five projects have nonuniform cash flows, and this severely limits the usefulness of the rate of return computed with these methods.

Project Rank	Project Evaluation Method			
	Internal Rate of Return	Net Present Value	Profitability Index	Payback
1	C and D	B	B	C and D
2	—	E	C and D	—
3	B	C	—	A
4	E	D	E	E
5	A	A	A	B

Figure 13-3
A ranking of the five projects using four evaluation methods. Each method suggests a different ranking of the investment alternatives.

the information provided by that method is the most useful for making capital budgeting decisions. Most financial analysts support the use of discounted cash flow evaluation methods because they incorporate the time value of money into the analysis. But internal rate of return, net present value, and profitability index are all discounted cash flow methods. A major differentiating variable is the assumption about the reinvestment rate for cash inflows generated by projects. The IRR model assumes cash inflows are reinvested at the IRR for that project, whereas the NPV model assumes cash inflows are reinvested at the cost of capital. Each reinvestment rate assumption has some advocates. In summary, there is no correct answer to the ranking question, only opinions of managers. Each must select the evaluation system and ranking method considered most useful.

Taxes and capital budgeting

Taxes affect cash flows and must be included in the analysis of investment projects

Taxes are expenses of doing business. Consequently, in making decisions, including capital expenditure decisions, managers must take tax effects into account when analyzing the alternatives. That is, projects should be evaluated using estimated after-tax cash flows. To illustrate, Baytown Plumbing Company is evaluating the installation of a radio communications system in its fleet of five trucks with a base unit in the company's office. In addition, the company would install a minicomputer with a cathode-ray tube terminal. Employees will use the radio to call in the arrival and completion time for each job. The dispatcher will use the computer terminal to develop quickly the correct charges for the job using standard times and charges for that type of job. The accounts receivable file will be searched by the computer to determine whether the customer in question has any outstanding balance with the plumbing company. The dispatcher will then radio the correct bill to the plumbers, and the customer will receive the bill for the job before the plumber leaves. With the radio equipment and minicomputer, the entire billing process will take less than two minutes. In addition, the dispatcher will be able to assign new jobs without the plumbers returning to the office. This will save many hours of travel time. The cost of the new equipment is $24,000, and installation cost is $1,000. A full-time radio dispatcher would have be to hired at a cost of $13,000 a year. The new dispatching system would minimize trips back to the office for new assignments and allow the firm to make an estimated 80 additional service calls a month. The average revenue per service call is $30, and average parts and supply cost is $5 per call. The company's income tax rate is 40 percent. All the new equipment has a ten-year useful life and no salvage value.

The cash outflows of $24,000 for the equipment and $1,000 for installation are made when the equipment is purchased. The cash flows associated with the project for each of the ten years of useful life are as follows:

Revenue	80 calls × $30/call × 12 months =	$28,800
Expenses:		
Parts and supplies	80 calls × $5/call × 12 months =	(4,800)
Dispatcher's salary		(13,000)
Net cash flows from project before taxes		$11,000

This part of the analysis is not different from earlier discussions except that revenue and expenses are identified separately. Note that the $11,000 is the net cash inflow from the project, ignoring taxes, and is not accounting net income. To calculate accounting net income, depreciation expense must be included. Then the tax expense can be calculated using the 40 percent tax rate. Assuming straight-line depreciation with a ten-year life and a cost of $25,000 for the equipment, the calculation of taxable income and tax expense is as follows:

Depreciation impacts on the amount of taxes paid and therefore on cash flows

Net cash flow	$11,000
Less: Depreciation	2,500
Taxable income	$ 8,500
Tax rate	× .40
Income tax	$ 3,400

Subtracting the taxes from the net cash savings yields the following:

Before-tax cash savings	$11,000
Less: Income taxes	3,400
After-tax cash savings	$ 7,600

The above illustrates an important point. A depreciation of $2,500 in the above example resulted in a tax saving of ($2,500 × .40 = $1,000) $1,000 which is called by some accountants the *tax shield*. As it can be seen without depreciation, the company would be paying $4,400 tax instead of $3,400. Depreciation does not require a cash outlay, but it does affect cash flows because of its effect on taxes. For this reason managers often used accelerated depreciation methods, such as double declining balance or sum-of-the-years'-digits, to reduce taxable income and increase cash savings in the early years of a project's life.

Once the net-of-tax cash flows are determined, the evaluation is made as before. If Baytown Plumbing's cost of capital is 14 percent, the net present value of the project is

Present value of annuity of 10 rents at 14% =	
5.2161 × $7,600 =	$39,642
Less: Present value of cash outflows	25,000
Net present value of the project	$14,642

The profitability index is

$$\frac{\text{Present value of cash inflows}}{\text{Present value of cash outflows}} = \frac{\$39,642}{\$25,000} = 1.59$$

Canadian income tax legislation requires use of a declining balance method of accelerated depreciation referred to as *capital cost allowance* (CCA). Basically, an asset is assigned to a particular class defined by the Income Tax Act, and a prescribed depreciation rate is allowed on the balance of the class. Considering the previous example of Baytown Plumbing Company, and assuming that this particular equipment is in a class that has 30 percent CCA rate and has zero beginning balance, the capital cost allowance computations for the next four years will be as follows:

Year	Opening Balance	Purchase	Disposal	Capital Cost Allowance	Ending Balance
1984	$0	$25,000	$0	$7,500	$17,500
1985	$17,500	$0	$0	5,250	12,250
1986	$12,250	$0	$0	3,675	8,575
1987	$8,575	$0	$0	2,573	6,002

Keep in mind that the capital cost allowance, though irrelevant to the investment decision, provides a tax shield and decreases the amount of cash outflow for that purpose. Baytown Plumbing Company, according to the above computations, will show the following after the tax income in 1984:

Net cash flow	$11,000
Less: CCA	7,500
Taxable income	3,500
Tax rate	× .40
Income tax	$ 1,400

Subtracting the taxes from the net cash savings, at this time, yields a much higher after-tax cash savings for 1984 as shown below:

Before-tax cash savings	$11,000
Less: Income taxes	1,400
After tax savings 1984	$ 9,600

Since capital cost allowance changes every year, we can no longer use a single annuity factor for varying cash flows; present value normally requires yearly computation. In order to remedy this tedious task, a simple formula can be applied to compute the present value of the tax shield for an investment on an after tax. Since Income Tax laws change every year, for specific application the reader is advised to use this formula after a thorough study of the current legislation. Given the present conditions the present value of the tax shield (PVTS):

$$PV\$\overline{5} = I\frac{t\,d}{r + d}$$

where I = is the initial investment
       d = capital cost allowance rate
       t = is the tax rate
       r = required rate of return.

For our Baytown Plumbing Company example where r = 14% and life of the asset 10 years,

$$PVTS = \$25,000 \times \frac{(.40) \times (.30)}{.14 + .30} = \$25,000 \times \frac{.12}{.44} = \$6,818.18$$

Assuming that Baytown Plumbing Company can expect $11,000 pre-tax cash inflows and $6,600 after tax (and before capital cost allowance effect) for the next 10 years from the dispatching equipment, the present value computation is:

PV of $6,600 per year for 10 years at
14 percent = $6,600 × 5.2161 = $34,426.26

Present value of the cash inflows	$34,426.26
Plus present value of the tax shield	6,818.18
Total inflows	$41,244.44
Less investment	25,000.00
Net present value	$16,244.44

Since the above example assumes no salvage value, no further adjustment is necessary. However, existence of a salvage value will require an additional calculation if we assume a salvage value of $1,000 at the end of the tenth year. The present value of reduction of the tax shield at the time of year 10 due to the salvage value is:

$$PVST = S\ (\text{salvage value}) \times \frac{t\,d}{r + d} = \$1,000 \times \frac{(.40)\,(.30)}{.14 + .30} = \$272.72$$

This figure is at time 10, so it must be discounted back to year 0 ($272.72 × .2697) = $73.55. The present value of the tax shield in this case becomes:

PVTS (investment) − PVTS (salvage value) = $6,818.18 − $73.55 = $6,744.63

The net present value is also affected by the recovery of the salvage value in year 10.

$$\$1,000 \times .2697 = \$269.70$$

The revised Baytown Plumbing Company problem now has a net present value of:

Present value of cash inflows	$34,426.25
+ Present value of the tax shield	6,744.63
+ Present value of the salvage value	269.70
Total	$41,440.59
Less: The initial investment	$25,000.00
Net present value	$16,440.59

Government assistance and capital budgeting

Various levels of government in Canada provide assistance in acquisition and operation of fixed assets. These programs are too varied in terms of their nature and duration. Some examples are the Regional Development Incentive Act of the Dominion of Canada, Shipbuilding Temporary Assistance Programme, Federal Department of Regional Economic Expansion Programme, commonly known as DREE, Travel Industry Development Subsidiary Agreement, known as TIDSA, between the federal government and the Government of British Columbia. Considering the importance of government assistance to firms, The Institute of Chartered Accountants of Canada issued Section 3800 of the *CICA Handook* in 1975. This section gives general guidelines about accounting treatment of governmental assistance for external reporting. A capital budgeting decision, if it is related to any form of governmental assistance, should consider the specific nature of the particular program.

Summary

Capital budgeting decisions typically are long-term commitments of large amounts of resources and thus involve long-term policy decisions. Consequently, they are a major factor in determining the long-range success of an organization. Major capital investments require a systematic decision procedure that includes the identification of investment alternatives, estimation of project benefits and costs, evaluation of capital budgeting projects in a systematic way, development of the capital expenditure budget, and reevaluation of projects after acceptance. Projects should be selected using decision criteria that are compatible with organizational goals.

With **discounted cash flow (DCF)** methods, the **time value of money** is used to evaluate investments. There are several discounted cash flow methods. The **internal rate of return (IRR)** is the rate earned by a project. It is the interest rate that discounts the cash inflows to a **present value (PV)** which is equal to the PV of cash outflows. If the IRR is higher than the company's cost of capital, the project is acceptable. **Cost of capital** is the amount a company must pay for the use of money. Another discounted cash flow method is the **net present value (NPV)** method in which all cash flows are discounted at the firm's cost of capital. If the net present value is positive, the project is acceptable. Projects with nonuniform cash flows are easier to evaluate using the net present value method than the internal rate of return method. The **profitability index (PI)** is an extension of the NPV method. It is used to convert all net present value computations to a measure of NPV per dollar of investment and thus provides a basis for comparing projects of differing sizes.

The **payback** method measures how quickly the original investment is recovered. It is a quick and easy method of project evaluation, but it ignores the time value of money and all cash flows after the payback period. **Payback reciprocal** is a rough approximation of the IRR and is computed as 1/payback period. For the payback reciprocal to be a reasonable estimate of IRR, the life of the project must be at least twice the payback period and only uniform cash flow can exist.

The **accounting rate of return (ARR)** method is based on accounting concepts of income measurement and investment base to compute a rate of return. The timing of cash flows is totally ignored as is the time value of money.

Sometimes only some of the profitable investment proposals are accepted. The process of selecting the most desirable projects is called **capital rationing.** Some factors affecting capital budgeting decisions are economic conditions, growth policies, risk evaluation, intuitive factors, and capital structure.

It is difficult to select the correct projects for the capital budget. Different evaluation methods may yield different rankings of the projects. Capital expenditure decisions should include calculations of tax effects, which in turn must involve depreciation calculations, although depreciation itself has no cash flow consequences.

List of important terms

accounting rate of return
  (ARR)   (536)
capital budgeting   (521)
capital cost allowance (CCA)   (543)
capital rationing   (539)
cost of capital   (527)
discounted cash flows (DCF)   (524)
government assistance   (543)

internal rate of return (IRR)   (525)
net present value (NPV)   (530)
payback   (533)
payback reciprocal   (535)
present value (PV)   (525)
profitability index (PI)   (532)
tax shield   (542)
time value of money   (525)

Appendix: Time value of money

Money available today is more valuable than money available at some future time. Money received today can be invested or spent. Money received in the future involves the sacrifice of waiting before it can be used or invested. The compensation for waiting is the time value of money, called **interest.**

Compound interest

Compound interest occurs when interest is earned and allowed to build up. The interest earned during the previous period itself earns interest in the next and subsequent periods. For example, if $1,000 is placed into a savings account paying 6 percent interest per year, interest accumulates as follows:

Principal invested in first year	$1,000.00
Interest for first year, $1,000 × .06 × 1	60.00
Amount available at the end of first year	$1,060.00
Interest for second year, $1,060 × .06 × 1	63.60
Amount available at the end of second year	$1,123.60

The interest earned in the second year is greater than $60 because it is earned on the principal **plus** the first year's interest, which remains on deposit.

Compounding of interest may take place more frequently than once a year. For example, if the savings account mentioned above pays 6 percent interest compounded quarterly, 1.5 percent interest is added to the account each quarter. The more frequent the compounding, the more interest is earned.

To deal with compound interest problems, we define the following terms:

P = the principal sum that earns interest
i = the interest rate per period
n = the number of periods during which compounding takes place. A period can be any length of time.

Future value of $1

A sum of money invested today at compound interest accumulates to a larger sum at the end of some future time period. The sum at the end of the future period is called the **amount** or **future value.** For example, the future value of $1,000 invested at 6 percent compounded annually for two years is $1,123.60, as shown above. The future value includes the original principal and the accumulated interest. Using the formula for simple interest, we see that the interest I at the end of one period on $1,000 at 6 percent is

$$I = P \times i$$
$$= \$1,000 \times .06$$
$$= \$60$$

The future value, abbreviated fv, must include the principal

$$fv = P + (P \times i)$$
$$= P + Pi$$
$$= P(1 + i)$$
$$= \$1,000 (1 + .06)$$
$$= \$1,060$$

The future value varies with the interest rate, the compounding frequency, and the number of periods. If we know the future value of a $1 principal investment, we can use it to calculate the future value of any amount invested. It is easy to construct a table of future values for a $1 investment for a variety of interest rates and time periods. For example, at 8 percent interest per period, $1 accumulates as follows:

Future value of $1 at 8% for 1 period = $1.00   × 1.08 = $1.08
Future value of $1 at 8% for 2 periods = $1.08   × 1.08 = $1.1664
Future value of $1 at 8% for 3 periods = $1.1664 × 1.08 = $1.2597
Future value of $1 at 8% for 4 periods = $1.2597 × 1.08 = $1.3605

The above table can be diagramed as follows:

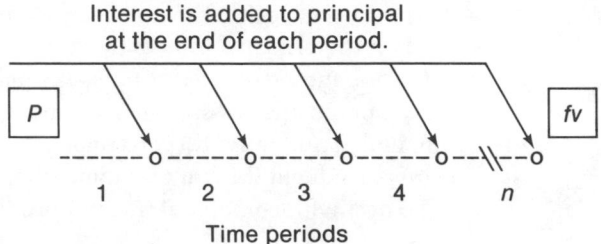

The end of each period is designated by a small circle (o). The arrows pointing to the end of each period indicate that payments are made into the investment. Later, you will see diagrams that show payments taken out of the investment, a process illustrated by arrows pointing away from the end of the period. Diagrams of this type are very useful for visualizing and solving compound interest problems.

Formula for future value of $1

The computations above show that at the end of the first period, the future value of $1 is $1.08; at the end of the second period, it is $1.08 × 1.08, or $1.08^2; at the end of the third period, it is $1.08^3, and so on. From this we derive the general formula for the future value of $1, with n representing the number of compounding periods

$$fv = (1 + i)^n$$

Using the formula for the future value of $1, a computer can easily calculate amounts for any interest rate and any number of time periods. Table 13-1 on page 572 shows values for many common interest rates and time periods. To obtain the future value of any principal other than $1, it is only necessary to multiply the principal by the factor found in the table for the future value of $1.

$$fv = P(1 + i)^n$$

or

$$fv = Pf$$

where f is the factor in the future value of $1 table, with interest rate i and number of periods n.

Use of future value of $1 table

The following problem and solution illustrate the use of tables of the future values of $1.

Problem 1. Palmer Company invests $2,500,000 in certificates of deposit that earn 10 percent interest per year, compounded semiannually. What will be the future value of this investment at the end of six years when the company plans to use it to build a new plant?

Solution 1. Since compounding is semiannual and there are six years, the number of half-year periods is 12. The semiannual interest rate is half of the 10 percent annual rate, or 5 percent. Using Table 13-1, with $i = 5$ percent and $n = 12$, the factor in the table is 1.7959. Multiplying this factor by the principal investment, we get

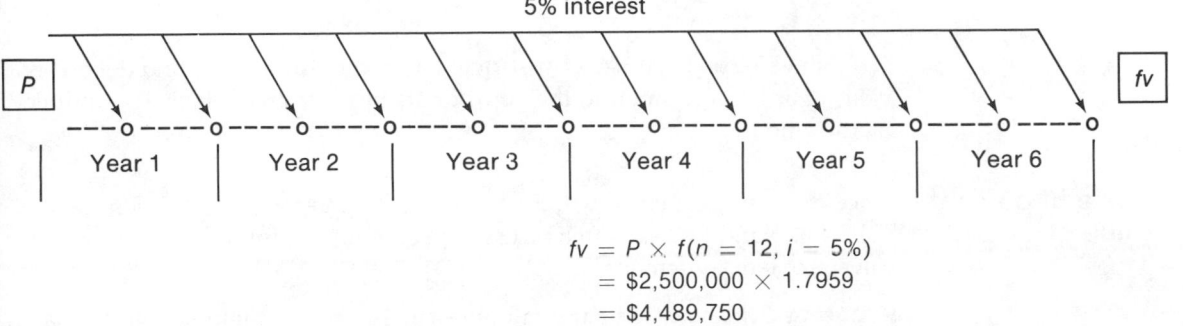

5% interest

Year 1   Year 2   Year 3   Year 4   Year 5   Year 6

$$fv = P \times f(n = 12, i - 5\%)$$
$$= \$2,500,000 \times 1.7959$$
$$= \$4,489,750$$

Compound discount

If $1 can be invested at 8 percent today to become $1.08 in the future, then $1 is the **present value** of the future amount of $1.08. The present value of future receipts of money is very important in business decision making. Frequently it is necessary to decide how much future receipts are worth today in order to determine whether an investment should be made or how much should be invested. Finding the present value of future receipts involves discounting the future value to the present. **Discounting** is the opposite of compounding. Instead of finding how interest accumulates, discounting involves finding the present value of some future amount of money that is assumed to include interest accumulations.

From the discussion of compound interest you know that the future value of $1 at 8 percent for one period is $1.08. Then the present value of $1.08 discounted for one period at 8 percent is $1. We can obtain the present value, abbreviated *pv*, as follows:

$$pv = \frac{fv}{1 + i} = \frac{\$1.08}{1 + .08} = \$1$$

Present value of $1

It is very useful to know the present value of $1 because then the present value of any amount can be computed merely by multiplying the amount by the present value of $1. To illustrate the computation of the present value of $1, assume an interest rate of 8 percent per period. A table of present values of $1 can be constructed as follows:

Present value of $1 discounted for 1 period at 8% $= \$1.00/1.08 = \$.9259$
Present value of $1 discounted for 2 periods at 8% $= \$ .9259/1.08 = \$.8573$
Present value of $1 discounted for 3 periods at 8% $= \$ .8573/1.08 = \$.7938$
Present value of $1 discounted for 4 periods at 8% $= \$ .7938/1.08 = \$.7350$
etc.

Formula for present value of $1

The first value is obtained by dividing $1 by 1.08. The second value is obtained by dividing $1 by 1.08^2, and so on. The general formula for the present value of $1 is

$$pv = \frac{1}{(1+i)^n}$$

Table 13-2 on page 574 is constructed from this formula. To find the present value of any future amount, the appropriate factor from the table is multiplied by the amount.

Use of present value of $1 table

Since the future value of $1 and the present value of $1 are closely related, Tables 13-1 and 13-2 can often be used to solve either a future value or a present value problem, as demonstrated below.

Problem 2. Albert Company can invest at 16 percent compounded annually. Beeble Company can invest at 16 percent compounded semiannually. Each company will need $75,000 five years from now. How much must each invest today?

Solution 2. With annual compounding $n = 5$ and $i = 16$ percent. With semi-annual compounding $n = 10$ and $i = 8$ percent. Using Table 13-2, we find the present value factors and multiply by the future value to obtain the present value. For Albert Company

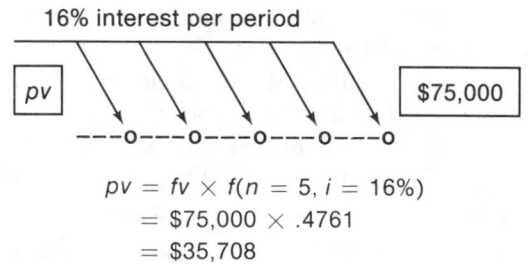

16% interest per period

$$pv = fv \times f(n = 5, i = 16\%)$$
$$= \$75,000 \times .4761$$
$$= \$35,708$$

For Beeble Company

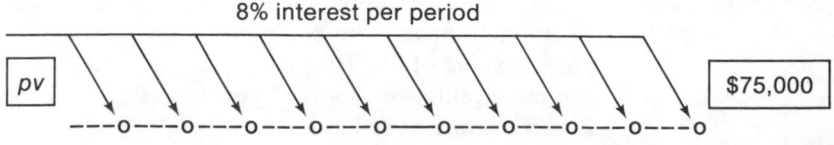

8% interest per period

$$pv = fv \times f(n = 10, i = 8\%)$$
$$= \$75,000 \times .4632$$
$$= \$34,740$$

The more frequent the compounding, the smaller the present value. Beeble Company needs to invest less than Albert Company because its investment grows faster due to more frequent compounding.

The solution can be obtained from Table 13-1 as well. For Albert Company you know the amount, but not the present value. To use Table 13-1, the formula is

$$fv = P \times f(n = 5, i = 16)$$
$$\$75,000 = P \times 2.1003$$
$$\frac{\$75,000}{2.1003} = P = \$35,709$$

The factor f previously came from the present value table; this time it is from the amount of $1 table. The slight difference in the answer is due to rounding of figures in the tables to 4 decimal places. For more accurate results, tables showing 6- or 8-place decimals are required.

Annuities

An **annuity** is a series of equal payments made at equal time intervals, with compounding or discounting taking place at the time of each payment. Each annuity payment is called a **rent.** There are several different types of annuities, but we discuss only ordinary annuities. In an **ordinary annuity** each rent is paid or received at the **end** of each period. There are as many rents as there are periods.

An example of an annuity is a contract with an insurance company that provides for future income in exchange for an investment today. With such a contract the buyer of the annuity pays a given sum of money to an insurance company. In return the insurance company guarantees the buyer a given amount of income each year, or each month, for a specified period of time, or for the remainder of the buyer's life. Each periodic payment of income is the rent of the annuity. Although most people think of annuities in terms of insurance contracts, annuities have much wider application. Installment purchases, long-term bonds, pension plans, and capital budgeting all involve annuities.

Future value of annuity of $1

If you open a savings account that compounds interest each month and at the end of each month you deposit $100 in the savings account, your deposits represent the rents of an annuity. After one year you will have made 12 deposits of $100 each, or a total of $1,200, but the account will have more than $1,200 in it since each deposit earns interest. If the interest rate is 6 percent a year compounded monthly, your balance is $1,233.56. The total sum of the account at the time the last rent is paid is called the future value of the annuity. The **future value of an annuity** or **amount** is the sum accumulated in the future from all the rents paid and the interest earned by the rents. The abbreviation

FV is used as the abbreviation for the future value of an annuity to differentiate it from the lowercase *fv* used for the future value of $1.

To obtain a table of future values of annuities, we assume payments of $1 each period made into a fund that earns 8 percent interest compounded each period. The following diagram illustrates an annuity of four payments of $1, each paid at the end of each period, with interest of 8 percent compounded each period.

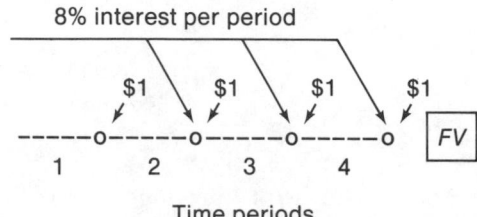

8% interest per period

$1 $1 $1 $1

1   2   3   4

Time periods

Notice that there are four rents and four periods, and each rent is paid at the end of each period. At the end of the first period, $1 is deposited and earns interest for three periods. The next rent earns interest for two periods, and so on. We want the amount at the end of the fourth period. It can be determined by calculating the future value of $1 as follows:

Future value of $1 at 8% for 3 periods = $1.2597
Future value of $1 at 8% for 2 periods = 1.1664
Future value of $1 at 8% for 1 period   = 1.0800
The fourth rent of $1 earns no interest = 1.0000
Total for 4 rents $4.5061

Formula for amount of annuity of $1

Using this approach the future value of any annuity can be calculated. However, this approach is not very efficient. The formula for the future value of an annuity of $1 can be used to produce tables for a variety of periods and interest rates. Without explaining its derivation, we present the formula here.

$$FV = \frac{(1 + i)^n - 1}{i}$$

It is not necessary to memorize the above formula. Table 13-3 on page 576 is derived from it, and you should just know how to use the table to solve annuity problems.

Use of amount of annuity of $1 table

Problem 3. In the beginning of 1980 the directors of Maple Corporation decided that plant facilities will have to be expanded in a few years. The company plans to invest $10,000 every six months, starting on June 30, 1980, into a trust fund that earns 10 percent interest compounded semiannually. How much money will be in the fund on December 31, 1984, after the last deposit has been made?

Solution 3. The first deposit is made at the end of the first six-month period, and there is a total of 10 periods. The last deposit, made on December 31, 1984, earns no interest. The investment represents an ordinary annuity, with $n = 10$ and $i = 5$ percent. From Table 13-3 we find that the amount of an ordinary annuity of $1 is 12.5779. The problem is diagramed and solved below.

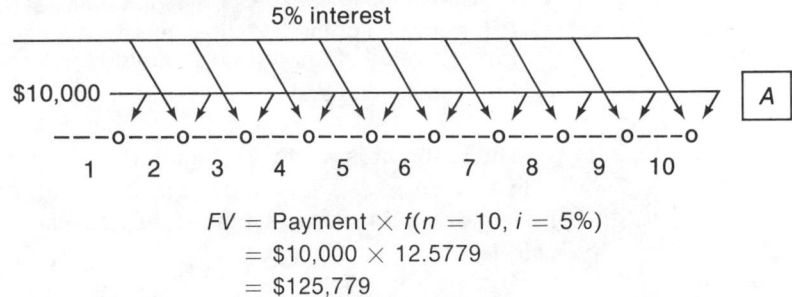

5% interest

$$FV = \text{Payment} \times f(n = 10, i = 5\%)$$
$$= \$10,000 \times 12.5779$$
$$= \$125,779$$

If the company needs a total of $150,000 on December 31, 1984, how much would it have to deposit every six months? Here we have to solve for the rent, given the future value, as follows:

$$FV = \text{Payment} \times f(n = 10, i = 5\%)$$
$$\$150,000 = \text{Payment} \times 12.5779$$
$$\text{Payment} = \frac{\$150,000}{12.5779} = \$11,926$$

The company has to deposit $11,926 each time in order to accumulate the necessary $150,000 by December 31, 1984.

Present value of annuity of $1

The present value of an annuity is the amount which must be invested today at compound interest in order to obtain periodic rents over some future time. Notice that we use the abbreviation *PV* for the present value of an annuity, as differentiated from the lowercase *pv* for the present value of $1. By using the present value of $1, we can obtain a table for the present value of an ordinary annuity of $1. We can then use the table to solve problems dealing with the present value of annuities. The present value of an annuity of $1 can be illustrated as follows:

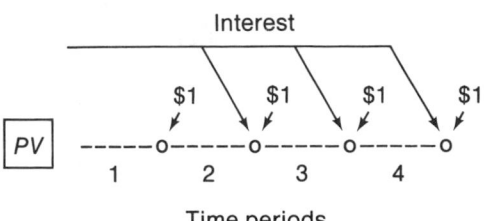

Interest

Time periods

With each rent available at the **end** of each period, when compounding takes place, the number of rents is the same as the number of periods. By discounting each future rent to the present, we find the present value of the entire annuity.

Present value of first $1 discounted for 1 period at 8%	= $ .9259
Present value of second $1 discounted for 2 periods at 8% =	.8573
Present value of third $1 discounted for 3 periods at 8%	= .7938
Present value of fourth $1 discounted for 4 periods at 8%	= .7350
Present value of annuity of 4 rents at 8%	$3.3120

The first rent is worth more than the others because it is received earlier. Table 13-4 on page 578 is derived in this manner and may be used to solve problems involving the present value of annuities. The formula used to construct Table 13-4 is

$$PV = \frac{1 - \dfrac{1}{(1 + i)^n}}{i}$$

Use of present value of annuity table

The amount and the present value of annuities are not related as nicely as the amount and present value of a single investment. The relationship is complex because the principal consists of rents paid at different times. The following problem illustrates the use of Table 13-4:

Problem 4. Jebson Corporation wants to establish a retirement plan for its president and only shareholder. The plan is to provide an income of $60,000 per year for the rest of his life. An insurance company calculates that his life expectancy is 24 more years and offers an annuity that yields 5 percent compounded annually. How much will the insurance company want from Jebson Corporation now in exchange for the future annuity payments?

Solution 4. The investment today is the present value of an annuity of $60,000 per year, with $n = 24$ and $i = 5$ percent. In Table 13-4 we find the factor 13.7986, which is the present value if the rents were $1.

$$PV = \text{Rent} \times f(n = 24, i = 5\%)$$
$$= \$60,000 \times 13.7986$$
$$= \$827,916$$

To assure its president an income of $60,000 per year, Jebson Corporation must pay the insurance company $827,916 today. The first rent will be paid at the end of the first period. What happens if Jebson lives longer than 24 years?[1]

Solution of managerial problems

Many business problems are solved by use of compound interest and present value tables. For example, Simon Corporation is investigating two possible investments. Project A is the purchase of an office building that is leased for 15 years. The lease calls for annual payments of $25,000 at the end of each of the next six years, and annual payments of $30,000 for the remaining life of the lease. The purchase price is $125,000. Project B is the purchase of a mineral deposit for $125,000. Net income from the sale of minerals is expected to be $29,000 per year for 10 years, at which time the deposit will be depleted. The property will then be sold at an estimated price of $45,000. Simon Corporation requires a 20 percent return on its investments. Which investment is preferable for Simon Corporation?

Solution. Project A can be diagramed as follows:

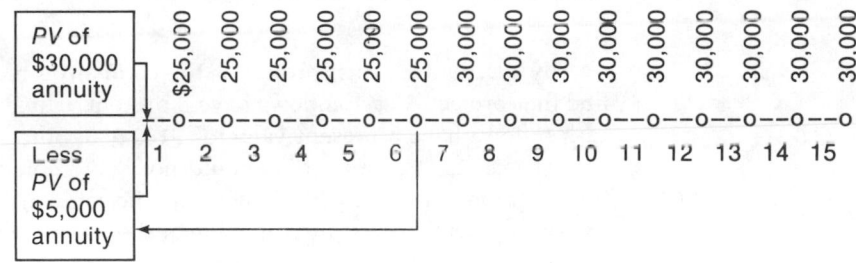

The problem can be broken down into two separate annuities, one with receipts of $30,000 per year for 15 years and the other with payments of $5,000 for 6 years. The present value of the two annuities can be found by computing the present value of an annuity of $30,000 for 15 years at 20 percent minus an annuity of $5,000 for 6 years at 20 percent.

PV of annuity of $30,000: $n = 15$, $i = 20\%$ is $30,000 × 4.6755 =	$140,265.00
PV of annuity of $ 5,000: $n -$ 6, $i = 20\%$ is $ 5,000 × 3.3255 =	(16,627.50)
Total present value of project A cash inflows	$123,637.50

Project B can be diagramed as follows:

---

[1]The insurance company keeps making the payments. Its calculations are based on probabilities. What it pays to those living longer than expected it makes up from those who die earlier than expected.

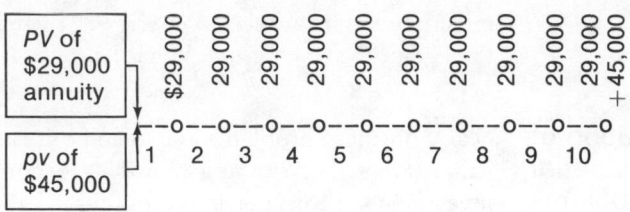

To evaluate the project, we need to find the present value of the future income stream of $29,000 per year plus the present value of the future sales price of $45,000, both discounted to the present at the company's required rate of return of 20 percent.

PV of annuity of $29,000: $n = 10$, $i = 20\%$ is $29,000 $\times$ 4.1925 =	$121,582.50
pv of $45,000: $n = 10$, $i = 20\%$ is $45,000 $\times$ .1615 =	7,267.50
Total present value of project B cash inflows	$128,850.00

By discounting each project at the company's required rate of return, we find that project A cash inflows have a present value of $123,637 and project B cash inflows have a present value of $128,850. Since the asking price of each project is $125,000, project A should not be accepted. The value of Project B is greater than the asking price, therefore the company should acquire project B. By paying less than the present value of the project, the company will obtain a rate of return greater than 20 percent.

Questions

1. What characteristics do capital budgets have that cause management to spend much time and effort preparing them?
2. Briefly describe the five activities involved in the capital budgeting process.
3. What is meant by discounted cash flow methods? Name two capital budgeting methods that are based on discounting of cash flows.
4. Define the internal rate of return.
5. What effects do nonuniform cash flows have on the manual computation of IRR?
6. Compare and contrast the net present value method with the internal rate of return method of evaluating capital projects.
7. Describe cost of capital and explain how it pertains to net present value and the internal rate of return.
8. What is the profitability index and why is it used?
9. Defend the use of payback as a capital budgeting evaluation method.

10. Is the timing of cash flows relevant to payback analysis? Discuss.
11. What is the payback reciprocal? What requirements must be met for the payback reciprocal to be of any use?
12. How does the accounting rate of return method differ from the other capital budgeting methods?
13. What does capital rationing mean?
14. Identify variables other than capital budgeting evaluation models that influence capital budgeting decisions.
15. Explain how it is possible to have a set of capital budgeting projects ranked differently by the different capital budgeting methods.
16. Depreciation is a noncash item and consequently does not affect the analysis of investment proposals using discounted cash flow methods. Comment.
17. How does government assistance affect capital budgeting decisions? Explain.

Exercises

Ex. 13-1 **Computing internal rate of return.** Rampus Manufacturing Company is evaluating an investment proposal to purchase two new machines to be used for quality control. The machines cost $47,500 each plus a 6 percent sales tax. There is a $2,293 total installation cost for the machines. The useful life of the machines is five years; there is no salvage value. Annual net cash savings from the two machines is $30,000.

Required:
Compute the internal rate of return for the proposed acquisition.

Ex. 13-2 **Computing net present value.** A company with a target rate of return of 15 percent is evaluating an investment proposal with an initial cash outlay of $80,000 followed by five years of cash inflows of $25,000 each.

Required:
Compute the net present value of the project.

Ex. 13-3 **Present value and profitability index.** Below are cash flow data for two investment projects that are being evaluated

| | Investment Project | |
Year	Machine X	Machine Y
0	− $250,000	− $100,000
1	+ 90,000	+ 45,000
2	+ 90,000	+ 45,000
3	+ 90,000	+ 45,000
4	+ 90,000	+ 45,000
5	+ 90,000	+ 45,000

The company uses a target rate of return of 20 percent for evaluating investment proposals.

Required:
a. Compute the net present value for both machines.
b. Compute the profitability index for both machines.

Ex. 13-4 Payback and payback reciprocal. A manager is evaluating an investment proposal that costs $100,000 and has expected annual cash inflows of $25,000 for eight years.

Required:
a. Compute the payback period.
b. Compute the payback reciprocal.

Ex. 13-5 Accounting rate of return. Sauna City Sales Company is evaluating a plan to expand its showroom space by 30 percent and its warehouse space by 10 percent. The expansion would cost $200,000 and would have a useful life of 20 years, with no salvage value. The firm uses straight-line depreciation. The expected increase in revenue is $55,000 a year, and cash expenses are $20,000 a year.

Required:
a. Compute the accounting rate of return.
b. If Sauna City requires a 15 percent accounting rate of return, should the project be accepted?

Ex. 13-6 Computing net present value. A company with a 12 percent cost of capital is considering the purchase of a machine used in production. The machine costs $90,000 and would provide the following cash savings in production:

Year	Cash Savings
1	$30,000
2	25,000
3	20,000
4	20,000
5	10,000
6	10,000

At the end of six years, the machine will be sold for $25,000.

Required:
Compute the net present value of the investment.

Ex. 13-7   Computing internal rate of return. Following are cash flow data for three investment proposals.

	Investment Project		
Year	Blue	Green	Red
0	− $99,352	− $74,765	− $92,096
1	+ 20,000	+ 25,000	+ 40,000
2	+ 20,000	+ 25,000	+ 40,000
3	+ 20,000	+ 25,000	+ 40,000
4	+ 20,000	+ 25,000	−
5	+ 20,000	+ 25,000	−
6	+ 20,000	−	−
7	+ 20,000	−	−
8	+ 20,000	−	−

Required:
Compute the internal rate of return for each of the investments.

Ex. 13-8   Project evaluation using net present value. J & J Radiator Repair has operated in an old garage for over 10 years. A reputation for quality service at a fair price has pushed business past current capacity. A. J. Jones, owner of the business, is considering the possibility of building a new facility that would double capacity. The total cost of the new facility, including equipment, would be $200,000, not including land of $25,000. The estimated useful life of the facility is 10 years; at the end of the period, the facility and land are expected to have a value of $50,000. The current garage can be sold for $60,000. Jones can obtain funds at 12 percent interest. Jones estimates that net cash receipts will increase by $32,000 a year as a result of increased capacity.

Required:
a. Compute the net present value of the project.
b. Should it be accepted? Explain.

Ex. 13-9   Computing net present value and the profitability index. The Mount Morgan Hospital is contemplating the purchase of a minicomputer system for use in its laboratory. The computer would cost $44,000 and would have a useful life of ten years and a salvage value of $8,000. Computer operating costs will be $18,000 a year, but $25,000 a year will be saved by eliminating the current manual record-keeping and order-entry system. The hospital is a private corporation and estimates its cost of funds at 12 percent.

Required:
a. Using the net present value method, determine whether the project should be accepted.
b. What is the profitability index for the project?

Ex. 13-10 Maximum investment to achieve a desired rate of return. The Webberville Toy Company is contemplating marketing a new toy. The company expects the product to be marketable for five years. Expected net cash inflows from the product are

Year	Net Cash Inflow
1	$ 40,000
2	60,000
3	50,000
4	30,000
5	10,000
Total	$190,000

The company uses 25 percent as the minimum required return on new products.

Required:
What is the maximum the toy company should invest in the production of the new toy, assuming no salvage value on any of the investment?

Ex. 13-11 Capital budgeting using different evaluation methods. Donlevey Hardware Store currently has four cash registers in the store, all of which are fully depreciated. The owner is evaluating the possibility of purchasing two new electronic cash registers at a cost of $10,000 each. The new machines are much faster than the old cash registers and would free some employees to help customers. The owner estimates that new cash registers will save $6,000 a year over their useful life in personnel costs. Maintenance and other operating costs will total $1,000 a year on the new machines. The machines have a useful life of ten years, with no salvage value. The current cash registers will be scrapped. The firm uses straight-line depreciation. Donlevey's cost of capital is 12 percent.

Required:
a. Compute the accounting rate of return based on total investment.
b. Compute the payback period.
c. Compute the net present value.
d. Compute the profitability index.

Problem Set A

P. 13A-1 Comparing alternative investments. J. C. Salt has been a commercial fisherman for 40 years. In that time he has managed to save $95,000. With five years to go until his retirement, Mr. Salt is faced with a career choice. His current fishing vessel is old and no longer safe. The engine and controls would bring $5,000 if scrapped, but a new fishing boat would cost $100,000. The fisherman can retire early, invest his cash in 8 percent certificates of deposit, and work at odd jobs that would bring $4,000 a year. Or he can buy the new boat and fish for five more years. His net cash flow from fishing would be $24,000 a year, and the boat could be sold for $50,000 in five years.

Required:
Should Mr. Salt remain a fisherman for the next five years? Use the net present value method to evaluate the investment.

P. 13A-2 Using five project evaluation methods. Following are cash flow data for an investment that is being evaluated by Carlisle Company.

Year	Cash Flow
0	− $114,200
1	+ 40,000
2	+ 40,000
3	+ 40,000
4	+ 40,000

The company's cost of capital is 12 percent.

Required:
Compute the:
a. Payback period.
b. Payback reciprocal.
c. Internal rate of return.
d. Net present value.
e. Profitabiliy index.

P. 13A-3 Project analysis using net present value. Sullivan Custom Welding is considering the purchase of an automatic spot-welding machine. It costs $10,000 and has an eight-year useful life. Annual net cash inflow of $2,500 is expected from new business, and it is expected the machine will have a salvage value of $1,000. Sullivan's cost of capital is 15 percent, and the company uses the net present value method of evaluating investments.

Required:

a. Should Sullivan Custom Welding acquire the welding machine?
b. The owner of the welding business is not confident of the estimated net cash flow from new business. If actual net cash flow turns out to be $2,000 a year, should the welding machine be purchased?
c. What is the minimum annual net cash flow from the investment that the company must have to accept the project?

P. 13A-4   **Evaluating two projects using payback and IRR.** Durango Corporation is planning to buy a new metal fabricating machine. Two models are being evaluated. Model 222 is a small machine that costs $80,000 and provides $20,000 each year in net cash savings for eight years. Model 444 is a larger and more expensive machine providing higher cash inflows in later years as volume increases. The company uses payback for most investment decisions.

Year	Model 222	Model 444
0	− $ 80,000	− $150,000
1	20,000	20,000
2	20,000	20,000
3	20,000	30,000
4	20,000	40,000
5	20,000	40,000
6	20,000	60,000
7	20,000	80,000
8	20,000	80,000
Total cash inflows	$160,000	$370,000

Required:

a. Compute the payback period for both projects.
b. Compute the payback reciprocal. Comment on your answer.
c. What is the internal rate of return for each project?

P. 13A-5   **Investment evaluation using net present value.** Moonlite Health Spas is evaluating the opening of a new spa this fall. The proposal calls for a ten-year building lease at $10,000 a year. Equipment purchases and leasehold improvements are expected to cost $50,000. The expected useful life of the equipment and leasehold improvements is ten years, and it has no salvage value. Other cash operating expenses are estimated at $25,000 annually. Moonlite will not open a new spa unless the expected return is at least 20 percent. The company has an effective tax rate of 40 percent. Based on past experience with new spas, the company thinks revenues should be $50,000 annually.

Required:

a. Evaluate the project using the net present value method and determine whether it should be adopted.

b. The proposed location of the spa is in a town not served by the company, and the company is not certain of its revenue estimates. What is your answer to *a* if revenue is 10 percent higher than estimated?

c. What is the minimum annual revenue the new spa can generate and still meet the firm's investment requirements?

P. 13A-6 **Project evaluation and ranking using different methods.** Little-Bit Candy Company needs new chocolate-moulding equipment to replace obsolete equipment that no longer meets the company's requirements. Three alternative types of machines are being considered. All meet the company's production and quality requirements, but each machine has a different life expectancy, different cost, and different annual cash savings. Straight-line depreciation is used; there is no salvage value. The company uses 15 percent as the estimate of its cost of capital. Cash flow data for the three machines are presented below.

	Machine		
Year	Cold-Mould	Warm-Mould	Hot-Mould
0	− $120,000	− $200,000	− $270,000
1	+ 40,000	+ 50,000	+ 60,000
2	+ 40,000	+ 50,000	+ 60,000
3	+ 40,000	+ 50,000	+ 60,000
4	+ 40,000	+ 50,000	+ 60,000
5	+ 40,000	+ 50,000	+ 60,000
6	−	+ 50,000	+ 60,000
7	−	+ 50,000	+ 60,000
8	−	+ 50,000	+ 60,000
9	−	−	+ 60,000
10	−	−	+ 60,000

Required:

a. For each of the three machines calculate:

1. The payback period.
2. The payback reciprocal.
3. The accounting rate of return using total investment.
4. The internal rate of return.
5. The net present value.
6. The profitability index.

b. Prepare a chart ranking the desirability of the projects using each of the six methods mentioned in part *a*.

P. 13A-7   Project evaluation with changing costs. Taccumpsa Drive Train Company manufactures automobile and truck parts in an old plant. A proposed new production facility would cost $6,000,000 and would have a useful life of 10 years, with a salvage value of $3,000,000. The old facility can be sold for $2,000,000. The new facility would be highly automated and far more efficient, eliminating 50 percent of the labour cost and 10 percent of the material cost. Labour cost was $800,000 this year, and material cost was $500,000. Management expects the labour rate to increase 8 percent a year and material prices to rise 4 percent a year regardless of whether the new plant is built. Taccumpsa has a 16 percent cost of capital. Ignore taxes.

Required:
a. Compute the annual cost savings with the new plant.
b. Compute the net present value of the project and decide whether the project should be accepted.

P. 13A-8   New-product capital investment decision. Headly Power Products is planning to create a new heat pump division to manufacture and market a quality, energy-efficient, heat pump. Headly is a respected name in the production of power tools and equipment, but heat pump production would be an entirely new line. Management believes a major promotional effort would be required to get good market penetration. Estimated promotional costs for the first 12 years of the product are

Year	Promotional Expense
1–3	$800,000
4–8	400,000
9–12	200,000

The product would have unit variable manufacturing costs of $1,200 and variable selling and administrative costs of $300. The selling price would be $2,500 each. Additional production and office facilities would be required at a cost of $12,000,000. Other divisional fixed expenses, including straight-line depreciation, would be $1,200,000 a year. The firm's income tax rate averages 45 percent, and 18 percent is the minimum acceptable rate of return on investments.

Management expects to sell the product for 12 years. The added facilities could be sold for $6,000,000 in 12 years. Expected annual sales are

Year	Sales per Year in Units
1	2000
2	5000
3–8	6000
9–12	4000

Required:
a. Prepare a report for the management of Headly Power Products describing and documenting the course of action you suggest.
b. What would your recommendation be if the company's cost of capital is 15 percent? Show supporting computations.

Problem Set B

P. 13B-1 **Analyzing alternative capital expenditures.** River Community College is considering two alternative plans for improving its student housing shortage on campus. Both involve dormitory construction. One plan calls for construction of a large dormitory that would not be fully occupied until the sixth year after construction. The second plan involves construction of two smaller dormitories five years apart. Both plans can be financed with 10 percent bond issues. The cost of the large building would be $3,800,000. The cost of the two smaller dormitories would be $2,000,000 for the first and $3,000,000 for the second. The two-dormitory alternative would provide lower operating costs and higher cash flows the first several years, but cash flows in the last five years would be identical using either option. Estimated net cash inflows from the project are

Year	Large Dormitory	Smaller Dormitories
1	$ 400,000	$ 500,000
2	450,000	550,000
3	500,000	600,000
4	600,000	600,000
5	700,000	600,000
6	900,000	900,000
7	1,000,000	1,000,000
8	1,000,000	1,000,000
9	1,000,000	1,000,000
10	1,000,000	1,000,000

Required:
Evaluate the two projects using net present value.

P. 13B-2 **Project evaluation using NPV, PI, and payback period.** Yard Beautiful Nursery has four employees who plant trees and shrubs on a full-time basis. Currently the company uses a large flatbed truck and a pickup truck for all planting deliveries. A new truck with a small hydraulic crane can be purchased for $54,000. It would have a useful life of eight years and a salvage value of $6,000. If the new truck is purchased, the company can maintain its current level of operations with only two employees engaged in full-time planting. The savings in personnel costs would be $9,000 per year for each employee. Operating and maintenance costs on the new truck are expected to be $4,000 per year higher than on the old trucks. The old trucks, which have a book value of zero, would be sold for a total of $2,000. The company has a tax rate of 40 percent and uses straight-line depreciation for all depreciable assets. Yard Beautiful requires a 15 percent return on investments.

Required:
a. Compute the net present value for the new truck.
b. Compute the profitability index.
c. Compute the payback period.

P. 13B-3 **Project evaluation and ranking.** A firm is evaluating three alternative investment proposals each requiring a $60,000 initial cash outlay. Each project has an expected useful life of six years. Below are expected net cash inflows over the life of the projects. Observing the data, one manager comments, "Clearly, Project C is the best choice; it yields far more cash than the others." The firm's cost of capital is 20 percent.

	Investment Proposal		
Year	A	B	C
1	$ 50,000	$ 20,000	$ 10,000
2	10,000	20,000	10,000
3	10,000	20,000	10,000
4	10,000	20,000	10,000
5	10,000	20,000	10,000
6	10,000	20,000	90,000
Total	$100,000	$120,000	$140,000

Required:
a. Evaluate and rank the projects using payback and net present value. Do you agree with the manager's evaluation? Discuss why you answered as you did.
b. Would your ranking of the projects change if the firm's cost of capital were 10 percent?

P. 13B-4 **IRR and payback reciprocal.** A computerized inventory control system can save Doolittle Department Stores $70,000 a year in lost inventory and inventory handling costs. The new system has an expected life of five years before technological changes and internal and external reporting requirements will force major changes in the system. The inventory system can be leased from a computer systems consulting firm for an initial fee of $60,510 plus an annual use fee of $8,000 a year. In addition, the store must purchase 12 cathode-ray tube computer terminals at a cost of $2,500 each. Other operating costs associated with the proposed system amount to $12,000 a year. The company has an effective income tax rate of 46 percent.

Required:

a. Compute the internal rate of return for the project.

b. Compute the payback reciprocal for the project. Is it a good estimate of IRR in this case?

c. Should the proposal be accepted if Doolittle's target rate of return is 18 percent? Explain.

P. 13B-5   Determining the maximum amount of an investment. The High Peaks Sporting Goods Store has been plagued by numerous burglaries over the last three years. To keep insurance premiums at a reasonable level and protect a $1,000,000 inventory, the store hired a night watchman. The watchman has solved the burglary problem, but he costs the firm $12,000 a year. He is occasionally absent from work due to sickness or bad weather. A security systems company has offered to sell the store a system that would eliminate the need for the night watchman. The system has an expected useful life of 15 years. The security systems salesperson is computing the cost of the system and will present a bid this week. The management estimates cost of capital at 16 percent.

Required:

a. What is the maximum bid the store should accept?

b. If the bid is $64,000, should the store accept it?

c. If the actual life of the security system is 12 years instead of 15, does it have any effect on your answer in *b*?

P. 13B-6   Using various methods to analyze four investments. Dune and Ryan, Incorporated, is evaluating four investment opportunities. The company estimates its cost of capital at 14 percent. Below are cash flow data for the investments.

	Estimated Annual Cash Flow			
Year	A	B	C	D
0	− $82,228	− $90,000	− $78,242	− $50,000
1	20,000	15,000	15,000	10,000
2	20,000	15,000	15,000	10,000
3	20,000	15,000	15,000	10,000
4	20,000	15,000	15,000	10,000
5	20,000	15,000	15,000	10,000
6	20,000	15,000	15,000	38,117
7	—	15,000	15,000	—
8	—	53,337	15,000	—
9	—	—	15,000	—
10	—	—	15,000	—

Required:

a. For each project calculate:
   1. The payback period.
   2. The internal rate of return.
   3. The net present value.
   4. The profitability index.
b. Prepare a schedule ranking investments in order of preference using each of the evaluation methods in part *a*.

P. 13B-7 **Project evaluation with increasing costs.** Starburg Manufacturing Company is concerned about the rising cost of labour. The assembly phase of its small appliance manufacturing business is almost totally manual. The engineering department has developed a plan to automate 80 percent of the assembly operation. The cost of the proposed project is $2.2 million. The expected life of the automated system is 10 years after which time the system will be scrapped without any salvage value. If implemented, labour cost should decline by 60 percent and direct material cost should fall by 5 percent due to greater production efficiencies. Current-year labour and material costs are $500,000 and $200,000, respectively. Over the life of the project, management expects labour costs to rise 10 percent a year and material costs 8 percent a year. Starburg's cost of capital is 15 percent. Ignore taxes.

Required:

a. Compute the expected cost savings for the life of the project.
b. Compute the net present value of the project.
c. Should the project be accepted?
d. If there were no cost increases at all, should the project be accepted?

P. 13B-8 **New-product project evaluation.** Graph-O-Tron, Inc., has acquired the patent rights to a new, very fast vector cathode-ray tube computer terminal. The terminal is very attractive to organizations, such as utilities, highway departments, and land-use planning organizations that use geography and geographic locations in their management information systems. Graph-O-Tron is operating near capacity and would require a new production facility to produce the new terminal. The cost of the plant and other facilities would be $6,200,000. The expected useful life is eight years, with an estimated salvage value of $1,400,000. Expected unit manufacturing costs are

Direct material	$280 per unit
Direct labour	270 per unit
Variable overhead	30 per unit
Variable selling and administrative	120 per unit

The product is expected to have an eight-year life cycle after which it will be technologically obsolete. At a selling price of $1,400 per unit, expected sales for the eight-year period are

Year	Expected Sales
1	2000 units
2	4000 units
3	5000 units
4	5000 units
5	4000 units
6	3000 units
7	2000 units
8	2000 units

Heavy advertising and promotional costs are required to penetrate the market quickly before competition reacts to the new product. During the first two years of the product's life, such costs would be $300,000 a year, and they would decrease to $100,000 per year for the last six years.

Other fixed costs, including straight-line depreciation, would amount to $800,000 a year. The firm's average income tax rate is 40 percent.

Graph-O-Tron requires a 25 percent return on investment for a product that is as risky as the new terminal.

Required:
a. Using the net present value method, evaluate the investment project.
b. If Graph-O-Tron, Inc., uses its normal required rate of return of 16 percent instead of the 25 percent rate for risky projects, would the project be acceptable?

Minicases

Minicase 13-1   (CMA Examination Question)

New West Company plans to replace an old piece of equipment which is obsolete and is expected to be unreliable under the stress of daily operations. The equipment is fully depreciated, and no salvage value can be realized upon its disposal.

One piece of equipment being considered would provide annual cash savings of $7,000 before income taxes. The equipment would cost $18,000 and have an estimated useful life of five years. No salvage value would be used for depreciation purposes because the equipment is expected to have no value at the end of five years.

New West uses the straight-line depreciation method on all equipment for both book and tax purposes. The company is subject to a 40 percent tax rate. New West requires an after-tax return of 14 percent.

Required:

a. Calculate for New West Company's proposed investment in new equipment the after-tax:
   1. Payback period.
   2. Accounting rate of return.
   3. Net present value.
   4. Profitability (present value) index.
   5. Internal rate of return.

   Assume all operating revenues and expenses occur at the end of the year. Appropriate discount tables are presented below.

b. Identify and discuss the issues New West Company should consider when deciding which of the five decision models identified in *a* it should employ to compare and evaluate alternative capital investment projects.

Minicase 13-2

(CMA Examination Question)

The Burnaby Company makes cookies for its chain of snack food stores. On January 2, 1983 Burnaby Company purchased a special cookie cutting machine; this machine has been utilized for three years. Burnaby Company is considering the purchase of a newer, more efficient machine. If purchased, the new machine would be acquired on January 2, 1986. Burnaby Company expects to sell 300 000 dozen cookies in each of the next four years. The selling price of the cookies is expected to average $.50 per dozen.

Burnaby Company has two options: (1) continue to operate the old machine, or (2) sell the old machine and purchase the new machine. No trade-in was offered by the seller of the new machine. The following information has been assembled to help decide which option is more desirable.

	Old Machine	New Machine
Original cost of machine at acquisition	$80,000	$120,000
Salvage value at the end of useful life for depreciation purposes	10,000	20,000
Useful life from date of acquisition	7 years	4 years
Expected annual cash operating expenses:		
Variable cost per dozen	$.20	$.14
Total fixed costs	$15,000	$ 14,000
Depreciation method used for tax purposes:	Straight-line	Sum-of-years'-digits
Estimated cash value of machines:		
January 2, 1983	$40,000	$120,000
December 31, 1986	$ 7,000	$ 20,000

Burnaby Company is subject to an overall income tax rate of 40 percent. Assume that all operating revenues and expenses occur at the end of the year. Assume that any gain or loss on the sale of machinery is treated as an ordinary tax item and will affect the taxes paid by Burnaby Company at the end of the year in which it occurred.

Required:

a. Use the net present value method to determine whether Burnaby Company should retain the old machine or acquire the new machine. Burnaby requires an after-tax return of 16 percent.

b. Without prejudice to your answer to *a*, assume that the quantitative differences are so slight between the two alternatives that Burnaby Company is indifferent to the two proposals. Identify and discuss the nonquantitative factors which are important to this decision that Burnaby Company should consider.

Minicase 13-3*   (CICA adapted)

Widgets, Ltd., a Canadian-controlled private corporation, manufactures and sells toys. The controller is considering the economics of replacing the firm's four automatic packaging machines early in the 1984 taxation year. At the end of the 1983 taxation year, the existing machines will all have been in operation for five years and will have been 50 percent depreciated based on an original life of ten years. A salesperson for the equipment supplier had recently suggested that the four machines should be replaced by two new machines which would give the same capacity as the existing four machines and would be more economical to operate.

The production manager estimated that the existing machines could be used for another five years, but would need considerable maintenance costs each year. He estimated that the combined operating costs and maintenance costs over the next five years would be $3,000 per year for each of the existing machines. These machines could be sold now for $1,100 each but would fetch only $50 each after another five years' usage. The net book value of the four machines represented about 10 percent of the net equipment on the balance sheet.

The salesperson had quoted a price of $12,500 for each of the new machines. It was estimated that the annual combined operating and maintenance costs of each of the new machines would be $2,500 per year if they were used for five years. After five years, the maintenance costs would rise significantly, making it more economical to scrap these machines for no residual value.

The company's net profit over the past five years has risen smoothly from

Reprinted, with permission, from Uniform Final Examination, 1976, published by the Canadian Institute of Chartered Accountants, Toronto, Canada.

Table 13-1

					Future Value of $1						
n	.5%	1%	1.5%	2%	2.5%	3%	3.5%	4%	4.5%	5%	*n*
1	1.0050	1.0100	1.0150	1.0200	1.0250	1.0300	1.0350	1.0400	1.0450	1.0500	1
2	1.0100	1.0201	1.0302	1.0404	1.0506	1.0609	1.0712	1.0816	1.0920	1.1025	2
3	1.0151	1.0303	1.0457	1.0612	1.0769	1.0927	1.1087	1.1249	1.1412	1.1576	3
4	1.0202	1.0406	1.0614	1.0824	1.1038	1.1255	1.1475	1.1699	1.1925	1.2155	4
5	1.0253	1.0510	1.0773	1.1041	1.1314	1.1593	1.1877	1.2167	1.2462	1.2763	5
6	1.0304	1.0615	1.0934	1.1262	1.1597	1.1941	1.2293	1.2653	1.3023	1.3401	6
7	1.0355	1.0721	1.1098	1.1487	1.1887	1.2299	1.2723	1.3159	1.3609	1.4071	7
8	1.0407	1.0829	1.1265	1.1717	1.2184	1.2668	1.3168	1.3686	1.4221	1.4775	8
9	1.0459	1.0937	1.1434	1.1951	1.2489	1.3048	1.3629	1.4233	1.4861	1.5513	9
10	1.0511	1.1046	1.1605	1.2190	1.2801	1.3439	1.4106	1.4802	1.5530	1.6289	10
11	1.0564	1.1157	1.1779	1.2434	1.3121	1.3842	1.4600	1.5395	1.6229	1.7103	11
12	1.0617	1.1268	1.1956	1.2682	1.3449	1.4258	1.5111	1.6010	1.6959	1.7959	12
13	1.0670	1.1381	1.2136	1.2936	1.3785	1.4685	1.5640	1.6651	1.7722	1.8856	13
14	1.0723	1.1495	1.2318	1.3195	1.4130	1.5126	1.6187	1.7317	1.8519	1.9799	14
15	1.0777	1.1610	1.2502	1.3459	1.4483	1.5580	1.6753	1.8009	1.9353	2.0789	15
16	1.0831	1.1726	1.2690	1.3728	1.4845	1.6047	1.7340	1.8730	2.0224	2.1829	16
17	1.0885	1.1843	1.2880	1.4002	1.5216	1.6528	1.7947	1.9479	2.1134	2.2920	17
18	1.0939	1.1961	1.3073	1.4282	1.5597	1.7024	1.8575	2.0258	2.2085	2.4066	18
19	1.0994	1.2081	1.3270	1.4568	1.5987	1.7535	1.9225	2.1068	2.3079	2.5270	19
20	1.1049	1.2202	1.3469	1.4859	1.6386	1.8061	1.9898	2.1911	2.4117	2.6533	20
21	1.1104	1.2324	1.3671	1.5157	1.6796	1.8603	2.0594	2.2788	2.5202	2.7860	21
22	1.1160	1.2447	1.3876	1.5460	1.7216	1.9161	2.1315	2.3699	2.6337	2.9253	22
23	1.1216	1.2572	1.4084	1.5769	1.7646	1.9736	2.2061	2.4647	2.7522	3.0715	23
24	1.1272	1.2697	1.4295	1.6084	1.8087	2.0328	2.2833	2.5633	2.8760	3.2251	24
25	1.1328	1.2824	1.4509	1.6406	1.8539	2.0938	2.3632	2.6658	3.0054	3.3864	25
26	1.1385	1.2953	1.4727	1.6734	1.9003	2.1566	2.4460	2.7725	3.1407	3.5557	26
27	1.1442	1.3082	1.4948	1.7069	1.9478	2.2213	2.5316	2.8834	3.2820	3.7335	27
28	1.1499	1.3213	1.5172	1.7410	1.9965	2.2879	2.6202	2.9987	3.4297	3.9201	28
29	1.1556	1.3345	1.5400	1.7758	2.0464	2.3566	2.7119	3.1187	3.5840	4.1161	29
30	1.1614	1.3478	1.5631	1.8114	2.0976	2.4273	2.8068	3.2434	3.7453	4.3219	30
31	1.1672	1.3613	1.5865	1.8476	2.1500	2.5001	2.9050	3.3731	3.9139	4.5380	31
32	1.1730	1.3749	1.6103	1.8845	2.2038	2.5751	3.0067	3.5081	4.0900	4.7649	32
33	1.1789	1.3887	1.6345	1.9222	2.2589	2.6523	3.1119	3.6484	4.2740	5.0032	33
34	1.1848	1.4026	1.6590	1.9607	2.3153	2.7319	3.2209	3.7943	4.4664	5.2533	34
35	1.1907	1.4166	1.6839	1.9999	2.3732	2.8139	3.3336	3.9461	4.6673	5.5160	35

$200,000 to $500,000. There is no significant difference between taxable income and accounting income. The plant is currently operating at capacity, but because competition is increasing and prices are soft, the controller is concerned whether the company will be able to maintain the net income level. The minimum acceptable after-tax rate of return on projects is 10 percent.

Assume that the firm's incremental income tax rate is 40 percent. Ignore effects of investment tax credit.

Required:

a. Based upon estimates the controller has put together, should the firm replace the packaging machines? Show the calculations to support your opinion.

n	6%	7%	8%	9%	10%	11%	12%	15%	20%	25%	n
1	1.0600	1.0700	1.0800	1.0900	1.1000	1.1100	1.1200	1.1500	1.2000	1.2500	1
2	1.1236	1.1449	1.1664	1.1881	1.2100	1.2321	1.2544	1.3225	1.4400	1.5625	2
3	1.1910	1.2250	1.2597	1.2950	1.3310	1.3676	1.4049	1.5209	1.7280	1.9531	3
4	1.2625	1.3108	1.3605	1.4116	1.4641	1.5181	1.5735	1.7490	2.0736	2.4414	4
5	1.3382	1.4026	1.4693	1.5386	1.6105	1.6851	1.7623	2.0114	2.4883	3.0518	5
6	1.4185	1.5007	1.5869	1.6771	1.7716	1.8704	1.9738	2.3131	2.9860	3.8147	6
7	1.5036	1.6058	1.7138	1.8280	1.9487	2.0762	2.2107	2.6600	3.5832	4.7684	7
8	1.5938	1.7182	1.8509	1.9926	2.1436	2.3045	2.4760	3.0590	4.2998	5.9605	8
9	1.6895	1.8385	1.9990	2.1719	2.3579	2.5580	2.7731	3.5179	5.1598	7.4506	9
10	1.7908	1.9672	2.1589	2.3674	2.5937	2.8394	3.1058	4.0456	6.1917	9.3132	10
11	1.8983	2.1049	2.3316	2.5804	2.8531	3.1518	3.4785	4.6524	7.4301	11.6415	11
12	2.0122	2.2522	2.5182	2.8127	3.1384	3.4985	3.8960	5.3503	8.9161	14.5519	12
13	2.1329	2.4098	2.7196	3.0658	3.4523	3.8833	4.3635	6.1528	10.6993	18.1899	13
14	2.2609	2.5785	2.9372	3.3417	3.7975	4.3104	4.8871	7.0757	12.8392	22.7374	14
15	2.3966	2.7590	3.1722	3.6425	4.1772	4.7846	5.4736	8.1371	15.4070	28.4217	15
16	2.5404	2.9522	3.4259	3.9703	4.5950	5.3109	6.1304	9.3576	18.4884	35.5271	16
17	2.6928	3.1588	3.7000	4.3276	5.0545	5.8951	6.8660	10.7613	22.1861	44.4089	17
18	2.8543	3.3799	3.9960	4.7171	5.5599	6.5436	7.6900	12.3755	26.6233	55.5112	18
19	3.0256	3.6165	4.3157	5.1417	6.1159	7.2633	8.6128	14.2318	31.9480	69.3889	19
20	3.2071	3.8697	4.6610	5.6044	6.7275	8.0623	9.6463	16.3665	38.3376	86.7362	20
21	3.3996	4.1406	5.0338	6.1088	7.4002	8.9492	10.8038	18.8215	46.0051	108.4202	21
22	3.6035	4.4304	5.4365	6.6586	8.1403	9.9336	12.1003	21.6447	55.2061	135.5253	22
23	3.8197	4.7405	5.8715	7.2579	8.9543	11.0263	13.5523	24.8915	66.2474	169.4066	23
24	4.0489	5.0724	6.3412	7.9111	9.8497	12.2392	15.1786	28.6252	79.4968	211.7582	24
25	4.2919	5.4274	6.8485	8.6231	10.8347	13.5855	17.0001	32.9190	95.3962	264.6978	25
26	4.5494	5.8074	7.3964	9.3992	11.9182	15.0799	19.0401	37.8568	114.4755	330.8722	26
27	4.8223	6.2139	7.9881	10.2451	13.1100	16.7386	21.3249	43.5353	137.3706	413.5903	27
28	5.1117	6.6488	8.6271	11.1671	14.4210	18.5799	23.8839	50.0656	164.8447	516.9879	28
29	5.4184	7.1143	9.3173	12.1722	15.8631	20.6237	26.7499	57.5755	197.8136	646.2349	29
30	5.7435	7.6123	10.0627	13.2677	17.4494	22.8923	29.9599	66.2118	237.3763	807.7936	30
31	6.0881	8.1451	10.8677	14.4618	19.1943	25.4104	33.5551	76.1435	284.8516	1009.7420	31
32	6.4534	8.7153	11.7371	15.7633	21.1138	28.2056	37.5817	87.5651	341.8219	1262.1774	32
33	6.8406	9.3253	12.6760	17.1820	23.2252	31.3082	42.0915	100.6998	410.1863	1577.7218	33
34	7.2510	9.9781	13.6901	18.7284	25.5477	34.7521	47.1425	115.8048	492.2235	1972.1523	34
35	7.6861	10.6766	14.7853	20.4140	28.1024	38.5749	52.7996	133.1755	590.6682	2465.1903	35

b. What other factors should management consider before making a final decision?

Minicase 13-4 (CMA Examination Question)

Quebec Products Company manufactures several different products. One of the firm's principal products sells for $20 per unit. The sales manager of Quebec Products has stated repeatedly that he could sell more units of this product if they were available. In an attempt to substantiate his claim the sales manager

Table 13-2

					Present Value of $1						
n	4%	5%	6%	7%	8%	9%	10%	12%	14%	15%	n
1	.9615	.9524	.9434	.9346	.9259	.9174	.9091	.8929	.8772	.8696	1
2	.9246	.9070	.8900	.8734	.8573	.8417	.8264	.7972	.7695	.7561	2
3	.8890	.8638	.8396	.8163	.7938	.7722	.7513	.7118	.6750	.6575	3
4	.8548	.8227	.7921	.7629	.7350	.7084	.6830	.6355	.5921	.5718	4
5	.8219	.7835	.7473	.7130	.6806	.6499	.6209	.5674	.5194	.4972	5
6	.7903	.7462	.7050	.6663	.6302	.5963	.5645	.5066	.4556	.4323	6
7	.7599	.7107	.6651	.6227	.5835	.5470	.5132	.4523	.3996	.3759	7
8	.7307	.6768	.6274	.5820	.5403	.5019	.4665	.4039	.3506	.3269	8
9	.7026	.6446	.5919	.5439	.5002	.4604	.4241	.3606	.3075	.2843	9
10	.6756	.6139	.5584	.5083	.4632	.4224	.3855	.3220	.2697	.2472	10
11	.6496	.5847	.5268	.4751	.4289	.3875	.3505	.2875	.2366	.2149	11
12	.6246	.5568	.4970	.4440	.3971	.3555	.3186	.2567	.2076	.1869	12
13	.6006	.5303	.4688	.4150	.3677	.3262	.2897	.2292	.1821	.1625	13
14	.5775	.5051	.4423	.3878	.3405	.2992	.2633	.2046	.1597	.1413	14
15	.5553	.4810	.4173	.3624	.3152	.2745	.2394	.1827	.1401	.1229	15
16	.5339	.4581	.3936	.3387	.2919	.2519	.2176	.1631	.1229	.1069	16
17	.5134	.4363	.3714	.3166	.2703	.2311	.1978	.1456	.1078	.0929	17
18	.4936	.4155	.3503	.2959	.2502	.2120	.1799	.1300	.0946	.0808	18
19	.4746	.3957	.3305	.2765	.2317	.1945	.1635	.1161	.0829	.0703	19
20	.4564	.3769	.3118	.2584	.2145	.1784	.1486	.1037	.0728	.0611	20
21	.4388	.3589	.2942	.2415	.1987	.1637	.1351	.0926	.0638	.0531	21
22	.4220	.3418	.2775	.2257	.1839	.1502	.1228	.0826	.0560	.0462	22
23	.4057	.3256	.2618	.2109	.1703	.1378	.1117	.0738	.0491	.0402	23
24	.3901	.3101	.2470	.1971	.1577	.1264	.1015	.0659	.0431	.0349	24
25	.3751	.2953	.2330	.1842	.1460	.1160	.0923	.0588	.0378	.0304	25
26	.3607	.2812	.2198	.1722	.1352	.1064	.0839	.0525	.0331	.0264	26
27	.3468	.2678	.2074	.1609	.1252	.0976	.0763	.0469	.0291	.0230	27
28	.3335	.2551	.1956	.1504	.1159	.0895	.0693	.0419	.0255	.0200	28
29	.3207	.2429	.1846	.1406	.1073	.0822	.0630	.0374	.0224	.0174	29
30	.3083	.2314	.1741	.1314	.0994	.0754	.0573	.0334	.0196	.0151	30
35	.2534	.1813	.1301	.0937	.0676	.0490	.0356	.0189	.0102	.0075	35
40	.2083	.1420	.0972	.0668	.0460	.0318	.0221	.0107	.0053	.0037	40
45	.1712	.1113	.0727	.0476	.0313	.0207	.0137	.0061	.0027	.0019	45
50	.1407	.0872	.0543	.0339	.0213	.0134	.0085	.0035	.0014	.0009	50

conducted a market research study last year at a cost of $44,000 to determine potential demand for this product. The study indicated that Quebec Products could sell 18 000 units of this product annually for the next five years.

The equipment currently in use has the capacity to produce 11 000 units annually. The variable production costs are $9 per unit. The equipment has a book value of $60,000 and a remaining useful life of five years. The salvage value of the equipment is negligible now and will be zero in five years.

A maximum of 20 000 units could be produced annually on the new machinery which can be purchased. The new equipment costs $300,000 and has an estimated useful life of five years with no salvage value at the end of

n	16%	17%	18%	19%	20%	22%	25%	28%	30%	35%	n
1	.8621	.8547	.8475	.8403	.8333	.8197	.8000	.7812	.7692	.7407	1
2	.7432	.7305	.7182	.7062	.6944	.6719	.6400	.6104	.5917	.5487	2
3	.6407	.6244	.6086	.5934	.5787	.5507	.5120	.4768	.4552	.4064	3
4	.5523	.5337	.5158	.4987	.4823	.4514	.4096	.3725	.3501	.3011	4
5	.4761	.4561	.4371	.4190	.4019	.3700	.3277	.2910	.2693	.2230	5
6	.4104	.3898	.3704	.3521	.3349	.3033	.2621	.2274	.2072	.1652	6
7	.3538	.3332	.3139	.2959	.2791	.2486	.2097	.1776	.1594	.1224	7
8	.3050	.2848	.2660	.2487	.2326	.2038	.1678	.1388	.1226	.0906	8
9	.2630	.2434	.2255	.2090	.1938	.1670	.1342	.1084	.0943	.0671	9
10	.2267	.2080	.1911	.1756	.1615	.1369	.1074	.0847	.0725	.0497	10
11	.1954	.1778	.1619	.1476	.1346	.1122	.0859	.0662	.0558	.0368	11
12	.1685	.1520	.1372	.1240	.1122	.0920	.0687	.0517	.0429	.0273	12
13	.1452	.1299	.1163	.1042	.0935	.0754	.0550	.0404	.0330	.0202	13
14	.1252	.1110	.0985	.0876	.0779	.0618	.0440	.0316	.0254	.0150	14
15	.1079	.0949	.0835	.0736	.0649	.0507	.0352	.0247	.0195	.0111	15
16	.0930	.0811	.0708	.0618	.0541	.0415	.0281	.0193	.0150	.0082	16
17	.0802	.0693	.0600	.0520	.0451	.0340	.0225	.0150	.0116	.0061	17
18	.0691	.0592	.0508	.0437	.0376	.0279	.0180	.0118	.0089	.0045	18
19	.0596	.0506	.0431	.0367	.0313	.0229	.0144	.0092	.0068	.0033	19
20	.0514	.0433	.0365	.0308	.0261	.0187	.0115	.0072	.0053	.0025	20
21	.0443	.0370	.0309	.0259	.0217	.0154	.0092	.0056	.0040	.0018	21
22	.0382	.0316	.0262	.0218	.0181	.0126	.0074	.0044	.0031	.0014	22
23	.0329	.0270	.0222	.0183	.0151	.0103	.0059	.0034	.0024	.0010	23
24	.0284	.0231	.0188	.0154	.0126	.0085	.0047	.0027	.0018	.0007	24
25	.0245	.0197	.0160	.0129	.0105	.0069	.0038	.0021	.0014	.0006	25
26	.0211	.0169	.0135	.0109	.0087	.0057	.0030	.0016	.0011	.0004	26
27	.0182	.0144	.0115	.0091	.0073	.0047	.0024	.0013	.0008	.0003	27
28	.0157	.0123	.0097	.0077	.0061	.0038	.0019	.0010	.0006	.0002	28
29	.0135	.0105	.0082	.0064	.0051	.0031	.0015	.0008	.0005	.0002	29
30	.0116	.0090	.0070	.0054	.0042	.0026	.0012	.0006	.0004	.0001	30
35	.0055	.0041	.0030	.0023	.0017	.0009	.0004	.0002	.0001	.0000	35
40	.0026	.0019	.0013	.0010	.0007	.0004	.0001	.0001	.0000	.0000	40
45	.0013	.0009	.0006	.0004	.0003	.0001	.0000	.0000	.0000	.0000	45
50	.0006	.0004	.0003	.0002	.0001	.0000	.0000	.0000	.0000	.0000	50

five years. Quebec Products' production manager has estimated that the new equipment would provide increased production efficiencies that would reduce the variable production costs to $7 per unit.

Quebec Products Company uses straight-line depreciation on all of its equipment for tax purposes. The firm is subject to a 40 percent tax rate, and its discount rate is 15 percent.

The sales manager felt so strongly about the need for additional capacity that he attempted to prepare an economic justification for the equipment, although this was not one of his responsibilities. His analysis, presented below, disappointed him because it did not justify acquiring the equipment.

Table 13-3

					Future Value of Annuity of $1						
n	.5%	1%	1.5%	2%	2.5%	3%	3.5%	4%	4.5%	5%	*n*
1	1.0000	1.0000	1.0000	1.0000	1.0000	1.0000	1.0000	1.0000	1.0000	1.0000	1
2	2.0050	2.0100	2.0150	2.0200	2.0250	2.0300	2.0350	2.0400	2.0450	2.0500	2
3	3.0150	3.0301	3.0452	3.0604	3.0756	3.0909	3.1062	3.1216	3.1370	3.1525	3
4	4.0301	4.0604	4.0909	4.1216	4.1525	4.1836	4.2149	4.2465	4.2782	4.3101	4
5	5.0503	5.1010	5.1523	5.2040	5.2563	5.3091	5.3625	5.4163	5.4707	5.5256	5
6	6.0755	6.1520	6.2296	6.3081	6.3877	6.4684	6.5502	6.6330	6.7169	6.8019	6
7	7.1059	7.2135	7.3230	7.4343	7.5474	7.6625	7.7794	7.8983	8.0192	8.1420	7
8	8.1414	8.2857	8.4328	8.5830	8.7361	8.8923	9.0517	9.2142	9.3800	9.5491	8
9	9.1821	9.3685	9.5593	9.7546	9.9545	10.1591	10.3685	10.5828	10.8021	11.0266	9
10	10.2280	10.4622	10.7027	10.9497	11.2034	11.4639	11.7314	12.0061	12.2882	12.5779	10
11	11.2792	11.5668	11.8633	12.1687	12.4835	12.8078	13.1420	13.4864	13.8412	14.2068	11
12	12.3356	12.6825	13.0412	13.4121	13.7956	14.1920	14.6020	15.0258	15.4640	15.9171	12
13	13.3972	13.8093	14.2368	14.6803	15.1404	15.6178	16.1130	16.6268	17.1599	17.7130	13
14	14.4642	14.9474	15.4504	15.9739	16.5190	17.0863	17.6770	18.2919	18.9321	19.5986	14
15	15.5365	16.0969	16.6821	17.2934	17.9319	18.5989	19.2957	20.0236	20.7841	21.5786	15
16	16.6142	17.2579	17.9324	18.6393	19.3802	20.1569	20.9710	21.8245	22.7193	23.6575	16
17	17.6973	18.4304	19.2014	20.0121	20.8647	21.7616	22.7050	23.6975	24.7417	25.8404	17
18	18.7858	19.6147	20.4894	21.4123	22.3863	23.4144	24.4997	25.6454	26.8551	28.1324	18
19	19.8797	20.8109	21.7967	22.8406	23.9460	25.1169	26.3572	27.6712	29.0636	30.5390	19
20	20.9791	22.0189	23.1237	24.2974	25.5447	26.8704	28.2797	29.7781	31.3714	33.0660	20
21	22.0840	23.2392	24.4705	25.7833	27.1833	28.6765	30.2695	31.9692	33.7831	35.7193	21
22	23.1944	24.4716	25.8376	27.2990	28.8629	30.5368	32.3289	34.2480	36.3034	38.5052	22
23	24.3104	25.7163	27.2251	28.8450	30.5844	32.4529	34.4604	36.6179	38.9370	41.4305	23
24	25.4320	26.9735	28.6335	30.4219	32.3490	34.4265	36.6665	39.0826	41.6892	44.5020	24
25	26.5591	28.2432	30.0630	32.0303	34.1578	36.4593	38.9499	41.6459	44.5652	47.7271	25
26	27.6919	29.5256	31.5140	33.6709	36.0117	38.5530	41.3131	44.3117	47.5706	51.1135	26
27	28.8304	30.8209	32.9867	35.3443	37.9120	40.7096	43.7591	47.0842	50.7113	54.6691	27
28	29.9745	32.1291	34.4815	37.0512	39.8598	42.9309	46.2906	49.9676	53.9933	58.4026	28
29	31.1244	33.4504	35.9987	38.7922	41.8563	45.2189	48.9108	52.9663	57.4230	62.3227	29
30	32.2800	34.7849	37.5387	40.5681	43.9027	47.5754	51.6227	56.0849	61.0071	66.4388	30
31	33.4414	36.1327	39.1018	42.3794	46.0003	50.0027	54.4295	59.3283	64.7524	70.7608	31
32	34.6086	37.4941	40.6883	44.2270	48.1503	52.5028	57.3345	62.7015	68.6662	75.2988	32
33	35.7817	38.8690	42.2986	46.1116	50.3540	55.0778	60.3412	66.2095	72.7562	80.0638	33
34	36.9606	40.2577	43.9331	48.0338	52.6129	57.7302	63.4532	69.8579	77.0303	85.0670	34
35	38.1454	41.6603	45.5921	49.9945	54.9282	60.4621	66.6740	73.6522	81.4966	90.3203	35

Required Investment		
Purchase price of new equipment		$300,000
Disposal of existing equipment:		
Loss of disposal	$60 000	
Less tax benefit (40%)	24,000	36,000
Cost of market research study		44,000
Total investment		$380,000

n	6%	7%	8%	9%	10%	11%	12%	15%	20%	25%	n
1	1.0000	1.0000	1.0000	1.0000	1.0000	1.0000	1.0000	1.0000	1.0000	1.0000	1
2	2.0600	2.0700	2.0800	2.0900	2.1000	2.1100	2.1200	2.1500	2.2000	2.2500	2
3	3.1836	3.2149	3.2464	3.2781	3.3100	3.3421	3.3744	3.4725	3.6400	3.8125	3
4	4.3746	4.4399	4.5061	4.5731	4.6410	4.7097	4.7793	4.9934	5.3680	5.7656	4
5	5.6371	5.7507	5.8666	5.9847	6.1051	6.2278	6.3528	6.7424	7.4416	8.2070	5
6	6.9753	7.1533	7.3359	7.5233	7.7156	7.9129	8.1152	8.7537	9.9299	11.2588	6
7	8.3938	8.6540	8.9228	9.2004	9.4872	9.7833	10.0890	11.0668	12.9159	15.0735	7
8	9.8975	10.2598	10.6366	11.0285	11.4359	11.8594	12.2997	13.7268	16.4991	19.8419	8
9	11.4913	11.9780	12.4876	13.0210	13.5795	14.1640	14.7757	16.7858	20.7989	25.8023	9
10	13.1808	13.8164	14.4866	15.1929	15.9374	16.7220	17.5487	20.3037	25.9587	33.2529	10
11	14.9716	15.7836	16.6455	17.5603	18.5312	19.5614	20.6546	24.3493	32.1504	42.5661	11
12	16.8699	17.8885	18.9771	20.1407	21.3843	22.7132	24.1331	29.0017	39.5805	54.2077	12
13	18.8821	20.1406	21.4953	22.9534	24.5227	26.2116	28.0291	34.3519	48.4966	68.7596	13
14	21.0151	22.5505	24.2149	26.0192	27.9750	30.0949	32.3926	40.5047	59.1959	86.9495	14
15	23.2760	25.1290	27.1521	29.3609	31.7725	34.4054	37.2797	47.5804	72.0351	109.6868	15
16	25.6725	27.8881	30.3243	33.0034	35.9497	39.1899	42.7533	55.7175	87.4421	138.1085	16
17	28.2129	30.8402	33.7502	36.9737	40.5447	44.5008	48.8837	65.0751	105.9306	173.6357	17
18	30.9057	33.9990	37.4502	41.3013	45.5992	50.3959	55.7497	75.8364	128.1167	218.0446	18
19	33.7600	37.3790	41.4463	46.0185	51.1591	56.9395	63.4397	88.2118	154.7400	273.5558	19
20	36.7856	40.9955	45.7620	51.1601	57.2750	64.2028	72.0524	102.4436	186.6880	342.9447	20
21	39.9927	44.8652	50.4229	56.7645	64.0025	72.2651	81.6987	118.8101	225.0256	429.6809	21
22	43.3923	49.0057	55.4568	62.8733	71.4027	81.2143	92.5026	137.6316	271.0307	538.1011	22
23	46.9958	53.4361	60.8933	69.5319	79.5430	91.1479	104.6029	159.2764	326.2369	673.6264	23
24	50.8156	58.1767	66.7648	76.7898	88.4973	102.1742	118.1552	184.1678	392.4842	843.0329	24
25	54.8645	63.2490	73.1059	84.7009	98.3471	114.4133	133.3339	212.7930	471.9811	1054.7912	25
26	59.1564	68.6765	79.9544	93.3240	109.1818	127.9988	150.3339	245.7120	567.3773	1319.4890	26
27	63.7058	74.4838	87.3508	102.7231	121.0999	143.0786	169.3740	283.5688	681.8528	1650.3612	27
28	68.5281	80.6977	95.3388	112.9682	134.2099	159.8173	190.6989	327.1041	819.2233	2063.9515	28
29	73.6398	87.3465	103.9659	124.1354	148.6309	178.3972	214.5828	377.1697	984.0680	2580.9394	29
30	79.0582	94.4608	113.2832	136.3075	164.4940	199.0209	241.3327	434.7451	1181.8816	3227.1743	30
31	84.8017	102.0730	123.3459	149.5752	181.9434	221.9132	271.2926	500.9569	1419.2579	4034.9678	31
32	90.8898	110.2182	134.2135	164.0370	201.1378	247.3236	304.8477	577.1005	1704.1095	5044.7098	32
33	97.3432	118.9334	145.9506	179.8005	222.2515	275.5292	342.4294	664.6655	2045.9314	6306.8872	33
34	104.1838	128.2588	158.6267	196.9823	245.4767	306.8374	384.5210	765.3654	2456.1176	7884.6091	34
35	111.4348	138.2369	172.3168	215.7108	271.0244	341.5896	431.6635	881.1702	2948.3411	9856.7613	35

Annual Returns

Contribution margin from product:	
Using the new equipment [18 000 × ($20 − 7)]	$234,000
Using the existing equipment [11 000 × ($20 − 9)]	121,000
Increase in contribution margin	$113,000
Less depreciation	60,000
Increase in before-tax income	$ 53,000
Income tax (40%)	21,200
Increase in income	$ 31,800
Less 15% on the additional investment required (.15 × $380,000)	57,000
Net annual return of proposed investment in new equipment	$ (25,200)

Table 13-4

					Present Value of Annuity of $1						
n	4%	5%	6%	7%	8%	9%	10%	12%	14%	15%	*n*
1	.9615	.9524	.9434	.9346	.9259	.9174	.9091	.8929	.8772	.8696	1
2	1.8861	1.8594	1.8334	1.8080	1.7833	1.7591	1.7355	1.6901	1.6467	1.6257	2
3	2.7751	2.7232	2.6730	2.6243	2.5771	2.5313	2.4869	2.4018	2.3216	2.2832	3
4	3.6299	3.5460	3.4651	3.3872	3.3121	3.2397	3.1699	3.0373	2.9137	2.8550	4
5	4.4518	4.3295	4.2124	4.1002	3.9927	3.8897	3.7908	3.6048	3.4331	3.3522	5
6	5.2421	5.0757	4.9173	4.7665	4.6229	4.4859	4.3553	4.1114	3.8887	3.7845	6
7	6.0021	5.7864	5.5824	5.3893	5.2064	5.0330	4.8684	4.5638	4.2883	4.1604	7
8	6.7327	6.4632	6.2098	5.9713	5.7466	5.5348	5.3349	4.9676	4.6389	4.4873	8
9	7.4353	7.1078	6.8017	6.5152	6.2469	5.9952	5.7590	5.3282	4.9464	4.7716	9
10	8.1109	7.7217	7.3601	7.0236	6.7101	6.4177	6.1446	5.6502	5.2161	5.0188	10
11	8.7605	8.3064	7.8869	7.4987	7.1390	6.8052	6.4951	5.9377	5.4527	5.2337	11
12	9.3851	8.8633	8.3838	7.9427	7.5361	7.1607	6.8137	6.1944	5.6603	5.4206	12
13	9.9856	9.3936	8.8527	8.3577	7.9038	7.4869	7.1034	6.4235	5.8424	5.5831	13
14	10.5631	9.8986	9.2950	8.7455	8.2442	7.7862	7.3667	6.6282	6.0021	5.7245	14
15	11.1184	10.3797	9.7122	9.1079	8.5595	8.0607	7.6061	6.8109	6.1422	5.8474	15
16	11.6523	10.8378	10.1059	9.4466	8.8514	8.3126	7.8237	6.9740	6.2651	5.9542	16
17	12.1657	11.2741	10.4773	9.7632	9.1216	8.5436	8.0216	7.1196	6.3729	6.0472	17
18	12.6593	11.6896	10.8276	10.0591	9.3719	8.7556	8.2014	7.2497	6.4674	6.1280	18
19	13.1339	12.0853	11.1581	10.3356	9.6036	8.9501	8.3649	7.3658	6.5504	6.1982	19
20	13.5903	12.4622	11.4699	10.5940	9.8181	9.1285	8.5136	7.4694	6.6231	6.2593	20
21	14.0292	12.8212	11.7641	10.8355	10.0168	9.2922	8.6487	7.5620	6.6870	6.3125	21
22	14.4511	13.1630	12.0416	11.0612	10.2007	9.4424	8.7715	7.6446	6.7429	6.3587	22
23	14.8568	13.4886	12.3034	11.2722	10.3711	9.5802	8.8832	7.7184	6.7921	6.3988	23
24	15.2470	13.7986	12.5504	11.4693	10.5288	9.7066	8.9847	7.7843	6.8351	6.4338	24
25	15.6221	14.0939	12.7834	11.6536	10.6748	9.8226	9.0770	7.8431	6.8729	6.4641	25
26	15.9828	14.3752	13.0032	11.8258	10.8100	9.9290	9.1609	7.8957	6.9061	6.4906	26
27	16.3296	14.6430	13.2105	11.9867	10.9352	10.0266	9.2372	7.9426	6.9352	6.5135	27
28	16.6631	14.8981	13.4062	12.1371	11.0511	10.1161	9.3066	7.9844	6.9607	6.5335	28
29	16.9837	15.1411	13.5907	12.2777	11.1584	10.1983	9.3696	8.0218	6.9830	6.5509	29
30	17.2920	15.3725	13.7648	12.4090	11.2578	10.2737	9.4269	8.0552	7.0027	6.5660	30
35	18.6646	16.3742	14.4982	12.9477	11.6546	10.5668	9.6442	8.1755	7.0700	6.6166	35
40	19.7928	17.1591	15.0463	13.3317	11.9246	10.7574	9.7791	8.2438	7.1050	6.6418	40
45	20.7200	17.7741	15.4558	13.6055	12.1084	10.8812	9.8628	8.2825	7.1232	6.6543	45
50	21.4822	18.2559	15.7619	13.8007	12.2335	10.9617	9.9148	8.3045	7.1327	6.6605	50

Required:

a. The controller of Quebec Products Company plans to prepare a discounted cash flow analysis for this investment proposal. The controller has asked you to prepare corrected calculations of

1. The required investment in the new equipment.
2. The recurring annual cash flows.

Explain the treatment of each item of your corrected calculations which is treated differently from the original analysis prepared by the sales manager.

b. Calculate the net present value of the proposed investment in the new equipment.

n	16%	17%	18%	19%	20%	22%	25%	28%	30%	35%	n
1	.8621	.8547	.8475	.8403	.8333	.8197	.8000	.7812	.7692	.7407	1
2	1.6052	1.5852	1.5656	1.5465	1.5278	1.4915	1.4400	1.3916	1.3609	1.2894	2
3	2.2459	2.2096	2.1743	2.1399	2.1065	2.0422	1.9520	1.8684	1.8161	1.6959	3
4	2.7982	2.7432	2.6901	2.6386	2.5887	2.4936	2.3616	2.2410	2.1662	1.9969	4
5	3.2743	3.1993	3.1272	3.0576	2.9906	2.8636	2.6893	2.5320	2.4356	2.2200	5
6	3.6847	3.5892	3.4976	3.4098	3.3255	3.1669	2.9514	2.7594	2.6427	2.3852	6
7	4.0386	3.9224	3.8115	3.7057	3.6046	3.4155	3.1611	2.9370	2.8021	2.5075	7
8	4.3436	4.2072	4.0776	3.9544	3.8372	3.6193	3.3289	3.0758	2.9247	2.5982	8
9	4.6065	4.4506	4.3030	4.1633	4.0310	3.7863	3.4631	3.1842	3.0190	2.6653	9
10	4.8332	4.6586	4.4941	4.3389	4.1925	3.9232	3.5705	3.2689	3.0915	2.7150	10
11	5.0286	4.8364	4.6560	4.4865	4.3271	4.0354	3.6564	3.3351	3.1473	2.7519	11
12	5.1971	4.9884	4.7932	4.6105	4.4392	4.1274	3.7251	3.3868	3.1903	2.7792	12
13	5.3423	5.1183	4.9095	4.7147	4.5327	4.2028	3.7801	3.4272	3.2233	2.7994	13
14	5.4675	5.2293	5.0081	4.8023	4.6106	4.2646	3.8241	3.4587	3.2487	2.8144	14
15	5.5755	5.3242	5.0916	4.8759	4.6755	4.3152	3.8593	3.4834	3.2682	2.8255	15
16	5.6685	5.4053	5.1624	4.9377	4.7296	4.3567	3.8874	3.5026	3.2832	2.8337	16
17	5.7487	5.4746	5.2223	4.9897	4.7746	4.3908	3.9099	3.5177	3.2948	2.8398	17
18	5.8178	5.5339	5.2732	5.0333	4.8122	4.4187	3.9279	3.5294	3.3037	2.8443	18
19	5.8775	5.5845	5.3162	5.0700	4.8435	4.4415	3.9424	3.5386	3.3105	2.8476	19
20	5.9288	5.6278	5.3527	5.1009	4.8696	4.4603	3.9539	3.5458	3.3158	2.8501	20
21	5.9731	5.6648	5.3837	5.1268	4.8913	4.4756	3.9631	3.5514	3.3198	2.8519	21
22	6.0113	5.6964	5.4099	5.1486	4.9094	4.4882	3.9705	3.5558	3.3230	2.8533	22
23	6.0442	5.7234	5.4321	5.1668	4.9245	4.4985	3.9764	3.5592	3.3254	2.8543	23
24	6.0726	5.7465	5.4509	5.1822	4.9371	4.5070	3.9811	3.5619	3.3272	2.8550	24
25	6.0971	5.7662	5.4669	5.1951	4.9476	4.5139	3.9849	3.5640	3.3286	2.8556	25
26	6.1182	5.7831	5.4804	5.2060	4.9563	4.5196	3.9879	3.5656	3.3297	2.8560	26
27	6.1364	5.7975	5.4919	5.2151	4.9636	4.5243	3.9903	3.5669	3.3305	2.8563	27
28	6.1520	5.8099	5.5016	5.2228	4.9697	4.5281	3.9923	3.5679	3.3312	2.8565	28
29	6.1656	5.8204	5.5098	5.2292	4.9747	4.5312	3.9938	3.5687	3.3317	2.8567	29
30	6.1772	5.8294	5.5168	5.2347	4.9789	4.5338	3.9950	3.5693	3.3321	2.8568	30
35	6.2153	5.8582	5.5386	5.2512	4.9915	4.5411	3.9984	3.5708	3.3330	2.8571	35
40	6.2335	5.8713	5.5482	5.2582	4.9966	4.5439	3.9995	3.5712	3.3332	2.8571	40
45	6.2421	5.8773	5.5523	5.2611	4.9986	4.5449	3.9998	3.5714	3.3333	2.8571	45
50	6.2463	5.8801	5.5541	5.2623	4.9995	4.5452	3.9999	3.5714	3.3333	2.8571	50

Chapter 14

The Public Sector and Not-for-Profit Budgeting

This chapter presents basic concepts for public sector budgeting and some fundamental concepts of public finance and governmental budgeting. When you have completed this chapter, you should understand:

1 The similarities and differences between public and private sector budgeting.

2 The concept of program budgeting.

3 Some basic public finance concepts.

4 The general impact of governmental activities on private-sector firms.

5 The concept and basic elements of the federal government budgeting system.

The **not-for-profit sector** of the economy comprises such entities as federal, provincial, and local governments, universities, foundations, and museums. Such organizations typically provide services, and occasionally products, for the general public or some designated group of society, with the primary intent of serving the public rather than generating a profit. The not-for-profit area is sometimes referred to as the **public sector,** but that term is not sufficiently broad because it includes only public institutions, such as governments, whereas not-for-profit entities include many private organizations as well, such as hospitals, universities, churches, and charities. Although our discussion focuses primarily on the public sector, much of it also applies to other not-for-profit entities.

580

The relative importance of not-for-profit organizations in the Canadian economy has changed dramatically in the last 40 years. We have been experiencing a fast growth both in its absolute dollar amount and in terms of its relative share of the economy. By far the most dramatic increase in size has come in governmental activities, with the federal government leading the way. It is estimated that today governmental and other not-for-profit activities account for nearly half of all economic activity in Canada. With not-for-profit spending approaching its highest levels in Canadian history, it is logical that we devote a portion of this book to this part of the economy.

The purpose of this chapter is to present the characteristics and procedures of budgeting that are unique to the not-for-profit area and to illustrate important basic budgeting concepts, introduced in Chapter 7, as they relate specifically to not-for-profit activities. In addition, we present an overview of the governmental financing and expenditure process, referred to as public finance, and discuss the governmental budgeting process. There are two reasons why a large portion of the chapter is devoted to public finance and governmental budgeting. First, the federal government is responsible for well over half of all not-for-profit expenditures; second, federal government financing and spending decisions have a significant effect on business decisions and activities in the **private sector.** Therefore, material in this chapter should be useful in understanding budgeting in the not-for-profit sector and also the impact of governmental activities on planning and decision making in the private sector.

The first part of the chapter deals with budgeting for not-for-profit organizations. Similarities and differences between not-for-profit and private sector budgeting are examined, and program budgeting is illustrated. Next, we present an overview of the important aspects of public finance, showing their effect on both public and private entities. Finally, after discussing the influence that government policies have on business, we examine the budgeting system used by the federal government and some provincial and local governments.

The budgeting process

The fundamentals of budgeting are very similar for both profit and not-for-profit organizations

In many respects the fundamentals of budgeting are identical for profit and not-for-profit organizations. In both cases budgeting plays a vital role in planning and monitoring the effective and efficient use of scarce resources. A key element of all budgets is budgeted revenue. Often it is the primary determinant of all the expenditures in the rest of the budget. In most profit-oriented firms, revenue is a key determinant of profit, which is the primary goal of the firm. However, in most not-for-profit organizations, revenue is not the prime benefit. Instead revenue is used to finance various activities that generate the desired benefits. For example, a city parks department's revenue is an appropriation made by the city council. The amount of the appropriation determines the size, quality, and quantity of the programs to be provided by the parks department. The benefits are derived by the citizens who use facilities,

The revenue budget

such as swimming pools and picnic grounds, and who participate in recreation programs and arts and craft lessons.

Revenues may be just a simple appropriation, such as the amount allocated to the highway department by the provincial legislature. Some entities may obtain revenues from several sources. For example, Figure 14-1 shows the revenue budget for the current year and the budgeted revenue for the coming fiscal year for Good City. The city has identified 11 different categories of revenue.

The detail in the revenue budget allows the city to evaluate each revenue source separately. Some revenue sources are more susceptible to prediction errors than others. For example, water sales, sewage service fees, and property taxes are less likely to fluctuate significantly with economic conditions than city sales tax revenue. Similarly the likelihood of receiving government grants

Good City Budgeted Revenue For the Fiscal Year 1984-85		
	Current Budget 1983-84	Approved Budget 1984-85
Taxes:		
Property tax	$3,040,000	$3,220,000
Other taxes	150,000	180,000
Total taxes	$3,190,000	$3,400,000
Fees and assessments:		
Licence fees	$ 6,000	$ 8,000
Recreational fees	3,000	3,500
Water sales	960,000	990,000
Sewage service	1,240,000	1,400,000
Refuse collection	660,000	680,000
Miscellaneous	48,000	31,500
Total fees and assessments	$2,917,000	$3,113,000
Other revenues:		
Provincial and federal government grants and appropriations	$ 540,000	$ 815,000
Investment income	32,000	32,000
Sale of city equipment	61,000	—
Total other revenue	$ 633,000	$ 847,000
Total revenue	$6,740,000	$7,360,000

Figure 14-1

Not-for-profit organizations must know the sources of their revenues just as profit-oriented organizations do. Good City personnel have developed a detailed description of revenue resources, which is useful in evaluating each revenue source separately.

may depend on political attitudes and on other variables outside the control of city officials. Like a business, the city must determine the probabilities that projected revenues may be different from actual revenues. Variances could have a serious effect on the operation of city services. City officials may attempt to identify a range of possible values for each revenue classification and establish alternate budgets for various amounts of revenue. Such budget plans identify which programs would be curtailed or eliminated in the event of revenue shortages and which programs would be expanded or added with revenue surpluses.

The expenditure budget

Expenditure budgets state how the organization plans to spend its resources during the budget period. As with private industry, the format of the budget and nature of the expenditures are dictated somewhat by the type of organization. Good City separates its expenditures into 12 major activities. The summary budget for these activities is presented in Figure 14-2, which shows the current budget year as well as the budget for the next fiscal year.

The summary expenditure budget provides an overview of the resources expended in each of the major activities of the city. However, this budget is of little use in planning and controlling daily operations in any one of the activities. Instead detailed operating budgets are required for each activity. Figure 14-3 illustrates the operating budget for the parks and recreation department. The total of $127,400 for the current year is the same amount shown for the department in the summary expenditure budget.

Figure 14-2
The summary expenditure budget identifies the major categories of expenditures, which are subsequently broken down into more detailed expenditure budgets.

Good City Summary Expenditure Budget For the Fiscal Year 1984-85		
	Current Budget 1983-84	Approved Budget 1984-85
Schools	$2,460,000	$2,800,000
Police department	946,000	994,000
Fire department	271,000	290,000
Water department	342,000	368,000
Sewage and treatment plant	440,000	512,000
Refuse collection department	480,000	524,000
Streets department	680,000	665,000
Parks and recreation department	127,400	139,000
Transportation department	335,000	346,000
City council	90,000	98,000
City office facilities	411,600	456,000
Court system	157,000	168,000
Total	$6,740,000	$7,360,000

Good City Parks and Recreation Department Budget For the Fiscal Year 1984-85		
	Current Budget 1983-84	Approved Budget 1984-85
Supervisory salaries	$ 41,000	$ 44,000
Lifeguards' wages	13,100	14,000
Instructors' wages	21,600	21,000
Clerical wages	11,000	11,600
Payroll taxes and fringe benefits	8,200	10,300
Maintenance expenses	8,000	9,500
Maintenance supplies	6,000	6,400
Utilities	3,000	3,900
Equipment operating expenses	2,600	2,700
Uniforms, trophies, prizes	1,100	900
Equipment purchases	7,800	11,200
Miscellaneous	4,000	3,500
Total	$127,400	$139,000

Figure 14-3
The total budget appropriation of $127,400 for the parks and recreation department is listed in the summary expenditure budget in Figure 14-2. Here the departmental budget is presented in detail.

Budgets should be used for control as well as a means of securing resources

Budgets provide an excellent means of controlling costs and operations of government or other not-for-profit units. All too often, however, they are viewed merely as devices for securing resources. Once the budget is approved, there may be a tendency to ignore it and simply use the resources provided by it in whatever way seems convenient. In such cases the benefits of control from the budgeting process are lost. The control aspects are important, however, because resources are scarce, and only a limited amount may be available for specific purposes.

To ensure that budgets are not forgotten once approved, the budget becomes an operating plan that must be followed by the governmental unit. For example, if a city council approves $2,800,000 for schools, city management cannot simply decide that part of these funds should be used for road maintenance. If planning is a worthwhile activity, then comparing actual results with the budget to see whether the plans were carried out is also worthwhile. Such comparisons are made by means of performance reports prepared by accountants to show how the planned activity was accomplished and how the accomplishment compared with the original plan. Figure 14-4 presents a performance report for the parks and recreation department for the 1983-84 fiscal year.

Program budgeting

In Chapter 7 the master budget example was developed along functional lines. Basic business functions, such as marketing, manufacturing, and administration, were major entities in the master budget. This form of budget is called a

		Good City	
	Parks and Recreation Department Performance Report		
	For the Fiscal Year 1983-84		

	Budget 1983-84	Actual 1983-84	Unfavourable (Favourable) Variance
Supervisory salaries	$ 41,000	$ 41,000	—
Lifeguards' wages	13,100	12,400	$ (700)
Instructors' wages	21,600	19,500	(2,100)
Clerical wages	11,000	11,400	400
Payroll taxes and fringe benefits	8,200	8,000	(200)
Maintenance expenses	8,000	11,300	3,300
Maintenance supplies	6,000	6,600	600
Utilities	3,000	3,800	800
Equipment operating expenses	2,600	2,200	(400)
Uniforms, trophies, prizes	1,100	1,000	(100)
Equipment purchases	7,800	4,100	(3,700)
Miscellaneous	4,000	5,500	1,500
Total	$127,400	$126,800	($600)

Figure 14-4
A detailed budget performance report provides managers with information useful in controlling and coordinating activities. Significant variances for any activity should be investigated.

Line budgets follow the functional lines of an organization

line budget or **functional budget.** Line budgeting is popular because it closely parallels the lines of responsibility in the organization chart, and it facilitates the performance measurement of responsibility centre managers. The budget provides a convenient framework for developing performance reports.

Program budgets are prepared for programs or outputs of an organization

Another form of budgeting is **program budgeting,** with each budget prepared for some program or output of an organization. For example, a police department may prepare budgets for programs such as crime prevention, stolen property recovery, and community education. As in line budgeting, the level of detail in the program budget depends on management's needs. For instance, the community education program may be divided into primary school safety education, secondary school drug abuse education, driver safety education, and burglar prevention education. Even these categories may be divided into more specific programs or objectives. The distinguishing characteristic of program budgeting is that the focal point in budget preparation and cost control is the program or goal rather than a functional or organizational unit. Later in our discussion of governmental budgeting we mention the idea that program budgeting may be instrumental in identifying changes in an organization's structure that would facilitate the achievement of goals. To contrast line and program budgeting, refer to Figure 14-5.

Deer Mountain School District Line Budget For the Fiscal Year Ending June 30		
	Adopted Budget 1983-84	**Proposed Budget 1984-85**
Teachers' salaries	$ 980,000	$1,050,000
Administrative salaries	120,000	132,000
Clerical salaries	70,000	75,000
Maintenance salaries	80,000	85,000
School supplies	90,000	105,000
Maintenance supplies	20,000	26,000
Utilities	38,000	46,000
Other facilities expenses	28,000	30,000
Miscellaneous expenses	24,000	25,000
Transportation	150,000	176,000
Total	$1,600,000	$1,750,000

Figure 14-5
The line budget is the type that is most commonly used in profit-oriented organizations. Program budgets identify costs and benefits for programs or goals of the organization. Many not-for-profit organizations find that program budgets provide a more effective method of evaluating costs and benefits.

Deer Mountain School District Program Budget For the Fiscal Year Ending June 30		
	Adopted Budget 1983-84	**Proposed Budget 1984-85**
Primary education	$ 655,000	$ 712,000
Secondary education	729,000	786,000
Student enrichment programs	90,000	98,000
Adult education	58,000	67,000
Athletic programs	53,000	62,000
Community service programs	15,000	25,000
Total	$1,600,000	$1,750,000

Figure 14-5 shows the current and proposed budgets for the Deer Mountain School District. The budget at the top is a line budget for the school system, and the budget at the bottom is a program budget. The line budget identifies ten functional activities of the school system. The program budget is divided into six programs. Costs are identified with programs rather than with functions. As with line budgeting, some costs may not be clearly identifiable with a single program in the budget. Such common costs are allocated to the appropriate programs in a logical manner using cost allocation concepts discussed in Chapter 4.

In business organizations most activities are intended to contribute to the firm's profit objective, and the benefits of the programs are measured in the income statement. In not-for-profit organizations there is typically no common denominator for measuring the success of programs. For example, a city government has many diverse goals that it attempts to achieve with a variety of programs. Included are educational goals, fire and police protection goals, cultural goals, recreational goals, etc. Success for the various programs cannot be measured in dollars, but rather with other statistics, such as the number of high school diplomas, reduced crime rates, enrollments in recreational programs, or attendance at symphony concerts. If resources are to be allocated among the various programs in ways that maximize total benefits to the citizens of the city, there must be a method of comparing program benefits with program costs. Since benefits are measured for programs rather than for organizational lines, it stands to reason that costs should be identified with programs also, so that direct analyses can be made.

Program budgeting facilitates cost-benefit analysis

The primary advantage of using program budgeting is that it facilitates cost-benefit analysis for programs in which benefits are measured in something other than dollars. For example, the benefit of a late-night police patrol through residential areas is a 20 percent reduction in burglaries, and the cost of the patrols is $200,000 annually. The benefits and costs are identified specifically for this program. If a program budgeting system were not used, the cost of the late-night patrols would be buried in personnel costs, gasoline costs, patrol car operating costs, and other accounts of a line budget. If benefits are measured for projects, then the costs should be identified for each project as well so that logical resource allocations can be made.

When costs are expressed in dollars and the benefits are described in other terms, such as decreased crime, the measures are not directly comparable. However, additional analysis might yield more useful statistics. For example, assume 20 percent fewer burglaries means 90 fewer burglaries for the city, and city crime statistics show that the average loss from a burglary is $2,600. Therefore, the estimated reduction in burglary losses from the program is $234,000 (90 × $2,600). Of course, there are other benefits as well, such as a feeling of security among citizens, a better image for the city in terms of crime rate, etc. Sometimes managers in not-for-profit organizations think that quantification of program benefits is of little use. General arguments praising the value of quality education, safer streets, or better recreational facilities have merit, but perhaps not enough merit to secure project funding when compared with specific quantified benefits of competing projects. In a world of scarce resources, not-for-profit entities must evaluate program costs and benefits just as businesses do so that intelligent resource allocation decisions can be made.

A combined line-program budget

A combination line-program budget may be prepared that provides cost information by function and by program. An example of this type of budget presentation is shown in Figure 14-6 using the data from the Deer Mountain School District in Figure 14-5.

Deer Mountain School District
Line-Program Budget
For the Fiscal Year 1983-84

	Primary Education	Secondary Education	Student Enrichment	Adult Education	Athletic Programs	Community Service	Total
Teachers' salaries	$392,000	$490,000	$58,000	$32,000	$ 6,000	$ 2,000	$ 980,000
Administrative salaries	65,000	40,000	6,000	3,000	4,000	2,000	120,000
Clerical salaries	34,000	28,000	4,000	2,500	1,000	500	70,000
Maintenance salaries	40,000	30,000	1,500	500	6,500	1,500	80,000
School supplies	38,000	43,000	3,000	4,000	1,000	1,000	90,000
Utilities	18,000	12,000	3,000	1,000	3,500	500	38,000
Maintenance supplies	8,000	6,000	700	500	4,500	300	20,000
Other facilities expenses	8,000	6,300	500	500	12,000	700	28,000
Miscellaneous expenses	1,000	1,700	300	12,000	6,000	3,000	24,000
Transportation	51,000	72,000	13,000	2,000	8,500	3,500	150,000
Total	$655,000	$729,000	$90,000	$58,000	$53,000	$15,000	$1,600,000

Figure 14-6
Line and program budgets can be combined to provide both types of budget information.

The program budget is presented in the columns and the line budget appears in the rows. The data presented in the combination budget provide much greater detail than either the line or program budgets separately. Notice that only the 1983–84 fiscal year is presented in Figure 14-6. Another budget is required to present the proposed budget for the 1984–85 fiscal year in a similar format. The combination budget provides cost information on both programs and functions and allows the determination of the amount of cost for each function devoted to each program.

Public finance

Public finance defined

Public finance involves the entire area of government economic activity. Included are resource allocations, income distributions to people, and the financing function of government. In total, public finance activities significantly affect both the public and private sectors. Our discussion of this topic should provide an understanding of the characteristics of governmental budgeting, and it should give you an understanding of the way that public finance activities impact on private-sector business.

In Chapter 7 we defined budgeting as a comprehensive quantitative plan for utilizing the resources of an entity for some period of time, and we stated that the budgeting process is very important in allocating scarce resources in a way that optimizes the achievement of organizational goals. To a large degree, actions of federal, provincial, and local governments determine resource allocations and income distributions with taxing and expenditure decisions. For example, a tax increase takes money out of the hands of the taxpayers, and a social security benefit increase puts money into the hands of recipients. Most people and businesses are affected by taxing and spending decisions. Realizing the impact of its economic decisions on individuals, businesses, and the entire economy, Parliament evaluates its decisions rather carefully.

The ability to tax is a very important power of government. To a large degree, taxing powers determine the amount of influence government has over the economy. Probably the most important taxes are the federal and provincial income tax which affect every individual and business in Canada. Other important taxes at the federal level include custom duties, excise taxes, and federal sales taxes. Provincial governments levy various taxes like payroll taxes, inheritance taxes, and licences, besides the income tax. Municipalities also levy taxes. Common municipal taxes are property taxes and various fees and assessments.

The function of the public sector

A logical question might be, "Why does the public sector exist and what does it do with the vast wealth of resources it collects?" The public sector exists to fill the voids not serviced by the private sector and to ensure that the private sector operates in a way that is acceptable to the society. Many governmental services, such as parks, highways, police protection, national defence, or national archives, are not available from the private sector. The market mechanism does not provide for regulatory agencies. Nor are most of the special programs of the Ministry of Industry, Trade, and Commerce, Ministry of Manpower and Immigration or other government departments and agencies available to society through the private sector. The Crown corporations also represent a good example of government activities in the Canadian economy. The government rules and regulations affect virtually every facet of business life, including external accounting reporting requirements, health and safety standards, transportation costs, routings and schedules, employee taxes, and countless other items. These governmental activities, rules, and regulations often have an impact on business decisions concerning investments, number and types of employees to hire, types of products to produce, plant locations, types of transportation systems used, and others. It is clear that currently the public sector commands a tremendous amount of resources, and directly and indirectly influences private-sector business in many ways. We must assume the government's significant role in the economy will continue in the future. Therefore, it is important to understand the processes of government budgeting and resource allocation.

Public finance objectives

The basic policy objectives of public finance are

1. Allocation
2. Distribution
3. Stabilization

What goods should be provided and in what quantity?

Allocation. The first objective deals with providing socially desirable goods and services not made available through the private sector. Allocation is concerned with what goods and services should be provided and in what quantity. In the public sector resource allocations are made primarily through the process of voting. Citizens vote for people to represent them in government, and the representatives in turn vote on projects and proposals in Parliament, provincial legislatures, and in city councils. These are the places where allocation decisions are constantly made that, in the aggregate, have a tremendous impact on our economy and on society. In the private sector the "voting" is done with dollars. Consumers tell suppliers how to allocate resources by the amount that consumers spend on the various products and services supplied by the private sector.

Who should receive the economic benefits of society?

Distribution. The second policy objective addresses the issue of who should receive the economic benefits of society. Of course, the private sector strongly influences income distribution by providing jobs and by distributing profits to owners. However, the impact of the governmental tax programs is significant. Graduated income taxes take a larger portion of a wage earner's income as wages increase. Payroll taxes are paid to the government by wage earners and distributed to recipients typically who are not employed or who earn a small amount. Many tax programs are designed to tax people earning higher incomes on the assumption that such people are better able to bear the tax burden. Many expenditures are designed primarily to help lower-income people because they are most in need of the services. Such governmental actions are based on distribution policies. Many distribution policy decisions are based on establishing a lower limit on poverty or an upper limit on wealth.

Stabilization. The objective of stabilization is to see that the economy runs smoothly. Economic theory implies that a stable economy characterized by an acceptable level of growth without widely fluctuating economic conditions is most conducive to high employment, stable prices, and reasonable income levels. To minimize fluctuations and wide swings known as depression, inflation, recession, or booms, the government has two basic instruments that may be used to stabilize the economy. They are fiscal policy and monetary policy.

The objective of stabilization is to keep the economy running smoothly

Fiscal policy pertains to the taxing and spending actions of government. Although taxing and spending together constitute fiscal policy, federal or provincial legislatures seldom specifically tie the two functions together. However, both taxing and spending may have important effects on the economy. For instance, during periods of high inflation Parliament may raise taxes to reduce the quantity of money available for the purchase of goods and services. Another possibility is to reduce government spending, thereby keeping money out of the economy.

Fiscal policy of the federal government is a powerful economic tool and has a strong impact on the economy. It is also not easy to implement very quickly since it takes time for Parliament to enact new tax legislation or new spending programs. When fast action is needed to stabilize the economy, or to counteract the poor timing of fiscal policy, the government has monetary policy at its disposal. **Monetary policy** deals with the quantity and the cost of money in the economy.

If both fiscal and monetary policy were in the hands of Parliament, serious abuses could take place, and even with the best intentions serious economic dislocations could occur if the same body attempted to use both economic tools. Monetary policy is carried out by the Bank of Canada, but the government always bears the ultimate responsibility for this policy, for it has the power to substitute its own policy at any time. The Bank of Canada is managed by a Board of Directors comprising the Governor and Deputy Governor, the Deputy Minister of Finance (with no vote), and 12 Directors appointed for three-year terms by the government. The Governor and Deputy Governor are appointed for terms of seven years by the Directors with the approval of the Governor in Council (in effect, the Cabinet). The Governor may only be removed from office before the expiration of his term by Act of Parliament.

Specific segments of the economy may be dealt with using fiscal policy. For example, at various times federal and provincial governments provided several incentives for first-time home buyers. The Registered Home Ownership Savings Plan permits a $1,000 per year tax exemption for those that intend to buy a home. Public work programs, private industry incentive programs to hire students, and training programs to improve workers' skills are all geared towards reducing unemployment. Investment tax credits are aimed at increasing productive capacity and reducing unemployment. Sometimes a program addressing one objective is not consistent with another program. For instance, expensive job-creation programs may reduce unemployment, but add to the problem of high inflation.

Fiscal actions may have dramatic impacts on the business environment and managers' attempt to make sound business decisions in light of fiscal policy decisions. For instance, a manager may postpone an investment because a special tax break on investments is expected shortly, or a company may buy more automated production equipment to avoid higher payroll taxes and a higher minimum wage. Fiscal decisions can create dramatic changes in economic conditions, particularly for certain segments of the economy. For example, energy shortages, government tax breaks, and energy policies brought boom times to insulating firms in the late 1970s.

Fiscal policy may have dramatic effects on the economy

The functions of the Bank of Canada can be divided into five categories:

1. The Bank of Canada holds the deposits, or reserves, of chartered banks which are required by the Bank Act.

2. The Bank of Canada is responsible for supplying the economy with needed paper currency.

3. It acts as banker and fiscal agent for the federal government. For example, collection of taxes, sale and redemption of government bonds.

4. The Bank of Canada and the Department of Finance supervise the operations of chartered banks.

5. The major task of the Bank of Canada is to manage the money supply in accordance with the needs of the economy as a whole. This duty entails making the amount of money available which is consistent with high and steadily rising levels of output and employment, and a relatively constant price level. It is through quantitative and qualitative credit controls that the Bank of Canada attempts to manipulate the supply of money in terms of short-run stability and long-run economic growth.[1] More specifically, monetary policy entails increasing the money supply during a recession to stimulate spending and, conversely, restricting the growth of money supply during inflation to constrain spending. The cause-effect chain between monetary policy and output and employment is summarized as follows:

Monetary policy may be used for "fine-tuning" the economy

Bank of Canada monetary policy influences the size of chartered
bank reserves
which
Influences the supply of money
which

[1]Campbell R. McConnell and William Henry Pope, *Economics*, First Canadian Edition (McGraw-Hill Ryerson Ltd., Toronto, 1978), pp. 308-309.

Influences the interest rate (the cost) and the availability of bank credit
which
Influence investment spending, output, employment, and the price level

Some economists strongly oppose the above Keynesian explanation and emphasize the capacity of the competitive market system to automatically allocate resources efficiently.[2]

The effect of governmental influence

Governmental taxing and expenditure activities affect our lives continuously and often in very significant ways. We may not be fully aware of the effect of some taxes because most taxes are not paid the way a utility bill or store charge account is paid. Instead, many taxes are somewhat hidden. Gasoline taxes are included in the price of the fuel; sales tax is part of the total cost of the purchase; income taxes and payroll taxes are withheld from paycheques; excise taxes are buried in the purchase price of certain products; and property taxes may be part of house payments. We therefore tend to think of the tax-inflated cost of items merely as the price of the item, and we think of wages as the amount of the paycheque rather than the gross wage amount. Taxpayers should not lose sight of the taxes they pay to governmental units. Taxes pay for governmental services and, like other outlays for purchases, there should be justification for the resources spent. Such justification is provided in the form of budgets, which elected officials must approve before tax money can be spent.

Many tax laws have a direct measurable effect on citizens. For instance, a $35 per-person tax credit has a direct effect on the tax burden of each taxpayer, whereas a tax credit on a new home has no effect on a taxpayer who is not in the market for a new home. Expenditure legislation often has a more indirect impact on people. While certain expenditures, such as Canada Pension payments and welfare payments, are direct benefits to individuals, many other expenditures have a more indirect effect on the population. Highway programs, regulatory agencies, national defence, education programs, and space programs all have value to some or all of the people. However, it is difficult for an individual to measure the benefits from such programs. It is easy to see that a monthly Canada Pension Plan cheque of $400 provides an annual income of $4,800 to the recipient. It is harder to determine the specific value of the national defence program or maintenance of public parks to that individual. Clearly such measures are very difficult and very individualistic, and most individuals do not have to assess them. But government officials must evaluate the benefits of programs and compare them with the costs of programs to make intelligent resource allocation decisions. The danger with nondirect benefit programs is

---

[2]Campbell R. McConnell and William Henry Pope, *Economics*, First Canadian Edition, (McGraw-Hill Ryerson, Toronto, 1978), p. 333.

that individuals often view the programs as costless. Services such as libraries and schools appear to be provided free to users, but the services clearly have a cost, and the taxpayer pays the bill.

Effects on businesses

Government policies have a decisive effect on businesses, as they do on individuals. Businesses are subject to many types of taxes in addition to income taxes. In order to continue earning profits, businesses must view taxes and other government assessments as part of the cost of doing business and must pass on these costs to customers in the form of prices. Pricing decisions are therefore greatly influenced by government actions.

The government has a significant economic impact on individuals and businesses

Fiscal and monetary policies can be used effectively by governments through their influence on businesses. As interest rates are increased by the Bank of Canada, businesses curtail new expansion or borrowing. When the government wants to stimulate the economy, it may induce expansion by providing tax benefits to businesses, such as the investment credit, additional depreciation on fixed assets, or other tax credits and benefits. Businesses react to such policies by shifting resources in directions that will minimize their tax burden or place them in a better competitive position.

In addition to influencing business by means of tax legislation, governments also affect business by demanding many reports and other information, the cost of which must also be reflected in the price of products.

Government demand for information from business

In the past ten years there has been a significant increase in the amount and types of information that businesses must provide to the government. Governments use business information for a variety of purposes. Some information is summarized and used to report general business conditions. Other information is used to monitor government rules and regulations. Some is used for research by government staffs or private individuals. In general, the government uses the wealth of data that it gathers from business in whatever way it deems necessary and appropriate.

There has been a large increase in the kinds and amount of information the government requires of businesses

The impact on businesses of government activities in requiring and analyzing business data is both indirect and direct. The indirect impact occurs when the analysis of business data results in new government rules and regulations that affect the operations of businesses. The direct impact occurs from specific reporting requirements that cause a business to modify the way it gathers and reports information. In most cases government information requirements are for financial data. Sometimes firms must modify their financial information system to satisfy government reporting requirements. Some common effects on a company's information system are

The effects of government information requirements on business information systems

1. More detailed data base
2. Different data base structure
3. Different reporting characteristics

More detailed data base. Numerous government reporting requirements have caused some businesses to develop a more detailed cost data base than they previously had. For example, during the price and wage controls of the mid-1970s, some companies were unable to get price increase approval solely because the cost data provided by the companies were not detailed enough to prove that the price increase was cost justified. As a result many companies started to accumulate more detailed cost data primarily to satisfy future information requirements the government might make. Similar examples can be cited for other governmental organizations, such as Statistics Canada and Revenue Canada, which require detailed reporting. It is likely that the government will continue to seek information that includes more and more detailed cost data.

Different data base structure. The accounting data base consists of the basic data elements from which internal and external reports are developed. The structure of the data base—that is, the way data are organized and stored—is determined by such factors as efficiency in updating the data base and retrieving needed data elements as well as by the reporting requirements supported by the data base. Whenever government requires information that is significantly different from the information normally generated by the business, there is a possibility that the company may have to modify its data base structure to satisfy the reporting requirement.

Different reporting characteristics. The purpose of the internal reporting function is to provide managers with the information necessary to manage the organization efficiently and effectively. The frequency, detail, and format of internal reports are dictated by the information needs of managers, which may change with new governmental requirements. For example, if very detailed product cost information is needed to justify price increases, a firm may change its cost accounting system and internal cost reporting system to provide management with necessary cost details on a timely basis.

The future role of government reporting requirements

It is always difficult to predict future actions, but currently there is no evidence to suggest that government reporting requirements for businesses will be reduced. In fact most evidence suggests that more reporting will be required in the future. In the last six to eight years there has been a significant increase in the government's demand for financial data from businesses, and few voices in government suggest a need to reverse the trend.

New-product warranty laws, pension laws, employee health and safety laws, special incentive programs for hiring hard-core unemployed, and countless other possible government actions loom on the horizon. Each may potentially have an impact on the detail or structure of a firm's data base or on its internal reporting process.

Federal government budgeting

All federal resource allocation (spending) decisions are made by Parliament. In obtaining these decisions the government plays an important role. It is often said that in British tradition the Parliament controls the purse strings of the nation. However, much of the supporting information for Parliament's decisions is provided by the federal government's budgeting process. The federal government's budgeting system also strongly influences the budgeting processes and procedures of many provincial and local governments.

Although government expenditures are financed basically by taxes, taxing and expenditure decisions typically are not specifically tied together. Usually the taxing and expenditure decisions only merge when total revenues (taxes) and total expenditures are compared to determine whether the budget balances. Frequently the federal government operates at a deficit, which means spending programs exceed tax revenues. Deficits are covered by borrowing money in the form of bonds or other government securities, most of which are sold to Canadians and companies within Canada. Seldom does Parliament specifically address the financing of projects except in the very broadest sense of how the project will affect the balancing of the budget or the budget deficit. Two exceptions are the CPP and UIC programs, which are specifically financed by CPP and UIC premiums. In general, however, Parliament possesses tax legislation and spending legislation separately without tying specific expenditures and tax laws together.

Canada's federal Crown corporations are also important allocators within the federal state. They account for considerable resources and expenditures. In addition to Crown corporations, commissions and boards wield considerable allocative, regulatory, and structural power with little or no Cabinet or ministerial influence until the minister decides to change their statutes. Since discussion of boards, commissions, and Crown corporations would be too lengthy, we will concentrate on the federal government's budgeting system.

In federal government's budgeting, it can be said that the Prime Minister's Office functions as a strategic source of political advice, while Privy Council Office is the key source of over-all governmental advice. The overview of government activity by the Privy Council is bolstered by the Department of Finance and the Treasury Board, but on a more functional basis. The latter two organizations are too complex to be examined fully here, although it should be mentioned that the Treasury Board is a Cabinet committee which functions in two distinct, if interrelated, areas of federal government: the Cabinet Committee on the Expenditure Budget and the Cabinet Committee on Management. The Department of Finance, on the other hand, tends to view matters in terms of their impact on: (a) the government's ability to extract resources; and (b) the fiscal and economic consequences of government activity on the Canadian society and economy. The Treasury Board seems more concerned with current resource allocations and with the internal financial administrative impact of proposed and established government activity.[3]

A major attempt to enforce central guidelines has been through the budget preparation reforms since 1967. In the mid-1960s the Glassco Royal Commission made certain criticisms and provided some recommendations for a budgetary reform. The Glassco Commission's main criticism of government planning and budgeting was that both had been designed around an approach which com-

[3]Thomas A. Hockin, *Government in Canada* (W.W. Norton and Company, Inc., New York, 1975), especially chapters 3 and 5.

pared only the two previous year's budget figures to the new budget year. This also meant that a department's efficiency was measured simply by comparing percentage increase in expenditure between two years; no scientific methods such as work measurement, cost analysis, or statistical techniques were employed. The Glassco Commission recommended among other things that:

> More objective standards for analysis and comparison be developed and employed by senior departmental management and Treasury Board in a process of over-all program review, and that all departments and agencies be required to prepare and submit to the executive long-term plans of expenditure requirements by programs. . . . Based thereon, an overall forecast of government expenditures and prospective resources for a period of five years ahead should be prepared annually.[4]

To meet this request the government of Canada adopted what is called a "Comprehensive Programme Budgetary System" in which overall government operations were divided into major functions, then subfunctions, and further on to a departmental program. The division into departmental programs was to permit the work of government to be assigned to different agencies. This movement was definitely in line with the Planning, Programming, Budgeting System (PPBS) movement started by other governments around the world in the mid-1960s.

PPBS is also identified as PPB. The purpose of the system is to provide a more systematic process for developing and analyzing budget proposals and for completing the final budget package. As the title implies, PPBS is based on program budgeting, but it encompasses more than just the concept of program budgeting. PPBS includes systematic procedures for the accounting, programming, and evaluation processes. It has been suggested that PPBS has five distinguishing features:

Features of PPBS

1. Program accounting
2. Multiyear costing
3. Detailed description of activities
4. Zero-base budgeting
5. Benefit-cost analysis[5]

Program accounting

The ability to attach accounting data to specific programs

A basic requisite of program budgeting is an ability to attach accounting data to specific programs to show the resources used or budgeted for each objective. The process of accumulating costs by programs is referred to as **program accounting.** It must be capable of accumulating historical costs by program as well as developing projected costs for programs. The PPBS system requires four types of costs to be accumulated for programs: past costs, current-year costs, budget-year costs, and future costs. **Past costs** refer to program costs for the last fiscal year. **Current costs** are program costs for the current fiscal year.

---

[4]Ibid., p. 149.
[5]Leonard Merewitz and Stephen H. Sosnick, *The Budget's New Clothes* (Markham Publishing Company, Chicago, 1973), pp. 2–108.

Budget-year costs are proposed program costs for the coming fiscal year, and **future costs** are anticipated expenditures for the program covering four or more years in the future.

Multiyear costing

Identifying costs for the life of the project

Multiyear costing refers to the process of identifying costs with a project for the life of the project rather than just the next budget year. Multiyear costing is not a new budgeting concept. It has been used for many years in business in evaluating capital expenditure projects. The logic for multiyear costing in capital expenditure decisions is that most projects require large outlays benefiting many future periods. However, in conventional budgets few items in the operating budget are evaluated in light of expected outlays beyond the current budget period. Thus some budget proposals may be accepted with only a small portion of the relevant cost data available for analysis.

Many government programs have life spans covering many accounting periods. Consequently, it is logical to evaluate projects based on costs and benefits over their entire expected life rather than just for one year. Like all long-range estimates, multiyear costing of programs becomes more subjective the longer the estimate. Nevertheless, multiyear costing is often cited as one of the major contributions of PPBS because it gives a better picture of program alternatives. Occasionally a proposed program requires very small expenditures initially, followed by very substantial outlays in later years. For example, the growth in social security payments since the start of the program has been tremendous.

Detailed description of activities

Uniform systematic procedures for evaluating all projects

PPBS is intended to provide uniform systematic data for evaluating ongoing programs and new programs alike by providing a detailed description of activity. An important attribute of PPBS is that systematic procedures are uniformly applied throughout the federal government budgeting system. Each program requires six specific steps, each resulting in information that helps to implement the program in accordance with the planning, programming, budgeting system. First, objectives must be established for each program. **Objectives** are the basic goals or desired outcome of the program. Next, each program must have **targets** that are specific short-term expectations for the program. Then the program director must identify the **selections made,** which are the specific operating plans of the program. The selections made must be supported by a description of the **alternatives reviewed** with a discussion of why the alternatives were eliminated in favour of the selected plans. **Outputs** are the current benefits or results achieved by the program and should relate directly to the targets. Finally, the detailed description of activities must include a discussion of **effectiveness,** which is the measurement of how well targets and objectives were achieved. Figure 14-7 illustrates a hypothetical set of detailed description of activities for the hypothetical Maritime Administration of the Minister of Transport.

Notice that all components of PPBS are included in the description of activities. Outputs are the measurable results of the programs. In this case 700

Maritime Administration Maritime Readiness Detailed Description of Activities	
Objective:	Maintain a well-rounded maritime capability to provide military support during times of crisis and to provide a strong commerce base for international trade.
Target:	Provide 1000 new shipbuildings jobs annually for Canadian citizens or residents.
Selection made:	Let $200,000,000 of new contracts to Canadian ship-builders for Navy ships.
Alternatives reviewed:	Offer a 20 percent wage subsidy to firms training new employees. Develop a government-training program to teach shipbuilding skills by repairing older Royal Navy ships.
Output:	A total of 700 new employees received skilled-labour classifications in the shipbuilding industry.
Effectiveness:	A total of 1300 people started company job-training programs in shipbuilding during the year. Of these, 600 dropped out, were terminated, or required more training before being classified as skilled labour.

Figure 14-7
Each program requires a detailed description of activities, which encourages managers to perform a thorough review of each program and its alternatives.

new skilled labourers were trained. In other programs outputs may be measured in higher reading levels of elementary students, improved grain prices, or many other variables. **Effectiveness** measures compare the output with input. In this example the inputs and outputs are people in a training program. In other cases they may be measured in dollars; for instance, a job-training program may cost $2,458 per graduate.

Zero-base budgeting

Governments operate on budgets that must be approved prior to the beginning of each fiscal year. Before PPBS each new budget was usually developed using the previous budget as a base. The previous budget was a convenient starting point because it consisted of revenues and expenditures that had already been approved once before. The new budget usually represented a revision of the old budget, with most of the items increased to allow for a growing economy, rising population, or inflation. Such a budgeting process is generally known as **incremental budgeting,** because the new budget consists of the old one with an increment. Budget increments based on the inflation rate, increases in appropriations, a fixed percentage, or any other across-the-board increment to the budget begs the question of a true budget evaluation process. As a result of incremental budgeting, there is a tendency for budgets to become ever larger, and it is difficult to eliminate unsuccessful or inefficient programs once they are included in a budget.

To justify government programs and costs, a relatively new budgeting concept known as zero-based budgeting has been developed. **Zero-base budgeting** means that each project or program must start the budget evaluation

With zero-base
budgeting each
program, new or old,
starts the budget
review process with
no commitment of
resources

process with no commitment of resources. Instead of using the old budget as a base, a zero base is assumed, and every item in the budget must be justified on its own merit, not simply because it existed previously. Each project must be proven worthy of funding, or it is eliminated regardless of whether the project is a new proposal or a program of long standing. With zero-base budgeting, it is conceivable, although unlikely, that major program classifications, such as national defence or the space program, could be terminated if they proved undesirable. Typically such major programs are sufficiently important to continue receiving federal support and funding without substantial modifications. Still there is a natural appeal to the idea that programs of all sorts and durations should be evaluated on a year-to-year basis. Obsolete or ineffective programs should be terminated and resources should be shifted to new justifiable programs. An important contribution of the zero-base budgeting concept is that it provides an alternative to incremental budgeting.

Zero-base budgeting is conceptually attractive but is not always easy to apply in practice. Programs currently in operation are hard to eliminate or curtail. They may involve long-term commitments or fixed investments that cannot easily be shifted to other areas. Program participants with vested interests in the program can cite prestige, hardship, tradition, or countless other reasons to maintain the program. Consider, for example, the following hypothetical situation in a zero-base budgeting environment.

A large provincial university has a prestigious foreign language department. The program in Russian linguistics has been nationally recognized for its achievement. Five prominent faculty members developed the program 12 years ago and still teach in it. During the last five years, however, there has been a steady decline in enrollments from a high of 400 students to a present enrollment of about 100.

With zero-base budgeting, the foreign language department must justify the Russian linguistics and other programs as if they have not been funded previously. If the program is to be continued, the department must present a case to maintain program funding near its present level simply because most of the funding is for the salaries of the five faculty members. When other departments have 50 students for each faculty member, it is difficult to justify funding a department that has only 20 students for each professor. On the other hand, it is also not possible to dismiss any of the faculty members since they are tenured. Moreover, the decline in enrollments may be temporary, and if the program is reduced, it may be impossible to handle larger enrollments in the years ahead with reduced faculty. If some of the current faculty leave now, it may not be possible to replace them with qualified teachers later.

In addition to the above practical problems, the department may argue that the program is too prestigious to be eliminated since it would diminish the overall reputation of the entire university. Such arguments often have merit, and alternatives to eliminating the program may have to be found. For example, some of the faculty are qualified to teach English and French, and their teaching assignments may be shifted to these areas where enrollments are higher. Arrangements may be made for one of the faculty members to take a leave and teach at another university for one or two years, or a promotional campaign may be used to attempt to increase enrollments in the Russian linguistics program.

With zero-base budgeting, no program is viewed as sacred, and there is no seniority system for existing programs. Each must stand on its own merits, and to be funded, must prove its worth. Even with the limitations outlined above, zero-base budgeting has advantages. It provides a logical conceptual framework for evaluating all programs and requires a thorough justification for each program periodically. Even if modifications are necessary in the way benefits are measured, zero-base budgeting serves a very useful purpose. An example of zero-base budgeting is given in the Appendix.

Benefit-cost analysis

Budgeting decisions are made based on cost-benefit relationships

Benefit-cost analysis integrates the previous four features of PPBS into a decision framework. Here the term *decision framework* is used somewhat loosely because often no formal decision model is developed. However, all of the program proposals are evaluated in terms of benefits and costs. It is logical that proposals with the highest benefit-cost ratios are accepted first, and other programs are delayed or canceled. The difficult question is, "How are benefit-cost ratios determined?"

Although program costs are sometimes difficult to measure, program benefits are even harder to determine for many government projects. How does one compare the value of a program that helps a few people a great deal with a program that helps many people a little? Similarly how do the benefits of cancer research compare with a 10 million-hectare national park in Ontario? What is the benefit-cost ratio of a program that reduces unemployment by 30 000 people and costs the government $90,000,000?

None of the above questions is simple, but they must be answered if government is to achieve policy goals effectively and efficiently. The entire budgeting system collapses if we arrive at the last step and cannot make sound resource allocation decisions based on solid benefit-cost analyses supported by relevant factual data.

The PPBS emphasizes quantitative benefit-cost analysis. Clearly quantitative analysis may be difficult, almost impossible in some cases, but quantitative measures of some sort are frequently available if intuition and persistence are applied. Quantitative analysis does not necessarily mean dollar-for-dollar benefit-cost comparisons. For example, many types of unemployment statistics may be evaluated in considering full-employment programs, and park visitation statistics, population densities, and changing recreational patterns may be cited in developing a case for new park facilities.

The status of PPBS

Probably no other budgeting phenomenon swept the country, even the world, as PPBS did in the late 1960s and early 1970s. Government officials and others raved about it as the new system that would ensure effective and efficient government. In 1966 California adopted the system and renamed it programming and budgeting (PAB). Many provincial and local governments rushed to pattern their budgeting system after PPBS, or at least to use some of its features. The rush to PPBS has been referred to as the "PPB epidemic."[6]

Unfortunately to date the planning, programming, budgeting system has not fulfilled all of the great expectations held for it. There have been some successes from time to time in various government agencies with parts of PPBS, but in aggregate the system has not produced as much improvement in governmental budgeting as was expected. The most common reasons cited for the difficulties with PPBS are costs, government size, government organization, and difficult measurement problems.[7]

PPBS costs. Any accounting and budgeting system must be benefit-cost justifiable. The PPB system with its intricate detail, devotion to full disclosure of all alternatives, need for justification of currently operating programs, and requirement for quantitative measures in benefit-cost analysis is very expensive and time-consuming. Some people feel the idea is superior, but the economic realities of operating the system are prohibitive.

Government size. The federal government is huge and growing larger every year. All private sector businesses, including General Motors and American Telephone and Telegraph, are dwarfed by the size of the federal government. The coordination of large businesses is very difficult; the coordination of all federal government activity is truly mind-boggling. The major purpose of PPBS was to help coordinate resource allocation decisions, but the sheer size of the federal government may preclude any chance of complete success. A comprehensive plan like PPBS for a small firm would require a lot of work, for the federal government PPBS is a massive undertaking.

Government size. The federal government is huge and growing larger every year. All private sector businesses are dwarfed by the size of the federal government. The coordination of large businesses is very difficult; the coordination of all federal government activity is truly mind-boggling. The major purpose of PPBS was to help coordinate resource allocation decisions, but the sheer size of the federal government may preclude any chance of complete success. A comprehensive plan like PPBS for a small firm would require a lot of work, for the federal government PPBS is a massive undertaking.

Difficult measurement problems. Many of the measurements required in PPBS are very difficult to make. Particularly difficult are long-range cost and benefit estimates. So many different benefit measures are used for the myriad of government programs that it is perplexing to attempt to integrate the benefit-

---

[6] Ibid., p. 2.
[7] Aaron Wildavsky, *The Politics of the Budgetary Process* (Little, Brown and Company, Boston, 1974), pp. 181–208.

cost analysis of each program into a logical structure for a comparison of all alternative programs.

The future of PPBS

Any criticism of PPBS must be tempered by the realization that planning, coordinating, and controlling an organization the size of the federal government is tremendously difficult. Any general criticism can be countered with the question, "What system would operate more effectively and efficiently than the PPB system?" For the near future it appears that the current PPB system will be continued, with only minor modifications from time to time to improve the system or to remedy perceived problems.

Auditor- General

Another frequent form of control over the public service is the expenditure audit. This audit is the responsibility of the office of the auditor-general and his staff of over 600. The auditor-general is an employee of Parliament and not of the public service or of the executive. He is responsible for reporting on the audit of the accounts of the Government of Canada (including departments, Crown corporations, boards, commissions and other federal public agencies). His report always attracts a fair amount of publicity each year. His revelations, however, are confined to an outline of failures to expend funds effectively or failures to spend as authorized. The auditor-general is not expected to report on expenditures in a larger policy context. His term of office is ten years. The auditor-general conducts a *comprehensive audit* which stresses *value for the public's money*. In short, the question "Is the public getting the full value of its tax money spent by various governmental ministries and agencies?" is examined and reported to parliament by the auditor-general.

Summary

Not-for-profit organizations are an important segment of the economy. By far the largest element in the not-for-profit sector is government, particularly the federal government. As with profit-oriented organizations, budgeting is vital to the effective and efficient utilization of resources. Most budgeting concepts and procedures are the same regardless of the type of organization.

The revenue budget strongly influences the number, size, and quality of programs in not-for-profit organizations. However, revenue is not a goal in itself. Revenue merely provides the means for operating various programs that in turn provide the desired benefits. The expenditures budget is the organization's plan for using the resources at its disposal. Budgets should be prepared in sufficient detail to provide adequate control over the resources of not-for-profit organizations. Typically control includes timely performance reporting.

The two basic approaches to budgeting are line budgets and program budgets. **Line budgets** are prepared using functional lines or the organization structure as the framework for the budget. Typical categories in a line budget include marketing, accounting, production, divisions, departments, and process centers. **Program budgets** identify costs and benefits for goals or programs. Budget entities include police protection, fire protection, parks and recreation, and bus service. The primary advantage of using program budgeting is the ability to compare the cost of a program with the benefits of the program.

Some organizations use both line and program budgeting and thereby benefit from the advantages provided by each system.

Governments play a vital role in the economy. **Public finance** refers to the financing of government activities as well as to resource allocations and income distribution. There are three basic policy objectives in public finance: allocation, distribution, and stabilization. **Allocation** is concerned with the quantity and types of goods and services to be provided. **Distribution** addresses the issue of who should receive the economic benefits of society and in what amount. **Stabilization** actions attempt to keep the economy running smoothly. Stabilization is accomplished by means of **fiscal** and **monetary** policies.

The government requires an ever-increasing amount of information from businesses and uses it to establish and monitor rules and regulations, report general business conditions, perform business research, or for other purposes. Government information demands affect businesses both directly and indirectly. Often reporting requirements cause businesses to modify their accounting system because a more detailed data base is required, the data base structure must be changed, or the reporting characteristics of government reports are different from those of the current system. There is no evidence to indicate that government demand for business information will decline in the near future.

The federal government's taxation and expenditure decisions have a large economic impact on most people. An important element of governmental decision making is its budgeting activity. In the mid-1960s a **planning, programming, budgeting system (PPBS)** was introduced in the federal government. It is a program budgeting system that has five distinguishing features: program accounting, multiyear costing, detailed description of activities, zero-base budgeting, and benefit-cost analysis. **Program accounting** is a system capable of accumulating costs by program or goal. **Multiyear costing** means identifying costs for the life of the project, not merely for the current budget period. **Detailed description of activities** refers to the careful delineation of the proposed program's goals, targets, selections, alternatives, output, and effectiveness measures. **Zero-base budgeting** requires all activities to be evaluated each year whether the activity is a newly proposed or an old program. **Benefit-cost analysis** requires all proposals to be evaluated in a quantitative systematic manner.

PPBS has had a dramatic impact on governmental budgeting, but the initial expectations of the system have not been entirely realized. Common reasons cited for the lack of complete success of the system are its high cost; the size of the government, which is too large to utilize comprehensive budgeting effectively; the fact that the government is not organized along program lines; and the large number of projects whose benefits are difficult to measure and compare.

List of important
terms

Auditor-general   *(603)*
allocation   *(590)*
benefit-cost analysis   *(601)*
comprehensive auditing   *(603)*
distribution   *(590)*
fiscal policy   *(592)*
functional budget   *(585)*
line budget   *(585)*
monetary policy   *(591)*
multiyear costing   *(598)*
not-for-profit sector   *(580)*

planning, programming,
  budgeting system (PPBS)   *(597)*
private sector   *(581)*
program accounting   *(597)*
program budget   *(584)*
public finance   *(589)*
public sector   *(580)*
stabilization   *(591)*
Treasury Board   *(596)*
value for public money   *(603)*
zero-base budgeting   *(599)*

APPENDIX: Application of Zero-Base Budgeting

ZBB Tailored for Thunder Bay*
by J.G. Rapino and D.L. Holmstrom, City of Thunder Bay

The City of Thunder Bay, Ontario, with its population of approximately 120 000 persons, is located in the geographic centre of Canada. The city's main industries centre on its busy port on Lake Superior handling grain from Western Canada and transporting and processing mineral and forest products which are extracted in the surrounding area.

Additionally, Thunder Bay's location in Northwestern Ontario means a nearby all-season recreational playground of forests, lakes and streams. Thunder Bay reached its tenth birthday in 1980, having been created in 1970 by the amalgamation of the former Cities of Fort William and Port Arthur, and the adjacent Townships of Neebing and McIntyre.

As the city enters its second decade, a backward look can be taken at its achievements, particularly the innovations and improvements that have come in the past few years. During this time, the city seemingly has "got its act together." The city administration has established itself as a front runner in municipal innovation in Ontario. Change has taken place, not for the sake of change alone, but to increase the organization's ability to make effective use of its available resources.

The innovations which have taken place over the past few years include:

- a new council/committee/manager form of government
- a high level of pay-as-you-go capital financing
- effective budget communication documents
- a comprehensive employee training and development policy

Reprinted from an article appearing in *Cost and Management* by J.G. Rapino and D.L. Holsfrom, September/October 1981 issue, by permission of The Society of Management Accountants of Canada.

- an employee suggestion and award program
- introduction of a system of ward meetings by ward aldermen
- review and investigation of a citizen survey program
- standardized council communication forms
- a financial assistance policy to administer grants to community groups
- the development of departmental performance measures
- the use of operational audits
- hosting of the 1981 Jeux Canada Summer Games in August, 1981.

In recognition of these innovations, the city's chief administrative officer recently received a 1980 Management Innovations Award from the International City Management Association in the category of Organization and Management.

Council/administration reform. In 1970, when amalgamation took place, there was an integration of the two different city management structures and similar organization segments of the former cities. The city appointed a city co-ordinator, along with two assistant co-ordinators, who each administered a functional grouping of the 20 departments.

In 1975, improvements were attempted with the organization of a team management system involving the creation of five functional groupings of departmental managers. These co-operative groups of equals were to achieve corporate co-ordination of services.

Unfortunately problems remained and early in 1978, following an extensive review of the organization by management consultants, city council approved a council/committee/manager form of government. A new chief administrative officer was hired and a concise organization structure of five divisions was created. Each division was composed of a functional grouping of departments headed by a director. These five directors form the senior management group and are responsible to the chief administrative officer for the effective and efficient delivery of municipal services and programs under their jurisdiction (see Exhibit 1).

At the same time, the city council committees were reorganized to complement the new administrative structure by aligning council committees with the appropriate division within the administration.

This system was instituted to provide more accountability, to co-ordinate corporate planning, and to give better control over functions (see Exhibit 2).

This new council/administrative structure has been working quite effectively since its inception two years ago.

ZBB implementation overview. During the early years of the new city, there was a clear need for management-oriented information as the various services and activities were amalgamated. The organization moved quickly from line-item budgeting to a form of program budgeting in 1973. Included at that time was the requirement of five-year projections for both capital and operating programs.

In 1978, the city began departmental ranking of operating programs based on a set of corporate criteria. In the same year, a management consultant's study observed that the city's budgeting system was one of the most advanced they had seen in any Ontario municipality. Some of the important elements relating to this budget process were:

• only two semi-autonomous outside boards and commissions existed and working relations with these bodies were effective
• council operated largely as a policy-making body and did not concentrate on line-item expenditure details

Although the city's previous budget system was very advanced, it was a traditional incremental budget. Its shortcomings were:

1. It focused on increases over prior years
2. There was insufficient justification of existing activities and programs
3. There was little evidence of cost-effectiveness
4. Inflexibility existed over alternative levels of funding
5. It did not detail service level information

Exhibit 1

CITY OF THUNDER BAY
ADMINISTRATIVE STRUCTURE

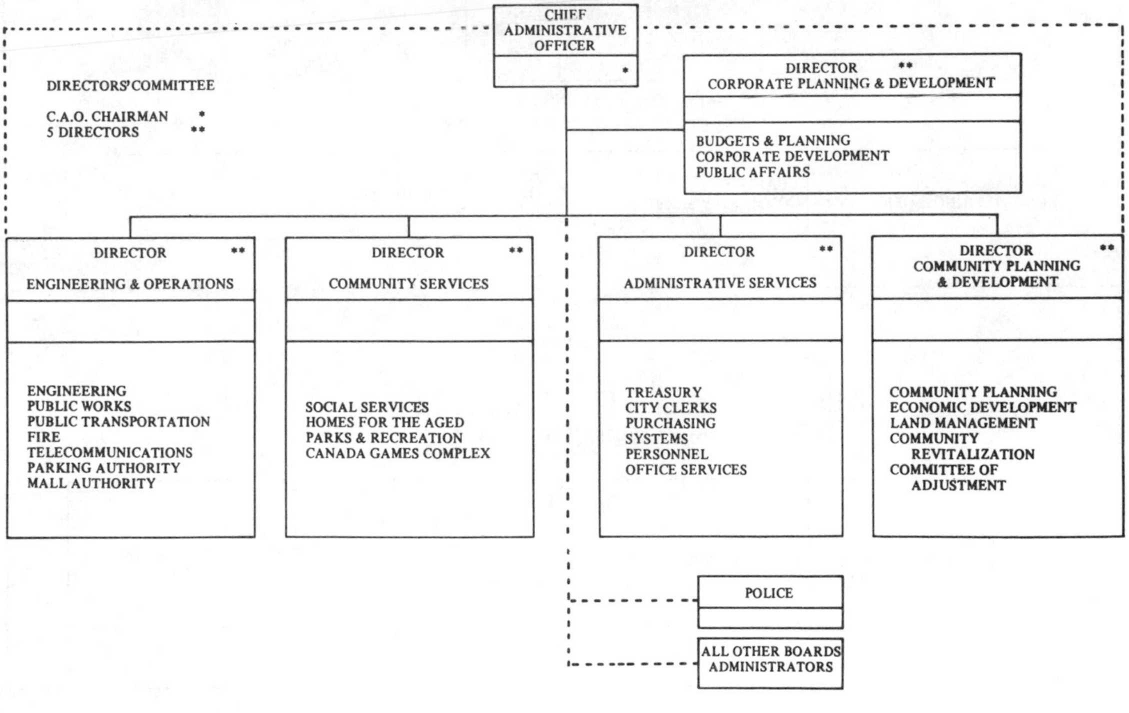

6. There were no clear priorities

7. It was departmentally oriented.

Later in 1978, council approved an administrative recommendation to implement Zero Base Budgeting for the 1979 budget. Its objectives were primarily to be a process that would encourage a thorough review of all elements of the organization, would achieve a corporate orientation in allocating resources, and would involve more managers in planning and analyzing their operations.

Like other municipalities, the city is now facing increasingly difficult budget years. With an operating budget of nearly $100 million and a full-time staff complement approaching 2,000 persons, the process has evolved in the face of a cost-revenue squeeze typical to most municipalities. As a management tool, the ZBB process:

Exhibit 2

CITY OF THUNDER BAY

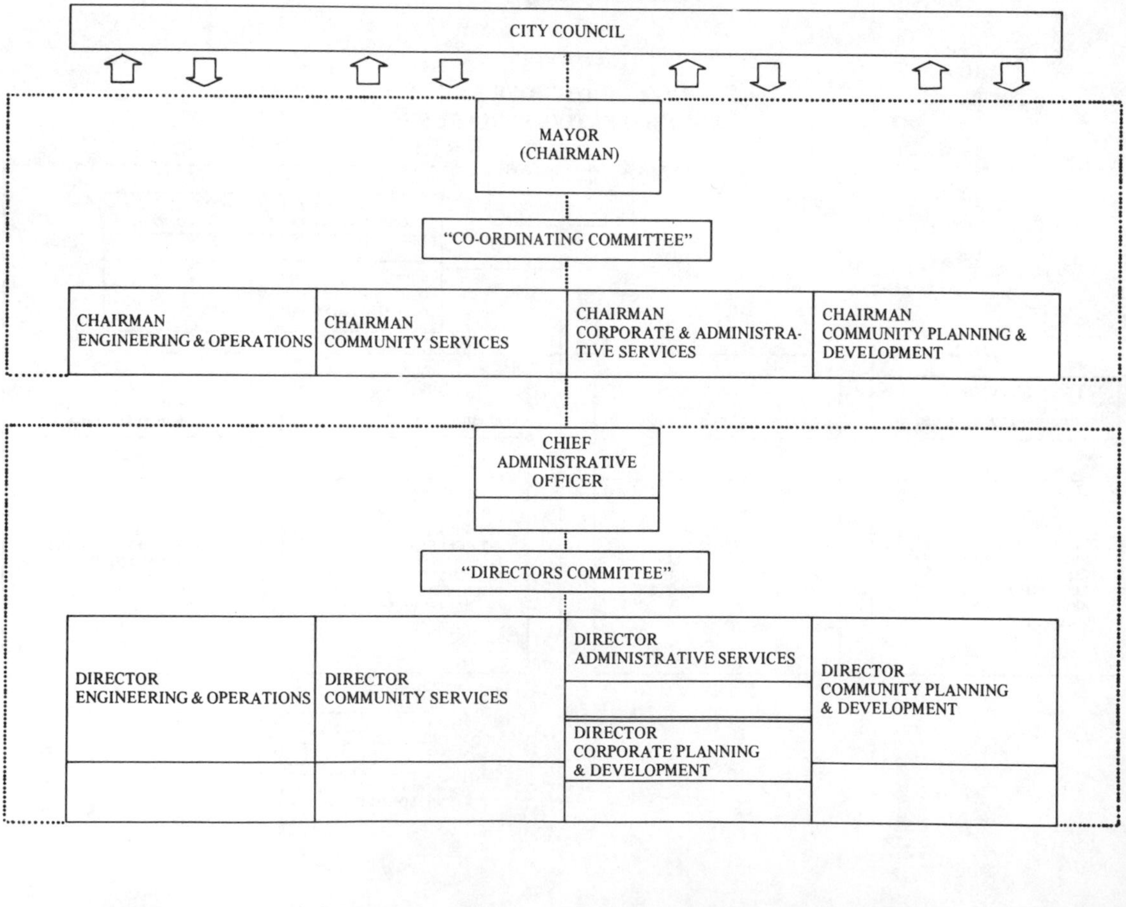

- assists in the re-examination of existing services
- encourages innovative thinking
- permits resource allocation recommendations by administration and decisions by council based on priorities
- involves more managers in the budget process
- emphasizes the development and use of performance measures
- encourages cost-effective budget proposals.

Many of these objectives have been achieved as the city has closely analyzed and justified both existing and new services. The final budgets have been settled earlier than in previous years and have given the new council and the new senior administration an in-depth look into all operations.

1979 ZBB process and outcomes. Following the decision to introduce ZBB for the 1979 budget process, design and implementation began. The two-man Budgets and Planning Department were involved as the project managers. Consultants were hired on a limited basis, involving about 72 man-days at a cost of $36,500, to act as advisers to senior staff. The consultants assisted at key points during the design, training, preparation, review and ranking stages.

In utilizing ZBB the first year, the process was supportive of both the councillors' and administration's roles.

The elected representative must continually reassess the service needs and demands of the community in order to establish a sense of priorities.

With the desired conditions in mind, comparisons must be made with current services to ensure they match the priorities and are being provided in a cost-effective manner.

Given that financial resources are always limited, the resulting tax burden must also be considered. Hopefully the end result achieves a balance between the service levels desired by the community and the citizens' ability or willingness to pay.

Managers also have a vital role in this process. They have a prime responsibility for the development of financial and operational plans consistent with council's goals, policies and guidelines. Then, after a decision on the service level, the manager is accountable for delivering the services efficiently and effectively.

A clear understanding and acceptance of these roles by these two major players in the municipal budget process is essential, particularly in a ZBB environment. Moreover, the process should be tailored to support these roles consistent with the organization's needs and conditions.

The implementation of the 1979 process began with the distribution of a Budget Manual and the holding of "how to" training sessions. More than 100 managers participated versus 30 to 40 persons in prior years.

For review and ranking sessions, the budget was organized into seven major budget task forces. Each group consisted of a functional grouping of departments. Outside boards and commissions were included in the appropriate task force.

For the administrative review that occurred first, the new chief administrative officer, two directors, the budget manager and respective department heads were gathered for each of the task forces. Each of these groups reviewed the department budgets which were developed into service levels and arranged in priority order.

Each budget group re-ranked the service levels and created a consolidated priority list. The ranking process used a scale from 1 to 6, with 1 being the lowest priority rating and 6 being the highest. The average vote was calculated to give the priority order.

Council review, ranking and decision-making took place next. The reviews were a joint effort by the councillors and the senior management team. Again the outside boards and commissions were involved. Following the same task force groups, each service level was reviewed and a ranking assigned by the participants.

A corporate priority list was created which was used as the basis for final decision-making.

Some of the beneficial outcomes of the first year's experiences were improvements to the efficiency and effectiveness of operations such as:

- financial and operational accountability in the police department was increased by matching the new organization structure and the budgets plans
- low-usage recreation programs were discontinued
- savings of $100,000 were made by curtailing holiday garbage collection
- an outdoor winter rinks policy was established.

During the budget reviews, 100 management study and improvement opportunities were identified. Later study resulted in some significant dollar savings and several method changes.

Budget proposals were more closely analyzed and reviewed, resulting in tighter, more accurate allocations. Also emphasized were performance measures and targets as part of the operational plans.

A much better understanding was gained of operations and service levels. Many councillors and the mayor commented that they had learned more about functions and services than during the past several budget cycles. This also represented the beginning of a dialogue on priorities, goals and objectives for the community.

1980 ZBB process Improvements were made to the ZBB process to tailor the system more closely to the particular needs of the organization. The improvements included:

- developing specific criteria for the priority ranking of service levels
- streamlining the design and format of documentation by combining service level alternatives on one page
- reducing the number of decision units slightly by combining related, smaller units from 1979
- simplifying council's review process by focusing their attention on lower priority items only

Exhibit 3

THE CITY OF THUNDER BAY
1980 OPERATING BUDGET
TRANSMITTAL MEMORANDUM

| DIVISION/_____ | The City of Thunder Bay
1980 BUDGET
TRANSMITTAL MEMORANDUM | PREPARED BY _____ |
| DEPARTMENT | | DATE _____ |

SUMMARY OF BUDGET SUBMISSION

CHANGES/IMPROVEMENTS/ISSUES

PROBLEMS/CONSTRAINTS

• incorporating proposed user charge increases into the budget process.

The key forms used by the city's departments in the ZBB process are:

• Transmittal Memorandum (Exhibit 3)
  A covering letter which presents an overview and summary of the budget proposal
• Priority Ranking List (Exhibit 4)
  A listing of the priority order of service levels facilitating resource allocation to the most important service areas first
• Decision Unit Summary (Exhibit 5)
  Provides the purpose, methods, resources and improvements of each separate budget "chunk" to the recommended level and in the most cost-effective manner
• Service Level Analysis (Exhibit 6)
  Presents and justifies each incremental/alternative service level within a decision unit, noting description, consequences of not funding, resources and performance measures
• User Charge Increase Proposals (Exhibit 7)
  Analysis and proposal recommending increased or new user charge fees for city services.

Exhibit 4

THE CITY OF THUNDER BAY
1980 OPERATING BUDGET
PRIORITY RANKING LIST FORM

DIVISION _____ Ⓐ				The City of Thunder Bay 1980 BUDGET PRIORITY RANKING LIST ($000's)				PAGE ___1___ OF ___4___ PREPARED BY K.F. Punch DATE September 20, 1979		

Ⓑ RANK	Ⓒ DECISION UNIT NAME & SERVICE LEVEL	Ⓓ CODE	Ⓔ NEW STAFF		CURRENT LEVEL F/T	INDIVIDUAL SERVICE LEVEL		CUMULATIVE	
			F/T	OTHER F/T		Ⓕ GROSS	Ⓖ NET	GROSS Ⓗ NET	
1	Systems − Administration 1/3	250 A1	−	−	3.0	79.2	60.0		
2	Personnel − Personnel Administration 1/3	280 A1	−	−	7.0	185.2	170.0		
3	Systems − Operations 1/3	250 B1	−	−	7.0	392.3	300.0		
4	Purchasing − Purchasing 1/3	270 A1	−	−	4.0	101.8	80.0		
5	Clerks − Legislative Service 1/3	240 A1	−	−	6.0	131.9	125.2		
6	Systems − Support Services 1/3	250 C1	−	−	2.0	44.3	35.0		
7	Treasury − Finance & Administration 1/3	260 A1	−	−	12.0	258.3	240.0		
8	Treasury − Telephone Billing & Collection 1/3	260 C1	−	−	15.0	345.3	320.1		
9	Treasury − Tax Collection 1/3	260 G1	−	−	7.0	148.0	148.0		
10	Treasury − Cashiering & Coin Counting 1/3	260 D1	−	−	9.0	151.4	140.0		
11	Treasury − Water Acc. to Billing & Collection 1/3	260 B1	−	−	4.0	99.5	−		
12	Treasury − Licensing & Insurance 1/3	260 E1	−	−	2.5	50.5	40.2		
13	Systems − Development 1/3	250 D1	−	−	3.0	72.3	60.0		
14	Treasury − Finance & Administration 2/3	260 A2	−	−	3.5	83.2	75.0		
15	Office Services − Printing 1/3	220 B1	−	−	4.0	117.8	117.0		
16	Office Services − Stenographic Services 1/3	220 A1	−	−	12.0	212.7	200.3		
17	Purchasing − Purchasing 2/3	270 A2	−	−	2.0	35.6	−		
18	Driver Training − Driver Training 1/3	210 A1	−	−	1.0	30.4	25.1		
19	Systems − Operations 2/3	250 B2	−	−	4.0	106.0	80.1		
20	Clerks − Election 1/3	240 B1	−	−	−	150.0	150.0		
21	Purchasing − Stores 1/3	270 B1	−	−	9.0	213.0			
Ⓙ	THIS PAGE TOTAL		−	−		THIS PAGE TOTAL	3,008.7	2,266.0	
	CUMULATIVE TOTAL					CUMULATIVE TOTAL	3,008.7	2,266.0	

The budget training, prior to budget preparation, focused on elements of the management process and on the development of performance measures. In previous years, the training usually focused on "how to" sessions related to the process and on forms completion.

After the proposed departmental budgets were completed, three members of the senior management team met with the respective department heads and reviewed their budgets. The purpose of the meetings was to ensure all budgets were cost-effective and were supported by senior management.

Although departmental priority lists were reviewed at these meetings, very few changes were made. Nor was any attempt made by administration to consolidate all departmental priority lists into a corporate priority list.

Further aspects of the senior management team's role in 1980:

Exhibit 5

THE CITY OF THUNDER BAY
1980 OPERATING BUDGET
DECISION UNIT SUMMARY

DIVISION Engineering & Operations DEPARTMENT Public Works	City of Thunder Bay 1980 BUDGET DECISION UNIT SUMMARY	DECISION UNIT NAME Garbage Collection CODE 620P

PURPOSE AND DESCRIPTION

To operate an efficient and effective garbage collection system which maintains community health, safety and cleanliness standards. Meets Health Unit regulations and City's collection By-Law. Uses 11 three-man crews, 3 two-man crews, and 20 rear-loading packers for once weekly residential and 3 times weekly commercial pick-up. Also roadside rubbish collection from May to November by 2 two-man crews using 2 extra trucks. Organized into 75 routes covering all urban and rural areas.

IMPROVEMENTS AND INNOVATIONS

1. A joint union-management committee will investigate in 1980 the use of 2 and 1 man collection crews using side loaders.
2. Under the 1979 program which eliminated holiday garbage collection, all new residents and residents that moved will receive the collection date calendars.

PERFORMANCE MEASUREMENT

FINANCIAL RESOURCES ($000's)	1979 BUDGET	1979 ESTIMATED ACTUAL	1980 PROPOSAL CURRENT LEVEL	1980 PROPOSAL EXPANSION LEVEL	1980 TOTAL
GROSS COST $	939.2	906.9	947.7	–	947.7
% OF 1979 ACTUAL	103.6	100%	104.5	–	104.5
ALL REVENUES	19.11	(10.5)	(10.0)	–	(10.0)
NET COST	930.1	896.4	937.7	–	937.7

MANPOWER RESOURCES

FULL TIME	r's	40.7	38.8	40.5		40.5
	NEW				–	–
TEMPORARY	F.T.E.'s	2.5	2.4	2.6		2.6
	NEW				–	–

AVERAGE HOUSEHOLDS PER MAN HOUR (HOUSEHOLDS axis: 30, 40, 50, 60; years: 1976 1977 1978 1979 1980)

PREPARED BY G.A. Boge DATE September 15, 1979	REVIEWED BY: DEPARTMENT HEAD R.U. Bish DIRECTOR D.Y. Ector

• began with recommending budget preparation guidelines to council. Considerations included the overall mill rate, labor settlement targets, user charge increases, capital out-of-current revenue, debt retirement provision and a freeze on program expansions and staff increases.

• next came individual involvement in the budget review of the departments reporting to them. Then followed the joint review sessions with at least two other senior managers as described above.

• later, as a senior management team, they met and jointly reviewed the 17 departmental priority lists. In total, the 1980 mill rate was 19 per cent above the 1979 municipal mill rate. This was much above council's 8 percent guideline increase. The team identified the lower priority service levels from the bottom of each priority list that would be reviewed and ranked by council.

• they also made broad corporate recommendations dealing with:
  • an overall mill rate target consistent with the earlier council guideline
  • proposed user charge increases
  • contingency and surplus treatments.

The council review sessions were next. Council heard a verbal presentation from individual department heads and their divisional directors. Departmental overviews were presented, but the presentation focus was on the lower priority service levels and any user charge increase proposals.

Exhibit 6

THE CITY OF THUNDER BAY
1980 OPERATING BUDGET
SERVICE LEVEL ANALYSIS

DECISION UNIT NAME Garbage Collection CODE 620-P	The City of Thunder Bay 1980 BUDGET		SERVICE LEVEL (S/L) ANALYSIS	
SERVICE LEVEL	S/L - 1 CURRENT	S/L - 2 CURRENT	S/L - 3	S/L - 4
BRIEF DESCRIPTION OF BENEFITS/ACTIVITIES/METHODS/RESOURCES Provide once weekly residential & 3 times weekly commercial collection. Use 15 two-man crews with 20 cu. yd. packers covering 75 urban & rural routes. Provides basic level of service for safety, health and cleanliness.	Add 6 months rubbish service from May to November & roadside debris pick-up. Uses 9 full-time & 4 sanitation loaders plus 2 rental trucks.			
CONSEQUENCES OF NOT FUNDING City would not provide garbage collection service & would result in a combination of private contracting by City and personal disposal in rural area. Probably lower levels of cleanliness in some lanes.	Roadside debris would not be collected. Some rubbish would be collected with garbage. Other disposed personally. Less property & lane cleanliness.			

FINANCIAL RESOURCES ($000's) / MANPOWER RESOURCES	SERVICE LEVEL	S/L - 1	S/L - 2	CUM	S/L - 3	CUM	S/L - 4	CUM
	GROSS COST $	812.2	135.5	947.7				
	% OF 1979 EST. ACTUAL	89.6	14.9	104.5				
	ALL REVENUES	(10.0)	–	(10.0)				
	NET COST	802.2	135.5	937.7				
	FULL TIME r's	14.2	6.0	40.5				
	NEW	/////	/////	/////				
	TEMPORARY F.T.E.'s	2.0	.6	2.6				
	NEW	/////	/////	/////				

PERFORMANCE MEASUREMENTS	S/L-1	CUM	S/L-2	CUM	S/L-3	CUM	S/L-4	CUM
1. Tons of Garbage		39,000		39,000				
2. Tons of Rubbish		1,000		1,000				
3. Cost Per Ton Garbage		$21.42		$23.31				
4. Cost Per Capita		$ 7.79		$ 8.48				
5. Average Households Per Man Hour		49		57				
6. Percentage of collection routes completed on schedule		43%		94%				
7. Percentage of households not reporting missed collections		70%		96%				
8. Number of valid citizen complaints per 1,000 households served		8		6				

In this manner, council relied on the senior management team to ensure the bulk of the budget proposals were cost-effective. Council's review concentrated on the key policy decisions they faced in choosing a balance between cutting current levels of services and increasing user charges. The priority list they generated was an effective method to deal with this situation.

Council reviewed and ranked only 129 out of a total of 450 service levels. These represented a net cost of $3.3 million which was 5.3 percent of the final approved net budget. In effect, the detailed review of the remaining budget was largely an administrative responsibility. Council's ranking was made on

Exhibit 7

THE CITY OF THUNDER BAY
1980 OPERATING BUDGET
USER CHARGES ANALYSIS & PROPOSAL

DEPARTMENT _____	The City of Thunder Bay 1980 BUDGET
USER CHARGE _____	USER CHARGES ANALYSIS & PROPOSAL PAGE ____ OF _____

BACKGROUND

ANALYSIS

ALTERNATIVES

RECOMMENDATION

Exhibit 8

THE CITY OF THUNDER BAY
1980 OPERATING BUDGET
PRIORITY RANKING PROCESS

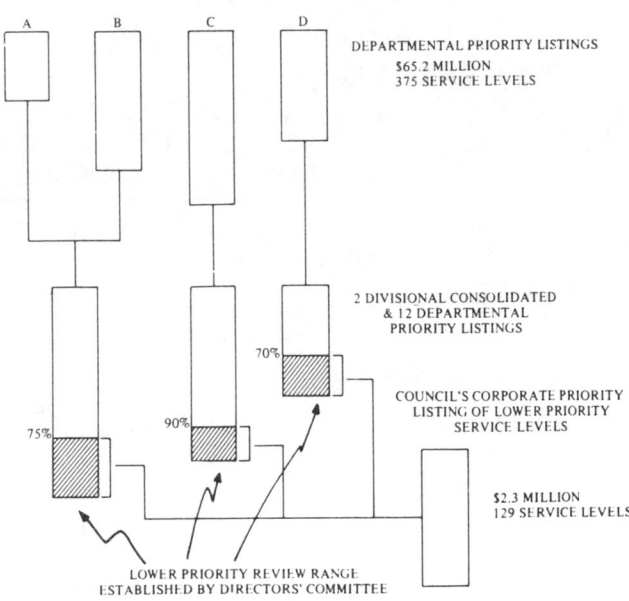

DEPARTMENTAL PRIORITY LISTINGS
$65.2 MILLION
375 SERVICE LEVELS

2 DIVISIONAL CONSOLIDATED
& 12 DEPARTMENTAL
PRIORITY LISTINGS

COUNCIL'S CORPORATE PRIORITY
LISTING OF LOWER PRIORITY
SERVICE LEVELS

$2.3 MILLION
129 SERVICE LEVELS

LOWER PRIORITY REVIEW RANGE
ESTABLISHED BY DIRECTORS' COMMITTEE

the basis of assigning a value of either 1 of 2 to each service. The "1" or "2" vote meant giving a low or high priority, or expressed another way, a "no" or "yes" in terms of funding.

Based on the calculated average vote of all the elected representation, a consolidated priority list of lower priority service levels from council's perspective was prepared.

In reviewing this list, council approved spending of all the high priority service levels and costs which were not re-ranked to a cost of $27.1 million. They also approved not funding the 22 lowest priority service levels worth about $1.5 million.

Then they re-ranked, for a second time, 53 service levels with a value of $850,000 critically positioned around their 8 percent mill rate increase funding cut-off line.

After finalizing user charge increases with a value of $0.5 million, and deciding to support a 9 percent average mill rate increase, the actual funding cut-off line was finalized (see Exhibit 8).

1980 budget outcomes The 1980 Approved Net Municipal Budget totalled $62.7 million. It was 10.8 percent above the 1979 budget and represented a 9 percent municipal mill rate increase. Some of the beneficial outcomes were:

• user charge increases were successfully integrated into the budget process
• effective use was made of the process by the directors' committee
• the first full-time staff reduction for existing municipal services since amalgamation was achieved
• few expansionary programs were proposed or approved
• some lower priority programs in several departments were terminated
• evaluation of the process by managers and budget preparers was generally favourable.

The detailed evaluation of review, preparation and budget administrative time is shown in this table:

THE CITY OF THUNDER BAY
BUDGET COMPARISONS 1978-1980

	Before ZBB	ZBB	ZBB
Review Meeting Manhours	1978	1979	1980
Administration	350	850	190
Council	200	320	140
Budget Staff Man Days			
Regular Time	325	480	380
Overtime	10	60	10
Budget Preparation			
Manhours	4,100	10,400	7,700
Cost	$45,100	$124,800	$100,100

Additionally, a firm of management consultants was hired to conduct a small independent evaluation of the process. Their recommendation supported the continued use of ZBB principles and further enhancement of the planning, review, reporting and performance appraisal aspects of the process.

1981 and beyond The city will continue to use ZBB principles in preparing its operating budget. The same simplified format developed in 1980 will be utilized.

Additional plans call for the development of a computer ranking program to streamline this aspect and further emphasis on improving performance measures.

ZBB in perspective There is nothing magical about ZBB. Conceptually the idea is very sound. It needs to be altered, however, to meet the needs and requirements of the organization using it. It is a change and, as with any change, there is a need for careful management and to anticipate problems and difficulties.

But it is an effective process to deal with budget allocations based on objectives, priorities and results. It reflects all aspects of the management process; accordingly, potential benefits lie beyond just the resource allocation decisions.

Questions

1. Distinguish between public-sector organizations and private-sector organizations. Give several examples of each.
2. "Look, Sam, we are a city government. We are not in business to make a profit. We do not want a lot of detailed data on revenue estimates; just give us your guess about how much total revenue we can expect next year." Comment on this statement
3. Describe program budgeting and compare it with line budgeting.
4. Performance reports are for profit-oriented firms; such reports are a waste of effort in public-sector organizations. Do you agree? Explain.
5. Define the term *public finance.*
6. What is the purpose of a public sector in a capitalistic society?
7. Briefly describe the three basic objectives of public finance.
8. Discuss the role of fiscal policy in stabilization. What characteristics does fiscal policy have?
9. What is monetary policy? How does it relate to fiscal policy and the stabilization objective?
10. What is PPBS? When and how was it started?

11. Briefly describe the steps in PPBS.
12. What is program accounting and what does it involve?
13. What is the purpose of a detailed description of activities and what information is included?
14. What is zero-base budgeting? What is its origin? What are its strengths and weaknesses?
15. Discuss the status of the PPB system.
16. What is the function of the auditor-general? Discuss.

Exercises

Ex. 14-1   **Identifying program benefits.** The fire chief and his employees are very eager to acquire a new, fast, efficient fire truck. The truck costs $260,000, and the city council has been reluctant to approve the request. In the past arguments in favour of the truck have always been general statements about the need, and the council has requested more quantitative measures of benefit. The fire chief hires you as a consultant to help prepare the department's case.

Required:
Discuss some possible measures of benefits. Be specific. Develop hypothetical data to illustrate your case.

Ex. 14-2   **Tax structure.** On the way home from work Frank heard an interview on the radio in which a researcher said the average citizen earning $25,000 a year pays nearly 40 percent of the earnings in taxes. Frank, who earns $24,500 a year, was shocked at that number and immediately went to his den to find copies of last year's tax return. After adding up his provincial and federal income tax payments, he finds that these two amounted to 24 percent of his salary. Frank wonders how his tax burden can be so different from what the researcher stated.

Required:
Discuss what might account for the difference Frank found. Use numbers to illustrate your point.

Ex. 14-3   **Identifying line and program budget items.** Below are costs that come from a school system that prepares separate line and program budgets.

Cost Item	Line Budget	Program Budget
a. Utilities	_____	_____
b. Teacher salaries	_____	_____
c. Special education	_____	_____
d. Transportation	_____	_____

e. Primary education   _____   _____
f. Physical education   _____   _____
g. Supplies   _____   _____
h. Administration   _____   _____
i. Student exchange   _____   _____
j. Continuing education   _____   _____
k. Textbooks   _____   _____
l. Equipment   _____   _____

Required:

For each cost determine if it most likely came from the line budget or the program budget and place a check mark in the appropriate column.

Ex. 14-4   Incremental budgeting. The intramural department of Nonsuch College has proposed the following changes in the current year's budget as the budget for the next academic year:

Item	Change	Current Budget
Administrative salaries	8% increase	$ 70,000
Student wages	4% increase	10,000
Supplies	15% increase	30,000
Equipment	10% decrease	20,000
Utilities	20% increase	12,000
Miscellaneous	10% increase	8,000
Total		$150,000

Required:

a. Prepare the intramural department's budget for the next academic year based on the proposal above.

b. Compute the total percentage difference between the current year's budget and next year's budget.

Ex. 14-5   Analyzing budget data. The management of the X-ray department of a municipal hospital prepared the following budget proposal in response to the hospital controller's request for departmental budget proposals for the coming year. The controller's budget memo informed department heads of a need to hold total budget increases to 7 percent or less. The X-ray department manager is pleased with the department's budget proposal because it shows an average increase of 5 percent. The proposal is presented below.

	Current Budget	Proposed Change
Salaries and wages	$800,000	12% increase
Supplies	250,000	10% increase
New equipment purchases	100,000	5% decrese
Maintenance	80,000	3% increase
Utilities	120,000	5% increase
Average increase		5% increase

Required:

As controller, respond to the X-ray department's budget proposal, specifically with reference to the percentage increase guidelines.

Ex. 14-6 **Program budgeting.** A line budget has always been used at Tidal Pool Provincial Park. A recent directive from provincial headquarters informed all park managers to prepare a program budget for the next year. Below is the proposed line budget for the coming year along with information about the percentage of line item cost assignable to each program.

Tidal Pool Provincial Park
Proposed Line Budget

Personnel salaries	$200,000
Housing costs	50,000
Utilities	25,000
Supplies	30,000
Vehicle costs	40,000
Clothing and other allowances	5,000
Total	$350,000

	Percentage of Cost Assignable to Each Program			
	Educational Programs	Park Protection	Repairs and Maintenance	Park Administration
Personnel salaries	30%	30%	20%	20%
Housing costs	20	30	20	30
Utilities	20	10	30	40
Supplies	40	10	30	20
Vehicle costs	15	50	30	5
Clothing and other allowances	20	30	20	30

Required:

Prepared a program budget for the next budget year.

Ex. 14-7 Combined line and program budget. The Good City Police Department typically has prepared a line budget. Now there is discussion about using a program budget as well in an effort to control activities better and do a better job of securing resources from the city council. Below is the proposed line budget for the coming year and estimated data concerning the percentage of line item cost assignable to each of the four major programs of the police department.

Good City Police Department Proposed Budget	
Salaries	$525,000
Patrol car costs	250,000
Supplies	125,000
Utilities	50,000
Miscellaneous	44,000
Total	$994,000

	Percentage of Cost Assignable to Each Program			
	Crime Prevention	Criminal Investigation	Criminal Proceedings	Community Education
Salaries	60%	20%	10%	10%
Patrol car costs	70	20	2	8
Supplies	20	30	20	30
Utilities	10	60	20	10
Miscellaneous	30	25	20	25

Required:
Prepare a combined line-program budget proposal for the coming year.

Problem Set A

P. 14A-1 Revenue budget. UBC University had the following revenue for the 1983–84 academic year:

Tuition 2000 students @ $2,500 per student	$ 5,000,000
Provincial appropriations	3,000,000
Contributions	1,000,000
Investment revenues	400,000
Fees and assessments	600,000
Total revenue	$10,000,000

For the 1984–85 academic year, student enrollments are expected to increase 5 percent, and student tuition will be raised 8 percent. Provincial appropriations are based on the estimated number of students enrolled, and it is estimated that state appropriations will rise 4 percent per student. Contributions are expected to rise 5 percent in 1984–85. A large portion of the investments was sold this year to finance the construction of a multipurpose centre; therefore, investment revenue will decline by 60 percent. Student fees and assessments will increase 25 percent per student to help pay for the cost of constructing and operating the new multipurpose centre.

Required:

Prepare a revenue budget for the university for the 1984–85 academic year.

P. 14A-2   **Revenue budget.** Below is the 1983 revenue budget for a municipal government.

Taxes:	
Property tax	$2,000,000
Other taxes	120,000
Fees and assessments:	
Water sales	800,000
Sewage charges	1,200,000
Recreational user fees	5,000
Refuse collection	500,000
Other revenues	
Provincial government grants	800,000
Investment income	25,000
Total revenue	$5,450,000

Currently the 1984 revenue budget is being prepared. The following information affects the revenue budget:

The property tax rate will increase 5 percent, and assessed valuation of property within the city will rise 20 percent by 1984. Other tax base for the city should grow 8 percent in 1984. A 9 percent water rate increase goes into effect January 1, 1984, and water use is expected to go up 12 percent. New industrial businesses will increase sewage use 18 percent in 1984, but a 5 percent rate reduction effective January 1, 1984, has already been approved by the municipal council. All charges for recreational programs and services are being dropped in 1984 to encourage participation in physical activities. Refuse collection fees will be raised 7 percent in 1984. A provincial grant of $450,000 a year runs out in 1983, but a new provincial grant of $300,000 a year for three years is expected to start in 1984. Other provincial government funds totaling $200,000 will be lost in 1984. No investment revenue is expected in 1984 since the bonds that generated the revenue mature January 3, 1984. Maturity value of the bonds is $312,500. The city plans to use the money rather than reinvest it.

Required:

Prepare a detailed revenue budget for 1984 for the city.

P. 14A-3 **Program budget.** The Barklay City Police Department has a highly respected residential patrol program that has resulted in an extremely low crime rate in residential areas. As a general rule, police need one patrol route for every 300 residences. A patrol route requires two patrol shifts, each with one officer. One police car is required for each patrol route. Total actual patrol time on a route is 14 hours a day. The following data are available for patrol costs for the program in 1983.

Patrol routes	32
Average salary of officers	$11,000
Gasoline cost per patrol car	$1.20/h
Annual maintenance cost per patrol car	$350

Six of the current patrol cars will have to be replaced in 1984. New patrol cars have a net cost of $8,200. The price the city pays for gasoline will increase 5 percent in 1984, and maintenance costs are expected to rise 8 percent. The wage agreement calls for a 7 percent increase in officers' salaries in 1984. New housing developments have added 900 new residences to the city's patrol area. One patrol car is required for each route.

Required:

Prepare the 1984 budget for this patrol program, identifying salary costs, gasoline costs, maintenance costs, and the cost of new patrol cars.

P. 14A-4 **Budget performance report.** Below is the expenditure budget for the 1983– 84 school year for the New West School District.

Item	1983–84 Budget
Administrative salaries	$ 180,000
Teachers' salaries	980,000
Other salaries	110,000
Maintenance costs	70,000
School supplies	80,000
Utilities	42,000
Transportation	210,000
Medical and legal	40,000
Furniture	80,000
Equipment	25,000
Miscellaneous	83,000
Total	$1,900,000

At the end of the school year, an office clerk prepared the following listing of account balances:

Item	1983–1984 Actual
Administrative salaries	$ 172,000
Teachers' salaries	1,004,000
Other salaries	104,000
Maintenance costs	126,000
School supplies	92,000
Utilities	38,000
Transportation	226,000
Medical and legal	34,000
Furniture	25,000
Equipment	27,000
Miscellaneous	89,000
Total	$1,937,000

Required:
a. Prepare a detailed budget performance report for the year for the New West School District.
b. What budget items appear to need investigation?

P. 14A-5 **Program budget.** Great North College is a liberal arts college that has never offered business courses. In recent years students have expressed a considerable amount of interest in taking some business courses. In response to this interest, the faculty have developed a proposed business minor. The faculty believe that the business minor will attract students to campus who might otherwise have attended other colleges. Thus any loss of student enrollments in other disciplines of the college because of students taking the business minor will be more than offset by new students attending the college. The minor would require the establishment of the following courses:

Course	Estimated Annual Student Enrollment
Accounting 101—Financial	180
Accounting 102—Managerial	150
Accounting 201—Intermediate	60
Accounting 204—Income tax	60
Marketing 101—Introduction	120
Marketing 103—Retailing	60
Management 101—Policy	120
Management 201—Production	60
Business Law 102—Contracts	270

The college averages one faculty member for every 120 student enrollments. The average cost of hiring faculty to staff the new business minor would be $18,000 each. In addition, health care, retirement program, and other fringe benefits amount to 25 percent of faculty salaries. Two secretaries would have to be hired for the business faculty at a cost of $6,500 each per year plus 12 percent in fringe benefits. Supply costs average $5.50 per student enrollment. Currently excess classroom space is available to handle the new business enrollments, but office space is at a premium. A large house on the edge of campus was willed to the college. It will be remodeled at a cost of $60,000 for faculty office space. Utility costs for the new offices will average $360 per month.

Required:
a. How many business faculty are required to staff the new program?
b. Prepare a detailed budget for the cost of the new program for the first year.
c. If student tuition for courses is $250 a class, does the program appear to be economically feasible?

Problem Set B

P. 14B-1   **Expenditure budget.** OUR University had the following expenditure budget during the 1983–84 academic year:

Faculty salaries	$ 3,500,000
Other employee salaries	1,640,000
Educational supplies	260,000
Buildings maintenance	2,600,000
Utilities	800,000
Miscellaneous	1,200,000
Total expenditure	$10,000,000

Faculty staffing will increase in the same ratio as student enrollments, and faculty raises are expected to average 6 percent for the academic year. Other employee salaries are covered by a labour agreement calling for an 8 percent raise during the 1983–84 academic year; however, new labour-saving equipment will allow a 10 percent decrease in the number of other employees. Rapidly rising paper costs and other supply items are expected to increase supply costs by 15 percent per student. Building maintenance costs should continue their trend of a 9 percent-per-year increase, and a major overhaul of the air conditioning system will increase costs an additional $450,000 in 1983–84. A 12 percent rise in utility rates will be in effect during the 1983–84 academic year. Miscellaneous items are expected to increase 8 percent. There were 2000 students in 1982–83. Student enrollment is expected to grow 5 percent in 1983–84.

Required:
Prepare an expenditure budget for OUR University.

P. 14B-2   Revenue budget. The Hadley City municipal council wants more detailed information on the city's revenue budget than has been available in the past. The city controller has been asked to provide the current-year revenue budget and additional information that is necessary to prepare a more detailed plan of next year's revenue budget. Below is the controller's response.

Hadley City Revenue Budget 1984	
Taxes	$3,000,000
Fees	2,400,000
Provincial money	300,000
Total revenue	$5,700,000

1. Tax revenue in 1984 is 95 percent property tax and 5 percent other tax. In 1985 it is expected that the assessed valuation of property will increase 10 percent and the property tax rate will go up 2 percent. Other taxes will continue to grow at the 6 percent rate achieved each of the last five years. The council plans to raise the other tax from .5 percent to 1 percent.
2. In 1984 fees consist of water use fees, 30 percent of total fees; sewage service fees, 45 percent; and refuse collection fees, 25 percent. Water and sewage use should increase 8 percent and refuse collection, 5 percent. A new water purchase agreement with another water company will force a 6 percent increase in the water rate in 1985. Provincial government water pollution standards have forced the construction of a large sewage treatment plant. The cost of the plant will be reflected in a 15 percent sewage rate increase January 1, 1985.
3. In 1984 the city received $300,000 from the provincial government for a low-income housing subsidy program. The city expects to receive 40 percent more than in 1984 for the program in 1985.

Required:
Prepare a detailed revenue budget for Hadley City for 1985.

P. 14B-3   Expenditure budget. Following are data relevant to the preparation of the 1985 budget for the refuse collection department. The department can provide weekly refuse collection for 1600 houses with one collection unit, which consists of one truck, one driver, and two collection people dumping refuse into the truck. Drivers receive $12,000 a year and collection people $11,000 a year. Each truck uses $3,600 a year in gas and oil and requires average annual maintenance costs of $600. Each year 50 percent of the trucks require new tires at a cost of $800 a truck. Total insurance costs are $26,000 a year. Administrative costs for 1985 are expected to rise 9 percent from their 1984 level of $210,000. In 1984 refuse is collected from 40 000 houses. That number is expected to increase 4 percent in 1985. Other items include:

Cost	1984 Budget
Electricity	$ 30,000
Building maintenance	65,000
Payroll taxes	140,000
Miscellaneous	25,000

Management expects electricity use to increase 10 percent because of a program to light up truck lots all night to discourage vandalism. In addition, the electricity rate is scheduled to rise 14 percent on January 1, 1985. A new building maintenance agreement has been signed with an outside contractor for 1985. It calls for more thorough cleaning and more preventive maintenance. The new agreement costs $87,000 for the year. Payroll taxes will go up 16 percent in 1985. It is expected that the miscellaneous category will continue its annual growth of 8 percent. A new truck costs $95,000.

Required:
Prepare a detailed expenditure budget for the refuse collection department for 1985.

P. 14B-4 **Performance report analysis.** This year, for the first time, the municipal council requires all city departments to prepare year-end performance reports. This requirement has generated considerable unrest since some department heads consider the report useless "busy work." One such manager is the director of the streets department who, on the day before the reporting date, told an office clerk to prepare the report. The accompanying letter and resulting report are presented below:

We respectfully submit the performance report for the streets department. We are proud of our very favourable performance this year. A couple of report notes require comment. First, new equipment purchases, marked*, shows a favourable variance of $220,000. This year we were able to acquire many new pieces of snow removal equipment at a very significant saving, which clearly will save the city money in future years. Two other items, cash and accounts payable, are marked†. Neither of these items appeared in the expenditure

Streets Department Expenditure Budget 1984			
	1984 Budget	**1984 Actual**	**Variance**
Administrative salaries	$ 265,000	$ 257,000	$ 8,000 F
Clerical salaries	120,000	126,000	6,000 U
Employee wages	520,000	488,000	32,000 U
Equipment maintenance	165,000	174,000	9,000 F
Gasoline and oil	140,000	121,000	19,000 F
Road supplies	95,000	76,000	19,000 F
New equipment purchases*	240,000	460,000	220,000 F
Miscellaneous	50,000	56,000	6,000 U
Utilities	28,000	31,000	3,000 U
Building lease	32,000	38,000	—
Cash†	—	86,000	86,000 F
Accounts payable†	—	174,000	174,000 U
Total	$1,600,000	$2,087,000	$425,000 F

budget approved by the municipal council, but we wanted to note that the department still has $86,000 in its cash account at year-end, which we believe is very favourable. However, we must present a complete and clear picture, so we feel compelled to point out that the department owes six different suppliers $174,000 on open account.

Required:
a. You are the chief financial advisor for the municipal council. Provide a **detailed** analysis and evaluation of the above report.
b. Prepare a corrected performance report in good form.

P. 14B-5 **Program budget.** The athletic department of Alberta College wants to start an intercollegiate basketball team for women. The department is trying to determine the first-year cost of such a program. Some relevant data follow:

The team will have 14 players, each on a scholarship costing $4,000. The new coach will be one of the current physical education teachers. She will become the full-time basketball coach in addition to her current duties and will receive 40 percent more than her current salary of $18,000 a year. Other costs include:

	Cost per Player
Uniforms	$260
Shoes	90
Supplies	150
Medical	60

In addition, an old locker room will be remodeled at a cost of $12,000. New equipment will cost $7,200. A trainer will work part-time for $4,500 a year. Travel costs should run about $1,200 per year per traveler. On average, 17 people will be traveling to games off campus.

Required:
Prepare a detailed budget for the first year of the new basketball program.

Minicases

Minicase 14-1   (CMA Examination Question)

Early in March 1984 the Anytown, Canada Administration presented a budget to the municipal council. This is four months prior to the start of the new fiscal year which begins July 1. Most of the important amounts must be estimated because the data upon which to base the final budget either will not be available until much closer to the end of the year, or are based upon estimates of events that occur in the next year.

The city revenues are a good example of the problem. The city obtains its cash revenues from four sources: property taxes, city income tax, parking fees and fines, and other revenues. The property taxes are based upon the assessed valuation of all the property in the city. The final assessment values for the 1984–85 fiscal year were not available until late May 1984. The income taxes withheld depend upon the income earned next year by the residents of the city. The parking fees and fines depend, to a large extent, on the size of the population.

The city administrator added an estimate of the monthly cash receipts and disbursements for the next year to the budget material he presented to the council. The cash receipts were estimated using a cash forecasting model developed in the controller's department. The model was the result of the statistical analysis of prior years results and is presented below:

$$C_i = mr_iA_t + \frac{(1 + I)T_{t-1}}{12} + \frac{(1 + G)P_{t-1}}{12} + \frac{(1 + G)R_{t-1}}{12}$$

where:

C_i = cash collected for the ith month (July = 1)
m = property tax rate per \$1,000 of assessed valuation
r_i = percent of property tax collected in the ith month
        (July = 1)
A_t = the assessed valuation of property in year t (t = budget year)
        in thousands of dollars
I = inflation rate (decimal)
T = income taxes withheld from taxpayers
G = population growth (decimal)
P = parking fees and fines collections
R = other revenues collections

The assessed valuation in thousands of dollars, A_t, was estimated from the regression equation:

$$A_t = 50,000 + 1.05A_{t-1} + 3S$$

where: S =

square metre of
new construction
since the last assessment

The numerical data shown below was available at the end of February when the budget for the fiscal year 1984–85 was constructed. The data for the 1983–84 represents either actual figures or data which was projected for the entire year based upon the first eight months of 1983–84. The data for 1984–85 represented either rates or amounts which would be experienced or were estimates of what was expected to be experienced.

1983-84	Population (actual)	100 000 people
1984-85	Population growth rate (estimated)	8%
1983-84	Assessed valuation (actual)	\$600,000,000 m²
1983-84	Square metre of new construction (projected)	30,000,000 m²
1984-85	Property tax rate per \$1,000 of assessed valuation (actual)	\$25
1983-84	Income taxes withheld (projected)	\$4,000,000
1983-84	Collections of parking fees and fines (projected)	\$1,000,000
1983-84	Other revenues collections (projected)	\$500,000
1984-85	Inflation rate (estimated)	11%

The collection pattern for property taxes that has been experienced the past three years is shown below. City officials expected this pattern to persist in the 1984-85 fiscal year.

July	20%	January	1%
August	60%	February	1%
September	10%	March	1%
October	5%	April	—
November	1%	May	—
December	1%	June	—

Required:
a. Determine the estimate of the cash receipts for the month of August 1984 that the Anytown City Administrator included in the budget material he presented to the city council in March, 1984. Use the cash forecasting model developed by the controller's department and the data available in February.
b. This is the first time the cash forecasting model has been used by the City of Anytown in its budget procedures. Explain what limitations regarding the cash receipt estimates generated from the cash forecasting model that the Anytown Administrator should have identified for the city council in his budget presentation for the coming fiscal year.

Minicase 14-2

Read the Appendix *ZBB Tailored for Thunder Bay* and answer the following questions:
a. It is said that ZBB is an effective process to deal with budget allocations based on objectives, priorities, and results and extends, in terms of benefits, beyond just the resource allocation decisions. What other decisions that ZBB made can be useful? Explain.
b. What benefits and costs do you see in using ZBB? Explain.
c. What would your reaction to ZBB be as the mayor of Thunder Bay; as the tax-paying resident of Thunder Bay? Explain.

part 4

Advanced Managerial Accounting Topics

The successful management of a business depends heavily on the managerial accounting fundamentals presented in earlier parts of this book. Managers rely on accounting information, measurements, and reports, but they also utilize experience and a good knowledge of business and economic conditions to guide the operations of a business. Considerable research has been done on management and decision making, resulting in new, more sophisticated managerial tools. Managers may use some of these new tools such as quantitative methods or other managerial techniques to supplement their intuition and experience. This section of the book presents some important concepts and tools used for cost evaluation and decision analysis.

Chapter 15 presents some quantitative models used in inventory management and illustrates methods for determining when and how much inventory to order. Standard cost-variance analysis, discussed earlier, is extended in Chapter 16 to include analysis of multiple material and labour inputs in manufacturing operations and also some advanced variance concepts used in nonmanufacturing operations. A number of important quantitative tools used in identifying cost behaviour patterns and forecasting future operations are presented in Chapter 17. This part of the book introduces a number of concepts useful to managers in analyzing and making decisions.

Chapter 15

Inventory Planning, Control, and Valuation

The valuation and control of inventories are important in planning business operations. When you have completed this chapter, you should understand:

1 The nature of inventory planning and control and the reasons it is important.

2 The procedures and methods used in inventory management.

3 Typical costs associated with inventory.

4 The methods used to determine the amount and timing of inventory orders.

5 The use of quantitative techniques in planning and controlling inventory.

6 The reasons for and the assumptions underlying the inventory valuation process.

7 The methods used in valuing periodic and perpetual inventory.

In many merchandising and manufacturing firms inventory is among the largest dollar investments. Consequently inventory must be carefully managed to ensure that it is being used as efficiently as possible and in accordance with management's policies. Determining the types of inventory to buy, the optimum inventory order size, and the best time to reorder inventory are common types of inventory decisions. Additionally, managers must plan the most efficient ways of storing, handling, and using inventories. Inventory management is an important activity involving production engineers, systems engineers, industrial engineers, financial managers, and accountants. The primary role of accountants is to provide relevant cost data to managers involved in the inventory management process.

In this chapter we discuss the general concept of inventory planning and control. We present the general model for choosing the best inventory order size and discuss the issues involved in selecting the optimum time to reorder inventory items. Finally, we discuss inventory valuation, which is essential to inventory costing procedures.

Inventory planning and control

All assets have economic value and require some planning and control to ensure that they are used in accordance with organizational goals. Engineers, for example, carefully schedule manufacturing activities to make the best use of production facilities, and information systems managers develop operating procedures and controls to maximize the company benefits from the computer system and ensure that unauthorized use of the system does not occur. Some assets require more management attention than others because of their nature or importance. For example, cash is essential to the operations and liquidity of the firm and is useful to everyone. Managers therefore expend much time and effort planning cash receipts and disbursements to ensure a desirable level of cash, and they take great care to prevent cash from being lost, stolen, or misused.

Two characteristics of inventory

Inventory is another asset that often commands the attention of management in merchandising and manufacturing firms. Two characteristics make inventory planning and control necessary. First, inventory usually represents a very large investment of resources, and the size of the investment warrants management's attention. Second, inventory constantly circulates. Unlike fixed assets, inventory is constantly being used and replenished. In manufacturing operations raw materials flow to work in process and are converted to finished goods that are then sold. In a merchandising firm the various inventory items are sold and new items are purchased to replenish the inventory.

The nature of inventory planning and control

By itself inventory is not an earning asset. It must be sold before it generates revenue for the firm. Additionally, in a manufacturing firm, raw materials must first be converted into finished goods before products can be sold. Since all firms operate with limited resources, money invested in inventory is money that cannot be invested in earning assets such as production or sales facilities.

The purpose of inventory management is to keep production and sales activities moving smoothly

The purpose of inventory management is to keep production and sales activities moving smoothly without interruptions caused by inventory shortages. Managers try to maintain an optimal investment in inventory that balances the cost of ordering and carrying inventory with the costs of not having enough inventory. This balance is achieved by determining the optimum size of an inventory order and the optimum time for placing each order. The quantity of inventory on hand and the frequency and size of inventory orders are directly related to inventory costs.

Inventory costs. Inventory decisions are affected by the cost of ordering inventory and the cost of carrying inventory, as well as by the costs of not having enough inventory on hand. Below are illustrations of each type of inventory cost:

Costs associated with inventory

Inventory ordering costs:
   Costs of acquiring recent price quotations
   Costs of preparing and approving a purchase order
   Costs of receiving shipments and checking against purchase orders
Inventory carrying costs:
   Cost of money invested in inventory
   Heat, light, power, and depreciation costs for inventory storage facilities
   Inventory handling costs
   Inventory insurance costs
   Cost of taxes on inventory
   Costs of spoilage, obsolescence, and deterioration
Inventory shortage costs:
   Cost of lost sales
   Cost of inefficient production runs
   Cost of substituting more expensive raw materials
   Penalty costs for late completion of a contract

Inventory **ordering costs** and inventory **carrying costs** are used to compute the optimum size inventory order, discussed in the next section. Inventory shortage costs are included in determining the optimum reorder point for inventory items. In addition to these two important inventory topics, several practical considerations are discussed, such as how sensitive the optimum inventory order quantity is to changes in the values of different variables.

Economic order quantity (EOQ)

The **economic order quantity (EOQ)** is the order size for some particular inventory item that results in the lowest total inventory cost for the period. Total inventory cost consists of inventory ordering costs and inventory carrying costs. An EOQ may be computed for each inventory item. Each inventory item may have a different economic order quantity.

The optimum order quantity for an inventory item is achieved when the total cost of inventory is minimized. The minimum cost occurs when the cost of ordering inventory is equal to the cost of carrying inventory. These inventory cost relationships are shown in Figure 15-1.

The EOQ occurs where the cost of ordering inventory equals the cost of carrying inventory

When the order size is small, total ordering costs are high because orders must be placed frequently, but total carrying costs are low because relatively small amounts of inventory are on hand at any particular point in time. When orders are large, total ordering costs are low but carrying costs are high because

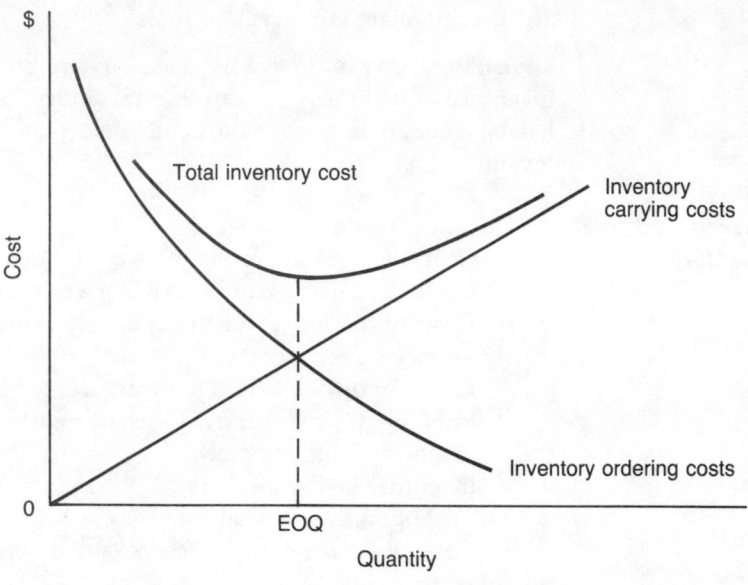

Figure 15-1
Diagram of inventory ordering and carrying costs. As the order size is increased, the total inventory ordering cost decreases and the total inventory carrying cost increases. Minimum total cost is reached at the order size for which ordering cost equals carrying cost. This order size is called the economic order quantity (EOQ).

the average amount of inventory on hand is relatively large. The total inventory cost curve, which is merely a combination of ordering and carrying cost curves, is lowest at the intersection of the ordering and carrying cost curves. Any point other than the EOQ yields a higher total inventory cost for the period.

Several methods for finding the EOQ are available. One is trial and error, which requires computing the total inventory costs at various order sizes. Eventually the EOQ can be found or closely approximated by repeating the computation enough times. Another approach is to graph the costs. In earlier chapters we noted the value of presenting relevant cost data graphically. Although both methods can be used, the first is very time-consuming and the second is difficult to use with precision.

A third approach is to calculate the optimum order size mathematically using a method called the economic order quantity (EOQ) model, which yields the optimum order quantity with a single set of calculations. The model is

The economic order quantity model

$$EOQ = \sqrt{\frac{2\,AP}{UI}}$$

where:

A = quantity of inventory required for the period
P = cost of placing one order
U = unit cost of item
I = inventory carrying costs expressed as a percentage of unit cost

The economic order quantity model is a mathematical equation that describes the relationships between ordering costs and carrying costs for inventory in reference to order size. The model rests on several important assumptions:

EOQ model assumptions

1. There is a known constant demand.
2. Ordering costs are known and remain constant.
3. Carrying costs are known and remain constant.
4. Production and inventory capacity is unlimited.

In spite of the somewhat restrictive assumptions, the model can provide managers with some useful information in planning inventory and making ordering decisions.

EOQ illustrated

To illustrate the computation of the economic order quantity, let us use the example of the Samplewood Wholesale Tire Company. The company is open Monday through Friday except for a two-week vacation period and ten holidays. The firm operates for a total of 240 business days a year. Below are demand and cost data for the most expensive steel-belted radial tire the company sells.

Average daily demand	50
Selling price	$95/tire
Cost	$60/tire
Ordering cost	$500
Carrying cost	20 percent of unit cost

It is easy to solve for the EOQ using the above data. The quantity required for the year (A) is 50 tires a day times 240 business days during the year, or 50 × 240 = 12 000 tires. The cost of placing one order (P) is $500. The carrying cost ($I$) is 20 percent or .2 of the $60 unit cost ($U$). Substituting the above values into the EOQ model, we have

$$EOQ = \sqrt{\frac{(2)(12\ 000)(\$500)}{(\$60)(.2)}}$$

$$= \sqrt{\frac{\$12,000,000}{\$12}}$$

$$= \sqrt{1,000,000}$$

$$= 1000 \text{ tires}$$

The economic order quantity—that is, the order size that minimizes the total inventory cost for this particular tire—is 1000 units. Total inventory cost for the year for this inventory item is merely the carrying cost plus the ordering cost. In this example ordering cost is $500 times the number of orders placed, and carrying cost is 20 percent times the cost of the average amount of inventory for the period. The number of orders placed during the year can be determined by dividing the EOQ into the number of units required for the period:

Inventory ordering cost

$$\text{Number of orders} = \frac{A}{EOQ}$$

$$= \frac{12\,000 \text{ units}}{1000 \text{ units per order}}$$

$$= 12 \text{ orders}$$

$$\text{Ordering cost} = \frac{A}{EOQ} \times P$$

$$= \frac{AP}{EOQ}$$

$$= \frac{(12\,000 \text{ units}) (\$500 \text{ per order})}{1000 \text{ units per order}}$$

$$= \$6,000$$

Inventory carrying cost

Carrying cost is a function of the average amount of inventory on hand multiplied by the carrying cost rate. The average inventory on hand is determined by dividing the order size by 2 and is expressed as

$$\text{Average inventory} = \frac{EOQ}{2}$$

$$= \frac{1000 \text{ units}}{2}$$

$$= 500 \text{ units}$$

$$\text{Carrying cost} = \frac{EOQ}{2} \times UI$$

$$= \frac{1000 \text{ units}}{2} \times (\$60)(.2)$$

$$= \$6,000$$

Total inventory cost for the period

As expected, at the EOQ, the cost of ordering for the period ($6,000) equals the carrying cost for the period ($6,000). By combining carrying cost and ordering cost, we can determine the total inventory cost for the period:

$$\text{Total inventory cost} = \frac{AP}{EOQ} + \frac{EOQ}{2} \times UI$$

The above equation can be generalized to find total inventory cost for any size order by substituting Q for EOQ. Q refers to any order size, not just the economic order quantity. The more general model is

$$\text{Total inventory cost} = \frac{AP}{Q} + \frac{Q}{2} \times UI$$

Substituting the values from the tire company example, we find the total inventory costs for the steel-belted radial tires at the EOQ of 1000 units.

$$\text{Total inventory cost} = \frac{(12\,000)(\$500)}{1000} + \frac{1000}{2} \times (\$60)(.2)$$

$$= \$6,000 + \$6,000$$

$$= \$12,000$$

The lowest possible inventory cost the company can achieve for this particular inventory item is $12,000. Any other order size yields a higher total inventory cost. To illustrate, Figure 15-2 shows inventory costs for several other order sizes above and below the EOQ of 1000 units. Note that each order size other than the EOQ causes a higher total inventory cost. Order sizes near the EOQ yield inventory costs near the optimum amount, illustrating the relatively flat nature of the inventory total cost curve near the EOQ point.

Cost estimation and model sensitivity   Often it is difficult to make precise estimates of the variables used in computing the economic order quantity. For instance, total demand for the year may fluctuate significantly from one year to the next, or carrying costs may be hard to measure. To determine the effect of incorrect estimates of variables used in the model, managers often compute the EOQ several times, each time substituting a new value for one of the important variables. By comparing the results of the several computations of EOQ, managers may be able to determine

Samplewood Wholesale Tire Company
Schedule of Inventory Costs at Various Order Sizes

Order size	400	600	800	1,000	1,200	1,400	1,600
Average inventory size	200	300	400	500	600	700	800
Number of inventory orders	30	20	15	12	10	8.6	7.5
Ordering cost	$15,000	$10,000	$ 7,500	$ 6,000	$ 5,000	$ 4,300	$ 3,750
Carrying cost	2,400	3,600	4,800	6,000	7,200	8,400	9,600
Total inventory cost	$17,400	$13,600	$12,300	$12,000	$12,200	$12,700	$13,350

Figure 15-2
Any inventory order size other than the EOQ yields a higher total inventory cost. However, order sizes close to the EOQ provide relatively low inventory costs, illustrating the relatively flat nature of the inventory total cost curve near the EOQ point.

how sensitive the model is to changes in the value of the model variables. For example, Samplewood is not confident about its demand estimate of 50 tires a day, but management is confident demand will be at least 40 but less than 60 tires a day. The two extremes of 40 and 60 can be substituted in the EOQ model, one at a time, to see what effect the difference in demand estimates has on the EOQ. We proceed as before:

40 tires a day.

$$A = 40 \text{ tires per day} \times 240 \text{ days} = 9600 \text{ tires}$$

$$EOQ = \sqrt{\frac{(2)(14\ 400)(\$500)}{(\$60)(.2)}}$$

$$= \sqrt{\frac{\$9,600,000}{\$12}}$$

$$= \sqrt{800,000}$$

$$= 894.4 \text{ tires}$$

60 tires a day.

$$A = 60 \text{ tires per day} \times 240 \text{ days} = 14\ 400 \text{ tires}$$

$$EOQ = \sqrt{\frac{(2)(14\ 400)(\$500)}{(\$60)(.2)}}$$

$$= \sqrt{\frac{\$14,400,000}{\$12}}$$

$$= \sqrt{1,200,000}$$

$$= 1095.4 \text{ tires}$$

These computations give management some information about what effect its demand estimate has on the optimum order size. But what impact do differing demand estimates have on inventory cost? Since the optimum order quantity is computed using estimates of demand, unit cost, ordering cost, and carrying cost, if any of the estimates are wrong the EOQ will be incorrect. If the incorrect EOQ is used for inventory decisions, the total inventory cost will be greater than if the correct EOQ had been calculated and used in managing inventory. To illustrate, suppose the actual demand for tires is 40 a day rather than 50. The optimum order size with demand of 40 tires a day is 894, which yields a total inventory cost of $10,733:

$$\text{Total inventory cost} = \frac{AP}{Q} + \frac{Q}{2} \times UI$$

$$\text{Total inventory cost} = \frac{(9600)(\$500)}{894.4} + \frac{894.4}{2} \times (\$60)(.2)$$

$$= \$5,366.7 + \$5,366.4$$

$$= \$10,733$$

If managers use the order quantity of 1000, which is the EOQ based on a demand estimate of 50 tires per day, when actual demand is 40 tires per day, the total inventory cost is $10,800:

$$\text{Total inventory cost} = \frac{(9600)(\$500)}{1000} + \frac{1000}{2} \times (\$60)(.2)$$

$$= \$4,800 + \$6,000$$

$$= \$10,800$$

The cost of estimation error

The difference between the total inventory cost using the correct EOQ—$10,733—and the total inventory cost using the incorrect order quantity—$10,800—is $67, which is the cost of incorrectly estimating the demand. The difference in inventory cost of $67 is the result of not placing the optimum size orders, which occurred because demand was incorrectly estimated.

The sensitivity of other variables can be tested as well. Assume that the carrying cost for our example is expected to be 20 percent with a possible range of 16 to 24 percent. What effect would these different carrying costs have on the EOQ? Again we substitute each of these two values in the EOQ model, leaving the other values in the model unchanged.

16 percent carrying cost.

$$EOQ = \sqrt{\frac{(2)(12\,000)(\$500)}{(\$60)(.16)}}$$

$$= \sqrt{\frac{\$1,200,000}{\$9.6}}$$

$$= \sqrt{1,250,000}$$

$$= 1118 \text{ units}$$

24 percent carrying cost.

$$EOQ = \sqrt{\frac{(2)(12\,000)(\$500)}{(\$60)(.24)}}$$

$$= \sqrt{\frac{\$12,000,000}{\$14.4}}$$

$$= \sqrt{833,333}$$

$$= 912.9$$

As before, we can determine the cost of incorrectly estimating the value of one of the variables in the economic order quantity equation. For instance, suppose the actual inventory carrying cost is 24 percent rather than the original estimate of 20 percent. Let us determine the effect on inventory cost of using the original estimate of a 20 percent inventory carrying cost if the actual carrying cost is 24 percent. The EOQ is 912.9 if carrying cost is 24 percent. The total inventory cost using this optimum order size is

$$\text{Total inventory cost} = \frac{AP}{Q} + \frac{Q}{2} \times UI$$

$$= \frac{(12\ 000)\ (\$500)}{912.9} + \frac{912.9}{2} \times (\$60)(.24)$$

$$= \$6,572.5 + \$6,572.9$$

$$= \$13,145$$

The EOQ of 1000 was calculated with the incorrect carrying cost estimate of 20 percent. The total inventory cost using the EOQ of 1000 and the actual carrying cost of 24 percent is computed as follows:

$$\text{Total inventory cost} = \frac{(12\ 000)(\$500)}{1000} + \frac{1000}{2} \times (\$60)(.24)$$

$$= \$6,000 + \$7,200$$

$$= \$13,200$$

The difference in total inventory cost of $55 ($13,200 − $13,145) represents the additional amount of total inventory cost caused by using a nonoptimum inventory order quantity, which resulted from not estimating inventory carrying costs correctly. If management had known carrying cost was 24 percent, the quantity ordered would have been 913 units each time an order was placed. However, the original estimates of 20 percent produced an EOQ of 1000, which is larger than the optimum order of 913, causing a $55-per-year higher total inventory cost for this particular inventory item.

In both situations just illustrated the model was not very sensitive to estimation errors. In the first case estimated daily tire sales were 25 percent [(50 tires − 40 tires)/40 tires] higher than actual sales. However, the total inventory cost, using an EOQ based on the incorrect demand estimate, is only .6 percent [($10,800 − $10,733)/$10,733] higher than the optimum total inventory cost. Similarly, the estimated carrying cost was 16.7 percent [(24 percent − 20 percent)/24 percent] lower than actual carrying cost. The resulting total inventory cost, using an EOQ based on the incorrect carrying cost, is only .4 percent [($13,200 − $13,145)/$13,145] more than the optimum total inventory cost.

When model sensitivity is very low, as in these two illustrations, managers cannot justify spending significant amounts of time and money refining estimates of demand and carrying cost. If the EOQ model is sensitive to estimation errors, however, such errors can cause significant unanticipated costs. In such cases, managers generally try to avoid excessive inventory costs by making more accurate estimates of the value of variables used in the EOQ model.

If the cost of estimation error is large, managers will devote time and resources to improving estimates

EOQ and not-for-profit organizations

In the Samplewood example the selling price of the tire was given, but it was not used in the computation of EOQ. It is an irrelevant bit of data for EOQ analysis. Its primary reason for inclusion is to distinguish between purchase price (cost) and selling price. Economic order quantity computations rest on

EOQ analysis rests solely on costs and quantities and therefore is applicable to not-for-profit organizations

cost and quantity data only. Consequently, EOQ analysis is applicable to all types of organizations interested in optimizing resources invested in inventory. For example, a municipal government uses a centralized purchasing and inventory system. Supplies for all city facilities are handled through this centralized system. One supply item is paper towels for use in all city buildings and public restrooms. The following data pertain to this inventory item:

Annual use	1800 cases
Purchase price	$20 case
Ordering cost	$90/order
Carrying cost	18% of purchase price

Solving for the optimum order size yields 300 cases as follows:

$$EOQ = \sqrt{\frac{2\,AP}{UI}}$$

$$= \sqrt{\frac{(2)(1800)(\$90)}{(\$20)(.18)}}$$

$$= \sqrt{90{,}000}$$

$$= 300 \text{ cases}$$

The municipal government can minimize its inventory cost for paper towels by placing six orders a year (1800/300 = 6), each for 300 cases.

The reorder point

The inventory level at which a new order is placed is called the reorder point

The economic order quantity is the optimum order size for a particular item of inventory, but the EOQ does not provide a manager with information about when the order should be placed. If a firm has the ability to buy and receive inventory items instantly, the reorder point is zero; that is, a new order is placed when there are no more units left in inventory. In such a case, inventory purchases and use would appear as shown in Figure 15-3 for the tire dealer. As soon as the company runs out of inventory, it orders the EOQ of 1000 units and receives instant delivery. The quantity of inventory on hand increases to 1000 units and declines at the rate of 50 tires per day until zero is again reached. Then the cycle begins anew.

Lead time and lead time demand

Unfortunately, few firms are able to get instant deliveries on orders. Some time is required between the time the order is placed and the time inventory is received. This time period is called **lead time** and is sometimes abbreviated LT. If the lead time is known and daily demand is known, the reorder point is easy to find. The Samplewood Wholesale Tire Company example has a lead time for tire orders of eight days. The daily demand is 50 tires. The **demand during lead time,** or **lead time demand,** is 8 × 50 = 400 tires. If Samplewood plans to receive a new tire shipment just as the inventory reaches zero, it

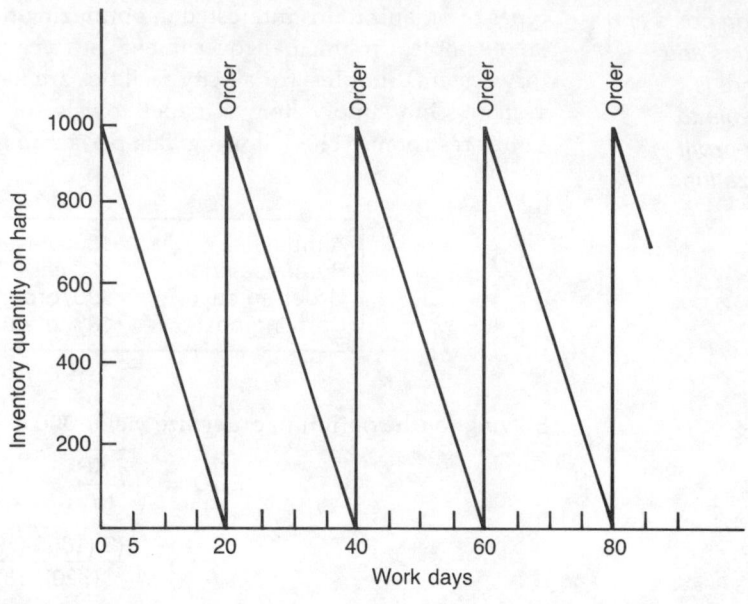

Figure 15-3
An order is placed when the inventory quantity reaches zero. The quantity on hand then increases to 1000, the EOQ. Then the quantity declines at the rate of 50 units a day until 20 days later when the inventory quantity has again reached zero. A new order is placed and the cycle begins again.

should place an order when the inventory level reaches 400 tires. The inventory flow and timing of inventory orders is shown graphically in Figure 15-4. A new order is placed at an inventory level of 400 tires, eight days before inventory reaches zero.

Inventory under uncertainty

Although the above discussion does include lead time and lead time demand in the analysis of reorder point, it still assumes a known constant demand and lead time. Often one or both of these fluctuate and are not known. Demand in particular is difficult to predict, since it often fluctuates from day to day. Also, delivery on inventory is affected by the supplier's inventory levels and operating efficiency, as well as by variations in delivery schedules of shippers and common carriers. When there is uncertainty about lead time and demand, the analysis of the inventory reorder point is complicated. A firm must consider *Stockouts* the possibility of running out of inventory, a situation known as a **stockout.** Typically stockouts have a cost. With merchandise inventory or finished goods inventory, **stockout costs** are likely to be lost profit on potential sales, customer ill will, or the loss of customers altogether. Raw material inventory stockouts

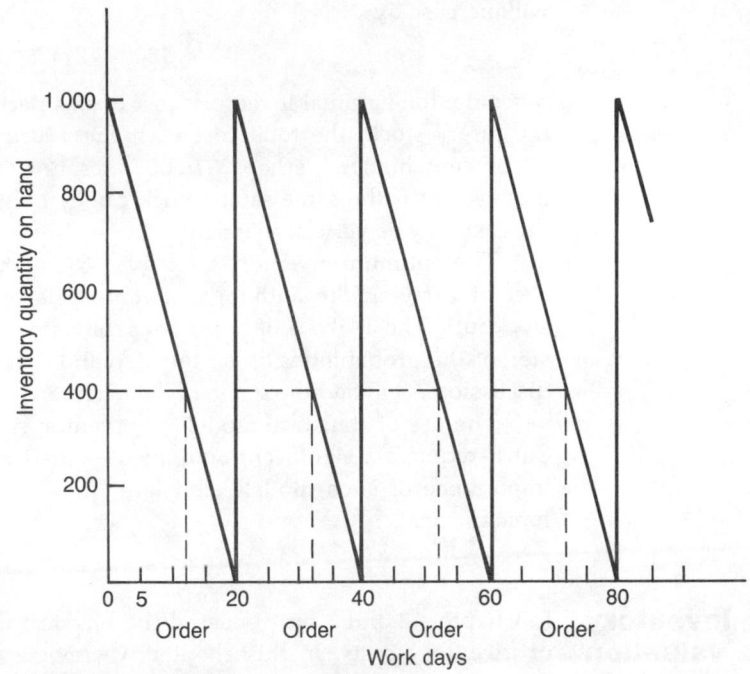

Figure 15-4
With daily demand of 50 tires and lead time of eight days, a new order must
be placed when the inventory level reaches 400 tires, eight days before
stockout.

may cause expensive new start-up costs, production inefficiencies, a switch to
more expensive raw materials, or penalty costs for late delivery of contracted
goods. Often it is difficult to estimate stockout costs. For instance, how does a
firm know exactly how many sales were lost rather than postponed because of
a stockout? Stockouts are very real costs even if they are hard to measure.

Uncertainty about lead time and demand may cause a firm to carry safety stock

   In an effort to avoid stockout costs, firms sometimes carry a **safety stock,**
which is an additional amount of inventory above what is needed for average
demand. Safety stock is a cushion that management uses to avoid an interruption of normal activities due to stockouts. Sometimes managers establish the
amount of safety stock arbitrarily. For instance, Samplewood may establish a
safety stock of 100 tires to guard against heavy demand or late deliveries of
orders. The firm places its order when the inventory level reaches 500 tires,
which is the average demand of 50 tires × 8 days' lead time plus the safety
stock of 100 tires.

The cost of carrying safety stock

   The establishment of arbitrary safety stocks can be a very costly proposition. We have already discussed the importance of carrying costs in computing

the EOQ. If a safety stock of 100 tires is established, the annual carrying cost will increase by

$$100 \times \$60 \times .2 = \$1,200$$

Since the total annual inventory cost of this particular item is $12,000 without the safety stock, the total cost with the 100-unit safety stock is $13,200 or 10 percent higher. Perhaps $1,200 does not sound like a large amount of money, but if the same safety stock policy is used for all items in inventory, the cost may be very large indeed.

The optimum inventory strategy is to increase safety stock as long as the cost of carrying the additional inventory is less than the expected cost of stockouts. The analysis of optimum safety stocks requires an in-depth discussion of the probabilities of various demand and lead time occurrences. Such a discussion is beyond the scope of this chapter.

The use of statistical models in inventory management is very important, but it requires a significant amount of statistical expertise. Note for now the importance of such models, and later in your studies you may pursue this topic further.

Inventory valuation

In Chapters 2 and 3 we discussed the physical flow of inventory and the flow of inventory costs. In this chapter we review those cost and physical flow concepts and discuss specifically the various inventory valuation methods. These methods are covered in the financial accounting text, but they are reviewed here because inventory valuation has a direct effect on many costing activities.

Physical flow of inventory

Accountants are primarily interested in inventory cost flows rather than in the physical flow of inventory

The physical flow of business inventories may occur in a variety of ways. Some businesses find it necessary to rotate their stock of inventory so that fresh goods are always available. For example, in a paint store, the oldest cans of paint are placed at the front of the shelves so that they will sell first, preventing inventory from spoiling or deteriorating with age. The usual rule for moving inventory is first in, first out. Some inventories, however, follow a last-in, first-out pattern. For example, if coal is stored in a pile, the inventory removed from the pile is the latest inventory purchased, because coal obtained earlier is at the bottom of the pile.

Cost flow assumptions

The physical movement of inventory is not of particular importance to the accountant in most cases. The flow of inventory **costs,** however, is of some considerable concern. Inventory cost flows affect the value of ending inventories and the amount charged to cost of goods sold. Consequently, both the balance sheet and the income statement are affected directly by inventory cost flows.

Accounting for inventory cost flows is relatively simple if the costs of raw materials and merchandise inventories do not fluctuate and the cost of producing finished goods inventory does not vary. However, it is common for inventory costs to vary, sometimes significantly. The accountant must decide which costs should be assigned to ending inventory and which should be charged to production or cost of goods sold. A number of costing alternatives can be used.

Inventory cost flow assumptions

It is possible to assign the most recent costs to the inventory on hand on the assumption that **first in, first out (FIFO)** is the appropriate flow of costs. On the other hand, it is also possible to assign the most recent costs to cost of goods sold. In that case a **last-in, first-out (LIFO)** flow of inventory costs occurs in the business. It is, of course, also possible to make other assumptions about cost flows, for example, using **average costs.** There is no need for the cost flow to follow the physical movement of inventory. Whether the accountant uses FIFO, LIFO, or an average cost depends only on the assumption about the cost flows and the best way to satisfy the matching concept.

Valuation of periodic inventories

In a periodic inventory system, which is used often by merchandising firms but seldom by manufacturing firms, purchases and sales of inventory are not recorded in the merchandise inventory account. Instead, all inventory acquisitions are recorded in a purchases account. When merchandise is sold only the sales revenue is recorded. Cost of goods sold is calculated only at the end of the accounting period, when financial statements are prepared.

In a merchandising firm the beginning inventory balance and the purchases account balance together represent the cost of goods available for sale. To calculate the cost of goods sold a physical count must be made of merchandise remaining on hand. Next the ending inventory must be valued by assigning to each unit a cost based on some cost flow assumption such as FIFO, LIFO, or weighted average. When the value of ending inventory is deducted from the cost of goods available for sale, the remainder is the cost of goods sold.

Periodic inventory valuation illustrated

To illustrate the effects of various inventory valuation methods we use the example of Boltek Corporation's inventory for the month of July. The beginning balance consists of eighteen units that cost $10 per unit. During July the company purchased 32 additional units as follows:

July 1 beginning balance	18 units @ $10.00	$180.00
July 11 purchased	10 units @ 10.50	105.00
July 25 purchased	12 units @ 11.00	132.00
July 30 purchased	10 units @ 12.00	120.00
Total goods available	50 units	$537.00

From the 50 units available for sale during the month, the company sold 30 units, leaving an ending inventory of 20 units on hand on July 31. Sales occurred as follows:

July 3 sale	8 units
July 17 sale	5 units
July 28 sale	17 units
Total sales	30 units

In order to prepare financial statements, Boltek Corporation must assign a value to the 20 units in ending inventory. The value depends on the inventory method used by the company and on the cost flow assumption adopted. We first consider valuation of periodic inventories. Perpetual inventory systems are covered later in this chapter.

First in, first out (FIFO) FIFO is logically appealing as a costing technique because it follows the actual physical movement of many kinds of goods. With a beginning inventory of $180 and total purchases of $357 during July, total cost of goods available for sale is $537. The physical count of inventory reveals 20 units remaining on hand. With FIFO valuation we assume that these 20 units consist of the **latest** units acquired. The ending inventory is

10 units from the July 30 purchase @ $12.00	$120.00
10 units from the July 25 purchase @ 11.00	110.00
20 units	$230.00

Cost of goods sold is $307 calculated as

Goods available for sale	$537
Less ending inventory	230
Cost of goods sold	$307

Last in, first out (LIFO) With LIFO inventory valuation in a periodic system, the 20 units remaining on hand are assumed to be the **earliest** units acquired. They consist of the beginning balance and part of the first units acquired in the current month, computed as follows:

18 units from the beginning balance @ $10.00	$180.00
2 units from the July 11 purchase @ 10.50	21.00
20 units	$201.00

Cost of goods sold is $336 in this case.

Goods available for sale	$537
Less ending inventory	201
Cost of goods sold	$336

Weighted average

The weighted average cost of the inventory available in July is obtained by dividing the total cost of inventory, including the beginning balance and July purchases, by the total units available for sale. In the example above, the calculation is

$$\frac{\text{Cost of goods available for sale}}{\text{No. of units available for sale}} = \frac{\$537}{50 \text{ units}} = \$10.74/\text{unit}$$

The cost of ending inventory is obtained by assigning the average cost of $10.74 to each unit in ending inventory. With 20 units remaining on hand, the ending inventory is valued at $214.80 (20 × $10.74). Note that the average cost of ending inventory and of cost of goods sold falls between FIFO and LIFO costs. Cost of goods sold in this case is $322.20.

Valuation of perpetual inventories

A perpetual inventory system is essential to timely cost accounting information in manufacturing businesses

In a perpetual inventory system, the inventory account contains a current record of all inventory transactions. Such a system is particularly useful in a manufacturing firm where current production cost data are vital. A perpetual inventory system allows the firm to charge inventory costs to production as soon as the inventory is used. Each acquisition of raw materials and each transfer to work in process is recorded in the inventory account as the transactions occur. The inventory account is current, hence the name perpetual.

As in a periodic system, purchases in a perpetual system are recorded at their invoice cost. When raw materials inventory is put into production, its cost is transferred from the raw materials inventory account to the work in process account. If the cost of raw materials is changing over time, some cost flow assumption must be made. Perpetual systems may be maintained using FIFO, LIFO, moving average, or specific identification. The examples that follow deal with merchandise inventory, but the discussion applies equally well to transfers of raw materials to WIP and to transfers of WIP to finished goods.

Specific identification

The specific identification method of inventory valuation requires an ability to follow the physical flow of each inventory item and its cost from acquisition through use or sale. The method is appropriate when each item of inventory can be separately identified and therefore has a cost that applies only to that item. Specific identification is used with unique and costly items, such as jewelry or custom-made products.

Boltek Corporation
FIFO Perpetual Inventory Record

Date	Explanation	Purchases No. of Units	Unit Cost	Total Cost	Sales No. of Units	Unit Cost	Total Cost	Balance No. of Units	Total Cost
July 1	Balance							18	$180.00
3	Sold 8 units				8	$10.00	$ 80.00	10	100.00
11	Bought 10 units	10	10.50	105.00				20	205.00
17	Sold 5 units				5	10.00	50.00	15	155.00
25	Bought 12 units	12	11.00	132.00				27	287.00
28	Sold 17 units				5	10.00	50.00		
					10	10.50	105.00		
					2	11.00	22.00	10	110.00
30	Bought 10 units	10	12.00	120.00				20	230.00

Figure 15-5
The FIFO cost flow closely approximates the physical flow of many inventory items. In a perpetual system each inflow and outflow of inventory is recorded at the time of the transfer.

First in, first out (FIFO)

Perpetual inventory valuation illustrated

The flow of costs with perpetual FIFO is illustrated in Figure 15-5. Notice that the units remaining in inventory are always assumed to be those purchased most recently. Thus after the July 17 sale of five units, the 15 units remaining on hand consist of the most recent 10 units acquired on July 11, and five units from the beginning balance. Similarly, the sale of 17 units on July 28 first exhausts five units from the beginning balance, then 10 units acquired next on July 11 and finally two units purchased most recently on July 25.

If you compare the ending inventory at FIFO for the perpetual system with the previous calculation for the periodic system, you will note that the two are the same. With FIFO valuation, periodic and perpetual systems both give the same ending inventory cost.

Last in, first out (LIFO)

With a perpetual LIFO system, when a sale takes place the cost of the latest acquisition is transferred from inventory to cost of goods sold. Figure 15-6 illustrates how perpetual LIFO is maintained. The first sale of eight units reduces the initial balance to 10 units, but subsequent sales all consist of the units purchased most recently. Therefore the sale of 17 units on July 28 consists of the 12 units obtained on July 25 plus five units obtained on July 11. Of the original 18 units, 10 units at a cost of $10 each still remain in inventory at the end of the period.

Notice the difference in ending inventory under the perpetual and periodic systems when LIFO valuation is used. The cost of ending inventory with the periodic system is $201. With the perpetual system the cost is $220 because some of the units on hand are valued at the most recent purchase costs. Perpetual LIFO and periodic LIFO often produce different inventory valuations.

Moving average

To maintain a perpetual inventory system using average costs, it is necessary to calculate the average cost for the units on hand each time an acquisition occurs. This moving average is calculated by computing a new weighted average of the units on hand after each acquisition. The procedure is illustrated in Figure 15-7. For example, the average cost of the units on hand after the July 11 purchase included 10 units at $10 each and 10 units at $10.50 each. The average cost is $10.25, calculated by dividing the total cost of $205 by 20 units.

The units removed from inventory are valued at average cost. With costs increasing over time, the moving average cost also increases, but it always lags somewhat behind the current cost of inventory. As usual, the average cost valuation falls somewhere between FIFO and LIFO valuation.

Summary and comparison of inventory valuation methods

The six inventory values obtained in the previous examples are summarized in Figure 15-8. Assuming total sales of $500, gross margin varies from $164 to $193, depending on the inventory system and the cost flow assumption applied in valuing the ending inventory.

It is clear that the selection of an inventory valuation method has a strong effect on product costs and the determination of net income. If managers could

Boltek Corporation
LIFO Perpetual Inventory Record

Date	Explanation	Purchases			Sales			Balance	
		No. of Units	Unit Cost	Total Cost	No. of Units	Unit Cost	Total Cost	No. of Units	Total Cost
July 1	Balance	18	$10.00	$180.00				18	$180.00
3	Sold 8 units				8	$10.00	$ 80.00	10	100.00
11	Bought 10 units	10	10.50	105.00				20	205.00
17	Sold 5 units				5	10.50	52.50	15	152.50
25	Bought 12 units	12	11.00	132.00				27	284.50
28	Sold 17 units				12	11.00	132.00	10	100.00
					5	10.50	52.50		
30	Bought 10 units	10	12.00	120.00				20	220.00

Figure 15-6
The primary advantage of LIFO is that current costs are matched with current revenues. Consequently, LIFO, if permitted by the tax authorities, has definite tax advantages during periods of rising prices.

Boltek Corporation
Moving Average Perpetual Inventory Record

Date	Explanation	Purchases			Sales			Balance		
		No. of Units	Unit Cost	Total Cost	No. of Units	Unit Cost	Total Cost	No. of Units	Unit Cost	Total Cost
July 1	Balance							18	$10.00	$180.00
3	Sold 8 units				8	$10.00	$ 80.00	10	10.00	100.00
11	Bought 10 units	10	10.50	105.00				20	10.25	205.00
17	Sold 5 units				5	10.25	51.25	15	10.25	153.75
25	Bought 12 units	12	11.00	132.00				27	10.5833	285.75
28	Sold 17 units				17	10.5833	179.92	10	10.5833	105.83
30	Bought 10 units	10	12.00	120.00				20	11.2915	225.83

Calculation of average costs:
July 11, $205.00/20 units = $10.25 per unit
July 25, $285.75/27 units = $10.5833 per unit
July 30, $225.83/20 units = $11.2915 per unit

Figure 15-7
The moving average inventory costs are between FIFO and LIFO costs. In a
perpetual system a new average cost is computed every time more units are
added to the inventory. Units transferred out of inventory are costed at the
most recently computed average cost.

Boltek Corporation Gross Margin Calculations			
Perpetual Inventory Systems			
	FIFO	Moving Average	LIFO
Sales	$500.00	$500.00	$500.00
Less cost of goods sold	307.00	311.17	317.00
Gross margin	$193.00	$188.83	$183.00
Ending inventory	$230.00	$225.83	$220.00

Perpetual Inventory Systems			
	FIFO	Weighted Average	LIFO
Sales	$500.00	$500.00	$500.00
Beginning inventory	180.00	180.00	180.00
Purchases	357.00	357.00	357.00
Goods available for sale	$537.00	$537.00	$537.00
Less ending inventory	230.00	214.80	201.00
Cost of goods sold	$307.00	$322.20	$336.00
Gross margin	$193.00	$177.80	$164.00

Figure 15-8
Of the three inventory valuation systems, only FIFO always yields the same inventory cost using either a perpetual or periodic inventory system. Can you explain the differences in inventory costs between perpetual and periodic inventory for LIFO and average inventory?

The selection of an inventory valuation method may have a significant effect on the determination of net income

select an inventory method at will and change methods whenever they wished, they could easily manipulate reported income, but the **consistency** principle prevents such manipulation. You should be aware of the strengths and weaknesses of each of the inventory valuation methods.

Specific identification. The advantage of specific identification is that it provides good matching of product costs and revenues. The disadvantage is the possibility of income manipulation. Managers may choose the amount of gross profit by deciding which item to deliver when merchandise is sold. Moreover, the method does not lend itself to many different types of inventories, and is generally limited to businesses that deal in expensive, or unique items.

First in, first out. By far the most popular method, FIFO has the advantage of being easy to apply. It tends to conform to the physical movement of inventory and results in reporting inventories on the balance sheet at a cost that is close to the current purchase price. During periods of rising prices the net income reported is higher than with other valuation methods.

FIFO valuation has several disadvantages. When prices are rising, the higher net income results in a higher income tax expense. Current revenues tend to be matched with old costs, implying that the company is able to earn a higher profit than is actually possible with current costs. To replace the

Inventory profits

inventory used or sold, the business must pay the latest prices. The higher profits reported by matching current revenues with older costs are known as **inventory profits.** During periods of rising prices, inventory profits make a company appear more profitable than is actually the case.

Last in, first out. The most important advantage of LIFO, if permitted, is the lower tax expense incurred during periods of rising prices. Net income tends to be stated more nearly in current terms, since revenues are matched with current rather than old product costs. The lower tax expense results in improved cash flows. However, current Canadian tax laws do not permit LIFO.

LIFO has some serious disadvantages. If it is used for a number of years, balance sheet inventory values tend to become grossly understated, since inventories are reported at costs that existed several years ago. If the company has to reduce its inventory below the amount normally on hand, product costs calculated with old values appear abnormally low. In that case, high profits result from the artificially low product costs.

During periods of rising prices, net income tends to be lower with LIFO. Although this results in a tax advantage, reduced earnings per share tend to be viewed unfavourably. In the United States where LIFO is permitted, the tax authorities require that companies choosing LIFO for tax purposes must also use it for reporting purposes. A company has no choice but to report the lower income if it wants the tax savings offered by LIFO.*

Average cost methods. Inventory valuation at average cost is one of the least popular methods. It seems to have all the disadvantages of LIFO and FIFO, and few advantages. Neither net income nor ending inventories is shown at current values.

Summary

Inventory is a major asset in many merchandising and manufacturing firms. Like other important assets, inventory must be monitored and controlled to ensure that the best use is made of the resources invested in inventory. Inventory analysis requires the use of relevant inventory costs: inventory ordering costs, carrying costs, and shortage costs. In addition, the costs of inventory must be determined by one of several cost flow assumption methods: FIFO, LIFO, or average cost.

The **economic order quantity (EOQ)** is the inventory order size that results in the lowest total inventory cost for the period. It is achieved at the point where the inventory ordering cost equals the inventory carrying cost. Trial-and-error computations and graphic techniques may be used to find the EOQ, but the most precise and efficient method is to use the EOQ model. The model is an inventory cost minimization technique that is equally applicable to businesses and not-for-profit organizations.

*For a detailed discussion see Matulich, Heitger, and Var, *Financial Accounting, First Canadian Edition,* McGraw-Hill Ryerson, 1982.

Estimation of model variables may be difficult. If a range of values is more realistic for some variable, the extreme values may be substituted into the model to find their impact on the EOQ. The cost of incorrect estimates can be computed and various sensitivity measures can be made by managers.

In addition to knowing how much to order, managers must know when to order. The **reorder point** is the inventory level at which management places a new order. Most firms must place an order before inventory reaches zero. The time between placing an order and its delivery is called **lead time.** The amount of units demanded (used) during lead time is called **lead time demand.** If demand and lead time are known, the order is placed when the inventory level equals lead time demand.

Often demand and lead time are not known and the determination of the reorder point is more difficult. With uncertainty there is the possibility of a **stockout,** or running out of inventory, which typically results in a **stockout cost.** To avoid stockout costs, firms maintain additional quantities of inventory called **safety stocks.** However, safety stocks add carrying costs to the total inventory cost. The optimum reorder point equates the cost of carrying safety stock with the expected stockout cost. A sophisticated analysis of the inventory reorder point problem requires the use of probabilities and statistical inference.

The valuation of inventories and calculation of the cost of goods sold depends on the cost flow assumption used in measuring inventory costs. **First-in, first-out (FIFO)** valuation assumes that the ending inventory consists of the goods acquired most recently. **Last-in, first-out (LIFO)** valuation assumes that the goods acquired most recently are the first goods used or sold, and the ending inventory is therefore valued at the earliest cost. It is also possible to adopt an **average** cost flow assumption, or to value inventories on a **specific identification basis.**

FIFO valuation produces the same results, whether perpetual or periodic inventory systems are used. With LIFO valuation, there can be a difference in value with different inventory systems. During periods of rising prices LIFO results in a close match between costs and revenues and produces a lower gross margin than FIFO. On the other hand, balance sheet valuation of inventory is usually out of date. FIFO produces balance sheet valuations that are close to current costs, but the method may not produce a good match between current costs and current revenues on the income statement and results in the reporting of **inventory profits.**

Questions

1. Why is inventory planning and control important?
2. Describe briefly the three types of inventory costs associated with economic order quantity and reorder point computations.
3. What is the economic order quantity and how is it computed?
4. Define inventory carrying cost, inventory ordering cost, total inventory cost, and average inventory size.
5. Discuss the limitations and assumptions of the EOQ model.
6. "Hey, we're running a city government here, not a business. We're not trying to make a profit, so forget this inventory management stuff." Reply.
7. What is meant by a reorder point? What factors affect the inventory reorder point?
8. How does uncertainty affect inventory management?
9. Discuss the relationship between inventory physical flow and cost flow, and relate them to the accounting function.
10. Describe perpetual inventory and periodic inventory.
11. Do FIFO perpetual and FIFO periodic always yield the same inventory valuation? Do LIFO perpetual and LIFO periodic always yield the same inventory valuation?
12. Distinguish between weighted average and moving average methods of inventory valuation.
13. Compare the effect of LIFO and FIFO inventory valuation on the income statement and balance sheet in periods of rising and falling prices.

Exercises

Ex. 15-1 **Economic order quantity.** Hoopston Baby Products sells a complete line of baby supplies and equipment including a quality national brand buggy-stroller. The normal demand for the product is 3000 units a year. The company pays $60 each for the buggy-strollers and carrying cost is estimated at 20 percent of unit cost per year. Ordering cost is $125 per order.

Required:
a. Compute the economic order quantity for the buggy-stroller.
b. Determine how many orders will be placed a year.

Ex. 15-2 **Economic order quantity.** Langley Manufacturing Company provides the following data for one of its raw materials.

Annual use	100 000 litres
Purchase price	$5 / litre
Ordering cost	$100
Carrying cost	25% of purchase price

Required:

a. Compute the economic order quantity.

b. Determine how many orders a year Langley should place.

Ex. 15-3 **Economic order quantity and inventory cost.** Below are cost and demand data for a china hutch sold by a large eastern furniture wholesaler:

Demand in units	800
Unit cost	$500
Carrying cost as a percentage of unit cost	25%
Cost of placing an order	$125

Required:

a. Compute the economic order quantity.

b. Determine how many orders will be placed during the year.

c. Find the minimum total cost of ordering and carrying inventory.

Ex. 15-4 **EOQ and ordering costs.** Folsom River Products is contemplating the use of economic order quantity analysis to optimize inventory ordering activities and minimize inventory cost. Below are data for three products the company sells:

	Product		
	RS2	**PM3**	**SNZ**
Annual demand in units	24 500	16 000	5000
Cost per unit	$50	$20	$10
Cost to place an order	$100	$60	$40
Carrying cost as a percent of product cost	20%	15%	16%

Required:

a. Compute the EOQ for each product.

b. Determine the number of orders placed annually for each of the products.

c. Compute the total annual inventory ordering costs for the three products combined.

Ex. 15-5 **EOQ and sensitivity analysis.** The Lake City School System purchases school supplies for the entire school system and distributes them from a central supply facility. Each year 10 000 packs of construction paper are used. The paper costs $2 a pack. Ordering costs are $22.50 and carrying costs are estimated at 10 percent of purchase price.

Required:

a. Compute the economic order quantity for construction paper.
b. If actual use for the year increased to 12 000 packs, find the cost of incorrectly estimating demand.
c. If paper use is actually 10 000 packs but the price of construction paper averages $2.50 a pack, determine the cost of incorrectly estimating the purchase price.

Ex. 15-6 **Cost of estimation error.** The Blusky Swimming Pool Company manufactures above-ground swimming pools of various sizes. Several large-model pools require XM42Z filter pumps, which the company buys from a supplier for $100 each. Estimated annual use of the pumps is 4000 units and carrying cost is estimated at 16 percent of unit cost. Ordering cost is $80 per order. Using the above estimates, the EOQ for the pumps is computed as 200 units. During the year extremely strong demand for large swimming pools pushed the need for the pumps to 6250 units.

Required:
Compute the cost of incorrectly estimating demand.

Ex. 15-7 **Cost of estimation error.** The Blusky Swimming Pool Company manufactures above-ground swimming pools of various sizes. Several large-model pools require XM42Z filter pumps, which the company buys from a supplier for $100 each. Estimated annual use of the pumps is 4000 units and carrying cost is estimated at 16 percent of unit cost. Ordering cost is $80 per order. Using the above estimates, the EOQ for the pumps is computed as 200 units. A shortage of filter pumps and rising production costs caused the unit cost of pumps to be $125 instead of the estimate of $100.

Required:
Calculate the cost of incorrectly estimating the cost of the pumps.

Ex. 15-8 **Periodic inventory system.** The Monroe Canning Company has developed the following data for one of its raw material items:

Purchases			Use	
Date	**Quantity**	**Price**	**Date**	**Quantity**
4/11	400	$50	5/11	300
12/11	300	52	13/11	100
19/11	800	54	21/11	500
28/11	500	55	29/11	300

Required:

If Monroe uses a periodic inventory system, determine the cost of ending inventory for this raw material item using

a. FIFO
b. LIFO
c. Weighted average

Ex. 15-9   Inventory valuation. Brackington Supply House is a wholesaler dealing in small appliances. Below are October purchase and sales data for 900-W hand-held hair dryers, one of Brackington's biggest sales items:

Purchases			Sales		
Date	Quantity	Purchase Price	Date	Quantity	Selling Price
2/10	1000	$ 9	5/10	500	$20
9/10	800	10	11/10	600	20
24/10	1200	11	21/10	500	21
			28/10	800	21

Required:

Compute the cost of goods sold and cost of ending inventory for October using both FIFO perpetual and LIFO perpetual inventory methods.

Ex. 15-10   Periodic FIFO, LIFO, and average. The beginning inventory balance of a certain item on February 1 and the purchases of this item during February were as follows:

Feb. 1	Beginning inventory	45 units @ $ .90	$ 40.50
Feb. 4	Purchase	60 units @ .95	$ 57.00
Feb. 11	Purchase	25 units @ 1.00	$ 25.00
Feb. 17	Purchase	100 units @ 1.01	$101.00
Feb. 25	Purchase	50 units @ 1.04	$ 52.00
	Totals	280 units	$275.50

The company uses a periodic inventory system. On February 28 ending inventory consisted of 125 units.

Required:

Determine ending inventory and cost of goods sold using

a. FIFO inventory valuation.
b. LIFO inventory valuation.
c. Weighted average inventory valuation.

Ex. 15-11   **Valuation of perpetual inventory.** The inventory account for 2-L cans of indoor house paint showed the following at the end of July:

		Cans	Cost Per Can
July 1	Beginning inventory	70	$2.00
July 10	Purchase	50	$2.05
July 12	Sale	100	
July 19	Purchase	90	$2.15
July 27	Sale	50	

Required:
Assuming a perpetual inventory system, determine the cost of goods sold and the cost of ending inventory using

a. FIFO
b. LIFO

Problem Set A

P. 15A-1   **Economic order quantity.** The Blufton Union Hardware Store currently uses seat-of-the-pants inventory management methods, but management is interested in using more quantitative inventory management methods. First the management of Blufton Union Hardware plans to compute the economic order quantity for each major product. Below are data for galvanized nails.

Quantity sold each year	100 kegs
Cost	$40/keg
Ordering cost	$25
Carrying cost	20% of cost

Required:
a. Compute the EOQ for galvanized nails.
b. If demand for nails doubled to 200 kegs annually, find the effect on the EOQ.

P. 15A-2 **Inventory analysis.** The Florida Outdoor Marina sells 10 000 cases of outboard motor oil a year. Oil costs $12 a case, inventory carrying costs are 10 percent of oil cost, and inventory ordering costs are $60 per order. Average lead time for orders is 10 days and average daily demand is 27 cases.

Required:
a. Compute the EOQ for outboard motor oil.
b. Determine the total inventory cost at the EOQ.
c. Determine the expected lead time demand.
d. If the marina wants a safety stock of five days' demand, determine the reorder point for outboard motor oil.
e. Compute the cost of providing the safety stock.
f. Compute total inventory cost with the safety stock.

P. 15A-3 **Inventory analysis for a public sector organization.** The Barnaby Highway Department uses a centralized fueling operation for all departmental vehicles. During the year the department uses 200 000 litres of gasoline. Gasoline is purchased for $1.00 a litre. Gasoline orders are made through the county purchasing department and the highway department is charged $60 per order for the purchasing service. Carrying costs are estimated at $.06 a litre per year. There are 250 work days in the year. Lead time on gasoline orders is five work days. Gasoline use is pretty constant, but some fluctuations occur because of crisis situations such as severe weather. To guard against gasoline stockouts during emergencies, the department keeps a 15-working-day safety stock of gasoline.

Required:
a. Compute the optimum order quantity for gasoline for the highway department.
b. Determine expected lead time demand.
c. Determine the reorder point.
d. Compute the annual inventory cost for the department.
e. A severe winter caused actual gasoline use to be 250 000 litres. Find the cost of the incorrect estimation of gasoline use.

P. 15A-4 **Cost of estimation errors.** Ellen's Camera Shop is a high-volume camera and photographic supply store. The store manager estimates a demand of 600 units for its most popular 35-millimetre single-lens reflex camera. The cost of placing an order is $60 and the carrying cost is estimated at 25 percent of unit cost. The store purchases the cameras for $320 each and sells them for $415 each.

Required:
a. If the actual demand for cameras is 384 instead of 600, determine the cost of incorrectly estimating demand.

b. If demand is 600 units a year, but high interest and insurance rates cause carrying cost to be 36 percent of unit cost, find the cost of incorrectly estimating carrying cost.

P. 15A-5 **EOQ and reorder point.** The Bloominggulch Paint Company sells 60 000 litres of latex house paint each year. Cost of the paint is $10 a litre. Management estimates that inventory carrying costs are 15 percent and the cost of ordering is $72. Order lead time averages five days and average daily demand is 200 litres per business day. Management wants a safety stock of 10 days.

Required:
a. Compute the EOQ for latex paint.
b. Determine how many latex paint orders the store should place per year.
c. Find the reorder point.
d. Compute the total inventory cost using the reorder point computed in *c.*

P. 15A-6 **Periodic and perpetual inventory systems.** Below are the January 1984 inventory purchases and sales data for the Morton Company:

Acquisitions			
Date	Units	Unit Cost	Total Cost
Beginning Balance	200	$2.00	$ 400
January 1	300	2.20	660
January 20	300	2.40	720
January 30	200	2.50	500
	1000		$2,280

Sales			
Date	Units	Selling Price	Total Sales Revenue
January 8	100	$4.50	$ 450
January 12	200	4.75	950
January 15	100	4.75	475
January 31	400	5.00	2,000
	800		$3,875

Required:
Determine the cost of goods sold **and** cost of ending inventory for each of the following:

a. Perpetual inventory, FIFO
b. Perpetual inventory, LIFO
c. Periodic inventory, weighted average
d. Periodic inventory, LIFO

P. 15A-7 **Perpetual inventory system.** Below are finished goods inventory data for January through May for the Finite Yo Yo Company.

Date	Transferred to Finished Goods (Units)	Unit Cost	Total
Beginning balance	400	$2.00	$ 800
January 9	200	2.10	420
February 20	400	2.20	880
April 30	200	2.30	460
May 10	800	2.35	1,880
	2000		$4,440

Date	Sales (Units)	Unit Selling Price	Total
January 5	100	$5.00	$ 500
January 19	200	5.00	1,000
February 15	200	5.00	1,000
March 25	300	5.50	1,650
April 21	100	5.50	550
May 12	400	5.50	2,200
	1300		$6,900

Selling and administrative expense = $2,500.00

Required:
Calculate net income for the period using a perpetual inventory system and

a. FIFO
b. LIFO
c. Moving average

Problem Set B

P. 15B-1 **EOQ and cost estimation error.** Jones Electrical Contractors buys electrical tape by the case. During the year the company uses 1200 cases of tape costing $50 each. Inventory carrying costs are 12 percent of unit cost and inventory ordering costs are $100.

Required:
a. Find the EOQ for electrical tape.
b. If the company's actual carrying cost is 16 percent rather than 12 percent, determine the effect on the EOQ.

P. 15B-2 **EOQ, reorder point, and estimation errors.** The I. M. Big Corporation has a centralized data processing system where all company information processing is performed. One service of the centralized operation is data preparation including keypunching. During the year the company expects to use 100 000 cases of punch cards, which cost $10 a case. The company estimates a carrying cost for the cards of 12 percent of cost. Ordering cost is $150. The company operates Monday through Friday and closes for 11 holidays. Lead time on orders averages three days and the use of cards is pretty much constant. The company chooses to keep a five-day safety stock of cards.

Required:
a. Find the EOQ for the punch cards.
b. Determine how many orders per year will be placed for cards.
c. Compute the expected lead time demand.
d. Determine the reorder point.
e. If actual use was only 80 000 cards for the year, find the cost of the estimation error.

P. 15B-3 **Inventory analysis.** The Ski-King Shop sells a variety of water skiing and other water sports equipment. An important sales item is a moulded life jacket. It costs $30 and sells for $50. The shop sells about 1000 life jackets in the 250 days the shop is open each year. Ordering costs are $37.50 an order, and carrying costs are 25 percent of purchase price. Lead time on ordering the jackets is five business days. The manager of the shop is very conscious of the problem of losing customers because of stockouts. Thus, he carries a 15-day safety stock of this type of life jacket.

Required:
a. Compute the economic order quantity for the life jackets.
b. Find lead time demand.
c. Find the reorder point.
d. Determine the cost of carrying the safety stock.
e. If actual demand for the year were 1500 jackets, compute the cost of estimating the wrong amount of demand.

P. 15B-4 **Sensitivity analysis.** Brewster Manufacturing Company's production supervisor was asked to provide some estimates on the expected use of one of the raw materials used in a plastic moulding process. She supplied the following data:

Annual use	100 000 litres
Purchase price	$5 per litre
Ordering cost	$100 per order
Carrying cost	25 percent of purchase price

Required:

a. If actual use turns out to be 120 000 litres instead of the 100 000 litres estimated, find the cost of the estimation error.

b. Assuming that use is 100 000 litres as estimated, but that the cost is $6 per litre and carrying cost is 30 percent of purchase price, find the cost of using the original estimates.

P. 15B-5   Inventory analysis under uncertainty. The Home-Grown Fence Company installs chain-link fences in southern Manitoba. In a year it uses 25 000 rolls of chain-link fence. Each roll costs $120. Orders for fence rolls are placed directly with the manufacturer and require 20 business days to fill. Ordering cost is $60 and carrying cost is estimated to be 10 percent of purchase price. The company operates 250 business days a year—five days a week except for two weeks a year when the company closes for vacation. The company experiences a reasonably stable demand for fencing. A two-week safety stock is desired by management.

Required:

a. Find the EOQ for the fence inventory.

b. Find the expected lead time demand for chain-link fence.

c. Determine the reorder point.

d. Compute the minimum expected stockout cost.

e. If the actual carrying cost is 18 percent, find the cost of using the 10 percent annual carrying cost in computing EOQ.

P. 15B-6   Perpetual inventory system. The Hardrock-Maple Furniture Company produces quality solid-wood furniture. Below are purchase and use data for lumber for the month of August.

Purchases			Put Into Production	
Date	Quantity	Price	Date	Quantity
1/8 balance	2000 bd m	$1.20	2/8	1000 bd m
5/8	4000 bd m	1.25	7/8	2000 bd m
12/8	5000 bd m	1.30	15/8	3000 bd m
22/8	4000 bd m	1.40	20/8	2000 bd m
			23/8	4000 bd m

Required:

a. Calculate the cost charged to work in process for lumber using the FIFO perpetual inventory method.
b. Calculate the cost charged to work in process for lumber using the LIFO perpetual inventory method.
c. If LIFO periodic had been used instead of LIFO perpetual, compute the charge to work in process.
d. Calculate the cost of August 31 lumber inventory using moving average.

P. 15B-7 Periodic and perpetual inventory. The J & J Fertilizer Company uses a chemical labeled XBZ2 in manufacturing a general purpose nitrogen fertilizer. Below are April purchase and use data for XBZ2.

Acquisitions			Use	
Date	**Quantity**	**Price**	**Date**	**Quantity**
April 1 balance	1 000 tons	$250/ton	April 9	800 tons
14	5 000 tons	260/ton	15	2200 tons
24	2 000 tons	280/ton	23	2000 tons
30	2 000 tons	300/ton	28	2000 tons
	10 000 tons			7000 tons

Required:
Calculate the ending inventory cost using

a. FIFO periodic.
b. FIFO perpetual.
c. LIFO periodic.
d. LIFO perpetual.
e. Weighted average.
f. Moving average.

Minicases

Minicase 15-1
(CMA Examination Question)

Hermit Company manufactures a line of walnut office products. Hermit executives estimate the demand for the double walnut letter tray, one of the company's products, at 6000 units. The letter tray sells for $80 per unit. The costs relating to the letter tray are estimated to be as follows for 1984:

1. Standard manufacturing cost per letter tray unit—$50.00.
2. Costs to initiate a production run—$300.00.
3. Annual cost of carrying the letter tray in inventory—20 percent of standard manufacturing cost.

In prior years, Hermit Company has scheduled the production for the letter tray in two equal production runs. The company is aware that the economic order quantity (EOQ) model can be employed to determine optimum size for production runs. The EOQ formula as it applies to inventories for determining the optimum order quantity is shown below.

$$EOQ = \sqrt{\frac{2 \text{ (annual demand) (cost per order)}}{\text{(cost per unit) (carrying cost)}}}$$

Required:
Calculate the expected annual cost savings Hermit Company could experience if it employed the economic order quantity model to determine the number of production runs which should be initiated during the year for the manufacture of the double walnut letter trays.

Minicase 15-2   (CMA Examination Question)

Canucks, Ltd., is a large wholesale distributor which deals exclusively in baby shoes. Due to the substantial costs related to ordering and storing the shoes, the company has decided to employ the economic order quantity method (EOQ) to help determine the optimum quantities of shoes to order from the different manufacturers. The EOQ formula is

$$EOQ = \sqrt{\frac{2C_oD}{PC_s}}$$

where

EOQ = optimum number of units per purchase order
D = annual demand
P = purchase price per unit
C_o = cost of placing an order
C_s = the annual cost of storage per dollar of investment in inventory

Before Canucks, Ltd., can employ the EOQ model, they need to develop values for two of the cost parameters—ordering costs (C_o) and storage costs (C_s). As a starting point, management has decided to develop the values for the two cost parameters by using cost data from the most recent fiscal year, 1984.

The company placed 4000 purchase orders during 1984. The largest number of orders placed during any one month was 400 orders in June and the smallest number of orders placed was 250 in December. Selected cost data for these two months and the year for the purchasing, accounts payable, and warehousing operations appear below.

	Costs for High Activity Month (June; 400 orders)	Costs for Low Activity Month (December; 250 orders)	Annual Costs
Purchasing Department			
Purchasing manager	$ 1,750	$ 1,750	$ 21,000
Buyers	2,500	1,900	28,500
Clerks	2,000	1,100	20,600
Supplies	275	150	2,500
Accounts Payable Dept.			
Clerks	2,000	1,500	21,500
Supplies	125	75	1,100
Data processing	2,600	2,300	30,000
Warehouse			
Foreman	1,250	1,250	15,000
Receiving clerks	2,300	1,800	23,300
Receiving supplies	50	25	500
Shipping clerks	3,800	3,500	44,000
Shipping Supplies	1,350	1,200	15,200
Freight out	1,600	1,300	16,800
	$21,600	$17,850	$240,000

The purchasing department is responsible for placing all orders. The costs listed for the accounts payable department relate only to the processing of purchase orders for payment. The warehouse costs reflect two operations—receiving and shipping. The receiving clerks inspect all incoming shipments and place the orders in storage. The shipping clerks are responsible for processing all sales orders to retailers.

The company leases space in a public warehouse. The rental fee is priced according to the square metre occupied during a month. The annual charges during 1984 totaled $34,500. Annual insurance and property taxes on the shoes stored in the warehouse amounted to $5,700 and $7,300, respectively. The company pays 8 percent a year for small amount of short-term, seasonal bank debt. Long-term capital investments are expected to produce a rate of return of 12 percent after taxes. The effective tax rate is 40 percent.

The inventory balances tend to fluctuate during the year depending upon the demand for baby shoes. Selected data on inventory balances is shown below.

Inventory, January 1, 1984	$160,000
Inventory, December 31, 1984	120,000
Highest inventory balance (June)	220,000
Lowest inventory balance (December)	120,000
Average monthly inventory	190,000

The boxes in which the baby shoes are stored are all approximately the same size. Consequently, the shoes all occupy about the same amount of storage space in the warehouse.

Required:
a. Using the 1984 data, determine estimated values appropriate for
   1. C_o—cost of placing an order.
   2. C_s—the annual cost of storage per dollar of investment in inventory.
b. Should Canucks, Ltd., use the cost parameters developed solely from the historical data in the employment of the EOQ model? Explain your answer.

Minicase 15-3   (Adapted from Certified Accountant, U.K.)

While three eccentric sisters, Alice, Betty, and Clair, were on holiday in Manitoba, they obtained the distribution rights for the Ontario market of a ready-mix flour which was packed in .2-kg bags for sale to bake French bread.

On January 1, 1984 the sisters put $1,000 from their savings into a bank account under the name of the Eccentric Sisters' Partnership which they had formed for the purpose of distributing the flour. Initially, they commenced operations from the rambling old house in which they lived and in discussion concluded not to charge overheads, nor to pay themselves a salary, but rather to share any profits that the partnership might make equally between them on a six-monthly basis.

Once their capital was in the bank they immediately made a purchase of 10 000 bags of the mix which exactly exhausted their initial capital. Although they understood from the supplier that the price they would have to pay for the flour was likely to fluctuate considerably, as they wanted to be able to offer

Reproduced from Certified Accountants Questions and Suggested Answers, including papers for Scottish and Irish Students, Professional Examination, June 1976. With permission of The Association of Certified Accountants.

their own customers a stable price on a six-monthly basis they set their sales price at 15 cents per bag for their launch period.

During the following six months of the partnership's trading the following transactions took place:

	Bought	Sold
January	—	5 000 bags
February	5 000 bags @ 12¢	5 000 bags
March	10 000 bags @ 10¢	—
April	—	10 000 bags
May	5 000 bags @ 11¢	5 000 bags
June	5 000 bags @ 12½¢	5 000 bags

Early in July 1984 each of the sisters independently prepared her own version of the partnership's first half-year performance. On July 10, 1984 the sisters held a meeting to decide on the amount to be distributed as their first profit shares.

Alice was more than happy about the situation, saying that each would get more than they originally hoped, and with her share of $450 would take a trip to Lake Louise. Betty said that Alice must have made some mistake in her calculations because she would only get $408.33 as her third share. Clair could not hold back her growing exasperation over her view of the ineptitude of her sisters at calculating profit and jumped in to say that none of the other sisters would ever make accountants. According to her, the correct distribution would be $421.43.

An argument started about who was right. When the sisters compared their statements they also found that as well as their income calculations being different, the valuation they had obtained for ending inventory on June 30, 1984 also varied in each case.

Required:

a. Showing the calculations to support your answer, provide information of which methods the sisters had used to price out inventories in their various assessments of the partnership's performance. Present your results in table form to show the total income for the partnership and the value of the closing inventories for each of the methods.

b. Discuss the major conceptual difficulties associated with pricing out inventories as far as the measurement of income and value are concerned. Refer to the sisters' calculations where appropriate.

c. Do any of the methods used by the sisters overcome the difficulties that you have discussed and can you make additional suggestions which might prove to be even more helpful to management in trying to measure the performance of an organization? Give reasons for your answer.

Chapter 16

Standard Costs Extended: Mix and Yield Variances

The variance analysis reporting concepts discussed in Chapter 8 can be extended to include the analysis of varying the proportion of inputs in the production and selling process. When you have completed this chapter, you should understand:

1 The different types of variance analysis reports used for manufacturing activities.

2 The computation of manufacturing variances.

3 The separation of material quantity and labour efficiency variances into their component parts.

4 The use of standards in nonmanufacturing activities.

5 The nature and use of marketing variance analysis reports.

6 The computation of marketing variances.

In Chapter 8 we introduced the basic standard cost concepts and described variance analysis for direct materials and direct labour. The material and labour variances are divided into two parts, one that isolates the effects of using more or less than the standard **amount** of material or labour and one that isolates the effects of paying more or less than the standard **price** of materials or labour. Such variances are very useful for identifying situations that require management's attention. However, not all manufacturing activities can be analyzed adequately by material price and quantity variances and labour rate and efficiency variances.

Some products can be manufactured using various mixes of material inputs; or various mixes of labour inputs. For example, steel may be produced using different proportions of hot iron and scrap metal. A brick wall may be built by two journeymen bricklayers and four apprentices, or by three journeymen

674

bricklayers and two apprentices. When the mix of material or labour inputs is different from the standard, the effect can be analyzed by dividing the material quantity variance or the labour efficiency variance into separate components called mix and yield variances. In this chapter we discuss mix and yield variances by presenting a manufacturing example for which we analyze material and labour variances including mix and yield variances. Later in the chapter we discuss and illustrate variance analysis for nonmanufacturing activities.

Performance reporting for manufacturing activities

Chapter 8 presents the fundamentals of standard costing systems and illustrates basic standard cost performance reports for a manufacturing business. Included are direct material and direct labour variance reports. This chapter briefly reviews the variance reporting concepts and extends the analysis to mix and yield variances. To illustrate the discussion of a comprehensive variance analysis that includes mix and yield variances, we use the Dixie Chocolate Company, a manufacturer of high-quality candy. First we illustrate the computation of direct material price and quantity variances and direct labour rate and efficiency variances. Then the direct material quantity variance is separated into mix and yield variances, and the direct labour efficiency variance is separated into its mix and yield components. One of Dixie Chocolate Company's specialty products is a dark chocolate cream, produced in 4000-kilogram batches. The company uses standard costs to set selling prices and to monitor production costs and activities.

Standard cost data

The Dixie Chocolate Company's dark chocolate cream candy is packaged in 10-kilogram cartons and shipped to stores in 100-kilogram cases. The product is priced at 250 percent of standard prime cost (direct materials + direct labour). A schedule of standard costs for the product is presented in Figure 16-1.

<table>
<tr><td colspan="3">Dixie Chocolate Company
Schedule of Standard Costs
For Dark Chocolate Creams</td></tr>
<tr><td colspan="3">Standards</td></tr>
<tr><td>Materials</td><td>Quantity
per 10 kg carton</td><td>Price</td></tr>
<tr><td>Cocoa syrup</td><td>5 L</td><td>$2.50/L</td></tr>
<tr><td>Milk</td><td>3 L</td><td>$0.40/L</td></tr>
<tr><td>Liquid sugar</td><td>1 L</td><td>$1.05/L</td></tr>
<tr><td>Flavouring</td><td>$1/2$ L</td><td>$1.50/L</td></tr>
<tr><td>Labour</td><td>Quantity
per 100 kg case</td><td>Rate</td></tr>
<tr><td>Skilled labour</td><td>4 h</td><td>$9.00/h</td></tr>
<tr><td>General labour</td><td>2 h</td><td>4.50/h</td></tr>
</table>

Figure 16-1
This schedule presents the standard costs and quantities for direct materials and direct labour.

Standard cost data may be expressed in whatever units management finds convenient and useful. Notice that in Figure 16-1 materials standards are in terms of 10-kilogram cartons and labour standards are in terms of 100-kilogram cases. To perform variance analysis, however, it is convenient to convert standards to identical measurement units.

Unit standard costs

Either kilograms, cartons or cases could be used as the unit for measuring costs. In this example we use the kilogram as the unit measure and convert the standards in Figure 16-1 to costs per kilogram of product. Material standards are expressed in terms of 10-kilogram cartons, so the amounts must be divided by 10 to find the standard cost for one kilogram.

Material	Quantity	Input Price	Cost per Kilogram
Cocoa syrup	5.0 L/10 = .5 L × $ 2.5/L		= $1.250
Milk	3.0 L/10 = .3 L × $ .4/L		= $0.120
Liquid sugar	1.0 L/10 = .1 L × $1.05/L		= $0.105
Flavouring	.5 L/10 = .05 L × $1.50/L		= $0.075
Total material cost per kilogram			$1.550

Labour standards are expressed in terms of 100-kilogram cases and must be divided by 100 to arrive at labour cost per kilogram:

Labour	Quantity	Hourly Rate	Cost per Kilogram
Skilled labour	4 h/100 = .04 × $9.00/h		= $.360
General labour	2 h/100 = .02 × 4.50/h		= .090
Total labour cost per kilogram			$.450

The total prime cost of the product is $2.00 per kilogram, which is the sum of the material and labour costs calculated above. Now that we have a standard prime cost per kilogram of candy, we can calculate the standard price of the product. At 250 percent of standard prime cost, the selling price of a kilogram of candy is $5.00, which is the $2.00 standard prime cost multiplied by 250 percent.

Standard cost data should be converted to common units to facilitate variance analysis

The conversion of standard cost data to a common unit of measure is frequently necessary to facilitate analysis. The data should be expressed in the most appropriate physical units. Note that when the costs are converted to common units as above, it becomes easy to see the relative proportion of the various costs. For example, you can see that sugar is a much cheaper input per kilogram of candy than cocoa syrup, and that general labour is much less costly than skilled labour. These relationships will become important when we analyze mix and yield variances.

Variance reports   Variance analysis measures the fluctuation of actual costs from standards, and managers usually attempt to explain the cause of variances, particularly if they are large. Generally, managers' ability to interpret variances is affected by the content and detail in the variance reports prepared by the accountant. To prepare such reports actual production data are required. The costs of producing 60 000 kilograms of candy in the first quarter of 1983 are shown in Figure 16-2. These data can be compared with the standards in Figure 16-1 and any variances computed can be reported to management in an appropriate report.

Material price and
quantity variances

Material variances. Material variances are typically divided into a price variance and a quantity variance. When there are multiple inputs, such as the four raw materials in this example, a variance must be calculated for each material. The **price variance** for each input is the difference between the standard and actual cost of the material times the actual quantity. The **quantity variance** for each material is the difference between the standard and actual quantity of material multiplied by the standard cost. Figure 16-3 presents the material variances for the period.

The standard and actual unit costs for each material are obtained directly from the standard cost schedule in Figure 16-1 and the actual cost schedule in

---

Dixie Chocolate Company
Schedule of Actual Costs for Dark Chocolate Creams
First Quarter, 1983

Actual Results for the Month of May

Production = 60 000 kg of candy

Materials	Quantity	Cost
Cocoa syrup	29 000 L	$2.70/L
Milk	20 000 L	$0.50/L
Liquid sugar	5 500 L	$1.00/L
Flavouring	3 200 L	$1.40/L
Total materials	57 700 L	

Labour	Quantity	Cost
Skilled labour	2500 h	$23,500
General labour	1050 h	5,040
Total labour	3550 h	$28,540

Figure 16-2
This schedule presents the actual direct material and direct labour costs for the first quarter of 1981.

Dixie Chocolate Company
Material Variances for Dark Chocolate Creams
First Quarter, 1983

Price Variance

Price variance = (Standard cost − Actual cost) × Actual quantity
Cocoa syrup   = ($2.50 − $2.70) 29 000 L = $ 5,800 U
Milk   = ($0.40 − $0.50) 20 000 L = $ 2,000 U
Liquid sugar = ($1.05 − $1.00) 5 500 L = $ 275 F
Flavouring   = ($1.50 − $1.40) 3 200 L = $ 320 F
Total material price variance $ 7,205 U

Quantity Variance

Quantity variance = (Standard quantity − Actual quantity) ×
                    Standard price
Cocoa syrup   = (30 000 L − 29 000 L) × $2.50 = $ 2,500 F
Milk   = (18 000 L − 20 000 L) × $0.40 = $ 800 U
Liquid sugar = (6 000 L − 5 500 L) × $1.00 = $ 300 U
Flavouring   = (3 000 L − 3 200 L) × $1.50 = $ 300 U
Total material quantity variance $ 1,900 F

Total material variance $ 5,305 U

Figure 16-3
A material price and quantity variance report. Price and quantity variances are computed for each material.

Figure 16-2. To obtain the standard quantities, however, it is necessary to refer to the unit cost data calculated earlier. The actual quantity of each input is given in Figure 16-2. The standard quantity is obtained by multiplying the standard quantity per kilogram of output by the production for the period of 60 000 kilograms. For example, the standard for cocoa syrup is .5 litre per kilogram of finished product. The standard quantity for the period's production level is .5 litre per kilogram × 60 000 kilograms, or 30 000 litres of syrup. The standard quantities for each of the other resources are calculated in the same manner.

Labour variances. Frequently businesses establish separate labour standards for different production operations, departments, or other differentiating characteristics of labour, the purpose being to facilitate control over the firm's labour activities. In the Dixie Chocolate Company example, labour is categorized as general and skilled. Skilled labour is used to operate all machinery and to perform quality control, while general labour is used for all other production jobs. Like multiple materials, multiple labour classifications require a rate and efficiency variance computation for each labour classification. The rate variance is the difference between standard and actual rates, multiplied by the actual number of hours worked. The **efficiency variance** is the difference between the

Labour rate and efficiency variances

```
┌─────────────────────────────────────────────────────────────────────┐
│                      Dixie Chocolate Company                          │
│          Direct Labour Variances for Dark Chocolate Creams            │
│                      For the First Quarter 1983                        │
├─────────────────────────────────────────────────────────────────────┤
│                          Rate Variance                                │
│  Rate variance = (Standard rate − Actual rate) × Actual hours         │
│  Skilled labour  = ($9.00 − $9.40) × 2500 hours = $1,000 U            │
│  General labour = (  4.50 −   4.80) × 1050 hours =    315 U           │
│  Total labour rate variance                              $1,315 U     │
│                                                                       │
│                        Efficiency Variance                            │
│  Efficiency variance = (Standard hours − Actual hours) ×              │
│                             Standard rate                             │
│  Skilled labour  = (2400 − 2500) × $9.00 = $  900 U                   │
│  General labour = (1200 − 1050) ×   4.50 =    675 F                   │
│  Total labour efficency variance                           225 U      │
│                                                                       │
│  Total labour variance                                  $1,540 U      │
└─────────────────────────────────────────────────────────────────────┘
```

Figure 16-4
A direct labour rate and efficiency variance report.

standard and actual hours for the output achieved times the standard rate. Figure 16-4 presents the labour variance report.

The schedule of actual results in Figure 16-2 provides the total labour hours for each labour classification for the period. Labour costs for each type of labour are expressed in total dollars. This is common since most firms have employees working for various rates in any particular labour classification. Labour costs for each labour classification are accumulated each pay period and the total is reported at the end of the period. Although some skilled employees earn more than others, for variance analysis we are concerned with the average cost of skilled employees, and not with their individual earnings. Similarly, we need the average cost of an hour of general labour. We can calculate these costs from the actual data given, and then use them to calculate variances. For the first quarter of 1983 the average rates paid for skilled and general labour were

Skilled labour rate: $23,500/2500 hours = $9.40 per hour

General labour rate: $ 5,040/1050 hours = $4.80 per hour

Now we can compare the actual and standard labour rates to arrive at the **labour rate variance**, as shown in the labour variance report in Figure 16-4.

The efficiency variance requires the computation of standard hours. Earlier we calculated the standard amount of labour per kilogram of chocolate cream candy. Now we can multiply these standard per kilogram costs by the total actual production to arrive at the standard hours of labour for production of the period. The calculations are shown at the top of page 680.

$$\text{Skilled labour} = .04 \text{ h/kg} \times 60\,000 \text{ kg} = 2400 \text{ h}$$
$$\text{General labour} = .02 \text{ h/kg} \times 60\,000 \text{ kg} = 1200 \text{ h}$$

The standard hours computed above are compared with actual hours in Figure 16-4 in order to arrive at the labour efficiency variance.

Extending variance analysis

With multiple inputs, quantity and efficiency variances can be separated into mix and yield variances

The material and labour variances just computed frequently provide very useful information for managers. However, in situations where there are multiple inputs used in the production of the product or service, additional information can be obtained by separating the material quantity variance and labour efficiency variance into two components. The purpose of this additional variance analysis is to provide information about the economic consequences of varying the relative amounts of inputs used in production. Figure 16-5 illustrates the relationship of mix and yield variances to the material quantity and labour efficiency variances. The diagram also shows the breakdown of total prime cost variances into its various component parts.

The Dixie Chocolate Company example has four raw materials and two labour classifications. The standard quantities of materials and labour per kilogram of candy were calculated earlier. It is, however, possible to produce a kilogram of candy with a different mix of material or with a different mix of labour. When the mix of resources changes, mix and yield variances can be calculated to determine the effect of these changes, as discussed on the following pages.

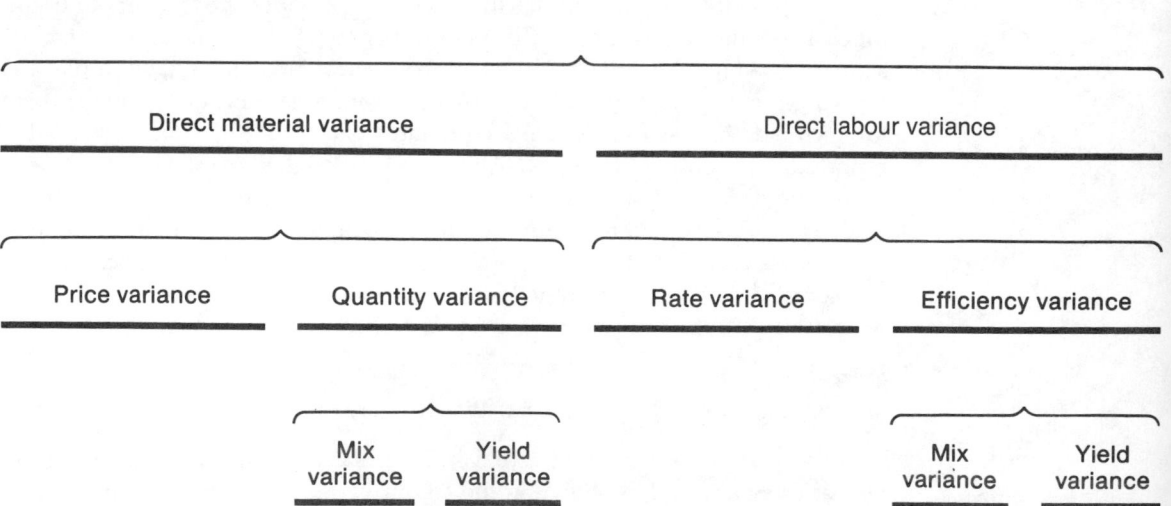

Figure 16-5
This diagram shows the component parts of direct material and direct labour variances. Notice that the material quantity variance and the labour efficiency variance can each be separated into mix and yield variance components that provide more specific information about the use of material and labour quantities.

Mix and yield variance

The total prime cost variance, which is the difference between standard prime costs of production and actual prime costs, is made up of separate material and labour variances. The material variance is further subdivided into a price and quantity variance, and labour variance is subdivided into a rate and efficiency variance. If materials consist of several inputs whose mix can be varied without changing the nature of the product, the material quantity variance can be further subdivided into two parts, called the mix and yield variances. Similarly, if labour consists of more than one classification and the same product can be manufactured with different combinations of labour, the labour efficiency variance can be subdivided into mix and yield variances also. The purpose of this additional variance analysis is to provide information about the economic consequences of varying the relative amounts of the different material or labour inputs used in production.

For example, a bakery may be able to reduce the amount of sour cream and increase the amount of milk in the production of a batch of danish pastry. The relative proportion of inputs may vary from standards for a variety of reasons, including:

Causes of input variances from standard

1. Shortages of a particular raw material.
2. Attempts by managers to reduce production costs.
3. Human error.
4. Random error.

Mix variance defined

Yield variance defined

Whatever the cause of variations in the relative proportions of inputs, managers often find it useful to analyze the cost effect of such variations by means of mix and yield variances. A **mix variance** measures the amount of cost variance attributable to using a different proportion of inputs than defined by the standards. The **yield variance** is the amount of variance caused by using more or fewer total inputs than standard. Unlike a quantity variance, total inputs are used to measure yield variance without regard to the composition of the inputs. Both mix and yield variances require data on the standard quantity and price of the mix of inputs. Remember that the mix and yield variances together make up the material quantity variance or the labour efficiency variance.

Mix and yield variances for materials

We repeat below the per-kilogram standards for material given earlier for the Dixie Chocolate Company:

	Standard Quantity per Kilogram of Output	Cost per Litre	Cost per Kilogram of Candy
Cocoa syrup	.5 L	$2.50	$1.250
Milk	.3 L	$ .40	$ .120
Liquid sugar	.1 L	$1.05	$ .105
Flavouring	.05 L	$1.50	$ .075
Total	.95 L		$1.550

The standard material cost of 1 kilogram of candy is $1.55 which results from the input mix described above. On the average .95 litre of input is required for 1 kilogram of output. Since .95 litre of input at the standard mix costs $1.55, the average cost of a litre of input at the standard mix is $1.63157 per litre, which is sometimes referred to as the **standard average cost** of inputs. With the above data, mix and yield variances can be computed.

Standard average cost of inputs

Mix variance. The **production mix variance** measures the dollar amount of variance caused by changing from the standard mix of production inputs to some other mix. In a mix analysis, a variance is favourable if less than the standard amount of a high-cost input is used **or** if more than the standard amount of a low-cost input is used.

In a mix variance the objective is to use less of high-cost inputs and more of low-cost inputs

What is a high- or low-cost input? High- or low-cost inputs are determined by the average cost of the inputs using the standard mix. Any input costing more than the standard average cost is a high-cost input, and any input costing less than the standard average cost of inputs is a low-cost input. In terms of the mix of inputs, the objective is to use more low-cost inputs and less high-cost inputs, thereby reducing the cost of production. For example, the standard average cost of raw material for 1 kilogram of candy is .95 litre of input, or $1.63157 per litre for the standard mix of raw materials. Any raw material having a standard cost greater than $1.63157 per litre is a high-cost input, and any input with a standard cost less than $1.63157 is a low-cost input. In our example cocoa syrup is a high-cost input, while liquid sugar, milk, and flavouring are low-cost inputs.

Materials mix and yield variance illustrated

A mix variance analysis is presented in the top half of Figure 16-6. The format for calculating the mix variance for an individual input is

Mix variance = (Standard quantity − Actual quantity) ×
(Standard cost of the individual input −
Standard average cost of all inputs)

The comparison of standard and actual quantity for each material in the mix variance is identical to that of a material quantity variance analysis. The standard quantity of each raw material is computed by multiplying output of the period by the per-unit standard quantity of each raw material. For example, the standard quantity of cocoa syrup is 30,000 litres (60 000 kilograms of output × .50 litres of cocoa syrup per kilogram of candy), and the standard quantity of milk is 18 000 litres (60 000 kilograms × .30 litre per kilogram of output). These per-unit standards were computed earlier; actual quantities used for each material are given in Figure 16-2 on page 677.

The difference between standard and actual quantities is multiplied by the difference between the standard cost of each material and the standard average cost of $1.55 per kilogram. For instance, during the first quarter of 1983 Dixie used 1000 litres less cocoa syrup than standard. Cocoa syrup is a high-cost input since it has a standard cost of $2.50 per litre which is $.86843 per litre higher than the standard average cost of $1.63157. The result of the computation is a $868.43 variance (1000 × $.86843 per litre difference). This variance is

---

Dixie Chocolate Company
Materials Mix and Yield Variance
First Quarter 1983

Mix Variance

Mix variance = (Standard quantity − Actual quantity) ×
  (Standard cost − Standard average cost)

Cocoa syrup	(30 000 − 29 000) ($2.50 − $1.63157) =	$ 868 F
Milk	(18 000 − 20 000) ($0.40 − $1.63157) =	$2,463 F
Liquid sugar	(6 000 − 5 500) ($1.00 − $1.63157) =	$ 316 U
Flavouring	(3 000 − 3 200) ($1.50 − $1.63157) =	$ 26 F
Mix variance		$3,041 F

Yield Variance

Yield variance = (Actual input × Standard average cost of inputs) −
  (Actual output × Standard cost of output)

57 700 L × $1.63157/L	= $94,141	
Less 60 000 kg × $1.55/L	= 93,000	
Yield variance		$1,141 U
Material quantity variance		$1,900 F

Note: All rounded to the nearest dollar

Figure 16-6
The direct materials quantity variance is separated into mix and yield variances. Notice that the total of the mix and yield variances equals the quantity variance.

favourable, because the company used less than the standard quantity of a high-cost input. If the company were able to substitute a low-cost input for cocoa syrup, a net cost saving should result. The second raw material, milk, has a standard quantity of 18 000 litres, but 20 000 litres were used. Milk is a low-cost item, costing $.40 per litre or $1.23157 a litre less than the standard average cost of inputs. In terms of mix, it is desirable to use more of a low-cost input. You may wonder how one can obtain a favourable variance by using more than the standard quantity of an input. Logic tells us that we would be better off if less milk had been used. However, a certain quantity of raw material is required to produce one kilogram of chocolate candy. The mix variance measures the effects of changing the relative amounts of materials, not the effect of changing the quantity of an individual material. If changing the proportion of material means reducing the quantity of a high-cost material and increasing the quantity of a low-cost material, the variance from this change in mix is favourable, since the cost per kilogram of output will be lower if other inputs remain constant. Therefore, the mix variance for milk is $2,463 favourable (rounded) (2000 litres × $1.23157 per litre less than the standard average cost of inputs).

The remaining two inputs are analyzed in the same fashion as cocoa syrup and milk. Dixie used less liquid sugar than standard, but sugar is a low-cost material relative to the average cost of inputs. Using less than average of a low-cost input yields an unfavourable mix variance. Finally, the company used more than standard quantity of flavouring, which is a low-cost resource. The result is a favourable mix variance for flavouring. If each variance computation is made in strict algebraic fashion, all positive outcomes are favourable mix variances (F) and all negative outcomes are unfavourable mix variances (U).

For example:

Algebraic solution
to mix variances

```
Mix variance =
(Standard quantity − Actual quantity)(Standard cost − Standard average cost)
Cocoa       =  (30 000 − 29 000)($2.50 − $1.63157)
  syrup              (1000)          ($.86843)       =     $868 =    $868 F
Milk        =  (18 000 − 20 000)($0.40 − $1.63157)
                   (−2000)        (−$1.231 57)       =   $2,463 = $2,463 F
Liquid      =     (6000 − 5500)  ($1.00 − $1.63157)
  sugar             (500)          (−$.63157)        =    −$316 =   $316 U
Flavouring  =     (3000 − 3 200) ($1.50 − $1.63157)
                   (−200)         (−$.13157)         =      $26 =    $26 F
```

The above approach works every time if the analysis is structured as above. If the order of any set of variables is reversed, however, the sign will be incorrect.

The yield variance is the difference between actual and expected yield for a specified amount of input

Yield variance. Yield can be described as the amount of output derived from a certain amount of input. A yield variance is the difference between the actual and the expected yield from some actual amount of input. For example, the Dixie Chocolate Company expects a yield of 10 kilograms of dark chocolate from each 9.5 litres of input, as calculated earlier. Production results can be measured against expected performance to determine whether the yield matched expectations. The yield variance for the Dixie Chocolate Company is presented in Figure 16-6. It is computed as follows:

Yield variance = (Actual quantity of inputs during the period ×
                  Standard average cost of inputs) −
                 (Actual quantity of outputs for the period ×
                  Standard cost of outputs)

The actual input of 57 700 litres is merely the sum of the quantities of the four materials used during the period. This amount is computed by summing the actual quantities used, as shown in the schedule of actual costs presented in Figure 16-2. Total actual quantity of inputs is multiplied by the standard average cost of the standard input mix. The yield variance is blind to the composition, or mix, of the inputs. Only the total amount of inputs is important for the analysis. Next, the actual output of 60 000 kilograms is multiplied by the $1.55 per kilogram standard cost of the output. The difference between the results of the two calculations is the variance.

If the cost of the inputs at standard average cost is greater than the cost of the outputs at standard cost, the yield variance is unfavourable, as in our example. The logic is that the standard cost of the outputs should be at least equal to the standard cost of the resources used. If the standard cost of the output exceeds the standard average cost of the inputs, the yield variance is favourable.

When the favourable mix variance of $3,041 and the unfavourable yield variance of $1,141 are combined, the result is the material quantity variance of $1,900 F shown in Figure 16-3. Often a favourable mix variance caused by substituting a lower-cost material for a higher-cost one is partially or entirely offset by an unfavourable yield variance. The lower-cost material may create more waste, shrinkage, or some other production problem.

Interpreting the variances. Price, mix, and yield variances help managers isolate the cost effects of modifying the mix of inputs. However, the mere calculation of variances does not complete the variance analysis process. Typically management wants to determine the cause of changes in the input mix and the effect of those changes on costs and product quality. The input mix may have been altered from standard because of temporary or permanent resource scarcity, changing resource prices, human errors, random errors, or attempts at improving production costs. Input mix changes may also affect product quality. The manager must determine the nature or cause of the variances before appropriate actions can be taken.

Investigation by managers may determine that product quality is adversely affected by a particular change in input mix. The savings in input cost is more than offset by the decline in gross margin from lost sales. Another investigation might indicate that a new material distribution system has been ineffective in supplying production operations with the correct type and quantity of materials. Machinery malfunctions, production employee errors, computer programming errors for the production activity, or faulty materials are other possible causes of input mix changes. Analysis of the causes of mix changes and the appropriate management action for such mix changes are determined by the nature of the situation being analyzed. However, in many cases mix and yield variances are an important part of the total variance analysis.

Mix and yield variances for labour

Mix and yield variances can be computed in some situations where there are multiple labour classifications

Sometimes managers are able to modify the mix of labour used to produce a product or service. A construction company may use apprentice carpenters instead of journeymen carpenters to frame houses, or a manufacturer may use less-skilled labour for assembly activities when standards call for skilled labour. Changes from the expected mix of labour resources may occur because of labour shortages, changes in production schedules, attempts to reduce costs, strikes, and for other reasons. Whatever the cause of using a mix of labour other than standard, it is usually desirable to know the effect of the changed mix. Often a labour efficiency variance is not informative enough, so it is divided into a mix and yield variance, as was done with direct materials, except that now direct labour data are used in the computations. Figure 16-7 presents the labour mix and yield variance for the Dixie Chocolate Company.

Mix variance. The standard hours for each classification of labour are

Standard hours = Standard quantity per unit × Output
Skilled labour   = .04 hours per kilogram × 60 000 kilograms = 2400 hours
General labour   = .02 hours per kilogram × 60 000 kilograms = 1200 hours

Figure 16-7
In some situations it may be appropriate to separate the labour efficiency variance into a mix and yield variance. The Dixie Chocolate Company had a favourable labour yield variance, but it was more than offset by an unfavourable mix variance caused by using a higher proportion of expensive labour.

Dixie Chocolate Company
Labour Mix and Yield Variance
First Quarter 1983

Mix Variance

Mix variance = (Standard hours − Actual hours) ×
(Standard rate − Standard average rate)

Skilled labour	(2400 h − 2500 h)($9.00 − $7.50) =	$150 U
General labour	(1200 h − 1050 h)($4.50 − $7.50) =	450 U
Mix variance		$600 U

Yield Variance

Yield variance = (Actual hours × Standard average rate) −
Output × Standard cost of output)

3550 hours × $7.50 per hour	= $26,625	
60 000 kilograms × $.45 per kilogram	= 27,000	
Yield variance		375 F
Labour efficiency variance		$225 U

The standard average rate for labour is the weighted average cost of labour. It can be determined in two ways. One approach is to weight the cost of each labour classification by the relative amount of hours used in production. In this example, for each hour of general labour two hours of skilled labour are used. Therefore, the weighted average cost of labour is:

$$
\begin{aligned}
2 \text{ hours} \times \$9.00 &= \$18.00 \\
1 \text{ hour} \times 4.50 &= 4.50 \\
3 \text{ hours} &= \$22.50
\end{aligned}
$$

Weighted average ($22.50/3 hours) = $7.50/h

Another method is to use the standard cost of labour for 1 kilogram of candy and convert the cost to a labour cost per hour.

	Quantity per Kilogram	Labour Rate	Cost per Kilogram
Skilled labour	= .04 hours per kilogram	× $9.00 =	$.36 per kilogram
General labour	= .02 hours per kilogram	× $4.50 =	.09 per kilogram
Total labour	= .06 hours per kilogram		$.45 per kilogram

Since labour cost using the standard labour mix is $.45 per kilogram for .06 hour of labour, then one hour of labour at the standard average rate is $.45/.06 hour or $7.50 per hour. By comparing the standard average labour cost of $7.50 per hour with the two standard labour rates, you can see that skilled labour is a high-cost resource, since the rate is greater than average, and general labour is a low-cost resource.

During the first quarter of 1983 Dixie used more skilled labour and less general labour than required by the standards. Since there was a greater proportion of a high-cost resource used, the skilled labour mix variance is unfavourable. Similarly, less general labour was used than standard, but general labour is a low-cost labour resource. Therefore, it also has an unfavourable mix variance. The total mix variance is $600 unfavourable.

Yield variance. The labour yield variance is similar to the material yield variance. The inputs, in this case total actual hours worked, are multiplied by the standard average wage rate. Subtracted from this amount is the output multiplied by its standard cost for labour. A special note of caution is needed here: The output is expressed in the same units as used in the material variance—a kilogram of candy in our example—**but** the standard cost of the output refers to the standard cost of the labour used to produce the candy. Therefore, we multiply the 60 000 kilograms of output by the $.45 per kilogram standard labour cost, whereas we used the $1.55 per kilogram standard material cost when computing the material yield variance. The 3550 actual labour hours are taken from the schedule of actual costs in Figure 16-2. The computation of the yield variance is shown in Figure 16-7. The $375 favourable yield variance indicates that the output achieved was greater than expected based on the hours of labour used.

Interpreting the variances. In this example the favourable **yield** variance of $375 is more than offset by the unfavourable **mix** variance of $600. The net result, of course, is the $225 unfavourable labour efficiency variance shown in Figure 16-4. Typically a higher proportion of skilled labour results in a favourable labour yield variance. The objective is to generate a large enough labour yield variance to more than offset an unfavourable labour mix variance. Just the reverse is true if management attempts to reduce production costs by substituting lower-cost labour for higher-cost labour. Under these conditions management hopes to create a large enough mix variance to more than offset an unfavourable yield variance that might occur.

Performance reporting for nonmanufacturing activities

Standards may be used for many nonmanufacturing activities

Most of the standard cost discussion in this and previous chapters has been illustrated with manufacturing examples. Although standards are widely used in planning and controlling manufacturing activities, standards are also very useful in many other types of business activities. Some marketing and administrative activities may be monitored using standard costs. The ingenuity of managers and the nature of the cost-benefit relationships are the primary limitations on the type and amount of standard cost information a firm can develop. The purpose of this section is to illustrate the use of standard cost variance analysis reports for nonmanufacturing activities. The example presented is for marketing activities.

Business firms can establish standards for marketing activities such as sales volume, unit prices, product sales mix, and contribution margin. To illustrate, consider the example of the Country Road Bike Shoppe, which sells three types

Bicycle Model	Unit Sales Price	Sales Volume in Units	Sales	Unit Variable Cost	Unit Contribution Margin	Total Contribution Margin

Country Road Bike Shoppe
Budgeted Sales and Contribution Margins
For the Year 1983

Bicycle Model	Unit Sales Price	Sales Volume in Units	Sales	Unit Variable Cost	Unit Contribution Margin	Total Contribution Margin
Ten-speed	$260	200	$ 52,000	$143	$117	$23,400
Five-speed	150	700	105,000	93	57	39,900
Single-speed	80	100	8,000	53	27	2,700
Totals		1000	$165,000			$66,000

Average unit selling price = Sales/Sales volume in units
= $165,000/1000 units
= $165 per unit

Average contribution margin = Total contribution margin/Sales volume in units
= $66,000/1000 units
= $66 per unit

Figure 16-8
The Country Road Bike Shoppe creates standards for sales volume, sales mix, and contribution margin. The standards are presented here.

of bicycles, a ten-speed, a five-speed, and a single-speed model. The company establishes standards for sales mix, sales volume, variable costs, and contribution margins. Standards for sales and contribution margin for 1983 are presented in Figure 16-8.

The unit variable cost includes product cost, marketing cost, and any variable administrative costs associated with the product. The unit contribution margin is the sales price less the variable cost, and the total contribution margin is the unit contribution margin times the expected sales volume in units. The average unit selling price is merely the weighted average price of the sales at the expected sales volume and sales mix. No single product sells for $165, but on the **average** a sale results in $165 of revenue. Similarly, the average contribution margin is the weighted average contribution margin on expected sales.

Figure 16-9 presents the actual results for the bicycle shop for the year. As is often the case, actual results are somewhat different from expectations. Sales volumes and contribution margins for each product differ from those expected, resulting in a lower average unit selling price and a lower average unit contribution margin than standard. However, the total contribution margin is $75,000, or $9,000 higher than expected. Although a manager can often obtain some information from the standard and actual data in reports such as Figures 16-8 and 16-9, systematic analysis of variances typically provides far more information for decision making. In this example we discuss three variances, a contribution margin variance, a quantity variance, and a mix variance.

			Country Road Bike Shoppe Actual Sales and Contribution Margin Data For the Year 1983			
Bicycle Model	**Unit Sales Price**	**Sales Volume in Units**	**Sales**	**Unit Variable Cost**	**Unit Contribution Margin**	**Total Contribution Margin**
Ten-speed	$260	300	$ 78,000	$150	$110	$33,000
Five-speed	145	600	87,000	92	53	31,800
Single-speed	90	300	27,000	56	34	10,200
Totals		1200	$192,000			$75,000

Average unit selling price = Sales/Sales volume in units
= $192,000/1200 units
= $160 per unit

Average unit contribution margin = Total contribution margin/Sales volume in units
= $75,000/1200 units
= $62.50 per unit

Figure 16-9
Actual sales results are presented above in the same format used to present the standards.

Contribution margin variance

The contribution margin variance is the difference between the standard and the actual contribution margin

Sales variances illustrated

A **contribution margin variance** measures the difference between the actual contribution margin and the standard contribution margin for each product. The contribution margin variance is computed as follows:

Contribution margin variance = (Standard contribution margin per unit −
Actual contribution margin per unit) ×
Actual units sold

The contribution margin variance analysis for Country Road Bike Shoppe is presented in Figure 16-10 together with the quantity and mix variances.

The standard and actual contribution margins are presented in Figures 16-8 and 16-9. The difference in contribution margin is multiplied by the actual quantity sold. Basically the contribution margin variance addresses the question, "Given the actual sales, how much different would profit have been if the expected contribution margin had occurred rather than the actual contribution margin?" For instance, if the contribution margin for ten-speed bicycles had been the standard of $117 a unit instead of the actual contribution margin of $110, the company's profit would have been $2,100 higher ($7 × 300 ten-speed bicycles). Likewise profit could have been $4 a unit higher if five-speed bicycles had attained their expected unit contribution margin. Since 600 five-speed bicycles were sold, the company's profit was $2,400 lower because of the lower-than-expected contribution margin. A higher-than-standard contribution margin is achieved for single-speed bicycles, which in total provide

Country Road Bike Shoppe
Sales Variance Analysis Report
For the Year 1983

Contribution Margin Variance

(Standard contribution margin − Actual contribution margin) ×
Actual units

Ten-speed ($117 − $110)(300 units) = $2,100 U	
Five-speed ($ 57 − $ 53)(600 units) = 2,400 U	
Single-speed ($ 27 − $ 34)(300 units) = 2,100 F	
Total contribution margin variance	$2,400 U

Quantity Variance

(Total expected sales − Total actual sales) ×
Average standard contribution margin

(1000 units − 1200 units) ($66)	13,200 F

Mix Variance

(Expect sales in units − Actual sales in units) ×
(Expected contribution margin per unit of product −
Average contribution margin per unit for all products)

Ten-speed (200 units − 300 units)($117 − $66) = $5,100 F	
Five-speed (700 units − 600 units)($ 57 − $66) = 900 F	
Single-speed (100 units − 300 units)($ 27 − $66) = $7,800 U	
Total mix variance	1,800 U
Total variance	$9,000 F

Figure 16-10
The performance report above isolates the contribution margin variance, the quantity variance, and the mix variance.

$2,100 more profit than would be the case with the standard contribution margin. The total of $2,400 U is the net result of all the contribution margin variances. It tells us that fluctuations from the standard contribution margins have decreased profit by $2,400 in 1983.

Quantity variance

Did we sell more total units than expected?

The **sales quantity variance,** like the yield variance, deals with total quantities rather than with specific products of the sales mix. Basically, the quantity variance addresses the question, "Did we sell more or less total units than expected?" This variance is basically an effectiveness measurement. More units than standard means a favourable variance, and less units than standard an unfavourable variance. The sales quantity variance should not be confused with the materials quantity variance, which is primarily an efficiency measure that asks, "Did we use more or less material than we should have given the amount of production?" The amount of the sales quantity variance is determined by the difference between expected and actual sales and the average contribution margin:

Quantity variance = (Total expected units of sales −
Total actual units of sales) ×
Average standard contribution margin per unit

The quantity variance in Figure 16-10 is a large favourable variance, because the bicycle store sold 20 percent more bicycles than expected. Notice that the quantity variance does not consider the mix of the units sold. High- and low-profit items are equally important in computing the quantity variance. Variances caused by selling a different product mix than expected are discussed next.

Mix variance

With a sales mix variance, the objective is to sell more of the high-profit items and less of the low-profit items

The **sales mix variance** measures the profit consequences of selling products in amounts different from the standard sales mix. In terms of sales mix only, managers generally want to increase the sales of high-profit items relative to the sales of low-profit items. For any particular volume of sales, managers want to sell more high-profit items and fewer low-profit items. Therefore, a favourable mix variance occurs, whenever sales of a high-profit item exceed expected sales **or** whenever sales of a low-profit item fall short of expected sales. Unfavourable sales mix variances occur when sales of low-profit items exceed the standard quantity. Note the characteristics similar to a production mix variance, where the object is to use more low-cost inputs and less high-cost inputs. The computation of the sales mix variance is as follows:

Sales mix variance = (Expected sales in units − Actual sales in units) ×
(Expected contribution margin per unit of product −
Average contribution margin per unit of all products)

Figure 16-10 includes the sales mix variance at the bottom of the report. The standard sales quantities and contribution margins and the average contribution margin are found in Figure 16-8. Actual sales quantities and contribution margins are presented in Figure 16-9.

One hundred more ten-speed bicycles were sold than expected, and the ten-speed bicycle is a high-profit item resulting in a favourable mix variance of $5,100. High-profit items are products that provide a higher contribution margin than the average. In this example, only ten-speed bicycles have a higher contribution margin than the $66 average. The low-profit five-speed bicycle falls 100 units short of standard sales, yielding a favourable mix variance of $900. More single-speed bicycles were sold than expected, but single-speeds are low-profit products. More-than-standard sales of a low-profit product means an unfavourable sales mix variance, in this case $7,800 U. The total sales mix variance is $1,800 unfavourable, indicating that the net effect of selling a product mix different from the expected one is $1,800 unfavourable.

Some people have difficulty understanding why selling more of a low-profit item yields an unfavourable variance. The point to remember is that the mix variance only measures the effect of selling a different sales mix from what was expected. The effect of sales volume changes has been dealt with in the quantity variance. Consequently, if a low-profit item sells more than the standard quantity, it appears as a favourable quantity variance and an unfavourable mix variance. To illustrate, the bicycle shop sold 200 more single-speed bicycles than expected. This resulted in an unfavourable mix variance of \$7,800 [200 bicycles × (\$27 − \$66 a bicycle)]. However, it also contributed \$13,200 of favourable variance (200 bicycles × \$66 a bicycle) to the quantity variance. The net effect is that selling the 200 additional single-speed bicycles contributed an additional \$5,400 of profit to the shop. Whenever variance analysis is performed, the analyst must constantly be aware of precisely what is being measured by the analysis.

Algebraic analysis of sales mix variances

Earlier we mentioned that if production mix variances are solved using algebraic rules, all positive answers mean favourable variances and all negative answers mean unfavourable variances. Just the **reverse** is true for sales mix variances. Positive outcomes are unfavourable variances and negative outcomes are favourable variances. The reason for the difference is that production mix attempts to minimize cost, while sales mix attempts to maximize profits.

Summary

Standard cost variance analysis reports provide managers with much detailed and useful information for planning and controlling many types of business activities. The material and labour variances presented in Chapter 8 are widely used and often provide managers with adequate variance information to make intelligent decisions about material use and about the management of production activities. However, sometimes when multiple inputs are used to produce a product and the mix of inputs can be varied, variance analysis reports may need to be expanded. The material quantity variance and labour efficiency variance can be divided into mix and yield variances.

A materials **mix variance** measures the cost effect of using a proportion of material inputs that differs from the standard. The **yield variance** measures the cost effect of using more or less total inputs than required by standards.

In terms of the mix of resources, managers would prefer to use more low-cost inputs and fewer high-cost inputs, which would result in a favourable mix variance. A high-cost input is one that has a standard cost greater than the **standard average cost** of inputs. The size of the mix variance is determined by the difference between the standard and the actual quantity and the difference between the standard cost of the input and the standard average cost of all inputs.

The yield variance is used to compare the inputs at standard cost with the outputs at standard cost. Actual inputs are multiplied by the standard average cost of inputs, and outputs are multiplied by the standard cost per unit of output.

Usually managers are interested in determining the cause of changes in the input mix and the cost effect of such changes. Factors influencing input mix are human error, random error, resource shortages, and attempts to reduce costs. Part of the information used by managers to determine the cause and cost effect of input mix changes consists of mix and yield variances.

Mix and yield variances can be computed for the labour efficiency variance if multiple labour classifications are used to produce the product. The computational process is the same except that labour data are substituted for material data.

Many nonmanufacturing activities can benefit from a good standard cost system. If standards are created for sales volume, sales price, sales mix, and variable costs, then several detailed variance analysis reports can be prepared. Included are a contribution margin variance report, a quantity variance report, and a sales mix variance report.

The **contribution margin variance** measures the difference in profit or contribution margin when actual contribution margins are different from expected contribution margins. The **quantity variance** measures the effect of selling more or less **total** units than expected. The variance is based solely on the total number of units sold regardless of the mix of units, and the computation is based on the weighted average profit of all products. The **sales mix variance** measures the impact on profits of selling a different mix of products from the standard sales mix. A favourable variance occurs when more than the standard amount of a high-profit product is sold or when less than the standard amount of a low-profit product is sold. High or low profit is determined by the profit margin of individual products compared with the weighted average profit margin for the standard product mix.

List of important terms		
	contribution margin variance *(689)*	**sales mix variance** *(691)*
	labour efficiency variance *(672)*	**sales quantity variance** *(690)*
	labour rate variance *(678)*	**standard average cost** *(682)*
	material price variance *(677)*	**variance analysis** *(675)*
	material quantity variance *(677)*	**yield variance** *(686)*
	production mix variance *(682)*	

Questions

1. Helen Morgan was hired recently as the controller in a manufacturing firm. One of her first actions was to develop a standard cost system for the company. Her first weekly standard cost variance analysis report, presented below, summarized the cost of variances for one of the company's products. The company president, not familiar with standard costs and variances commented, "I cannot tell what it cost to produce this product." Explain briefly the meaning of the variances and compute the product cost for the president.

Units produced	1000
Standard cost	$80 per unit
Material price variance	$1,500 U
Material quantity variance	$2,500 U
Labour rate variance	$2,000 U
Labour efficiency variance	$1,800 F

2. How do mix and yield variances relate to material quantity or labour efficiency variances?

3. What kind of situations lend themselves to mix and yield variance analysis? How does a mix and yield variance analysis assist managers in such situations?

4. How can using more than the standard amount of some resource produce a favourable variance?

5. Cite several reasons why the actual mix of production resources used may differ from the standard mix of production resources.

6. The monthly variance analysis reports have just been released. The assembly line report shows:

| Labour mix variance | $26,000 U |
| Labour yield variance | $37,400 F |

The assembly line supervisor states, "I knew we should not have hired all those skilled workers. Look at the horrible labour mix variance we generated." Do you agree with the supervisor's assessment? Explain.

7. "Standard costs are for manufacturing activities, not for marketing and administration. Standards for nonmanufacturing activities serve no useful purpose and waste a lot of time." Respond to the preceding remarks.

8. Describe the nature and use of a contribution margin variance analysis.

9. A regional sales manager just received a monthly sales performance report and is concerned about having an unfavourable sales mix variance on a product for which sales were double the expected amount. How can there be an unfavourable variance on a product whose sales were significantly higher than standard?

10. A sales mix variance and a production mix variance are the same variance for two different types of activities. Respond.

Exercises

Ex. 16-1   **Direct material and direct labour variances.** Following are standard and actual cost data for the production of a driveway sealer compound that is sold in 20-litre cans.

```
Standards
  Materials
    Silicate compounds      3 kilograms per can @ $.80 per kilogram
    Petroleum solvents      2 litres per can @ $.50 per litre
  Labour
    Skilled                 1/4 hour per can @ $9.00 per hour
    General                 1/10 hour per can @ $4.50 per hour
Actual Results
  Production                25 000 cans
  Material
    Silicate compounds      72 000 kilograms, cost $61,200
    Petroleum solvents      51 000 litres, cost $24,480
  Labour
    Skilled                 6000 hours, cost $55,500
    General                 2400 hours, cost $11,040
```

Required:

a. Compute the material price and quantity variances.

b. Compute the labour rate and efficiency variances.

Ex. 16-2   **Materials mix and yield variances.** A company produces a high-fibre axle grease for high-speed bearings. The grease is produced in 5000 litre vats. Below are standard cost data for materials for 5000 litres of output:

Material	Quantity	Input cost	Total Cost
MQ	1000 litres	$3.00/litre	$ 3,000
MR	3500 litres	1.50/litre	5,250
MZ	1500 litres	2.50/litre	3,750
Totals	6000 litres		$12,000

During the month of April, 24 000 litres of axle grease were produced and the following material costs were incurred:

Material	Quantity	Input cost	Total Cost
MQ	5 000 litres	$3.20/litre	$16,000
MR	18 000 litres	1.40/litre	25,200
MZ	6 000 litres	3.00/litre	18,000
Totals	29 000 litres		$59,200

Required:

Compute the mix and yield variance for the April production of axle grease.

Ex. 16-3 **Material quantity, mix, and yield variances.** A company produces an adhesive compound by mixing two substances together. Material standards for the product are

8 litres of petroleum distillates ZG7	@ $ .60 =	$4.80
2 litres of ketone compound YG7	@ 1.20 =	2.40
10 litres of standard mix		$7.20

Each 10 litres of standard mix yields 9 litres of adhesive.

In the month of October, 18 000 litres of adhesive are manufactured using 14 500 litres of petroleum distillates and 4600 litres of ketone compounds.

Required:
a. Calculate the material quantity variance.
b. Calculate the mix and yield variances.

Ex. 16-4 **Labour efficiency and mix and yield variances.** Downtown Plumbing Company uses plumbers and apprentices to perform many jobs. Plumbers command a higher wage and are more efficient than apprentices. The company has determined the following labour standards for septic tank installations, a major service of the firm:

Labour Classification	Hours	Rate
Plumbers	4	$15 per hour
Apprentices	8	6 per hour

During the last month the company installed 15 septic tank systems using 45 hours of plumbers' time and 150 hours of apprentices' time.

Required:
a. Compute the labour efficiency variance for the month.
b. Compute the labour mix and yield variances.

Ex. 16-5 **Material price mix and yield variances.** Sunshine Fruit Drinks has prepared the following material standards for 1 kilogram of its orange-flavoured powdered fruit drink mix:

Material	Quantity	Input Cost per Kilogram	Standard Cost of Output
Ascorbic acid	.02 kg	$2.50	$.05
Sugar	.50 kg	.14	.07
Flavouring	.38 kg	1.50	.57
Preservatives	.10 kg	.40	.04
Total	1.00 kg		$.73

In the month of December the company manufactured 20 000 kilograms of the drink mix. The following production costs were incurred:

Material	Quantity	Total Cost
Ascorbic acid	380 kg	$ 1,064
Sugar	10 500 kg	1,680
Flavouring	7 800 kg	10,920
Preservatives	2 200 kg	924
Total	20 880 kg	$14,588

Required:
Compute the material price, mix, and yield variances.

Ex. 16-6 **Sales variances.** Fern decides to open a lemonade stand in her front yard during summer vacation. Her mother builds her a stand of spare lumber she found in the garage. Fern plans to sell two drinks. Her estimate of sales for the summer are presented below:

Product	Price per Glass	Sales in Units	Unit Variable Cost
Lemonade	$.30	600	$.21
Fruit punch	.20	400	.06

Based on the above Fern expected to earn a profit of $110 during the summer. However, her actual profit was $124 in spite of the fact that she sold much less of the high-price drink and sold fewer total drinks than she expected. Being a fifth-grader, Fern has not had any accounting, and she asks you to explain why she made more money with fewer sales. Actual sales data are presented on page 698.

Product	Price per Glass	Sales in Units	Unit Variable Cost
Lemonade	$.30	300	$.19
Fruit punch	.20	650	.06

Required:

a. Prepare a variance report including contribution margin, quantity, and mix variances.

b. Explain to Fern what your variance report means to her in terms of the performance of her business.

Ex. 16-7 **Mix and yield variances for labour.** The Longly City School Board has decided to establish an extensive achievement testing program for all students in the third, sixth, and ninth grades. The purpose of the program is to measure the performance of students in the school system against provincial-wide averages. Teachers will do some of the testing, but outside help must be hired to handle much of the individual testing. Substitute teachers or teachers' aids can be hired to assist in testing. Substitute teachers and teachers' aids are less efficient at testing because they are not as familiar with each student or with the testing procedures as regular teachers. Expected time and personnel costs for testing the estimated 1500 students are:

	Hours	Rate
Teachers	600	$7 per hour
Substitutes	2100	6 per hour
Aids	3300	4 per hour

During the school year 1700 students were tested. A shortage of qualified substitute teachers required the use of more teachers' aids in the testing program than expected. Actual costs for the year are

	Hours	Cost
Teachers	600	$ 4,680
Substitutes	1400	9,100
Aids	5100	21,675
Total	7100	$35,455

The school board is interested in data on the cost of the program compared with the original cost estimates. Also, the board would like to know the effect of the necessary modification in the staffing of the program.

Required:

a. Calculate the standard average labour cost, standard hours per student, and expected labour cost per student based on original estimates of cost.
b. Calculate the total variance of the labour cost for the program.
c. Compute labour rate and efficiency variances.
d. Prepare a labour mix and yield variance report and explain the meanings of these variances to the school board.

Ex. 16-8 **Marketing variances.** Lakeside Marine Products has just secured the local distributorship for Salt-Spray boats, a recognized name in quality fishing boats. The manager of Lakeside has the following sales and cost expectations for the new product for the coming season:

Boat	Sales Units	Price	Unit Variable Cost
3 m	30	$ 500	$320
4 m	50	800	480
5 m	20	1,200	750
	100		

When the season is over the manager accumulates the sales and cost data presented below, but he would like a more systematic analysis of the data. He asks you to help.

Boat	Sales Units	Price	Unit Variable Cost
3 m	28	$ 490	$300
4 m	55	780	500
5 m	12	1,250	760
	95		

Required:
Prepare a detailed analysis of variance report for the manager showing contribution margin, quantity, and sales mix variances.

Ex. 16-9 **Materials price, quantity, mix, and yield variances.** The Northside Lacquer Company uses four inputs in its production of hard-gloss lacquer. On page 700 are standards for a typical production run of 1000 litres of lacquer:

Material	Litres	Unit Cost	Total Cost
Alkyd solutions	480	$2	$ 960
Calcium carbonate	360	3	1,080
Petroleum distillates	240	5	1,200
Pigment	120	8	960
Total	1200		$4,200

During January 1984, 22 000 litres of lacquer are produced and the following production data are accumulated:

Material	Litres	Unit Cost	Total Cost
Alkyd solutions	11 000	$1.80	$19,800
Calcium carbonate	7 500	2.90	21,750
Petroleum distillates	5 500	5.40	29,700
Pigment	2 100	9.00	18,900
Total	26 100		$90,150

Required:
a. Compute the price and quantity variance for Northside Lacquer Company.
b. Compute a material yield and mix variance.
c. Suppose you were the production manager. Would you use the standard mix of materials or the January mix to manufacture February production? Explain.

Ex. 16-10 **Material price mix and yield variances.** The Industrial Solvents Company prepares the following standards for a typical production run of 2000 litres of its lightweight solvent:

Material	Quantity	Unit Cost	Total Cost
Acetate	300 litres	$8 per litre	$ 2,400
Acetone	800 litres	6 per litre	4,800
Ketones	400 litres	5 per litre	2,000
Petroleum distillates	1000 litres	4 per litre	4,000
Total	2500 litres		$13,200

During the last quarter of 1983 the company manufactured 31 000 litres of lightweight solvent, incurring the following material costs:

Material	Quantity	Unit Cost	Total Cost
Acetate	3 700 litres	$8.50	$ 31,450
Acetone	14 000 litres	6.40	89,600
Ketones	6 800 litres	5.10	34,680
Petroleum distillates	14 500 litres	3.70	53,650
Total	39 000 litres		$209,380

Required:

a. Determine the total material variance for the last quarter of 1983.

b. Compute the material price, mix, and yield variances for the period.

c. Given the actual cost of the materials used during the last quarter of 1983, determine the material cost of a litre of solvent if the standard mix of inputs had been used.

Problem Set A

P. 16A-1 **Price mix and yield variances.** Iram K. Whiplash, an inventor, has developed a powerful racing fuel. He has prepared the following set of standards for a typical production run of racing fuel.

Standards			
Raw Material	**Quantity in litres**	**Price/litre**	**Total Cost**
Alcohol	100	$8.00	$ 800
Flite-fuel	600	3.00	1,800
Xzote	300	6.00	1,800
Total	1000		$4,400

Standard yield = 20 barrels

Actual Results			
Raw Material	**Quantity in litres**	**Price/litre**	**Total Cost**
Alcohol	150	$7.00	$1,050
Flite-fuel	600	4.50	2,700
Xzote	400	6.50	2,600
Total	1150		$6,350

Actual yield = 25 barrels

Required:

Using the data above to analyze the price, mix, and yield variances.

P. 16A-2   **Labour mix and yield variances.** Elec-Tec-Instruments, Ltd., plans to re-view and evaluate all product engineering specifications and standard costs for all its products. The purpose of the review is to detect errors or omissions, up-date requirements to reflect the current production environment of the firm, and provide more uniform decisions on standards and engineering specifi-cations that had been developed over a number of years. This rather large project cannot be undertaken solely by the company's current personnel without disrupting normal business activities. Therefore, college juniors studying engineering and accounting will be hired for the summer to help with the job. In addition, some of the company's clerical staff will be used. Professional staff from the engineering department and accounting depart-ment will supervise student and clerical employees and will make all evalu-ations and modifications of standards and specifications. Students and clerical employees will cross-reference standards with engineering speci-fications, check for numerical errors, classify data by product type and production activity, and generally serve the professional staff in whatever capacity possible for completing the project. Elec-Tec-Instruments estab-lishes the following labour standards for the project:

Type of Labour	Expected Labour Time	Expected Labour Cost
Professional staff	3000 hours	$45,000
Clerical	1200 hours	6,000
Students	7800 hours	31,200

Products to be reviewed = 300

In early September the project is completed. The company accumulates the following data related to the project:

Type of Labour	Actual Labour Time	Actual Labour Cost
Professional staff	2 800 hours	$39,200
Clerical	1 400 hours	7,350
Students	10 000 hours	42,000

Products reviewed = 320

Required:
a. Compute unit standards for input and output.
b. Compute the labour rate and efficiency variances for the project.
c. Compute labour mix and yield variances from the data.
d. During the project, management decided to train students to perform some of the easier evaluation functions in an effort to relieve professional staff members for daily activities. Compute the economic consequence of the labour shift.

P. 16A-3   Sales variance analysis. Miscellaneous Industries produces and sells four products. Budget and actual production and sales data are presented below for each product and in total.

				Budgeted Data			
Product	Units	Unit Price	Sales	Unit Var. Cost	Total Var. Cost	Contribution Margin
A	2 000	$20	$ 40,000	$8	$ 16,000	$12
B	6 000	10	60,000	6	36,000	4
C	8 000	8	64,000	6	48,000	2
D	4 000	15	60,000	5	20,000	10
Total	20 000		$224,000		$120,000	

Fixed cost = $35,000
Budgeted net income = Sales − Variable cost − Fixed cost
= $224,000 − $120,000 − $35,000 = $69,000

				Actual Data			
Product	Units	Unit Price	Sales	Unit Var. Cost	Total Var. Cost	Contribution Margin
A	3 000	$20	$ 60,000	$9	$ 27,000	$11
B	5 000	9	45,000	6	30,000	3
C	9 000	8	72,000	5	45,000	3
D	4 000	15	60,000	6	24,000	9
Total	21 000		$237,000		$126,000	

Fixed cost = $35,000
Actual net income = $237,000 − $126,000 − $35,000 = $76,000

Required:
Compute the contribution margin variance, quantity variance, and sales mix variance.

P. 16A-4   Production variance analysis. Jackson Food Processing Company produces a variety of convenience foods and canned products. A popular product is beef stew, which is packaged in 2-kilogram cans. Production standards for beef stew are presented on page 704 for a normal cooking vat of 2000 kilograms of stew:

Material	Quantity in Kilograms	Cost per Kilogram	Total Cost
Beef	500	$1.71	$ 855
Beef broth	800	.20	160
Potatoes	500	.12	60
Tomato paste	300	.40	120
Sugar	100	.15	15
Total	2200		$1,210

Labour	Hours	Rate	Total Cost
Mixing	24	$5	$120
Cooking	16	8	128
Total	40		$248

In the past month 7000 cans of beef stew were produced. The following production costs were incurred:

Material	Quantity in Kilograms	Cost per Kilogram	Total Cost
Beef	3 200	$1.80	$5,760
Beef broth	6 000	.18	1,080
Potatoes	3 000	.09	324
Tomato paste	2 200	.44	968
Sugar	600	.15	90
Total	15 600		$8,222

Labour	Hours	Rate	Total Cost
Mixing	150	$5.20	$ 780
Cooking	125	8.40	1,050
Total	275		$1,830

Required:
a. Calculate the standard prime cost for one can of beef stew.
b. Compute the material price and quantity variances.
c. Determine the labour rate and efficiency variances.
d. Find the material mix and yield variances.
e. Compute the labour mix and yield variances.

P. 16A-5 **Contribution margin, sales quantity, and sales mix variances.** Vergouven Home Appliance Store sells three types of refrigerator-freezer units. The standard model is a .4 cubic metre model with a freezer at the top. The deluxe model is .5 cubic metre and frost-free and has an ice maker. The side-by-side model is .7 cubic metre and frost-free and has an ice maker and .3 cubic metre of freezer space. In an effort to plan and control operations better, the store has prepared the following schedule of expected sales of refrigerators:

Refrigerator	Sales in Units	Price	Sales	Unit Variable Cost	Unit Contribution Margin	Total Contribution Margin
Standard	100	$400	$ 40,000	$300	$100	$10,000
Deluxe	300	600	180,000	420	180	54,000
Side-by-side	100	900	90,000	600	300	30,000
Total	500		$310,000			$94,000

During the year the store had the following refrigerator sales:

Refrigerator	Sales in Units	Price	Sales	Unit Variable Cost	Unit Contribution Margin	Total Contribution Margin
Standard	120	$410	$ 49,200	$290	$120	$14,400
Deluxe	360	560	201,600	420	140	50,400
Side-by-side	70	880	61,600	620	260	18,200
Total	550		$312,400			$83,000

Required:
Prepare a variance analysis report for the store isolating the contribution margin variance, quantity variance, and sales mix variance.

P. 16A-6 **Material, labour, and overhead variances.** Murphy Manufacturing Company uses a standard cost system for all its production activities. Below are standard and actual cost data for the production of an industrial lubricant sold by the barrel.

Required:
a. Compute the material price and quantity variances.
b. Determine the labour rate and efficiency variances.
c. Compute manufacturing overhead variances using the two-variance method.

Standard Costs per Barrel	Actual Results

Materials:
  A   10 kg @ $.60./kg
  B   15 kg @ $.25./kg
Labour:
  Blending   .6 DLH @ $8.50/h
  Packaging   .4 DLH @ $5.00/h
Overhead:
  Variable $10 per direct labour hour
  Fixed $40,000
  Budgeted activity level   10 000 direct labour hours
	Output = 10 500 barrels
	Materials:
	  A 106 000 kg @ $.50/kg
	  B 150 000 kg @ $.30/kg
	Labour:
	  Blending 6760 @ $8.20/h
	  Packaging 3900 @ $5.40/h
	Overhead:
	  Actual $131,000
	  Applied ?

Problem Set B

P. 16B-1   Price, mix, and yield variances. Smedly Smalsh has been producing high-quality garden fertilizer for many years. Until recently he never worried about production variances. But tough economic conditions are causing him some concern. He therefore called in a consultant to help him set production standards. But just looking at the standards for a typical 4-ton production run does not help. He calls you in to analyze April production data. Below are the standards as well as the production data for April 1984.

Standards			
Raw Material	**Price / Kilo**	**Kilo**	**Total Cost**
B	$ 2.00	800	$1,600
Y	12.00	300	3,600
Z	8.00	100	800
			$6,000

Expected yield from inputs = 4 tons

Actual Production			
Raw Material	**Price / Kilograms**	**Kilogram**	**Total Cost**
B	$ 2.20	4,600	$10,120
Y	11.00	1,200	13,200
Z	9.00	700	6,300
			$29,620

Actual yield = 20 tons

Required:
Analyze the price, mix, and yield variances using the above production data.

P. 16B-2 **Labour rate, mix, and yield variances.** The Campbell TV Cable Company is a five-year-old company with a rapidly expanding business. A major cost of the company is labour used to install cable service to new customers. The process involves laying the cable from the line near the street to the house of the new customer and then getting the cable into the house and attaching it to the television set. The cable connections at the main line and television set must be done by skilled electricians. Most of the other work can be done by general labour although the electricians may perform other activities in the installation process. The company has established the following labour standards for installing a cable:

Type of Labour	Time Required	Hourly Rate
Electrician	1 hour	$14
General labour	2 hours	5

During the first six months of 1983 the company experienced the following results:

Cable installations	3000
Electrician labour	$48,000 for 3200 hours
General labour	28,600 for 5200 hours

Required:

a. Compute the rate mix and yield variances for labour.

b. If the shift in labour inputs from the standard mix is caused by management's decision, determine whether it was a good decision. Discuss your opinion.

P. 16B-3 **Contribution margin, sales quantity and sales mix variance.** Hard-time Incorporated sells three products with varying profit margins. Below are the budgeted and actual sales and cost data for fiscal 1983–84.

Budget						
Product	Units	Price	Sales	Unit Variable Cost	Total Variable Cost	Contribution Margin
X	6 000	$25	$150,000	$ 8	$ 48,000	$17/unit
Y	12 000	10	120,000	6	72,000	4/unit
Z	2 000	15	30,000	12	24,000	3/unit
Total	20 000		$300,000		$144,000	

				Actual		
Product	Units	Price	Sales	Unit Variable Cost	Total Variable Cost	Contribution Margin
X	7 000	$23	$161,000	$9	$ 63,000	$14/unit
Y	15 000	9	135,000	5	75,000	4/unit
Z	2 000	14	28,000	9	18,000	5/unit
Total	24 000		$324,000		$156,000	

Required:

Compute the contribution margin variance, sales quantity variance, and sales mix variance.

P. 16B-4   Multiple input variance analysis. The By-Cracky-Snacky Company manufactures a variety of snack foods, including pretzel sticks, whose production standards are listed below for an 800-kilogram batch:

Materials	Quantity	Unit Cost	Total Cost
Flour	600 kg	$ .14/kg	$ 84
Shortening	250 kg	.48/kg	120
Butter	100 kg	1.20/kg	120
Yeast	10 kg	1.40/kg	14
Salt	40 kg	.15/kg	6
Total	1000 kg		$344

Labour	Hours	Rate	Total Cost
Skilled	4	$8 per hour	$32
General	2	4 per hour	8
Total	6		$40

The company packages pretzel sticks in 1-kg bags and sells them to wholesalers for 175 percent of standard prime cost. In the month of November the company produced 9000 bags of pretzel sticks. Actual production costs were:

Material	Quantity	Total Cost	Labour	Hours	Total Cost
Flour	7 000 kg	$ 840	Skilled	40 hours	$336
Shortening	3 000 kg	1,500	General	30 hours	126
Butter	1 000 kg	1,350	Total	70 hours	$462
Yeast	110 kg	132			
Salt	420 kg	63			
Total	11 530 kg	$3,885			

Required:

a. Compute the material quantity and price variances.

b. Find the labour rate and efficiency variances.

c. Determine the material mix and yield variances.

d. Compute the price to wholesalers per bag of pretzels.

P. 16B-5   Sales variances. A department store sells three different types of air conditioning units. Expected sales and cost data for the first six months of the year are presented below:

Air Conditioner	Sales in Units	Selling Price	Sales	Unit Variable Cost	Unit Contribution Margin	Total Contribution Margin
6 000 BTU	500	$300	$150,000	$180	$120	$ 60,000
10 000 BTU	300	400	120,000	240	160	48,000
25 000 BTU	200	800	160,000	420	380	76,000
Total	1000		$430,000			$184,000

Summaries of sales and cost data for the period show the following actual results:

Air Conditioner	Sales in Units	Selling Price	Sales	Unit Variable Cost	Unit Contribution Margin	Total Contribution Margin
6 000 BTU	400	$280	$112,000	$180	$100	$ 40,000
10 000 BTU	400	400	160,000	250	150	60,000
25 000 BTU	300	825	247,500	440	385	115,500
Total	1100		$519,500			$215,500

Required:
Compute variances for contribution margin, sales quantity, and sales mix.

P. 16B-6   Comprehensive standard cost variance analysis problem.
Rainbow Paints, Inc., uses a standard cost system to control costs and to provide data for product pricing decisions. Below are standard cost data for one of its products. The standards data are followed by actual results data for the fiscal year ended March 31, 1984.

Standards		
Materials	**Quantity (for 5L can)**	**Cost**
Base	.4 kg	$1.50/kg
Hardener	.25 L	$10.00/L
Colour	.50 L	$ 6.00/L
Labour	**Quantity (for 10 can case)**	**Rate**
Mixing	6h/10 can case	$5.00/h
Packaging	2 h/10 can case	$4.00/h

MOH	
Fixed MOH cost	$96,000
Variable MOH cost	$2.00/DLH
Expected (Budgeted) activity level	32 000 DLH

Actual Results for the Fiscal Year		
Output = 40 000 cans		
Materials	**Quantity**	**Cost**
Base	165 000 kg	$264,000
Hardener	9 800 L	$9.00/L
Colour	21 000 L	$7.00/L
Labour	**Hours**	**Cost**
Mixing	24 500	$134,750
Packaging	7 600	$30,400
Actual MOH		
$161,400		

Required:
a. Calculate the material quantity and price variances.
b. Determine the labour rate and efficiency variances.
c. Compute the overhead variances using the two-variance method.
d. Calculate the standard cost of one can of paint.
e. Find the actual cost of one can of paint.

Minicases

Minicase 16-1   (CMA Examination Question)

The Felton Company manufactures a complete line of radios. Because a large number of models have plastic cases, the company has its own moulding department for producing the cases. The month of April was devoted to the production of the plastic case for one of the portable radios—Model SX 76.

The Moulding Department has two operations—moulding and trimming. There is no interaction of labour in these two operations. The standard labour cost for producing ten (10) plastic cases for Model SX76 is as follows:

Moulders	.50 h @ $6.00	= $3.00
Trimmers	.25 h @ $4.00	= $1.00
		$4.00

During April, 70 000 plastic cases were produced in the Moulding Department. However, 10 percent of these cases (7000) had to be discarded because they were found defective at final inspection. The Purchasing Department had changed to a new plastic supplier to take advantage of a lower price for comparable plastic. The new plastic turned out to be of a lower-quality plastic, and resulted in the rejection of completed cases.

Direct labour hours worked and direct labour costs charged to the Moulding Department are shown below.

Direct Labour Charged to the Moulding Department		
Moulders	3800 h @ $6.25	= $23,750
Trimmers	1600 h @ $4.15	= $ 6,640
Total labour charges		$30,390

As a result of poor scheduling by the Production Scheduling Department, the foreman of the Moulding Department had to shift moulders to the trimming operation for 200 hours during April. The company paid the moulding workers their regular hourly rate even though they were performing a lower-rated task. There was no significant loss of efficiency caused by the shift. In addition, the foreman of the department indicated that 75 hours and 35 hours of idle time occurred in the moulding and trimming operations, respectively, as a result of unexpected machinery repairs required during the month.

Required:

a. The monthly report which compares actual costs with standard cost of output for the month of April shows the following labour variance for the Moulding Department:

Actual labour cost for April	$30,390
Standard labour cost of output	
(63 000 × $4.00/10)	25,200
Unfavourable labour variance	$ 5,190

This variance is significantly higher than normal and management would like an explanation. Prepare a detailed analysis of the unfavourable labour variance resulting from (1) labour rates; (2) labour substitution; (3) material substitution; (4) operating efficiency; and (5) idle time.

b. The foreman of the Moulding Department is concerned with the large variances charged to his department. He feels that the variances due to labour substitution and change in raw materials should not be charged to his department. Does the foreman have a valid argument? Briefly justify your position.

Minicase 16-2 (SMA of Canada adapted)

Monson Company manufactures a special assembly which requires three different types of labour inputs: E1, E2, and E3. The standard inputs of labour for the assembly units are: 2 hours of E1, three hours of E2, and 5 hours of E3. Standard wage rates per hour are $10, $12, and $8 for E1, E2, and E3, respectively.

In the month of February, 1000 assembly units were produced. Recorded inputs of E1, E2, and E3 were 900 hours, 1800 hours, and 2100 hours, respectively. Wage rates for E1 and E2 remained at standard, but E3, being in short supply, was paid $8.50 per hour.

Required:
Determine the labour-wage rate, mix and yield variances, if any.

Minicase 16-3 (SMA adapted)
King Corporation manufactures a special type of metal alloy. Budgeted sales for 1984 were 10 000 kilograms at $50 per kilogram. Standard variable production and selling costs were $30 per kilogram. Fixed costs were budgeted at $50,000 for 1984.

Actual fixed costs in 1984 were $50,000, but the market price realized was $55 per kilogram due to an international shortage. Operating income was below the static budget figure amount by $50,000. Revenue volume variance for 1984 was $100,000 unfavourable. Contribution margin price variance was $20,000 unfavourable.

Required:

Determine the following:

a. Revenue price variance.

b. Variable cost price variance.

c. Variable cost efficiency variance.

d. Contribution margin efficiency variance.

e. Variable cost volume variance.

f. Contribution margin volume variance.

g. Operating income volume variance.

Minicase 16-4   (CMA Examination Question)

The Lenco Company employs a standard cost system as part of its cost control program. The standard cost per unit is established at the beginning of each year. Standards are not revised during the year for any changes in material or labour inputs or in the manufacturing processes. Any revisions in standards are deferred until the beginning of the next fiscal year. However, in order to recognize such changes in the current year, the company includes planned variances in the monthly budgets prepared after such changes have been introduced.

The following labour standard was set for one of Lenco's products effective July 1, 1984, the beginning of the fiscal year.

Class I labour 4 hours @ $6.00	$24.00
Class II labour 3 hours @ $7.50	$22.50
Class V labour 1 hour @ $11.50	$11.50
Standard labour cost per 100 units	$58.00

The standard was based upon the quality of material that had been used in prior years and what was expected to be available for the 1984-85 fiscal year. The labour activity is performed by a team consisting of four persons with Class I skills, three persons with Class II skills, and one person with Class V skills. This is the most economical combination for the company's processing system.

The manufacturing operations occurred as expected during the first five months of the year. The standard costs contributed to effective cost control during this period. However, there were indications that changes in the operations would be required in the last half of the year. The company had received a significant increase in orders for delivery in the spring. There were an inadequate number of skilled workers available to meet the increased production.

As a result, the production teams, beginning in January, would be made up of more Class I labour and less Class II labour than the standard required. The teams would consist of six Class I persons, two Class II persons and one Class V person. This labour team would be less efficient than the normal team. The reorganized teams work more slowly so that only 90 units are produced in the same time period that 100 unit would normally be produced. No raw materials will be lost as a result of the change in the labour mix. Completed units have never been rejected in the final inspection process as a consequence of faulty work; this is expected to continue.

In addition, Lenco was notified by its material supplier that a lower-quality material would be supplied after January 1. One unit of raw material normally is required for each good unit produced. Lenco and its supplier estimated that 5 percent of the units manufactured would be rejected upon final inspection due to defective material. Normally, no units are lost due to defective material.

Required:

a. How much of the lower quality material must be entered into production in order to produce 42 750 units of good production in January with the new labour teams? Show your calculations.

b. How many hours of each class of labour will be needed to produce 42 750 good units from the material input? Show your calculations.

c. What amount should be included in the January budget for the planned labour variance due to the labour team and material changes? What amount of this planned labour variance can be associated with the (1) material change; and (2) the team change? Show your calculations.

Chapter 17

Cost-Finding Tools and Techniques

Many sophisticated techniques have been developed for the purpose of providing managers with better data on which to base their decisions. This chapter discusses a number of such techniques. When you have completed this chapter, you should understand:

1 The strengths and weaknesses of quantitative managerial tools.

2 The meaning of central tendency measures.

3 The use of dispersion measures such as the standard deviation.

4 The use of the powerful quantitative technique known as regression-correlation analysis.

5 The use of the results of regression-correlation analysis.

6 The basic aspects of learning curves.

7 The basic concepts of trend analysis using moving averages and exponential smoothing.

Cost behaviour patterns have played an important role in the discussion of many different concepts in previous chapters. Cost-volume-profit, alternative choice decisions, flexible budgeting, variable costing, and manufacturing overhead variance analysis are some of the topics that require the use of cost behaviour data.

Identifying cost behaviour patterns is among the more difficult tasks facing an accountant. Yet it is an important one because of the frequent use of costs in managerial analysis. In Chapter 5, we discussed cost behaviour and described several fairly simple techniques for identifying behaviour patterns such as the high-low method and scatter diagram method. In this chapter we discuss and illustrate several more sophisticated methods for identifying and analyzing cost behaviour patterns. The purpose and applicability of each method are described, followed by a simple illustration. For each method the computational process is carefully explained and finally more complex applications are discussed. An appendix to the chapter provides computer programs for some of the analysis methods.

The use of quantitative methods

Few business topics generate stronger opinions than the use of quantitative methods in business. Advocates argue the virtues of being able to describe and analyze business activities in quantitative terms. Dissenters maintain that there is no substitute for understanding the intricate interrelationships of a business and that quantitative models often miss the central issues of a problem. Part of the controversy arises from the fact that many quantitative tools have been introduced into business by people who found a technique and then went looking for a problem that fits it. The logical approach is to identify a problem and then look for an effective way to solve the problem. In this chapter we discuss several solution techniques that are useful in certain situations.

Quantitative methods do not always yield correct or useful data. Our purpose in this chapter is to present some quantitative tools that are **potentially** useful in planning and control activities, as well as in managerial analysis and decision making. You should attempt to become proficient with these tools and use them when they prove fruitful, and you should have the courage and wisdom to ignore them when they are not useful. Wise managers fill their arsenal with a wide variety of tools that may be utilized when the situation requires. Quantitative tools should be part of that arsenal.

Statistics

Statistical data provide information

The mere mention of the term *statistics* causes some people to envision complicated numerical analyses that are difficult to understand. Although some statistical analyses are complex, many statistical measures and analyses are not difficult and can provide managers with information useful in making decisions. In its simplest form, a **statistic** is merely a numerical representation or description of something. For instance, a person's age is a statistic that provides some information about the person. Additional statistics such as height, weight, grade point average, and others provide a more complete description of the person. Many statistics are used in business, both externally and internally. Earnings per share and dividend payments are two important statistics that investors, lenders, and others use to help evaluate the performance of businesses. Such statistics provide external users with descriptive measures of performance that may be compared among several firms or for a single firm over a period of time. Internally there are many different statistics that are used for planning, control, and decision making. Included are statistics on inventory turnover, daily cash receipts, average production costs, and many others.

In the course of developing the cost accounting data base, managers accumulate a wealth of data, much of which is assimilated and analyzed to provide relevant information for decision making. Much of the analysis involves statistical measures of central tendency and dispersion.

Measures of central tendency

One of the most commonly used business statistics is a measure of central tendency called an average. The average represents a central number, a middle value that is representative of a set of data. For decision making an average is often the most important characteristic of a set of data. For example, daily cash receipts for a retail store during the past year ranged from $500 on the day of a blizzard to a high of $8,500 during peak sales, with an average of $5,200. The range of daily cash receipts may have some information value, but the average is more useful in predicting cash receipts for some future period. Averages such as average unit costs, average hourly wage rate, and average inventory size are widely used in all areas of business.

There are several different ways of calculating averages. Each provides a different **measure of central tendency.** We use the data in Figure 17-1 to illustrate the calculation of several types of averages. The data consist of weekly cash receipts of the Streeter Company for a period of nine weeks.

Averages are useful statistics

Mean. The most commonly used average is the **mean,** which is determined by adding up the value of each element in a set of data and dividing the total by the number of data elements in the set. The mean of the cash receipts data is computed as follows:

$$\text{Mean} = \frac{x_1 + x_2 + x_3 + \cdots + x_n}{n}$$

$$= \frac{\Sigma x_i}{n}$$

where

x_i = individual values for the data elements with $i = 1, 2, \ldots, n$
n = number of data elements
Σ = summation sign indicating that the values of x_i are added together

$$\text{Mean} = \frac{\$5,800 + \$4,300 + \$6,500 + \$7,000 + \$6,800 + \$5,500 + \$5,400 + \$6,500 + \$6,200}{9}$$

$$= \frac{\$54,000}{9}$$

$$= \$6,000$$

The mean of the nine weeks of cash flow data is $6,000. The mean, usually denoted as $\overline{X}$, is a very important value for many statistical calculations.

Streeter Company Weekly Cash Receipts	
Week	**Cash Collected**
1	$5,800
2	4,300
3	6,500
4	7,000
5	6,800
6	5,500
7	5,400
8	6,500
9	6,200

Figure 17-1
Nine weeks of cash receipts data for Streeter Company. The range of values is $2,700, but what is the expected amount of cash receipts each week?

Median. Another type of average is the **median,** which is the middle value of the data set. There is an equal number of values below and above the median value. The easiest way to determine the median value is to list all the values in the data set in either descending or ascending order. For example, the cash receipts data in ascending order are

$4,300
5,400
5,500
5,800
6,200
6,500
6,500
6,800
7,000

Since there are nine values in the set, the middle value is the fifth value or $6,200, with four values above the median and four values below.[1] The median is useful when the middle value is an important measure. For example, a few very low test scores can make the mean of a test much lower than the median. Often students are more concerned with their relative class standing; thus the median may be more informative than the mean.

Mode. A third measure of central tendency is the **mode,** which is the most frequently occurring value in the data set. In the Streeter Company example in Figure 17-1 only the value $6,500 occurs more than once. Therefore, this amount is the mode. Like the median, the mode is determined by observing the data rather than by computing it mathematically. The mode is not used in statistical

[1]If there is an even number of data elements, the median is the mean of the pair of middle values.

computations, but as the most frequently occurring value it may suggest business patterns or other characteristics of the business. For example, the manager of a shoe store would be interested in knowing the most commonly purchased shoe size so as to order more shoes of that size for any given style. The mean or median shoe size is not as significant as the mode. Note that in any set of data there may be no mode, or several modes may exist. The mode is most useful as a qualitative measure and is seldom used in statistical analysis.

Measures of dispersion

Another very important type of statistical measure is **dispersion,** which refers to the amount of variation in the values of data elements about the mean. The amount of variation can be very important in planning. For example, look at the weekly sales volume data in Figure 17-2 for two fast-food restaurants.

Both stores have total sales for the ten-week period of $60,000 and mean weekly sales of $6,000. However, store B has significantly greater fluctuations in the amount of weekly sales. Such fluctuations affect planning for cash flows, employee staffing, inventory requirements, and other factors. A mere glance at the data in Figure 17-2 indicates the much greater dispersion of weekly sales for store B, but how much greater is the dispersion? Two measures of dispersion are the variance and the standard deviation.

Variance. The **variance** is a measure of how much the items of data vary from the mean. It is computed as follows:

$$\text{Variance} = \frac{\Sigma(x_i - \bar{X})^2}{n - 1}$$

The difference between each value and the mean is found and squared, and the sum of the squared amounts is divided by the number of data elements

Figure 17-2
Two fast-food restaurants have identical mean weekly sales for a 10-week period, but one restaurant has significantly more fluctuation in weekly sales.

Streeter Company Weekly Sales Data		
Week	Store A	Store B
1	$ 5,600	$ 7,400
2	6,100	4,900
3	5,700	8,600
4	5,900	4,200
5	6,300	9,100
6	6,200	8,300
7	6,400	3,700
8	5,900	4,800
9	5,800	5,600
10	6,100	3,400
	$60,000	$60,000

Mean = $\bar{X}$ = $60,000/10 = $6,000

minus one. The differences are squared to eliminate the problem of negative numbers. The value $n - 1$ is used because the calculation of variance is made using the mean $\overline{X}$, a value already computed from the same data, which causes a loss of a **degree of freedom.**

A discussion of the theory behind degrees of freedom is beyond the scope of this chapter, except to note that adjusting for degrees of freedom gives a less biased statistic. The variances, denoted S^2, for the weekly sales data of the two stores in Figure 17-2, are computed as follows:

$$S^2 = \frac{\Sigma(x_i - \overline{X})^2}{n - 1}$$

Store A	Store B
($5,600 -- $6,000)² = $160,000	($7,400 − $6,000)² = $ 1,960,000
($6,100 − $6,000)² = $ 10,000	($4,900 − $6,000)² = $ 1,210,000
($5,700 − $6,000)² = $ 90,000	($8,600 − $6,000)² = $ 6,760,000
($5,900 − $6,000)² = $ 10,000	($4,200 − $6,000)² = $ 3,240,000
($6,300 − $6,000)² = $ 90,000	($9,100 − $6,000)² = $ 9,610,000
($6,200 − $6,000)² = $ 40,000	($8,300 − $6,000)² = $ 5,290,000
($6,400 − $6,000)² = $160,000	($3,700 − $6,000)² = $ 5,290,000
($5,900 − $6,000)² = $ 10,000	($4,800 − $6,000)² = $ 1,440,000
($5,800 − $6,000)² = $ 40,000	($5,600 − $6,000)² = $ 160,000
($6,100 − $6,000)² = $ 10,000	($3,400 − $6,000)² = $ 6,760,000
$620,000	$41,720,000
$S^2 = \$620,000/9 = \$68,889$	$S^2 = \$41,720,000/9 = \$4,635,556$

Standard deviation. The variance for weekly sales data is much larger for store B, but the numbers are difficult to understand because the squaring of the differences made them so large. By taking the square root of the variance we find the **standard deviation,** S, which is a very useful statistic. For our example:

Store A	Store B
$S^2 = \$68,889$	$S^2 = \$4,635,556$
$S = \sqrt{\$68,889}$	$S = \sqrt{\$4,635,556}$
$= \$262$	$= \$2,153$

The calculation of the standard deviation using the square root of the variance formula can be quite cumbersome. It is far easier to use the following

Formula for standard deviation

formula for the standard deviation, which we present without explaining its derivation:

$$S = \sqrt{\frac{n\Sigma x_i^2 - (\Sigma x_i)^2}{n(n - 1)}}$$

This formula yields the same results and requires squaring each of the data elements, a far easier task than squaring the differences between each data element and the mean.

The standard deviation has some very useful statistical properties. As will be explained shortly, under certain frequently occurring conditions, it is known that about 68 percent of the data can be found within one standard deviation on each side of the mean, and about 95 percent of the data can be found within two standard deviations of the mean. These characteristics enable managers to make estimates of the probability of certain events occurring based on the mean and standard deviation calculated from the data. For example, the mean and standard deviation of the above data indicate that 68 percent of the time sales for store A will be between $5,738 and $6,262, calculated as:

$$\overline{X} \pm 1S$$
$$\$6,000 \pm \$262$$

Similarly, 95 percent of the time sales revenue for store A will be within two standard deviations of the mean, or between $5,476 and $6,524, calculated as $6,000 ± 2($262). This kind of information is of obvious value to managers trying to project future sales revenue for the purpose of planning business operations. For example, in fast-food restaurants, sales revenue is usually the same as cash inflows, and knowledge of the range of future cash flows can help managers to plan when to borrow cash and when to invest idle funds or repay loans.

The estimate of weekly sales revenue for store B is much less precise. Store B has the same mean sales revenue of $6,000, but revenue fluctuates much more. The standard deviation of store B's revenue is $2,153. Therefore, 68 percent of the time sales revenue should be $6,000 ± $2,153 or between $3,847 and $8,153. Two standard deviations from the mean or approximately 95 percent of the time, weekly sales should be in the range from $1,694 to $10,306 [$6,000 ± (2)($2,153)]. From the data it is clear that even though the two fast-food restaurants have identical average weekly sales revenue, they face significantly different planning problems.

Sample characteristics

The above estimates of sales, obtained from the mean and standard deviation, are based on two important assumptions:

1. The sample is representative of the population.
2. The population is normally distributed.

Representative sample. The total set of data from which the sample data are collected is called the **population.** To provide good statistics the sample of data taken from the population should be representative of the population in order for the mean and standard deviation calculated from the sample to be meaningful. We used 10 weeks of sales data as our sample of sales revenue. If the sample data are not representative of weekly sales revenue in general, the estimates of probabilities will be wrong. Most statistical analyses of accounting data are based on a sample of the total data. For example, quality-control programs frequently utilize sampling techniques to select every tenth or every

A sample should represent the population

twenty-fifth item to test for quality. Testing every item is too costly and sampling often provides very good quality control. Most business statistical analyses use sample data from which sample means, variances, and standard deviations are computed.

Normal distribution. The second assumption underlying estimates of the probability of various sales' occurring is the normal curve assumption. The **normal curve** assumption means that we assume the data are normally distributed in a systematic and uniform pattern about the mean. There is an equal probability that a value will fall on one side of the mean as the other. The symmetrical characteristic of a normal distribution results in a bell-shaped curve illustrated at the top of Figure 17-3.

Many populations are normally distributed

Not all data generate a bell-shaped curve, but a normal distribution is assumed for many business statistical analyses, because the data are often close enough to a normal distribution to provide useful statistics. The mathematical properties of the normal distribution have considerable practical value, such as enabling us to estimate easily the probabilities of the occurrence of many events.

Use of the normal curve

The area under the normal curve represents the probability of the occurrence of an event that comes from a normally distributed population. The area under the curve on each side of the mean amounts to 50 percent. You can now see where the 68 percent and 95 percent values mentioned earlier come from. The first normal curve shown in Figure 17-4 indicates a shaded area within one standard deviation of the mean. In the table in Figure 17-3, the area between the mean and one standard deviation is given as .3413. Since the shaded area in the first normal curve in Figure 17-4 is on each side of the mean, the value must be doubled to obtain the total shaded area, and you see that 2 × .3413 = .6826 or slightly more than 68 percent. Similarly, the table gives the value .4772 for the area between the mean and two standard deviations away, or .9544 for the area on both sides of the mean as illustrated by the second normal curve in Figure 17-4. This means that an item of data falls beyond two standard deviations away from the mean less than 5 percent of the time. The table can also be used to find the probability of an item's being at least as large as some value, or at least as small as some value.

For example, store B may want to know the probability that weekly sales revenue will fall between $5,000 and $7,000. These amounts are $1,000 on either side of the mean value of $6,000. One thousand dollars is only a portion of one standard deviation of $2,153. In fact it is $1,000/$2,153 = .46 standard deviation from the mean. The .46 value is found in the table by finding .4 in the left column and going across that row to the .06 column, giving the value .1772 in the table. This value means that there is a 17.7 percent chance of being within .46 standard deviation of the mean. But this table only measures the probability of being away from the mean in one direction. The 17.7 percent is the probability of being between $5,000 and $6,000 **or** between $6,000 and

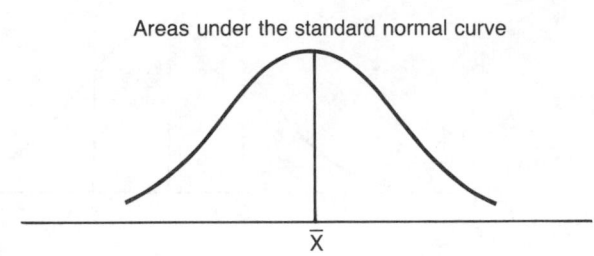

Areas under the standard normal curve

The following table provides percentage areas under the normal curve on one side of the mean.

Standard Deviation	.00	.01	.02	.03	.04	.05	.06	.07	.08	.09
0.0	.0000	.0040	.0080	.0120	.0160	.0199	.0239	.0279	.0319	.0359
0.1	.0398	.0438	.0478	.0517	.0557	.0596	.0636	.0675	.0714	.0753
0.2	.0793	.0832	.0871	.0910	.0948	.0987	.1026	.1064	.1103	.1141
0.3	.1179	.1217	.1255	.1293	.1331	.1368	.1406	.1443	.1480	.1517
0.4	.1554	.1591	.1628	.1664	.1700	.1736	.1772	.1808	.1844	.1879
0.5	.1915	.1950	.1985	.2019	.2054	.2088	.2123	.2157	.2190	.2224
0.6	.2257	.2291	.2324	.2357	.2389	.2422	.2454	.2486	.2518	.2549
0.7	.2580	.2612	.2642	.2673	.2704	.2734	.2764	.2794	.2823	.2852
0.8	.2881	.2910	.2939	.2967	.2995	.3023	.3051	.3078	.3106	.3133
0.9	.3159	.3186	.3212	.3238	.3264	.3289	.3315	.3340	.3365	.3389
1.0	.3413	.3438	.3461	.3485	.3508	.3531	.3554	.3577	.3599	.3621
1.1	.3643	.3665	.3686	.3708	.3729	.3749	.3770	.3790	.3810	.3830
1.2	.3849	.3869	.3888	.3907	.3925	.3944	.3962	.3980	.3997	.4015
1.3	.4032	.4049	.4066	.4082	.4099	.4115	.4131	.4147	.4162	.4177
1.4	.4192	.4207	.4222	.4236	.4251	.4265	.4279	.4292	.4306	.4319
1.5	.4332	.4345	.4357	.4370	.4382	.4394	.4406	.4418	.4429	.4441
1.6	.4452	.4463	.4474	.4484	.4495	.4505	.4515	.4525	.4535	.4545
1.7	.4554	.4564	.4573	.4582	.4591	.4599	.4608	.4616	.4625	.4633
1.8	.4641	.4649	.4656	.4664	.4671	.4678	.4686	.4693	.4699	.4706
1.9	.4713	.4719	.4726	.4732	.4738	.4744	.4750	.4756	.4761	.4767
2.0	.4772	.4778	.4783	.4788	.4793	.4798	.4803	.4808	.4812	.4817
2.1	.4821	.4826	.4830	.4834	.4838	.4842	.4846	.4850	.4854	.4857
2.2	.4861	.4864	.4868	.4871	.4875	.4878	.4881	.4884	.4887	.4890
2.3	.4893	.4896	.4898	.4901	.4904	.4906	.4909	.4911	.4913	.4916
2.4	.4918	.4920	.4922	.4925	.4927	.4929	.4931	.4932	.4934	.4936
2.5	.4938	.4940	.4941	.4943	.4945	.4946	.4948	.4949	.4951	.4952
2.6	.4953	.4955	.4956	.4957	.4959	.4960	.4961	.4962	.4963	.4964
2.7	.4965	.4966	.4967	.4968	.4969	.4970	.4971	.4972	.4973	.4974
2.8	.4974	.4975	.4976	.4977	.4977	.4978	.4979	.4979	.4980	.4981
2.9	.4981	.4982	.4982	.4983	.4984	.4984	.4985	.4985	.4986	.4986
3.0	.49865	.4987	.4987	.4988	.4988	.4989	.4989	.4989	.4990	.4990
4.0	.49997									

Figure 17-3
The normal curve shows the symmetrical nature of a normal distribution. The table allows us to make probabilistic statements about a set of normally distributed data once the mean and the standard deviation have been computed.

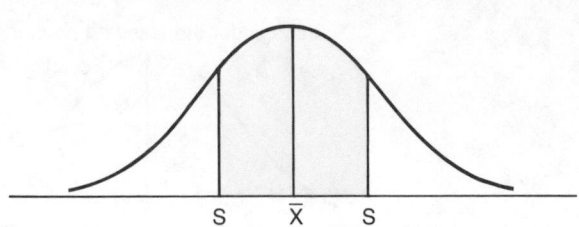

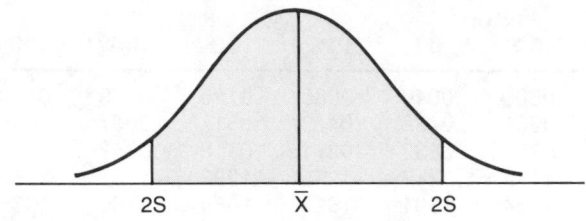

Figure 17-4
The normal curve with the shaded portions showing the areas under the curve for one and two standard deviations from the mean.

$7,000. To find the probability of being between $5,000 and $7,000, the 17.7 percent is merely doubled to yield 35.4 percent.

Often managers are far more concerned about fluctuations in one direction than in another. For instance, assume the management of store B wants to know the probability of sales being **at least** $5,000. The probability of sales revenue being between $5,000 and the mean of $6,000 is 17.7 percent. The probability of its being above the mean with a normal curve is 50 percent. Therefore, the probability of sales being at least $5,000 is 17.7 percent + 50 percent or 67.7 percent.

Regression-correlation analysis

Another important type of statistical analysis used in business is regression-correlation analysis. It is used in cost planning and control to relate costs to activity levels for both actual costs and budgeted costs. Changes in costs as different activity levels occur have a significant impact on the planning and control functions. Some costs appear to be relatively fixed over a relevant range of activity, some vary with activity level changes, while still others defy accurate description of the nature and magnitude of their change with fluctuating activity levels or over time. Quantitative methods are especially useful for analyzing such varied cost behaviour.

Regression-correlation analysis is used to determine the nature and strength of the relationship between costs and activity measures. Probably no other quantitative tool has as wide an applicability to accounting data analysis as regression-correlation analysis. Its appeal stems from its ability to use one

Regression analysis is a prediction tool

or more variables to predict the value of another variable. The prediction problem surfaces in many facets of budgeting, planning, and control. For example, in Chapter 5 we discussed separating mixed costs of production into fixed and variable components. This process is easily accomplished by regression analysis. Regression-correlation analysis is a two-step process, involving:

1. Determination of the nature of the association between two or more variables
2. Determination of the strength of the relationship between the variables

First we discuss simple linear regression and later we illustrate a more complex form of regression analysis.

Simple linear regression deals with two variables; the first is the **independent variable.** Typically it is derived from historical data. The second variable is the **dependent variable** whose value depends on the value of the independent variable and on the relationship between the two variables as described by a mathematical equation. For example, employee fringe benefits are related to the number of hours worked by employees. A company may use regression-correlation analysis to measure the relationship between the two variables. Here the independent variable is labour hours, and the dependent variable is employee fringe benefit cost. It is the dependent variable because its value depends on the number of labour hours and the relationship between labour hours and the amount of fringe benefit costs.

Computing the regression line

The **regression line** is a line whose equation best describes the linear relationship between the independent variable and the dependent variable. The linear regression line has the traditional form of the equation for a straight line, which is

$$Y_c = a + bX$$

where:

Y_c = the value of the dependent variable computed from a specific value for the independent variable

a = the constant which is the point where the regression line crosses the Y axis. It is the value of Y_c when $X = 0$.

b = the slope of the regression line. It describes the change in the value of Y_c for each unit change in the value of X. If Y_c increases when X increases then the slope of the regression line is said to be positive. If Y_c decreases when X increases, the slope of the regression line is negative.

X = the value of the independent variable

Figure 17-5 illustrates a regression line described by the equation $Y_c = 5 + 2X$. In this case $a = 5$, and $b = 2$. For any value of X, Y is equal to $5 + 2$ times the value of X. The regression line was computed from the 10 data points shown on the graph. The line is the straight line that minimizes the

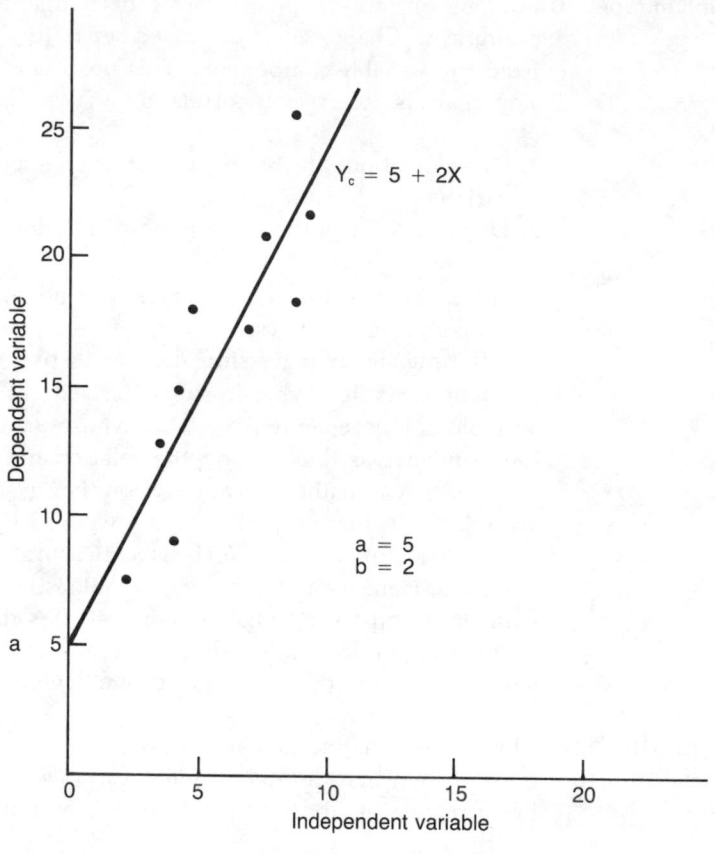

Figure 17-5
Graph of a regression line showing the constant, *a*, where the regression line crosses the *Y* axis and the slope of the regression line, *b*, which is the change in the value of *Y* for each unit change in the value of *X*.

absolute vertical distance between the line and each data point. In other words, no other straight line can be drawn through the set of data that would reduce the total vertical distance between the data points and the regression line, so the line is referred to as the **line of best fit**.

Illustrative example of regression-correlation analysis

To illustrate the computation and use of regression-correlation analysis, we present an example of the Wheat City General Hospital. A schedule weekly indirect costs and activity data is presented in Figure 17-6 for the hospital's emergency room.

These are historical data for six weeks of operating the emergency room. The indirect costs are given in column 1. Three different measures of activity

	1	2	3	4
	Indirect Cost per Week	**Patients Served**	**Direct Labour Hours Staff**	**Direct Labour Hours Medical**
Week				
1	$ 22,500	110	600	150
2	25,800	132	620	180
3	28,000	184	760	190
4	23,400	115	570	170
5	21,500	91	550	140
6	24,000	148	610	135
Totals	$145,200	780	3,710	965

Wheat City General Hospital
Weekly Emergency Room Cost and Activity Data
January 1—February 12, 1984

Figure 17-6
This schedule provides six weeks of data for indirect costs and three activity measures for a hospital emergency room.

are given in columns 2 through 4. In an effort to plan for and control the indirect costs of this patient care program, the hospital would like to be able to relate indirect costs to some measure of activity.

Regression analysis There are many ways to analyze these data, some more meaningful than others. For example, we could calculate the mean and standard deviation of the emergency room indirect costs. The mean is merely the sum of the weekly costs divided by the number of weeks, or $145,200/6 = $24,200 and the standard deviation is $2,361. As discussed earlier, this information can be used to help plan activities and make decisions. However, even more useful information can be obtained if emergency room indirect costs are mathematically related to one of the activity variables presented in the schedule.

In simple linear regression only one independent variable can be related to the dependent variable. The hospital wants to predict indirect cost, which is the dependent variable. The independent variable can be any one of the three activity measures listed in Figure 17-6. For this illustration we choose patients served as the independent variable. Most regression lines are computed from some type of historical data such as monthly, weekly, or daily cost data, as in the hospital example. Here six weeks of emergency room data are used. This is a relatively small amount of data, but it suffices for purposes of illustrating the computational process. Later we deal with significantly larger data bases, whose regression lines may be found easily with a computer.

Definition of variables. Several terms must be defined before proceeding:

Y_i are the observed (actual) values of the dependent variable used in the computation of the regression line. In the example the Y_i values are the six weekly observations of the total indirect cost. For example, Y_1 is the $22,500 indirect cost for week 1, and Y_2 is the $25,800 cost for week 2. X_i are the observed (actual) values of the independent variable. Here X_i is the number of patients served each week. For example, X_1 is 110 patients in week 1 and X_2 is 132 patients in week 2.

n is the number of observations used in computing the regression line. In our example there are six weeks of data, so $n = 6$.

There are a number of different approaches to computing the regression line. One approach, known as **the least-squares method,** is to solve the following set of simultaneous equations:

Formulas for calculation of intercept and slope

$$\Sigma Y_i = na + b\Sigma X \qquad (1)$$
$$\Sigma XY_i = a\Sigma X + b\Sigma X^2 \qquad (2)$$

At first glance these two equations may look complex, but in fact they are easy to solve and require very basic algebra. First, we explain the terms that are used in the two equations.

$\Sigma Y_i =$ the total of all the observed values of the dependent variables Y_i, in this case the total of the weekly indirect costs

$\Sigma X =$ the sum of the observed values of the independent variables X_i, in this example the total number of patients served weekly

$\Sigma XY_i =$ the sum of the products of each pair of X_i and Y_i

$\Sigma X^2 =$ the sum of the squared values of the independent variables X_i

Figure 17-7 provides all the necessary data to calculate the regression line equation. In addition, it contains values for Y_i^2, which are not needed to compute the regression line but are needed later. Note that once these values are substituted into the two equations, the only variables without values are a and b, which are the two values necessary to describe the regression line.

Figure 17-7
A schedule of data necessary for computing the regression line relating indirect costs with number of patients served.

Wheat City General Hospital
Schedule of Data for Regression · Correlation Analysis
January 1–February 12, 1984

Week	Indirect Cost Y_i	Y_i^2	Patients Served X	X^2	XY
1	$ 22,500	$ 506,250,000	110	12 100	$ 2,475,000
2	25,800	665,640,000	132	17 424	3,405,600
3	28,000	784,000,000	184	33 856	5,152,000
4	23,400	547,560,000	115	13 225	2,691,000
5	21,500	462,250,000	91	8 281	1,956,500
6	24,000	576,000,000	148	21 904	3,552,000
Totals (Σ)	$145,200	$3,541,700,000	780	106 790	$19,232,100

Solving for *a* and *b*. Since there are two unknowns, *a* and *b*, and two equations, a solution is possible. The process is not difficult. The first step is to substitute the known values into the equations as follows:

$$\$145,200 = \quad 6a + \quad 780b \qquad (1)$$
$$\$19,232,100 = 780a + 106\,790b \qquad (2)$$

These two simultaneous equations may be solved either by substitution or by subtraction. We choose the latter method. The coefficient of *a* is smaller in each equation than the coefficient of *b*, so we eliminate *a* simply as a matter of convenience. When we multiply each term of equation (1) by 130, the coefficients of *a* in both equations become identical, and we can subtract one equation from the other.

$$(130)\$145,200 = (130)6a + (130)780b$$

or

subtract

from

$$\$18,876,000 = 780a + 101\,400b \qquad (1)$$
$$\underline{\$19,232,100 = 780a + 106\,790b} \qquad (2)$$
$$\$\quad 356,100 = 0 \quad + \quad 5\,390b$$

$$\frac{\$356,100}{5390} = b$$

$$b = \$66.06679$$

The value of *b* is the slope of the regression line. It means that for every unit increase in X, there is a $66.06679 increase in Y. Since X is the number of patients served and Y is indirect costs, we can say that for each additional patient served indirect costs rise by $66.07.

Once we have found *b* it is a simple matter to find *a* by substituting the value of *b* into equation (1) or (2). Again equation (1) is selected for computational ease, although either equation yields the same answer.

$$\$145,200 = 6a + 780(\$66.06679)$$
$$6a = \$145,200 - \$51,532.096$$
$$6a = \$93,667.904$$
$$a = \$15,611.317$$

The term *a* in the regression line equation is the Y intercept and represents the fixed component of indirect costs. The regression line equation is:

$$Y_c = \$15,611.32 + \$66.07X$$

or total indirect cost is equal to the $15,611.32 fixed cost plus $66.07 for each patient served. Later you will see how the regression line is used for predicting, budgeting, or just helping managers better understand costs and their relationships to other variables.

Correlation analysis   The regression line describes the relationship that exists between the dependent and the independent variable, but it does not say how good the relationship is. The regression line is the best-fitting straight line that can be drawn through the set of data, but it is possible that no regression line does a very good job of fitting the data. We saw such a case in the scatter diagram in Chapter 5, Figure 5-10. Statistical techniques exist that measure the **strength of the relationship.**

Coefficient of correlation. One important measure is called the **coefficient of correlation,** denoted as r, which measures the degree of association between the dependent and the independent variables. It ranges in value from $+1$, representing perfect positive correlation, to -1, representing perfect negative correlation. Positive correlation means that as the independent variable increases or decreases so does the dependent variable. Negative correlation means that as the independent variable increases, the dependent variable decreases, and vice versa. Figure 17-8 illustrates the general relationship between r, the regression line, and the data.

Positive and negative correlation

There are several computational approaches for finding r. One is to solve the following equation:

Formula for coefficient of correlation

$$r = \frac{n\Sigma XY_i - (\Sigma X)(\Sigma Y_i)}{\sqrt{n\Sigma X^2 - (\Sigma X)^2} \cdot \sqrt{n\Sigma Y^2 - (\Sigma Y)^2}} \qquad (3)$$

All the data necessary for solving equation (3) are presented in Figure 17-7. Substituting the required data into equation (3), we get

$$r = \frac{(6)(\$19,232,100) - (780)(\$145,200)}{\sqrt{(6)(\$106,790) - (780)^2} \cdot \sqrt{(6)(\$3,541,700,000) - (\$145,200)^2}}$$

$$= \frac{\$115,392,600 - \$113,256,000}{\sqrt{\$32,340} \cdot \sqrt{\$167,160,000}}$$

$$= \frac{\$2,136,600}{\$179.83326 \cdot \$12,929.037} = \frac{\$2,136,600}{\$2,325,070.7}$$

$$= .9189398$$

The closer r is to 1 or -1, the stronger the relationship between the dependent and the independent variables. The above calculation indicates a strong positive relationship. As r gets closer to zero it indicates a weaker relationship. The sign of r does not indicate the strength of the relationship but only the direction. One must be careful in interpreting r; it measures the strength of the **linear** relationship between the dependent and independent variables. It is quite possible for r to be small, indicating a weak linear relationship, when the actual relationship between the variables is quite strong although it may not be linear. For example Figure 17-9 shows two variables strongly related but having a weak linear relationship.

Correlation measures the strength of linear relationships

Different values of r must be interpreted carefully. An r of .8 does not indicate twice as good a linear relationship as an r of .4; the larger value actually indicates a relationship that is four times as strong as the smaller value. Similarly an r of .75 is nine times as strong as an r of .25. You can see that as r doubles, the relationship increases by 2^2, and as r triples the relationship increases by 3^2. To make the interpretation of r more meaningful, therefore, the coefficient of correlation is often converted to the coefficient of

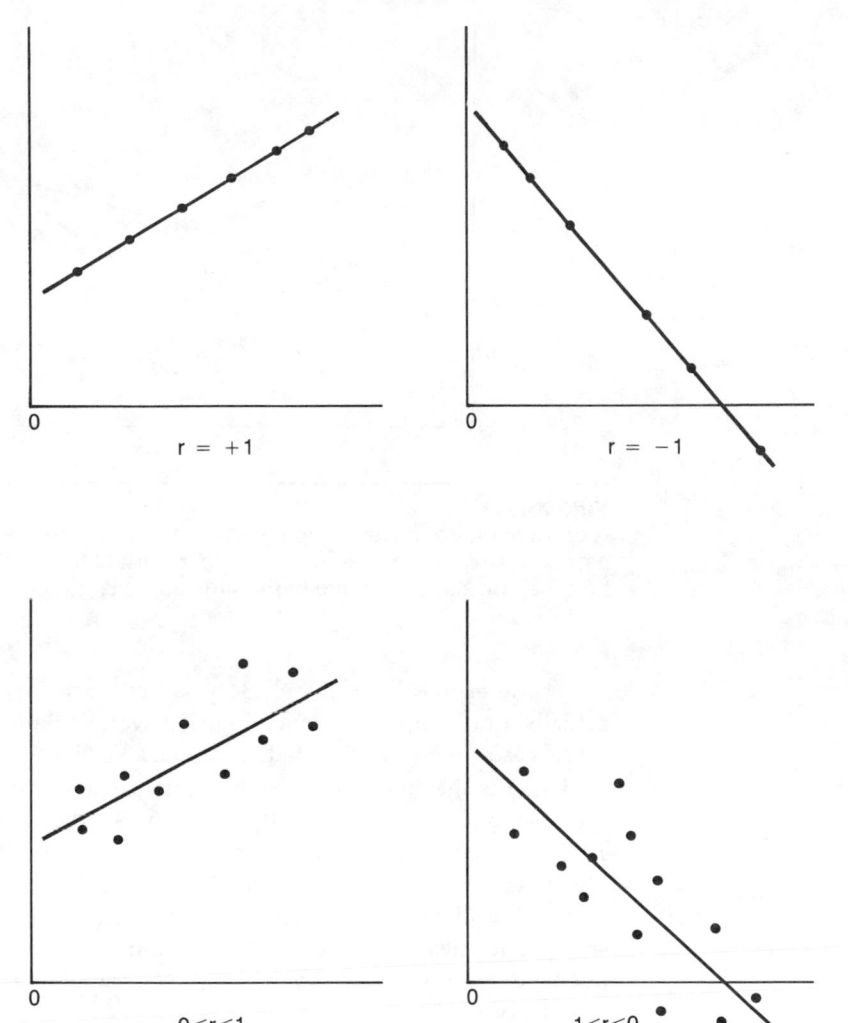

Figure 17-8
Graphs showing the general slopes and data distributions for correlations ranging from perfect positive correlation, +1, to perfect negative correlation, −1.

determination, which is calculated as r^2, thereby eliminating the sign of r and enabling a comparison to be made between the resulting values that is more easily understood.

The **coefficient of determination** is another measure of the goodness of fit of the regression line to the data used in computing the regression line. It is a measure of the degree to which the two variables X and Y are related linearly. In the example above,

*r^2 measures
goodness of fit*

$$r^2 = .9189398^2$$
$$= .84445036$$
$$\approx .84$$

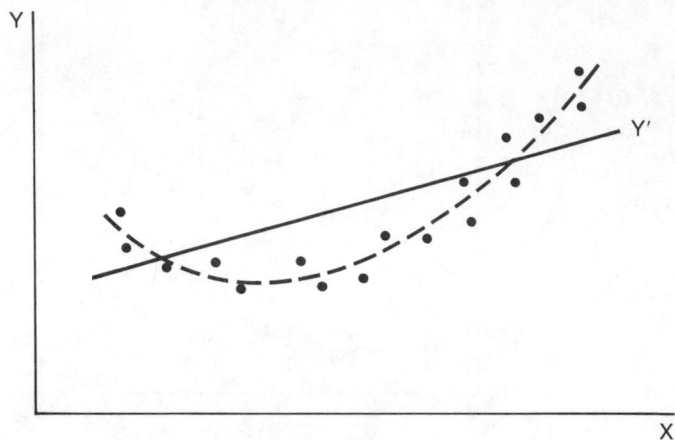

Figure 17-9
A correlation coefficient calculated for the linear regression line Y' may indicate a poor correlation between the X and Y variables, but the broken line shows that the correlation is quite high, although it is not linear.

To interpret this value of .84 it is first necessary to understand that r^2 is actually a ratio of two variances. Earlier we calculated the mean of emergency room costs of $24,200 and the standard deviation of $2,361. The standard deviation is the square root of the variance, and the variance is a measure of the fluctuation of costs about the mean, illustrated by diagram A in Figure 17-10. The costs also fluctuate about the regression line that we calculated as illustrated by diagram B in Figure 17-10, and the coefficient of correlation told us that the fluctuation of actual data about the regression line was relatively small. The mean and standard deviation give no indication why the costs fluctuate from week to week. The regression line relates the costs to the number of patients served in an attempt to explain some of the week-to-week fluctuations. The coefficient of determination of .84 indicates that of the total variance of indirect costs about the mean of $24,200, 84 percent of the fluctuation can be explained by knowing the number of patients served during the week.

Diagram C of Figure 17-10 shows the variation of the regression line Y_c about the mean $\bar{Y}$. You can see that where the vertical lines in diagram B are short, the vertical lines for the same data in diagrams A and C are similar in length. The coefficient of determination r^2 is actually the ratio of the variance of the regression line about the mean value of $24,200 to the total variance of the actual data points about the mean. In other words, r^2 is the ratio of the variance in diagram C to the variance in diagram A. Mathematically, it is expressed as:

$$r^2 = \frac{\Sigma(Y_c - \bar{Y})/(n - 1)}{\Sigma(Y_i - \bar{Y})/(n - 1)}$$

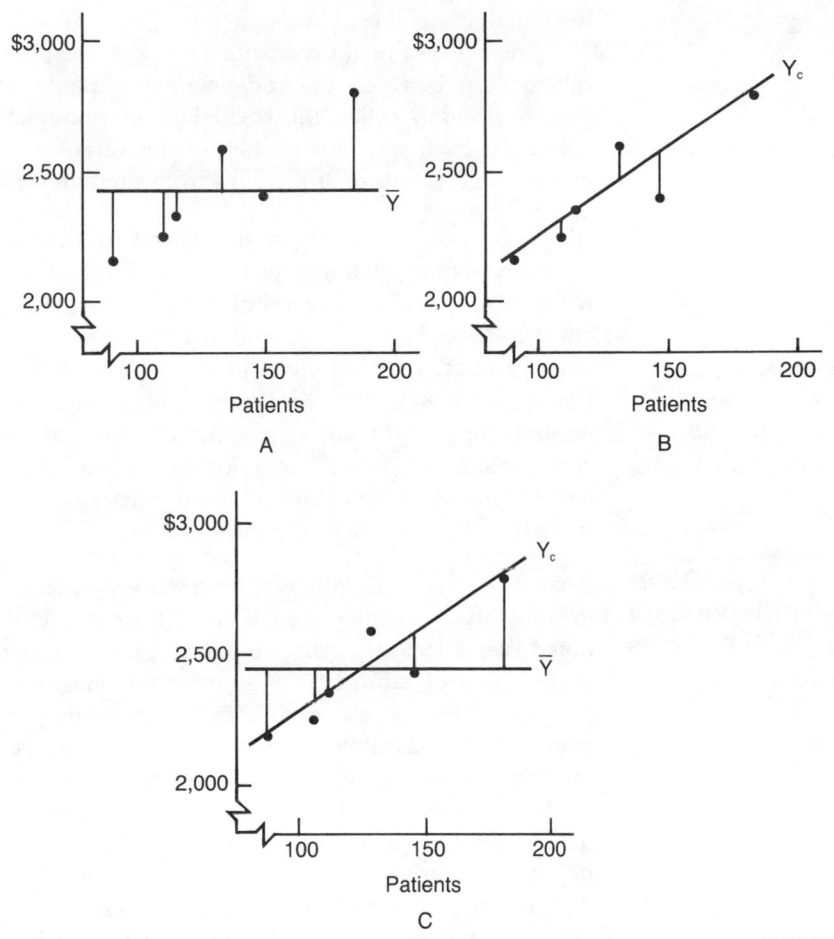

Figure 17-10
The indirect costs of Wheat City General Hospital's emergency room are plotted against the number of patients served in each of six weeks. The same data are plotted in each diagram. The variance of the data around the mean are shown in A, the variance about the regression line in B, and the variance of the regression line about the mean in C.

The numerator of the equation is the variance of the regression line about the mean (diagram C); the denominator is the variance of the data about the mean (diagram A). If the data all fell precisely on the regression line, that is, if $r = 1$, the variance of the regression line about the mean would be equal to the variance of the data about the mean, and ratio r^2 would be equal to 1, which would mean that all the variance of indirect costs about the mean results from the number of patients visiting the emergency room. In our example, 84 percent of the variance is explained by the number of patients, and the remainder is due to other factors.

The portion of the variance that is not explained by the regression line relationship between the independent variable and dependent variable is $(1 - r^2)$ and is called the **coefficient of nondetermination,** whose value is .16 in our example. This portion of the variance must be explained by other independent variables or it results from random fluctuations.

Association versus causation

Regression-correlation analysis requires careful interpretation

Many business decisions are influenced by managers' perceptions about the cause-and-effect relationships between activity variables and cost movements. Much of responsibility accounting rests on an ability to determine cause-and-effect relationships in business. Regression-correlation analysis measures the nature and association between two variables, usually based on historical data, but association—even strong association—does not prove cause-and-effect relationships. Many strong statistical associations exist that certainly suggest causal relationships but do not prove them. Regression-correlation analysis can provide much useful evidence, but the manager is the judge who must determine the ultimate use of the information.

Other independent variables

A coefficient of determination of .84 is very good. In practice r^2 of .5 or even lower is often considered good enough to be useful to managers. It should be noted that a lack of strong correlation or even negative correlation does not mean a lack of information value for a manager. Frequently it is very useful to know that no relationship exists between two variables, particularly if managers have assumed a positive relationship in decision making. When the relationship is disproved, managers may look for better relationships. If an r^2 value is considered too low, a manager may choose to evaluate another independent variable to see whether it has a stronger relationship with the dependent variable. The Wheat City General Hospital emergency room data in Figure 17-5 presented three different measures of activity. Patients served was the activity measure used as the independent variable in the illustration, but either of the other two activity measures may be used as the independent variable.

It is possible that one or both of the other two variables have a strong relationship to indirect emergency room cost, that is, a higher r^2, than number of patients served. The only way to find out is to proceed as before. Each of the other activity measures can be evaluated one at a time. Using direct labour hours for staff we compute a new regression line and r^2. Figure 17-11 presents the data necessary for the solution.

Solving the two simultaneous equations to determine a and b for this regression line, we get

$$\Sigma Y_i = na + b\Sigma X \tag{1}$$
$$\Sigma XY_i = a\Sigma X + b\Sigma X^2 \tag{2}$$

$$\$145{,}200 = 6a + 3710b \tag{1}$$
$$\$90{,}579{,}000 = 3710a + 2\ 321\ 500b \tag{2}$$

	Indirect Cost		Direct Labour Hours		
Week	Y_i	Y_i^2	X	X^2	XY
1	$ 22,500	$ 506,250,000	600	360 000	$13,500,000
2	25,800	665,640,000	620	384 400	15,996,000
3	28,000	784,000,000	760	577 600	21,280,000
4	23,400	547,560,000	570	324 900	13,338,000
5	21,500	462,250,000	550	302 500	11,825,000
6	24,000	576,000,000	610	372 100	14,640,000
Totals (Σ)	$145,200	$3,541,700,000	3,710	2 321 500	$90,579,000

Wheat City General Hospital
Schedule of Data for Regression · Correlation Analysis
January 1–February 12, 1984

Figure 17-11
This schedule provides the data necessary for computing the regression line, as well as measures of correlation that describe how well the regression line fits the data.

The multiplier is 3710/6, or 618.3333.

$$\$89,782,000 = 3710a + 2\ 294\ 016\ 7b \tag{1}$$
$$\$90,579,000 = 3710a + 2\ 321\ 500b \tag{2}$$
$$\$797,000 = \qquad\qquad 27\ 483.3b$$
$$b = \$28.999429$$

To solve for a, we substitute the value of b into equation (1).

$$\$145,200 = 6a + (3710)(\$28.999429) \tag{1}$$
$$\$145,200 = 6a + \$107,587.88$$
$$6a = \$37,612.12$$
$$a = \$6,268.6867$$

The regression line using direct labour hours for staff is

$$Y_c = \$6,268.6869 + \$28.999429X$$

To find the value of r and r^2 we use equation (3):

$$r = \frac{(6)(\$90,579,000) - (3710)(\$145,200)}{\sqrt{(6)(\$2,321,500) - (3710)^2} \cdot \$12,929.037^*}$$

$$= \frac{\$543,474,000 - \$538,692,000}{\sqrt{\$164,900} \cdot \$12,929.037}$$

$$= \frac{\$4,782,000}{\$5,250,208}$$

$$= .910\ 821\ 06$$

*Note that this term, composed entirely of Y values, does not change when other independent variables are used and need not be computed again.

The coefficient of determination is

$$r^2 = .910\ 821\ 06^2$$
$$\approx .83$$

Medical direct labour hours may be used as an independent variable also. By substituting the necessary data into the analysis, we can compute the following regression line:

$$Y_c = \$10{,}546 + \$84.96X$$

The coefficients of correlation and determination are

$$r = .806\ 226$$
$$r^2 = .65$$

You may want to compute both the regression line and r^2 to be certain you can arrive at the same answer for medical direct labour hours. Because r^2 for number of patients served is higher than for either medical or staff direct labour hours, we can state that the relationship between costs and number of patients is stronger than the relationship between costs and the other two variables. We now discuss how this information is used.

Using linear regression A primary use of regression-correlation analysis is to aid in the planning process. Often accountants analyze historical cost data using various measures of activity in an attempt to determine the activity variable which has the strongest relationship to cost. Then the variable is used as a basis for budgeting and other planning and analysis activities.

Since the number of patients served provides the highest coefficient of determination of the three activity variables analyzed, the hospital may use that variable as a basis for projecting emergency room indirect costs. With the regression equation available, management can project expected costs for any level of activity. It is only necessary to substitute the desired activity level into the equation for the value of X and calculate the value of Y. For example, to estimate indirect emergency room costs for a week when 150 patients are treated, we use this calculation:

$$
\begin{aligned}
Y_c &= \$15{,}611.32 + \$66.07X \\
&= \$15{,}611.32 + \$66.07(150) \\
&= \$15{,}611.32 + \$9{,}910.5 \\
&\approx \$25{,}522
\end{aligned}
$$

The computations required in regression-correlation analysis can be made easily using inexpensive hand calculators. Many medium-priced calculators have internal programs that automatically compute a, b, and r^2. Many people have access to computers with regression-correlation programs as part of the available program package. A regression-correlation computer program written in BASIC programming language is provided in the appendix to this chapter.

The advantage of regression-correlation analysis is that it provides far more precision than the methods discussed in Chapter 5. For instance, the high-low method provides the following results for the emergency room data:

Patients served		Using High-Low Method	Using Regression Line
$b = \dfrac{\$28,000 - \$21,500}{184 - 91} =$		$\$\ \ \ 69.89$	$\$\ \ \ 66.07$
$a = \$28,000 - 184(\$69.892473) =$		$\$15,139.79$	$\$15,611.32$
Staff labour hours			
$b = \dfrac{\$28,000 - \$21,500}{760 - 550} =$		$\$\ \ \ 30.95$	$\$\ \ \ 29.00$
$a = \$28,000 - 760(\$30.952381) =$		$\$\ 4,476.19$	$\$\ 6,268.69$
Medical labour hours			
$b = \dfrac{\$28,000 - \$21,500}{190 - 140} =$		$\$\ \ \ 130.00$	$\$\ \ \ 84.96$
$a = \$28,000 - 190(\$130) =$		$\$\ 3,300.00$	$\$10,546.00$

In the first case the *a* and *b* values are reasonably close to those of the computed regression line; in the second case the *b* values are close but the *a* values are not; in the case of medical hours, the high-low estimate is poor. If high-low yields results similar to the regression line values, why not use the easier method? Because there is no way of knowing when high-low provides a good estimate and when it does not. There is no r^2, the goodness-of-fit measure. One of the real advantages of regression-correlation analysis is the knowledge of how strong the relationship is between the two variables.

Two points of caution should be mentioned. One is that the regression line and r^2 are typically based on historical data. The resulting measures of the relationships may or may not hold in the future. Past data are often the best indicators of the future, but not always, and seldom is the past a perfect predictor of the future. Second, although there may be a strong cause-and-effect relationship between many linear regression variables, such as between utility bills and production output, regression-correlation analysis does **not** **prove** that there are causal relationships, only that the data seem to be related.

Multiple linear regression

A dependent variable may be related to many independent variables

An extension of simple linear regression is **multiple linear regression** where two or more independent variables are used simultaneously to predict the value of the dependent variable. The motivation for using multiple regression is that in some instances using more than one independent variable can improve the forecast of the dependent variable by better explaining the past variations of the dependent variable. For example, if in the previous example the number of patient visits and number of medical staff hours could be related simultaneously to indirect labour costs, we may find that together they provide a stronger relationship than either of them alone.

Multiple regression is the same two-step process as linear regression analysis: Compute the regression line and compute the strength of the relationship. The regression line takes the general form of:

$$Y_c = a + b_1X_1 + b_2X_2 + b_3X_3 + \cdots + b_nX_n$$

where a is the Y intercept or the value of Y when **all** X terms have a zero value, and $b_1, \cdots, b_n$ each represent the relationships between the dependent variable and one of the independent variables. Note that each independent variable has its own b coefficient and that the number of terms in the regression line equation depends on the number of independent variables used in the analysis.

The strength of the relationships is measured by the **multiple coefficient of determination,** which is determined by

$$r^2 = \frac{\text{Explained variation}}{\text{Total variation}} = 1 - \frac{\Sigma(Y - Y_c)^2}{\Sigma(Y - \overline{Y})^2}$$

However, the computation of multiple r^2 is much more complex and tedious than that of r^2. Likewise, the complexity of computations for determining the regression line preclude solving multiple regression problems manually, but multiple regression programs are available on most computer systems.

Learning curves and cost analysis

In financial planning and control and in managerial decision analysis, there is a tendency to force all costs into fixed or directly variable categories. Clearly, this is convenient, and often it approximates cost behavior well enough to suffice for many purposes. However, there are situations in which cost behavior characteristics dictate a more precise analysis.

One such class of cost behaviour is known as **learning curves** (mentioned briefly in Chapter 5). Many organizations have found and documented a learning effect in the production of goods or services. In other words, they have found that the amount of effort required to make a product or to provide a service declines over time. This is particularly true for new products. The improvement in labour efficiency produces unit cost reductions in labour costs and it reduces other costs related to labour. Many products have relatively short life cycles, such as 2 to 5 years. If learning curve effects occur for a year or more, product costs for a good portion of the product's life may be declining. In such cases learning curve cost analysis may be useful for estimating production costs and establishing product prices. Learning curves may be used to aid managers in predicting costs and in interpreting cause-and-effect relationships between activity measures and costs.

As learning takes place, labour efficiency improves

While learning is taking place, total labour time—and therefore total labour-related costs—continue to rise as units of output rise, but the labour time and costs rise at a decreasing rate. If this relationship were graphed with units of service or product on the horizontal axis and total cost on the vertical axis, it would look like Figure 17-12.

The broken line OA represents a directly variable cost whereby each unit change in activity level causes exactly the same change in total variable cost regardless of what the level of activity is. The solid line OB is the cost curve describing a learning curve cost function. Although the total cost increases with activity, it is increasing at a decreasing rate.

Although Figure 17-12 shows the general shape of a cost curve with a learning effect, it does not give the precise shape of a particular learning curve. Depending on the degree of learning, the **learning rate,** and the time period involved, the learning curve can have a somewhat different slope than the one in Figure 17-12.

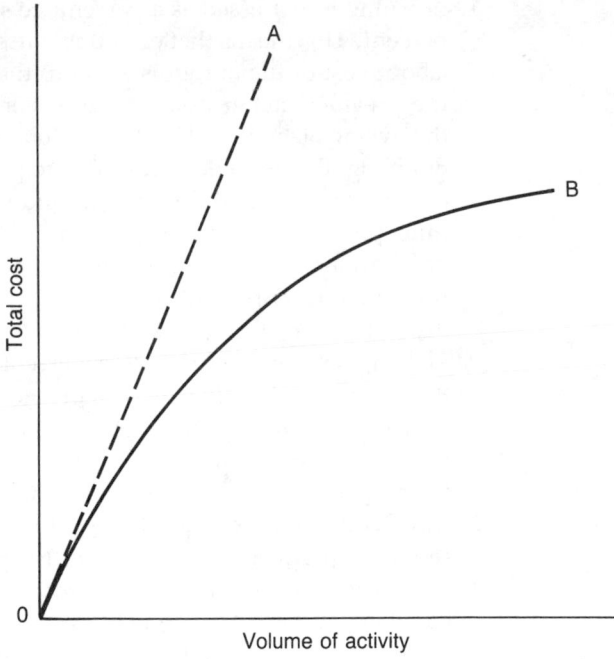

Figure 17-12
Learning curves are semivariable costs that increase at a decreasing rate.
The dashed line OA is a directly variable cost, and the curved line OB is a
learning curve that bends toward the X axis as the learning effect takes place.

Computing
learning curve
costs

In order to use the learning curve phenomenon for planning and control purposes, one must be able to express the cost function with a learning effect in mathematical terms. The general form of the equation for a learning curve is

$$Y = aX^b$$

where:

Y = the average amount of time or cost per unit of output
a = the time or cost required to produce the first unit or batch of units
X = cumulative number of units or batches produced
b = the learning effect (index) = the logarithm of the learning rate divided by the logarithm of 2

Note that a and b have a different meaning in the notation for a learning curve than they do for the regression line. Be careful to use them correctly in each situation.

Substituting values into the equation makes it possible to determine specific values for labour time or cost for a particular situation. Some terminology should be discussed before we work an example.

1. Learning is expressed as a percentage such as 70 percent, 90 percent, or 98 percent. This means that each time output doubles, the cumulative average labour cost of the output is equal to the learning curve percentage of what the previous labour cost was. In other words, when production doubles, the average labour cost of the product is a percentage of the cost at the last doubling. For example, it cost $100 to produce the first unit and the learning curve is 95 percent. When the second unit is produced, the cost of the two units produced so far is 95 percent of $100 or $95 per unit. When two more units are produced, output has again doubled and the cost of each of the **four** units is 95 percent of $95, or 95 percent of 95 percent of the original $100 cost. The average cost of the four units is therefore $90.25.
2. The **higher** the learning curve percentage, the **lower** the learnings effect. An 80 percent learning curve represents significantly more learning than a 95 percent learning curve. Also, note that a 100 percent learning curve represents no learning at all. In that case cost is directly variable and learning has reached what is known as a steady state.
3. The term a may represent a group of units rather than a single unit of service or product, such as the first 100 patients using a new service.
4. X is expressed in multiples of a for computational purposes. If production has doubled once, X is 2; if it has doubled twice, X is 4; if it has doubled three times, X is 8; and so on. X can also be a figure like 3, or 4.7, representing a fraction of a doubling.

We now turn to a simple example using these learning curve concepts.

An illustration   The Saverine Boat Company is a family-owned manufacturer of quality boats. It started as a producer of handmade canvas canoes and has branched into several specialized boat types. The most recent product line addition is a small bass boat that sells for $1,350. Like all Saverine's products, it is primarily manually produced except for basic fabricating processes. Consequently, labour and labour-related costs comprise a large part of the product's total cost. The first quarter of 1984 was the first period of production for the new boat. Production data for the period are:

Boats produced	500
Direct materials	$200,000
Labour-related costs	120,000
Allocated fixed overhead	100,000

With the last three new boats added to the company's line, Saverine Boat Company has experienced a 90 percent learning effect for labour-related cost for the first several years of production. A similar learning curve effect is expected with the bass boat. The company would like to project product costs for this boat for the rest of 1984. The company estimates cost will remain stable for the nine-month period except for the learning curve effect, and production is expected to remain at 500 boats per quarter.

In order to prepare the budget for boat production for the last three quarters of the year, the company needs fixed and variable cost data. Fixed costs for the first quarter are $100,000, so for the last three quarters they are expected to total $300,000. Direct material is easily found by finding unit variable costs from the data above:

$$\text{Direct material cost} = \$200,000 \text{ for 500 boats}$$

$$\frac{\$200,000}{500} \text{ boats} = \$400 \text{ per boat}$$

Direct labour cost poses a problem because it changes as learning takes place. To complete the budget for the last three quarters of the year, the company must first calculate expected labour-related cost for production, using the learning curve.

Finding labour costs with learning curves. The labour-related costs are expected to have a 90 percent learning curve effect, which means that each time the output doubles the **cumulative average cost** of labour-related costs is 90 percent of what it was during the previous doubling. Therefore, for the first doubling of production from 500 boats to 1000 boats, the cumulative average labour-related cost is 90 percent of the original cost. For the second doubling, from 1000 boats to 2000 boats, the cumulative average cost becomes 90 percent of 90 percent or 81 percent of the original cost. A schedule of labour-related costs for the production of the first 2000 bass boats is presented in Figure 17-13.

		Saverine Boat Company			
		Schedule of Labour-Related Costs for Bass Boats			
Cumulative Number of Units	Incremental Number of Units	Cumulative Cost	Incremental Cost	Total Average Unit Cost	Incremental Average Unit Cost
500	500	$120,000	$120,000	$240.00	$240.00
1000	500	216,000	96,000	216.00	192.00
2000	1000	388,800	172,800	194.40	172.80

Figure 17-13
This schedule identifies the cumulative and incremental labour-related costs
for producing the first two doublings of the original 500 units of production.

The learning curve is an exponential function

The labour-related cost for the first 500 boats is $120,000 or an average of $240 per boat manufactured during the first quarter of the year. The first doubling of output, from 500 to 1000 boats, occurs during the second quarter. The cumulative average cost of production should be 90 percent of $240 or $216. The total cumulative cost should be 1000 units × $216 or $216,000. However, the cost of production for just the second quarter is $96,000 or an incremental average cost of $192 per boat. The next doubling, from 1000 to 2000 boats, will occur during the third and fourth quarters of the year. The cumulative average cost should be 90 percent of $216 or $194.40.

Another way of computing the same cost is to use the original cost and raise the learning effect to an exponential power equal to the number of doublings that have occurred. For instance, the cost for the second doubling is calculated as:

$$\$240 \times (.9)^2 = \$240 \times .81 = \$194.40$$

If the cost of the third doubling were to be calculated it would be

$$\$240 \times (.9)^3 = \$174.96$$

Total cumulative labour-related cost for production of the first 2000 boats is

$$\$194.40 \times 2000 = \$388,800$$

As Figure 17-13 shows, the cost of production for the last two quarters only is $172,800 or an incremental average cost of $172.80. As you can see, the cost of producing the last boat is much less than the cost of producing the first boat. The learning curve formula, however, does not give the cost of producing the last unit. It gives the average unit cost of producing **all** units.

In Figure 17-13 the cumulative average cost is determined using the cost relationships described by the learning curve. The incremental cost is the cost of producing the additional increment of units. For example, the cumulative cost of producing the first 1000 boats is $216,000. The cost of the first 500 is $120,000, therefore the remaining $96,000 is the labour-related cost of producing the second 500 boats. Dividing the $96,000 by the 500-boat increment yields an incremental average unit cost of $192.00 for the 500-unit increment. The incremental average unit cost of the last 1000 boats is similarly computed and is shown in Figure 17-13 as $172.80 per boat.

Saverine Boat Company has already produced the first 500 boats and the calculations in Figure 17-13 are made for the purpose of budgeting production for the last three quarters of the year. The cumulative labour-related cost is $388,800 for the first 2000 boats, but that amount includes the $120,000 for the first 500 boats. Consequently, the labour-related cost for the 1500 boats to be produced during the last nine months of 1984 is $268,800 ($388,800 − $120,000). Dividing $268,800 by 1500 boats yields a labour-related cost of $179.20 per boat for the 1500 boats. The budget for the last three quarters of 1984 for the 1500 bass boats is

Direct materials	1500 boats @ $400	= $ 600,000
Labour-related costs	1500 boats @ $179.20 =	268,800
Allocated fixed overhead	=	300,000
Total budgeted cost for last three quarters		$1,168,800

Using logarithms to compute learning curve costs

In the boat company example, learning curve cost computations were quite simple, because the expected production precisely matched an exact doubling of the original production amount of 500 boats. The first doubling covered the second quarter and the second doubling matched expected production for the third and fourth quarters. But what if the expected production level is not an exact doubling? Suppose Saverine wants to budget costs for the first six months of 1985. At the current production level of 500 boats a quarter, it will produce 1000 new boats in the first six months of 1985, which will be 3000 in total since the first boat, but the next doubling of output occurs at 4000 boats. A simple linear approximation can be made, but by definition learning curves are not straight lines, so some error will occur. This and other learning curve problems can be solved using logarithms since learning curves represent a power function—a number raised to some exponential power. The general form of the learning curve equation is

$$Y = aX^b$$

Using logarithms we can transform this to the linear form:

$$\ln Y = \ln a + b \ln X$$

If we know or can estimate a and b, it is possible to solve for any value of Y given any value of X regardless of whether X is a doubling multiple of the initial unit represented by a. Not long ago the calculation would have been considered cumbersome, but today many inexpensive hand calculators have log function capabilities that make the computations very simple.

To illustrate, we again look at the boat company example. To solve the problem using logarithms, we must change the variables to the logarithm form expressed earlier.

Y is the average amount of labour time or cost to produce X number of boats. It is the unknown value for which we want to solve.

Learning is computed in multiples of initial production

The number of units of service or product, in this case 3000 boats, is expressed by X. However, X is not 3000 boats; in our example the value of X is 6. This is because the first batch of boats produced consisted of 500 units and not just one. X in the learning curve formula is actually a multiple of the initial number of units. To solve for 3000 boats when the initial number was 500, we use X to represent 3000 / 500 boats, or 6. If we wanted to solve the learning curve formula for 3250 boats, X would be 6.5 (3250 / 500).

The value a is the average unit cost or labour time needed to produce a unit of service or product in the initial observation period. In this case it is $240 per boat as shown in Figure 17-13.

The value b is the learning effect that is equal to the log of the 90 percent learning rate divided by the log of 2 (ln .9/ln 2).

Any learning curve problem with a 90 percent learning effect has a b value of $-.1520$, calculated as follows: the log of $.90 = -.1054$, and the log of $2 = .69315$, so $b = -.1054/.69315 = -.1520$. Values of b for any given learning effect are constant, so to eliminate computing them for each situation they are often given. Below are b values for some common learning rates:

Learning Rate	b value
.70	−.5146
.75	−.4150
.80	−.3219
.85	−.2345
.90	−.1520
.95	−.0740
.98	−.0291

To summarize, the initial production run of 500 boats had average labour-related costs of $240, and the company uses a 90 percent learning curve. We first repeat the previous calculation using logarithms to find the cost of production of 1500 boats in the last three quarters of 1984. Then we calculate the cost for the first half of 1985 when 1000 more boats are produced.

To compute the budgeted labour-related cost—Y in the learning curve equation—for the last three quarters of 1984, we merely substitute the necessary values into the equation presented on page 743:

$$\ln Y = \ln a + b \ln X$$
$$= \ln (\$240) + (-.1520) \cdot \ln 4$$

where:

$\ln Y$ = the logarithms to the base e, or natural log, of the cost which is expressed as Y

$\ln (\$240)$ = the natural log of the original unit cost of $240

$-.1520$ = the value of b for a 90 percent learning curve

$\ln 4$ = the natural log of the multiple of the initial quantity. Production for three quarters is 1500 boats. Five hundred boats were already produced in the initial production run. Therefore, at year-end 2000 boats will have been produced. Since 500 were in the initial production run, 2000 is four times the initial amount, so the value of X is 4.

We can now substitute the appropriate values into the above equation and solve for the log of Y and then for Y.

$$\ln Y = 5.480\ 638\ 9 + (-.1520)\ 1.386\ 294\ 4$$
$$= 5.480\ 638\ 9 - .210\ 716\ 8$$
$$= 5.269\ 922\ 2$$
$$Y = \$194.40$$

The value of Y is the antilogarithm of 5.269 922 2 and may be obtained from tables of natural logarithms or by means of a calculator.

Common or natural logarithms may be used in learning curve calculations

Logarithms to the base e, or natural logs, are used here because they are most commonly found on hand calculators. However, logarithms to the base 10, or common logs, may be used just as easily.

Note that the cumulative average cost for labour activities is the $194.40 computed earlier and shown in Figure 17-13. The analysis is easily extended to compute the labour costs of boat production for the first six months of 1985. One thousand boats for the six-month period means a total of 3000 by the end of June 1985, which is six times the original production quantity of 500, so the value of X is 6. Substituting:

$$\ln Y = \ln a + b \ln X$$
$$= \ln (\$240) + (-.1520)\ \ln 6$$
$$= 5.480\ 638\ 9 + (-.1520)\ 1.791\ 759\ 5)$$
$$= 5.480\ 638\ 9 - .272\ 347\ 4$$
$$= 5.208\ 291\ 5$$
$$Y = \$182.78$$

The cumulative average labour-related cost for 3000 boats is $182.78. The total cumulative labour-related cost is $182.78 × 3000 boats, or a total of $548,340.

The cumulative labour-related cost for 2000 boats completed in 1984 was computed earlier as $194.40 \times 2000 = $388,800$. The difference between the total cost of $548,340 and the first-year cost of $388,800 is the incremental labour-related cost for the 1000 boats to be produced in the first six months of 1985. The estimated amount the firm will have to spend for the labour-related costs of producing 1000 boats in the first six months of 1985 is

Total labour cost for 3000 boats	$548,340
Less labour cost for the first 2000 boats	388,800
Labour cost for the last 1000 boats	$159,540

Figure 17-14 shows the bass boat data presented in Figure 17-13 with cost estimates for 2000 additional boats. As before, cumulative costs are presented along with the incremental cost of producing an additional amount.

The steady state

In the steady state no learning takes place

Most new activities do not experience an indefinite learning phenomenon. Instead, learning occurs for a period, and then the **steady state** is achieved where the costs become directly variable, causing the curve to become a straight line at that point. Figure 17-15 shows a learning curve that reaches the steady state at production level X_1. When the steady state is reached the labour-related costs become directly variable and act in the manner of other variable costs. Once the steady state has been reached, the budgeting process becomes one of evaluating the directly variable costs in the same manner as before.

Saverine Boat Company
Schedule of Labour-Related Costs for Bass Boats

Cumulative Number of Units	Incremental Number of Units	Cumulative Cost	Incremental Cost	Total Average Unit Cost	Incremental Average Unit Cost
500	500	$120,000	$120,000	$240.00	$240.00
1000	500	216,000	96,000	216.00	192.00
2000	1000	388,800	172,800	194.40	172.80
3000	1000	548,340	159,540	182.78	159.54
4000	1000	699,840	151,500	174.96	151.50

Figure 17-14
The schedule of labour related costs presented in Figure 17-13 is extended here to include production of the next 2000 units in increments of 1000 units.

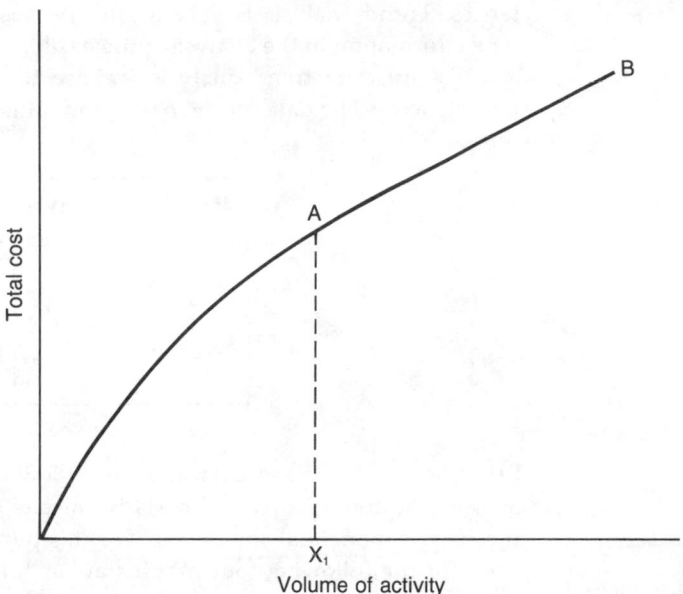

Figure 17-15
A plot of learning curve data. The learning curve is quite steep and does not decrease at a rapid rate because it represents a value of 90 percent, which is a relatively low rate of learning. Note the point where the steady state is reached, when the curve becomes a straight line, representing a directly variable cost.

Trend analysis

Forecasting methods are available that provide an easier means of updating the forecasts than regression analysis. Two such methods involve the use of moving averages and exponential smoothing for analyzing trends in data. These methods are designed to facilitate and improve continuing forecasts by adding new data points as they become available over time. Moving averages and exponential smoothing are forms of forecasting that are part of a general class of models called **time series analysis.** The general purpose of time series analysis is to identify trends and to use the trends for planning and to improve decision making in general.

In regression analysis all data points have equal weights in the analysis. With exponential smoothing, more recent data may be given more or less weight than older data. Often more recent data are better predictors than older data because the more recent values result from current conditions that are more likely to approximate future conditions.

Trend analysis is used for forecasting

The primary use of trend analysis in business and economics is forecasting. Managers may use moving average data or exponential smoothing data to predict sales, costs, cash receipts, activity levels, and other items. For example, a firm may use a moving average of monthly sales to predict the next month's sales, and a hospital may use exponential smoothing to predict weekly admittances. Trend analysis is very useful, because it allows managers to include new information in the analysis quite easily.

To illustrate trend analysis we use the following example of monthly payroll taxes. The data for the past six months consist of the following:

Month	Payroll Costs
1	$83,000
2	80,000
3	88,000
4	91,000
5	90,000
6	96,000

We use the above data and the following four month's payroll costs to analyze the trend in payroll costs by means of moving averages and also by means of exponential smoothing. For this purpose we assume that the payroll costs for the following four months are as follows (but of course these values only become available as each month passes):

Month	Payroll Costs
7	$95,000
8	93,200
9	98,800
10	97,000

Moving averages The mean value of the first six months of payroll costs is $88,000, but if the costs are plotted for each month, as in Figure 17-16, you can see that there is a general trend upward. Therefore, the mean value may not be the best predictor of future costs. However, it is a good start. Now if we observe the cost at the end of the seventh month, we can calculate the new mean of the seven available values, or we can calculate the **moving average** by dropping the first value of $83,000 and using only the six latest values. The new moving average after adding month 7 data is $90,000. Each succeeding month, as a new value becomes available, a new moving average is computed from the six latest values. For month 8 the moving average value is $92,200; for month 9 it is $94,000; and it is $95,000 for month 10.

The actual data points and the moving average values can be plotted together to visualize the relationship of trend lines to actual data. The moving average can be plotted along with the most recent data point, which is shown in the top of Figure 17-16. For example, the moving average of $90,000 for month 7 can be plotted with the $95,000 actual cost for month 7. However,

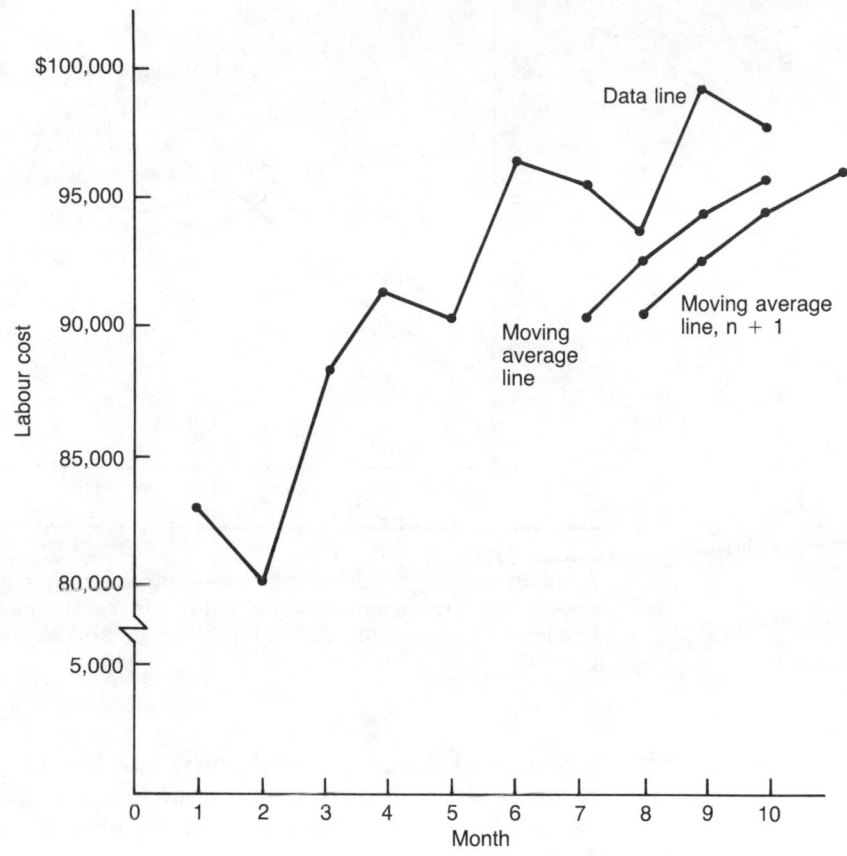

Figure 17-16
Actual data are plotted along with the moving average line for the last four months. The moving average line is also plotted one time period ahead ($n + 1$) to compare with the next period's actual data.

the moving average computed with month 7 data will be used to forecast month 8 labour cost. Therefore, a logical graph of the data is to plot the moving average of one month with the actual data point of the next month to see how well the moving average predicted the actual results. This comparison is graphed in Figure 17-16 also, and the line is identified as the $n + 1$ moving average curve.

When plotted with the latest data point, the moving average is always below the data if the trend is up, and above the data if the trend is down. This means that the moving average always lags behind the actual data, and this fact must be kept in mind when the moving average is used in making predictions. The latest value of the moving average is not necessarily a good

The moving average lags behind the data from which it is computed

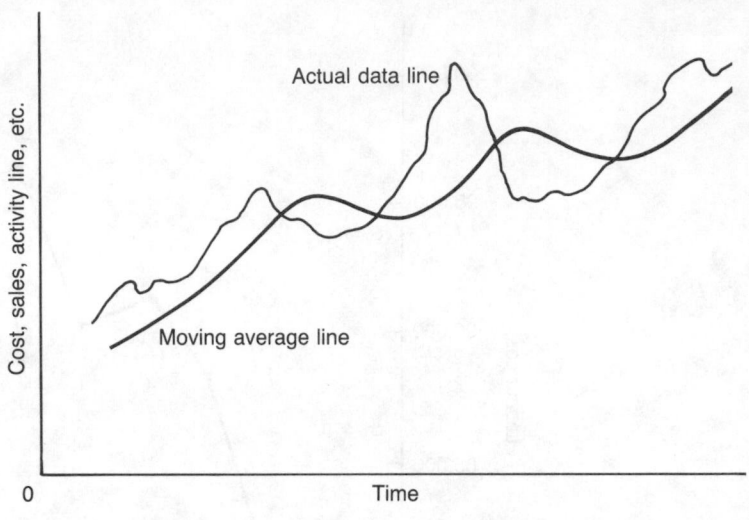

Figure 17-17
A moving average plotted over a long period of time along with actual data shows the general smoothing effect of the trend analysis. Note that the trend line lies below the data during rising trends and above the data during falling trends.

prediction of the next value of actual data, but it is usually a good prediction of the trend, or direction, in which future data elements can be expected to go. Figure 17-17 presents the moving average plotted over an extensive set of data, showing its smooth flow above or below the more erratic data. Sometimes the point where the moving average crosses above or below the data can be used to predict a change in trend direction.

Exponential smoothing　A method of trend analysis that has some advantages over the moving average is called **exponential smoothing.** Exponential smoothing is easier to calculate than a moving average, especially if there is a large number of data items. It may also assign more weight to the most recent value, so that the lag characteristic of the moving average can be minimized. A theoretical explanation of exponential smoothing is beyond the scope of this book, but it is not necessary to know the mathematical theory in order to understand and use this method of trend analysis.

To illustrate the use of exponential smoothing, we start with the first six months' data used in the moving average and the first mean of $88,000 calculated on page 748.[2] When the next month's value of $95,000 becomes

[2]We use the $88,000 for convenience. The exponentially smoothed value for month 7 could actually be different.

available, it is made part of the next calculation. We assume that the old data represent 70 percent of the available information, and the new item represents 30 percent. Therefore the new information and the old are weighted and combined to yield a new point to add to the trend line:

$$\$88,000 \ (.70) + \$95,000 \ (.30) = \$90,100$$

When the value for the eighth month becomes available we again assign 70 percent to the old value and 30 percent to the new. The new exponentially smoothed trend line value is

$$\$90,100 \ (.70) + \$93,200 \ (.30) = \$91,030$$

The next value of the trend line is calculated using the previous value and the latest data item as follows:

$$\$91,030 \ (.70) + \$98,800 \ (.30) = \$93,361$$

Finally, the value for month 10 is

$$\$93,361 \ (.70) + \$97,000 \ (.30) = \$94,453$$

Both moving average and exponential smoothing adjust to accommodate new data. With a moving average, the oldest data item is dropped and the most recent data item is added, so, in effect, this trend analysis method recognizes the impact of new information by dropping the oldest and adding the newest information. No data are dropped using exponential smoothing. Instead managers adjust for the importance of new information by assigning different weights, called **alpha factors,** to the most recent data element. Heavier weights make the most recent datum more important, which means that a high alpha factor causes the exponential smoothing curve to react more quickly to changing trends. However, it also causes the curve to move away from the true trend when an unusual data point is encountered. For instance, a strike may cause payroll costs to drop to zero for a short period of time.

The exponential smoothing curve looks quite different if we assign a different alpha factor to the most recent data. For example, assume an alpha of .6 for the payroll cost example. That means the weight for the old data is .4 (1 − alpha). Computing the values for the exponential smoothing curve we arrive at:

Month 7: $\$88,000 \ (.4) + \$95,000 \ (.6) = \$92,200$

For the other months the values are

Month	Value
8	.4 ($92,200) + .6 ($93,200) = $92,800
9	.4 ($92,800) + .6 ($98,800) = $96,400
10	.4 ($96,400) + .6 ($97,000) = $96,760

Both the .3 alpha and .6 alpha exponential smoothing curves are plotted in Figure 17-18 along with the moving average curve.

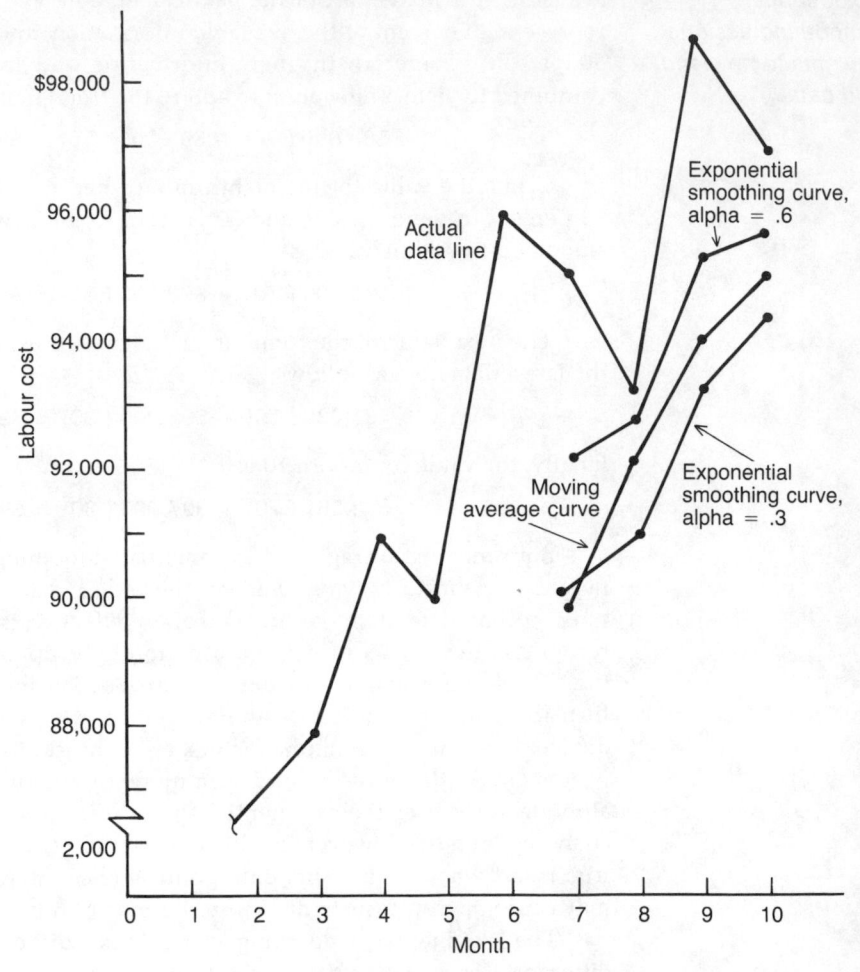

Figure 17-18
A data line is plotted for months 3 through 10 along with the moving average
line and exponential smoothing lines with alphas of .3 and .6. The appropriate
alpha factor must be determined for each situation.

There is no generally accepted value for alpha. Managers should choose
the value that appears to supply them with the most useful information over
time.

Trend analysis is a very useful management tool that can be very complex.
Here we have only provided a very brief introduction to the topic. In other
courses you may study trend analysis in more depth and apply it to accounting
activities.

Summary Information about cost behaviour patterns is important for many management accounting analyses and reporting activities. Many accountants believe that identifying cost behaviour patterns is among the more difficult tasks facing accountants. Simple techniques such as high-low and scatter diagram analysis are useful sometimes, but their information value is relatively limited. More sophisticated quantitative techniques may be used in planning and control. Quantitative methods do not provide useful information automatically. Managers must learn to use those techniques that are useful in each particular situation.

Many types of statistical analyses are used in business to help managers plan operations and make decisions. Among the more useful statistics are measures of central tendency and measures of dispersion. The **mean** is the average of a data set. It is computed by summing the values in the data set and dividing by the number of data elements. The **median** is the middle value in a data set and the **mode** is the most commonly occurring value.

Measures of dispersion describe the amount of fluctuation of the values in a data set about its mean. The **variance, S^2,** and the **standard deviation, S,** are two commonly used measures of dispersion. The standard deviation together with the mean may be used to make estimates about the probability of occurrence of certain values or events.

Use of the mean and standard deviation often assumes that the **population** from which the sample data are selected is normally distributed. A **normal distribution** of data means that the data are distributed symmetrically about the mean and satisfy certain statistical properties of the **normal curve.**

Among the more powerful quantitative tools for planning and controlling costs is **regression-correlation analysis.** One form, called **simple linear regression,** relates a single dependent variable to a single independent variable. The **independent variable** is given or derived from historical data. The **dependent variable** is so called because its value depends on the value of the independent variable and the relationship between the two variables as described by an equation.

Regression-correlation analysis is a two-step process. The first step is to compute the **regression line,** which is a line whose equation best describes the linear relationship between the dependent and the independent variable. It is also called the **line of best fit.** The regression line can be computed by means of **least squares method** and, once computed, can be used to predict any value of the dependent variable, given some value of the independent variable.

Correlation analysis measures the strength of the relationship between the two variables. The **coefficient of correlation** is denoted as r whose value ranges between -1 and $+1$. Positive correlation means that X and Y move in the same direction. Negative correlation means that X and Y move in opposite directions. The relationship between X and Y is strong if the value of r is close to -1 or to $+1$, and it is weaker as r approaches zero. To make interpretation of r easier, we usually convert it to r^2, which is called the **coefficient of**

determination. Its value shows the percentage of fluctuation in the data that can be explained by the relationship between the dependent and the independent variable. The amount of fluctuation due to other factors is explained by the **coefficient of nondetermination.** If one independent variable does not yield a satisfactory r^2, another independent variable may be found to have a better fit.

With **multiple linear regression** more than one independent variable is used to predict the dependent variable. The purpose of using multiple independent variables is to improve the prediction process. The computation of the regression line and the coefficient of determination is significantly more complex than with simple linear regression.

Learning curves are a class of semivariable costs that increase with activity levels but at a decreasing rate. The term learning curve comes from the fact that such cost behaviour is most commonly found in labour and labour-related costs as employees become more and more familiar with the production of a product or service. Learning curves are used to help managers predict the labour related cost of producing products or providing services. Learning curves are particularly useful in estimating labour costs for new products or services. Usually the learning effect lasts only for a period of time, after which the **steady state** is reached and the cost becomes directly variable.

Trend analysis is used to help managers identify trends in sales costs activities, or other items, and can be very useful for budgeting and forecasting. Trend analysis allows new data to be incorporated easily into the analysis. With a **moving average,** one form of trend analysis, the most recent datum is added and the oldest datum is dropped each time a new average is calculated. Another form of trend analysis, called **exponential smoothing,** does not drop any data values but weights the relative importance of the old and the new data. The weight assigned to the new data may range from zero to 1 and is called the **alpha factor.** The weight assigned to the old data is always (1 − alpha). The higher the alpha factor, the more importance management assigns to recent data.

Appendix A: computer programs

Following are two computer programs that may be used for solving some of the end-of-chapter problems and for analyzing actual data. The first program calculates the mean and standard deviation of a set of data. Up to 100 items can be analyzed with this program.

The second program calculates the regression line, the coefficient of correlation r, and the coefficient of determination r^2. It may be used with up to 80 pairs of data. Problems 17A-7 and 17B-7 are intended to be solved with this program.

```
100 REMARK. PROGRAM TO CALCULATE MEAN  AND STANDARD DEVIATION
110 REMARK. OF 100 ITEMS OF DATA.
120 DIM X(100)
130 PRINT
140 PRINT 'MEAN AND STANDARD DEVIATION CALCULATION.'
150 PRINT
160 PRINT 'HOW MANY ITEMS OF DATA ARE THERE';
170 INPUT N
180 PRINT
190 S1 = 0
200 S2 = 0
210 PRINT 'TYPE IN EACH VALUE, FOLLOWED BY A COMMA OR CARRIAGE RETURN.'
220 PRINT
230 FOR I = 1 TO N
240 INPUT X(I)
250 S1 = S1 + X(I)
260 S2 = S2 + X(I)*X(I)
270 NEXT I
280 S = S1/N
290 D = SQR((N*S2 - S1*S1)/(N*(N-1)))
300 PRINT
310 PRINT '    MEAN                = '; S
320 PRINT '    STANDARD DEVIATION = '; D
330 PRINT
340 STOP
350 END
```

```
100 REMARK. A PROGRAM TO CALCULATE LINEAR REGRESSION LINE INTERCEPT
110 REMARK. AND SLOPE, AS WELL AS THE VALUE OF R AND R SQUARED.
120 PRINT 'THIS PROGRAM PERFORMS A SIMPLE LINEAR REGRESSION ANALSYS.'
130 PRINT
140 DIM X(80), Y(80)
150 PRINT 'HOW MANY OBSERVATIONS ARE TO BE ANALYZED';
160 INPUT N
170 PRINT
180 'TYPE YOUR X AND Y VALUES WITH A COMMA AFTER THE X.'
190 'STRIKE THE RETURN KEY AFTER EACH PAIR OF VALUES.'
200 PRINT
210 FOR I = 1 TO N
220 INPUT X(I), Y(I)
230 NEXT I
240 S1 = 0
250 S2 = 0
260 S3 = 0
270 S4 = 0
280 S5 = 0
290 FOR I = 1 TO N
300 S1 = S1 + X(I)*Y(I)
310 S2 = S2 + X(I)
320 S3 = S3 + Y(I)
330 S4 = S4 + X(I)*X(I)
340 S5 = S5 + Y(I)*Y(I)
350 NEXT I
360 B = (S1 - S2*S3/N)/(S4 - S2*S2/N)
370 A = S3/N - (B*S2)/N
380 Q = (N*S1 - S2*S3)
390 T = SQR(N*S4 - S2*S2)
400 U = SQR(N*S5 - S3*S3)
410 R = Q/(T*U)
420 R2 = R*R
430 PRINT
440 PRINT ' ','Y INTERCEPT','SLOPE','R','R SQUARED'
450 PRINT ' ',' A, B, R, R2
460 STOP
470 END
```

Appendix B: The growing role of computers in management accounting

Computers are a relatively recent innovation in business. In the 1950s computers were first used in business to take over very mundane clerical activities. By the early 1960s computers had become widely used and began to play an important role as the centre of information systems activity. Computers had an impact on accounting activity in several ways by:

1. Reducing manual clerical work
2. Having the ability to store greater quantities of data
3. Providing easier access to the accounting data base
4. Providing the ability to generate more timely reports
5. Requiring an integration with other segments of the firm's information system
6. Requiring new kinds of data for external users and internal data for new types of management analysis and decision models

Evolving computer technology

It is difficult to predict future developments in a field as dynamic as computer systems. In the past some developments have been almost revolutionary in effect, such as the advent of multiprogramming, which allowed many computer jobs to share the resources of a computer system rather than one job's monopolizing the entire system until it was complete. Multiprogramming changed the nature of computer systems in a short period of time. However, most change, even in the computer field, has been more evolutionary and that will probably be true in the future.

There seem to be several areas in which changing computer technology will affect accounting information in the near future. These are

1. Reduced equipment cost
2. Specialized equipment
3. Minicomputers

Reduced equipment cost

During the last ten years, a period of rapidly rising prices in general, computer prices have dropped significantly. By any measure of computing capacity or power, computing capacity costs far less today than it did ten years ago. Most firms have not experienced a decline in their total computer-related cost, however, because they have increased their use of the computer and their hiring of computer personnel and because supply costs have risen.

The decreasing cost of computer power has had an important effect on accounting information systems. It has allowed firms to store data more economically, to retrieve data more frequently, and to prepare reports that previously were not economically feasible. The promise of continued declines in computer costs will certainly lead to many new types of information, a more detailed data base, and an expansion of management accounting activity. One of the most important cost factors in many computer-based accounting systems is the cost of on-line or real-time storage. On-line storage means that data are stored in the computer in such a way that they may be retrieved instantly.

With older computer systems, on-line storage was limited and expensive, and most data were stored on magnetic tape that required considerable time to be wound and rewound in order for users to gain access to the stored information. When stored on magnetic disks, data can be retrieved instantly, but disk storage space was very expensive. On-line retrieval is necessary for direct-access information systems such as airline reservation systems. As the cost of such on-line storage decreases, direct-access computer systems become more popular because managers start demanding more timely information. With on-line storage costs continuing to decline, there should be a very significant impact on the development of more and more real-time management reporting systems.

The cost of computer terminals has also declined, providing an inducement to management to supply more terminals for the use of more managers. As terminal costs drop, it becomes feasible to provide terminals for managers for even limited uses.

Specialized equipment

Some specialized equipment provides an impetus for the development of new managerial reports or other modifications of the accounting system. For instance, electronic scanners made possible very rapid storage of large volumes of hand-prepared data such as daily sales tickets, inventory change slips, and other documents that could be input, summarized, and reported on a very timely basis. New vector cathode-ray tubes are now available that allow users to plot geographic data quickly as well as to use the terminal for alphanumeric data. The result is that organizations like utilities can integrate traditional accounting data, such as customer accounts receivable, with engineering and operating data, such as load flow studies, meter and transformer locations, and power outage data. The integration of the accounting data base with other data bases allows utilities to relate revenue and expense data with engineering and operating data to evaluate efficiency and effectiveness measures. Surely terminals and other equipment developments will continue to affect management accounting activities.

Minicomputers

Minicomputers are relatively small and inexpensive computers that are used by small businesses, or, for specific purposes, by larger businesses. A manufacturing firm may use a minicomputer for scheduling and monitoring of production activity. For larger firms minicomputers provide an alternative to expanding a large centralized computer system. For some computer applications that do not require the resources of a large computer system, a minicomputer may be more effective and efficient than larger, more centralized computing facilities. With a minicomputer available for the specific uses for which it was intended, there is no need to compete for the centralized computer resources. The problem of allocating the cost of centralized computer facilities may also be reduced by using minicomputers. Typically the cost of operating a mini-computer can be identified more clearly with specific activities of the firm.

Perhaps the biggest impact of minicomputers is that many more firms can justify having their own computer. Many businesses that used manual accounting systems or purchased computer resources from time-sharing companies now find that an in-firm computer system is economically feasible. The result is that firms are better able to meet their management information needs. Instead of relying on information-reporting formats of computer programs available from time-sharing firms or from firms that sell standardized computer programs, the firm may develop programs that provide precisely the information needed to manage the business. The increasing capabilities of minicomputer systems and the declining cost of such systems promises to have a most significant effect on management accounting. In general, we can expect that more and more management accounting activities will be computer-based and that many smaller firms will be able to expand greatly their managerial accounting functions, because minicomputer costs have reduced the cost of accumulating, analyzing, and reporting management accounting information.

Growth of operations research

Before computers became widely available most statistical analyses and most mathematical programming methods, such as linear programming, were impossible to do manually in any reasonable time period, or they were just far too costly to use. Computers have made possible the use of more sophisticated management analysis tools and decision models. The entire field of quantitative business analysis is often referred to as **operations research.** The continued expansion of the use of computers will surely result in even more utilization of operations research methods. Much of the data necessary for such analysis methods are provided by the management accounting system. Information such as inventory carrying costs, unit production costs, and detailed nonmanufacturing costs are but a few examples of data inputs necessary for some operations research models.

Forecasting

Business forecasting is an integral part of management's activity in most well-managed firms. We have talked extensively about the budgeting process and the use of forecasts in other activities such as inventory management. Historically, business forecasting has been an important but internal part of the accounting reporting activity. Forecasts were used externally only for specific purposes such as forecasted sales and profit data used to support an application for a bank loan. Recently there has been growing support for more extensive business forecasts by management that might be made public as part of the company's formal financial statements. In addition, it has been suggested that independent auditors—certified public accountants—attest to the reasonableness of the forecasts. This would be a significant extension of the current role of the audit opinion.

Of course, the extension of forecasting to external financial statements is not part of management accounting itself, but it is a direct extension of management accounting activity. It is likely that the management accounting activity will be modified to ensure that both internal and external forecasting requirements are met. It may be that more extensive and more reliable forecasting models will be developed.

Questions

1. "These numbers just do not seem to make any sense, but they came out of our multiple regression model, so I guess they must be right." Comment.

2. Define the mean, the median, and the mode. What are all three called?

3. Name the two common measures of dispersion and discuss why such measures are important.

4. In statistics, what is meant by a population and a sample? Give an illustration.

5. What is the purpose of using regression-correlation analysis?

6. Explain the two steps in regression-correlation analysis.

7. Trymore Horticulture Laboratories, Inc., is attempting to develop new strains of carrots from seeds bought for that purpose from two different suppliers. The company wants to develop a strain that yields miniature carrots for use in preparing gourmet delicacies, and also a strain of giant carrots for making canned carrot juice. The process involves cultivating carrots from seeds that come from the largest or smallest carrots of subsequent plantings. In testing samples of seeds from the suppliers, the company finds that the mean length of carrots from supplier A is 5 centimetres with a standard deviation of 2.3 centimetres, while the mean length of carrots from supplier B is 5.2 centimetres with a standard deviation of 1.2 centimetres. Which supplier's seeds are more likely to produce the desired results?

8. In order to compare two brands of tires, a research organization tested five tires of each brand, measuring the mileage provided by each tire. The results of the test were

Mileage	
Brand A	**Brand B**
26 800	25 600
22 300	23 400
27 400	21 000
24 000	26 000
23 500	25 000

After the test, each tire manufacturer claimed that "on the average" its tires held up better than the other brand. Comment on these claims by discussing the meaning of the term **average** as used by the tire manufacturers.

9. A boat manufacturer builds boats of the following lengths, in metres: 10, 12, 14, 16, 18, 22, 23, 28, and 37. To plan next year's production, the company decides to hire a surveying firm to determine what size boat the public prefers. When the surveying firm quotes a price of $30,000 for the survey, the company decides to conduct the survey with its own staff. After some time, the surveying staff makes the following report: 22 percent of respondents preferred the mean size of the boats, which is 20 metres. Only 12 percent preferred the median size of 18 metres. Forty percent

expressed a preference for 16-metre boats, 12 percent preferred boats smaller than 14 metres, and 13 percent preferred boats larger than 32 metres. Which measure of central tendency is most significant to the boat manufacturer? Why?

10. During a slack time in the personnel office, a clerk performed a regression-correlation analysis between shoe sizes of the company's employees and their salaries, with salaries as the dependent variable. She found that shoe sizes were negatively correlated with salaries with an r^2 of .64, and she consequently recommended that in order to save money, the company should reject all employment applicants with small shoe sizes. Comment on the nature of the relationship between shoe sizes and salaries. What is the value of the coefficient of correlation? What do you think of the clerk's recommendation?

11. What is meant by a 90 percent learning curve? Does a 90 percent or a 70 percent learning curve show the greater learning effect?

12. "I've been looking over your 80 percent learning curve calculations on the cost of the new compressor. It says the steady state will be reached at a labour cost of $263 per unit. That is a bit too high. Why don't we switch to an 85 percent learning curve and a steady state of $250? Reducing the $263 by 5 percent yields about $250, giving us a lower labour cost for the compressor." Comment on the validity of the above statement and explain its fallacy by reference to learning curves and the steady state.

13. What is the purpose of using a moving average and exponential smoothing? How is exponential smoothing different from a moving average?

Exercises

Ex. 17-1   Measures of central tendency. Following are data on the average number of births per week in a hospital.

Week	Births
1	67
2	72
3	43
4	56
5	39
6	48
7	52
8	56
9	54
10	49
11	69

Required:
Compute the mean, median, and mode of births per week.

Ex. 17-2   Central tendency and dispersion. A drugstore has the following daily cash sales for a ten-day period:

Day	Receipts
1	$350
2	260
3	410
4	385
5	440
6	325
7	370
8	310
9	290
10	360

Required:
a. Compute the mean.
b. Compute the standard deviation.

Ex. 17-3   Use of normal curve. A manufacturer of carpenter and power tools has developed some statistical data on the use of 700-watt electric motors in the production of several power tools. Management wants to manage inventory better than in the past. Use of the motors has averaged 1000 a week with a standard deviation of 200. The company believes the use of motors approximates a normal distribution.

Required:
a. Find the range of motor use for 95 percent of the weeks.
b. Compute the probability that use will be between 900 and 1100.
c. Determine the probability that motor use will exceed 1100 a week.

Ex. 17-4   Use of mean and standard deviation. The management of a company believes that its cash receipts are normally distributed. The mean daily cash receipts are $5,500 and the standard deviation is $500.

Required:
a. Compute the probability that cash receipts for a day will be between $5,000 and $6,000.
b. Compute the probability that cash receipts will be at least $4,500 for a day.
c. Find the probability of daily cash receipts being greater than $6,000.
d. Determine the probability of cash receipts being between $5,200 and $6,200.

Ex. 17-5   Graph of a regression line. Following is the equation for a regression line:

$$Y_c = 1500 + 80X$$

Required:

a. Graph the regression line.

b. Use the graph to predict Y if $X = 20$.

Ex. 17-6   Calculation of regression line. Below are machine hours and utility cost data for the Oolitic Chain Saw Company:

Month	Machine Hours	Utility Costs
January	1200	$8,500
February	1500	9,100
March	1600	9,400
April	1700	9,500
May	1300	9,000
June	1100	8,400

Required:

a. Compute a regression line from the above data using machine hours as the independent variable.

b. Use your solution to predict the expected cost of utilities when 1800 machine hours are used.

Ex. 17-7   Coefficient of correlation and determination. Use the data in Exercise 17-6 to calculate the coefficient of correlation and coefficient of determination.

Ex. 17-8   Calculation and use of regression line. Below are production and diesel fuel consumption costs for a coal mine:

Month	Diesel Fuel Used (in Thousands of Litres)	Coal Production (in Thousands of Tons)
1	144	96
2	133	84
3	126	72
4	145	88
5	160	105
6	158	101

Required:

a. Compute the regression line using coal production as the independent variable and diesel fuel use as the dependent variable.

b. Predict fuel consumption for producing 150 000 tons of coal and also for 50 000 tons.

Ex. 17-9   **Calculation of *r* and *r*^{2}.** Use the data in Exercise 17-8 to calculate the coefficient of correlation and the coefficient of determination.

Ex. 17-10   **Use of learning curves.** The Red Clay Pottery Company manufactures attractive handmade pottery items. New lines of pottery require some learning time and the management has noted a decline in labour time and cost as employees become used to the production of new products. The learning effect seems to approximate an 85 percent learning curve. Last summer the company produced 50 sets of a new line of pottery. The total labour cost was $3,000. This fall the company will produce an additional 150 sets for Christmas orders.

Required:
Find the labour cost for the 150 sets of pottery using an 85 percent learning curve.

Ex. 17-11   **Use of learning curves.** Gedson, Inc., uses a learning curve of 90 percent for all new products it develops. A trial run of 1000 units of a new product shows total labour-related costs of $150,000. Management plans to produce 3000 units of the new product during the next year.

Required:
a. Compute the expected labour-related cost for the year to produce the 3000 units.
b. Find the unit cost of production for next year for labour-related costs.
c. Answer parts *a* and *b* again using a learning rate of 80 percent.

Ex. 17-12   **Moving average.** The Old Time Barbecue Restaurant experiences considerable fluctuations in sales, with lowest levels occurring in midweek and increasing to high levels on weekends. The company uses trend analysis to project sales for purposes of planning purchases and cash flows. Following are sales data for a two-week period:

1	Monday	$1,260
2	Tuesday	1,120
3	Wednesday	970
4	Thursday	1,010
5	Friday	1,330
6	Saturday	1,580
7	Sunday	1,490
8	Monday	1,300
9	Tuesday	1,170
10	Wednesday	1,030
11	Thursday	990
12	Friday	1,480
13	Saturday	1,650
14	Sunday	1,590

Required:
Calculate a seven-day moving average of sales revenue for the last eight days of data.

Ex. 17-13   Exponential smoothing. Refer to the data in Exercise 17-12 on the sales revenue of the Old Time Barbecue Restaurant. The company uses exponential smoothing to predict average sales revenue for the purpose of planning cash flows and purchases. The average revenue projected on day 6 is $1,266. The weight assigned to the old value of the exponentially smoothed trend line is .70 and the weight assigned to the latest day's revenue is .30.

Required:
Calculate the exponentially smoothed value of average daily revenue for days 7 through 14.

Problem Set A

P. 17A-1   Use of mean and standard deviation. Marge owns two different neighbourhood movie theatres, the North and the South. Frequently the North Theatre has very large weekly revenues and sometimes it experiences poor revenues. Marge engages you to analyze the data and suggest how they may be used to forecast future revenues.

Week	Admissions Revenue, North	Admissions Revenue, South
1	$1,200	$1,100
2	900	1,050
3	800	1,000
4	1,100	900
5	1,400	960
6	1,300	1,000
7	1,000	1,050
8	700	1,000
9	600	950
10	900	990

Required:
a. Compute the mean and standard deviation for weekly admission revenues for the two theatres.
b. Find the range of admission revenues for the two theatres 95.4 percent of the time, assuming a normal distribution.
c. Determine the probability that weekly admission revenue at the North Theatre would be below $600.

P. 17A-2 **Regression-correlation analysis.** A West Coast city has been experiencing an increase in major crime over the last five years, which has concerned city officials. One official argues that the increase in crime is attributable to the growth in city population and presents the following data in support of the contention:

Year	City Population (in Thousands)	Major Crimes
1979	165	2400
1980	175	2300
1981	190	2700
1982	200	3000
1983	240	3200

Required:
a. Perform a regression-correlation analysis to find the nature and strength of the relationship between population size and major crimes.
b. Discuss the meaning of the results of your analysis.

P. 17A-3 **Calculating regression line, *r*, and *r*².** Lakeport Recreational Vehicles Company treats all material-handling costs as part of overhead. Recently a manager noted that such costs have been increasing for the last several years and suggested that they may be strongly related to production output. To test his theory, the manager has accumulated the following data:

Month	Material-handling Cost	Units Produced
January	$4,600	100
February	5,100	110
March	5,800	120
April	6,800	130
May	5,900	110
June	5,200	90
July	4,400	70
August	4,000	50

Required:
a. Compute a regression line relating material handling costs to units produced.
b. State how strong the relationship between the two variables is.

P. 17A-4 **Regression-correlation analysis.** An electric utility is concerned about the number of customer complaints it has been receiving. Management is attempting to isolate the causes of rising customer complaints by investigating several suggested problem areas. One manager believes that most customer complaints are related to equipment failure or human errors made during periods of heavy demand for electricity. To support her idea, the manager submits the following data for the first eight days of the month.

Day	Complaints	Electricity Generated (in Thousands of Kilowatt Hours)
1	670	2300
2	590	2100
3	500	1900
4	540	2000
5	680	2900
6	590	2400
7	860	3300
8	770	2600

Required:
a. Compute a regression line equation for the data above using complaints as the dependent variable.
b. Compute the coefficient of determination.
c. Based on the results in parts *a* and *b*, agree or disagree with the manager's opinion of the relationship between the two variables. Tell management why you answered as you did, explaining carefully the meaning of the information you used in reaching your conclusion.
d. Based on the regression line you computed, find the expected number of complaints if the utility generates 3.8 million kilowatt hours in a day.

P. 17A-5 **Use of learning curves.** Stahley Electronic Products Company finds that new-product production is affected by an 80 percent learning effect, and it takes at least two years to reach the steady state. A new digital CB radio had labour-related costs of $20 a unit for its initial production run of 2000 units. During the first year of production the company expects to produce 6000 new radios in addition to the initial run of 2000. In the second year the company expects to produce 10 000 more radios.

Required:
a. Compute the labour-related costs of producing the radio for the first year.
b. Compute the labour-related production costs for the second year.
c. Find the average unit cost of labour-related costs for each year.

P. 17A-6 **Trend analysis of sales.** The Sanfran Company wants to use trend analysis methods to help forecast monthly sales on a month by month basis. Below are

January through December sales data. Starting with August, the company uses trend analysis in forecasting.

Month	Sales
January	$18,000
February	22,000
March	24,000
April	27,000
May	28,000
June	30,000
July	27,000
August	24,000
September	22,000
October	20,000
November	30,000
December	33,000

Required:

a. Calculate the moving average for each month from August through December, using eight months in the average.

b. Using an alpha of .2, calculate the exponential smoothing values for August through December assuming the July estimate was $25,200.

c. State which method provides the better estimate of monthly sales for September through December. Explain.

d. Determine whether an alpha value of .4 provides a better exponential smoothing model for predicting monthly sales in this problem.

P. 17A-7   Regression-correlation analysis (by computer). The Union City Shoe Factory has used direct labour hours to apply manufacturing overhead for the last ten years. During the same period of time the company has experienced rapidly rising total overhead costs, even though production activity has only increased modestly. Below are data for the ten-year period:

Year	Direct Labour Hours	Manufacturing Overhead Costs
1972	10 000	$148,000
1973	10 600	152,000
1974	10 900	155,000
1975	11 700	168,000
1976	11 000	166,000
1977	9 800	158,000
1978	12 200	174,000
1979	12 600	178,000
1980	13 000	183,000
1981	13 400	186,000

Required:

a. Compute the regression line, using direct labour hours as the independent variable and overhead costs as the dependent variable.

b. Compute r^2 for the regression above.

c. Compute the regression line and r^2 using time as the independent variable.

d. Discuss the results of your analyses with special reference to forecasting overhead costs for the shoe factory.

Problem Set B

P. 17B-1   Use of mean and standard deviation. Curve-Ball Concessions operates the hot dog concession at a major league baseball park. The hot dogs sell for $.80 each and are a high-profit item, but sales fluctuate from game to game and it is hard to plan for adequate inventories without having some spoilage. Below are hot dog sales data for the first 11 games of the year.

Game	Hot Dogs Sold
1	24 000
2	18 000
3	16 000
4	28 000
5	25 000
6	14 000
7	9 000
8	12 000
9	19 000
10	18 000
11	15 000

Required:

a. Compute the mean, the mode, and the median for the hot dog sales.

b. Compute the standard deviation of hot dog sales.

c. If the concession wants to have enough hot dogs so it does not run out 85 percent of the time, determine how many hot dogs it should have available for each game.

d. Based on the data, determine what the range of hot dog sales is for 95.4 percent of the games.

P. 17B-2   Regression-correlation analysis. The manager of plant No. 3 is complaining that the plant is uncomfortable to work in and should be air conditioned. She claims that on warm days production tends to decline and that the company could save money by installing an air-conditioning system. To test her claim, the vice president collected temperature and production data for one week, obtaining the following results:

Day	Mean Daily Temperature	Production in Units
1	24.4°C	560
2	26.7	520
3	23.9	550
4	27.8	540
5	25.0	520

The vice president agrees with the manager that if there is a strong correlation between temperature and production, air conditioning will be installed in plant No 3.

Required:
a. Calculate a regression line relating production as the dependent variable to daily mean temperature.
b. Calculate the coefficients of correlation and determination.
c. Discuss the results and decide whether air conditioning is warranted for the plant based on these data.

P. 17B-3   **Regression-correlation analysis.** The director of marketing of a large automobile dealer is trying to convince the owner to give away free tickets to a local dinner-theatre to every person visiting the dealership. The plan is expensive, but the marketing director is convinced that there is a high correlation between the number of people visiting the business and the number of cars sold. To test this belief the marketing director has gathered the following weekly visitation and sales data:

Week	Customer Visits	Car Sales
1	700	44
2	550	41
3	600	36
4	800	49
5	890	57
6	750	44

Required:
a. Compute the regression line using customer visits as the independent variable.
b. Compute the coefficient of determination.

   c. Explain what your analysis in parts *a* and *b* means in terms of visitations and car sales.
   d. If the cost of the dinner tickets is $6 and each visitor receives one ticket, what is the average cost per sale of the program?

P. 17B-4   **Use of regression line and r^2.** The Fishing Shack is a general-purpose fishing tackle store that also rents fishing boats at a nearby lake. The heaviest rental times are on weekends, although the number of rentals varies from one weekend to another. The manager of the Fishing Shack thinks that boat rentals may be related to the number of campers staying at the campgrounds around the lake or to the number of visitors entering the provincial park located on the lake. To test his theory the manager gathered campground occupancy and provincial park visitation data for the last six weekends, which are presented below:

Week	Boat Rentals	Campers	Park Visitors
1	45	200	1020
2	54	260	1380
3	63	280	1570
4	68	320	1440
5	60	320	1500
6	52	270	1300

Required:
   a. Compute the regression line using campers as the independent variable and boat rentals as the dependent variable.
   b. Compute the regression line using park visitors as the independent variable and boat rentals as the dependent variable.
   c. Compute r^2 for both regression lines.
   d. State which of the two independent variables you would suggest using as a predictor of boat rentals. Explain why.

P. 17B-5   **Learning curve analysis.** McGavren Manufacturing has recently started manufacturing a new industrial air compressor. During the first six months of the year 1000 units are produced with average unit labour costs of $100. The firm expects to continue production of the air compressors for the next several years at the same level of output. The expected learning rates for labour costs are 70 percent for the rest of the current year, and for the next year.

Required:
   a. Calculate expected labour for the first year.
   b. Calculate expected labour cost for the second year.

P. 17B-6   **Trend line analysis.** Each quarter Belmor Company computes the average unit cost for manufacturing labour for each of its products. Below are data for the last 10 quarters for one product.

Quarter	Unit Labour Cost
1	$80
2	84
3	83
4	86
5	90
6	88
7	92
8	94
9	91
10	95

The company decides to use trend analysis to estimate labour cost for products for the next quarter. Five quarters of data that follow the ones above are

Quarter	Unit Labour Cost
11	$100
12	98
13	97
14	102
15	105

Required:

a. Using a ten-month moving average compute the moving average for quarters 10 through 15.

b. Compute the new average for quarters 10 through 15 using exponential smoothing and an alpha of .2, assuming that the exponentially smoothed value for the tenth quarter is $88.

c. Repeat part *b* using an alpha of .4.

d. Of the three trend lines computed in parts *a*, *b*, and *c*, determine which appears to be the best predictor of unit labour cost.

P. 17B-7   **Regression-correlation analysis (by computer).** Warren Metal Products uses direct labour cost to apply overhead to production. The controller believes that other activity measures may be more closely related to the movement of overhead costs. The controller has decided to use regression-correlation analysis to test his belief. He has accumulated the data shown below for his analysis.

Year	Direct Labour Cost	Direct Labour Hours	Machine Hours	Overhead Cost
1971	$100,000	30 000	19 000	$300,000
1972	110,000	31 000	18 500	340,000
1973	120,000	31 000	19 000	350,000
1974	125,000	31 500	20 000	380,000
1975	130,000	30 500	20 000	360,000
1976	160,000	32 000	20 500	410,000
1977	180,000	33 000	21 000	470,000
1978	200,000	32 500	20 800	460,000
1979	220,000	34 000	21 000	490,000
1980	240,000	34 500	21 500	520,000

Required:

a. Compute three regression lines using overhead cost as the dependent variable and each of the activity variables as independent variables.

b. Compute the coefficient of determination for each regression line.

c. Using the data determine which activity measure appears to be most closely related to overhead costs. Use regression-correlation information to support your answer.

Minicases

Minicase 17-1 (CMA Examination Question)

The Toronto Company, Ltd., has pooled information from salesmen, customers, sales managers, and its economic research group to make a demand forecast for a new product line. From this information, annual demand in kilograms (x) is forecast to be normally distributed with a mean of 500 000 kilograms and standard deviation of 100 000 kilograms. It is expected that the Toronto Company, Ltd.'s new product line will have a selling price of $30 a kilogram, variable costs of $20 a kilogram and attributable fixed costs of $3,500,000 per year.

Mr. John Smith, Jr., the president of the Toronto Company, Ltd., would like to know more about the expected annual profit from this product line and called Mr. James W. Wong, the newly appointed accountant, to prepare an analysis of the whole situation.

Required:

a. Given the above information, what is the expected profit of this new product line? What is its standard deviation?

b. As Mr. Wong, comment about the procedure used in this case.

Minicase 17-2

Var Brothers Maintenance Services has been performing technical maintenance service on a wide variety of business machines in the Vancouver area for many years. The management of the company has been considering a change in its fee structure. Oral Var, who is in charge of service planning, suggested establishing the distribution using the relative frequency of various numbers of weekly service calls over the last four years. The following tabulation was prepared:

Number of calls	Number of occurences
801-850	4
851-900	10
901-950	80
951-1000	40
1001-1050	20
1051-1100	12
1101-1150	12
1151-1200	10
1201-1250	8
1251-1300	4

Dennis Var, marketing manager, disagreed with his brother, arguing that the number and size of companies with which they held maintenance contracts had changed recently. He concluded that this past experience therefore was not relevant and the firm would be better off recognizing its ignorance of the future in the rate restructuring. Dennis Var proposed the assumption of a uniform distribution with every possible number of calls from 801 to 1300 being equally likely. Both brothers are interested in knowing the probability of experiencing more than 1150 calls for service during a given week because this would mean certain extra measures should be taken by the management.

Required:
a. Find the probability of experiencing more than 1150 calls for service during a given week by using Oral Var's suggested frequency distribution.
b. What would be your answer if you used Dennis Var's suggestion?
c. How would you reconcile your answers? Comment.

Minicase 17-3

The Alma Plant manufactures the industrial product line of CJS Industries. Plant management wants to be able to get a good, yet quick, estimate of the manufacturing overhead costs which can be expected to be incurred each month. The easiest and simplest method to accomplish this task appears to be to develop a flexible budget formula for the manufacturing overhead costs.

The plant's accounting staff suggested that simple linear regression be used to determine the cost behaviour pattern of the overhead costs. The regression data can provide the basis for the flexible budget formula. Sufficient evidence is available to conclude that manufacturing overhead costs for each month of the last three years were used in the linear regression analysis.

The three-year period contained various occurrences not uncommon to many businesses. During the first year production was severely curtailed during two months due to wildcat strikes. In the second year production was reduced in one month because of material shortages and substantially increased (overtime scheduled) during two months to meet the units required for a one-time sales order. At the end of the second year employee benefits were raised significantly as the result of a labour agreement. Production during the third year was not affected by any special circumstances.

Various members of Alma's accounting staff raised some issues regarding the historical data collected for the regression analysis. These issues were as follows:

1. Some members of the accounting staff believed that the use of data from all 36 months would provide a more accurate portrayal of the cost behaviour. While they recognized that any of the monthly data could include efficiencies and inefficiencies, they believed these efficiencies / inefficiencies would tend to balance out over a longer period of time.

2. Other members of the accounting staff suggested that only those months which were considered normal should be used so that the regression would not be distorted.

3. Still other members felt that only the most recent 12 months should be used because they were the most current.

4. Some members questioned whether historical data should be used at all to form the basis for a flexible budget formula.

The accounting department ran two regression analyses of the data—one using the data from all 36 months and the other using the data from the last 12 months. The information derived from the two linear regressions is shown below.

Least Squares Regression Analyses		
	Data from all 36 months	**Data from most recent 12 months**
Coefficients of the regression equation:		
Constant	$123,810	$109,020
Independent variable (DLH)	$1.6003	$4.1977
Coefficient of correlation	.4710	.6891

Required:

a. From the results of Alma Plant's regression analysis which used the data from all 36 months:

    1. Formulate the flexible budget equation that can be employed to estimate monthly manufacturing overhead costs.

    2. Calculate the estimate of overhead costs for a month when 25 000 direct labour hours are worked.

b. Using only the results of the two regression analyses, explain which of the two results (12-months versus 36-months) you would use as a basis for the flexible budget formula.

c. How would the four specific issues raised by the members of Alma's accounting staff influence your willingness to use the results of the statistical analyses as the basis for the flexible budget formula? Explain your answer.

Minicase 17-4
(SMA adapted)

The management of Sanders Corporation has found that direct labour cost *variances* fluctuate in response to production volume. Each unit of product requires standard input of two hours of direct labour at a standard wage rate of $5 per direct labour hour. To check this, actual direct labour costs were recorded for a sample of recent production volumes as shown below.

Production Volume in Units	Actual Direct Labour Costs in Dollars
105	$ 990
44	460
61	600
42	440
77	740
78	760
87	850
31	330
103	1,000
84	810
53	540
40	430
56	560
37	390
69	670
93	930

Let y denote the actual direct labour costs and x denote standard direct labour costs of production. The relationship between x and y is given by:

$$y = a + bx$$

where a = \$60.48 and b = \$0.8955, calculated from the data given above. It is also determined that the r^2, the coefficient of determination, is .999.

Required:
a. What total labour cost variances would you predict when the production volume is:
  i   80 units
  ii 75 units
  iii 50 units
b. The actual labour costs will differ from the predicted values. Will most of the actual labour costs fall within a narrow or wide interval of the predicted values? Give reasons.
c. Is standard cost a good predictor of actual costs in this particular situation? Give reasons.

Minicase 17-5   (CMA Examination Question)

Xyon, Ltd., has purchased 80 000 pumps annually from Kobec, Inc. The price has increased each year and reached \$68 per unit last year. Because the purchase price has increased significantly, Xyon management has asked that an estimate be made of the cost to manufacture the pumps in its own facilities. Xyon's products consist of stamping and castings. The company has little experience with products requiring assembly.

The engineering, manufacturing, and accounting departments has prepared a report for management which included the estimate shown below for an assembly run of 10 000 units. Additional production employees would be hired to manufacture the subassembly. However, no additional equipment, space, or supervision would be needed.

The report states that total costs for 10 000 units are estimated at \$957,000, or \$95.70 a unit. The current purchase price is \$68 a unit. The report recommends a continued purchase of the product.

Components (outside purchases)	$120,000
Assembly labour[1]	300,000
factory overhead[2]	450,000
General and administrative overhead[3]	87,000
Total Costs	$957,000

[1]Assembly labour consists of hourly production workers.
[2]Factory overhead is applied to products on a direct labour dollar basis. Variable overhead cost vary closely with direct labour dollars.

Fixed overhead	50% of direct labour dollars
Variable overhead	100% of direct labour dollars
Factory overhead rate	150% of direct labour dollars

[3]General and administrative overhead is applied at 10% of the total cost of material (or components), assembly labour, and factory overhead.

Required:

a. Was the analysis prepared by the engineering, manufacturing, and accounting departments of Xyon, Ltd., and the recommendation to continue purchasing the pumps which followed from the analysis correct? Explain your answer and include any supportive calculations you consider necessary.

b. Assume Xyon, Ltd., could experience labour cost improvements on the pump assembly consistent with an 80 percent learning curve. An assembly run of 10 000 units represents the initial lot or batch for measurement purposes. Should Xyon produce 80 000 pumps in this section? Explain your answer.

part 5

Developing a Financial Accounting Foundation for Managerial Accounting

Students using this book normally have completed a course in financial accounting. Such a background is a useful prerequisite to the study of managerial accounting. Often the previous course cannot cover all necessary materials, and the topics not covered are completed in the following course. This part of the book contains the financial accounting material most likely still required of students prior to starting their study of managerial accounting. It consists of topics that integrate the students' financial accounting background and apply it in two areas. Chapter 18 covers the statement of changes in financial position, a report that normally cannot be understood well until a significant amount of accounting knowledge has been accumulated. Chapter 19 covers financial statements analysis, providing an understanding of the information that can be obtained from accounting reports, and the ways such information is used by managers, investors, analysts, and others. Students who have covered these two topics in a previous course will usually not cover them again, but for those whose background is lacking, this part of the book provides the necessary material.

Chapter 18

The Statement of Changes in Financial Position

The statment of changes in financial position is one of the basic financial statements found in the annual report of companies. When you have completed this chapter, you should understand:

1 The nature of financing and investing activities of businesses reported in the statement of changes.

2 Two definitions of funds.

3 The difference between net income and funds provided by operations.

4 What is meant by sources and uses of funds and how they are reported.

5 How the statement of changes is used in decision making.

6 The concept of nonfund items and the way they are used to convert net income to fund flows.

7 The concept of all financial resources.

8 The use of working papers for preparing the statement of changes.

The actions of management and the consequences of managerial decisions must eventually be reflected in the financial accounting reports that businesses provide to their owners, and to other interested users of external statements including governments, creditors, investors, and financial analysts. In recent years financial analysts have insisted on the presentation of a statement of changes in financial position, a report that was not included with the balance sheet, income statement, and retained earnings statement until recently but was usually available to management. Financial analysts find this report—in addition to the other financial statements—useful in evaluating the past performance and future potential of a business. In this chapter we discuss the concepts of fund flows and the way they are reported in the statement of changes in financial position.

Financing and investing activities of a business

The statement of changes in financial position, often referred to as the **funds flow statement,** describes the financing and investing activities of a business enterprise. **Financing activities** include transactions such as borrowing money or selling merchandise, resulting in a flow of financial resources **into** the business. **Investing activities** include transactions such as the purchase of equipment or the repayment of debt, resulting in the flow of financial resources **out of** a business. The financial resources, or funds, obtained from financing activities are used to pay for the investing activities.

The statement of changes reports the sources from which funds were obtained and the uses to which the funds were put. In addition, it explains why the amount of funds on hand at the end of the accounting period is different from the amount on hand at the beginning of the period.

The nature of changes in financial position

Because **funds** may be defined in several ways, it is important to understand which definition is being used before the statement of changes in financial position can be prepared. We consider two definitions:

1. **Funds** may be defined as **cash.**
2. **Funds** may be defined as **working capital.**

Two definitions of funds

The definition used determines the form of the statement of changes in financial position. When funds are defined as cash, the statement of changes explains how cash changed from the beginning balance reported in the previous period's balance sheet to the ending balance reported in the current period's balance sheet. When funds are defined as working capital, the statement of changes explains how the amount of working capital changed from the beginning balance to the ending balance.

For purposes of reporting to external users of financial statements, funds are usually defined as working capital. Investors, shareholders, analysts, and other external users are usually not concerned with the detailed operations that are disclosed by cash flow information. The statement of changes with funds defined as cash is generally prepared for internal use by managers. Managers are usually interested in the day-to-day operations of the business and must manage the flow of cash carefully. They accomplish such management by monitoring current operations and controlling the flow of current assets and liabilities, as well as by planning and controlling other sources and uses of funds.

Sources and uses of funds

There are four major financing activities that provide funds:

1. Operations that generate net income are the most important source of funds for most businesses.
2. Capital contributions by owners during the accounting period represent a major source of funds.
3. Funds provided from borrowing, such as the issuance of bonds, represent a significant source.
4. The sale of assets normally not held for sale is a source of funds, although usually not the most important source.

The funds made available by financing activities are put to use by making investments. Investing activities are represented by the following major uses of funds:

1. The expansion of the business by investment in additional fixed assets
2. The repayment of debt to creditors
3. The payment of dividends to shareholders
4. The reacquisition of capital stock

If the amount of funds flowing into the business is greater than the amount needed to purchase assets, repay debts, and distribute assets to shareholders, the balance increases working capital or the company's cash. When total sources are greater than total uses of funds, the situation is described algebraically as follows using hypothetical figures for the equation:

Sources − Uses = Increase in funds
$100,000 − $90,000 = $10,000 increase

If the resources available to the business are not sufficient to purchase assets, repay debts, and pay dividends, cash or working capital must be reduced to provide the balance of the needed funds for these purposes. In that case the situation is described algebraically as follows:

Sources − Uses = Decrease in funds
$92,000 − $100,000 = $8,000 decrease

The statement of changes in financial position reports all the sources and uses of funds and is frequently prepared showing the change in funds as the difference between the sources and the uses, as follows:

Sources	$ 92,000
Uses	100,000
Decrease in funds	$ 8,000

Some accountants prefer to prepare the statement in balanced form, with the change in funds viewed as if it were itself a source or use of funds, so that the algebraic representation becomes

$$\text{Sources} = \text{Uses}$$

When the statement is viewed as a balanced equation, an increase in cash or working capital is reported together with the uses of funds, and a decrease is reported together with the sources. To illustrate the first example above in the balanced form, we have

$$\begin{aligned}\text{Sources} = & \qquad\qquad \text{Uses}\\ \$100,000 = & \;\$90,000 + \$10,000 \text{ increase in funds}\end{aligned}$$

On the other hand, the second example with a decrease in funds appears in the balanced form as

$$\begin{aligned}\text{Sources} & \qquad\qquad = \; \text{Uses}\\ \$92,000 + \$8,000 \text{ decrease in funds} & = \$100,000\end{aligned}$$

The balanced form of the statement of changes in financial position is prepared as follows:

Sources	$ 92,000
Decrease in funds	8,000
Total	$100,000
Uses	$100,000

It does not matter which form is used, as long as you understand that the difference between total sources and total uses of funds represents the change in funds for the period.

The information used to prepare the funds flow statement is obtained from the beginning and ending balance sheets and from the statements of income and retained earnings. In Figure 18-1 we illustrate how the statement of changes is related to the other three statements. As the name of the statement implies, it reports the **changes** in financial position that took place between the beginning and ending balance sheets. The business employs its assets to operate in order to earn more assets. Operations are the primary source of funds that can be used to repay debts, acquire new assets, and pay dividends. In addition the company also obtains funds by selling old assets, issuing new stock, and incurring new debts. These financing and investing activities change the balance sheet accounts, and the changes are explained in the statement of changes in financial position. In addition, the statement of changes shows the amount of funds provided by the operations reported in the income statement, and the amount of funds used to pay dividends, as reported in the retained earnings statement.

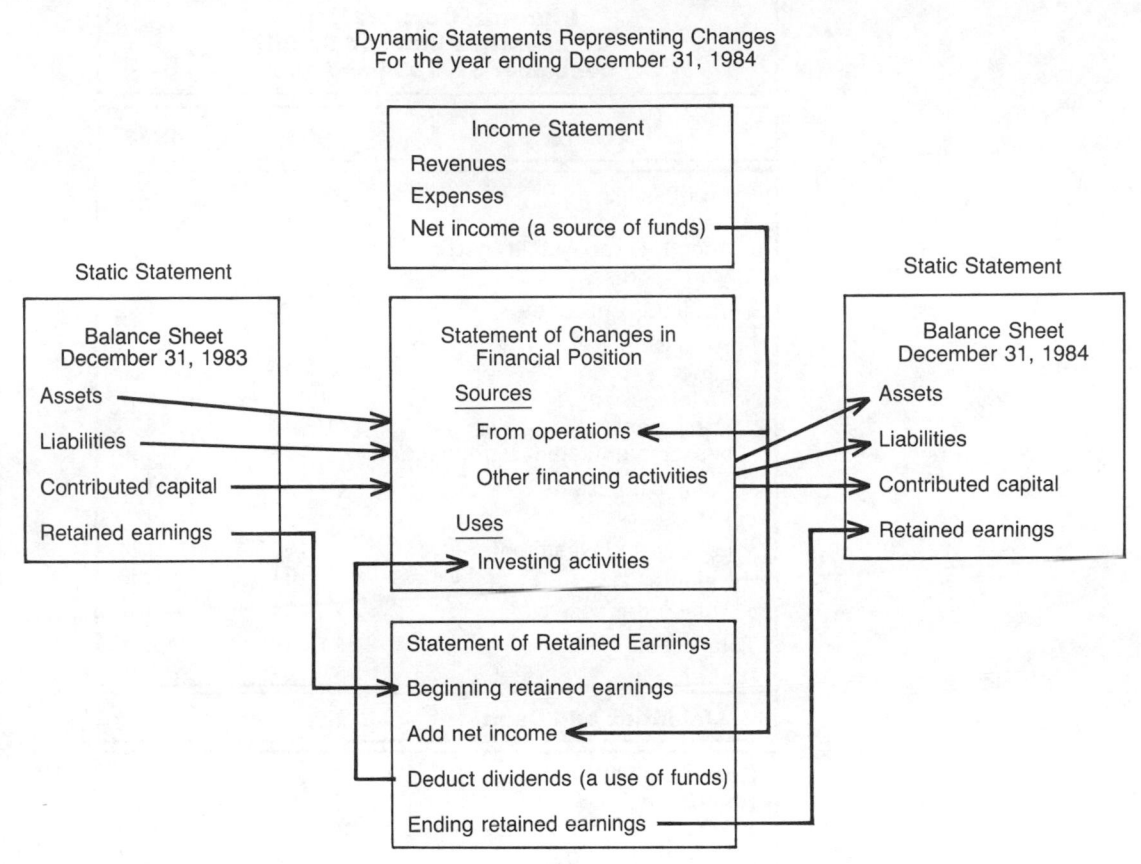

Figure 18-1
Relationship between static balance sheets and dynamic statements
representing changes. The statement of changes in financial position describes
the financing and investing activities of the business.

The statement of changes covers one accounting period

Note that the income statement, the statement of retained earnings, and the funds flow statement are dynamic statements that report changes occurring during one accounting period, while the balance sheet is a static statement that reports financial position at one specific point in time.

Now that we have discussed the basic concepts and definitions of funds, we can proceed to an illustration that demonstrates how funds are reported in a statement of changes in financial position, and the differences between the definitions of funds. For this purpose we use the comparative balance sheets, income statement, and statement of retained earnings of Phoenix Corporation illustrated in Figure 18-2.

Phoenix Corporation
Comparative Balance Sheet
December 31, 1984 and 1983

Assets	1984	1983
Current assets		
Cash	$ 70	$ 64
Accounts receivable (net)	128	101
Merchandise	72	87
Total current assets	$ 270	$ 252
Fixed assets		
Land	$ 60	$ 60
Buildings	1,000	987
Equipment	940	800
Less accumulated depreciation	(706)	(660)
Total fixed assets	$1,294	$1,187
Other assets		
Long-term investments	$ 100	$ 124
Patents	34	38
Total other assets	$ 134	$ 162
Total assets	$1,698	$1,601

Liabilities and Capital		
Current liabilities		
Accounts payable	$ 92	$ 74
Salaries payable	21	30
Income taxes payable	30	13
Total current liabilities	$ 143	$ 117
Long-term liabilities		
Notes payable, due 1988	$ 44	
Bonds payable, due 1998	450	$ 450
Premium on bonds payable	16	18
Total long-term liabilities	$ 510	$ 468
Total liabilities	$ 653	$ 585
Capital		
Preferred stock		$ 48
Common stock, $1 par	$ 510	500
Contributed surplus-premium on common	260	220
Retained earnings	275	248
Total capital	$1,045	$1,016
Total liabilities and capital	$1,698	$1,601

Phoenix Corporation
Income Statement
For the Year Ending December 31, 1984

Sales		$2,340
Less cost of goods sold		
Beginning inventory	$ 87	
Add purchases	1,389	
Goods available for sale	$1,476	
Less ending inventory	72	
Cost of goods sold		1,404
Gross margin		$ 936
Less expenses		
Administrative	$ 219	
Rent	98	
Salaries	306	
Depreciation	60	
Amortization of patent	4	
Interest	38	
Total expenses		725
Income from operations		$ 211
Other income		
Gain on sale of investments	$ 5	
Loss on sale of equipment	(3)	2
Net income before tax		$ 213
Less income tax		96
Net income after tax		$ 117

Figure 18-2
The income statement, statement of retained earnings, and the comparative balance sheet on page 786 are accompanied by a statement of changes in financial position to make a complete annual report. The statement of changes developed from the statements in this figure is presented in Figure 18-4 on page 797.

Phoenix Corporation
Statement of Retained Earnings
For the Year Ending December 31, 1984

Retained earnings, 1/1/84		$ 248
Add net income		117
		$ 365
Deduct dividends		
2 percent stock dividend	$ 50	
Cash dividends	40	90
Retained earnings, 12/31/84		$ 275

Analysis of balance sheet changes

The cash balance of Phoenix Corporation changed from $64 on December 31, 1983 to $70 at the end of 1984 and the statement of changes must explain this $6 increase if funds are defined as cash. Working capital is the difference between current assets and current liabilities. Phoenix Corporation's working capital on December 31, 1983, was $135 ($252–$117), and at the end of 1984 it was $127 ($270–$143). If funds are defined as working capital, the statement of changes must explain the $8 decrease in working capital.

Since cash increased by $6 from the beginning of the period to the end, it is evident that the total financing activities provided $6 more cash than was needed to pay for total investing activities. Similarly, the $8 decrease in working capital indicates that financing activities provided $8 less working capital than was needed to pay for total investing activities. The statement of changes in financial position must show the nature and amount of financing and investing activities and thereby explain the change in funds, however funds are defined.

The most significant of the fund changes is the amount of **funds provided by operations** that result in net income. We first discuss the concept of funds provided by operations and explain why the fund inflow from operations is not the same as net income. Later we use the same example to illustrate preparation of the entire statement of changes with funds defined as working capital and as cash.

To explain the change in funds, we must analyze the change that took place in every balance sheet account from the end of 1983 to the end of 1984. These changes are analyzed in Figure 18-3 in the two columns next to the comparative balance sheet data, indicating the increases or decreases in asset and equity accounts from one year to the next. The change in cash is a $6 increase denoted by a debit in Figure 18-3; the change in accounts receivable is an increase of $21, denoted by a debit; and the change in merchandise is a decrease of $15, denoted by a credit. All other changes are similarly calculated. Increases in liabilities are credits and decreases are debits. Obviously, since the balance sheets balance, the changes from one balance sheet to the next must also balance.

Operations are a major source of funds

Net income is measured in accordance with the accrual concept rather than on the cash basis, so it must be converted to a fund inflow by appropriate adjustments. Transactions that affect the income statement also affect the balance sheet, so an examination of business operations should explain some of the balance sheet changes calculated in Figure 18-3. Any other balance sheet changes are the result of other financing and investing activities that are not necessarily reported in the income statement.

Cash provided by operations

The income statement of the company shows the various revenues, gains, expenses, and losses that resulted in a net income of $117. However, retained earnings did not increase by the amount of net income because the company paid $40 of cash dividends during the year and a $50 stock dividend as reported in the statement of retained earnings.

We now look in detail at some transactions that occurred in 1984 as a result of operations. Note that these transactions were **already recorded** during the year. They are **reproduced here to explain cash flows,** and many identical transactions are aggregated into a single entry so that the overall effect on cash

Phoenix Corporation Comparative Balance Sheet December 31, 1984 and 1983				
Assets	**1984**	**1983**	**Uses dr.**	**Sources cr.**
Current assets				
Cash	$ 70	$ 64	6	
Accounts receivable (net)	128	101	27	
Merchandise	72	87		15
Total current assets	$ 270	$ 252		
Fixed assets				
Land	$ 60	$ 60		
Buildings	1,000	987	13	
Equipment	940	800	140	
Less accumulated depreciation	(706)	(660)		46
Total fixed assets	$1,294	$1,187		
Other assets				
Long-term investments	$ 100	$ 124		24
Patents	34	38		4
Total other assets	$ 134	$ 162		
Total assets	$1,698	$1,601		

Liabilities and Capital				
Current liabilities				
Accounts payable	$ 92	$ 74		18
Salaries payable	21	30	9	
Income taxes payable	30	13		17
Total current liabilities	$ 143	$ 117		
Long-term liabilities				
Notes payable, due 1988	$ 44			44
Bonds payable, due 1998	450	$ 450		
Premium on bonds payable	16	18	2	
Total long-term liabilities	$ 510	$ 468		
Total liabilities	$ 653	$ 585		
Capital				
Preferred stock		$ 48	48	
Common Stock	$ 510	500		10
Contributed surplus–premium on common	260	220		40
Retained earnings	275	248		27
Total capital	$1,045	$1,016	245	245
Total liabilities and capital	$1,698	$1,601		

Figure 18-3
Changes in balance sheets that must be explained by the statement of changes in financial position are shown as debits and credits.

may be seen. From the income statement we know that sales were $2,340, recorded as follows:

Accounts Receivable	2,340	
Sales		2,340

All revenues are not fund inflows

Although operations provided $2,340 of revenues, only $2,313 was collected in the form of cash. This is evident from an examination of accounts receivable, which increased by $27. The beginning balance in accounts receivable was $101, and $2,340 was added as a result of the current year's sales. Since the ending balance is $128, only $2,313 of accounts receivable was collected during the year. The collection of receivables is recorded as:

Cash	2,313	
Accounts Receivable		2,313

The above two entries are posted in the account below:

Accounts Receivable

Bal 31/12/83	101	1984 Collections	2,313
1984 Sales	2,340		
Bal 31/12/84	128		

It should now be clear that the amount of revenue earned and the amount collected are different, and that the difference is due to the change in accounts receivable. The sales revenue figure can therefore be converted to a cash inflow figure as follows:

Sales	$2,340
Less increase in accounts receivable	27
Cash collected from sales	$2,313

By deducting the increase in accounts receivable, we converted sales revenue to a cash inflow. If accounts receivable had decreased, the decrease would be added to sales. It is also possible to convert the net income figure to a cash inflow the same way.

The amounts recorded for some expenses are not the same as the amounts actually paid. For example, salaries required more cash than is reported on the income statement as salary expense; depreciation required no cash; and income taxes required less cash than reported as tax expense.

The journal entries to record salaries are given on page 791. The payment of salaries includes not only the current year's salaries paid in cash, but also the payment of the accrued salaries of $30 from the previous year. The adjusting entry at the end of the period records salary expenses which have not yet been paid but which have been accrued as salaries payable of $21.

Salaries Payable	30	
Salaries Expense	306	
Cash		336
To pay current salaries and salaries accrued in 1983		
Salaries Expense	21	
Salaries Payable		21
To accrue salaries at end of 1984		

Salaries Payable

1984 payments	30	Bal 12/31/83	30
		12/31/84 accrual	21
		Bal 12/31/84	21

All expenses are not fund outflows

The use of cash to pay salaries is clearly not the same as the amount of salaries expense reported. The amount of cash paid for salaries is larger than the reported expense because the company decreased its liability to its employees by $9 from $30 to $21. By adding the decrease in the current liability to salary expense, we converted the expense figure to reflect the actual cash outflow. Or we can convert the net income figure itself to a cash inflow by deducting from it the $9 decrease in salaries payable.

The depreciation expense reported on the income statement does not require the use of either cash or working capital, since no current assets or liabilities are affected by the recording of depreciation.

Depreciation Expense	60	
Accumulated Depreciation		60

Depreciation is neither a source nor a use of funds

Depreciation is a **nonfund item,** an expense that requires no funds. It was deducted in the income statement to arrive at net income. Adding it back to net income changes that figure to a net fund inflow.

The payment of taxes resulted in the use of $79 cash, although tax expense is reported as $96. The difference is the result of the change in Taxes Payable, which was $13 at the end of 1983 and $30 at the end of 1984. The tax expense is recorded as

Tax Expense	96	
Taxes Payable		96

This entry increases the Taxes Payable account to $109, and to leave a $30 balance in Taxes Payable, the following cash payment must have been recorded:

Taxes Payable	79	
Cash		79

To arrive at net income, the company deducted more for tax expense than was actually paid. By adding the increase in tax liability to net income we convert the net income figure to a net cash inflow.

It is possible to analyze each change in current assets and current liabilities in a similar way, and to determine how they affected the amount of cash provided by operations. As you have seen from our analysis of sales and the change in accounts receivable, an increase in current assets must be deducted from net income in order to convert the net income figure to a cash inflow. Conversely, a decrease in current assets must be added to net income to convert the figure to a cash inflow. With the salary and tax examples, you saw that an increase in current liabilities decreases the amount of cash used to pay expenses and should therefore be added to net income to convert it to a cash inflow, whereas a decrease in current liabilities must be deducted from net income since more cash was used to pay the liability than was recorded as an expense. In addition, nonfund items such as depreciation that are deducted on the income statement are now added back to net income, and nonfund items such as gains that are added on the income statement are now deducted from net income. When all nonfund items and changes in current assets and liabilities have been added to or deducted from net income, the net income figure has been converted to the amount of cash provided by operations.

The amount of cash used in operations and obtained from operations clearly depends on the changes in the current asset and current liability accounts that make up working capital. As you will see later in the chapter, the amount of cash provided by operations is $199, although net income is only $117. On the other hand, the amount of working capital provided by operations is $177. The difference is due to the fact that changes in working capital accounts affect the amount of cash provided by operations, but not the amount of working capital, as explained below.

Working capital provided by operations

With funds defined as working capital, most of the revenues and expenses in the income statement represent increases and decreases in working capital in the amount actually reported in the statement. For example, sales revenue was recorded as

Accounts Receivable	2,340	
Sales		2,340

Subsequently, $2,313 of accounts receivable was collected, but the collection of receivables does not change the amount of working capital. Consequently, sales provided $2,340 of working capital, whether the goods were sold for cash or on open account, since both cash and accounts receivable are components of working capital.

Operations change the balances of working capital accounts

Similarly, salaries and taxes decreased working capital by the amount of salary and tax expense reported on the income statement. It does not matter whether the salaries and taxes are paid or accrued; the change in working capital is the same. On the other hand, depreciation expense had no effect on working capital, just as it had no effect on cash. Depreciation is a nonfund item and does not affect funds whatever definition of funds is used. Other nonfund items are discussed below.

You can see now that with funds defined as cash, the income statement must undergo considerable modification before the net income figure can be converted to a cash inflow figure. On the other hand, relatively little conversion is required if funds are defined as working capital. Only the nonfund items require adjustments.

Nonfund items on the income statement

Net income measured under the accrual concept is not the same as the amount of funds obtained from operations. Some expenses and losses are deducted from revenues to arrive at net income, although they do not require the use of funds. Depreciation expense is an obvious example. Other nonfund deductions include amortization of intangibles, losses, deferred taxes, and amortization of bond discount. To convert the net income figure to a figure representing fund inflows from operations, such nonfund deductions must be added back to net income.

The income statement also contains items that are added in arriving at net income but that did not provide funds. Amortization of premium on bonds payable, gains, and revenue from stock investments accounted for at equity are examples. Since such nonfund items do not represent fund inflows, they must be deducted from net income to convert the net income figure to an amount representing fund inflows. Some of these nonfund additions and deductions are explained below.

Depreciation and amortization. You already know that depreciation does not require the use of funds. No one writes a cheque to pay for depreciation expense. Amortization of intangible assets and depletion of natural resources similarly require no use of funds. Because such items are added back to income in the funds flow statement, many users of financial statements mistakenly believe that depreciation is a source of funds. Some people mistakenly believe, in fact, that accumulated depreciation represents the accumulation of a fund intended for the purpose of acquiring new assets when the old ones need to be replaced. Such misconceptions arise from a lack of understanding of fund flow concepts.

Nonfund items on the income statement neither provide nor use funds

Premium on bonds payable. When bond discount or premium is amortized, the amount of interest expense reported in the income statement is not the same as the amount of cash paid for bond interest. You may remember that interest expense on bonds sold at a premium is smaller than the required interest payments. Phoenix Corporation's interest expense is reported at $38, and from the balance sheet you see that $2 of bond premium was amortized. Therefore the entries to record interest expense must have been

Bond premium or discount amortization is a nonfund item

Interest Expense	40	
Cash		40

Cash paid to bondholders was $40, but the income statement reports only $38 of interest expense because at the end of the year interest expense was adjusted when bond premium was amortized:

Premium on Bonds Payable	2	
Interest Expense		2

The $40 outflow of funds for the payment of interest was greater than the $38 of interest expense deducted to arrive at net income. The difference, represented by $2 of bond premium amortization, is therefore deducted in order to convert the net income figure to the amount of funds obtained from operations.

If bond discount had been amortized instead of premium, the amount of amortization would have to be added back to net income to arrive at funds provided by operations. A similar treatment is necessary for discount or premium amortization on long-term bond investments, because the amount of interest revenue recorded is not the same as the amount of cash received.

Gains and losses. When transactions result in gains or losses, only the net effect on owners' equity is reported in the income statement. The fund flow effects of such transactions are quite different from the amount of gain or loss. Transactions on which gains or losses are recorded usually involve important financing or investing activities. For example, the sale of fixed assets is a financing activity that may result in a gain or loss. Gains or losses may also occur with such investing activities as the retirement of bonds payable. A gain or a loss from the sale of assets or the retirement of bonds is only a part of the transaction. It would be incorrect to show a part of the transaction as the fund flow. The entire amount of funds provided or used as a result of such financing or investing activities should be reported in the statement of changes, whereas only the gain or loss portion is shown in the income statement. Such gains or losses are nonfund items that must be added back to, or deducted from, net income to convert the net income figure to a number representing fund flows from operations.

Gains and losses are nonfund items

For example, Phoenix Corporation's sale of fixed assets for $8 cash was recorded as follows:

Cash	8	
Accumulated Depreciation	14	
Loss on Sale of Fixed Assets	3	
Equipment		25

Deducting a loss in the income statement has the same effect on net income as deducting an expense for which a cheque was issued. Yet the loss transaction actually provided $8 of cash because there was a transfer of $8 from fixed assets to current assets, whereas most expenses use funds. Therefore the loss must be added back to net income in the funds flow statement, and the entire amount of proceeds from the sale of the asset is reported among the sources of funds.

If gains occur from sales of assets, they must be deducted from income to arrive at funds from operations. The gain itself does not represent an increase in funds; the proceeds from financing activities represent the increase.

Other nonfund transactions

Changes sometimes occur in capital accounts that appear to be sources or uses of funds when in fact they are not. The issuance of new stock provides a source of funds if assets are received when the stock is issued. However, if stock is issued as a result of a stock split, there is no effect on funds. Changes from stock splits do not appear on the statement of changes in financial position. Similarly, the issuance of a stock dividend neither provides nor uses funds. Therefore the 2 percent stock dividend distributed by Phoenix Corporation is not disclosed in the funds flow statement, although it appears in the statement of retained earnings.

The concepts discussed above are important for your understanding of the difference in the amount of funds provided by operations with different definitions of funds. In addition to funds provided by operations, other sources and uses of funds are reported on the statement of changes in financial position. Below we describe some of these and show how they are presented in the statement of changes, using the two definitions of funds.

Other sources and uses of funds

The changes in balance sheet accounts shown in Figure 18-3 indicate that fixed assets were acquired, long-term investments were disposed of, long-term debt was increased, and capital stock was issued. Such changes result from financing and investing activities other than usual business operations and must be explained on the statement of changes. Before showing how these financing and investing activities are reported, we present a list of the transactions that will help to clarify the amounts reported in the statement of changes:

a. The company sold, for $8 cash, fixed assets that had a cost of $25 and a book value of $11 at the time of sale.

b. Preferred stock was redeemed at its book value and retired.

c. A 2 percent stock dividend was paid on the common stock, in addition to the cash dividends.

d. New equipment was acquired for $121 cash and a $44 long-term note payable.

Examine carefully the statement of changes to see how the fund flows from these and other transactions are reported. Figure 18-4 is the statement of changes with funds defined as working capital. Figure 18-5 is the statement with funds defined as cash. Other than the amount of funds provided by operations, the sources and uses of funds are the same in both statements.

Note that the statement in Figure 18-5 is in the balanced form Sources = Uses, while the one in Figure 18-4 is in the form Sources − Uses = Change in funds. Both forms are commonly employed. The statement with funds defined as cash has a separate schedule detailing the source of funds provided by operations. This schedule may be made a part of the statement as in Figure 18-4 and need not be presented separately. The statement with funds defined as working capital has a section detailing changes in working capital for the period. The main difference between these two statements is the treatment of working capital. When funds are defined as cash, changes in working capital affect the amount of cash provided by operations, and such changes are therefore reported in the schedule showing how net income is converted to a cash inflow. In addition to working capital changes, this schedule shows the various nonfund items found in the income statement. When funds are defined as working capital, the conversion of net income to a fund inflow involves only the nonfund items.

The concept of all financial resources

Exchanges represent both sources and uses of funds

Many transactions take place during an accounting period that do not affect cash or working capital. For example, common stock may be issued in exchange for land and buildings. Or a new 10-year bond payable may be issued in exchange for an old bond payable that is about to mature. Although such transactions do not affect funds, they nevertheless represent resource changes that must be disclosed in the statement of changes in financial position. The ability of a company to issue additional common stock represents an important resource. The acquisition of new land and buildings represents an important use of the company's resources. The concept of **all financial resources** requires the disclosure of the financing and investing aspects of exchanges.

As an example of the way exchanges are treated, let us examine the acquisition of new equipment by Phoenix Corporation in exchange for cash and a long-term note payable. The transaction was recorded as follows:

Equipment	165	
Cash		121
Notes Payable		44

Phoenix Corporation
Statement of Changes in Financial Position
For the Year Ending December 31, 1984

Sources of Working Capital

Funds provided by operations		
Net income		$117
Add items not requiring use of working capital		
Depreciation	$60	
Amortization of patents	4	
Loss on sale of fixed assets	3	67
Less items not providing funds		
Amortization of bond premium	$ 2	
Gain on sale of investments	5	(7)
Total sources from operations		$177
Other sources		
Sale of equipment		8
Sale of investments		29
Additional long-term borrowing used to finance		
purchase of new equipment		44
Total sources of working capital		$258

Uses of Working Capital

Payment of dividends	$ 40	
Retirement of preferred stock	48	
Addition to buildings	13	
Purchase of new equipment, partly financed by		
new long-term borrowing	165	
Total uses of working capital		266
Decrease in working capital		$ 8

Schedule of Changes in Working Capital	Working Capital	
	Increase	Decrease
Current assets		
Increase in cash	$ 6	
Increase in accounts receivable	27	
Decrease in merchandise		$15
Current liabilities		
Increase in accounts payable		18
Decrease in salaries payable	9	
Increase in taxes payable		17
Total changes	$42	$50
Net decrease in working capital	8	
	$50	$50

Figure 18-4
Statement of changes in financial position, with funds defined as working
capital. In addition to the sources and uses of working capital, the statement
presents a schedule of changes in working capital, showing the change in
each working capital component.

Phoenix Corporation
Statement of Changes in Financial Position
For the Year Ending December 31, 1984

Sources of cash	
Cash provided by operations (see schedule)	$191
Other sources of cash	
Sale of equipment	8
Sale of long-term investments	29
Long-term borrowing to finance purchase	
of new equipment	44
Total sources	$272
Uses of cash	
Retirement of preferred stock	$ 48
Payment of dividends	40
Purchase of equipment, partly financed by	
new long-term debt	165
Addition to buildings	13
Increase in cash	6
Total uses	$272

Phoenix Corporation
Schedule of Cash Provided by Operations
For the Year Ending December 31, 1984

Net income	$117
Add items not requiring use of cash	
Decrease in merchandise	15
Increase in accounts payable	18
Increase in taxes payable	17
Depreciation expense	60
Amortization expense	4
Loss on sale of fixed assets	3
	$234
Less items not providing cash	
Increase in accounts receivable	$ 27
Decrease in salaries payable	9
Gain on sale of investments	5
Premium on bonds payable	2
	$ 43
Total sources of cash from operations	$191

Figure 18-5
Statement of changes in financial position, with funds defined as cash. This statement is shown in balanced form. Note the separate schedule of funds provided by operations. In Figure 18-4 this schedule is part of the main body of the statement.

It is clear that only $121 of working capital was needed to acquire the new equipment. The company was able to obtain $44 of long-term financing for the acquisition of these assets. Although the note payable did not provide working capital, it does represent the ability to borrow funds. Also, the purchase of assets represents $165 of investing activities, not just $121 represented by the use of cash.

If only the working capital effects of the above transaction were disclosed in the funds flow statement, the result would be to hide part of the company's investing and financial activities. Instead, as illustrated in Figures 18-4 and 18-5, such activities are reported and described in the statement to indicate that they do not involve working capital.

Use of the funds flow statement

Phoenix Corporation's statement of changes in financial position illustrated in Figure 18-4 shows that most of the company's funds were provided by business operations. A relatively small amount came from the sale of fixed assets, indicating that the business did not depend on such sales for its major source of funds. At the same time, the disposal of old assets and investment in new ones indicates that the business is updating its plant and equipment and expanding its operations. The sale of long-term investments and retirement of preferred stock may also indicate that management is revising its asset and equity structure to meet changing business conditions.

Funds defined as working capital are useful to financial analysts

By examining the detailed changes in working capital we see that funds have become much more liquid, with cash and receivables increasing, and the less liquid merchandise balance decreasing. The company is in a good position to improve its current ratio, finance expansion by means of new long-term investments, and increase the volume of current operations, thereby possibly improving future profits.

Managers are especially interested in the detailed analysis of the changes in current assets and current liabilities. They need information about cash flows in order to maintain good control over business operations and resources and to ensure adequate working capital. Managers undertake financing and investing activities that are eventually reflected in the financial statements that will be evaluated by external users of the company's annual report.

Funds defined as cash are useful to managers

Before we examine the techniques for preparing the statement of changes, it is important that you have a clear understanding of the nature of changes that are reported in the statement. We therefore start by illustrating why debits may be viewed as uses and credits as sources of funds, and by explaining the nature of nonfund items that are frequently found in the income statement.

The nature of balance sheet changes

The financial statements of Phoenix Corporation on pages 786 and 787 are used to illustrate the technical aspects of preparing the statement of changes in financial position. The resulting funds flow statements are shown in Figures 18-4 and 18-5, but here we show how they are derived. To review briefly the concept of sources and uses of funds, examine again the comparative balance sheet and the income statement in Figure 18-2.

Uses and sources as debits and credits

The changes in the balance sheet accounts are calculated in Figure 18-3 and are entered in the two columns headed debit and credit. The headings of these two columns also indicate that debits are uses of funds and credits are sources. Why should this be the case? The reason is made evident by reference to a change in a fixed asset or a long-term liability.

For example, as shown in Figure 18-3, Phoenix Corporation did not have notes payable outstanding in 1983 and has them outstanding in 1984. It is therefore clear that the company borrowed money by issuing notes payable. When it did so the following entry was made:

Cash	44	
Notes Payable		44

Sources of funds are recorded by credits

The issuance of the note provides funds and requires crediting a liability. The note payable is the **source** of the funds received and it is recorded by a credit. If instead a liability had been reduced, it would have required the **use** of funds, and the decrease in the liability would be recorded as a debit. Therefore, in the case of a liability, sources are credits and uses are debits.

The same reasoning applies to a change in an asset. Phoenix Corporation acquired buildings in 1984 making the following entry:

Buildings	13	
Cash		13

Uses of funds are recorded by debits

Funds were used to acquire the building and to increase the Building account with a debit. Therefore uses of funds are debits. Similarly, selling an asset provides funds. The decrease in the asset account is a credit, so sources of funds are credits.

The concept of nonfund items

The most important source of funds is from operations. Revenues are sources and are recorded by credits; expenses are uses and are recorded by debits. In the statement of changes in financial position we do not detail all sources and uses from operations but only the net difference between revenues and expenses, that is, the source arising from net income. Since net income includes a number of nonfund items, the net income figure must be adjusted to eliminate the effects of the nonfund items and to reflect actual net sources and uses of funds from operations. The adjustments required to convert net income to net fund flows from operations include those in the following list:

Nonfund items added to net income:
   Depreciation of fixed assets
   Depletion of natural resources
   Amortization of intangibles
   Discount amortization on bonds payable
   Premium amortization on bond investments

Nonfund items are used to convert net income to fund flows

Increases in deferred tax credits
Decreases in deferred tax charges
Losses
Nonfund items deducted from net income:
Premium amortization on bonds payable
Discount amortization on bond investments
Decreases in deferred tax credits
Increases in deferred tax charges
Revenue from investments carried at equity
Gains

Data for statement preparation

The primary source of information for preparing the statement of changes is the set of financial statements. In addition to the statements presented in Figure 18-2, additional data may be helpful in analyzing the way specific transactions affect funds.

The procedure for preparing the statement of changes consists of a series of mechanical steps. They are designed to convert the information available above and in the company's financial statements into a statement of changes with a given definition of funds. The procedure consists of preparing working papers, which may be either a set of T accounts or a columnar worksheet. Entries are made in these working papers so that information is organized into a form from which the formal statement of changes in financial position may be prepared. None of the entries illustrated become part of the accounting records of the company. They are made in the working papers only, and not in the books of account. Most of the entries are simply duplicates of entries that were prepared in the books previously. The entries are duplicated so that their effect on funds can be observed and entered onto the working paper.

By following the steps illustrated below, we first determine how much each balance sheet account changed. Each change came about as a result of transactions that were recorded in the books. When the transactions were originally recorded, they were analyzed to determine their effect on the accounting equation. Now we need to analyze these same transactions to determine their effect on fund flows. The easiest way to analyze each transaction is to reproduce the journal entry that describes it and then put the entry into the worksheet. Each entry explains how some of the account balances changed. When the change in each account in the working papers has been explained, sufficient information is accumulated to prepare the statement of changes.

Funds defined as working capital

The techniques employed in preparing the statement of changes depend to some extent on the definition of funds. With either definition, the concept of all financial resources is used. We first discuss the techniques for preparing the statement when funds are defined as working capital, because use of this definition is somewhat easier to understand.

Phoenix Corporation
Worksheet for Statement of Changes in Financial Position
For the Year Ending December 31, 1984

	Beginning Balances 12/31/83	Balance Sheet Changes dr.	Balance Sheet Changes cr.	Ending Balances 12/31/84
Debits				
Working capital	135		k. 8	127
Land	60			60
Buildings	987	j. 13		1,000
Equipment	800	d. 165	a. 25	940
Long-term investments	124		h. 24	100
Patents	38		f. 4	34
	2,144			2,261
Credits				
Accumulated depreciation	660	a. 14	e. 60	706
Notes payable	—		d. 44	44
Bonds payable	450			450
Premium on bonds payable	18	g. 2		16
Preferred stock	48	b. 48		—
Common stock, $1 par	500		c. 10	510
Contributed surplus–premium on common	220		c. 40	260
Retained earnings	248	c. 50	x. 117	275
		i. 40		
	2,144			2,261
Sources of working capital from operations				
Net income		x. 117		
Loss on sale of equipment		a. 3		
Depreciation of equipment		e. 60		
Amortization of patent		f. 4		
Amortization of bond premium			g. 2	
Gain on sale of investments			h. 5	
Total sources from operations		177		
Other sources of working capital				
Sale of equipment		a. 8		
Increase in long-term debt		d. 44		
Sale of long-term investments		h. 29		
Uses of working capital				
Retirement of preferred stock			b. 48	
Payment of dividends			i. 40	
Purchase of equipment			d. 165	
Addition to buildings			j. 13	
Decrease in working capital		k. 8		
		266	266	

Figure 18-6
Worksheet used to prepare the statement in Figure 18-4. The bottom portion of the worksheet is divided into two parts, one for sources of funds from operations, and the other for other sources and uses of funds.

| Steps in preparing the statement of changes | The following step-by-step procedure is employed in the preparation of the statement of changes in financial position using a worksheet. Keep in mind that these are **mechanical procedures** whose logic becomes clear only after some proficiency with them is developed.

The completed worksheet is presented in Figure 18-6 and is discussed in the following pages. |

Setting up the worksheet

Step 1. A four-column worksheet is established, with beginning and ending balances in the extreme left and right columns respectively and the two middle columns blank. The middle columns are used to explain the changes that occurred as illustrated in Figure 18-6.

Step 2. A space is provided at the bottom of the worksheet to accumulate funds from operations, and for other sources and uses of funds.

Note that current assets and liabilities are shown in the worksheet as working capital. This simplifies the worksheet when funds are defined as working capital, but there is, of course, no requirement to show current items condensed into one figure.

Treatment of net income

Step 3. One of the more important sources of funds is from operations that provide net income. The net income figure, however, is calculated on the accrual basis, and adjustments are necessary in order to convert this figure to the amount of fund inflows for the period. Net income originally changed retained earnings when the Income Summary account was closed. We now reproduce the entry to observe the effect on retained earnings, and also to determine where to show the change in the worksheet.

| x. | Income Summary | 117 | |
| | Retained Earnings | | 117 |

The debit part of the entry is the net income that represents a source of funds from operations. Sources from operations are accumulated in the part of the worksheet established for that purpose. The credit part of the entry explains part of the change in retained earnings and is entered in the worksheet on the retained earnings line as entry *x*. Since this credit to retained earnings does not explain all the retained earnings change in the worksheet, other transactions must have affected this account. We shall deal with them shortly.

Treatment of given transactions

Step 4. Transactions that affected funds and caused changes in financial position can now be journalized. Transactions *a* through *d* described on pages 795 and 796 are now analyzed for their effects on funds. Prior to recording these transactions it is necessary to examine the financial statements to obtain the relevant facts. For example, for transaction *a*, the sale of fixed assets, it is possible to see from the income statement that a $3 loss occurred when fixed assets were sold, and we know the cost and book value of the asset. We can, therefore, examine the following journal entry:

a.	Cash	8	
	Accumulated Depreciation	14	
	Loss on Sale of Equipment	3	
	Equipment		25

The sale of equipment resulted in an inflow of funds of $8, but on the income statement there is a deduction of $3 for the loss. Clearly, the $3 loss did not result in an outflow of funds, yet this amount was deducted in arriving at net income. To convert the net income figure to the amount of funds flowing into the company, we must add this loss back to net income. The loss is automatically added to net income in the worksheet when the journal entry is entered in the worksheet according to the following rules:

Rules for entering amounts in the worksheet

1. All temporary accounts are entered in the section designated as funds from operations.
2. Permanent accounts are entered on their respective lines if the account exists in the worksheet.
3. Permanent working capital accounts represent fund flows and are entered in the portion of the worksheet designated for other sources and uses of funds.

You can see that these rules were followed in posting entry x. Income summary is a temporary account and was therefore entered as funds from operations. Using the above rules, entry a to record the sale of fixed assets is modified and entered in the worksheet as follows:

a.	Cash (Source of funds)	8	
	Accumulated Depreciation	14	
	Loss (Funds from operations)	3	
	Equipment		25

Transaction b, the acquisition and retirement of the preferred stock at its book value, is recorded as follows:

| b. | Preferred Stock | 48 | |
| | Cash (Funds used) | | 48 |

Preferred stock started with a balance of $48 and had no balance at the end of the year. When entry b is made, the debit of $48 and the original credit of $48 result in a zero balance, showing that the change in the preferred stock account has been explained. The explanation is in the lower part of the worksheet as the credit part of entry b.

Transaction c, and 2 percent stock dividend, is reported in the statement of retained earnings as a reduction of $50. Originally, 500 shares of $1 par common stock were outstanding as shown in the 1983 balance sheet, and an additional 10 shares were issued as a stock dividend. The entry to record the stock dividend is reproduced below:

c.	Retained Earnings	50	
	Common Stock		10
	Contributed Surplus — Premium on Common Stock		40

The payment of a stock dividend has no effect on funds. When the entry is made in the worksheet, it changes the balance of the common stock and contributed surplus accounts from the amount shown in the first column to the amount shown in the last column. But the change in retained earnings is not yet fully explained. The difference between the beginning and the ending balance in retained earnings still cannot be reconciled with the changes recorded thus far. Additional changes must affect the Retained Earnings account.

Transaction *d,* the acquisition of equipment in exchange for cash and a note payable, illustrates the all financial resources concept. Originally the transaction was recorded as follows:

d.	Equipment	165	
	Cash		121
	Notes payable		44

The all financial resources concept applied

If this transaction were journalized as above, equipment would be debited $165 and the notes payable change would be explained by the $44 credit, but funds used would be credited only $121. If all financial resources are to be shown on the funds flow statement, the company's ability to borrow funds for the purpose of acquiring assets must be fully disclosed. We therefore separate the above transaction into two components: one to record the source of funds from borrowing and the other to record the use of funds for buying plant and equipment. In the working papers the two component transactions are

d.	Funds Provided	44	
	Notes Payable		44
	Equipment	165	
	Funds Used		165

These two entries have the same effect on the asset and liability accounts as before, but now the funds provided and used show all financial resources involved in this transaction.

Examination of income and retained earnings statements

Step 5. We now turn our attention to the financial statements and examine them for clues as to other transactions that affected funds. The balance sheet accounts are already listed in the worksheet; therefore, there is no need to examine the balance sheet itself. The income statement is examined to determine whether there are any nonfund items requiring adjustments of net income.

Since funds are defined as working capital, most of the revenues and expenses represent inflows and outflows of working capital. The first obvious nonfund item is depreciation expense. The entry to record depreciation is

e.	Depreciation Expense (Sources from operations) 60	
	Accumulated Depreciation	60

Because Depreciation Expense is a temporary account, it is entered among sources from operations. Depreciation must be added back to net income to convert the net income figure to a cash inflow, and both numbers therefore appear in the same column of the worksheet. The credit to Accumulated Depreciation eliminates the remaining change in the Accumulated Depreciation account.

Amortization of patents also does not require the use of funds, as can be seen when amortization expense is recorded. This entry explains the change in the Patent account and adds the amortization expense back to net income.

f.	Amortization Expense (Sources from operations) 4	
	Patents	4

The payment of interest expense resulted in an outflow of funds, but the amount of interest expense reported on the income statement is not necessarily the amount of cash used to pay the interest. This is because the amortization of bond discount or premium may have affected the entry by a year-end adjustment. The payment of interest is normally recorded as follows:

	Interest Expense	40
	Cash (Use of funds)	40

The cash payment was an outflow of working capital and interest expense appears on the income statement as a deduction, so we do not need to do anything with this entry, just as we do not need to make an adjustment for the payment of salaries or rent. However, at the end of the accounting period, the following adjusting entry was made to record the amortization of premium on bonds payable:

g.	Premium on Bonds Payable	2
	Interest Expense (Sources from operations)	2

It is clear from this entry that the interest expense recorded on the income statement is smaller than the amount of cash actually paid by the company for interest. Since less was deducted as interest expense than was actually paid, the difference must be deducted from net income. Entry *g* adds $2 to the credit side of sources from operations and the debit of $2 explains the change in the Premium on Bonds Payable account.

Proceeding further in our examination of the income statement, we find that a gain on the sale of investments of $5 was recorded. Although this amount was added in arriving at net income, the inflow of cash from the sale of investments was not $5. The Investment account requires a credit of $24 in order to explain its change. The sale of long-term investments, therefore, must have been recorded as follows:

h.	Cash (Funds provided)	29	
	Gain on Sale of Investments (Sources from operations)		5
	Long-Term Investments		24

The sale of the investments resulted in a cash flow of $29 that is not related to operations. The $5 gain added in the income statement is deducted from net income because it did not provide any working capital. The $24 credit explains the change in long-term investments.

The next item on the income statement is the loss on sale of equipment, which was already recorded as entry *c*. Finally, the income tax must be examined because the amount of tax paid may be different from the amount reported. This could happen if a tax deferral occurred. Since a deferred tax account does not exist, the amount of tax reported must be the amount actually paid, and no adjustment is needed.

Examination of the statement of retained earnings indicates a cash dividend of $40, which used working capital when it was declared. The entry, reproduced below, eliminates the retained earnings balance and shows $40 for the payment of cash dividends as a use of funds. Note that the $40 credit was originally recorded as dividends payable. The payment of dividends payable uses cash but has no effect on working capital.

i.	Retained Earnings	40	
	Dividends Payable (Uses of funds)		40

Examination of remaining account balances

Step 6. When the examination of the income statement and the statement of retained earnings is complete, only the Buildings account still remains unexplained. With access to the accounting records, the accountant can easily find out why the Buildings account changed, but even without looking at the underlying records it is clear what occurred. To explain the Buildings account change, a debit of $13 is required. This implies that buildings were acquired or that additions were made to existing buildings, and such transactions require the use of funds. The change in the Buildings account is explained with the following entry:

j.	Buildings	13	
	Use of Funds		13

Step 7. The final worksheet procedure is to transfer the change in working capital to the lower part of the worksheet and find the total of funds provided by operations. Entry *k* is entered as follows:

k.	Working Capital	8	
	Sources of Funds		8

The credit part of the entry is the amount needed to balance the debits and credits in the lower part of the worksheet. The balance is verified by adding both sides to obtain total sources and uses of funds.

Preparation of the statement

Step 8. The data in the lower part of the worksheet are used to prepare the formal statement of changes in financial position. The section of sources from operations provides the details necessary to explain the amount of working capital provided by operations that may be shown in a separate schedule as in Figure 18-5 or included in the body of the statement as shown in Figure 18-4.

Funds defined as cash

When funds are defined as cash, the statement of changes in financial position becomes somewhat more complex, because every change in the balance sheet, including changes in current assets and current liabilities, must be explained to show the effect on cash. Changes in the current asset and current liability accounts affect cash primarily through operations. As illustrated earlier, the change in accounts receivable affects the amount of cash provided by sales. Likewise, changes in accounts payable and merchandise affect the amount of cash used to pay for the sold goods.

Not all changes in current accounts are related to the operations of the company. For example, if equipment is purchased on open account a portion of the increase in accounts payable is due to the purchase of fixed assets rather than the purchase of merchandise. A careful analysis of current accounts is necessary to determine whether changes in them affect the amount of cash provided by operations or result from nonoperating transactions. In general, however, current assets and liabilities are handled as follows in converting the net income from operations to a cash flow figure:

Items added to net income:
    Decreases in current assets
    Increases in current liabilities
Items deducted from net income:
    Increases in current assets
    Decreases in current liabilities

In addition, the nonfund items discussed and listed earlier are added or deducted as illustrated previously.

Steps in preparing the statement of changes

Steps 1 and 2. Steps 1 and 2 are the same as in the previous example and result in the worksheet illustrated in Figure 18-7 on page 810. Note, however, that this worksheet contains all current asset and liability accounts.

Step 2a. Changes in current assets and current liabilities affect the amount of cash provided by operations. Previously the changes in these accounts were used to determine the net change in working capital. Now, instead of finding the change in working capital and transferring the change in working capital to the lower part of the worksheet as in step 7 previously, we must transfer the changes in all working capital accounts except cash to the sources from operations part of the worksheet. These changes affect the amount of funds provided by operations when funds are defined as cash. The current accounts are transferred to funds from operations with the following entries:

With funds defined as cash, current accounts are transferred to Operating Summary

1.	Sources from Operations	15	
	Merchandise		15
2.	Sources from Operations	18	
	Accounts Payable		18
3.	Sources from Operations	17	
	Income Taxes Payable		17
4.	Accounts Receivable	27	
	Sources from Operations		27
5.	Salaries Payable	9	
	Sources from Operations		9

These entries are made separately because each of the individual amounts is later used to explain the amount of cash provided by operations. If the entries were combined, much valuable information would be lost. The only remaining current account is Cash. Now you see the main difference the two definitions of funds make in the preparation of the statement of changes in financial position. When funds are defined as working capital, all the current asset and current liability accounts are combined into one figure representing the change in working capital. When funds are defined as cash, the current asset and current liability accounts that affect operations are transferred into the part of the worksheet that summarizes funds from operations. Aside from these differences, the remainder of the procedure is the same as already described. We now go through the entire example again with explanations only where necessary to illustrate the differences between the two approaches. Remember that the following entries are not recorded in the books. They were originally recorded when the transactions took place. Now they are simply reproduced for the purpose of analyzing their effect on funds.

Treatment of net income

Step 3. The Income Summary account is closed in order to transfer net income to retained earnings.

Phoenix Corporation
Worksheet for Statement of Changes in Financial Position
For the Year Ending December 31, 1984

	Beginning Balances 12/31/83	Balance Sheet Changes dr.	Balance Sheet Changes cr.	Ending Balances 12/31/84
Debits				
Cash	64	k. 6		70
Accounts receivable	101	4. 27		128
Merchandise	87		1. 15	72
Land	60			60
Buildings	987	j. 13		1,000
Equipment	800	d. 165	a. 25	940
Long-term investments	124		h. 24	100
Patents	38		f. 4	34
	2,261			2,404
Credits				
Accounts payable	74		2. 18	92
Salaries payable	30	5. 9		21
Income taxes payable	13		3. 17	30
Accumulated depreciation	660	a. 14	e. 60	706
Notes payable	—		d. 44	44
Bonds payable	450			450
Premium on bonds payable	18	g. 2		16
Preferred stock	48	b. 48		—
Common stock $1 par	500		c. 10	510
Contributed surplus–premium on common	220		c. 40	260
Retained earnings	248	c. 50	x. 117	275
		i. 40		
	2,261			2,404
Sources of cash from operations				
Net income		x. 117		
Decrease in merchandise		1. 15		
Increase in accounts payable		2. 18		
Increase in income taxes payable		3. 17		
Increase in accounts receivable			4. 27	
Decrease in salaries payable			5. 9	
Loss on sale of equipment		a. 3		
Depreciation of equipment		e. 60		
Amortization of patent		f. 4		
Amortization of bond premium			g. 2	
Gain on sale of investments			h. 5	
Total sources from operations		191		
Other sources of cash				
Sale of equipment		a. 8		
Increase in long-term debt		d. 44		
Sale of long-term investments		h. 29		
Uses of cash				
Retirement of preferred stock			b. 48	
Payment of dividends			i. 40	
Purchase of equipment			d. 165	
Addition of buildings			j. 13	
Increase in cash			k. 6	
		272	272	

Figure 18-7

Worksheet used to prepare the statement in Figure 18-5. The changes in current assets and current liabilities are transferred to the portion of the worksheet used to accumulate funds from operations. Cash appears in the lower portion of the worksheet as a balancing item.

x.	Income Summary (Sources from operations)	117	
	Retained Earnings		117

Treatment of given transactions

Step 4. The sale of fixed assets at a loss is recorded.

a.	Cash (Funds provided)	8	
	Accumulated Depreciation	14	
	Loss on Sale of Equipment (Sources from operations)	3	
	Equipment		25

Preferred stock is acquired and retired.

b.	Preferred Stock	48	
	Cash (Funds used)		48

A 2 percent stock dividend is declared and paid and there is no effect on cash.

c.	Retained Earnings	50	
	Common Stock		10
	Contributed Surplus — Premium on Common		40

The purchase of equipment for cash and a note payable is recorded using the concept of all financial resources.

d.	Cash (Funds provided)	44	
	Notes Payable		44
	Equipment	165	
	Cash (Funds used)		165

Examination of income and retained earnings statements

Step 5. The income statement is examined for any nonfund item needed to convert the net income figure to a cash flow figure. Depreciation and amortization expense do not result in an outflow of cash and are added back to net income.

e.	Depreciation Expense (Sources from operations)	60	
	Accumulated Depreciation		60
f.	Amortization Expense (Sources from operations)	4	
	Patents		4

Bond premium amortization is treated as before.

g.	Premium on Bonds Payable	2	
	Interest Expense (Sources from operations)		2

The sale of investment provided a $29 cash inflow. The gain added in the income statement must be deducted because it did not provide an inflow of cash from operations.

h.	Cash (Funds provided)	29	
	Gain on Sale of Investments (Sources from		
	operations)		5
	Long-Term Investments		24

The effect of dividends payable on fund flows

The loss on sale of equipment is already recorded as item *c*. The payment of cash dividends is recorded with the following sequence of entries:

i.	Retained Earnings	40	
	Dividends Payable		40
	Dividends Payable	40	
	Cash (Funds used)		40

The dividend payable entries cancel each other and the funds used indicate that $40 of cash was used to pay dividends.

Examination of remaining account balances

Step 6. Two accounts remain whose balances have not yet been eliminated. The following entry eliminates the balance in the Buildings account:

| j. | Buildings | 13 | |
| | (Cash) Funds Used | | 13 |

Step 7. The change in the Cash account is now transferred to the lower part of the worksheet. The total of cash provided by operations is found, and the worksheet columns are added to ensure that they balance. The change in cash is, of course, the balancing item.

| k. | Uses of Funds | 6 | |
| | Cash | | 6 |

Preparation of the statement

Step 8. Preparation of the cash flow statement is a matter of using the information in the worksheet to make up the formal report shown in Figure 18-5. Because the cash provided by operations is a fairly complex computation, it is reported in a separate schedule with a reference in the statement of changes in financial position.

Summary of worksheet approach

The steps in preparing the funds flow statement using the worksheet are summarized below.

Step 1: Establish a four-column worksheet and enter account titles and beginning and ending balances.

Step 2: Establish space for funds from operations and other sources and uses of funds in the worksheet.

Worksheet approach summarized

Step 2a: If funds are defined as cash, transfer all working capital account changes, except cash, to the part of the worksheet designated as funds from operations.

Step 3: Transfer net income to funds from operations and to retained earnings.

Step 4: Enter transactions to adjust balances and to record fund flows.

Step 5: Examine income statement for nonfund items and adjust accordingly. Examine retained earnings statement for cash and stock dividends and record these dividends.

Step 6: Examine account balances for any accounts whose changes have not been fully explained. Adjust accounts by recording fund flows.

Step 7: Transfer cash or working capital to lower part of worksheet and find totals.

Step 8: Prepare formal statements.

Summary
The **statement of changes in financial position** describes the **financing** and **investing activities** of a business. Such activities are viewed as inflows and outflows of **funds,** which may be defined either as **cash** or as net **working capital.** Sources of funds are obtained from business operations and from such financing activities as the sale of fixed assets, the issuance of capital stock, and the borrowing of money. Funds obtained from financing activities are used for investment in new fixed assets, for the repayment of debts, and for the distribution of assets to shareholders in the form of dividends or by the reacquisition of capital stock. The difference between total sources of funds and total uses represents the change in cash or working capital.

The statement of changes in financial position is also known as a **funds flow statement.** It is a **cash flow statement** if funds are defined as cash. In either case the funds flow statement must be prepared in accordance with the concept of **all financial resources.**

One of the most important sources of funds is business operations. Net income is not the same as funds provided by operations, because the income statement includes some expenses, revenues, and other deductions and additions that do not use or provide funds. Such **nonfund items** include depreciation and amortization expense, gains and losses, amortization of bond premium and discount, and tax deferrals. The net income figure must be modified to be converted to a figure representing fund flows from operations.

When funds are defined as **working capital** the net change in working capital is detailed in a separate schedule of the funds flow statement to show

how the working capital components changed during the period.

In most annual reports the funds flow statement is based on changes in working capital. External users of the statement analyze the relationships among the various sources and uses of funds to determine the effectiveness of management's investing and financing activities. For managerial purposes it is more useful to define funds as cash, because managers are interested in the more detailed day-to-day operations of the business. The components of working capital, and the way they affect cash, are of more interest to managers than is working capital as a whole.

Changes in balance sheet accounts represented by debits are uses of funds. Changes represented by credits are sources of funds. The source from operations is the net result of revenue credits and expense debits. Sources of **funds from operations** are important and should be reported in sufficient detail to explain how the net income figure is adjusted for nonfund items and converted to a figure representing net inflows of funds from operations.

To disclose fully a company's ability to obtain and use funds, exchanges must be accounted for using the concept of **all financial resources.** In the preparation of the funds flow statement, such transactions may be divided into two components. One component shows financial resources provided by the transaction and the other shows financial resources used. The source and use of financial resources is then reported on the funds flow statement as if the transaction had provided and used funds.

List of important terms		
all financial resources *(796)*	**investing activities** *(782)*	
cash flow statement *(782)*	**nonfund items** *(791)*	
financing activities *(782)*	**statement of changes in financial position** *(787)*	
funds *(782)*	**working capital** *(792)*	
funds flow statement *(782)*		
funds provided by operations *(788)*		

Questions

1. What are the four major categories of financing activities?
2. What are the four major categories of investing activities?
3. What happens to funds if the amount available from financing activities is greater than the amount needed for investing activities?
4. List some of the nonfund items that must be added back to net income in order to arrive at funds from operations.
5. List some of the nonfund items that must be deducted from net income in order to arrive at funds from operations.
6. Why is depreciation added back to net income in order to arrive at cash generated by operations? Why not do the same with other expenses such as salary expense?
7. Define working capital.

8. Describe why sales provide cash and working capital in different amounts? Under what circumstances do sales provide an equal amount of cash and working capital?

9. A company sold fixed assets at a loss. Describe the fund flow aspects of such a transaction and explain why the loss is added back to net income in the funds flow statement.

10. Equipment with a cost of $1,600 and a book value of $600 is sold for $250 cash and a $500 note receivable. Describe the effect of this transaction on the accounting equation. Describe the effect on funds with funds defined as cash. Describe the effect on funds with funds defined as working capital.

11. During the year a company declared dividends of $2,000. Of this amount $500 remains unpaid at the end of the accounting period. Describe the effect of the dividends on the accounting equation, on cash, and on working capital.

12. Faltas Corporation pays interest of $45,000 cash to its bondholders and amortizes bond discount in the amount of $3,000. How much interest expense is reported in the income statement? What is done with discount amortization in the funds flow statement?

13. What is meant by the concept of all financial resources? Describe a transaction that illustrates the concept.

14. Why does the increase in long-term notes payable affect working capital but an increase in a short-term note payable does not?

15. Explain why a purchase of merchandise on open account does not affect working capital, while a sale of merchandise on open account does?

16. A company issues 1000 shares of common stock in exchange for land. What is the effect of funds, and how is this transaction reported on the statement of changes in financial position?

Exercises

Ex. 18-1 Change in working capital. The working capital account balances of Golbasto Corporation at the beginning and end of the accounting year were as follows:

	Beginning	Ending
Cash	$1,260	$2,120
Accounts receivable	3,050	3,490
Merchandise	7,680	6,930
Supplies	370	420
Accounts payable	2,300	2,490
Notes payable	1,980	1,710
Salaries payable	2,400	2,730

Required:
Calculate the change in working capital for the year.

Ex. 18-2   Effect of transactions on income and funds. For each item below, indicate the effect on income, cash, and working capital. Use a + or − to show whether cash or working capital increased or decreased, and show the amount of change.

Transaction	Income	Cash	Working Capital
a. Sold merchandise costing $600 from perpetual inventory for $900 on open account.			
b. Sold land with a book value of $9,000 for $4,000 cash and a $10,000 mortgage note.			
c. Sold a patent with a book value of $5,000 for $1,200 cash and a $3,000, 90-day note receivable.			
d. Bought equipment for $2,500 cash and a $5,000, 60-day note payable.			
e. Received $1,000 cash and a $3,000 30-day note from a customer for her $4,000 account receivable.			
f. Paid $980 of accounts payable recorded at gross amount of $1,000 and recorded discount taken.			
g. Wrote off $750 uncollectible account against allowance for bad debts.			
h. Declared a cash dividend of $9,500 payable next month.			
i. Paid the $9,500 dividend payable.			
j. Accrued interest receivable of $350 on bond investment at end of year.			
k. Paid $7,000 semiannual interest on bonds payable and amortized discount of $120.			
l. Sold a temporary investment with a cost of $10,000 for $13,500 cash.			
m. Paid $1,000, 30-day, 6 percent note payable.			
n. Purchased merchandise on open account for $1,780 for perpetual inventory.			
o. Used supplies costing $35 bought on open account last month.			

Ex. 18-3   Calculating funds from operations. Following are data from the income statement of Complasize Corporation and changes in working capital accounts. For each item indicate whether it is added or subtracted in order to calculate the amount of cash and working capital provided by operations. The first two items are given as examples.

		Definition of Funds	
		Cash	Working Capital
a. Reported net income, $28,000		$ 28,000	$ 28,000
b. Increase in accounts receivable, $1,600		($1,600)	0
c. Decrease in merchandise, $3,500			
d. Increase in accounts payable, $2,100			
e. Decrease in wages payable, $1,200			
f. Decrease in prepaid expenses, $700			
g. Depreciation expense, $4,100			
h. Gain on sale of land, $900			
i. Total provided by operations		$	$

Ex. 18-4   Recognizing nonfund items. To convert net income to a figure representing fund inflows from operations, certain nonfund items must be added or deducted. Indicate whether each item in the list below should be added to net income, deducted from net income, or neither if the item does not affect funds from operations. Use the following codes:

    0   Neither add to nor deduct from net income
    +   Add to net income to arrive at fund flows
    −   Deduct from net income to arrive at fund flows

a. Increase in bonds payable
b. Depreciation expense
c. Amortization of discount on bond investment
d. Gain on sale of land
e. Loss on redemption of bonds payable
f. Issuance of common stock
g. Amortization of intangibles
h. Retirement of preferred stock
i. Amortization of discount on bonds payable
j. Dividend revenue from temporary equity investments
k. Decrease in deferred tax credits
l. Loss on sale of equipment
m. Increase in deferred tax charges
n. Amortization of premium on bonds payable
o. Purchase of land
p. Revenue from investment carried on equity basis
q. Depletion of natural resources
r. Acquisition of treasury stock

Ex. 18-5   Recognizing nonfund items. To convert net income to a figure representing cash inflows from operations, certain nonfund items and changes in current assets and liabilities must be added to or deducted from net income. Indicate whether each item in the list below should be added to net income, deducted from net income, or neither if the item does not affect the amount of cash provided by operations. Use the following codes:

    0   Neither add to nor deduct from net income
    +   Add to net income to arrive at cash flows
    −   Deduct from net income to arrive at cash flows

a. Amortization of intangibles
b. Increase in merchandise inventory
c. Decrease in preferred stock
d. Decrease in accounts receivable
e. Interest revenue from temporary bond investments
f. Decrease in prepaid expenses
g. Increase in cash
h. Gain on bond redemption
i. Decrease in payroll taxes payable
j. Increase in salaries payable
k. Amortization of premium on bond investments
l. Decrease in raw materials inventory
m. Increase in dividends payable
n. Loss on sale of buildings
o. Increase in deferred tax credits
p. Sale of treasury stock for less than cost
q. Depreciation expense
r. Increase in intangible assets

Ex. 18-6   **Cash receipts and payments.** Grether Company had sales of $12,000 and cost of goods sold of $7,500 in 1983. Working capital account balances were as follows:

	Beginning	Ending
Cash	$9,000	$9,800
Accounts receivable	4,000	4,400
Merchandise	6,300	6,000
Accounts payable	3,000	3,200

Required:
a. Calculate how much cash was collected from customers in 1983.
b. Calculate how much was paid for merchandise in 1983.

Ex. 18-7   **Cash collection and payments.** Singleton Company's fee revenue amounted to $18,000 in 1983. Salary expenses were $10,600 and supplies expenses were $1,700. Working capital balances were as follows:

	Beginning	Ending
Cash	$1,250	$1,760
Accounts receivable	2,160	2,840
Supplies	890	780
Accounts payable	1,170	1,050
Salaries payable	1,350	1,560

Required:

a. Calculate the amount of cash collected from clients.

b. Calculate the amount of cash paid for salaries and supplies, assuming that all accounts payable are owed for supplies.

Ex. 18-8 Interpretation of statement of changes. Examine carefully the following statement of changes.

Marston Company, Ltd.
Statement of Changes in Financial Position
For the Year Ending December 31, 1984

Sources of Funds		
From operation		
Net loss	($3,000)	
Add depreciation expense	12,000	
Add loss on sale of land		
and equipment	2,000	
Total		$11,000
Other sources		
New two-year note payable		15,000
Sale of land		30,000
Sale of equipment		10,000
Change in funds		9,000
Total sources		$75,000
Uses of Funds		
Repayment of mortgage		$40,000
Payment of dividends		5,000
Purchase of new equipment		30,000
Total uses		$75,000
Changes in Funds		
Cash decrease		($23,000)
Accounts receivable increase		8,000
Merchandise increase		16,000
Accounts payable increase		(15,000)
Notes payable decrease		5,000
Change in funds		($ 9,000)

Required:

a. What is the definition of funds? Explain.

b. Did funds increase or decrease and by how much?

c. What was the company's main source of funds?

d. Explain how operations produced $11,000 of funds when the company operated at a loss.

e. What was the company's main use of funds?

f. What problems do you perceive with respect to the composition of liabilities? The composition of working capital? The company's ability to generate funds in the future?

g. Discuss the soundness of the decision to pay a dividend.

Ex. 18-9   **Interpreting a funds flow worksheet.** The controller of Elmer Corporation prepared the following worksheet on December 31, 1984:

	Beginning Balance	Changes dr	cr	Ending Balance
Debits				
Working capital	$ 200	g. 20		$ 220
Fixed assets	2,800	f. 581	b. 35	3,346
Long-term investments	1,500			1,500
	$4,500			$5,066
Credits				
Accumulated depreciation	400		c. 23	423
Long-term debt	1,000			1,000
Common stock	2,000		d. 400	2,400
Retained earnings	1,100	e. 17	a. 160	1,243
	$4,500			$5,066
Sources and Uses of Funds				
Net income		a. 160		
Loss on sale of fixed assets		b. 5		
Depreciation		c. 23		
Sales of fixed assets		b. 30		
Common stock		d. 400		
Dividends			e. 17	
Fixed assets			f. 581	
Change in working capital			g. 20	
		1,236	1,236	

Required:

a. What definition of funds is used in this worksheet? Explain.

b. Is it possible to determine the cost of the sold assets from the above data? Is it possible to determine the book value? Explain.

c. Did funds increase or decrease and by how much?

d. What was the amount of funds provided by operations?

Ex. 18-10 Use of funds flow worksheet. Refer to the worksheet presented in Exercise 18-9.

Required:

Use the data in the worksheet to prepare a statement of changes in financial position with funds defined as working capital.

Ex. 18-11 Interpretation of funds flow worksheet. BZB Company's internal auditor prepared the following worksheet on June 30, 1984.

	Beginning Balance	Changes dr	cr	Ending Balance
Debits				
Cash	$ 200	m. 48		$ 248
Accounts receivable	900		a. 73	827
Merchandise	1,300	b. 105		1,405
Fixed assets	3,900	j. 332	c. 170	4,062
Patents	600		f. 10	590
	$6,900			$7,132
Credits				
Accumulated depreciation	800		d. 72	872
Accounts payable	600		e. 30	630
Long-term debt (net)	1,500	l. 150	g. 5	1,355
Preferred stock	1,300	i. 300		1,000
Common stock	2,000		h. 400	2,400
Retained earnings	700	k. 40	x. 215	875
	$6,900			$7,132
Sources of Funds				
Net income		x. 215		
Accounts receivable		a. 73		
Merchandise			b. 105	
Gain on sale of land			c. 5	
Depreciation		d. 72		
Accounts payable		e. 30		
Amortization		f. 10		
Bond discount		g. 5		
Land		c. 175		
Common stock		h. 400		
Uses of Funds				
Preferred stock			i. 300	
Equipment			j. 332	
Dividends			k. 40	
Bonds			l. 150	
Cash			m. 48	
		1,955	1,955	

Required:

a. What definition of funds is used in this worksheet? Explain.

b. What was the cost of the land that was sold? What was the selling price? Explain.

c. Which stock was retired, and which stock was issued during the period? Explain.

d. Was the amount of interest expense reported on the income statement greater or smaller than the amount actually paid to bondholders? Explain.

e. Calculate the change in working capital.

Ex. 18-12   Use of funds flow worksheet. Examine the worksheet presented in Exercise 18-11 for BZB Corporation.

Required:
Use the data in the worksheet to prepare a statement of changes in financial position with funds defined as cash.

Ex. 18-13   Interpretation of statement of changes. Examine the following statement prepared by Faron Company's new treasurer:

Faron Company **Statement of Changes in Financial Position** **December 31, 1984**	
Sources	
Net income from income statement	$ 3,000
Accounts receivable decrease	6,000
Merchandise increase	(9,000)
Accounts payable increase	2,000
Depreciation	7,000
Total	$ 9,000
Cost of land sold at loss of $4,000	24,000
New three-year note	10,000
Change in funds	8,000
	$51,000
Uses	
Debt	$30,000
Equipment	12,000
Dividends	9,000
	$51,000

Required:

a. Does the statement present information adequately? Explain.

b. What is the definition of funds? Explain.

c. Did funds increase or decrease and by how much?

d. What was the company's main source of funds?

e. What amount of funds was actually provided by the sale of land? Where should the loss on the sale appear?

f. What amount of funds was actually provided by operations? How could funds from operation be so much greater than net income? Explain.

g. Does the statement indicate that current assets are becoming more or less liquid? Explain.

h. What was the main use of funds?

i. Does the decision to pay dividends appear to be sound?

j. Does the statement indicate the presence of potential problems for the company? Explain.

Ex. 18-14 **Recasting a statement of changes.** Examine the statement of changes in financial position presented in Exercise 18-13 and note any deficiencies in the presentation.

Required:
Recast the statement in its proper form assuming it covers a 1-year period.

Problem Set A

P. 18A-1 **Change in working capital.** Comparative trial balances of Blefrisco Corporation are presented below.

Blefrisco Corporation Trial Balances December 31		
	1984	**1983**
Cash	$2,120	$1,160
Accounts receivable	3,390	3,150
Merchandise	6,520	6,780
Prepaid expenses	860	950
Equipment	9,950	9,800
Accumulated depreciation	(4,450)	(3,500)
Accounts payable	(2,390)	(2,200)
Taxes payable	(880)	(1,060)
Salaries payable	(3,720)	(3,500)
Unearned revenue	(1,710)	(1,980)
Bonds payable	(5,000)	(5,000)
Common stock	(3,200)	(3,000)
Retained earnings	(1,490)	(1,600)
	$ 0	$ 0

Required:
Prepare a schedule of changes in working capital.

P. 18A-2   Funds provided by operations. The income statement of Platona Corporation is provided below.

Platona Corporation Income Statement For the Year Ending December 31, 1983		
Sales		$175,000
Less cost of goods sold		103,200
Gross margin		$ 71,800
Less expenses		
Salaries	$28,900	
Administrative	19,700	
Depreciation	5,800	
Amortization of patent	1,500	
Other	4,600	60,500
Operating income		$ 11,300
Other income and expenses		
Rent revenue	$ 1,000	
Loss on sale of equipment	(300)	700
Net income before tax		$ 12,000
Less income tax		5,100
Net income after tax		$ 6,900
Extraordinary gain on bond redemption (net of tax)		600
Net income		$ 7,500

Required:
Prepare a schedule showing the amount of working capital provided by operations.

P. 18A-3   Statement of changes in financial position. Following is a list of transactions and their amounts of Flaster Corporation for the year 1983 as collected by the company's internal auditor.

Transaction	Amount
Total revenues	$300,000
Depreciation expense	18,000
Other expenses	180,000
Amortization of patents	3,000
Increase in inventory	5,000
Purchase of land	60,000
Decrease in receivables	7,000
Increase in payables	9,000
Redemption of bonds payable	35,000
Sale of equipment at book value	22,000
Issuance of common stock	16,000
Purchase of other fixed assets	57,000
Increase in cash	17,000

Required:
Prepare a statement of changes in financial position, working capital basis, for 1983.

P. 18A-4 **Recasting a statement of changes.** The following statement was prepared by Loudell Company on December 31, 1983.

Loudell Company Funds Flow Statement For the Year 1983		
Funds Provided		
Net income		$16,860
Depreciation		1,530
Amortization		600
Accounts receivable		120
Accounts payable		150
Bond discount amortization		90
Sale of land		1,880
Sale of investments		1,090
Sale of stock		4,000
		$26,320
Funds Applied		
Dividends		$15,000
Merchandise		430
Notes payable		200
Gain on sale of land	$480	
Less loss on sale of investments	210	270
New buildings		6,100
New equipment		4,100
Change in cash		220
		$26,320

Required:
Recast the statement using proper accounting terminology and form, with funds defined as cash.

P. 18A-5 **Recasting a statement of changes.** Refer to the statement provided by Loudell Company in Problem 18A-4.

Required:
Recast the statement using proper accounting terminology and form, with funds defined as working capital.

P. 18A-6 **Simple statement of changes.** Comparative financial statements of Mars Company are provided below. Net income for the year was $3,980 and the company paid $5,000 in dividends.

Mars Company
Balance Sheets
December 31

	1984	1983
Assets		
Cash	$ 680	$ 500
Accounts receivable	1,440	1,250
Merchandise	2,070	2,130
Land	7,700	5,600
Buildings	15,200	15,200
Accumulated depreciation	(5,300)	(4,100)
Total assets	$21,790	$20,580
Equities		
Accounts payable	$ 1,160	$ 930
Bonds payable, due 1999	10,000	8,000
Common stock	5,000	5,000
Retained earnings	5,630	6,650
Total equities	$21,790	$20,580

Required:

Prepare a statement of changes in financial position for the company, with funds defined as working capital.

P. 18A-7   **Simple cash flow statement.** Use the data in Problem 18A-6 to prepare a statement of changes in financial position for Mars Company, with funds defined as cash.

P. 18A-8   **Statement of changes.** Below are the changes in account balances taken from the December 31, 1983 and 1984 balance sheets of Sirius Company:

	Changes dr (cr)
Cash	($ 440)
Accounts receivable	240
Merchandise	(860)
Long-term investments	2,600
Land	(10,000)
Buildings	4,000
Equipment	1,100
Accumulated depreciation	(3,060)
Patents	1,200
Notes payable	(400)
Accounts payable	300
Bonds payable	2,400
Premium on bonds payable	180
Common stock	0
Retained earnings	2,740
	$ 0

The income statement reported $3,060 depreciation expense, $200 amortization of patent, a gain of $600 on the sale of land, and a net loss of $2,700 for the year ending December 31, 1984. Dividends in the amount of $40 were paid in 1984.

Required:
Prepare a statement of changes in financial position for Sirius Company with funds defined as working capital.

P. 18A-9 **Statement of changes.** Use the data in Problem 18A-8 to prepare a statement of changes in financial position for Sirius Company, with funds defined as cash.

P. 18A-10 **Funds defined as working capital.** The financial statements of Saturn Corporation are given below. During the year the company sold a parcel of land that had a cost of $2,000, and it also paid cash dividends of $358.

Saturn Corporation Comparative Balance Sheet December 31			
	1984	**1983**	**Changes dr (cr)**
Assets			
Cash	$ 1,586	$ 2,064	(478)
Accounts receivable (net)	3,676	2,980	696
Merchandise inventory	1,688	1,960	(272)
Prepaid expenses	149	138	11
Property plant and equipment	30,582	26,670	3,912
Accumulated depreciation	(10,710)	(9,870)	(840)
Total assets	$26,971	$23,942	
Liabilities			
Notes payable	$ 710	$ 639	(71)
Accounts payable	2,147	2,190	43
Taxes payable	317	308	(9)
Bonds payable	5,000	3,000	(2,000)
Mortgage note payable	3,000	3,500	500
Total liabilities	$11,174	$ 9,637	
Capital			
Common stock	$ 8,000	$ 8,000	
Retained earnings	7,797	6,305	(1,492)
Total capital	$15,797	$14,305	—0—
Total liabilities and capital	$26,971	$23,942	

Saturn Corporation
Income Statement
For the Year Ending December 31, 1984

Sales		$39,290
Less cost of goods sold		25,537
Gross margin		$13,753
Less expenses:		
Selling and administrative	$5,360	
Wages and salaries	4,025	
Depreciation	840	
Interest	520	10,745
Operating income		$ 3,008
Gain on sale of land		72
Net income before tax		$ 3,080
Income tax		1,230
Net income after tax		$ 1,850

Required:
Prepare a statement of changes in financial position, working capital basis, for Saturn Corporation for the 1984 fiscal year.

P. 18A-11 Funds defined as cash. Refer to the information for Saturn Corporation in Problem 18A-10. Prepare a statement of changes in financial position, cash basis for the Saturn Corporation for the year ending December 31, 1984.

Problem Set B

P. 18B-1 Change in working capital. Below are comparative trial balances of Fleximat Company.

Fleximat Company
Trial Balances
December 31

	1984	1983
Cash	$ 16,300	29,700
Accounts receivable	44,100	47,400
Merchandise	94,900	91,300
Prepaid expenses	13,300	12,000
Fixed assets	130,000	145,000
Accumulated depreciation	(49,000)	(62,000)
Patents	7,000	6,000
Accounts payable	(30,000)	(33,400)
Taxes payable	(14,800)	(12,300)
Salaries payable	(47,000)	(52,000)
Unearned rent	(27,700)	(24,000)
Long-term debt	(70,000)	(70,000)
Capital, Flexin	(34,000)	(37,600)
Capital, Matthew	(33,100)	(40,100)
	–0–	–0–

Required:
Prepare a schedule of changes in working capital.

P. 18B-2 **Working capital provided by operations.** The income statement of Chin Hu Li, Incorporated is provided below.

Chin Hu Li, Incorporated Income Statement For the Year Ending December 31, 1983		
Sales		$297,000
Less cost of goods sold		175,000
Gross margin		$122,000
Less expenses		
Salaries	$49,100	
Administration	33,500	
Depreciation	9,800	
Amortization of patent	2,500	
Other	5,400	100,300
Operating income		$ 21,700
Other income and expenses		
Rent revenue	$ 1,700	
Loss on sale of equipment	(500)	1,200
Net income before tax		$ 22,900
Less income tax		8,700
Net income after tax		$ 14,200
Extraordinary gain on bond redemption		1,000
Net income		$ 15,200

Required:

Prepare a schedule showing the amount of working capital provided by operations.

P. 18B-3 **Statement of changes in financial position.** Following is a list of transactions and their amounts of Flaster Corporation for the year 1983 as collected by the company's internal auditor.

Transaction	Amount
Total revenues	$300,000
Depreciation expense	18,000
Other expenses	180,000
Amortization of patents	3,000
Increase in inventory	5,000
Purchase of land	60,000
Decrease in receivables	7,000
Increase in payables	9,000
Redemption of bonds payable	35,000
Sale of equipment at book value	22,000
Issuance of common stock	16,000
Purchase of other fixed assets	57,000
Increase in cash	17,000

Required:

Prepare a statement of changes in financial position, cash basis, for 1983.

P. 18B-4   Interpreting a statement of changes. Below is a statement taken from the annual report of Bardot Corporation.

Bardot Corporation **Statement of Changes in Financial Position** **For the Year Ending December 31, 1983**		
Sources of Funds		
From operations		
Net income	$10,000	
Add depreciation	7,000	
Amortization of patents	3,000	
Increase in accounts payable	2,200	
Decrease in inventories	2,800	
Loss on sale of investments	2,400	
Less increase in accounts receivable	(900)	
Decrease in wages payable	(600)	
Gain on sale of equipment	(1,500)	$ 24,400
Other Sources		
Sale of equipment		58,000
Sale of investments		10,000
Issuance of stock		30,000
Total		$122,400
Uses of Funds		
Payment of dividends		$ 45,000
Retirement of bonds		65,000
Building improvements		11,000
Change in funds		1,400
Total		$122,400

Required:

Examine the above statement and answer the following questions:

a. What definition of funds is used?
b. What was the major source of funds?
c. Did funds increase or decrease and by how much?
d. What was the book value of the sold equipment?
e. What was the book value of the sold investment?
f. What was the book value of the retired bonds?
g. How much cash was required to retire bonds?
h. What was the main source of funds from operations? Explain and discuss in detail.

i. Assess the soundness of the dividend.

j. Do you perceive any problems with this company? Explain.

P. 18B-5 **Interpreting and recasting a statement of changes.** The following schedule was provided by Black Company.

<table>
<tr><td colspan="3" style="text-align:center">Black Company
Schedule of Funds Provided by Operations
For the Year Ending November 30, 1984</td></tr>
<tr><td>Net income</td><td></td><td>$4,700</td></tr>
<tr><td>Add items not requiring the use of funds</td><td></td><td></td></tr>
<tr><td>Depreciation expense</td><td>$2,900</td><td></td></tr>
<tr><td>Decrease in accounts receivable</td><td>1,000</td><td></td></tr>
<tr><td>Increase in notes payable</td><td>200</td><td></td></tr>
<tr><td>Increase in wages payable</td><td>12</td><td></td></tr>
<tr><td>Loss on sale of equipment</td><td>600</td><td></td></tr>
<tr><td>Increase in deferred income tax liability</td><td>50</td><td>4,762</td></tr>
<tr><td></td><td></td><td>$9,462</td></tr>
<tr><td>Less items not providing funds</td><td></td><td></td></tr>
<tr><td>Increase in merchandise inventory</td><td>$ 206</td><td></td></tr>
<tr><td>Increase in prepaid expenses</td><td>11</td><td></td></tr>
<tr><td>Decrease in unearned rent</td><td>5</td><td></td></tr>
<tr><td>Bond premium amortization</td><td>20</td><td></td></tr>
<tr><td>Gain on sale of land</td><td>300</td><td>542</td></tr>
<tr><td>Total funds provided by operations</td><td></td><td>$8,920</td></tr>
</table>

Required:

Examine the above schedule and answer the following questions:

a. What is the definition of funds?

b. Did the change in accounts receivable cause an increase or a decrease in working capital?

c. Was the amount of tax expense reported by the company larger or smaller than the amount actually owed to the government? Explain.

d. Assume that cash increased by $10. Calculate the change in working capital.

e. Is Black Company a sole proprietorship, a partnership, or a corporation? Explain.

f. Recast the schedule to reflect funds from operations with funds defined differently than in the schedule shown.

P. 18B-6 **Simple statement of changes.** Listed below are changes in account balances for Venus Company calculated from December 31, 1983 and 1984 balance sheets. During 1984, the company had a net loss of $990, the owner withdrew $30 during the year, and land was sold at a gain of $300.

	Changes dr (cr)
Cash	($ 180)
Accounts receivable	(190)
Merchandise	60
Land	(2,100)
Plant and equipment	360
Accumulated depreciation	(1,200)
Accounts payable	230
Mortgage payable	2,000
Capital, Venus	1,020
	$ 0

Required:
Prepare a statement of changes in financial position for the company, with funds defined as working capital.

P. 18B-7 **Simple cash flow statement.** Use the data in Problem 18B-6 to prepare a statement of changes of financial position for Venus Company, with funds defined as cash.

P. 18B-8 **Statement of changes.** The financial statements of Javol Corporation are presented below.

Javol Corporation Balance Sheets December 31		
	1984	**1983**
Assets		
Cash	$ 1,120	$ 900
Accounts receivable	2,710	2,830
Merchandise	5,180	4,750
Long-term investments	7,700	9,000
Land	6,000	7,400
Buildings	27,800	21,700
Equipment	21,340	17,240
Accumulated depreciation	(10,890)	(9,360)
Patents	5,000	5,600
Total	$65,960	$60,060
Equities		
Notes payable	$ 1,800	$ 2,000
Accounts payable	2,310	2,160
Bonds payable	30,000	30,000
Discount on bonds payable	(660)	(750)
Common stock	14,000	10,000
Retained earnings	18,510	16,650
Total	$65,960	$60,060

Net income for the year was $16,860. The income statement reported $1,530 depreciation expense, $600 amortization expense, a gain of $480 on the sale of land, and a loss of $210 on the sale of investments. The company paid $15,000 in cash dividends.

Required:
Prepare a statement of changes in financial position for the company, with funds defined as working capital.

P. 18B-9 **Statement of changes.** Use the data in Problem 18B-8 to prepare a statement of changes in financial position for Javol Corporation, with funds defined as cash.

P. 18B-10 **Funds defined as working capital.** The financial statements of Nebula Corporation are given below. During the year the company sold a parcel of land that had a cost of $2,000, and it also paid cash dividends of $308.

Nebula Corporation Comparative Balance Sheets November 30			
	1984	**1983**	**Changes dr (cr)**
Assets			
Cash	$ 2,984	$ 3,464	(480)
Accounts receivable (net)	4,678	3,980	698
Merchandise inventory	3,690	3,960	(270)
Prepaid expenses	748	738	10
Property plant and equipment	30,583	26,670	3,913
Accumulated depreciation	(10,710)	(9,870)	(840)
Total assets	$31,973	$28,942	
Liabilities and Capital			
Liabilities			
Notes payable	$ 1,710	$ 1,639	(71)
Accounts payable	3,146	3,190	44
Taxes payable	2,320	2,308	(12)
Bonds payable	6,000	6,000	
Mortgage note payable	3,000	3,500	500
Total liabilities	$16,176	$16,637	
Capital			
Common stock	$ 8,000	$ 6,000	(2,000)
Retained earnings	7,797	6,305	(1,492)
Total capital	$15,797	$12,305	–0–
Total liabilities and capital	$31,973	$28,942	


```
┌─────────────────────────────────────────────────────────────┐
│                    Nebula Corporation                         │
│                     Income Statement                          │
│            For the Year Ending November 30, 1984              │
│                                                               │
│   Sales                                            $44,290    │
│   Less cost of goods sold                           25,537    │
│                                                               │
│   Gross margin                                     $18,753    │
│   Less expenses:                                              │
│      Selling and administrative        $8,360                 │
│      Wages and salaries                 6,025                 │
│      Depreciation                         840                 │
│      Interest                             520       15,745    │
│                                                               │
│   Operating income                                 $ 3,008   │
│   Gain on sale of land                                  72    │
│                                                               │
│   Net income before tax                            $ 3,080   │
│   Income tax                                         1,280    │
│                                                               │
│   Net income after tax                             $ 1,800   │
└─────────────────────────────────────────────────────────────┘
```

Required:

Prepare a statement of changes in financial position, working capital basis, for Nebula Corporation for the 1984 fiscal year.

P. 18B-11   **Funds defined as cash.** Refer to the information for Nebula Corporation in Problem 18B-10. Prepare a statement of changes in financial position, cash basis, for the Nebula Corporation for the year ending November 30, 1984.

Minicases

Minicase 18-1   (CMA Examination Question)

The Ontario Furniture Company is an established firm specializing in the manufacture of wood furniture. The company is well-known nationally for its high-quality furnishings.

The company's accounting department is in the process of preparing the financial statements for the fiscal year just completed on December 31, 1984. The comparative statements of income and financial position for 1983 and 1984 appear below.

Ontario Furniture Company
Income Statement
For the Years Ended December 31, 1983 and 1984
(000 omitted)

	1983	1984
Revenue		
Sales (net)	$5,850	$6,320
Interest and dividends	20	8
Total revenue	$5,870	$6,328
Costs and expenses		
Cost of goods sold	$4,330	$4,470
Selling expenses	610	620
Administrative expenses	510	5151
Interest expense	90	83
Loss on sale of investments	—	10
Total costs and expenses	$5,540	$5,968
Net income	$ 330	$ 360

Ontario Furniture Company
Statement of Financial Position
December 31, 1983 and 1984
(000 omitted)

Assets	1983	1984
Cash	$ 220	$ 46
Marketable securities	80	40
Accounts receivable (net)	960	1,152
Inventories	1,580	1,802
Current assets	$2,840	$3,040
Investments	320	135
Property, plant, and equipment (net)	1,320	1,370
Total assets	$4,480	$4,545
Liabilities and equities		
Short-term notes payable	$ 350	$ 430
Accounts payable	450	450
Cash dividends payable	—	30
Accrued and other liabilities	120	130
Current portion of long-term debt	200	200
Current liabilities	$1,120	$1,240
Serial bonds payable	1,000	800
Convertible bonds payable	150	95
Total liabilities	$2,270	$2,135
Common stock, $4 par	$1,120	$1,164
Contributed surplus	280	291
Retained earnings	810	1,020
	$2,210	$2,475
Less treasury stock	—	65
Total stockholder's equity	$2,210	$2,410
Total liabilities and equities	$4,480	$4,545

The state of the furniture industry is influenced greatly by the economy and the number of housing starts. Consequently, the industry as a whole has been suffering the past few years.

Ontario Furniture Company was able to show a modest increase in sales over 1983 levels. The company's management expects that its operations in 1985 will be similar to those in 1984. Even if the economy and housing starts should improve during 1985, Ontario will not benefit from the recovery until 1986.

Ontario's manufacturing process is labour intensive. The present labour contract has an additional 18 months to run before it expires. The cost of lumber, especially high-quality hardwoods, has risen in recent years, but company officials expect that these costs will stabilize at their present levels.

The following additional data regarding Ontario's operations have been assembled by the accounting department:

1. The allowance for uncollectible accounts had a balance of $50,000 on December 31, 1983, and a balance of $63,000 on December 31, 1984. A total of $52,000 in accounts receivable were written off as uncollectible during 1984. Provisions for uncollectible accounts amounting to $60,000 in 1983 and $65,000 in 1984 were included in the selling expenses.
2. The company liquidated some of its investments during 1984 in order to raise cash. Marketable securities were sold at their recorded cost of $40,000. In addition, Ontario sold its interest in Nova Products Company, a promising new company in contemporary furniture and related accessories, for $175,000. Management regretted this action, but this was the only long-term investment which could be sold easily and quickly.
3. Equipment costing $215,000 was purchased during 1984 as part of management's project to improve the manufacturing facilities and to replace obsolete equipment. This upgrading of the manufacturing facilities, which was started in 1983, is expected to be completed next year when a similar amount will be expended on equipment. Used equipment was sold at its book value of $25,000. Annual depreciation on plant and equipment included in the operating expenses amounted to $130,000 and $140,000 for 1983 and 1984, respectively.
4. At the end of the current year holders of Ontario's short-term notes agreed to extend the maturities through 1985. The serial bonds are being retired on schedule at the rate of $200,000 per year. A total of 55 convertible bonds were exchanged for common stock during 1984.
5. The company purchased $65,000 of its own common stock.
6. It declared cash dividends of $150,000 during 1984; a total of $120,000 was actually paid during 1984.
7. A large operating loss was incurred by the Ontario Furniture Company in 1980. As a result of this loss, the company has not had to pay any federal or provincial taxes on its earnings for the past three years (1981-1984).

Required:

a. Using the data provided, prepare a Statement of Changes in Financial Position for the year ended December 31, 1984.

b. Using the Statement of Changes in Financial Position prepared, above, and the data provided in the problem, identify and briefly discuss the significant funds movements which should be the concern of the management of Ontario Furniture Company.

Minicase 18-2

(CMA Examination Question)

Motel Enterprises operates and owns many motels throughout Canada. The company has expanded rapidly over the past few years, and company officers are concerned that they may have overexpanded.

The following financial statements and other financial data have been supplied by the controller of Motel Enterprises.

Motel Enterprises Income Statement for years ending October 31 (unaudited) (000 omitted)		
	1982	**1983**
Revenue	$1,920	$2,230
Cost and expenses		
Direct room and related services	$ 350	$ 400
Direct food and beverage	640	740
General and administrative	250	302
Advertising	44	57
Repairs and maintenance	82	106
Interest expense	220	280
Depreciation	95	120
Lease payment	73	100
Total costs and expenses	$1,754	$2,105
Income before taxes	$ 166	$ 125
Provision for income tax	42	25
Net income	$ 124	$ 100

Motel Enterprises Statement of Financial Position as of October 31 (unaudited) (000 omitted)		
Assets	**1982**	**1983**
Current assets		
Cash	$ 125	$ 100
Accounts receivable (net)	200	250
Inventory	50	60
Other	5	5
Total current assets	$ 380	$ 415
Long-term investments	$ 710	$ 605
Property and equipment		
Buildings and equipment (net)	$2,540	$3,350
Land	410	370
Construction in progress	450	150
Total property and equipment	$3,400	$3,870
Other assets	$ 110	$ 110
Total assets	$4,600	$5,000
Liabilities and Stockholder's Equity		
Current liabilities		
Accounts payable	$ 30	$ 40
Accrued liabilities	190	190
Notes payable to bank	10	30
Current portion of long-term notes	50	80
Total current liabilities	$ 280	$ 340
Long-term debt		
Long-term notes	$2,325	$2,785
Subordinated debentures due May 1989	800	800
Total long-term debt	$3,125	$3,585
Total liabilities	$3,045	$3,925
Stockholder's equity		
Common stock ($1 par)	$ 300	$ 300
Contributed surplus	730	730
Net unrealized loss on long-term investments	—	(105)
Retained earnings	165	150
Total stockholders' equity	$1,195	$1,075
Total liabilities and Stockholders' equity	$4,600	$5,00

Other Data

1. *Accounts Receivable.* The allowance for uncollectible accounts had a balance of $3,000 on October 31, 1982 and $4,000 on October 31, 1983.
2. *Long-Term Investments.* Motel Enterprises has investments in preferred stocks of public utilities which are carried on the books at the lower of cost or market. The market value of the investments were as follows:

> October 31, 1982 — $725,000
> October 31, 1983 — $605,000
> December 1, 1983 — $670,000

3. *Property and Equipment.* Motel Enterprises acquires parcels of land for future sites and disposes of land if the site does not prove to be advantageous; this is a frequent and regular activity of the company. In addition, the company acquires existing motels, constructs motels on new sites, and builds additions to motels at existing sites.

During the 1982-83 fiscal year, construction was completed on building additions at a total cost of $350,000.

New buildings were purchased during the year at a cost of $620,000; 40 percent of the purchase price was paid in cash and the balance will be due in two years. A total of $40,000 of the purchase price was allocated to land.

Land no longer needed was sold on June 15, 1983 for $100,000; the land had a basis of $80,000.

Motel Enterprises has several operating leases which are not capitalized; this is the proper accounting treatment for the leases. The present value of the minimum lease commitments was $430,000 on October 31, 1983 and $520,000 on October 31, 1983.

4. *Long-Term Notes.* The long-term notes of Motel Enterprises consists mainly of term loans and mortgage loans. A major portion of the property and equipment and investments of Motel Enterprises are pledged as collateral for long-term notes.

Long-term notes become due as follows:

> by October 31, 1984 — $ 80,000
> by October 31, 1985 —   150,000
> by October 31, 1986 —   550,000
> by October 31, 1987 —   350,000
> by October 31, 1988 —   425,000
> over five years   1,310,000

5. *Dividends.* The company declared and paid to its stockholders $115,000 of cash dividends during the 1982-83 fiscal year.

Required:

Prepare an estimated Statement of Changes in Financial Position for the y
ending October 31, 1983.

Chapter 19

Financial Statement Analysis

In this chapter much of the material you studied in financial accounting is synthesized. To perform a financial analysis you must draw upon your past knowledge of accounting. When you have completed the chapter, you should understand:

1 The meaning of financial analysis.

2 How to perform a horizontal and vertical analysis.

3 How to perform a ratio analysis.

4 What is meant by tests of liquidity and solvency.

5 How profitability is measured.

6 The purpose of market tests.

7 That a real appreciation of the value of accounting information requires a good knowledge of accounting and considerable experience with financial statement analysis.

External accounting reports contain **historical** information about a business firm's financial condition, operations, and financing and investing activities. Decision makers, however, make decisions that affect the future. A good starting point in most decision making is an understanding of events that occurred in the recent past. Merely reading financial statements provides a considerable amount of information, but to make good decisions, one needs to make a thorough analysis of the statements. A complete **financial analysis** and interpretation of financial statements involves the assessment of past business performance, an evaluation of the present condition of the business, and predictions about the future potential for achieving expected or desired results.

Financial analysis
requires experience

It is not possible to become an experienced financial analyst by studying one chapter in an accounting textbook. We can only introduce the topic of financial analysis and discuss some of the information that emerges when financial statements are thoroughly analyzed. The integration of such information into a complete coherent analysis can be accomplished only after much experience and further study of this and related topics.

The value of most figures in financial statements is enhanced significantly when the figures are compared with other data in the same or other financial statements. Such comparisons may reveal trends, highlight important relationships, or provide other types of information. For this reason corporations

Comparative figures
enhance analysis

provide annual reports with comparative financial statements for at least two consecutive accounting periods. In addition, annual reports contain a great deal of information in the notes that accompany the financial statements. The notes explain many aspects of business operations that cannot be shown clearly with the figures alone. They include such information as the accounting principle selected when more than one is available, details of items that may be shown as a single figure in the statements, information on various contingencies, and other data necessary to make the report more informative.

Although companies must present comparative financial statements, there is no requirement for them to provide an analysis of the statements. The analysis is left to the financial analyst, who uses the data in the statements to develop a more comprehensive picture of the financial status of the firm by performing one of the following types of analyses:

1. Horizontal analysis
2. Vertical analysis
3. Ratio analysis

To illustrate the three types of analysis, we use the financial statements of Dominion Corporation for 1983 and 1984 shown in Figure 19-1.

Horizontal analysis

Horizontal analysis involves comparing figures reported in the financial statements of two or more consecutive accounting periods. The financial analyst calculates the difference between the figures of one year and the next and computes the percentage change from one year to the next, using the earlier year as the base period. Much additional information is obtained from financial statements in this manner. For example, in Figure 19-1, 1984 net income of $95,300 is a significant item of information, but it becomes more significant when it is seen as representing an increase of $7,700 or 8.8 percent over the previous year. In addition, the examination of the remaining changes and percentages in the statement shows that the 8.8 percent increase in earnings was accomplished with a 3.3 percent decrease in total sales. This indicates that management was able to operate more efficiently in 1984 than in 1983. The increase in net income was obtained by a reduction in cost of goods sold and operating expenses.

The base period for calculating percentage changes is usually the earlier year. For example, the balance sheet in Figure 19-1 shows that cash increased from 1983 to 1984 by $5,070. The percentage increase is calculated as follows:

$$\frac{\text{Most recent value} - \text{Base period value}}{\text{Base period value}} = \text{Percentage change}$$

$$\frac{\$38,570 - \$33,500}{\$33,500} = \frac{\$5,070}{\$33,500} = .151 \text{ or } 15.1\%$$

Absolute and percentage changes

The absolute changes and the percentage changes between reported amounts must be carefully interpreted. For example, if the base period amount is very small, the percentage change may appear extremely large, although the absolute change is not especially material. An example is the change in temporary investments in Dominion Corporation's balance sheet, which shows an absolute change of $12,400. Although the percentage change of 221.4 percent appears very large, the amount of temporary investments in either year is not unusual for a corporation with total assets of over $1 million. Note that the percentage change cannot be calculated if the base year amount is zero, since division by zero is not defined.

Horizontal analysis can provide an indication of significant trends in financial statement items. For this reason corporations often provide comparative data for longer periods of time such as five to ten years so that a number of year-to-year comparisons can be made.

Long-term comparisons are often more significant than comparisons for only two accounting periods, because data from more time periods can indicate the presence of trends in the figures. A change from one period to the next is not necessarily part of a longer trend, because it could be caused by unusual economic conditions or a few transactions that cannot be expected to recur. For example, a sharp increase in earnings per share for one year may occur as a result of a profitable sale of investments that were acquired years earlier at a very low cost. Since such transactions may not occur again in the future, a similar increase in earnings cannot be expected to continue.

In addition to data for long-term comparisons, summaries of items such as total sales, total expenses, net income, earnings per share, and other important figures may be provided in tables or graphs in the annual report to highlight the company's operations. Graphic presentations often illustrate financial relationships that are difficult to perceive by reading the statements alone. In addition, graphs can convey a large amount of information at a glance. Some examples of graphic illustrations are shown for the Dominion Corporation in Figure 19-2. Note the obvious presence of upward trends in sales and income, and the corresponding trend in earnings and dividends per share.

Vertical analysis   Vertical analysis involves comparing figures in the financial statements of a single period. Figures in a statement are converted to a common unit, which makes comparisons more meaningful. Conversion to a common unit is accomplished by expressing all figures in a statement as a percentage of an important item such as total sales or total assets. For example, Figure 19-3 shows the income statement of Dominion Corporation with each item expressed as a

Dominion Corporation Income Statements For Years Ending December 31				
			Increase (Decrease)	
	1984	**1983**	**Amount**	**Percent**
Sales	$1,210,000	$1,251,400	($41,400)	(3.3)
Less cost of goods sold	666,500	713,800	(47,300)	(6.6)
Gross margin	$ 543,500	$ 537,600	$ 5,900	1.1
Less expenses				
Selling	$ 142,800	$ 158,100	($15,300)	(9.7)
Administrative	150,700	155,400	(4,700)	(3.0)
Other expenses	69,900	67,500	2,400	3.6
Total operating expenses	$ 363,400	$ 381,000	($17,600)	(4.6)
Interest expense	33,500	21,800	11,700	53.7
Total expenses	$ 396,900	$ 402,800	$ 5,900	1.5
Net income before tax	$ 146,600	$ 134,800	$ 11,800	8.8
Income tax	51,300	47,200	4,100	8.7
Net income after tax	$ 95,300	$ 87,600	$ 7,700	8.8
Earnings per common share	$9.53	$8.76	$.77	8.8

Dominion Corporation Statements of Retained Earnings For Years Ending December 31				
			Increase (Decrease)	
	1984	**1983**	**Amount**	**Percent**
Retained earnings, Jan. 1	$139,600	$ 96,000	$43,600	45.4
Add net income	95,300	87,600	7,700	8.8
	$234,900	$183,600	$51,300	27.9
Less preferred dividends	(3,000)	(3,000)	0	—
Common dividends	(45,500)	(41,000)	(4,500)	11.0
Retained earnings, Dec. 31	$186,400	$139,600	$46,800	33.5

Figure 19-1
Horizontal analysis of financial statements. The change in each item from one year to the next is computed both as an absolute and as a percentage amount.

Dominion Corporation
Balance Sheets
December 31

Assets	1984	1983	Increase (Decrease) Amount	Percent
Current assets				
Cash	$ 38,570	$ 33,500	$ 5,070	15.1
Temporary investments	18,000	5,600	12,400	221.4
Accounts receivable (net)	91,280	79,700	11,580	14.5
Merchandise inventory	78,300	68,100	10,200	15.0
Prepaid expenses	9,350	18,200	(8,850)	(48.6)
Total current assets	$ 235,500	$205,100	$ 30,400	14.8
Investments				
Bond sinking fund	$ 42,000	$ 36,000	$ 6,000	16.7
Investments in securities	182,000	181,300	700	.4
Total investments	$ 224,000	$217,300	$ 6,700	3.1
Long-lived assets				
Land	$ 30,000	$ 30,000	$ 0	0
Buildings	330,000	280,000	50,000	17.9
Equipment	670,700	526,300	144,400	27.4
Total	$1,030,700	$836,300	$194,400	23.2
Less accumulated depreciation	427,900	376,200	51,700	13.7
Total	$ 602,800	$460,100	$142,700	31.0
Intangible assets	40,200	44,700	(4,500)	(10.1)
Total long-lived assets	$ 643,000	$504,800	$138,200	27.4
Total assets	$1,102,500	$927,200	$175,300	18.9

Liabilities and Capital

	1984	1983	Amount	Percent
Liabilities				
Current liabilities				
Notes payable	$ 23,000	$ 30,000	($ 7,000)	(23.3)
Accounts payable	42,100	53,200	(11,100)	(20.9)
Taxes payable	12,600	10,700	1,900	17.8
Unearned revenues	38,400	43,700	(5,300)	(12.1)
Total current liabilities	$ 116,100	$137,600	($ 21,500)	(15.6)
Bonds payable 9% due 2000	350,000	200,000	150,000	75.0
Total liabilities	$ 466,100	$337,600	$128,500	38.1
Capital				
6% preferred stock $100 par	$ 50,000	$ 50,000	$ 0	0
Common Stock $ par	100,000	100,000	0	0
Contributed surplus–premium on stocks	300,000	300,000	0	0
Retained earnings	186,400	139,600	46,800	33.5
Total capital	$ 636,400	$589,600	$ 46,800	7.9
Total liabilities and capital	$1,102,500	$927,200	$175,300	18.9

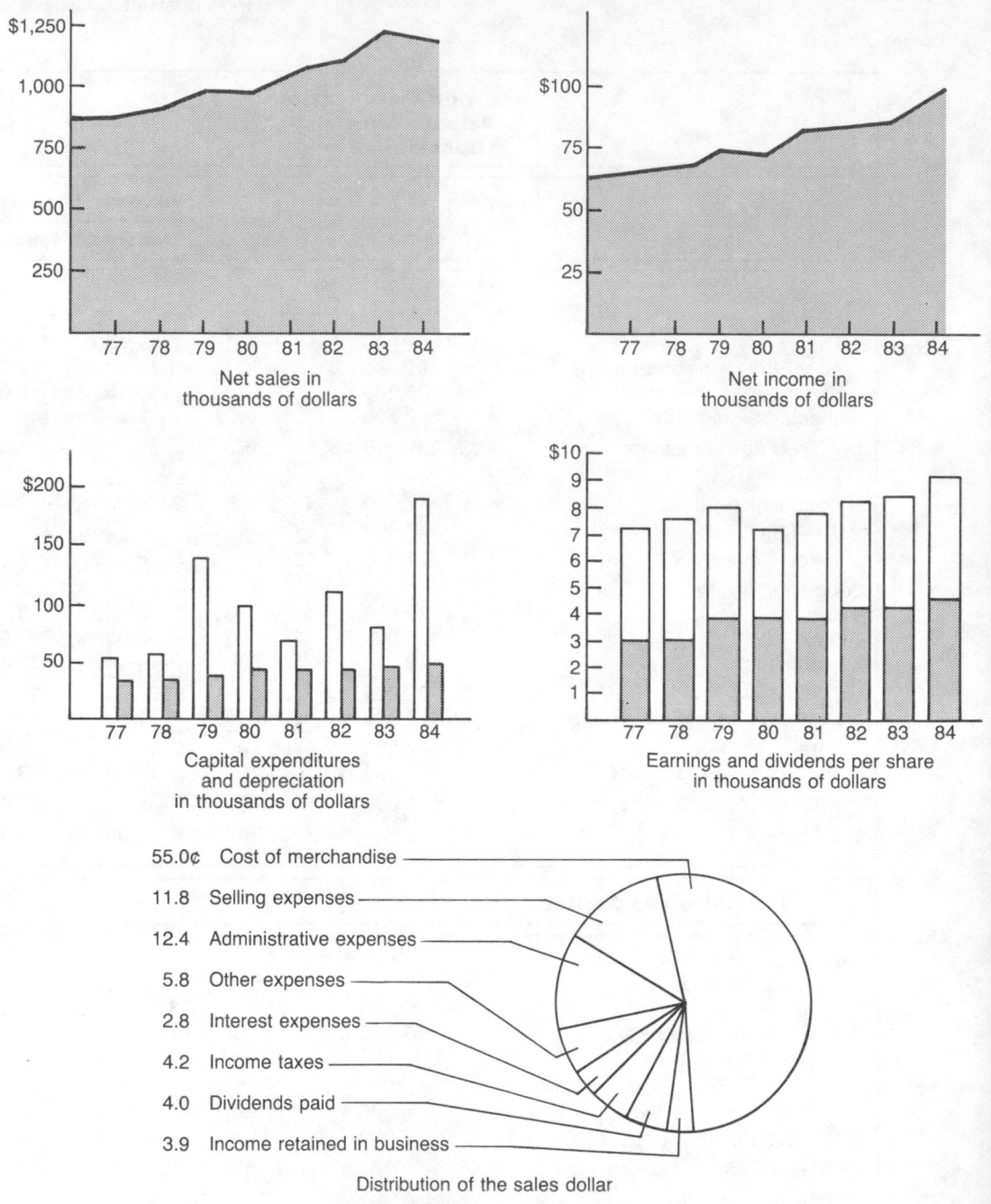

Figure 19-2

Many significant relationships and highlights of important financial data can
be shown graphically in annual reports to supplement financial statements.
The graphs here represent only a small sample of the ways information can
be presented. Capital expenditures and earnings per share are not shaded
in the bar graph; depreciation and dividends are shaded.

Statements can be converted to common units

percentage of sales. The individual percentages may reveal important proportional relationships among income statement items for each year or between the two years' figures. For instance, cost of goods sold as a percentage of sales decreased from 57 to 55 percent. Total expenses increased from 32.2 to 32.8 percent. Net income as a percentage of sales was 7.9 percent in 1984 compared to 7.0 percent in 1983; thus, despite a decrease in net sales, the company earned a higher net income primarily by reducing product expense. The implication is that management is controlling operating and product costs carefully to counteract an adverse sales trend that may be the result of temporary economic conditions.

Balance sheet items are usually expressed as a percentage of total assets, as shown in Figure 19-4 for Dominion Corporation. The component percentages indicate that current assets in 1984 are 21 percent of the total, whereas current liabilities are only 10.5 percent of the total. A comparison of the current asset components in the years 1983 and 1984 shows that the company reduced both receivables and inventories as a percentage of total assets. Although the total amount of investments increased in 1984, total investments are a smaller percentage of total assets in the previous year. The company is relying more heavily on creditors for its financing in 1984 than it did in 1983, and there has been a shift toward more long-term financing, as indicated by an increase in total liabilities as a percentage of total assets and a decrease in current liabilities. Reducing current assets as a percentage of total assets is consistent with the reduction in sales and shows careful management of working capital.

Figure 19-3
Vertical analysis of the income statement. The items in each statement are reduced to a percentage of sales, facilitating comparisons within a statement and between statements.

Dominion Corporation Income Statement For Years Ending December 31				
	1984	**Percent**	**1983**	**Percent**
Sales	$1,210,000	100.0	$1,251,400	100.0
Less cost of goods sold	666,500	55.1	713,800	57.0
Gross margin	$ 543,500	44.9	$ 537,600	43.0
Less expenses				
Selling	$ 142,800	11.8	$ 158,100	12.6
Administrative	150,700	12.4	155,400	12.4
Other expenses	69,900	5.8	67,500	5.4
Total operating expenses	$ 363,400	30.0	$ 381,000	30.4
Interest expense	33,500	2.8	21,800	1.7
Total expenses	$ 396,900	32.8	$ 402,800	32.2
Net income before tax	$ 146,600	12.1	$ 134,800	10.8
Income tax	51,300	4.2	47,200	3.8
Net income after tax	$ 95,300	7.9	$ 87,600	7.0

Dominion Corporation Balance Sheets December 31				
Assets	**1984**	**Percent**	**1983**	**Percent**
Current assets				
Cash	$ 38,570	3.5	$ 33,500	3.6
Temporary investments	18,000	1.6	5,600	.6
Accounts receivable (net)	91,280	8.3	79,700	8.6
Merchandise inventory	78,300	7.1	68,100	7.3
Prepaid expenses	9,350	.8	18,200	2.0
Total current assets	$ 235,500	21.4	$205,100	22.1
Investments				
Bond sinking fund	$ 42,000	3.8	$ 36,000	3.9
Investments in securities	182,000	16.5	181,300	19.5
Total investments	$ 224,000	20.3	$217,300	23.4
Long-lived assets				
Land	$ 30,000	2.7	$ 30,000	3.2
Buildings	330,000	29.9	280,000	30.2
Equipment	670,000	60.8	526,300	56.8
Total	$1,030,700	93.5	$836,300	90.2
Less accumulated depreciation	427,900	38.8	376,200	40.6
Total	$ 602,800	54.7	$460,100	49.6
Intangible assets	40,200	3.6	44,700	4.8
Total long-lived assets	$ 643,000	58.3	$504,800	54.4
Total assets	$1,102,500	100.0	$927,200	100.0

Liabilities and Capital				
Current liabilities				
Notes payable	$ 23,000	2.1	$ 30,000	3.2
Accounts payable	42,100	3.8	53,200	5.7
Taxes payable	12,600	1.1	10,700	1.2
Unearned revenues	38,400	3.5	43,700	4.7
Total current liabilities	$ 116,100	10.5	$137,600	14.8
Bonds payable 9% due 2000	350,000	31.7	200,000	21.6
Total liabilities	$ 466,100	42.3	$337,600	36.4
Capital				
6% preferred stock $100 par	$ 50,000	4.5	$ 50,000	5.4
Common stock $10 par	100,000	9.1	100,000	10.8
Contributed surplus–premium on stocks	300,000	27.2	300,000	32.3
Retained earnings	186,400	16.9	139,600	15.1
Total capital	$ 636,400	57.7	$589,600	63.6
Total liabilities and capital	$1,102,500	100.0	$927,200	100.0

Figure 19-4
Vertical analysis of balance sheets. Each item is reduced to a percentage
of total assets.

A shift to longer-term liabilities will preserve working capital and may improve financial leverage.

Ratio analysis

Different ratios are useful to different users

A ratio is the relationship of one number to another. Many ratios calculated from financial statement data provide users of the statements with important information about the liquidity, solvency, and profitability of the business. Long-term creditors are interested in the solvency of the corporation, while short-term creditors are more interested in liquidity. In either case they are concerned with the company's ability to repay its debts when they mature. On the other hand, shareholders and potential investors are interested primarily in the company's profitability and in the way the company's stock behaves in the stock market. Managers are typically concerned with all aspects of business operations to ensure that the financial statements reflect results that will be viewed favourably by creditors, shareholders, and potential investors. By maintaining adequate liquidity and an appropriate balance between assets, liabilities, and owners' equity, managers attempt to keep the company solvent and profitable over a long period of time. As a history of profitable operations develops, investors tend to view the company favourably, and their views are reflected in the market price of the company's stock.

Ratio analysis can be useful to many types of decision makers, and usually is classified into four general categories. However, a specific ratio may fit into more than one category. The four categories are

Tests of Liquidity
1. Current ratio, or working capital ratio
2. Acid test, or quick ratio
3. Receivables turnover
4. Inventory turnover

Tests of Solvency
5. Times interest earned
6. Debt-equity ratio
7. Debt ratio
8. Equity ratio

Tests of Profitability
9. Return on sales, or profit margin
10. Return on total assets
11. Return on owners' equity
12. Earnings per share

Market Tests
13. Price-earnings ratio
14. Dividend yield
15. Dividend payout

We illustrate many of the more commonly used ratios, but other ratios can be calculated as required for specific situations. The ratios listed on page 849 are discussed in connection with our analysis of Dominion Corporation for the year 1984. A more complete analysis requires the calculation of comparative ratios so that trends can be examined as well as the ratios themselves. Our purpose, however, is not to perform an analysis but to show how each ratio is calculated and used. We round our calculations to one decimal place as more precision is not warranted.

Tests of liquidity

Liquidity refers to the company's ability to meet its current obligations as they mature. The assets that make up working capital are converted into cash, which in turn is used to pay current liabilities.

1. Current ratio. The components of working capital are used to calculate the **current ratio,** which measures the number of times that the current liabilities could be paid with the available current assets. For the Dominion Corporation, the current ratio, or **working capital ratio,** is calculated as

$$\text{Current ratio} = \frac{\text{Current assets}}{\text{Current liabilities}}$$
$$= \frac{\$235,500}{\$116,100} = 2.0 \text{ times}$$

The ratio indicates that there are enough current assets to repay the current liabilities twice. For many types of businesses this is considered to be an adequate current ratio. If the ratio is considerably smaller, such as 1.2, sufficient cash may not be available to pay current liabilities when due. If the ratio is much larger, such as 3.6, the company may have an excessive investment in current assets that do not produce a return. How does the current ratio in 1983 compare with the 1984 ratio calculated above?

2. Acid test ratio. Not all current assets are readily convertible into cash to pay debts. For example, prepaid expenses are not converted to cash but are instead used in operations. Inventories are usually converted to receivables before the receivables can be converted to cash. Therefore some of the current assets are considerably less liquid than others. To test the company's immediate ability to meet its current obligations the **acid test ratio,** or **quick ratio,** is computed as follows:

$$\text{Acid test ratio} = \frac{\text{Liquid assets}}{\text{Current liabilities}}$$
$$= \frac{\$147,850}{\$116,100} = 1.3 \text{ times}$$

The liquid, or quick, assets include cash and other assets that can be converted to cash quickly, such as temporary investments and notes and accounts receivable. In our example merchandise inventory and prepaid expenses are excluded from current assets to arrive at quick assets. Many analysts believe that an acid test ratio of 1 indicates an adequate ability to satisfy current

*Adequate values of
ratios depend on the
company and the
type of industry*

obligations, but one must beware of such general rules since they do not apply to all situations. A more significant evaluation is obtained by comparing the current and acid test ratios. For example, a company whose current and acid test ratios are 2.3 and 1.5, respectively, is much more liquid than one whose ratios are 2.3 and 1.1, but whether the former or the latter represents a more favourable situation depends on many other factors. The industry in which the business operates, or the type of credit terms it grants and receives, may require more or less liquid positions. For instance, a company that grants credit terms of 30 days but is allowed 60 days to pay its accounts payable does not need as high an acid test ratio as one that grants 60-day terms but must pay its own debts within 30 days. The former company collects its accounts faster and can get by with less cash on hand than the latter.

3. Receivables turnover. Another measure of liquidity is receivables turnover, which measures how quickly notes and accounts receivable are converted into cash. **Receivables turnover** is the time required for one complete cycle from the time receivables are recorded, through collection, to the time new receivables are recorded again. The faster the cycle is completed, the more quickly receivables are converted into cash. Receivables result directly from credit sales and their turnover depends in part on the credit terms granted to customers. Ideally, only credit sales should be used to calculate receivables turnover. However, this information often is not available in the financial statements, and net sales must be used instead. For the Dominion Corporation the calculation is

$$\text{Receivables turnover} = \frac{\text{Net sales}}{\text{Average receivables}}$$

$$= \frac{\$1,210,000}{(\$91,280 + \$79,700)/2} = \frac{\$1,210,000}{\$85,490} = 14.2$$

Notice that the average of receivables for the period is used in the calculation rather than the ending balance of receivables. Income statement information covers an entire accounting period, but balance sheet data are for a point in time. When it is to be related to income statement data, balance sheet information should be averaged in order to represent the entire accounting period as well. Therefore, to calculate receivables turnover for 1983 would require the use of 1982 ending balance of accounts receivable, which is not available in Dominion Corporation's statements. The use of the beginning and ending balances to calculate averages may not provide the best average figure. Year-end balances may not be representative of account balances during most of the year due to seasonal variation in business volume. Therefore, when available, the current year's monthly or quarterly data should be used to calculate averages.

4. Inventory turnover. The liquidity of inventories is measured by the number of times that inventory is replaced during the period. **Inventory turnover** may be calculated by dividing average inventory into cost of goods sold.

For the Dominion Corporation inventory turnover is

$$\text{Inventory turnover} = \frac{\text{Cost of goods sold}}{\text{Average inventory}}$$

$$= \frac{\$666,500}{(\$78,300 + \$68,100)/2} = \frac{\$666,500}{\$73,200} = 9.1$$

Each time merchandise is sold a profit is usually realized; therefore a high inventory turnover is generally desirable. However, too high a turnover may mean that sufficient goods are not on hand, and the company may be losing some sales because merchandise may be out of stock. Conversely, a low turnover may mean that merchandise is lying idle, representing unproductive resources.

Whether a particular turnover figure is too high or too low depends on the type of business. Inventory turnover rates vary tremendously by the type of merchandise that businesses sell. If the merchandise is perishable, a higher turnover is required than if the company sells durable goods. Consequently, businesses that sell perishable merchandise usually have lower profit margins on each item. A high turnover compensates for a lower margin on each item, producing a normal profit for the business. On the other hand, a business that sells slow-moving goods must make up for the low turnover by having a higher profit margin on each item sold. For example, a grocer may charge $1.00 for an item that cost $.90, but a jeweler may charge $100 for an item that cost $45. However, the jeweler may have to hold the $100 item for a year before it is sold.

Tests of solvency

An insolvent company cannot pay its bills

Liquidity is a measure of a company's ability to pay its current debts. **Solvency** refers to a company's ability to pay all its debts as they come due, whether such obligations are current or noncurrent. **Tests of solvency** generally focus on the company's ability to satisfy its long-term creditors. In order to be able to service its bond indebtedness, a company must earn sufficient income to pay its interest expense in addition to paying all other expenses. When the bonds payable mature, the company must have the ability to repay the debt from its own funds or from newly borrowed funds. The ability to obtain and to repay long-term debt often depends on the firm's ability to obtain capital from shareholders. Therefore the relationship between shareholders' equity and creditors' equity usually must be evaluated.

5. Times interest earned. If earnings before interest and taxes are divided by interest expense, the result is an indication of how many times the interest has been earned. The company that earns only enough to pay its interest and other expenses, with little or nothing left for net income, is less solvent than the company that can pay all its expenses and have a large net income. Bondholders can assess the company's ability to continue paying interest in the future by calculating the number of times interest is earned in each period. For Dominion Corporation the calculation is

$$\text{Times interest earned} = \frac{\text{Net income before tax} + \text{Interest expense}}{\text{Interest expense}}$$

$$= \frac{\$146,600 + \$33,500}{\$33,500} = 5.4 \text{ times}$$

In the calculation above, interest expense is added back to net income before tax, because the interest paid has also been earned in addition to the remaining income. The before-tax figure is used because it is the maximum that could be paid as interest, since interest is a tax-deductible expense. Net income before tax plus interest expense is frequently abbreviated as **EBIT,** derived from Earnings Before Interest and Taxes. EBIT is used frequently in financial analysis.

6. Debt-equity ratio. The assets of a business are provided by owners and by creditors. The larger the portion provided by owners, the less risk is assumed by creditors. Liabilities expressed as a percentage of owners' equity indicates how much capital is provided by creditors relative to that provided by owners. If this ratio is 1, each group provided an equal amount of capital. As the ratio increases above 1, the amount of risk assumed by creditors increases, since the ratio indicates decreasing solvency. In our example the ratio is

$$\text{Debt-equity ratio} = \frac{\text{Total liabilities}}{\text{Total owners' equity}}$$

$$= \frac{\$466,100}{\$636,400} = .732 \text{ or } 73.2\%$$

For the Dominion Corporation more capital is provided by owners than by creditors. The relative amounts of debt and equity are also measured by the debt ratio or the equity ratio, as indicated below.

7. Debt ratio. Dividing total liabilities by total equities indicates the percentage of total assets provided by creditors. In our example the calculation is

$$\text{Debt ratio} = \frac{\text{Total liabilities}}{\text{Total equities}}$$

$$= \frac{\$466,100}{\$1,102,500} = .423 \text{ or } 42.3\%$$

8. Equity ratio. Subtracting the debt ratio of 42.3 percent from 100 percent yields 57.7 as the percentage of assets provided by owners. The ratio can, of course, be calculated as

$$\text{Equity ratio} = \frac{\text{Total owners' equity}}{\text{Total equities}}$$

$$= \frac{\$636,400}{\$1,102,500} = .577 \text{ or } 57.7\%$$

The relationship between owners' equity and liabilities is an indication of the company's use of financial leverage. The more debt, the more highly levered is the company. Leverage is an indication of the use a company makes of borrowed funds to increase the return on owners' equity. If the borrowed money can be invested to return a yield higher than the interest rate paid on the borrowed money, the difference increases the profit for the owners. However, interest expense must be paid whether or not the company earns a profit, and with large amounts of debt the company runs a greater risk of not having enough income to service the debt.

Tests of profitability

The goal of business is to earn a profit, without which it is impossible to attract investment capital from owners or creditors. The long-range survival of a business depends on its ability to earn enough revenue to satisfy all obligations and still provide a return on the owners' investment. Several **tests of profitability** are available to measure whether the amount of income is adequate.

The basic calculation of return expresses the amount of income earned as a percentage of the amount of investment used to earn that income. Return is therefore calculated as a percentage rate as follows:

$$\text{Rate of return} = \frac{\text{Income earned on investment}}{\text{Amount of investment required}}$$

A complete analysis of financial statements involves the calculation of several rates of return, with different definitions of income and investment.

9. Return on sales. The amount of net income provided by the average dollar of sales revenue is called the **return on sales** or the **profit margin.** Return on sales is calculated as a percentage of net sales as follows:

$$\text{Return on sales} = \frac{\text{Net Income}}{\text{Net sales}}$$
$$= \frac{\$95,300}{\$1,210,000} = .079 \text{ or } 7.9\%$$

From each dollar of sales $.079 or about 8 cents was available for profit. Whether this profit margin is considered adequate depends on the type of business the company operates, and on the amount of assets invested in the business. If the assets turn over rapidly, the return on sales is usually lower than for businesses with slow turnovers. A business that holds slow-moving assets assumes more risk that those assets will become obsolete, more costly to replace, or less productive. The results obtained from assets with a high turnover are easier to predict, and holding such assets involves less risk. To compensate for high risk businesses must earn higher returns.

High profit margins compensate for high risk

10. Return on total assets. Income is earned by using assets productively. The more efficiently assets are used, the more profitable the business. Assets perform their function whether they are obtained from borrowed money or from owners, therefore the return on assets should be calculated before deducting interest expense. If interest is not deducted income taxes should not be deducted either, since taxes are calculated on income after interest deductions. Consequently, EBIT is usually used to measure the return on assets.

$$\text{Return on total assets} = \frac{\text{Earnings before interest and taxes (EBIT)}}{\text{Average total assets}}$$

$$= \frac{\$180,100}{(\$1,102,500 + \$927,200)/2} = \frac{\$180,100}{\$1,014,850}$$

$$= .177 \text{ or } 17.7\%$$

The above result indicates that, on the average, every dollar of assets earned 17.7 cents of income, from which interest and taxes must be paid. When interest and tax data are not available because condensed statements are presented, the analyst has no choice but to calculate return on total assets by using net income instead of EBIT.

11. Return on owners' equity. The amount earned on the owners' investment is often called **return on owners' equity** or **return on investment.** Return on owners' equity is considered an important indication of the company's profitability because it indicates how well the company is doing with the investment contributed by its owners. For Dominion Corporation return on owners' equity is calculated as follows:

$$\text{Return on owners' equity} = \frac{\text{Net income}}{\text{Average owners' equity}}$$

$$= \frac{\$95,300}{(\$636,400 + \$589,600)/2} = \frac{\$95,300}{\$613,000}$$

$$= .155 \text{ or } 15.5\%$$

Net income is not shared equally by common and preferred shareholders. The return to preferred shareholders is limited to their preferred dividend. All remaining income belongs to the common shareholders, whether or not it is paid to them in the form of dividends. For the common shareholder, therefore, return on investment should be calculated separately as:

$$\text{Return on common equity} = \frac{\text{Net income} - \text{Preferred dividend requirement}}{\text{Average common equity}}$$

$$= \frac{\$95,300 - \$3,000}{(\$586,400 + \$539,600)/2}$$

$$= \frac{\$92,300}{\$563,000} = .164 \text{ or } 16.4\%$$

12. Earnings per share (EPS). EPS is considered one of the most important indicators of profitability because it can easily be compared to previous EPS figures and to those of other companies, and investors find it convenient to see the amount earned for a single share of stock. To interpret this ratio properly requires a good understanding of how basic and fully diluted earnings per share are calculated, concepts that are beyond the scope of this book. Since Dominion Corporation does not have a complex capital structure, the calculation of earnings per share is simple:

$$\text{Earnings per share} = \frac{\text{Net income} - \text{Preferred dividend}}{\text{Weighted average number of common shares}}$$

$$= \frac{\$95,300 - \$3,000}{10\ 000 \text{ shares}} = \frac{\$92,300}{10\ 000 \text{ shares}} = \$9.23$$

As with all ratios, the absolute value of EPS for the year is not as significant as the change from the previous years. Therefore, financial analysis should include calculations of ratios for comparative statements.

Market tests   Investors and shareholders are usually interested in the market price of a company's common stock and in the ratios that describe the stock's market performance. Since an investor has to pay the market price for a share of stock, most market tests are based on the current price of the stock. Dominion Corporation's common stock sells in the market at $70 per share.

13. Price-earnings ratio (P/E). The price of a stock alone does not indicate whether the stock is cheap or expensive. A $60 stock may be a better buy then a $25 stock. To indicate value, the price should be related to the amount of income the company earns. The price-earnings ratio (P/E) reduces the stock to a common unit of measure for comparison with other stocks. It indicates how many dollars are required to buy one dollar's worth of earnings. In our example the calculation is

The P/E ratio facilitates comparisons between different-priced stocks.

$$\text{Price-earnings ratio (P/E)} = \frac{\text{Price per share}}{\text{Earnings per share}}$$
$$= \frac{\$70}{\$9.23} = 7.58$$

This calculation indicates that it costs $7.58 to buy $1 of Dominion Corporation's annual earnings. Typically companies whose earnings exhibit a rapid rate of growth have higher P/E ratios than those whose earnings are stable. Investors are willing to pay more for current earnings if they anticipate that future earnings will be higher. There is a very wide range of P/E ratios in the stock market. The average in the past few years has been between 6 and 12, but P/E ratios of over 100 can occasionally be found.

14. Dividend yield. Investors often buy common stock in order to earn dividend income. The dividend yield is one measure of a rate of return on the investor's stock investment and is calculated as

$$\text{Dividend yield} = \frac{\text{Dividend per share}}{\text{Price per share}}$$
$$= \frac{\$4.55}{\$70} = .065 \text{ or } 6.5\%$$

If the company has a policy of paying regular dividends, the investor can expect a yield of 6.5 percent on an investment in the common stock of Dominion Corporation. There is, of course, no guarantee that the company will continue to pay dividends. Many companies, however, try to maintain a stable dividend and to increase the dividend when possible, so that investors can depend on receiving a steady income from their shareholdings. Some companies, on the other hand, pay little or no dividends, since they attempt to grow by retaining and investing their earnings. Investors buy the stocks of such companies for their growth rather than for their dividend yield. Dominion Corporation's dividend history illustrated in Figure 19-2 indicates that current dividend rates will probably continue into the future.

15. Dividend payout. The portion of net income not paid to shareholders in the form of dividends is retained by the company for the purpose of financing growth and expansion. Retained earnings do not provide a direct yield to the shareholder, but the shareholder can benefit from this portion of the company's income through growth in the market value of stock caused by the growth in retained earnings. The dividend payout is the percentage of net income distributed by the company and provides an indication of the proportion of net income retained by the business.

$$\text{Dividend payout} = \frac{\text{Total dividends}}{\text{Net income}}$$

$$= \frac{\$48,500}{\$95,300} = .51 \text{ or } 51\%$$

Slightly more than half the income was distributed as dividends. The dividend payout can also be viewed from the point of view of common shareholders by relating common dividends to net income less preferred dividends. The calculation can be made on the basis of total dividends and income, or on a per-share basis as follows:

$$\text{Dividend payout} = \frac{\text{Common dividend per share}}{\text{Earnings per share}}$$

$$= \frac{\$4.55}{\$9.23} = .49 \text{ or } 49\%$$

With approximately half its income retained by Dominion Corporation, the company is providing for its future growth and increased earnings. Such increases in earnings should be reflected in the price of common stock.

All the ratios discussed above are summarized in Figure 19-5, which indicates how the ratios are calculated and what their interpretation means.

Interpretation and use of financial ratios

The ratios presented in this chapter represent some of the more common ones used by decision makers to assess the performance and future potential of a business. Other ratios can be calculated, and some of the ones presented may be calculated differently from the ways shown here. Sometimes it is necessary to calculate only a small number of ratios in order to arrive at a decision about a business. More important than calculating the ratios is interpreting them. Evaluating ratios allows the analyst to determine whether specific areas of the business warrant further investigation. An adequate financial analysis involves more than an understanding and interpretation of each of the individual ratios. An insight into the meaning of the interrelationships among the ratios and financial data in the statements is also needed. To gain such an insight and understanding requires considerable experience in the analysis and interpretation of financial statements. Moreover, even experienced analysts cannot apply their skill equally well to all financial statements. Every industry has its

Name of Ratio	Method of Calculation	Interpretation
Tests of Liquidity		
Current ratio	$$\frac{\text{Current assets}}{\text{Current liabilities}}$$	Ability to pay current debts from current assets
Acid test (quick) ratio	$$\frac{\text{Liquid assets}}{\text{Current liabilities}}$$	Immediate ability to pay current debts from liquid assets
Receivables turnover	$$\frac{\text{Net sales}}{\text{Average receivables}}$$	Ability to convert receivables to cash measured by the number of collection cycles
Inventory turnover	$$\frac{\text{Cost of goods sold}}{\text{Average inventory}}$$	Ability to sell inventories measured by the number of purchase and sales cycles
Tests of Solvency		
Times interest earned	$$\frac{\text{Earnings before interest and tax (EBIT)}}{\text{Interest expense}}$$	Ability to service long-term debt
Debt-equity ratio	$$\frac{\text{Total liabilities}}{\text{Total owners' equity}}$$	Proportion of assets provided by creditors compared to that provided by owners
Debt ratio	$$\frac{\text{Total liabilities}}{\text{Total equities}}$$	Proportion of total assets provided by creditors
Equity ratio	$$\frac{\text{Total owners' equity}}{\text{Total equities}}$$	Proportion of total assets provided by owners
Tests of Profitability		
Return on sales	$$\frac{\text{Net income}}{\text{Net sales}}$$	Profit margin earned on each dollar of sales
Return on total assets	$$\frac{\text{Earnings before interest and taxes (EBIT)}}{\text{Average total assets}}$$	Efficiency with which managers use total assets to operate the business
Return on owners' equity	$$\frac{\text{Net income}}{\text{Average owners' equity}}$$	Rate of return earned by owners on their investment
Earnings per share (EPS)	$$\frac{\text{Net income} - \text{preferred dividend}}{\text{Weighted average no. of common shares}}$$	Amount of net income earned by each common share
Market tests		
Price-earnings (P/E)	$$\frac{\text{Price per share}}{\text{Earnings per share}}$$	Number of dollars required to buy \$1 of earnings
Dividend yield	$$\frac{\text{Dividend per share}}{\text{Price per share}}$$	Return to owner on the investment required to buy one share of stock
Dividend payout	$$\frac{\text{Total dividends}}{\text{Net income}} \quad \text{or} \quad \frac{\text{Dividends per share}}{\text{Earnings per share}}$$	Proportion of earnings distributed as dividends

Figure 19-5
Summary of financial ratios discussed in the chapter.

own characteristics with which analysts must be familiar, and it is not possible for any one individual to understand all industries equally well. Several financial services compile data and provide information about Canadian and American industries and business corporations. *Financial Post Corporation Service; Blue Book of CBS Stock Reports;* Canadian Business Service, *Investment Reporter;* Moody's Investor Service's *News Reports* and *Manuals* on Banks and Finance, Industrial, Municipal and Government Public Utility, and Transportation; Standard and Poor's *Corporation Records;* and Arnold Bernhard's *Value Line Investment Survey* are publications that provide large amounts of financial data, ratios, and financial analyses to help decision makers evaluate businesses. Dun & Bradstreet, Inc., compiles lists of ratios that represent averages for many industries. While published industry averages, ratios, and financial analyses can be helpful, the individual analyst must still rely on skill, insight, and even intuition, in order to interpret the financial statements of a corporation and arrive at a decision. Often a comparison of historical ratios for a single company can indicate important trends and can be more useful than published averages that obscure significant variations among companies.

Financial analysts have been instrumental in bringing about changes in the way accounting data are reported. For example, the statement of changes in financial position was not a part of the annual report of corporations until financial analysts began to demand that it be provided. More recently, financial analysts have been requesting that corporations publish forecasts and pro-

Financial forecasts may be included in future annual reports

jections of future operations. Such **pro forma** financial statements are available only to management, and companies have been reluctant to provide them to external users. Managers prepare pro forma statements by adjusting the data in the current period's financial statements to reflect expected changes. For example, if sales are $100,000 currently and management expects a 15 percent increase in sales, the pro forma income statement shows sales of $115,000. Other figures are similarly obtained from estimates, projections, and educated guesses. Pro forma statements can obviously prove to be quite different from actual results. The accounting profession is concerned about the way that such statements should be verified and certified. There is a danger that forecasts could be viewed as actual expectations by external users who may feel misled if the forecasted performance is not achieved. Nevertheless, in the future we may see annual reports containing pro forma financial statements in addition to historical data.

Summary

Analysis of financial statements requires a thorough understanding of the principles that govern the measurement and reporting of financial data, and of alternative accounting methods that may be selected by management to present historical information. An adequate analysis requires the comparison of at least two accounting periods, and preferably more, in order to perceive trends in the figures presented. A complete financial analysis may involve horizontal analysis, vertical analysis, and ratio analysis.

Horizontal analysis involves the calculation of differences between account balances in the statements of two accounting periods. Such differences may be computed in absolute and in percentage amounts and, if calculated for several accounting periods, can indicate significant trends in the figures. **Vertical analysis** involves the comparison of figures within a financial statement of one period. To facilitate such comparisons, the figures are expressed in common terms by converting them to a percentage of a significant value. In the income statement all amounts are usually converted to a percentage of sales. In the balance sheet they are usually converted to a percentage of total assets. **Ratio analysis** involves the calculation of the relationship between two figures that can come from the same statement or from two different statements. Ratios may be classified into tests of **liquidity, solvency, profitability,** and **market tests.** The most common of these ratios are summarized in Figure 19-5.

The interpretation of financial statements requires skills and insight that can only be achieved through experience. Published ratios and analyses may be helpful, but they form only a part of the input that is needed to assess the past performance and future potential of a business.

List of important terms

financial analysis   *(841)*
horizontal analysis   *(842)*
market tests   *(856)*
pro forma   *(859)*
ratio analysis   *(849)*

tests of liquidity   *(850)*
tests of profitability   *(854)*
tests of solvency   *(852)*
vertical analysis   *(843)*

Questions

1. Discuss what is meant by external and internal decision makers.
2. Discuss the main purposes of analyzing financial statements.
3. What are some of the reasons for presenting comparative financial statements in annual reports?
4. Explain the main difference between horizontal and vertical analysis of financial statements.
5. Describe what is meant by ratio analysis of financial statements. What kind of tests can be performed with ratio analysis?
6. What advantage is offered by presenting financial statements of the past five to ten years compared to presenting financial statements for only the current and previous year?
7. Discuss the concepts of financial leverage. What advantage can be derived by owners from financial leverage? What are the risks involved?
8. Stock A trades in the market at $60 per share. Stock B trades in the market at $20 per share. The price-earnings ratio of A is 9 and the price-earnings ratio of B is 12. While talking to her stockbroker, Miss Smith said, "I can't afford Stock A. It's too expensive. Buy 100 shares of Stock B." Discuss Miss Smith's statement.
9. The president's letter to shareholders in the annual report of a corporation stated, "Return on sales this year increased to 9 percent from 8 percent last

year. The company's net income was $98,000 this year down from $112,000 last year." Did sales increase or decrease since last year?

10. The current ratio of a company is 1.6 and working capital is $30,000. The company uses $8,000 of cash to repay a short-term note payable. Will the current ratio increase or decrease?

Exercises

Ex. 19-1 **Measures of liquidity.** Samar Company's current ratio is 2 and its quick ratio is 1.2. Listed below are several independent events or transactions, some of which affect the company's liquidity. Indicate how each transaction would affect the ratios given in the table. Use a + to show an increase, a − for a decrease, and a 0 if the ratio is not affected or if the effect cannot be determined.

Transaction	Current Ratio	Quick Ratio	Inventory Turnover	Receivables Turnover
a. Purchased merchandise on open account.				
b. Declared a cash dividend payable.				
c. Changed from terms of n/60 to 3/10 n/30 on accounts receivable.				
d. Purchased equipment on open account.				
e. Reduced selling price of merchandise and advertised special sale thereby increasing volume of sales.				
f. Paid account payable.				
g. Sold merchandise for cash.				
h. Changed from FIFO to LIFO inventory method because prices are rising.				
i. Wrote off uncollectible account against allowance for bad debts.				
j. Collected account receivable.				
k. Paid dividend previously declared.				
l. Issued stock in exchange for land.				
m. Sold temporary investment at a profit.				
n. Added new line of durable goods to present line of perishable goods.				

Ex. 19-2 **Measures of solvency and profitability.** Below is a list of independent transactions or events each followed by some measures of solvency or profitability. Indicate what effect each transaction would have on the ratio. Use a + or − to show an increase or decrease, and a 0 to show no change or that the change cannot be determined.

a. Issued capital stock for cash
   1. Debt-equity ratio
   2. Return on sales
   3. Debt ratio
b. Declared and paid cash dividend
   1. Equity ratio
   2. Return on owners' equity
   3. Debt-equity ratio
c. Notified by city of decrease in property taxes
   1. Return on sales
   2. Return on total assets
   3. Return on owners' equity
d. Bondholders converted bonds into common stock
   1. Equity ratio
   2. Return on total assets
   3. Debt-equity ratio
e. Inventory turnover increased with no change in costs or selling prices
   1. Return on sales
   2. Return on total assets
   3. Times interest earned
f. Operating income increased 15 percent; interest expensed increased 5 percent
   1. Return on owners' equity
   2. Times interest earned
   3. Return on total assets

Ex. 19-3 **Effects on market measures.** Below is a list of independent transactions or events, some of which affect market ratios of Zebo Company. Indicate the probable effect each transaction or event would have on the ratios in the table. Use a + or − to show an increase or decrease, and a 0 to show no change or that the change cannot be determined.

Transaction	Book Value per Share	EPS	P/E	Dividend Yield
a. Declared regular quarterly cash dividend.				
b. Issued common stock for cash at market price, which is double the book value.				
c. Effected a 2-for-1 stock split.				
d. Won large court award in patent infringement suit.				
e. Declared and issued 5 percent stock dividend.				
f. Acquired profitable subsidiary in a pooling of interests. Prior to acquisition, P/E ratio was 20 for Zebo stock and 6 for subsidiary stock.				

Transaction	Book Value per Share	EPS	P/E	Dividend Yield
g. Board of directors declared an increased dividend, payable next month.				
h. Return on assets is 12 percent. Issued 8 percent bonds at a discount.				
i. Net income increased but the market price of the stock remained unchanged.				
j. Earnings increased 20 percent; dividend payout remained unchanged.				
k. Sales decreased and return on sales is unchanged. Market price of stock remains the same.				

Ex. 19-4   Profitability and solvency. Lancer Company has total assets of $300,000 and owners' equity of $120,000. Net income after interest and before tax is $20,000, and interest expense is $8,000. The company is subject to a tax rate of 40 percent.

Required:
Calculate the following ratios
a. Times interest earned
b. Return on assets
c. Return on equity

Ex. 19-5   Turnover ratios. Below are related financial data of Billmore Company.

Sales	$385,000
Cost of goods sold	170,000
Gross margin	215,000
Average inventory	21,250
Average receivables	27,500

Required:
Calculate the following ratios:
a. Inventory turnover
b. Receivables turnover

Ex. 19-6   Horizontal analysis. Following are comparative financial statements of Walsch Corporation in condensed form.

Walsch Corporation
Statement of Income and Retained Earnings
For the Years Ending December 31

	1984	1983
Sales	$225,000	$210,000
Less cost of goods sold	130,000	128,000
Gross margin	$ 95,000	$ 82,000
Operating expenses	(59,800)	(54,800)
Interest expense	(5,200)	(5,200)
Income before taxes	$ 30,000	$ 22,000
Income taxes	9,000	6,400
Net income after tax	$ 21,000	$ 15,600
Add beginning retained earnings	16,000	8,000
	$ 37,000	$ 23,600
Less dividends	17,000	7,600
Retained earnings ending balance	$ 20,000	$ 16,000

Walsch Corporation
Balance Sheets
December 31

	1984	1983
Cash	$ 12,000	$ 16,000
Accounts receivable (net)	19,000	23,000
Inventories	46,000	43,000
Fixed assets (net)	80,000	70,000
Total assets	$157,000	$152,000
Current liabilities	$ 25,000	$ 24,000
Bonds payable, 10 percent	52,000	52,000
Common stock, 6000 shares	60,000	60,000
Retained earnings	20,000	16,000
Total equities	$157,000	$152,000
Year-end market price of stock	$31.50	$25

Required:
Perform a horizontal analysis of Walsch Corporation's financial statement by completing two additional columns, one for the amount of increase or decrease for 1984 over 1983, and the other for the percentage increase or decrease.

Ex. 19-7   Vertical analysis. Refer to the financial statements of Walsch Corporation in Exercise 19-6. Perform a vertical analysis on these statements by converting the statements to common units. Convert the income and retained earnings statement to components expressed as percentages of sales. Convert the balance sheet to components expressed as percentages of total assets.

Ex. 19-8 **Ratio analysis.** Refer to the financial statements of Walsch Corporation in Exercise 19-6. Perform a ratio analysis for Walsch Corporation for 1984 by calculating each of the ratios discussed in this chapter.

Ex. 19-9 **Horizontal analysis.** Following are comparative financial statements of Adrian Company in condensed form.

Adrian Company Statement of Income and Retained Earnings For the Year Ending December 31		
	1984	**1983**
Sales	$400,000	$390,000
Less cost of goods sold	245,000	220,000
Gross margin	$155,000	$170,000
Operating expenses	(104,000)	(105,000)
Interest expense	(10,000)	(9,000)
Income before taxes	$ 41,000	$ 56,000
Income taxes	12,000	17,000
Net income after tax	$ 29,000	$ 39,000
Add beginning retained earnings	40,000	19,000
	$ 69,000	$ 58,000
Less dividends	19,000	18,000
Retained earnings ending balance	$ 50,000	$ 40,000

Adrian Company Balance Sheets December 31		
	1984	**1983**
Cash	$ 30,000	$ 21,000
Accounts receivable (net)	44,000	33,000
Inventories	82,000	76,000
Fixed assets (net)	140,000	150,000
Total assets	$296,000	$280,000
Current liabilities	$ 46,000	$ 50,000
Bonds payable, 10 percent	100,000	90,000
Common stock $10 par	100,000	100,000
Retained earnings	50,000	40,000
Total equities	$296,000	$280,000
Year-end market price of stock	$25	$35

Required:

Perform a horizontal analysis of Adrian Company's financial statement by completing two additional columns, one for the amount of increase or decrease for 1984 over 1983 and the other for the percentage increase or decrease.

Ex. 19-10 **Vertical analysis.** Refer to the financial statements of Adrian Company in Exercise 19-9. Perform a vertical analysis on these statements by converting the statements to common units. Convert the income and retained earnings statement to components expressed as percentages of sales. Convert the balance sheet to components expressed as percentages of total assets.

Ex. 19-11 **Ratio analysis.** Refer to the financial statements of Adrian Company in Exercise 19-9. Perform a ratio analysis for Adrian Company for 1984 by calculating each of the ratios discussed in this chapter.

Problem Set A

P. 19A-1 **Horizontal analysis.** Below are condensed financial statements of Carter Company for the years ending December 31, 1983, 1984, and 1985.

Income Statement	1985	1984	1983
Sales	$40,000	$40,000	$42,000
Cost of goods sold	15,000	17,000	18,000
Gross margin	$25,000	$23,000	$24,000
Expenses	20,000	19,000	20,000
Net income	$ 5,000	$ 4,000	$ 4,000
Balance Sheet			
Current assets	$14,850	$12,600	$ 8,000
Investments	9,000	7,500	10,800
Fixed assets (net)	26,150	24,900	23,200
Total	$50,000	$45,000	$42,000
Current liabilities	$ 6,750	$ 7,000	$ 5,000
Long-term debt	12,000	10,000	11,000
Common stock $5 par	25,000	25,000	25,000
Retained earnings	6,250	3,000	1,000
Total	$50,000	$45,000	$42,000

Required:

a. Perform a horizontal analysis on the statements.

b. Discuss any trends that appear to be significant.

c. Discuss any significant improvements you perceive in operations or financial position over the years presented.

P. 19A-2   **Vertical analysis.** Refer to the financial statements of Carter Company in Problem 19A-1.

Required:
a. Perform a vertical analysis for each of the three years.
b. Discuss any significant changes you perceive in the statements over the years presented.
c. What seems to be the primary reason for the increase in net income?

P. 19A-3   **Ratio analysis.** Refer to the financial statements of Carter Company in Problem 19A-1.

Required:
a. Calculate the following financial ratios for the two most recent years:
   1. Debt-equity ratio
   2. Debt ratio
   3. Equity ratio
   4. Return on sales
   5. Return on assets
   6. Return on equity
b. Discuss any significant trend you perceive in the rates of return.
c. Do the solvency measures indicate any significant trends? Discuss.

P. 19A-4   **Market tests.** Refer to the financial statements of Carter Company in Problem 19A-1. The company paid cash dividends in 1985 and 1984 but not in 1983. The year-end market price per share of the company's stock was $6.50 in 1983, $7.25 in 1984, and $10.75 in 1985.

Required:
a. Calculate the amount of dividends paid by the company in 1984 and 1985.
b. Calculate the following ratios for each of the three years:
   1. Current ratio
   2. Earnings per share
   3. Price-earnings ratio
   4. Dividend payout
   5. Dividend yield
c. Explain any significant trends you perceive in the ratios you calculated.

P. 19A-5   **Complete financial analysis.** Shown below are the comparative balance sheets of the W. Kelso Company, Inc., and its income statement for 1984.

W. Kelso Company, Inc.
Balance Sheet
December 31

Assets	1984	1983
Cash	$ 11,500	$ 10,000
Investments	7,500	8,000
Accounts receivable	9,500	11,000
Merchandise	45,000	42,000
Prepaid expenses	1,500	2,000
Fixed assets	120,000	100,000
Accumulated depreciation	(40,000)	(35,000)
	$155,000	$138,000
Equities		
Accounts payable	$ 28,500	$ 27,500
Accrued expenses	11,500	12,000
Long-term debt	20,000	30,000
Common stock	60,000	60,000
Retained earnings	35,000	8,500
	$155,000	$138,000

W. Kelso Company, Inc.
Income Statement
For the Year Ending December 31, 1984

Sales	$200,000
Cost of goods sold	95,000
Gross margin	$105,000
Expenses	78,500
Net income	$ 26,500

Required:
a. Perform a horizontal analysis of the balance sheets.
b. Perform a vertical analysis of the statements for 1984.
c. Calculate the following ratios for 1984:
   1. Current ratio
   2. Acid test ratio
   3. Inventory turnover
   4. Receivables turnover
   5. Return on sales
   6. Return on total assets
   7. Return on owners' equity
   8. Debt-equity ratio
   9. Gross margin percentage

P. 19A-6 **Reconstruction of balance sheet.** Below is the December 31, 1983 balance sheet of Delindi Company and its statement of changes in financial position for the year ending December 31, 1984.

Delindi Company
Balance Sheet
December 31, 1983

Assets		Equities	
Cash	$ 225	Accounts payable	$ 1,030
Accounts receivable	650	Bonds payable, due 1990	3,500
Merchandise	1,185	Preferred stock	1,250
Land	4,900	Common stock	3,000
Equipment	4,500	Retained earnings	2,780
Accumulated depreciation	(1,000)		
Patents	1,100		
Total	$11,560	Total	$11,560

Delindi Company
Statement of Changes in Financial Position
For the Year Ending December 31, 1984

Sources		Uses	
From operations			
Net income	$ 600	Payment of dividends	$ 180
Depreciation	200	Retirement of preferred stock	1,250
Amortization	100	Retirement of bonds	700
Gain on sale of land	(40)	Purchase of equipment	1,500
Total	$ 860	Increase working capital	170
Issuance of common stock	2,000		
Sale of land	940		
Total sources	$ 3,800	Total uses	$ 3,800

Delindi Company had the following financial ratios at the end of 1983 and 1984:

	1984	1983
Current ratio	2.20	2.00
Acid test ratio	.80	.85
Return on ending total assets	.05	.05
Return on sales	.03	.04
Turnover of average receivables	32.00	22.23
Dividend payout	.30	.31

Required:
Prepare the December 31, 1984 balance sheet for Delindi Company without adding any new accounts.

P. 19A-7   **Analysis of pro forma statements.** Below are the financial statements of Alexander Corporation. The company was established six years ago and management has decided, based on market studies and demand for the company's products, that it is time for a major expansion. To accomplish the expansion, the company needs a $60,000 infusion of capital. Two alternatives are considered by management: The company can issue additional common stock for $60,000, or it can obtain the same amount by issuing new 9 percent bonds. The funds are to be used to buy new equipment for $40,000 and to increase working capital. The company pays no dividends and is subject to a 40 percent income tax rate. The stock or bonds are to be issued in early December 1983.

Alexander Corporation
Balance Sheet
November 30, 1983

Assets		Equities	
Current assets	$ 25,000	Current liabilities	$ 14,000
Fixed assets	115,000	Note payable 8% due 1988	30,000
Accumulated depreciation	(40,000)	Common stock $10 par	40,000
		Retained earnings	16,000
Total assets	$100,000	Total equities	$100,000

Alexander Corporation
Income Statement
For the Year Ending November 30, 1983

Sales	$112,500
Selling and administrative expenses	$ 88,800
Depreciation expense	5,500
Interest expense	3,200
Total expenses	$ 97,500
Net income before tax	$ 15,000
Income tax	6,000
Net income	$ 9,000

The following projections are made for the next year of operations:

a. The old equipment includes a machine that cost $5,000 and is fully depreciated. This will be disposed of with no salvage value. The remaining equipment is depreciated at an annual rate of 5 percent.

b. The new equipment will be depreciated at 10 percent per year with no salvage value. The equipment will be acquired in December 1983.

c. Sales are expected to increase by 40 percent and selling and administrative expenses by 30 percent over the current year.
d. Interest expense will remain the same if the stock is issued. If the bonds are issued, interest expense will increase.
e. Current liabilities are expected to increase by $20,000 by November 30, 1984.

Required:
a. Prepare pro forma financial statements for the year ending November 30, 1984 for each alternative method of financing the expanded operations.
b. Perform as complete a ratio analysis as possible on the 1983 statements and on the pro forma statements.
c. Recommend which alternative you prefer. Support your recommendation by the findings in your analysis.

Problem Set B

P. 19B-1 **Horizontal analysis.** The condensed financial statements of Kloverton Company are presented below for three years ending January 31.

Income Statement	1985	1984	1983
Sales	$ 57,000	$ 62,000	$ 60,000
Cost of goods sold	28,000	30,000	27,000
Gross margin	$ 29,000	$ 32,000	$ 33,000
Expenses	11,000	12,500	13,000
Net income	$ 18,000	$ 19,500	$ 20,000
Balance Sheet			
Current assets	$ 46,000	$ 40,000	$ 32,000
Fixed assets (net)	56,000	50,000	48,000
Intangibles	18,000	19,000	20,000
Total	$120,000	$109,000	$100,000
Current liabilities	$ 28,000	$ 23,000	$ 17,000
Notes payable, due 2001	40,000	40,000	40,000
Capital, Klover	27,000	24,500	22.000
Capital, Overton	25,000	21,500	21,000
Total	$120,000	$109,000	$100,000

Required:
a. Perform a horizontal analysis on the statements.
b. Discuss any trends that appear to be significant and any significant changes in operations or financial position over the years for which data are presented.

P. 19B-2   Vertical analysis. Refer to the financial statements of Kloverton Company in Problem 19B-1.

Required:
a. Perform a vertical analysis for each of the three years.
b. Discuss any significant changes you perceive in the statements over the years presented.
c. What seems to be the primary reason for the decline in net income?

P. 19B-3   Ratio analysis. Refer to the financial statements of Kloverton Company in Problem 19B-1.

Required:
a. Calculate the following financial ratios for each of the two latest years:
   1. Debt-equity ratio
   2. Debt ratio
   3. Equity ratio
   4. Return on sales
   5. Return on total assets
   6. Return on owners' equity
   7. Book value of the company
   8. Current ratio
b. Discuss any significant trends you perceive in the ratios.
c. State whether the book value is increasing faster or slower than net income.

P. 19B-4   Measuring liquidity. The current portions of the balance sheets of Babich Tool Corporation and Cleever Cutlery, Inc., are shown below.

Current Assets	Babich	Cleever
Cash	$ 870	$ 790
Temporary investments	1,000	520
Notes receivable	490	390
Accounts receivable	1,380	1,150
Merchandise inventory	780	2,140
Prepaid expenses	250	950
Total current assets	$4,770	$5,940
Current Liabilities		
Notes payable	$ 580	$ 470
Taxes payable	300	320
Accounts payable	930	1,360
Salaries payable	840	970
Total current liabilities	$2,650	$3,120

Required:

a. Calculate the current ratio and the amount of working capital for each company.

b. Compare the current ratios and working capital for the two companies and discuss each company's ability to meet current obligations.

c. Calculate the acid test ratio for each company.

d. Discuss each company's liquidity in terms of the acid test ratio.

e. What additional information did you gain by calculating the acid test ratio?

P. 19B-5 **Complete financial analysis.** The comparative balance sheets of K. Weinbaum Company and its income statement for 1984 are presented below.

K. Weinbaum Company
Balance Sheet
October 31

	1984	1983
Cash	$ 2,500	$ 11,500
Accounts receivable	9,500	9,500
Merchandise	36,000	52,500
Prepaid expenses	1,000	2,500
Fixed assets	90,000	100,000
Accumulated depreciation	(32,000)	(35,000)
	$107,000	$141,000
Accounts payable	$ 20,000	$ 37,000
Accrued expenses	15,000	19,000
Note payable due 1983	55,000	55,000
Capital, K. W.	17,000	30,000
	$107,000	$141,000

K. Weinbaum Company
Income Statement
For the Year Ending October 31, 1984

Sales	$500,000
Cost of goods sold	367,000
Gross margin	$133,000
Expenses	136,000
Net loss	($ 3,000)

Required:

a. Perform a horizontal analysis on the balance sheets.

b. Perform a vertical analysis on the statements for 1984.

c. Calculate the following ratios for 1984:

    1. Current ratio

    2. Acid test ratio

    3. Inventory turnover

    4. Receivables turnover

    5. Return on sales

    6. Return on total assets

    7. Return on owners' equity

    8. Debt-equity ratio

    9. Gross margin percentage

P. 19B-6   **Reconstruction of financial statements.** Following is the balance sheet of D-Tek Company on December 31, 1983.

D-Tek Company Balance Sheet December 31, 1983	
Assets	
Cash	$ 600
Accounts receivable	3,000
Merchandise	11,000
Prepaid expenses	230
Fixed assets	110,000
Accumulated depreciation	(30,000)
Total assets	$ 94,830
Equities	
Accounts payable	$ 11,580
Bonds payable	30,000
Common stock $1 par	10,000
Contributed surplus	30,000
Retained earnings	13,250
Total equities	$ 94,830

The company did not buy or sell any fixed assets nor issue any stock during 1984. On December 31, 1984 the company's accountant obtained the following ratios and other data based on the 1984 operations:

Current ratio	2.0
Acid test ratio	.8
Inventory turnover	5.0
Receivables turnover	25.0
Equity ratio	58.8
Debt ratio	41.2
Times interest ratio	6.0
Return on total average assets	9.4%
Return on sales	7.0%
Gross margin percentage	52.0%
Book value per share	$ 5.88
Market price per share	$10.00
Earnings per share	$ .875
Dividend yield	3.2%
Income tax rate	30.0%
Depreciation rate	4.0%

Required:

a. Use the above data to prepare the company's income statement for the year ending December 31, 1984. The following form is suggested:

D-Tek Company
Income Statement
For the Year Ending December 31, 1984

Sales		$
Less cost of goods sold		_____
Gross margin		$
Less expenses		
Depreciation expense	$	
Interest expense		
Other expenses	_____	
Total expenses		_____
Net income before tax		$
Federal income tax		_____
Net income after tax		$

b. Prepare the company's balance sheet on December 31, 1984.

P. 19B-7 Analysis of pro forma statements. The financial statements of Erika Corporation are presented below. The company's management has decided to acquire a new piece of equipment that should help the company to expand its operations. The equipment can be financed by the issuance of common stock or bonds at an interest rate of 10 percent. $100,000 is to be obtained, with $80,000 to be used for the new equipment and the remainder to increase working capital. Erika Corporation is subject to a tax rate of 40 percent of income and pays no dividends.

Erika Corporation
Balance Sheet
May 31, 1984

Assets		Equities	
Current assets	$125,000	Current liabilities	$ 50,000
Fixed assets	320,000	Long-term debt	60,000
Accumulated depreciation	(90,000)	Common stock, $10 par	180,000
		Retained earnings	65,000
	$355,000		$355,000

Erika Corporation
Income Statement
For the Year Ending May 31, 1984

Sales		$153,000
Cost of goods sold		66,700
Gross margin		$ 86,300
Depreciation expense	$16,000	
Other expenses	38,966	
Interest expense	6,000	60,966
Net income before tax		$ 25,334
Income tax expense		10,134
Net income		$ 15,200

The following projections are made by management for the year ahead:

a. Sales are expected to increase by 30 percent. With a larger volume of purchases, cost of goods sold is expected to decline to 43 percent of sales.
b. Depreciation on the new equipment will be 5 percent of cost. Other expenses will increase 25 percent over the current year. Interest expense will increase only if bonds are issued.
c. Current liabilities should increase to $80,000 by the end of the fiscal year with the increased volume of business.

Required:

a. Prepare pro forma financial statements for the year ending May 31, 1985 for each alternative method of financing the expanded operations.
b. Calculate whatever ratios are possible on the current and pro forma financial statements to help you to evaluate the alternatives.
c. Recommend to management how the planned expansion should be financed. Support your recommendation with your analysis.

Minicases

Minicase 19-1   (SMA of Canada adapted)

Roberts Company, which currently has credit sales of $1,200,000, is considering a change in its credit policy. Under the present policy, the average collection period is one month and default losses average 1 percent of sales. Two proposals are under consideration: under the first, sales are expected to increase 25 percent, but the collection period and default losses would become two months and 3 percent, respectively; under the second proposal, sales are expected to increase by $33^1/_3$ percent while the average collection period would become three months and default losses 5 percent.

Roberts Company requires a return of 20 percent before tax on an additional investment of this type. Variable costs amount to 70 percent of sales.

Required:
a. Which policy should the Roberts Company adopt? Show all calculations.
b. Is the present policy more profitable than the policy that increases sales by $33^1/_3$%? Show calculations.

Minicase 19-2   (CMA Examination Question)

Turvar, Ltd., was formed five years ago through a public subscription of common shares. Lucinda Street, who owns 15 percent of the common shares, was one of the organizers of Turvar and is its current president. The company has been successful, but currently is experiencing a shortage of funds. On June 10, Street approached the Royal Bell Bank, asking for a 24-month extension on two $30,000 notes, which are due on June 30, 1983 and September 30, 1983. Another note of $7,000 is due on December 31, 1983, but she expects no difficulty in paying this note on its due date. Street explained that Turvar's cash flow problems are due primarily to the company's desire to finance a $300,000 plant expansion over the next two fiscal years through internally generated funds.

The Commercial Loan Officer of Royal Bell Bank requested financial reports for the last two fiscal years. These reports are reproduced below.

Required:
a. Identify and explain what financial reports and financial analyses might be helpful to the commercial loan officer of Royal Bell Bank in evaluating Street's request for a time extension on Turvar's notes.
b. Assume that the percentage changes experienced in fiscal year 1983 as compared with fiscal year 1982 for sales, cost of goods sold, gross margin, and net income after taxes will be repeated in each of the next two years. Is

Turvar's desire to finance the plant expansion from internally generated funds realistic? Explain your answer.

c. Should Royal Bell Bank grant the extension on Turvar's notes considering Street's statement about financing the plant expansion through internally generated funds? Explain your answer.

Turvar, Ltd.
Income Statement
For the Fiscal Years Ended March 31

	1982	1983
Sales	$2,700,000	$3,000,000
Cost of goods sold[1]	1,720,000	1,902,500
Gross margin	$ 980,000	1,097,500
Operating expenses	780,000	845,000
Net income before taxes	$ 200,000	$ 252,500
Income taxes (40%)	80,000	101,000
Income after taxes	$ 120,000	$ 151,500

[1]Depreciation charges on the plant and equipment of $100,000 and $102,500 for fiscal years ended March 31, 1982 and 1983 respectively are included in cost of goods sold.

Turvar, Ltd.
Statement of Financial Position
March 31

	1982	1983
Assets:		
Cash	$ 12,500	$ 16,400
Notes receivable	104,000	112,000
Accounts receivable (net)	68,500	81,600
Inventories (at cost)	50,000	80,000
Plant & equipment (net of depreciation)	646,000	680,000
Total assets	$ 881,000	$ 970,000
Liabilities and Owner's Equity:		
Accounts payable	$ 72,000	$ 69,000
Notes payable	54,500	67,000
Accrued liabilities	6,000	9,000
Common stock 60,000 shares ($10 par)	600,000	600,000
Retained earnings[1]	148,500	225,000
Total liabilities and owner's equity	$ 881,000	$ 970,000

[1]Cash dividends were paid at the rate of $1.00 per share in fiscal year 1982 and $1.25 per share in fiscal year 1983.

Minicase 19-3

Barrie, Ltd., is a major regional retailer. The Chief Executive Officer (CEO) is concerned with the slow growth of both sales and net income, and the subsequent effect on the trading price of the common shares. Selected financial data for the past three years are presented below.

Barrie, Ltd. (in millions of dollars)			
	1983	**1984**	**1985**
1. Sales	$187.0	$192.5	$200.0
2. Net Income	5.6	5.8	6.0
3. Dividends declared and paid	2.5	2.5	2.5
December 31 balances:			
4. Owner's equity	63.2	66.5	70.0
5. Debt	30.3	29.8	30.0
Selected year-end financial ratios:			
Net income to sales	3.0%	3.0%	3.0%
Investment turnover	2x	2x	2x
6. Return on equity	8.9%	8.7%	8.6%
7. Debt to total capital	32.4%	30.9%	30.0%

The CEO believes that the price of the stock has been adversely affected by the downward trend of the return on equity, the relatively low dividend payout ratio, and the lack of dividend increases. In order to improve the price of the stock, he wants to improve the return on equity and dividends.

He believes that the company should be able to meet these objectives by:

1. Increasing sales and net income at an annual rate of 10 percent a year.
2. Establishing a new dividend policy which calls for a dividend payout of 50 percent of earnings or $3,000,000, whichever is greater.

The 10 percent annual sales increase will be accomplished through a new promotional program. He believes the present net income to sales ratio of three percent will be unchanged by the cost of this new program and any interest paid on new debt. He expects that the company can accomplish this sales and income growth while maintaining the current relationship of total investment to sales. Any capital needed to maintain this relationship that is not generated internally would be acquired through long-term debt financing. The CEO hopes that debt would not exceed 35 percent of total capital.

Required:

a. Can the CEO meet all his requirements if a 10 percent per year growth in income and sales is achieved? Explain your answer.

b. What alternative actions should the CEO consider in order to improve the return on equity and support increased dividend payments?

c. Explain the reasons the CEO might have for wanting to limit debt to 35 percent of total capital.

Glossary

The number in parentheses after each term refers to the chapter in which the term is described.

absorption costing *(10)* A product costing method in which all costs of production, direct and indirect, fixed and variable, are included in the cost of products. Also called full costing.

accounting information *(1)* Financial information that is relevant, timely, and accurate.

accounting rate of return (ARR) *(13)* A method of capital expenditure investment analysis that uses accounting measures of income and investment as the basis for evaluating investment projects.

accuracy *(1)* A characteristic of accounting information referring to the correctness of accounting information, free from error.

activity costing *(2,10)* The process of determining costs for activities of a business other than manufacturing.

actual cost *(2,11)* The cost actually incurred in producing a product or providing a service. Also called historical cost.

administrative expense budget *(7)* Estimated administrative expenses for a specified time period, such as a month or a year.

all financial resources *(18)* The concept of reporting all financing and investing activities in the statement of changes in financial position including those that do not affect cash or working capital, such as exchanges of stock or long-term debt for fixed assets.

allocation *(4)* The process of assigning common costs to cost objectives in some systematic manner in accordance with the matching principle. *(14)* One of the three basic objectives of public finance, it deals with providing socially desirable goods and services in the right amount.

allocation base *(4)* An activity measure or ratio used for allocating a cost to a cost objective.

alpha factor *(17)* A number ranging from zero to 1 used for weighting the latest item of information to be used in calculating an exponential smoothing curve, with larger values for alpha assigning more importance to the most recent data.

alternative choice decision *(6)* A decision involving the choice between two or more decision alternatives or courses of action.

application base *(4)* An activity measure used to apply manufacturing overhead to products. Direct labour hours, machine hours, and direct labour cost are common application bases.

Auditor General *(14)* The office that is in charge of auditing expenditures of the federal government. The Auditor General is responsible to Parliament.

average cost inventory method *(15)* A method of inventory valuation in which the total cost of inventory is divided by the number of units to determine the weighted average cost. This cost is used for valuing ending inventory and for charging product costs to cost of goods sold.

bail-out *(13)* A capital budgeting project evaluation method that measures how quickly the project's investment can be recovered from the combination of cash savings and the salvage value of the investment at any point in time.

basic standards *(8)* Long-term standards created for a period of two to five years or more. Used as a benchmark for long-term comparisons.

break-even point *(5)* The activity level that yields zero profit. Revenue equals total costs.

budget *(7)* A comprehensive quantitative plan for utilizing the resources of an entity for some specified period of time.

budget variance *(7,9)* The difference between budgeted data and actual results.

budget variance report *(7,9)* An internal report that shows the difference between budget data and actual results.

budgeted activity level *(4)* The estimated amount of activity for the coming accounting period expressed in terms of the application base, for example, 10 000 direct labour hours. The budgeted activity level is estimated before the accounting period begins.

budgeted income statement *(7)* Estimated revenues and expenses for an entity for some specified time period in the form of a pro forma income statement.

budgeted overhead cost *(4)* The estimated amount of overhead costs determined before the accounting period begins. Used in the computation of a predetermined overhead rate.

budgeted overhead rate *(4)* A rate for applying overhead to production during the accounting period, for example, $5 per machine hour; the rate is determined before the accounting period begins. Also called a predetermined overhead rate.

budgeted statement of financial position *(7)* An estimated statement of financial position for some specific future point in time. Also called a budgeted balance sheet.

by-product *(4)* A product of relatively small economic value that results from the production of a main product or group of products, e.g., particle board made from sawdust in the production of lumber.

CA *(1)* Chartered accountant.

Canadian Institute of Chartered Accountants *(1)* Commonly abbreviated as CICA, is the association of provincial institutes. CICA confers the CA designation and safeguards professional standards and ethics.

capital budgeting *(13)* The systematic process of identifying and evaluating capital investment projects to arrive at a capital expenditure budget.

capital cost allowance (CCA) *(13)* A deduction, similar to depreciation, allowed in computing income for income tax purposes.

capital expenditure budget *(7,13)* The report identifying an organization's plans for investing in capital projects with lives typically exceeding one accounting year and representing relatively large expenditures.

capital rationing *(13)* The process of selecting the more desirable projects from a series of profitable investments.

carrying costs *(15)* Costs such as inventory storage and handling costs that are essential in maintaining an inventory of goods ready for sale or for use in the production process.

cash budget *(7)* Estimated cash receipts and disbursements of an entity for some specified time period, starting with the expected beginning cash balance and ending with the expected ending cash balance.

cash flow statement *(18)* The statement of changes in financial position with funds defined as cash; primarily used for internal purposes.

Certified General Accountant *(1)* A professional accountant who has completed the requirements of the Certified General Accountants' Association of Canada and certified to practise public accounting.

coefficient of correlation *(17)* A statistic known as r whose value ranges from -1 to $+1$ and that explains the strength of the relationship between the movement of two sets of data. If r has a value close to -1 or $+1$ it represents a strong relationship; a value close to zero represents a weak relationship.

coefficient of determination *(17)* A statistic, known as r^2, that is obtained by squaring the coefficient of correlation. Its value ranges from zero to 1 and it measures the strength of the relationship between two sets of data, with the stronger relationship designated by values closer to 1 and the weaker relationship designated by values closer to zero.

coefficient of nondetermination *(17)* A statistic calculated as $1 - r^2$, where r^2 is the coefficient of determination. The coefficient of nondetermination explains random fluctuation in a set of data and fluctuations caused by variables other than the independent variable.

committed fixed costs *(5)* The fixed costs of providing production facilities and other relatively long-term commitments of resources. Fixed costs that cannot be easily or quickly eliminated.

common cost *(2,4)* A cost that is not identifiable with a single cost objective but instead is shared by, or common to, more than one cost objective, e.g., the salary of a production plant manager shared by all producing departments in the manufacturing plant.

contribution approach *(10)* A cost reporting approach that highlights cost behavior characteristics rather than functional cost characteristics. Variable costs are deducted from sales to determine the amount contributed toward covering fixed costs and providing profit.

contribution approach pricing *(12)* A form of cost-plus pricing using variable costs plus an amount or percentage as the basis for setting the price.

contribution margin *(5,10)* The difference between the selling price and the variable cost of a product or service. Both the per-unit manufacturing and non-manufacturing variable costs are deducted from the selling price to determine the contribution margin. In aggregate contribution margin is the difference between total sales and total variable costs.

contribution margin variance *(16)* A measure of the difference between the standard contribution margin and the actual contribution margin generated by a product for some time period.

control *(7)* The concept of monitoring activities and taking action to correct undesirable performance, often using budgets as a basis for measuring performance.

control account *(2,3,4,9)* An account whose balance represents the total of all balances in accounts of a related subsidiary ledger. Accounts receivable is the control account for the individual accounts of amounts owed by customers.

controllable cost *(2,11)* A cost over which a manager has direct control or significant influence.

controllable variance *(9)* The difference between actual manufacturing overhead and a flexible overhead budget based on actual output in the two-variance method of overhead variance analysis. Equal to the sum of the spending and efficiency variances in a three-way overhead variance analysis.

conversion cost *(2)* Direct labour cost and manufacturing overhead cost combined.

cost *(2)* The amount of resource given up for some product or service.

cost accounting *(1)* The process of determining the cost of some product or activity.

cost after split-off *(4)* The joint-product production cost that occurs after the split-off point and therefore is identifiable with a specific product.

cost allocation *(2,4)* The process of assigning common costs to cost objectives in accordance with the matching principle.

cost analyzing *(1)* A basic activity in cost accounting dealing with the systematic evaluation of cost data to solve problems and to provide relevant information.

cost behaviour *(2,5)* The way a cost changes with respect to changes in the level of activity. Usually classified as fixed, variable, semifixed, semivariable, or mixed.

cost-benefit analysis *(1,3,8,17)* The process of analyzing the benefits derived from some project or activity with the costs necessary to do it. To be acceptable the benefits must be greater than the costs.

cost of capital *(13)* The amount that an organization pays for the capital that it uses.

cost centre *(11)* A responsibility centre in which managers are held responsible for the costs under their control.

cost-of-estimation error *(15)* The cost that arises from incorrectly estimating the value of variables used in management decision making.

cost finding *(1)* A basic activity of cost accounting dealing with the determination of costs for some specific product or activity.

cost of goods manufactured *(2)* The cost of the products transferred from work in process inventory to finished goods inventory during a period. Usually reported in a cost-of-goods-manufactured schedule showing beginning work in process, current-period production costs, and ending work in process.

cost indifference point *(6)* The activity level at which the total costs of two alternatives are identical. At this level of activity managers are indifferent between the two alternatives in terms of cost.

cost objective *(2)* The product or activity whose cost is being determined.

cost of production report *(3)* A report used to summarize production costs in a process centre of a process costing system.

cost-plus pricing *(12)* A type of pricing model using costs plus an amount or percentage as the basis for determining the price.

cost recording *(1)* The process of recording cost data in the formal accounting records of an organization.

cost reporting *(1)* Communicating cost information in the form of internal and external reports.

cost-volume-profit *(5)* Analyses that deal with how costs and profits change in relation to changes in the volume of activity.

cost-volume-profit chart *(5)* A graphic presentation of cost-volume-profit relationships. Often called a CVP chart. Frequently useful for presenting complex cost relationships.

Crown corporations *(1,14)* Corporations that are owned by various governments and accountable to Parliament.

CPP *(3)* Abbreviation for Canada Pension Plan.

currently attainable standards *(8)* Standards that describe desired levels of performance but that reflect the problems of the operating environment, such as machine breakdowns.

daily time ticket *(2)* A document used by employees to record how they spent their workday. A source document used to identify labour cost with cost objectives.

data *(1)* The basic facts and figures that constitute a data base; the building blocks of an information system.

data base *(1)* The foundation of data elements supporting an information system or a portion of an information system; the data drawn on by users to meet information needs.

decentralization *(11)* The process of delegating decision authority to various levels in the organization.

decision model *(1)* A description of how a particular decision is made.

decision theory *(1)* The body of knowledge concerning the process of decision making.

demand *(12)* The total amount of product or service all purchasers are willing to buy at all possible prices.

demand curve *(12)* A graph of demand showing the amount buyers in aggregate are willing to buy at all possible prices.

departmental job cost sheet *(3)* A job cost sheet that identifies manufacturing costs by department or production function as well as by cost elements.

departmental overhead rates *(4)* Manufacturing overhead rates created for individual departments or groups of departments rather than one overhead rate for an entire production plant. The purpose of departmental rates is to do a better job of matching overhead costs with the revenues generated by the sale of products.

dependent variable *(17)* The variable whose value is to be predicted by means of a linear regression line and that depends on the values of the independent variable.

differential cost *(6)* A cost that is different between decision alternatives.

direct allocation *(4)* A method of allocating service department overhead costs directly to producing department without any allocation to other service departments.

direct costing *(10)* See *variable costing.*

direct labour *(2,3,4,7,8,16)* Labour that is directly identifiable with a specific product or activity.

direct labour budget *(7)* Estimated direct labour costs and quantities of an entity for some time period.

direct material budget *(7)* A formal plan describing the use of direct materials for some specific time period. Part of the master budget.

direct materials *(2,3,4,7,8,16)* Raw materials used in the production process that can be identified with specific products.

discounted cash flows (DCF) *(13)* Capital budgeting and other types of analyses that rely on the time value of money. All cash flows are discounted at some interest rate to their present value.

discretionary fixed costs *(5)* Fixed costs that can be eliminated at managements' discretion in a relatively short period of time, e.g., some administrative salaries, research and development, and new systems development.

distribution *(14)* A basic objective of public finance concerned with who should receive the economic benefits of society and in what amount.

divisional contribution statement *(10)* A contribution report identifying the amount of contribution margin provided by each division of a company.

divisional income statement *(10)* An income statement identifying net income by division.

dynamic budget *(9)* See *flexible budget.*

economic order quantity (EOQ) *(15)* The optimum order size that results in the lowest total inventory cost for some specific inventory item.

efficiency variance *(9)* The difference in variable manufacturing overhead caused by using more or fewer hours than standard. Also used to describe labour variances caused by using more or fewer hours than standard.

equivalent units *(3)* A measure of the amount of production in a process centre. The amount of equivalent whole units that would have been produced if all efforts had been devoted to starting and completing units rather than completing units in beginning inventory and starting units in ending inventory.

estimated activity level *(4)* See *budgeted activity level.*

estimated overhead cost *(4)* See *budgeted overhead cost.*

exponential smoothing *(17)* A statistical technique of trend analysis using an alpha factor to assign weights to new data for the purpose of calculating a trend line.

external reporting *(1)* See *financial accounting.*

factory burden *(2,4)* See *manufacturing overhead.*

factory overhead rate *(2,4)* See *manufacturing overhead rate.*

favourable variance *(8)* The amount by which standard costs exceed actual costs. Any variance in which actual cost is less than standard cost.

financial accounting *(1)* Accounting for the financial affairs of entities for the purpose of reporting such affairs to those outside the entity. Also called external reporting.

financial analysis *(19)* The interpretation of financial statements for the purpose of assessing past business performance, evaluating present business conditions, and predicting future potential for business success.

financial budget *(7)* The set of budgets including capital expenditures budget, cash budget, budgeted balance sheet, and budgeted statement of changes in financial position.

financing activities *(18)* Business activities that provide funds. Examples include operations that generate net income, investment by owners, borrowing, and sale of noncurrent assets.

finished goods *(2)* Products in a manufacturing firm that have been completed and are ready for sale.

first in, first out (FIFO) *(3,15)* The inventory valuation method that assumes that the inventory acquired earliest is the first to be used or sold. The method refers to the flow of costs rather than to the physical flow of goods.

fiscal policy *(14)* Pertains to the taxing and spending actions of government. One of the two instruments of economic stabilization policy.

fixed budget *(7,9)* A budget prepared for a single expected level of activity. Also called a static budget.

fixed cost *(2,5)* A cost that does not change with the level of activity. Described by the general formula $Y = a$.

fixed overhead *(7,9)* The portion of manufacturing overhead that does not change with changing levels of activity.

flexible budget *(9)* A budget prepared for more than one level of activity, covering several levels within the relevant range of activity. Also called a dynamic budget.

full costing *(10)* See *absorption costing.*

functional budget *(14)* See *line budget.*

funds *(18)* Cash or working capital whose change is reported in the statement of changes in financial position.

funds flow statement *(18)* See *statement of changes in financial position.*

funds from operations *(18)* The amount of cash or working capital provided by operations and reported in the statement of changes in financial position, generally consisting of net income adjusted for nonfund items.

gross profit allocation method *(4,6)* A method of assigning joint product costs to products so that each product contributes an equal percentage gross margin on sales.

high-low method *(5,17)* A method of estimating the fixed and variable cost components of a mixed cost. Based on the difference between the highest and lowest costs experienced in a specific time period and the difference in activity level.

historical costs *(2)* Costs that have already occurred. Also called actual costs.

horizontal analysis *(19)* Financial analysis involving the comparison of figures in financial statements of two or more consecutive accounting periods.

ideal standards *(8)* Very tight, hard-to-achieve standards assuming ideal production conditions.

independent variable *(17)* The variable whose value is used in linear regression analysis to predict the value of the dependent variable.

indirect costs *(2,3,4)* Costs that cannot be identified directly with a cost objective.

indirect labour *(2,3,4)* Manufacturing labour necessary for the production process, but not identifiable with specific products.

indirect material *(2,3,4)* Material necessary for the production process, but not identifiable with specific products.

inferior goods *(12)* Products whose demand is the inverse of normal products. Price increases cause an increase in demand, and price decreases cause a decrease in demand.

information *(1)* Data assembled in usable form. It should increase a person's knowledge or decrease the risk of making an incorrect decision.

internal reporting *(1)* See *managerial accounting.*

inventoriable cost *(2)* Necessary cost of production that increases the value of a product and becomes part of the cost of the product.

inventory control *(15)* The process of planning and monitoring inventory.

inventory profits *(15)* Profits higher than normal caused by matching current revenues with older inventory costs.

investing activities *(18)* Business activities that require the use of funds, such as acquisition of assets, repayment of debt, payment of dividends, and reacquisition of stock.

investment centre *(11)* A form of responsibility centre in which managers are held responsible for the return on assets invested in that segment of the organization.

job cost sheet *(3)* A report used to summarize the production costs for a specific production job in a job order costing system.

job number *(3)* An identification number assigned to each job cost sheet. The number may be designed to allow accountants to analyze costs easily in a variety of ways.

job order costing *(3)* A cost accounting system used to accumulate costs for products produced in batches or intermittent production runs. Job order production is characterized by an identifiable starting and completion time for the batch of production. Production costs are summarized on a job cost sheet.

job time ticket *(2)* A source document used to identify labour costs with cost objectives. Employees prepare this document for each job on which they work.

joint cost *(4,6)* Production costs associated with joint products before the split-off point and allocated to products by means such as the gross margin method or the physical units method.

joint cost allocation *(4,6)* The process of assigning joint costs to products.

joint product *(4,6)* A product that is produced as part of a group of products and not distinguishable as a separate product until the split-off point.

kinked demand curve *(12)* A demand curve occurring in oligopolistic markets in which the action of one supplier causes a kink or sharp break in the demand curve for products of other suppliers.

labour distribution report *(2,3)* A report summarizing the use of labour for some time period, such as a week or month.

labour efficiency variance *(8,16)* A variance caused by using more or fewer labour hours than standard.

labour rate variance *(8,16)* A variance caused by using labour costing more or less than standard.

last in, first out (LIFO) *(15)* Inventory valuation method that assumes that the goods purchased most recently are the first ones sold. The method refers to the flow of inventory costs and not to the physical flow of the goods.

lead time *(15)* The time between placing and receiving an order.

lead time demand *(15)* The amount of inventory required during lead time.

learning curve cost *(5,17)* A semivariable cost that increases at a decreasing rate. It indicates the cost effect of labour becoming more efficient as new tasks and processes are learned.

learning curves *(5,17)* A class of semivariable costs that increase at a decreasing rate, such as labour costs resulting during a period when a new task is being learned.

learning rate *(17)* The rate at which learning takes place, expressed as a percentage that determines the shape of the learning curve.

least-squares regression line *(17)* See *regression line.*

line budget *(14)* A budget prepared along organizational or functional lines, such as marketing, administrative, and manufacturing.

loss leader *(12)* A product priced very low, perhaps below cost, intended to attract customers to the business to buy products at normal prices as well as the loss leader items.

make-buy decision *(6)* A decision involving the choice between buying a product or service or producing it.

management by objective *(8)* A management method whereby managers establish specific performance criteria and investigate situations only when actual performance varies significantly from the performance criteria. Also called management by exception.

managerial accounting *(1)* The accounting and reporting of information to managers within the organization. Also called internal reporting.

manufacturing contribution margin *(10)* The difference between sales and the variable manufacturing expenses.

manufacturing overhead *(2)* All necessary costs of manufacturing other than direct labour and direct materials. The indirect costs of manufacturing.

manufacturing overhead applied *(2,3,4)* The account used to accumulate the amount of overhead applied to production. The account normally has a credit balance. The term also refers to the amount of overhead charged to a particular cost objective.

manufacturing overhead budget *(4,7)* The estimated amount of manufacturing overhead costs for an entity for a specific time period. Estimated indirect manufacturing costs, both fixed and variable.

manufacturing overhead control *(2,4)* The account used to accumulate actual manufacturing overhead costs as they are incurred. The account normally has a debit balance.

manufacturing overhead rate *(2,4,9)* A predetermined rate used for applying manufacturing overhead costs to products, for example, $6 per direct labour hours.

manufacturing overhead variance analysis *(9)* The systematic process of analyzing the difference between actual manufacturing overhead and applied manufacturing overhead. The two-variance and three-variance methods are common ways of analyzing overhead variances.

margin of safety ratio *(5)* A measure of the relative amount that actual activity differs from break-even activity. The difference is expressed as a ratio of actual activity, with a range of possible values from $-\infty$ to $+1$. Values above zero indicate the firm is operating above the break-even point.

marginal cost *(12)* The amount of increase in total cost caused by a one-unit increase in output.

marginal revenue *(12)* The amount of increase in total revenue caused by a one-unit increase in sales.

market equilibrium *(12)* The intersection of the supply and demand curves; it occurs when the amount buyers are willing to buy at a particular price coincides with the amount sellers are willing to supply at that price.

market price *(11)* The price for some product or service determined by the market mechanisms external to the business.

market tests *(19)* That part of financial analysis that involves the calculation of financial ratios such as dividend yield, price-earnings ratio, and others derived from stock market data.

marketing expense budget *(7)* Estimated marketing costs of an entity for a specific time period.

master budget *(7)* The total budget package of an organization, including both the operating and financial budgets. Sometimes referred to as the profit plan.

material price variance *(8,16)* A variance caused by paying more or less than the standard price for a raw material.

material quantity variance *(8,16)* A variance caused by using more or less material than the standard quantity.

materials budget *(7)* Estimated materials use for an entity for some specified period.

materials requisition *(2,3)* A document sent to the inventory storeroom area to start raw materials into the production process.

mean *(17)* A measure of central tendency calculated by adding all items in a set of data and dividing by the number of items.

measures of central tendency *(17)* Statistics that describe average characteristics of a set of data, such as the mean, the median, or the mode.

measures of dispersion *(17)* Statistics that describe how data fluctuate around some measure of central tendency.

median *(17)* A measure of central tendency calculated as the middle value of an ordered set of data.

mixed cost *(5,17)* A cost composed of both fixed and variable cost components. Described by the general equation $Y = a + bX$. Y is the total cost, a is the fixed component, and b is the variable cost per unit of activity.

mode *(17)* A measure of central tendency representing the value of a set of data that occurs most frequently.

modified cost *(11)* A form of transfer price based on cost and modified to reflect special conditions or management's attitudes.

modified market price *(11)* A transfer price based on market price and adjusted to reflect such factors as the absence of marketing costs in interdivisional sales.

monetary policy *(14)* Deals with the quantity of money and the cost of money in the economy. One of the two instruments of economic stabilization policy.

monopolistic competition *(12)* A market in which there are many suppliers of similar, but not identical, products.

monopoly *(12)* A market with only one supplier.

moving average *(17)* A mean calculated for a set of data by deleting the oldest data element and adding the newest data element as it becomes available.

multiple-alternative choice decision *(6)* A decision involving more than two alternative courses of action.

multiple linear regression *(17)* A statistical technique using two or more independent variables to predict the value of one dependent variable.

multiyear costing *(14)* The process of identifying costs with a project for the life of the project rather than just the next budget year. An element of PPBS.

negative correlation *(17)* The relationship described by the coefficient of correlation when increases in the values of the independent variable are accompanied by decreases in the values of the dependent variable.

negotiated price *(11)* A form of transfer price in which the buying and selling parties negotiate the transfer price.

net present value (NPV) *(13)* A capital budgeting analysis method that is used to discount all cash inflows and outflows from a project to their present value. The firm's cost of capital or target rate of return is used as the interest rate.

nonfund items *(18)* Those expenses, revenues, gains, and losses reported on the income statement that do not provide cash or working capital. Items that are added to or deducted from net income to arrive at funds from operations.

nonmanufacturing activities *(10)* All activities other than manufacturing, e.g., marketing, accounting, and administration.

normal capacity *(9)* The expected activity level for the accounting period assuming normal operating conditions. The activity level is expressed in units of output, direct labour hours, machine hours, or some other measure of activity.

normal curve *(17)* A symmetrical bell-shaped curve describing the normal probability distribution found in many types of statistical data.

not-for-profit sector *(14)* The sector of the economy comprising governments, universities, charities, and other organizations that provide services to the public without attempting to generate a profit.

oligopoly *(12)* A market in which there are several large sellers that dominate the market and compete with one another.

operating budget *(7)* The set of budgets for the normal operations of a business, including all activities involved in generating operating income.

opportunity cost *(6)* The benefit forgone by rejecting one alternative so that another can be accepted.

ordering costs *(15)* The total cost associated with ordering a particular inventory item, typically including the costs of obtaining current prices, securing order approval, preparing purchase documents, and receiving the order.

overapplied overhead *(2,4,9)* The amount by which applied overhead exceeds actual overhead.

overhead *(2,3,4,7,8,9,10)* See *manufacturing overhead.*

payback *(13)* A capital budgeting analysis method that is used to determine how long it will take to recover the initial investment of a proposed project.

payback reciprocal *(13)* A capital budgeting evaluation method that is an estimate of the internal rate of return. Payback reciprocal is computed by dividing the payback period into 1.

perfectly competitive market *(12)* A market in which there are many buyers and sellers, none of whom can affect the market price by their individual actions. The product or service sold in the market is homogeneous, resources can flow freely into and out of the market, and all market participants have perfect knowledge of prices and costs.

performance reporting *(7,8,9,11,16)* The comparison of actual results with the expected results embodied in the budget, often resulting in the reporting of variances.

periodic inventory system *(2,15)* A method of accounting for inventories in which the inventory account is adjusted only at year-end after a physical count of the inventory. Inventory purchases are recorded in a purchases account and the cost of goods sold is determined at the end of the accounting period by summing beginning inventory and purchases and subtracting ending inventory.

perpetual inventory system *(2,15)* A method of accounting for inventories in which all inventory increases and decreases are recorded directly in the inventory account. Cost of goods sold is determined at the time of sale.

physical units allocation method *(4,6)* A method of joint cost allocation in which each unit of product in the joint-product group receives the same amount of joint cost.

planning *(7)* The process of developing the set of budgets used in achieving organizational goals. A design or scheme for achieving specific goals or objectives.

planning, programming, budgeting system (PPBS) *(14)* A comprehensive review, evaluation, and preparation process first initiated in federal government in mid-1960s and subsequently used in similar forms in various provincial and local governments.

positive correlation *(17)* The relationship described by the coefficient of correlation when increases in the values of the independent variable are accompanied by increases in the values of the dependent variable.

predetermined overhead rate *(4)* See *budgeted overhead rate.*

present value *(13)* The current value of an amount to be received in the future.

price indifference point *(6)* The activity level at which the new price produces a profit identical to the profit generated by the old price and activity level.

pricing *(12)* The process of assigning a selling price to products or services sold by the organization.

prime cost *(2)* Direct materials cost and direct labour cost combined.

private sector *(14)* The sector of the economy consisting of privately owned organizations primarily engaged in providing services and selling products to earn profits.

problem definition *(1)* The process of determining precisely what problem is being addressed.

process centre *(3)* A separate identifiable production activity characterized by homogeneous output and by work that is identical for each unit.

process costing *(3)* A cost accounting system used to accumulate costs of products manufactured in continuous flow production processes. There is no identifiable starting and completion time for production activity, so production costs must be summarized periodically in cost of production reports.

producing department *(4)* A department that is directly involved in furthering the production of products by performing some production process, such as drilling, assembly, or finishing.

product contribution statement *(10)* A contribution report that identifies the amount of contribution margin provided by each product.

product cost *(2,3)* All costs, both direct and indirect, of producing a product in a manufacturing firm or the cost of acquiring a product in a merchandising business and making it ready for sale.

product profitability report *(10)* A report identifying profit by product.

production budget *(7)* Estimated production quantities and costs for an entity for some specified period of time.

production mix variance *(16)* A measure of the dollar amount of variance caused by changing from the standard mix of production inputs to some other mix.

profit centre *(11)* A form of responsibility centre in which managers are held responsible for both expenses and revenues.

profit plan *(7)* A company's total budget used in achieving a desired profit goal. Sometimes the term refers only to the operating budget, and sometimes it is used synonymously with the term *master budget.*

profit-volume chart *(5)* A special form of cost-volume-profit chart that highlights the break-even point and profit. The horizontal center line of the chart is the zero profit line.

profitability index (PI) *(13)* The ratio of the present value of cash inflows to the present value of cash outflows. A capital budgeting evaluation method that adjusts for the dollar amount of projects.

program accounting *(14)* An accounting system with an ability to attach accounting data to specific programs to show the resources used or budgeted for each objective.

program budget *(14)* A budget prepared for programs or outputs of an organization.

public finance *(14)* The entire area of government economic activity including resource allocation, income distribution to people, and the financing function of government.

public sector *(14)* The portion of the not-for-profit sector consisting of publicly owned organizations and institutions, such as city governments, provincial universities, federal parks, and others whose purpose is to provide services to the public without earning a profit.

purchase order *(2)* A business document prepared by the purchasing department to order some resource or service.

purchase price *(12)* The amount paid for some resource acquired by a firm.

purchase requisition *(2)* A business document indicating that some item or service needs to be ordered.

quantity variance *(8,16)* See *material quantity variance.*

raw materials *(2)* The basic materials used in production by a manufacturing firm. Most raw materials are direct materials, but some are indirect materials.

receiving report *(2)* A business document indicating the receipt of some item or items and the amount received.

reciprocal allocation *(4)* A method of allocating service department costs to producing departments; requires the use of linear algebra.

regression-correlation analysis *(17)* The analysis of statistical data performed by calculating a regression line, the coefficient of correlation, and the coefficient of determination and then interpreting the results of the calculations.

regression line *(17)* A straight line that best fits through a set of data by minimizing the absolute distances between the data points and the line. Also called the line of best fit and the least-squares regression line.

regression line equation *(17)* The equation that describes mathematically the intercept and slope of the regression line.

reinvestment rate *(13)* The rate at which cash inflows from capital projects can be invested.

relevance *(1)* The characteristic of accounting information requiring that information meets the needs of users.

relevant cost *(6)* A cost useful in the decision-making process; it has two characteristics: it is an expected future cost and a differential cost.

relevant range assumption *(5,17)* The assumption that the identified behaviour pattern of a cost may exist only for a certain range of activity. At an activity level above or below the relevant range the cost may have a different behaviour pattern.

reorder point *(15)* The inventory level at which a new order is placed for some specific inventory item.

residual income *(11)* The difference between actual net income and a specified target net income.

responsibility accounting *(11)* The process of reporting on how well managers meet their responsibilities.

responsibility centres *(11)* Clearly identified segments of an organization in which managers are held responsible for the performance in the organizational segment. Cost centres, profit centres, and investment centres are the three common forms of responsibility centres.

return on investment *(11)* A measure of the amount earned on an investment project.

Revenue Canada *(1,14)* The tax collecting arm of the federal government.

RIA *(1)* Registered Industrial Accountant.

safety stock *(15)* An additional amount of inventory in excess of lead time demand intended to minimize or eliminate the possibility of a stockout.

sales budget *(7)* Estimate of sales volume of an entity for some specified period of time. Prepared first because most other budgets are derived, at least in part, from the sales budget.

sales mix variance *(16)* A measure of the profit consequences of selling products in different amounts from the standard sales mix.

sales quantity variance *(16)* A measure of the amount of variance in profits caused by selling more or less units than standard.

sample *(17)* A set of data collected from a population so that the set is representative of the population.

scatter diagram *(5)* A chart or graph used to plot cost data that may provide managers with a visual representation of cost trends or patterns.

segmental reports *(10)* Reports that identify costs, revenues, profits, contribution margin, or other variables for parts or segments of an organization.

selling the budget *(7)* The process of convincing the budget review committee of the merits of some budget proposal.

selling price *(12)* The amount charged by an organization for some product or resource that it sells to others.

semifixed cost *(5)* A cost that increases with activity in jumps or steps. It remains constant for a range of activity and then jumps to a higher amount. Also called a step function cost.

semivariable cost *(5)* A cost that increases continuously, but not proportionately, with activity. Learning curve costs increase at a decreasing rate. Other semivariable costs increase at an increasing rate.

sensitivity analysis *(15)* The process of determining how sensitive the output of a model is to changes in the inputs or changes in the model parameters.

service department *(4)* A department, such as maintenance or inventory storeroom, that facilitates or supports production activities, but is not directly involved in producing products.

simple linear regression *(17)* Regression analysis involving one dependent variable and one independent variable.

SMA *(1)* Society of Management Accountants of Canada, formerly SIA, Society of Industrial Accountants.

special orders *(6,12)* An order that has characteristics different from regular orders. Typically a one-time order that provides the opportunity to utilize unused capacity.

spending variances *(9)* The difference between actual manufacturing overhead cost and a flexible budget based on actual inputs. One of the variances isolated by using the three-variance method.

split-off point *(4)* The point in the production process when a by-product separates from the main product or when joint products become identifiable as separate products.

stabilization *(14)* An objective of public finance aimed at keeping the economy running smoothly with acceptable growth and few economic fluctuations. Fiscal and monetary policy are the two instruments of stabilization.

standard average cost *(16)* The average cost of inputs calculated as the standard mix of inputs at the standard cost of each input.

standard cost *(8,16)* A carefully predetermined cost. A measure of what a cost should be.

standard deviation *(17)* A measure of dispersion describing the variation of data from their mean.

standard setting *(8)* The process of establishing standard costs.

standards committee *(8)* A group of people within an organization whose function is to establish standards and reevaluate them periodically.

statement of changes in financial positions *(18)* One of the basic financial statements presented in an annual report describing the financing and investing activities of a business enterprise.

static budget *(9)* See *fixed budget.*

statistic *(17)* Any item of information that describes some characteristic of a subject under investigation.

steady state *(17)* The point on a learning curve when no more learning takes place and each subsequent repetition of the learned task requires as much time or cost as the previous repetition.

stockout *(15)* The zero inventory level for some specific inventory when there is demand for the item.

stockout cost *(15)* The cost associated with running out of inventory which includes lost sales, customer ill will, and production inefficiencies.

subsidiary ledger *(2)* The set of individual accounts that are summarized by a control account in the general ledger, e.g., individual accounts receivable for each customer that sum to the balance in the control account for accounts receivable.

sunk cost *(6)* A cost that has already been incurred and cannot be changed and therefore is not relevant to the decision process.

supply *(12)* The total amount all suppliers are willing to sell at each possible selling price.

supply curve *(12)* A graphic presentation of the amount suppliers in aggregate are willing to sell at each possible selling price.

target income *(5,11)* A desired level of income expressed as an amount or a percentage of investment or sales.

target profit pricing *(12)* The process of establishing prices based on desired profit levels.

tests of liquidity *(19)* That portion of financial analysis that involves the calculation of ratios such as the current ratio, quick ratio, and various turnover ratios that provide an indication of a company's liquidity.

tests of profitability *(19)* That portion of financial analysis that involves the calculation of ratios, such as rate of return, that provide information about the profitability of a business.

tests of solvency *(19)* That portion of financial analysis that involves the calculation of ratios, such as the debt-equity ratio, and other tests that provide

an indication of a company's ability to pay its debts as they mature.

three-variance method *(9)* A method of overhead variance analysis that isolates three variances — spending, efficiency, and volume.

time assumption *(5)* The assumption that cost behaviour patterns may change over time and an identified pattern may be valid only for a specific period of time.

timeliness *(1)* An information characteristic requiring that accounting information be very current.

total net assets *(11)* Total assets less any contra asset accounts, such as accumulated depreciation.

total net assets employed *(11)* Total assets less contra asset accounts less any assets not currently employed in generating net income.

transfer pricing *(8,11)* The process of pricing the transfer of goods and services between segments of an organization.

trend analysis *(17)* A statistical technique using moving averages or exponential smoothing to determine the trend in a set of data, usually for the purpose of predicting future values of the data.

two-variance method *(9)* A method of overhead variance analysis that isolates two variances — controllable and volume.

UIC *(3)* Unemployment Insurance Commission.

underapplied overhead *(2,4,9)* The amount by which actual overhead exceeds applied overhead.

unfavourable variance *(8,9,16)* The amount by which actual costs exceed standard costs. Any variance in which actual cost is greater than standard cost. cost.

unit cost *(2,3)* The cost of one unit of product. Typically an average unit cost of producing the product during some time period, such as a month.

variable cost *(2,5,6)* A cost that increases proportionately with the level of activity. Described by the equation $Y = bX$ where Y is total cost and b is the variable cost per unit of activity.

variable costing *(10)* A product costing method that includes all variable costs of manufacturing in the cost of the product and excludes any fixed costs. Also called direct costing.

variable overhead *(7,9)* The portion of manufacturing overhead costs that vary directly with the level of activity.

variance *(17)* A measure of dispersion describing the fluctuation of data items about their mean.

variance analysis *(8)* The systematic process of identifying, reporting, and explaining variances.

vertical analysis *(19)* Financial analysis that involves the comparison of figures within a financial statement or between financial statements of a single period.

volume variance *(9)* The amount of overhead variance caused by operating at an activity level different from budgeted. The difference between applied overhead and a budget based on actual output.

work in process *(2, 3)* Inventory that is in the process of being manufactured. Partially completed inventory.

yield variance *(16)* The difference between the standard and actual output obtained from a given amount of inputs.

zero-base budgeting *(14)* A method of budget review and evaluation that requires all projects and programs, new and old, to justify all resources. Each project starts the budget evaluation process without a resource commitment even if it is an ongoing project.

Index

P 11B–3 Transfer price based on target profit = $.75
P 11B–4 ROI on total net assets in 1981 = 17.5%
P 11B–5 Transfer price (a) = $82.60
P 11B–6 Mining division net income using target profit = $4,557,000
Ex 12–3 Equilibrium price = $8 per ton
Ex 12–4 Net income at optimum strategy = $1,600
Ex 12–5 Dry food price = $1.62 per bag
Ex 12–6 Price using full cost plus 25% = $22.75
Ex 12–7 (a) Profit from special order = $6,000
Ex 12–8 (c) Price including opportunity cost = $145 per house
Ex 12–9 Number of students per lesson = 8
Ex 12–10 Reject the national distribution offer
P 12A–1 Amount supplied = 900 bags
P 12A–2 Maximum variable manufacturing cost = $270
P 12A–3 Price using total cost plus 20% = $768
P 12A–4 (d) Effect on net income = (1,000)
P 12A–5 Required sales volume for discount store option = $350,000
P 12A–6 (d) Price for 7-day trip = $570
P 12B–1 Equilibrium price = $13
P 12B–2 Price using normal price formula = $210
P 12B–3 Price based on total standard cost plus 15% = $8.05
P 12B–4 (b) Effect on net income = $20,000 increase
P 12B–5 Required sales quantity for desired profit = 2 624 tractors
P 12B–6 (a) Required admission price = $.80 per visitor
Ex 13–1 IRR = 14%
Ex 13–2 NPV = $3,805
Ex 13–3 PI, machine X = 1.08; machine Y = 1.35
Ex 13–4 Payback = 4 yrs.; payback reciprocal = 25%
Ex 13–5 ARR = 12.5%; reject project
Ex 13–6 NPV = $7,068
Ex 13–7 IRR, Blue = 12%; Green = 20%; Red = 14.5%
Ex 13–8 NPV = $31,906.40; accept project
Ex 13–9 NPV = ($1,872.60)
Ex 13–10 Maximum amount that should be invested = $111,565
Ex 13–11 PI = 1.41
P 13A–1 NPV of fishing boat = $13,884
P 13A–2 IRR = 15%
P 13A–3 (a) NPV = $1,545.15
P 13A–4 IRR, model 444 = 19%
P 13A–5 Minimum revenue = $54,876.77
P 13A–6 IRR ranking = cold, warm, hot
P 13A–7 NPV = ($274,659)
P 13A–8 NPV (b) = $1,194,306
P 13B–1 NPV, small dormitories = $576,840
P 13B–2 Payback period = 4.47 yrs
P 13B–3 Project ranking, NPV (b) = C, B, A
P 13B–4 IRR = 15%, payback reciprocal = 29.9%
P 13B–5 Maximum bid = $66,906
P 13B–6 Project rankings, PI = D, C, A, B
P 13B–7 Total cash savings = $5.415.801
P 13B–8 NPV using 25% = ($1,057,704)
Ex 14–4 Total budget for the next year = $161,700
Ex 14–5 Actual percentage increase in the budget = 9.2%
Ex 14–7 Educational programs total budget = $94,000
Ex 14–8 Total budget for crime prevention = $533,200
P 14A–1 Total budgeted revenue = $10,943,500
P 14A–2 Total revenue = $6,268,940

P 14A–3 Total program costs = $1,136,281
P 14A–4 Total variance = $37,000 U
P 14A–5 Total budgeted cost for the program = $287,320
P 14B–1 Total budgeted expenditures = $11,279,530
P 14B–2 Total budgeted revenue = $6,731,316
P 14B–3 Total budgeted expenditures = $1,667,520
P 14B–4 Total variance = $172,000 U
P 14B–5 Total budgeted costs = $115,140
Ex 15–1 EOQ = 250
Ex 15–2 Number of orders = 25
Ex 15–3 Total inventory cost = $5,000
Ex 15–4 Total inventory ordering costs for the three products = $5,100
Ex 15–5 (b) Cost of incorrectly estimating demand = $1.36
Ex 15–6 Cost of incorrectly estimating demand = $100
Ex 15–7 Cost of incorrectly estimating product cost = $22.29
Ex 15–8 Cost of ending inventory, weighted average = $42,520
Ex 15–9 Cost of goods sold, LIFO perpetual = $24,000
Ex 15–10 Cost of goods sold, LIFO = $158
Ex 15–11 Cost of goods sold, FIFO = $307
P 15A–1 EOQ at demand of 100 kegs = 25
P 15A–2 Reorder point with safety stock = 405
P 15A–3 Expected lead time demand = 4 000 L
P 15A–4 Cost of incorrectly estimating demand = $48
P 15A–4 Total inventory cost = $6,600
P 15A–6 Cost of ending inventory, LIFO perpetual = $440
P 15A–7 Net income, LIFO perpetual = $1587.05
P 15B–1 Cost of estimation error = $14.36
P 15B–2 Reorder point = 3 200 cases
P 15B–3 Cost of carrying safety stock = $450
P 15B–4 Cost of incorrect price and carrying cost = $100
P 15B–5 Cost of estimation error = $350.16
P 15B–6 Ending inventory, moving average = $4,042.50
P 15B–7 Cost of ending inventory, LIFO perpetual = $858,000
Ex 16–1 Total labour variance = $960 F
Ex 16–2 Material yield variance = $400 U
Ex 16–3 Total material mix variance = $468 U
Ex 16–4 Total labour efficiency variance = $45 F
Ex 16–5 Total material price variance = $412 F
Ex 16–6 Contribution margin variance = $6 F
Ex 16–7 Total labour mix variance = $2,500 F
Ex 16–8 Total sales mix variance = $840 U
Ex 16–9 Yield variance = $1,050 F
Ex 16–10 Total material variance = $4,780 U
P 16A–1 Total material mix variance = $340 U
P 16A–2 Standard cost of output = $274 per unit
P 16A–3 Sales mix variance = $4,800 F
P 16A–4 Total material quantity variance = $396 F
P 16A–5 Total contribution margin variance = $14,800 U
P 16A–6 Total labour variance = $1,942 U
P 16B–1 Total material mix variance = $3,300 F
P 16B–2 Total labour variance = $4,600 U
P 16B–3 Sales quantity variance = $31,200 F
P 16B–4 Price to wholesalers = $.84
P 16B–5 Total variance = $31,500 F
P 16B–6 Total labour variance = $13,150 U
Ex 17–2 Standard deviation = 55.13
Ex 17–3 (c) Probability = 30.05 percent
Ex 17–4 Probabilities: (b) = 97.7 percent; (d) = 64.5 percent

TRADE ROUTES
IN THE DAYS OF LEHI

(LEHI'S CUTBACK TRAIL TO AQABA)

FRANKINCENSE TRAIL

MOUNTAIN ROAD TO AQABA

MIDIAN

AQABA

COASTAL PLAIN

(AARON AND TOBIT'S PURSUIT OF LEHI)

AQABA BRANCH

FRANKINCENSE TRAIL

JABAL AL LAWZ
(MT. HOREB?)

To BOUNTIFUL
(SOUTHERN ARABIA)

HAQL

(LEHI'S ROUTE TO VALLEY OF LEMUEL)

BORDERS NEAR THE RED SEA

WADI IFAL

BORDERS NEARER THE RED SEA

VALLEY OF LEMUEL
(WADI TAYYIB AL-ISM)

Fountain of the Red Sea
Gulf of Aqaba

...SULA

Gulf of Suez

Jane Harward

PLACE of
REFUGE

OTHER BOOKS AND BOOKS ON CASSETTE
BY DAVID G. WOOLLEY:

The Promised Land Series:

Vol. 1: Pillar of Fire

Vol. 2: Power of Deliverance

VOLUME 3
THE PROMISED LAND

PLACE *of* REFUGE

A NOVEL

DAVID G. WOOLLEY

Covenant Communications, Inc.

Cover painting, *Lehi's Dream* © Greg Olsen. By arrangement with Millpond Press, Inc.
Cover design copyrighted 2003 by Covenant Communications, Inc.

Published by Covenant Communications, Inc.
American Fork, Utah

Printed in Canada
First Printing: December 2003

11 10 09 08 07 06 05   10 9 8 7 6 5 4 3 2 1

ISBN 1-59156-411-5

The third volume in the *Promised Land* series is the story of faithful Jews in search of a *Place of Refuge* from the storms of history that terrorized their faith and threatened the foundations of Jewish society around the turn of the sixth century before Christ. Some Jews remained in the capital city and witnessed the events leading up to its destruction, while many others sought refuge in the secluded deserts of the Arabian Peninsula during the years prior to that ruinous war. Lehi and his family were among those who abandoned their homes and wealth to find refuge in a secluded mountain valley deep in the Border Mountains along the shores of the Red Sea. The harsh clime, deep narrow canyons, and rugged terrain with few year-round water sources to support the life-giving fruit of the date palm inspired Lehi's revelatory dream of a tree of life, giving them hope that they were correct to exchange the earthly comforts of their inheritance at Jerusalem for the fruits of eternal joy hidden in a *Place of Refuge* from the storms that swirled around their lives.

Lehi and his family left Jerusalem during a time of escalating conflict with Babylon and, after suffering threats from the ruling classes of Judah, they ventured into the insufferable heat, waterless desert climes, and rugged mountain borders south of Jerusalem, finally taking refuge in the shadows of an obscure valley beside a river of continually running water. The modern-day discovery of the upper and lower valleys of "Wadi Tayyib al-Ism"—the Pleasant Valley—provides evidence of the only continually running river of water on the Arabian Peninsula, hidden for decades from the view of geologic satellite surveys by two-thousand-foot-high canyon walls shrouding the small year-round river on the canyon floor. Lehi named this valley after his second son Lemuel. This shoreline enclave was a cool, water-filled respite amidst the harshness of the desert Border Mountains surrounding them. It was a God-blessed find for a travel-weary family hidden beyond the reach of man. This secluded valley was the back-drop and possibly the inspiration for Lehi's dream of the Tree of Life, fulfilling the words of Isaiah and later quoted by Nephi that God would 'open rivers in high places, and fountains in the midst of the valleys' (Isaiah 41: 17–18,) ". . . and there shall be a tabernacle for a shadow in the daytime from the heat, and for a *place of refuge* . . . from storm" (Isaiah 4:6; 2 Nephi 14:6).

Numerous explorers, scientists, archaeologists, and scholars of religious texts have explored the ancient trade route along the Arabian Peninsula, searching for evidence of Lehi's trails, and their work, particularly along the east coast of the Gulf of Aqaba in the split Jabal Mountain Range of the Northern Hijaz—known anciently as well as in modern times as the northern borders, similar to the name given them by Nephi (1 Nephi 2:5)—has added depth to the geographic and historical accuracy of this novel. The multitude of geographic, archeological and historical information written into the plot lines and settings in *Place of Refuge* would not be possible without the efforts of so many hardy, gifted, and faithful seekers. These intrepid Saints provide a wealth of evidence documenting the route of Lehi's early travels immediately after leaving Jerusalem, and I offer my sincere thanks for their past and current efforts. Historical notes summarizing their explorations and discoveries, as well as notes on other historical material, appear at the end of this novel.

A project of this scale requires the efforts of many. I offer my sincere thanks to Bonnie Arbon. She has been the first hearer and reader of *Place of Refuge* as she was for the first two books in the series, *Pillar of Fire* and *Power of Deliverance*. Three additional readers, Susan Wilson, Jane Harward, and Patty Jolley have joined Bonnie in this project and together they have been instrumental in preparing this work for submission to the publisher. I also offer sincere thanks to Jane Harward for her fine drawings of the maps of the Valley of Lemuel and the ancient trade routes leading from Jerusalem to the Gulf of Aqaba.

The editorial staff, design group, and management team at Covenant Communications have again been peerless partners in producing a work worthy of the sacred accounts this book portrays. The Covenant Team has been extraordinarily patient and supportive.

Since I began writing this series of historical novels, my previously excellent health has suffered a series of setbacks that have made writing and researching a very difficult undertaking. I owe a debt of gratitude to Bill Bodine for having the spiritual sense to be in the right place at the right time to administer a priesthood blessing that set my feet on the path to recovery. I am thankful to Heather Bodine for her insight, coupled with much prayer, which led me to the proper remedies and doctors. I offer my sincere thanks and appreciation to them for their medical guidance, and for nutrition recommendations that have helped me understand the infinite wisdom and gift of health embodied in the Word of Wisdom. I also offer sincere thanks to my sister and brother-in-law, Jane and Steve Harward of Springville, Utah, for nursing me day to day, over many months, back to full health. Through this battle to reclaim my health, I have gained a deeper appreciation for the direction of the Spirit, for the blessing of personal revelation, and for the protecting care of a wise and loving Heavenly Father. I live a God-blessed life and I share with you my deep personal understanding that our Father in Heaven is aware of our trials and our triumphs, our bitter struggles, and our sweet victories, and with His guidance and help we can happily endure to the end.

Preserved within the pages of the Book of Mormon is the prophetic knowledge of our Savior and Redeemer, Jesus Christ. I have felt His presence, inspiration, and sustaining power throughout the writing of this book and I pray it is acceptable to Him. The task of producing *Place of Refuge* has drawn me to reflect daily on the eternal truths taught in the Holy Scriptures. May God bless your life as you study them.

David G. Woolley
Springville, Utah
November 2003

*There shall be a tabernacle for a shadow in the daytime from the heat, and for a **place of refuge** . . . from storm.*

2 NEPHI 14:6; ISAIAH 4:6

List of Characters

While this is a work of fiction, and all of the characters have been fictionalized, many are based on what we know of the historical figures of the time period. In cases where the names of historical characters are not known, the author has created names. These are marked with an asterisk (*).

HISTORICALLY BASED CHARACTERS:

The Family of Lehi the Olive Oil Merchant
Lehi, *Former Olive Oil Merchant, Prophet of God*
Sariah, *Lehi's Wife*
Rachel*, *Eldest Daughter*
Leah*, *Daughter*
Laman, *Eldest Son & Former Pressmaster*
Lemuel, *Son & Former Stablemaster*
Sam, *Son & Caravanmaster*
Nephi, *Youngest Son & Former Keeper of the Oil*

The Royal Family of Judah
Zedekiah, *King of Judah*
Miriam*, *Queen of Judah*
Mulek, *Prince and Heir Apparent of Judah*
Dan*, *Prince of Judah*
Benjamin*, *Prince of Judah*

The Family of Lord Yaush, Exiled Governor of Southern Judah
Lord Yaush, *Former Commander of Fort Lakhish*
Sophia*, *Wife*
Setti*, *Son & Former Captain of the Night Watch*

The Family of Ishmael the Vineyard Master
Ishmael, *Vineyard Master*
Isabel*, *Ishmael's Wife*
Nathan*, *Eldest Son & Master of Olive Culture*
Seth*, *Son & Watermaster*
Nora*, *Eldest Daughter*
Abigail*, *Daughter*
Hannah*, *Daughter*
Mary*, *Youngest Daughter*

The Family of the Prophet Jeremiah
Jeremiah, *Prophet of God*
Eliza*, *Jeremiah's wife*
Zoram, *Keeper of the Keys*
Hanameel, *Cousin and Seller of Properties*

The Family of Tobit the Babylonian Inspector
Tobit, *Inspector of the Babylonian Occupation*
Darius, *Son & Chief Babylonian Map Maker*

Other Historical Characters
Ezekiel, *Chief Accountant & Lawyer of Jerusalem*
Laban, *Captain of the Guard*
Zadock, *Chief Elder of the Jews at Jerusalem*
Shechem, *King of Robbers*
Ebed-Melech, *Ethiopian Sailor, Egyptian Merchant Vessel, The* Viceroy

FICTIONAL CHARACTERS:

The Family of Jonathan the Blacksmith
Jonathan, *Blacksmith, Elder of the Jews*
Ruth, *Wife & Weaver*
Elizabeth, *Eldest Daughter*
Aaron, *Eldest Son & Former Firemaster*
Daniel, *Son & Former Forgingmaster*
Sarah, *Youngest Daughter*
Joshua, *Youngest Son*

The House of Josiah the Potter
Josiah, *Former Second Elder of the Jews*
Rebekah, *Josiah's Only Child*
Mima, *Ethiopian Handservant*

The House of Moriah, the Scribe
Moriah, Former *Apprentice Scribe at Fort Lakhish*
Hagoth, *Boat Builder and Uncle to Moriah*

Other Fictional Characters
Beuntahyu, *Aaron's Horse*
Phineas, *Tax Collection Station Guard, King's Highway*
Jesse, *Prince of Sidon*

JERUSALEM

Summer.
Six hundred years before
the birth of the Anointed One.

CHAPTER 1

Ezekiel hid himself in the fading shadows that clung to the Citadel Building's steps before dawn. The glow of morning colored the limestone façade and towering columns of the entryway a dirty gray and Ezekiel hurried up the steps, his fingers brushing over the dampness of morning dew that coated the timbers in the tall cedar doors and scented the air with the minted smell of pine strong enough to clear his head of everything but worry over the unpaid Babylonian tax. He unlatched the main door, careful not to wake the night watchman sleeping in his stoop over along the edge of the porch—the man's head propped against the stone column and his arm supported by the hilt of his sword. It wasn't a comfortable bed, but at least the watchman was getting some sleep, something Ezekiel hadn't had since the day he changed the Babylonian tax notice from one quarter to three quarters of a man's income. He took a deep breath and let the pine-scented air prick his lungs. If it weren't for Zadock's order to alter the tax he'd not have to suffer these worries. He stepped beyond the doorpost and into the darkness. Why did he ever listen to the Chief Elder? His part in Zadock's scheme plagued the farthest retreats of his mind, and his only recourse was to be rid of the tax and pray that his part in this never returned to haunt him.

Ezekiel pulled shut the thick cedar door slowly to keep the wood slats from banging against the post. He didn't need to sneak past the night watchman. Ezekiel was the kingdom's Chief Accountant and his office was housed within, but he had to finish tallying the tax before dawn and there was precious little time to wait for his name to be written into the entry log. Better to let the man sleep away these hours before the building opened for the business of the day while Ezekiel prepared the tax for transport to the Babylonian inspector at Jericho. When this morning ended, every gold coin, kernel of grain, and cup of olive oil would be gone from his care and he could forget his part in Zadock's foolish tax revolt that never was.

The brass lamps of the main lobby hung black and cold from the ceiling beams, watching over Ezekiel like ravens perched on nighttime stoops, waiting for him to strike a flint and light their wicks, but there were not enough lamps in all of Judah to drive away the shadows of deception that shrouded this chamber and shed light on the multitude of cunning surrounding the collection of the Babylonian tax, and Ezekiel left the lamps unlit. Zadock had bound him by an oath not to tell any of the Jews at Jerusalem that he'd ordered an increase to the original tax and Ezekiel was foolish enough to honor Zadock's bidding, altering the levy without any of his many assistants to witness the matter—a breech in accounting protocol he never allowed with any of the kingdom's other finances.

Ezekiel lifted the hem of his robe and hurried into the darkness beneath the cold watch of the hanging lamps. He skirted around the main stairs, beyond a run of pillars, and down the hall to the tax storeroom at the back of the Citadel Building. The door to the store-room vault was recessed into the wall, hinged with thick metal posts and held together with iron bars thick enough to discourage the most enterprising thief from prying them back. Ezekiel removed the key from his pocket. It was a long finger-of-a-key, fashioned of brass and tarnished from years of use, and Ezekiel was the only one to possess it. No one in the kingdom except himself had power to enter the storeroom and if anything went missing, only he was left to answer for it. Ezekiel reached the key into the lock, turned it against the pull of the pin and—

The door fell away from his grasp, the metal bars ringing against the inside wall, and Ezekiel marched into the opened vault. How did this door get left open? Was he foolish enough to leave it unlatched last night after he finished his accounting? Ezekiel locked the door behind him to keep anyone from following him inside. He had to be alone if he were to finish accounting for the tax and have it ready to leave the city this morning. He inched through the darkness until he felt the square wooden corner of the counting table near the front of the chamber. Heaven help him if any portion of the tax was missing. He'd spend the rest of his days in a debtor's prison for thievery that was not his doing. What a nightmare this tax collection was becoming, and the sooner he signed it over to the Chief Elder for delivery to the Babylonians at Jericho the sooner he could be free of this charade. No more sleepless nights. No more tossing and turning. No more complying with the Chief Elder's requests to raise the tax from one quarter to three quarters of a man's income—an increase he and his accountants never collected.

Ezekiel felt for the lamp on the counting table and lit it with a flint, the flickering yellow light casting a pale glow over the tax stored in this chamber. The cisterns of sweet wine stacked along the far wall stood exactly where he left them last night, and the hundreds of smaller bottles were unmoved from yesterday's accounting. Ezekiel walked the lamp down past the wine and around a stone pillar to check on the wheat. Seven hundred burlap bags sat on wood slats to keep the dampness of the limestone floor from rotting the grain. Stacks of barley and lentils stood between the stone columns in the middle of the storeroom without a single bag gone missing, and when he raised the clay lids on the cisterns of olive oil set near the back, none of the large vessels were missing even a single precious cup. The sacks of almonds were fine, the dates sat in the corner untouched, and the tanned leather covers sealing the jars of cinnamon, clove, garlic, and basil were tied in place as tight as skin stretched over a drumhead. Everything was accounted for except—

"Is this money what you were looking for?"

The rasping voice came from the front of the storeroom and Ezekiel swung the lamp around, the light playing over the black-robed form of Zadock, Chief Elder of the Jews. Gray hair hedged out from under the brim of his black turban and when Ezekiel raised the lamp higher, Zadock's pale complexion took on a flickering yellow hue. How did the man get inside this vault? Ezekiel rubbed the brass key between his fingers before dropping it into his pocket. The door was locked and no one came in or out without his knowing, unless Zadock was already here, waiting in the darkness before Ezekiel arrived, not uttering a word or making a sound. The Chief Elder stood at the counting table, his long forefinger pausing over the gold coins left out overnight and waiting to be registered in the official tally.

Ezekiel hurried around the sacks of wheat and down past the last column to the counting table. He scooped the remaining coins into a leather pouch, noted the amount in his ledger and sealed the satchel with a cord before stacking it with forty other saddlebags of gold and silver. He said, "I didn't expect you this early, sir."

Zadock walked out from behind the counting table. "This trip to Jericho is not going to be pleasant."

"I wish you Godspeed."

"The only speed we need is that of a good horse, a fast moving mule train, and a well-built carriage. Early summer is far too warm a season to be traveling with slow animals, wouldn't you agree?" Zadock adjusted his shawls back over his shoulder. "I want all this packed onto the mule train immediately. We leave for Jericho before the heat of the morning sun makes this journey any more unpleasant than it already is."

The Chief Elder spoke in a loud, demanding voice, but there was no one in this chamber to take his orders. They were alone without a manservant or soldier to pack these cisterns of oil, vessels of wine, and bags of grain onto the mule train gathering in the alley outside the Citadel Building.

Zadock reached for Ezekiel's arm. "You do have everything accounted for, don't you?"

"I believe I do, sir."

"I don't care for you beliefs. I need an accounting. Is your ledger correct? I can't submit your parchments to the Babylonians only to find out something has gone missing among this, this . . ."

"The tax?"

"This isn't tax." Zadock raised his arm to the chamber filled with goods. "It's blood money stolen from the sweat and tears of Hebrew workers, and as soon as the Babylonians are gone from this land, we'll not have to pay their wretched tariffs."

When did the Chief Elder ever concern himself with the workers and vineyard keepers of Israel? It was as if he were addressing a crowd, but there was no one in this chamber to hear his lies. He had no more concern for his fellows than a vulture has for a carcass. Ezekiel pressed the curled leather ends of his ledger flat against the counting table and started the tip of his pen over the entries to make one final accounting.

Zadock said, "Do you have everything in order or do you simply believe you do?"

Ezekiel kept his gaze down on his parchment. "If you'll allow me, sir."

"It isn't like you to make errors with your record keeping."

Ezekiel brought his head up from going over the ledger. "There were ten other accountants who assisted with this tally, sir."

"So many details. So many chances for error." Zadock leaned over Ezekiel's shoulder, close enough that his warm breath streamed past Ezekiel's neck. It was impossible to work with Zadock peering over him like this, but he couldn't ask the man to step away. The Chief Elder did as he pleased and Ezekiel hurried through the accounting record without telling Zadock how much he disliked having him that close.

The penmanship on the number of bags of wheat was difficult to read and Ezekiel wrote over it to make the poorly formed letters legible. The number and size of wine and oil vessels were entered properly, the other grains and herbs were accounted for correctly, and the lines detailing the collection of gold didn't appear to have any errors. Ezekiel certified the tally with his mark near the bottom of the ledger and—

"Add another line here." Zadock stabbed the tip of his finger into the ledger below Ezekiel's mark. "Write that Zadock, Chief Elder of the Jews, was responsible for ending the tax revolt by imprisoning the man who engineered this evil."

"But sir, no instigator has been imprisoned."

"Do it."

Ezekiel got out his pen and wrote the line of affirmation at the end of the scroll, but it wasn't accurate. Zadock hadn't imprisoned anyone over the tax revolt. The Chief Elder and Captain Laban were the perpetrators of this failed scheme and Zadock certainly wasn't going to imprison himself. The tax Ezekiel and his accountants collected was exactly what the Babylonians had asked in their original levy—Ezekiel was certain of it. He'd received the tablet the day it arrived by courier and it required a one-quarter tax to be delivered to Tobit, the Babylonian Inspector at Jericho, and not a single shekel more. Ezekiel finished the Chief Elder's dictation in a flowing Hebrew script and lifted his pen from the only inaccuracy on an otherwise accurate accounting parchment.

Zadock said, "Do you read many documents in your work?"

Of course he did. Ezekiel rolled the tax notice and tied it off with a leather cord. But why did Zadock care if he read often? He said, "Mostly numbers, sir," and daubed a bit of soft wax along the end of the parchment before pressing his ring into it, fastening it shut with his seal—a rendering of a moneychanger's scale, the rod balanced on a fulcrum and the money bowls hanging by chains from both ends.

Zadock said, "But you do read other things, don't you?"

What did he mean by *other things?* Ezekiel said, "I don't usually have time, sir."

"What about your favorite writings?"

"I have none."

"Not even your books from heaven?"

Ezekiel lowered his ring finger from the sealed parchment. How did Zadock know about his vision of the book of heaven? "I don't know what you mean, sir."

"You study the prophecies, don't you?" Zadock raised the thin, black eyebrow over his left eye. "Why don't you recount some of your personal prophecies for me?"

"I read the law like every good scribe."

"Not that drivel. I want to hear your new prophecies."

Ezekiel spoke without looking directly at the Chief Elder. He couldn't look directly at a man he mistrusted more with each passing day. He said, "New prophecies, sir?"

"That's right. The ones detailing the coming together of the records from the tribes of Joseph and Judah into some book on a future day many years distant from our time." Zadock cut his words short and raised the pitch of his voice. "It's just the sort of heady stuff men with the strength of *flint* would conceive."

Ezekiel stepped back from the Chief Elder. How did he know about Ezekiel's visions? He was recounting word for word what Ezekiel read from the Book of Heaven and his revelation of the two records of the Hebrews coming together in the last days—visions he'd not made known to anyone but Lehi. Ezekiel was alone in the palace livery last month when he spoke to the olive oil merchant immediately after Uriah's trial. At least he thought he was alone. Ezekiel slowly tightened his grip on the writing pen. There was no way the Chief Elder could know such things unless he sneaked into the livery the day Ezekiel spoke with Lehi and hid among the shadows. And he never repeated to anyone the promise Lehi gave him that afternoon outside the horse stables—that Ezekiel was to become as strong as flint and a watchman over Israel.

"The notice isn't entirely accurate." Ezekiel handed the tax notice over to Zadock. "There was never a tax revolt except the one you asked me to create by changing the—"

"You didn't write that into the official ledger, did you?" Zadock held on to the word "official" and let it ring amid the sacks of wheat and cisterns of oil and wine, his voice rising through his stiffening body, the flesh about his eyes narrowing like a fox peering out of its hole—a very dark hole. He tore back the seal on the document and turned his gaze onto it.

"It's not in there, but it should be." Ezekiel nodded his head, his dark ringlets dancing over his brow. "You had me alter the—"

"You and your accountants posted a three-quarter tax on every gate in this city."

"Of course we did." Ezekiel reached for the ledger, but Zadock pulled it back and stuffed it under his arm. "I altered the Babylonian tablet when you asked me to—"

"Are you saying you lied about the tax when you posted it to the citizens of Jerusalem?"

"I was acting on your—"

"Answer me."

Ezekiel pointed to the tax notice under Zadock's arm. Did he have such a poor memory he couldn't remember ordering Ezekiel to alter the levy? He said, "Certainly you haven't forgotten that you—

"I'm leaving this morning to meet with Inspector Tobit to negotiate the tax down from three quarters to one quarter . . ."

There he went again, insisting he was going to Jericho to negotiate a tax that was never any higher than one quarter.

Zadock said, ". . . and you tell me that the tax was never that high. What did you hope to gain by spawning a tax revolt among the Jews?" He began to pace in front of the counting table. "It is sheer treason to think you could start another war."

Ezekiel raised his hands. "I was following your—"

"Guards, take this man to the palace prison."

"We're alone."

"You should know me better. I never accuse a man of treason without witnesses present." Zadock pointed the end of the tax record toward the far corner of the storeroom where a troop of soldiers burst from the shadows. They surrounded Ezekiel with their swords drawn. The largest man bound Ezekiel's wrists with cords while two more tied his feet in stone shackles. He tried to pull free of the half-tied knots, but a soldier pressed the edge of his blade against Ezekiel's neck, cursing him a traitor to the kingdom and warning him not to move or he'd force the weapon clean through his throat.

Traitor? Ezekiel kept his neck still against the sharpness. Betraying his homeland was the last thing Ezekiel would ever do. He was a fool to have ever trusted the Chief Elder and alter the levy on the man's orders. Zadock was the author of this scheme and Ezekiel would not allow this charade to continue. He said, "I'll tell the Babylonian Inspector everything."

"A confession?" Zadock stepped past the circle of soldiers surrounding Ezekiel. "The Babylonians aren't interested in your guilt. They want you to pay for your insurrection."

"They'll want to know the details and I'll tell them everything."

"Do you really think I'd let the Babylonians put you on trial?" Zadock pulled the blade back from Ezekiel's throat. "I learned my lesson with Uriah, sir. The Babylonians will listen to me. They don't have time to try Hebrew prisoners, especially ones foolish enough to instigate a tax revolt."

"I was doing your bidding."

"Please, no more of your lies." Zadock turned to the soldiers. "This man is the rebel responsible for instigating the tax revolt. Take him to the palace prison. *That* should make him as strong as flint." He nodded to Ezekiel. "Isn't that what God told you—that He would make you strong as flint and a watchman over Israel?" He patted

Ezekiel on the cheek with his long, bony fingers. "You zealots are all fools."

Ezekiel tried to pull free, but the lead soldier hit him across the side of the head with the butt of his sword and he fell back into the grasp of his captors. What a fool he was for letting the Chief Elder follow him to the palace livery after Uriah's trial and overhear his words with Lehi. Ezekiel had seen a vision of the Book of Heaven and he couldn't deny that Lehi would have some part in bringing the sticks of Joseph and Judah together—he'd seen it in vision and he could never deny it. A line of blood streamed over his left ear and he pressed his hand against the gash in the side of his head. If going to prison would give him the strength of flint God intended him to have, then so be it; he was prepared to suffer whatever fate was his, but how was he to be a watchman over Israel if he were locked away in the catacombs? The lead soldier pushed him toward the door of the storeroom with such force that he fell to the ground, his hands skinning over the stone, and the expensive silks and linens in his robe ripping at the elbow and knees.

"Watchman over Israel?" Zadock spat in Ezekiel's face, the spittle spraying into his eyes. "Take him away."

CHAPTER 2

Captain Laban pushed the nursemaid back from leaning over his bed and cursed her for waking him. Couldn't she see he was winning back a portion of the sleep he lost last night? The woman's soft white robe was half-hidden beneath nursing aprons and she raised her hands in the dim light of the shuttered room, begging his pardon and urging him back to sleep while she fetched him his morning tea.

Tea? Laban felt for the bottle of strong wine on the stand next to his bed and when he found it he shook the uncorked lip at the nursemaid and cursed again. Her teas were nothing more than ill-fated potions, and none of her ointments and powders would ever mend his broken shoulder. It was ale he needed, a cistern full whenever the pain inspired a drink, and his broken shoulder was cause for a good deal of inspiration at this ungodly hour of the morning. The pillows the nursemaid placed under his back last night didn't ease the throbbing, and he tossed and turned until just before dawn only to be wakened by her insufferable care. He should have slept the night on a straight hardwood table at the Jawbone Inn and drowned his pain in a bottle instead of convalescing on the feather cushions in this bed and waking to her impotent cures. There was not a tea in her cupboard that could dull the pain of his shoulder like a good drink from the cool recesses of the Jawbone's cellar.

Laban scratched his chest and caught a fistful of the untied ends of a linen sling. So that's what the nursemaid was doing when she woke him—fixing a support beneath his arm and over his shoulder— and when she leaned over to finish her knots, he pushed her aside. She had the touch of an ox and if she tried one more time to tie that sling on, he was going to break her arm and let her enjoy the unpleasant company of a fractured bone. He paid her a fine price for her nursing, but that didn't give her the right to poke at his shoulder like a cook tending a fire. He was not some weaver's needle cushion. For the love of Moses, she treated his shank bone like the shoulder of an ass. He may have a thick chest and powerful arms, but his strength didn't numb him to the pain her mulish prodding inflicted.

Laban turned on his side to remove the sling, but the sudden movement shot a bolt of pain through his shoulder. The nursemaid insisted he lay back and let her remove the linen, but he couldn't, not with the fierce pain stopping his breath. He arched his back and cried out, the groan starting deep in his bowels and rising out of his lungs with enough force to scare the nursemaid back a step.

"Cursed son of the blacksmith!"

Laban pressed the bottle to his lips and poured a swig of warm wine over his tongue, swishing it between his teeth before lying back and swallowing. All his troubles would be over if the son of the blacksmith had bled to death in the bushes at Beit Zayit, but somehow Aaron survived long enough to follow him back to Jerusalem and keep Laban from killing Lehi. Laban blew the air out of his lungs and let his shoulder settle against the pillows. The boy couldn't have lived much longer than that, not after losing so much blood, and with the ensuing infections that were certain to finish what Laban's arrow began. He took another long drink from the bottle, the wine spilling out the side of his mouth and staining the pillows red. Aaron was dead, he had to be, and soon Lehi would join him. Laban would see to that. No one escaped him and lived to tell of it—certainly not an olive oil merchant who claimed prophethood to cover his secret designs. The sword and brass plates belonged to Laban and no one would take them from him, not even the rightful heir to the royal relics.

There was no telling what direction Lehi fled. He wouldn't have gone toward the rising sun. The Babylonians patrolled the Empty Quarter, and beyond Jericho the trade route led south into the deserts of the Arabian Peninsula—a forsaken land Lehi would never enter, no matter that every tax evader, religious zealot, and traitor to the kingdom took refuge in that part of the world. The deserts and mountains of Northern Arabia—those towering barren borders separating civilization from the harsh extremes of the Peninsula—couldn't provide the opulent life to which Lehi was accustomed. Laban forced his head back into the soft, down pillow and drank the wine bottle dry. A wealthy man like Lehi would have led his family to Bethlehem, through Hebron, and then west through the hill country past Fort Lakhish, and across the Sinai to Egypt. Lehi had friends and a host of business associates there, and he traveled that way often enough that he knew every sand dune and wadi between here and the Nile Delta. There was no question Lehi fled that way. He and his well-heeled family were far too inclined to the comforts of this world to go anywhere but the land of the Pharaohs.

The pain in Laban's shoulder ebbed somewhat and he stripped the sling off and threw it at the nursemaid's feet. Did she really think he would wear this for others to see? This injury never happened. It was a simple fall from the saddle that broke his shank bone, not an arrow from the feeble-handed bow of the blacksmith's son. And he'd tell anyone who asked that his horse reared while riding in the hills east of the city. He was returning from an evening ride when his horse got away from him and . . .

No, Laban was too good a horseman for anyone to believe he suffered a simple fall, but he couldn't tell his lieutenants that an arrow from Aaron's bow made him unfit to train in the wrestling pit, or unable to wield a sword, or practice his bowmanship. Better to tell them he was thrown to the ground when his horse came across a serpent in the trail and he was lucky to escape without suffering a snakebite. That was a sensible explanation for everything except for the scar on his back. Laban craned his neck and reached for the wound high on his shoulder. The doctor removed the bandage last week and he lightly touched his fingers over the dark red scab, careful not to pull it up and make it worse. His other scars were for show— the ones he'd gotten saving the brass plates in his treasury—not this foolish wound made by a boy who didn't have the strength to pull a string to a full draw. This small scar on his shoulder would never inspire the respect he'd won with the wounds suffered at the hands of Babylonian swords. Those were the stuff of legends and he slowly raised his arms to inspect the two-year-old war wounds. The first cut deep across his left bicep and ran up his arm and over his shoulder, and the other shot across his chest before disappearing under his arm. These were a testimony to his bravery—a reminder to every Jew that he'd saved the relics of his royalty and kept the Babylonians from confiscating his treasures. He hadn't been entirely successful. The Babylonians managed to get his sword, but since the blacksmith made a perfect copy there was no reason that Laban's scars of bravery couldn't cover the heroic rescue of both national treasures. He moved his fingers slowly over the new scar on his shoulder. There was little boasting he could make of this wound except to prove he'd done what Lieutenant Daniel failed to do. Laban killed Daniel's brother and there was no doubt Aaron lay buried in a shallow grave somewhere along the trail of Lehi's flight to Egypt.

The thick smell of frankincense left burning in the brass incense bowl overnight stifled the air and Laban ordered the nursemaid to open the shutters and freshen the room. She undid the latch, pushed open the wooden slats and let the gray predawn glow brighten the cushions and blankets on Laban's—

"What hour is it?" Laban threw off the lambskin blanket, swung his feet onto the stone floor, and stood with nothing on but a leather kilt. He raised his hand to his brow to shield his eyes from the glow of morning. "Did the Chief Elder stop by?"

"You didn't say you were expecting visitors this morning." The nursemaid turned her gaze to the floor away from Laban.

"The Chief Elder is no visitor in this house. Before he left for Jericho we were to speak about . . ." Laban stepped closer to the nursemaid, his powerful body towering above her bent-over frame. "What are you staring at, woman?"

"I'm sorry sir, but . . ." She kept her gaze down and pointed toward the shelf along the far wall. "Your clothes are folded over there."

"You've seen me in less than this." She'd been Laban's maidservant since the day he was born and he didn't need a lecture about proper dress. He was Captain of the Guard and he would wear whatever suited him.

The nursemaid said, "You've been drinking a good deal these past few nights, sir."

"Get me another bottle and meet me in the courtyard." He marched into the hall, crossed through the anteroom, and threw open

the main doors of the estate. The front gates were latched and Laban
called to the watch, asking if the Chief Elder had passed by in the
early light of morning. They answered that he hadn't, and there was
no telling if Zadock had left for Jericho before consulting with him
on the matter of Lehi's escape. Laban stormed across the courtyard
toward the livery, his kilt sagging about his hips with each stride, and
the morning light silhouetting his nakedness. How did he ever allow
Lehi and his company to leave the city alive? They may not be a
threat any longer, but they were an embarrassment. No one ever
escaped Laban, and he pulled open the livery doors with his good
arm. His shoulder was healed enough that he could saddle his horse
and ride to the Citadel Building to see if the Chief Elder had left the
city. He threw the silver-studded saddle over the horse's haunches,
draped the bridle in place, and teased it into the animal's mouth with
three short jerks on the end of the—

Mother of Moses! A sharp pain flashed through Laban's shoulder.
Where was the nursemaid with his wine? He pulled himself up into
the saddle with his good arm and brought the Arabian around into
the courtyard, swearing by heaven and earth he'd see Lehi suffer
greater pain than this.

The nursemaid stood on the front steps of the estate, holding a
new wine bottle in one hand and offering a cloak with the other,
telling Laban he should cover himself before going out, and if he
didn't do as the doctor told him and stay off his horse until his shank
bone mended, it would heal improperly.

Laban sidled in next to the nursemaid, leaned over the saddle and
snatched the wine bottle from her grasp. Did she think she was his
mother? The woman hadn't spent the past weeks lying on a bed
searching for the perfect pose that would keep the pain from driving him
to insanity and beyond. Laban tipped the wine bottle to his lips, the wine
spilling down his neck and dripping onto his shoulder like an ointment
that could cure him. It wasn't the broken bone that turned him to
drinking. It was Lehi's escape that plagued him more than any lame limb.

The nursemaid said, "Don't you think that's enough for one
morning, sir?"

"I'll decide when I've had enough." Laban threw the bottle at the
steps, the clay splintering in a thousand pieces, and cherry-red wine

splattering over the stones. He took the cape, draped it over his shoulders and tied it about his neck, the poorly knotted bow rising and falling with each painful breath. "Have another bottle ready when I return." He reined across the courtyard and the day watch pushed open the gates.

"Captain, sir." The nursemaid's voice trailed behind him. "What shall I tell the Chief Elder if he should pass this way?"

Laban came around in the street, his Arabian arching her neck against the pull of the reins, and the ends of his cloak rising on the air about his unclothed frame. "Tell Zadock I'm going to finish what we started if I have to go to the gates of hell and back to do it." He cradled his bad arm against his belly and spoke in a low, penetrating voice. "The olive oil merchant will never find a place of refuge!"

CHAPTER 3

Captain Laban veered sharp, past the shuttered carts in the Upper City market, the sudden turn pulling his arm away from his belly and the pain in his shoulder begging him to slow his pace. Curse his broken shank bone and curse the nursemaid for warning him not to ride until he was healed, no matter how right her caution.

The market stood empty this early in the morning without any shoppers to slow his way through this maze of stone walkways and overhanging balconies, or stare at his half-clothed frame. He spurred his horse beneath the low archway at the top of the market and into the government district, the clap of his Arabian's hooves echoing across the empty sprawl of the open plaza and reverberating off the limestone walls of the temple before dying amid the columned entrance of the Citadel Building opposite the sanctuary. There was not a single lawyer climbing the steps of the government building, no accountants milling about with scrolls beneath their arms and no mass of priests congregated about the gates of the temple.

Laban brought his mount around. What a fool he was. He'd missed the Chief Elder's departure for Jericho and he slowly reined his Arabian back toward home when the snap of a whip and the order to prepare to mount beckoned him toward a narrow gate along the far side of the Citadel Building. He squinted to focus his wine-blurred gaze on the alley where a line of mules stretched down the length of the passageway, disappearing behind the government headquarters. He cantered over and sidled in close enough for his Arabian to rub its muzzle against the gatepost. Each animal in the mule train was packed with cisterns of olive oil strapped atop a sea of grain sacks.

Lieutenant Daniel sat in the saddle at the head of this armada of mules with a whip hanging from his grip. The brown steed he rode was the wrong color for a boy who was fast becoming Laban's most trusted officer, and he made a note to find another white Arabian like his—one Daniel could be proud to ride about the city. A long, black cloak was draped over Daniel's square shoulders, and the collar of his tunic hedged out from beneath the coat, hiding his thick neck. The square turns of his brow and the rugged dark color of his cheeks commanded respect, but the black patch on his left eye was an ugly reminder that his brother, Aaron, had robbed him of his sight. It was a waste of a perfect man, but it wouldn't keep the boy from rising in the military. A war wound gotten defending the kingdom wouldn't keep Daniel from rising through the ranks of his officers, no matter how false the claim to courage.

Daniel's riding boots were worn beyond what a Lieutenant in the military should wear and Laban was going to have to get the boy another pair when he returned from this mission, regardless of Daniel's affection for the touch of worn Egyptian crocodile against his skin. The boy couldn't wear whatever pleased him, not if he was going to become Laban's heir. Daniel wasn't just any officer in this military; he was a sturdy lad with the same powerful frame Laban possessed and they shared a love for the power that officer life afforded. Daniel was the son Laban did not have and one day, once the throne of Judah belonged to Laban, the boy would make a fine Captain of the Guard. He may not be well-known among the common soldiers— Daniel rose to a commission too quickly to have fostered any low-ranking friendships—but it was foolishness to waste the boy's preparatory years in the company of men less able than he. Laban would see that Daniel had more than enough experience to qualify for the highest post in the military.

Daniel was assigned to escort the tax to Jericho with the entire second cavalry under his command—fifty of the finest horsemen in the military. It was twice the number needed for a short trip through safe country. They had little trouble with robbers on the descent from Jerusalem to the low-lying lands around Jericho along the north rim of the Dead Sea, but this was Daniel's chance to prove himself to the rank and file. As long as the delivery went without issue, the boy was certain to gain the affection of these soldiers, and word of his command would spread until he was known among Laban's ten thousand. All the boy had to do was deliver the tax to Inspector Tobit in Jericho, a short thirty-mile jaunt from here, and he'd return a successful commander—a title Laban would see he earned often before it was time for Daniel to stand in his stead.

Laban nudged his Arabian into the alley, but not far enough inside to be seen by Daniel. The boy raised his hand to the cavalrymen, his cloak falling away from his thick arms, and signaled the riders to mount up and form a double-file column down both sides of the mule train—his low, powerful voice resonating off the high walls of the alley. He was right to tell the men to keep the mules from wandering out of line—the trail to Jericho was a steep descent through hill country, and cavalrymen made poor shepherds unless they were ordered to keep the animals organized. None of the men complained when Daniel told them they wouldn't break for water except on his word and they nodded when he told them not to approach the high-bearing, four-wheeled rig at the front of the caravan. The bags of gold and silver were sealed behind the leather canopy covering the carriage, and no one but the eight riders assigned to guard it were allowed to approach.

Laban nodded his approval with each of Daniel's orders, and when the boy asked if any soldier had anything to say about their mission to Jericho, Laban spurred into the alley and sidled in next to Daniel. He said, "There is one thing, Commander."

"Captain Laban?" Daniel turned in the saddle, the leather creaking under his weight. "I didn't expect you here this morning."

Laban spoke loud enough for the entire cavalry to hear. "I don't let my finest commander leave the city without wishing him well."

Daniel adjusted the black patch over his eye. "Thank you, sir."

Laban sat back in the saddle and surveyed the cavalrymen and mules. The packs were secure, the riders well supplied—their saddles bags stocked with food, their water skins full, and their riggings in good repair, but they lacked one thing before they were ready. Laban lowered his voice and said, "The men are waiting for an inspection, son." He tipped his head down the long line of cavalrymen and smiled at the boy. "Go on; it's your duty."

Daniel reined slowly down the alley and when he nodded to the men near the front, they sat to attention. The next pair of soldiers grunted their approval of his command and he spurred his mount faster, tipping his head to each pair of soldiers until he reached the end of the mule train, came around and galloped back to Laban. "Everything's in order, sir."

Laban leaned over the saddle. "Did you speak with your father?"

"Not yet." Daniel patted the neck of his horse to settle her down. "There wasn't time."

Laban inched his mount closer. "He should know before you leave the city."

"What does it hurt if he hopes Aaron will come home one day?"

"Ride by your father's house."

"Now, sir?"

"You've plenty of time."

"But—"

"Go on; that will give me time for a word with the Chief Elder."

Daniel turned in the saddle to face Laban. "Is it true what you told me about Aaron?"

"I've never deceived you, son. Now go. Your father shouldn't hold on to false hopes any longer." Laban adjusted his cloak to cover his bare shoulder. "It's time Jonathan the Blacksmith knew the fate of his firstborn son."

"My men, sir." Daniel shifted back in his saddle. "They're ready to ride to—"

"They're not ready to ride until you say they're ready."

Laban raised his voice to the cavalrymen, his words resonating off the alley walls. He ordered them to groom their horses and repack their supplies. They'd done a poor job tying down the tax and what were the mules doing preparing to leave when the animals weren't watered enough to get them much beyond the city gates? Didn't they know they were headed east and it was certain to be a much warmer day at the low elevations around Jericho than it was here in Jerusalem? Laban barked his orders. They were to get it right this time or he'd have them do it again until everything was in order.

Laban turned back to Daniel. "You see. They aren't ready until you give the word. No go speak with your father." He leaned over and swatted Daniel's horse, sending him trotting out of the alley toward the Lower City, then reined over to Zadock's carriage at the head of the mule train. The cavalrymen guarding the four-wheeled transport stepped aside and let Laban dismount just outside the stoop. Thick leather canopies covered the top of the carriage, and the unsecured flaps along the sides lifted on the morning breeze. Laban pulled back the leather veil and found Zadock leaning over a saddlebag counting gold coins. When he noticed the light streaming in through the opening, he spun around on his bench seat, his hand in front of his pale face, his eyes squinting between his fingers. "What's the meaning of this interruption? I told you, Lieutenant, I don't want to be bothered until we arrive at Jericho and I mean what I . . ." He slowly lowered his hand from in front of his eyes. "Laban? You should be in your bed."

"I'm well enough to ride."

"Dressed like that?"

Laban ripped his cloak off his back, draped it over the sideboard and leaned his bare chest against the cart. "I'm going to Egypt."

"It's over, Captain. Lehi's not a threat as long as he stays in Egypt."

"And if he returns?"

"We're done with him." Zadock slipped down along the bench seat and leaned out the side of the carriage, the leather flaps of the canopy brushing against the point in his black turban and his stale breath streaming over Laban's face. "As long as he doesn't return to Judah he's none of our concern."

Laban stood away from the carriage, his bare shoulders stiffening in the morning light. "No one escapes me."

"Your pride will ruin both of us."

"Lehi will ruin us."

"The captain of Judah's military can't go searching about the kingdom of Egypt for an olive oil merchant."

Laban gripped the side of the carriage. "It's time we improved our relations with the Egyptians."

"That's sheer foolishness." Zadock called to the soldiers standing by to busy themselves with watering horses and let him speak with Laban in private. He waited until they disappeared behind the Citadel Building before speaking another word. "If the Babylonians get news you're negotiating an alliance with the Egyptians, there will be another war."

"I never said anything about an alliance. I call it a friendship. Our ties to Egypt should be something more than the trading of olive oil for gold."

Zadock pulled himself back inside the cart. "When did you ever concern yourself with the merchant trade?"

"A certain olive oil merchant inspired me."

"What will you do, question every Egyptian to ever purchase olive oil from Lehi?"

"That's a start."

"Stop this. Now." Zadock shook his head and his gray hair curled up around his reddening cheeks. "If you go to Egypt you'll need permission from King Zedekiah and neither of us can afford to push the limits of his trust after what happened at Uriah's trial. Our friend Lehi was not kind with his accusations."

"Curse Lehi and curse the king to—"

"Silence!" Zadock raised his hand. "Curse the king again and we'll both end up in prison with Ezekiel."

"Did you take care of him?"

"Early this morning and I don't want either of us to share his fate, do you understand me?"

"What are you afraid of?"

"Your newfound fascination with Egypt, your unbridled passions, your . . ." Zadock turned his gaze over Laban's half-clothed frame. "Your lack of clothing."

"Have you lost your ambition?"

"We haven't time for ambition." Zadock leaned forward and sniffed the smell of wine rising from Laban's breath. "You're to stay in Jerusalem and let your shoulder heal. We'll discuss Lehi when I return from Jericho."

"I'll do as I please."

"And exactly what will you do after you question every merchant and royal between the Nile Delta and Pharaoh's palace at Tanus and find nothing to lead you to Lehi?" Zadock sat back against the bench seat and stared at the leather canopy. "The only thing worse than *not* finding Lehi is . . ."

"Is what?"

"Finding him." Zadock folded his arms across his chest, the large cuffs falling down over his narrow middle. "We were fools to have brought Uriah back from Egypt to stand trial. We should have let him stay in exile and not suffer the humiliation. Let Lehi live out his days in Egypt where he can't bother us."

"He'll be coming back."

"He won't risk his life to return and enjoy his wealth."

"This was never about wealth, sir. It's a matter of kingship." Laban mounted his Arabian, but before spurring out of the alley he said, "Lehi knows of our lineage."

CHAPTER 4

Elizabeth reached for the lamp left overnight on the windowsill. The early-morning drizzle didn't douse the light, but there was no reason to keep the flame lit with sunrise breaking through the gray mist. She grasped the lamp between her hands, the rough clay sides warm from the flickering flame that had burned in the window for almost a month. Mama kept it alive, but she was fooling herself if she thought keeping this small lamp lit would lure Aaron home. She was frittering away expensive oils on a brother who didn't deserve anything better than a good kick across the backside. Aaron knew the way home and as soon as he came to his senses he'd return without any help from this lamp.

The lamp's holding vessel was full to the brim and there was no doubt Mama trimmed it during the night. Poor woman. She'd been up pacing as she had every night since Aaron went missing nearly two months before—running to the front door and leaning out the moment she heard a stir about the house. Elizabeth told her a hundred times it was the wind, or a passing mule cart, or the creaking of the roof beams, but Mama would not listen to her logic. It was not Elizabeth's son who had gone missing and Mama would not surrender the constant trimming of the lamp for other rituals, no matter that it was time they ended their wondering about Aaron and got on with life without him.

Elizabeth tightened her hold around the clay vessel. Foolish brother of hers! Did he not understand what pain his secret exodus caused them? He could not have fled on a more hurtful night, leaving on the Feast of Passover without confiding in anyone. Beyond Papa,

Aaron was their last blacksmith, the only other able body left to run the shop and he never should have disappeared like this. Elizabeth stared at the flame dancing between her hands. No, Aaron didn't disappear, he stole away in the middle of the night and he took a part of Elizabeth's heart with him. Of all her siblings it was with Aaron she confided most and he could have at least had the good grace to say good-bye. Elizabeth pressed her palms tight against the lamp's holding vessel, her hands trembling against its coarseness. Aaron was selfish, and cruel, and petty, and he'd done an awful thing to them running off like he did. Elizabeth leaned over to blow out the—

"Not the lamp, dear." Ruth reached around Elizabeth and covered the flame with her hand. "You know why I keep it lit."

Elizabeth raised her lips away from the flame. Of course she knew, but must they keep lit this reminder that Aaron didn't love them any longer? She said, "Why did he leave us, Mama?"

"I don't know what lure keeps him from home." Ruth lowered her head. Her dark black hair was tied up behind her head, but she'd done the ribbon in such a hurry the strands fell down around her neck and hedged about her cheeks. She slowly nodded. "We must keep a flame lit for him deep in our souls." Her lower lip began to tremble and she quickly daubed back a tear. "He has to know we want him home with us."

"It's my doing." Jonathan sat at the kitchen table. His thick black hair fell down into his eyes as he spoke, but he didn't bother to push it back off his brow. "I drove the boy away."

Elizabeth said, "That isn't so, Papa."

"I've always been suspicious of his faith." Jonathan held an empty cup between his hands, but he didn't tap it on the table to tell Ruth he wanted another round of warm goat's milk. It wasn't like Papa to show any patience early in the morning, but there he sat, his stare wandering across the table until it rested on Joshua. The boy's light brown hair was wet and combed back behind his ears. He was dressed in the thickest tunic Mama could find and she told him not less than three times he was to stay away from the ovens, not lift anything that would strain him and he was only to help gather tools for Papa, nothing else, no forging, and certainly no tending the ovens. Mama didn't want another of her sons scarred by the heat of blacksmithing or crippled by the dangers of working too close to the fires—especially a son as inexperienced and untrained as her little Joshua. Sarah sat next to him. She was a full hand taller than Joshua and her long, red hair fell down over her shoulders and brushed across Joshua's face, tempting him to give a tug, but he didn't bother, not this morning. Joshua sat stiff against the back of his chair, his bowl of pottage untouched and his eyes filled with a certain apprehension. He nodded to Papa and mumbled he was ready to go to the shop before lowering his stare into the bowl of pottage and stirring it with a spoon. Joshua was a good many months away from his eighth birthday and three years too young to spend his days at the shop lifting a forging hammer or stoking the ovens, but Papa needed an assistant and with Aaron gone, Joshua was to be Papa's last hope to pass on the secrets of his blacksmithing.

Jonathan tapped the side of his cup. "I thought I'd mended my differences with Aaron until now."

Elizabeth said, "What happened?"

"What does it matter?" Jonathan lowered his head. "The boy's gone."

"Not forever, Papa." Elizabeth came down along the kitchen table careful not to let the lamp go out. She placed her free hand on Papa's shoulder, his body tensing against her soft touch. "He'll come—"

"He's never coming home." Daniel stepped into the kitchen from the main room. He'd slipped in the front door without making a sound, all the time listening to them. He was dressed in his lieutenant's tunic, his sword holstered at his hip and a small cape hanging from his thick arm. He adjusted the black patch over his bad eye— the one he said he injured at the military grounds during a training exercise. It was a shame he'd lost the use of his left eye, but it didn't seem to bother him, except when Elizabeth asked him to tell the details of a story he said didn't have any details. He hurt his eye in archer training and that was more than enough detail for the family. Daniel nodded to Ruth and said, "I'm sorry Mama."

"Sorry for what, son?"

"I should have told you sooner." Daniel's powerful body stiffened and he worked the sole of his boot into the stone floor. "I wanted to be sure."

Elizabeth said, "Sure of what?"

"Captain Laban sent me with a report."

"You're not leaving on another assignment are you, son?" Jonathan leaned back in his chair. "I may need some assistance for a time until Joshua learns to be of help."

Ruth reached for Daniel's shoulder, but she pulled back before touching him and held her hand to her mouth.

Daniel said, "I'll only be gone to Jericho for a few weeks, nothing more Mama."

Ruth sighed. "You'll be careful. I couldn't bear it if anything happened to any of my sons."

Jonathan said, "Go on, tell us what you came to tell us."

Daniel cleared his throat before saying, "Captain Laban informed me that Aaron is—

"They found him?" Ruth took Daniel by the arm. "Is he well? Where is he?" She tugged on the sleeve of his tunic. "My prayers have been answered."

Daniel pulled free of Ruth's grasp and backed into the archway between the kitchen and main room, his face hidden from the glow of the lamp. His lone brown eye was difficult to read and Elizabeth raised the lamp until she could see he was without the mischievousness that once filled his gaze. It could be that his unflinching stare was part of his military training, but there was a certain longing in his look, his single eye slowly turning about the kitchen to Joshua and Sarah, then past her to Papa and finally resting on Mama. Daniel would never return to be the playful taunt she knew before he left home to live at Captain Laban's estate, back when he wasn't beholden to the military commander—the man who had forever removed the light of Daniel's soul from his eye.

Elizabeth said, "What are you keeping from us?"

"Nothing." Daniel wrapped the small cloak over his shoulders and pulled the collar up around his neck. "Captain Laban thought it was time I informed you."

"Informed us?" Jonathan turned in his chair and pushed the hair out of his eyes. "We're your family, son. You don't inform us of things." He motioned for Daniel to come back to the table. "You tell us whatever's on your mind."

Daniel didn't come back into the kitchen. He said, "There was a struggle at Beit Zayit the night of Uriah's trial last month."

Jonathan said, "What does this have to do with Aaron?"

"He tried to stop Captain Laban from interrogating Lehi." Daniel slowly backed toward the front door, the heel of his boots clipping the stone.

Jonathan said, "Go on."

"Aaron stepped in the way of Captain Laban's arrow and—"

"No, it isn't so!" Ruth shook her head so hard her hair came loose from its ribbon and the long strands fell over her cheeks and covered the tears welling up in her eyes. "Aaron's gone for a season, but he's coming back. I've prayed him home and God will grant me at least that." Her voice faltered, but before her words were lost in a deep sigh she managed to say, "I will see him again in this life." She bent over, her arms wrapped around herself.

Elizabeth hurried over and held Mama with her free hand and balanced the still-burning lamp with the other. She pulled Mama against her to keep her from collapsing and when Daniel softly said that Aaron was dead she could feel Mama gasp for breath. A river of tears flooded her cheeks, the drops falling from the end of her chin and landing on the lamp in Elizabeth's hand.

The flame went out.

CHAPTER 5

Inspector Tobit ordered the butler to fill his cup with imported tea from the Orient. The man nodded and told Tobit he would do as the good inspector wished. The butler was the oldest manservant at the governor's mansion in Jericho. He had a steady hand, a slight but firm frame, and he made the finest tea this side of the Jordan—a river that ran close enough to the mansion house for Tobit to see its blue-green waters flowing east of Jericho from the terrace of this dining-room chamber and to enjoy the miles of lush, green date palms that grew along its banks, surrounding this oasis city with green foliage in the middle of a desert.

The butler was the finest help Tobit had hired among all the Jews living in Jericho, but he could do without the man's odd habit of saying "as you wish" after his every request. It didn't matter if Tobit asked him to bring him his tea, prepare a warm bath, or dance under the light of the moon until it rained on these barren plains of Jericho, the butler always replied that he would do as the good inspector wished. Tobit could ask him to pick up some fruit in the market and while he was out could he see to having the sky fall to the earth and the man would offer his well-rehearsed line—as you wish—and get on with his duties. Just last week when the butler informed him that military supplies from Babylon had been delayed for a week, Tobit, in a fit of frustration, told the butler to jump off the balcony, flap his arms and fly about the gardens and see if he could find some replacement supplies to tide them over, and the old fool didn't hesitate to respond that he would do as the good inspector wished. Then he went on straightening the rugs on the chamber floor and fluffing the red linen cushions on the anteroom chairs without going near the balcony. He was a fine old butler and his dry wit settled the most unsettling circumstances, but couldn't he at least give a little hint, a smile, a raise of the brow, or a slight shake of the head that he understood the difference between a sensible order to fill Tobit's cup with tea and a foolish command to stand in the corner on his head?

Inspector Tobit asked the butler to sweeten the tea and after replying he would do as the inspector wished, the butler stirred in three spoons of honey and leaned a cinnamon stick against the rim. The butler had prepared another fine brew for entertaining Tobit's yet-to-arrive Jewish guest, though this was no tea party. It was the last hope of détente with rogue Jews a good three months delinquent paying their taxes, and his request that the butler prepare a round of Tobit's favorite cinnamon tea on this warm, summer evening in Jericho was entirely out of place. Tobit took a sip of the brew. It was surprising the butler bothered to make this tea at all, but the man had learned which of Tobit's orders were foolish ramblings and which were to be obeyed, and preparing a tea for this evening's meal was not a joking matter regardless of the heat on this early summer evening. Tobit unbuttoned the collar of his blue dress military tunic and let the tight-fitting cloth fall away from his neck, though it would do little to relieve the heat that was certain to accompany these negotiations.

Inspector Tobit sat at the end of a long cedar dining table in the company of ten empty place settings for a meal that should have been served hours before. The plates were fired in the pits of Babylon's finest potter, the wine goblets fashioned by a Babylonian silversmith on the banks of the Tigris, and it was a shame there was no one to enjoy these decorations. Tobit sent his military lieutenants away to attend to their duties with instructions that he'd send for them if their visitor from Jerusalem ever arrived. The cooks took away the baskets of bread to keep warm near the ovens along with a roasted lamb garnished without a single bit of seafood from the shipment that arrived from the Persian coast yesterday. Babylon had the finest clams and mussels in the world, but Tobit would never prove to his visitor just how fine, and he ordered the cooks to keep them out of this evening's menu. It was too difficult to know which sea creatures a good Jew ate and which ones were to be shunned. And how was Tobit to decide if his visitor was a good Jew or a bad one? Was he a kosher sort of man or was he a creature of more tangible pleasures? It was impossible to know. Jews thought themselves the people of God and it was better to let heaven deal with their odd eating habits and their arrogance.

Tobit stirred the tea with his cinnamon stick before breaking it in half and letting it sink to the depths of his cup beneath the warm, brown brew. All he needed was the tax paid in full, then he could turn his attention to more important matters and let these Jews squabble about their claims to holiness. Tobit took another sip of tea. His only religion was his assignment to oversee this territory, and his only God was Nebuchadnezzar, King of Babylon. Tobit did not come to Jericho to find a spiritual awakening—he came here to find money for the good of Babylon, and God help the Jews and any others traveling through these territories if they didn't pay their tax. The hot sands of the Judean Wilderness were not dry enough, the vineyard country of Moab's high plateaus were not populated enough, and the endless maze of steep, narrow canyons of the Jabal Mountains along the shores of the Red Sea were not secret enough to keep Tobit and his men from tracking any who passed through this territory without paying their dues. He'd trained five hundred soldiers in the art of tracking men through narrow gorges and washed-out wadis, he'd instructed them in the tactics of patrolling the checkpoints along the traveled routes, and they could hunt down a man hiding in a city of ten thousand without a single witness. They could pick a tax evader out of a horde of travelers, they knew how to interrogate the most unwilling informants, and they could find clues where most men couldn't find a footprint in the sand. From the lush, date palm groves at Jericho to the six-thousand-foot peaks of the Jabal Mountains along the Arabian border on the southern extreme of the Babylonian territories, Tobit and his men oversaw the world's most lucrative merchant route—the mighty Frankincense Trail. Jerusalem may be a more inviting location to set up his command and enjoy the comforts of city life, but there was no better place to govern this ungovernable trade route than the Frankincense trailhead at Jericho—the oldest city on earth.

Tobit turned in his chair, set his feet up on a wooden footstool, and leaned against the backrest, cradling the cup of tea in both hands while steam streamed past his cheeks. What was the name of this emissary from Jerusalem? Tobit took a long sip. Zadock. That was the man the Jews were sending. It wasn't a common Hebrew name and it didn't appear in any of the logs his spies had collected since the war. Zadock wasn't a member of the royal house of Judah with blood ties to the king; at least none of Tobit's reconnaissance mentioned any. He wasn't a member of the military—he was never mentioned in any of Captain Laban's public matters, and Tobit had no word from any merchants or caravaneers passing this way from Jerusalem about the visitor expected this evening. Zadock was an enigma, without a past and less of a present, and if Tobit didn't get a chance to meet this shadow of a man face-to-face, he may never assemble an accurate profile for the emissary he would have to deal with through the duration of his tenure at Jericho. He was appointed for eight long years to the post of Chief Inspector of the Arabian Trade Route leading to the frankincense groves of the southern peninsula, and he should at least know something about a man who could be key to either his success or his failure. Tobit set his cup down, the fired clay bottom rattling against the saucer. For the love of the gods of the Euphrates, how was he to negotiate with a man he knew nothing about? He didn't even know if Zadock liked tea with his meal.

The Jewish tax caravan arrived hours ago. They set up camp on a ridge across the hill from the main gates of Jericho, and Zadock sent word he would arrive for dinner well before sunset, but look at it now. The sun had set and the heat of the first hot summer day at Jericho warmed the brick lining the garden terrace balcony with only a weak evening breeze to cool the dining room. Inspector Tobit ordered the butler to shut the curtains and the man answered that he would do as Tobit wished before pulling the cloth shut across the windows. Old fool, he'd never be able to drop the phrase from his speech. Tobit turned sideways in his chair and fanned himself with one of the empty plates. Warm summer nights in this new territory passed slowly and if he were to endure a commission in this part of the kingdom without going mad, he would do it with the windows shut up to a night view of the rugged moonlit cliffs and sandstone plateaus near this governor's mansion. During daylight the sun-washed foliage of a hundred date palm groves growing against the gray-brown cliffs were a colorful hedge against the heat. But with the sun gone and the call of wild animals carried on the night breeze, it was like listening to the voices of a hundred Jewish outpost commanders from centuries past telling him that a Babylonian military man was not welcome here—especially a commander of Tobit's genius. He adjusted his feet on the footstool, lifted his cup of tea to his lips and took a long, warm sip. Tobit didn't need a welcome from Jews long since dead, but the eerie silence of the night called out, telling him that he should not trust his instincts to anyone but—

"Zadock, sir. Chief Elder and emissary of the King of the Jews."

A man in a long black robe with a matching turban passed into the dining chamber, his thin, high-pitched words escaping his mouth like steam from a narrow-necked pot. Tobit choked on his tea and tapped his chest with a fist before setting aside the cup and standing to greet the man. How did Zadock get inside the governor's mansion without the watchmen announcing his arrival? They had instructions to report to Tobit at the first sighting, but there he stood, unannounced, his robe hanging from his thin body like a cobweb wrapped around an insect. Tobit lowered his head. It wasn't proper to think such contempt for the emissary from Jerusalem and he kept his head down until the vision of an insect left his mind. Zadock was to be Tobit's link to the kingdom of the Jews, his concierge, his confidant on matters Jewish, and he wasn't going to question his appearance or why a holy man was sent to negotiate the tax. If the Jews wanted to send an elder to confer on matters of their national fate, so be it. At least Tobit had done right by this evening's meal and instructed the cooks not to garnish the lamb with seafood. Zadock was certain to be a kosher man, an ally, a colleague who could win him success in this territory. Tobit raised his head and offered Zadock a smile. He would think of this man in respectful terms—at least for now.

"Please, have a seat." Tobit motioned for Zadock to take his place and the Chief Elder crossed the room with a slow gait, a leather parchment poking out from under his arm, the wooden dowel jabbing at the air with each measured stride. Before fitting his frail frame into the high-backed chair on the far end of the dining table, Zadock handed over the document and told Tobit he would find everything in order.

The leather parchment was scrolled around a single wooden dowel—nothing as solid and well fashioned as a Babylonian clay tablet, but it did have the virtue of not weighing down the hands. Tobit picked away the wax seal and let the soft leather fall open, the end of the long document reaching to the floor. It began with a detailed account of the levy paid by Jerusalem's merchant traders, artisans, and vineyard owners. Every gold coin, basket of grain, and vessel of oil and wine was listed followed by a certification in the careful pen strokes of a man named Ezekiel, Chief Accountant of the Jews, proclaiming that every Jew at Jerusalem had faithfully paid the levy of a one-quarter tax. Tobit moved to the last portion of the document where the final receipt of the tax was written, announcing that Zadock had quelled the tax revolt and imprisoned the man responsible. Tobit brought his head up and peered around the goblets to where Zadock sat. Prisoner? Tobit heard nothing about the imprisonment of anyone responsible for the delinquent payment of taxes. Capturing the conspirators of the tax revolt was his duty, not to be left to this vassal Zadock.

Tobit said, "Did your caravan deliver everything listed here?"

"You'll find it stocked and accounted for in your storehouse."

"You're wise not to challenge our one-quarter tax." Tobit affixed his mark to the scroll and rolled it around the dowel. "We're accustomed to having our way."

"We never intended to pay anything less, sir. I can assure you."

"Then why did you travel all the way to Jericho to negotiate a tax that needs no negotiation?"

"You're Babylon's most trusted military officer sent here to oversee her most vital interests." Zadock set his forearms on the table, the wide cuffs of his robe falling over his hands. "Interests I'm prepared to ensure are not threatened."

"What threats?" Tobit slowly walked down along the table and set the scrolled tax notice on the tabletop next to Zadock. "Does this have anything to do with the prisoner you're holding?"

"There are men who would overthrow your rule and keep you from collecting taxes." Zadock took a cup of tea from the butler's tray and held it with both hands, his gaze turned down into the steaming brew. "Men who delight in your ruin."

"Do you have names?"

"Ezekiel sits in our prison awaiting punishment."

"How can that be?" Tobit took back the tax notice and found Ezekiel's name in the document. "That man is your Chief Accountant."

Zadock nodded and the ends of his shawls lifted from his shoulders. "The man published a false, three-quarter levy, hoping to keep the excess for himself."

"A three-quarter tax is too much for one man to hide."

"Greed, sir, is just as difficult to conceal."

"You're certain he started this revolt?"

"Thank God we found him out before this went any further." Zadock gripped the edge of the table with both hands. "He altered the Babylonian tax notice with his chisels and pens and published the alterations to every citizen in Jerusalem. His crime is worthy of the severest punishments."

Tobit returned to his chair and ordered the butler to fill his cup and stir in another stick of cinnamon. And before the man could say as you wish, Tobit said, "Do you really want me to put to death a man of his education? Certainly you have use for—"

"For the future of the New Babylonian Territory, I advise you allow us to remove Ezekiel's head for instigating an uprising."

"Very well. Keep him in your prison for now." Tobit dabbed the tea from his lips with a cloth. "As soon as I'm able, I'll ride to Jerusalem to meet with this—"

Zadock dropped his cup, the noise cutting off Tobit's words. Hot tea splashed over the brim and stained the cloth on the table. Zadock said, "There's no reason for you to waste your time with him. Ezekiel is a rebellious fool, a renegade of the worst sort, a man of little consequence and even less honor. He can't be trusted, but he's not such a difficult man we can't take care of him—with your permission of course. We'll see he's put to death on your word."

"I never order a man's execution without a proper interrogation."

Zadock wiped away the spilt tea around his cup. "I'll send you a record of my interviews."

"A matter like this requires my personal attention." Tobit pressed both hands flat against the tabletop. "Rebellion must not be tolerated in these new territories. Not even the slightest revolt from a greedy accountant."

A Jewish military officer entered the chamber. He introduced himself as Daniel, lieutenant in charge of escorting the Jewish tax and he informed Inspector Tobit that his men were setting up a camp outside the city walls and could they water their animals from the city wells before bedding down? He was a young man with thick arms, a straight chin, and black hair cut short above the ears with a long thatch combed forward over his brow. He was strong as a mule and he stood with his shoulders back, chest forward, and his unmoving gaze riveted on Tobit, his only weakness a bad left eye covered with a black patch with a matching cord tied around his head and holding it in place. He said, "Could I have a word with the Chief Elder, sir."

Tobit waved his hand. "Do as you like."

Daniel leaned his head in next to the Chief Elder and spoke in a low voice, but before he finished delivering his message Zadock raised himself out of his chair and said, "What's he doing here?"

Daniel said, "He's waiting at the main gates of the mansion now."

"Will you excuse me for a moment?" Zadock nodded to Commander Tobit. "There's a matter that requires my attention." He started across the chamber in company with Daniel, but pulled up in the entryway when Tobit asked what was the matter.

Zadock stood beneath a hanging lamp, the yellow light casting over his pale skin. "Captain Laban has come to Jericho."

Zadock followed Daniel down a winding path through the date palms. The stones had collected the summer heat during the day and now that night had settled over the garden they gave off enough warmth that Zadock had to lift the hem of his robe to keep the hot air from bothering him more than the news of Laban's arrival in Jericho. Why did Laban follow them here? Zadock had enough troubles with Commander Tobit wanting to interrogate to Ezekiel, and he didn't need any more. Whatever bad news Captain Laban brought with him, he couldn't allow it to complicate his efforts to stop the inspector from traveling to Jerusalem to interrogate Ezekiel. He would not be embarrassed like he was at Uriah's trial. These self-proclaimed prophets were a curse!

Zadock pulled on the collar of his robe to loosen the cloth and let the air pass beneath. The highlands he left behind in Jerusalem made for more comfortable evenings than these in Jericho and thankfully he wasn't going to suffer the heat of this low-lying valley much longer. One day at Jericho, possibly two, should be enough to convince Commander Tobit that Zadock could be trusted in every matter of détente between the Babylonians and the Jews—including Ezekiel. And hopefully whatever word Captain Laban brought didn't require a longer stay in this infernal city set on the northern rim of the Dead Sea. He did not have the disposition to endure the heat in this sink-hole of a valley they called the plains of Jericho. Zadock brushed the shawls off his shoulders and pushed the brim of his turban back off his brow. There was not a hotter place in all of Judah to wither away his days and he should have waited here and had Captain Laban come up into the gardens to speak with him, but he kept following Lieutenant Daniel down past the date palms that lined the path. It was hardly early summer and there was no telling how dreadfully scorching this wilderness would become in the months ahead. The path skirted around the main fountains and Zadock stopped long enough to let the evening breeze filter across the water and stream past his cheeks. That was better. There was nothing like an evening breeze to cool his temperament, but no matter how refreshing these fountains, he wasn't going to let whatever news Captain Laban brought slow his return to the highlands of Jerusalem. What was the man doing here anyway? Zadock left him in Jerusalem with instructions to stay home and heal, not ride about the countryside with a broken shank bone.

"Over there, sir." Daniel pulled up beside Zadock and pointed to a man just inside the main gates, just beyond a run of eucalyptus trees, the smell of pungent oil rising from their evergreen leaves. Captain Laban stood beside a brown steed—not his usual white

Arabian. He wasn't wearing a sling and when his mount sidestepped, the captain pulled on the reins and stroked the animal with what should have been an injured arm. His beard was trimmed along his straight jaw in the usual fashion, but his hair was longer than Zadock remembered, though in his hurry to leave Jerusalem, he hadn't bothered to take much note of Laban's grooming. The captain stood below a tall gate pillar, the white limestone gathering the light of the moon and reflecting it over his powerful frame, his thick chest rising and falling with each breath. He wasn't dressed in his military uniform. No breast plates, no sword sheathed at his hip, and no riding boots to protect his feet—an odd thing for a man who never traveled anywhere without the trappings of his captainship. His steed was rigged with a small leather saddle, nothing like his usual riggings with metal rivets decorating the surface, silver threads trimming the seams and long flaps trailing down either side. There was nothing military about Captain Laban's appearance except his stature—strong enough to wrestle three men to the ground.

"What are you doing here?' Zadock pushed through the eucalyptus trees and stepped from the gardens. "I didn't send for you."

"I came on my own." The captain turned and when the direct light of the moon flashed across his face Zadock pulled up, the soft brush of his sandals falling quiet on the stone. This wasn't the captain. He had the same stature, the same dark complexion and square chin. Nearly every distinction was similar—the broad shoulders, the narrow line of beard, the penetrating dark eyes, the high bones in the cheeks and the forward brow—though Zadock wasn't fooled by the son of Lehi the olive oil merchant. The boy's face was covered in dust, his longer-than-the-captain's hair matted to his scalp.

Zadock said, "How did you get past the guards?"

Laman removed the leather band holding his hair back off his brow, and his dark locks fell down into his eyes. "Your men mistook me for Captain Laban and let me inside."

"You should have told them who you were."

"I had to speak with you, sir." Laman wiped the sweat off his brow with the sleeve of his tunic.

"How did you know I was here?"

"Word travels quickly in Jericho's markets."

"You rode all the way from Egypt to buy wheat and pulse in this city?"

"I never said I was buying wheat, sir."

"Then what? Melons or potatoes? Or did you come here to buy dates?" Zadock raised his hands toward the date-palm groves east of Jericho. "They grow the finest dates in the world here. Is that what brought you all the way from Egypt?'

"It wasn't the dates, sir."

How infuriatingly vague! Zadock slapped the sand from the coat of Laman's horse, the animal backstepping away from his harshness. This boy wasn't going to give him any clue about his family's where-abouts, but one thing was certain—he didn't just happen through the market and by chance hear news of Zadock's coming to Jericho, not if he was escaped with his family to Egypt. Zadock adjusted his robe over his narrow shoulders and hid his hands beneath the large cuffs. There was no reason for Laman to travel across two nations to purchase a sack of grain and a bottle of wine in the markets of Jericho unless he and his family never fled to the land of the pharaohs. Zadock stepped closer to Laman and peered through the shadows into the boy's eyes. Could they really be here, somewhere close to Jericho, possibly hiding in the Judean Wilderness? Every Jewish outlaw and renegade to flee Jerusalem found refuge in the wide swath of sands and cliffs wedged between Judah's hill country and the western shores of the Dead Sea—a long corridor of the most unin-habitable tracts in all this barren territory. If Lehi was living near Jericho, would he really risk the harsh discomforts of life in the Judean Wilderness just south of here, a land fit for only the most unfit Jews in the Kingdom?

Zadock worked the end of his chin between his fingers. This was an awful predicament. Commander Tobit planned to interrogate Ezekiel in Jerusalem and now this. Captain Laban was right. Lehi was still a threat, and the longer the man was allowed to gather his strength in the wilderness, the harder it would be to root him out. Lehi was not gone to Egypt, he couldn't be, not with Laman standing in front of him, his legs washed in sand, his brow dusted with the fine gray powders of the Judean Wilderness, and his hair matted from the sweat of a ride from their hiding place. Zadock worked his lower lip between his teeth. Worst of all, there was no reason for Lehi to take refuge in this wilderness unless he had designs to return to—

"All we want is to go home." Laman cleared his throat. "That's all we've ever wanted, sir."

"Home?" Zadock pushed the muzzle of Laman's horse aside. "You have no home."

"Reason with me, sir. We can make peace on whatever terms you choose."

"Tell me where your father is."

"Will you let us return to Beit Zayit?"

"You miss your wealth, do you?"

"Please, sir. Have pity on our desperation."

"You've lost your appetite for desert life, haven't you?" Zadock raised his hand toward the desolate cliffs and sands beyond the walls of Jericho. "You've seen the dreariness of the Judean Wilderness, the desolation, the impossible heat, the lack of water, and you want to return to the privileged life you left behind in Jerusalem. Are you enjoying your stay in the Judean Wilderness?"

Laman's head came up quickly, startling his steed with the sudden movement. "I didn't say where we were hiding."

"You didn't have to." Zadock leaned his head in close to Laman. "Tell me where in this wilderness your father's hiding or I'll see that you're chased deeper into the wastelands of Arabia where you'll never find a place of refuge."

"We'll not cause you any trouble if you allow us to return." Laman came around in front of Zadock. "Not ever again."

"You'll never return to Jerusalem." Zadock grabbed Laman by the cloth of his tunic. "Not until you rid yourself of your father."

"What are you saying?" Laman pulled free of Zadock's grasp and backed toward his horse, his gaze fixed on Zadock—on what the Chief Elder had just said. "How do I rid myself of Lehi?"

"Purge him from your life, then you can come back to your lands and your inheritance and your precious olive groves. You want to enjoy your wealth don't you? Or would you prefer living in this wilderness the rest of your life?" Zadock tipped his turban toward the gates of the city. "Bring me the head of your father and you're free to return to Beit Zayit."

Laman pulled himself up into the saddle and brought his horse around without answering. He started his steed toward the gate, his head down and his shoulders hunched forward.

Zadock walked alongside the animal, the hem of his robe swirling about the horse's hooves. He said, "Will you do it?"

Laman kept his horse cantering slowly over the cobblestones.

"Answer me, son." Zadock reached for the reins, but couldn't get hold of them. "Do you want to return to Jerusalem or not?"

Laman turned out of the gate and onto the street, and Zadock slowed his steps at the entrance, calling into the darkness, his rasping words chasing after the fading clap of horse hooves. "Do you hear me? You must be rid of Lehi."

"I'll get my horse." Lieutenant Daniel brushed past Zadock on his way to the livery across from the main gates, but Zadock took him by the arm and stopped him from taking another step.

Daniel said, "I can follow him. Find out exactly where he's hiding."

"I want you to find someone else who hides in this wilderness."

"We're not searching for anyone else, sir."

Zadock let go of Daniel's arm. "No one knows the Judean Wilderness better than Shechem."

"But, sir, Shechem's a—"

"The King of Robbers can be trusted."

"To do what?"

"I'll see that Captain Laban is summoned here to Jericho, and you see that Shechem finds Lehi's hideout in this wilderness and brings me word." Zadock started back through the gardens toward the mansion house. He had to keep Tobit from coming to Jerusalem to interrogate Ezekiel and there was no better way than to send him hunting about the Judean Wilderness for Ezekiel's conspirator, the man who inspired Ezekiel to begin the tax revolt, the mastermind behind the uprising, an unassuming olive oil merchant turned renegade. He said, "Finding Lehi isn't *our* dilemma, son."

"Then whose is it?"

"This task is worthy of the finest desert scout to ever grace this wilderness." Zadock slowed his speech and said, "Inspector Tobit will find Lehi for us."

"He doesn't have any interest in Lehi."

"He will, son. Trust me, he will." Zadock turned his gaze toward the garden terrace off the main dining room. The lamps cast a bright yellow light from inside the chamber and warmed the stone columns with the inviting glow of the evening meal. "Lehi will become the Babylonian Inspector's most pressing concern."

"Why would Tobit bother with Lehi? He's nothing but a—"

"A renegade, a menace, an outlaw bent on destroying Babylonian rule and the inspector has good reason to rid his territory of such men." Zadock removed his turban and the black shawls fell to his shoulders. "Tobit will silence Lehi. Forever."

"You want me to do what?" Commander Tobit settled into his chair at the head of the dining table and pushed aside the full wine goblets separating him from a view of the Jewish Elder. Zadock didn't lower his head, didn't blink, didn't act as if his suggestion that Tobit join with Laban, Captain of the Hebrew Guard, and begin searching the Judean Wilderness was anything out of the ordinary. "I can't send my men after every Jewish criminal to flee into the desert."

"I wouldn't suggest you do this for an ordinary thief, sir." Zadock leaned forward, the cuffs of his robe brushing over the dinner plates filled with sliced lamb and garnished with onions. "But this Lehi is no ordinary criminal."

"I thought you said Ezekiel was the renegade who started this rebellion over the tax."

"Ezekiel is nothing but a pawn in all of this." Zadock took a long drink from his goblet of wine. "We were interrupted before I could explain the depth of this insurrection."

"And this Lehi; you say he's the one who inspired Ezekiel?"

"He's a pernicious evil, sir. He'll stop at nothing. He's devious, without the least bit of respect for governance or the rule of our laws. He's ruthless, cunning, and without the slightest dignity for human life. He's a wretch of the worst kind."

"And this Ezekiel is simply one of Lehi's—"

"Let that man rot in our prison while you turn your attention to Lehi. He was the instigator of this revolt and he's more dangerous to you than a full garrison of Egyptian soldiers."

"I don't fear the Egyptians."

"You should fear Lehi. If he's not dealt with, his rebellion will grow."

"How do you know he's hiding in the Judean Wilderness?"

"We have our spies."

"How could one man be so dangerous?"

"That one man nearly caused a war between our nations." Zadock nodded slowly. "He's not alone in this wilderness. He's gathering zealots to his cause every day. Think what evil he could work along the trade route with an army of zealots at his command."

Tobit pushed aside his plate of lamb. "This Lehi wouldn't dare interfere with the merchant trade."

"Desperate men commit desperate acts."

Tobit crossed to a large wooden case standing in the corner of the dining room. He unlocked the latch, and the leather hinges holding the ornate cabinet doors in place gave up a soft squeak. He removed a detailed map of the New Babylonian Territory, beginning with the land of Jerusalem on the north all the way to the Red Sea on the south. He marched it over to the table, cleared away the empty plates, and laid the drawing in front Zadock with the wine goblets holding down the corners, the cherry-red drink spilling over the lip and down the polished brass. The map was drawn on four large leather parchments sewn together with gold threads, with every mountain peak, plateau, wadi, valley, and canyon laid out in perfect detail by Babylon's finest artists and scribes. They weren't complete—there were some wilderness areas that remained uncharted—but Tobit had a personal mapmaker, his son Darius. He was among the finest mapmakers in the Babylonian army, and with the boy's skills he'd soon have a complete charting of these lands.

"Tell me, sir." Tobit motioned to the map. "Where do you propose we begin searching for this renegade Lehi?"

Zadock came down along the table and leaned over the map. He studied it for a moment, his long forefinger quickly moving down from Jerusalem on the northern edge of the parchment, east across to Jericho, and then immediately south to the barren desert between Judah's hill country and the Dead Sea. It was a long corridor of sand dunes, one hundred and thirty miles long and sixty miles wide, without town or arable land noted on the map. There were no springs emptying into the Dead Sea; at least there were none marked anywhere along the edges of the Judean Wilderness where the sand gave way to the shores of the Salt Sea. And there were no markings to indicate any wells in the endless sand that covered this portion of the territory. The word "uninhabited desert" was written in large Babylonian letters from where the hills of Judah quickly descended into the depths of this sand-filled basin. A Hebrew subscript appeared below the Babylonian words naming this place the Judean Wilderness of the former kingdom of Judah. Zadock ran his finger in a circle around the entire length and width of the wilderness and said, "You'll find him somewhere in here."

"Somewhere in there?" Tobit leaned in next to Zadock. "Do you have any idea how large a territory that is? It could take my men a year to search that much territory."

"Our soldiers will help."

"It will still take months."

"I've sent for a man who knows this part of the Judean Wilderness. He'll shorten your search."

"I haven't agreed to a search."

"You and your men with the aid of Captain Laban and his cavalry will make quick work of this." Zadock returned to his chair and leaned against the backrest. "I'll need accommodations. Do you have any that are cool during the heat of the day?"

"You're planning to stay here?"

"Only as long as it takes to organize this two-nation search party."

Tobit scrolled the map, stuffed it beneath his arm and called for the butler. The man hurried into the chamber, bowed quickly, and asked what was wanted. Tobit said, "Bring the good Elder's things inside."

The butler said, "Will he be staying long, sir?"

Tobit walked past Zadock without looking down at him. He crossed to the wooden case along the far wall and returned the map to its shelf. He said, "Only as long as it takes to sift through every grain of sand in this wilderness."

The butler said, "As you wish, Inspector Tobit."

CHAPTER 6

Ezekiel pushed aside his half-eaten ration of dried bread and set the cup of sullied water on the prison floor. He lay down, searching for a bit of rest on this thin mat of thatched reeds that didn't have power to soften his sleep. What was to become of him? He was a lawyer, not a criminal, and Zadock's false accusations over the tax could not hold him here against the will of heaven unless God had reason for this insanity. He turned on his side, his back to the other prisoners and his feet curled up beneath the hem of his robe. Would it defy some eternal plan if he were to be a free man?

Food was sparse, but no more meager than the sleep Ezekiel missed since coming to the upper palace prison. Had he been here a week, or was it two? He couldn't remember and he adjusted the cloth of his robe over his shoulders and closed his eyes to the flickering torchlight reflecting off the thick limestone wall. Cool evening air drafted through the vents cut into the wall just below the ceiling and Ezekiel wrapped his arms around himself, rubbing his robe to chase away the chill. How many more days must he endure this place until the Babylonians came to Jerusalem to decide his fate? There had to be a reason the inspector of the occupying army hadn't come to judge him for his part in the tax revolt, but for the mercy of heaven what was it? And when Inspector Tobit did arrive, would he believe Ezekiel innocent when Zadock accused him of embezzling the tax and inciting an uprising?

The cold metal edge of a sword fell against Ezekiel's neck and a rasping voice ordered him to get up, but he was to do it slowly, no tricks, no sudden movements, just get up with his hands overhead.

Ezekiel turned onto his back and rubbed his eyes until the hunched-over outline of the jailer came into focus. The man was alone, without the usual escort of guards to protect him. His sword hand trembled under the weight of the blade and he scanned the prison like a nervous rat searching for a morsel of food before scampering back to its hole. His hair was parted down the middle of his scalp and the long scraggly strands fell over his brow and mixed with the withered lines in his face. His back was bent from years of shuffling about on a lame leg without a cane to straighten him upright. He couldn't be the answer to Ezekiel's prayers, could he? Heaven would not send such a man to help him unless . . . ?

Ezekiel sat up. "Are you come to free me?"

"Freedom?" The jailer smiled and the whisper of a laugh escaped from deep in his throat. He glanced over his shoulder to the far side of the prison. "I'm taking you to see a man who believes he can free everyone."

Ezekiel stood and peered into the dimly lit chamber, but there was no one standing by to speak with him. "Where is he?"

"Walk this way." The jailer shook his lantern, throwing wild streams of light over the stone floor. Ezekiel didn't resist when the man poked the sword into his backside, marching him past the open washing pool and over beyond the other prisoners sitting at a wooden table beneath the light of a solitary lamp, but when he forced him past the door leading out of the prison, he struggled to turn back against the sharpness of the blade. Where was the jailer taking him? This wasn't the way out of the prison. The door to his freedom was back there and he wasn't going to walk past it without—

"Keep marching." The jailer jabbed the cold metal tip of his sword through the cloth of Ezekiel's robe. "Nothing foolish, do you hear? Or I'll run you through."

The jailer escorted him to the door leading to the Lower Prison. It was recessed into the wall with iron bars holding thick cedar timbers in place and round metal rivets bolting the wood together. Not here, not the door to that awful place. He was not a criminal worthy of the Lower Prison. The jailer was mistaken and as soon as he came to his senses he'd escort Ezekiel back to his sleeping mat in the corner and let him enjoy whatever refinements could be found in this unrefined place. Ezekiel hadn't had a change of clothes since he came

here and he'd need a good tailor to mend the tears the jailer cut in
these fine linens, or possibly he could send for some of his things
from home. That would certainly ease the burden of his confinement.

Ezekiel turned around from facing the lower prison door. He said,
"There's been a mistake."

"No mistake. Your liberator awaits." The jailer smiled and his
yellow teeth shimmered between the gaps. "None of the others lasted
long with him. He's mad, he is." He pointed the tip of his sword at
the door. "He isn't right in the head, not right at all. He's always
spouting off about his strength, something to do with the powers of
earth not stopping him."

"Stopping him from what?"

"You'll see." The jailer poked him with the tip of the blade. "Get
along. I have my orders."

"From whom?"

"Make you strong as flint, that's what Zadock told me to do, he
did." The jailer spoke through wide gaps in his teeth, his words
whistling from between his lips. "Make Ezekiel strong as flint before
he pays for his crimes." The jailer spit on the ground and rubbed the
spittle into the stone with the toe of his boot. "There's only one place
with the power to make you that strong."

The thick prison door came open with a rush of damp air
filtering up from the catacombs, and a rat skittered across the steps
before running down into the darkness. The jailer prodded him into
the stairwell and down a run of winding circular stairs cut from thick
slabs of limestone, the light of the upper prison fading behind them
with each turn in the staircase. Faint smoke rose off the jailer's lamp
and mixed with the musty smell oozing up from beneath the foundations of the palace, the moist air streaming past his cheeks. Mercy of
heaven, he was the chief accountant of Judah, hired to serve the royal
house, but now he was confined in the belly of this royal place.
Ezekiel slowly felt his way around the stair, pressing his hand to the
cold stone wall. Dear God of Heaven, what was the reason for this
awful twist of fate and where was the strength of flint he needed to
endure whatever test lay below?

The stairs ended at an iron gate and the jailer quickly unlocked
the latch and forced Ezekiel inside. They stepped over the

outstretched legs of a host of prisoners chained to the walls, down a wide corridor and around a tall foundation footing where a solitary prisoner sat alone on the stone-covered ground, his legs pulled up to his chest and his brow pushed down onto his knees. It was impossible to see his face, but his hands betrayed an obvious fierceness. They were thick and powerful—the skin of his fingers calloused like the worn fibers of a hanging rope that had power to wrap around Ezekiel's neck and choke the breath of life from him. Was it not enough that Ezekiel had to endure imprisonment on the lies of Zadock; must he also endure the misery of the lower prison in the company of a cellmate with a maniacal disposition? The man was chained to a pillar of stone and the jailer pushed Ezekiel onto the floor next to him, chaining them together with the same length, latching the metal around Ezekiel's neck to near suffocation and pinching the skin about his ankles and wrists until he was locked in place next to this man the jailer called the—

"Fool, you have a guest." The jailer pushed the lamp next to the prisoner's face, but he didn't raise his head from his knees, didn't flinch, and didn't make any movement no matter how close the heat came to searing the skin of his neck. "Fool, did you hear me? I say you have a guest." He didn't respond and the jailer took back the lamp, the flame flickering out at the sudden movement before roaring back to life and casting its light over Ezekiel. "I told you he's gone daft in the head, but not so daft he doesn't know you're here with him now." He laughed through his teeth and wished Ezekiel a good rest before starting back down the corridor, mumbling something about Ezekiel biding his time with a cellmate of a dreadful temperament, then disappearing around the corner, his lamplight slowly fading to darkness.

Ezekiel sat as far away as the chains allowed. He kept still, not moving his head so as not to disturb the metal hanging from his neck, and holding his feet and hands steady. If he didn't bother this wild man, maybe he'd leave Ezekiel alone. But how was he to protect himself from this animal when he was sitting close enough to feel the warmth of his body and the rise and fall of his breathing? If he wasn't careful, the man could reach out in the darkness and snap Ezekiel's neck. He slowly leaned back, bracing his head against the unyielding stones in the wall. What inspiration was there from heaven to save him from this awful circumstance? He lowered his head and waited for a word or a thought, anything that would tell him what action he should take to save himself from—

"I have something to tell you." The wild man crawled past Ezekiel on his hands and knees like an ape circling its prey, the holes in his tattered robe revealing the bones of his withered torso. Their shared chains pulled taut, stopping the wild man beside the foundation pillars. He peered around the thick stone and down the corridor where the jailer disappeared. He said, "Something no one can hear but you."

Heaven have mercy on Ezekiel's soul, what was he to do? His cellmate's crawling about was pulling the chains tight around his neck, cutting off his breath, but he kept silent about the choking and pried the metal back from his throat. This prisoner was deluded and Ezekiel couldn't ask mercy of a man who did not have any to offer. What if this beast-of-a-man were provoked to greater delusions and he lashed out at Ezekiel in anger?

"I knew you'd come." The wild man crawled back to his place against the foundation stones, his long, wiry legs and arms working his body over the ground. "Do you remember what I told you last time?"

Last time? There had never been a last time and he kept still, not showing any sign he heard the man's peculiar conversation. Ezekiel may be forced to sit shoulder-to-shoulder with this feral soul, but he would not risk answering the questions of a madman.

The wild man reached out and Ezekiel pulled away from his reaching, but the chains held him there and he could not escape without choking. The man raised his voice, his words echoing off the massive foundation stones. He said, "Oh that I had a lodging place in the wilderness, I would go far away from this assembly of treacherous men for they make this people to trust in a lie."

Those were words Ezekiel heard at Uriah's trial and he leaned closer to his companion, the slack coming back into the chains. He peered through the dimness at his cellmate, past the loneliness in his words to see the shadow-fettered face of Jeremiah.

"Is that you, Jeremiah?" Ezekiel blinked in the darkness. "You're alive?"

"I am, son." Jeremiah laid his thick, calloused hand on Ezekiel's shoulder.

"They accused you of Hannaniah's murder. I thought there was no hope of ever seeing you alive again, not after Uriah was murdered."

"My life has been preserved from day to day." Jeremiah coughed, the tattered cloth of his collar lifting with each spasm of his chest. This lower prison was a musty, moldy place and the dampness had infected his breathing. He said, "God kept me alive until you came."

"You have no reason to trust me." Ezekiel shook his head. "I'm with the Elders of the Jews. I allowed your imprisonment. I didn't stop Zadock from sending you to this awful place. I . . ."

Jeremiah raised his hand to silence him. He coughed again and cleared his throat before saying, "I trusted you since the day I saw you last year."

"It's only been two months since Uriah's trial."

"I knew you before that." Jeremiah nodded and the chains about his neck rattled with the rise and fall of his speech. "God showed me your part in this work long before Uriah came to trial."

"My part in what work?"

"Preserving the covenants."

Ezekiel leaned forward in the darkness. "What covenants?"

"The ones we're to preserve for our children and our children's children. The very covenants God made with our fathers." The words fell from Jeremiah's lips in a slow, whispered stream of eloquence spoken by an uneducated vineyard keeper and Ezekiel could do nothing but relish the words of heaven delivered by this consecrated courier. "If we fail, our children will be cast off forever."

"And if we succeed?"

"For our children's sake, I promise you we shall. They must know that we knew of covenants that will preserve our families forever." Jeremiah wrapped his arms around his knees, the chains encircling him with metal links. "Do you know of Laban's royal relics?"

"What Jew doesn't? They're national treasures."

"The captain hides the codex of brass plates in his treasury and permits no one to read it." Jeremiah lowered his voice to a whisper. "They're not from the kingdom of the Jews."

Ezekiel worked his fingers over his brow. "What do you mean, not from this kingdom?"

"The brass plates were fashioned in the blacksmithing fires of Egypt by the patriarch Joseph and delivered to the Northern Kingdom in the days when there were two Hebrew nations. They've been kept over the centuries by the prophets and kings of that lost kingdom of Hebrews to the north until, just before the fall of Samaria, they were delivered to Laban's treasury."

Ezekiel lowered his fingers from his brow and softly said, "Joseph the Patriarch fashioned the brass plates?"

"That's right. And his descendants have kept the record ever since."

Ezekiel leaned back against the wall, his head propped against the stone. The seriousness in Jeremiah's voice supported his claim that the brass plates were much more than relics of kingship or treasures from the ancient past and Ezekiel rubbed his brow, searching his mind for the possibilities. Could these brass plates have anything to do with Ezekiel's vision—the one that came to him nearly three months ago and hadn't left his mind since? The memory of it filled his thoughts by day and his dreams by night. He remembered every detail. He was sitting before the dying embers of a late evening fire studying debtors law when he thought he saw two men standing beside his chair, one holding the records of the Jews and the other man—a man he was certain was Lehi the olive oil merchant—carrying the record of Joseph. It was odd that Lehi would be carrying the record from that tribe. He was a Jew, not a Hebrew from the tribes of Ephraim and Manasseh. But of one thing he was certain—Lehi was charged with carrying the stick of Joseph. The vision was so powerful, so absolutely real he could never forget that when the two record keepers handed their records to a third man—a prophet far in the future, living in the last days of the earth—the leather of the scrolls of the Jews fused with the fibers of the records of the descendants of Joseph until they became one in the hand of that latter-day prophet, like the waters of two rivers flowing together into one. Ezekiel rubbed the back of his neck, the chains rattling against the pull of his movement. Could these brass plates have anything to do with the record he saw Lehi carrying? Were they the reason Ezekiel was brought to this prison?

Jeremiah didn't look up from staring at the darkness in front of him. He said, "I must write my prophecies into Laban's plates of brass."

"We're prisoners." Ezekiel leaned back and rattled his chains. "We haven't the power to walk three steps."

"My son can get us into Laban's treasury."

"We have to get out of here first."

Jeremiah leaned his face in close enough to Ezekiel that he could feel the breath of his words. "I must write my prophecies into the plates before they're taken from the city."

"Taken by whom?"

"I don't know." Jeremiah slowly shook his head, the chains rattling below his chin like a beard of metal. "The Lord hasn't shown me that."

Ezekiel leaned back, stunned by the force of Jeremiah's words. Could this be the meaning of his vision, the reason he'd been plagued by it all these days? Was Lehi the man who was going to take the plates from Laban's treasury and preserve them for the prophets of the last days? Ezekiel slowly whispered the name Lehi. It fell from his lips with hardly enough power to cross the distance between them, the name falling muted against the stone.

Jeremiah turned his ear to him. "What was that?"

"Lehi." Ezekiel turned to face Jeremiah and repeated the name louder, Lehi's name echoing off the columns. "Lehi will be the one to take the plates from Laban's treasury."

"The olive oil merchant is gone." Jeremiah shook his head. "The man fled the city months ago."

"He'll come back. He's the man chosen to preserve the covenants for our children so they're not cast off forever." Ezekiel laid his hand on Jeremiah's thin arm. "And God has chosen you to prepare that record."

Jeremiah held Ezekiel's face with both hands. "How do you know this?"

"Thus saith the Lord." Ezekiel pulled free of Jeremiah's grasp and stared up into the darkness of the catacombs. "I will take the stick of Joseph, which is in the hand of Ephraim and put it with the stick of Judah, and make them one stick, and they shall be one in thine hand."

"Dear God of Heaven." Jeremiah leaned against the wall, the chains dragging over the stones behind his retreat. "Make way our escape from this prison!"

CHAPTER 7

Jonathan quickened his stride down through the afternoon shadows of Beit Zayit's hillside vineyards, the olive trees arching their twisted, leaf-laden branches over the dusty road, like vines on a forgotten gravestone. He carried a large satchel pressed against his chest. It was an awkward way to walk, but this was no ordinary journey and he let the sweet smell of tanned leather fill him with the emptiness of the task ahead. The satchel was fashioned from four large skins, tanned and dried on the roof and sewn together with the finest threads from the basket beneath Ruth's foot loom. And instead of fixing cords along the length of the opening to seal it, she attached polished brass buttons to keep the empty satchel shut—she said it was the least she could do to honor their firstborn son.

A tear streamed down Jonathan's cheek and fell onto the leather, but since there was little sunlight filtering through the thick vineyard canopy he didn't bother to brush away his grief. In this silent place he could bear his soul, but bear it to whom? There was no God to understand his grieving heart and he was left to console himself. If there was any mercy left in the heavens then he should never have to suffer the task of filling this satchel with the bones of his dead son. But he'd not bothered heaven with the things of his heart in such a long time there was little he could do now to attract her gaze. And what balm would he ask if he knew how? He was not a beggar and he did not need the alms of heaven to remove this pain and heal his heart.

Jonathan pushed his shoulders forward and hurried his stride, the clip and fall of his sandals slapping at the shadows in the road. No father should have to bury his firstborn twice. Aaron died once when he embraced the foolish traditions of Lehi's faith, and again when he stood in front of an arrow that was not strung for him. Jonathan lowered the satchel and draped it across both arms like a high priest carrying an incense bowl in a funeral procession, but there was not a holy man in all of Judah who would offer a blessing on the grave of his son. Aaron was a rebel in life, seeking after a renegade religion, and Jonathan would have to offer whatever blessing he could conjure up to pay his last respects to a boy he loved more now in death than he ever had courage to show in life. What more could he do now that Aaron was gone but purchase a small plot in Jerusalem's cemetery, high on the plateau with a good view of the valley. The boy's remains belonged there, where Jonathan could tend to the weeds and Ruth could place a flower to mourn his passing, not here at Beit Zayit where only ghosts were left to care for the grounds and there was no one to mourn the flesh of his flesh.

The dusty road gave way to cobblestone and Jonathan lengthened his stride up the rise leading out of the green canopy of summer leaves and hurried past the burned-out grove. No matter how many times the story of Daniel's part in this fire fell on Jonathan's ear, it was a mistaken rumor. These charred and withered trees were not the doing of his son, and curse the merchants of Beit Zayit for blaming the destruction on Daniel. The whirlwinds that stirred the skies of early summer uprooted the blackened trees from their burned moorings and Jonathan turned his gaze away from the fallen ruins, his sandals brushing quickly over the cobblestones. Daniel had no hand in this crime and Jonathan would not pause on his journey to examine the devastation of vandals. Daniel was a fine man, an officer in the military, an honor to Jonathan's good name and he would not look at a lie.

The road leveled beyond the burned-out vineyard, turned past a fountain of gurgling water and ended in front of the gate to the estate that belonged to Lehi the Olive Oil Merchant. The mansion house stretched back so deep into the trees that Jonathan couldn't see where it ended. Shuttered, arching windows graced the upper floors, and a canopy of vines shaded a host of balconies. The yard stood quiet, without a soul to disturb the chirping birds in the branches of the sycamore trees lining the far edge of the gardens. There had to be someone about to care for these manicured grounds, but there was no gardener chasing about the yard, no maidservant sweeping the walks, no one with whom he could divide the haunting serenity of Aaron's burial ground. There was not a stray leaf along the maze of footpaths leading through the gardens, each branch bordered by neatly trimmed low-growing hedges. The leafy foliage lining the main path up to the front porch was freshly blocked this morning—the shoots rounded to a perfect arching half circle. There were no weeds growing in the garden. No dust had collected on the limestone path, and fresh water gurgled from a spout near the top of the yard—piped from lake Beit Zayit—and it gave life to the blossoms of white, purple, and red poppies filling the estate with the colors of early summer. It was a peaceful resting place, but Jonathan would find no rest as long as Aaron lay in these grounds. He ran his hand over the leather satchel. The cords were strong enough to hold the rotted dust of his son, the seams were sewn tight and the leather was thick enough to keep the stink of two months of death from turning his stomach to vomit.

Jonathan tried the metal latch, but the iron bars refused his push. Cursed gate! He kicked at the metal rods, but they would not budge. There was no reason for it to be locked. Lehi and his family were gone from Beit Zayit and with any luck they took their religion and their foolishness with them. A sign hung from the gate. It was written in bold Hebrew letters warning that intruders would suffer the wrath of the groundskeeper, but there was no watchman looking after this estate and he turned the warning sign on its face before climbing the gate, his powerful arms hoisting him over the top and onto the garden path. His intrusion didn't arouse any notice from the neighboring estate on the other side of the wall of trees and when he started up the path to the main house no groundskeeper emerged from the side gardens and no maidservant hurried out the front doors to shoo him away.

A swinging chair hung by four lengths of rope near the edge of the long limestone porch. The windows were barred with iron rods and tied with thick curtains without any gap except the last one near the far side of the porch. There was a small opening in the canvas and Jonathan pushed his face to the bars. A blue Egyptian vase sat on the floor against the far wall of the anteroom waiting to be trimmed with flowers and placed on the cherry-wood table set near the entry. Three Persian tapestries hung from the walls and a fourth sat atop the table with hooks and a hammer beside it, waiting to be nailed in place alongside the others. This wasn't an abandoned estate, not with so many repairs underway. The banister capping the rails along the length of the stairwell was missing, but there was a carpenter's trowel set beside a rough-hewn piece of black wood, half shaped into the form of a new hand-rail for the steps. The floors were freshly cleaned, the brass lamps polished, and the scent of incense lingered on the air. There was only one reason the servants in this estate would busy themselves with so many preparations. If the master of Beit Zayit were planning to return, Jonathan would make certain Lehi felt the grief of an arrow that should have been his.

Jonathan stepped back from the window. Daniel said it was here, near the entry to the house, where Aaron took the arrow, but there was no sign of a struggle. The thick doors of the estate hadn't been forced, the wood planks were not damaged, and the trim around the frame didn't look to have been repaired, or cleaned or changed to conceal any . . .

Jonathan's gaze stopped at the base of the door, down near the threshold. The stones at the foot of the entry were stained a deep red. The color was faded and some of it lifted away from the scratching of a tool, but there was no doubt it was a dried pool of blood. It was the same ugly rust-red color left on the floor of the blacksmith shop the day Aaron's feet were burned, and Jonathan fell to his knees and ran his fingers over the stain. How did he ever let this happen to his son? He never should have allowed Aaron to blacksmith for Lehi. The man filled the boy's head with his odd faith, won Aaron's heart with his wealth, and what did Aaron get in return? Jonathan's hands began to tremble. Beit Zayit brought Aaron nothing but death.

"I'm sorry about your son."

Jonathan glanced over his shoulder to find a man standing at the far end of the porch, but his eyes were blurred with tears so that he couldn't make out the face, couldn't read his height, couldn't even see the clothes he wore except for the blur of green, red, and yellow stripes in the colorful cloth. Jonathan turned his gaze to the ground to clear his vision. He couldn't face another with grief welling in his eyes.

"I trust he's healing well." The man spoke in a steady voice without his words running too fast and little of the sing-song lift and fall that littered the speech of most men, and immediately Jonathan recognized the constant manner of Ishmael, the cousin of Lehi the olive oil merchant. "I was heading to the city this morning. I didn't see your horse and I thought I should offer you a ride back, possibly stop in and see Aaron. Maybe wish the boy well. We certainly think highly of him. He's a fine blacksmith. You certainly have every right to be pleased by him."

Jonathan kept his head down. "I can walk, sir."

"Really, it isn't any trouble." The soft fall of Ishmael's leather sandal on the stone drew closer until his shadow cast across the bloodstains. "I'd be pleased if you'd allow me to accompany you to the city. I would very much like to wish Aaron well."

"He isn't getting well." A run of tears streamed from Jonathan's eyes and before he could stop them, they landed on the bloodied stones. He pressed both hands to his eyes to stop the tears. No man knew his grief and he would not share it with this cousin of the one who should be dead in Aaron's place. Ishmael was an accomplice and there was every reason to loathe his kindness.

Ishmael said, "I'm sorry to hear that. I really should stop by and see if there's anything I could do for the boy. He liked pickled olives. Maybe I could send a jar of them with—"

"He's dead." Jonathan stood and pushed his face close enough to Ishmael he could feel the man's breath. "Do you hear me? He died here on your land."

"That isn't so, it can't be." Ishmael stepped back from Jonathan's stern words. "There was some blood on the porch the day after Aaron was here. I thought he might have been hurt." He raised his hand toward the gardens. "There was a trail of blood leading into the trees over there, but I can assure you, no one died there. I walked the grounds to check for him. I would have known if—"

"You people think you know all the answers." Jonathan grabbed Ishmael by the arm. "You preach your foolish faith to my son, fill his head with your ideas about God, and you show off your riches like they were some sort of blessing from heaven, but when my son needed your help where were you?" He tightened his grip on

Ishmael's arm. "Aaron stepped in the way of an arrow to save your cousin Lehi. Where were you when he was bleeding to death? You could have saved him." Jonathan's shoulders began to shake. He forced his hand to his mouth and spoke through his trembling fingers. "You could have saved my son."

Ishmael shook his head "Lehi was gone from here long before Aaron or Captain Laban passed by."

"Don't lie to me, coward." Jonathan stood on the bloodstained stones, his hands curled into fists. "You let my son die here."

"I'm telling you, it didn't happen, not here." Ishmael slowly backed down the length of the porch and onto the garden path. "I didn't even get word about the boy's burial."

"There hasn't been one." Jonathan followed Ishmael into the garden, the leather satchel raised between them and the brass buttons shimmering in the afternoon sun. He pushed the leather satchel at Ishmael. "Help me fill this bag."

"You should go now." Ishmael kept backing away, the hem of his robe brushing over the hedges and the heel of his sandals catching on the stones. "We can discuss this another time, once you've calmed yourself."

"You want me to be calm?" Jonathan shook the satchel, the leather straps slapping about his hands. "You let my son die on this porch and now you hide his body to cover your sins. I'll calm myself as soon as you lead me to Aaron's grave."

Jonathan threw the leather bag at Ishmael. Curse him for his part in Aaron's death, and curse his family and his lands and his olive groves for taking his son from him. The force of Jonathan's voice scared the robins from beneath the cover of the sycamore branches, the flutter of their wings drowned by his railing against Ishmael, telling him he was no better than the others who beguiled Aaron. He was the first to come to their shop and hire Aaron away to this evil place and Jonathan spit on the ground next to Ishmael's feet. If it weren't for his white beard and his colorful red, green and yellow robe—the same white beard and traveling robe Aaron said was like the appearance of an angel the day they first met at the shop—Jonathan never would have trusted the life of his son into Ishmael's care. Angels? What did Ishmael know about heavenly things? He pushed Ishmael back against the gate, his shoulders rattling against the stiff metal. If there was a God, then why would a merciful being let his son—his innocent, believing, deluded son—die for no reason? Jonathan gripped Ishmael's robe by the collar and pulled hard enough to rip the cloth down to his chest. Ishmael tried to push away, ordering Jonathan to take his satchel and leave Beit Zayit before he called for his sons to escort him off their land, but Jonathan swung his fist, striking Ishmael across the cheek, sending the back of his head reeling against the gatepost. Ishmael wasn't going to threaten him, not after he let Aaron die. He swung again, landing a blow across Ishmael's brow and another under his chin and two more into his stomach. Ishmael fell against the gate and slowly slid down the metal bars to the ground, blood seeping from a cut over his eye and his hands pressed to his stomach. That would teach him to never bother Jonathan for blacksmithing again. He didn't need the man's work or his money—he'd never need this man for anything, not ever! Jonathan picked the empty satchel off the ground and stepped past Ishmael's fallen body. The gate was open, left unlocked from Ishmael's coming, and he let himself onto the road and started down past the charred remains of the burned-out olive grove. He was not a man to keep bitterness in his heart, but Ishmael was the only living reminder of his loss and he could never let go of that hatred.

Ishmael was his enemy.

CHAPTER 8

Miriam opened the door to Mulek's bedroom for the first time since she sent the boy away under the protecting care of Mima, her trusted Ethiopian handservant. The twelve windows running the length of the room were shuttered, and only a narrow shaft of late afternoon sunlight brightened the sills. There were no cobwebs gathered in the corners of the dark chamber and none on the valance above the hanging wall tapestries. The treasure-filled bowls of feathers and rocks on the table near Mulek's bed lay untouched since his leaving. The robes tailored to fit his long-boned body hung on hooks in the closet waiting for him to return to dress himself in the cloth and traipse about the palace, leading his younger brothers in search of another imagined adventure.

Not less than once each day Miriam asked the maidservants to run their plumes over the chairs and tables, replace the linens with freshly washed bed coverings, and brush what the feather dusters couldn't reach with the coarse ends of a reed broom. But no matter how often she saw to the straightening of this room and the scenting of the air with incense, there was no young boy to spoil the tidiness. No forgetful twelve-year-old hands to leave a tunic hanging over the backrest, no feet muddied from mucking about the backwaters of the Gihon Spring to track over the stone floor, and no sign of a concealed frog beneath the bed coverings lying in wait for the maidservant to come across the poor creature and, in a fit of discomposure, refuse to clean again until the room was rid of every living thing—including Mulek. He was the Prince of Judah, but there were days when the maidservants referred to him as the heir apparent of foolery. Miriam leaned against the bedpost. How many times did she tell Mulek his bedroom was not a stable for the creatures he packed home? She could only hope that Mima required better comportment than she ever had power to enforce before she sent him from her under the wings of her care.

Miriam leaned over the sideboard and smoothed the blankets in Mulek's bed. He was gone—hidden far away at the palace of Prince Jesse of Sidon on the coast of the Great Sea. But how was the boy sleeping in Sidon? Were they feeding him well? He was gaining a healthy appetite before she sent him away in the middle of the night on a chariot with a strange driver whom she paid to keep silent the details of the boy's flight. She couldn't keep him here any longer. Not with the dangers posed to him by Captain Laban and Zadock and, heaven help him, his own father.

Miriam snatched the pillows from against the headboards and fluffed them full. She arranged the trim along the sideboard, hiding the wood with a covering of lace. Mulek couldn't have grown too much in the short time he was gone, though these two months had passed as slow as a lifetime, and no matter how hard she tried to keep alive every detail of the boy's image, the vision of his playful smile was slowly fading. How much of his life would she forfeit before she dared bring him home to sleep in his own bed? Miriam sat herself on the feather mattress, her body sinking into its soft recesses and her hands clasped in her lap. Did he know how much he was missed? Did he understand the emptiness he left behind? And more than anything else, did Mulek miss his mother?

Miriam stood at the window, pushed open the shutters and let the late afternoon sun cast its warmth over her. The cry of merchants and farmers delivering their wares to the palace storehouse filtered up from below. Across the wall, stable boys saddled horses in the palace livery, and over the other wall white-robed temple priests milled about the outer courts of Solomon's Temple. No wonder Mulek loved this window. He sat here for hours, his skinny legs and thin arms curled into the square frame of this windowsill like a cocoon, preparing to emerge into manhood. In this window he was a silent observer of all he could survey and she wished him to return and curl himself here again and let her be the mother of the little boy she sent away. One day he would come home, but would it be such a long time coming that his body would no longer fit in this windowsill? And would the rattle of farmers' carts and the snorting of horses in the livery cease to attract his imagination? Not a day passed that Zedekiah didn't ask her to end this foolishness and send for the boy. He claimed he would do Mulek no harm for his spying, but she could not trust her husband's words. Men more powerful than Miriam held sway over Zedekiah, and she kept the knowledge of Mulek's hiding place from the king until she was certain Mulek could return and claim his royal place without facing whatever revenge lay dormant in Captain Laban's heart.

A knock sounded at the half-opened bedroom door. It was a faint tapping and Miriam hurried over and pulled back the tall timbers to find the bent-over frame of the jailer standing in the hall. His cheeks were red from climbing the steps, and the end of his long beard pushed against his chest when he spoke. He reached his hand out, his palm open like a beggar asking alms. He said, "I did what you asked."

Miriam checked the hall and when she was certain there were no maidservants to see her doings, she quickly ushered him inside and closed the door. "Is Jeremiah safe?"

"I keep him away from the other prisoners. No one can hurt him there."

"Not even one of your guards?"

"I'm the only one who goes near the man. They know that."

Miriam said, "What about his food?"

"Three warm meals from the palace kitchen every day."

"Does he sleep well?"

The jailer said, "I'll see that he gets a mat."

"Can't you find him something better than reeds?"

The jailer lowered his head. "It's a prison, My Lady."

"Very well." Miriam took three pieces of silver from her purse. "Thank you for—"

"I have another offer." The jailer's words whistled between the gaps in his teeth. "For another piece of silver I'll see to protecting the other prophet. I can't make any promises, mind you. I'm at the mercy of Captain Laban and Zadock, but I'll see that he's well fed and kept away from the other prisoners. He'll have plenty of fresh water and—"

"What other prophet? "

"Ezekiel, My Lady." The jailer quickly counted the silver coins in his palm before hiding them in a small leather pouch strapped about his waist. "The man accused of stirring the tax revolt."

"Who told you that?"

"The soldier who brought Ezekiel to the prison said he has ties to Lehi, the olive oil merchant who started the tax revolt." The words rushed out of the jailer's mouth. He said, "Captain Laban left for Jericho this morning to help the Babylonians hunt Lehi down."

Miriam began to pace in front of the jailer. She had to do something to protect these men of God, but what? There was little she could do to warn Lehi. She had no contact with the man and little knowledge of where he'd gone. And what of Ezekiel and Jeremiah? She couldn't simply let them rot in prison, or worse, let them wait on the unmerciful whims of Zadock and Laban. She lifted the skirts of her robe, turned about and paced across the path of the jailer, softly speaking aloud her frustration over the treatment of the prophets, and possibly might the jailer somehow find it in his heart to help her in her effort to help the . . . ?

"Don't ask me to do any more for you." The jailer stepped back from her words.

Miriam stopped her pacing. "I can pay you a good sum."

"It's enough what I'm doing. There's no harm in feeding them." The jailer lowered his head. "But I won't do any more. I could never do any more. Laban would have my head."

"See that you watch over Ezekiel." Miriam held out two more pieces of silver. "I want the same care for him as for Jeremiah."

The jailer nodded and took the money. "I've already seen to that."

The voice of Zedekiah sounded in the hallway and Miriam told the jailer to wait there while she led her husband away. When they were gone, he could let himself out. She hurried out the bedroom door and found Zedekiah standing on the main palace steps leading up from the anteroom. He was dressed in a formal blue robe with silver trim and he started toward her, but pulled up when she suggested they go downstairs and have a cup of tea.

"I didn't come in search of your company." Zedekiah pushed his straight hair off his brow.

"I'm sorry." Miriam crossed the distance between them with her gaze turned to the floor. "I didn't mean to presume you wanted—"

"What were you doing in Mulek's room?" Zedekiah peered past her down the hall.

"Nothing, really." Miriam took him by the arm and started him down the stairs. "I was looking through some of Mulek's things to see if they needed mending."

"There's nothing to mend." Zedekiah pulled free from her grasp and stopped in the middle of the first flight of steps. "The boy hasn't worn his clothes for going on two months. Or did you forget you sent him away?"

"Why must you question everything I say?" Miriam slowly turned on the stone step. "Do you think it your duty to investigate everything I do?"

"None of this would have happened if I had questioned you more often."

"About what?"

"Visionaries, dreamers, you know what I'm talking about. Protecting men who think they have power to peer into heaven. Holy men who have answers to questions that have no answer. That's what I should have asked you about before any of this happened. But then I forgot. You believe heaven will answer every one of your prayers."

Miriam turned away from her husband. Where did he misplace his faith? He hadn't lost his devotion, only replaced it with an allegiance toward men she could never trust. She said, "I'm sorry."

"Sorry for what?"

"We no longer share the same convictions." Miriam started down the next flight without him, but he hurried to catch her stride. He said, "Your meddling with these prophets could ruin us."

"Don't you mean it could ruin *you?*" Miriam gripped the thick marble railing.

"I'm concerned, that's all."

"Concerned about what? Your prestige before Zadock and the princes of the city?" Miriam turned around the post and on to the last run of steps opening onto the main palace lobby, the hem of her robe brushing over the stone. "I thought the faith of the King of Judah was the faith of every Jew."

"These men, these prophets of yours, they're not good Jews."

"Why don't you tell me what makes a good Jew?"

"When did you become such a difficult woman?" Zedekiah reached for her hand, but Miriam pulled away from his reaching. She said, "I do what I must."

"Is that your excuse for sending Mulek away?"

"I'm his mother."

"And I'm his father." Zedekiah stepped in front of her, stopping her descent. "When will you come to your senses about the boy?"

"If you think me mad, then fine, I'll be mad." Miriam stepped past him and continued down the last run of steps. Her husband seemed earnest, but she couldn't risk Mulek's safety on the sincerity of Zedekiah's voice or his pleading words. She said, "I'll claim whatever insanity you think me to have until the day Captain Laban is dead."

"Don't speak like that." Zedekiah scaled down the steps behind her. "Captain Laban means Mulek no harm."

"You don't know him like I do." Miriam reached the anteroom floor and started toward the main doors of the palace. "If I were king, I'd be rid of him."

Zedekiah's voice echoed off the high limestone walls of the vaulted anteroom. He said, "I'm bringing Mulek home from Sidon."

The hem of Miriam's robe gathered about the ankles on her sudden stop. She held the latch to the main doors in her hand, but she didn't turn it open. How did Zedekiah know Mulek was in Sidon? She slowly turned around. She had not told him where she'd sent the boy. Zedekiah stood one step above the anteroom floor, his arm raised and the wide cuffs of his blue robe falling down over his wrist. He said, "I'm taking this matter into my own hands."

"You're wrong if you think you can trick me into telling you where I've sent him."

"This is no trick." Zedekiah slowly shook his head, his straight, dark hair pushing down over his brow. "You never should have hired a driver to take the boy to Sidon in company with Mima. Word among my men may travel slowly, but it does travel."

Miriam started back toward him. "You can't—"

"You have no say in the boy's future any longer." Zedekiah held his hand up to quiet her protest. "I'm sending Captain Elnathan with a troop of soldiers to bring the boy home. He leaves this evening."

"You don't need Mulek here."

"I'll deal with the boy as I see fit."

"It isn't safe for him."

"I'll decide what is and isn't safe."

Miriam lowered her head, her hands holding tight to the pleats in her robe. What was she to do? Did not heaven see she was alone without anyone to help her? And if there were anyone who could aid her now, how would she find them? There was not a soul in the palace that didn't watch her every step with suspicion, and when she left the palace an escort of soldiers stayed by her side. Zedekiah insisted it was for her own protection, but she knew differently. He didn't trust her, not even to go to market for a bottle of perfume or take a private stroll through the upper-city walkways away from the confines of these thick royal walls. She was the mother of the palace informant. The treacherous queen who could not be trusted with anything beyond the list of invited palace guests expected for a visit and the menu of what was for dinner. There was enough suspicion hanging over her that it would not be long before the cooks stopped asking her opinion on how long to roast the lamb and what kind of wine to serve before evening meal. What was she to do? She was a captive of her own shadow. She'd lost the trust of her husband, the potter and his daughter were gone from this place, and Mima was fled to Sidon with Mulek—Miriam's only son old enough to be of any help. She was alone in her designs, a prisoner in her own home, and there was no telling when her husband would punish her for her part in Uriah's trial and Mulek's spying. She was at his mercy and every day she prayed he would not conclude she was no longer fit to be his wife. She was the Queen of Judah, but she was trapped in this royal station—no more than a pauper quietly begging heaven that her husband would not penalize her for her faith in the promised Messiah. The prophecies of the Anointed One burned in her soul and she clung to her unwise ways when reason begged her to submit to men more powerful than she, and she prayed that she could find someone, anyone who had the wisdom and power to guide her through these troubles.

Miriam slowly fitted herself into the square frame of the bench seat at the base of the stairs and let go her hold on the skirts of her robe, her hand pressed against her breast. The soft voice in her soul rose like a familiar melody on a flute, lifting and growing stronger until it was as powerful as a song choired by angels, quietly speaking to her mind the answer to Mulek's safety. She lowered her hands to her side and quietly said, "Ruth, the weaver?"

Zedekiah leaned over the marble hand railing. "What was that?"

"Your clothes, dear." Miriam didn't look up from her bench seat. She kept her gaze fixed on the doors to the palace entry. "Do you have need of a tailor?"

"What sort of question is that? Of course not. Why do you ask?"

"Nothing dear. I was simply gathering a few thing to take to the weaver's for a stitch or two."

"Take an escort with you if you leave the grounds." Zedekiah started up the stairs to their living quarters. "Something could happen, you know."

"Yes, dear. Something could happen." Miriam spoke slowly, her words filled with the same determination that fired her soul. She raised herself from the bench without help from the armrest, and as soon as Zedekiah disappeared around the last run of stairs, she started for the main doors.

Dear God, give her the strength to make the right thing happen.

Jonathan draped the leather satchel over his shoulders and turned onto High Street, the hill hurrying his tired stride. It was a long walk from Beit Zayit, but it was neither the length of the journey nor the making of an enemy of Ishmael that wearied his feet. It was the loss of his son, and he kept in the shadows away from the last rays of summer sun, over where the high walls preserved a breath of cool air against the heat of the day. He'd walked this street in the company of Aaron many times, but now he'd have to find his way to the black-smith shop alone. Foolish boy. Aaron was naive to believe he could stand in front of an arrow and live to see the fruits of his misplaced courage.

High Street turned down a sharp incline and veered to the left before coming out in front of Jonathan's home. He rounded the bend and, standing there, in front of the gate was a group of soldiers milling about. They were dressed in breastplates, their heads were covered with polished brass helmets, and their tunics were dyed in the deep purple color of the palace guard. The officer in charge stepped to Jonathan, the metal rivets in his kilt clanging against his sword. He reached for Jonathan's shoulder. "I'm sorry sir, you can't pass. Not until we're finished delivering—"

"This is my house." Jonathan pushed the officer's hand off his shoulder and stepped through the gate. He ducked beneath the grapevines, the summer growth hiding the entrance in a stand of healthy leaves, and found a powerful brown steed pawing at the stones in the yard. It was a young animal, with nimble legs and strong haunches and when Jonathan reached to stroke its coat, the beast jumped with a feistiness fit for only the swiftest horses. Silver studs decorated the seams in the leather saddle, and the animal was rigged with a single water skin and two saddlebags. Jonathan started inside to find out what sort of visitor owned such a beast. He reached for the latch, but when the sound of voices filtered around the corner, he started down along the front of the house, past the kitchen windows, and stopped before turning into the side yard. It was Ruth and she was speaking with Miriam. It had to be the queen. There was not another woman in all of Jerusalem who spoke with such a refined tongue and her worry poured out of her like a flood of water after a summer storm. She feared for the life of her son Mulek, and Jonathan turned his ear to get every word of their conversation. Miriam said she sent the boy to Sidon two months ago to protect him from Captain Laban's revenge. The man hated Mulek for his spying and now her husband was sending Elnathan and a company of men to find Mulek in Sidon and bring him home. Miriam's voice caught and she cleared her throat before telling Ruth that she didn't know who else to turn to for help. She feared the worst for her son and she could never bear to lose him.

Jonathan leaned against the side of the house, his shoulder pressed into the stone. Why must this woman bring her worries to their home? Didn't she understand they were still suffering the loss of their own son? Jonathan made a fist and pressed it into the foundation wall. He would not agonize over another firstborn son. It was pain enough that Jonathan didn't find Aaron's body and he tightened his grip on the empty leather satchel under his arm. Miriam may be the Queen of Judah, but she was not welcome to make *her* fears *their* fears. This was Jonathan's home and he was going to put an end to these worries.

There would be no more death in this house.

Ruth took the basket of weaving from Miriam and leaned it against the side of the water basin—wedged between her leg and the coarse stone. There was a large blue tunic with a tear in the collar, a white robe ripped at the cuff, and a linen veil with loose threads in the seam. It wasn't anything Ruth couldn't fix, but these self-inflicted tears and rends were not the reason for Miriam's coming and she did not know if she could mend the queen's heart as easily. How could she find comfort for fears that did not show any hope of relief? Tears streamed from Miriam's eyes and Ruth set aside the basket, took her by both hands, and promised her she would do something to remedy this awful dilemma, but what could she do? Miriam could not risk going to Sidon. She'd packed a horse with water and supplies for the long journey, but she'd never make it beyond the Jordan River before her husband's men—the soldiers who followed her about the city like shadows she could not elude—caught her and returned her to the confines of the palace. Miriam was watched at every turn, and no matter how much Ruth desired to make this journey in her place, she'd never ridden a beast as powerful as a horse. She could steer a mule, but not the galloping, trotting, unbridled power of a steed from the king's stables. She could never hope to reach Sidon ahead of the king's men and warn the prince he was hunted.

Miriam said, "I don't know why I came to you, but my heart told me I should."

Ruth tightened her grip on Miriam's hands. "We'll think of something."

"What shall we do?" Miriam let go of Ruth's grasp and brushed the tears from her cheeks. "Once Elnathan and his men are away, there's nothing we can do to get word to Mulek."

"If God sent you here, then this is where you'll find the answer to your prayers."

Jonathan appeared from behind the corner of the house holding an empty leather satchel in one hand and swinging his other hand to the rhythm of his marching, his shoulders pushed forward and his sandals slapping the stone path. Miriam pulled the hood of her robe over her head and across her face and tried to step back beneath the shadows of the house, but Ruth would not let her go. She pulled the woman next to her, whispered for her to be calm, and then she offered a prayer she hoped would register quickly in the heavens. If God sent Miriam here, then surely He would provide, and would He please send whatever grace there was reserved for them soon. There was so little time.

Ruth said, "Jonathan, come meet the—"

"I know who she is." Jonathan spoke in a stern voice. "I heard everything."

Ruth raised her voice to match the firm resolve of his speech. "There's no reason for you to be angry."

"I have every reason." Jonathan stopped in front of Ruth. There was somberness deep in his eyes. It was the dark, lonely look of loss and it spilled out of him when he said, "No mother should ever have to worry about the life of her son." He was angry, but not over Miriam's visit. Something else inspired his marching stride and his bristling frame and she could only thank heaven's hand when he tipped his head toward the front of the house and said, "Can your horse make it to Sidon without much rest? I know the best roads, the shortest back ways, but Sidon is still a good hundred-and-fifty-mile journey from here."

Miriam took Jonathan by the arm. "You would risk this for me?"

"Where can I find Mulek?"

"Mima is watching over him in the royal palace of Jesse, Prince of Sidon. Do you know it?"

"Jonathan can find anything in Sidon, we lived there for . . ." Ruth raised her hand to her mouth. She didn't mean to interrupt her husband's discussion with the queen, but her relief for his sudden change of heart sent a thrill through her. What had come over him? He was not given to help anyone who sided with the prophets, and Ruth finished speaking softly between her fingers, keeping back the wonder that carried on her voice. "We lived in Sidon many years before moving to Jerusalem."

Jonathan said, "I can find my way about the palace. I made a good many blacksmithing deliveries there." He started out of the side yard back toward the horse, but stopped when Miriam said, "Will you take a message to Mima about the prophets?"

Jonathan didn't turn back to speak with the queen. He kept facing the courtyard and spoke in a low voice over his shoulder. "What sort of message?"

"Jeremiah and Ezekiel are held in the palace prison. We must do something to ease their suffering."

"Mima can't do anything for them. The woman is in Sidon."

"She can pray for them."

Jonathan turned back from facing the courtyard, his hands tight at his side and his brow furrowed. "It's enough I'm warning her to hide your son, but I'll do nothing to save the men you call prophets." He spit on the ground and rubbed the heel of his sandal into the dust. "Their doings are as cruel as any revenge Captain Laban would inflict on Mulek."

Ruth and Miriam quietly followed Jonathan back down the side of the house and into the courtyard. He inspected the riggings on the saddle, pulled on the bridle, checked the supplies of food and water in the saddlebags and then mounted the steed, the animal jumping against his weight. He stroked the horse on the neck and told her to be calm. He said, "I'll leave by the back gate. If the soldiers ask about the horse, tell them you're leaving the animal while I fit her with some shoes. That should keep them from suspecting anything." He trotted over next to the obscure back gate that led into a narrow alley and waited for Miriam to open the latch.

Ruth stepped in next to him and laid her hand on his leg, but before she could ask about Aaron's body, he leaned over the saddle, handed her the leather satchel and said, "I'm sorry. I didn't find him."

Ruth lowered her gaze from his stare. "Why are you doing this for Miriam?"

Jonathan started the horse inching out the back gate. "No mother should have to endure the loss of her eldest son."

Jonathan left for Sidon.

CHAPTER 9

Nephi adjusted his sleeping mat and lay on his side to salvage what sleep he could before dawn in this desert where summer nights began hotter than the coals of a campfire and ended with a deep chill that only a good lambskin blanket could cure. It wasn't Aaron's breathing on the far side of the tent that kept Nephi awake. The blacksmith hardly made a noise during the night and even if he snored as loud as Lemuel he wouldn't send the man off. There were four additions to the family tent, one for each son, and since this one was the largest with three center poles to support the roof and a good twenty stakes to moor her in place to the back of Lehi's tent, inviting Aaron to make his home in these quarters was the least Nephi could do for the blacksmith who risked his life to save theirs.

A soft groan filtered over from Aaron's side of the tent and Nephi quickly sat up, peered into the darkness, and asked if all was well. There was no answer and he raised his voice, the words rushing out of him. If there was anything Nephi could do to ease the pain, would Aaron please say it? He wouldn't let Aaron endure anymore than he already suffered. The blacksmith took the only arrow in their escape from Jerusalem, and if it weren't for his bravery none of them would have survived Captain Laban's drunken wrath. They nearly lost him to infections twice and it wasn't until last week that some color came back into his cheeks and he had the strength to get out of bed and use the crutches Nephi whittled for him out of the twisted branches of a Joshua tree. It was a shame to see Aaron have to use them again. It wasn't right for one man to have to suffer so much pain—first his burned feet and now the head of an arrow lodged deep in his thigh where they couldn't remove it. The wound was healing, and with time Aaron would be rid of the walking sticks and he could climb the cliffs above their hideout at Qumran without this awful pain to hold him back. But until he was whole, he would shuffle along a while longer, supported by the dead branches of a tree.

The steady rhythm of the blacksmith's breathing returned and Nephi stopped asking if there was anything he could do to ease his suffering, but he'd never stop thanking Aaron for saving them—even in the dark, early hours of morning when there was no one to hear his thanks. Nephi pulled the edge of his lambskin blanket up under his chin and turned onto his other shoulder, but it was no use. He was never going to get back to sleep as long as Laman was gone. Had it been three days or four since his brother left camp to negotiate their return to Jerusalem? No, it was five this morning—five long days since Laman left for Jericho to seek out the Chief Elder of the Jews. And if by some good fortune he found a way to convince Zadock to let them return to harvest their olive groves, then Nephi could go back to tending the storage vats instead of eking out a living in this barren desert. Nephi rolled onto his back, stuffed his hands beneath his head, and stared at the dark ceiling. Would he ever return to be keeper of the olive oil at Beit Zayit on the lands his father and grandfather worked their whole lives to cultivate, or was there another future for him and his family beyond the land of their inheritance?

The sand beneath the animal-skin floor made for a comfortable bed, but not comfortable enough to bring Nephi any sleep, not with the matter of his family's future nagging at him, begging him to make certain Laman was right, that they should seek the mercy of the Chief Elder and Captain Laban and request a peaceful homecoming. But how could they ask mercy of men who neither dealt in mercy nor possessed the sympathy to grant them an end to their hiding at Qumran, deep in this Judean Wilderness? Nephi felt about in the darkness until he found the blue linen tunic folded beside his sleeping mat. He pulled it on, the seams coming tight about the collar. Six months ago this shirt was more than large enough to fit his frame, but now his wide shoulders and thick chest were pulling up the stitches, and without any weavers within miles of this desert hideout he would wear this tight-fitting tunic until the family returned home and mother could get him another shirt to cover his bulkiness.

Sariah lectured him not less than three times a day that he was growing like a weed, that he was stronger than an ox, and she always wanted to know was he sleeping well? And he would answer that a weed didn't look anything like an ox and then wait for her to laugh, but not too much in her delicate condition. He could never tell her he'd not slept through the night since coming to Qumran—not with the undecided question of their return hanging over his mind like a dark tempest pouring into his thoughts by day, storming his dreams by night and rousing him from his sleep. It was the first thing he asked his brothers each morning before they left to quarry stone for building the city that was to become their new home and they told him not to lose sleep over their troubles; they would not forfeit the land of their inheritance because of a misunderstanding with Captain Laban and the Elders of the Jews. Return was all they ever talked about over meals; it filled every conversation, and it was the last thing they mentioned before going to sleep. They would return home, but every time Nephi asked them when, all they could tell him was to be patient—it would come soon enough.

Nephi tucked the ends of his shirt beneath the waist of his leather kilt and straightened the cloth over his shoulders. Laman told him he was certain that by next year in Jerusalem they would have forgotten this foolish foray into the wilderness. Lemuel counted the passing days with olive pits, placing one into an empty jar at sunrise every morning. He said they would be home before the pits reached the brim or he would not eat the next Passover meal. But Lemuel was a thin boy; it was not a good thing for him to gamble away his meals, so Nephi refused his wagers. Sam spoke of celebrating Passover next year in Jerusalem more than he ever spoke about building a corral for the large herd of caravan camels under his charge. For all of them, it was always next year in Jerusalem.

Nephi set aside his lambskin blanket and felt about in the darkness with his toes until he found his sandals, then latched them to his feet. Why was he the only one uncertain about returning home? No one need know of his doubts, especially Mama what with her carrying a baby that she could lose any day. If anyone needed to hope they would leave this barren place and return to the luxury of maidservants to care for her pain and doctors to look after her unborn child, and to storehouses filled with food to nourish the life growing in her womb, it was Sariah. Her condition hadn't improved in this wilderness and it was best for her to believe that this hideout was nothing more than a place of waiting until the storm Captain Laban rained down on them had passed, and all was well in Jerusalem and they could go home. But there was a nagging deep in Nephi's soul telling him that for all his sensible reasoning and for all his longing to return to the way things were before they fled their home, it was not to be. No matter how he tried to ignore the pestering, it would not leave him in peace.

Nephi turned his ear to listen for Sariah's voice filtering through the thick leather skins separating his sleeping quarters from the main tent. All was quiet on the other side, Mama was still resting and Papa wasn't moving about. There was still time before the family stirred from their rest to search for the answer to the question that woke Nephi early from his sleep every morning since the day he left Beit Zayit. Until he was certain his older brothers were right he would continue reading the scrolls, hoping beyond hope he could find some guidance in the writings he kept in his tent.

Nephi lit a small reading lamp and lifted it until its light illuminated a stack of parchments set beside the corner tent pole. Father told him to bring the most precious documents from their library at Beit Zayit and these parchments with the words of Isaiah written into them were the ones he packed away in saddlebags before any other records. They were the words he'd read a hundred times under the tutelage of his teachers. Until now they were nothing more than words from an ancient prophet a hundred years dead, but since fleeing Jerusalem there was something about the writings of Isaiah that drew Nephi to read them like he'd never read them before.

Nephi sat beside the tent pole, spread the parchment over his legs, and leaned forward like a man grinding wheat, gleaning the scroll for every bit of meaning, searching for any help recorded here. The edges were worn and some of the letters faded from use, but the ink wasn't so weak he couldn't read them quickly, his finger hurrying to keep up with his gaze. He was to the middle of the parchment when he found the place where he left off yesterday, the part that had him believing they could never leave the land of his inheritance. Jerusalem was the capital of Nephi's homeland. It was the place where his family had built their estate. They had their inheritance there and olive groves and more wealth than they could ever hope to gather out of this wilderness. They lived a comfortable life at Jerusalem and why would they ever want to leave a place where the very God of heaven was to be born? Nephi slowly read through the passage from Isaiah's writings that unto the people in Jerusalem would be born a child and his name would be wonderful, counselor, the mighty king, the everlasting father, and the prince of peace. Nephi raised his gaze from the scroll and stared into the darkness. If there was a center place under all the heavens, Jerusalem was that place. And if there was a land where they could live in comfort it was their home at Jerusalem. It was the land of Nephi's birth. He'd grown up at Beit Zayit and there was no reason to want to leave the place where Yeshua the Anointed One—the very Messiah—was to be born. But Isaiah was speaking of a distant future, not this day when Babylonians occupied Nephi's homeland. And if there was anything in these parchments that spoke of this present day he would keep reading until he found it—some allusion to his family's escape into this wilderness, some phrase speaking of their plight, any heavenly clues detailing the fate of . . .

Nephi stopped at a passage he'd not noticed before. He'd studied this scroll more times than he could count, but he'd not read with the same searching as he did now and he backed up to the beginning of the phrase and read: *Harken all ye that are broken off and are driven out because of the wickedness of the pastors of my people; yea, all that are broken off and scattered abroad.* Nephi placed the end of his finger on the phrase "pastors of my people." Was Isaiah talking about them? There was no doubt about Captain Laban's wickedness. And he, along with the Chief Elder were certainly pastors of this people, but was Isaiah speaking of their flight from Jerusalem? Nephi knew well the prophecies of the scattering of the House of Israel—he could recite the words of the prophet Zenos and his Allegory of the Olive Tree from memory. But were these pastors like the tops of the olive trees that were to be lopped off? Were they the same pastors who threatened the lives of Nephi and his family? There was no way to know unless Isaiah was speaking of the present day when . . .

There it was, the piece of history he was searching for. But this wasn't history. Isaiah was speaking of Nephi's day, warning him that these pastors were living at Jerusalem during the Babylonian occupation. Nephi pressed his finger against the leather parchment. Right here it said that some Jews would be broken off and scattered and they would flee Jerusalem with a voice of singing and rejoicing because the Lord had redeemed them. That's exactly how they arrived at Qumran, rejoicing and singing after Aaron had saved them from Captain Laban's wrath. They had traveled through the night to this desert hideout thanking heaven they were alive.

Nephi pulled the reading lamp closer, the flame warming his leg and throwing shadows over the scroll. He slowly read over Isaiah's prophecies of the scattering of Israel in the days of the Babylonians as if that dead prophet were in this tent with him, describing the very troubles the Jews faced with Babylonian rule and the deportation of Jews that accompanied their occupation.

Nephi reached the end of the scroll and quickly took out the next one, laying it overtop the first, gripping the ends of it like a chariot driver holds the reins on a team of mighty steeds. There was more about these scattered Jews Isaiah saw in vision. They were to be led through the deserts—not just one desert, but many deserts. Nephi slowed his reading, carefully going over each word, his lips moving to the whispered rhythm of Isaiah's writings, that *God would lead them through the way they should go. They would pass through a furnace of affliction to purify them and bring them to depend on God more deeply than they had ever done before. And though their travels through this desert wilderness were to be long and difficult, they would not thirst nor hunger, neither would the heat nor the sun smite them, but by springs of water would he guide them. And O that thou would hearken unto the commandments of the Lord, then your peace shall be as a river, and your righteousness as the waves of the sea.*

"Did you find what you're looking for?" Aaron sat up on one elbow and peered across the tent at him. "You've been reading from the same scrolls every morning since we arrived."

"I didn't mean to wake you." Nephi set the lamp aside with one hand, but kept a tight hold on the edge of the scroll with the other. "It's nothing really. I've been reading these things for years."

"Not like that you haven't."

"Like what?"

"As if you were holding on to life." Aaron pointed to Nephi's tight grip on the scroll and his bent-over posture that allowed him to peer down at the parchment like a doctor examining a patient. "You read as if every word had a sealed meaning you were trying to unlock. You know what I mean, like a merchant lost in the desert, searching a map to decipher the right directions."

Nephi loosened his hold on the parchment and leaned his head back against the tent pole. "I couldn't sleep."

"What is it in those scrolls that holds your interest?" Aaron sat up and the pain of moving his leg flashed across his face.

"You really should stay down."

"I've got to walk the pain out of this wound or I'll be limping the rest of my life." Aaron reached for the crutches next to his sleeping mat and hoisted himself up onto the long timbers. He hobbled to the entrance and pushed back the tent flaps, the cool air streaming in from the dark morning. He stood silent at the entrance, his gaze turned out onto the sand-swept hillsides surrounding Qumran and the morning stars still visible before dawn, the breeze lifting the short sleeves of his tunic about his arms, and his grip firmly set on the hand holds of his crutches.

"You don't think they're right, do you?" Nephi set aside the scroll. "You don't agree with my brothers that we'll go home to Beit Zayit anytime soon, do you?"

Aaron disappeared out of the entrance and returned with the graft he'd taken from the old olive tree at Beit Zayit—the one they called the House of Israel, the oldest olive tree on the plantation. He had cut it the night Papa shared with him the Allegory of the Olive Tree and had nurtured it since they arrived at Qumran, keeping the grafted end in a bulb of olive mash and wrapping it with a cloth and dipping it not less than three times a day in water. It was still alive; there was a bud near the tip and the limb was still green. Aaron said, "It isn't so much that we won't be able to go home, but that we were never meant to go back." He turned back to the entrance, his gaze searching the stars in the morning sky before dawn. "There's something out here for us."

"There's no place to plant your graft in this barren desert. There's nothing here but sand and a Salt Sea."

"Not here, but somewhere." Aaron held the graft in the palm of his hand, the cloth ball pushing through his fingers. "Somewhere there's got to be a place prepared for us."

Nephi said, "You don't believe we're ever going back home, do you?"

"I believe we'll make our home wherever we find a place of refuge."

Aaron disappeared past the tent flaps, the shuffle of his crutches over the sand slowly fading into the darkness of morning, and Nephi turned back to his reading. Were there any clues in these ancient writings, anything that would quiet his questioning heart? He raised the lamp over the scroll and started down through the lines of narrow Hebrew script, his gaze hurrying over the words until the flickering light gathered around a passage in the middle of the leather skin. It was a short verse, short enough that he'd passed over it without much thought before, but now it stood out on the parchment with power to speak to his soul and he read it again—for the first time: *There shall be a tabernacle for a shadow in the daytime from the heat, and for a place of refuge from the storm.*

Nephi set down the lamp. Aaron was right. There was a place of refuge for them, but where? Was Isaiah speaking to him, telling him that God had prepared a tabernacle in the middle of this hot desert to shade them from the heat and give them refuge from the storms that raged in Jerusalem? And if there was a place of refuge prepared for them, was Qumran that place, or would they have to travel deeper into the deserts of Arabia to find refuge? It was as if Isaiah had written these words in a letter and sent them by courier to travel through time a hundred years for Nephi to read, but why didn't he send more details, the name of the territory or any other clue that could lead them to a new home?

Nephi quickly turned to the top of the scroll, back to the passage that said God would lead them through the way they should go, not Isaiah. If God spoke to Isaiah about Nephi and his family's flight into this wilderness, couldn't He speak to Nephi now? He set aside the soft leather scroll, got up on his knees, lowered his head and asked God to answer the one question he could not answer for himself.

Would there ever be a *next year* in Jerusalem?

Sariah refused to prop herself against such a large stack of pillows and she told Lehi two was more than enough—she could lean against the center pole of the tent and see out the front entrance just fine without him collecting every pillow between here and the Orient. Where did he find so many? They certainly didn't pack all these from Beit Zayit, did they? She was certain she left the finest pillows and bedding at the estate with instructions to her daughters to run the feather dusters over every room and change the linens from time to time until they returned.

Sariah waved her forefinger at Lehi and reminded him that he had his writing to worry about and if he didn't get about recording the events that brought them to hide in this wilderness, the day would get away from him and he'd be far too tired to push a pen over the parchment. Sariah could sit up and watch the sunrise without the help of any pillows, but Lehi insisted on a mountain of feathered support stacked atop a foundation of lambskin blankets. It was like watching a child build a fortress with Lehi flitting about, fluffing pillows and folding blankets and stuffing them one atop the other until he'd built a mound of comfort she could not possibly enjoy in a lifetime of bearing his children. He was losing his head over nothing. She hadn't had any bleeding for days, or any of the pains that accompanied it. The back of her scalp was healing, though she still suffered headaches. But she didn't wear a bandage around her head and the bald spot where the nursemaids cut away her hair was growing in, almost four fingers long the last time she measured. If she kept herself down and didn't strain too much, she would keep this precious spirit maturing in her womb—she was certain of it.

Sariah may not be well enough to help with the chores of desert dwelling, but with a few more days of rest she'd be out grinding wheat instead of leaving those tasks to her sons. Laman could hardly prepare a bowl of dates, Lemuel burned every morsel of lamb he set his hand to, Sam did not have the sense to season anything he served, and Nephi preferred to eat ground wheat mixed with goat's milk than spend time cooking flat bread over an open fire. She'd suffered two months of their cooking and as soon as she was well she would not be confined to the culinary tastes of these men any longer.

Sariah begged Lehi to end his fussing, but he would not listen to her plea. If Sariah was well enough to watch the sunrise from her bed, then he would see that she had the support of as many pillows as he could gather from every corner and compartment of this maze of tents they called home. He told her no less than twice a day that he had brought her into this wildness with few of the luxuries she enjoyed at Beit Zayit, and the least he could do was provide her with a few simple comforts.

The tent was woven from the coarse, brown hair of camels. The dry, straight fibers allowed the tent to breathe, swelling only in times of rain to keep out the moisture, before drying and allowing the air to pass through the walls. The camel-hair tent was cooler than the sweltering heat of an animal-hide tent, and much more durable than a dwelling of reeds or palms. But no matter how spacious they wove it—adding a new partition each time another child was born into the family—it was nothing compared to the grandeur of their abandoned estate; though it was certainly much grander than the small, single-room tents in this city of makeshift Bedouin dwellings. And thank heaven her husband was an experienced caravaneer or they never would have had any tent at all to call their own, or camels and provisions at the ready to quickly slip into this wilderness. Her husband's merchant trading prepared him well for this flight, to say nothing of his knowledge of the trails leading through this country.

Sariah tried to ignore Lehi's fussing, but how could she not enjoy all the selfless to-do he made over her. And this from a man who had every reason for conceit. He knew every byway leading from Jerusalem all the way to the tip of the Arabian Peninsula, and he had a host of maps drawn by his own hand to prove his knowledge of these territories. And when they returned to Beit Zayit he'd have more details to add to his map collections after exploring the lay of the land along these barren western shores of the Dead Sea. Sariah eased back against the softness, her husband's strong hands guiding her into a mountain of pillows, but the most comfortable thing was to have the touch of his hand on her shoulder and to know that he was there, watching over her. Before Lehi was ever an olive oil merchant or an expert caravaneer or a wealthy man of business, he was her husband. And never a day passed that she wasn't grateful for a kind, humble soul to look after her—forever.

Sariah touched his outstretched arm and said, "I'm fine, dear. Really I am."

"Are you in any pain?"

Sariah waved her hand. "I don't feel a thing."

"You're not hungry are you?"

"Lemuel will bring us plenty to eat once he's got a fire going. He's a fine cook."

"You don't really mean that." Lehi shook his head. "The boy could burn air if he could conjure a way to keep it over a fire long enough."

"Go on, get on with your records." She pointed to the saddlebags stacked along the north wall of the tent. "Your writing box is over there."

Lehi slowly backed away from hovering over her. "You're certain you're comfortable?"

"You have more important things to see to than the comfort of an old woman."

"You're not old my dear. You're just now blooming into the finest rose I've ever known."

"Look at you, making such a fuss." Sariah raised her hands to the pillows rising up either side of her. "I couldn't be more comfortable."

That wasn't entirely the case. Sleeping in a tent with a sand dune for a mattress was not the same comfort she enjoyed at Beit Zayit. And having Lemuel prepare flat bread on an open fire was certainly nothing like the hosts of cooks who prepared meals in her kitchen at home with two hearths, bins of flour and grain, and every spice known to man, but they were safe here on the shores of the Dead Sea where none of their enemies could find them.

Lehi picked through the stack of leather saddlebags until he found the one where he stored his writings. He reached inside with both hands and slowly lifted out a wooden box. It was five hands wide and three deep. The lid was fastened along the spine with bright brass hinges and it was sealed shut with a matching brass lock. It was a bulky thing to haul into this wilderness on the back of a camel when they could have carried bags of wheat or barley in its place, but Sariah never complained. This writing box was more important than a storehouse full of grain. The yellowish olive wood was still new without any of the dark color that was certain to turn a deep, golden brown with the passing of time, but hopefully they would be in this wilderness such a short time that the box would have to age on the library shelves of the map room at Beit Zayit.

Lehi cut the wood for the box from one of the trees in his vineyard, but he didn't decorate the lid or the sides with the etching of an olive tree—a decoration Lehi burned into every leather saddlebag used in his caravanning. He imprinted the olive tree emblem into the mud bricks he formed for the main hearth of their estate home, and he branded it into the hide of every camel in his herd. But on this box he whittled the portrait of a large date tree. His library at home was filled with his writings, and accountings, and the histories of their life at Beit Zayit, but his life had changed so much the past year he decorated this writing box to remind them both of the worth of what lay within. Sariah ran her fingers over the wood etching. There was not a better reminder of the fruits of the spirit that had come to Lehi than the picture of the golden-colored, life-giving dates ripening on the tree. So much had changed so quickly, but Sariah would return to Beit Zayit to live a peaceful life, away from the hurry of Jerusalem and protected by the surrounding hills where she could enjoy her children and her children's children.

Lehi unlatched the box and slowly lifted the lid. Two leather parchments sat on the upper shelf of the two-tiered box. The scrolls were a sacred, personal record sealed with cords and half hidden beneath a red silk wrap. He began the first parchment last year immediately after his vision, filling it with the details of his prayer at Raphia and the appearance of God on the cliffs above his camp, followed by his three days of visions when she was certain she'd lost him to death, only to realize that God had found him and called him to be a prophet. He finished the second parchment a short time before they left Beit Zayit, detailing his attempts to free Uriah and chronicling the powerful warnings he left with the people of Jerusalem during the trial. And these last two months since arriving here, he'd begun writing of the dream that inspired him to flee into this wilderness on the night of Passover, but he'd not finished that record, at least not with the detail that met with her approval. And not a day passed that she didn't encourage him to finish his record.

Lehi lifted away the two completed parchments and removed the small wooden shelf, revealing a supply of virgin parchments lying in the bottom of the box, waiting for him to begin his account of their time in this desert. The unwritten parchments sat next to a corked jar of ink and a single writing pen with a bronze metal tip. There was enough ink to last him until they found another source, and if they couldn't purchase it, then Sariah would crush her own coal and mix it with powders and make ink for her husband to write his record. She pressed her hand against her womb. She wouldn't let their lives slip away like a dream without recording the important events to pass on to their children. This unborn babe would have a record of this desert, and when the child was enjoying the comforts of their estate at Beit Zayit the babe would come to know the courage of Sariah's husband and the long suffering of her sons. It would be a story she would not let anyone forget, no matter how short a time they spent in this place before returning home.

Lehi prepared this writing box well before they fled Beit Zayit, but with so much to attend to in the days before their flight he'd not written anything beyond the first two parchments. And if he didn't get about keeping his record, he was going to forget the details of their coming here and they'd be lost forever. Sariah leaned over the pillows, lifted out an unwritten parchment from the box along with a writing pen and ink bottle. She said, "Open the tent for a bit of morning light and get on with your writing."

Lehi stood at the entrance and pushed back the tent flaps to let the cool morning air filter over Sariah. She pulled the hood of her robe back to let the breeze lift her long black hair off her shoulders and handed Lehi his pen and ink. "I'll tend to making sure the sun rises while you tend to your writing."

Sariah turned her gaze outside, but she couldn't entirely forget the sound of Lehi's pen scratching over the parchment. It was a soothing sound and it had the same lift and fall as the rock doves flying through the gray mists before dawn, graceful like Lehi's pen strokes— the birds gliding through the air in flowing circles with soaring arches at the top of their flight and sharp-edged turns at the bottom. The encampment spread out below the birds like a sea of animal-skin roofs dotting the sands in this cliff-protected alcove. This secluded city of tents was set in straight, neat rows with the front of every dwelling facing east and waiting with Sariah for the sun to rise over the Dead Sea. It was a perfectly secluded place to build this secret community, and this spot Lehi selected above camp was the only one left to pitch a tent this size. And though the winds were stiffer here, they had plenty of stakes to moor it to the ground and enjoy the view from higher up.

Sariah leaned forward away from the pillows to see the expanse of Qumran beginning at the north cliff, past the plumes of smoke rising up from the camp's first fires of morning, then down to the south end where the first permanent structures grew out of the sand. The wall of a main building stood a good three stones high and the foundation of a storehouse was a large outline in the sand. The beach fell slowly toward the mighty Salt Sea, the calm water waiting in the dim light for the first rays of orange sun to rise over the horizon and bake her surface with the stifling desert heat of summer. But in the cool before the sun there was not a more captivating sight than the mysterious wide blue water stretching all the way across to the shores of Moab.

The sound of Lehi's pen scratching over the parchment fell silent and there was not the tinkling of the stylus against the lip of the bottle to draw up more ink. Sariah waited for Lehi to continue, but when she didn't hear him writing, she turned back from her view of Qumran and found him staring at her, the parchment hanging from his hand with the fresh ink drying on the breeze. He said, "I don't want to you to be frightened by this."

"Nothing you write frightens me."

"Read this." Lehi handed his writing over and Sariah quickly glanced over it, his familiar firm pen strokes were bolder than she remembered. They filled the parchment with the power of his convictions and she hurried her gaze back to the top of his journal record and began a careful reading. There was some detail about Uriah's trial and his concern for the man and his family, nothing she already didn't know and it certainly didn't frighten her. He mentioned going to the fort south of Jerusalem and the awful discovery he made of Captain Laban's and Zadock's evil designs written in the Lakhish Letters, something she'd discussed with him many times, and she was pleased he wrote that it would be better that both of those men perish rather than to have the entire Hebrew nation suffer them leading this people to doom.

But what doom was Lehi writing of? Sariah hurried her reading of the parchment. She'd heard Lehi speak of the destruction of Jerusalem during Uriah's trial and he referred to it in passing from time to time, but that was a spiritual death, a destruction of the soul of the city that awaited evildoers. Lehi didn't actually mean to write that Jerusalem would be destroyed, at least she didn't think he did, until she read the passage about his recent dream—the one that came to him while he was at Fort Lakhish and Lehi heard the voice of God warning him that there were men who sought to take away his life and commanding him to take his family and depart into the wilderness. That wasn't anything she didn't already know, but this part about the fate of Jerusalem was new. He'd seen the abominations of Jerusalem, not only the evil he confronted in Captain Laban the night they fled the city, but a future evil, one that awaited an entire nation, and he wrote that it plagued his mind and he could not escape its certainty. Captain Laban and men like him were leading this people into mists of darkness from which they could never . . .

Dear no, not this. Sariah held her hand to her mouth and slowly read on. How could Lehi write of such awful things about his homeland? The horrible details of death and ruin filled the parchment. There were sieges of the capital with such horrible starvation to cause men to eat the flesh of their children. And there were many dead from lack of water and food and, mercy no, from horrible sickness that ate the skin and caused men to shake and vomit and die in the streets, and their bodies were stacked one upon the other and the stink filled the city. Sariah started to hand the scroll back to Lehi, but there was more and she returned it to her lap and read on about the coming of the Babylonian armies, toppling the walls, destroying the temple, and leaving not even one stone upon the other, until every building was leveled, every vineyard for miles round about burned, and those who were not killed or who did not escape were carried off captive to Babylon.

Sariah set aside the scroll. She said, "How certain are you of this?"

"I see it all the time." Lehi slowly shook his head. "It turns my sleep to nightmares and haunts me by day. It will not leave me in peace."

"When will it be?" Sariah's body stiffened against the pillows. "How soon will this come to pass?"

"Well before our days on this earth end."

"What about our family? We still have children in Jerusalem." Sariah turned her gaze back outside to the tent city of Qumran. "Are you saying it's too dangerous for us to hope to return home?"

"We're safe here for now."

"For how long?"

Lehi turned his gaze to the ground. "Not long enough for us to build this city in this desert."

"What's to become of us?" Sariah leaned over and set the scroll in the writing box next to the unwritten volumes of their history waiting for the touch of Lehi's pen. "Are we to roam in these desert forever?"

Lehi took her by the hand and held it against his cheek, the small tuft of black beard at the end of his chin prickling her skin. He said, "I wish I had an answer for you."

Lehi put away his writing box.

Lemuel hunched over the flat stone set in the middle of red-hot coals and held his hand to his eyes to shield them from the smoke shifting in the wind. Cursed breeze. Why couldn't it stay put long enough for him to bake the bread dough? During the afternoons there was a constant stream blowing off the sands of the Judean Wilderness, and in the evening it filtered up from the Dead Sea as certain as the water was wet; but the morning breeze was as obedient as a thirsty mule headed away from a watering place and he waved his hand at the swirling smoke, telling it to stay put while he sidled around to the other side of the fire. The breeze shifted again, driving the smoke back into Lemuel's face. Why did it always follow him? It didn't matter if he stood upwind or downwind or on his head, he could never get away from the stinging it caused his eyes. If it were true that smoke followed beauty then he was the loveliest man in all of Qumran, but beauty did not dress in a shirt that hung on narrow shoulders like wash drying on a line, and there was nothing beautiful about his white skin as pale as the morning sky before sunrise. Lemuel was a tall, thin lad and if he had to spend too many more months in this forsaken place he was certain to die from the heat, or contract some wretched illness from eating his own miserable cooking. Lemuel quickly formed three rounds of flat bread, clapping the brown wheat dough between his hands and setting them on the rock in the center of the fire-pit, careful not to let his fingers touch the—

Cursed cooking stone! The hot surface burned his knuckles and he dropped the flatbread into place before spitting on the back of his hand and waving it in the breeze. He was a useless cook and his bread never turned out anything like the breads the maidservants prepared at Beit Zayit. Lemuel's bread had the taste of fire smoke and there were flecks of black ash collecting on the uncooked side, and he never turned the bread in time to keep if from burning and where was Laman anyway? If his brother didn't get back soon with word of an immediate return home, Lemuel was certain to poison himself with ash or burn himself in a fire, or worse, starve to death in this wasteland. The top of the flat-bread began to bubble and Lemuel leaned over the fire to pull it up, but it was stuck to the rock and he wedged the end of a stick against the stone to pry it free before it burned. The smoke shifted and he sidled back around the fire pit to miss the worst of it, one hand covering his eyes from the stinging smoke and the other hand feeling the way ahead of him to keep from running into . . .

Lemuel hit against something hard, his shoulder taking the brunt of the blow. He reached out in the smoke, both hands wrapped around a thick, powerful—

"Would you let go?" It was Laman and he stepped back from the fire, shaking his leg to loose himself from Lemuel's grasp. The smoke lifted and there, standing before the fire, was Laman. His tunic and kilt were covered with sand, and the coat of his horse was salted from riding through the night. The saddlebags road high on the animal's haunches, filled with supplies—but they didn't need wheat or barley or dates, not nearly as much as they needed word from the Chief Elder.

"What took you so long?" Lemuel licked his burned knuckles. "Did you meet him?"

"Look at you." Laman walked a circle around his brother. "Are you that hungry that you need to chew your knuckles?"

"They're burned." Lemuel fanned his fingers in the air. "What do you think I'm doing?"

Laman turned his gaze to the rounds of bread cooking on the stone "That's not all you're burning."

Black smoke filtered up from beneath the flatbread and Lemuel cursed the burning bread, he cursed the day they came to this place, and he kicked at the sand. He'd done it again. The flat bread was too long on the rock and it was gone black and caked to the stone.

Lemuel said, "When do we go home?"

"I don't know."

"You don't know?" He fell to his knees, wedged the end of the stick under the burnt bread and began prying it away. "You met with Zadock, didn't you?"

"I found him with the Babylonians."

Lemuel worked the stick under the bread and black bits of it flew into the fire and raised a cloud of ash around him. "What did he say?"

"He wasn't prepared to make a decision."

"What kind of an answer is that?" Lemuel scraped the stick over the cooking stone, cleaning away the burned bread and preparing it for another round. "How difficult can it be to tell us we can return to our home in peace?"

"I did what I could."

"Don't say we're cursed to wander in this wilderness any longer."

Laman took a deep breath and his shoulder raised on his breathing. "With time we can convince Zadock."

"Time? We don't have any time." Lemuel stood and shook his burned fingers at his brother. "We can't stay in this desert forever."

"We don't have many choices right now."

"Didn't Zadock say anything more?"

Laman lowered his head and spoke in a halting voice, mumbling something about it being a short conversation with the Chief Elder before starting his horse past the fire and up the sandy rise toward the family tent. Lemuel came around in front of him and said, "You're not telling me everything."

"What do you want me to tell you?"

"We don't keep things from each other. You know that. We never keep things from each other." Lemuel held his ground, his thin body stopping Laman from climbing the hill. "Tell me what Zadock told you."

"Not so loud." Laman raised his hand. "You'll wake the family." He lowered his voice to a whisper, his chin forced down into the collar of his tunic. He said, "Zadock gave us his blessing to return home."

"But I thought you said—"

"Under one condition."

"You agreed, didn't you?"

"It isn't that simple."

"Don't tell me you refused his offer."

"Hear me out." Laman glanced up the rise to the family's tent and when he came back to Lemuel his dark eyes had grown darker. He said, "I'm telling you this only because I may need your help."

"I'll do anything to get back home."

"Even if we go back without Father?"

"What do you mean without him? We can't leave him out here."

"That wasn't part of Zadock's offer. The man didn't mean for us to leave him anywhere." Laman spoke in a steady, methodical voice, without any rise or fall in his speech. "He wants Father dead."

Lemuel dropped his cooking stick and the tip stuck in the sand like a driven arrow. "You're not going to . . ."

"I didn't agree to anything."

"Wonderful. Absolutely wonderful." Lemuel rubbed the back of his head with both hands, his skinny elbows rising and falling with his rubbing. "We're never going home." He kicked at the sand and Laman's horse backstepped away from the spray of grit. "We'll die in this forsaken place. A lonely and forgotten people."

"Listen to me." Laman took him by the collar and pulled him close enough that Lemuel could feel his brother's breath pulse over him. "We send word to Captain Laban. Let him know where we're hiding."

Lemuel pulled free. "You can't betray Father."

"You want to return home, don't you?" Laman began to pace in front of Lemuel. "All we do is let Captain Laban come and take him prisoner."

"You said they wanted him dead."

"We'll make arrangements with the captain. He'll listen to us and once he sees that father isn't a threat, he'll let all of us return home."

"What if the captain kills him?"

Laman pressed his lips close to Lemuel's ear. "Would that be any worse than watching Father lose his mind?"

"He's as strong as any of us. He's not going to lose his mind."

"*They* did." Laman turned his brother around to face the rows of camel-hair tents dotting the sand below the rise, his hand still gripping the collar of Lemuel's robe. "These zealots left Jerusalem with no reason to leave. They can go back any time they choose. Have you ever asked yourself why they don't? They stay here because of their delusions."

"Exactly what do you mean by delusions?"

"Thinking they can live the Law of Moses better here without a temple than they could have lived it in Jerusalem. That they're some sort of chosen people waiting for the Messiah to save them from this wilderness. That's what I mean by delusions, willing to throw away all the joys and pleasures they could have in this life for something better they think will be theirs when they die. They've all lost their minds and the longer we stay here, the more Father is becoming like them. Have you listened to his words, the thoughts he lets slip out in idle conversation when he doesn't think we're listening carefully?" Laman tapped this side of his head. "I tell you, he isn't right. This desert sun has played on his mind. He thinks God speaks to him, telling him not to return home."

"When did Father say that?"

"He didn't have to. I can see it in his eyes. They way he keeps the caravan camels fed and ready for flight at any moment. That isn't the sign of a man preparing to return home."

Lemuel pulled his collar free and faced his brother. "You're not really serious about this, are you?"

"Everything we've worked all our lives to gain is back in Jerusalem—all our wealth, our inheritance, all our comforts. Do you just want to walk away from that?" Laman turned his gaze back up the rise to the entrance of Lehi's tent. "We won't let any harm come to him, not unless we're certain."

"Certain of what?"

"Certain he's gone mad."

"How do you know when a man has gone mad?"

"It's simple. He starts thinking wrong."

"But he's our father. What thinking could be so horribly wrong you would even consider betraying him?

"Father's a sensible man, wouldn't you say?"

"Of course he is." Lemuel slowly nodded. "He knows these lands better than any caravaneer that works the trade routes."

"It was Father's dreams that caused him to leave our lands and come to this forsaken place." Laman pointed his finger at Lemuel and shook it to the rise and fall of his words. "If Father follows his dreams and visions instead of his good sense, that's when we'll know he's gone mad."

"You would kill him because of a dream?"

"I didn't say anyone would kill him."

"But it could happen, couldn't it?"

Laman slowed his speech, his lips hanging on every word. He said, "If I thought betraying Father was our last hope to return to—"

"You're home!" Sam stood at the entrance of the side tent pushing back the flaps to air it out with one hand and holding his tunic in the other. "I thought I heard familiar voices out here." He rubbed the sleep from his eyes and shook his head, his dark brown hair falling over his brow. He was a long sleeper and if they didn't wake him he'd sleep past midday. Sam yawned, stretched his shoulders and said, "What a beautiful day."

Sam pulled his shirt on, but before he started down the rise toward them Nephi came around the back of the tent carrying a leather scroll. He waved a greeting with the end of a long parchment before stuffing it under his arm. That boy read more than a scribe in a treasury house, but what in the name of Moses could be so interesting he would spend the early morning hours poring over ancient scrolls? And he didn't read just once in a while. Every morning since coming here, Lemuel found him reading by lamplight. It wasn't right that a boy his age should spend so much time reading, especially one as stout as Nephi. There were better things he could spend his strength on than withering away in his tent with a stack of ancient writings. It would only fill his head with nonsense, the same sort of nonsense that caused these Rekhabites to forsake their homes in Jerusalem to live in this place.

Lehi turned out of the entrance of the main tent with Sariah walking slowly beside him, telling him she wouldn't wait inside for Laman to come greet her. She'd gone too long without seeing her eldest son. She steadied herself against his sturdy frame, the two of them standing at the entrance of the tent and Nephi and Sam joining them there, all of them waiting for Laman and Lemuel to climb the sandy rise.

Lemuel spit on his burned fingers and fanned them in the air. He spoke softly. He said, "What are you going to tell them?"

"The same thing you're to tell them." Laman started up the rise, pulling his horse behind him. "Next year in Jerusalem."

CHAPTER 10

Only ten pieces of silver? The paltry sum of money inched closer to the edge of the writing table with each irritated stroke of Hanameel's pen and he steadied his foot against the table leg to keep the stack of coins from going over. Lamplight filtered over his shoulder and cast a yellow glow on the property deed—a two-acre parcel of land that should have brought him twice the money. Cursed cousin of his! He could have gotten three times these ten pieces of silver for the sale of the plot of land located on the southern edge of Anathoth, but no one wanted to put in a new vineyard near the grape arbors that belonged to the prophet Jeremiah—not until his cousin was released from the palace prison in Jerusalem and the shame of owning property beside a traitor was forgotten.

Hanameel dipped his pen in the inkwell. What a disgrace Jeremiah had become. He had warned his cousin not to publicly criticize the crown. There were two things that a good Jew, if he wanted to remain a good Jew, never did. One was disagreeing with the royals over matters of national defense, and the other was taxes, and Jeremiah's prophethood offended both those unwritten laws and did little to increase the value of land around his vineyards—land that Hanameel purchased with the certainty he'd double his investment in short order. If Jeremiah didn't get out of prison, denounce his former pronouncements, and return to his vineyard in Anathoth without further public displays of disaffection, there was no telling how low the value of the piece of property on the other side of the prophet's vineyards would drop.

Hanameel scratched the pen over the parchment, careful to twice record the sale price and the transfer of the property to the new owner—once at the top of the parchment and again at the bottom. That was the only way to do business in these days of rascals. A double-sealed document may require a few more trips to the tannery and there was no end to the amount of ink he used to double-copy everything, not to mention the hours he spent preparing identical versions of every legal description on the top and bottom portion of each deed, but he was a buyer and seller of properties and this most secure of documents tempered the fears of his customers. Hanameel set aside his pen, scrolled the top portion of the deed into a small package no larger than a walnut, tied it with cords, and sealed it shut with a daub of beeswax. As long as the seal remained unbroken, the customer buying this land was certain not to question the authenticity of the sale.

Hanameel laid the unsealed portion of the document open on the table and got out his stamp—a rounded piece of metal with the impression of a grapevine etched into it. He placed his seal below the description of the property and it was finished; the document was ready for the closing ceremony. It was an odd tradition, but one that Hanameel attended without fail. He was to sign the unsealed portion of the deed right there below his seal, and he was to do it in front of the family and gathered friends of the buyer. Once that was finished, these ten pieces of silver were his and the new property owner was welcome to unseal the scroll to be sure the terms of the transaction were double-copied properly. There wasn't really a need for making these double-sealed documents, not when the property deed wasn't to be sent by courier or handled by any scoundrels who might alter it, but there were odder tales of sons absconding with the property of their fathers, and a good double-sealed document stored in a clay vessel was a fine hedge against deceit.

Hanameel was a respected buyer and seller of property and issuing a double-sealed deed won him a good deal of business. No customer purchased property from a trader who didn't ensure the legality of the sale and there was no better way to appease the fears of a buyer than to keep tradition and use this double-sealed document as proof of purchase. If it was properly prepared, and Hanameel issued the very finest, then the new owner of this land would make his home on that plot of ground now and forever with all the rights of ownership so long as the Jews possessed this kingdom.

Hanameel set aside the deed and started on the description for the two-acre parcel of land that sat on the other side of Jeremiah's property, over beyond the creek. It was a good square piece, with hardly a sloping hill or an uneven ridge to slow a farmer's plow, and he wasn't going to let this land go for as little as the first two acres. The vineyard keeper who purchased this parcel was going to have to pay a premium price for the location, not to mention the fine condition of the land. Hanameel adjusted the lamp to cast a good light on the document, his pen hurrying over the parchment, his written words delineating the length and width of the parcel and its location next to Jeremiah's barns. There weren't too many rocks that required clearing on the land. It stood next to the main road leading through Anathoth and whoever purchased this property owned a fourth of the water rights in the small creek shared with Jeremiah's vineyards. Hanameel finished the last of the description with a line about the goodness of the soil before setting aside his pen. He'd not let this piece go for anything less than fifteen pieces of silver. All that remained was to find a buyer foolish enough to purchase property next to his cousin. That fool was going to ruin his business, to say nothing of the size of his treasury. If only he could fine someone— anyone—to buy this property adjacent to Jeremiah's home.

A knock sounded at the front door and Hanameel dropped his writing pen, the stylus clicking over the polished wood tabletop. He set aside both scrolls and hurried from the study and down the hall to the front entry. The caller knocked again, this time with a hurried stroke and with enough force to rattle the door on its hinges. Hanameel undid the latch, pulled open the door, and found Zoram framed between the doorposts. What was he doing here? Hanameel stepped onto the porch, the cool evening air lifting his gray hair off his brow. The road was dotted with estate homes and he glanced toward the main square of Anathoth before checking the way down past his closest neighbors.

Hanameel quickly said, "Did anyone see you?"

"No one, sir."

"You shouldn't come here. You could lose your job in Laban's treasury if anyone knew you were related. It's hard enough to sell property with your father speaking his mind against the throne and everyone in Anathoth knowing my kinship to the man." Hanameel took him by the hand, quickly ushered him into the light of the lobby, and closed the door behind him before latching it shut.

"I don't mean to intrude, sir, but if—"

"If it weren't for your father's public utterings neither of us would have reason to hide our heads." Hanameel paced across the foyer. "What are we going to do with the man?"

"May I make a suggestion?"

"Certainly you didn't come to speak about your father." Hanameel stopped pacing. "Now tell me, what brings you to Anathoth this late in the day?"

"Actually, sir, I did come to see you about my father." Zoram removed his white turban and held it with both hands. "I was hoping you could—"

"Don't bother yourself with his troubles, boy. He's been in prison before and he'll no doubt find himself there again until he learns to keep his thoughts to himself."

"It's his heart, sir, that brings him trouble—a very sincere heart." Zoram ran his fingers over the crisp, freshly pressed white cloth of his turban. "His words have a way of agitating others."

"Agitating? He's a traitor and you're kind not to call him one."

"He's my father."

"That doesn't lessen the charge of treason, son." Hanameel walked over next to Zoram. "Now don't misunderstand. I'm fond of the man. He's been a good father to you, a fine husband to your mother, and he's done nothing but right by the land I sold him, at a very good price, mind you." He shook his head. "But God bless his soul for not ever learning the finer art of silence. Do you understand what I'm telling you? Jeremiah never could keep quiet. The moment his heart felt or his mind thought, he couldn't help but tell the world about it." Hanameel waved his hand in the air in front of him. "Jeremiah shares his most intimate thoughts as if it were gossip among women at the well. If he must speak so much, couldn't it be of more peaceable things than war and taxes?" He laid his hand on Zoram's shoulder. "Now tell me what you came to tell me. Are you looking for work, son?" He took back his hand. "You're a fine scribe, but can you do numbers like an accountant? You'll need to do numbers if you calculate my taxes. I could certainly use some help with my record keeping, but what would Captain Laban say? Have you spoken to him about this? Does he know you're leaving his treasury? That's a man I wouldn't want to cross, not ever. I couldn't bear to—"

"No, sir. I don't need work." Zoram turned his green-eyed gaze down into his turban. "I need your help."

"For the love of Moses, boy, what help could I possibly provide?"

"The property next to Jeremiah's vineyards. Do you know it?"

"Know it? I'm just now preparing a document of sale for the—"

"You haven't sold it, have you?" Zoram stepped closer.

"I don't think I'll ever sell that property, not for what I'm asking."

"How much do you want?"

Was Zoram serious? The boy couldn't afford to pay the fifteen pieces of silver he was asking for it, could he? Hanameel tugged on the end of his long gray beard before crossing his arms over his chest. "I couldn't let that piece of land go for anything less than, oh, seventeen pieces of silver."

"Very well."

"Do you have that kind of money?"

"I can get it, sir."

Hanameel scratched the back of his neck. "Do you want me to prepare documents in your name?"

"Not in my name."

"Then whose?"

Zoram replaced the turban on his head. "How soon do you need the money?"

"Well, I . . ."

"I can deliver it to you by midday tomorrow."

Hanameel raised his eyebrows. "So you're giving up your duties as a scribe to become a vineyard owner, are you?"

"The land isn't for me."

"I'm going to need the name of the buyer." Hanameel rubbed his hands together. "I have to make arrangements for the ceremony of purchase, invite all the lords, princes, overseers, and anyone else associated with the buyer, to say nothing of the family. Can you get me the names of everyone involved? We can't leave anyone out who has anything to do with the buyer. You know the law, and I can't afford not to follow it to the letter. You don't sell property in this land without making an insufferably large celebration of it." He kept rubbing his hands and slowly shook his head. "To think how much money I could make if I didn't have to spend my days celebrating the purchase of every sale. You do know you'll need to have a scribe representing the buyer who can attest to the sale and I don't know any better than yourself. Should I put your name on the documents as the attending scribe?"

"No." Zoram declined with such force that his voice echoed about the entry with the power of ten men. There was no doubt in his resolve. He did not want to attest to the sale of this property.

Hanameel stared down the end of his nose at Zoram. "Is there a reason, son?"

Zoram stepped back a step from Hanameel's questioning. "My name can't be seen on the same document with the buyer."

"It's a formality son. There's nothing to concern yourself with. You attest to the purchase price, weigh the money in the balances to make sure I get all seventeen pieces of silver, without any poorly minted pieces, mind you, and that's all you have to—"

"I'll find another scribe in the city to attest to the sale."

"Why pay another scribe for work you can do yourself?" Hanameel wagged his finger at Zoram. "Scribes these days are more expensive than lawyers. You should know that better than any."

"Money isn't a concern."

"Not a concern?" Hanameel let a soft whistle escape between his teeth. "Who exactly is this buyer, son? I don't know anyone in these parts who doesn't count the cost of every venture before they part with their money."

"She isn't from around here."

Hanameel worked his chin between his thumb and forefinger. "I'm selling property to a woman?"

"There are two buyers." Zoram offered a quick nod of the head. "One name will go on your documents and the other buyer wishes to remain unnamed."

Hanameel raised both his hands to Zoram. "I can't prepare a document without a—"

"Jeremiah." Zoram lowered his head. "Put his name on your documents."

"My cousin?" Hanameel slowly shook his head. "For the love of Moses, the man is in prison. He hasn't earned a shekel since last growing season and if he doesn't get out of prison and get home to his vineyards and his poor wife, it will be another year before he has any crop to take to market. I don't know if I can risk this sale without the money in hand."

"The unnamed buyer will pay for everything." Zoram found the latch with his hand, opened the door, and backed out onto the porch.

"I can't sell this property without knowing who's paying for it."

"I'll see that she contacts you."

"When?"

"The first day of the week."

Hanameel stepped out onto the porch. "Where do I go to get my seventeen pieces of silver?"

"She'll meet you at the palace dungeons in Jerusalem." Zoram started down through the courtyard to the open gate. "Near the main doors at midday."

"What's her name? You can at least give me that much."

"She'll find you, sir." Zoram's voice disappeared with him out the front gate, leaving Hanameel standing on the porch. Hanameel rubbed his brow, working the trouble out of his mind. He should give up his selling of property. This business was becoming more difficult every day. He leaned against the doorpost, his arms folded across his chest and his gaze turned down to the stone beneath his feet. Seventeen pieces of silver—

Was it worth all this trouble?

CHAPTER 11

Aaron leaned his crutches against the sandstone outcrop and inched his injured leg onto the edge of the cliff above his new desert home. The rows of camel-hair tents sat nestled a hundred feet beneath him in a protected alcove where no thief could enter in and deny them safe haven. There was no reason for anyone to stake claim to this land. It was the most uninhabitable place in all of Judah—fit for nothing but a hard life. Qumran was an impossible place to build a city to God, but these Rekhabites had already set the foundation around a main hall, started a bakery with two ovens, and set the footings on a sanctuary in the middle of camp. Over there below the north cliffs they had the beginnings of a livery, a cobbler shop and, for Josiah, a pottery yard complete with what was to become a kiln, though now it was only outlined by a single ring of bricks laid in the sand. And below where Aaron sat was the aqueduct. One, maybe two more weeks of tiling and mortaring the canal walls with stone and it was ready to carry water from the spring deep in these cliffs without any of the precious liquid seeping between the seams and disappearing into the sands.

The call to morning work hadn't sounded and there was still time before Aaron was off to carry water to the stonemasons and bricklayers that he could sit for a while in the cool morning breeze and wait for the sun to rise over the Dead Sea. From atop these rugged cliffs above Qumran he could see across the water to the shores of Moab's high plateau country. It was too far across the wide blue expanse to see merchant traders traveling the trade route, but he'd heard Lehi speak of the long trains of caravans wending their way out of the harsh heat of the deserts of Arabia and up into the green valleys and fertile farmlands of Moab. Aaron came here every morning in the soft light before dawn to forget the pain Laban inflicted on his limb and imagine the lush hillsides on the far side of the Dead Sea. Hardly anyone traveled the shores on the Qumran side. It was too hot here and there were no hills in the Judean Wilderness to trap the passing rain clouds and milk a bit of water out of heaven. But over there, high in the Moab countryside, there was plenty of rain and a land peopled with farmers selling grains, and vineyard owners peddling pulse. On the other side of these waters, merchant traders shepherded their caravans teeming with gold and silver and frankincense, all of them headed around the north shores of the Dead Sea and then west past Jericho toward Jerusalem, the land of his . . .

Aaron lowered his head. He shouldn't think of home. He left his family there without word of his leaving, and Aaron slowly turned his gaze up along the shoreline until the brown sand and blue water disappeared into the gray sky on the northern horizon. Why did everything in this desert point him back toward home, reminding him of a family he'd left without even a word of farewell? Would Papa forgive him for running off like this? There was no one but little Joshua to help him run a smithy that should have the blessing of three hard-working brothers to make a go of blacksmithing. That was Papa's dream—to build the finest smithy in the land with the help of his three sons. And what about Elizabeth? Would she ever excuse him for his disappearance? Aaron shared everything with his oldest sister, but there wasn't time to tell her of his leaving, and she would never allow him any penance for his desertion, and neither would young Sarah. And then there was Mama. Did she know he was still a faithful son? There was no pain more piercing than to think he'd troubled his mother's heart. Surely she wouldn't think him gone in anger. Aaron lightly touched the bandaged wound on his thigh. Somehow he had to get word to his family that he was well, that it was not hatred that caused him to leave. But by going back to heal the wound he opened in their hearts, would he bring them more harm? It was Laban who forced Aaron to flee and he could never allow his homecoming to turn the wrath of the captain onto the ones he loved more than his own life. He would return, but only after he was certain Laban could never harm his family for Aaron's offense against the man. And he prayed one day Laban would be gone from Jerusalem and allow Aaron to walk the city's streets without fear of retribution.

Aaron turned his gaze away from a view of the way across the desert sands leading toward home and back to the harsh shores of the Dead Sea spreading out below him. He was without anyone to call family in this desert and it was only by the good graces of Lehi that he was kept from poverty, the man feeding him day to day, offering him a place to sleep by night, and allowing him to heal while all others about him eked out a living in this desert. It was Josiah the Potter who doctored his wound. He got the shaft out, but the arrowhead came loose and it was better to let the wound heal than to poke about in search of the metal lost in his leg. With time, his body would absorb the arrowhead and he'd walk with a steady gait. It was the powers of heaven that healed his burned feet, and it was by the grace of heaven that Aaron survived the loss of blood from Laban's arrow and lived through the desperate flight into this wilderness where he enjoyed the company of . . .

Rebecca slipped onto the rock next to him without a sound beyond the brush of her robe against the sandstone and the fluttering of her sashes on the breeze. She set her legs over the edge and covered them with her robe, the hem reaching all the way to her ankles, before pulling back her hood and letting her long, dark hair lift on the breeze, fall back to her shoulders, and lift again about her cheeks. She turned her gaze east toward the first orange-yellow rays of sunshine piercing the morning sky, as bright and full and warm as was the comfort of her sitting next to him. She didn't go on about the preparations for morning meal at the tent of her father, or the jars of water she had yet to draw and carry from the spring. She didn't speak of the wheat that waited for her on the grinding stone or the spool of wool in need of a good batting and combing before she could turn it to thread to patch her father's clothes. There was no idle talk of Aaron's wound or his limp, or whether his crutches were supporting him well enough. Those were the daily discussions of camp, and somehow she knew not to bring them here to Aaron's sanctuary and spoil the sharing of a silent moment up where the rock doves hung on the sea breeze and they could think the same thoughts without a word between them to spoil the sound of their silent conversation.

Aaron may not have any family in this wilderness, but he had Rebecca, the woman who waited on his heart when there was no reason to linger any longer on his stubbornness. He'd not been joined with the Rekhabites by baptism, but one day, when his leg was healed and with his family beside him, he would share the life-giving hope of Rebecca's Messiah. Aaron lived a God-blessed life, beyond any a man could hope for. He was alive, and there was no greater balm to ease the loss of leaving his family than the company of Rebecca. Aaron kept his gaze looking out over the sea, but he set his hand on the rock between them, and Rebecca laid her hand on his. One day he would return to Jerusalem and ask his father's blessing to marry this woman, and if Papa agreed and Rebecca would have him, then he would stand on these cliffs and shout across this Dead Sea that he'd never felt more alive.

Rebecca said, "Are you thinking of your family again?"

Aaron tightened his hold on her hand. "They don't know what's become of me."

"We can send word that you're well."

"I could never leave that message to a courier."

"There's no other way. You can't go back; it's too dangerous. This is your home now."

"This will never be home until I get a blessing from my father."

Rebecca took back her hand and held it to her mouth, her gaze turned away and her words falling silent on the gentle morning breeze.

"What is it?" Aaron leaned close.

"Nothing." Rebecca brought her hand to her mouth. "Nothing at all."

"I know you well enough to know that nothing means something, and nothing at all means something maddening."

Rebecca lowered her hand from her mouth, but kept her gaze turned toward the cliffs on the far side of camp. Her voice was soft, but her words had power to open old wounds. She said, "It was your father who told you I was dead."

Aaron steadied his hands on the rocky edge of the cliff. "He was only trying to protect me."

"Is that what you call his lies?" Rebecca's words rushed out. "He told you I was dead and he let you believe it at every turn. Is that the sort of man you would tell about our secret city in this wilderness?"

"You don't trust him."

"Do you?"

Aaron said, "I would never tell the location of Qumran to anyone, not even my father."

"He'll want to know why you don't stay in Jerusalem to help him with his blacksmithing."

"He'll allow me my freedom."

"He'll want to know where you're going, where you plan to live, how you plan to make a living, and he'll not accept anything less than your telling him about this city of Rekhabites in the wilderness." Rebecca slowed her words. "We've suffered so much, I could never bear to bring more suffering on these people. You must promise me you'll never let anyone know of this place."

Aaron straightened on the cliff, his body in line with the sheer rock wall stretching down below him. "Do you really think I would betray you or your father or anyone who lives here?"

"Your father will try to pry it from you." Rebecca lowered her gaze to the stone ledge where they sat, her heels softly tapping against the wall of the cliff. "He'll do anything to stop you from returning here."

"I have to tell them I'm well. I can't let them worry over me."

"Your father let you mourn my death without reason."

"He was doing what he thought right."

"Right for whom?"

"I've got to believe my father is a good man. I won't lose hope in him. I can't." Aaron squared his shoulders and turned his gaze out over the sun-washed surface of the Dead Sea. Some day his father's heart would soften and Aaron was as certain of his part in the conversion of his father's soul as he was of the sun rising over Moab across the waters. He'd seen it in his dreams as clearly as he was breathing the morning air. Jonathan the Blacksmith was going to seek the blessed comfort of a faithful life just as Aaron sought it, and in some way Aaron was to be part of that change. He didn't know how it would be done, but it would come to pass; Aaron would see to it. There was too much at risk. He would not let his father suffer the consequences of the prophecies of the Allegory of the Olive Tree and be damned. Papa was not like the other Elders of the Jews.

Aaron said, "I have a duty to him."

Rebecca slowly shook her head. "It's too much of a risk."

"It's one I'm willing to take."

"I lost you once. I won't lose you again." Rebecca reached for Aaron's arm. "Not after what we went through to get you here, safe and away from Captain Laban. Don't you see? You've risked your life one too many times. You can't play with death like a child plays pitch and toss. One day you're going to lose and you won't get to play another day. Do you understand that? Life will not always be kind to you and I do not want to witness that cruelty."

Aaron didn't answer. He pulled his arm free from Rebecca and stood on the rock with his crutches stuffed under his arms. He leaned forward, peering down along the ridge, past a craggy outcrop and over beyond a run of sand where the dunes had drifted over the rock, pushing the borders of the wilderness closer to camp.

"What is it?" Rebecca stood next to him. "What's wrong?"

"Over there. Do you see?" Aaron pointed with the end of his crutch down along the ridge. Half hidden behind the uneven outcrops of stone stood two steeds, their muzzles pushing out from behind their hiding places and their riders leaning over the saddle and looking down on Qumran, studying every tent and noting every building mapped by foundation stones in the sand. They were dressed like wild men with red bandannas tied to the brow to hold back the long hair that hung down past their shoulders. There were no tunics covering their nakedness, nothing but a water skin strapped over one bare shoulder, a bow with a quiver of arrows hanging from the other, and a short sword strapped about the waist of their loin cloths.

Aaron got down off the outcrop, quietly telling Rebecca to stay put. He'd deal with the intruders, but she would not be still. She scrambled down the rock next to him, telling him not to go another step closer, he was injured and what if they tried to hurt him or worse, what if they were . . . ?

Rebecca reached for Aaron's arm. "I've heard Papa speak about the robbers who hide in these deserts." She stepped past Aaron and started down the trail leading around the switchbacks to camp. "I'll get the others to come and—"

"No." Aaron grabbed her hand. "I don't want these men to be scared away before we get close enough to find out what they want."

The clatter of horse hooves pounded over the rocky plateau behind them and Aaron spun around on his crutches to see a third rider coming at them at full gallop. He leaned his naked body forward in the saddle, his long, thick legs wrapped around the dark-coated Arabian's middle like the cords of a saddle. Leather straps tied his riding boots to his shins, and the sinew in his legs strained to spur his mount forward with sharp heel jabs. The animal stampeded across the ridge and the rider's long hair streamed out behind him, down past his shoulders, the tangled ends lost below the level of the horses haunches. It was longer than any hair Aaron had seen on a man, and immediately he knew the legends of the great robber band weren't legends at all, but until now he'd not ever believed there could be a man as powerful, nor as feared as the myths of Shechem, King of Robbers. He was a ghost riding across these cliffs at the break of dawn, the orange light silhouetting his terrible form.

Shechem steered toward Rebecca, but Aaron jumped in his path, swinging his crutch to shield her from the robber's sword, the wood taking the brunt of the blade and the timbers splintering in his hand like chaff in the wind. Rebecca screamed, her voice echoing about the cliffs, calling for help from camp.

Shechem came around, his horse raising a cloud of dust around them, and the man swearing by heaven and earth he'd not let either of them live to speak of his coming to Qumran. He jumped from the saddle, sword in hand, closing the distance between them like a hunter cornering its prey, the leather of his loincloth slapping against his legs.

Aaron reached to pull Rebecca to safety, but they were bound by the edge of the cliff, a hundred-foot fall trapping them from escape, and he could do nothing but tighten his grip around her and shield her from the pain of Shechem's blade.

"Please, sir." Aaron held Rebecca close. "Have mercy."

"I have none to give, boy." Shechem raised his sword over them like an executioner and spoke with a deep voice, his words pulsing out of him with each breath. "Captain Laban and the Babylonians will find your camp, but it will be too late for you." He jabbed the sword at them, pushing them a step closer to the edge of the cliff. "Your friends will never know I was the reason for your dead bodies falling from these cliffs."

Nephi cleared the last turn in the trail leading up from camp, his sandal-shod feet quietly running over the rocky cliffs, and when Shechem prodded his sword at Aaron and Rebecca to force them the last step over the edge, Nephi dived for the robber, knocking the sword from his hand and pulling the man to the ground, their bodies rolling along the ledge. Shechem struggled to come out on top, his powerful arms pinning Nephi against the stone. He was reaching for the sword when Sam turned the last switchback in the trail, yelling at Shechem, calling him a yellow-brazen, flea-bitten, snake-bellied, weak-armed coward hiding behind the metal of a sword. He slowly stepped along the edge of the cliff, holding onto the word coward and letting it ring about the cliffs, while balancing himself on the edge, his feet spread and his arms out, his precarious stance inviting Shechem to rush at him. Sam pushed his brown hair up off his brow and spoke in a steady voice. "Throw down your sword and make this a fair fight."

"You little fool." Shechem turned the tip of the blade toward Sam, his knee pressed into Nephi's throat, choking him against the stone ledge. "I don't need to prove my strength to you."

Josiah the Potter and Lehi rounded the bend in the trail and ran down along the cliffs before halting next to Sam.

"Stay back or I'll kill the boy." Shechem raised the sword over Nephi. "I'll kill all of you." He slowly stood, removing his knee from Nephi's throat and letting the boy gasp for breath. He slashed the air with his sword, driving Sam and Lehi and Josiah back a step and cutting a path to his horse. His men joined him, galloping across the plateau and coming alongside, their horses pawing at the ground and their swords raised. Shechem pulled himself up into the saddle and spit in the sand, telling Josiah and Lehi that one day very soon they would come to curse the day he found their camp. "Do you hear me? All of you will regret I found you here." He spurred around and galloped into the endless sea of shifting desert sands, his men riding after him and disappearing over the mountains of drifted dunes like ghosts riding into a dream, their horses cutting a wide swath in the sand.

Josiah watched the desert sands long after Shechem was gone. He said, "We can't defend our camp against a man like that."

"I'm not afraid of three robbers." Aaron gathered the broken pieces of his crutches. Their secret hiding place wasn't a secret any longer, but that didn't mean they couldn't stand against Shechem. He threw the splintered wood into the sand next to the horse tracks. "Shechem doesn't own this desert."

Lehi stepped in next to Aaron. "Did he say why he was angry with us?"

"He cursed us for coming here." Aaron wiped away the wood splinters stuck to his sweat-covered brow. "What right does he have to tell us we're not welcome?"

"Was there anything else?" Josiah laid his hand on Aaron's shoulder. "Try to remember."

"He said he was going to force us over the edge and none of you would ever know why we fell to our deaths." Aaron rubbed the back of his head, his brown hair sticking up on end. "It all happened so fast. He had a sword. He came at us with his horse and . . ."

"There was one thing." Rebecca lifted the hem of her robe and picked her way over the rocky cliff to her father's side. "It frightened me, caused me to worry about the future of our camp."

Josiah said, "What was it, daughter?"

"He said Captain Laban and the Babylonians would find us."

Lehi said, "Babylonians?"

"That's right, sir."

"This isn't good." Lehi lowered his voice to a whisper and slowly repeated the word *Babylonians* before turning his gaze back out toward the desert sands where the king of robbers and his two men disappeared. "Shechem isn't foolish enough to spend his strength driving us from Qumran unless . . ."

Nephi said, "Unless what, Father?"

"Heaven help us, you don't mean . . . ?" Josiah walked to the edge of the cliff and looked out over the rows of tents below.

"What is it, Papa?" Rebecca followed him to the edge.

"Call for the men of the camp to gather. There's only one thing we can do." Josiah started down the trail toward camp, the hem of his brown robe swirling about his sandals.

Rebecca said, "Papa, where are you going?"

"We have work to do." Josiah kept his sandals slapping down the steep, rocky trail toward camp. "We must hide this place from the eyes of all men."

CHAPTER 12

Where was that voice coming from? Jonathan pulled up in the saddle and came around to peer back down the trail—a still, small voice telling him there was no time to waste and urging him to keep going and not stop until he reached Sidon. The cedars lining the way shrouded the light of a full moon and cast an uneasy shadow across his path. It was his imagination. There was no one following him, telling him to keep going, at least not anyone he could see. The trail winding through the wide lowlands of the Jezreel Valley stood dark and quiet and Jonathan started his horse trotting again, her hooves clapping over the dusty trail with a tired rhythm. Did he really need to keep such a hurried pace? The men following him certainly didn't know he was riding ahead of them. Since leaving Jerusalem, Jonathan kept to himself, never uttering a word of greeting to travelers bound back the other way toward the capital city, though at this hour there was not a solitary soul to share the silence shrouding this trail. He passed a train of mules early this morning, ran across some wine merchants watering their animals at midday, and he crossed the path of a company of Persian skin traders just before dusk, but he didn't strike up a conversation with them or ask about the trail to Sidon. He stayed close to the cedars when travelers passed and he waited until the watering places were empty before he watered his horse. He couldn't risk a traveler headed back to Jerusalem remembering him to the king's soldiers, no matter how far ahead he'd gotten.

Dried sweat stuck the cloth of Jonathan's tunic to him like snake-skin he could not shed, but there wasn't time to stop and bathe in the gurgling waters of the Kishon River flowing beside the trail, not if he were to win this race. Saving Mulek from his abductors was all that mattered. The long nights of riding, the dust-covered trail that choked his breathing, the poor meals, and the bone-deep weariness— it was all worth the trouble as long as he kept Mulek from suffering the same fate as Aaron. His son was dead and he would not let the prince become the second casualty in this battle of faith. The cedars lining the trail gave way to a run of open country and Jonathan spurred his mount out from under the shadows and onto a moon-swept meadow of wild oats and chia grass. He would do right by his dead son and see that Mulek lived to an old age.

The trail crossed through the gurgling water of the Kishon River and Jonathan spurred through it, the steed Miriam loaned him from the royal herd kicking up a spray and the mist mixing with the cool night air that hung over this riverbed. He reined around the largest rocks glowing white from the light of the moon and pulled up in the middle of the river when he heard something stirring on the trail behind him. Someone was back there. He could feel it deep in his soul, the same soft whisper he heard in his heart urging him to keep riding on to Sidon and not stop to sleep the night, the voice warning him of unseen eyes he should avoid if he were . . .

Stop it! There was no one to avoid. The king's men couldn't be within miles of this place, not with the pace Jonathan kept. His weary mind was playing tricks and he wasn't about to let exhaustion get the best of him. There was nothing in the shadows—no cavalry, no men traveling the trail on foot, nothing but an owl in the branches of a cedar along the banks, the fowl hooting her unwillingness to divide the serenity of this summer evening between them. She was a large, wise bird nestled on a thick middle branch, and her hooting begged Jonathan to stop and rest. He could use a good meal or he'd lose whatever good judgment that . . .

There he went again, talking nonsense to an owl—the most foolish thing he'd done since leaving Jerusalem, but it wasn't foolish-ness to want a rest. Whatever sleep he was fortunate to steal, he got hiding behind the trunk of a tree or in the shadows of a rocky outcrop, his head propped against the legs of his steed, the reins draped in his hands and his ear turned to the clatter of hooves passing by on the trail. There was no telling how far ahead he was, but the king's men had to be a good two days behind him. A night's sleep would do Jonathan good, no matter how much the voice in his soul begged him to keep pushing and not stop for anything. Jonathan spurred up the bank, his mount grunting her disapproval at another night on the road, but he stroked her mane and whispered not to worry. They'd find a place to rest up ahead, somewhere they could spend the night, then finish the last leg of this journey come morning.

Jonathan left Jerusalem two days ago, stopping at Jericho only long enough to water his mount before heading north through the Jordan River Valley. He stayed off the main road and away from the best watering holes. Early this morning, before the sun rose, he veered west out of the Jordan River Valley and into the lush green pastures and verdant hillsides of the Jezreel Plain long before the main trail turned that way, cutting a good three miles out of the ride. Jonathan's horse strained against the bit and she arched her neck. The shortcut through the foothills this morning wearied her legs and Jonathan let her slow, but not stop. There was an inn ahead, the lamplight from the windows filtering through the branches. The building stood around the bend and down at the end of a long stretch in the road, nestled in a stand of tall trees, and his horse had the strength to get them that far—their first full night's rest since leaving Jerusalem.

Jonathan steered his steed through the growth of cedars lining the banks and let the cool breeze lifting off the river course over them, rousing their strength for one last push toward the inn. They could overnight there, descend to the coast come morning and, if his horse had enough strength to push one more day, they could make Sidon by nightfall tomorrow—a three day ride that should have taken six. Jonathan spurred down through a stand of cat's claw waving in the breeze and over a rise before turning along the southern slopes of the valley and coming onto the stretch of road leading to the inn. The sight of the square roof, limestone front, and flickering lamps soothed his aching legs, and his steed picked up her pace, racing for the trough of freshly drawn water beside the entry.

The Kishon River Inn stood among cedars at the base of Mount Carmel, the high walls of Fort Megiddo rising on the foothills directly above the inn and overlooking the main road. The ancient fortress built by Solomon stabled a thousand steeds in its underground livery. The torches on the towers and parapets burned orange into the night sky, and the watchmen making their rounds atop the catwalks forced Jonathan to ride among the trees, out of view of their lookout towers to keep his coming to the Kishon River Inn from the sight of any Hebrew soldiers.

The yard outside the inn stood quiet, without any horses or mules tethered to the posts. Jonathan paid the stable boy two shekels to feed and curry his steed and one more for the boy's trouble before climbing the stone steps and pushing through the cedar door. A row of round tables ran the length of the main parlor, all of them empty at this hour. Jonathan didn't take a seat. He kept his gaze turned to the floor—avoiding the stare of the innkeeper standing behind the bar—and found his way to the far side of the inn, over beyond the wooden pillars separating the main room from a darkened parlor. Four tables stood in the corner, but with all the lamps put out and only the light from the main room streaming around thick pillars, he couldn't tell if there were more tables obscured in the dark shadows along the walls.

The innkeeper followed him to the parlor and stood beside the pillars, his short, wide frame silhouetted by the glow of light streaming around him from the main room. "Are you wanting a meal or glass of wine?"

"This should be enough for a glass of wine, some roasted lamb, and a room on the upper floor away from the notice of your other guests." Jonathan set a piece of silver on the table and the innkeeper snatched it up, replacing the silver coin with a tall bottle of wine and a drinking cup. "The rooms on the upper floor are filled for the night." He glanced into the shadows of the parlor before coming back to Jonathan. "I had some unexpected arrivals this evening."

"Arrivals?"

'That's right."

"I didn't see any horses stabled outside." Jonathan reached for the wine bottle. "Do you rent your rooms to ghosts?"

"So long as they pay in silver." The innkeeper glanced about the darkened chamber again, his gaze flitting from one corner to the other, but never resting too long on any shadow. He spoke in a deliberate tone, his words directed more to the shadows than to Jonathan. "For another piece of silver you can have the private room on the main floor. They'll see you coming and going, but it's a good room, reserved for our finest guests."

The inn was empty, without another soul eating a meal or drinking from a bottle and it was impossible to know exactly what guests the innkeeper was referring to. And why was the innkeeper speaking past him, addressing the wooden pillars and the rafters. There was no one here but the two of them and he could at least speak directly to Jonathan if he hoped to sell the private room on the main floor.

The innkeeper said, "It comes with a perfumed bath before you retire and a second meal in the morning."

"See that the water is hot and that the morning meal is served before sunrise." Jonathan handed over another piece of silver and the innkeeper scurried off to the kitchen, assuring Jonathan he was going to fetch the finest cut of lamb for his supper and start the bath water boiling.

Jonathan uncorked the wine bottle and downed half of it before wiping his lips on the sleeve of his tunic. It wasn't the finest wine, but it had enough of a bite to take the pain out of his weary bones. He was thirsty and if the bottle were filled with the juice of a turnip, he'd drink it and thank the innkeeper for the refreshing drink after so many days on the—

"The trail from Jerusalem to the Kishon River Inn usually takes five days."

The voice came from the corner of the parlor and Jonathan slowly lowered the bottle and peered into the darkness, over where there was little light to chase away the shadows. He squinted until he found the form of a man leaning over a darkened tabletop, his elbows firmly planted in the planks. "You made it in less than three."

Who was this man and how did he know Jonathan had come from Jerusalem in such a short time? The stranger moved away from the table and stepped closer, the shadows retreating from his face, and the light from the main parlor casting a soft yellow glow over Captain Elnathan, the finest scout in the Hebrew army. He was Daniel's commanding officer on his first mission to Egypt to capture the fleeing Uriah, and his skill for tracking men through the worst territories and under the most impossible conditions was the stuff of legends.

"You're a long way from home." Elnathan removed his riding gloves and set them on the table in front of Jonathan. "Why such a hurry?"

"I like the wine here." Jonathan poured a round into the empty cup and pushed it across the table at Elnathan, his gaze steady as an iron rod, not hinting at the concern that swelled within. Captain Elnathan suspected him; he had to. There was no other reason for him to ride at such a harried pace up the Jordan River Valley and into the Jezreel plains unless he was smart enough to know there was a horseman riding ahead of his company, making the same turns, stopping at the same wells, and passing the same travelers headed back toward Jerusalem. What Elnathan didn't know was that Jonathan was racing him to Sidon to save the life of Prince Mulek.

Elnathan pushed the cup back at Jonathan, the clay bottom scratching over the wood surface. "I drink with my men."

There wasn't another soul with Elnathan; At least Jonathan didn't see anyone until the captain raised his hand and waved his companions forward. Five cavalrymen appeared out of the darkened corners of the inn, their gray tunics spotted with dried sweat, and the luster of their brass-studded kilts tarnished with a thick layer of dust.

"Tell me, blacksmith." Elnathan leaned forward over Jonathan's table. "Where are you headed?"

"I came for the wine, sir." Jonathan took another drink from the bottle. "And business of course."

"You don't sell steel to patrons this far from your shop."

"Steel-making secrets, Captain. Surely you've heard of them." Jonathan let his gaze run over the dusty faces of the men in Elnathan's patrol. "My patrons are willing to pay for what I know. Even patrons this far from Jerusalem."

Elnathan sat in the chair across the table and leaned back on its legs. "Exactly what secrets bring you to Sidon?"

"I didn't say I was headed there."

"You didn't have to." Elnathan brought the front legs of his chair down, the wood clapping against the stone floor. "When was the last time you were in Sidon?"

Now! For Subscribers Only!
Subscribers Save Over
~~25% 40%~~ **60%*** Off
the cover price!

▲ Detach this card and mail today! ▲

Get 2 FREE† Gifts!

TV GUIDE

Save Over 60%*

☐ **YES!** Send me 52 issues for just 4 easy monthly payments of only $10.66** each! Plus send my FREE† Mystery Gift with my order and **Curve Calculator** upon receipt of full payment.

☐ Send me 24 issues for just 4 easy monthly payments of only $4.92** each!

Name: _____

please print

Address: _____

City: _____

State: _____ Zip: _____

53185A2*B1

THE NEWLYWEDS
Is Jessica really that stupid?

TV GUIDE
We See...

Oprah Opens Up!

"Why I Never Married"
"Why I Never Had Kids"

PLUS
The Book Club Returns

HURRY!
R.S.V.P. for your Special Savings!

Your first issue will be mailed within 3-5 weeks.
*Savings based on newsstand cover price
of $2.49 per issue †Mystery Gift will
be shipped upon receipt of order and
Curve Calculator is shipped upon receipt of full
payment of 52 issue subscription.
**Plus 17¢ per issue shipping
and handling.

LOT L

For Subscribers Only!

Get 2 Free† Gifts!

Save Over <u>60%</u>

Off the $2.49 Cover Price!

▼ Detach this card and mail today! ▼

"I don't recall."

"And these patrons of yours, who are they?"

"Surely you have better things to do than to pass the evening hours in idle conversation with a blacksmith." Jonathan called to the kitchen for the innkeeper to bring him his dinner before saying, "If you like, you're welcome to join me.

"You make for fine company, sir."

Elnathan started out of the darkened parlor, but before he disappeared out the front doors with his men he turned back and said, "We'll discuss your secret another time, blacksmith."

The fall of footsteps and the muffled din of voices above the main-floor bedroom fell silent and Jonathan put out the flickering lamp and sat on the end of his bed. Sleep had most likely come to Elnathan and his men quartered on the second floor of the inn, but he turned his ear to the ceiling and waited in the quiet until he was certain they were gone to sleep and he could get away without their seeing.

The perfume from his bath scented the air around him. His hair was combed back with olive oils, and his weary body begged him to stay the night and curl up on this bed, but he could not indulge his need for sleep. He had to reach Mulek before Captain Elnathan did, and he slung the saddlebag over his shoulder, stood at the small window, and unlatched the shutters.

The horse stable stood in full view of the second-floor windows. It was a short run of thirty cubits through a small garden and he tossed his saddlebag out the window before shimmying up onto the sill and forcing his body through the narrow opening. He landed quietly on bent knees and hurried down through the rows of melons and artichokes before slipping around to the front of the stable, his back pressed against the tall timber doors. The latch was sealed and Jonathan broke it away from the timbers with the heel of his boot before tying the saddle onto his horse and leading her out into the night and down the road beyond a stand of cedars. He was away without causing a stir or raising the innkeeper from his bed to open the stables, and if he made good time through the Kishon River Pass to the sea and up the coast, he'd reach Sidon by morning, long before Captain Elnathan found him gone. Jonathan got up into the saddle and circled around once to make certain no lamps came on after his leaving. The inn stood dark and he spurred down the road toward Sidon without fear of being followed.

What he didn't know was that Captain Elnathan stood in the shadows of his second-floor bedroom window, watching Jonathan sneak out.

CHAPTER 13

Ruth the weaver stood in the gate of her home and showed the queen her newest creation—a sample of the twenty blankets Miriam hired her to weave for the beds and benches of the royal sleeping chambers. It was a large project, one of the most ambitious she'd undertaken since moving from Sidon, and she handed Miriam the only blanket she had finished for inspection. The queen stood in the street just outside the gate with an escort of soldiers surrounding her. It wasn't the finest place to entertain a guest of her stature, but Miriam insisted. They were to discuss the weaving here and not destroy the solitude of Ruth's home with the company of so many soldiers escorting her about like a child. It was a kindly consideration, but Miriam didn't need to worry; there was plenty of room for these men in the courtyard. But when she offered, Miriam's body stiffened and she shook her head quickly, her finger wagging with the rushed words of her refusal. She lowered her voice soft enough so that the soldiers couldn't hear and told Ruth she wouldn't allow these men to traipse about her house without Jonathan here, and if she had her wish she wouldn't have to traipse anywhere with these men. They were like millstones tied about her neck.

Miriam said, "Jonathan is still away, isn't he?"

"We haven't heard from him in days."

"You'll let me know when he returns, won't you?" Miriam held he hand to her breast. "I do so worry about you being on your own."

That wasn't the only thing that worried the poor woman. Ruth could tell by the concern that furrowed her brow and played across her eyes. Soldiers were riding to find her son in Sidon and bring him home to an unknown fate and all Ruth could say in front of these soldiers was, "You'll be the first to know when I get word of Jonathan's return." She pointed out the finely stitched hems in the blanket. "Step closer and look at what I've weaved for you."

The cloth was dyed to match the Persian rugs and wall hangings in the palace bedroom chambers. It was exactly what the queen ordered—a double-stitched blanket with blue cloth, no visible stitches to spoil the intricate star pattern weaved into the cloth, and a hem hidden beneath an off-white border with silver threads to decorate the edges—a perfect addition for the royal bedrooms.

Miriam tugged at the hem and ran her hand over the pattern in the cloth before saying, "This simply won't do."

Ruth brought her gaze up from going over the patterns in the blanket. Had she heard right? Did Miriam say this wouldn't do? This sample was one of Ruth's finest, but Miriam shook her head and instead of speaking directly to Ruth, she held the blanket up to the soldiers standing behind her, their stiff bodies leaning forward and their untrained gaze moving over the cloth. What did soldiers know about weaving? If they were anything like her son Daniel, they couldn't judge between a finely weaved cloth and a sack for grain, but that didn't stop Miriam from telling all these men that this blanket wasn't what she wanted by any measure and she was going to have to leave it with Ruth for alterations and return another day to see if she could get it right the next time.

Get it right? Ruth took back the blanket and draped it between her hands. She'd spent weeks crafting the fine patterns in this cloth and where did Miriam get the nerve to speak publicly about her dislike of this most likeable blanket. Ruth said, "It's exactly what you—"

"You'll have to try again." Miriam's voice echoed in the street. "The hem is wrong, I want the gold thread in the center, not silver thread, and could you have another sample completed by the end of next week?"

Ruth said, "I haven't the time to—"

"Your daughter Elizabeth is good with hems, and her suitor, what is that boy's name?"

"Are you talking about Zoram?"

"That's the lad." Miriam snapped her fingers in the air and the soldiers beside her pulled back from leaning in around the gatepost. "I've spoken to him already. He's making some preparations to help with these blankets. He has a Cousin Hanameel in Anathoth who has just what you need to finish these off. Do you know the man? I understand he's very good with details, just the details we need. I asked Zoram to come see your next sample three days from now. He's very good with threads. I think it best he work on this project with you and with the help he's gotten from his cousin, we'll simply have the finest blankets to ever grace the palace bedrooms."

Zoram? Good with thread? And who was this cousin Hanameel? Was he a tailor or a weaver or thread spooler? Ruth folded the blanket under her arm. Was Miriam losing her mind? Where did she get her logic? Zoram was a hard worker, but his talents were for writing and languages and the work of a scribe. He'd learned some of the art of blacksmithing the past year working at the shop, but smelting steel and forging plowshares was hardly the same as guiding a weaver's needle through cloth or threading a spool on a foot loom. Zoram was a learned man, but his education did not include the skills of a weaver and Miriam was mistaken if she thought the boy could offer any assistance.

Ruth said, "I don't think you really want Zoram to—"

"Nonsense. He's a fine spooler and I want him working with you, do you understand? I'll stop by the end of next week to speak with all of you." Miriam ran her hand over the blanket stretched between Ruth's arms. "You'll see that both he and your daughter are here, won't you?" She slowed her speech. "I'm going to need all your help with my project at the palace." Her gaze moved slowly about the yard before coming back to Ruth. "You do understand what I'm trying to say, don't you dear?"

"Well, I—"

"It's settled then. I'll be here no later than midmorning the first of next week and we'll go over everything with you and your assistants." Miriam took Ruth by the arm and she could feel the trembling in the woman's hand—deep-to-the-bone trembling. She spoke in a low, unsteady voice, the corners of her words clipped short with concern. "Tell me you do understand." She glanced at the solders standing beside her and offered a weak smile, her mouth infected with the same unsteady trembling as her hand, but hidden by the red pomegranate she used to color her lips. "We'll talk more of the details when I come to see the new blanket."

Ruth set her hand on Miriam's and lowered her head. How could she be such a fool not to understand the pleading in Miriam's voice until now? The queen wasn't unkind or unreasonable; she was a trusted friend and Ruth was Miriam's confidante. How did she miss the woman's silent plea for help? A plea she couldn't make in the company of these soldiers? But what trouble could there be that Miriam needed the help of Elizabeth and Zoram and this other fellow, cousin Hanameel?

"I'll see that everything is in order." Ruth patted the back of Miriam's hand, her gaze turned onto the soldiers surrounding Miriam. "And I'll see to preparing something for your escorts. They'll be much more interested in eating than discussing the weave and hem and stitching of a blanket. Wouldn't you agree?"

Miriam forced a nervous laugh and leaned her head back. "I knew you'd understand."

Ruth tightened her grip on Miriam's hand, telling her with a gentle squeeze that of course she understood, and if there were any burden Ruth could lift, any aid or comfort she could lend, she was prepared to offer it freely. What an awful predicament for Miriam. The poor woman confined to the palace under the suspecting eye of her husband and sentenced to be followed about the city by this escort of soldiers—never allowing her out of the palace precincts without accompanying her to every destination and listening to her every word. Miriam never left the palace without an escort at her side and she told anyone who asked that it was for *her* safety—her husband didn't want any harm to come to her when she was about the city. But Miriam didn't need protection as much as she needed freedom. Ruth could see the longing in her eyes. She couldn't go to market without dragging these men with her and if it wasn't for her requisition of a new set of blankets for the royal sleeping chambers, the queen wouldn't have an excuse to come here and see Ruth.

Miriam pulled free of Ruth's hand, but before she started out the gate, she lowered her voice and said, "I'm going to need your very best, most courageous help, my dear." Miriam pulled the hood of her robe over her head. "These blankets will be a great escape from the drudgery of spending my days in the confines of the palace."

Dear no, Miriam wasn't telling her she was planning her own escape from the palace, was she? That would only add to her husband's suspicions, and if she got away he'd hunt her down and there was no telling what would become of this lovely woman with long black hair, deep brown eyes, and a smile that had all but disappeared from her once-shining countenance. Ruth held the blanket close against her breast. Dear God of heaven, was there no blessing of relief for this woman who risked everything she held dear to protect His prophets?

Miriam left Ruth standing in the gate with the unwanted blanket draped over her arm. It wasn't really rejected and she was going to present the queen with the same blanket when she returned in three days. The soldiers would never see that it was the same cloth. Ruth watched the street long after the queen turned on to Main Street at the top of the hill. Miriam was planning an escape; She had to be by the way she spoke. But whose escape? And if she needed help, why did she come here? Ruth was not a subversive soul and her talents were better suited to cooking and cleaning and looking after her children, not defying soldiers. But if Miriam had need, Ruth would leave her kitchens long enough to help her friend. She laid the blanket over her shoulders and started inside. Miriam lived a secret life in the company of her husband, and Ruth was just now daring to become an actor in that play and the only way she knew to cover her part in it was to continue living the life of a mother. Sunflower-seed bread— that's what she'd prepare for Miriam's return visit—sunflower-seed bread with honey, some berry wine, and a bit of roasted lamb. That's what her son Daniel enjoyed, and the queen's escorts were sure to enjoy the same food or she wasn't as good a mother as she thought herself. Ruth pulled open the door to the house and hurried inside. She may be a very dull accomplice, but dullness afforded her one advantage—

No one would dare suspect a mother of sedition, would they?

CHAPTER 14

Ebed Melech pushed past the crew of the *Viceroy* and spit off the end of the wharf, the spittle falling to the white foam lapping between the dock moorings and the Egyptian merchant vessel. The ship's first mate held out three silver coins and Ebed snatched them from his palm. He'd take the bet and scale the ship's gangplank with a full water cistern on his back and he'd do the crew one better to win the pot—he'd walk the gangplank blindfolded. That was a challenge certain to sweeten the meager wagers thrown in by crewmates who knew too well his strength and nimbleness. The narrow bridge of timbers spanning the watery gulf to the ship was weathered from the salt of the seas they sailed, but Ebed had sure feet and he'd never fallen overboard, though a good many of his mates knew the shame of losing their footing, to say nothing of the cargo that went into the water with them.

Ebed tore a piece of cloth from the sleeve of his shirt, shook the remnant at the crew milling about the dock and told them he was going to cover his eyes and cross the gangplank blind—a promise that gleaned him two more pieces of silver from the ship's cook, an Egyptian farthing from the cabin boy, and three Greek copper coins from the sail masters. There was nothing to lose in this wager. The ship was docked at Sidon only long enough to take on enough drinking water to sail for Athens, and spilling a cistern of water wasn't as costly as falling from the gangplank with a crate of pomegranate, a sack of fine linens, or a round of wines. Ebed leaned over the edge of the pier, the seawater swirling below him in the shadows of the *Viceroy* and the end of the gangplank lost above him in the brightness of the morning sun. He wasn't going to fall from this perch above the water; he was too strong a ship hand to let a cistern unbalance him. Ebed was the spryest sailor in the entire fleet of Egyptian merchant vessels and he didn't win that honor mending sails, swabbing the deck or coiling rope. No matter the port and no matter the weather—rain, hail, wind, or torrent—Ebed was the first to climb onto the gang-plank and cross the wooden bridge in the shortest time and with the heaviest loads on his back. He gleaned his sense of balance climbing the ridges and canyons in the mountain jungles of his home in Ethiopia and he could scale the *Viceroy's* gangplank as easily as a gorilla walks the branches in the treetops surrounding his home village. Ebed tightened his grip around the money. If anyone could win this pot of money, it was he.

Ebed turned away from the edge of the pier, his black-skinned shoulders pushing his Egyptian crewmates back. He raised his fistful of coins like a merchant hocking wares, his powerful arms stretched overhead and the heat of the sun drawing a line of sweat from beneath the coarse black curls in his tightly woven cap of short hair. The gulls roosting on the highest mast of the *Viceroy* took to flight on the sound of Ebed's deep voice challenging his crewmates to double the pot. They were fools if they thought this small pittance-of-a-wager was enough. A water cistern was the work of two men and if the crew wanted him to carry it up the gangplank blindfolded and without any help they'd have to pay for the show.

The pot-bellied navigator pushed to the front of the crew and shouted that he wasn't about to risk even a half-day's pay on a water cistern. Ebed was too strong a man to put a wager on anything less than an elephant. A rumble of laughter filtered through the crowd of sailors and Ebed quieted the navigator before he said anything more to discourage the new lads from anteing up. They didn't know Ebed's strength like the navigator—not after twenty years together sailing the Great Sea. The two sailors who came on board at the port at Athens last month and the three ship hands they hired in Crete stood near the front, shaking their heads and insisting no one, not even Ebed, could carry a load meant for two, no matter how broad his shoulders, thick his arms, or powerful his legs. They dug deep in their purses to the jeers of their mates and doubled the wager to—

"I'll triple the pot." The *Viceroy's* captain stepped from the deck and onto the gangplank, balancing himself with both arms out like a bird taking to flight, but the poor man would never fly, not with the large paunch bulging at his middle and the double chin weighing him down. He slowly navigated his way over from the ship, careful not to lose his balance on the narrow bridge of wood. If the man would only invest in a wider plank, loading the ship wouldn't be such a difficult chore, but the captain of the *Viceroy* was a frugal man and the narrow gangplank did provide a good deal of entertainment with new deckhands falling into the water at every port.

The captain held out twelve pieces of silver—more money than Ebed would make in months of voyages to every port along the shores of the Great Sea.

"You'll have to do more than carry a single water cistern up the gangplank for this." The captain's words whistled through the holes in his teeth. "Two cisterns, no blindfold, and the money is yours."

The crew fell quiet, their shoulders forward and their heads leaned in with only the sound of lapping water beneath the wharf and squawking gulls circling above the ship to fill the silence. Ebed scratched the back of his head. Two cisterns? That was an impossible load to carry up such a narrow gangplank. One wrong step, one off-balance placement of his foot and the load was sure to pull him into the harbor along with the load.

"You're on, sir." Ebed stuffed the silver into the leather pouch he kept cinched around his chest before crouching next to the water cisterns. The first mate stepped up to help lift them onto Ebed's back, but the captain ordered him to stand down—the wager was from pier to deck and Ebed was going to have to do this on his own if he wanted to keep the money.

The first mate retreated back with the others and let Ebed tip the heavy cisterns against his back before wrapping his powerful arms around the neck of the vessels and coming up out of his crouch with a mighty grunt, the drinking water rising off the ground in a powerful push from Ebed's thick legs. He stepped out over the harbor, the gangplank bowing but not breaking under the weight, and he kept his head forward, his gaze set on the prow of the ship, away from the intoxicating swirl of seawater below. The weathered timbers were rough underfoot and he felt his way along with his toes, his stance as wide as the narrow bridge allowed and his powerful shoulders hunched forward, but not so far as to unbalance him.

The ship's crew stood at the edge of the pier, cheering and jeering Ebed's careful steps. The navigator cupped his hands to his mouth and told Ebed he'd never reach the other side, and the ship's cook untied his apron and waved it in the air like an ensign, asking if Ebed could swim with cisterns on his back. The breeze filtered through Ebed's torn shirt, the short sleeves flapping against his thick arms and his tattered sailing knickers pulling taut against his straining thighs. The cistern on his right shoulder slipped on the sweat streaming down his back and Ebed steadied his foot sideways on the gangplank and curled his toes around the edge of the weathered wood to keep from losing his balance. He leaned forward, shifted the cistern back into place and tightened his grip before slowly pushing further out over the water. He was halfway across when his right leg gave out and he fell to his knee, his mates hooting their approval and Ebed careful to steady the cisterns against the small of his back to keep them from taking him over the edge. He was a fool for going down like this. He wasn't so tired that he shouldn't be able stay upright and he slowly lifted himself to his feet, trained his gaze on the end of the gangplank and started across, placing one foot in front of the . . .

A rock flew across his path, then another and still another.

"You missed him." The small, high-pitched voice rising up from the water below begged Ebed to look that way. It was a young lad's voice, nothing like the gruff speech of his shipmates and he quickly glanced down at the water. A dizzying white foam churned on the surface between the ship's wooden hull and the pillars holding up the pier. In the center of the swirling water, half hidden beneath the shadows of the gangplank were the faces of two lads, their heads bobbing atop the surface and their arms treading water to keep afloat.

The cisterns shifted on Ebed's sweat-laden back. He leaned forward, his body bent over to balance them, but he was too long looking down at the water and he lost his upright sensibilities. The clay vessels began to slide off Ebed's back. One foot came up and the crew hooted. He let go of the cisterns to keep from falling, the heavy vessels crashing around the young swimmers below like rocks launched from a giant catapult. Ebed swung his arms for balance, but he couldn't stay upright and he went off the side of the gangplank head first, his powerful body turning head over feet, falling down between the ship and pier and hitting the water with a stinging splash.

Ebed came back to the surface and shook the water from his head, cursing his lost wages while his crewmates jumped from the dock and into the harbor around him, their jeering voices echoing off the hull of the ship and mixing with the sound of their laughing over his failed crossing of the gangplank. He rubbed his eyes clear of the salt water and looked past them, searching the shadows for the lads who lost him the pot of money. They weren't swimming alongside the *Viceroy* and he stroked about the water, hunting for them amid his mates. They couldn't be drowned; Ebed was careful to throw the cisterns clear of them before he fell overboard.

The sound of youthful giggling turned Ebed back toward the dock. The lads were climbing out of the water and up onto the rock foundations of the pier. They pulled their tunics on over their shoulders before quickly starting up the pillars, telling each other to hurry away before they were caught meddling with the sailors. A gold chain glistened around the neck of the taller lad with light brown hair. He climbed the pillars hand over fist with the skill of a monkey climbing a tree. The second boy wasn't as quick. He faltered on the timbers and he was slow to lift the weight of his thin body up the sheer side of the dock. The older boy reached the top and came around on his belly, reaching his hand over the edge to help the dark-haired lad to safety before the two of them disappeared beyond the planks of wood.

Foolish lads. They lost Ebed a goodly sized pot of money and he stroked to the water's edge. They were going to hear a word from him about their foolery and he pulled his large body up onto the moorings and scaled the pillars, cursing them for the money they lost him.

Ebed reached the top of the dock and found the boys headed farther out onto the pier, toward the royal navy ships in the harbor. They were more foolish than Ebed believed, going to watch the navy ships set sail when they should have been hiding from him among the fish vendors and merchants lining the shores. Ebed started after them, water spraying from his clothes and—

"Let them go." The harbormaster slapped his tide stick against the floor of the dock, the tip of the marked pole he used to measure the height of tides clicking against the timbers. He stepped into Ebed's path and twisted his face into a frown. He said, "You don't want any trouble with those boys."

"They lost me a pot of money."

"Forget them." He tapped his stick twice more. "I'm warning you, son, they aren't worth your trouble."

"Those boys could use some trouble they won't soon forget."

"Not those lads." The harbormaster took Ebed by the arm and held him back. "The brown-headed one is Jesse, Prince of Sidon. You cause him any trouble and you'll end up in prison if you're lucky."

"What about the thin lad, the one that unbalanced me?" Ebed leaned around the harbormaster and watched the boys disappear beyond the prow of a ship. "What about him?"

"They say he's from Jerusalem. He speaks the language of the Jews. He and the prince explore the docks nearly everyday. He lives with the royal family along with a handservant, a woman like yourself, son."

Ebed turned his gaze out across the harbor. The domed rooftops and marbled walls of the palace of Jesse, Prince of Sidon, rose above the masts and sails of the moored sailing vessels, the magnificent columns and granite walls built out into the harbor on a man-made point of rock and earth. The palace was a many-terraced structure, with arched doorways and steps leading down to the water's edge from every floor of the elegant five-story building. A white-plastered wall sealed off the pristine life of the royals from the hurly burly harshness of the docks without sacrificing a view of the ships that passed before the balconies and terraces of the royal precincts. A small boat launch graced the seaside entrance to the palace and a long land bridge led from the mainland to the palace entrance.

"A handservant like me?" Ebed pulled free of the harbormaster's grip. "What are you talking about?"

"I see her in the fish markets every morning, right about this hour. If you head that way, you'll no doubt find her buying fish or shopping for clothes in the main market. You can't miss her." The harbormaster tugged on the cloth of his tunic with one hand and pulled on his ear lobe with the other. "She wears that green and red clothing all your people wear, with baubles hanging from her ears and an odd cloth tied in her hair to raise it up off her head. She speaks the language of the Jews, just like the boy, but she isn't Hebrew, not with skin as black as yours. She's Ethiopian like you son, there's no question about it."

"Are you sure the woman's from Jerusalem?"

"She speaks like a Jew, you know, with that deep hacking sound in the back of the mouth, like she was clearing her throat. She's good with her Hebrew."

"You're certain?"

"No mistaking it. There's not another people in all the world who speak like the—"

"I mean the woman—are you certain she's an Ethiopian from Jerusalem?"

"I don't know what to be certain of anymore." The harbormaster scratched the side of his head. "It's all so odd—an Ethiopian woman speaking like the Jews and the Prince of Sidon lodging a boy from Jerusalem. Very odd indeed."

Ebed started down the pier toward land without another word to the harbormaster. He skirted past his shipmates with his head down and his stride full, jumping over the end of the gangplank and then down past a merchant trader loading his cart from the next ship over. The Captain of the *Viceroy* called after Ebed, telling him not to leave the pier. They had drinking water to bring aboard and if he weren't back before they finished he'd set sail without him. Ebed may be the hardest working sailor in the crew, but the captain wouldn't wait on him.

Ebed tucked the wet tails of his shirt into his sailing knickers before breaking into a run down past a crew unloading another merchant vessel and in between the mule carts waiting to take on cargo. He was risking his post on the *Viceroy* to chase after his heart, but he had to find this Ethiopian woman. The life of a sailor was all that mattered since the day nearly twenty years ago when the *Viceroy* floundered back into homeport at Tanis two months behind schedule with the ship's mast broken and the bow taking on water from a winter storm fierce enough to have the ship and its crew declared lost at sea. Ebed's betrothed wife-to-be departed Tanis on the news of his death, leaving word with friends that she was going to start a new life among the Jews, far away from the painful memories of the docks and boat builders of Tanis, but there was no telling if she traveled to Judah or Athens or back to her home in Ethiopia. Ebed combed his fingers through his tightly woven locks of black hair and hurried his stride down along the pier. It was so long ago she left him, he'd nearly forgotten the beauty of her smile or the firm resolve of her voice. An acquaintance told him she left Tanis a brokenhearted woman, not knowing she left Ebed a lone man with only the life of a sailor to keep his heart from breaking.

Ebed skirted past three more carts and onto the shore, the sea breeze flapping the wet ends of his sleeves against his arms. The stares and glances from the fish merchants and shoppers didn't slow his stride. Hadn't they ever seen an Ethiopian of his stature before? Ebed wasn't a thin, long-boned man like so many from his village. He had the strength to keep these curious folks at a respectable distance and he pushed his way through the crowd, his gaze searching for any sign of the woman he lost so many years before. He passed the silversmiths without stopping. The woman he knew wouldn't shop for that sort of jewelry. There wasn't enough color in the precious metal and he turned his gaze to the tailors in the next cart. She was nowhere to be found among these drab garments. The woman he remembered wore nothing but colorful clothing and if she was here in Sidon, she'd be shopping for clothes colored with greens and yellows, not these drab brown and off-white robes. Ebed checked the fruit vendors on his way past, but there was no black woman purchasing produce, no head of tightly curled, coarse hair bobbing amid the straight-haired men and women of this Phoenician market and no brightly colored robes to attract his gaze. He had to find her, but where? Ebed stepped past a potter, the man's spinning wheel spattering red clay over his legs. Was this Egyptian handservant the woman who left him for dead twenty years ago? He hurried around a bend in the street and past a perfume merchant, his gaze searching the crowd for any sign of his long-lost love. Could it be true or was he only dreaming this dream?

Was Mima living in Sidon?

Jonathan pulled back the hood of his black riding cape and slowly reined around a shoal in the coastline and onto a wide strand, his horse plodding over the warm sand. There was no need to cover his head against the cool coastal breeze with the sun coming up over the hills and chasing away the fog that hovered over the waters in early morning, and he let his hood fall away, the point of the black cloth playing about his shoulder. The riding cloak was weaved on Ruth's looms and on this ride from Jerusalem it was a blanket by night, a cover from the sun in afternoon, and a protection from the summer coastal storms along the Great Sea.

Jonathan reined around a rocky point and came onto the last sandy strand of beach leading to Sidon, the homes and shops of the city coming to view, nestled among the Cyprus and Cedars of these seaside hills like a string of elegant pearls accented by the glow of morning. He leaned forward in the saddle and squinted through the rising sunlight to find his former smithy—a small, gray, stone building in the middle hills of the city a little down from the columned estate entrances and white plastered walls of the wealthiest neighborhoods. He kept his steed trotting over the sand without spurring her faster. There was no need to hurry, not with Captain Elnathan and his men rising this morning to find Jonathan gone from the Kishon River Inn. And as soon as he found Mima and Mulek, he could rest from his travels and fill his belly with a good helping of boiled fish and baked clams from the market across from the city's main docks. There was nothing finer than a meal from the Great Sea. Shellfish may not be the most kosher foods for a Jew, but Jonathan ate Phoenician cuisine without suffering the guilt of Hebrew creeds.

A flock of seagulls took to flight on Jonathan's passing, fluttering from their perch atop a lush green bluff overlooking the sea, and the sound of the surf mixed with the flapping of their wings. How fine was his return to this place he once called home without the rush of the king's men following him. The worry of not reaching Prince Mulek faded with the rising sun. He was free of concern for Mulek. The lad would not suffer the same fate as his own son, Aaron, and Jonathan reined his steed at a restful pace over the beach, remembering his former life in Sidon before he moved his family to

Jerusalem, back in the days when he was nothing more than an apprentice among the steelmaking smiths of Sidon. There were no finer artisans in the entire world and Jonathan was the only Jew to ever join their ranks and share their secrets.

The sandy trail turned to cobblestones before rising to Sidon's main entrance—a limestone wall twenty cubits high with pomegranates etched into the stonework and an archway towering above a watchman guarding the opening. There was hardly a reason to guard the gates except to catch an occasional thief or seal the entrance on a feast day against the crowds that grew too large around the city's marbled sanctuaries built to pagan gods. There were so many temples Jonathan couldn't remember all the deities' names. There were temples to the gods of fertility and gods of harvest, not to mention the spacious seaside temple built to the gods of the sea, and the ones high on the hillside in honor of the gods of the sky. Jonathan spurred up the cobblestone way, the clap of the steed's hooves filling the morning air with the sound of his arrival. Thank heaven he was Hebrew with claim to only one God. More than that was too much bother. It was chore enough to offer a prayer to a single God, and if he had to worry about so many, he'd not ever consider petitioning heaven. It was less confusing to beg the attention of a single Father than to think so many unknown gods watched over the wealth of this city, the fine buildings, the expert artisans, and the treasuries filled with gold and silver. Sidon survived a good many years without a single invader coming to these shores, but it wasn't the large temples adorned to a host of stone Gods that protected this place. It was the high mountains surrounding this narrow strip of coastal land like a fortress wall that kept back aggressors. And the king's navy with countless vessels moored in the harbor repelled conquerors from sailing into this port and making these wealthy lands their own.

Phoenicia was the true conqueror, exporting her blacksmithing and learning to every corner of the earth. The architecture of Sidon charmed the courts of Egypt with columns and circular stairways, graced the Hebrew temple at Jerusalem with vaulted ceilings, lined the streets of Nineveh with statues, and watered the floating gardens of Babylon with aqueducts engineered by men from this city. And after so many years of peace there was no need for a standing army, at least not a large one. There were no watchmen on the towers surrounding the city and no garrison marching about the entryway. The watchman at Sidon's main gate waved Jonathan to a halt and when he answered the man's questions with a perfect Phoenician dialect, telling him he was a blacksmith come to seek out his mentors in the smithing district, he let Jonathan pass beneath the archway and through the shadows into the square.

The pounding approach of horse hooves up the beach filled the archway with the muffled beat of an approaching band. Jonathan came around the high-columned entrance shading him from the morning sun. Off in the distance, riding up off the sand and onto the cobblestones was a garrison of riders. Jonathan leaned forward in the saddle and squinted into the sunlight. How could this be? Jonathan backed his steed out of the shade of the archway and into the square, the columned entrance framing his view of Captain Elnathan and his men. Jonathan left them at the Kishon River Inn and there was no way they could get here this soon.

Jonathan scanned the streets. The narrow roads branched out from the main gates like spokes on the wheel of a mule cart, some meandering up through the homes on the hillsides and others cutting through the middle hills toward the market. Mulek could be anywhere, and with Captain Elnathan and his men coming onto the cobblestone approach leading to the gates, Jonathan had to find the boy. But where should he look? The race was on, but where was the prize?

Captain Elnathan spurred his mount at full gallop, his men racing over the sand behind him and onto the cobblestone road leading to the main gates of Sidon. The black-cloaked rider passing beneath the archway had to be Jonathan. They tracked him through the night from the Kishon River Inn, down the pass to the sea and north along the coastal plain. They lost time in the descent through the Kishon river gorge without the moon to light the way, but they gained on Jonathan in the early morning ride over the beaches, and now Elnathan had the man in his sights. He let go his hold on the reins and strung an arrow, his steed racing full out. Foolish black-smith. If he was come to Sidon to warn the prince, he'd pay for his doings, no matter that he was an Elder on the council. No one lied to Elnathan without paying a price and the sting of an arrow was only the first pain he would endure. Blacksmithing was good reason for him to come here, but not at such a harried pace, and if it wasn't blacksmithing that brought him here, Elnathan would report the man to Zadock and make certain he lost his shop. Elnathan sat straight in the saddle, his shoulders back and his body stiff against the stride of his steed. He scanned the gate over the horse's head, the blacksmith coming to view sitting on his steed beneath the stone archway of the . . .

Where did he go? Elnathan squinted in the morning sun. The blacksmith was gone, disappeared beyond the shadows of the archway and Elnathan reached for his bow. They had to hunt him down. He wasn't a threat to their mission if he was meeting with smiths in the smithing district, but if he interfered with Mulek, he would deal with the man. There was no other option. Prince Mulek was to be returned to his father, and Jonathan the blacksmith would not be allowed to meddle. Elnathan strapped his bow over his shoulder and leaned forward in the saddle, leading his men up the cobblestone rise. The tall timber gates of Sidon were drawn open and the watchman stood in the opening, his sword raised to their approach. He was an older man, with graying hair hedging beneath his brass helmet and a bulging paunch about the middle, pushing his silver trimmed tunic against a wide leather belt. He waited until the riders came to a full stop before announcing they were required to enter their names in his log and answer his questions about the nature of their coming to Sidon.

Elnathan came around next to the watchman. They didn't have time to sign a log and he quickly uttered a plea for the man to hurry and he did it in broken Phoenician, clipping the ends of his words like a butcher cutting a carcass, his gaze turned beyond the man, over past the archway to the streets of Sidon, searching for any sign of the blacksmith in the shadows of the entryway, but Jonathan was gone, disappeared in the labyrinth of winding streets spreading out from these seaside gates in every direction.

The watchman came around in front of Elnathan, clicking his tongue and telling him to repeat his words slowly enough so he could understand the nature of his business in Sidon. Elnathan brought his gaze back to the watchman, the man standing directly below the snout of horse. He said, "Can we get on with this? I have business in the city."

"What sort of business, sir?" The watchman tapped the tip of his pen against the ledger.

Elnathan slowed his speech to keep this poor excuse of a soldier from misunderstanding his words. If the people of Sidon wanted to protect their city, they should post a host of soldiers at their gates and not place their safety in the hands of a single watchman toting a pen and parchment. Elnathan repeated his name, his voice echoing about the tall stone parapets of this watch post and telling the guard he was sent by the king of Judah with business for the royal house of the Phoenicians.

The watchman said, "What business have you with the king of Sidon?"

"The usual documents." Elnathan patted the saddlebags lashed over the animal's haunches. "An agreement on water rights in the hill country in the hills above Samaria, some letters detailing the sale of horses from the herd of Judah in exchange for shipping rights on the Great Sea. Nothing out of the ordinary."

The watchman circled around behind the five riders in Elnathan's troop and when he came back to the front he said, "It doesn't take this many soldiers to deliver the mail."

Elnathan steadied his mount. "We're couriers."

"Outfitted like this?" The watchman turned his gaze over their swords sheathed in leather slips and tied to the saddles, the daggers sprouting from the lips of their boots, the bows strapped over their saddlebags, and steel-tipped arrows peaking above the soft leather brims of long quivers. Elnathan reined across the watchman's gaze. Cursed man. Why did he have to linger so long on their instruments of death?

Elnathan reined forward. "Are you going to let us pass or not?"

The watchman backed toward the gates, the parchment of his log falling over his forearm "You say you're couriers?"

"That's right. All of us."

The watchman turned his head into the parchment and made a note in his ledger. "Do you have any other business in the city beyond delivering mail?"

"Nothing." Elnathan started his horse trotting beneath the archway, motioning for his men to follow.

"I haven't released you."

"We have mail to deliver, sir."

The watchman walked alongside Captain Elnathan's horse. "I'll expect you to check here when you leave the city."

Elnathan reined through the main gates without answering. He came in past the shadows of the archway, through the plaza and into a narrow side street before coming around. He ordered one of his men up into the homes on the hills overlooking the city and another to check the markets. They were to search the streets for Jonathan the Blacksmith and any tall, thin boy resembling the prince with black hair cut straight across his brow. Elnathan hurried through his orders. If they found the prince, they were to bind him and ride out of the city without stopping for anyone. Elnathan glanced back at the main gate, his voice low enough that his men leaned forward in their saddles to hear his words. They weren't to stop, not even for the watchman at this gate. Nothing was to keep them from getting Mulek back to Jerusalem. He sidled in next to the largest soldier—the strongest man among the company, with a long, black cape hiding his broad shoulders and thick arms. The soldier pulled back his black hood, exposing his cap of dark hair. He was good with a bow, he knew how to use his sword, and he could chase down a fleeing child and pick him out of a crowd without getting out of the saddle, to say nothing of his skill at meting out a lethal dose of death. He was the best choice to send among the ruffian sailors and deckhands of Sidon's piers in search of the prince.

"You search the docks, and if you find the prince we'll meet you down the coast in the Cyprus groves where the creek empties into the sea." Elnathan came around in front of the remaining two soldiers in the company and ordered them to follow him. They had a mail delivery for the palace.

The dark-cloaked soldier reined across Elnathan's path. He said, "What about the blacksmith; what if he interferes with our taking of the prince?" He steadied his horse in the middle of the road. "What do we do with him?"

Elnathan kept one hand on the reins and he gripped the end of his bow with the other. He said, "Kill him."

Mima carried a steaming pot of tea out the side door of the main palace kitchens and down a run of white marble steps to the veranda, the hem of her new green and yellow wrap fluttering about her ankles. It was a perfect Ethiopian garment, and to think she got it in a Phoenician market. She ran her hand over the comfortable fitting gown. She may be the personal handservant to the Queen of Judah, but her tastes in clothing were far from drab Hebrew brown or boring Israelite gray. Mima pressed the cloth between her fingers. Color was the essence of life, and this new wrap certainly had power to cultivate her sensibilities of good dress to say nothing of flattering her rather large, fashionable frame. In the Ethiopian village of her childhood, a full-bodied girth was a sign of well-being and she dressed her robust health in the finest, most colorful cloth she could buy at market.

Mima stirred three spoons of honey into the mid-morning tea before sitting at the table on the edge of the veranda. Her chair faced the fish markets on the shoreline, over beyond the tall masts that hovered above the moored ships like skeletons waiting for sailors to pull up anchor, unfurl the sails, and clothe their dry bones with the meat of a hefty sea breeze. Mima leaned forward in her chair, straining to see through the timbers and ropes and pulleys of a hundred vessels. Where were Mulek and Prince Jesse? There was no sign of them walking along the point toward the palace amid the carts and riders headed this way. They couldn't have spent the entire morning at the fish market no matter how much the vendors enchanted Mulek by throwing their catch to the highest bidder. Mima shielded her eyes from the morning sun with her hand. She left Mulek with enough money to barter on a single fish, but catching it out of the air didn't require the entire morning, and the boys should have been well on their way across the man-made land bridge leading to the palace entrance. Mima shifted in her veranda chair, her gaze riveted on the road leading over from shore. Mulek loved the fish market as much as watching the sailing ships arrive in the harbor. The fish vendors threw their fresh catch to anyone who offered a price high enough to attract their tossing, and Mulek was certain to stay until he offered enough to attract the throw of a fish vendor. It was an odd custom to be sure, but the flying fish delighted the prince and he told Mima not less than three times this morning that today was the day he would catch her the largest one in the market. Foolish boy. He wasn't keen on the taste, but she could have the cooks hide whatever he brought home in a soup or bake it with some lamb. They certainly didn't need to purchase their own food, not while living among these royals where their every need was attended to by a host of servants and cooks and butlers, but Mulek would not return to the palace until he caught a fish. Mima allowed him this morning adventure, just so long as he returned before his tea went cold. He may be the prince of Judah, but she couldn't let him squander the day. There were reading and writing lessons to finish and a music lesson from the royal harpist. Mima poured some tea from the pot and raised it to her lips. How fortunate they were to enjoy the kindness of Jesse, Prince of Sidon. If Mulek hadn't befriended the boy the last time he was in Jerusalem, they could never hope to enjoy the luxury of this palace home. The tea was too hot and Mima set the cup down and fanned it with the back of her hand. Where were the two princes? They had until this tea went cold before she went to the markets to fetch them home and make sure they got their education.

A man in a black riding cape and boots started through the gardens beyond the veranda. He marched past the main steps, around a run of stone statues, and in beside the trees growing up along the edge of the wall, the morning breeze lifting his black hair off his brow. His strong stride carried him quickly over the marble porches and when he rounded the trunk of the last tree in the arbor Mima pushed away the pot of tea and stood. What was Jonathan the Blacksmith doing in Sidon? This wasn't good, not good at all, and she lowered her head. She had to keep the knowledge of Mulek away from this man who could betray them to Zedekiah and destroy the peace of this paradise they enjoyed far away from the strife in Jerusalem. Mima started down along the veranda toward the stairs leading to the lower balcony to escape his coming. Where was Mulek? She leaned over the railing to see if the prince was returned from the fish market without her seeing, but he was nowhere to be found playing about the boat launch. He wasn't running along the water's edge or swimming in the sea and she prayed he stayed in the fish market until she could send Jonathan on his way without him finding out that Mulek was here.

Jonathan cut off Mima's retreat, his hand gripping the veranda railing in front of her. "Where is he?"

"Jonathan the Blacksmith? What on earth are you doing here?" Mima primed the bright yellow bow in her hair. "You're so far from home, dear."

"Tell me what you've done with the boy." Jonathan stepped closer. His face was covered with sweat and his dark eyes narrowed on her. "There's little time to hide him."

Hide him? Why did Jonathan want to hide the boy? That was the very reason Mima brought him to Sidon.

Mima said, "I don't know what you're talking about, sir."

"I didn't ride from Jerusalem to play games with you. Now tell me . . ." Jonathan leaned over the railing and scanned the gardens below. "Where is the boy?"

"Who told you he was—"

"The boy's mother sent me ahead of a troop of Zedekiah's soldiers come to take Mulek back to Jerusalem." Jonathan nodded and his black hair fell over his brow.

"No one knows we're here."

"Listen to me." Jonathan took Mima by both arms. "We must hide the boy where they'll never find him."

Mima rushed across the veranda to the shore-side railing. She leaned up on her toes and scanned the land bridge leading over from the city. "Where are the soldiers?"

"They're not that far behind." Jonathan followed her across the veranda. "We should take Mulek away from the palace before the captain comes here looking for—"

"Mulek isn't here." Mima held her hands to her mouth and spoke through her fingers. "I left him in the fish markets with Prince Jesse."

"You what?"

"You've got to help me find him." Mima dried the tears from her cheeks. "We can't let them take the boy."

"Stay here and hide yourself until I return." Jonathan started across the veranda toward the steps and Mima hurried after him. She said, "I'm going with you."

"It isn't safe." Jonathan waved his hand in the air between them. "Captain Elnathan is searching for you as much as he's looking for the prince."

"Looking for me? Who told you that?" Mima hurried around in front of Jonathan, stopping him at the top of the steps leading down to the side gates of the palace. "Did Miriam tell you they were coming for both of us?" She set her hands on her hips. "Tell me everything Miriam told you."

Jonathan started past her, but Mima took him by the arm. "Tell me what the queen told you." She reached for his cheek and turned his face back toward her. His skin was wind blown and his lips chapped from so many days in the sun, but deep inside his dark eyes there was a kind, gentle expression that begged her to trust him. She said, "There's more, isn't there?"

"She wanted you to pray."

"For what?"

"Do you want me to find the boy or not?"

Mima tightened her grip on Jonathan's arm. "Not until you tell me the reason for my prayers."

"Jeremiah and Ezekiel are held in the palace prison, and Miriam wanted you to pray for them." Jonathan spoke slowly, the words catching in his throat. He lowered his head.

Jonathan pulled free of her grasp, scaled down the steps and marched across the gardens without another word about the prophets, but there had to be a reason Miriam wanted her to pray for the men of God. The Queen didn't send such petitions without needing help and though Jonathan didn't say Miriam needed Mima's help, there was more to this than the offering of a prayer. Mima scaled halfway down the steps, her hands gripping the railing. She had to do something—anything.

But what more could she do than pray for these men of God?

The smell of fish filtered through the open market and Jonathan prodded his steed through the crowd, the basket-laden women parting to let him pass. The fish carts lined the winding street, the shoppers shouting their offers and the fish merchants throwing their catch to the highest bidder. Jonathan kept his horse moving in behind the shoppers, scanning the crowd for Mulek, but there were no lads standing near the fish carts, no young boys running between the vendors or waiting their turn to catch the flying fish, and no high-pitched young voice making an offer. Jonathan reined past the last cart and into the main market where wheat- and pomegranate-laden carts stood alongside tables filled with linen, and when he cantered beyond the last cart in the row he spied one of Elnathan's men dressed in the gray military tunic of the Hebrew army entering the market on the far end.

Jonathan spurred into the shadows of a narrow side street and came around. The soldier didn't give any indication he'd noticed Jonathan. He moved slowly among the shoppers milling about the farmer's carts, scanning the faces in the crowd, his gaze stopping on every child in the market. Mulek was somewhere among these shoppers, but he couldn't continue his hunt for the prince with this man here. The rider drew closer, but before he passed by the alley, Jonathan sidled in against the limestone wall of the alley and lowered his head like a man bowed in reverent prayer.

He wasn't really praying. He was only hiding from this Hebrew soldier. No matter how strong the feeling deep inside his heart, praying wasn't one of his talents. It may have come easily to his son, but Aaron was dead and praying brought him nothing but heartache. Jonathan tightened his grip on the reins and steadied his horse against the cold stones in the wall. What good could come of begging the help of heaven? He had to search the city and find Mulek before Captain Elnathan caught the boy, not hope for some miracle from . . .

What was that voice? Someone called his name, he was certain of it and he brought his head up. It wasn't the Hebrew soldier. He was reining his horse a few paces from the alley, but his gaze was turned the other way and Jonathan quickly lowered his head. The voice that called his name had a quiet timbre, hardly audible, but he'd heard someone speak to him as clearly as the voice of a father calling his son. He steadied his horse. Whoever it was didn't approach him. There were no footsteps hurrying over the cobblestones, no one walking up the alleyway behind him, only a warmth penetrating to the center of his heart, begging him to ask God for help, but was it possible to ask such a thing? Did God bother himself with the troubles of men? And if He did, would He guide Jonathan to Mulek?

A farmer's cart loaded with grains and fresh vegetables turned out of the market and clattered down the alley past Jonathan, and since he was left with his head bowed, he could try to utter a prayer, couldn't he? Jonathan clasped both of his strong, calloused hands around the reins and offered the only plea he could think to utter. *For the good of Mulek, didn't God see the boy needed help and if there was any being in the heavens able to help, would He please send it now.* Jonathan kept his eyes closed, his lips slowly mouthing the silent words of his heart. Please God, if he were worthy of any mercy then help him to help Mulek. The creaking wheels of the farmer's cart startled Jonathan's horse and the animal sidestepped away from the wall. Jonathan tightened his hold on the reins, his head still down and his heart still turned toward heaven. He'd never had any need of help before now. He built his blacksmithing shop on his own and he provided for a family of seven without help from anyone, but finding Mulek was beyond what he could do for himself and the only place he could turn was heaven, pleading for the inspiration to find the boy before Elnathan and his men found him. Dear God, if there *was* a God, where could he find . . . ?

"Blacksmith?" The Hebrew soldier called from the market and Jonathan brought his head up to find him stringing an arrow onto his bow. The crowd kept the man from reining closer and Jonathan came around, spurring his horse down the alley. He reached the first turn when an arrow slashed through the air past his head and died against the stones in the wall before falling to the cobblestones. He never should have bothered to pray. The only attention his petition got was an arrow aimed at his head. He turned down an incline, past the gated entrances to these high-walled homes and out onto a small plaza with five narrow paths leading away in every direction. There was only the clatter of an approaching horse to force his hand.

Dear God, which way should he ride?

Mima hurried along the main palace hallway toward the servant's quarters where she was assigned a single room on the main floor with the window looking out onto the palace gardens. It wasn't as large as her room at the palace in Jerusalem, but she was a guest here and there was nothing but gratitude in her heart for the safety of this place. She set the key in the latch, turned the bolt, and as she pushed open the door the latch flew out of her hand and a man stepped from the shadows of her bedroom. He pressed his hand over her mouth and forced her inside, pulling the door shut with his foot and lighting the small lamp beside her bed with his free hand, the faint yellow light filtering over the stout frame of . . .

Captain Elnathan? Mima pulled his hand from her mouth. "What are you doing here, sir?"

"I think you know the answer." Elnathan stepped to the shuttered window and spoke through the wooden slats, asking the two soldiers in the courtyard if the way was clear. They answered there was no sign of the palace guards. The passageway leading to the side gates where they left the horses was clear, and there didn't appear to be anyone who could stop them from escaping.

The scuffle of shuffling feet and grunting voices filtered in through the window, and Elnathan leaned over the shuttered windowsill. "What's going on out there?"

There was no reply and Mima said, "I'm not going with you and neither is Mulek."

Elnathan pointed the tip of a dagger at her. "You'll do exactly as I say or you'll never see the boy alive again."

"You'll never find him."

"Don't play me for a fool." Elnathan pressed the edge of the blade against Mima's neck. "You're going to tell me where the prince is hiding or I'm going to—"

"He's gone."

"Take me to him."

"I'm telling you . . ." Mima leaned away from the sharpness of the blade. "The boy left early this morning and he's not returned."

"Where did he go?"

"He could be anywhere in Sidon."

"You're coming with us." Elnathan wrenched Mima's arm behind her back and walked her out the bedroom door and down the hallway. The white marble corridors of the palace were empty without a soul about to come to her aid or call for the palace guards to save her from this madman. He ushered her around the corner, out a small door at the end of the hall, and into the gardens where he said his men were waiting to . . .

"Where are they?" Elnathan pushed Mima ahead of him. "They were right there, outside your window."

Mima smiled. "They must have been frightened away."

"My men don't scare." Elnathan pulled Mima's arm higher on her back, and the pain wrenched through her shoulder. He started her walking across the gardens, past the palm trees growing in the shadows of the palace walls amid a canopy of white and red impatiens. They turned out of the gardens and under a stone-covered esplanade leading to a remote palace entrance when a man stepped onto the porch on the far end, the bright midday sun streaming under the stone arch and backlighting his tall, powerful figure, but it was impossible to see his face or his dress.

"There you are." Captain Elnathan pushed Mima along the esplanade, his voice echoing beneath the stonework. "Did you ready the horses?" He kept the dagger pressed to Mima's neck and said, "Where's your companion?"

"Put down your weapon, sir."

The man spoke with an eerily familiar voice, beyond the smooth rhythm of his brogue or the inflection that drawled his speech like the short, clipped language of the Phoenicians. Mima squinted into the light, searching to see the speaker's face, but she couldn't make out the details of this man with the sun streaming in behind him and falling down over his broad shoulders. There was no telling if this was a Hebrew soldier or a Phoenician palace guard or a man from any of a hundred nations bordering the Great Sea, though one thing was certain—he was her only hope to be free of Elnathan.

The captain stopped in the middle of the porch, the dagger still pressed to Mima's neck. "Out of my way or I'll see—"

"See that you let the woman go or you'll end up like your men." The man pointed over the edge of the porch to the side gates. Bound to the gatepost and gagged with the torn ends of a linen cloth were two Hebrew soldiers, half conscious and groaning from their bruises.

Elnathan pushed Mima away, throwing her against the stone column in the archway. He waved the dagger in the air between them. "Out of my way or I'll kill you."

The stranger started toward Elnathan, and the bright light of the sun faded in the shadows enough that Mima could see the face of . . .

Ebed-Melech? Mima held her hand to her breast, her heart beating quickly beneath her palm. It couldn't be him. The stranger had the same black skin, straight jawline, and powerful shoulders she remembered on Ebed, but it couldn't be her betrothed of so many years ago. Ebed was dead, lost at sea years ago, and though this stranger was dressed in the clothes of a sailor, this wasn't Ebed's ghost. He lunged for Elnathan, dodging the slashing of the captain's knife, grabbing him around the waist and throwing him down the short run of steps, his body twisting and turning over the hard marble and coming to rest against the trunk of a palm tree in the courtyard below. Ebed jumped over the railing, coming down beside Elnathan's sprawled body and landing three powerful blows across the man's jaw before dragging him to the gate. He bound the captain alongside the two other soldiers, tying his hands and feet with cords and telling him he and his men were going to spend the rest of their lives in a Phoenician prison cell, hundreds of miles away from Jerusalem and God be merciful to them—the Phoenicians were not kind to Jewish prisoners. Ebed wiped the sweat from his brow, his words ringing about the courtyard. "You're a fool for trying to harm this woman. No one will ever hurt her as long as I'm alive to protect her, don't you understand?" He leaned over the captain's dazed face. "If you ever try such foolishness again, you'll not live to tell about it."

"Ebed Melech?" Mima hurried down from the porch with her hand still pressed to her chest. "Is it really you?"

He smiled up at her in the soft light of morning sun, his white teeth gleaming between his dark lips. He said, "Where have you been hiding these past twenty years?"

Hiding? Mima ran to him, her green and red wrap rising about her legs. It was her betrothed, the man she never stopped loving, no matter how many years had passed since she thought him lost at sea. She fell into his arms and she would have leaned her head against his shoulder and savored this reunion, but the matter of her heart would have to wait a while longer.

Ebed said, "Are you happy to see me after so many—"

Mima pressed her finger to his lips and stopped his speaking. Of course she was pleased. He had no idea what joy this reunion caused. Having him close to her again filled her heart with unspeakable happiness. He was the man she loved, but there was one thing they must do before they could rekindle their love. It had been so long since she'd lost hope of ever seeing Ebed again, she'd stopped praying for that blessing. But Queen Miriam never stopped her prayers and could it be that God sent Ebed here in answer to the woman's cries for help. Mima was certain of it.

Mima gripped Ebed's strong arms. The prophet Jeremiah and Ezekiel needed the help that only a strong, courageous man like Ebed could provide. He may be a sailor, but this seaman of hers had the strength to deal with the king of the Jews. Mima stepped back from him, her hands in his calloused palms and her gaze rising and falling over his stout frame.

Mima said, "Will you go to Jerusalem for me?"

Mulek balanced his footsteps on the edge of the pier and held his arms out to keep Jesse from slipping ahead of him. This was the best game they had invented since throwing mud clods over the palace walls and onto the fishing boats passing in the harbor. One foul step off the narrow timber nailed along the edge and he'd forfeit this race to Jesse. And one misplaced step the other way and he'd end up in the water. Jesse may be older and faster, but Mulek had better balance, and he stayed ahead of his friend by a good three strides, hurrying toward the wooden pillar near the end of pier where the last of ten navy ships was untying from its mooring and setting sail into the deep blue waters of the Great Sea.

The worn timbers along the edge of the pier were coming up from the lashings and crumbling under Mulek's foot, but he kept moving like a bird skittering across the palace eaves with Jesse plodding behind him. The prince of Sidon climbed walls faster than Mulek, he scaled hills at twice Mulek's speed, and he jumped onto the bed of a mule cart without a running start, but his taller, thicker body didn't balance nearly as well as Mulek's.

Jesse caught up and pushed against Mulek, but he used the large fish he bartered for in the market this morning to counter the shoving and kept from falling over the edge.

"That's an awful smell." Prince Jesse tried to step past, but Mulek swung the tail fins at him, fending off his friend's attempt to get by. The fish smelled to the highest heaven, but he couldn't let go of it after promising Mima he'd bring home the largest fish from the market. And how would he ever convince her to add swimming to the reading and writing lessons he missed this morning if he returned to the palace without bringing home this prize? To say nothing of keeping Jesse from getting ahead of him.

Mulek held the fish out. "Stay back."

Jesse grabbed Mulek's fish-filled hand long enough to keep his balance and jump past Mulek.

"Why you . . . " Mulek hurried to keep up with Jesse, his sandals plodding in behind him. "You can't grab hold of me. It's against the rules."

"I took hold of the fish."

"Taking hold of the fish and taking hold of me is the same thing."

Mulek hurried to keep up with Jesse's longer strides. The wooden pillar marking the finish line to their race stood a few cubits down from a crowd of navy seamen unlashing the gangplank, throwing out the mooring ropes and shoving away the tall vessel. The unfurled sails and the rising anchor captured Jesse's attention long enough for Mulek to swing the fish around Jesse's waist, the weight of it holding him upright so he could jump ahead and take the lead on the narrow timber.

"You can't use the fish like that," Jesse shouted in Mulek's ear, loud enough that Mulek could feel his friend's breath streaming past.

Mulek kept his feet hurrying over the railing. "Swinging a fish isn't the same as taking hold of it."

"I should push you over."

"You can't." Mulek shook his head, but not so hard as to unbalance his steps. "It's against the rules." He lowered the fish to his side. "You're to make sure nothing ever happens to me. Remember what Mima tells you every morning? You're supposed to protect me from . . . "

Jesse's footsteps quieted, his quick breathing faded, and Mulek slowed but didn't stop. This could be a trick. It wouldn't be the first time Jesse found a way to jump ahead of him on the race down the dock and he kept going, hurrying over the narrow timber. He couldn't feel Jesse's closeness or see the length of his shadow along the pier. Jesse was falling behind and Mulek was going to win this race. He was three strides from the finish line when he glanced over his shoulder to find Jesse facing the shore, his shoulders pulled back and his gaze fixed on the horseman racing toward them.

Mulek spun around, his feet falling from the timber. He forfeited the race, but it didn't matter, not with the rider bearing down on Jesse. The rider's face was hidden in the shadows of the hood, his dark hair streaming out the side of the cloth. The powerful hooves of the steed thundered over the timbers, and the silver threads in the saddle outlined the pattern of the royal house of Judah in the leather. No, it couldn't be! Mulek slowly backed away, his shoulders coming up against the wooden post that was the end of the dock. He'd beaten Jesse, but this was a race they never should have run, not with this rider coming at them with the devices of death hanging from his saddlebags. The pleats and hems of his black riding cape rose and fell over the bow and arrows strapped to the horse's haunches, and the dockhands hauling their cargos jumped out of his unswerving path. There was no doubt. This rider was coming at them and Mulek gripped the wooden post. He wouldn't go back to Jerusalem and face the dangers he left behind in the kingdom of his father. Two more riders turned onto the pier off Harbor Street. They were dressed like the first, their black capes masking the Hebrew military tunics beneath. Their bows hung from their hands, notched with steel-tipped arrows and ready to fire.

Jesse turned around, his face white and his eyes wide as seashells. "Run Mulek! It's the men Mima warned us to watch for." He started down the pier toward Mulek, but his feet went out from under him, the decayed wood giving way and his body sprawling over the dock. Jesse picked himself up, his bleeding hands filled with splinters, and started running, but the first horseman came alongside and scooped him off the ground and set him on the saddle, his powerful arms holding him there.

The other two riders let go their arrows, one driving into the wooden pier short of Mulek and the other flying past and into the waters below. Jesse's broken cry filled the air. He said, "Run to the ship. Get help from the captain of the vessel."

Jesse's captor came around hard, the sudden turn throwing his head back and stopping his speech. The rider spurred toward Mulek, the powerful steed bearing down at full gallop. Mulek ran for the navy ship. The gangplank was drawn up, and the ship was pushing away from the pier, but it was wasn't so far away he couldn't beg the help of the sailors aboard and plead with them to lower the anchor and send out the gangplank and get the captain to come and save them from—

The rider grabbed Mulek by the collar of his shirt, lifted him off his feet, and without pulling up, the animal took the last lengths of the dock in two powerful strides before leaping off the edge of the pier. The blue water of the harbor came beneath Mulek with only the frail cloth of his shirt collar to keep him from falling from the grasp of his captor. They cleared the ship's railing hardly a hand length above the wooden palings and came down on the deck, a host of sailors gathering around them with their swords drawn. The navy captain marched down from the stoop, his cap in his hands and his beard brushing against his chest with each step. He pressed in past his sailors and pushed the muzzle of the horse aside. He said, "What's the meaning of this, sir? This is a ship of the king's navy."

"And this, sir . . ." The rider lifted Jesse down from the saddle and stood him next to Mulek. "Is the king's son." He pulled back his hood and there, emerging from the darkness of the black cloth was Jonathan the Blacksmith, the father of Sarah, the pretty girl from Jerusalem's Lower City.

"Your highness." The captain bowed.

Jonathan said, "How long are you going to sea?'

"A year, possibly longer."

"Take these boys with you."

"I can't do that."

Two arrows shot across the portside and the captain turned to the railing to find a pair of black-caped riders firing from the edge of the pier. "Who are those men?"

"That's not important. They'll be captured before they get out of Sidon. But there will be others."

"Others? I can't allow this to go unreported. Where did they come from and what do they want with Jesse and this other boy?"

"Listen to me." Jonathan got down from the saddle. "You can let me off at the next port down the coast, but these boys need you to take them far away from here for a season until it's safe for them to return to Sidon."

"This is highly irregular." Another arrow shot across the stern and the captain turned from the railing and ordered his men to return fire. He fitted his cap over his graying hair and straightened his navy tunic on his shoulders. "And you, sir. Why do you risk your life for these boys?"

Jonathan ran his hand through Mulek's straight black hair before pulling him close enough for Mulek to feel the warmth of the black-smith's body against his own. He said, "Because God once gave me a son like this."

CHAPTER 15

Jeremiah sat in the darkness of the lower prison, his arms wrapped around his knees and his stare riveted on the same foundation that for three months filled his view with nothing but gray stone. It had to be close to morning. A good while had passed since the prison hands left the unleavened scraps of dinner and it wouldn't be long before the water boy made his morning rounds ladling out a drink and offering them a taste of poorly cooked pottage.

Jeremiah shifted his weight to keep from leaning too long against the same damp stone. How much longer must he sit here wrapped in chains without standing to stretch his legs, and barred from adding his prophecies to the brass plates? Jeremiah coughed on the damp air. He had to find a way out, and God willing, he would find it before he went mad staring at the same three-cubit square of mold-infested limestone.

The oil-soaked rags of a torch offered the only light to this forgotten corner, the flame flickering from over behind the rounded pillars of this human vault, and the oil smoke smothering what little fresh air he shared with his cellmate. Ezekiel lay next to him, his head propped against the wall, his back supported by rough-hewn stone and his arms tangled in chains that wrapped about him like a fisher's net. The rise and fall of his chest pushed against the metal links and the sound of it filled the chamber with the chiming of his sleep. Somehow Ezekiel managed to rest at night, though it was hard to know nightfall from dawn and there was no way to tell exactly how long the man slept while Jeremiah coughed through the night. He rubbed his brow to rid himself of the pain that accompanied his fevers. Thank heaven Ezekiel hadn't yielded to the same hacking that had plagued Jeremiah since coming to this basement vault. The aching in his limbs never ceased and he rocked back and forth with his knees drawn up close to his chest, his eyes closed and his mind searching for an escape. It was the only way to keep his head clear of the sickness that tempered his vigor. How could he get out of here? There was only one stairwell leading to the upper prison and from there a single doorway to his freedom. And what about the sewer and water tunnels running below the prison? There had to be an access from within this chamber, but where was it, and if he found it where would it lead him? Jeremiah kept rocking, his eyes closed to the dimness around him. He had to carefully plan his escape. The prison water boys with their buckets of cool water passed at midday and again in the evening, ladling out their rations; the prison help threw them their food at midmorning and again in late afternoon. And then there were the guards. As best he could tell, they changed by the light of the sun, but in this dark chamber there was no telling if it were dawn, midday, or dusk and he was going to have to find another way to calculate their movements about the prison and slip past them—a task that was becoming more impossible with the weakening of his body. Jeremiah coughed on the bad air of the vault. And what about these chains? He rattled them against the stone. They were so tight about his wrists he couldn't slip his thin hands through, and only the jailer had a key. He was a hobbled man but with a terrible temper, and he kept the keys to the prison doors tied around his neck, never letting them out of his sight. Jeremiah set his chin on his knees, his body slowly rocking and the chains of his confinement dragging over the ground beside him. How would he ever get out of this prison to fulfill his . . .

What was that? Jeremiah brought his head up and scanned the shadows, but there was no one in this alcove at the back of the catacombs to speak the name of Hanameel. That was his cousin, a wealthy landowner in Anathoth, but why would Hanameel's name come to him with such power when he was thinking so deeply about escaping? Hanameel was not given to Jeremiah's dislike of the Kingdom—it wasn't a profitable venture. For a good many years Jeremiah had asked his cousin to sell him the field adjacent to his vineyards and every year Hanameel declined to come down off an unspeakable sum of money for the sale. Hanameel was as unyielding on the price as he was on his opinions in support of the kingdom. What an odd thing his cousin's name would come to his mind deep in the depths of this prison—a place the wealthy Hanameel would never venture.

Jeremiah lowered his head back to his knees, the cold chains hanging from his limbs. Hanameel's name came again, this time more forcefully than before, telling him that his cousin would sell the field he had refused to sell for so many years. Jeremiah turned to his cell-mate, but it wasn't Ezekiel speaking. He was still sleeping and there was no one standing in the corridor leading from the main chambers of the lower prison to speak these unbelievable words. The solitary torchlight flickered without any shadows of men passing beneath its light, and Jeremiah leaned back against the wall, coughed on the damp air, and closed his eyes to rest before the water boys came to offer him a . . .

There it was again, but Jeremiah didn't open his eyes to search the prison for the source of the words. He let the soft, soothing voice fill his mind with the message that Hanameel would come to this prison and ask Jeremiah to purchase the field for the price of seventeen pieces of silver. The voice was hardly audible to his mind, but before it faded, it told him that the sale of this property was a sign that, though the Jews would suffer seventy years of captivity in Babylon, they would return to build houses and fields and vineyards in this land again. Jeremiah leaned back against the stone, his eyes still closed to the dimness around him. Could this be? Was Hanameel really going to sell Jeremiah his property while he was languishing in the prison without even the means to purchase a drink of water or a morsel of—

"Jeremiah, wake up, sir." A hand shook him by the shoulder and he opened his eyes, blinked in the dimness, and found a dark-cloaked figure standing above him, the light of the torch silhouetting the outline of narrow shoulders and a high pointed hood. It was a whispered voice, barely audible, with the words dying against the stone. The long black hair of a woman cascaded out from under the hood and over her shoulders. She parted the vents of black cloth in her cloak to uncover a basket of food, revealing the finely tailored royal vestments beneath, her white pleats and skirts sewn with silver threads, trimmed with lace, and tied with elegant sashes. It was Miriam, Queen of Judah, and she held out a pot of steaming tea and told Jeremiah it would ease his suffering until she could get him out of this damp place where he could heal. Ezekiel stirred from his rest and she offered him the basket with a jar of fresh goat's milk, two rounds of warm bread from the palace kitchens, a bit of cheese, a bowl of dates, fresh lemons, and nuts. It was more food than they'd been fed in weeks and Ezekiel pressed the lemons to his lips before taking a drink of goat's milk, his shaking hands spilling the life-giving liquid down his chin.

The jailer stood behind the queen, over beneath the torch, the oily smoke swirling about his bent-over frame. Miriam said, "Is he treating you well?"

Jeremiah lowered his rasping voice to a whisper. "You must deliver us from this place. I have to finish the plates, My Lady."

Miriam brushed back a tear from her cheek. "I am doing what I can."

"Please, help us." Jeremiah reached for the hem of Miriam's robe, but his chains held him back, the sudden clang bringing the jailer down the corridor.

"Stand aside My Lady. I told you he was a violent man." The jailer pointed his sword at Jeremiah and ordered him to back away or suffer the piercing of cold metal.

Miriam said, "Must you keep them chained like this?"

"You don't want to risk it any other way." The jailer shook his head, and graying thatches of uncombed hair fell into his eyes. He passed his hand over the ring of keys around his neck—the only keys to the doors and vault and shackles of these catacombs. "You unlock their chains, give them a little freedom and you're asking for more trouble than any of these creatures are worth. They'll try to escape I tell you, and when they do, it won't be a pretty sight watching Captain Laban remove my head."

Miriam handed the jailer two pieces of silver and asked if he would allow her to speak with Jeremiah in private, but the man didn't leave. He stared at the coins in his hand until Miriam added two more to his palm.

The jailer stuffed the money into his purse and backed down the corridor, the tip of his sword pointed at Jeremiah. "No tricks, do you hear me? I'm watching you. I don't want any trouble from this or I'll see both of you thrown into the well of the prison. The queen was kind enough to bring you food and water and . . ." He tapped his purse and the coins jangled about. "You see you give the woman the respect she's paid for."

Miriam waited for the jailer to disappear around the last stone column before turning back to Jeremiah. She said, "I have a plan."

Jeremiah peered past her to where the jailer disappeared, then turned back to Miriam and said, "Does it have anything to do with my land?"

"How did you know that?"

Jeremiah slowly rocked back and forth, his hands around his knees. "Go on, tell me what you came to tell me."

"Do you know the custom around the sale of land?"

Jeremiah nodded. "The Ceremony of Sale."

"There will be a grand ceremony in the chambers of the upper prison. All the princes and nobles and lords of the palace will attend. The law requires it of them."

"A ceremony in this prison?" Jeremiah leaned forward to see past Miriam, but there was no one waiting to spy on them. "Is there a reason for such a thing?"

"You're buying land."

Could it be? Were the words of his revelation coming to pass so quickly? Jeremiah said, "How will this free us."

"The sale is a diversion." Miriam leaned over, close enough to whisper. "It should distract the guards from their regular duties long enough for us to unlock your chains and open the sewers to get you out of here."

Jeremiah grabbed Miriam by the arm. He spoke breathless words. "Do you have keys to the sewers?"

"Not yet."

"But you know someone who has keys."

"The jailer."

Jeremiah let go of her hand and leaned back against the stone wall. No prisoner had ever wrestled the keys from the jailer without paying with his life. "You'll not get them from him. The only time he ever removes them from around his neck is when he's locking a prisoner into these." Jeremiah held up his shackles. "He's not the sort of man to leave them about unattended."

"Except when he drinks his wine."

"How do you know that?"

"I know everything about everyone who works in the palace." Miriam glanced back into the corridor and when the jailer wasn't anywhere to be seen she said, "We'll have plenty of wine for the man when the time comes." She leaned forward, her hands clasped and the pleats of her cloak falling over her wrist. "We're going to need a good scribe to attest to the transaction. I've asked Zoram to—"

"No, not him. You can't ask him to help. I don't want him to have anything to do with this. They could find out he's my son and then . . ."

"She already has, Father." Zoram stood beside the stone pillar, his dark-skinned face silhouetted by the torchlight. He stepped past Miriam and fell down on his knees next to Jeremiah, his strong arms wrapped around his father's bony frame. "What have they done to you?"

"You shouldn't be here, son." Jeremiah's wrapped his trembling arms around Zoram's white-robed frame. "They can never know. No one can ever . . ."

"That isn't for you to worry about." Zoram leaned back from holding Jeremiah, his green-eyed gaze piercing the shadows. "I have another scribe, a man we can trust to help us in this matter."

"Trust no one, son. You must be certain before you put your faith in any scribe but yourself. There are treacherous men everywhere in this city."

"Do you know Baruch?"

Ezekiel stirred from his sleeping place in the shadows. "Baruch is a man you can trust." He leaned in close to Jeremiah. "He's one of the only men in this city I would ever trust again."

Jeremiah said, "Trust him to do what?"

A man stepped down along the corridor, a leather parchment hanging from his hand. He was dressed in fine blue and white linens with gold rings about his fingers and a silver amulet hanging from his neck. His black hair was combed in place with costly olive oils and he was freshly bathed, the scent of frankincense crowding out the musty smell of this basement vault.

Jeremiah said, "Hanameel? Is that you, Cousin?"

"It is." Hanameel stood away from the shadows, careful not to let his garments brush against the filthiness of the stone pillars. "I never thought we'd finally agree to do business in a place like this, Cousin."

Jeremiah said, "What business are you talking about?"

Miriam said, "You've wanted to purchase the land next to your vineyards for years."

Jeremiah sat up straight and peered at his cousin through the shadows. Could it be? Was God fulfilling the very words whispered to him this morning? He said, "I can't afford to purchase your land."

"What? I thought we had an agreement?" Hanameel came around in front of Miriam. "I won't sell my land for anything less than the selling price." He shook his head. "I never should have believed I could sell property to a prisoner."

"I have your money, sir." Miriam handed Hanameel a purse, the coins jangling about inside. "Now go on, recite the words required by law."

Hanameel opened the purse and once he'd counted the money inside he cleared his throat, his gaze flitting between Miriam and Jeremiah. He spoke quickly, the words falling from his lips in a hurried rhythm of rehearsed recitation—words Hanameel uttered in his profession every time he offered property for sale. He said, "Will you buy my field, I pray thee, that is in Anathoth, in the country of Benjamin?" He waved his hand in the air as he spoke. "The right of inheritance will be yours, the right of redemption will be yours, and you are free to buy it for yourself and for your—"

"Exactly how much do you want for the land, cousin?"

Hanameel shook the money purse, the coins softly jangling inside the leather pouch. "Exactly this much."

Jeremiah leaned forward, his ear turned to his cousin's speech. "And exactly how much is that?"

Hanameel turned to Zoram. "We agreed on seventeen pieces of silver, didn't we?"

"Glory be to God!" Jeremiah clasped his hands together, the chains clattering about his arms and forcing Hanameel back a step.

Not an hour had passed since Jeremiah heard the voice of heaven telling him he would purchase Hanameel's property for that very amount. "The Jews will be conquered and held captive for seventy years, but they will return to inhabit this place again and build houses and own vineyards—the sale of this land is witness of that." Jeremiah closed his eyes and offered his silent thanks to God for confirming to his heart that none of his prophecies need be changed. All that he'd spoken of the destruction of Jerusalem, the deportation of the Jews to Babylon and their return seventy years later would come to pass. He was as certain of that as he was of his release from this prison. The word of God would be fulfilled.

Jeremiah tugged on the hem of Hanameel's robe. "Do you have the documents?"

"Of course I have them. I never conduct business without preparing the finest." Hanameel waved the double-sealed scroll in the air, the top portion sealed with a splattering of beeswax and the bottom portion hanging open, the description of the property written across the front and waiting for the final seal and signature to finalize the purchase. "I've already begun preparations for the purchase ceremony." He glanced about the confines of the lower prison. "We can't host it down here. There isn't enough light, it's far too damp to be comfortable, and I don't know a single prince in this city who would dare set foot in this place." He nodded. "I've made arrangements to use the court of the upper prison and with so many invited guests, there will have to be plenty to eat." He turned to Miriam. "There will be food and wine, won't there?"

"More than enough, sir." Miriam nodded. "That's something my husband *will* allow."

"Very well." Hanameel stuffed the double-sealed document under his arm. "I've had enough of this place."

Miriam called for the jailer and when he came down the corridor she told him to see that the prison was in order to conduct a sale of property in two weeks' time.

"I don't like this." The jailer scratched the side of his head, the keys to the prison jangling about his neck. "I don't like this at all."

"What isn't there to like?" Hanameel started down the corridor through the shadows, his voice fading with each step. "This will be the finest Ceremony of Sale of my career and to think it's going to take place in a prison."

The jailer hurried after him, the man limping into the dimness and his lantern raised ahead of his faltering stride, telling Hanameel what foolishness this was.

Miriam leaned her head in close to Zoram, Jeremiah, and Ezekiel. She turned her gaze between them and whispered that all would be well, she would see that they got out of this place. She said, "Be ready. You'll need all your strength. It will come swiftly."

The queen disappeared with Zoram down the narrow corridor, the sound of their leaving fading like the dripping of water through these seeping stone walls and leaving Jeremiah with his thoughts. God would deliver the Jews, of that he was certain, and this purchase of property was further proof of God's watchful eye over the details of their lives. But Miriam was making more of this purchase of property than a simple reminder that God was keeping watch over His people. She was going to turn the sale of property into the deliverance he'd prayed, the deliverance that would allow him and Ezekiel to finish recording his prophecies on the brass plates.

The queen was arranging their escape.

CHAPTER 16

Josiah the Potter stood on the salt-laden shores of the Dead Sea. The sun hung above the cliffs of Qumran, the last hot rays of afternoon angling over him and casting a dying shadow across the men from camp gathered in a circle about him. The beach was an odd place for a meeting of the council, but it was far enough from the ears of camp that they could speak their mind.

Lehi the Olive Oil Merchant stood with his arms folded and his ear turned to his eldest son, Laman. The boy mumbled something about not wanting to waste his time listening to Josiah preach another sermon, but Lehi quieted him with a wave of his hand and turned his gaze toward Josiah, nodding his support for this hasty gathering of the council. Three carpenters sidled into the circle next to Lehi, pushing shoulder to shoulder along with the stonemason and his eldest son. The bricklayers, two architects, and a host of laborers found their way down the beach, the low rumble of voices filling the air with muted questions over the reason for calling the council together at this hour when there was still enough light to keep working.

These men toiled in the heat of the desert day after day to raise a city out of sand. Only yesterday water began flowing in the canal running down from the cliffs and into a string of four pools—one for drinking, another for bathing, and two more for watering animals and irrigating the grains they were to plant in the higher soils away from the saltiness of this shoreline. With the aqueduct finished, they could turn their efforts to raising the buildings from their foundations and, God willing, one day they would build a city here, but not now, not after Schechem found their camp.

"Is it true, sir?" The stonemason leaned forward, a chisel hanging from one hand and a hammer from the other. "Is Captain Laban coming?"

"This is Babylonian territory." The carpenter waved his finger in the air. "He'd not dare bring his armies into this wilderness and risk angering them."

"We can't hope that the Babylonians will keep him from hunting us." Josiah ran his gaze over the council, their heads leaning in. "We need to leave Qumran."

A murmur of voices passed over the gathering, their questions filling the late afternoon air with concern. The bricklayer wanted to know if there was no other way? They'd risked so much to come here, couldn't they stand and defend this land or pray the Babylonians would keep Laban from venturing into this desert?

The stonecutter said, "How soon could Laban mount a patrol to this land?"

"I have a young family." The brick mason pushed his dark hair off his brow. "We came here to begin a new life."

The stonemason dropped his chisels in the sand. "How will we ever start over again?"

"No one's starting over." Josiah raised his voice above the din of conversation and when the gathering fell silent he said, "We're coming back to this place. Do you hear me?" He stepped into the center of the circle, turning slowly around to face each man in the council. "We're going to hide this city from the eyes of men for a season, and when we get word that Captain Laban is no longer hunting us, we'll come back here and we'll build this city. It may not be right away. We may wander in these deserts for a time, but our dreams will rise on this desert shore and we'll write on scrolls of leather and metal and clay so that our children who come after us will know of our faith in God." Josiah raised his hands to the cliffs behind him. "One day we'll preserve in the caves above our homes a record that we lived and we looked forward to the coming of the Messiah." He slowed his speech before reciting the words of the *Shema*. If there was ever a time that required the speaking of that powerful verse recorded by Moses, this was the moment. Josiah spoke it twice daily in his morning and evening prayers, but until he faced abandoning this outpost in the desert, he'd not had reason to depend so completely on heaven. These ancient words of Moses had power to point his heart toward divine help and Josiah lowered his head, both hands raised in the air in front of him. He said, "And when we return to build this city we'll do it with all our hearts and all our souls and all our might."

The men in the circle quietly repeated the *Shema*, intoning their love of the Lord and committing to show that love with all their hearts and all their souls and all their might, and when they finished reciting the verse the stonemason retrieved his chisels from the sand. He said, "How will we hide this city from Captain Laban?"

"We'll use what we have before us." Josiah stabbed his toe into the ground, kicking up a flurry of sand. "You sir, with your sons and help from the other masons and bricklayers will cap the spring with stones and fill in the aqueduct." He laid his hand on the carpenter's shoulder. "And you along with the other artisans will cover the building foundations on the north end with more sand while the rest of us do the same with the foundations on the south side." He raised his forefinger in the air. "Remove any sign of what we've built on this ground. Qumran must appear untouched by the hand of man until we return and start again where we left off." He reached down and picked up a handful of sand, the grains sifting between his fingers. "When Captain Laban and his armies come, they'll find nothing but dry earth where now stands the beginning of our dream."

The bricklayer said, "Where will we go?"

A rush of possibilities rose from the crowd, the carpenter asking if he should take his family and return to Jerusalem? No one in the capital city knew he was a Rekhabite and they could fit themselves back into life there without any trouble. The brick mason spoke above the sound of the carpenter's questions, telling him that it was too dangerous for some of them to think they could return to Jerusalem after leading their neighbors to believe they were dead. Jericho was a fine place to live. It stood at the head of the trade route and if there was any need to escape into the southern wilderness, it wasn't more than a few days ride into less governed territories. The stonemason spoke of his desire to return to a better life and if he couldn't do it in Jerusalem, then why not Hebron or Bethlehem?

There was plenty of work for a trained artisan and he could make a good wage and bide his time in the peaceful company of—

"There will be no peace in Jerusalem or any of the cities round about her." Lehi the Olive Oil Merchant stepped inside the circle next to Josiah, the breeze lifting the end of his robe about his legs. He raised his hands, and wide cuffs fell down about his arms. "This is a large wilderness. You have your sheep and your tents and you can make a good life for yourselves until it's safe to return here."

The stonemason said, "Are we to live the life of Bedouins?"

Lehi nodded. "That would be better than what will become of you in Jerusalem or anywhere in her borders."

"But sir, we had a comfortable life there."

"You'll find little comfort in the years ahead." Lehi raised his voice above the breeze rolling off the Dead Sea. "You're better off living the life of a nomad in these deserts than living at Jerusalem."

Josiah said, "It should take us two days to cover the foundations with sand, maybe three. As soon as you've finished your part in this, you are free to leave with your family."

Lehi said, "No large groups that will attract the attention of Captain Laban and the Babylonians. Let them think you're nothing more than Bedouins searching out lands to graze your sheep. There's plenty of water in the southern hill countries of Judah where you can live comfortably."

"What about our family?" Laman pushed past the stonemason and stepped inside the circle of men, his thick shoulders squared to his father. "Are you taking us to the southern hill country of Judah?"

"Son." Lehi raised an open palm to Laman. "We can discuss our plans later."

"Why not now?" Laman slowly turned his gaze over the circle "These men deserve to know our plans."

Lehi said, "We'll stay here with Josiah until the camp is cleared. We can't leave behind any evidence of where we've gone."

"Do you fear Captain Laban that much?"

Josiah stepped closer to Laman, close enough to see into the boy's eyes. When did the eldest son of Lehi become so outspoken? He'd hardly uttered a word since arriving here a few months back, and now look at him, questioning his father in front of the council, no less. Josiah said, "The only one your father fears is God."

Laman turned the force of his words onto Josiah. "Then why don't you have heaven deal with Captain Laban and let us go home and live in peace?"

Josiah said, "It isn't that simple, son."

"Do you think living in this desert is a simple thing?" Laman raised his voice so loud that the sparrows nesting in the cliffs above them took to flight.

"Enough of this." Josiah raised his hands to the men of the council. "These are difficult decisions for all of us. Go to your tents. Speak with your families and decide where you'll go to find safety."

The circle of men dissembled and started up the beachhead, but Laman didn't join them. He pushed past Josiah and stepped in next to his father. "You're wrong about Captain Laban. He'll let us live as we please." He raised his voice loud enough that the men of the council slowed their departure and listened from the sandy paths leading up the shore to camp. "As long as we don't bother the man, we're safe to return to our homes." He raised his hand to the departing council. "I say we go back to Jerusalem—return to our lands and our inheritance and live out our lives in comfort instead of wasting away in this desert."

"Please, son. You don't understand." Lehi reached for his arm, but Laman backed away from Lehi's reaching and said, "I'm not forsaking the comforts of our life in Jerusalem for this, this . . ." He kicked his boots at the sand, raising a cloud of grit in the air. "What's to become of us?"

Lehi came around in front of Laman, the man's gaze riveted on the boy—on Laman's dark, narrow eyes.

"Don't look at me like that." Laman turned away from Lehi's staring. "I don't like it when you look at me like that."

Lehi lowered his voice soft enough that only Laman and Josiah could hear him say, "We face a fate much worse than Captain Laban if we return to Jerusalem."

Lehi left his son standing on the shores of the Dead Sea and started past Josiah. Poor man, he'd come to Qumran to save his family from Laban and he certainly didn't need his eldest son questioning his resolve, no matter what fate he feared. How long had this rebellion festered in the boy? Josiah slowly followed after Lehi, the olive oil merchant's footsteps brushing over the sandy beach, the sound of it unable to break the trance of council members, as their gaze followed each step and their eyes betrayed a silent longing to know what Josiah wanted to know.

Josiah pulled up near the top of the beach and let Lehi disappear over the rise. He couldn't bother Lehi with more questions, not after his son's public pestering, but he couldn't let go of Lehi's words. They stayed in his mind and penetrated to the very center of his soul.

What fate could be worse than Captain Laban's revenge?

The desert sun fell behind the hills and cast long shadows across Sariah's view. She stood in the entrance to the family tent, waiting for Lehi to return. Where was that man? The council meeting should have ended by now, but there was no sign of her husband returning home. Daylight was fading to darkness, but Sariah would not be left to worry in the shadows of evening. She pulled the leather flaps shut and lit the large oil lamp that hung from the center pole. Lehi told her the council was deciding on the future of Qumran and she prayed that future wasn't anything like what her husband recorded in his journal. The saddlebags sat in the corner of the tent and Sariah picked over the stack of leather straps and pouches until she found the one holding Lehi's parchments. She lifted out the writing box and let the dim lamplight cast over the drawing of a date tree etched into the yellow olive wood. The new leather hinges on the lid didn't squeak when she opened it and the smell of freshly cut wood filtered up from inside the long wooden compartment.

Two completed scrolls sat on the top shelf and a third one Lehi had yet to finish was wrapped in a red silk—the one recording the coming desolation of Sariah's precious homeland. She lifted the unfinished scroll from the box, leaned back against the center pole of the tent and pressed the parchment against her breast. If her husband's prophecy was to be believed, and she had no reason not to trust his judgment, then what would become of their home at Beit Zayit? Her two eldest daughters still lived there with Ishmael's family and they couldn't simply abandon them to an unspeakable fate. Sariah lowered her head, her chin resting on the scrolled end of the soft leather document. There must be something she could do to warn them.

The tent flap pulled aside and a gust of air rushed in with Lehi. He didn't offer a smile or a word of greeting. His brow was furrowed and when he saw the scroll she held against her chest he moved toward her.

"What did the council decide?" Sariah stood away from the tent pole and secured the parchment under her arm.

Lehi didn't answer. He slowly took the scroll from her, found a pen from the writing box and sat down beside her, the soft leather scroll spread over his legs, his back set against the tent pole and the pen quickly scratching over the parchment. Sariah stood above him, careful not to block the lamplight and cast a shadow over his scroll. The words he wrote a few days back were still inked across the top of the parchment. The details of a looming Babylonian war were set in dark ink as black as were the horrible predictions of sieges and the leveling of Jerusalem. Sariah quickly passed her gaze over those awful warnings and stopped on the fresh words forming in the wake of Lehi's pen. There was a line about Shechem's discovery of their hideout at Qumran and another about waiting with Josiah the Potter to see the camp was cleared of every evidence of their living here before heading north around the Dead Sea, then east to the King's Highway and south through Moab to find safety at a small outpost city called—

"You must take us home to Beit Zayit." Laman stood in the tent entrance, his shoulders squared to Lehi.

"Son, why don't you call your brothers?" Sariah got out five rounds of bread from a basket. Her hands began to tremble, and she quickly set down the bread, together with a jar of goat's milk, before letting her hand slip down across her womb. She was a good many months along and if they had to make another journey farther from home, could she endure the hardship? Sariah adjusted her robe across her front. This poor unborn child had endured so much in the first months of life, how could the babe possibly endure more? Sariah said, "We can talk about the future over evening meal."

"There's no future to talk about." Laman stepped so close she could feel his breath against her cheeks. "Father's already made his decision without asking any of us." He sidled in next to the tent pole, his thick body shielding the lamplight and casting a shadow over Lehi's parchments. "Isn't that right, Father?"

The shadows didn't deter Lehi from his writing. He turned his head down and moved his pen quickly over the scroll, stopping only long enough to ink the tip before adding more lines to the record.

Laman said, "I asked you a question, Father."

"You know we can't stay here any longer." Sariah stepped between them, her soft voice mixing with the scratching of her husband's pen. "Captain Laban knows we're here."

"Do you believe everything Father tells you?" Laman leaned forward to see past her, his voice filling the tent with the harshness of his speech. Her eldest son was an independent soul, but he wasn't disrespectful; she wouldn't allow him that. She'd raised him better.

"Laman." Sariah took him by the arm. "Why don't you speak with your father once he's finished with his writing."

"I'll speak with him now." Laman pulled free. "It's time he took us home."

"It isn't safe at Beit Zayit, son. You know that." Sariah shook her head. "Captain Laban won't allow it."

"He's after father, not us." Laman shook his forefinger at Sariah. "You should be home at Beit Zayit with Rachel and Leah and a host of nursemaids to care for your unborn child. Not here in this good-for-nothing wasteland." He kept his finger jabbing at the air between them. He said, "Is it too much to ask that we return home?"

Sariah slowly turned to her husband, the hem of her robe brushing across his sandals, but not disturbing his hurried writing. His head was still down and he worked the pen over the parchment like a scribe rushing to finish a tax record.

Sariah said, "Dear, why don't you share with Laman what you shared with me?"

Lehi finished two more lines of writing before setting aside his pen and standing with the scroll draped over his arms, the ink soaking into the parchment fibers. He held it out to Laman and the boy snatched it from him, the soft leather stretched between his hands. He hurried his gaze over the writings beginning near the top where only last week Lehi recorded his predications of the coming destruction to their homeland.

"This is foolishness." Laman brought his head up. "The Babylonians will never destroy Jerusalem. Where did you get these ideas?" He shook the parchment. "Tell me this isn't another of your dreams."

"Read on, son." Sariah patted Laman on the hand.

Laman ran his gaze over Lehi's freshly penned words and when he reached the last phrase he said, "Bozrah?"

"That's right." Lehi came around and stood next to his son. "It stands at the crossroads of the trade route leading into Arabia."

"You don't mean this." Laman lowered the scroll to his side. "That's farther from home."

"It's a reasonably safe place. We can replenish our supplies there and bide our time."

Laman ran his hand through his hair, the black locks pressed between his fingers. "You can't do this to Mother. Look at her. She's in no condition to travel about the country like a bedouin."

Sariah said, "I'll do whatever your father thinks best."

Laman rolled Lehi's parchment into a tight scroll. "Is this your last word?"

"This is what's best for us."

"How do you know what's best for any of us?"

Lehi stepped to the door of the tent and held back the flaps. The last rays of sun colored the sky orange, the light silhouetting the distant six-thousand-foot peaks of the Jabal Range marking the borders of Arabia, the blue-black mountains a small swell on the southern horizon. The Jabal Range bordered the beginning of the Arabian Peninsula like a giant wall, warning any who ventured beyond it that here lay the harshest lands on earth. Lehi said, "Somewhere out there we'll find a place of refuge."

"No man can live in that country." Laman threw the parchment at his father's feet. "It was a dream that brought us to this awful wilderness and now your dreams will take us farther from home and deeper into madness."

"Laman." Sariah bent to pick up the parchment, but a sharp pain shot through her womb and she stayed upright, her hand pressed against her side. "You're to respect your father, do you hear me?"

Laman turned his gaze between Sariah and Lehi, his lower lip trembling and his fists clenched at his side. He was a powerful boy, but he would never used his strength against them—would he? Sariah reached to take him by the arm, but he backed out the entrance of the tent. He said, "Father's making a mistake. A very dangerous mistake."

Laman disappeared into the evening.

CHAPTER 17

A single lamp hung from the wall of the registry, but Darius, chief mapmaker of the New Babylonian Territories, didn't complain about leaving the open windows of his office on the main floor of the governor's mansion to work in this dimly lit vault. It was a hot summer afternoon in Jericho and the cool recesses of this underground archive were a refreshing relief from the heat of the day.

A chest of leather parchments sat on the shelf in the corner and Darius walked the vessel back to the table under the faint, yellow lamplight, removed the sealed lid, and began his search for the map detailing the southern frontier. The inspector asked to see it today, but it was the last map of this conquered kingdom of the Jews Darius had yet to finish and he couldn't let the inspector have it until it was complete, or at least until he ferreted out the inaccuracies.

Eight months of exploring these territories, finding the water sources, and traveling the trails was plotted into these newly rendered maps, every pen stroke calculated to steer a supply company down the proper route or reassure a military patrol they could find water exactly where his map indicated. And then there were the couriers— the true test of his mapmaking skills. If they cursed the inaccuracies of his maps then he'd spend a good many more months revising and rewriting these parchments; but if they praised the trueness of the distances between the cities, lauded the exactness of his plotting of the water supplies, and commented on the fine orientation of the roadways and trails through the mountain passes, then Darius was certain to have finished the finest rendering of these Babylonian possessions to ever see the ink of a pen, at least every possession but the ones that remained a mystery—the uncharted lands of the Arabian Peninsula.

Darius carefully removed the map of the territory northwest of Jericho and spread it across the table. None of his ink lines detailing the coast along the Great Sea had faded, his illustration of the shipping docks at the seaport in Sidon held its ink nicely, and the elevations of Mount Carmel were without errors. Darius lifted the next scroll out of the cistern—the one detailing the lands directly north of Jericho—and laid it over the first. The ink lines depicting the Jordan River Valley were faded, sopped into the new leather like water into sand, and he uncorked an ink bottle and sketched over the banks, widening the lines in the main channel and touching up the shoreline around the Sea of Galilee before setting it on the drying shelf. If this leather didn't hold the ink better, he was going to have to switch from ox hide to sheepskin.

Darius slowly lifted the third map from the clay jar, careful not to mar the edges. He spread the large leather parchment over the table, the corners of it falling over the edges of the wooden planks and revealing little more than a few detailed lines near the top around his plotting of the city of Jericho marked with the star of Babylon, and noting the place as the headquarters of the New Babylonian Territories. Darius gripped the edge of the table and leaned over the map, his shadow casting over the leather. What was he going to tell Inspector Tobit? This map was dreadfully incomplete, with hardly any detail and none of the plotted wells, wadis, or mountain passes were checked for accuracy. He charted the King's Highway properly, but that was a route that the cooks in the kitchen could draw—everyone knew the twists and turns of the hundred-mile stretch of trade route between Jericho and the military outpost city at Bozrah to the south. It was an odd name for a well-traveled roadway through the plateau country of Moab, but since he'd not been told by his superior officers to find another name, he wrote King's Highway in bold letters down along his map, the words paralleling the shores of the Dead Sea like the highway, all the way south to Bozrah.

There were two more routes leading south past the Dead Sea to Bozrah, but they were such obscure trails of little consequence that it didn't seem like he should detail them on this map. No sane caravaneer would travel those waterless desert trails simply to avoid paying the tax on the King's Highway; but some caravaneers had little more sense than a mule and he made certain to detail the two alternate routes south— his pen strokes carefully marking the way of the Red Sea through the Judean Hill Country. The third route that lay farther east of the King's Highway, out in the deserts of the Empty Quarter, and Darius added the title in letters small enough not to detract from the main route it paralleled, his pen strokes lightly printing the name "Way of the Wilderness" over the leather.

Darius moved his pen down to the empty portion of his map. The parchment was blank here, without a single pen stroke detailing the way through the six-thousand-foot peaks of the Border Mountains of Midian. He'd not traveled that region and until he did, these charts would remain woefully lacking. Inspector Tobit refused him permission to mount an inspection of the southern extremes of the Kingdom's possessions, and without exploring the territory he might never complete this map. There was no other way than through his expert eyes to record the rise and fall of the land, properly orient the branches off the main trade route south into Arabia, or mark the location of wells. Darius lowered his pen from the unfinished portion of his map. He may never see the Border Mountain of Midian—the split range standing between the Dead Sea and the deserts of the Arabian Peninsula. It was dangerous territory. There were tales of hidden valleys and deep, dead-end canyons where travelers lost their way never to return. These were the mountains of the ancient prophet of the Jews, the place where Moses lived for forty years with the hosts of Israel. It was land he had to see, not only for his charts, but for the chance to say he'd been to Midian and seen the mountain the Jews called *The Lord's House.* But without exploring the region he would never know which peak to call Horeb, which cluster of twelve springs to name the waters of Moses, and which way to orient the trails through these mountains the Jewish merchant traders called the Borders. Darius set down his pen and rolled the map of the southern territory into a scroll. He may be the chief mapmaker of the New Babylonian Territories, but he was also the inspector's son, and Father refused to approve an expedition into the uncharted lands south of here.

"Darius, are you in there?" Inspector Tobit pushed open the door to the registry and marched inside, the smell of beeswax rising from his polished riding boots.

"Good afternoon, sir." Darius stuffed the map of the south under his arm before backing away from the table, his shoulders back and his stance straight.

"Where is it, son?"

Darius stepped aside and let his father stand at the table. "The finished maps are right here, sir."

"Not these, boy." Tobit looked over the two maps on the table. "I want the map of the south."

"It isn't finished." Darius patted the leather parchment under his arm. "I can't let you have it until I—"

"I decide what's finished and what isn't." Tobit snatched the map from Darius and held it beneath the light of the lamp. "It's hardly uncharted, son. Look at this; you have the shoreline of the Dead Sea detailed nicely."

"There's a good deal more to the southern territory than that, sir."

"All I need is the western shore of the Dead Sea."

"I'm not certain if it's accurate. I have to travel the shoreline to make sure I rendered it exactly as I have it recorded in my logs."

"You're not traveling anywhere, not until the area is secure."

"Secure from what?"

"Renegades, son. We have a problem in that region."

"When did you ever worry about Jewish renegades?"

"Ever since Zadock arrived with news of trouble." Tobit stabbed his finger at the leather map, stopping down along the western shores of the Dead Sea, twenty miles south of Jericho. "There could be a settlement right here."

"No one lives in the Judean Wilderness."

"Renegades do, son."

There he went again, talking about renegades as if they had power to come against Babylon. There were no renegades in these deserts, at least not any that should concern Tobit, and if he didn't stop letting Zadock dictate his priorities as governor of these territories, Darius was going to have to speak plainly on the matter. No renegade could live in the deserts south of here. It was too hot and too dry for anything but sand dunes and rock doves. There were no wells on the western shoreline. Maybe a few scattered reports of fresh water springs, but those were nothing more than seasonal winter runoff. There was simply no reason to believe anyone could live in that awful stretch of land for any length of time—not even a renegade fleeing for his life.

Darius took back the map of the southern territory. "I can't let any of your officers use this. It isn't finished, its not been tested. Whoever plans to use this to navigate through uncharted territory is a fool. Who's leading this patrol?"

Tobit said, "I am, son."

Darius softened his voice and said, "Where did you get the notion to chase renegades into the desert? We have plenty of work patrolling the King's Highway without traipsing off into the Judean Wilderness on the words of a man like Zadock. He's never seen that territory."

"It isn't a notion son. There's a renegade planning an uprising against Babylon. His outpost is located somewhere along the western shores of the Dead Sea."

"Did Zadock convince you of that?"

"The rebels were sighted not a day ago."

"Then take me with you." Darius handed the map of the southern territory to his father. "I can check the accuracy of this map, while you capture your renegade."

"That isn't a good idea. There could be trouble."

"I know how to ride a horse better than the men in your cavalry."

"I don't want you coming with me, do you understand?" Tobit waved his hand at the jars of sealed maps lining the shelves. "Stay here and draw your maps."

"I have nothing more to draw, not until I see the south."

"I won't have you out on the trail with me, not this time, son."

Darius held his pen out to his father. "I can wield a sword as well as I use this pen."

"We don't know what kind of threat awaits us."

"Then you'll need more men with you."

"You're as stubborn as your mother."

"I'm much worse than she ever was, God rest her soul." Darius straightened his shoulders. "If you don't take me with you, I'll explore these lands on my own."

"I'm ordering you to stay here until I return."

"You'll have to chain me to the wall."

"You and your mother." Tobit handed the map of the southern territories back to his son and started for the door.

Darius said, "You're going to need this map, Father."

"Bring the map along." Tobit stopped on the threshold of the registry, and before starting up the stairs to the main floor he said, "You'll need it if you're coming with us."

Inspector Tobit rode out of the livery, spurred his horse across the dusty street and in through the gates of his Governor's mansion. He brought his horse around in the main yard and faced the cavalrymen waiting on his arrival, the shoulder-length linen ends of his white turban rising on the breeze. A white, long-sleeved tunic shielded his arms and a long kilt fell over his knees—the leather tanned thick enough to keep the rays of the sun from burning his skin, but not so long as to hinder the comfort of the long ride ahead. His riding boots were laced with cords up his shins to let the breeze cool his limbs and keep this journey from growing any more distasteful than a midday summer ride into the Judean Wilderness was certain to be. Tobit stroked his horse's mane and spoke into her ear, telling her to calm herself—they wouldn't push any harder into the wilderness than what she could endure.

There was not a single cloud in the blue sky to shield them from the brightness of this summer afternoon and Tobit tucked the end of his turban under his collar and wrapped it with double the number of turns beneath his chin and triple the number of turns around his brow, the thick brim protecting him from the intense desert sun and the loose end of the turban falling down the back of his neck and onto his shoulders like locks of long white linen hair. He never wore this turban about Jericho, and never within the precincts of his governor's mansion, but there was no telling how long he'd be exposed to the mind-numbing sun of the Judean Wilderness, not to mention the sand storms that stirred in that desert, and there was not a finer headdress among his attire than this official military turban. It was fashioned of the finest linen cloth woven in the mills of Babylon, decorated with rubies mined in Nineveh, and adorned with two heron feathers rising from the back of his head. The sight of the plumes brought his cavalrymen in the main yard to attention, all fifty of them sitting straight in the saddle and steering their Arabians into orderly rows. Babylonian captains were permitted a single plume, but Tobit was Inspector of the New Territories and there was not another officer in the military permitted two feathers in his turban. His men could not mistake his entrance into the yard for any soldier other than the highest commander under the king of Babylon. Tobit was the head of this expedition and these heron feathers distinguished him above all the other turban-headed men in this company of sword-bearing soldiers.

Tobit leaned forward in the saddle, the polished leather squeaking under his sudden movement. He raised his voice loud enough that the men in the last row straightened their shoulders on the strength of his words, Tobit telling them that the Hebrew military commander camped outside the walls of Jericho had received notice from a scouting expedition early this morning that an outlaw had been sighted in the Judean Wilderness. Tobit tightened his hold on the reins, his voice booming about the yard. The outlaw was holed up with a group of renegades along the northwest coast of the Dead Sea, not too far into the desert from Jericho. Their mission was to ride in company with the Hebrew soldiers, put an end to whatever insurrection these renegades planned, disband the group by whatever means necessary, and capture their leader, a man by the name of Lehi, a wealthy olive oil merchant turned rebel. It would take two, maybe three days to capture the man and return him to Jerusalem, but they should have packed enough food for a full month's expedition into the desert and the means to carry a good supply of water in case they had to extend their search beyond this short jaunt down the shores of the Dead Sea. The Judean Wilderness was an unpredictable land, the watering places were uncharted, it was the middle of the hottest season of the year, and the sand storms were a constant threat in summer. Tobit ran his gaze over the company and he cleared his throat before asking if there were any questions.

The first lieutenant of the cavalry inched his mount forward. He pulled the cloth of his turban back and asked Tobit why they would leave in the middle of a hot afternoon—wasn't it better to wait until after sunset when their horses wouldn't labor against the heat? Before Tobit could answer, a cavalryman in the second column wanted to know why this renegade Lehi was a threat to their rule in the New Territories, another rider asked for a detailed description of Lehi in case they had to find him in a crowd, and a fourth soldier called out from the back of the company asking why Lehi was such a dangerous man and should they be prepared to use their weapons when the encountered him?

"Keep your hand on your sword when you deal with that rebel." The familiar, grating voice of Zadock, Chief Elder of the Jews, filled the main yard and Tobit turned in the saddle to see the Hebrew Elder standing on the main steps of the governor's mansion, his black robes lifting about his sandals. "He's a snake who can never be trusted." Zadock stayed beneath the cover of the veranda, the shade hiding his pale complexion and his words hissing from the shadows, branding Lehi a serpent with power to lure a man into a pit of words before striking with venom more powerful than death itself. Lehi was to be treated as a rebel bent on overthrowing Babylonian rule, a liar and traitor willing to risk the lives of his friends and family to save his own. Zadock stepped closer to the edge of the shade, but didn't leave the shadows, his piercing voice penetrating the farthest reaches of the yard and stirring the horses to arch their manes. The Chief Elder described Lehi as slightly taller than most men, with a tuft of beard growing on his chin if he hadn't shaved it off for disguise. And he was mounting an insurrection in the Judean Wilderness, the likes of which none of them could imagine.

Tobit quietly reined his horse alongside the porch. It didn't seem possible that one man could be such a danger to an entire kingdom, but Zadock continued railing against Lehi, insisting that the man was the incarnation of evil, belittling him for his arrogance, ridiculing him for his defiance, and mocking him for his foolishness. They were to capture him—no matter if they had to kill him to do it—and with God as Zadock's witness, they would save both nations the terrible price of a war Lehi hoped to foment between them. Zadock leaned forward in the shadows and peered out at the Babylonian soldiers in the yard, his voice cracking at the end of each phrase. In the two weeks Zadock had lodged here he never raised his voice beyond a scratchy monotone, preferring to sip wine in the cool recesses of the governor's mansion. But this afternoon he was filled with a vengeance for Lehi—a man Tobit had never heard tell of until Zadock came to Jericho. Who was this Lehi and what had he done to raise the wrath of Zadock to such a fevered pitch beyond tampering with the tax levy that was now paid in full?

Zadock carried a traveling satchel in one hand and he set it on the porch next to his feet before turning back to the cavalrymen in the yard, commending them for mounting this patrol into the wilderness. Instead of dividing their two nations, the renegade Lehi would bring them together under the banner of a single purpose and turn their warmongering into a peace solidified by mutual trust.

Tobit came around in front of the porch next to Zadock's traveling satchel. He said, "Will you be riding with us, sir."

Zadock pulled the shawls of his turban close to his face, protecting his eyes from the light of day. "I have no training in the art of cavaliering. I'm traveling to Jerusalem ahead of you to see that Ezekiel remains in our prison until you bring Lehi to join him." He leaned his head out from under the veranda. "Beware, my friend. Lehi mentored Ezekiel in the art of lies. Whatever you do, don't let him fool you with his cunning."

Tobit said, "I'm not easily convinced of anything, sir."

Zadock picked his traveling satchel off the ground. "Lehi will claim to speak in the name of heaven, prophesying in the name of a Messiah come to liberate your subjects and wrest control of your kingdom from you and the king of Babylon." He wrapped his arms around the satchel, tightening his grip on the leather bag. "You'll find out very quickly how large a liar he is and why both he and Ezekiel deserve to be executed to save us from their tyranny."

"We'll capture him, sir." Tobit nodded and the white linen ends of his turban lifted off his shoulders. "And with any luck, we'll be headed to meet you in Jerusalem within a few days' time to see to this Ezekiel."

"I'll be waiting." Zadock started down the porch and into the full light of day, the hem of his black robe dragging behind his stride, and his traveling satchel pressed against his side. The chief Hebrew Elder was never a nervous man, but this afternoon he was anything but calm. There was a tension in his stride and the rough edges in his voice bordered on fear. How could a desert renegade engender such emotion in a man of Zadock's distinction? Perhaps this Lehi was more powerful than Tobit believed, but with as many soldiers as he'd assembled, there was nothing to fear. They would capture this criminal and take him to Jerusalem to be judged with Ezekiel for their part in this tax fraud and then be done with it.

A horse-drawn chariot turned into the yard and steered up to the porch. The driver got down from the stoop, pulled back the leather canopy and helped Zadock inside before returning to his post and steering the cart out through the gates, raining down a cloud of dusty brown earth on a regiment of Hebrew cavalry that entered the yard, passing Zadock on his way out. The Hebrew horsemen came around in five straight columns, their dark-gray uniforms filling the far side of the yard with their presence. They faced the white-robed Babylonian riders, leaving a path from the gate to the main porch between them and allowing enough space for Captain Laban to ride in from the street. His short, dark hair was groomed with olive oil and it glistened in the light of afternoon from the brow of his head and down along the narrow band of beard gracing his jawbone. The man's thick shoulders pushed against the polished brass breastplates strapped to the chest of his black tunic. The matching cloth of an unwrapped black turban hung about his neck, the ends streaming out behind him and waving above the white coat of his Arabian.

Two riders accompanied Laban into the yard. The first one, a lieutenant named Daniel, was dressed in proper Hebrew military dress, his powerful shoulders pushing against his gray tunic and his body erect in the saddle. The long hair of the second rider fell in a tangled cascade down his back before disappearing beyond the level of his saddle. Shechem wore a short black cape, the end of it flapping on the breeze, the cloth of the shoulders rising and falling with the stride of his horse and the front of it open, exposing his nakedness. He wore nothing but a leather loincloth about his waist without any robes shielding him from the scorching rays of the sun. He wasn't part of the Hebrew military, not dressed like that.

Tobit leaned forward in the saddle. "We agreed, Captain. Hebrew and Babylonian military only." He tugged on the reins and his mount backed a step. "Who is this man dressed like a—"

"I dress how I please." Shechem spurred across Tobit's path and came around. He spoke out of the side of his mouth, his lips hardly moving. "I'm the only one who can lead you to the renegades, unless you prefer to find them on your own."

Laban said, "Shechem comes with us."

Tobit said, "I'm leading this expedition."

"And I'm advising you, sir, that we would be fools not to have Shechem with us."

Tobit came around next to Shechem, the man's long, powerful legs wrapped around the body of his horse like a noose. "If you know the lay of land well, I want you working with my mapmaker."

"I don't draw on parchments." Shechem tapped the point of his dagger against the side of his head. "I keep everything right here."

"I gave you an order."

"I don't take orders from anyone but—"

"Tobit's leading this patrol." Laban released his tight grip on the reins and his mount shook its mane. "You're to listen to him on these matters."

"We don't need maps." Shechem spit on the metal of his dagger and rubbed it against the leather strap tied around his loincloth. "A man who uses a map doesn't have the sense to remember where he's traveled and what lay in his path."

The main doors to the governor's mansion pushed open, the tall timbers slamming against the outside stones in the wall. Darius marched out, carrying the leather satchel filled with pens and inks and the unfinished parchment waiting for the touch of his hand to complete the charting of the south. He was dressed in the same white riding robes as the other Babylonian soldiers, but his untied turban hung over his shoulder, and his straight black hair fell into his eyes. He came down the steps, set his bag of maps on the ground next to Tobit's horse, and pushed his hair back off his brow. He said, "I believe I have everything."

Shechem said, "I don't work with scribes."

"I'm no scribe, sir." Darius turned his brown-eyed gaze onto Shechem and straightened to his full height, his wide shoulders back and his black hair lifting on the breeze. "I don't copy the words of other men. I make maps."

"He's my son." Tobit reined his horse in a slow circle around the longhaired man. "Chief mapmaker of the New Babylonian Territories."

Darius said, "Who is this man?"

"He's a—"

Laban said, "Shechem's a scout and he knows the Judean Wilderness better than any man in your army or mine."

"Son." Tobit leaned over the saddle. "He can help you with the charting of the lands south of here."

"I don't need his help." Darius picked his satchel off the ground and started for the livery to get his horse, but Shechem spurred across his path, blocking his way. He flashed his dagger in the sunlight and polished the metal on his cape. "You never know what sort of help you may need from me, boy."

"Put that away." Tobit reined between them. "That's enough from both of you. You're going to work together on the charting of this territory. Is that clear?"

Shechem grunted his approval and Darius nodded while tying on his white turban, his black hair hedging out beneath the cloth on his brow and the breeze lifting the ends of the turban off his shoulders. Darius was a good son, an intelligent boy, but he was going to have to work with Shechem no matter what. They had to chart a detailed map of the southern frontier, and this expedition to find the renegade Lehi was their best chance to explore at least a portion of the shoreline.

"So tell me, sir." Tobit leaned forward in the saddle, his words directed at Shechem. "How do we approach the renegade camp without giving away our coming?"

"Along the shoreline." Darius dug down into his satchel and pulled out the map detailing what little he knew of the western shores of the Dead Sea. "That's the best way to travel. It's a wide shore, with beaches all the way to the Arabah. We can make better time that way than any other approach."

"You're a fool, boy." Shechem hid his dagger under the leather of his boot. "We approach them from the west."

"No, no, not that way." Darius held the map between both hands. "There's nothing but endless mountains of sand. We'll have to circle a good ten miles west of the Dead Sea in order to approach them from the desert side."

Shechem said, "The Rekhabites have watches posted along the shoreline."

Lieutenant Daniel reined forward. He had a deep voice and powerful frame and there was no doubt he had the trust of Laban, the captain turning his ear to the boy and allowing him to speak his mind. "We could ride down the beach and circle inland before we reach their camp."

Shechem said, "That won't work. They'll be expecting us to come at them from the beaches."

"I don't like this." Darius turned his head into his map. "Too many things could go wrong. There's no water supply in the desert."

Laban said, "There isn't any water in any part of that desert."

"It's much hotter inland than along the shoreline." Darius ran his finger over the surface of his map. "The animals will travel better along the beaches and there's always a chance of sandstorms this time of year."

Shechem sidled in next to Captain Laban. "Why does this boy think he knows the Judean Wilderness better than I? He spends his days with pens and ink, not riding these lands."

"I know the lay of the land, sir." Darius brought his head up from his map, his brown eyes filled with resolve. "The shoreline is the best way for us to—"

"That's enough from both of you." Tobit rode down between the dual companies of Hebrew and Babylonian cavalry before coming around in the center of the yard. He nodded to Shechem. He said, "We'll do as you say and surprise them from the desert side."

CHAPTER 18

The sound of knocking at the front gate hurried Ruth from the kitchen and out into the courtyard. That couldn't be Miriam and her soldier-escorts already. It was too early and she hadn't finished preparing the tables. Ruth set a basket of bread on the table next to a jar of honey, the aroma of fresh baked bread filling the courtyard with the smell of her deception. A heaping bowl of dates sat on one end of the table next to some nuts, and Ruth arranged bottles of wine around them, the strongest she could purchase from the Jawbone Inn. The innkeeper guaranteed it powerful enough to deaden a man's senses in less than ten swallows, but she didn't intend to intoxicate them, only test the power of the wine to see if it could help them win Jeremiah and Ezekiel's freedom. If there was any way to divert the attention of a man, it was through his stomach and she'd prepared more than enough diversions to keep them from suspecting Ruth and Miriam of anything beyond a discussion of weaving. Ruth quickly dusted a wet cloth over the lips of five large glasses and stood them beside the wine bottles. Five. That's how many soldiers escorted Miriam about the city and she prayed there weren't more than that this morning or she'd not have enough wine to distract their ears.

Another knock sounded at the gate and Ruth hurried back to the house and leaned through the kitchen window, announcing that Miriam and her escorts had arrived and would they hurry with the last of the preparations? The front door flew open and Zoram emerged, back-stepping the kitchen table out the entrance with Elizabeth holding up the other end. Ruth directed them over near the food table, but not so near they couldn't make their plans without the soldiers hearing. They couldn't suspect Ruth and Miriam guilty of anything beyond weaving. Ruth spread out three choices of blue cloth from her weaving basket, five spools of gold and silver thread, weavers' needles, hooks, batting boards, spooling baubles, and a selection of flax, wool, and goose feathers—more than enough weaving decisions to keep them engaged in discussion for as long as it took Miriam to explain why she needed their help.

Zoram tied a length of thread to the wrong end of a weaving needle and pulled it through the hem of the remnant of cloth. "Is this how it's done."

"No, no, not like that. You must look like you know what you're doing. If any of these soldiers have ever seen a spooler or threader tailoring their work, they'll spy you out." Elizabeth sat him down at the end of the weaving table, set the needles beside him and said, "Don't pick up any of these. Just run your hand over them like this." She brushed her fingertips over the first needle, tested the point of the next one with the tip of her finger, but she never held any of them. "The moment you pick these up they'll know you've never threaded a single piece of cloth."

Ruth set the spools of gold thread beside Zoram. "You'll want to recommend this thread to the queen. It's thicker than the others, and it has a better luster in the cloth."

"What if she asks a question I can't answer?"

"Don't worry, boy." Ruth touched him on the shoulder. "The help Miriam needs from us has nothing to do with weaving. She'll not ask anything about weavers' work."

"The poor woman can't leave the palace without a horde of soldiers following her." Zoram reached for the weaving needle, but took his hand back when Ruth wagged her finger at the boy.

"Just nod your head and say as little as you can." Elizabeth sat across the table from Zoram. "And don't say anything about weaving. You don't want to give these soldiers reason to think you're anything but the finest spooler in the city."

A flurry of knocking sounded at the gate and the deep voice of a soldier called from the street announcing the Queen of Judah had come to the house and would they please answer their knocking? He didn't demand the gate be opened immediately, but the tone of his voice was not kind. Ruth quickly pressed the creases out of her apron. She checked the wine glasses, uncorked the seal on the jar of honey, and raised both hands to Elizabeth and Zoram, telling them to be calm and not panic, everything was going to be all right. She hurried across the courtyard, retying the sash on her apron as she went. Calm? How could she ask Zoram and Elizabeth to be calm when she was anything but? They were gathering here to speak of subversion, disguised as the talk of weavers. Ruth reached the gate, but before opening she turned back to Elizabeth and Zoram, raised her hands to them again, and mouthed the words: *peace, be at peace.* And then she offered a prayer to calm her troubled heart. She was not an experienced conspirator and could heaven please send whatever blindfolds they had to cover the eyes of these soldiers to her doings and keep her home a safe haven away from the troubles that brewed in this city.

Ruth opened the gate and the Chief of Escort barged in ahead of the other four soldiers. The escorts were dressed in the colorful blue tunics of the palace guard, with gold hems about the sleeve and silver studs sewn into their leather kilts. They formed a line just inside the gate, and the Chief of Escort stuck his brass helmet under his arm before announcing Queen Miriam's arrival and asking them to bow low and let her—

"That will be all, sir." Miriam pushed aside the grapevines growing up around the gate and stepped in from the street, her white outer robe covering the blue sashes and bows of her royal robes. She took Ruth by the hand and started across the courtyard to the tables. She spoke in a loud voice, her words filling the courtyard with her questions. She said, "So tell me dear, have you made the changes to the blankets? I do so want to—"

"Gentlemen." Ruth stopped in the middle of the courtyard and turned back to the soldiers. She raised her hand to the table of food. "I've prepared a few things for you. Please, come, enjoy your visit while the Queen makes her final decision on the weaving."

The men gathered around the table, but before the Chief of Escort allowed them a drink, he uncorked a wine bottle, poured the dark red wine into a glass, swished it about, and took a long sip. It was strong wine, undiluted and with the power to cloud the clearest mind. The man slowly lowered the glass to the table, his stare riveted on the wine bottle. *This wasn't good, not good at all*, thought Ruth. *Look at him eyeing the brew.* He lifted the clay vessel off the table, held it out to his men and told them to enjoy the feast, then broke into a wide grin.

Ruth hurried Miriam over to the weaving table and sat down at the end near the finished blanket—the same one Miriam rejected two weeks before. "Tell us before they finish drinking"

Elizabeth raised a spool of thread and said, "Do you like the color?"

"That's wonderful. Do you have anything with more silver in it?" Miriam smiled and lowered her voice. "Has Zoram already told you about the arrangements for the Ceremony of Sale?"

Ruth nodded and said, "I used a smaller weave on the hem. Is that the weave you were hoping for?" She lifted the needles off the table before whispering, "How do we get the keys from the jailer?"

"It's a perfect weave." Miriam ran her hand over the finished blanket, and between comments about the quality of the weave she said, "Elizabeth, will serve him some wine. He takes the keys off from around his neck whenever he takes his wine. You'll only have as long as he's drinking to open the sewer doors and unlock Jeremiah and Ezekiel from their shackles."

Elizabeth lowered her gaze into the weaving needles. "And if I fail?"

"You won't fail getting the keys to . . ." Zoram fell silent when the Chief of Escorts walked over with a glass of wine and stood directly behind him, his hands on the backrest of his chair and his scented breath hanging on the air. Zoram picked up a spooling bauble and pointed it at Elizabeth. "I say, you won't have any trouble weaving with this spool. My threads tie nicely into the blankets."

No, that wasn't right. You don't tie threads into blankets. Ruth leaned over the table and took the spooling bauble from Zoram. Didn't he know you were to *sew* them into the cloth? And you don't weave with a spool; you keep your thread with it. Ruth held her lip between her teeth, silently telling the boy he was giving them away with his talk of weaving, but it was no use. Zoram said, "There aren't a lot of spools that can do what this one does."

The Chief of Escorts said, "So you're a spooler are you, son?"

"Among other things, sir."

"Exactly what does your spool do that others won't?"

"Can I pour you some more wine, sir?" Ruth reached for his glass, but he pulled back and said, "I'll get my own." He came around to the end of the table and stood next to Miriam. "Do you see anything you like, My Lady?"

"I'll be a while longer." Miriam didn't look up at him. She kept her gaze straight ahead, turned out over the courtyard.

"Very good, My Lady." The man backed from the table holding the wine glass out to Miriam. He stumbled slightly, caught himself and told her he'd keep the men occupied until she was ready. He turned back to the table and poured himself another round of wine.

Elizabeth said, "How will I get the keys down to the sewers without the jailer noticing they're gone?"

"Your mother, dear. You'll keep the jailer supplied with as much wine as he'll drink while Ruth takes care of the sewers." Miriam handed Ruth a remnant of weaving. "I do so like the pattern in this cloth. Can you add it to the small, foot-warming blankets and pillows you're weaving?"

"I'm not sure I can do this." Ruth lowered her gaze into the goose feathers and flax. "I'm a weaver, not a spy."

"You most certainly can weave anything you like, do you understand me?" Miriam took Ruth by the hand until her bones stopped trembling and she looked up from the flax. "You're my only hope." She cleared her throat. "I'll see that you're paid double for your work."

"Oh, the foot warmers, yes, I think we can make that change, can't we?" Ruth turned her gaze between Elizabeth and Zoram until they all nodded. "Of course we can."

Miriam said, "Do you have a good, strong wine?"

Ruth tipped her head toward the soldiers gathered around the other table. One was leaning over rubbing his head, another steadied himself by the table edge, and two more were sitting on the stone wall near the water cistern, their helmets pushed back from their brows. "I think we've found just the right brew for the ceremony."

"Very well." Miriam stood from the table, the legs of her chair grating over the courtyard stones. "That settles everything for the new blankets." She spoke loud enough to bring her escorts to attention. They gathered beside her, forming a line behind her chair.

Ruth said, "When do you want them, My Lady?"

Miriam leaned forward over the table, her hands holding the edge of the worn wood. "I'll take the delivery of your services the end of next week."

CHAPTER 19

Sam paced across the highest outcrop on the cliffs above Qumran like a soldier standing watch over a walled city. These rocky crags and uneven cliffs were a poor protection against attack and thank heaven they were pulling out tonight or they'd never fend off an assault. Sam turned his gaze slowly across the dune covered desert floor north of camp. There were no horses riding over the earth stretching out before him, no approaching band of robbers climbing the ridges, and not a single soldier headed toward Qumran with a terrible banner waving in the breeze. There was nothing but a harmless whirlwind whipping across the desert and he wasn't about to mistake the sudden appearance of a column of twisting brown dust for an attack on Qumran. Sam leaned forward and squinted out across the uneven desert. Was Captain Laban really foolish enough to want to search for them in this wilderness? A man of his station should have more important business than chasing about this desolate place after a group of harmless outcasts.

Sam turned down along the outcrop to the south end, scanning the desert for any sign of trouble. There was nothing to warn of the arrival of danger. There was no trail of dust rising in the distant sky behind an advancing platoon. And no cavalrymen riding down the faraway ridges to the south. No horses galloping past the three sand-covered stone columns—their tall peaks marking the location of Qumran on the cliffs above camp. There was not a single bit of movement to the south beyond the beginnings of another small twister rising like a fountain of sand and shifting about the desert floor. What an odd coincidence. There'd never been two errant twisters dancing along the desert floor on the same afternoon. They were small pillars of dust and they didn't offer a hint of a breeze to break the sultry calm of this desert nor stir the stagnant air to cool him, and Sam had a mind to end his watch over the Judean Wilderness and attend to the animals. He was caravan master, not chief of the afternoon watch, and though he made sure to feed the camels enough grain to prepare them for a full night of desert travel before climbing these cliffs to keep watch, he couldn't expect his brother Nephi to prepare the caravan without his help. Nephi was a strong boy, but he didn't know the first thing about packing mules and bridling camels for a journey through the desert. Sam started back along the edge of his sandstone parapet. He curried the animals last night, watered them twice this morning, and if he only had the jar of balm he left on the top shelf in the stables at Beit Zayit, he could rid the lead camel of a festering leg sore before they started this journey. And there were three bridles he left hanging from a hook on the stable wall, a horse blanket on the top shelf of the commissary, and five water skins they certainly could use for tonight's flight into the desert. Of all the things to leave behind, why did he have to forget water skins? Father told him not to worry. They had more than enough water for their journey and what they lacked, God would provide. Sam pulled up in the middle of the rock outcrop, the toes of his sandals hanging over the edge. Since when did Father depend on divine help to water a caravan? Sam had to convince Father to lead them closer to home until this trouble passed—a place where he could ride back to Beit Zayit from time to time and check on the animals they left behind and see that Ishmael and his daughters were well. That was the wise thing to do and as soon as his watch was finished, Sam was going to have a word with him. Lehi would listen to his logic, wouldn't he? There was no reason to travel farther from home. Laban would forget about them soon enough and until he did, they could camp in the hill country south of Beit Zayit as safely as they could hide in the uncharted quarters of Arabia.

A sudden wind rushed over Sam, raising the collar of his robe and turning him toward the setting sun. The small twisters were gone, replaced by a swirling cloud of brown sand, rising and falling at the head of a desert storm. The giant swell of dust filtered the sun through dirty brown shadows and Sam lowered his brow to meet the gusting breeze, his loose-fitting traveling robe flapping in the air behind him. Where did this storm come from? Desert twisters never turned into sand storms, at least nothing like this pillar of dust as wide as this desert was long. Winds plagued the desert afternoons in early summer, but Sam had never seen one as large as this sudden blast that ballooned his sleeves around his forearms and pressed the pleats of his robe against him like wind-weathered skin pulled taut across his body.

Sam jumped from the outcrop and slowly backed toward the path leading down the cliffs to camp. The storm was stalled a few hundred cubits from his lookout, the churning earth rising out of the desert floor and surrounding Qumran like a wall around a city. They couldn't travel in weather like this, not with the clouds of sand growing higher and wider with each gust of wind. Sam started down the switchbacks to warn the others, leaving his lookout without anyone to keep watch over the desert. There was no need to post a watch.

A storm was coming.

Daniel jumped his steed over the edge of a washed-out gully and down the sandy embankment before letting the animal go full out across the wide expanse of this low-lying wadi, his lone-eyed gaze set on the far side of this desert wash and his animal racing over the strand. The black patch over his left eye didn't keep him from leading the cavalry across the last obstacle separating them from the man responsible for beguiling Daniel's dead brother. Lehi was hiding in this desert and he'd stolen Aaron's steel bow—the only remembrance Aaron left behind after his death. Lehi may have charmed Aaron in life, but he'd not live to enjoy his deceit. The sultry summer sun beat down on his brow, but a strong breeze streamed across the wadi from the steep bank on the other side and the growing breeze was a welcome relief, the force of it lifting the ends of Daniel's turban off his shoulders and cooling his neck. Daniel jumped two deep crevices and skirted around a sand bar left from the winter rains before reaching the far side of the wadi at full gallop, his shoulders forward and his boots spurring his steed up the steep embankment, leading the expedition closer to the secret camp where Daniel was sure to exact his brother's revenge. He was going to claim for Captain Laban the sword he failed to get for him on Passover.

Daniel spurred onto the sandy ridge top above the wadi, his steed rearing at the sight of what lay beyond. He adjusted the black patch tight against his bad eye before shielding his good eye with the palm of his hand, peering between his fingers at the roiling wall of earth rising out of the desert floor like a fortress wall built without hands. The storm rose along the length of the Judean Wilderness with clouds reaching high into heaven, sealing off their advance to the Dead Sea. Daniel came around, his hands raised to the riders following him up the rise, telling them to hold off and take cover in the lowest-lying spot of ground they could find in this wadi. The wind blasted across his face and he raised his voice loud enough to pierce the gale, telling this mixed company of Hebrew and Babylonian soldiers that there was an approaching storm the likes of which he'd never seen before.

Inspector Tobit reined up the embankment next to him and when he saw the reason for Daniel's retreat he spurred around and repeated Daniel's instructions, warning the men that desert storms were fickle. A gust raced over the desert floor and Tobit held the ends of his turban over his face, crying the last of his instructions through the cloth, telling them that these storms went where they pleased and they should stay put until he gave them orders that it was safe to proceed.

"We're going on." Captain Laban reined over the top of the wadi's bank and sidled in between Daniel and Tobit, sand pelting the brass of his breastplates. He raised his head to the storm and spoke through the cloth of his bandanna, but it was impossible to make any sense of his words with the wind twisting about him and salting his short black hair with desert sand.

Daniel came around in front of Captain Laban and Inspector Tobit, all of them falling silent at the sight of swirling clouds of brown earth stalled a few hundred cubits away.

Inspector Tobit leaned over the saddle and said, "We could lose some animals, maybe some men in a storm like this. What do you say, Lieutenant?"

Daniel tightened his hold on the reins to keep his horse from back stepping away from the force of the wind. "Lehi's camp is somewhere in that storm."

Tobit said, "That isn't what I asked. I want to know the risks to our men."

Daniel said, "It's hardly a mile from here."

"You can't be certain of that." Darius climbed the dune and stood beside his father's horse, his map stretched between his hands to keep it from flapping about. He moved his gaze quickly between the drawings on his leather scroll and the late afternoon sun, its dim light piercing through the sand-filled sky. "There's no telling where we're at until these winds die down and we get our bearings."

"We don't need more bearings." Shechem reined up the rise, his long hair snapping in the wind behind him, the skin of his bare chest red from the pelting sand. He faced into the gale, his stare riveted on the stalled clouds. "This is the place."

Darius said, "How can you be sure?"

"Those three hills." Shechem brought his horse around and faced her south. "They're all the same height."

Darius said, "Sand dunes are always changing, always shifting. They're no good to us."

"Those aren't dunes, boy." Shechem sidled in next to Darius and leaned over his saddle. "They're solid rock columns marking the approach to the renegade camp." He grabbed a dagger from inside the brim of his boot and pushed the tip of it into the sparsely charted map, the metal cutting the leather fibers and marking the location of the three sand-covered stone columns.

Darius pulled his map away from the dagger's tip. "Keep your blade away from my maps."

"Curse your maps. You wanted my help with your charting, didn't you?" Shechem replaced the dagger in his boot. "I was following orders."

Tobit said, "Do we ride on or do we hunker down until this storm passes?"

"If Captain Laban orders us to ride on, then I say we ride." Daniel came around in front of Captain Laban, the sand whipping across his cheeks like a thousand pin pricks. "What are your orders, sir?"

"I'm leading this expedition." Inspector Tobit sidled his mount between Laban and Daniel, the end of his white turban whipping across his mouth. "We're not going anywhere until I say we go, is that clear?"

Laban said, "We can't let Lehi get away."

"He can't travel in this weather."

Laban said, "There's no way to know that without riding through it."

Inspector Tobit leaned forward in the saddle and pulled his turban tight across his face to keep it from snapping into his eyes. "This renegade Lehi you have us chasing—if he's worth chasing at all—is he worth risking our lives and lives of our men?"

"Capturing Lehi is worth any trouble." Laban gritted his teeth, the muscles along his jawline taut like a cord.

Daniel said, "Captain, sir. What are your orders?"

Laban turned his gaze over the height and width of the storm. "The inspector has charge of this expedition, son."

A stiff wind blew across the empty confines of Qumran, and Nephi quickly lashed the tent poles together. The silence of so many people fled from this place hurried his fingers over the knots. He cinched the poles in place on the lead camel, the wooden ends running alongside the animal's neck and ending just behind the ears like the harness on a mule cart. The pole-bearing camel balked at the load on her back, shaking her head and backing away from Nephi's cords, but he was strong enough to keep her from jumping, one arm wrapped around her side and the other holding fast to the long timbers to keep them from falling to the ground. Why wasn't Sam here when he needed him? His brother was caravan master and he knew which camels spooked easily, which mules were stubborn beyond hope, and which sheep couldn't be trusted to wander free about the shoreline, though it didn't seem to matter with the entire flock of fourteen scattered beneath the camels' legs, taking refuge from the wind that picked up across the abandoned camp and showered them with a fine coating of sand, the grit spilling over from the cliffs above. Sam was gone standing watch and Nephi was left to oversee the packing of supplies and the organizing of the animals into two caravans—one of mules and the other of camels. It was an odd request. There was no reason for Lehi to tell him to divide the caravan, not when Father said they were taking Josiah the Potter, his daughter Rebecca, and Aaron with them to Bozrah and there was only one route to get there, at least only one comfortable route with plenty of water and not nearly as much heat. A sane traveler would only take the route north along the shoreline toward Jericho, around the north end of the Dead Sea, then south on the king's highway to the southernmost settlement at Bozrah.

Odder still was Father's insistence they pack the family tent with the camels, when the mules always carried that load. And why was he to pack so much grain and water with the camels and so little with the mules? The sacks of wheat, barley, and oats were lashed into place on the middle camels with thirty freshly filled water skins bulging at the sides of the rear camels, leaving only a few sacks of grain and water skins to pack on the two lead mules.

A shrill whistle of wind blew down over the cliffs and streamed along the shoreline, the camels and mules grunting their pleasure at the cool relief on this hot summer afternoon, no matter that it stirred enough sand to blur the view across camp. Nephi and his family were alone here, with only the company of Josiah the Potter, Rebecca, and Aaron to divide the loneliness between them. Mother sat on a flat stone beyond the line of mules, over where they corralled the horses, their large bodies protecting her from the brunt of the blowing sand. Sariah held the hem of her traveling robe down with one hand and supported her womb with the other. She was a small woman, with hardly the constitution to endure another journey. She kept her shoulders down and her head hidden beneath her hood. And though she appeared unfit for travel, she had the resolve of ten stout men and never once did she waver from supporting Father's decision. When Lehi announced they were traveling deeper into the wilderness, she agreed without a word of complaint, and that from a woman who had reason to complain with the pain of this unborn child slowing her stride, weakening her frame, and turning her stomach ill at every turn. Sariah ran her gaze slowly about camp and when her eyes rested on Nephi, he felt the concern in her stare. He'd never seen that sort of worry in his mother, but they were fleeing for their safety a second time and she could only be fretting over the same concerns that troubled Nephi. Were they to be condemned to wander through these deserts the rest of their lives, a forgotten and lonely people, without any place to call home? Nephi forced a weak smile and Sariah returned the gesture before he could no longer endure the sadness of her concern and he turned back to checking his knots and securing the tent poles.

The sooner they escaped these desolate shores along the Dead Sea, the sooner Nephi could forget how much this tent-packing and water skin filling reminded him of their first flight from Beit Zayit. They were outcasts, despised by their own people, and this nomadic life was harming more than their own family—they were taking others with them. Nephi stepped to the water skins on the last camels, lashing them with double cords to keep them from coming loose, his gaze half-turned over his shoulder, stealing another glance at Mother. The young blacksmith sat beside her, his crutches set at his feet. How many more times would Aaron be required to risk his life to protect them? The arrow wound in his leg was healing, but it would never heal enough to make up for the pain he suffered to save them. And then there was Aaron's love, the quiet, well-mannered Rebecca. She sat on the other side of Mother, her long, black hair hedging out from under the hood of her traveling robe, the ends flirting with the breeze. Would there ever be enough peace in their lives so she could enjoy the company of Aaron like other women enjoyed the company of a proper suitor, or was she destined, like the rest of them, to wander in this desert in search of an ordinary life that may never be theirs?

In the distance, down along the strand, her father, Josiah the Potter, and Laman and Lemuel walked the length of camp, removing the last signs of their living here, brushing away footprints with the ends of reeds, burying the remains of a fire pit with their hands, discarding the dried bones of a yearling into a pit, and removing every trace of their existence along these shores. The foundations of buildings and the aqueduct carrying water into the center of camp were gone, buried below the sand that transformed the hope of a rising city into a desolate run of flat ground. Any sign they lived here or had any hope of returning was stamped out. Nephi gathered the tent stakes and ropes into a saddlebag and lashed it onto the back of the lead camel. The family tent came down with a few hours' work, but their lives—the ones they left behind at Beit Zayit—were so much fuller than this empty pile of leather and cords. It was a fine tent, more spacious than the other dwellings that once dotted these shores, but it was nothing like the comfort of the estate they left behind. These camel-hair walls were all they had to show for generations of vineyard keeping and olive oil pressing, a shadow of the comfortable estate they once called home. Nephi folded the tent and hoisted it onto the middle camels in the caravan, the large bundles riding above the sacks of grain like extra humps, then lashed them into place with a good ten turns of cord to keep the stiffening breeze from blowing them free.

The family possessions sat on the ground waiting for Nephi to tie them in place on the mules. There were blankets bundled by cords, sacks of medicines, and Sariah's cooking herbs and seasonings. They hadn't used many while they were here, but Mother said that once they were settled and she was finished carrying this unborn child, she'd cook them a meal they'd never forget, just like when they were home. The large stack of pillows sitting by the feet of the rear camel was a luxury, but wherever their mother was concerned, such things were not a luxury. Every bottle of perfume, box of powder, and jar of lotion and ointment was essential, and Nephi packed those items deep into the saddlebags where they wouldn't break. The steel bow Aaron crafted for Nephi stood leaning against the rock cliffs, its polished metal gleaming in the afternoon sun, and a quiver of steel-tipped arrows lay on the ground beside the invention. Nephi kept it away from his other packing, leaving it out until his horse was saddled and he could stow it across the animal's back. It was a precious weapon—there was not another steel bow in all the earth—and with Father leading them into hostile territory, there was no calculating its value. The wooden box holding Father's writings sat in the sand beside an open saddlebag waiting for Lehi to come and stow it inside the protective leather pouch and lash it to his horse. Father kept his journal close when he traveled, packing it atop his saddlebags with a pen and ink ready and waiting to write of their journey, though there didn't seem to be anything worth remembering in this flight that was taking them farther from home.

Another blast of wind streamed over the cliffs above Qumran raising a cloud of dust and darkening the sky. The lead camel jumped at the sudden pelting of sand, sidestepping into the line of mules and tearing free a sack of grain, the wheat spilling to the ground and mixing with the sand. As Nephi pulled on the harness to keep the camel from bolting, he heard Sam calling to him from the cliffs. His brother turned down the last switchback and started across the emptiness of camp, a twisting cloud of sand rising above him and hovering over the cliffs, the dark mass filtering out the light of the sun. Sam waved his hands overhead and called to Nephi, telling him to get the animals up against the steepest part of the cliffs in the alcove, out of the worst of the storm. He cupped his hands around his mouth and called to Lehi and the others to hurry over and help them unpack the tent and supplies from the animals before the gale winds reached camp.

Lehi marched over, his head leaning into the wind and his traveling robe flapping against his legs. He met Sam at the front of the two caravans, his voice muted by the storm. "Son, we're not unpacking."

"We can't leave the animals like this." Sam steadied the lead animals, pulling hard on the reins to keep them from jumping at the rush of wind. "They'll bolt if we leave them loaded down in this storm."

Josiah the Potter raced up from checking the shoreline, his hands protecting his face from the force of the wind. He stepped in next to Lehi, telling him they could wait until morning before breaking camp. Rebecca fought through the sand, guiding Sariah over and shielding her with a blanket. Aaron limped behind them, his crutches holding up his tall, thin frame. He could walk without the help of the timbers, but the pain still had power to hobble his gait. Laman and Lemuel fought through swirling columns of sand that swirled about the far side of camp and shrouded them in pillars of dust, both of them holding their forearms over their eyes and Laman shouting above the howl of the wind that they should abandon their plan to leave Qumran and take cover before the storm grew any worse.

A blast of sand rained down over Lehi, swirling grit about his face. He turned to the cliffs, his head raised to the sky and his gaze fixed on the twisting clouds looming above.

"Dear." Sariah stood beside Lehi. "We can't stay out in this much longer."

Sam shouted above the whistle of wind. "Get the animals behind those rocks."

"Gather your things and follow me to the caves above camp." Josiah started for the blankets packed on the back of a mule. "We'll be safe there until the storm subsides."

"We're not staying the night." Lehi kept his gaze fixed on the clouds swirling just beyond the top of the cliffs, the worst of the storm a few hundred cubits from engulfing them. "I want all of you to mount your horses. We're leaving now." He pointed at Laman. "I want you to lead the family and these mules north toward—"

Laman said, "We can't travel in this storm."

"This isn't a storm, son."

"What do you call this?" Laman raised his hand to the sky, the sleeve of his tunic flapping in the rush of wind.

"A blessing from heaven." Lehi turned his gaze down along the shoreline. In both directions leading north toward Jericho and south toward the rift valley deserts of the Arabah, the beaches were without any of the blowing sand that swirled about them at Qumran. The storm was stalled a hundred cubits from the Dead Sea, the high wall of sand forming a calm corridor along the shoreline in either direction, like a tunnel carved into the storm by the hand of heaven. The only place the storm reached the water's edge was here at Qumran, the swirling sand covering every remnant of their footprints like a giant reed broom brushing away the last bit of evidence that they lived here. The force of the storm was urging them to leave this place and find refuge elsewhere and Nephi turned his gaze to the saddle-bags where he had packed the parchments of Isaiah's writings. Could it be that the words of that dead prophet were guiding them again in this journey? Only last night, by the light of flickering lamp he read the passage near the end of the fourth scroll, the careful pen of Isaiah calling to him through words over a hundred years of time, assuring him that God would open rivers in high places, and fountains in the midst of the valleys, and that there would be a tabernacle for a shadow in the daytime from the heat, and for a place of refuge from the storm.

"He's right." Nephi stepped in next to his brothers. "Father's right."

Laman said, "What do you know about desert storms?"

"This isn't a storm, it's a . . ." A gale raged across the abandoned camp, showering them with sand and Nephi held his arm over his face and spoke through the harshness of the wind. "It's from God."

Lemuel said, "Have you lost your mind?"

Laman stepped around in front of Nephi and said, "We don't know how long the storm will stall like this. We could get trapped along the shoreline."

"We don't have a choice, son. We leave now." Lehi took Sariah by the hand, led her to the horses tethered to a rock and helped her up into the saddle. He motioned for Rebecca and Josiah the Potter to mount their horses, and he held Beuntahyu steady while Aaron pulled himself onto her back, his injured leg slowly swinging over her white coat, the animal careful not to jostle her rider until he secured his crutches on her backside. Somehow Beuntahyu understood that Aaron's limp had returned and she was to be his legs until he healed again. Lehi led the horses to the front of the mule caravan, heading them north down along the beach and telling Laman above the rush of the wind that he with his brother Lemuel were to take Sariah and their friends north to Jericho, then down the King's highway to Bozrah.

"Not Bozrah." Laman found his father's writing box set in the sand beside the camels and pulled out the stack of scrolls. He hurried through them until he found the newest one and shook it at Lehi. "You don't really mean what you wrote on this parchment. Only a fool would take us farther from—"

"Laman." Sariah reined her horse forward, close enough not to lose her voice to the wind. "Don't speak to your father like that."

"Then you speak to him." Laman raised his father's scrolls in the air, the wind whipping the leather ends about the rolled documents. "Tell him you don't want to go farther from home. Tell him you're not able to travel in your condition. He'll listen to you."

"Your father knows what he's doing." Sariah held her hand to her womb to keep her robe from flapping against the unborn child. "If he says we go to Bozrah for a time, then to Bozrah we will go."

"This is foolishness Mother, don't you see that?"

"Son." Sariah shook her head. "No more."

Laman marched down along the line of mules, his stout, powerful body cutting a swath through the storm. He wedged his father's scrolls under his arm before pulling on the ropes tethering the mules together and testing the strength of the knots holding the supplies of food and water in place, then mounting his steed and coming back to the head of the caravan of mules. The wind streamed over Laman's black hair, but he didn't turn away from the sand blowing across his face. He pressed his father's leather scrolls against his ribs and said, "What about you and the camels? There's only one route to Bozrah from here."

"I'm taking Sam and Nephi with me." Lehi turned his gaze south along the shoreline toward the Arabah. The Dead Sea sat in a low rift valley with cliffs rising along the eastern shore, and these sandy hills along the west shore. And where the waters ended on the south shoreline, the low-lying desert valley—the Arabah—continued all the way to Aqaba on the coast of the Red Sea. There were no wells or springs in the Arabah, no creatures to hunt for food, and during the days of summer the sun heated the sand so hot no man dared set his foot on the burning ground. Nephi had never traveled the wide rift valley of the Arabah, but he'd heard stories of men who tried to reach Aqaba that way in summer to avoid paying taxes on the King's Highway and were never heard of again.

Lehi said, "Your brothers and I will take the camels around the south end of the Dead Sea."

Sam said, "We can't go that way. No one can travel the Arabah in summer. You know that. It's a winter route only."

"We can't risk taking the camels down the King's Highway, not with Laban and his men watching that trade route for us." Lehi patted a mule on the backside. "They won't pay much attention to these mules and sheep, but this many camels are sure to draw the attention of the captain."

"You don't know that. Laban and his men have better things to do than patrol the trade route for us." Laman leaned over the saddle. "He's forgotten about us."

"We can't take that chance." Lehi took Sariah by the hand. "Splitting the caravan is the only way to be sure we get you safely to Bozrah."

"Not through the Arabah, not in summer." Sam stepped around in front of Lehi, the wind blowing through his curly cap of light brown hair. "You know that better than any of us. If the lack of water doesn't kill us, the heat certainly will."

"I'll not parade these camels down the King's Highway and I won't risk taking your mother or our friends across the Arabah." Lehi placed his hand on Sam's shoulder. "If we travel quickly, we have plenty of water to get three of us through to Bozrah."

"And what if we can't travel quickly? What if this storm slows us?"

"We'll travel by night and use the tent for shade by day." Lehi took a bag of money from his belt and handed it over to Laman. "There's enough money to get you to Bozrah comfortably. The trade route between there and Jericho is dotted with inns. I want your mother staying in the finest lodgings and eating the best foods. Do you understand?"

"All the money in the world won't make this journey comfortable." Laman stuffed the bag under his belt, but before he started the mule caravan across the beach, Lehi took the boy's steed by the bridle and kept him from pulling away. He said, "I want you to stop in the date groves east of Jericho and buy as many sacks of the fruit as you can load onto these mules."

Laman pushed his father's scrolls under his riding robe, hiding the writings from view before shouting through the howling wind. "Why do we need so many dates?"

Nephi stepped closer, his hand cupped about his ear to keep the hissing wind from drowning his father's words. Did he really mean to have Laman buy so many dates? They were a fine food, the golden brown fruit filled with the strengthening sustenance of lamb, the whole goodness of vegetables, and the roughage of grains. There was not another food with the power to sustain life in the desert wilderness like a simple date. It stored well, it didn't require much space, and caravaneers headed through the remote wastelands of the Arabian Peninsula and stocked their caravans with large supplies from the groves at Jericho before heading out. It was the eternal fruit—sweet above all others—and for a man traveling the peninsula, it was desirable above any other fruit, with power to make a hungry traveler happy beyond measure. But they weren't headed to the southern extremes of Arabia, and Father's order to gather dates at Jericho was certainly not delightful news. They were fleeing for their lives and they didn't need dates to get them to Bozrah. There was more than enough food along the King's Highway and unless father planned to go beyond Bozrah, through the Border Mountains of the Jabal Range, and into the uninhabitable deserts that lay beyond, there was no reason to pack so much of this essential fruit for an unnecessary journey.

"We don't need that many dates unless . . . ?" Laman pulled on the reins hard enough to free his horse from Lehi's grip. "You're not taking us farther than Bozrah. I won't let you take us through the Border Mountains."

"I want us ready for whatever comes."

Laman came about, his horse snorting at the sand driving past its muzzle. "I've been ready for what's coming for some time now." He spurred his horse north along the shoreline, with Rebecca, Aaron, and Sariah reining in behind him. The mules trudged into line and Lemuel and Josiah the Potter followed at the rear, herding the animals toward calmer beaches where the roiling clouds and twisting sands hadn't penetrated to the sea and where they could find a way through this storm to Jericho.

Nephi watched the mule caravan head north through the blowing sand, the outline of the horses fading and the white hood of Mother's robe disappearing in a cloud of brown earth. This storm was dividing his family a second time. They were separated once when they left Ishmael's family at Beit Zayit and again in this wilderness. It didn't seem they would ever be reunited and he offered a silent plea for heaven to help Laman find a way to get Mother and Josiah the Potter and Rebecca and Aaron down the well-guarded King's Highway without attracting the attention of any who might report them to Captain Laban. They were fleeing again, forsaking their newfound home in search of another. But no matter where they wandered, Beit Zayit would always be the place of Nephi's inheritance and he couldn't keep from carrying the memory of that beautiful land in his heart. One day, by the grace of heaven, he would stake claim to a land that would be an inheritance for his family—forever.

The force of the storm swirled over them and Lehi started back toward the camels, telling Sam and Nephi to mount up and start the lead animals down along the beach while he followed behind, making sure they left nothing behind. Nephi didn't go to his horse immediately. He stayed watching long after the mules were gone around the bend in the beach and out of sight beyond the cliffs of this seaside alcove that had been their home for nearly three months. Didn't Father understand they would never be able to take everything with them, not with their family split up between every quarter of this land.

Father didn't understand that somewhere in all this fleeing Nephi was leaving behind his heart.

Laman reined ahead of the caravan, leading the mules around the bend from Qumran and out of the worst of the storm. The desert floor was a cloud of blowing sand, but none of it reached the sea where gulls glided on the updraft and squawked at their passing, the fowl calm and unfettered in the face of the approaching storm that refused to move closer to the shoreline. Laman kept the mules up away from the water's edge, their caravan cutting a wide path of footprints in the beach. He should have steered them through the water lapping along the shore, but there was a chance Captain Laban would come searching for them, and if the coming storm didn't ruin the evidence of their passing here, the captain and his scouts would know they traveled these shores toward Jericho. The scrolled ends of Father's leather parchments stabbed against Laman's side and he pulled them out from under his riding robe. The parchments he took from the writing box were his father's journal—the scrolls recording father's plans to flee to Bozrah. Laman kept his horse plodding through the sand, the hooves pressing an easily tracked path deep into the sand. He unrolled the soft leather of the newest scroll. Father's flowing pen strokes ran across the brown parchment, filling it with his foolish ideas of Babylonian conquest over Jerusalem and his plans to lead them to Bozrah. Laman tightened his grip on the scroll, folding the writings into his powerful hand. Lehi was a fool for taking them on this flight deeper into the southern territories and if he kept up this insanity, Laman was going to have to stop him from ruining their lives—forever.

Laman quickly rolled the scroll and checked to see if Mother was watching. Sariah rode with her head down, the hood of her robe bobbing to the stride of her horse like a seabird riding the surf. Aaron was over riding beside Rebecca, and Josiah the Potter was watching the storm that raged a few hundred cubits inland but without the power to push closer to them. He turned his gaze on Lemuel and when his brother saw him looking in his direction, Laman pressed his finger to his lips, telling him to keep quiet about what he was about to do. If these animal tracks didn't provide Captain Laban enough information to track them, Father's scrolls held more than enough. Laman lowered the writings down along the side of his saddle and let them fall into the sand amid the churning of his steed's hooves. Captain Laban was their best hope to keep Father from abandoning their home at Jerusalem. He would not let Father squander his wealth.

Beit Zayit was Laman's inheritance.

CHAPTER 20

Inspector Tobit reined his horse across the empty alcove, the morning sun rising over the Dead Sea and casting an orange glow over his search. The desert storm left the cliffs and stones surrounding this renegade hideout salted in a layer of sand, but there was nothing worth hiding and he ordered his men to fan out between the bluff along the north edge of this deserted place all the way to the caves in the cliffs to the south. They were to search everywhere. Tobit got down from the saddle, unwrapped the turban from around his face and let the band of white cloth fall to his shoulders. If this was the home of the Rekhabites, there had to be some sign of them living here.

Tobit walked along the top of the beach, scanning the lay of the land. The ground sloped down to the shore in perfect proportion without any irregular rise or fall. There was no sign of anyone digging in the sand, no footprints—nothing that indicated anyone lived in this remote place. Where was the evidence of a city that was rumored to thrive here? There were no stone walls rising out of the ground, no footings or foundations laid out across the strand, no sign at all that renegades built an outlaw city in this wasteland or had any intentions to base their subversions in this deserted headquarters. Tobit pushed the toe of his boot into the ground, the leather sinking deep into the sand. There were no fire pits left in the sand, no bones from the devoured carcass of a cooked lamb, no seeds or kernels of grain and not a single bit of horse or camel dung mixed into the sand. Where were the supplies to mount an attack against the New Babylonian Territories, the weapons to overthrow Babylonian rule, and the living quarters to house the mercenaries recruited to come against the armies of Nebuchadnezzar? This was neither a place of revolt nor the hideout of a renegade. It was a barren stretch of sand among thousands of square miles of wasteland, and if they didn't find any evidence of rebellion Tobit was going to call off this search and return home to the comforts of his mansion at Jericho.

The glint of morning sun reflected off the surface of the water and Tobit marched down the beach to the water's edge, his stride hurrying him to the south end of the alcove. The reason for his haste was there in the water, hardly a step beyond dry ground. Tobit pushed the end of his turban back from his face to keep it from obscuring his view. He leaned over the brackish water, his gaze fixed on the sandy bottom a hand's length beneath the calm surface. This Lehi was shrewder than Tobit thought him. The man hid the only evidence of their living here under the surface of—

"We have them!" Captain Laban spurred his white Arabian down along the strand, the animal racing over the beach and kicking up sand in its wake. He leaned forward in the saddle, driving the sleek animal at full gallop down through a cluster of soldiers, over the rise in the beachhead, and down to Tobit. He jumped from the saddle, his powerful legs landing firm in the sand. "Here it is, the evidence we need." He handed over a stack of leather parchments. "These writings came from the pen of the rebel leader, Lehi."

Tobit unraveled the document and wiped the sand from the leather, revealing the words of some sort of journal, or personal log. No, not a log. These were religious writings and they read like the words of a holy man. The first entry dated back a full three months. There were some extensive notes about a recent trial in Jerusalem of a man named Uriah and some quaint Hebrew observations about the customs of Babylonian rule among the Jews.

Laban said, "We should have ridden through the storm and not camped in that infernal desert." He paced down along the beach and when he came back to Tobit he said, "They can't have gotten far. There's a host of footprints running north along the beach. Horses, mules, sheep; there's even the mark of a milking goat." He stabbed his finger at another entry in the scrolls. "They're headed south by way of the King's Highway. We can send word for your soldiers to secure the route. I can provide them with detailed descriptions of the men they're looking for. Every outpost on the trade route should be notified. They won't be traveling fast with that many mules."

Tobit turned his head into the writings, quickly assessing the bits of information hidden between the lines of Lehi's writing. These were some sort of prophecies detailing the future of Jerusalem. They were recent writing, the last entry dated to only yesterday.

Tobit said, "Are you certain about Lehi?"

"Of course I am." Laban turned back, the heel of his boots digging into the sand. "He's headed to Bozrah by way of Jericho."

"Not his escape." Tobit lowered the scroll. "I mean his motives. Do you really think him to be the rebel you've made him out to be?"

Laban lowered his voice. "Why do you ask?"

Tobit raised the scroll draped between his hands. "These aren't the words of a man bent on overthrowing Babylon." Tobit steadied the scroll for Laban to read the first entries, the ones detailing Lehi's certainty that the Babylonians would destroy Jerusalem and deport the Hebrews as slaves.

"I told you he's a troublemaker, a warmonger." Laban tapped his fingers against the parchment. "He uses these sorts of claims to incite a rebellion. That's why he started the rumors of tax revolt. It's all part of his lies and tricks." Laban untied his black turban and wrapped the cloth around his forearm. "I tell you, he's a madman. He's headed north along this beach and the longer we waste our time here the less chance we have of capturing him."

"A rebel wouldn't be headed deeper into the deserts."

"What are you talking about?" Laban began to pace in front of Tobit. "Of course he's running away. He wrote it right there in his own handwriting."

"I don't care what this scroll says. If Lehi's the agitator you say he is, he's headed back to Jerusalem with plans to cause another uprising."

"Don't be a fool." Laban stood next to Tobit and pointed out the final entry in the journal. "He's fleeing to Bozrah."

"Then take your men and that longhaired scout of yours and follow their mule caravan down the trade route to Bozrah." Tobit took the reins of his horse and started into the water, his boots splashing against the gentle surf. "And see that you notify the outpost at the trailhead of the King's Highway. I want every soldier in my army to have a detailed description of the men we're looking for."

"Why don't you inform your men yourself?"

Tobit moved farther out from the beach, the water rising up to his shins, and his horse kicking a spray. "I'll meet you in Bozrah once you've secured the main trade route."

"What about you?" Captain Laban stayed out of the water, picking his way along the wet sand and guiding his white Arabian by the reins, following Tobit down along the shoreline. "Where are you going?"

Tobit stood in the knee-deep water, his gaze turned to the south. "I'm taking my men that way."

"Listen to me." Laban stepped forward, but the water lapped around his new leather boots and chased him back to dry ground. "Lehi and the rest of his party are headed north. Their tracks lead that way. You're chasing ghosts if you think anyone is foolish enough to head south. You can't get to Bozrah that way. It's impossible in summer."

"Maybe Lehi headed to Bozrah, and maybe he's headed back to Jerusalem, but wherever he's going, he went south from here and I'm going to track him step for step." Tobit stuffed the leather parchments of Lehi's journal under his arm and reached down under the surface until his hands felt the muddy bottom. Just as he thought. There were deep imprints running across the sea floor and he let his fingers slowly pass over them. The tracks couldn't be more than a day old, maybe two. The mud was beginning to break up, but he could feel the cloven double toe mark left by camels and the rounded imprint of horse hooves—probably three riders on horseback. He kept moving down along the sea floor, his feet moving slowly through the water to keep from stirring the surface and cloud his view of the bottom. He was right about the horses, there were three steeds and about twenty camels, all head south.

Captain Laban got up into the saddle and brought his Arabian around, the animal kicking up a spray along the water's edge. "Do you hear me? You're chasing ghosts if you think any fool would travel south. No one crosses the Arabah in summer."

Tobit brought his mud-covered hands out of the salty waters, the slime dripping off the end of his fingers and the smell of brine water scenting the air around him. He said, "Ghosts don't hide their tracks on the bottom of the sea, Captain."

CHAPTER 21

Laman led his band of weary travelers down a narrow path through the protective shadows of the date palms, choosing the thick cover of trees that grew on the plains east of Jericho farthest from the city gates. Lemuel, with the help of Aaron, Josiah the Potter, and Rebecca rode near the back, herding the sheep and goats from wandering among the trees while Sariah stayed directly behind him, her horse following like an animal tethered to a short rope, though there was nothing forcing Mother to stay so close.

Sariah rode with her hood pulled down over her eyes, her shoulders forward, and a hand across her womb and it was impossible to know if she were steering her horse this close or if she'd fallen asleep from the weariness and let the animal find its own way. Mother hardly moved in the saddle with the burden of carrying a child and it was sheer foolishness to lead her farther from home. They reached these date palm groves east of Jericho in less than two full days and if they headed west from here they could be home in two more. Laman reined his horse between the trunks of two close-growing trees and kept moving through the cool shadows beneath these branches. The tired troop of riders followed Laman around a bend in the narrow trail, up a gentle slope toward the back of the grove where the vineyard owner said they could camp for the night and harvest whatever they needed, so long as they paid him for the dates come morning. A small irrigation channel crossed Laman's path and he steered his mount through the trickle of water, the animal's hooves sloshing through the water-soaked earth. The Jordan River Delta branched out across this desert plain in a web of small tributaries, the blue-green waters running dirty brown across this dusty vineyard and seeping into the parched soil to nourish the roots of a thousand acres of date palms. The insufferable heat of Jericho baked the ground hot enough to choke life out of the dust, but with the life-giving waters of the Jordan irrigating this delta, the date palms thrived, basking in the heat along the north shore of the Dead Sea and covering the desert floor with the lush green color of life.

Laman turned past another stand of trees and came into an opening where the rays of the afternoon sun found their way past the thick canopy of palms, the light chasing away the shadows and casting rays over the fruit clustered beneath the branches. The sunlight penetrated the clear skins of the dates, the fruit glowing like a thousand flickering oil lamps hanging from the branches, and Laman cursed the beauty of it under his breath. The dates decorated the trees like festive ornaments on a feast day, but no amount of dressing or trimming could change the foolishness that brought them here. What sort of insanity was Father plotting by sending them to harvest fruit from these groves? They didn't need dates for a journey to Bozrah and they weren't going farther into the wilderness of Arabia. They would never survive that journey, not with Mother in her condition and none of them prepared for the harshness of traveling beyond the civilized borders of Bozrah. And if Lehi intended to take them much beyond that outpost, Laman would have no other choice than to stop him and save his family from the hell these dates were certain to bring upon them. They were nothing like the dates Laman purchased in the markets at Jerusalem and packed on caravans to Egypt—none of them were gone black. These unpicked dates had an unearthly glow like—

"The fruit of heaven it is." Josiah the Potter reined past Laman and circled in next to the tallest tree. He sat up in the saddle, plucked a ripening date from the cluster and took a bite. "The most heavenly dates I've ever tasted." He picked a handful of the glowing fruit and came around next to Laman. "Go ahead, boy, have one, they'll help you forget the long ride from Qumran." He popped another date into his mouth and spoke between bites. "Nothing brings a hungry traveler greater joy than a tree-ripened date fresh from the—"

"I don't want one." Laman pushed Josiah's hand aside and ordered Lemuel to help Sariah and Rebecca off their horses and under the shade of the trees.

"Have some fruit, boy." Josiah inched his mount closer. "They have a wonderful flavor like nothing you've ever tasted on this earth. It's like eating the fruit of—"

"For the love of heaven, I told you, I don't have an appetite for dates." Laman backed his horse away from Josiah's offering. "I may never have one."

"Come now, son, you don't know what you're missing."

"I know exactly what I'm missing."

"You really should—"

"Enough about dates."

"Is there something wrong, Laman?" Sariah pulled back the white hood of her riding robe revealing her travel-weary face gone pale from the long ride up the coast of the Dead Sea, and she sat in the saddle with her shoulders forward, not uttering a word about her discomfort. Laman prodded his mount around next to her. What utter foolishness was this? If Father would only let him take Mother home she'd be in the care of nursemaids and doctors to see to her unborn child. Laman reached for her hand. "You're in no condition to travel to Bozrah or any other place in this wilderness. We're hardly two days' ride from home. Why don't you let me take you back to the comfort of home?"

"No dear, I'll not hear of such a thing." Sariah took back her hand and sat as straight as her weak body allowed. "Your father told us to harvest a supply of these dates and we'll not do any other thing but what he asked of us."

"It isn't safe here." Laman spurred his horse in a circle, squinting through the long stand of branches and searching for any sign of soldiers passing on the main road. "We should abandon this foolishness before someone is hurt."

Aaron spurred over next to Laman. "Do you think you'll be safe from harm at Beit Zayit?"

"Safer and certainly more comfortable than we are in this desert."

"The comforts of Beit Zayit aren't worth the trouble Laban will visit on your doorstep."

"We can defend ourselves from him."

"Captain Laban commands armies, son." Josiah the Potter reined around the trunk of a date palm. "You can't defend against that kind of force no matter how many menservants you have at your plantation."

"Laban won't come with an army if he can kill you with his own hands." Aaron ran his hand over the bandages wrapped tight around his thigh. "He'll come in the dark of night with a bow or a knife or whatever instrument of death suits his fancy and wait on your porch until he finds a way to sneak into your home; and while you're sleeping he'll steal your mortality with about as much remorse as a thief who steals a lemon from the market." He slowly shook his head, his brown hair falling down into his blue eyes. "I've seen into Laman's soul when he has death on his mind. He's hungry to kill and he'll hunt you quietly. Laban is a hunter and he'll hunt you like he hunted me and he'll not stop until he's caught his prey." His hands began to tremble and he steadied them against the wound in his thigh. He turned in his saddle toward Laman, his blue eyes filled with the steeliness of a man who'd faced death and won. "You can talk all you want about going home and enjoying your possessions, but what sort of joy do you think you'll have when every shadow in the halls and corridors of Beit Zayit could be hiding Captain Laban? Say whatever you like about returning to the comforts of your wealth and your lands, but the good life you so desperately want to find again will escape you."

Laman said, "Captain Laban won't harm us."

Aaron leaned forward and patted Beuntahyu's neck with an open palm. "Lions never lose their thirst for blood."

Laman said, "Have you gone mad as well?"

"As well as who?"

Laman didn't answer. He couldn't tell them he thought Lehi possessed of the same insanity that afflicted Aaron. It was better to counsel with his brother Lemuel in private on the matter of Father's foolishness. Lemuel was the only right-minded soul in this sorry company of travelers. He said, "We'd be no worse off returning to Beit Zayit than we are hiding like outcasts in this wilderness."

"You can think that way if you like, but I prefer the safety of this desert to the comforts of home." Aaron inched his Arabian back from Laman and steered her toward the golden glow of the tallest date palm. "Captain Laban is hunting us."

"He wouldn't be if it weren't for Lehi."

Sariah said, "No son. You'll not speak ill of your father."

"I won't lie. It's Father he's after."

"If we must live in this desert to protect your father, then so be it. We'll suffer this place." Sariah pulled her hood back in place, shrouding her eyes. Laman was certain those eyes reflected her longing for the comforts of home—a longing she kept hidden from him, locked away in the deepest recesses of her heart. She didn't really want to follow her husband into this place; she couldn't want that, not after what they left behind in Jerusalem. Sariah said, "It's time we saw to harvesting these dates. That's what your father wants of us."

Josiah sidled between them, his horse chomping at the bit. He offered another handful of golden-white dates to Laman and said, "Go on, boy. Have something to eat. It's good for cheering your spirits. It'll settle your mind and—"

"I don't need your precious fruit to cheer me." Laman shoved Josiah's hand aside, throwing the dates from his hand and scattering them over the ground. "Do you understand? This whole venture will bring us nothing but misery." He came around and started out of the grove. "You can pick all the fruit you like and pack it onto the mules, but I haven't the stomach for this, not when this fruit has the power to take us further from our inheritance."

Laman reined out of the clearing, spurring between the close-growing trunks of the date palms, over the shallow irrigation channel, and down a long row of trees until he came out onto the dusty main road running past the vineyard. He rode far enough to clear the branches of date palms and check the way west. The grove stood within sight of Jericho—the headquarters of the occupying Babylonian army—and it was foolishness for him to stay on the road any longer than to check for soldiers. There were none he could see riding out the gates of the city and he came around and headed to the other side of the groves, the palm branches giving way to a view of the ride east. A caravan of camels traveled the king's highway making a long, slow descent out of the plateau country of Moab to the level plains of Jericho. It was a long way off, the caravan nothing larger than a line against the gray brown earth of the hills, but there weren't any military patrols on the road. Nothing moved fast enough to be anything but the plodding of merchant traders traveling the trade route from Arabia to Jerusalem.

Laman started back into the cover of trees, when the pounding of horse hooves over the dusty road drew his gaze back toward Jericho.

Where did those soldiers come from? The road was clear not moments before, but now ten Hebrew cavalrymen spurred around the bend, the troop racing down along the shaded edge of the grove, and Laman quickly reined in behind a stand of trees.

"Captain Laban. Is that you, sir?" The lead rider stopped about three trees down from where Laman hid, then prodded his horse into the shadows beneath the branches, but not far enough to find Laman's hiding place.

"Lieutenant, sir." A second rider sidled in next to the officer. "We left Captain Laban in Jericho."

"I know that, but . . ."

"But what, sir?"

"Who else could it have been?" The lieutenant stepped his mount down to the tree next to the one where Laman hid. He pushed the bands of his black turban back off his brow and squinted to see into the shadows, his gaze moving over the grove like an eagle perched on a branch, searching its prey. "The man I saw had the same thick shoulders and dark complexion as Captain Laban. I've known the man for years, worked with him since the day he was appointed Captain of the Guard after his father and brothers were killed in the first Babylonian conflict, God rest their souls." He reined back out onto the road. "I'm certain it was Captain Laban."

"Lieutenant, sir." The quartermaster trotted forward from the back of the company. "Captain Laban isn't scheduled to leave Jericho until late this afternoon."

The first rider said, "That's right, sir. He's headed for a meeting at the tax collection station on the King's Highway with details about a caravan of mules we should watch for."

The lieutenant shook his head. "It was him right down to every detail except . . ."

"Except what, sir?"

"The hair." The lieutenant passed his hand over his scalp. "The man I saw along here had longer hair than Captain Laban. It was the same dark black, mind you, but it was longer than Captain Laban's."

"Sir, we should be on our way." The first rider urged his horse to the middle of the dusty road and the troop fell into line behind his lead. "We're to be at the tax collection station before the night watch."

The lieutenant gave him permission to lead out and he would follow at the rear, but when the company pulled away from the grove in a thunder of galloping horses, the lieutenant didn't fall into line at the back. He sidestepped his mount down to the stand of trees where Laman hid. It was a run of thick-trunked trees with close-growing shoots coming up around the base, providing enough foliage to obscure Laman from the closest inspection. The lieutenant lingered three lengths from Laman, his gaze examining the date palms as if he could see through the green leaves to where Laban sat, his horse pressed up against the trunk, his body crouched forward in the saddle like a cobra ready to strike. Laman slowed his breathing and peered back at the man like a lion peers through the brush, his eyes set behind the vents in the palm leaves. The lieutenant reined past the trunk, and Laman jumped him, pulling him from the saddle. They rolled in the dusty road and Laman landed a barrage of blows across the man's face, silencing him before he could summon his men for help. He dragged the man's unconscious body beneath the cover of date palms, removed his gray Hebrew officer's tunic, his silver-studded kilt and high strung riding boots, leaving him without a single shred of clothing to cover his body, before leaping back into the saddle and spurring into the grove to warn the others.

Their plans had changed.

"Steady, girl."

Aaron steered Beuntahyu with a gentle prod from his knees while working his fingers over the fruit that hung from the branches of the date palms like lanterns in the darkness—the sunlight filtering down over the clear amber skin and brightening them to the very center. He stuffed a cluster in his harvest sack and then he cut another bunch from the next highest branch. These weren't dried dates gone dark after sitting in the sun. They were fresh-picked without shriveled skin and it was like harvesting nuggets of transparent gold. Aaron plucked a single date and worked the fruit between his teeth, the sweetness tantalizing his tongue beyond any taste he'd ever known. It was like food from another world, but since the lands of Jerusalem and Sidon weren't hot enough to ripen dates with such flavor, he'd never known the heavenly taste he was missing. How had he lived nineteen years on this earth and never enjoyed the taste of tree-ripened dates? Aaron picked another cluster from the tree with the enthusiasm of a young child finding a treasure for the first time in his life.

They had till morning to harvest as many dates as they could pack onto the backs of their mules, but with the sweetness of this fruit begging Aaron to keep eating, a good many of them would never see the inside of this harvest bag—not with Josiah the Potter eating them as quickly as he could pick them.

"Enough of this." Laman galloped past a stand of trees and jumped down from the saddle. He hurried over to a mule, found the sharpest knife in the saddlebags and began cutting away his hair, lifting the long strands and whacking it off in large clumps, throwing his long black locks at his feet.

"Laman?" Sariah stepped from beneath the shade of a date palm. "What are you doing, son?"

"Get everyone mounted up." He shook a fistful of hair at Lemuel before throwing it aside and scraping the sharp blade over the back of his neck, shaving the hair down to stubble. "We have to get past the first checkpoint on the King's Highway before it's too late."

Josiah set aside his bag of dates. "Too late for what?"

"What's come over you?" Lemuel reached for the knife, but Laman pulled away from his reaching and shaved away the hair above his ear.

Rebecca helped Sariah over, holding her hand and guiding her over the unevenness of the ground. "Whatever are you doing, son?"

Aaron came in next to Rebecca, and lowered his half-filled sack of dates to the ground. "Have you lost your mind?"

Laman threw a clump of hair at Aaron's feet. "Don't ever accuse me of that, do you understand? Insanity is not my trouble." He worked the blade up the side of his scalp. "Captain Laban knows we're traveling this way with a caravan of mules. We have to split up."

"What?" Josiah stepped in between Aaron and Rebecca, his arms wrapped around both of them. "You don't really mean that."

"It's the only way if you want to get to Bozrah." Laman dropped another fistful of hair to the ground. "I'll take Mother down the King's

Highway. Any other route is too difficult for her. The soldiers are looking for a caravan of mules, not a man and woman on horseback."

Lemuel said, "What about the rest of us?"

"You'll take the mules farther east through the wide-open deserts of the Way of the Wilderness. The trail headed that way branches from the main route a few miles from here."

Josiah said, "We can't split up. The Way of the Wilderness is too hard a journey."

"It's either that or we go back to Jerusalem." Laman pointed the tip of the knife at him. "Which do you choose?"

Josiah didn't answer and Laman said, "We leave now." He bent over, quickly shaving off the last remnants of his long, flowing, black hair.

"What about the dates?" Aaron held out his sack. "Lehi wanted the mules packed with them.

"We don't have time for dates. We have to be past the first check-point before Laban arrives."

Sariah said, "We can't leave without the dates."

"We can't afford not to leave." Laman dusted the hair off his blade and stuck it under the brim of his boot. "What is that you're always telling me about our troubles, Mother?"

"That God will provide?"

"That's it. We're going to take care of ourselves and let God provide whatever dates we may need once we reach Bozrah."

"But son, that isn't what I meant by—"

"Whatever you intended by it, we're not staying here longer to pack the mules."

Josiah said, "What makes you think you can take your mother down the King's Highway without Captain Laban catching you?"

Laman took out a Hebrew officer's uniform from his saddlebags and held the gray tunic beneath his chin, the cloth falling down over his thick chest, the silver-threaded stripes glimmering in the light. He possessed the same stature as Captain Laban, the same dark eyes, the same short shaved hair, and now the same dress. Laman stepped into the kilt before throwing off his traveling robe and pulling the tunic on over his powerful shoulders. He cinched the belt around his waist and stood next to his horse with the military saddle lashed around the animal's belly. He was the image of the captain, a perfect replica down to the height of his head, the twist of his lips, the turn of his nose, and the thickness of his arms. It was like seeing the ghost of Captain Laban appear in the date grove. He ordered Aaron out of the saddle, telling him that he needed a white Arabian that matched Captain Laban's horse and the blacksmith could have her back when they reached Bozrah. Then he mounted Beuntahyu and came around in front of them. "I won't have any trouble getting Mother down the King's Highway." He straightened his officer's tunic over his shoulders and reined in next to Sariah.

He said, "No soldier will question Captain Laban and his riding companion."

CHAPTER 22

Darius reined up the sandy rise while his father ordered the company to fan out around the abandoned campsite and see what they could find before the sun set. He inched his horse to the edge of the hill and took in the full breadth of the deep-rift valley of the Arabah spreading out below the encampment. It was wider and deeper than he believed and he quickly took out his parchment and added this detail to his map. The desolate waste of the Arabah began where the southernmost waters of the Dead Sea turned to a dried, cracked plain, the moisture evaporating into the heat of the desert sun, leaving nothing but an endless expanse of salty white deposit over the flat earth—the lowest, flattest stretch of earth in all the known world. Darius made note of the unpredictable shoreline, using a dotted line over the soft leather map. These salty waters ended here, but the Arabah grew wider and deeper all the way to the Fountain of the Red Sea, and Darius sketched into his map what details he could see, the orange light of the dying sun casting shadows across this desolate valley.

The low-lying rift valley of the Arabah attracted the most insufferable heat in the territory and the impassable clime chased away any who dared believe they could descend down into this sixty-mile-wide canyon, cross the barren rift between the highlands of the Judean Wilderness and the plateaus of Moab on the far rim and live to tell of the journey. A whirlwind kicked up across the flat expanse, driving the sand and mixing it with the salty ground before blowing up the rise. Darius covered his face with the soft leather map and waited for the stir to pass. This was a place even God had forsaken and he was going to tell his father that he was wrong; no matter what Lehi's journal said, the rebel wasn't going to Bozrah, at least not this way. It was sheer foolishness to think Lehi would dare cross this infernal pit where the sun baked the ground so hot that no man or beast set foot on it during the heat of the summer. And he was going to tell him before he gave the order to follow Lehi into this valley of death.

Darius cantered over to the other side of the encampment, the westward-rolling sand dunes of the Judean Wilderness reaching up out of this rift valley toward the cool blue mountains of Southern Judah and on to the highlands surrounding Jerusalem. Lehi went that way—he had to. It was the only sane choice. Darius got down from the saddle, stood over the burnt remains of a fire, and rubbed the charred ends of a branch between his fingers. Father would be along later to check the neatly arranged stones, but for now he was busy down the ridge searching for footprints in the sand, and Darius tested the latent heat of the dead fire. The rocks around the pit were warm and the ashes fairly new. They were gaining on Lehi, but how close were they? The man couldn't be more than a day ahead of them, but in which direction?

Darius rolled his map and stuffed it under his arm. He walked a large circle around the fire pit, scanning the ground for any clue revealing where Lehi had gone from here, but there were no tracks leading away from this place. If Lehi wanted to cover his escape from here, he never would have left this fire pit intact. But why go to the trouble of removing the footprints and brushing away the animal tracks, only to leave the most obvious clue in full view? Darius ran his hand through his hair and held onto the ends. None of this made any sense, not unless—

Tobit said, "Do you have a map of the wells between here and Bozrah?" He stood on the edge of the rise a little way down from the fire pit. He kept his back to Darius, his hands on his hips, the loose ends of his white turban fluttering in the early evening breeze, and his gaze turned out over the Arabah.

Darius walked over, wiping the ashes of the fire pit and the sweat from his brow. Tobit stood next to his father, both of them looking out across the Arabah. "You don't really think Lehi would try to cross this wilderness do you? It'll take him three days. He'll have to hunker down his animals under whatever shade he can make for them, and once the cool of the morning burns off, his herd will go through water like cheap grain in a stockyard at feeding time. And once the water's gone, he's a dead man."

"The wells, son. Tell me about the water."

"There aren't any." Darius took out his map and quickly scanned over the drawings. "There's no sweet water between here and Bozrah and if he tries to cool his thirst with brine from the Dead Sea, he'll go more insane than he already is."

"What about the heat?"

"As bad or worse than the deserts farther south in Arabia."

"And the lay of the land?"

"Flat as a snake's belly, at least until you reach the steep cliffs of the plateau country of Moab on the far rim. If Lehi makes it across before his water supplies run out, he can't get up the other side. He can climb out with ropes, but there's no way his caravan of camels can scale the eastern rim of the Arabah. The cliffs are a good two hundred feet high. He's trapped in this rift valley."

"He can ride south, can't he?"

"He'd have to go at least twenty-five, maybe thirty miles to find a way up and out."

"That would add another full day of—"

"Two days, sir. He still has to ride to Bozrah. Lehi can't cross here and he knows it. There isn't enough water on the backs of his camels for that long a journey."

"That should tell us a good deal about the man."

"It tells us he's a fool if he attempts it."

"He may well be that, son." Tobit started toward the fire pit and stood over the ring of rocks around the ashes. "Take a message to the men. They're down over the hill looking for tracks."

"What's the message?"

"Tell him we're all fools." He stared down at the fire pit. "We cross the Arabah tonight."

"We can't ride seventy miles through that heat. It will take us . . ." Darius turned his head into his map, quickly calculated the exact distance and when he looked up he said, "We don't have enough water for three days out there."

"Then we cross it in two days."

Darius marched around in front Tobit, his map raised between them. "Do you know what you're asking?"

"I'm asking you to capture a fugitive, and we're going to hunt him down—wherever he leads us."

"What if we run out of water?" Darius lowered his map. "We can't just climb out of the Arabah for a drink."

"Neither can Lehi." Tobit played the toe of his boot through the ashes in the fire pit. "My instincts tell me he's headed that way."

"What else do your instincts tell you?"

Tobit shook the ashes off his boot. "Check the fire pit, son."

"I did."

"Check it again."

"For what?"

"A message."

"You can't leave a message in ashes."

Tobit said, "There aren't any footprints in the sand. No animal tracks, nothing that would tell us which way Lehi went from here. But he left this fire pit in full view."

"That doesn't tell us anything."

Tobit folded his arms across his chest. "It should tell you the man intended for us to find it."

"Why would he do such a foolish thing?"

"Go on, check the stones, son. And tell me how long ago Lehi left this fire to die out on its own."

Darius went to his knees and felt the rocks. They were slightly warm, the surface cool, but there was enough heat permeating from deep inside to make an intelligent guess. "I'd say mid-morning, but no later than midday."

"The man is talking to us."

"He's trying to steer us off his path. Don't you see that?"

"There's more here than you think, son." Tobit got down on his knees with Darius. He ran his hands over the warm stones, stirred his fingers through the ashes. "If Lehi was using this fire pit as a decoy, how did he know to leave it? The man would have to be a prophet of the most incredible order to know we're tracking him. For all he knows, we never went to Qumran, and if he thought we did go there, he certainly doesn't think he left any sign of his escape. Why would he risk leaving a message for a scout he couldn't be certain was following him? No, son, the hunted don't disguise their tracks as decoys; they hide them."

"Do you think he doesn't know we're following him?"

Tobit tightened his grip on the stones around the fire pit. "He knows, and he's trying to tell us something."

"What if this fire pit is a trick? Lehi is playing with us. Why else would he leave something for us to find?"

"He could be telling us something more than what hour of the day he left here."

"What do we care? He's an outlaw."

Tobit stirred the charred end of the stick about the fire pit. "We care because we need the answer to one question."

"What's that?"

Tobit didn't provide an answer. He sat on a protruding rock and set his feet up on the firestones. "What do your maps tell you about Lehi?"

"Maps don't speak." Darius put away his drawings of the southern territory. "But if they could, they'd tell me only a fool would head any other direction but west, back through the Judean Wilderness toward Jerusalem."

"Desperate men do foolish things."

"I don't think Lehi is desperate."

Tobit said, "Then what is he?"

"He's what Captain Laban said he is. A rebel. An outlaw. A fool bent on starting an uprising against the kingdom." Darius sat on the rock beside his father. "Isn't that what you think he is?"

"I never brand a man before I know him." Tobit took a long breath. "But I will say that if Lehi's an outlaw, then he's a very methodical one, and if he's a renegade then he's a careful one. And if he's a fool, he's the most intelligent one I've ever known." He took the map from Darius and slowly rolled the leather around itself. "If you want to catch a man, you don't study the routes of his exodus. You look inside his heart and get inside his mind."

"We don't know the man. We've never met him. We hardly know what he looks like. How do you get inside the mind of ghost?"

"Lehi's a very serious man."

"Serious?"

"That's right. He didn't make his enemies without calculating the cost. Only a serious man would dare such things as he dares."

"Exactly what daring things are you talking about?"

"Defying the rulers of his people, accusing them of being murderers, claiming that God revealed their doings to him, and then eluding their very best efforts to capture him."

"Where do you come by all this?"

Tobit opened the satchel strapped to his side, took out Lehi's journal, and handed over the soft leather parchment. "You should read this."

Read it? Darius had gone over every word of Lehi's journal so many times he could quote from it. Lehi wrote he was headed to Bozrah, but it was all a trick, no matter that Captain Laban believed he was headed that direction. Lehi left his parchment at Qumran, hoping they'd rush off to Bozrah on a wild chase while he headed back to his home in Jerusalem. "Lehi didn't cross the Arabah to Bozrah."

Tobit spread the scroll out in front of Darius. He said, "Read, son."

"I've already—"

"Then read it one more time."

Darius quickly moved his finger over Lehi's words. The first part of the scroll was nothing more than an account of caravanning. That much Darius already knew and he didn't need to read it again. There was a long list of cargo caravanned to Egypt on Lehi's most recent trip last growing season, his careful pen strokes accounting for every cistern of olive oil, bottle of wine, and bag of grain on the back of fifty camels. Darius quickly scanned the cargo list until he found the entry on the animals. That was the right number. Lehi owned fifty camels in his merchant trade and with a herd that size, the man could sell his caravan and live off the wealth. Darius brought his head up. "What does this have to do with capturing Lehi?"

"Keep reading."

Darius moved farther down the meticulous business record of this outlaw. Line after line detailed every bend and twist along the trade route between Jerusalem and Egypt. There was a description of the high-mountain water conditions, miniscule details about a washed-out section of the trail above the Bezor River, and a perfect accounting of every well through the southern hill country of Judah all the way to the Great Sea.

Darius said, "So the man knows the trade route."

"He knows it better than anyone." Tobit leaned over his son's shoulder. "Look at that. He includes more detail in a few words than you have in an entire map."

"What are you trying to tell me?"

"This Lehi is no fool when it comes to these territories. There isn't a trail he hasn't traveled or a hidden valley he doesn't know about. Our knowledge of these lands is nothing compared to his understanding."

"Lehi is lying. All his writings are lies." Darius skipped to the end of the parchment, down to where the most damning words of Lehi condemned him a traitor, just like Captain Laban claimed. "Here, look at this. Only a rebel would write something like this."

"I've already read it."

"Then what do you make of it?"

Darius leaned over his father's shoulder and together they read again the entry of Lehi accusing Captain Laban and Zadock of plotting the murder of King Zedekiah. That was most certainly a lie. Captain Laban and Zadock may not be the most likeable men, but they weren't murderers and they certainly wouldn't kill Zedekiah—not without good reason. Their king gave them their powers and without him they were nothing more than commoners without any claim to royalty or the power that flowed from royal lineage. Darius ran his finger farther down the parchment to where Lehi wrote all sorts of odd warnings about the Babylonian army destroying the Jews and carrying them away captive. It began with a line explaining that these were the words given to Lehi by God and he used a prophetic language, speaking of the future as if it had already come to pass. There was a detailed description of some future starvation and slaughter from a siege of Jerusalem, followed by the destruction of the Jewish capital and the deportation of thousands of Hebrew slaves. It was nothing more than the ranting of a madman bent on destroying the New Babylonian Kingdom, and if Father didn't see this man for who he was, then Darius was going to have to insist that Lehi be treated as a threat not only to Captain Laban and the Jews, but to every peace-loving Babylonian between here and the Tigris.

Darius said, "These are the words of a man with a mind to provoke an uprising."

"That, or . . ."

"Or what?"

"Look at this, son." Tobit brought his finger back up to the middle of the scroll where Lehi wrote about setting camp for his caravan at Raphia, and immediately his writing changed from a merchant trader's account to the telling of a very personal story. Lehi described his worry over a young prophet named Uriah with the words *"deep anguish,"* and *"utter concern."* The man, Uriah, was captured in Egypt and on his return to Jerusalem he passed Lehi's caravan at Raphia. The Hebrew military inflicted a good deal of hurt on the man and it caused Lehi so much concern he climbed to the top of the hills above his camp along the shores of the Great Sea and pleaded with his God to spare Uriah's life, and that wasn't all. Darius kept his finger moving over the description of the appearance of a pillar of fire on a rock and—no, that couldn't be. Darius set aside the scroll. God didn't speak to men, not like this. And if He did, he certainly wouldn't speak to an outlaw. Where did Lehi get the outlandish sense to write that he'd seen a light, and in that light he saw a being he called the Messiah—the creator of the whole earth? Lehi was a rebel worthy of execution, and Darius turned to his father. "Do you really believe this?"

"That isn't the right question, son. If Lehi's journal is a lie, then he made it all up to fool us, send us the wrong way, and his writings are nothing more than an elaborate scheme to elude us at every turn."

"And if what he recorded isn't a lie?"

"You're still not asking the right question."

"Then what is it?"

A smile pulled at Tobit's lips. "You should ask, 'Does Lehi believe he's a prophet?'"

"Does he?"

"Tell the men we ride at sundown."

"You haven't answered me, sir."

Tobit stabbed the toe of his boot into the ashes, the gray-white powder covering the stones of the fire pit he said were the best clue to Lehi's mind—a charred passage through the portals of the man's soul—and the recollection of his words rushed through Darius's mind. If Lehi was using this fire pit as a decoy, how did he know to leave it? For all the man knew, they never came to Qumran. Why would he risk leaving a message for a scout he couldn't be certain was following him? The hunted didn't disguise their tracks as decoys— they hid them.

Tobit said, "Lehi is either a rebel or he's a prophet."

CHAPTER 23

Phineas turned his back to his Babylonian companion sharing the watch post, pulled his brass helmet down over his ears, and leaned against the doorpost on the guard station. If he had to listen to anymore poorly spoken Hebrew, he was going to take the sword the soldier was polishing and silence him with it. The banners of the king of Judah and the king of Babylon snapped in the breeze above the awning of this small, mud-brick guard post set alongside the dusty road. The Babylonian soldier collected the taxes and Phineas translated for the merchant traders, and since nearly all of the caravaneers traveling the King's Highway didn't speak a barley corn's worth of Chaldean, he did most of the talking while his tax-collecting companion took their money. This may be the New Babylonian Territory, but in these parts, the local Hebrew dialect was the international tongue.

The Babylonian soldier tapped Phineas on the shoulder and mumbled something about the sword he was polishing, but he butchered his words so badly it was hard to know if he was practicing his Hebrew or whether he simply possessed an insufferable case of poor diction. Couldn't he polish his weapon in silence and not fumble with words he didn't know? It wasn't swaddling cloth, for the love of Moses; the man was using a chamois to polish his blade. And fish oils were for cooking, not shining metal. Couldn't he get anything right? Phineas spoke the words "resin oils" aloud and he would have ordered the soldier to repeat after him, but the Babylonians commanded this outpost and if Phineas had the nerve to order the man around the guard post, he might as well tell him to get on his horse and ride back to Babylon where he came from and let the Hebrew army take care of the business of operating the King's Highway. Why did they need foreigners to run a trade route they'd operated for three hundred years?

The Babylonian soldier rubbed his belly, pointed to his mouth and said, "I am good morning."

Phineas rubbed the back of his head. This poor soul was no doubt learning his Hebrew from the jesters in the company assigned to this outpost and he wasn't speaking a greeting. The man was hungry. "Can you say: I am hungry?"

"Happy?" The soldier's tongue twisted over the sounds of his newfound word. He nodded and kept rubbing his belly. He said, "I very, very happy." He said, "You happy too?"

"I was born happy."

Phineas left the shade of the guard post and crossed the dusty road to do his watching of the King's Highway from the other side, where the only thing pricking his ears was the breeze blowing up the rise to the top of this hill overlooking the Plains of Jericho. He could endure the heat of the late afternoon sun better than the foolish blathering of his companion.

The tax collection station stood behind his guard post, lost in the harsh light of afternoon. The hot sun beat down on the main building's columned entrance and tall façade—a structure very much out of place along this trade route where nothing but sagebrush sprouted on the hills surrounding Mount Nebo. It stood like a sentinel on the windswept bluff above the northeast shores of the Dead Sea. There was a good view of the Jordan River Delta spreading out over the Plains of Jericho, and Phineas dug his boots into the hard-packed dirt in the road. This was the perfect location to collect taxes from merchant traders running the King's Highway. The rugged foothills of Mount Nebo on one side of the road and the steep cliffs overlooking the rift valley of the Dead Sea forced every caravaneer running the trade route down this road.

Phineas leaned against a large boulder sitting at the side of this roadway crossing. There wasn't a single merchant trader guiding his caravan up the winding stretch of the King's Highway from Bozrah. There were no mule trains packed with perfumes, no camels grunting and spitting their cud, and not a single courier with bags of mail to deliver. Two hours, maybe three, and Phineas could end his watch and go back inside to a conversation with his mates over evening meal that went beyond the grunting and pointing of this Babylonian tax collector.

The plains of Jericho spread out below the hillside to the west, and Phineas held his hand over his brow to shield it from the afternoon sun and see if there were any riders coming up out of the valley. Jericho was nestled against the far west rim of the valley, with the blue water tributaries of the Jordan River Delta circling about the walled city half hidden among the bright-green date palm groves. The trail leading across the valley floor was empty, without a line of camels moving across the dusty plain. And down at the bottom of the bluff, where the trail started up into the foothills of Mount Nebo there was no cloud of dust to give notice of a coming traveler. The trade route disappeared below the horizon, the road twisting up into the hills before coming past an outcrop near the top and out onto the . . .

Where did those horses come from? Phineas stood away from the boulder and counted fifty riders rumbling around the ridge, pounding up the trail from Jericho, the ground trembling underfoot. They were Hebrew soldiers, all of them dressed in the finest desert dress and turbans of the king's army. They were outfitted for a long ride with water skins strapped on their haunches above the bows and swords on their saddlebags. The lead rider was a powerful man, with thick shoulders, black hair cut short from the top of his head to the sides of his ears and a narrow beard along the jaw. He was flanked by a longhaired man with only a loincloth, and a bow strapped over his shoulder to protect him from the burning rays of the sun, his skin without a single burn for all his nakedness. A square-shouldered lieutenant flanked the lead rider on the other side, his youthful face and pitch-black hair hiding the menace of his gaze. There was no mistaking this troop, not with the lead rider decorating his white Arabian with a silver-studded saddle. This was Captain Laban and his men.

Phineas hurried to the middle of the road, snapping his fingers at his Babylonian companion and telling him to fetch the commanding officers and summon the soldiers in formation in front of the main building. The least they could do was offer the captain a military welcome, but the Babylonian tax collector hurried across the road snapping his fingers back at Phineas and asking him what was meant by this odd making of noise. Fool. He was creating a scene in the middle of the road with the highest military commander in the kingdom approaching. Phineas grabbed his companion's hand to quiet his snapping fingers and when he told him it was the Hebrew Captain of the Guard, the Babylonian raised his curved scimitar to his face before kissing the metal and lifting it in the air.

"Put that away." Phineas pushed the blade down.

"You'll say nothing. Do you understand? Not a word. I'll do the talking."

Captain Laban slowed to a canter, then pulled up a good twenty strides before reaching them.

Laban removed his black turban from around his head and wiped his brow with the cloth. "Have you any reports of renegades on the King's Highway?"

"None, sir."

Laban's gaze was directed at Phineas, but he was looking past him to the longhaired rider. He said, "They must not have passed here yet."

Phineas said, "Who, sir?"

Laban sidled in next to Phineas, the Arabian's muzzle pushing against his shoulder. "Four outlaws are driving a caravan of mules this way. There are about twenty, although we're not certain exactly how many."

"What cargo are they smuggling?"

"No cargo, soldier."

"Is there a tax we should collect from them?"

"If they come this way, hold them and send me word."

"Exactly where should we send word?"

Captain Laban pulled back and started his Arabian past the guard station and onto the King's Highway, his cavalry falling into line behind him. He said, "We'll be waiting for the renegades in Bozrah."

The setting sun fell below the western hills, casting long shadows across the Plains of Moab and cheering Phineas after a cheerless afternoon. Finally, he could turn his duties over to the next watch and head inside, but the men assigned to relieve him were still nowhere to be found and he leaned against the boulder still hot from the heat of the long afternoon. He nodded across the road to his companion standing in the doorway of the guard post, but Phineas wouldn't cross back over, not until the Babylonian stopped rubbing his belly and pointing at his mouth. They were both hungry and as soon as this watched ended they could head to the kitchens and pray the Babylonian cook prepared something better than last evening. Phineas glanced up into the sun-washed sky. Please Lord, let it not be the same as last night. There were twenty-five Hebrew soldiers assigned to this joint collection station under the command of half as many Babylonian officers and it was a travesty they didn't hire a cook from Jerusalem. The Babylonian cook prepared stew seasoned with sage gathered from the hills surrounding the tax collection office, and in spite of the peppers, salts, basils, onions, and every other spice known to man stored at the commissary, the cook insisted on adding a pinch of mystery to his creations. Phineas turned his gaze over the weeds and grasses growing along this hillside and shook his fist at the brown stand of wild pig-wheat waving in the breeze down where the trail from Jericho came over the rise. He had a mind to torch the whole hillside. There was nothing mysterious about bitter roots and bland grasses and he was going to insist the cook consider sprinkling a few of the more tolerable spices into his concoctions. These grasses certainly didn't have power to add anything but bitterness to a meal, and if he didn't get a good plate of lamb seasoned with onions and basil with a hint of lemon, he was going to desert to Jerusalem before his six-month tour of duty ended.

Phineas stood away from the boulder at the edge of the road and began pacing in the orange light of sunset. Where was the night watch? There were only a few moments of daylight left and as soon as the sun was gone below the hills, Phineas was done for the day. His Babylonian companion could stay if he liked, but there were no taxes that required their supervision and there was certainly no need to enter Captain Laban's passing in the log. They weren't going to charge him and his men a levy for riding the King's Highway. There was nothing to report for the afternoon watch, and it was time they headed in for evening meal.

The last crescent of sun fell below the horizon and Phineas crossed the road and told his companion to leave the tax log where the night watch could find it.

"We leave?"

"That's right." Phineas pointed to the man's belly. "You're happy aren't you?"

The man didn't answer. He was staring past Phineas, his gaze turned to the riders trotting up the last stretch of road in the twilight of evening. The first rider was dressed in a black traveling cape, and his woman companion wore an expensive white silk robe, her hood pulled down over her face against the gusting late afternoon winds. They came up the rise and onto level ground, the distance between them closing quickly and there was no mistaking the short-shaved hair, straight jaw and broad shoulders of . . .

Captain Laban? What was he doing riding up the same hill he scaled not three hours before? And how did he get past this guard station without Phineas noticing? Laban was a good horseman, but there was no way he could ride through the hills above the tax collection station without the guards seeing them. He rode the same Arabian. At least the white coat was the same, but the plain, brown leather saddle without any silver studs wasn't nearly as impressive. What an odd thing. Why would the Captain change saddles on the same journey? This second coming of Captain Laban was a strange thing indeed. There were no escorts accompanying the man, no cavalry to protect him, and not a single banner carrier nor drummer to announce his passing. There had never been a return journey headed in the same direction and Phineas blinked in the twilight shadows. Maybe it was the lack of food. He'd not eaten since morning and there was no sane explanation for this other than his own insanity. Captain Laban was come to the tax collection station—again.

The Babylonian raised his blade in the air and pointed the tip of it at Laban. It was an odd Babylonian greeting, but before he scared the captain's riding companion, Phineas took the scimitar and whispered for him to keep quiet or he'd use the weapon on him. He clicked his boots together and stood to attention with the sword pressed firmly against his side, the tip pointed at the ground.

Captain Laban said, "We're headed down the King's Highway."

"I expected that, sir. Will you be spending the night this time? It's late to be traveling."

"Not this time." Laban turned in the saddle and peered past Phineas down into the lengthening shadows across the King's Highway. "We're chasing some renegades."

"Yes, sir. I knew that."

"Have you seen any?"

"None, sir. Not since we spoke."

The Babylonian soldier nodded.

"Will you be eating before you head out? I'm sure the commanding officers would like a word with—"

"No word with anyone."

"Can I get the good lady anything? Something to drink or possibly a—"

"We haven't time." Laban's thick, powerful voice silenced the crickets chirping in the grass beside the road.

"Very well." Phineas stepped aside and the captain quickly rode past, the woman coming in close behind him and the two of them heading down the King's Highway as quickly as they arrived.

"This isn't good. Not good at all."

Aaron went down on his belly next to Lemuel and parted the dry, brown grasses with his hand to get a good view up the hill toward the tax collection station. He left the mules in the company of Josiah and Rebecca behind a large outcrop while they hid on the grassy slope of Mount Nebo's foothills far enough down that the afternoon watch couldn't see them, but not so far they couldn't get a good view of Laman and Sariah riding up the hill toward the outpost. They were still below the bend in the road, out of the view of the soldiers, but one of the men shook his fist in their direction. He wasn't pointing directly at them. It was as if he were mad at the grasses growing on the hillside.

Aaron said, "Is he pointing at us?"

"Stay down." Lemuel dropped his head. "Move toward the mules slowly, on your hands and—"

"We can't leave now." Aaron took back his hand from holding the tall grasses and turned on his side. "We have to see Laman and Sariah get past the outpost."

"There's nothing we can do to help them now." Lemuel spoke into the grass, his head still down. "We don't have a choice. We have to get out of here before they call for reinforcements."

"We can't abandon them."

"We have to get out of here."

"We can't outrun them on mules."

"We're taking the side trail." Lemuel played with the stalks of dead grass in front of him. "If we go now we'll be into the Way of the Wilderness while the soldiers follow the main road back to Jericho searching for us."

"This side trail is the first place they'll look. Every traveler avoiding the tax goes this way."

The Way of the Wilderness trail split off the main road here, just below the tax collection station. It meandered through the foothills of Mount Nebo before dropping down onto the wide, low plains of the Empty Quarter. It was a harsh journey, with wells that went dry by midsummer, no farmers selling grains or fruits, and no soldiers to protect them from robber bands and desert nomads. Only the most intrepid merchant traders dared travel this way to avoid the high taxes collected along the King's Highway, though it wasn't taxes that forced their band of four riders and a host of mules into the east desert. Aaron was in charge of their journey now that Laman had taken Sariah down the King's Highway, and he was going to have to lead them through the great expanse of the Empty Quarter with only the sun and stars as his guide. None of them had ever traveled this route, but Laman insisted that if they stayed on the fringes of Moab, far enough east to stay out of sight of Babylonian patrols, but not so far they couldn't follow the lay of the highlands, they'd meet up with the main road just outside of Bozrah, eighty miles south of here. They had a good supply of water packed on the mules, and they could travel by night to avoid the heat. Aaron parted the brown grass to peer through it again. He was a blacksmith, not a caravaneer, but with any luck he'd get them through to Bozrah alive.

"Look at that." Rebecca inched out from behind the rocky outcrop and crawled up through the tall grasses. "The soldier isn't shaking his fist anymore."

"It's worse than a fist." Lemuel raised his head, his long, thin body coming out of the grass like a chameleon searching for a rock to sun his cold-blooded body. He said, "Look at that soldier running across the road pointing his sword at Laman. They've found him out, they've found us all out." He dropped back down below the grass. "We're all dead men."

"Don't say that." Aaron took Lemuel by the shoulder.

Rebecca started to get up, but Aaron held onto her robe and kept her from standing up. He said, "Stay down."

"But . . ."

"Don't draw their attention this way."

"It's no use hiding from them. They know everything." Lemuel buried his head in his hands. "Laman made sure Captain Laban knew we were headed to Bozrah."

"What in the name of . . . ?" Josiah the Potter left the mules tethered to the rock outcrop and quickly crawled up the grassy slope. "What did your brother do?"

"It was a foolish thing." Lemuel spoke through his fingers. "He left Father's scroll in the sand at Qumran."

Aaron pulled Lemuel's hands away from his thin face. "Why did you let him do it?"

"I couldn't stop him." Lemuel pressed his lower lip between his teeth. "Laman thought we could make a peaceful surrender at Bozrah and end this charade. All he wants is to go home."

"Go home?" Josiah shook his balding, sunburned head. "You'd be dead now if you were still living at Beit Zayit."

"That isn't so." Lemuel shook his finger at Josiah. "My father and his wild chasing through these deserts is what will get us killed. Look at us, sneaking about the desert, heading to where? The Way of the Wilderness? We should be home enjoying a fine meal, not wondering if we can live through this journey."

Josiah crawled closer to Lemuel, his face pushed up close to the boy. "Did it ever occur to you that Captain Laban will kill you before he'll ever let you go home?"

"He wouldn't do that. He's an honorable man."

"You're a fool." Josiah blew out a deep breath, the tall grasses bending away from his exasperation. "You have no idea what evil you've unleashed."

"Take another look, all of you." Rebecca helped Aaron to his feet, held his chin in her hand and turned his gaze to the tax collection station. Laman and Sariah rode on past the checkpoint and down the King's Highway, one soldier waving them on with his hand raised, wishing them well.

Aaron started back toward the mules, the brown grass stinging his legs.

Lemuel said, "Where are you going?"

"We have to get to Bozrah."

"We can't go there. Captain Laban knows."

"That's exactly why we need to get to Bozrah before the rest of them." Aaron marched around the rock outcrop and began untying the mules. "There will be a full garrison waiting for Laman and Sariah in Bozrah—more men than your brother's disguise could ever ward off."

"My brother can take care of Mother."

"He's leading her into a trap that could get both of them killed."

Lemuel took Aaron by the arm. "We'll never make it through the Way of the Wilderness in the middle of summer."

"We're going through the Empty Quarter to Bozrah and we're going to do it before Laman and Sariah get there."

"You're a fool. You're going to get us all killed."

"It's you and your brother who are the fools." Aaron untied the mules from the outcrop and handed the reins of the most stubborn animal to Lemuel. "Leaving that scroll in the sand may have already gotten all of us killed."

CHAPTER 24

"Son, you're drifting!"

Lehi's voice boomed from the back of the caravan, invading Sam's sleep like a cock crowing at dawn. But it was too early for dawn and if Sam were to get out of bed now, Mother wouldn't have the morning meal ready. He adjusted his weight in the saddle and kept his eyes shut, trying to keep his dream alive to the end, the lace hem of his blanket playing about his neck, begging him to sleep in the safety of his dream, but there were chores to do and the lure of morning meal pulled him from the comfort of his room. The blue Egyptian vases lining the marble floored corridor were real enough that he reached out and touched the fresh-cut pansies from Mother's gardens. The anteroom below the mezzanine was filled with the smell of roasted almonds and baking bread that filtered to the front of the estate from the kitchens. The doors leading to the gardens behind the estate were open and he thought he could hear the sweet sound of Sariah humming a melody and picking roses in bunches. Red ones, white ones, yellow ones and . . .

"Son, turn your horse back on course."

Sam pressed his eyelids shut to keep the vision from fading. Couldn't Father wait a moment and let him reach the end of his dream? Just a little more sleep on this uncomfortable leather saddle to take the edge off his tired bones and then he'd open his eyes, roll out of bed, and wash his face in the freshly drawn basin of cool water sitting on the bed stand. Sam wiped the back of his hand beneath his nose to chase away an itch and sniffed at the air. Where was the smell of Mother's baking bread? Not a morning passed at the plantation

when she didn't have plenty of fresh bread for her sons, and Sam
sniffed the air again, but there was nothing to remind him of the
warmth of the home fires burning in the ovens. It was fading with the
images in his mind, turning to darkness, and Sam leaned forward in
the saddle that for two days had been his bed, lingering on the last
vision of home, searching in the darkness for the aroma of a new day
to lure him out from under these blankets so he could start his chores
around the plantation. There were camels to feed, horses to water, a
missing plank to replace in the gate to the stable, and—

"Sam, you're off course!"

He opened his eyes and blinked. Where was he? There was darkness
all around and he rubbed his eyes, but the darkness didn't fade to light.
The powerful strides of his steed shook him out of the saddle and he
pulled hard on the reins that were no longer in his grip. The leather
straps were gone, dropped from his hands, and dangling from the
mouth of his horse. How did he ever nod off like that? He righted
himself in the saddle and raised his hand to signal Father that all was
well. He'd get the camels back on course as soon as he figured out
exactly which way they had strayed and how long he had been sleeping.

The moon was gone, replaced with nothing but the thin glow of
morning stars to give light to his foolishness. He'd never fallen asleep
in the saddle before, but he'd not ever led a tired band of riders by
night across a flat, salty desert, and after three full days sleeping
during the hot hours and traveling in the cool after dark he had good
reason to fall asleep, no matter that he was the lead rider in this
caravan. Sam wiped his mouth on his sleeve, but there was no drool
to clean away, not with his swollen lips parched and cracking from
three days in this insufferable desert inferno. The camels were still
following him in single file, his horse was plodding at the same slow
canter as before, but the stars weren't in the sky where they should be.
For the love of Moses, how did he get this far off course? His horse
had drifted, but thankfully it was to the south. And since they had to
turn that way to get out of this rift valley he didn't bother to redirect
the steed back in line with the bearings of their previous—

"Sam!" Lehi's voice thundered above the din of plodding hooves.
"Get us back on course, son." It was too dark to see anything beyond
the faint outline of twenty camels and two riders following him, but

there was no doubt Father could sense his wandering ways. Lehi's watchful eye tracked every deviation from their charted course and his instructions were to be followed without question. Sam was to travel due east toward the Cliffs of Moab, the rock wall rising into the dark morning sky and growing taller with their approach.

The Cliffs of Moab ran along the eastern rim of the Arabah, from Mount Nebo on the north end of this hundred-and-fifty-mile-long valley down the eastern shores of the Dead Sea toward the Fountain of the Red Sea. The Cliffs were an impassable wall of rock without any trail traversing the face. A steady climber could find a way up on foot, but none of the camels or horses in this caravan could ride up the twisted face that separated the well waters of the King's Highway from the dry, salty plain of this rift valley.

Sam urged his horse faster, his heels prodding the animal into a strong gait. They were across the Arabah but they weren't out of trouble. Two and a half cisterns of water from now they'd be in serious need and if they didn't get out of this infernal pit this morning and find a good well in the plateau country above, they'd never get out. The sky was brightening with the first light of day, and once the rays of this hot desert sun chased away the cool of morning there wouldn't be enough water to go around—not with so many thirsty animals. If they were forced to set up camp for another day and wait out the heat, they'd not live to travel in the cool of another evening. Sam loosened his hold on the reins and spurred his steed to a canter. They had to go faster to get out of the Arabah before they ran out of water, or this deep desert pit would be their tomb.

The dark morning sky softened into shades of blue, the light silhouetting the dark Cliffs of Moab with a back glow, the jagged ridge cutting into the heavens like the skyline of Jerusalem at dawn with a hundred uneven spires reaching upward. Sam leaned forward in the saddle, pushing the caravan toward the towering rock wall as fast as he could get them to run, and veering toward the south. Father would let him head that way, wouldn't he? It was the only way out of here and since they were going to turn south as soon as they reached the cliffs, there couldn't be anything wrong with straying that way a few hundred cubits early and saving the extra distance.

"Sam! Come back due east."

Lehi's voice was insistent, no matter how odd his instructions. Sam asked him not less than five times since starting across the Arabah if they could push toward the south, back when they could have saved a good ten miles on their journey and come out of the Arabah down where these cliffs were nothing more than a gentle sloping sand dune. And Lehi always answered that things were not as they appeared. Sam scanned the steep cliffs coming into relief beneath the light of morning. The gray-blue twisted rock face towered above them, the slope far too steep for the most nimble-footed beast to climb. There was no way up this face and Sam could only pray they would find a way out of the Arabah farther south before it was too hot to travel. They could ride in the shade of the cliffs until midday when the sun crested over the plateaus. That would get them eight, maybe ten miles to the south before it was too hot to travel, and if by some good fortune they found a way up onto the King's Highway, he'd forgive Father his foolishness for keeping a strict course to the east. But if they failed to find a way out by midday they'd have to set up camp and hope they could last another day on a few cisterns of water. Sam ran his tongue over his parched lips. It was either find a way out or hope for a miracle, but with morning breaking over the cliffs, they were growing desperately short on miracles.

"Slow down, son. You'll run the water out of the camels and get them wanting a drink." Lehi spurred from the back of the caravan and reined in alongside Sam, his turban untied and hanging from his shoulders, the ends of the cloth rising on the breeze. His windblown cheeks were chapped red and his brow salted with the remains of dry sweat. He studied the cliffs for a long, silent moment, squinting into the dawn through the ends of his dark black hair that fell over his eyes, the strands of gray hardly visible against his tanned skin. He was studying the rise and fall in the rugged face of the rock wall before letting his gaze fall to the base of the cliffs, down where the cool darkness of night still clung to the desert floor. He said, "We're too far south; turn your horse back toward the dark rift in the outcrops. That should keep us on course."

Too far south? What did it matter? They were nearly to the cliffs and then they'd have to turn south and Sam didn't bother to change directions. They should have headed south two days ago. This was sheer foolishness and Sam spurred his horse faster, the camels grunting their displeasure at the pace. There was every reason to hurry their flight, but no reason to alter their course.

Lehi spurred across his path, forcing him back due east, the same direction they'd charted since leaving their camp along the west rim of the Arabah. The twisted rock face engulfed them, the rock tortured in a hundred directions, with jagged inlets and hidden alcoves among the deep shadows rising around them. The steep face dwarfed them like grains of sand in a giant sea of stone, the caravan heading in among the weathered columns, fractured slabs, and overhanging outcrops of sandstone. The soft floor of the Arabah underfoot gave way to solid bedrock, the final approach to the cliffs without any sand to capture a footprint, and the camels balked at leaving the supple surface and placing their soft cloven hooves on the hard surface. Sam spurred to the back of the caravan, telling Nephi to get them up onto the bedrock floor with his whip, the sound if it cracking in the air and echoing against the face of these cliffs. In a rush of hooves clapping against the stone, the camels came onto the narrow strip of bedrock up off the desert floor.

Sam said, "Why are we stopped?"

Lehi said, "How much water do we have?"

"Two full cisterns on the lead camel." Nephi nudged his horse through the animals. His light olive skin was gone dark from so many months of desert living and his eyes were bloodshot from the winds of the Arabah. "There may be some packed onto the last camel."

Lehi said, "Exactly how much more, son?"

"A little more than two-thirds full."

"That should do."

Sam said, "Do for what?"

"Them." Lehi pointed back toward the wide expanse of the Arabah, the murky light of morning spreading over the salty plain.

Sam turned in the saddle and squinted into the half-light. "I don't see anyone."

"They're out there and they're closing on us." Lehi got down from the saddle, untied the two full water cisterns with help from Nephi, the two of them setting the heavy load on the ground, up against the cliff wall. "This should be enough to get them out of the Arabah."

Sam said, "We need the water."

"Not nearly as much as they will."

"What are you talking about?"

"Trust him." Nephi got back up in the saddle. "Father's been running caravans through these deserts since long before we were born. If he says they'll need this water more than we do, then we leave it for them."

Sam said, "There's no one following us."

"Let me show them to you, son." Lehi reined his horse around to the north. "Keep the animals on the bedrock and stay close or you'll miss the turn. We can't leave any tracks."

What in the name of heaven was he doing? Lehi left the last of their water for pursuers who weren't there and now he was leading them the wrong way. They had to ride south if they were ever going to get out of this infernal abyss.

"This isn't right." Sam spurred up alongside Lehi and raised his voice loud enough that it echoed up along the cliff wall. "Have you lost your mind?"

Lehi didn't answer. He kept his horse moving at a steady clip, riding a good mile or more along the base of the cliff in silence, and Sam turned in the saddle to make sure the camels kept up with Father's galloping. They weren't losing ground and Nephi was keeping them from straying off the bedrock and leaving tracks in the sand, but they were headed in the wrong direction and Sam turned back to try to convince Lehi that . . .

Where did he go? Sam only looked away for a moment and when he brought his gaze back, Father was gone.

Disappeared into nowhere.

Inspector Tobit stayed ahead of his troop of Babylonian cavalrymen, leading them at full gallop across the last stretch of the Arabah, the towering Cliffs of Moab rising from the valley floor and blocking the rising sun with its rugged summit stretching the length of this rift valley. Two nights of riding was more than enough to catch Lehi's slow-moving caravan, but where was he? The scouts found his trail near dawn yesterday and they were still following the man's tracks. These were fresh marks, hardly an hour old, and Tobit kept his men pushing toward the cliffs. He was right about Lehi not heading back to Jerusalem, but did that mean he was leading them on a wild chase deep into the wilderness only to return to his home once he eluded them; or was it Captain Laban and Elder Zadock who were leading him on a wild chase? Tobit coaxed his horse faster, whispering into the animal's ears and telling her they'd rest once they reached the cliffs, but all his whispering didn't answer the terrible question. Were they chasing an outlaw or a prophet?

Morning had come to the Arabah and the brightening sky was sure to unmask Lehi. He couldn't stay hidden any longer with the shadows of night ebbing and the wide plain of the Arabah ending at this wall of gray-blue rock rising out of the valley. Tobit leaned forward in the saddle and scanned the desert floor, but there was no sign of animals moving against the backdrop and dark shadows of these towering cliffs and Tobit called to his men, telling them to ride shoulder to shoulder in a wide band to see if there were any other tracks beyond the single file column they were following across the salty plain. Lehi was a fool for keeping due east, but they followed him into the cliffs, the twisted rock rising up around them, and the cool of morning still hanging about the jagged face.

The soft sand of the valley floor gave way to bedrock, the camel tracks disappearing in a run of hard stone. Tobit pulled up, his men sidling in beside him. What sort of trick was this? The column of camel tracks they found last evening was gone without leaving the slightest indication of which way Lehi turned. Tobit rode in a circle over the bedrock, before trotting back to where the sand met stone. He got down out of the saddle and fell to his knees, his hand running through the last cloven-hoofed track left by Lehi's camels. The edges were sharp and the prints deep. None of the sand had crumbled away to fill the marks. Tobit stood and slowly walked his horse north over the narrow strip of bedrock before coming around and walking the animal south, checking the cool shadows for any sign to tell him which way Lehi escaped from here. Where had the man gone? There were no animals heading north and none he could see going south from here, and he walked his horse back to his men, the animal chomping its bit next to Tobit's ear. There was no way out of here without heading south and if Lehi thought he could trick Tobit into thinking they hadn't gone that way, he was fooling himself. Tobit hadn't explored this land, but his son was the chief mapmaker for the New Babylonian Territories and he knew this country well enough to know there was only one route out of here.

What was that? An odd-colored rock sat against the cliff wall and Tobit left his horse and walked closer until he could make out two clay water cisterns sitting in the shade. It was like a child's game, finding a treasure at the end of the trail, but this was no game and Lehi was no child. The cisterns stood directly at the end of Lehi's camel tracks without deviating even the slightest from his due-east course. Tobit removed the tightly fitted beeswax seal, the clay lip coming away with a rush of air, and he ladled out a handful. It smelled good, there wasn't any rancid odor, and when he touched his tongue to the tepid water there wasn't the slightest taste of poisons.

Darius inched forward past the other cavalrymen, pulled the white cloth of his turban back from his mouth and said, "Why would the man leave his water here?"

Tobit doused the back of his neck with it. "He knows we're following him."

"That's a foolish way to tell us. He'll need every drop to get out of here."

"Lehi is anything but a fool." Tobit replaced the lid and checked the rock around the cisterns, searching for anything that could tell them where Lehi went from here. What was Lehi trying to tell him?

Tobit walked in a large circle, slowly moving farther and farther from the water cisterns. He pushed aside the cavalry horses and kept moving, his gaze down in the bedrock. There were no other marks in the stony ground, no holes chiseled for tent pegs, no rocks used to hold tent poles in place, and no sign of a fire pit. Tobit came back to the water cisterns. This was no campsite and a hurried caravan master did not leave these water cisterns in error. There was nothing to indicate Lehi stopped here for any other reason than to unload the water. But why in the name of heaven would he leave . . . ?

Tobit said, "The water. How much do we have left?"

Darius said, "The men have enough rations to get out of the Arabah."

"And what about the horses?" Tobit walked between the steeds, checking the water skins set aside for the animals. Just as he thought, the men had enough, but they didn't have near the water these horses were going to need if they were to stay alive through another day in this desert, and once the sun passed over the top ridge of these cliffs they'd be exposed to the worst heat in the Arabah. They were certain to lose their animals without this added supply.

"Fill your water skins from these cisterns, all of you. You'll need it for your horses." Tobit fell to his knees beside the vessels, his hand running over the rough clay sides. Could it be possible? Did Lehi leave this water for them as some sort of peace offering? And if he was trying to tell Tobit he wasn't an enemy, the man shouldn't leave his water for them even if he had enough to get his men and animals out of this valley. Better to let them die in this valley than to leave them water so they could live to hunt another day. Lehi was either a fool or he was a—

"Father." Darius strapped the filled water skin to his saddle. "Which way do we go?"

"South, son, around these cliffs." Tobit slowly pulled himself up into the saddle. "It's the only way out."

Sam slowed his steed at a cleft in the cliff where the towering rock wall gave way to a narrow opening—a small break in the stone like a hidden door hardly wide enough for a single camel to shimmy through, but hundreds of cubits high, the opening reaching up into the brightening skies of morning. He inched his horse through the passage, Nephi and the camels following him into an opening until they were surrounded by tall cliffs and hidden from view of the valley floor. A cool breeze blew down the slope on the far side of this secluded alcove, and running across the face of it was a trail traversing the rocky slope with switchbacks cut into the rock to the top of the ridge, the end of it disappearing beyond the crest. How did Lehi know about this place north of where they left the water cisterns? Sam never overheard any caravaneer speak of a trail leading out of the Arabah through these cliffs. There was no way out and every merchant trader traveling this country knew it—no one could get their animals up these cliffs, but here it was—an engineering wonder rising out of this rift valley that no one, not even the most experienced caravaneers knew about.

Sam pulled up alongside his father at the base of the trail leading up the side of the cliff. He was studying the switchbacks, checking the rocks, verifying the cracks and fissures in the stone beneath each turn in the trail. Father was a good merchant trader and he ran a fine caravan to Egypt with his oil trade, but how did he know the secrets of these southern territories?

Lehi said, "Some things, son, are not as they appear."

That was all he needed to say. Sam wasn't going to question him again. Lehi knew things the most traveled caravaneers never learned. This secret trail was a miracle, hidden from view behind a façade of steep cliffs with a trail wide enough to drive a single-file line of animals up into the high plateau country of Moab. Lehi reined his horse up the first switchback, testing the firmness of the trail and checking higher up before backing his steed down to the valley floor and announcing that the way up didn't look to be washed out or damaged, but to be sure, he'd go first with Sam following behind him, then the camels, and finally Nephi bringing up the rear.

Lehi got down from the saddle and started his steed up the rise, ordering Sam and Nephi to do the same. It was too great a risk to stay in the saddle. One misplaced hoof or one start from a frightened animal and they'd go over to their death. Sam led the camels onto the narrow trail, coaxing the lead animal up the steep incline rising quickly off the valley floor. They rounded the first switchback to where the trail shot across to the opposite ridge overlooking the alcove below, then around two more switchbacks until the Arabah came into view over beyond the false front of cliffs, the façade giving way to a view of the wide expanse of the rift valley spreading out below them. Lehi pulled up near the top and pointed to a line of dust rising off the valley floor behind a wide line of cavalrymen riding shoulder to shoulder, heading south and into the shadows down along the cliffs of Moab, searching for a way out.

Lehi said, "Those men need our water, son."

CHAPTER 25

Zoram knocked on the front door of the one-story structure that sat at the top of a narrow street in Jerusalem's wealthiest neighborhood. It had neither the marbled entryways nor columned terraces like the many-storied limestone estates that towered up either side of the property. Footsteps sounded beyond the thick cedar planks before the hinges turned in the well-greased pivot stone and Baruch the Scribe stepped from the shadows of the foyer and onto the porch, his head clearing the dark walnut door beam by three fingers.

Baruch was dressed in a plain brown evening robe. His cheeks were gone red from the warmth of the summer evening, his eyes were narrow teardrops beside a thin nose, and a gray band of hair ran about the sides of his balding head. He said, "I've been waiting for the day when you'd return to see me, son."

"Me, sir?"

"You're Zoram, the scribe from Captain Laban's treasury, aren't you?"

"I am, sir, but I've never been here before."

"Your cousin Hanameel is selling more property I see. Did you bring the documents for the property sale? I'm to represent his interests at the Ceremony of Sale and you . . ." Baruch passed his gaze over Zoram like a jailer searching a prisoner, beginning from the top of Zoram's white-turbaned head to the latches of his brown leather sandals. "You're representing the interests of the King and the Elders of the Jews."

How did the man know Hanameel was his cousin? That was a secret only slightly more guarded than Zoram's relation to Jeremiah. He said, "How did you know that?"

"A better question, son, would be: how do I know that Jeremiah is your adopted father?"

Zoram removed his white turban and slowly shook his head, the black locks of hair falling onto his brow. This man wasn't supposed to know that. It could ruin everything Zoram had worked his whole life to conceal. "Hanameel told you that?"

"He didn't need to, son." Baruch ushered Zoram inside. "Follow me."

Baruch started down the dimly lit hallway without further introduction. He didn't inquire about the nature of Zoram's visit and he didn't seem the least bit annoyed at the late hour of Zoram's coming. The cool limestone walls of the corridor were adorned with aging leather scrolls of Baruch's making. His penmanship was flawless, his flowing script filling parchment after parchment with his artistry. There were two copies of the words of Isaiah on goat leather, another written by the prophet Micah on what had to be gray ox hide, one of Elisha's, and two more quoting the words of Zenos. A run of royal letters graced the opposite wall of the hallway. There was a letter copied from the original border dispute between King Solomon and the Assyrians, another letter of psalms copied from the personal effects of the ancient King David, and letters from every monarch down to the reign of Josiah, the father of King Zedekiah—all of them copied onto newly tanned lambskin hides. Zoram slowed without letting Baruch get too far ahead. This man was much more than a skilled keeper of documents or a gifted manipulator of a stylus. His home was the repository of the finest writings to grace the Hebrew nation since the days of the first Passover.

Baruch stopped at the end of the hall, his gaunt body framed by the entrance to the writing room and his long, thin fingers motioning Zoram to follow him inside. A large oil lamp hung from the rafters and cast a strong light over the shelves of scrolled documents and sealed urns filled with a lifetime of scribing, the sheer volume of records enshrining this writing room with the efforts of his pen. Three scrolls sat atop a pedestal near the entrance, and Zoram stepped closer to examine the work. Red tasseled cords lay untied and hanging from the edges of the partially opened parchments and the bright light from the large oil lamp shone over the opening phrase of each document.

No—it couldn't be. Zoram leaned over the pedestal and quickly read through as much as he could. How did Baruch ever come to possess a personal copy of the law written by the hand of Aaron, the brother of Moses, and recorded onto what looked like several-hundred-years-old parchment? The ends of the documents were dark with age. The fibers were wearing thin, but they weren't coming apart and the surface was polished with olive oils to preserve the ancient words, the light reflecting off the leather like the shimmering of polished stone tablets.

"Your father unlocked the mystery of these scrolls for me," Baruch said in answer to Zoram's staring.

"My father, sir?" Zoram stepped back from the pedestal.

"He brought you here when you were a very young child. You and your brother both needed records of adoption."

"My brother? You know my brother?"

Jeremiah and Eliza never told Zoram anything about his brother. They didn't even know his name, only that he was one year younger with the same green eyes, dark curly hair, and the same mild disposition. Zoram stared across the room, his turban stretched between both hands. He always hoped he'd find a man with the same carriage, the same dark complexion, the same laugh or voice or affinity for the work of a scribe or skill with a pen, but until today he'd not found anyone who knew anything about his lost brother—the only blood relation he had left on the face of this earth. He came here to beg the help of this man on behalf of Jeremiah and Ezekiel, but now he found himself begging help for himself. "Tell me what happened to my brother, sir."

Baruch came around in front of Zoram, the pedestal filling the distance between. He ran his hand slowly over the scrolls of the Law, the words of Moses passing beneath his fingers. "I've read these a thousand times, copied them onto countless leather parchments, but I never understood them until your father opened them to my understanding."

Zoram said, "Do you know anything about my brother?"

"This record is filled with covenants."

"What about his name? I never knew his name."

"The record of Moses has a single purpose." Baruch laid his hand on the scrolls. "Isn't that why we both became scribes, son? To preserve the covenants for generations of families yet to follow?"

"What about my brother? Do you know where he—?"

"I'm trying to tell you, son. This record will help you find your lost family." Baruch played his fingers along the edge of the record of Moses. "Your father helped me come to know the promises recorded in this document. He put my feet on the path to unlocking the secrets of heaven." He cupped his hands together, his long, skillful fingers intertwined like the strings on a fine harp. He lowered his voice. "Moses wrote that it was God's work and his glory is to bring to pass our immortality and eternal life, son."

"My brother's dead, isn't he? That's why you're telling me this." Zoram leaned over the scroll, searching for some word, some phrase recording the name of his lost brother, some detail indicating where he could find his sibling, anything that would lead him to what was left of his family, but there was nothing in the parchment.

Baruch said, "The covenants preserved in these parchments will help you find him."

"Is there nothing more you can tell me?"

"I wrote out the adoption arrangements over there." Baruch nodded toward the writing table. It stood along the far wall with eight pens—each one sprouting from the well of different textured inks. Baruch's secret recipes held their color longer, never disintegrating the leather like the other, more caustic preparations of lesser scribes, and there wasn't a man in the city who wouldn't pay dearly for the recipes. A half-finished leather scroll lay open across the table and immediately Zoram understood he'd interrupted Baruch in the middle of his work. This was a bad time to stop at the home of this renowned scribe, and Zoram would have begged the man's pardon and excused himself for coming, but he couldn't go now. There may never be a good time to come here and ask Baruch to be his accomplice, but he couldn't leave without asking Baruch to help him with his family.

Zoram said, "May I see the adoption records of my brother?"

"I gave them to his new parents and there's so little I remember beyond that. It was so many years ago and your brother was so young, just an infant." Baruch rubbed his brow. "I don't recall the name his new parents gave him, but I believe the father was a boatbuilder."

"In Jerusalem?"

"As I recall, it was at the port in Aqaba on the Fountain of the Red sea, but that was so long ago, he may not live there now." Baruch ushered Zoram to a chair beside his writing table and poured a cup of tea from a steaming pot. "Would you like some?"

Zoram thanked him, but refused the offer. He couldn't drink anything with his mind reeling. "What else did uncle Hanameel tell you about me?"

"Only that you may need to ask my help." Baruch came around and stood beside his writing table, his hand pressed against the wood-plank top. "Exactly what sort of help did you need, son? Is it about tanning good parchments or is it the inks you're having trouble with? I can help you mix a good ink with a mixture of—"

"It's brass, sir. I'm transcribing my father's records onto brass. He's obsessed with preserving them for a very long time." Zoram glanced at the decaying leather scrolls sitting on the pedestal. "Longer than records written on parchments."

"Brass?" Baruch sat on his writing stool and tapped his long fingers against his chin. "What sort of record is this, son? Brass is a difficult medium, to say nothing of the cost."

"I've smelted some of the plates, but the writing is impossible. The tools are always breaking, the chisels go dull, and it requires hours of work to engrave a single phrase."

Baruch rummaged through the pens on his writing desk until he found a hard metal stylus with a small, hand-held hammer. "You'll need something like this. It takes a good deal of practice, but you'll get used to the small neck and the placement of the hammer atop the chisel. And if it breaks, come see me. I have another."

Zoram refused the stylus. "I haven't done any engraving for months, sir."

"Then I insist you at least try the tool."

"It isn't that." Zoram lowered his head. "It's my father. With him in prison, I can't finish this record in time."

"In time for what?"

"All I know is that his record must be finished very, very soon before it's taken from the city." Zoram held his turban like a priest holds an incense bowl. He leaned forward in the chair and lowered his voice to a whisper to soften the blow of what he was about to say.

"During the Ceremony of Sale in the Court of the Prison, we need you to help us stall for time."

"Time for what, son?"

"Time for Jeremiah and Ezekiel to escape so my father can finish his record."

Baruch leaned back against the edge of his writing table, the wood planks supporting his weight.

Zoram worked his lower lip between his teeth. "Will you help us?"

CHAPTER 26

Sariah held the reins with one hand and supported her womb with the other. She leaned forward in the saddle to see the trail ahead, but it was no use. The King's Highway wandered through the hill country of Moab and there was no telling how much farther to Bozrah. The first days of this journey weren't nearly as difficult as the last hours of this one, but she didn't slow her horse or tell Laman of the discomfort begging her to take a day of rest. They couldn't stop, not even for this unborn child. Lehi, Sam, and Nephi were to meet them in Bozrah tonight and she kept her horse galloping over the dusty road, down a rise, and through a grassy meadow. Small herds of grazing sheep and wandering goats dotted the arid grasslands bordering the King's Highway, the cry of strays braying at the setting sun, and a family of goats meandering over a rocky outcrop.

Laman reached the summit of the next hill and without saying a word he pulled up, his horse chomping at the bit. Sariah reined up the incline behind him, the dust of their ride settling out of the air. The hood of her traveling robe hung down into her eyes and she pulled back the brim.

"Bozrah?" Sariah turned in the saddle to Laman. "Are we there, son?"

Laman didn't answer her question. He nodded without even a hint of a smile and kept his stare riveted on the settlement glimmering in the distance beneath the shadows of the dark, dusky-blue sky of early evening. This city without a wall was the end of their flight, and the King's Highway ran down out of these hills from this summit into the center of whatever humanity lay waiting to receive them.

Bozrah was the last outpost of civilization on the King's Highway before lawlessness replaced the patrols of the Babylonian and Hebrew armies. Every merchant trader who trafficked in frankincense knew the risks of traveling beyond Bozrah to the perfume groves at the end of the Frankincense Trail. The trade route into the wilderness of the Arabian Peninsula was ruled by nomadic tribes and governed by the law of the wilderness. Bozrah was the gateway to the dangers of an uncharted land, the six-thousand-foot gray-blue summits of the Jabal Mountain Range rising behind the city like a great wall, daring any traveler to ride through her peaks into the deserts of Arabia that lay beyond. Sariah offered a silent prayer in her heart, thanking the God of Heaven her husband wasn't taking them any farther into this wilderness than this outpost. Bozrah was a good place to end this fleeing. There were sturdy brick homes here and children playing in the streets and, heaven bless this place, doctors to tend to her needs. There were vegetables in the market, a supply of well water, and if she must bear a child so far from home, she could do it in Bozrah without too much concern for the health of her unborn. Sariah's back ached from bearing the weight of her baby, but she sat straight in the saddle and said, "How much longer, son?"

"We're not going any farther." Laman came around and sidled in next to her, his horse rubbing against her leg. "You're not up to it."

"Nonsense. I rode this far; I can certainly make it another few miles."

"I don't want you traveling at night."

"We're nearly to Bozrah."

"Bozrah can wait."

"What about your father?"

Laman said, "He's not going anywhere. If he made it across the Arabah to Bozrah he can wait another day."

"What do you mean, if he made it?" Sariah lowered her voice. "Where's your faith in him, son? Of course he made it across."

"It isn't lack of faith, Mother."

"Then what is it?"

"Good judgment. Father seems to have less and less of it these days." Laman turned his gaze down the hills toward Bozrah and spit. He sat with his shoulders forward, one fist around the reins and the other clenched at his side. "If Father made it across, we can hope he doesn't have any more foolish plans beyond this place."

A breeze filtered across the hillside meadow and Sariah pulled her robe close, her body shivering against the sudden coolness of Laman's words. What was the source of his contempt? She said, "You shouldn't speak about your father like that."

Laman rode away, steering his horse off the main road and down through a farmer's flat. Night was come to the hills above Bozrah and a lamp burned bright in the windows of an inn over beyond a pasture, the flickering flame announcing the vacancies. Sariah followed in Laman's path, slowly guiding her horse over an irrigation channel, past the mouth of a sealed well with the capstone fitted in place, and down along a line of fruit trees before coming out in front of the main entrance of the inn. A long porch graced the front with a run of thick cedar doors wrapping around the building like a sash on an expensive robe. Smoke filtered out the chimney and the smell of roasting lamb from the kitchens filled the night air. A stable boy hauled a cartload of hay through the open doors of a barn, and another boy watered three oxen from a trough. This was a fine place to lodge for the night, but Sariah couldn't rest until she finished telling Laman he shouldn't let his strong will get in the way of his heart. He should get beyond his pride and not complain so much about his father. He was her firstborn son and he owed his father his allegiance, not to mention thanks for the good education Lehi provided him from the finest Egyptian teachers, and a birthright few could ever hope to inherit. They lived a God-blessed life and forsaking their opulent living for a short few months wasn't such a difficult task for the multitude of blessings Lehi provided them.

Sariah got down from the saddle and followed Laman to the main door of the inn, one hand supporting the heaviness of her womb and the other reaching for his sleeve. She wasn't a large woman, but she was strong enough to deal with this boy's heart. She caught him before he knocked, turned him around to face her and said, "What is the cause of all this?"

"The cause of what?"

"You know exactly what I'm talking about." Sariah straightened her shoulders. "Your father's done nothing to garner so much of your contempt."

"I'm tired, Mother. Can we speak of this come morning?" Laman turned back to the door, but before he could make a fist, she took him by the hand and turned him back to her. "Tell me what it is, son. Why have you drifted so far from your father?" She stood on her toes and peered into his dark eyes. There was a time when she could see through them into his heart and read the silent words written there and know his deepest thoughts, but that was when Laman was a boy and he wore his heart on his sleeve without so much darkness obscuring his eyes. When did he learn to hide the unspoken thoughts of his soul from her? Sariah slowly lowered from standing on her toes. Did he lose the openness of his heart all at once or did it come like the maturing of a tree as he grew from a boy into manhood? If she could only find the light that once brightened his spirit, she would know the source of this division between father and son, but there was nothing beyond the silence of his eyes without the least bit of life to tell her what trouble festered deep inside his soul.

"If we wait to speak of this until tomorrow I fear . . ." Sariah lowered her gaze.

Laman said, "You fear what?"

"Son." Sariah held the cloth of his sleeve tight. "You can't hold this anger any longer."

"It isn't anger." Laman tried to pull his arm free, but Sariah wouldn't let go. She said, "Then what is it?"

"You can't tell me all this fleeing about these lands doesn't bother you as well." Laman pulled his arm free of her grasp. "Don't you think our journey through this wilderness is a foolish venture?" He turned away and faced the door. "Father's a dreamer. You know that better than any of us and he's invented these dangers to keep us from home."

"Invented them? Have you forgotten Captain Laban's arrow? That was not a dream." Sariah pulled her hood back off her head and let her long, black hair fall down past her neck. She laid her hand on Laman's back and slowly stroked his powerful shoulders. "Why would your father invent such things?"

"I don't know. Maybe it's because he . . ." Laman made a fist and pressed it against the door, but didn't knock.

"Go on, son."

Laman quickly said, "Maybe it's because he's losing his mind."

Sariah took back her hand. How could he think such a thing? She held her hand to her mouth. Twenty-two years Laman lived under the same roof with his father—his talented, hardworking, intelligent father who never raised his voice to the boy, did nothing but treat him with longsuffering, gentleness, and kindness. And what did Laman return to his father except contempt for his way of life. And what was there to hate about their life? Could it be Lehi's visions that irked the boy? She said, "I'm sorry you feel that way."

"And I'm sorry you don't." Laman spoke his words at the door, his voice echoing back off the thick timbers. "Haven't you ever wondered if Father's dreams and visions are nothing more than the fantasies of a frenzied mind? I've seen it happen to men whey they grow old. It could be happening to Father."

"No more, son. Your father is as healthy as the day I married him." Sariah shook her head. "I'll not hear anymore of this."

"Don't you want to be certain?"

"Of what?"

"That we're not following a strange mind into stranger lands." Laman turned from facing the door. "Shouldn't we be certain he's not gone mad before we—?"

"Enough." Sariah pulled her hood back over her dark hair, the white cloth brim hiding the tears that wet her cheeks. "If you only knew what I know about your father. If you only knew his heart, you'd not speak as you do."

"It's not his heart that should worry you." Laman turned back to the door and knocked, the wood slats coming up off the threshold with his pounding. The latch clicked open, the door creaked on its hinges, and a man with graying hair and a bent-over stride stepped out, his small oil lamp flickering in the breeze. He was dressed with a cap on his head and a white sleeping robe that fell to just below his knees, without enough length to cover his knobby shins. He raised the lamp to Laman's face and let the light wander over his thin line of beard and short-shaved hair. He said, "You look familiar boy. What's your name? Are you from around here?"

Laman turned his head from the lamplight. "We've never met, sir."

"Look at me, boy." He held the lamp out, the yellow glow casting over Laman's face and he spoke with a heavy accent like those hailing from the Capital, and there was no doubting this man had frequented Jerusalem. "I'm sure we've—"

"There was a light in your window, sir." Sariah stepped in front of Laman. "Do you have a room for the night?"

"Oh that . . ." The innkeeper shook his lamp and the flame flickered, before coming back to life. "I've got a good room here inside on the main hall right next to the—"

"We'd prefer a room with an outside door." Sariah took out her purse and offered the man a piece of silver—double what they'd pay for a room in the finest inns of Jerusalem. "Do you have something that would be suitable?"

"What she means is we don't want any trouble." Laman leaned around Sariah. "No trouble from anyone."

The innkeeper took the money and stuffed it under his belt. "What sort of trouble were you hoping to avoid?"

Laman said, "Meddlers, men who ask too many questions."

"I know who you are. You're the Captain of the Hebrew Guard." The innkeeper pushed his lamp at Laman's face. "Weren't you headed to Bozrah after passing through here?"

Laman said, "Well, I . . ."

"No need to tell me why you're back so soon." The innkeeper wagged a finger in front of Laman's face. "You saw what a nice inn we have here—much nicer than any in Bozrah, mind you—and you decided coming back here for the night wasn't such a long ride after all. All the merchant traders tell us the same thing. Nicest inn on the King's Highway." He stuck his head out the door and peered past them. "Where are your men? That rider with the long hair; he was certainly an interesting sort. Didn't speak a word when I served him his meal, just sat over there and stared." He stepped back from the door and pointed his lamp across the main room, over past the wooden pillars to a table set along the far wall. "And that lieutenant Daniel of yours, my granddaughter couldn't keep her eyes off the man the way he sat under the window and stared back at her between drinks on a bottle of wine. I gave him our strongest brew from the root cellar and it didn't slow him, not for a moment. And what ever happened to the boy's eye that he wears that black patch over it? My granddaughter, the poor girl, she's been talking about the soldier with one eye ever since you rode out of here." He shook his head. "Women. They see a man dressed in a uniform and they lose their heads, they do." He brought his lamp back to Laman. "So Captain, are you certain you don't want the large room on the upper floor? There's a caravan master in there right now, but I can move him out. Once I tell him the Captain of the Hebrew Guard is here, he'll not utter a word of complaint. And your lovely wife deserves the best." He raised his lamp to Sariah, the white cloth of her hood taking on the yellow glow of the flame. "I can prepare you both a late dinner in the main hall if you like. We still have plenty of lamb and a good round of—"

"No dinner in here." Laman handed him another piece of silver and stepped back, his gaze running down along the porch to the first door. "Is that room taken?"

"Sir, you don't want a room with an outside door." They aren't nearly as safe as the rooms inside."

"I didn't ask if it was safe, I asked if it was—"

"Empty, yes, but dreadfully lacking in the finer comforts and you've paid more than enough for the very finest." The innkeeper rubbed the silver coin between his thumb and forefinger. "There's not a key for the door, just an iron rod to wedge across the doorpost and you don't really want your wife to have to worry about—"

"We'll take it."

Laman started Sariah moving down the porch when the innkeeper said, "Would you like dinner in your room, sir?"

"Keep it warm in the kitchens. I'll be by to pick it up once I stable the animals." Laman tossed him one more piece of silver. "Remember, no trouble."

"None, sir." The innkeeper held the money in the palm of his hand and stared at the glimmering pieces. He slowly said, "No trouble at all."

The door to the room was left ajar and Sariah stood beside the entrance while Laman pushed inside and marched across the threshold into the darkness. He struck a flint and lit the wick on a small lamp, the light hardly bright enough to chase away the shadows.

"Doesn't what the innkeeper said worry you?" Sariah stepped in from the porch, her hands wrapped around herself.

"I don't have time for worry, Mother." Laman handed her the lamp before carrying the saddlebags inside. He sat on the end of it and tried to untie the leather cords binding the saddlebags.

"But dear, what he said about the captain is cause for concern." Sariah walked to his side, the lamp in her hand flickering on her movement and the light casting a glow over Laman's sunburned cheeks. "Do you think Laban is already come to Bozrah?"

"You know how innkeepers are; they boast to have served, slept, and fed every important man in the kingdom." Laman picked at the knots on the saddlebag, but he couldn't get them undone. "The innkeeper was dreaming all that up about Captain Laban stopping here with his men. And when he saw how much I looked like the man, he went on, didn't he? He doesn't know the first thing about Captain Laban visiting this inn."

"He wasn't telling you about Captain Laban's visit, son. The man was welcoming you back to his inn." Sariah sat on the end of the bed next to Laman. "How would Captain Laban know to follow us here?"

"I told you, put it out of your mind." Laman tightened his grip around the ends of the knots and pulled, the leather cords snapping in his hands. The seam split and dried lamb and nuts spilled over the floor. "Cursed thing!"

"You don't know your own strength, son." Sariah quickly gathered the food back into the pouch and set it in Laman's lap. "What will we do if—?"

"I'll get us some food from the kitchens."

"Not the food, son. It's Captain Laban I worry over. What will we do if the man has come to Bozrah?"

Laman kept his gaze down in the torn saddlebag draped between his hands. "I don't bother to think about such things."

"Your father was certain the man wouldn't follow us to Bozrah."

"I don't try to understand the foolish things Father thinks." Laman fiddled with the cords, trying to mend his tearing. "Captain Laban isn't following us. He could come to Bozrah for any number of reasons. There may have been a dispute among merchant traders, or maybe there's been trouble with renegades. They always have trouble with renegades in this territory."

Sariah returned to sit on the bed next to Laman. "Captain Laban thinks us renegades."

"Neither of us know the man's thinking. I've never met him and I'm not his butler nor his nursemaid." Laman rubbed his hand over his short-shaved scalp. "I'm his imposter." He dropped the saddlebag at his feet and kicked it away, the dried lamb scattering over the floor and falling between the cracks in the timbers. "Here, take this." He found the iron rod leaning against the wall and handed it to Sariah, telling her to wedge it across the doorjamb and lock herself inside until he got back from stabling the horses. There was feed to get, water to haul, and if the stable boy was gone for the night, Laman would have to do it himself. He marched from the room, kicking the pieces of dried lamb out of his way and jumping down from the porch. Sariah followed him to the door and pulled it closed, the thick timbers shutting off her view of Laman rounding the corner of the inn, leaving her with troubles wedged into her heart like this thick iron rod across the doorpost. Sariah set the lamp on the table. Its uneven legs wobbled on the cold stone floor, and its pale light threw shadows across the far wall like spirits haunting this lonely room. What was she to do with Laman? He was a good boy, caring for her these many days on the trail, not letting her want for anything, but how could she ebb his tide of anger that raged against Lehi?

Laman had the strength of two men, but the heart of none and if she could only find a way to soften his strong will then she'd not have to endure the thought of losing him, no matter how persistant the premonition. Sariah leaned against the door. The back of her head pressed against the timbers, the hood of her robe fell down past her shoulders, and her eyes closed. Laman was the child who whittled her a ladle out of the wood of an olive tree, telling her that her cooking deserved only the finest spoons. He was the boy who helped her down from every horse and carriage out of fear that the animal might spook and hurt her. Laman was the young man who brought her cisterns of cooking oils from the farthest storehouses, and fetched her the finest olives from the pressing yard before his brothers devoured them. Sariah rubbed her brow, forcing away the image of Laman walking a forbidden path to never be seen again, but the vision would not leave her. He'd taken the horses around the corner of the inn to water them, that's all. And he was coming back as soon as that work was finished. She took hold of the iron rod that was braced across the door jamb, locking the door shut. It was a thick rod, cold to the touch, but no matter how hard she held it and tried to replace the vision of Laman turning his back on the family and washing his hands of their faith, the image would not depart. Sariah grasped the iron rod with both hands, the thick metal bearing her up against the weight of this disturbing image. Was she really going to lose her eldest son to the darkness?

The faint sound of footsteps on the porch outside the door filtered through the cracks in the wood slats and Sariah turned her ear to it. Whoever it was moved slowly, carefully placing his sandals along the porch and slowing in front of her door. She tightened her grip on the iron rod, holding the door latch shut against any intruder who might be lying in wait. The footsteps stilled directly outside her door and she could hear heavy breathing on the other side of the timbers.

"Son? Is that you?"

"Mother?"

Thank heaven. Sariah took a deep breath. Laman was back, but why was he standing on the porch? It wasn't like him not to try the latch or knock with a loud fist. She pulled up the iron rod from the doorpost and swung open the door to find him standing in the darkness. The light from the room filtered out onto the porch, but without the strength to light his face. And in the shadows of night he appeared as Captain Laban, with the same square stance, broad shoulders, and thick arms. His straight chin was like the captain's and the gaunt cheeks were identical. He stepped to the threshold and when the shadows of night fell from his face she said, "Nephi?"

How did he find her here? Sariah took him by the arm and pulled him close. He was a strong boy, grown stout enough these past months that she could mistake him for Captain Laban, and he did look like the man. His thick, red lips had narrowed, and though his chin was without a beard, he had a strikingly similar stance. How was it that Laman and now Nephi could look so much like the Captain of the Guard, yet be completely unrelated to him?

A slight shaking trembled through Nephi's body, and Sariah let go of the boy, stood him in front of her and said, "You're not well."

"Do you have any water?"

"Drink this." Sariah carried a vessel over from the bedstand. "Where's your father?"

Nephi tried to speak between gulps, but the water only coursed down his chin and—

"Hello, Sariah." Lehi stood in the doorway, his traveling robe covered with dust and the dried sweat of so many days on the trail caked to his brow. He took Sariah in his strong arms, the strength of his presence driving away her fears. She said, "How did you know to find us here?"

Sam backed through the doorway in short, hurried steps, his gaze flitting back and forth across the porch, scanning the approach to the inn. He said, "We've been going from inn to inn, along the King's Highway, hunting for you the whole day."

Lehi said, "Are you strong enough to travel?"

"Well I . . ."

"What is it?" Lehi took her by the hand, his rough, calloused skin soothing her spirit. "You're not—"

"I'm well enough." She propped her shoulders back and let her robe drape over her growing womb, hiding the reason for her weariness. "After a good night's rest I'll be as fit as any of you."

Sam slowly shook his head. "We can't rest here."

"It's Captain Laban." Nephi came around and stood next to her. "He's come to Bozrah. Somehow he knew to look for us here."

It was true. The innkeeper wasn't telling stories. But of all the cities in the world, why would Captain Laban think they would seek refuge in Bozrah, a city on the edge of civilization without any of the comforts they could easily purchase in a score of other lands more habitable than this wilderness?

Sariah said, "How did he find us?"

"It doesn't matter now." Lehi marched back to the door and peered out into the night. "He's here and once he's finished searching the city he'll start with the inns along the trade route."

"He doesn't know we're here, does he?"

Sam said, "Not yet."

"We have to leave tonight." Lehi came back from looking out the door and draped his arm around Sariah's shoulder. "Can you travel?"

"Where will we go?"

"The Mountain Road nearer the Red Sea. They'll not follow us through that pass."

"Aqaba?" Sam stepped to his father. He ran his hand through his sandy brown hair. "When did we decide that? You never said anything about going farther south than Bozrah."

"It's our only hope to find some peace." Lehi paced across the room. "We can't go back across the Arabah. The King's Highway is patrolled by too many soldiers and . . ." He pulled up on the far side of the room. "Where are the others?"

Sariah said, "Laman's gone to stable the horses."

"And the rest?"

Sariah sat on the end of the bed, her hands folded in her lap. "We couldn't bring all the mules down the King's Highway. It would have drawn too much attention."

Lehi said, "Where are they?"

"I told them it was too dangerous." She brought her head up and slowly said, "The Way of the Wilderness is a difficult journey."

Sam said, "How much water did they take with them?"

Sariah said, "Just what they could carry in the water skins. We didn't have time to get more. It all happened so fast."

Sam said, "Which route did they take?"

Lehi said, "There's no route through that desert, son. You know that. It's a wide, flat wilderness."

Sam said, "They could have stayed close to the hills of Moab country."

Nephi stood next to Sam. "Not if they ran into a military patrol that pushed them farther east into the Empty Quarter."

"I never should have let them do this." Sariah cupped her hands together. "Not in summer with the wells gone dry."

"Water isn't the worst of it." Sam leaned over the side of the bed and spoke quickly, his thoughts spilling out of him like a merchant selling his wares. "Caravaneers take that route to avoid paying the tax, and every robber band between here and Babylon knows it."

Sariah said, "You don't think they're in danger, do you?"

"That desert isn't safe, not with so many outlaws preying on the poor souls who dodge the tax collection stations on the King's Highway."

"Sam . . ." Lehi started for the door. "How many full water skins will you need to get the family to Aqaba?"

Sam stepped in Lehi's path. "Where do you think you're going?"

"Someone has to bring them to Aqaba."

"I'm the one who should go after them."

"You don't know what route they took."

"Didn't you just say there wasn't a route through the Empty Quarter?"

Lehi held Sam by the arm. "It's too great a risk."

"I stopped calculating risks the day we left Beit Zayit, Papa." Sam stepped past his father and marched out into the night, his last words ringing on the cool air. "If we're not in Aqaba in three days, come looking for us."

"Sam, no . . ." Sariah hurried to the door and watched him jump down from the porch and untie four camels from the herd of twenty in front of the inn. He checked the water skins on their backs before starting the animals down the trail, the sound of their hooves dying on the night. She softly said, "Three days son, no more than three days."

Nephi stood beside Sariah. He said, "Sam's a good caravan master. He'll bring them to us at Aqaba and then we'll find some peace before we go home."

Sariah turned her gaze onto her youngest son. He was taller now, taller than she ever remembered him being, and she pressed his thick, strong hand in hers. Why did so much have to change so quickly, including the stature of her youngest son? She said, "Will we ever return home?"

"One day, Mother." Nephi nodded. "One day we'll be home."

The life within Sariah kicked. It was a slight movement, hardly enough to draw her attention, but it was the first time she'd felt the child so alive and she quickly pressed her hand to her side. If this unborn could hear the thoughts of her heart, then please Lord, let the child know she was doing all she could to bring him into this world with a healthy body, strong beyond measure, and without having to endure the harshness of the wilderness her sons endured.

"Mother." Nephi laid his hand on her shoulder. "If you're not able, we can wait until morning."

"I'm ready to go whenever your father thinks it best."

Lehi started for the door, telling them he was going to fetch Laman from the stable, but Sariah took him by the arm before he could go. She said, "Let Nephi bring Laman back with the horses. There's something you should know."

"Are the horses lame?"

"I wish it were that." Sariah offered a faint smile and nodded to Nephi, her silence telling him to do as she'd said and fetch Laman back from the stables. She waited until the boy marched down the porch and was out of earshot before saying, "It's Laman. Something isn't right with him." She picked the iron rod off the floor and walked it back to the corner where she found it, but she didn't set it in place. She held the cold metal close against her heart and said, "It's something deep in his soul."

"He's growing older, dear. We have to let him become a man in his own way."

"It's more than a child becoming a man." Sariah shook her head. "We're going to lose him."

"You don't really think he'd abandon us, do you?"

"Not now, but I worry Laman will take another path in life, follow another way."

"What did Laman do to cause you so much worry?"

"He's done nothing, not yet."

"Then why all this fuss over the boy?"

"Because I can't rid myself of a vision of his future." Sariah straightened her shoulders and held the iron rod with both hands. "I fear for the boy. If his heart doesn't change, we're going to lose him."

"Laman's a strong boy and he isn't easily swayed."

"All his strength doesn't have power to save his soul."

Lehi gathered the saddlebags over his shoulder. "With time you'll get over these fears."

"I don't want to get over this, not until these fears are put to rest." Sariah leaned the iron rod against the wall in the corner of the room. "Don't you see what I see? With every passing day the boy grows angrier, more torn within, more . . ."

"More like a man?"

"This isn't a sign of any manhood we should want for him. It's . . ."

"Go on, say it."

"Laman is forgetting God."

Sariah pulled the hood of her robe over her head. She couldn't put aside her premonitions about their son. The fear of him choosing the wrong path in life was growing stronger, and her ride down the King's Highway with only the company of Laman to divide the journey between them added to her concerns. Somehow she was going to have to convince Lehi her fears were founded on more than a mother's worry. Lehi helped her out onto the porch and down the steps. She squeezed his hand. Dear God, please help her husband see what she was seeing in their eldest. And if there was room to ask help beyond that, let him know what they could do to save the boy.

Lehi quietly led her down the porch steps and around the corner of the inn, careful to walk in the shadows away from the flickering light of the lamp that beckoned evening travelers to this place. They couldn't let any of the patrons see them leave in the middle of the night. It would only take a single witness to remember them to Captain Laban, and all their midnight fleeing would be in vain.

What Sariah didn't know, was that Laman had paid the innkeeper one more piece of silver to stand in the shadows, down along the porch near the door to their room and watch over her.

The innkeeper knew of their flight to Aqaba.

CHAPTER 27

Inspector Tobit pulled up near the base of a steep incline, his horse chomping at the bit and pawing the hot ground under hoof. A narrow neck of sand rose out of the low-lying plain of the Arabah Valley between two steep rock walls—the first break in the Cliffs of Moab since they turned south yesterday—and Tobit wasn't about to ride past this chance without testing it. They had to find a way out of this valley before the stifling heat of another day and the waterless land entombed them.

There were no tracks leading up the steep hillside, no indication that Lehi or anyone else had tried to get out of the Arabah this way. The base of the incline was a gentle rise, but near the top it turned sharply uphill, the sand giving way to a narrow rocky way set between two sheer faces on either side and ending at the ridgetop a hundred cubits above the valley floor.

Darius sidled in next to his father, the cavalrymen raising a cloud of dust and sand in the wake of their coming. The horses lined up at the base of the hill, all of them studying the way up. Darius leaned over the saddle and said, "You're not thinking we can get up this ridge, are you?"

"We've got to try." Tobit inched his mount a stride up the incline. "We could be searching for another break all the way to the Red Sea, son. Our water's gone and the only wells are up there, beyond that ridge. I want you to lead the rest of the men up once I'm over the top."

"And if you don't make it?"

"You won't have to come for me." Tobit turned in the saddle. "My body should fall most of the way down these cliffs."

Tobit dug his boots into the horse's side and he was away, driving the animal at full gallop up the gentle slope before slowing near the sharp upturn. The sand gave way to rocky ground and the steed reared on its hind legs, the steep way spooking her to a stall. Tobit leaned forward, his body coming out of the saddle and his chin pushing against the horse's mane, yelling for her to jump to the next ledge. The animal reared again, but Tobit spurred his heels into her haunches, forcing her to leap higher, her powerful legs pushing them past the wall of weathered sandstone and cracked outcrops, over the ridge and onto level ground.

Darius came next, his horse leaping over the ridge, followed by a line of cavalrymen, all of them clearing the rise, the ends of the their sweat-covered turbans flapping in the breeze and their white riding robes glimmering in the morning sunlight.

Tobit pulled in alongside his son. "How far are we from Bozrah?"

Darius took out his maps and unrolled the ends of the parchment. He ran his finger over the leather, plotting the distances, his gaze shifting between his careful sketches and the lay of the land spreading out before them. He said, "See those foothills leading south into the Jabal Mountains?"

Tobit inched his mount in line with his son's forefinger and sighted down the boy's arm. "I see them."

"There's a faint brown line rising and falling through the foothills."

"I see it clearly, yes."

"That's the Mountain Road to Aqaba. You take it south through those high mountain peaks and you end up on the shores of the Fountain of the Red Sea."

"Go on."

"If we take it we'll reach Bozrah come morning."

"What about well water?"

Darius turned back to his map and stopped his finger next to a small marking with a note sketched beside it. "We should find the first capped well right here at the crossroads where the Mountain Road and the Frankincense Trail split."

Tobit pulled the cloth of his turban back from his mouth and took a drink from the small water skin he carried over his shoulder. It was the last of their precious supply and he tilted his head back and let it wet his dry throat. If it weren't for the water Lehi left for them, they'd never have lasted long enough to find this break in the cliffs. What sort of man was he? Tobit wiped the sweat from his brow. This was a harsh, unforgiving desert suited to outlaws and renegades, not the kindheartedness Lehi managed to mete out in a heartless place, leaving them just enough water to save their lives. Curse him! What sort of game was he playing? Was this water a kindness or some sort of trick?

"We ride to the Crossroads, men. Keep your eyes open." Tobit raised his hand and pointed toward the Mountain Road in the distance—the only trail leading them back to Bozrah.

He said, "Find me this Lehi!"

Captain Laban spurred into Bozrah's main square, with Lieutenant Daniel and the long-haired Shechem reining alongside. They cantered through the ranks of the poorly rested Hebrew cavalry. The men had spent a difficult night sleeping in the streets of the city, but there was little he could do to ease their discomfort. The inns of Bozrah barely had room for Captain Laban and his officers, but as soon as these soldiers did their duty, he'd see they got their respite. A week's rest at the hot springs near Hebron, or a few days on the shores of the Great Sea at Joppa should keep these men in saddle until Lehi and his family were wiped from the face of this earth.

The cavalrymen sat at attention as Laban came into the square, the clapping and pawing of animal hooves falling silent on the cobblestone—the only paved road in this dusty outpost town. Laban nodded to the first column of men—a troop of twenty good riders with two scouts who knew this country well. His voice echoed off the one-story, mud-brick buildings ringing the plaza, telling them to search the trails leading into the pastures and vineyards around the city. They were to check every stable, search every dwelling, and look anywhere a caravan of mules could hide.

Laban turned in the saddle to the next column of fifteen soldiers. These men were outfitted with enough bows and swords and slings to do his bidding. They were to obey every order of the Babylonian Inspector Tobit except one. No matter what the good Inspector wanted, they were to kill the olive oil merchant first and beg Tobit to forgive their quick bowstring second. Lehi was not to speak a word to Tobit. Lehi was a traitor and he was to die as a traitor, and neither Tobit nor any other man must know the real reason for Laban's hatred for the olive oil merchant. The knowledge of Lehi's lineage would die in this desert outpost.

"You men work your way through the homes along the market and then into the hills along the King's Highway. You know what we're looking for and you know what to do."

Captain Laban came around to face the last column of fifteen cavalrymen when a short, squatty man with graying hair worked his way down between the horses. He pushed aside the muzzle of the last animal in the column, and immediately Laban recognized the innkeeper from the hill country north of Bozrah where they stopped for midday meal the day before last. The man ambled over in front of Captain Laban's white Arabian and offered a deep bow, his heavy paunch unbalancing him enough that he took a step forward to regain his composure.

Laban said, "What is it, innkeeper? What brings you to Bozrah this early in the morning?"

"I walked through the night to tell you of an outlaw."

"Did he steal your chickens?"

A round of laughter broke out among the soldiers until Laban quieted them with a wave of his hand. He said, "We don't have time to hunt down every outlaw in this country."

"This isn't any ordinary thief, sir."

"There are hundreds of unusual men that pass through this city." Laban turned to give the third column of cavalry their orders when the innkeeper reached for the Arabian's muzzle. "I suppose Lehi the Olive Oil Merchant is simply another ordinary caravan master."

The square quieted and Laban leaned over the saddle. "What did you say?"

"I walked through the night to tell you that the man you're hunting stopped by my inn last evening."

Daniel reined in behind the innkeeper. "Is he still there?"

"That depends."

"On what?"

"It was a very long walk, sir." The innkeeper opened his hand.

"Pay the man twenty pieces of silver." Laban waved the quarter-master over. "And twenty more when he leads us to—"

"I'm not leading you anywhere." The innkeeper took the small purse, counted the silver and told the quartermaster that this was enough. He hid the money under his belt before saying, "You can find Lehi on the trade route headed south. He passed through Bozrah during the night while you were sleeping, and he's taking the Mountain Road to Aqaba."

Shechem reined over, his long hair braided down his back and the ends of it playing about the saddle. He stared at the innkeeper and held onto his words like a dying man holds onto life. He said, "Why Aqaba?"

"Lehi's looking for some peace."

"He'll not find any there." Shechem pulled a dagger from inside his boot and pointed it at Captain Laban. "There's a good-sized port at Aqaba, and the city is large enough that Lehi could lose himself among the hordes of fishermen and boatbuilders."

"Then we stop him before he gets through the mountains." Laban rode out in front of the cavalry and stood in the saddle, his boots notched in the stirrups. "When you catch this fox on the Mountain Road, you know what to do with him."

Nephi inched his steed to the edge of the last vineyard in the foothills, pushed aside the branches of the Joshua tree, and peered down the main road leading out of Bozrah. From this distance there were no military patrols he could see leaving the city, but with a good eight miles separating them it was difficult to see every twist and turn along the trail. There were no soldiers marching over the dusty trade route and not a single traveler coming up the rise out of the city in the cool of morning before the sun baked the trail with the heat of summer. Nephi's steed pawed at the ground and he slowly stroked the animal's mane, whispering in her ear they'd be on their way as soon as he was certain all was clear.

"Any soldiers?" Laman's strong, deep voice carried on the morning breeze, chasing away a meadowlark from the grasses growing up by the last arbor. His call from the back of the caravan was the first word he'd uttered since leaving the inn north of Bozrah late last evening, and amazingly it wasn't a complaint. Not a week before, Laman swore he'd not travel deeper into the Border Mountains beyond Bozrah, but here he was, guiding the camels toward Aqaba without carping over the length of the journey or the foolishness of the ride. Something was wrong with his eldest brother, but what was it? Thankfully there were no mules to herd and no sheep or goats to trouble Laman anymore than he must already be troubled with having to travel beyond Bozrah. Whatever Laman's reservations, he kept silent his dislike for this journey to Aqaba.

Could Beuntahyu be the reason Laman didn't complain about traveling farther? She was a fine horse with a steady temperament, and if an Arabian with a white coat had the power to calm his brother's heart, Nephi would buy him a full herd of like-colored horses. But Beuntahyu belonged to Aaron, and though she was good to carry Laman on this leg of the journey, she didn't respond well to his constant spurring and whipping. Laman was a hard master and he used the lash more often than he ever spoke a soothing word in the poor animal's ear, and if he didn't soften his temper, Beuntahyu was going to rear him out of the saddle and teach him the respect she was accustomed to at the hand of Aaron.

Laman never rode at the rear of the caravan—a dusty, dirty unlikable task he left to his brothers—but last night he voluntarily herded the camels without Father even asking him to stay back in the foul wake of the caravan and keep the tired animals moving along. He didn't protest Father's decision last night to drive the caravan through the outlying vineyards to keep off the well-traveled routes. And he didn't grouse one bit about the slow pace of travel through the low-lying wadis out of sight of the military patrols—a journey that took three times as long as driving the caravan along the charted routes through the city. And when Nephi took a wrong turn in the dark before morning and added two miles to their journey skirting around Bozrah, Laman didn't grumble about the loss—he simply brought Beuntahyu around and followed Nephi back through the sagebrush and dry grasses until they reached this vineyard and found the main trade route.

Nephi turned his steed onto the dusty road, leading his travel-weary family away from whatever fate Captain Laban planned for them and toward the safety of the Jabal Mountains. The line of sixteen camels slowly lurched into step behind him, past a stand of Cyprus trees, and lumbered onto the trade route headed away from Bozrah—the square rooftops and mud-brick walls of the city fading on the distant horizon. They were in the open expanse of the last mile on the King's Highway without any trees or fully-grown arbors to conceal their journey.

The revealing light of morning spread across the foothills with the rising of the sun, the soft orange light exposing them like driftwood bobbing atop the surf of the Great Sea. Nephi sat up in the saddle and checked the road ahead. They were a good ten miles from entering the mountain pass leading through the Jabal Range, and with any luck they'd not be sighted until they reached the cover of those steep rock walls, and leave the threat of Captain Laban behind forever.

The caravan herd was a cantankerous lot after traveling through the night and with the towering peaks of the Jabal Mountains rising before them, the animals balked at the sight of the rigorous climb ahead, the caravan stretching along the incline rising up into the foothills in a long train visible for miles. Nephi slowed the lead camel and called to Lehi and Laman to gather the straggling animals closer. Sariah's steed wandered out of line and came alongside Nephi. Mother had fallen asleep in the saddle. Her head leaned forward and the brim of her white robe covered her eyes. Nephi took her horse by the reins, pulling the animal back into line and letting her dream a little longer before the rising sun woke her and reminded her that the ascent through the Jabal Mountains separated her from the respite she sought at Aqaba on the shores of the Red Sea. Their journeying took them a good distance across the civilized world—nearly one hundred and fifty miles from their home at Jerusalem—and Aqaba would be a final resting place suitable to Mother's needs. Where else in this wilderness could they take her to find the refuge she so desperately needed?

The trade route rose to the top of a hill before turning down to the Crossroads, the Frankincense Trail—the main branch of the trade route—veering east of the Border Mountains of the Jabal Range and running inland away from the coast. The Frankincense Trail meandered south along the foothills, never heading up into the majestic six-thousand-foot peaks dividing the Arabian Peninsula from the Red Sea. It was an easier trail for caravans headed to the frankincense groves of southern Arabia than driving up the Mountain Road, but Nephi and his company of weary travelers weren't trading in perfumes or spices. They were headed no further than Aqaba on the other side of these blue-gray mountains that reached into the heavens, the summit of each peak capped with green foliage up where the air was light and the heat of the day didn't brown the grasses of summer. These mighty peaks protected the less-traveled Aqaba Branch of the trade route like a thick gate defends a city and, with the help of heaven, these mountains would bring them the seclusion they sought. There was not a better name than *Aqaba* for this trail—Mountain Road was a perfect name for the stretch of trail through these high peaks and rugged terrain, and as soon as they traversed these Border Mountains near the Red Sea they were certain to find peace in the city of Aqaba—the city of the Mountain Road.

Nephi cantered down to the crossroads, slowly leading Sariah by the reins, careful not to disturb her sleeping. The capstone of the well marked the fork where the trail split—the Aqaba Branch leading through the Borders near the Red Sea and the Frankincense Trail heading inland down along the eastern slopes of the Border Mountains—and Nephi steered the lead camel onto the Aqaba Branch of the trade route, positioning the animals for the journey over the summit before pulling up and coming around. They could wait for the rest of the caravan camels to clear the rise and come down into this wadi. They were spread out over a good distance, and this low-lying alcove was a fine place to water the animals, away from the eyes of men before starting the climb into—

"Midian."

The hushed voice of Sariah carried on the morning breeze and Nephi turned in the saddle to find Mother taking in the view ahead, the hood of her white traveling robe pulled back and her black hair falling down over her shoulders. She sat straight, her head forward like the prow of a ship heading into stormy seas, her gaze set firmly on the way ahead.

Nephi said, "Mother, did you rest well?"

"As well as I could riding in the saddle all night." Sariah didn't turn away from looking up into the mountains, her gaze fixed on the run of peaks near the Red Sea. "The Borders, son. Do you know of them?"

"I know what I see ahead, what father tells me of these mountains, what I read in his maps, and a little of what I hear from merchant traders."

Sariah leaned back in the saddle, relaxing her hold on the reins and letting her steed take a step forward. "And exactly what have you heard?"

"You know, the usual talk of merchant traders losing themselves in the maze of narrow canyons and steep-walled wadis that run through these Borders."

"Is that what your father's maps tell you about these mountains?"

"See that pass through the Borders?" Nephi pointed up the Mountain Road running between two distant peaks. "We're going through there. It's the only way to Aqaba."

"No, son, I wasn't asking about the way through these Borders to Aqaba. I was meaning the history. Do your father's maps tell you anything of the past these mountains have witnessed? Do they teach you what these Borders mean to us?"

"They're high mountains." Nephi rubbed the back of his neck. "A good five thousand cubits above the surface of the—"

"Your father didn't tell you, did he?"

"Tell me what?" Nephi turned in the saddle and glanced back up the hill toward Bozrah where the camel trail was slowly coming over the crest. "Father should be along soon."

"When your eldest sister, Rachel, was born, your father didn't bring me a new robe or new linens or any such thing." Sariah smiled and laid her hand on the life maturing within her. "He brought me an old leather map done in his own hand. The fibers were worn, the ink was faded, but it was the finest gift he could have given me."

"A map?"

"That's right." Sariah slowly nodded. "A map of these borders, the same one you've studied so many times in the map room at Beit Zayit. A detailed chart of the Mountains of Midian, the place where Moses married and where he brought the children of . . ."

The plodding and grunting of the camels falling into line behind them drowned Sariah's words and Nephi reined down along the caravan steadying the arriving animals into line headed up the Mountain Road before coming back to Sariah and saying, "Go on; tell me what Father told you about this place."

"This is Midian, son."

"I've seen them in Father's maps."

"What the maps don't tell you is that hidden deep within the narrow valleys of the Borders near the Red Sea is sacred land." Sariah folded her arms, the pleats of her robe falling down over her front. "High in these mountains is the place where Moses spoke with God face-to-face, where he received revelation of the covenants God makes with men—covenants that bind families together throughout all generations. The same covenants revealed to Adam and Noah and Moses and to every prophet since the world began." She turned her gaze up into the peaks rising before them. "I've always hoped to see the Mountains of Midian, but I never dreamed they were in such an uncivilized country as this and surrounded by such a wasteland. How did Moses ever support so many lives in this barren land without any water?"

Nephi sidled in next to her and turned his gaze up into the mountains, both of them admiring the rugged beauty of the Borders near the Red Sea. Could this be the place Isaiah spoke of in his writings? Were these the mountains where God promised to open rivers in high places, and fountains in the midst of the valleys, and make for them a tabernacle for a shadow in the daytime from the heat, and for a place of refuge from the storm? Nephi softly repeated the phrase from the writings of Isaiah, the words he'd read over and over again by the lamplight of early morning at Qumran on the shores of the Dead Sea. Back then he didn't understand there could be a place prepared for them, preserved over centuries for their flight from Jerusalem, but the whisperings deep in his soul begged him to believe that God heard their pleadings, understood their plight, and he was guiding them, however haphazard their flight may be, to these mountains where Moses once dwelt to find a place of refuge. It was a faint stirring, hardly noticeable, but it was sweet enough to bring Nephi the peace that had escaped him since leaving Jerusalem. Nephi was to be still and know that God was God—He was mindful of them, no matter that it seemed he'd forsaken them. Nephi let his gaze run over the bulwark of mountains, the mighty rock towering in the horizon. He lowered his voice to a whisper and said, "We'll find refuge in these mountains, Mother."

"This land is a land of renegades, son." Sariah slowly shook her head. "Moses may have led the children of Israel through these mountains, but he didn't stay here forever and I fear we may never leave."

"Bring the animals back onto the main route." Lehi rode over the rise and past the last arriving camels. He slid out of the saddle and stood in the center of the Aqaba Branch leading up the Mountain Road, his hands on his hips and his gaze studying the rise and fall of the trail leading up through the Borders near the Red Sea before marching over to the Frankincense Trail and examining the main route running inland along the base of the eastern slopes of the range.

"What is it, dear?" Sariah leaned over the saddle. "Is there something wrong?"

Lehi came back down along the line of camels and studied the Mountain Road again, his hand over his brow to shield his eyes from the morning sun.

"You can't take us on the Frankincense Trail. You gave your word." Laman hurried the last camel down the rise and into line, facing up the Mountain Road toward the Borders near the Red Sea before spurring over next to Lehi. "You said we were headed to Aqaba."

"We are, son." Lehi took the reins of the lead camel and started her around, leading her back down past the capstone of the well and around onto the Frankincense Trail. "We're going to Aqaba this way."

Laman jumped from the saddle, his landing raising a cloud of dust about his sandals. He marched over to his father and leaned his head in. "You know this country better than any of us. There's only one charted route to Aqaba, and it's up the Mountain Road."

"We're not following the charts." Lehi pointed down along the Frankincense Trail running inland of the Border Mountains, but before his forefinger reached the horizon where the trail disappeared, he brought his hand back west across the foothills to the pass leading over the summit. "We'll cut back to the Aqaba Branch down that way."

"We can't ride that way. There could be ridges we can't cross or wadis that keep us from cutting back." Laman raised his hands in the air. "The Mountain Road is the only route." He took Lehi by the arm. "Tell me this isn't one of your foolish dreams."

"Father's dreams are not foolish." Nephi got down from the saddle and joined them near the capstone of the well, with Sariah reining in behind him, but before he could say anything more, Lehi turned the full force of his gaze onto Laman, his deep green eyes filled with a power Nephi had never seen in his father. It was a penetrating stare, as if he could see into Laman's deepest thoughts and read them like a man reads from a scroll. The longer Father stared at Laman, the more his teardrop-filled eyes fell to saddened half circles, and the chapped flesh of his lips began to tremble, betraying the sadness of seeing into the heart of his eldest son.

Laman said, "I don't like it when you look at me like that."

Lehi lowered his head. "And I don't like what I see."

"I'll get the animals." Nephi reached for the reins of the closest camels to start them around when Laman stepped in his way, blocking him from bringing the animals onto the Frankincense Trail. He stood straddling the two ways—one foot planted in the dust of the main trail and the other set firmly in the Mountain Road, like a man undecided about which way he should go. He said, "Why are you doing this?"

"We left the Babylonian soldiers with enough water to find their way out of the Arabah." Lehi stepped to the capstone of the well, turned it on its side and rolled back the stone, the hole in the ground giving up a soft rush of air. He let down a cistern on the end of a rope. "They'll be traveling north on the Mountain Road on their way back to Bozrah and we're not going to meet them on the trail when they pass."

"You don't know they'll come this way."

"They'll be stopping at this well, son." Lehi raised the cistern, the cool water dripping from the bottom of the vessel. "They need water as much as we do."

Laman marched away, down along the caravan camels, and when he reached Nephi's horse at the far end, he started unpacking the riggings, removing the saddlebags and calling to them, telling them he was finding the nuts and seeds packed on Nephi's horse and they should all eat something before they started off on this uncharted route to Aqaba. Nephi didn't follow Laman to tell him there wasn't any food packed on his horse—at least he didn't remember packing any. There was nothing but some ropes, a water skin, and his steel bow—the weapon half hidden beneath the saddlebags and wrapped in a blanket to keep the shimmering recurved arms from attracting the gaze of travelers on this route. There could be nothing worse than to have a merchant trader or a vineyard owner remember them to Captain Laban by this steel bow, and he kept it hidden under the blanket. Let his brother find out for himself there was nothing in those saddlebags to comfort his belly.

Laman stayed behind Nephi's horse going through the saddlebags a good while before stepping off the trail beside a stand of Joshua trees, kicking at the dust and snapping free a long stick from the gnarled branches. Laman was a temperamental man, but there was no need for such a fierce reaction to Father's decision to take an uncharted route to avoid a chance meeting with their pursuers.

Laman stepped from behind the line of withered Joshua trees, wrapped what appeared to be the steel bow in a blanket and arranged it beneath the saddlebags as it was before, strapping the weapon back in place with leather cords. He was a long way off and it was difficult to see if he'd found any food among Nephi's things, but whatever he found it tempered his ill will. He took the reins of two camels, came back down along the caravan and started them onto the main trade route leading inland, telling Father he was sorry for the disagreement and he was ready to head to Aqaba in whatever direction Father pleased.

They finished watering the camels, replaced the capstone covering the well, and headed down the wide, well-traveled inland route of the Frankincense Trail. The route pushed close to the Borders near the Red Sea, the foothills rising alongside their path like a steep wall blocking the way back to the Mountain Road. They kept a good pace, the camels following without complaint, and it wasn't until the morning sun reached well overhead, a good two hours past midday that Lehi signaled for them to turn off the Frankincense Trail and cut back across the Borders toward the Mountain Road. It was a steep climb over a ridge and Nephi went first, his steed churning the sand under hoof. It wasn't the easiest climb for the camels. They didn't do well on steep inclines and Nephi came around to signal Father to send the lead camel up the hill slowly. The ground was uneven and they'd lose her along with the possessions she carried if they didn't keep her from—

What was that? The ends of the blanket hiding Nephi's steel bow came lose and slapped against his leg. He reached to secure the weapon beneath the saddlebags when his hand slipped beneath the covering and his fingers brushed against the course, unforgiving, curved end of—

A tree branch? Nephi pulled back the blanket to find a curved piece of wood in place of his steel bow. He felt under the blanket for the polished metal of his weapon, but it was nowhere to be found and Nephi turned his gaze over the trade route, searching for the shimmering metal fallen in the wake of their wandering. There was no sign of the bow along the main trail, nothing glittering between the large brown bodies of the camels, and no indication of where his bow had gone until his gaze rested on Laman at the back of the caravan staring up the rise at Nephi, a subtle smile pulling at his lips. Nephi took the branch of the tree out from beneath the blanket and threw it on the ground.

What did Laman do with his steel bow?

"Over here."

Inspector Tobit's son called from behind a stand of Joshua trees, but he didn't respond to the boy's pleading. Darius could wait with his maps and pens and compasses until Tobit examined these far-too-familiar prints in the sand. The suspicious tracks surrounded the well at the Crossroads and he stayed at the watering place, his gaze quickly going over the ground. They came to this fork in the trade route seeking water on the way back to Bozrah, but found much more than a drink to wet the tongue. The sand that usually collected around the seal of the capstone was gone, removed earlier in the day by a thirsty traveler— nothing out of the ordinary if not for the fresh footprints identical to the ones they tracked across the wastelands of the Arabah.

Inspector Tobit fell to his knees, ordering his men to secure the area and keep their horses off the road until he examined the prints.

There was nothing worse than a stray horse from his company meandering about and destroying whatever clues were hidden in the dust. There were sixteen distinct camels in this caravan—four less than what they tracked across the Arabah—and there were four riders on horseback where before there were only three. Tobit crawled over the ground, the tips of his fingers tracing the outline of the marks left by the horses. There was no mistaking these narrow cloven hoofs with metal shoes. The width of the crosspiece and the placement of the nails were exactly the same as the ones they tracked through the Arabah. And what merchant trader could afford a blacksmith to hammer metal shoes onto a horse except a wealthy man like Lehi?

"Inspector, sir." Darius hurried over, placing his boots well away from any tracks. The boy understood there were clues where other men saw only dust, and the less he disturbed the area the more they could glean from this road. "Over there behind a stand of Joshua trees, up the Mountain Road. I've found something you should—"

"Not now, son."

"But it's—"

"Not until I've examined these prints. You know that." Tobit crawled along the road studying each track with Darius walking beside him. "When we track a man there isn't anything more important than the prints he leaves behind."

"Not even if we—"

"If we don't examine these prints before the wind blows sand over them or a stray animal destroys them, we'll lose them." Tobit pressed his thumb into the deepest print and slowly moved up the side of the concave marking. The ridges were sharp without any sand falling back into the center of the cloven hoof. These tracks were fresh, left here about the same time the capstone was removed, and it was safe to conclude Lehi watered his caravan earlier in the day, sometime this morning, possibly around sunrise. They were onto his trail again and Tobit stood, brushed the sand from his hands, and marched down along the Mountain Road with Darius hurrying to keep up. They were to the stand of Joshua trees where his son had discovered something of interest.

Darius said, "It's right back there.

"Not yet, son."

"But, sir, I—"

"Not until I check the change of direction."

"Change of what?" Darius marched alongside his father, the ends of his leather map flapping against his stride.

"You see here." Tobit motioned to the wide turns in the road. "The caravan master wasn't certain which route to take. Lehi started his caravan headed up the Mountain Road toward Aqaba, before turning around and heading inland down the Frankincense Trail." He pulled his turban back from his brow and scanned the camel tracks leading off into the distance in an unbroken line. "This doesn't make any sense."

Darius said, "What doesn't?"

"Let me see your maps." Tobit took the soft leather drawing from Darius and draped it between his hands, slowly studying the ink lines charting the trade route through these parts. His son's careful pen strokes outlined the perimeter of these mountains, but there was scant detail of the canyons and wadis running through them. Darius knew enough about this area to draw the mountains as a split range. The ridge of peaks they could see were the Borders near the Red Sea and beyond them, down where they couldn't see along the coast, the range split into two—the Borders near and nearer the Red Sea—but beyond the drawing of those dual ranges, there was no description of the width or depth of any canyons, no sense of which gullies were dead ends and which led to higher mountain valleys. The title of this region was written in Darius's flowing pen, designating these mountains as the Northern Hijaz— the Borders—and there was not a more suitable name for these mountains separating the inland deserts from the coast of the Fountain of the Red Sea. These mountains were the southernmost possessions of the New Babylonian Kingdom, the extreme ends of Tobit's commission, and his son had carefully used a double ink line to mark the end of the territory at the south end of this run of mountain peaks. They were a majestic sight, but for the love of the gods of the Euphrates, they didn't have any accurate charts of these mountains, not a single marked well, no wadis or springs, nothing to help them through this territory. The only thing Darius marked with a thick pen stroke were the two trails splitting here at this well, the Mountain Road leading to Aqaba and the Frankincense Trail running inland down along the eastern slopes of these Mountains to southern Arabia.

Tobit ran his fingers over the surface of the map, searching for any clue that would tell him why Lehi took the Frankincense Trail. There was every reason for the man to take the less-traveled Mountain Road to Aqaba. There were a good many Jews living in that city on the sea; there were renegades avoiding the tax, and refugees believing the Babylonians were come to war with the Hebrews, but it didn't appear Lehi was headed to join with them, not with his caravan heading down the Frankincense Trail. They had to capture Lehi before he escaped past the frontier of the territories of the Babylonian Kingdom and beyond Tobit's reach.

Tobit said, "It isn't like Lehi to vacillate."

"How do you know it isn't? We hardly know the man. We've never met him. All we have are some of his writings. For all we know he doesn't exist."

"He's real son, very real." Tobit rubbed the sweat from his brow. "And I have met him."

"You what?" Darius rolled his map into a tight scroll. "You never told me you'd seen the man."

"Every night since we started this expedition." Tobit kept his gaze fixed out over the Frankincense Trail, peering into the horizon where Lehi's caravan had gone. He hardly moved his parched lips when he spoke. He said, "In my dreams I see Lehi dressed in riding robes, with a white turban held in place with an ivory-studded black band and decorated with a single feather sprouting out the back. He rides with a company of sons like a troop of renegade soldiers storming across the country and when he pulls up on his horse at the top of a rise and turns around in the saddle I can see . . ."

"You see what?"

"Nothing, son. That's where I wake every morning. Lehi's face is nothing but a shadow." Tobit lowered his gaze from looking out over the desert. "If I could only get a look at the man, see into his eyes, peer into his soul and ask what drives him, then I'd know what sort of a man we were tracking." He worked his lower lip between his teeth.

"There's a deeper reason Lehi left his life of wealth and the comfort of his estate at Jerusalem for this desert and I'm going to find it out." He fitted his turban back in place. "Something beyond our chasing is driving this man deeper into—"

"It's Captain Laban, sir." A cavalryman galloped down from the top of the rise surrounding the wadi. "The Hebrew military commander is arriving from Bozrah."

The sound of horses pounding across the desert grew louder until it shook the ground, and Captain Laban appeared on the rise leading a troop of soldiers down to the watering place. Lieutenant Daniel and the long-haired scout Shechem rode double-file behind Laban with a company of cavalry spurring into line. Captain Laban reined past the well and onto the main road, the hooves of his white Arabian destroying the fresh tracks, and what he didn't run over with his horse, the Hebrew cavalry ruined in the wake of their coming.

Fool! What was he doing, riding over these carefully preserved tracks? Tobit ran toward them, waving his arms to keep Captain Laban back, but it was no use. The man galloped across the watering place, his horse kicking up a flurry of sand. This Captain Laban may be a powerful man, with his broad shoulders and thick arms, but he certainly didn't understand the subtleties of tracking a man through the desert.

"We tracked Lehi to this well." Tobit came alongside Laban's horse and peered up at the captain through the rays of the afternoon sun. "I believe he's headed to—

"Aqaba." Laban sat straight in the saddle. "I already tracked him that direction."

"What tracks are you following?"

"We have information."

"From whom?"

"An innkeeper."

"Do you trust him?"

"I paid him twenty pieces of silver."

"You may want to get your money back. Lehi's headed into Arabia down the Frankincense Trail."

"There's no reason for him to head that way. Where do you come by your information?"

"I don't deal in information."

Laban got down from the saddle, his boots landing on the last fully formed camel track left in the sand and destroying it from heel to toe. "What evidence do you have?"

"You're standing on it." Tobit turned his gaze to the camel tracks under Laban's boots. "Lehi's tracks begin at the edge of a vineyard back on the other side of the ridge. You passed them on your way in."

"I didn't see any tracks."

"They're subtle prints, sir. The ground is harder back up on that rise. Lehi traveled through fields and wadis during the night until he ventured out onto the trade route and stopped at this well before heading down the Frankincense Trail to Arabia."

Captain Laban shook the sand from his boots. "How do you know these prints were left by Lehi?"

"Merchant traders don't hide in vineyards."

"I still say he's headed to Aqaba."

Tobit stepped down along the Frankincense Trail. "These are the same tracks we've been following since we left Qumran. Lehi can't be more than a half day ahead of us and if we ride hard, we should capture him before he gets beyond these mountains." Tobit held his hand over his brow to shield his eyes from the afternoon sun. "I want to speak with the man. Find out exactly what drives him to run from us with such fury."

"There's no need to question him. He's a rebel bent on inciting an uprising against Babylon. All we need to do is stop him."

"You mean kill him?"

"If I have to."

"I want Lehi taken alive."

Darius stepped in between Tobit and Laban. He said, "The trees, sir. You have to see behind the Joshua trees."

Darius led them past the well, around the turn in the fork, and down the Aqaba Branch of the trade route in behind the gnarled trunk of a withered Joshua tree. The glimmering light of midday reflected off the curved outline of polished metal lying in the sand.

Lieutenant Daniel rode over and jumped from the saddle. He pushed in ahead of Tobit and Laban. "That's Aaron's steel bow, the one he was forged for Lehi."

Tobit leaned over the bow to study it, but not move it from its resting place. The upper and lower arms were balanced in perfect symmetry, the recurved arches of metal polished to a fine luster, and despite the sand that dirtied the handgrip, the leather covering was tanned to a perfect suppleness. He'd strung bows of cedar and black wood, shot arrows with bows fashioned of cherry and olive, but never a bow of steel. It was an impossible feat for any blacksmith and Tobit came around and knelt behind the bow. An arrow lay across the handgrip, the fletching knocked in place against the string, and Tobit sighted down the shaft. The metal tip was set like the needle on a compass, pointing precisely where the Mountain Road entered the pass through the Jabal Mountains on the way to Aqaba. Someone was trying to tell them something, but what? Only a desperate man would leave a precious weapon on the ground to fool them.

Tobit slowly lifted the bow off the ground and wiped away the sand. The metal was bright, the surface smooth to the touch, and when he pulled on the string it had the tension of three wooden bows. He drew it to a full draw, flexing the arms as far as he had strength. The metal held its shape. There were no cracks forming along the surface, no indication that this metal was too brittle to endure the pull of an archer's arm. Tobit held in his hands the finest invention of his lifetime—the world's first steel bow—and any military armed with a host of these weapons was certain to reign over the entire earth. Tobit tightened his grip. Captain Laban was right. If Lehi had a blacksmith who could smith a weapon of such power, he was planning an uprising of untold proportion. Renegades outfitted with bows of this strength were unbeatable. But the answer wasn't simply to apprehend Lehi. Tobit had to find the blacksmith who perfected the art of imbuing a weapon with the power of steel.

"I'll take that, sir." Daniel reached for the bow, but Tobit pushed his arm aside. "Don't touch this."

"The bow belongs to me." Captain Laban leaned his head in. "If you don't mind, I'll take it back to—"

"This weapon is the property of the King of Babylon." Tobit raised his hand, forcing Laban back a step. He pointed the steel tip of the bow at Daniel. "You said your brother smithed this."

'That's right, sir."

"I want to meet this boy, do you hear?"

"That isn't possible." Daniel shook his head. "You can't meet him."

"I gave you an order and I expect you to obey it."

"He's dead, sir."

"Dead?"

"That's right" Captain Laban nodded. "He took an arrow trying to save Lehi the night the man fled from Jerusalem. Before he died he must have given that bow to Lehi."

"Did he smith any others?"

"That's the only one." Daniel reached for the bow and ran his finger over the bright metal. "This was Aaron's first attempt."

Tobit pulled the bow away from Daniel's stroking. Why would Lehi leave this weapon on the trail when he should be using it to pattern more bows? Tobit plucked the bowstring, ran his hand over the recurved arches in the metal. He was beginning to understand Captain Laban's urgency. If Lehi recruited a smith capable of fashioning a bow of steel, there was no telling what sort of designs he possessed for raising an army.

"We ride after Lehi." Tobit pointed the tip of the arrow down along the Frankincense Trail where the camel tracks led over the horizon.

"This rebel must be stopped."

CHAPTER 28

The hood of Rebecca's traveling robe fell from her head, but she didn't have the strength to replace it and keep the unforgiving rays of the sun from burning her mind. The brightness blurred her sight, and the heat ached like the fury of a blacksmith's anvil pounding against her skull, but it did not have power to remove the vision of the life she hoped to live. Death would not be her companion in this desert. She'd lived the life of a dead woman once before and it did not suit her well. This was not her time to part this earth and she slowly pulled the hood of her robe back over her head to shield it from the worst of the sun.

The sands of The Way of the Wilderness sapped her strength, the dry heat swelled her tongue to near choking, and the lack of water turned her hands to shaking branches. They lost four camels and two sheep to the harshness of the Way of the Wilderness, but she would not let this thief-of-a-desert steal her vision of what would be, and she tightened her grip on the reins to keep from falling out of the saddle, clinging to the dream of finding a well or another traveler with a supply of water to share or, heaven help them, the sighting of the city Bozrah on the other side of this long, sandy dune rising ahead of the mule caravan's slow push to the top.

The Empty Quarter stretched endlessly to the east. The plateaus of Moab were a distant swell on the western horizon, but Rebecca kept her horse headed south up the incline. It was longer than the other dunes they crossed this morning and there was a rocky ridge near the top with a Joshua tree sprouting on the uneven horizon, giving her hope that the end of their trek was near, but there was no way to know until she reached the top and scanned the land beyond. They should have stopped riding at midday and waited until nightfall, but they ran out of water late yesterday and if they didn't reach Bozrah soon, Rebecca may never wake from another night's rest to enjoy her life in company with Aaron.

Where was Aaron? Rebecca rode second behind him, with Papa and Lemuel riding at the back of the mule train, but it had been so long since she'd heard anyone speak, there was no telling if the others were suffering the same light-headedness. She blinked, but she could see nothing but bright lights dancing in her sun-dazed mind. The struggle to ride a full day without water weakened her body and before she could get her bearings and find Aaron in the brightness, her head reeled back, her eyes taking the full force of the sun and blinding her to . . .

"Aaron?" Rebecca lost hold of the reins, her arms waving about to keep from falling out of the saddle. "Are you there, Aaron?"

There was no answer and Rebecca wrapped her trembling hands around the horse's neck to steady her frail body in the saddle. She shielded her eyes with the brim of her hood, the cloth doing its blessed work and keeping her from the piercing light until she found Aaron a little to the right of her. He'd strayed, his horse veering along the side of the sand dune. They were nearly to the top, but the mules were following him the wrong way. His body was slumped forward in the saddle and when she spurred her slow-plodding, travel-weary horse to come alongside, she could see his swollen lips with blood seeping between the cracked skin. Why did she allow him to give away his rations? He never should have gone without water longer than the rest of them. He needed it as much as any of them and she never should have believed him yesterday when he told her he was thinner and didn't need as much. His parched body trembled out of control, his body falling from the saddle and—

"Someone help us."

Aaron's long body sprawled over the sand and his horse pulled up beside him, poking its muzzle at his head the way a vulture picks at a corpse. Rebecca slipped from the saddle and her knees gave out, but she would not so easily let go of this man whose life she was to share, and she crawled through the sand, pushed the horse back from

Aaron's fallen form, and took his head in her hands. His body trembled and despite the heat of this desert he was gone cold like the chill of a winter storm. Rebecca rocked back and forth with Aaron's weak body cradled in her arms. She turned her gaze to see into his eerily opened blue eyes, eyes that for months had given her the courage to live a frugal life at Qumran and guide her soul through their travels in this desert, but it was as if she were staring at a blind man. The sun had worked its evil, blurring his vision and filling him with the chilling foreshadows of death.

The mule train slowed to a stop behind them and Rebecca cried out with enough force to overcome her swollen tongue and parched lips. "Papa, help me with Aaron. Something has gone terribly wrong and I need your . . ."

Josiah's horse meandered past and pulled up just below the top of the rise, the animal seeking what little shade there was beneath the branches of the Joshua tree. Papa was slouched forward in the saddle, his arms hanging at his side like a dead man. Lemuel's horse stopped below Rebecca, but the boy's body wasn't anywhere to be found. The relentless heat of the sun blurred her vision, but she'd seen enough and she slowly laid her body over Aaron, protecting him from the heat.

Was she cursed to live long enough to watch them die?

Sam replaced the capstone of the well and tied the last water skin onto the backs of his four camels before steering the animals out of camp and down along the base of a sand dune, which had a rocky ridge near the summit and a withered Joshua tree sprouting from the top. He had more than enough water to meet the needs of the mule train, and saddlebags packed with grains and seeds and dried pulse, but there was no telling which way Aaron was leading the mule caravan through this Way of the Wilderness. Sam could climb this dune and check the way north, or head further east out into the Empty Quarter, but which way should he try first?

Sam left Bozrah last night and traveled a few miles up the King's Highway before leaving the highlands and heading down through this wadi in the early morning hours. He slept during the hottest part of the day beneath the clustered branches of three date palms—the last oasis before the burning sands of The Way of the Wilderness replaced the arid lands leading up into the hill country of Moab—and now that the hot afternoon was ebbing, he turned his horse away from the dune and spurred further east, deeper into the Empty Quarter.

What was that? He heard a voice as clearly as if a man were riding alongside him, telling him he'd selected the wrong route. But there was no wrong route in these endless sands. He could go up over that dune and past the withered Joshua tree to see the desert directly north of here, or he could go this way, farther east into the deserts of the—

There it was again, that deep, penetrating voice ordering him to stop heading east and ride up over that hill past the Joshua tree and have a look north. Sam slowed his horse to a stop, the large frames of the four camels lumbering to a stop behind him, and the water skins swaying on his sudden turn. There was no one behind him ordering him the other way. He was alone in this desert and he shook his head. Was his mind playing tricks on him? He wrapped the loose cloth of his turban around his brow to keep the sun from getting any deeper into his mind. It didn't make sense to check the other side of that dune. Aaron was too clever to risk running the mules this close to the King's Highway, not with so many soldiers searching for their caravan, and Sam turned back toward the east, leading the camels away from this hill of sand with an outcrop near the top. He scanned the flat desert floor for any sign of his friends. He had to find them and lead them past Bozrah and on to—

No more! Sam turned in the saddle. He wouldn't let his sun-stroked mind convince him to turn around. The voice was as loud as a man screaming in his ears, demanding he go check the other side of the dune. Sam reined in a circle, looking up at the lone Joshua tree, then turning around to scan the way east out over the flat deserts, and then back to see up the rise to the withered tree. His indecision was nothing but foolishness. He was wasting time here and he had to choose. Which way was he to go? He turned another circle, studying both directions. It shouldn't matter where he looked as long as he was looking. What Sam didn't know was that his friends lay dying on the other side of this dune.

Sam's decision mattered to heaven.

CHAPTER 29

That had to be the outside entrance to the prison. The Ethiopian, Ebed-Melech, pressed his face against the iron bars of the back gate to the palace at Jerusalem. A watchman walked the catwalk above the gate and two more stood at the parapet, looking over into the alley where Ebed stood. On the other side of the gate was a door sealed with three latches and buttressed with metal rivets and crosspieces. Mima told him he'd find it here, but breaking it down wasn't nearly as difficult a task as dealing with the two soldiers standing guard. Ebed had more than enough strength to overpower them, but he had to find a subtle way if he were to keep faith with Mima's request and gain the good favor of King Zedekiah in order to win the release of the prophets.

Ebed tightened his grip around the iron bars. How was he to win the favor of the king while breaking into this prison and sneaking away the monarch's most closely guarded prisoners? Ebed folded his arms across his thick chest, the torn cloth of his sailor's tunic pulling taut against his dark skin. There had to be a better, quieter way to the inside of this prison and he had to find it before—

"Move along, sir." A palace guard marched through the gardens, across a small plaza, and stepped to the gate. He forced the butt of his sword through the bars and pushed the metal into Ebed's backside. "Move along before I call for the palace watch to remove you."

"I'm moving." Ebed backed into the alley away from the soldier's poking. "Is that how you treat your prisoners?"

"Keep moving or you can join them in the dungeons."

"Is that where you keep them?"

"Keep who?"

Ebed tipped his head toward the sealed prison door. "The prophets."

"Why do you want to know?"

"I'm looking for work. I make a good prison hand."

The soldier ran his gaze over Ebed's dark-skinned Ethiopian frame, from his thick neck, down past his wide shoulders and arms, to his feet shod in sailor's boots. "We don't have need of your help."

Ebed raised his fist. "I'm a hard worker with a good—"

"Move along!" The guard pointed the way out of the alley before starting back through the palace gardens to his post and leaving Ebed alone without anyone to keep him from walking deeper into the alley. Mima told him to try this gate first and if that didn't get him inside the prison, he should try the tunnels. She said Mulek escaped at night through the sewers, and Ebed walked along the outside wall of the palace to where the alley narrowed near the back and turned sharply downhill. The walkway ended at the bottom of a steep decline with a wooden trap door recessed into the base of the limestone wall, the narrow opening reinforced with a metal frame. When Ebed took hold of the latch it refused his pulling. The trap door was locked tight from inside and he turned his ear along the edge of it, the sound of rushing water passing by the seam. This had to be the way in. Where else could the prince escape the palace than through an underground aqueduct passing below the prison? Ebed tried the trap door with both hands, his powerful legs straining to force it open and his back arched, but it wouldn't come up. The watchman walking the catwalks above the alley started toward him and Ebed quickly backed into the narrow shaft of midday shadows that clung to the palace wall, waiting for the man to reach the end of his march and start back the other way. How was he ever going to get inside with soldiers watching over this alley? He had to find a way, and the only other instruction Mima gave him was to pray if everything else failed. Ebed shook his head and smiled. Where did that woman come by her faith? When he knew her, she wasn't a praying, God-fearing soul, but twenty years had softened her heart and Ebed did the only thing he could think to do. He lowered his hands to his side, bowed his head and offered the first prayer he'd uttered in his life.

Heaven help him to gain the favor of the king.

Ruth hid in the back of the palace kitchens, over beyond the ovens gone cold overnight. It was still too early to fire them for evening meal, and she with Elizabeth were safe to change into the disguises Miriam left for them without the cooks finding them here. She helped Elizabeth tie the sash on her robe—a light blue maidservant's dress identical to those worn by the other servers carrying food down the back corridor to the prison. It was a perfect disguise and Ruth slipped the robe on over her linen skirts before lifting the collar against her cheeks and doing the same with her daughter's robe. A thick hood was a much better way to keep them from recognition, but none of the other maidservants covered their faces and she couldn't turn their disguise into an oddity. This was not a wedding and they were not brides. They were to serve the guests arriving at the palace prison for the ceremony of property sale, and veiling their face would only draw attention where none was wanted.

Three wicker baskets sat on the floor at Ruth's feet, filled with wine purchased from the Jaw Bone Inn—the strongest wine the innkeeper had in his cellar. It was fermented from last year's harvest and none of it diluted, not even by a sixteenth of water, and thankfully she was able to sneak these bottles into the palace without the guards asking the reason for carting in so much when the palace storehouse was stocked with more than enough for the ceremony. She couldn't tell them she needed a brew strong enough to divert the attention of the palace guards. They needed the help of this wine if they had any of hope of beguiling the jailer. Ruth lifted the baskets from the floor.

"How will I recognize the jailer?" Elizabeth took the basket from Ruth and adjusted it against her hip. "Are you certain he's the one with a cane?"

"Not a cane, dear. The man has a limp, but you won't see him walking about the Court of the Prison. He doesn't mix with guests."

"Did Miriam tell you that?'

"The jailer shouldn't be too difficult to find."

"Is he a short man?"

"He's bent over."

"What of his eyes? Are they brown or—"

"Don't worry yourself." Ruth patted Elizabeth on the arm. "You'll recognize him."

"What if someone recognizes me?"

"The nobles don't look at the maidservants." Ruth pressed her palm against the girl's cheek. "It isn't proper."

"It isn't propriety that concerns me." Elizabeth took a quick, short breath. "I'm worried about—"

"There's nothing to worry about. Do you hear me? Everything is going to be fine."

"How can you be so sure?"

Ruth pulled her cuffs down past her wrists. She wasn't certain of anything, but she managed to softly say, "We can be sure we're doing what's right."

"Does the jailer wear his hair uncombed or does he care for it with a—"

"It's the keys you're looking for." Ruth lowered her voice to a whisper to keep her words from filtering from their hiding place behind the ovens and into the serving room where the other maidservants gathered food onto trays. She fiddled with the sash on Elizabeth's robe, but all the priming of her daughter's clothes didn't have power to chase away the fear that shook her fingers, and she let go of the girl's pleats before Elizabeth felt the concern that turned her hands to jelly. She said, "Look for a man carrying keys."

"Is there nothing more you can tell me? What if I serve the wrong man?" Elizabeth took Ruth by the arm and she could feel the girl's shaking—deep-to-the-bone trembling. They both suffered an insufferable bout of edginess and all Ruth could think to say was, "Look at you, as perfectly dressed as any of the palace maidservants." She stepped back from Elizabeth and let her gaze pass over the girl's disguise. She had to say something more—anything to take Elizabeth's mind off dangers that were impossible to forget. "My, you're beautiful in that robe."

"You don't know, do you? You don't have any idea what the jailer looks like." Elizabeth took back her hand and held it to her lips. "You don't even know if the jailer will be in the Court of the Prison when we arrive and if he's not there then our entire plan will be ruined."

"Zoram will be in the chamber. He'll not let any harm come to you. You know what to look for." Ruth took Elizabeth's hand and placed it over the girl's heart. "If anything goes wrong, Zoram will signal with his hand over his heart and you'll know to drop your basket and get out. Do you understand? Stay calm and watch Zoram, He'll not let us fail."

"How can I stay calm?" Elizabeth rubbed her hands together. "We're looking for a man we don't know, stealing keys to unlock doors in hidden parts of the palace where we've never been."

"The jailer keeps the keys on a chain about his neck. That's all you have to remember."

"I can't do this." Elizabeth shook her head, the ends of her long, black braids lifting about her shoulders. "What if we're caught? What will become of Zoram if they find him helping Jeremiah escape? And what about you? You have the hardest part in this. What if the guards won't let you down into the Lower Prison?"

"Why wouldn't they?" Ruth lifted the other two baskets of wine from the floor. "The men guarding this prison are going to want a drink as much as any of the nobles attending the ceremony." She patted Elizabeth on the hand. "See that you get me the keys and I'll take care of the rest." She started Elizabeth walking toward the voices of cooks and maidservants filtering over from the serving chamber. "Go along, dear. Mix with the others."

"Aren't you coming?" Elizabeth pulled up near the last oven.

"I'll be along."

"I can't do this alone."

"The keys, dear. Get me the keys." Ruth squeezed Elizabeth on the arm before ushering the girl past the ovens and into the serving chamber where a host of cooks hurried about long tables, preparing plates of cooked lamb wrapped in flat bread and garnished with chestnuts and basil. It was best they not be seen together and she let Elizabeth take her wine basket and join the company of servers heading into the hall while she stayed a good distance behind. The robes Miriam left for them matched the light blue color of the palace help, the white sashes were the perfect width, and the hems reached to just below the ankle. A maidservant stepped into stride next to Ruth. She carried a plate of lamb on her shoulder and Ruth slowed to

let her pass, distancing herself from Elizabeth, but not losing sight of
the girl. She kept her head down with the heavy baskets of wine
riding against her hip. Why did she ever agree to this? There had
never been an escape from this prison and it was foolishness to hope
to be the first. Neither Ruth nor her daughter were practiced at
deception and they didn't have the soul for subversion, but Ruth kept
walking in the company of these unsuspecting maidservants, her face
pressed against the collar of her robe.

Dear Lord, they couldn't shrink from this now.

Water gathered on the ceiling stones like dew on the underbelly
of a dark cavern, the moisture collecting on the walls of this tunnel
corridor outside the Court of the Prison, but soaking into the seams
between the limestone blocks before any drops could fall at Zoram's
feet. The nobles of the city stood outside the sealed prison doors,
waiting under the flickering flame of a solitary lamp for the jailer to
come and open the door and let them inside to conduct the ceremony of property sale. Zoram stayed hidden in the shadows, a narrow
limestone pilaster blocking the light of a lone yellow lamp burning
above the main entrance. What was taking such a long time? The
jailer shouldn't keep so many nobles waiting. The man knew about
the ceremony of property sale for weeks and he didn't require a fort-
night to prepare the chamber.

The invited guests spoke in round, pear-shaped tones, and Zoram
stayed in his half-shadowed hiding place, close enough to hear their
hushed conversations, but not so close so as to oblige his inclusion.

The city's Chief Money Changer stood nearest the thick, metal-
reinforced timbers of the main doors, surrounded by a sea of black-
robed elders discussing the oddness of the ceremony. The perfume
merchant leaned his head in and wondered aloud the reasons for the
king permitting a prisoner to purchase property. The gold merchant
removed the ring on his middle finger and polished it to a perfect
shine before fitting it back in place with his ten other rings, while
asking his companions why Zedekiah would ever entertain such a
ceremony for a man like Jeremiah the Prophet, a rebel who did

nothing but vilify the princes and nobles of the city with false accusations of selfishness. Zoram stepped deeper into the shadows along the corridor wall at the mention of Jeremiah, the pens in his satchel shifting about inside his soft leather satchel. Father's sermons were powerful indictments, but only the uncharitable need sting at any bite in Jeremiah's preaching, and if these men had reason to be stung—so be it.

Zoram was hired by these nobles to represent the king's interests in the sale of Hanameel's property to Jeremiah and make certain nothing suspect transpired. If they only knew that everything about this ceremony was suspect and Zoram was the cause of everything suspicious, they'd never have hired him to oversee their interests in this matter. They detested the prophet above all the prisoners incarcerated in these precincts, and Zoram kept behind the limestone pilaster, his face veiled in shadows, away from the searching gaze of these nobles. The less he spoke with them, the less chance he would let on that Hanameel was his cousin. They couldn't know that the scribe they hired to represent their interests in Jeremiah's land transaction had any conflict of interest with Hanameel the seller of properties—the very cousin to his father. And heaven help all of them if Zoram, by some slip of the tongue or a poorly timed glance, or a nervous disposition, provided these men with even the slightest hint that this ceremony was a façade, an illusion, a ruse engineered to cover the escape of the prophets Jeremiah and Ezekiel from the musty, moldy confines of the palace prison. Zoram kept his hands at his side, held his head steady, and kept his gaze from shifting too quickly. A calm demeanor was certain to deflect any suspicion he couldn't shroud in the darkness of this stone tunnel. It was an odd circumstance indeed—Zoram keeping company with the very men who would see his father rot in these catacombs.

Zoram leaned around the stone pilaster to get a better view of the nobles standing beneath the glow of the yellow lamp. Where were cousin Hanameel and his scribe Baruch among these eloquent men? Without them, the nobles were certain to call Jeremiah from his cell before they could work their plot. Hanameel and Baruch weren't stooped over in this low-ceilinged hallway and there was not a single soul milling about the entryway to the Court of the Prison carrying the double-sealed deed of property sale for approval. He pressed his writing satchel against his side, the tips of the pens poking through the leather pouch and pinching his ribs. How could he hope to stall the ceremony long enough for Elizabeth and Ruth to make a go of this? He turned back down the hall, quickly walking the length of the tunnel, his gaze shifting from side to side, checking the branching corridors. Hanameel and Baruch were nowhere to be found in any of these dark alcoves, and Zoram came back down the hall and slipped into place behind the shadows of the pilasters. What was he to do without them?

The quick clip of boots against the stone floor sounded in the corridor and the jailer stepped around the corner in the company of a troop of prison guards. The man favored his left foot with a heavy limp, his keys rattling about his neck with each labored stride. There were seven, possibly eight keys on the end of a silver chain—far too many for Ruth to find the right one unless Zoram allowed her enough time.

That's what their plot depended on—the perfect timing of every step, and without Hanameel and Baruch, there was no telling if they could be perfect.

The jailer scanned the gathering of nobles and princes crowded into this small space before ordering them to step back and let him at the door, his words hissing through the holes in his yellow teeth. He was the only one with keys and if they wanted to get out of this narrow hallway, they were going to have to make way. The man didn't demonstrate the least bit of deference for these wealthy men and he pushed his way past as if they were prisoners chained to the wall of this tunnel, his guards following in his wake. They marched past Zoram's hiding place, unlocked the prison chamber doors, and held them open for the nobles.

Zoram lingered in the corridor while the others shuffled in. What was he to do? Should he let Elizabeth and Ruth carry on with their plan or should he place his hand to his heart and signal them to abandon this ruse and try again another day? That was the signal they agreed to. If they were in danger of being caught, Zoram was to place his palm to his chest as if adjusting the pleats in his shirt, telling them to abandon their doings and get out of the palace before they were caught. But if they deserted their design, there may never come another day to free Father from this horrible prison. Zoram rubbed his brow, but it didn't have power to remove the indecision that plagued his mind. Without the help of Hanameel and Baruch there was only one decision to make—

Was their scheme still on?

Elizabeth followed the other servers through the wide palace halls, past the main lobby to the west wing, and then down through the never-traveled hallway of the lions—the statues of a hundred crouching beasts staring at her, their silent growling warning her against doing what she was about to do, the wild beasts whispering in muted stone voices that she should turn back before she was captured. Elizabeth lowered her head and kept walking. She wouldn't let the imagined words of these stone statues keep her from her mission. She let a maidservant hold open a thick timber door leading off the hall of lions and into a narrow corridor. A musty smell hung on the air like moss on the underside of a river stone. The tunnel turned and twisted to an ironclad door at the end where two prison guards stood beneath a solitary lamp, admitting the palace help inside the Court of the Prison.

Four brass incense bowls greeted her just inside the main door. They sat atop tall metal stands with frankincense burning into a light fog and disguising the musty air with an expensive scent. The company of maidservants busied themselves serving their plates of bread and lamb, but Elizabeth moved deeper into the chamber, keeping her basket close to her hip and not serving a single nobleman.

"The nobles, dear. Over there." A maidservant leaned over her shoulder and nodded toward the gathering of overly dressed men milling about the center of the chamber. "Pass around your basket to them first, then you can worry about the others. The princes of the city are a finicky lot and you don't want them reporting you to the royals or you'll not be employed long."

Elizabeth forced a smile. "I was just headed there."

"You're new here, aren't you?"

"Fairly new."

The maidservant offered a quick laugh. "You'll learn soon enough who you need to impress in order to get along here and you'd do well to put the nobles at the top of that list, along with the Captain of the Guard and Zadock. You cross those men and you'll not last long in the palace."

"I would expect not."

"Off you go then, and smile when you serve them, but don't stop to chat, not even a word of greeting. You don't want any of them to remember you."

Elizabeth quickly nodded. "I wouldn't want that, not at all."

"That's it, girl. You'll get along well here."

Elizabeth waited for the maidservant to disappear beyond a stone column before she skirted through a group of nobles and lost herself in the sea of pleated robes and expensive ox-hide-leather sandals. She came around a tall stone pillar near the center of the chamber and found Zoram seated at a writing table near the front. He was alone, but where was his cousin Hanameel or the scribe Baruch? Zoram's white turban sat on the table next to his pens and ink, his dark curling locks falling down over his brow, and when he felt her lingering gaze on him, his head came up and their eyes met. He didn't nod, didn't smile, and didn't give any indication that all was well and she looked to see if he was holding his hand over his heart. He wasn't, at least not yet. He shifted his gaze to the back of the chamber where a short man sat alone in a chair. He had a beady-eyed stare and when the keys hanging by a chain around the jailer's neck caught the light of the oil lamps and reflected a glint over the chamber, Zoram took a deep breath and nodded, before lowering his head into his hand. That had to be the jailer and she took a deep breath—the same deep breath she'd seen Zoram take—quickly smiled back at her beloved and started toward the jailer, walking in behind the man and uncorking a bottle of strong wine.

The jailer turned at the sound of the bottle opening, his body spinning on his wooden stool. He spoke with a gruff voice, his words troubled by a cough deep in his throat. He said, "What do you want, girl?"

"Wine, sir?" Elizabeth reached the bottle toward him.

"I'm not a guest."

She set the bottle on the chair beside him. "Go ahead. There's plenty for all."

"Not now, not with so many nobles milling about my prison. Look at them." The jailer pushed aside the bottle and kept his gaze moving over the gathering of nobles. "When did the princes of this city ever conduct a ceremony in my court?"

Elizabeth pushed the wine bottle back toward the jailer. "I'm sure they'll enjoy the ceremony."

"It isn't my job to entertain them. I have prisoners to guard." He pushed the bottle away, but Elizabeth set another beside him and said, "Go ahead, have two. It's a fine berry wine."

"The only wine I drink is straight from the cellars of the—"

"It's from the Jaw Bone Inn, sir." Elizabeth's mouth trembled slightly and she pressed her lower lip between her teeth before saying, "We've spared no expense."

The jailer slid off his stool and limped around in front of the wine bottle. He bent over, rubbed his hands together and said, "Are you certain?"

"Purchased this morning, sir."

"Well then . . ." The jailer removed his keys and when he set them on the chair, Elizabeth lowered her basket over them. She uncorked four more bottles, set them on the chair beside the wine basket and waited for him to sit on his stool and start drinking. He tilted his head back and lifted the bottle to his lips, a line of red berry wine sneaking down the corners of his mouth. Elizabeth started across the chamber, telling the jailer she was leaving her basket with him and he was to drink as much of the wine as he liked until she returned with more. What she didn't tell him was that she'd slipped his prison keys out from beneath the wine basket before the wicker met the rough-hewn wood planks of the chair and hidden them in the folds and pleats of her robe. Elizabeth pressed the keys close against her ribs.

She had to get them back before the jailer found them missing.

Ruth entered the incense-laden Court of the Prison, handed a bottle of wine to the first nobleman standing beside the entry, and poured a glass for another before moving beyond the crowd and down along the wall to the far corner where a guard stood beside the door to the Lower Prison. He was a robust man with thick arms folded across his chest and a gaze that didn't deviate from staring forward. The door was recessed into the wall, with iron bars holding the thick cedar timbers in place and round metal rivets bolting the wood together.

"Please, sir . . ." Ruth came around in front of the man, nodded toward the latch and said, "Would you be so kind as to hold the door?"

"You can't go down there." The guard kept his stare directed past Ruth, his eyes never meeting her stare. "No one goes down into the catacombs without permission."

"I wouldn't ask your help if I didn't already have it, son. Now would you please be so kind as to stand aside and hold the door?"

"On whose orders?"

"King Zedekiah, of course."

The guard slowly turned his gaze onto Ruth, his body still erect and his stance wide and unyielding. "The king sent you?"

Ruth handed him a bottle of wine from her basket. "Zedekiah wants everyone to enjoy this ceremony. Now go on, drink up, will you?" She waved the back of her hand at him. "This is a celebration."

"The jailer said no one was to—"

"I take my orders from the king, not the jailer." Ruth adjusted the two wine baskets in her arms and counted the number aloud. "Fourteen. Will that be enough? How many men are guarding the lower prison?"

"I can't tell you the size of the watch."

"Of course you can, son." Ruth ran an arm beneath the wine baskets to support the weight of so many bottles. "I'm not taking all these down there if I don't have reason."

The guard pushed his brass helmet off his brow. "You don't expect me to—"

"Now, now, young man." Ruth uncorked a second bottle and stuffed it into his other hand. "Drink up."

"But . . ."

"How many, son?"

The guard took a sip of wine and wiped his lips on the sleeve of his tunic. "There's one at the base of the stairs."

"What about the men guarding the catacombs?"

"There's only one and he won't be making rounds. Not without anyone to look after him and see that he's doing his job. He's no doubt holed up down there in some corner sleeping." The guard took another swig. "He was the lucky one. The rest of us were assigned to the Upper Prison to make a show for these royals."

"I certainly won't be needing all these." Ruth set one basket on the floor beside the prison door. "Have as much as you like. It isn't every day you get a delivery of wine from the Jawbone Inn."

The guard uncorked another bottle and ran the opening below his nose, the hint of a smile pulling at his lips. He turned around to unlatch the metal pins latching the door to the Lower Prison when Elizabeth hurried through the murkiness of the incense-filled chamber, her servant's robe rising and falling about her sandals. She walked past Ruth without slowing her stride and dropped the keys into Ruth's basket. She didn't nod, didn't offer a smile and didn't speak a word before turning back into the crowd of nobles and disappearing into the sea of black robes as quickly as she appeared.

The Lower Prison door came open in a rush of damp air filtering up from the catacombs below. The prison guard stepped aside and let Ruth pass with a warning to beware of the prisoners below. They were not the kind of men to treat a woman with respect. A run of circular stairs led down into the belly of the palace prison, and with each winding turn the din of voices from above gave way to the dim light of this underground vault. Putrid air streamed past Ruth's cheeks and the musty smell of rotting flesh stung her lungs. She felt her way around the stairwell, one hand on the cold stone wall and the other covering the keys in her basket, hiding them between the bottles of wine away from the view of—

"Who goes there?"

The prison guard stood at the bottom of the steps holding a small lamp, the light casting a weak glow over the landing at the bottom. Ruth slowly descended the last run of stairs and stepped into the yellow glow. She pulled her dark, black hair back off her shoulders and said, "Wine, sir?"

"Who let you down here? This place is off limits to everyone."

"It's a fine berry wine."

"Woman, these are prisoners and—"

"And two very brave prison guards who shouldn't be left out of the ceremony." Ruth handed over a bottle of wine. "Where is the other?"

The guard pointed the lip of the wine bottle through the iron-barred gate sealing off the catacombs from the stairwell. "You can't go back there."

"You don't want your companion to go without a good wine, do you?" Ruth ran her fingers over the wine bottles sprouting from the brim of her basket. "This is some of the best."

"Leave one and I'll see he gets it." The guard leaned over to take another bottle, but Ruth pulled back, drawing the basket out of his reach. She said, "He deserves to be served like the rest. It isn't right not to treat him well."

"We don't treat anyone well in this prison."

Ruth stood to the bars in the gate. "Are you going to open or not?"

"You ask too much." The guard handed Ruth the oil lamp and started up the stairwell out of the Lower Prison, the sole of his boots slapping against the cold stone.

"Sir . . ." Ruth came back to the stairs and followed him up around the first flight, the light flickering in her hand. "Where are you going?"

"The keys, woman." The guard didn't stop, his thick body disappearing up into the dark shadows and his voice echoing down the spiraling steps. "The jailer's the only one with keys."

Ruth backed down the steps and lifted the prison keys from her basket. How could she be so foolish as to send the prison guard off to fetch these keys? She hurried over to the gate, fumbled with the ring until she found the one that fit the latch and pushed open the gate, the iron bars slamming against the inside wall. The other prison guard was nowhere to be found in the main catacomb and she hurried deeper into the shadows.

There was little time for this escape.

Zoram sat at the writing table near the front of the Court of the Prison. He had no documents of sale, no double-sealed parchment describing the property transaction, nothing but useless pens and inks. Without Hanameel and his property deed, there was nothing Zoram could do to keep the nobles from declaring this sale void and sending for Jeremiah, and he couldn't let them call for the jailer to bring his father from the lower prison, not with his keys missing and Ruth down there somewhere.

The main prison doors swung open and the palace crier entered, announcing the arrival of King Zedekiah. The monarch wore a deep blue cloak over his narrow shoulders and he carried a gold scepter in his right hand, the rod decorated with jewels. He stood before the assembly and waited for Miriam to follow him into the Court of the Prison. The white-laced linen hid her face and it was impossible to see her expression until she removed the veil long enough to find Zoram at his writing table. Miriam didn't usually wear a veil, but it wasn't proper for a woman of her distinction to go uncovered in the presence of criminals. Zoram rubbed the tip of his pen between his fingers. If Ruth did her work in the catacombs below, Jeremiah would never make an appearance in this chamber and the queen wouldn't have need of her veil.

Chief Elder Zadock followed behind the royals, the man's long, black council robe flowing down past his feet and gathering on the stone floor. He was recently returned from paying taxes to the Babylonians, and for his success in quelling the revolt—a rebellion the man blamed on Ezekiel and Lehi—the king promoted him to a position of trust. His first public duty was the administration of this ceremony and Zoram lowered his head to keep from offending the Chief Elder with his staring. Heaven help this Kingdom if Zadock gained more influence over Zedekiah than he already possessed.

Zadock called the assembly to order before pointing at Zoram down along the length of the writing table, the wide sleeves of his black robe hanging from his arm like the wings of a raven. "Have you a judgment on the land documents?"

"I'm sorry, sir." Zoram stood, his gaze shifting between the Chief Elder and the door to the Lower Prison. "I haven't any documents."

"Where are Hanameel and his scribe? Have they lost their stomach for this sale of land?"

"They should be along."

"We haven't time to wait on them. They knew the hour."

"But, sir, could you at least allow them—"

"Do you want to keep the king waiting?"

"That was not my intention, sir." Zoram returned to the writing table while the Chief Elder called for the jailer to bring Jeremiah from his cell and tell the man his request to purchase land was denied. A hush fell over the men in the chamber as the jailer reached to move the wicker basket off the chair beside him and—

"Don't call for Jeremiah, sir."

Hanameel pushed through the main prison door, his voice echoing off the walls. He was dressed in a black robe like the other nobles, his large belly pushing on the pleats about his middle and a parchment hanging from his hand. "There's certainly no need to call for Jeremiah until your scribe renders a judgment on this deed."

Zoram leaned forward over the writing table to see the jailer lower the wine basket back to the chair without reaching beneath it to find his keys missing. They were spared for a time and he let his glance pass over the relieved face of Elizabeth hiding in the shadows of the prison perimeter before taking the deed from Hanameel and slowly spreading the leather over the tabletop.

"Zadock, sir." Zoram looked up from the deed. "May I have a moment to review this?"

"You'll not waste precious time."

"I wouldn't think of delaying any longer than I must."

The description in the top half of the scroll detailing the land for sale in Anathoth was duplicated word-for-word in the bottom section. The dimensions and size of the property were exact, the location precise, but there was no mention of water rights from the small creek flowing along the backside of the property, and Zoram stopped his finger on the missing line and—

"If you want the water rights, you'll have to change the deed." Hanameel sat beside Zoram. He leaned over and spoke in a whisper hardly audible above the din of voices in the chamber. "You're a scribe. That's what they pay you for, isn't it?"

"You know I can't do that." Zoram kept his finger moving over the lines of writing while he spoke. "Your scribe has to make those changes."

"You need time; I'm giving you time." Hanameel spoke softly, his words hardly spanning the distance between them. "Change the document and you'll have all the time you need to carry out whatever you've planned."

"This had better not be another of your schemes." Zoram stared at the document, his palms pressed against the surface. Hanameel had already been paid the seventeen pieces of silver for the land and the water rights and if this was a trick to get either back without forfeiting his money, then shame on him. Zoram hid his pen beneath his hand and quickly struck the phrase "property only," replacing it with "property and one fifth of the water flowing in the adjacent creek" without anyone seeing the quick movements of his hidden pen. He was taking a huge risk. He could only change the top portion of this double-sealed document. The bottom portion was tied with cords and sealed with wax to protect against the very forgery he was committing.

The outstretched legs of prisoners littered the way through the main catacomb and Ruth jumped her way over the bodies strewn about in the dimness, holding the lamp overhead until she found the narrow corridor over beyond the third pillar. This had to be the way, and she had started into the narrow opening when a prisoner grabbed the hem of her robe. She screamed, but it didn't save her from his grasp and she yanked on the skirts to free herself, the cloth tearing along the hem. What a fool she was for crying out like that. It would only alert the prison guard roaming these catacombs and she could ill afford to deal with another watchman.

Ruth stumbled past two more sleeping prisoners before reaching the narrow opening leading off the main catacomb. Two tightly placed limestone walls framed the passageway and Ruth turned sideways, shimmying through to a sloping decline that opened onto a run of narrow steps. Water soaked the base of a thick cedar door at the bottom of the stairs, and the large metal latch locking it shut was rusted from years of dripping and seeping. She tried the first key on the ring, but it didn't fit the opening. The second key was too long and the third entered the latch, but wouldn't turn the bolt. She tried the fifth, sixth, and seventh keys until the lock started to turn before rusting to a stop. She rattled the key, but it was no use. It had been months since Mulek escaped through these passageways and the bolt was stuck beyond what Ruth could budge. What was she to do? There was so little time, and in her frustration she kicked at the door. The rusted bolt clicked and the weight of the key turned the latch. It was nothing less than a miracle and she put her shoulder to the small door, budging the swollen wooden timbers free of the frame and falling headfirst into the rushing waters of a stone channel, the current whisking away her wine basket, and the submerging oil lamp, shrouding the watery chamber in pitch darkness.

Ruth struggled to her feet. How was she ever going to find the door leading out of these dungeons without light? All was lost with the dropping of the oil lamp, but she would not give up, not yet. She walked against the rushing water, her stride pushing through the force of the current and her fingers brushing the coarse stone of the low-lying ceiling. She felt past a thick foundation stone arching overhead, a long gap of smooth stone, and then her hand came upon a metal frame. This had to be the way out. The casing held four wood planks in place and she slipped the tip of the last key into a latch before forcing the door up with her fist, the bright light of midday filtering down into the chamber and brightening the water tunnel with the light of freedom. She'd done it! She'd found the way out through the aqueduct, just as Miriam had said she'd find it—the same water tunnel Mulek used to sneak out of the palace.

Ruth left the trap door propped open, hurried back through the water tunnel and into the catacombs, her drenched hems dragging along the stone floor. The main chamber stood dark, and the snoring of sleeping prisoners and the groaning of sick men led her deeper into the maze of corridors and stone cells to a hallway lit by a torch burning the remnants of an oil-soaked linen. A small alcove stood at the far end and Ruth picked her wet hems off the ground and sprinted down through the passage. She turned past a wide pilaster and there, sleeping in the flickering of the torchlight lay the two prophets, their frail, thin bodies leaned against the wall. The color in Jeremiah's face was gone white, and Ezekiel's expensive robes were torn at the sleeves and collar. Ruth fell to her knees beside them, hurried through the ring of keys until she found the one to unlock the iron shackles.

"You must hurry or all is lost."

Jeremiah began to speak, but the hacking in his throat stopped his words and he turned away until the flurry passed and he said, "Praise God for sending an angel to save us from our suffering."

Ruth said, "Do you know the sewer doors off the main catacomb?"

Ezekiel nodded. "We can find it."

"Follow the aqueduct to the light at the end of the tunnel to freedom." Ruth started back down the hallway.

"Where are you going?"

Ruth came back and helped him with the shackles, ripping them from their hands and feet and throwing the iron bindings in the corner. She tightened her grip around the keys. I have to go." She stepped back to let them stand, but they'd been locked so long in chains neither could get up on his own power and Ruth knelt beside Ezekiel, rubbing his legs and working the stiffness out of his joints. "There's a prison guard somewhere in these chambers. Do you understand? You have to avoid him and get out of here on your own."

Ezekiel pulled himself to his feet with a mighty groan, but his left leg faltered and he fell against Ruth, pushing her down. He righted himself, held the stone pillar for balance and kicked aside the last link in the chain that bound him these many days. He tried to lift Jeremiah to his feet, but he was too weak to lift him on his own.

Ruth came around Jeremiah and pulled on one arm while Ezekiel pulled on the other until the prophet slowly came up off the floor, his legs trembling, his knees buckling under the weight, and his thin arms draped over Ruth. The man was buoyed up by what little strength she had to offer. What was she to do? She could save these men, but by saving them would she curse Elizabeth and Zoram?

Ezekiel peered through the shadows, his pale face drawn out and his brow furrowed. He stumbled with his speech, his parched tongue hardly able to form the words. "Help us please. We must prepare the plates before they're taken from the city."

Ruth wrapped her arms around Jeremiah's hip.

She said, "Follow me."

Zoram slowly brought his head up from studying the property deed and he was about to give the Chief Elder approval when the door to the Lower Prison inched open and a guard appeared. Where was Ruth? The man stayed by the door, speaking with the soldier standing guard. He raised and lowered his hands with the ebb and flow of his speech and thankfully his words elicited nothing more than a smile from his mate. The guard from the Lower Prison started across the chamber toward the jailer. What could have gone wrong in the Lower Prison that this man would come seeking his overseer? He turned past three stone columns and down through the gathering of nobles, slowly working his way across the crowded chamber.

Zadock said, "Will you render your judgment on the deed?"

Zoram glanced at Hanameel, his cousin holding his cupped hands to his mouth. Was there nothing he could do to stop the prison guard from reaching the jailer? Zoram said, "The deed appears to be in order. It meets all the requirements of the—"

"This is unacceptable." Hanameel snatched the deed from Zoram. "This document has been altered."

Zoram shook his head at Hanameel. What was he doing? The prison guard was nearly to the jailer.

"You pose serious allegations, sir." Zadock pointed his long, bony finger at Hanameel. "Have you any proof?"

Hanameel said, "I want my scribe to review this."

"You haven't a scribe with you."

The prison guard came around and stood beside the jailer, the chair with Elizabeth's basket of wine bottles dividing the distance between them. He leaned his head over the basket to address the jailer and—

"He most certainly does have a scribe."

The main door banged against the inside wall and Baruch the scribe stepped in from the corridor. The chamber fell silent and the jailer warned off his prison guard with the wave of his hand, the man leaning forward on his stool with a bottle of wine in each hand and straining to see the reason for the silence descending across the chamber.

The elderly scribe crossed to the writing table with his pens in one hand and his inkwell in the other. He was dressed in a plain brown robe. The hair of his head was thinning and a bald spot in the center of his scalp reflected the light of the lamps. He took the deed from Zoram, sat erect in a chair and slowly moved his forefinger over the neat Hebrew characters, nodding at the end of each line, the white bald spot at the top of his head bobbing in rhythm to his reading. He finished reading the opened portion of the document before picking away the cords sealing the bottom of the double-sealed parchment. He shook his head, furrowed his brow and returned to the top to check whatever phrase bothered him, skipping down to the bottom portion of the double scroll, back to the top then back to the bottom again.

Zoram turned his gaze out over the chamber and found the prison guard whispering in the jailer's ear when Ruth burst through the Lower Prison door. She paused for a moment, long enough to pull the bands of wet hair out of her face before hurrying across the chamber, pushing her way through the crowd.

The jailer spun on his stool. He put aside the wine bottles and reached for the wicker basket just as Ruth came around the last pillar behind him. She bumped his arm and threw the keys to the ground as if she'd knocked them off the chair where they had never been, the metal clanging against the stone and the jailer snatching them up.

"We've had enough reading of this deed for one day." Zadock took the parchment from Baruch, rolled it tight and pointed the end at the jailer seated at the back of the chamber. He said, "Send your guards to fetch the—"

"The prisoners are escaped!"

The guard from the catacombs burst through the Lower Prison doors and raised the empty shackles overhead that for so many months had bound Jeremiah and Ezekiel in their cell.

The jailer pushed his way through the nobles, waving the prison keys in the air and shouting at his men to follow him to the catacombs. They ran to the Lower Prison door when the deep, thundering voice of a broad-shouldered, thick-armed Ethiopian echoed about the chamber, stopping them in their rush.

The Ethiopian said, "There's been no escape."

The eyes of the crowd turned toward the main doors leading from the palace. The man stood in the entrance holding the weak, frail frames of Jeremiah and Ezekiel by their tattered, wet robes. He marched them to the front of the chamber, their clothes dripping water onto the floor and pooling at their feet. He bowed low to King Zedekiah, the prophets still held in his grasp, and he didn't come up out of his bow until Zedekiah raised his scepter and said, "What is the meaning of this?"

"Your highness." The man stood, his black skin reflecting the light of the lamps. "My name is Ebed-Melech, come to serve you and your house as a keeper of the prison."

"We don't need your help." The jailer limped over and threw the shackles at Ebed's feet. "No one escapes from my prison."

Zedekiah said, "Where did you find these men?"

Ebed said, "I caught them crawling out the aqueducts."

"That's impossible." The jailer shook his keys. "I never open the doors to the tunnels."

Ebed said, "I am at your service, sire."

"There has never been such a faithful servant among all the Jews." Zedekiah took the keys from the jailer and handed them to Ebed. "From this day forward you will be the keeper of this prison."

Jeremiah pulled free of Ebed's grasp. He reached his trembling hand beneath the soaked rags of his robe and took out a small leather purse. He stepped to the writing table and weighed out seventeen pieces of silver in the balances before exchanging the money for the property deed. He read over the parchment, sealed the bottom portion with leather cords and handed the document to Baruch, telling him that the Lord instructed him to purchase this land as evidence that though the Jews would be subjected to seventy years of captivity by the Babylonians, they would return to Israel again and own land and cultivate fields and prosper in this land. His hands trembled from want of food, but he raised the double-sealed scroll to the noblemen gathered in the chamber. "Take this evidence of purchase, both that which is sealed and this evidence which is open, and put them in earthen vessels that they may continue many days; for houses and fields and vineyards shall be possessed again in this land and—"

"We will never have need to return to this land." Zadock took the property deed from Jeremiah and threw it on the ground. "Do you hear me? The Jews will never be deported by the Babylonians."

Jeremiah turned his gaze up into the ceiling. "Oh Lord God, thou hast said to me, buy this field from Hanameel as evidence, for the city of Jerusalem will be given into the hands of the Babylonians."

Zadock turned to Ebed-Melech the Ethiopian. "Take these men to the well of the prison and let them rot there."

"Not the well, sir." Jeremiah shook his head. "Have mercy on us."

"There will be no mercy for men who attempt escape." Zadock shook his fist at Ebed. "See that they're put in the well immediately."

The Elders erupted in cursings against Jeremiah for his preaching against the city and against Ezekiel for supporting the man, their fists rising and falling with their oaths. Zoram stood from the writing table as his father passed. He was close enough that the cloth of Jeremiah's tattered robe brushed his hand. Amid the shouting Jeremiah whispered, "The plates, son. Ask Baruch to help us with the brass plates." Then he was gone, marched along by a platoon of angry guards with the jailer cursing Jeremiah for the loss of his prison.

Zoram turned to see to the back of the chamber where Elizabeth stood in the shadows of a pillar beside Ruth. And when Elizabeth felt the gaze of Zoram on her, she turned her eyes to meet his. Why hadn't they abandoned this scheme before now?

Zoram held his hand over his heart.

CHAPTER 30

Moriah pulled four fully shaped timbers out of the brine and replaced them with straight ones, holding them under while the air bubbled to the surface and the salty water seeped into the fibers, softening the wood enough so he could tie them into an arc and bend them to the shape of the hull. The fishing boat stood down from the bending vats in the center of his father's shipyard like the carcass of a beached whale, waiting for Moriah to carry over the newly bent timbers to the stitchers and fill in the gaps. The hull was a skeleton with curved wooden ribs rising out of the boat's spine, the wooden slats filtering the late afternoon sun like shutters on a window and casting long shadows across the white sands of the shipyard. It was a single-mast boat without a deck, no galleys and no portholes for a gang of oarsmen.

Brine splashed over the sides of the bending vat, soaking the front of Moriah's long-sleeved white tunic. The wet cuffs sagged down past his hands like the shirt of a boy too young for his clothes, and though this was the home of his youth, he was no longer a boy—not after what he'd suffered at Fort Lakhish. Moriah's tunic was better suited to his former work as a scribe, not the hard labors of a boat builder, but he returned here to find the safety he could find nowhere else on earth. The cloth of his tunic was stained with boat resins, the high collar was torn from catching on the coarse timbers of nag wood protruding from the small quarter deck near the stern of the unfinished fishing boat, and two of the silver buttons had gone missing, the shirt coming open at the chest. His shirt was the last vestige of a forsaken career as a scribe in the Hebrew military, the tattered white cloth reminding him every day of the future he left behind at Lakhish. The potsherd copies he made of Captain Laban's letters were burned and gone, but he was alive and he thanked God every day that he had escaped to this secluded harbor at Aqaba on the southern extremes of Judah's borders, away from the eyes of any who might report him.

None of the patrons in his father's shipyard recognized the finely tailored cloth of Moriah's apprenticeship. He tore the gold embroidered head of a lion off the cuffs the day he arrived home. The matching gold stripes along the shoulder were covered with boat resins, and the stripes on the shoulder were stained with enough sweat to hide their color. Father didn't announce Moriah's return to any of the neighboring boat builders along this crowded shore that littered the sky with the single masts of a hundred unfinished vessels. The sands were covered with half-finished hulls, and an army of men scurried over the beach with all lengths, sizes, and shapes of timbers to fasten to their boats and sell to the highest bidder. The beach—all the way to the first brown-brick buildings of the city's bustling market— was peopled with rope makers, stitchers, wood benders, sail makers, mast cutters and rudder fitters. The air bristled with the cry of men at work, the hammering of anvils, the cutting of wood, and the sweet smell of moist, salty air rushing ashore off the surface of the Fountain of the Red Sea and cooling them in late afternoon.

The mud brick buildings of Aqaba lined the main road beside the shipyards, the cry of farmers from the market mixing with the sounds of boat building and the squawk of seagulls circling overhead, waiting to swoop down and snare a fish from a fisherman's cart. Beyond the shipyards stood the corrals of animal traders, waiting to buy and sell camels and mules to the merchant traders passing through Aqaba, and beyond the stabled animals rose the main buildings of the city, two- and three-storied structures reaching into the sky.

Moriah quickly wrung the water from his sleeves before dragging the curved timbers across the yard to the fishing boat, the droplets from his wide cuffs leaving a watery trail in the sand.

"This should keep you until sunset." Moriah dropped the timbers near the stitchers who stood inside the skeleton-hull like prisoners behind the bars of a cell, but they were not incarcerated here. They were free men still wearing the clothes of a forsaken life. Setti wore a dark-gray officer's tunic of the night watch at Fort Lakhish, Commander Yaush was dressed in a blue dinner tunic, and Moriah stood outside the hull with the long-sleeved vestments of an apprentice scribe—all of them wearing the same clothes they wore four months before on the night of Passover when they escaped Lakhish. They were three men dressed in the worn rags of their former lives, and as soon as they sold this fishing boat they could afford new clothes from the weavers in Aqaba and be rid of these remnants of Fort Lakhish they wore on their backs.

"We're getting faster." Setti quickly bored a hole in the end of a timber.

Commander Yaush smiled through the gaps in the hull before carving a hole in the end of the plank opposite his son. "Another month of boat building and you'll not bend enough wood in all your vats to keep us busy."

They hoisted the timber overhead and started their hands rushing over the knots. They were apprentice stitchers, but they set the perfectly formed plank in place, fit it along the spine and stitched it to the frame like seasoned boat builders, quickly tying the plank with coconut ropes and tightly lashing the ends with leather caps to seal the wood from splintering in the salty waters of the Fountain of the Red Sea. Setti daubed a thick, milky coat of boat resin between the seams while Yaush steadied the board flush with the rest of the hull.

Sophia, the wife of Commander Yaush, pushed out the front doors of the house with a dinner basket in hand. She didn't usually come outside during the day, except at this hour to quickly feed them and return to the protecting shadows within the walls of the seaside home next to the shipyards. She scurried down along the narrow rocky point between the house and the sea, the surf lapping against the shoal and splashing across her path. The tide was coming in and with it came the light spray off the waves. Sophia reached the beach, hurried over the sands to the fishing boat, and passed a drink of cool water to them before handing around a basket of bread, dates, and nuts. Boat building was a simpler life than these nobles were accustomed to living, but at least they had a place to call home and forget the fears that once troubled their lives.

The shipyard stood a rock's throw from the waters of the Fountain of the Red Sea on the east end of Aqaba and there wasn't a finer place to build a sailing vessel among all the shipyards. Moriah's father was the only boat builder to own this much property. And he built his home—a two-story stone structure—on the rocky point beside the yard. The home had a fine view of the sunset, the west windows opening onto the seaside city with a backdrop of tall cliffs. At high tide Moriah could dive off the rocks near the porch and into the deep pool that filled all the way level with the back door in early morning. But as soon as the high tides shifted into daylight hours Moriah would forfeit the swimming to keep from the view of others. The less people knew of his return from Lakhish, the less he'd have to fabricate an explanation. He couldn't tell anyone about the lost Lakhish Letters and their owner Commander Yaush, not with the man and his family living under the same roof a short walk from this shipyard.

A mule cart clattered down the Mountain Road and Moriah quickly returned to stand behind his bending vats, hiding the remnants of his tattered military tunic from view. The large oval basins were fashioned of fired clay and they hid him from the Mountain Road that descended into Aqaba through a narrow canyon—the only opening in the rim of steep red-brown cliffs surrounding the city like a wall surrounds a fortress. The Mountain Road divided at the shipyard, one fork leading to the markets of Aqaba and the other heading along the coast toward Haql, a small fishing village farther down the shoreline.

"Stand away from the road, son." Hagoth marched around the palm trees growing up in the center of the shipyard, the white bands of his half-tied turban falling down over his brow. Not a day passed that Hagoth didn't jump at the sound of a cart, or bristle at the passing of an horseman. Since Moriah had returned home in company with Commander Yaush and his family, Father had found little peace. His wind-burned face was gone red from passing so many summer days in this shipyard. He was a tall, thick-shouldered man with hands calloused from years of working boat timbers—nothing like the soft skin of Moriah's long fingers gotten from a full year of working a pen over military parchments. Hagoth and Moriah were father and son, but they looked nothing alike. Moriah had dark black hair that curled about his ears and over his brow, while Hagoth had a cap of straight brown hair that flopped forward into his eyes. Moriah was tall and slender. Hagoth was as thick-boned as the center mast on a mighty merchant vessel. Moriah had green eyes. Hagoth's were brown. Moriah spoke with a refined tongue. Hagoth preferred the gruff speech of the other ship builders on these beaches. But they were family, the only family either of them had left on earth.

Hagoth wasn't Moriah's natural father, but since the day of his adoption at three months of age, Hagoth was the only man he knew to call father. And when Moriah showed more interest in learning the art of writing than the skills of boat building, Hagoth told him it was no doubt a talent he inherited from his parents—family he never knew in this life. Moriah was ten years old when Hagoth secured his first private lessons in the art of languages. And though Hagoth didn't understand Moriah's affection for writing, he had more than enough love for the boy to help him become a scribe, hiring teachers to train him in five languages and win an apprenticeship for him at Fort Lakhish.

Hagoth wore a plain brown robe that danced about his shins with each stride and he waved his hands as he spoke, his powerful voice filling the shipyard with his hurried warning. "Did you hear? Get back, son, away from the road." He marched past Moriah, around the bending vats and onto the Mountain Road, his hands on his hips and his gaze turned up into the canyon descending out of the high peaks of these Borders near the Red Sea.

Moriah said, "You shouldn't worry so much."

"I only want you and your friends to be safe."

"We're safer than we had ever hoped to be." Moriah pointed up the Mountain Road above the shipyards. "Lakhish is a hundred and fifty miles from here."

"That isn't far enough." Hagoth's gaze darted back and forth along the Mountain Road. "That place will never be far enough away from here."

Moriah said, "Why don't you tell me about your boat-building dreams?"

"I don't dream anymore." Hagoth came back around the bending vat next to Moriah, his hand on the coarse clay rim. "For the love of heaven, I hardly sleep."

"I'm sorry, Papa." Moriah rubbed his long, writing fingers together. "I didn't mean to cause you so much worry. You were always such a . . ."

"A carefree man?"

"Happy. You were always happy."

"I still am, son."

But he wasn't, not really, and Moriah had to do something to dispel the cheerlessness of his soul. He said, "Remember how you always said you were going to leave the shipyards in my care and sail the seas to a new world?"

"I am and I'm taking you with me." Hagoth slapped the brine water with the palm of his hand. "After what happened to you at Lakhish, a new world is exactly where you belong."

"Stop your worrying." Moriah slapped the water back at his father, the spray splashing across his front. A grin pulled at Hagoth's mouth, the playfulness Moriah once knew returning like the rising sun, and Father shoved both hands under the water and sent a wave splashing over the sides and soaking Moriah before he jumped behind a brine vat, out of sight. Moriah held his hands over the brine, waiting for Hagoth's head to come above the rim so he could—

Two strong arms wrapped around Moriah's waist, pulling him to the ground and laying him on his back. Hagoth hovered over him, his finger pressed to his lips telling Moriah not to say a word. His grin was gone, replaced by a furrowed brow, and his lips were pressed together tighter than two planks in the hull of a ship. There was no reason to be silent, at least there didn't seem to be any until Moriah heard a caravan of camels plodding down the last stretch in the Mountain Road. The sound of the caravan mixed with the lashing of stitchers, the hammering of carpenters, and the flapping of sail makers in the shipyards separating the Mountain Road from the sea, and Moriah leaned around the bending vat to get a glimpse of the lead rider. There was something familiar about the dark black hair tied back off his brow with a red bandanna, his straight jaw, narrow nose, and broad shoulders. A woman wearing a white veil followed on a brown steed ahead of a line of slow-moving camels, the animals raising a cloud of dust about the fork in the road. A third rider passed in the wake of the large beasts, his head down to keep from choking on the dirty air. He reined in at the back of the caravan in company with a man wearing a long, pleated traveling robe with a matching white turban, the ends of the headpiece flowing over his shoulders and when he reached the crossing in front of the shipyard and turned off the Mountain Road headed toward Aqaba, Moriah recognized the weary, sun-burned face of—

"Lehi." Moriah stepped from behind the bending vats and onto the road. "Is that you, sir?"

Hagoth followed Moriah through the dusty air, grabbing for his arm to draw him back to the cover of the bending vats, but Moriah pulled free. The last rider had to be Lehi—the same man who helped him decipher the terrible meaning hidden in the phrases of the Lakhish Letters. Moriah called to Lehi through the dusty air until he came around and there was no mistaking the penetrating green-eyed stare of the olive oil merchant, looking at him from behind the cover of a bandanna drawn over his mouth. He swung around, pulled the cloth back from his face and slid from the saddle, taking Moriah by both hands, the man's rough, calloused fingers rubbing against the soft skin of Moriah's grip and his voice praising heaven that Moriah was still alive. He said, "I worried Captain Laban would have tried to harm you."

Moriah said, "He failed, sir."

"Bless you, boy. Bless us all." Lehi wrapped his powerful, wiry arms around Moriah, pulled him close and said, "What of Commander Yaush and his family? Are they still at Fort Lakhish or did they—"

"Right here, sir." Yaush stepped onto the road, his hand extended to Lehi, his son Setti following behind with a length of coconut rope draped over his shoulder, and his wife, Sophia, carrying a dinner basket. "All of us are safe and a very long way from harm."

"Not as far away as you might think." Lehi removed the white turban from his head and let his black hair fall onto his brow. "We left Captain Laban in Bozrah last night."

"Curse that man!" Hagoth stepped in next to Moriah, his hand on his son's shoulder. "Why did he come to Bozrah?"

Nephi reined back from the front of the camels and sidled in next to Hagoth. The boy had a powerful carriage but a mild, calming voice. He said, "Laban refuses to stop hunting us."

Laman said, "Don't you mean he's hunting our father?"

"No, boy." Commander Yaush wrapped his arms around Setti and Sophia, drawing them close to him. "Captain Laban is hunting all of us."

Moriah said, "What about your other sons, sir?"

"We're not certain. They travelled the Way of the Wilderness. We sent Sam to find them in the Empty Quarter." Lehi fitted his turban back in place. "They should be along in time."

"We pray they'll be along soon." Sariah pulled back the white hood shielding her face from the late afternoon sun. She was a slight woman with a deep, penetrating gaze and a warm smile. She softly said, "We pray for the safety of us all."

Hagoth said, "What were they riding?"

Laman said, "What does it matter?"

"It matters, boy."

Lehi said, "Five horses, four camels, a caravan of twenty mules and a small herd of sheep. Why do you ask?"

"See those animals?" Hagoth pointed up the canyon, beyond the cleft in the red-brown cliffs, past the switchbacks to where a line of dust rose up off the trail a hundred horses long, the earth churning up into the sky and thundering down the Mountain Road like a monsoon in summer. "Mules and sheep don't move that fast."

Hagoth lifted Sariah from the saddle as carefully as a man of his size could lift a woman off her horse and stood her next to Sophia, telling them to hurry across the shipyard and get inside his house. He started Nephi and Laman's horses to the front of the caravan, yanking the animals by the bit and ordering the boys to take the camels to the animal trader in Aqaba. The man was a good friend and since they couldn't tie their caravan up in his shipyard without attracting the notice of Captain Laban—and Hagoth was certain, if not obsessed, that everyone descending the Mountain Road was the Hebrew Commander—they were to stable the camels with the animal trader and find their way back across the city without drawing attention.

Hagoth came back to Moriah and said, "Get up into the hills above the Mountain Road." He took the white cloth of Moriah's sleeve in his hand—the cloth that had power to betray him to Laban. "I don't want the captain to see you, do you understand?"

"I won't hide from him while the rest of you risk your lives."

"You're not hiding, son. You're waiting."

"For what?"

"Lehi's other sons." Hagoth tightened his grip on Moriah's tunic. "If you see a caravan of mules heading down the Mountain Road, keep them from turning toward Aqaba."

Nephi and Laman started the caravan of camels into the city, raising a cloud of dust around Moriah, but not so thick that he couldn't see Sophia leading Sariah across the shipyard. Lehi stood in the middle of the road long after the dust settled, watching his family hide from the evil that had chased them from their lands, all the way south to this port on the Fountain of the Red Sea.

Hagoth said, "On any other day, sir, you'd be a wealthy olive oil merchant come to purchase a sailing vessel from my yard, but today you're a boat builder like the rest of us." He tossed Lehi a hammer and chisel. "Welcome to my shipyard."

***

Inspector Tobit reined around a narrow switchback, his horse galloping onto a stretch of uneven gravel, losing its footing, and slipping to the edge of the cliff. He veered back to the inside canyon wall, steering his steed away from danger. The Mountain Road was only wide enough for a single horse and he turned in the saddle to make certain his mixed company of Hebrew and Babylonian cavalry followed his lead. They kept a swift pace and rode in a long, single file column, the cavalry stretching back around three switchbacks, their dust rising into the sky like a thunderhead at the front of a storm.

Tobit steered around two more switchbacks, the hooves of his steed obliterating the camel tracks in the trail. He didn't need to study them any longer. These were the same tracks he'd followed since he began this odyssey at Qumran and there was no reason to compare these metal-shod hooves with any others. These were the fresh tracks of Lehi, the cleanest they'd found in weeks.

Tobit veered hard across a ridge before the canyon opened onto a view of the Fountain of the Red Sea below. The soft orange rays of late afternoon shimmered off the deep blue waters, welcoming him to

this valley on the sea. The Mountain Road descended through a
narrow gorge and out of the high ridges of these Borders and onto
lower ground—the first stretch of straight road since starting into
these mountains. The steel bow Tobit found at the crossroads south
of Bozrah slapped against his saddlebags, the metal arm reaching
around past his knee, reminding him of the danger Lehi posed. What
sort of rebellion drove the man to create a weapon like this?

The road widened through the final stretch in the canyon and
Darius pulled alongside Tobit, his pouch of leather maps rising and
falling at his side. Captain Laban came up the other flank, and Daniel
with Shechem pushed through the gaps between the front riders to form
a troop of five horsemen racing toward the sea, their gaze set on the end
of the Mountain Road, down where the trail turned past the shipyards
along the beach. They spurred past the opening in the cliffs, the red-
brown sandstone ridge giving way to a view of Aqaba. The city sat along
the beach a quarter mile west of the Mountain Road, the square rooftops
and mud brick homes of this fishing village bordering on the edge of the
Fountain of the Red Sea like seaweed washed ashore. It wasn't a jewel-of-
a-city like Jerusalem or Sidon. There were no high walls protecting this
place, no guards making rounds above the city entrances, and not a
single cobblestone in the streets to keep the dust from swirling over the
homes and shops of three thousand residents. It was a forgotten city on
the extremes of the newly charted territories of Babylon. Tobit called to
his son above the pounding of the horse hooves, telling him to be certain
to make a detailed map of these lands for their archives at Jericho—they
were finished with their chase through these deserts and once they
captured Lehi, they weren't coming back again.

Tobit reached the shipyard at the end of the Mountain Road, but
before turning toward Aqaba, he swung around, the cavalrymen
falling into four straight columns, their horses pawing the ground. He
pulled alongside Captain Laban and said, "Take your men to the far
side of the city and seal off the road west to Egypt. I'll have my men
do the same on this end."

"We won't find Lehi without going house to house."

"It's a small city, Captain." Tobit faced his mount toward the sea,
his gaze turned down to the shipyards running beside the Mountain
Road. "If Lehi's here, he can't hide forever."

Laban said, "This is foolishness."

"It would be more foolish to force our entry into these homes. These people will welcome us with a sword if we're not careful."

"Then we burn their homes."

"We didn't come to destroy this city, Captain." Tobit raised his voice, but he didn't turn in the saddle to face Laban. He kept his gaze directed down over the white sands of the beach, scanning the unfinished hulls and the growing masts in the shipyards below the road. "We came here to find one man and I suggest you take your men and secure Aqaba."

There was something odd about the boat builders in the shipyard, but what was it? He left Captain Laban to accompany his men into the city while he reined off the road and past the bending vats. He got down from the saddle, slung the metal bow over one shoulder and the pouch of scrolls he found in the sands at Qumran over the other—the only clues he had to help him understand the mind of Lehi. He led his horse by the reins over the white sand and paused next to a cluster of palm trees, leaning around to see down where three stitchers gathered around the unfinished hull of a fishing boat, fitting bent wood into place. Two of them were familiar men. He couldn't remember exactly where he'd seen them, but somewhere, buried deep in his memory, he recognized the young, black-haired boat builder lashing intricate knots through a hole in a plank and the other man with graying hair fitting a board into the hull. They reminded him of two soldiers in the Hebrew military, but he'd met so many rank and file soldiers since coming to the New Babylonian Territories, he couldn't remember who they resembled. The third boat builder stood on the other side of the hull, his frame half hidden behind the skeleton of boards rising out of the boat's spine like the ribs on a carcass. He didn't attract Tobit's investigating gaze as much as these two familiar men, not until the third boat builder walked down along the far side of the hull, a glimpse of his regal dress flashing between the gaps in the hull. Tobit adjusted his position behind the trunk of the palm tree to see through the openings better. The hammer and chisel hung idle from the man's hands and his gaze was turned into the sand. An ivory-studded band held his white turban in place and he wore a long riding robe with a leather sash tied about his waist—the same dress Tobit imagined Lehi would wear. The headpiece wasn't decorated with a feather sprouting out the back and there were no rubies along the cuffs and collars of his clothing, no gold rings on his fingers, but his appearance matched the images of the olive oil merchant that peopled Tobit's dreams. This boat builder matched the description gotten from Zadock and Captain Laban, and Tobit waved for Darius to join him, the boy ordering the rest of the company to head into the city and secure the streets while he ventured into the confines of this shipyard.

Tobit kept peering around the palm trees. He said, "Bring me five men."

"I just sent them—"

"Bring them back to help."

"Help with what?"

"Do as I say." Tobit dropped the reins of his horse and stepped down from the palm trees toward the boat builders, coming in near the ship, the boards of the hull filling the distance between them. He leaned his hand between the gaps in the boards and shouted, "Lehi!"

The boat builder spun around, the breeze off the Red Sea lifting the ends of his turban about his shoulders, the cloth playing across his gaze. Tobit could not get any closer, not with the planks in the hull separating them, framing the unearthly light shining in Lehi's deep green eyes and his dark black hair that hedged out beneath the brow of his turban. This was the man he'd been chasing since Qumran, the ghost that eluded him and Tobit would have offered his hand through the planks and honored him for his brilliant crossing of these deserts if he weren't a criminal. What a shame to imprison a caravaneer of his skill. Lehi's face was windblown—gone red from so many days on the trail. The tuft of beard on the end of his straight chin moved with the slight trembling of his lips and when Lehi's gaze fell on Tobit's military turban and then to his dagger, he started sidestepping down along the fishing boat, the gaps in the unfinished hull casting shadows across his face like the bars of a prison cell.

"It was you, wasn't it?" Tobit sidestepped along the hull, matching Lehi's step, stride for stride. "You left water for my men."

The two other boat builders set aside their knot tying and picked up their hammers and chisels, holding the blunt tools like weapons and following Tobit from inside the hull like guards protecting their prisoner. Where was Darius with the cavalrymen? He was outnumbered and all he could think to do was take the steel bow off his shoulder and hold it up between the planks. "How many of these weapons do you have?"

Lehi dropped his hammer and chisel in the sand and turned to run from the hull, down toward the beach, but Tobit said, "No, wait. I won't hurt you." He threw down the bow and fumbled with the straps on the satchel sealing away the scrolls of Lehi's journal and when he got it open he snatched one out, the leather pouch falling to the ground at his feet and the parchment hanging from his hand, the end of it unraveling to reveal the strong, steady pen strokes that belonged to Lehi the Olive Oil Merchant. He said, "This is yours isn't it?"

Lehi came back to the hull and peered through the boards, and the other boat builders eased their hold on the tools.

"You left these in the sands at Qumran." Tobit softened his voice and offered the journal through the timbers. Lehi leaned through the hull and snatched the parchment from Tobit, holding it like a newborn babe, the leather draped between his hands and his eyes quickly scanning the words.

Tobit said, "It's yours isn't it?"

Lehi began to answer, and Tobit cocked his ear to hear every word above the crashing of the surf down along the beach, but the hissing of an arrow masked his speech, the weapon slashing through the air and landing in the plank beside Lehi's head, splitting the board from deck to spine. Tobit spun around and found Captain Laban standing on the rise near the bending vats, stringing another arrow. That fool! Tobit came back around. The leather scroll was thrown in the sand and Lehi was sprinting down through the shipyard. Tobit chased after him past the masts in the next shipyard and around the tables of the sail makers one yard further over, his feet thrashing through the soft sand and his riding robes streaming out behind his run. Captain Laban and Darius spurred down along the road on the far side of the shipyards, the masts and hulls keeping them from joining the footrace.

Lehi reached the first line of buildings on the outskirts of Aqaba and darted into an alley. The narrow street ran in a horseshoe away from the sea, past the doors of twenty homes before turning back toward the blue waters and coming out onto a long dock extending into the harbor. Tobit ran onto the floating boards. Curse that man! How did he get away? Three fishing boats moored to weathered posts sat empty and a fourth was setting sail. Tobit waved the fisherman down, calling to him and asking if he'd seen a man run onto the dock, but he was too far out to sea to hear the cry. A line of mule carts stood near the dock waiting to gather the day's catch, but there was no sign of Lehi hiding among the wooden wheels or behind the animals. The harbor was still, without another fisherman or merchant to point out where Lehi was hiding.

Captain Laban turned through a narrow opening between the fence posts of the last shipyard and came alongside the dock with Darius reining in behind. Laban said, "I had him in my sights."

"I want him alive," Tobit said.

Laban said, "It doesn't matter how we take him."

"Men don't plot uprisings alone, Captain." Tobit paced along the shoreline in front of the narrow wooden dock. "I have to find out what Lehi knows about this uprising. I must have him alive if we're to ferret out all the conspirators."

"I know what he's planning."

"Wonderful. Why don't you share his plans with me—the names of every accomplice, the blacksmith who fashions their steel bows, and the location of their headquarters in these deserts?" Tobit kicked the ground, spraying sand in the air. "If we knew that, we could end our chase through this wilderness and go home."

Darius said, "You're tired, Father."

"Of course I'm tired." Tobit kicked the sand again, this time throwing the grains high into the air. "I'm tired of getting close to capturing Lehi and then failing. We ride through every forsaken desert between here and Jerusalem, we nearly have the man, and then this happens."

Captain Laban swung his Arabian around. "I'll have my men seal off the area."

Tobit removed his turban and ran his hand through his hair. He walked back out over the dock again, scanning the harbor. Next time he wouldn't be such a fool and try to reason with Lehi. Tobit worked the heel of his boots into the pier, forcing the dust and sand from his leather sole down between the tightly fitted boards to the water beneath. He'd had Lehi as close as two men standing in a market, bartering over melons, and now he was gone, vanished into the moist afternoon air of this harbor.

"All right. We do it your way." Tobit turned to Captain Laban. "Take Lehi however you can."

The grinding of the inspector's riding boots over the dock timbers overhead filled the narrow space under the dock with sand and grit and Lehi went under to shield his eyes, holding his breath. He steadied himself against a waterlogged post, careful not to interrupt the swaying of the small pier beyond the normal rise and fall of the surf in this protected harbor. The lone fisherman headed out to sea never saw him jump into the water and swim beneath this boardwalk, and he slowly raised his head for a breath of air and peered up through the gaps in the swollen dock timbers. Inspector Tobit scratched the back of his head, worked his chin between his fingers and cursed his foolishness. Soldiers poured into the alley from the streets of Aqaba, sealing off an escape, and Lehi turned in the water and peered down along the beach through a notch in the sideboard. Hagoth's home stood on a rocky point jutting out into the harbor down near his shipyard. Another cascade of sand fell from under Tobit's boot and Lehi closed his eyes until it settled into the water.

Merciful heaven, how was he to escape from this?

CHAPTER 31

Moonlight flashed past the shuttered windows of Hagoth's house and he hurried over to peer between the slats. There were no soldiers standing near the darkened door and no cavalrymen riding along the rock-strewn point in front of the house. It was nothing more than moonlight that brought him to this window, and he let the shutters fall back in place before returning to sit in the hardwood chair in the dark corner of the main room. Lehi's wet riding robe hung on a skewer beside the dying embers of a fire, drying from his swim through the harbor. He returned well after dark, without drawing any suspicion to the house, but to be sure, Hagoth posted himself to the night watch and told the others to get some rest. Lehi and his wife were sleeping in the bedroom on the second floor. The olive oil merchant's two sons, Laman and Nephi, returned from the animal traders at sunset with word the man would help with whatever was needed, and the boys waited with their mother, Sariah, until Lehi returned and they could find some peace amid all this tumult. The boys were sleeping in the corner bedroom across from Commander Yaush, his wife Sophia, and their son Setti. It was the room that belonged to Moriah, but since the boy was still hiding on the ridge above the Mountain Road waiting for Lehi's son Sam to arrive with a caravan of mules, there was no reason not to let Nephi and Laman rest in that room.

There was not another bed left in the house for Hagoth, no space to throw out a sleeping mat, not even a secluded corner where he could prop his head. He nestled the butt of his weapon against his side and stared across the room, his ears cocked to the constant crashing of waves against the shoal outside, searching for any odd sounds hidden in the surf. There were none and he leaned back in the chair to wait for night to pass and hope that Laban's men never took interest in his home. There were no horses or camels on the property, no saddlebags filled with provisions, nothing that would attract the attention of . . .

A rustling sounded beneath the back window and Hagoth hurried over to pull aside the shutter and peer into the moonlight. There was a shadow in the distance, down along the shoal where the point gave way to the sandy beach, but with a line of palm trees filtering out the moonlight there was no telling if it were a single man on horseback or twenty riders hiding in the shadows. Hagoth rubbed his eyes and when he checked back along the shoreline there was nothing but the form of the unfinished fishing boat sitting like the shell of a tortoise in the sand. He was a fool to think anyone was watching the house and he—

A man on horseback spurred past the window, his long hair flowing out behind him in ratted thatches, and the silhouette of his half-naked frame glowing in the starlight. He galloped down the point, disappeared into the darkness along the beach, and Hagoth let the frame of the shutter slap against the window frame. He checked the latches. The one leading to the shipyards was locked and the one turning out onto the tide pool was sealed shut. They were safe in here and he slowly backed to the comfort of his chair and fitted himself down onto the cushion, his sword pointed at the window where the night rider passed, waiting for . . .

Laman? What was the boy doing, quietly stepping down the stairwell and into the main room? He hurried his thick frame to the back door and when he reached for the latch Hagoth said, "You don't want to go out there."

Laman spun around. "What are doing up at this hour?"

"I was going to ask the same." Hagoth jabbed the end of his sword at the door. "They're watching the house."

"There's no one out there."

"Check again, son."

"I need some air." Laman reached for the latch, but didn't turn the pin.

"You go outside, son, and you'll get more than a breath of air." Hagoth slowly stood from his chair and crossed the room to Laman. "You don't seem nearly as worried about Captain Laban as the rest of your family.'

"You have no idea what we've suffered." Laman tightened his grip on the door latch. "We left our home in Jerusalem. All our wealth, all our possessions, everything we've worked our lives to earn and for what? To save the life of a prophet whose body lies in a pauper's field on the flats south of the city?" He moved his hand off the latch long enough to make a fist. "I worry every day about how we're going to claim our inheritance after this is over."

"It may never end, son."

"You're wrong. This is going to end very soon." Laman turned to the door, but before his hand touched the latch, it rattled on its own power, the noise sending the boy back a step. The door jangled again, the planks coming up off the hinges before settling back against the posts.

Hagoth motioned for Laman to stand aside and he quickly raised his sword. He removed the pin, the timbers creaking open with the sea breeze and there, standing between the doorposts, was the soaking frame of Moriah, water dripping from the cuffs of his white tunic. His hair was matted against the sides of his head and a strand of seaweed was wrapped around his neck. He said, "There are patrols all along the road."

Hagoth glanced at Laman before saying, "Come inside before you're seen."

Moriah didn't come in immediately. He turned around and helped another man out of the tide pool and when the stranger entered the house Laman said, "Sam, is that you?"

"I found them alive. Aaron, Rebecca, Josiah, and Lemuel. They're all alive." Sam shook the saltwater from his hair. "I started past them headed deep into the Way of the Wilderness, but something told me to come back and check beyond a ridge of sand and there they were, nearly dead from lack of water."

"We prayed you'd find them, son." Lehi came around the landing at the base of the stairs, his hair still wet from swimming through the harbor. He took Sam in his arms and held the boy's wet body close. "Heaven led you to them."

Hagoth stepped to Moriah. "Where did you hide them?"

"Down the shoreline a mile where the coast opens onto a wide plain. We couldn't bring the mules and sheep any closer to Aqaba." Moriah pulled the seaweed from his neck. "You still have the boathouse in Haql don't you, Father? We can take them to the fishing village. They'll be safe there until—"

"Until what?" Commander Yaush turned down the stairs in company with his son Setti and Nephi, the two boys rubbing the sleep from their eyes. They gathered into the main room, hardly large enough to hold so many. Yaush said, "What are you thinking of doing?"

Moriah said, "All of you have to leave Aqaba until the danger passes."

Laman said, "And what if it's never safe to come back here?"

Lehi said, "We don't know where this is going to lead us, son."

"I want you to go with them." Hagoth took Moriah by the hand. "Just until it's safe. You can show them the way down the coast to Haql, help them set up camp beside the boathouse." He turned to Lehi. "Your wife is too frail to travel."

Lehi said, "What other choice do we have than to take her with us?"

Hagoth said, "Captain Laban has no war against me. I'll stay behind and watch over her until she's stronger. By then, God willing, all this will have passed and we'll send for you."

"What about our animals?" Laman came around in front of Hagoth. "They're stabled in the center of the city."

Hagoth said, "I'll have the animal trader meet you down the coast with your camels. The soldiers won't question him. He takes caravans that way all year long."

Laman said, "And exactly how do we escape this house?"

Hagoth cracked open the door overlooking the tide pool, the water high enough to lap against the bottom stones of the step. "Take a deep breath, son." He inched Laman toward the opening, the dark surface of the water shimmering in the moonlight.

"We don't want you to drown."

CHAPTER 32

Sariah sat up in bed. How did she rest so soundly with the stifling heat of late afternoon turning her room into an oven? She should be up fretting over her family's escape down the coast to Haql, not sleeping away the day. She let her long, black hair down onto her shoulders, pulled the collar of her robe away from her neck, and fanned her cheeks with her hand. The air was heated beyond what she could breathe and all the waving of her hand didn't have power to cool her. The journey from Qumran to the Fountains of the Red Sea had tired her more than she knew. Sariah threw back the linen. The water jar next to her bed was empty and she started down the hall to the stairs. Hagoth warned her to stay on the upper floor until he returned, but the fierce heat of the day was collecting in these upper rooms and she left them to find relief in the cool recesses of the main floor.

The wooden stairs creaked under her shifting stride and when she reached the last step, she peered over the railing and into the main room. It was hardly as large as the entryway to her estate at Beit Zayit. There were no blue Egyptian vases to decorate the main doorway, no hardwood railing to accentuate the marble floors, no Persian rugs to color the rough-cut stone in the walls, and not a single fresh flower to perfume the musty air of this seaside home. They left behind so much to travel to this place, but as long as the windows remained shuttered and the doors latched she was safe here and she could wait until her family returned.

Sariah quickly crossed to the clay cistern sitting on the small wooden table opposite the hearth. The water was tepid from sitting out since early morning and she tipped the cistern to her lips and let the warm water wet her parched throat. This wasn't the finest of homes nor the largest, but there was reason to be grateful for these four narrow walls giving her shade against the sun and hiding her from view.

Sariah and her unborn child were safe here.

Hagoth bored a hole in the end of a curved boat timber. The wood was still wet from the bending vats and he pressed the chisel into the wood, without forcing too hard. Shavings flew past his cheeks and fell into a growing pile at his feet and he kept the chisel moving, one-quarter turn for each tap of the hammer. The chisel punched through and Hagoth left the tool hanging in the board without routing or smoothing the notch and marched up the yard to the bending vats, dragging a timber back over the sands to tie into the fishing boat. And before boring a hole in the wood, he hurried over to the stand of palm trees and weaved three lengths into a square wicker sail, before heading back across the yard to bore another hole. He was the only man working today, but if he kept moving about, the shipyard would look like all the other shipyards along the beach—busy with the work of building a boat, not hiding the escape of his ship hands to Haql.

The afternoon heat softened into the warm orange light of evening, but boat building didn't end on these beaches until sundown and Hagoth didn't dare leave his yard idle and attract unwanted notice. Another hour and he'd go inside and see to Sariah's needs, and heaven help him if she needed more than a morsel of bread or a drink of water. He was a boatbuilder, not a midwife, and caring for a woman expecting to deliver a child in less than two months was not one of his talents. Why, with all her traveling from Jerusalem, she could deliver this child anytime.

Captain Laban turned into the shipyard and headed toward the house. Hagoth threw down his chisel, marching across the man's path and blocking him from riding out onto the rocky point. He waved the man to a stop and said, "Can I help you find a boat, sir? I have one finished and another nearly ready for—"

"We've here to inspect your home." Captain Laban leaned forward in the saddle, the thin line of beard in his chin moving slowly with each word. His eyes were dark and he squinted in the waning light of day.

Tobit clenched his fists at his side. Curse this man for the trouble he caused so many. He said, "Can I get you something cool to drink?"

"You are the boatbuilder, aren't you, sir?"

"There's a good many on this beach."

"There was a man sighted in your shipyard about this time yesterday." Laban held the reins of his white Arabian tight, the animal arching its neck against the pull on the bit. "Tell me what you know about the stranger."

"I didn't really take note of the man. He stood with the stitchers right over there asking about the art of boatbuilding." Hagoth pointed to the hull of the fishing boat. "And then he ran off."

"You won't mind if we search the house then."

"I have nothing to hide, sir."

Captain Laban spurred his Arabian forward, forcing Hagoth back a step. He turned up the rocky path to the front doors, ordering his men to search the house. Hagoth hurried to catch them with the key, calling to Laban and telling him he'd unlock the doors and let them inside, but the Captain reached the entry first and kicked it open with the heel of his boot, the wood planks splitting from threshold to door beam. Laban started inside as Inspector Tobit reined down the point and came around in front of the house.

"Captain, I told you no inspections." Tobit raised his voice above the surf crashing along the shoal.

"We can't wait any longer."

Tobit said, "Lehi's not in there."

"How do you know that?" Laban came back to the door and peered out.

"He escaped Aqaba early this morning."

"What?"

"I questioned three witnesses. They each saw a caravan of camels leave the city in company with the animal trader."

"An animal trader leading a caravan of camels isn't anything out of the ordinary." Laban returned back inside the main room, and the

sound of him pushing aside chairs and tipping over a table streamed
out the door.

"The animal trader returned to Aqaba this morning." Tobit
marched back down the steps to his steed and pulled himself up into
the saddle. "He came back without a single camel."

Laban came back to the doorway. "Did you interrogate the man?"

"He's nowhere to be found. His stable hands insist he left the city
on business."

Laban stepped over the broken planks in the door. "Which way
did they head?"

"Haql. A day's ride down the coast."

Laban stepped over the broken planks in the door, followed Tobit
down the rock steps, and mounted his Arabian, reining her away
from the house as quickly as he'd arrived. Hagoth waited until they
were out of sight and heading down the road toward the city before
going inside and climbing the steps to the second floor. He turned
into the small bedroom on the west side, calling ahead to warn Sariah
of his coming, but when he entered the room it stood empty. The
linens were pulled off the feather mattress and Sariah was nowhere to
be found. He checked the other rooms and she wasn't there. He
hurried back to the main floor taking the steps two at a time. Sariah
wasn't hiding behind the large grains sacks on the far side of the
kitchen. She wasn't beneath the stack of pillows on the floor and she
wasn't hiding behind the bench seat pushed up against the far wall.
She was gone, but where? There was no place she could go on this
narrow neck of rocks extending into the sea except . . .

The back door creaked open on the breeze before banging into
place against the doorpost. It had come unlocked and Hagoth threw
it open and stood on the porch overlooking a sharp drop into the tide
pools, gone low this time of day. Sariah body's lay among the rocks
and with such a low tide there were a good many rough places to
bruise her body. She lay face down, the sleeves of her robe torn away
from her arms, her apron and sashes floating in the water beside her
feet and the waves rushing over her, tossing her against the shoal.
Hagoth jumped down the ledge and plucked her from the rocks. A
long gash cut across her brow, her arms were bruised, her cheeks
scraped, and her clothing torn from collar to hem. Her body trem-

bled and when she slowly opened her eyes and turned her gaze up the shoal to the house, she said, "Are they gone?"

Hagoth said, "You could have killed yourself."

"I was hurrying to hide from them in the water, but I lost my footing and—"

"Curse Captain Laban for scaring you like this and curse him for chasing your family." Hagoth bit on his lower lip. "We have to warn them." He carried her up the shoal toward the back door. "You can sail, can't you?"

"Can we beat Captain Laban's horses by boat?"

"You heard the winds last night didn't you?"

Sariah nodded, her gaze turning out to the sea.

"We get a strong gale like that every summer night. Sometimes it lasts an hour, sometimes until morning, and with any luck tonight it will last long enough to carry us down the coast ahead of Captain Laban." He ushered Sariah inside to pack her things, board up the windows, and collect some provisions.

Hagoth said, "Tonight we sail to Haql."

CHAPTER 33

Sand pelted the walls of the tent like a tanner's whip softening leather, and Aaron turned away from the grains blowing beneath the tent flaps. He rubbed his eyes clear and pulled the blanket up around his neck—an odd chill filling the tent in the middle of a summer night. The poles shifted against the rush of wind, pulling the ropes taut, and Aaron braced his foot against the side. Would he ever get any sleep? The constant blowing was more tiring than their forced one-day march to Haql.

The tent was still dark in the early-morning before dawn, but Aaron didn't dare move away from the entrance to find a better place to sleep, not with so many crowded inside the main compartment. They didn't have time last night to raise more than a single section of tent and the snoring of Laman rose and fell like the breathing of a lion over near the center pole. Lemuel mumbled in his sleep in the corner. Sam and Nephi slept on the far side, their steady breathing rushing from them but it was difficult to know exactly how steady with the winds howling past their tent and covering whatever stirring there was to hear from Josiah the Potter, Moriah the scribe, Commander Yaush or his son Setti—all of them sleeping too quietly to be heard above the rush of wind.

It took a good portion of the night to raise this tent, but at least they had a place to sleep away from the blowing sands that plagued the beaches along the coast in late summer. Aaron pressed the ends of the blanket to his ears, but it didn't quiet the howling wind and he let go of it and rested his aching arms, tired from digging a pit in the beach. They had to keep the tent from blowing over, and burrowing a large hole in the sands was the only way to keep it upright through the night. The entrance was pushed up against a waist-high wall of sand and the backside of the tent stood flush with the far side of the pit. The poles hardly rose above the ground and the stakes were set beneath large rocks. Aaron rolled onto his side to keep the wind from blowing another round of sand into his . . .

Where was the wind? There were no grains of sand blowing beneath the sealed leather flaps and he sat up, his ears turned to the entrance. The roar of wind was gone, the poles were still, and the creaking of the ropes against the drag of the stakes was suddenly silent, the gale disappearing as quickly as it arrived. Aaron untied the flaps and climbed out of the protective depths of the hastily dug pit and up onto the flat white strand of beach. A thick, cool fog hovered along the shoreline, blown here on a ferocious wind, and Aaron wrapped his arms around himself against the coolness of morning in the middle of summer. What an odd thing for the desert to feel like winter, but no more odd than Aaron's coming to this Fountain of the Red Sea so far from home. Not long from now the heat of the desert sun was certain to bake these shores, but now, in the light before dawn the mist of morning dripped from the end of his desert-burned nose.

The mud-brick boathouse that belonged to Hagoth the boat-builder sat down the beach a short walk from the tent. Rebecca and Sophia were asleep inside. The rickety wooden door was shut, with nothing more than a rope to seal it in place. There was an idle spout running off the square roof to drain it of the monsoon rainwaters that raced across the Fountain of the Red Sea on late summer afternoons. A quick movement flashed across the small peephole—the opening cut into the bricks at eye level to see the boats coming ashore. It was too dark to know if Rebecca stood on the other side peering back at him, but to be sure he waved at the building and waited for the door to swing open, and when it stayed shut, he turned down along the strand and let the surf wash over his unshod feet, allowing Rebecca more sleep.

Haql was quiet this early in the morning, the square roofs of eight single-story mud-brick homes rising against the mists. The buildings stood on the other side of the springs, the water bubbling up out of the sand and trickling down past Aaron, the overflow meandering across the beach before seeping back into the ground. Two springs flowed with sweet water, but the third was gone salty, and last night before retiring, Sam tied the camels and mules a good distance away from the watering place to keep them from breaking out of their riggings and bloating on bad water. They grunted in the early-morning stillness, calling to Sam to rise out of his bed and come lead them to water, but they were wasting their breath. Didn't these creatures know, after all these years, that Sam was Caravan Master, not a stable boy?

Aaron walked a brisk walk through the cool surf. He was alive because Sam saved him from wasting away in the insufferable heat of the Way of the Wilderness along with Rebecca, Josiah, and Lemuel. The headaches lingered still; Aaron's nose was burned, his lips swollen, and he leaned his head back to let the cool mists off the sea gather on his face and rid him of the sting. They were fools to try to cross the wide expanse of the Way of the Wilderness with so little water, and Sam never would have found them if not for listening to the quiet whisperings of heaven, directing him back over a rise of sand to where they lay dying. Not a day passed since their rescue that Aaron wasn't grateful that Sam possessed a listening heart. A strong-willed caravaneer never would have found them languishing behind a remote sand dune among hundreds of miles of sand dunes in the Way of the Wilderness, but Sam had a good heart and thankfully the boy put his faith in a God wiser than any of them or they'd not be camped along these shores—alive.

Aaron turned back to the sea, his mouth open to collect a drink out of the air, the cool water healing his blistered lips and his heart raised in thanks for bringing them to this shoreline where they were blessed to find—

Sariah? What was she doing appearing through a breach in the fog, coming ashore on a small vessel? The square sail sagged on the riggings and there was not a breath of air to push them the last cubits to shore. Hagoth worked the oars, bringing them in against the undertow, the small schooner fighting the pull of the sea. The craft paused atop the surf like driftwood before breaking over the waves and rushing aground in a wash of white spray. Aaron ran to the vessel, but before he closed down the last few strides, he pulled up at the sight of Sariah. Her robes were torn away from her arms, the rent cloth hanging limp about her wrists. A large blue-black bruise started along the side of her skull just above the jawbone, ran up the side of her face and across her brow before disappearing beneath her cap of dark brown hair. A bloody gash cut across her brow, her cheeks were scratched, but when she leaned over the boat railing and reached for Aaron's hand she spoke nothing of pain.

Sariah said, "Are you well, son?"

Was he well? How could she ask such a thing when she'd spent so many days on the trail with hardly a rest? Her body was weak from carrying a child and now she suffered these painful cuts and bruises. Aaron placed his hand beside her face, but didn't touch the bloodied skin of her cheeks, not with the memory of his own injuries welling up inside him and reminding him of pain so fierce the whisper of a touch stirred him with fear. Too few months had passed since the molten metal of the smelting oven burned his feet and he had suffered the torment of scars unable to heal, sinew pulling away from bone, and infections bloating what skin he had left to the size of melons. He suffered again at the hands of Laban's arrow, the metal head lost in his thigh, reminding him with every step of that bloody night when he escaped the captain's hatred, hiding among the trees of Beit Zayit away from the threat of another arrow. And he could never forget the long, slow pain of dying from thirst in the Way of the Wilderness. What awful things they'd both suffered. Aaron drew back his hand from Sariah's bruised face, the depths of his soul shuddering with understanding. He said, "What happened?"

"It was Captain Laban, son." Hagoth stowed the oars, banging the long lengths against the inside of the hull. "That's all I need say."

Aaron gripped the edge of the boat, the rough-hewn wood splintering into his skin. "Captain Laban did this to you?"

"A few days and it should heal." Sariah reached for the railing and laid her hand on his. "I fell along the shoal below Hagoth's home. It's nothing, really."

"If it weren't for Captain Laban, she wouldn't have had reason to fall." Hagoth jumped out of the vessel and pulled the boat from the surf, beaching the schooner as close to the boathouse as he could without the help of a larger crew. He raised his gruff voice, the sound of it resounding through camp and scaring the gulls walking along the shoreline to flight. "Wake Lehi and tell him Laban's coming to Haql."

"Not here." Rebecca pushed open the doors of the boathouse, tying her hair back off her shoulders with nothing more than a length of cord. Sophia followed her, holding the hem of her robe out of the sand. They started toward the boat, Rebecca asking Hagoth if he was certain Captain Laban was headed to Haql, and Sophia wanting to know if he was coming anytime soon, but when they saw Sariah they fell silent and pulled up short of the hull—their unshod feet sinking into the wet sands. "Captain Laban can't have followed us here."

Aaron said, "He did this to you?"

"I'll heal." Sariah forced a smile.

Rebecca said, "How does Laban know about us?"

"He has a Babylonian working with him." Hagoth removed the square wicker sails and brought down the mast. "A very cunning man."

"That would be Inspector Tobit." Lehi crawled out of the waist-deep pit surrounding the family tent. He held the leather flap back for the other men waking to the sound of Hagoth's arrival. Laman, Lemuel, Nephi, Moriah, Yaush, Setti, and Josiah gathered on the beach around Lehi.

"That's right, sir." Hagoth turned in the boat to face Lehi. "He has charge of all the New Babylonian Territories."

Lehi started down the short distance of beach separating them. He pushed his dark hair off his brow and rubbed the sleep from his eyes while Hagoth recounted Inspector Tobit's clever piecing together of clues that started them down the coastal plain after them.

Lehi came alongside the boat and when he saw Sariah—her body down below the level of the hull and her shoulders slumped against the boards—Hagoth lowered his voice and said, "I'm sorry, sir. I should have taken better care."

Lehi jumped over the boat railing and sat beside her, resting her head on his arm and passing his fingers lightly over her bruises. A single tear fell down his cheek and landed on her head like the healing oil from a priest's vessel—the same cap of dark brown hair that only months ago was shaved away to make room for the frequent changing of bandages on a gash in the back of her skull gotten at the hands Lieutenant Daniel. Aaron's brother didn't cause Sariah her new pain, but the memory of what he did to her festered inside him. How could Daniel have been so cruel to a woman as gentle as she? Aaron gripped the side of the boat so hard the nails of his fingers dug deep into the wet wood fibers. Sariah suffered more than any woman should ever have to endure.

Lehi turned his swollen eyes up into the patchy mists of fog filtering over from the sea, his cry raised to heaven. "Dear merciful God, I will suffer whatever lot is cast across my path, but spare my family the pain of this journey."

Laman pushed in past Aaron, sleep still lingering in his gaze. "We never should have left her behind."

"Laman?" Sariah sat up and reached over the side for his hand. "Are you well, dear?"

Laman said, "I'm sorry you've had to suffer. I'm sorry any of us have suffered this foolish journey."

"There's no telling how much time we have left." Hagoth moored his sailing vessel to the boathouse with lengths of rope. "Captain Laban headed this way in the early hours this morning."

Rebecca took Aaron by one hand and Josiah by the other. "Will this fleeing never end?"

"I warned you." Laman stepped to the prow of the boat. "I warned all of you." He raised his hand to the circle of fourteen weary travelers gathered around. "We never should have run from Captain Laban to begin with."

Rebecca said, "Where will we go from here?"

Aaron said, "We can escape farther down the coast."

"Not that way, son." Hagoth turned down along the shoreline, his hand raised to the way south. "These wide-open beaches narrow the farther you travel down the shoreline until the Borders nearer the Red Sea push you right into the surf. You can't see them for the fog, son, but down that way there are two thousand foot peaks rising out of the sea." He shook his head and came back to the moored sailing vessel. "We have to head east across the coastal plain and through the Borders near the Red Sea to the Frankincense Trail on the other side."

"I'll gather the animals; the rest of you pull down the tent." Sam started up the beach, but Laman took him by the arm and said, "We can't outrun Captain Laban."

"We can try, son." Hagoth pointed east across the coastal plain, the flat stretch of sand running a full mile inland to the towering range of the Borders near the Red Sea. The sun rose over the distant summit and chased away the cover of morning mists, quickly melting the fog into spotty patches. He said, "The Aqaba Branch heads back through those mountains to the Frankincense Trail. It's our only chance."

Laman said, "If we stay here we can make peace with Captain Laban and give him what he wants."

Josiah said, "Exactly what do you think he wants from us?"

"My father. That's all he's ever wanted."

Setti stepped to Laman, his shoulders pushed forward. "What are you saying?"

Commander Yaush held his son back. "The boy's saying we should sacrifice Lehi in exchange for our lives."

"I never said Captain Laban was going to kill anyone." Laman glanced at Lehi before turning his gaze into the ground. "Father could ride up the coast, make peace with the man, and beg his mercy."

"Mercy?" Setti leaned his head in close to Laman. "Do you have any idea what sort of man you're dealing with? He tried to kill my family."

Laman said, "I have an idea what sort of man he is."

Setti said, "Captain Laban will do anything to get what he wants, sacrifice any loyalty, destroy anyone who gets in his way."

Laman said, "I told you what he wants."

Josiah said, "You don't really think he would stop pursuing us if we sent him your father, do you?"

"My father could arrange a truce."

Setti said, "You're a fool."

"All of us have reason to fear Captain Laban." Hagoth laid aside the riggings of his boat. "We have to break camp and try our luck in those mountains. It's a two-day ride, maybe three, over the Borders near the Red Sea to the Frankincense Trail."

Lehi turned down along the beach, studying the coastline, his hand over his brow to shield against the rising sun, and when he came back to the gathering he said, "I'm taking the camels and heading south along the shoreline with my family down to the Borders nearer the Red Sea. I want the rest of you to head east to the Frankincense Trail."

Hagoth stood next to Lehi. "You can't go along the shoreline more than twenty miles before the mountains stop you."

"We leave Haql together, all of us, is that understood?" Lehi spoke quickly. "We head down this beach until we're out of view of the village then I want the rest of you to turn inland toward the Borders near the Red Sea." He took Aaron by the arm. "You be sure to cover their tracks when we part company."

"What about you?" Aaron pulled free of Lehi's grasp. "What are you going to do to cover your escape?"

"Better that Captain Laban follows us than you." Lehi turned to Hagoth. "How long will it take us to reach the end of this shoreline?"

"Less than a full day if you push hard."

Commander Yaush said, "Don't condemn yourself and your family like this. You'll end up trapped down by those mountains with Captain Laban on your heels." He took Sophia and Setti by the hand. "Come with us. There's a chance we can get through the Borders near the Red Sea and onto the Frankincense Trail before Captain Laban catches us." He shook his head. "You're riding into a trap if you head south into the Borders nearer the Red Sea."

"I would never lead my family into a trap." Lehi lowered his voice. "We'll find a way through these coastal mountains."

"Not down where the coast narrows you won't." Hagoth shook the end of the boat riggings at Lehi. "You try to escape up into the narrow canyons and wadis in the foothills of the Borders nearer the Red Sea and you'll not get more than a few hundred cubits before you run up against steep mountain cliffs."

Lehi said, "Moses found a way in through the Borders nearer the Red Sea. And he struck his staff on the ground to call up springs out of the sands to quench the thirst of Israel."

Hagoth said, "No one knows exactly where that happened. It could be on the mountains of Sinai or any of the Borders between here and Egypt."

Sam came back to his father. "I've heard caravaneers tell of a passage leading through the Borders nearer the Red Sea, down along the coast where the mountains push into the sea."

Hagoth said, "Have you ever traveled it?"

"No, but I—"

"It's too dangerous to risk your life on a trail that doesn't exist." Hagoth shook his head. "There are thousands of passages winding through the narrow canyons south of here, and all of them will lead you nowhere but to your death. There's only one way out of here." He pointed across the wide coastal plain to where the trade route started up into the Borders near the Red Sea. "Come with us and we'll leave this place together."

Nephi said, "What if it's true? What if there is a place hidden in these Borders nearer the Red Sea where we can find water and refuge from Captain Laban?"

"This isn't the time to go exploring." Hagoth rubbed the back of his head. "The stories of the waters of Moses and a land of bounty deep in the belly of the Borders nearer the Red Sea mountains are the stuff of late nights around caravan campfires, told by men with sun-baked minds who've had too much strong wine. They're nothing more than legend."

Laman said, "I say we stay here at Haql and negotiate with Captain Laban."

"Don't be a fool, boy. You'll dig your own grave if you stay here." Commander Yaush took Laman by the arm. "Captain Laban will come after you with the same vengeance he has for your father."

"I'm not doing this to save myself." Laman pulled free of Yaush's grasp. "I'm thinking of all of you. If we want to return to our homes at Jerusalem, we don't have any other choice but to bargain with Captain Laban."

Hagoth said, "The only choice we have is to keep moving."

"Until when?" Laman kicked his foot through the sand. "Until we're all dead men?"

"Until we find a place of refuge." Lehi stepped to the center of the gathering and turned in a circle, his eyes moving over his friends and family. "I've dreamed a dream."

Laman said, "I've had enough of your dreams."

"Son." Sariah stood next to Laman. "Let your father finish."

Lehi said, "I was lost in a dark and dreary wilderness."

"I've had the same nightmare, Father." Lemuel leaned his head into the circle and smiled. "Every night I see these forsaken deserts that never end. It's time we found a way home and end this awful dream."

Lehi raised his hand to quiet his son. He said, "A man dressed in a white robe stood beside me and led me through a dark and dreary waste." He rubbed his brow, his face drawn out, his gaze looking far off, beyond the gathering around the boat and into the mist covering his view of the way south. "I prayed to the Lord that he would have mercy on me according to his tender mercies, and after I prayed I came to a large, spacious field and after traveling to the end of the field I found a tree of delicious fruit and a river of water running alongside it and—"

"What does this have to do with us traveling down the coast?" Laman pushed on the side of the moored boat. "What do any of your dreams have to do with anything but leading us into foolishness?"

"The dark and dreary wilderness I saw in my dream, son—the one the robed man led me through . . ." Lehi pointed down along the coast to the winding, impassable foothills at the base of the Borders nearer the Red Sea—the same mountains that blocked their journey south along the coast. He said, "The passages through those foothills are the same dark and dreary waste I saw in my dream."

Laman said, "What else does your dream tell you?"

"I don't know yet."

"What do you mean, you don't know yet?"

"That's where I wake every night, just barely beyond those foothills and up in a wide canyon behind the Borders nearer the Red Sea, in a large spacious field, with a river running beside a tree whose fruit was desirable to make one happy."

"There are no rivers in this desert. None. There never have been." Laman glanced up the beach to the spring flowing with fresh water. "Haql has the only water between here and the Frankincense Trail and you know it. If we're to go anywhere it should be with the rest of them, up through the Borders near the Red Sea, not down the coast on some chase through the belly of these Borders nearer the Red Sea."

"Father." Lemuel slowly shook his head. "Only in a dream will you ever find a date palm in these mountains. There's plenty of heat, but without any water they'll not have a chance to—"

Laman said, "What he's trying to tell you is that we didn't harvest any dates in Jericho."

Lehi said, "You defied me."

"I had no other choice."

"I told you to pack the mules with as many dates as you could carry."

"We didn't have time. We had to leave or risk losing our lives." Laman raised both his hands to Lehi. "We don't have food to support us in these Borders." He began to pace in the sand. "Even if we found a fabled passage through the mountains along this coast, we'll die in whatever large and spacious field you think you see in your dreams. The saddlebags on our mules are empty. We have no dates. Do you hear me? There is no fruit to satisfy our souls when we're starving."

Lehi said, "I don't know where it is and I don't know how we'll find it, son, but—"

"Find what?"

Lehi glanced at Aaron and when their gaze met, he said, "God wouldn't lead us this far from home without opening rivers in high places, and fountains in the midst of these valleys."

Aaron turned to Nephi, both of them staring at each other. Those were the words of Isaiah, the ones Aaron and Nephi read together in the early morning hours in their tent at Qumran. They were writings they never dared share with anyone—not with Laman and Lemuel both insisting they should return home, and certainly not in the presence of Sariah with her holding onto hope that on some future day they would quietly find their way back to Beit Zayit. The harsh desert life turned their thoughts always toward home, the comforts of the estate they abandoned begging them to resolve their troubles and end this fleeing. But Aaron together with Nephi was slowly coming to share Lehi's conviction—no matter how impossible it seemed—that they might never see their homeland again. Somehow Isaiah saw their flight from the land of their inheritance and when that dead prophet wrote of opening rivers in high places and fountains in the midst of valleys, Aaron could only pray he was writing about these Borders nearer the Red Sea. Somewhere hidden within the maze of impassable wadis and uninhabitable valleys was a fountain of life-giving water, and Aaron with Nephi likened the words of Isaiah to their plight. There had to be a way through to a place of refuge—they had no other hope.

The full force of the morning sun broke over the peaks, burning off the last remnants of fog and revealing the length and breadth of the shoreline running south and opening up the full view of the Borders nearer the Red Sea, cutting off their retreat down the coastline a day's ride south of Haql. Lehi took Sariah in his arms and Aaron inched closer to hear him whisper in her ear. It was a private moment, but he couldn't keep from wanting to know what words of comfort the prophet was speaking to her and he leaned his head in to hear.

Lehi softly said, "Somewhere in these borders nearer the Red Sea, my dear, there is a canyon tabernacle prepared to give us shade in the daytime from the heat, and for a *place of refuge* from this terrible storm."

They were living the prophecies of Isaiah.

CHAPTER 34

Inspector Tobit spurred past the last mud-brick building at the far end of Haql and spit in the sand. Where were the signs of Lehi's coming to this outpost? There were no camels tethered to ropes, no mules braying in the light breeze off the sea, and no sheep scattered along the shady side of these single-story homes, hiding from the heat of afternoon. He came around and studied the sands leading down from the village to the surf of the . . .

What did fishermen call these waters? He turned in the saddle, found Darius riding near the front of the cavalry arriving at Haql and waved him over. He pointed to the pristine blue sea, but before he could ask the name, his son said, "Fountain, sir. They call this the Fountain of the Red Sea."

Darius reined over, holding out his map, the ends of the parchment hanging down between their two horses. The careful strokes of his son's pen charted the shoreline and it did have the appearance of a fountain, this long gulf extending off the main body of the Red Sea and dividing the coastal plain of Haql from the Sinai Peninsula with a deep, fifteen-mile-wide trough of crystal-blue water shimmering in the sun. Tobit handed back the map and leaned forward in the saddle, peering across the sea to the desolate shores of Sinai, the stark beauty of this place belying the hostile desert with little fresh water, and insufferable heat that burned these sands in the late summer afternoon.

Tobit cantered over to the spring percolating up through the ground. Three women hovered over the fresh water, dipping their clay jars, but when they saw him approach with a metal bow tied to his saddlebags and the two feathers of his office sprouting out the top of his military turban, they stepped back and pulled the cloth of their robes across their faces. Haql was an isolated place that caravaneers frequented, but where the military never traveled, and Tobit pulled up on the far side of the spring without asking them if they'd seen Lehi's caravan. These women could have information he lacked, but a pair of tracks in the sand was a better witness than the testimony of any two of these villagers, and he slowly reined about the spring, searching for any sign of Lehi's passing.

"Where is he?" Captain Laban rode over, his gruff voice chasing the women back to the safety of their mud-brick homes.

Tobit got down from saddle and walked a circle about the spring. There were no tracks surrounding the watering place, no indication that any caravan had stopped to get water here or camp along the—

What was that? Tobit fell to his knees in the sands below the spring and ran his fingers over the surface. There were animal tracks here. They were difficult to see, half blotted out and raked over by some sort of reed broom or . . .

Tobit leaned forward and pressed his nose into the sand, the faint scent of animal skins lingering among the white grains. Camel hair. What an ingenious man this Lehi. He dragged the wall of his tent over the sand to hide his tracks, but he wasn't going to escape that easily—not this time.

"What is it?" Captain Laban brought his Arabian around in front of Tobit, the horse's hooves destroying the half-hidden tracks. "You told me we'd find Lehi here."

"I said nothing about finding him at Haql." Tobit brushed his nose clean of the sand before pushing aside the muzzle of Captain Laban's Arabian and marching down the beach, past the line of one hundred cavalrymen gathering on the south end of Haql. He pulled his steed by the reins and Captain Laban steered in behind him. Tobit said, "I never expected to find Lehi here. He's too smart to be captured on an open beach like this."

Laban said, "What did you expect to find?"

"This." Inspector Tobit jumped down into a sandy pit dug into the beach, the four sides surrounding him with a waist-high wall. "See those deep holes in the corners, the ones just wide enough for a wooden pole? There was a tent staked here last night and it was pulled up early this morning."

"How do you know it was this morning?"

"The wind, Captain. It hit here last night as hard as it hit us up the coast. These holes in the sand never would have survived unless the poles came out after the wind died."

"I'll interrogate the villagers." Captain Laban came around in the sand, but Tobit grabbed hold of the bridle and kept the Arabian from pulling away. "No interrogations, Captain. We don't need the villagers. They aren't going to tell us what they know. These people depend on caravans for their support." He pointed to the gold stripes in Captain Laban's tunic. "You're not a caravaneer, sir."

"If we don't question them, we'll lose Lehi."

"We'll find the man on our own." Tobit mounted his steed. "Lehi needs a good tent in this wilderness. He won't have dragged the animal skins too far in the sand."

Tobit spurred off down the beach, his shoulders forward and the ends of his white turban flapping about his head. Laban chased after him, the cavalry falling into line behind their sudden departure, the line of horses churning over the sand, up a gentle rise in the coastal plain and out of sight of the villagers at Haql. Tobit pulled up just beyond the crest of the sandy rise and came around. Just as he thought—Lehi covered his tracks until he was beyond the view of Haql. He slowed his mount and jumped from the saddle, carefully studying the markings of twenty camels, twenty mules, some sheep, and fourteen horses. The tracks were fresh and Tobit hovered over them like a doctor over a patient, studying every nuance.

Tobit said, "How many in Lehi's family?"

Laban sat back in the saddle. "What does it matter if he—"

"How many, sir?"

"There's Laman, the eldest."

Tobit walked down the rise, his gaze turned to the wide swath of animal tracks. "Go on."

"He has a brother Lemuel, a sickly boy with hardly a shekel's worth of skin on his bones. Then there's the wily one, Sam, and the youngest one they call Nephi—a good wrestler, strong lad, he's—"

"I didn't ask for their names."

Laban said, "Lehi brought four sons with him."

Tobit pulled up near the base of the rise, well beyond the view of Haql. "Are you sure?"

Laban came in behind him with the cavalry gathering in a large circle, the horses pawing the sand. Laban said, "They have their mother with them, but you could hardly call that woman a threat to any of—"

"That's it." Tobit marched back up the rise in the coastal plain until he could see the mud-brick homes of Haql in the distance. "The tracks of fourteen riders started out of the village along with a caravan of camels and mules. And they continue down until . . ." He marched back toward the circle of cavalry. ". . . Until they reached here." He pulled up where the tracks in the sand narrowed from a band of fourteen riders to only six, and where the mules completely disappeared. "From here there are only six horses and a line of camel tracks headed south."

Darius reined in next to his father, the leather map hanging from one hand. "They wouldn't go south, sir." He spread the parchment across the horse's mane. "The Borders push right into the gulf and there's no way out from there but by sea."

"The boy's right." Shechem pulled in next to Darius, his long hair streaming past his shoulders and falling over his steed's backside. "If they traveled south to where this coastline ends, they're trapped by the mountains with no way out."

Laban sidled in next to Tobit. "Are you telling me that Lehi took his family down the coast, into a trap?"

"These are the tracks I've been following since we left Qumran."

Laban counted the riders on his fingers, softly speaking the name of each one headed south—Lehi, Sariah, Laman, Lemuel, Sam, and Nephi.

Tobit pulled himself up into the saddle and came around. "They left Haql early this morning."

Captain Laban turned out of the circle of cavalrymen, ordering his men to follow, but when Inspector Tobit didn't join him, he turned back. "We haven't time to lose, Inspector. The sun will be gone soon."

Tobit said, "What about the other tracks?"

Laban said, "There aren't any others."

"Eight riders and twenty mules don't disappear into nothing, sir." Tobit turned his gaze to where the tracks narrowed from fourteen riders to six. There were faint impressions of a tent or some sort of bundle veering off across the coastal plain toward the Border Mountains, the same impressions he found around the springs at Haql. A portion of Lehi's caravan was headed toward the high peaks rising out of the coastal plain a mile inland from the pristine blue waters of these shores like a backdrop reaching into heaven, coloring the sky with dark blue and purple rock. Tobit snapped his fingers and said, "The map, son."

Darius leaned over the saddle, orienting his map to the mountains in the distance, letting Tobit sight down along the base of the range. The Border Mountains farther from the Red Sea were a formidable fortress with steep inclines and a web of deep, narrow canyons. It was no wonder the local Bedouins and merchants called these mountains Hijaz—there was not a more foreboding border along the trade route than the high peaks and endless rugged sandstone gorges through the split range of the Jabal Mountains.

"Eight riders are headed that way." Tobit pointed to the wide canyon opening in the distant range. "If they cross the summit and join with the Frankincense Trail, we'll never catch them."

Laban said, "Forget them. Lehi's riding into a trap down along the coast."

"We can't let the other go. We don't know what part they have in Lehi's uprising."

Captain Laban reined forward. "We're nearly done with this chase and I need you to help us finish it."

"You can follow Lehi's tracks without my help." Tobit straightened in the saddle. "Set a base camp down where the shoreline narrows and pushes into the sea. I'll find you when this is over."

"Help us capture Lehi and you can force him to lead us to the others. He's the only one who knows the details of this uprising."

"There is one other, sir." Tobit started his horse slowly moving inland away from the shore, toward the distant mountains.

Laban reined alongside Tobit's slow-moving horse. "What are you talking about?"

"The man who issued the tax levy."

"Ezekiel?" Laban uttered the name in a low voice that resonated from deep in the pit of his stomach.

"That's right; Lehi's accomplice in all this." Tobit glanced at the steel bow strapped to the back of his horse—the most powerful weapon he'd ever come across. He said, "Ezekiel could help us put down this insurrection."

Laban spurred ahead and came around in front of Tobit, stopping the inspector from riding further inland. "We've already questioned him."

"A month in one of your prisons may have righted his memory."

"You don't need to question him."

"I'll be the judge of that." Tobit reined around Laban. "I'll meet you at the end of the shoreline."

"How long?"

"Three days, Captain. No more."

Tobit spurred out across the coastal plain, his fifty cavalrymen parting from the company of Laban's men and following him toward the mountains in the distance. Whoever covered these tracks in the sand was hiding something and Tobit was going to find the reason for the concealment. The obvious tracks heading south along the coast were a decoy, and Tobit dug the heels of his boots into the horse's side. What were these eight riders hiding? What secret did they carry with them? The answer begged Tobit to follow them back up into the Borders near the Red Sea and leave Captain Laban to chase after Lehi and his family down to where the Borders nearer the Red Sea were certain to stop Lehi from going any farther. It was a deep, powerful feeling and it worked on his heart like the swelling of a seed before it sprouts, pulling him toward the distant peaks on the horizon to find the answer to his question.

What was this still, small voice luring him up unto the Borders near the Red Sea, away from the hunt for Lehi?

CHAPTER 35

"Riders on the trail!"

The cry carried up the high mountain pass from the back of the caravan, piercing the pristine air like an arrow racing past Sophia's ears and turning her in the saddle to search down the line of mules for her son. Setti called to them from the far end of the pass, back on the ridge they had cleared a good while before. She couldn't see him, but she could hear his voice streaming around a sandstone outcrop that separated them like a great window shutter sealing off her view of the Aqaba Branch. The warning couldn't have come at a worse time with the caravan of mules and horses trapped in this pass, the towering rock walls void of even a trace of vegetation to soften the terrible cry that cut to the very center of Sophia's soul. Why must this conflict follow them into the wilderness? They fled Fort Lakhish to be rid of this senselessness and now the very evil they left behind was chasing them through these Border Mountains.

Setti's cry grew louder, warning them of the men he spied on the Aqaba Branch below the pass. The boy was well suited for the duty of watchman after so many years on the night watch at Lakhish, but there were not five thousand soldiers posted in this canyon to call to arms, no regiments to direct about the walls of this valley, and if a battle came to them in this pass, there were no watchtowers where they could take refuge. Setti and his father would have to fend them off with an army drafted from the ranks of a boatbuilder, a scribe, a potter, a blacksmith, and two women.

"They're coming!"

Setti raced around the sandstone outcrop and jumped a stand of rock. His father, Yaush, followed at full gallop, the pounding hooves of their return mixing with the echo of their voices. Setti didn't glance at her when he passed, his shoulders forward. The boy spurred beyond Rebecca and Josiah the Potter, around past Moriah and Hagoth, and came in beside Aaron.

"How far back?" Aaron brought Beuntahyu around hard.

Setti said, "It's the Babylonians. They're without Captain Laban or his men."

Yaush pulled in beside Setti. "They're riding hard. There isn't much time before they reach this pass."

Aaron said, "How many men?"

"A good fifty soldiers or more." Setti spoke between hurried breaths, his dark hair falling into his eyes. "They're all over the face of the mountain, climbing the steepest inclines without slowing."

Hagoth said, "We can't outrun them."

"All we need is time." Yaush pointed to the mule at the back of the caravan. "Unleash her and leave her on the trail to catch their attention. That should give us enough time to get off this mountain and down where we have a chance among the rocks." He wiped the sweat off his brow and turned his gaze to the sun falling low on the horizon. "Once night falls, they can't track us."

Setti quickly lashed a leather bundle behind his steed, stroking the animal's mane, and telling her to pull the load over the ground as hard and as swift as she'd ever pulled a load. They had to cover their tracks one more time, enough to confuse these soldiers and fool them into investigating the side canyons. Josiah, Rebecca, and Sophia gathered the water skins from the mule. Moriah and Hagoth removed the provisions off her back and Yaush and Aaron started the mule back down to greet their pursuers.

Yaush was the first to reach the summit, coming around a rocky outcrop above the valley floor and looking down the trail, calling for Sophia and the others to hurry along. Hagoth and Moriah herded the mules up the last stretch to the top, followed by Josiah, Aaron and Rebecca. Sophia spurred up the approach alongside Setti, over a narrow ridge and out onto the plateau overlooking the valley. The trade route meandered below them, turning a wide path around tall outcrops, over patches of sand and across the open stands of brush gone brown in the heat of summer, and when the first Babylonian soldiers cleared the ridge at the far end of the valley, silhouetted by the setting sun, Sophia inched her steed back from the summit's edge. It wasn't a long line of cavalry, not nearly as many soldiers as Setti reported seeing. There were ten, possibly fifteen riders, but despite the smaller numbers, Sophia couldn't keep her body from going weak at the sight of their enemies. Twenty years she cleaned her husband's sword with a chamois of perfumed olive oil—a task she did in secret since he never approved of a sweet-smelling sword—but no matter how often she cleaned her husband's many weapons, she never conquered the panic that gripped her soul when men brandished the instruments of death. The soldiers spurred in two columns up the pass, galloping between a cleft in a large outcrop before falling out of line to jump a stand of rocks strewn across the valley floor, then coming together along a stretch of flat sand in a double-file line headed up the trail toward . . .

Mercy no! The riders veered around the stray mule without the slightest pause in their pursuit. The animal didn't attract the least attention from the riders and Sophia inched her steed in next to Yaush and Setti. What were they to do? They needed more time to hide themselves among the rocks and brush on the leeward side of this Border near the Red Sea. There were a hundred paths heading down from here, past tall sandstone outcrops that stood like sentinels warning them of dangers that waited in this game of chase and catch. They could lose themselves down over there where the main trail split into many paths, or they could take an obscure route along the far ridge and bide their time until the cover of evening hid them from these soldiers, but they had to go quickly. There wasn't any time to waste. They had to get off this mountain before—

"Don't move, any of you!" A man with two feathers sprouting from his turban reined out from behind the nearest outcrop, a fully drawn bow aimed at them. He rode a horse powerful enough to carry him in the ridges above the pass with enough speed to get ahead of their caravan. The animal was outfitted for fleetness without any silver studs in the saddle to weigh it down, and only a single water skin wrapped in a blanket to keep the animal from tiring. The rider wore a flowing white robe, tied close against his body, and he rode his mount with a nimble carriage.

"*We* took the high route over the ridge," the man said in answer to Sophia's staring. He was alone on this mountain without any companions to keep them from fleeing his single arrow and Sophia had no way of knowing who his *we* included.

He aimed the full force of his weapon at her and sighted down the shaft, the power of his steel bow ready to propel the metal tip into her flesh with nothing more than the release of his first two fingers. It was a terrible weapon, fiercer than any bow she'd seen among her husband's five thousand soldiers. There had never been a steel bow at Fort Lakhish, not that she remembered seeing among the ranks of archers or stored at the commissary. If there had been, Yaush would certainly have told her about the invention. The metal was polished to a fine luster, the arms forged into a recurved shape like the halves of the moon. The hand grip was made of ox hide as supple as the skin of a newborn, and in the orange light of afternoon Sophia saw the mark of a serpent etched into the metal just above the notch—the same sign Covenanters used to signify their faith in Yeshua the Anointed One.

Sophia inched her horse forward. "Are you one of us?"

Yaush said, "Sophia, no."

The man aimed his bow at Yaush, the steel pulled back to a full draw, the metal arms quivering against the force. "Ah yes, the Commander of Lakhish and his wife. We meet again."

Yaush said, "Good evening, Inspector Tobit."

Somehow her husband knew this man, and by the way Yaush sat at attention in the saddle she could tell he was a powerful man.

"So you've joined the renegades, have you?" Tobit inched his mount closer to Yaush, relaxing his draw to examine the Commander's Hebrew officer's dress, the cloth faded after so many months of working in the sun of Hagoth's shipyards.

Yaush said, "We mean you no harm."

"No harm?" Tobit tapped the side of the steel bow with his forefinger. "Lehi recruits you from the Hebrew military to direct his uprising and you tell me you mean no harm?"

"It's true." Aaron stepped toward Tobit. "You heard him. We don't mean you any—"

"Back away or I'll send this arrow through your heart." Tobit pulled the string to a full draw, the tip of the arrow rattling against the metal notch, the sharp end pointed at Aaron's chest.

"Please, no. Don't hurt him." Rebecca reined beside Aaron and he shifted his aim between them, moving quickly from Aaron, then to Rebecca and back again to Aaron, telling all of them to get down out of the saddle, and do it now, before he let go of his arrow on whomever he pleased and ended this foolishness once and for all. He said, "Who makes these bows of steel for you?"

"Don't say anything." Yaush raised his hand, his gaze resting on Aaron longer than the others, an uncomfortable tension jumping the distance between them. "Do you understand, not a word about—"

"The bow!" Tobit brandished the weapon at all of them. "Tell me what you know about this."

"It isn't a weapon." Rebecca took Aaron by the hand, the two of them standing in front of Beuntahyu. "It was fashioned as a gift."

Aaron pulled her close to him, his long arms wrapped around her slight frame. "Don't say more."

Tobit leaned over his saddle and held the tip of the arrow a hand's length from Rebecca's face. "How do you know that? Tell me everything you know about—"

"I'm the blacksmith." Aaron stepped away from Rebecca, pulling Tobit's aim onto him. "You can let the others go. In this wilderness you have no authority to keep them."

The boy was wrong. Sophia had seen her husband's maps of the New Babylonian territory, the occupied lands reaching down beyond these Borders to where the Fountain of the Red Sea emptied into the main channel. This mountain summit stood near the extreme south end of the territory, but in these lawless lands, the final word was the strength of a man's hand and the size of his clan. There were no courts here, no monarch to extend mercy, no soldiers to enforce the law, nothing but the sheiks of the desert, and Inspector Tobit was chief among sheiks, a governor with power to execute whatever judgment he saw fit.

Aaron said, "Let the others go or I'll not fashion you another steel bow for your armies."

Tobit inched his steed forward, the animal's powerful body pushing the boy back a step, unbalancing him. "How many weapons like this one have you forged?"

"Only one."

Tobit said, "You don't expect me to believe that, do you?"

"All we want is to be free."

"Free to do what? Plot an uprising?"

"Your armies are the ones plotting war." Aaron raised his chin and pushed his chest forward. "I know what you're going to do at Jerusalem—destroy the entire city until there's not one stone standing on another."

Tobit lowered his aim. "Did the olive oil merchant tell you that nonsense?"

"He's more than a merchant, sir. He's a prophet."

Tobit laid the bow across his saddle and said, "Take these people prisoner."

Twenty Babylonian cavalrymen spurred out from the cover of outcrops and ridges spread across the leeward face of the mountain. The first soldiers to reach them led away their horses, and the others surrounded them.

Tobit said, "Feed them before the light of day is gone and prepare a watch to look after them while they sleep. All of them but this one." He pointed at Aaron. "Tie the blacksmith up and put him in front of a hot fire, away from the others. He doesn't eat, he doesn't sleep, he doesn't speak with anyone until I interrogate him further."

The soldiers bound Aaron's hands behind his back and Sophia was helpless to do anything but stand in the protecting graces of her husband and Setti and watch the Babylonians march Aaron off over beyond a run of sandstone, cursing him and pushing his long, slow stride along by the tip of their swords. Sophia took Yaush by the hand, both of them watching long after the soldiers forced Aaron around the outcrop, out of sight.

What was to become of them?

CHAPTER 36

"Curse the olive oil merchant!"

The cry of Captain Laban's oath was lost among the roar of waves and he reined deeper into the rocky shoal, following the last prints of Lehi's trail through large rocks fallen from the sheer walls of the Borders nearer the Red Sea, the surf crashing against the base of the mountains and the spray misting across his face. Impossible, this was simply impossible. Lehi couldn't disappear into the sea like this. The footprints he tracked from Haql ended where the waves washed over the last narrow strand of beach, the marks of six riders and twenty camels trailing off into the surf. It was an eerie sight, like the footprints left on the shores of the Red Sea after the children of Israel had gone through on dry ground and the parted waters fell back in on the chariots and cavalrymen of Pharaoh's army. Laban spit into the surf, the spittle mixing with the white foam and washing back out to sea. This wasn't a second parting of the Red Sea and Laban spit again, the breeze catching the spittle and driving it down into the prints of Lehi's horse. The man didn't vanish into the water with his family, no matter how much Lehi wanted Laban to believe he had the mystical powers of Moses. Curse him! He was a man, not a prophet, and he had as much power to part the Red Sea as Laban had to fly. What a fool he was to think Lehi might have ventured into these waters with his animals. They couldn't swim around these mountain borders with the sheer cliffs dropping directly into the sea. Lehi was taunting him, daring him to find him— and he *would* find the man. Moses may have eluded Pharaoh along these shores, but Lehi was not Moses and Laban was not fool enough to go in after him and suffer the same fate as Pharaoh.

Laban turned down along the beach toward where the Borders pushed into the sea, the mountains rising out of the shoreline like the immovable stone wall of a city barring passage down the coast. Lehi didn't travel that way, no matter that the camel tracks led off into the sea. There was no trail Lehi could travel along the shore, no flat land for the camels to get their footing, nothing but the surf crashing against the base of these mountains, and it was impossible to think he'd escaped down along the shores of the Fountain of the Red Sea. The hypnotizing rhythm of the waves slowed Laban's stride along the shoreline and he pulled up, his thoughts lost in the sound of the waves, his mind wandering over the possibility that Lehi could have found a way down along the coastal mountains to some alcove or beach farther down the shore where—

Stop it! Laban rubbed his thin line of beard between his thumb and forefinger and started pacing through the sand again. Lehi didn't travel down along these coastal mountains. There was nothing but water pushing against these steep walls of rock, and he was a fool to think Lehi could have taken his caravan that way. Camels didn't swim.

This had to be another of Lehi's tricks. Laban mounted his horse and reined out into the surf, his steed striding knee-high against the waves before coming around and backtracking through the water, past his cavalrymen waiting for orders. Lieutenant Daniel and Shechem followed on dry ground, staying with Laban's run through the water, his Arabian heading back toward Haql, his gaze scanning the beach for any sign that Lehi backtracked through the surf before coming out and heading inland into the maze of dead-end canyons, narrow wadis, and steep-walled gorges that snaked through the foothills of these Borders nearer the Red Sea.

It wouldn't be the first time the olive oil merchant tried to hide his tracks in the sea, and Laban spurred farther north where the beach opened onto a wide coastal plain, his horse kicking up a spray. Lehi had to come out of the sea along here somewhere, but there was no sign the man hid his track under the surf. There were no subtle markings in the sand, nothing like what Tobit found at Haql. Where was the inspector when he needed a good eye to decipher the secrets left in the sand and find Lehi's lost trail?

Laban got down from the saddle and knelt in the surf, the water washing over him and soaking his tunic. He felt along the bottom, searching for the deep footprints of camels the same way Tobit searched for them at Qumran along the shores of the Dead Sea. But the sand was unstable here, without any of the mud that covered the bottom of the Dead Sea to hold the imprint of camels and horses against the surf. Another wave washed over Laban, spraying water up his nose, but he shook his head and kept his hands moving over the bottom. The surf was strong here without any calm waters to preserve the tracks and it washed over him again, the sand rushing from beneath his hands. He'd lost the trail and he stood in the surf, his gaze turned toward the foothills. Lehi was up in those narrow gorges hiding—he had to be—and Laban was going to root him out. He mounted his Arabian, spurred out of the surf, up the beach past his men and along the base of towering mountains to where they gave way to the first narrow canyon, the opening hardly wide enough for two horses to ride side-by-side. The sandstone walls of the wadi was worn smooth by the flood of summer monsoons, and Laban turned up into the twisting maze, the rock partition rising quickly around him and sealing off the orange light of late afternoon. The soft white sand under hoof made travel easy for camels and there were no steep inclines to keep a caravan from heading deep into this mountain, but when Laban reined around the next turn, the trail turned up a sharp incline and the sandy ground gave way to rock before ending in a steep wall. Curse Lehi! Where did the man go with his caravan? He didn't disappear into the sea and he couldn't fly over these cliffs through these Borders nearer the Red Sea to the trade route on the other side—not past these high rock walls. And that's what every wadi and ravine in these parts was like, a thousand twisting, turning gorges, leading nowhere.

Laban reined back down the wadi and out onto the beach, spurring farther inland along the base of the mountains to the next wadi. His cavalrymen followed him, and when Lieutenant Daniel came alongside and asked if he should order the men to help in the search, Laban spurred away without answering. He was responsible for losing Lehi's trail and he was going to find it. He turned past the entrance of a wider gorge, leaving his men behind. Steep sandstone walls rose higher around each turn in the narrow canyon, the wadi running deep into the belly of this mountain range. He kept his horse galloping around another turn and still another, the sandy trail slowly turning steeper and the sand giving way to some rocks, but not so many that a caravan of camels couldn't travel this way. He kept his horse running, the orange light of dusk reflecting off the rim above him and the shadows of evening darkening the lower reaches of this canyon. He wound through three more turns and when he came to the next, the wadi forked into three canyons, each of them winding off into a new direction with high walls and a narrow opening hardly wide enough for his horse. Lehi could have gotten his camels through the tight-fitting passage, but there was no telling if these wadis split into more gorges deeper in these mountains or ended in a cliff of sandstone farther up the trail. These were the foothills where men lost themselves in the maze of canyons that ran through these Borders nearer the Red Sea, and he was a fool to think he could find Lehi without the help of his men. Laban spurred back down the narrow gorge and came out onto the beach to find Lieutenant Daniel, Shechem, and his fifty cavalrymen waiting at the wadi entrance.

Daniel said, "Should we mount a search party, sir?"

"No searches, son. Not in these foothills." Laban steered his Arabian out onto the beach, away from the base of the mountains before coming around and studying the Borders nearer the Red Sea. There were hundreds of narrow wadi inlets and gorges opening onto this shoreline, some only a few hundred cubits long and others winding for miles up into these mountains. Lehi was lost in these twisted canyon foothills, hiding in a rock-walled coffin from whence no traveler could return.

Daniel came alongside. "Should I post a watch along the base of the foothills?"

"Tell the men we're headed home." Captain Laban turned his Arabian north, up along the coastline. "I have to see to an accountant in Jerusalem."

CHAPTER 37

Aaron forced his head down, his cap of dark brown hair shielding him from the flames. He sat perched on a boulder, the heat rising off the campfire like ripples on a pond, bending the air and blurring his vision. Sweat streamed off the end of his nose, but, with his mouth gagged by a dirty length of linen, he couldn't complain to his captors. The fire was as hot as an open hearth, but this wasn't the familiar confines of his father's smithy in Jerusalem where he could set aside the forging hammer and ladle a cup of cool water over his head. He was a prisoner, with three Babylonian soldiers keeping vigil over him from their post in the shadows.

The captain of the night watch marched over and added three long pieces of nag wood to the fire, stoking the flames higher while his first lieutenant threw on an armful of brown mountain grasses, the dry fuel shooting orange sparks into the air. The soldiers forced Aaron to stay on this perch long after the others retired. They whistled every time his head nodded off and clapped their hands whenever he closed his eyes.

Aaron shook the sweat from the end of his chin. Why did he ever smith a bow of steel? The weapon was to blame for Inspector Tobit's interest in him and there was little he could do to convince the man he and his friends weren't a threat to his rule over these territories. Aaron worked the linen gag between his teeth, gnawing a small hole in the cloth. If he could only get it out of his mouth and speak some sense to these men, convince them he wasn't a renegade—none of them were renegades. He managed to finally cut through the gag, the cloth hanging from his mouth, when he spied Inspector Tobit sitting on the other side of the fire, his blue-eyed gaze peering back at him through the flames. How did he get there without Aaron's seeing? He let the gag fall from his lips and said, "Why are you treating me like this?"

"I would think a blacksmith would enjoy sleeping beside the heat of a fire."

"I'm a steelmaker, sir." Aaron spit the taste of the gag from his mouth. "I work beside a smelting oven; I don't sleep beside it."

Tobit ordered the night watch away and he waited until the last soldier turned out of sight beyond the ridge before coming around the fire with the steel bow over his shoulder and a number of leather scrolls stuffed under his arm. He sat next to Aaron, propped the bow against the rock between them and unrolled the scrolls, spreading them out before the brightness of the firelight.

Aaron said, "What are those?"

"I was hoping you could tell me that."

Aaron leaned over to get a better view of the documents, the parchment filled with familiar pen strokes. It was Lehi's journal, the same parchments Laman left in the sands at Qumran, the ones revealing their plans to escape to Bozrah, but they were more than a log detailing their flight into this wilderness. These scrolls contained Lehi's most personal moments and there had to be some evidence, some phrase in Lehi's own hand to prove they were not renegades. The first entry dated back many months, detailing the trial of Uriah when Lehi accused Captain Laban and Zadock of plotting the murder of King Zedekiah.

Aaron brought his gaze up from reading. "That's exactly how it was. I heard the testimony against these men, sir."

"You heard wrong, boy."

"I was there, in the king's court when—"

"You don't really think I'm going to believe you when King Zedekiah still trusts these men. They work for the man; they're his closest advisers." Tobit set aside the first scroll and went on to the next. It was difficult for Aaron to lean over with his hands and feet bound together, and he inched down along the rock, close enough to see over the Inspector's shoulder. The second scroll began with a line explaining that these were the words given to Lehi by God, and it detailed the starvation and slaughter of the Jews at Jerusalem followed by the destruction of the capital city and the deportation of thousands of Hebrew slaves to Babylon.

"Your friend Lehi is a troublemaker." Tobit tapped his fingers against the parchment. "He uses these stories to incite rebellion."

"A rebel wouldn't be headed deeper into the wilderness."

"That's exactly where he'd go to plot an uprising."

"He's only seeking his own safety. That's all any of us want in this wilderness. To be left in peace."

"I can't allow that, not after finding out what I know about Lehi."

"You'll never catch him. He knows this land better than any caravaneer."

"Is that why the man rode into a trap this morning down along the coast?"

"He knows a way out."

"You should stop hoping for a miracle son, and tell me the details of your plotting against the kingdom. Lehi will never escape beyond the coastline. Captain Laban will have captured the man by now."

"No he won't. There's a . . ." Aaron lowered his head. He couldn't tell Inspector Tobit about Lehi's dream of a trail leading through the belly of the Borders nearer the Red Sea.

Tobit said, "I know the legends, son. There are no secret trails through the mountains south of here and if Lehi tries to find a passage, he'll be marching into a sandstone sepulchre."

Aaron said, "Lehi's gone from these territories and he's never coming back."

"If Lehi never returns, then he's dead—lost in the wadis of these Borders." Tobit stopped his finger on the last line of the document. "Don't you see? These are the words of a renegade. Lehi's fooled you into believing him and he brought you into these deserts to fashion bows of steel and outfit an army for his uprising."

"There's more. There's got to be more to prove otherwise." Aaron tried to reach for the scrolls but the leather cords held him back, the tight bindings digging into his wrists. Foolish cords! If he could only be rid of these bindings and examine the scrolls, study them, find an explanation for what Lehi meant when he wrote that Jerusalem was to be destroyed, then he'd prove to Tobit that . . .

The cords tying Aaron's wrists fell away, cut by Tobit's sharp knife. The Inspector returned the blade to the leather holster on his belt and handed over the scrolls. "Go ahead boy; show me what you want to show me."

Aaron rubbed the pain out of his wrists before taking the scroll in his hands and letting his gaze stray between Tobit's dagger and the steel bow before coming back to read Lehi's carefully penned words. This document was far too personal an account for Lehi to have shared it with Aaron and he glanced down over the edge of the parchment to the dagger half-hidden below the level of the leather scroll, the arm of the bow nestled in next to it. It was simpler to escape than to try and prove Lehi's innocence, but he had to try a peaceful solution before risking an escape to save his friends, and he hurried his finger over the scroll down to the middle section where Lehi recorded his vision received at Raphia on the cliffs above the shores of the Great Sea. He said, "You see, it says right here. Lehi's a prophet, not a renegade."

Tobit inched in close enough so Aaron could feel the man's dagger press against his side. Tobit said, "This man's prophecies and visions aren't anything more than a lie to get you to follow him."

"I was there, sir."

Tobit said, "Did you see the same vision Lehi saw?"

"I was there when he first told of it."

"Don't you understand, boy? It isn't possible to know if Lehi or any other man is called by God."

Aaron turned his gaze to his bound feet, the ones Lehi healed by the power of heaven. There was nothing he could show Tobit to prove Lehi was a prophet. There were no documents he could read beyond the testimony of Lehi recorded in these parchments. There were no witnesses he could call, and the unscarred, unblemished skin of his feet would never convince Tobit that Lehi had power to heal. Aaron rolled the parchment back into a scroll and handed it to Tobit, the loose leather ends brushing over the man's dagger and touching the upper arm of the steel bow. If the Inspector could only experience what Aaron had experienced. If he could only hear Lehi speak the words of life and salvation and let them penetrate to the very center of his soul. If he could see the power of heaven bestowed on a humble olive oil merchant. If this Babylonian officer could be still for one moment and know that God was God, then he could come to know that Lehi was a servant of the Almighty the way Aaron knew it. But all Tobit wanted was a thousand steel bows to outfit his army, and Aaron glanced at the weapons set between them, the firelight dancing off the polished metal arms of the bow and casting across the dagger. Escape was his only recourse and he turned his gaze back toward the fire. The flames had weakened, the nag wood was nothing more than hot coals. Aaron could free himself with Tobit's knife, silence the man with the threat of death, and escape with his friends in the dark of . . .

The cords binding Aaron's feet together fell away from his ankles and Aaron turned his gaze down to find Tobit kneeling beside him, cutting him free. He pointed the tip of his dagger at Aaron and said, "You can run off if you like, but if you're still here come morning, I'll know what you say is true."

Aaron rubbed the pain out of his ankles and watched Tobit start around the outcrop, but before he disappeared beyond the reach of the firelight Aaron said, "I know Lehi's a prophet the same way I know God is God."

Tobit turned around, the firelight dying across his face. "What was that, son?"

Aaron said, "I'll be here come morning, sir."

CHAPTER 38

Inspector Tobit tucked the end of a blanket under his chin and turned on his side to steal another moment of rest before dawn broke across this mountain summit. The rocky ground troubled his back during the night and the fatigue of the forced march from Aqaba lingered in his bones. Tobit's horse grunted in the early-morning shadows, telling him she was tired of their long trek, and he pulled the blanket up around his ears and turned on his side. One more day, girl. That's all that remained of their journey into this wilderness. One more day to get these prisoners down out of the Borders near the Red Sea, meet up with Captain Laban where the Borders nearer the Red Sea pushed into the coastal waters, and then this hunt was over. It took them two days from Aqaba to find these prisoners, and all he needed was a third day to meet Captain Laban along the coast of the Fountain of the Red Sea and start these renegades back to a prison cell in Jericho. Tobit closed his eyes, shutting out a view of the sandstone outcrop where last night he left Aaron.

Tobit sat up and peered through the soft, gray light of early morning. The blacksmith wasn't sleeping with the other prisoners—there were only seven bodies lying still on the ground under close guard. Tobit threw off the blanket, pulled on his boots, and cinched his dagger in place around his waist before marching down the rise, past the sleeping soldiers, beyond the prisoners, and in behind the outcrop where he left the campfire to burn down to . . .

Curse the boy! Aaron was gone, run off in the night. Tobit paced in front of the fire pit, his head down and his boots kicking through the sand. He never should have indulged his petty interests in the boy's claims of Lehi's prophethood, no matter how powerful the still small voice that begged him to believe. Tobit's allegiance was to the king of Babylon, not the pious words of a young blacksmith. He stopped his pacing and stood beside the ring of cold rocks surrounding the fire pit. There was not another blacksmith in the entire world with power to smith bows of steel, and Tobit had let him escape because of a personal need to coddle his religious curiosity.

The leather cords Tobit cut away from Aaron's hands and feet lay on the ground beside the fire pit, exactly where they fell last night. A line of footprints led over the sandy ground away from the cold ashes of this dead fire, and Tobit followed them up a steep, sand-covered ledge to the ridge above camp, past some dead brown grasses growing in a rocky crag and around a large boulder opening onto a view of . . .

Aaron? The blacksmith sat at the top of a ridge that spanned the distance between the Borders near the Red Sea and the coastal range of Borders nearer the Red Sea. Thankfully, Aaron couldn't escape down the ridge. Impassable narrow canyons and deep wadis ran down along the north side of the ridge, and steep rock walls on the south side blocked any flight deeper into the Borders nearer the Red Sea. Aaron was trapped here, without another way down off this mountain except north toward Haql on the Aqaba Branch. The ridge ran a good five miles due west, traversing the south rim of the coastal plain all the way to the Borders nearer the Red Sea, their majestic peaks and towering rock walls rising out of the coast, down where Captain Laban was sure to have trapped Lehi.

Tobit quietly stepped in behind the blacksmith, careful to walk lightly and keep from alerting the boy to his approach. He crept in behind Aaron and reached for—

"Lehi's out there somewhere." Aaron turned his deep, penetrating brown-eyed gaze onto Tobit, the boy's sandy brown hair falling in thatches over his brow, and Tobit quickly lowered his hands. Aaron wasn't going to run away, not down this ridge. Aaron spoke with a soft voice, like a man mourning the loss of a friend, and his eyes were red, the stinging rash of tears lingering about the corners of his eyes. He brushed his cheeks with the back of his hand to hide the depth of his loss and said, "I stayed the night for you, sir." He turned back toward the view of the ridges and canyons below and said, "You need to know what I know about the prophet Lehi."

"Son." Tobit inched down along the ledge closer to Aaron. How could he tell the boy that Lehi was likely dead at the hands of Captain Laban? He said, "There's something you should know about your friend."

"Lehi escaped, I know that now." Aaron pointed to the coastal mountains in the distance. "He fled into the Borders nearer the Red Sea."

"Listen to me." A breeze filtered up from the coast, lifting Tobit's hair off his brow. "Your friend can't get up into these mountains. The foothills are impassable."

"He found a way. I'm sure of it."

"Your friend rode into a trap." Tobit laid his hand on Aaron's shoulder. "Captain Laban snared him down where the coastal mountains rise out of the shoreline."

"You don't believe me, do you? You don't think Lehi's a prophet."

"What I believe isn't important."

First light broke across the ridge, casting a red glow over the blacksmith, the brightness forcing Aaron to turn his eyes away from Tobit—away from what Tobit was saying. There were no clouds in the west, no thunderheads rolling over the Sinai Peninsula from Egypt and out over the Fountain of the Red Sea, but with the sky taking on such a strong blood-red hue there was sure to be a storm today as terrible as the tempest of telling Aaron that Lehi could be dead.

Aaron said, "Lehi knows a way through the foothills. He's seen it."

"What?" Tobit fell to his knees next to Aaron. "You never told me Lehi traveled this country before."

"I'm telling you now—the man's seen this place. He knows of a large, spacious field in the belly of these mountains. There's a river running beside a date palm and—"

"Look at me." Tobit took Aaron by the arm and stood him on the ledge, his tall, thin frame reaching a full hand above Tobit's head. "Your friend is either lost in a narrow canyon down along the coast or . . ."

"Or what?"

"I'm sorry, son. Your friend Lehi may not have survived the night." Tobit lowered his voice. "I gave Captain Laban and his men permission to kill him on sight."

"No." Aaron shook his head and backed away a step, the edge of the cliff stopping his retreat. "God wouldn't bring Lehi into this desert to die. He escaped to a place where no one can find him. Not you, not Captain Laban, no one. God is leading him through these mountains."

Tobit pulled Aaron away from the edge of the cliff before his passion unbalanced him. "You really believe that, don't you?"

Aaron lifted his hands and let the early-morning light shine over his wrists—the skin swollen from the cords that had bound him last night. "If I didn't believe Lehi was a prophet, sir, I'd be gone from this place."

Tobit worked his lower lip between his teeth. Was it really possible for God to speak to Lehi? The deities of Babylon were chiseled of stone, or lost in a mysterious cloud of smoke rising from the incense burners of a holy man. God was a figment of imagination conjured by zealots, and a lifeless being of stone and smoke didn't have power to lead Lehi through this wilderness without a map. Tobit ran his fingers through his hair. Why couldn't he let go of the battle raging deep in his soul? His duty was to take these renegades back to a prison cell in Jericho, not listen to the words of this young blacksmith. God couldn't speak with Lehi or any man, not unless . . .

"Darius!" Tobit turned toward camp, his hand cupped to his mouth. "The map, son, bring your map!"

Darius sat up in the sand, his father's voice spoiling the last moments of a poor night's rest. What was Tobit doing on the cliff above camp, asking to see the map? Darius grabbed the leather satchel he used for a pillow and climbed to the plateau, stuffing the end of his tunic under his kilt and retrieving the map from inside the pouch.

Tobit met him on the ridgetop, pointed to the distant peaks rising along the shores of the Red Sea and said, "Tell me what you know about the way through those mountains."

"There isn't much to tell, sir." Darius held his map up to the morning light for Tobit to see the detail he added last night. The parchment still held the smell of ink, and his bold strokes marked the switchbacks leading up the Aqaba Branch to this summit. But farther south of this ridge, the parchment was empty. They simply didn't know anything about the lands down between the Borders near the Red Sea and the Borders nearer the Red Sea, and without making the precarious descent down this ridge, it was impossible to know exactly what lay hidden deep within the belly of these Borders.

Darius said, "You're not taking us down this ridge, are you?"

"Take another look, son. You've seen lands like this before." Tobit turned Darius around by the shoulder, directing his gaze over the mountain terrain below. "Could there be a valley in those Borders, or possibly a large field?"

"A field, sir?"

"That's right. Some arable land where a man could cultivate, say, a date palm?"

"It takes a river to grow a tree." Darius shook his head. "You know that. You've seen the groves near Jericho. The Jordan river flows through there, but in this wilderness, well . . ."

"There's a river in these mountains." Aaron stepped in close between them. "A river that runs all year round."

"Not in these Borders." Darius stepped back from Aaron's words. "Maybe some seasonal flows from a summer monsoon." He glanced up into the western sky, the sunrise painting the horizon in a deep red glow. "We may get one later today, but beyond that, there are no rivers of water in this territory. It's too hot and dry in this country."

Aaron took the map from Darius and quickly ran the tip of his finger down to the uncharted portion. "There's a grove of date palms in the Borders nearer the Red Sea. And a spacious field with a river running through it."

Tobit said, "Exactly where did Lehi say he'd seen a river in these mountains?"

"He didn't exactly see it with his eyes, sir."

"What are you talking about? How else does a man see this territory?"

"It was a dream. Lehi is following a dream into these mountains."

"Give me that." Darius snatched the map out of Aaron's hands. "You can't find your way through these mountains on a dream." He rolled the parchment back into his satchel. "You need a map plotted by an experienced mapmaker or you'll never return from this place alive." He strapped the leather pouch over his shoulder. "Your friend is a dead man if he thinks he can flee from us without a map of these territories."

"You didn't chase Lehi into this wilderness." Aaron turned back to look out over the distant mountains. "God led him here, and if there's a river in this high place or a fountain in the midst of these valleys where you say there is no valley, then Lehi is the prophet I'm telling you he is."

Darius said, "Don't be a fool."

"That's enough, son." Tobit took Darius by the arm and said, "Prepare the men to ride."

"I'll tell them we're headed back down the Aqaba Branch to Haql."

"Tell them we're heading into a mirage."

"A mirage, sir?"

"That's right." Tobit stepped in next to Aaron and together they scanned the uncharted lands down between the Borders. He said, "We're riding into the valley of Lehi's dreams."

CHAPTER 39

Tobit led the cavalrymen and prisoners down a steep incline and out onto a level plateau. They were an odd company of travelers traversing the ridges high above the coastal plain like mountain goats finding their way among the arid cliffs. The Border Mountains along the coast grew larger past each turn in this trail, their two-thousand-foot peaks rising out of the blue waters of the Fountain of the Red Sea and dominating the horizon like mighty sentinels, guarding within their bulwark of stone Lehi's hidden valley of dreams. These ridges were the dividing line, the height Lehi had to cross if he were to get up through the foothills from the coastal plain and venture in behind the Borders nearer the Red Sea to a secret, unknown river of . . .

What was he thinking? There was no river in this desert and if Lehi found one in the Borders nearer the Red Sea, then Tobit's interest in this man was more than a curiosity—it was a serious matter for his soul.

Darius rode past Tobit before reining in along the north edge of the ridge, guiding his horse with his knees and working his pen over the leather map. The boy was a cautious lad, but with his mapmaking he was nothing but foolhardy. Tobit spurred after him, but before he could warn the boy to stay back from the crumbling edge of sandstone and risk falling into the twisting maze of canyons below, Darius said, "We're fools if we believe the blacksmith." He steered his horse farther down along the cliff edge. "Lehi needs a map to navigate this wilderness, not a dream." He raised his pen from the parchment. "Beyond the map I'm creating here, there isn't another one charting this wilderness."

"Lehi's a caravaneer. He could remember the lay of the land, son."

"There are no landmarks in this wilderness." Darius pointed out over the hundreds of the narrow canyons twisting in every direction below the ridge. "You'd need an angel from heaven dressed in white to lead you through a wilderness like this, no matter how many times you traveled it."

Tobit nodded. "That may well be how Lehi got through, son."

"You don't mean that." Darius inched his mount closer to Tobit. "You don't really believe the blacksmith's stories about Lehi's dream, do you?"

"I'll believe whatever I see."

Darius tipped his head over the ridge, past the foothill wadis over to where the Borders nearer the Red Sea pushed into the coastline. "Captain Laban already captured the olive oil merchant down that way."

"Make your maps, son, and let me decide where to lead this company." Tobit reined forward, picking his way over the uneven brown rock of this high mountain traverse.

"You can't let the blacksmith influence you like this." Darius spurred alongside him. "We should be headed back to the coast to meet Captain Laban."

Tobit swung around to inspect the company following them down the ridge, the line of horses strung out along the slope. Aaron rode near the front of the cavalry with five soldiers escorting him while the rest of the prisoners—Josiah the Potter and Rebecca, the boat builder Hagoth and his son Moriah, Commander Yaush with his wife Sophia and their son Setti—rode under close guard in the middle of the cavalry, each one flanked by two of the regiments finest swordsmen.

Tobit came back around and started his horse slowly traversing a steep rise along the ridge. "If we find Lehi's river in these mountains, I want a detailed map of how to get to it."

Darius rode behind Tobit up the rise and out onto a level stretch. "Then you believe the blacksmith?"

"You make your maps and I'll do the rest."

"I can't map a dream." Darius spurred past Tobit. He disappeared around a run of rocks further down the trial and Tobit let him go.

The boy had drawings to make, distances to chart and as long as he didn't meddle in Tobit's harmless decision to explore these mountains, he wasn't going to tell Darius how to make his maps. The sun rose up into the midday sky, but they were shielded from the hot rays of afternoon by an uncommon cover of clouds dragging across the horizon ahead of the coming storm. If Lehi was lucky enough to find a way up onto these mountain ridges he couldn't travel in behind the Borders nearer the Red Sea. The south side of these ridges were nothing but sheer walls of rock without any opening leading down behind the Borders—there was no belly inside these mountains, no open valley, no wide spacious field with a river running beside a . . .

For the love of heaven! The rocky cliffs blocking the way south gave way to a u-shaped valley and Tobit pulled up along the rim, his horse pawing at the sandy slope. The valley ran in behind the coastal mountains as far as Tobit could see. It was nearly a mile wide, like a large field spacious enough to capture the moisture from the summer monsoons and winter rainwater. A thick layer of sand covered the valley floor reaching to just below this ridge, and it was deep enough to insulate the groundwater from drying in the insufferable heat of this desert wilderness. There were no date groves with lush green foliage growing on the valley floor, but hidden from sight at the end of this valley, down where it leveled off to a flat plain, there could be a spring, some sort of seasonal run-off, or possibly an oasis with a stagnant pool—not a river, but at least some fresh water to support a tree.

Aaron broke free from his escort of soldiers and reined in beside Tobit. The lieutenant of the first company ordered him back, but Tobit waved the officer off and let the blacksmith come alongside to the see down into this sand-filled wadi.

Aaron said, "This is it, sir. Just like Lehi told me."

"There's no vegetation, son. No date palms." Tobit turned in the saddle. "Where is the river your friend Lehi was so certain he'd find in this desert?"

"It could be down there, somewhere."

"We can't go any deeper into these mountains." Tobit slowly shook his head. "Not without some evidence that Lehi found his way up onto this ridge and down into—"

"Over here!"

Darius called from the other side of the ridge, and Tobit and Aaron spurred over at full gallop, the cavalry pulling into rank behind them. The boy stood beside his horse and worked his pen over the map, the tip of his stylus furiously drawing the outline of a narrow wadi coming up onto the ridge from the coastal plain below. It rose out of the foothills like a conduit rising into heaven, coming out of the maze of sandstone wadis and onto this height above the sea. The ground was without any rocks to impede the soft cloven hooves of camels, and running up the middle of the wadi there were—

"Camel tracks, sir." Darius pointed his pen at the ground. "Twenty of them by my count and six horses."

Tobit came around beside the impressions and leaned over the saddle. The ends of Tobit's turban lifted around his eyes and he pushed the cloth aside from his studies. The tracks were in perfect condition. Not even the stiffening breeze of the coming monsoon altered the grains of sand in the cloven prints. Tobit swung around in a circle, his gaze searching the ridge for any sign of a caravan. If Lehi made it this far, there had to be some sign of his passing, but this ridge was nothing but solid sandstone, the camel tracks disappearing where the wadi reached up onto the ridge like the end of a dream at morning. Somehow that fool Lehi found a way up through these wadis from the coast and onto this ridge, but there was no telling where he went once he reached this height.

Tobit spurred down into the wadi and Aaron and Darius followed him, their horses galloping around the first sharp bend in the trail, down into the cool reserves of this deep canyon leading them back toward the coast. They rode past three more twisting turns, the high rock walls rising above them and the camel tracks leading them deeper into the foothills before pulling up at a fork in the trail. Three wadis no wider than the width of a pair of camels split off from the one bearing Lehi's tracks. How did the olive oil merchant ever find his way through this maze with so many paths begging for him to follow?

Tobit leaned over the saddle to Darius and said, "This is where you'd need your angel, son."

Aaron said, "That's what Lehi said, sir."

Darius inched his horse back next to Aaron. "What are you talking about?"

"There was an angel in Lehi's dream." Aaron reined down past the fork in the trail and when he came around he said, "When Lehi reached this dark and dreary wilderness there was a man standing before him dressed in a white robe, telling him to follow him through." He sidled in between Tobit and Darius, the canyon walls towering above them, shielding the light of day and leaving them in the dark, cool shadows, deep in these foothills. The blacksmith spoke quickly, telling them what Lehi's dream said of this place—that Lehi traveled for many hours in darkness until he was overcome with the fear of being lost and he prayed to the Lord that He would have mercy on him according to the multitude of His tender mercies.

Aaron said, "An angel led Lehi through this maze of canyons or he'd not have found his way to the—"

"An angel? How can you believe such foolishness?" Darius stuffed his map and pen into the satchel. "Lehi will need a good deal more than an angel if he thinks he can find a river in this desert." Darius swung around, spurring his horse up the wadi toward the ridge and Aaron and Tobit followed him, back to where the camel tracks disappeared onto the rocky plateaus above the foothills.

Darius said, "Why don't you show us where the angel took Lehi from here?"

"That way." Aaron pointed to the south side of the ridge, over where the u-shaped valley led in behind the Borders nearer the Red Sea.

Tobit was first across the ridge. He slowly cantered along the rim of the valley, but there was no sign a caravan had descended the gentle decline down into this basin of sand, not until . . .

Mercy! A line of tracks appeared on the slope where the bedrock met the sandy walls of the valley and Tobit waved Aaron and Darius over. "Look at this."

Darius got down from his horse and examined the camel tracks. "They're from the same animals that came up out of the wadi, sir." He dusted his fingers clean before getting out his parchment and pen. "Lehi must have traveled this wilderness before."

Aaron said, "It was a dream that led him here."

Darius stabbed the tip of his pen at Aaron. "You're a fool."

"That's enough." Tobit reined in front of his son.

Darius said, "There must be some other way for the olive oil merchant to know the secret trails through these mountains."

Aaron said, "Lehi doesn't keep any secrets."

Darius pushed aside the muzzle of Tobit's horse and came around next to Aaron. He peered up at the blacksmith sitting back in the saddle of his white Arabian. "Why do you believe the man's lies?"

Tobit said, "No more, son. Leave the boy alone."

"Father, you can't let him go on like this. Lehi was a merchant trader, he could have traveled this route a good many times over the years."

"You're wrong." Aaron straightened in the saddle. "Lehi would never come this way unless God led him here." He turned his gaze down over the wadi stretching south, in behind the coastal mountains. "There's no one in this wilderness to buy his olive oil."

Tobit started his horse slowly down the slope of the U-shaped valley. He said, "We'll settle this at the other end of this wadi, down where the ground water comes above the sand."

Tobit ran his horse at a good clip, following the camel tracks and leading the company of soldiers and prisoners deeper into the wadi. They traveled due south for a long stretch before the valley forked. The camel tracks stayed in the wadi closer to the coastal mountains and Tobit followed their path, his gaze moving quickly across the valley from one slope to the other, searching for any sign that Lehi disguised his tracks and climbed out of this wadi and into another.

The sun hung just above the peaks and ridges of the Borders separating them from the sea, the withering afternoon rays softened by dark clouds streaming over from the coast on a stiff breeze, the whisper of rain falling from the sky like the spray off the surf. They couldn't see the coming storm down in this valley, but there had to be one brewing on the coast with the first drops of rain cooling the hot sands of this desert floor. Tobit spurred his horse faster, following Lehi's trail before the summer monsoon washed it away.

The valley floor turned up a gradual sandy crest. It was a gentle incline, hardly noticeable to the eye and if Tobit weren't watching the ground underfoot he would have followed the camel tracks over a gentle divide and into the next wadi without noticing the subtle change in elevation. He got down from the saddle and lay on his stomach, ordering his men to stay back while he closed one eye and sighted up along the valley floor, back where they came from. He was right. The wadi descended for ten, maybe twelve miles before leveling off here. This was the low point and Tobit stayed on his belly, his hands pressed against the sand still hot from a morning in the sun despite the gray clouds and the stiff breeze blowing over from the Fountain of the Red Sea. Where was the vegetation of an oasis clustered around a spring? The underground waters of this long valley should be bubbling above ground here, but there was nothing. The wadi was dry. There was no river, no well, not even a hint of a dried spring where there should be some evidence of water. If this was the valley Lehi saw in his dream with a river running beside a date palm tree, then the man was a foolish dreamer, but he certainly wasn't the prophet Aaron thought him to be, not unless . . .

Tobit spun around on his belly, the buttons of his tunic digging into the sand. He sighted west from here, toward the Border Mountains. The tall peaks stood a mile away, but instead of the sand-covered valley floor rising up to meet the mountains, it sloped ever so slightly toward the Borders nearer the Red Sea. It was a subtle decline, the gradual descent veering toward the coast hardly noticeable from the back of a horse, and if Tobit hadn't gotten down from the saddle he would have led the cavalry up out of this low spot without noticing the turn toward the sea.

Tobit stood and brushed the sand off his front. What about Lehi? The man's trail continued south and Tobit pulled himself back into the saddle and spurred down along the camel tracks until Lehi's trail came around, veering west toward the Borders nearer the Red Sea. Somehow the olive oil merchant found the same change in elevation, the same subtle shift in the valley floor beckoning him back toward the low point in this wadi. Was it possible that back among the rocky ridges of these coastal mountains, beyond what he could see from the middle of this wadi, lay a spring or a well or some sort of underground water rising to the surface?

"Darius, come with me." Tobit veered back to the cavalry and swung around, his mount kicking up a spray of sand. "The rest of you keep watch over the prisoners. If we're not back before sundown, come looking for us."

The sandy way leading toward the Borders nearer the Red Sea narrowed, the outcrops closing in on them, the brown porous sandstone giving way to walls of gray granite—the only place among these mountains where the rock had power to hold back the underground waters and keep them from seeping through to the sea on the other side of these mountains. The granite was an impermeable barrier, damming the underground water from . . .

Mother of Mercy! Tobit reined around a bend, the tall cliffs and peaks of the borders towering over a lush green stand of date palms at the entrance to a secluded valley.

Darius started his pen over the parchment. "I never would have—"

"Quiet, son." Tobit turned his ear to the wind carrying up from these groves to hear the faint sound of voices. He pointed toward the ridge above the valley and motioned for Darius to follow. They reined up a steep incline, onto a rocky ridge above the valley floor, and out onto a butte overlooking the lush green foliage of a valley covered with groves of date palms—the trees as thick and mature as any growing in the Jordan River delta at Jericho. The trees were clustered around twelve springs, the water bubbling up onto the surface, mingling together to form a river that ran toward a tall granite border before disappearing into a narrow chasm in the mountainside.

A caravan master watered twenty camels and six horses, leading them four at a time from a makeshift corral of ropes and over to the lowest spring in the valley. A large camel-hair tent stood on a swell of earth like an estate rising in the wilderness, the many compartments staked high enough off the valley floor to keep safe from floodwaters. On a ridge above the tent a man stood beside an altar of rocks. It was Lehi—it had to be him. He had the same white traveling robe and turban he wore at Aqaba and he tended a skewered lamb cooking over the red-hot coals of a fire while his sons gathered wood from the fallen date-palm groves to fuel his cooking. The smell of tender meat roasting over the heat filtered up onto the ridge and Tobit let his nose savor the aroma. A woman sat on a rock near the altar, one hand braced against the stone and the other over her womb. A light sprinkle of rainwater fell across the valley and Lehi helped the woman with the hood of her robe before returning to the altar to tend to his cooking.

A clap of thunder echoed across the sky, but there was little wind rushing down into this alcove. The towering mountain walls protected this valley from the winds of a summer monsoon as much as they provided Lehi a refuge from the tumult he left behind in Jerusalem. There was no other explanation for Lehi coming to this secret valley hidden in the Borders nearer the Red Sea—Lehi was no renegade.

Darius leaned over the saddle, cradling the map in his arm and starting his pen across the—

"No, son." Tobit took the pen from him.

"You want a good map of this wilderness, don't you?"

"I want the most accurate map you can draw, son, but not of this place. It doesn't exist." Tobit secured the leather parchment beneath his arm. "Let them have their place of refuge."

CHAPTER 40

Lehi cut into the center of the skewered lamb and the tender meat fell away from his blade, a line of fat coursing down the skewer and sizzling over the hot coals. Smoke encircled him before rising into the light rain, the smell trapped from going higher by the light drizzle of an approaching storm. The cooking of this lamb wasn't like any of the peace offerings Lehi prepared at Beit Zayit. There were no maidservants bringing bowls of diced onion and minced garlic to baste over the roast. There were no menservants tending the fire, and there was no butler standing by with a platter to carry the roast to the table with a garnish of basil. Lehi was his own servant in this desert, and the open air of this newfound home was their only dining room.

The altar teetered under the shifting weight of Lehi's cutting and he grabbed the top of the skewer to keep the lamb from sliding to the ground. He never should have trusted this hastily built altar. It was nothing more than a heap of rocks thrown together without mortar and none of them cut to fit like the seamless stone alters built by the seasoned stonemasons at Jerusalem. But he couldn't wait and let their first day in this valley pass without making a peace offering to thank heaven for the blessed vision leading him through the dark and dreary maze of foothills on the coast of the Fountain of the Red Sea, in behind the Borders, and through a large spacious field to this valley with a river of water running beside countless date palms. He'd seen the rise and fall of the trail along the coast and up into these Borders nearer the Red Sea, but it wasn't until they split with their friends at Haql and started down the coast that he understood how carefully

God was guiding them. It was a marvelous dream, but he always awoke before it played to the end, leaving him with the impression there was more to be learned, but this peace offering wasn't a plea to ask for more from heaven. He was thanking God for granting him enough guidance to lead his family to the safety of this valley.

Lehi lifted the morsel of lamb to his mouth and let the meat melt on his tongue before cutting away another slice, skewering it on the point of his knife and raising the food to his—

"That's enough, dear." Sariah climbed the rise and set a basket of freshly gathered dates on the edge of the altar beside the lamb. "Why don't you have some fruit? They'll do you good."

These dates were heaven-sent manna. A daily fare of lamb and water was certain to cripple their health, but with the nourishing goodness of the fruit of these date palms, they could hide in this wilderness forever. How blessed it was to find these groves clustered around twelve springs. Laman had failed to harvest a supply of dates at Jericho and they fled here without a single satchel of the fruit to keep them from returning to . . .

No, it couldn't be. Lehi took a handful of dates from the basket. Laman wouldn't betray his order to harvest dates to force them out of this wilderness, would he? The boy said he didn't collect the dates at Jericho because they were being pursued, and Lehi had no reason not to believe his words, at least not until now.

Laman was a mildly defiant son, but it was his nature to speak his mind. He complained something fierce when Lehi instructed him to harvest a supply of dates at Jericho. He opposed their flight by night around Bozrah to elude Captain Laban's soldiers, he was a stubborn mule at Aqaba when they discussed their flight down the coastal plain, and he was simply out of line to suggest that Lehi give himself over to Captain Laban at Haql. Lehi tightened his grip around the dates. Laman wasn't the most yielding of souls, but he wouldn't risk their lives for a sack of fruit, would he?

Lehi stared at the dates held in his open palm. They weren't more than a few moments picked from the trees, but already the clear, golden white color was fading, replaced by a dark hue in the center. The skin was turning thick and opaque, without the clear, bright translucence of dates fresh from the vine. Was it possible? Could it be that his own son hated him enough to betray him, or was he blaming the boy for nothing?

Lehi returned the dates to the basket. "I've had my fill."

Sariah said, "You didn't eat a single one."

"Tell me what happened at Jericho."

"Go on, dear, eat your dates."

Lehi came around the altar and stood beside her. "Why did Laman leave Jericho without harvesting fruit for our journey?"

"We have plenty now." Sariah sat on a rock near the altar and adjusted the hem of her robe over her feet. "More than enough."

She was avoiding his question the way she always did when her answer would only make things more unpleasant. Lehi said, "Why did Laman—"

"He said he didn't like dates, dear."

"That isn't so. The boy eats bushels of them."

Sariah raised her hand out over the secluded mountain valley, the lush green of the date palms rising against a backdrop of brown rock cliffs. She took Lehi by the hand and sat him down next to her. "Remember when you found Laman and me at the inn north of Bozrah?"

"You said he was growing angrier with every passing day, that he was forgetting God."

"I thought he was, but it may be that Laman never really knew God well enough to keep him from starting down another path." Sariah tightened her grip around Lehi's hand. "He blames you for his lack of faith."

"I've never compelled the boy to believe anything." Lehi pulled his hand free. "I've taught him well."

"You forced him into this desert."

"Captain Laban and the Elders of the Jews forced us into this wilderness."

"It's your dreams he despises, your reliance on guidance from a God he isn't certain exists." Sariah lowered her head. "There's something wrong deep in Laman's soul and whatever turmoil is troubling him, whatever thing he's done to darken his faith, it's turned him against you."

Lehi stood to the altar, his hands gripping the stones and his face taking the heat of the coals. "Are you saying Laman betrayed me?"

"The boy is confused. He wants to go home."

"He isn't a child any longer. He knows why we came here."

"Then ask him what it is that's gone wrong. Find out why he didn't harvest the dates at Jericho. Maybe you can soften his heart where I failed."

Lehi turned from the altar, cupped his hands to his mouth and called to his sons, telling them to come celebrate their first meal in this valley before the approaching storm dampened their plans and they were forced to take cover inside the confines of a musty tent. Sam marched over with two camels, the animals tethered on a short rope. His duties of Caravan Master weren't ended after a three-day forced march down the coast from Aqaba, and he told Lehi he couldn't stay long—he had to water the herd before nightfall. Nephi finished securing the last tent pole with a double length of rope and placed a stone over the stake to keep it from pulling free of the sandy earth before climbing the rise to the altar, assuring them it could stand against whatever winds the monsoon carried. Laman and Lemuel were the last to head over, the two of them stepping from deep in the date groves with firewood gathered from the fallen branches of the date palms and tied into bundles. There was no reason to gather so much firewood. They wouldn't need it in the morning with so many ripe dates to harvest, and once the storm passed there was sure to be more than enough heat to dry the dead timber. But there Laman stood, holding the bundle of firewood close to his chest like a child holding a newborn lamb, protecting the dry branches from the light sprinkling of rain that fell over them.

The boys quieted around the altar and Lehi peered through the hot coals at Laman, the heat bending the air between them, blurring a good view of his firstborn son. How was he to go about asking Laman if he were a traitor? The question would only anger the boy and with this journey already straining the bond between them, he could only think to offer a silent plea to heaven for wisdom to know what to say.

Laman adjusted his grip on the firewood. "Are we going to eat or not?"

Sariah touched the rock beside her. "Why don't you stack that firewood beside the altar and come sit here with me, son."

"I can hold it until we're finished."

Sariah said, "Now, son. Come and enjoy the—"

"I said, I'll hold the firewood." Laman spoke with enough force that Sariah lowered her head from his words.

Sam said, "You're not making fires anywhere else in this valley. Too much smoke will attract the notice of—"

Laman said, "I'll take care of the firewood."

Lehi gathered his sons close to the altar before lowering his head, the sporadic rain spattering over the coals and mixing with the sound of his soft words of thanks to God for leading them to this valley, but he kept silent the words of another, more private prayer. This was to be a celebration of joy, but deep in his heart he hid the suspicion of Laman's unfaithfulness. Lehi offered aloud his gratitude for the blessing of finding these dates, for the peace of protection this valley provided, and for the joy of arriving safely in this hidden sanctuary amid a hostile wilderness. His words were filled with joy, but his heart was joyless. How could he offer thanks when his mind was muddied by Laman's deceit? Could he ever trust Laman with—?

What was that?

Lehi's head came up and he turned his ear to the growing cry of voices descending down through the date palms and echoing off the canyon walls like the cry of an army heading into war. A company of horses burst past the last cluster of trees, and Lehi recognized the awful white Arabian leading the pack. He stepped in front of Sariah to protect her from whatever evil found them in this valley. How could this be? They traveled into the wilderness to escape the Jews at Jerusalem, but now they'd been found by . . .

Aaron? The blacksmith was the first to pass the stand of date palms—there was no mistaking his long, slight frame leaning forward in the saddle. He guided Beuntahyu over the river, leaping her across the narrow fountain of water with Rebecca splashing beside him, her long, black hair streaming out behind the swift run of her horse. Josiah the Potter spurred down through the grove and out onto the open run of valley, flanked by Moriah and Hagoth on one side and Commander Yaush, Sophia, and Setti on the other—all of them shouting a greeting that echoed through the canyon like the trumpeting of shofar horns on a feast day.

Aaron got down from the saddle, marched past Lehi and around the altar, his shoulders forward and his arm wrapped around five leather scrolls. It was Lehi's diary—the one he'd kept since leaving Jerusalem. How did Aaron come by them? Lehi stowed them on the back of the lead camel the day they fled Qumran and they were sealed safely away, weren't they?

Aaron dropped the scrolls at Laman's feet. "You left these for Captain Laban to find."

Laman said, "Who told you that lie?"

Lemuel stepped alongside his brother. "What matters is that they've been returned. We have Father's scrolls back." He quickly turned his gaze around the circle of fourteen travelers gathering to the altar. "You see, all of father's scrolls are accounted for."

"Keep silent, you fool." Laman spit on the ground in front of Lemuel, his arms still wrapped around the bundles of firewood.

Aaron said, "Captain Laban found these on the shores at Qumran, right where you left them."

Laman said, "Where's Captain Laban?"

"He can't help you now. He's camped up the coast with his men, back where these Border Mountains first push into the sea. He isn't close enough to help you now. He can't find you here."

"Laman?" Lehi came around the altar, picked the scrolls off the ground, and unrolled the first one, his careful pen strokes filling the leather with the sacred accounts of his prophethood. He pressed the parchments to his chest and slowly shook his head. "Did you . . . ?"

'Tell him, Laman." Sariah reached for her eldest son. "Tell your father why you did what you did."

"I haven't done anything."

Lehi said, "What about the dates at Jericho? Why didn't you harvest any for our journey?"

Sariah said, "Tell your father what you told me at Bozrah, about what angers you so."

Nephi walked around the altar, and the gathering stepped back from his thick-shouldered frame that moved like a priest before a congregation. He leaned his head in next to Laman and said, "Are Father's scrolls the reason Captain Laban and his soldiers were waiting for us at Bozrah?"

"This is foolishness." Laman pushed Nephi aside. "I've not done anything to harm any of—"

"That's a lie." Aaron untied the leather flaps on his saddlebag, revealing the gleaming polished metal of Nephi's steel bow strapped to Beuntahyu's back. He handed the weapon to Nephi and said, "I checked the metal. There aren't any cracks in the steel and the arms still have their spring."

"Where did you . . . ?" Nephi turned the bow in his hands, inspecting its shape, running his fingers over the finish and placing his hand on the grip fitted perfectly to his thick palm. He slowly raised his gaze to Laman and said, "You left this at the crossroads south of Bozrah, didn't you?"

Sariah took Lehi by the hand. There was a look of worry in her eyes, the same concern he'd seen at the inn north of Bozrah—the worry of a mother over her willful children—but this time he didn't dismiss her concerns over Laman as the gruff exterior of a boy learning to become a man. There was something much deeper troubling their firstborn son, something that cankered his soul enough to turn him against them, and Lehi could only pray that the redeeming balm of the Messiah would somehow penetrate his heart. Sariah tightened her grip around Lehi's hand and she whispered for him to do something, anything, to end this peacefully and keep Laman from traveling into forbidden paths. She did not want these accusations to chase off her son, no matter that there was no place for him to run. They'd abandoned their inheritance at Jerusalem to venture into this wilderness, and she lowered her voice to a whisper and softly told Lehi she did not want to count her eldest son among the losses.

"Leave Laman be." Lemuel pointed his long, thin finger at Nephi, the sudden movement dislodging a dead timber from his bundle of firewood. "He was only doing what he thought best."

"Your brother did nothing but harm us at every turn." Aaron reached over and ran his hand along the arm of Nephi's steel bow. "For the love of heaven, Inspector Tobit thinks we're gathering an army to come against him."

"Why, Laman?" Lehi tightened his grip around the scrolls. "Why did you—?"

"Someone had to save us from your foolish dreams." Laman spit at Lehi's feet. "You've become like the other zealots at Jerusalem. You're nothing but *Piqqeah*—a foolish visionary man."

Sariah said, "Son, that's enough. It wasn't a foolish vision that led us to this valley."

Laman stepped back from his parents, his sandals catching on a rock and faltering his stride, but not unbalancing his thick frame. "It's time we forsake this journey and return to enjoy our—"

The sky erupted in thunder before Laman could finish his words. The light sprinkling of warm rain turned to a torrent of cold water soaking Laman's head and dripping off the end of his thinly bearded chin. He wrapped his arms around the stack of wood, angling his shoulders over the timbers to keep the rain from rendering the firewood useless. He leaned his head in close enough that Lehi could feel the warmth of his breath across his face. Laman said, "Captain Laban will finish this."

Lehi stepped close to his son and peered into his bitter dark eyes, a hidden hatred seething just beneath the surface. "Finish what, son?"

Rain streamed down Laman's cheeks and spit off his lips as he spoke. "We'd be better off if you were . . ."

A gust of wind rushed over the peaks and down through the valley, masking Laman's words.

Lehi said, "If I were what?"

Laman pushed out of the circle, and the gathering parted to let him run past. He started down along the river, calling for Lemuel to join him and together they headed toward the cleft in the granite Borders, down where the river disappeared into a narrow chasm, both of them protecting their bundles of firewood from the rain and disappearing into the mountain where the river left the valley.

Lehi scaled down the rise from the altar and started along the narrow riverbank, his hand shielding his eyes from the driving rain. The mountain chasm was no wider than five camels riding side by side, and the river flowed down the middle. Sheer walls of granite rose up either side, the towering chasm cliffs protecting him from the monsoon that raged above. It was quiet here, without the sound of rain or wind and only the babbling of this river flowing deeper into these narrows. Lehi skirted around a large boulder the height of a camel's head and down past a run of pools, the water cascading over the bedrock before it gathered back into a channel in the sand. The narrows veered south onto a long stretch and he spied Laman and Lemuel running toward the far end. He called to them, his voice echoing against the sheer rock walls, begging Laman and Lemuel to come back, but they would not heed his pleading, the two of them disappearing around the bend without looking back. The river veered to the right, spilled over a run of moss-covered rocks and spread out into . . .

The Fountain of the Red Sea? Were they camped this close to the coast without knowing it? The roiling surf crashed against the rocky shoal, and the monsoon winds carried the wet spray across the sand. Rain pelted Lehi with stinging drops and he covered his face before stepping out onto the beach to overlook the deep blue waters gone gray with so much churning. A towering, massive granite mountain wall reached out of the north shoreline like a large, spacious building rising above the alcove and blocking Lehi's view of the way back up the shore to where Captain Laban was camped. The river flowed down from the mouth of the chasm and spread over the beach like the delta waters of the Jordan, and Lehi splashed through it, searching this small beach enclave for his sons. His sandals sunk into the wet sand and the hem of his robe dragged behind his stride. They had to be here somewhere and Lehi pulled up in the middle of the small river delta and turned his gaze over the alcove, the cool river waters running over his feet. Laman and Lemuel couldn't go south with the sea crashing against the shoal, and the way north was blocked by this mammoth mountainside.

The rain eased and in the lull of the storm, gray mists pushed ashore, encircling the base of the twenty-five-hundred-foot granite border, the fog swirling around the mountain like clouds circling a large, spacious building floating in the air above the ground. He called for Laman and Lemuel, but there was no answer. They were gone, disappeared into the tossing, churning waters of the sea—at least that's what it seemed until the last rays of the setting sun found their way through the banks of clouds, casting a dull orange light over Laman and Lemuel climbing the granite face. Bundles of firewood were strapped to their backs and they pulled themselves up one jagged ledge at a time.

"Boys, the storm isn't over." Lehi's voice echoed off the mountain. "Come down and we can settle this."

Laman's voice broke through the sound of the crashing surf, his deep laugh echoing off the mountainside. He pulled himself up onto a ledge and turned around on the narrow precipice, the low-lying rush of mists swirling about him, half hiding his expensive traveling robes—the same costly apparel Lehi had purchased for the boy on his last caravan trip to Egypt. He pointed his finger down at Lehi and laughed again, his howling louder than before, scoffing at Lehi for asking him to come down. He repeated Lehi's words, mocking the offer to work out their differences. He said, "This won't be settled until we go back to Jerusalem."

Lehi splashed closer to the towering rock face, kicking through the river water with each stride. "This mountain will get you no closer to home."

"Is that what your dreams tell you? Or do you only dream of abandoning our inheritance at Jerusalem to perish in this wilderness?" Laman climbed to the next ridge, his laughter mixing with the swirling clouds. "You can't deceive us into believing Jerusalem will be destroyed. I won't let the foolish imaginations of your heart lead us any farther from our wealth."

A flurry of mists passed across the face of the mountain, and when it cleared, Laman was gone, disappeared with the fading of his laugh on the wind. Another bank of fog engulfed this floating mountain of granite and Lehi waited for it to clear, but the mists settled into the alcove, filtering out the last light of the setting sun and casting a dark shadow over the sand.

Lehi fell to his knees, the cool river waters coursing over his legs. He raised his voice loud enough to penetrate the darkness of these evening mists. What had he done to turn his eldest sons against him? Did they not know the dealings of that God who had created them? He said, "O Laman, that thou mightest be like unto this river." Lehi was speaking to his sons climbing among these dark mists, but he was addressing heaven, his words filled with the language of prayer, pleading before God to turn his watchful eye toward his willfull children. He looked down at the cool waters flowing over him before lifting his gaze out toward the churning waters of the Fountain of the

Red Sea. He said, "O Laman, why will you not be like unto this river, continually running into the fountain of all righteousness?" He raised his arms to the towering cliffs where his sons disappeared into the dark mists. "O Lemuel, that thou mightest be like unto this valley, firm and steadfast, and immovable in keeping the commandments of the Lord."

"Father, they're gone." Nephi rushed out of the mouth of the narrow gorge and down the beach to Lehi's side. He walked him out of the river and let the sand drip from the hem of his robe. "There's nothing you can do to bring them back."

"We can't stay here any longer." Aaron followed Nephi out onto the beach. "The river's swelling. We have to get back to the Upper Valley before we're stranded here."

A thick mist pushed against the coastal mountains, warning of a larger storm headed across the sea. It shrouded the entrance to the narrow chasm, and Lehi pressed his hand along the cold stone of the coastal mountains like a blind man, feeling his way back to the date groves in the Upper Valley. The swirling fog filled the narrows and with the light of day turned to evening it was impossible to find the twists and turns in this mile-long canyon without holding fast to the cool rock wall. Lehi kept a firm grip on the immovable stone and pushed through the mists, slowly ascending the chasm back toward his family and friends camped above, and leaving Laman and Lemuel to pursue their rebellion. The canyon twisted north and Lehi kept his hands feeling along the wall, the firm rock guiding them through the mists. Why did Laman and Lemuel let go of their faith and turn against him? Would they ever repent of whatever dealings caused them to betray him? All he wanted was for them to take hold of the Messiah with a grip as firm as his hold on this canyon wall, guiding him through the mists of this storm back to the date groves above. A deep, despairing fear welled up inside his soul—the fear of a parent for his children—and in the depth of these narrows, without a light to lead them out, Lehi begged the help of heaven, asking God to remove whatever evil cankered Laman and Lemuel's soul, and bring his sons back to him. O, that they would return and partake of the fruit of the tree of life—the Anointed One—and know that Lehi's love for them was like the redeeming love of God. He was their father and they would find no greater love on the face of this earth than the love of a tender parent for his children.

Did his sons never feel that joy in their souls?

Cursed wood!

Laman knelt on the cliffs above the sea and struck the flint, but the sparks turned black and cold on the timber. He angled his body against the wind that gusted over this mountaintop and tried again, striking the flint over the wood, but the sparks failed to catch fire. If they could only light a signal fire before the second wave of this storm reached these mountains, they could guide Captain Laban to them. Laman struck the flint again, raising a faint rush of sparks into the wind, but there was no flint strong enough to overcome the force of the storm.

"It's no use." The wind whipped over Lemuel, the cloth of his robe slapping against his legs. "The wood won't take fire in this storm."

Laman struck the flint again and again, but a cascade of rain rushed across the cliffs, dousing the spray of sparks. "We're not going back, not until we—"

"Stop it." Lemuel pulled the flint from Laman's hand and he cried above the howl of the wind. "We have to get down off these cliffs before the storm gets any worse."

A bank of clouds rolled across the night sky like the angel of death, shrouding the light of the moon and bringing another torrent of rain, the water cascading into pools atop the cliff. Lemuel started over the side, inching himself off the edge with water coursing over his arms and streaming down the rock face. He spoke through the water running over his head. He said, "I'm going back to camp."

Laman reached for Lemuel, but it was too late. His brother disappeared over the side and he shimmied down over the summit after him, gripping the twisted granite wall, his head turned down into his shoulders to fend off the driving rain. He lowered himself from ledge to ledge until the steep face gave way to the rocks near the base and he could pick his way over the beach. The river ran deeper than before, surging out of the chasm like the spray of a waterfall, carrying sand and earth in its muddy water. Lemuel was gone from the alcove, disappeared up into the chasm and Laman hurried after him up into the narrows.

Water filled the chasm from wall to wall and Laman trudged through the torrent. Dirty, sand-filled water reached past his knees and covered his thighs with a thick film of mud, but it wasn't enough to force him back until he turned around a bend in the river where the canyon walls closed in and the rush of water rose past his waist with enough force to push him downstream. He grabbed a large boulder, but the force of the current pushing against him was too much and it pried his grip off the—

Lemuel reached down from the top of the boulder and yanked Laman out of the torrent and onto the rock. The river coursed past, washing mud over them and chilling them to the bone. They hunkered down on the rock, their bodies pressed against each other to keep the chill of night from leaving them dead in this canyon.

Laman took out his dagger and shouted above the raging rush of the river. Mud streamed into his eyes and he spit the taste of it off his lips. He said, "Father has lost his mind."

CHAPTER 41

Lehi threw off the lambskin blanket and sat up on his sleeping mat. Was that the sound of Laman and Lemuel returning to camp? He peered across the tent, searching the shadows for the outline of their frames in the entrance, but the flaps were tied shut and the only sound reaching his hearing was the rush of the river surging through the valley below. The monsoon rains and wind pelted the sides of the tent, but there was no worry of it going over. The poles were secure, the stakes set firmly in the ground, and the ropes were double tied to protect against the winds. It was his dream that gave him reason to fear over Laman and Lemuel and he slowly lowered his head to the pillow, but he would not let himself fall back to sleep. His eldest sons abandoned them in this wilderness and the fierce reality of his dream plagued his mind with that loss. Lehi shook his head to chase away the sleep that hung in the wings of his mind to haunt him with the memory of Laman and Lemuel climbing out of sight over the coastal mountains. He would not suffer the loss of his eldest sons twice in the same night.

Lehi tucked the lambskin blanket across his chest, but not high enough to pull the warmth of the covering off Sariah. She needed the comfort of this blanket more than he, and he listened to the steady breathing of her rest, the constant rise and fall of her breathing beckoning him slowly back to . . .

No! He was not going to sleep tonight. Not with this dream waiting to carry him back to memories he was trying so hard to forget. Lehi stared at the animal-skin ceiling, but he wouldn't count the pelts of leather or the seams sewing them together and let the monotony of numbers draw him into a trance. He was to stay awake until morning and calculate exactly what more he could have done to save his sons. He brought them to this place in the wilderness to protect them from Captain Laban, only to find out that Laman and Lemuel had betrayed him to the very man they were fleeing. Lehi rubbed his brow to keep his mind from drifting back to . . .

Where did that light come from? It was a small, bright spot, half-hidden among the leather folds in the ceiling above his bed like the flickering flame of an oil lamp, but there were none lit in the tent. He blinked his eyes, but the light grew brighter until the dream he'd dreamed so many times before appeared like a vision before him. The dark and dreary waste of winding canyons and wadis on the coastal plain played across his mind, and he would have turned the caravan around and headed back to Jerusalem if not for the man in a white robe, telling him to follow him into the foothills of this wilderness, the dream carrying him back to the three-day forced march from Aqaba to this valley in the midst of the Borders nearer the Red Sea. Tall sandstone walls rose above him, cutting out the light of day, and endless, twisting canyons forked into unknown paths, leaving him without knowing which way to lead his family. He pulled the lambskin blanket over his face, but that didn't keep the deep, pressing darkness from surrounding him, thick enough that he could feel the shadows against his face, the cold vision of losing his way passing through his blanket and chilling him to the bone. The dream was back more powerfully than on any night before this, the vision penetrating the deepest recesses of his mind, carrying him back to travel through the darkness of this wilderness again. Lehi curled his knees up into his chest. "Dear Lord have mercy on me, according to the multitude of thy tender mercies."

He cleared the foothills and came onto a large, spacious valley, the wadi appearing on the animal-skin ceiling of his dreams. He rolled onto his side, the blanket still pulled over his head and led the caravan down the wide, sand filled valley. And when he turned back toward the Borders nearer the Red Sea he found a tree with fruit ripening in the sunlight, turning it white above the whiteness of anything he'd ever seen. It was sweet to the taste and it chased away the fear of finding himself lost in this wilderness. He was filled with the joy of God for leading him and his . . .

Where was his family? Lehi pulled the lambskin blanket away from his face, but he couldn't force his eyes open to find them. He was fixed in this dream, searching the images of his mind until his gaze cast down along the river to the far end of the valley. Sariah was there, with Nephi and Sam, and he called to them, leading them to the tree of life, telling them that this fruit was the reward for holding fast to the iron rod of Yeshua the Anointed One—the savior of all men. They found their way up along the river, but where were Laman and Lemuel? Lehi turned his head against the pillow, hunting through his dream, searching the faintest images of his mind. His eldest sons had to be here somewhere and when he turned his gaze down to where the river disappeared into the lower canyon through a narrow chasm in the mountainside, he found them standing in mists of darkness. He called to them, telling them to follow his directions and feel their way over to the iron rod and come up along the river to enjoy the fruit of this tree, but they would not take hold of it. Numberless concourses of people emerged from the lower canyon, took hold of the iron rod, and started on the path, but Laman and Lemuel wouldn't join them. Lehi pressed the back of his head into his pillow and tightened his grip on the hem of the lambskin blanket, but he could not rid himself of the image of his eldest sons turning away from the iron rod. Didn't they understand what they were rejecting? Lehi raised his voice above the rush of the river, urging them to embrace the Messiah and let his atoning blood refine their souls. He begged them to hold fast to the rod of iron and let forgiveness and mercy follow them all the days of their lives and not let the mists of the storm keep them from feeling their way through the narrows, back to this tree. Please sons, take hold of the . . .

Dear God of heaven! Lehi pressed his face into the pillow. Must this dream include the image of the mountainside down on the coast where Laman and Lemuel disappeared last night? Lehi knelt in the river, the cold water coursing past and numbing his legs. His sons were pointing their fingers at him, laughing and scoffing and mocking him for eating the fruit of the tree, telling him he was a fool, a *piqqeah*, a man who dreamed foolish dreams. Hordes of people joined them, all of them stepping out onto the verandas and balconies of this mountainside. The rocky cliffs were as the great halls of a large, spacious building. There were no windows in the lower floors, no oil lamps to brighten the base of the structure, and with the mists pushing ashore and gathering around the foundation, the building appeared to float as it were in the air. It was peopled with old and young, both male and female, and the manner of their dress was exceedingly fine—like expensive traveling robes purchased from the finest Egyptian weavers. Lehi turned onto his back and gripped the pillow with both hands, the blanket pressed against his face. They were pointing their fingers at him—at anyone taking hold of the iron rod, mocking them for holding fast to their faith in the Anointed One. Some let go of the rod and were drowned in the depths of the river, and others were lost from view, wandering in strange roads. And a great multitude let go of the iron rod, left the path and felt their way toward the large, spacious building to join those who were mocking and pointing their fingers at Lehi—scorning him for eating the sweet fruit of the tree. But he would not let go of his faith in the Anointed One. He'd spoken with God face-to-face and he could never deny it, no matter how painful it was to see his eldest sons leave the only path that had power to lead them to . . .

No! Not that. Lehi tried to open his eyes and wake himself, but he was held there in his sleep long enough to see the deadly vision slowly creeping from deep in the recesses of his mind, showing him the reason Laman rebelled against him. It was the image of his two sons betraying Lehi in exchange for . . .

Lehi sat up, his hands still gripping the pillow and his head turning about, searching the tent for more images of his eldest sons, but only the dim light of morning filtered through the open flaps of the entry. Sariah was gone; the pillows she used to soften her bed were neatly stacked in the corner. The rains were stopped, the wind gone quiet, and the rush of the river was replaced by a quiet babbling filtering up the rise and through the open entrance. The sound of rock doves chirped the arrival of morning in the cliffs above the tent, and when Lehi stepped to the entry he spied Sariah down the rise standing beneath the largest date palm in the grove, holding a basket while Nephi and Sam harvested their morning meal.

The river had settled back into its narrow channel during the night, the clear water bubbling up from the underground springs, untroubled by the rush of muddy water from farther up the wadi. Their friends were still asleep in the side compartments of the tent and Lehi quickly pulled on his sandals and hurried down the rise. He stepped across the river and came in next to the trunk of the tree, plucking a date from the nearest frond. It was soft against his tongue and sweeter than any of the dates sold in the open market of Jerusalem—the fresh, golden-white skin melting in his mouth, and the meat of the fruit awakening his sensibilities to the joy of heaven. Lehi ran his hand over the trunk of the tree, its symmetrical limbs rising into the air like the crown on the head of a great king. The fruit of the tree were jewels in a crown and Lehi turned to tell his family that this tree was like the prophet the Lord God would raise up among the Jews—even a Messiah, or, in other words, a Savior of the world. And dates were like the fruit of eternal life he would shower on all who—

"Father!"

Lehi spun around to find Laman and Lemuel trudging out of the chasm of the lower valley, mud clinging to their sandals. Their hair was filled with sand, their arms and legs coated with a film of silt, and their faces caked with a layer of mud thick enough to hide their expression behind a mask of mire, but it wasn't difficult to find the anger in Laman's stride. He marched ahead of Lemuel's plodding, up along the bank of the river, his shoulders forward, one hand swinging at his side and the other hidden under the mud-soaked cloth of his tunic.

"They're back." Sariah turned with a full basket of fruit under her arm. "Look, dear. They've come home to ask your—"

"Stay back." Lehi reached his arm in front of her. "It isn't safe."

"What isn't safe?" Sariah pushed his arm aside, but Lehi said, "All of you stay back. I dreamed a dream last night."

Nephi dropped the dates at the trunk of the tree and hurried in next to Lehi. He wore a red band around his black, flowing hair to keep it back off his brow. The seams in the cloth of his shirt were pulled taut across his chest and with Sam flanking him on the other side, they had enough strength to fend off—

"Father, it's you I want." Laman pointed his free hand at Lehi, the other hand still hidden beneath his tunic. He was halfway up the canyon and closing down quickly, the mud kicking up behind his sandals.

"Get behind me. All of you." Lehi stepped in front of his family and started down along the river. He raised his hands to Laman and said, "Not another step, son. Do you hear me? I know what you've come to do and I'm warning you to stay back until you've lost your anger or you'll regret this day the rest of your life."

Laman pulled up across the narrow river from Lehi, his hand gripping the hilt of a dagger beneath his robe. Father had lost his mind and it was time to end this wandering in the wilderness. He said, "I've regretted every day since we left Beit Zayit."

Lehi said, "Take your hand out from under your shirt and we'll talk about this."

Laman started across the river, but pulled up when Lemuel said, "He knows." He splashed into the water alongside Laman, the two of them standing in the middle of the channel. "Did you hear that? He knows."

Lehi raised his hands to Laman, the wide cuffs of his robe hanging down from his wrists. "Why must you be like the Jews at Jerusalem?"

"I'm nothing like them." Laman spit into the river. "All I've ever wanted is our inheritance."

"That isn't everything son. I know why you seek to take away my life."

Laman tightened his grip on the dagger. That was impossible. Father couldn't know the details of his collusion with Captain Laban, not unless . . .

"Why, you little fool!" Laman turned on his brother Lemuel and pulled his dagger out from under his robe. "You told him, didn't you?"

"No, I never . . ." Lemuel backed away from the dagger, his foot catching a river stone and tripping him into the water at Laman's feet. He wrapped his thin arms around his head and said, "Please Laman, no. I'm your brother."

Laman raised the dagger over Lemuel and—

"Son." Lehi shouted loud enough to shake Laman to the very center, his cry echoing off the canyon walls. "In the name of heaven, put that weapon down."

Laman's shoulders began to shake and the trembling spread to his arms. He tightened his grip on the dagger, but his hand shook out of control and the blade fell from his grip in among the river stones. He bent over to fish it out, the trembling in his body dropping him to his knees. The river rushed over him, but there was no water cold enough to quench the fire burning in his soul. How did Lehi know of his doings? He tried to speak, but his lips would not form the words. His anger was trapped inside him, welling up like the heat of a great inferno burning hot enough to melt the very crucible that held the flame.

Laman was confounded.

CHAPTER 42

Ruth poured Jonathan a lukewarm glass of water and served it with a round of day-old flat bread. Her husband sat at the kitchen table for the first time in a month and the celebration of his return merited more than a drink of water and some dry bread. Jonathan was home and she would have sweetened a bowl of pottage with dates, picked the finest melon from the garden, and roasted a leg of lamb for morning meal, but Jonathan didn't have time to wait for any more than water and bread. He arrived home in the early hours this morning and immediately fell asleep, promising to tell her the details of his ride to Sidon when he awoke.

Jonathan sat on the edge of his chair, his elbows planted on the tabletop and his head down in the bread, hurrying through his meal. There were plows to mend, a host of bridles and chains to repair, but she couldn't let him leave the house until he told her about—

"Mulek will be safe at sea with the Phoenician navy," Jonathan said in answer to Ruth's staring from across the table.

At sea? Ruth dropped the jar of honey and the sound of it echoed about the kitchen. Thankfully the clay vessel didn't break in two and spill its contents over the table. She righted the bottle and set a spoon beside it. How could she report to Miriam that her son was sailing the Great Sea? Visions of storms and shipwrecks were certain to worry the woman more than the fear of her husband and his men bringing the boy back to Jerusalem to suffer whatever harm Zadock and Laban could conjure.

"He'll be treated like royalty." Jonathan dipped a spoonful of honey onto his flatbread. "He sailed in company with Prince Jesse of Sidon."

Ruth washed her hands in a basin of water in the corner and wiped them dry on her apron. What was she going to tell—?

"Tell Miriam he's learning the art of sailing." Jonathan spoke between bites of flat bread. "That should pacify her."

Oh my. Ruth held firm to the cloth of her apron. The queen didn't want to be pacified. She wanted to know that her son was safe and out of harm's way. She said, "Is he well?"

"Well enough I suppose." Jonathan finished the bread and reached for another round. "Mulek was in good spirits when the ship's captain let me off with my horse at the port at Tyre."

Ruth came back to the table. "Exactly how did you decide to put the boy on board a sailing vessel along with your horse?"

"The prince is safe; that's all you need to know."

Ruth worked the cloth of the apron between her fingers long after they were dry. "Is there nothing I can tell Miriam to ease her mind?"

"Not until the boy's back safe with his mother. If I tell you more, you'll worry over things you can't possibly change."

Jonathan tore the bread in half, dipped it in the honey and chased it with a drink of water. He spoke quickly, his words rushing from him like they did whenever he didn't want her to see too deeply into his soul. He said, "Tell Miriam that it was God who put the boy aboard ship."

Ruth let go of her apron and the cloth fell down her front over the girded pleats of her robe. Did she hear him right? She pulled a chair back from the table, the legs grating over the stone floor and sat across from Jonathan. Did he say God had a hand in placing Mulek aboard a sailing vessel? Jonathan was not given to the language of faith. He was silent on the matters of heaven. Her husband had a good heart and somewhere deep in the recesses of his soul he guarded the fruits of the spirit, hidden where no one but he could reap them, but if he ever did decide to make public his very private sentiments, Ruth wanted desperately to be at that harvest and gather in the light of her husband's budding faith.

Ruth said, "What was that, dear?"

"You heard me." Jonathan downed another round of flat bread and poured himself a half glass of water. "I never would have found the boy if not for the help of heaven."

Ruth leaned back in the chair until her shoulders pushed flush with the timbers. She lowered her head, but her heart was turned up toward heaven. Somehow, for whatever purpose God had in mind for them, her husband—her kind, wise, stubborn husband—had been touched by the power of the Eternal One. Jonathan was not given to prayer. He never celebrated his faith except on feast days a few times each year. Not once in their marriage of twenty-one years did the words of faith enter into his speech, but he'd said it was the power of heaven that directed him to save Mulek. She'd heard it as clear as the sun was shining over the windowsill and it kindled a faint hope that somehow, someway, Jonathan's heart would be softened enough for him to enjoy the quiet whisperings of—

A knock sounded at the door, the suddenness of it raising Ruth out of her chair. Who could that be to disrupt this remarkable moment? Jonathan's heart was taking root in the things of faith and she did not want to leave him and risk never hearing him speak of this again. She touched Jonathan on the hand, told him she'd see to the visitor while he finished his meal. She righted the pillows on the bench seat in the main room, straightened the small rug near the entry, and when she turned the latch and pulled back the thick wooden planks she found Ishmael the Vineyard Master standing in the full light of morning. He wore a colorful Egyptian traveling robe, the red, blue, and green stripes reflecting off the weathered doorpost and adding a heartwarming splash of color to their meeting. His white hair was parted to the side and his beard was shaved close to his chin, covering his cheeks with a thin growth of pure white, as pristine as the foam atop the surf of the Great Sea. He carried two vessels of olive oil under his arms. The lids were sealed with beeswax and they were large enough to weigh down his arms, the man's fingers going red from the strain of holding them.

Ishmael said, "I told your husband I'd drop off some olive oil."

"I didn't know we ordered any."

"We didn't." Jonathan stepped into the main room from the kitchen, his shoulders forward and his stance chasing Ruth back a step. His eyes were dark and he tightened his fists at his side. "Did you hear me? We don't want anything from your plantation in this house."

"I'm sorry, sir." Ishmael's gaze flitted between Ruth and Jonathan like a moth caught over the searing heat of an oil lamp, its wings singed. He held the cisterns out to Jonathan and said, "I've come to ask forgiveness for any part I may have had in Aaron's—"

"We don't need your olive oil."

"It's an offering of peace, dear." Ruth took the cisterns from Ishmael and held the heavy vessels in her arms. How could he refuse a heartfelt request for mercy?

Jonathan said, "We don't accept offerings from enemies."

"Jonathan." Ruth stepped between them. "The man came all the way from Beit Zayit to bring us this oil."

"Where was he when Aaron was dying on the porch of Lehi's estate, bleeding to death?" Jonathan leaned his head in next to Ishmael. "You're not welcome here. Do you hear me? I don't want you or your olive oil in this house."

Jonathan knocked the oil vessels out of Ruth's hands, throwing them down at Ishmael's feet, the red clay splintering into a thousand pieces against the threshold and splattering olive oil over the hem of the vineyard master's robe. He marched back to the kitchen, leaving Ruth standing in the doorway with their visitor. All she could think to do was remove her apron, fall to her knees, and clean away the oil, working the cloth over his sandal-shod feet and sopping up what she could of the mess her husband made. Jonathan may still be grieving, but it was time he mended this rift with Ishmael and let the healing begin. They couldn't remain bitter enemies forever and she prayed a silent prayer that heaven would help her understand how to heal this ill will over Aaron's death. Ruth turned the cloth over to finish sopping up the spill around the vineyard master's feet. When would Jonathan's heart be softened?

"I'm sorry, sir." Ruth kept her head down, away from Ishmael's gaze. "My husband hasn't gotten over the loss." She pulled the hem of his traveling robe away from his legs, but before passing the apron over the bright-colored cloth to clean away what she could of the stains, she turned her gaze up to meet his. Ishmael stood in the entry looking down at her, not uttering a word of rebuke, not reproving Jonathan for his unspeakably awful behavior. And when his gaze met hers and she felt the compassion of his eyes, her mind flooded with understanding like the opening of a window onto a view of the purposes of heaven. There was a reason for this animosity—a reason beyond her understanding and deep in her soul she knew to let heaven lead in the matter of her husband's unforgiving heart and not enter this fray. She was to keep silent her loathing for Jonathan's unyielding will and wait for the day when her husband stood in the threshold of Ishmael's dwelling and begged for the same forgiveness he was unwilling to offer. She could see it as clearly as the light of morning bending around the doorposts and silhouetting Ishmael's sturdy frame. Jonathan was to come full circle, passing through the crucible of his own refining to stand where Ishmael stood and seek forgiveness for sins that were not entirely his own. Ruth quickly worked the cloth over the hem of Ishmael's robe. Aaron's death was the cause of this bitterness and though she didn't know how, their dead son would be the balm to heal Jonathan's hatred and admit him into the encircling arms of heaven.

Ruth said, "You will forgive him, won't you, sir?"

King Street turned up a rise in front of the main palace gates, and Zadock hurried up the middle of the cobblestone street and around a slow-moving group of white-robed temple priests. He was to meet with Zedekiah today and offer advice regarding a trade alliance with the Kingdom of . . .

A thundering troop of cavalry galloped past him, the powerful horses riding close enough to push him off the street. Fools. Zadock gathered himself along the outside wall of the royal precincts. These soldiers should have the courtesy to let him pass, not cut across his path like starving knaves to a bowl of pottage. The animals were caked in desert sands and the riders covered with the dust of a long journey, but that was no excuse for these men not to pay him the respect due him. Zadock marched down along the column of horses, pushing aside the wide bodies of the animals. He came around in front of the lead rider and said, "Captain Laban?"

The man's thin line of beard had grown thick and full across his chin, hiding the square lines of his jaw. His short hair had grown longer, the dark, black hair falling over his brow and hiding his ears. He got down out of the saddle and stood before the gate, his riding boots salted with the sands of his ride. He said, "We must deal with the prisoner now."

Zadock glanced past him, straining to find a prisoner chained among the double-file column of cavalry, but there was no one tied with cords or under heavy guard. They were fifty riders dressed in the dusty riding tunics and kilts of the Babylonian army, and without Lehi or his sons in custody it was impossible to know what prisoner he was referring to.

Laban left his Arabian with Lieutenant Daniel, ordered him to take the men and horses around to the livery, then told him they were dismissed for a week of rest. The pivot stones on the main gates ground open, the iron bars creaked open, and Captain Laban marched inside with Zadock hurrying along beside him.

Zadock said, "What prisoner?"

"Lehi's dead."

"You killed him?"

"He did himself in, hiding like a coward in the Border Mountains."

"You're certain?"

"No man comes out of there alive."

"Then it's over."

"Not yet."

Zadock let the hem of his robe fall to the cobblestones. He followed Laban down through the side gardens, around a stand of juniper, and up a stone path to the west-wing doors. "We should celebrate your return from—"

"There isn't time for celebration." Laban waited for the palace guards to open the doors to the west wing before turning inside the dimly lit hallway and marching down past the long line of lion-head statues lining the wall, the stone animals quietly observing their conversation. "Ezekiel knows our secrets."

Zadock said, "The man mounted an escape."

"What?" Laban pulled up in the middle of the hall, the echo of his boots falling silent on the stone. "You let him go?"

"We caught him before he got out through the sewers."

"Where is he?"

"The well of the prison."

"Is he alive?"

"He can't last much longer down there."

"We're not waiting this time, not like we did with Uriah." Laban started down the hallway, the rushed rhythm of his boots echoing about the vaulted passageway.

"Why such a hurry, Captain?"

"Inspector Tobit."

"The Babylonian isn't concerned with these matters."

"He will be if he's allowed to interrogate Ezekiel. I nearly let Lehi ruin us by not dealing with him swiftly. I'll not make the same mistake twice." Laban reached the prison door, but before he turned the latch he said, "It's time we end this foolishness. Dead prophets receive no revelation, sir."

Laban forced open the prison door.

What was that?

Ezekiel sat up in the mud, his torn accounting robes hanging like rags from his mold-infested skin. Footsteps sounded in the chambers above this dark well, hidden deep in the bowels beneath the palace. It couldn't be the prison hands come with evening meal. It was too early for them to toss down rotted scraps of potatoes into this pit. The flickering light of a torch passed over the opening above and the stir of men filtered down, but it was impossible to know why so many gathered to this forgotten hole beneath the catacombs of the lower prison; then the harness of ropes around Ezekiel's body pulled taut, plucking him out of the mire and lifting him off the ground like a net snaring a fish from the sea. He flailed about, his arms and legs covered with the mud that for a full month engulfed him in the putrid slime of this intolerable cell.

The cursing of prison guards echoed down through the opening, the men pulling him higher with each rhythmic, hoisting chant, like a leaf tossed on the unseen cords of the wind until his head cleared the hole in the stone, and the light of ten torches blinded his eyes. A rush of cool air passed over him, stinging his lungs and tightening his stomach. He was free of the foulness that plagued him below, but it had been so long since he'd breathed fresh air, he vomited on the many sandal-shod feet surrounding the edge of the pit. The prison guards jumped back from his retching and the cords went slack, sending Ezekiel falling back into the darkness until the ropes pulled taut about his waist, and his body arched in mid-air, his back straining to near breaking against the pull of the cords.

"Fools, get him up here."

The grating voice of Zadock echoed down into the well, ordering the prison guards to do it quickly—they had little time to dispose of the chief accountant.

Ezekiel hung at the end of the rope like a gnat caught in a spider's web, his body hovering in the air. Dear God of heaven, was this the end? Was Zadock come to take his life?

A narrow shaft of yellow torchlight filtered down into the well, past Ezekiel, and onto Jeremiah lying in the mire below. He was huddled against the wall, his knees pulled up into his chest and his body shivering in the dampness. There was nothing Jeremiah could do to save him and he tried to untie the ropes and fall back into the muddy cell to join his friend, but the cords were too thick and his arms too weak. Flashes of torchlight danced around his spinning head and in the confusion of hanging above the ground he heard the voice of a great rushing, telling him to *be strong as flint—he was to be a watchman over Israel among the people of the captivity.* The rope spun him around and around again, and there was no telling who was speaking. He caught another glimpse of Jeremiah in the flickering light below. His friend was still huddled against the wall, his body covered in mud and shivering in the dampness. Jeremiah was silent and there was no doubting the source of these words. It was the voice of God speaking to his mind, telling him that he was to be a watchman over Israel, to the children of his people who were taken captive.

The pull of the ropes inched him upward out of the dark pit and into the light of the lower prison. Zadock peered over from beyond the circle of prison guards gathered around the hole to pluck him out of the pit. The open cuffs of the Chief Elder's black vestments fell down around his long fingers and his gray hair hedged out from under the brim of his shawls. Captain Laban stood beside him, his dark hair salted with the dust of a long ride, and his narrow line of beard grown thick around his jaw.

Laban said, "Tie his hands with cords and bring him with us."

Captain Laban and Zadock marched from the catacombs, and the prison guards escorted Ezekiel in stride behind them. They carried him to the top of the circular stairs to keep from waiting for his feeble legs to function, before setting him on his feet to limp out the doors of the upper prison and down an empty corridor with only the hushed voices of Zadock and Laban to fill the silent stone hall. Captain Laban dismissed the prison guards to return to their posts, telling them he could take the prisoner from here. Laban led Ezekiel down another corridor that ended at a narrow entry. He unlocked the latch, his deep voice resonating about the doorposts and assuring Zadock they could get Ezekiel out through the back alleyway without anyone—

"Is that him?"

Ezekiel blinked in the bright afternoon sunlight streaming under the door beam until the image of a man riding down the alley came into focus. He was dressed in a flowing white Babylonian riding robe with two heron feathers sprouting from a turban, and he rode at the head of a company of fifty like-dressed Babylonian cavalrymen—their horses trotting down the long corridor from the front gates.

The lead rider reined in across Laban's path. His horse was salted with a thin film of sandy brown earth from a long journey, his lips were cracked from the wind and sun of a parched country, and his cheeks were tanned dark brown. He said, "Is that the man who altered the tax levy and spread revolt among the Jews?"

"What about Lehi?" Captain Laban stepped in front of Ezekiel and strained to see past the Inspector to the cavalry behind him. "Did you find the man?"

Tobit said, "Forget the olive oil merchant and his sons. They're never coming back to Jerusalem. They should be the least of your worries."

Laban said, "Capturing Lehi is our only worry."

"Then you won't mind me taking Ezekiel into custody." Tobit motioned for one of his men to lead a horse over. The animal's coat was freshly curried, the saddle polished with beeswax, and the silver studs decorating the leather were shined to a brilliant luster. Three Babylonian soldiers got down from their mounts and took Ezekiel by the arms, helping him up into the saddle.

"This man is our prisoner." The rasping voice of Zadock echoed about the alley. "There's no better place for Ezekiel to be tried for his part in the tax revolt than by our judges."

"It's for me to decide what's best." Tobit leaned over the saddle and cut away the cords binding Ezekiel's wrists, the leather straps falling into the dust. He said, "Get this man something to eat."

The Babylonian quartermaster brought Ezekiel a round of flat bread, and the water master offered him a drink from a freshly filled skin.

Tobit said, "There are some Jews living in the north of Babylon at a place called Tel-abib, up along the Chebar River. Do you know of them?"

Ezekiel lifted the water skin to his lips and let the cool refreshing liquid pour down his throat and spill over his cheeks. He nodded to the inspector. He knew about the refugees. They were deported from Jerusalem after the first Babylonian war. They were good, educated Jews, some lawyers, a few doctors, a good many blacksmiths—all of them taken from their homes with their families to provide the skills of their trade to the Babylonian empire.

"There's enough inside here to keep you a good while." Tobit handed over a leather satchel. There was a new robe inside, a supply of food, and a money purse jingling with silver Babylonian dinars. Tobit ordered five cavalrymen to gather around Ezekiel. He said, "These men will escort you to Tel-abib, see that you're received well among the Jews there, and find you a good dwelling with plenty of food. I want you to be a watchman over the Jews at Tel-abib. The captives in that part of Babylon have need of a man like you. Will you do it?"

Ezekiel lowered the water skin from his lips. The man used the word captives—Ezekiel heard it with his own ears. Inspector Tobit asked him to be a watchman over the captive Jews along the Chebar River and he turned his gaze up into the blue skies above the palace, the bright sun blinding his vision. God was watching over him, guiding him and opening this window where before there was nothing but sealed prison doors holding him back. This Babylonian officer was offering him kindness when his own countrymen offered him nothing but evil. Tobit was fulfilling the very word of God.

Tobit turned in the saddle to Laban. "Have your men let Ezekiel out."

"We can't let him go."

"Open the gates, Captain."

"I must protest." Zadock came around in front of the inspector. "This man is a rebel."

"What uprising has he led?"

Zadock said, "Have you forgotten the tax revolt?"

Laban took Inspector Tobit's horse by the bridle. He raised his voice, the words stinging off his lips. He said, "Why are you doing this?"

Inspector Tobit got down from the saddle, the two men standing face-to-face.

Tobit said, "Because Ezekiel is a prophet—like Lehi is a prophet."

HISTORICAL NOTES

Author's Note: *Place of Refuge* is a fictional work based on events recorded in the opening chapters of *The Book of Mormon: Another Testament of Jesus Christ*. The story, settings, and, in some instances, the plot lines were developed from historical research of the period. Though it is impossible to review all the sources that contributed to the preparation of this novel, the following notes summarize the historical basis of elements in the story.

CHAPTER ONE

Ezekiel was called as a prophet to the captives taken in the first Babylonian war. We have no record of when he left Jerusalem to join the Jews living at Tel-abib on the Chebar River in Northern Babylon, and at the opening of this novel he is found still living at Jerusalem a few years after the first captives were taken from the city (Ezekiel 3: 15–17). Beyond Ezekiel's prophetic writings and his ordination as a priest, we have little detail about his livelihood. It is possible that he was supported in his priestly duties by offerings, but it is more likely that he had some other occupation within Jewish society. King David and the prophet Ezekiel both attempted to standardize weights and measures during their lifetime, and it is possible that Ezekiel was an accountant or a lawyer in Jerusalem, charged with the task of dealing with the monetary system (The Church of Jesus Christ of Latter-day Saints, *Old Testament Student Manual: 1 Kings–Malachi*). His association with the standardization of the monetary system may have raised him fairly high in the accounting hierarchy of the capital city, and in this chapter, as well as in the previous volume in this series, *Power of Deliverance*, he is depicted as the chief accountant and chief lawyer with specific duties of finalizing the payment of tribute tax to Babylon (William F. Allbright, "The Seal of Eliakim and the Latest Preexilic History of Judah, With Some Observations on Ezekiel," 148).

* * * * *

In Lehi's day Judah was a vassal state paying tribute taxes to Babylon. There is no record of the amount of taxes paid; however, there are some references to the in-kind payments. This chapter describes some of those payment options, including wine, grains, gold, silver and olive oil. During the final ten years of Babylonian occupation, beginning around 600 B.C., Zedekiah threatened to stop paying tribute to Babylon on three different occasions (John Bright. *A History of Israel),* and this chapter fictionalizes Ezekiel's involvement in the preparation of the tax payment immediately following the first tax revolt of the Jews (*Great People of the Bible and How They Lived;* see also Hugh W. Nibley, "Dark Days in Jerusalem: The Lakhish letters and the Book of Mormon," in *The Prophetic Book of Mormon).*

* * * * *

In Ezekiel's personal account of his call to prophethood—a call fictionalized in *Power of Deliverance,* volume two of this series, and continued in subsequent chapters in this book—he declared that God would make him "hard as flint" in order to serve as a watchman over a group of very rebellious Jews in Tel-abib in Northern Babylon. In this chapter his prophetic call is reiterated (Ezekiel 3:8–9).

* * * * *

There were multiple styles of head coverings employed by the Jews at Jerusalem. Unmarried women typically wore a cloth covering over the head that reached down over the shoulders without any cords to bind it in place, while married women often wore a hood incorporated into their robe that covered the body from head to foot. Their guidelines governing modesty were societal norms and not enforceable by any formal punishment, but rather imposed by cultural and religious norms. The informal head covering for men included a cloth band around the brow to keep the hair back out of the eyes. This was usually worn by men working in active, vigorous labor, or by young boys. In this chapter, Zadock wore the customary turban of religious and political leaders of Lehi's day. It was not like the full turbans of desert dwellers, but rather composed of two layers of black and white cloth or shawls laid over the head and reaching down to the shoulders. A black cap, rounded at the top or with a point, was fitted over the shawls and head, and the brim was often decorated with silver threads or some sort of jewels. The turban Zadock wears was inspired by artistic renderings of Jewish religious leaders of the period (Florence E. Petzel, *"Textiles of Ancient Mesopotamia, Persia and Egypt"*).

CHAPTER TWO

There are a number of wilderness areas east and south of Jerusalem, each one distinct from the other, but all of them considered wilderness—some mountainous, others wide open deserts, and still others parched, barren ground. Wandering Bedouin tribes inhabit a number of these harsh climes, and Hugh Nibley as well as other Book of Mormon scholars suggest that the rugged terrain provided safe haven for criminals, outlaws, robbers, religious objectors, and political defectors fleeing the rule of the Jews and the Babylonians (Nibley, "Lehi in the Desert," in *Lehi in the Desert/The World of the Jaredites/There Were Jaredites.* ed. John W. Welch. See also John W. Welch, "Theft and Robbery in the Book of Mormon and Near Eastern Law"). In the months and years leading up to the destruction of Jerusalem that took place about seven years after the time period depicted in this novel, more and more Jews fled into these wilderness areas to avoid the escalation of hostilities between the two nations. Despite the geographic differences of these varied wilderness areas, they all share a common scarcity of water, and in this chapter, Laban discounts Lehi's flight into those lands due to the harsh conditions and the belief that Lehi would seek the comforts of civilized society in Egypt rather than head out into the uncivilized wilderness (Nibley, Voices From the Dust," in *The Old Testament and Related Studies.* See also: "The Jerusalem Scene." See also: "Lakhish letters" in Noel B. Reynolds and Charles D. Tate, eds., *Book of Mormon Authorship: New Light on Ancient Origins).*

* * * * *

Many scholars suggest that the sword and brass plates Laban kept guarded in his treasury were national treasures, and the Babylonians would have attempted to confiscate them as a sign of conquest over Judah, just as the Egyptians carried the Ark of the Covenant back to Tanis after their invasion of the kingdom (Daniel N. Rolph, "The Sword of Laban as a Symbol of Divine Authority and Kingship"). In this chapter, Laban reminisces over the battle scars he received during the first Babylonian War while attempting to save the royal relics.

* * * * *

The fate of the sword of Laban at the time of the first Babylonian incursion into Judah—eight months prior to the opening of this series of novels—is unclear. There is evidence supporting two possibilities. First, the sword was protected in Laban's treasury from the Babylonian soldiers. The second possibility suggested by Book of Mormon scholars, and the one preferred for developing the character of Jonathan the Blacksmith, is that the Babylonians confiscated the sword as part of the spoils of war. We do know that ancient armies seized religious and political relics after their conquests, and it could be that the sword was one of those spoils the Old Testament tells us were carried off to Babylon. Scholars indicate that if the Babylonian army took the sword, another would have been smithed as a replacement. Laban echoes this theory in this chapter. Based on these conclusions, the sword of Laban could have been an original or a replica of one of the national treasures (Rolph, "Prophets, Kings, and Swords: The Sword of Laban and its Possible Pre-Laban Origins, 73–79").

CHAPTER THREE

There is a good deal of evidence supporting Egypt as Israel's major trading partner, regardless of the Babylonian rule over the Jews. If Lehi traded in the lucrative olive oil markets of Egypt he likely had a good number of ties with the merchants of the Nile. Hugh Nibley suggests that the economic ties between the two countries were much stronger than previously believed by most Middle East scholars (Nibley, "Lehi in the Desert," in *Lehi in the Desert/The World of the Jaredites/There Were Jaredites.* ed. John W. Welch). In this chapter, both Captain Laban and Elder Zadock logically assume that Lehi, because of his wealth and his business ties to Egypt, would have taken his family and traveled across the Sinai Peninsula toward the Nile to seek refuge among his business contacts and friends in that part of the world, where they would enjoy the luxury and opulence of their wealth and their wealthy friends rather than heading south into the wilderness of the Arabian Peninsula.

* * * * *

Birthright treasures, or treasures of inheritance, were commonly passed from father to son in the royal families of both the Old Testament and Book of Mormon, and usually included an inheritance of land as well as the authority to preside. Based on scripture and the diaries of early LDS Church members who were with the prophet Joseph Smith when he discussed the sword of Laban and the brass plates, it is likely that Joseph who was sold into Egypt prepared these treasures for his sons before his death and that they served to designate Ephraim and Manasseh as his heirs, who were worthy of a royal birthright (Brett L. Holbrook, "The Sword of Laban as a Symbol of Divine Authority and Kingship," 39).

* * * * *

Without the genealogy recorded in the brass plates, we cannot be certain how close the lineage relationship was that existed between Laban and the royal blood-line of Joseph who was sold into Egypt, but we do know that such a relationship did exist. By virtue of his ownership of the royal relics, Laban was most likely a very close blood relative (Rolph, "Prophets, Kings, and Swords: The Sword of Laban and its Possible Pre-Laban Origins"). The Book of Mormon tells us that Laban and his family kept the brass plates (1 Nephi 5:16) and the sword of Joseph—possibly re-named the sword of Laban by Book of Mormon authors. Joseph Smith told the early Saints that the sword was a symbol of kingship in ancient Israel and was anointed by prophets as such (Rolph, "Prophets, Kings, and Swords: The Sword of Laban and its Possible Pre-Laban Origins"). Swords were intended to symbolize the mantle of royal authority. It is likely that the sword of Joseph was used in the coronation ceremonies of Northern Israel's kings, much like monarchs of the middle ages used crowns. Because Laban possessed this heirloom, it is possible that he was part of the direct father-to-birthright-son bloodline of Joseph and had a strong claim to some sort of kingship.

CHAPTER FOUR

Among ancient Jews, the flame of an oil lamp and the olive oil used to fuel it were steeped in imagery. The famous menorah of Solomon's temple was intended to burn continually until the Messiah came. The Jews called it the eternal flame and took great care to keep it lit. There is no record that the flame was ever extinguished previous to the destruction of the temple, about seven years after this novel ends. The olive oil and the light of the lamp were employed in countless stories and parables among the Jews from the time of Abraham to the ministry of Jesus. Lamps and their light were often used as a metaphor for messengers—typically heavenly messengers—as well as for the presence of God (Exodus 3:2; Hebrews 12:29; 1 Nephi 1:6). Darkness in scriptures is a metaphor for blindness and loss. In this chapter, the flame of the lamp is used in much the same way as the Jews viewed this very important light source—as a metaphor for life and for the loss of life.

CHAPTER FIVE

Jericho is considered one of the oldest cities on earth. The ancient walled city was located at the north end of the Dead Sea. The Jordan River empties out of the Jordan Valley near Jericho and onto the wide expanse of the Arabah—the deep-rift valley where the Dead Sea is located. The hot, low elevations around Jericho—about 825 feet below sea level—coupled with the constant flow of the Jordan River have allowed for the cultivation of large date palm groves near the city. Over the centuries, Jericho has become famous for its date production.

* * * * *

Inspector Tobit was an ancient Babylonian commander, but we know nothing beyond his name, and his role in this novel is fictionalized. We do, however, know the nature of his assignment, based on Babylonian and Jewish geopolitics of the time period. Babylon—similar to Egypt—exercised three spheres of influence. The first was direct control of military and government institutions. The second was a wider geographic control in foreign lands where the presence of military regiments and army officers was enough to insure compliance to the will of Babylon. The third sphere of influence had a much wider geographic reach, with only the threat of future military action obliging the sometimes-infrequent payment of tribute tax (Nibley, "Lehi in the Desert," in *Lehi in the Desert/The World of the Jaredites/There Were Jaredites.* ed. John W. Welch). During Babylon's occupation of the Jewish homeland, the Jews fell into the second tier of Babylonian occupation. Army captains and their regiments were stationed about the country providing a visual presence, but it does not appear that the Babylonian army conducted a full occupation the country after the first war, but rather operated as overseer of the Jews. In this chapter, Inspector Tobit personifies the political and military relationship that existed between the Jews and Babylonians during Lehi's day. The Jews were permitted to raise an army, control the police forces within their cities, operate their governmental institutions, establish laws, provide judges, and oversee their economic and religious practices with little or no Babylonian interference. They were required to pay tribute to Babylon, and a good many of the educated classes as well as the artisans—blacksmiths, stonecutters, silversmiths, carpenters—were repatriated to Babylon to provide their expertise to the people and king living along the Tigris river. Tobit's character personifies the relationship that existed between Babylon and Israel in Lehi's day.

* * * * *

The Judean Wilderness was a barren, hundred-mile-long swath of sand between the west shores of the Dead Sea and the southern hill country of Judah. It received little rain due to its low elevation. In comparison, the hill country directly to the west and the plateau region of Moab across the Dead Sea on the east shores received substantially more rain, the higher elevation milking out any possible moisture from passing storm clouds. John the Baptist lived in the harsh deserts of the Judean Wilderness as did the Essenes of Dead Sea Scroll fame. Desert dwellers call these geographically definable wilderness areas Hijaz—an Arabic term for some sort of geographic boundary that translates roughly into the English word "partition," or "barrier." The most common use of the word Hijaz is in reference to the wide desert separating the inland cities of Mecca and Medina—sites sacred to present-day Muslims—from the Red Sea; and some English-Arabic dictionaries list this particular desert as the first meaning of Hijaz. In the more general application of the term, there are numerous Hijaz or geographic boundaries or borders south and east of Jerusalem—the Judean Wilderness, the Arabah, the Empty Quarter farther east of the Dead Sea, the Jabal Mountain Range south of the Dead Sea, and the inland deserts of the Arabian Peninsula (Joseph Catafago, "Arabic-English Dictionary." See also: The New Roget's Thesaurus, Revised Edition, ed. Norman Lewis, "Boundary," 49).

* * * * *

When Nephi wrote that his father Lehi left his house, land, gold, silver, and precious things and departed into the wilderness with his family and took only provisions and tents, he may have been referring to one of these geographically identifiable wilderness areas, or he may have been referencing all of them together since they are all located south and east of Jerusalem, between the capital city and the Red Sea, and they lie along the generally traveled routes between those two destinations (1 Nephi 2:4).

CHAPTER SIX

We know that Jeremiah was incarcerated on several occasions for his insistence that the Jews were to be vassals to Babylon for a period of seventy years. Because of his prophecies, he was regarded as a traitor to the Jews, was reviled, spit upon, and jailed by the king and the princes of the city. In this chapter, Jeremiah's opening words of dialogue include a reference directly from his writings, calling the Elders of the Jews an assembly of treacherous men (Jeremiah 9:2). There is, however, no record that the Jews imprisoned Ezekiel. His writings in the Old Testament do not begin until after he migrated from Jerusalem—or was taken captive—and repatriated to Tel-abib in northern Babylon along the shores of the Chebar River. It is possible that prior to Ezekiel's departure he had some contact with the prophet Jeremiah; however, it is unlikely that they were jailed in the same prison cell. Ezekiel is known for his prophecy of the sticks of Joseph (Book of Mormon) and Judah (Bible) coming together in the last days of the earth, and in order to foreshadow the story lines for volume four of this series, *Day of Remembrance*, it is critical that Ezekiel share with Jeremiah his revelation of the coming forth of the latter- day Book of Mormon scripture (Ezekiel 37: 15–20). Portions of the dialogue spoken by Jeremiah were taken directly from his writings in the Old Testament, and Ezekiel's closing words are direct quotes from his prophecy of the sticks of Joseph and Judah (Ezekiel 37: 19).

* * * * *

We do not know where Ezekiel was living when he received all of his prophecies but it is clear he recorded most of them while living in Babylon, and he may have been familiar with the practice of Babylonian cuneiform writing when he penned his revelations regarding the sticks of Joseph and Judah. Babylonian scribes pressed a wedge-shaped stylus into moist clay tablets—the most preferred writing medium among ancient Babylonian scribes—and prior to finding another writing medium, archeologists believed clay tablets were the only writing medium used by Babylonian scribes. San Nicolo theorized that the Babylonians may have also used wooden tablets for their writings, similar to the tablets used by Roman and Greek scribes. The wooden boards were covered with a thick wax coating and the edges raised to allow for the wooden tablets to be placed one atop the other. Archeologist Max Mallowan made the first discovery supporting this theory of wooden tablets rather than clay when he found some preserved in a layer of sludge at the bottom of a well in the city of Nimrud in what was ancient Babylon (Keith H. Meservy, "Job: Yet Will I Trust in Him"). The cover boards had hinge marks on both sides, making it evident that all the tablets had been joined together, and Mallowan announced his discovery as the oldest known example of a book. The Hebrew word *etz* has been translated in the English King James version of the Bible as stick or rod, a very strange departure from the basic and more common meaning of wood. Latter-day Saints interpret Ezekiel's prophecy (Ezekiel 37:15–20) as the joining of two scriptural records in modern days into one volume of scripture: the Book of Mormon as the stick of Joseph, and the Bible as the stick Judah. It is possible that Ezekiel described his revelation of the stick (wood tablet) of Joseph, based on his

Babylonian experience of seeing scribes writing on the wax surface of ancient wooden books called sticks or wood (Messervy "Job: Yet Will I Trust in Him").

* * * * *

In this fictional account of Ezekiel and Jeremiah in prison, the importance of preserving information regarding eternal covenants through the preservation of records that will ultimately become part of the Book of Mormon scripture is mentioned in the dialogue. The title page of the Book of Mormon tells us that one of the scripture's main objectives, in addition to testifying of Christ, is "to show unto the remnant of the House of Israel what great things the Lord has done for their fathers; and that they may know the covenants of the Lord, that they are not cast off forever." Lehi prophesied that the brass plates would "go forth unto all nations, kindreds, tongues, and people who were of his seed," and that they should "never perish; neither should they be dimmed any more by time" (1 Nephi 5:18–19). It may be that Joseph Smith fulfilled Lehi's words in the publication and distribution of the Book of Mormon, which today numbers in the hundreds of millions of copies, since much of what was written in the brass plates was also re-written into the gold plate record Moroni prepared for translation by Joseph Smith (William J. Hamblin, "Sacred Writings on Bronze Plates in the Ancient Mediterranean"). The brass plates served a very important purpose for Lehi's descendants. They preserved the written language as well as providing a hard copy of religious covenants and doctrine that would not have been preserved beyond one or two generations if written on leather parchment. The title page of the Book of Mormon indicates that the covenants were of eternal consequence and that by not knowing them a man could be cast off forever. It may be that some important insights regarding temples or temple covenants were preserved in the brass plates and, if so, would have assisted Nephi when he built a temple after Lehi's colony arrived in the Americas about 580 B.C. (Daniel H. Ludlow, "The Title Page," in *The Book of Mormon: First Nephi, The Doctrinal Foundation, papers from the second annual Book of Mormon Symposium*, eds. Monte S. Nyman and Charles D. Tate, 5–11).

* * * * *

Nephi records that Lehi found the writings of Jeremiah inscribed into the plates (1 Nephi 5: 13). Captain Laban was a ranking member of the noble class of Jerusalem that despised Jeremiah, it is unlikely that Laban knowingly allowed Jeremiah's prophecies to be recorded in the brass plates. Jeremiah may very well have understood the urgency of recording his prophetic words into the brass plates. In this chapter, Jeremiah persists in his efforts to include them in the brass plates prior to Nephi's return to the capital to secure the record and take it out of the city. Lehi informs us that the brass plates contained the first five books of Moses, similar to the first books of the Old Testament that give the account of the creation of the world and the biography of Adam and Eve, the parents of the human family. Scholars of religion suggest that the first books of Moses written on the brass plates would have been in a less altered state than the books of the Old Testament, since they would not have endured centuries of abridging and rewriting. The brass plates also included a history of the Jews from the beginning down to the reign of King Zedekiah. Nephi also tells us that they included a record of Lehi's and Laban's shared genealogy (1 Nephi 5: 10–20).

CHAPTER SEVEN

Ancient Jews washed the corpse, covered it with spices to hide the odor of decaying tissue and organs, and wrapped it with long strips of linen or other material. In this chapter, Jonathan's private journey through the olive groves of Beit Zayit to collect the body of his dead son is intended to supplant a public funeral procession that would have been conducted, complete with hired wailers and expressions of grief by family members. With the exception of the death of a parent, the body of the deceased was buried on the day of death. However, in this chapter, Aaron is believed to have been dead for almost two months, and Jonathan, with help from Ruth, has prepared a leather satchel to collect whatever decayed remains he can find of his eldest son. For this reason, he does not employ the customary burial rituals.

The funeral procession of ancient Jews included laying the body without a coffin on a bier and carrying it out beyond the town walls to the place of burial, which was either a cemetery or, if circumstances allowed, the private grounds owned by the family. Women—mothers, daughters, and sisters of the deceased— led the procession, and the hired mourners followed, expressing sorrow with music, praises of the dead, loud wailings, beating of the breast and rending of garments (Bible Dictionary, The Church of Jesus Christ of Latter-day Saints). The Jews detested cremation and either buried the body in the ground or in a rock-hewn tomb. Gravesites were carefully marked and often whitewashed to keep people from defiling the tomb by walking over it (Matthew 23:27; Luke 11:44).

CHAPTER NINE

Nephi indicates that the writings of the prophet Isaiah were among his most cherished reading materials (1 Nephi 19:23; 2 Nephi 11:8). He quoted extensively from Isaiah and included a good deal of Isaiah's writings in the gold plate record once he arrived in the New World. In this chapter, Nephi quotes numerous passages from Isaiah, including the reference to the birth of Christ at Jerusalem (Isaiah 9:6), the promise that God would open up rivers in the midst of the valleys (Isaiah 41:18), and that He would make a river in the desert (Isaiah 43:19). Nephi may have copied Isaiah's writings from the brass plates. He may also have had an alternate source for Isaiah's writings beyond the brass-plate record, and in this chapter, Nephi reads from Isaiah scrolls brought from his family's personal library. Isaiah began his ministry at Jerusalem 158 years before Lehi escaped the city, and it is possible that Nephi was immersed in the writings of Isaiah long before he left

Jerusalem. Isaiah's writings may have been part of Nephi's studies as he learned to read and write during his youth.

We do not know what records, if any beyond the brass plates, Nephi brought with him into the wilderness, but his education, reading and writing abilities, and his familiarity with Isaiah suggest he may have carried records into the wilderness beyond the codex of plates recovered from Captain Laban's treasury—an event that will be treated in volume four of this series, *Day of Remembrance.* In this chapter, Nephi reads a text of Isaiah he carried into the wilderness from his home. In his new surroundings in the Judean Wilderness and after their flight from Jerusalem, Nephi begins to see his family's escape in terms of Isaiah's prophecies. Nephi borrows numerous phrases and expressions from Isaiah that are mixed with his own writings, which demonstrates how deeply he appreciated that prophet. Nephi writes about a "marvelous work that will be of great worth to his seed" (1 Nephi 22:8), he uses the title "Holy One of Israel" and "Savior" which are also employed by Isaiah, and, when an angel visits Nephi, the messenger uses phrases from Isaiah that would have been very familiar to Nephi (1 Nephi 21:1; Isaiah 49:22–23; & S. Kent Brown, *From Jerusalem to Zarahemla).*

* * * * *

Scholar S. Kent Brown in his literary and historical studies of the Book of Mormon, suggests that Nephi included chapters 48 and 49 of Isaiah at the end of his first book to clarify the prophetic message of the scattering and gathering of Israel when he quotes "Hearken all ye that are broken off, that are scattered abroad, who are of my people, O house of Israel," (1 Nephi 21:1; Isaiah 49:22–23; & S. Kent Brown, *From Jerusalem to Zarahemla).* Dr. Brown points out that Nephi likely believed Isaiah was speaking about their family as being part of the exodus from Jerusalem and viewed his posterity as taking part in the future gathering. These Isaiah prophecies are similar to the prophecies of scattering and gathering suggested in the Allegory of the Olive Tree by the prophet Zenos (Paul Y. Hoskisson, "The Allegory of the Olive Tree in Jacob," in *The Allegory of The Olive Tree,* eds. Steven D. Ricks and John W. Welch, 186–247), and included prominently in the writings of Nephi's younger brother, Jacob, both brothers viewing the scattering in intensely personal terms, since they saw their family's flight from Jerusalem as a partial fulfillment of these prophecies.

* * * * *

In this chapter, Aaron reminds Nephi that he and his family are part of God's carefully orchestrated scattering, and he produces an olive graft cut from a tree at Beit Zayit and carried into the wilderness as a reminder of the personal significance of the Allegory of the Olive Tree to their exodus from Jerusalem (Jacob 5: 11–14). This chapter combines the prophecies of Isaiah that Nephi features prominently in the Book of Mormon with the Allegory of the Olive Tree written into the Book of Mormon record by his younger brother, Jacob. The remainder of this historical note summarizes the significance of the Allegory of the Olive Tree. A more extensive summary of the first fourteen verses of the allegory appears in the previous novel: *Power of Deliverance.*

The Allegory of the Olive Tree presents seven identifiable periods of Jewish and world history, with Lehi and his family living about the time of the closing of the second period. The allegory is similar to Isaiah's prophecies of that time period; however, hidden in the allegory's allusions are many more details about the scattering than in Isaiah's writings. The allegory details God's attempt to reclaim the House of Israel from apostasy by sending prophets like Moses, Samuel, Elijah, and Isaiah to dig about the olive tree, prune it, and nourish it. The Lord of the vineyard met with minimal success, with the tree putting forth "somewhat a little, young and tender branches," while most of the tree continued to deteriorate (Jacob 5:6). This portion of the allegory (Jacob 5: 4–14) makes clear that the ruling class, the "main top" of the tree was for the most part beyond recovery (Jacob 5:6), and in this fictionalized account, Nephi is portrayed as beginning to understand the ominous, destructive ramifications of the leadership of his people.

At some point during this second historical time period described in the Allegory of the Olive Tree, the Lord of the vineyard directs the servant to take three vineyard keeping measures to preserve some of the fruit of the tree by: cutting out those parts of Israel in apostasy (Jacob 5:7); grafting other people into the House of Israel (Jacob 5:9); and grafting or planting some of the young and tender branches from the House of Israel into other parts of the vineyard (Jacob 5:8).

The first step in this process (Jacob 5:7) may have occurred when the Assyrians destroyed the Northern Kingdom of Israel in wars beginning around 734 B.C. and culminating with the fall of that kingdom in 721 B.C., when many of the inhabitants of that land were carried away captive. The Babylonians completed this phase of scattering by destroying the Southern Kingdom in battles between 605 B.C. and 586 B.C. and taking captive the remaining inhabitants of Judah (Hoskisson, "The Allegory of the Olive Tree in Jacob," in *The Allegory of The Olive Tree,* eds. Steven D. Ricks and John W. Welch, 186–247).

The second instruction given in this portion of the allegory (Jacob 5:9)— grafting other people into the House of Israel—may have been completed by the Assyrians who, after carrying away captive the ten tribes of the Northern Kingdom and intermingling them with other nations along the upper Mediterranean, imported people from many nations under their control into Northern Israel. This immigration led to intermarriage among the Israelites who remained in the land (2 Kings 17:24; Ezra 4: 2, 10).

The third instruction given in this portion of the allegory of the olive tree— grafting or planting some of the young and tender branches from the House of Israel into other parts of the vineyard (Jacob 5:8)—involved transporting to other lands Israelites who were faithful to the laws of Moses and their covenants made in the holy temple at Jerusalem. Lehi and his family qualify as some of the young and tender branches described in the allegory.

* * * * *

In addition to fulfilling the prophecies of scattering, S. Kent Brown indicates that Nephi's other "stated" reason for quoting Isaiah was to: "more fully persuade [his people] to believe in their Redeemer" (1 Nephi 19:23). However, Brown also suggests that Nephi may have had an "unstated" purpose for inserting chapters 48 and 49 of Isaiah at the end of his first book, due mostly to the painful separation he felt from leaving his homeland (Brown, *From Jerusalem to Zarahemla*). Nephi never explicitly states his longing to return home, but through the eyes of his younger brother Jacob, who was born in the wilderness and never knew Jerusalem, we get a sense of the sentiments that may have lingered in family discussions regarding their flight from Jerusalem when he wrote: "The time passed away with us, and also our lives passed away like as it were unto us a dream, we being a lonesome and a solemn people, wanderers, cast out from Jerusalem, born in tribulation, in a wilderness, and hated of our brethren, which caused wars and contentions; wherefore, we did mourn out our days" (Jacob 7:26). In this chapter, Nephi's longing to return to Jerusalem is personified, particularly in his unanswered question—would there ever be a *next* year in Jerusalem?

* * * * *

Nephi tells us that Lehi was a dedicated scribe whose influence set a pattern for record keeping throughout Nephite history, and he begins his own writings by giving a summary of his father's record (1 Nephi 5–15). When Nephi inscribed his record on metal plates after arriving in the new world (1 Nephi 9), it appears that he used an already-existing journal or daily log kept during their travels from Jerusalem that contained Lehi's writings, some sort of family genealogy, and a diary of the family's eight-year odyssey in the wilderness of Arabia (1 Nephi 19:1–2). Dr. S. Kent Brown points out that after the receipt of the Liahona compass, Nephi narrates the events of their travels through a number of third-person-plural "we" passages, which bear the distinct marks of the author summarizing the diary-record of a second author—most likely Lehi in this case—which begins with the phrase: "*We* did sojourn for the space of many years, yea, even eight years in the wilderness" (1 Nephi 17:4).

We do not know what materials Lehi used to make his diary record; however, it is likely he used leather parchments made from the skins of animals rather than a more difficult writing medium like potsherd, clay tablets, or metal plates. As an adult, Jacob, Nephi's brother, had possession of Lehi's journal as well as the brass plates, and he may have been referring to the deteriorating condition of his father's diary when he wrote that he knew what was written on plates would remain, but what was written on any other material would vanish away (Jacob 4: 1–2). In this chapter, Lehi begins his diary in the wilderness on leather parchments—a diary that would guide Nephi and Jacob many years later when they recorded the events of their family's journey to the new world on the gold-plate record, possibly quoting and summarizing directly from their father's writings.

* * * * *

Caravaneers weaved their tents from animal hair, preferably from camels. Weaving a tent was a time-intensive task that required months of weaving, usually by the hands of a number of weavers. The camel fibers darned seamlessly into place, and the coarseness of the hairs allowed air to pass through the wall of the tent, but swelled in times of rain to produce a watertight surface that kept out moisture. As each child was born to a merchant trader, a room was added to the tent to accommodate the growing family (Lynn M. and Hope Hilton, *In Search of Lehi's Trail*). Explorer George Potter weighed a small, traditional camel-hair tent with dimensions of approximately ten square feet. Without any bedding or floor rugs, the tent weighed 250 pounds. Lehi's tent was likely much larger than ten feet square, and required a good many camels or mules to carry it into the desert (Potter & Wellington, *Lehi in the Wilderness*).

In ancient times, a tent was a substantial investment since it required a good number of walls and a substantially large roof sewn from the hair of camels over a period of many years. For Lehi to escape Jerusalem with little notice and take a tent with him meant that he had most likely had a tent ready for the journey, and it also indicates that he may have traveled often enough to justify the time and cost of owning a large tent. The Book of Mormon tells us in the first chapter that "Lehi went forth," a possible reference to travel along the known trade routes of the ancient world (Nibley, "Lehi in the Desert"; also Lynn M. and Hope Hilton, *In Search of Lehi's Trail*). Hugh Nibley suggests that Lehi's ability to slip out of Jerusalem with a tent—most likely a camel-hair tent—indicates he made heavy investments in the merchant trade—possibly olive oil—and he used his tent on his merchant travels to Egypt and other Middle East locations.

* * * * *

On numerous occasions, Laman reviles his father for his dreams and visions, and on at least one occasion he may have plotted to kill Lehi for leading them so far from their wealth at Jerusalem (1 Nephi 2:13). In this chapter, Laman begins considering the murder of his father, or at least consenting to the act, in order to comply with Zadock's decree that he and his family will not be allowed to return to Jerusalem as long as Lehi remains alive.

CHAPTER TEN

Hanameel is an historical character introduced in the Old Testament as the prophet Jeremiah's cousin (Jeremiah 32:7). He was involved in the sale of land to Jeremiah, though it is not clear whether he owned the land or acted as an agent to sell the property in Jeremiah's hometown of Anathoth. He was involved in the final purchase that took place in the prison at Jerusalem for the price of seventeen pieces of silver. There is no record of how Hanameel was recruited to prepare the documents of sale and we do not know how Jeremiah obtained the money to make the purchase. We do know that a double, sealed scroll was prepared for the sale of property to Jeremiah and that Hanameel was most likely responsible for its preparation. In this chapter, Zoram's visit to Hanameel is a fictionalized event that occurred prior to events recorded in the Book of Jeremiah where Hanameel goes to Jeremiah in prison (Jeremiah 32:9–11).

* * * * *

The practice of preparing two identical documents and then sealing one of the two was common practice in the ancient world, and the use of a double, sealed parchment described in this chapter is based on an ancient legal practice common in Israel at 600 B.C. (John W. Welch, "Double, Sealed, Witnessed Documents: From the Ancient World to the Book of Mormon," in *Mormons, Scripture, and the Ancient World,* ed Davis Bitton). The documents had two parts: one was left open, while the other was sealed for later consultation or to be used by a judge. When the prophet Jeremiah purchased land near his home in Anathoth (Jeremiah 32:9–10), he signed a document, part of it sealed and another part left open. Jeremiah writes that he acted according to the custom and law of his time (Jeremiah 32: 11), and technical terms of law are part of Jeremiah's description of this document and the transaction of his land purchase (John Bright, "Jeremiah" in *The Anchor Bible,* 237). There are many examples extant today of double, sealed documents. They were typically written on one side of a single sheet of papyrus or parchment with the text copied twice, once at the top and again toward the bottom, with a space about 2–3 centimeters wide between the two renderings of the text. In some instances, the sealed copy was an exact copy and in other cases it was an abridgement. The open portion allowed for parties to orient themselves with regard to the terms of the contract while the sealed copy guarded against tampering (Elisabeth Koffmahn, "Die Doppelurkunden aus der Wuste Juda," 19). A standard sealing procedure included folding the sealed portion, then threading bands through holes punched along the middle before affixing a wax or clay impression over the bands. In this chapter, Hanameel prepares a double, sealed document on parchment that was commonly used for legal and otherwise important documents in Lehi's day (Nibley, "Lehi in the Desert"; also Lynn M. and Hope Hilton, *In Search of Lehi's Trail;* also Potter & Wellington, *Lehi in the Wilderness*).

CHAPTER ELEVEN

Qumran is located along the northwest shores of the Dead Sea, about twenty miles south of Jericho. It was a secluded location, surrounded by long stretches of sand dunes, and the harsh climate repelled all but the most hardy of desert dwellers. A group of Jewish religious dissenters lived at the historic community of Qumran and left us the now-famous Dead Sea scrolls, the writings dating back to between 250 and 350 B.C. and ending about A.D. 73. Hugh Nibley suggests that this community may have started long before the scrolls were written, possibly as early as Lehi's day or earlier (Nibley, "More Voices From the Dust"). It is possible that the religious refugees of Lehi's day, the Rekhabites, were some of the founders of the group that ultimately wrote the Dead Sea Scrolls. In this chapter, the description of their community is based on archeological evidence uncovered at the site.

The remains of the ancient community of Qumran are located along the northwest shores of the Dead Sea and are surrounded by rocky outcrops and cliffs. Archeologists have found a series of pools fed by a freshwater spring and connected by aqueducts; the existence of those structures is attributed to a community called Covenanters. The first pools were used for ritual washings and baptisms, the next pools for drinking water and storage, and the remaining pools were for livestock. There were homes, meeting rooms, and what appears to be a large communal kitchen and eating area. In this chapter, the people at Qumran live in tents and are only beginning to erectstructures that will ultimately be finished centuries later by the community responsible for writing the Dead Sea Scrolls (Nibley, "More Voices From the Dust," in *The Old Testament and Related Studies*).

* * * * *

Pulse is a Hebrew word meaning seeds and vegetables—particularly leguminous vegetables. When the prophet Daniel was taken captive to Babylon during Lehi's day, he challenged his captors to give him pulse to eat (seeds and vegetables), and water to drink, and then monitor his health for ten days to see if he were physically stronger and healthier than the Babylonian soldiers and servants whose diet included large portions of the king's meat (Daniel 1: 12, 16). Daniel's prescription for the consumption of vegetables and seeds and his proscription against meat is similar to the recommendations for good health found in the Doctrine and Covenants (D&C 89: 10–13)—the scriptural reference to "herbs" includes wholesome plants of every kind. In this chapter Aaron refers to vineyard owners selling pulse to the merchant traders and caravaneers passing through Moab where there was enough arable farmland and rainwater to grow seeds and vegetables in an otherwise desert region.

* * * * *

The 224-mile journey from Jerusalem to the Valley of Lemuel began an eight-year odyssey for Lehi and his family. We do not know how long Lehi traveled and camped in the wilderness areas between the capital city and the secluded valley that was to serve as a base camp for many years. A direct journey, driving the animals as hard as conditions permitted, and without any stops to collect food, observe the Sabbath, rest, or find water would have required about 9–14 days. It is unlikely, however, that Lehi would have pushed his family and their animals that hard, unless they had a compelling reason to travel that quickly. The only time-distance reference Nephi gives in his record is the three-day march along the shores of the Fountain of the Red Sea—an ancient name for the Gulf of Aqaba—to a valley Lehi named after his second son, Lemuel. Some readers of the Book of Mormon mistakenly attribute the three-day journey in the wilderness (1 Nephi 2:6) as a time-distance reference for the entire 224-mile journey from Jerusalem to the valley of Lemuel. A careful reading of the previous verse (1 Nephi 2:5), however, indicates that Lehi and his family traveled for an undisclosed amount of time before arriving at the Gulf of Aqaba. They may have camped in numerous wilderness areas north of the Fountain of the Red Sea before making a forced march of three days down along the coast, through the Jabal Mountain Range that Nephi refers to as the Borders *near* and *nearer* the Red Sea. The final leg of the journey to the Valley of Lemuel appears to have been a forced march, since Lehi and his family drove their animals about twenty-five miles every day, covering the 72 miles between Aqaba and their final camp in three days' time. There are numerous possible wilderness areas where Lehi may have set up camp after leaving Jerusalem and before reaching the Fountain of the Red Sea. In this chapter, the site selected for his first camp is at Qumran in the Judean Wilderness along the northwest shores of the Dead Sea.

CHAPTER TWELVE

The journey from Jerusalem to Sidon on the shores of the Mediterranean Sea was not a direct northwest route. Travelers departed Jerusalem and headed east to Jericho, then north through the Jordan River Valley until they reached the Jezreel Valley. This is the same valley where Nazareth is located and where Jesus lived as a child among the homes and shops dotting the tree-lined community among the hills. Travelers turned west past Nazareth, through the Jezreel Valley along the Kishon River until they reached fort Megiddo, and then down through the forested mountainous country known as the Cedars of Lebanon to the shores of the Mediterranean, and finally up along the coast, past the city of Tyre and on to the famous port city of Sidon. In this chapter Jonathan has traveled as far as Fort Megiddo, where he takes refuge at a trailside inn. King Solomon built Fort Megiddo at the top of the Kishon Pass and stabled more than a thousand horses there. Some of the stables can still be seen in excavations at the site (*Great People of the Bible and How They Lived*).

* * * * *

Captain Elnathan is an historical character introduced in volume one of this series, *Pillar of Fire* (Jeremiah 26: 21–24). He was assigned to return the Prophet Uriah from Egypt and his mission is mentioned in both the Old Testament and the Lakhish Letters ("Lakhish Letters" in Noel B. Reynolds and Charles D. Tate, eds., *Book of Mormon Authorship: New Light on Ancient Origins*). We do not have any other records regarding Elnathan's military exploits. In this chapter and chapter 14, Elnathan's pursuit of Jonathan is fictionalized. The Old Testament references to Elnathan show him acting under orders from a monarch previous to Zedekiah's rule; however, Bible scholars point out that, based on references to Elnathan in the Lakhish Letters, those events were incorrectly recorded in the Old Testament and that Elnathan most likely performed his military mission during the reign of King Zedekiah (Nibley, "Dark Days in Jerusalem, The Lakhish Letters and the Book of Mormon").

CHAPTER THIRTEEN

We do not know the name of Zedekiah's wife or what role she may have played in the events of the time. In this novel she has been given the name Miriam, which means exalted. The name for this character was partly influenced by the role played by the sister of Moses, also named Miriam, who watched over her infant brother in the bulrushes along the Nile River. In this novel Miriam shares a function similar to the sister of Moses—watching over the prophets of God and ensuring their safety at the peril of their own lives. Hugh Nibley suggests that Zedekiah's wife was most likely responsible for saving her son Mulek from execution by the Babylonians eight years after Lehi left Jerusalem (Nibley, "Dark Days in Jerusalem"). We are certain that Zedekiah was married, but the written records are silent with regard to details about the Queen of Judah. She likely played a central role in rearing and protecting Mulek and her other sons. In this chapter, she is portrayed in that light.

CHAPTER FOURTEEN

Sidon is the most common place-name in New World Book of Mormon geography—most likely borrowed from the ancient port city along the Mediterranean Coast. Hugh Nibley suggests that the common use of the name in the New World is tied to Lehi's familiarity with the ancient Old World city of Sidon. It was the largest port on the eastern seaboard of the Great Sea, and if Lehi was a merchant olive oil trader in the years leading up to his departure from Jerusalem, he may have caravanned his oil to Sidon for export to other nations bordering the Mediterranean. During winter months, sand storms across the Sinai Peninsula made travel difficult, and Nibley suggests that some of the olive oil shipped from Lehi's groves was sent to Egypt by ship from Sidon rather than over land on the backs of camels traveling across the Sinai Peninsula. Lehi may have caravanned his olive oil to Sidon and shipped it aboard merchant sailing vessels bound for Egypt

(Nibley, "Lehi in the Desert," in *Lehi in the Desert/The World of the Jaredites/There Were Jaredites.* ed. John W. Welch).

*　*　*　*　*

Sidon was named after its founder, the grandson of Ham. It was the northernmost city in Canaan and was the birthplace of Jezebel who introduced Baal worship among the Hebrews (1 Kings 16: 30–33). Sidon was the oldest of the Phoenician cities and reached the pinnacle of economic prominence during Lehi's day, due mostly to the dominance of the merchant traders sailing from its ports. The merchant traders were known as the "great ones" (cf.Revelations 18:23; Isaiah 23:8), and though the city of Tyre, down the coast from Sidon, would eventually rival the economic power of Sidon, in Lehi's day there was no rival—Sidon was the jewel of ports on the Mediterranean (*Old Testament Student Manual: 1 King–Malachi*).

*　*　*　*　*

The Phoenicians were known for their boatbuilding. King Solomon, centuries before Lehi's day, hired Phoenician boatbuilders to travel south of Judah to Aqaba (Ezion—Geber) on the Fountain of the Red Sea (Gulf of Aqaba) and build a port to establish merchant trade by water where before there was only over land trade (*Great People of the Bible and How They Lived*). Hugh Nibley suggests that the Phoenicians were responsible for helping Mulek and the royal family of Judah find their way to the New World by outfitting them with sailing vessels, and by teaching the royal entourage how to sail the high seas (Nibley, "Lehi in the Desert"). In this chapter, Mulek begins his training as young sailor, forced by circumstance aboard a Phoenician navy vessel in company with his young friend, Prince Jesse of Sidon.

*　*　*　*　*

Ebed-Melech the Ethiopian is an historical figure who served in the royal court under King Zedekiah. He appealed to the king for clemency on behalf of the imprisoned prophet Jeremiah, when he was in prison and was instrumental in freeing the prophet from the well of the prison (Jeremiah 38). In this chapter, Ebed-Melech is characterized as a sailor prior to his arrival in Jerusalem, as recorded in the Old Testament. When he is reunited with Mima—the fictional Ethiopian handservant—she asks him to go to Jerusalem and seek the favor of King Zedekiah in order to help the imprisoned prophets. Mima's plea prefigures the beginning of Ebed-Melech's relationship with King Zedekiah, as recorded in the Book of Jeremiah.

CHAPTER FIFTEEN
The Old Testament records that while Jeremiah sat in prison, the voice of the Lord came to him, telling him that his cousin, Hanameel, would visit him in prison

and ask Jeremiah to buy his property—a field located in Anathoth (Jeremiah 32:7). Hanameel fulfilled that revelation and offered to sell his property for seventeen pieces of silver (Jeremiah 32:8). We do not know if Hanameel owned the property outright, or if he was selling the property on behalf of a family trust or another seller. However, the Old Testament indicates that Hanameel was the agent of sale, telling Jeremiah that the right of inheritance belonged to him. Jeremiah's purchase of property was intended to accentuate his prophetic pronouncements that Israel would suffer seventy years of captivity under the rule of Babylon, but that they would return to the land of their inheritance. Jeremiah stored the record of the sale of this property in a sealed clay jar to show his faith that God would allow the Jews to return to this land and possess houses, fields, and vineyards again (Jeremiah 32: 14–15). For more information regarding this event, see the historical notes for chapters 25 and 28.

CHAPTER SIXTEEN

In this chapter, Josiah the Potter prepares his followers to leave Qumran; however, he also indicates that either he or his descendants will return to this place and store the records and scrolls of their people in the caves above the shoreline of the Dead Sea. Many years after this fictional event, a group similar to the Rekhabites inhabited Qumran, built a series of baptismal and water pools from the spring, raised a communal kitchen and cafeteria, and carved out an existence in this desert outpost similar to the one Josiah the Potter and his Rekhabite followers began in this novel. The Dead Sea scrolls written by members of this community do not date back to Lehi's day. However, Hugh Nibley suggests that the community itself may have begun long before the records were made and stored in the hills above the encampment. In 1964, the Dead Sea scrolls were found by a shepherd boy in the caves above Qumran and Josiah's words in this chapter are intended to foreshadow that future event (Nibley, "Qumran and the Waters of Mormon," in *An Approach to the Book of Mormon;* also "More Voices From the Dust," in *The Old Testament and Related Studies).*

* * * * *

Josiah the Potter is a fictional character based on the life of a historical figure who was responsible for founding the community at Qumran centuries after Lehi's day. He claimed divine guidance for his people, taught them what he knew about the Messiah, required strict observance of the Law of Moses, and introduced among them the idea of baptism, a sacrament or holy supper, and many other doctrines. Among the writings in the Dead Sea Scrolls are numerous references to a man who either founded the community of Covenantors at Qumran or who was revered by them enough to be considered their leader. His teachings are part of the *Manual of Discipline*. As prolific as the writings are, there is no mention of his name. The only title given him in the written record of the Dead Sea Scrolls was Teacher of

Righteousness, a code name used to protect the man from persecution and discovery (Nibley, "More Voices From the Dust").

* * * * *

The Rekhabites were not the only group of religious dissidents in Lehi's day, but their doctrines were similar to many groups (Jeremiah 35). The prophet Jeremiah and other prophets of his time were not typically associated with any religious faction within Judaism, but they did champion the cause of Rekhabites and others who shunned the popular religious and political fads of their day and called for a return to strict observance of the Law of Moses in anticipation of the coming of the Messiah. The Rekhabites were, in essence, a "Church of Anticipation" (Nibley, "Dark Days in Jerusalem: The Lakhish Letters and the Book of Mormon," in *The Prophetic Book of Mormon*, 380–406).

* * * * *

Among Jews, the *Shema* is an affirmation of the love of God and a commitment to his purposes to love and serve him with all their hearts. Jews often refer to the *Shema*—Hebrew for the command to Israel to hear the word of God—as the acceptance of the Yoke of the Kingdom of Heaven (*Encyclopedia Judaica, Jerusalem,* 1372). Christ may have been quoting the Old Testament *Shema* when he taught that loving God was the greatest commandment and adding that a similar, second commandment was to love your neighbor as yourself (Matthew 22:36–37). The entire *Shema* (Deuteronomy 6:4–5) is recited twice daily by devout Jews as part of evening and morning prayer similar to Josiah the Potter's prayers in this chapter. Jewish martyrs are expected to face death with the *Shema* on their lips, and parents are to teach their children to cultivate an attitude of love toward God with the belief that it will change society, guiding men toward righteous living and blessings from heaven (*Encyclopedia Judaica, Jerusalem,* 1373). Restoration scriptures contain similar affirmations of love and commitment to God (D&C 101:35–38). The sixth chapter of Deuteronomy, where the *Shema* is found, includes a figurative command to the faithful to bind the words of this prayer to their foreheads and hands and to put them on the doorposts of their homes (Deuteronomy 6:8–9, 11:18, 20). This decree led to the dual Jewish custom of wearing a *tepillin* around the forehead and upper arm, and placing a *mezuzah* on the doorposts of Jewish homes. Jews inscribed scriptural passages on parchment, including the *Shema* but not limited to it, folded them into tiny leather boxes less than two inches square, and wore the *tepillin*, Hebrew for phylactery, on the forehead and the left bicep, suggesting that they would fulfill the law with the head and the heart (Samuel Fallows, *The Popular and Critical Bible Encyclopedia and Scriptural Dictionary* vol. 3, 1344). Years after Moses first encouraged Jews to love God and bind his word to their hearts, some Jews, without the guidance of living prophets, viewed the *tepillin* as an amulet or charm with power to ward off evil spirits. At the same time, the use of the *mezuzah* gained popularity. Scriptural passages and the words of the *Shema* were inserted into a tiny, cylindrical box and attached to the door frame. It was customary for Jews to touch or kiss the *mezuzah* each time they left or entered, reminding all who pass to do the will of God as they go out among their fellow man (*Old Testament Student Manual: Genesis–2 Samuel,* 218).

* * * * *

The opening chapters of the Book of Mormon record Lehi's prophetic assurances that Jerusalem would be destroyed. In this chapter, he verbalizes the first of those prophecies in the presence of his eldest son. Nephi indicates that Laman and Lemuel did not believe their father's statements about the coming destruction of Jerusalem, and in this chapter, Laman shows his initial contempt for his father's unsubstantiated claims as well as his disregard for Lehi's personal record keeping (1 Nephi 2:13).

CHAPTER SEVENTEEN

Ancient cartography was known among Semitic peoples during Lehi's day, and remnants of maps charted on parchment, potsherds, metal plates and chiseled into stone markers and statues have been recovered from antiquity. Mapmakers do not appear to have used accurately scaled distances in their maps, due, in part, to the difficulty of collecting reliable measurements. Distances between cities, the length of mountain ranges, and the width of bodies of water were calculated in terms of days of travel—a practice that often skewed the distance scales and added to their inaccuracy. The distance for one day of travel on the ancient trade routes varied between ten and twenty-five miles, depending on the terrain and the state of the animals making the trip—some packed with heavy loads and others with light burdens. Lynn and Hope Hilton indicate that a typical caravan traveled about twelve miles in one day; however, the maximum distance for a forced march was close to twenty-five miles (Lynn M. and Hope Hilton, "In Search of Lehi's Trail"). Book of Mormon explorer, George Potter, analyzed the cartographic directions written by Nephi (1 Nephi 2:5–6) and determined that the Valley of Lemuel was located within seventy-five miles of the port city of Aqaba, about the maximum distance traveled over a three-day journey. Those mapmaking assumptions, along with other research, proved helpful in directing Mr. Potter and his search team to discover Wadi Tayyib al-Ism—The Pleasant Valley—the most likely candidate for the Valley of Lemuel (Potter & Wellington, *Lehi in the Wilderness*).

* * * * *

In this chapter, Inspector Tobit is dressed in a full desert turban. The white cloth was wrapped multiple times around the skull, forming a wide brim as a shield from the sun, and covering the head. It was tied loose enough to allow cool air to pass over the scalp, while the cloth captured the moisture from sweat and acted as an additional cooling mechanism. Military captains and royalty fixed a heron feather to the back of the turban to signify their station. In this chapter, Tobit wears a turban with two feathers, distinguishing his high place in the Babylonian military.

CHAPTER NINETEEN

In this chapter, the members of Lehi's traveling party divide into smaller groups and begin an odyssey that will take family members and friends down numerous possible routes that ultimately lead to the Fountain of the Red Sea. We do not know which route Lehi took to reach the Gulf of Aqaba—Nephi is silent on the matter except to say that they traveled in the wilderness—nor do we know how long they took to reach the Red Sea. What we do know is that Lehi and his family headed southeast of Jerusalem and reached the shores of the Fountain of the Red Sea after traveling for an undisclosed amount of time. In this novel, the various routes leading from Jerusalem to the Red Sea are tightly integrated into the story line with members of Lehi's family and their friends traveling all the known ancient routes in order to highlight the possible trails they could have taken.

The least-traveled route between Jerusalem and the Red Sea ran through the hill country south of Jerusalem, past Hebron (or farther south past Bersheba), then east onto the sands of the Judean Wilderness, past the southern extreme of the Dead Sea, and into the rift valley called the Arabah, following the contour of that low-lying basin all the way to the Gulf of Aqaba. This route—particularly through the Judean Wilderness and down the rift valley of the Arabah—presented a rather difficult journey due to the lack of water during the hot summer months, making passage on foot or by camel nearly impossible (I. S. Kawashti, and M. M. Omar, "Water Economy and Water Metabolism of Camels and Donkeys, Under Desert Conditions").

The King's Highway appears to have been the preferred route, heading east from Jerusalem, past Jericho along the north shores of the Dead Sea, before turning south along the east side of the Dead Sea. This route passed south through the plateau country of Moab and Edom where caravaneers found frequent well water, arable farm land, and a good many sheepherders and vineyard owners selling food in small markets along the route.

The third route to the Fountain of the Red Sea, known anciently as The Way of the Wilderness, runs parallel to the King's Highway, between five to twenty-five miles farther east of the preferred route, on the sandy, desert lands of the Empty Quarter. There is less water and food available farther east along the Way of the Wilderness; However, many merchant traders preferred this more difficult route and risked the lack of water and the possibility of robber bands attacking them rather than pay the high tariffs collected along the King's Highway. Arabian explorers George Potter and Richard Wellington suggest that Lehi may have determined to travel the Way of the Wilderness rather than the King's Highway, since it lay farther from Jerusalem than the other routes and may have provided Lehi some insular advantages from any member of the ruling classes who might have been following him. In this chapter and subsequent chapters, the story line is designed to allow characters to demonstrate that all routes lead to Aqaba and the Fountain of the Red Sea (Potter & Wellington, *Lehi in the Wilderness*).

* * * * *

Frequent sandstorms and dust storms occur in the wilderness areas between Egypt and the Arabian Peninsula. They are hazardous to land transport, sea navigation, and human health. In mid-March 1998, sandstorms in the same location where this chapter is set claimed four lives, left 29 people injured, and forced the Suez Canal, airports, and seaports to close. The storm bathed the entire region in an eerie yellow light. The arid regions of the Arabian Peninsula experience the highest frequency of dust storms with over 30 per year. In Egypt, sandstorms are called khamsin (fifty) for the number of days on which they typically occur during the year. In 1997, eighteen Egyptians died in what was believed to be the worst sandstorm in three decades. Dust storms occur on a variety of spatial scales from mesoscale (limited to an area around a city), regional areas (extending over large portions of a nation), and continental storms. Sandstorms remove large quantities of surface sediments and topsoil along with nutrients and seeds. In this chapter, the sandstorm that saves Lehi from capture is characteristic of the size, wind speed, and tendencies of storms in that region.

CHAPTER TWENTY-ONE

The date palm groves growing in the Jordan River Delta east of Jericho date back many centuries before Lehi's day and are still widely known today for their prolific fruit production. Date palms thrive in hot, dry climates and grow throughout the Middle East, flourishing where few plants can grow. The date palm is one of the world's oldest crop plants, and early civilizations began cultivating them over four thousand years ago, the fruit still forming an important part of the diet of many desert peoples. Date palms provide shade, nourishment, building materials, and fuel. Muslim legend names the date palm as the "Tree of Life" (*World Book*, vol. 5, p. 40), and the Qur'an alludes to the date-palm imagery of the tree of life as representative of the son of god, proclaiming that "Seest thou how Allah sets forth a parable of a *good word* [son of God] as a *good tree* [date palm]" (Qur'an 14:29–31). Numerous Middle Eastern tribes held a similar regard for the date palm as the "Tree of Life" long before the rise of the prophet Mohammed, six hundred years after the birth of Christ. In pre-Islamic times (pre A.D. 600), the date palm was worshipped by the people of what is today modern Yemen, along the southern extremes of the Arabian Peninsula, where they adorned their temple with numerous depictions of the date palm as the "Tree of Life" (R. L. Playfair, *A History of Arabia from the Commencement of the Christian Era to the Present Time*).

Three genus of date palms are extant today, with the *Hyphenae thebaica* producing the largest fruit—the dates growing to the size of lemons. Explorer George Potter indicates that all three varieties of date palm, including the large lemon-sized variety, can be found in the date palm groves east of Jericho as well as at Wadi Tayyib al- Ism—the site he discovered and corroborated with numerous other Book of Mormon scholars as the most likely location of the Valley of Lemuel (Potter & Wellington, *Lehi in the Wilderness*). Potter indicates that the different varieties of fruit vary in color from red to yellow. The *Khulas* are considered the best commercial varieties, particularly in what is called the *rutab* stage when it is pale yellow, touched with amber, and filled with sweetness (S. A. Amin, "Fresh Dates Will Soon Be Ready to Harvest," 1). These sweet, pale-yellow, clear-skinned, amber-touched dates growing in the Valley of Lemuel may have influenced the imagery of Lehi's dream. In this chapter, the date is foreshadowed as the "fruit sweet above all other fruits," and the date palm is prefigured as the "Tree of Life" that would eventually appear in Lehi's dream symbolic of the Son of God (the date palm) bearing the fruits of eternal life (the date).

CHAPTER TWENTY-THREE

The King's Highway was the preferred route from Jerusalem to Aqaba and points farther south in Arabia. The King's Highway began a few miles beyond Jericho, running up into the foothills of Mount Nebo and traversing through Amman, Moab, and Edom. The northern portion of the King's Highway runs through plateau country high above the shores of the Dead Sea. This route, particularly through the region of Moab, was an island of arable land capable of supporting year-round crop production and sheep grazing, surrounded by less productive wilderness lands. When Moses led Israel north out of Midian on the way to Jerusalem, he sent word to the King of Moab, asking permission to cross through his kingdom. The King of Moab denied the request and forced the Israelites to travel farther east in the hot, waterless deserts of the Empty Quarter known as the Way of the Wilderness. He feared that this large group of wandering Israelites would see the bounties of his desert kingdom and decide to stay as squatters on their land rather than simply pass through the region as travelers.

Over the centuries, caravaneers and merchant traders charted the best routes of travel. This route through Moab country was known as the finest way to reach the Arabian Peninsula. Most nations that controlled this route collected taxes from merchant traders, and in Lehi's Day it was not uncommon for caravaneers with large cargoes to avoid the tariffs by traveling the less desirable routes through Wadi-al Araba in the winter (the rift valley of the Arabah), or in summer months, the Way of the Wilderness east of the King's Highway.

CHAPTER TWENTY-FOUR

The Arabah is a deep rift valley that runs from Jericho to the Red Sea. Impassable rock cliffs and plateaus on the eastern slopes make an east-west crossing

with camels, mules, or horses impossible except near the southern extremes of the
rift valley, down near the Fountain of the Red Sea (Gulf of Aqaba). The Dead Sea,
fed by the Jordan River, occupies about a quarter of the rift valley at the north end,
while the remaining three quarters is a dry, low-lying, flat plain, 1300 feet below sea
level and covered almost entirely by sand and salt residues. The southern shore of
the Dead Sea is a stretch of shallow evaporation pools that leave the rift valley floor
stained with rings of salt deposits.

One of Lehi's possible routes from Jerusalem to the Fountain of the Red Sea
could have taken him through the rift valley of the Arabah (Wadi al-'Araba). This
route is sometimes referred to as the Way of the Red Sea, and in this chapter, Lehi
crosses the Arabah, but doesn't follow the rift valley south to the Fountain of the
Red Sea. Instead, he descends into the Arabah down the traversable western slopes,
travels due east, and finds a relatively unknown path up off the valley floor and
through what is thought to be an impassable ascent. This account was inspired by
the geography of the rift valley.

Explorers Lynn and Hope Hilton point out that the Arabic name "Arabah"
translates into the English "wilderness" (Lynn M. and Hope Hilton, *In Search of
Lehi's Trail*). They suggest that this route from Jerusalem to Aqaba—the Way of the
Red Sea—was the wilderness Nephi names in his record when he wrote that they
departed into the wilderness (1 Nephi 2: 4). Explorer George Potter, however,
points out that the ancient route taken by merchant traders through the Arabah
passed through a small portion at the south end of the rift valley near the final leg
of the journey to Aqaba, after traveling parallel to the rift valley for much of the
distance high in the plateau country of Moab along the King's Highway. Lehi, if he
were to travel this route, would have descended into the rift valley from the western
slopes for the very end segment of the trip (Potter, & Wellington, *Lehi in the
Wilderness*).

In chapter 27 of this novel, Lehi does not take this route to the Red Sea—
preferring instead to travel through the Jabal Mountains. Thus, Inspector Tobit is
left with no other option than to ride down through the Arabah, at the risk of his
life due to the heat and lack of water in summer, and search for a way out of the rift
valley down near the southern portion. This was where merchant traders were
known to descend into the Arabah and take the Way of the Red Sea over the final
distance to Aqaba and avoid driving their camels up through the Jabal Mountains
Range to reach the port.

Alois Musil writes that the entire length of the rift valley of al-'Araba (the
Arabah) was never traveled by merchant traders between Jerusalem and Aqaba due
to the extreme summer heat, the waterless environment, and the steep ascent in and
out of the valley. He further explains that ancient transport routes were charted
through regions that posed the fewest obstacle, and the wadi al-Araba was not
without numerous hindrances, though it is not impossible that Lehi could have
traveled the Way of the Red Sea during the cool of winter (Alois Musil, "The
Northern Hijaz—a Topographical Itinerary"). Without a written record detailing

which route Lehi traveled between Jerusalem and the Fountain of the Red Sea, it is impossible to suggest, with any certainty, which route he selected; therefore, in this novel, all routes are suggested as possibilities.

CHAPTER TWENTY-FIVE

Baruch is a historical character who served as a scribe to the prophet Jeremiah (Jeremiah 32: 12–16). It is not clear if he was a long-time friend to Jeremiah or if he was employed by Jeremiah's friends to assist the prophet with his record keeping later in life. In this chapter, Baruch' s introduction as an elderly, respected scribe in Jerusalem begins a long-standing relationship with Jeremiah that will become critical to the story line in volume four of this series, *Day of Remembrance*. There are a number of errors in the Book of Jeremiah where King Zedekiah's nephew, Jehoakim, is mistakenly named as king. Hugh Nibley suggests that Baruch, acting as editor for Jeremiah, may have inadvertently dated the events incorrectly as having occurred during the wrong dynasty when he recorded the account of Uriah's flight to Egypt, his capture, and his subsequent trial in four short verses in the Old Testament (Jeremiah 26: 20–24). Scholars originally believed that Uriah's trial occurred much earlier than the date attributed to it in this series of novels, since Jehoakim is named as the King of Israel, not Zedekiah who later replaced him as king. The Lakhish Letters, however, indicate that Zedekiah was actually on the throne at the time of Uriah's trial. Scholars now believe that the ancient scribe, Baruch, mistakenly wrote the former king's name in the Old Testament record when the intended king was actually Zedekiah (Nibley, "Dark Days in Jerusalem: The Lakhish Letters and the Book of Mormon," in *The Prophetic Book of Mormon*).

CHAPTER TWENTY-SIX

Hugh Nibley points out that common to the dreams of desert dwellers are images from their daily experience as well as representations of the events occurring in the family groups ("Lehi in the Desert," in *Lehi in the Desert/The World of the Jaredites/There Were Jaredites*. ed. John W. Welch). The dream of the Tree of Life is filled with the imagery of Lehi's disobedient sons. In this chapter, Sariah presents concerns to Lehi about her premonitions over Laman, concerns that will ultimately become part of his well-known dream of the Tree of Life (1 Nephi 8). We do not know how much influence Sariah had on Lehi's dreams; however, it is possible that Sariah's concerns found expression in the revelatory dreams of her husband.

CHAPTER TWENTY-SEVEN

The city-outpost of Bozrah, near the south end of the King's Highway, is an ancient Hebrew name that dates back to the reign of Kings Solomon and David and is the name preferred in this series of historical novels over the modern Arabic name Ma'an. In present-day maps, Bozrah is most likely the Arabic town Ma'an in the Kingdom of Jordan, located near the crossroads where the ancient King's Highway divides into two routes and where the closing scenes in this chapter are set. Anciently, the main trade route—called the Frankincense Trail—ran inland of the coastal mountains parallel to the Gulf of Aqaba. The less-traveled Aqaba Branch led through the six-thousand-foot peaks of the Jabal Range and then down to the shores of the Red Sea. The Aqaba Branch of the trade route is about a one-hundred-and-twenty-five-mile loop off the main route, beginning at Bozrah and running southwest through the Jabal Range to the port of Aqaba. It then runs south along the coastal plain to the fishing village of Haql, east across the mile-wide coastal plain of the Fountain of the Red Sea, and back through the Jabal Mountains to join with the main Frankincense Trail about eighty miles south of the crossroads at Bozrah.

The Jabal Mountains run parallel to the east shore of the Gulf of Aqaba and have been referred to for centuries as The Northern Hijaz or Northern Borders. During the British occupation of these territories, military mapmakers used the name "Northern Hijaz" in their maps, journals, and geographic explorations as the proper name for the range (David George Hogarth, "Hejaz before World War I, a Handbook").

Hugh Nibley indicates that Nephi's use of the word "borders" was a logical choice when he penned what to him were obvious directions detailing the route his family followed to the Valley of Lemuel. Somewhere between Joseph Smith's verbal translation of the word "borders," to his scribe Oliver Cowdery, and the printer's typeset version of the first printing of the Book of Mormon, the case-sensitive (capitalized) word "Borders"—a proper name for the Jabal Mountains—may have been lost and replaced by the lower case word "borders." The uppercase usage of "Borders" implies the proper name for the mountain range running along the Gulf of Aqaba, while the lowercase usage connotes any geographic boundary (desert, plateau, wadi). In this chapter, as well as in subsequent chapters, the word "Borders" is printed in uppercase, suggesting the Jabal Mountains as the range Nephi and his family traversed in their journey. Nibley suggests that Joseph Smith and Oliver Cowdery may have left the word in lowercase, since neither of them were aware of the proper names in that region of the world (Nibley, "Lehi in the Desert," in *Lehi in the Desert/The World of the Jaredites/There Were Jaredites*. ed. John W. Welch).

There are numerous transliterate evidences pinpointing the Jabal Mountains or Northern Hijaz along the east coast of the Gulf of Aqaba as the mountains Nephi referred to in his record as borders (1 Nephi 2: 5). The Arabic word "Hijaz" translates into the English meanings for partition or barrier. In addition, the Arabic "Jabal" or mountain cognates to the word "Gebul," Hebrew for border (Joseph Catafago, *Arabic-English Dictionary*. See also: *The New Roget's Thesaurus*, Revised Edition, "Boundary," 49).

* * * * *

The Jabal Mountains are a split range with dual peak elevations running side-by-side and extending north-south through the region anciently known as Midian, parallel to the Gulf of Aqaba. The dual nature of this range is not immediately evident on examination of spatially flat, one-dimensional maps, but it is readily apparent to travelers making their way through these mountains. One array of summit-peaks lies inland from the coast. The inland range shelters the second "split" chain of mountains that run directly along the coast. The inland chain extends north beyond the port city of Aqaba. In this chapter, they are the borders *near* the Red Sea barring Sariah and her family from reaching the Fountain of the Red Sea. The "sheltered" second chain of mountains begins about forty miles south of the port city of Aqaba along the coast. This second chain of mountains—the borders *nearer* the Red Sea—presents an imposing array of mountain peaks with two-thousand-foot elevations rising directly out of the sea in an impressive bulwark of sheer cliffs. These *nearer*-to-the-coast mountains block passage for about thirty miles, making uninterrupted travel along the shoreline by camel, horse, or mule virtually impossible.

In this chapter, Sariah cannot see past the inland chain of mountains to the nearer-to-the-coast chain many miles south of her location at the fork in the trade route, but she mentions the existence of the borders *nearer* the Red Sea and she explains that Moses passed through those mountains many hundred years before. Nephi refers to borders *nearer* the Red Sea when he gives the directions his family followed in their journey to the base camp at the Valley of Lemuel (1 Nephi 1:5). A few years later, when Nephi and his family leave the Valley of Lemuel, he writes about traveling in the fertile parts of the borders *near* the Red Sea (1 Nephi 16:14). It is likely that Nephi was referencing the split range of the Jabal Mountains when he wrote about the borders "nearer" the Red Sea and the other borders "near" the Red Sea. Hugh Nibley was the first to point other scholars to searching among the Jabal Mountains of Midian as the Border Mountains described by Nephi. Explorer George Potter was the first to successfully identify major landmarks in that split mountain range, supporting the theories of Nibley and other scholars (Potter & Wellington, *Lehi in the Wilderness*).

* * * * *

The actual location for Mount Horeb, more popularly known as Mount Sinai, is not known. Old Testament scholars, cartographers, and geographers disagree as to the exact location. The maps in the Latter-day Saint publication of the King James Version of the Bible place Horeb (Sinai) on the Sinai Peninsula with a question mark listed in parentheses to indicate that this site is one of many possible sites proposed as the location where Moses was visited by Jehovah and received the Ten Commandments along with numerous covenants that allowed him to construct a tabernacle-like tent in the wilderness and administer temple ordinances, many of which are recorded in the books of Deuteronomy and Leviticus. The covenants and instructions Moses received over many days atop Mount Horeb guided the practice of Jewish temple rites during their time in the wilderness, as well as for centuries after Solomon built a more permanent edifice to house the sacred ceremonies.

Moses and the wandering Hebrews camped in the valleys surrounding Mount Horeb for more than a year before continuing their journey (Bible Dictionary, The Church of Jesus Christ of Latter-day Saints). Numerous geographers indicate that there are no locations on the Sinai Peninsula with enough water and arable land to support the Hebrews of Moses' wandering camp, and climatic conditions have not changed dramatically since that time (Exodus 15 and 16). More than half of the proposed sites for Mount Horeb are located across the Gulf of Aqaba from the Sinia Peninsula in the mountains of Midian, commonly referred to today as the Jabal Mountains or Northern Hijaz—the same mountain range where Nephi writes that his family made their camp beside a river of continually running water. George Potter indicates that a number of sensitive military radar installations are located in the peaks and ridges of these mountains today. However, he, as well as other researchers secured permits to conduct explorations and they report the discovery of compelling archeological and geographic evidence for placing Mount Horeb in the mountains Nephi called the Borders (Potter & Wellington, *Lehi in the Wilderness*).

Local Bedouins living in and around the mountains Nephi called the Borders *nearer* the Red Sea have for centuries referred to the twelve fresh water springs and the river they feed at Wadi Tayyib al-Ism as the waters of Moses. Wadi Tayyib al-Ism is considered the only candidate in the Border Mountains of Midian for the Valley of Lemuel, and Lehi's base camp is described in great detail in chapters 39 and 40. It is possible that Lehi made his camp in the same mountain valleys where Moses camped with his wandering nation of Israelites, hundreds of years before Lehi escaped Jerusalem (Exodus 15: 27). Nephi's record is replete with references comparing his exodus from Jerusalem with the exodus Moses led out of Egypt, particularly when he confronts his older brothers (1 Nephi 4: 23 & 1 Nephi 17: 23–43). It is possible that both these wandering prophets spoke face-to-face with God, received dreams, revelations, and covenants from heaven while living in the same Border Mountains. In this chapter, Sariah tells her son Nephi that Mount Horeb—the mountain where Moses talked face-to-face with God—is located in the mountains of Midian and her comments in this chapter foreshadow the major storyline of the next volume in this series.

CHAPTER TWENTY-EIGHT

The Way of the Wilderness passes through the transitional lands between the high plateau country of Moab and the deserts of the Empty Quarter. Merchant traders often refer to this area as the lands of Bedouins, where desert dwellers move in roving bands in search of enough foliage to feed their animals. In contrast, the King's Highway is often called the land of settlers where there is enough water and arable land to support farming and vineyard keeping.

CHAPTER TWENTY-NINE

The Old Testament indicates that Jeremiah was a prisoner when he purchased land from his Cousin, Hanameel. The prophet was taken to the court of the prison where the double-sealed parchment was reviewed. Jeremiah affirms his prophecy that the Jews will return to their homeland after seventy years of captivity in Babylon by sealing the documents of the property sale in clay jars. Much of the dialogue attributed to Jeremiah, as well as the actions of Hanameel and Baruch, are taken directly from the Old Testament (Jeremiah 32).

CHAPTER THIRTY

Aqaba is about one hundred and fifty miles from Jerusalem. In Lehi's day, the road leading to the port city was called Aqaba, but the town was called Ezion-geber. The Arabic name "Aqaba" translates into "the mountain road" or "the road leading up a mountainside," which is most likely a reference to the trade route that traversed through the mountain passes of the Jabal Range before descending to the coast. In this chapter, Hagoth refers to the trade route as the "Mountain Road." The reference to "Mountain Road" appears in uppercase in this chapter since the Arabic equivalent—"Aqaba"—is a proper name and should appear capitalized in English usage.

Aqaba was a port city for thousands of years. King Solomon hired Phoenician ship builders from the Mediterranean Sea to build the original port at Aqaba prior to the Queen of Sheba (modern day Yemen) docking her ship there on her famous trip to Jerusalem to pay tribute to Solomon's wisdom and greatness (*Great People of the Bible and How They Lived,* (Pleasantville NY: Readers Digest Association, 1974).

The boatbuilding described in this chapter is based on the accepted practices of the day. Metal nails were not used in the hulls of ships due to the corrosive nature of the waters of the Gulf of Aqaba—the highest salinity content of any ocean on earth, due mostly to the salty sea bed. Inefficient square sails were common on fishing boats and sailing vessels in Lehi's day. Shipbuilders were familiar with the proper woods used to construct ships, the preparation of resins and glues to bind boards together, as well as the use of ropes and wooden nails to secure the hull (Liionel Casson, "Ships and Seafaring in Ancient Times").

Hagoth is a fictional character, but his shipbuilding yards at the Port of Aqaba are based on what we know of shipbuilding during that time period. His name was inspired by the New World shipbuilder mentioned in the Book of Mormon centuries later.

CHAPTER THIRTY-THREE

Ship captains routinely refuse to sail the Gulf of Aqaba due to winds that plague those waters. The winds have enough power to dash ships against the coral reefs and break the hull of smaller sailing vessels. Evening windstorms are often followed by fog that pushes ashore and fills the low-lying wadis along the coast with a thick blanket of mist. Explorers and travelers record finding mists in the seaside canyons and about the cliffs of the Nearer-to-the-coast Mountains mentioned by Nephi. This chapter begins with a common night windstorm along the shores of the gulf, followed by a morning cover of fog (Potter & Wellington, *Lehi in the Wilderness*).

* * * * *

The shoreline immediately south of Aqaba opens onto a wide coastal plain. At its widest point it measures about one mile. This wide, relatively flat, sandy plain ends about forty miles south of the port city of Aqaba where the Border Mountains *nearer* the Red Sea rise out of the shoreline and block travel farther down the coast.

In Lehi's day, the fishing village of Haql was likely the only small settlement along the coastal plain and marks the point where the trade route running south from Aqaba turns east across the flat coastal sands and up into the borders *near* the Red Sea. Caravaneers headed south into the Arabian Peninsula traveled inland away from Haql and the Gulf of Aqaba, through the Jabal Mountains, and down onto the eastern slopes to follow the main branch of the trade route known in Lehi's day as the Frankincense Trail. Travelers did not follow the coastal plain along the shores of the Gulf of Aqaba past Haql since there were no charted routes leading through the Borders *nearer* the Red Sea. Thus, there was a very good chance of getting lost among the narrow canyons of the foothills in those mountains. There are three springs that percolate up through the sands at Haql; two of them are known to be contaminated by salt water, while the third spring flows with sweet water .

* * * * *

The last seventy-two-mile portion of Lehi's 224-mile journey to the Valley of Lemuel was most likely along the coastal plain of the Fountain of the Red Sea and in through the Borders *nearer* the Red Sea. Lehi made this final leg of the journey in company with his wife Sariah and their four sons (1 Nephi 2:6). It is likely that they came into contact with numerous other travelers, desert dwellers, farmers, settlers, merchants, and city dwellers on their journey between Jerusalem and the Red Sea, as well as in subsequent travels through the Arabian Peninsula. It may be that these six members of Lehi's family traveled the entire route without any other traveling companions. However, it is not impossible to suggest that others accompanied Lehi as far as the shores of the Red Sea. When Lehi's party reached the coastal plain of the Fountain of the Red Sea, Nephi listed the members of his traveling party by name, including himself, his parents and three brothers (1 Nephi 2: 5). It is not clear whether Nephi was listing the traveling party that made the entire 224-mile journey from Jerusalem or if some event occurred along the shores of the Red Sea that caused nonfamily members to leave the group. If Lehi and his family parted company with other traveling companions after arriving at the Fountain of the Red Sea, they most likely would have split at the fishing village of Haql south of Aqaba.

In this chapter, Lehi and his family part with the nonmembers of their family and head twenty miles further south along the coastline to the Borders *nearer* the Red Sea—a route leading to what in Lehi's day was most likely believed to be a dead end where the Nearer-to-the-sea Mountains blocked passage down along the shoreline. Aaron, Josiah, Elizabeth, Moriah, Hagoth, Sophia, Yaush, and Setti take

the Aqaba Branch of the trade route east over the Borders *near* the Red Sea to join
with the main Frankincense Trail.

* * * * *

We do not know if Lehi was pursued in his journey to the Valley of Lemuel or
if he simply left Jerusalem to avoid persecution at the hands of the Jews. In Nephi's
description of their travels to the base camp, he makes mention of a three-day
journey that could be interpreted as a forced march (1 Nephi 2:6). Camels without
any load to bear and headed for winter pastures traveled up to forty miles per day
(Alan Keohane, "Nomads of the Desert"); however, Explorer Nigel Groom indicates
that loaded camels traveled about 2.5 miles per hour and did not exceed twenty-five
miles in a single day of travel—a maximum distance commonly observed by
ancient merchant traders (Nigel Groom, "Frankincense and Myrrh: A study of the
Arabian Incense Trade").

In order to cover the seventy-two miles from Aqaba to the proposed site of the
Valley of Lemuel at Wadi Tyyib al-Ism in three days, Lehi and his family would
have had to travel the maximum of about twenty-five miles per day with heavily
loaded animals through mountainous terrain. It is possible that some sort of pursuit
prompted Lehi and his family to make the final leg of this journey in three days. In
this chapter and the following chapter, the fictionalized forced march of Lehi and
his family with Captain Laban in pursuit is based on Nephi's statement that once
his family reached the Fountain of the Red Sea—most likely descending the Aqaba
Branch of the trade route near the port of Aqaba—they covered the distance to
Wadi Tayyib al-Ism in less than seventy-two hours (1 Nephi 2: 5–6).

* * * * *

In this chapter, Lehi shares essential information from a portion of a dream
that will ultimately become his dream of the Tree of Life once it is received in its
entirety and recorded in the Book of Mormon. To this point in the novel, Lehi has
only received a portion of his now-famous dream and he indicates that there is
more he has yet to discover, telling his traveling companions that he awakes prior to
the dream running to its conclusion. This fictionalized retelling of a portion of the
dream of the Tree of Life with Lehi waking before he sees all the images that will
ultimately be part of the entire dream is similar to the way in which Joseph Smith
Sr. received a dream of a tree beside a river with the fruit of eternal life growing in
its branches. Joseph Smith Sr. received a total of seven dreams over an eight-year
period between 1811 and 1819—the last dream coming to him one year prior to
his fourteen-year-old son, Joseph Smith Jr., receiving a revelation he describes as his
First Vision (Lucy Mack Smith, *The History of the Prophet Joseph Smith by His
Mother*). In at least two of Joseph Smith Sr.'s dreams, he indicates that he awoke
before critical information was given to him by his spirit-guide who accompanied

him in his dreams, and in a third dream he awoke before the dream moved to its climax, depriving him of the final understanding of the dream.

We do not know when Lehi's dream of the Tree of Life was given to him. The Book of Mormon records that Lehi *shared* the entire dream with his family after they arrived at the Valley of Lemuel and conducted two return trips to Jerusalem (1 Nephi 8). However, Nephi does not indicate *when* Lehi received the dream or dreams. The later dreams received by Joseph Smith Sr. continue with themes and images begun in his earlier dreams, and in this chapter, Lehi is shown following a similar pattern of reception as did Joseph Smith Sr.—receiving a portion of the dream of the Tree of Life that will ultimately be added to in later dreams. Lehi may have received his Tree-of-Life dream all at once, but it is also possible that he received that celebrated vision over the course of several dreams until he knew the end from the beginning and determined to share it with members of his family (1 Nephi 8: 2)—similar to the manner in which Joseph Smith Sr. received continuing portions of the same dream over a period of time and shared them with his wife, Lucy Mack

* * * * *

The winding passes through the Borders nearer the Red Sea south of Haql—in this chapter referred to as the foothills—are an uncharted web of convoluted canyons and dead-end wadis. It is possible that Lehi's decision to travel down the coast and through the Borders *nearer* the Red Sea was prompted by revelation rather than reason, since there is little evidence to suggest that travelers risked the possibility of getting lost by venturing farther south than Haql along the shores of the Fountain of the Red Sea. It may be that the image in Lehi's dream of a man dressed in a white robe is a dream representation for the revelation or the inspiration Lehi received that prompted him to travel a route that he would otherwise have avoided. Hugh Nibley indicates that the greatest fear of desert travelers, more intense than the fear of lack of water, lack of food, or contact with roving hordes of robber bands, was the fear of getting lost in the desert (Nibley, "Lehi in the Desert," in *Lehi in the Desert/The World of the Jaredites/There Were Jaredites,* ed. John W. Welch). The uncharted Borders *nearer* the Red Sea posed the threat of getting lost in the desert and may have weighed heavily on Lehi's mind when he considered the direction the family would ultimately travel. In the fictionalized events in this chapter, Lehi indicates that it was revelation, in the form of a dream, which aided him in making the decision to risk traveling through the foothills of the Borders *nearer* the Red Sea.

* * * * *

Nephi indicates that he "likened the words of Isaiah" to himself, and he may have seen references in Isaiah's writings to their actual trek in the wilderness. In this chapter, Nephi foreshadows his family's arrival at the Valley of Lemuel when he reads that God would open rivers in high places, and fountains in the midst of the valleys (Isaiah 41: 17–18) . . . "and here shall be a tabernacle for a shadow in the daytime from the heat, and for a *place of refuge*... from the storm" (Isaiah 4:6; 2 Nephi 14:6).

CHAPTER THIRTY-FOUR
The Book of Mormon indicates that Lehi and his family traveled from Jerusalem to the *Fountain* of the Red Sea (1 Nephi 2: 9). The word "fountain" defines a font of water that empties into a larger body of water, similar to the Gulf of Aqaba that empties into the larger Red Sea. Anciently, the Gulf of Aqaba—the body of water separating the Sinai and Arabian Peninsulas—was referred to as the Fountain of the Red Sea. In this chapter, Inspector Tobit reminds himself of that name with help from his mapmaking son, Darius.

CHAPTER THIRTY-FIVE
The mountain pass described in this chapter is the major trade-route artery leading from the coast of the Gulf of Aqaba, southeast through the Borders *near* the Red Sea to the Frankincense Trail on the eastern slopes of the Jabal Mountains. Travelers through this region were very familiar with the charted routes of the day. It is likely that Lehi knew of this route but for some reason determined not to use it. The historical notes for chapter 33 and 39 discuss the image of an angel-guide in Lehi's Dream of the Tree of Life as representative of revelation leading Lehi away from the route described in this chapter.

CHAPTER THIRTY-SIX
In this chapter, Captain Laban is frustrated from following Lehi farther down the coast by the foothills at the base of the Borders *nearer* the Red Sea. It is possible that the deep, narrow canyons that wind through these mountains, and that conjure, for desert travelers, the fear of getting lost inspired the images of a dark and dreary wilderness or waste described by Lehi in his dream of the Tree of Life (1 Nephi 8: 4–7).

CHAPTER THIRTY-NINE
Nephi recorded his father's dream of the Tree of Life many years after Lehi recounted it to his children (1 Nephi 8). It is likely Nephi copied it from a journal his father kept during their travels through Arabia (Brown, *From Jerusalem to Zarahemla*h). Hugh Nibley indicates that Nephi may not have been aware of the depth of his father's anxiety, but the fears are subtly apparent in the images of his dream. Lehi's dream of the Tree of Life has an authentic undertone of a man burdened with worries over the journey he is undertaking, as well as the responsibility over the misbehavior of his two eldest sons ("Lehi in the Desert," in *Lehi in the Desert/The World of the Jaredites/There Were Jaredites.* ed. John W. Welch). Explorer George Potter indicates that travel through the Mountains of Midian on

the northwest frontier of Saudi Arabia is cause for concern, since the Valley of Lemuel is beyond the traveled routes of the day without any known water supplies (Potter & Wellington, *Lehi in the Wilderness*). Hugh Nibley indicates that the images dreamers see while awake often influence their dreams—even those inspired by heaven—and Lehi's dream of the Tree of Life appears to fall into that category. Lucy Mack Smith records in her journal that her husband, Joseph Smith Sr., had a series of seven dreams, some of them similar in nature to Lehi's vision of the Tree of Life (Lucy Mack Smith, *The History of the Prophet Joseph Smith by His Mother*). Lehi saw a "dark and dreary waste" or wilderness in his dream, while the setting for most of Joseph Smith's Sr.'s dreams appear to be eighteenth-century frontier America in a field of "dead, fallen timbers."

In this chapter, Inspector Tobit tracks Lehi along the route he may have taken through the Borders *nearer* the Red Sea using directions gleaned by Aaron from portions of Lehi's dream related to him in chapter 33. It is possible that some of the images and events of Lehi's dream of the Tree of Life represent a map or daily journal detailing the final leg of Lehi's 224-mile journey from Jerusalem to the Valley of Lemuel. A careful comparison of the route Lehi traveled through the Borders *nearer* the Red Sea to his dream of the Tree of Life suggest that the images Lehi saw in his dream were inspired by the landmarks he encountered while traveling on a three-day, forced march down the coast of the Fountain of the Red Sea, up through the narrow foothills, along a wide, high mountain wadi, and eventually to a secluded mountain canyon with a river growing beside a grove of date palms.

* * * * *

The first image Lehi sees in his dream of the Tree of Life is a dark and dreary waste (1 Nephi 8:4). The foothills of the Borders *nearer* the Red Sea are a maze of winding, dead-ending canyons with high walls and numerous branches that lead nowhere. Travelers who venture into those canyons lose themselves deep in the shadows of rocky corridors, and it is possible that these forbidden wadis inspired the image of a dark and dreary wilderness recorded in Lehi's dream. Explorer George Potter indicates that Lehi may also have traveled this route in the cool of night if he passed through Midian during the hot months of summer, and the evening shadows may have intensified Lehi's reference to a dark and dreary waste. The tall canyon corridors, however, provide enough shadows, even during daylight hours, to inspire the imagery of darkness and dreariness.

* * * * *

The second image Lehi sees in his dream of the Tree of Life is a man dressed in a white robe—possibly an angel or guide—who instructed Lehi to follow him into a dark and dreary waste. The historical notes for chapters 33 and 35 discuss the possibility that the angel in Lehi's dream may represent heavenly guidance, inspiring

Lehi into uncharted territory that he may not have traveled if not for that inspiration. Merchant traders turned east at the fishing village of Haql and traveled through the borders *near* the Red Sea back to the main inland Frankincense Trail. They never continued farther south along the coastal plain past Haql, since the borders *nearer* the Red Sea blocked passage down the coast, and the foothills leading in behind the coastal ridge of mountains were an impassable maze. Based on the geography of the coastline and the known trade routes of Lehi's day through this area, it is possible that Lehi would never have traveled through the borders *nearer* the Red Sea without some guidance from heaven. The man dressed in a white robe in Lehi's dream (1 Nephi 8:5–7) may represent some sort of heavenly prompting or guidance Lehi received to forsake the known, safe trade route of his day and travel through impassable mountain country at the risk of getting lost and leading members of his family to their death.

Guides were not uncommon in heavenly dreams. Nephi reports the aid of a heavenly guide in his personal dreams (1 Nephi 11, 12, 13 & 14). Joseph Smith Sr. also indicates the presence of an angel-guide in nearly all of his seven dreams. Early in his married life—about six years after his son Joseph Smith Jr. was born—Joseph Smith Sr. received his first dream that was later recorded by his wife, Lucy Mack Smith:

> "I was alone in this gloomy desert, with the exception of an attendant spirit, who kept constantly by my side. Of him I inquired the meaning of what I saw, and why I was thus traveling in such a dismal place. He answered thus: "This field is the world, which now lieth inanimate and dumb, in regard to the true religion, or plan of salvation; but travel on, and by the wayside you will find on a certain log a box, the contents of which, if you eat thereof, will make you wise, and give unto you wisdom and understanding.
>
> "I carefully observed what was told me by my guide, and proceeding a short distance, I came to the box. I immediately took it up, and placed it under my left arm; then with eagerness I raised the lid, and began to taste of its contents, upon which all manner of beasts, horned cattle, and roaring animals, rose up on every side in the most threatening manner possible, tearing the earth, tossing their horns, and bellowing most terrifically all around me, and they finally came so close upon me, that I was compelled to drop the box and fly for my life. Yet, in the midst of all this I was perfectly happy, though I awoke trembling. (Smith, Lucy Mack, "The History of the Prophet Joseph Smith by His Mother," Covenant: American Fork, UT, 2000)."

Joseph Smith Sr. concluded from his dream that there were no religionists of any faith that knew anything more concerning the Kingdom of God than did men who did not make a profession of religion. In that same year, 1811, Joseph Smith Sr. received a similar dream that could be considered a continuation of his first dream:

> "I was traveling in an open, desolate field, which appeared very barren. As I was thus traveling, the thought suddenly came into my mind that I had better stop and reflect upon what I was doing, before I went any farther. So I asked myself, what motive can I have in traveling here, and what place can this be? My guide, who was by my side, as before, said, 'This is the desolate world; but travel on.'
>
> "The road was so broad and barren that I wondered why I should travel in it; for, said I to myself, 'Broad is the road, and wide is the gate that leads to death, and many there be that walk therein; but narrow is the way, and strait is the gate that leads to everlasting life, and few there be that go in thereat.'
>
> "Traveling a short distance further, I came to a narrow path. This path I entered, and, when I had traveled a little way in it, I behold a beautiful stream of water, which ran from the east to the west. Of this stream, I could see neither the source nor yet the mouth; but as far as my eyes could extend I could see a rope, running along the bank of it, about as high as a man could reach and beyond me was a low, but very pleasant valley, in which stood a tree such as I had never seen before. It was exceedingly handsome, insomuch that I looked upon it with wonder and admiration. Its beautiful branches spread themselves somewhat like an umbrella, and it bore a kind of fruit, in shape much like a chestnut bur, and as white as snow, or, if possible, whiter. I gazed upon the same with considerable interest, and as I was doing so, the burs or shells commenced opening and shedding their particles, or the fruit which they contained, which was of dazzling whiteness. I drew near and began to eat of it, and I found it delicious beyond description. As I was eating, I said in my heart, 'I cannot eat this alone, I must bring my wife and children, that they may partake with me.' Accordingly, I went and brought my family, which consisted of my wife and seven children, and we all commenced eating and praising God for this blessing. We were exceedingly happy, insomuch that our joy could not easily be expressed.
>
> "While thus engaged, I beheld a spacious building standing opposite the valley, which we were in, and it appeared to reach to the very heavens. It was full of doors and windows and they were all filled with people, who were very finely dressed. When these people observed us in the low valley, under the tree, they pointed

the finger of scorn at us, and treated us with all manner of disre-
spect and contempt. But their contumely we utterly disregarded.

"I presently turned to my guide and inquired of him the
meaning of the fruit that was so delicious. He told me it was the
pure love of God, shed abroad in the hearts of all those who love
him, and keep his commandments. He then commanded me to
go and bring the rest of my children. I told him that we were all
there. 'No', he replied, 'look yonder, you have two more, and you
must bring them also.' Upon raising my eyes, I saw two small
children, standing some distance off. I immediately went to
them, and brought them to the tree; upon which they
commenced eating with the rest and we all rejoiced together. The
more we ate, the more we seemed to desire, until we even got
down upon our knees and scooped it up, eating it by double
handfuls.

"After feasting in this manner a short time, I asked my guide
what was the meaning of the spacious building which I saw. He
replied, 'It is Babylon, it is Babylon, and it must fall. The people
in the doors and windows are the inhabitants thereof, who scorn
and despise the Saints of God because of their humility.' I soon
awoke clapping my hands together for joy" (Smith, *The History
of the Prophet Joseph Smith by His Mother*).

* * * * *

The third event Lehi reports in his dream of the Tree of Life is kneeling in
prayer in the midst of a dark and dreary waste and begging the Lord for mercy
according to the "multitude of His tender mercies" (1 Nephi 8: 8). This prayer
image, coupled with the image of the man in a white robe leading Lehi into the
dark and dreary waste from the previous verse (1 Nephi 8: 7), may be a reaffirma-
tion of Lehi's faith in the heavenly guidance he received, leading him through this
uncharted land.

It is noteworthy that only one of many narrow canyons leading up off the
coastal plain allows a traveler to reach a mile-wide "large, spacious field" or wadi
that runs south, behind the peaks of the coastal mountains *nearer* the Red Sea. The
other wadis and canyons in these foothills dead-end in steep cliffs or lead off into
other remote, waterless valleys.It is possible that the image of Lehi praying in his
dream of the Tree of Life was inspired by his actual supplication for help to find a
way through these foothills in order to reach the long wadi local Bedouins call Wadi
Tayyib al-Ism—the Pleasant Valley.

Directly behind the coastal peaks of the Borders *nearer* the Red Sea lies the 12-
mile-long Wadi Tayyib al-Ism that runs south from the foothills down to a secluded
portion of this rather long, "spacious field." This mile-wide field acts as a large

aquifer, collecting the rainwater runoff from mountain tributaries during the winter months and directing the ground water beneath the sands and along the gradually south-sloping incline of Wadi Tayyib al-Ism until it reaches its low point. There, the wadi turns west back toward the coastal mountains leading to the proposed site for the Valley of Lemuel where date palms groves grow in abundance clustered around twelve springs, and where a year-round river runs through the wadi to the sea.

The mountains along the coast of the Gulf of Aqaba in this region are composed almost entirely of sandstone—a permeable rock without the capacity to seal water in an underground aquifer. However, the mountains directly surrounding the extreme south end of Wadi Tayyib al-Ism are composed of granite capable of keeping the ground water from seeping beneath the Borders *nearer* the Red Sea and into the Gulf of Aqaba. It is possible that when Lehi indicates he saw a large, spacious field in his dream, it was representative of the 12-mile-long aquifer-wadi he traveled after receiving inspired help to find his way off the coastal plain and through the foothills.

After offering a prayer in his dream of the Tree of Life, Lehi reports that he saw a large, spacious field (1 Nephi 8: 9). There is no indication that Lehi initially saw a tree until the next verse (1 Nephi 8: 10). The second verse in this pair is separated from the first verse with the words "And it came to pass," an ancient writing form signifying a new thought, similar to the modern usage of a paragraph. In the Book of Mormon, a paragraph is placed between Lehi's vision of the large spacious field and his view of the tree. This sequence in Lehi's dream follows how a traveler would have arrived at the Valley of Lemuel, first traveling south down a long wadi—Lehi's large, and spacious field—then west into the secluded portion of this wadi where date palms can be found growing in what was considered to be one of the most barren deserts on earth:

> 9. And it came to pass after I had prayed unto the Lord I beheld a large and spacious field.

> 10. And it came to pass that I beheld a tree, whose fruit was desirable to make one happy.

CHAPTER FORTY

Wadi Tyyib al-Ism—Arabic for the Pleasant Valley—is located seventy-two miles south of the port at Aqaba, about the distance of a three-day forced march with a caravan of heavily packed camels. The Pleasant Valley consists of an "upper valley" located on the inland—east side of the coastal Border Mountains—and a narrow "lower valley" created by pre-historic seismic activity that likely split the coastal mountains, producing a descending path to the shores of the Red Sea.

The upper valley covers an area of about one square mile. The walls are composed of red sandstone, and the cliffs and overlooks above the valley often crumble underfoot. The upper-valley floor is composed of sand and gravel. Twelve springs percolate above ground, watering clusters of date-palm groves as well as irrigating seven identifiable strains of grain and numerous varieties of seed-bearing plants. A small river emerges out of the sandy ground farther down from the springs. In Lehi's dream he sees a tree and tastes of its fruit (1 Nephi 8: 10–12) before he casts his eyes round about and sees a river of water (1 Nephi 8: 13). This sequence of images is similar to the way Lehi may have viewed the Pleasant Valley upon entering it from the east end, where he would have seen the clusters of date palm trees before he found a river emerging out of the sandy ground about two thirds of the way down the upper valley. The river flows from the upper canyon into a narrow opening in the coastal mountains referred to by explorer George Potter as the lower valley (Potter & Wellington, *Lehi in the Wilderness*).

The lower valley is composed of solid gray granite—an immediate change in the appearance of the rock—and Lehi may have been referring to this lower valley when he counseled Laman to be as "firm and steadfast and immovable in keeping the commandments of the Lord" as was this valley of gray granite (1 Nephi 2: 10). The lower valley is about 1.3 miles long. It runs west, bends south for a good distance, and then turns abruptly west again before emerging on the shores of the Red Sea. The river runs gradually down the middle of the lower valley over worn, eroded beds of granite, while the canyon walls rise higher until the lower valley reaches sea level and the granite walls stand over 2,500 feet above the valley floor in an impressive bulwark of gray stone. It is common for windstorms along the coast to blow fog in around these impressive granite coastal peaks and up into the lower valley. George Potter suggests that the physical appearance of this wadi may have provided Lehi with the dream images of a large, spacious building floating in the air (1 Nephi 8: 26), mists of darkness (1 Nephi 8: 23), sheer canyon walls running alongside a river like a rod of iron (1 Nephi 8: 20), flash floods through the upper and lower valleys with the power to drown many in the depths of a fountain (1 Nephi 8: 32), date palms representing the tree of life (1 Nephi 8: 10–12), and a river of water (1 Nephi 8: 13). Nephi's description of the Valley of Lemuel, Lehi's exhortations to his sons, and the images of Lehi's dream are combined in the narrative and storyline of this chapter, effectively merging the physical descriptions of Wadi Tayyib al-Ism with the events, revelations, and descriptions recorded in chapters 2 and 8 of First Nephi.

* * * * *

The Red Sea is not visible from the upper valley. It is likely that Lehi was unaware his family was camped slightly over a mile from the Fountain of the Red Sea until he explored the lower valley. Nephi records that his father didn't lecture Laman to be "like unto this river, continually running into the fountain of all righteousness," and he didn't compare Lemuel to granite walls of the lower valley and advise him to be "firm and steadfast and immovable in keeping the commandments of the Lord" until he discovered how close they were to the sea (1 Nephi 2: 9–10). In this chapter, Lehi follows the description recorded by Nephi in the Book of Mormon, and doesn't lecture his two oldest sons until they reach the shores of the Fountain of the Red Sea after emerging from the lower canyon of Wadi Tayyib al-Ism.

* * * * *

Numerous Book of Mormon scholars suggest that the Valley of Lemuel was located in the Mountains of Midian. Intrepid explorers have traveled that region in search of evidence of a more exact location for Lehi's base camp in the Borders *nearer* the Red Sea, but for decades their efforts to substantiate Lehi's claim of a valley with a river running through it located in one of the world's driest, hottest deserts proved fruitless (1 Nephi 2: 6–9). Bedouins likely knew of the springs and river of Wadi Tayyib al-Ism for centuries, and the locals today use this obscure mountain valley to water their herds. As recently as 1984 the *Saudi Arabian Ministry of Agriculture and Water* listed that nowhere in the entire Kingdom were there any continually running rivers of water. After an exhaustive 44-year survey of the water resources of the Kingdom of Saudi Arabia, conducted jointly by the *United States Geologic Survey* and *Saudi Arabian Ministry of Agriculture and Water*, the report found no continually running rivers anywhere within the kingdom (*Water Atlas of Saudi Arabia*).

When Joseph Smith Jr. translated the Book of Mormon there was little written material about the Arabian Peninsula available in the libraries near his home in Canandaigua, Ithaca, or Rochester in western New York. English professor Eugene England suggests that what books did exist at the time were incorrect and, if Joseph Smith were to use them as source material, they would have alerted him not to include mention of any river or water source anywhere among the Borders *nearer* the Red Sea (Eugene England, in Noel B. Reynolds and Charles D. Tate, eds., *Book of Mormon Authorship: New Light on Ancient Origins*). For a hundred and fifty years, critics of the Book of Mormon have claimed that it contained geographic errors since there were no rivers in Arabia and that the Valley of Lemuel was likely a fictitious setting.

Hugh Nibley and other apologists of the Book of Mormon have defended the description of a river in the Valley of Lemuel as consistent with seasonal runoff or flash floods responsible for the many gullies, washes and wadis in the mountains throughout Midian. However, those explanations fall short of a year-round water source similar to the one described in the Book of Mormon (1 Nephi 2: 9). It wasn't until explorer George Potter identified Wadi Tayyib al-Ism with its underground aquifer, twelve springs, and a year-round river running through a narrow mountain valley emptying into the Red Sea along the coast of the Gulf of Aqaba, did Joseph Smith's translation of Nephi's description of the Valley of Lemuel find astounding current-day corroboration.

George Potter was the first to propose Wadi Tayyib al-Ism as the most likely candidate for Lehi's base camp in the Borders *nearer* the Red Sea, and the account of his 1995 discovery is recorded in his writings (Potter & Wellington, *Lehi in the Wilderness*). The most recent 2001 satellite survey maps of the east shoreline of the Gulf of Aqaba now include Wadi Tayyib al-Ism listed by name, and a marker indicating date palms and a river—the only location on the entire west coast of Saudi Arabia with that designation (U.S. Geologic Map Service, "Gulf of Aqaba Southwest Asia," (AMS K502, Sheet NH 36-4, 2001). George Potter points out that the river running through Wadi Tayyib al-Ism was most likely hidden from the view of lands at satellite photos, surface and aerial surveys, and seismic readings by the sheer mountain peaks surrounding the valley (Potter & Wellington, *Lehi in the Wilderness*).

Wadi Tayyib al-Ism meets all the physical criteria of the Valley of Lemuel described by Nephi (1 Nephi 2). Today, however, the Saudi Arabian government has placed a number of wells down into the aquifer. The springs produce less water. They are still able to maintain the clusters of date palms growing beside the percolating water source; however, new trees must be planted three to four feet into the ground in order to preserve the roots, and it is possible that the date groves that have grown there for possibly thousands of years may not continue to survive. The flow of the river that comes above ground about two-thirds of the way down the upper valley and flows into the narrow canyon of the lower valley is substantially smaller today than it was in recent years. Currently it is about the size of a creek and supports year-round flora, fauna, and some small freshwater fish. The erosion along the granite floor and the walls of the lower valley as well as the sediment deposits in the upper valley indicate that the river flow was recently much larger than it is today.

* * * * *

The Old Testament indicates that to give thanks for a safe journey through deserts or over water, the traveler was to make a peace offering of a male or female animal from the flock or herd (Psalms 107: 22). S. Kent Brown indicates that the proper translation of "peace offering" means an offering of well-being, and it is possible that Lehi made an offering to give thanks for their safety in traveling through uncharted desert lands that caused Lehi enough fear to fill his dreams with images of a dark and dreary waste (1 Nephi 8:4–8). This chapter opens with Lehi preparing a peace offering that would normally begin a celebration that lasted well into the night until all the food was consumed according to tradition. In this fictionalized account, however, Laman and Lemuel's rebellious natures cut short the festivities, ending what normally would have been a much longer peace offering celebration (Brown, *From Jerusalem to Zarahemla*).

* * * * *

When Martin Harris lost the translation of the first 116 pages of the Book of Mormon, Joseph Smith was instructed not to re-translate it since it had fallen into the hands of men who were conspiring to defame the prophet's translating abilities (D&C 10: 620).

The notes that appear at the beginning of section ten of the Doctrine and Covenants indicate that the lost pages comprised the Book of Lehi. In subsequent verses in that same section of the Doctrine and Covenants, Joseph Smith is instructed that much of what was contained in the Book of Lehi was reiterated in the record made by Lehi's son, Nephi (D&C 10: 38–46). Through careful examination of Nephi's writings we find recollections of his father's life, Lehi's call as a prophet, his visions and dreams, and his prophesies (1 Nephi 1:16–17, 1 Nephi 8:2, 1 Nephi 18:23, 2 Nephi 4:12, 2 Nephi 5:29, Jacob 2:23–33). A number of Lehi's teachings, dreams, and admonitions appear as large quotations in Nephi's account, most likely taken directly from Lehi's writings (1 Nephi 21:1; Isaiah 49:22–23; and Brown, *From Jerusalem to Zarahemla*). Kent Brown points out that Nephi's account of finding the Valley of Lemuel (1 Nephi 2: 6–8), his father's admonitions that Lemuel be "firm and steadfast and immovable" like the mountains surrounding them (1 Nephi 2: 10), as well as his plea that Laman be like the river flowing into the fountain of righteousness (1 Nephi 2: 9), are a mixture of Lehi's words and Nephi's words. They are essentially observations from both authors, which demonstrates that Nephi may have been reading from his father's journal when he made that account in his record (1 Nephi 2:1–24). A similar mixing of Nephi and Lehi's observations is found in the summary of Lehi's dream (1 Nephi 8:30–33, 8:35–9:1), and in the exhortations that follow the summary of the dream, which closes with: "And all these things did my father see, and hear, and speak, as he dwelt in a tent . . . and also a great many more things, which cannot be written upon these [small] plates" (1 Nephi 9:1). Nephi also tells us that many of the revelations he received were actually based on revelations given to his father, which then spurred his desire to receive the same heavenly instructions that his father had received. In this chapter, Lehi's admonitions to his sons in the Valley of Lemuel, as well as portions of his dream, are not filtered through the narration of Nephi, but are portrayed directly through the eyes of Lehi as they may have unfolded. It is likely that Nephi copied the events that unfolded in the Valley of Lemuel directly from his father's record many years later, once the family arrived in the New World.

* * * * *

From the Lakhish Letters we learn that the Hebrew slang *piqqeah* (pronounced pee-kay-ah), translated into English as visionary, dreamer, or one whose eyes have been opened by God, may have been used as a derogatory reference to the prophets in Jerusalem at 600 B.C. Though it is not certain how vulgar the term was, high-ranking military and government officials used the word in derision and it could be equated with obscenities common in the modern world. In this chapter, Laman's dialogue employing this slang term is taken directly from the Book of Mormon (1

Nephi 2:11). Laman and Lemuel blamed the forfeiture of their property, riches, and comfortable lifestyle on the fact that their father was a visionary man and they used the derogatory slang *piqqeah* to verbalize their insinuations against their father (1 Nephi 17: 21–22). The Book of Mormon also records (1 Nephi 5: 1–4) that when Sariah complained to Lehi about her sons' absence after returning to Jerusalem for the brass plates she called him a visionary man. Lehi's response was stern and so strikingly out of character from what we know of his normal treatment of Sariah, it is possible that in her anguish she employed the word piqqeah derogatorily. In Lehi's rebuttal to Sariah he may have referred to himself using the more respectful usage of the word, ha-piqqeah. He told her that he knew he was a visionary man and blessed of God to have seen a vision of their sons' safe return and of obtaining a future land of promise (Hugh W. Nibley, "The Jerusalem Scene"). Other scholars have suggested there are other Hebrew word forms that could have been used in reference to Lehi as a visionary man (John A. Tvedtnes, "Was Lehi a Caravaneer?" in *The Most Correct Book: Insights from a Book of Mormon Scholar,* Salt Lake City: Cornerstone, 1999, 76–98).

CHAPTER FORTY-ONE

When Nephi was shown a similar vision to Lehi's dream of the "Tree of Life," he was told that the tree—not the fruit—represented the Son of God (1 Nephi 11: 4–11). Jeanette Miller indicates that for thousands of years among Middle Eastern peoples, the date palm was representative of royalty. The king was considered to be part human and part god, and the son of the king was sent to fight the evil that threatened his kingdom. The perfect symmetry of the tree with its fan-shaped branches personified kingship. These ideas are very similar to the instruction the angel gave to Nephi that the tree of life—possibly represented by the date palm— was an allegorical representation of Jesus Christ (1 Nephi 11:7), and numerous Book of Mormon scholars have pointed out the symbolism of Christ in Lehi's dream of the Tree of Life (Jeanette W. Miller, "The Tree of Life, A Personification of Christ").

Date-palm imagery appears to be evident during the ministry of Jesus Christ on earth when faithful Jews took branches of palm trees and went out to meet the Savior, crying Hosanna shouts and blessing Christ as the King of Israel who came in the name of the Lord (John 12:13). Scholar Simo Parpola writes that early Mesopotamian cultures expressed the image of kingship allegorically through the sacred image of a tree, represented in stone drawings and other iconographic forms, as a palm tree growing on a mountain. This decorative tree-of-life motif was common in expressions of Assyrian royal art (Simo Parpola, "Sons of God: The Ideology of Assyrian Kingship"), and is very similar to the geography of the Valley of Lemuel with its date-palm groves surrounded by mountains. In this chapter, Jesus Christ—the Messiah—is personified by the tree of life and the date palms growing at Wadi Tayyib al-Ism.

* * * * *

In this chapter, Laman and Lemuel attempt to murder their father so they can return to their home at Beit Zayit. Soon after Lehi scolds his sons in the Valley of Lemuel, Nephi indicates that Laman and Lemuel displayed some sort of murderous tendency toward their father, writing that: "They were like unto the Jews at Jerusalem who sought to take away the life of my father (1 Nephi 2: 13). Nephi prefaces Laman and Lemuel's plot against Lehi with a list of the reasons they likely wanted to murder him. Nephi's summary inspired the closing scene in this chapter where Lehi confounds Laman and Lemuel before they carry out their planned homicide (1 Nephi 2: 11–14):

CHAPTER FORTY-TWO

The first chapter of the Book of Ezekiel details a revelation the prophet received after he was exiled to the northern provinces of Babylon and was living among the captives by the Chebar River. This was about four years after King Jehoakim was taken by the Babylonians, and his uncle, Zedekiah, was appointed vassal king of Judah (Ezekiel 1: 1–2). For this reason, Ezekiel is considered to be the prophet to exiles. The Book of Ezekiel, like the Book of Jeremiah and the Doctrine and Covenants, is not a chronological account of visions and revelations, and it is not certain whether the vision in the opening chapter of the Book of Ezekiel was his first. We do not know when Ezekiel was deported from Jerusalem, nor do we know why he was deported to the northern provinces, other than it fulfilled the purpose of God to have a prophet among the captive Jews in that part of the world. It is possible that Ezekiel was still living among the Jews at Jerusalem in the first few years after Zedekiah was made king. In this chapter, Inspector Tobit releases Ezekiel from prison and sends him to northern Babylon, fulfilling the revelation that Ezekiel would be a prophet to the exiled Jews at Tel-abib along the banks of the Chebar River.

LIST OF REFERENCES

Allbright, William F. "The Seal of Eliakim and the Latest Preexilic History of Judah, With Some Observations on Ezekiel." *The Journal of Biblical Literature*, vol. 51, 1932, 148.

Amin, S. A. "Fresh Dates Will Soon Be Ready to Harvest." Arabian Sun Dhahran, Saudi Arabia, July 16, 1997, 1.

Bright, John. *A History of Israel.* Philadelphia: Westminster Press, 1981.

————. "Jeremiah" in *The Anchor Bible.* Garden City, NY: Doubleday, 1965, 237.

Brown, Kent S. *From Jerusalem to Zarahemla.* Salt Lake City: Bookcraft Inc., and Provo: Religious Studies Center at Brigham Young University, 1998.

Casson, Lionel. "Ships and Seafaring in Ancient Times." Austin, TX: University of Texas Press, 1994.

Catafago, Joseph. "Arabic-English Dictionary." Beirut: Librairie de Liban, 1975.

Old Testament Student Manual: 1 Kings–Malachi, second edition. Church Educational System, The Church of Jesus Christ of Latter-day Saints, 1982, 33–34.

Old Testament Student Manual: Genesis–2 Samuel, second edition. Church Educational System, The Church of Jesus Christ of Latter-day Saints, 1982.

Clark, Adam. *The Holy Bible with Commentary and Critical Notes*, vol. 6. New York: Abingdon-Cokesbury Press, n.d.

Encyclopedia Judaica. Jerusalem: Keter Publishing House, vol. 14, 1972, 1372.

England, Eugene, in Noel B. Reynolds and Charles D. Tate, eds., *Book of Mormon Authorship: New Light on Ancient Origins.* Provo: Brigham Young University 1982.

Gee, John, and Peterson, Daniel C. "Graft and Corruption: On Olives and Olive Culture in the Pre-Modern Mediterranean," in *The Allegory of The Olive Tree*, eds. Steven D. Ricks and John W. Welch. Salt Lake City: Deseret Book, and Provo: F.A.R.M.S., 1994, 186–247.

Great People of the Bible and How They Lived (Pleasantville NY: Readers Digest Association, 1974).

Groom, Nigel. "Frankincense and Myrrh: A Study of the Arabian Incense Trade." London: Longman, 1981.

Hamblin, William J. "Sacred Writings on Bronze Plates in the Ancient Mediterranean." F.A.R.M.S. preliminary report, 1994.

Hilton, Lynn M. and Hope. *In Search of Lehi's Trail.* Salt Lake City: Deseret Book, 1976.

Hogarth, David George. "Hejaz before World War I, a Handbook" second edition, 1917. Cambridge England: Falcon-Oleander Press, 1978.

Holbrook, Brett L. "The Sword of Laban as a Symbol of Divine Authority and Kingship." *Journal of Book of Mormon Studies,* vol. 2, no. 1, 39–72.

Hoskisson, Paul Y. "The Allegory of the Olive Tree in Jacob," in *The Allegory of the Olive Tree*, eds. Steven D. Ricks and John W. Welch. Salt Lake City: Deseret Book,and Provo: F.A.R.M.S., 1994, 186–247.

Kawashti, I. S. and Omar, M. M. "Water Economy and Water Metabolism of Camels and Donkeys, Under Desert Conditions." Conference on the biological aspects of Saudi Arabia, Mathematics and Science Center. Riyadh: Riyadh University Press, 1977.

Keohane, Alan. "Nomads of the Desert." London, Stacey International, 1994.

Ludlow, Daniel H., "The Title Page," in *The Book of Mormon: First Nephi, The Doctrinal Foundation, papers from the second annual Book of Mormon Symposium,* eds. Monte S. Nyman and Charles D. Tate. Provo: Brigham Young University, 1986, 5–11.

Meservy, Keith H. "Job: Yet Will I Trust in Him," in Sydney B. Sperry Symposium. Provo: Brigham Young University, 1978.

Musil, Alois. "The Northern Hijaz—a Topographical Itinerary. New York: Oxford University Press, 1995.

New Roget's Thesaurus, Revised Edition, editor: Norman Lewis. New York: Berkeley, 1976, "Boundary," 49.

Nibley, Hugh W. "Dark Days in Jerusalem: The Lakhish letters and the Book of Mormon," in *The Prophetic Book of Mormon.* The Collected Works of Hugh Nibley, vol. 8. Salt Lake City: Deseret Book, and Provo: F.A.R.M.S. 1989.

———. "Qumran and the Waters of Mormon," in *An Approach to the Book of Mormon.* The Collected Works of Hugh Nibley, vol. 6. Salt Lake City: Deseret Book, and Provo: F.A.R.M.S., 1988.

———. "Portrait of Laban," in *An Approach to the Book of Mormon.* The Collected Works of Hugh Nibley, vol. 6. Salt Lake City: Deseret Book, and Provo: F.A.R.M.S., 1988.

———. "Israel's Neighbors." F.A.R.M.S. Reprint, 1984.

———. "Lakhish Letters" in Noel B. Reynolds and Charles D. Tate, eds., *Book of Mormon Authorship: New Light on Ancient Origins.* Provo: Brigham Young University Department of Religious Studies, 1982.

———. "Lehi in the Desert," in *Lehi in the Desert/The World of the Jaredites/There Were Jaredites,* ed. John W. Welch. The Collected Works of Hugh Nibley, vol. 5. Salt Lake City: Deseret Book, and Provo: F.A.R.M.S., 1988.

———. "More Voices from the Dust," in *The Old Testament and Related Studies.* The Collected Works of Hugh Nibley, vol. 1. Salt Lake City: Deseret Book, and Provo: F.A.R.M.S., 1986.

———. "The Jerusalem Scene." F.A.R.M.S. Reprint, 1980.

———. "The Lesson of the Sixth Century B. C." F.A.R.M.S. Reprint, 1984.

———. *Since Cumorah,* second edition, ed. John W. Welch. Collected Works of Hugh Nibley, vol. 7. Salt Lake City: Deseret Book, and Provo: F.A.R.M.S., 1988.

Offord, Joseph. "Archeological Notes on Jewish Antiquities," in *An Approach to the Book of Mormon.* The Collected Works of Hugh Nibley, vol. 6. Salt Lake City: Deseret Book, and Provo: F.A.R.M.S., 1986.

Parpola, Simo. "Sons of God: The Ideology of Assyrian Kingshi." Archeology Odyssey Archives, Nov.–Dec., 1999.

Petzel, Florence E. *"Textiles of Ancient Mesopotamia, Persia and Egypt."* Corvallis Oregon: F. E. Petzel, 1987.

Playfair, R. L. "A History of Arabia Felix or Yemen from the Commencement of the Christian Era to the Present Time." Westmead, England: Gregg International Publishing, Ltd., 1970.

Potter, George and Wellington, Richard. *Lehi in the Wilderness.* Springville: Cedar Fort, 2003.

Rolph, Daniel N. "Prophets, Kings, and Swords: The Sword of Laban and its Possible Pre-Laban Origins." *Journal of Book of Mormon Studies,* vol. 2, no. 1, 73–79.

Smith, Lucy Mack. *The History of the Prophet Joseph Smith by His Mother.* Covenant: American Fork, UT, 2000.

Starkey, John L. "The Discovery," in *The Lachish Letters*, ed. Harry Torczyner. Oxford University Press, 1938.

———. "Summary," in *The Lachish Letters,* ed. Harry Torczyner. Oxford University Press, 1938.

Thompson, J. A. "The Book of Jeremiah," in *The New International Commentary on the Old Testament,* ed. R. K. Harrison. Grand Rapids, MI: William B. Eerdmans Publishing Company, 1980.

Tvedtness, John A. "Was Lehi a Caravaneer?" in *The Most Correct Book: Insights from a Book of Mormon Scholar.* Salt Lake City: Cornerstone, 1999, 76–98.

U.S. Army Map Service, "Jerusalem Southwest Asia." AMS K502, Sheet NH 36-4, 1958.

U.S. Geologic Map Service, "Gulf of Aqaba Southwest Asia." AMS K502, Sheet NH 36-4, 2001.

Welch, John W. "Lehi: The Calling of a Prophet," in *The Book of Mormon: First Nephi, The Doctrinal Foundation, Papers from the Second Annual Book of Mormon Symposium,* eds. Monte S. Nyman and Charles D. Tate. Provo: Brigham Young University, 1986.

———. "Theft and Robbery in the Book of Mormon and Near Eastern Law," F.A.R.M.S. Reprint, 1992.

———. "Double, Sealed, Witnessed Documents: From the Ancient World to the Book of Mormon," in *Mormons, Scripture, and the Ancient World,* ed. Davis Bitton. Provo: F.A.R.M.S., 1998.

World Book, "Homing Pigeons," vol. 8. Field Enterprises Corporation, 1961, 276.

Water Atlas of Saudi Arabia. Riyadh: Saudi Publishing, 1984.

World Book, vol. 5. Scott Fetzer Corporation, 1988, 40.

LAND DIVIDED

HOUSE OF ISRAEL VOL. 2

Prologue

Jerusalem, October 1841

Elder Orson Hyde walked out of Stephen's Gate and stared up at the city wall. Though he knew these were not the same walls Jesus had looked upon anciently, he felt awed at the sight of their harsh, firm beauty bathed in the light of a nearly full moon. They had seen hundreds of years of war and turmoil, peace and promise, and much more was yet to come, for there was much prophesied about Jerusalem and its role in the world. These walls would yet see the final destruction of the wicked and the coming of the Son of Man.

He walked down the poorly maintained road into the Kidron Valley, across the stone bridge, up a winding, rock-strewn path, and through an old gate in a wall of stone. Here in the Garden of Gethsemane, he delayed briefly, his thoughts on Christ and His sacrifice. Shedding a few tears, he took a small branch from one of the trees and climbed to the crest of the Mount of Olives.

It was from here that the Lord ascended to Heaven and, according to prophets older than the walls of the city across the Kidron, the place where Jesus would come again to save His people from their enemies one last time.

And he was here. To the west he could see the distant Mediterranean Sea; to the east, the Dead Sea valley. It was not an unfamiliar sight. He had seen it all in a vision eighteen months earlier—witness that he was to come, witness to the need to begin something new for the house of Israel.

He sat down on a large rock and watched the city come to life as the sun rose behind him. Over the last few days he had mingled with Arabs in traditional bright colored garb, Turks in their conical hats and loose pantaloon trousers, and Jews in more European attire. It was a city of twenty thousand people with dingy, narrow streets, each emitting a thousand different smells. It had all been strange, but then most of his trip had been that way.

Taking out a piece of paper, he smoothed it flat and dipped his pen in an inkwell he had brought and began writing his prayer. Now he must do what he had come to do. He cleared his mind then began to write the prayer God had revealed to him.

"O Thou! Who art from everlasting to everlasting . . ."

His greeting petitioned God to listen to his words. Then he consecrated the land under and around him for the gathering together of Judah's scattered remnants, the building up of Jerusalem again—though now trodden under the feet of Gentiles—and the rearing of a temple that would honor God's name and work.

Pausing for a brief moment, he thanked God for his safety in the midst of a tumultuous land and asked for that continued kindness on his return home. He then spoke of the promises the Lord had made to Abraham, Isaac, and Jacob wherein He would remember their scattered seed who waited for the fulfillment of these promises. He asked that God grant removal of the barrenness and sterility of the land and let springs of living water break forth to water its thirsty soil that it might flow with plenty to eat when possessed by its rightful heirs, those returning prodigals who would come home.

He concluded his prayer by remembering the Saints at home, especially his family. He then prayed for the Saints and the leaders of the

Church who were being persecuted. Finally he spoke words that would bless members of the Church forever. "And let this blessing rest upon every faithful officer and member in thy Church. And all the glory and honor will we ascribe unto God and the Lamb for ever and ever. AMEN."

Standing, Orson piled stones, that by ancient custom established by Jacob and Joshua would witness that he had fulfilled his mission.

As he viewed the city from his lofty position one last time, he knew Jerusalem would never be the same. Slowly but surely the hearts of the dispersed of Judah would turn to this dusty, dry, and sparsely-inhabited land, and it would become "a cup of trembling unto all the people round about, . . . a burdensome stone for all people" (Zech. 12:2–3). Though the entire world would be gathered against them, they would survive this time. They would prevail.

The words of Zechariah came to mind wherein that ancient prophet said that the governors of Judah would reestablish a nation that would become "like an hearth of fire among the wood, and like a torch of fire in a sheaf; and they shall devour all the people round about, on the right hand and on the left" (Zech. 12:6). With only seven thousand Jews in all of Palestine and its ancient beauty all but gone, Elder Hyde wondered how they could become that nation.

He took a deep breath. He did not know, but he knew it would be. Somewhere, somehow— even now—the hearts of dispersed Judah would begin to change until Judah returned like a flood to this land. It would not be pleasant; it would certainly not be without war and mayhem in the lives of both Jew and Gentile, but it would happen. The hardships she would endure to prepare this land for the return of her King would make the Jews shudder if they were able to see them. What lay ahead to bring them home would be as difficult as anything Judah had ever endured in her history. Eventually, she would become a humble nation prepared for the Gospel by the coming of the Lord to drive away both her pride and her enemies.

Elder Hyde started down the slope toward the road. Once on it, he turned south and began a final trip around the city.

Chapter 1

November 29, 1947

Silently unfolding the first slip of paper, Assembly President Oswaldo Aranha paused, the heaviness of the impending vote weighing on him. This vote—the vote for partition—would establish separate Jewish and Arab states in Palestine. It had already been delayed once, leading to a three-day break of intense lobbying and promise making. Aranha himself had lobbied hard with the Catholic countries of South America. The moment of truth was at hand.

"Guatemala."

Aranha's heavy silence now transferred to the old skating rink, the improvised assembly hall of the United Nations. For this one moment, the delegates, the spectators, even the reporters in the press gallery, were silent, almost in awe.

Quietly, Dr. Jorge Garcia Granados rose from his seat. As he rose, a piercing cry in Hebrew came from the spectators' gallery. *"Ana Ad Hoshiya!"* O Lord, save us.

"Guatemala votes for partition."

Almost 5,700 miles away, Hannah Daniels squeezed Naomi Stavsky's hand. They stood huddled around an old radio with a number of their fellow outcasts in a small garden in Tel Aviv, concentrating on the most important moment in Jewish history since Joshua crossed the Jordan River to capture the Promised Land.

The United Nations' vote to partition Palestine, if successful, would effectively give them the opportunity to create a Jewish state. It had not come easily. Over the last two years Hannah had watched as Britain had remained intractable in its policy, Foreign Secretary Ernest Bevin insisting that British interests were more closely linked to Arab nationalists than to Jewish Zionism. Most in Israel considered the arguments he spewed forth dirty water—nothing but a cover for a deeply ingrained anti-Semitism. Regardless, much of the world had slowly turned against the British, the United States especially.

"The United States of America votes for partition." There was applause by all those who gathered to hear the news as it blared from the radio in the garden.

"That's nearly enough," Naomi said to Hannah.

Hannah could only nod. It was going well; they were close! She put her arm around her young friend and pulled her in. Naomi had only recently arrived from Europe where she had been a part of the underground for nearly two years now. She and dozens like her had led Jews out of Displaced Persons camps to the shorelines of the Mediterranean where they had put them on boats similar to—and even larger than—the one on which Hannah had escaped, sending them on their way to Palestine. Though hundreds had made it to Israel's shores, many more had been caught by the British and interred on the island of Cyprus where more than fifty thousand waited in camps similar to those they had escaped in Europe. Still more continued to wait in those DP camps hoping the doors of legal immigration would finally open and they too could escape the squalor of the camps of postwar Europe. Though all such people would not come to Palestine, many would, and their ability to do so without further British interference depended on this vote!

She glanced at her young friend. Her hair was lighter, but her eyes dark brown, set to the side of an aquiline nose. Taller than Hannah, she was thin with no sign of any fat, though she had matured in recent years. More noticeable to Hannah was the way Naomi carried the emotional and spiritual growth gained by literally walking thousands of miles over valley and mountain to lead others out of the camps. Smart, determined, and confident, Naomi was a far cry from the self-protective introvert Hannah had first led out of Berlin. She and Hannah had grown close those last few months in Italy, and even closer through their constant letters to one another. Now she was here. It was wonderful!

Hannah would not be in Tel Aviv were it not for Naomi coming in by ship that morning. Her own home was in Jerusalem where she and Ephraim had found a place in the Jewish Quarter of the Old City. It wasn't much, but it was home, and David and Elizabeth were there now, anxiously awaiting Hannah and Naomi's return.

"England abstains."

"Fancy that," said one man cynically.

"Still want to hold on do they. Well, we won't let them," cried another. With that there was applause.

Though Britain had announced two weeks prior that it would withdraw all its troops from Palestine by August 1, 1948, many Jews—especially the leaders—were doubtful they would actually go. Palestine was the most important part of the British Empire's tenuous hold on the Middle East. To walk away might cause them to lose their grip entirely, and few believed that was what they intended. If partition were successful, many Jews were afraid the disgruntled British would allow disorder, either to show their displeasure or to try and force a reconsideration. After all, if Jews and Arabs started massacring one another, someone would have to step in. With the British already here, the UN would surely give them what they wanted—a trusteeship and the freedom to clean out the rebels.

"The Brits at least stayed out of the vote," Naomi said.

"Tonight. Tomorrow they vote with their favors." By giving the Arabs the advantage in the coming fight, the Brits could still beat back any Jewish national home.

"When will Ephraim be back?" Naomi asked.

"In the next few days," Hannah grinned. Just the sound of his name gave her joy. He was the miracle in her life. She missed him terribly, but the Jewish Agency, the representative government for the Jews in Palestine under the British Mandate, had sent Ephraim to contact old friends in postwar Europe to help open the doors for arms purchases, especially planes. Without such weapons, any Jewish State promised by the UN would never become a reality, would never survive the coming war.

War. She dreaded even the thought of it. The Arabs were armed with weapons her people could only dream of. To survive the next few months would be critical. While the British prepared to leave, while the Jews still had some peace, they must buy and ship an array of weapons to Israel or lose their state to the Arab nations the moment they crossed the borders.

Another vote, another celebration. A vote for partition would only open the door for statehood, not guarantee it. The Jews would have to come to a peaceful solution with the Arabs, who would not even speak of peace, or they would have to fight. And if they could not show the world that they had the ability to hold such a state, the

UN could reverse its position as easily as it had granted it.

"How much arm twisting did the Americans have to do to push this vote through?" Naomi asked.

"A great deal, and because of it those countries would be glad to have a clear chance to reverse their vote."

"I hear that the President had trouble with some in his own cabinet."

"Secretary of Defense James Forrestal is the most opposed. But there are others, and they are avid Arabists for the same reason as the Brits—influence and oil. Ephraim thinks they've already laid plans for bringing about reversal and may have even secretly promised the Arabs to try." The cry of a baby immediately turned her toward the house as another round of applause greeted words announced by the radio. Inside she found the twins still lying on the bed in her host's bedroom, Jacob wide awake. She picked him up and cradled him in her arms, her warmth giving him immediate comfort.

When planning their marriage, she and Ephraim had wondered if they would ever have children. Who really knew the effects of the Holocaust? She smiled. The twins had been a double gift from God, but a challenge to care for. She glanced at Joseph where he lay on the bed. Alike down to the shape of their nose and the length of their feet, even she had difficulty at times knowing the difference. Only the slight cowlick in Joseph's hairline gave him away.

She pulled Jacob even closer as she returned to the yard. How she loved them!

As she left the house, a clock on the cupboard revealed that it was near midnight. The crowd in the yard had doubled and was overflowing into the street. All were silent, straining to hear the radio. A barrel-chested man with a bald pate turned to her and said hello as she approached.

"Yitzhak, nice to see you." Hannah smiled.

"I see Ephraim has not returned."

She shook her head. "If we win tonight, his work may take even longer."

Yitzhak only smiled agreement. Yitzhak Perlman worked as an arms procurement agent for the underground Jewish army known as the Haganah. Because of those connections, he knew of Ephraim's mission to Europe and how such missions would make the difference between victory and defeat. It would do no good to have the UN resolution if they must fight the Arabs with little more than rocks and sticks.

"What will happen tomorrow, Yitzhak?"

"Haj Amin will start a strike, then a riot, then a war. What else?" He forced a smile.

"Yes, what else," she replied.

For months the Jews had continued to hope for a peaceful solution, but with the Arabs, especially Haj Amin el Husseini, Mufti of Jerusalem and self-proclaimed leader of the Palestinian Arabs, making rash statements about never allowing a Jewish state in their midst, it was difficult.

"He began fanning the flames of passion against Jews years ago. Now his men—his Holy Strugglers, he calls them—train and arm guerillas both here and across the border. He will set them loose on partition, and by their violence, they will make it hard for the UN to resist reversing what happens tonight," Yitzhak said.

"He is a butcher," Hannah said through a granite jaw.

"He is a nationalist, just like you and me. And he hates Jews because we threaten to take what he thinks belongs to him."

"He sided with Hitler in the war, Yitzhak. That makes him more than a nationalist patriot. Do not forget that he called for the absolute annihilation of the Jews and supported the Nazi resolution to the Jewish problem."

"No one said he was a patriot, Hannah," Yitzhak smiled. "He is Mufti, a holy man to all Islam, a defender of the faith who is justified in fighting the infidel and destroying them all. We are next on his list. He has been planning this for years, and even though the British recognize him as the butcher you know him to be and will not allow him into Palestine, he runs things here for the Arabs through the Arab Higher Committee. It is him we have been fighting since 1920, and now he will see the chance he has always wanted. He will not miss it, and it will be him and his beliefs we will have to defeat more than all other Arab Armies. Until we do, we will not have peace in this land."

JABAL AL-LAWZ
(MT. HOREB?)

NORTH

LEHI'S LARGE AND
SPACIOUS FIELD

River of Laman

B O R D E

LOWER VALLEY
OF LEMUEL

FOUNTAIN OF
THE RED SEA
GULF OF AQABA